$60.00
D1479486
DISCARDED

# PREFACE

The need for an encyclopedic book on hunting, a work offering detailed information on the game birds and animals of this continent, the successful methods of hunting them, and the development of the firearms and equipment required, has long been recognized. In the past decade many publishers have considered a project of this scope, but when preliminary surveys revealed the magnitude of the task it has always previously been abandoned.

To be of real and lasting value to the sportsman, such a volume would have to include detailed information on every phase of hunting, the areas in which the various game birds and animals were most abundant, and a thorough treatment of the subjects allied to the sport. In brief, this work would constitute a complete hunting library carefully compressed into one volume. It was not until 1946 that Chester R. Heck, convinced of the need and the demand for such a book, began the first definite steps for its creation.

No individual, regardless of his age or experience in the field, could turn out a book of this scope. Each section, large or small, called for the selection and development of material from a number of individuals, each a recognized expert in his particular field. In addition to the zoologists, biologists, botanists, ballisticians, and other scientists, it was necessary to obtain definite contributions from artists, craftsmen, gunsmiths, hunters, and shooters from all parts of the continent. Each of these experts in the varied scientific and sporting fields played an important part in the development of the finished work. Even the casual reader will recognize the extent of the direction, research, and editing required to present this complete picture of North American hunting.

The very form of the outline followed in presenting the varied subjects was not without its problems, and it was finally decided to group the subjects in logical divisions, each following a definite alphabetical sequence. Thus, with a complete and detailed index, the reader will be able easily to locate any subject matter in which he is interested.

The compilation of the material itself occasionally presented a high and difficult hurdle, for scientific opinion is not without its differences, and the decision reached by one expert does not always coincide with that reached by another in the same field. In such instances, it was our policy to follow one of two courses, depending upon the circumstances and the extent of the disagreement involved. Either both opinions are offered, leaving the decision to the reader, or the opinion of two or more recognized authorities is accepted.

Shooters have almost as many theories as to the best caliber, gauge, or load for the various forms of hunting as there are individuals. This constituted another problem, which was solved by offering complete data on the performance of every type of hunting weapon employed in the field, and in instances where recommendations are made, the firearms listed have been compiled from preferences expressed by leading authorities. Authenticity and clarity were the guides followed in the preparation of The Hunter's Encyclopedia. Long experience as a rod and gun editor, gun crank, and hunter convinces me that this book will be acceptable to the individual who is interested in all forms of hunting and shooting.

In gathering the material we received the wholehearted support from the legion of authorities who made its creation possible. We should be remiss indeed if we did not mention here some of the individuals whose interest, advice, and painstaking effort made my own work not only easier, but more pleasant. In addition to the members of the advisory board, whose names are listed elsewhere, a large share of the credit for this volume must go to Luis M. Henderson, M. L. Fuller, Wilbur G. Gaffney, William Depperman, and Henry P. Davis.

While it would be impossible to list every individual who contributed advice and information during the production of the Encyclopedia, the following pages give recognition of special co-operation not otherwise acknowledged within the conduct of this volume.

*June 1, 1948*

Raymond R. Camp, *Editor*



202944

# The HUNTER'S ENCYCLOPEDIA

EDITOR

RAYMOND R. CAMP

CARNEGIE LIBRARY
OF
NASHVILLE

STACKPOLE AND HECK, INC.

HARRISBURG, PA. NEW YORK, N. Y.

COPYRIGHT, 1948
STACKPOLE AND HECK, INC.

ALL RIGHTS RESERVED

This book may not be reproduced in whole or in part in any form or as a translation without permission in writing from the publisher, except brief passages included in a review to be printed in a magazine or newspaper.

Ref
799.2
H94

CARNEGIE LIBRARY
OF
NASHVILLE

*Printed in the United States of America*
*at the Telegraph Press, Harrisburg, Pa.*

# THE HUNTER'S ENCYCLOPEDIA

# EDITORIAL ADVISORY BOARD

Nash Buckingham
Dr. Ira N. Gabrielson
Frank Dufresne
Bob Becker
Archibald Rutledge
Captain Philip B. Sharpe
Seth Gordon
J. Hammond Brown


# CONTRIBUTORS

## ARTISTS

T. M. Shortt—*Original paintings on Waterfowl, Grouse, Partridges, and Pheasants.*

Luis M. Henderson—*Original paintings on Quail, Ringneck Pheasant, Chukar Partridge, Woodcock, Wild Turkey, and Decoys.*

## WRITERS AND EDITORS

(With topics to which each contributed)

Barrett, Peter — *Photography*
Becker, Bob — *Dog Health and Care*
Benson, Ray — *Waterfowl Conservation*
Bridges, Henry — *Small Game*
Cahalane, Victor H. — *National Parks*
Coble, Don — *Muzzle Loader Shooting*
Comeaux, C. Stewart — *Firearms*
Connor, Jack — *Big Game and Pheasants*
Costley, Richard J. — *National Forests*
Cummings, Dr. C. S. — *Ballistics*
Davis, Henry P. — *Dogs*
Day, Albert M. — *Wildlife*
Decker, Maurice — *Woodcraft*
Depperman, William — *Arms and Ammunition*
Dufresne, Frank — *Big Game, Grouse, Pheasant*
Elliot, David D. — *Dogs*
Elliot, Robert — *Waterfowl*
Feeney, W. S. — *Falconry*
Fuller, M. D. — *General editorial*
Gabrielson, Dr. Ira N. — *Wildlife*
Gasque, Jim — *Wild Boar*
Gillham, C. E. — *Waterfowl*
Goodwin, George — *Big Game*
Gordon, Seth — *Foreword*
Hagie, C. E. (The late) — *Big Game*
Heilner, Van Campen — *Geese*
Henderson, Luis M. — *General editorial*
Hightower, John — *Quail*
Hill, Howard — *Archery*
Hochbaum, Albert H. — *Waterfowl*
Klewer, Lou — *Cooking*
Knight, John Alden — *Woodcock*
LeTourneau, Gene L. — *Hounds*
Ludlum, Stuart D. — *Kentucky Rifle*
Lytle, Horace — *Dog Training*
Mackey, Wm. J. Jr. — *Decoys*
Marshall, Thomas — *Rail Shooting*
Newell, David M. — *Cat Predators*
O'Connor, Jack — *Big Game*
Ormond, Clyde — *Trophy and Meat Preservation*
Pugsley, Edwin — *Shot Guns*
Randall, Charles E. — *National Forests*
Riddle, Maxwell — *Spaniels and Retrievers*
Robinson, Ben C. — *Small Game*
Robinson, Jimmy — *Trap and Skeet*
Rutledge, Archibald — *Upland Game*
Seagears, Clayton B. — *Fox Hunting*
Sharpe, Philip B. — *Arms and Ammunition*
Wheeler, Charles E. — *Waterfowl*
Whelen, Col. Townsend — *Camping and Woodcraft*
Wulff, Lee — *Big Game and Airplane Hunting*
Young, Stanley — *Predators*

# ACKNOWLEDGMENT

The editors and the publisher acknowledge with sincere appreciation the generous aid and support in the preparation of this work contributed by the following:

O. Lytegraff
Redfield Gun Sight Co.

Henry H. Lyman
Lyman Gun Sight Corp.

Robert Abercrombie
D. T. Abercrombie Co.

Allen M. Schauffler
Abercrombie & Fitch

E. W. Averill
American Britanny Club

Charles S. Morgan
Golden Retriever Club of America

Miriam L. Steyer
Gordon Setter Club of America

G. D. Godwin
German Shorthaired Pointer Club of America, Inc.

Francis Gerstner
St. Louis Beagle Club, Inc.

Vincent Monacelli
New Jersey Beagle Club, Inc.

Thomas Q. Stabler
The English Springer Spaniel Club of Michigan, Inc.

J. Gould Remick
Labrador Retriever Club, Inc.

Charles S. Goodall
English Springer Spaniel Field Trial Club of Illinois, Inc.

Frederick C. Walcott
American Wildlife Institute

Albert H. Blum
Bausch & Lomb Optical Co.

H. S. Harper
Belding & Mull Co.

The Hon. D. Leo Dolan
Canadian Travel Bureau

David W. Griffiths
New Brunswick Tourist Bureau

Mrs. Jane Mayer
Metropolitan Museum of Art

E. C. Herkner
E. C. Herkner Co.

Lyle S. Corcoran
Hollywood Gun Shop

Sheldon M. Smith
Ithaca Gun Co., Inc.

Charles T. Haven
Johnson Automatics, Inc.

Major Donald M. Kellett
U. S. Army

A. E. Mashburn
Mashburn Arms Co.

O. B. Morman
Modern-Bond Corp.

Ted Mulliken
Wildfowler Decoy Co.

Richard Borden
National Audubon Society

George E. Brewer
New York Zoological Society

I. Bailey
Norman Ford & Co.

Philip S. Olt
Pekin, Ill.

E. F. White
Poly Choke Co., Inc.

E. L. Moynihan
Savage Arms Corp.

Herbert G. Croll
Swain Nelson Co.

W. R. Weaver
W. R. Weaver Co.

P. D. Johnstone
Griffin & Howe Co.

Emil J. N. Ott, Jr.
California Division of Fish and Game

Edward Hunter
Denver *Post*

Dr. R. P. Hunter
Connecticut Board of Fisheries and Game

Frank A. Lawson
Delaware Game and Fish Commission

I. N. Kennedy
Florida Game and Fresh Water Fish Commission

James H. George, Jr.
Georgia Game and Fish Commission

Cedric G. d'Easum
Idaho Fish and Game Department

Frank Phipps
Kentucky Division of Game and Fish

Isaac Chapman
Louisiana Department of Wildilfe and Fisheries

Earle Doucette
Maine Development Commission

Frank L. Bentz
Maryland Game and Inland Fish Commission

James F. Power
Massachusetts Department of Conservation

Jesus J. Rulfe
Forestal y de Caza y Pesca, Mexico Departamento

Cliff Ketcham
Michigan Department of Conservation

Alfred L. Nelson
Minnesota Department of Conservation

H. W. Clover
Missouri Conservation Commission

D. M. Gish
Arizona Game and Fish Commission

C. G. Hixon
Alabama Department of Conservation

Roald Amundson
Nebraska Game, Forestation, and Parks Commission

Ralph G. Carpenter, 2nd
New Hampshire Fish and Game Department

Hiram B. D. Blauvelt
New Jersey Department of Conservation

Elliott S. Barker
New Mexico Department of Game and Fish

H. F. Curry
Oklahoma Game and Fish Commission

F. B. Wire
Oregon Game Commission

Leo A. Luttringer, Jr.
Pennsylvania Game Commission

E. C. Hayes, Jr.
Rhode Island Department of Agriculture and Conservation

A. A. Richardson
South Carolina Game and Fish Department

Elmer Peterson
South Dakota Game, Fish and Parks Department

Charles J. Chance
Tennessee Department of Conservation

R. M. Busfield
Texas Game, Fish, and Oyster Commission

R. L. Turpin
Utah Fish and Game Commission

George W. Davis
Vermont Fish and Game Service

B. W. Stras, Jr.
Virginia Commission of Game and Inland Fisheries

Jack Shipman, Director
West Virginia Conservation Commission

R. M. Freeman
Mississippi Game and Fish Commission

A. A. O'Claire
Montana Fish and Game Department

E. J. Vanderwall
Wisconsin Conservation Department

Lester Bagley
Wyoming Game and Fish Commission

D. E. Forsland
Alberta Department of Lands and Mines

F. R. Butler
British Columbia Game Commission

G. W. Malaher
Manitoba Game and Fisheries Branch

R. A. Gibson
Northwest Territories Administration

George E. Herman
Nova Scotia Bureau of Information

W. J. K. Harkness
Ontario Department of Lands and Forests

Harrison F. Lewis
Canadian Department of Mines and Resources

Charles Fremont
Département de la Chasse et de la Pêche
Province of Quebec

W. A. Hartwell
Saskatchewan Department of Natural Resources and Industrial Development

J. E. Gibben, Esq. K. C.
Yukon Territory

Richard W. Westwood
*American Nature Magazine*

Bill Geagan
Bangor *News*

Lurton Blassingame
New York, N. Y.

William Sharpe
North Carolina News Bureau

Ted Kesting
*Sports Afield*

Hugh Grey
*Field and Stream*

Ray Brown
*Outdoor Life*

Ray Trullinger
New York *World Telegram*

Commissioner Richard N. Reed
Maine Sea and Shore Fisheries

Henry Moore
Boston *Herald*

Allen Corson
Miami *Herald*

Jack Meehan
Stoeger Arms Co.

Jack Hill
Stoeger Arms Co.

Perry Duryea
New York State Conservation Department

C. Stewart Comeaux
Sporting Arms and Ammunition Manufacturers' Institute

Jack Wilson
Manotak Lodge

Alex M. Wilson, Publisher
Northwestern Ontario Sportsman

Larry Hasbrouck
New York *Herald Tribune*

Herman P. Dean
Standard Printing & Publishing Co.

Richard R. Smith
New York, N. Y.

The American Museum of Natural History

W. S. Allen
Western-Winchester

J. M. Davison
Western-Winchester

Charles S. Hopkins
Western-Winchester

A. G. Ormsbee
Western-Winchester

M. A. Robinson
Western-Winchester

V. J. Tiefenbrunn
Western-Winchester

The Canadian National Railways

Canadian Pacific Railway Co.

# TABLE OF CONTENTS

**Upland Game Birds (Continued)**



## PART VII—SHOREBIRDS



## PART VIII—WATERFOWL

## PART IX—COLOR SECTION



## PART X—FIREARMS



## PART XI—AMMUNITION

# FOREWORD

Hunting is the oldest, and by all odds the most diversified, sport known to man.

The chase began long before the dawn of recorded history. It is the only major sport, born of grim necessity, which now continues as a recreation enjoyed by millions.

The first hunters resorted to the chase to provide at least two of the three essentials to human existence—food, clothing, and shelter. The families of the mighty hunters survived; the others starved.

But why do *we* love to hunt? Why will a man periodically desert home and family to enjoy the chase? Why will he leave a warm bed on a bitter-cold morning, long before the crack of dawn, to slosh to his favorite duck blind, and then freeze until it is lawful to shoot? Why will he put up with discomforts and physical hardships such as he would not tolerate at home—just to go hunting?

The answer is simple. The thrill of the chase has been inherited from our primitive ancestors, and is still one of the fundamental passions of man.

In this modern era hunting has largely become a social pastime—an opportunity to enjoy the companionship of kindred spirits, and to commune with nature. Yes, and also, to a certain extent, an opportunity to revert to the primitive. The meat we bring home for the family larder, if any, is purely secondary.

Today more men engage in this strenuous, yet ever thrilling, form of recreation than in any other personal sport. In the United States alone there are almost 15,000,000 hunters afield annually. The gentle art of angling attracts a like number of enthusiastic participants. The two groups release into the channels of commerce and trade over $4,000,000,000 every year—one of the nation's major industries. Canada and Mexico collect comparable golden harvests from hunting and fishing, totaling upward of another billion dollars.

No one has ever attempted to put a dollar value on the human or social benefits derived from hunting, or what the sport means to a nation in time of stress. These factors are far more important than the average statesman would willingly admit.

Hunting has long received more attention from legislative bodies and governmental agencies than any other sport. A virtual army of people are engaged in protecting and propagating game, in conducting wildlife research, in providing refuges and other places for game to live, and in administering a multitude of statutory regulations governing its pursuit.

But let us take a peek into the dim past, and trace briefly this phase of man's social development.

Scientists tell us that many thousands of years ago primitive man wandered through the forest picking up nuts and fruits for food. He wore no clothes and had no tools or weapons. At night he climbed into a tree for security while he slept.

The first great step toward civilization was the discovery of fire, and its use. This enabled man to leave the tree tops, for wild beasts were frightened by his flaming brands. From being hunted, man became the hunter. He could now cook meat for his food.

Next man learned to use snares and traps, to throw stones, to make clubs, stone axes, and finally rough stone spears for hunting. This gave him his first advantage over wild beasts. But these were poor weapons against sabertoothed tigers, cave bears, mammoths, and wild bulls.

Another great stride forward was when man discovered that wild animals could be tamed. This probably came about by accident when some hunter brought home a young animal as a pet for his children, doubtless a dog. And thus man's canine companion, his most capable aide for the chase, came into use.

Then some savage genius developed the bow, and man was able to slay the larger game animals and to drive off his fiercest enemies. For the first time he was sure of plenty of food. Much later the crossbow was developed, but it was found to be less effective, except in warfare.

According to the findings of scientists, hunters long, long ago banded together in clans or groups, much as do our sportsmen today. They obviously had secret rituals for admission of those deemed worthy to join their coveted circle. These supermen of the chase evidently used caves as secret meeting places. Artistic drawings, all having to do with hunting and the constant fight for survival, made something like 25,000 years ago, have been found in these caves.

It is apparent that these groups devised their own "rules of conduct," in the form of tribal taboos, to safeguard their food supply. The tribes which observed taboos effective in preserving the game supply were more likely to survive and prosper than the tribes which did not. Professor Aldo Leopold in his excellent textbook on *Game Management* concludes that "Hunting customs, like plant and animal species, were evolved by a process of selection, in which survival was determined by successful competition. Game laws grew out of these hunting customs."

Who made the first game laws? The first known written restrictions on the taking of game are found in the Mosaic Law. In Deuteronomy 22:6, among the covenants which Moses decreed shall be observed, we find that when a bird's nest is found with eggs or young (and we assume he referred to those of the size which were commonly taken for food), the dam shall in no wise be taken. Apparently the intent was to preserve the dam, or hen, to raise her brood. Taking the latter was not forbidden.

"The Mosaic game law," says Professor Leopold, "was evidently an advance beyond that of his Egyptian taskmaster, whose spirited depiction of hunting scenes shows them to have been keen sportsmen, but whose records reveal no worries over the conservation of sport."

The origin of man's social structures was based upon family nomadic groups who obtained their living from the forests and waters by hunting, fishing, and grazing. These groups were not concerned with growing crops, or with land ownership. As civilization advanced, and the cultivation of crops became the mode of life for those who could make a living thereby, new problems arose. The cultivated lands were constantly subjected to encroachment of the wilderness dwellers, many of whom became bands of criminals. As large landholding families developed, and early systems of social order evolved, they also had to control the near-by wilderness and its inhabitants. These landlords became the rulers and nobility. About this time the common man lost control of his right, as well as a place, to hunt. But his inborn desire to enjoy the chase could not be quelled, and poaching became a common practice.

The Greeks and the Romans had game laws, but they were not intended to conserve the sport. Their purpose was, rather, to keep their people from idling away their time on the chase instead of devoting themselves to the mechanical arts. However, Xenophon, the Greek historian and general (about 430-355 B.C.) felt differently about hunting. He believed that "Men who love sport will reap therefrom no small advantage. . . . It is an excellent training for war . . . such men will not break down . . . they will be able to sleep on a hard bed and keep good watch over the post entrusted to them . . . they will be able to save themselves . . . in marshy, precipitous, or otherwise dangerous ground, for from experience they will be quite at home in it."

Xenophon clearly recognized hunting as an asset to the health and well-being of the individual, and therefore an asset to society. Many public leaders since his day have encouraged hunting, but even to this day there are those who argue that in modern society hunting is of no value, and should be abolished as a sport.

The Roman law classified things into public and common. The latter embraced animals *ferae naturae,* which, having no owner, were considered as belonging in common to all citizens of the state, and became the property of those who captured them. The Roman Emperor Justinian recognized the right of an owner of land to forbid another from killing game on his property, which was merely a matter of trespass, not conservation. It may well be said, therefore, that game laws are in part based upon the old Roman law, and that our trespass laws date back to Justinian's reign (527-565 A.D.).

The first clear record of a system of game management, and the first man-made laws to protect game, is found in the Mongol Empire, not Europe. According to the writings of Marco Polo, the Venetian traveler, recorded almost 700 years ago, Kublai, "The Great Khan" (1216-1294) was not only a great hunter but one who appreciated the fact that wildlife must have a place to live, with plenty of food, and that it must not be taken during the breeding season if it is to survive and increase. Marco Polo wrote:

> "There is an order which prohibits every person throughout all the countries subject to the Great Khan from daring to kill hares, roebucks, fallow deer, stags, or other animals of that kind, or any large birds, between the months of March and October. This is that they may increase and multiply; and as the breach of this order is attended by punishment, game of every description increases prodigiously."

The Great Khan spent about three months each year in his hunting camp, where he used both hounds and falcons for his sport. The use of trained falcons for hunting small game in China dates back to about 2000 B.C. The Khan required a great retinue of servants for his hunts. Marco Polo found on the Great Khan's hunting preserves, near the city of Changanoor in Cathay, that patches of millet and other grains were being sown for the pheasants, partridges, quails, and other birds, which no person was allowed to harvest "in order that the birds may not be in want of nourishment. Many keepers are stationed there for the preservation of the game, that it may not be taken or destroyed, as well as for the purpose of throwing the millet to the birds during the winter."

Although the Khan's ideas of sport were not democratic, he allowed his subjects to hunt so long as they kept away from his preserves; he prohibited hunting during the breeding season; and he initiated steps in game management which many of us erroneously assume to be of recent origin.

A hundred years after the era of the Mongol Khans the feudal lords of Europe had not yet learned how to increase the game supply, but they had developed to a high degree restrictions on hunting in favor of the ruling classes. Their inhibitions against pursuit of the chase by the peasantry are said to be one of the main forces which later overthrew the feudal system.

Before the Norman Conquest in England there apparently were no restrictions against the hunting of game, except on Sundays. Later a law prevented monks from hunting in the woods with dogs, but all other classes of society were permitted to hunt throughout the country, so long as they did not interfere with the king's sport. When the king desired to hunt all his subjects had to leave the forest until he and his party were through.

English hunting preserves for the privileged, described in *Grouse and Grouse Moors* (1910) by Malcolm and Maxwell, were first recognized in a charter of the forest granted by Canute the Dane in 1062.

After the Norman Conquest (1066) and before the Magna Carta of King John, as summarized in *Wild Game—Its Legal Status* (1931), it seems that the ownership of wild game in England was vested in the English king, who claimed such ownership in his individual capacity and as a personal prerogative. Under such a system no one could acquire ownership in or title to game except by reason of a special license of the king, which was rarely granted. Enjoyment of the chase became the privilege of the nobility. The common people were excluded and penalties were severe. A writer on that period says: "To gain the right of killing a partridge required 50 times the amount of property as to vote for a

Knight of the Shire, and under the Conqueror it was as great a crime to kill one of the King's deer as to kill one of his subjects."

These oppressive game laws drove the people into rebellion. Many of them, as in the case of the famous Robin Hood, became outlaws who had to be quelled or organized society would have fallen.

In the early 1200's the barons at Runnymede exacted from King John the Magna Carta, or Great Charter (June 15, 1215). A change seems then to have taken place in the ownership of game. It was recognized as a great victory for the common people of England, and the charter was reissued in modified form in 1217 by Henry III. The clauses relating to forests were omitted and embodied in a separate Forest Charter granted the same day (Nov. 6, 1217). The Forest Charter reached its final form in a reissue of February 1225, and in March 1299 Edward I confirmed it. It remains on the statute books of England today.

Most informed people know about the Magna Carta, but comparatively few are acquainted with the Charter of the Forest, which was a grant of "hunting freedoms" from the king, given in consideration of a substantial tax. A study of it shows that over 700 years ago an important document was adopted containing basic principles of forest and wildlife management which many of us are prone to believe were of much later origin. The conditions under which the chase might be enjoyed by all citizens constituted an important part of this charter.

Since the Magna Carta the King of England has owned all wild game, not reduced to possession, in his sovereign capacity. He holds such property as the representative of and in "sacred trust" for the people.

The colonists who settled in America brought with them these common-law concepts of England to govern their dealings, and in this country wild game is owned by the State in its sovereign capacity for the people. An individual may acquire an absolute property right in game only as a matter of privilege, not as a matter of right, and only under the conditions decreed by the proper legislative body. More of this later.

During the century after the Magna Carta there seems to be a dearth of information concerning hunting developments throughout the Old World. But it is certain that the hunting methods, in addition to the age-old snare, pit, or trap, were still confined to the use of hounds, falcons, and the bow and arrow. Small game as we now know it was hunted primarily with falcons, big game with hounds and archery.

Gunpowder was not discovered until late in the 13th and early in the 14th century, the honor being shared jointly by Roger Bacon, the Englishman, and Berthold Schwartz, a German. Its use in a cannon is apparently first mentioned in the records of the city of Florence (1346). Its first important use is said to have been in blowing up or battering down castle walls of rebellious barons, later in hunting weapons.

During the 1400's Frederick II, Holy Roman emperor, practiced game management on a considerable scale to improve his opportunities for falconry. His book, *De Artibus Venandi* (On the Art of Hunting) is recognized as a classical treatise on the chase. The falcon was still the "sporting weapon" of that period for taking small game.

What is said to be the most famous hunting book of all times was written by the renowned Frenchman, Count Gaston de Foix, whose *Livre de la Chasse* (Book of the Chase) was started in May 1387. The Count came to his end on a bear hunt about four years later.

Deer apparently were the first game animals to be protected and increased (managed) in Europe. This practice became general about 1400 on the royal forests and feudal estates. The methods employed were rigid patrol, heavy fines against poaching, increase of the deer food, limitations on the kill, and the control of predators. In hunting, the deer were driven into nets with hounds, then killed with bows and arrows.

The first book on hunting *written* in the English language is the *Master of Game,* by Edward, second Duke of York, in 1413 (before the art of printing was invented) while he was in prison. It was largely a translation of Count Gaston's *La Chasse,* with five additional original chapters on English hunting practices and game-management methods. This is recognized as one of the most important early works on the art of hunting, though it was not printed until 1904, when President Theodore Roosevelt wrote a pungent foreword for it.

There are numerous arguments extant today relative to the age at which a lad should be taught the rudiments of hunting, especially the safe handling of hunting weapons. In passing let us cite the English philosophy of that period, as recorded by the Duke of York:

> "First he must be a child past seven or eight . . . for every man knoweth well that a child of seven . . . is more capable . . . of such things that he liketh to learn than . . . a child of twelve . . . therefore I put him so young thereto, for a craft requires all a man's life ere he be perfect thereof. And also . . . that which a man learns in youth he will hold best in his age."

A considerable portion of the Duke of York's book dealt with fox hunting, the origin of which has been lost in antiquity. In England it developed rapidly into a top-ranking sport of kings. In reality, "riding to the hounds" became the regal group participation sport, a social function of the highest order. It still thrives as such in the British Isles.

Within a few years after the first settlers came to America, English immigrants introduced fox hunting to the New World. George Washington was an active participant, and maintained kennels of imported hounds and stables of spirited horses for the sole purpose of pursuing sly Reynard. Today this sport of the centuries still has a sizable following in America, even though constantly increasing handicaps and opposition from small-game shooters make it difficult to maintain on the grand scale of former years.

The earliest English book *in print* on hunting is *The Book of Hawking, Hunting, and Heraldry,* printed at St. Albans, England, in 1486. It is generally credited to a somewhat mythical Dame Juliana Berners. According to the Library of Congress, there are only four copies of the original volume in American libraries.

As already mentioned, gunpowder came into use

during the early part of the 14th century. However, firearms (the matchlock rifle) were not developed until the following century. The first fowling pieces for the purpose of shooting at flying birds apparently were not made until about 1580. Previously guns had been so clumsy, and locks so uncertain, that wing shooting was next to impossible. The development of suitable guns for this purpose gave falconry a big setback, but did not eliminate the sport of hunting with trained hawks, as we shall later see. Incidentally, the first picture of wing shooting in an English book did not appear until 1683, a full century after suitable guns were first made.

The development of hunting preserves in England brought new problems. Henry VII (1485-1509) recognized the wisdom of granting landowners protection from trespass. He forbade the taking of pheasants and partridges on the land of others without permission of the owner, apparently to protect the hunting preserves and to encourage the production of more game. Comparable action had been taken by the Romans almost a thousand years earlier, for a somewhat different purpose. James I (1603-1625) extended this no-trespass edict to all shooting on all land, and says Professor Leopold, "Here was the first 'owner's permission' trespass law" —one of the moot questions of modern times.

Artificial pheasant propagation had its beginning in England during the reign of James I (1523); in Bohemia, as early as 1598. As better sporting arms became available, more men became expert in the art of shooting. More game had to be provided, new breeds of dogs were necessary. Hounds alone no longer sufficed. Dogs for bird hunting were developed, another step which brought greater pleasures to hunters.

The demand for more game not only gave birth to the science of game propagation, but to the intensive management of shooting estates. Large numbers of men with special training and ability were employed as gamekeepers or forest wardens, their designation depending upon the kind of game they were employed to produce or manage. They not only propagated game, or increased herds of deer, for their masters, but they patrolled the shooting preserves to prevent poaching. They controlled predators, provided food for the game, trained and handled the dogs for their employers, and directed the employees engaged to conduct the drives. They also determined when enough game had been removed from the property under their care, thereby avoiding overshooting.

Laws for the protection of the Scottish grouse moors date back to 1694, and cover improvement on them began about 1850.

While hunting as a sport for the select few had been developed to a high degree on the large estates of Europe long before the shooting-preserve era of the British Isles, nowhere did it gain the prominence it attained in England and Scotland.

The standards of skill and sportsmanship (ethics of the hunt) developed by the English sportsmen became widely recognized as the paragon of perfection. The excellence of their sporting arms, their mass game-production methods, the superior performance of their hunting dogs, and the management of their shoots were in a class all their own.

Englishmen have long been recognized as superior hunters; among them were those who sought out remote parts of the world in pursuit of their recreation. Many of them were explorers and scientists; some were prolific writers who contributed greatly to the early sporting literature of the civilized world.

The English and Scottish shooting preserves, after hundreds of years, still provide superlative sport for the fortunate few who can afford to maintain, or to rent, such expensive establishments. The masses, for economic and other reasons, are unable to participate, except as hirelings. In normal times, however, the man of average means is able to purchase for food in the public markets, at reasonable prices, the game killed on the shooting estates. The lucky hunters can not begin to use the enormous quantities bagged, and the sale of the surplus in the markets helps to finance the preserves. Efforts to have the English system of game husbandry developed in America have always met with strenuous opposition, because it is felt to be anti-democratic.

When the first settlers reached our shores they brought with them their inborn love of the chase. Most of them had been denied the opportunity to hunt in their native lands; many of them, and their forebears, had long been poachers on the estates of England and Europe.

Here they found game in abundance; it was a hunter's paradise. This was most fortunate, as otherwise they would have starved long before they could have cleared the land and tilled the soil. In the beginning, they hunted and trapped game only for food and clothing, much as did the Indians. Wildlife, like the forests, was believed to be inexhaustible; it was free for the taking. But as settlements developed, and channels of trade were opened, game and the hides of valuable fur-bearers quickly became important articles of trade. That was the beginning of oblivion for several important game species.

It is commonly believed that settlers desiring to till the soil were the trail blazers into the North American hinterland. This is wrong; fur-traders, trappers, and hunters were the pioneers. The settlers followed in their wake. Conflicts over the possession of the wildlife resources of the new land made a bigger impact upon the history of both the United States and Canada than did the desire to possess and till the land.

As the vanguard of the settlers trekked westward from the Atlantic coast, extermination of the vast herds of buffaloes (American bison) became inevitable. The flesh and the valuable hides of these "cattle of the plains" did not spell their doom. Great herds of buffaloes and the crops and fences of the settlers could not survive together. Finally, in order to whip into submission roving bands of Indians, the United States Army hastened the extermination of the remaining bison herds. Cutting off the Indians' chief source of food was more effective than small detachments of soldiers far from an operating base.

The commercialized slaughter of the wildlife resources of North America was by no means confined to the fur-bearers, or to the buffalo. The former myriads of passenger pigeons were exterminated by wholesale trapping (netting) and other methods of the greedy market hunters. Carloads of these magnificent birds went to the city markets to satiate the demand. The late William B. Mershon, in his book *The Passenger Pigeon,* estimated that during the last great nesting in Michigan (late seventies) from three to five million pigeons were slaughtered. Efforts to save them came too late, and the last bird died in the Cincinnati Zoo on September 1, 1914.

Hunting as a business accounted for many millions of game birds and mammals between 1840 and 1910. Dr. William T. Hornaday, an early crusader for game protection, mentions a single professional market hunter who admitted having killed more than 139,000 game birds and animals.

The buffalo, passenger pigeon, antelope, elk, deer, wild turkey, ruffed grouse, and many other species were persecuted and destroyed by the wagonload, later by the carload, to fill the growing demands of city markets. Professional killers also kept lumbering crews and railroad construction gangs supplied with meat. Market shooting unquestionably was one of the most devastating factors in the ruination of a sportsman's paradise.

Hunting for sport had little effect on the game supply in that early period, even though terrific kills were made. The advancement of civilization, the development of agriculture, the drainage of 100,000,000 acres of marshland, the pollution of our waters, and the destruction of our forests, jointly did more to destroy the wildlife than did the hunting weapons of the sportsmen. Game must have a place to live, and thrive.

In the beginning there were no game laws in America. Game was so abundant that restrictions were not needed. But gradually restrictions were imposed.

As already indicated, the common law of England governed the colonists in their approach to this phase of their new social order. The first game law in America was to protect deer in Rhode Island (1646). Next came Massachusetts with a closed season on deer in 1694. In 1739 the first game wardens in America were appointed in the Bay State as "deer wardens." Delaware denied Sunday hunting in 1750.

These were only the initial steps. By the time of the Revolution most of the colonies had a few game laws. After its conclusion the question arose as to whether the newly independent colonies had a common law. It was decided that the common law of England, plus all English statutes prior to the Revolution applicable to our conditions, constituted the common law of the states. The net result is that all game belongs to the states, held in trust for their people, but the landowner has the right to determine who may come upon his property to hunt it. Laws for the protection of migratory game, enacted pursuant to treaties between the Dominion of Canada, the Republic of Mexico, and the United States, supersede the laws of the states and the provinces.

Here it should be recorded that New York, in 1864, was the first state to adopt a hunting license, and Iowa, in 1878, was the first to fix a bag limit on game. California established the first game refuge in 1870; 33 years later (1903) Indiana became the second state to create a wildlife refuge; third was Pennsylvania (1905), which now has the largest state system of game refuges in North America. The year 1903 also marked the beginning of the Federal wildlife refuge system in the United States, the biggest maintained by any government.

Hunting as a sport gradually increased after the Revolutionary War. The first book on shooting in this country was published in 1783, six years before George Washington was inaugurated as President of the United States. This was *The Sportsman's Companion,* dealing largely with wing shooting, training dogs, "and the necessary precautions to guard against many accidents that attend this pleasant diversion," by a gentleman (unidentified) "who has made shooting his favorite amusement upwards of 26 years in Great Britain, Ireland, and North America."

The next book on the subject apparently did not appear until 1827; this was *The American Shooter's Manual, by a Gentleman of Philadelphia County.*

It is significant to note that in those early days hunting for sport was evidently not a very popular, or publicly respected, pastime. Both of the books mentioned were published anonymously. Even the best-known writer in early American sporting literature used the pen name "Frank Forester." He was Henry William Herbert, a well-educated Englishman who came to this country in 1831. Forester was passionately devoted to shooting, and is recognized as the first really capable American sporting writer. Now there are dozens of them.

By 1850 many books on shooting began to appear in America, and the authors gladly identified themselves. *The American Sportsman,* by Dr. Elisha J. Lewis (1856), of Philadelphia, was a fine volume of over 500 pages, an amazing storehouse of information on dogs, guns, game birds, cooking game, etc. Dr. Lewis, like Xenophon, strongly recommended hunting as an invigorating recreation, Said he:

> "There . . . far away from the busy throngs of men . . the mind of the most grave and studious becomes truly unbent, and freed from its labors . . the heart beats with renewed vigor . . . and the whole animal . . . becomes sharpened and revivified. . . . We invite you to . . . participate in these innocent enjoyments so captivating to a true sportsman."

During the latter half of the 19th century sportsmen's publications became more popular, and there appeared on the horizon a few courageous crusaders determined to save North America's wildlife. In addition to Forester, there were such stalwarts as Theodore Roosevelt, George O. Shields, George Bird Grinnell, George Shiras 3d, William Brewster, William B. Mershon, William Dutcher, Dr. William T. Hornaday, John M. Phillips, and others of like stature.

Hunters began to organize into militant groups. The first organization of its kind was the New York Association for the Protection of Game, a local group founded in 1844, but the first to organize on a state-wide basis was the Massachusetts Fish and Game Association, in 1874. This pioneer state organization is still functioning. No national organization appeared until the Boone and Crockett Club, composed of big-game hunters, was organized by Theodore Roosevelt in 1887. It also is still on the firing line.

Other organizations, national in scope, formed around the turn of the century, were The League of

American Sportsmen (1898), organized by G. O. Shields, long since discontinued; the National Audubon Society, the American Bison Society, the Camp Fire Club of America, the American Game Protective and Propagation Association, and the Izaak Walton League of America.

From meager beginnings, these early crusaders made progress. In the national field the first man in high official position to give wildlife conservation real impetus was President Theodore Roosevelt, who by his example and leadership brought the need for conserving wildlife forcefully to public attention. In May 1908 he called the governors of the states to the White House and had a serious talk with them about the manner in which the nation's natural resources were being wasted. The following December delegates from all over the country came to Washington for a Joint Conservation Conference, the first of its kind in America. Thereafter, things began to move, although slowly. But President Roosevelt, by executive order, set aside many of the early wildlife refuges in the United States before his term of office ended.

We mentioned President Roosevelt's foreword to the *Master of Game*, dated "the White House, February 15, 1904." That foreword should be studied by every hunter, because it gives the "hunting psychology" of one of the great leaders of modern times. After reviewing the development of the chase in Europe and Great Britian, he said:

> "The great lords . . . followed the chase in ways which made scant demands upon the hardier qualities either of mind or body. . . . The absence of all demands for the hardy virtues rob any pastime of all title to regard. . . . The chase is the best of all national pastimes. . . . Laying stress upon the mere quantity of game killed, and publication of the record of the slaughter, are sure signs of unhealthy decadence in sportsmanship."

Early in the present century it became clear, at least to a few farsighted individuals, that there was considerable doubt about the possibility of continuing shooting for the masses in America. In one of his first official utterances John B. Burnham, president of the newly organized American Game Protective and Propagation Association (1911, later known as the American Game Association) warned that "This country stands today at the parting of the ways in the matter of field sports. It faces today the question of whether free shooting shall continue, or whether the European system of preserves and posted lands is to become universal." We shall comment on this later.

In the beginning of the active wildlife restoration movement in America the principal emphasis was upon stopping market hunting, setting restrictive seasons and bag limits, and enforcing laws. Today every state in the United States, and every province in Canada, has modern laws to conserve the game and fish supply, with a staff of officers to enforce them. The hunting seasons have progressively become shorter, and the bag limits smaller. All of the departments are actively conducting wildlife research to learn how to produce more game with constantly shrinking habitats; they are creating more and more wildlife refuges and acquiring or leasing lands for public hunting grounds; many of them are propagating and stocking game in constantly increasing quanties; and doing many other things in an effort to continue hunting for the masses.

As the native small-game supplies began to shrink alarmingly, especially the game birds, numerous individuals and public agencies began importing stock from the Old World. Thousands of pheasants were brought from China and England, Hungarian (European Gray) partridges from Europe, bobwhite quail from Mexico, and later chukar partridges from Asia.

Most of the imported stock was released, but considerable quantities of the birds were retained on public game farms for propagation purposes.

Of all the imported exotics, the most successful has been the ringneck pheasant, a bird which prospers on fertile farm lands, and today provides the bulk of the wing shooting in many states north of the Mason-Dixon Line. The pheasant also is doing well in some of the Canadian provinces.

For a time it appeared that the Hungarian partridge would be a great success in North America. Recently the territory where it thrives on a shootable basis has been shrinking, and hunting for this excellent little foreigner is now limited to a few states and provinces. The chukar partridge was an utter failure, except in a few limited spots. Even there doubt still prevails.

The only native game birds that have been raised successfully in captivity are the bobwhite quail, the valley quail, the Gambel quail, and the eastern wild turkey. A number of states raise thousands of bobwhites for stocking purposes, but pen-raised birds seem to have difficulty in adjusting themselves to existence in the wild. A few states produce excellent wild turkeys in quantities for release annually.

Attemps to raise such grand native birds as ruffed grouse and prairie chickens in captivity failed miserably. This was also true of efforts to produce in confinement the wild cottontail rabbit, the number one small-game animal in a large part of the country.

The most notable success in game restoration has been the country-wide increase in the herds of big-game animals. The several species of deer, the elk, the antelope, have all done well where conditions are favorable, and big game now provides shooting for an unbelievable number of hunters annually.

These activities are financed almost exclusively by license fees contributed by those who enjoy hunting. In the United States alone the official expenditures by the state game departments now run close to $30,000,000 a year. To maintain angling they spend another $20,000,000. Canadian provinces have similar agencies and are spending increasing sums to provide good hunting and fishing. The big difficulty is that *we are spending only about* $50,000,000 *to maintain hunting and fishing in the United States as against* $4,000,000,000 *spent in killing game and catching fish*—80 *dollars to one!* The sportsmen of America must wake up and either provide their departments with adequate funds to maintain good hunting and fishing, or roll up their sleeves and do much more work themselves than they have been doing in the past.

The first Federal law to protect wildlife in the United States was the Lacey Act (1900) to stop illegal interstate shipments of game for the markets. But market shooting had scarcely been brought under control when the problem of conserving the migratory game birds arose. Ducks and geese know no state or international boundary lines, and few of the states were willing to do anything about it. Most of them did their utmost to kill all they could while the birds were in their midst.

It was not until 1913 that Congress passed the Weeks-McLean Act asserting Federal jurisdiction over migratory game. To make it stick in the courts a treaty was negotiated with Canada (1916); two years later the Migratory Bird Treaty Act was passed to make it effective.

Within a year after enactment of the Migratory Bird Treaty Act the country was warned that unless adequate funds were provided to enforce the new regulations, and to restore a large part of the 100,000,000 acres of waterfowl grounds which had been drained for agriculture, the plight of the ducks and geese would be pathetic. It also became evident that unless suitable action was taken promptly the remaining good ducking grounds would be lost to the general public.

Various proposals were advanced. Congress was persuaded to authorize purchase and development of two important waterfowl areas. Finally, realizing that a piecemeal approach would be wholly inadequate, Congress in 1929 passed the Norbeck-Andresen Migratory Bird Conservation Act, which authorized appropriations totaling almost $8,000,000 over a ten-year period to acquire feeding, nesting, and resting areas for waterfowl. It also established a Migratory Bird Conservation Commission to pass upon purchases. But unfortunately this Act made no provision for public hunting grounds.

Although our government was at last committed to a broad waterfowl restoration program, Congress failed to adhere to its own schedule of appropriations to restore the waterfowl breeding grounds. Finally, in 1934, the Duck Stamp Law was passed, requiring waterfowl hunters to purchase a $1 stamp to attach to their state licenses before shooting ducks and geese. This produced slightly over $600,000 in the beginning, and since World War II has increased to about $2,000,000 annually. Most of this money has gone into refuges and the restoration of breeding and feeding marshes in the United States.

The biggest single appropriation by Congress for this work was $6,000,000 in 1936. So far about $30,000,000 have been spent for waterfowl restoration in the United States; much more remains to be done. Canada has made excellent progress to the same end, partly through funds contributed by sportsmen in the United States, but a still bigger job remains to be done in the Dominion (the principal waterfowl breeding grounds of the continent) to assure future duck and goose hunting.

The total acreage in wildlife refuges of all kinds in the United States and Alaska now aggregates about 25,000,000 acres; in Canada 30,000,000 acres.

A treaty comparable to the one with Canada was negotiated with the Republic of Mexico in 1937. Another important Federal venture to provide more game for the hunter was the Pittman-Robertson Federal-Aid Program (1937), under which the excise tax on sporting arms and ammunition was earmarked to aid the several states. Under this program the 75% of the cost of approved projects is Federally provided, and the states supply the remaining 25%. Almost $9,000,000 is currently available to the states for a single fiscal year, and a backlog of over $13,000,000 has accumulated. This is the biggest single forward step ever taken in the wildlife restoration program of this country; it enables many of the states to undertake projects never before possible; it provides money for essential research work and to acquire lands for wildlife purposes, including public hunting grounds. It has also greatly improved the general standard of performance by the participating states.

The number of hunters in the United States has more than doubled within the past 15 years; the number of anglers has more than trebled. The $4,000,000,000 they spend has become big business.

Besides the sport, the companionship, the healthful recreation, what do the hunters bring home? In 1942, according to statistics collected by the U. S. Fish and Wildlife Service, the game bag exceeded 141,000,000 pieces, weighing 255,404,000 pounds (dressed). This was the first time such national figures had been compiled; they amazed everybody. The big-game animals totaled 647,000, and included 598,000 deer, 34,000 elk, 9000 antelopes, and 5000 bears. There were 71,000,000 small-game animals, which included 46,000,000 rabbits and 22,000,000 squirrels. The upland game birds aggregated over 41,000,000, including 22,000,000 quail; 15,000,000 pheasants; 3,000,000 grouse; 900,000 partridges; and 47,851 wild turkeys. Migratory game birds, other than waterfowl, aggregated 11,500,000, among them being over 11,000,000 doves and 203,000 woodcocks. There were over 16,000,000 ducks and 440,000 geese in the waterfowl bag. The trappers that year collected almost $100,000,000 for their furs. The harvest of game meat was enough to provide a pound daily for 700,000 soldiers for an entire year—not bad for a country that was "shot out" at the turn of the century.

What of future hunting for the average American sportsman? As already indicated, wildlife habitats have been shrinking, especially on the 6,000,000 farms and ranches, where certain species of small game thrive best. Modern transportation permits a hunter to cover many times the ground he did at the turn of the century. Firearms and other equipment are far superior. Despite the efforts of public agencies and sportsmen's organizations, hunting ethics, and respect for the landowner's rights and property, are at low ebb in many parts of the country. Landowners are becoming more restive and trespass laws more severe.

Why this growing mistrust by farmers? How far-reaching is it? What is the danger to our American way of providing hunting for the masses?

The fault lies chiefly with groups of thoughtless, sometimes greedy, strangers from distant places who annually invade the farms and ranches. They are mostly urban dwellers who do not understand farm problems. Some of them ignore the common courtesies which should be extended to every host.

The farmers and ranchers of America can easily increase game crops on their lands. By the same token they can make them barren of game, or practically so. The hunting fraternity must regain the good will of the landowners. Unless they do, in a few decades our hunting will revert to the European system. Then only those with private shooting preserves will enjoy good hunting for pheasants, rabbits, quail, and other species which prosper on cultivated lands.

The current situation is reminiscent of that which faced hunters in the Old World five or more centuries ago. In the present instance the "wilderness dwellers" are those who live in large centers of population. The sport of hunting for the masses is truly "at the crossroads" now. It is far more serious than when the president of the American Game Association made his dire prediction almost 40 years ago.

All game departments are gravely concerned. Many of them are spending large sums to set up public hunting grounds in co-operation with farmers and ranches. Encouraging progress is being made, but the hunters themselves must help to save the American system. If they fail to eradicate the troublesome elements in their midst, their country cousins will do it for them—and in a way they will not like.

What else is graying the temples of game officials? Probably one of the most disturbing is disregard for the common rules of safety. Recklessness with firearms is alarming all concerned. Far too many present-day hunters lack an intimate knowledge of their weapons. The information available in this *Encyclopedia* should materially aid them to understand the functions of each part of a shotgun or rifle. How to hunt safely is fully as important as what kind of firearm or ammunition to use.

So long as hunters are greedy to make kills, and will in their haste endanger their own lives, there is cause for concern. But when they will maim or kill a fellow hunter for a deer, a bear, or even a woodchuck or squirrel, *it is time to call a halt!* These things happen; they are not imaginary. Many hunters even fail to use the safety mechanisms which thoughtful manufacturers have provided, and self-inflicted injuries are common. Safety campaigns must be intensified. Offenders who shoot others must be ferreted out and prevented from hunting again. But notwithstanding the recklessness of the few, *hunting is still the safest mass-participation sport in America.*

With increasing gun pressure hunters must practice more self-restraint; each must kill less than in former years. They must each do more to assure a game supply. And those worthy to be called true sportsmen must see to it that those who are irresponsible or unsafe are forced to conduct themselves properly, or that they are eliminated from the field.

Fortunately, more and more hunters are enjoying trap, skeet, rifle, and pistol shooting as off-season sports. More of them are getting deeper satisfaction from their camping trips, their outdoor cookery, their gunsmithing, than they do from the game they bag. And increasing numbers of them every year are reverting to the weapons of Robin Hood to get more sport from their hunting. Some are even trying to revive one of the oldest of hunting methods, falconry. These are all evidences that the spirit of true sportsmanship still lives.

Incidentally, the measure of a "true sportsman," written anonymously in 1835, is worth repeating.

> "The true sportsman is confined to no particular rank in society, but may be found in the lowest as well as in the highest circles. He hunts . . . because he has an innate and ardent love of healthful exercise. . . . He is a philosopher. . . . The same *discriminating judgment* which he exhibits in the ordinary affairs of life he carries with him into the field".

And we might add, he respects the rights of his fellow man, he observes the rules of safety, and he sees to it that those who come after him may also enjoy good hunting.

Numerous magazines and books are now published for the sportsman, and special columns in our best daily newspapers. The literature on the subject of hunting is voluminous. But in spite of the ramified history of the world's oldest sport, there apparently has never been for this field of human interest a multiple standard reference work presenting the basic factual information to which every hunter can turn for instruction, for the establishment of fact against myth.

THE HUNTER'S ENCYCLOPEDIA is, to the best of our knowledge, the first attempt to assemble, within the covers of a single volume, this nucleus of basic information. To its compilation have been drawn the resources of research institutions, industrial organizations, governmental agencies, and the pens of a great staff of distinguished writers and editors.

The development of this *Encyclopedia* represents an effort of international co-operation which has functioned smoothly. The Dominion Government of Canada and its several provinces have co-operated freely, as have the Federal and state agencies of the United States and of Mexico. They have contributed generously, and otherwise facilitated the development of this unusual reference volume.

This *Encyclopedia* is more than a manual of instruction in the techniques of hunting. In a larger sense it is an instrument of education in conservation precepts and the elements of intelligent sportsmanship. For the novice, as well as the old-timer, here is the information on how, where, and what to hunt; which weapons to use and how they may be used safely; how to dress, how to camp and cook, and what to do with trophies.

It will serve as an authoritative reference for all phases of hunting, and give those who love the chase a broader and more intimate acquaintance with the biological and ecological relationships of our wild creatures. Based on my observations as a game administrator for a quarter of a century, I predict that this unusual volume will occupy in hunting literature a position comparable to the great reference works in the professions.

THE HUNTER'S ENCYCLOPEDIA is destined to become the silent, though ever useful and entertaining, companion of every sportsman who is fortunate to number it among his cherished possessions. The publishers are to be congratulated upon having added this long-needed volume to the literature of the sporting field.

SETH GORDON.

*Harrisburg, Pennsylvania*
*June 1, 1948*

# BIG GAME

## HISTORY OF NORTH AMERICAN BIG GAME

**Rise of the Patriarchs.** Generally, only the external appearance and the obvious facts register with the human conscience. The construction, the mechanism under the surface, and the origin, even of familiar things, are accepted usually at face value. Only the specialist can determine true values because he alone knows something of the source, the time, and the labor involved to accomplish the finished product. Before any slight conception of the infinite value of North American big game can be visualized, it is necessary to learn something of its origin. Our splendid sleek animals of the present day did not just happen so; Nature toiled through countless ages to produce them, her efforts often retarded by failure or the progress of centuries completely wiped out by world catastrophes.

The rise of mammals from the ranks of lower vertebrates began to be noticeable in the early Eocene Age, more than 60,000,000 years ago, but the actual dawn of mammal life came much earlier. Evolution during the early stages was rapid, and soon all great land masses were teeming with life.

North America was a relatively stable continent with a warm climate, both factors conducive to the production of a large and varied fauna. All Eocene mammals bore the stamp of great antiquity. There were some rhinoceroslike creatures and small primitive horses, but most of the animals were grotesque archaic monsters. By the beginning of the Oligocene there had evolved a decided predominance of the modernized mammals over the archaic forms and patterns were now in the making for the magnificent North American big-game animals. But the Oligocene mammals were experimental or in a transitional stage and all were eventually discarded and became extinct. There were many ungulates, both even and odd-toed, and the saber-toothed cats were common.

The Miocene Age brought a great advancement in the variety and the development of hoofed mammals, including many horses, camels, and deer. Native peccaries appeared and the first elephants reached America. Native rhinoceroses died out but were replaced by immigrants from the Old World.

The real modernization of North American big game, however, did not begin to take definite form until the Pliocene. The herds of strange creatures that teemed on the vast plains and in the great forests were going through a stage of modification. The extreme exotic forms were discarded and a competitive race for the survival of the fittest weeded out the weak points. Characteristic of this age was the modernization of the horses, the dying out of the camel-llama type, and the extraordinary migration of the Proboscidea from Asia, the first appearance of American bears, and the presence of a hornless deer, an immigrant from Asia, probably the ancestor of our Virginia deer.

The climax in evolution came when the great drought exterminated the greater part of our North American big game. The broad plains and prairies became burning deserts, the life-giving waters of the lakes and rivers were drained by hot, dry winds and not replenished. Year after year the drought continued in increasing severity until the last remaining water-holes, dried up, were strewn with countless carcasses of the dead. This marked the end of the magnificent fauna of the Pliocene Age. The survivors, gaunt, hardy, resourceful creatures, aided by immigrants from the Old World, replenished this great continent with game.

The passing from the Pliocene to the Pleistocene marked the final link between the primitive types and the direct ancestors of the modern, progressive, big-game animals of this present age.

North American life from the early to the mid-Pleistocene was by far the grandest and most varied mammalian era that ever existed on this continent and equaled, if it did not surpass, that of Africa and Asia. There were deer, elk, moose, pronghorns, peccaries, mastodons, elephants, llamas and camels, yaks, horses, tapirs, American lions, saber-toothed cats, dire wolves, and wild dogs, as well as our modern puma, lynx, wolves, and coyotes.

A land-bridge stretched across the Bering Sea, connecting North America and Asia. Invaders over this open road were bison, musk-ox, caribou, moose, wapiti, mountain sheep, mountain goats, and bears.

The most spectacular of the North American Pleistocene fauna was the *Proboscidians*—the mastodons and the elephants or mammoths, emigrants from the Eastern Hemisphere. Mastodons were the most common, especially in the forests east of the Mississippi and on the Pacific coast. Three different elephants roamed the continent from Alaska south and east to New England; all belonged in the mammoth group. They were cold-country creatures, the largest being the Imperial mammoth.

The *Perissodactyla* or the odd-toed ungulates were abundant in the North American Pleistocene and included tapirs and at least ten different horses, but the rhinoceros had disappeared in the Pliocene Age. The tapirs roamed both coasts but were not found on the plains of the Middle West. The smallest horse, *Equus tau*, was about the size of a Shetland pony and was in marked contrast with *Equus gigantus of* Texas which exceeded the heaviest modern draft horse. The forest horse was a modern-sized species.

Of the *Artiodactyla* or even-toed ungulates, some were indigenous types that had descended from a long line of American ancestors. Some, however, were descendants of ancient emigrants from Asia. The peccaries or American pigs were indigenous, as also were the llamas. The typical American deer, blacktail and Virginia deer, were descendants of a Miocene emigrant. The giant elk-moose was the most outstanding deer of that age but is now extinct. Today, there is only one species of pronghorn, also a descendant of a Miocene emigant, but during the Pleistocene there was a large group, some with four horns. Several different bison were then dominant on the plains as in recent times; most of them were larger than the existing buffalo and some were gigantic like the regal bison, that had a spread of horns over 6 feet. Strangely enough, none of the true antelopes, so abundant in Asia and Africa, were ever included in the American fauna, but the saiga, an aberrant antelope, was here.

This great concentration of big game was easy prey for the hordes of terrible destroyers, many of them larger and more ferocious than any that exist in this present age. The most specialized and formidable of the Pleistocene carnivores was the saber-toothed tiger that spread over practically the whole of North America. It was not only the most treacherous creature of its day but the commonest of the flesh-eaters. Another great cat, the American lion, also preyed on the Pleistocene ungulates. It was larger than any of the living big cats of Africa or Asia but, unlike the saber-toothed tiger, was an immigrant and restricted in distribution. Also found at this time were the pumas, lynxes, and other cats. The great dire wolves, larger than any existing wolf, ranged over the entire continent as well as the gray wolves, the coyotes, and the dogs.

The Pleistocene fauna was cosmopolitan—a great assembly of Old World neotropical and North American types that had a great expectation for a mighty future. Great size was one of their characteristics, but the largest, fiercest, and most grotesque were the forms that disappeared. By mid-Pleistocene the forests and plains of North America teemed with countless herds of big game animals; their numbers were legion. Natural food resources were taxed to the limit.

The first world catastrophe's burning heat and drought came when mammalian fauna had reached a peak. After recovering itself and reaching new heights in development, a second scourge of violent climatic change had an even more disastrous and far-reaching effect on North American big-game animals. This came gradually in an era of ever-increasing cold. The waters of the oceans were transformed into snow and deposited on the polar ice cap. Year after year the great glacier moved southward until it covered some 3,000,000 square miles and in Canadian centers reached a maximum thickness of 10,000 feet. There were four successive glacial invasions and three interglacial periods. After the final retreat, less than one-third of the great Pleistocene mammalian fauna had survived the Ice Age. All elephants, mammoths, and mastodons were gone, as were the American lion, saber-toothed tiger, great dire wolf, giant elk-moose, yak, regal bison, two genera of musk-ox, camels, saiga, four genera of pronghorns, all the horses and tapirs. Six kinds of bears survived, but a huge species related to the spectacle-bear of South America did not.

Great catastrophes where readjustment and resourcefulness are taxed to the limit for existence usually produce improvement and advancement for the survivors. All living big-game animals of North America are the direct descendants of survivors of this glacial age. They have, it would seem, reached the ultimate perfection in every form of beauty, grace, strength, speed, and form.

Hunting prehistoric big game is not a random, haphazard procedure. The geological history of the prospective fields must be known and studied. It is true that collecting fossil vertebrates began in an entirely unsystematic way. Specimens were found on the surface weathered out of the ground by erosion, but such material was fragmentary and incomplete. Present-day palaeontologists, with their skilled workers, go below the surface and excavate huge blocks of matrix containing whole skeletons. Crumbling sections are reinforced and the whole section is carefully transferred to the laboratory. The preparators go to work on freeing the bones from the matrix—a task requiring the utmost skill and care.

Pleistocene mammals lie near the surface, under the topmost layer of earth, and are widely spread over the continent. Their fossil-bearing beds are readily detected by the trained hunter from fragments of semi-fossilized bones that are brought to the surface by erosion or excavation. Gold miners and prospectors have brought to light many well-preserved deposits of prehistoric creatures that had long since perished in quicksands and mire. Many well-preserved Pleistocene specimens have been recovered from the tar or asphalt pits or pools of Southern California. Around the border of these pools the tar hardens by evaporation but there is an indefinite boundary between the hard and soft portions. Many large prehistoric animals frequently found themselves sinking in the tenacious material. The cries uttered in their death struggles as they tried to escape brought many carnivores which, in turn, were caught in the death trap. Individual small pools have recorded hundreds of specimens, mostly wolves, but the bones are disarticulated by the action of the pit and mixed in a mass. Nothing actually remains of the pre-Pleistocene mammals, but as Scott aptly put it, "the original material of the bone or tooth has been more or less completely removed and some mineral substance, commonly silica, has been substituted for it. The substitution has been effected molecule by molecule and so perfectly that the most minute microscopic structure is exactly reproduced." While there is no mathematical ratio, it is generally true that the greater the geological antiquity of a bone, the more completely petrified it is and the greater its fluorine content. Skeletons from the Paleocene and Eocene are usually heavy and dark colored from the infiltration of iron compounds, while Miocene and Pliocene fossil bones are usually light colored. There are many exceptions to this rule;

Valentine fossils (upper Miocene, or lower Pliocene) are often black, and John Day fossils are generally dark brown, while those of the preceding White River are buff, or white. The soft parts of Tertiary mammals are very rarely preserved, but in the Brown Coals of Germany some very interesting examples of carbonized hairs have been found. Recognizable impressions of birds' feathers have been found several times in Mesozoic and Cenozoic shales.

Duration of the Pleistocene Age preceding the glaciers is estimated as 600,000 years. The 12,000 or 15,000 years that have elapsed since the retreat of the last glacier is designated by palaeontologists as "Present Time." How long the present era will last is anyone's guess, but American big game is now living on borrowed time and its future is dependent on the grace of human interest.

## THE LAST STAND

It is well to remember that man himself was cradled and brought up in the lap of nature and that conditions of his emotional sanity instinctively draw him back to the old home. There is an uprush of feeling above the level of average consciousness when he allows the magnetic influence of nature to restore the feeling of peace found on the hunting grounds.

The natural instinct in man to hunt and pit his skill against the cunning of wild creatures was born not only from the necessity to kill that he might eat but also for self-preservation. Today, nature's depleted pastures may seem of little importance to the united labor and scientific world of the great cities, but even here all are dependent on the precarious supply of Nature's bounties. Only time will tell if she will always be able to meet the ever increasing drain on her resources.

Man's struggle for supremacy over the beasts of the fields started some 400,000 years ago. At that time, and for many centuries, he was less destructive to wild life than his competitors the carnivores, and no doubt he himself knew what it was to be hunted. Even in those primitive days man needed a weapon to protect himself and to kill game for food and clothing. He used clubs, dug pits, rolled down rocks, and eventually constructed spears and arrows shot from bows. From primitive times up until the beginning of the 19th century there was game enough in North America for all, and enough on the plains and prairies to feed a nation if it had been carefully husbanded. Away back in the Pliocene Age a great drought had almost annihilated American game; centuries later, in the Pleistocene, glaciers swept the continent again and again, destroying the majority of North American wildlife. But all the catastrophes that nature ever dealt this land never so completely stripped the continent of its fauna as the white man's invasion.

Hunting big game in North America is fast passing into the past tense. Even now in the United States it is practically restricted to a few deer or an occasional bear. The age of big game is approaching its final close. Education and conservation may help delay this day, but the inevitable spread of civilization is rapidly converging over the very last stronghold of wildlife.

Elimination of American big game, as would be expected, began in the northeastern states and soon spread westward. Game was surprisingly abundant until the beginning of the 19th century, but its decline from then on was so rapid that by 1850 practically all the big game in the northeastern states had disappeared except in northern New England.

**Moose.** Published records of the stragglers and rare fugitives missed in the massacre bring vivid memories of the loss that can never be recovered. Moose were one of the first to go in the East. In the Adirondacks moose were numerous in the forties and even the sixties of the last century but were rapidly diminishing in numbers. They apparently survived until 1874, and one was killed on the eastern inlet of Raquette Lake during August 1861. The last moose killed in the Adirondacks seems to have been in 1863. Moose were once common in the Catskills but have been gone since the beginning of the 19th century. Rhoads omitted moose from his list of *Recent Mammals of New Jersey,* but Dr. Schoepf, the distinguished German traveler, mentioned the black moose as having occurred in Northampton County in 1783. The doctor also reported it as numerous in the Allegheny Mountains between what are now Altoona and Pittsburgh. At the beginning of the 18th century moose ranged south into New England, at least as far as southern Massachusetts. Accounts of early travelers give no indication that moose were ever found in Connecticut during historic times. William Wood in his *New England Prospect* (1634) said that there were not many moose at Massachusetts Bay but that 40 miles to the northeast there were many. This was in the vicinity of Plymouth, which is so close to Connecticut that some must have crossed over the border. Moose continued in northern Vermont and New Hampshire until about 1900. There is an official report of moose killed in Wenlock, Essex County, Vt., in 1900. C. F. Jackson in a letter to Ernest Thompson Seton, dated Dec. 12, 1921, wrote, "During the last three weeks a young bull moose has been seen frequently in the town of New Ipswich, N. H. A fairly good photograph was secured and there can be no doubt of the record." Moose now have absolute protection in Maine. In Michigan and Wisconsin moose were comparatively common in recent years and it is not unlikely that individuals are to be found in both states. An estimate of the number of Wyoming moose was set at 1600 in 1924. In Minnesota moose are still found in limited numbers. Colorado had its share of moose but records are only from the remains of animals long dead. In Canada, moose are still common over most of their original range. How these great deer can go galloping up a steep mountainside at high elevation, over the top and down the other side without a single pause, is nothing less than a miracle.

**Wapiti.** The American elk or wapiti were common in New York until about 1836. De Kay wrote in 1842: "The stag is still found in the State of New York but very sparsely and will doubtless be extirpated before many years." A set of wapiti antlers at Letchworth Park, N. Y., were from an animal said to have been killed in Genesee Valley about 1843. Another set, formerly at the Albany Museum, from Cattaraugus County, was also taken in 1843. Wapiti disappeared in the Adirondack wilderness somewhere about 1847. Wapiti survived a little longer in the mountains of Pennsylvania than in New York, and it was here that the eastern wapiti made its last stand. In the Blue Mountains they disappeared about 1800 but were fairly common in the Allegheny Mountains during the early part of the 19th century. In the Academy of Science, Philadelphia, is a set of wapiti antlers from an animal shot by Sherman Devers supposedly in 1853 near Teutonia, McKean County, but they may have come from Cherry Springs in Potter County in 1858. Two bulls were reported killed as late as 1878 but this record is unsubstantiated. John G. Hamersby, apparently a careful observer, reports seeing live wapiti in 1869 and 1870. An Indian, Tim Jacobs, killed a bull in the headwaters of the Clarion River in 1867, but the last individual reported for the state of Pennsylvania appears to have been a young bull killed by John Decker in 1877. The wapiti of the Carolinas, once abundant, disappeared early, leaving no records. In West Virginia wapiti were found at the headwaters of the Tygart and Greenbrier Rivers up until 1875. According to the pictorial accounts of Daniel Boone there were plenty of wapiti when he went there in 1769. Oklahoma was fortunate, as the wapiti lasted there until about 1891. In Tennessee there was a splendid herd of wapiti near Nashville in 1894. General William H. Jackson supervised the herd on his estate, "Belle Meade," and did much to preserve the natural fauna of Tennessee. Henry W. Shoemaker, famous historian and authority on vanishing game, saw the herd when he was a guest of the general at that time. The eastern wapiti was fast approaching extinction. It held on in Missouri, its last stand, until about 1898, but all are gone now; not a single complete specimen was preserved for posterity. A few sets of their antlers, it is true, found their way into museums but no one thought to preserve skulls, skeletons, or even the hides. There are still a few wapiti in Arkansas but they were, in all probability, imported from Wyoming. The vast wilderness of the Rocky Mountain chain saved the western wapiti until they were given protection, and where they are still hunted it is under supervision. They have long since gone from the plains and prairies and most of the West Coast region except in parks and reservations.

**Caribou.** Caribou are herd animals, easily killed, and owe their present existence to a northern habitat. Practically all the caribou have been extirpated south of the Canadian border. In the east, south of the St. Lawrence, there are still a few small bands on the Shickshock Mountains in the Gaspé Peninsula, Quebec. They persisted in New Brunswick until recent years but the native stock has apparently all gone now. Originally caribou ranged south to Grafton, Maine. Although this state provided absolute protection for the caribou, they disappeared in 1901; their last stand was at Mount Katahdin. Caribou have been reintroduced in Maine. Percy B. Falding, a veteran guide in the Serpentine River and lake region of New Brunswick, stated that he saw more caribou in the winter of 1927-1928 than he had previously seen for about 20 years. An article in *Forest and Stream* in 1928 stated that in 1927 guides and camp owners in the Moosehead Lake district of northeastern Maine reported having seen an increasing number of caribou during the three previous years. The same article stated that in 1927 over a dozen fair-sized herds of caribou were reported as seen in the district. The thing that most forcibly impressed the man who saw these animals was their excellent condition. In the Allegash River section of northern Maine, also in the winter of 1927-1928, more caribou were reported than at any time during the preceding 25 years. For many years prior to this time caribou were exceedingly scarce in this section, and it was not until 1924 that they began to return. These caribou seem to have been following the rivers from their sources. Particularly is this true of the St. John River. In 1927 a few caribou were seen on the upper reaches of this stream. By 1928 they had extended their range over almost two-thirds of the course of the river, or about 350 miles. It is likely that they will soon be found near its mouth, as the movement is surely southward by easy stages. Some of the caribou apparently have deviated from the paralleling river systems in favor of a more southerly course, and are heading into eastern Maine. From the above accounts by Percy Falding it seems likely that caribou are increasing in numbers in the sparsely-inhabited sections of northern Maine, and the future bears a certain amount of assurance for the perpetuation of the animal in this state. In Newfoundland, caribou are still found on certain parts of the island. In Massachusetts, Vermont, and New Hampshire the caribou have been gone for more than a century. Caribou probably still persist on the Upper Peninsula in Michigan and if given careful supervision may last for some time. The caribou that occurred in northern Wisconsin in the early days are all gone now. Minnesota has reintroduced caribou but the original animals were fairly common in their day. Herrick encountered caribou about the headwaters of Whiteface River and along the St. Louis River near Knife Falls in 1884. The original stock was extirpated in this state about 1930. Caribou are still plentiful and still hunted in the Canadian Rockies. They are also fairly abundant in Quebec and Ontario but the greatest concentration of caribou—and of all American wild game, for that matter—is on the great barrens of northern Canada.

**Bison.** The Pennsylvania bison, like the Eastern elk, has gone, leaving nothing but a sorry list of records. No specimen was preserved and not even a hide or skull found its way into a museum. Henry W. Shoemaker, the best living authority, states that the last buffalo in Pennsylvania was killed in 1810 by John Yutsey, a Bessarabian pioneer in the glades of Somerset County. Earlier that same year Frederick Stamm killed a bison on the Juniata River near Lewistown and Jacob Stower killed several here at an earlier date. Some records have it that the last Pennsylvania buffalo was killed in Somerset County by Joseph Shank in 1810. The forests of Pennsylvania contained thousands of buffalo as late as 1750, but 50 years later the great herds had gone. In 1704 Buffalo Springs, 55 miles west of Philadelphia, was the eastern boundary of the range, and many bones have been excavated from near the springs. One of the favorite fording places for the bison to cross the Susquehanna River was Buffalo Creek, about 20 miles north of Harrisburg.

The bison lingered a little longer in West Virginia than in Pennsylvania. The last record for the state was a bison shot in 1825 on the headwaters of the Tygart and Greenbrier Rivers. In Virginia bison are recorded as seen in Tidewater at the beginning of the 18th century, 150 years ago.

The plains of central and western New York teemed with bison in the early days. A salt deposit at Onondaga was a favorite visiting point for the herds. The great slaughter of New York buffalo, when 10,000 were massacred, occurred in 1790. Thomas Ashe, who witnessed the destruction, placed the locality as a salt spring in Clarion County but many other writers locate the slaughter at Syracuse.

Kentucky also teemed with bison in the early days, and they were still plentiful in that state until 1769. The Oklahoma bison were destroyed at an early date. Texas had a large share of bison but they were all gone by 1890. Indiana was not so fortunate with its bison, and although herds of about 500 animals still persisted in 1792, as recorded by John Heckewelder, a Moravian missionary, there were none left by 1835.

How the countless herds of bison were banished from the plains and prairies in so short a time is an example of man's lust to kill and his greed for personal gain. The American Indian for centuries depended on the bison for a livelihood and although he annually took a large toll of the bison they not only held their own but the herds increased. To the white man the herds of bison were commercially valued for hides, tongues, and tallow. The building of the Union Pacific and Kansas Pacific railroads from the Missouri River westward cut right through the bison country and brought the beginning of the most drastic and wasteful slaughter of big game that the world has ever known. The railroads now not only furnished convenient access to the bison but transportation for the hides, meat, and tongues. At the auction sales of buffalo hides at Fort Worth, Texas, in 1870, hundred of thousands were sold in a few days. Buffalo killing became a profession. Some killed only for the tongues, while others slaughtered for the hides or meat. Professional buffalo killers slaughtered from 40 to 60 buffalo a day and from 1000 to 3000 in a season. In the Medicine Lodge district alone, 210,000 buffalo were reported killed in two months. By 1873, there were thousands of buffalo hunters. The market was glutted with buffalo products, hides fell to $1.25, the best cuts of meat to one cent a pound—and the rest of the meat was valueless.

The Indians complained bitterly of the wanton slaughter of bison by the white man and they hated the hunters. In 1867, they obtained a treaty whereby no white hunter should trespass in the territory south of the Arkansas River. The Indians zealously fought for the right to preserve the bison in their territory, but the treaty was soon broken. The enormous slaughter north of the Arkansas soon made buffalo hunting unprofitable. In 1874, the hunters invaded the Indian Territory and when attacked were given military protection. The mighty southern herds were eliminated during the winter of 1877 and 1878, when over 100,000 were slaughtered. Except for a few individuals, there were no survivors. The last individual in Kansas was killed in 1879 at "Point of Rocks" along the old Santa Fé Trail west of Dodge City; its skull is still in the Beeson Museum at Dodge City.

In the fall of 1878, the valley leading to Buffalo Springs, Texas, was teeming with buffalo, but that fall the hide hunters moved in. The last survivors here were four killed in 1889. After the complete annihilation of the southern herds, buffalo hunters turned their attention to the northern herds or the bison north of the railroad. Destruction here was more rapid. As early as 1876, one-year consignments from Fort Benton numbered 80,000 hides, but it was in 1880 that the shameful slaughter got under way. The extension of the Northern Pacific Railroad went through the very center of the remaining buffalo country, lands formerly dedicated to the Indians. The Indians objected and, as usual, military support was given to the white man and the buffalo hunters. Fifty thousand buffalo hides were shipped on the Northern Pacific in 1881 and the number jumped to 200,000 in 1882, but had dropped to 100,000 in 1883.

The gruesome story of a herd, comprising 50,000 or 80,000 buffalo, that was slaughtered crossing the Yellowstone at Fort Keagh in 1883 has been told many times. In the fall of that year the last herd, numbering about 10,000 head, was found in North Dakota. The first day, more than 1000 animals were killed; by the middle of November the herd had been ruthlessly slaughtered. This marked the end of the great herds; a few scattered individuals survived for a few years longer.

At the head of Dismal River in Nebraska, Captain Luther H. North discovered a band of 36 bison in 1882 and although he and his party succeeded in killing only one, Indians finished the job in the fall of the same year.

In 1889, about 30 bison were seen in Wyoming, east of the Red Desert, all were promptly killed except a few that escaped into Yellowstone Park. The last of the wild plains bison was probably a small herd that ranged Lost Park near Bison Peak, Park County, Colorado. They were protected by ranchers and cattlemen but poaching of individuals had wiped them out by February 1897.

The bison reached its lowest ebb in 1895 when the total number of plains bison was reduced to about 800 including those in captivity. A census of pure-blood bison in North America, taken in 1929, showed the herds had increased to 18,376. Calculated estimates of the original numbers of bison in North America have placed the figure at between 60,000,000 and 75,000,000.

**Deer.** Deer reached a low ebb in the middle of the 19th century. By 1880 the whitetail was almost unknown in Pennsylvania and had been practically exterminated in Connecticut about 1850. Given reasonable protection, the whitetail has re-established itself in Connecticut and in most of the eastern states. Pennsylvania unfortunately restocked with animals from widely separated regions, resulting in an inferior representation of its native whitetail deer.

**Musk-ox.** The original number of musk-ox in the American Arctic was never very great, probably less than 1,000,000 at their peak. That the musk-ox continued on the tundra of northern Alaska until about 1850 is a conclusion based on reports by reliable Eskimos and on remains found in native middens. The last musk-ox seen west of Dolphin and Union Straits were killed in March 1902 by a party of Alaskan Eskimos who made a long trip southeast to Darnley Bay where they killed two herds totaling 27 musk-ox. In 1930 a herd of white faced musk-ox from Greenland were imported by the United States Biological Survey and repatriated in Alaska. This herd is now located on Nunivak Isle in the Bering Sea and seems to be increasing in numbers. Although given total protection, Eskimos and Indians continued to poach on the musk-ox preserves. Probably the greatest concentration of musk-ox today in continental Canada is along the Hanbury and Thelon Rivers. Goodwin in 1936 counted 200 head of musk-ox in this region including two herds numbering 50 and 60 individuals. The present status of the musk-ox:

| | |
|---|---|
| Continental Canada | 500 |
| Prince of Wales Island | 1,500 |
| Axel Heiberg Island (east side only) | 1,000 |
| Melville Island | 4,000 |
| Cornwallis Island | 200 |
| Bathhurst Island | 1,500 |
| Victoria Island | 20 |
| Devon Island (north side only) | 200 |
| Ellesmere Island | 4,000 |
| Greenland | 10,000 |
| TOTAL | 22,920 |

**Pronghorn.** Fortunately the American antelope or pronghorn, having little or no commercial value, fared better than the bison. Its meat was not desirable for marketing nor did it carry a head of horns to be coveted by trophy hunters. What was considered a conservative estimate of pronghorns in 1800 placed the number of animals in North America at about 40,000,000. The inevitable shrinkage in numbers during the 19th century, however, was so rapid that by 1908 Dr. T. S. Palmer of the Biological Survey calculated, on figures obtainable at the time, a total of the United States, Canadian, and Mexican pronghorns as less than 30,000. A 1922-1924 census, published in detail by Dr. E. W. Nelson, given in the table below shows that there were approximately 30,000 pronghorns still in existence at that date. (See also p. 14.)

| REGION | NUMBER OF PRONGHORNS | REGION | NUMBER OF PRONGHORNS |
|---|---|---|---|
| Arizona | 651 | Canada: | |
| California | 1,057 | Alberta | 1,030 |
| Colorado | 1,233 | Saskatchewan | 297 |
| Idaho | 1,485 | | |
| Kansas | 8 | TOTAL, Canada | 1,327 |
| Montana | 3,027 | Mexico: | |
| Nebraska | 187 | Coahuila | 600 |
| Nevada | 4,253 | Chihuahua | 700 |
| New Mexico | 1,682 | Sonora | 595 |
| North Dakota | 225 | Lower California | 500 |
| Oklahoma | 23 | | |
| Oregon | 2,039 | TOTAL, Mexico | 2,395 |
| South Dakota | 680 | | |
| Texas | 2,407 | Summary: | |
| Utah | 670 | United States | 26,604 |
| Wyoming | 6,977 | Canada | 1,327 |
| | | Mexico | 2,395 |
| TOTAL, United States | 26,604 | GRAND TOTAL | 30,326 |

**Mountain Goat.** The mountain goat is the one exception that defied man's attempt to eliminate North American big game. It still inhabits most, if not all, of its rightful range and in numbers comparable to those of 400 years ago. A census for 1922 by the Bureau of Forestry gives the number of goats in National Forests as Washington 1550, Idaho 4148, Montana 2525, and to this can be added Glacier Park 3500, making a total of 11,721. This does not include the total of all goats ranging in North America or the United States. In 1925, Seton placed the white goat population in the United States at 15,000 and the total in North America as 1,000,000 for primitive times; the 1946 big-game census gave a United States total of 15,700.

**Bighorn Sheep.** The primitive number of bighorn in North America has been estimated at between 1,500,000 and 2,000,000. This does not include the slender horned sheep of the north. In some districts the bighorn have been extirpated. The Black Hills was formerly sheep country and the bighorn continued there until about 1887; the last survivor, according to Howard Eaton, was killed here in 1899. The Boone and Crockett Club of New York made a census of the American bighorn in 1915 and published the following valuable statistics:

"In the fall of 1913, probably 3000 or 4000 or more exist in the Desert ranges of Arizona. Some still remain in the Santa Catalina Mountains, north of Tucson. Though protected by a close season, prospectors, Indians, and others going into the mountains indifferently shoot them for meat. In spite of this, they are holding their numbers. More investigations in the Grand Canyon corroborate the numbers suggested in the Committee's last report.

"In California, Nelson's sheep exist in numbers in the mountains about Death Valley, and in less numbers along the lower Colorado River. Here, for 30 years the sheep have at least held their own. In the high Sierras running through Inyo County, some 200 sheep have been observed in different bands. There are probably many more. There are sheep in the San Jacinto Mountains.

"Mountain sheep were formerly abundant in the Warner Mountains and the Steen Mountains in south central Oregon, but a careful search in these ranges in 1914 failed to discover any traces of them—only vague reports of their presence. In limited areas in eastern Oregon there are still fair numbers of them in certain localities. In Nevada, small numbers exist in nearly all the desert ranges in the southern part of the state. Small numbers are also known to range in the Toiyabe range in central Nevada, but conditions there are not hopeful for their survival.

"In Colorado, sheep seem to be increasing, and in some parts of the state, have become extraordinary tame, even coming down the mountainsides in winter to feed in the towns and about the ranches with the cattle. These sheep may eventually afford a supply to restock other areas of the country. The Forest Service estimates that there are 7230 sheep in the National Forests of Colorado.

"In Wyoming, sheep are believed to be slowly increasing, especially in the north and south forks of the Shoeshone River in the game preserve. In the Booneville National Forest, the severe winters, poor winter range, and predatory animals seem to be causing a decrease. The Forest Supervisor there reports that he commonly finds coyote tracks following the trail of sheep in the snow. A small band still exists, and there are about 160 on the Big Horn Mountains. They appear to have become extinct with the last year on the Medicine Bow Peak. In the Yellowstone Park, the number is about what it was [300].

"A few sheep still exist in Texas and New Mexico. For the present sheep should enjoy a close season everywhere in the United States. Large numbers of sheep occupy the desert ranges of Lower California, extending almost the entire length of the Peninsula. Large numbers are found also on nearly all the ranges of western Sonora, growing scarcer a hundred miles south.

"It is clear that, in the United States, desert sheep hold their numbers better than the northern variety.

"At present the desert sheep is apparently increasing in some sections of its range, notably the desert ranges in Inyo County [California] and stationary or decreasing in others, as in the desert portions of the more southerly counties, San Bernardino, Riverside, and Imperial. There are, fortunately, some large bands which promise well, and which at least indicate that there is no cause for concern over the immediate future of the species within the state."

Seton added estimates from official census figures of the game in National Forests in 1922 and estimated the number of bighorn sheep in the United States as follows (see also p. 91):

| | |
|---|---|
| Arizona | 3,500 |
| California | 3,500 |
| Nevada | 500 |
| New Mexico | 500 |
| Utah | 1,000 |
| Colorado | 8,000 |
| Texas | 500 |
| Wyoming (incl. Yellowstone) | 4,000 |
| Montana (incl. Glacier Park) | 5,000 |
| Idaho | 1,500 |
| TOTAL | 28,000 |

**Peccary.** As late as the beginning of the 1880's peccaries were abundant in Texas, Arizona, and New Mexico. In the early 1890's, according to Mearns, they were still common though their numbers had been greatly reduced in southwestern Texas and in Pima County, Arizona. This was many years ago and it can be assumed that only a few stragglers are now left north of the Mexican border.

**Carnivores.** With the rapid destruction of big game, especially in the East, the large predators turned to domestic stock for sustenance. Large bounties were soon offered and paid for their destruction and it was not long before they too were among the missing. The black bear has fared better than most carnivores, partly because he is less predatory than most of the flesh eaters, partly because he hibernates when he would be most easy to hunt. He has, of necessity, departed from thickly populated districts and his numbers have been greatly reduced over his range south of the Canadian border. In fact, his status in most states could be briefly summed up in the statement: "Once common but now almost but not quite exterminated."

**Mountain Lion.** The Adirondack wilderness appears to have been the last stronghold of the mountain lion in the northeastern states. Several were reported killed about 1877. G. S. Miller stated that from 1871 to 1897, 107 mountain lions were officially killed in the Adirondacks. The last record for the state was 1894 when game protector R. B. Nicholas saw a cougar seven miles above Indian Lake Corners on the Cedar River. In the Catskill Mountains there were lions until about 1865. In 1814 one was reported killed near White Plains in Westchester County, N. Y.

In Pennsylvania bounties were paid for "panther" in 1866 and two were killed in Clearfield County in 1891; the last recorded kill of a mountain lion in this state was in 1904. Mountain lions have not been found in New Jersey for over 100 years; the last was destroyed between 1830-1840. Their favorite range in New Jersey was in cedar swamps along the coast. In Massachusetts and Connecticut mountain lions were gone by the beginning of the 19th century. A few remained in Vermont and New Hampshire until about 1888, but the last cougar reported killed in Vermont was shot by Alexander Crowell near Brainard, November 24, 1881. This specimen weighed 182 pounds and is in the State Collection at Montpelier. Two were reported in 1907 as having been seen 50 miles from Norcross, Maine, and one was shot in that state September 1, 1906. Two men, while hunting near Andover, Maine, in 1891 saw and shot at a cougar.

Mountain lions were plentiful in the Carolinas up to the early 1860's but they continued in West Virginia until 1882. Florida is the only state in the east where the mountain lion still has a general distribution, but even here the country is being drained and the mountain lion will be the first of the big game to go. In Louisiana the mountain lions were not particularly rare in 1904 and one was occasionally seen in Arkansas up to 1920. A few mountain lions still haunt the Texas ranges but bounty hunters will eventually eliminate them.

The Black Hills of South Dakota was a great range for the mountain lion until 1887; very few, if any, now remain in even the wildest parts. Theodore Roosevelt, when he visited Colorado in 1901, killed 12 mountain lions at Meeker, and in 1906 Henry Honenkrat killed eight in Idaho. In Utah, Wyoming, and Montana, as well as the other Rocky Mountain states, the mountain lion is verging on the border of extirpation.

The record on elimination in California is a sample of the rapidity with which the mountain lion is disappearing in the West. Between 1907 and 1919, 3628 individuals were officially killed in the state. For the year 1918, 85 were destroyed and in 1919, 111 California mountain lions were killed in three months. The population of mountain lions in California is now estimated at about 575; for all of North America, north of the Rio Grande, at less than 5000.

**Jaguar.** This big spotted cat once ranged north to California and probably Colorado. North of the Mexican border it is now restricted to southern Arizona, southern New Mexico, and southern Texas, and even here it is considered a rare fugitive. In California, Merriam wrote of an old chief of the Kammeri tribe who told him that in the Cuyamaia Mountains in San Diego County, the "tiger" was well known to the Indians. James O. Pattie killed a jaguar on December 12, 1829, on an island of the Colorado River below its junction with the Helay, and in 1855 "Grizzly Adams" (J. C. Adams) discovered a family of jaguars in a rocky cavern on the south side of Tejon Pass in the Tehachapi Mountains. In Colorado, Rufus B. Sage stated that while camped on Soublet's Creek on the headwaters of the Platte in December 1843 one of his party saw a strange animal which from the description could have been a jaguar. In Arizona, I. E. Roberts saw a jaguar cross the Silver Bell Highway three miles north of Tucson in September 1920. In January 1920, Stanley R. Graham or one of his party from Chicago killed a large jaguar at Riricon Mountain,

Arizona. In New Mexico, Nat Straw killed a jaguar on Taylor Creek, Socorro County, N. M., in May 1900. In Texas, the jaguar was common until 1857. Vernon Bailey killed a specimen near London, Kimberly County, Texas, in the spring of 1910. Jaguars were still found along the Rio Grande as late as 1915.

**Wolf.** The timber or gray wolf (not to be confused with the coyote) originally ranged over the entire North American continent. Wolves appear to have persisted in the northeastern states in fair numbers until toward the end of the 19th century. Between the years 1871 and 1882 bounties were paid in New York State for 45 wolf scalps. Reuben Cary killed a wolf at Brandreth Lake, Hamilton County, in November 1893. This apparently, was the last survivor of the Adirondack packs. The following three later records of wolves killed in New York are probably of stray animals from Canada: one at Stephentown, November 21, 1902; one at Port Byron, 11 miles north of Auburn, November 21, 1906; and one near Whiteface Mountain, Wilmington, about February 1923. In Pennsylvania wolves were not uncommon in the 1880's. Stragglers were killed or reported as seen prior to about 1898. In southern New England they disappeared about 1850. The last wolf in Connecticut was killed near Bridgeport in 1839 by Moses Berkley; one other had been killed in 1832 at Newtown by Aaron Glover. The last New Hampshire individual was killed in the White Mountains in 1887. A wolf was shot by J. W. White at Norway, Maine, during the winter of 1908-1909. This, according to acounts, was the third wolf killed in Oxford County within a few years. Recently examined old records for Butler County, dated from 1807 to 1845, but omitting the ten years from 1815 to 1825, show that from 1807 to 1831 bounties were paid in this county on 235 wolves and one cougar. After this date wolf payments terminated abruptly, except for one paid for a wolf killed in 1840. The records showed payments up to 1845, however, for large numbers of wildcats, and for red and gray foxes. The largest number of wolves brought in on one day was on May 20, 1825, when bounties were paid for ten, killed by John Pollock.

Elimination of wolves in the Rocky Mountain region from the Canadian border to Mexico was so rapid that while not uncommon over the whole region in 1915, they were completely wiped out by 1941. A few still persist in northern Minnesota, Wisconsin, Michigan and Oregon. Red wolves, west of the Mississippi, are sparsely distributed over Texas, Arkansas, Missouri, Oklahoma and Louisiana. The Forest Service in 1939 estimated the following number of wolves in the National Forests: Montana, 28; Idaho, 48; Wyoming, 1; Arizona, 25; New Mexico, 30; Nevada, 10; Utah, 20; California, 48; Oregon, 130; Washington, 10; Arkansas, 87; Louisiana, 95; Oklahoma, 50; South Carolina, 2; Texas, 237; Michigan, 140; Minnesota, 610; Missouri, 450; Wisconsin, 230; Alaska, 1110.

Some idea as to the former abundance of the gray wolf can be gleaned from the records of numbers killed. George Smith, a noted Pennsylvanian hunter, killed 500 wolves during his lifetime (1827-1898) and 13 wolves in one day. Items in *Trappers of New York,* by J. R. Simmons (1850), show that Thomas Meacham of Hopkinton, N. Y., killed 214 wolves and Nathaniel Foster of Herkimer County collected bounty on 300 wolves. Between 1901-1905, 498,000 wolf pelts were taken in the United States and Canada. In four months ending October 9, 1909, 1581 wolves were taken in Minnesota. In Wyoming, bounties were paid on 2140 wolves each year for 1897 and 1898. Wyoming paid bounties on 20,819 wolves in the 11 years prior to 1908. Seton placed what he considered a conservative estimate of the primitive number of wolves in North America at 2,000,000.

**Grizzly Bear.** The original range of the grizzly once extended through the West from Mexico north to Alaska, but today it is not found south of the Canadian border except in parks and reservations. Dr. C. H. Merriam in 1922 published an estimate on the grizzlies left in the United States at that time, and in summing up listed a total of 800 grizzlies left in Wyoming, Montana, and Colorado. The history of the grizzly in the United States is not clearly recorded. Pioneers and hunters claimed they saw a dozen of these monsters in a day's march. Newberry wrote of the grizzlies in 1857 and remarked: "They are rather unpleasantly abundant in many parts of the Coast Range and Sierra Nevada; in California, where large numbers are killed by the hunters, and where not a few hunters are annually killed by the bears." Rogers' *History of Colusa County* states that when the county was first settled it was not uncommon to see 30 or 40 grizzly bears in one day. In Canada and the Northwest, the range of the grizzly has shrunk but it is far from exterminated. In British Columbia, one can still count on getting a grizzly, and in the Yukon conditions are even better. Alaska still has a fair number of grizzlies as well as brown bears, but the future here is not too bright; the population increase is having its usual effect in annihilating the big game.

## BIG GAME OF TOMORROW

How, when, or why American big game vanished is past history. Regrettable and shameful as it must now seem even to those left who aided in its destruction, neither remorse nor wishful thinking can make restitution. American big game in its entirety has gone, never to return. The bison and the pronghorn can never roam the plains and prairies again in countless millions. These once-rich, fertile lands are now dedicated to the raising of grain for the hungry people of the world and no one could wish it otherwise. The howl of the timber wolf will never again awaken the echoes among the rocky crags of our mountain peaks, nor will the scream of a cougar again freeze the blood of those who wander in the wilderness. The future from a sportsman's point of view is not bright. At present the whitetail will continue to give sport to the hunter for many years to come. Somehow this ubiquitous deer has responded quickly to protection and actually thrives better on abandoned farm lands than in the forests that once covered the same territory.

Bear, at least in the eastern states, are only an occasional trophy. Mule deer, while still plentiful in some areas, have a doubtful future. They are migrating animals and at present do not have an adequate method of protection to assure a permanent breeding stock. There is an open season on elk in some states but only a favored few hunters can hope to get an elk. It is hoped, however, that the future will not be quite so dismal. The human race, it is assumed, is intelligent enough to cease the waste of wildlife that has gone on in this country since the white man came. But can we reverse our destructive policies before it is too late, and start replenishing the dissipated portions of the renewable resources? It is obvious that the present measures of restrictive conservation laws cannot restore game nor halt its gradual shrinkage of numbers.

There is a new era of carefully planned and scientifically organized measures slowly taking form for game management. Powerful organizations are putting renewed efforts behind this scheme to save American game. Included are such institutions as the American Museum of Natural History, the New York Zoological Society, the Boone and Crockett Club (one of the most active), the American Game Protective Association, the American Bison Society, the National Association of Audubon Societies, the United States Fish and Wildlife Service, the National Park Service, the United States Department of Interior, the American Society of Mammalogists, the Emergency Conservation Commission, and many others. To the efforts of these splendid protectors of wildlife can be credited the remnants of the game we have today. Had this same school been given a free hand 60 years ago, supported by the power of the United States Government, to administer the management of wildlife, the story would be a different and pleasanter one.

Times are so forcibly and rapidly changing that unless a united and unrestricted national or continental organization system for game economy is adopted in the near future it will be too late. The usefulness of individual enterprises, private organizations, clubs, and scientific institutions and societies as a means to conserve wildlife is not enough to meet the emergencies that continually crop up. All too often the combined efforts of these organizations, teamed together with their wealth of information and experience, are overruled by big commercial combines. Forests are denuded and the game destroyed to meet a temporary demand, and shortsightedness causes watersheds to be destroyed, inviting drought, erosion, famine, and poverty for many farmers.

No one can entirely foresee the future necessity or the value of our wildlife resources either from a recreational or monetary point of view, but no one can deny the fact that once American forests and wildlife are gone not even time can restore the damage. Given all the factors and support necessary for adequate management of big game, the husbandry of wild life is a manifold business that is neither stable nor progressive. Its followers must be kept constantly in touch with life as it is lived in nature. In what may perhaps be called the keenly analytic atmosphere of modern zoology there is no risk that anyone will fail to appreciate the abstractions made when studying conservation problems or solutions to parts of it; but there is all too often a risk of the original picture's being forgotten. In short, wildlife, its drama of life and relation of the living creature to its environment, is not taken into consideration.

Given proper protection and handling, game will grow and replenish itself. Man can co-operate and assist to some extent but his well-meant interference in the actual process is harmful. He cannot restore wildlife once it has gone nor can he revive a species that has shrunk below the danger point. Air, sunshine, soil, and water are the basis of animal life, but it took millions of years to produce the forests and prairies with the co-ordinated wild game. When the natural conditions in an area are disrupted the result is great changes in the entire animal population and usually its complete annihilation. It matters little whether the change is due to overgrazing by stock on the forest ranges, a forest fire that sweeps for miles destroying all in its path, or man's remaking the earth's face to suit his needs—cutting down a forest, draining lakes and marshes, or plowing grasslands; all wild game must suffer by it. The management and building of a national game conservation program is an intricate, complex task. Until it is fortified with the good will of the public and given government support unhampered by political influence, progress will be slow.

Reforestation as a game-sanctuary measure is much more than planting a large area with trees. Such an area would be negative, or at least passive, and could not begin to support the life expected of it. Obviously there must also come all the leaf- and fruit-bearing shrubs that under natural forest conditions would be there. To hold the game population to the number that can be supported in a given area might not seem particularly difficult; but such a problem is often complex and cannot be measured by any set, fast rule. Many regions have an overabundance of forage in the summers but a great shortage of winter forage. In the case of non-migrating game, the population must be gauged by the available winter forage and not the summer bounty.

There is one abstract in the propagation of wild life, especially among the deer, that has received little or no attention and will not be popular with the sportsman. The aspiration of every hunter is to get the largest head. Killing of the big bucks each year must, of necessity, in regions where hunters are numerous, eliminate to a great extent most of the older animals and leave an abundance of young bucks for breeding and restocking purposes. This should, it would seem, have a tendency to improve the breeding stock, but, as it happens, it has the reverse effect. The young bucks come into rut at a later date than the older sires; nature intended it that way. But in the absence of the fully mature bucks the does are mated late, the fawns also arrive late, and by the following fall they have not developed sufficiently to cope adequately with a hard winter.

Reforestation is a necessity, but restocking of game often is worse than no game at all. If careful husbandry of natural resources is coupled with protection, game will usually return to an area if it is possible to exist there. It will take time, but the prospects are promising where a species has not been exterminated. This is well illustrated in Connecticut. Fifty years ago the whitetail was completely extirpated in this New England state. Today, through careful husbandry, the native whitetail deer can be seen at any time in almost any part of the state. They are fine animals, returned of their own volition from neighboring states. Pennsylvania deer disappeared at about the same time as those in Connecticut, but Pennsylvania restocked, bringing in purchased animals secured in states all the way from Maine to Florida. They have interbred and multiplied, but this mongrel breed is but a poor copy of the original Pennsylvania stock; the antlers are small and puny.

The future prospects of big-game hunting in Canada are brighter than in the United States. Though the conservation measures of our northern neighbor were enacted at a later date than ours, in terms of animal population they are far ahead of us. Canada had and still has the advantage of having a comparatively small population. There is real big-game hunting to be had in Canada and with the possible exception of Alaska, the finest outside of Africa in the world today. Having learned from our experience the disastrous results of leaving wildlife unprotected, Canada set aside great areas for the safeguarding of its big game—vast reservoirs of wildlife that will assure these animals a refuge for many years to come.

Canada's natural refuges cover thousands of square miles. Wood Buffalo Park, the largest preserve on the continent, covers an unbroken wilderness area 176 miles in length, approximately 100 miles in width and embraces an area of 17,300 square miles. The establishment of this park was primarily for the protection of 1500 wood buffalo that were known to inhabit the region. Unfortunately, in 1925 and during the succeeding four years 6673 plains bison from the Wainwright herd were liberated in the park. Many were unable to withstand the extreme winters at this northern latitude, but some survived and the pure-blooded wood bison have given place to hybrids.

Alaska has many remote and not easily reached areas where big game is to be found in diminishing but still fair numbers. Current accounts indicate that this Arctic area is headed for a scarcity of game in the near future. The rapidly increasing population and the lack of public sentiment are the chief factors causing the decline in Alaska's big game.

The destruction of the big carnivores as a precautionary measure to insure a millennium for other game animals is a subject of considerable controversy between factions of the government and out-and-out naturalists. It should be borne in mind that through the ages Nature entrusted the mighty task of administering her unwritten laws to the fearless carnivores. They not only were empowered to maintain law and order in every field but successfully controlled disease and improved physical fitness of all races. They regulated living conditions, checked overcrowding, and operated an efficient sanitary system. Ever since man fought the carnivores in prehistoric times for supremacy he has waged a relentless war against all the flesh eaters and still gloats over the murder of the "fierce and ferocious creatures," as he likes to label them. The vital necessity for the carnivores is confirmed when it is realized that they have been placed in every field for a purpose. Some are modified for a life in fresh or salt water, others are at home in the trees, still others must laborously dig in the soil to fulfill their purpose, and many are runners. They range in size from the pigmy weasel to the great brown bear and in versatility vary from the ponderous bulk of the bear to the high-tension muscles of the cat. Some are gifted with a keen sense of smell and can follow a trail, in total darkness long after the prey has passed, as clearly as a posted highway. Others depend on sight.

The complete annihilation of the wolves in the Rocky Mountain regions was not brought about as a measure to protect wildlife that had thrived through the ages without the interference of man. Rather, the wolves and most of the cougars were destroyed because of their supposed raids on domestic stock, many of which could actually be traced to feral dogs.

Times, it is true, have changed, and there is obviously a necessity to control overabundance of the predators. A limited number is essential in this experimental age.

No one can question the disastrous results effected by forest fires. There is no more deadly enemy of both forest and wildlife than the careless traveler who drops a lighted match or cigarette butt, or empties the burning ashes from his pipe, onto the ground—in forest, field, or swamp. There is no surer way to destroy or drive out from a region all wildlife than to start a forest fire that sweeps forward with terrific heat leaving nothing but the gaunt, charred remnants of a beautiful, peaceful countryside behind.

The first method and what will ultimately prove to be the most effective one, to insure big game for the future is education. The children of today will be the hunters, foresters, and conservationists of tomorrow. In big communities like Greater New York such a program is being effectively exercised but the smaller towns throughout the states are neglected. The National Audubon Society realizes this and is now extending its activities from coast to coast. An educational program should be such that it will interest as well as instruct and engage the affections, and thus enlighten the child. Wildlife does affect man and his interests in many ways and his attitude to game, for good or bad, is governed by the presentation to him of accurate facts or faulty information.

There are no strictly harmful or beneficial creatures. All life works together in a chain like the mechanism of a clock. The strings of nature are so finely tuned and co-ordinated that they readily respond to the slightest change of natural conditions. From this marvelous biological procession of nature alone evolved the fertile soils, giant forests, and teeming game found on this continent by our predecessors. It is, therefore, vitally important to man's best interests that the process of nature be permitted to continue and the communities of wild life be free to fulfill their intended purpose.

## WEAPONS OF THE MIGHTY

The first thought that comes into the mind of a sportsman when he sights his big game is the horns or antlers. In his mind's eye he gages their size and beauty—which may determine the fate of the animal.

Horned big game are the most coveted and most prized of all trophies by sportsmen. For a head that has the prospect of being a record, the hunter will toil in rarefied air over steep mountain ridges and fearlessly skirt gaping chasms that normally he would shun with horror.

Horns were adopted by animals at an early date in geological time and are known to have occurred on some species as far back as the Eocene. They must have proved beneficial to the wearers, as they were considerably more general in the Oligocene, and from that time on horns became more and more characteristic of the herd animals. Pleistocene ungulates had a great variety of fantastic headgear. From the appearance of many types it would seem that they were more ornamental than useful. Some antelope-like species had four horns, and the peculiarly fashioned horns of the great elk-moose would be enough to make anyone sit up and take notice. In recent mammals the horns are more tailored and conventional and constructed so as to be most useful for the particular species. The common white-tail deer has small, low antlers as compared with the tall, many-tined antlers of the elk. While American ungulates do not have the largest horns in the world, and the head of a bighorn is smaller than that of the Poli sheep, the Alaskan moose has the largest antlers of all the deer.

Horns and antlers of game animals have been utilized by man for various purposes. Fortunately, their commercial use has been discontinued for some time. Primitive man made good use of horn material and fashioned it into various useful instruments. To the animals themselves they serve a two-fold purpose, but their primary objective is sexual. The bull with the bigger horns wins in competitive battles for the females. Secondary in use to some, but a vital necessity for others, the horns—or antlers, as they are termed among the deer—are weapons of defense.

Horns may be briefly defined as hard, excrescent outgrowths on the heads of mammals. The term horn as now applied customarily distinguishes the hollow type that is found on the sheep, goats, and cattle from the solid, branched antlers of the deer. These horns are simple and consist of a hollow horny sheath, growing over a pointed bony core which arise from the frontal bones. Horns continue to grow throughout the life of an animal and are never shed. Usually both sexes are horned. In the bovine world there is a remarkable diversity in the pattern of the horns. The horns of the bison are evenly tapered to a point and directed forward and upward. In musk-ox the horns are flattened at the base and spread out in a protective shield across the frontlet, then curve abruptly down each side of the face and hook upward to a pointed tip. Characteristic Rocky Mountain sheep horns are massive at the base and spiral outward, often making more than a complete turn. The ewe has no such fanciful ambitions as the ram but is satisfied with a simple, rather flattened, spiked horn, somewhat similar to the cylindrical, short, daggerlike horns of the mountain goat.

Antlers are perhaps the most characteristic feature of the deer. They are solid, usually branched, and sometimes palmated bony outgrowths of the skull and are lost or shed—usually in midwinter—and replaced annually. Antlers are typical male appendages. Certainly they find their best development on the male, although it is true that in one group, the caribou, both sexes bear them. About two weeks after the old antlers have been cast off, a soft rounded ball of fur begins to show on the pedicels left by the former antlers. This is soft, spongy, and full of blood. Gradually elongating, it takes on the form of, and encloses, the growing antlers, remaining more or less soft and vulnerable. It also retains its supply of blood, furnishing the antlers with nourishment until they are fully grown. This is the period when the animal is said to be "in the velvet." During the velvet stage the animal shows the effect of a considerable drain on its vitality and is often thin and enervated. This can be appreciated when we learn that the enormous palmated antlers of one individual moose have actually turned the scales at 60 pounds. When the antlers are fully grown the supply of blood and nourishment conveyed by the "velvet" ceases and the antlers harden to their normal bonelike consistency. By the middle of August, the antlers are fully developed and the bulls begin to rub the now useless "velvet" off against the branches or trunks of trees. Occasionally there are freak or abnormal antlers, such as multiplicity of tines, misdirected and stunted growths. These are due either to some internal injury or to elimination from sexual activity. In either case it is caused by an unbalanced physical condition of the animal.

Differing conspicuously from the horns of cattle and the antlers of the deer, the pronged weapons on the head of the pronghorns are the most aberrant type of horns found on any American animal—and, for that matter, in the entire world. The horns of the pronghorn resemble those of sheep and oxen and goats, in that they are hollow and grow over a permanent bony core; but, unlike any of these, the horn sheaths are not only branched but are actually shed annually. These peculiarities are not shared with any other living animal. The new horn covering, produced by epidermal cells, is formed first at the tip and grows downward, just reversing the growth in the sheep, goats, antelopes, etc. The new tip begins to form before the change is made. The pressure of the new growth serves to loosen and forces the old sheath from the core.

It is apparent that the antlers of the deer are almost, if not entirely, sexual. From early spring until August, during development, they are not only useless and a drain on the animal's vitality but must be guarded against injury. When a stag passes its prime and is no longer useful as a sire the development of the horns is retarded. Antlers are in their prime at the height of the rutting season but are dropped in midwinter when the mortal enemies of all deer, wolves and cougars, driven by cold and hunger, are the most treacherous.

In one exception, where the female deer has antlers, the sex-linked character is not so obvious. The female caribou has a good head and though the antlers are conspicuously slenderer and smaller than those of the male they are carried for a longer period. The female does not shed until after the calves are born in the spring. The theory has been proposed that the possession of antlers is an advantage to the caribou in scraping the frozen snow from the vegetation beneath and so providing free access to its food. No other species of deer range so far north as the caribou, and so this theory may eventually prove the real significance of antlers. South of the polar regions and in the warmer countries the female deer in all species are hornless.

In combat, antlers are formidable weapons that can wreak frightful havoc on an adversary. Given an even chance, a stag can rout any carnivore in its own territory. Not even the grizzly can withstand the mighty head-on charge of a giant moose, and the duels fought between moose during rutting season for possession of the females are the most terrific battles in the history of wildlife. So forceful are the head-on impacts that occasionally the tines of the antlers are sprung momentarily and the heads of the opponents are interlocked. The sequel of such a catastrophe is always inevitable: At the foot of a mountain in the Macmillan Range was a small spring-fed lake, the outlet carrying a fair head of water which disappeared down a sinkhole. Deep down in the crystal-clear water could be seen the whitening skeletons of two gigantic moose with locked antlers. As Ernest Thompson Seton said, "The end of every wild animal is a tragedy." These great creatures had fought a mortal battle on the frozen lake, and both had either died in combat or eventually succumbed to starvation. When the spring thaw came they were slowly lowered to their last resting place.

The spiral horns of the bighorn sheep are put into service as battering rams when the mating season comes along. The rams in battle dispense with all preliminary vocal embellishments. One eyes the other in silence and knows exactly what each is thinking. They back off for a good start, perhaps 100 feet or more, and let go. At a velocity of 20 miles per hour they meet with a frightful impact. The crash of the horns can be distinctly heard two miles away on a clear day. Each ram is a 300-pound missile hurled with all the fury and hate of sexual violence. That their skulls and neck bones can survive such an impact is nothing less than miraculous. Weight and endurance are what count, and both must be proved to the satisfaction of both animals before the battle is ended.

The massive horns of the buffalo, tapered to a piercing point, are sufficient to safeguard the herd from attack by any four-footed foe. A herd bull is dependent on these weapons to retain his harem. Battles between an aspiring young blood and a reigning bull are long and furious, often continuing far into the night and lasting for days. Paying no attention to the hungry wolves waiting for the final pay-off, the battling giants charge and fence, bellowing and working around to drive a deadly thrust at each other's vulnerable flanks. After hours of combat, gored, ripped, frothing, and bleeding at the nose, both sink in exhaustion to the ground and continue to battle on their knees. If the intruder is vanquished he will ultimately turn tail and seek safety in flight. But an old conqueror of many such a battle will fight and defend his rights to the finish.

For the infliction of mortal wounds the short black daggers of the mountain goat are the most effective. From his dizzy heights the humpback of the mountains commands the passes that lead downward. A pack of hungry wolves may venture along the narrow part that winds upward through the precipitous crags in hopes of a possible feast. Unhurriedly, without one hasty step, the goat slowly descends to meet his unwelcome guests, perhaps at a narrow pass where the cliff rises sheer up on one side and a yawning gulf below. He pauses and waits calmly. Those polished, ebony-black daggers, curved slightly backward to serve their deadly purpose more effectively, can hold the pass against great odds. As the foremost wolf rushes forward with bared fangs he is struck by a lightning jab and impaled on the goat's piercing horns. Momentarily he hangs, and then a sharp twist of the defender's neck sends him flying over the precipice. Quick to strike when the right moment comes, this calm mountaineer repeats the performance as fast as the daring members of the oncoming pack can muster courage.

Wild animals are not limited to teeth and horns for defense and attack. The bears, especially the grizzly, can deliver death-dealing blows with their mighty paws. With one quick stroke the grizzly can crush in the skull of a bull. In a test of his might, a grizzly has slain six fighting bulls in one afternoon. As each bellowing bull in turn charged, the grizzly reared up on his hind legs and at an opportune moment struck the bull dead with a blow between the eyes.

Hooked talons, with their needle-sharp points carried carefully guarded in a sheath, are the deadly weapons of the cougar. The spring of this great cat at the climax of his hunt drives the searing talons deep into the flanks of the fleeing foe and four long white fangs sink into the victim's neck, a great paw reaches forward and four claws hold firmly on the nose as the head is twisted back until the neck snaps.

Teeth are the wolf's sole weapons. Once his jaws, armed with a gleaming array of piercing ivory points, clamp onto the throat of his prey, they tighten and hold like a vise. The wolf is perhaps the most sportsmanlike hunter of all the big predators. He does not hide in ambush or attempt to sneak up and seize his quarry unaware, but gives full warning of his presence and loves the chase as much as any huntsman.

# ANTELOPE

*Antilocapra americana*

The antelope, in common with many other forms of North American big-game animals, was misnamed by the early explorers, and such errors are long-lasting. In most of the areas in which it is abundant, this animal is known as the "Pronghorn Antelope" or merely the "Pronghorn." The latter, at least, is accurate, for the pronghorn is neither an antelope, nor a goat, nor an "antelope-goat" which the Latin term specifies. The pronghorn is a true American, with no relative in any other part of the world, and is the lone descendant of a genus that during the Pleistocene Age was broken up into several species and sub-species.

**History.** Only 25 years ago the future of the pronghorn was in some doubt, for of the millions of these animals that once roamed the plains from Kansas to the foothills of the Rockies, the Biological Survey census of 1924 revealed that approximately 26,000 remained in this country, with an additional 5000 scattered over the rest of the continent. Many conservationists predicted that the pronghorn was due to join the extinct moorhen and passenger pigeon.

During the past 20 years the pronghorn has made one of the greatest revivals in the history of conservation, and has given proof positive of the value of adequate protection from predators and overshooting. At present there are approximately 175,000 pronghorns in the United States, and they have also shown an increase in both Canada and Mexico. The hunter success ratio in pronghorns runs as high as 70 per cent in many of the western states, which is considerably higher than that of any other big-game animal. Wyoming is the major pronghorn state, with the present census somewhere between 45,000 and 55,000 animals.

**Identification.** The pronghorn is one of the easiest big-game animals to identify, even at a great distance, because of its distinctive coloration and its habit of using its white rump patch to signal. The pronghorn is able to erect the hairs of this rump patch, causing them to flash. It is a HORNED and not an ANTLERED animal (see Glossary), but is unusual among horned animals in that it sheds these horns each year. Many who have seen the pronghorn only at a distance insist that the horns are not shed. The outer, pronged sheath is shed early in Autumn, but the bony, fibrous core remains.

**Characteristics.** Probably the most outstanding characteristic of the pronghorn is his speed, and next to this, his keen vision. These animals have been paced by automobiles and airplanes, and while many bucks have been paced at 60 miles per hour, several motorists have reported pacing does at as much as 68 and 70 miles per hour. They are by far the fleetest of all North American game animals. Many experienced hunters have made careful studies on the vision of the pronghorn, and the general opinion is that the average pronghorn can see as far as a man equipped with eight-power binoculars.

Another distinction of the pronghorn is its feet. Unlike the deer, for example, the pronghorn has on each foot only two hoofs rather than the conventional four, as the dew claws are missing.

In coloration, the pronghorn is among the brightest of his race. His white belly and rump merge to a glistening tan, buff, and dark brown, and the throat is sharply marked by brown and white bars. The average pronghorn weighs about 80 pounds, and a 100-pound buck is an exception. Does are small, in comparison, weighing about 65 pounds, and the horns are much shorter.

The record head, with horns measuring just over 20 inches, was taken about 50 years ago in Arizona, but there seem to be no scarcity of 18- and 19-inch heads. Unlike the deer, the older the pronghorn the larger the horn, and while the old bucks make strong, tough eating, the average hunter will sacrifice flavor to a good trophy.

Courtesy U. S. Fish and Wildlife Service.

PLATE I. Pronghorn Antelope a Victim of Curiosity.

**Breeding.** The mating season of the pronghorn runs from early August until mid-September. The period of gestation of the doe is longer than that of sheep. The young normally are born during May and June, and twins are the rule rather than the exception.

Immediately after their birth, the fawns are carefully hidden by the doe. She feeds in that general area but returns to the fawns only to let them suckle. During this period the greatest predation losses occur from coyotes and eagles. The only other period in which their predators cause large losses is during the early spring, when the pronghorn is weak after winter privations.

The fawns are able to follow the doe after about ten days. Then the does that have left the herds of their own sex during bearing once more gather into small groups accompanied by the fawns. The fawns normally remain with the doe until the following year. When the time arrives for her to bear more young she drives the yearlings from her.

**Range and Distribution.** The range of the pronghorn is much broader than many realize. The states in which they are most abundant include: California, Colorado, Montana, North Dakota, South Dakota, and Wyoming. They are found in reasonably large numbers in Idaho, Nebraska, Nevada, New Mexico, Oregon, Texas, and Utah. There are a few herds as far north as Alberta, Saskatchewan, and Manitoba, and herds in Chihuahua and Sonora, in Old Mexico, are on the increase. It is estimated that there are approximately 230,000 of these animals on the North American continent, with the number increasing each year. The latest big-game census (1946) shows the following distribution:

| | | | |
|---|---|---|---|
| Arizona | 7,200 | Oklahoma | 77 |
| California | 4,700 | Oregon | 9,600 |
| Colorado | 7,300 | South Dakota | 9,700 |
| Idaho | 10,500 | Texas | 12,000 |
| Montana | 37,800 | Utah | 1,300 |
| Nebraska | 2,000 | Washington | 50 |
| Nevada | 8,700 | Wyoming | 80,600 |
| New Mexico | 39,900 | | |
| North Dakota | 2,500 | TOTAL | 233,900 |

Although normally a *browser,* the pronghorn also is a *grazer* (see Glossary). The preferred food, however, is low shrubs and weeds, although they feed heavily on various forms of cactus during the flowering stage of these plants. They prefer rolling plateaus and plains that are cut by gullies and ravines and dotted with occasional thin forest growth. Normally they seek out high ground during the summer and are driven to the low valleys only by snow and cold. Although the herds seem to scatter into smaller groups during the summer, large herds seem to form during the winter, possibly for protection from the elements and predators. As a rule a herd will have a definite range, encompassed by a circle from 10 to 15 miles in diameter. Unless driven from this range by drought, severe storms, or unusual hunting pressure they may be found on this range year after year.

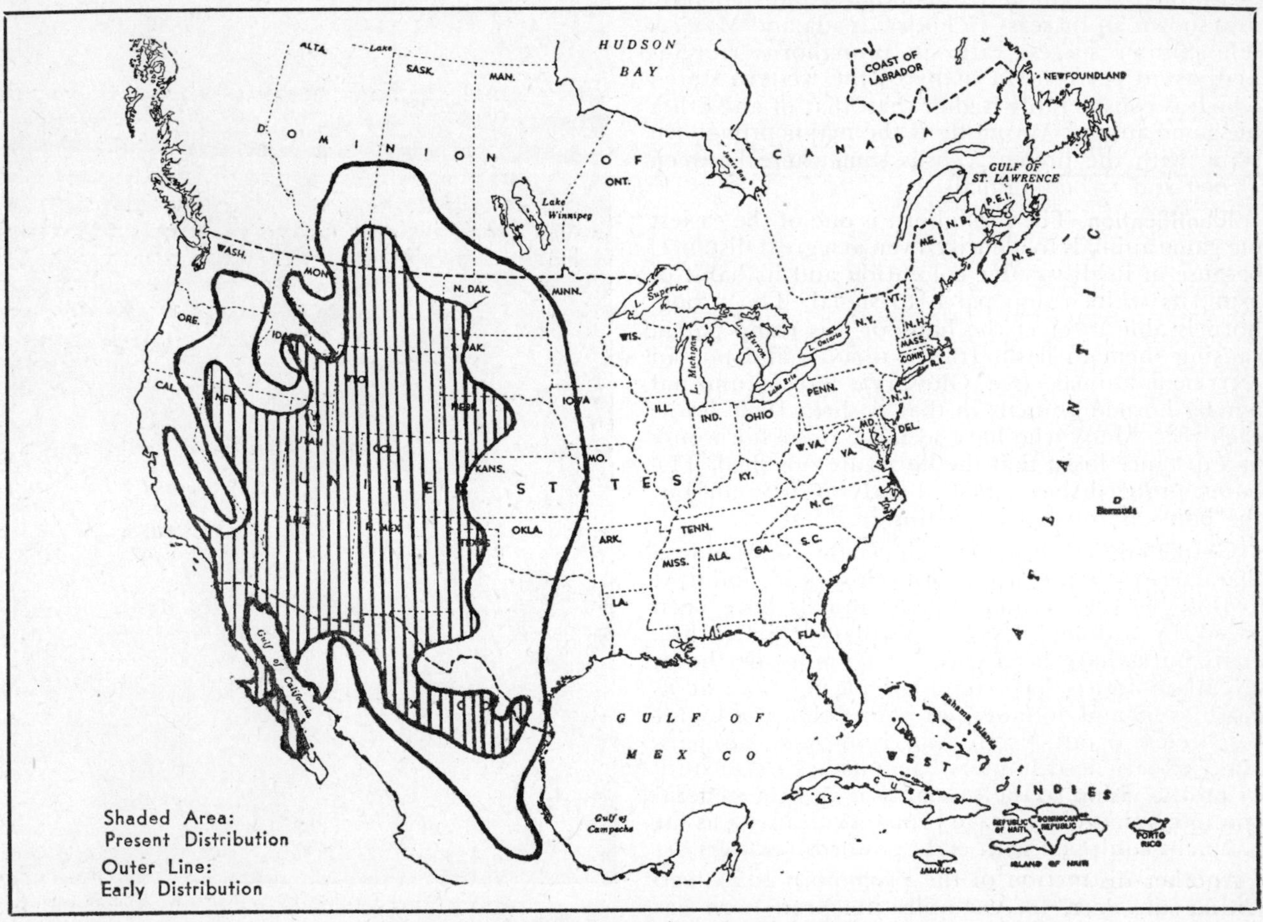


**Plate II.** Distribution of Pronghorn Antelope.

Courtesy U. S. Fish and Wildlife Service.

PLATE III. Pronghorn Antelope at a Water Hole.

The curiosity of this animal often is its undoing, for it seems impelled to investigate anything it cannot classify. On the other hand, it is extremely nervous, and is very easily frightened. This faculty, in part, atones for the curiosity.

Among other unusual characteristics is the tendency of age groups to herd together, namely, two-year-olds with two-year-olds, etc. Except during the mating season, which runs from early August to mid-September, the bucks and does do not run together, and as the best hunting period is during May, June, and July, the hunter has little difficulty in differentiating between sexes.

The coyote is the pronghorn's worst enemy, running just ahead of the illegal poacher. In areas where experimental coyote trapping has been carried out, the herds have shown remarkable increases. The greatest inroads by coyotes are made on the fawns, for the adult pronghorn can outrun the coyote with ease. In areas where doe herds are found with but one fawn to two does, excess predation is apparent, and it is a clear sign that coyote control is required if the pronghorn is to survive. Herds with a ratio of three fawns to two does indicate satisfactory predator control.

**Hunting Methods.** Pronghorn hunting methods are as varied in interest as they are in type. In those areas where hunters as well as antelope are fairly plentiful, the average hunter follows the line of least resistance and effort. He seeks out an elevation with reasonably good cover and waits for other, more active hunters to move herds or individuals within range.

Many sportsmen frown on this method. They point out that it results in a high percentage of wounded animals that are never recovered, and results in the wasteful killing of large numbers of does and yearlings. A pronghorn, when frightened, can suffer a severe wound and continue to run for more than a mile. In many instances this deceives the hunter into believing that he did not connect with his bullet. Therefore, he may wound several before making a clean kill. The tendency of the average hunter to misjudge range and LEAD on long, running shots is partly responsible for the losses this method brings about.

Many sportsmen prefer to STALK the pronghorn, for under normal conditions this method not only is more sporting, but offers the hunter an opportunity to get a better trophy. Arrived at the range, the hunter leaves his transport and finds a vantage point from which he can "glass" the surrounding country. For this job, 8-power binoculars are best, although many hunters also carry a 20-power spotting scope to insure the quality of the trophy before beginning the stalk.

After locating a herd or individual, the hunter then begins the stalk; and under normal conditions it is not an easy one. He must take advantage of every mask in the terrain, for the pronghorn, though he depends little upon his nose, has telescopic vision, and can spot a moving object at almost unbelievable distances.

The rolling terrain enables an experienced hunter to approach within reasonable range of his selected quarry, although he must often cover several miles and devote from two to three hours to completing the stalk. He *must* follow a route, no matter how devious, which will keep him completely hidden from the animal until he is ready to shoot.

At this point, the task becomes a matter of range determination, shooting ability, and target selection. And if the pronghorn sees the hunter first, it is all of these plus a good knowledge of "lead."

Another method, but one which is forbidden by law in some areas, is that of hunting on horseback. This usually is a group method. A dozen mounted hunters, upon locating a suitable herd, separate and form a wide circle around the herd. Then on signal, the hunters approach the herd from all angles. Seeing their enemies approaching from all directions, the herd often mills around for several minutes, then breaks up, each individual taking a separate course. In most instances, at least half of the hunters will get a shot. The results of this shooting, of course, depend upon the factors outlined above.

A method which is practiced in a few areas is often the easiest, but certainly not the most sporting. A hunter will drive an automobile into an area where herds are known to exist. When the herd runs he will follow a parallel course so far as the terrain permits. The antelope, overconfident in their speed, often will cross in front of the automobile. The hunter then slams on the brakes, leaps from his vehicle, and tries to get in a telling shot before they are out of range. This method also is forbidden by law in many areas.

**Rifle and Sights.** Several things are required of the proper rifle for this hunting. In order of their importance, they are: flat trajectory, shocking power, and long range. Although the first requirement often embodies the third, this is not always the case. Sights are next in importance, and although iron sights, open or peep, are satisfactory for big game in many areas, telescopic sights are a MUST for the pronghorn hunter.

A poll of a large number of experienced pronghorn hunters reveals a surprising preference for one caliber and load for this shooting. The preferred rifle is the .270, using the 100-grain soft-point bullet.

Second on the preferred list is the .250/3000 with the 87-grain soft-point bullet.

Next comes the .257 with the 87-grain bullet. (See Ammunition section for ballistics and trajectory for these.)

Many who expect to hunt pronghorn only one season will not want to invest in a rifle that will be of slight use to them on the game they normally hunt, although devotees of the .270 will insist that this rifle is at the top of the "all-around" category. These hunters, provided they already own a .30 '06 or a .300, will find these rifles adequate for pronghorn shooting provided they are scope-mounted. With the .30 '06 the 150-grain open-point or soft-point bullet is best. If the .300 is used, the 150-grain soft point is favored.

Ranges for pronghorn shooting can not be figured to a mean, for they run from 150 yards to 400, the success of the latter depending upon the rifle and the shooter's knowledge of his rifle, the load, and the sights, as well as his ability to estimate range with reasonable accuracy. The flat-trajectory, high-velocity, light bullet is a definite asset, but successful shooting depends upon the human as well as the mechanical factors concerned.

The telescopic sight is of great importance to the pronghorn, mountain sheep, and mountain goat hunter, but nowhere has it greater value than to the pronghorn hunter. The preferred scope is one of 3 power, although many hunters hold out for more magnification and a few for less. Extremists often use a scope of from 10 to 12 power, and those who happen to have a rifle with 2¾-power scope which they use on other game do not care to risk a change. The scope mount should be low, and of the quick-detachable type. The scope reticule is a matter of personal choice, but here again there is a general preference for one type: the tapered post. (See Telescope sights.)

The high-power spotting scope, of 20 to 25 power, is a real asset to the pronghorn hunter who is interested in a good trophy as well as meat, especially if he has a limited time to spend in getting this trophy. Even after locating a buck or a herd with binoculars, it is often impossible to calculate the value of any individual head because of insufficient magnification. By using the spotting scope, however, the trophy may be examined in detail. This often eliminates the necessity for a long and arduous stalk with an unsatisfactory trophy at the end of it. (See "Sights and Optical Aids.")

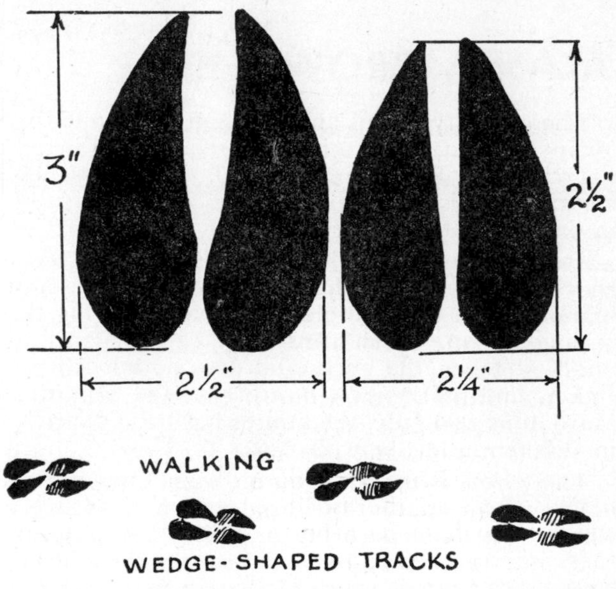

PLATE IV. Typical Hoofprints of the Pronghorn Antelope.

The mere fact that a hunter has the proper rifle, adequately sighted, is not sufficient to insure even a fair chance of success in pronghorn shooting. First, and most important, is the hunter's familiarity with that rifle and its performance at ranges of from 100 to 500 yards. Long shots are the rule rather than the exception in this shooting, and the man who is unfamiliar with the trajectory of his rifle at any distance within these extremes is unlikely to become ill from eating pronghorn steaks.

Many pronghorn hunters sight in their rifles at 200 yards. Knowing the trajectory of the bullet they are using, they know just how high or how low to hold when the target is at 450 or 100 yards. The shoulder area is the target, and any spot farther back or lower reduces the chances of making a clean kill. Windage also is of some importance, especially on long shots, and the pronghorn hunter should have some knowledge of the drift of his bullet as a result of normal winds.

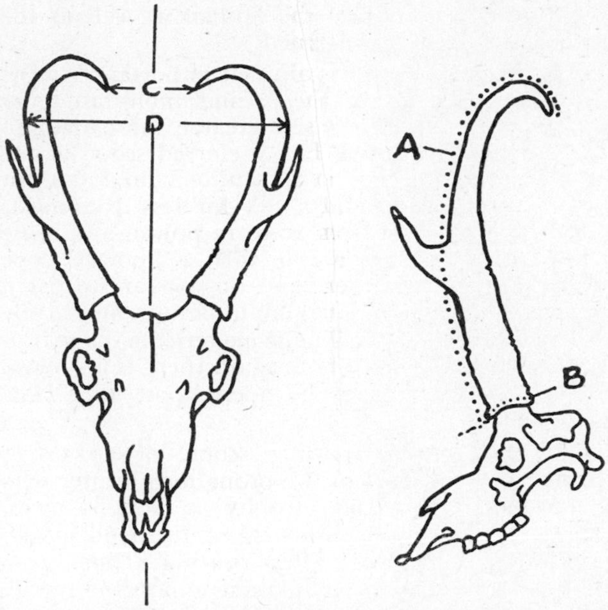


PLATE V. Trophy Measurements, Antelope.

A-Length of outside curve. B-Circumference at base. C-Tip to tip. D-Greatest spread.

On running shots, especially when the animal is crossing directly in front, LEAD is of major importance. The pronghorn moving at 40 miles per hour—not an unusual speed for this animal—covers about 58 feet of ground in one second. This gives you an opportunity to practice some rapid calculation, for your time lag as a result of swinging for the LEAD, pulling the trigger, the fall of the hammer, the explosion of the powder, and the speed of the bullet all enter into the problem. In the last analysis, only experience can supply the answer. And luck as well as reasonably accurate calculation are factors in success. Only the rare pronghorn hunter overleads the pronghorn, and usually the dirt flies several feet behind the running animal. Leads of from 12 to 15 feet are not unusual.

The buck with the good head usually is the old-timer, who has had experience with man and is extremely wary and difficult to deceive. Also, he is difficult to stalk. This means that the average really good trophy is obtained as a result of a long-range shot. Most long shots can best be made from the prone, and the use of the sling becomes important.

# ALASKA BROWN BEAR

*Ursus*

**History.** Evidence in the form of fossils, hair, and flesh, buried deep in the Alaskan icebox, proves the existence of the giant brown bear in the Pleistocene Age, and it proves that the world's largest carnivore has not changed materially in size or nature. The secret of his existence lies in the abundance of fish along the Alaskan coast, and this abundance has insured food for the big animal throughout the year. Zoologists believe that he arrived in Alaska via the Bering Straits and, finding food plentiful and conditions right, remained there.

Prior to the past 50 years he was virtually unknown to hunters and zoologists due to the inaccessibility of his range. He lives only along the coastal regions and on the isolated rim of Kamchatka where "You land on a beach that no man knows, bleak, storm swept, alone." The remoteness of the brown bear's range, which is not only expensive but difficult to reach, is one of the reasons for this bear's continued existence.

In the days of the open carriage, the rare, warm brown bear robe was a fashionable luxury. The demand for buffalo robes had swept the bison almost into oblivion, but the brown bear was protected by distance, and eventually by a Federal law which prohibited traffic in the hides.

To many the brown bear is widely known under a misnomer, that of "Kodiak" bear. This error arose as a result of the large numbers of these animals on Kodiak Island and from the location of a trading post on the island which received pelts from other areas.

**Identification.** Like the grizzly, the Alaska brown bear varies in size and weight in different areas. The technical variation in species also is the result of geography. The average brown bear weighs in the neighborhood of 800 pounds. The record hide, from an animal killed in 1930 by D. S. Hopkins on Kodiak Island, measured 10 feet 4 inches in length and 10 feet 11 inches in width. As few hunters are equipped with scales capable of weighing a big brown bear, the weight is often estimated, although a few of these animals have been weighed in at 1600 pounds.

The largest members of the family seem to be on the Peninsula and on Kodiak Island. There the climate is milder than in the other areas where this bear is located, with less snowfall and more food. The streams teem with spawning Pacific salmon from early July until late fall, which means a full stomach for the big brown bear.

Sexual differences also vary according to species and area, although normally the males are much larger than the females. On Kodiak Island, where the *middendorffi* are found, it is not at all difficult to differentiate between sexes on the basis of size, but the *kidderi* of the Peninsula offer something of a problem as there is very little difference in size between the male and female.

Although the zoologists have not completed the breakdown of the various species and sub-species of the brown bear, 16 species have been identified and named. These include: *kidderi kidderi, kidderi tundrensis, eximus, innuitus, cressonus, alexandrae,*

Courtesy Jonas Bros.

PLATE I. Alaska Brown Bear—life-size mount, 11 feet tall, weight 1600 pounds.

*townsendi, dalli, hoots, sitkensis, shirasi, uchek, gyas, middendorffi, kenaiensis,* and *sheldoni.*

**Characteristics.** The sober, dignified brown bear has the characteristic typical of other members of the bear family, namely, an unpredictable behavior. He is a combination of astute caution and suspicion, and betrays a complete indifference to most of his enemies. At one moment he will carefully check the wind. The next moment he will exhibit complete indifference, even after picking up the scent of man.

He has been reported by many as dangerous, with a high record of raging attacks, of mauling and killing men, but it is a matter of record that no hunter, protected and prepared with guide and gun, has been injured. The brown bear uses his great strength, size, and speed when escape is impossible, or when called upon to protect a mate or cubs, but he will not normally charge a hunter. In fact, most hunters report that the individual bear will not even fight back. He prefers to elude rather than fight.

Like other bears, he is omnivorous, but his vegetable diet of grass and kelp is abandoned with the first appearance of the salmon run.

Just prior to hibernation he leaves the streams and ceases eating. This is his method of purging himself prior to the long hibernation. At this period his body is encased in a two- or three-inch layer of fat. Late in the fall he climbs to a den on the mountainside, the coldest part of his range, and does not emerge until early in May.

**Breeding.** The mating season begins about mid-May and continues through June. At this period the brown bear does most of his traveling, mainly at night. Except during this period the male is a solitary animal, and though he seeks the company of a mate, he is far from gregarious, and the cubs which may have remained with the female are soon taught to keep their distance.

The female breeds only every other year, and normally has two cubs. Occasionally there is but one, and less often three, but only in rare instances four. Like the grizzly, the cubs are blind until about six weeks old, and weigh but a few ounces at birth, but grow rapidly, and when they emerge with the mother from the den they weigh from 15 to 25 pounds.

An interesting check was made in Alaska on the growth of a brown bear, the *Ursus gyas,* one of the larger species. The following table of weights was prepared:

| | | |
|---|---|---|
| May | 1901 | 18 pounds |
| January | 1902 | 180 " |
| January | 1903 | 450 " |
| January | 1904 | 625 " |
| January | 1905 | 770 " |

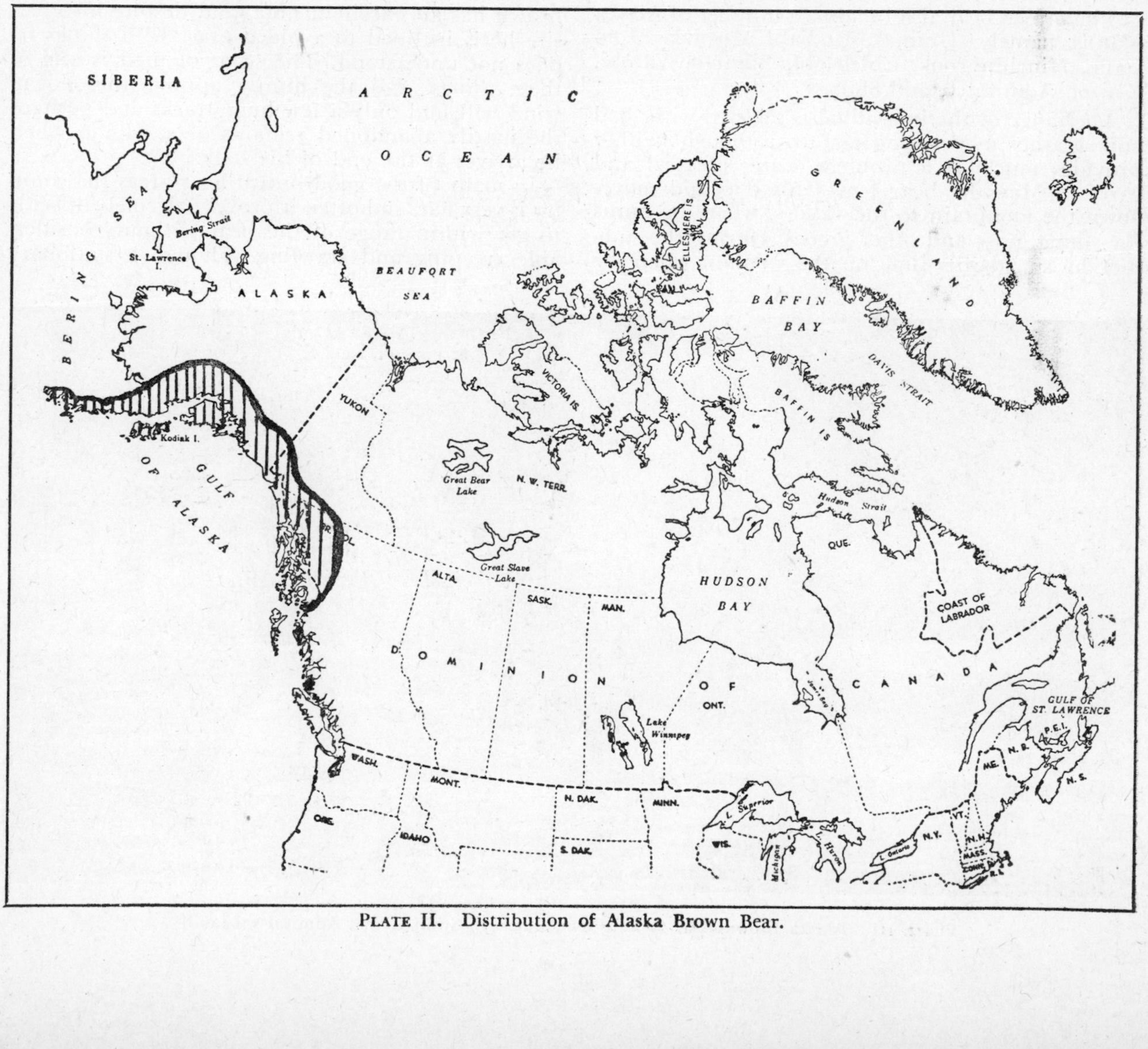


**Plate II.** Distribution of Alaska Brown Bear.

| | | |
|---|---|---|
| February | 1906 | 890 pounds |
| March | 1907 | 970 " |
| March | 1908 | 1050 " |
| December | 1910 | 1200 " |

The female brown bear is a good mother and a painstaking instructor. She teaches the cubs to swim and to fish, and when the cub exhibits a fear of the water she will take it by the neck and carry it across the water. The yearlings den with her the first winter, and she leads them to the lowland the second spring. Once the male appears and begins his courtship, however, she permits him to drive them off. Often the twin cubs remain together during the summer and fall and den together the following winter, but in their third year they go separate ways.

**Range and Distribution.** The range of the brown bear has been termed a primeval bear paradise, with special emphasis placed on the area in the vicinity of the Pavlof Volcano. Brown bears are found over a wide area on the Alaskan mainland; up the Alaska Peninsula east to Cook Inlet and north to Norton Sound; from Unalakleek north to Seward Peninsula; west to the Iliamna region from the Chugah Mountains; within the Kenai Peninsula and along the Malaspina Glacier; by the Clearwater Creek of the Stikine River; Prince William Sound and throughout the southeastern mainland.

The brown bear also inhabits a number of Alaska islands, namely: Unimak, Kodiak, Afognak, Montague, Hinchinbrook, Chichagof, Baranof, Yacobi, Kruzof, Admiralty, and Shuyak.

The range of the individual is selected with food and weather as deciding factors, although neither provides much of a problem. Late in April and early in May the bear leaves his den and moves down the mountain to the valleys, where he hunts for young grass and other greens. During the summer he spends his time on the streams, where he lives on the salmon which he sweeps to the shore with a flailing paw.

He feeds heavily all summer, but in the fall he seems to become partially sated, and eats but twice a day, usually late in the afternoon and during the night. He grows fat and sleek with but little effort. Zoologists point out that the greater weight of the brown, as compared to the grizzly, is the result of this plenitude of food and the ease with which it is obtained.

**Hunting Methods.** The habits as well as the habitat of the Alaska brown bear are so similar to those of the grizzly that the methods of hunting the two are similar in almost every area. The browns, however, seldom venture far inland, for their favorite food is the salmon. As this fish abounds in the areas where the bear is most plentiful, locating a big one is not too difficult.

The Alaskan bear hunter is required by law to employ a guide, and the intelligent hunter will let this guide decide on the area to be hunted and the methods to be followed. The pelt is in its finest condition early in the spring, immediately after the bear emerges from hibernation. As this season usually is a wet one, with rain and heavy fog almost a daily occurrence, the hunting is not so comfortable or easy as the fall hunting, but often is productive of a much finer trophy.

Like other members of the bear family, the big brown has an excellent nose, and despite his great size he is inclined to avoid contact with things he does not understand. The scent of man is one of these things, and the hunter approaching downwind will find only a few huge tracks and perhaps the hastily abandoned remains of a salmon when he arrives at the end of his stalk.

In many of the good brown bear areas the country is very flat, and often it proves extremely difficult to get within range of the bear without considerable creeping and crawling. Though a stationary

**Plate III.** Alaska Brown Bear Fishing for Salmon in Swan Creek, Admiralty Island.

Photo by Fred Hollender.

**Plate IV.** **Fred Hollender with a Really Fine Alaska Brown Bear.**

object often is ignored, the brown bear, despite his poor vision, seems readily to detect any movement. Often when a good trophy is spotted, the terrain may be of such nature as to make a successful stalk up-wind extremely difficult if not impossible. In this case the guide often tries a procedure that is as old as hunting. Placing the hunter at a vantage point, the guide will make a wide circle and move down-wind on the bear, hoping to "spook" him past the hunter at a range which will offer a reasonably good shot. While this ruse occasionally works, too often the bear follows a departure route that is wide of the hunter.

The nature of the brown bear is as unpredictable as that of his smaller cousins. Experienced hunters claim he has much in common with the grizzly, in that he is not inclined to charge unless cornered or unless he has been badly wounded at rather close range. In the latter event, especially where the quarry happens to be a female with cubs, the grizzly is no more ferocious. Also, as it normally is larger and heavier, the brown is much harder to put down. In stopping a charging brown the point of aim should be the same as for the grizzly, namely, the shoulder or foreleg.

The hunter who takes a snap shot at a brown bear gives indisputable evidence of inexperience and foolhardiness. The experienced hunter will wait until conditions are right before squeezing off the first shot. No one can predict the reactions of a wounded bear, whether he be black, grizzly, or brown, and while the record of the Alaskan guides is a fine one, there have been many occasions when cool thinking and quick shooting on the part of the guide were the factors responsible for the preservation of this record.

Few guides, and fewer hunters, have ever been able to remain sufficiently calm during the charge of a big brown to make a reasonable estimate of his speed during this anger-inspired rush. One veteran guide summed it up as: "A charging brown covers ground just about twice as fast as appearances indicate, and at least five times as fast as the hunter believes."

The range of each brown is apt to be criss-crossed with numerous well-defined trails, made by him in the course of routine trips to various feeding grounds. In the early spring, immediately after emerging from hibernation, the brown will be found feeding on the coastal flats, bare meadows, and occasionally on the higher ground near the tree line. Often a hunter, moving carefully over the rolling terrain, will arrive on the crest of a low hummock to find a brown feeding in the shallow valley on the far side. The range of the first shot may be 50 yards or 200, and it is extremely important to know the exact zero of the rifle at both ranges or any distance in between. In most instances there will be no opportunity to change the sight

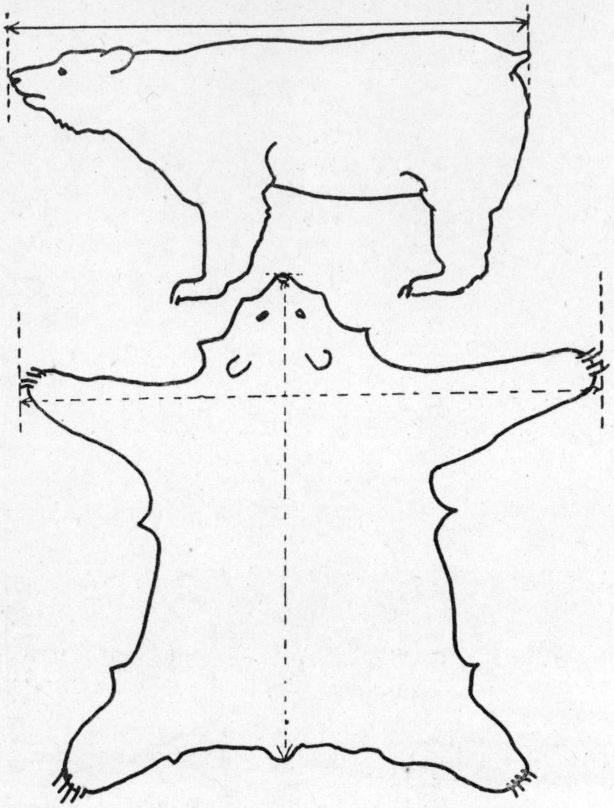

PLATE V. Method of Measuring Hide.

setting, and in many cases the problem of range estimation and rifle zero is one which must be solved in a matter of seconds.

Good binoculars are of tremendous importance, for they enable the hunter to seek out a high point and glass the country well before (otherwise) barging through it in hit-or-miss fashion. Many a hunter, however, having located the trophy he wanted and begun the up-wind stalk, has been brought face to face with another brown while en route to his selected quarry. After locating his bear, the experienced hunter will not rush off immediately, but will carefully map out his route, following it on the ground through his glasses and checking to determine whether any disturbing element lies along his route. Many a hunter, almost within range of his bear, has lost his opportunity by having flushed up a squawking flight of waterfowl from a pothole he did not see. Normally, the brown interprets any disturbance of his area as being a potential danger, and he departs from the vicinity in a hurry.

The brown that is wounded and does not charge, but manages to get away before a fatal shot can be registered, constitutes something of a problem for both the hunter and the guide. No hunter, if he is a sportsman, will abandon wounded game without first making every reasonable effort to complete the job. Normally, when badly wounded, the bear will seek out extremely thick cover, which not only serves to hide him but warns him of the approach of his enemy.

Taking up the trail of a wounded brown is a job calling for courage, considerable skill, a knowledge of the bear's habits and of the terrain, plus a set of calm nerves; also, it demands slow and studied movement. The bear that did not charge on being wounded is very apt to change his mind upon being trailed, and few hunters can approach within range of the wounded bear without the animal's knowledge. When light conditions become bad the trail should be abandoned, and the quest postponed until the following morning. Many guides, having decided the course taken by the wounded animal, will move to higher ground paralleling this course. This procedure is followed for several reasons. First, it offers an opportunity to locate the possible hiding place of the bear, and, in the event the animal decides to charge, it forces him to charge up-hill.

**Rifles and Sights.** The hunter who can afford the incidental expenses entailed by a hunt for this bear can afford to equip himself with a rifle that is really adequate for the job. Brown have been killed with the bow and arrow, and several have been killed with rifles of calibers as small as .22. The theory that there is a direct relation between the small-caliber rifle and sportsmanship is one that has been exploded too many times for serious discussion in this volume. The most sporting rifle is the rifle that kills quickly and with the minimum of suffering on the part of the game.

The rifle that is adequate for most hoofed game, even the one that the black bear hunter finds completely satisfactory, often proves not only inadequate but very unsatisfactory for hunting the grizzly and brown bear. Many experienced guides, hunters, and woodsmen kill both of these big bears with rifles intended for killing caribou, sheep, deer, or wolves, but the ability of these "one gun" men normally is much greater than that of the hunter whose grizzly and brown bear hunting has been of a vicarious nature.

Every experienced hunter has emphasized the need for extremes in bullet weight, velocity, and long-range accuracy for this hunting. There are several calibers that have proved their excellence for this shooting. They are:

.375 H. & H. Magnum, with 300-grain bullet.
.300 H. & H. Magnum, with 220-grain bullet.
.348 Winchester, with 250-grain bullet.

(See "Ammunition—Rifle.")

The majority of those who have a rifle such as one of the above prefer to have it equipped with telescopic sights, with the 2½-power scope, and the tapered post reticule is favored. A pair of 8-power binoculars proves a tremendous asset in this hunting. (See "Sights and Optical Aids.")

The method of dressing and skinning out the trophy is given under "Preservation of Trophies."

# BLACK BEAR

*Eurarctos americanus*

**History.** Long before prehistoric man came to this continent, man and bears were enemies. The primitive people in Europe recorded in drawings on their cave walls the struggle which existed between them and the greater bears. The black bear has been no exception in this long feud. As civilization moved westward the warfare between man and bear grew in intensity and the bear was the loser. In many sections of the eastern seaboard states, where once he was plentiful, the black bear approached extinction. A few survivors, crowded into the relatively small islands of wilderness that today form a part of our National and State park system, continued to exist and, during the past 20 years, even to multiply. During the period of colonization thousands of bears were killed annually by fur traders and by farmers who resented their inroads on livestock.

The bear population rises and falls, although in a less ordered chronological cycle than those of other big and small game animals. Many of the eastern and central states have protected them by law and others have granted protection except for a brief hunting season. In eastern Canada, however, they have approached the pest stage in many areas, and hunting and trapping the black bear is encouraged by a bounty. New Brunswick, for example, offers a free bear-hunting license to the nonresident anglers who visit the province for the spring fishing.

The last census of big-game animals made by the U. S. Fish and Wildlife Service in 1946, though not complete, revealed that there were more than 155,000 black bears in the United States. This census was far from complete as it related to Alaska, which abounds in bears of several species. Studies conducted between 1941 and 1943 indicated an increase in black bears of 28.6 per cent in the states, which is a hopeful sign for the future.

**Identification.** The term "black bear" often is misleading, for this bear may be anything *but* black. He varies in coloration from black to gray-black on through cinnamon, blue-gray, and creamy-white. This factor has resulted in many arguments as to species, not only by the non-scientific hunter but by some zoologists. One well-known zoologist has advanced the theory that, since any departure from the black in eastern bears is a rarity, the color phases result from an infusion of Asiatic blood via the Bering Straits which did not have time to spread eastward.

Normally, the black bear keeps the coloring to which he is born, although there may be slight seasonal variations in the length and glossiness of the pelage. The offspring of a black bear may show a mixture in coloration. A cinnamon mother, for example, may have one black and two cinnamon cubs, and in some areas—Mississippi, for example—there may be several shades of cinnamon brown.

The glacier bear *(Eurarctos emmonsii)* constitutes one of the most unusual color phases of the black bear group, ranging from pale gray to a Maltese blue. As a result of this coloration it is called "blue bear" by some of the natives who have encountered it among the coastal glaciers west of the St. Elias Range in Alaska. The glacier bear is a rarity, and is greatly prized as a trophy. It is estimated that there are but a few hundred of these bears in existence, and zoologists have been anxious to obtain skulls and exact measurements of the animals. Although the bear has a definite black-bear skull, the teeth are smaller and in most instances the claws are shorter and more curved. It is an excellent swimmer, and seems more at home in the water than other members of the group. It is not unusual to see a Maltese mother with one Maltese cub and one coal-black one.

Variations in size and general appearance are also dependent upon the region. The North Carolina and Tennessee black bear, for instance, is stockier than the rangy Florida species, and the Rocky Mountain species vary in conformation from long, narrow skulls to a distinctly broad-shaped skull. The black bear looks deceivingly awkward, but is, in reality, swift and coordinated in his movements, especially in speedy tree climbing.

The establishment of an average weight is impossible, but the range is normally between 200 and 500 pounds. The average bear, however, is about 60 inches in length and stands 25 inches high at the shoulder. The Smokies in Carolina occasionally produce an unusually large specimen,

PLATE I. Black Bear.

scaling as much as 500 pounds, and several are killed each year in New Brunswick that tip the scales at more than 600 pounds. The largest black bear on record weighed 916 pounds, but as the skull of this bear was not examined by an experienced zoologist, there is a possibility that there was an error in classification. The hide of the record North American black bear measured 7 feet in length and 8 feet in width. It was a male, killed in Alaska by E. O. McDonnell in 1933. The black bear is

Courtesy U. S. Fish and Wildlife Service.

PLATE II. Black Bear Cub.

free of markings except for a white patch on the breast. Other identifying characteristics are the short-curved claws of the front paws (which leave a wide five-toed imprint only when he is running) and nearly straight profile of the skull.

**Characteristics.** The black bear is not a gregarious but a solitary animal, and except for a female with her cubs it is unusual to see more than one at a time. The mother (or *sow*, as she is called in some sections) normally permits her cubs to remain with her until a new set of cubs is born, and as the normal female mates only every other year, the cubs often attain considerable size before she drives them off to fend for themselves. Except for the protection offered by the mother for her cubs, there is no record of an adult bear going out of its way to aid another of his kind.

Although omnivorous, the black bear is inclined to be vegetarian. Primarily he is a root and berry eater, but lack of this preferred food, or hunger, or circumstance, can bring about rapid change to a meat diet. This is especially true in farming and ranching areas; having found a liking for a meat diet, the black bear often causes high losses in cattle, colts, pigs, and sheep. He kills his prey with sweeps of his mighty forepaws and tearing claws (*not* by hugging, as is popularly thought).

The normal diet covers a wide variety of foods. This includes grass, fruit, berries, grubs, insects, fish, and carrion. In the north, the black bear finds a shorter growing season and consequently is more of a meat eater, which has a definite effect on his nature, making him more vicious and more easily aroused. In the south, he is inclined to be a vegetarian, and is therefore more amiable and indolent.

Upon emerging from hibernation in the spring the bear is hungry and cold, and immediately begins feeding on grass, snow lilies, various starchy plant bulbs, cow parsnips, and skunk cabbage. If his range is near a mountain farm, he often indulges his love for young corn. Often a bear will peel bark from a tree from the base to a point five feet up the trunk in order to get the succulent cambium under the bark. They are especially fond of tamarack. The unfortunate ground squirrel is another staple in the bear's diet during the late fall. As this animal hibernates about a month before the bear, he is dug out of his burrows and helps build up the bear's fat for the long sleep.

Although he has extremely poor vision, the black bear has acute hearing and a keen sense of smell, and the hunter moving down-wind often finds nothing but a bear track for all his effort. The poor vision accounts for most of the sudden meetings between the hunter and the bear. As the bear normally is a timid animal, he will attempt to escape without a fight if possible. Many experienced bear hunters attest to the fact that a bear will always run unless cornered, but many admit that "no one can tell when a bear thinks he is cornered."

The black bear, though a very fast runner on occasion, uses this speed only when frightened, except in rare instances. When on a meat diet he hunts from ambush, depending on surprise rather than a foot race with his prey. Normally he does not fall in the predator class, although hunger often drives him to make inroads on the moose, calf, and fawn population. He, in turn, has three major enemies other than the human hunter: the cougar, the grizzly, and the porcupine.

The bear mortality due to porcupines is much larger than many would suppose, but the reason for it is rather difficult to determine. The bear is, by nature, both curious and playful, and these attributes may account for his ultimate death due to quills. Many hunters have described instances in which the black bear, passing near a porcupine, gave the animal a sweeping pat with one paw. The result was a paw full of quills. This often so angers the bear that it snaps at the offending porcupine. The quills that become imbedded in the mouth and tongue often result in a slow death due to starvation.

Hibernation usually begins late in the fall and ends early in the spring. With the first frost he becomes a voracious eater, and gorges himself at every opportunity, often throwing caution to the winds. During this period he will drive off all interlopers from what he considers to be his private range. After a springtime of eating, a summer spent lolling in cool, swampy areas and a fall of gorging, he is glossy and sluggish and, with no more food to eat, he is ready to hibernate. In areas where this tree grows, the bear seeks out the mountain ash just before hibernation. He eats of the bright red berries and after this thorough cathartic he dens up. While he sleeps, he breathes very slowly and has an equally slow pulse beat.

It would be impossible to describe a typical *den,* for these shelters range from a cave to a clump of thick brush, depending upon the terrain and the temperature. The black bear's idea of a comfortable spot in which to hibernate seems to depend upon the individual. Many curl up in the hollow at the base of an uprooted tree, which offers shelter from the winter blasts. In the warmer but wetter climates, the bear normally seeks a den that offers merely cover and concealment.

**Breeding.** The black bear mates in the late spring and early summer. The period of gestation is about seven months, and the cubs are born late in January during the hibernation. The mother sleeps through this natural function and the cubs—blind, helpless, and almost hairless at birth—alternately suckle and sleep during the rest of the hibernation. At birth they weigh about eight ounces, and when they emerge from the den with the mother they average about five pounds. Normally the cubs remain with the mother the first year and den up with her prior to their first winter, but when the new cubs arrive they are driven off, often by force, although it is not unusual to see a mother with two generations of cubs. At no time is the father bear concerned with his progeny, though he usually begets several litters on the same range.

**Range and Distribution.** The range of the black bear is a wide one. Formerly he was present in large numbers over almost all of the wooded area of the continent. Although this range is now spotty as to population, it has lost little in extent. The animal is found in very large numbers in a half-dozen states. The latest big-game inventory gives total U. S. population as 155,100. (This does not include Alaska, which has a black bear population estimated at 75,000.)

| | | | |
|---|---|---|---|
| California | 21,500 | Montana | 8,400 |
| Colorado | 10,800 | New Mexico | 5,800 |
| Idaho | 8,000 | North Carolina | 7,300 |
| Maine | 20,100 | Oregon | 9,900 |
| Michigan | 7,100 | Washington | 21,100 |
| Minnesota | 8,200 | Wyoming | 5,300 |

The states where the black bear is less plentiful are as follows:

| | | | |
|---|---|---|---|
| Alabama | 125 | Ohio | 12 |
| Arizona | 1,300 | Oklahoma | 10 |
| Arkansas | 73 | Pennsylvania | 3,500 |
| Florida | 1,800 | South Carolina | 456 |
| Georgia | 925 | Tennessee | 630 |
| Louisiana | 900 | Texas | 210 |
| Maryland | 25 | Utah | 985 |
| Mississippi | 25 | Vermont | 910 |
| Nevada | 40 | Virginia | 1,500 |
| New Hampshire | 1,400 | West Virginia | 1,300 |
| New York | 1,000 | Wisconsin | 4,500 |

The states which had no black bear living in the natural state were:

| | |
|---|---|
| Connecticut | Massachusetts |
| Delaware | Missouri |
| Illinois | Nebraska |
| Indiana | New Jersey |
| Iowa | North Dakota |
| Kansas | Rhode Island |
| Kentucky | South Dakota |

Food and temperature usually guide the selection of the individual's range. Normally, he selects wooded areas, but within this range he frequents the sections where food is most plentiful. The normal home range of the black bear covers a 15-mile radius. When this range abuts on civilization the black bear is inclined to fall into habits which often result in his death by a bullet. He is notoriously playful in a boisterous, destructive way, and has been known to destroy food caches and cabin kitchens with a thoroughness that is almost unbelievable.

**Hunting Methods.** Bear hunting is unlike most other forms of American big-game hunting. This is especially true where the black bear is concerned. This difference is due to several factors recognized only by the sportsman who has made a study of bear habits.

All members of the bear family are inclined to be solitary in their habits, and only unusual circumstances bring them together in groups of more than two. Even when two are seen together, the chances are that they are a mother and cub. There are, of course, a few exceptions to the rule. When food is unusually scarce several bears may gather at the carcass of a large mammal that has died or been killed, but in every instance they return to their individual range when the bones have been picked clean. During the mating season a male and female may be seen together, but this period falls in the late spring or early summer, when the animal is not in prime condition and when it is protected by law in many states.

Another factor which makes bear hunting more difficult than the hunting of hoofed game is the tendency of the bear to be here today and 20 miles away tomorrow. The bear's excellent hearing and excellent nose conspire to keep him out of range, not only of the rifle, but of the vision, of the average hunter.

Except in a few areas, where the black bear is unusually plentiful, this animal is hunted in conjunction with some other big-game animal, with the latter supplying the primary reason for the hunt. The methods of hunting vary greatly, depending upon the area and the nature of the terrain.

In several of the Southern states, and in other areas where neither law nor prejudice prevent the use of dogs, black bear are hunted with hounds. This method can be good sport, or it can be extremely unsporting, depending upon the hunters themselves.

The hunters may follow the hounds by sound, and wait until the bear has been treed or brought to bay before moving in to make the kill. The kill under such circumstances is just about as exciting as shooting a fat hog in a pen, and entails the same amount of skill.

In many areas, however, the dogs are employed merely to keep the bear moving. When the cry of the hounds indicates that a bear has been located, the hunters separate and locate vantage points which promise an unobstructed shot at reasonable range and wait for the bear to appear. The bear, in its effort to keep well ahead of the hounds, offers a fast-moving target under such conditions, and has a sporting chance of making an escape.

Many states, desiring to protect a fine game animal from extermination, have initiated laws to prevent the hunting of bears with hounds. As the average bear hound is inclined to run deer as well as bear, such laws usually are based on sound conservation.

In the West it is common practice to take an old and ailing horse to a known bear range, kill it, and wait for the carcass to ripen. The hunter then takes up his position down-wind from the bait and waits for Bruin to arrive. This method entails little skill on the part of the hunter, and is frowned upon by many sportsmen.

The stalking method is by far the most sporting, and calls for a display of real skill on the part of the hunter, as well as some knowledge of the terrain and the habits of the bear on that range. This hunting usually is carried out in the fall, and the hunter seeks out berry patches, scrub oak thickets, or other areas where there is a natural food concentration. Having located evidence of a bear *using* the area, the hunter moves slowly and carefully up-wind, being careful to avoid unnecessary noise.

In some areas bear are not hunted until the first snowfall, when they may be tracked. This method is not so easy as many have believed, for the bear

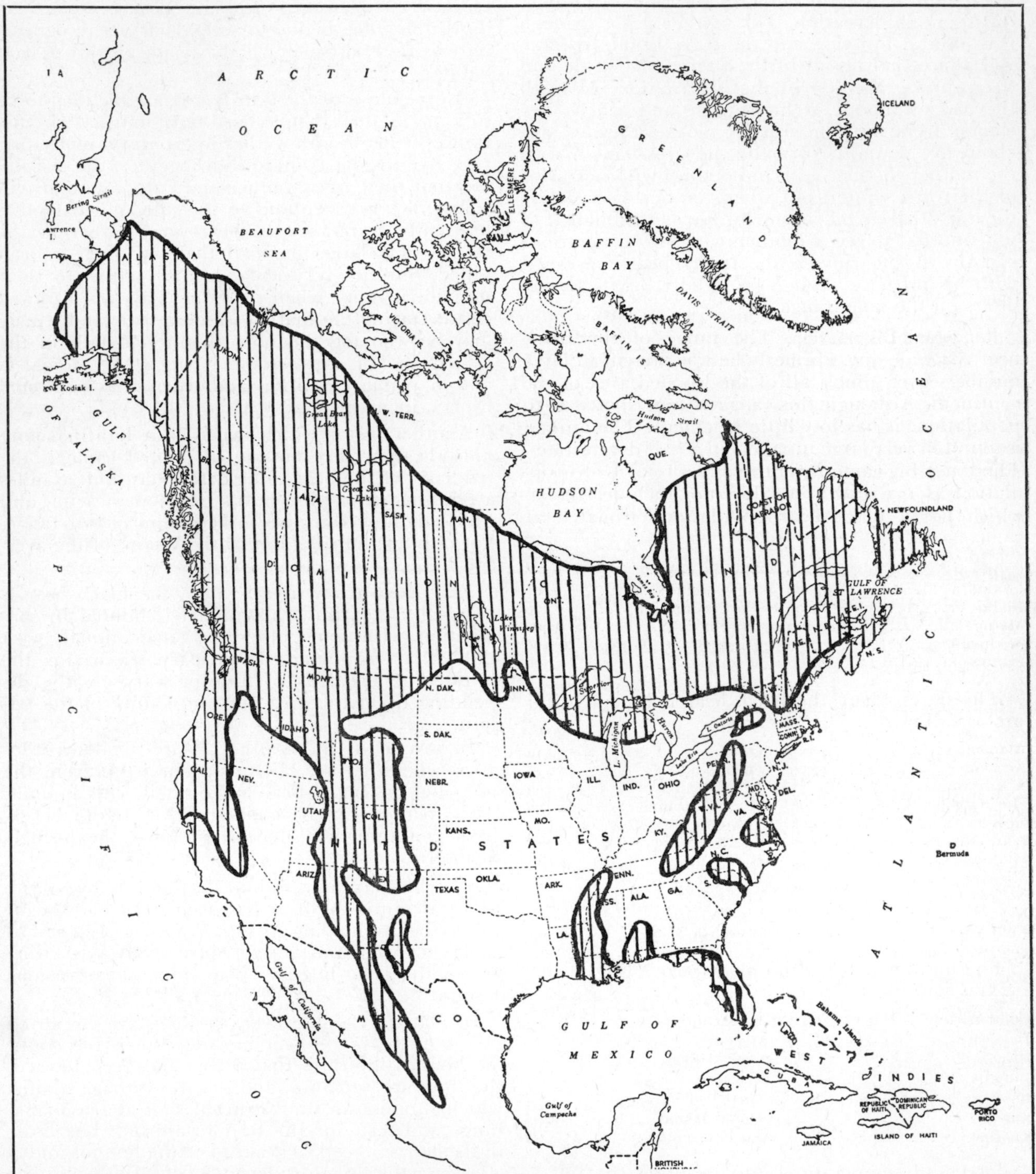


**Plate III.** Distribution of Black Bear.

is about to den up at this period and is covering considerable ground in order to stuff himself in preparation for his long hibernation.

By far the greater number of black bears are killed in the fall while the hunters are seeking deer, elk, and other game. Normally there are more hunters moving through the woods at this time. Therefore the bears are kept on the move, and many of them are unfortunate enough to run into some lucky hunter with a high-power rifle. Killing a bear under such circumstances often is about 99 per cent luck and one per cent skill.

There have been many arguments regarding the dangers involved in hunting the black bear, especially concerning the tendency of this bear to charge a hunter. Experienced bear hunters insist that the black bear will, in almost every instance, run rather than fight. The exceptions occur when the animal is cornered, or thinks he is cornered, or when he has been badly wounded by a hunter who is in close proximity. It is generally agreed, however, that no hunter can tell when the bear considers himself to be cornered, and there have been several recorded instances of hunters killed by black bears without having fired a shot.

In some instances what hunters believe to be a charge is merely an effort on the part of the bear to escape, and his accidental movement in the direction of the hunter is the result of confusion and poor vision. Often a bear is unable to locate the direction from which a shot came, due to echo or the reflection of sound from a rock face. In many instances, when the bullet misses or inflicts a minor wound, a bear will rise up, frantically swing around, and then make off in the direction which he believes leads to safety. When this happens to be toward the hunter, the latter is certain the animal is charging him.

The tendency of the black bear to follow the lines of least resistance also results in amplification of the charging theory. A bear shot or disturbed on a side-hill, for example, may swing downhill immediately, heading directly for the hunter he is trying to avoid.

The wise hunter, having downed a bear, will not immediately rush in to look his trophy over. He will throw another shell in the chamber, be ready to shoot instantly, and watch his downed bear for a few minutes from a safe distance before moving in to look the animal over at close range. A bullet near the spine or a grazing head shot often will knock a bear down for the count, and too often hunters have been injured or killed by bears that were knocked out but not killed.

A New Brunswick hunter, believing he had made a clean kill, was seated astride his bear and about ready to begin skinning operations when the animal recovered, jumped to all fours, and ran for heavy cover. The surprised hunter had a ride for several yards before rolling from the animal's back. Fortunately for this hunter the bear had but one thought—escape.

In areas where spring bear hunting is not prohibited, many hunters prefer this season for their hunting, especially in mountainous regions. When emerging from hibernation the bear seeks out a vegetable diet, and usually can be found feeding on succulent plants and grasses on open hillsides. At this time the pelt is in its finest condition, and usually the meat is more palatable.

**Rifles and Sights.** The rifle used by the hunter in killing deer, elk, or other hoofed game normally has sufficient shocking power for all except unusually large members of the black bear family. The average black bear is not hard to kill, and although many have been killed by .22-caliber bullets, and several with the small-caliber, high-velocity "varmint" loads, such rifles are not recommended for the hunter who hopes or expects to get a shot at bear.

Among the calibers and loads widely used are:

.30 '06 with 150-, 180-, or 220-grain bullet.
.30/30 with 150- or 170-grain bullet.
.30 (Remington) with 160- or 170-grain bullet.
.300 (Savage) with 150-, 180-, or 200-grain bullet.
.303 (Savage) with 180- or 195-grain bullet.
.35 (Remington) with 200-grain bullet.
.32 (Remington) with 170- or 180-grain bullet.
.270 with the 130- or 150-grain bullet.

For details on above loads see "Ammunition—Rifle."

The type of bullet, whether open point, soft point, or belted, depends upon the individual hunter and his preference, but the full-jacketed bullet and the hand-loaded lead or alloy bullet should be eliminated. The former is inclined to bore a clean hole without delivering the punch necessary to knock the animal down, and the latter is inclined to "blow up," resulting in a bad wound but not necessarily a fatal one.

The loads listed as preferred are all "factory" loads, most of them available at any shop handling rifle ammunition. When selecting the cartridge you intend using, be SURE you zero your rifle (sight in) with this cartridge, as the ballistics of each of the loads is different from any other, and a clean kill with the 170-grain bullet, for example, may result in a clean miss with the 200-grain bullet, unless the shooter is familiar with the "zero" of his rifle for the various loads used. No two rifles will have the same zero with the same bullet, so *make certain* you know the zero of the rifle you are firing for the cartridge (load, bullet weight, and bullet type) you are using. For dependability, use cartridges by the same maker. Although all our leading cartridge manufacturers turn out dependable ammunition, there is likely to be a considerable variation in the same caliber and type of cartridge turned out by two different makers.

While few eastern hunters equip their bear rifles with telescopic sights, the 2½- to 4-power scope is popular with many western and northern hunters. (See "Sights and Optical Aids.")

For complete details on skinning out and dressing the trophy, see "Preservation of Trophies."

# GRIZZLY BEAR

*Ursus horribilis*

When the Lewis and Clark expedition, sent out to explore the Louisiana Purchase, arrived at the foothills of the Rocky Mountains, the Indians they encountered told tales of a great bear, an animal of tremendous strength, great shyness, and unusual ferocity. Even then, the "facts" were influenced by legends born of fear.

As late as 1857 even the naturalists and hunters believed *Ursus horribilis* to be the only member of the grizzly family. Since then, zoologists have made careful studies of this animal, and C. Hart Merriam made the initial extensive breakdown by species. His record included about 30 recognizable species and sub-species, but present authorities believe there are about half that number.

Courtesy U. S. Fish and Wildlife Service.

PLATE I. A Toklat (Alaskan) Grizzly. The typical "hump" is clearly shown.

Despite the existence of many different species, each of the subdivisions remains aloof from the others, and although some zoologists have written to the contrary there is no evidence of habitual inter-breeding. It does occur, in isolated cases, and the hybrids in most instances are the result of breeding while in captivity and are not representative of the animal in its natural habitat.

Due to the wide distribution of the animal in the West and North, details on the different species and their ranges will be listed under "Range and Distribution."

**History.** The American grizzly, defined as the "king of North American game animals," dates back to the Pleistocene Age. Through the years he has changed in numbers and in size. In the early days his range covered the greater part of western North America, from northern Mexico northward and into western Canada. He was especially numerous among the foothills of the Rockies and its bordering plains. The sweep of civilization drove him from these plains to isolated pockets in the mountains. As the varied species which ranged the plains were reduced in numbers and forced to the mountains, several species were crowded into one range.

Changes in climatic conditions through the ages brought about a slow change in the size of the bear. On the plains he had easy access to food, there were few enemies, and the climate was temperate. This resulted in his attaining maximum growth. The struggle for existence which has been his lot for the past 50 years has reduced both his life span and his size and has resulted in a lengthening of his period of hibernation.

Both the hunter and the zoologist have found it difficult to differentiate between the aggressive grizzly and the mild big brown bear, and there has been considerable confusion. Only in recent years has there been even a partial clarification of the differences in these species. A typical grizzly differs from a typical brown bear in color, claws, skull, and teeth. The brown bear is more uniform in color, has a darker pelage, and shows less admixture of the silver-tipped hairs. Also, the brown has shorter claws and a more massive skull. (See diagram of footprints.)

The strength and courage of the grizzly are the features which make him the most sought-after animal, and it has been necessary to protect him from hunters in several areas in order to insure his existence. The larger national parks, such as Mount McKinley and Yellowstone, have proved to be the most certain refuges for this bear, for in them he is permitted to live and thrive in a natural habitat.

**Identification.** Because of the many species, it is difficult to describe a "typical" grizzly. His coloration may vary from almost black to a light cream, although the average grizzly has the coloration his name implies—grizzled: a dark brown undercoat with grayish, silvery tips to the hairs. While a cub he has a characteristic white collar around his neck, which he loses at the age of three.

By the time he has reached this age he has gained maturity in size but not in strength. His skull, which is used as a means of identification by zoologists, is still changing at this age, and he does not reach full maturity until about seven years old. An average lifetime is 25 years, but unconfirmed records indicate that some have lived to be 50 years of age.

The track of an average mature grizzly will measure about 6½ to 7 inches in width and from 12 to 14 inches in length. The length varies with species and with individual members of a species. Though the typical adult male weighs 500 pounds, a most unusual kill was reported in 1908 in Colorado. This bear weighed approximately 1800 pounds, and the hide measured 11 feet 7 inches in width and 12 feet 6 inches in length. This kill has not been confirmed.

As a result of the inability of zoologists to establish a definite line between the grizzly and the big brown bear, the present records are not broken down as to species. The largest grizzly on record is the animal killed by C. Craven in 1938, while hunting in the Tetons in Wyoming. This bear measured 7 feet 4 inches in length by 8 feet 1½ inches in width.

While the grizzly has poor vision, his sense of smell and his hearing are very acute. In many instances hunters have worked up-wind in stalking a grizzly, only to find, on arriving at the place where he had been spotted, that he had departed in great haste in another direction. His actual vision is not so poor as many believe, but the fact that his eyes are set very close together makes his field of vision extremely limited. He sees very well directly ahead, but badly at even slight angles. Often, when surprised, he will swing his head from side to side and often turn in a complete circle in an effort to locate the enemy he senses to be near.

**Characteristics.** By nature, the grizzly is a peaceful individualist, desiring only to be left alone, but he will fight viciously to maintain his solitary way of life. Because of his great size and strength, he requires a vast quantity of food; consequently he finds it necessary to protect a wide range against constant challenge by other animals. One sweep of his huge paw is capable of crushing the skull of a range bull, and he can mangle a man or beast as thoroughly as a lion with his almost straight claws. He flips over a boulder that a strong man would find difficult to move by an apparently effortless sweep of one paw. One of his enemies, the black bear, finds his only safety from his big cousin by climbing a tree. The grizzly though able to climb during his cub days, is unable to get up a tree when he reaches maturity because of the stiffening of his wrists.

In the spring the grizzly drops down to the foothills where he feeds on green grass. rock-chucks, gophers, and mice, but with the arrival of warm weather he retires to the shade of mountain forests, where his major diet is made up of roots, nuts, and berries. Like other members of the bear family he is omnivorous, but is a vegetarian by preference. He is not above eating the kill made by another animal, and is an avid fish-eater.

The early farmers and cattlemen found him a ruthless enemy and a pest, and his inroads on stock were severe in many instances. While he lived on the plains he did not begin his hibernation until mid-December, and often emerged from his den in March. Driven to the mountains, however, he often dens up late in October remaining until April.

**Range and Distribution.** The grizzly is found in large numbers in Alaska and British Columbia, but in this country his range is concentrated in the Rockies and a few isolated areas west of the mountains. No evidence exists of his ever having existed east of the Mississippi. The last big-game inventory made by the Federal Government shows a total population of 1400 of these animals in the States, with most of them located in Montana, with 772, and Wyoming, with 487.

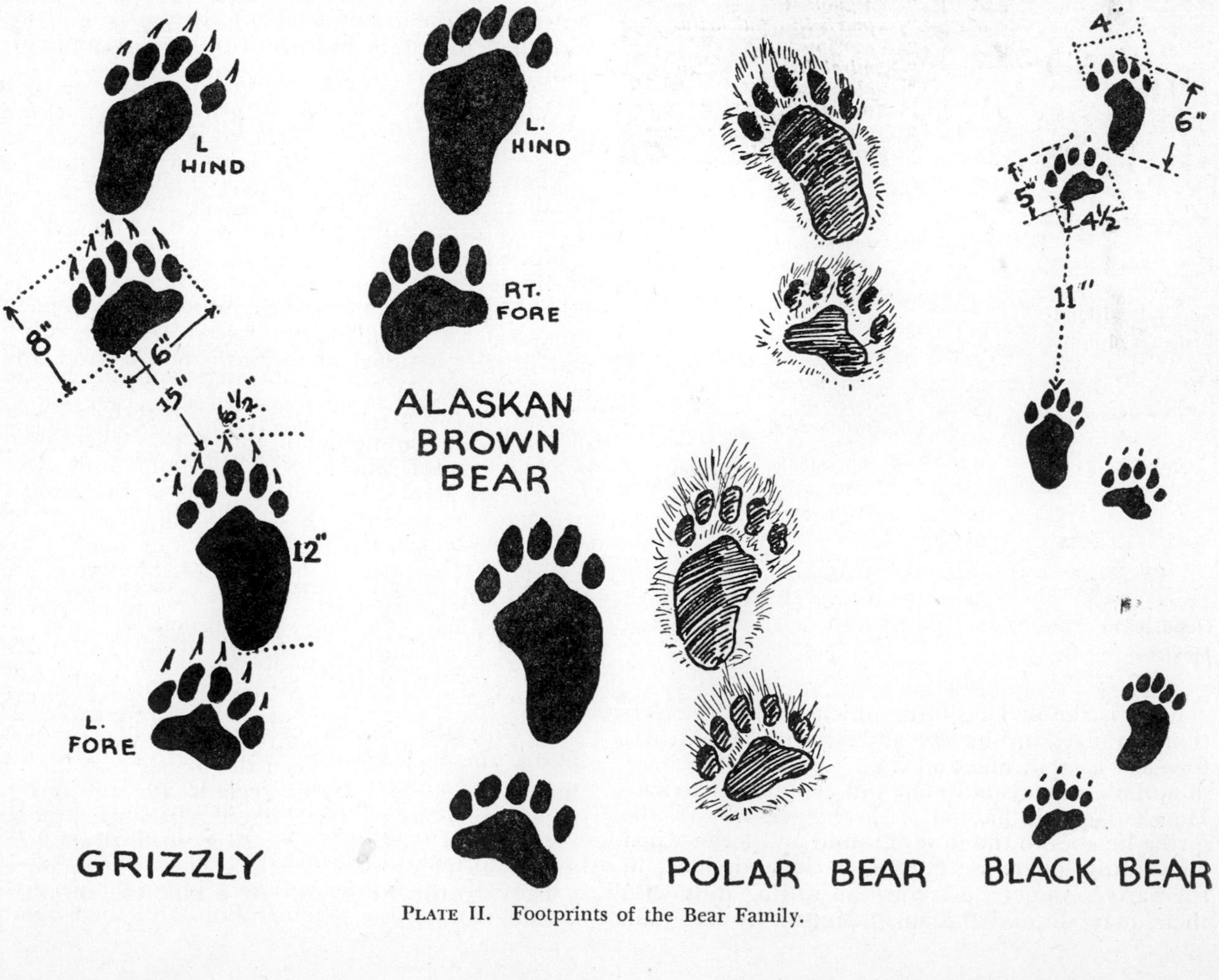


PLATE II. Footprints of the Bear Family.

A breakdown of the range of this bear, by species, is as follows:

| *AREA* | *SPECIES* |
|---|---|
| Arizona | *Ursus texensis navaho* |
| | " *arizonae* |
| | " *apache* |
| California | " *californicus* |
| | " *tularensis* |
| | " *colusus* |
| | " *klamathensis* |
| | " *mendocinensis* |
| | " *magister* |
| Colorado | " *horribilis bairdi* |
| | " *planiceps* |
| | " *macrodon* |
| | " *shoshone* |
| Idaho | " *idahoensis* |
| Montana | " *horribilis horribilis* |
| | " *absarokus* |
| | " *mirus* |
| Nevada | " *henshawi* |
| NewMexico | " *perturbans* |
| | " *horriaeus* |
| Texas | " *texensis texensis* |
| Utah | " *utahensis* |
| Washington | " *chelan* |
| Wyoming | " *horribilis imperator* |
| | " *rogersi rogersi* |
| | " *washake* |
| | " *rogersi bisonophagus* |
| | " *rungiusi rungiusi* |
| Alaska | " *nortoni* |
| | " *pallasi* |
| | " *rungiusi sagittalis* |
| | " *orgiloides* |
| | " *pulchellus pulchellus* |
| | " *caurinus* |
| | " *mirabilis* |
| | " *alascensis* |
| | " *toklat* |
| | " *phaeonyx* |
| | " *internationalis* |
| Canada | " *dusorgus* |
| | " *hylodromus* |
| | " *latifrons* |
| | " *macfarlani* |
| | " *andersoni* |
| | " *russelli* |
| Admiralty Island | " *eulophus* |
| British Columbia | " *chelidonias* |
| | " *atnarko* |
| | " *warburtoni* |
| | " *kwakiutl* |
| | " *canadensis* |
| | " *tahltanicus* |
| | " *purchellus ereunetes* |
| | " *oribasus* |
| | " *crassodon* |
| | " *pervagor* |
| | " *kluana impiger* |
| | " *stikeenensis* |
| | " *ophrus* |
| Hood River | " *richardsoni* |
| Mexico | " *nelsoni* |
| | " *kennerlyi* |

Food is the driving force which guides his selection of range, and his size and strength permit him to select a large one and hold it against the invasion of all animals but man and his repeating rifles. He changes his habitat with the seasons. In the spring he goes to the lower ground and feeds, when opportunity offers, on grasses, cattle, and game; in the early summer he favors the rolling hills with their quamash and Indian turnip; in the late summer he prefers the berry growth along the river flats, and in the fall he moves to the pine woods. Each spring, after winter winds and snow have erased his signs, he renews his "mark" on the trees bordering his range by rearing to his full height and stretching himself against a tree trunk, where he rubs his itching skin. This not only aids in the removal of his heavy winter coat but identifies that area as *"his."*

**Breeding.** June of every other year is the mating period for the female grizzly. The cubs, normally twins, but occasionally triplets or quadruplets, are born in late January or early February while the mother is in hibernation. Despite the great size of the mother, these cubs weigh but a few ounces when born.

The female is a gentle, wise mother, carefully instructing her cubs in all the tricks of eating and living, and guarding them with a savagery which few other animals dispute. Few of the predators that prey on the young of other animals are inclined to annoy the grizzly cub.

**Hunting Methods.** Grizzly hunting has much in common with black bear hunting, for due to the relative scarcity of these animals today the great majority of them are killed by hunters in search of hoofed game. The major exceptions to this rule will be found in Alaska, British Columbia, and in the mountainous area of Northwest Canada, where visiting sportsmen often set out with the express purpose of hunting grizzlies.

Although the grizzly tends to be more of a carnivore than the black bear, he is no less an individualist and tends to shun the company even of his own kind. Also, he is inclined to remove himself much farther from the haunts of man than is his black cousin.

There are a few places, even today, where the grizzly is hunted with dogs, but in most instances this procedure is limited to areas where the grizzly is hunted as a stock-killing pest, and the object of the hunt is not sport but the elimination of the bear. In most instances such hunts are extremely rough on the dogs, for one sweep of the grizzly's paw usually is sufficient to crush the life from the largest hound.

Most of the grizzlies in this country have been driven to the remote mountain retreats where man is a rare visitor. Sheep, goat, elk, and mule deer hunters are most likely to get shots at the animal that has, through the passage of time, earned the title of the "most dangerous American game." His very name, *Ursus horribilis* (the horrible bear), has led thousands of sportsmen to seek him out, and there are many instances of hunters devoting as much as two months a year for several consecutive years in order to look at one grizzly over their sights.

As with the Alaska brown bear, his gigantic cousin, the best hunting for the grizzly is in the spring, immediately after his emergence from hibernation, for his feeding habits at this time make it much easier to locate him. Also, the pelt is in its best condition at this time.

Normally the hunter will pack into a known grizzly range, establish a main camp, and then climb to some vantage point that offers a wide view of the surrounding country. Here he will sweep the terrain with powerful binoculars in an effort to locate his quarry. Upon emerging from the den after his winter fast, the grizzly normally shuns the heavy cover and frequents sunny slopes and mountain meadows where the warm sun has melted the snow and where grass, roots, bulbs, rock-chucks, and mice are more plentiful. The best period for this hunting usually is from daybreak until 9 A.M. and from 3 P.M. until sundown, for the grizzly, still in his heavy winter coat, does not welcome the heat of the warm sun.

Once a grizzly is located the real work begins, for extreme care must be used in making the stalk. Like the other members of his family, the grizzly has imperfect vision, but unusually keen nose and ears. A down-wind stalk is hopeless from the start, which often means that the hunter must detour in a wide circle in order to approach up-wind. As scent, except in unusual instances, is carried up-hill during the day, the cautious grizzly hunter often crosses to the far side of a valley or canyon and makes a wide circuit before ascending the slope on which his bear has been located.

Until the hunter has the grizzly in his sights and

PLATE III. Distribution of Grizzly Bear.

Photo by Fred Hollender.

PLATE IV. Two Grizzlies Hunting for Trouble.

is ready to squeeze off the shot, he must practice every stalking trick in his knowledge. Any rattle of equipment, a rolling pebble, the rasp of a hob-nailed shoe on rock, will normally eliminate the possibility of getting a shot. For this reason, many hunters favor the corrugated rubber or composition soled shoe-pac for this kind of hunting. Also, having located their bear, many hunters welcome wind and rain which, despite the discomfort it entails, will serve as a cover for their movements.

Having located the bear, the experienced hunter will not move until he has taken numerous bearings and cross-bearings on the relation of his quarry's position to adjacent landmarks. This permits him to make his stalk and at the same time avoid any possibility of his being observed by the bear, for he can check his progress from time to time by means of the landmarks.

A hurried stalk too often proves to be an unsuccessful one. A grizzly located late in the afternoon often is marked down but not hunted until the next day, for if he is not disturbed the chances are that the animal will return to the same area to feed. It is always a sound practice, having located a bear, to estimate the time it will require to make the stalk and kill, dress out the skin, and return to camp before dark. Spring nights can be cold, and the experienced hunter prefers a comfortable night in camp to an uncomfortable one in the open.

On the coastal areas, especially on those drained by a good salmon river, the grizzly is often found in the vicinity of water, for like the Alaskan brown, he loves fresh fish, or perhaps it would be more accurate to say he loves "fish," for many seem to consider "ripe" salmon a delicacy. Experienced hunters scoff at the popular legend of a grizzly standing in a stream cuffing out salmon left and right, then emerging to the shore for a feast. Only in very narrow, shallow streams crowded with salmon will the bears follow this practice. Instead, they stand in shallow water and wait for a salmon to pass close, whereupon they pounce, using both tooth and claw to hold the fish, then carry it ashore to be eaten. In brief, the grizzly is not nearly the expert fisherman legend would have one believe.

Another method of grizzly hunting is similar to the one practiced in hunting the black bear, that is, the use of bait. A winter-killed elk or caribou, uncovered by the melting snow, will attract a grizzly by the scent. Often, upon eating his fill, the bear will scrape up leaves and brush to cover the remainder of the carcass, which normally he will revisit twice a day, early morning and late afternoon, until it has been consumed. In some instances, as in hunting the black bear, an old horse or cow is sacrificed to serve as bait.

The most sporting method, but one that is not so widely practiced, is by tracking. This requires a

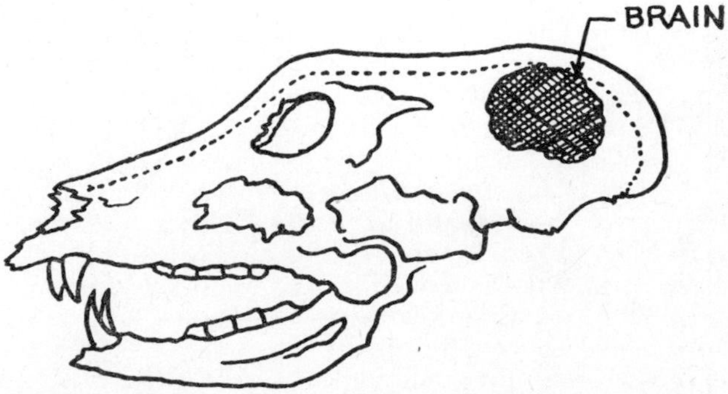


PLATE V. Drawing showing small brain area of bear, dotted line indicating thickness of skull.

thorough knowledge of woodcraft and of grizzly habits as well as considerable endurance. In many instances it calls for rapid and extremely accurate shooting as well.

The grizzly bear is constantly alert, even when he seems to be relaxing over his food or just resting. Hundreds of experienced hunters have related examples of the wariness of this animal. A hunter stalking a grizzly will arrive at the point where he had located the animal only to find very apparent signs that the bear has learned of his approach and departed from the place in a hurry, although other game, feeding between the bear and the hunter, had not been disturbed.

Only a foolhardy hunter will ignore the dangers involved in hunting this bear, for an aroused grizzly is not only dangerous, but can cover ground at an incredible speed although mortally wounded. Several hunters have found snap shooting to be a fatal error. Many instances are known in which a grizzly, his heart completely shattered and his lungs torn badly, managed to cover 50 to 100 yards and maul or kill a hunter. Only two wounds are certain to stop him: one which shatters the spinal column, or one through the brain.

The hunter who is a good shot and who is thoroughly familiar with his rifle, should try for a shot from an angle that will smash the shoulder and hit the heart, one which will smash the spine, or one which will hit the brain. (See vital area diagram.) The sensible hunter, unable to get in such a shot, will hold fire until the animal moves to a position where this is possible. The hunter not certain of his marksmanship or his rifle would be well advised not to shoot at all.

The hunter who has wounded a grizzly and is being charged by the animal would do well to concentrate on breaking a fore-leg or the shoulder, rather than try for a head shot. The curved, thick skull of this bear serves as excellent armor. Also, few hunters are sufficiently cool and capable to make an effective brain shot while a half-ton of grizzly is moving toward them at high speed. The bear, contrary to the belief fostered by many wildlife artists, charges on all fours and not erect.

Veteran grizzly hunters report that not one out of

Courtesy U. S. Forest Service.

PLATE VI. Mother Grizzly and Cubs, checking up on an intruder.

20 grizzlies encountered, wounded or not, will charge a man. Ned W. Frost, who probably has been in at the kill of more grizzlies than any other hunter in the world, insists that of the 350 grizzlies he has killed or seen killed, not more than a dozen of the animals charged the hunters. But he urges extreme alertness in grizzly country. Getting in the first shot at a grizzly already charging is a hair-graying job, and one which places the odds very definitely in the bear's favor.

**Rifles.** The preferred calibers, bullets, and loads for this hunting are similar to those for hunting the Alaska brown bear *(q.v.)*.

# POLAR BEAR

*Thalarctos maritimus maritimus*

**History.** The polar bear, having selected for his home the harsh Arctic land regions, has, by the very remoteness of his habitat, been comparatively unmolested by man. He is seldom hunted, except by the Eskimos, who enjoy the flavor of a meat which is too strong for the average white man's palate. Fur traders find no demand for the coarsely furred pelt, and when taken by an occasional hunter the pelt serves primarily as a wall decoration or a rug.

During the past 20 years only 1300 polar bear pelts have been reported shipped from the Arctic. Never as plentiful as other members of the bear family, the polar bear population has fluctuated but slightly in recent years, and it has been estimated that approximately 3000 inhabit the northern coast of Alaska.

**Identification.** This monarch of the ice is one of the largest of the surviving members of the bear family, with big males often weighing 1500 to 1600 pounds, and the females scaling from 850 to 900 pounds. The male often reaches 9 feet in length, while the average female is about 6 feet 6 inches long. The record polar bear, killed by Captain Bob Bartlett in 1914, had a skin which measured 12 feet in length.

In the winter this bear's coat blends perfectly with the white ice floes. In the spring he begins to shed this white mantle, assuming a yellowish coat, but his camouflage remains excellent, for he merges with the yellowed ice in the summer pack.

The general appearance of the polar bear is somewhat different from that of the other big bears, not

Courtesy Nature Magazine.

PLATE I. Polar Bear.

only by reason of his white pelage but by his longer neck, comparatively small head, narrow skull, and small molars for grinding. His feet are broad and hairy, and serve as natural snowshoes, enabling him to move over the snow with comparative ease. (See Plate II, p. 29.) His claws are long and sharp, because of the honing they receive when he moves over the hard ice, and they are black-tipped, as is his nose.

Like other members of his family, his vision is not good, and his hearing is little better. His acute sense of smell, however, more than atones for his other sensory defects, and he can pick up the scent of a stranded whale from a point 20 miles distant.

**Characteristics.** In his frozen habitat, the polar bear spends most of his time roaming a tremendous range in search of food. He travels almost without pause over the land and ice floes, giving careful attention to everything edible. His pace is rapid and tireless, and, as the only truly aquatic bear, he swims great distances, at three to six miles an hour, often many miles from land, using only his forelegs to propel himself.

Largely carnivorous, his favorite food is the seal, but he will turn to fish, porpoise, a stranded whale, roots, seaweed, and grass when no other sustenance is available. There is no indication that his grass-eating is the result of hunger, however, for analysis of the stomach contents of many polar bears shows that grass often is eaten on top of a full meal. The inference is that he craves a vegetable balance for health reasons.

He is a highly skilled stalker, and the animal on which he gets most practice is the wily seal. When he winds or sights a seal napping on an ice floe, the polar bear will move at a fast, noiseless shuffle over snow or ice and slide into the water with hardly a ripple. He paddles gracefully and quietly, with only the top of his head showing. When a few yards from the edge of the floe he submerges, then emerges from the water with a remarkable rush and kills the seal with the rapid sweep of a paw.

He hunts eider ducks and scoters with equal efficiency, and eats them, as he does the seal, completely. The bones, skin, hair, and teeth of such prey pass through his stomach undigested.

The attitude of the polar bear toward man, its only enemy, is unpredictable. On one occasion it will defend food, habitat, and cubs with real ferocity, and will wage a roaring attack when cornered. On other occasions the vaguest scent of man sends this bear rushing away at top speed.

There is some conflict among zoologists as to the hibernation tendency of the polar bear. Some maintain that only the pregnant female hibernates; others contest this, pointing out that in many areas pregnant females have been killed during the hibernating season, and that during this season as many females as males are seen. The denning, or holing-up, of both male and female is the same. They select a jumble of shore ice, or dig a hole in deep-drifted snow. These holes are about 7 feet long and 3 feet wide, with at least a one-foot thick roof and a small ventilating hole.

**Breeding.** The male and female polar bear go their solitary, lonely ways except during mating season, which extends from late May into July. The cubs, normally just one, but occasionally two and rarely three, arrive late in December or early in January. They are about the size of an adult guinea pig, and are born naked and blind. The mother is asleep when they are born, and they instinctively burrow into the warm fur and suckle. By April they have increased greatly in both size and strength, and have a heavy coat of white, woolly fur which is heavy enough to protect them from the rigors of an Arctic spring, which normally is well below zero.

Zoologists report that in some areas the bears have two mating seasons, one in early March, the other in August, but the gestation period is the same in each instance, namely between ten and 11 months.

The polar bear mother is one of the most devoted in all wild life. She guards her cubs with ferocity, and teaches them the art of survival with extreme patience. It is her body which protects them against the piercing storms, and she tows them or rides them on her back across lanes of open water. She teaches them how to stalk and kill the fat hair seals and how to catch fish. The female is inclined to be more wary than the male, and her range is not so wide as that of the male. She is inclined to have a definite range, normally not too far from land, and this trait is intensified when she has cubs.

When a female with a cub is killed, the task of catching the cub is not so simple as it is with other members of the bear family. The cub will run away with amazing speed, and if captured is vicious in the extreme, using both claws and teeth in an effort to win freedom. Like the parents, a cub has a tremendous tenacity for life, and even a serious wound often fails to bring death.

**Range and Distribution.** The entire length of the Arctic coast comes within the distribution range of the polar bear. It is a wet, cold, and bleak climate, with temperatures often dripping to 60 degrees below zero, but it is a preferred habitat. Food is always a problem, and exposure to the climate frequently causes the bears to suffer from bone and muscle ailments.

Polar bears have been seen as far south as Newfoundland, but the supposition is that they were swept to this southerly area aboard ice floes. Often these bears will drift along on a big berg because of its large seal population. Such floes sometimes drift far, and as they move southward they disintegrate, occasionally leaving the bear stranded miles from the nearest land. Because of his great endurance as a swimmer the bear often manages to reach shore. The polar bear population of Iceland as well as Newfoundland has been increased through this means.

The peregrinations of the bear usually are restricted to the ice floes, and he moves from one to the other in search of his favorite food. Occasionally, however, one will be found from 18 to 20 miles from the nearest open water, crouched near a seal-hole.

**Hunting Methods.** Only the hunter with a top-heavy bank balance, plenty of idle time, and the willingness to undergo a lengthy period of hardship and some discomfort will be interested in hunting the polar bear.

The advent of the airplane has reduced the cost and time element to some extent, but not the discomfort, for the airplane can be employed only to *locate* the bear. The expedition must then set forth by boat in order to reach the area where the bear was seen. Normally this requires from several days to two weeks of movement among the floe ice, a procedure which proves too dull for the majority of sportsmen. Also, the cost usually is far too great for the trophy obtained.

No one who has hunted this bear has denied the element of danger involved, not only from the bear but as a result of the dangers involved in taking a small boat among floe ice. The wounded polar bear can be a dangerous enemy, and even when mortally wounded has amazing vitality. Several instances have been recorded in which a polar bear, shot through the heart, covered from 60 to 80 yards *toward* the hunter, being stopped only by another bullet which smashed the spine or shoulder and made further travel impossible.

To kill a bear that is swimming in the open water is no feat, of course, and such a procedure reflects

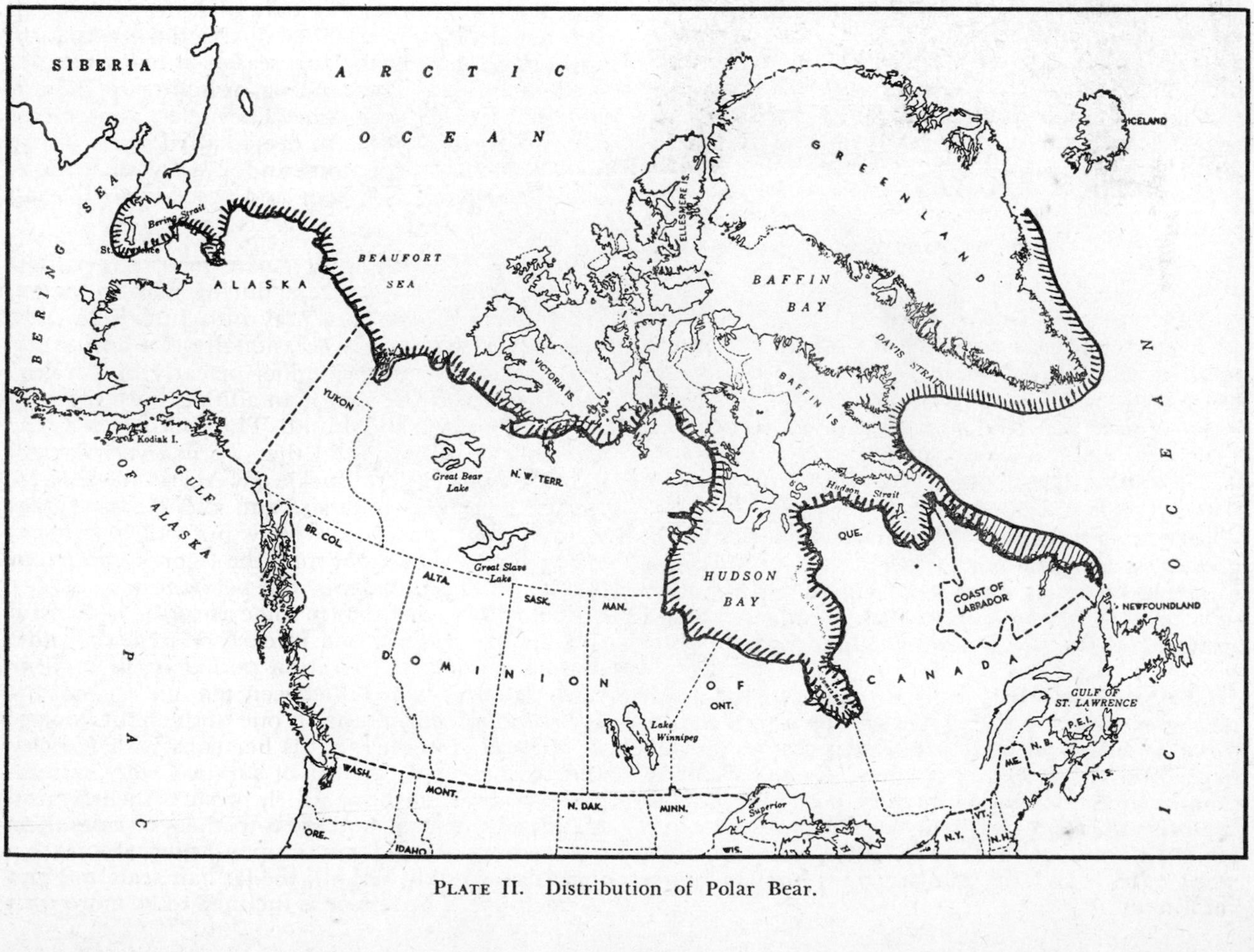


PLATE II. Distribution of Polar Bear.

no credit to the hunter. In such instances the range normally is *point blank,* and the bear does not have a chance.

**Rifle.** For the most satisfactory rifle for this hunting, see the rifles recommended for hunting the Alaska brown bear.

# BISON

*Bison bison*

**History.** Buffalo is the common name for the American bison, although in strict usage "buffalo" applies only to the larger species of Asia and Africa. Within the ox family *(Bovidae),* our species *(Bison bison)* is more closely related to the European bison *(Bison banasus).* There is no evidence of descent from the great *Superbison* of the American Tertiary Period. More probably the short-horned American buffalo was an immigrant from Europe or Asia, arriving in North America in the middle Pleistocene.

At one time the buffalo's range extended over about a third of the continent, between Great Slave Lake in Canada, and northeastern Mexico. It reached west of the Rockies to the Blue Mountains in Oregon and the Sierra Nevadas in the Southwest. East of the Mississippi it was shallower, running from the Great Lakes to central Georgia. Although buffaloes may never have been numerous east of the Alleghenies, they were found as far east as the Tidewater section of Virginia.

A century and a half ago they were plentiful in the central part of New York and in Pennsylvania. History records the slaughter of a herd of 10,000 in this part of the country in 1790, and in 1792 one animal was killed on the street in Harrisburg, Pa. By 1820, however, buffaloes were rare east of the Mississippi.

Three sub-species are generally recognized; the plains bison *(Bison bison bison),* the wood bison *(Bison bison athabascae Rhoads),* and the eastern bison *(Bison bison pennsylvanicus).* Some mammalogists distinguish a fourth race, the mountain bison *(Bison bison haningtoni Figgins),* which was peculiar to the mountains of Colorado. The eastern race of Pennsylvania, Maryland, and Virginia was extinct by 1815.

The history of the bison in Canada parallels that of the animal in this country. Where scores of thousands roamed the country in the vicinity of Morley and Calgary, the major haunt of the animals in

Courtesy U. S. Forest Service.

PLATE I. The Largest Bison in the World, now with the Wichita herd.

Canada, not a one remained by the turn of the century. Far to the north near Great Slave Lake, a small isolated herd of wood buffalo remained. Through the Dominion Government a reasonably successful attempt was made to re-establish the plains buffalo there. Between 1906 and 1912, 716 bison were distributed in small herds among several national parks. The animals multiplied and since that period it has been necessary to kill off more than 27,000 of the surplus population. The principal herd in Canada is now at Elk Island Park in the vicinity of Edmonton and numbers approximately 1000.

It was the plains or prairie bison which made up the tremendous herds of the Great Plains. Their total number has been estimated at 60 to 75 million. During the spring migration, wagon trains and later railroad trains often were surrounded by herds reaching as far as the eye could see; because of the danger of stampedes, trains were stalled on the track, in one instance for eight hours. The classic account, however, was given by Colonel Richard Irving Dodge, who in 1871 rode for three days through a herd which he judged to be 25 miles wide for at least part of its length, with 15 to 20 animals grazing to the acre. He estimated the length of this herd at 50 miles, from the fact that it took five days to pass one point. This was an army of perhaps four million animals.

But already the great herds were dwindling rapidly. The plains Indians, depending primarily on the buffalo for food and on its hide for their bedding and shelter, abhorred waste, and usually killed judiciously. White men, however, killed thousands of animals for the tongues alone. Dried or smoked tongues became a commodity, shipped down-river from St. Louis. With cheap rail and steamboat transportation, the bulky hides gained a commercial importance formerly held by beaver skins during the vogue of the beaver hat. Buffalo robes were widely used as rugs and as substitutes for blankets, and the demand spurted in 1870 when an English firm began processing the tough hides for leather. Professional buffalo hunters, followed by teams of skinners with wagons, left acres of rotting carcasses behind them.

Bone-gathering became a profitable occupation. The Santa Fe railroad made Dodge City in Kansas a boom center of the hide and bone trades. In 1875 some stations in this region were handling buffalo bones at the rate of a carload a day. When pulverized, the bones were used as fertilizer or processed for carbon for sugar refining.

By the turn of the century the plains bison was in imminent danger of extinction. The completion of the Union Pacific Railroad in 1869 had divided the buffalo masses into northern and southern herds. In 1895 only 800 animals remained of the northern herd. In 1888 Colonel C. J. ("Buffalo") Jones had rescued a few calves of the southern herd, keeping some on his ranch in the Texas Panhandle and presenting some to neighbors. But a scientist making a careful survey in 1903 discovered only 969 individuals in the United States.

Thanks are due largely to the New York Zoological Society and the American Bison Society for preventing the extinction of the buffalo. Theodore Roosevelt played an important role in persuading the Federal government to establish the protected herds which today number more than 6000.

**Identification.** The massive head and the hump on its shoulders give the buffalo its characteristic outline. Long, woolly hair on head, hump, and shoulders, contrasting sharply in texture with the short hair on the rest of the body, adds to the bulky effect. On the head the hair grows 10 to 14 inches long, and the ears are practically hidden in this woolly pompadour. A distinctive feature is the 8 to 10 inch beard. Twelve inches is the record length, but zoo animals may have equaled or surpassed this, since their beards are not worn short by grazing.

Both sexes have permanent horns, short, thick at the base but tapering sharply. These curve out and upward at the sides of the head, suggesting handles. The horns of the cow are smaller at the base and more sharply pointed than the bull's, and curve inward farther toward the head. The young calves have straight horns which gradually acquire the curve.

A grown plains bison five or six years old stands from 5½ to 6 feet high at the hump, and may be from 9 to 12½ feet long from nose tip to tail tip, with 20 to 36 inches of this length in tail. The average weight is between 1800 and 2000 pounds, although there is a record of a Kansas bull which weighed 3000 pounds. The cow is considerably smaller, weighing about 800 pounds. The average height is about 5 feet, the length about 7 feet, including 16 inches or so of tail.

In the bull the horns average 18 inches long, with an average circumference of 13 inches at the base. The record measurements are: length, 22⅜ inches; circumference at base, 14⅞ inches; greatest spread, 35⅜ inches.

Though often described as brown, over most of his body the plains bison is more nearly the dark tan of saddle leather. In spring the woolly mantle over the bull's hump becomes a lighter, yellowish tan. The head, throat, forelegs, and tail are dark, however. Especially with the spring pelage, the contrast of the dark head with the lighter shades is striking. The cows, generally darker in the body, show less contrast. The calves are very light at birth, with the brown showing only on the nose and around the eyes. In about six months they acquire the coloring of the adults, and at two years are considerably darker. From this point on the coloring grows lighter as the animal grows older.

The wood bison was much darker than the prairie buffalo, and showed its dorsal strips. It was also a larger animal, with long legs, a higher hump, and a more massive head, broader between the base of the horns. The horns were an inch or so shorter than those of the southern race, but thicker at the base, and they curved in closer to the head.

The mountain bison of Colorado was distinguished for its soft, fine coat of a reddish color and for its creamy muzzle. The horns were large and spread comparatively wide.

We have no detailed description of the eastern bison; writings of the 18th-century observers indicate that it resembled the wood bison, but was very dark, and perhaps nearly black, and that the hump was poorly developed or lacking altogether.

**Characteristics.** The plains bison likes open country. It is primarily a grazer, preferring short, fine grasses like grama, bluestem, buffalo, and bunch grass. If hard up, though, it will browse on sagebrush. The wood bison was more of a browser; in winter it depended heavily on willow twigs. In spite of its name, the wood bison was not associated with heavy timber.

On the plains, roads and railroads have been laid along trails made by buffalo herds going to water. The animals water once a day, sometimes traveling 20 or 30 miles. Like sheep, they string out in single file; some of their trails were worn a foot deep.

Shallow basins, where the animals have torn up the earth with horns and hoofs and rolled, are a feature of buffalo country. Apparently a good coating of mud gives relief or protection in the mosquito season. Since buffalo wallows become pools after rain, they saved lives in frontier days; in some cases troops of cavalry found enough water for both men and horses.

Buffaloes seem to itch a good deal in summer. They rub the bark off trees, and have been credited with wearing stones smooth and knocking down telegraph poles with their scratching.

When they had the freedom of the open prairies, they normally traveled from 200 to 400 miles between their winter and summer feeding grounds. The great herds, which were made up of numerous distinct smaller groups of 50 to 200 animals each, were seen only in spring and summer, during the northward migration. The plains Indians believed that each year an entirely new set of buffaoes appeared, released by a benevolent god from an underground cavern in the Staked Plains of Texas. Drifting southward in the fall, the animals were seen only in comparatively small herds, some of bulls only.

Buffalo calves are born in April or May, after a gestation period of about nine and a half months. In a day they can follow their mothers. They and the wary cows make up the front ranks or center of a herd, which usually is led by an old cow. The bulls, forming a scattered fringe, are described by some observers as sentinels. A few old bulls may be stragglers. Aged or disabled bulls often are seen alone.

In spring the animals are very nervous; it has been said that they will stampede from a cloud shadow. During the rutting season in July and August they are more easily approached, but also are more irritable. Buffaloes generally are timid, but their temperament always is uncertain. One never knows when a bull will decide to charge.

The usual attack is a head-on ramming charge in which the horns do not come into play. In the rutting season, however, the bulls rake their rivals. In

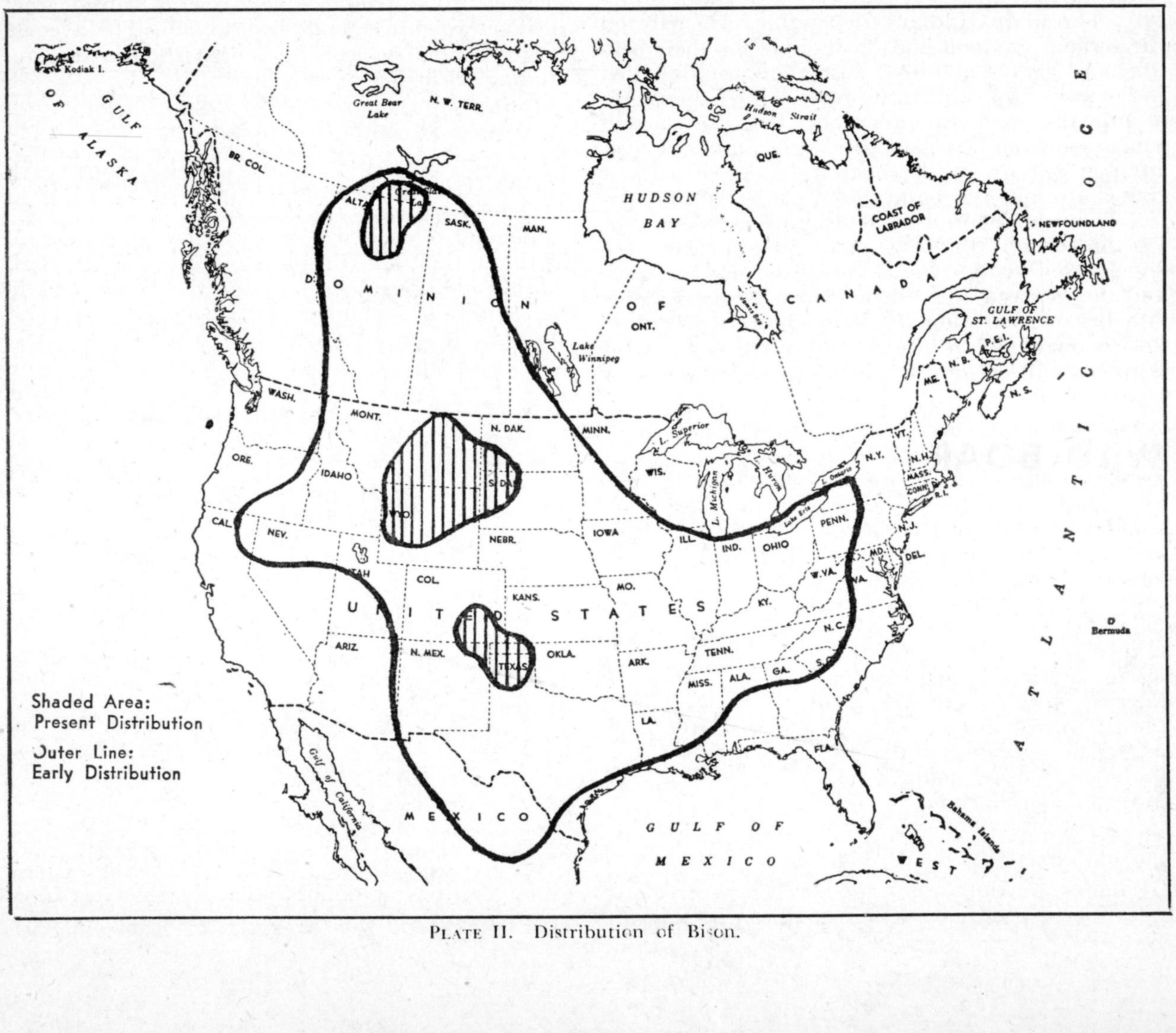


PLATE II. Distribution of Bison.

butting they may knock each other out, but their fights are seldom fatal.

Buffaloes have poor eyesight, but their hearing and sense of smell are quite acute. When vaguely alarmed, they walk slowly into the wind. One unusual characteristic is the fact that they face a blizzard. They are famous for endurance—old-timers of the plains vowed that a running buffalo could tire three horses—and they are strong swimmers.

Besides man, the buffalo's chief enemy has been the gray wolf, though it is doubtful that wolves ever did much worse than to pick off the weaker specimens and the aged. So far as is known, the species is not subject to any epidemic diseases.

**Range and Distribution.** Because of the establishment of the protected herds at the beginning of this century, there is no question of the buffalo's survival. Its present numbers are limited, however, by the available range. The big-game inventory of 1946 showed the following distribution:

| | |
|---|---|
| Arizona | 208 |
| Colorado | 26 |
| Montana | 1,300 |
| Nebraska | 358 |
| New Mexico | 18 |
| North Dakota | 27 |
| Oklahoma | 676 |
| Pennsylvania | 60 |
| South Dakota | 915 |
| Texas | 300 |
| Utah | 50 |
| Washington | 25 |
| Wyoming | 1,000 |
| TOTAL | 4,963 |

The Big Delta region of Alaska, where 23 buffaloes were released in 1928, also has a herd which in 1946 was estimated at several hundred.

**Hunting Methods.** In most of these states the species is completely protected. Texas permits the shooting of males over ten years old, or of any stags or steers, though this could hardly be called sport. Arizona, however, permits about 50 hunters to take part in an annual midwinter hunt which holds the herd down to the 250 or so which the available range can support. This herd is the only one in the country living free on unfenced land, and its members have acquired an impressive reputation for cussedness. Hunting them on horseback, in frontier style, is no parlor game. Arizona's game commission keeps a number of cowboys standing by, however, to rope any wounded animal which seems about to charge.

The Indian methods of hunting required daring and superb horsemanship. Sometimes it was possible to head off a stampeding herd and force the animals to mill; in such a "surround" the hunters rode around the herd, shooting at selected targets. In the chase the hunters rode among the buffaloes, each brave choosing a particular animal and closing in on the right side (unless the hunter was left-handed) for a shot at close range. Many Indians were able to sink their arrows in a buffalo up to the feathers.

This type of hunting was extremely dangerous. If a wounded buffalo got close enough to use his horns, if horse and buffalo collided, or if the horse stepped in a gopher hole, the rider would almost surely be trampled by the herd. Old-time frontiersmen preferred Indian-trained horses for the chase. A good buffalo horse, identified by a split ear, usually was a prized and pampered animal used for no other work.

Another group of great buffalo hunters were the Mexicans of the Southwest. For many years they stuck with the six-foot lance equipped with a three-inch blade, on the grounds that the lance was "always loaded."

The method most used by the professionals who nearly exterminated the buffalo was the still hunt. When within 1000 yards of a herd, the hunter dropped out of sight in a ravine or behind a ridge, taking care to stay up-wind, and tried to approach within 100 yards. Professionals rarely tried shots longer than 50 or 75 yards. If the first victim was neatly dropped, the rest of the herd usually moved on no more than 50 yards or so before they began to graze again, and an expert shot, if he could stay up-wind and out of sight, might kill 20 or more buffaloes without causing a stampede. By this method some bunters got as many as 250 a day.

# WILD BOAR

*Sus scrofa*

**History.** The American wild boar, which is not to be confused with the *peccary* or *javelina (q.v.)* of the Southwest and Old Mexico, is an animal whose origin in this country and true species is a mystery. This huge boar, which now roams the dense thickets of the Great Smokies, and is confined almost entirely to North Carolina and eastern Tennessee, has been the subject of considerable debate, not only among the natives of this area but among zoologists. The origin of the animal in this area is a matter of some speculation. Some contend that they were captured in Germany's Black Forest and imported to America by an adventurer named Barnes. Others claim that two North Carolina brothers imported several of both sexes from Russia about a year after the First World War. While the country from which they were imported remains highly doubtful—and the truth may never come to light—the facts concerning the time and place of their introduction into this region have been quite well established.

In the early part of this century, an Englishman named George Moore leased a large area of mountain wilderness adjacent to and surrounding Hooper's Bald, a wild and practically impenetrable area, just southwest of the Great Smokies. He had long dreamed of establishing a huge game preserve here and at once enclosed a large timbered tract with a great fence. One day in the year 1910, a mob of curious mountaineers from the surrounding country gathered on the mountain top. The sight of heavily bolted crates being transferred to the Bald had stimulated an inquisitive and speculative interest among these natives. Included in the Englishman's menagerie were several wild boars which attracted more attention than any of the other animals released. The spectators stood about awed by the monsters as they scrambled into the forest. Thus the opening of the big crates on the mountain top was the beginning of American history of the wild boar.

**Identification.** The physical make-up of this hardy animal is unlike that of the domestic hog. He does, however, bear some resemblance to the wild razorbacks of both the swamps and mountain country of the Southeast. The average boar (unless fat from

Courtesy U. S. Forest Service.

PLATE I. A real tusker at bay, and ready to take on the hounds.

mast) has a narrow body which slopes from mighty shoulders to almost nondescript hind quarters. Underneath their long dark brown or brownish-black bristles, which in adult hogs are usually split at the ends, there is a thick wool-like undercoat, that gives evidence that Nature had intended them to live in cold regions. Prevalent with adult animals is the heavy tail, sometimes bushy, with thick, matted bristles hanging several inches long. Other distinctive features of their physical make-up are: the red glint in their eyes, which reminds the beholder of the expression "blood in his eye"; and their sharp, protruding, razorlike tusks, the chief weapon of attack, which in adults range anywhere from 3 to 6½ inches. The size and ruggedness of the boar distinguishes him from the rest of the hog family. He is superior to the wild boars of India and Malaya. Most hunters on their maiden trip into the boar country are utterly surprised to learn of the immense size to which they grow. There are, of course, many small pigs in the 125- or 150-pound class to be found (yearling pigs that become wilder with age), but 200- to 350-pound specimens are quite common. The largest one ever killed in this great wilderness was reported to weigh 600 pounds; almost every fall, boar ranging upwards of 350 pounds are killed.

**Characteristics.** Big-game hunters claim that in the heat of battle these boars are the most vicious of all animals that roam the American forest. They reign supreme in their territory and even the black bear is no match for this powerful, belligerent brute. Mother bears selecting one of these pigs to feast their cubs have been found with bellies ripped inside out and littered on the battle ground in the boar's own inimitable manner of destruction. When he is first jumped by dogs it is uncertain just what he will do. He may stand his ground and fight it out on the spot where he is first routed from his bed; it may be a vicious running fight, or it may be a fleet chase of many miles before he comes to bay. Short-sighted and ill-tempered, the Russian fights at close range, and when he decides to fight where jumped he usually springs boldly into action, charging head-on with a series of lightning-like thrusts of the head. The tusk-blades fly into action, in rapier fashion, and the damage is done in the flash of a second. These wild boars take the greatest toll of dogs of any American big game, and the hounds surviving battle carry more scars than hunting dogs in any other part of the country.

When he elects to run for it, instead of fighting it out, he may run the open ridges as does the mountain deer, but frequently he criss-crosses the ledges and slopes indiscriminately. They have terrific speed, and are as fast as a young deer—a statement that hunters not familiar with the animal have refused to believe. With incredible agility they can blaze a path through the roughest sort of country. In the rhododendron thickets that are impassable for man and even difficult for the best of dogs, they have an uncanny way of splitting through undergrowth to gain distance on the hounds, leaving them behind to chase by scent instead of sight.

While most big-game hunters agree that a shot through the heart or brain is instantly fatal to most animals, in the case of the boar there is much evidence to the contrary, particularly the shot through the heart. After absorbing quantities of lead in vital spots, his reported ability to move through the forest at a rapid pace or to stay on his feet and fight until the last breath is not without basis. His capacity to keep running for some distance after a direct shot through the heart or after his intestines have been riddled through and through—and until he finally drops dead from combined exhaustion and loss of blood—is common knowledge. Quite significant is the unyielding courage that is an intrinsic characteristic of this animal. In battle with dogs there is never a complaining squeal, neither will he grunt or squeal when mortally wounded. Regardless of death wounds inflicted, he maintains his unique Spartan courage to the end. Amazing as it may seem, one huge boar, after three bullets had been pumped through his ribs near the heart at close range, and after he had been chewed by a pack of hounds for some minutes, at the sight of man, sprang to his feet, and shaking off dogs as if they were no more than dry leaves, continued what had seemed an impossible race.

**Breeding and Feeding.** From data available, it seems well established that the boar's breeding habits are not timed as seasonably as with the bear and most other wild animals. Reports show that the mating season is spread over a longer period of months. On most occasions when a sow and young pigs have been discovered, it has been more commonly during the spring and summer months. Frequently, however, sows, heavy with pigs, have been killed during the December hunting season. On such occasions, due to the weight of the unborn offspring, they are found to be lacking in the usual speed, thus coming to bay much quicker. The litter may number anywhere from three to eight, but four or five are most common. Before the young litter comes the sow usually dens up in the recess of a ledge or cliff, or in some high thicket of rhododendron jungle, almost impenetrable and away from all potential danger. With primitive alertness she keeps a constant vigil while the young brood are confined to bed. Reports from those Santeetlah mountaineers most familiar with their breeding habits give evidence that the sow always bears her litter in a region where food will be readily available during the suckling period; thus she will not have to range far until the young brood are of a size to follow.

During the Russian boar's 37-year existence in the mountain jungles, there have been occasional instances of interbreeding with a native strain of wild razorbacks, which in their own right are rugged animals. Evidence of this native blood is present in various degrees, ranging from the barely noticeable changes in the Russian to the more obvious physical characteristics of the razorback. As a result of this occasional interbreeding, boars leaning to the native blood are not quite so speedy afoot.

In the combined Santeetlah and Tellico Plains Forest areas there is a wide variety of food composed of various fruits and mast. Perhaps from necessity, the boar is largely a vegetarian; one of his most common characteristics, however, is a willingness to accept almost anything edible—which includes everything from a chick-grouse to fox grapes. The various foods normally available are wild fruits, of which there is a wide variety, namely, mountain grapes, blackberries, huckleberries, dewberries, wild apples and cherries, and other kindred fruits. Included in his menu is green corn from the high-up mountain fields, which has caused many complaints from the ridge farmers. With no pretense to a fancy appetite, he will eat the eggs from wildfowl nests, grubs, frogs, crustaceans from the stream. Edible roots are acceptable, and last, acorns, which are perhaps the most substantial in the fattening part of his winter diet. When the food crop of some particular locality fails (as it does occasionally) this self-sufficient animal readily changes his habitat to a farther range—as food conditions may necessitate.

Although the boar is characteristically a nocturnal feeder, a sow and her litter—or some solitary boar—are occasionally seen feeding during daylight hours. Of the varied food, more or less of it is available throughout the year. This fact, combined with suitable climate, offers a logical reason why this remote range is so well suited to the wild hog.

The life span of the boar may range anywhere from 7 or 8 years to about 15. There is some difference of opinion, however, as to the maximum age. Several factors support the common belief that 10 to 12 years is the normal span of life. Individual animals, however, may exceed that by several years. Some who believe the maximum age to be 15 years

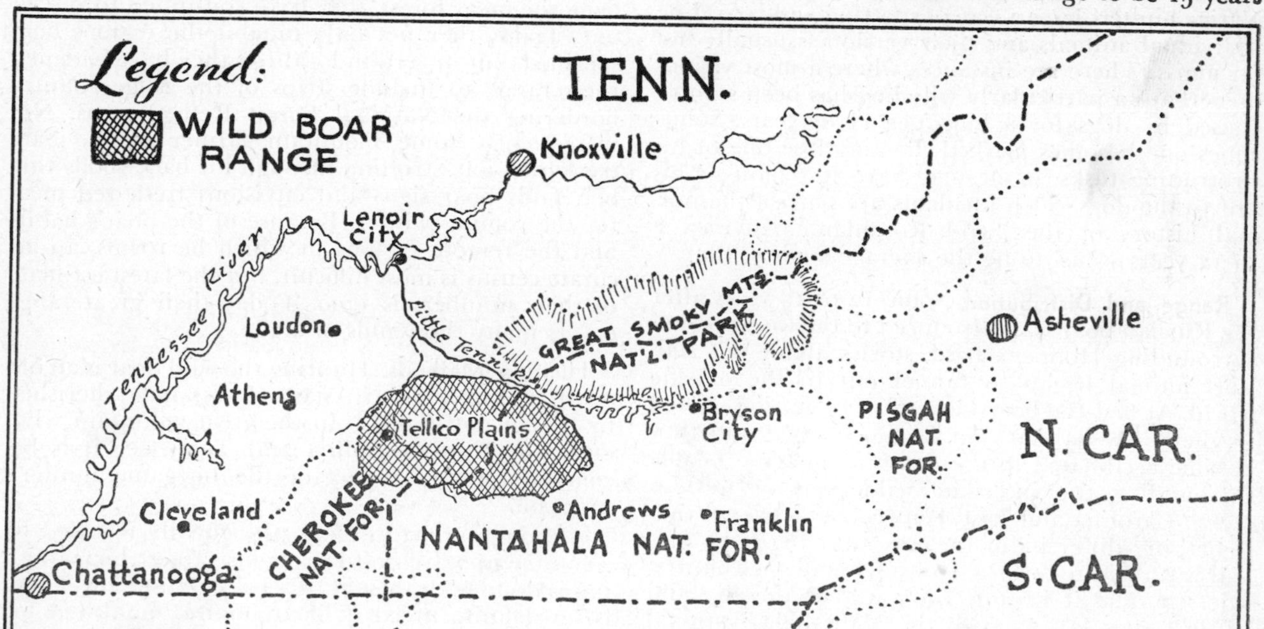


PLATE II. Distribution of Wild Boar.

Courtesy Tenn. Conservation Dept.

PLATE III. A Sow with Three Young Pigs. They will lose their stripes when grown.

base their theory on the fact that the hogs do not reach maturity for several years, after which they still continue to build frame and take on weight. Native hunters have a way of spotting and recording individual animals and their version is usually not far amiss. There are instances where a most vicious or perhaps a particularly wily hog has been seen or chased by dogs for a long period of years. Sometimes one becomes marked—he may lose one of his protruding tusks, or he may have lost most of his tail to the dogs. Such incidents are part of the normal history of the "wild Rooshian." Anyway, 8 to 12 years seems to be the average span of life.

**Range and Distribution.** Some 12 to 15 years after the Russian boar was introduced to the forest region surrounding Hooper's Bald, stories about this stalwart animal began to funnel out to the outside world. At first the boars were slow in getting started in their new habitat, but as time passed and they became acclimated to the dense region, the people surrounding the interstate wilderness of western North Carolina and East Tennessee discovered that something different in the way of a big-game animal was roaming over wide stretches of the countryside. In time it became evident that the Big and Little Santeetlah areas of the Nantahala National Forest on the western North Carolina side, and the Tellico Plains area of the Cherokee National Forest on the eastern Tennessee side, were those best suited to the propagation of the wild boar. In the mid to late 1920's, the beast was so solidly established in this wildest range of eastern America that his presence began to attract hunters from many parts of the country. For 25 years now, the animal has been hunted by men and dogs. Despite indiscriminate hunting before proper regulations were applied, and predictions that in time the boars would vanish from the great forest, they have continued to spread out. Today they not only inhabit the regions here specified, but in certain localities they have widened their range to include strips of the ridge country bordering the National Forest Refuge areas. Not infrequently some mountain farmer of the Santeetlah region, strolling through his backwoods timber, finds boar signs and envisions fresh red meat for the coming winter. Because of the boar's habits and the remote regions in which he roams, an accurate census is most difficult, but the latest estimate of their numbers is 1700. Today their great range covers many thousands of acres.

**Hunting Methods.** Hunting the wild boar is an old sport in Europe and Asia and was long cherished by the ancient Greeks. In the great mountain wilderness of North Carolina and Tennessee it is becoming a popular part of the big-game hunter's program.

Although a chance boar occasionally is killed by a hunter in search of deer or bear, most boar hunting is done with the aid of a pack of hounds. There is no definite breed of boar hounds employed for this, although many of the hill farmers do breed hounds primarily for boar hunting. As a rule, any hound, or other breed (airedales are used quite extensively) that has encountered a boar, has survived the encounter, and can be persuaded to hunt this animal again, is added to the pack.

Normally a group of hunters, four to eight in number, participate in the boar hunt, and the pack often numbers from 12 to 15 dogs of assorted breeds. On arriving at an area which a boar is known to be using, the dogs are cast and the hunters take it easy until a "Rooshian" is jumped.

There is no mistaking the outcry of the pack once this has happened, and usually the chorus is drowned a few seconds later by the piercing cry of one hound that has made the mistake of getting too close to the boar. When jumped, the boar does not follow a straight course, but seems to run at random, and often will pass within a few yards of the place where he was jumped a few minutes after the chase has started. Occasionally, if the chase becomes too heated, the boar will turn and attempt to dispose of his nearest pursuers. Too often he is successful, and it is a rare hunt that does not result in the death or serious injury of about 40 per cent of the pack.

When the boar is finally at bay the hunters move in, but with much more caution than they would use if approaching a big black bear that had been cornered by the dogs. A boar will stand at bay and fight dogs and often will charge a man immediately on sighting him. Most boar hunters, like squirrels, prefer their hunting to be in an area with plenty of trees.

Special boar hunts are now conducted under the direction of the U. S. Forest Service and the conservation departments of Tennessee and North Carolina. Qualified guides with dogs are supplied to the hunting party at a $50 fee, which for a party of five or six makes the cost negligible. The hunt

Courtesy Tenn. Conservation Dept.

PLATE V. A Rare Trophy and a Really Big Boar.

Courtesy Tenn. Conservation Dept.

PLATE IV. A big "Rooshian" at bay and making trouble for the hounds. The hound by the tree has had enough.

limit, like the season limit, is two boars, but few hunters manage to get a limit on one hunt. These hunts may be held between October 15 and January 1, and although there is no limit as to the number of hunters that may participate, no party may use more than eight dogs. As the bear season also is open at this time, each hunter is permitted to kill one bear and one boar, or two boars.

The North Carolina Conservation Department now conducts supervised boar hunts on the refuge. The hunter desiring to participate files an application with the Department, accompanying this application with a check for $15. In the event the applicants are too numerous, and if the applicant's name is not drawn, his money is refunded.

**Rifles.** The average boar hunter normally uses the same rifle for this hunting that he uses for deer, but the majority favor a heavier bullet than the average deer load. The shooting normally is at ranges of less than 50 yards, and the boar hunter normally zeroes his rifle in at that range. Because of the heavy brush in which the boar lives, long shots are a rarity. The important thing is to get in a fatal shot at close range and be ready to follow it up with a second shot without delay.

Calibers and loads are as follows:

.30 W.C.F. with 170-grain bullet.
.30 Remington with 170-grain bullet.
.300 Savage with 180-grain bullet.
.30/40 (Krag) with 220-grain bullet.
.30 '06 (Springfield) with 180- or 220-grain bullet.

.303 Savage with 190-grain bullet.
.32 with 170-grain bullet.
.35 with 200-grain bullet.
6.5 with 160-grain bullet.
7 mm. with 175-grain bullet.
8 mm. with 236-grain bullet.

For details on above loads see "Ammunition—Rifle."

**Sights.** Open or aperture sights are preferred. Due to the short range, telescopic sights are not required, and in heavy brush the scope would be undesirable in any case. (See "Sights and Optical Aids.")

# CARIBOU

*Rangifer*

Caribou are members of the *ungulate* group, and date from the Pleistocene times. Each of the three species has been broken down as follows:

| | |
|---|---|
| **Barren Ground Caribou** | |
| Barren Ground Caribou | *Rangifer arcticus arcticus* |
| Labrador Barren Ground Caribou | *Rangifer arcticus caboti* |
| Dwarf Caribou-Dawson Caribou-Queen Charlotte Island Caribou | *Rangifer dawsoni* |
| Grant Caribou | *Rangifer arcticus granti* |
| Greenland Caribou | *Rangifer arcticus groenlandicus* |
| Peary or Ellesmere Land Caribou | *Rangifer pearyi* |
| Stone's Caribou | *Rangifer arcticus stonei* |
| Osborn Caribou | *Rangifer arcticus osborni* |
| **Woodland Caribou** | |
| Woodland Caribou | *Rangifer caribou caribou* |
| Richardson Caribou | *Rangifer caribou sylvestris* |
| Newfoundland Caribou | *Rangifer terroenovoe* |
| **Mountain Caribou** | |
| Mountain Caribou | *Rangifer montanus* |
| Rocky Mt. Caribou | *Rangifer fortidens* |

**History.** The Indian-named caribou, incorrectly called "reindeer" by the general public, has been separated into three distinct species—Barren Ground, mountain, and woodland—but the general characteristics are the same in all three.

At the present time the caribou is the most numerous of the big-game animals in Alaska, and is protected by large refuges. At the turn of the century, there were millions, but the present population has dwindled to about one-half million. This animal is still retreating to the peaceful, vast Arctic regions. No longer do winter herds of thousands upon thousands migrate hundreds of miles southward from the Arctic for food and shelter at the timber line.

Man, the wolf, and the reindeer are rapidly reducing his numbers, for he is widely hunted for food by trappers, Indians, and Eskimos, as his succulent meat is considered the "beef of the Arctic." Because he travels in the open and is readily seen, he is easily hunted. He also is sought for his hide, which often is the primary source of clothing to the natives of the Far North. The Barren Ground caribou was particularly affected by encroaching farmlands, since his habit of extensive wandering requires a large range. The present-day influx of road and airport building has further restricted him. When his range has been eliminated, he must move or die.

The timber wolf has always been the enemy of the caribou, and where he runs, the wolf follows. The Eleventh North American Wildlife Conference of 1946 reported an unusual abundance of wolves in Canada and Alaska and there was no explanation for their numbers except the mysterious rise and fall in the natural cycles of species.

Between 1891 and 1902 great numbers of reindeer were imported from Siberia for food and clothing for the Indians and Eskimos. The smaller, domesticated reindeer, a cousin from Asia and Europe, was put on the same range with the wild caribou, and the spotted and white hybrid of this extensive interbreeding is an unfit offspring of the wild caribou. The real danger lies in the overgrazing of the same range, where the prolific reindeer eats the food from his neighbor's mouth.

At one time, great herds of woodland caribou were found in the northern states, especially Maine, where they were common about 1870-1890. They were exterminated in Connecticut about 1870, in Massachusetts about 1760, in New Hampshire about 1870, in New York and Vermont about 1860. Some authorities believe the reason for the drastic decrease and migration was due to the shortage of preferred food. Others attribute his disappearance to unchecked hunting and deforestation which left the caribou without shelter or food.

Courtesy U. S. Fish and Wildlife Service.

PLATE I. Stone's Caribou.

**Identification.** The identifying characteristic of the caribou is his magnificent antlers. The caribou is the only member of the deer family in which both male and female are antlered, with even a one-month-old fawn bearing a spike. The length, weight, and palmation of the antlers vary with different species, but on the average they are slightly palmated on both sexes and have distinctive "shovel" of brow tines projecting down over the face. The main beams bend back, then forward and up, in "rocking-chair" fashion, ending in a palm with small tines. The antlers of the male average much larger than those of the female; the male's are larger in proportion to his body than those of any deer.

Each year the antlers are shed, with the old bulls losing them in early winter or late fall, the young males and does keeping them up to May.

The general appearance of all three caribou species is not very distinctive one from the other, and often it is difficult to differentiate between them. An average weight might be put at 300 to 400 pounds, length 76 inches, and height at shoulders 42 to 48 inches for the male, which is typically larger than the female, though in Alaska some animals scale from 500 to 600 pounds. The female averages from 150 to 250 pounds.

Coloration among the caribou does not vary to an extensive degree, but is more pronounced with the change of seasons. Brown is his normal coloration and all seasonal changes are variations of that color, with the white trimmings. In winter, his grayish-brown coat is typically whitish along his belly, with a yellowish-white neck, throat, and muzzle, and clean white circling just above his broad flat hooves, and a white rump patch. In spring, this generally-brown tone fades and becomes more whitish, but again in summer and fall is darker.

I. The Barren Ground caribou, smallest of the three species, with an average length of about 7 feet and weight of 200 to 300 pounds, is characterized by his size and his pale, rangy antlers with three to four palmations.

The Barren Ground caribou is identified by subspecies as follows:

BARREN GROUND CARIBOU: Smaller in size and paler in color (especially in the summer) than other members of the species, having slender horns with little palmation.

GRANT CARIBOU: Smaller and darker than average.

GREENLAND CARIBOU: Small and pale with simple antlers.

LABRADOR BARREN GROUND CARIBOU: More true to its type than the Barren Ground, but having a distinguishing characteristic of recurving tips of well-formed brow and bez tines.

OSBORN CARIBOU: Authorities differ as to its classification. It has been considered by some as belonging to the mountain caribou, and the greatest of all the caribou by virtue of its size and its massive flattened antlers. Its weight is not typical of this group, since the bulls often weigh from 500 to 600 pounds. It is the largest and darkest of the species.

Stone's Caribou: Second in size and darkness to the Osborn is this species, often from 300 to 400 pounds; large antlers.

Peary Caribou: Lightest of all caribou, almost white with "a small patch of light grayish brown (almost lilac) along back from shoulders to rump"; about 7 feet in length.

Dwarf Caribou: Some authorities consider it extinct. Small, with poorly developed antlers; different

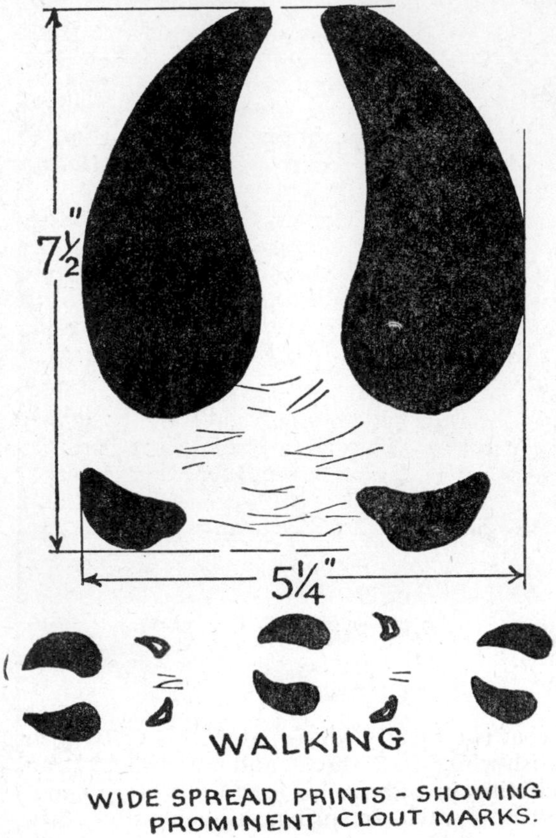


Plate II. Typical Hoofprints of the Caribou.

from other caribou by color which is an even, dull brown, free of white or black.

One of the largest kills of Barren Ground caribou officially confirmed was made on the Kuskokwim River in Alaska by Rev. J. A. Wilemski, in 1933. The antlers measured: length of outside curve, right 65½ and left 62¼ inches; greatest spread, 42 inches; length of brow antlers, right 16 and left 0 inches; number of points, right 14 and left ten.

II. The woodland caribou is midway in size, larger than the Barren Ground with darker, almost black, coloration, and heavier, though shorter, antlers, more heavily palmated and flattened. In the early fall, the dark antlers fade.

Newfoundland Caribou: Paler than average, with antlers unusually low, spread, and forked.

Richardson Caribou: An average caribou except for darker coloration on ears and neck.

Woodland Caribou: Typically of darker pelage and greater size than Barren Ground, with antlers characteristic of species.

One of the largest woodland caribou recorded was killed in 1881 by Frederick Brooks in Newfoundland. The antlers were: length of outside curve, right 49⅜ and left 0 inches; greatest spread, 43½ inches; length of brow antlers, right 15¼ and left 14¼ inches; number of points, right 12 and left 13.

III. Mountain Caribou: The mountain caribou is distinguished by his large size, his blackish-brown coloration, and many-pointed, great antlers. This is the darkest of all the caribou, with a near-black coloring except for the lighter grayish-brown of the neck. He averages the greatest in size; the bulls usually scale from 450 to 600 pounds (sometimes 800) and stand about 5 feet at the shoulder. His heavy, large antlers are not so massive, however, as those of the Osborn caribou.

Rocky Mountain Caribou: Thought the largest of all mountain caribou, varying in color from the rich brown to black of the white-maned bulls, to the dark gray of the cow. On both sexes the necks are lighter. The antlers of the bull are heavily palmated, but the female's are small and light, often not appearing at all.

The largest mountain caribou kill on record was made by D. W. Bell in 1923 at Cassiar, British Columbia. The length of the outside curve was: right 65⅛ and left 62¼ inches; greatest spread 54½ inches; length of brow antlers, right 27¼ and left 24⅝ inches; number of points, right 23 and left 15.

**Characteristics.** The caribou has been characterized by many as stupid, but that term has been applied because he has never learned to distrust man. Unlike the confined, easily accessible whitetail deer, he lives on a wide, changing range primarily in Alaska and the Arctic tundra. He often advances to investigate a man, curious and unafraid, and friendly fawns have followed canoeing hunters along the river bank.

Since he is herd-bound, he does not develop the wariness of the solitary animal. The most gregarious of all the deer family, he relies on the safety of numbers. However, caribou are characteristically unpredictable and sometimes bolt at the scent of man, especially the restless bull just before the rutting season.

Some naturalists report the movement of caribou herds as being aimless wanderings, without purpose or direction, but other authorities defend their rangings on the grounds that they are seasonal migrations, dependent upon food and climate. Of all the caribou, the Barren Ground moves about the most, when herds of many thousands travel from one range to another in search of food. The mountain caribou is less migratory because his range is more limited, and he confines himself to feeding on the mountains at timberline, leaving only to seek the shelter of the lower ground in bad weather. He does not travel in the large herd, typical of the Barren Ground, but bands in winter in small groups of a dozen, or less, and in the summer often runs alone.

One of the most interesting features of the caribou is his striking running gait. He usually goes at an easy trot, a pace which he can effortlessly maintain for as far as 60 miles over swamps and rocky ground. However, he tires easily at a gallop. While in his typical mincing pace, he holds his head erect, his back straight, and his tail level. A running herd makes a peculiar clicking noise which has never been convincingly explained. Some think it is from the ankle joints knocking together, others that it comes from the joints within the feet. While running, the cows and calves call to each other with a grunting sound, and while running the tails often are held high, similar to those of the whitetail deer.

Wide hoofs take caribou with ease over difficult terrain that would make any other animal flounder. He has enormous, even-toed hooves which spread, enabling him to stay atop deep snow. If he breaks through hard-crusted snow, the large hole made by his foot provides enough room for his slim leg to follow unharmed by the cutting crust. For this reason, he does not "yard" as do other members of the deer family less fortunately endowed.

An equal advantage for good traveling is the caribou's coat, which extends to his hairy muzzle. He is an excellent swimmer, and the hollow hairs of his pelage make him more buoyant in the water. Since these air-filled hairs hold the body heat, he can easily adapt himself to various temperatures.

Much has been written about the caribou's love of the fungus growth, lichen, popularly called reindeer moss. It has been said that his wanderings are a constant search for it, but, though it is a favorite food, there are areas where many caribou exist and in which only scanty amounts of lichens grow.

In the summer he eats green grasses, plants, and shrubs and in the winter dead grass, mosses, and lichens. He has been known to eat shed antlers for the sake of the calcium to balance his diet. He often eats as he runs, taking a bite about every five yards, gathering it in with his tongue, and cutting it off with the bottom teeth since he has no upper ones.

He has poor eyes, but a good sense of smell protects him to some extent from his natural enemy, the wolf. Wolves are ever present, lurking on the forest fringe, waiting for a straggling, old, or wounded animal. Bears and wolverines also prey upon the herd, but they take a limited number—usually fawns.

**Breeding.** The rutting season usually is in September and October, but in some areas of Alaska it starts in late July. With a herd bull in the lead, caribou travel in large numbers hundreds of miles. A large bull often collects as many as 20 females for himself, and fights any challenger after he has carefully bunched all his cows in a group. Younger bulls often drive an old bull, too old to fight, completely out of the herd.

The period of gestation is about eight months. The fawns, usually just one, are born in June. They are brownish-red with a black nose and a black face halfway up to the eyes. Within two hours after birth they are walking, and soon are ready to follow along with their mothers, especially in the ever-moving Barren Ground group.

**Range and Distribution.** The caribou is primarily a northern animal. Though he has advanced far into the bleak Arctic, a region too cold for other members

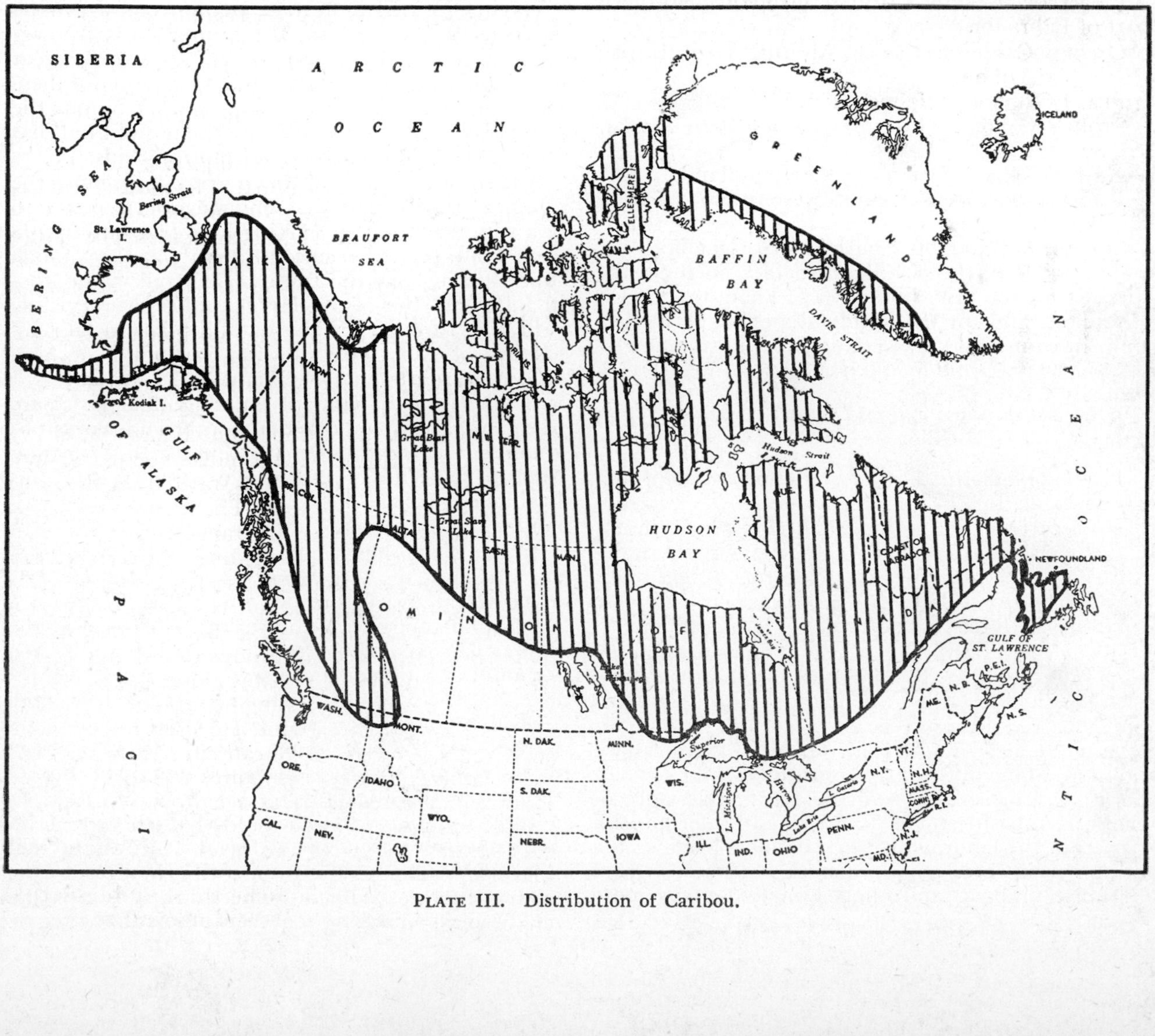


PLATE III. Distribution of Caribou.

of the deer family, he once ranged extensively through our more temperate northern states. Today there are only 40 caribou left in this country; they are of the woodland species, inhabiting Minnesota, Idaho, and Washington.

The caribou adjusts himself well to his range. On the treeless tundra of the Arctic his heavy, adaptable coat protects him, and his wide hoof is suited to pawing through snow for lichens and dead grass, or for traveling over the snow. The mountain caribou goes even higher than the goat to range, just as long as there is soil.

His coloration varies with each locale, since those of the far north are far lighter, almost white, in color, as compared to the dark types of forest regions.

The caribou has the problem characteristic of every ruminant—where to find enough vegetation to keep filled a large, fast-emptying stomach. His range changes with the food supply, with a special emphasis on lichens.

The range of each species has been listed thus:

Barren Ground Caribou: Circumpolar in range; Barren Grounds of Canada from the Mackenzie Basin east to Hudson Bay from the Arctic coast.

Dwarf Caribou: Possibly extinct; Graham Island in Queen Charlotte Island group.

Grant Caribou: Alaska Peninsula and Unimak Island.

Greenland Caribou: Greenland.

Labrador Barren Ground Caribou: Northern part of Labrador.

Osborn Caribou: Cassiar Mountains of British Columbia; Yukon.

Peary Caribou: Ellesmere Land.

Stone's Caribou: Interior and northern Alaska; Yukon.

Newfoundland Caribou: Newfoundland.

Richardson Caribou: Southwestern part of Hudson Bay.

Woodland Caribou: Southeastern Canada.

The range of the woodland caribou includes the forested regions, and high slopes. There the food is abundant, and on the windy slopes there are less snow in winter and fewer mosquitoes in summer.

Mountain Caribou: Selkirk Range of British Columbia.

Rocky Mountain Caribou: British Columbia and Alberta.

**Hunting Methods.** The most important step, and the first one, for the caribou hunter is the selection of an area in which to hunt. Although many hunters plan their trips for the sole purpose of obtaining a caribou, the majority select an area which offers an opportunity to hunt sheep, goats, bear, or moose in addition to one of the three types of caribou.

The airplane, although it has cut down the elapsed time once spent in reaching good caribou territory, whether this happens to be in Canada or Alaska, is only a partial means to the end. Without pack horses waiting at the wilderness air terminal there can be no hunt. Many of the larger outfitters send pack outfits to certain isolated hunting areas in advance of the season, basing them near a lake of sufficient size to permit the landing of a float plane. This saves the hunter from three days to a week of arduous travel by horse or boat, and offers him that many more days of active hunting. Also, as a result of the present low charter rates, using a plane often means economy in money as well as time.

The hunting of caribou also is a matter of *selection.* The hunter in good caribou country will find plenty of opportunities for a shot. The duration of the hunt is limited, not by the number of caribou present, but by the hunter's desire for a good trophy; the average man is at least as much interested in the head as he is in the meat.

The most interesting caribou to hunt are the woodland or mountain species, not only from the standpoint of size but because of more interesting hunting methods and more picturesque terrain. The man who enjoys imposing scenery and isolation will seek this species rather than the Barren Ground member of the family.

During the early part of the season these caribou will be found on the high ground, primarily in areas where there is a reasonable balance between rock and soil, and where reindeer moss and other food is plentiful. During this period the big bulls begin moving from the timber to the open, higher ground, where they start the process of rounding up their harems.

The fact that he can remain in one spot and count more than a hundred caribou is no excuse for carelessness on the part of the hunter who seeks a good trophy. The man who ignores the wind direction seldom obtains a good trophy, except by accident.

Having located a vantage point from which he may survey a wide area, the hunter finds 8-power binoculars or even a 20-power spotting scope a great help in making trophy selection. Also, either of these visual aids can be of great help in working out the route of the ultimate stalk, once the desired bull has been located. (See"Sights and Optical Aids.")

A hasty stalk, across or down wind, can reduce the number of caribou in a given area from 100 to zero in a very few minutes. Having located a bull with a good head, the experienced hunter spends as much time working out the route of his stalk as he does in following the route. He examines every visible yard of it through his glasses, and plans to take advantage of every gully or wash that will hide him. If, on the route tentatively laid out, he discovers it will take him up-wind of an individual or group of caribou, he abandons that course and works out another. One whiff of man scent is all a caribou needs to send him off at his mile-eating trot, and his frightened whistle often will scatter the other caribou in the immediate vicinity.

In the event the coveted bull happens to be feeding in the open, with so little adjacent cover as to make it impossible for the hunter to get within reasonable range, two courses remain open to the hunter. He can go back to his binoculars and search for another bull, or he can sit quietly and watch his first choice, hoping the caribou will move to a more accessible position. Occasionally, under such circumstances, a bull will lie down. This reduces the range of his vision and often offers the hunter an opportunity to get within range.

If the bull happens to have an unusually fine head and conditions seem stacked against the hunter, it is a sound move to withdraw quietly and return the next morning. If the animal is left undisturbed, there is a good chance that he will be in the same general area the next day.

Once the stalk has been made, the problem of range estimation comes up. This is not the simple problem that many novice hunters believe it to be. To one unfamiliar with the estimation of range at high altitudes, the normal tendency is to under-estimate distance. Many a record caribou, bear, sheep, or goat, estimated to be about 250 yards distant, has proved to be 350 to 400 yards, and disappeared after the first shot kicked up the dirt a foot or two low.

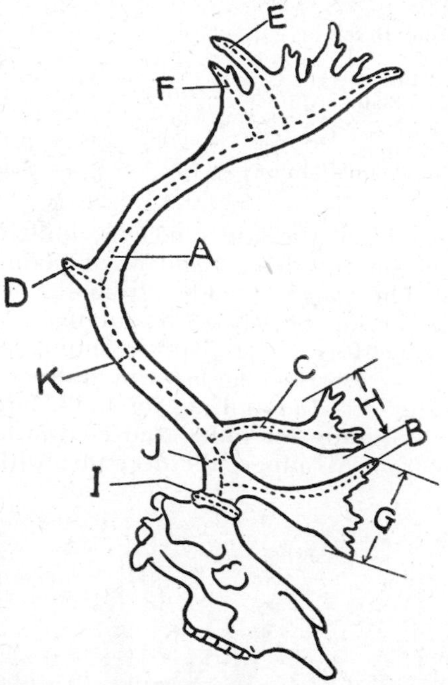


With the range determined, if the bull is in a good position for the shot, hold high and just behind the shoulder. (See vital area diagram, Plate IX, p. 63.) But be ready to get in another shot without delay.

A heart-shot caribou can, on occasion, travel several hundred yards before dropping, which offers some risk of causing damage to the antlers. Many fine heads have been ruined when the animal, mortally wounded but not dropped in its tracks, managed to travel far enough to fall down a slide or off the edge of a ravine.

Too often such loss is caused by an impatient hunter who cannot wait until the animal is in a good position for a shot. A head-on shot, for example, often fails to put the animal down. The preferred shot is one in which the animal is approximately two-thirds broadside to the hunter. This angle permits him to put the bullet through the heart, lungs, and shoulder, and a caribou so shot usually does little traveling.

(For details on skinning out and preserving trophy and meat see "Preservation of Trophies.")

The Barren Ground caribou usually are hunted while they are moving to their winter feeding grounds. Hunting them often proves about as interesting as leaning against a fence and shooting a cow.

The great herds, often numbering more than a thousand, move in a rather aimless manner, and it is seldom difficult for a hunter to locate a position which will bring a good portion of the herd past him, provided he remembers to keep down wind. The tendency of these animals to range widely is the most troublesome factor in hunting them, for they may be here today and far away tomorrow. In hunting them you may quarter the territory for a week, examining the ground carefully for fresh signs, and never see one. The next morning, upon emerging from your sleeping bag, you may look across a valley and see a thousand of them. During September and October the herds often cover hundreds of miles.

Unless frightened, they offer no shooting problems, and the hunter's greatest problem is to decide

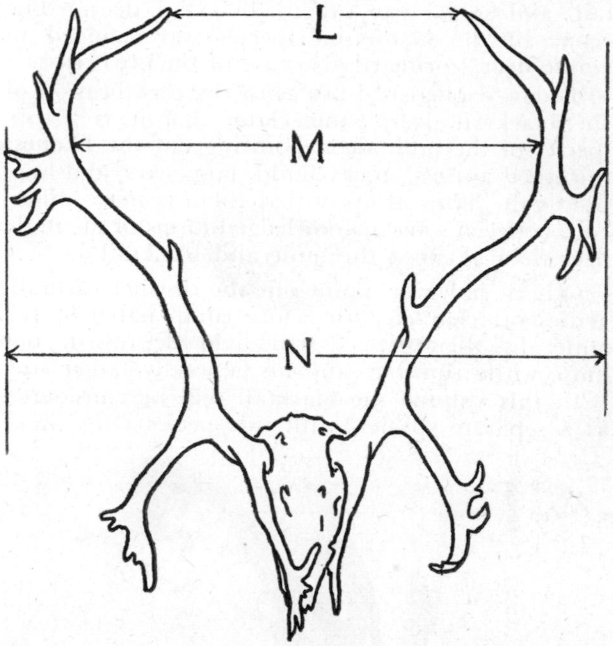


PLATE IV. Trophy Measurements, Caribou.

A-Length of antler.
B-Length of brow palm.
C-Length of bez palm.
D-Length of rear prong.
E-Longest top point.
F-Next longest top point.
G-Width of brow palm.
H-Width of bez palm.
I-Circumference of burr.
J-Circumference of beam at smallest place between brow and bez palms.
K-Circumference of beam at smallest place between bez and head prong.
L-Tip to tip spread.
M-Greatest spread inside main beams.
N-Extreme spread.

which one of the hundreds that pass will provide the best trophy.

**Rifles and Sights.** Although a high-velocity, heavy load is not required for caribou, and great numbers have been killed with rifles similar in caliber and power to the .30/30, the majority of caribou hunters are equipped with rifles intended for use on larger game. The high-velocity rifle is an asset to the trophy hunter, for it offers him an opportunity to select a target at ranges which would make a clean kill uncertain with the lower-powered rifle.

The most popular calibers and loads are:

.30 '06 with 180-grain bullet.
.300 Savage with 150-grain bullet.
.348 Winchester with 150-grain bullet.
.270 with 130-grain bullet.
.300 H. & H. Magnum with 180-grain bullet.
7 mm. with 175-grain bullet.

For details on above loads see "Ammunition—Rifle."

NOTE: The above rifles, for long-range accuracy, should be equipped with 2½- to 4-power telescopic sights. For these sights the tapered post reticule is preferred. (See "Sights and Optical Aids.")

# BLACKTAIL DEER *Odocoileus hemionus columbianus*

# MULE DEER *Odocoileus hemionus hemionus*

Since the time of their discovery by Lewis and Clark in the early 19th century, there has been confusion concerning the nomenclature of the blacktail deer and mule deer. The mule deer was found first along the Missouri River and was named a blacktail, but a year later, by the Columbia River, explorers came upon another deer, with a true black tail, and so he was called "blacktail deer." The name of the first-found species was changed to "mule deer," primarily because of the great ears.

Today, zoologists differ as to the classification of the blacktail deer. Some claim that it is a subspecies of the mule deer, pointing out the likeness in forked antlers, stocky build, large ears, and hopping gait. They also say that there is more difference between some acknowledged forms of the mule deer than between the mule and blacktail.

Others, however, point out the distinct dissimilarities of: characteristic white rump patch of the mule, his black-tipped tail—held depressed, not limp, while running—and his generally larger size.

In this volume the blacktail will be considered as a separate species, with sub-species *Odocoileus hemionus columbianus* (Columbian Blacktail or Coast Deer) and *Odocoileus hemionus sitkensis* (Sitka Deer).

The recognized sub-species of the mule deer are:

| | | | |
|---|---|---|---|
| California Mule Deer | *Odocoileus* | *hemionus* | *californicus* |
| Gray Mule Deer | " | " | *canus* |
| Cactus Buck | | | |
| Desert Mule Deer | " | " | *eremicus* |
| Burro Deer | | | |
| Southern Mule Deer | " | " | *fuliginatus* |
| Eastern or Plains Mule Deer | " | " | *hemionus* |
| Inyo Mule Deer | " | " | *inyoensis* |
| Rocky Mountain Mule Deer | " | " | *macrotia* |

**History.** Until the late 1800's the mule deer was numerous on the deserts and open plains of this country. The range extended from the Southwest to either side of the Rocky Mountains.

The same forces that cut the numbers of the whitetail deer worked against the mule deer. With the advent of settlers killing for food, hunters destroying wantonly for hides, and civilization pushing him from his range, the deer met with virtual

Courtesy Jonas Bros.

PLATE I. Record Columbian Mule Deer Head, with 46-inch spread, 24 points. Count them.

extinction in some sections. For instance, he once thrived east of the Rockies, but where he was exterminated he has been replaced to a large extent by the whitetail, which is more adaptable to settlement and the ways of man. Instead of making a compromise with civilization, the mule deer retreated, leaving the plains to domesticated sheep and farming, and sought refuge in the mountains. This complete change in habitat has puzzled zoologists.

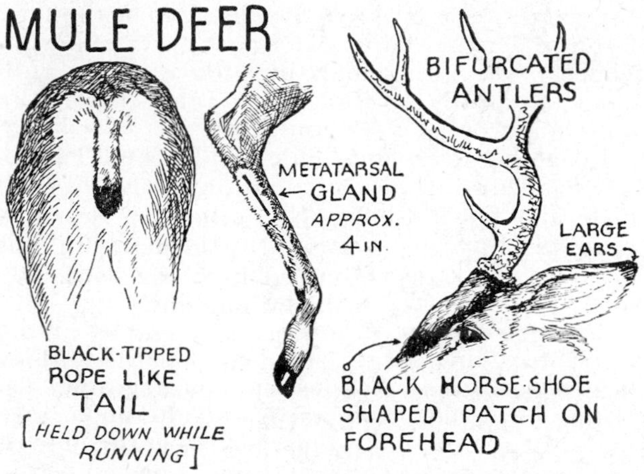


Plate II. Mule Deer Identification.

The changes in the life history of the blacktail have been less drastic, though he suffered from the inroads of civilization as did all the other deer. The blacktail is confined specifically to the Pacific Coast and there are no records of his having left his range, in spite of man and wolves.

Before Alaskan game laws were established, there was unchecked killing of blacktails by commercial hunters on some of the Alaskan islands. They were an easy mark, because winter snow forced them down from the high slopes to seek food at the shoreline, and those not killed by hunters in so confined an area were attacked by wolves. The deer of those islands were almost completely annihilated.

Today's game laws and management protect and regulate the population of the blacktail and mule as efficiently as that of the whitetail.

**Identification.** The general appearance of the blacktail and mule deer is very similar. They are both chunky and rugged in build, but the mulie, the largest of the genus, is about a fifth heavier, with longer, sturdier legs, and is more awkward in manner.

The size of either type is largely dependent upon the food supply of his range. The weight is consequently variable, but a blacktail averages 150 pounds, with large bucks scaling about 200 pounds. Some of the largest specimens are found in northern Washington and British Columbia, but a record kill was made in Tehama County, California, in 1927 by Gus Nordquist. The length of the right outside curve measured 30½ inches, and the greatest spread 23½ inches, with three points on either antler.

Although the blacktail is considered to be generally much smaller than the mule deer, there are notable exceptions in some areas. In one section of Oregon, for example, a large area was burned off. Because of the number of deer killed as a result of the fire, the Game Commission closed the area to hunting for four years. When it finally was opened, the deer kill was not especially large, but the individual bucks were unusually large and heavy, and in perfect physical condition.

The average mulie weighs 250 to 300 pounds. British Columbia produces the largest animals, which range between 300 and 400 pounds. The record kill for mule deer was made in Glenwood Springs, Colo., by V. T. Newton. The length of outside curve of the antlers was: right 32½ inches and left 33⅛ inches, with a spread of 32½ inches, and 11 points on both right and left antler.

The white-lined ears of the blacktail are almost as large as the tremendous, broad ones of the mule deer, and the hearing of both is excellent.

The tail of the blacktail is as distinctive as the name implies. It is black on the outside and white underneath. It is bushier and wider than the mule's, which is shorter and hairless on the inside surface and is typically white with a black tip. While running, the blacktail sometimes holds his tail erect like a whitetail, but usually it droops, as opposed to the mule deer's, which is pressed against the body and never raised when startled.

The metatarsal gland of the mule averages 5 inches, that of the blacktail 3 inches. Both have the scent glands on the outside of each hind leg.

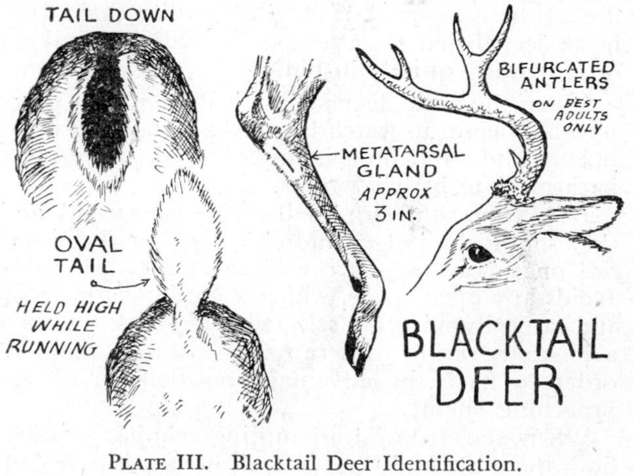


Plate III. Blacktail Deer Identification.

The coloring of the blacktail resembles that of the whitetail. It is alike in both sexes. The winter coat is brownish gray with a darker forehead, and the summer coat is a yellowish brown. In both seasons there is a dark stripe running down the length of the back.

The coat coloration of the widely distributed mule deer varies with the particular section. It varies more noticeably in the summer when the dull yellow of the mule deer of Sonora contrasts with the rusty red of the race in Arizona. Between the summer and winter seasons a black coat is worn for a short period, being replaced by the winter one of brownish gray with its common marking of a dark "horseshoe" on the forehead. In both seasons, though, the tail and gray legs remain the same color, as does the important identifying characteristic of the white rump patch.

Only the buck bears antlers, though an occasional freak female, usually incapable of producing young, carries a poorly-developed rack. The antlers of the mule and blacktail are typically forked, but those of the mule tend to be larger and more widely spread. There is much individual variation, however, in the antlers of the mule deer, and many are high and narrow, extensively palmated or heavy with points.

Antler formations are a most uncertain means of telling age in these two species, unless a mature buck has begun to decline. The yearlings, for instance, have two to three points while those of any other deer have only spikes. Between two and five years of age the bucks usually have four points, but a four-pointer could be anywhere from three to nine years old. After the bucks pass their prime at about six years of age, the antlers "go back" to two points or flatten and palmate and often have a freakish number of points. This retrogression occurs at an earlier age than with any other deer.

The buck sheds his antlers about February or March and new ones start forming almost immediately. Since he usually drops both at once, he is left for a brief period without any protection in a fight except his forefeet.

**Characteristics.** The wariness of the blacktail is much like that of the whitetail. He is cautious and careful as he moves through his timbered country, showing little of the notorious curiosity of the mule deer. If he is pursued, his flight is, unlike that of the mule deer, brief. He attempts to elude by skulking or remaining quietly in hiding.

When the mule deer picks a bed, he pauses every now and again to watch his tracks, as he does when pursued, to see if he is being followed, and usually backtracks to his chosen spot.

Deer vary. Some are intelligent, some stupid, and they should be judged individually; but the blacktail on the average is considered more canny. He avoids any open space, which a mulie would cross, and carefully skirts the selected bed, which is always a lookout station over canyon, valley, or plain in order to have the advantage position on an approaching enemy.

When alarmed and attempting a quick getaway, both the mule and the blacktail use a peculiar stiff-legged hop which has given them the name "jumping deer." This gait is spectacular but quickly tires them. They jump high with all four feet drawn together and land on all four at once. They cover about 15 feet with each leap. The fawns are the most skilled at leaping, scarcely seeming to touch the ground between bounds.

The mule deer utilizes this gait on the rough terrain of his habitat, but when the blacktail is calm, he uses a moderate gallop for speed. Both species have a clumsy, shuffling walk.

As described in some detail under "Whitetail" *(q.v.)*, the first enemy of all deer is the timber wolf. The blacktails of the Alaskan islands will swim five to six miles, from island to island, in order to escape pursuit.

The cougar also takes a high toll, particularly of the mule deer, which he is said to kill at the rate of over 100 a year for each adult lion. Here naturalists are eager to point out that they see no "nature's stabilizer" in these predators, since a mature lion is a capable judge of the fattest, finest deer of the herd, and kills them by preference to the weak and old. His killing, therefore, weakens the stock by destroying the best breeding specimens.

The coyote has *developed* into an enemy of the mule deer. At one time the coyote was a plains animal, but he followed the sheep into the hills and rougher country where he became stronger and heavier and eventually capable of deer killing.

Deep winter is considered by many to be the chief factor of deer mortality. After near starvation in his winter yards, spring finds him too weak to withstand the deadly attrition of parasites (ticks, nose bots, lung worms, tapeworms, etc.).

Like other deer, both mule and blacktail habitually band up in the winter with a mixing of both male and female, but with spring they separate, going off alone or in twos and threes. The bulls often form larger groups of about six to ten. A common combination among the mule deer is a large bull with a smaller one.

Their feeding habits have been likened to those of grazing cattle—eating in the morning and then resting until they eat again in the afternoon. Like the whitetail, the mule and blacktail graze on grass and other vegetation, and browse on numerous types of foliage and shrubs. The northern Sitka blacktail eats kelp when forced down to the salt-water edges in the winter season.

**Breeding.** The breeding habits and the birth and care of the fawns of the mule and blacktail deer are much like those of the whitetail *(q.v.)*.

Rut begins in late fall, at which time there occurs the characteristic swelling of the buck's neck, which in the mule deer is tremendous; his neck becomes almost as big around as his body.

The bucks will fight viciously to collect a harem which averages from five to seven does, but sometimes as many as 15. Once a harem is established, however, the violent question of ownership dies down somewhat, for it is not uncommon for a buck with his does to be followed by from one to three young bucks which the successful conqueror has little trouble keeping in line.

In some areas, where the deer are actively hunted, the bucks remain at a higher level during the daytime, coming down to the does only during the night.

**Range and Distribution.** The range of the blacktail deer is one of the most confined of all our American deer. It is restricted to the Pacific Coast, from Sitka, Alaska, to Southern California, extending east to the crest of the Sierra Nevada and Cascade Mountains, and remaining within the rain belt.

The 1946 Big-Game Inventory shows the population of the blacktail deer as 402,300, with a breakdown by states as follows:

| | |
|---|---|
| California | 220,100 |
| Oregon | 86,000 |
| Washington | 96,200 |

The blacktail is a typical "edge" dweller, a lover of the broken country, of heavy underbrush and dense forest borders. In the north he seeks cedar, spruce, fir and in the south he is found in the chaparral country and among firs and redwoods. His preference for the redwood forests of California has given him the nickname of "redwood deer." He thrives in the humid areas of the coast where the heavy rainfalls provide an abundant undergrowth upon which he can browse.

The blacktail is migratory and changes his habitat with the seasons. On the inland ranges winter drives him from the upper levels of the mountains to the lowland shelters of timbered country. He travels as much as 100 miles when he makes these yearly trips. At one time, when civilization did not obstruct their line of march, the deer would stamp out a set path leading down from the mountains which they used every year, with the does and fawns in front, then the young bucks, followed by a guard of old bucks in the rear. In the spring the deer go back once again to the mountains, where they remain all summer. Such a migration is not necessary, however, for the blacktails of the coastal ranges, where there are no severe weather changes to affect the food and shelter of the area.

The mule deer ranges over rough country along the Rocky Mountains from British Columbia to Mexico.

The population of the mule deer in the United States as reported by the 1946 Big-Game Inventory totaled 2,008,060, and is listed below by states:

| | | | |
|---|---|---|---|
| Arizona | 102,400 | North Dakota | 760 |
| California | 342,000 | Oregon | 172,600 |
| Colorado | 384,000 | South Dakota | 6,800 |
| Idaho | 147,000 | Texas | 7,500 |
| Montana | 104,200 | Utah | 220,000 |
| Nebraska | 4,400 | Washington | 79,700 |
| Nevada | 113,200 | Wyoming | 149,000 |
| New Mexico | 174,100 | | |

His range is wide and he is at home on plains, foothills, and mountainsides. He inhabits the wooded river bottoms of the Great Plains, mountain forests of California, and deserts and plains of Sonora.

Large herds, often numbering as many as 1000, gather in the fall to start the winter migration. The food crisis comes about the end of December; then they travel 100 miles or more from the craggy mountain slopes to sheltered lowlands. It is the heavy snowfall, not the cold, which forces this migration.

About 50 years ago, herds of mule deer were found wintering far out on the open sage flats, but today they usually venture no farther than the fringes. This inadequacy of winter ranges, often grazed and browsed clean by sheep and elk, curtails the mule deer's numbers in the Rockies.

With the oncoming spring they retreat to the mountains, keeping about three miles below the snow-line where the coyotes lie in wait to force a lone wanderer onto the crust.

**Hunting Methods.** See under "Whitetail Deer."

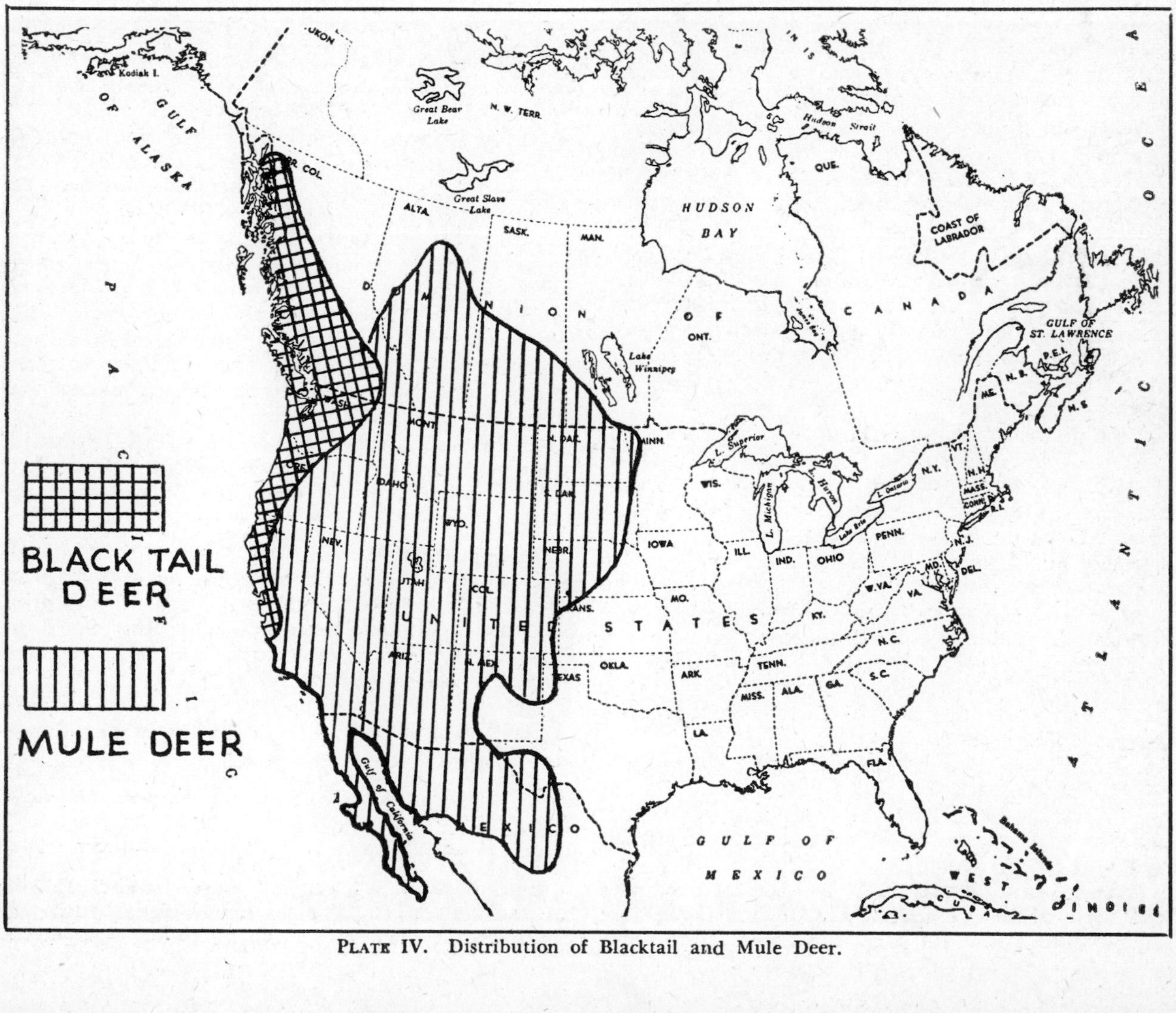


PLATE IV. Distribution of Blacktail and Mule Deer.

# WHITETAIL DEER

*Odocoileus virginianus*

**History.** The genus *Odocoileus* of the deer family, comprising the whitetail, blacktail, and mule deer, is the most populous and popular of the big-game animals on this continent, and according to the latest estimates are very nearly five million strong. Although the present representatives emerged during the Pleistocene Age, there is no evidence of any direct relation to the deer of the Old World. The three species are exclusively North American animals except for the whitetail, which is found in small numbers in Peru, Bolivia, and Brazil, having migrated there during the Tertiary period when the continents of North America and South America were more solidly joined.

The Indians and early settlers relied heavily on the whitetail as a source of both food and clothing, and the expansion of this country would have been considerably retarded had it not been for the deer. In many states, especially in the East, deer are believed to be more plentiful today than they were before the white man arrived on the continent. Records of early explorers indicate that in many instances they were forced to kill their horses for meat while passing through areas that are now heavily populated with deer.

In the past many estimates made of the early deer herds and total populations were noted primarily for their inaccuracies. One well-known naturalist, for example, estimated that at one time there were approximately 40,000,000 deer on this continent, an estimate based on an average of 20 deer per square mile.

The deer's ability to adapt itself to the encroachment of farm lands is a guarantee of its position and numbers on this continent. Other big-game animals died or were driven from their natural ranges by man, but deer continue to thrive, and even increase, on the fringes of settlements. Difficult as it may be to believe, whitetails have been killed within sight of the skyscraper towers of New York City. In Ontario, to cite another example, their numbers increased greatly as the woodlands were thinned out.

**Identification.** The antlers, as well as the white tail, are the identifying characteristics of the so-called "whitetail." These antlers have a basal "snag," and each beam bends back slightly, then sweeps forward, with the individual tines or points emerging from a *single* beam. The antler beams of the blacktail and mule deer branch and re-branch, forming forks.

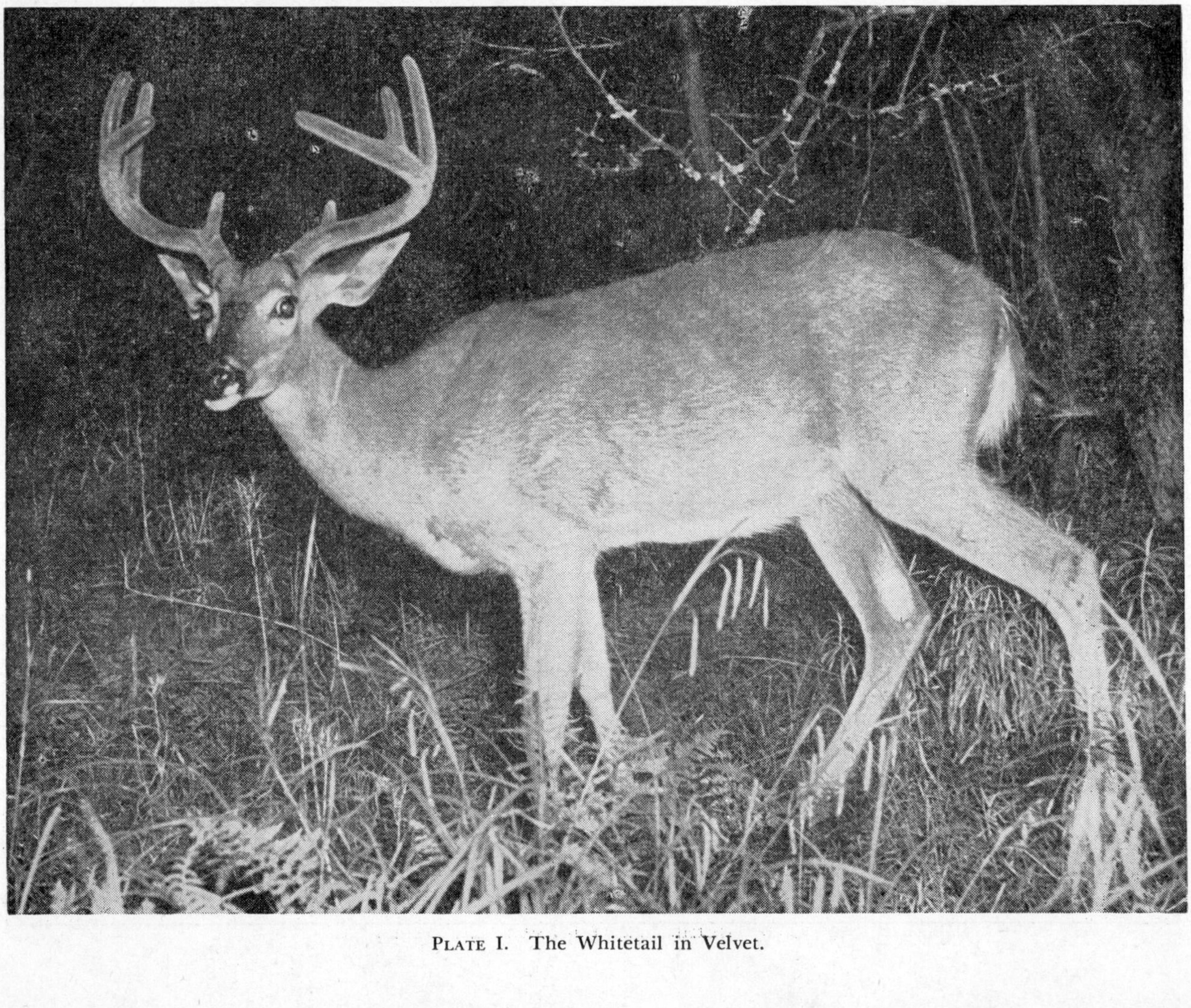

PLATE I. The Whitetail in Velvet.

As a result of the many antler formations within the species, and because antlers are worn only for a limited time each year, plus the fact that does are antlerless, many zoologists claim that antlers are not a satisfactory means of species identification. Many insist that the metatarsal gland on the middle of the leg is a more certain means of identification; they point out its consistency in size in each species and its presence on both sexes. However, it has been proved that there is some size variation of this gland within the species. There is, normally, a similarity of appearance in this gland among one species. The whitetail, for example, has a fringe of white hairs around the gland, which is lacking in both the mule deer and blacktail.

Although it is abnormal, there are many recorded instances of does bearing antlers. Each hunting

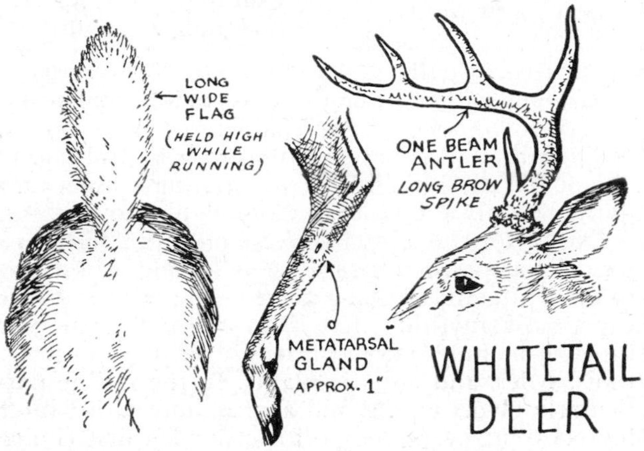


PLATE II. Whitetail Deer Identification.

season finds several antlered does killed by mistake, but such antlers usually are underdeveloped and freakish in appearance and have few points.

Additional identifying factors of the whitetail are smaller, narrower ears and, of course, the white tail. The latter is the distinctive feature, for it is erected as a "flag" when the animal is excited or frightened.

The whitetail buck is larger than the doe, but due to size and weight variations in different localities, it is impossible to establish an average weight for either the buck or the doe. The most striking size variation occurs in the Coues deer of Mexico, which also is found in fairly large numbers in southern Arizona. This deer, known locally as the *fantail, Sonora whitetail, Arizona whitetail,* or, near the border, *venado,* is a small edition of the normal whitetail, with the average buck weighing from 75 to 85 pounds and the doe from 55 to 65 pounds. Hunters have reported killing even smaller whitetails in Sonora, Mexico, believed to be a subspecies of the Coues deer, but as yet these deer have not been officially classified by zoologists. According to reports, the bucks of this sub-species average around 35 to 40 pounds and the does 25 to 30 pounds.

The average southern whitetail is considerably smaller than the northern representative. The whitetails of Florida, coastal Louisiana, Southwest Texas, and Arizona are among these smaller specimens, and their antlers or "racks" are correspondingly smaller. The whitetails of northern New York, Michigan, Maine, and the eastern provinces of Canada are the big examples of the species, with mature bucks often weighing in the neighborhood of 300 pounds.

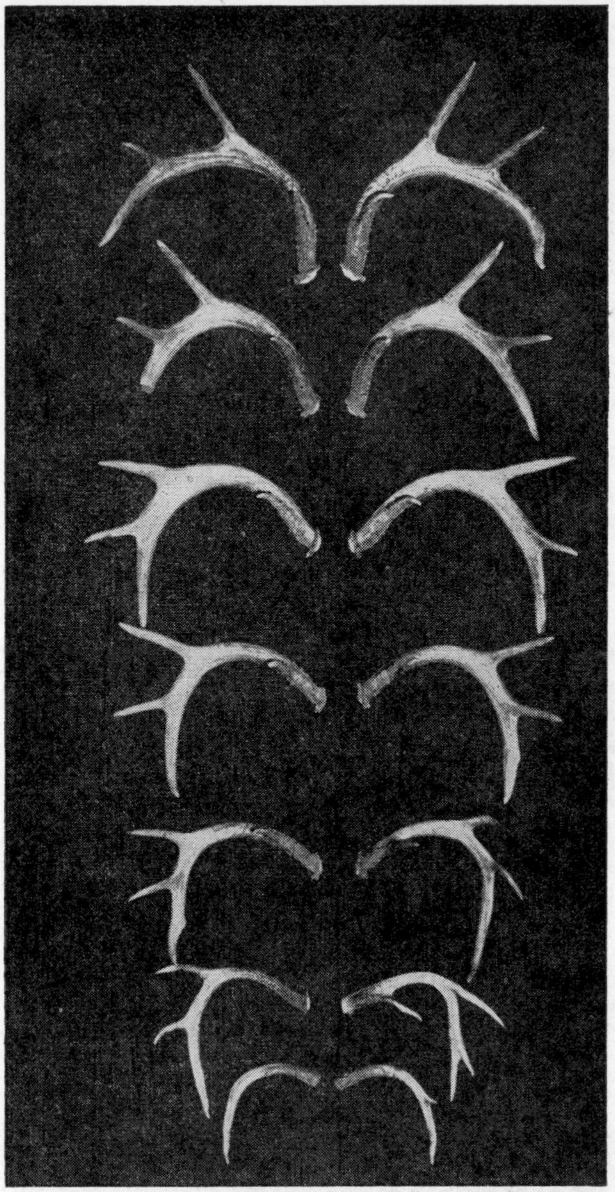

Courtesy New York Conservation Dept.

PLATE III. This should settle the argument on "points" and age. The antlers were all from the same whitetail buck over a nine-year period.

The Virginia deer is considered to be the largest of the whitetails, and has the most extensive range and the largest population. The record whitetail, killed by James C. Brewster in the Elk River area of British Columbia, had a remarkable head. The length of curve was: right antler 30¾ inches, left antler 27½ inches, greatest spread 33½ inches, with 14 points on the left antler and 12 points on the right.

The color of both male and female is similar, and normally there are two seasonal variations. In summer the coat is a reddish-tan, which fades to grayish-tan in the winter. This color difference is noted less among the deer of the south, and the coat is paler among those living on the plains. The Coues is the one exception, for its coat is brownish-gray all year.

The whitetail is even-hoofed, with a narrow heel and a typical white band above each hoof. It is the long, narrow shape of this hoof which confines the northern whitetail to a "yard" in the winter, for he sinks deeply into the snow and the crust cuts his slender, delicate legs.

Many have erroneously believed that the number of points and size of the antlers indicate the age of an individual deer. The only scientific means of determining age is by the condition of the teeth, which are 32 in number (no canines), and this method requires considerable study and experience as well as knowledge of local conditions. In areas where there is considerable sand, age-determination is more difficult, as the teeth are worn down more rapidly by destructive grinding.

The buck sheds his antlers each year, usually by late December. The new antlers begin showing in early May, when food is once more abundant, and the excess vitality from eager eating goes into this new bony growth. The yearling whitetail has "spikes," and normally does not have mature antlers until he is four years old. The antlers grow from permanent pedicels on the forepart of the skull.

During the first stage these pedicels are filled with blood and tissue, which forms and deposits the bony matter from which the antlers grow. For several months the antlers, nourished by blood vessels, are covered with a soft, spongy tissue called "velvet." At this time they are sensitive, and the buck avoids contact with trees and heavy brush which might injure them and affect their development. By August they are fully formed, and the velvet begins to peel. This peeling process is speeded up by the mature bucks, who rub their antlers against trees. The desire for perfected antlers is stimulated by the sex urge, for this period marks the beginning of the "rut."

**Characteristics.** The whitetail normally is a shy, timid animal, given to hiding in thickets and swamps to avoid his enemies. Although often bold during the "rutting" or mating season, he normally is more wary than the doe. Both sexes are skilled at skulking, and at times they will "creep" close to the ground, but at a remarkable speed, in order to circle an enemy.

When startled, the buck "blows." This is a whistling sound which in many instances seems to be an involuntary warning to other deer in the area. He then takes off in a spurt of speed, which has been estimated to be as much as 40 miles per hour. The first rush seems to be a combination of four or five leaps followed by a great, high jump, often covering from 15 to 20 feet.

The natural gait is a smooth-paced trot, at a speed ranging from 10 to 20 miles per hour. The whitetail also has a fast, low gallop, but is unable to maintain this pace for a great distance. The endurance of the deer is not great, and many records by early settlers indicate instances of Indians running down deer on foot, the process normally requiring four to six hours. The whitetail is an excellent swimmer, however, and like other members of the deer family he has air-filled hairs which cause him to ride fairly high in the water. He can swim a steady four miles per hour and has confidence in his ability in the water.

Although the whitetail's vision is far from good, he can pick up movement at considerable distance. Nature, to atone for the poor vision, has given the deer excellent hearing and a fine nose.

The deer is not migratory, and most of his traveling is done over a four- or five-mile radius, except that bucks, during the rutting season, often travel more extensively in their search for does. In summer the deer follow regular routines in moving from the resting to the feeding grounds, and in winter they are inclined to seek out thicker cover. In the north, where deep snow makes travel on narrow hoofs difficult, and makes escape from predators a problem, deer normally "yard up." Often as many as 50 or more deer will band together in one small area, usually a dense growth of evergreens, where they will trample the snow to a hard, packed surface.

The whitetail is not gregarious, for he lives alone except for the brief rutting or mating season, and normally only deep snow will cause him to yard up.

Except for the winter season, and the limitations fixed by a specific range, food is seldom a problem to the whitetail, for has a goatlike appetite and will eat almost anything that is green. In the summer his food includes grasses, leaves of shrubs and trees, roots, twigs, and aquatic plants. In the fall he particularly favors apples and acorns, and with winter he seeks out evergreens, with cedar his first choice and balsam and spruce secondary.

The highest rate of mortality occurs in the early spring, when the deer is weakened from the hard winter. By spring, the lower branches have been browsed clean, and disease finds an easy victim. The average life span is about 12 years, with a buck reaching his prime between the ages of five and eight. By the time he is ten he is going downhill rapidly.

The major enemies of the whitetail are wolves, coyotes, members of the wildcat family, and, of course, man.

**Breeding.** The whitetail buck first feels the rutting urge in late summer or early fall, and the first evidence of this is the swelling of his neck. Within a six-week period the neck of the mature buck often has swelled to a degree that has increased its circumference by 10 inches.

Although much has been written of the "death fights" of bucks, among whitetails these battles are not nearly so spirited as those carried on by other members of the deer family. The buck's primary interest is the doe, and as the whitetail normally is concerned with an individual doe, and not with a harem, as is the elk, he is not inclined to be overpugnacious. When two bucks do contest for the favor of a doe, the first jarring rush ordinarily is the hardest. After crashing together headlong, the rest of the fight usually consists more of jostling and pushing than of serious fighting, and usually after a brief encounter one will quit and leave the field of battle at a run.

Instances in which antlers become firmly locked

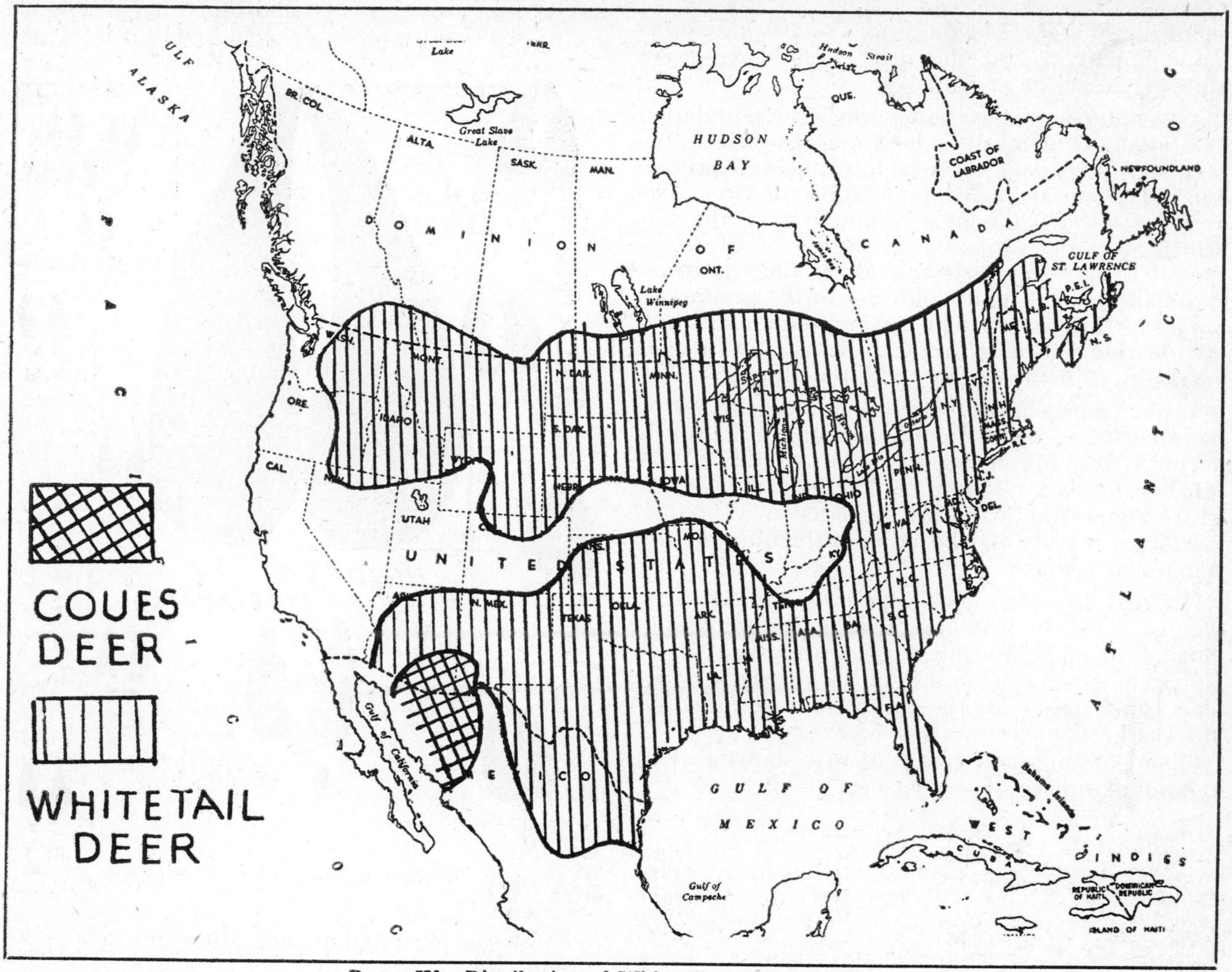


PLATE IV. Distribution of Whitetail and Coues Deer.

as a result of these encounters are rare, but due to the roughly circular formation of the rack, a temporary locking of antlers is not unusual.

The whitetail buck is considered among the most monogamous males of the deer family, but he is no outstanding example of fidelity. He is in almost constant pursuit of a doe during the rutting season, but remains with each conquest only about three days, and then departs in search of another.

The period of gestation of a doe is about 210 days, and the fawn is produced in the late spring. The whitetail fawn weighs approximately four pounds at birth, and is endowed with a natural camouflage. The spots which enable the fawn to merge with sun-dappled leaves remain about four to five months, and disappear when the first coat is shed.

For the first month the fawn is rather weak and helpless, and is carefully hidden by the doe, who returns to it five or six times each day for feeding. Normally the fawn is not fully weaned for about eight months. It is not unusual for a male fawn to remain with the mother for a year, and for the female fawn to remain for as much as two years, or until the young doe's initial mating.

**Range and Distribution.** In recent years it has been a common practice to transplant deer from one state to another, both for the sake of herd improvement and to stimulate the production or quality of a particular group. As little care was taken to insure a unity of species, many hybrids have resulted, some of which defy exact classification.

Among the majority of deer, however, set geographical areas separate individual species. Below is the accepted listing of the members of the whitetail species.

| | | | |
|---|---|---|---|
| Virginia Deer | *Odocoileus* | *virginianus* | *virginianus* |
| Eastern whitetail Deer | | | |
| Northern Virginia or | " | " | *borealis* |
| Whitetail Deer | " | " | |
| Key Deer | | | *clavium* |
| Coues Deer, Sonora | " | *couesi* | |
| Deer, Fantail | | | |
| Louisiana Deer | " | *virginianus* | *louisianae* |
| Plains whitetail Deer | " | " | *macrourus* |
| Northwestern Whitetail | " | " | |
| or Yellow-tail Deer | | | *ochrourus* |
| Florida whitetail Deer | " | " | *osceola* |
| Texas whitetail Deer | " | " | *texanus* |

The range of the whitetail is chiefly east of the Mississippi, from the wooded slopes of the east, extending north to Canada, through most of the Maritime Provinces, thence across to British Columbia and Oregon. They do not prefer the deep, timbered woodlands, or the wide plains, but are inhabitants of the margins or forest edges.

Because of increased land utilization, forest spoliation, forest fires, and market hunting, the whitetail population showed a dangerous trend at the turn of the century, and there was little improvement for 20 years. Then a process of adaptation became apparent, and the deer population began showing a definite increase.

Given a reasonable chance, the deer population of almost any area can be held to a reasonable constant, for no animal seems able to recover quite so rapidly from a serious population decline. The reason for this is the great productivity of the doe, which gives the whitetail the largest breeding potential of any big-game animal on the continent. Normally an 18-month-old doe will produce a single fawn from her first mating, but each successive mating normally produces twins, and in some instances, as many as three and four fawns.

Game management practices now are based on sound science, which, more than any other single factor is responsible for the great increase in the size of the nation's deer herd during the past 20 years. Pennsylvania and Michigan are two excellent examples of what may be accomplished by scientific game management.

In 1920 less than 3000 whitetails were killed in Pennsylvania. In 1940 more than 30,000 were killed during the open hunting season without making an apparent dent in the seed herd. In Michigan, where deer once faced almost complete extermination, the last big-game census showed 872,700.

The U. S. big-game census of 1946 shows a whitetail population of some 4,965,000.

| | | | |
|---|---|---|---|
| Alabama | 32,500 | Nebraska | 200 |
| Arizona | 34,000 | Nevada | 0 |
| Arkansas | 45,300 | New Hampshire | 57,800 |
| California | 0 | New Jersey | 29,000 |
| Colorado | 0 | New Mexico | 36,600 |
| Connecticut | 6,800 | New York | 300,100 |
| Delaware | 135 | North Carolina | 48,200 |
| Florida | 38,400 | North Dakota | 15,500 |
| Georgia | 19,200 | Ohio | 8,500 |
| Idaho | 28,600 | Oklahoma | 9,500 |
| Illinois | 5,100 | Oregon | 500 |
| Indiana | 3,300 | Pennsylvania | 676,000 |
| Iowa | 2,000 | Rhode Island | 500 |
| Kansas | 0 | South Carolina | 33,600 |
| Kentucky | 2,100 | South Dakota | 22,400 |
| Louisiana | 51,300 | Tennessee | 4,600 |
| Maine | 303,200 | Texas | 511,100 |
| Maryland | 1,500 | Utah | 0 |
| Massachusetts | 15,000 | Vermont | 74,800 |
| Michigan | 872,700 | Virginia | 46,600 |
| Minnesota | 609,700 | Washington | 20,300 |
| Mississippi | 21,800 | West Virginia | 120,000 |
| Missouri | 22,000 | Wisconsin | 791,000 |
| Montana | 37,500 | Wyoming | 5,900 |

**Hunting Methods—Whitetail.** Although there are but three generally accepted methods of hunting the whitetail, the STILL hunt, the DRIVE, and the STALK, there are many variations of each, the exact method depending upon the nature of the terrain and local custom. There are several factors which govern the general method: density of the woodland, character of the woodland, number of competing hunters, proximity to civilization, the deer population of the area, and, finally, the habits of the deer.

In a section where deer are reasonably plentiful and the cover quite thick, as it is in many parts of the East and Southeast, and where hunters also are plentiful, still hunting and driving are the most popular methods. In more open country, where the terrain is rolling or even mountainous, stalking is

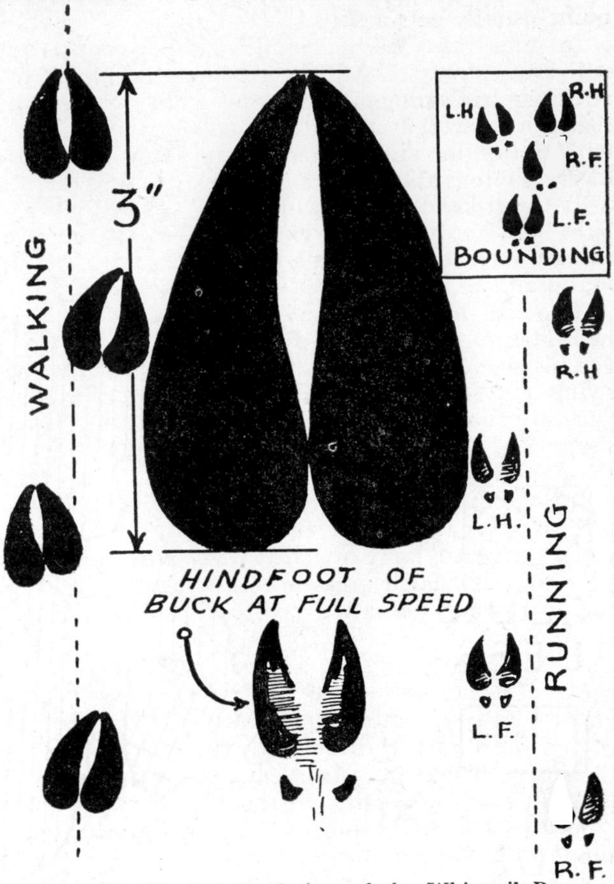


PLATE V. Typical Hoofprints of the Whitetail Deer.

not only the preferred method but seems to be more productive.

The still hunter, in order to be consistently successful, must have a reasonably good knowledge of the terrain, the game trails, and the habits of the local deer. In some areas in the late fall this proves to be cold sport, for the hunter's task is to locate a vantage point in an area where runways and browse indicate deer are present, and then stand or sit quietly until one passes within range. To be successful requires constant vigilance and absolute lack of movement. In an area where the temperatures hover well below freezing during the early morning hours, it is cold work, and the still hunter is denied the solace of a cigarette or pipe. From dawn until about 9 A.M. is the best period; from 9 A.M. until 2 P.M. the still hunter would do just as well to return to camp for an early lunch and a nap before returning to his lonely post.

In approaching as well as leaving his vantage point, the still hunter moves as quietly as possible, and slowly. For the lone hunter, this method is the most practical, and it seems especially successful in areas where other hunters are constantly on the move, and even where large drives are being conducted by hunting groups. The average hunter, on the move, sees about one deer out of the 20 that are within his range but undetected. Also, regardless of the number of "drivers" employed in a deer drive, a number of deer manage to pass through the line of drivers. These deer normally move to an adjoining area where there is less noise and movement, and the still hunter who has selected a strategic point usually gets a shot.

In some parts of the South and Southwest, the still hunter may take along a pair of antlers. After selecting his vantage point, one which offers concealment as well as a view of near-by game trails, he will rattle the antlers together at long intervals. Deer, having almost human curiosity, often will drift toward the sound, which they believe to be a fight between two bucks. Even in the event they are not attracted by the sound, it is a "natural" sort of sound and so it does not frighten them away.

The still hunter who hears a deer approaching behind him must, unless he believes the deer will get his scent, restrain his impatience until he can swing and shoot without loss of time and without encountering obstacles. Impatience has lost more shots, and the resulting venison, to still hunters than any other one factor.

In some areas the still hunter finds prospects best on the very fringe of the farmlands, especially where there are large orchards partially surrounded by woodland. Such areas are best during the very early morning, just after daybreak, and late in the afternoon.

In the West the still hunter often seeks out a vantage point overlooking a small valley or even a narrow canyon which he knows is inhabited by deer. This often requires considerable patience, and binoculars as well as a telescopic sight are valuable aids. Success also varies, in this instance, with the shooting skill of the hunter and his knowledge of where to "hold" at various ranges.

The DRIVING method, although more widely practiced in almost all sections, except in the north, where great tracts of dense woodland make it impractical, is one of the least interesting forms of deer hunting. To stage a deer drive requires from 3 to 60 hunters; those who may think this latter number an exaggeration have never witnessed a big drive in southern New Jersey. In some of the southern states the use of hounds eliminates the necessity for a number of drivers, but the use of dogs in hunting deer is forbidden in most states.

The average deer drive, especially as practiced in the East and Southeast, requires about a dozen hunters, a few of whom must have a sound knowledge of the country as well as of the habits of local deer. One requisite for a successful deer drive, many groups fail to recognize, or, if they recognize, do not put it in practice. That is: *one man in charge.* Nothing can ruin a drive quite so thoroughly as several dissenting opinions on how it should be run. The hunter most familiar with the country and its deer population should be the "boss," and if his organization fails to produce, then he may be dethroned.

Normally, the group is broken up into two sections, one to do the driving, another to be posted on "stands." The ratio of each varies with the type of terrain to be driven.

The method itself is quite simple, but its practice calls for considerable tactical maneuvering. For example, the area to be driven may be roughly wedge-shaped, with the point of the wedge down-wind. This condition would call for about twice as many drivers as standers.

Normally, in driving such an area the drivers would be posted from 50 to 100 yards apart, the distance depending upon the denseness of the wood-

PLATE VI. Waiting for the Drive to Come Through.

land. Each driver should be able to see or hear the driver on either side during the progress of the drive. Otherwise, deer will manage to work between them and sneak behind the line.

The first problem is the posting of the "standers," who must be placed on vantage points which not only should command a view of the terrain more than half the distance between them, but which must offer COMPLETE safety from a bullet from the gun of an adjoining stander. Once in position, a stander should not move. In effect, he is a still hunter. Movement not only will cost him a chance of getting a shot, but may bring a shot his way. The head of the drive, in placing the standers, takes these points into consideration, and in many clubs any stander who moves more than a gun length from the spot on which he was placed is forced to contribute to the club fund.

The drivers, advancing on a general line toward the standers, may move at a normal pace, with no special emphasis on noise, or they may, as is done in some areas, blow whistles, toot horns, beat pans, and shout. The purpose of the driver is not to kill deer, but to keep them moving ahead of him in order to give one of the standers a shot. Drivers and standers alternate until all have had a chance at each function.

In large woodland areas, drives are organized according to the wind direction and the terrain. An old logging road, a long clearing, parallel valleys or gullies, or any natural terrain offering a long vista may serve as boundaries for the drive. Standers may be placed in a line or in U formation, with the drivers moving in a rough crescent (the ends in advance) toward the standers.

In some areas—in the New Jersey pine barrens, for example—as many as 50 or 60 hunters participate in a drive; often 20 men are put on stands with 30 or 40 driving. In most instances the deer killed are pooled at the end of the hunt, and divided by lot among the hunters, regardless of who did the shooting. In other instances, the deer all are placed in storage and the hunters, their families and friends gather later for a venison dinner.

In those states where dogs are permitted to run deer, the percentage of standers can be much higher than that of the drivers, for the dogs do the work. The usual procedure is for the "head" of the drive to place the standers, and then move well up-wind with the dogs and dog-handlers. When the dogs jump a deer the drivers follow them, usually shouting encouragement, and the deer move toward the standers.

This method is frowned upon in many areas, where it is charged that the use of dogs often results in deer being killed that are never recovered, and tends to bring about a rather high mortality rate among does and fawns.

The driving method can be extremely dangerous, regardless of the particular form practiced, if there happens to be one careless or "trigger-happy" hunter in the group. Excitement, coupled with tension, often causes a man to shoot at a movement in the brush which he believes to be a deer, regardless of the fact that this movement may be another hunter or a doe. Each year scores of hunters are killed or wounded by companions who shot before they saw antlers. One Adirondack guide, who takes groups of deer hunters to his camp each fall, claims this job to be the most "hazardous occupation in the world."

"On one occasion," he explains, "I was shot at by three standers before I could drop behind a log, and while I lay there two of them continued to shoot, riddling the brush, until their guns were empty. At that point, if I had had my rifle with me, I'd have done some shooting back."

Stalking, though one of the least practiced methods, undoubtedly is the most interesting, and requires the greatest amount of skill and woodcraft. This method is not necessarily a lone one, for often two men will hunt as a team, although separated by two or three hundred yards or more.

Lone stalking, to be successful, requires considerable experience in the woods, a knowledge of deer habits, a knowledge of the terrain, and the ability to shoot quickly and accurately. The man who is unable to move quietly through various types of cover, or who is unable to maintain a reasonably accurate sense of direction, should stick to still hunting or driving, for his success in stalking is not going to be consistent.

The experienced stalker moves up-wind, and very slowly. He must know "where" to look, what type of cover the deer will be in at all times of day, and must be able to cover the area with his eyes. He must be familiar with the vagaries of the wind and its relation to his movement. Normally, he will pause a few seconds every 15 or 20 paces, in order to take a more careful look ahead and on either side and to listen.

Many novices make the mistake of paralleling the course of a noisy stream, under the illusion that this *natural* sound will cover the noise of their movement. Although this is true, the deer, being an alert and wise animal, normally will avoid an area that would permit an enemy to approach unheard.

Stalking during an extremely dry spell often proves unsuccessful, even for the experienced hunter, for it is impossible to move through the woods without the sound of the movement going ahead to the sharp, listening ears of the deer. At such times the experienced hunter will engage in still hunting, selecting a low, well-watered area where the deer will come to avoid the heat and get water.

Perfect stalking conditions result when there has been a light rain for a few hours, followed by about an inch of snow. This not only permits the stalker to move quietly through the woods, but gives him a chance to do some tracking. Such conditions, however, also aid the deer, for a moving object shows up sharply against the white, and the experienced hunter moves slowly.

Deer blend very well into the brush, and they know it. Many a stalker has approached to within four or five feet of a buck, which lay quiet in a patch of brush confident that the camouflage was sufficient to hide it. Often a hunter, halting to look around, has been considerably startled by having a deer jump from a clump of laurel or rhododendron almost under his feet. Many a buck has been killed on his bed due to a twitching ear or a blinking eye.

When two hunters engage in the stalking method together, there are several forms that may be fol-

PLATE VII. Blacktail Deer in the Late Fall.

lowed. In some instances the rough course, up-wind, will be decided upon in advance. One will then follow the top of a ridge-line, the other the valley. In some instances they move three or four hundred yards apart, but with one as much as a hundred yards in advance.

During the afternoon, in the late fall, deer often seek out a sunny slope with sufficient cover to offer concealment and at the same time to give them a chance to watch the avenues of approach. On a sunny slope, the wind normally carries the scent toward the crest. Therefore, the hunter moving along the ridge usually lags slightly behind his companion in the valley. The deer, scenting and hearing the hunter in the valley, normally will attempt to cut high and behind him, offering the other hunter a shot.

Knowledge of deer habits is important to the stalker. For example, a deer jumped on the fringe of an open area often will cross the open in long, high jumps, offering an almost impossible shot to the hunter. However, in many instances a deer, unless badly frightened, will halt immediately upon reaching cover, and look back. Unless the cover is extremely thick, this will offer the hunter a standing shot.

The stalker who is alone often will get a shot by following along the sunny slope of a ridge about one-third the distance between the crest and the base. This seems to be most productive between the hours of 9 A.M. and 2 P.M.

**Blacktail and Mule Deer.** While all of the methods outlined previously for the hunting of the whitetail are practiced in some areas where the blacktail are found, members of the mule deer family normally are found in rougher, wilder terrain.

The mule deer, unlike his cousins, has a decided preference for more open terrain, which permits him to detect the approach of his enemies by means of his eyes as well as his nose and ears. This characteristic undoubtedly has developed as an adaptation to environment, for the mule deer is most plentiful in the high and rugged mountain areas, where the country is broken, sparsely timbered, and cut with ravines and gullies. Most hunters claim that the mule deer's vision is considerably superior to that of the whitetail and blacktail.

When too heavily hunted, the mule deer will take to the thick timber or tangled windfalls and brush of the ridges.

The mule deer hunter should be prepared to locate his game a good distance ahead, and therefore should be equipped with good binoculars and a rifle with a telescopic sight. When jumped, the mule deer is apt to make a big circle and end up in a good cover only a few hundred yards from his starting point. This tendency to emulate the rabbit has resulted in increasing the mortality rate of the animal. Often, after jumping one of these animals, but failing to get a shot, a hunter will move a few hundred yards beyond the jumping point, seek out an elevation, and wait in hopes that the deer will return. Unless too often disturbed, the chances are excellent that the deer will feed in the same area the following day, even though he fails to return before dark on the day he was jumped.

The mule deer often will be found in open parks, and on most occasions he seems to base his safety factor on yardage, and will not take off in haste if a hunter is seen as much as three hundred yards distant. The man with a good telescopic sight, who is familiar with his rifle and the sight setting for extreme ranges, often has an excellent chance of eating deer liver for supper.

In the Western mountains one of the favorite haunts of these deer is under the steep rimrocks along ridges, where with two or three bounds they may reach the cover of wooded slopes. Another likely place is an aspen thicket at the head of a steep gully. As a result, one of the best hunting methods is to move along a ridge, keeping well hidden, and halt for occasional surveys of the lower country through glasses.

Often, a hunter will be offered a clear, open shot at a range of about 200 yards. However, as from 100 to 150 yards of this distance may be straight down, most hunters score more misses than hits due to their lack of knowledge of ballistics. Rifles that are sighted in with the belief that the bullets will be traveling roughly horizonal to the pull of gravity, must be sighted quite differently when the angle of the shot is acutely high or low. (See "Shooting at Acute Angles.")

In hunting the aspen thickets, the method often used somewhat parallels driving. Two or three hunters will station themselves at avenues of departure from a thicket, and two others will walk or ride horses through the thicket, thus pushing the mule deer out toward the standers.

In the fall the big mule deer seem to gather on the upper edge of timberline, and still hunting is the approved method. Here the best periods are early morning and late afternoon.

Hunting mule deer on the sagebrush flats, or the broken slopes, normally is a job for the mounted hunter. The popular procedure is for several hunters to line up, a few hundred yards apart, and advance in a line. When a buck is jumped, the hunter normally dismounts to shoot, and usually is offered a moving target that is a good test of his skill.

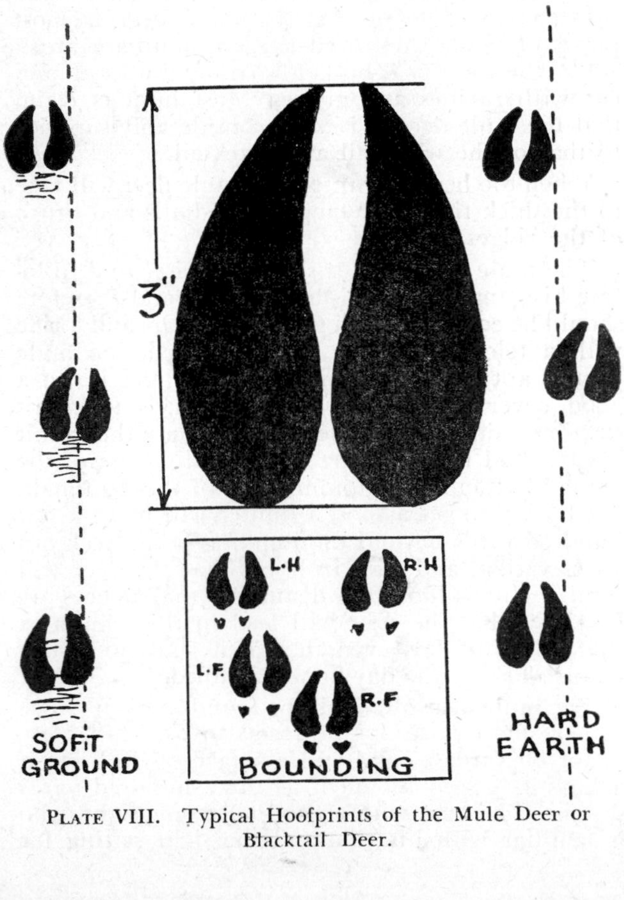


PLATE VIII. Typical Hoofprints of the Mule Deer or Blacktail Deer.

Regardless of terrain, the mule deer will be easier to locate when he is moving around or feeding, which means early morning and late afternoon. If the nights are dark and moonless, the mule deer are inclined to bed down and not feed, which means they will be out early the following morning. On bright, moonlight nights they often feed before sun-up, then seek out their beds during the day. While bedded down they are extremely alert, and in many instances they are able to sneak off long before the hunter arrives.

The novice hunter who sees a deer "sneak" for the first time usually is amazed at the speed the animal can make with its belly almost scraping the ground, and neck outstretched. The deer under such circumstances seems able to take advantage of every low spot in the ground, and can move unseen along an extremely shallow ditch or gully.

The blacktail, like his whitetail cousin, normally is found in the heavy cover, and is even less inclined to feed or move in the open than the whitetail. Normally, the hunting methods follow those used in hunting the Eastern whitetail, especially on the West Coast between the Cascade Range and the Pacific.

Large numbers are to be found on the coastal marshes, provided there is sufficient heavy cover adjacent to such marshes. In western Canada, still hunting and stalking are the most common methods employed. They usually are found in considerable numbers on burns, for these offer good browse and excellent cover.

Experienced Western hunters remark on the sharp dividing line that seems to separate the mule deer from the blacktail. It is possible to hunt blacktail up to the rim of the Cascades; then, on the eastern slope the blacktail seems to have disappeared and the mule deer takes his place.

There have been many long, heated arguments concerning "where to hold" on the various species of deer. The majority of hunters, confronted with a short-range shot, will try to put the bullet high in the neck just forward of the shoulder. A shot here not only spoils less good meat, but usually shatters the spine and eliminates trailing a wounded animal. On longer-range, standing shots, the experienced hunter holds just back of the shoulder, aiming a little high rather than low. This usually puts the bullet through the heart and upper lungs, and if the animal does not drop in its tracks it normally is able to travel but a short distance. What every hunter wishes to avoid is a gut shot, for in too many instances this means a long job of trailing a wounded animal with no assurance that success lies at the end of the trail.

When a deer has been wounded, the novice is inclined to take up the trail immediately. This is a mistake. The experienced hunter will wait until the deer has made its first run and has stopped to lie down. After 20 or 30 minutes, he takes up the trail, moving very slowly and keeping careful watch on either side, for the wounded deer often circles back to a point where it can overlook its trail. Every minute the deer lies down means increased stiffness,

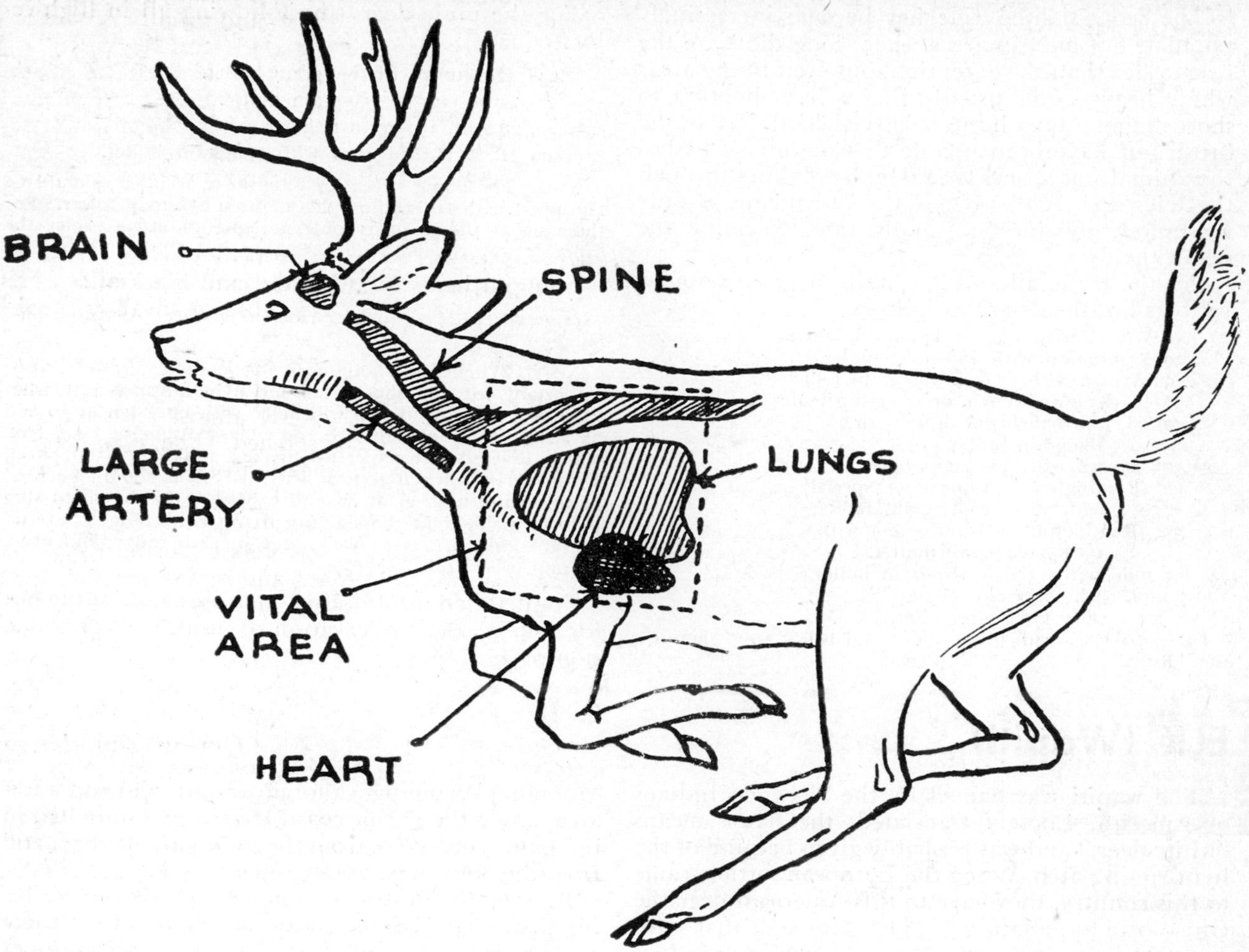


PLATE IX. Vital Areas, Deer.

and when jumped the second time a wounded deer usually offers an easy shot.

**Deer Rifles.** The term "deer rifle" is something of a misnomer, for in many areas, especially in the extreme eastern and western portions of the country, shotguns, with buckshot or rifled slugs, are used in preference to rifles. In many instances, however, the use of the shotgun for deer hunting is directed by law rather than by the hunter's choice, the major exception being supplied by "one gun" hunters, who make a shotgun do double duty.

No two hunters, if forced to hunt under varied and varying conditions, would ever agree on any one action and caliber of rifle or bullet weight, type and powder load of cartridge for *all* deer hunting. And this is not unusual or unreasonable.

In the extreme eastern and western sections, where the hunting primarily is for the whitetail and blacktail, and where the cover is heavy and short-range shooting is the rule rather than the exception, the carbine is favored. And with sound reason. For brush hunting, the short-barreled rifle is lighter, easier to carry through heavy cover, and does just as effective a job at short range as the longer-barreled, heavier, scope-sighted rifle that is preferable for the open country favored by mule deer.

For the average deer a bullet is required that has sufficient weight and shocking power to stop the animal quickly, but without the high velocity that damages meat. Here also, there is a common belief that has absolutely no basis in fact, to the effect that the small-caliber rifle is more "sporting" than the large caliber. Nothing could be more removed from the truth. The small-caliber, high-velocity rifle, except in the hands of a real expert, is decidedly "unsporting," for it results in the wounding of many deer but the recovery of few. As with all other game, the arm which results in the quickest and most merciful death is the most "sporting" arm.

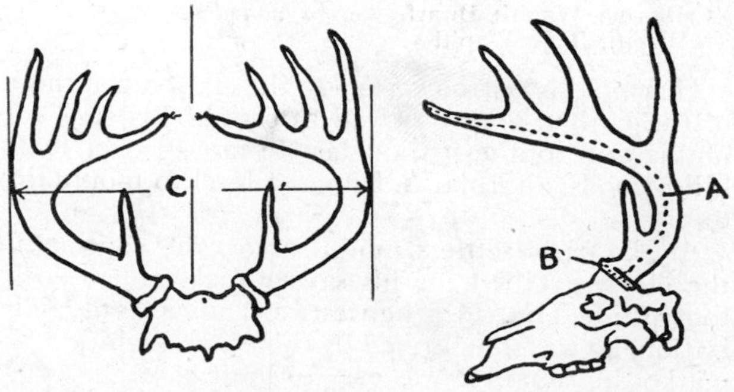


PLATE X. Trophy Measurements, Whitetail Deer.
A-Length of outside curve. B-Circumference at base.
C-Greatest spread.

The scope-sighted rifle has become increasingly popular, not only in areas where long shots are the rule rather than the exception, but even in the areas where heavy cover usually limits deer shooting to short ranges. Many hunters have sighted deer in the brush but have been unable to determine whether the animal was a buck or a doe. By looking through the telescope sight, even if the instrument is only 2¼-power, the hunter usually can determine the sex of the deer.

For the whitetail and blacktail, the most popular calibers and loads are as follows:

.30 W.C.F. with 150- or 170-grain bullet.
.30 Remington with 170-grain bullet.
.300 Savage with 150- or 180-grain bullet.
.30/40 (Krag) with 150- or 180-grain bullet.
.30/'06 (Springfield) with 150- or 180-grain bullet.
.303 Savage with 180-grain bullet.
.32 (Remington or Winchester Special) with 165- or 170-grain bullet.
.35 (Remington or Winchester) with 150- or 200-grain bullet.
6.5 mm. with 150- or 160-grain bullet.
7 mm. with 170-grain bullet.
8 mm. with 170-grain bullet.

For details on loads given above and below see "Ammunition—Rifle."

For the mule deer (the following all in **high-velocity loads**):

.256 (Newton) with 140-grain bullet.
.270 with 130-/or 150-grain bullet.
.30/'06 with 150-grain bullet.
300 H. & H. Magnum with 180-grain bullet.

NOTE: The above rifles, for long-range accuracy, should be equipped with telescopic sights of from 2½ to 4 power. For these sights the majority of experienced hunters prefer the tapered post reticule. (See "Sights and Optical Aids.")

Shotgun loads for whitetail and blacktail:

12 gauge, with oo buck or rifled slug. (See "Ammunition—Shotgun.")

NOTE: When the shotgun is to be used for deer, it is important for the shooter to know in advance just what kind of a pattern his gun will make with buckshot at 50 and 75 yards. It is advisable to construct a frame, 4 by 5 feet, which, covered with paper will make a suitable pattern sheet. Using an improvised rest, at least five shots should be fired at this pattern sheet at 50 and 75 yards. If the rifled slug is to be used, sight the shotgun in with this slug at 50 and 75 yards, firing at least five rounds at each range, and using an improvised rest.

For detailed information on dressing, skinning out for trophy, and preservation of meat, see **"Preservation of Trophies."**

## ELK (Wapiti)

*Cervus canadensis*

The wapiti was named by the Shawnee Indians of America. Loosely translated, the name means "white deer," and was probably given because of the light rump patch. When the European settlers came to this country, they gave to this American deer the Old-World appellation of "elk" although that term properly belonged to the Scandinavian moose. It is by this incorrect name, however, that the animal is commonly known.

The wapiti is the only member of genus *cervus* in North America, but there are numerous smaller relatives in Asia and Europe. He is allied to, but larger than, the European stag, or red deer. He is almost a duplicate in appearance of some large stags of China and Siberia, a few of which also are called wapiti.

A breakdown of the wapiti into sub-species is as follows:

| | |
|---|---|
| American Wapiti | *Cervus canadensis canadensis* |
| Manitoba Wapiti | *Cervus canadensis manitobensis* |
| Olympic Wapiti; Roosevelt Wapiti; Western Wapiti | *Cervus canadensis occidentalis* |
| California Wapiti; Dwarf Wapiti; Tule Wapiti | *Cervus nanodes* |

**History.** About 100 years ago the elk roamed most of the United States as well as central British Columbia and southern Canada. He ranged over foothills, woods, and plains, from sea level to mountain tops.

As the early settlers moved across the continent, the elk was killed for his savory meat and useful, tough hide, and with the westward advance of civilization, he was slaughtered by thousands by hide and market hunters. He was easy to hunt because of his large size and because he inhabited the open plains.

Eventually, he was virtually destroyed in every part of his home range except for sections of Canada, Montana, Wyoming, Colorado, and Idaho and a few areas along the Pacific coast. He was exterminated in the East about 1860, from the plains about 1870, and from the Southwest about 1890.

By 1900 the drastically reduced numbers were being protected in some states, but at this time there arose a clamor for "elk tusks," the two useless upper canine teeth of the elk. Poachers ruthlessly killed the elk (usually in the winter migrating season) by thousands and left the bodies of the animals to spoil where they fell.

Pushed back from the plains by ranchers and farmers, the elk has become a mountain animal in the West. During the winter season he comes down for food to the foothills, where he finds grass over-grazed by domestic sheep and trees over-browsed by deer. Within the last 40 years, food shortages during the winter have caused many thousands of elk to starve.

The chief remnants of these formerly tremendous herds are now prospering in the Yellowstone Park area. They are of sturdy, prolific stock and the main problems are a too-rapid increase within a limited range, and an inadequate winter range. The National Park Service plans to cut down the present herd in order to allow a rejuvenation of the foliage and vegetation.

To prevent the elk from making desperate sorties on the lands of the stock grower and farmer, and to help them survive the winter, authorities in many areas provide an abundant supply of hay.

Elk have been successfully reintroduced into Arizona and New Mexico and other sections of the country where they formerly abounded, and where the conditions are still favorable for them. They also have been transplanted into Afognak Island where they prosper on the luxuriant growth of grasses and vegetation. The eight that were originally imported there have multiplied to 300.

**Identification.** The bull elk gives the appearance of being tall, even taller than the moose, the largest of the deer family, primarily because of his slender, towering antlers, which often rise a majestic 5 feet above his head. They are round and widely-branching, and a bull in his prime will carry from five to seven points with the heavy racks extending 66 inches along the beam. He bears a brow tine, bez tine, tres-tine, sur-royal, royal, etc., tine with the terminal tines forming a fork. He is typified by the fourth tine.

A record head was taken by Colonel Archibald Rogers in the Wind River Mountains, Wyoming. The length of the right outside curve was 64¾ inches with the greatest spread 49⅝ inches, and the antlers bore seven points on each side.

The male is much more handsome than the female. He is graceful in spite of a massive weight, which ranges from 700 to 1000 pounds and is carried on slender legs. He stands about 5 feet at the shoulder, with an average length of over 9 feet.

The female is plain and much smaller by comparison. She is antlerless and more awkward in appearance, usually swaybacked. She weighs between 500 and 600 pounds, has a height at the shoulders of just under 5 feet, and measures about 7 feet in length.

Both sexes have a neck mane, a muzzle (barren of hair), a small head, and large ears. The canine teeth of the male are much larger than those of the female.

The elk has a generally tan coloring which is a darker brown on his head and a grayish-brown along the sides, back, and legs. The female is paler. Both male and female have a characteristic light (pale buff or white) rump patch and tail.

The summer pelage is more reddish than the winter one which is of lighter color with longer hairs.

**Characteristics.** The elk is gregarious, migrating in large herds in the winter, and banding together in a typical group of several cows with their young along with two or three bulls in the summer season. Often the cows and bulls may separate into small groups.

He is very curious and will approach any strange, motionless object. A story has been reported of a herd of over 30 elk coming within 50 yards to investigate a stationary hunter. The elk which inhabit the foothills are more wary of man, however, and they rely on their keen senses to warn them of the enemy. These same distrustful animals put aside their canny alertness in the winter season, when they are forced to eat the hay provided by man on the refuges or die of starvation.

Though he grazes to some extent on grass, he is primarily a browser, preferring twigs and leaves, especially those of the quaking aspen tree, which in some sections never reaches maturity. In some areas he has been known to survive on aspen bark only when no other food was available in the winter.

His enemies are the same as those of other deer—the cougar, bear, wolf, and coyote. The adults can

Courtesy U. S. Forest Service.

PLATE I. A Good Bull, but Worried.

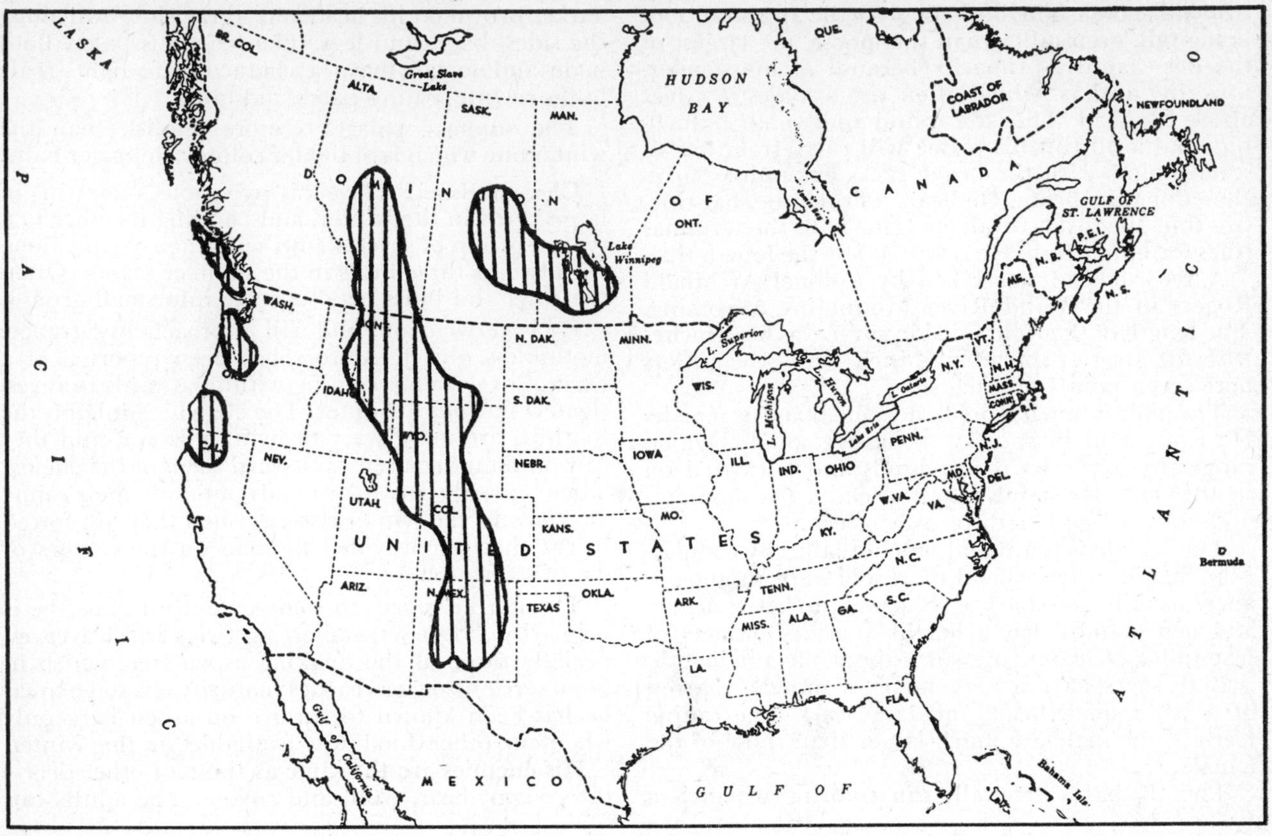


PLATE II. Distribution of Elk.

usually defend themselves against attack, often using a 35-mile-an-hour gallop, but the fawns normally are easy prey.

The elk usually fights with his forefeet, viciously attacking and defending with quick, hard blows of his slashing hoofs. With one blow he can break the back of a wolf.

**Breeding.** The bull elk starts the rutting season in late September or October when, antlers hard and white-tipped, he stalks the forest giving his call to battle. His martial trumpet is a challenge to other bulls to fight for the cows. This "bugling" is not like the harsh bellow of the moose, but is melodious, yet piercing. The same bulls that spent the summer in peaceful bunches of three to 20 now seek each other out for violent combat. The elk is the most polygamous of all the deer family and he will fight viciously to collect and hold his harem, which may number as many as 30 to 40 cows. As the rutting season advances they form into herds and start for the wintering grounds, like the other migratory deer.

The gestation period is around 8½ months and usually only one fawn is born in May or June, though sometimes there are two, and rarely three. The fawns are yellowish and spotted at birth. The color remains, but the spotted coat is shed in about 12 weeks.

The fawns are able to follow the cow in three to four days and the careful mother teaches them to lie still and quiet when danger is near. The call of a mother to her young sounds like the bark of a dog.

**Range and Distribution.** The range of the elk is within the western part of North America, chiefly in the Rocky Mountain region, with some in the Far Western states. The largest concentration of herds, numbering about 40,000, is in the Yellowstone National Park area. From here they move north and south in the winter season. They also inhabit Manitoba in moderate numbers and a few rugged specimens live in their natural habitat in Northern British Columbia, unaided by the government.

The latest big-game inventory accounts for the elk distribution within the United States as follows:

| | | | |
|---|---|---|---|
| Arizona | 6,600 | North Dakota | 52 |
| Arkansas | 175 | Oklahoma | 268 |
| California | 729 | Oregon | 20,600 |
| Colorado | 55,800 | Pennsylvania | 17 |
| Idaho | 36,200 | South Dakota | 2,300 |
| Michigan | 250 | Texas | 500 |
| Minnesota | 160 | Utah | 7,900 |
| Montana | 40,700 | Virginia | 175 |
| Nebraska | 119 | Washington | 20,800 |
| Nevada | 655 | Wisconsin | 20 |
| New Hampshire | 25 | Wyoming | 88,700 |
| New Mexico | 6,100 | | |
| North Carolina | 5 | TOTAL | 288,830 |

The spring and summer are spent on the mountain meadows, or high, treeless plains, or along the mountain ridges. At this high altitude they are free of flies and insects and flourish on the rich vegetation because of the heavy, mountain rainfall. About the time of the first frost in late fall, the elk starts to merge the small bands into larger herds in preparation for the migration from the snow-covered mountains to the sheltered valleys. On their winter range at the foothills they contest with the antelope, bighorn, and deer for the limited amount of forage. About 75 years ago the elk used to go far out onto the plains for winter feeding, but today's ranchers and farmers keep him pressed back to the foothills.

**Hunting Methods.** The American elk is one of the most magnificent of the world's big-game animals. Many consider it the number one antlered trophy, even passing the moose in this respect. Except for the antelope, bighorn, and Rocky Mountain goat, the average range at which elk are killed exceeds that of any other North American big-game animal. Ranges of from 150 to 300 yards are probably the rule rather than the exception, and shots at 500 yards or more are not unusual. This merely indicates that they are frequently seen at excessively long ranges, and that many hunters yield to the temptation to shoot at much greater distances than they can reasonably hope to place a bullet in a vital area. Entirely too many animals are wounded and lost due to this practice on many elk ranges. One of the reasons for this is that the elk is so large in proportion to the smaller members of the deer family, to which he belongs, that many well-intentioned hunters misjudge distances.

In the early days the wapiti occupied a range stretching practically across the entire United States, and seems to have been as much at home on the plains as in the woods and mountains. Today, wherever he has been hunted he has sought refuge in only our roughest mountain areas. As his favorite food consists as much of grasses as of browse he is fond of open parks and alpine meadows above timberline. But during daylight he seldom goes so far from timber that he can not reach it with a comparatively short run in the event that his principal enemy, man, appears unexpectedly upon the scene.

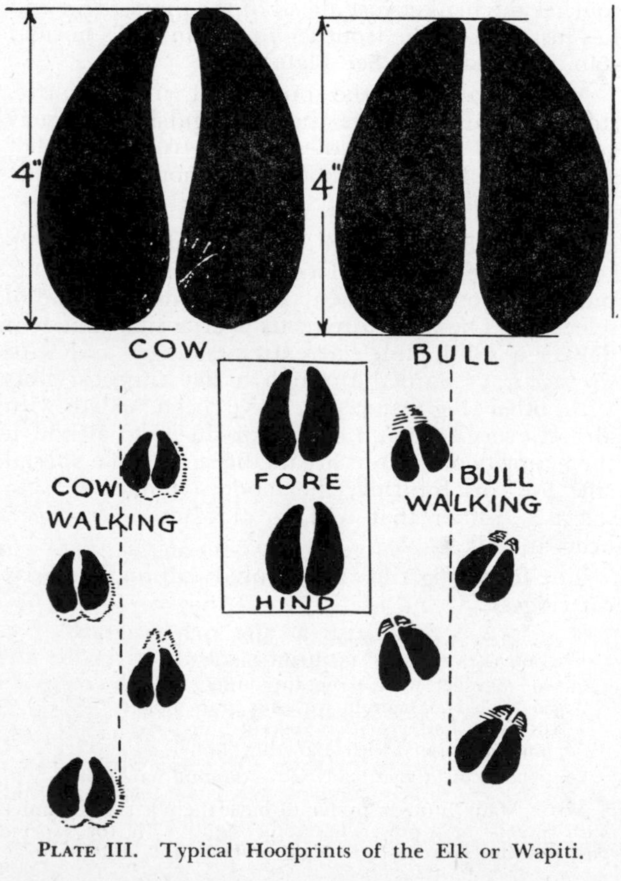


PLATE III. Typical Hoofprints of the Elk or Wapiti.

Many herds of elk in the Rocky Mountain region spend practically the entire year above timberline and just at the upper edge of timber, where protective cover can be reached when occasion requires. These animals depend upon the cutting winds of winter to keep the snow swept from their favorite foods along the ridgetops, and upon the upper fringe of stunted timber to provide shelter against the severest storms. Other herds yield to the temptation to drift toward livestock ranches at the approach of deep snow and become a menace to fences and haystacks. Ordinarily hunting seasons find them in the prime of condition and prepared to match wits with the sportsman in rugged, timbered areas far from automobile roads and the haunts of men.

It is inconsistent to think of hunting elk without thinking in terms of saddle and pack horses. In the first place, the carcass is too heavy to bring to camp without the aid of a horse (a single quarter is too heavy for the average man to pack), and in the second place, the elk is altogether unlike the deer in that he does not seem to feel tied to any particular locality that he must call home. Elk herd up into bunches of considerable size, sometimes as many as several hundred together, and tomorrow they may be found many miles from where they were yesterday or today. The man on foot has little chance of being able to keep up with their wanderings and the country over which they roam precludes the use of any transportation other than the horse. The prospective elk hunter should first assure himself that horses are available before arranging the other details of a hunt. Every year witnesses a considerable number of well cared-for carcasses left hanging in remote areas where hunters depending upon rubber tires and sole leather have been unable to bring out their meat. Unless horses have been arranged for in advance it is frequently impossible to rent them for love or money after the hunting season gets into full swing. No sportsman dares risk postponing arrangement for pack horses until he needs them. If horses can not be assured in advance it is usually better to cancel or postpone hunting plans.

In hunting from horseback there are two general procedures. Many prefer to dismount and hunt on foot as soon as fresh elk signs indicate that the animals are in the immediate vicinity. This has the advantage of being much quieter than continuing on horseback. It is often possible to come upon the animals entirely unaware and get in the first shot with real deliberation—provided they are approached from down wind. The elk's sense of smell is as keen as that of the most sensitive member of the deer family, and once they get the human scent they seldom remain to locate their natural enemy by sight. They usually break for the closest cover, but they are not so speedy as the smaller members of the deer family. This, coupled with the fact that they constitute a much larger target, makes them much easier to shoot on the run than either the whitetail or mule deer. A guide who knows the country, and the habits of the animals of that particular terrain, usually can forecast just where a herd of elk will go in attempting to escape from a given locality. By detailing members of the hunting party to cover these natural avenues of travel it is usually possible to assure shooting for at least some of the members of a party—provided, of course, that wind currents are favorable to such an approach.

Many successful guides prefer to hunt elk by a combination of men on horseback and men on foot. Where this strategy is used, the hunters who are to be on foot will ride their horses to positions down wind from where elk are likely to be located in heavy timber cover. They will tie their horses out of sight and distribute themselves at intervals in small open parks or natural passes where the animals, when disturbed, are most likely to pass. Those on horseback then ride down wind, and far enough apart to cover the width of the timber belt, yet close enough together to prevent the elk from getting back between them without being seen. Frequently, an elk will prefer to try this rather than to move

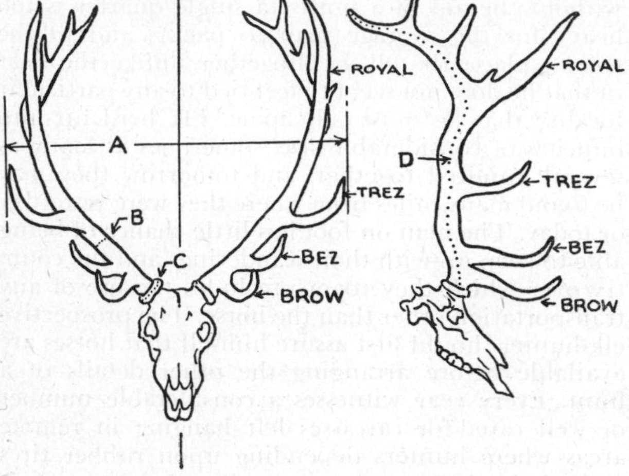


PLATE IV. Trophy Measurement, Elk or Wapiti.

A-Greatest spread.
B-Circumference midway bez and trez.
C-Circumference at base.
D-Length of outside curve.

into the wind for any considerable distance. They seem to realize their disadvantage in traveling down wind where they cannot detect, by scent, what is before them.

A great many westerners prefer to hunt entirely from horseback, dismounting only to shoot after the quarry has been sighted within certain killing range of the particular rifles in use. Residents of the mountains are usually much less likely to take chances on out-of-reasonable-range shots than the people who classify themselves as sportsmen. An old bull elk (or any other elk, for that matter) can carry a lot of lead without going down, if the lead is not in exactly the right place—and it is truly surprising how much blood they can spill and still keep going. A great many elk are lost to the hunter because he fails to follow them far enough after they have been shot. A couple of miles is not an unreasonable distance to follow an elk that fails to lie down after the hunter has drawn blood. Many an elk has gone five miles or more before being picked up by the man who shot him, or by another hunter who took up his trail.

The elk hunter should carry a good pair of binoculars (see "Sights and Optical Aids"), and be prepared to spot his game at distances of a mile or two across canyons and on the slopes of high, sparsely timbered mountain ridges, where they may be feeding shortly after sunup or shortly before sundown. If there is good grass range they are almost certain to take chances on feeding there rather than depending entirely upon browse in thick timber, but during the middle of the day they are very likely to be in the thickest cover they can find, among steep cliffs and heavy windfalls. Where they have been hunted intensively they are as wary and as difficult to hunt as any other species of hoofed game. The success ratio among hunters of elk is notoriously low in comparison with that of deer hunters over comparable terrain. The probable reason is that the elk are by nature more cautious. Then, too, they are taller and can see farther and spot their enemies at greater distances than can the smaller species. The man who has the idea that hunting elk is like shooting cows in a farmer's back pasture had better stay at home and get his meat across the counter and his trophy from a taxidermist's shop.

If one cannot be sure of breaking an elk's neck, the next best place to aim, if the elk is standing or running broadside, is at the shoulder. If both shoulders are broken an elk will not travel far. There are a good many records of bull elk recovering from a bullet entirely through the lungs. Of course, these were cases where the sportsman failed to follow up the trail long enough and the animal had an opportunity to get plenty of rest. A shot high in the lungs is more likely to be fatal than a low one because death usually comes from suffocation, and the low shot allows the blood to drain off instead of accumulating to clog the lungs. A heart shot is a good choice for the person who can locate its position. The tip of the heart almost touches the brisket just ahead of the diaphragm and lies just back of the front leg in the animal's normal standing position. (See Plate II.)

A shot that severs the spinal cord will, of course, stop any animal in its tracks. A gutshot elk may go for days before it dies. Every true sportsman should avoid such a shot, even though he must forego shooting entirely.

**Rifles and Sights.** There are several factors concerned in the selection of a good rifle for elk hunting, but the major requirements tend to limit the field of selection. These requirements are: a rifle that will deliver a solid punch at extreme ranges and with the accuracy gained through a flat trajectory. As with other big game, elk have been killed with almost every type and caliber of rifle, and although the majority of hunters are unable to afford a special rifle for this hunting, the modern tendency is to select a caliber that will be satisfactory for deer, bear, and elk.

The following rifles are favored (all high-velocity cartridges):

.270 with 130- or 150-grain bullet.
.30 '06 with 150- or 180-grain bullet.
.300 (Savage) with 180-grain bullet.
.300 H. & H. Magnum with 180-grain bullet.
.348 (Winchester) with 150-grain bullet.
7 mm. (Mauser) with 150-grain bullet.

For details on above loads see "Ammunition—Rifle."

NOTE: Many hunters prefer to have the elk rifle mounted with a 2½- or 4-power telescopic sight, with the tapered post reticule favored. (See "Sights and Optical Aids.")

# ROCKY MOUNTAIN GOAT (White Goat) *Oreamnos montanus*

The Rocky Mountain goat, or white goat, is not a goat at all, but a type of antelope. The zoologist terms it the *Oreamnos montanus* and explains that it is a member of the ox family *(bovidae)* and is the only member of its sub-family *(rupicaprinae)* or its genus *(oreamnos)* in North America.

It is believed that this animal crossed to this continent via the Bering Sea bridge in the middle Pleistocene period, leaving his Eurasian relatives, including the chamois, goral, takin, and serow. His closest relative is the serow of Asia. In this country the mountain goat is broken into four sub-species, the *Americanus, Kennedyi, Columbiae,* and *Missoulae.*

**History.** The mountain goat, as his name implies, is a dweller of the peaks, and because of the remoteness of his range few of these animals were seen by the early explorers. Hence, no detailed information was available on the goat for several decades after the settlers moved in on the fringes of his domain. Where there is a scarcity of fact, often there is a mass of rumor, and so myths and legends were the chief records on the existence of the animal for several years, and some biologists actually indicated their doubt of his existence. By 1800, however, a thorough account of the animal's life and habits was compiled following a study made in Montana.

Before 1884, and the classification of the Dall sheep, the goat was often mistaken for this mountain animal of the same coloring and approximately the same size, which also ranged high on the mountains.

Civilization has had little effect on the range or distribution of the goat, and he is molested less than any other member of the big game family. Biologists who have studied this animal believe that his survival potential is as good as that of the whitetail deer. In the first place, the haunts of the goat are far removed from civilization, and to reach them is a test

Courtesy Nature Magazine.

PLATE I. White Goats Alerted.

of the lungs and stamina of even the strongest hunters. Also, the meat of the mountain goat is strong and tough, and his horns do not make nearly so desirable a trophy as many other big-game animals that are much easier to hunt. Finally, he is comparatively unmolested by predators because of the ruggedness of his habitat.

In a few areas the goat's chance of survival has been threatened, as it was not many years ago by the Indians of southern British Columbia, who killed more of these animals than they needed for food. The Indians sought the animal for the fine under-wool, which they spun into yarn and made into blankets which rivaled Cashmere in quality. These blankets, known as Chilkat robes, are still being produced by the Indians, but the trade fortunately has not been commercialized, and the authorities have limited the kill of the animals.

In the States, only Montana and Idaho now have open hunting seasons on this animal. The goats that were transplanted into the Black Hills of South Dakota in 1943 had multiplied into a herd of 200 by 1946. The few goats introduced on Baranof Island also have thrived, and Alaska has established refuges in the southeastern area as well as on the Kenai Peninsula, where they are granted full protection.

**Identification.** The goat, because of his shoulder hump, somewhat resembles a miniature buffalo, and his beard and shaggy coat make him appear much larger than he is. He is awkward in build, and averages about 250 pounds in areas where food is plentiful. The weight varies with the area, however, and in some regions the goat will average as little as 150 pounds.

There is but little difference in size between the male and female, and since both are horned their appearance is so similar that in sections where they may be legally hunted both male and female may be killed. The average hunter attempts to differentiate between the sexes by assuming that a group of goats represents nannies with kids and young billies, whereas the chances are that a single goat will prove to be an adult male.

The coat of both sexes is white throughout the year, which makes this animal distinctive from all ruminants except the Alaskan sheep. A few specimens have been found with brown hair markings on the mane and tail, which some zoologists theorize may be an indication that in ancient times the goat was darker in color and inhabited the lower country of rocks and woods.

The horns of the goat, as well as its lips and hoofs, are black, and the eyes are yellow. The hair is longer in the winter season, especially on the neck and chest. Beneath the long, outer guard hairs lies a soft under-wool about 3 inches long. The white coat serves as a natural camouflage in the peaks where there is eternal snow, but in the spring, summer, and fall, when the goat moves down to the lower areas he shows up in great contrast.

This animal is credited with being the most surefooted of all the hoofed animals on this continent. His selection of a habitat, which requires his movement from one infinitesimal ledge to another along a sheer cliffside, makes certain footing vitally important.

The horns, like those of his kinsman, the serow of Asia, are hollow and are a polished black, bending back slightly. There is little difference between the male and female in the length of horn, but those of the female are more slender. They average around 9 inches in length, with 10-inch horns qualifying as record trophies. The record horns were taken from a nanny shot by A. B. Williams in British Columbia, with a left horn measuring 12¼ inches and a right measuring 12½ inches, and a spread of 7 inches. Although short and brittle, the horns often are dagger-like in sharpness, and are extremely effective in close-in fighting. It is a matter of record that a grizzly has been killed by a goat.

Since it is not a true goat, this animal does not have the numerous musk glands typical of the goat family, but does have a distinctive black gland, approximately 2½ inches in diameter, behind each horn. Both sexes are equipped with this gland, which secretes an oil that is most noticeable during the mating season.

**Characteristics.** The goat is a solitary animal by nature, and his lonely life is rarely challenged, for he relies on his inaccessibility for safety from enemies. Occasionally small family groups form, or a number of goats will gather at a good feeding place, a water basin, or a salt lick.

He is inclined to have a rather calm nature, and is said to be one of the most difficult of the big-game animals to arouse. It is this slow reaction to danger that has induced some hunters to term him stupid. His natural enemies are the bear, wolf, coyote, and eagle. Only the eagle can meet the goat on his own range, and these birds account for many young kids. The kills of the bear and wolf are few, and usually are made when the goats cross a valley in order to reach an adjoining mountain.

The goat rarely is pugnacious among his own kind, and prefers to elude all enemies by putting to use his seemingly unlimited wind and strength to climb. In defense, however, he fights courageously and savagely.

Possibly because his ears are almost constantly assailed by roaring winds, tumbling rocks, and slides, his sense of hearing is indifferent. His vision also is only fair, but his sense of smell is acute.

If food and water are sufficient, the goat is inclined to remain in one small area for several days, and his average range is an area about 5 miles in diameter.

Although his pace is slow and deliberate, he has a clumsy, ungainly appearance. Despite his apparently casual shuffle, he seems able to move with complete safety along a narrow ledge on a sheer rock face which even a sheep, considered a skillful mountaineer, would not attempt unless frightened.

Although he uses a stiff gallop when startled, the goat's normal pace is a slow amble. Unlike the mountain sheep, which is known for its swift jumps, the goat moves rather slowly, and frequently uses a characteristic muscling maneuver when he moves from one ledge to another. Often he will stand on his hind legs, place his forefeet on the ledge above him, and inch his way up slowly and carefully, somewhat as a man would climb.

He is a ruminant, with 32 teeth, and is primarily a browser, feeding on buds and twigs. He also eats moss and lichens, and in late winter or early spring, when faced with a shortage of his preferred food, will descend to the lower levels to feed on withered grasses. It is during this period that he suffers his greatest losses from his natural enemies.

**Breeding.** The rutting season begins in November, and during this period both billy and nanny keep on the move. During this period the glands behind the horns give off such a quantity of oil that the horns often are softened, leaving permanent ridges when the horn again hardens. The goat is considered a polygamous animal, although monogamy is not uncommon.

The period of gestation is about six months, and one kid, born in April or May, is the rule, with twins quite rare. On the average, a kid will weigh about seven pounds at birth. For about two weeks the nanny keeps the kid well hidden, but a three-week-old kid seems as undisturbed by heights as its parents, and is capable of moving across a narrow ledge without fear or hesitation. Normally the kid remains with the nanny until it is two years old. Three- and four-year-old goats are inclined to group together, but older ones seek solitude.

**Range and Distribution.** Being a dweller of the dizzy heights, sheer peaks, and nearly unsurmountable ridges, his distribution is limited to the mountain ranges which offer this type of terrain. The mountains along the Pacific Coast are not steep enough for him, and he is found in greatest numbers on the peaks of the northwestern Rockies and the mountains on the Alaskan coast. He is most plentiful in British Columbia and Alberta, where many hunters have reported seeing as many as 100 goats in a day. He also is present in fair abundance on the Kenai Peninsula.

The latest big-game inventory of the United States shows a goat population of about 15,700. In addition to the estimated 325 in South Dakota, there are about 3700 in Idaho, 5300 in Montana, and 6400 in Washington.

Severe winter weather seldom forces the goat to leave the high peaks for the lower but protected forests. Often storms force him higher rather than lower, and he manages to eke out a living on these frigid heights where only small dwarfed patches of vegetation offer him food.

In the southern ranges, however, the goat often comes down to the valley to feed during the winter, and may be seen feeding in proximity to sheep and caribou on the mountain meadows during the summer. But he never strays far from his home cliffs, and when threatened it is to these cliffs he turns. In early fall, when many of the streams have dried up, goats often are found in the vicinity of a water basin, and

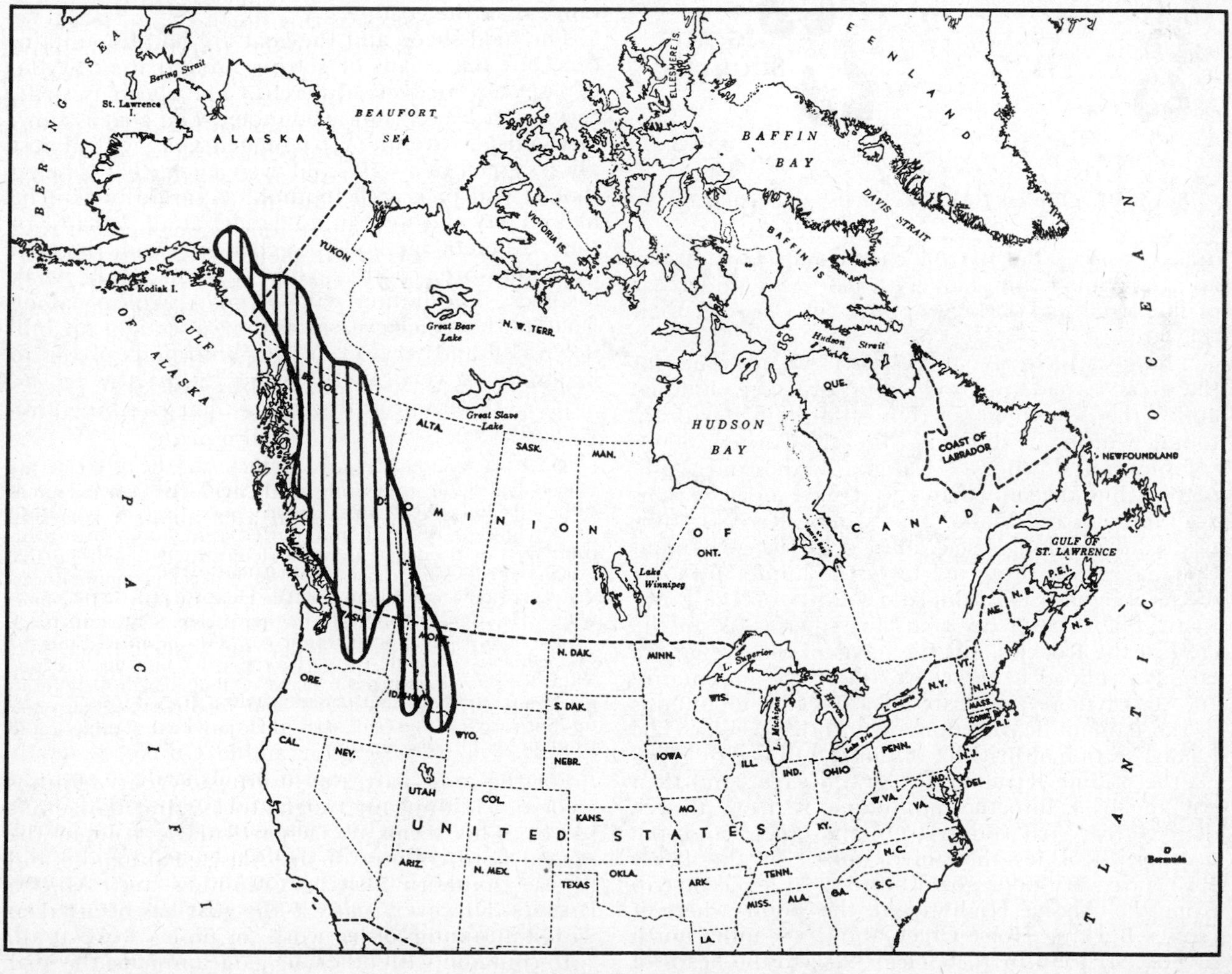


PLATE II. Distribution of Rocky Mountain Goat.

it is in such places that they gather in larger numbers than is their normal habit.

**Hunting Methods.** People who have never seen a Rocky Mountain goat think of him as a slim, slender, spry creature on the order of the domestic goat. Actually the Rocky Mountain goat is a large, heavy, phlegmatic animal. He does not skip gaily from crag to crag. Instead he is seldom seen out of a walk. Many fat old billies weigh 300 pounds or more. They

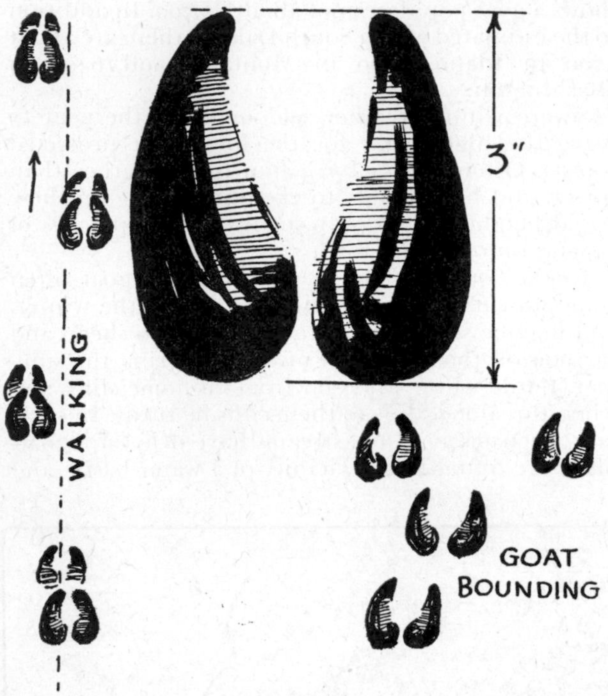


PLATE III. Typical Hoofprints of the Mountain Goat.

have very deep but narrow chests, and heavy bones, and their long white hair with its downy undercoat of fine wool makes them appear even heavier than they are.

The goat is, today, almost entirely an animal of the great Canadian province of British Columbia, and perhaps 85 to 90 per cent of all living goats are found within its borders. In the United States colonies spill down into Montana, Idaho, and Washington; but the only states that have open seasons are Montana and Idaho. The Salmon River country of Idaho has long been famous for its goats, and they have been protected from the hunter by some of the roughest, most difficult country on the continent. There are many goats in Alberta east of the crest of the Rockies, but the goats of the Yukon are largely confined to the coast side of the mountains. In Alaska there are goats all along the mountains of the Panhandle, but none in interior Alaska. The Cassiar section of British Columbia, reached by going up the Stikine River to Telegraph Creek and then packing back into the mountains, is, from all evidence, great goat country. On the other hand, the northern Rockies themselves north of the Peace River are very poor goat country. In a recent trip from the Alaska Highway at the point where it crosses Bucking Horse Creek about 125 miles north of Fort St. John in 1946, clear back to the heads of the Muskwa and Prophet Rivers, one hunter saw altogether no more than a dozen goats during a 40-day trip. In real goat country he would have seen hundreds if not thousands.

The finest remaining goat country is along the Smoky River and its tributaries in Alberta and the adjacent country across the line in British Columbia. A hunter camped on the Muddy River in Alberta about a dozen miles from where it runs into the Smoky would practically never be out of sight of goats, and it would not be unusual to see anywhere from a dozen to a hundred at any time of day.

In the old days before white men overran the country, mountain sheep used to come right down into the foothills and were even found on isolated little buttes and mesas out on the plains. The goat, however, was always a high-country animal, and for this reason it was many years before its distribution was correctly worked out. Stories about the strange creature came through from trappers and mountain men for years before their authenticity was proved by actual specimens. As late as the 1890's, in a book on American big game, Theodore Roosevelt listed Rocky Mountain goats as being found in *California* and *Colorado,* and in the mid-1920's Colonel Townsend Whelen in his book, *Wilderness Hunting and Wildcraft,* said that they were found in the Teton range of Wyoming. Actually they have never been found south of the Salmon River country of Idaho. The various species of wild sheep have a far greater range than the goat.

The wild sheep and the goat are both mountaineers, but the means of getting around used by the two species are very different. The sheep is swift, reckless, a leaper and a bounder. The goat is slow, methodical, careful. A frightened goat will almost always go off in a walk, and even a goat that is being shot at will pick each foothold as carefully as if he had all day and were in no danger at all. Because of their different methods of getting around, the goat can climb over country where a sheep would break his neck. The hunter will see goats strolling along what, to the naked eye, seems to be a straight up-and-down cliff and what even with binoculars proves to be an *almost* vertical cliff with a few narrow ledges.

Jack O'Connor, in discussing their climbing ability writes:

> "Once in Alberta I came around a point and saw a big lone billy feeding on a slide at the bottom of an enormous cliff. The billy didn't care for my looks. He slowly walked to the foot of the cliff and started going up, putting his front feet on the ledge above, and muscling himself up like a man. Because I was astounded at his feat of mountaineering, I sat down and watched the performance with binoculars. He would test each foothold before he put much weight on it, then up he would go. Two or three times he stopped, looked at me earnestly, the wind blowing his long white whiskers, stirring the mane of long hair which forms his hump. It took him a half hour to climb 500 feet or so up the face of that cliff, but that any living thing could climb it at all was amazing."

For the most part, the hunting of goats requires a lot of climbing in rough, rocky, and dangerous places. This seems to be particularly true in the rugged fiord country of the Alaska Panhandle and in the southern British Columbia and Alberta Rockies. However, many a fine goat has been taken with a minimum of leg work—or no leg work at all.

In common with other big-game animals, the goat is an unpredictable creature. On many occasions a hunter finds it impossible to get within reasonable range of a goat, despite skillful stalking. On other occasions a hunter may approach within a few yards. One well-known big game hunter gives an illustration of this.

"On one occasion I caught a big billy in a position where I could have ridden him down with a horse and killed him with a revolver—if I had wanted to, and if I had had a revolver. I had ridden up a long slope to the top of the mountain right on the British Columbia-Alberta border and known as Coffin Top or Casket Mountain. While the others were skinning out the head of a caribou, I took my horse and rode over to the cliff side of the mountain to look for other game. There was a big fat billy, feeding up on the flat top of the mountain. I trotted the horse up to him, but he grunted, ground his teeth, and lowered his head threateningly. My horse shied, so I drew off a little way, dismounted, and watched the goat. In spite of the fact that it was frightened, it never got out of a quick walk. It headed for the cliffs where it felt safe, and the next time I saw the old boy, he was lying on a ledge about 100 feet below at peace with the world and gazing out over a few hundred miles of vast, empty country."

In some areas, goats will be found in rough but relatively small canyons where the hunter can actually do his hunting on horseback, riding along the rim, and picking out a billy bedded either below or on the opposite side. Hunting with a camera, rather than with a rifle, it is possible to make some magnificent movies of goats by this method.

In spite of the fact that there is little difference in appearance between the billies and the nannies, there is not much excuse for killing a nanny—particularly one with a kid. During the hunting season, the old billies, the trophy goats, are, unlike mountain sheep, almost always alone. If in September or October, the hunter sees a bunch of goats he can just about bet on it that they are all nannies, kids, or young billies with poor heads. If, on the other hand, he sees a lone white speck up on a ledge a thousand feet above a slide, the chances are that it is a billy—and a big one. The little black horns of the nannies with their wicked sharp points are just as long as those of the billies. Actually the world record goat head is that of a nanny. Heads of the billies usually have thicker, heavier bases, however.

Picking out a good goat head is not easy, as the difference between a fair head and a good head really does not amount to much. The world record goat, a nanny, had a horn-length of 12½ inches. Nothing less than 10 inches in length is listed in the records—only 2½ inches between the top and the bottom of the list. However, a respectable trophy goat should go over 9 inches certainly, and there is not much excuse for bringing back the little 7- or 8-inch heads so often seen. One way to judge a good goat head is to determine whether the horns are as long as the distance from the base of the horn down to the hair at the point of the jaw. That will mean a horn-length of from 9 to 10 inches. The goat makes an interesting but not a particularly impressive addition to the trophy room. Perhaps the best goat trophy is not the head at all, but a rug, soft, snow-white, luxurious-looking, made from the incomparable hide.

Some hunters claim to like goat meat. They say the flesh of nannies and kids is excellent and even have a kind word for the meat of an old billy goat killed before the rut. Most goat hunters, however, insist that the person who said "meat was so tough one couldn't stick a fork in the gravy" had the billy goat in mind. The mountain men of Alberta and British Columbia have scant use for goat meat. As one wrote: "If we had to choose between eating a grizzly and a goat, I'd pick the grizzly any day!"

Except for the climbing involved, goat hunting is not considered difficult. On a long trip, the guide and the sportsman will usually concentrate on getting the more difficult species, like sheep and grizzly, and pick a goat when a good one comes along and when it is convenient.

As in sheep hunting, the first step in securing a goat is to see him. In the hunting season, it is wise to pass up *bunches* of goats, as these are composed of nannies, kids, and young billies. Instead, the hunter should strive to find a lone goat in a spot where stalking will not be too difficult or climbing too arduous.

The goat is not nearly so wary as the sheep, and many claim that his eyesight is not nearly so good. Furthermore, the goat is an introvert. He is interested in himself and what goes on immediately around him. For the most part he doesn't even bother to look at whatever is away over there across the canyon.

Actually, an old billy has few natural enemies. He lives in rough, steep country, where predators seldom penetrate. Eagles will kill small kids, and now

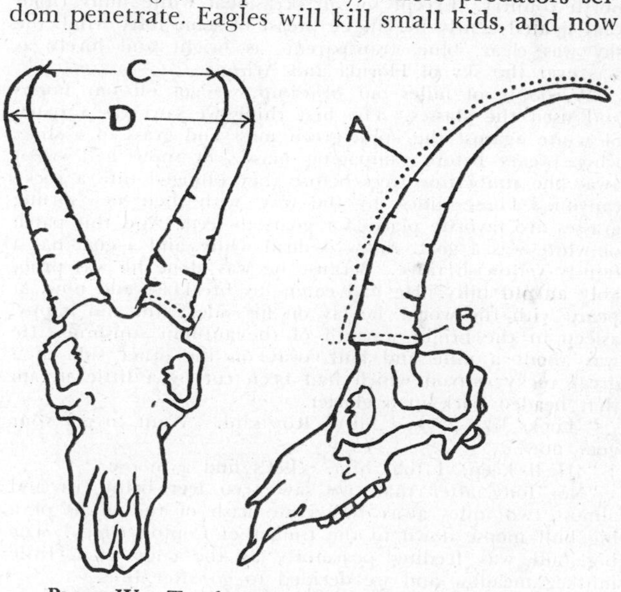


**Plate IV.** Trophy Measurements, Mountain Goat.
A-Length of front curve. C-Tip to tip.
B-Circumference at base. D-Greatest spread.

and then wolves or perhaps grizzlies will cut down goats when they are at a lowland lick. The goat, however, is a long way from being defenseless. He is powerful and courageous, and his dagger-sharp black horns are wicked weapons. Wolves and even grizzlies have been killed by them. Man is really just about the only important enemy the goat has, and because his flesh is not very good to eat, he has never really been hunted hard. The sportsman trophy-hunter has yet to kill off a species.

A hunter *above* a goat will frighten him and usually make him climb up to regain his lost advantage, but a goat above a hunter usually is not worried.

His instincts tell him that he can climb in places where no other thing in the world can come to him. As a consequence, finding the right goat may not be easy and, when the goat is found, climbing to him may be difficult. The stalk itself, however, usually does not amount to much.

As in sheep hunting, it is wise to watch the goat for a while to find out if he is going to stay put. Even a tough old billy may decide to feed in a spot where he would not feel secure enough to take a nap. Then, when his stomach is full, he may go off a mile or so to lie down. If the stalk is begun before the goat fills up, the goat may be gone and hard to locate by the time the hunters have completed their stalk.

In Alberta, a moose often has a higher place on the priority list than a goat, and many get a goat as a sort of by-product of moose hunting. The experience of Jack O'Connor is a typical example.

"Roy Hargreaves and I started out one morning from our camp at the head of Copton Creek in the Alberta Rockies not far from the British Columbia line. We had pitched our tents right at timberline. All around us lay a series of parklike basins, smoothly lush with grass, moss, and lichens. In the creek bottoms timber grew to fair size but the stunted little Alpine firs had marched in thick ranks only a little way up the mountains' sides. Then they had stopped in a sharp, abrupt line. Above them only moss, lichens, and a few stunted willows grew; and still higher there were only the bare gray rocks, crumbly slides, snow patches, and glaciers. The day was a lovely one—Indian summer in the north country. Except for an occasional white fluffy cloud that floated gently by on the breast of some lofty wind, the sky was clear, blue, transparent, as bright and lovely as was ever the sky of Florida and Arizona.

"A couple of miles out of camp, we got off our horses and used the glasses. The first thing we saw was a patch of white against the apple-green moss and grass of a slide, where years before rampaging masses of snow had swept away the timberline trees before they plunged into a rocky canyon. These slides, by the way, with their new-sprung grasses are favorite places for goats to feed. And this patch of white was a goat. Snow is dead white, and a goat has a faintly yellowish tinge. Because he was alone he was probably an old billy. He had eaten his breakfast and now, at peace with the world, he lay on his side, calm and happy, asleep in the bright warmth of the autumn sunshine. He was about a mile and half away on the other side of a great rocky canyon which had been cut by a little stream that headed back in a glacier.

"'Looks like a good billy,' Roy said. 'Want to get your goat now?'

"'He'll keep,' I told him. 'Let's find a moose.'

"Not long after that, we saw 1500 feet below us and almost two miles away the white flash of the horns of a big bull moose down in the timber of Copton Creek. The big bull was feeding peacefully at the edge of a little muskeg meadow and we decided to go after him.

"That is really game country, and as we led our horses down the steep hill through the stunted spruce and jackpine, we caught a glimpse of a big white-necked caribou bull, but we were moose hunting. . . . The wind was right, so when we reached the creek, we tied our horses and worked as quietly up-wind as possible. When we got to the meadow, however, the moose was gone. I don't think he had smelled or heard us. He had simply filled up and then gone back to lie down in heavy timber. We could never find him.

"At noon we gloomily devoured our sandwiches and washed them down with the teeth-chilling waters of Copton Creek.

"'Well,' Roy asked presently, 'want to go try for that big billy now?'

"By this time I was ready.

"We were not far from the mouth of the side canyon where the goat was, and although we had not seen him for some hours, the chances were that he was still there. We could go up through the timber and try a shot at about 450 yards across the canyon, or we could go up the bottom of the canyon, then try to climb closer. We chose the latter course. Using our horses only as a means of crossing the creek and keeping our feet dry, we tied them in the timber and set out along the creek bed. At first we were among thick trees, but presently the timber thinned out and walls of the canyon rose higher and higher around us. It was very cold down there out of the sun. Dank spray from the brawling, turbulent little stream eddied around us, and we could see big chunks of glacial ice caught in the boulders.

"Finally we could see our billy. He was still lying on the slide, asleep and at peace with the world. In all the time since we had seen him last, the only thing he had done was to swap ends. As so often happens in stalking, the country was a bit different from the way it appeared through the glasses and a couple of miles away. Instead of being within easy shooting distance from the bottom of the canyon, the goat was about 1500 feet above us and probably 400 yards away. We could get no closer without being seen by going up the canyon. The thing to do, we decided, was to climb up, get opposite him, and then shoot him across a side canyon at about 300 yards or so.

"So we started up. When I say up, I mean UP. I strapped my rifle across my back and literally pulled myself up by clinging to the little Alpine firs which grew on the canyon wall. When we were about halfway to the spot we had selected to shoot from, a colony of marmots across the canyon spotted us and began to utter that shrill rusty whistle of theirs.

"'Damn those whistlers!' Roy said. 'They'll spook that goat as sure as shootin'!'

"I was in the lead and I cautiously poked my head above the dwarfed little trees. The goat had awakened. He lifted his head and looked around. Then he got to his feet. I was going to have to shoot quickly. I scrambled up out of the timber to a smooth lichen slope, then gently slid a cartridge into the chamber of my .270. When I tried to aim, though, I slid gently down hill. Roy got his feet on the trunk of a little fir below us and signaled me to put my feet on his shoulders. So there I was, my elbows in the ground of that almost straight-up-and-down slope, my feet on Roy's shoulders.

"When the crosshairs of the scope settled against the billy's snow-white coat, I touched off a shot and saw him flinch. I worked the bolt, shot rapidly once more. This time I could see hair fly and a big red spot appear. The goat turned slowly around then and stood there weaving, with his rump toward me. My next shot was high. It creased the billy along the back and sent a shower of long white hair 20 feet into the air. Again he turned broadside and I fired my fourth shot. This was another lung hit—and this time he went down.

"'I'm glad you got him before he fell into the canyon,' Roy said. 'If you hadn't, his horns would have been all busted up!'

"We climbed down into the main canyon, then, and went up to the goat by pulling ourselves hand-over-hand through the stunted Alpine fir. He was a big fellow with 9¾ inch horns, fat, heavy, massive, his coat in perfect condition."

The goat is a phlegmatic animal that can stand a terrific amount of punishment without going down, and almost all experienced Rocky Mountain hunters agree that he is as hard to kill as a grizzly and harder to kill than the much heavier moose. He does not seem susceptible to shock and he will walk slowly off even when mortally struck in the lung-heart area with a bullet from the powerful .270 or .30 '06. Because his instinct is to take to rough country when in danger, a goat will almost always head for the cliffs when wounded, and then when he goes down he will fall hundreds of feet to skin up his scalp and dash his fragile little black horns to pieces. A high percentage of all goat heads received by taxidermists are pretty badly beaten up, and if the truth were known, probably many hunters have to shoot two or three goats before they recover one in condition to mount.

Furthermore, the goat has a very tough hide, a heavy layer of fat, and a thick mat of hair. He should be killed quickly, and often he must be shot at fairly long range.

**Rifle and Sights.** As in hunting other big game, the average hunter is inclined to place confidence in the rifle he knows and can shoot best, but the requirements of a *good* goat rifle are rather rigid, for it should be capable of producing a quick kill at extreme ranges. The calibers preferred are as follows:

.270 with 130-grain bullet.
.30 '06 with 150-grain bullet.
.300 Savage with 150-grain bullet.
.300 H. & H. Magnum with 180-grain bullet.

For details on above loads see "Ammunition—Rifles."

The bullet types preferred are the P.E. (pointed expanding) or P.S.P. (pointed soft point).

NOTE: As in sheep hunting, the telescope sight, from 2½ to 4 power, is almost essential, and the hunter in search of a good trophy will not be without a pair of good 8-power binoculars or a spotting scope. (See "Sights and Optical Aids.")

# MOOSE

*Alces americana*

**History.** The moose, North America's largest game animal, is the largest member of the deer family *(Cervidae)* in the world. It has been estimated that this species was a million years in the making.

We can assume that the moose had a common ancestor with the giant elk-moose *(Cervalces)* of the American Tertiary Period. The modern species, however, apparently did not come to this continent until about the middle of the Pleistocene Age. It is a comparatively recent citizen of Alaska; on the Kenai Peninsula, where the great Alaska moose now are plentiful, there were natives still living in 1939 who could remember the days before the moose came. From this fact, and from old records indicating a concentration of moose in the East, some authorities reason that the species spread gradually across North America from east to west. Others, however, believe that the moose came from Siberia over a land bridge at Bering Strait.

One "circumpolar" species embraces the moose and the elk *(Alces alces)* of northern Europe and Asia. Although the moose is larger and darker than its European relatives, one observer believes that if a typical specimen were transported to the forests of Norway or Sweden, it would not be recognized as a stranger. Perhaps the moose should be called the American elk. But the early French and English settlers on this continent, though they had heard of the great elk of the north, had never seen any. Mistakenly they gave the name "elk" to the wapiti,

**PLATE I. A Good Bull, Still in Velvet.** Courtesy U. S. Forest Service.

and the moose therefore has had to keep its Algonquin name.

In French Canada the animal is called *l'orignal.* Some writers assume that is was so named because of its fantastic appearance, because it is *un original,* a "character." But in New France at the beginning of the 17th century, the animal's name was spelled also *l'orignat* or *l'orignac.* Since many of the early trappers were Basques, it seems more likely that the name comes from the Basque word *orenac,* for deer.

As with many other species, the advent of white men was bad news for the moose. They are forest-dwellers needing a cold climate—their range extends into the Arctic—and today are associated primarily with Canada and Alaska. At one time, however, they were plentiful in several sections of the northern United States. But they had to move out of the way of agriculture. They also were relentlessly hunted for meat and hides, as well as for sport. The French in Canada early began exporting hides, and at about the time of the Civil War commercial hunting was taking a heavy toll.

Long before this time the moose had lost much ground in the eastern United States. From New York, where they had been plentiful at the time of the Revolution, they migrated to Pennsylvania, but practically disappeared from that state before the end of the 18th century. History records the death of the last moose in Massachusetts in 1780. In the following century they were exterminated in Vermont and, except for a handful, in New Hampshire. In the Great Lakes region they fared no better. The last moose in Wisconsin was killed in 1865, and a few years later the moose were gone from the forests of Michigan, except for the northern peninsula and for Isle Royale in Lake Superior.

In this century they seemed headed for extinction even in Maine, where formerly they inhabited all the northern lakes region. A few were left on Isle Royale, in northern Minnesota, and in the Rockies, where the moose range extends in a thin strip like a drooping tail from Alberta and British Columbia down to the Yellowstone Park area.

Protective legislation—initiated in Michigan as early as 1889—stopped the indiscriminate killing. It has not, however, accomplished all that was hoped for. True, the moose have increased in the Rockies; for some years Wyoming has permitted hunting under a special license, and more recently Montana has followed suit.

Elsewhere in the United States the species has complete legal protection. Even so, the game surveys of 1938 and 1943 showed that in Maine moose were barely holding their own. The danger is not from wolves and panthers, which have been gone from this area since the Civil War. Poaching and the moose disease account for some casualties. In New Brunswick, the moose in losing out in competition with whitetail deer for the available food supply.

Fortunately there is another side to the coin; in the western and northwestern sections of the continent the moose have increased in numbers and greatly extended their range. They are more plentiful in Wyoming now than when white men first arrived there. They have moved into Alaska, where a new sub-species, providing the outstanding trophies, has developed apparently in little more than half a century. In the Alaskan moose country numerous forest fires destroyed great stretches of evergreens, which were succeeded by willow, birch, aspens, and alders. This abundant supply of browse at least partly explains the migration, and according to some authorities also accounts for the fact that here moose have increased in size as well as in numbers. Old burns on the Kukwaus Plateau in British Columbia have attracted a moose population since World War I.

**Identification.** The moose is an absurd-looking animal, but still most impressive. He is taller than a large horse; a full-grown Canadian bull stands from 6 to 6½ feet high at the shoulder, and an Alaskan specimen 7 feet or more. The antlers, spreading perhaps 5 or 6 wide, may reach to 8 or 10 feet above the ground, and with their solid pelvis may weigh as much as 60 pounds. The bull moose carries more weight on his head than any other horned or antlered animal.

In proportion to height he weighs less than a horse, for his long legs support a short, rather chunky body. A typical Canadian bull, with a total length of 8½ or 9 feet, may weigh anything between 900 and 1400 pounds. The Alaskan type, however, may attain a length of 10 feet or more and may weigh 1700 or 1800 pounds. Cows are about three-quarters the size of bulls.

From the high shoulders the animal's back slopes to lower hindquarters. The tail is a mere stub, no more than 4½ inches long, with no long hairs. The head, supported by a short, thick neck, has large ears rather like a mule's, and an exaggerated muzzle, long and broad, with a decided hump. This is decorated with a hairy nasal pad. The upper lip or muffle, about 3 inches long, is extremely flexible; its owner can use it almost like a hand to strip leaves and twigs from a branch.

Like most ruminants, the moose has sharp lower incisors but none in the upper jaw. Farther back in the jaw are heavy molars, 12 on each side, which can grind up twigs half an inch thick. The animal is equipped to eat and run, for he chews the cud at leisure.

A distinctive feature is the bell, a bag of skin, with long hair, which hangs under the jaw. Its function is not known. On young animals it is slender and long —10 to 15 inches on a bull, and often 20 inches on a cow. One cow was found whose bell measured 38 inches in length. With age the bell becomes shorter and broader; on an old bull it may be an inconspicuous bulge no more than 4 inches deep.

Unlike the elk, the moose has pointed hoofs. He leaves a cloven track, easily distinguished from the deer's by the size, for a bull's track is about 7 inches long.

The color is the same in both sexes—dark brown or brownish-black, with some gray on the muzzle. A lighter, rather dull brown appears on the lower legs and on the belly. In summer the coat appears faded, especially on the legs, but it becomes dark and glossy again in the fall. The coarse hair is dark only at the tips; close to the skin it is nearly white.

Undoubtedly the most distinctive feature is the antlers of the male. In winter, when the moose needs weapons against other species than his own, he uses his hoofs. The antlers are a secondary sexual characteristic, grown fresh each year for the contests of the rutting season. Growth begins in April. In late summer the bone hardens and the velvet—the tissue covering with its network of blood vessels—dries and begins to peel. The bull works hard to scrape his antlers clean in time for the rut in mid-September. At first they are very pale, in the distance appearing almost yellow, but as the season progresses they acquire a brown coloring, darker in the young bulls than in the old. A prime bull drops his antlers about the first of January, though immature animals keep them longer.

A bull calf has knobs, a yearling mere spikes 8 or 10 inches long. A two-year-old becomes a "crotchhorn," with two prongs, and a three-year-old has three prongs. In the fourth year the antlers have the adult pattern, but it is not until the sixth or seventh year that they reach their full glory of palmation. Then they are great palms, often described as shovels, spreading wide and curving upward, with a number of points along the outer edge. Smaller brow palms with three or more points branch out from the main beams, pointing forward. With advancing years the main palms show greater width, filling in the spaces between the points; the antlers of an old bull may show mere jagged edges.

Past his prime, after about the tenth year, the moose grows heavier, but the largest tracks do not always lead to the finest trophy, for the antlers lose in size and symmetry. They are also lighter in color, like the coat.

Trophies are judged not only by spread, but also by the length and width of the palms. Symmetry also is important. The number of points is considered less important than the width of the palm. Because the upward curve varies, in the record lists this figure is an average of the measurements of both surfaces.

Three sub-species on this continent are generally recognized.

### CANADIAN MOOSE

*Alces americana americana (Clinton)*

This is the typical form, also called the American or common moose. It is found from Maine and Minnesota to Hudson Bay; in the Northwest its range extends into southeastern Alaska and north into the Arctic. This group includes Lydekker's *Alces columbae,* a questionable classification.

A 5-foot antler spread is considered quite good, but the record head, owned by the Canadian Bank of Commerce in Edmonton, has a spread of 73 inches. The right palm is 37½ inches long and 12¼ inches wide. The right antler has 14 points, the left 15. This animal was killed in the Peace River area of Alberta in 1922.

### WYOMING MOOSE

*Alces americana shirasi Nelson*

The Wyoming or Shiras moose are a smaller race peculiar to the Rockies of Wyoming, Idaho, and Montana, although specimens have been found in Minnesota. They have small hoofs, and show a light brown on the ears and along the back. The antlers are usually spread no wider than 4 feet, although the record pair have a 54-inch spread, with the right palm 3 feet long and 9 inches wide. There are 11 points on each side. This trophy was taken in Minnesota in 1890 by E. L. Brown, and it is now owned by the museum of the University of Kansas.

Courtesy Nova Scotia Dept. of Lands and Forests.

**PLATE II.** Day-Old Moose Calf.

### ALASKA MOOSE

*Alces gigas Miller*

This is the giant race identified with the Kenai Peninsula, from which they have spread eastward, and northward into the Yukon. They are blacker than the Canadian type. Some observers doubt that the average bull has an antler spread of more than 5 feet, but a number of trophies measuring more than 6 feet are recorded. The record is 77⅝ inches; the larger right palm is 45⅜ inches long and 20 inches wide, with 18 points. This animal, mounted in a fighting stance, is on display at the American Museum of Natural History. He was killed on the Kenai Peninsula in 1938.

**Characteristics.** The Algonquins called the moose "wood-eater." He likes the leaves and twigs of many varieties of trees and shrubs, including hardwoods. Often he straddles young trees to force the trunks down and bring the branches within reach. In winter he depends heavily on willows wherever the tips show above the snow. Using an upward jerk of the head, he strips the bark from young trees—but on one side only; the trees do not die.

Though primarily a browser, the moose does not disdain weeds and grasses, and his diet includes lichens, moss, and mushrooms. In summer the favorite food is water plants, especially pond lilies. Moose are strong swimmers, and will wade far out in lakes or streams. Often they are seen standing with their heads under water, and sometimes they submerge altogether. The water serves as a refuge from mosquitoes, ticks, and gnats.

The moose feeds by day as well as by night. Through the middle of the day he likes to rest in a thicket.

Many hunters) have marveled that in a standing position so large an animal can conceal himself in low brush, but he knows the technique of freezing, and often escapes notice at very close range. Where hunted, he is extremely cautious and alert; moose have lived in a particular area for years without being discovered. Although their eyesight is poor, their keen ears and noses keep them informed of danger at a distance. A deep-rooted instinct to travel down-wind sometimes is their undoing, however, for it enables the hunter to guess his quarry's route.

When confronted by man, the moose hesitates for a few seconds. There is considerable debate on whether this pause is a deliberate survey of the situation, showing courage and intelligence, or whether it is merely a sluggish reaction. Once under way, the animal uses a lumbering gait, with none of the deer's grace. He never hops like a deer.

He may decide to charge. Though ordinarily placid, the bulls in rut are definitely dangerous, and there are some year-round rogues. In heavy undergrowth the moose's long legs give him a considerable advantage over man, and not a few hunters have been killed.

Moose make docile pets, however, and in several cases have been driven in harness. But they do not survive long in confinement or outside their natural habitat.

Timber wolves are the most important predators, especially where they can find the moose yarded up in deep snow. But if a wolf can hamstring a moose, a moose can trample a wolf. Other enemies are the bear, and in the southern tip of the moose's range, the cougar. Both are more dangerous to calves than to adults. Wolverines and coyotes occasionally take a calf.

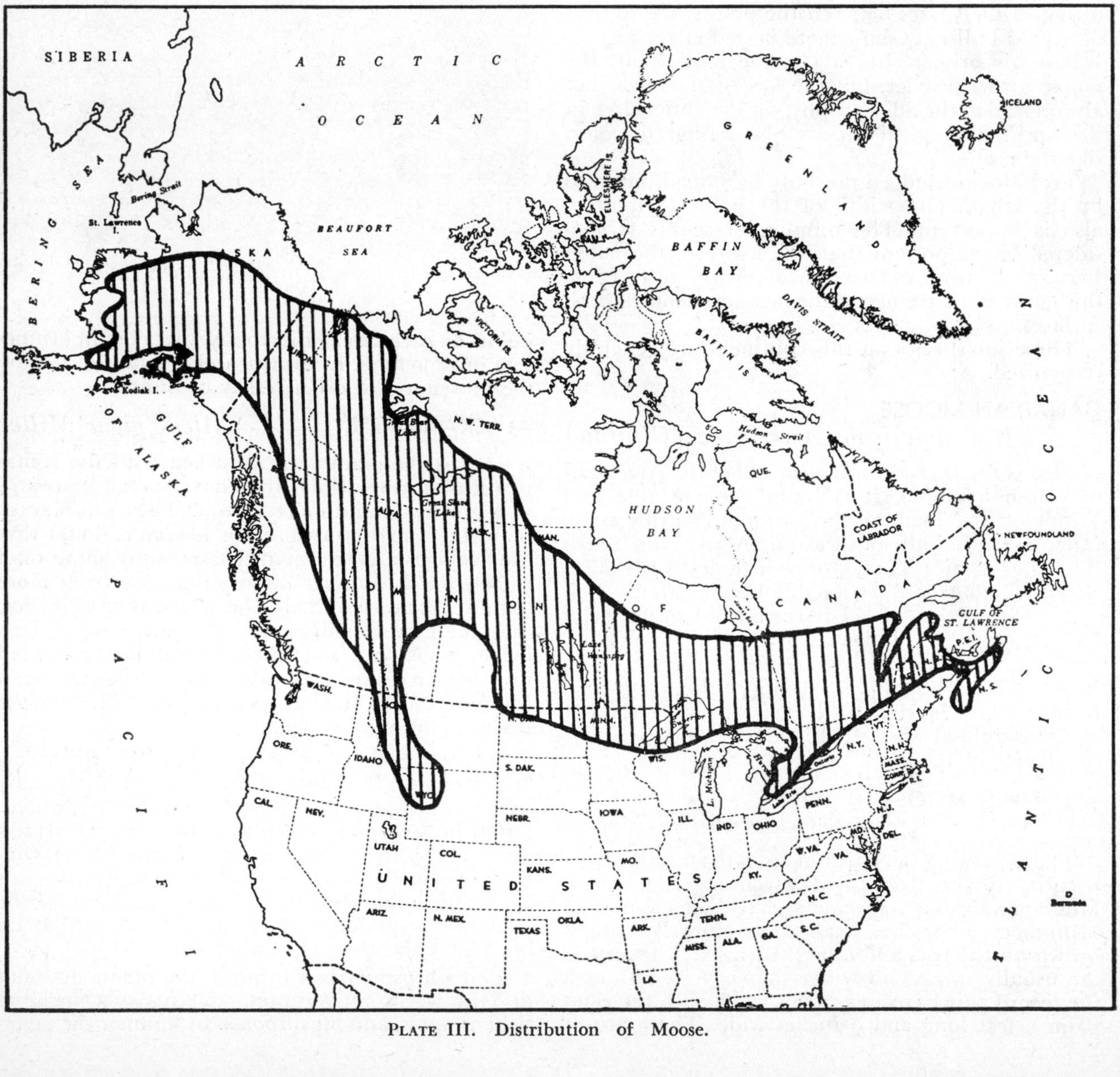


PLATE III. Distribution of Moose.

**Breeding.** Early in September the bulls get restless; through the rutting season, which lasts until November, they are constantly moving. They acquire a strong musky odor. This is the season when they are hunted for their antlers, but unfortunately at this time the meat has a rather disagreeable flavor. A rutting bull makes a shallow wallow in the earth which has a strong odor of urine.

The call of the cow he answers with a deep grunt, or sometimes with a bellow which can be heard several miles away. This may be accepted by another bull as a challenge. Though ordinarily moose can move almost silently, the rivals for a cow go crashing through the brush to their meeting.

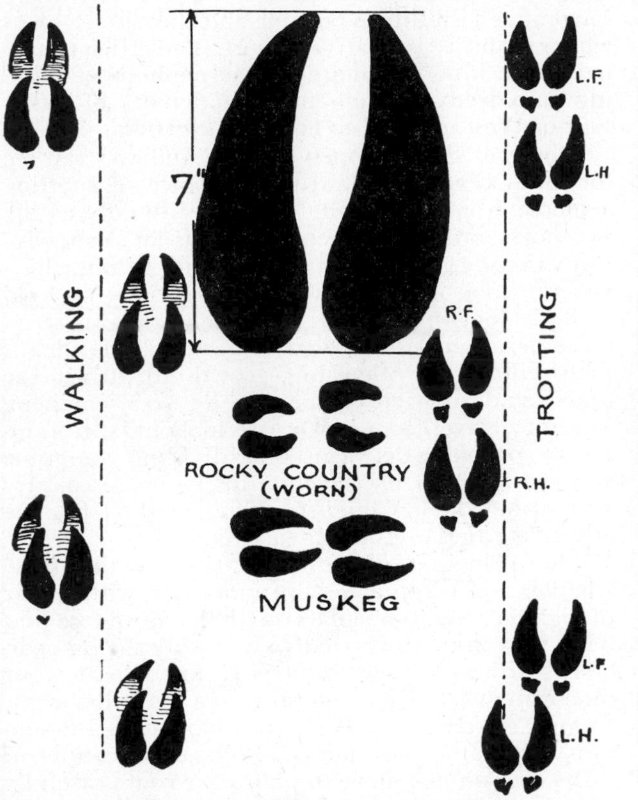


PLATE IV. Typical Hoofprints of the Moose.

There seems to be a preliminary period when bulls meet with a great noise of clashing antlers, but are merely sparring. But as the season grows older, the combats become serious. Most old bulls show the scars of many battles on their hides. The object of the charging bull is to knock his opponent sideways, so that another thrust of the antlers can reach through the ribs to a vital organ. The weaker of two adversaries may give up and retreat. In rare cases the two sets of antlers interlock; then both animals die of thirst and starvation. This is not so common, of course, with the shovel-horned moose as with caribou and common deer, but it does happen.

The victorious bull and the cow remain together for perhaps a week or ten days, and then separate. There is a legend that moose are monogamous; probably in a section where moose are rare, by accident or for lack of other opportunities the same pair have been seen together in succeeding seasons. Actually there is no reason to believe that a bull will not seek a second mate in one season, and in Alaska especially strong bulls have been seen with harems of several cows at once. There is evidence that the cow is not too faithful to her mate, and may accept service from more than one bull.

During the mating period a yearling calf or two may be hanging around, for the cow does not drive her calves away until the second year, when a bull calf becomes a crotch-horn and a female is about ready to breed.

Late in April or early in May the cow seeks a hiding place safe from bears and other predators. She may choose an island, for a calf will go into the water at an early age. Twins are produced in a high percentage of cases, but triplets are rare.

A new calf has woolly hair, sandy or reddish in color, without the spots which occur in most other species of deer. The characteristic moose nose and limber upper lip are undeveloped. Although adult moose can eat moss or mushrooms at ground level by straddling their legs wide, the calf has a neck so short that it must kneel to reach the ground. But the moose calf grows amazingly fast. In the first week it is something less than 3 feet tall, and weighs about 65 pounds, but in six weeks, although its weight is still less than 100 pounds, it gains the height of a grown whitetail buck. At five months it may stand more than 5 feet tall.

**Range and Distribution.** The total moose range, running as far north as the timber line, covers a tremendous area. It includes nearly all of Canada, where moose are found in every province. Most of the provinces have generous open seasons. The animals are most numerous in the midwestern and western sections, but Nova Scotia also has a large moose population and they are present in Newfoundland. In New Brunswick they are making a comeback, although poaching is a serious problem.

In Alaska the range is still expanding. The great *gigas* are most plentiful on the Kenai Peninsula, in Rainy Pass, and along the far shores of Cook Inlet. They also are found in the Yukon and in the Tanana and Kuskokwim Valleys. The moose seen above the Arctic Circle near the coast, and in the southeast in the Chilkat, Taku, Stikine, and Unuk Valleys, are of the Canadian type.

From Alaska the range follows the Rockies down into Montana, Wyoming, and Idaho. In the Yellowstone area the moose are thick, but the population is controlled because of limited winter forage. Idaho has quite a number in the Bitter Root Mountains.

Today in Minnesota moose are seldom seen outside the border counties. Michigan still has its small group of survivors on Isle Royale. In Maine the moose inhabit the marshes in the extreme north, and strays wander into New Hampshire.

The distribution of moose in the United States, according to the latest game census, was as follows:

| | |
|---|---|
| Idaho | 2,200 |
| Maine | 5,000 |
| Michigan | 600 |
| Minnesota | 4,500 |
| Montana | 3,900 |
| New Hampshire | 40 |
| Vermont | 3 |
| Wyoming | 7,100 |
| TOTAL | 23,343 |

In 1946 the Alaskan population was estimated at 30,000. The moose likes wooded lake shores and swamps where his favorite foods are abundant. The lifetime of the animal is estimated at 18 to 20 years, and if conditions are favorable he will spend his life in the area where he was born. He may cover considerable territory, however, in search of the foods he prefers. Wyoming moose winter in the valley and spend their summers high in the mountains. Here and in the Canadian Rockies moose are often seen in summer above timberline. In the rutting season, bulls roam for miles looking for cows.

A muskrat colony, taking over a good lily pond, may force a moose to move elsewhere. In the North, in a year when very heavy snows bury the willows to their tips, snowshoe hares may be serious competitors for the available browse. But since the hare population rises and falls in cycles, this happens only at long intervals.

The moose's long legs are a decided advantage in snow. Some observers say that it takes 3 feet of snow to make these animals yard up. In certain sections where the snowfall is not so heavy as might be expected, as in Nova Scotia, the Rockies, and the Far North, they yard seldom or never. But where the snow becomes deep and crusted, several moose, perhaps half a dozen, may join forces. Using each other's trails between good browsing spots, they pack down the snow in a network of deep trenches. Such a group is likely to consist of cows, calves, and immature bulls, for older bulls are inclined to live alone.

Moose country usually shows plenty of tracks. A cow's tracks are more pointed than a bull's. Moose droppings are larger than those of deer or elk. A common sign is young trees stripped on one side, or bent by the straddling process.

**Hunting Methods.** Moose are the largest living members of the deer family, but hunting for moose is seldom like hunting for deer. The deer have been able to survive almost in our back yards while the moose are rarely found in settled country. They are big animals and their mere size makes it difficult for them to avoid detection. The sight of a moose by a hungry settler, either in season or out, more often than not means death. As a result, the moose are wilderness animals and give promise of maintaining themselves only in wild country or where conservation control can be rigidly enforced.

Moose hunters seldom have need to wear conspicuous red clothing. When hunting pressure for moose in a given area is great enough to require protective garb for the hunter the moose will be almost extinct. Nor are there any moose drives similar to those organized for deer. Moose hunting remains, as it always has been, a problem of still hunting and of calling. They are wilderness game and hunting them takes the gunner into wild and beautiful country.

Hunting for moose differs still further from deer hunting in that a licensed guide is normally required for each hunter. Consequently much of the problem of stalking or decoying the moose falls on the shoulders of that worthy individual. But the hunter, or "sport," as his guide may refer to him, should be a full-fledged partner in the enterprise, capable of doing the job on his own if need be, which means that the hunter should have a good sound knowledge of the animal and his habits as well as the ability to stalk and shoot.

In moose hunting we are concerned only with the bulls, those magnificent animals that wear the most massive antlers in existence, antlers that grow to full size from April through August and are shed around the first of the year. The bulls run larger than the cows by about 50 per cent and a mature bull will weigh from 1000 pounds upward to the occasional 2000-pound mark reached only in the famous moose-hunting grounds of Alaska.

Moose-hunting territories fall into two main classifications: the mountain country of the West where long-range visibility is possible and the eastern areas where visibility is relatively short. These two factors have a deciding influence on the methods of hunting employed although individual parts of either East or West may fail to fit into the general pattern.

Wherever there is open country and you can see for miles there is an excellent chance of spotting a moose from a lookout. They are literally as big as a horse and can be seen equally as far. Your visibility may be gained by traveling a ridge from which you can look into the valleys that flank it or from a single lookout stand from which you can see a meadow, a long stretch or river bottom, or a sidehill with willows or other low growth to attract the moose and sufficiently open to let you see them. You may travel from lookout to lookout, still hunting as you move between them, dividing your time as you wish between traveling likely moose country and sitting on lookout; the latter method has the advantage if the visible area is large.

The principle of sight hunting is the same whether you sit on a western mountain with a pair of high-powered binoculars or climb a dead tree that will give you unobstructed view of only the immediately surrounding bog country. You may locate your moose anywhere from 100 yards to a few miles away. From there on you stalk. If your lookout is a mountain ridge and your moose shows up a couple of miles off, you may have to plan your route carefully before you leave your point of vantage since you will be out of sight of the meadow in which he stands from the moment you leave the lookout until you approach the spot an hour later. During that time the moose may or may not have stayed put. He may conceivably have moved out of the place as far and as rapidly as you have approached it. But the chances are that if he was feeding or had lain down he will be just about where he was when you saw him last. Make allowances for his movements. Swing wide if necessary to approach him from down-wind with allowance for his possible movement in that direction. Too little caution at this point may nullify the work and caution of days of hunting. If you spot your game at close range, the problem is simplified. Knowing where he is, you can begin your approach certain of his position in relation to yours.

The moose depends predominantly on his ears for his safety, relying secondarily on his senses of sight and smell. His keen hearing will warn him of all but the stealthiest approach. His sight is good, particularly in regard to any movement. His sense of smell is essentially keen, but apparently moose realize the difficulty of moving around much without being seen. Unlike smaller game animals, it is very difficult for him to hide his huge bulk or to move without being detected, so that his chances of deploying unobstrusively to get down-wind for a whiff of you are slim, and he knows it.

Although the moose does find it hard on occasions to hide himself, he manages surprisingly well much of the time. His grayish-brownish-blackish fur lets him merge with the shadowy tree trunks of the deep woods. It fades into the pattern of the dry alders, brown leaves, and autumn grasses. Oddly enough, when you are trying to spot a bull among the shadowed trunks of mixed evergreens, he may be so well hidden that only his slender legs will finally give him away. Although his big body and massive horns are indiscernible as they are half hidden and camouflaged by the lower branches, his legs will stand out among the trunks since they taper the wrong way. They get bigger as they rise from the ground instead of growing smaller.

In spite of his great size, the moose travels the thickest timber and goes through interlacing branches and trunks that will keep a man ducking and weaving. How he gets his big body and spreading antlers through the woods at all, the soundlessness with which he can move through the forests, is amazing. You may look up suddenly to discover the dim outline of a bull only yards away or see the head of a cow peering at you from the fringe of alders, the rest of her body seeming ethereal or non-existent. The sight of a moose is often the first warning of his approach, but when traveling through the woods casually or when answering the call of a cow moose at rutting season, the bull may throw caution to the winds and make about as much commotion as a bulldozer traveling the same route.

The broad hooves and long spindly legs of the moose equip him beautifully to travel the wet, boggy country that produces so much of the food he loves. He wades easily through places where a hunter would mire down or find himself swimming. In

Photo by Fred Hollender.

**Plate V.** **Moose, Alerted.**

traveling their customary routes, however, the moose follow the harder ground and develop trails which offer good, solid going for them and for hunters as well.

Moose like the water and feed on the marshy growth and lily pads. Their natural liking for water is enhanced by the pressure of flies, ticks, and other insect pests which drive them to semi or complete immersion as a means of escape. Paddling through a waterway by canoe may give sight of a great number of moose and make the locating and killing of a bull seem a simple matter. A prospective hunter making a canoe trip through a good fishing territory in August may be so impressed by the number of moose he sees that he will decide to return in September to find the biggest bull and shoot him, a project that looks as if it should require only a day or two at most. A week or so later, after a cold snap has eliminated the insect menace, only a few moose may remain near the river and most of them may be back on the high ground. The angler may return as a hunter to see only a few cows and calves with perhaps one fleeting glimpse of a bull after he finally leaves the main river and works up toward the higher ground on the last day of the hunt.

In the early hunting, the bulls are likely to be found in the same place day after day. They are at the peak of condition and food is plentiful everywhere. It makes sense then to hunt for a good bull for several days in the same location once you have sighted him. But later, when the rutting season has begun, a bull is likely to be here today and gone tomorrow. Then the bulls will be on the move.

Moose tracks are unmistakable because of their size. The sharp cloven hoofprints are about 7 inches long; those of the cow are smaller and perhaps a trifle more pointed than the bull's. A light tracking snow is always a boon to the hunter. The animals are much more conspicuous in snow-covered country, appearing very dark against the white background, and there is the added advantage of seeing the story of their movements imprinted in the snow for easy reading. A snow covering facilitates the tracking of a wounded and bleeding animal and in general acts in the hunter's favor.

The cold weather that brings snow may bring danger as well as better hunting conditions. When traveling by canoe there will be the chance of a freeze that will make it impossible to move on by river, since even a thin sheeting of ice will cut a canoe to rags in almost no time. The rivers may freeze enough to make canoeing impossible but not enough to let the ice carry a man's weight and become an easy trail back to civilization. At the time of the first snows it is hard to know whether you will need a canoe or a sled and the day or method of your return may be uncertain.

A bull moose packs a lot of meat on his tall frame. This meat is best in late August or early September before the rutting season starts, because bulls in rut develop a strong flavor that makes the meat less desirable. However, in almost every case there is an obligation to see that the meat is packed out and utilized. The hindquarter of a bull will weigh in the neighborhood of 250 pounds, which is more than a sizable load for any packer. It is natural, then, that where no pack horses are included in the outfit, the guides prefer to kill the moose near some sort of transportation. This may be within reach of old logging roads which are passable for a team of horses or oxen, but it is more likely to be near nature's natural highways of canoeable water.

Since moose like the water and the lush growth that goes with it, hunting by canoe becomes one of the most common methods. Still another factor in the use of the canoe is its stealth: A canoe moves through the water with a silence unequaled by any other transportation. A moose standing on the shore might well be unapproachable without detection through the timber because of his keen sense of hearing, yet a canoe could glide up into easy range without making a sound to disturb him in his feeding.

The hunting season usually begins in advance of and continues well into or through the rutting season. As the mating instinct grows stronger, the opportunity to call the bulls develops. Calling is often done from a canoe to gain at one time the advantages of silence, good visibility, and mobility. The call of the cow is made, usually with a birchbark horn to make the sound. The bull's answer will be a low or heavy grunt. Calling moose, like calling ducks, is a thing to be learned from hearing the sounds and knowing the animals that make them, and success depends not upon the birchbark horn but upon the inflection of the caller. The young bulls, stirred by the sex urge, tend to let their eagerness overcome their natural caution, and crash right

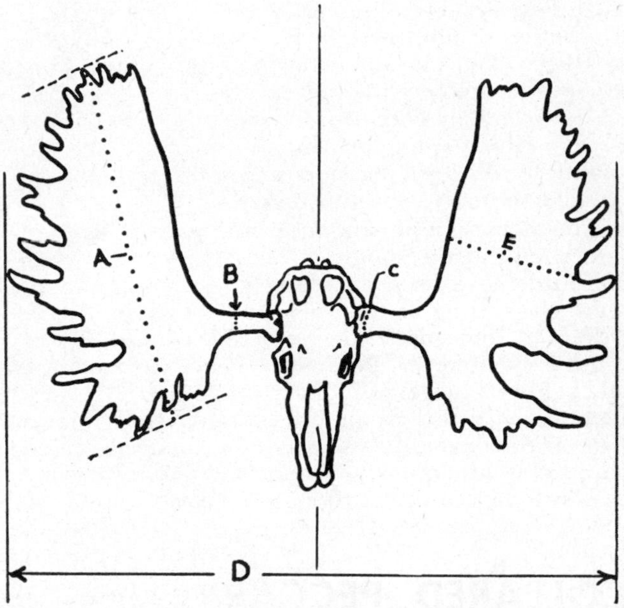


**Plate VI.** Trophy Measurement, Moose.

A-Length of horn. Measured between perpendiculars which are at right angles to the axis of the longest horn.

B-Circumference *above* burr. Measured around the largest main beam two inches above the base of the burr.

C-Circumference of burr.

D-Greatest spread. Measured between perpendiculars at right angles to center line of the skull.

E-Breadth of palm. Measured in a straight line across the upper side of the palm at right angles to the rear edge of palm, to a dip between tines at the greatest width of palm.

up to the caller for an easy shot. But the old-timers with the broad palms and the heavy horns are almost certain to be wary. They will circle for scent, they will approach silently for a visual inspection, and they will spend long minutes, even hours, in the process. It takes a good caller to work a suspicious old bull up to his downfall! A canoe can be a valuable aid, enabling the hunter to stay down-wind as the bull approaches and to select the spot offering the best cover for the hunter and the best view of the approaching moose. Although calling may be effective at any time of the day, the best time is the evening and on into the night if it is moonlight. The grunt or challenge of the bull may prove effective, too, to draw another bull in close enough for a shot.

If the object of the hunt is a trophy, it behooves the gunner to look a bull over carefully, preferably with binoculars, before lining up the sights and pulling the trigger. All moose antlers look big to anyone not accustomed to judging them. To a hunter experienced only on lesser game even a small bull will seem like a magnificent animal at first glance. Your faith should rest in your guide. Tell him what you hope to get and, unless you are well versed in the moose woods and moose ways, take his advice as to whether or not to shoot. He cannot, of course, be infallible. You may shoot at his bidding and later see several moose with bigger antlers, or may pass up a moderately good trophy and go on for days or weeks without seeing anything to match it. But the situation calls for a decision, and your guide should be the one to give you the answer.

The moose is a big target. A bull will stand about 7 feet high at the shoulder. He is big—and easy to hit. Bulls have been missed at 30 yards, but in essence the hitting of the animal is not as difficult as with other and smaller big game. To kill him swiftly is not easy, however. Because he is big and tough, it takes either a bigger gun or a more accurately placed shot. Perhaps this factor has also added to the decline of the moose. It is so easy to wound him and so hard to kill him quickly. Wounded by an insufficient or poorly placed bullet that caused almost no bleeding where it entered his body, he may later die of the wound while the gunner hunts on to take another trophy.

Your guide, living in moose country, may use a .30/30 rifle and kill his moose, even bragging truthfully that he kills them with a single shot. The difference is that your guide has the whole season in which to shoot his moose. He knows the animals and he knows the woods. When he lifts his rifle it is usually on a short shot with the animal standing. You, too, could do the same thing in a similar situation. But the chances are that your shot will not be as short as his, since it is harder to get two men as close to a moose as one can go. Your time of hunting will be limited and you will have only a longer shot, perhaps at a moving animal, and a shot that sends the bullets through branches where a light one, traveling at high speed, may be deflected.

Moose hunting is not for every hunter; there are too few of them to go around. It takes money and travel to put a gunner into moose country, and the prospect is that it will take more of both as the years go by. The highways will bite deeper into the mooseland, the settlers will continue to move into his country, and the airplanes will cut down the travel time required to reach his haunts. The opportunity to hunt this magnificent animal in his natural wilderness may be a more or less fleeting privilege for American hunters who have already lost that hunting on much of his original habitat. Hunt him with a little reverence for what he is and what he represents as you stalk him through the pine and spruce. And when you lift your gun to kill him, shoot hard and clean.

**Rifles and Sights.** For moose, the following rifles are recommended (all with high-velocity loads):

.35 Remington Express, with 200-grain bullet.
.270 with 150-grain bullet.
.30 '06 with 220-grain bullet.
.300 H. & H. Magnum with 180-grain bullet.

NOTE: The above rifles, for long-range accuracy, should be equipped with telescopic sights of from 2½ to 4 power. For these sights, most experienced hunters prefer the tapered post reticule.

## COLLARED PECCARY (Javelina)

*Pecari angulatus*

The peccary *(Dicotyles* or *Tayassu),* a distant relative of the domestic pig and the European wild boar, is an animal peculiar to the Western Hemisphere. Its range extends from southern Texas, Arizona, and New Mexico south to Patagonia. In the area where it is found in the United States, as well as south of the border, it is commonly called the javelina (pronounced *haveleena*). It is sometimes known also as the musk hog, from the gland on its back. The excretion from this gland gives the animal a characteristic and most unpleasant smell, often strong enough to be detected by a man 100 yards away. The family name *Dicotylidae* comes from the fact that opening of the gland resembles a navel.

There are two living genera, the collared peccary *(Pecari angulatus)* and the white-lipped *(Tayassus pecari spiradens),* but only the smaller collared peccary is found as far north as the southwestern United States. Within its great range there are many local types varying in color from light grizzled-gray to nearly black.

**History.** Formerly peccaries were considered a subdivision of the swine family *(Suidae),* but because neither living nor extinct *Tayassuidae* have ever been found outside the Western Hemisphere, paleontologists have conceded them full family status. Some authorities believe pigs and peccaries had a common ancestor in the Eocene Age. Peccaries rank higher than pigs in the evolutionary scale because of their more complicated stomachs. They are distinguished from the pig family also by the fact they produce no more than two shoats at one birth, that the hind foot has only three toes, and that the upper tusks turn downward.

Extinct forms of *Tayassuidae* have been placed in North America as far back as the Miocene, but in South America their remains have been found only in deposits of later periods; from this fact comes

Courtesy U. S. Fish and Wildlife Service.

PLATE I. Adult Peccary with Young.

the theory that peccaries came to this continent during the Upper Oligocene Age, and spread southward. They were common in North America in the Pliocene and Pleistocene Ages. Peccaries have been found in Maryland, West Virginia, Pennsylvania, Illinois, Indiana, Kansas, and Mexico.

The present-day collared peccaries once ranged as far north as the Red River in Arkansas, but gradually lost ground with the settling of the West. In the 1930's they were exterminated from much of their former range because of the commercial demand for "pigskin," even though the hides at that time brought only 25 to 50 cents each. The wholesale slaughter is illustrated by the fact that in one town, Nogales, Ariz., 85,000 hides from south of the border were sold in a single year. The prospect was extinction in the United States; the 1938 game survey showed fewer than 44,000 individuals. Finally, the southwestern states adopted protective legislation, and in recent years the peccary population has increased considerably.

**Identification.** In build, the peccary resembles a small pig, except that it seldom takes on fat. The collared peccary averages about 3 feet in length, and from 2 to 2½ feet in height at the shoulder. There is little difference in size between the sexes. A full-grown animal may weigh from 50 to 70 pounds, but not more than 75 pounds.

Though at a distance these animals look black, at close range the color usually is a dark gray, with a pepper-and-salt effect; the individual hairs are banded light and dark. The collar is a light band running over the shoulders from the sides of the neck. At birth the shoats are a light yellowish shade and lack the collar.

The head has small, erect ears and a rather long snout which closes to hide the tusks almost entirely. These are well developed, from 1½ to 2½ inches long, with razor edges. There are two in the upper and two in the lower jaw. Well-defined grooves show where the uppers contact the back surface of the lowers.

The forefoot has four toes, the hind foot three. The legs are slender, and the hoofs small. The tail is represented on the peccary by a slight bump. Seven or 8 inches higher on the rump, and between the hips, is the musk gland, which may be rather prominent. Its internal structure is oval, about 3 inches long, and lies just under the skin. The function of the gland is not definitely known, but it is said that the odor helps the young to find their mothers. One observer speculates on its possible value in keeping off mosquitoes.

The white-lipped peccary of Mexico and Central and South America is perhaps 6 inches longer than the collared, has coarser hair of a rusty black, and is marked with a light band on the lower jaw. Its musk gland is relatively larger than that of the collared peccary, and the odor is said to be even more offensive.

**Characteristics.** Peccaries are gregarious. As many as 265 of the white-lipped genus have been counted in one band. A band of collared peccaries, however, usually numbers no more than a dozen. In most cases the leader is an old boar. The females produce one shoat each a year, though twins are seen occasionally.

Early morning and late afternoon are the preferred feeding times, with a midday siesta. Apparently these animals will eat anything available; their diet includes roots, acorns, nuts, fallen fruit, berries, and also insects, toads, snakes, and small lizards. They root for worms and grubs. Arizona's cactus thickets provide both food and shelter. They like plenty of good cover handy, and dash for their hiding places when alarmed. Often they bed at night in caves or hollow stumps or logs.

**Range and Distribution.** Apparently peccaries can make themselves at home in any kind of country. In Central America they inhabit the tropical rain forests, and in Texas are found in swampy lowlands. Most of their northern range, however, is desert or brush country. In Arizona they are found on mountainsides at elevations as high as 6500 feet, and in the Sierra Madres of Chihuahua and Sonora in Mexico at elevations as high as 7500 feet.

The assumption is that individual bands move about very little, if they are reasonably safe and if the food supply is good. The most obvious signs of their presence are the rooted-up earth where they have been feeding, and the characteristic smell which hangs over their feeding grounds and hiding places.

In the United States their range includes all the brush country of southwest Texas, and practically all the southeastern quarter of Arizona. A mere handful live in the sandy uplands of southern New Mexico. The game census of 1946 showed 1800 there, but Arizona had 14,600 and Texas 100,200. Total peccary population in the United States was estimated at 116,600.

**Hunting Methods.** Many a hunter who, over a period of years, has acquired quite a reputation as a deer, elk, antelope, or sheep hunter often finds his laurels slipping from his brow after a few days stalking the peccary, or javelina. That is, if he tries *stalking*. Hunting these desert pigs with dogs is no difficult task, and normally is hard only on the dogs, for a cornered peccary is a vicious character, and after his first encounter many a hound will decide he has had enough.

Stalking these animals along the desert fringes, through the sparse thickets of the valleys, is a pursuit that calls for good eyes, a knowledge of *sign*, constant attention to wind, and, when the game is sighted, quick and accurate shooting. Seldom does the hunter locate a single peccary, for these pigs are extremely gregarious and normally travel in a herd of from 6 to 40, and often their numbers are nearer the latter than the former. They are alert, even while feeding or resting, and with several pairs of eyes checking the open approaches, the hunter is required to do some real stalking.

On their range, the peccaries may be found from desert level to as much as 6000 feet or more, although they seem to prefer the low ground and warm temperatures. Like a wild razorback, the peccary will eat almost anything from snakes to vegetable matter, and will not pass up an offer of carrion. This adds to the stalker's difficulties, for he cannot limit his search to areas where they might be feeding. One thing he must remember, however, and that is to hunt up-wind.

By hunting up-wind the hunter often will be able to scent the peccary herd and plan his stalk accordingly. Hunting down-wind he will hear his game, as they race through the brush, but will seldom see them. The hunter who moves slowly and quietly often may approach a herd or band of pigs without knowing it, and suddenly find himself almost surrounded by racing forms. This is where the quick and accurate shooting comes in, for the short legs of the peccary can carry him to the safety of thick cover in an amazingly brief period of time.

Experienced peccary hunters snort loudly at the stories concerning hunters being charged by a herd or band of these pigs after one of their number has been wounded. Often a wounded pig may turn and charge, but his friends and relatives have but one thought in mind—to escape from the sight, scent, and sound of man. When wounded or cornered, however, the peccary could do considerable damage to a hunter who was too confused to get in another quick shot, or who was a bit slow on his feet. The peccary has a good set of tusks and knows how to use them. This is evidenced by the respect granted them by predators and dogs. A mere whiff of the peccary's musky scent will send many a hound scurrying to his master's heel.

Hunted with dogs, the peccary does not have much of a chance, and although he is fast, he has little endurance. Normally the dogs will single out one pig and run him a few hundred yards. Having put on a burst of speed, the pig will cast about for a rock or other obstructions to keep his pursuers off his back. Then he will turn and face the pack.

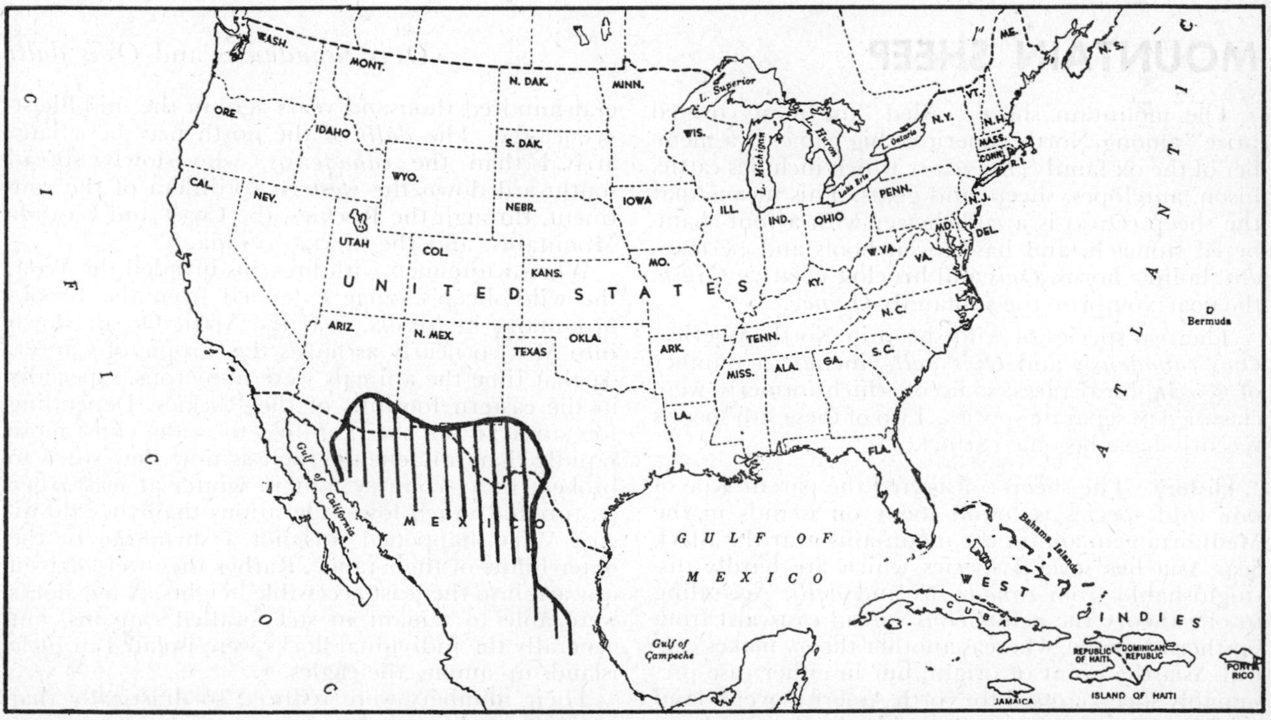


PLATE II. Distribution of Collared Peccary.

Well-trained dogs will keep the pig at bay but not attempt to close in, for experience has taught them this can be fatal.

Once the peccary is at bay, the hunter can approach him to a point only a few yards distant, which calls for no remarkable shooting skill. A brain or spine shot is necessary, however, if the hunter is interested in avoiding injury to his dogs, for even with a mortal wound the peccary can inflict severe wounds on several dogs.

Once you have killed a peccary, you are faced with the problem of what to do with it, for no matter how carefully the flesh is prepared, it holds its odor. A very young piglet is said to be extremely palatable, but no one has come forward with a recipe for the preparation of an appetizing dish from the flesh of an adult peccary. You can remove the scent gland within two minutes, hang the dressed pig for any length of time, soak a cutlet for two days, in salt water, vinegar, or wine, but when you put it on the stove you will not want to remain in the kitchen.

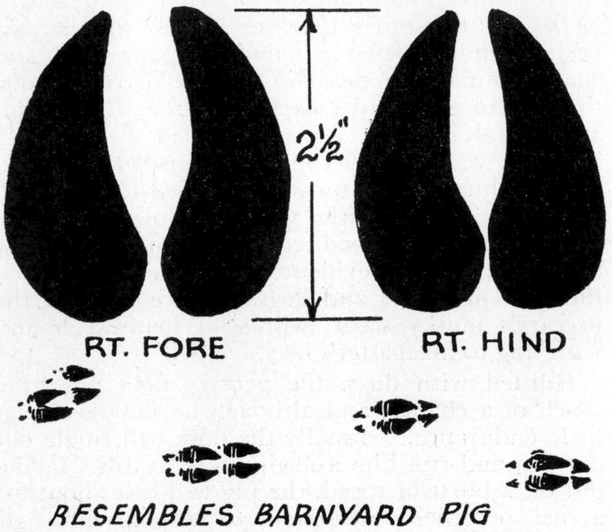


PLATE III. Typical Hoofprints of the Peccary or Javelina.

Many hunters seek out the peccary primarily as a test of their skill, and in an effort to obtain an interesting trophy. Once they have been successful, however, they are inclined to close the book on that chapter and resume hunting for a more edible species of game. Some have the hide tanned and made into gloves, for no finer pigskin is obtainable.

The illegal hide industry has been the major factor in reducing the peccary population, and it has been estimated that about 100,000 hides are used for this purpose annually. The majority of the hides come from Mexico, where this traffic has made heavy inroads on the peccary population. Some hides, unhappily, come from border states where the peccary is protected due to the sharp decline in its population. At the present time Texas is the only state which has an open season for the hunting of this animal.

**Rifle and Sights.** The average hunter prefers a deer or varmint rifle for this shooting, and as the range usually is short and there is no interest in avoiding damage to meat, the type and weight of the bullet is not important. The following calibers and loads are satisfactory.

.30/30 with 150-grain bullet
.30 Remington with 170-grain bullet
.300 Savage with 150-grain bullet
.30 '06 with 150-grain bullet
.303 with 180 grain bullet
.270 with 130-grain bullet
.250/3000 with 100-grain bullet

For details on above loads see "Ammunition—Rifle."

NOTE: The telescopic sight is not needed for this shooting, and most of the experienced hunters prefer the sight which can be aligned with the greatest speed and ease, which is the open iron sight or a wide aperture peep (see "Sights and Optical Aids.")

# MOUNTAIN SHEEP

*Ovis canadensis* and *Ovis dalli*

The mountain sheep, called "the most coveted prize" among North American big game, is a member of the ox family *(Bovidae)*, which includes cattle, bison, antelopes, sheep, and goats. This means that the sheep *(Ovis)* is a cud-chewer with a four-chambered stomach, and has cloven hoofs and permanent, hollow horns. *Ovis* and his close relative *Capra*, the goat, comprise the subfamily *Ovinae*.

The two species of wild sheep in North America, *Ovis canadensis* and *Ovis dalli*, include a number of geographical races, some of which formerly were classified as separate species. Two of these sub-species recently have become extinct.

**History.** The sheep considered the parent type of our wild species is found today on islands in the Mediterranean and in the mountains near the Black Sea. Asia has several species which are hardly distinguishable from *canadensis* and *dalli*. According to one theory the genus *Ovis* spread eastward from southern Europe, whereas another theory makes central Asia the point of origin, but in either case presumably sheep crossed to North America over a land bridge at Bering Strait . Probably this occurred several hundred thousand years ago, in the mid-Pleistocene Age. The *dalli* of the north may be a later arrival than the *canadensis*, who slowly spread southward down the western cordillera of the continent, through the Rockies, the Coast and Cascade Mountains, and the Sierra Nevada.

When white men with firearms invaded the West, the wild sheep's range extended from the Brooks Mountains in Alaska, near the Arctic Ocean, down into Mexico nearly as far as the Tropic of Cancer. At that time the animals were numerous, especially in the eastern foothills of the Rockies. Depending for survival on their ability to scale cliffs more rapidly than any enemy, then as now they stuck to broken, rocky country. But in winter at least, they pastured at much lower elevations than they do today. What happened was not a shrinking of the outer limits of their range. Rather they were driven upward into the least accessible heights. A few flocks were able to remain in steep-walled canyons, but generally the individual flocks were isolated in little islands up among the eagles.

Their numbers were reduced so drastically that in the United States they came very near extinction.

They were hunted mercilessly. Many people consider wild mutton the finest of game meats, and in some of the metal-mining areas, mountain sheep were the only big game—that is, the only important local meat supply. During the most active period of market hunting, after the Civil War, it was a common practice for the hunter to lie in wait near a favorite water hole or salt lick, where often it was possible to bring down a whole flock in short order. Some prospectors and sheepherders with small respect for game laws still use this method.

Domestic stock soon were competing with the mountain sheep for their upland ranges. The introduction of domestic sheep brought new parasites and devastating epidemic diseases. In some areas sheepmen killed off the wild flocks in an effort to check the spread of scabies among the domestic flocks.

Two sub-species were completely exterminated. The rimrock bighorn *(Ovis canadensis californiana Douglas)*, which inhabited the lava beds of eastern Oregon, northeastern California, and northwestern Nevada, probably was extinct by 1912. The Badlands bighorn *(Ovis canadensis auduboni Merriam)*, of western Nebraska, the Dakotas, and eastern Montana and Wyoming, became extinct about 1926. Both these races were distinguished from the typical Rocky Mountain bighorn by heavier teeth. The Badlands type had comparatively long and slender horns, and the rimrock bighorn had wide-spreading horns set rather far apart on the head.

Today, the survival of mountain sheep in the United States hangs in the balance. They have complete legal protection everywhere except for a few counties in Idaho and Wyoming, where they are hunted under special license. Even in these states, whose combined wild-sheep population totals more than 7500, the annual kill in recent years has been held down to fewer than 100 rams. Such a light kill could hardly account for the decrease noted recently in Wyoming. Indeed, some observers believe that since ewes and lambs suffer most under adverse conditions, complete protection of the rams upsets the sex ratio and weakens the stock. In Arizona the sheep have decreased steadily, although there has been no open season for 40 years.

Courtesy Jonas Bros.

PLATE I. A Fine Stone Sheep Head (near record).

Poaching undoubtedly is a serious problem. Predators may play a role, especially since the coyotes have extended their range to higher elevations. In most states there is a shortage of winter range. This shortage, concentrating the flocks in small areas, increases the danger from parasites and epidemics. It is believed by some biologists that inbreeding is seriously weakening the small isolated flocks.

The picture is not completely dark. The game census of 1946 showed a total of 23,863 individuals in the United States, and this meant an increase of more than 5000 since a survey of several years before. This increase was spread over several states. The latest reports indicate that increased protection pays definite dividends where sheep are concerned. Research on conservation methods has been instituted which may save the bighorns, but there are no grounds yet for cheerful predictions.

In Canada, where the sheep were given early legislative protection and where they have prospered in the great chain of national parks, their survival seems assured and in many sections the hunting is good. In recent years, however, they have noticeably decreased. Some hunters are alarmed by an increase of predators, also protected in the park areas. Many conservation experts, on the other hand, argue that the numbers of predators and their prey work out to a natural balance in the course of time.

The flocks have been shrinking also on some areas of central Alaska. Control of predators and less generous hunting seasons have been suggested as the remedy. Sheep are still numerous in Alaska, however, especially above the Arctic Circle, where they are seldom molested by man.

**Identification.** The mountain sheep has a sturdy but not ungraceful build. His coat is short hair, not wool, although in winter he wears an undercoat of short, rather scanty fuzz close to the skin. Except for the white sheep of Alaska and the Yukon and the so-called "saddlebacks," there is a common pattern of markings though the colors vary. Usually the color is some shade of gray or dull brown. It is darkest on the back, fading to a light shade on the belly and on the nose and ears. Pale streaks run down the insides of the legs. The rump is marked with a large, very conspicuous patch of creamy white. Often this is divided by a brown or blackish line running down to the dark, stubby tail. The new pelage of autumn is darker than the coat of spring, when the pigmented tips of the hairs show signs of wear. Ewes generally are lighter in color than rams.

The eyes are usually gold or amber, the horns dark brown. The hoofs are black. Each encloses four toes, and is equipped with a rubbery pad with very valuable non-skid properties. There are musk glands on all four feet.

Ewes and yearling rams have short, slender, backward-curving horns resembling those of a goat. An old ewe's horns may measure 8 or 10 inches. But 3 feet is not an extraordinary length for ram's horns; the record length is 51⅝ inches for Stone sheep and 49½ inches for bighorn. Growing longer each year, the ram's horns curve back, then out, then spiral upward. From the side view, the horns of a ram in his prime, at the age of six or seven, form the better part of a circle. On trophy heads the circle is completed, and in old rams with really exceptional heads the tips continue up past the nose, sometimes as far as the eye.

Throughout their length the horns show shallow ridges, but it is the series of deeper encircling creases which tell the ram's life history. It is said that each of these marks a year's growth. In the declining years, the rate of horn growth slows down and these rings come closer together. Still the varying distances between them tell which were the fat years and which the lean. From the rings a ram's life span is estimated at 12 years, although it is doubtful that many animals live that long.

There are two general types of horns, the close-curled and the flaring. Those curled close to the head are associated with *canadensis,* the bighorn; the widespread form is considered typical of *dalli,* the comparatively slender-horned species of the north. Both types, however, occur in both species, often in the same flocks.

There is room for different tastes in trophies. Many hunters of *dalli* value width of spread and perfect points, but the system of recording which gives credit for spread does not do justice to the bighorn. And the finest horns of the close-curled type commonly are "broomed off" at the tips. As they grow beyond a complete circle, the tips may block the animal's vision to the sides; old rams have been seen busily filing down their horns on rocks.

Bulk, the most important quality, is measured by adding the length of each horn along the outer curve to the circumference at the base and at points one-quarter, one-half, and three-quarters of the way from base to tip. The penalty for lack of symmetry is the difference between the totals for the two horns, subtracted from the grand total.

The bighorn, the species found in the United States, fall into two groups, the Rocky Mountain bighorns and the Desert bighorns.

### ROCKY MOUNTAIN BIGHORN

*Ovis canadensis canadensis Shaw*

The typical form, *Ovis canadensis canadensis Shaw,* is called simply Rocky Mountain bighorn. This is the largest mountain sheep in North America. Well-developed rams run 5 to 6 feet long, with about 5 inches of this length in tail, and stand about 40 inches high at the shoulders. Many weigh 250 to 300 pounds, and individuals weigh well over 300 pounds. The ewes are considerably smaller, from 4½ to 5 feet long, weighing from 125 to 175 pounds. The autumn coat is a dark brownish gray. This type is widely distributed, from southern Alberta and British Columbia down through Colorado. In the past it was common in eastern Washington and Oregon, and was found as far south as New Mexico and central Arizona.

A race far less numerous is the Sierra Nevada bighorn, *Ovis canadensis sierrae* (Grinnell). This is a somewhat smaller animal with more slender horns and paler coloring, not so warm in tone. The pelage is short, like that of the desert bighorns. Formerly these sheep lived in the Sierras of California from Mono County as far south as Mount Whitney, but today they have disappeared from much of their old range.

A good pair of horns for Rocky Mountain bighorn should measure at least 3 feet along their outer curves, and from 15 to 18 inches around at their bases. On the record head the right horn is 49½ inches long, with a base circumference of 16 inches. The left horn, which has a broomed tip, measures 48¼ inches. This animal is displayed in a habitat group in the American Museum of Natural History. It was shot by James Simpson in 1920 at Sheep Creek in British Columbia.

### DESERT BIGHORN

The desert bighorns, in Mexico called *cimarrones,* live in a most unfavorable environment and average smaller than the Rocky Mountain sheep. There is less contrast in size, however, between rams and ewes. The *cimarrones* have rather long ears, but on the whole their lines are cleaner than those of their Rocky Mountain relatives. Their colors usually are paler, and definitely brown in tone.

Their horns, though comparatively short, are quite respectably massive at the bases. A length of 33 inches is good for desert horns, and 36 inches is considered excellent. The record head, however, has a right horn 44 inches long and a left 43½ inches long. The base circumference of each is 17 inches. This trophy, owned by Dr. Henry M. Beck, was taken in Lower California.

Half a dozen races of desert bighorns have been described.

### NELSON BIGHORN
*Ovis canadensis nelsoni Merriam*

This type, found in the desert sections of southeastern California and southern Nevada, is relatively small, with rather slim horns, nearly triangular at the bases. The general coloring is very pale, although the rump patch is marked with a dark dorsal line.

### ARIZONA BIGHORN
*Ovis canadensis gaillardi Mearns*

This race, found in western Arizona and northwestern Sonora, is the one which inhabits the Grand Canyon of the Colorado. The Arizona bighorn is small, like the Nelson, but has heavier horns, usually close-curled, spaced 2 or 3 inches apart at the base. He is darker than *nelsoni,* with less color contrast between the nose and the rest of his face, but not as dark as the Rocky Mountain type.

The classification of *Ovis sheldoni Nelson* as a separate species probably is not valid, for it seems likely that the specimen which Nelson described was merely an undernourished Arizona runt.

### LOWER CALIFORNIA BIGHORN
*Ovis canadensis cremnobates Elliot*

This sheep, lighter in color than any other bighorn, is found in the desert of the extreme southern part of California, and in the northern part of Lower California. He is larger than the Nelson and Arizona types.

### SOUTHERN LOWER CALIFORNIA BIGHORN
*Ovis canadensis weemsi Goldman*

*Weemsi* inhabits the Sierra de la Giganta and sections farther north in the southern half of Lower California. As desert bighorns go, he is quite large, with long horns. His pelage is rather dark.

Courtesy Glacier National Park (Photo by Hileman).

PLATE II. Rocky Mountain Sheep.

## TEXAS BIGHORN

*Ovis canadensis texiana Bailey*

The range of the Texas bighorn once included the San Andres Mountains in New Mexico and the Guadalupe Mountains in New Mexico and Texas, and from west Texas extended into eastern Chihuahua. Only remnants of the race survive, however. This sheep has slim horns and a narrow muzzle, but large teeth like those of the extinct badlands bighorn. His coloring is like that of the Arizona sheep.

## MEXICAN BIGHORN

*Ovis canadensis mexicana Merriam*

This *cimarrone* of southwestern New Mexico and northwestern Chihuahua is very light in color, and his horns, comparatively slim are usually of the flaring type.

The *dalli,* the species found in Alaska, the Yukon and Northwest Territories, and northern British Columbia, characteristically have comparatively slim horns whose cross section is a triangle with one corner rounded off. They run much smaller than Rocky Mountain bighorns. Formerly the *dalli* were thought to comprise several distinct species, but it has been observed that although they never intergrade with bighorns, within the group local varieties intergrade freely, so much so that in spite of wide color variations, only two sub-species can be definitely classified. These are named for the two extremes, the white sheep and the black sheep.

## WHITE or DALL SHEEP

*Ovis dalli dalli Nelson*

The white sheep has a year-round pelage to match the snow, and in spring and summer, against dark cliffs or green mountain meadows, can be seen from miles away. The effect in sunlight has been described as dazzling. At close range he often shows a sprinkling of dark-tipped hairs on the back, and sometimes a definite dark line on the rump and tail. The lambs, however, are pure white.

Alaska's Kenai Peninsula has pure white flocks with a high proportion of close-curled rather than flaring horns. But these sheep cannot be easily distinguished from the all-white sheep found in central Alaska and farther east.

Around Dawson City in the Yukon the saddlebacks or Fannin sheep occur. In these flocks some individuals have dark tails, some gray on their backs, and pale gray on the legs. Here the white sheep have interbred with the closely related black or stone sheep.

The white sheep are the smallest on the continent. Rams usually are a bit under 5 feet long, and weigh about 200 pounds.

The record horns for this type belonged to an animal killed in Alaska in 1927 by Patsey Henderson. The right horn is 47½ inches long, with a base circumference of 13 inches; the left is 47 inches long. This trophy is owned by Dr. Henry M. Beck.

## BLACK or STONE SHEEP

*Ovis dalli stonei Allen*

The Stone sheep, found near the headwaters of the Stikine River in British Columbia and farther north and east, is larger than the white. His color pattern is that of the bighorns, but with sharper contrast, for the white rump patch is set off against a body color of brown or gray so dark that it sometimes approaches black. Local varieties found at the head of the Skeena River, around Mount Logan, along the Liard River, and in the Samilkameen Mountains are all considered identical with *stonei.*

The longest pair of horns recorded for any North American wild sheep belonged to a Stone sheep shot by L. S. Chadwick in 1936 in the Muskwa River region of British Columbia. The left horn is 51⅝ inches long, with a base circumference of 14¾ inches; the right measures 50⅛ inches long and 15⅛ inches around the base.

**Characteristics.** On a high point stands a sentinel guarding the flock which grazes in a little mountain meadow well above timberline. The sheep make no effort to avoid being seen. Unless some enemy has sneaked up quite close, they are not disturbed by a shift of wind. Some hunters believe that mountain sheep have no sense of smell. This has been disproved, but it is true that scent gives them warning only at close range. Their ears are good, but it is their remarkable eyesight on which they place reliance.

The sentinel watches a suspicious-looking object in the far distance. Until the object moves, he shows no signs of alarm. Then he takes to flight. Instantly the whole flock follows. A quick series of bouncing leaps takes them up the near-by cliffs, and in the wink of an eye they are around on the other side of the mountain, or are looking down from the highest peaks, where no other mammal can follow, at least without long hours of climbing.

Perhaps in the middle of the day the sheep have been lying down on a rocky ledge above a sheer drop of several hundred feet. As the afternoon wears on, one sheep rises and steps off the ledge. The cliffs are so nearly perpendicular that apparently only a fly could descend safely. But the other sheep confidently follow. They are not committing suicide; they have only decided that it is time to graze a while. Their feet touch the cliff occasionally as they drop in zigzags. Knowing every inch of their territory, they are taking advantage of inch-wide ledges, small projections, cracks, and the like to check their descent; their spongy hoof-pads act as brakes.

Such amazing performances are not acts of desperation, for this is their everyday method of locomotion. Sheep have been seen bounding at top speed across rocky slides where a slower pace or a split-second's pause would mean a fatal fall. They leap chasms as a matter of course.

Rarely are they seen where they cannot instantly escape to the heights. Even so, they nourish many predators. Wolves, bears, mountain lions, lynxes, wolverines, coyotes, and foxes take a heavy toll of lambs each year. Baby lambs often are the prey of the golden eagle, which in the Subarctic does more damage to the flocks than any other predator. But not only lambs are killed. Coyotes can bring down a pregnant ewe. In the mountain lion's range, he is the number one enemy next to man. Though at night the sheep bed in the heights on narrow ledges or in caves, the big cats, climbing silently, manage to surprise them. Rams in the rutting season travel from one mountain to the next, and often wolves get them en route, in the valleys. In winter snows, when the flocks come down to timberline, the predators pick off the weak ones and the old. In the south, the *cimarrones* must watch out for scorpions and rattlers.

All but the desert sheep graze through the summer on the tender mountain grasses found at higher levels. A small portion of their diet consists of leaves and buds from the variety of plants and shrubs growing at high altitudes. But in winter the sheep seek more sheltered slopes and canyons below timberline. Then they must browse on whatever shows above the snow. They also use their hoofs to paw under the snow. Sometimes a slope is left stripped down to bare earth and rock, where the sheep have eaten off a carpet of moss and lichens.

Sometimes the going is hard. The sheep will not share their range with any other species, and if they find intruders—cattle, or possibly elk—on their winter pastures, they prefer to stay high and go hungry. The same thing happens if they are too much hunted by men or carnivores. Then they escape the heaviest snows by climbing to the highest windswept ridges.

In winter they quench their thirst with snow. But in summer, notwithstanding possible risks, they must come down from the heights to water. They make the trip once and sometimes twice a day, always to a favorite stream or water hole. In this season they also make two or three trips a month to a salt lick, or perhaps to a spot where salt has been left for domestic stock.

The desert sheep necessarily live rather differently. Grass is scarce on their arid range, and so they must browse a good deal throughout the year. They have no problem with snow. But through about half of each year they have no water. Yet they have managed to adapt to such conditions. Body moisture is conserved if they can spend their siestas in a cave. Careful search sometimes reveals a little water left in some natural cistern in the rock. But when potholes and water holes are bone dry, there is always cactus, providing liquid as well as food. *Cimarrones* have been seen nipping the spines off cacti in order to eat the flesh. A ram may butt a barrel cactus a few times to persuade it to give up its juice more readily.

Through most of the year the mature rams live apart from the main flocks of ewes, lambs, and young rams. In some sections the home range of the rams is some miles from that of the main flock, although this is rather unusual. Among the *dalli*, far more numerous today than the bighorns, the main flock may number a hundred or more. This once was true of bighorns too, but now a good-sized flock is one of 30 or so. Rams are seen in smaller groups of perhaps three or four, sometimes of 15 or more. Where the sheep are numerous, the rams tend to split up according to age levels, but where sheep are few, all ages live together. Occasionally an old ram, slow-moving and with a bad disposition, probably due in part to bad teeth, is seen alone.

**Breeding.** In spring and summer, when their sole occupation is eating and storing up fat, the rams are all good friends, but when the restlessness comes on them in the fall, the battles begin. They may join the ewes as early as September, though the rut is usually most active in late November, and lasts well into December. In their contests the opponents leap at each other, and are balanced on their hind feet when the horns meet. The clash may be heard some miles away. Chips and flakes of horn are left to litter the battleground. Through such contests a strong ram may reserve for himself 40 or 50 ewes. Winning and servicing such a harem keeps him too busy to eat much, and drains his energy. At the end of the season he is gaunt, and may have a hard time getting through a severe winter. It is believed that in winter the horns stop growing, to start again in the spring, and that this cycle produces the so-called annual rings.

In late May or early June, after five months of gestation, the lambs are born. Twins are the general rule. The ewe goes into hiding to give birth. Observers believe that when the lambs are first seen skipping after her, they are only a few days old. In a month they are strong enough to follow her to the highest pastures. Although adult mountain sheep are rarely heard uttering any sound, and then only snorts, the lambs bleat like the offspring of domestic sheep.

Where the main flock is a large one, the ewes with their new lambs may form a separate group for a while, leaving the mixed flock of yearlings and two-year-olds, but later in the summer the adolescents usually rejoin the ewes.

**Range and Distribution.** The big-game census of 1946 showed the following distribution of mountain sheep within the United States:

| *Rocky Mountain Bighorns* | |
|---|---|
| California | 460 |
| Colorado | 5,900 |
| Idaho | 2,100 |
| Montana | 1,500 |
| New Mexico | 107 |
| Oregon | 10 |
| South Dakota | 8 |
| Utah | 435 |
| Washington | 20 |
| Wyoming | 5,500 |
| TOTAL | 16,040 |

| *Desert Sheep* (Nelson, Arizona, and Texas Bighorns) | |
|---|---|
| Arizona | 2,200 |
| California | 1,500 |
| Nevada | 3,400 |
| New Mexico | 468 |
| Texas | 75 |
| TOTAL | 7,643 |

The Taryall Mountains of Colorado probably are better stocked than any other section. Since an epidemic in the 1920's, the sheep have been increasing, and recently numbered an estimated 750. Lately the Colorado game commission has experimented with trapping some of these sheep and transplanting them to other parts of the state.

No figures are available for Canada, but the Dominion has plenty of good hunting areas, in some of which the sheep population has been perennially replenished by the overflow from national parks. One section is not far north of the Montana border, in British Columbia and Alberta east of the Kootenay River. Another lies northward in Alberta, adjacent to Jasper and Banff National Parks. Further north there is more extensive sheep country along the Smoky and other streams flowing into the Peace River. Sheep are still found in smaller numbers here and there in the Cascade Range in British Columbia near the Washington border, for example, in the Ashnola Range and in country along the Lillooet River.

Alaska's sheep population was estimated in 1946 at 30,000. The white sheep are widely distributed through central Alaska. Among the best sections are the Kenai Peninsula, the Chickaloon Mountains, and the area around Mount McKinley Park, and also the Rainy Pass region and that of the headwaters of the Kuskokwim. Eastward, the range of the white sheep extends into the Yukon and Northwest Territories almost to the Mackenzie River. There is good sheep country along the White River and around Kluane Lake, but that in the Mackenzie Mountains is rather inaccessible.

Stone sheep are found in the Cassiar District near the head of the Stikine River in British Columbia, and east of the Rockies in large areas drained by the Sikanni Chief river and the Muskwa and Prophet Rivers. Their range reaches northward into the Yukon Territory to about the 64th degree of latitude.

Mountain sheep are home-loving creatures and slaves of habit. At the price of great danger and hardship they will remain in the same small area inhabited for centuries by the ancestors of their particular flock. They migrate only in extreme emergencies, as when their water supply is completely cut off—although this has not discouraged them in the cactus country. If they are driven from their home range by an invasion of domestic stock or by persistent hunting, they return as soon as possible. Most sheep, then, live out their lives within a few miles of their birthplace. Within this area they shift with the seasons, following their food supply. Only heavy snows bring them below timberline.

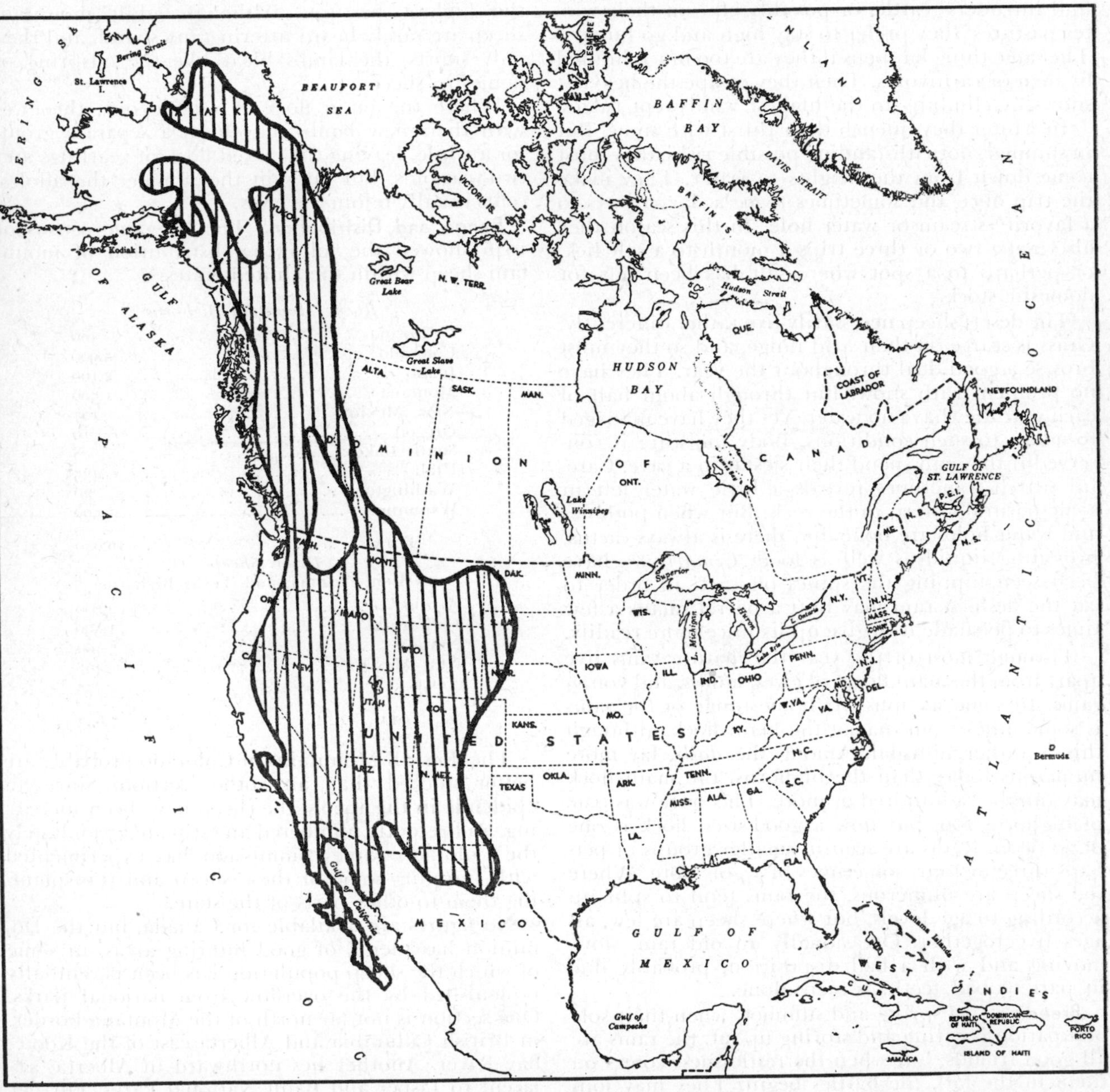


**Plate III. Distribution of Mountain Sheep.**

Sheep range is usually well marked with trails. A flock of ewes and lambs wears deep, narrow trails along the easier grades; even in snow these show a line of shadow. Wide-spaced, zigzag tracks in snow mean that a single animal or a small group, probably of rams, has passed.

**Hunting Methods.** Wherever he is encountered, the mountain sheep has more or less the same habits. Tactics that will get him in the Sierra Azul de los Indios on the Sonora coast also will get him in Alaska. Hunting the wild sheep is, to many sportsmen, the grandest and most difficult of all types of hunting. The sheep hunter works high, in the north usually above timberline and often above the clouds. Always he has a vast panorama of wild, lovely country spread out below him, and often the climbing he has to do is not only difficult but dangerous.

The giant moose, the great many-pointed head of the caribou, the skin of the mighty Alaska brown bear make magnificent trophies; but all in all, the wild sheep is the Number One North American trophy to many, and there is nothing that can compare with the heavy, massive head of a fine old ram. Many have found that the only times they were in actual danger while hunting came through climbing for sheep. On occasion the country is so rough that survival is only a matter of chance—and inches. In such hunting a competent guide is as good as a high insurance policy.

The wild sheep is found from Alaska clear down through the western mountains of the North American continent to Sonora on the Mexican mainland and to Lower California. There are two main divisions of the American wild sheep—the bighorns and the thinhorns. The bighorns are found south of the Peace and Skeena rivers in British Columbia clear to the mountains opposite Tiburon Island on the Sonora coast and almost to the tip of Lower California. The bighorns are relatively plentiful in Canada, with the finest rams coming from the type locality, which is the crest of the Rockies. Particularly famous for great ram heads is the Brazeau section of Alberta, where *Ovis canadensis canadensis* is found at his best. In the United States, the sheep have been badly thinned out over most of their range, and the only state which still has an open season on special license is Wyoming. In those areas where sheep are making a less rapid recovery than in Colorado and Nevada, biologists are satisfied that the losses are due to several factors, including illegal hunting, poor winter range, inbreeding, and disease brought in by domestic sheep. The sheep of Arizona, once one of the greatest bighorn states, are just about gone, and even those of Sonora have been thinned by illegal meat-hunters.

For the sake of convenience, the bighorns south of the Peace and Skeena are divided into the Rocky Mountain bighorn and the desert sheep. Properly, all are bighorns, but the desert sheep are smaller, more thinly haired, lighter in color, and have smaller horns than the sheep of the high Rockies.

The thinhorn sheep range from the absolutely pure white Dall *(Ovis dalli dalli)* through sheep with a few black hairs in their saddles and black tails, to the sheep with snow-white heads and necks and gray or black saddles which were formerly called *Ovis fannini,* to the Stone sheep *(Ovis dalli stonei)* with black saddles and medium gray necks and faces. The farther south the thinhorn sheep go, the darker they get. In the western Yukon and Alaska, they are pure white. Around Dawson City, Y. T., they have a good many dark hairs in their saddles. In the Pelly Mountains of the southern Yukon most of the sheep are of the "Fannin" type, but even in the same band rams will be found almost light enough to be classed as pure Dalls and almost dark enough to be Stones. Bill Barthman of New York once shot a ram in the

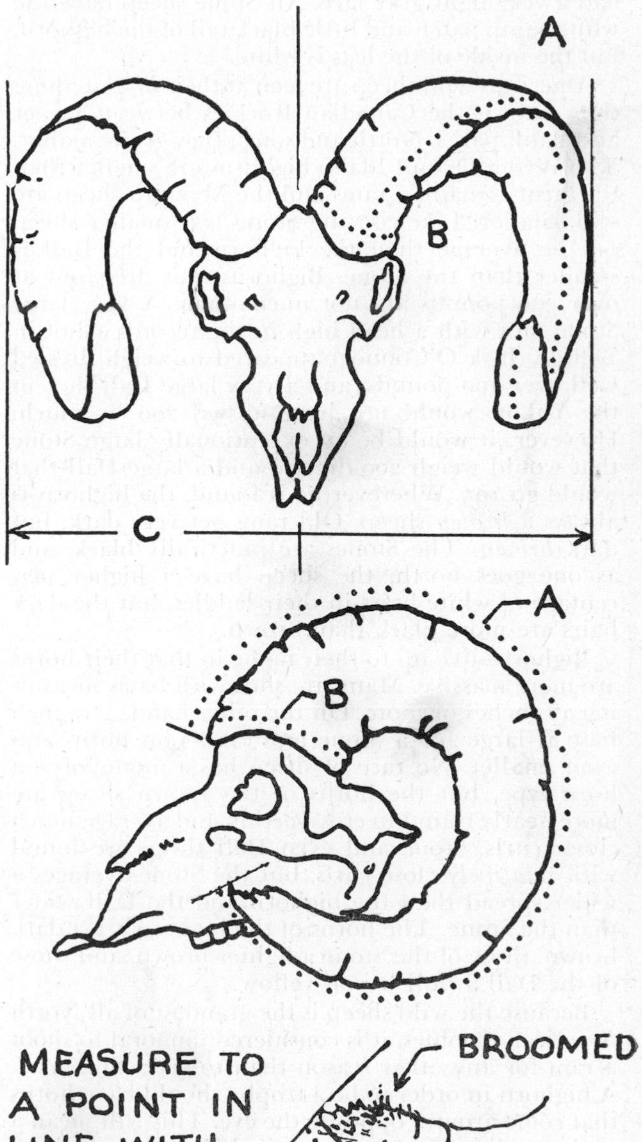


PLATE IV. Trophy Measurement, Bighorn Sheep.

A. Length of front curve. Measured on outside curve from base to tip.

B. Circumference at base. This is not a measurement following the hair line. The lower edge of the steel tape should be held at the edge of the horn in the center of skull. A plane through this point at right angles to the center axis of horn should mark the line around the horn which the tape should follow.

C. Greatest spread. Measurements at perpendiculars, at right angles to the center line of the skull.

Pellys that was as dark as the "true" Stones found around the heads of the Prophet and Muskwa rivers in British Columbia.

In the Cassiar district of northwestern British Columbia the Stone sheep vary all the way from very light to very dark. Around the heads of the Muskwa and the Prophet rivers in British Columbia, far to the east of the Cassiar, the Stone rams evidently average darker. One hunter on a 40-day trip saw only two rams there that appeared to have pure white heads and necks. However, about one in four or five had a very light gray face. All Stone sheep have the white rump patch and little black tail of the bighorn, but the inside of the legs is white.

American wild sheep are seen at their largest along the comb of the Canadian Rockies between Jasper and Banff parks. North and south they grow smaller. The Wyoming and Idaho bighorns are smaller than the great Canadian rams and the Mexican sheep are still smaller. Likewise the Stone is a smaller sheep on the average than the bighorn and the Dall is smaller than the Stone. Bighorns that dress out at over 300 pounds are not uncommon. A very large Stone ram with a head high in the records (shot in 1946 by Jack O'Connor) appeared to weigh dressed well over 200 pounds, and a very large Dall shot in the Yukon would not have missed 200 by much. However, it would be an exceptionally large Stone that would weigh 200 dressed and a large Dall that would go 195. Wherever he is found, the bighorn is always a *brown* sheep. Old rams get very dark, but dark *brown.* The Stones are practically black, and as one goes north, the sheep have a higher percentage of white hairs in their saddles, but the dark hairs are more black than brown.

Bighorns live up to their name in that their horns are more massive. Many are shot with bases measuring 17 inches or more. On the other hand, a 15-inch base is large for a Stone and Dall ram horns run even smaller. No race of sheep has a monopoly on horn type, but the horns of the brown sheep are more nearly round in cross section and average much closer curls. Stone and even Dall sheep are found with *relatively* close curls, but the Stone averages a wider spread than the bighorn and the Dall wider than the Stone. The horns of the bighorn are a dark brown, those of the Stone a lighter brown, and those of the Dall a dull lemon yellow.

Because the wild sheep is the grandest of all North American trophies, it is considered immoral to shoot a ram for any other reason than to get a fine head. A bighorn in order to be a trophy should have horns that come around opposite the eye. This will mean a curl, usually of from 36 to 37 inches. If the ram is an old one the ends of the horns should be blunted and broomed. Many prefer a massive, broomed 37-inch head to a longer one that is more slender and tapered. If the horns go up to form a complete curl with the tips even with the base, the head will measure from 38 to 40 inches and will be in the record class. If it goes beyond this it is in the very highest class.

To be a good trophy, the head of a thinhorn ram should make a complete curl and the tips of the horns should be seen *beyond* the nose. To be well in the record class, the horn tips should project *well above the nose.*

Wherever he is found, the wild sheep is a *rough country* animal. He depends more on his eyes for protection than on anything else, and above all it is necessary for the hunter to see the ram he wants before it sees him. Many good sheep hunters swear that the animals have noses that are no more efficient than those of human beings and in hunting sheep they disregard the wind. The nose of a sheep is not as keen as those of deer, moose, and caribou. Nevertheless there is plenty of evidence that they can smell and many stalks go sour because rams catch a man scent carried on some unpredictable, eddying mountain current. Because sheep live in high rough country where stones are always breaking loose and tumbling down, they are not particularly bothered by ordinary noises. As compared to the deer and the caribou, their ears are small.

Once the hunter grasps the basic fundamentals of sheep hunting, he will find it simplicity itself. First, he must hunt ram country. Rams come together with the ewes in the mating season, which is December in the north and late August and September in the deserts. After the rut the rams will hang around with the ewes for awhile, and then they go off by themselves. In the hunting season on sheep, which ranges from August 1 in the Yukon to September 1 in Alberta, the rams are off by themselves, and if any good ram is found close to ewes it is by accident. Sometimes, big rams will be just over the ridge or in a near-by basin from the ewes with whom they consort during the rut. At other times they will be miles away.

Mexican sheep travel widely to take advantage of the sparse grasses and weeds that follow the spotty rains in that arid country, but the northern sheep are pretty much creatures of habit, and a band of rams will use the same summer range year after year. When they migrate to the winter range they will follow the same routes.

This is where a good guide comes in. He knows ram country, he knows the migration routes. One particular mountain may produce good rams year after year. Another mountain near by, which to anyone else looks as "sheepy" as the other, may never have rams on it at all. Knowing the country is half the secret of a successful hunt.

Young rams two or three years old stay with the ewe herd. When they begin to become big boys, the old rams chase them off during the rutting season. Where sheep are relatively scarce, one will find rams of all sorts in the same bunch, little three- and four-year olds as well as great old patriarchs with trophy heads and from 11 to 14 years old. Where sheep are plentiful, however, the rams tend to associate with other rams in their own age group. One herd will be all young rams, another all old rams.

In the Yukon one hunter spent a whole day stalking a large group of rams which had been seen at a distance of about three miles. When he came close to them he found that not a single one was over seven years old—not a trophy head in the lot. A hunter on the Prophet River in British Columbia, reported climbing 3000 feet to ram country. He saw about 50 rams, but there were no outstanding heads, as the oldest ram in the group was not more than eight. About ten days later he was on the same mountain. All the young rams had moved on and their place was taken by the old patriarchs. With a companion, he took two heads that day that went over 40 inches, and they saw one ram at a distance through a spotting scope that must have had a 45-inch head!

It is often said that sheep are gregarious animals and that a ram is never found alone. That is not strictly true. Sheep are gregarious and rams usually run in bunches, but now and then one will find a very old ram with a head in the highest class off by himself. As a ram gets old, his teeth decay and drop out. He suffers from what would be called pyorrhea in a human being. His teeth must pain him terribly. He gets cross, quarrelsome, crotchety, and is evidently unable to get along with other rams.

One of the largest Mexican rams reported was off by himself in country where no other sheep were to be found. He had been living alone at the head of a canyon and eating great quantities of Indian wheat and a pealike vine that had come up following the winter rains. It appeared that in a couple of months he had not moved more than a quarter of a mile. Because of the rich, abundant food, he was very fat; but it is doubtful that he could have survived the coming dry months. He had lost most of his teeth and those remaining were so loose that they could be pulled out with the fingers.

One of the largest rams recently shot in the Yukon was all alone, although he was in the same basin with a flock of ewes and lambs. Like his very distant Sonora relative, he had been staying in a limited area for a long time. His annual rings showed him to be 13 years old, about as old as a sheep ever gets. This sheep was taken by Jack O'Connor, and his description of the hunt is an interesting one:

> "The taking of this ram is a strange and improbable story, but I'll tell it nevertheless. Field Johnson, my Indian guide and I, had thoroughly glassed the basin and had seen no sheep except the ewes and lambs. We decided to cross it to look into the one beyond. About halfway across, I suddenly knew I smelled a ram. I stopped, told Field that I did. A moment later that big old ram, who had been lying on a point, jumped and ran. I shot him. The wind had been blowing directly from him to us. A ram has a musky, sweetish, heavy smell, and on several occasions I have smelled them at a distance. This, however, is the only time I ever located a ram by my nose *first.*"

The really good sheep hunter has to be a skillful and patient user of binoculars. A sheep has marvelous eyesight, but a man who knows what to look for and who has a good pair of 8-, 9-, or 10-power binoculars can see even better. The first step after getting into ram range is to go to a point of vantage and then carefully to look over all likely spots, not only for sheep but for signs of sheep. Rams travel over bad places in single file, and if the country is being used it is easy to locate sheep trails on the shale slides. Rams like to bed down in fine shale because they can paw out comfortable beds and also because they can run faster over slides than any of their natural enemies—the wolf in the north and the mountain lion and coyote farther south. They also like to bed near rough cliffs because they can bound up an escarpment where a wolf would break his neck. Rams also like to bed on points from which they can see in every direction. They like to feed in the great basins above timberline, basins adjacent to steep rocky country where they can flee to safety. In many sections they will bed in rough, cliffy country and feed *above* on rolling, grassy mesas.

The snow-white Dall sheep is easy to locate except in the winter because his beautiful coat will gleam like a diamond against green grass and lichen slope or against dark shale. Hunters report having seen Dalls at least seven miles away! The Stones and bighorns are less easy to see because they are less conspicuous, but at great distances their white rump patches give them away. Unlike the deer, the elk, and the moose, the wild sheep nearly always beds out in the open.

The good user of binoculars will first give a more or less hasty look to see if anything is conspicuous; then, if he sees nothing, he gets into a very steady position sitting down with his back against a tree or a rock or with his glasses rested on a stone or log and looks the country over sector by sector, examining systematically *everything* that might be a sheep. Here is a group of light spots against green lichen. Are

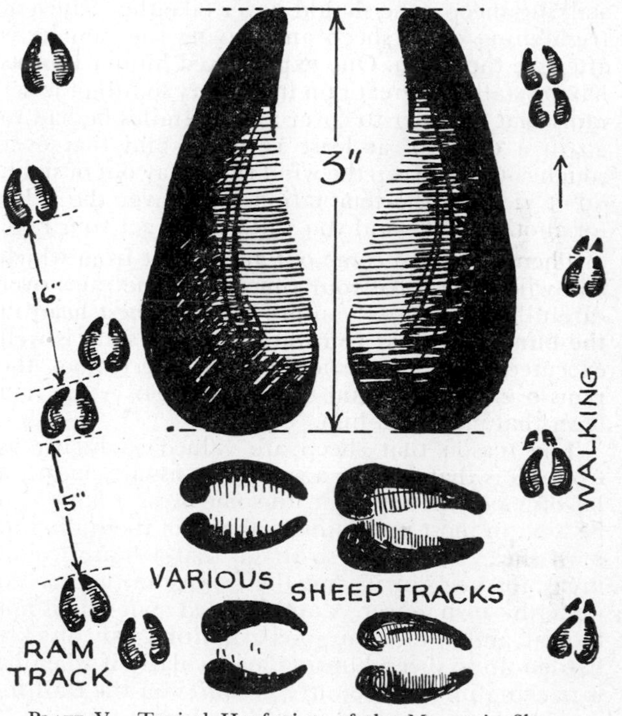


PLATE V. Typical Hoofprints of the Mountain Sheep.

they stones or the rumps of rams? Here is something dark over on that point that might be the side view of a ram lying down.

When the hunter's suspicions are aroused, he should lay the glass on something so it will be absolutely steady and *watch, watch.* The sheep hunter's binoculars should be of the very highest quality, as there is no poorer investment than a poor pair of binoculars. German Zeiss and Hensoldt glasses of suitable specifications are excellent, as are the latest British Ross glasses, and, of course, the American Bausch & Lomb binoculars. The big 7 x 50 glasses as made by various concerns are too heavy and bulky for sheep hunting. The 6 x 30 glasses, though far better than nothing, do not have enough power. The 7 x 35 Bausch & Lomb glass is a beautiful all-around glass, but for sheep hunting where the air is clear and the light good, the glasses preferred by many are the 8 x 30, Bausch & Lomb and Zeiss, and the 9 x 35 Bausch & Lomb, which—power, definition, and weight considered—are considered the best to be found.

Once rams are located, a good spotting scope, either draw-tube or prismatic, will aid greatly in evaluating the head. The hunter can carry binoculars and the guide can keep the spotting scope in the rucksack.

When the hunter puts his finger on a ram, the stalk should be planned carefully so that the hunters will never be in sight of the sheep. If the ram is seen feeding, it is usually best to wait until he beds down. Then he will stay put and the hunter can begin the stalk assured that unless something frightens him he will stay put for several hours. On the other hand, a feeding ram may go a mile or two to bed and when the hunter comes out at where he expected to see the ram his quarry will be gone and perhaps he can never again locate him.

The greatest care and patience should be used in stalking sheep. One should never take the chance of frightening other sheep and having the ram he is after see them run. One experienced hunter reports having stalked a great ram in country so full of lesser rams that in order to cover about 2 miles he had to go in a circle of at least 12 miles—and that over rough country. Keep the wind right, stay out of sight, don't yield to the temptation to go over the ridge for another look—and you will usually get your ram.

Then when you come out at the spot from which you will shoot, take your time. Look the rams over carefully; make *sure* you are after the best head in the bunch and that you want it. If the stalk is well executed, the hunter should have time to look the rams over, get his wind back, and get over the ram fever that may beset him.

The reason that sheep are valued so highly as trophies is that getting a good ram usually means a lot of good stiff leg work. In some areas a horse can be used in most preliminary phases of the stalk, but most sheep country is so rough that a horse would break his neck in it, and the hunter must proceed under his own power. A middle-aged man who is not too fat and who is in good condition can quickly harden up to sheep hunting, particularly if when he is packing into the country he *walks* on the trail instead of sitting on his horse like a bag of potatoes.

Jack O'Connor's story of the stalking of a Mexican ram is typical of sheep hunting:

"I rode with one Mexican over from camp about nine miles away to the base of a sheep range. In five minutes I had with binoculars found rams on a crest about two miles away. The rams had seen us too, but we were so far away they were not worried. I set up the 20x spotting scope and saw that one of them was a trophy ram. Telling the Mexican to stay with the horses, I dropped into an *arroyo* that led in the general direction of the sheep. I kept out of sight until I was within a half-mile of the rams, then I found that there was a place I couldn't cross without their seeing me. There was nothing for me to do but to wait until the rams had all fed over to the other side of the ridge and then make a break for it before another came over to see what the Mexican and the horses were doing two miles away.

"Finally all the rams were on the far side of the ridge. I ran as hard as I could until I got around a shoulder of the mountain. I then stopped and got my wind and made my last climb as quietly as I could sheltered from their sight by a rimrock. When I came to the place from which I had planned to shoot, seven rams were within 35 yards of me, and I killed the largest instantly with a shot through his heart!"

Sheep hunting is usually thought of as long-range shooting, but if the stalk is well executed, there is usually not much reason for taking long-range shots. The average kill is made at slightly over 200 yards, and some are killed at around 35 yards.

**Rifle and Sights.** There is always a possibility that the hunter may have no recourse other than taking a long shot, and hence his rifle should have a high velocity and flat trajectory. In addition, the rifle should be as light as is consistent with accuracy and power.

The following calibers and loads are preferred.

.270 with 130-grain bullet.
.30 '06 with 150-grain bullet.
.300 H. & H. Magnum with 180-grain bullet.
.300 Savage with 150-grain bullet.

For details on the above loads see "Ammunition—Rifle."

The bullet type should be selected with care, for the primary concern is to get the utmost in shocking power, and the damage to meat is not important. Therefore, the "pointed expanding," the "hollow point," or the "hollow copper point" are favored.

NOTE: The telescope sight, preferably of four power, is almost a *must* for this shooting, and there is a difference of opinion as to the most acceptable reticule. Many prefer fine crosshairs for this hunting, while others hold that the tapered post is most satisfactory. (See "Sights and Optical Aids.")

# SMALL GAME

## OPOSSUM

*Didelphis virginiana*

The opossum (or possum), whose common name is of Algonquin origin, belongs to the order of mammals named for the marsupium, the pouch in which the mother carries her young. Australia has a variety of marsupials, but only a few families in this group are found in the Western Hemisphere. Among the *Didelphidae,* the opossum family, the pouch often is poorly developed or lacking altogether; the tiny mouse opossum *(Marmosa)* of Mexico and Panama, for example, is pouchless. It is characteristic of marsupials, however, that the young are born at a very early stage of development. For some time after birth they have the appearance of embryos, and are nearly as helpless; whether protected by a pouch or not, they merely cling to the mother's body.

Another characteristic of marsupials is the simple structure of the brain. The opossum, which has an extremely small brain case, is described as a primitive mammal; and it is one of the most primitive types found in the Americas.

Central and South America have several genera of opossums, including the woolly type *(Philander),* and the water opossum *(Chironectes)* of Panama, with webbed hind feet. Mouse opossums, about the size of rats, often come to the United States in bunches of bananas. The only genus native to the United States, however, is *Didelphis,* from which the family takes its name. The species is called *Didelphis virginiana,* since the Virginia opossum is considered the typical form.

**History.** Fossil remains show that members of the opossum family were common in the Oligocene Age, and that, like elephants, they once had a vast range extending over many parts of the world where later they became extinct. Today the family has no representatives in Africa. But *Didelphis* is one of the relatively small number of mammals surviving in North America from the Pleistocene Age.

The spread of civilization on this continent may have reduced the number of opossums, as woodlands were cleared for agriculture. Yet today they are plentiful even in some thickly populated sections. Because the opossum is shy and wary and ventures from his den only at night, his presence in a particular locality may be unsuspected for some time, and few people have any idea how common this animal is.

Probably no other American fur bearer of comparable commercial importance has maintained its numbers so well. A high birth rate and the opossum's great adaptability in relation to variations in the food supply help to compensate for very heavy hunting. Thousands of animals are killed each year for sport, or simply for food, and enormous quantities of skins reach the fur market. This fur trade flourishes despite the fact that the return to the hunter

N. Y. Zoological Society.

PLATE I. Opossum Carrying Young.

or trapper is very small; in recent years 50 cents has been considered a good price for even the finest of northern skins. Through night hunting with hounds, the opossum is easily taken, and in many areas the market is supplied principally by rural youths of school age. Before the war, many skins were exported to Europe, where generally they were dyed to resemble skunk fur and used as trimming on low-priced cloth coats.

**Identification.** The typical Virginia opossum *(Didelphis virginiana virginiana Kerr),* familiar throughout the greater part of the United States, is about the size of a house cat, though with shorter legs. An adult may weigh 9 pounds, sometimes more. The total length is about 2½ feet, including 12 or 13 inches of tail. The tail, slim and tapering, is naked, with a scaly appearance. Wrapped around a branch, it can support the owner's weight as a monkey's tail does.

The large, erect ears also are naked. In northern states the tail and ears may be frostbitten if the opossum leaves his den in near-zero weather. The muzzle is long, rather pointed, and is furnished with 50 teeth.

Like the other small animals which spend much of their time in trees—the tree squirrel, raccoon, skunk, and marten—the opossum has five-toed feet strongly resembling human hands. The long, flexible toes easily grasp branches. On the hind feet the first toe, which is clawless, can be opposed to the other toes like a human thumb; the opossum leaves a distinctive track very like a hand print. All the other toes are equipped with sharp claws for climbing.

The female *Didelphis* has a well-developed pouch with strong muscles to close the opening.

On the body long white guard hairs overlie softer under fur of dark-tipped hairs. The short fur on the head, throat, and toes is pale, practically white, and the tail and ears are white or creamy, except for black tips on the ears and some black at the base of the tail.

Along the Atlantic coast southward from Charleston, S. C., and westward through the Gulf region, will be found the Florida opossum *(Didelphis virginiana pigra Bangs).* This is a slightly smaller subspecies with a longer and more slender tail. It is generally darker than the Virginia opossum, with less white on the toes.

**Characteristics.** The opossum makes his home in a hollow log or tree, or in a snug cleft in the rocks, and lines his nest with leaves. He sometimes makes use of a woodchuck's burrow. In winter he stays home and sleeps through the severe cold, but, like the bear and the raccoon, he is not a true hibernator, for though his breathing slows down when he is denned up, he maintains a high body temperature. Like the raccoon but unlike the bear, he dens up for no more than two or three weeks at a time. As soon as the weather moderates a little he is abroad searching for food. Occasionally opossums are seen out on very cold nights.

Like bears and raccoons, they eat practically anything. The contents of opossum stomachs have been found to include insects, small snakes, baby turtles, bats, crabs, and the like, as well as berries and fruits. Apparently this animal has a special weakness for corn in the milk stage, and for persimmons; often a hunt starts at a persimmon tree.

A peculiar trait is the opossum's trick of feigning death when cornered: of "playing possum." He falls on his side, often with eyes closed and tongue hanging out; if picked up and dropped from not too great a height, he falls limp. He may remain in this condition for some minutes. But the hunter or dog who turns his back, assuming that his prey is dead of heart failure, may turn again to find the opossum gone.

Men and dogs are the opossum's worst enemies, but he is hunted also by owls and by most of the larger predators. He is subject to tularemia or "rabbit fever," which may be transmitted by the wood tick to man, and also to sheep.

**Breeding.** Two broods per year are not unusual in the South, although in northern states one brood only is more likely. The gestation period is only 12½ days. A brood of 18 may be gathered in a tablespoon, for at birth a baby opossum is scarcely the size of a honey bee. The blind, round-mouthed head has a wormlike appearance. The tail is curled under the belly, and the hind limbs are hardly more than bumps. The fore limbs, however, are well developed, with strong claws. With a hand-over-hand stroke, the infant pulls itself through its mother's fur into her pouch. There it fastens firmly on a teat, to remain for several weeks.

Normally the female has but 13 teats, and when the brood exceeds this number, some inevitably die. After a month the pouch usually contains no more than seven or eight young. They remain in the pouch for about two months. When they have reached the size of mice they may go exploring over their mother's body, but will scurry back into the pouch at the slightest alarm. After the second month they travel clinging to the mother's fur. A female with two rows of passengers on her back appears twice her normal size.

**Range and Distribution.** Open woodlands, swamps, marshes—almost any kind of wasteland—are this animal's habitat; opossums have been seen some distance from the nearest trees. They are found in practically every state in the Union. Their numbers are likely to fluctuate in any given area.

It has been observed that the species is extending its range northward; opossums are plentiful now in northern states where early in the century they were rare. Today they are common in the southern sections of Vermont and New Hampshire, and recently a few have been seen as far north as southern Ontario.

**Hunting Methods.** Possum hunting is the chase reduced to its simplest and most primitive form. No gun is needed and even a club is unnecessary if the participants are agile. (The plural is used advisedly here because it is much more fun to hunt with a companion, or a group, than alone.) All that is required is a capacity for walking, plus a dog that can follow a trail and bark "treed" at the right time.

The opossum is a nocturnal creature and the hunting is therefore done between nightfall and daybreak—often beginning with the former and ending with the latter. For some reason, or so it seems, the darker the night the better the hunting; for the possum needs no moon to light his way around.

The prime requisite is a hound, but almost any "pot-licker" of doubtful ancestry will do. Possums have been trailed and treed by a greater assortment of lop-eared "houn'-dawgs" than possibly any other animal in North America. The average coonhound will also work on opossum—and often does, to the annoyance of the hunters.

Possum hunting is more a matter of luck than skill. The dog, or dogs, is turned loose where it is hoped he will pick up a trail and the hunters stand around until "hound music" tells them he has been successful. The run is seldom a long one and the dog is usually barking "treed" soon after he catches a fresh scent. One hunter generally carries a lantern or an electric torch, and all of the party should be armed with flashlights. As soon as the treed signal is heard, all start for the sound. Not infrequently it becomes a mad scramble through briars, uphill and down, jumping small streams, and plowing through swampy morasses in the eerie darkness of the woods. Woe to him who forgets to bring a flashlight or who loses it in the scramble.

When the hunters reach the tree where the eager hound is standing on his hind legs, looking up into the branches and telling the world of his success, the business of bringing the opossum to bag begins. There are several methods for this—and each to his own notions. If the tree is slender, and it often is, the opossum can be shaken from his perch. Before doing so, however, it is wise to tie up the dog or have one member of the party hold him to prevent his tearing the future dinner.

A small-caliber rifle is an asset for picking Br'er Possum out of the higher trees. The wavering, uncertain light beam from a flashlight makes for tricky shooting. The more athletically inclined can shinny up the tree and either grab the possum by the tail or knock him down with a club. The end result is the same; the possum goes in a bag and the hound is cut loose to run again.

Aside from meat in the pot, the rewards for possum hunting are a lot of healthy exercise and the ringing music of the eager hounds which, to the man who enjoys the long bugle note or the quick, bell-like chop coming back through the stillness of the night, is enough.

PLATE II. A good possum hound is eager.

## PRAIRIE DOG

*Cynomys ludovicianus*

The prairie dog is an animal of the prairies, but he is not even remotely connected with the dog, as his common name deceivingly implies. He is a member of the squirrel family, but the genus, of six species and sub-species, is found only in the New World. The marmot and spermophile are related to him. Early explorers on this continent—Lewis and Clark, Pike, Brackenridge, and others—wrote in their journals of the prairie dog and sometimes referred to him as "barking squirrel," "petit chien," and by the Indian name "wishtonwish," given to imitate his characteristic shrill whistle.

**History.** The pioneer explorers wrote idealistically of the triumvirate of mammal, bird, and snake exemplified in the prairie dog, burrowing owl, and rattlesnake, all of which shared the same hole. This theory of friendship was disproved when better observation indicated that the snake was in the burrow to eat the prairie dog young, the burrowing owl used any hole for emergency protection, and remained in an abandoned one, and the prairie dog entombed the snake and ate the young of the owl.

The explorers also were amazed at the size of the prairie dog "villages" which extended for many acres, numbering thousands of individuals. Through the years, however, the numbers increased in many sections of the plains because of land cultivation and extermination of natural enemies, though many large colonies were broken up by ranches. It was not unusual for a dog town to cover miles of land with thousands and occasionally millions of individuals. A town existed in Texas which was reportedly 100

N. Y. Zoological Society.

PLATE I. Common Prairie Dog.

miles wide and 250 miles long with 400,000,000 animals.

By 1900 the prairie dog had multiplied to such an extent that he was declared one of the most destructive forces to agriculture and ranching. The loss in crops, especially in grain and alfalfa, was great. Irrigation ditches were inadvertently drained by the burrows. The holes, made larger by predatory badgers, tripped up cattle and horses. Texas was one of the most violently protesting states. Millions of acres of grassland had been destroyed. It was estimated that the ratio of an animal's grass-consuming potential was 32 prairie dogs to one sheep, and 256 prairie dogs to one cow. The annual loss was in millions of dollars. Large-scale poisoning and fumigating was advocated, and the movement spread from farmer and rancher to section and state. The Biological Survey in Washington aided the extermination of hundreds of millions of prairie dogs and today the animal is virtually extinct in some states (Kansas, for example).

**Identification.** The short-legged prairie dog is heavy-bodied and sturdy, usually appearing rather fat. The length ranges between 14 and 16 inches, but the male is heavier by about a pound.

He has a broad head and cheek pouches with ears set low and rounded. The short, hairy tail is flattened.

The coarse-haired coat varies in coloration from dark pinkish hazel to black and buff. The undersides are whitish. In winter the pelage becomes thicker, smoother, and grayer. Both male and female are colored alike. The pelage molts and is renewed from March to May and August to November.

**Characteristics.** The prairie dog is a sociable animal, and makes large burrows near one another, forming one colony in a locality. The number of individuals in each hole is variable, but there are usually a pair to each burrow, with the numbers increasing when the young are born. The count in a colony is estimated as 25 prairie dogs to the acre, but that is often an inaccurate measure since many holes in old towns are abandoned.

The size and construction of the burrows are widely variable, often depending on the size and age of the animal. Typically, there is a mound of earth about one foot high and 3 to 4 feet wide at the mouth of each burrow, and the size of the mound grows with usage. The primary purpose of this built-up rim is to protect the hole from being flooded during heavy rains. If the mound is injured, the prairie dog repairs it by scratching up earth around it and packing it down with his nose.

The width of the hole is around 4½ inches in diameter. The tunnel goes down from the surface for about 15 feet, then turns and extends horizontally for about 9 feet. The grass nests are about 11 inches in diameter and 9 inches high, branching off the main part of the tunnel in circular chambers.

The burrows are built in the midst of a food supply or very near to one. The chief source of food is the bunch grass of the plains, but the prairie dog prefers a more succulent diet of vegetation and cultivated crops. When a large colony has eaten bare a surrounding area, and, exposed to predators, is forced to travel some distance for food, the town usually abandons the site and digs new burrows near a fresh supply.

Like other members of the rodent order which live in semi-desert or desert country, the prairie dog can live on little water. A small amount is derived from his diet of grasses, roots, and seeds, but the burrows do not strike water, as has sometimes been supposed. In prairie-dog land, engineers have unsuccessfully driven artesian wells 1000 feet.

The prairie dog is diurnal in habit, usually feeding in the morning and afternoon, and spending the heat of the day in his burrow.

When an enemy is in sight, the spotter gives an alarm note—a piercing whistle—and all the prairie dogs run for their burrows. They characteristically do not enter the burrow at once, but sit or stand at the edge of the hole, barking and chattering and repeating the alarm whistle while the danger is present. Each individual goes down only when the enemy is upon him.

The keen-eyed prairie dog is ever on the alert for the enemy and manages to escape many of them, but the coyote, badger, black-footed ferret, and rattlesnake are most relentless and successful predators. The coyote relies on stalking and concealment, but the badger and ferret go down into the hole. The rattlesnake also invades the burrow, usually in late spring, in search of the young. The snake is equally terrified of the prairie dog, for he lives in fear of being smothered, and a light sprinkling of loose earth will often send him hastily to the surface. If a returning parent finds the snake in his hole, he reportedly barks to attract the attention of his neighbors and together they push earth down into the hole until it is plugged.

The prairie dog is usually ridden with vermin and the tick-borne tularemia is often fatal.

Those of the colder ranges hibernate briefly and erratically, interrupting the winter's sleep periodically to check on weather conditions, coming out when the snow is off the ground.

**Breeding.** The prairie dog has a high reproduction rate, with an average of four, and sometimes six or eight, to a litter. The number of young is variable with the range, as influenced by weather and food. The young are born in late May or early June and mature quickly. By fall, if they have managed to live that long by escaping their numerous natural enemies, they are of adult size.

**Range and Distribution.** The range of the prairie dog is limited to the Great Plains region, from the easternmost fringe of the Mississippi Valley west to the Rocky Mountains, and from Montana and North Dakota as far south as Mexico.

In the case of the prairie dog, climate is a more powerful distributor of his numbers than food. The arid prairies and plains are mostly treeless, with little vegetation other than small shrubs and grasses. The prairie dog prefers succulent foods, as evidenced by the great damage done to crops, but he will not leave the sunshine and dryness. His numbers decrease the nearer he gets to the rich vegetation of the humid Mississippi Valley.

About 1900, however, two pairs were transplanted into Nantucket, and within ten years they numbered in the thousands. A town meeting was finally called in a desperate attempt to rid the island of such constant destruction. The residents then successfully killed off all the prairie dogs on the island.

**Hunting Methods.** The prairie dog of the western plains is a sort of pocket edition of the eastern woodchuck, but he is more gregarious than *monax* and lives in towns with others of his kind. This tiny "sod-poodle" offers a tempting target as he sits on a mound above his burrow and hunters west of the Mississippi River test their rifles on him just as the eastern shooter practices on the 'chuck.

As with the eastern 'chuck, the main idea is to get close enough for a shot, but stalking the prairie dog is a somewhat different proposition. His natural habitat is the open plains and there are no stone fences, hedgerows, or convenient trees to shield the approaching hunter. Furthermore, much of his range is shared by the rattlesnake and attempting to crawl up to him is not recommended.

The best time to hunt for prairie dogs is early morning or late afternoon, as the animals are more active at those times. During the heat of midday the whole village may appear deserted.

While above ground the colony relies on posted sentinels to sound the alarm at approaching danger. Immediately upon hearing the shrill whistle every prairie dog dashes to the mouth of his burrow. Unlike the 'chuck, however, he does not dive from sight but sits erect on the mound and repeats the piercing whistle of alarm and protest. This is the moment for the rifleman to make his shot. The crack of the rifle will likely send the closer animals below ground, but if the hunter remains motionless for a time and is fairly well concealed, a few cautious heads will reappear. If the coast seems clear the dogs will climb on their mounds for a better view and the fun begins again. In large towns they will often dive into their holes as the hunter approaches and come up again when he has passed. Experienced hunters take advantage of this trait and profit by walking boldly through the edge of the town and then turning to pick their targets in the rear.

In some sections the little animals may be approached close enough for the ordinary .22 to be effective, but in areas where they have become wiser and more gun-shy killing them successfully is a job for the longer-range "varmint" rifles.

A scope-sighted rifle is not a *must,* but a good scope is a great advantage for this type of hunting. The tiny animals offer but a small target at best and when the heat waves are dancing over the prairie it is difficult to see them clearly over iron sights. As with 'chuck hunting, a scope with very fine cross-hairs is preferred.

# RABBITS AND HARES

## Rabbits

*Genus Sylvilagus* and *Genus Brachylagus*

Our North American "rabbit" is commonly known under a misnomer. The true European rabbit *(Cuniculus)* is native to southern Europe and northern Africa and has been transplanted to various countries, but not to this continent. The Department of Agriculture has forbidden its importation for fear of its becoming a serious economic pest as in Australia, but a few individuals have illegally brought some European rabbits into this country from Austria. They have proved themselves dangerous pests on Fisher's Island, specifically, and are now scattered throughout various localities in the New England states.

The European rabbit is characterized by burrowing and living in colonies, but our native cottontail *(Sylvilagus)* usually nests above ground in land depressions and is more or less solitary in habit. The Idaho pygmy *(Brachylagus)* is the nearest in form to the European rabbit and can be called a "rabbit" for want of a better name.

The term "rabbit" has also been used to include the jack rabbit and snowshoe rabbit which are hares *(Lepus).*

### COTTONTAIL *Sylvilagus*

**History.** The ubiquitous cottontail ranges throughout this continent and is more hunted, by boy and skilled sportsman alike, than any other North American animal. In spite of the hunter's yearly toll, as well as the high death rate due to numerous natural enemies, and sweeping scourges of disease, the rabbit has escaped extinction largely because of its fecundity. In most species several litters are born each year with about four young to each litter.

In varying degrees, dependent upon their numbers and food supply, the cottontail is considered a pest by farmers and ranchers. Losses suffered are compensated in some measure, however, by the business done in meat, felt, and fur. Modern methods of preparing fur have stimulated successful shearing and dyeing of rabbit fur ("coney") to the likeness of beaver, ermine, chinchilla, etc.

In almost all areas the cottontail is influenced by a "rabbit cycle." This cycle is a period of about ten years during which time there is a gradual rise in rabbit population to a peak of *over*abundance, followed by a sharp decline to near-extinction, lasting a year or two. One of the controlling factors in this rise and fall is a disease recently identified as tularemia. Other animals carry this disease, and often it is passed from one to another as well as to man by the infected deer fly and tick.

If a rabbit is infected, it appears to be in a stupor, is sluggish, and does not run when the hunter approaches. If an animal is found in that condition, it should be killed and not touched. Once the animal is killed, the disease also can be detected by the yellowish or whitish flecks on the liver and spleen. Even though the disease is not detected, if an infected animal is thoroughly cooked, the germ is rendered harmless.

Since the germ is transmissible to human beings, primarily through open cuts, the hunter is advised to wear gloves while dressing the carcass and to wash his hands thoroughly afterward.

**Identification.** The distinctive characteristic of the cottontail is, as the name implies, his short, bushy tail. It is elevated when he runs and shows white on the underside. It is this feature which distinguishes him throughout the species.

Both sexes of the cottontail are colored alike in brown coats with white undersides. The size of the animal varies according to the food supply of each locale, but he weighs from 2 to 3 pounds and averages about 13 inches in length. His ears are about 3 inches long. He has the gnawing teeth typical of the rodent family.

**Characteristics.** The cottontail is very timid and is easily frightened into flight. His first swift spurt is not sustained, however, for he relies on hiding rather than running. When closely pursued, he will often run into the abandoned hole of a woodchuck, prairie dog, or badger. Usually the hole in which the cottontail is found is not one of his own making since he does not characteristically burrow. When he picks a hiding place to rest in, it usually has two exits, to observe an approach of the enemy and to make sure of a getaway.

When terrorized, the adult often squeals. Also, when alarmed, he will commonly beat out a warning to others in the neighborhood by thumping on the ground with his hind feet.

His enemies are numerous and millions are killed each year by hunters and predators. His natural enemies are the owl, fox, brown rat, hawk, coyote, and other small carnivores to which he is the chief food supply. His greatest and least-mentioned enemy is the common house cat, which is a skilled and stealthy stalker, usually prowling through the woods at night.

Of his senses his eyesight is the best. His eyes are bulging, allowing him to see to the front, to both sides, and partially to the rear without changing position.

In summer he feeds primarily on herbs, short shrubs and his favorite clover. Since he does not hibernate like the woodchuck, he must seek winter food, which is usually the bark and twigs of low trees and shrubs.

**Breeding.** The prolific nature of the rabbit has been mentioned. Breeding begins at about six months and continues at the rate of several litters per year with an average of four young to a litter until

Pennsylvania Game Commission.
PLATE I. The Cottontail, most sought-after game in the United States.

the rabbit dies at about seven years of age. The gestation period averages 28 days.

The number of young produced is relative to the state of abundance or scarcity in the "cycle." Seven young are often dropped at the peak of a cycle abundance, three offspring are common in the low point of population.

In the more southerly ranges young are born all during the year, but in northerly ranges there are seldom any young in the winter.

The young are dropped naked and blind into a nest which is built in a depression in the ground. It is often lined with the fur of the mother. The doe suckles her litter, and after a few days they have grown a protective fur and are strong enough to leave the nest in her company. The doe often moves them about by picking them up by the neck as a cat does kittens.

The mother casts off her innate timidity when her young are threatened. She is a courageous protector and will place herself between them and larger animals. She has been known to ward off and chase away a marauding weasel.

**Range and Distribution.** The cottontail has the widest range of any American rabbit. He inhabits all types of country from the Atlantic to the Pacific, from Canada to South America.

There are three distinguishable groups: (1) The Eastern cottontail ranging from Florida north to the New England states; (2) the Rocky Mountain group; and (3) the Western cottontail of the Pacific coast.

The cottontail prefers the cultivated areas, especially where there are farms and orchards, but he also thrives on the desert lands of southern California. He usually travels over a network of paths which can be readily detected.

## BRUSH RABBIT *Sylvilagus bachmani*

The brush rabbit is of the same genus as the cottontail but does not have the white underside of the tail characteristic of the cottontail species. He is typically small in size, with a small tail and short legs. His coat is even and dark.

The habits of the brush rabbit closely resemble those of the cottontail, but, as his name denotes, he is a lover of the brush and shies from open country altogether.

## SWAMP RABBIT or MARSH RABBIT

*Sylvilagus palustris*

The swamp rabbit is similar to the cottontail, but also lacks the white underside of the tail which identifies the cottontail. He has a short tail and has a dark pelage. He is small with slender legs.

He is reportedly the only rabbit in the world which lives in and along the margins of water. He inhabits the swamp areas, and near-by higher ground, of the southeastern United States, and is found in large numbers in south and western Florida. He is distinguished by the webbing of his hind feet which makes him a good swimmer. To escape pursuit he will head for the water and lie totally submerged except for his nose.

## IDAHO PYGMY RABBIT

*Brachylagus idahoensis*

The Idaho pygmy rabbit, smallest of the North American rabbits, resembles a midget cottontail in form. Despite the lack of the distinguishing tail, many confused the Idaho pygmy with a baby cottontail primarily because so few were seen. The rarity proved to be a lack of knowledge of where to find them, not a scarcity in numbers.

He varies between 10 and 12 inches in length. His ears are short and wide and he has a short tail.

He differs from the cottontail in assuming a distinct seasonal change of coloring. In summer his coat is a brownish-gray, but in winter it varies to a wine color. Both colors are protective and blend with his peculiar habitat in the sagebrush plains. He creeps with ratlike closeness to the ground, not bounding like the cottontail. His habits are much like those of the cottontail. He feeds on various plants and grass and the leaves of shrubs. His range is very confined and is limited to the area where California, Nevada, and Oregon meet, extending into the southern part of Idaho. His long pelage keeps him warm in Nevada, where he inhabits areas 7000 feet above sea level.

**Hunting Methods.** Number One position among popular North American small game goes to the cottontail rabbit, and it is unlikely that any runner-up will ever oust him from that place. Every game species has its loyal followers, but it is the lowly bunny who furnishes more gunning each year than most of the other game combined. He may not be as sporting an opponent as the wilier and faster-moving upland game, or the speedy ducks, but he can and does provide both sport and food to millions of hunters annually.

The real reason for his popularity, aside from his being a very tasty dish, is that he is available. From Maine to Florida, from the Atlantic to the Pacific, he is found in virtually every one of the United States and parts of southern Canada. Unlike most other species he suffers not at all from the encroachments of civilization; in fact, he benefits thereby and is as much at home in a suburban garden as a distant swamp. He is here, there, and everywhere a ready quarry for the scattergun enthusiast.

Some states do not even class him as a game animal; in those that do the open season is a long one and a hunter may go after rabbits when there is no other game which he may legally pursue. Grouse may disappear from favorite covers; the woodcock flight is uncertain and of short duration; pheasant shooting is spotty and nonexistent in many localities; the duck season becomes shorter and the birds fewer with the passing years; but the prolific cottontail continues to thrive and prosper all over the country.

No expensive paraphernalia is required for the sport of rabbit hunting. A gun, some shells—and usually a hunting license—are all that are necessary in the way of equipment. The confirmed rabbit hunter needs no advice regarding the proper clothing but the tyro may profit by the following suggestions: In most sections of the country good bunny hunting comes after the first frost and continues right on through the winter. There will be mild days of Indian summer when the lightest of clothing will seem too warm, and there will be days of bitter cold when the right mitten is removed only when it is time to shoot. The amount of clothing and its protective warmth will be dictated by the thermometer, but regardless of what is worn the outer garments should be resistant to briars.

The cottontail is keenly aware of his many natural enemies and for protection against them he relies chiefly on patches of briars, tangled weeds, underbrush, and dense thorny growths which are difficult to penetrate. Such cover will make shreds of a sweater in no time at all and is destructive to all soft fabrics. The ordinary hunting coat, made of tough drill or some other closely woven fabric, is ideal. Heavy cotton overalls or dungarees serve to cover the legs, but a pair of hunting pants or breeches with special reinforcement in front will be more comfortable because they prevent scratches from the briars. Since rabbit hunting usually entails a lot of walking it is well to wear a good grade of heavy wool socks and comfortable shoes or boots. Some hunters make a practice of wearing a glove on the left hand even in warm weather because it saves the hand from a lot of nasty scratches when fending the way through cover. The rest of the clothing problem is a matter of individual taste.

The cottontail has been killed with everything from a slingshot to a high-powered rifle. Many a budding hunter has tried out his first mail-order gun on a convenient bunny, and each season an army of eager gunners sallies forth with a varied assortment of leadslingers in search of rabbit stew. It is not within the province of this section to deal with the question of the proper gun for the purpose. Any problem regarding that matter will be answered fully in the section on firearms. The choice of a gun is entirely up to the individual shooter. The preferred weapon, and the one which puts meat on the table most regularly, however, is the shotgun.

Gauge is not very important. The majority of hunters prefer a 12 gauge, probably because the majority of hunters own but one gun—but the smaller gauges can be just as deadly when properly aimed. It is well to bear in mind that a rabbit can carry a lot of lead unless hit in a vital spot, and, like any other animal or bird, he is entitled to a quick, humane death. Any shotgun which will kill cleanly at reasonable ranges is suitable for the job.

Although the rifle is generally used in hunting the larger hares and jack rabbits, it is not recommended for bunny shooting. Br'er Rabbit has a habit of "freezing" in hopes he will not be seen—and most of the time he isn't—but when he decides to go, his bobbing, twisting getaway is fast and he offers a slim target to the rifleman. There is another angle regarding the use of a rifle for rabbit shooting that deserves some consideration. Good cottontail hunting is frequently found in fairly well-settled communities where the distance between houses and farms is not great. The printed warning on a box of .22 cartridges that they are dangerous at a mile is no myth. The possible danger involved is obvious. Even a .22-caliber bullet has a nasty way of ricocheting at weird angles from a rock, a tree branch, or frozen ground, and it can do a lot of damage when it hits. Among sportsmen, of course, the chief argument against the use of the rifle is that it can be employed only to pot sitting bunnies—which hardly seems like giving them a fair break.

Perhaps one of the greatest charms about rabbit hunting is that there are no hard and fast rules. Each hunter may develop his own technique as he gains experience. The cottontail is found in so many different places and types of cover that certain sections use methods which are more or less local in character. Unfortunately for the rabbit, however, he follows much the same general pattern of behavior no matter where he is found, and so some knowledge of his habits will help in hunting him anywhere.

The cottontail does a lot of aimless wandering in his search for food but in his favorite cover he uses the same trails day in and day out until they become well defined and obvious to even the unpracticed eye. When put to flight he may circle in any direction but as soon as possible he will get onto one of these favorite runways. The wise hunter takes up his position where two or more of these paths converge, while his companion or a dog works the cover, for it is reasonably certain that any rabbits in the vicinity will eventually come loping along that way.

Typical rabbit cover embraces a wide variety of different terrain. Patches of thick brush with open spaces in between are usually productive. Hedgerows, swamps and swales, sassafras thickets, briar clumps, old orchards, weedy patches, line fences, and open fields near wooded areas all harbor cottontails. Clumps of juniper, evergreens, and cedar swamps are favored winter hangouts in the northern states. Any place that has a good growth of underbrush and vines is likely to be home to one or more bunnies. All piles of brush should be thoroughly trodden and kicked in passing, for they are the favorite hiding places of the cottontail.

Rabbit hunting reaches its peak as a sport when one or more dogs are used, but the time-worn custom of "walking 'em up" is still popular with millions of hunters who have no dogs. Two or three gunners make an ideal combination both from the standpoint of companionship and the fact that one man is likely to put out rabbits for the others. However, a lone hunter can bag rabbits successfully and have a lot of sport in doing it. The quest for cottontails is, or should be, a leisurely procedure. The old axiom that haste makes waste is especially true in this game, and he who burns up the miles is not likely to see many rabbits. Br'er Rabbit relies on two stratagems for survival. One is absolute immobility, and the other is headlong flight. He generally tries the former before he resorts to the latter. Crouched in a clump of dried grass, or among the brown leaves, he flattens his body, lays back his ears, and hopes to remain unnoticed. As a rule he blends so well with his surroundings that it takes a keen eye indeed to detect him. His large dark eyes are the only giveaway to his otherwise excellent camouflage. When thus concealed he will almost allow himself to be stepped on before getting under way. The fast-moving hunter passes many rabbits unknowingly in the course of a day afield. Now the bunny, like most animals, believes himself invisible as long as the hunter keeps moving rapidly along. Approach him slowly, however, or stop in his vicinity and he becomes unnerved and bolts from his hiding. It is an excellent practice in rabbit hunting as well as when after other game to pause briefly after every few steps. Many a well-concealed animal or game bird has been urged into giving away his whereabouts simply because he thought the motionless hunter had spotted him.

In heavily matted undergrowth the rabbit will often skulk along unless actually forced into the open. This is especially true of swamp rabbits and those found in the heavy swale grass. Of course with a dog this maneuver is of no avail, but they often outwit the gunner alone.

There are some who scoff at the rabbit as being a target unworthy of their skill. Perhaps they have yet to hunt him in the proper cover. It is true that a cottontail bounding across an open field presents little difficulty, but the same bunny in close cover becomes a highly elusive target. He usually leaves his hiding place as though jet-propelled and flaunts his powderpuff tail for a matter of seconds before he is lost to sight. Where the cleared spaces between covers are small he can leap from one shelter to another with amazing speed. It takes fast thinking, fast shooting, and excellent co-ordination to hit him under these conditions. Some gunners hold their fire if their quarry disappears, but the experienced rabbit shooter estimates about where the rabbit should be and fires into the cover, often with the desired effect.

Some states ban rabbit hunting when there is snow on the ground but in those places where it is permissible it is good sport. It has been noted that the cottontail is a wanderer; the tracks he makes during the night may be a veritable maze, but they are a definite indication of his presence in the vicinity and encourage the search for their maker. The story is told of a squaw who handed a very young buck his tiny bow and arrows, pointed to a rabbit track, and said, "At end of track is your breakfast." And so it is with winter hunting. One has only to follow the telltale sign and sooner or later there will be fried rabbit for supper—or a miss.

During severe storms and periods of bad weather rabbits go underground, or seek shelter in hollow tree roots, or beneath overhanging banks. They emerge from these places as soon as the weather clears, and that is the best time to hunt them. The cottontail is fond of comfort and during the cold, windy season he is most likely to be found on the lee side of a hill. On sunny days in winter he will remain in the open spots where he can absorb all the warmth possible.

The sport of cottontail hunting really reaches its zenith with a dog. Three breeds of hounds are commonly used for this purpose, namely, the beagle, the basset, and the dachshund. More recently the springer spaniel has also become popular. Each breed has its loyal adherents and it is a matter of personal choice. The respective merits of each are covered at length in the section on hunting dogs and so only their general qualifications will be mentioned here. Numerically the beagle hound is the most popular, but any of the breeds mentioned is admirably suited for rabbit hunting.

The ideal rabbit dog must possess certain characteristics in order to meet the requirements peculiar to his job. First in importance, in the case of a hound, is a good nose; for a hound should run rabbits by scent only. He must be able to pick up a cold trail and puzzle out the right track from the welter of haphazard cross trails left by a feeding bunny. He must be determined on the trail but not too fast. A fast-running dog will crowd his quarry so much that the rabbit either seeks refuge in a hole or is too close to the dog to permit safe shooting. The dog should be small in stature to work in the tangled cover through which the rabbit will lead him. A moderately slow dog with a merry tongue keeps the rabbit moving but does not frighten him unduly.

A rabbit, if not pressed, will bound along at what he considers a safe distance ahead of the dog and may even stop for brief rests while the hound patiently works out the scent track. Though he may start out on a straight line he does not hold such a course for long. Within a hundred yards or less he usually swings to the right or left and begins to circle back to the spot where he was originally put up. This trait works to the advantage of the knowing hunter, who has only to station himself on a hummock, stump, or some other elevation where he can obtain a clear view of his surroundings and await the arrival of Br'er Rabbit.

The hound music following the course taken by the rabbit tells the gunner from which quarter his quarry is likely to arrive and as the sound of the hound gets closer he knows the bunny is not far ahead of it. The voice of the hound changes by degrees from the tentative *"yip"* when he first finds a trail to an excited, eager baying when the trail gets warm. Rare indeed is the hunter whose pulse fails to quicken in response to the song of his dog on a hot trail. Some hunters declare that two hounds work better than one, but that seems to be a matter of personal opinion.

The springer spaniel flushes the rabbit out of his cover and immediately gives chase. The cottontail has little trouble in keeping well ahead of the dog, although he may have to run somewhat faster than he would from a hound. When a well-placed shot up-ends the rabbit the springer completes his job by retrieving the game.

The possibility of infection from rabbits having tularemia (rabbit fever) cannot be overlooked. Active, healthy-appearing rabbits seldom are suffering from this disease but it is a wise precaution to treat all of them as though they were until certain. Hunters invariably have scratches on their hands and it is through these tiny breaks in the skin that the germ enters the bloodstream. The use of gloves when cleaning and skinning a bunny and thoroughly washing the hands thereafter is sufficient protection.

All rabbits should be cleaned and the head removed as soon as possible after shooting but should not be skinned until ready to cook. Shot usually penetrate the viscera and allow the juices to escape into the body cavity; these will ruin the meat if left too long. A rabbit shot in the lungs will bleed readily when freshly killed but is hard to clean when cold. Caution should be taken to prevent the dog from eating rabbit entrails because they often contain tapeworms which will then infest him.

# Hares

*Genus Lepus*

**History.** The history of the hares is much the same as that of the rabbits. They have suffered a comparable loss from predators and hunters but revived their numbers because of the prolific rate of breeding. The jack rabbit and snowshoe rabbit also are victims of tularemia, and the effect of this plague on the northerly-ranging snowshoe rabbit is particularly serious. The resultant scarcity of rabbits sets off a cycle in other carnivores which depend on the small animal as a chief supply of food.

The jack rabbit is perhaps a more dangerous pest, particularly in the Southwest, than any other member of the rabbit or hare family, but, like the rabbit, the hare compensates for some of these losses because its fur is used in felt and the imitation of more valuable furs.

Pennsylvania Game Commission.

PLATE II. Varying Hare or Snowshoe Rabbit.

## SNOWSHOE RABBIT (Varying Hare)

*Lepus americanus*

The snowshoe "rabbit," also called "varying hare," has a distinctive seasonal variation in pelage. Both sexes have two protective seasonal pelages; one is brownish for summer, and the other white for winter. The sub-species *"washingtoni"* is the exception, having a dark brown coat in winter.

The snowshoe is a hare of medium size, about 19 inches long, weighing from 3 to 4 pounds. Neither his ears nor his hind legs are as long as those of the jack rabbit, but he is differentiated from the cottontail by his larger size, longer hind legs, and large hind feet.

He inhabits areas of deep snows and harsh winters, but does not hibernate. He is well adapted to such a climate because of his heavy, thick fur—pure white in winter except for dark-tipped ears. It is a natural camouflage from his enemies, the owl, coyote, hawk, lynx, etc. He does not typically hole up when pursued, and usually is able to escape an enemy by running on top of soft snow. He can travel without difficulty where other animals flounder because his long-haired, broad feet spread, providing the natural snowshoes which give him his name.

Like the cottontail, he sends an alarm to others by beating his feet on the ground. When greatly excited or frightened he often makes a strident squealing noise.

He feeds primarily on green plants and clover in the summer, and on willow bark and twigs in the winter. As the snow deepens, he is raised higher to a fresh source of buds and bark, and in some areas competes with the deer and moose for the food supply.

The snowshoe is a woods hare. He inhabits the northern part of North America, and during the peak of a cycle there are millions in Alaska. From Prince William Sound he ranges north to the spruce forests. There are some rabbits scattered along the southeastern mainland of Alaska and in 1934 he was introduced into the Kodiak-Afognak Island group.

The mating period is about March or April, and four to six leverets form the average litter. The gestation period is 30 days. This northerly hare usually rests in "forms" in the snow, but in the warmer mating season makes an open nest of leaves. The doe usually drops only one litter a year, but in times of plenty commonly has two litters, with the second one coming later in the summer, and producing about eight young each time. In times of scarcity and poor health the doe drops about two leverets.

A distinguishing characteristic between the hare and the rabbit is that the young of the rabbit are born naked and blind, while those of the hare are born fully-furred with their eyes open. The young hares lose their brownish-gray coat and take on a white one in the season of the first snows.

## JACK RABBITS

All the jack rabbits are large hares and heavy-bodied, with long ears and long hind legs.

They are shy and timid and crouch quiet and still in their "forms" during most of the daytime with their ears and tail held close to the body.

They depend partly on protective camouflage and partly on their running speed to escape their enemies. They are paced second only to the antelope among North American animals, and the greyhound is the only dog which can overtake them. They often cover from 12 to 15 feet with each leap. Intermittently, they take great leaps into the air to observe their progress and locate the enemy, using their keen sight and hearing. They are capable of leaping as high as 6 feet. They also are skilled in doubling back on their own tracks, and often jump wide of the path into a hiding place to throw off the pursuer.

Most of the jack rabbits are gregarious, living together in groups averaging about 15.

Their favorite food is alfalfa and young fruit trees, but they eat any kind of vegetable matter as well as bark and the leaves of shrubs and cactus. When there is a food shortage, they sometimes make daily food migrations, often traveling as far as 10 miles, and in some sections, they make seasonal migrations. In the Southwest thousands of black-tailed jack rabbits have been reported gathered in a concentrated area of fruit trees. The damage done by jack rabbits to alfalfa fields, fruit orchards, grain supplies, and winter haystacks makes up the greatest economic losses. The ranchers and farmers cannot depend on the natural animal enemies of the jack rabbits to keep the numbers controlled, and they often must resort to gun and poison.

Among their natural enemies are the wolf, owl, eagle, and coyote.

The jack rabbits have a wide range and are distributed throughout the western plains of the United States and extend from Canada south into Mexico. Some species are found in the mountains.

In the mating season the jack hares often fight for a female. They stand upright and hit each other harmless blows for a brief period, often pausing to eat between rounds.

The number of litters born to the hares is dependent upon the climate of each range. The average is two a year, but in the northerly ranges usually only one is produced. In the southerly ranges there are as many as three and sometimes four. The gestation period is 30 days, and the doe starts producing young before she is a year old.

As with all hares, the young are born furred, and with their eyes open. The nest is a simple opening, usually made in dense brush. It is used for a brief time, since the young of hares are more sturdy than those of cottontails. In about five weeks they are weaned and independent of the doe, which is a bold fighter in defense of her young.

## WHITE-SIDED JACK RABBIT *Lepus alleni*

## WHITE-TAILED JACK RABBIT *Lepus tounsendi*

The white-sided jack rabbit is the most striking of the North American hares. His sides are white from shoulder to rump. When he is running, and the sun is reflected upon his showy side, it makes a perfect target.

Among the various sub-species is the antelope jack rabbit, one of the largest and fastest of the hares. He averages 24 inches in length and ten pounds in weight, and is called "burro" and "donkey" jack rabbit because of his tremendous ears which often are 8 or 9 inches long and 3 inches wide. His more common name of "antelope" hare is descriptive of his running speed, which approaches that of the antelope. The white-tailed jack rabbit ranges the desert areas of Mexico and southern Arizona. He is identified by his flashy white tail. Some varieties share the characteristic common to other hares of the sub-genus *lepus* (snowshoe rabbit,

N. Y. Zoological Society.

PLATE III. Jack Rabbit.

arctic hare) of adopting a white winter pelage in the areas where there are severe winters.

He is larger than the blacktail rabbit and a fast runner, making 12- to 20-foot leaps.

## BLACK-TAILED JACK RABBIT *Lepus californicus*

The range of the black-tailed jack rabbit varies from the prairies and open plains to mountain heights up to 10,000 and 12,000 feet in the Sierra Nevada and the Rocky Mountains.

The black-tailed jack rabbit is distinguished, as his name denotes, by his tail which is black above. He is large, averaging 23 inches long. He abounds on the plains of the West and is seen by the hundreds during the times of abundance. He is the most numerous and widely distributed of the hares.

## ARCTIC HARE *Lepus arcticus*

The husky arctic hare is the largest of all the American hares. An average length is 24 inches, and some weigh as much as 12 pounds. He is equipped with tough claws to dig through the crusted snow for food.

A seasonal change of pelage occurs; in summer it is brownish-gray, and in winter is all white except for black-tipped ears. In winter his thick, puffy coat is so like the snow that he is most difficult to detect, even when running. Often it is only the black-tipped ears, which appear to be moving by themselves, that give him away.

The lynx, fox, weasel, and great snowy owl depend on him as a main source of food. He has successfully defended himself from a pursuing owl by hitting it a hard blow with his forefeet, and has been known to send an owl sprawling with a thrust of his hind feet.

The arctic hare is not numerous in any area, but his range is primarily the arctic region, north of the spruce growth. He ranges from the Alaskan Peninsula north to the Arctic along the Bering Sea coast.

He is normally solitary but in the mating season (in April or May) the hares band in groups of 20 or more. After a gestation period of 30 days, five to seven leverets are dropped in some concealing brush. In less than a month the band has dissolved.

**Hunting Methods—Snowshoe Rabbit (Varying Hare).** The snowshoe rabbit, or varying hare—erroneously called jack rabbit by the natives in some regions—is a big hare of the north country. He is a strange paradox of stupidity and sagacity. Often he will squat under a bush or log until he is literally kicked out, but put a hound on his trail and he becomes one of the most artful of dodgers. Normally he displays little concern over a hunter who moves quietly through the woods. His penchant for sitting makes him an excellent target for the archer and hunting him with the longbow is becoming increasingly popular.

Despite his protective white winter coat he is not too difficult to spot on the snow; the black-tipped ears and the large shoe-button eyes are readily visible. When the first snow lies in patches on the brown earth and leaves he is just changing to his winter overcoat and is partly white, partly brown, a condition which often makes him easier to see. Some years when the snow is late in arriving he has already donned his white coat and is extremely conspicuous.

The best hunting is generally in fir or cedar swamps, and the thicker the growth the more the snowshoe seems to prefer it. He often displays a tendency to slip quietly through the tangled thickets like a wraith. The best time to hunt him, as expressed by one old-timer, is—whenever you can get an opportunity—from autumn through midwinter. A great many hunters prefer the latter season when the trees are mantled in a heavy blanket of snow and the thickets stand out bare and dark against the stark white background.

It is well to choose a dull, overcast day, and if a few snowflakes are tumbling down so much the better. The going will be tough and it is advisable to wear snowshoes. The big hare is already equipped with his and he can skim over the light snow almost as well as though it were firm ground.

Still hunting, or merely walking through the woods hoping for a pot shot, has its attractions, and is the sport for the longbow fan. The real thrill, however, comes when a hound or two is turned loose on the trail. The snowshoe then becomes a quarry to test the mettle of dogs and man. He is fast and practically tireless. He may run a mile or more on his first circle and then begin all over without a pause for breath.

Often he will lead the dogs out of hearing for a time, and if the cover is thick and the hounds have the stamina to stay with him he may keep ahead of them for hours before coming within range of the gun. The hunter tries to determine from the baying of the dogs what course the hare is taking, and lucky is the man whose guess is accurate. The usual procedure is to get to an open spot or clearing where there is as much visibility as possible and hope that the hare will come that way. He exhibits an uncanny judgment in passing just out of range from where the hunter is standing or else slipping silently past to the rear.

Many hunters, experienced at this game, believe that the beagle hound is inadequate for the job. In deep snow the short-legged dogs flounder pitifully and it is grueling punishment at best. Nevertheless, a good beagle that is not too short in the legs can deliver a wonderful performance. Long-legged dogs of the foxhound, or cross-bred, variety have an advantage. A hound with a fighting heart will stay on the trail to the end but he is up against fierce odds because his quarry is so much better equipped for running over the snow.

A coon will eventually tree; the cottontail, or even the fox, will go underground if tired or hard pressed; but not the snowshoe. He runs as long as there is breath in his body. A running hare is a target for the shotgun, and usually at long ranges. He is able to carry considerable lead and "sixes" are a good load.

**Jack Rabbit.** The jack rabbit does not rate very high as a game animal and his flesh is far from being a delicacy, but he furnishes some sporty shooting at times. Doubtless young Indian braves practiced their marksmanship on him, and since the white man introduced firearms to the West he has been shot at with everything that would burn powder. He *can* be killed with a shotgun but at the present time it is usually difficult to get within that range except in very remote sections. Here is a sport made to order for the rifle addict. Running jacks are an elusive target and the man who can score on them consistently has every right to be vain about his ability. If he serves no other purpose, the jack furnishes the best possible practice for running shots at more important game.

Although by no means as plentiful as in former years, the jack rabbit still abounds in many sections west of the Mississippi River and is a familiar sight on the western plains. Civilization has crowded many of them out of their open range and back into the brush country. Up in the hills they can be hunted with hounds in the same manner as the varying hare.

In the hands of an expert, or where the cover is such as to permit short ranges, jacks can be killed with a .22 but something a bit more powerful is generally preferred. Any of the so-called varmint rifles with high velocity and low trajectory are satisfactory for the purpose of hunting these rangy, leaping animals. A wide variety of shots will be offered

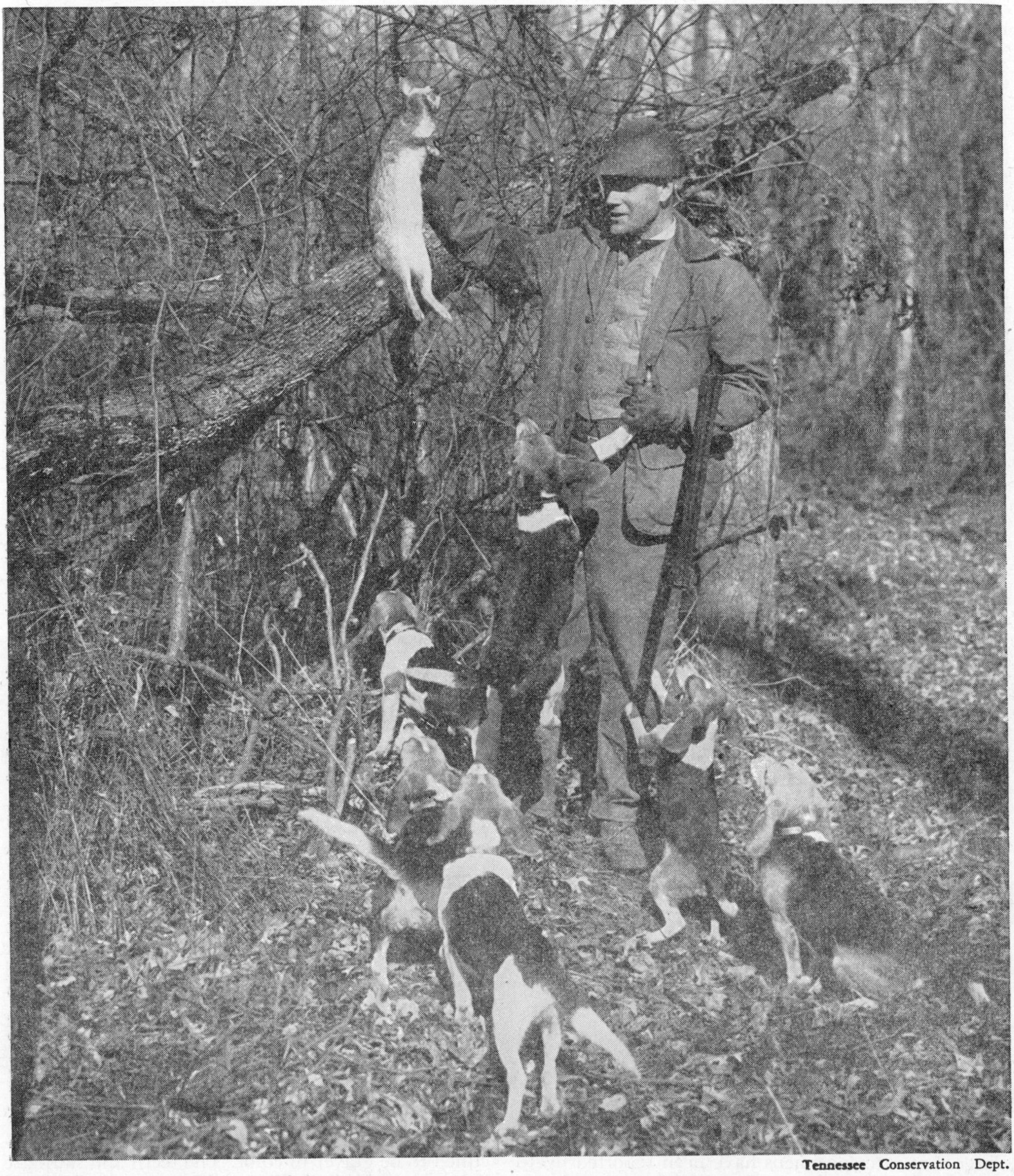

Tennessee Conservation Dept.

PLATE IV. Hunting rabbits with good beagles is real sport.

in a day's hunting and the rifleman can select his own type of shooting. By far the most sporting, of course, is to try potting a jack while he is en route for other parts under a full head of steam. The hunter who likes to peer through a scope for some fine and far off shooting may also have his innings, for the jack has an insatiable curiosity which prompts him to stop when he thinks he is safe and sit up for a look-see. That is the time to figure windage and elevation and center the cross-hairs on his chest.

The jack rabbit can run rings around most of the hounds and except in some of the hill country he does not offer much in the way of sport with the long-eared trailers. In open country he is sometimes hunted with greyhounds—the only dog he cannot outrun—and even then it usually takes two of them to head him off and make the kill.

Few sportsmen would go out of their way to hunt jack rabbits deliberately, but as incidental targets they furnish fun and excitement. There need be no compunction about killing these animals because they are everywhere rated as pests and do considerable damage in cultivated areas.

# RACCOON

*Procyon lotor lotor*

Common Names: Coon, Ringtail.

**History.** The raccoon is another animal whose early history is obscure because he was native to this country long before any white men arrived. The Algonquin Indians called him *arakun,* from their word *arakunem,* meaning, literally, "he scratches with his hands." Considering how much the coon's forepaws resemble tiny hands, the name was well chosen. Our "raccoon" was the white man's attempted spelling of the Indian word. Popular usage soon shortened this to the more familiar "coon."

The scientific name *lotor*—meaning "a washer"—sprang from the early belief that raccoons always washed their food before eating it.

There are some who claim that coon meat is very palatable, but Ringtail has always been chiefly valued for his pelt. Pioneer woodsmen found that a single skin made an excellent head covering, and a coonskin cap became an identifying mark of a frontiersman. While never of great value as compared to many other skins, the pelt of the raccoon is used in a variety of ways and thousands are trapped each season. Natural coonskin coats were very popular at one period, especially in collegiate circles, but the fur is commonly dyed and marketed under various other names.

**Identification.** The coon is a medium-sized animal with rather short legs and a bushy tail. His long, thick fur coat makes him appear more stocky than he really is. The color varies rather widely from grayish-brown or grayish-black to a dull yellowish-gray. Some specimens are very dark. The hair is usually darker along the back and many of the guard hairs are black tipped, thus giving the coat a grizzled appearance. The under parts are dull gray or slightly yellowish and the feet are white or nearly so. The tail is about one-half the length of the body and is banded with four to six black or dark brown rings which are not clearly defined on the underside.

The face is lighter in tone than the rest of the body, except for a black streak on the forehead. The most outstanding marking is a well-defined black mask extending from the eyes to around both cheeks. The muzzle is slender and the prominent, rather pointed ears add the final touch to the appearance of inquisitiveness so characteristic of the coon.

The weight of raccoons seems to vary as much as their coloring. They commonly weigh from 15 to 18 pounds. Coons of 22 to 24 pounds are considered large, but rare specimens have been reported up to 50 pounds.

There are a number of sub-species sufficiently different in size and appearance to warrant separate mention here:

### FLORIDA RACCOON *Procyon lotor elucus*

This animal is similar in general appearance to the common type but not so large. However, the limbs are longer so that when on all fours the animal appears to stand higher than a normal coon. The feet are larger and the ears less pointed than in most types. The coat is inclined to be more yellowish in color and there is a distinct patch on the shoulder which in some specimens is nearly orange, or rufous. The fur is short and rather harsh in texture. This species commonly weighs from 10 to 15 pounds. They are found from the south-central part of Georgia and West Florida down to the Keys.

### UPPER MISSISSIPPI VALLEY RACCOON *Procyon lotor hirtus*

This specimen, found chiefly in Wisconsin and the northern peninsula of Michigan, is the largest and darkest of all the eastern coons. *Hirtus* often attains a weight of 30 pounds, and his long, soft fur makes his pelt more valuable than those of most of his cousins.

### ALABAMA RACCOON *Procyon lotor varius*

*Varius* is similar to the common raccoon but not so large. His fur is shorter and usually paler in color. He ranges from western North Carolina and western Georgia to western Kentucky, Tennessee, Alabama, and Mississippi.

### ST. SIMON ISLAND RACCOON *Procyon lotor litoreus*

This type closely resembles the Florida coon, but the pelage is shorter and rather more bristly. Characteristic is the heavier cranial structure and the heavier teeth than either the common *Lotor* or *Elucus.* As the name implies, such coons are typical of St. Simon Island, Glynn County, Georgia, although they range the coastal islands of Georgia, southern South Carolina, and the adjacent mainlands.

### HILTON HEAD ISLAND RACCOON *Procyon lotor solutus*

This is a small raccoon similar to *Litoreus* but inclined to be grayer in color. The teeth and skull are lighter in structure. These differences are believed partly due to an isolated habitat. The range of *Litoreus* surrounds that of *Solutus* but the latter is found only on Hilton Head Island, Beaufort County, South Carolina, and is barred from the mainland by a wide, deep channel.

Some additional sub-species are found along a chain of "keys" bordering the southwest coast of Florida—known as the 10,000 Islands—and on a series of islands from Biscayne Bay to Key West (commonly called the Florida Keys). These raccoons are notable results of isolation and the exposed conditions under which they live. Such conditions have resulted in producing well-marked types which are below natural size and development as the result of a near-starvation diet. The following four types are found in this region:

## CHOKOLOSKEE RACCOON

*Procyon lotor marinus*

These animals are a small race, dull gray in color and weighing about 8 pounds. The skull is very light and more depressed in the frontal region. The cheek teeth are larger than usual. These animals are restricted to the keys of the 10,000 Islands. Since many of these keys are completely covered at high tide, it is presumed that the coons take refuge on the mangrove roots.

Pennsylvania Game Commission.

PLATE I. Raccoons in a Warm Home.

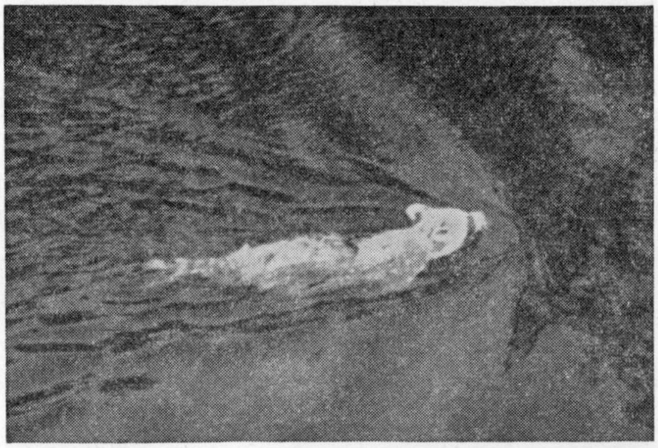

Gene Letourneau, Waterville, Me.
PLATE II. A coon in the water spells trouble for dogs.

## MATECUMBE RACCOON

*Procyon lotor inesperatus*

This is a type similar in color and weight to *Elucus* of the mainland but which has a smaller skull with the frontal area much depressed. The hind feet are notably smaller than other species. These coons inhabit a group of islands beginning with Virginia and Biscayne Bay Keys on the north side of the entrance to Biscayne Bay and ranging south to the southern point of lower Matecumbe Bay.

## KEY VACA RACCOON

*Procyon lotor auspicatus*

This is the smallest raccoon found in the Florida Keys. This type weighs only 5 to 6 pounds. It is somewhat like *Marinus* in appearance except that the upper parts are grayer. The range is restricted to Key Vaca and the keys in that immediate vicinity.

## TORCH KEY RACCOON

*Procyon lotor incautus*

This is the lightest in color of all the key raccoons. The top and sides of the head are nearly white and the black mask is smaller and less distinct—in some specimens almost nonexistent. The coat has a worn appearance and is generally either a dingy white or dirty yellowish color. The range of this type is restricted to the keys of the Big Pine Group, from Big Pine Key to Key West.

**Characteristics.** Probably the outstanding characteristic of *Lotor* is his insatiable curiosity. He is particularly attracted by bright and shiny objects, such as colored stones, bits of glass, bright tin, or almost anything which reflects light. Trappers aware of this trait often use it to their advantage by placing a piece of bright metal on the pan of the trap in lieu of bait.

Raccoons are expert climbers and have five strong toes on both fore and hind feet to aid in this purpose. Being *Plantigrades,* or "sole walkers," the soles of the hind feet are naked. Like the squirrel, they can descend from a tree either head or tail first but generally climb down catlike in the latter position.

Home, to a raccoon, is usually a hollow tree although at times he may use a large fissure in a cliff, or a small cave as a den site. If hard pressed he has been known to use a woodchuck hole as a sanctuary.

Coons are nocturnal in habits and are seldom seen during the daytime. Occasionally one may be spotted in the early morning on his way to a tree den after a night of foraging. They are extremely wary and well versed in the art of eluding pursuit. Their chief enemy is man and his dog, and a wise old coon has many tricks for throwing a pack of hounds off his trail. Chief among his tactics is the practice of wading for some distance in shallow water to destroy the scent. If finally overtaken by a pack of hounds he climbs a tree rather than take refuge in the ground and the sound of the dogs barking "treed" is sweet music to the ears of a coon hunter. A fully grown male coon is no mean adversary and it takes a very good dog indeed to get the best of him in single combat. He will often lead the dog into the water and then turn to attack and attempt to drown his pursuer.

The raccoon sleeps soundly during severe winter weather. His metabolism is not lowered as is the case with the woodchuck, bear, and others, so he cannot be said to hibernate, but he does lie dormant for considerable periods. He will often be found abroad during mild spells of weather in December and January.

*Lotor* is decidedly omnivorous in his feeding habits. He consumes a wide variety of plant and animal matter with equal relish. He is particularly fond of crawfish and spends hours along the bank of stream turning over the stones in shallow water and grabbing for these creatures. Frogs and fish are high on his list of foods also. In season he devours hosts of grasshoppers and crickets. His fondness for green corn is well known by many a farmer, and he likes acorns as well. Various fruits, grains, nuts, and berries round out his diet.

**Breeding.** The urge to mate comes in the latter part of January or early February. In their natural wild state the males are inclined to be polygamous. (There is some controversy about this, but the weight of evidence supports the belief that the male consorts with more than one female.)

The gestation period is 63 days and from three to six young are born in early April. The baby coons are covered with fur at birth and soon display the same markings as the adult. Their eyes open when they are about three weeks old and shortly thereafter they are able to get about with the mother. The female is very devoted to her young and teaches them to hunt, to climb, and to be crafty in escaping their enemies. The family (mother and young) remains together well into the fall and often for part of the winter. By midwinter the young weigh from 7 to 12 pounds. They attain nearly full growth and often mate before they are a year old.

**Range and Distribution.** Raccoons may be found quite generally throughout the eastern portion of the United States from northern Maine to the mangrove swamps of the Florida Keys, west to Wisconsin and down in the bayou country of Louisiana. They are at home wherever the country provides acceptable food and den sites. In the North they prefer the forested regions and in the South they frequent the swamps and the mangrove thickets.

**Hunting Methods.** Whoever coined the phrase "night holds a thousand mysteries" must have been a coon hunter. For of all the entertainment which the great out of doors provides, none, certainly, is as mysterious, as downright puzzling, and as uncertain as coon hunting.

Undoubtedly one of the most fascinating attractions of coon hunting is the fact that whether in the river-bottom country of the South or the hilly terrain of the North, the hunter who strikes out with the fall of one day does so with a wide open mind as to what may happen before the following dawn.

But not all coon hunting is confined to the hours of darkness. The development of cold-nosed hounds has resulted in the sport's going on a round-the-clock basis. But before dealing with coon dogs and coon hounds, which today are generally considered two distinct types, let us take stock of the brazen, game, cunning animal around which coon hunting revolves.

The primary-grade child usually associates the ring-tailed raccoon with soap and water and a trip to the washbasin to remove that telltale dirt accumulated on his hands while at play. Debunking that much overemphasized theory—that the raccoon washes everything it eats—would require a nationwide campaign today, so deeply has it been rooted. To intimate that the raccoon does not exercise some degree of caution and selectivity in what it eats would be more than unfair to the animal. But to suggest that a raccoon, once having invaded a farmer's cornfield, will strip an ear off the stalk and then rush to the nearest brook to wash it before nipping at the kernels would be ridiculous.

The coon hunter who familiarizes himself with the type of feed available each season to raccoons will be well repaid for the effort. And, with few exceptions, the feed usually is different each year.

The raccoon is classified as carnivorous, or a flesh eater. But its menu is as varied as its range, which includes all of the United States, Mexico, and the southern part of Canada. What it eats depends greatly on availability. It will search river bottoms for aquatic life such as frogs and crawfish, thrive on the shellfish it can find along coastal regions, feast on many varieties of wild nuts and on cherries, enjoy raids on the farmer's cornfields and apple orchards, feel satisfied with a meal of angleworms, and in lean years will raid garbage cans around sporting camps and frequently within the city or town limits.

Although largely arboreal, coons frequently make their homes in ledges or underground. The selection of ledges has increased in modern times, particularly because they afford better protection against the hunter and the dogs he uses.

It is not uncommon today to find families of coons —they number from four to six—living in old quarries, rock piles, and other places where only an atom bomb could rout them out. It is these sanctuaries that insure future propagation of the ringtails.

Once any particular ledge or den becomes overcrowded, coons will pair up and find new homes. It has been learned through observation that from one particular ledge, areas within 15 miles of it will be stocked naturally.

In most sections of the country raccoons go through a period of semi-hibernation during the coldest months of winter. They will come out during a mild period. The mating season varies in different sections of their range but occurs early in the spring. Litters average five in number and families do not break up until forced to do so during the hunting season.

The death rate is relatively low as coons are courageous and vicious fighters, having few natural enemies.

No better example of how quickly they will propagate can be found than on the offshore island of North Haven, 14 miles from Rockland on the Maine coast. In 1935 five pair of raccoons were liberated on the island, which is 6 miles long and 4 wide. Ten years later, despite some hunting, they became a nuisance and the Maine legislature was asked to remove all protection from them until such time as they could be controlled. It was estimated that from the original five pair, at least 400 coons were roaming the island ten years later.

In 1945 raccoons were introduced into Alaska, several pair being released on an island near Ketchikan. While it will be some time before hunting is permitted, it already has been established that the coons are reproducing rapidly and have acclimated themselves to that territory.

Although considered nocturnal in its habits, the raccoon will roam during the day. Ordinarily, however, it will be either in its den or sunning itself in a treetop or crow's nest during the day and start its prowling as the sun sets. If there is plenty of feed available, it will be homeward bound with a stomachfull before daylight. During lean years it becomes necessary for it to spend more time in the search for feed. For that reason it is not surprising to see coons crossing roads long after daylight.

There are two different types of raccoon in the United States. The southern or warm-climate coon

Gene Letourneau, Waterville, Me.

**Plate III.** Treed!

Gene Letourneau, Waterville, Me.

PLATE IV. These coons, all males, were taken during a week's hunting in Maine. They weighed from 25 to 30 pounds each.

has a light coat of fur. His northern brother has a dense pelage and long hair. The southern pelt is used for coats while that from the north goes for trimmings. In recent years heavy northern pelts have been trimmed to imitate beaver, the shearing process opening a new avenue for the marketing of this type of pelt.

On an average a mature raccoon will weigh 16 pounds. A 30-pounder is rare, a 40-pounder the exception but not an impossibility.

Within ten years raccoons have increased their range naturally. While rare in the northeastern tip of the United States in 1937, they have been showing up along the Maine-New Brunswick borders in increasing numbers since then.

Men who hunt with hounds have argued long and loud about the relative cunning of the raccoon and the fox, each claiming that one is more difficult to track down or chase than the other. Unlike the fox, whose foot is heavily furred, the raccoon's paw is bare and cold. The coon moves more closely to the ground, its long fur undoubtedly leaving considerable scent as it touches vegetation.

But there is nothing clumsy about the tactics of a wild coon once it becomes aware that it is being chased. It can and will take to water like a duck. It will take advantage of every physical opportunity to shake off one or a pack of dogs. It will run narrow stone walls or stay on slash or hurricane-felled timber for hours, jumping from one pile to another, backtracking itself, resorting to hundreds of tricks to escape.

That brings the matter of coon dogs and hounds to the front.

Considering coon hunting purely as a sporting proposition, there are four distinct features to look for in the selection of a coon hound. They are striking ability (which is ability to locate tracks), trailing, courage, and honesty.

The silent trailer, which is a distinct type of coon dog, can be of almost any breed or combination of breeds. He will sneak up on his quarry, using the element of surprise to corner or tree his coon, giving tongue only when he has accomplished one or the other. There is little doubt that the silent trailer will be more effective under certain conditions. Where coons are hunted hard and have access to impregnable ledges, the silent trailer will corner more game than the open trailer.

But the hound with the open mouth is the symbol of coon hunting for sport. He learns to speak a language understandable by his master. Every tone is a message and the chase becomes an unfurling story as the voice of an open trailer tells of hardships through bogs, hurricane timber, or easier going over dampened duff and finally the cry at the tree to come and get him.

In recent years a serious effort has been made to have coonhounds recognized as a distinct breed. The United Kennel Club now registers Redbones, Blueticks, Black and Tans, and Treeing Walkers. There is no doubt that but coonhound blood is becoming blue and that in the not too distant future the registered coonhound will be the rule rather than the exception.

The silent trailer usually is not a cold-trailing coon dog. There are exceptions, but primarily the silent performer is hot-nosed and will not work up the trail of a coon that may be old in terms of hours. And while this type of dog always uses the element of surprise, he can be fooled by a wise old coon.

What can happen, and does, is that once forced to escape sudden attack, the coon will make for the nearest tree. But defeat is only temporary. Its eyesight far superior to that of the dog that is baying below, the coon will move out on a limb, watch for the ideal moment, then take off, usually springing so that it will land from 30 or 40 feet away from the base of the tree.

How a 25-pound coon can hit the ground so lightly from heights up to 50 feet is one of the many mysteries of coon hunting. But as the dog bays at the tree, the light thud is buried in the night. And the moment the coon alights it is running and running hard. Even the experienced silent trailer—which will, like an experienced open trailer, frequently check around the outer limbs of his tree—may not discover that his coon has bailed out in time to overtake it before it has reached the safety of a ledge or den tree.

In the selection of a coon dog or coonhound, one of the primary points to look for is treeing ability, for without that there can be no climax to coon hunting. It may not necessarily hold throughout a litter born from treeing parents, but treeing undoubtedly is inherited and when it shows up strongly in the bitch and the sire, it is more likely to be retained in the bloodline.

Color or markings are a matter of personal choice. It is obvious that the hunter will enjoy companionship of a handsome dog more than one that seems just a step ahead of being a stand-in for a side-show freak. But coon dogs or hounds do not run with their looks.

Training the coonhound can be easy, or it can be a long and tedious task. Much depends upon the type of country being hunted, and the abundance or scarcity of raccoon and other game.

The fact that the five- to six-year-old coonhound demands the top price on the market is sufficient evidence to show that until a dog has reached that age he has not reached his peak nor has his training been fully completed.

Two different methods of hunting are followed by coon hunters in this country. One is to walk a selected piece of territory, allowing the dogs to range; the other is roading, or allowing the hound to run ahead of an automobile, jeep, or truck.

In the first method, the hound should be able to cover the territory thoroughly and locate a coon track if one has traversed the area. In the other method, the hound must be able to pick up the scent of a track that has been laid across the road. The smart roader will not only strike the trail that crosses his path but will also catch the rising scent of tracks or the game itself within the woods. It is not uncommon for finished roaders to strike trails a quarter of a mile off the road, provided, of course, that conditions, principally wind, are ideal.

After the track has been located the ideal open trailer should tongue along as he pushes ahead. He should not take a back step, even though many good coonhounds will frequently backtrack; that is pardonable if only they correct themselves before running the trail to the den from which the coon has emerged.

While most coonhounds have a distinct tree bark, which even the novice can detect from trail, there are some who change very little when the trail has reached its destination. For that reason the hunter must acquaint himself thoroughly with his dog if he hunts single rather than with a pack. He should be able to distinguish the tree bark readily and answer the call, letting no barrier interfere with his progress.

Coonhounds are made at the tree. If they have completed their part of the job, the hunter should not be found wanting. If streams must be waded, yes, even if they are waist high, the hunter who always has good coonhounds will wade them. No matter how tough the going, a hound at tree should have his plea answered. He never should be called away.

A hound that is never let down by his master will stay treed for hours. Some have been known to stay a day, tongueing spasmodically and refusing to give up. The ideal tree dog is the one that will keep barking, directing his master at all times toward the end of the chase.

As it is always a good policy to carry a compass, it can be used not only as a guide eventually to emerge from the woods, but also to walk to a treed hound. If the hunter has not followed the chase through—a custom which in many places is becoming a lost art—he can use the compass to locate the position of the hound, especially if the dog is not a steady tree barker. Most dogs will pick up courage as they hear the crashing of hunters approaching them. Thus the compass will prove a valuable piece of equipment in reaching the coon tree and also will prove helpful in returning to the field or road from which the hunter entered the woods.

Unless the hunter is thoroughly familiar with the country being hunted, he should write down the compass points before entering the woods. If he travels south to the tree, he necessarily must travel north to come out. Basically, that is how the compass is used; the points vary, of course, but never change when established from a set point.

After reaching the treed hound, encouragement should be given the dog for a job well done. Some dogs are vicious killers; others, because of age, loss of teeth, or size, cannot handle even a spring kitten.

Some hunters will not shoot coons, preferring to climb the tree and shake them out for the dog or dogs to kill.

A good killer has its advantages, but more than one outstanding coonhound has never killed a coon without some help. A mature coon is a rough scrapper. An old boar or bitch coon can often be a match for an average dog, especially in water.

If there is to be a kill, it is recommended that the coon be shot with whatever type of weapon is allowed in the area being hunted. Many a smart killer has been lost for several hunting nights, sometimes the entire season, due to infections resulting from wounds inflicted by the sharp teeth of a maddened coon.

Shooting is certainly more humane, and equally satisfactory to the dog or dogs, for the taste of hot fur has been provided, and it is primarily for that climax that the hound has completed his job and done it well. And one kill is sufficient at any tree. That is where sportsmanship can be shown, especially if an entire family has been treed. Leaving a few for seed is always a good policy, whether in Maine or in the State of Washington.

The product of a finished cooner has been outlined in the foregoing paragraphs. But a finished or straight cooner today is just about the last word in a hunting dog.

Such a dog must be made. The easiest method to follow is to start the hound early in life. Seven months is none too early to take the prospective coonhound afield. The training task is rather simple if there is an older, experienced dog to serve as the tutor.

It is wise to allow the straight cooner to do the striking before giving the pup its freedom. He will usually answer the call and join the tutor. He may even begin treeing at the end of his first chase. And it is probable, too, that several seasons will be necessary to make him tongue freely at tree.

Bear in mind that hunting dogs do not learn while at the end of a chain or in the pen. They must be given all the work possible. There will be stages when they will test one's patience, principally by going off-game—which is chasing other animals than that for which they are being groomed.

Should a young dog insist, after a sufficient number of trials, upon running fox, or rabbit, or deer, especially if a kennel mate is trying to teach him how to become a coonhound, it is better to work on another prospect.

Coon hunting is just what it implies. It requires a straight coonhound, and that means a dog that will run nothing else but raccoon. There can be no enjoyment in having a coon hunt end up by trying to round up a hound or hounds driving other game.

There is no finer, smarter, more intelligent hunting dog than the straight cooner. Let us see what can happen on a coon hunt in Maine, for example.

The late November night is chilly, the temperature a few degrees below freezing. The drizzle has stopped and ice has coated the deciduous trees.

The car turns off a paved highway onto a narrow dirt road. The fall has been one of plenty for game, with oak and beech trees carrying a peak crop of acorns and beechnuts, tasty morsels for the ringtail.

The car stops at the foot of a ridge and out goes Tippy, a black, tan, and white hound of eight seasons' experience. He is in top shape, a condition which requires a month of training for a dog of that age.

In the party are an ex-Marine freshly out of the service, a salesman, and a newspaperman. Six eyes are glued on the hound as he trots out in the glare of the headlights.

As Tippy moves up the road, checking the ditches, the car follows. Suddenly the hound jacks up, head high, tail flagging. He bounds off the road. There is a bedlam of baying almost instantly. The woods crash as three deer suddenly appear in the lights, which are still on. Tippy is a straight cooner and he is driving farther into the woods. The deer just happened to be in the way. They scamper into the night.

Before there is time to park, Tippy is barking treed. The chase, less than five minutes, is over. The hunters walk in to him quickly, for this is an open ridge, where wide lanes divide the rows of hardwood trees.

Icicles clinging to the limbs of the beech tree where Tippy says he has got the coon sparkle as the rays of the two-cell flashlight strike them.

Sure enough, in a crotch above is the ringtail, eyes shining like balls of fire as the lights are played upon him.

The .22-caliber pistol, only legal weapon for coon hunting at night in Maine, is loaded. There is a shot, and down comes the coon, an old 28-pound boar that probably gave the hound more than one merry chase during the earlier nights of the season.

"Is this easy!" one remarks.

"Simple," the salesman comments.

The newspaperman, 20 years a coon hunter, has no comment to make. The hunters return to the car, enthusiastic for another chase. But tracks are scattered just before the season is ready to button up. It is well past midnight before Tippy shows signs of game again. This time he checks both sides of the road carefully. This track is old, not the hot, steaming trail that was his earlier in the night.

The hound has taken to the woods now. A long, but anxious, bay breaks the silence. This is a cold trail, warns Tippy with that message, meaning that it may take hours to catch up to this coon.

It is one A.M., and getting colder. Perhaps, the hunters agree, it would be warmer to follow the chase.

They light a kerosene lantern and check the compass. The dog is going north from the road, which runs east and west. That means the party will have to travel south to come out again.

So the party follows, through bent birches mixed with pine, spruce, and fir, making some places almost impassable barriers. But the hound is moving ahead, slowly, to be sure, but moving, and the hunters stay with him.

There are losses, when barks come five minutes apart. But this is another type of a coon hunt, a cold-trailing task that requires patience, trust in the dog, and willingness to stay as long as he will.

Through a mile of cuttings where one must walk on fresh tops, sometimes ten feet off the ground, to keep the pace, the chase progresses. The eastern sky is graying. Dawn is breaking. The chase is now along an overflowed stream. First Tippy is on one side, then on the other bank. The hunters keep to one side, hoping that this will end in their favor, for crossing the stream seems an impossibility.

The morning brings a fresh clearing. The sun is showing up now, and though the hunters are warm when walking, it takes only a minute's inactivity to bring chills down their backs.

"Say," asks one hunter, "how long will this last? Sure it's a coon?"

"Sure," the salesman replies. "It's a coon, all right." He doesn't elaborate on the time element. He has hunted coon before.

Tippy's tongueing grows steadier now, making progress, too. He is almost leaving his hunters even though they are on the double.

The chase heads into swampland bordered by groves of old, rugged pines and hemlocks. Tippy circles once. There is a pause and then comes the familiar tree bark. He has done his part of the job.

The three hunters move toward him. They hit the stream again. Sure enough, Tippy is on the other side. There is a felled tree downstream that just misses linking both banks. You can cross here, if you are willing to get wet over your knees.

The hunters are willing. One by one they wade to the tree, slide on the ice that coats it, and reach the opposite bank by groping on the natural bridge on their hands and knees.

Tippy is elated when the trio walks up to him. He has marked the tallest pine in the whole area. He places both front paws on the trunk and in coonhound language says, "There it is, boys, you get him."

The first limb is 15 feet off the ground. The ex-Marine is young and in good shape. He is willing to climb. So the other two make a human ladder, one standing on the shoulders of the other. The ex-Marine completes the pyramid, his fingers just able to grab that limb. He pulls himself up and on. He is warned to respect every limb, for pine is brittle and dangerous. That tree is tall, thick at the top, and even in the daylight there is no sign of a coon from ground view.

It seems like hours, but finally the climber has gained the uppermost reaches of that 80-foot tree.

"I see him, what do I do now?" he asks, excitedly.

"Load the pistol and shoot him in the head," advises the salesman.

But Tippy is barking and in the bedlam the climber crosses the signal. He crowds the coon, or something.

"Watch out!" he yells. "He's jumping out!"

There is a thud over toward the stream. All rush over as Tippy, now aware of what has happened, passes the group like a streak. He picks up the hot scent, drives away in full cry, once again across the stream.

Even as he changes to a tree bark again, the dead limbs of a hard, rustic oak can be seen in that direction.

The climber comes down, slowly, disheartened. Three hunters again get wet, but cross the stream and make for the new finish. It is an old den tree.

"What do we do now?" the ex-Marine asks.

"We call it a day," the salesman replies. "This is where one coon will most likely spend the winter. Simple, isn't it?"

Quite simple. One big coon in five minutes, no coon in five hours. That is coon hunting—never the same, always coming up with the unexpected. It is a great sport, shared by the experienced and the novices in 48 states, some sections of Canada, and Mexico.

While much depends upon the hound's ability in outwitting the coon, a chase can last five minutes or five hours. Daylight hunters—and there are more of them each year—do not expect a cold-nosed hound to cover a 3-mile run in two minutes. If the strike comes where the coon may have passed several hours before the hound came upon it, the dog must unravel the puzzle and follow it to the end.

Honesty in the coonhound is revealed at the tree. If he errs in the location of his coon, he is false-treeing, a fault which must be condemned, for it will mean tiring walks through the brush with no ringtail at the end of the trail.

Coon hunting is older than the Pilgrims' landing. The "cat with the rings in his tail" was a favorite with the Indians along the Kennebec River in Maine. They caught him in traps both for his warm fur and for his flesh, which they considered highly palatable.

In the late fall the coon acquires heavy layers of fat which will serve him well as insulation during hibernation. In preparing a coon for cooking, all of this fat should be removed. There are several ways to cook coon meat. A favorite method is to parboil it until all or most of the remaining fat has melted.

Gene Letourneau, Waterville, Me.

PLATE V. A Successful Night's Hunt.

The meat is then transferred to another pan, placed in the oven, and roasted slowly. It can be seasoned with any of several kinds of fruit juices, or if you prefer, pineapple slices or some favorite wine.

Coon flesh is like dark meat of chicken. It has the combined features, taste, and texture of both chicken and lamb.

The value of coon fur depends upon the market and women's styles. Pelts have gone from a high of $18 during the era of the popularity (in the 1920's) of raccoon coats to the record low of $4 for extra-large pelts following World War II.

There are two methods used in preparing a pelt for market, casing and boxing. In preparing a pelt for casing, skinning follows the conventional method of pulling the entire hide from the carcass without cutting except opening the tail. The hide is then stretched on a smooth board, inside out, and fleshed.

For boxing, the hide is opened and stretched, flesh out, on either a wide board or wall, being tacked at the extremities so that it will be almost square as laid out.

As with any other fur, over-stretching will decrease its market value. While most fur dealers pay the same prices for cased or boxed pelts, some of the houses in the metropolitan areas prefer the cased skins.

That is the story of coon hunting. Field trials throughout the country have increased interest in the sport and also have resulted in an improvement in the types of dogs used for it. Such trials attract thousands of spectators, many of whom eventually fulfill their desires to see the real thing and are stricken with the virus that makes a coon hunter. When that happens the ailment is likely to become permanent.

# GRAY SQUIRREL

*Sciurus carolinensis*

COMMON NAMES: Bannertail, Silvertail, Fanitasho (Choctaw), L'Ecureil Gris et Noir.

**History.** Despite various changes in coloration in different parts of the country, this animal is known from coast to coast as the gray squirrel. His scientific name *Sciurus* describes his most common attitude, for it is comprised of two Greek words: *Skia* (shade) and *Oura* (tail)—literally, "shade-tailed," or "he who sits in the shadow of his own tail"—a characteristic pose of the squirrel family.

Little is known of his origin in this country, but he was here in vast numbers to greet the first white men who arrived and he has been an important contribution to the game bag ever since. Early writers and naturalists were far from exact in estimating his numbers and were given to describing "myriads" and "hordes" as astounding, incredible, etc. Some indication of numbers is gained from the records of those states where he was deemed a nuisance and a bounty was paid for his scalp. Such records show annual kills of over the half-million mark!

"Bannertail" shares with the American bison the unwelcome distinction of having had a rifle especially designed for his speedy demise. The noted "Kentucky squirrel rifle" was evolved because of his popularity as a food item for the early settlers.

Old game books record daily takes running into the hundreds, but it was the woodsman's axe rather than his rifle which ultimately affected the squirrel population. The gray squirrel is a lover of dense woods and heavy forests; as soon as these began to disappear his food supply was seriously affected and his numbers decreased. Undoubtedly excessive hunting did play some part in reducing the original population, but the clearing of the land was a more deciding factor.

Early naturalists referred to bannertail as the "migratory squirrel" because, like the Scandinavian lemmings, periodic migrations of great magnitude were observed. Undoubtedly such movements were directly connected with the shifting food supply and indicate the decline in abundance.

*Sciurus* no longer exists in "incredible" numbers, but there are enough of his kind scattered over the country to keep him high on the list of small-game favorites.

**Identification.** Somewhat smaller than his cousin the fox squirrel, *Sciurus niger,* the common gray squirrel weighs about one pound and measures (average) 19 inches long, of which about 9 inches are tail. The general color is a pepper-and-salt gray. The under fur is lead colored and the longer guard hairs are often tan near the base, black in the center, and white-tipped. On the top of the head, back, legs, and saddle the gray is tinged with brownish yellow. On most specimens the cheeks, muzzle, ears, and upper parts of the paws are a clear tan. The chin, throat, underside of legs, and under parts are white, or nearly so. The long tail hairs, like those of the body, end in white and give the tail a silvery appearance. In winter the tan markings are less apparent; the fur is longer and more silvery gray.

Black squirrels, or *melanos,* are merely a color phase of the common gray and not a distinct species as is sometimes supposed. This melanism ranges from glossy black to any gradation between black and gray. The all-black phase increases in frequency in the northern range. In Canada, for example, black is the rule and gray the exception.

Albino squirrels are found occasionally over all parts of the range.

The color variation of *Sciurus carolinensis* is so slight that one should have little trouble in identifying him anywhere, but five races have been recognized:

*Sciurus leucotis*: Larger and more silvery gray; found in the region between Toronto, Ontario, and Lake Simcoe.

*Sciurus hypohoeus*: Also larger than the common gray, darker on the back and has very little white below. Typical locality is around Elk River, Minn.

*Sciurus fuliginosus*: A large specimen; never white below but often shows a reddish tinge. Typical locality is around New Orleans, La.

*Sciurus extimus*: Rather small in size, pale gray in

color, and has a short tail. Typical locality around Miami, Fla.

Some western squirrels, while members of the gray squirrel family, are sufficiently different in appearance to warrant a separate description. Listed below are the more notable exceptions to the common coloration:

### CALIFORNIA GRAY SQUIRREL *Sciurus griseus*

Common Names: West Coast Gray Squirrel, Western Gray Squirrel, Gray Tree Squirrel.

This squirrel is much like the eastern gray except for being generally more bluish-gray in color. Three races are recognized:

*Sciurus griseus*: Typical locality The Dalles, Wasco Co., Ore.

*Sciurus nigripes*: Rather dark-brownish in color with nearly black feet. Typical locality, coastal region, San Mateo, Calif.

*Sciurus anthonyi*: A paler specimen often tinged with brownish-yellow on the back. The upper surfaces of the feet are intermediate in color between the other two races. Typical locality, Laguna Mt., San Diego, Calif.

### TASSEL-EARED SQUIRREL *Sciurus aberti*

Common Names: Tufted-Eared Squirrel, Abert's Pine Squirrel, Saddle-Backed Gray Squirrel, Black Squirrel, White-Tailed Squirrel, Silver-Tailed Squirrel.

On account of its likeness to Old World squirrels some naturalists suggest that this may be of Asiatic origin, while others contend that the species may have migrated from the eastern part of this country. There are two kinds, varying enough in appearance to be considered by some authorities as separate species. Both of these have outstanding features: tufted ears, and enormous tails.

*Aberti* is leaden gray on the upper body with a reddish-brown saddle, and all white on the under parts, including the underside of the tail. A black stripe running along the sides separates the gray of the upper body from the white below. The top side of the tail is gray and black and has a black tip. In winter the tufts on the ears are slightly more than one inch long and blackish in color. These tufts turn to brown before being shed in early summer.

Like the eastern gray, these squirrels are chiefly melanistic along their northern ranges, melanism being rare in the south.

The second specimen, *Sciurus kaibabensis,* is like the *Aberti* except that the under parts are mainly black instead of white and the tail is usually white all over.

Typical locality of these squirrels is along opposite sides of the Colorado River, particularly in the Bright Angel country. The fact that each kind preserves its individual markings demonstrates how a river acts as a natural barrier to non-swimming, non-flying creatures.

### FOX SQUIRREL *Sciurus niger*

Common Names: Yellow-Bellied Squirrel, White-Nosed Black Squirrel, Big Red Squirrel, Red-Tailed Squirrel, Le Coquallin (French).

The fox squirrel is the largest of the squirrel family, measuring about 25 inches over-all, including a 12-inch tail. The average weight is from 2¼ to 2¾ pounds. The typical form and the one from which the species derives its names is marked as follows: Upper part of the body, pepper-and-salt gray. Face, paws, under parts of body, and tail are a rich, reddish fox color. The breast is a striking shade of orange. The long hairs of the tail are alternately banded orange and black and from the underside this shows as a broad black band near the tip.

Other color phases exist in varying degrees and often blend into each other. The black squirrel of South Carolina is merely a melanistic phase of the common fox squirrel and may be readily identified by the always white ears and nose.

The buff phase is distinguished by the pinkish-buff upper body and the rich, warm buff of the under parts, feet, and underside of the tail.

The gray phase most nearly approaches the color of the common eastern gray squirrel. The upper parts and the tail are gray and the under parts are white, but the crown of the head is black and the nose, ears, and feet are white.

Perhaps the size is the most distinguishing feature in many cases. The fox squirrel, never as numerous as the common gray, has become extinct in many of its former haunts and is rapidly becoming scarce in many parts of the South. A typical locality for this species is southern South Carolina.

**Characteristics.** The common gray squirrel probably is the least aggressive member of the whole

N. Y. Zoological Society.

**Plate I.** Bushytail at Lunch.

squirrel family. Unlike his arch-enemy, the pugnacious red squirrel, he is content to live at peace with his neighbors and only occasionally will he fight to preserve some section which he deems his private domain. He usually spends more time aloft than on the ground, but this seems to depend largely on the food situation.

When frightened he takes to the nearest tree and is expert in keeping the trunk between himself and his enemies. By skillful dodging he often eludes pursuers and when pressed he does not hesitate to leap from the highest branches. On such occasions his bushy tail serves as both a rudder and a parachute. Should he miss a branch—which he rarely does—and come hurtling to the ground it does not seem to matter, for he dashes to the nearest tree without a pause.

His enemies are numerous and only his watchfulness and agility have enabled him to survive. The larger hawks, the great horned owl, and the barred owl include him in their diet although they are not often successful in capturing him. Hawks hunting in pairs are able to come at him from both sides at once, thus giving him little chance to dodge, but a single hawk has great difficulty in cornering him. Besides the winged threats, the weasel, fisher, mink, red fox, gray fox, bobcat, and wolf all prey upon him; so he must be ever on the alert whether aloft or aground.

The squirrel's second line of defense is his ability to "freeze," that is, to lie motionless along a limb for long periods at a time. In this position he is well-nigh invisible to even the sharpest eyes.

The red squirrel, or "chickaree" *(Sciurus vulgaris)*, is his particular Nemesis. Although fully twice as large as the red, he is no match for the little fellow in speed and ferocity. He rarely tries to defend himself but resorts to headlong flight with the red in hot and noisy pursuit.

This clash between the red and the gray often has a painful ending for the latter. The red has a particularly vicious habit of seizing the gray by the scrotum and tearing it open. This practice has led many to contend that the red castrates the gray deliberately. It cannot be denied that the red does bite into the scrotum, possibly because it is the most convenient part to grab, but naturalists generally attribute this to accident. The fact that many castrated grays have been shot also lends some support to the contention but hardly offers conclusive proof. In some cases, possibly because of immaturity, the testes of squirrels so found may have been in the abdominal cavity.

The botfly warble *(Cuterebra emasculator)*, commonly called "wabbles," is believed to produce this same result in many cases. In several instances the botfly grub has been found in scrotums where the glandular tissues of the testes were wholly consumed. Thus, despite considerable apparent evidence against him, the red squirrel may not always be the culprit that many believe him to be.

Several instances have been cited of gray squirrels pilfering the nests of birds and eating the eggs and young. It is possible that certain members of the species may develop abnormal tastes, just as all mammals do, but for the most part the diet is strictly vegetarian. Gray squirrels are particularly fond of nuts and these in some form are a staple food item. Acorns from both the black and white oaks, hickory nuts, butternuts, and beechnuts make up the bulk of the diet and these are supplemented by seeds of various kinds. In the spring the squirrels eat the buds of the maple, elm, and other trees. They are also fond of sap and will gnaw through the bark of sap-trees to get the sweet liquid. The gray squirrel also consumes a lot of water and will drink several times a day when it is available.

During storms or severe weather the gray holes up in his nest or a hollow tree for short periods, but, since he does not hibernate like the bear or woodchuck, he must be assured of a food supply during the winter. Each autumn he gathers and hides large quantities of nuts and acorns. However, he does not store large caches of food in any one place. At times he may hide a handful of nuts or acorns in a hollow limb or tree, but usually he plants them singly in the ground or hides them haphazardly in the rough bark of a tree trunk.

Despite his keen sense of smell—and squirrels can detect buried nuts under more than a foot of snow—it is doubtful that more than half of the hidden stores are ever recovered. Thus he unconsciously aids nature in reforestation; for while acorns virtually plant themselves in falling from the trees, hickory nuts, butternuts, and walnuts must be planted in order to germinate.

**Breeding.** The mating season is in the early spring, with some variance in time between the extreme northern and southern limits of the range. At this time the males fight savagely for the female of their choice and often severely wound an opponent. The victorious male then pairs off with his hard-won mate for an extremely brief honeymoon. Within a day or two he either returns to his bachelor ways or looks around for a new mate. His erstwhile spouse has no further interest in his existence.

The gestation period averages 44 days. In northern New York the first litter is often born in March, and seldom later than early April. Farther south the first litter may come in February or early March. Generally from two to four are born; more rarely a litter may be from one to six. The second litter arrives about mid-July—depending somewhat on the latitude and season. In the wild state the second litter is likely to be sired by a different male because the mating is only temporary.

For the first litter the mother fashions a nest in a hollow tree or a convenient hole in a large limb, but for the second she prefers the built nest or "dray" in the crotch of a tree. Such outdoor nests resemble that of a crow or hawk when seen from below; in fact, abandoned hawk nests are often used as a foundation. The "dray" differs from the usual nest, however, in that there is a waterproof roof and the entrance is on one side. The nest is built of twigs, bark, and dead leaves and has fewer large sticks than a crow or hawk nest. Within the nest the mother prepares a clean soft bed, and here the young are suckled and kept warm during the first weeks of their lives.

Baby squirrels are blind at birth and remain so for about five weeks. The tiny bodies are hairless, without ears, and have only rudimentary tags for limbs. They first emerge from the nest at the end of six weeks and by the eighth or ninth week they begin to take regular food such as buds, leaves, etc.

Thus it is about 12 weeks from the time of conception until they open their eyes. At the end of this period they weigh around one-quarter pound. The youngsters become fully adult in 12 months. They are fully grown by the second year and in their prime between two and six years. The probable life span is estimated at 15 years.

The breeding, number of young, and general habits of all the squirrels are so similar to those of the common gray that they do not warrant individual mention.

**Range and Distribution.** The common gray squirrel is found over a wide range of the United States and Canada in the various forms given under "Identification" (pp. 118-119). His less numerous cousins such as the fox squirrel, the California gray squirrel, and the tufted-eared squirrel occupy a more restricted range.

The periodic migrations mentioned above are less frequent now than in former years. When they do occur, however, they are likely to affect the range areas materially.

Many remarkable migrations have become a matter of record. As mentioned previously, such movements are frequently caused by food shortages, but there is no proof that all migrations are for this reason. Overpopulation sometimes results in mass movements, and some naturalists are inclined to believe that when increases in density occur in certain areas nature prompts emigration to preserve the race.

During the great squirrel year of 1935, for instance, when several mass migrations were observed (notably the one from New England into New York State), it was also noted that three litters were produced that year instead of the usual two. It is possible that three litters may have occurred in the previous year as well.

Whatever the reason, immense numbers of squirrels congregate in the autumn and move off as though at a signal. The directions of the movements may vary but the squirrels do not turn aside from obstacles. Although poor swimmers, they do not hesitate to attempt the crossing of large streams.

Observers have noted squirrels swimming for almost 150 miles along the Ohio River. Similar crossings have been seen on the Niagara, Hudson, and other streams. In the autumn of 1933 more than 1000 squirrels swam the Connecticut River between Hartford and Essex, a distance of about 40 miles.

In 1935 a more extensive movement took place in western New York. Thousands of squirrels were killed on the highways or drowned while attempting to swim the large lakes in central New York. After this migration squirrels were seen in places where they had been absent for many years. Another movement of note was one from Wisconsin to the southwest which lasted four days, and a similar exodus occurred at five-year intervals over a long period of time.

This migratory trait often accounts for the scarcity of squirrels in a given place one year and an abundance the next. The general distribution however, remains about the same.

**Hunting Methods.** In many sections of the country squirrel hunting runs a close second to rabbit shooting in popularity. The elusive grays and reds challenge the sportsman's shooting ability and his knowledge of woodcraft. The formula for success in this particular sport is "to be where they are," and to be able to hit them. Some knowledge of their feeding habits will help greatly in locating good squirrel grounds. As mentioned earlier, they show a preference for the various nuts, acorns, and the buds of such trees as the beech and poplar.

A stand of shagbark hickory, a beech flat, an oak ridge (particularly white oak), a grove of walnut or pecan trees all offer opportunities as a base of operations. Old stone walls and rail fences are popular squirrel highways and will always bear watching. Old orchards are frequently productive, especially if they are near the woods.

The best time of the day for finding squirrels active is just after daylight when the first rays of the morning sun are glinting in the treetops. Later in the morning, if there is a stream in the vicinity squirrels will often be found going to and coming from the water. Of course a few squirrels may be found all during the day, but as a rule they lie close in their nests during the warmer part and resume feeding again in the evening. Rainy and stormy days are usually unproductive because the squirrel likes his comfort and normally does not venture forth in bad weather. On clear cold days he may often be spotted taking a sunbath in the topmost branches of a tall tree.

There are two common methods of squirrel hunting. The first is still hunting or walking slowly and as silently as possible through likely places while keeping on the alert for a flash of gray or red. The second is the "watchful waiting" method in which the hunter, having found a patch of cover with squirrel sign (such as discarded nut shells), seats himself at the base of a tree or stump where he commands a good view of his surroundings and waits for the squirrel to come within range.

Discounting pure luck, to be successful by the first method the hunter must have some knowledge of squirrel habits and an eye trained to catch the slightest movement around him.

When employing the second method the hunter should endeavor to be as inconspicuous as possible and remain motionless. Some hunters even claim that smoking while on a stand reduces the chances for a shot because the squirrels can detect an unnatural odor and will not move around. Be that as it may, the waiting is likely to be long and tedious and it is up to the smoker to decide whether he prefers the solace of a pipe or cigarette at the possible cost of a shot or two. After taking his position, and after all has quieted down in the woods, the sitting hunter has the advantage of being able to hear his game as well as see it. Feeding squirrels, while often invisible in the foliage, drop their cuttings and the outer husks of nuts. Even small fragments of these when falling from a height make a considerable pattering noise on the leaves or ground. Often too, the grating of sharp teeth against the tough shell of a nut can be plainly heard for some distance. The rasp of claws on bark as the squirrel moves about is also clearly audible. All these sounds indicate the presence of squirrels and their general location.

Sometimes the hunter must move a bit in order to see them in the trees. It is generally considered better, however, to be patient and wait for the squirrel to show himself. A move to get one squirrel may cause several others to hide. A frightened squirrel will flatten himself on a limb or dodge into a hole in a tree and not stir for a long time.

The sound of a shot does not seem to disturb the squirrels for long. They may cease their activity for a few minutes but they appear to forget the noise quickly. The sight or sound of a hunter produces quite a different effect, however, and usually the entire squirrel population within the area goes into hiding. Wounded squirrels should be dispatched quickly, of course, but clean kills may be left where they fall and retrieved when the hunter is ready to move on.

There are, naturally, exceptions to every rule, and all squirrels do not behave in the same manner. Occasionally the sight of a hunter will cause one or more to set up a great chattering and scolding. Such squirrels, however, usually have an uncanny way of being just out of range and flee when the hunter tries to approach them.

Wary as he is, the squirrel can be outwitted at times. Often he will be found sitting in such a manner that only his bushy tail is visible. In order to get a shot at his head—which is the only proper place to shoot him with a rifle—the hunter may simulate his chatter by pursing the lips and making a noisy, exaggerated kissing sound. This usually arouses the squirrel's curiosity and causes him to show himself more fully. (This trick applies only to such squirrels as are unmindful of the hunter's presence, however, for a frightened squirrel loses his curiosity.)

Squirrels have a habit of dodging around a tree trunk as the hunter circles the tree trying to get in a shot. When one is hunting with a companion this trick avails the squirrel nothing because both sides of the tree can be covered at the same time, but when one is alone it can be decidedly annoying. Frequently the squirrel can be fooled if the hunter hangs a coat on a bush in plain sight under the tree. The hunter then gets close to the trunk on the opposite side and by backing up carefully and quietly can line his sights on the squirrel that is watching the garment.

The sound caused by striking two stones rapidly together often produces an answering chatter from some squirrel whose presence was unsuspected and sometimes he will come loping along a fence or through the trees to investigate.

A den tree or a tree nest can usually be spotted without much trouble, and it often pays to keep careful watch on such a tree for a time. If two or more hunters are working together it is a good plan for one to hide where he has a good view of such a tree while the others scout the woods. In escaping the others a squirrel will try to slip quietly through the treetops to the security of the den and thus provide a shot for at least one of the party.

Hunting squirrels with a dog is often effective—if the dog knows his business. Breed is not important for this work and some mongrels are as efficient as the best pedigreed dogs. Small dogs of the terrier type are excellent for squirrels. It is, however, an acquired art with the dog and one which he seems to develop either naturally or not at all. It is difficult to train a dog for this type of work, and it is usually best merely to encourage any natural tendencies which he may display.

Some hunters prefer a dog that will bark when the squirrel trees, while others incline toward the silent worker that simply stands and watches at the base of the tree. This is largely a matter of personal choice, although the barker is more easily located in thick woods.

The theory of hunting with a dog is that the squirrels, once up a tree, have little fear of their four-footed pursuer, but the dog attracts their attention and permits the hunter to approach and get in a shot. A dog with a good nose will often find squirrels in a section where the hunter alone would seldom be aware of them.

The choice of a gun for the bushy-tails is a matter of great controversy among those who hunt them. One school considers it definitely unsporting to use anything but a .22 caliber rifle and loudly protests that the shotgun is for meat hunters only. The scattergun enthusiasts rise in their own defense with the contention that a leaping, fast-running squirrel is as tricky a target as a flying bird. The argument will never be settled, and so each individual must decide the issue for himself. The walking hunter will find few suitable targets for his rifle, whereas the patient watcher does not need a shotgun to pot a sitting squirrel.

In choosing a rifle nothing more powerful than a .22 is recommended, and regular short, long, or long-rifle cartridges are adequate. The hollow-point bullets usually damage the carcass so that it is unfit for food. A scope-sighted rifle aids in accuracy, especially in long shots, and many hunters prefer the scope to iron sights.

Caution: Rifle bullets, especially those of low velocity like the .22's, have a tendency to ricochet off rocks, and other hard surfaces, even hard ground. Therefore, it is dangerous to shoot at squirrels on the ground or on fences and other low places. A miss may send a bullet flying off into the woods where others are hunting or where stock is grazing. When using a rifle for squirrels it is best to confine your shots to high angles in the trees, where a possible miss is unlikely to matter.

Shotguns of any gauge from 12 to .410 are in common use and No. 6 shot is the favored load.

The old-time method of "barking" squirrels is still used by some hunters whenever possible. This calls for extremely fine shooting and is a game for experts only. First, of course, the target must be in the right position—which means stretched out flat and tight against a limb (one of the squirrel's favorite methods of hiding). Careful aim is then taken just *below* the body. The impact of the bullet erupts the bark on the limb and the resultant concussion stuns the squirrel. Knocked from his perch in a stunned condition, his fall to the ground usually kills him and there is no shot damage to his carcass.

# WOODCHUCK

*Marmota monax*

When the early Devonshire settlers came upon a fat, woodland animal, they called him a "woodchuck" after their word "chuck" meaning "little pig." This name is commonly used in the northern states, but "groundhog" is more familiar in the southern states. The French-Canadians called him a *"siffleur,"* meaning "whistler." He is the American representative of the European marmots, belonging to the squirrel family and the genus *Marmota.*

The 28 species and sub-species of the genus compose three distinct groups, the common, eastern woodchuck *(Marmota monax),* the yellow-footed marmot *(Marmota flaviventris),* and the hoary marmot or rockchuck *(Marmota caligata).*

**History.** Before the white settlers came to this country, the woodchuck was an active, free animal of the woods and deep forests, but he also had to grub for food and fight his many carnivorous enemies. When the colonists cultivated an easy food supply, of rich pasturage, fruit orchards, and vegetable gardens, the woodchuck left the forests to feed and burrow in this rich land. His lord was his stomach.

When he gave up woodland independence, he took on the life of the hunted. The woodchuck has been declared an enemy of agriculture and has been continuously persecuted, especially in the eastern states. Besides the food he eats, his burrow is a menace. Cattle and horses often step into the holes, breaking a leg or otherwise injuring themselves, and the mound of dirt about the hole interferes with farm machinery. The damage done in farming regions is not actually so extensive as it is persistent.

The woodchuck's chances of survival are high since, like the rabbit, he is a rigid vegetarian and man continues to supply him with an easy access to food. Also, now that he has left the forests, his natural enemies are fewer.

Though woodchucks are not eaten to any extent by man, they are palatable and young, lean ones are quite tasty. The Indians of Canada, British Columbia, and Alaska relish their meat and use their fur for making robes. Some marmots of Europe and Asia figure in the fur trade, but there is no commercial use of them on this continent though the yellow-footed marmot has an attractive pelt.

**Identification.** The woodchuck has the typical appearance of a large ground squirrel, heavy-bodied and thickset. At all times of the year he looks plump. The average length is 2 feet, with males slightly larger than females. He is short-legged, with hind legs between 3 and 5 inches in length and a hairy, flattened tail averaging 6 inches. The claws, except for nearly vestigial thumbs on the forepaws, are long and strong and are as well adapted for digging as his 22 chisel-like teeth are for cutting and grinding.

His pelage molts yearly, but there is no set time when this takes place. Usually the new coat grows back around August. His coat has an outer covering of coarse guard hairs and beneath it is a shorter, dense under fur. The coloration is highly variable, but is commonly brownish or yellowish varied with black and rust above, with the underside ranging from whitish to brownish. The rockchuck is grayer. The fur stops at the wrist joint, giving the dark feet a tight-gloved look.

**Characteristics.** The woodchuck is shrewd by nature and in regions where hunted down and harassed, he becomes more cunning. He is terrestrial, though he sometimes climbs a stump to sun himself or goes about 10 feet up a tree, usually to escape pursuit.

He lives in burrows, which he digs himself, in the ground, in wood or rock piles, and in stone walls. These are dug near a food supply, preferably clover or grass. He often tunnels into crops of corn and alfalfa and burrows into fruit orchards, where he strips the bark from young trees. It is characteristic that there are usually two or three entrances to the burrow, and it is provided with an observation post with an eye to the enemy. It opens near a hillock in a pasture, a summit among rocks, or a log in the woods.

There are two main types of burrows. One goes several feet down from the surface, and has no loose dirt about the entrance. The other type has a mound of earth by the opening of the tunnel which extends for 3 to 4 feet downward then slants upward and continues horizontally from 10 to 25 feet. The nest, made of leaves and grasses, is about one foot in diameter and is in a roundish chamber in a side tunnel.

The burrows are distributed over a wide area, usually with one adult to each burrow, in sharp contrast to the sociable prairie dog which lives in colonies. The rockchuck, however, who makes his home in piles of slide rock, is more gregarious than the woodchuck.

U. S. Fish & Wildlife Service.

PLATE I. The Woodchuck, target for thousands of varmint hunters.

U. S. Forest Service.

PLATE II. Young Woodchuck in an Unguarded Moment.

The woodchuck is diurnal in habit, though he sometimes feeds in the evening. He usually goes only short distances from his burrow, and makes a run for it when pursued by one of his enemies, the mountain lion, coyote, wolf, bear, eagle, hawk, or fox. Since most of his numbers have left the woods, and many of their enemies have been killed or died off, the present-day woodchuck of field and pasture does not suffer from predation to a large extent. His chief enemies, besides man, are the fox, which digs him out of his hole, and the hawk, which kills the young. He is also susceptible and a prey to tularemia.

If he is cornered by a small hunting dog, he will put up a good fight, but his aim is to get to his burrow. He often manages, while facing a dog and clicking his teeth in warning, to back successfully into his hole.

The woodchuck is bold but alert, and few dangers escape his keen eyes. When he sights an enemy, he gives a shrill, whistlelike alarm. The whistle of the rockchuck is particularly strong and piercing, carrying as far as a mile.

When food becomes scarce and the woodchuck is rolling in his own fat, after a summer of glutting himself on succulent vegetation, he is ready for winter hibernation. He goes into a *true* hibernation, a deep, deathlike sleep, as contrasted to the characteristic hibernation of the bear, which is a light sleep, a semiconscious state. In the woodchuck, all normal body functions cease, whereas the bear gives birth and suckles her young, for example, while denned up. The body temperature of the burrowing woodchuck drops as low as 40° F.; the bear, on the other hand, sleeping on the surface of the ground, maintains a high body temperature and heat production in relation to the temperature of the air. The heartbeat of the woodchuck is about seven per minute with respiration averaging one per minute.

The woodchuck stays in hibernation four to six months, depending on the coldness of the range. His wakening is abrupt and for about a half hour his normal bodily activities are abnormally accelerated.

The woodchuck periodically emerges to test the weather and earth, making a permanent exit when the snow is gone and the ground is soft.

**Breeding.** The mating season begins with the males battling for the females. From four to six young are born in the spring, late April or early May in the more northerly ranges and about March in more southerly climates. Their coloring resembles the adults, but is not so rich.

Authorities differ on the maternal attitude of the mother. Some cite evidence of extreme selfishness or indifference, others report examples of frantic defense and general self-denial.

When very young, the offspring emerge from the burrow to feed and sun themselves. When the mother sees approaching danger she runs to the burrow and whistles, and the young run after her. They learn the association of whistle and danger so perfectly that imitators of the whistle have brought the young woodchucks scurrying to the hole even while they were feeding next to their mother. At a very early age, the young ones are forced to leave the burrow and fend for themselves.

**Range and Distribution.** The woodchuck inhabits most of North America, ranging from the Atlantic coast west to Oklahoma, and north from British Columbia to Alaska. He is most numerous in the eastern United States, where he is known to every farm boy and is hunted widely.

The yellow-footed marmot inhabits the western United States, British Columbia, and Alaska. The hoary marmot, or rockchuck, ranges the mountains of western North America and thrives in the Rocky Mountains.

The few animals who remain in the real forest are commonly found living in hollow logs or at the foot of trees. They are not so fat or sluggish as the field dwellers who have an abundance of rich food at their disposal.

**Hunting Methods.** Few other small animals can tax the hunter's patience or challenge his shooting ability more than can the educated woodchuck. In the more settled communities he has learned that his life depends on eternal vigilance and he is determined to go on living if possible.

A few states have accorded him the status of a game animal, and protect him during certain seasons, but generally he is classed as vermin and a fair target at any time. The 'chuck relies on no man-made law for protection, however, and his sharp eyes and natural caution are his best life insurance. Occasionally 'chucks, like all other animals, will do some pretty stupid things which upset the general pattern of their behavior, but the grizzled veteran of the pasture got that way because he was smart. Getting within range of a wise old 'chuck often calls for as much stalking ability as would be needed for a mountain goat or a bighorn ram.

There are two ways to hunt the woodchuck. One is to locate an area where there are several dens within sight and range—usually on a rocky hillside—and simply sit or lie quietly until the 'chucks appear.

The other way is to roam through likely 'chuck territory, spot the game, and then try to get within range before the 'chuck becomes suspicious and dives into his den. He never ranges far from a convenient hole and it takes him only a split second to disappear therein.

Some hunters save footwork by driving slowly along the highway until they spot their quarry through the glasses and then piling out of the car for a shot. In a few sections of the country it is still legal to shoot at vermin from a car on the highway, but most states tend to disapprove of this practice and it is well to be informed regarding the local laws. By and large, it is the hunter who is willing to tramp the back country who gathers the most 'chuck tails as trophies.

No matter which method is favored, a good pair of binoculars or a spotting scope is a definite asset in this sport. Many a woodchuck appears through the lenses that would never have been noticed with the naked eye, and many a rock or stump which resembles a 'chuck from a distance may be properly identified.

The woodchuck has a special fondness for clover and so will often be found near clover fields. Open fields, meadows, pasture land, rocky ledges, old stone fences, and along the edges of woodlands all are good places to find *monax* at home. Originally a woods animal, he still may be found deep in the backwoods of some sections, but generally he has transferred his activities to the more cultivated areas. Except in those communities where he has been excessively hunted there are few large farms in the East and Midwest where at least one or two 'chucks cannot be found.

*Monax* emerges from his winter sleep about the same time that the pussywillows burst forth and the first tender green shoots herald the spring. He forages above ground until late September, or even October if the weather is mild. He may be sought at any time during that period (but for exceptions provided by local laws) but it is late summer when 'chuck shooting is at its best. The 'chuck is not fond of rain and during bad weather he seldom shows himself above ground for long. Bright, sunny days find him basking outside his burrow and his favorite eating periods are early morning and late afternoon.

Once the 'chuck has been spotted it is time to begin the careful stalk which is usually necessary to get within good shooting distance. Sometimes the hunter gets a lucky break and discovers an unsuspecting 'chuck within easy range, or may be hunting in one of the few places where *monax* is still a little careless, but such occasions are few and far between in the average 'chuck country today. The 'chuck's keen eyes are alert to everything that moves and he seldom waits to find out what a strange movement is. His nose is not especially sensitive but he can detect danger if the wind is in his favor. His hearing is reasonably acute and a cracking twig will at least put him on the alert if it does not send him scurrying to a hole. With most of the advantage in favor of the 'chuck, the hunter has to play the game out to the best of his ability. Stalking becomes a matter of taking advantage of every bit of cover, of inching forward on the belly with the elbows and toes doing the propelling, and of "freezing" whenever *monax* sits up for a look-see. The approach should be made to windward if possible, and care must be taken not to make any noise. When the shooter has reached the best possible position from which to fire he must be doubly cautious about his movements. The sun glinting on a rifle barrel is a red light of danger to a 'chuck. A careless head thrust above a rock will defeat the most patient stalk, and even the snick of a rifle bolt may result in the loss of a shot.

Curiosity is seldom the 'chuck's undoing. When he suspects that all is not well he is usually content to dive into the most convenient hole and stay there until he is pretty sure the danger is past. Once in a while, however, if not badly frightened, a 'chuck will go down but after a minute or so he may thrust a cautious head part way out of the hole and take a look around. If the coast seems clear he often inches his way along until he is in full view. Sometimes it pays to wait a few minutes after a 'chuck has holed up in the hope that he may reappear. At other times a 'chuck may be feeding in long grass or in a spot where he offers little in the way of a target; frequently a low whistle will cause him to sit upright long enough for the cross-hairs to be centered on his chest. A trick that is often effective with two hunters is for one to remain in plain view of the 'chuck but well out of range while the other makes the stalk. The 'chuck is apt to center his attention on the first hunter and be less alert to the second.

**Rifle and Sights.** This is a rifleman's sport, and several guns have been developed in recent years for the primary purpose of woodchuck shooting. These so-called vermin (or "varmint") rifles come in a variety of calibers and each caliber has a fairly wide choice of loads. They all have one feature in common, high velocity and flat trajectory. Any one of them can be deadly if properly aimed and choosing from the many is a matter for the shooter.

Many a farm boy has killed 'chucks consistently with his single-shot .22. That little caliber is still popular with thousands of 'chuck hunters because it makes little noise, the ammunition is inexpensive, and there is no recoil. However, except where the 'chucks are less wary than usual it takes a lot of patient stalking to get within a range where the low-velocity bullet is effective. The modern hollow-point bullet is the best 'chuck load for the regular .22; standard long or long-rifle cartridges usually lack the force necessary for a clean kill. A 'chuck dies hard and can carry a lot of lead before he gives up the ghost. Even a mortally wounded 'chuck frequently manages to kick himself into his den before he dies. It takes nothing less than a head or spine shot with the .22 hollow-point to insure a clean kill.

One disadvantage of the low-velocity bullet is its tendency to ricochet off any solid object, or even the hard ground, and go whining across the landscape at odd angles. The safest load in populated communities is the high-velocity type because such a bullet "powders" or destroys itself on impact. These bullets tear a 'chuck wide open, and a hit on almost any portion of his anatomy is instantly fatal.

Any rifle used for this sport will be better if equipped with a telescope sight, for most of the shots offered will be at ranges where iron sights are inadequate. The scope selected may be of much higher magnification (as much as 10 power) than one used for ordinary offhand hunting, because the shooting is usually done while prone and with the barrel on some convenient rest. Scopes with very fine cross-hairs are generally preferred. Many shooters also add a sling to the rifle to aid in steady holding.

Here only two types of rifles have been suggested; one because it is commonly used and readily available, the other because it is becoming increasingly popular with a growing army of hunters who demand great accuracy at long ranges. Thousands of hunters, however, keep in practice between seasons by using their regular big-game rifles on woodchucks. Since the actual days afield are all too few and far between this idea permits the average hunter to keep his hand and eye in training. So long as the shooter exercises the proper precautions in regard to safety there is no reason why his pet deer rifle may not serve a double purpose.

Preferred calibers and loads in 'chuck shooting are:

.220 Swift with 48-grain bullet.
.219 Zipper with 46-grain bullet.
.22 Hornet with 45-grain bullet.
.22 Highpower with 70-grain bullet.
.257 Roberts with 87-grain bullet.
.250-3000 with 100-grain bullet.
.270 with 130-grain bullet.
.30 '06 with 110-grain bullet.

For details on loads see "Ammunition—Rifle."

NOTE: Many big-game hunters go 'chuck shooting primarily to become more familiar with their rifle, and these men will prefer to use the 2½- or 4-power telescope sight with which they may have equipped the rifle. Others invest in special vermin rifles, which normally they equip with a 10- or 12-power telescope sight. The fine crosshair reticule is almost standard equipment with the latter, although the former seem to prefer the tapered post. Most 'chuck hunters also go equipped with 6- or 8-power binoculars or a 20-power spotting scope. (See "Sights and Optical Aids.")

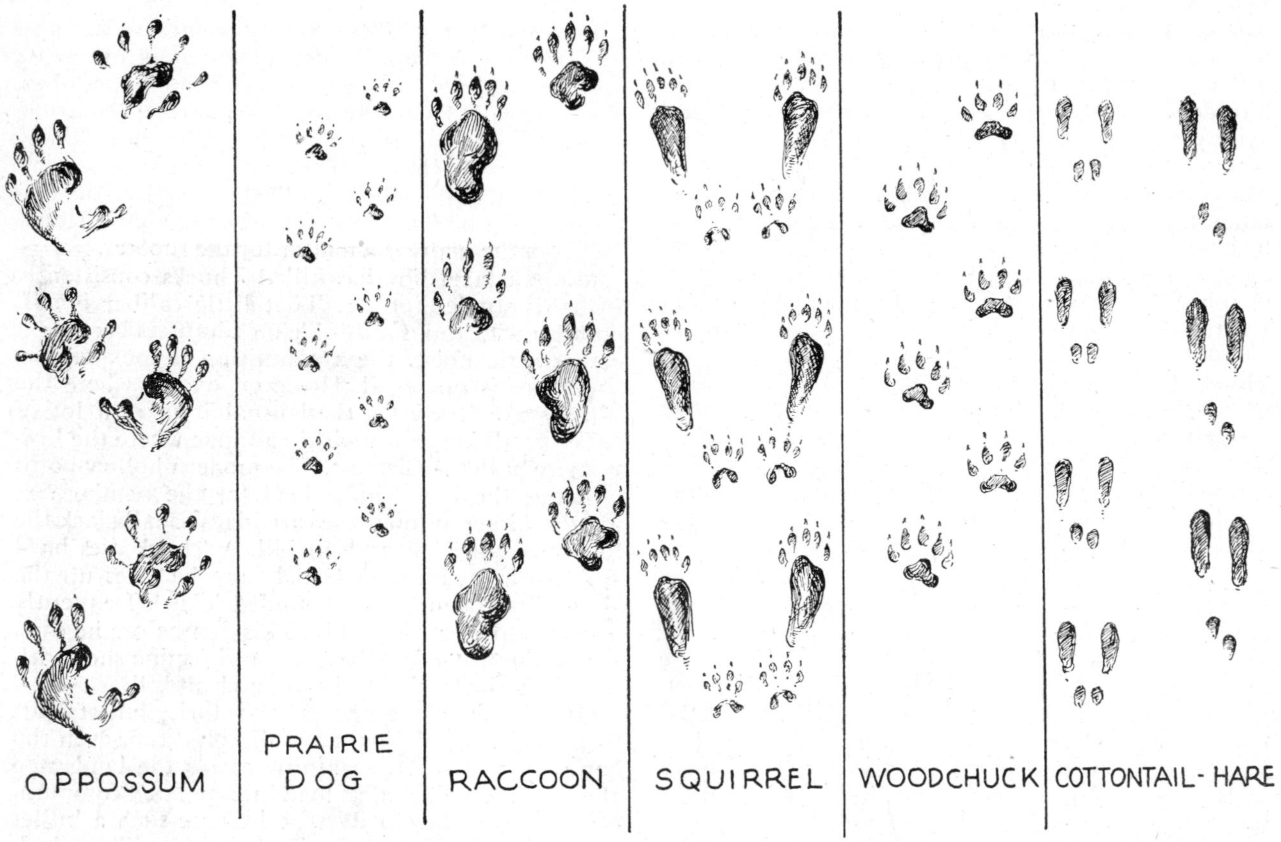

# ANIMAL PREDATORS

## BOBCAT

*Lynx ruffus*

Common Names: Bay Lynx, Red Lynx, Wildcat.

**History.** The bobcat differs from the Canadian lynx in that it is somewhat smaller, its tail is slightly longer, and the tufts on its ears are not so pronounced. Its feet are large in proportion to its size but not so much so as with the Canadian lynx.

**Identification.** There are several related species and considerable variation in color and size. In general, the animal is tawny-brown and spotted with dark brown spots on the back and sides. The under parts are yellowish-white, spotted with black, and the long legs are spotted on the outside and barred with black on the inside. The lips, chin, and underside of the neck are white and the mouth is edged with black. The Florida bobcat *(Lynx ruffus floridanus)* is darker in color and the desert bobcat *(Lynx ruffus eremicus)* is paler. But, in spite of slight differences in markings between these and other related species, the main characteristics of the animal remain the same.

In size bobcats also vary considerably. The average weight of the full-grown male is 20 to 25 pounds. But specimens of *Lynx gigas* from Nova Scotia have been reported weighing as much as 50 pounds. Very large ones have also been taken in New Brunswick. As is the case with all the cats, the female is somewhat smaller than the male.

**Breeding.** There seems to be no set mating season for these animals, and the young may be born at any time of the year. There are from two to four kittens in a litter and the den is in a hollow tree or log, rock cave, or dense thicket. During mating season and occasionally while they are hunting, bobcats give vent to loud yowls, sounds which are often wrongly attributed to cougars, which are generally silent creatures. (See "Cougar," p. 129.)

**Range and Distribution.** Bobcats are found from southern British Columbia to northern Mexico and from Nova Scotia to Florida and seem to be equally at home in mountains, deserts, pine forests, and swamps. In the swamp country of Florida, Georgia, and South Carolina, for instance, they do not hesitate to take to water when pursued by hounds and are excellent swimmers. In unsettled areas the bobcat preys on rabbits, small rodents of all kinds, fawns, and whatever birds it can catch. It is particularly destructive to young wild turkeys. In Maine, New Brunswick, and Nova Scotia, bobcats occasionally kill grown does when they catch the deer at a disadvantage in deep snow. The heavier deer, with its small, sharp hooves, breaks through the crust, over which the bobcat can travel with ease.

In sheep country bobcats kill many lambs; they are also very fond of small pigs and poultry. Although nocturnal and wary of man, bobcats are often seen in the early morning hours close to well-settled communities. Unlike cougars, they do not seem to require vast stretches of wilderness areas but are content enough to live wherever there is an abundance of food, even though it may be close to some farmer's house. As a matter of fact, the clearing and planting of fields attracts rats, mice, and rabbits, which in turn attract the bobcat.

**Hunting Methods.** The only way a bobcat may be hunted successfully is with hounds and in the South, particularly, it puts up a great chase, often running for several hours ahead of a fast pack of foxhounds before it is treed or caught. In some parts of the country it will tree readily, but the Florida species, especially, will usually run and dodge until it is exhausted. Then it will stop to fight. Not one out of 20 will climb a tree—whether pursued by two dogs or a dozen. To the man who is hunting cougars a bobcat is merely an incidental diversion, but in parts of the United States bobcat hunting is a sport in itself—and good sport at that.

U. S. Forest Service.

Plate I. The Bobcat, high on the list of predators.

U. S. Fish & Wildlife Service.

PLATE II. Watching the back trail to decide whether to run or climb.

For hunting these little cats in the southeastern United States, where they seem to put up a better run than anywhere else, a pack of fast foxhounds is desirable. Although a bobcat will not ordinarily make as large circles as a red fox, for instance, it is an expert dodger and when it gets into thick cover it is hard to catch. In one instance a big Florida bobcat ran for 7 hours ahead of a pack of 14 hounds—and they were blooded foxhounds, dogs which would kill a gray fox in an hour or less.

There are two methods of hunting the bobcat with dogs. One is for the hunters to take stands in likely spots and shoot the cat as it comes by. The other is to take no gun and leave the fate of the hunt with the hounds. This latter was the creed of the late Paul J. Rainey, who used to say, "I have no use for the man who will shoot a bobcat ahead of hounds. If the critter can outrun the pack, more power to him."

A big bobcat will put up a vicious fight when overtaken by the hounds, but four or five experienced dogs will soon finish it off without serious damage to themselves. Needless to say, there is no danger to the hunter, and the wild stories of bobcats springing on people are totally without basis. A bobcat in a trap, however, should be approached carefully, for it will often leap without hesitation to the end of the chain and there are many authentic cases of men having been badly clawed. In many respects the bobcat shows more nerve than the much larger cougar.

Bobcats are very fond of following old trails, logging roads, etc., and it is in such places as these that the hunter should take his stand. Almost invariably the dogs will strike the scent in some such old road or trail—where the bobcat has been noiselessly prowling along in search of rabbits—and very often

U. S. Forest Service.

PLATE III. A mule deer fawn which had been badly mauled by a bobcat, but finally recovered.

the cat will run these trails and roads for a short distance after the hounds have him up and running. Since a bobcat is comparable with a small hound in size, the hunter should bear this fact in mind and be very careful of his target, particularly in early morning light. When the pack is coming head-on, in full cry, the natural assumption is that the first object to make its appearance will be the cat, but this may not be the case. The cat may double back at a sharp angle just before reaching open ground and the dog which is in the lead may not be barking at the moment. Of course, there is always considerable excitement at such a time and the hunter should beware of an itchy finger. Better to let the cat escape than to cripple or kill a good dog, particularly if the dog belongs to some old swamp hunter who thinks as much of it as he does of his wife!

In the Maine woods the same system is used in bobcat hunting that is used for hunting red foxes through New England. Only a couple of dogs are necessary and the hunter, with his rifle or shotgun, tries to keep ahead of them, which is not too difficult because the quarry usually runs in circles. If the animal trees promptly, so much the better, for it is generally hunted for its pelt rather than for the sport. Early morning is the best time for hunting this animal and many hunters start out well before daylight in the hope of striking a hot trail and jumping the cat before sunup. Bobcats leave considerably less scent than the larger cougar and jaguar and, consequently, are more difficult for hounds to trail. If a good running trail can be had before the early morning dew is gone, so much the better. Some hunters who do not wish to shoot the cat, run the hounds on moonlight nights and get their thrill from the music of the chase.

Throughout the West the range of the bobcat usually coincides with that of the cougar and the same method of hunting is used. For some reason bobcats in the West tree much more readily and fast dogs are not required. The same hounds which are used in cougar hunting—preferably bloodhound-foxhound cross—are equally effective on bobcats.

**Rifle.** The hunter who is in the country where he is apt to find both cougars and bobcats will carry a rifle suitable for the larger cats. (See "Cougar," p. 133.) Otherwise, light rifles in .25-20, .25-35, and .32-20 calibers are amply powerful and many hunters prefer a shotgun loaded with No. 2 shot or BB's, particularly for shooting at cats which are running ahead of the dogs.

# COUGAR

*Felis concolor*

COMMON NAMES: Mountain Lion, Panther, Puma.

**History.** The cougar probably is the subject of more misinformation than any other animal in North America, with the possible exception of the wolverine. During the early days of colonization the animal also was known as painter and catamount, but these names are seldom used today.

At one time the cougar had a much broader range, running from northern Washington through mid-Alberta, across southern Quebec to Maine, and then extending south as far as the Strait of Magellan. Today this range has been sharply reduced, and in many areas the animal is found only in small "islands" of terrain that offer them the degree of isolation they require.

The cougar has no really close relative among the cats of other continents, but it is so closely allied in bone structure and teeth to other members of the cat family that biologists are inclined to list it as "sub-genus" rather than award it the status of a separate genus.

**Identification.** This big, tawny cat, fourth largest member of the cat family, and second largest member of the family on this continent, is characterized by its very long tail, heavy legs, and proportionately small, round head. Although the cougar actually weighs less than the jaguar, largest of our cats, it gives the appearance of greater size because of its longer legs and comparatively rangier build.

A big male cougar attains a maximum weight of slightly over 200 pounds and an over-all length of 8 to 9 feet. Of this length, the tail comprises approximately one-third. The average full-grown male, however, weighs around 140 pounds, and the average female not over 90. Average over-all measurements range from 6 to 8 feet.

In color the cougar grades from light tawny gray to almost "red" and a sub-species, *Felis coryi*, found in Florida, is occasionally almost chocolate brown. The tips of the tails are generally dark, sometimes almost black. The backs of the ears are black with gray-white patches and there are black patches on the upper lips. There is also considerable variation among cougars according to the season. As is the case with deer, these big cats are much grayer in the winter and more tawny in the summer.

**Characteristics.** Regardless of where he is found, whether in the heavily timbered mountains of Oregon, the rocky, arid canyons of Arizona, or the jungles of Central and South America, the habits of this big cat remain the same. His favorite natural food is venison and it has been estimated that a grown cougar will kill, on an average, one deer per week the year around. In ranching areas he prefers a colt to any other food, even venison, and will, on occasion, kill grown horses. He also preys on calves and sheep and has been known to kill and drag off sizable boars. In fact, one cougar collected in Florida had just killed a wild boar which was estimated to weigh well over 200 pounds. This was just a wild razorback but it had tusks 4 inches long. Notable, however, was the fact that this formidable fighter had been killed by the cougar after a very brief struggle, during which the big cat had not received a scratch!

Contrary to popular belief, the cougar rarely if ever leaps on its prey from the limb of a tree. All evidence indicates that it either lies in wait along a trail or ledge, or stalks its prey. Then it makes a quick dash, leaps onto the animal's withers, pulls its head down with one paw, and bites into the neck or throat. Having made its kill, the cougar covers the carcass with pine needles, sticks, leaves, or dead grass, often after first dragging it to a more secluded or shady spot. Sometimes an old male, who is traveling, will not cover the kill but will eat what he wants, leave the rest, and move on.

Unlike the timber wolf, cougars rarely kill just for the love of killing, although a few such individuals have been reported. One in particular, an old male, killed and maimed 19 sheep in one night! As a general rule, however, a cougar will make its kill, cover the carcass, and remain in that vicinity for several days until the meat is gone or becomes putrid, when it will leave to look for other prey. The cougar does not like putrid meat.

Many experienced cougar hunters will stoutly maintain that a cougar never makes any other sound than to growl and spit at the hounds when brought to bay. In fact, Ben Lillie, probably the greatest cougar hunter of them all, answered the question this way: "Well, a mountain lion may scream, but *I've* never heard one!" And it must be remembered that "Old Man" Lillie had accounted for over a thousand of the big cats during his lifetime of hunting them. On the other hand, several cougars in a zoo at Bonito Springs, Florida, have been known to utter high, shrill, whistling calls, and the keeper reported that on occasion they gave vent to loud, snarling screams which could be heard for some distance. Dale Lee, a professional cougar hunter and guide, observed a cougar screaming in a zoo in Oregon, although he admitted that he had never heard one scream during his hunting in the wilds, which included most of the western states and Mexico. It must be concluded, therefore, that cougars can and do scream on occasion, but that it is not typical of the animal as is the howling of a coyote or the roaring of an African lion.

There is also much argument as to whether or not a cougar will attack a man. They have been known to do so on occasion, but the occasions have been rare. As a general rule, these big cats are cowardly where man is concerned and will not usually attack even when brought to bay or treed. In fact, some government hunters kill their "lions" with pistols at very close range—even climbing up into the tree at times, with no fear of a charge. Here is a cat, larger than a leopard and able to kill grown horses and cattle, but possessing a strange fear of man.

In spite of its apparent fear of human beings, however, the cougar will often follow a man for considerable distances, as many hunters and ranchers will testify. Whether this habit arises from curiosity or whether the cougar wants to attack and does not quite have the nerve is something we probably will never know. The big cat is rarely seen on such occasions, and only his tracks, following the human tracks, remain as evidence.

In hunting any animal it is necessary to know its habits and habitat. Cougars live in communities, so to speak. An old male will range through a certain valley which may include over 100 square miles of territory. In this area there may be half a dozen females. The old tom makes regular trips through his range, visiting his harem. He has no interest

Jonas Bros., Denver, Colo.

PLATE I. Cougar.

Jonas Bros., Denver, Colo.

PLATE II. A realistic mount of the cougar killing a deer.

whatever in his offspring, however, and will, in fact, kill them if he has a chance. The females do not travel far from their dens, especially when the cubs are very young, and they will fight savagely in defense of these cubs, driving off the old male. As the cubs grow older, she takes them on hunting forays and teaches them to kill. Sometimes the cubs remain with the mother until they are a year old. Then they leave her and shift for themselves, seeking their own range.

During their travels, cougars make "scratches" and "sign heaps," usually near where each has made a kill. They visit these scratchings regularly when making their rounds, checking up on each other, so to speak, in much the same way that a dog uses a tree. A knowledge of the terrain and the location of sign heaps and scratchings is of great aid to the cougar hunter.

**Breeding.** There appears to be no regular mating season and the cubs may be born at any time of year. There are usually two and sometimes three in the litter, and cases have been reported of litters of four. The cubs are spotted with large splotches of dark brown and their little tails are ringed with black like a tiger's tail. As they grow older the spots and tail rings gradually disappear and are almost gone by the time the animal is six months old.

**Range and Distribution.** The cougar has a greater range than any other member of the cat family, being found from British Columbia to southern Argentina. In past years it was widely distributed throughout the United States but today is almost extinct east of the Rockies. As a matter of fact, many scientists claim this animal to be virtually extinct in the eastern United States but this is offset by the fact that nine cougars were taken during expeditions into the Big Cypress Swamp of Florida in 1933 and 1935. There are still quite a few of these big cats left in the Big Cypress Swamp, the Everglades, and the mangrove swamps of the Ten Thousand Islands. Since much of this area is very difficult to hunt, the cougar, or panther, as it is called down there, will undoubtedly remain a part of the Florida wildlife picture for some years to come.

**Hunting Methods.** Very few men have ever seen a cougar, which has not first been treed, being brought to bay by hounds. The big cats are nocturnal, lying up in rock bluffs or other inaccessible places during the day, and are so wary and stealthy that they can easily slip away well in advance of any intruder. It is obvious, therefore, that to hunt them successfully well-trained hounds are essential. Since deer, coyotes, and foxes are usually also present in cougar country it is necessary that the dogs be proof against the scent of these other animals and trained to trail only the big cats. Most cougar hounds will also take the trail of a bobcat—especially a very hot trail—but some old, experienced cougar dogs apparently lose all interest in the smaller cats; lucky indeed is the hunter who owns such a dog. Through its enthusiasm or lack of enthusiasm on a trail, he is able to tell whether his pack is after a cougar or a bobcat and thereby save considerable time. The little cats are harder to run and harder to tree, as a general rule, and the hunter who is after cougar does not like to waste time on bobcats.

Training a pack of cougar hounds is a specialized job requiring much patience and hard work. There are comparatively few really good packs in the country, and these are owned by professional guides and government hunters. For a successful cougar hunt it is almost imperative to obtain the services of such a hunter and his hounds. Without dogs a man could spend ten years in the best cougar country and never get a shot at one. There are a number of professional cougar hunters in the Southwest who occasionally combine hunting with the business of serving as guides.

A cougar is one of the fastest animals on earth for the first hundred yards, but it has very small lungs and is short-winded. Often, when jumped by hounds, it will climb the first sizable tree it can find, and, in any event, rarely runs far. The average chase does not last over 10 or 15 minutes, although occasionally a big male will give the hounds some trouble in the bluffs and ledges, sometimes refusing to tree and coming to bay in the rocks. There are many cases of cougars being jumped and treed by one dog—shepherd dogs, mongrels, airedales, and even wire-haired fox terriers having accomplished the feat—for it is not difficult to tree a cougar after it has been jumped from its bed. The real job lies in trailing the animal to its bed.

It would be safe to say that 90 per cent of cougar hunting is working out a cold trail. It follows, therefore, that hounds must have keen noses and great perseverance. Occasionally foxhounds possess the necessary qualities, but the ideal cougar dog seems to be a bloodhound-foxhound cross. Purebred bloodhounds rarely make good hunters as their feet will not stand up in the rocks and they are inclined to potter around on hopelessly cold trails. Good voice is a valuable asset in a cougar hound, as it is through his baying that he keeps his master advised of the progress of the hunt. In big, rugged country it is often impossible for the hunter to keep up with his hounds and many times they will go out of hearing and tree their quarry on the other side of a big mountain or canyon. Often several hours will elapse before the hunter is able to locate them. It is at such a time as this that training really counts. Experienced dogs will sit right there under the tree "telling the news" until their master arrives, whether it be one hour or ten. In fact, some famous dogs have been known to stay at a tree for 14 hours! It is obvious that such patience and perseverance can come only through long experience, during which the dog has learned that eventually his master will arrive and shoot out that big, snarling cat.

The man who hunts cougars should be prepared for some long, hard days in the saddle—breakfast before daylight so that he can be hunting at the crack of dawn, for it is a great advantage to strike a trail early, before the sun has burned off the dew. Moisture intensifies the scent, as evidenced by the fact that hounds can always handle a trail better in the snow on the north hillsides than they can on the southern slopes where the snow has melted off and the rocky ground is dry.

Many times hounds will work all day on the cold trail of a traveling cougar, leading the hunters many miles from camp. If the weather is not too severe it often pays to tie the horses, build a fire, roll up in the saddle blankets, and take the trail again next morning. It is surprising how hounds can go to work again on the same trail with which they were having much difficulty the evening before. And it must always be remembered that what may seem to be a hopelessly cold trail can suddenly develop into a smoking-hot scent, for the cougar must eventually make a kill and lie down. A day and a half of cold trailing may suddenly be climaxed by a wild burst of music from the hounds and five minutes later a treed cat. So never give up hope as long as the dogs can follow the scent.

Although there is little danger to the hunter, it must be remembered that the cougar is a big, powerful cat which can do plenty of damage to the hounds. If a cougar falls out of a tree crippled the dogs will rush in with disastrous results. The big cat can disembowel a dog with those raking hind claws or kill it by biting through its skull. Therefore, the hunter should take plenty of time and get close enough to be sure of his aim. A head or neck shot is preferable because it will kill instantly.

There is no need to hurry when approaching a treed cougar, for even if it should jump out it will run only a short distance before climbing another tree. When the big cat has been shot out, let the dogs have their fun and worry the carcass to their heart's content. It may look as if they are tearing that fine trophy to pieces but, as a matter of fact, their teeth rarely puncture the tough hide.

In cool, dry climates the skin should be spread out on the ground flesh side up, thoroughly salted, and then either rolled up or tacked on the side of the cabin, flesh side out. If the animal is killed in low, humid country it is desirable to stretch the skin in a frame of poles so that the air may circulate freely around it. (This method is later described in the section on jaguars, pp. 159-160.)

The meat of a cougar is good to eat and has no wild flavor whatsoever, tasting a good deal like a cross between veal and lamb. The South American Indians prefer the meat of both the cougar and the jaguar to any other game, including venison. It is juicy and palatable, and if a man can just forget that he is eating cat he will find this meat an excellent addition to his camp fare.

Cougars are often taken alive, and, because the big cat fights purely a defensive fight, this is not a particularly difficult or hazardous operation, but it is preferably a two-man job. The hounds should be tied up, well back from the tree. Then when a noose has been gotten over the cat's head it can be pulled to the ground—if it does not jump of its own accord. The next step is to get a rope on one or both of its hind legs and stretch the animal between a couple of trees, after which it can be hog-tied and effectively muzzled by tying a stick in its mouth or by using a regular strap muzzle similar to the ones used on dogs. Unlike jaguars or bobcats, cougars, when captured young, can be tamed to some extent.

**Rifle and Sights.** A light carbine is all that is required for cougar hunting. There is seldom any real danger to the hunter, and the shot usually can be made at very short range. A .30-30, a .32 special, or any good saddle gun has ample killing power for this animal. The following calibers and loads are normally used:

.30-30 with 150-grain bullet.
.32 Special with 170-grain bullet.
.35 with 150-grain bullet.
.30 '06 with 170-grain bullet.
.300 with 150-grain bullet.

For details, see "Ammunition—Rifle."

NOTE: Iron sights are all that are required, due to the short range, and normally the rifle will be sighted in at 50 yards.

## AMERICAN COYOTE

*Canis latrans*

**History.** The name coyote comes from the Spaniards, and is a modification of the Aztec word *coyotl.* Eighteen races of the coyote have been described since 1823, when Thomas Say, an early American zoologist, first named the animal, calling it *Canis latrans,* the "barking dog."

**Identification.** Coyotes are relatively small animals. An adult male will weigh about 35 pounds and reach nearly 4 feet in length, including the tail, or brush. In appearance a coyote resembles a small dog. Novices often mistake German shepherd dogs for coyotes and vice versa; but the observant hunter soon learns to recognize at least three characteristic marks of identification: the sharply-pointed ears, which never droop, or fold over, as with some dogs; the equally sharp and pointed nose; and the long heavy brush, which appears to float behind the animal when in flight.

The coyote's color changes slightly with changes in season. In summer, a coyote is predominantly gray, the color washing out into a light tan along the belly and lower legs—which makes the beast blend well with the weeds and summer grasses through which it slinks. In winter the pelage thickens and becomes lighter in color, making detection difficult when the animal is in winter snow, sage, or brush.

**Characteristics.** In a den, similar to that of the wolf, it produces a litter of young averaging seven in number, but there are specific instances on record of individual litters as large as 15, 17, and 19. They weigh, on an average, 21 pounds at full maturity.

U. S. Fish & Wildlife Service.

PLATE I. Coyote.

U. S. Fish & Wildlife Service.
PLATE II. Coyote Depredation on Sage Hen Nest.

Coyotes are not highly selective as to food. They eat birds, insects, carrion, rabbits, and what larger game, both wild and domestic, they can overcome or catch at a disadvantage. They are predacious by nature and transient to the extent of following their food supply. They prey on poultry yards and sheep flocks in outlying districts. In packs they can kill animals of the deer class, in heavy winter snow or when such game is caught upon the ice of rivers or lakes. They follow desert concentrations of jack rabbits.

In addition to its ability to perpetuate itself, even in direct conflict with man—by whom much of its habitat has been greatly modified—and the tenacity with which it can do this, the American coyote has become our outstanding North American predatory mammal. Like wolves, coyotes also use a runway (see p. 168), but it is of more limited extent. The animal tends to localize itself, generally ranging but short distances from the den where it was born. Food is a factor that has much to do in controlling the coyote's migratory movements. Present field studies indicate that scarcity of food coupled with its constant persecution by man are reasons for the spread of its range. It is the only American carnivore known that has been able to do this.

The coyote also seemingly possesses an anatomy that can withstand much in the way of shock and pain, as shown by its ability to overcome severe physical disability to the point of complete recovery. Coyotes have been trapped that had all four feet missing, the result of trapping injuries received previously. The stubbed feet in such instances were found to be all healed, nor did the animal appear to be greatly handicapped in moving around in its habitat. Often, too, but one foot or two feet will be found missing, the animal thus becoming what the coyote trapper, in western range parlance, dubs "peg-legs." In cases of this kind under observation, the coyote that is minus from one to four feet, or maintains broken elbows, the result of a rifle bullet, or is otherwise badly shot up, invariably turns out to be a worse depredator on domestic stock than the coyote which is in normal condition. This is probably because of the greater ease with which domestic stock can be killed by the coyote when laboring under such physical handicaps. It requires more strength to capture and kill wild prey such as deer and their young, or fast-running rabbits and rodents. Judging from field experiences, very few of the smaller carnivores, such as the fox and badger, ever recover from trap injuries after escape. Seldom are any of those recaptured minus one or more feet, nor do they otherwise show previous injury. The supposition is that such injuries, so remarkably withstood by the coyote, soon cause the death of the smaller carnivores following their escape.

More adaptable to a modified habitat than its near relative the wolf, which is practically disappearing from its former western ranges, the coyote will long remain a part of our western fauna. Whether it will ever be lessened in numbers, like the present-day wolf, can only be conjectured. So far, it has been able to persist in appreciable numbers. Its present-day habitat, however, is being subjected to more and more intense modification, and more modern instruments are being brought into use against it, such as hunting from airplanes and motor cars. Confined habitat and modern methods of extermination will no doubt severely handicap the coyote. That it has little place in a habitat shared by man engaged in livestock production has long been recognized, and to this end its control is constantly sought. Even where not in direct conflict with man, its habitat is being intensely worked most of the time for the monetary returns that are derived from the creature's pelt. Before the depression, the pelt brought a handsome price, but in later years an average of $5 a pelt has been considered excellent.

Possibly expanding industry and the opening up of new jobs may take some of the pressure off the animal, thereby giving it a chance to build up its numbers throughout its range to the extent it did following the poison onslaught of the 1860's and onward for the following quarter-century. If so, more intense control may be required in the livestock areas and game ranges of the West, where it never has been and never will be willingly tolerated. Further impetus might likewise be given toward more intensive coyote control in livestock-producing areas than at present on the part of the Federal Government as a national measure. The nation's meat supply looks better hanging in the nation's larder than it does as meat abandoned and lost on the ranges as a partial toll to the coyote. No one will shout this louder than the producer of beef and mutton.

Through the years our western coyote has contended with ups and downs. A distinguished naturalist once wrote:

> ". . . Theoretically he [the coyote] compels a certain degree of admiration, viewing his irrepressible positivity of character and his versatile nature. If his genius has nothing essentially noble or lofty about it, it is undeniable that few animals possess so many and so various attributes or act them out with such dogged perseverance. . . . The main object of his life seems to be the satisfying of a hunger which is always craving; and to this aim all his cunning, impudence, and audacity are mainly directed."

That was our North American coyote in 1873. Through the succeeding years it has changed but little; if anything, it has become tougher, though not to the extent that we cannot deeply admire it and hope that in its proper place it will continue to form a part of our western fauna. Judged by everything about the animal in the past, the coyote, of all the mammals in North America, appears to be the most permanent.

This versatile wild dog of the western prairies, deserts, and mountains, possesses one particular characteristic by which it is best remembered by those becoming acquainted with it for the first time. That is its several calls, particularly those made late at night or just near the break of day. One western man aptly described the coyote's cry as a "prolonged howl which the animal let out and then ran after and bit into small pieces."

**Range and Distribution.** It may be that the possession of such recuperative powers as shown by the coyote also accounts for its remarkable ability to extend its range; to hold its own as to numbers; and to obtain a livelihood in mountain, valley, or desert habitats in spite of every hand's being turned against it. Unknown in Alaska before the famous gold rush of 1898, latest wild-animal estimates there show it now ranging throughout the greater portion of Alaska in numbers estimated at 10,000. Therefore, the present remarkable range of the coyote extends from near Point Barrow, Alaska, in the frozen north to tropical Costa Rica in Central America—a north and south range of approximately 7200 miles. Then, too, it has the outstanding dietary habit of subsisting on a large variety of items, consisting in part of carrion, insects, birds, domestic stock, rodents, reptiles, and at times full-grown deer and their young.

Many of the coyotes that have been captured to date, or reported in the eastern United States, have come as prospective pets in the autos of returning tourists, only to escape from their owners. Others have been planted inadvertently by fox hunters who, unknowingly, had coyote pups shipped to them by wild-animal dealers for planting, instead of young foxes. The young of the fox and the coyote are at times hard to distinguish by the average layman. The fact was apparent in one of the southern states when fox puppies supposedly were introduced by sportsmen as an aid in replenishing the diminishing supply of foxes for hunting. The release of these took place in 1924. Five years later, in 1929, these animals began to make themselves known by the livestock depredations they were committing on the ranches or farms in the locality of their original liberation.

Some coyotes have been deliberately turned loose. In reporting upon the coyote's recent appearance in one eastern state, the state's game department stated: "This is not an unusual case, as several coyotes have been introduced into the state by persons purchasing them from the West for pets, eventually getting tired of them and then turning them into the wild." Coyotes reported in northwest Florida were believed to have been the result of a liberation by a man from Idaho who, on abandoning his farm in Gadsden County, liberated 11 coyote pups that he had kept on the farm as pets.

The occurrence of the animal in New Jersey was proved by the taking of a female of the species in 1938 near Ringoes. Several reported crosses between the coyote and dog were also captured. As a consequence of the depredation that had occurred on livestock in that state, legislation was enacted making anyone liberating a coyote liable to a fine of $100 for each offense, as well as making it illegal to possess the animal except under certain regulations. The violation of this latter clause called for a similar fine for each coyote illegally possessed in New Jersey.

Only the future will tell whether the plantings of the coyote will result in the species establishing itself in the eastern United States where it has never been known or reported as occurring naturally in all of our history. Many of the far eastern and

PLATE III. Coyote and Dog, mortal enemies in spite of close family relation hip.

southern states contain suitable habitat for it. If the present eastern extension of its range and that northward into Alaska in the past 40 years are any criteria, it may well establish itself in the East and South if given enough encouragement. Wherever the animal has shown itself to date in the eastern states, it has created huge excitement in the locality where seen or killed, judging by the efforts that have been made by the local inhabitants, or in some cases by personnel of state game departments, to get rid of it—and generally with success.

**Predation.** There is no North American predator that can compare, up to the present time, with the coyote in its ability to hold its own in the face of the many factors with which it must contend. The first great hazard which it faced on the North American continent took place more than 80 years ago when, together with the wolf, it was subjected to probably the greatest mass poisoning ever instituted by man. This poisoning program began in the late 1850's and continued for the following quarter-century. It was conducted over much of the animal's prairie range from southern Saskatchewan, Canada, southward to the Texas Panhandle. This episode was contemporary with the so-called "tongue and tallow period" of the Plains buffalo. Thousands of coyotes were taken for their pelts around the strychnine-poisoned carcasses of buffaloes and antelopes. The professional wolf poisoner came prominenty into the picture at the time. He was the successor in many respects of the beaver trapper who, because of the diminished supply of beavers, turned to wolf and coyote poisoning for a livelihood. His income was from the sale of the skin. In spite of the thousands of coyotes killed by poison during this interval, enough of the species survived this onslaught so that by the close of the last century coyotes appeared to be in as great numbers as ever before.

**Hunting Methods.** Coyote hunting as a sport is gaining in popularity. This is due partly to the combination of more hunters and a dwindling game supply, and largely to the coyote's own intrinsic possibilities as a sporting quarry. Hunters who pursue coyotes on the same terms they would accord big-game animals find that it takes perhaps even greater skill to bring these little prairie wolves consistently to bag.

By trial and error, luck, and intelligent persistence, coyote hunters have learned a variety of methods which will produce results. These methods, in turn, are based upon the coyote's characteristics, habits, and the terrain over which he roams. The first step in using, or evolving, any technique of hunting the coyote, is a basic understanding of the animal itself.

Coyotes are both prolific and ubiquitous. Generally speaking, the varmints are to be found in all game areas, wilderness sections, and sparsely-settled regions the country over. Despite the fact that encroaching settlement has driven the animals from all strictly urban areas, they have, nevertheless, demonstrated the capacity to live, thrive, and multiply, virtually in civilization's back yard. They are intelligent, wary, and cunning beasts. They are fleet of foot and only such dogs as the greyhound, wolf hound, or other dogs bred especially for coursing, can overtake them. For the hunter, coyotes represent a quarry hard to spot, and, once seen, an elusive, distant, and difficult target.

Perhaps the most widely used method of coyote hunting might loosely be called "incidental" coyote hunting—that is to say, hunting coyotes in conjunction with game animals. This type of coyote hunting can be as casual, or as intense, as the hunter wishes. Game country is almost without exception coyote country, since the beasts are both vegetarian

Clyde Ormond, Rigby, Idaho.

PLATE IV. Coyotes are often killed "incidentally" by hunters after deer, elk, and other big-game animals.

and carnivorous, and scavenge on the remains of diseased game, weakened animals, etc.

In this type of hunting, the hunter's main interest is game, but he keeps alert also for sign and sight of coyotes. The same binoculars or telescope sight he expects to use on deer, elk, or other game, will be used for locating the occasional coyote; and the same rifle the hunter carries for game will naturally be used on any coyote spotted. Many of the little prairie wolves are killed in this incidental fashion. The deer hunter, motionless along a game trail, suddenly detects a movement in the brush which resolves itself into the gray slinking form of a coyote—and slowly raises his rifle for a lucky shot. Or the elk hunter listening for an elk bugle at daylight, sees the slight motion of a doglike animal, trotting and silhouetted upon a ridge-top across the basin, recognizes the beast as the maker of that weird, plaintive "yodeling" of the night before, and makes a lucky shot from prone.

These incidents may almost be called "accidental" coyote hunting, just as youngsters hunting rabbits occasionally come across a wandering coyote and shoot it with a .22 rifle or shotgun, or as a cattleman, fence rider, rancher, or other outdoorsman may happen upon a chance coyote while engaged in other pursuits. Many such people carry scabbarded rifles for just such opportunities.

However, "incidental" coyote hunting need not be that haphazard. Many veteran game hunters go at it with more forethought and chance of success. They plan hunting trips so as to include a day or so of coyote hunting, as such, either before or after the main hunt. They often alter routes of travel to and from the hunting field so as to cross desert country or other areas where coyotes are known to be. They plan to "take" this country either in the hours shortly after daylight or at dusk—the two periods of daylight when a coyote does most of his own hunting and is, consequently, on the move. While crossing such country one of the party will drive, the others watch the rolling buttes, promontory points, and desert flats for any slinking form, or pair of upright, inverted V's, which may resolve itself into a coyote moseying about, or a pair of ears.

While hunting deer or other game, the hunter still keeps his eye peeled on the high ridge-crests, old game trails, and the early-morning, sunny side of canyon humps from which a coyote may be watching.

With other game down, the hunter (after coyotes incidentally) has his best chance of getting one of the little prairie wolves. Coyotes will scent a game kill within a matter of hours. Any of them within the general area will gravitate toward the smell of fresh blood and meat. While there is any man-smell about such a kill, the beasts will not approach too closely though they will circle the area at a distance of a few rods. Many coyotes are killed by the hunter who noiselessly approaches his game kill each morning at daylight until the meat is removed, with his rifle and senses alert for the presence of the little gray predators. Many other coyotes are killed by hunters watching the "ripe" offal of game kills for several days after the meat has been packed away and all man-scent is gone.

It is safe to say that the majority of hunters who can boast of having killed coyotes will have killed their first one "incidentally."

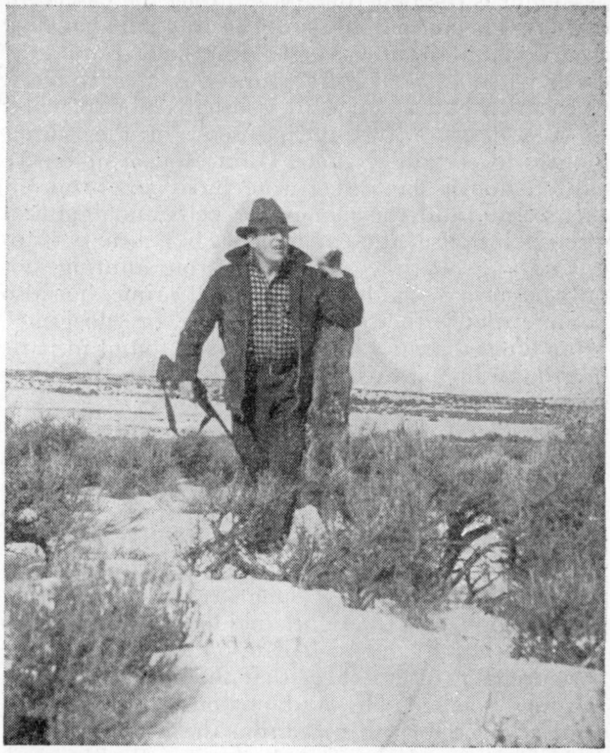

Clyde Ormond, Rigby, Idaho.

PLATE V. It is good sport to go out after a coyote on his own ground and bag him under the same conditions as other game.

One of the most interesting and commonly used methods of pure coyote hunting might be termed "running the desert." This manner of hunting coyotes presupposes large areas of desert or prairie land free of fences, a vehicle capable of negotiating such sections of terrain, and a known coyote population. There are many such areas in the West. Usually they are semi-barren tracts of arid land, covered with sage, rabbit-brush, or tumbleweeds, which are far from settlements and have not been used except, perhaps, for summer range for sheep.

These desert regions often contain large jackrabbit populations, rodent infestations, and game birds such as sage grouse. As a consequence, they are ideal coyote grounds. The little wolves can freely prey on the smaller animals, den and reproduce in the rocky bluffs adjacent to such areas, and range over great stretches of terrain—all free of human molestation. Running the desert simply means going out into such country and hunting the coyote on his own terms, and in his own bailiwick.

A rugged car is a "must" for such desert travel. More often than not the only roads are the ones the hunters themselves make through the sage, up and down the gullies, across rocky flats. Occasionally an old road made by a sheep outfit, or wood hauler, can be found. But only a car in first-class mechanical condition can be expected to take such desert punishment. Half-ton pick-up trucks, equipped with chains, shovel, spare tires, extra gas and water can, are favored. So are army jeeps and weapons carriers having four-wheel drive.

Winter is the best time for running the desert for coyotes. The animals are more easily spotted against a background of snow than against the sage and gray earth of summer. Desert country is arid country. Consequently, the snowfall is usually not sufficient to stop desert travel during most of the winter months in certain sections. Hunters also prefer the winter months because coyote hides are prime at this season, and the money for pelts and bounties often helps offset the expense. Early February is an especially good time for desert coyote hunting, not only because of the hides being still prime, but also because that is the season of mating, or "dogging." More often than not, the animals are found in pairs or groups during this period; and at such time they seem less wary of the presence of man.

The actual hunting procedure in this type of hunting is simple. It consists largely in driving leisurely and for great distances through desert country, utilizing all possible roads and routes so as to make the coverage complete. Usually, hunters go in pairs. One man drives, the other watches for suspicious-looking objects, such as sagebrush that doesn't look exactly right, odd-looking clumps of lava, brush, and weeds. It is upon the skill and experience of this "watcher" that the success of desert running is based. He must not only have the eyesight and practice to pick from the literally thousands of desert objects that look virtually identical, the one which "doesn't seem to belong there"; but, in addition, he must have the further capacity to interpret this particular object, as to both contour and color, in terms of a possible coyote.

If a first suspicion seems verified, the hunters stop the car and put binoculars or telescope sight upon the object. Nine times out of ten it is but another sagebrush or jutting lava. The tenth time, perhaps, the glass reveals that it *isn't* sage, but a pair of ears attached to a coyote, watching from behind the sagebrush.

Once an actual dog is seen, the hunters try to get in a shot before the animal flees. Coyotes are aggravating in this respect. They seem able to divine a hunter's intention of doing them harm; to break and run at precisely the instant before he is ready to shoot; to flee in a direction which inevitably puts every obstruction upon the terrain between themselves and the shooter. Coyotes have the further characteristic of habitually stopping on the *last* crest within sight of the hunter (unless the hunter is pursuing them), for a second or so, to look back. Many coyotes are shot by hunters who are ready and waiting for this instant.

Some hunters shoot from the car, after shutting off the motor, and use the seat, wheel, and seat cushions for a rifle rest. Others, with a different code of hunting ethics, prefer to pile out of the car before shooting.

A variation of this type of hunting is hunting from a winter camp in the desert. The same heavy-duty, rugged car is used, but only to get an outfit deep into the desert, and to make frequent camp changes, since coyotes are suspicious to the extreme and hastily quit a known camping spot.

Winter camp-hunting for coyotes is a rugged business which only the physically hardy and eager should attempt. Equipment calls for an easily set up tent, down sleeping-bags, woolen clothing with plenty of extras, scope-sighted, precision rifles, ample food, and a ten-gallon can of water for "dry-camping." This is all in addition to the car extras mentioned before.

The actual terrain influences the spots picked for this type of hunting. Experienced coyote hunters favor the country which marks the boundary between vast desert flats, and the extending bars, promontories, and gullies where such flats "break" into the higher plateaus above. Coyotes love such places—points, tiny buttes, ridges, etc.—from which they can at once watch the desert flats below, and the plateaus above, both for their own prey and possible danger to themselves. If coyotes are in an area, veteran hunters know they will be found at such points at daylight.

Camp is set up as close to such likely places as possible without actually invading the country to be hunted. Available fuel supply determines the camp site, also, since the desert is "woodless," and the campfire must be of sage. The main consideration is sufficient dry sage for a fire, and a spot in some broken gully where the car and tent cannot be seen by coyotes for any great distance.

In this type of hunting, the hunters take off on foot after the animals, with rifle, binoculars, and possibly webs if the snow is deep. Hunting in this manner is not merely tramping away from camp, in any old direction, until something is spotted. It is planned hunting. Camp is made only upon the discovery that coyotes are in the vicinity. Such discovery is made either from reliable information obtained in advance (such as information from sheep-herders, etc.), the presence of fresh coyote tracks in the snow, or from actually having heard the beasts "yodel." Weather has a great influence on this type of hunting. Veterans choose a time, if possible, when there has been recent and light snow, when it is frosty, and when there is no wind. Coyotes travel more just after a snowstorm which has kept them huddled. They howl more during frosty, clear weather. They dislike to move about during windstorms.

If, while driving a desert "road," a pair of hunters locate either broken, rolling country (which their experience labels "likely"), or see fresh coyote tracks (similar to tracks of a small dog) in the snow, or happen to hear the weird howl of a beast, then a hurried camp is in order. Camp is simply made—just a light tent, quickly erected, and a tiny fire of sagebrush. No undue noise is made, and the remaining hours of that day, at least until dusk, are spent in marking down any possible coyotes in that area.

Locating the animals is done either with binoculars, by watching and scrutinizing every possible ridge, promontory, and bluff in the general area, or by listening for the animal's howling. One coyote, to the inexperienced, sounds like many. The successful hunter must determine, from perhaps ten seconds of "yodeling," not only how many dogs are calling but where each is located. In clear, cold, and frosty weather, noise carries far. Once a single coyote howls, all animals within a mile area may be expected to answer.

With all possible beasts marked down, the hunters wait for morning. By daylight, they are at the spot, or spots, where coyotes are known to have been the evening before. They move slowly, sit for long periods glassing every possible object, and are often rewarded by the sight of a prairie wolf moseying about, beginning his own day's hunting. Long shots are the rule. The hunter usually will shoot from prone or sitting, the two best possible shooting positions. His rifle must be a precision instrument, correctly sighted in to strike "on the nose" from a cold barrel. The first shot ordinarily must do the trick. Succeeding shots are invariably harder, since the target will (after the first shot) be instantly in motion—and nothing dodges faster, or vanishes more completely, than a scared coyote in high sagebrush.

With the coyotes spooked or luckily killed from one area, camp is hurriedly broken and set up again, perhaps miles away, at another likely area.

Running coyotes with horses is another method, perhaps the most thrilling of all. Hunting coyotes in this fashion presupposes several fundamental and ideal conditions. The area to be coursed must contain a reasonably "heavy" coyote population. It must be an area of at least several miles diameter, free of fences, gullies, and boulder areas over which a good saddle horse cannot cross—usually at a good stiff gallop. Another prerequisite is a recent heavy fall of snow, which, at the time of hunting, is yet unfrozen. Several storms in a series will suffice if a combination of thawing-and-freezing weather has not intervened. The ideal is about a foot or more of fresh fluffy snow, which tires a running coyote but which a good running horse can negotiate at a good pace for several miles. Dogs in this type of hunting are neither used nor necessary.

Many desert areas which are adjacent to the periphery of recently settled ranching country make good country for this kind of hunting. Especially good are elevations over 4000 feet, where considerable snow-depth in winter may be expected.

Saddle horses are either trailer-hauled to the area (once the combination of conditions appears ideal) or are arranged for beforehand, as close to desert-edge as available. The riders are ready, at the edge of coyote country, at daylight. In instances of reasonable snow-depth, hunting begins at once. The riders spread out, fan-shape, within "hollering-up" distances of each other. They head into the desert area, eyes scanning the fresh snow for possible coyote tracks. Fresh coyote tracks in fresh snow at daylight ordinarily mean that the beast is not far off. Occasionally a rider spots an actual beast before he discovers a track, but this is rare.

Once a fresh track is located the hunt begins. One or a pair of hunters strike off on the coyote's trail. Experienced hunters can tell from the tracks whether it is fresh, and whether the animal has merely been hunting or is suspicious. A short-stepped, meandering trail in the snow means the animal is unsuspicious. The point where such a trail straightens out, heads in a predetermined direction, and the sets of footprints extend to a galloping stride, is the spot where the varmint discovered himself to be pursued. Hunters can tell from this how long ago such discovery has been made, what difference in miles separate the hunter and the hunted, and in what general direction the chase will be.

At such a point the race quickens. Veteran riders can tell how much a good coursing horse can stand,

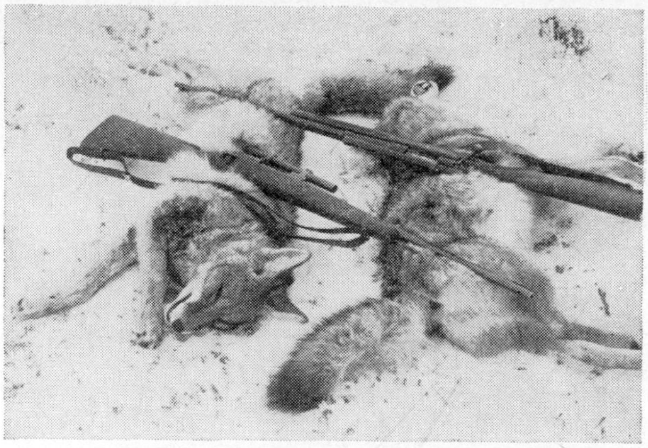

Clyde Ormond, Rigby, Idaho.

PLATE VI. The best coyote rifles are the modern, high-velocity, super-accurate models, with medium-power, low-mounted telescope sights.

and still retain enough energy for a final burst of speed. Usually the pace is alternated between a quarter-mile of mild galloping, and a similar distance of trotting while the horse catches its wind. Snow-depth, terrain, and condition of the horse all influence the length and possible outcome. Under ideal conditions an experienced horseman can overtake a coyote in from 2 to 4 miles after the beast straightens out. When the pursued coyote actually comes within view, usually at about one-half mile, the rider pushes his horse for all the speed it has. At this point, the coyote tires rapidly; and when the intervening distance is cut to less than 100 yards, the beast is apt to go around in circles as if insane, and simply lie down exhausted.

The dispatching is done usually with a rifle or pistol. Some men kill the beast with a heavy iron weight, swung onto the skull at the end of a rope. Even though exhausted, such a beast is still dangerous and may grab onto either horse or rider if he gets too close.

More often than not, the coyote in such a chase gets away. He knows the most rugged terrain in the area, as well as any possible dens or holes he may run down. Invariably he will head for such spots the moment he discovers pursuit. Riding rapidly after him over broken terrain covered with perhaps a foot of snow calls for horsemanship of the first order; and the thrills of such hunting are augmented by the sporting fact that all odds are in the coyote's favor.

Often, in instances of greater snow-depth, a team and bob-sleigh is used in conjunction with the saddle horses. The team "breaks trail" into the desert until a fresh track is located. Riders ride in the sleigh; the saddle nags are led behind and their strength saved until the actual chase begins.

Coursing coyotes with hounds is done in much the same manner. The dogs are hauled to desert-edge and turned loose in coyote country. The hunters follow on horses. When a fresh track is located the hounds take off, coursing either by scent or sight. Only especially bred coursing dogs such as the greyhound or Russian staghound can overtake a coyote in full flight. And unless any dog can outrun a coyote within a mile after spotting him the pursued beast is very apt to get away.

The riders follow the dogs and direction of chase as fast as possible. Usually the dogs will have killed the coyote by the time the hunters arrive—often by bowling the running beast from its feet, then hastily breaking its neck by biting.

The advantage of this type of coursing is that it may be done in summer as well as winter. The disadvantage is the general absence of suitable coursing dogs among average hunters.

Snow-planing for coyotes is rapidly developing into an accepted form of winter hunting in large dry-farm areas or prairie sections which in winter are snow covered and free of all surface foliage. The ideal here is large areas of semi-level or rolling country, or inland lake bottoms, which would allow for a mile or so of unimpeded racing in any direction, but interspersed with canyons or mild gorges containing cover for the rabbits, rodents, and birds upon which coyotes winter-feed.

Two hunters usually work together. One drives the snow-plane, the other shoots the overtaken beast —ordinarily with a 12-gauge shotgun, loaded with goose loads or buckshot.

The trick is to cruise about over such big rolling country until a coyote is spotted in an open area, and then overtake him before he can get to the protection of a gully, or brush, through which the snow-plane cannot go. Some of these outfits will travel up to 60 miles per hour, on fairly level going and crusted snow. Coyotes caught in the open under ideal conditions of travel can often be outrun within a mile.

Two kinds of vehicle have been developed: the snow-plane and the snow-toboggan. The snow-plane consists of a closed-in cabin or fuselage, usually two-place; a light airplane motor of radial design, with a short propeller; and an undercarriage consisting of three laminated-plywood skis, two of which are set widely-spaced beneath the forward part of the plane, and a third set at the tail containing the steering apparatus. The ski runners are set at great width to prevent tip-overs upon uneven terrain. The short propeller is to clear short foliage or snow when traveling in light, fluffy snows.

The snow toboggan is more of a sled. It consists of a toboggan-shaped sled, about 2 feet wide and perhaps 12 feet long, turned up at the front end. A small gasoline motor of the motorcycle class turns an endless tread of cleats, operating in the rear center of the vehicle. The toboggan is built for one or two passengers, has an open cockpit, and is equipped with levers and transmission for different speeds and different traction-depth.

Both outfits are capable of overtaking coyotes under ideal snow and terrain conditions. Neither works satisfactorily in wet or melting snows.

Another thrilling way to hunt coyotes is with a light airplane. The general technique is similar to that of snow-planing for the beasts. With the plane, however, much rougher country can be hunted, and vastly greater areas can be scanned. Pilot and hunter operate as a team; often when fur prices are high, a third man follows the hunting on a saddle horse and peels off the pelts.

Since the speed of even the lightest plane greatly exceeds that of the fastest coyote, the difficulty is in spotting the coyote, inducing him to break into a straightaway course, and coming upon him from behind—all before the low-flying ship overtakes the animal. The pilot often has to bank and circle several times before he can get the beast to do this. Once this is done, the plane comes rapidly and low up from behind, the pilot banks over and veers slightly away, and the gunner is allowed a quick shot under the plane's wing, just as the beast quarters away.

Since the plane's speed exceeds the beast's, the

Clyde Ormond, Rigby, Idaho.

**PLATE VII. After a fresh, heavy snowfall, coursing for coyotes in heavily-infested areas often is done with saddle horses.**

Clyde Ormond, Rigby, Idaho.

PLATE VIII. A two-place snow-toboggan like this one often is used for racing after coyotes on inland lakes and snow-covered prairies.

animal must be "led" from behind. A 12-gauge automatic shotgun, loaded with buckshot, is standard ordnance.

Some states permit airplane hunting of predators. Many others prohibit all kinds of airplane hunting. The hunter wishing to hunt coyotes from a plane naturally ascertains the legality of it beforehand.

Hunters possessed of great love of the outdoors and physical stamina often set out on foot to hunt coyotes in wintertime. They travel on webs or skis and carry light packs on their backs. Late February or March is the time generally chosen, since travel is easiest on snow-crust. The actual hunting procedure is similar to that of desert camp hunting—distances between likely country, however, being traversed on foot. Danger from the elements and weather are extreme, usually, and the hunter must go prepared for any eventuality. In addition to his rifle, he must carry concentrated food, a down sleeping-bag, snow-glasses, etc. Often he can hunt in semi-settled areas where some kind of shack or building is available for an overnight shelter.

Many interesting and ingenious techniques have been developed in diverse localities for hunting the little prairie wolves. In wild-hay and meadow sections which contain large coyote populations, hunters often kill a worthless animal out in an open meadow and use it for bait. Such a carcass is never approached afterward. The hunter has arranged to kill it on the windward side of a convenient haystack, wherein he hides each morning until the coyotes smell the "ripe" carcass and begin arriving. Either a rifle or a shotgun is used, depending upon the hunter's skill and his proximity to the carcass.

Sheepmen sometimes dress in white and bed down at dusk with their flocks—and rifle-shoot many a coyote which comes snooping, as they do, about the outskirts of a sheep flock.

Another method used in brushy country where coyotes are known to travel game trails, but are seldom seen because of underbrush, is to climb a high tree overlooking such game trails, sit for long periods of time at dusk and dawn, and then shoot the unsuspecting coyote as he wanders down the trail below. Coyotes seem not to fear any danger or enemies from above.

**Rifle and Sights.** Perhaps every kind of gun has been used on coyotes. But most guns are not suited to the serious coyote-sniper. Except for snow- and airplaning for coyotes, wherein a shotgun is necessary, the only really suitable weapon for coyote hunting is a precision rifle, accurate to the extreme, equipped with the finest of telescope sights, stocks, and gunsling, and shooting bullets possessed of very flat trajectory, so shaped as to retain their high muzzle velocity. The reason is that the coyote is a small animal—a minimum target. Peeled down, a coyote represents about 6 inches of target vertically, and perhaps 18 inches horizontally. Generally speaking, the coyote is a far-distant target. If not, then he is a moving target, elusive of definition, baffling as to course or intention, and extremely difficult to hit "in front of the belt."

Clyde Ormond, Rigby, Idaho.

PLATE IX. These snow-toboggans can make up to 40 miles per hour.

More shots at coyotes are to be had at 200 yards than at 100. More shots may be had at 400 yards than at any lesser range. Coyotes seem to feel, at this great range, that they are safe from rifle-fire, and as a consequence will often stand and watch the hunter.

The best coyote rifles commercially manufactured at present are: the .270 Winchester, shooting either 100-grain or 130-grain bullet; the .257 Roberts, shooting 87-grain or 100-grain bullet; the .30 '06, using 150-grain bullet; the .300 H. & H. Magnum, using 180-grain bullet; the 7-mm. with 139-grain bullet; the .300 Savage, with 150-grain bullet; the .250-3000, with either 87-grain or 100-grain bullet; and the .220 Swift, with a bullet of 46 to 56 grains weight. (See also "Ammunition—Rifle.")

"Wildcat" (uncommercialized) cartridges, and the heavy-barreled rifles built to use them, are sometimes better, though more costly, instruments for serious coyote sniping. The Varminter, Kilbourne Hornet, Lovell, Ackley Magnums, and Weatherby Magnums are among the very best of these.

The best sights for the coyote rifle are telescope sights, since it is possible only with such sighting equipment to take full advantage of the rifle's inherent possibilities. Scope sights for coyote hunting should be of from 3 to 6 power, mounted low and rigidly, have coated lenses, and micrometer adjustments for both windage and elevation. The best reticule is either a fine or a medium-fine cross-hair. Post reticules will usually subtend a chord of from 4 to 6 inches per hundred yards; at average coyote ranges this is sufficient to blot out most of the target, and also makes holding over the animal extremely difficult. The sight should be set for from two-thirds to three-fourths of the longest range at which shots are expected to be taken. That is, the rifle should be sighted for approximately 200 yards, if shots are to be taken at 300. Once sighted in, the adjustments should be tightened down and left unchanged during actual hunting.

Experimenters in ballistics, rifle makers, and veteran hunters agree that the ideal coyote rifle would be one capable of shooting minutes-of-angle (inch groups per 100 yards); which would have a muzzle velocity of between 4000 and 5000 foot-seconds in its bullets; whose bullets would have the sustained velocity necessary to shoot over 400 yards of range, without trajectory height at any point midway excessive enough to miss a coyote—if such a rifle were sighted for, and held on the target at 400 yards.

This ideal has not as yet been reached in a commercial rifle, but may shortly be reached.

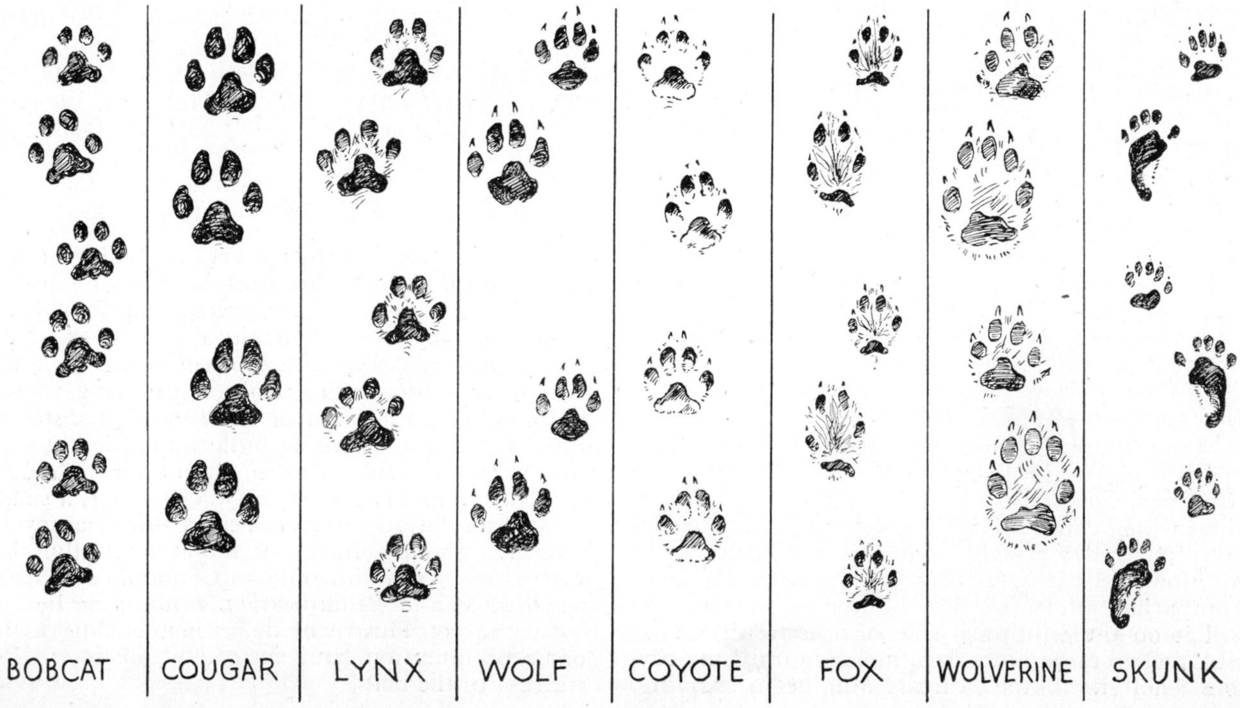

# GRAY FOX *Urocyon cinereoargenteus*

COMMON NAMES: Fox of Virginia, Grayback, Mane-Tailed Fox, Tree-Fox.

**History.** The gray fox, whose scientific name is *Urocyon cinereoargenteus* (a name taken from the Greek meaning tail and dog, "dog tail," a tail under which exists a mane of stiff hairs, ashy-silver in color), was first described by Schreber in 1775, its type locality being eastern North America. Besides the typical form, 20 geographic races have been described. In addition to these, there are four dwarf forms on the Santa Barbara Islands off the coast of California. The outstanding character of these forms are the possession of pygmy-like tails or "brushes."

Its range is similar to that of the red fox which it overlaps in many areas, but in the United States its range extends much deeper into the South than the red (see distribution map). It does not like the extreme cold of the North, but endures the hot, dry climate of our Southwest, particularly within an elevation from 3000 to 7500 feet. It is more of a denizen of forests than is the red fox; often its habitat will be composed of an intermixture of rocky, brushy, and lightly timbered forest land interspersed with small open glades and parks, as well as wide and rocky canyons, and dry arroyos or washes. In warmer regions it will often use swampy areas.

In the last several decades, it has extended its range into northern New York, Vermont, and parts of New Hampshire.

**Identification.** The gray fox is a grizzled gray on its upper parts, mixed with buffy to light brick red; the under parts are white to ashy-gray, and the tip of the tail is dark gray. In the higher elevations of its range, the buffy, bricklike red at times becomes a cinnamon color occasionally noted in the upper reaches of the Huachuca Mountains of southeastern Arizona.

In weight it ranges between 7 to 11 pounds, generally averaging about 8.

Its habits and bodily characteristics in many ways parallel those of the red fox, but at the same time show marked differences. One of the greatest outward differences is the gray fox's tail. Close examination reveals an arrangement of guard hairs, producing a manelike appearance, that lack almost entirely any soft underfur. The other great differences are in the configuration of the muscle ridges of the skull and the contour of the lower jaw (see Plate II, p. 148). These cranial characteristics readily enable one to distinguish between the two species whenever the skulls are compared side by side. Why this great difference in skull structure on the part of two species, so much alike in many of their mannerisms, is one of the mysteries of evolution. It is these skull characters that are mainly used in determining whether a fox is of the red or the gray species, particularly when examinations are made from fragmentary bone material obtained from archaeological bone sites.

**Characteristics.** The gray fox is just as shy as the red, and in many ways is just as cunning, but judging from the antics of trapped or bayed red and gray foxes, the gray fox puts forth a greater fight for its life. Some trappers aver that the gray fox exceeds the red fox in cunning, particularly when it comes to stealing bait put out with steel traps or snares for its capture. Some instances are on record in southeastern Arizona where this trait is almost human in its cleverness. Some trappers in certain gray fox habitats are forced to change their trapping technique constantly if they are to outwit the animal. The gray fox seldom makes a domestic pet.

Like the red fox, the gray uses a den. This, however, is seldom a burrow, though occasionally it may be in the hollow of a decayed tree; oak is one of its favorites. It prefers, where possible, a rocky habitat for denning, often among large boulders that form rugged talus slopes. Typical were a number of such gray fox dens that were observed at an elevation of 5500 feet near Canelo Pass, the Canelo Hills of southeastern Santa Cruz County, Arizona. Granite boulders of large proportions formed the talus slope in this instance, and close by was a game trail used mainly by the pygmy white-tailed deer of the Southwest, the Coues deer. Bordering both sides of the trail were a profusion of manzanita bushes, and juniper, heavy with berries in various stages of ripeness. Several years of observation revealed that this was a gray fox paradise, for here were not only ideal denning sites, but the necessary food in the form of manzanita and juniper berries. In addition there were many small rodents. The consistency with which this trail was used showed that the gray fox is more inclined to use a den continuously than is the red. Droppings along this trail, of all ages and conditions, proved that it had long been used in traveling to and from the den sites.

**Breeding.** In such a den, the young numbering two to five are born, beginning about the middle of March in the South and Southwest, and in late April to June 1 in its more northerly habitat. Female dogs of the small breeds such as the fox terrier have been known to adopt motherless gray fox cubs and permit them to suckle.

Like all the dog tribe of the wild, the male gray fox assists in feeding the young, beginning at the time they appear at the den's entrance when approximately 1½ months old. The food consists of small rodents and other typical fox food that the parents gather in their forays and pack to the den's entrance for the young cubs to feed upon. As with the red fox, the family tie is very strong during the rearing of the young, which continues until the break-up of the family in the early fall. Comparable to the large gray wolves, there seems to be more permanency of mating after once the female chooses her mate. After the young are matured and separate their respective ways from the adult parents, the old male and female stay on together. The observations made in the Canelo Pass area previously mentioned bore out this conclusion. These dens were used for rearing the young, but new ones would also be established and occupied later on, apparently for use in colder weather. In this trait, the gray thus differs materially from the red fox.

The life span of 23 gray foxes kept in captivity

averaged 5¼ years, but it is probable that in the wild the life span is similar to that of the red fox—8 to 10 years.

Of the two species, the gray fox is more adept at climbing trees, and shows no hesitancy in doing so, particularly when closely crowded by coursing hounds. It uses its claws in climbing much as do the members of the cat family. An interesting comment on this trait was given by the late Vernon Bailey, writing about the animal in Texas:

"These foxes go up the trunk of a tree with almost cat-like ease. I have found them looking down at the dogs from 20 to 40 feet up in the branches of nut-pines and live oaks, and have known of their climbing a yellow pine *(Pinus ponderosa)* where 20 feet of straight trunk over a foot in diameter intervened between the ground and the first branch. More often they take to live oak or juniper, where the lower branches can be reached at a bound, and then, squirrel like, hide in the swaying topmost branches. On the approach of the hunter, they become anxious and seem to doubt the security of their position, sometimes making a flying leap to the ground. Stones and clubs will usually dislodge them from the treetop."

**Feeding.** Like the red fox, the gray is omnivorous in what it eats: All the wild berries which grow in its habitat, all the small rodents (particularly field mice, rabbits, woodchucks, moles), every bird it can catch (including all of the domestic fowls), snakes, horned toads, shrimps, clams, crayfish, grasshoppers, frogs, fish, young turtles, field corn, nuts, acorns, melons, and grapes of the vineyard. At times the gray fox can be a real detriment to newly born lambs. After killing a young lamb, instead of eating at any place on the carcass, it will at times open up a hole in the side of its victim large enough so that it can stick its sharp-pointed nose inside and remove only the liver. After doing this, the rest of the lamb prey is abandoned and left unmolested for some other carnivore or bird of prey.

Since so much of fox prey consists of wild rodents, a large number of which have been found to be carriers of tularemia, some authorities hold the opinion that possibly further and more widely conducted field investigations will find the wild foxes infected with it or their ectoparasites.

In obtaining its food, it prefers the oncoming twilight, though, as with all the carnivores, it will often feed in daylight, especially if food is scarce.

The voice of this creature consists of a short, snappish, and rather deep, harsh bark. Like the red fox's bark, this is sometimes heard just at the beginning of twilight, and is emitted in somewhat rapid succession. When in pain, however, such as shortly after being trapped, it emits a high lyric-soprano tone of long duration, much like the final "sound

Pennsylvania Game Commission.

PLATE I. Gray Fox.

off" of the coyote's yap or howl. It leaves a never-to-be-forgotten impression upon one, especially when heard echoing up some remote, wide, dry canyon wash located in a wilderness area far removed from civilization.

Among the diseases of the gray fox, rabies probably is the most important in relation to man and his economic pursuits. The outbreaks mentioned as occurring among red foxes also occur among the gray. Encephalitis also occurs in both species. This, caused by a filtrable virus, is believed to be the disease, or at least one important factor, that is responsible for the occasional low decline in fox population from a high cyclic peak.

Among their parasites, both the red and the gray carry large numbers of fleas on their bodies and throughout their fur. It is believed that one reason why both the red and gray foxes will at times change dens is the heavy flea populations that invariably infest the floor of the den. They become afflicted at times with the skin mite that produces mange. Ticks are also a common fox parasite.

Like the red fox, the gray has similar enemies. In a coyote habitat, seldom does the trapped gray fox remain alive. Coyotes literally tear it to pieces.

Salmon poisoning, a virulent poison to domestic dogs and to wolves and coyotes, is also fatal to foxes. The gray is at times a fish eater and is subject to this hazard. What causes salmon poisoning among some of the carnivores long remained a mystery. Within recent years, however, research has established the fact that in the Pacific Northwest, where it is so prevalent, there are watercourses inhabited by trout and fresh-water salmon that at times are infested with an intestinal parasite. A final summary of these findings, the work of scientists connected with the Oregon Agricultural Experiment Station, stated among other things: ". . . The cause of so-called salmon poisoning in dogs and foxes is an intestinal fluke," and "A cystic form of this parasite occurs in the muscles, kidney, liver, and gills of trout and fresh-water salmon." Carnivores feeding upon such food thus become afflicted and often die. This situation was first noted nearly 100 years ago by the naturalists connected with early government railroad surveys that got under way during the middle of the 19th century. Still more recent research on chastek paralysis in captive foxes, which has been identified as a nutritional deficiency resulting from feeding raw fish to the extent of 10 per cent or more of the diet, gives a further explanation of salmon poisoning.

All foxes are keen scented and cautious. Their taste for fish is taken advantage of by many trappers who use ground-up eel, trout remains, or other oily fish, thoroughly rotted, as one of the scents for trap scenting.

Though it has always had a place in the fur markets, gray fox fur is much inferior to red fox fur, and as a result generally brings a low price. Its wearing qualities are not good. When worn as a finished garment—muff, coat, scarf, or trim—it tends to rub badly, and in a short time loses its guard hairs plus the underfur.

While the local habitat of both the red and gray foxes is of comparatively small size, comparison of the two shows that the gray appears to be the more unstable. Nevertheless, both species are inclined to have well-established runways over the area. Where such areas or habitats are criss-crossed with trails, dry sand ditches, logged over and partially cleared spots, old roads, ditches, terraces in cultivated fields and meadows, both species will use one or a combination of the foregoing for runways. Such runways are not followed with the counterclockwise regularity of wolves and coyotes. The fox may follow such a path for only a short distance, and then may cross to another ditch, old road, or trail, follow that for a way, and then zigzag back across to the original trail it had begun to travel upon, and so continue its travel. Fox dung is voided at more or less definite spots along the runways, as is also the urine. It is at these scent posts that fox trappers conceal traps for catching the animals. Along dustier portions of such runways may often be found the telltale fox tracks. Those of the front foot of the red are approximately 1¾ inches in width; the gray has a slightly smaller front foot, averaging about 1½ inches. The foot pads generally show distinctly, as do also the claws.

As with most mammals among the carnivorous group, all foxes possess a scent gland located on the upper side near the base of the tail. This gland functions to emit a scent when foxes meet, and is much stronger among red than gray foxes. The odor of the dung and urine of both species is fairly strong and pungent when first voided.

In a straightaway short sustained run, both red and gray foxes have been clocked at speeds of 26 to 30 miles per hour. They cannot keep up such speed, however. When coursed, the fox will often use a defensive measure for avoiding continued full speed. This is its ability to get into more or less impenetrable cover. Here it adopts such a zigzag course within such cover that it will even circle back unknown to its pursuers, so that it is not only able for a long time to delay its becoming winded, but at the same time it will throw hounds off its track and scent.

**Hunting Methods—Trapping.** When any fox control is essential, resort is made to the use of traps, coursing with dogs, locating and destroying dens and cubs, and still hunting with the rifle. Trapping is the more common form of fox control.

Every wild animal possesses some form of defense against danger or harm to itself. In foxes, these defenses are their acute sense of smell, alert hearing, and keen eyesight. To trap either the gray or red fox successfully, the trapper must work to defeat these highly developed senses when placing traps. Success will come only with a full knowledge of the habits of the two species and after repeated experiments with trap sets. Probably, if a poll were made, the majority of fox trappers would say that of the two species, the red fox is the more difficult to trap. Its cunning at times in avoiding set traps becomes almost uncanny.

When using traps, the fox trappers generally resort to the sizes known as the No. 1 single spring, the No. 2 coil spring, or the No. 2 double spring.

Throughout their habitat, foxes have selected runways or hunting routes. Fox sign, such as tracks, droppings, and scent posts will be noted along such routes. Whenever found, scent posts are commonly selected for points to set traps. If they cannot be found, they can be readily established on a known runway by placing fox scent on likely looking scent posts and bedding traps near them. One of several favorite fox scents is concocted from the urine, excreta, anal glands, and gall bladder of the fox; to every 3 ounces of this mixture, an ounce of glycerin is added to give it body, together with 1 grain of corrosive sublimate to keep it from spoiling. This scent is dropped on a low shrub, near which a set trap has been placed. Suitable trap sites are found at the junction of runways, a natural bend in the runway, or natural scent posts where foxes urinate in the course of their travel.

Fox traps should be clean and with no foreign odor. In making the set, a hole the length and width of the trap with jaws open is dug with a trowel, piece of angle, or a prospector's pick. While digging, a good fox trapper stands or kneels on a "setting cloth" about 3 feet square, made of canvas, or a piece of sheep or calf hide. Human scent must be removed from this cloth by previously burying it in an old manure pile. The dirt removed from the hole dug to bed the trap is placed on the setting cloth. The trap is then bedded in the hole. Some traps are anchored by a stake pin a foot long that is driven flush with the ground; they may also be attached to a drag-hook fastened by a swivel to a 4-foot chain linked to the base of the trap. Drag-hook and chain are buried beneath the base of the trap. Extreme care is taken in burying the trap and building up of a so-called shoulder around and under the trap pan. When this stage of the set is completed, the shape of the ground within the spread trap jaws resembles an inverted cone, in order to give a foundation for the pan cover, or "trap pad."

The "trap pad" may be made of slicker cloth, or ordinary wire fly screen cut in circular shape. When this is in proper place, the entire trap is carefully covered with the remaining portion of earth on the setting cloth. Surplus earth not needed on the setting cloth is taken a good distance away from the set and evenly scattered. The art of successful fox-trap setting is attained when the ground that has been disturbed in bedding the trap is, on the final burial of the trap, left just as natural as humanly possible. An expert fox trapper leaves no evidence whatever.

Scenting follows the foregoing procedure. A few drops of the concoction described above is placed on any obstacle from 6 to 8 inches away from the chosen trap site such as the base of a low bush, an old fox excrete, an old bone, a stick, or weed clusters. Rescenting of such spots is done every three to five days, depending on the weather. Wet weather necessitates scenting more often because of the rain-washing.

The actual trapping of a fox by the foregoing method (which is only one of many, but quite commonly used by many fox trappers) occurs when the animal comes over its runway and is attracted to the post by the scent that has been dropped. In approaching the spot for a smell the animal invariably puts a foot on the concealed trap pan, the jaws are thus released, and the foot is securely held. The place where a fox has been caught affords an excellent location for a reset after the animal has been removed. At such points, natural scent permeates the ground touched by the animal while in the trap.

**Range and Distribution.** Archaeological collections from bone-pit sites and caves show that the gray fox has long been a common part of our American fauna, and particularly so in the eastern United States. Moreover, it has shown periodic increases and decreases within this area. Why it continued as a part of the fauna in the West following the poisoning onslaught it was subjected to for the period from 1860 to 1885 is a moot question. A concluding statement on this poisoning is apropos here.

With the decline in the numbers of beaver throughout the West, beaver trappers took on a new avocation, called "wolfing," which soon became a recognized industry for practically a quarter of the 19th century. Wolf skins, which for many years had been little valued, rose in price. The "professional wolfer" of the western plains was a person who made a business of killing wolves that followed the vast buffalo herds. Many others joined him, such as homesteaders, discharged soldiers, and ne'er-do-wells, for the venture was most profitable at times. In the early 1850's, strychnine sulphate began to make its appearance on the shelves of the frontier stores for sale to trappers for killing wolves. The bait used was freshly killed carcasses of buffalo and antelope, killed purposely for such use, and into which the strychnine was liberally inserted. Vivid accounts of this calling and descriptions of the individuals concerned with it have been left us. One of the best chroniclers was J. H. Taylor, who narrated:

> "With a full knowledge of his game, the wolfer rigs up an outfit similar to that of the hunter or trapper with the exception of traps and baits. In place of these, he supplies himself liberally with strychnine poison.
>
> "If it was in the autum, he moved slowly in the wake of a buffalo herd, making open camp, and shooting down a few of the beasts, and after ripping them open, saturating their warm blood and intestines with from one to three bottles of strychnine to each carcass.
>
> "After his line of poisoned buffalo had been put out to his notion, the wolfer makes a camp in a ravine or coulee and prepares for the morrow.
>
> "With the first glimmer of light in the eastern sky he rises, makes his fire, and cooks his coffee, then hitches up, if he has a team, or saddles up if with packs, and follows his line to the finish. Around each buffalo carcass will probably be from three to a dozen dead wolves, which he packs off some distance from his baits and skins them."

Other smaller mammals, such as the coyote, gray and swift foxes, skunk, and the large, beautiful race of the prairie red fox (*Fulva regalis*) that was in time practically wiped out from the plains, which also took the poisoned baits so carelessly strewn, all served to augment the total monetary returns the wolfer received from the sale of his pelts at the end of each poisoning season.

The area these wolfers covered was an immense stretch of land extending from the plains of Saskatchewan in Canada on the north and southward to and including the Staked Plains of Texas. In width, the area extended from the eastern base of the Rocky Mountains thence to the Missouri River. As Granville Stuart commented: "The wolfer's lines of bait extended from far up into Canada to Colorado and Nebraska. Their principal trading posts were Fort Peck, Fort Benton, Fort Hawley, Fort Brown, the Crow Agency, Fort Pease, and Bozeman."

With regard to the profits from this business, those

recorded by Robert Morris Peck and two companions who took to wolf poisoning after they had been mustered out of the United States Army in the 1860's at Fort Wise, Colorado, is typical. During the winter of 1861-62, they poisoned bait carcasses of buffaloes and antelopes in Walnut Creek Valley, in Rush County, Kansas. Their entire poison kill for this period of practically only four months was more than 3000 animals, composed of wolves, coyotes, and foxes, for which they received over $2600, a tidy sum for those times.

Thus in this era the western country was subjected to one of the strangest chapters in the history of killing mammals. It seems unlikely that this slaughter was ever exceeded in North America unless by the slaughters of the buffalo and the antelope. Throughout this entire period of the onslaught, both *Vulpes fulva,* the red, and *Urocyon cinereoargenteus,* the gray fox, made up a good part of each wolfer's daily bag. At the time, fox skins were marketed in such numbers that they brought the hunter an average of only 25 cents apiece.

# RED FOX

*Vulpes fulva*

**History.** Through the centuries, the red fox has left a record symbolizing cunningness, sagacity, courage, and much pro and con in its role as a predator—is it harmful, beneficial, or neutral? It has left a mark on the pages of literature and legend, even to modern slang, which applies the name to sly, sharp-witted people: for example, "He is a foxy fellow," or "He out-foxed me."

Who, in his youth, failed to read the classic Aesop's Fables—Aesop the slave from the island of Samos, who is believed to have lived about the sixth century before Christ? Fables which he is credited with using specifically for political purposes, when the reign of Greek tyrants made unveiled speech dangerous, and are generally associated with a moral, frequently included the fox. "The Fox and the Crow," "The Fox and the Mask," "The Fox and the Stork," "The Fox and the Grapes," "The Fox and the Cat," "The Fox, The Cock, and The Dog," pointed morals still practical today, as "Do not trust flatterers," "Outside show is a poor substitute for inner worth," "One bad turn deserves another," "It is easy to despise what you cannot get," "Better one safe way than a hundred on which you cannot reckon," and "Cunning often outwits itself."

Many other interesting legends, not credited to Aesop, are also to be found. Of particular interest is that concerned with the wolf, an ancient enemy of the fox against which the fox has no known defensive armor. Legend reported that the fox used squill as a protective measure. It was believed that if a wolf trod upon the flower of the squill bulb, it soon be-

N. Y. Zoological Society.

PLATE I. Red Fox.

came torpid and could not bend its head back. Hence the fox, to protect itself in a wolf country, would strew squill flowers in the wolf's runway to produce the desired effect. The antiquity of this legend in bringing out the cunningness of the fox becomes obvious, when we consider that natives in the squill-growing sections of North Africa today use pulverized squill bulbs in sacks for sinking to slight depths in their fishing operations. The juices given off from the bulbs produce a toxic effect upon the fish coming in contact with the immersed sacks, and they then become temporarily stunned, rise to the surface, and are clubbed to death or netted without difficulty.

Scientifically the red fox is known as *Vulpes,* from the Latin, "a fox," and *fulva* from the Latin meaning "yellow." It was first described in 1820 by Desmarest, who used as a basis a red fox skin that came from an unknown locality in the eastern United States. Colloquially, *Vulpes fulva* was called "Renard" by the French-Canadians, "Wah-Kus" by the Cree Indians, "Wah-gush" by the Ojibwa and Sauteaux, "Nak-ee-they" by the Chipewyan, and "Songkee-na" by some of the Sioux tribes.

Red fox skins began to play an important role in the fur industry after the first quarter of the 19th century. Hudson Bay Company records for the 85 years between 1821 (when this company amalgamated with the Northwest Company) and 1905 show a turnover of 1,536,420 pelts. In the years 1919-1921, a total of 1,295,258 American red fox skins were marketed. The price of red fox fur has fluctuated greatly, for like other fur, its value is decreed by milady's annual whims as to what is going to be fashionable to wear. Red fox skins from the Far North woods area generally command the top prices. As an example, one Canadian sale during the early 1920's averaged close to $23 per pelt. The pelt has long been used for scarfs, muffs, coats, coat trimming, and robes. It was often used by the early day Indian tribes of the West. Today, one Indian tribe, the Hopi of northeastern Arizona, uses the skin as adornment when performing its famous Snake Dance.

Red fox fur is more valuable than the fur of the gray fox. Silver and cross foxes, the red fox color phase, while found in the wild, are generally not common. These command higher prices, because of their novelty and all-around richness. Generally speaking, prime fur of the red fox occurs from November through January in its northern range of the United States, and from December through January in the south.

Fox hunting in the United States, "riding to the hounds," is almost as old as the Union. George Washington spent many happy hours running foxhounds over the wooded areas of his Mount Vernon plantation. In colonial Virginia the recorded expert horsemanship got some of its impetus from foxcoursing. As a result, there has come down through the years a feeling, particularly in the South, that the red fox is the top sort of huntable game. In some areas, the fox trapper has been legislated against. Certain outdoorsmen consider it a sin to kill a red fox; such enthusiasts view it solely as a coursing animal, and are content to let it remain such forever.

In some states it is unlawful to trap foxes with steel traps except when done on private land by the owner, members of his famiy, tenants, and those obtaining permits from the owner or his agent.

Lancaster, New Hampshire, symbolizes the pioneer struggle in the conquering of the wilderness by a bronze statute of the fox, which is located in the central part of that city. This is the only known in-

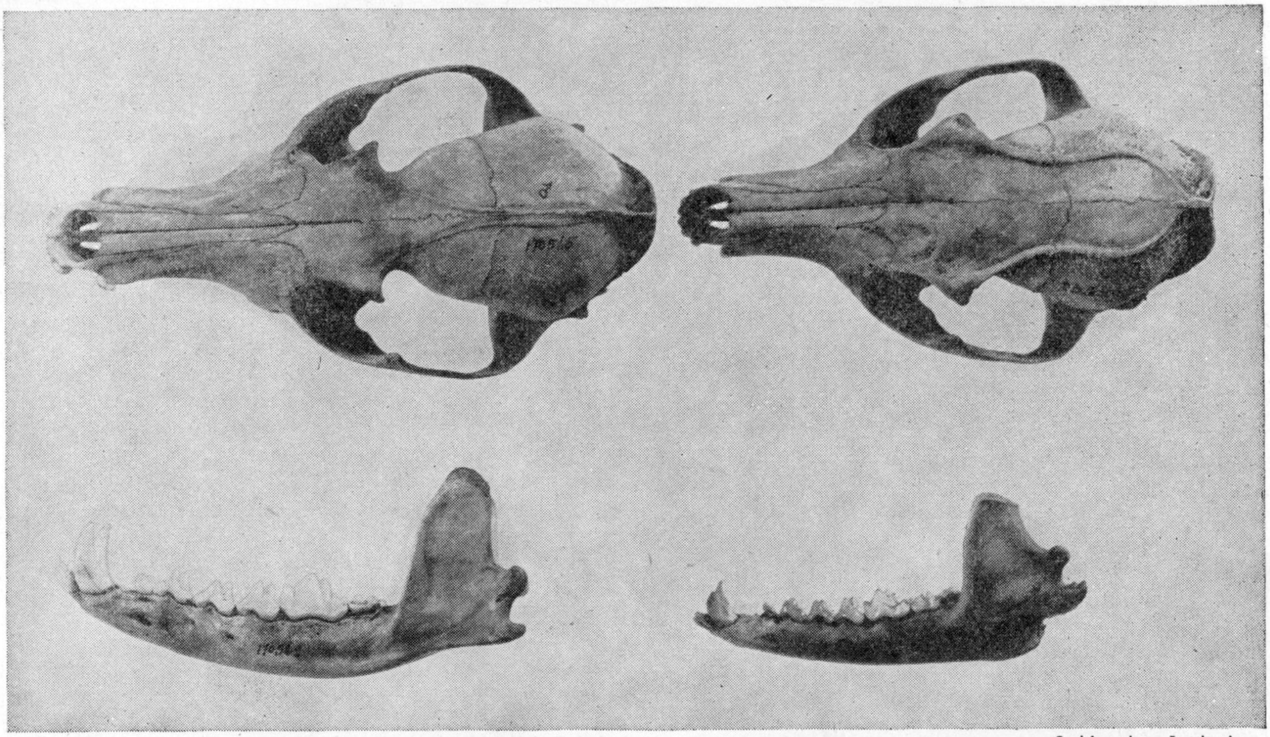

Smithsonian Institution.

PLATE II. Skull and lower jawbone of adult red fox (left) and gray fox (right), showing difference in configuration of the muscle ridges of the skull and the contour of the lower jaw.

stance of a statue to the animal anywhere in present-day North America.

**Identification.** The red fox belongs to the dog group, with teeth which, though much smaller and different in detail, are still the same in number, totaling 42. Its voice is that of a short, coarse, snappish bark, not unlike that emitted at times by the small fox terrier, though not as loud. Over-all length of the animal's body runs approximately 40 inches, of which its tail will average between 12 and 14 inches. The animal's weight is between 8 and 14 pounds, with 10 pounds considered the average. The red foxes are divided into two groups, the kit and the desert foxes; the latter are known as *Vulpes velox,* and are sometimes called the "swift fox." All told, there are 23 recognized races of the red fox, ranging from the typical form *fulva,* common in Virginia, to other types occurring in Nova Scotia, Labrador, Newfoundland, Minnesota, Utah, Mexico, California, Washington, British Columbia, and Alaska.

The general color of all red foxes is a reddish yellow. Certain parts of its habitat seem to bring out a more definite reddish hue. If the area is free of thick underbrush the fur appears to be softer, because of less rubbing on the animal's body when traveling over its runways in quest of prey. Local temperatures are also a factor in the quality of the pelt. The extreme northern cold ranges make for a heavier bushy tail, or "brush," as it is often called.

Three distinct color phases exist in the red fox. These are red, black or silver (generally black with silver-tipped hairs), and the cross, an intermixture of red and black. In the so-called silver phase there occur varying percentages of silver. Pale silver is 75% silver; silver, 50% silver; dark silver, 25% silver; extra-dark silver, 10% silver; and finally the black fox containing no silver. The tip of the tail is white in all phases from the typical red to the pure black. All of these color phases may occur in the same brood or litter of the young. Often the cross fox will have a dark cross near its shoulders. Because of this oddity some authorities believe the name "cross" was coined as the name thus applied to this color phase. Among red and other foxes such as the gray, a freakish pelt sometimes occurs, which gives rise to the name "Samson fox." In such a pelt, no long guard hairs occur whatsoever, a condition that some credit to a deficiency in diet. Such a pelt resembles the "wool" occurring on wild North American sheep, and has no commercial value whatever.

**Characteristics and Breeding.** From early February to the end of May is the breeding and rearing season of red foxes. The litter or brood varies from three to ten, the average seems to be five. Only one litter is produced annually.

The young are born in a den. When about five weeks old they appear at the entrance, which may have more than one opening. The den is usually located in the sunny side, and may be a burrow which the female fox has dug, or a hollow log, or a small rocky cavern that it appropriates. During winter months, portions of woodchuck burrows are occupied by the red fox when woodchucks are not active. As with wolves and coyotes, the den is the center of all activity during the rearing season, and until the break-up of the fox family by early fall, there is a strong social tie. The family sociability is not so strong as among the large wolves, but from late spring to early fall closely parallels it. Also, like the large wolves, red foxes maintain "loafing places," which are selected spots within the habitat, containing the den, and are used after the young foxes are old enough to leave the den, when between eight and ten weeks old, and the start of the family break-up begins. Foraging from and return to these loafing places may be done when the parent foxes, as with parent wolves, are moving the young to a new den site. Like its cousins the large wolves and coyotes, the fox's den entrance often contains evidence of the prey brought to the young such as feathers and bones of small song and game birds, and mammals. Dens are seldom used in the wintertime, but there is an exception to this trait during periods of heavy snow, when the red fox will resort temporarily to an old den for protection. Like wolves and coyotes, foxes will return, year after year, to the same denning area if not too greatly interfered with.

The gestation period varies between 49 and 52 days. The female at the period just before birth of the young is very irritable, and seldom countenances any close association with the male. The young are born blind, and the eyes of the young do not open for approximately nine days. By this time the female has overcome her irritability, the male is again tolerated, and the family life is sociable once more. Both parents, like wolves and coyotes, forage food for the young. When very young, red foxes are difficult to differentiate from young coyotes. Their brown, sooty, close-cropped fur has fooled some sporting enthusiasts, so much so that those desiring to replenish their fox population for hound coursing have ignominiously had coyote pups shipped to them for red fox cubs because of their inability to tell the difference. In one case, some five years after release, it became evident that coyotes had been inadvertently introduced because of the resultant severe damage to poultry and livestock. An S.O.S. emanated from the county agricultural agent in this section requesting coyote control because of poultry and calf losses.

The life span of 14 foxes held in captivity averaged something over six years. In the wild they probably average from eight to ten years.

The red, silver, and cross foxes occasionally make domestic pets, and tend to show a friendly disposition. In the wild, their friendly associations with other mammals are of record. One of these recorded by the late hunter-naturalist Charles Sheldon occurred while sheep hunting in Alaska between Tustamena Lake and the Kenai River on September 18, 1912. At this time, he states,

> "We saw . . . a most remarkable and unusual sight. Three rams were on the side of a hill, walking along in single file, and a cross fox was walking with them, he jumping up and biting their faces in play, and they butting him gently along in front. When they lay down, he lay down too, and they were evidently traveling together and the best of friends. We watched them for fully 15 minutes through the glasses at about 300 yards."

Another instance, recorded by the late Donald R. Dickey, concerns the friendly relationship between a red fox and caribou on the marshes of Sandy River, Newfoundland, on November 6, 1916. Here the caribou were migrating, and in one herd a red fox was seen to "zigzag casually through the middle of the band. The caribou seemed to be on perfectly good terms with the fox, and all in all, his actions and their response reminded me exactly of a sheep-dog working through a band of domestic animals." Dickey believed that a possible reason for all this might have been that the migrating caribou stirred up meadow mice upon which this particular red fox was feeding.

Other than man, the red fox has numerous enemies. Foremost are the large wolves, coyotes, bobcats, lynx, and fishers. In some parts of its northern range the red fox shows a decrease with increased coyote population. Seldom is it found alive in a trap placed in a wolverine habitat. Under such circumstances the wolverine is an habitual killer of the animal.

**Feeding.** One of the most intriguing sports is to trail a red fox that has been hunting its food in the snow. Though it generally hunts at dusk, there come times when it hunts in broad daylight, particularly if food is scarce. Its course is much like that of the large gray wolf, though it zigzags more, hunting under this cover and that cover, poking its sharp nose into weed clusters or low shrubs in the hope of finding a mouse or other prey. At such spots, a telltale triangular snout depression is often left in the snow. Very often along its hunting routes it will make temporary caches of food, to which it will return after a lapse of a few days to feed therefrom. In the course of its wanderings it will void feces or urine much as do wolves and coyotes; it prefers, however, wind-blown knolls, hillocks, or mounds where it may have previously dropped its sign. Thus its sign posts are like those of the other members of the dog family.

Among the main food items of the red fox, in order of importance, are field mice, rabbits, particularly the cottontail, ground squirrels, birds, poultry, and insects, such as grasshoppers. It will also eat almost any form of carrion. The animal is likewise very fond of wild and domestic fruits such as grapes, figs, dates, cherries, and wild berries. It occasionally takes cold-blooded vertebrates, such as the blue racer and garter snakes. Among the invertebrates, the crayfish has been observed taken by red foxes, and also carrion beetles, the giant water bug, and diving beetle. Game birds, such as the ring-necked pheasant and sage grouse, become vulnerable at times, as does the muskrat, when extreme drought conditions prevail.

There are occasions when red foxes can become exceedingly destructive to poultry and livestock such as turkeys, chickens, and young lambs. In the month of July during 1944, foxes killed a total of 205 turkeys and 104 chickens on 4 ranches located in Yamhill County, Oregon. Thus, like the coyote, the red fox is most omnivorous in its food habits. As one authority aptly puts it, "It can eat everything but the garbage can."

**Predation.** As a predator, the red fox is loudly maligned by some, held neutral by others, and loudly praised by others. Whether the individual considers it a first-class predator, a menace in a game-bird habitat, or just a good all-around denizen of the wild often depends on "whose ox is being gored." There is no question about its beneficial food preferences for mice and rabbits, at times two outstanding orchard pests. Its insect diet also is on the beneficial side. When its favorite prey, such as mice or rabbits, is absent, red fox predations on farm poultry can be most severe. An observation recently made deals with fox forays on farm poultry in the Peoria district of Linn County, located in the Willamette Valley, Oregon. Here, a single fox "killed 17 hens during successive visits to a henhouse," and on another farm in the same area, "a dozen young pullets were lost from outdoor coops." Thus, when red foxes become overabundant in farming areas they often become very detrimental to poultry, game, and newly born livestock such as lambs. Under such conditions local control often becomes a decided necessity. In some areas, however, local control can be minimized as far as poultry is concerned if intelligent poultry husbandry practices are followed, such as housing and penning broilers and laying hens.

There are situations, however, where it is not possible to put such practices into effect, any more than it is practical to build a wolf- or coyote-proof fence surrounding large areas. Illustrative of this was the case of two farmers in a Mississippi Valley state who had sold their outlying pasture lands to the U. S. Army to be used for important military experimental work. The purchased lands were fenced, became inaccessible to anyone without proper credentials, and were closely guarded. For many years, these farmers had carefully carried on fox control over these holdings to alleviate poultry and other damage. However, with the selling of the outlying lands, fox control abruptly ended. After one year, the fox population increased heavily on the purchased lands, and accordingly, poultry depredations correspondingly increased on the adjoining farm holdings. The farmers threatened damage suits unless some form of reparations could be granted by the Federal authorities for fox damage. This situation was finally compromised by tht Army's leasing, for the duration of the war, the abutting lands upon which the poultry was raised, thus relieving the farmers from their fox losses. So even the red fox played its role in World War II.

A recent fox-control program has been inaugurated co-operatively by the Oregon Game Commission. With a budget of nearly $7000, and employing six trappers, the area chosen for the work is the Willamette Valley. Here, it is hoped to learn to what extent the fox is a menace to the Chinese pheasant. While both the red and gray foxes occur in the state, the red fox is considered the more harmful of the two species.

Among diseases of the foxes affecting man, rabies or hydrophobia is probably the most important. Of late years, this disease seems to be more evident among foxes than in earlier times. Since 1940, outbreaks have occurred in Georgia, Alabama, Mississippi, Louisiana, Arkansas, and Maryland. In Burke County, Ga., during 1940, many people were bitten by rabid foxes, and livestock suffered heavy losses before the outbreak was suppressed. An outstanding outbreak occurred in Clark County, Ala., during 1944. In the course of 3½ months of rabies control work, a total of 1188 foxes were removed from an area comprising 1216 square miles. This is considered a very exceedingly heavy fox population. At this time, 15 people in Clark County took Pasteur treatment. Corresponding heavy losses from rabies occurred to cattle, horses, mules, hogs, and goats. During this same year a similar rabies outbreak occurred in 12 counties and parishes of Louisiana, Mississippi, and Arkansas. Rabid foxes in this instance were responsible for the death of 405 domestic animals, valued at approximately $29,000, and besides, necessitated Pasteur treatment for 98 people.

**Range and Distribution.** With the exception of the large gray wolf, the red fox has one of the widest ranges of all the American mammals (see distribution map). Wooded regions form its main habitat from coast to coast, extending northward to the Arctic regions and southerly to near the 30th parallel.

Within its habitat, which is fairly open country with not too dense cover, in contrast to heavy forest, its home range is small, provided there is sufficient food. Five to six miles is considered the average range, but should food become scarce it will cover a larger range in its wanderings. What fox concentrations on a small area can be at times is indicated by the statement of F. H. Bezdek of Ohio, that a professional fox trapper trapping an area only five miles square near Marietta, Ohio, has taken over 100 foxes a year for eight consecutive years.

In a small way, it parallels the ability of our large American cat, the puma, or mountain lion, in adapting itself to the extreme cold of our northern latitudes and to the other extreme, the hot, humid, sticky heat of the South. The beautiful brush or tail with which it is adorned on most of its northern ranges is much smaller in proportion when found in its southern habitat. The tail is one of the most important parts of the animal's anatomy, because it forms a protective blanket, or muff, for the remainder of its body when curled up in sleep, or resting.

For many years, two schools of thought have existed as to whether the red fox of the eastern United States was native to that part of our country during pre-Columbian times. One school of naturalists holds the affirmative, and the other, the negative.

The red fox of the eastern United States of today is believed to have developed from red fox stock imported from England during colonial days for use in the sport of coursing with dogs. Long ago (1857), Professor Spencer F. Baird, the first secretary of the Smithsonian Institution, in his Pacific Railroad Report upon the mammals said:

"It is not a little remarkable that there have as yet been no remains of the Red-fox detected among the fossils derived from the Carlisle (Pa.) and other bone caves. The Gray-fox is abundantly represented, but not a trace of the other. This would almost give color to the impression, somewhat prevalent, that the Red-fox of eastern America is the descendant of individuals of the European Red-fox imported many years ago, and allowed to run wild and over spread the country."

Through the years, the accumulated evidence seems to bear out Professor Baird's contention. Because of its importance it is appropriate to quote from the remarks and opinions expressed in 1946

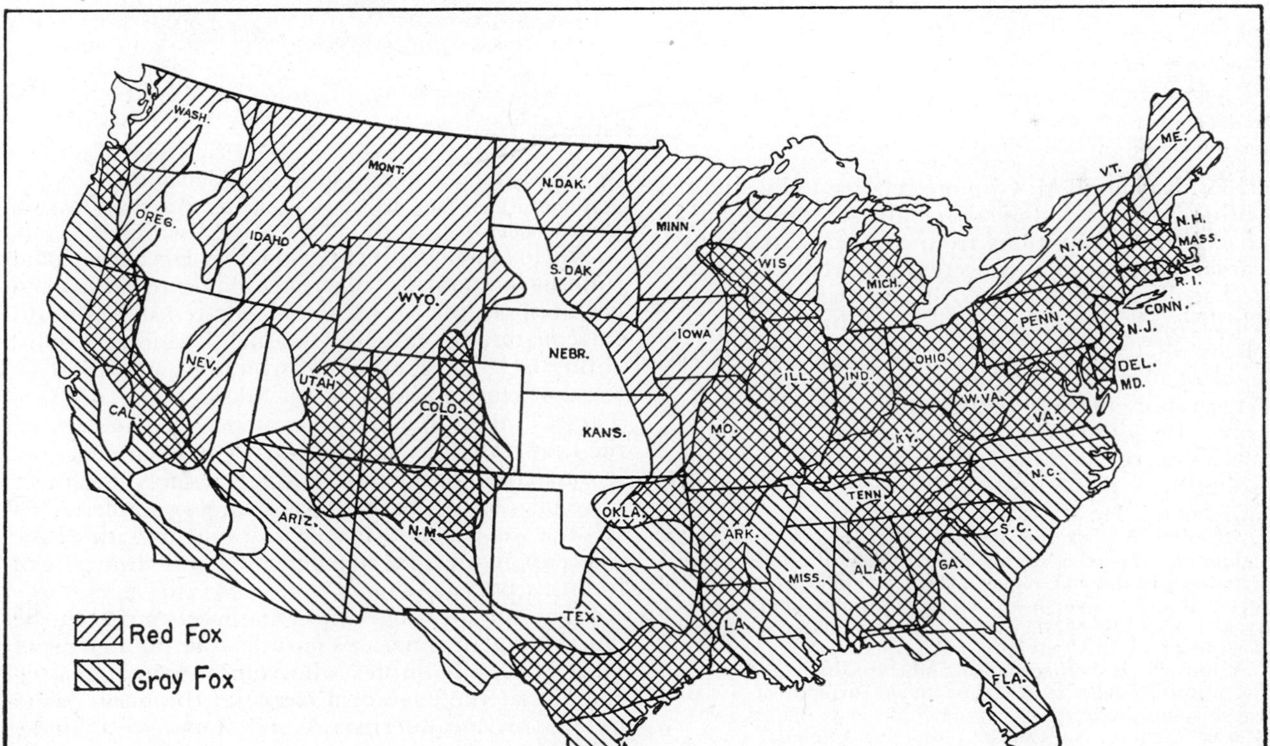


**Plate III.** Distribution of Red and Gray Foxes in the United States.

Pennsylvania Game Commission.

PLATE IV. Red Fox Kits Playing in Front of Den.

by Dr. Raymond M. Gilmore relative to his findings with respect to mammal remains examined in archaeological collections from southeastern Pennsylvania. These remains were recovered from three archaeological sites located at Fort Hill, Martin, and Phillips, all situated in the hill country of the Allegheny Plateau. In his bone identification from a total of over 3000 fragments, Dr. Gilmore found a large representation of the fur-bearers, larger carnivores, the deer family, and rodents. All told, 26 species were identified, two of which were post-Columbian domesticated livestock, such as cattle and horses. He states:

"The absence of the red fox *(Vulpes fulva)* is highly significant. There is strong evidence that the native American red fox did not range into the middle eastern United States from the north in aboriginal times, and that the present red fox of the central eastern states is a direct descendant of the European red fox *(Vulpes vulpes)* which was introduced between 1650 and 1750 from England for fox hunting. The case against the occurrence of a native red fox in the eastern United States was stated well by Rhoads [Samuel N. Rhoads, 1903, *The Mammals of Penn? sylvania and New Jersey*, Philadelphia, 1903, pp 146-147] and the absence of any red fox remains from these southeastern Pennsylvania sites corroborates this view. Thus, the red fox may be an important faunal time-marker for eastern archaeology. Any alleged remains of red fox in archaeological sites in the eastern United States should be scrutinized carefully. Fortunately, many skeletal characters (foremost of which is the top of the skull) distinguish this fox from the gray fox, which long has been an inhabitant of the eastern United States."

The fox has a distinct personality. His exceptional cunning, amounting sometimes almost to genius, has been responsible for many exaggerated stories of his extreme resourcefulness. One such legend relates his ability to rid himself of fleas by holding a piece of wood or cloth in his mouth while he gradually submerges himself in a body of water. As he goes under, the fleas crawl forward and finally up to the last object remaining above the surface, namely, the piece of wood. As the fox finally submerges completely he sets the wood adrift, loaded to capacity with fleas—whereupon the fox emerges and trots away, freed from his parasites.

Whatever his range, and whatever his species, he remains one of America's most fascinating sources of sport. The still hunter who comes upon him accidentally at the edge of a clearing; the hunter who follows his meanderings by the tones of a bugle-voiced hound; or the resplendent red-coated hunter on horseback—all testify that the fox is not only one of wildlife's wiliest creatures but one which offers the most diversified forms of pursuit. And in addition to these methods of hunting, the trapper also rates him high as a source of income.

# FOX HUNTING

Fox hunting, next to falconry, is perhaps the oldest of all field sports. In the British Isles it was practiced probably prior to 1300. In America it made its formal bow soon after the Virginia colonists got their land opened and their horses saddled. By the time George Washington was running his own pack of gray foxes, the sport was well established. In New England, meantime, fox hunting had taken on a new aspect. No horse and no hound entered this picture. But the flintlock and the red fox did, a combination born of cold weather and a practical desire for fur.

Fox hunting begins with the fox.

The Old World red fox averages about 14 pounds. Its fur lacks length, density, and luster, and hence is of little commercial value. But it possesses just as much cunning as Aesop claimed for it. Also, it runs for long and devious distances.

The American red fox is considerably smaller than his British brother. Vixens (females) average 8 pounds. Dog foxes (males) weigh a pound or so more. Built like an elongated whippet, he also is faster and, it is said, even trickier than his overseas counterpart. That fact is important, for it led to the development of the world's greatest nose—owned by the American foxhound. He also has a gorgeous, long-furred pelt, normally worth enough to make him sought for his hide. That also is important, for it resulted in a diversity of hunting practices. The American red fox also is a noted open-field runner. In fact, he seldom holes up, even in winter, unless at the end of his rope or unless pups are occupying the woodchuck burrow usually acquired and refurbished for domestic activities. This is a northern fox. It was not until the 1850's that fox hunters recorded extension of his range south into Maryland and beyond. In fact, the newcomer was believed to be the result of previous importations of the English red fox.

The American gray fox bears comparatively distant kinship to the red. He stems from another group of foxes. He is different in color and structure, possessing a much shorter muzzle. His grizzled fur is coarse by comparison. His habits are different and he even has a different smell. The common gray is a southern fox. This is the one which Washington hunted. But he slowly spread northward. He was a rare visitor in New England before 1890 and did not begin to filter into the Adirondacks of New York until 1930. The gray is a poor runner, usually being driven in within an hour, even in swampy, brushy lowlands, which he seems to prefer. Often he will run up a tree, demonstrating surprising agility. As a sporting fox, he is not in the same class with the red. But he is still good enough to provide plenty of sport, especially at night when he runs his best, or in February when he is out looking for a mate.

In general, this is the quarry; now the chase.

Originally, the English term *hunting* meant pursuit with hound and horse. Fox hunting merely specified the quarry. This was the hunting referred to by Gervase Markham 350 years ago when he wrote: "Of all the field pleasures wherewith old time and men's invention hath blest the houres of our recreation, there is none to excelle the delight of hunting."

Fox hunting, supreme among British field sports, for centuries has been bound closely by tradition and is generally considered an integral part of English country life. It unquestionably influenced strongly the breeding of horses and hounds. Prior to the World Wars, nearly 200 packs of foxhounds were maintained in the British Isles. In 1878, the English authority on dogs, "Stonehenge," wrote that "Numerous instances have occurred where forty or fifty thousand dollars a year have been spent . . . upon a fox-hunting establishment. . . ."

Although fox hunting in its strict British sense is primarily a diversion for the wealthy, it has remained for generations a catholic sport, since virtually anyone able to beg or borrow a horse may ride to the hounds.

A pack of foxhounds may consist of up to 120 dogs—60 couples—preferably bred as alike as possible in both looks and action. In traditional general supervision is the Master (M.F.H.), an amateur of long apprenticeship, while under him are the professional Huntsman (kennelman and trainer who directs the dogs' activities afield) and the Whippers-in (his assistants). Usual procedure is for the riders—some of whom, especially the M.F.H., may be garbed in traditional "pink"—to gather at a given point near a covert in which the pack is likely to locate a fox. Once the fox breaks cover, the rallying cry "Tally-ho" sets the pack and the field off in chase. The hounds often may "fault," or lose the scent, whereupon a "check" occurs until it is regained and they are off again "in full cry" if the scent is hot and the pack in tongue together. The hounds may catch the fox. If so, the first rider in at "the death" may claim the brush, or tail, as trophy.

Often, when foxes are scarce, the hounds are lashed off and the animal is saved to be "let down" in front of the pack another day. Sometimes, when foxes cannot be found or when a hunt is designed to take riders over a planned course, a bag of scent (which may be turpentine and anise) is dragged along the route ahead of the hounds.

In the United States, formal fox hunting with horse and hound has been far less popular than in England. However, before World War II, the Master of Foxhounds Association of America listed about 150 affiliated clubs from nearly half the states. Most of the formal hunts, however, are spread along the Atlantic seaboard states northward from the Carolinas, with major activity in Virginia.

In every organized hunt club there are two types of members—those who ride to hunt and those who hunt to ride. To the former the chase is the thing and the horse is a necessary adjunct to it. To the latter the ride is the thing, and the hounds and fox merely provide the incentive for the ride. To these it is always, "What a glorious race we had today." Masters of Fox Hounds are constantly endeavoring to "educate" these members to a fuller appreciation of the chase. The Master of Fox Hounds is responsible for the hunt, and is always anxious to improve the performance of his pack. These hounds are carefully selected not only for nose and endurance but also for gait, willingness, and pack and cry. It is absolutely essential to good sport that the pack work as a team and not as a group of individual stars. The organized, formal hunt clubs give to American fox hunting the color and glamour which gain wide publicity for the sport.

Some of the better-known American Hunt Clubs are the Grafton, the Middlesex, the Brandywine, the Meadow Brook, the Orange County, the Genesee Valley, the Piedmont, the Brunswick Foxhound Club, the Myopia, the Harford, the Fairfield and Westchester, Hitchcock Hounds, Radnor, Patapsco, Warrenton, Deep Run, Iroquois, Rockaway, Rose Tree, Aiken, Pine Hill, Keswick, Norfolk, Shelburne, Cheshire, Mr. Joseph B. Thomas' Hounds, Mr. Newbold Ely's Hounds, and the Millbrook. There were, and still are, many other packs, both privately owned and hunt club property, far too numerous to mention here. These packs were all schooled and disciplined and hunted from horse over country well adapted to riding to hounds.

The American hunting packs for the most part are composed of English or half-English hounds, trained in good manners and, also, to move in a compact group around the Huntsman's horse when not trailing.

In formal fox hunting it is questionable whether the major emphasis is on the hound or on the horse. But fox hunting, American style, leaves no room for doubt. The hound is the whole show.

In 1947 the number of pedigreed American foxhounds was estimated to exceed 150,000, with many of them registered in the International Foxhunters' Stud Book, Lexington, Ky.

The American foxhound, adjudged the finest trail dog the world has ever known, was at least indirectly developed as a result of the spread of the red fox into the South's hunting cover. The English hound, able to handle the gray fox in this country, as he was the comparatively easygoing European red in the open inland areas at home, could not match speed, stamina, and drive with the American red in rugged terrain, especially on a cold scent over rocks. So foxhunters began to develop a hound that could. Generations of careful breeding produced several noted strains—all with a common attribute: a remarkable nose. These hounds are the Walkers, most famous strain of all, and the Triggs, both of which were developed in Kentucky; the Julys, Trumbos, and a few others. Higher at the shoulder and racier than the English type, they far outclass their European cousins in independence and scenting ability.

Also, they have been developed to run on snow, a special attribute only attained satisfactorily since 1930 by such packs as the famous snow-going Walkers, owned by Fred Streever in New York.

Of course, there are hundreds of thousands of other foxhounds in America—native hounds. These are the redbones, the black and tans, the blue-ticks. Thousands of them have noses capable of as many miracles as their more carefully bred brothers. But all have one thing in common—voice. On this voice, plus its variations of tone and tempo, depends much of the intense interest in American fox hunting. The southern style of hunting and the northern style, though they differ, are both largely based on the voice of the hound.

Hound voices are individual voices. There are the so-called bell-toned or bugle-voiced hounds for which small fortunes have been paid. There are the silver tonguers of the tribe—the "Bugle Anns." There are squealers and choppers, deep organ-throated basses, high-pitched clarinets, foggy drum-like beaters, and those which merely sigh, sounding like some exotic wood-wind as it echoes back from some distant hill. Each pack is a veritable orchestra of sound, yet within individual messages of trail performance for the expert ear. Every subtle change of pitch or cadence telegraphs a meaning back far down-wind where the hunter stands.

There may be many dogs, or only one; many hunters, or just one man. But the true values of foxhunting reach general climax in the big trials when scores of hounds are cast at one signal.

The November National in the South may provide the spectacle for eye and ear of 150 crack hounds unleashed simultaneously and leading off in one vast bedlam of sound and movement. The famous Brunswick Foxhound Club Trials in New England or the annual New York State Foxhunter's Association meeting produce some of the most outstanding examples of rugged American individualism possible in the name of sport.

One of the most stirring moments in foxhunting annals occurred during a New York trial in 1946 when nearly 100 hounds, lined up on a Catskill peak, were cast as one. Immediately a fox was started and for a quarter-mile the flying animal and streaming pack were silhouetted against the great red-gold backdrop of a sunrise sky. There were crags to roll back the echoes and half a thousand men to stand, silent, ears cupped to hear the monumental swirl of sound.

The fox ran up an old stone wall into a tumbled mass of granite far up the mountain and got away. But for three days men stood high on the summits, fox horns to lips, calling to their hounds, still running other foxes on a score of far-flung hills.

Fox hunting customs vary by regions.

In the South, usually, the social aspects are emphasized. Men—all kinds of men—gather on some likely knoll at night. Then the hounds are loosed and the owners, who may have come by car, or muleback, or on foot, gather round the pitchpine fire. There the spinning of yarns about dogs—and foxes—is interrupted only when the pack swings within earshot and the men move silently from the crackling logs the better to tell the position of old Thunder, or Driver, or Mandy-Lee. Once in a while a hound may sneak into the campfire circle or stay, spooky and panting, out where the faint shadows lap against the leaves. It is only then that some luckless owner is silenced, crestfallen, hardly bearing the friendly jibes of those whose hounds are still driving through the night.

In the South it is virtual heresy to *shoot* a fox. This is left to the pack—if it is good enough. Here the fox enjoys the greatest measure of legal protection. Some states, like South Carolina in 1947, entirely prohibit the trapping of foxes. Others limit hunting to certain months.

In the North it is different. The fox hunter normally shoots the fox. Sometimes, for one reason or another, foxes become so scarce that it is difficult for the hounds to get a "race." In that event the hunter is likely to hold fire, saving the fox—and his sport—for another day. The true northern fox hunter condones the shooting of the quarry by pointing out that in the South the hunt is merely a match between hound and fox with chances likely enough in that open country that the pack itself will make the kill. But in the North, he points out, the fox has all the advantage of the rugged going and it is just as much of a sporting feat to get in a shot as it is for the southern hound to make the kill.

Northern fox hunting is distinctly tinctured with frostbite and aching backs. It is a hardy sport, perhaps the hardiest of all.

The method, normally, is this: The hound or hounds are led, leashed, into red fox country. This usually means remote, thinly settled hills where nature has taken back farms abandoned in the 1880's and where wild, rocky old pastures reach high toward the scudding clouds.

Often snow is underfoot, preferably a new snow. When a reasonably fresh fox track is discovered (and the hunter usually knows about where that will be) the dogs are unleashed. If the ground is bare, the hounds are cast to do their own looking. But when the first tonguing indicates that they have struck a "line," the hunters scatter to take up stands where they believe the fox is most likely to pass, usually on the highest, windiest area of good visibility at hand.

The hunter may wait two hours before the fox brings around the hounds. And then it may be down the opposite ridge; or, often as not, the fox may take the hounds clear into the next county and lose them during the night. Northern hounds have been known to run a fox three days and end up, lost, 40 miles away.

PLATE V. Fox hunting in New England can be a cold sport.

The job of regaining the dogs is, in fact, an important aspect of fox hunting, particularly in the North. First, the fox horn enters the picture. Usually it is a cow horn with mouthpiece, often laboriously carved in one piece by the owner. These horns are prized, especially for tone—and not everybody can blow them. Usually, the straighter the horn, the more mellow the tone. Lacking a horn, the houndsman may have mastered the art of blowing down his gun barrel to produce a similar far-reaching sound. In any event, each dog normally is trained to come in at the sound of the master's horn. But invariably some hound is out of earshot at day's end, or he just will not respond. He may be worth $1000 or $15—it matters little, the true houndsman does what he can to get the dog back. Usually he leaves his coat or an old cloth, carried for the purpose, where the hound first was cast. On this the returning dog may curl up and await the coming of his owner next dawn. But the sound of the fox horn through the night is common in good hunting country when there is a new snow on the hills and a full moon helps the wanderer wearily back from the race.

By 1947 use of the foxhound had all but vanished from many areas. The spread of the white-tailed deer was one reason, since deerproof hounds are scarce. Another was what hunters described as an increasingly high mortality in hounds in settled areas. This was attributed to mounting highway hazards and to less inclination by the public to return strayed hounds. especially since the demand for game dogs of any kind exceeded the supply following the end of World War II. Houndsmen invariably affix names and addresses to the collars of their animals.

Often because of the lack of dogs, thousands of northern hunters have learned to hunt the fox without him. Still hunting is the major method. Requisites are a fresh fox track in soft snow, and patience. Usually, the fox beds down by day—the red in the open on a rock or some slight elevation, the gray in a hole or under tree roots. The method is to follow the track noiselessly, looking well ahead and to each side, since the fox usually goes off to watch his backtrack before bedding. Opportunity for a successful shot usually occurs only when the fox is jumped from the bed. Foxes so jumped within a few hours of dusk rarely bed down again before the following day. Also, if pursued immediately after being routed the first time, Reynard is likely to move an excessive distance before curling up again.

Another method of fox hunting, born of an overabundance of foxes in the northern states during the 1940's, is by means of the drive.

The common practice is for as large a number of hunters as possible to surround a given area. Thus they are presumed to be in position to shoot the fox as it attempts to elude the "drivers" who, usually keeping abreast for safety's sake, rake through the area. Sometimes a dog or two—it matters little what kind—is brought along to help out.

Some fox drives, however, are carefully planned for up to a dozen participants. Half the men quietly take up stands at the down-wind side of the area to be driven, usually a swamp or square of woods. They remain hidden and motionless. Meantime, two of the remaining men start toward the standers from the other end of the area, walking down opposite sides. They talk naturally back and forth, refraining from unusual noises. When they have proceeded 50 to 75 yards, the remaining men also start toward the standers and in between the flankers. These late starters also walk along naturally, usually looking for tracks in the snow. The object is to make the fox sneak slowly out of the area past the standers, being prevented from moving out the sides by the advance flank men.

At best, fox drives can be termed merely Sunday diversions, with their effectiveness limited by the amount of teamwork, and luck. In 1945 one Buffalo sportsmen's club staged an enormous hunt in which nearly 1000 men and several dogs participated one wintry Sunday. Net results: two foxes, one woodchuck, and many tons of exercise.

One little-known method of fox hunting remains. It has been practiced by a handful of New England individualists for generations. It is called belling. It requires two hunters, a fresh fox track in soft snow, a liberal amount of humor, a gun, and a dinner bell. The fox also must possess an overwhelming curiosity and a nervous temperament. It is almost certain the fox will possess both.

The hunters jump the fox. One man then proceeds down the trail uninterruptedly ringing the bell. After a half-mile, the other goes on around in a wide circle to get down-wind of the fox. By then his general direction probably has been determined. Sooner or later the fox, apparently impelled by curiosity, begins to backtrack, switching his tail. Before long a normal animal seems almost overcome. His antics slow him to a virtual halt. At this point the hunter with the gun is supposed to be handy.

Fox belling, as can be seen, cashes in on the predictable vagaries of what is considered one of the wiliest of all mammals. That the fox never is a victim of routine, especially when pursued, is a characteristic on which, after all, fox hunting is based.

Mix the guile of the fox with the music of some bell-tongued hounds, or with a campfire and friends, or with the majestic sweep of winter hills, or even with the lift of a handy hunter as he soars over a brushy hurdle—and sportsmen will tell you that you have in fox hunting a sport as enduring as the slyest old dog fox himself.

## JAGUAR

***Felis onca***

**History.** The jaguar, once found in small numbers in Southern California, New Mexico, and southwest Texas, is virtually extinct in these states today and is only rarely encountered in southeastern Arizona. From Arizona south, through Central America and as far south as northern Argentina, the animal is more plentiful, but the Matto Grosso in Brazil is the home of the largest of these cats and there also they seem most plentiful. Like other carnivores, the jaguar retreated as civilization advanced, but in some instances the retreat was not so far or so rapid as to prevent the animal from making occasional forays against the invader's cattle, horses, and pigs.

**Identification.** The jaguar, which is broken down into 16 sub-species (see "Range and Distribution"), is the largest of the North American cats and ranks third among the cats of the world, only the lion and tiger being larger. In general coloration and markings they resemble the leopard, but are heavier, and where the leopard has a small, narrow head, the jaguar's is broad and boxlike. It differs from the leopard also in that the spotted markings are in the form of large black rosettes with one or more black spots in the center.

*El tigre,* as the animal is called throughout Mexico and Central America, does not stand as high as the average cougar, but is heavier and much more powerful. There is considerable variation in size among the various sub-species or geographical types. The Matto Grosso jaguar is the largest, with one specimen recorded at 307 pounds. The maximum weight of the jaguars found in the northern part of their range is around 250 pounds for the males and 150 pounds for the females, but the average weight would fall well below these figures.

In parts of its range, notably Central America and northern South America, the jaguar occasionally shows melanistic phases and black specimens are occasionally found. These are known as *tigre negro.* In northern Brazil such black specimens are called by the Portuguese *onca prieta.* Although the pelts of these animals appear coal black, the spots may be seen, almost like watermarks, in certain lights.

**Characteristics.** The jaguars seem to have adapted themselves equally well to arid, mountainous, and jungle areas. In the low country of marshes and swamps they do not hesitate to take to the water, and are excellent swimmers. They prey indiscriminately on whatever living thing is available in their range, from peccaries, their favorite food, to tapirs, capybaras, turtles, turtle eggs, and alligators, and they make an occasional raid on livestock in areas where their outer ranges touch on farming lands. The tropical lowland is the favorite habitat of this animal.

They do not exhibit the ferocity of the leopard, but they will attack human beings. Although there is a slight overlapping of the ranges of the jaguar and the cougar in a few areas, the jaguar kill usually can be distinguished from that of the cougar. The cougar covers its kill with grass, sticks, and leaves, and may lie up some distance away, but the jaguar is inclined to bed down near its kill, where it can drive off intruders.

The jaguar, being a night marauder, and preferring the almost inaccessible tangle of jungle, probably stands in little danger of extinction over a large part of its range, provided it receives some protection from excessive hunting.

Like the lion, tiger, and leopard, the jaguar is able to emit deep, guttural roars of considerable volume.

**Breeding.** The very nature of its existence and habitat has prevented zoologists from acquiring much definite information about the breeding habits of the jaguar. Like many of the animals whose range is primarily in sub-tropical and tropical areas, the jaguar seems to have no definite breeding period. In one section young will be born late in December and through January, and in others the majority of the young seem to be born during April and May. The period of gestation, determined through animals which have been observed in zoos, is approximately 100 days, and from two to four young are produced.

**Range and Distribution.** Today, jaguars are rarely found north of the Rio Grande, but are reasonably plentiful in parts of Mexico and Central America as well as in Brazil. The various sub-species or typts are found in the following areas:

| | |
|---|---|
| *Felis onca arizonensis* | Arizona |
| " " *boliviensis* | Bolivia |
| " " *centralis* | Costa Rica |
| " " *coxi* | Brazil |
| " " *goldmani* | Mexico |
| " " *hernandesii* | Mexico |
| " " *major* | Surinam |
| " " *madeirae* | Brazil |
| " " *mexianae* | Brazil |
| " " *milleri* | Brazil |
| " " *onca* | Brazil |
| " " *paraguensis* | Paraguay |
| " " *paulensis* | Brazil |
| " " *peruviana* | Peru |
| " " *ucayalae* | Peru |
| " " *veraecrusis* | Mexico |

**Hunting Methods.** As is likewise true of most of our North American cats, the most successful way of hunting the jaguar is with well-trained hounds, although in some areas it is occasionally "called up" and shot in much the same manner as the moose. When prowling, especially during mating season, jaguars often utter deep, coughing roars and certain Indians have learned to imitate this roar with horns made of bark. In the marsh country of Brazil, where the jaguar frequents the water, the Guato Indians often went out in dugout canoes, hid in the grass, and when the jaguar swam out in answer to their call they killed him with a big spear. In recent years the Lee Brothers, big game hunters of Tucson, Arizona, have developed a similar method of hunting in Mexico. They have learned to use the bark

N. Y. Zoological Society.

PLATE I. Jaguar.

horn in imitating the roar of the jaguar, but only to locate the big cat so that they may place their hounds on the trail the next morning.

Needless to say, the success of a jaguar hunt depends on the hounds. The big cats are nocturnal in their habits and a hunter rarely sees one which has not been treed or brought to bay by dogs. Ordinarily, hounds which are good cougar dogs will prove to be good jaguar dogs, although hunting *el tigre* is a far grimmer task. For whereas a cougar nearly always climbs a tree, rarely stopping to fight on the ground, a jaguar will often come to bay in thick brush, boulders, or rocky caves. And whereas the cougar generally fights an entirely defensive fight, the jaguar will not hesitate to make determined charges at his harassers—if cornered either by dogs or men. As a matter of fact, there are several well-authenticated instances of jaguars making unprovoked attacks on humans. Therefore, when the hunter approaches a jaguar at bay he should proceed with caution and be sure that his gun is ready for use. These big cats are very fast and since they usually come to bay in very thick cover, the hunter must approach sometimes to within a few feet before getting a shot. There is no time to make a mistake in case of a charge.

This is not meant to imply that all jaguars will show fight. Very often they will tree or, even if

Fred Hollender.

Plate II. Mexican Jaguar.

brought to bay on the ground, will run at the approach of the hunter. In fact, it is probably safe to say that 60 per cent of these big spotted cats will make every effort to escape. On the other hand, some individuals will fight savagely, killing dogs and charging without hesitation. It is well for the jaguar hunter to keep this in mind at all times.

It is obvious that the hunter should not be undergunned, not only for his own safety but for the sake of his dogs. Even though the big cat may not charge the hunter, it can wreak havoc among the hounds if crippled by an ineffective shot. When the gun fires the dogs usually become very excited and overconfident and will rush in on their quarry. There is, of course, much controversy in every field of hunting over the proper gun for the job and each hunter has his own particular favorite. A head or neck shot from as light a rifle as a .30-30 will kill a jaguar, but it is not always possible to make such a shot. Therefore, a heavier load is recommended.

While the big cats are thin skinned and do not take as much stopping as a grizzly, for instance, they nevertheless have tremendous vitality and, particularly the jaguar, present a certain element of danger. Therefore, the hunter should make every effort to kill the cat instantly. Whenever close enough to be sure of his aim he should shoot for the head or neck. A body shot—even a heart shot—will not always stop one of these big cats in its tracks.

Since the jaguar is nocturnal in its habits, it follows that the earlier a hunter can get out in the morning the better chance he will have of striking a fresh trail. Also, the hounds will be able to follow the trail much better in the cool of the morning before the hot sun has dried off the dew and burned up the scent. When a hound gets hot he loses 50 per cent of his trailing ability.

Invaluable to the jaguar hunter is a well-trained, experienced "strike" dog—a hound which will not pay attention to any trail but that of the big cats. It is most discouraging to try to hunt jaguar with a pack of dogs which will go dashing off on the first trail they strike, whether it be deer, peccary, or *coati*. For this reason it is always advisable to secure one or two "strike" dogs before going into jaguar country. Many ranches in Mexico maintain a *Tigrero,* or tiger hunter, with a pack of dogs whose job it is to hunt down cattle-killing jaguars. These packs are usually composed of nondescript mongrels which, although they undoubtedly account for a considerable number of jaguars, are, nevertheless, usually unreliable and will run whatever animal they come across first. Here is where the strike dogs will help you. Furthermore, a mongrel cannot begin to handle as cold a trail as a well-bred hound, and very often this means the difference between success and failure on the hunt.

The ideal hound for hunting any of the big cats is a foxhound-bloodhound cross. The foxhound gives speed and the bloodhound gives added scenting ability and generally better voice, which is an important angle in hunting big, rough country where the hunter must be able to course his dogs from a long distance.

In fox hunting with hounds, 70% of the dog's job is driving the fox after he has been jumped. Trailing the fox to the jump is not over 30% of the job. In hunting jaguar and cougar, 70% of the job is trailing. The big cats are short winded and ordinarily do not run far after being started. Consequently, speed is far less important than the ability to follow a cold trail through all kinds of terrain.

In following the hounds on a jaguar trail the hunter should always keep in mind the fact that a very cold trail can suddenly turn into a very hot trail. The big cat may be traveling, holding a pretty straight course over considerable distance, but at any time may make a kill and lie down. If, for example, the hounds are following an early-morning trail which was made at midnight, it is obvious that the animal has a 6- or 7-hour start. The trail may lead straight away and the hounds may carry it so fast that the hunter will have difficulty keeping in hearing of them, particularly in brushy country. Perhaps, however, the big cat killed a deer or calf just before daylight, ate his fill, and lay down near by. The hounds reach this kill, jump the jaguar from its bed, and the 6- or 7-hour-old trail immediately becomes a sight race, or at least a smoking-hot scent. It is the ever-present hope of such a break which keeps both hunter and his hounds working away on a cold trail, even although almost exhausted.

The jaguar is very fast for a short distance but has small lungs and quickly tires. When crowded by the hounds it will either climb, come to bay, or seek refuge in a rocky cave. In parts of Mexico jaguars often go into deserted mines.

When approaching a treed jaguar the hunter should take his time, trying to reach the tree from an angle which will give him an unobstructed shot. The big cat's attention is focused on the dogs below, and with caution it is often possible for the hunter to approach to within 50 or 75 feet of the tree, depending on the cover. At such a distance, where a man can be sure of his aim, a head shot is recommended. A clean miss is better than a crippling shot, for even if the animal jumps out unhit it will often tree again within a short distance. If crippled it will fall out into the dogs and is sure to do considerable damage before it can be finished off.

Although the jaguar does not put up a long chase after it has once been started by the hounds, it often travels long distances and whenever possible hunting should be done on horseback. It is grueling work to try to follow a pack of hounds on foot, especially when on the trail of a cat which is traveling and may lead out straight away for several miles through rugged country. For this reason it is best to hunt the jaguar in cattle country where horses may be obtained from the ranches. The big cats take a heavy toll of livestock and ranchers naturally are glad to have them killed and will generally do everything possible to be of assistance. Local hunters, or *vaqueros* (cowboys), are invaluable as guides and in their knowledge of the habits and habitats of the jaguars in the vicinity.

Naturally the hunter who secures a fine specimen will be anxious to preserve the skin as a trophy. Perhaps the best method is that of the Indians. A frame of poles should be made in a rectangular shape 8 or 9 feet tall and 6 or 7 feet wide, depending on the size of the animal. When the skin has been removed from the carcass, make small incisions with the point of a knife around the edge of the skin. These incisions should be about 6 or 8 inches apart. Lay the frame of poles on the ground and stretch out the skin inside the frame. Then, with cord or rawhide, tie the nose midway of the top pole and fasten the tail midway of the bottom pole. Then tie out all four paws to the side poles.

After the skin is thus laid out in the desired shape, lace and stretch it all the way around, passing the cord through the incisions, out around the pole, back through the next incision, out around the pole, etc. In this way the full size of the trophy can be preserved and it can be set up where air can circulate freely around it. All flesh and fat should be removed from the skin and it should be well salted. Particular care should be taken to skin out the lips and ears completely as these parts are where the hair is most apt to slip. Jaguars are often killed in hot humid areas and the above method will keep the skin in good shape. When the skin is thoroughly dried it can be rolled up and sent to the taxidermist for finishing.

## CANADIAN LYNX

*Lynx canadensis*

**Identification.** The Canadian lynx is an awkward-appearing cat with very long legs, very short tail, large paws, and long tufts on its ears. It has also a pronounced ruff on the cheeks. In color it is a soft, warm gray, occasionally mottled with indistinct brownish patches. The tail is tipped with black and there are black markings on the head and throat. As with all our North American cats, the backs of the ears are black with a grayish-white patch.

Generally, the Canadian lynx is larger than the bay lynx or bobcat, an adult male weighing up to 35 or 40 pounds. The female is somewhat smaller. Because of its long legs, this animal looks larger than it really is, standing about as high at the shoulders as an Irish terrier. When running it has an awkward, "rocking-chair" gallop.

**Characteristics.** The broad paws of the Canadian lynx are peculiarly adapted to traveling in the snow and it preys successfully on varying hares, ruffed grouse, and ptarmigan, as well as on mice, small birds of all kinds, and occasionally fawns. The varying hare, however, makes up its main diet, just as the cottontail rabbit or swamp rabbit is the favorite food of the bobcat.

The Canadian lynx is a shy, stealthy creature which is rarely seen by man in the wild state. It is

N. Y. Zoological Society.

PLATE I. Canadian Lynx.

nocturnal and makes its lair in heavy thickets, rock ledges, or caves. Two kittens are usually born in a litter.

When captured very young, a lynx kitten may very often be tamed, as these animals do not appear to be as intractable as bobcats.

The pelt of the Canadian lynx makes a beautiful trophy and the flesh is palatable, being light in color and tasting much like veal. It is often eaten by the natives. It is almost identical in taste with the flesh of a bobcat, having no strong, wild taste whatsoever.

**Range and Distribution.** The range of the lynx extends from Newfoundland to Alaska, but it is rarely found very far south of the Canadian border. Unlike the bobcat, it does not like civilization, preferring the wilderness forests. The animal found in Newfoundland, *Lynx subsolanus,* has the same general appearance but is slightly darker in color. The Alaska cat, *Lynx canadensis mollipilosus,* is somewhat browner.

**Hunting Methods.** Very little hunting is done for this animal by sportsmen as it is nowhere plentiful and is usually found in country where horses are either not available or cannot be used because of the heavy timber and deep snow. Since the job of following hounds on foot is a very arduous undertaking, and since the use of dogs is essential, the average sportsman prefers to leave such rugged work to native hunters and guides. Even these men, however, rarely hunt the lynx for sport, pursuing it mainly for its pelt, which is long, soft, and has excellent commercial value. As a matter of fact, most of these cats are taken by trappers, either in steel traps or in snares—this latter method being much in use by the Indians, who attract the lynx to the snare by using a scent made of beaver castors.

Any hounds which will run bobcats will be equally good after the Canadian lynx as the scent seems to be very similar. When started by dogs the lynx will tree readily, rarely running far. It travels considerable distances, however, and it is the difficulty of keeping up with hounds on such a traveling trail which makes lynx hunting strenuous work.

There is no danger to the hunter from the animal itself and when treed it can be killed easily with any light rifle such as .25-20, .25-35, .32-20, or .30-30. For the sake of the dogs, however, the hunter should make sure of his aim so that the cat will be dead on hitting the ground.

## OCELOT

*Felis pardalis*

COMMON NAMES: Leopard Cat, Spotted Cat, Tiger Cat.

**Identification.** The ocelot is one of the most beautifully marked of all the cats. The fur is soft but short and is marked with black spots and stripes on a tawny background. No two skins are alike but the spots and stripes combine to form beautiful patterns. The throat and under parts are white against which the black bars stand out sharply.

N. Y. Zoological Society.

**PLATE I. Ocelot.**

In size the ocelot is about the same as a bobcat but the general build is somewhat different. The ocelot has a longer, heavier body and somewhat shorter legs. It also has a long tail and resembles the common house cat in general conformation. The average male weighs around 35 pounds. the female slightly less. There is no noticeable seasonal variation in color among ocelots as is the case with the lynx and cougar, for ocelots are mainly creatures of the tropics or the subtropics.

**Characteristics.** In its general habits it may be compared with the bobcat, as it often frequents areas close to settlements and ranches and does considerable damage to poultry and livestock, being especially fond of lambs, kids, and young pigs. In the wilds it preys on birds of all kinds and in Mexico undoubtedly kills many wild turkeys, particularly the young birds. It also catches small mammals and occasionally fawns. It is an excellent climber.

Ocelots often travel in pairs, particularly during the mating season, and the young are usually born in the fall, usually two, occasionally three, kittens to a litter. In parts of their range, such as the marshes and jungles of Brazil, ocelots do not hesitate to take to water and are good swimmers.

Ocelots have a very strong, musky scent, resembling that of the African leopard, and the flesh is not commonly eaten, even by the South American Indians.

**Range and Distribution.** Today this handsome member of the cat family is rarely found in the United States, although a few specimens are occasionally taken in southern Texas. It is fairly common in Mexico and its range extends on down into South America, through southern Brazil and Paraguay.

**Hunting Methods.** The most sucessful way of hunting any of our North American cats is with a well-trained pack of dogs, and the ocelot is no exception. It is very often treed during a cougar or jaguar hunt, just as the bobcat is a by-product, so to speak, of a cougar hunt in the more northern latitudes. Like the bobcat, in most of its range, the ocelot does not usually run long before taking to a tree.

Many ranchers in Mexico and Central and South America maintain packs of dogs for hunting down stock-killing cats of all kinds—jaguars, cougars, and ocelots. Although these packs are usually composed of nondescript mongrels, they account for a good many cats. A well-trained hound, however, with experience on cougar, is always a welcome addition to such a pack and is invaluable for striking and working out cold trails.

Since ocelots are usually killed incidentally to jaguar hunting and are usually found in the same area, it is evident that the hunter should be armed with a rifle powerful enough to handle one of the larger cats. So it is not recommended to carry a light rifle. An ocelot is not dangerous to the hunter but a jaguar occasionally is. Therefore, carry a gun powerful enough for either job. (See "Jaguar.")

## STRIPED SKUNK (Canadian Skunk) *Mephitis mephitis*

COMMON NAMES: Big Skunk, Common Skunk, Large Striped Skunk, Line-Backed Skunk, Polecat, Wood-Pussy.

**History.** Aside from the porcupine, the skunk is the only North American mammal endowed with special protection which makes him virtually immune to attack from other animals. The "porky" relies on his quill armor, the skunk on a defense that is much more effective because he can defend himself from a greater distance. Because of his unique method for discouraging his enemies he is seldom molested, but occasionally he is killed by the great horned owl, and even some of the larger predators will brave his terrible weapon if hard pressed by hunger.

His pelt is used extensively in the fur trade where, after a certain processing treatment, it is often known as "Alaska Sable." Being rather stupid animals, thousands of skunks are trapped annually and their pelts furnish a considerable income to both amateur and professional trappers. The pelts with the least white are considered the most valuable.

**Identification.** There is little likelihood of confusing skunks with any other North American mammals because they alone possess a shiny black coat with distinctive white stripes and have a long bushy tail. They are squat, compact, heavily built animals about the size of a large house cat. The males are about 24 inches long over-all, with an 8-inch tail, and weigh about 8 pounds. The females average slightly smaller but are identical in coloration, and there are no seasonal variations in pelage. The head is relatively small, the legs short, and the tail large and bushy. The forefeet are equipped with long claws for digging.

The fur is composed of two coats; a soft underfur covered with long, glossy guard hairs. The pelage is entirely black except for a narrow streak of white running from the nose to the crown, where the white area expands to a wide patch extending to the shoulders. There it divides into two white streaks which continue to the base of the tail. These lateral stripes enclose a black area along the top of the back. The width of these stripes varies with different specimens, being quite wide on some animals and practically nonexistent on others. The tail hairs are all white at the base but the amount of white visible on that appendage varies with the individual specimens. As a rule the tip of the tail is white.

**Characteristics.** Although *Mephitis* does most of his hunting after dusk he is not strictly nocturnal and may sometimes be seen in the daytime. His appetite is cosmopolitan and he eats about anything that is available. Small mammals such as rats, mice, and moles form a part of his diet. He is also fond of eggs and young birds, a fondness which sometimes leads him to raid poultry pens and which plays havoc with the eggs and young of the pheasant, quail, and grouse population. He rounds out his menu with frogs, lizards, crayfish, snakes, and large insects. In regions

U. S. Forest Service.

PLATE I. Skunk.

where hops are grown he feeds on the large grubs found among the roots.

Knowing that he is reasonably safe from attack, his movements, like those of the porcupine, are slow and deliberate. He does not use his defense mechanism unless provoked and will sometimes make every effort to escape before resorting to his only defense. The musky liquid is stored in two glands near the anal opening. It is pale yellow in color, vile in odor, and highly volatile. A small amount at a time is discharged in the form of a fine spray by means of a special apparatus which is projected through the anus. By muscular contraction this spray can be ejected for a distance of nearly 10 feet, but may be carried by the wind for a much greater distance. So powerful is this liquid that even a small amount will contaminate everything for several feet in all directions. It is highly acid in its reaction and especially painful if it gets in the eyes, where it may cause temporary blindness. Clothing which has thus been affected will retain the odor for weeks, although burying such clothing in the ground will help to remove the odor more quickly.

There is a popular legend that the skunk sprays this liquor by saturating his tail and then swishing it in the direction of his attacker. This is not true. When the animal is ready to dispense the spray, the tail is held erect with all the hairs bristled and well out of the way of the discharge. The skunk keeps his own fur clean and free from odor at all times. The usual danger sign is when his head goes down and his tail comes up, for he is then in position to let go, and within certain limits he can direct the spray in any desired direction.

Experts claim that a skunk can be captured without danger of ejection if the tail is grasped and held down, possibly on the theory that the animal will not foul his own tail, but this is hardly a stunt for an amateur. Trappers often manage to take a skunk without experiencing any dire consequences but there is always an element of risk. Skunks may be safely killed by drowning. Shooting is uncertain unless the spinal cord is severed.

Young skunks, although as fully equipped for defense as the adults, may be more readily captured and are easily tamed to make fine pets. A simple surgical operation renders them harmless and they are as playful as kittens and much more affectionate. A pet skunk is a much better mouser than any cat.

The den is usually a burrow in the woods. Sometimes an abandoned woodchuck or badger den is taken over, but if neither of these is available the skunk will dig his own. Less often the den may be located in a small cave, a stone wall, or a hollow log. The female makes a large bed of grass and leaves before the young arrive. The average litter is from four to six but may number as high as ten. The young are born in April or early May, and when about one-fourth grown they accompany the mother on nocturnal forays for food. On these travels they follow the mother from place to place in single file about 20 inches apart.

Generally the skunk is mute but under certain conditions can utter a whining grunt or a tiny squeal.

The skunk hibernates, or at least lies dormant, for part of the winter but his sleep is neither as deep nor unbroken as that of the other sleepers. In all but the most northern latitudes he may emerge from the den any time during the winter if there is a spell of mild weather.

**Range and Distribution.** Skunks are widely distributed throughout the United States and Canada from southeastern Alaska in the west to Nova Scotia in the east.

There are several species and subspecies of the genus *Mephitis* bearing slight variations in markings, length of tail, and size. These occur over more or less definite ranges and are listed as follows:

### ARIZONA SKUNK *Mephitis estor*

This skunk is similar to the typical species but has broad dorsal stripes which sometimes meet across the lower back to form a wide white patch. The white on the upper tail predominates and the tail ends in a narrow white tip. The range is not clearly defined, but these animals are commonly found in Arizona, western New Mexico, northern Lower California, and northern Mexico.

### BROAD-NOSED SKUNK *Mephitis platyrhina*

This is somewhat like the typical California skunk but has a broader skull. The lateral stripes are of medium width and the tail is all black except for a faint white band on the upper surface. The range is limited to Kern County in California.

### CALIFORNIA SKUNK *Mephitis occidentalis occidentalis*

The California skunk is a rather large specimen with a long tail and markings like the typical *Mephitis*. The white lateral stripes seldom exceed medium width. It is commonly found in northern California from Monterey through the Sierra and Cascade Mountains to the Willamette Valley of Oregon.

### CASCADE SKUNK *Mephitis occidentalis notata*

This animal is similar to the California skunk except that the lateral stripes are narrower and sometimes broken toward the rear. The dorsal stripes often end short of the tail. The tail is shorter than on the typical specimen and shows very little if any white. The exact range is not well defined, but this type occurs in northern Oregon, east of the Cascades, and extends into southern Washington.

### EASTERN SKUNK *Mephitis nigra*

On this animal the white dorsal stripes are usually broader than on the typical *Mephitis*. The tail is longer and totally black with a white tip. This is the skunk common to the New England and eastern states as far south as Virginia and west to Indiana.

### FLORIDA SKUNK *Mephitis elongata*

The Florida skunk is distinguished by a very long tail with white markings on the sides and a long white tip. The lateral stripes vary in width but are generally wide. The range includes the mountainous regions of West Virginia south through North Carolina to Florida and west along the Gulf of Mexico to the Mississippi.

### GREAT BASIN SKUNK *Mephitis occidentalis major*

This is a large skunk with wide white stripes which do not split until they reach the middle of the back. These stripes extend slightly into the tail, which is otherwise black. The range includes northern California, eastern Oregon, Nevada, and east as far as Utah.

### ILLINOIS SKUNK *Mephitis mesomelas avia*

This is a small skunk similar to the Louisiana type and somewhat variable as to markings. The range includes the prairie sections of Illinois, eastern Iowa, and western Indiana.

### LONG-TAILED TEXAS SKUNK *Mephitis mesomelas varians*

This is a large specimen with a long tail. The markings are like those of a typical *Mephitis* but the tail lacks a white tip. The range includes much of the Southwest through southern and western Texas, New Mexico, Oklahoma, Colorado, Nebraska, and Kansas.

### LOUISIANA SKUNK *Mephitis mesomelas mesomelas*

This skunk is a small type which is highly variable in marking. The white streaks may not reach to the base of the tail. The tail is short and generally without any white hairs. It is found from southern Louisiana to Missouri on the west side of the Mississippi Valley, westward to Texas and north to Kansas.

### NORTHERN HOODED SKUNK *Mephitis macroura milleri*

The hooded skunk belongs to the subgenus *Leucomitre* and, unlike the typical *Mephitis*, occurs in two color phases. In one the upper body is almost all white, and in the other the upper parts are black with narrow white lateral stripes and much white on the underside of the tail. There are many gradations between these two phases, in which the black and white markings occur in varying degrees. The range is limited to southern Arizona southward into Mexico.

### NORTHERN PLAINS SKUNK *Mephitis hudsonica*

This is a large skunk with markings similar to the typical *Mephitis* but has a large bushy tail without any white on the tip. This western variety is found chiefly in western Canada and southward into the United States to Colorado, Nebraska, and east as far as Minnesota.

### PUGET SOUND SKUNK *Mephitis occidentalis spissigrada*

This is similar to the typical California skunk but generally has a greater area of white on the body. The short tail has more white than black. It is found along the coastal region of northern Oregon and Washington.

### SOUTHERN CALIFORNIA SKUNK *Mephitis occidentalis holzneri*

This specimen is almost identical in appearance to the typical California skunk but somewhat smaller. The range extends from Southern California into Lower California, eastward to the San Bernardino Mountains and thence southward indefinitely.

## SPOTTED SKUNK (Alleghenian Spotted Skunk) *Spilogale putorius*

COMMON NAMES: Little Spotted Skunk, Little Striped Skunk, Polecat, Spotted Skunk.

**History.** The spotted skunk belongs to the genus *Spilogale* and is distinguished from *Mephitis* not only by the markings of the pelage but also by being slimmer and much smaller than the latter species. These graceful animals are more like a weasel than the common heavy-bodied skunk, and although widely scattered throughout the United States they occur most frequently in the open plains and desert country.

**Identification.** The average body length is about 20 inches, the females being slightly smaller. The basic body color is black but this is broken by irregular spots and streakings of white. There are four white stripes, sometimes interrupted and of varying widths, running parallel from the nape to beyond the middle of the back. The crown is irregularly spotted with white, as are the rump and the hindquarters. There is a lateral stripe on each side extending from the shoulder to the lower back where it curves upward and sometimes meets the dorsal stripe. The markings on the hindquarters commonly appear as transverse white bands. The tail is black with a white tip. The under parts are totally black. The pelage is long and thick and the tail is quite long and bushy.

**Characteristics.** In habits this little skunk is more inclined to be completely nocturnal than his larger cousin, *Mephitis,* but is very similar in other respects. His diet includes some fruit as well as the foods eaten by his larger relative. His scent glands are highly efficient and he uses them in the same manner as *Mephitis.*

**Range and Distribution.** Including the various species and sub-species listed below, this little skunk is found throughout most of the United States.

### ARIZONA SPOTTED SKUNK

*Spilogale arizonae arizonae*

The white markings are pronounced, the lateral stripes being especially wide. The tail is white about one-half its length from the base and much of the tip. It is found in Arizona, especially the central and southern parts, in southwestern New Mexico and south into Mexico.

### CALIFORNIA SPOTTED SKUNK

*Spilogale phenax phenax*

This animal is similar to the typical *Putorius* but its dorsal stripes extend between the ears. There are large white spots on the forehead and in front of the ears. The white area on the rump is usually smaller than on the typical specimen. The shorter tail is white on the lower half and white for some distance at the tip. The range includes most of California with the exception of the northern part and the southeastern desert country.

### CANYON SPOTTED SKUNK

*Spilcgale gracilis gracilis*

This is a small, slender skunk with extensive white markings but with less white on the tail than the typical specimen. The white area on the forehead is long and narrow. It is commonly found on the eastern side of the Rocky Mountains through Colorado and New Mexico.

### CHIHUAHUA SPOTTED SKUNK

*Spilogale ambigua*

The markings on this variety are similar to those on the canyon skunk, but the lateral stripes are broader and there is a distinct white band on the thighs. The range extends from central Arizona southward into Mexico.

### FLORIDA SPOTTED SKUNK

*Spilogale ambarvalis*

This is a smaller animal than the typical variety with considerable white on the pelage. The black and white along the back is about equal in area. The white on the forehead is extensive and the white spot in front of the ear continues until it meets with the lower dorsal stripe. The tail is about one-third white above and one-half white below. The range includes the eastern half of the Florida peninsula.

### GREAT BASIN SPOTTED SKUNK

*Spilogale gracilis saxatilis*

This animal is considerably larger than the canyon skunk and is usually minus the lateral stripe. If such stripes are present, they are not prominent. The range includes Utah, western Colorado, Nevada, Idaho, and northeastern California.

### GULF SPOTTED SKUNK

*Spilogale indianola*

This type appears more spotted because the striping is not continuous but broken and generally narrower, giving the animal a blacker pelage. The tail is white for about one-quarter of the terminal end. It is found along the Gulf Coast region of Louisiana and Texas.

### OREGON SPOTTED SKUNK

*Spilogale phenex latifrons*

This variety is smaller than the typical California skunk with more black than white in the pelage. The dorsal stripes are narrow and the lateral stripe is missing or nearly so. The white areas on the rump and flanks are smaller. It inhabits the coastal regions of California and Oregon.

### PRAIRIE SPOTTED SKUNK

*Spilogale interrupta*

This type most nearly resembles the typical skunk but shows more black and lacks the broad white tip on the tail. The dorsal stripes are broken by black, the spot on the forehead is smaller, and the white area in front of the ear rarely runs into the lower lateral stripe. The range extends from Minnesota through Iowa, Nebraska, Kansas, Missouri, and Oklahoma southward into about central Texas.

### PUGET SOUND SPOTTED SKUNK

*Spilogale phenax olympica*

The markings on this animal are about the same as those on the Oregon spotted skunk, but this type has a shorter tail and the white on the forehead is long and narrow. It occurs on the Olympic peninsula and along the shores of Puget Sound, sometimes as far north as British Columbia.

### RIO GRANDE SPOTTED SKUNK
*Spilogale leucoparia*

This type is distinguished by having more white than black on the upper parts. The spotted areas are more extensive and the stripes are broader than usual. It is found throughout the arid regions of the Southwest including western Texas, central Arizona, southern New Mexico, and southward into Mexico.

### ROCKY MOUNTAIN SPOTTED SKUNK
*Spilogale tenuis*

This is similar to the Rio Grande skunk but has somewhat less white. The range includes the eastern sides of the Rocky Mountains through Colorado and northern New Mexico and is not definitely limited.

### HOG-NOSED SKUNK (MEARNS)
*Conepatus mesoleucus mearnsi*

Common Name: White-Backed Skunk.

**History.** As the name denotes, this skunk has been provided with a hoglike snout, devoid of hair, with which to root out much of his food. He belongs to the genus *Conepatus* but is similar in size and general habits to *Mephitis.*

**Identification.** Adult males average about 27 inches in length; the females are somewhat smaller. Both sexes are alike in coloration and there is no seasonal change of pelage, but individual specimens display a rather wide variation in markings.

Unlike *Mephitis,* the dorsal area is clear unbroken white from the crown to the tip of the tail. This broad white band is sometimes tinged with pale yellowish and is narrower over the shoulders than on the back. The tail is not so bushy as that of the other species, and except for a few dark hairs it is white on the underside.

**Characteristics.** This skunk is similar in every respect to the more common *Mephitis,* but the diet includes more insects and grubs which this animal roots out of the ground.

**Range and Distribution.** This skunk occurs principally from western Texas southward into Mexico.

The following species and sub-species of the genus *Conepatus* are found in limited numbers north of the Mexican border.

### ARIZONA HOG-NOSED SKUNK
*Conepatus mesoleucus venaticus*

This specimen closely resembles the hog-nosed skunk but has a slightly different skull formation. The range is limited to southern Arizona and the bordering regions of New Mexico.

### SWAMP HOG-NOSED SKUNK
*Conepatus mesoleucus telmalestes*

This animal is similar to the common type but has a greater area of white on the top of the head. The skull is more slender and the teeth smaller. The range is confined to a small area in Texas, including the counties of Montgomery, Hardin, Harris, Liberty, and San Jacinto.

### TEXAS HOG-NOSED SKUNK
*Conepatus leuconotus texensis*

This is a larger specimen than any of the other hog-nosed skunks, and has much less white. The stripe along the back is narrower and often ends short of the hindquarters. The underside of the tail shows more black than white. The range is limited to the coastal area of Texas from about Aransas County to the mouth of the Rio Grande River.

## NORTH AMERICAN WOLF
*Canis lupus*

**History.** The wolves of North America, members of the dog family, reached their greatest size during the late Pleistocene period. Preserved skulls and skeletons from the famous La Brea tar pits of Southern California and fossil remains from eastern limestone caves show that our present-day wolf is smaller than its prehistoric ancestor. As will be noted later, only three races of our present gray wolf—all occurring in the Arctic—approach the Pleistocene wolf in size.

Two species of wolves occur in North America, the red and the gray. At one time during early colonial settlement these were represented by a total of 26 sub-species or races. Of these the red was composed of 3 and the gray of 23 races.

**Identification.** The red wolf was first described by John James Audubon and the Reverend John Bachman in 1851. Its type locality has been set at a point approximately 15 miles west of Austin, Texas. It was found throughout the range of eastern and northeastern Texas and southeastern and central Oklahoma. Here it joined with the other red wolf race, the so-called Mississippi Valley red wolf that formerly ranged north to Warsaw, Ill., and Wabash, Ind. The other red wolf race, known as the Florida red wolf, probably now extinct, occurred in Florida, Georgia, Alabama, and probably South Carolina. The group of red wolves is distinctly North American, having no Old World connection as does the gray wolf group.

Anatomically, the red wolf resembles the coyote, particularly the head and the teeth, so that it is only with difficulty that even the expert can at times distinguish between the two species. The smallest of the North American wolves, the red wolf, averages between 30 and 35 pounds in weight, has an over-all length between 48 and 53 inches, and has a shoulder height of 19 to 22 inches. However, some male red wolves have been captured in Louisiana that weighed from 50 to 80 pounds. Its appearance can be likened to that of the greyhound dog, as it is inclined to have long, spindly legs. As a result of this leg structure, it is a good long-distance runner. It takes its name "red" from its beautiful coat, particularly when in full winter pelage. The hairs of the coat when in this condition take on a light yellow hue at the roots ending in red tips. Sprinkled throughout will be found irregular black hairs. During the moult of the pelt in the late spring that produces a shorter summer coat, the reddish hue of the animal fades considerably and is thus paler. A color phase of black is common in this wolf, and predominated in the red wolf that formerly ranged throughout Florida—whence the name "Florida black wolf."

The gray wolf tends to be heavier in its northernmost range. Its weight varies between 60 to 175 pounds. The latter weight is attained in Alaska and the Mackenzie River district of Canada. Here are found the three largest races of the gray wolf in the world, known by the common name of Interior Alaskan wolf, Kenai Peninsula wolf, and Mackenzie Valley wolf. These three races of wolves will at times measure 84 inches long and 38 inches high at the shoulder, and weigh 175 pounds, nearly 100 pounds heavier than the largest of the red wolves. Shoulder heights of gray wolves vary between 26 and 38 inches.

The coloration of the gray wolf varies greatly, so much so that on no part of its range does it tend to be uniform. Gray may be said to predominate. However, individual wolves on the same range or in the same family may vary in color from gray to pure white to black, with intermediate stages of coloration such as brindled brown to yellow. Some authorities believe that this great variation may be caused by varying intensities of light coupled with temperature and humidity in the wolf's respective habitat. They also believe that these factors that make the varying colors are natural phenomena that tend to provide protective coloration against enemies, and serve as an asset in obtaining prey—exemplified by the black and white wolves occurring in the Arctic where perpetual snows and darkness are found in the extreme. Commercially prime wolf pelts are of value in providing both leather and fur utilized by man.

**Characteristics.** Wolves generally mate for life. They do not breed until approximately three years of age. The gestation period is similar to the dog's, 60 to 63 days, and they give birth to an average litter of seven whelps during the months of April, May, and June. They are generally born in a den such as holes in eroded sandstone or limestone, stumps of rotted trees, or in holes dug in cut-banks. The young are sooty-brown when born, though in the Arctic where the white color phase of the parent wolves at times predominates, the color of the young is a dull slate. At times severe fighting takes place among

U. S. Biological Survey.

PLATE I. Gray Wolf.

PLATE II. Tracks of Pleistocene wolf occurring in sandstone quarry, Carson City, Nev.

wolf whelps in the same litter; this often causes young wolves to mature with bob tails, the result of biting. Young male wolves are well grown when approximately 1½ years old and reach full maturity by the end of three years. Female wolves are fully matured at the end of two years. Wolf families exhibit a strong affection that continues until they begin to break up when individual members mate with other wolves.

On the open ranges wolves have what are commonly referred to as "scent posts," or places where they come to urinate or defecate. These posts are established along runways on stubble of range grasses, on bushes, or on old bleached-out carcasses. Ground conditions being right, wolf scent posts may be detected from the toenail scratches on the ground made by the animals after they have urinated. This habit of having scent posts and of scratching is similar to that noted in dogs.

Wolf runways, roughly circuitous in shape, are confined to open and more or less broken country. In seeking prey over a runway, the animal may use a combination of trails of cattle or sheep, canyons, old wood roads, dry washes, low saddles on watershed divides, or even dirt highways in thinly inhabited sections. Such runways have been found more than a hundred miles in extent, and families of wolves have been observed passing by a certain spot every nine days with almost the regularity of a clock. The time it takes to complete the circle of the runway depends upon the available food. Regularity of habits is the weak point in the wolf's defense. It has been the main cause of the wolf's diminution in numbers by trapping in spite of its acute sense of smell, alert hearing, and extremely keen eyesight.

The intelligence of wolves is comparable in every respect to that of dogs. In some individual wolves, they excel the dog's. The cunning and ability of some wolves to avoid capture at times has caused considerable wonderment.

Wolves and dogs are so closely related that hybridization is not uncommon, and it has been practiced for many centuries with the idea and hope of improving upon the breed of domestic dogs. Breeding of a female wolf and a graded collie dog through four generations is on record, as well as countless successful cross-breedings in the Arctic regions, in the hope thereby to improve upon the build and stamina of the dog as a sledge dog or cross-country packer.

Wolf parasites are the relapsing-fever tick, the biting louse, the skin mite that produces mange, and the tapeworm. Diseases that affect wolves are that spread by sheep, known as gid; also encephalitis, rabies, tularemia or rabbit fever, salmon poisoning. They are also susceptible to smallpox, and arthritis has been detected in old wolves.

When large numbers of wolves are traveling together, they are commonly called a "pack." This is generally the intermingling of several wolf families, and is of short duration. More commonly the "wolf-pack" is a pair of wolves and their yearling or two-year-old offspring.

Wolves take a wide variety of foods, ranging from the musk-ox to the mouse. Buffalo, antelope, elk, deer, caribou, and moose, in the order named, are the preferred foods of the wolf. All forms of livestock are substituted when the foregoing are not readily available. At times they can be most irregular in their feeding habits. Equipped with great power to kill, the wolf prefers large prey in order to sustain its large body. There are few animals that can gorge food to the extent the wolf does. Feeding experiments show that the wolf can gorge its stomach with raw meat at a single meal whereupon that organ, capable of great stretching, will weigh one-fifth of the body weight.

**Range and Distribution.** The gray wolf forms a compact circumpolar group that ranges across North America and Eurasia. These large North American predators are geographic races of *Canis lupus* found on the Scandinavian peninsula, first described by

U. S. Fish & Wildlife Service.

**PLATE III. The Red Wolf of Texas, Oklahoma, Louisiana, and southern Mississippi Valley states.**

PLATE IV. Hybrid Wolf-Collie Dog, nine months old.

the famous Swedish naturalist, Carl von Linné, in 1758. There is much evidence that *Canis lupus,* the true wolf, is the progenitor of our domestic dog. The original distribution of the North American gray wolf extended northward from the plateau of central Mexico to the polar regions to the most northern point of land in the world, Cape Morris Jessup, approximately 380 miles south of the North Pole. It occurred in the coastal fringes of Greenland, and had an east-west distribution, excluding the southern and southeastern United States, from the Atlantic to the Pacific. This included the islands of Newfoundland and Vancouver. It avoided the extreme desert regions of southwestern Arizona, southern Nevada, and southern California as well as Lower California in Mexico.

Thus, with the foregoing exceptions, the gray wolf occurred in all the Mexican states northward from Mexico City, and through all the Canadian provinces and territories, the coastal fringes of Greenland, and Alaska, while the red wolf was confined mainly to the areas bordering the Mississippi Valley south of Wabash, Indiana, including the extreme southern and Gulf coastal states of the Union.

With the passing of time, which has caused vast modification in habitat, the red wolf's distribution has become confined to the Ozark Mountains in Missouri, Arkansas, southeastern Oklahoma, eastern Texas, and scattered portions between northeastern and southwestern Louisiana. Similarly the gray wolf has been extirpated in the United States east of the Mississippi, except in Wisconsin and Michigan. Necessity, reward, sport, and nature all combined to shrink this animal's distribution. They are scarce in eastern Canada, and have disappeared from all of Newfoundland. West of the Mississippi they are confined mainly to Arizona and New Mexico where they cross the international line as invaders from Sonora, Chihuahua, and Coahuila, Mexican states where the gray wolf population does not seem to diminish. This "Mexican wolf" is the smallest race of the gray species. It also occurs in small numbers in the Cascade Mountains of Oregon; the animal's range at present in the United States is thus vastly restricted as compared to earlier times.

North of the Canadian border the gray wolf is well represented in British Columbia, Alberta, the Northwest Territories, Yukon, and Alaska, and sparsely so on the coastal fringes of Greenland. In these areas, naturalists opine that it will long remain a part of the northern fauna in spite of every hand turned against it. Climatic conditions and rough terrain are two factors in the north country that afford the gray wolf considerable respite from hunting or trapping pressure.

**Predation.** During the early settlement of America, wolf depredations became too severe on domestic stock and wild life, such as deer. Therefore, as early as 1630, a decade following the Pilgrim landing at Plymouth Rock, Massachusetts established the first American wolf-bounty law. Virginia followed suit in 1632, and other colonies did likewise during the 17th century. In addition, all sorts of schemes and devices were used to encourage wolf killing.

The records show that constant warfare between man and wolves has been carried on for centuries,

PLATE V. Alaskan Wolf.

because stock raising has always been incompatible with great numbers of wolves. It is in this connection that wolves have been the greatest of predators. Over a vast area, the wolf at times was a scourge to the stock interests. On one range in Wyoming comprising an area of 35 square miles, 500 wolves were killed. Here 50 per cent of the calf crop had been killed by wolves.

To a more limited extent, the same holds true for wildlife, especially when numerical numbers of a wildlife species are threatened with near extinction. A preponderance of wolf populations in such an area generally calls for surplus wolf removal. In recent years, in Mount McKinley National Park, in Alaska, the dwindling herds of Dall mountain sheep were believed to be caused by heavy wolf depredations. An intensive study by field biologists of the wolf-sheep relationship, however, showed but 15 wolves in that immense area, and indicated that other factors, possibly more important than wolf depredations, were probably the main causes of the sheep die-off. The Alaskan sheep, one of the hardest preys for the wolf to capture, have probably come through a normal cycle, and now give every assurance of surviving in present numbers, with annual increases to bring the herds back to their normal levels. A late wolf census of Alaskan wolves put their numbers at approximately 6600 for the entire territory.

It was officially reported in 1940 that wolves were a serious menace to the reindeer herds of northern and western Alaska, and therefore a serious menace to the economic life of the Eskimo of the region. A typical example was the so-called Kivalina herd which decreased from 42,000 in 1932 to 6000 in 1939. Two other herds in the same vicinity, numbering 17,000 and 12,000 respectively, were completely wiped out.

Canadian naturalists estimated that there were 36,000 wolves in the area of the Canadian Barren Grounds in 1940. Here, the home of the caribou, they were credited with killing 400,000 caribou annually. It was believed, however, that the wolves fluctuated materially each year as to population, up or down, and accordingly the caribou depredations would fluctuate.

In British Columbia, the wolf question is constantly prominent, particularly as regards sheep and moose, but no tangible finding has yet been forth-

U. S. Fish & Wildlife Service.

PLATE VI. Musk-oxen, Arctic prey of wolf packs, assuming their circular defense position against wolf attack.

coming. In this province the game authorities have wildlife technicians in the field hoping to ascertain the extent to which wolves may affect these two game species.

Occasionally a single old wolf may become an outstanding killer of domestic stock and big game. This happened in the early spring of 1941, with a lone male wolf in Becker County, Minnesota, at the headwaters of the Ottertail River. This animal had a cruising range of approximately 20 miles. During this period it killed 139 sheep and 18 deer, which included two does with unborn fawns and a large buck with horns. Because of this animal's liking for venison, it was often called the "deer wolf" in early New England.

Trapped, hunted, and poisoned through the centuries, always with a price on its head, no other carnivore rivals the wolf in the profound effect exerted on man. Nevertheless, as the science of modern game management progresses, wildlife technicians, biologists, and game managers are beginning to realize that this great killer, under a suitable measure of control, deserves a permanent place as a wilderness animal when far enough removed from areas producing domestic stock that it can do relatively little economic damage.

## WOLVERINE

*Gulo luscus*

Common Names: Carcajou, Glutton, Loup-Garou, Skunk Bear.

**History.** The wolverine, largest and fiercest of the weasel tribe, was once found over a much wider range and in greater numbers than at the present time. He was at home throughout the great forests from the Arctic down to the heavily wooded areas of the New England states, New York, and across the northern tier through Michigan, Wisconsin, and Minnesota to the Rocky Mountains and the Sierra Nevadas.

His cunning and sagacity made him an almost legendary creature with the Indians, who regarded him as supernatural and believed that he embodied the Evil Spirit. Among the more superstitious trappers and woodsmen there was a profound conviction that "carcajou" bore a charmed life which only a silver bullet could end. Some Eskimos of the Far North are said to wear bits of wolverine fur in hopes that the strength of the beast will be magically transplanted to themselves.

The passing of the great forests where he formerly roamed meant that he must confine himself more and more to the still untouched or inaccessible regions of the North Country. He is still to be found over a widely scattered range from coast to coast but is nowhere numerous.

**Identification.** The adult male wolverine is about 36 inches long and weighs between 25 and 30 pounds. Some specimens reach a length of more than 40 inches and weigh over 35 pounds. The female is shorter and generally weighs no more than 22 to 27 pounds.

The pelage, composed of a short, woolly undercoat covered by long, straight guard hairs, is a deep, rich brown—nearly black—with broad bands of paler chestnut-brown running down each side of the body and extending into the short, bushy tail. The outer hairs are coarse and shaggy.

The legs are short and sturdy, giving the animal a squat, heavy appearance, and the feet end in large sharp claws. The skull is broad and rounded, the small round ears are set close to the head, and the jaws are heavy and powerful.

In general appearance this animal might be said to resemble a small brown bear with short legs.

**Characteristics.** The wolverine is one of the most dreaded animals in all North America. He not only strikes terror into the hearts of all the smaller creatures but even the moose is afraid of him. The bear and the mountain lion will give up a fresh kill to him, and even a pack of wolves have been known to give ground at his approach.

He is a compact bundle of steel-hard muscle wrapped in fur. Incredibly powerful for his size, he also possesses more cunning, more courage, more meanness, and more ferocity than any other animal in the wild. If he may be said to have any weakness it is his vision. His eyes are not strong and he has the almost human habit of shading them with his paw in bright light. His sense of smell is very keen, however, and compensates for his poor eyesight.

He fears nothing and shows no hesitation in attacking any other animal if the occasion warrants a fight. His teeth and long sharp claws are the instruments of his abnormal strength, but it is not his fighting prowess alone that overawes his opponent. The viciousness of his attack is aided by his indomitable spirit. He rushes into the fray grunting and snarling with but one intent—to kill—and he never retreats no matter how great the odds. It is a fight to the death, either for himself or his adversary, and a wolverine seldom loses.

Not only is he a terror to all the four-legged creatures around him but he is almost equally dreaded by trappers and woodsmen. Their fear, however, is not of physical harm, but because of his depredations on trap lines or on food and supplies.

Because of his incredible cunning and stealth, few people, even seasoned woodsmen, have ever seen a live wolverine on his native heath. (Even the rare animals that have been captured alive did not thrive well in zoos.) So he remains a mysterious presence, unseen, but the trapper becomes acutely aware that the animal is dogging his footsteps by day and robbing his traps by night.

Where the wolverine learned how to avoid the modern steel trap is a matter of speculation. It would hardly seem that instinct alone could account for his ability to outwit all but the cleverest of traps. Even in remote regions where traps appear for the first time, the carcajou displays an uncanny ability to deal with them. One by one he visits the sets made by the trapper. If the set is untouched he eats the bait, if any, then destroys the set, and often carries away the trap and hides it. If the trap holds some animal he eats what he wants and destroys the remainder. Out of sheer deviltry

N. Y. Zoological Society.

PLATE I. The Wolverine, seldom seen and a master of stalking.

he will destroy or befoul every pelt so that it is valueless.

The carcajou is equipped with anal glands which secrete an evil-smelling fluid. He cannot dispense this in the same manner as the skunk, but he uses it to spoil anything he cannot eat.

Not content with robbing the trap line, he sometimes invades the trapper's cabin during his absence and destroys everything within. What he does not eat or carry away he tears to shreds and sprinkles with offensive scent. He often plagues hunters and lumbermen in the same manner.

The appearance of a wolverine in a trapper's district is the signal for a feud that must end in the death of the beast or ruin for the trapper. At the first sign of this wily demon along his trap line the trapper ceases all other activity and concentrates on getting rid of his tormentor. If he is finally successful his efforts are rewarded more by the savings thus effected than by the value of the wolverine's pelt.

The pelt of the wolverine is not so commercially valuable as many other furs but it is highly prized by those who winter in the North Country because of all the furs it is the least susceptible to "hoaring," or frosting up when breathed upon. For this reason it is extremely good for trimming that portion of a parka hood which surrounds the wearer's face.

The carcajou is an inveterate wanderer and sometimes goes 50 miles or more from his den. Although mostly nocturnal in habits, he often roams abroad in daylight as well. With his short legs and heavy body he does not attempt pursuit of most animals but relies chiefly on the kills of others for his food. He often stealthily follows a bear, wolf, lynx, or cougar until they make a kill, then he rushes in, drives the killer from his prey, and gluts himself on the carcass. What he cannot eat he occasionally buries for future use, but more often he simply befouls the remains so that no other animal will touch it.

**Breeding.** For most of the year the wolverine leads a solitary existence. He mates toward the end of March, and usually from three to five young are born in June. The young remain with the mother throughout the summer but all go their separate, criminal ways in the autumn. The wolverine, for all his courage and ferocity, does not normally attack man, but a female in defense of her young knows no fear and is not likely to hesitate in such an attack.

**Range and Distribution.** The present range of the wolverine is throughout the North from the Arctic limit of trees to slightly south of the Canadian border in some of the United States. In the West it follows down the Rocky Mountains to Colorado and northern California. The animals are widely but thinly distributed over all the big timber areas within this range.

# WINGED PREDATORS

## EASTERN CROW

*Corvus brachyrhynchos brachyrhynchos*

COMMON NAMES: American Crow, Carrion Crow, Common Crow.

**History.** The crow, one of the highest types of birds in regard to intelligence and body conformation, is found throughout most of the world and is represented in North America by several species. The most common type is *Corvus brachyrhynchos,* which is found over the greatest part of the continent and includes four sub-species, the eastern, southern, Florida, and western crow. The most widely distributed and therefore the best known of these subspecies is the eastern crow *(C. b. brachyrhynchos)* which is typical of all the American crows and from which the other varieties do not differ basically. The three other species in North America are the northwestern, Florida, and fish crows, all of relatively limited range. The hooded crow is a casual visitor to eastern Greenland. Crows are of the same genus as ravens or rooks and the three birds often are confused because of their resemblance in appearance and habits. The general term "crow" sometimes is applied to these close allies as well as to the entire family *Corvidae* which includes the jays and magpies besides the crows. This family is of the sub-order *Oscine,* which is the grouping of singing birds (of which the crow is perhaps one of the least melodious members) and includes about 5000 species of the 7000 specimens which compose the order *Passeriformes.*

In the English-speaking lands, the crow apparently has always been called by that name. The common crow of England is known as the carrion crow, and the common eastern crow of the New World is popularly, but incorrectly, known by the same appellation, though that name officially belongs to the American black vulture. The early settlers learned that each Indian tribe had a name for the ubiquitous black bird, and today it is one of the best-known birds in America. It is far from secretive in habit, and is familiar to the most casual observer. The large size of the bird, its glossy-black plumage, and raucous call readily identify it.

Early historical records reveal that "crow" has long been synonymous with "despicable predator." King Henry VIII put a public bounty on the crow, along with its relations, the chough and rook. Today, wherever the species is discussed, whether by ornithologist or sportsman, the emphasis is invariably on the degree to which the bird should be controlled. Many sportsmen believe that abundant game and no predators go together, but the ornithologists claim that annihilation of any species is unwise and unnecessary. The matter of natural balance has long been a controversial issue, and is still so much a matter of theory that it is difficult to arrive at a definite conclusion and solution, since there are many unknown quantities involved. The general, unqualified opinion is that where crows are excessive they should be checked.

Though the most common means of killing off large numbers of crows is by combing the winter roosts (a procedure usually supervised by a Federal-State combination), crow shooting is good sport and takes a heavy toll of the crow population. Where the birds are concentrated, one gunner can bring down 500 in a day and is rewarded with the gratitude of the neighboring farmers, who often suffer extreme crop damage, especially to corn. Unlike its close kin, the raven, the crow favors agricultural areas and has advanced as far north as cultivated lands exist. Beside this extension of its original range, and its developed accent on crops, the crow has come into closer association with the great waterfowl nesting grounds of the Prairie Provinces. Where there is overlapping of ranges, the crow-waterfowl relationship is serious, and the destruction of eggs and young is high, but the major part, about five-sixths, of the waterfowl breeding grounds is beyond the northern limits of the crow abundance.

More than any other bird, the crow has been persecuted unremittingly by man, but has managed to survive throughout its hereditary range and has adapted itself to new environment and conditions. Since his success is largely an application of resourcefulness and intelligence, the species warrants objective admiration.

**Identification.** The male and female crow are indistinguishable, both being entirely black in plumage as well as in bill, legs, feet, and claws. The body plumage is glossed with violet, the wings with bluish violet and greenish blue. The brighter the day the brighter the reflections, for they pick up their colors from the spectrum. The long, pointed wings are much longer than the tail. A complete post-nuptial moult takes place at the end of the breeding period and the worn, brownish feathering of both adult sexes is replaced by the glossy black winter plumage. Albinism frequently occurs among crows, but scientists assume that the number reported is large as compared with many other species because of the commonness of the bird and the striking contrast to its natural coloring. Crows are large, measuring about 20 inches long and about one pound in weight, but the eastern crow is the largest member of the species. The southern crow and western crow are very similar in appearance, both being much smaller than the eastern crow and having slenderer bills. They are smaller than the Florida crow.

The crow is better known for its various types of calls than for its musical range though it has well-developed vocal muscles. When in captivity, the combination of imitative powers and natural muscular construction develops new calls, the most famous of which is an imitation of human laughter, though its own high-pitched *"ha-a-a-a-a"* sounds like a laugh. To the amateur gunner most of the crow calls sound alike, and often, in an attempt to imitate and lure in the birds, he inadvertently drives them off in terror by sounding an alarm call instead of a seductive love note. The wide emotional range includes notes of despair, cheer, and chastisement. The most common call is the familiar *"caw, caw"* which has several modifications: *"gnaw, gnaw," "orr, orr,"* and *"ah, ah."* The warning note of a bird doing sentinel duty over a feeding flock is a loud, prolonged *"caw, c-a-a-w,"* and it can be heard a great distance. The typical courtship call of the male is a rattling song, but often, at the end of this unpleasant *"grr-r-r,"* is one of the most melodious tones of the crow's repertoire—a soft, pigeonlike coo, either double-noted, *"coi-ou"* or single, *"cou."* The single note is repeated several times, and sometimes this languid coo is sung independent of the preliminary rattle. A second mating call of the male is a prolonged *"carr-a-c-k"* to which the female responds with a slow *"car, car"* which is repeated more rapidly as the male approaches her. Young birds calling for food sound very much like adult birds making love calls.

**Characteristics.** The adult crow is naturally wary and suspicious of everything strange and new, particularly those things near or concerning man, its chief enemy. Such extreme caution is sharpened through the year, for the crow is regarded as a predator and treated accordingly. Few crows fail to become involved at some time during the year with the violence of gunning, poisoning, trapping, dynamiting or some other concentrated attempt to kill them; and there is no closed season to steady their nerves or revive their losses. In fact, it is officially advocated that the birds be killed on their breeding grounds. Neither sharp wits nor timidity is inherent, however, and young birds taken from their nest at two weeks,

Allan D. Cruickshank, from Natl. Audubon Society.

PLATE I. Eastern Crow.

or under, make excellent pets, reacting so completely to the interest and care of their owners that they treat them as parents. They will beg food from them and show little interest in crows living near by. Pet crows are taught to pronounce simple words with comparative ease, and because of the bird's natural ability to learn quickly are capable of distinguishing the sizes and shapes of blocks—in much the same way as mankind is tested in intelligence problems, and overenthusiastic crow owners often claim the birds can do it as fast. The penchant for destruction, however, becomes a dominant trait when the bird is in captivity.

"As the crow flies" generally is considered the shortest distance between two points; the origin of this expression is the crow's direct fashion of flight. Though the flight formation is haphazard, the birds keep to a steady course, usually flying high at a cruising speed between 20 and 30 miles an hour, though they are capable of making 60 miles an hour. The wings, neither as pointed as a hawk's nor rounded as a grouse's or quail's, are large in comparison to the body weight, and the birds normally maintain a steady, moderately slow, flapping when in flight. Sailing and planing are not part of the flight pattern. Though the birds can walk well, they spend most of their time off the ground, either perched in trees or on the wing.

Although crows in captivity live to be 20 years of age and older, a bird in the wild averages only about four years of life. The constant and violent persecutions by man keep the life cycle a brief one. The crow has few natural enemies, for it is primarily arboreal by habit, roosting and nesting in trees, and is therefore inaccessible to most animals. In the Midwest, where the crows frequently build their nests on low bushes and occasionally on the ground, foxes are known to prey on them. Among its enemies are the larger hawks (red-shoulderd, red-tailed, and goshawks) and owls (horned and snowy). The relationship between the crow and hawks and owls is another example of predators preying on each other. A group of crows will "mob" an owl (a stuffed owl is sometimes used by gunners as a lure) and eat the owl's eggs. Owls snatch crows from off their roosts. Biologists offer examples like this mutual depredation as one of the underlying forces maintaining the balance of nature. Kingbirds and redwings harass crows by attacking a lone bird in the air or attempting to drive off the crows which nest too near to their breeding grounds, but these small birds qualify as an annoyance rather than an enemy.

Crows have suffered from epidemics of tuberculosis and roup. They also are susceptible to tropidocerca, intestinal cestodes, filaria, and several different types of nematode parasites. Crows commonly harbor lice and ticks. In sub-zero temperature many of the birds die of starvation when they are blinded by the freezing of the corneas of their eyes.

During the breeding season mated birds tend to isolate themselves in pairs, and the family group acts as an independent unit, but at the end of the season, or in late summer, the groups merge into flocks. Many of the birds migrate from the inland breeding grounds to the coast to spend the winter, and there they gather into communal roosts which number into the thousands and even hundreds of thousands. Food is the main force which drives the crows from the inland grounds, where the food supply is covered by snow and ice, to the coast, where there is a constant supply of food from the sea. During the winter they feed primarily on fish and mollusks. They frequently drop clams, scallops, and mussels from a height onto rocks or a paved highway in order to break open the hard shells.

The population in a winter roost often is composed of three distinct groups; those which are stationary in the vicinity for both winter and summer, those which migrate to the point from a more northerly breeding range, and those which are passing through to a more southerly region. Roosts located in thick evergreen forests are well protected in cold weather, but in more southern sections where some roost in willow thickets, the crows have been known to desert them in severe winters to roost on snow-covered sand banks. The birds leave the roosts in early morning to search for food, taking off in all directions in groups of 3 to 20, and return before dusk. In a roost of about 12,000 birds the morning departure was completed in about a half an hour, from 6:25 to 7:00 A.M. The return flight was more prolonged, with the first birds on a short winter day beginning to drift in at 1:00 P.M. and coming in subsequent waves until dusk, at 4:45 P.M.

Enormous numbers of birds are killed by bombing with dynamite when they are concentrated in these winter roosts. In 1937, 26,000 birds were killed in one roost in Oklahoma. In 1940, 328,000 were killed in roosts in Illinois. Partial or complete extermination of a roost does not guarantee annihilation of the crow from one locality, for the bird is highly mobile and resourceful and will return to a favorable section unless operations are continued. Aside from bombing the roosts with TNT and dynamite, quick and economic methods of attacking a concentrated area are by the use of gunning, trapping, and poisoning.

**Breeding.** The average farmer or gunner knows the crow as a raucous-voiced thief or scavenger, but the bird is faithful and tender in its home life. The male characteristically is monogamous and shares domestic chores with his mate. The breeding season begins with an active courtship, with usually two, but as many as five, males chasing one female. With much speedy circling and twisting the rivals vie against one another for the attentions of the resisting female. There are frequent noisy fights among the suitors which occasionally end in a struggle on the ground. The typical courtship of an interested male usually begins by his facing and bowing low to an apparently uninterested female. In displaying, he opens his wings and tail feathers slightly and puffs out the feathers of his body. This performance is followed by his rattling song of love which is repeated several times—and has been heard over 50 times in succession. As with most birds, the love call sometimes is uttered throughout the year, but since it is primarily to attract a mate, it is most frequently used in the spring breeding season. Though it is sometimes given while in flight, the call usually is uttered from a perch. Once the birds pair off, they drive off the rivals together and start the search for a suitable nesting site. Crows characteristically pair off and scatter over a large breeding range, but the western crow often nests in small colonies. Since the range of the crow is wide and highly diversified, the nesting site generally is dependent on the locality. Though the preferred place to build the nest, on both the northern and southern parts of the range, is in coniferous trees (especially pine, spruce, and fir) between 18 and 60 feet from the ground, the bird will nest in hardwood trees if they are more numerous than evergreen in a region. The bird adapts itself well in the western sections where much of the land is cultivated, or other parts of the range which are treeless, and there they will nest in shrubs, hedges, bushes, among the tules and reeds in swamps or on the ground—the more unusual places being selected, as a rule, because of a favorable food supply at hand. Generally, nest building takes place in the morning, between 7 and 11 A.M., and, after feeding and resting, begin work again in late afternoon, continuing until about dusk. The male helps the female build a nest by bringing sticks and other material to her and she arranges them. The nest is consistently a large, sturdy structure, and a typical nest is placed on several horizontal branches close to the tree trunk. The rough, outer nest is made of twigs, some as large as 1/4 inch in diameter and 12 inches long, but the inner nest or nesting bowl is formed from smaller, finer twigs which are twined with pieces of bark, etc. The particular material used to make the soft, warm lining varies with availability and is made from an assortment of bark fibrils, mosses, reeds, grasses, feathers, twine, hairs, rags, or similar substances. The foundation of the nest is 9 inches deep, but the nesting cup is 4 1/2 inches in depth. The number and coloring of crows' eggs vary, but an average clutch numbers between four and six, and they are bluish-green to olive green with brownish and grayish spots or blotches either evenly or irregularly distributed on them. Where there are as many as eight to ten eggs in a nest, they usually belong to two females, for crows occasionally share their nests. The male often assists his mate in the 18-day incubation period. Both parents raise the young, which when hatched are pinkish-colored and scantily covered with grayish down. When they are five days old, their eyes open, and by the tenth day they apparently develop an insatiable demand for food, and call loudly and constantly for it. When about four weeks old, they commonly stand on the edge of the nest while waiting for their food, and at five weeks can make weak flights from the nest. Normally, the sheaths of the young birds are open when they are about a month old, and this immature plumage is similar to that of the adults. Intense, glossy black has a tendency to give off green and violet light, but the young crows are grayish and duller in plumage than the coal-black adults and consequently are lacking in the colored reflections. Another difference between mature and juvenile crows is the coloring of the bill and feet, which are grayish black. Their first winter plumage follows the partial summer moult, and the young look very much like the mature birds but are less glossy.

**Feeding.** The economic status of the crow is largely dependent on several features of its feeding habits. The bird is an omnivorous feeder, with not only the desire to eat voraciously, but, more important, an exceptionally large capacity. Under normal conditions, adult crows glut themselves eight to ten times daily, and immature birds need to eat about half their own weight in food each day. The economic status of the crow refers to its relation to agriculture, and the question of predation on the eggs and young of other birds, especially waterfowl, is of importance to agriculture since waterfowl are among the chief destroyers of insects. An analysis of the food habits of the crow over the continent as a whole shows that the amount of harmful insects he eats does not compensate for the damage he inflicts on farming areas.

The diet of the crow is roughly divided into 28% animal matter and 72% vegetable substance, but the percentages vary according to the availability of particular foods on a range. Although the birds eat spiders, crustaceans, snails, the eggs and young of wild birds and poultry, the largest part (two-thirds) of the animal food is insects. They feed primarily on beetles, grasshoppers, locusts, and crickets, and to a lesser degree on wireworms, caterpillars, grubs, cutworms, and moths—all of which are classed as insect pests, and which, where numerous, are threats to the farmer's crops and pasturage. Where these noxious insects occur in abundance, and the crows are at hand to destroy or control their numbers, the birds are beneficial to the farmer. But the cases where large pastures are revived by the reintroduction of crows to save the grass from root-destroying grubs or a cornfield is rid of cutworms by the insatiable birds are examples of the good crows in action. Such cases of extreme crow benefits are few in comparison to the harm done by the birds in the over-all picture of crow feeding in North America.

The western crows have the worst reputation for crop damage, specifically because of their habit of congregating by the thousands to feed on cultivated fruits and nuts. Frequently, they end a day of gorging by invading a near-by watermelon field, either ripe or green, in order to save themselves the trip to a distant watering place. Under such conditions there often have been cases of complete crop destruction. Since neither the southern nor the Florida crow is as abundant as the eastern or western crow, these birds are not capable of gathering in enormous numbers to feed, and less damage occurs. For the Florida crow, there is less crop availability, and the birds are confined primarily to frogs, lizards, grasshoppers, snails, and small snakes, with some predation on the eggs and young of waterbirds during the breeding season. The southern crow apparently does more good than harm in its relation to the farmer by consuming quantities of rodents and harmful insects.

The amounts of eggs and young of wild birds destroyed by crows vary with the region and the proximity of predators to nesting grounds. A study made by the U. S. Biological Survey discounts many exaggerations of the degree of crow predation by reporting that only about one-third of one per cent of the animal food of adult birds and 1 1/2 per cent of the food of nestlings is derived from wild birds and their eggs. The Department of Agriculture in a survey of Canadian duck-nesting marshes in proximity to crow abundance in agricultural areas reveals that crow depredation on eggs under these highly adverse conditions is as high as 31 per cent of the season's laying. In 1938 the province of Alberta began the payment of a bounty of three cents for a pair of crow's feet and one cent for each egg. In that year there were an estimated 3,000,000 crows in that province. From 1938 to 1940, over 1,000,000 eggs and birds of the crow and magpie species (mostly crow) were destroyed, at a cost to the government of about $28,000. The government field study points up the advantages of killing these crows which frequent waterfowl nesting grounds and are confirmed egg stealers and killers of young birds. Shooting, trapping, and poisoning (usually by inserting strychnine in a hen's egg) individual crows within their extensive breeding grounds next to nesting ducks takes more time, money, and skill than attacking them in their winter roosts when they are not paired and scattered but concentrated in a confined area, but the method is more efficient and worth while. Many of the birds which collect in a winter roost do not breed near waterfowl areas and are not addicted to waterfowl destruction.

Crows are scavengers, feeding on the carcasses of cows, dogs, cats, skunks, snakes, squirrels, rabbits, pigs, seals, etc. Groups of eight to ten crows often are seen along the side of a highway in early morning feeding on whatever animals have been killed by cars during the night. Indigestible parts of animals (bone, teeth, fur, etc.) are regurgitated in the form of pellets. As scavengers, crows carry disease.

Over half of the 72 per cent vegetable food is corn and the crows feed on this favored food when it is sprouting, "in the milk," or when stacked in shocks before being removed from the field. The most extensive damage is done when the corn is in the milk, for then water enters and injures the immature ear. Individual counties in the great corn states have lost thousands of dollars a year from the crow's destructive feeding. Where wheat replaces corn in abundance, it is damaged when sown and when sprouting. Other favored foods are sorghum (especially milo and kafir), oats, and buckwheat (usually waste in the stubble). Fruits, such as apples, pears, figs, and cherries, are eaten and injured to a minor degree. Some wild fruits are taken, but the seeds of many are not destroyed in digestion and the crow is an important distributor of such noxious plants as poison ivy and poison oak.

**Range and Distribution.** The range of the eastern crow is wide and highly variable. It is found over the greater part of North America, but is rare in Mexico. It lives in many different climates from Alaska to the Gulf of Mexico. There is much overlapping of summering and wintering grounds and migrations often are difficult to follow, while many birds are known to remain in the same location throughout the year.

Spring migration to the breeding range begins about February when the first hardy birds set out, but the main movement takes place around early March. The nesting grounds extend from Florida and the Gulf States, along the coastal states of the Atlantic to Newfoundland, west to California and north into Canada and up the Pacific Coast toward Kodiak Island.

The flight south for the winter includes the majority of the crows, though some stay as far north as southern Canada, Maine, and Vermont. The birds from the Great Plains regions are the true migrators. Banded birds have been traced in direct flights from Saskatchewan south through the Dakotas to Texas. Crows of the northern Atlantic coast apparently migrate very short distances (about 100 miles) if at all, for (see under "Characteristics," p. 175) the search for food is the main force which drives the birds from the snow-covered interior regions to the coast. During the winter season, crows are found from the southern sections of the breeding range, north to southern Canada.

The southern crow *(C. b. paulus)* is found in Alabama, Mississippi, Louisiana, southeastern Texas, Georgia, and South Carolina, north to the District of Columbia and southern Illinois. The Florida crow *(C.b. pascuus)* is confined to Florida and is distributed throughout that state among the pine woods, cypress swamps, oak and palmetto hummocks, and on the prairies. The range of the western crow *(C.b. hesperis)* is in the western part of North America and extends from British Columbia, Saskatchewan, and Montana, south to Lower California and Mexico.

**CROW-SHOOTING METHODS.** Shooting crows on the wing is far more complex than most newcomers to the sport realize. The birds are tricky, deceptive targets and are often maddeningly unpredictable in flight as they approach the hunters. Their unusually keen eyesight requires that hunters take special precautions to conceal themselves. Moreover, crows are naturally suspicious of man, so that even a car parked conspicuously on a country road is cause for them to detour the area.

There are two ways of attracting the birds to waiting hunters. One method is visual, requiring the use of a stuffed owl—a bird that is a traditional enemy of crows—or crowlike decoys. The other method is vocal, wherein hunters use crow calls to "talk" in the manner of real crows, and lure them to within shotgun range. An owl or crow decoys are most practically used in areas having a large concentration of crows, with promise of prolonged shooting at one spot. The simple crow call may be used anywhere, but is best suited to a trip with many short stands in country with average bird populations.

Crow calling is the more popular method because there is no cumbersome equipment to set up, and because of the change of scene it provides during an outing; therefore it will be discussed first. Calls cost but a dollar or two. Most are fashioned of hardwoods, with a few models made of plastic material or hard rubber. The reed may be of metal, plastic, or even the cane of wind instruments.

An important feature is whether a call has a fixed or movable reed, for this controls the tone. If the reed cannot be moved in the mouthpiece, the tone cannot be altered, even for improvement. A call with a movable reed is usually capable of producing a range of calls from the high falsetto of a young bird to the gruff guttural of an old-timer, and hence this type is much preferred. At the time of purchase, blow a call several times to see if the reed is going to stick to the mouthpiece. If this happens, do not buy the call, as it will probably fail you whenever your breath has moistened the reed.

Also to be avoided are instruments which require a lot of wind for each note. "Windy" calls will make a man hoarse in a short time. If the purchaser is new to the game, he will do well to listen to, and perhaps buy, a phonograph record of expert crow calling.

It is difficult to hold a call in the teeth while shooting, and so many owners of wooden calls notch the mouthpiece for secure gripping by the teeth. As a further precaution against loss at a crucial moment, the call should be attached to a looped cord worn around the neck.

A still day with bright sunshine is best for calling. Windy days are apt to be poor for the simple reason that the call does not have much range then. And on cloudy, oppressive days the birds seem loath to fly any distance to the caller, particularly just before a rain.

Though one person can call and shoot crows successfully, it is less wearing and more productive if two callers operate as partners. The usual plan is for the hunters to cruise about the countryside in a car, looking for good spots from which to call. Just what constitutes good crow country will vary somewhat with the locale, but certain types of land are generally productive wherever they may be found. Among these are the environs of farmland, woods near a garbage dump, and the wooded outskirts of towns. Lake shores are often excellent also.

As mentioned earlier, crows are unusually wary and are quick to apply a hostile meaning to cautious or unnatural human actions. Thus when cruising hunters spot some crows feeding in a field not far from the road, their best plan is to drive past the birds without a pause. Feeding crows almost invariably post a sentinel—a lone bird perched high in a tree which provides a good view of the surrounding countryside. When a car stops suddenly within sight of a sentinel crow and hunters jump out with guns, this bird is sure to give the alarm call—three or four staccato cries repeated at short intervals—and the whole flock will take to the air.

It is usually hopeless to call when this happens, for then the crows like nothing better than to sit in trees out of gunshot and mock the calling hunters. The car should be parked well away from the crows—say 200 yards—and out of sight, entirely off the road if possible, and preferably under a thickly foliaged tree. The car doors should not be slammed, nor should the hunters talk in audible tones, as carelessness in these matters may ruin a perfect setup. Take a stand a good 100 yards away from the car—always a symbol of danger to crows—and 20 yards or so in from the road's edge. It will pay dividends if such precautions are *always* taken.

One of the best types of cover for calling is a patch of low trees with an open space in the center, forming a sort of natural amphitheater. Hunters crouched on opposite sides of the opening beneath the branches will get shots at birds as they approach and depart, and as they circle overhead. Shooting from the edge of cover often works well, but care must be taken to screen each gunner's movement from the *side* as well as from above. Crows have very sharp eyesight and can detect even slight movements from afar, especially silhouetted movements. Many a promising shot has been ruined by a gunner's parting the bushes or peeping up over the top of cover while the birds were still 100 yards out. If a man must reveal himself to get a shot, he should do it *after* the crows have come well within range.

There is just one way you can call safely from the open, and that is by keeping in deep shade. A hunter standing in the shadow of a tree such as a spruce, back against its branches so as not to be silhouetted, can be practically invisible to approaching or circling crows. Of course, the man must not be wearing a white or light-colored shirt, but this goes for all styles of crow shooting. Also, he must be motionless much of the time. In other situations, the main idea is to pick a spot that will hide you, yet provide an ample view of the birds.

No matter how many hunters are present, it works out best if only one sounds off at first, so as to set the pace and keynote the calling. When there are no crows in sight, the alarm call is an excellent attention-getter, and it carries exceptionally well. The brand of "talk" that follows is up to the individual. One method is to plunge into a series of harsh cries in imitation of a crow that has just come face to face with an arch-enemy like a hawk or an owl. The hoped-for effect is to summon to the fray all crows within hearing.

If there *are* birds in the vicinity they usually give voice promptly and head for the caller. This is the time for his partner to join in and swell the clamor with the same type of cawing. It is highly effective to increase the tempo and raucousness as the crows approach to give them the impression that a battle royal is in progress and nearing its peak. Crows hurrying to the scene apparently become so excited at the prospects of a free-for-all that they frequently throw away their natural caution and fly boldly to the callers, affording them fine shooting.

The other method starts much more calmly, almost as if a crow were investigating a situation that promises excitement. In this the calls are individually longer and raucous; also, their tempo is not fast. Picture a man cussing out a baseball umpire mildly at the beginning of a game, and you have got the general tone of this "talking." Calling in this manner has two things in its favor: It is not tiring to the caller, and if the answering birds are far off at first, it gives him time to build his tempo leisurely and save wind for frantic cawing when the crows are almost upon him. In both cases it is appropriate for the second caller to join in at any time after crows have answered.

The procedure is different when birds are known to be feeding in a near-by field. The alarm cry in this instance often serves merely to stampede the crows. Instead, a single questioning caw, followed a couple of seconds later by some semi-indignant calling, will frequently draw the whole flock like a magnet.

Another good opener for this setup is querulous, high-pitched calling, such as might be made by a young crow in sudden distress. This is especially persuasive during and for a few weeks after the spring nesting season, when young birds still have falsetto voices.

Whether or not to shoot when the birds first come in is a matter that is impossible to advise upon. At their first approach you can be sure that the crows will be scanning the hide-out carefully, and hence may notice any movement of the hunters. This is particularly true in the case of gunners in sparse cover, or at the edge of cover. So, if approaching crows are fired upon, one or two may be bagged, but the hunters may reveal themselves and so turn away the rest of the flock.

On the other hand, if the birds are permitted to fly over unmolested, they very often swing back above the callers—who should still be at work—and circle the area, sometimes even hovering in one place above the calling while they scan the trees. There will be times when some crows will actually land in the near-by treetops, while their fellows swoop down through the branches at the hunters. This makes for fast, exciting shooting and when it occurs, it is well worth while. Unfortunately, the crows may never return above the gunners after the initial pass, and may leave the area entirely; or, at best, may circle tantalizingly just at the extreme edge of shotgun range. Thus, *when* to shoot first can be a problem.

The uninitiated usually quit calling after the first round of shots has been fired, on the theory that intelligent birds such as crows could not be expected to offer themselves as targets again. This is a grave mistake. If the quality of the calling has been good, crows will often swing over the hunters two and three times.

Small bands of four or five birds are not too likely to return a second time if two or three of their number have been shot down. However, a flock of about a dozen crows often seems to think nothing of losing a couple of members at each of two or three passes.

Various theories explain this. It has been proved time and again that crows are poor mathematicians. For example, if there is a permanent blind set up in a cultivated field adjacent to a woodlot and two people head for the blind while crows are feeding in the field, the birds will, as expected, probably fly to the woods. But if, after the pair has entered the blind, one of them leaves shortly afterward, it is safe to bet that the crows will return to the field not long after this man's departure. So perhaps a fair-sized flock simply does not miss any of its members at first.

It is also argued that dead birds which pitch down when shot may be thought by their excited brethren to be *landing* in the trees or on the ground. This is borne out by the fact that crows often continue to dive down into an opening in the branches, into which dead crows have just fallen to the shot of gunners below. Also, a few dead birds in plain sight on the ground do not seem to have a frightening effect on the others above, particularly when they are diverted by competent calling. All this shows the necessity for continuous calling right along with the shooting.

There will be times when a largeish flock will make a single pass at the hunters, and then retire to the treetops a safe distance away, there to talk back to the callers, but not to budge. Continued calling will sometimes draw young and foolish birds, but not many. A better plan seems to be several minutes of silence. Then, as the crows start to leave, calling should begin again. Now a change in pace to the pleading cries of a young bird will often bring the whole flock over again. Frequently these same birds may be called again if the hunters will drive down the road some 400 yards and circle in *behind* the crows. This change in the direction of the calling is often successful.

It usually takes but ten or 15 minutes for a good workout at a stand. By then the birds will have become wary or will have left the region entirely, whereupon the hunters should return to their car and look for another cover from which to call. Generally a drive of half a mile is sufficient to bring the hunters into undisturbed territory.

Just how long to call at a stand is a moot point when there are no answers. Crows do not *always* reply while they are flying toward the callers. Sometimes the birds will come a considerable distance in complete silence, and then burst upon the hunters, cawing frantically. Again, they may never call at all. Such birds often approach *through* the trees, dodging the branches like partridges. For these reasons it is advisable to run through at least one complete "spiel."

Veteran hunters usually wait for two or three minutes after the initial effort, listening and waiting. Then they try a different brand of talk and will, if there is no action, quit the stand soon afterward. Old-timers at the game vary their routes so as not to call from the same locations too often. It is wise to "rest" crows for at least a week—and two are much better—for too-frequent calling makes them wary.

The second, or visual, method is most effective when there are several flocks in an area. Then the use of a stuffed owl will insure good shooting. Sporting-goods stores usually sell this item as part of a set —a great horned owl with wings that may be flapped by means of a pull cord, and a 20-foot, takedown pole on which to mount the bird. The owl should be set up on a knoll or other high place so that it is higher than surrounding trees, but well within shotgun range of the hunters concealed by natural cover or by a permanent or portable blind.

Permanent blinds of the lean-to variety, with a three-quarter front, are easy to make. Care should be used to build each hideout of strictly local brush, corn stalks, and so on. A type of blind you can buy at large sporting-goods stores and carry easily in your car usually rolls up, and has panels made from painted matting, rushes, or reinforced burlap. Also made along lean-to lines, this blind can be rigged up quickly and uses only four poles.

If the owl is put up near a garbage dump frequented by bands of crows, good shooting may be enjoyed for an hour or more, and sometimes for a whole morning or afternoon. Crows often spot the owl while it just sits motionless. At other times an occasional flap of the owl's wings will attract their attention. Calling must sometimes be used to draw the birds to the area. When the owl is spotted, the crows fly to it quickly and then stage a sort of mock battle, diving and screaming at the owl, but rarely touching it.

Shooting will be fast and furious until the remainder of the crows retreat. When they fly only to the nearest trees, a short rest and then renewed flapping of the owl's wings, accompanied by some calling, will often bring them back again. When the birds quit the area, however, it is wise to hurry out and retrieve the dead crows. Some hunters tie these together in pairs—one at either end of a yard of cord —and toss them up into the trees, where they serve as crude decoys.

Hunters fortunate enough to know the location of

a crow roost can put a stuffed owl to excellent use in the early morning and evening, when birds leave or return to the roost. This shooting must be done at intervals of several days, though, or else the roost may be abandoned. A cat tied out in a field near a couple of dead crows also makes a fine come-on near a roost. It should be mentioned that these attraction devices will be effective *anywhere,* and their importance when used near a roost, garbage dump, or other concentration point has been stressed only because it hardly seems worth the bother to rig up the equipment where but a few birds will be found.

In farmland especially, crow decoys set out in a field near a blind will often work well. The same holds true for the environs of a garbage dump, particularly when the land is level and clear of brush and trees. Homemade profile decoys are easy to make from sheet metal and are fairly good. The more lifelike commercial decoys are also inexpensive and effective. A stool of from five to ten decoys is usually sufficient. Dead crows should be removed from among them during lulls in the action.

Fair and even good wing-shots find that the crow is not the easiest of targets. When diving below the branches to fly near hunters, the birds appear to be traveling faster than they really are, and overleading often results. Overhead passing shots are particularly deceptive. And the twisting, sideslipping flight of a crow attacking an owl decoy has baffled many an expert. Killing five or six crows for each ten shells is excellent shooting.

Gun preference should rest with the individual. Nevertheless, it should be pointed out that the 12 gauge is the most efficient killer, as it handles the heaviest loads and does the job best. And No. 6 shot is the best all-round size, bar none. Crows can be killed a little farther out with fours, perhaps, but most hunters cannot point that well. No. 7½ is good for shots up to 30 yards, and usually ineffective beyond.

# FISH CROW

*Corvus ossifragus*

**History.** The fish crow is common along the coast of the Atlantic and Gulf states, and also is distributed about several of the larger rivers and several lakes. Though it is not primarily a fish eater, its popular name is derived from its habit of feeding on fish, either those washed ashore or taken alive from the water. This bird averages smaller in size than the common crow, but size is not a dependable means of identification since both species are highly variable in their measurements. The most certain means of distinguishing the two birds is by the difference in voice. The fish crow has a high-pitched, nasal-sounding voice, and its familiar call is an abrupt *"cor"* or double-noted *"caa-ah,"* as contrasted to the common crow's loud, clear *"caw."*

The fish crow is not very different in appearance or habit from other American crows. The feeding habits of the crows decide their economic status, and since the majority of these birds inhabit a coastal range, they feed primarily on the marine and aquatic life which is available and abundant throughout the year. The natural advantages of its range bring about a near-exclusion of feeding on cultivated lands, though there is some crop destruction, particularly to fruit and nut crops, in localized areas. The fish crow, however, is a serious predator on nesting seabirds, especially in Florida where the eggs of entire heron colonies sometimes are taken from the nests.

**Identification.** The plumage of the fish crow is a glossy black, but is of a richer coloring than that of the common crow. The upper parts are highlighted with a bluish-violet coloration, and the under parts with a bluish-green. Its compressed bill and heavy feet are black, and, as with the common crow, the only color relief on a dull day comes from the brown eyes. An average bird measures 14 inches in length, and usually is smaller and lighter than the common crow.

Among the hoarse, variable calls of the fish crow are, besides those previously mentioned, a querulous *"maah, maah"* or *"whaw, whaw"* and a clear-sounding *"cah"* which is repeated for about a half-minute at a time.

**Characteristics.** The nature of this bird is much the same as that of the other crows; it is bold where unmolested and exceptionally wary where persecuted. It is faster in flight than the common crow, and, though the basic flight patterns are all very much alike, the fish crow is given to more sailing and hovering, especially when searching for food, and at such times resembles the gull. A flock of several hundred birds often will interrupt a straight flight to indulge in circling aerial maneuvers. The fish crow is the most gregarious of all the American crows, and habitually moves with a group throughout the year. Though they sometimes nest in pairs, they more often gather in small colonies, and in the fall and winter congregate in large roosts, numbering many thousand individuals. Birds which feed in the vicinity form the roost, which usually is near the water (in marsh rushes by a river or lake or among willow bushes at the edge of a lake), or in the interior within traveling distance of the water (among pine trees about 30 miles inland).

The fish crow suffers more from harassment from small birds, attempting to protect their eggs from the larger, predatory bird, than from true, natural enemies.

**Breeding.** Breeding falls between April and June, but nesting activity is dependent on the climate of each particular range. Courtship is an active pursuit of, generally, two males after one female. In courting the male slightly opens his wings and bends backward on his perch with his beak open, and in flight often touches wings and heads with a desired mate. The nesting site is variable, but usually is chosen for its nearness to a food supply, especially the rookeries of herons, and is preferably near to water. Colonies of birds have built high among the tall trees of swampy, wooded areas, and at low or medium heights in the red cedars and pitch pines of salt marshes. They consistently nest off the ground, however, whether 7 feet up in a braccharis bush or 150 feet in a towering sycamore tree. They frequently build in holly trees between 12 and 30 feet from the ground, and also nest in cedar, oak, and chestnut trees. In Florida they are almost exclusively pine-tree nesters. As a rule the nest is placed in the crotch of the tree, and, like those of all the crows, it is a well-built structure. The platform of dead sticks and twigs sometimes is mixed with bark and averages about 14 inches in diameter. It is lined with material at hand which may be strips of grapevine bark, horsehair, feathers, grass, or leaves and in Florida often is Spanish moss. The four to five eggs are smaller, but otherwise indistinguishable, from those of the other crows and are incubated in 16 to 18 days by both parents. The young are hatched blind and naked, but the nestling soon develops a grayish-brown down. By the time the young bird is capable of leaving the nest, the dull, brownish-black juvenile plumage is nearly finished. From July to September the young go through an incomplete moult, but the resultant plumage still is duller than that of the mature birds and not until the next summer, with the second, post-nuptial moult, do the young appear mature.

**Feeding.** Fish crows will eat almost anything, but feed primarily on the offerings of the coastal, stream, and lake waters of its range. They will eat dead fish, seal, or any other carrion brought in by the waves, but will also snatch up live fish. They feed on crabs, shrimps, and crawfish left exposed in low tide. They prey on the eggs of herons, ibises, spoonbills, anhingas, and cormorants, and are often on hand when nesting colonies are disturbed by photographers, or other visitors. As the wild birds desert their nests, the crows drop down to carry off the eggs, and the action is repeated as often as the man returns, or until the eggs are all gone. To a lesser degree, they pick up grubs, ants, grasshoppers, and lizards. Several types of berries, fruits, and seeds make up a high percentage of their vegetable intake. They have damaged ripe figs and peanut crops in some areas, but the grain they consume is largely waste.

**Range and Distribution.** The range of the fish crow extends along the Atlantic and Gulf coasts and includes the larger rivers, such as the Hudson, Delaware, and Potomac. It is confined to the United States, its northern limit being southern Massachusetts, and its southern boundary southeastern Texas. The species is not migratory in the true sense, but in the winter severe weather forces temporary or seasonal withdrawals from the northerly sections.

Allan D. Cruickshank, from Natl. Audubon Society.

**Plate II.** Fish Crow.

# NORTHWESTERN CROW

*Corvus caurinus*

**History.** The classification of the northwestern crow has been a changing one, but in 1946 biologists lifted it from the status of sub-species to species. It is very similar to the western crow in appearance and some of its habits, but being an inhabitant of the coastal areas, from Alaska to Washington, it has ways distinctive to the range.

**Identification.** Both sexes have the coal-black plumage typical of all the crow group. The northwestern crow is smaller than the western crow (one of the smallest of the species *brachyrhynchos*), but the feet of this specimen are relatively smaller.

Like all the crows, the northwestern variety has a wide range of calls. Though the voice of this bird resembles that of the western crow, it is hoarser and lower, and the vocal difference is a partial reason for its being classed as a separate species. One characteristic note has the hollow sound of a cork being pulled from a bottle. A strange call, accompanying display and a dance, apparently is a love song and is *"kow-wow, koo-wow"* repeated several times with an intermittant, hoarse *"caw, caw."*

**Characteristics.** Of all the American crows the northwestern bird is most tame, wandering about the Indian villages with little attention to man. The Florida crow, like the northwestern crow, has little chance to do damage to cultivated land and consequently seldom is persecuted by man and is less shy of him, but the northwestern crow inhabits a still more isolated range and does not have constant contact with numbers of human beings.

**Breeding.** Like the western variety, this crow often nests in small colonies. A typical rookery is composed of a clump of trees with six to seven birds in a tree. The nesting area is variable, depending on the availability of nesting places. Though many nests are built in coniferous (especially spruce, fir, and hemlock) and deciduous trees (such as apple and cherry), between 10 to 20 feet from the ground, they often nest low to the ground in shrubs or second-growth trees. Sometimes the nests are placed on the ground under boulders on the beach, beneath bushes, and in the side of a sandy bank. Nests have been found in holes in the side of a cliff. The appearance of the nest is very different from that of *brachyrhynchos,* for it is rounder, basketlike in shape, and smaller. The material is less coarse. Generally, this crow lays four or five eggs which—typical of the crow family—vary widely in size, shape, and color. The young birds are well cared for by both parents, and, since fledglings have been seen in early spring and nestlings in late summer, presumably two or even three broods are reared in one breeding season.

**Feeding.** These coastal birds feed primarily on the beaches. As scavengers, they eat the refuse thrown out by fishermen and dead fish as well as small mollusks, shore crabs, shellfish, sand fleas, and other vegetable or animal matter washed up to shore. Crows commonly carry mussels, cockles, and other mollusks to a considerable height and then drop them on rocks in order to break the hard shells. This habit is common among many birds, especially the herring gull. In summer, the birds favor the dead fish and eggs of the clear-water salmon streams, and in late summer and fall they eat berries (wild cherries, wild blackberries, and saskatoon) and fruit (pears and apples). They search for food in the fields, picking up grasshoppers and other insects and sometimes follow the plow. They are fond of carrion, feeding on the carcasses of dogs, cats, and horses when they are available.

These crows habitually steal eggs from many nesting seabirds, and they are always on the hunt for an unguarded nest. Since they have little fear of man, they boldly move in to plunder when gulls, cormorants, murres, and pigeon guillemots rise in fright from their nests. Added to this damaging factor is the record of the birds in some areas on Vancouver Island. During the winter they gather in large flocks to feed on cultivated land.

**Range and Distribution.** This crow species is found along the northwest coast of the Alaskan mainland, from a point opposite Kodiak Island south to the Puget Sound region of the State of Washington. Apparently Vancouver Island has a complete shift in its population. The majority of these birds breeding on the island leave for a more southerly clime in the fall, and those which migrate onto the island for the winter return to the mainland in the spring to breed.

# OWLS

*Strigidae*

**History.** With exception of the barn owl *(Tyto alba pratincola)* which is described separately, all the owls belong to the family *Strigidae.* This huge family includes nearly a hundred species and subspecies found in North America, ranging from the great gray owl to the tiny elf owl.

The chief differences between the two families are that the *Strigidae* have round facial disks, not oval or heart-shaped like the *Tytonidae,* and that the leg feathers, when present, slant downward like a hawk's instead of being reversed like the barn owl's.

Various species and sub-species display individual traits and habits which will be considered under their separate headings, but all have certain general characteristics.

Their large, keen eyes are set so that both look in the same direction and the birds must turn their heads toward anything they wish to see. The very short neck is so flexible, however, that the head may be turned almost completely backwards. The eyes are surrounded by a ruff or facial disk of small short feathers; this disk is framed by a rim of short, stiff feathers which in some species, notably the horned and eared varieties, may be erected on the top of the head.

The bill is short and often nearly concealed by feathers but is strong, hooked, and very sharp. The feet are large, powerful, and equipped with long, curved claws of needle sharpness.

The plumage is extremely soft and even the wing

feathers lack the stiffness found in most primaries. This permits the owl to fly silently and to swoop down on his prey with no telltale swish of wings.

The owls are nocturnal hunters. They begin their foraging at twilight and seek shelter at the coming of daylight. Like all the *Raptores* they capture their prey with their strong talons and tear it to pieces with their bills. If the quarry is small enough it is swallowed whole, larger victims are eaten piecemeal, but in either case every bit is swallowed. After the digestible portions have passed through the stomach, the residue of bones, hair, fur, and other matter is ejected through the mouth in the form of compact wads or pellets. Food habits, in so far as they differ, will be noted with each species.

Both sexes are alike in appearance and the coloration is generally of a protective nature. Like the barn owls, the *Strigidae* are subject to many phases of coloration from very light to very dark, and these phases occur in both sexes at all ages. The young are covered with thick white down, but after attaining their first full plumage their color remains constant regardless of what phase it may be.

Nesting habits differ somewhat with the various species; these will be given under their proper heading.

North American owls are widely distributed and their combined ranges include practically all of the North American continent. Individual ranges will be noted under the section given to each species.

## AMERICAN HAWK OWL *Surnia ulula caparoch*

COMMON NAMES: Canadian Owl, Day Owl, Hudsonian Owl.

**History.** This bird is the American counterpart of the European hawk owl *(Surnia ulula ulula)*, which only occasionally strays to Alaska. The common name of hawk owl is applied because of the bird's hawklike appearance as well as his hunting methods, which are similar to those of the hawks.

**Identification.** Adult males average about 16 inches in length and have a wingspread of 34 to 36 inches. The females are slightly larger than the males. The upper parts are a dark grayish-brown, speckled with white on the top of the head and neck. There are no ear tufts and the facial disk of white, bordered on the sides with black, is not as prominent as on most owls—thus giving the face a more hawklike appearance. The eyes are relatively small; the iris is yellow. The bill is yellow with a black area beneath it. The tail, unusually long for an owl and rounded at the tip, is marked by six or seven narrow white bands.

The under parts are white. The sides of the neck and the chest are finely barred with grayish-brown, and the abdomen is barred with heavier brown markings. The feet are well feathered.

**Characteristics.** The hawk owl is one of the very few members of the owl family that hunt in daylight. His methods are similar to those of most hawks, and he often perches motionless on some point of vantage from which he can swoop down upon his prey. His food consists chiefly of ground squirrels, mice, other small rodents, and some birds.

The nesting site is often a deserted woodpecker hole, but other cavities in stumps or trees are used as well as the relined nests of other birds. Eggs vary from three to seven and are chalky white.

**Range and Distribution.** Like the snowy owl, the hawk owl is somewhat migratory and is only a winter visitor to the United States. These birds seldom range west of Montana, but from Newfoundland to southern New York they occur in varying numbers during the winter. In some years they are very scarce, but occasionally they appear in great numbers throughout the northeastern sections of the United States. They breed to the limit of trees in the Far North.

## BARRED OWL *Strix varia varia*

COMMON NAMES: Night Hooter, Hoot Owl, Rain Owl, Round-Headed Owl, Swamp Owl, Wood Owl.

**Identification.** The barred owl's average length is about 20 inches and the wingspread is from 43 to 45 inches. The females are slightly larger than the male.

The upper parts are dark grayish-brown with numerous small bars of whitish or yellowish-white. The facial disks are marked with a series of grayish-brown rings. There are no ear tufts and the head presents a rounded appearance. The large eyes are dark brown, the bill yellow.

Allan D. Cruickshank, from Natl. Audubon Society.
PLATE I. Barred Owl.

Allan D. Cruickshank, from Natl. Audubon Society.
PLATE II. Burrowing Owl.

The under parts are grayish or buffy white, finely barred on the throat and breast, while the abdomen is irregularly streaked with elongated dusky-brown markings.

**Characteristics.** The barred owl frequents the densest growths along lakes or rivers or in impenetrable swamps. At times he may take up residence close to civilization where his eerie hooting has earned him one of his common names.

During the mating season he is particularly vociferous and his questioning *"whoo, whoo, whoo, whoo, who, who, hoo-hooooaaww"* resounds through the forest. This call usually begins at twilight, ceases later, and is taken up again before sunrise, although on bright moonlight nights it may occur more or less continuously. Besides the familiar *"who, who, whoooo,"* these birds utter a variety of snarls, clucks, or cackles, and infrequently give vent to a hair-raising scream.

They are definitely nocturnal in habit, although they may call or move about on rainy or cloudy days. Their menu consists largely of mice and other small rodents but they also eat large insects, frogs, lizards, and small birds.

The nesting site is usually in a hollow tree. No attempt is made to construct a nest; the eggs are simply deposited on whatever material is present. Sometimes the abandoned nest of a hawk or crow is used without any rebuilding. The number of eggs varies from two to four, the lesser number being common in the southern range and the larger number more frequent in the north.

**Range and Distribution.** These birds are distributed throughout eastern North America. They breed from Newfoundland, southern Quebec, and northern Ontario west to Colorado and southward to most of the southern states except those bordering on the Gulf of Mexico.

There are several sub-species of the barred owl, similar in appearance but occupying more definitely limited ranges.

### FLORIDA or ALLEN'S BARRED OWL *Strix varia alleni*

This bird is very much like the typical specimen except for less feathering on the toes. The range is limited to the extreme southern states from South Carolina to Texas.

### SPOTTED OWL (California Spotted Owl) *Strix occidentalis occidentalis*

### NORTHERN SPOTTED OWL *Strix occidentalis caurina*

These are western prototypes of the common eastern barred owl and are often known as western barred owls. They are somewhat smaller than the typical barred owl. The spotted owl is marked with dusky spots instead of bars, although the general coloring is much the same as that of the eastern species.

The California spotted owl ranges throughout the mountainous regions of southern California, Arizona, New Mexico, and southern Colorado, southward through lower California to northwestern Mexico.

The northern spotted owl is similar to his southern relative but much darker in plumage with comparatively little white showing. The range extends along the Pacific coastal area from British Columbia through Washington and Oregon to northern California.

### TEXAS BARRED OWL *Strix varia albogilva*

This is a western counterpart of the Florida barred owl but is much lighter in color. The barred markings are very conspicuous and the banding on the tail is more pronounced. The extremely limited range of these birds embraces the central-southern portion of Texas.

### BURROWING OWL (Western Burrowing Owl) *Strix cunicularia hypogaea*

COMMON NAMES: Billy Owl, Ground Owl, Western Burrowing Owl.

**Identification.** Adult males average about 10 inches in length. The upper parts are a dark sooty-brown marked with bars and spots of pale buff and tawny white. The under parts are pale buff tinged with deeper tones and barred and spotted on the breast and upper abdomen with darker brown. The leg coverings, lower abdomen, and under-tail coverts are generally plain.

The head is rather small and round, and there is a grayish or buffy white streak extending from under the chin along the front of the neck on both sides. The eye is bright yellow.

The legs are unusually long for an owl, and covered over most of their length with short feathers. The bare portions of the legs and feet are grayish-brown.

**Characteristics.** The burrowing owl is a native of the western plains, where he lives among the prairie dogs and often uses one of their deserted burrows for a home. The nest is always a hole in the ground. If the owl cannot find a convenient old badger, prairie dog, or fox hole, he digs a burrow for himself. The birds are inclined to be gregarious and several of them may occupy one burrow. It is not an uncommon sight to see a group of these owls standing around a burrow or perched on a nearby bush or fence.

Although this owl does most of his hunting after dusk and before sunrise, he is also active at midday and apparently can see as well in the sunshine as any daytime creature.

These birds have voracious appetites and will eat almost anything they can catch. Ground squirrels, chipmunks, or any of the several small mammals in their habitat form a large part of their diet, but they also consume quantities of insects such as grasshoppers, as well as horned toads, lizards, and frogs.

The nest is composed of scraps of dried dung, pieces of skin, weed stalks, and other convenient material. The eggs, usually five to seven, are deposited on this mass. Such nests are situated well back (sometimes as much as 10 feet) from the entrance of the burrow, but they are often so near the surface that horses and cattle break through from above.

**Range and Distribution.** The range includes the open plains country of the western United States and southwestern Canada from the Pacific coast to the western part of Minnesota. They breed through the southern Canadian provinces and range throughout the Southwest.

### FLORIDA BURROWING OWL
*Speotyto cunicularia floridana*

This is a close relative to the western burrowing owl. It is somewhat paler, with more white showing on the upper parts, and a trifle smaller in size. It is found on some of the islands along the southern coast of Florida and on the flat lands of the interior.

### ELF OWL *Micropallas whitneyi*

COMMON NAME: Whitney's Owl.

**Identification.** The elf owl is the smallest of the owl family, being no more than 6 inches in length. The plumage is dichromatic. In the light phase the upper parts are gray or gray with a brownish tinge and are finely spotted with shades of brown and buff. The tail is usually browner than the upper body and is marked with five or six irregular transverse bars of light brown.

The under parts are basically whitish but mottled with grayish-brown and streaked with longitudinal splotches of rufous and dark brown.

The head is round and without ear tufts. Conspicuous white feathers form "eyebrows," and the lower cheeks and throat are white bordered by a ring of brown. The eyes are lemon-yellow.

In the dark phase the upper parts are nearly sepia and the mottling less pronounced.

The legs are not feathered but are sparsely covered with coarse hairlike bristles.

**Characteristics.** These tiny owls are at home in the desert sections of the southwestern United States. They are nocturnal in habits, and if found during the day they appear quite stupid and permit close approach. They nest in abandoned woodpecker holes in cactus or trees and they use these same holes as a hideout in the daytime. Their food consists almost entirely of insects; grasshoppers and beetles form the bulk of the diet.

**Range and Distribution.** The range includes most of the arid regions from southern California and Lower California to southern Texas and northern Mexico north through Arizona and New Mexico.

### SANFORD'S ELF OWL
*Micropallas whitneyi sanfordi*

This is a paler version of the elf owl, having upper parts with more grayish and darker markings. The range is limited to the southern portion of Lower California.

### TEXAS ELF OWL
*Micropallas whitneyi idoneus*

This owl is not unlike the typical species but is somewhat browner of plumage, without any gray tones. The tail is broader and the transverse bars lighter in color. The "eyebrows" and the lower cheeks are pale brown and the spot beneath the ear is yellowish-brown.

The northern limit of the range is the lower part of the Rio Grande Valley; the southern limit extends well into Mexico.

### GREAT GRAY OWL
*Scotiaptex nebulosa nebulosa*

COMMON NAME: Spectral Owl.

**Identification.** The body length is about 3 inches and the tremendous wings reach a spread of about 5 feet. The head and face appear unusually large. In general, this bird seems to be one of the largest of the owls. The bulky appearance is due largely to the thick and fluffy plumage, however, and the bird is actually much lighter than it looks. While this owl exceeds the great horned owl in over-all measurements, the body size and weight are much less.

The upper parts are a dark brownish-slate color, spotted with white and with wavy markings of dusky. The huge head is round and without tufts or "ears." The facial disk is white but heavily marked with concentric rings of black. The eye and bill are yellow.

The under parts are whitish, heavily streaked on the chest and breast with vertical markings of dark grayish-brown. The abdomen is streaked and marked with transverse bars of the same.

**Characteristics.** This bird is at home on the wastelands and tundra of the Far North. Since there is no real night over much of its range, the great gray owl hunts in daylight. Like the snowy owl, whose range

U. S. Fish & Wildlife Service.
PLATE III. Great Gray Owl.

it shares, its food consists of small mammals, including hares, and various birds up to and including the ptarmigan.

Those who have had opportunity to study these birds at close range consider them rather stupid. They seem to be singularly unwary and may sometimes be taken with the hands.

The nest is usually located near the top of a tall conifer, and like the hawk's, it is constructed of sticks, twigs, moss, and grasses and lined with feathers.

**Range and Distribution.** These owls are distributed throughout northern North America from the limit of timber to the southern portions of the Canadian Provinces. In the winter the birds often migrate southward to the northern sections of the United States. During especially severe northern winters they sometimes occur in numbers along the southern limits of their range.

### GREAT HORNED OWL

*Bubo virginianus virginianus*

COMMON NAMES: Big Hoot Owl, Cat Owl, Virginia Horned Owl, Virginia Owl.

**Identification.** The body length is about 2 feet and the wingspread about 5 feet. The upper parts are basically brownish-black but are heavily mottled with grayish-white, light brown, and buffy yellow. The head is large and the ear tufts or "horns" are conspicuous. The facial disks are pale brown margined with black. The bill is black and the large eye is deep yellow.

The under parts are grayish-white finely and thickly barred with dusky-brown except for a whitish patch across the foreneck and a whitish streak down the center of the breast.

The legs, feet, and part of the toes are feathered; the bare part of the toes is grayish-brown, the claws are horn-colored at the base and terminate in black.

**Characteristics.** *Bubo,* meaning "eagle-owl," is an appropriate name for this greatest killer in the owl family. A fierce, persistent, and powerful marauder, he strikes terror in the hearts of all the smaller wild creatures in the woods. His appetite is enormous and he is not too particular about what he eats. All small mammals, including the skunk, are on his bill of fare, and he does not hesitate to argue with a fox over a kill. Rabbits and game birds such as the grouse, pheasant, and turkey are eagerly sought by this aerial pirate and his depredations on game preserves and poultry ranches are notorious. Although widely distributed over eastern North America, it is fortunate that he is nowhere abundant.

The booming call, *"hooo, hooo, hooo, hooo, hoo-o-o-o-o,"* once heard is not likely to be forgotten. There are several variations of this hoot, one being a rather drawn-out *"oooo, tooo, hoooo,"* and another a coupling of the notes, as *"hoo-hoo, hoo-hoo, hoo-hoo."* Added to the more familiar hooting calls, these birds also utter a series of sounds not unlike the yapping of a dog, a cat-like meow, and a sudden piercing scream which if heard in a dark forest is apt to make the stoutest heart beat faster.

**Breeding.** These owls mate earlier than other owls. It is not uncommon to find one on the nest in February, or earlier if it has been a mild season. Two eggs seem to be the rule, and incubation is begun as soon as the first egg is deposited, so that there is usually a time interval between the arrival of the fledglings.

The nest is usually one formerly occupied by a crow, hawk, eagle, or osprey, but the eggs are often deposited on a ledge, in a small cave, or in a hollow tree. At times they may be laid on the bare ground in the midst of a mess of old bones, fur, and feathers.

**Range and Distribution.** This owl is distributed throughout northeastern North America from Labrador to western Ontario and south from Texas to Florida. Some birds winter as far south as Central America.

### ARCTIC HORNED OWL

*Bubo virginianus subarcticus*

or

*Bubo virginianus wapacuthu*

The Arctic horned owl is a much lighter colored bird than the great horned owl but otherwise similar. The upper parts are whiter and show very little black. The under parts are lightly barred and the covering on the legs and feet is unmarked buff or tawny-white.

They are distributed through the central part of

the Arctic from the Mackenzie River to the Rocky Mountains. During the winter these birds often reach as far south as Wisconsin, northeast Illinois, North Dakota, Montana, Idaho, and Colorado.

### DUSKY HORNED OWL
*Bubo virginianus saturatus*

This is similar to the typical specimen but is much darker on the upper parts and a trifle smaller in size. These birds range from the interior of Alaska along the Pacific coast to central California and in the Rocky Mountains, reaching as far east as New Mexico and Arizona.

### DWARF HORNED OWL
*Bubo virginianus elachistus*

This is a smaller version of the typical great horned owl, having considerably darker plumage. The range is confined to southern Lower California.

### LABRADOR HORNED OWL
*Bubo virginianus heterocnemis*

This owl is rather like the dusky variety, the basic coloration being dark sooty-brown. The lower abdomen is lighter and the leg and foot coverings are pale and lightly mottled. The breeding range includes Labrador and Ungava, and in winter the birds are found in Newfoundland, Nova Scotia, Quebec, and Ontario.

### PACIFIC HORNED OWL or CALIFORNIA HORNED OWL
*Bubo virginianus pacificus*

This is smaller than the typical horned owl, with more white and less brown on the upper parts. It is found from central California north to central Oregon and eastward to Arizona.

### NORTHWESTERN HORNED OWL
*Bubo virginianus lagophonus*

This owl is somewhat larger than the Pacific horned owl, and with darker plumage. It ranges from Idaho and eastern Washington and Oregon through British Columbia to the central interior of Alaska. Stragglers reach as far as Colorado in winter.

### ST. MICHAEL HORNED OWL
*Bubo virginianus algistus*

This is a slightly larger bird than the Pacific specimen. The under parts are a deeper buffy-brown. One of the most northerly owls, its range extends along the northern Alaskan coast from the region of Bristol Bay and the Yukon Delta to the North.

### WESTERN HORNED OWL
*Bubo virginianus pallescens*

This is smaller than the common eastern species and lighter in coloration. The range is western North America (except for the high mountainous regions) from Oregon to Minnesota and southward through southeastern California, Arizona, New Mexico, and into Mexico.

### LONG-EARED OWL
*Asio wilsonianus*

Common Names: American Long-Eared Owl, Cat Owl, Lesser Horned Owl.

**Identification.** The body length is about 15 or 16 inches and the wingspread about 40 inches. Both sexes are alike in coloration but the female is slightly larger. Their long wings and tail give the birds an appearance of size which is deceptive.

The upper parts are a mixture of sooty-brown, grayish-white, and buffy-yellow. The facial disks are pale reddish-brown framed by a black border which becomes broken and irregular on the throat. The bright yellow eye is surrounded by black or dusky-brown. The "eyebrows" and the front cheeks are whitish. The prominent ear tufts are black with buff edges blending to white.

Bert Popowski, from Natl. Audubon Society.

Plate IV. Great Horned Owl.

The under parts are whitish tinged with buff. The breast is heavily streaked with blackish-brown. The abdomen and flanks are streaked and barred with heavy markings of the same.

**Characteristics.** The long-eared owl is classed as one of the most beneficial members of the family because his diet consists mainly of rodents.

These birds are quite gregarious and it is not uncommon to find them in fairly large groups. They are nocturnal in habits, but unlike most owls they do not seek dark holes in which to rest by day. They perch in thick conifers or densely leafed trees, and if discovered they have a habit of compressing their body feathers and raising the ear tufts until they resemble a stub or broken limb. The elongated body with its protective coloration makes them very difficult to distinguish while in this position. If

Hal H. Harrison, from Natl. Audubon Society.
PLATE V. Long-Eared Owl.

forced into flight they fly as uncertainly as a nighthawk and seldom travel very far. However, their flight is as noiseless as that of the other owls.

The name "cat owl" is given them because one of their most familiar cries, *"eeeeeeow,"* resembles the meowing of a kitten. At other times their call is like the yelping of a small dog, or a shrill, querulous *"eeeyoooo."* During the mating season they frequently utter a soft, resonant *"hoo-oooo."*

**Breeding.** The nest is placed in thick coniferous trees at varying heights above the ground. Like those of most owls, it is rather haphazardly constructed of sticks and lined with grass, old vegetation, and feathers. Sometimes a squirrel's nest or a hawk's nest is made over to suit the new owner. The eggs generally number four or five and are dead white.

**Range and Distribution.** This owl is generally distributed throughout temperate North America. The northern boundaries of the range include Newfoundland, Quebec, northwestern Ontario, British Columbia, and the coast of southern Alaska. The birds breed as far south as Virginia, Arkansas, and northern Texas. They winter over most of their range but some birds travel as far south as Mexico.

## PYGMY OWL *Glaucidium gnoma gnoma*

COMMON NAME: Gnome Owl.

**Identification.** As the name implies, this small owl seldom attains a length of more than 6 inches. Both sexes are alike in coloration but the females are apt to be larger than the males. The plumage is dichromatic. In the light phase it appears grayish-brown above with numerous irregular spots of buff and white. The under parts are whitish with transverse spottings of brown. In the dark phase the upper parts appear more brownish and the spots are pale reddish-brown or cinnamon. The under parts are pale tawny brown.

**Characteristics.** This is the only member of the owl family whose flight is not soundless. The beating wings produce a whistling sound. The flight is spasmodic and uneven, especially when the bird is hunting. The chief food items are small rodents and birds, and this owl attacks and kills prey larger than himself. At times insects form a part of the diet.

These birds are diurnal in habits and do considerable hunting by daylight, although they are most active at dusk and before sunrise.

They are unsuspicious birds and will often decoy to an imitation of their common call of *"klook, klook."*

**Breeding.** The usual nest is in a hollow stump or in an abandoned woodpecker home. A site well protected by surrounding conifers seems to be preferred. The three or four white or creamy-white eggs are laid on a lining of grass, moss, and other dried vegetation.

**Range and Distribution.** These birds are generally distributed from British Columbia southward through the mountains to southern Mexico. The eastern limits of the range extend to Colorado, Montana, and New Mexico.

## CALIFORNIA PYGMY OWL

*Glaucidium gnoma californicum*

This sub-species is similar to the pygmy owl but occurs in a darker phase with spots of brownish on the upper parts. The range extends from British Columbia southward along the Pacific coast to central California.

## COAST PYGMY OWL

*Glaucidium gnoma grinnelli*

This owl is very like the California pygmy owl but has a much richer plumage. The range extends from southeast Alaska along the coast to central California and inland to Mount Shasta. Casual visitors occur in eastern Washington.

## HOSKINS' PYGMY OWL

*Glaucidium gnoma hoskinsi*

This owl is somewhat similar to the California sub-species but is slightly smaller. The plumage is paler in tone, with a greater amount of white about the head. The range is confined to the southern portion of Lower California.

## ROCKY MOUNTAIN PYGMY OWL

*Glaucidium gnoma pinicola*

Slightly larger than the typical pygmy owl, this little owl is dark gray above in the light phase and dark reddish-brown in the dark phase. The head is liberally speckled with fine white markings. The tail is sooty-brown with transverse bars of white. The under parts are whitish densely streaked with dark slaty-brown. The flanks are pale brown spotted with paler tones of buff or ashy-brown.

As the name implies, these birds are found throughout the Rocky Mountains from British Columbia as far as northern Mexico, except in the more humid coastal regions.

## RICHARDSON'S OWL

*Cryptoglaux funerea richardsoni*

COMMON NAMES: American Sparrow Owl, Arctic Saw-Whet Owl, Sparrow Owl.

**Identification.** The body length is 10 or 11 inches and the wingspread is about 24 inches. Both sexes are alike in coloration but the females are slightly larger.

The upper parts are brown or brownish-gray generously spotted with white. These spots are round on the head and roughly heart-shaped or irregular on the body. The head is rounded, without ear tufts, and the facial disks are grayish-white. The tail is brownish-gray with four or five imperfect, irregular transverse bars of white. The under parts are whitish thickly marked with streaks of grayish-brown.

**Characteristics.** This owl is strictly nocturnal in habits and unlike some of the others is virtually blinded by the sunlight. The call is a low musical note suggestive of water slowly dropping from a considerable height.

It will be noted that this owl shares two of the common names with the saw-whet owl. There is some similarity between the two birds and they commonly share much of the same range, but the saw-whet is a smaller bird and the call note is rasping and unmusical.

The Richardson's owl nests in hollow trees, often using a deserted woodpecker hole for the purpose. Less frequently the nest is built in bushes or in the branches of a tree. The eggs vary in number from two to seven and are pure white.

**Range and Distribution.** These birds are fairly well distributed over the northern portion of North America. Their breeding grounds extend from the Arctic limit of trees to the northern parts of the Canadian provinces. In winter they come southward to the northern tier of the United States, occurring in varying numbers from the New England states to Washington.

## SAW-WHET OWL

*Cryptoglaux acadica acadica*

COMMON NAMES: Acadian Owl, Kirtland's Owl, Sparrow Owl, White-Fronted Owl.

**Identification.** The body length is about 8 inches and the wingspread is around 18 inches. Both sexes are alike in coloration but the females are a trifle larger than the males.

The plumage is dark brown above liberally spotted with white on the crown, nape of neck, and shoulders. The facial disks are grayish with narrow radial streaks of brown. The "eyebrows" are buffy-white; the eye is bright yellow. The tail is marked by three or four fairly regular transverse bars of white.

The under parts are whitish with broad longitudinal markings of rich reddish-brown. The legs and feet are covered with pale buff feathers and the bare portions of the toes are pale yellow.

**Characteristics.** This owl is strictly nocturnal and sleeps so soundly by day that it may easily be captured if found on the roost. The birds often perch near the trunk of some tree in dense foliage to sleep, but prefer to hide in a hollow tree or stump where there is less chance of their enemies pouncing on them during their slumber. The chief enemy of this bird is the barred owl but hawks and other predators also menace its existence. The saw-whet in turn preys viciously on squirrels, small rabbits, and other small mammals and birds. Its chief food item, however, is the white-footed mouse.

The name "saw-whet" refers to their most common call, a harsh, rasping, three-noted *"scree-haw, scree-haw, scree-haw"* which is most often heard during the mating season. This sound is suggestive of someone filing the teeth of a large saw. Other calls include a variety of cooing noises, gurgles, clucks, and occasionally a subdued scream.

Though non-migratory, these birds are inveterate wanderers. They travel widely in search of food, particularly during the autumn and winter, and may suddenly appear in a locality where they were previously unknown.

Their flight is very much like that of a woodcock, and hunters occasionally mistake this bird for a flying woodcock.

The nest, like that of most small owls, is usually located in an abandoned woodpecker or squirrel hole. The three to six eggs are pure white.

Allan D. Cruickshank, from Natl. Audubon Society.
PLATE VI. Saw-Whet Owl.

**Range and Distribution.** These birds are widely distributed across northern North America. They breed from southern Alaska to Nova Scotia and (in summer) reach as far south as Maryland in the east and Southern California on the west coast. In the winter the birds occur southward to Georgia, Louisiana, and Texas.

### SCREECH OWL (Eastern) *Otus asio asio*

COMMON NAMES: Gray Owl, Little Dukelet, Little Horned Owl, Mottled Owl, Red Owl, Shivering Owl.

**Identification.** The body length is about 9 inches and the wingspread about 22 inches. The female is larger than the male. Both sexes are colored alike. The plumage is dichromatic. In the light or gray phase the upper parts are brownish-ash finely streaked with black and mottled with yellowish-white.

The ear tufts or horns are well developed and may be erected to the perpendicular. Prominent whitish "eyebrows" and large yellow eyes give this bird a sinister appearance.

The under parts are whitish finely barred with black and irregularly streaked with dusky-brown.

In the dark phase the upper body is a rich reddish-brown. The "eyebrows," foreface, and chin are whitish. The chest is white marked by four or five longitudinal streaks of black. The breast is washed with cinnamon-brown on each side and finely streaked with black pencilings. The abdomen is whitish or buffy-white and spotted with cinnamon-brown.

**Characteristics.** The term "screech owl" is really a misnomer, for the call of this bird is a querulous, plaintive, mournful wail rather than a screech. In the South this bird is known as the shivering owl, a name more suggestive of the quavering, doleful notes. It is a friendly little bird and not at all averse to living in or close to man's dwellings. Its favorite foods are noxious insects and rodents, of which it consumes a great quantity.

Unlike other owls and most other birds, the screech owl is thought to be monogamous. Observers claim that these owls mate for several seasons, if not for life. The pair remain together throughout the year and both parents take part in caring for the young. The nesting site is similar to those chosen by other small owls. The eggs, three to six in number, are chalky-white.

**Range and Distribution.** These birds are fairly common and widely distributed over most of eastern North America from New Brunswick to Minnesota, south to Florida and west to eastern Texas.

There are several variations of the screech owl distributed over North America. They differ slightly in size and coloration but are much alike in habits.

### AIKEN'S SCREECH OWL *Otus asio aikeni*

These birds are similar to the typical screech owl described above but have more gray in the plumage and more extensive black markings on the under parts. These birds are found from Colorado south to New Mexico and eastward to northeastern Arizona.

### BREWSTER'S SCREECH OWL *Otus asio brewsteri*

This owl is like the common type but has more brown in its plumage. The range is confined to Oregon and parts of Washington and California.

### CALIFORNIA SCREECH OWL (Bendire's Screech Owl) *Otus asio bendirei*

The plumage of this bird is like that of the eastern screech owl in the gray phase but the darker pencilings on the under parts are finer and more closely spaced. These birds are not dichromatic. The range is confined to Southern California.

### FLAMMULATED SCREECH OWL *Otus flammeolus flammeolus*

This owl is slightly smaller than the typical screech owl, and has very short tufts. The upper parts are very gray in the light phase and cinnamon-brown, finely marked with dusky, in the dark phase. The facial disks are bright cinnamon or dark brown. It is found commonly in Arizona and northern Colorado south to southern Mexico.

### FLORIDA SCREECH OWL *Otus asio floridanus*

This bird is slightly darker than the eastern variety, with denser markings on the under parts. This type is found along the Atlantic coast from South Carolina to Florida and west along the Gulf of Mexico to Texas.

## KENNICOTT'S SCREECH OWL
*Otus asio kennicotti*

This is a larger and darker bird than the eastern specimen. This sub-species is generally conceded to be the darkest of the screech-owl family and seldom occurs in the gray phase. It is commonly found along the coastal region from Sitka, Alaska, to Oregon.

## MacFARLANE'S SCREECH OWL
*Otus asio macfarlanei*

This is somewhat similar to the California screech owl but larger. These birds occur from British Columbia to Washington and Oregon and eastward to western Montana.

## MEXICAN SCREECH OWL
*Otus asio cineraceus*

This owl is smaller and grayer than the eastern type and more densely barred on the under parts. The common range is New Mexico, Arizona, Lower California, and northwestern Mexico.

## ROCKY MOUNTAIN SCREECH OWL
*Otus asio maxwelliae*

This owl is like the eastern screech owl, but is the lightest of all the screech owls in coloration. The white areas and the gray tones very pale. It is found in the foothills of the Rocky Mountains and adjacent plains from Montana southeastward into Colorado.

## SPOTTED SCREECH OWL *Otus trichopsis*

This owl is a close relative of the other screech owls and is somewhat similar to the Mexican screech owl, but is inclined to darker coloration and is slightly smaller. A distinguishing feature is a collar of white spots on the back of the neck and a well-spotted crown. These birds are found from southern Arizona to southern Mexico.

## SHORT-EARED OWL *Asio flammeus flammeus*

COMMON NAMES: Marsh Owl, Prairie Owl, Swamp Owl.

**Identification.** The body length is about 14 inches and the wingspread around 42 inches. Both sexes are alike in coloration but the female is larger than the male.

The upper parts are a mixture of yellowish-white, ochraceous brown, and dusky. There is a wide variation of color in these birds but the plumage is heavily mottled with dusky, white, and buffy marking.

The under parts are pale buff or yellowish-white with broad streaks of dark brown on the throat and chest, and finer, narrower streakings of the same on the abdomen.

The buffy facial disks are not prominent and the ear tufts are extremely short and dark.

**Characteristics.** These owls hunt in much the same manner as the marsh hawk and, like that bird, frequent marshes and fens, both fresh and salt. They may sometimes be seen during the day, especially on cloudy days, skimming silently over the meadows, pasture lands, and sand dunes in search of their favorite fare, the meadow mouse. About three-quarters of their food consists of mice and other small rodents such as ground squirrels and moles.

Their sense of hearing is remarkably well developed and it is likely that they rely as much on sound as on sight to locate their prey. They are extremely gregarious, for owls, and during the migratory period and in winter they may be seen in flocks of considerable numbers.

The nest is a haphazard affair of sticks and grass, lined with feathers. It is built on the ground, in clumps of grass or under a bush. The four to seven eggs are plain white.

**Range and Distribution.** These owls are widely distributed over all of North and South America. They breed over most of their northern range from the Arctic coast to the northern part of the Mississippi Valley. In the winter they spread through the southern states and southward to Chile.

## SNOWY OWL *Nyctea nyctea*

COMMON NAMES: Arctic Owl, Ermine Owl, Great White Owl, Harfang, Wapacuthu.

**Identification.** The body length is about 2 feet and the wingspread around 60 inches. The body color is pure white but the crown, back, shoulders, and tail of the males are marked with transverse barrings

Allan D. Cruickshank, from Natl. Audubon Society.
PLATE VII. Screech Owl.

Natl. Audubon Society.
PLATE VIII. Short-Eared Owl.

of grayish brown. The head is rounded and without ear tufts.

The female has much heavier markings of dark brownish-gray. The facial disks, throat, center of the breast, and feet are pure white.

The feet of both sexes are covered with fine bristle-like feathers which nearly hide the black claws. The eye is yellow and the bill is black.

**Characteristics.** Like the hawk owl, these great birds hunt in daylight as well as before dawn and after dusk. Their prey consists chiefly of small mammals and birds, but they are capable of killing the larger northern hare and such game birds as the ptarmigan and ducks. These birds are swift of wing and it is claimed they can catch a grouse. Instances have been noted where they have attacked wooden decoys in the belief that they were real ducks.

The nest is but a depression in the ground, usually on a knoll, and is thinly lined with grass and some feathers. The eggs, varying from three to ten, usually number from five to seven, and may be white or tinged with creamish.

**Range and Distribution.** These owls are fairly well distributed throughout the northern part of the Northern Hemisphere. The North American range extends from British Columbia and Manitoba eastward to Quebec and northward to the end of trees. In the winter these birds occur irregularly in the northern portions of the United States; their numbers at such times varying with the severity of the winter over their usual ranges.

## BARN OWL *Tyto alba pratincola*

COMMON NAMES: American Barn Owl, Golden Owl, Monkey-Faced Owl, Monkey Owl, White Owl.

**History.** Although belonging to the order *Raptores,* or birds of prey, the barn owls are of a separate family, *Tytonidae,* and differ in some respects from the typical owls. The family is distinguished by a rather heart-shaped face made prominent by a conspicuous ruff. This odd feature has earned them the name of "monkey face" by which they are commonly known in many localities. There are about 30 species and sub-species distributed throughout the world but only the one referred to above is found in North America.

**Identification.** Adult birds are about 18 inches long and have a wingspread of 40 to 44 inches. The females are often slightly larger than the males, rarely smaller.

The plumage, like that of other owls, is often dichromatic, with light and dark phases occurring regardless of age or sex, but the so-called normal or average coloration is as follows: The basic color of the upper parts is a yellowish-buff, but this color is so broken by markings of black, white, and gray that the general effect presents a very mottled appearance.

The roughly heart-shaped facial ruff is white or creamy-white often tinged with brownish. The area immediately in front of and surrounding the eye is a deep reddish-brown. The facial area is framed by a narrow border of ochraceous-brown. The rather small beady eyes are dark brown. The bill is dull yellowish.

Allan D. Cruickshank, from Natl. Audubon Society.
PLATE IX. Snowy Owl.

The under parts are white, tinged with buffy-yellow, and marked with small black dots. The unusually long legs are covered with short feathers which turn inward at the back of the legs instead of slanting downward as on the other owls. The claws are long and sharp.

**Characteristics.** The barn owl gets its most common name from its fondness for roosting and nesting in or near barns and other outbuildings. During the day these birds seek out a dark corner in some barn, church steeple, old tower, or deserted building and sleep until twilight. If flushed from their hiding place in daylight, they seem confused and take off in awkward, uncertain flight.

There is a popular misconception that owls can see in total darkness. This, of course, is not true, but their vision is extremely acute at twilight and in the moonlight. Unlike most birds, the eyes are set in such a manner that the owl can see in only one direction at a time, but the head can rotate so that the bird can look almost straight backwards between his shoulders. He is also equipped with a pair of sensitive ears attuned to the slightest rustle or squeak.

The plumage of the owls is very soft and downy, even the primaries lacking the stiffness found in most pinions. For this reason their flight is as noiseless as a moth's and they seem to glide through the air like small phantoms. To add to his eerie, ghostlike flight, the owl frequently utters a peculiar hissing scream.

This owl has a voracious appetite and feeds almost entirely on rats and mice. He will eat more than his weight in these rodents in a single night if he can find them, and a pair of these owls with ravenous young to feed will kill more rats, gophers, moles, shrews, and mice than all the cats in a community.

Like the hawks, owls swallow their prey whole, if possible; or if the creature is too large to be swallowed in one gulp, they hold it in their strong talons and tear it to pieces with their sharp beaks. Everything is eaten, and after the nutritious portions have been digested, the bones, fur, and other indigestible matter still in the stomach is formed into wads or pellets and disgorged through the mouth. Such discarded pellets may often be found about the nest or roost, and upon examination will show exactly what the bird has been eating.

**Breeding.** The barn owl is less particular about nest location than most birds and is apt to select from any number of possible sites. Often the deserted nest of a woodpecker or flicker is chosen, sometimes a hole in a large stump or tree, less frequently a cavity in the ground, and occasionally the abandoned nests of hawks or crows serve the purpose. The nest is a crude mass of sticks, leaves, grass, paper, string, rags, or other available material loosely thrown together. The number of eggs seems to vary widely from 3 to 11, with 5 to 7 being about average. These are a dull white, chalky in appearance and without markings.

**Range and Distribution.** These owls range throughout the greater part of the United States and Mexico, breeding as far north as southern Ontario, and from Oregon to the New England states. In winter

Wray H. Nicholson, from Natl. Audubon Society.
PLATE X. Barn Owl.

the range extends through Lower California and Mexico well into Central America.

**Summary.** It is well to emphasize that the hunter should be aware of the distinctions between the harmful and the beneficial habits of owl predators. While some members—e.g., great horned owl, hawk owl, and certain others—destroy such game as grouse, rabbits, and pheasants, other species help reduce the population of destructive insects and rodents and to that degree are friends rather than enemies of the hunter and the farmer.

The owl's natural enemy the crow is a much greater menace to game birds, and his permanent enmity for the owl is still another blackmark on his dark reputation. As in the case of hawks, the owl family cannot be generally praised or damned. The hunter should learn to identify the local species and be able to distinguish between those that are useful and should be protected and those that are menaces to game and therefore on the hunter's blacklist.

## BROAD-WINGED HAWK

*Buteo platypterus platypterus*

COMMON NAME: Broad-Winged Buzzard.

**History.** The broad-winged hawk may be numbered among the more valuable birds of prey because, like most of the *Buteo* clan, his diet consists chiefly of small rodents and insects. He seldom molests poultry but he does eat frogs, toads, and snakes that are chiefly insectivorous. A study of the food habits of these birds shows them to be largely beneficial to man and they should not be classed with the voracious *Raptores.*

**Identification.** This hawk is one of the smaller *Buteos,* the males being about 14 inches long with a wingspread from 33 to 36 inches. Both sexes are alike in coloration. The upper parts are dark grayish-brown, and the crown, back of the head, and neck are more dusky. The feathers on the upper body have a black shaft line with plain dark brown centers. The tail is marked by three narrow transverse bars of grayish-white. The sides of the head and a line behind the eye are grayish-white with fine streaks of dusky. A dusky marking extends from the corners of the bill down each side of the throat to the breast. The breast is pale buff blending into whitish on the under parts. The breast and upper abdomen are thickly marked with wide arrowhead spots of rufous, such markings being wider on the sides and flanks than on the thigh coverings. The cere, legs, and feet are yellow; the claws are black, and the bill is dark horn-color.

Edward A. Hill, from Natl. Audubon Society.
PLATE I. Broad-winged Hawk.

In the immature young, the upper parts are blackish-brown, each feather margined with chestnut or grayish-white. The sides of the head and streaks above and behind the eye are pale buff streaked with brown. The throat is white, but the under parts are yellowish-white washed with pale brown and boldly marked on the sides and flanks with elongated and arrowhead-shaped markings of brown. The tail is dark brown with six or eight transverse bars of lighter tone. All the tail feathers are tipped with white.

**Characteristics.** By preference a frequenter of the deep, forested areas, the broad-winged hawk exhibits remarkable patience in obtaining his food. He often remains motionless on his perch for hours, apparently asleep, but the slightest motion below arouses him to action and he can plunge swiftly upon his victim.

He is more silent than the other *Buteos,* and his call somewhat resembles that of the wood pewee, being only a trifle louder and less plaintive.

Insects form a large part of the diet of these hawks, especially the larger caterpillars, crickets, beetles, and cicadas. Meadow mice, chipmunks, red squirrels, snakes, frogs, toads, and occasionally small birds round out the menu.

**Breeding.** The nest, typical of the *Buteos,* is constructed with sticks and twigs, and is placed in a crotch at varying heights from the ground. The eggs, usually numbering from two to three, are pale grayish or greenish-white thickly spotted with brown.

**Range and Distribution.** These hawks are widely distributed over eastern North America from New Brunswick and Saskatchewan westward beyond the Mississippi and southward to the northern part of South America.

## COOPER'S HAWK

*Accipiter cooperi*

COMMON NAMES: Big Blue Darter, Chicken Hawk, Pigeon Hawk, Quail Hawk, Striker, Swift Hawk.

**History.** A glance at the common names given to this member of the *Accipiters* will show both his fondness for game and poultry and his mode of flight. The Cooper's hawk is the most destructive demon of the air. He is no fiercer or more deadly than the goshawk, but he occurs in greater numbers over a much wider range, and thus becomes a much greater menace to game and domestic fowls.

**Identification.** This hawk is generally larger than the sharp-shinned hawk, the females averaging about 20 inches and the males a couple of inches less. The wingspread is from 29 to 36 inches. Size is not always a definite means of identification, however, because small Cooper's hawks (males) may look very much like large female sharp-shinned hawks. The *rounded* tail of the Cooper's contrasts with the *squared tail* of the sharp-shin and usually enables the observer to determine which is which. There is less chance of mistaking a Cooper's for a goshawk because the latter, although somewhat similar in coloration, is considerably larger.

There is very little difference in plumage between the Cooper's and the sharp-shinned hawk. The head of the Cooper's is usually darker and a more even,

W. E. Shore, from Natl. Audubon Society.
PLATE II. Cooper's Hawk.

slaty-blue. The immature birds of both species closely resemble each other.

**Characteristics.** The similarity between the birds mentioned above extends to habits as well as color. The Cooper's hawk usually keeps to the woods, or near them, but does not hesitate to make dashing raids on near-by poultry pens or farmyards. These hawks are extremely bold and often dive on young chickens in the presence of humans. All three accipiters bear the common name of "chicken hawk," but the Cooper's hawk is the most deserving of that opprobrious title. Besides the larger game birds and fowl, these hawks also kill rabbits and the various squirrels.

**Breeding.** The nesting site is the same as that of the goshawk or the sharp-shinned. The eggs, usually two to five, are pale bluish and generally plain, but may sometimes be spotted faintly with light yellowish-brown.

**Range and Distribution.** These hawks are generally distributed throughout North America and are one of the most common hawks from northern Canada to southern Mexico. They breed from British Columbia in the west and Prince Edward Island in the east, southward to Florida and Texas. They winter from the south-central portion of Canada as far south as Costa Rica.

# DUCK HAWK

*Falco peregrinus anatum*

COMMON NAMES: American Peregrine, Great-Footed Hawk, Peregrine Falcon, Tercel (male), Wandering Falcon.

**History.** The peregrine falcon of Europe was the bird most commonly used in the ancient sport of falconry. Noted for its courage and superior flight powers, it was trained to kill partridges, doves, and ducks for its master. The American duck hawk is a close relative to the falcon of Old World fame and differs only in the coloration of the throat and breast.

The scientific name of the American species aptly describes its habits: *Falco,* meaning "sickle," presumably refers to the deadly accuracy of its strike. *Peregrinus* means "wandering," a trait for which this hawk is noted, and *anatum,* "of the ducks," refers to the bird's favorite prey.

**Identification.** The males vary in length from 16½ to 18 inches and have a wingspan from 38 to 45 inches. The females are an inch or two longer. Both sexes are alike in coloration.

The uppper parts in general are a dark bluish-gray. All feathers on the upper parts are margined with pale gray, but such markings are very faint on the rump and upper tail. The tail has five or six narrow bands of black, the one nearest the end being much wider, and the tail feathers are tipped with white.

The feathers on the forehead, just above the cere, are whitish, the crown and upper sides of the head to below the eyes are a darker slate-color. The bill is yellow at the base blending to bluish-black at the tip. The eye is dark brown. The lower sides of the head are yellowish, and a black streak extends from the base of the bill backward and downward to form a "mustache." The throat and breast are whitish

W. Bryant Tyrrell, from Natl. Audubon Society.
PLATE III. Duck Hawk (Peregrine).

and unmarked. This is the one feature which distinguishes the American duck hawk from the Old World peregrine which has dusky markings on those parts.

The under parts, except for the breast, are yellowish or creamy buff, closely barred and spotted with black. The dark markings are more pronounced on the sides and under-tail coverts. The thighs are finely marked with transverse bars of black. The cere, corners of the mouth, feet, and legs are yellow; the claws black.

On the young birds the forehead and sides of the head are pale, unmarked brownish-white. The crown, stripe back of the eye, "mustache," and all the remainder of the upper parts are dusky brown, the feathers edged with a lighter tone. The tail is grayish, ending in pale creamy white, and has four or five narrow bands of light gray. The under parts are pale buffy-brown or yellowish-white, heavily spotted and streaked with wedge-shaped markings of dark brown. The bill is entirely bluish-brown in color, the cere and feet ochre, and the claws black.

**Characteristics.** The duck hawk is a streamlined, powerful bird and wonderfully adapted for the business of killing. It is doubtful if any other bird of prey can equal its speed and agility in the air. The wing-beats are rapid, like those of a pigeon, and so unlike those of other hawks that this bird may be readily identified in the air.

When in pursuit of food, the duck hawk rises in spirals above its intended prey and suddenly "stoops" in a powerful dive on its target. No matter how the terrified victim twists and dodges, the relentless hawk is more than a match in speed and maneuverability. One mode of attack is to strike the quarry with the talons closed into a fist; so powerful is such a blow that it usually kills instantly. Another method, depending on the size of the selected victim, is to swoop down alongside or ahead of a bird in full flight and grasp it with the sharp, curved talons. In either case the result is sudden death to the pursued.

Duck hunters claim to have witnessed instances where this hawk mistook wooden decoys for the real thing and struck them so hard that the heads were broken off.

**Breeding.** Duck hawks locate their nests in such inaccessible places that they have little fear of being molested. Little or no attempt is made to build a nest, and the eggs are generally deposited in a crevice or depression on a high cliff. Two or three young are an average brood, and both parents share the task of feeding and caring for their offspring. While the young are growing, the parents prey on grouse, pigeons, and the larger songbirds. Later, when the birds leave the nest, they move with their parents to a marine area and the chief food items change to ducks, snipe, and other shore birds.

**Range and Distribution.** Fortunately for the duck population, these hawks are not abundant over their range which includes most of North America and the northern portion of South America. They breed from Norton Sound, Alaska, southward to Lower California, eastward to about central Greenland, and thence south to Connecticut and Pennsylvania. The winter range extends from British Columbia to New York and New Jersey, and south through most of the United States from Texas to the Atlantic coastal states, the Gulf of Mexico, and down through the West Indies and Panama to northern Chile.

### PEALE'S FALCON *Falco peregrinus pealei*

Common Name: Black Hawk.

This is similar to the typical duck hawk, but is a darker slate-color above with the under parts, especially the breast, more heavily marked with dusky. The range is confined to the Pacific coastal area from Oregon to the Aleutian Islands.

## (EASTERN) GOSHAWK

*Astur atricapillus atricapillus*

Common Names: American Goshawk, Blue Darter, Blue Hen Hawk, Chicken Hawk, Dove Hawk, Grouse Hawk, Partridge Hawk.

**History.** The name goshawk is believed to stem from "goose hawk," although it is doubtful that the North American variety ever tackled a bird as large as a goose. Goshawks belong to the order *Raptores,* the suborder *Falcones,* and the family *Accipitridae.* The accipiters, or true hawks, include several of the short-winged hawks such as the Cooper's hawk, sharp-shinned hawk, and the goshawk. The latter comes under a separate classification bearing the generic name *Astur.*

In the Old World the term "hawks" applied only to the diurnal bird-killers, but in common usage the name is given to almost all *Raptores.* Actually there are many North American varieties that belong to the genus *Buteo* and are not accipiters, or true hawks, at all. The *Buteos* soar at high altitudes with very little wing motion, while the true hawks, which are woodland birds, fly with short, quick wing-beats interspersed with periods of sailing.

**Identification.** The goshawk is the largest of the accipiters in North America, with a total length of from 22 to 26 inches, and a wingspread from 40 to 47 inches. The female is somewhat larger than the male. The tail is long and broad, the wings rounded.

Both adults are alike in coloration. The crown and back of the head are black. A wide, conspicuous streak extends from the base of the bill over the eye to the back of the head. This streak is finely penciled with black. The eye is red and the stout, curved bill is a slaty horn-color. The upper cheeks from behind the eye are slaty-gray. The lower cheeks, chin, and throat are white with very fine black pencilings. The back, scapulars, and secondaries are bluish-gray. The primaries and the tail are a darker slate-gray, the latter barred with five wide bands of blackish and tipped with white. The legs and feet are yellow; the long, hooked claws are black. The under parts are grayish-white crossed with narrow bands of dusky brown except on the under-tail coverts, which are plain. The barring on the breast is somewhat irregular, but on the flanks and thighs it is even and well defined.

The immature birds (up to the second season moult) have upper parts of dark brown, but each feather is edged with pale reddish-brown and the general appearance is mottled. The margins on the neck and shoulder feathers are much lighter, sometimes whitish or dull yellowish-brown. The wings and tail are barred with light and very deep brown, the barring being more conspicuous than on the adults. The under parts are creamy-white thickly speckled with spear-shaped streaks of deep brown. The legs and feet are a duller yellow than on the older birds, the eye is yellow, and the bill more brownish.

**Characteristics.** Of all the hawks, the goshawk is the most rapacious and destructive to game birds, small mammals, and poultry. These birds are particularly destructive to the northern grouse. Were it not for the fact that they normally come southward only in the winter, their toll on quail, grouse, pheasants, and rabbits would be much greater.

Most predatory birds depend on catching their prey in flight, in the open, and give up the chase when their quarry gains the protection of cover, but the goshawk is a more determined hunter. He often follows his game into the thickest covers, alights, and chases them into flight. Once in the air, few game birds can evade his swift, darting attack. His loud, piercing cries strike terror in the hearts of all small creatures. His fierceness is matched by his bold nature, and when driven by hunger he has been known to dive on a wounded or fresh-killed bird right in front of the hunter.

The kill, as with most *Raptores,* is made with the sharp claws, aided by the strong, curved bill. Small victims are sometimes swallowed whole, and the larger ones are torn into convenient pieces. The goshawk has a voracious appetite and a digestive tract capable of rapid assimilation; he gorges whenever possible and ordinarily consumes a large quantity of food daily. When all the nutritious elements have been extracted, the indigestible parts such as feathers, bones, hair, scales, and other residue are formed into solid balls, or pellets, by the action of the stomach muscles. These pellets are then regurgitated before more food is eaten. It is from the examination of such pellets that the food habits of the goshawk have been determined, for they contain all the evidence of what he eats.

During the nesting season both parents are kept busy bringing food to their ever-hungry young as well as feeding themselves. At this time their depredations in game covers are particularly great.

**Breeding.** The usual nest is in a tall conifer, deep in woods. It is made of twigs, sticks, bark, and leaves, and lined with grass, strips of bark, and sprigs of hemlock. The number of eggs varies from two to five, and they are a pale bluish-white, infrequently spotted with yellowish-brown. The young remain in the nest until fully feathered and ready for flight.

**Range and Distribution.** In summer, the goshawk breeds from northern Canada to northern Michigan, northern New England, and northern New York. A few birds breed as far south as the mountainous regions of Pennsylvania. During the winter they range from Alaska and the Canadian provinces as far south as Mexico, occurring in varying numbers in Texas, Oklahoma, Missouri, Indiana, Virginia, and Kentucky.

Photo by George Goodwin.
PLATE IV. Goshawk.

## (WESTERN) GOSHAWK
*Astur atricapillus striatulus*

**History.** This is a western counterpart of the eastern goshawk.

**Identification.** The western goshawk is similar in appearance to the eastern variety but has darker upper parts. The back is a very dark gray, nearly blackish. The wavy lines on the under parts are more numerous and darker.

**Characteristics.** Its characteristics are in general, the same as those given for the eastern goshawk.

**Range and Distribution.** These birds range from arctic Alaska to California along the Pacific coast. The breeding grounds extend from northern Alaska to the Sierra Nevada Mountains of California. In summer the range includes southern California and extends east as far as Colorado.

## MEXICAN GOSHAWK
*Asturina plagiata plagiata*

**History.** This smaller relative of the eastern raider is a goshawk in coloration only. He is generally considered as beneficial and has few, if any, of the bad habits associated with others of his clan.

**Identification.** The total length is about 17 inches and the wingspread from 32 to 38 inches. The upper parts are faintly bluish-gray, streaked or barred with black. The head is lighter in color and the rump darker. The upper tail coverts are white. The tail is very dark gray, nearly blackish, and banded with two or three broad white bars. The tips of the tail feathers are white. The chin and under-tail coverts are plain white; the remainder of the under parts are barred gray and white.

**Characteristics.** This bird prefers the open or broken country and is most often seen near streams and in the more moist regions. Pellet examinations disclose a low percentage of bird remains and the food is principally small rodents and injurious mammals. Insects such as beetles and grasshoppers form a large part of the diet, and some lizards and fish are also eaten.

**Range and Distribution.** These goshawks range throughout the southwest from southern Arizona and southern New Mexico along the lower valley of the Rio Grande, through Mexico to Guatemala.

## HARRIS' HAWK

*Parabuteo unicinctus harrisi*

COMMON NAMES: None so far as known.

**Identification.** Males average about 20 inches in length, the females an inch or two longer. The general coloration is a dark sooty-brown with lighter brown reflections. The wings and tail are usually darker than the back. The wing coverts and the leg coverings are a rich reddish-brown.

The lores are yellow and nearly bare, having but few bristly feathers. The cere, legs, and feet are yellow. The bill is horn-colored and the eye is brown. The upper and lower tail coverts and the base of the tail are white. The tail ends in a broad band of white.

The plumage of immature birds is more generally brownish in tone and the head and neck are streaked with yellowish-brown. The back and scapulars are mottled with chestnut and reddish-brown. The white band at the base of the tail is less conspicuous and the white tip is narrower or missing entirely. The under parts are buffy-white with wide streaks of dark brown and blackish. The feathers on the thighs are barred with white.

**Characteristics.** Harris's hawk is friendly and unsuspicious of man. Its food consists chiefly of small mammals but it also eats snakes and offal. On occasion it joins with the vultures and caracaras for a meal on carrion. The normal flight is rather slow and seldom more than a few feet above the brush and thickets where the wood-rats and chipmunks hide. When the occasion demands, however, this hawk can strike swiftly.

**Breeding.** The nest is made in a tree or bush and is constructed of sticks, twigs, moss, roots, and grass. The size of the nest and its construction vary in the different localities. The eggs, usually two to four in number, are greenish-white and may be either plain or sparsely spotted with yellow-brown or lavender.

**Range and Distribution.** This hawk ranges from southeastern California through southern Arizona, New Mexico, and southern Texas southward through Mexico and Panama. Occasional birds appear in Louisiana and Mississippi, but seldom reach as far north as Iowa.

## MARSH HAWK (Harrier)

*Circus hudsonius*

COMMON NAMES: Blue Hawk (adults), Bog-Trotter, Frog Hawk, Harrier, Marsh Harrier, Mouse Hawk, White-Rumped Hawk.

**History.** Although generally considered as a hawk, the true name of this species is *harrier* and in habits they differ considerably from the rapacious accipiters. The so-called marsh hawk is numbered among the more beneficial *Raptores* and is granted legal protection in many states and provinces.

**Identification.** The harrier is a fairly large hawk with a total length of about 19 to 20 inches and a wingspread from 44 to more than 50 inches. The wings are fairly broad and rounded. The most distinguishing feature is the white patch of the upper tail coverts.

As with nearly all birds of this nature, the female is somewhat larger than the male. In flight the wings of the male appear white on the under side and the under parts are whitish; the wings of the female show barred markings and the breast and under parts are streaked with dark markings.

The sexes differ in coloration, the male being a pale ashy-gray above and white below with scattered spots of reddish brown. The tail is bluish-gray with five or six transverse darker bars. The bar at the end of the tail is widest and darkest, and is mottled with white at the tip.

The under parts of the female are brownish. The head and neck are streaked with yellowish-rufous. There are pronounced creamy-white streaks running above and below the eye, separated by a dusky stripe from behind the eye rearward. The under parts are yellowish-brown, heavily streaked with lateral markings of dark brown.

Both sexes have a partial ruff surrounding the face, somewhat resembling that of an owl.

Immature birds closely resemble the adult female but are darker in general coloration and have but four bands on the tail.

**Characteristics.** The marsh hawk, as the name implies, does most of his hunting over wide meadows, marshes, and low-lying pasture lands. His flight is extremely graceful as he glides buoyantly a short distance above the ground. He veers and tilts, rises or drops according to the nature of the terrain, with scarcely a perceptible motion of the wings.

His chief prey is the meadow mouse, and as he quarters back and forth across a field few of those creatures escape his sharp eyes. When the quarry is spotted, he checks his flight with a sudden wing motion, hovers momentarily, and then plunges to the ground. He misses as often as he makes a capture, but if he is successful the prey is eaten then and there.

Food habits vary according to localities and the seasons. Although field mice constitute the bulk of the diet, the harrier eats small birds when other food is scarce, and occasionally dives on rabbits, squirrels, lizards, snakes, or frogs.

The courtship of the male is an interesting display of aerial acrobatics. He sweeps back and forth in wide semicircles which gradually lessen in diameter until he stops abruptly, folds his wings, and plummets toward the ground. In the course of his fall he makes two or more complete somersaults, pulling out of the last one just before he reaches the ground and soaring aloft again for a repeat performance.

**Breeding.** The mated pairs share the task of nesting and caring for the young, and are fearless in protecting them.

Unlike other *Raptores,* the harrier builds a nest on the ground. The site chosen is generally a grassy hummock or a tangle of vegetation. The nest is made from dried grass and is more carefully constructed than is usual with hawks. The number of eggs to a setting varies widely from two to eight, but an average clutch is four to six. The eggs are dull white tinged with bluish or greenish. Sometimes they are plain, but often are spotted with light brown or brownish-gray.

Lewis Wayne Walker, from Natl. Audubon Society.
PLATE V. Marsh Hawk (Harrier).

**Range and Distribution.** These birds are widely distributed over North America. The summer range extends from northwestern Alaska to Prince Edward Island and southward to the southern borders of the United States. In winter the range is from the southern Canadian regions throughout the United States to Central America.

## PIGEON HAWK

*Falco columbarius columbarius*

COMMON NAMES: American Falcon, Bullet Hawk, Little Blue Corporal, Pigeon Falcon.

**History.** The mated pairs share the task of nest-appearance, but much smaller, the pigeon hawk gets its name not from preying on doves and pigeons, but because in flight and body structure it resembles those birds. What it lacks in size it makes up for in ferocity and, like its larger relative, its principal food is birds. The family *Falconidae* has several representatives in North America, none of which are more deadly than the pigeon hawks.

**Identification.** Adult males are little more than 10 inches long; the females are slightly larger. Both sexes are alike in coloration throughout most of the year, but the males undergo a pre-mating change of plumage which differs somewhat from that of the female.

The normal coloration (i.e., the stage in which these birds usually appear, is a very deep brown above with most of the features having dark center lines and pale edges. The neck is marked by narrow whitish streaks. The primary feathers are dusky with lighter tips and there are scattered oval spots of cinnamon-brown on the inner webs. The tail is the same color as the upper body, but is crossed by four or five bars of dull yellow and ends in a white tip.

The under parts vary from grayish-white to a deep creamy buff and, except for the throat, they are heavily streaked with elongated markings of very dark brown or blackish. The throat is sometimes plain white but is often finely streaked with dark pencilings. The sides of the head are light buff marked with narrow streaks of dark which merge into a "mustache" from the corners of the mouth to the lower throat. The forehead, above the cere, and a small area in front of the eye are whitish. A dark streak occurs above and behind the eye. The iris is brown, the bill bluish-brown, the cere, legs and feet yellow, and the claws black.

In full plumage the adult male appears as follows: The upper parts, including the crown, back, shoulders, and rump are a purplish-gray. The crown is narrowly streaked with black, and the other feathers of the upper body have a conspicuous dark center. The forehead, space between the bill and the eye, and a line over the eye are white. This white line over the eye extends to the back of the neck. The sides of the head, neck, throat, and all under parts are a reddish-buff, narrowly streaked with dusky on the sides of the head and more heavily marked with the same on the neck, breast, and abdomen. The dusky "mustache" is narrower. The thigh feathers are narrowly marked with fine streaks of black. The cere, a narrow circle around the eye, the legs and feet are yellow; the claws are black.

The young birds closely resemble the adults, but during the first year are generally lighter colored and have broader margins of light brown on the upper parts.

**Characteristics.** The pigeon hawk often hunts along the edges of timber, in more or less open areas, and along the shores of open water. He is especially deadly to snipe, plovers, and other shorebirds. His powers of flight are almost equal to those of the larger duck hawk, or the goshawk, and his prey is killed in the same manner. Some indication of this

PLATE VI. Pigeon Hawk.

hawk's flying ability is revealed by the fact that it captures dragonflies on the wing.

**Breeding.** Typical of hawks in general, the nest is made from sticks, twigs, weed stems, grass, and moss, but unlike most such nests the pigeon hawk's nest is usually lined with feathers and soft bark. Such nests are sometimes located in the branches of a tall tree, less often in a hollow tree, and frequently on a bare ledge. In the latter case, the nest is a more haphazard affair with little material used in the construction. The eggs, averaging three, are whitish and often so heavily splotched with rich, warm brown that the ground color is barely visible.

**Range and Distribution.** The range extends from northwestern Alaska through to northern South America and encompasses most of the provinces and states. In the summer the birds seldom go south of northern Maine, northern Michigan, and northern California. In winter they range through the Gulf states, south through Mexico, Central America, and the West Indies.

### BLACK PIGEON HAWK

*Falco columbarius suckleyi*

COMMON NAME: Black Merlin.

This is a darker version of the eastern pigeon hawk, having similar habits and characteristics. The upper parts are sooty or dusky. The white throat is streaked with black and the under parts are brownish-black with deep brown and whitish markings. The lower parts of the female and the immature males are thickly spotted with dusky brown.

The range extends along the northern coastal regions from Sitka, Alaska, to northern California. These birds occur only in limited numbers in the southern portion of their range.

### RICHARDSON'S PIGEON HAWK

*Falco columbarius suckleyi*

COMMON NAMES: Richardson's Merlin, Pale Merlin.

This is a paler variation of the eastern pigeon hawk, similar in characteristics, habits, and breeding. The chief difference in coloration is the lighter tone of the plumage. The markings are the same as those on the eastern pigeon hawk except that the tail of the Richardson's has five transverse bars of dusky brown and six bands of pale gray.

The range covers the region of the Great Plains from southern Saskatchewan and Alberta to North Dakota and Montana. In the winter the range extends to southern Lower California, southern Texas, and northwestern Mexico, including Colorado and New Mexico.

### WESTERN PIGEON HAWK

*Falco columbarius bendirei*

This is a sub-species of the eastern pigeon hawk, having somewhat lighter upper parts and a black tail crossed by three bands of very pale gray. The range extends from Alaska and northwestern Canada southward into the Sierra Nevada Mountains. In winter this range is increased southward through New Mexico and southern Lower California to northwestern Mexico. Occasional birds occur in Louisiana, Florida, and the Carolinas.

## RED-SHOULDERED HAWK

*Buteo lineatus lineatus*

COMMON NAMES: Big Chicken Hawk, Hen Hawk, Red-Shouldered Buzzard, Winter Hawk.

**History.** The common names of "chicken hawk" and "hen hawk" are misleading and should never have been associated with this species. Actually, domestic poultry and game comprise less than 2 per cent of the diet. The red-shouldered hawk is one of the most beneficial of all hawks and is especially valuable to the farmer.

Like the red-tailed hawk, the red-shouldered is common in many places, but is less often seen because it is more retiring and prefers the dense woods and swampy areas. Because of their proved value as destroyers of noxious insects and injurious rodents these hawks deserve to be spared and not regarded as enemies by the sportsman.

**Identification.** Both sexes are alike in coloration, but, as with other hawks, the female is a couple of inches larger than the male. Adult males average 20 inches in length and have a wingspread of from 44 to 48 inches. The wide tail and broad wings help to identify this hawk as one of the *Buteos*.

The upper parts are a deep reddish-brown, each feather having a dusky center and lighter edges of yellowish-brown, grayish-brown, or white. The shoulders are usually a rich reddish-brown, and it is from these shoulder patches that this hawk derives its name, but they are often inconspicuous and of little aid in identification. One mark which occurs most frequently with the red-shouldered hawk is a diffused, light-colored patch at the base of the primaries; this mark is particularly noticeable in flight. The four outer primaries are barred with black and white. The tail is brownish-black or grayish-brown, barred with five or six narrow bands of white; the terminal bar is slightly wider than the others.

The chin, throat, and cheeks are a dull white with indistinct dusky markings which appear heavier and darker on the throat than elsewhere. The under parts are a light reddish-brown barred with white and pale gray. The lower tail coverts are plain whitish. The bill is a bluish-horn color; the cere, legs, and feet are yellow and the eye is brown.

In common with most young hawks, the immature birds are more or less heavily streaked below. The upper parts are a plain dark brown. The tail is brown, crossed by numerous transverse bars of lighter and darker tones. The eye is *yellow*.

**Characteristics.** Like all the *Buteos,* the red-shouldered hawk is much given to soaring, but when in search of food he perches motionless on a stump, fence, or dead limb close to the ground. He may remain perfectly still for long periods and will usually permit a fairly close approach before taking flight.

His tastes are more cosmopolitan than those of most hawks; although mice and large insects form the bulk of his diet, he also eats fish, frogs, crayfish, snails, centipedes, earthworms, and snakes. Because of his food habits he is more often found in the marshy lowlands than in the mountains or high hills.

The voice of the red-shouldered hawk is more musical than the others, and his shrill *"kee-yoo, kee-yoo"* sounds somewhat like the call of the blue jay.

**Breeding.** Red-shouldered hawks generally travel in pairs. They mate and remain together throughout the year and it is possible that they mate for life. The nest is generally located in the crotch of a tall deciduous tree, such as the birch, beech, elm, or maple, rarely in a conifer. Composed almost entirely of sticks, the nest is a large, bulky affair and may be used for more than one season.

The eggs usually number from three to five, and are white or bluish-white with irregular splotches of dark brown and yellowish-brown.

The young birds generally remain with the parents until early winter.

**Range and Distribution.** These hawks are widely distributed throughout the eastern United States. The breeding grounds extend from Manitoba and southern Keewatin eastward through southern Quebec, Prince Edward Island, and Nova Scotia southward to southern Florida. The western limit reaches as far as Oklahoma.

## FLORIDA RED-SHOULDERED HAWK

*Buteo lineatus alleni*

This hawk is identical to the variety described above except for being somewhat smaller. The range is confined to the southern tier of the United States from southern Oklahoma through Arkansas, Alabama, Louisiana, South Carolina, and Florida, and reaching into Mexico along its southern limits.

## INSULAR RED-SHOULDERED HAWK

*Buteo lineatus extimus*

This is a sub-species similar to the typical variety but its upper parts are darker and more inclined to grayish. There is no brown on the head and the under parts are generally paler. These hawks are a trifle smaller than the northern red-shouldered hawk. The range is confined to the Florida Keys.

## RED-BELLIED HAWK *Buteo lineatus elegans*

This variety is distinguished from the northern

Karl H. Maslowski, from Natl. Audubon Society.
PLATE VII. Red-Shouldered Hawk.

red-shouldered hawk by having under parts of rich, dark reddish-brown without markings or with such markings as do occur being very indistinct. The rufous-colored breast fades into a paler tone on the abdomen. The range extends from the Rocky Mountains to the Pacific coast as far north as British Columbia and southward into Mexico.

### TEXAS RED-SHOULDERED HAWK

*Buteo lineatus texanus*

This variety is similar to the above, with the head and back a more reddish-brown and the breast spotted with yellowish-brown. The range covers southern Texas and northeastern Mexico.

## RED-TAILED HAWK

*Buteo borealis borealis*

Common Names: Chicken Hawk, Buzzard Hawk, Eastern Hawk, Red-tailed Hawk, Red Hawk, Redtail, Red-Tailed Buzzard, White-Breasted Chicken Hawk.

**History.** Because of its abundance and the fact that it occurs over most of North America, the red-tailed hawk is probably the best known of all the larger *Buteos.* The name "hen hawk" or "chicken hawk," so carelessly applied to this species, is somewhat misleading. The redtail, in common with many other hawks, does prey on poultry on occasion, but rarely when other foods are available. Individual members of this species sometimes develop a taste for domestic poultry, and these should be quickly destroyed, but for the most part the species is considered beneficial in keeping down the rodent population and also consume huge quantities of noxious insects.

**Identification.** The average length (male) is 20 to 22 inches; the females are slightly larger. The long, broad wings have a spread of from 49 to 56 inches.

Both sexes are alike in coloration. The upper parts are dark brown mottled with various shades of reddish-brown, buff, gray, and white. The upper body feathers are irregularly marked with these colors to create a margined appearance.

The under parts are whitish, or grayish-white, washed with pale buffy-brown on the sides of the breast. The upper breast is heavily streaked with grayish-brown, the lower breast is very lightly streaked with the same, or may be plain. The abdomen is irregularly barred or streaked with dark brown, the markings often appearing as broken bands. The lower belly is usually plain white.

Fran Hall, from Natl. Audubon Society.

Plate VIII. Red-Tailed Hawk.

The upper surface of the broad tail is a bright rusty-red; the under surface is paler and more faded in appearance. There is a distinct black transverse bar at the end of the tail and the feathers are tipped with white.

The curved bill is dark horn-color; the eye is brown; the cere, legs, and feet are yellow, and the claws black.

The young differ from the adults in that the tail is grayish and banded by six or eight narrow bars of dusky brown. The eye and bill are yellow, as are the legs and feet.

**Characteristics.** The redtail belongs to the group of soaring hawks which are generally considered more beneficial than harmful. These birds may often be observed describing ever-widening circles as they ascend higher and higher until they are lost from view in the sky. Such soaring must be accomplished with little effort on the part of the bird, because they have frequently been known to remain aloft for many hours without alighting for a rest. Just why the redtail and others such as the broad-winged and red-shouldered hawks perform these soaring flights has not been definitely established. Contrary to a popular conception, they are not hunting for food at such times.

When in search of food the redtail perches motionless on a limb or on some other vantage point and silently waits for his quarry to come within range. He then plunges suddenly and silently to the kill. Unlike the goshawk and other accipiters, such kills are nearly always made on the ground, for the bulk of the redtail's food consists of ground-dwelling species. Small mammals, such as the various squirrels, mice, gophers, moles, shrews, and rats form a large part of the diet. Snakes, particularly the blue racers and garter varieties, as well as grasshoppers, beetles, and crickets, are also eaten. When other food is scarce, carrion and offal is acceptable, and the redtail has been known to eat dead crows. Poultry killing is more prevalent among the young hawks presumably because they lack the skill to catch other prey.

Although generally silent when attacking his prey, the redtail is by no means voiceless and frequently utters a piercing, whistling scream, sounding somewhat like a shrill *"k-e-e-e-e- e-e-e-r, K-e-e-e-e e-e-e-er."*

**Breeding.** The redtail breeds over most of its range. The nest is usually situated well up in the forks of a tall tree and is built of sticks and lined with bark, small twigs, moss, and often bits of hemlock. The birds use the same nest year after year, adding more material annually until it becomes a very bulky structure.

The eggs, usually two to four, are whitish or

bluish-white, sometimes plain but more often heavily splotched with irregular markings of brown, red, or gray.

**Range and Distribution.** The range extends along the Canadian North, from Saskatchewan to Newfoundland and down the Great Plains in the West to the Gulf of Mexico. In the East it extends southward to the Greater Antilles.

The following sub-species have the same general habits and characteristics as the foregoing type. They differ chiefly in coloration or in limited ranges.

### ALASKA RED-TAILED HAWK *Buteo borealis alascensis*

This sub-species is somewhat larger and darker colored than the typical redtail. The range is confined to southern Alaska from Yakutat Bay to the Sitka Islands.

### FLORIDA RED-TAILED HAWK *Buteo borealis umbrinus*

This sub-species is similar to the common eastern redtail but is slightly larger. The tail is marked by broken bands of dark brown and the throat and center abdomen are heavily striped or banded with deep brown. This bird is confined to southern Florida, the Isle of Pines, and Cuba.

### HARLAN'S HAWK *Buteo borealis harlani*

This is a southern version of the common eastern redtail. The upper parts are a darker grayish-brown and the under parts are white or nearly so, irregularly spotted on the abdomen with grayish-brown. The tail is densely mottled with black, brown, and white. These hawks are widely distributed from southern Pennsylvania, Illinois, and Kansas south to the Gulf of Mexico, and eastward to northern Florida.

### KRIDER'S HAWK *Buteo borealis krideri*

This hawk is very similar to the common eastern redtail except for being nearly all white on the under parts. The range extends from Minnesota to Texas, through the central states eastward as far as Illinois. This hawk has upper parts similar to the eastern redtailed, gray with irregular markings of brown, buff, and white; but a marked distinction is in the under parts, which on Krider's hawk is nearly all white. The range of the Krider's hawk extends northward from Texas to southern Canada, and eastward at times to Illinois.

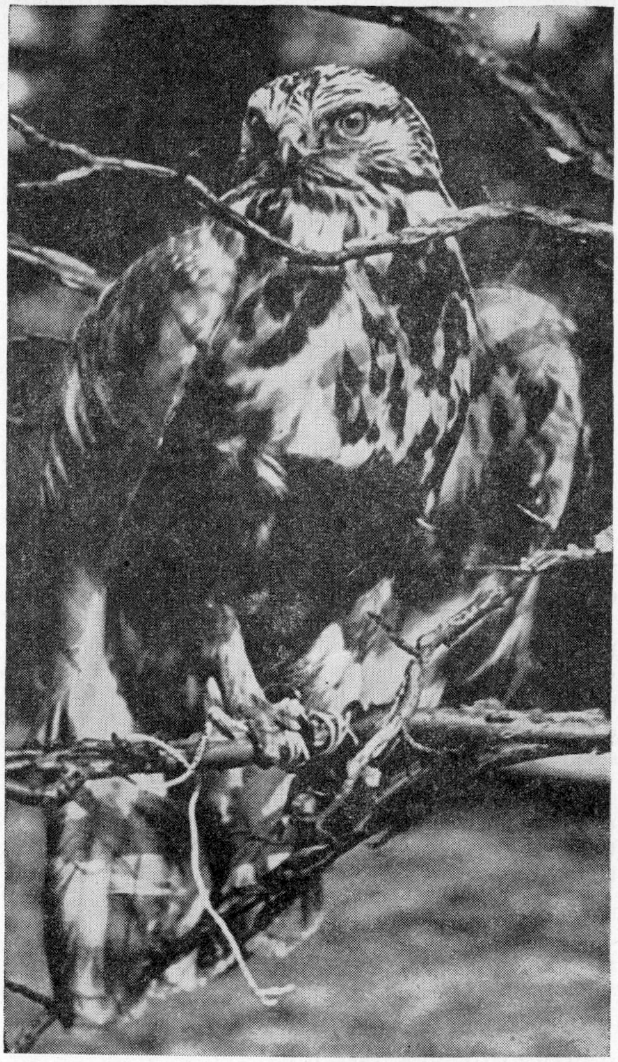

Natl. Audubon Society.
PLATE IX. Rough-Legged Hawk.

### WESTERN RED-TAILED HAWK *Buteo borealis calurus*

The plumage of this sub-species is generally darker in tone and the tail shows two or three dark bars. The under parts are darker and much more heavily marked with bars and spots of dark brown. The range is generally confined to the western coast from Alaska southward to Central America. A few birds occur from time to time as far east as Ontario and Illinois.

## (AMERICAN) ROUGH-LEGGED HAWK *Buteo lagopus sancti-johannis*

COMMON NAMES: American Rough-Legged Hawk, Black Hawk, Mouse Hawk, Rough-Leg, Rough-Legged Buzzard.

**History.** The rough-legged hawk differs from all other American hawks by being a truly migratory bird and nearly nocturnal in habits. These birds leave their summer homes in the Far North and travel southward in advance of the heavy snows. They are not affected by cold and can withstand severe northern winters if the snow is not too deep to rob them of meadow mice and ground squirrels which are their chief items of food.

**Identification.** These hawks achieve their most common name by having the legs completely feathered to the toes. The males average about 21 inches in length, the females about 23 inches. They are slender, slightly built hawks with longer and more pointed wings than the other *Buteos*. This species is more inclined to melanism than any others of the hawk family, and there are many variations in plumage between the established normal phase and the dark or melanistic phase. These variations are common to both sexes and occur at all ages.

The normal adult male and female are grayish-brown above, each feather margined with light reddish-brown, and whitish. The base of the tail is white or light buff blending to grayish-brown toward the end where it is marked by two or three transverse bars of gray and white. The wings are similarly barred with gray and whitish.

The under parts vary from dull white to reddish and are irregularly streaked and spotted with dusky. These dusky markings become an almost solid patch across the abdomen. The leg coverings or "pants" are finely streaked with elongated dusky markings.

In the various stages between the normal and the dark phase, the plumage tends to become progressively darker in tone and the markings less conspicuous.

The plumage in the melanistic phase is entirely dull black or brownish-black except the primaries and the tail feathers, which are crossed by grayish or whitish bars.

The young are similar to the adults except that the tail is plain grayish-brown unbroken by transverse bars and ends in a narrower white tip. The under parts have heavier dusky markings, and the dark band across the abdomen is wider and more solid in color.

**Characteristics.** The rough-legged hawk frequents meadows or areas lightly covered by brush and low trees. His flight is as noiseless as an owl's and, like that bird, he prefers twilight or semi-darkness for his hunting. These birds frequently travel in pairs, and on moonlight nights may be observed sweeping silently over the snowy wastes and swooping down to pick up field mice that run over the crust.

Because of its semi-nocturnal habits, the rough-legged hawk is rarely seen by the casual observer. Its flight is more labored than that of most hawks and is accomplished by much wing motion as though it were an effort to stay aloft.

The rough-legged hawk rarely utters a sound except during the mating and nesting season, at which times he gives vent to a short, piercing call at intervals.

It is extremely unfortunate that these hawks are not more plentiful, for they are of inestimable value to the farmer and do not prey on game birds or mammals.

**Breeding.** The nest resembles that of other hawks and is constructed of large twigs, grasses, and other vegetable matter cleverly laced together. It is usually located in a tall tree but may sometimes be built on a rocky ledge. The average two or three eggs are a dull grayish-white to buffy, and are sprinkled with deep brown.

**Range and Distribution.** The rough-legged hawk breeds from the Aleutian Islands, northwestern Alaska, the Arctic coast, and northern Ungava, south to British Columbia, southern Mackenzie, and Newfoundland. During the winter months only, these birds descend into the United States where they range in limited numbers as far south as Virginia in the east and westward through the central states to central Colorado.

## FERRUGINOUS ROUGH-LEGGED HAWK

*Buteo regalis*

COMMON NAMES: Same as those used for the American rough-legged hawk.

This hawk is similar in habits and appearance to the American rough-legged hawk, but is a larger western variety which rarely occurs east of the Mississippi River.

The name *ferruginous,* meaning resembling iron-rust in color, refers to the plumage of this bird. The markings are similar to those on the American rough-legged hawk but the under parts are lighter.

Like its western relative, it feeds on mice when they are available, but throughout most of its range ground squirrels are the chief item of food. Rabbits, prairie dogs, and pocket gophers are also eaten.

**Range and Distribution.** These hawks breed from southern Washington, southwestern Saskatchewan, and Manitoba to southern California, Colorado, Utah, and Kansas. In the winter they range over most of the western United States as far south as northern Mexico.

## SENNETT'S WHITE-TAILED HAWK

*Buteo albicaudatus sennetti*

COMMON NAME: Whitetail.

**History.** This member of the *Buteo* clan is better known in Mexico than in the United States, although numbers of the birds occur in Texas. It is one of the most beautiful of hawks, and like most of its relatives, it does more good than harm by preying on rodents and insects.

**Identification.** The males of this species average about 23 inches in length and have a wingspread of more than 50 inches. The female is an inch or two longer and has a correspondingly greater spread of wings. An adult male has upper parts of slaty ash-gray, tinged on the shoulders with a conspicuous patch of reddish-brown. The lower back, or rump, and the tail are white. The latter carries a wide black band near the tip and is generally marked by irregular transverse bars of blackish. The under parts are dazzling white faintly barred with dark on the sides and thigh feathers. The corners of the bill and the feet are yellow; the claws are black. The bill is dusky horn-color and the cere is greenish.

Adult females are similar in coloration but the general tone is darker and the reddish-brown wing patch larger.

The young birds are clear, deep brown above, the sides of the head and the area over the eye being narrowly streaked with white. The throat is also streaked with whitish. There is a wide streak of white below the eye and the leading edges of the wings are white. The under parts are white with irregular heart-shaped markings of dark brown. The tail is ashy-gray blending to brownish-gray toward the end and is tipped with white. The tail is sometimes marked with faint transverse bars of dusky. The legs and feet are yellow, the claws black. The cere is red.

**Characteristics.** In general characteristics and feeding habits of this hawk are very similar to those of the other *Buteos.* The nest is typical of the genus, but is usually built closer to the ground than that of other hawks and is rarely lined. The two or three eggs are grayish white lightly splotched with yellow-brown.

**Range and Distribution.** These birds range from southern central Texas southward through Mexico and Central America into the northern part of South America.

## SHARP-SHINNED HAWK

*Accipiter velox velox*

COMMON NAMES: Bird Hawk, Bullet Hawk, Chicken Hawk, Little Blue Darter, Pigeon Hawk, Sparrow Hawk.

**History.** This rather small hawk is readily acknowledged to be one of the most destructive birds in North America. Along with his larger relatives, the Cooper's hawk and the still larger goshawk, he forms a trio of marauders that carry on a relentless war against game birds, songbirds, and domestic poultry.

**Identification.** Not much larger than a robin, the female of this species measures from 12 to 14 inches and the smaller male rarely exceeds 11 inches. The short, rounded wings have a wing-span varying from 22 to 28 inches. The rather long tail ends in a square tip which appears slightly notched, especially when folded. (NOTE: Large specimens of the sharp-shinned hawk closely resemble small Cooper's hawks, but the latter has a rounded tail.)

The upper parts are dark bluish-gray; the tail and primaries often inclined to brownish. The tail is barred by four wide and conspicuous brownish-black bands. The terminal band is wider than the others and the first band is so hidden by the upper tail coverts that only three bars are generally visible.

Under the dark feathers on the crown there is a layer of pure white feathers which show through

Allan D. Cruickshank, from Natl. Audubon Society.
PLATE X. Sennet's White-Tailed Hawk.

Photo by George Goodwin.
PLATE XI. Sharp-Shinned Hawk.

when the crown feathers are erected. The eye is yellow, as is the cere at the base of the bill. The upper sides of the head are a pale reddish-brown. The lower cheeks, chin, and throat are white penciled with fine blackish shaftings. The lower parts are white marked with numerous transverse bars of reddish-brown. These barred markings are more predominant on the flanks and leg coverings where they appear as connected arrowhead shapes.

The bill is dark yellow-brown, the legs and feet yellow, and the claws are black.

The young, even after reaching the hunting stage, appear so different from the adults as to warrant a separate description. The upper parts are dull brown, the feathers being edged or bordered with dull, light reddish-yellow brown. The rump and shoulders are marked with white spots. The tail is similar to that of the adults but generally more brownish. The under parts are dull white or tawny light buff, heavily streaked with either dull or reddish-brown. The cheeks and neck bear very narrow streakings and there is a conspicuous light stripe over the eye.

**Characteristics.** The list of birds upon which the sharpshin preys is too long to be included here. He commonly feeds on all small birds from the various quail and doves to the tiny wrens and warblers. Unfortunately, the bulk of his diet is made up of the most beneficial, insect-killing birds within his range.

In general, his hunting technique is the same as that of the goshawk and the Cooper's. His swift darting attack, usually accompanied by shrill cries, has earned him the name of "bullet-hawk" among others. A glance at the common names above will give a good indication of his activities. Although not so great a menace to poultry as the larger Cooper's hawk, he does prey on enough small chickens to share one of the common names with the latter.

**Breeding.** The nest, like that of the goshawk, is usually located near the very top of a tall conifer; more rarely it may be built on a rocky ledge. The usual four or five eggs are dull greenish or bluish white, heavily spotted with various shades of brown.

**Range and Distribution.** This hawk is widely distributed throughout the United States and Canada. It breeds from northern Alaska to Newfoundland, southward over the entire range as far south as Panama.

## SPARROW HAWK

*Falco sparverius sparverius*

Common Names: American Kestrel, American Sparrow Hawk, Grasshopper Hawk, Killy Hawk, Mouse Hawk, Rusty-Crowned Falcon, Short-Winged Hawk, Windhover.

**History.** The sparrow hawk is not only the smallest and most beautifully colored of all the hawks but is the only member of the falcon tribe which may be considered as almost wholly beneficial.

**Identification.** These hawks seldom exceed 10 inches in length and the female is a trifle larger than the male. There is color variation between the sexes.

Males. The upper part of the head is slaty-blue except for a patch of reddish-brown on the crown. The chin and sides of the head are whitish with a black streak below the eye and a dusky streak bordering the white area behind the eye. The nape of the neck is buffy with a dusky spot on each side. The back is a rich reddish-brown barred with black. The wing coverts are bluish-gray marked with wedge-shaped spots of black. The primaries are brownish-gray barred with yellowish-white. The tail is a warm reddish-brown with a wide bar of black near the end and a white tip.

The chest and breast are creamy buff, the under parts whitish. The lower breast and abdomen are dotted with round black spots. On the flanks these markings become paler and more wedge-shaped. The under-tail coverts are pure white. The cere, a ring around the eye, and the legs and feet are yellow; the claws are black. The bill is bluish horn-color and the eye is deep brown.

Females. The head covering is similar to that of the males except for the addition of fine black streaks on the upper head and nape. The entire upper body, including the wing coverts, is a rich cinnamon-brown with regular barrings of black. The tail is reddish-brown with five or six broken bands of black and a wide black band at the terminal end. All the tail feathers are tipped with white.

The chest and lower parts are creamy-white or pale buff marked with elongated streaks of light brown. The thigh coverings are whitish and without markings. The legs, feet, and other features are the same as those of the male.

**Characteristics.** This common little hawk is often seen perched on a pole, wire, or dead tree overlooking a meadow where it finds the grasshoppers, crickets, and other large insects which are its chief source of food.

Pennington Sefton, from Natl. Audubon Society.
Plate XII. **Sparrow Hawk.**

The term "windhover" refers to the peculiar manner of flight while hunting, for these birds can hover or remain almost stationary over a spot for a considerable time. A fixed position is maintained by the rapidly beating wings while the bird scans the ground below for some choice morsel of food.

In the summer the bulk of the diet consists of various insects, and in the late autumn and winter field mice and common house mice replace the insects as food. During the nesting season when these hawks have less time to hunt for food, they eat some small birds and occasionally they may pick up a young chicken but for the most part their food habits are beneficial to man.

Another common name, "killy hawk," stems from the shrill, ringing call, *"killy, killy, killy, killy,"* which these birds frequently utter.

**Breeding.** Unlike most hawks, these do not bother to construct a regular nest and the four or five eggs may be deposited in unusual places. Hollow trees in an old orchard are often favored, but abandoned woodpecker homes, cavities in rocks, a hole in a bank, cornices of buildings, or even birdhouses may be used. The eggs vary in color from creamy-white to reddish-ochre and are irregularly marked and spotted with various shades of reddish-brown; sometimes the markings are so thick as to virtually obscure the basic color of the shell.

**Range and Distribution.** These hawks enjoy a wider distribution than almost any other species. They range from the upper Yukon and Hudson Bay area to the Gulf of Mexico east of the Rocky Mountains. They are common throughout the eastern states and winter from New Jersey southward and across the United States to Texas and the Gulf states except Florida.

### DESERT SPARROW HAWK
*Falco sparverius phalaena*

This is a larger and lighter-colored variation of the eastern species. The range embraces a strip from British Columbia and Montana southward through southern California, New Mexico, and western Texas into northwestern Mexico and eastward to Colorado, Wyoming, and western Nebraska.

### LITTLE SPARROW HAWK
*Falco sparverius paulus*

The little sparrow hawk is a southern relative of the common eastern variety, being smaller in form and darker in coloration. The wings and tail are shorter than in the typical specimen. The range includes central Alabama, westward across the southern portions of the Gulf states and into Florida.

### SAN LUCAS SPARROW HAWK
*Falco sparverius peninsularis*

This is similar in nearly every respect to the eastern sparrow hawk but is smaller in size and paler in color. The range is limited to the southern portion of Lower California.

## SWAINSON'S HAWK
*Buteo swainsoni (Bonaparte)*

Common Names: Black Hawk, Brown Hawk, Hen Hawk.

**History.** Like the red-shouldered hawk which it often resembles, this western variety belongs to a class of truly beneficial hawks. It is comparatively tame and unsuspicious of man, and lives at peace with its smaller neighbors. It is not uncommon to find smaller birds nesting in the same tree with a pair of these hawks, which is evidence that they have no fear of being eaten.

**Identification.** Few birds of any species exhibit a wider variation in plumage than Swainson's hawk. Not only are the sexes different in coloration, but there are various phases ranging from light to dark for both the male and the female. The birds found in the northeastern states are especially of the darker phase.

What has been established as normal plumage for the adult male appears somewhat as follows: The upper parts are a dark grayish-brown, the feathers having buffy edges which create a slightly mottled appearance. The tail has numerous narrow, grayish-white bars and a narrow white tip. The forehead, chin, and throat are white, the upper breast is light reddish-brown with black shaftings, and the rest of the under parts are whitish or pale flesh-color barred and spotted with brown. The eye is brown, the legs, feet, and cere yellow, and the claws and bill are bluish-black.

The average adult female is similar in coloration except for the breast, which is grayish-brown.

In the dark phase both sexes are colored alike. The entire plumage is a deep, dusky brown.

Immature birds have dark brown plumage above with each feather margined with light yellowish-brown. The head, neck, and under parts are creamy buff or buffy white. The wings and tail show distinct barrings of darker brown.

**Characteristics.** Swainson's hawk frequents the broad plains and open country of the West where it cruises in slow circles over the prairie in search of

Natl. Audubon Society.

Plate XIII. Swainson's Hawk.

its favorite prey, the spotted gopher and various mice. Other small rodents, as well as grasshoppers and large black crickets, round out its somewhat restricted menu.

**Breeding.** These hawks are less particular about the location of their nests than is usual with *Buteos*. Generally the nest is placed well out toward the end of a horizontal limb in a tall tree, but it may also be built on a ledge, on the ground, or in fairly low bushes. Small branches and twigs are used in the construction and it is lined with grass, leaves, and occasionally a few feathers. Old nests are often reused for several seasons.

The eggs, usually two to four, are white, buffy white or greenish, and are sometimes spotted with reddish-brown, but may often be plain.

**Range and Distribution.** This bird breeds from the arctic regions of North America southward to the Argentine. It is one of the most common hawks of the western plains and is particularly abundant over the sage wastes of Oregon, Washington, Colorado, and Idaho.

## ZONE-TAILED HAWK

*Buteo abbreviatus cabanis*

COMMON NAMES: None so far as known.

**Identification.** The zone-tailed hawk is a slim, slightly built hawk about 19 inches in length with an unusual wingspread of from 45 to 53 inches. The females are slightly larger than the males, but both sexes are alike in coloration.

The whole body is shiny black except for a whitish forehead. The upper surface of the tail is marked by three transverse bars of bluish-gray and ends in a narrow white tip. The under-tail surface shows three pure white markings and the undersides of the wings are barred and spotted with white. The legs and feet are yellowish, the bill dark horn-color.

Immature birds are similar to the adults, but the body feathers have white bases which partially show through the dark plumage. The tail is banded irregularly with numerous bars and the inner webs of the feathers are mostly white.

**Characteristics.** Not much is known about the habits and characteristics of these birds. They are said to prefer the canyon country where a small stream flows between the steep, narrow walls. Their food consists chiefly of small mammals, large insects, frogs, and lizards. They frequent the banks of streams and nest in cottonwoods or other trees near the water. The nest is placed at varying heights above the ground, seldom lower than 15 feet and sometimes as high as 50 feet. The construction is typical of the hawk family, chiefly sticks and twigs and of a coarse, bulky appearance, but the nest is usually lined with grass or Spanish moss. The two to four eggs are dull white splotched with warm brown at the large end.

**Range and Distribution.** These birds are found chiefly in southern Arizona and southwestern Texas, and range southward through Mexico and Central America to Venezuela and British Guiana.

# SMALL MAMMALS

In addition to the small mammals which furnish sport for the upland game hunter, and those which can definitely be classified as predators, there is another group which play an important part in the wildlife picture. These mammals are extremely important to the trapper, but are not hunted with gun and dog, and therefore cannot properly be included under the broad, general heading of "Small Game."

No volume such as this would be complete without details on the characteristics, habits, and identification of these small mammals, for they play an important role in the life of the game birds and animals with which the hunter is concerned. Most of them are guilty of predation, to a greater or lesser degree, whereas some of them—the beaver, for example—tip the balance wheel of nature in the opposite direction. The porcupine, vandal that he is, can be important to the woodsman on occasion, and there are many recorded instances in which the tough, strong flesh of this animal has kept life in a hunter when other resources have failed. The man with no weapon other than an ax or club can always knock a "quill-pig" in the head, and for this reason many hunters permit these pests to go their grunting, complaining way unmolested.

Although many of these small mammals—the weasel and mink, for example—take a rather high toll of small game, many biologists insist that the part they play is important to the over-all game picture. Kill off all these predators, it is explained, and the very animals and birds you desire to protect by such measures will suffer greater losses due to disease. The weak and the diseased are the easiest prey for the predator, and in eliminating them the predators insure the survival of the fittest.

## BADGER

*Taxidea taxus*

Common Names: None so far as known; possibly some purely local terms.

**History.** The name badger is a modern version of the earlier term *badgeard,* which was thought to be of probable French origin and a combination of "badge" and "ard" in reference to the white marking on the animal's head.

During the early 19th century the spectacle of "badger baiting" or "badger drawing" was quite popular in Great Britain. One or more dogs were turned loose in a pit where a small barrel or other artificial hole was provided for the badger. The objective for the dogs was to pull or "draw" the fighting badger from his hole. This form of

U. S. Forest Service.

**Plate I. Badger.**

"sport" was banned in the British Isles about 1850. The term "to badger," meaning to worry unmercifully, was a figure of speech derived from this ancient game.

*Taxus* is a member of the family *Mustelidae,* the genus *Taxidae,* and is the second largest of the weasel tribe in North America. Originally he roamed from the Peace River country in Canada all the way to Mexico and from Michigan and Kansas to the Pacific coast. He gradually became extinct over much of this area and is greatly reduced in numbers over his remaining range.

**Identification.** The badger is built along somewhat the same lines as the wolverine, with short, stout legs and a thick, heavy body. The average adult is about 28 inches long and weighs around 15 to 20 pounds. The feet are equipped with strong sharp claws which aid the animal in his constant digging. The long and shaggy pelage is grizzled-gray above and black below. The head is black with a white stripe running from the nose, over the top of the head and down the nape of the neck. The lower muzzle, under jaw, and lower cheeks are white, as are the inner ears and an area just in front of each ear. The legs and feet are dark and the short, bushy tail ends in black.

**Characteristics.** Although the badger has somewhat the same physical characteristics as the wolverine he is neither so vicious nor so cunning, and he lacks that animal's capacity for pure cussedness. Left to his own devices, he keeps busy digging out the gophers, prairie dogs, and ground squirrels on which he feeds. He is not lacking in courage, however, and if brought to bay he will charge fearlessly at man or dog and he fights savagely. The badger is especially equipped to put up a determined fight by virtue of having a lower jaw which locks into a cavity in his cranium and permits him to maintain a death grip on his opponent.

Unlike his skulking cousin of the woods, the badger prefers the open plains, prairies, the thinly wooded areas, and farming country. In addition to the rodent pests mentioned above he also eats mice, insects, roots, and occasionally young birds. Actually he renders a great service to the farmer and rancher by keeping down the rodent population, but his services are little appreciated and he is dubbed a nuisance. He captures his prey by digging them out of their dens and holes and in so doing he leaves larger holes, which are often a menace to horse and rider. For this reason ranchers detest him and he is invariably shot whenever they run across him. His hair is used in the manufacture of brushes and for various other purposes; and therefore he is also trapped to some extent for that reason and is becoming very scarce over most of his range.

In the northern part of their habitat badgers hibernate during the winter months. By autumn they become quite fat and before the ground is frozen they dig deep burrows in which to sleep until spring. In the more southerly regions they are usually active the year around.

The young are born late in the spring and cared for by the mother during the early stages of their career. The family breaks up when the youngsters are nearly full grown and each goes his separate way.

Badgers are usually nocturnal in habits but are sometimes seen during the day while foraging for a meal.

**Range and Distribution.** The badger is rather widely but thinly distributed over most of the plains and prairie country west of the Mississippi River. The northern part of the range extends into the Prairie Provinces and the southern portion reaches into Mexico.

# BEAVER

***Castor canadensis***

Common Name: American Beaver.

**History.** To the beaver goes the distinction of having played a greater role in the exploration and settlement of North America than any other wild animal. His fur was so much in demand that companies like the Hudson Bay Company were formed to organize his capture. Of course, other fur-bearers were included in their plans but beaver pelts were the staple of trade. Trappers pushed farther and farther into the wilderness, to be followed shortly by settlers. Explorers made long journeys in search of new beaver country and settlements sprang up in their wake.

The Hudson Bay Company did a very profitable business with the Indian trappers and the ever-popular Hudson Bay blanket was made especially for purposes of barter. Then as now, these blankets were made in various "points" and were known as "one-point," "two-point," "three-point," or "four-point," the difference being largely a matter of size. Originally such blankets were made only in bright colors to attract the Indian fancy, red, yellow, and "candy stripes" being the most popular. Each "point" had a value of one beaver pelt; thus an Indian could have a "two-point" blanket for two pelts, a "three-point" blanket for three pelts, etc.

Fortunes were made by trafficking in the pelts and whole industries became dependent on the beaver as a source of raw material. At one time the hat industry (men's) would use nothing but beaver fur to make fine felt, and the demand became so great that it was trapped to extinction in many places.

When the supply was all but exhausted other animals, notably the muskrat, replaced the beaver as a staple fur for the trade. In sections where he has been given a chance, *Canadensis* has staged a remarkable comeback, and while there will never be anything like the former abundance it is quite possible that he will again assume an important place in the annual fur harvest.

**Identification.** The beaver is the largest of North American rodents. The compact, heavyset body is covered with soft, brown fur, the legs are short and sturdy, and the tail very broad, flat, and scaly. The ears are small, rounded, and set close to the head. The large hind feet are webbed and the claw on the second toe is split, or double. The forefeet are comparatively slender and handlike.

Government of Nova Scotia.

PLATE I. **Beaver—Woods Engineer.**

The average total length is about 45 inches, counting the 10- to 12-inch tail, and the weight averages about 40 pounds. Weights vary according to conditions and time of year. Some adult beavers weigh no more than 30 pounds, while some old males may go over 60 pounds.

The sexes are the same in appearance and although there is no definite seasonal variation, the summer coat often appears worn and dull. The beaver undergoes a "moulting" or shedding process each year in which the long, glossy guard hairs are replaced.

In common with nearly all mammals that spend much time in the water, the beaver has been provided by nature with two coats. The soft, thick undercoat, for warmth, is dull brown to bluish at the base, while the long, shiny overcoat is a rich chestnut or reddish-brown. The head is generally a shade or two lighter than the upper body and the under parts are paler and without the reddish tinge. The tail is blackish and the large front teeth are brilliant orange.

**Characteristics.** The beaver is a model of industry, sagacity, and engineering know-how. These clever animals can quickly change a community to suit their particular mode of living. Aquatic by nature, they seldom venture far from water, but a large portion of their food is obtained on land near a stream, lake, or pond.

*Canadensis* insists upon having a home where the water level will remain consistent, or nearly so, throughout the seasons. Unlike the muskrat, he is capable of creating this desirable condition for himself. To insure the proper level he builds a dam across a stream or at one end of a pond to control the flow. Such dams may vary in length from a few feet to several hundred yards, depending on the terrain and how large an area the beavers wish to flood. Human engineers have long marveled at the beaver's uncanny ability to build such dams at exactly the right point to accomplish his purpose. The structures are made of small logs—which the beaver cuts—reinforced with branches, saplings, and stones. The whole mass is held together with mud, the cement of Beaverdom. The larger logs are towed or floated to the proper place and anchored to the bottom, smaller sticks are carried in the animal's mouth, and the mud, stones, and smaller material are carried in the forepaws.

When completed these dams are many feet thick at the base and so sturdy as to be well-nigh indestructible. The beaver has a keen sense for determining beforehand just how large an area he wishes to flood and the dam is constructed accordingly. This establishes a quiet pond or backwater where the current is sluggish and a mean level is easily maintained.

In the pond thus created the beavers build their houses, or "lodges," of the same kind of material that was used for the dam. They start a foundation on the bottom of the pond and patiently add sticks, stones, mud, and rubbish until a domelike pile rises several feet above the surface of the water. At this point the future home is a solid mass of tightly interlaced logs, twigs, and other material, varying in size from 10 or 12 to more than 20 feet at the base.

Now the beavers return to the bottom at the base of the house and begin cutting two tunnels which will serve as both entrance and exit. These tunnels are started from the outside, and cut through the solid pile at an angle which eventually brings them near the center at a point slightly above the water line. One tunnel curves upward but the second is straight in order to permit the beavers to bring in the lengths of poplar and other saplings upon which they feed during the winter. Where the tunnels nearly converge inside the sticks and debris are gnawed away to form a chamber or room large enough to accommodate the number of beavers that will occupy the house. The room is roughly circular in shape, the ceiling is domed, and the floor is a platform, or shelf, raised above water level and surrounding the water admitted by the two tunnels. This shelf is usually covered with drier rushes and shavings from the peeled sticks (after the beavers have eaten the bark) and serves as a bed or resting place. When the animals wish to go outside they merely plunge into the water in the center of their home and swim out through one or the other of the tunnels.

No air hole is left, but the very top of the house is never plastered with mud and so enough air filters through the lacing of sticks and branches to supply their needs. Thus they have a protective ceiling several feet thick which admits air but shuts out all light and their enemies. In the late autumn the outside of the house is given a fresh coating of mud; when this has frozen the beaver "castle" is virtually impregnable. Once inside, warmed by the heat of their own bodies, the beavers are snug and secure from any attack.

The beaver's principal food is bark, and that of the alder or poplar is preferred. However, he will eat the bark of almost any deciduous tree, as well as the tuberous roots of aquatic plants, grass, and other vegetable matter. After he has eaten the bark from a sapling the remainder is used for construction work on the dam or house. In the autumn the beavers cut a large number of trees having edible bark and store them on the bottom of the pond near their houses. During the winter they swim out beneath the ice and fetch these into their lodges as needed.

The beaver is slow and awkward on land and he dislikes to go far from the security of his pond in order to get food; therefore, when a colony has eaten the trees near the water they often dig canals leading into the woods, down which they can float a fresh supply of logs. The common saying, "busy as a beaver," must be accepted with reservations, for despite the popular belief, a beaver never works unless he has to. When building a dam, or a house, or laying in the winter harvest he toils long and earnestly, but as soon as the chores are finished he can be as lazy as a sloth. Much of his idle time is taken up with grooming his fur. This is not for the sake of appearance but to get rid of the lice with which he is invariably infested. The double toes on the hind feet serve as combs to straighten the hair and comb out the insect pests.

Another popular fallacy is the belief that a beaver always cuts a tree in such a way that it will fall into the water. Smart as he is, *Canadensis* often makes the mistake of picking out a tree which after hours of patient gnawing merely leans against the surrounding trees and refuses to topple, or else falls the wrong way so that he is forced to cut it in several pieces in order to get it to the water. The felling of a single tree represents considerable labor. The beaver approaches the base of the tree, squats on his haunches with his broad tail for a prop, and begins to gnaw. His strong, sharp teeth bite deeply into the wood and he pries out good-sized chips with a violent, jerking motion of his head. When the tree begins to creak and lean he usually gives a warning slap with his tail and scrambles out of the way until it hits the ground. He or his companions do not always escape, however, and occasionally one is pinned beneath a falling tree.

A colony of beavers set a fine example of true community spirit. It is "all for one and one for all" in their daily life. The first beaver to scent or sight danger sounds the alarm for all. If swimming, or in the water, his broad tail spats the surface with a resounding slap and every beaver within earshot immediately disappears. While the colony works, sentinel beavers stand guard against surprise attacks. Each member of the colony is ready at all times to do whatever is necessary for the welfare of the whole group.

The beaver is nocturnal in habits but may sometimes be seen during the day, especially if repairs are needed on the dam or there is some other emergency. In communities where they are not molested they become accustomed to man and often go about their business of living without fear.

Nearly all the larger predators are beaver enemies. The wolverine, bear, lynx, wolf, coyote, and otter are among the worst, and hawks and eagles sometimes swoop down on the young beavers. Except for the otter, of course, the beaver escapes most of his foes by diving into the water. During the winter, although he does not hibernate, he remains more or less inactive within his stout fortress and offers little opportunity for a meal.

**Breeding.** Being a solid citizen, the beaver is monogamous and mates for life. Mating usually takes place in late January or the first part of February and the kits are born in April or May. While the mother is busy with her brood the male leaves the lodge and either wanders aimlessly about or goes to visit another colony. Sometimes he digs a bank den and sets up bachelor's quarters for the summer. He returns to the lodge in the autumn and the family remains together until after the kits are born the following year. The average litter consists of four but may be any number from two to six, and rarely eight. The young beavers leave the home pond in their second summer and go in search of mates. They may return to the colony, mated, but more often they select a new site and begin a colony of their own.

**Range and Distribution.** The range extends over most of North America from Labrador and Alaska to southern Texas. The distribution is scattered and spotty over much of this area.

There are several species and sub-species of the genus *Castor* that differ slightly from the typical *Canadensis* in coloration and size, and occupy different ranges. They are as follows:

## CANADIAN BEAVER

*Castor canadensis canadensis*

This species is most widely distributed throughout North America and is the beaver that was the backbone of the early fur trade. History, pelage, and characteristics are as described above.

The range extends from all but the northern tip of Labrador across to the Arctic coast of the Yukon and reaches as far south as North Carolina on the east coast and to northern Oregon in the west.

## ADMIRALTY BEAVER *Castor canadensis phoeus*

In this species, the pelage on the upper parts is dark brown, the long hairs nearly black. The head and shoulders are somewhat lighter; the ears are black. Total length is about 40 inches; the tail is 10 inches long by about 5 inches wide. Its range covers only Admiralty Island, Alaska.

## BROAD-TAILED BEAVER; SONORA BEAVER

*Castor canadensis frondator*

In this species the pelage has upper parts russet, and sides duller. The feet are reddish-brown. This variety is larger than the typical *Canadensis* and has a broader tail. Total length is 45 to 46 inches; the tail is 11½ inches long by over 6 inches wide. It ranges over the southwestern states from Mexico northward to Wyoming on the east and through Montana to central Idaho on the west.

## CAROLINA BEAVER

*Castor canadensis carolinensis*

The Carolina beaver's pelage is light brown on the back, blending to reddish-yellow toward the tail. Total length is 45 inches; the tail is about 11 inches long by 6 wide. It ranges from North Carolina to northern Florida, along the Gulf coast to eastern Texas.

## GOLDEN BEAVER

*Castor subauratus subauratus*

The golden beaver has a pelage that is ochreaceous-brown above, darker below. Total length is 47 inches; the tail about 13 inches long by more than 6 wide. Its range is confined to the San Joaquin Valley, California.

## MISSOURI RIVER BEAVER

*Castor canadensis missouriensis*

In this species the upper parts are pale brown, under parts dull brownish-gray. It is somewhat smaller than a typical *Canadensis,* averaging only about 30 inches. Its range is along the headwaters of the Missouri River, north from Nebraska and as far west as Montana.

## NEWFOUNDLAND BEAVER *Castor coecator*

This beaver resembles the typical *Canadensis* in coloration, but the body is slightly smaller than typical. Its range is Newfoundland.

## PACIFIC BEAVER *Castor canadensis pacificus*

The pelage of this species is glossy, dark reddish-brown above, with under parts duller. It is the

Government of Nova Scotia.

**PLATE II. The beaver can build a warm house as well as a good dam.**

largest of the beavers, measuring over 46 inches total length; its tail is nearly 12 inches long by 5 wide. It ranges along the Pacific slope from Alaska to southern Oregon.

### RIO GRANDE BEAVER *Castor canadensis mexicanus*

This beaver's upper parts are at all seasons a dull russet or reddish-brown, relatively bright on the top of the head and normally a rather pale russet on the cheeks and lower back. Its total length runs from 43 to 44 inches; the tail is 12 inches long. It ranges along tributaries of the Rio Grande through New Mexico and Texas.

### SHASTA BEAVER *Castor subauratus shastensis*

The Shasta beaver's pelage is similar to that of the golden beaver. Its range is believed limited to Shasta County, California, along the eastern slope of the main Sierra Nevada range.

### TEXAS BEAVER *Castor canadensis texensis*

This beaver's pelage and size are very similar to those of the broad-tailed (or Sonora) beaver. It ranges along tributaries of the Rio Colorado in eastern Texas.

### VANCOUVER ISLAND BEAVER *Castor canadensis leucodonta*

This beaver's pelage is similar to that of the typical *Canadensis* but is usually paler, inclined to cinnamon. Total length is 46 inches. Its range is limited to Vancouver Island, British Columbia.

### WOODS BEAVER *Castor canadensis michiganensis*

The pelage of this beaver is a dark, somber brown on the upper parts, and deep reddish-brown on the top of the head and cheeks. The ears and feet are blackish. Total length runs from 47 to 48 inches, and average weight about 58 pounds. Its range is the Upper Peninsula region of Michigan.

## FISHER *Martes pennanti pennanti*

Common Names: Black Cat, Black Fox, Fisher, Marten, Pekan, Pennant.

**History.** The fisher, although actually a large marten, earned his name because of his fondness for fish. Like his smaller cousin, he once enjoyed a much wider range over the wooded regions of North America but is now becoming scarcer as the forests disappear.

**Identification.** The fisher is similar in structure to the American marten but is much larger, more powerful, and of a darker color. The fur is long, coarser than the marten's, and very durable.

U. S. Fish and Wildlife Service.

Plate I. Fisher.

The color of the coat varies with different specimens from an ashy-brown to nearly black and is darkest along the dorsal portion. The legs and feet are blackish and the tail, which is longer than the marten's, is bushy, black, and tapering. The shoulders, back of the neck, and top of the head are gray with a mixture of darker hairs and the throat, chest, and belly are dark brown.

An adult male is from 36 to 38 inches long and weighs from 8 to 12 pounds. Some large specimens, however, weigh as much as 17 or 18 pounds. The females average somewhat smaller. Both sexes are alike in coloration and there is no obvious seasonal change in the pelage.

**Characteristics.** The fisher prefers to be near a stream, lake, or swamp although he is by no means so aquatic as the mink. In fact, it is said by some observers that the fisher has no more liking for water than the average house cat. However, he does like fish and frogs and manages to get them without swimming like the mink or otter. The bulk of his diet consists of small mammals and birds, with possibly a few nuts and berries when other food is scarce. He is adept at killing the porcupine without getting full of quills and so agile that he can catch and kill his cousin the pine marten. He can leap from limb to limb like a squirrel and spends as much time aloft as he does on the ground.

When chased by dogs he will tree like a raccoon but if cornered he puts up a terrific battle and can kill a dog. It is claimed that he can also kill the raccoon, the fox, and even a grown lynx.

He is nocturnal in habits and seldom goes about in the daylight. He is cunning and difficult to trap, but like his larger relative, the wolverine, he sometimes raids a trap line and destroys animals that have been caught.

Except for man he has few enemies because he is too quick and agile for the larger predators and he is so powerful that none of the smaller animals dare to attack him.

**Breeding.** The female makes her den or nest in a hollow tree some distance from the ground. About the first of May she bears from one to five young; the average litter is three. Like those of the pine marten, the young are blind at birth and the mother cares for them until they are nearly full grown.

**Range and Distribution.** These animals range from the State of Maine northward through the Province of Quebec, and westward through Saskatchewan where they go as far north as the sixtieth parallel. They reach to the Pacific coast through British Columbia and range southward along the Rocky Mountains to Yellowstone National Park. They are becoming extremely rare throughout their entire range.

## MARTEN

*Martes americana americana*

Common Names: American Marten, American Sable, Hudson Bay Sable, Pine Marten.

**History.** The American marten is a close relative of the Russian sable and, as may be noted from the common names above, is frequently referred to as sable in the fur trade. The pelt is valuable and these animals contribute a considerable amount to the trapper's income annually. Like many other forest creatures, they were once found throughout the heavily wooded portions of northern North America but they resented the presence of man and quickly disappeared from the settled areas. Today they are found only in the more remote sections of the timber lands.

**Identification.** The marten is one of the weasel clan, with a body slightly smaller than the common house cat and a medium-short bushy tail. Like the weasel's, its body is long and lithe, the limbs are short, and the five toes on each foot end in sharp slender claws. The soles of the feet are covered with a dense growth of hair. The head is small, and the ears are broad, rounded, and prominent.

The soft, rich pelage is a shiny yellowish-brown mixed with dark brown hairs. The color varies somewhat with different specimens and may be any shade from a warm yellow-brown—almost olive—to a pale buffy-brown. The legs and tail are invariably darker than the rest of the body. The ears are edged with whitish and the top of the head varies from brown to nearly white. The under parts are warmer in tone and there is an irregular area of buffy-yellow on the throat and chest.

There is an obvious seasonal change in the pelage and the sexes resemble each other in coloration. The males, however, are nearly one-third larger than the females.

**Characteristics.** The marten is largely arboreal in habits although he does take some of his prey on the ground. His long slender claws and agile body permit him to climb and travel through the treetops as well as the squirrel upon which he feeds. His agility is his best protection from his enemies and he manages to escape from all but his cousin the fisher, and more rarely the lynx and the great horned owl.

Besides the squirrels that furnish much of his food, he also feeds on other small rodents such as mice, chipmunks, and rabbits. Grouse and other birds form part of his diet, as do a few reptiles, frogs, and insects. He is said to feed on nuts, fruits, and berries to some extent, with a preference for the berries of the mountain ash, but since he is almost wholly carnivorous by nature it is doubtful that he resorts to such food unless nothing else is available.

One of his favorite haunts is the dense pine forest, hence the name pine marten by which he is commonly known. He is both nocturnal and diurnal in habit, but he is so shy and secretive in his movements that he is seldom seen. Although he is extremely wary of man he has a streak of innate curiosity which makes him rather easy to trap. He does not seem to connect a trap with mankind and is singularly unsuspicious and ready to take the bait.

He possesses the same evil temper as the rest of his tribe and is ferocious in his killing. Observers claim that he snarls, growls, and hisses when angry and is dangerous when trapped or cornered.

Martens mate in the late winter or early spring and the young are generally born toward the end of April. The litter varies from one to five, with three or four being about average. The female builds a nest in a hollow tree, often enlarging the den of some squirrel that has furnished a meal. On rare occasions she may select a ground burrow, but the tree nest is most common. The young are born blind and are helpless for about four weeks, during which time the mother nurses and cares for them. When they are able to get about she instructs them in the rudiments of living and as soon as they are fully grown the family splits up. The juveniles closely resemble their parents in their first autumn.

**Range and Distribution.** Martens are found in limited numbers throughout the forested parts of northern North America. The American marten ranges across eastern North America from Labrador to the shores of Hudson Bay as far north as there are thick forests and south to the mountains of Virginia. The western limit of the species is about Minnesota.

There are several sub-species which differ somewhat in minor details of appearence and have definite ranges as follows:

### ALASKA MARTEN *Martes americana actuosa*

This variety is distinguished from the typical *Americana* by being larger and paler in color. The upper parts are a light brown blending to a darker shade toward the rear of the body. The shoulders are inclined to grayish and the head is a mixture of gray and brown. The chest patch is a pale creamy-buff. The range of this type extends from the coastal mountains of British Columbia and Alaska eastward to Saskatchewan and as far north as the Barren Grounds.

### BRITISH COLUMBIA MARTEN *Martes americana abietinoides*

This type is somewhat similar in appearance to the Hudson Bay variety but the upper parts are a richer seal-brown and the entire head is grizzly-gray. This type is commonly found in the Gold and Selkirk Mountains and the interior regions of British Columbia.

### HUDSON BAY MARTEN *Martes americana abieticola*

The specimen is larger than the typical *Americana* and somewhat darker in coloration. The fur down the middle of the back is quite dark and the tail is nearly black at the tip. The face and cheeks are a grizzled grayish-brown. The ears are edged with white and there is an irregular yellowish patch on the chest. These martens are found from Saskatchewan to the western shores of Hudson Bay as far north as the Arctic limit of timber.

### KENAI MARTEN *Martes americana kenaiensis*

This is a smaller variety than *Actuosa,* with a longer tail and shorter feet. The pelage is darker and there is no light patch on the throat. The top of the head is grizzled and the under parts are darker than the upper. The range is limited to the Kenai Peninsula, Alaska.

U. S. Fish and Wildlife Service.

PLATE I. Marten.

### NEWFOUNDLAND MARTEN *Martes atrata*

This species is about the same size as the typical *Americana* but is much darker colored. The upper parts are a deep rich brown similar to the mink, with the darkest tone on the head, along the back, legs, and tail which is nearly black. The ears are edged with a grayish-white and there is a patch of yellowish-white in front of each opening. Irregular patches of yellowish-buff appear on the throat and belly. As the name implies, its range is confined to Newfoundland.

### NORTH LABRADOR MARTEN *Martes brumalis*

This is a larger and darker marten than the typical *Americana,* with upper parts sometimes blackish. The head is lighter than the back. These animals inhabit the coastal areas of northeastern Labrador and Ungava Bay to the Straits of Belle Isle.

### PACIFIC MARTEN *Martes caurina caurina*

This species is similar to the typical *Americana* but the upper parts are a richer shade of brown and the patches on the throat and breast are larger and brighter. There is usually a sprinkling of white hairs on the upper body; the head is a pale brown, and the under parts are irregularly marked with buffy-orange from the lower jaw to the tail.

The common range is along the coastal areas of northern California, Oregon, Washington, and British Columbia as far east as the Cascade River.

### QUEEN CHARLOTTE MARTEN
*Martes nesophila*

This variety is larger than the typical species but otherwise resembles the *Caurina.* They are usually light colored and have shorter hair. They are to be found only on the Queen Charlotte Islands off British Columbia.

### ROCKY MOUNTAIN MARTEN
*Martes caurina origenes*

In this species the head is darker than the foregoing variety and the top of the head is inclined to grayish. The ears are edged with light tan instead of white. The under parts are brown but marked with large irregular areas of buffy-yellow on the throat, chest, and belly.

The range comprises the southern Rocky Mountain region from New Mexico through Colorado.

### SIERRA MARTEN
*Martes caurina sierrae*

This species is smaller than the preceding ones and paler in color than the typical *Caurina.* The cheeks are much lighter and there is a large patch of light orange-yellow on the chest.

The range includes the forested regions of the Sierra Nevada Mountains northward to the vicinity of Mount Shasta, California.

# MINK
*Lutreola vison*

COMMON NAMES: None.

**History.** The mink belongs to the family *Mustelidae,* along with the martens and weasels. They are placed in a distinct sub-genus, *Lutreola,* which is sometimes given generic rank.

From the very beginning of the fur-trade history of North America the mink has played an important role. One of the larger weasels, this prolific animal was much sought after for his valuable pelt and though not so important as the beaver in the early days, his fur was always highly prized in both America and Europe. The demand finally became so great that fur ranches were established for the sole purpose of breeding and raising these animals in captivity. Much of the present-day fur comes from pen-raised animals but wild mink is still a trapper's prize and constitutes an important part of the fur catch each year. Within recent years coats made of mink fur have become nearly synonymous with diamonds as symbols of wealth and high fashion.

**Identification.** The wild adult mink is about 24 inches long, including a fairly bushy tail which accounts for about one-third of his length. The body is slim and his movements are snakelike. The head appears rather small and the ears are small, rounded, and nearly hidden in the fur. The neck is long and the legs short. The feet are partially webbed and there are five toes on each foot. The female is slightly smaller than the male and weighs correspondingly less.

N. Y. Zoological Society.

PLATE I. Mink.

The pelage of the natural mink is a rich, dark brown. The fur on the back is darker than that on the other portions and the tail is nearly black. The chin is white and there are usually some white spots on the chest. The underfur is soft and thick and the longer guard hairs which are mixed with it have a lustrous sheen.

**Characteristics.** The mink is an excellent swimmer and spends much of his time either in the water or along the banks of streams where he finds his food. On land he either travels with short, quick, nervous steps or lopes along with his back arched like an angry cat. He is carnivorous and his menu consists of frogs, fish, ducks (especially little ones), and occasionally a muskrat. He also eats mice and other small rodents, birds and their eggs, and rabbits. He shares the vicious streak common to all the weasel tribe and does not hesitate to attack an animal larger than himself. Like the skunk and some other members of his clan he possesses a musk-gland through which he emits an offensive odor when angry or frightened. He cannot project this secretion as does the skunk, but it is an effective means of discouraging his enemies. Of his few enemies, the great horned owl is the most serious.

**Breeding.** The home is usually a hole on the bank of a stream. Often it is a muskrat burrow whose original owner furnished a meal for the new occupants. Sometimes the den may be in a hollow log, or in a pile of rocks, but in any case it is usually located near water. Mink are noted for their fecundity and even in the face of persistent trapping the animals are so prolific that they manage to hold their own. Five or 6 young is the average litter but it is not unusual for a female to bear as many as 10 or 12. The young are born early in the spring and the mother takes care of them during the summer. They are blind and naked at birth but they mature a little more rapidly than the common kitten.

**Range and Distribution.** Mink, though seldom plentiful in any area, are found all across the continent from Labrador to the Aleutians and as far south as the Gulf of Mexico, excepting, of course, the arid regions within that range.

## COMMON MUSKRAT

*Ondatra (syn. Fiber) zibethicus zibethicus*

COMMON NAMES: Marsh Hare, Musquash, 'Rat.

**History.** The muskrat gets his name from a pair of perineal glands which secrete a very strong and penetrating, but not unpleasant, odor of musk.

He is an overgrown relative of the tiny meadow mouse but to the fur trade he has replaced the beaver in importance. His pelt is the basic staple of the industry and the annual figures on his abundance become a barometer for the trade. In the hands of the furrier, common muskrat often becomes "Hudson seal" (the standard trade name) or "river mink." By plucking out the long, shiny guard hairs and dyeing the fur the furrier gets a fair imitation of the more costly seal.

The lowly 'rat furnishes a considerable income to rural boys and professional trappers each year. He is trapped in 47 states, Canada, and Alaska. The annual harvest is about 10,000,000 pelts, of which number the State of Louisiana contributes more than half. Despite this remarkable total there is small danger of depleting the muskrat population because they are so prolific and so widespread.

**Identification.** The muskrat has a squat, thick body, short legs, and broad hind feet which are partially webbed. The tail is long, narrow, scaly with a sparse covering of hair, and flattened laterally to a thin edge on top and bottom.

The average adult male measures about 23 inches, of which 10 inches are tail, and weighs from 2 to 2½ pounds. Large specimens sometimes measure 26 inches and weigh over 3 pounds. The female is slightly smaller. Both sexes are alike in coloration and seasonal changes in pelage are not obvious.

The fur is composed of two layers. The undercoat is dense, soft, and bluish-gray at the base. The outer coat of long guard hairs is dark brown on the head and back and inclined to chestnut-brown on the sides. When the pelt is prime the outer guard hairs are strong and glossy. The under parts of the body are usually lighter in appearance, often grayish on the throat and belly. There is a dark spot on the chin, the tail is dull black, and the lower legs are blackish. The feet are blackish-brown. There is also a black color phase in which the animal appears black above and very dark below.

The size of the animal and the condition of the pelt seems to be determined largely by its environment. Generally those animals that live in better marsh areas where food is plentiful are larger, heavier, and have a higher quality fur than animals from inferior habitats.

**Characteristics.** The muskrat is essentially a water animal. Nature has provided him with webbed hind feet for swimming and an outer covering that repels water like the feathers on a duck. He spends some time on land, of course, but it is in or near the water that he finds both food and shelter.

Along the coastal areas he lives in the salt or brackish marshes and farther inland he is at home in the swamps, lakes, ponds, and streams wherever there is aquatic vegetation. Musquash prefers a marshy area, be it fresh or salt water, or a quiet, sluggish stream. In such places he usually builds a rough domelike house of rushes and other water plants, mixed with mud and rubbish. Sometimes these houses are quite near the shore, but they may be out in the middle of the pond or marsh. The tunneled entrance and exit is on or near the bottom and inside the house there is a shelf or bed which is raised above the water level. The number of houses in a given area usually indicates the extent of the muskrat population.

Any considerable change in the water level affects not only his home, but if the change is prolonged it is likely to destroy the vegetation upon which he depends for food. Therefore the muskrat, lacking the beaver's intelligence in maintaining a mean level, prefers those waters where the level is naturally constant.

Muskrats that live along moving streams generally make bank dens rather than houses. Such dens are merely holes in the bank in which one tunnel starts on or near the bottom and after some distance curves or slants upward to a point above the water line; there the hole is enlarged to form a small room or den, the floor of which is usually covered with dried rushes for a bed. A second tunnel above the water line connects with this den and provides a convenient entrance or exit as well as admitting air. Often the outside entrance is concealed among the roots of a tree growing on the bank.

The muskrat eats a wide variety of foods but aquatic plants furnish the bulk of his diet. In the early spring he feeds on the tender sprouts of cattails and other marsh grasses and the tuberous parts of such plants as sedges, and arrowheads *(Sagittaria latifolia)*. Rice cut-grass is a favored item and pondweed ranks high on his list. During the winter he survives on roots, stalks, and such vegetation as he can grub from the bottom. In addition to the above he consumes some animal food such as mussels, salamanders, and fish—the latter not in any quantity, however.

Protected by his warm fur coat, the muskrat braves the toughest winter and does not hibernate. He is active throughout the year and when the surface of the water is frozen he goes about beneath the ice. If not molested he may be seen at any time of the day, but his favored feeding hours are early morning and just before sundown.

Slow-witted and unwary as compared to most wild creatures, he is the natural prey for many predators, including foxes, hawks, minks, otters, owls, weasels, and wolves. Young muskrats are often taken by snapping turtles, pike and pickerel. Musquash never seems to learn about traps and he may be readily taken even by those with little experience.

**Breeding.** The annual toll of muskrats taken by predators and trappers would be alarming were it not for the fact that musquash is so prolific. The female has at least two, and often more, large litters every year. The average number of young in each litter is 6 or 8, but 12 or more are by no means rare. Muskrats living in the better habitats have been observed to have a higher breeding potential than those in the less favorable areas.

There is a widespread belief that muskrats breed and produce young in their first year, but there is little evidence to support this theory and most naturalists consider it unlikely.

The first litter is usually born about mid-April, but young are common between May and August, and sometimes later. The young kits have a pelage of dusky bluish-gray, which changes with their growth to the thick, shiny pelt of the adult. They mature rapidly and by early winter about 80 per cent of the population are sub-adults. During the trapping season the larger percentage of the take is made up of animals born that year.

**Range and Distribution.** The muskrat is widely distributed over nearly all of North America south of the Barren Grounds. It will be noted that the range of *Zibethicus zibethicus*, the common musk-

Penna. Game Commission.

PLATE I. Muskrat.

rat, covers all or at least a part of all the eastern and central states except Florida, and extends northward through Canada to Hudson Bay.

The following species and sub-species differ slightly from the common muskrat either in size or coloration. Their individual ranges, as given, will aid in classifying them.

### ALASKA PENINSULA MUSKRAT
*Ondatra zibethicus zalopha*

The pelage is blackish-brown. Males reach a total length of about 21 inches; the tail is 9 inches long. The hind feet are smaller than those of the typical muskrat. Its range is along the southwestern coastal area of the Alaskan Peninsula as far east as Cook Inlet and north to Nushagak.

### ARIZONA MUSKRAT
*Ondatra zibethicus pallida*

The Arizona muskrat's pelage is reddish-brown without long black hairs on the dorsal region. Total length in males is 17 inches, with a tail about 7 inches long. Its range covers California, Lower California, and Arizona, east in New Mexico to the Rio Grande Valley.

### GREAT PLAINS MUSKRAT
*Ondatra zibethicus cinnamomina*

This specimen's pelage is cinnamon-brown above, with sides and lower parts paler in color. Males reach a length of 20 inches, the tail is about 9½ inches long. Its range covers most of the Great Plains region from northern Texas to Manitoba, east to central Iowa and west to the eastern base of the Rocky Mountains.

### HUDSON BAY MUSKRAT
*Ondatra zibethicus alba*

The Hudson Bay's pelage is generally paler in color than that of the typical *Zibethicus,* but otherwise similar. Males average 21½ inches long, the tail 9½ inches. It ranges from the southwest shore of Hudson Bay to eastern Saskatchewan, south to Lake Winnipeg and north to the Barren Grounds.

### LABRADOR MUSKRAT
*Ondatra zibethicus aquilonia*

The Labrador's pelage is very similar to that of the common muskrat but is more richly colored. Its range is Labrador and Ungava.

### LOUISIANA MUSKRAT *Ondatra rivalicia*

This is a slightly smaller species than the common muskrat. Its total length is 21 to 22 inches, its tail about 9 inches. The pelage is a dark brownish-black inclined to be duller and having little or no reddish tone. Its range is the marshes and bayous of the coastal region of Louisiana.

### NEVADA MUSKRAT
*Ondatra zibethicus mergens*

Pelage: Grayish-brown above, pale under parts. Total length, 22 inches, tail 10 inches. Range: Northeastern California, southeastern Oregon, Nevada, and western Utah.

### NEWFOUNDLAND MUSKRAT *Ondatra obscura*

The Newfoundland's pelage is very dark brown, sometimes nearly black on the upper parts. Its total length is 20 inches, its tail 9 inches. Its range is limited to Newfoundland.

### NORTHWESTERN MUSKRAT
*Ondatra zibethicus spatulata*

This specimen's head and back are a rich glossy brown; its sides are lighter in tone, the under parts are grayish-white tinged with pale brown. It ranges through northwestern North America, the Yukon Valley, Alaska, south into Alberta and British Columbia, and eastward to the Anderson River.

### OREGON COAST MUSKRAT
*Ondatra zibethicus occipitalis*

This muskrat has a pelage of a rich brown with a reddish tinge. Its total length is 23 inches, its tail 10½ inches. Its range is the coastal region of Oregon and the northern Willamette Valley.

### PECOS MUSKRAT
*Ondatra zibethicus ripensis*

The pelage is a deep, dark brown. The total length is 17 inches, tail about 8 inches. Its range is Texas and New Mexico through the Pecos Valley.

### ROCKY MOUNTAIN MUSKRAT
*Ondatra zibethicus osoyoosensis*

This specimen's pelage is dark brown to blackish above, with under parts whitish washed with cinnamon. Its total length is 23 to 24 inches, its tail 11½ inches. Its range covers the Rocky Mountains from northern New Mexico to southern British Columbia, including Idaho and Montana.

### VIRGINIA MUSKRAT
*Ondatra zibethicus macrodon*

The pelage is somewhat lighter, with less black than the common type. Its total length is about 25 inches (the largest of the muskrats). Its range is the middle Atlantic coastal region from Delaware Bay to Pamlico Sound, inland to central Virginia and North Carolina.

# OTTER

*Lutra canadensis*

COMMON NAMES: Common Otter, Land Otter, River Otter.

**History.** From the earliest days of fur trading otter pelts were a profitable source of income or barter to the trapper. Never so abundant or easy to catch as the beaver, the otter played a less spectacular role in the history of fur but has always ranked as one of the more valuable fur-bearers.

The fur is long-wearing and very serviceable. When dressed it resembles beaver fur and is used in many ways by the fur industry. Two types of pelts are in demand, the soft, silky pelt from the interior regions and the larger bluish-brown variety from the coastal areas.

**Identification.** The otter is a large member of the weasel family with the characteristic long, lithe body and short legs common to that species. The head is fairly broad and flat, the ears are tiny, and the whiskers on the muzzle are long, stiff, and bristly. All four feet end in five toes and are webbed. The soles of the feet are covered with hair. The tail is long, thick, and tapering toward the tip.

As with most aquatic mammals, the pelage is composed of an inner and outer layer. The former is short, soft, and very dense, while the outer coat consists of long, glossy guard hairs. The upper body is a dark, rich, shiny brown blending to brownish-gray on the mouth and cheeks. The under parts are lighter than the upper and inclined to grayish.

The total length of an adult otter averages about 43 inches, including a 13- to 14-inch tail, and the weight is around 20 pounds. Large specimens weigh up to 25 pounds or more.

**Characteristics.** The otter spends more time in the water than any other member of the weasel tribe. Although an inveterate wanderer, he travels close to lakes or waterways at all times. His principal source of food is fish and he is such an excellent, swift swimmer that he can capture his prey with ease. The dense fur and a thick layer of fat beneath it permit him to remain in even icy water for long periods without discomfort. The long, thick tail serves as a rudder and the snakelike body is extremely maneuverable either above or below the surface.

*Lutra* is strictly carnivorous. Besides a variety of fish, he feeds on crawfish, small mammals such as muskrats and young beavers, and occasionally on ducks, poultry, and frogs.

He is neither as bloodthirsty as his tiny cousins the weasels nor as ferocious as his larger relative the wolverine; nevertheless, he can give a good account of himself in a fight. He is a match for all but the best dogs on land and more than a match for any dog in the water. Aside from man he has virtually

N. Y. Zoological Society.

PLATE I. Otter.

no enemies to worry about. Smaller predators do not dare attack him and he can easily escape the larger ones.

He is gentle by nature and readily tamed. Otters in captivity have been trained to retrieve ducks and other game, make excellent pets, and seldom exhibit any of the vicious traits so characteristic of their close relatives.

The otter is active all year round and in the winter his search for food often requires long journeys to places with open water, such as falls and rapids.

Most wild creatures go about the business of living in deadly seriousness, but the otter has a playful streak in his make-up. Wherever these animals are found, "otter-slides" are not uncommon. In the summer such a slide is made on a steep bank—preferably clay—by smoothing and patting the earth and wetting it with their bodies until it offers a slick, even surface. The animals climb to the top of such a slide and coast into the water on their breast and belly with the feet tucked backward, much in same manner as children doing "belly-whoppers" on a hillside. As they are somewhat gregarious, it is not uncommon for several otters to use the slide in turn, and they seem to get as much pleasure from playing in this manner as any child. In the winter such slides are made in the snow and when frozen become very hard and glassy, permitting the animals to plunge swiftly into the water.

The otter utters a variety of sounds, from loud, birdlike chirps to a piercing whistle. Perhaps the most common is the loud sniffling sound resembling that of a swimmer clearing his nostrils. When alarmed there is often a menacing snarl and in captivity they have been heard to chatter, growl, or grumble like a raccoon.

**Breeding.** These animals are not very prolific. There is but one litter a year and the young vary in number from one to four. Two or three is about average, however, and five are rare. The youngsters arrive in late April or early May and mature at about the same rate as beavers. The home den is generally in the bank of a lake or stream with the entrance below the water line. More rarely it may be in a hollow log close to the water.

**Range and Distribution.** The range of the otter includes most of North America but distribution is extremely spotty and at no point can these animals be said to be very numerous.

There are several species and sub-species which differ slightly from the typical in either size or color variation, but in most instances their range is limited to definite localities. They are as follows:

### CANADA OTTER *Lutra canadensis canadensis*

This species is as described above and is the most common and generally best known of all the otters. The range extends from Labrador to beyond the Arctic Circle in Yukon and Alaska, and reaches as far south as South Carolina on the eastern coast.

### CALIFORNIA OTTER *Lutra canadensis brevipilosus*

This otter is a dark sooty-brown above with a sprinkling of light-tipped hairs along the back. The sides of the body are paler, the under parts lighter in tone. Throat, chin, and upper lip are light yellowish-brown. Its range is limited to the Sacramento and San Joaquin drainages, California.

### CAROLINA OTTER *Lutra canadensis lataxina*

The Carolina otter has upper parts of a deep brown, tinged with ochre on the sides of the head and neck. The lower parts are paler. It is a smaller animal than the typical *Canadensis,* and has less hair on the soles of the feet. It is found principally in the Carolinas, but the exact extent of the range is not defined.

### FLORIDA OTTER *Lutra canadensis vaga*

The Florida otter is a glossy reddish-brown above, paler below. Chin, throat, sides of the neck, lips, and cheeks, are a grayish-yellow-brown. It is slightly larger than the typical otter, being about 51 inches over all. Its range covers Florida and eastern Georgia.

### INTERIOR OTTER *Lutra canadensis interior*

This is similar to the Canada otter but larger, having a total length of 53 inches. Its range is principally in Nebraska and neighboring states; the exact extent of the range has not been recorded.

### NEWFOUNDLAND OTTER *Lutra degener*

The pelage of this otter is very dark brown to blackish above and lighter on the sides of the head and neck. It is smaller than the typical *Canadensis,* having a total length of only 40 inches. Its range is Newfoundland.

### PACIFIC OTTER *Lutra canadensis pacifica*

This otter's upper back is dark reddish-brown. The sides of the head, neck, and breast are a pale brown. The under parts are lighter in tone than the back. It is fairly large, with a total length of about 43 inches. It ranges through the Pacific Northwest from Oregon to the coastal area of Alaska.

### QUEEN CHARLOTTE OTTER *Lutra canadensis brevipilosus*

This is a little-known sub-species on which no definite information is available. It is probably similar to the Pacific otter but may possibly be larger. Its range is limited to the Queen Charlotte Islands, British Columbia.

### SONORA OTTER *Lutra canadensis sonora*

The Sonora otter's upper body is brown but so grizzled with light hairs that it appears pale brown. The sides of the head and neck are a pale yellowish or creamy and the under parts are pale grayish-brown. Its total length is 52 inches. Its range is Southern California and Arizona.

# PORCUPINE

Family *Erethizontidae*

**History.** The name porcupine comes from two sources: the Latin *porcus,* meaning "pig," and the French *épine,* which in turn stems from another Latin word, *spina,* meaning "thorn" or "spine"—thus, literally, "spiny-pig." It is easy to recognize the derivation of the colloquial term "quill-pig" from the combination.

There are two recognized species in North America. The most common is the eastern variety known as the Canadian porcupine *(Erethizon dorsatus)*; the other is the yellow-haired porcupine *(Erethizon epixanthus epixanthus)* of the Northwest and Rocky Mountain area. Both belong to the order *Rodentia,* and live up to their name by gnawing practically anything into which they can sink their big, sharp front teeth.

## CANADIAN PORCUPINE *Erethizon dorsatus*

COMMON NAMES: Porky, quill-pig; in some sections erroneously called "Hedgehog," a term confused with the European animal of that name.

**Identification.** The porcupine is a stout, heavily built animal with a short, rounded head. Specimens vary from 30 to more than 36 inches in length and weigh from 15 to 40 pounds, the latter weight being when they are very fat. The "porky" is the second largest rodent in North America, being next in size to the beaver. The pelage is composed of long, soft underfur of black or brownish tone and stiff spines or quills of varying lengths which form a protective outer covering. These spines are creamish-white with black tips and are more numerous on the back and tail than elsewhere over the body. The body quills, especially those on the back, are long and dangerous looking, but it is the shorter quills on the stubby tail that are most deadly. The head, belly, and feet do not have the spiny covering and the belly is nearly bare, or sparsely covered with coarse hair. The thick, stumpy tail is about 6 inches long, covered on the top and sides with short stiff quills, and the underside has a tough, scaly covering. The legs are short and stout. The front feet have but four toes, the back feet five, and each toe is equipped with long sharp claws for easy climbing.

**Characteristics.** Nature has endowed certain animals with special protection to enable them to cope with their enemies. The armadillo has his armorplate covering, the skunk his offensive spray, and the "porky" a bristling array of sharp needle-like spines which usually discourage any attack on his person. He has no other means of defense, but secure in his belief that few foes will molest him he waddles his clumsy way in comparative indifference.

The porcupine is strictly vegetarian and does not prey on a single living creature, yet despite his formidable covering he is often attacked and eaten by predators, large and small. With the possible exception of the fisher, however, it is doubtful that any animal attempts to make a meal of the porcupine except from dire necessity.

He is by nature a solitary creature who prefers to travel alone and mind his own business. Normally his quills lie flat against the body when he is relaxed, but when alarmed or angry he bristles them out at right angles, turns his head away from his pursuer, and presents little opening for an attack. He is too slow and clumsy to attempt flight, although he will climb a tree to escape if there is time. If caught on the ground he tries to stick his unprotected head under a log or some other cover and trusts to his quills to protect his rear.

With the exception of the dog few animals care to brave those possibly deadly spines. "Man's best friend" usually rushes in without caution and emerges from the attack a sadder and (sometimes) wiser dog. With his muzzle and throat painfully studded with quills there is but one way to prevent his probably agonizing death. Quick action with a pair of pliers will usually get out all the quills before they have had a chance to do any damage. The danger comes from not being able to find them all, especially the shorter ones which may have lodged in the mouth or throat.

Each quill has hundreds of tiny barbules slanting to the rear or base of the quill (these may be seen under a magnifying glass, or felt by drawing the fingers up the quill) and these barbs force the quill to travel in but one direction. Thus when the quill is inserted into live flesh the muscular action causes it to move and the barbs assure that such motion will be forward at all times. Once imbedded the quills are difficult to remove and continue to penetrate farther and farther with each movement of the victim. Often they travel until they strike a vital organ, thus causing death, or if no vital organ happens to be in their path they continue to work clear through the animal and become extremely painful.

Bears, mountain lions, and wolves have all been victims of these quills although they often attack and eat the porcupine when other food is scarce. Such attacks are not always fatal and the more skillful predators get away with but few quills in their paws. There are many instances on record where some of these animals have later been killed by man and quills have been found imbedded in their flesh.

The fisher has been mentioned as the particular Nemesis of the porcupine because he alone of all the animals seems able to dine on porky with little danger to himself. Not only is he extremely skillful in avoiding the quills while killing a porcupine but those which he does acquire in the process appear to do him little, if any, harm. The fisher is a specialist in porky slaying and he outwits his stupid prey at every turn. He is as agile as a squirrel; so it does the porcupine no good to seek refuge in a tree. If the slow-witted porky goes out on a limb the fisher comes up on the underside where there are no quills and his mission is soon accomplished. On the ground he maneuvers his victim into a position where he can get at the unprotected portion of his anatomy. But it is on the snow that the fisher is at his best. The porky gets his head under a log, or between some roots, bristles his quills, and squats in fancied security. The fisher merely tunnels in the snow, comes up under the soft belly, and one more porcupine trail is ended.

In some quarters the popular belief still exists that the porcupine can *throw* his quills. This, of

N. Y. Zoological Society.

PLATE I. Porcupine—Pig of the Woods.

course, is not true. It is quite possible that the fallacy originated from the fact that the porky can and does flip his short tail with great speed and vigor. He tries to strike his attacker with this appendage and the action is so fast that it may have appeared to some that he was actually throwing the quills. Each quill is rather loosely attached to the skin and readily comes free upon contact.

**Feeding.** The porcupine will eat almost anything in the nature of green vegetation but he has an especial fondness for the inner bark of pine trees. Buds and foliage form a part of his summer diet, but the bulk of his food comes from the spruces and the lodgepole, limber, and white-barked pine trees. He may gnaw the bark from ground level or any distance from there to the top of the tree. He often "girdles" a tree well up from its base, thus killing the top, or gnaws all the bark of some of the limbs, causing them to die and resulting in malformation of the tree. For this reason, and because he is very destructive to plantings of young pines, the lumber interests detest him and in many states there is a bounty on his head.

The porky has one weakness which makes him a nuisance to campers and woodsmen, and that is his fondness for salt. Human perspiration leaves a salty deposit on any articles that are handled frequently, such as canoe paddles, ax handles, tent guy ropes, gun stocks, pack straps, and other gear. To get the salt with which these things are impregnated porky will gnaw them to slivers. He will gnaw through floors and the sides of buildings where the human hand has touched the wood. In camps he often raids the grub box to get at the bacon and salt pork. Where these animals are abundant it is very difficult for the camper to keep everything beyond their reach.

In some places he is protected on the grounds that he is the only animal which an unarmed and hungry woods traveler could kill with a club. While this is undoubtedly true, it still leaves him of questionable value because he may be very difficult to find in such an emergency. However, if one is lost and without food, and *can* find a porky, all that is needed is a fire.

The Indian method of cooking one is extremely simple. Kill the porky by hitting him over the snout or head with a club. (He gives up the ghost easily.) Then, with no further preparation, put him on the coals and pile more coals over the body until it is covered. Let it roast for about 30 minutes; then remove it from the fire. The outer skin with burned quills will readily come away from the white meat. The flesh is said to be very tender, but likely to have a flavor of pine bark. It would supply nourishment and ward off starvation, but is not considered an epicurean delight.

The porcupine is largely nocturnal in habits but may often be found feeding or wandering about by day.

**Breeding.** Porcupines are apparently influenced by cyclic changes. They often increase slowly in many areas until they hit the peak abundance and then gradually decline in numbers until they are scarce. They mate in the late winter or early spring and the female bears from one to four young, the average being two. The young are fully covered with stiff hair and develop their quills early in life.

**Range and Distribution.** This species is found in the forested areas over the greater part of Canada and in the eastern part of the United States north of 40 degrees latitude.

### YELLOW-HAIRED PORCUPINE
*Erethizon epixanthus epixanthus*

COMMON NAMES: Same as for Canadian porcupine.

**Identification.** In this species the underfur is yellowish or tawny and the quills are a tannish-white. These animals are usually a little larger than the Canadian variety, sometimes being about 40 inches in length and some specimens weighing close to 50 pounds. Except for color and size, what has been written regarding the Canadian species also applies to the yellow-haired porcupine.

**Characteristics** are virtually the same as those given for the Canadian species.

**Range and Distribution.** This species is found throughout the Rocky Mountain regions as far south as Mexico.

# WEASEL
*Mustela cicognani*

COMMON NAMES: Ermine, Ferret, Stoat, Weasel.

**History.** The weasels are the smallest members of the family *Mustelidae* and the sub-family *Mustelinae*. They are also the most numerous and widely distributed; for their clan numbers 36 species and sub-species throughout North America. As a group they represent a high degree of development in predatory and carnivorous tendencies and are notorious for their wanton killing.

Their winter coat (typical with most species) of pure white with a black-tipped tail has earned them the name of ermine, but there is only one species, *Arctica,* which is most closely related to the true Old World ermine that furnished the robes of royalty.

The weasel plays a relatively minor part in the annual fur harvest because the pelts are so small as to be hardly worth the trapper's efforts.

### BONAPARTE WEASEL
*Mustela cicognani cicognani*

**Identification.** This is a small, slender animal with a long neck, long body, and short legs. The head is small; the ears are rounded and set close to the skull. The soles of both fore and hind feet are furred.

Both sexes are alike in appearance but the males are invariably larger than the females. An adult male is about 11 inches long, the female about 9 inches.

The fur consists of a short, dense undercoat covered by long, shining guard hairs. In summer the pelage is a warm brown on the upper body and yellowish-white below. The top of the head is somewhat darker than the rest of the body and the feet are tinged with yellowish-white. In winter the coat

Penna. Game Commission.

PLATE I. **Weasel.**

is pure glistening white except for a slightly yellowish tint along the rump and under parts and a black tip on the tail.

**Characteristics.** It seems incredible that so small a body could house such a vicious nature. Most predators, large or small, kill in order to eat, but the weasel goes beyond the law of survival and often kills for the mere pleasure of killing. It is doubtful whether a more bloodthirsty creature exists.

The term bloodthirsty is aptly applied to this tiny animal because warm blood is his normal food. To get it he attacks his prey in the neck or at the base of the skull and sucks the blood from a main artery. The smaller mammals, from mice to rabbits, and birds up to the size of the grouse are all on his list of victims. When the occasion offers he will kill as many as possible. It is a matter of record that a single weasel has slaughtered as many as 30 to 40 hens in one night. Obviously no one weasel needs, or could consume, that much blood, and such acts bear out the utter savagery and viciousness of his nature.

The weasel, in turn, probably falls prey to such creatures as the fox, lynx, larger owls, and his near relatives the mink, marten, and fisher, but his size and agility make him so hard to catch that he has less to fear from other predators than most small animals. As an additional protection he, like his fierce cousin, the wolverine, is equipped with an anal gland which secretes a strong, obnoxious odor.

He is both curious and bold by nature. He will instantly disappear at the sight of man but a squeaking sound—such as might be made by sucking against the back of the hand—will usually cause him to show himself immediately. He seems to be unsuspicious of a trap and is not difficult to catch. Baits, even old ones, seem to attract him, but it is thought that he investigates such traps from curiosity rather than for food because he prefers only a fresh kill.

All his senses are highly developed and he is a remarkable example of efficiency when it comes to killing. Although most of his activity is on the ground, or beneath it when he invades the burrows of other animals, he can climb trees if necessary. He is most active during the night but he is an indefatigable hunter and may be seen at any time of the day. Once he takes up the trail of a victim he is usually successful in making his kill and is thus a source of terror to all the small creatures in his vicinity.

**Breeding.** The weasel is one of the most prolific of his tribe. A female bears from four to six young as a rule but eight is not an uncommon litter. The home den is generally a burrow under a rock pile, stone fence, boulder, or some such secure spot. Once they are furred the immature animals resemble their parents. While the young are under the mother's care she is utterly fearless and will defend them with her life.

**Range and Distribution.** The Bonaparte weasel is the most widely distributed and therefore the most representative of all the weasel clan. It is common over a great portion of the United States and Canada. It occurs from the New England states through New York and the northern parts of Michigan and Wisconsin, to the timbered areas of Minnesota, north from Labrador to the coast of southeastern Alaska and thence south through the Rocky Mountains to Colorado. In some regions this species is replaced by others, or a sub-species, and in many instances its range overlaps that of other varieties.

A brief description of the other species, including their approximate range, follows:

## ALABAMA WEASEL

*Mustela peninsula olivacea*

This is a sub-species of the *Peninsulae* with a distinctly olive-green tinge in the pelage, and having less yellow on the feet than a typical specimen of that species. The coat does not turn white in winter, but is creamy-brown above with pale chrome-yellow under parts and a black-tipped tail. It is confined chiefly to the central portion of Alabama.

**ALASKAN LEAST WEASEL** *Mustela rixosa eskimo*

This is one of the smaller varieties similar to the typical *Rixosa* but of a duller coloration. The females are much smaller than the males. The summer coat is a reddish-brown above, the under parts are white. The winter pelage is all white with no black tip on the tail. It inhabits the region around Point Barrow, Alaska.

**ALLEGHENIAN LEAST WEASEL** *Mustela allegheniensis*

This is a trifle larger than other least weasels and of darker coloration. The summer coat is a rich brown above, white below, and the tail has but few black hairs, or none. In winter this animal is totally white. It is found in the Allegheny Mountain region of Pennsylvania.

**BLACK HILLS WEASEL** *Mustela alleni*

This is a medium-sized weasel about 15 inches in length with a summer coat of golden-brown above and orange-yellow below. The chin and upper lip are white. It is found in the Rocky Mountains as far as British Columbia and in parts of the Sierra Nevada range.

**BRIDLED WEASEL** *Mustela frenata frenata*

This variety has a longer tail than the typical weasel and is distinguished by having a white streak between the eye and the ear (hence the name "bridled"), and a white spot on the forehead. The upper parts in general are a pale brown; the top of the head is darker, and there is a dark spot back of the corner of the mouth. The under parts are a rich creamy-yellow blending to nearly white on the throat and chin. The range extends from southern Texas to well into Mexico.

**CALIFORNIA WEASEL** *Mustela xanthogenys xanthogenys*

This is a medium-sized weasel with a long tail. In summer the upper parts are a deep, dull brown with some golden tones, and the face has whitish markings. The under parts are light yellow-ochre. In winter the dull brown coat lacks the golden tints. The head is darker, being nearly black on the top of the nose. There is a wide slanting streak of whitish between the eye and the ear and a spot of the same on the forehead. The under parts, including the forelegs and feet and the inner side and toes of the hind legs, are buffy-yellow or yellow-orange. The chin is white. It is found in California both east and west of the Sierra Nevada Mountains.

**CASCADE MOUNTAIN WEASEL** *Mustela saturata*

This is a large weasel (males measure 17 inches) with a long tail. The pelage in summer is a very deep dark brown with the darkest portion on the head. There is a conspicuous spot of brown at the corner of the mouth. The chin is white and the under parts vary from pale orange to yellow. This variety is found chiefly in the Cascade and Siskiyou Mountains from Oregon into British Columbia.

**DWARF WEASEL** *Mustela streatori leptus*

The dwarf weasel is one of the smallest of weasels, with very little black on the tail tip. The summer pelage is dark brown above and white below. In the winter the coat is pure white except for the black tip on the tail. This type is found in the Rocky Mountains from Colorado into Alberta.

**FLORIDA WEASEL** *Mustela peninsulae peninsulae*

This is a fairly large weasel (males measure about 15 inches) with upper parts of a rich deep brown and the under parts yellowish. There is a dusky spot behind the mouth and the upper lips and chin are white. The actual range is not well defined but it is believed that this species is distributed throughout the Florida peninsula.

**GREENLAND WEASEL** *Mustela audax*

The Greenland weasel is short-tailed and of medium size. In summer the medium-brown upper parts are separated from the white under parts by a definite line of black. The range is limited to northern Greenland.

**JUNEAU WEASEL** *Mustela cicognani alascensis*

This sub-species measures about 13 inches (males) in length, and has a summer coat of chocolate-brown above and yellowish-white below. The feet usually show more white than those of a typical weasel. As the name implies, this variety is found near Juneau, Alaska.

**KODIAK ISLAND WEASEL** *Mustela kadiacensis*

This is a sub-species similar to the *Arctica* but slightly smaller. The range is limited to Kodiak Island, Alaska.

**LEAST WEASEL; BANGS WEASEL** *Mustela rixosa rixosa*

This is the smallest of the weasel tribe. In summer the upper parts are reddish-brown and the under parts white. The tail lacks the usual black tip. In winter the coat is totally white. Ranges to the Arctic limit of trees from Hudson Bay to the Alaskan coast, south to Montana and northern Minnesota.

**LITTLE WEASEL; SIERRA LEAST WEASEL** *Mustela muricus*

This is another very small member of the tribe, with a short black-tipped tail. In summer the upper body is a dull brown inclined to olive-green and the under parts are white. It is found in some sections of the Sierra Nevada Mountains, California.

**LONG-TAILED WEASEL** *Mustela longicauda longicauda*

This is one of the largest weasels (males measure

about 18 inches), with a longer than usual tail which has a short black tip. In summer the upper parts are light yellow-brown. The head is darker than the body and the upper lip and chin are white. The under parts are warm yellow. The winter pelage is pure white except for the black tail tip. This species inhabits the plains country from Kansas to the north.

**MINNESOTA WEASEL** *Mustela longicauda spadix*

On this large weasel (males measure about 18 inches) the upper parts are chocolate-brown and lower parts buffy-yellow. The upper lip and chin are white. In winter the pelage is totally white except for black on the tip of the tail. It is found along the northern timber belt of Minnesota.

**MISSOURI WEASEL** *Mustela primulina*

In summer this weasel is a very rich deep brown above and the under parts are strikingly yellow. The tail is tipped with black and the chin is white. Typical range includes Jasper County, Missouri.

**MOUNTAIN LONG-TAILED WEASEL** *Mustela longicauda oribasus*

This is a fairly large weasel with dark brown upper body and under parts of brownish-yellow. The upper lip, chin, and tops of the feet are white. It is found in British Columbia, especially in the region of the Kettle River.

**MOUNTAIN WEASEL** *Mustela arizonensis*

This weasel is smaller than the mountain long-tail, and has upper parts of somber brown, darker on the head, and under parts varying from orange to yellow. The upper lip and chin are white. It is found in the Rocky Mountains from Colorado to British Columbia and in parts of the Sierra Nevada Mountains.

**NEWFOUNDLAND WEASEL** *Mustela cicognani mortigena*

This is a medium-sized weasel (males measure about 13 inches) with a rather short tail. The summer soat is brown above and white below with very little white on the feet. It is found only in Newfoundland.

**NEW MEXICO BRIDLED WEASEL** *Mustela frenata neomexicana*

This variety has a wide whitish streak between the eye and the ear which resembles a bridle. The upper body is a pale brownish-yellow and the head is brownish-black. Besides the "bridle" there is a splotch of white between the eyes. The under parts are somewhat lighter than the upper body and the latter half of the tail is black. It is common to the Mesilla Valley region of New Mexico.

**NEW YORK WEASEL** *Mustela novaboracensis novaboracensis*

This is a fairly large type (males measure about 16 inches) which has a summer coat of rich, dark brown above and white below. The under parts are tinged with yellow. The winter pelage is white in the northern part of the range. This so-called New York weasel actually ranges widely throughout the eastern United States from southern Maine to North Carolina and as far west as Illinois.

**NORTHERN LONG-TAILED WEASEL** *Mustela occisor*

This is very similar to the New York weasel in coloration but has a narrower tail with a very short black tip. Males average about 18 inches in length. Typical range covers northern Maine and possibly Province of Quebec.

**OREGON WEASEL** *Mustela xanthogenys oregonensis*

The Oregon weasel is rather large (males measure about 18 inches) and has face markings similar to those of the California weasel but less conspicuous. The upper parts (in summer) are pale reddish-brown, under parts yellowish. The tail is briefly tipped with black. The limits of the range are not clearly defined but this sub-species is typical of the Rogue River Valley, Oregon.

**PLAINS LEAST WEASEL** *Mustela campestris*

This is a very small weasel (males measure about 7½ inches) with a summer pelage of soft brown above and very light under parts. The tail has no black tip and the white below extends onto the fore-feet. The range extends indefinitely through the plains country of Nebraska.

**POLAR WEASEL** *Mustela arctica polaris*

This is a large type with a summer pelage of rich golden brown above and light yellow below. The upper lips, chin, and throat are pure white. The winter pelage is totally white except for black on tip of tail. It inhabits the northern part of Greenland.

**QUEEN CHARLOTTE WEASEL** *Mustela haidarum*

This is a typical-sized weasel (males measure 11 inches) with a summer coat of very dark brown above and yellow below. The tail is black for more than half its length. In winter the pelage is white, tinged with yellow on the lower back and under parts. It is found principally on Graham Island in the Queen Charlotte Group, British Columbia.

**REDWOODS WEASEL** *Mustela xanthogenys munda*

This species does not change to white in the winter. The winter pelage is a deep, tawny brown, darker on the head and nose than elsewhere. The under parts are buffy-orange. In summer the brown is darker and duller and the under parts rather faded. Its range is along the coastal region of northern California.

**RICHARDSON WEASEL** *Mustela cicognani richardsoni*

This weasel is about 15 to 16 inches long and is similar to the typical Bonaparte weasel in coloration but has a longer tail. Its range covers the wooded regions from Hudson Bay to the interior of Alaska and British Columbia.

### SMALL-EARED WEASEL *Mustela microtis*

This is similar to the Richardson weasel but is only about 12 inches long. The upper body (in summer) has a golden-yellow tone and the white under parts are tinged with deep yellow. The ears are exceptionally small. It is found in British Columbia, particularly around Shesley.

### SOUTHERN WEASEL *Mustela novaboracensis notia*

In this large weasel (males measure about 17 inches) the summer coat is dark chocolate-brown on the upper portion and yellow on the lower. The tail is black for nearly half its length. It ranges from North Carolina to northern Virginia.

### TUNDRA or ARCTIC WEASEL *Mustela arctica arctica*

This variety is the weasel most clearly related to the Old World ermine. In summer the pelage is deep yellow-brown above and the under parts are distinctly yellow, including the first half of the underside of the tail. In winter the pelage is pure white except for a wash of yellow on the rump and a black tip on the tail. It is found largely along the Arctic coastal areas and in the tundra country of northern Alaska.

### WASHINGTON WEASEL *Mustela washingtoni*

The males of this type average about 16 inches, the females about 14 inches. The tail is longer than the typical variety and has a brief black tip. In summer the upper body is a rich brown and the lower parts white washed with yellowish. As the name denotes, its range is within the State of Washington—particularly around the Mount Adams region.

### BLACK-FOOTED FERRET *Mustela nigripes*

This animal belongs to the sub-genus *Putorius* and is larger and more like a mink than the other weasels. The males average about 22 inches in length and the females slightly smaller. The upper parts are a pale straw color with an admixture of dark brown hairs on the top of the head and along the back. The under parts are cream colored and the feet are dusky. The short tail is the same color as the body except for a short dark tip. There is a wide black marking across the face like the "mask" on a raccoon. The range comprises most of the Great Plains region from western North Dakota and northern Montana to Texas, west to the beginning of the Rocky Mountains.

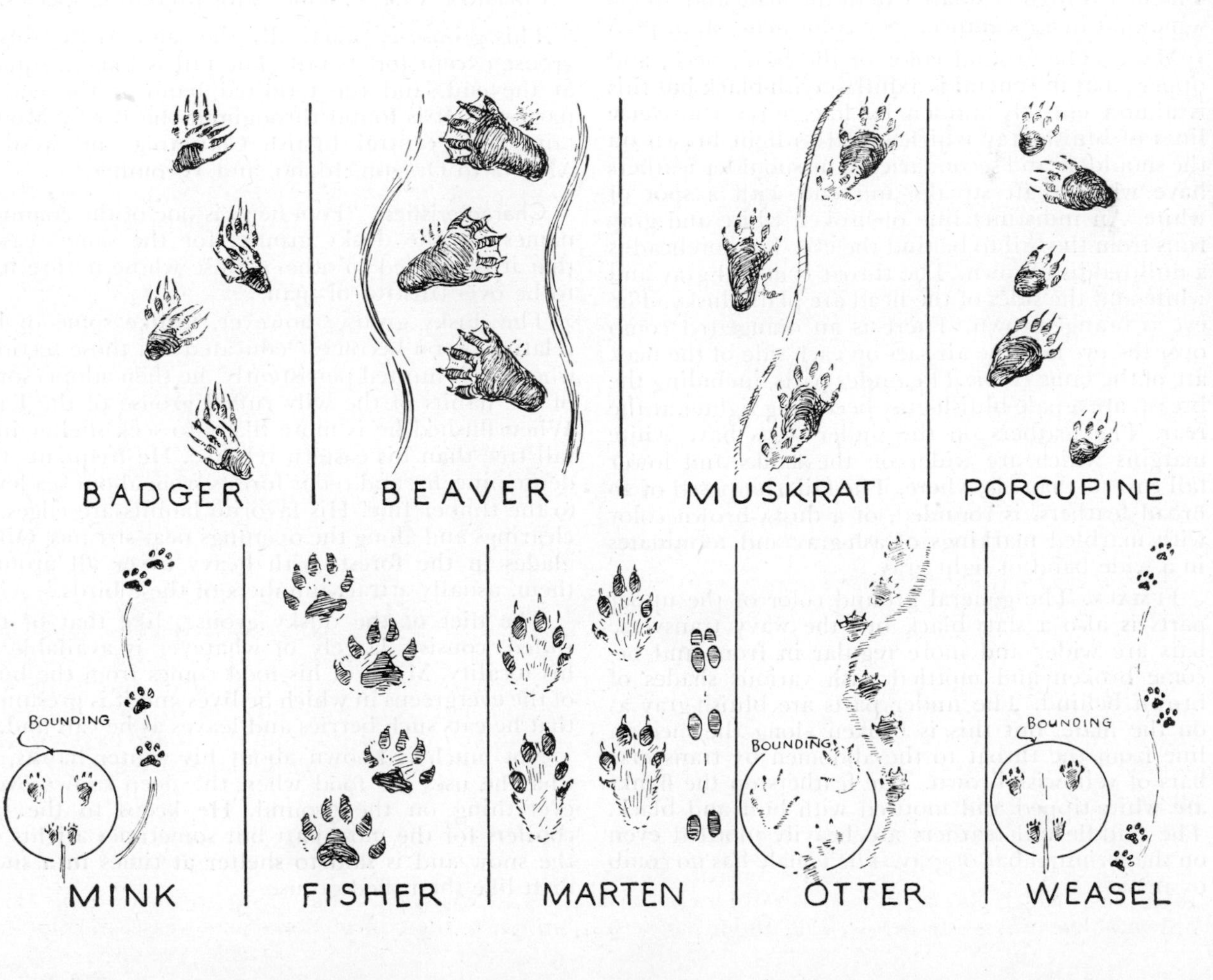

# UPLAND GAME BIRDS

## DUSKY GROUSE

*Dendragapus obscurus obscurus*

COMMON NAMES: Blue Grouse, Fool Hen, Gray Grouse, Mountain Grouse, Pine Grouse, Pine Hen.

**History.** The dusky grouse, a strictly western variety, was an inhabitant of the huge pine forests long before the first white man came to North America. Brief mention of him is found in some of the earliest notes made by explorers but the records are sketchy at best and all too little was handed down to succeeding generations.

In spite of the same characteristic trust in man that he shares with some of the other species, he has managed to cope with the inroads of civilization and is still found in considerable numbers in his native habitat.

In many sections of his range he is better known as blue grouse than under the official term of dusky.

**Identification.** The dusky grouse is the largest of the wood grouse, often weighing up to 3½ pounds. The hen is slightly smaller than the male and differs somewhat in appearance. (See color plate on p. 482.)

MALE. The ground color of the head, neck, and upper parts in general is a dull grayish-black but this is almost entirely hidden by fine, wavy transverse lines of bluish-gray which blend to light brown on the shoulders and secondaries. The shoulder feathers have white shaft streaks and end with a spot of white. An indistinct line of broken white and gray runs from the bill to behind the eye. The forehead is a dull reddish-brown. The throat is mixed gray and white and the sides of the head are plain dusky. The eye is orange-brown. There is an orange-red comb over the eye and the air sacs on each side of the neck are of the same color. The under parts, including the breast, are a pale bluish-gray becoming lighter at the rear. The feathers on the under parts have white margins which are wider on the flanks and lower tail coverts than elsewhere. The tail, composed of 20 broad feathers, is rounded, of a dusky-brown color with marbled markings of ash-gray and terminates in a wide band of light gray.

FEMALE. The general ground color of the upper parts is also a slaty-black but the wavy transverse bars are wider and more regular in front and become broken and mottled with various shades of brown behind. The under parts are bluish-gray as on the male, but this is broken along the median line from the throat to the abdomen by transverse bars of yellowish-brown. The feathers on the flanks are white-tipped and mottled with buff and black. The middle tail feathers are heavily mottled even on the terminal bar of gray. The female has no comb or air sacs.

Ornithologists now recognize two sub-species of the dusky grouse but these are so nearly identical that they can be included here. As with most sub-species the difference is more a matter of range than of coloration.

### FLEMING'S GROUSE

*Dendragapus obscurus flemingi*

COMMON NAMES: Same as for dusky grouse.

This bird is simply a darker variation of the dusky grouse and has the same general habits and characteristics. Its range is more northerly than the dusky as it is commonly found in northern British Columbia, southern Yukon Territory, and southwestern Mackenzie region.

### RICHARDSON'S GROUSE

*Dendragapus obscurus richardsoni*

COMMON NAMES: Same as for preceding species.

This grouse is practically the same as the dusky grouse except for its tail. The tail is longer, square at the end, and the terminal band at the end is narrower. It is found throughout the Rocky Mountains from central British Columbia and western Alberta to Oregon, Idaho, and Wyoming.

**Characteristics.** "Fool hen" is one of the common names for the dusky grouse, for the same reason that it is applied to other grouse whose nature it is to be over-trustful of man.

The dusky grouse, however, unlike some of his relatives, soon becomes "educated" in those sections where he is hunted persistently; he then adopts some of the habits of the wily ruffed grouse of the East. When flushed he is more likely to seek shelter in a tall tree than his eastern relative. He frequents the dense pine, fir, and cedar forests from about sea level to the timber line. His favorite haunts are edges of clearings and along the openings near streams. Open glades in the forest, with heavy cover all around them, usually attract numbers of these birds.

The diet of the dusky grouse, like that of the ruffed, consists largely of whatever is available in his locality. Much of his food comes from the buds of the evergreens in which he lives and it is presumed that he eats such berries and leaves as he can find.

Not much is known about his winter habits, or what he uses for food when the deep snow covers everything on the ground. He keeps to the tall conifers for the most part but sometimes alights on the snow and is said to shelter at times in a snow drift like the ruffed grouse.

His love-making follows somewhat the same general pattern of all the other grouse but he, like his close relative the sooty grouse, is especially equipped to show off before the hen. He is provided with an air sac on each side of his neck and when he becomes amorous he inflates these sacs until the feathers surrounding them spread and turn outward. The undersides of the neck feathers are white and when the red sacs are distended these feathers form a white ring, or rosette, around them.

With these sacs expanded he mounts a fallen log or some other slight elevation and struts about with drooping wings and tail held stiffly erect. The comb-like "eyebrows" are also distended as he approaches the hen. When directly in front of her he lowers his head to the ground as though making a bow and suddenly expels the air from the swollen sacs on his neck. This deflation produces a resonant *"boom, boom, boom."* Like the drumming of the ruffed grouse, this has a peculiar ventriloquistic character which makes it difficult to tell whether the sound comes from near or far and therefore difficult to locate the bird.

The males occasionally battle over the same hen but their efforts are directed chiefly toward a display of their individual charms as a means of winning a mate.

**Breeding.** After courtship and mating the hen goes into seclusion and proceeds with her nest building and egg laying.

The nest, like that of the other grouse, is little more than a crude collection of grass and pine needles placed in a depression in the ground. It is often located beneath a log and usually at the edge of the timber. The eggs, from seven to ten in number, are cream or pale buff, speckled all over with reddish-brown spots.

The hen is a close sitter and does not leave the nest unless in imminent danger of being stepped on. She makes no attempt to cover the eggs during her absence from the nest and they are quite conspicuous. Neither is she so skilled in the "broken-wing" trick often used by the female ruffed grouse.

It has been stated that the male aids in caring for the young, but if that is true it is an uncommon trait among grouse. It is known that the parents and young remain together in the autumn, however, which indicates that the dusky may be more inclined to monogamy than the ruffed grouse.

**Range and Distribution.** The dusky grouse is found wherever there are evergreen forests throughout the Rocky Mountains from Colorado and northern Utah to Arizona and central New Mexico and east as far as Nevada.

## FRANKLIN'S GROUSE

*Canachites franklini*

Common Names: Fool Hen, Franklin's Spruce Grouse, Mountain Grouse, Tyee Grouse, Wood Grouse.

**History.** The Franklin's grouse, named after the English explorer, Sir John Franklin, was first reported by Lewis and Clark in an account of their travels to the Pacific Coast in 1804-1806. Despite the intervening years and the remarkable tameness of the bird there seems to be comparatively little known about its breeding or nesting habits. Ornithologists report that these habits are virtually the same as those of the spruce grouse to which it is closely related.

The difference in appearance between this bird and the Hudsonian spruce grouse is small indeed, but it has been accorded a separate classification instead of being listed as a sub-species.

**Identification.** In general appearance the Franklin's grouse is identical with the Hudsonian except for having a longer tail which lacks the orange tip. The tail of the female is tipped with white.

**Characteristics.** The term fool hen, which is also used for all the spruce grouse tribe, is even more applicable to the Franklin's grouse. It would be difficult to find a more trusting bird, and its refusal to become alarmed and fly when encountered practically eliminates it from the list of "game" birds.

Like all the grouse, the male stages a special show at mating time to attract the hens. His performance differs slightly from that of the other species. The bare red patches, or "eyebrows," over the eyes are distended until they almost meet over the top of the head. Meanwhile he struts and prances around the object of his affections with trailing wings and his tail spread to its greatest width. From time to time he closes one-half of the spread tail, first on one side and then on the other, and the movement of the feathers gives a clearly audible rustling sound.

Like their close relatives, these birds prefer dense spruce and fir growths, but they are likely to be found higher up on the slopes than some of the other species.

**Range and Distribution.** The Franklin's grouse is fairly evenly distributed over an area from southern Alaska, through central British Columbia and Alberta, south to Oregon, Idaho, and Montana.

## HUDSONIAN SPRUCE GROUSE

*Canachites canadensis canadensis*

Common Names: Black Grouse, Canada Grouse, Cedar Partridge, Fool Hen, Spotted Grouse, Swamp Grouse, Swamp Partridge, Wood Grouse, Wood Partridge.

**History.** The Hudsonian spruce grouse is the most plentiful of all the grouse clan. As the scientific name denotes, he is strictly Canadian.

Like all grouse, he belongs to the order *Gallinae,* the sub-order *Phasiani,* and the family *Tetraonidae.* In order to avoid any possible confusion three sub-species have been classified, all very much alike as to habits but differing somewhat in plumage and range. These sub-species will be included here under "Identification." Together they cover practically all of the wooded regions of Canada and Alaska with the exception of one area where the Franklin's grouse *(Canachites franklini)* is most commonly found.

The spruce grouse is commonly referred to as the spruce partridge in an effort to distinguish it from the birch partridge (ruffed grouse), but the term partridge is a misnomer for the bird is actually a grouse.

**Identification.** The Hudsonian and the various sub-species are slightly smaller than the ruffed grouse. Unlike the latter, they have no ruff and no crest on the head. The sexes differ in coloration.

MALE. The head, neck, and shoulders are gray, barred with wavy markings of black. The male carries a narrow comb of bare red skin over the eye. The throat and sides of the head are a sooty black bordered with a broken line of white around the edges. The back and wings are grayish-brown crossed with wavy black and gray lines, and bear some markings of dark brown. The chest is sooty black with light margins and the under parts are boldly barred with black and white crescent-shaped markings. The under-tail coverts are tipped with white. The tail, composed of 16 feathers, ends in a wide orange-brown band. The feet are completely feathered right down to the toes.

FEMALE. The entire upper parts, including the wings, are brown, variegated with tawny yellow and deep buff and barred with wavy black lines. The under parts are dull white streaked with tawny brown, especially on the breast. The tail is mottled with buff and carries a narrow band of orange-brown at the tip.

## ALASKA SPRUCE GROUSE

*Canachites canadensis osgoodi*

COMMON NAMES: Same as those for Hudsonian spruce grouse.

Both sexes are paler in coloration than the Hudsonian and the tails end in buff instead of orange. They are otherwise identical in appearance and general habits. These birds are found along the Mt. McKinley range and in the Yukon Territory east to Great Slave Lake.

## CANADIAN SPRUCE GROUSE

*Canachites canadensis canace*

COMMON NAMES: Same as for preceding species.

The sole difference appears in the females, which are gray on the back instead of brown. The males are identical with the Hudsonian spruce grouse.

This sub-species is the only one of the group which finds its way into the United States, where at times its range may overlap that of the ruffed grouse. It is generally distributed throughout southern Manitoba, Ontario, Quebec, New Brunswick, and Nova Scotia, and is not uncommon in the northern parts of Minnesota, Wisconsin, Michigan, New York, and New England.

## VALDEZ SPRUCE GROUSE

*Canachites canadensis atratus*

The Valdez is somewhat darker than the Alaska spruce grouse but the real distinction lies in the olive-colored plumage. It is the only member of the family having plumage of a brownish-green hue. The range is limited to southeastern Alaska and the bird is therefore not well known to the average sportsman.

**Characteristics.** One of the common names, fool hen, refers to this bird's characteristic trust in man. When flushed he seldom flies beyond the most convenient limb where he perches in utter confidence and watches the intruder with friendly curiosity. Shooting does not seem to disturb him greatly and often a bird will remain on the same limb after being narrowly missed by a bullet. Woodsmen frequently kill them with a stick.

The name spruce grouse denotes the bird's favorite habitat, among the dark spruce forests and the tamarack swamps of the north country. His staple diet is spruce and fir buds and for this reason the flesh is dark and generally considered unpalatable although there are those who think it fine-tasting. During the summer the diet is varied with berries and some insects and at this time the flesh is said to be less strong, but since that is the rearing season it is hardly the time to kill any birds.

The cock does not drum in the same manner as the ruffed grouse but he indulges in a similar practice during the mating season. Instead of using a log he walks slowly up the trunk of a leaning tree as he fans the air with rapidly beating wings. Sometimes he varies the performance by flying straight upward and then hangs in the air as though suspended while his wing-beats create a drumming sound not unlike that of the ruffed grouse. This display may be at treetop height or only a few feet off the ground. The purpose, as with the ruffed grouse, is to attract a mate. While on the ground he struts like a turkey cock with his feathers distended, head held high, and tail raised and expanded to its full width to impress the hen of his choice.

**Breeding.** The breeding habits of the spruce grouse are very similar to those of the ruffed grouse. (see pages 237-238). The hen is a devoted mother and the young are well cared for during their downy stage.

The juveniles somewhat resemble the hen until after the first moult when they take on the distinctive plumage of their sex.

**Range and Distribution.** The spruce grouse is generally distributed from the eastern base of the Rocky Mountains to Labrador, north to Alaska and south through Canada wherever there are good stands of spruce. As mentioned under "Identification," only one member of the group, the Canadian spruce grouse, is found south of the Canadian border.

# PINNATED GROUSE (Prairie Chicken) *Tympanuchus cupido americanus*

Common Names: Pinnated Grouse, Prairie Chicken, Prairie Grouse, Prairie Hen.

**History.** The prairie grouse was once abundant throughout the prairie provinces of Canada and the Great Plains of the United States. Their former range extended from just east of the Rocky Mountains and through the eastern central states. Just how far east these birds came is difficult to determine because their easterly range probably overlapped that of the heath hen, a bird which they resemble very closely. The latter, now extinct, was believed to have ranged as far west as the Kentucky barrens, but early records made no distinction between the two birds and so it is impossible to state definitely where one range ended and the other began.

The heath hen, unable to adapt itself to the changes brought by intensive cultivation, gradually diminished in numbers until the lone surviving member died on Martha's Vineyard, Massachusetts, where remnants of a once numerous species had made a last stand for survival.

The pinnated grouse, with more territory at its disposal, was able to avoid the fate of the heath hen by moving westward before the advance of civilization. On the vast plains these birds found food, shelter, and breeding grounds where except for natural enemies they were unmolested during the all-important nesting season. The tremendous areas of grazing land provided ideal conditions under which the birds could thrive and multiply.

Then came a world-wide demand for wheat and grain. The sod was broken and much of the former grassland went under cultivation. When the demand for grain lessened the fields were left idle and the top soil, once anchored by grass roots, was lifted and blown away in great storms of dust. Areas which once provided excellent pinnated grouse grounds became nothing but arid wasteland.

In those regions outside the dust bowl other dangers threatened the grouse. The spring harvesting of the winter wheat destroyed many nests. Spring plowing likewise broke up the nests and cover, and the practice of burning the old stubble before starting a new crop took a huge toll of eggs and young birds.

Under such adverse conditions the pinnated grouse is making a valiant stand and is still numerous in some sections, but it is a losing battle. The great flocks of these birds are a thing of the past and unless more of their former range is returned to grazing land their future is not very bright.

**Identification.** The pinnated grouse is also known as the prairie chicken, but this name is also used in reference to its close relative, the several species of sharp-tailed grouse. Locally the former are referred to as "chickens" and the latter as "sharptails" to distinguish between the two. In order to avoid any possible confusion the ornithological name of pinnated grouse will be used here. (See color plate on p. 481.)

These grouse are about the same length (18 inches) as the ruffed grouse, but because of their much shorter tails more of that length is body and they are a larger and heavier bird.

The over-all color of the upper parts is a yellowish-brown or buff, but this is heavily overlaid with transverse bars of deep brownish-black. These give the bird a somewhat barred effect; closer examination, however, reveals that the markings are irregular and actually a series of broken lines.

The forehead, crown, and sides of the head are a rich buff. The crown feathers are thickly mottled with black and brown spots and can be raised to a short crest. A stripe of brownish-black runs from the bill beneath the eye to the nape of the neck. The throat is plain buff bordered by a streak of dull black on top which creates a second stripe on the lower side of the head.

On either side of the neck there is a tuft of stiff, quill-like feathers about 3 inches long, reddish-brown and buff at the base, shading to deep black at the ends. These resemble small wings and can be raised over the head like horns. The cock (only) has an orange-colored sac on each side of his neck directly below this tuft of feathers. It is from these peculiar feathers that the bird gets his name of "pinnated."

The breast and under parts are dull white thickly barred with well-defined bands of blackish-brown. The primaries are plain brownish-black with round spots of pale buff on the outer webs. The tail, which has 18 feathers, is short, rounded, and of the same color as the wings. Each tail feather is narrowly tipped with white.

The legs and feet are feathered to the toes and the toes are webbed at their base.

Except for the shorter and less conspicuous neck tufts and the absence of air sacs on the female, both sexes appear the same, although the hen is often smaller and somewhat lighter in color.

**Characteristics.** The pinnated grouse, unlike most members of his family, is a lover of the wide open spaces. He finds cover where wood grouse would feel exposed and his habits fit his mode of life on the wide prairies. He does not run as swiftly as the pheasant but he gets over the ground very well. His flight is powerful and moderately fast considering his size. He begins with a series of powerful wing-beats—a trait common to all heavy-bodied, short-winged birds—and when air-borne he alternates between gliding and flying. When flushed, a flock of these birds get up with a loud, unnerving *"whor-r-r-r"* almost as startling in effect as the initial rise of a ruffed grouse.

The pinnated grouse is more gregarious than his woodland cousins and good-sized flocks are not uncommon. This is especially true in the autumn when huge "packs," as they are known locally, get together for the trek southward. The pinnated grouse, like the sharp-tailed grouse and the sage hen, is migratory to a degree. The urge to migrate is especially strong in the northern limits of their range. With the coming of winter weather there is a restless gathering of the packs before they begin to work their way toward a more temperate climate. Some ornithologists claim that such packs are made up of young birds and hens. The adult and hardier cocks are said to form packs of their own and remain on the home range all winter.

**Breeding.** The mating urge occurs in March and may last until early in May. During this period the cocks put on a remarkable demonstration of courtship. A number of cocks—varying from 4 or 5 to nearly 50—gather before sunrise at a cleared space known as the dancing ground. A cock inflates the air sacs on his neck until they resemble two oranges and then with a violent jerking motion of the head he expels the air. The resultant sound is a loud, resonant *"boom-ah-b-o-o-o-m,"* or, according to some observers, *"chika-oomboo-oo-oo-ooh, chika-oomboo-oo-ooh,"* which can be heard for over a mile.

One after another, or perhaps several at a time, the other cocks follow the lead of the first and soon the prairie resounds with their booming. This attracts the hens, who slip shyly through the grass to where they can watch the performance. Gradually the cocks work themselves into a frenzy. The feather tufts on each side of the neck are raised until they look like horns. With wings drooping and tail raised and spread the birds rush around for a few steps and then pause to emit more booming.

As his ardor mounts a cock may give a hoarse cackle and spring from the ground in a series of hops. Eventually these hops bring him in contact with a rival cock doing the same thing and then the feathers fly. At intervals between fights and booming the cocks strut and dance before the hens. The whole show ends abruptly after about an hour and the rival cocks feed peacefully together until the next morning when the performance is resumed. Toward the end of the mating season the cocks get more and more excited and fight more frequently. About this time the hens steal away and begin their nesting and the display of male vanity and prowess is over for that season.

The nest is made in a slight hollow on the ground and is sometimes concealed by bushes or tufts of grass. It is but thinly lined with grass and a few feathers. The eggs, from 8 to 12, are a light drab or buff, generally plain but sometimes flecked with brown.

The young, as with all grouse, are precocial and leave the nest at once. They feed chiefly on insects and are soon able to fly for a short distance. So far as is known the male takes no interest in helping to raise the brood. Immature birds resemble the hen and acquire full plumage after the first year.

**Feeding.** From early spring until late autumn their diet consists largely of insects, mostly grasshoppers. In the fall and winter they feed on a variety of grains, seeds, fruit, leaves, and flowers. Wild sunflowers and goldenrod come high on the list, and the birds are very fond of rose hips.

**Range and Distribution.** The pinnated grouse is fairly distributed over suitable areas from southern Saskatchewan and Manitoba to Colorado, Idaho, North and South Dakota, south to Texas, Arkansas, western Kentucky and Indiana.

There are two other species of pinnated grouse whose differences in range and appearance are as follows:

### LESSER PINNATED GROUSE

*Tympanuchus pallidicinctus*

COMMON NAMES: Lesser Prairie Chicken, Lesser Prairie Grouse, Lesser Prairie Hen.

These are somewhat smaller birds than the common pinnated grouse, being from 3 to 4 inches shorter and correspondingly lighter in weight. The markings are similar but the general coloration is much paler than that of their larger cousins.

The lesser pinnated grouse is found in parts of Colorado, western Oklahoma, Kansas, New Mexico, and south into the central part of Texas (particularly in Beaver, Texas, and Cimarron counties).

### ATTWATER'S PINNATED GROUSE

*Tympanuchus cupido attwateri*

COMMON NAMES: Attwater's Prairie Chicken.

This species is even smaller than the lesser pinnated grouse. The feathers on the neck tufts end in square tips and the legs are feathered only halfway down the feet. Coloration is very similar to that of the common pinnated grouse. The range of these birds is restricted to the coastal areas of southwestern Louisiana and Texas.

## RUFFED GROUSE

*Bonasa umbellus umbellus*

COMMON NAMES: Birch Partridge, Drumming Grouse, Grouse, Long-Tailed Grouse, Partridge, Pa'tridge, Pheasant, Mountain Pheasant, Shoulder-Knot Grouse, Tippet, White-Flesher, Wood Grouse.

**History.** The Latin name *Bonasa,* meaning bison, probably was suggested by the wild, headlong flight of this bird when flushed, although it may have come from his "drumming" which rolls like the distant thundering of a herd of buffalo. *Umbellus* refers to the neck ruff which can be raised and spread like an umbrella. The name ruffed grouse stems from this collar.

This hardy native was not always as shy and crafty as he is today. The Indian hunted him with trap and snare and bow-and-arrow, and his reputation as a welcome addition to the menu was well established before the earliest settlers arrived. When the first Pilgrim Father shouldered his blunderbuss and went out to get some meat for the table it is not unlikely that he returned with a brace or two of ruffed grouse.

Later the market gunners slaughtered these fine game birds along with all the other species. Pennsylvania and New England were the two greatest centers and thousands of birds were sold in Philadelphia and Boston as cheaply as 50 and 75 cents a pair. Among the common names, the term "white-flesher" was popularly used where these birds were formerly sold, probably to distinguish them from the prairie chicken—a darker-meated variety also on sale at that time.

*Bonasa* was a trusting bird with little fear of man—in very remote sections he is still comparatively tame—but he was by no means stupid and soon learned to adapt himself to a changing situation. He was, and still is, essentially a bird of the forest. Clearing the land for agriculture reduced his range and affected his numbers but he refused to be pushed out of the picture. He retired to the rocky hillsides and inaccessible places and when the virgin timber had been cut over he found that the slashings provided both suitable cover and food.

As time went on he discovered that the fringes of old orchards and abandoned farms made an ideal habitat, and he adopted the wily habits which permitted him to survive within sound of the woodsman's axe and sight of the farmer's plow. The more he was crowded the wiser he grew, and despite the many factors working toward his extermination he managed to escape the fate of the heath hen, the passenger pigeon, and other species now extinct.

Despite the cyclic thinning of his ranks and the terrific odds against a young grouse reaching maturity—because of disease and predators—there are favorable indications that *Bonasa's* drumming will continue to resound through our woods.

**Identification.** One of the largest of the upland game birds, the ruffed grouse is about the size of a small chicken. An adult male measures about 18 inches long and weighs from 24 to 30 ounces. The female is usually a bit smaller and generally averages no more than 17 to 22 ounces in weight. (See color plate on p. 482.)

The head, back of the neck, and upper parts of the body are a light chestnut brown spotted with buff, gray, white, and black. The feathers on the crown are more or less evenly barred with black and rise to a crest. This crest is usually smaller on the hen than on the cock. A line of light buff beginning at the bill extends beyond the eye to the rear of the head. The bill is fleshy-brown or bone color, and the eye dark hazel.

The throat is light buff very faintly barred with brown. At the base of the neck on each side, tufts of long, broad, black feathers, sometimes tipped with brown, form the ruff or collar. These feathers have a metallic, iridescent sheen. Just above this ruff and extending across the chest below the throat is a series of irregular dark narrow rings—usually four or five—separated by light buff. In some specimens the ruff is distinctly reddish brown without any markings and lacking any metallic sheen. The ruff feathers on the hen are generally shorter and of a brownish black without any sheen. In rare instances the ruff is entirely lacking on the female.

The lower back and rump are usually washed with dark-reddish brown and marked with a series of oval buff spots encircled with black.

The scapulars and wing coverts are streaked with pale buff and rufous in a pattern roughly resembling a series of notches. The primaries are grayish brown with a pale stem through each feather, and the outer webs are barred with creamy white.

The long tail may be brown or gray. In the latter case it is finely mottled with black and usually crossed by six or seven narrow bands of blackish brown, the subterminal bar being much wider than the rest and each of the 18 feathers ending in a light mottled-gray tip. The brownish tails are crossed by irregular buff bands, bordered above and below by narrow bands of black. The subterminal black band is bordered on each side by gray mottled with black. The tail of an adult cock is usually about an inch longer than that of an adult hen. The color band at the end of a cock's tail is unbroken across the entire width, but the band on the tail of the hen is generally broken in the two center feathers—especially on the undersides.

The breast is whitish washed with pale brown or ochre and boldly marked with transverse bars of dark brown. The sides and abdomen, also of pale whitish-ochre, are marked with large, wedge-shaped spots of dark brown. The under tail coverts and thighs are plain light buff, sometimes tinged with gray, and the legs are feathered to the hind toes. The feet are brownish black.

In the winter the feet are equipped with tiny hair-like feathers which act as snowshoes and permit the birds to travel over soft snow.

The plumage description above will serve as a general guide but the color phases are so variable, even with birds in the same area, that some discrepancy will occur in different specimens. There are gray grouse and brown grouse, some almost reddish in tone, and a wide range of combinations between these two colors. All are true ruffed grouse, however, and are easily distinguished from the other species.

The two sexes closely resemble each other and despite the general differences noted above it is often impossible to distinguish between them except by dissection.

The following sub-species are so similar in habits and appearance that only a brief description is deemed neccsary.

### CANADA RUFFED GROUSE

*Bonasa umbellus togata*

A bird practically identical with the common ruffed grouse except for heavier barred markings on the under parts, and a grayer back; the tail is usually gray. Commonly found through the central portions of Canada and as far south as New York and New England and west to northern Oregon.

### NOVA SCOTIA RUFFED GROUSE

*Bonasa umbellus thayeri*

A sub-species similar to the others but inclined to a dark sooty-gray. As the name implies, these birds are found only in Nova Scotia.

### GRAY RUFFED GROUSE

*Bonasa umbellus umbelloides*

A sub-species which is very similar to the Canada ruffed grouse but grayer and generally lighter in color. It is found chiefly in the Rocky Mountain regions of the United States, as far north as Alaska and east to Manitoba.

### OREGON RUFFED GROUSE

*Bonasa umbellus sabini*

This sub-species is found in northern California, Oregon, Washington, and British Columbia and as far north as Alaska. It is a bird with much more reddish plumage than the ordinary ruffed grouse, but is the same in other respects. It is sometimes called Sabine's ruffed grouse, or, from its coloring, red ruffed grouse.

## YUKON RUFFED GROUSE

*Bonasa umbellus yukonensis*

This bird is the grayest of all the ruffed grouse and also the largest. Their range is the most northerly of all the ruffed grouse family, for they are found only in the interior of the Yukon Territory.

**Characteristics.** One's first acquaintance with a ruffed grouse is apt to be a very startling experience. At one moment all is quiet; the next moment a blurred brown-gray form explodes from the ground almost underfoot and rockets into the air with a thunderous roar of wings. A few scattered leaves settling slowly back to earth mark the spot where he was concealed, and falling twigs are likely to mark the route of his hasty departure. With uncanny skill he flies so that a tree or some other obstruction looms between the intruder and his line of flight. In a matter of seconds he has disappeared from sight, leaving the novice observer bewildered.

This is probably the most used of his many strategies, but *Bonasa* has a bagful of tricks to suit any occasion. He often waits until the intruder has passed and then whirrs up from behind to be gone almost before one can turn around. If he thinks the situation calls for an earlier departure he may flush far ahead and only the telltale whirr of wings will mark his going.

He can, and often does, fly as silently as an owl. Usually the silent take-off is from a tree where he has been hiding close to the trunk, body erect and motionless to resemble a branch. At such times he pitches out on set wings and coasts to the next cover.

The flight is generally in a fairly straight line and seldom more than 200 to 300 yards; often it is much shorter, particularly in the case of young birds or in those sections where there has been little disturbance from shooting. As a rule the flight does not exceed 30 to 40 feet in altitude and may be much lower. High-flying birds are more likely to alight in a tree, usually a conifer, than the low flyers. The wide tail is fanned out in flight and acts as a rudder, thus permitting the bird to skim through heavy growth at high speed. The term "high speed" is purely relative, however, for the grouse seems to fly more rapidly than is actually the case. The cover in which he is generally flushed and his ability to disappear quickly lend an illusion of super-speed which is deceiving.

Any statement regarding his flight must necessarily be general, for it is impossible to predict what he will do at any time, but it is usually a safe bet that he will do the unexpected.

The ruffed grouse is non-migratory and seldom moves beyond a one-half-mile radius from a chosen spot. Unless too frequently disturbed he is likely to be found in the same locality from year to year.

The search for food governs his movements to some extent. In the spring and summer he usually frequents the sunny hillsides and in the winter he generally drops down into the lowlands. Little-used roads in the back country attract him for their dusting beds. Old orchards and abandoned farms have a special attraction because he finds there the tender green shoots and plant life which do not grow in the more shaded portions of the woods. One of his favorite haunts is a cut-over stand of hardwoods interpersed with some evergreens. On rainy or stormy days he seeks the shelter of tall conifers where he nestles against the trunks for protection from the elements.

He feeds from daylight to about noon and then seeks some sheltered spot to dust and rest. About mid-afternoon he resumes feeding and continues until time to seek a roost at dusk.

On stormy days he is usually more wary, and when the wind is high he becomes extremely wild. The theory has been advanced that this extra wildness is caused by the fact that he cannot hear the approach of danger under such conditions.

Ruff is a capable walker and generally uses that method of locomotion in his search for something to eat. During his travels any old moss-grown log that occurs in his path draws him irresistibly and he will walk the length of it even though it might be just as easy to go alongside.

The most unique characteristic of the grouse is his habit of drumming, or "beating," as is was once called. This habit serves a triple purpose and is practiced throughout the year, although much less frequently during winter than in the other seasons. In the spring it is both a mating call and a challenge to rival cocks; at other times it seems to serve as an outlet for excess vitality. Generally it is done in the early morning but it may take place any time during the day and even at night, especially if there is a full moon. Most of the autumn drumming is done by young cocks.

The cock selects a site for his drumming with some care and returns to it, often year after year, if not molested. The chosen spot is most often a fallen log, but it may be a large rock, an old stone fence, or a stump. It is always situated in a spot which affords a fairly clear view of his surroundings, for the cock is most wary and cautious at this time.

The actual drumming sound is produced by a rapid beating of the wings while the body is held in an erect posture. Some early naturalists got the impression that the sound was caused by the wings beating on a hollow log; others thought that the wings struck each other on the back stroke; and still others contended that the noise was created by the wings beating against the breast. More recently, with the aid of fast lenses and movie cameras it has been established that the rush of air through the opened primary feathers of the wing is responsible for the sound which has been likened to "little thunder," or a roll on a muffled drum.

The grouse mounts his chosen site and begins with a few tentative wing flaps such as a barnyard rooster might make when about to crow. The wing beats are then speeded up until the wings become a blur; as the sound increases in volume the wing-beats become shorter. Suddenly the beating ceases. The cock then stands very erect, listening and watching intently for some results of his announced presence. His hope, in the spring, is to attract a hen; but a rival cock may also be drawn to the sound, or one of his many enemies. The wary grouse is ready to cope with any eventuality. If an enemy appears he springs into instant flight; if another grouse shows up he prepares for battle until he learns whether the stranger is a rival cock or a hen. The drumming lasts but a few seconds—seldom more than ten—and if there is no response the performance is repeated frequently with short periods of silence between each drumming.

The sound has a peculiar ventriloquial quality which makes it difficult to locate exactly. On quiet days it can be heard for more than half a mile and it echoes and re-echoes through the hills in such a way that its origin is lost. A drumming grouse often seems close at hand when actually he may be a good distance from the listener.

Incredible as it seems, the cock is not always able to determine whether the grouse that responds to his call is male or female. The drummer takes no chances and is ready for a fight or courtship as the occasion demands. He stalks toward the other bird with ruff extended, wings trailing, tail erect and fanned out to its greatest extent. As he nears the stranger he shakes his head rapidly and emits a sort of hissing sound. When but a short distance away he makes a fierce rush and brings up in front of his possible opponent with a drawn-out *"h-i-s-s-s-s."* This routine is sometimes referred to as his "intimidation display" and is intended for that purpose.

If the newcomer proves to be a cock and is not frightened by the display of truculence there is likely to be a battle royal. Rival cocks fight long and valiantly but seldom with serious results to either contestant. The drumming cock seeks to defend his territory and to drive the rival bird away, but he rarely picks a fight with a cock that is physically superior.

Should the newcomer prove to be a hen, the cock's demeanor changes abruptly from belligerence to courtship. He walks in a sort of strutting attitude around the hen, with his tail fanned and dragging on the ground, now and then giving her gentle pecks on the bill. The hen is generally receptive to his attentions and mating may occur soon after his "intimidation act."

Some mention has already been made of the predators which threaten the existence of the grouse. The complete list is a long one, and it is a tribute to the bird's sagacity that he contrives to elude so many enemies. Chief on the list is the great horned owl. The big snowy owl is just as deadly, but fortunately his normal range is farther north and he is only an occasional winter visitor to the major portion of the ruffed grouse country. All of the owls prey on grouse at times. The hawks crowd the owls for first place on the list of killers and practically the entire hawk family comes under suspicion. Fiercest and deadliest is the goshawk. Like the snowy owl, he commonly ranges farther north, but when driven down by food shortage he is a terror in grouse cover. The soaring hawks, such as the marsh hawk, broad-wing, and red-shouldered hawk sometimes pick up a young grouse, but they are not persistent grouse hunters and their normal diet of mice and other vermin more than makes up for an occasional lapse in conduct. The smaller hawks generally select smaller victims, but if food is scarce they will not hesitate to attack a full-grown grouse and are perfectly capable of killing one.

House cats, wild cats, and the bay lynx account for many birds each year. The latter, being comparatively few in numbers, are not so great a menace as the common wood-roving tabby who preys chiefly on young birds. Foxes take enough birds annually to be regarded as dangerous enemies. Weasels, martens, fishers, and the Canada lynx also kill grouse whenever the opportunity offers. These, in addition to the egg destroyers previously noted, make up a formidable array of predators which a grouse must outwit if he is to survive. It has been estimated that but three out of every hundred eggs produce grouse to be bagged by the sportsman.

Although the grouse is non-migratory there is a period in the early autumn when nature seems to take a hand in redistributing the grouse population. During this time, which the Indians called the "mad moon" or "crazy moon," the grouse, for no apparent reason, goes on wild, haphazard flights. He flies into all kinds of man-made obstructions—buildings, light wires, radio towers, poles, fences, and even the windshields of automobiles. Grouse killed by this apparently blind flying are picked up on roads, in streets, and in all sorts of unusual places. It is believed that nature impels them to disperse in this manner in order to relieve overstocked covers and to prevent inbreeding.

During the winter when the snow is deep, grouse often leave the evergreens and use a snowbank for a resting place. Generally they dive into the snow from flight and thus leave no trail for a predator to pick up, but sometimes they merely walk to a suitable drift and tunnel their way inside. There they remain snug and warm until the next morning. On rare occasions a hard crust forms over the opening and the grouse, unable to peck his way out, dies of starvation; but the site selected is usually on a southern exposure where the sun will soften any crust that might form during the night.

**Breeding.** The cock is polygamous and will mate with as many hens as he can attract. The hens disappear after mating and do their own nest building in secret. The cock takes no part in raising the family and is probably unaware of their existence.

The nest is crudely made of dead leaves, small twigs, and dried grass, with a few feathers sometimes added for good measure. It is usually located under a fallen tree, log, overhanging rock, or some other protection. Often a thick clump of bush affords a sufficient hiding place.

The clutch varies from eight to 14 eggs, with ten or 11 being about the average setting. The eggs vary in color from pale cream to pale brown and are sometimes blotched or spotted with dusky markings. The hen does not begin incubation until the entire clutch is laid, and so all the chicks hatch at the same time. The hen seems to be able to tell which eggs are fertile, for after about a week she begins to remove the infertile eggs from the nest. Fortunately the percentage of infertile eggs is low and seldom more than one or two at most need to be discarded. During the early stage of incubation the hen covers her back with leaves and grass which not only render her less conspicuous on the nest but fall on the eggs when she leaves and help to hide them until she returns. As the hatching time approaches she is less fussy about hiding the nest.

Various predators take a much heavier toll from the eggs than from the young chicks. Snakes, particularly rattlers and blacksnakes, skunks, raccoons, opossums, and the ever-vicious red squirrels destroy the eggs. Even chipmunks have been known to play havoc with them, although in the latter case it appears that the chipmunk hides the eggs but does not eat them. The red squirrel is not so much an egg eater as some of the other predators; he prefers those eggs which have completely developed chicks inside. However, he destroys a good many eggs in the course of his search. If the setting is destroyed the hen generally gives up for that season, but sometimes she will complete a second but smaller nesting.

The young leave the nest as soon as they are dry and begin a precarious existence under the watchful eye of a doting mother. For the first month of their lives they are subject to many perils. As they try to follow the mother they fall into depressions with vertical walls such as ruts, potholes, etc. Since many of these depressions contain water at that time of the year, the young chicks are drowned, as the mother seems powerless to extricate them from their plight. The chicks are low in vitality, and cold, wet weather is usually fatal to many. The mother does her best to cover them during the rain and chill but despite her devoted care a number usually succumb to the elements.

The downy young are also subject to parasites and disease. Some writers believe that their inability to withstand illness stems from the egg-forming stage within the hen. At that time of year the food supply is low in both quality and quantity, and although just what food is required to produce strong, healthy chicks is not known, it is assumed that the hen lacks sufficient nourishment for her task of egg building. It has been learned from surveys that the hen is generally in a much poorer condition during the egg-laying period than at any other time.

Added to their natural perils, the automobile has become a menace to both the chicks and the older birds. Roads provide an ideal combination of all the things a mother grouse seeks for her young. There are dusting places to keep down the ever-present parasites, and because roadsides are usually open to the sun they produce the lush green plants which in turn attract the insects upon which the young chicks depend so largely for food. At the approach of a car the little family scatters in every direction and many of the chicks run directly into the path of the vehicle. Sometimes the mother is killed, and her death usually means the loss of the entire brood.

No game bird does the "broken wing" trick better than a mother grouse. She relies on this ruse to distract attention from her family and gives a very convincing performance. Usually she drags one wing as though it were broken and for good measure adds a decided limp. Fluttering and hobbling along, just out of reach, she leads the intruder away from the chicks, who meanwhile have scurried to hiding places under leaves and roots where they remain absolutely motionless until she returns with the all-clear signal.

Chicks that survive the rigors of babyhood mature rapidly and in less than a month usually have sprouted enough feathers to enable them to fly a short distance. As soon as possible they fly up into the trees to roost and part of the mother's care is over. Their covering at this time is partly down and partly pin feathers. When the down is replaced by feathers the immature birds resemble the hen.

Late in July the adult birds have a moulting period. Like many other species, they lose the power of flight at this time. While the moult is in progress they seek shelter in the heaviest cover possible, to escape their natural enemies, and do not move about any more than is necessary. By September they have new plumage and emerge from their hiding to resume normal habits. The cocks then mingle peacefully with each other and with the hens and young birds. The cocks return to their drumming logs from time to time, but drumming is less frequent than during the breeding season. It is now more of a display of male vanity than a mating call. Young cocks must learn to drum, and they are more often heard in the autumn than the adult birds.

**Feeding.** Broadly, he is omnivorous, but the bulk of his diet, in season, consists of berries; he is not particular as to what kind. In winter he eats poison sumac, apple, birch, aspen and hemlock buds, or mountain laurel with impunity. Some claim has been made that when the birds are forced to feed largely upon the poisonous leaves of the laurel their flesh is contaminated and unfit for human consumption. This has never been proved and remains a matter of opinion; but since the birds feed on this substance only during the scarcity of other foods in the winter when they are not legal game it makes little difference to the sportsman.

It is hardly possible to enumerate all the items that a grouse classes as food, but the partial listing below will give some idea of his wide range in tastes: Apples (a few), barberries, bayberries, blueberries, chokeberries, dewberries, grapes (summer, frost, and fox), huckleberries, raspberries (wild), rose hips, snowberries, strawberries (wild), thorn apples, wild cherries (red and black), and wild plums.

In the autumn he feeds on mast, acorns, beechnuts, chestnuts, etc. During the winter his food list is limited to what he can find above the snow. Birch, poplar, and beech buds are favored when available.

In addition to the foods listed above he consumes quantities of green leaves and the tender shoots of such plants as asters, teaberries, fern tips, and hawthorn haws, to name only a few. Live creatures such as ants, beetles, crickets, cutworms, grasshoppers, leafhoppers, and locusts add further variety, although these are usually eaten by the young birds and not in any quantities by the adults.

With such catholic tastes, the grouse is obviously better equipped to survive, from a food standpoint, than most other game birds. He suits his appetite to whatever is available at the time in his locality.

**Range and Distribution.** The ruffed grouse is found throughout the eastern provinces of Canada and the northern tier of the United States. The greatest concentration, relatively speaking, is in the northeastern states. They range from southern Minnesota through southern Wisconsin and Michigan to New York and the New England states, south through Pennsylvania to northern Georgia and Alabama. If the sub-species listed on pp. 235-236 are included, it will be noted that the ruffed grouse family is widely distributed through Canada and the United States except in the south and southwest.

# SAGE GROUSE

*Centrocercus urophasianus*

Common Names: Cock of the Plains, Sage Cock, Sage Hen.

**History.** When westward-bound pioneers passed the fertile plains and entered the sagebrush country they came in contact with a grouse much larger than any they had ever seen before. These birds were the sage grouse, or sage hens, the largest of all the grouse family. Doubtless they were abundant over all the dry alkali plains and even at considerable altitude wherever there was sagebrush for food and cover.

Unlike their close relatives the prairie grouse, they shunned the more fertile grasslands and preferred the wilder and less inviting terrain which is still their habitat. Because their range was less conducive to cultivation than the lush prairies they suffered less disturbance than other members of their group. Although their former numbers have been greatly reduced they are still comparatively plentiful, and so long as a considerable portion of the western range remains covered with sage the species will probably continue to survive, for only the destruction of their desolate habitat can seriously affect their future.

**Identification.** The sage grouse is the largest true grouse in the world. Adult males measure close to 3 feet in length and weigh around 8 pounds. Next to the wild turkey these are the largest gallinaceous birds in North America. (See color plate on p. 481.)

Males. The basic color of the upper parts is an ashy-gray, but this is so variegated with black, brown, and yellowish-white that no one color can be called predominant. The darker markings take the form of rather narrow transverse bars, broken by the lighter areas. The wing coverts are streaked with dull white. The rump and central feathers of the tail are barred in such a manner as to produce a marbled effect, and the 20 tail feathers taper off into very thin points. The outer tail feathers are black barred with gray.

The entire head is marked with fine dusky bars but these are more conspicuous on the crown. On each side of the neck there is a patch of feathers about 3 inches long having very stiff shafts and ending in fine hairlike tips. Just in front of these feathers there is a patch of bare skin, varying from pale reddish brown to dull yellow, which can be greatly distended into air sacs. The lower portions of these sacs are covered with short white feathers and are very irregular and warty in appearance. When inflated they are not smoothly round like those of the pinnated or sharp-tailed grouse but can be distended to remarkable proportions. When filled with air they sometimes protrude above the head and far out in front of the body. Above the sacs on each side there is a tuft of white down covered by longer plumes of black. The throat is black, speckled with gray, and generally has a distinct white border at the rear.

The under parts are a yellowish-gray except for a black patch on the abdomen. They are lightly barred in front and heavily barred at the rear with dark brown markings. The legs are feathered to the toes.

Females. The hen is somewhat smaller than the cock; otherwise she is similar in appearance, but has a white throat, lacks the peculiar neck feathers and air sacs, and has a much shorter and narrower tail.

**Characteristics.** The sage grouse seems to be one species of which the ornithologists have been unable to discover any sub-species. Wherever found, these birds are the same in size, coloration, and habits. As the name implies, they abound only in the sagebrush country, where they find both food and shelter.

The bulk of their diet consists of sage leaves which, especially in the old birds, impart a decidedly strong and unpleasant taste to their flesh. Adult birds are as tough as they are unpalatable. The younger birds consume more insects and grains and are much preferred for the table. This preference is merely comparative, however, for most authorities on the matter agree that the sage grouse is no delicacy. In some sections all the birds eat alfalfa, grain, and garden plants when available and often devour quantities of berries.

Just how their food is digested is a matter of conjecture because, unlike other scratching birds, they have no gizzard. Lacking this organ, they do not take in gravel to aid in pulverizing their food, and it is assumed that they rely on strong digestive juices for this purpose.

Apart from their size, their peculiar nuptial demonstrations are their chief outstanding characteristic. In general their behavior at mating time is similar to that of the prairie grouse, but the sage grouse stages a more elaborate display.

The birds are gregarious and sometimes more than 100 cocks gather at a chosen site on some barren flat. Like the sharp-tailed grouse, they perform at sunrise and sunset and the hens gather from all around to admire the wooing of the males. The cocks are highly polygamous and endeavor to attract as many hens as possible.

This "drumming"—or "croaking," to describe it more accurately—begins very early in the spring. It may even begin in late winter if the weather is mild. The males are in full mating plumage and vigor as early as February along the southern portions of their range.

The male begins his remarkable antics by standing stiffly erect with drooping wings held away from his sides. He raises and spreads his tail and often works it from side to side like the opening and closing of a fan. At the same time the loose skin on the neck is drawn in and out like a bellows and the huge air sacs are distended until the feathers surrounding them bristle at right angles to the neck. Often the inflated sacs almost obscure the head. The skin between the sacs is then drawn in with a sucking motion which brings the two sacs nearly together in front of the throat. The air is then expelled with a coarse croaking or grunting sound which, being difficult to describe, has been likened to various noises. One observer thought it sounded like the purr of a giant cat, another claimed it resembled the sound of an old pump. There is considerable disagreement over the sound because it is so difficult to describe accurately.

During the alternate filling and deflation of the air sacs the cocks strut and dance about in a pompous attitude. As their excitement increases they often fight viciously with other males, but such battles are usually brief and result in little damage to either contestant. As a climax to their other actions the cocks inflate their necks until the sacs resemble small balloons and then, bending forward as though the sacs were too heavy to carry, they lower them to the ground and throw their whole weight upon the distended portions. They then push themselves along over the bare ground for some distance before expelling the air in a series of rumbling cackles and chuckling sounds. After this practice has been continued for a time all the feathers on the lower neck become worn down to mere bristles.

Toward the end of summer the hens and young birds are often found near streams or water holes. It is presumed that this is from choice, or possibly in search of different food, rather than the necessity for water, as the birds seem able to thrive in arid sections where no water is available. There is little or no succulence in their natural diet of sage and it is probable that dew provides whatever moisture is necessary.

Like the prairie grouse, they assemble in large "packs" in the autumn and, though they do not migrate in the same sense as do other migratory species, they often leave the open spaces and seek the shelter of valleys, or even the timber. They are hardy birds and can withstand the elements, although hailstorms sometimes kill both young and old.

They blend so well with their surroundings that it is not uncommon to walk into a flock without seeing a single bird and then have them whirr up on all sides. In sections where they are frequently hunted they become more wary and often flush well beyond range and fly for a long distance. When flushed they utter a sharp cackle of alarm which sounds like *"kek, kek, kek."* Their flight is labored at the start but they fly well and fast when under way.

**Breeding.** The mating period is of longer duration than that of other species and often lasts until early May. When the mating has been accomplished the hens retire and begin nesting. They usually select a site near a stream or spring hole if possible. Here they scratch out a depression under a sage bush and deposit from seven to nine dull greenish-brown eggs marked with round spots of sepia. Incubation requires about 22 days and the young birds are ready to run when no more than 15 minutes old.

The downy young resemble little turkeys and utter a similar *"peep."* They also give voice to a rather plaintive whistle. During the cool nights they nestle under the mother's wings until their own feathers provide sufficient covering. By late autumn the young birds are fully grown and resemble the hen except for being lighter in color.

**Range and Distribution.** These birds are widely distributed over the sagebrush plains from southern British Columbia, southern Saskatchewan, and northwestern North Dakota, south to middle-eastern California, northwest New Mexico, and northwestern Nebraska.

# SHARP-TAILED GROUSE

*Pedioecetes phasianellus phasianellus*

COMMON NAMES: Black Foot, Northern Sharp-Tailed Grouse, Prairie Chicken, Pin-Tailed Grouse, Pin-Tail, Sharp-Tailed Prairie Chicken, Spike-Tail, Spike-Tailed Grouse, Sprig-Tailed Grouse, White-Bellied Grouse, White-Belly, White Grouse, Willow Grouse.

**History.** The story of the sharp-tailed grouse family, of which there are three members, is like that of the pinnated grouse. In the early days these birds were plentiful throughout the western and northwestern plains country but suffered from the destruction of their cover and breeding grounds. The passing of the grazing lands sounded the death-knell for thousands of sharptails just as surely as it did for the other species.

As the flocks diminished there was a clamor for legislation to protect them, but drought and erosion, coupled with the destruction of their winter foods, were the real factors in reducing their numbers. With the planting of windbreaks and the restoration of the land in some sections the birds gained a new lease on life, and, while it is unlikely that they will ever regain their former state of abundance, there is some hope that complete extinction may be avoided.

**Identification.** The sharptail is slightly larger than the pinnated grouse, being about 20 inches in length. He is sometimes confused with the latter but is easily distinguished by the longer, spikelike middle feathers of the tail and the absence of feather tufts on the neck. Both species share the common name of prairie chicken, but this term generally refers to the pinnated rather than the sharp-tailed grouse. (See color plate on p. 482.)

The two sexes are identical in coloration but the tail of the female is considerably shorter and she lacks the air sacs of the male. The head and neck are a rich buff with a whitish patch on each side of the neck and a whitish streak behind the eye. The cocks have orange-colored air sacs on each side of the neck which are hidden by plumage when not inflated. The crown, which is slightly crested, and the nape of the neck are marked with narrow transverse bars of blackish-brown. The throat is plain light buff. The upper mandible is a dark horn-color and the lower bill is flesh-colored. The iris is pale brown.

The upper parts are yellowish-buff heavily flecked with brownish-black, dull chestnut, and gray. These markings are closely and evenly distributed and produce a variegated effect. The back has a more reddish tone and the markings on the rump are smaller. The wing coverts are the same coloring as the back but each feather bears a prominent, rounded spot of white. The primaries are plain dusky but the secondaries have square yellowish-white spots with white tips.

The under parts are buffy-white on the chest blending to nearly pure white below and the breast is generously marked with broad V-shaped pencilings of very dark brown. The rest of the under parts are marked with scattered spots of the same color except on the middle of the belly, which is plain.

The tail is marked with black and buff. The outside feathers are white on the inner webs and mottled on the outer. The middle tail feathers extend some distance beyond the rest to form the spike from which the bird gets many of its common names.

The legs are feathered to the first joint of the toes and in the winter the toes have a fringe of horny growth which serves as snowshoes.

**Characteristics.** The habits of the sharptail are similar to to those of the pinnated grouse. Both species eat the same foods and prefer the wide prairies for living space. The sharptail, however, ranges farther north than the pinnated grouse and modifies his habits to suit his environment.

The mating habits differ sufficiently from those of the other species to warrant a description. As soon as spring arrives on the prairies the males, like those of the pinnated grouse, congregate at the "walking" or "dancing" grounds and send forth their booming calls to attract the hens. The pinnated grouse performs his courtship antics early in the morning, but the sharptail performs twice a day, at sunrise and at sunset. When the birds first gather they stand quietly about, then a cock half spreads his wings horizontally, lowers his head, fans out his tail, and with air sacs distended runs across the meeting ground. He stamps his feet on the hard earth so rapidly that they produce a drumming sound and at the same time he utters a rumbling crow of *"cac, cac, cac . . ."* His wing-beats increase rapidly and his tail vibrates with a low rustling sound.

His excitement is contagious and immediately all the other cocks follow his example. They circle right and left, charge back and forth, and pass each other with stiffly bristled feathers. They bow, squat, and strut in a variety of postures until their antics resemble an Indian war dance. As their ardor increases the birds jump wildly about, sometimes leaping over the backs of their companions. Occasionally two cocks engage in battle but the prime motive seems to be for each bird to make as much noise and show as he can. The strange dance is continued twice daily until the entire mating season is over.

A similar display sometimes takes place in the autumn but since it has no connection with mating at that time it is probably, like the drumming of the ruffed grouse, merely a release of excess vitality.

In the fall the birds gather in large "packs" and alight on trees and haystacks. When disturbed and about to fly they utter a loud cackling sound which is often repeated during flight. The more northern birds are believed to migrate to some extent although numbers remain on the home range all winter. During this time they seek the protection of shrubbery and the edges of timber. In the winter they feed on buds from the willow, birch, and other trees.

**Breeding.** The nest is a thinly lined ground hollow, sometimes sheltered by a clump of grass, sometimes in the open. The eggs number from 10 to 16 and are grayish-olive with fine spottings of brown.

The hen sits very close and blends so well with her surroundings as to be practically invisible. The young birds leave the nest as soon as hatched and depend on their natural camouflage for protection.

**Range and Distribution.** The sharp-tailed grouse is the most northerly of the three races and its range is confined to Canada and Alaska. These birds are found from northwestern British Columbia to central Alaska and south to the Great Lakes.

### PRAIRIE SHARP-TAILED GROUSE
*Pedioecetes phasianellus campestris*

This sub-species is the most plentiful in the United States. It is identical in markings to the sharp-tailed grouse but there is more buff in the plumage which gives the bird a more yellowish appearance. They are found in the prairie country east of the Rocky Mountains from New Mexico to Manitoba and as far east as Wisconsin and Illinois.

### COLUMBIAN SHARP-TAILED GROUSE
*Pedioecetes phasianellus columbianus*

These birds are much grayer than the preceding birds and the dark markings are less conspicuous. They range from central British Columbia and central Alberta south to California (now becoming rare in that state), Utah, and Colorado.

# SOOTY GROUSE
*Dendragapus fuliginosus fuliginosus*

COMMON NAMES: Many of the same terms used for the Dusky Grouse.

**History.** This bird was formerly classed with the *obscurus* group but was later given a classification of its own. There are but few differences between the sooty and the dusky grouse, the chief variance being in size. In order to avoid any possible confusion ornithologists now list them separately.

**Identification.** The sooty grouse is about 2 inches shorter than the dusky and correspondingly lighter in weight. In general appearance the two birds are quite similar. The sooty grouse is a trifle darker than the dusky and the comb and air sacs are yellowish instead of red. Otherwise the plumage and markings are identical.

The group is subdivided into four classifications and the three other members will be described here. The range is the chief reason for subdivision, because the plumage changes are minor.

### SITKA GROUSE
*Dendragapus fuliginosus sitkensis*

In this sub-species it is the hens which vary by being much more reddish-brown in color, especially on the upper parts. The males are identical with the cocks of the sooty grouse. The range is restricted to the islands of southeastern Alaska.

### SIERRA GROUSE
*Dendragapus fuliginosus sierrae*

These grouse are generally paler in tone than the sooty grouse. The feathers on the shoulders show more white and the throat is lighter. They are fairly evenly distributed from southern Washington to Fort Klamath, Oregon, and thence south into California along the Sierra Nevada Mountains.

### MOUNT PINOS GROUSE

*Dendragapus fuliginosus howardi*

Grouse of this variety are even paler in tone than the Sierra grouse and the breast is reddish rather than gray. They range from Mount Pinos and southern California east through the Tehachapi Range, and north to the Sierra Nevadas.

**Characteristics.** What has been stated regarding the dusky grouse (pp. 230-231) also applies to the sooty variety. The habits of feeding, breeding, nesting, etc., are virtually the same.

**Range and Distribution.** Sooty grouse are found along the northwest coastal mountain ranges from Alaska to Oregon and northwestern California.

### HUNTING METHODS

**Ruffed Grouse.** Although the quail is a more widely distributed bird, and for that reason more widely known and more popular, and though the wild turkey, at least so far as size is concerned, is a grander bird, the ruffed grouse is the favorite of all American sportsmen who know him well. There is about him a constant patrician elegance that few other birds, even of the finer game species, possess. He is a bird of amazing speed and grace; and, loving the wilderness as he does, he has a personality that invests the forest with much of its mystery, beauty, and glamour.

Wherever he is much hunted, he develops a wildness and a wariness that are often more than a match for the stealth and craftiness of the hunter. In certain parts of his range he is so tame that it is no trouble to walk up to him and shoot his head off with a .22; sometimes he can even be killed with a stick. But he is a bird quickly educated; and where he is regularly hunted, the best sportsman's art is taxed to secure decent shots. And, except occasionally, as when the bird may be caught in the brush along some meadow stream, or in low-growing laurels or huckleberries on a mountain plateau, the shooting is going to have to be done in the woods, often in a dense stand of timber, or amid conifers; it bears no relation to shooting ducks or geese under the open sky, or quail above the stubble. It is distinctly a touch-and-go business, swift and sudden, with the advantage usually with the regal bird rather than with the hunter. And not only is the grouse supplied with what might be called the natural interference that the forest supplies, but he takes most amazing advantage of it. If there is a bush or a tree behind which he can veeringly dash in his dazzling flight, the hunter should count on him to do so. He may not, but he is likely to. It is in his nature.

In flight the grouse is likely to speed away low and dodgingly, putting, if possible, some natural obstruction between himself and his pursuer, or else he will tower to the treetops. In either case the hunter has to calculate, without a second's loss of time, the direction of flight and the angles of change. So exacting are the requirements that many otherwise good hunters simply do not try for grouse. They admit with blunt frankness that they simply cannot hit them. In fair grouse country, where the birds have taken a postgraduate course in the ways of sportsmen, if a man can bag on an average of two in a half-day's hunt, he has done well. It might be said that if a hunter kills 50 per cent of the birds he shoots at he need not be ashamed. The chances against him are a little more than even.

Many men hunt grouse without a dog, many use a dog. Which method is best will depend entirely on the qualities of the dog. A fast, careless, brash, wide-ranging dog is of little use in grouse hunting. This bird flushes much more easily than a quail, and his flight may take him much farther. Quail rarely fly more than 200 yards. Grouse, especially when flushed from the top of a hill or the high slope of a mountain, after once clearing the timber, have been known to fly clear across a valley more than a mile wide. When flushed, quail occasionally but rarely alight in trees; grouse frequently do so, especially in dense evergreens such as the pine and the hemlock. When, therefore, a somewhat hard-to-control dog flushes a grouse, it is often impossible to know where the bird has gone.

There seems to be no particular choice between the pointer and the setter; but the setter, being gentler by disposition and more easily managed, is more frequently employed. As a general rule, the older and slower the dog, the better he is for grouse. His value also depends to a considerable degree on his knowledge of the game he is hunting. It takes much longer to train a dog thoroughly on grouse than it does on quail. The terrain is usually more difficult, and the birds are wilder. Dogs of the flashy field-trial type will hardly ever be good grouse dogs. One veteran grouse hunter reports that the best dog he ever worked on this difficult game was a cripple, so slow that he could hardly keep up with the hunter. In working a dog on grouse the hunter should be exceedingly deliberate, and he should do all in his power to train his dog on close hunting. It might be added that as a rule the best grouse dog is used on no other kind of game. He has a very special kind of work to do, and does it less well if his game and his routine are varied.

The experienced hunter usually knows where to look for grouse; in old, abandoned mountain orchards and clearings; by tangles of grapevines and greenbriar thickets; in little valleys which have alder thickets. He should always hunt where natural grouse food is found. Among the favorites are wild grapes, sumac berries, haws, rose hips, and berries of the briar. This, of course, applies to the autumn and winter, which coincide with the hunting season. In the late winter, when seasons are usually closed, the grouse does a great deal of budding, and at that time it is more likely to be more widely distributed. Perhaps wild fox grapes are the favorite food of the grouse, for it is known that to obtain these he will come long distances. He sometimes covers these distances by flying.

Like quail, grouse feed in the morning and in the forepart of the afternoon, using the noon hours for drowsing and dusting. Unlike quail, they frequently feed on trees and bushes rather than on the ground. Not infrequently a grouse will be flushed from a dogwood tree or from a tangle of grapevines. Occasionally one will alight in a bare tree, but this is most unusual, and happens only if there are no evergreens in the vicinity.

Grouse are to be found in a variety of types of cover; yet they always are essentially birds of the woods. Occasionally one will be found far from its native hills, perhaps along a wooded stream wandering out of the mountains. When they are discovered in odd places, the time of the autumn "migration" is probably at hand; not that this bird migrates, for it never does, but it has been observed to display an unwonted restlessness when the members of other species are making heroic flights.

One favorite place for grouse is along little brushy streams in valleys. With good grouse dogs to work close, and with a hunter on either side of the damp thickets, the hunting is likely to be very sporty, the hunter's chance coming when the birds clear the underbrush. In certain parts of grouse country there will be high plateaus with a low growth of laurel or huckleberry; when they are found in such cover, there is really no excuse for a man's missing a grouse. The target is large, and the shot is a clear one. The difficulty always increases in proportion to the density of the cover. The most difficult grouse terrain is a hillside, with a heavy stand of trees, and jungles of briars and grapevines. Often, in such country, the birds may be heard and not seen; also, in making a shot, the hunter has to take into account the angles posed by the upward and downward slopes.

The closeness with which grouse will lie depends to some degree on the nature of the cover: it varies with the individual bird; and the weather has some control over it. Usually in dry, bright weather the birds will be wild; then, of course, they easily detect the hunter's approach. In damp, misty weather they are far more likely to lie close, both because they appear disinclined to move under these conditions, and because the coming of the hunter upon them may be noiseless. In windy weather, grouse, like all other game, are uniformly wild. A wind makes all game skittish; for it appears to realize that the noise made in the woods by the wind drowns out the approaching footsteps of an enemy.

It is only natural to think of a wild creature in relation to and in connection with its native habitat. We think of the king cobra and India, the lion and Africa, the red deer and the moors of Scotland. And it is difficult to think of ruffed grouse without having as a background some of the wilder and more beautiful aspects of nature: lichen-etched craggy boulders; dense pine thickets, dusky and aromatic; old hillside clearings; primeval gorges down which gush and babble crystal streams, overhung by birches and hemlocks; airy wildwoods of the autumn, gaudy with the tattered gold of yet unfallen leaves. Though this noble game bird is quite matchless for magic, yet his environment is altogether worthy of his beauty and his patrician elegance. He is the prince of his princely domain.

In some ways the grouse is a strange bird, for although at times he can be the wildest, at other times he can be the tamest. Perhaps a considerable difference in caginess is due to age. Young though full-grown birds, that have had no experience with hunters, may at times appear so tame as to be almost stupid. But no bird learns more quickly; and birds of a second season, or even late in the first season, are uniformly very wise. However, even if he happens to be tame, his flight is never so; and once he is a-wing, he presents as sporty a target as can anywhere be found.

The range of the grouse is so very wide that the hunter will have to study the nature of the terrain in order to discover the best places in which to find the birds. Though food, water, and favorable cover are essential, it must be remembered that the birds think nothing of traveling several miles for food they love, water they must have, and cover that they like. It is generally a good plan to look for grouse along the edges of thickets, especially where alder-runs extend out into fields; around abandoned farms and orchards; or in swamps within the woods. It is a wise precaution never to approach an old apple tree without being ready to shoot. The grouse loves all fruits, tame and wild, and is partial both to apples themselves and to the buds of this tree. Beechnuts are among his favorite foods.

Perhaps more than any other game bird, grouse should be hunted with patience and great deliberation. It pays to scan the ground and the trees. Unless he moves, a grouse is a very difficult bird to detect on the ground, for the blending of the colors of his plumage with those of the fallen leaves, the rocks, the mosses, and other natural objects is almost perfect. It is difficult also to see him in a tree, especially if he sees you first, as he is likely to do. He can draw in all his feathers so that he looks no more than half his normal size. But, since one's success in killing this bird depends to a great degree on a moment's warning of his presence, it is well to hunt for him with your eyes as well as by just merely ambling along. And it is amazing and gratifying how a hunter can train his eyes to see game, even motionless and half-hidden game.

Not only does the grouse employ the ruse of hiding; he is crafty as well in that he will sometimes deliberately let the hunter pass him before he flushes. When after this princely bird, a man should expect the unexpected; and he should not attempt to use as an alibi for a miss the fact that the bird got up behind him and went back. He should be prepared for just such a maneuver. Always keep in mind that wherever the grouse is found, he is a bird of the highest intelligence, fully capable of matching man's when he becomes used to the ways of hunters. True, in some of the remote provinces of Canada, the grouse is so unfamiliar with human beings that fishermen have been known to tie slipknots on the ends of their fishing rods and pull the birds out of trees. But when we speak of hunting grouse, we are naturally thinking of those that have had some experience in the matter of being pursued with dogs and guns.

Before hunting any territory for grouse, it is wise to ascertain beforehand whether there are any birds in that locality. The hunter will do well to inquire of friendly natives; and before the season opens one should take some preliminary rambles in likely country. Both the quail and the wild turkey leave more signs of their presence than does the grouse. When scattered, both of the latter birds do a lot of calling, and can be located in that way; the hunter can easily find quail roosts and dusting places. One can readily find also where wild turkeys have roosted by discovering their droppings; and these birds leave wide trails where they have raked and torn up the leaves and trash with their scratchings. It is not so with the grouse. Except for his drumming (which is commonly to be heard in the springtime, though it may also be heard on warm still days in the autumn), and except for a certain subdued, excited chittering when the bird is alarmed, the grouse is singularly silent. It is sometimes possible in the hunting season to locate one by his drumming; but no hunter should count on this possibility. Keep in mind also that this muffled sound is of a peculiar nature, somewhat ventriloquistic in its quality; for, whereas a man can go straight to the call of a quail or a wild turkey, he will usually have some difficulty in deciding exactly the direction from which the drumming proceeds.

If grouse have been using a certain locality, the careful hunter, scouting for signs, can usually find their washes in sunny sand beside old stumps and logs, in old orhards, or beside sawdust piles at abandoned mill-sites. Sometimes he can find the tracks in damp soil; and the tracks of the ruffed grouse are unmistakable. But perhaps the hunter can discover grouse most easily if, granted that the birds are in a certain territory, he will hunt where the birds come to feed. Veterans at this game know what they are talking about when they say, "This place looks like grouse, smells like grouse." Perhaps wild grapevines, laden with misty purple clusters, will riot over an old mossy stone wall or a sagging stake-and-rider fence bordering the woods. Beyond the fence may be an ancient orchard of gnarled apple trees, with an undergrowth of sumac, up which bittersweet vines clamber. A stream may be near, purling valleyward, with alders shadowing it, and beech trees rising on the higher ground.

It is generally true that, while a covey of quail may literally live in a field, retiring from it only as far as a little adjacent thicket or a bushy ditchbank, grouse really live in the woods, but come to clearings and semi-clearings to feed. Although it is unusual for quail to fly unless startled or unless they wish to cross a gully or a stream, the grouse makes pretty constant use of his wings. Time and again they have been observed flying far down a mountainside to feed in a favorite place, and been seen returning in the same manner. Neither quail nor turkeys make so much use of their wings; but they make far more use of their legs. The legs of the grouse are comparatively short; and while, if startled, he may run in a tall and upright position, he ordinarily travels low to the ground, with his body horizontal to it. He does not appear to be so active and restless a bird as many of the other game species.

Of course, if a man is hunting with a dog or with dogs, he will naturally depend on them to find the birds for him. But, as has been said before, grouse do not lie nearly so close for dogs as quail will. As a rule, unless a dog has faulted by running unexpectedly into quail, usually down-wind, the birds will always lie to him. But it is not so with his lordlier cousin. Therefore, in grouse hunting, the working dog has to be watched with especial care. If he gives the least sign of making game, the hunter should be ready, taking particular note of any possible obstructions such as trees and bushes, in case the bird flushes and dodges behind one of these objects, as it is his nature to do. In some cases even a good dog, under conditions adverse to scenting, will pass by a grouse, and it will be flushed by the hunter. While his quest should always be deliberate, he should remain constantly alert. Apparently this prince of the woodland has no low or second gear. He starts in high; and though he may make a little run before doing so, thus making the hunter aware of his presence, he is as likely to rise without running; and his sudden thunder of wings is disconcerting in proportion to the preparedness of the hunter. When after this bird, the hunter should give to the business at hand all his thought and attention. This is because the getaway of the grouse is blinding in its speed, and the gunner is afforded no time to come to his senses and at the same time make a creditable shot. The real chance that he is going to be afforded will be but momentary. In pursuing this patrician of the wilds, cool and constant preparedness alone insures success.

It is probably true that most men hunt grouse without a dog. As has been suggested, a really good grouse dog is comparatively rare. Although as a rule an old, steady dog, thoroughly familiar with grouse, is best, some hunters have had good luck with mere puppies, which have not yet attained wildness or speed, or hunted any other kind of game. But let us consider the case of a man going into the woods alone, with no kind of dog as an ally, to hunt grouse. If he is experienced, he will know, to begin with, that the flight of the grouse is harder to handle than that of the quail; it may not be swifter, but it certainly is more impressive, and it is far more enigmatic. Besides, it is a smashing flight, as a general thing, through the woods or through thickety underbrush. Because the ruffed grouse is a bird of the forest, and must needs do constant maneuvering and veering in flight, he handles himself more deftly than the bobwhite. He presents a larger target, it is true; but his nature is to present it in such a way that it is sometimes as difficult to get the gun on him as it would be to cover a hummingbird on the wing with a .22. A grouse may usually be expected to rise, though there may be endless variety in the flight itself, in one of three ways: One is the occasional silent rise, the big bird making his getaway low to the ground with hardly a sound; indeed, he might not be seen but for the dancing leaves that he has stirred up. Another is the instinctive habit, upon the detected approach of a hunter, of making a little run so that he gets near a tree, especially an evergreen, behind which he can rise unseen. The third is his love of speeding almost straight up to clear the trees, and then tearing away over their tops. The time to take a shot when the bird resorts to this last maneuver, granted that he is within reasonable range, is just when he reaches the apex of his rise. To shoot at him rising almost vertically will probably be to miss him; and when he is once in the clear heavens it will be too late for a shot.

If a bird gets up out of range, or is missed, the hunter should watch him with the greatest care as long as he is within sight. Although, at times, a grouse may fly a prodigious distance—especially when, flushed high on a hillside, he takes out across a valley—as a general thing, the grouse will fly only from 100 to 400 yards; a great deal depends on the degree of his fear and also on the presence of a suitable place to alight. If the hunter takes very careful bearings on the direction the bird has taken, the chances are that he can be flushed again, with a chance of a good shot. The hunter's success will then depend to a great degree on the manner of his approach.

It is a well-established fact that the hunter who eases along nonchalantly has a far better chance of coming close to any kind of game than one who tries to sneak up on it, or one who approaches it boldly and openly, his very attitude denoting his purpose. In following a grouse, it is a wise plan to begin by taking ten paces or so to the right before beginning to advance. The chances are that this will not only put the bird on the hunter's left, where his chance at it is going to be better than if it got up directly in front of him or to his right, but it also suggests to the grouse that the man, while coming in its general direction, may pass it. The chances are that in that case the bird will be far more likely to permit a close approach than if it were come at directly.

The hunter, though keenly on the alert every second, should avoid all appearance of being so. Nor should he always expect the bird to rise from the ground. If, after a flight of reasonable length, the bird should have come to a pine or a hemlock or a spruce, he may alight in it. The sportsman should therefore scan such trees carefully. If there are no conifers in the vicinity, the grouse will be on the ground. However, on alighting, the bird is not going to stay in the open, upon bare ground. He will likely run under a smother of vines, seek shelter under a low bush, or beside an old log or stump. Hunters who have watched grouse alighting have nearly always mentioned this tendency to seek cover before pausing to await events.

The ruffed grouse is a bird that never loses for the hunter his magic thrill. Despite all commercialism and despite all the advances of civilization, he remains what he has always been, a prince of the blood. His presence invests the wildwoods with mystery and wonder. He is what the marvel and the beauty of the wilderness means. Always he remains a patrician—in appearance, in character, at rest, and in flight. When once a man has tasted the tang of ruffed grouse hunting, he is committed to a lifelong love of it. Its wild romantic haunts, its princely bearing, its cyclone speed upon the wing, the marvelous and blinding dexterity with which it unerringly executes its aerial maneuvers, its poise and its rare distinction of carriage, its keenly bred woodland intelligence, the beauty and appropriateness of its plumage—all its characteristics proclaim it without a peer among the game birds of America. And the hunter who has once enjoyed this sport will always be dreaming of it; he will see the resplendent glory of the autumnal hills; he will inhale the aromatic fragrances of dewy mosses and fallen golden leaves, and he will hear the sudden thunder of aristocratic tawny wings.

**Prairie Chickens.** The upland bird shooter whose treasured techniques have been developed on New England partridge or woodcock must alter both style and equipment when he goes west for prairie chickens. The snap-shooter from the brush patches of eastern cut-over lands, keyed to split-second blasting through leaves and vines to reach a bird sighted but for a flash as it explodes into the air only a few yards away, adjust himself to new values out on the wide open grasslands and wheat stubbles.

Take a typical prairie-chicken shoot. On the first day of the open season the birds may hold well to the dogs, flushing within reasonable distances from the sea of grass that extends as far as the eye can see in all directions. But overnight something may happen. There is no explaining it, but next morning the square-tailed chickens take to wing and go cackling away at average distances of 45 to 50 yards. Give the whirring targets another 5 yards while the gun comes to shoulder, and the result is likely to be a delicate gamble. The birds may have slipped beyond the perimeter of good shotgun performance, or may yet be barely within scratching range. Partridge gunners from the tangled lairs of their favorite bird have been known to pray earnestly for built-in range finders on their scatterguns when confronted with these spooky hens of the prairies.

In the first place, the cylinder bore which serves so well on rocketing ruffed grouse does not have the "stretch" for open grassland shooting; it sprays too thinly. Obviously, the answer is to arm with guns choke-bored for waterfowl. The old reliable 12-gauge is none too heavy, although here as elsewhere, there are some who do remarkably good work with their 16's and 20's. Loads should run to the heavy side as well; some of the highest-scoring chicken shooters use long-range duck loads.

Most important is the ability to judge distances in the wink of an eye, and, if the prairie bombshell has not already passed out of range, to place the exact center of the shot charge just where the fast-flying chicken will run into it. There will be lucky days, of course, when close-up birds may permit some pretty ragged shooting and will come spinning down to grass if only nipped with the edge of the pattern. They are fairly tender in this respect. But when the prairie chickens are taking to the air over in the next quarter-section the scratch shooter might just as well rack his gun for the day. He will do more damage than good. His aim must be dead on, or else.

Time was when the pinnated grouse, prairie chicken, square-tailed chicken, prairie hen, heath hen, and other names given to this bird, ranged widely and abundantly over America. The several forms flocked in unbelievable numbers form Alberta and Massachusetts southward to the coast of Texas. Early colonists rated it a nuisance in their gardens and young orchards. The prairies of Kansas, eastern Colorado, Nebraska, and northward into the Canadian flat lands held millions of them. Arkansas, Illinois, and Indiana had big populations. All through the Great Plains region they were shot and shipped to market by the barrels. Gunners riding out over the rolling bunch-grass country with their strings of dogs fanning out ahead of them, loaded their horse-drawn buckboards between daylight and dark. Like the passenger pigeons and the buffaloes, their numbers seemed endless.

But now, like the Old Gray Mare, prairie-chicken

shooting "ain't what she used to be." Today, scattered flocks are all that remain of their colorful millions. The thunder of their wings as they rose half a thousand at a time ahead of the gunner is but a memory in the minds of the old-timers. Of the true prairie chicken, largest of the group, only remnants are encountered in the strip from Alberta and Manitoba south to Arkansas. Attwater's prairie chicken, smallest and darkest of the family, is carefully nurtured in Texas and Louisiana in efforts to bring it back. The northeastern pinnated grouse, or heath hen, once found from southern New Hampshire to New Jersey, is completely wiped out. The last one died on Martha's Vineyard, Massachusetts, in 1931.

The man with the shotgun cannot be blamed for all that happened. Uncurbed by laws, his toll was heavy, though not fatal. Mostly, it was the man with the plow who robbed the prairie chicken of the native grasslands without which it cannot thrive. In the early days of farming the square-tail appeared to benefit. Its numbers actually increased for a time. A certain amount of wheat stubble, cane, and kaffir corn was to its liking. But when too much of the bunch-grass plains came under the plow and the reaper, the prairie chicken began to fade.

Several of the states that now offer prairie chickens on the shooting list do so only because their intermixture with the similar-appearing sharp-tailed grouse makes it impossible to gun one without bagging a few of the other. When held in the hand there is, of course, a difference. A man does not need to be an expert ornithologist to note that the prairie chicken has a barred breast, while that of the sharptail is white with V-markings. Another distinguishing point in the prairie hen is the square tail—the two middle feathers in the other bird's tail are longer than the rest, hence the name "sharp-tailed." In flight the sharp-tail has a whitish rump and is generally lighter in color than the prairie chicken. But under field shooting conditions many state game departments wisely recognize that honest mistakes may be unavoidable.

Those who have known prairie-chicken shooting in the good old days, and who may be lucky enough in the current slimming years to locate a few coveys, are likely to esteem it above all other forms of upland scatter gunning. There is a feeling of bigness, of exhilaration, as one stands out on the windswept prairies. The dogs range free and wide. This is their kind of going, and they love it. Far in a thick swale the birds are located. The dogs converge to the point. Guns at ready, the hunters move in, and suddenly the startled chickens roar out of the short grass and go whirring and cackling away in the prettiest flight a man ever saw. There is a grandness to it, a feeling of vast space, of endless vistas of yellow grass bending and swaying under the crisp winds.

After he has gunned the prairies a partridge hunter will return to his alder patches and grown-old apple orchards with no less eagerness. But never again will it seem like the ultimate in upland bird shooting.

**Sharp-Tailed Grouse.** "Chickens?" echoes the Dakota farmer. "Plenty of 'em. They been comin' back strong these past four, five years. Shove over in the car, and I'll show you where you can fill your limit in an hour."

From the little prairie town of Timber Lake the farmer points a way along narrow, dusty roads that swing at sharp angles around cornfields and wheat stubbles, out into the rolling grasslands, then finally to a series of brushy gullies and thickets sloping steeply down from the bare plateau to the poplar-grown banks of the Missouri River.

"This is it," says the farmer. "This is sharptail country—the best. You can go down there now and rout 'em out in singles, or you can do what we do—wait till the chickens start flocking into the cornfields just before sundown."

It is early November and there is a tang of frost in the air. Flights of waterfowl move like drifting skeins of dark lace against thin layers of clouds, high above the glistening Missouri which is their beacon. As the late afternoon sun begins painting the clouds with pink and red, the waterfowl start dipping down in ragged patches from the high sky.

"Watch that corn patch," says the farmer, pointing to a field some half a mile distant. Presently the hunters make out the birds sailing low across the grasslands to drop down among the rows. "Chickens," he adds.

For this kind of shooting the dogs have no duties beyond that of fetching the birds. Much as in pheasant driving, the hunters form along one end of the field and start down the rows. The birds rise in singles and doubles at average distances of 30 or 35 yards and soon the bag limit of 4 is filled by each hunter. For every bird that crashes out of the dry stalks in full flight another comes sailing in from surrounding brush country to drop behind the drivers. It is incredible and wonderful; it is almost too easy.

It was not always like that, of course. Although the sharptail has been making a notable comeback in recent years, it is subject to cyclic changes which may reduce it from plenty to scarcity in a single season. Yet, unlike its close cousin, the prairie chicken, the sharp-tailed grouse has shown good ability to cope with increasing settlement. In its range—which extends, for the three sub-species, from Illinois to Oregon, and from New Mexico north into central Alaska—the pintail grouse has a much brighter future than the squaretail. While its chosen range overlaps that of the prairie chicken in many areas, the sharptail generally likes a brushier country. It can do with less of the short-grass country and it has learned to take fullest advantage of the table spread for it by corn growers and wheat farmers.

Look for sharptail grouse in rolling hills interspersed with plum and rose thickets and among willows and poplars. The brakes along the upper Missouri are much to its liking; it is doing well in parts of upper Michigan, through Wisconsin and Minnesota, and of course in the Dakotas. Where it can be choosy in its particular habitat it likes to linger along the margins of small streams. With a good dog leading the way, a hunter will do well to follow the meanderings of brush-bordered creeks, especially during the bright daylight hours. In late afternoon it is likely to move out into wheat lands and corn patches in early season. Later in the year it may take to the trees for a good part of its living.

The sharp-tailed grouse is a great game bird, qualifying on every count. It holds well to dogs, and except in late season, roars into flight within reasonable shooting range. Its dark flesh is an epicurean delight. One of our great naturalists has said that a sharptail split in two, doused well with bacon drippings, and broiled over a bed of cottonwood coals exceeds in flavor that of any other game bird.

Hardiest of the group is the northern sharptail, found from the Lake Superior shores north and west to upper Quebec and deep into the Yukon Arctic. This sub-species often lives far from the nearest farm lands, subsisting in summer on a variety of berries and seeds, and in winter flying into the trees for dried fruits and buds. Often it associates with the snow-white ptarmigan, and like that bird it burrows into the loose snow for protection against temperatures which may fall to 60 degrees below zero. Around Fairbanks, Alaska, it is a popular game bird, known there as "speckled chicken."

The Columbian sharptail, found along our northern states, and the prairie sharptail of Alberta and Manitoba, supply the bulk of present-day shooting for the species. While it may be gunned without the use of dogs, it is both comforting and more productive to watch a good setter scout the way, see it settle into the point, then walk in until the bird suddenly explodes into view with a great clapping of wings. And one never knows whether it will be a single, or a roaring flock of 200.

**Sage Grouse.** It is a strange place to go grouse hunting. A rolling, gray-green sea of sagebrush extends in all directions from horizon to horizon, and as the hunters stand knee-deep, aromatic odors rise to their nostrils. A jack rabbit bobs into sight from nowhere and goes bounding away in characteristic turns and switchbacks. Around the shores of a shallow alkaline lake shimmering in the sun, a herd of white-rumped antelope stands silent and watchful. A few mourning doves whip overhead.

Without warning, a huge bird in size more like a turkey than a grouse rattles heavily into the air and lumbers away with deceptive speed. As far as the eye can follow in the desert air the great gray bird flies fast and true. There is no hope of marking it down for a second try. The hunters must find another. "Besides," consoles the more experienced hunter, "that was an old rooster. Couldn't eat him if we wanted to; only the young 'uns are any good."

Colored remarkably like the sheltering gray brush, another bird sneaks furtively across an open space just ahead. When a half-dozen heavy bodies come hurtling out of the cover, a short guttural note coming from each bird, the gunners are ready. One grouse falls with a solid thump, but the other merely flinches and does not finally scale down until hit for the third time.

"That load of 3's did it," says the older gunner. "Toughest game bird in the country to knock down."

He picks up the fallen game and hefts them, one in either hand. "This little fellow we can eat; won't weigh no more'n 4 or 5 pounds." He shakes his head over the larger bird. "Another old rooster; he'll tip the scales at 8 pounds if he'll go an ounce. Flavor? Try mixing some strong duck dressing, rubber heels, and moosehide moccasins."

There is, honestly, not much to be said in favor of gunning this largest of all American grouse. For one thing, the birds are none too plentiful. In most parts of their range they are facing a hard struggle to survive. Unless one hunts in the Great Basin from New Mexico and California north into Saskatchewan, staying always within sight and smell of the sage, he may never see one of these giant, fan-tailed birds. And if he does, the event might well be regarded as an interesting sight rather than opportunity to pull down on another feathered target. In all the world there is no other bird like this Cock of the Plains. It is unique, an integral part of the rolling sagebrushed hills.

Young birds taken in early August are passable eating, but at any other time there is not even the excuse of needing camp meat because only the hungriest of men will put one in the pot. The grains and seeds which put flavor in most game birds cannot even be digested by the Cock of the Plains. Its gizzard, so thin-walled as hardly to be regarded as such, has been geared, by generations of living, for handling leafy plants, and in the parched land where it chooses to live the bitter sagebrush is its staff of life.

**Blue Grouse.** Up in Juneau, Alaska, a father and his 12-year-old son have worked out a good team for blue grouse hunting. The father carries his favorite 20-gauge double, the son a .22-caliber rifle. They walk the near-by mountain trails through the dark evergreen timber together, and this is their understanding: All grouse that take to wing are fair game for the shotgun; those that will not fly after reasonable shooing and throwing of clods become targets for the little rifle, likewise those that flutter foolishly into the nearest tree and stand craning their silly necks in tragic innocence. And such are the ways of the blue grouse that on most days junior's bag is the larger.

In the remoter areas of its range this big grouse has little fear of man. Many a deer hunter toiling upward through the heavy timber of the western mountains has come face to face with one of these beautifully marked birds as it struts confidently on a downed log scarcely 10 feet distant. But in some localities where hunted regularly it has learned to flush, and to rocket noisily away through the green forest on its stiff-feathered wings. Eastern gunners who may be inclined to contrast the behavior of this doltish bird with their beloved ruffed grouse should bear in mind that the partridge, too, is tame to the point of stupidity when encountered in the wilder portions of America. Indeed, there are several places in the north where the bigger blue grouse appears to be the more elusive of the two species.

The range of the two principal blue grouse forms, the dusky and the sooty, extends from Arizona and California northward along the Rocky Mountains to the southern Yukon, mostly confining itself to high elevations except in British Columbia and Southeastern Alaska where it works down to sea level. During the early fall season the gunner will find it around timber line and in high open glades of the forest. At this period its diet is mostly wild berries, small leaves, and insects. It is then a delectable bird.

In winter, however, the blue grouse goes into an

odd state of hibernation. For days at a time it remains practically motionless high in coniferous trees, bestirring itself only long enough to gorge on the resinous tips of spruce, pine, and fir. Few are killed, or often seen, at this time of year, and this is just as well, because its flesh becomes strong, all but nauseous to the taste.

Now wisely outlawed is "hooter hunting." In the spring the dark, slaty-blue cock with its fancy plumage is given to the habit of perching on a stout limb and summoning its harem by somber booming sounds, strangely ventriloquial in quality. Poachers take advantage of this trait to sneak up on the unsuspicious bird. Waterfowlers who wailed when spring shooting of ducks was prohibited a generation ago outnumbered, but did not outwail, the "hooter hunters" when faced with a similar curb.

**Spruce Grouse.** Out in the Northwest the Indians have a name for the Franklin grouse. "Tyee-kulla-kulla," they call it—the "gentleman bird." Taking a more realistic view, the white men of covered-wagon days conferred upon this grouse the unlovely name of "fool hen." The name has stuck. Fool hen it is, rarely taking advantage of its wings, which are capable of swift, twisting turns difficult to catch up with over the sights of a shotgun. Even if it is startled enough to get off the ground the chances are that it will first serve warning by clucking; then, after it has crash-landed in the nearest tree, it will cluck once more to make sure you have it located. "Gentleman bird"—"fool hen." Take your choice!

There are two distinct species of the fool hen. More widespread of the pair is the spruce grouse found in northern coniferous forests from Labrador and upper New England west and north to the limit of spruce timber in Arctic Alaska. It is well and favorably known to trappers and woodcutters who call it the wood, Canada, black, or spotted grouse, fool chicken, and many other names. To most of them it is a "pistol" bird, one to be potted at close range with .22-caliber revolver or rifle. But occasionally it has developed enough knowledge of man to be classed as a real "shotgun" bird, and when it does, it becomes fully as sudden and tricky in flight as any other member of the grouse clan. Since it is often encountered in thickly grown areas, the gunning of a scary spruce chicken calls for fast snap-shooting, preferably with an open bore and No. 7½ chilled shot.

Although this is not the type of grouse best adapted to the use of pointing dogs, there are many times when the springer or cocker spaniel may be employed to good advantage in locating ground-feeding birds, getting them into the air, and retrieving the downed game. But in northern spruce forests where snowshoe hares abound, one cannot expect his dog to be completely selective. More rabbits than grouse are likely to be jumped in a day's hunt.

The western counterpart of the spruce chicken, known as the Franklin grouse, is largely confined to mountainous forests of the Rockies from Idaho to British Columbia. Where the range of the two birds spills over the hunter may identify his bag largely by the tail feathers. The Franklin grouse has a black, not brown, tail. The Franklin's coverts bear distinctive white bars; the tip is not orange-barred as in the spruce chicken. The size is the same, slightly smaller than a ruffed grouse. In the fall season they are excellent pan birds, but in winter when spruce buds become the chief source of living, the flesh is strongly resinous.

Like the varying hare with which it is so often associated in the Far North, the spruce grouse is subject to rapid decline in numbers. From a period of extreme scarcity occurring about once in every ten years, the spruce chicken populations slowly build to a high peak, then fall off with drastic suddenness. For this reason the hunting is spotty through the years. In some seasons a man may travel for miles without seeing a bird. Then, on another September day, the graveled country roads will be lined with grouse. Some will fly, some will flutter into the nearest branches, some will strut. And the hunter may choose his favorite weapon—scattergun, rifle, or pistol.

**Guns.** As to the guns and ammunition for ordinary grouse hunting, there is so much variation in preference that it is not wise to attempt to lay down any laws concerning these matters. It seems reasonable that a hunter should use his regular gun; for he is always more likely to handle best the weapon with which he is most familiar, and it is with that that he is most likely to be able to coordinate, especially in the fast shooting required, with the best chance of success. Some sportsmen hold to the conviction that the smaller the bore, the sportier the shooting. Some use the 20 gauge; but this is rather too light a gun for forest shooting that may be of the long-range variety. A 16 gauge is good; so is a 12. Perhaps there is no choice between these two. As to the bore, the right-hand barrel should be open or modified, and the left, choke. The distance at which the shot is made will determine which barrel should be used.

The size of shot used varies all the way from 2 to 9. As a rule 7½ is recommended; but one veteran hunter uses that size in his open barrel, and 2's in his left. He has had great success; for the 2's permit a more deliberate aim, and will reach a grouse effectively far beyond the killing range of 7½. For rather clear open shooting the smaller or medium-sized shot are recommended, whereas, where the brush is heavy, so that the charge often has to smash through an obstruction before reaching its target, the larger size is more to be relied upon. The veteran hunter, from long experience, already knows the kind of gun and ammunition best suited to his purpose; the amateur might be advised to experiment until he discovers what is best suited for his own individual needs. If he kills grouse with a certain gun and a certain load, why, that is the answer for him.

# CHUKAR PARTRIDGE

*Cacabis chukar*

COMMON NAMES: Chickore, Chuckare, Chukru, Chukar Red-Legged Partridge, Indian Chuckor, Kau-Kau, Keklik.

**History.** The chukar is a comparative newcomer to the shores of North America. The particular species *(Cacabis chukar)* which has been introduced into the United States comes from the foothills of the Himalayas where they have been common for centuries.

Chukar has several close relatives in western Asia and southern Europe so close, in fact, that only the experts can distinguish one from the other. In France it is the red-legged partridge, *Cacabis rufa,* that represents the clan. Other members are the Greek partridge, *Cacabis saxatilis,* from southern Europe, the Barbary partridge, *Cacabis petrosa,* and the Arabian partridge, *Cacabis synoica,* from Smyrna. All are considered excellent game birds and are widely hunted in their respective countries.

Many attempts have been made to introduce this exotic species in North America, but most of them have been unsuccessful. In recent years sportsmen have shown a decided interest in the liberation of chukars, and a majority of the states have made attempts to establish these birds in their local covers. Complete results of such attempts cannot be accurately reported at this time, for there is still a great deal of uncertainty about how the released birds will thrive and breed.

Those states which have been able to report some success and where the birds have apparently caught on are California, Minnesota, Nebraska, Nevada, North Dakota, Washington, and Wyoming. Definitely unsuccessful plantings were made in Georgia, New Jersey, Ohio, Pennsylvania, Rhode Island, Virginia, West Virginia, and New York. In other states no plantings have been made, or, where planted, the bird's situation is still uncertain.

From past experience and current successes, it is apparent that this species stand a better chance to establish themselves west of the Mississippi River.

California has been particularly successful in efforts to establish the species, and it is now reported that the birds are doing very well in the more arid regions of that state. Other western states are optimistic about the outcome but decline to state definitely that they have established the chukar as a game bird.

**Identification.** In size the chukar partridge is about midway between the common bobwhite and the ruffed grouse. The plumage is a combination of pale slaty-blue and tan. The upper parts are bluish-gray without conspicuous markings. The throat and cheeks vary from white to tan, and this area is boldly margined by a band of brownish-black. The under parts are whitish, often washed with buff. The sides and flanks are white with prominent diagonal bars or streaks of brown and black. The bill, legs, and feet are bright vermilion. (See color plate on p. 482.)

**Characteristics.** In its native haunts of India and China the chukar prefers the cultivated areas, areas along streams, and barren hilly regions. In America the birds have shown a preference for stubble fields, open prairies, and even deserts.

It has not been possible to study the food habits of these birds very thoroughly. In captivity they thrive on the same food as the bobwhite, i.e., ragweed, sorghums, and lespedeza. Grasshoppers are also a favored food. It is assumed, therefore, that this same fare will appeal to the birds after release. The question of competition with native birds has not been decided. Some officials report that no competition has been noted, and instances have been cited of chukars and bobwhites feeding peacefully in the same field. However, it is admitted that some instances of competition may result if the chukars become really numerous.

Definite information on the breeding and nesting habits of the chukar is currently lacking, but it is likely that on the whole they resemble those of the native quail.

**Range and Distribution.** It is not possible to give facts concerning either the range or distribution at the present time because of the scattered planting attempts now in progress.

**Hunting Methods.** The chukar, like the ringneck pheasant and the Hungarian partridge, is an exotic species introduced to supplement the native population and provide the gunner with more game. The future of the ringneck is well established. The Hun already has earned a place of honor and his tribe is increasing. The chukar is not yet in sufficient numbers to take his place beside these other two, but there is every reason to believe that he may soon do so.

"Red-legs" has a long sporting history elsewhere in the world. His close relatives in Europe are considered top-flight game birds and the chukar has furnished sport for centuries on his native heath. On the Continent and in the British Isles the common method of hunting these birds is by driving, a form of shooting which has never been popular in America.

"Red-legs" is strong of wing and although twice as large as a bobwhite offers no easy target on the getaway. The birds usually feed and travel in groups or coveys and flush like quail. They are reported to lie well to a good dog when there is any cover, but like the Hun they are inclined to sprint and flush wild in the open country. They seem to thrive best in the more arid regions or on prairie lands, and since introduced species have a way of adapting themselves to their new environment, the chukar probably will be hunted in the same way as the western quail.

In a few of the private preserves in this country where the chukar has been tried, the bird has proved to be very popular. Reports indicate that covey shooting is similar to that on quail. Locating the singles, after the covey has been flushed, is not quite so easy, for the chukar is inclined to make a flight about twice as long as the quail. In open areas, such as wide fields, the flight may be from 400 to 700 yards. In areas bounded by wooded borders the birds normally drop in just short of the trees.

The favorite quail gun should answer the purpose, but considering the relatively larger size of this bird and its ability to carry more lead a heavier load is recommended. Chukars not only fly rapidly but are inclined to climb, and it will be necessary to reach out to get many of the birds.

The double gun, with one barrel bored improved cylinder and the other modified choke, is the most popular gun for this shooting. The average shooter will find a standard load of No. 7 shot in the "open" barrel, and No. 6 shot in the modified barrel most practical. A few shooters prefer the long-range load in No. 6 shot for the barrel bored modified choke.

With the pump gun or autoloader, the shooter is advised to have a standard load of No. 7 shot in the chamber and a long-range load of No. 6 shot in the magazine.

When these birds have increased enough to warrant more general shooting, the upland gunner of today has a treat in store with the chukar partridge of tomorrow.

## HUNGARIAN PARTRIDGE (European Gray) *Perdix perdix perdix*

Common Name: Hun.

**History.** The Hungarian partridge, more correctly known as the European gray partridge, is a comparative newcomer to the North American sporting scene. These birds originated in Central Europe and were first imported to the United States about 50 years ago. They were most common on the great agricultural plains of Hungary and it was from that country that most of the importations were purchased; hence the familiar term "Hungarian," or "Hun."

Various attempts have been made from time to time to introduce exotic species in the Western Hemisphere, and some, as in the case of the ringnecked pheasant, have proved successful. Other species thrived briefly and then disappeared; many failed in some sections and thrived in others. A brief history of the effort made to establish the "Hun" as a game bird in North America will demonstrate the difficulties encountered with this species.

In the year 1899 about two dozen birds were placed on a private preserve at Lynnhaven, Va. A little later another planting was made at Montague, Essex County, Va. By 1906 more than 180 birds had been released in those areas but they quickly disappeared. On the West Coast similar plantings met with greater success. In 1900 nearly 100 birds were liberated in the Willamette Valley, Ore., and by 1906 the counties of Spokane, Yakima, Adams, and Kittitas in the State of Washington released about 5000 Huns. From these birds, by natural propagation only, the Hun population multiplied within ten years until the range was extended through nearly all of eastern Washington, well into Oregon, Idaho, Montana, and a part of British Columbia. The latter province had experimented with the release of more than 50 birds in 1904 but there seems to be no record of how they fared.

The Province of Alberta became interested in the introduction of Huns to supplement the rapidly diminishing flocks of sharp-tailed grouse there. In 1908 and 1909 over 500 Hungarian partridges were released south and west of Calgary. The results of that planting were little short of phenomenal. The birds seemed to find ideal conditions in the great wheat empire of Alberta, Manitoba, and Saskatchewan. Being of a hardy nature, they withstood the rugged winter, food was plentiful, and nature appeared to aid their productivity. They spread in considerable numbers throughout the provinces and down through the border states of Washington, Oregon, Idaho, Montana, and the Dakotas. The entire population of Huns in those regions today is credited with having stemmed from the original planting of the birds around Calgary.

Meanwhile, back in the East, like efforts continued to meet with failure. In 1904 about 200 birds were liberated on Hilton Head Island, S. C., but they did not do well. In 1905 some 20 Huns were liberated on a preserve in Massachusetts and 91 on a North Carolina preserve; neither of these plantings met with success. By 1906 more birds were tried on the Virginia preserves and plantings were made on preserves in New York, New Jersey, Pennsylvania, North Carolina, and Mississippi. The New Jersey birds were released on the great pine barrens between Trenton and the sea; they simply disappeared. Subsequent plantings met with a little better success in that state. Pennsylvania liberated close to 10,000 Huns over a 15-year period, but the results were far from satisfactory, considering the cost. Some birds did take hold in the wheat section of the Cumberland Valley and the flat country in the northern part of the state, and as early as 1939 there were enough Huns to warrant a brief shooting season with a daily limit of five birds. New York State met with failure, as did North Carolina and Mississippi. In 1906 the State Game Commission of Illinois imported 1000 Huns, and the State Game Warden of Kansas liberated 200. By 1907, 2500 more birds were purchased for the same purpose. By 1909 the various states engaged in experimenting with the Hun as a game bird included California, Connecticut, Delaware, Illinois, Indiana, Kansas, Nebraska, New Jersey, and Washington. By that time the official importation totaled about 27,000 birds, and the total for birds imported from the turn of the century was close to 45,000.

The majority of these plantings showed good results in the initial stages only to be followed by disappointment in most cases later on.

While early attempts were being made to introduce the Hun there was considerable feeling against the idea in many sections of the country. The local gunners feared that the new birds might drive out many of the local species, just as certain other exotic importations had played havoc with local fauna in the past. It was contended that the Hun would drive out both the square- and sharp-tailed grouse; contrary to some expectations, however, these latter species staged a comeback in the very regions where the newcomer was most populous.

In sections where he seems to find conditions ideal to his well being, notably the prairie provinces and the northern border states, the Hun is well established as a valued game bird. It is to be hoped that future experiments east of the Rockies will be more successful and that, like the ringneck pheasant, another "furriner" will become a welcome addition to our list of game.

**Identification.** The European gray partridge, commonly known in North America as the Hungarian partridge, is about one and one-half times as large the bobwhite quail and smaller than the ruffed grouse. Huns are from 12 to 14 inches long and weigh from 12 to 13 ounces. (See color plate, p. 482.)

As the true name denotes, gray is the predominant color in the plumage. The upper parts, including the top of the head, nape of neck, back, shoulders, breast, and tail are varying shades of gray. The gray on the breast and shoulders is a soft, pastel tone, similar to that on a dove, while the gray on the back is more brownish. The wings are brown with white lines running lengthwise through them. The pale-gray flanks are barred and splotched with markings of chocolate brown. There is a horseshoe-shaped patch of dusky on the breast.

Both sexes are practically identical in appearance. Unlike the ruffed grouse, the red color phase rarely occurs in the gray partridge.

**Characteristics.** The Hun is a bird that can stand drought and rather severe winters. These two characteristics make him well qualified to complement—or to replace, if necessary—the prairie grouse of the great wheat belt.

Huns are gregarious at least part of the year and travel in coveys like the bobwhite. Such coveys are generally led by an old bird. They also roost like the quail, on the ground and in a circle with their heads pointing outward. When flushed they go up in a group, scatter in all directions, frequently uttering squeaks or squeals, and their wing-beats whirr as noisily as those of grouse.

They habitually prefer the wide open spaces and are seldom found in wooded areas. Like the pheasant, they are fleet-footed birds and often inclined to run rather than take wing, although they generally lie well to a trained dog. In flight their wing-beats are rapid and at top speed they are fast flyers. It is not uncommon for a covey or even a single bird to travel a half-mile or more before alighting.

In common with other ground-feeding, ground-nesting birds they suffer from predators such as cats, foxes, weasels, rats, coyotes, and the predatory crows, hawks, and owls. One of their chief enemies, however, is the modern mowing machine, and thousands of birds are killed annually by the sharp, moving blades.

**Breeding.** The cock is monogamous by choice and a devoted mate and father. At mating time his voice is harsh and raucous and he is extremely pugnacious. He guards his chosen territory and will viciously attack any intruder of his own kind.

The birds pair from mid-January to late February, depending on the locality and the weather. After pairing and mating they separate from the rest of the covey and seek a place for nesting and the rearing of their young. If the weather turns unseasonably severe, however, they again form in groups—presumably for mutual warmth and protection—until the cold spell is gone.

Nesting usually begins in late April or early May. The number of eggs is variable; it is thought that food supply and weather both play some part in the fecundity of the birds. Normally they are prolific breeders and under favorable conditions large clutches are the rule. Some observers believe that reproduction is stimulated by cyclic conditions, and they point out that transplanted species such as the pheasant often develop abnormal fecundity.

The nest is an extremely simple affair, being no more than a depression in the ground with a few dry leaves and a little grass for lining. Sometimes two or more hens lay in the same nest. The eggs are pointed-oval, olive-green in color, and about midway in size between those of the bobwhite and the ruffed grouse. Incubation requires from 21 to 26 days, with the former being the usual time.

The faithful cock remains close to the nest while the hen is sitting. Some believe he even takes part in incubating, but this has not been clearly established. He does however, help the hen to brood, shelter, and find food for their young.

In captivity both sexes show a marked tendency to adopt and rear birds that have been hatched by others. Unmated cocks are sometimes given orphaned or left-over chicks to raise.

In the natural state most young are hatched around mid-June. It is possible that there may be two broods a season, but this second nesting is most likely to occur if the first attempt is wiped out. June is normally a month of considerable rain and frequently nests in the lowlands are flooded, destroying the eggs or drowning the young chicks. In July thunderstorms sometimes drench the immature birds and they die from cold and exposure.

**Feeding.** Their food consists of both grain and insects. In season they consume quantities of various insects and their larvae, including locusts, grasshoppers, and potato bugs. The downy young feed chiefly on ants and ant pupae. Wheat, millet, clover, cabbage leaves, and other green food, and the various berries make up a portion of their diet. In winter, like the sharptail grouse, they survive on buds and such foods as they can find above the snow. The Hungarian, although a bird of the cultivated plains by choice, is less dependent on arable land than some other species.

**Range and Distribution.** The Hungarian partridge does not migrate but remains fairly constant over his entire range. These birds are widely distributed throughout the wheat belt of Saskatchewan, Alberta, British Columbia, and the states of Washington and Wisconsin. They are also plentiful in some sections of Oregon, Idaho, Montana, Illinois, and Minnesota. They are scattered in the Dakotas and found to a lesser degree throughout small areas in some of the eastern states.

**Hunting Methods.** The Hungarian partridge is another exotic species which has finally taken root on the North American continent and has won a place in the hearts of upland gunners. Each year increasing numbers of hunters get a chance to test their skill against the hardy Hun and thenceforth become voluble in their praises of this bird. Alien no longer, in those areas where he has found things to his liking he has become as much a part of the local fauna as any native bird. He flies like a quail, only faster, runs like a pheasant, and is smart enough to outwit all but the best dogs.

The pheasant legs it down a fence row, a drainage ditch, or even through the swale or stubble in a fairly straight line, but the Hun doubles and twists and circles until none but a wise and keen-nosed dog can unravel his route of escape.

Quail will often take to the thickets or the woods but the Hun prefers to play the game in the open. Rarely does he seek the protection of cover. A covey that has been repeatedly flushed in one field is apt to fly over intervening woods to get to some field beyond.

The Hun *can* be hunted without a dog but not very satisfactorily. He can give a pheasant cards and spades at sprinting and skulking, and if he does flush it is likely to be at extreme gun range or beyond.

A smart dog, particularly one that has learned to handle pheasants, can lock up a covey of Huns very nicely. The covey is usually under the leadership of an old bird that knows all the tricks in the book. The birds will sprint ahead of the dog if possible, but the pheasant-wise pointer or setter will circle, and when the birds come head on to the dog they seem to lose the power of locomotion and will sit as tight as quail.

The following states and provinces now have open seasons on the Hun: Idaho, Indiana, Iowa, Montana, Ohio, Pennsylvania, Wisconsin, Alberta, British Columbia, Nova Scotia, and Prince Edward Island. This indicates the bird's ability to thrive and multiply under favorable conditions. Other states are still experimenting; some are meeting with success and will doubtless be able to declare an open season in the near future. The great wheat belt seems to be the region in which these birds are most at home, and that is where the best shooting is found at present. Although subject to cyclic fluctuations like the grouse and other upland game birds, the future of the Hun now seems assured. His favorite habitat may not be as picturesque as the haunts of the ruffed grouse, or as interesting as the home of the bobwhite, but the Hun is a target to test the mettle of any gunner, and when he finally reaches the table his flesh is a gourmet's delight. What more could be asked of any game bird?

On the vast prairies or in the comparatively small wheat fields farther east, the Hun behaves pretty much the same. He rarely permits close approach and the initial range is likely to average 30 yards or more. A close-shooting gun with loads that will deliver a wallop is a must if these birds are to be bagged consistently. Shot size smaller than No. 7 or 7½ is not likely to be effective, for the Hun has an amazing vitality and can absorb a good deal of lead before he tumbles. Literally a blue streak, he must be squarely hit in order to stop him. Since the second, if offered, will be a long one, a good double gun for this type of hunting would be one with the right barrel of modified and the left barrel full-choke. Pump guns and autoloaders may be either modified or full. Gauge is a matter of choice, and as small a bore as the 20 will be adequate if correctly pointed.

## RINGNECK PHEASANT

*Phasianus colchicus torquatus*

Common Names: China Pheasant, China Torquatus Pheasant, Chinese Pheasant, Chinese Ringneck, Chink, Denny Pheasant, John Pheasant, Mongolian Pheasant, Oregon Pheasant, Ringneck Chinese Pheasant.

**History.** The ringneck pheasant is of the order *Gallinae,* a large group of fowl-like birds which embraces domestic fowls, pea fowls, argus pheasants, partridges, and other gallinaceous varieties. It is further identified as belonging to the family *Phasianidae,* specifically to the sub-family *Phasianinae* which includes about 48 genera and 149 species. The genus *Phasianus,* of which the ringneck is a member, is representative of the entire sub-family. The pheasants (20 genera and 48 species) are native to Asia. *Phasianus colchicus* was distributed from the Black Sea across the central regions to Japan and to Formosa, but the Chinese ringneck pheasant, *Phasianus colchicus torquatus,* was confined to China. The American ringneck bears the same scientific name as its chief ancestor, the Chinese ringneck.

The first known record of game preservation provided for protection of the Chinese ringneck pheasant. During the rule of the great Kublai Khan (1259-1294) a law was established forbidding the killing of pheasants. Food and shelter were provided for them, and for other animals and birds. Pheasants were limited to Asia until about 1250 B.C., when they were successfully introduced into western Europe by the Romans, and legend tells that it was the Roman conquerors who carried them from Europe to England. The bird originally was taken from the banks of the Phasis (now Rion), a river in the Asiatic province of Colchis. From the names of this river and territory, the English ringneck pheasant received its scientific name, *Phasianus colchicus colchicus.* The bird thrived in England, both wild and in captivity, and was raised in numbers for shooting purposes. Through the years, three or four other pheasant species were brought into England, and readily intermingled with the original import, producing a fertile hybrid, or a mongrel bird. The principal species involved was the *Phasianus versicolor* from Japan (via Europe), which was introduced into England in 1840 by the Earl of Derby. This hybrid, still called English ringneck, is a larger and better bird for table food and makes sportier shooting. It ranks higher than any single member of its basic stock.

In 1790, an Englishman, married to the daughter of Benjamin Franklin, imported some of the English ringnecks for his estate in New Jersey, but the experiment in propagation was a failure as the birds died the next spring. The first successful transplant to the United States was made in 1881 by the United States Consul-General at Shanghai, who shipped 28 Chinese ringnecks to the Willamette Valley of Oregon. The terrain, climate, and feed of the region so suited the brilliant-plumaged foreigner that, with the help of some additional stock, the numbers warranted a cut-back within 11 years. Fifty thousand birds were reported killed on the first day of the shooting season.

The West had a new sport as well as a new commercial interest in raising and marketing pheasants. The earliest attempts to transplant the English ringneck to the eastern states failed. Several theories have been advanced for such failures. Some zoologists maintain that since the pheasants were thinly distributed the few specimens in each area rarely or never synchronized in a sex cycle and failed to reproduce themselves. Eventually, a fertile hybrid between the English ringneck and Chinese ringneck was introduced into the New England states and thrived there and across the northern section of the United States and up to southern Canada. By the early 1900's, the pheasant was abundant in the north central United States and scattered throughout all the other states but nine. Five of the barren states were in the South, below the Mason and Dixon line. To this date incessant efforts to plant pheasants throughout the South have failed. The reasons are not definitely known, but theories regarding distribution are discussed under that section (p. 257). The ruffed grouse is mistakenly known as a "pheasant" in some Southern locales.

The history of the foreign-born ringneck pheasant in the New World is an American success story. This game bird, familiar today to thousands of gunners in the United States, is an import of the last 60 years or so. Naturalists and sportsmen have made repeated attempts to introduce game birds into the United States, but the ringneck is the first successful transplant. Presumably, it has thrived by virtue of its natural ability to adapt itself to the new environment and because it lends itself readily to artificial propagation. An estimated 5,000,000 pheasants are killed each year by sportsmen, a figure which indicates that the popular ringneck has little competition from the native bird specimens.

Though this pheasant is commonly called the Chinese ringneck, perhaps it should be more correctly identified as a distinct American variety, for though it is a blend of several pheasant species, it is, as it exists today, a fairly static hybrid. There is little additional admixing within the population as a whole. The ringneck is primarily a composite of closely allied types of pheasants, principally the sub-species, English ringneck, Chinese ringneck, and the Mongolian pheasant. A pure Chinese ringneck is a rarity, but the American type is a surprising facsimile of that bird, having retained most of the markings and general plumage coloring. The Chinese is similar to the English and Mongolian races, and they frequently interbreed. All three bear the distinctive white ring about the neck. The English is the smallest of the three sub-species, and the female is dark while the male has a reddish-colored rump. The Mongolian looks like the English, but is larger. The Chinese, however, is distinguished by the greenish back of the male and the brighter body plumage of the female, and is midway between the other two in size.

The abundance and ever-increasing numbers of the ringneck pheasant are dependent, to a great degree, on its ability to adjust itself to civilization; in that respect it is like the whitetail deer. Both have a high survival potential. Whereas cultivated fields drive away other birds, such as the native ruffed grouse, they become the home of the pheasant. When the heavily wooded habitat of the ruffed grouse is destroyed by lumbermen, the bird is automatically exterminated or driven away, for it cannot learn to live in really close proximity to settlements and man. Consequently, the pheasant has supplanted the ruffed grouse in many sections, particularly in several eastern states. Most sportsmen consider the grouse sportier shooting, but the pheasant has a larger range, and is more readily available.

**Identification.** (See color plate on page 485.) The ringneck cock is a gaudily plumaged bird, and his haughty manner is no doubt a result of the extreme brightness of his coloring and general handsomeness. Red wattles and green head top the white collar circling his neck, and his multi-colored body plumage terminates in a sweeping tail. The spurs on his long, black legs intensify the effect of a confident-looking strut. His plumage is most vivid during the mating season, but the main seasonal moult of July and August has a relatively mild effect on the coloring. The moult is inconspicuous, for the feathers are gradually replaced on the body and wings so that there is only a slight loss of beauty or flight power.

The female is a mottled brown, drab in comparison to the male. She carries a fairly long tail of an awkward length which gives her an ungainly look. She is chunky in comparison to the graceful cock. Except for the long, pointed tail, which is characteristic of the species, she has some resemblance to the ruffed grouse, but a closer likeness to the sharp-tailed grouse.

The ringneck is a large bird, built somewhat like a chicken. Weight varies according to the section and its particular food supply, but the bird normally is heaviest in the fall, after a summer of easy feeding. The male averages about 2¾ pounds; a 3½-pound bird is considered big, and a 5-pounder is an exception. The female is lighter, about 2 to 3 pounds. Male and female are both about 3 feet in length.

The mature cock is heard more often than the female, but is not a voluble bird, normally calling only when startled or courting. When flushed, only the cock emits a series of loud, harsh cackles, *"Cak! cak! cak!"* as he takes to the air. The call does not continue during flight. In courtship his crow is a loud, double-noted squawk. The female voices the same type of sounds, but she rarely talks, and the calls are neither so loud nor so strident.

**Characteristics.** The ringneck is an intelligent bird with a cool-headed, natural wariness and caution. Its wildness is inherent and is its chief asset as a game bird, for those raised in and released from captivity to restock game areas are good shooting within a week's time. The outstanding characteristic of the ringneck is its ability to skulk under conditions that would rattle the nerves of the average bird. It will run silently and as fast as a galloping horse for as far as several yards through heavy cover and take advantage of the scantiest concealment. It resorts to flight only when pursued to the limit of cover or flushed by a dog. The pheasant will seldom take to the air to escape a man on foot. If pressed, or wounded, it sometimes will swim short distances.

When running along the ground, the ringneck habitually circles back and around its pursuer. Since the bird normally is frightened or flushed into the air, the take-off often is a distracted, noisy one, accompanied by an indignant cackle and a rush of wings. It is a heavy bird with small wings and needs a lot of power to get airborne. The vertical spring directly from the ground is like that of the mallard. The ascent is not fast in spite of the bound and rapid wing-beat, because of the wing-to-body ratio which will not permit either swift flight or sustained flight. They are good fliers for short distances but, since they do not migrate, they do not need great powers of flight. Pressed past their limit, some exhausted birds drop into the water and drown when unable to make it to the other side. Though some go off directly into flight after thundering up from the ground, the ringneck usually towers to its highest point, about 20 to 30 yards, in order to seek a line of flight. The height to which the bird rises often is dependent on the terrain. If there are trees, for example, it must see above them. Once the course is set, it flaps and sails, then sets its wings and planes, usually to a landing, since the pheasant rarely maintains a level flight. The ringneck has been known to fly three miles, but an average flight is 200 to 300 yards. When seen in the air, it is usually rising or descending. The planing or scaling often gives an illusion of being level, but the bird is really pitching. The average speed is from 35 to 40 miles per hour. In rare cases the ringneck flies into a treetop for safety when flushed, but it is seldom found in trees except during the winter season when deep snows force it to roost in the trees rather than on the ground. When roosting on the ground during the winter, their tails, especially the cock's, sometimes freeze to the ground and the helpless birds starve to death.

**Breeding.** The breeding season is variable according to the range, but an over-all date would be from April to June, inclusive. The sexes frequently separate in the winter, and during this time the cock's genitals are shrunken and non-functional. During the courting time the cocks begin the break-up of the distinct sex bands, for the testes of the males develop rapidly during the pre-mating phase, and the action reaches its peak in the establishment of "crowing areas," and then general fighting among the cocks as they seek out hens. The pre-mating or "crowing" phase provides one of the common sounds accompanying the first signs of spring. Males, having moved up to higher ground, select their restricted territories for crowing to attract hens. At this time each cock fights off all other males who intrude on his territory. His courting methods are similar to those of the domesticated rooster, as he calls the hens with a low cluck, picks out bits of food for them, struts to display his plumage, and gradually acquires his harem.

The size of this harem depends only on the number of hens in the neighborhood and the male competition for them. The cock-to-hen ratio in the wild normally stands at 1 to 3, and it should never be greater than 1 to 6 or 7 for the best egg fertility. Old males usually establish the same crowing areas year after year. Younger cocks, sometimes vanquished by stronger foes in their search for mates, often move to new but adjacent crowing areas or become wanderers.

During the mating phase, ear tufts of the cock are erected and the bare skin around the eyes becomes extremely red. The male, on his crowing area, struts before interested hens, turns in all directions, and walks with exaggerated bobbing. Occasionally he will run around the female with short steps, wing tips partly outstretched and dragging in an arc on the ground. Then he will stop before her, the feathers of his upper and lower back, rump, and tail shifting over to the side nearest the hen. At this point the tail is partly spread, neck bent and head low. The pose is maintained for several seconds. Finally plumage is allowed to fall back to normal position and the cock gives a low hissing sound before copulation takes place.

Along with the other gallinaceous birds, ringnecks rate with the cottontail rabbits as the fastest breeders in the entire bird and animal kingdom. Both males and females are capable of breeding when one year old and the cock is polygamous. This type of relationship is not a harem in the true sense, however, for the hens are not collected, but each seeks out an individual nesting site and is independent of the other females. A group of these sites forms a "hen territory," or a "crowing area." When the post-nuptial phase occurs, the cocks go into moult. At the same time the genitals decrease rapidly, and cocks become solitary and silent. This is the precursor of the non-sexual interphase which extends through the fall hunting season.

Though it is not the normal or usual procedure, the pheasant sometimes mates with other gallinaceous birds. Not only has an aggressive, or rejected, cock invaded the barnyard, fought and successfully driven off a domestic rooster to acquire his hens (the offspring is called a "pero"), but has also hybridized with turkeys and pea fowls.

The favorite nesting place of the pheasant is in a hayfield, but the site chosen varies and is dependent upon available and suitable locations in the section. Fence-rows, alfalfa fields, grain fields, and the woodland edges often are selected to conceal the nest. Within a slight depression in the ground, the nest is built of dried weeds and vegetable debris, and occasionally is given a scant lining of vegetation. The 8 to 16 olive-buff eggs are incubated in 23 days. If a clutch is destroyed by predators (skunks, jays, crows, snakes, etc.) or accident such as fire or flood, the eggs are laid again, though they are fewer in number in the second series. In some instances, the re-laying is repeated a third time. The juveniles of this third clutch usually have the least chance to survive because of the winter cold and snow. The strong determination to nest is an important factor in their high survival potential. Normally, the hen performs the incubation duty alone, but occasionally the cock incubates the eggs. The periods when the hen leaves the nest for rest and feeding are usually at dawn and 4 P.M., and the nest is not covered over for protection or warmth as are duck nests. Before incubation begins the eggs are bunched in layers, but once brooding begins the hen carefully rolls them into a single layer around the nest cup. She turns them with her bill once a day to distribute her body heat equally. In the early stages of incubation, a hen will desert her nest if threatened with danger, but as hatching time approaches, she becomes more and more reluctant. Just before hatching, the hen lies so closely that she often is killed in an attempt to save her eggs. The death rate is high among the sitting hens when fire, mechanical harvesters, or fast mowing machines destroy both her and the nest. The hen raises one brood each year, though the Chinese ringneck sometimes rears two sets of young in her native Asiatic habitat.

The young, about evenly divided as to the number of each sex, weigh slightly under an ounce at birth, and mature at about the same rate as the domestic chicken. They weigh about 5 ounces in one month and 20 ounces at two months of age. The chicks are precocious, and capable of running a short time after they emerge from their shells. When eight to ten weeks old, they can make brief flights, and at three months are nearly mature in flight power. The yellowish-buff feathering of the chicks develops into near-adult coloring by their first winter. The hen is a good mother in wild life, reportedly even counting her brood, checking and waiting for each member, before making an enforced departure. In captivity her maternal efforts are indifferent to fair, and the cock often is the guardian of the young. Old, sterile hens in captivity have destroyed eggs and chicks. The hen and young habitually keep a family unit until fall, though the cock leaves for the late summer moult. By the end of the fall season, the sexes usually separate for the winter.

The number of offspring is strongly affected by the weather. (See "Distribution," pp. 256-257.) Heavy spring rains cause drownings and once the chicks get wet they are susceptible to pneumonia, like the turkey young. If they escape death fom accidental or natural causes, they must attempt to elude numerous predators, such as skunks, raccoons, weasels, minks, rats, owls, and hawks. Evidence indicates that, when extremely young, they do not give off scent if they remain quiet, just as young fawns are scentless when lying in their beds. The most vicious enemies of young and adult birds alike are foxes (gray and red), stray dogs and cats, skunks, owls, and crows. Though birds in captivity average an eight-year cycle, those in the wild have a much shorter existence, though they are tougher and stand a better chance of survival in comparison to a pen-raised pheasant released with them.

Three-quarters of the cocks are bagged yearly by gunners in some areas (there is rarely an open season on hens), but the stocking of game areas usually allows and plans for such a high kill. There is a high yearly loss among pheasants due to crippling, especially in the corn states where a wounded bird can hide in the tall stalks. The Iowa Game Survey of 1931 reported a toll of 968 birds crippled in one season against 2964 actually bagged. Additional reasons for such a high ratio of crippled to bagged were the fast-running ability of the bird and the confusion of a brief shooting season.

The chicks feed primarily on insects, and the effects of certain insecticides, such as DDT, are probably not directly responsible for the deaths of any really great numbers of young, but the interruption of the cycle of insect life theoretically would interfere with the feeding and existence of the birds. Among all the upland birds, pheasants are least susceptible to disease, and this immunity has contributed considerably to their remarkable increase in favorable habitat. One of their few known diseases is lacellary white diarrhea or "pullorum disease," and even this is uncommon. Young and adult suffer from tapeworms and the parasitic nematode worm which lodges in the windpipe. Ringnecks develop well-worn "dusting" sites as an aid in the control of lice and mites, for plumage development through shedding of downy feathers, and to cleanse feathers of oil and dirt. Perhaps the greatest threat to the pheasant, however, is deep snow which covers up their food supply.

Since about 1900, artificial propagation of pheasants has proved to be a success for marketing and stocking, and the Fish and Wildlife Survey of 1940 reported 2029 licensed breeders in North America.

**Feeding.** The ringnecks are omnivorous feeders, and are especially fond of corn as well as other grains and seeds. They also feed on insects, berries, shoots, worms, wild plants, fruits, and various small animals such as baby field mice. They peck and move from place to place, seeking out the most delectable morsels. When fattened on grain in the fall, they make especially fine eating. Their feeding time depends on the weather. If it is poor weather, they are likely to eat on and off at different hours throughout the day, but normally the schedule is to look for food early, about an hour after sunrise, and then settle down on the chosen spot for a couple of hours, rest until late afternoon, and then feed for around three hours or up until sunset, finishing the process with gravel before going to roost. The supposition that as the quality of the land goes—and the resultant quality of the plant life—so goes the condition of the bird life, applies specifically to the ringneck.

The reports of damage inflicted by pheasants on farm and fruit crops are justified in some areas and exaggerated in others. The general opinion of scientists and some farmers is that the amount of good that the bird does in eating the seeds of noxious weeds and destroying injurious insects (cutworms, codling moths, plant lice, tree borers, etc.) outweighs the damage to crops. The majority of grain taken is waste, picked up in the dropping after harvesting, and this habit prevents the development of much volunteer grain that could carry over crop diseases from one year to the next. The most populous of all the pheasant states, South Dakota, has reported that the birds follow the sower and pick up the seeds or pull up the shoots with the germinating kernel, necessitating two and three replantings, but such cases are extreme and isolated. A survey was run in Pennsylvania to ascertain pheasant damage to commercial tomato crops. Because of the difficulty in segregation, the pheasants were included in the same group with other birds known to feed on the fruit—crows, starlings, grackles, and domestic chickens. It was learned that the bulk of the loss of tomatoes was due to rot, being 2.19% of the 45,710 counted. 1.28% were damaged by insects, and only 0.19% by all the birds as grouped. Pennsylvania can be considered an average pheasant state.

Winter feeding is one of the major problems of the pheasant, for when the ground is covered over with deep snow, its food is covered, and the pheasant is not adapted to obtaining it from anywhere but the ground. Starvation causes a high mortality rate. The ringnecks of the corn belt states are the most fortunate, for stray stalks often stick above the snow and tide them over until the ground is clear. They will enter barnyards, corn cribs, or barns in search of grain.

Ringnecks need little water and the minimum amount, dew and succulence, sustains them during the nesting season. In early fall when the young are grown they move adjacent to a water supply.

**Range and Distribution.** The ringneck is found over a large range in North America, but the areas of abundance are across the north central section of the country, as far west as the Rockies. The land is largely agricultural, above the Mason and Dixon line. Eighteen states have an open season, but the birds are virtually nonexistent in the far southern states, despite repeated attempts to plant them. Of the 5,000,000 birds bagged each year, the top kill is in South Dakota, with 1,500,000, followed by Minnesota, with 1,000,000, and with declining numbers come Nebraska, North Dakota, Iowa, Wisconsin, and Illinois. Pennsylvania leads among the eastern states with an approximate 250,000 kill, then New York with 185,000, New Jersey, 100,000 Connecticut, 50,000, and Massachusetts, 40,000.

The pheasant population is variable within a region, and there are several theories regarding population control, but the natural habitat of the ringneck is fairly consistent. They thrive in agricultural areas which furnish suitable food and cover, but shy from deep forests and mountainous, snowy regions. Like most game species, they are lovers of the "edges" which provide a choice of habitat, such as an eating place near a hiding place. They roam an approximate distance of 1/8 to 1/2 mile a day with a maximum of 3 miles, over a range which is a variation or combination of boggy swales, gullies, fields of weeds, thickets and marshes. In the course of a year the pheasant's individual range usually is within a 6-mile circle. Where neat farmers scythe around fence-rows and roadside workers clean ditches and cut away the thick weeds, the pheasants are left exposed to predation or their nesting areas are destroyed.

South Dakota is the most populous pheasant state, but only a part of its magical appeal to the ringneck is understood and that is changeable. The ringneck fattens on the fields of corn, wheat, and oats, and in the winter keeps from starving to death where cornstalks tower above the snow. The climate is temperate throughout the year. The 4000 birds introduced into South Dakota in 1915 thrived until the numbers were the envy of sportsmen throughout the country, but in the bitter winter of 1936-37 there was a serious setback when 50 to 90 per cent of the birds died. The population revived quickly, however, and by 1942 they were over-abundant. In the winter of that year the Game and Fish Commission declared an open season on them in 37 counties and the annual kill was 4,500,000. By 1944, the total yearly bag was up to

Warren Boyer

"Don't shoot! It's a hen!" The hunter out in front is rather worried, and with cause, for if the man behind is "trigger happy" he is certain to get some of the rear man's shot pattern. The scene was staged to show how accidents *can* happen in open-field shooting.

17,000,000. Plans were initiated to form a shelter belt as a soil conservation measure, and the Forest Service began the planting of trees. Later this activity was taken over by the soil conservation agencies and private citizens, and did much to improve wintering conditions of pheasants.

The antithesis to this fertile area of South Dakota is New York State. Where South Dakota raises grain and corn, favorite foods of the bird, New York favors dairy farming and fruit orchards. South Dakota has flat land with adequate coverage, while New York abounds with hills. South Dakota, then, provides the best in food and coverage. Several scientists have chosen New York State to illustrate or advance the theory that climate, precipitation, and temperature, take a major part in controlling the pheasant population, specifically during nesting time. The climatic conditions were the same for the Dakotas, Minnesota, Michigan, Wisconsin, Ohio, and Pennsylvania, during the crux of the testing time—the spring of 1945. In the fall of 1946 a good gunning season was expected because fewer hunters had been active during the war, but 1946 proved to be one of the worst pheasant seasons in New York's history. An analysis of the breeding season of the spring of 1945 was in order. The heavy spring rains were excluded because they came before nesting was actually started or chicks hatched, so that losses were not caused by flooding of nests and drownings. Moreover, in 1942, there had been a good fall gunning season although rains were heavy during the actual nesting time. Predation was ruled out after examination of the stomachs of 28 foxes, one of the chief natural enemies. However, study revealed that many hens were dropping eggs promiscuously without making a nest, for the nesting urge never culminated in the majority of them. The reason guessed was the abnormally low temperature. If this theory is proved, some ornithologists assert that it will explain the latitudinal confinement or distribution of the ringneck.

A second important theory regarding the distribution of the ringneck concerns nutrition, or the need for certain minerals or vitamins. The hypothesis is that there must be some specific explanation for the density of pheasant distribution and that reason might be the nature of the soil. Climate was proved to be a subordinate factor influencing distribution. Planted birds will thrive in a temperate locality (the southern states) when first introduced, then lag, or wane in production, but revive upon additional plantings, and die out altogether if new additions are not made. The areas selected for stocking had food and cover with predators, poachers, and disease in the same approximate proportions as in those regions where the ringneck was abundant. But the soil of the north central region, where the bird is numerous, is glaciated. The proposed theory, therefore, is that a relationship exists of soil and plants to food and pheasant. The minerals and vitamins of any area, then, could affect the health and survival of the bird and the abundance or scarcity of its distribution.

For the year 1938, the United States Fish and Wildlife Service supervised a survey of a given number of birds on a representative tract. There were 950 pheasants in 1675 acres in the fall before the opening of the shooting season. Gunners took 266 cocks, 133 were crippled, 15 birds were killed accidentally (by cars, etc.), 35 were taken by poachers, and 20 were driven from the area—under the pressure of gunning. By winter there were 300 left. Of those, 3 were killed by acident, 40 by harvesters, 38 left the area to search for better range, and 10 were destroyed by predators, which reduced the total to 209 by February 1. Of the 209, predators killed 30 more, but 25 birds came in from other areas. Between February and July, 24 were lost to predators and the breeding season began about mid-July with only 180, about 1 cock to 6 hens. The loss of the original stock was 870. Of the 301 nests made that spring, 20.3% were productive. Of 22 built by the roadside, 2 were successful, 1 out of 10 succeeded by the fencerow, 25% of those in the wasteland (a high rate of predation from skunks and weasels), 27.2% of the ones placed in the hayfields, and 29.17% in the grain fields. Man was blamed for the depredation of 50% of the nests; less than 10% was attributed to accidents or roadside cleanups, and 40% to mowing. Of the 301 nests, 776 chicks emerged from the 80 clutches, and 96 chicks died. Ten more adults were killed and by September 20, 1939, there were 850 birds in the total population after a severe winter.

Sportsmen do not have to rely solely upon native birds, however, because of the stocking from birds raised in captivity. The main reason ringnecks are steadily increasing in numbers is primarily because of artificial propagation, or machine methods employed by state and private game farms. These birds are released and thus increase the natural breeding stock. Where one hen can hatch from eight to 16 eggs, the incubator heats and hatches hundreds. One pen can supply birds for a pheasantry of many acres. Some states raise them for stocking public lands, preserves, and aviaries. In other cases individuals or associations rear them for their private preserves. There are game farms open to the public where birds may be shot for a fixed price per head.

On one Michigan game farm 750 hens lay 600 to 700 eggs per day which total 24,000 a season. To this number are added 27,000 bartered from the state of Wisconsin in order to try to keep the stock strong and free from interbreeding. The 51,000 eggs are then distributed to sportsmen's clubs and private individuals. Those that are left are hatched at the game farm and the chicks are then distributed. The remaining chicks are raised and released shortly before the opening of the shooting season.

**Hunting Methods.** The car with a wire container clamped to its top stopped briefly at the upper edge of the Dakota cornfield while three red-shirted gunners bundled out. While they were slipping shells into their shotguns the car left them to bump along an adjoining grain stubble a half-mile to the other end of the corn patch. The two remaining hunters got out and took up their positions as "stoppers" at each corner where rustling stalks merged with a thicket of ragweed. Before squatting out of sight one of the hunters waved his long-visored cap in signal to the first group. In a moment the drive was under way.

Spaced 20 corn rows apart, the three red-shirted gunners began their march down through the dry, frost-sered stalks, guns held at ready. Hardly had they moved into the shoulder-high corn when a brightly colored cock bird crashed into full flight near one driver, swerved into the sun to become all metallic brilliance for a second, and, to the accompaniment of twin explosions from a hastily fired shotgun, flashed over a low hilltop unscathed. The gunner, grunting in disappointment, his face redder than his shirt, blew a pair of smoke rings from his double and loaded up again.

The drive continued. Two brown hens got up ahead of the middle gunner and split away to offer easy shots to the outside men but were not fired upon. Although the bag allowed one hen a day, most non-resident hunters preferred all cock limits. This field held plenty of birds, they knew. Ears of yellow corn, hanging downward from the stalks or lying on the ground, had been picked clean of kernels by the birds. Their tracks formed networks in the dry, dusty soil. Pheasants were ahead—many of them—skulking along just out of sight. Action would come as always when the drivers neared the end of the field and the two stoppers rose to their feet to complete the cordon.

Fifty yards to go. The gunners waited, tense in the prairie sunshine. This was the moment they had dreamed about for an entire year; this the exciting moment for which they had driven across a half-dozen states; this the moment of thrilling suspense, the heart-stopping instant before the fireworks started.

One of the gunners shifted his weight nervously from one foot to the other. His thumb clicked the safety on his shotgun. It was like striking a match to a skyrocket. Instantly, a red-faced rooster roared out of the dry cornstalks a dozen feet away, its boisterous *"Cuk! Cuk!* CUK! CUK!" cut short by a charge of chilled sixes. For a short second the yard-long, glistening bird seemed to hang suspended while a puff of feathers drifted away from it. Then it fell heavily into the field. The air became alive with birds. The constricted space between the gunners erupted with brilliantly flashing wings. Every gun was emptied within 30 seconds. And while the gunners fumbled hastily for more shells, more pheasants came buffeting up out of cover to go sailing away, their long tails curving behind them, like comets against the golden Dakota sky. When it was all over the gunners picked up their birds, tossed them up into the wire container, and headed for the next field of waving corn.

While most pheasant hunters are confirmed cornfield addicts, and while the majority of birds in the Midwest states are taken by driving these fields, there are many other fruitful types of cover for ringneck shooting. The pheasant is a seed-eater. Although corn stands high on its list of favored foods it does well on many kinds of cereals such as wheat, rye, and barley. Away from the fields it survives on a wide variety of weed seeds, rose apples, and other wild and cultivated fruits. Grasshoppers are a favorite summer food, and it further helps pay its board bill to the farmer by destroying noxious insects, including the potato bug. The skilled pheasant gunner seeks his quarry in many other places besides the cornfield. He learns that the wily ringneck follows a fairly regular morning to night routine, and to know this routine will help him fill his bag.

At sun-up the pheasants troop in from the open meadows and wheat stubbles where they have roosted overnight to assemble along the roadsides, perhaps to replenish the supply of sharp-cut gravel in their gizzards. Where sunrise shooting is permitted, country lanes and byways are good places to find these long-tailed birds. Indeed, the early morning shooting is so productive that many state game departments have set the daily opening late enough to allow the birds to disperse into the fields.

Not long after daylight the flocks slip quietly into convenient cornfields where they do the bulk of their feeding during the fall season. Some of the birds may remain among the rustling rows nearly all day, but certainly a great many of them will have filled their craws to the bursting point and vacated before midday. By high noon they will have moved into other types of cover, the weed and briar patches, grass-grown swales and brushy tangles. Here they have come to rest during the heat of the day. Here they will lie close, flattening themselves into practical invisibility as the hunter crashes by, thundering up and away only when he has all but stepped on them, or perhaps after he passed their hiding spot, so that he must pivot and shoot quickly in an awkward stance. Tramping the weed patches is hard, hot work under the high sun, though it often produces the best kind of shooting for the man who hunts alone. Another good place is uncut swamp grass, tules, and cattails along watercourses. Here again every square yard of cover must be worked carefully if all the birds are to be flushed. And lucky is the gunner who finds a dense, low thicket of willows, Russian olives, or box elder in the big corn country, for during the heat of the day it may hold such concentrations of pheasants as he never expected to see in a lifetime.

Their noonday period of resting and dusting ended, it is the habit of pheasants to feed industriously into the hours of dusk. The cornfield drivers have their innings once more. With the setting sun the ringnecks start leaving the corn, showing up along the roadsides again, or often flying long distances to reach safe roosting places far out in the stubbles. In South Dakota the game department live-caught many pheasants for transplanting to other counties and states by equipping light trucks with searchlights and combing the open wheat stubbles after dark with long-handled nets. These birds, never tamed by captivity, proved much more adaptable to new surroundings than hatchery-reared chicks.

However pheasants have been seeded over the continent, it has been learned that ample food supplies are not alone sufficient to yield good shooting. The matter of good cover is paramount. The birds must have thickets, swamps, and weed patches for hiding during the heat of the day, for nesting, and for protection against the storms of winter. Where cultivation of soil is carried to the very edges of the fields, where meadows are cut clean by mower and scythe, no amount of good feeding will produce desirable stocks of ringnecks. There must be plenty of waste land provided through unuse of the soil, through cooperation between farmer and sportsman, or through deliberate purchase and management by game departments for that specific purpose. Wholesale hatching and liberation of young pheasants in areas not generously sprinkled with natural, uncut cover is a gross waste of time and money. The cost of rearing a single pheasant may even cost more than a resident hunting license. The loss between time of liberation and opening of the shooting season may run from 50 to 90 per cent where conditions are unsuitable to natural propagation.

Wilderness is not essential, or even desirable. The ringneck has no fear of the farmer, the rancher, or the settler. Give it a fair supply of grain foods, provide it with near-by hiding places, and it will furnish shooting to the very edge of city limits. It will even come into the barnyards on a winter day to squabble with domestic poultry for its share from the feed bucket. The red-faced cock will match its rusty-pump crowing with that of its close cousin, the Leghorn rooster. The pheasant is no shy denizen of the forests, but a bold swashbuckler ready to match its wits with man in order to share some of his comforts in the way of cultivated grains and fruits. That is why the ringneck is such a favorite with gunners; that is why this gaudy exotic furnishes more shooting today than any other upland game bird; that is why more pheasants find their way into the pot than all native species of grouse combined.

Not all parts of the country are suitable for pheasants, whether they be Chinese, Mongolian, English Blackneck, Versicolor, Mutant, or any mixture of the combination—such as most of them are. South of the Mason-Dixon Line, south of the once glaciated regions of America, it dwindles quickly. Mostly, the pheasant is a cool-weather bird, notwithstanding sizable flocks in some parts of southern California. Nearest to its ideal choice of habitat is the grain-belt area comprising the Dakotas, Nebraska, Montona, Minnesota, Iowa, and parts of Michigan, Ohio, Illinois, Utah, Oregon, and Washington. Pennsylvania and New York boast surprising numbers, and altogether the ringneck furnishes sport to millions of gunners in 28 of our northern states. Sub-zero weather offers no insurmountable hazards if generous amounts of food and cover are available. The grain-growing provinces of Canada are well populated from the region of the Great Lakes west and northward into British Columbia. In Alaska, farmers in Matanuska Valley successfully introduced them. But in the yellow and brick-colored soil of the south the pheasant simply will not take root. Where quail flourish best the ringneck cannot thrive. Where Southern gentlemen ride behind bird dogs there are no pheasants to confuse the well-trained setters and pointers. Perhaps it is just as well because the crafty ringneck plays strange pranks with hunting dogs.

**Dogs.** There is the gunner who will claim that he owns the perfect pheasant dog; that his dog knows all the tricks and will pin a long-tailed cock to earth with precision beautiful to behold. But for every one of this fortunate guild there are a dozen who will throw their hats on the ground and stamp upon them with exasperation; who, instead of trying to appreciate the poor dog's dilemma, will shout orders and condemnations loud enough to be heard across three Dakota cornfields. Inconvenient as it may be, there is no understood orthodox behavior between a pheasant and a bird dog. The dog knows its duty, but from the pheasant there is little in the way of cooperation. Instead of lying still and docile at the setter's proper point, the pheasant is quite likely to take one look at the quivering nose and then leg it out of there like a race horse on the quarter turn. It is just as likely to stand high on its spurred legs, regard the creeping setter appraisingly, and then take to wing while the gunner is yet a good rifleshot distance away. Or, if it thinks it is well hidden, it may enter into the spirit of the game long enough to let the harassed dog rest its tired jowls across its flattened tail. It is all very confusing, all very likely to "unlearn" a good quail dog of all its carefully schooled qualities.

But a dog is an essential part of pheasant shooting, nonetheless. Without a retriever, for example, the crippling loss is both shameful and staggering. A wing-tipped ringneck has no peer in the art of illusory disappearance. In cover appearing too thin to hide a meadow mouse a downed cock will vanish from the eye in a flash. A desperately wounded rooster, brought down solidly in a cloud of feathers, will somehow summon its last ounce of strength to burrow under a pile of trash, or maybe scuttle down a badger hole. A survey conducted among typical hunter groups afield without dogs indicates that three or four pheasants out of every ten brought down by scattergun fire are never recovered.

Obviously, therefore, every pheasant hunter needs a dog. To go gunning for these tricky, tenacious-of-life birds without one is to invite needless, almost wanton, waste. But what kind of a dog? In the first place, not every man can afford a blueblood. His pheasant shooting may not carry through a single week of the entire year, and certainly this brief period does not seem to warrant the purchase and training of a dog for that particular purpose. It does not; nor is it necessary. It is surprising how many kinds of dogs can be taught to do a job of simple retrieving, and in pheasant hunting that is the main chore.

Setters and pointers, once the owners have learned not to expect the same high standard of performance on pheasant as on quail or grouse, probably lead the field as partners in the cornfields. Irish, Llewellin, English or Gordon, Liver and White, or German, the setter-pointer breeds are hard to beat. When hunted principally on ringnecks, these clean-limbed dogs sometimes develop marvelous sagacity in combating the sly maneuvers of a wise old cock. One favorite trick they have learned is to range swiftly past the skulking bird and then swing quickly to pin it down in front of the gunner. Always, of course, these two breeds can be depended upon to do a classy job of retrieving crippled and lost birds. But there are other notable contenders for honors. The springer spaniel seems exceptionally well adapted to pheasant hunting, seems, in fact, to have been bred for that specific purpose. Moving cautiously, not too fast, ahead of the gun and scenting carefully all the time, this big spaniel lets its master know when birds are near. More, it generally springs them into the air within reasonable range of the scattergun. Except in young, inexperienced springers there is no great tendency to race wildly ahead as is too often the case with leggier breeds when the air is full of bird scent. They retrieve nicely and with a tender mouth. Another less-known spaniel is the Brittany, favored by some hunters for its deliberate work afield. Other pheasant shooters swear by their little cockers. To see one of these pint-sized fellows come out of the brush, his stumpy tail vibrating happily, head held high to keep the crumpled ringneck from dragging on the ground, is to bring forth words of praise. If there is a camera man in the crowd he can never resist this appealing sight of a little man doing a big man's work, and doing it well.

When duck and goose hunting forms a part of the autumn sport, as it does over much of the United States, Labradors, Chesapeakes, Irish water spaniels, and cross-breeds developed between these water-loving strains do creditable jobs in pheasant cover. They are highly intelligent breeds and most of them take quickly to trailing and retrieving on the uplands. So do some of the so-called non-hunting dogs. One man in the state of Washington will pit his dachshund against any of the highbrows; a game warden in South Dakota has a cross between a fox terrier and a beagle whose performance on crippled ringnecks comes close to perfection. An elderly gentleman from Chicago never takes to the field without his apartment-dwelling French poodle. The choice is wide. The idea is to get a dog. And get that cripple. There are none to squander as lost birds.

**Guns.** To ease any dog's work in pheasant country the hunter must also play his part. Sloppy shooting and wrong ammunition can result in such a conglomeration of near misses and wing-tipped birds that no dog, however proficient, should be expected to cope with the situation. Buy a gun that fits, one that swings naturally to the shoulder without humping and straining and squinting. It does not make much difference whether it is a conventional double, an over-and-under, repeater, or autoloader. These are matters of personal preference. In the hands of the right man they will all make sharp, clean kills. Correct gauges vary from 12 to 20, with the bigger 12 getting the most nods from experienced field hands. The matter of proper shot sizes has helped while away many an evening in camp, but when all the pipe smoke has drifted away the chances are that chilled 6's remain as general favorites. Early in the season, though, when birds are lightly feathered and flushing in the moderately close ranges there is no denying the pulverizing effects of 7½'s; nor of 5's when the big cocks have donned their heavy winter underwear near the tail end of the season and go winging away at Magnum distances.

Choke or open bore? The best average lies somewhere between the two. For the double gun a good combination is an improved cylinder for the right barrel, modified choke on the left. Gaining increasing popularity in the repeaters and autoloaders are the various screw-on gadgets whereby a twist of the wrist, a turn of the screwdriver, quickly produce every bore from full choke to complete cylinder.

Given the proper gun and ammunition, there is still the major operation of raking the pheasant down out of the sky where the retriever can lay tooth on it. There are such matters to consider as effective ranges, angles, and correct leads, for instance. Not that perfection is possible, or even probable, because every day afield may pose a new problem, may teach a new lesson. But there are a few fundamentals.

Mostly, be it remembered, the pheasant roars up out of thick cover with a great clattering of cupped, rounded wings and heads noisily for other places, often straight away on a slightly rising incline. This is without doubt one of the simplest of all shots at near range. Because of the shock-absorbing qualities of the big, stiff tail and the heavy padding of downy feathers beneath, however, this fast-disappearing target is likely to result in heavy crippling loss after the pheasant has passed beyond the 40-yard range. This kind of crippling no retrieving dog can do much about, for the reason that the stricken bird may fly for a mile or more before scaling to earth. But when a rising pheasant swings either to right or left the gunner has a good chance to score a dead-in-the-air bird, a chance to swing just ahead of the speeding target and to center the charge in the vulnerable head and neck region.

A man has to keep reminding himself that the rear two-thirds of his ringneck rooster is mostly tail—that it doesn't count. The eye that looks down the barrel rib should try to see only head, neck, and wings.

"Stoppers" at the ends of corn rows have a different perspective of pheasant shooting. Their shots are for the most part on rising game and always on birds drawing rapidly nearer until they whizz overhead like projectiles from a battery of bazooka guns. In the British Isles more blackneck and Reeves pheasants are gunned this way than by any other method. Specially trained beaters are engaged to do the driving. In this country, perhaps the most comparable kind of pointing occurs in pass shooting at waterfowl. It is tricky gunning, especially when the hunter permits the bird to reach the almost overhead position before catching up with it.

Although the pheasant is not the fastest of flying game, its average speed of 36 miles an hour carries it quickly across the 20- to 35-yard range where the shotgun does its most effective spraying. The time, roughly, is slightly less than a second. No time to waste, granted, but still enough for a smooth, fast swing onto the target, then slightly ahead, gun following through as the trigger is touched off. If a man does this over and over again he will eventually, perhaps, down enough birds to retain the respect of his dog. But certainly often enough to keep his hat from fitting too snugly he will be completely dumbfounded by completely unaccountable misses. It happens to the best of hunters, and if it were not so the sport might have languished long ago.

There has been a tremendous increase in the number of pheasant preserves now operating throughout the country, especially in the East. While the cost of a day's shooting on one of these preserves is somewhat more than the average gunner can afford, except for perhaps one or two sorties a year, the preserves seem to be doing an excellent business.

The normal procedure is for the hunter to arrange with the preserve operator in advance, giving the number of shooters in his party and stating the number of birds he wishes to have put out. Some preserves demand that each shooter buy not less than five pheasants for release. Although most of the preserve operators supply good pheasant dogs and a handler for each party of three or more hunters, many hunters prefer to use their own dogs. Early in the morning of the day set, the operator puts out the birds. Normally, he selects typical pheasant cover, and "spins" or "rocks" the bird before putting it down. When the hunters arrive everything is in readiness.

Though many birds would not be satisfactory for this practice, the pheasant is a natural. The "preserve" birds are just as fast on the wing as "natural" birds, and usually they are in better condition. They react no differently to a dog or to man than does the "natural" bird, and most hunters have found them just as difficult to hit.

**Summary.** How long will this outstanding game bird continue to dominate wing-shooting in the United States? Probably always. The trend has been gradually upward ever since Oregon declared the first open season on them back in 1892. While most native species have been fading, while the prairie-chicken millions have all but been swept into oblivion, while the shy ruffed grouse finds fewer and smaller places to hide, the colorful Chink has been digging in here for keeps. In the Deep South it will never encroach on little Bob White's domain, but in the more temperate zones of America it is definitely the principal upland game bird. Moreover, it lends itself so well to game management that it numbers may even be further increased.

In the first place, the pheasant is the only upland game bird in which the shooting harvest may be limited by law to cocks, and it is the only one of the group in which this is a decided advantage. Our native quail and grouse, as well as the transplanted Hungarian and chukar partridges, tend to split into pairs during the mating season. Not so with the pheasants. Their close kinship with the jungle cock, progenitors of domestic poultry breeds, results in the most promiscuous polygamy. Seventy-five per cent of the cock birds, perhaps more, may be shot during each open season as surplus to breeding needs. They may be regarded as purely extras, and their removal from the flocks will have no appreciable effect on the annual increase. From the game management and hunter standpoint this is a tremendous advantage.

But there are even more desirable features about the pheasant. Cultivation of the soil by man attracts rather than repels it. There is only the need for game management to provide adjoining cover in order to increase their populations. This calls for understanding and partnership with landowner, rancher, and farmer, because only through them is it possible to arange resting places. Food, the farmer supplies, willingly or otherwise. His corn, wheat, and other grains and general crops form a large part of the ringneck's diet. But to persuade the farmer to provide uncut swales, wide, brushy fence borders, water, and safe nesting sites is quite another matter. In the Dakotas and throughout much of the prairie grain belt these shelter areas occur naturally. In the more heavily tilled regions of the East and Midwest they must come about as a result of deliberate planning.

Many game departments already have acquired submarginal lands in the farming sections and have seeded them to preferred pheasant cover. They have learned the extravagance, the folly even, of releasing hatchery-reared birds where protection from natural enemies and the elements is lacking. The milenium toward which they are striving is the creation of an environment good enough to take care of hunter needs through natural propagation. This is an ideal which probably never will be brought to complete realization in the more congested states, though it clearly points the way to better things ahead. Year-around food and shelter—not one but both—are the ingredients from which improved pheasant hunting in more places will evolve. Individual gunners, sportsmen's clubs, game departments, landowners—these must pool their interests, must work together to that end.

# PIGEONS AND DOVES

Family *Columbidae*

**History.** The family *Columbidae* (order *Columbiformes*) is composed of pigeons and doves, but all members of the group are commonly known as pigeons, a word taken from the French *pigeon,* derived from the Latin *pipio* meaning a chirping bird. Though the names are virtually interchangeable, the tendency is to refer to the larger species as "pigeons" and the smaller as "doves." Of the 475 species distributed throughout the world in temperate and tropical sections, two types are found in North America, those with square tails (i.e., domestic pigeon) and those with pointed tails (i.e., mourning dove). Of the several species occurring in North America, three are well known and of real interest to the sportsmen as game birds. They are the wide-ranging mourning dove, the white-winged dove of the South, Southwest, and Mexico, and the band-tailed pigeon of the West. Other specimens, either indigenous or introduced into North America, are too small in size, too limited in range, or too few in number to qualify as popular game birds of the continent. The native ground dove, for instance, is about the size of a sparrow. The transplanted ringed turtle dove is approximately as large as the mourning dove, but its North American range is localized around Los Angeles, California. The famous passenger pigeon, at one time one of the most abundant bird species in America, is now extinct. Many different types of pigeons have been developed in captivity, with the rock dove as the basic breeding stock. A few of the most common hybrids are the pouter, carrier, homer, and fantail.

Formerly many ornithologists grouped the pigeons in the order *Gallinae,* but later a distinction was made and the pigeon was classed in a separate order from the fowl-like birds primarily because of one distinctive characteristic—both sexes secrete a curd-like substance in the crop to feed the squabs. This is known as "pigeon milk" and is fed by regurgitation. Also the young of the gallinaceous birds are fully developed at birth and capable of following the parent soon after hatching, but the young pigeons are completely dependent on the parents at birth and are brooded for about two weeks to a month, and even after leaving the nest rely on the adults for food and cannot fly far.

# BAND-TAILED PIGEON *Columba fasciata*

Common Names: White-Collared Pigeon, Wild Pigeon.

**History.** The band-tailed pigeon receives its common name from its identifying tail marking, for across the brownish-gray tail is a band of darker gray. The Indians called it *"hubboh"* in imitation of its call. There are two races of bandtails in North America. The typical *Columba fasciata fasciata* is found throughout the range of the species, which inhabits the western part of the continent, but the paler variety, *Columba fasciata vioscae* (Viosca's pigeon) is confined to the southern part of Lower California and apparently is non-migratory.

At one time the band-tailed pigeon was numerous, and thousands of birds migrated in flocks so large and constant that the flights from British Columbia to California, and other southern wintering grounds, darkened the skies. Their abundance was likened to that of the passenger pigeon, and the extinction of that species perhaps forewarned the near-extermination of the large band-tailed species which is likewise excellent table food. The habits of the bird, particularly during the winter season, made it vulnerable to market hunters who ruthlessly slaughtered them by gun and by net, shipping thousands of them to restaurants in big cities. The majority of the pigeons wintered in California, and fed in concentrated areas according to the supply of piñon nuts and acorns, their chief fall and winter food. It was a comparatively simple task to destroy the birds congregated in such large flocks, especially when the characteristic of the bird is to remain in a feeding area even when heavily hunted. The activities of the market hunters of the 1900's were culminated in the fall and winter season of 1911 to 1912 when extensive killing was estimated by ornithologists to have represented about one-half of all the band-tailed pigeons. Around one-half million birds had gathered in the oak forests in the vicinity of Santa Barbara, California, to feed on the heavy acorn crop.

The wanton destruction provoked the Federal Government to declare a closed season on the bird, beginning in 1914 and to last five years. There was then a marked increase in pigeon population, but once gunning was allowed again the numbers sharply declined until 1932 when the bird was saved once more by the government from excessive depredation. Though the bird can easily be exterminated because of its habit of concentrating in feeding and watering places and its slow rate of breeding, it reacts very favorably to protection. By 1933 it had staged a return and with good game management will continue to increase. Eventually, it is hoped, a longer season will be allowed for the many sportsmen who consider this true game bird among the sportiest shooting.

**Identification.** The North American band-tailed pigeon gives the general impression of being a stout bird, and its plump appearance normally is maintained throughout the year. It is larger that the domestic pigeon, being 16 inches from wing-tip to wing-tip and 16 inches in length, and is sometimes confused with the now nonexistent passenger pigeon. The bill, typical of the pigeon family, has a horny tip, but a soft cere at its base. The legs are comparatively short and the feet small in relation to other fowl-like birds, from which they distinctly differ by not scratching for food

The rather dense plumage is smooth, and, though not colorful, is handsome. The upper parts are brownish and bluish-gray while the under parts and head are purplish drab, with a glossy iridescence on the side of the neck. Besides, the peculiar band across the middle of the squared tail, which divides the darker section from the lighter, this species has a conspicuous white marking across the nape of the neck which gives the bird its popular name of white-collared pigeon. The female is similar to the male but drabber.

The male bandtail has several calls, perhaps the most common of which is *"coo-coo, coo-coo,"* or *"tuck-oo, tuck-oo."* Other less languid notes are the hollow, owl-like notes, *"who-who-hoo"* and *"hop-ah-who,"* but all the calls are loud and clearly audible at considerable distance. They are monotonously repeated at irregular intervals, about seven to eight notes to a series, and habitually given in the early morning and again in early evening. As with other pigeons, the bill is opened slightly, and the bird looks as if it were "singing through its nose."

**Characteristics.** They are not wary except where actively hunted and then are not easily approached. They are gregarious and gather in large flocks during the year except for the breeding season when the birds tend to scatter in pairs in a large area. Presumably the breeding trait influences the behavior of the flock during the fall and winter seasons. If a flock of band-tailed pigeons is startled while feeding, the birds rise a few at time, like the mourning dove, which also scatters when nesting, but, unlike the white-winged dove which nests in colonies and is flock-bound in all seasons, acting as one bird.

As a rule the take-off from the ground is accompanied by a noisy flapping of wings, but the pigeon is capable of making a virtually silent landing on a slender branch in a forest. The large, pointed wings are powerful, and the strong, direct flight is rapid, with an average cruising speed of 45 miles per hour. Variations in flight habits are circling, spiraling, and planing, with occasional use of a short wing-beat and then sailing. They are more at home in the air or in trees than on the ground, though they walk easily. They roost in trees and are fond of perching on the top of tall trees, preferably those with dead limbs at the top so there will be no foliage to hamper a quick getaway, specifically from the prairie falcon and Cooper's hawk, which snatch the adult birds right off their perches.

**Breeding.** The breeding season varies with the range, but is prolonged, and on some ranges lasts ten months of the year—November and December being the only non-breeding months. During the season from one to three or four broods are raised. The birds are capable of mating at one year of age, and they are monogamous as a rule, though some males are fickle. Beside the male's courtship display on the ground which includes head ducking and stretching to show his markings, he often takes to the air, with wing and tail spread, on odd nuptial flights, after which he circles back to his perch. On his return flight he utters a peculiar wheezing noise. His loud, owl-like coo is repeated frequently from his perch.

The mated pairs usually are well distributed over a large area, but sometimes a group of 30 to 40 birds form a loose colony over a large section with one bird to three or four acres. The preferred nesting areas are in large gulches filled with thick foliage at the bottom and sides which provide natural concealment, and, if filled with seed-bearing trees, such as alders, furnish them with an abundant food supply, particularly for the young. The pigeon is adaptable to many different kinds of nesting sites. Though the nest usually is placed on the lower branches of fir or oak trees, or about 20 feet above the ground, they often are found from 8 to 30 feet, and sometimes 8 to 180 feet, from the ground. They may be made on the ground among bushes, between the roots of trees, or without a nest near a stream. Wherever the chosen spot, it is characteristic of the band-tailed pigeon to return to the same nesting place each year.

Nest-building proceeds at an unhurried pace in the morning hours, and as the male brings sticks, the female arranges them, though she often must be prodded by her mate to continue the slow process which lasts about six days and may involve the laying of just six sticks. The shallow nest of dead twigs is a crude structure, so poorly made that in most cases it will fall apart if moved by hand. It is similar to the mourning dove's but larger. The eggs are kept from rolling by the rough nature of the twigs, which are not woven together but placed one on the other to form a platform 6 to 8 inches in diameter. Occasionally, the nest is lined with pine needles.

As a rule just one porcelain-white egg is laid, but sometimes two. When as few as 6 to 18 twigs are used in building a lofty nest (though there may be as many as 100), the job of incubation on so airy a spot is a wondrous thing. Both sexes sit on the eggs, which hatch in 18 to 20 days. During incubation the sitting bird will stand upright when approached and give away its nesting location, usually deserting when frightened.

The nestlings, like all the members of the pigeon family, are practically helpless at birth, being blind and unable to stand or peck, but their rate of growth is second to that of no other bird for the first 20 days of their existence. When hatched, they weigh about one-half ounce, and that amount is doubled in two days. At six days of age, they weigh about 4 ounces, and at one month, after being carefully brooded, guarded, and stuffed by both parents, the squab often is larger than the adult bird. The bill of the nestling is adapted to the sucking motion used in feeding by regurgitation. It is thick and large in relation to the body size, and its soft and fleshy quality changes as the bird matures, and gradually becomes hard and contracts.

The pigeon milk, which is furnished by both sexes, begins to form about the eighth day of incubation, and presumably is stimulated in the crop by a hormone near the brain. The fluid is derived from cells of mucous membrane lining the crop, which grow larger and multiply upon stimulus, and secrete fat globules. The cells are shed, and are a partial ingredient of the whitish liquid, which is high in fat and protein content but totally lacking in sugar. The production of this milklike substance continues for about 20 days. At the end of that time the squab is able to take soft foods, seeds, etc., which are partially digested by the parents and fed to the young by regurgitation or a vomiting-like action which takes about three minutes. When a month old, the young are ready to leave the nest.

When hatched, the squabs are scantily covered with white down through which the yellow skin is easily seen. The spiny quills, first indication of true feathering, are about one inch long when the young are ten days old. The quills burst from their sheath into juvenile plumage which is similar to that of the mature birds, but without the white bar on the upper hind neck and lacks the iridescence on the side of the neck and vinaceous tints. After the first fall moult takes place, the plumage coloring of the juveniles is nearly adult.

This pigeon can hold its own against its natural enemies, and now is reasonably protected from overshooting by its chief enemy, man. The fact that it is susceptible to nematode parasites, which lodge in the intestines and kill off the birds in some numbers, is of importance primarily because of the danger of transmitting the parasite to new hosts.

**Feeding.** Normal feeding time for the pigeons begins shortly after dawn and continues to about 8 or 9 in the morning, then the birds return to eat later in the afternoon, about 4 P.M., and eat until dusk. The feeding grounds vary with the range and seasonal abundance of preferred foods. The chief sources of food for this species are nuts and berries, and, since the supply of both is seasonal and varies in a particular locality from year to year, the birds often roam from one area to another. Often, as the nut and berry crop goes, so goes the pigeon abundance or scarcity. Hazels, piñons, and acorns are favored, but of these nuts the acorns, particularly from the live oaks, golden oaks, and black oaks, are perhaps the most important food item, because a good crop normally lasts through the fall and winter. They eat various kinds of fruits or berries, such as manzanita berries, wild cherries, wild grapes, wild mulberries, elderberries, chokeberries, blueberries, and blackberries. Seeds make up a good percentage of the diet, with the emphasis on grain (barley, oats, and corn), largely waste, picked up in the stubble after harvesting.

The flock normally bunches together while feeding in grain fields. The birds intermittently walk (not hop) and fly, the ones in the back flying over the group to the front, and in this manner they keep constantly on the move and cover the ground quickly. The habit of congregating in large flocks where food is abundant has caused some crop damage, mainly because of their pulling of grain and pea shoots for the purpose of getting at the kernel. During the late winter in some locales when the nut and berry supply is depleted, they turn to toyon or Christmas berries, and in early spring to the sycamore balls. A small number of insects are taken during the year, mostly grasshoppers.

There is a daily intake of gravel into the gizzard which helps grind the food swallowed whole. The lining of the gizzard is corrugated and tough, like a washboard, and when food is admitted, it is rubbed against it with an alternately contracting and expanding motion which is a substitute for mastication. The action is set off by the presence of food. There is no true digestion with the forming of digestive juices. Unlike a chicken, the pigeon does not have a true crop but an enlargement of the esophagus. This bird also has no gall bladder.

Like the rest of the pigeon family, the bandtail drinks in a unique manner. Liquid is not raised up in the lower part of the bill and, with head lifted, allowed to flow down into the crop, but the bill is held in the water and the water is flicked or sucked in with a quick tongue action.

The band-tailed pigeon generally is excellent eating, especially when the bird has been killed after feeding on piñon nuts, but the flavor of its flesh varies with the type of food eaten. If it has been feeding over acorns, the flesh will have a bitter taste, and the bird should be soaked overnight in salt water or water with vinegar or lemon. Recommended cooking is by broiling or baking in a pot pie.

**Range and Distribution.** The band-tailed pigeon species ranges from British Columbia, down western United States, south to Central America. They inhabit thickly wooded ranges of oaks, pines, firs, and other trees.

The Viosca's pigeons of the oak forests of the southern part of Lower California are confined in their range and presumably are non-migratory since few birds consistently have been identified as wanderers from that region.

The typical bandtail variety, however, is found from the northern to the southern extremes of the range for this species. The breeding grounds extend from northern British Columbia down the Pacific Coast, through Washington, Oregon, and California, east to New Mexico, and south to Lower California. Fall migration south takes place about September to November and the birds move down to the southern sections, with the majority of those living north of California journeying into California to spend the winter. In the winter season they live north to California and are found in Arizona, south to New Mexico and Lower California, and on south to Guatemala. The return trip north in the spring to breed is made around April and May. These pigeons seldom are found outside of their normal range.

**Hunting Methods.** Relatively few gunners, except those who live near the autumn flyways of these birds, are familiar with bandtail shooting, and the novice is usually in for a chastening experience. As his pile of empty shells becomes larger with no birds to balance the account, the tyro may well ask some old hand at the game, "How far should I lead 'em?" The answer is likely to be, "About twice as far as you'd naturally figure—and then double it!" The bandtail sweeps down over a ridge at high speed, and the matter of correct lead is the chief factor between hits and misses. This is pass shooting at its literal best and the gunner with experience on high-flying canvasbacks over a windy marsh will fare better than the average upland shooter.

The flights of these birds are sporadic. They do not always use the same flyways and they may appear by the thousands one season and be extremely scarce the next. The flights seem to be governed by the local food supply. Bandtails are very fond of piñon nuts, and during the years when these nuts are abundant the pigeon shooting is excellent; when the nut crop is poor the birds shift their flight to other quarters. The same applies to acorns and other crops.

Each season the arrival of the flight is the signal for a holiday to the local gunners. In former years this shooting was spread over a longer period, but with the present short season it is more concentrated and in some localities opening day sounds like the beginning of a battle.

The incoming birds select a low spot or pass between the hills, and streak through in flocks varying from a few birds to several hundred. In areas where there are several ridges the birds usually follow the contours of the land, rising over the high ground and pitching into the valleys in undulating flight. The flight speed is usually less when the birds are climbing or before they start on the downward angle, and for this reason—as well as to get in the first shot—wise hunters prefer to be near the tops of the ridges. Those lacking the fortitude or ambition to climb must be content to take their chances at a lower level.

By dawn the favorite ridge is reminiscent of "where the embattled farmers stood," with gunners hiding behind trees, rocks, brush, and other places of concealment, for the bandtail has extremely keen vision and he who is careless about showing himself is not likely to collect many birds.

As the first birds come into sight there is an excited yell of "Here they come!" and a general tenseness grips the expectant gunners. Almost invariably some trigger-happy enthusiast overestimates the possibility of his gun and cuts loose at birds obviously out of range. This simply causes the birds to swerve and climb before zipping off on a new tack and usually draws a flood of profanity from his neighbors.

The birds come in waves at varying intervals, but the shooting is apt to be fast and furious most of the time. A shooter runs out of shells and frantically tries to borrow from those around him. Another suddenly realizes that his too-light loads are merely dusting feathers and clamors for some "sixes." In the lulls between flights the gunners retrieve their dead birds and the less skillful—or less lucky—bolster their alibis.

There is no "best" gun for this type of shooting, but the average gunner will be likely to collect more birds by using a typical duck gun. A hard-hitting 12-gauge double-barreled shotgun with a modified right barrel and a full-choke left barrel loaded with No. 6 shot should be a good all-around bet. Pump guns and autoloaders bored full choke are likely to produce better results than those with more open barrels. Express loads are preferable in any case.

# MOURNING DOVE

*Zenaidura macroura*

COMMON NAMES: Carolina Dove, Turtle Dove, Wild Dove, Wild Pigeon.

**History.** The mourning dove, *Zenaidura macroura,* is represented in North America by two of its three sub-species. The eastern variety, *Z.m. carolinensis,* is distributed through eastern United States and Canada, and the western type, *Z.m. marginella,* is found in western United States, Canada, and Mexico. The third sub-species, *Z.m. macroura,* is believed to be non-migratory and is restricted to the Caribbean islands. The soft, plaintive call of the mourning dove is its most commonly recognized characteristic, and has given the bird its name. The eastern and western varieties are similar, differing primarily in range, and only slightly in size and color.

This dove is distinctive among all game birds of the United States in that it breeds in every state. Its numbers have been sharply reduced, especially in the southern New England states, since the early settlers found the bird in such abundance. By the early 1900's the population had reached such a low in the northeastern states, that, in 1908, Massachusetts began the movement to save the dove from extermination in that region by passing a state law giving it permanent protection. Today, most of the northern states completely protect the dove, and there has been a gradual but slow increase in population. In these northern states it is regarded as a songbird, but in the southern and western states, where it is more numerous, it is hunted as a game bird. Sportsmen find the small, swift dove a difficult shot and tasty eating.

In relation to other popular game birds, there has been little game management extended to the doves, on which 25 states have a shooting season. Only the annual kill of quails, pheasants, or ducks (which have been given much state and Federal aid) exceeds that of the doves. Eleven million doves were taken in 1942, but there are few active state projects in existence to make certain of a continued dove population for shooting purposes or even for its very survival. Four or five states have extensive research projects, but at the present date, the solution to the diminishing dove population is carefully controlled shooting, especially in the southeastern states where many of the birds migrate for the winter.

The mourning dove has been established as an international migratory species. Though it often spends both winter and summer seasons on its southern range, many breed in Canada and winter in Mexico, so the bird comes under the protection of the United States Federal Government, which has established migratory-bird treaties with Great Britain (1916) and Mexico (1937). Its migratory status removes it from individual state decisions. Its nearly perennial breeding habits in the southern

Hal H. Harrison.

PLATE I. Mourning Dove.

parts of the range make dove management difficult. The shooting season should be after the month of September, since October and November normally are the only non-breeding months. According to a survey made by the Fish and Wildlife Service, 25% to 50% of the birds bagged in September are immature, and 15% of the adults are brooding on nests.

**Identification.** The male mourning dove is a slim bird and with subdued plumage coloration. The upper parts of the dense plumage are a light grayish-brown with olive-colored overtones, and under parts are pinkish-brown to buffy. The 5- to 6-inch blue-gray tail, longer than the brown wing, is margined with black and has white spots which are clearly visible when the bird is in flight and a good identifying feature in the field. On the side of the buffy head is a distinctive small, black spot. The crown is a bluish-gray, and the sides of the pale vinaceous neck are iridescent. The small, slender bill, which is curved and dips slightly in the middle, is typical of the pigeon group. The mourning dove is similar to the passenger pigeon, having the same trim body lines and general plumage coloring. Amateur bird spotters have mistakenly reported flights of the extinct pigeon during the last 20 years because of its resemblance to the dove. Besides the size difference, the rump of this species is a gray-brown, while that of the passenger pigeon is slate-gray, and the pigeon lacks the black marking below the ear. The mourning dove is further distinguished by the whistling sound which its short, pointed wings make in flight, for the pigeon was reportedly silent on the wing.

The female mourning dove looks very much like the male, but is duller and usually is without iridescence on the side of the neck. Also, her tail is shorter than the male's. Both adult sexes have a complete moult which generally takes place in the autumn and winter or when the mating season is finished.

The western mourning dove is similar to the eastern mourning dove but is a little larger in size and slightly paler in plumage coloring.

Male and female measure both between 11 and 13 inches in length, with a wingspread of 17 to 19 inches. Both weigh about 4 ounces.

The well-known call of this dove has been described in various fashions, for the sound apparently is strongly dependent on the mood of the listener. It is generally considered to be a sad, mournful tone, but pleasant and soothing to the ear. It sounds more soft at a distance, but is still a clear *"cooah, cooo, cooo, cooo"* at 250 yards, the last three notes being more drawn-out and usually more distinct. The male is the artist at calling, for it is a feature of courting time. He is silent during the winter. As a rule the call is repeated at irregular intervals, with the song lasting about 3 to 4 seconds each time. The suitor stands still and taut when cooing. The female is capable of calling, but she does so infrequently, and gives a poor, weak imitation, abrupt by comparison.

**Characteristics.** The nature of the dove varies by seasons, because of the pressure of shooting, plus the natural make-up of the bird. It becomes increasingly gentle and unsuspicious as the breeding season approaches and will feed with domesticated fowl in barnyards. In autumn and winter, however, it returns to its wild and timid ways, which are intensified in relation to the amount of shooting. Except for the breeding season, when the birds pair off, the dove is found in loose flocks, but they are not flock-bound—that is, the unit does not react and move as one bird, which action would make it as vulnerable as the passenger pigeon, which even nested in large colonies. When a flock of this species is frightened, they do not rise together, but according to individual reaction—though usually by twos, which probably is a throwback to the mating habit of traveling in pairs.

As a rule when the birds are startled they take off into an odd, swerving flight. The ascent is quick and neat and they gain altitude rapidly. Once on the wing their flight is swift and direct, with a cruising speed of about 40 miles an hour and spurting into an unsustained pace of 60 miles an hour. The powerful, rapid wing-beat makes a whistling sound, much like that of the golden-eye. The bird also bears some resemblance to the sparrow hawk in the air because of its slim body as well as its long tail, pointed wings, and manner of flight.

The mating season varies with the climate of each particular section of the range, but it is invariably a long one since only one nesting for a mated pair is rare and two are normal even in the most northerly breeding grounds. The breeding period averages six to seven months in the south, but ten months is not uncommon, with December and January being the only non-breeding times. Since the making of the nest, egg incubation, and raising of the young all take only about six weeks, the job is not a difficult or long one.

The "dove of peace" is a common association of words and ideas, but is not a true statement of the ways of the dove, particularly during courtship when rival males clash over a prospective mate. When a fight begins, the female in question vanishes. The male's courtship display on the ground includes strutting, nodding, puffing out of neck feathers, and spreading of tail feathers as the wings are dropped with tips touching the ground. At this time the male also indulges in a strange aerial flight which is assumed to be a nuptial display. With a strenuous flapping of wings, which appear to hit over his back, he rises to a height of about 100 feet, then glides in wide, sweeping curves back to his perch. This performance generally is repeated four to five times at 2- to 3-minute intervals.

**Breeding.** With some exceptions, this species is monogamous, and a mated pair bills and coos with affection throughout the year while the male takes an equal share of the female's chores of nesting and rearing the young. The pair leaves the flock to find a nesting site, which normally is upland in a woodland clearing, orchard, or field bordered with trees, but occasionally is in a marsh or swampy area. The mourning dove builds its nest in a variety of places, practically any place as long as it is a level prop and capable of holding up a flimsy nest. Sometimes the doves take over the deserted nests of other species, such as the English sparrow, robin, or kingbird, but usually their nest is built on a tree branch, or crotch, from 5 to 10 feet above the ground, but the extremes are 3 to 20 feet. The nest also is constructed in holes of trees, on tree stumps, or in bushes. In treeless areas the eggs occasionally are laid on the ground, in a bunch of grass, and no nest is made. Nest building generally occupies the early morning hours when the male brings the material to his mate and she constructs the nest. It is a flat platform loosely made of sticks and lined with straws or softer twigs and sometimes weeds or roots.

Two eggs are the average number laid, though one, three, or four are dropped. They are white or creamy-white, and are hatched in 12 to 14 days, with both sexes participating in the incubation. Generally, the incubation is a constant process since the female sits from evening to morning and the male relieves her to sit from morning (about 8:30) to evening (about 4:30). For second and successive broods, a new nest usually is made, though the old one occasionally is used a second time.

The newly hatched squabs are nearly naked, having a thin covering of short, white down, and are helpless. They are brooded by both parents for 11 to 14 days, and are completely dependent on them until ready to leave the nest. During the greatest part of their nest life they are fed by regurgitation. Their first food is "pigeon milk," a whitish liquid secreted in the crop of both parents. The male produces more of this glandular secretion than the female and actively participates in feeding the young. As the young grow, the liquid is supplemented and eventually replaced by the regurgitation of partially digested food, such as seeds, insects, and worms. When a squab wants to eat, it raises its head from beneath the brooding parent and as the adult opens its beak, the young bird inserts its smaller one into the side of it. By rhythmically working the body and head back and forth, a motion which is reciprocated by the squab, the adult successfully ejects the food. The feeding time varies from about 15 seconds to one minute.

By the time the squab is ready to leave the nest it is fat and the stiff quills have developed into the first juvenile plumage. In this plumage the young are very similar to the mature female, being duller in coloration than the mature male. By their first winter, after the fall moult, they are nearly adult. In the southern sections of the range the young mature at a very fast pace, and some born in the spring are ready to breed in the late summer or when about five to six months of age.

Like the average game bird, the mourning dove suffers a sizable nesting loss due to forest or marsh fires when the nests are burned and nests or young are destroyed, and also during heavy rains when the nests are flooded and the eggs roll out or the young are drowned. One of the major reasons for nest failures among this species is stormy weather, when high winds pull loose the carelessly constructed nests. A three-year survey of nesting failures in Iowa revealed that 25 per cent of the losses could be attributed to this cause. Snow also takes a high toll by covering the food supply, and during the severe winter of 1940, which included much of the southern range, thousands of birds starved to death.

**Feeding.** The mourning dove is primarily a ground feeder, seeking fields, gardens, and wooded clearings, but as a rule shying from the deep forest. About 99% of the dove's diet is vegetable matter, and seeds make up the major food item. The preferred seeds are grain, mainly wheat and buckwheat, which along with oats, rye, corn, and barley form about 30% of the food intake. Seeds of weeds are the principal food, however, since they are available throughout the year. In the winter, mast, especially beechnuts and acorns, is eaten, and in the South the birds congregate in large numbers around peanut fields. The small percentage of animal matter is mostly insects, especially grasshoppers, and worms. Regardless of the type of food, the eating is concluded with a supply of gravel which helps to grind and digest. Drinking water also is needed each day, and flocks are habitually seen making their daily flight to water at dusk, just before roosting. It is a peculiarity of the entire pigeon and dove family that while drinking they keep the head in the water up to the nostrils, and take one continuous draught rather than raise the head at intervals to swallow as most other birds do.

The farmer's opinion of the dove as a crop destroyer is dependent to a great degree on the dove population in the particular locality. Where there is a concentration of doves near a favorable food supply, such as peas, corn, or buckwheat, where thousands of birds have been known to gather, there is sometimes serious crop damage The general agreement of farmer and scientist, however, is that the bird does enough good to justify the harm done over its range as a whole, since the greatest part of the grain is waste, picked up in the stubble after harvesting, and most of the weed seeds are of the harmful variety.

**Range and Distribution.** The range of the mourning dove is very extensive, and the hardy bird adapts itself well to the extremes of climatic conditions. It is found from Canada to Mexico in North America, and down to Central America and the West Indies. In spite of its wide distribution, it is not an obvious bird, because of its pale coloring and shy habits.

The two sub-species are separated by differences in range, being on the eastern and western side of North America, as their names indicate. Despite the fact that the bird breeds in every state, and some birds winter in the northerly nesting areas, the breeding grounds tend to be in the North and the wintering grounds in the South. The eastern variety breeds from New Brunswick, Nova Scotia, southern Maine, Ontario, and Manitoba west to eastern Iowa, eastern Arkansas, and Louisiana south to the Gulf coast. Its wintering grounds extend from Kentucky and North Carolina southward to Central America.

On the eastern edge of the Great Plains and at the Gulf of Mexico, the eastern sub-species meets the western. The western bird ranges from the Great Plains to the Pacific coast and south to Panama. It breeds from Manitoba, Saskatchewan, and British Columbia south through Mexico and winters as far south as Panama.

Where the species breeds in the south, there is little or no shifting of the population for the winter months, but generally those which nest in the north, from New Jersey to California, travel to warmer climes in the fall. The birds of eastern United States and Canada are among those which prepare for the fall trip about July, or when the mating season is over, and band together in large flocks of 500 to 600. These birds normally migrate to the southeastern United States between October and November and go to South Carolina, Georgia, northern Florida, Alabama, Mississippi, and Louisiana. Few of the eastern variety go farther south than the Gulf states. The return trip in the spring takes place between March and mid-May. The migrating habits of the western bird, like the eastern, are largely dependent on the nesting range, but whereas the eastern bird seldom leaves the United States for winter, many of the western ones go south to Mexico.

The mourning dove is a bird of the open country, of sandy plains, of broad cultivated fields. The activities of man have forced many of the birds from their preferred natural habitat into thinly wooded hillsides or into forests where they retreat in order to nest in unmolested seclusion. The eastern variety lives on cultivated land (80%) and marshland (20%), but the bird of the west lives primarily on the open plains and semi-arid regions, though it roams to mountains 7000 feet in altitude.

# WHITE-WINGED DOVE

*Melopelia asiatica*

COMMON NAMES: Singing Dove, Sonora Pigeon, Whitewing.

**History.** The white-winged dove, found along the southern part of North America, is divided into two sub-species which are separated primarily by regional distribution since the differences in size and coloring are minor. The eastern whitewing *(Melopelia asiatica asiatica)* inhabits the eastern part of the range, and the western whitewing *(Melopelia asiatica mearnsi)* lives in the western section. The bird of the West is better known, because it is more numerous and is common in the deserts and mesquite valleys of the southwestern United States and Lower California. There it is popularly called "Sonora pigeon."

**Identification.** In over-all appearance, the adult male whitewing is a small, trim bird with brownish-gray plumage coloring and a pointed tail. There is a bluish-black patch on the side of the head as well as a metallic golden-brown spot. It is similar to the mourning dove but heavier and resembles tht zenaida dove, but the tail is pointed, not squared, and the whitewing has a large white wing patch which is conspicuous in flight and readily identifies it and gives it the popular name.

The mature female is similar to the male but is smaller in size and duller in plumage coloration. Both sexes measure about 11 inches in length.

The most common calls of the dove sound more like the hoot of a commanding owl than the coo of a sad-voiced dove. The male is the talkative sex in this species, and his various notes range in tone from soft and sonorous to bold and harsh. Sometimes one call includes all the tonal qualities he is capable of making. Often there are variations in each love song, but two of the most distinct ones are changes on *"Who-hoo who hoo-oo."* The call most frequently heard is the male's *"who cooks for you"* which is repeated in a monotonous fashion in the early morning hours and begins again at dusk. When calling, the bills are opened very slightly, if at all, and the noise appears to come through their nostrils. When a whole colony of doves sings at one time, the amplified sound may carry as far as a mile or more.

**Characteristics.** The whitewing is naturally shy and this characteristic is intensified wherever man is at hand to frighten or shoot it. This species is neither arboreal nor terrestrial, but a combination of both, and so is at home in either place. It roosts in trees but feeds on the ground, and usually does both in large, sociable flocks, often nesting in colonies. The dove is airborne with about the second flap of its wings, and the wings beat rapidly and clap noisily, making a whistling sound as the bird rises. In normal flight there is no whistling wing-beat like that which characterizes the mourning dove on the wing. The whitewing is a rapid flier and holds to a direct course.

**Breeding.** The breeding season is long and allows for two and more broods to be raised yearly. The length of the season and number of broods varies with the range, the birds in the most southerly part averaging more than two broods in their prolonged nesting time. The whitewing is capable of breeding when one year old.

The males are monogamous and usually remain with the same female throughout the year, but many bloodless fights take place among the suitors before the birds are paired. When courting on the ground, the male repeats a loud *"kroo-kroo"* to attract the female, and his display includes bobbing and ruffling of neck feathers and a particular maneuver when he tilts forward, fans out his tail to show the white bands, then rapidly closes it and returns to normal position. His nuptial flights take him 30 to 40 feet in the air, then he planes and circles back to his perch.

The nesting pairs scatter over a large area or gather in large colonies, but in spite of their sociable ways, do not bunch together though two or three nests sometimes are built in the same tree. As many as 2000 birds congregate in one colony, or rookery, which spreads over one-quarter to one-half a square mile among mesquite or blackberry bushes, cottonwood or willow trees, and on cultivated lands. Of all these nesting sites the mesquite is perhaps the preferred location in the Southwest, for the spiny little tree is a natural protection from predators, especially the dreaded Cooper's hawk. As a rule the nest is made off the ground—from 4 to 20 feet, but averaging about 8 feet—and usually is placed on a branch or in the midst of a dense bushy growth. They sometimes take over the old nests of other bird species. The nest is of more durable construction than that of the mourning dove, but is still a frail structure. It is a flat platform made of twigs and lined with softer, finer twigs and other material in the location such as straws, grass, and weeds.

Two eggs are the average number dropped, and one or three are rare. They are pure white or creamy white and hatch in about 18 days. The male aids the female in incubation, but not with the regularity of the male mourning dove. The dove is easily flushed from the nest, and rarely allows an approach closer than 25 feet. Even when hatching time is near the female seldom attempts to divert the enemy with pretenses of injury and deserts the eggs instead .

When the young are born, the male remains by the female to help rear them, and he perches near the mother as she broods her young. The first food of the young is "pigeon milk," and when they are about four days of age, regurgitated solid food, usually seeds, is added to the liquid food. The squabs are not able to leave the nest until they are three or four weeks old, and though very fat they are small and weak and rely on their parents to get food for them. They are capable of short flights at this time. The early feather development of the young birds is an unattractive process. The long, full down of the new-born is supplanted in a week by spiny quills which grow quite long before opening into smooth feathers. The first juvenile plumage is similar to the adult birds' but grayer.

**Feeding.** The doves habitually feed in flocks, and are very alert while eating. If they are startled, they rise as one bird, not in ones, twos, or threes as do the mourning doves. Flocks vary in size but are largest in the fall, just at the conclusion of the breeding season when the family groups merge, but before the fall migration. As many as 700 birds have congregated around a favorable food supply, and this habit has caused serious damage to crops in certain localities. Though the dove prefers waste grain, where wheat and barley have been cut but not threshed the bird will eat the grain in the shock. Besides different grain seeds, the doves eat weed seeds, berries, mesquite beans, fruits of giant cactus, and insects. A supply of grit is taken each day to aid digestion, and the birds often are seen on graveled roads at dusk before roosting.

Unlike the average upland game bird, the whitewing is not able to survive on dew and succulence during the nesting period, for it drinks water daily in every season. Daily flights are made to drinking places, and are a common sight in the arid southwestern range. Apparently from habit, flights to water are made even when it rains.

**Range and Distribution.** The eastern whitewing is found from Texas south to Mexico and Costa Rica, and east to the West Indies. It is occasionally seen in southern Louisiana and Florida. The western bird ranges across the southwestern United States and western Mexico, and winters as far south as Panama. Many of the birds spend the winter on the nesting grounds, since the range for the species is entirely southern, but there is some migration southward in the fall (about September and October) and back northward in the spring (about April.)

**Hunting Methods.** Dove shooting, according to many upland game hunters, is an excellent way of "separating the men from the boys." Probably no other game bird, with the possible exception of the grouse and the snipe, can so undermine the morale of a novice to that particular shooting. Only the snipe can exceed the dove when it comes to twists, turns, and dives, and as one famous wing shot remarked after his first trip for doves: "I kept shooting where the dove was, but he wasn't."

The easiest form of dove shooting, as well as pigeon shooting, is that termed "water-hole" shooting. Normally, the hunter who limits his dove or pigeon hunting to this form is himself limited to a brief period each day. In dry areas, both doves and pigeons hunt out a water hole, usually in the late afternoon. The shooter merely stations himself in good cover adjacent to a water hole known to be used by the birds and awaits their arrival. This limits him to anywhere from 15 minutes to an hour of shooting daily, depending upon the terrain and the bird population.

Shooting at a water hole or a roost is somewhat easier than walking up the birds in stubble fields, cornfields, or "burns," for the doves come in more slowly, and normally are in straight flight. Roost shooting, however, is much less productive than it was in the past, for the law sounds a curfew at sunset, and in most areas the doves do not really approach the roost in numbers until the sun has disappeared.

The most interesting, widely practiced, and at the same time most difficult method of dove shooting is to be found in the organized, or, in some instances *disorganized,* dove shoot. This practice merely calls for the assembly of from 6 to 20 shooters in a field where the birds are known to be feeding. The *organized* shoot will be conducted by one man, who will assign shooters to various positions around the perimeter of the field, then dot the center with an occasional shooter. The job of the organizer is to place the shooters to insure that each is a gunshot—but not much more—from the next. This will keep the birds moving and at the same time insure that they will pass within reasonable range of at least two shooters, once while entering and once while leaving the field. In the event the organizer has a "minimum" rather than a "maximum" eye, the chances are that a few of the shooters will get dusted with shot during the course of the day, when some over-anxious but heedless hunter is unable to resist a salute at a low bird.

In the days before the Wildlife Service assumed control of migratory bird regulations, a common practice was to bait a field for doves, which insured a large number of birds for the shoot. Today baiting is illegal, but in many areas it is debatable as to just what constitutes a "baited field." The term normally covers the deliberate scattering of grain in a field for the purpose of attracting birds. In several states where dove shooting is legal and popular, farmers will have a field that is "naturally" baited, rather than deliberately. Along rows of corn they will plant soybeans or some other cover crop, and after the corn is harvested they will turn hogs loose to fatten on this cover crop. The fact that this crop is extremely attractive to doves is merely incidental.

The visiting hunter who is invited to one of these informal but rather traditional shoots is certain of an interesting and exciting day. The number of doves he contributes to the bag depends upon his knowledge of this form of shooting as well as his shooting eye, for many an expert grouse, duck, pheasant, or quail shooter has found dove shooting a quick means of losing confidence in his shooting ability.

In many of the Southern states these shoots take on all the aspects of a combined barbecue-drinking-shooting-talking event, with several jugs, a roasting pig, and a big pot of Brunswick stew to keep the participants occupied when the doves are laggard. In areas where birds are really plentiful, and large turnouts are the rule, it is not unusual to hear almost constant gunfire for several hours. The number of shells fired in comparison to the doves killed often must be seen to be believed.

Those who consider this form of shooting to be unsporting have never attended one of these shoots. If a good wind happens to be blowing it is not unusual to see more than half of the doves fly the length of the field, saluted on every hand, and depart without having been touched by a pellet. Nor is it unusual to see one of the shooters literally surrounded by empty shells, with one or two doves to show for his efforts. The noise merely serves to stimulate the dove to greater speed and a more complex flying pattern.

By far the highest percentage of misses occurs as a result of under-leading the bird, which is traveling at a much greater speed than the novice to this shooting is aware. Incoming descending or ascending birds account for additional misses, and the twisting, diving turns account for the rest. The experienced duck shooter seems to accommodate himself to this shooting more rapidly than the upland game hunter, for he soon recognizes the fact that he is shooting behind the birds and he changes his lead to accommodate for the speed of the dove.

Often a wing-tipped bird will scale down to a point 2 or 3 feet from the ground and, with apparently no loss in speed, skim down the line of shooters. Under normal conditions at least one or two of the shooters will be unable to resist a shot, and too often the immediate response will be shouts of rage from a near-by shooter who has been stung by the pellets. Shooting glasses are a distinct asset to the shooter on one of these turnouts, for they are excellent insurance against a few stray pellets in the eyes. Thanks to the interval of the shooters, stray pellets fired by enthusiasts seldom do more than sting, but one in the eye might very well be serious.

Walking up birds in the stubble fields, peanut fields, or cornfields will prove productive in areas where the birds have not become wild through heavy shooting. Two hunters, moved down a field from 100 to 200 yards apart, will find the shooting more productive than a single hunter, as birds flushed by one often will pass near the other.

The large wheat fields of the Midwest, which once produced excellent shooting right after the harvest, today often prove barren of doves, for the agricultural methods have changed and the plow follows the combine, leaving no gleaning for the birds. Pea fields, bean fields, and peanut fields, however, usually offer plenty of food for the doves, and they grow fat on this fare.

As a table delicacy, the dove leaves nothing to be desired, and in many areas these birds rate high in the upper bracket. For dove recipes see "Game Cookery."

**Dogs.** A retriever is an asset in all forms of dove shooting, and while the spaniel, either cocker or springer, seems to be favored, many dove hunters use the same dog they employ in their regular upland shooting. The majority prefer the dog to remain at heel, and use it merely as a retriever and do not permit it to range ahead. The dove gets away quickly, and a dog that moves ahead of the hunter will flush birds out of range. Also, the dove normally skims along close to the ground for some distance after being flushed, and often the dog would be in line and so prevent the hunter from getting a shot.

**Guns.** The best gun for dove shooting often serves as the major topic of conversation and debate at the shoot The majority of experienced shooters prefer a double gun, bored with one barrel full choke and the other modified choke. Others contend that the barrels should be bored cylinder and modified. Still others insist that any suitable duck gun is satisfactory for doves. "You don't get too many close shots," they contend, "and if you do you can always wait the bird out and get in a shot when the pattern is best."

Shot size is another source of argument among this fraternity, with some holding that quail load is best, while others insist that No. 8 shot is too small for such a "tough" bird, and that the heavier 6's are more successful. All seem to agree, however, that in almost every instance the long-range load is best. Experience will convince most shooters of this fact, for it is not unusual to see a handful of feathers drift off from a dove without slowing the bird down to a noticeable degree. This experience seems more prevalent when smaller shot is used than when No. 6 shot is employed.

# PTARMIGAN

*Lagopus*

**History.** The ptarmigan of North American are close relatives of the red grouse so popular in Scotland. The origin of the birds in this country is obscure but it is believed that all of them are indigenous to this continent. Probably no group of birds is subject to more difficulty in classification, for at the present writing there are some 30-odd species and sub-species, with more being added annually.

Only four species or sub-species will be considered here, for these are the only ones an American sportsman would be likely to find. In order to meet with even these four he would have to cover a lot of country from the Rocky Mountains to Newfoundland and as far north as the Arctic Circle.

Two of the better-known species, the willow and the rock ptarmigan, are found in the lowlands, usually close to sea level in those sections where the mountains form a backdrop against the sky. The third species, the white-tailed ptarmigan, is almost invariably a bird of the high places and rarely comes down to timber line. Of the three, the willow ptarmigan is the most widely distributed. The rock ptarmigan is second in numbers, and the white-tailed ptarmigan is the least populous of all. The fourth member of the group is classed as a sub-species, known as Allen's ptarmigan, and is found only in Newfoundland.

The entire group are the smallest members of the grouse family and the only representatives of that clan in North America that display a completely different plumage in winter.

Both the willow and the southern white-tailed ptarmigan are found in the United States. The former is more widely distributed from coast to coast along the northern border states; the latter is confined solely to the Rocky Mountains. Ptarmigan are fast disappearing in the United States and where once abundant over a wide range are now found in depleted numbers over relatively small areas.

## WILLOW PTARMIGAN *Lagopus lagopus albus*

COMMON NAMES: Common Ptarmigan, Snow Grouse, Snow Partridge, White Grouse, Willow Grouse.

**Identification.** No more than a very general description can be offered in this case because it is rare that two birds ever bear the same markings. They moult three times each year and the plumage undergoes a more or less constant change. It is this trait which adds confusion to any attempt to classify them definitely into the various sub-species. In many cases the difference between the several races are so minute as to be negligible. (See color plate on page 481.)

The *summer plumage* of an adult male is somewhat as follows: Head, neck, and breast is a rich chestnut or cinnamon brown. The crown is spotted with black and the neck and chest are barred with the same color. The back and upper parts are more reddish-brown and are broadly and thickly barred with black. This area and the wing coverts are always blotched and spotted irregularly with varying-sized areas of white. The under parts are white, or nearly so.

The female in summer plumage is a mixture of tawny-brown and gray, heavily barred and spotted with dusky markings. The wings are mostly white with very little brown between the light areas. The under parts are white with uniform barred markings.

The legs and feet of both sexes are completely feathered.

In *winter plumage*, the entire body is snowy white. Only the tail feathers are black with white tips. The upper tail coverts reach to the end of the tail and these, as well as the two middle feathers are white. Both sexes adopt this change for a short time each year and while in this phase they are identical.

**Range and Distribution.** The willow ptarmigan breeds across the northern tundra from Greenland to the Aleutian Islands. In winter the birds come to northern British Columbia, Saskatchewan, and Quebec, and thence down through Canada to North Dakota, Montana, Wisconsin, and Michigan. A few birds have been recorded in New York, Massachusetts, and Maine, but these are regarded as accidental visitors. In former years the birds were more common in New Brunswick and the lower St. Lawrence region than at the present time.

## ALLEN'S PTARMIGAN *Lagopus lagopus alleni*

**Identification.** Many ornithologists question the reason for giving this bird a separate classification because it varies so slightly from the willow ptarmigan. About the only difference is that the shafts of the primaries and secondaries are usually black or mottled with that color.

**Range and Distribution.** These birds occur only on the rocky barrens of Newfoundland and live chiefly on berries, seeds, and lichens.

## ALEXANDER'S PTARMIGAN *Lagopus lagopus alexandrae*

This is a sub-species, similar in every respect to the willow ptarmigan; it is merely another variation of that species.

These birds are found chiefly on the Baranof, Porcher, and Shumagin Islands of Alaska.

## SOUTHERN WHITE-TAILED PTARMIGAN *Lagopus leucurus altipetens*

COMMON NAMES: Mountain Quail, Rocky Mountain Snow Grouse, Snow Grouse, White Quail.

**Identification.** This is the smallest member of the tribe, being no more than 13 inches long.

Adults in *summer* have the head, neck, back, and breast finely marked with grayish-brown, white, and black. These markings vary widely with every specimen: so there are many variations of the white-tailed ptarmigan. The tail, most of the wings, and the lower parts from the breast down are pure white. The tail coverts reach to the end of the tail. The legs and feet are entirely feathered.

Adults in *winter* have the entire plumage snowy white; only the bill remains black. The juveniles are all white except the tail, which is gray.

**Range and Distribution.** This is the alpine bird, sometimes found at dizzy heights in the Rocky Mountains from British Columbia south to northern Montana, Colorado, and northern New Mexico.

There are three sub-species of this race which are classified as follows:

## KENAI WHITE-TAILED PTARMIGAN *Lagopus leucurus peninsularis*

This is a variety found in central Alaska, Yukon, Mackenzie, and Kenai Peninsula.

## NORTHERN WHITE-TAILED PTARMIGAN *Lagopus leucurus leucurus*

This species is found in the Rocky Mountains from British Columbia and Alberta south to Vancouver Island.

## RAINIER WHITE-TAILED PTARMIGAN *Lagopus leucurus rainierensis*

The range of this species is limited to the Cascade Mountains of Washington.

## ROCK PTARMIGAN

*Lagopus rupestris rupestris*

**Identification.** These birds are slightly smaller than the willow ptarmigan, whose range they often share, and a trifle larger than the white-tailed ptarmigan.

Adults in *summer* have upper parts, except the wings and tail, brownish-yellow barred with blackish-brown. The lower parts of the male, except the breast and sides, are white. Lower parts of the female and the wings and tail of both sexes are white.

Adults in *winter* have a winter plumage which is pure white except for black tail feathers and a black line from the bill to behind the eye.

**Range and Distribution.** This species is fairly well distributed from northern British Columbia, southern Yukon, and south on the barrens from Alaska to Ungava. In the winter they move as far south as southern Mackenzie and southern Ungava Peninsula. In earlier times they were often found in Quebec and upper New Brunswick, but few if any stragglers now reach those sections of the country.

No less than ten variations of this species are currently recognized. The main reason for division is range rather than plumage or habits.

## CHAMBERLAIN'S PTARMIGAN

*Lagopus rupestris chamberlaini*

This sub-species is confined to Adak, one of the Aleutian Islands.

## DIXON'S PTARMIGAN

*Lagopus rupestris dixoni*

This bird is commonly found on Admiralty, Baranof, and Chichagof Islands of Alaska.

## EVERMAN'S PTARMIGAN

*Lagopus rupestris evermanni*

This variety inhabits Attu, one of the Aleutian group.

## KELLOGG'S PTARMIGAN

*Lagopus rupestris kelloggae*

This is a more widely distributed variety found in the interior of Alaska, northern Yukon, along the western Arctic coast, and east to northwestern Greenland.

## NELSON'S PTARMIGAN

*Lagopus rupestris nelsoni*

This is another Aleutian variety found chiefly on Unalaska, Akutan, and Unimak Islands.

## REINHARDT'S PTARMIGAN

*Lagopus rupestris reinhardi*

The range of this species is confined to southwestern Greenland.

## SANFORD'S PTARMIGAN

*Lagopus rupestris sanfordi*

This bird's range is confined to Tanaga, one of the Aleutians.

## TOWNSEND'S PTARMIGAN

*Lagopus rupestris townsendi*

This bird's range is confined to Kiska, one of the Aleutian Islands.

## TURNER'S PTARMIGAN

*Lagopus rupestris atkhensis*

This bird is found on Atka, in the Aleutian Islands.

## WELCH'S PTARMIGAN

*Lagopus rupestris welchi*

This is a sub-species confined to Newfoundland.

**Characteristics.** Nature has equipped the ptarmigan for life in the frozen North and the snow-capped heights of the Rocky Mountains even to the extent of providing a special winter coat to match his surroundings. His legs and feet are completely feathered to protect him from the cold, and the feathering on his toes keeps him from sinking in the soft snow. (The scientific name *Lagopus* means "rabbit-footed.")

In the summer when the tundra and muskeg are bare he wears a rich coat of mottled brown, which is equally inconspicuous.

In habits he is much like other members of his family but he has adopted certain characteristics to conform with his surroundings.

**Breeding.** Of all the grouse, only the ptarmigan is monogamous. He selects a mate, remains with her, and is ready to fight all comers to protect her and their brood.

He does not indulge in such fantastic courtship demonstrations as the prairie grouse or the sage grouse, but he battles savagely with other males to win his spouse and keep her. These battles are apparently nature's way of selecting only the stronger birds to carry on the race in a country where strength and vigor are essential to survival.

During the mating season the male is as noisy as he is pugnacious. His calls are loudest and most insistent during the midnight hours when there is the least daylight in the "land of the midnight sun." His voice is far from musical and he gives vent to hoarse, squeaky croaks which often sound as though he is suffering from croup. Living as he does in a land of almost perpetual fog, wind, rain, and snow, it is no wonder that his "song" is harsh.

Whether or not he assists in incubation is not definitely established but he does remain on guard close to the nest at that time. The nest is no more than a depression in the ground lined with leaves and grass, and possibly a few feathers. The number of eggs ranges from 7 to 12, and they vary in color from pale yellow to chestnut-brown, heavily spotted with deep brown and black. It has been claimed that the color may be washed from a freshly laid egg until only the pale cream of the shell remains.

The willow ptarmigan is the most prolific of the three major species. The rock ptarmigan lays from six to ten eggs, and the white-tailed ptarmigan seldom deposits more than eight.

Incubation is believed to take about 21 days, and the young are able to run about soon after leaving the shell. Both parents look after their brood until the youngsters are well grown. In early autumn the young attain full growth and the birds then begin to "pack" in readiness for their migration.

The willow ptarmigan comes down into the valleys and the shelter of willow groves for the winter. The rock ptarmigan, who usually frequents the highest and most barren slopes in the summer, drops down to the more sheltered slopes. The white-tailed ptarmigan migrates less than his cousins and spends both summer and winter in the bleak, alpine fastnesses of the mountains.

The flight of the ptarmigan is strong and fairly rapid when once in the air and they may fly for a considerable distance before coming to earth again. They are sturdy runners also and often prefer to run rather than take wing. When flushed they usually go up one or two at a time instead of rising in a flock, and they rely a great deal on their protective coloration to conceal them from their enemies.

Foxes, the great snowy owl, and other predators take some annual toll from their numbers but they are less preyed upon than many other members of their family.

Like all the other species of American grouse and the northern hares and rabbits, the ptarmigan is subject to cycles of population. It has not yet been established whether these cycles of fluctuations are periodic or irregular, nor is there any positive determination of their cause. It is well known that in some years the birds are plentiful in a certain locality and the next year there may be none, but just why such cycles occur is still a matter of study.

**Feeding.** In early summer he feeds on various insects and herbs; later on he eats blueberries, huckleberries, cranberries, mossberries, and seeds. In the winter he subsists on rock moss, lichens, and the buds and terminal ends of willows and dwarf alders. The young, like those of other grouse, devour a great many insects. The diet of the various species and sub-species is similar and varies only because of the availability of certain foods.

The white-tailed ptarmigan is very fond of a leguminous plant called cassia, and because he lives mostly above the timber line he is more inclined to feed on mossberries and lichens than on tree buds.

**Hunting Methods.** To the gunner with some experience in shooting prairie chickens, sage grouse, or Huns, the ptarmigan will offer no particular problem. Likewise the inveterate quail hunter will find some similarity to his favorite game and an agreeably larger target.

Unfortunately these birds are so limited as to range and distribution that comparatively few gunners ever have an opportunity to hunt them. The alpine, or white-tailed, ptarmigan is familiar to those hardier souls who stalk the high places after sheep and goats. Hunting them is seldom deliberate but more likely to be incidental to the search for bigger game. This type of hunting is rugged work, and it is the rare hunter who would care to be burdened with the excess poundage of a shotgun; therefore, such birds as do reach the pot are generally killed with a rifle *after* the sportsman has obtained his trophies. A .22, preferably equipped with a scope sight, is an excellent little weapon for the purpose if the guide can be persuaded to pack one, but most of the birds that help to round out the menu at those elevations are decapitated by the same gun the hunter is using for his main purpose.

The rock and willow ptarmigan, however, are found on the barrens and tundra where they are not only more accessible but offer even sportier shooting. As with all upland birds, reference to their feeding habits will provide the knowledge of where to look for them.

Early in the season the birds may be found in groups of a half a dozen or more, and since such groups are often single families the percentage of young birds is usually high. At this time the birds, especially the young, lie well to a dog when in cover but are often inclined to run when on comparatively open ground. Later in the season, when the groups begin to "pack" and larger flocks are encountered, they become much wilder, flush wide, and are more difficult for a dog to handle.

It is impossible to give more than a general pattern of ptarmigan behavior. In those sections where they have been heavily hunted they are apt to be extremely wary and refuse to lie close. In other areas they may burst from almost underfoot with all the breathtaking abruptness of a ruffed grouse. Ptarmigan of the alpine slopes are not only inclined to flush wilder but generally fly farther than the birds of the lowlands. Coveys break suddenly, like quail, rise to the accompaniment of raucous croaking, and scatter in all directions. The initial flight is accomplished by a rapid beating of wings which later gives way to a sailing or scaling movement. Single birds often squat on the edge of cover rather than in it, or on a patch of snow, and depend on their protective coloration to remain unseen.

**Dogs.** Ptarmigan may be "walked up" in the same way as other grouse but the sport of shooting them reaches its zenith over one or more good dogs. At least a good retriever should be used whenever possible, for these birds blend so well with their surroundings that downed game is almost impossible to find. In the late fall, when the plumage change has begun, dead birds are easier to locate.

The right dog for the purpose is largely a matter of individual choice and, as with all other upland bird shooting, is always a matter of controversy. In some covers, such as the Newfoundland Barrens, either a setter or a pointer may turn in a wonderful performance. In the dense willow runs where the birds congregate late in the season, many experienced gunners claim that a spaniel is more efficient for routing the birds out into the open. In very open country a fast-going, wide-ranging dog will find more birds, but in the heavier covers the slower-moving dog working within effective gun range will likely provide better shooting.

**Guns.** Ptarmigan hunting needs no special equipment beyond that used in the pursuit of grouse or other upland game birds. The upland game gun of any gauge which suits the gunner's preference is perfectly adequate for the purpose. There is also some latitude in the selection of loads, but No. 6's are a good average choice. Number 5 shot will come in handy at those times when the birds are flushing wild and "far off," and No. 7 is excellent for close-lying coveys. Although not a large bird, the ptarmigan can carry more lead than a quail and shot smaller than No. 7 is likely to produce too many wounded birds.

# BOBWHITE QUAIL

*Colinus virginianus*

COMMON NAMES: Bob-White, Partridge, Quail, Virginia Partridge.

**History.** The large and popular quail family is represented in the United States by five distinct genera; the crested, eastern upland, plumed, spotted, and western upland quail, which in turn are divided into various sub-species. They cover a great part of the country, with an emphasis on the southern regions, and live from the Atlantic coast to the Pacific. Other types are found in Mexico, and south through Central America, but all of the quail varieties of the United States are similar in appearance and habits. A typical member of the group is the bobwhite quail which is perhaps the best known of them all. It has the widest distribution, ranging from southern Manitoba to Texas and Mexico, but its area of abundance is in the southeastern United States. In the rural sections of the South its clear, musical call, *"bob-white,"* is common, and gives the bird its identifying name, although, like the other quails, it is frequently called a "partridge" in the South. The quails and partridges share the same family, *Perdicidae.*

The quail is very secretive in all its ways and is not well known in the true sense. Because of its popular appeal, many legends about the bird have been carried down through the generations. A study of the bobwhite was made in the southeastern United States with the combined efforts of the United States Department of Interior and a group of sportsmen of the Southeast, and, since it was the first such study made in the United States, many facts are now in their rightful place and the quail story is a more complete one. The report on the habits of the bird in the wild and in captivity provided much-needed information on the requirements of the bird, especially in regard to food and coverage—a knowledge which is essential if man wishes to increase the numbers of any species. There is no shortage of bobwhite on its southeastern range, but there has been a steady decrease, and the co-operation of all sportsmen is mandatory if an annual surplus for shooting is desired.

There are several reasons for the cutback in the quail's numbers. In pioneer times the bird multiplied under the most favorable conditions because of the settler's crude type of agriculture. There was an abundant food supply in the weedy fields, and much grain was left after imperfect harvesting. There was a good deal of open cover and many of the bird's natural enemies were destroyed by man. As the cultivation of the land became more intensive, however, precise machines left little grain on the ground, fence rows and other protective coverings were scythed to give the farm a neat look, and cattle and other domesticated animals trampled quail food and nests. Later, with over-working of the land, came soil infertility, which meant that less food was produced for the quail. As the quail status weakened, there was an ever-increasing number of hunters. Since the quail has received its share of gross depredation from the traps, guns, and nets of early market hunters, has been neglected by man in regard to the maintenance of its natural habitat, and has been constantly attacked by numerous natural enemies, in addition to the serious menace of the dog and cat brought by civilization, it is a wonder that this highly vulnerable species still exists.

The quail, however, is very adaptable, with specific reference to its breeding potential. The bird normally has a strong nesting urge and is a fast breeder, averaging 14 offspring each year. Under abnormal conditions, such as when losses to a covey narrow the survivors to a lone pair, nature provides that the maximum potential is reached, and a reasonable number of birds are maintained in that area. However, where the birds are abundant, predators concentrate (often by-passing an area where the birds are few) and whittle down any excess. Because of this natural leveling-off action in either extreme, there is a fairly consistent quail population from one year to the next.

Despite the fact that more quail are hunted and bagged each year than any other game bird in North America, there are as many quail killed today, where ideal conditions exist, as there were during the time of commercialized hunting. Notable examples are in the "red hills" of Tallahassee, Florida, the "blacklands" of Alabama, and in the Piedmont country of North Carolina. Where shooting is properly regulated to insure a sufficient breeding stock, shooting within the annual increase is possible.

Depleted quail areas sometimes are restocked with wild birds transplanted from areas of abundance. As a result of an annual importation of about 100,000 Mexican quail, many of the bobwhites have hybridized. Although most of the imports go to sections other than the Southeast, where quail are few and attempts are made to revive or introduce them, some are kept in that region. Beside this method of restocking, pen-reared birds are released. Artificial propagation of quail on game farms and by private individuals has not been fully developed. It is an expensive and technical process requiring extensive experience, but since one hen in captivity is capable of producing as many as 150 eggs in a season, as contrasted to 12 to 16 in the wild, the method is certainly a most important one. Many birds reared in captivity are not able to survive life in the wild, however, often because of uncontrolled predation. Most replanting and restocking by this means has been done in the East, where the emphasis is on maintaining or establishing a breeding stock. On many southern plantations the owner of the land is both farmer and sportsman who recognizes the bird as an aid in the cultivation of his crops and an unrivaled sporting bird, and is therefore inclined to leave both food and cover for the bird and provide ideal breeding ground.

Of great interest to sportsmen is the propagating experiment on the rare, red bobwhite. This bird is a color phase of the bobwhite, and an average bird in all other ways. The over-all plumage coloring is a bright rusty-red, with the throat marking on the cock being black, and on the hen a deep bronze. They are gradually increasing on the Ames Plantation at Grand Junction, Tennessee.

**Identification.** (See color plate on page 483). Consistent with the quail as a group, the bobwhite is a small bird, built like a chicken, with a plump body, short, curved wings, and a short, dark tail which folds into a rounded point. The loose head feathers form a modified crest, capable of being spread and erected, but which lacks the showy, distinctive plumes of the valley and mountain quails. Differing from those of the grouse and ptarmigans of the same gallinaceous order, the strong legs are without feathering.

The full winter plumage of the adult male and female are very much alike and though the cock normally is distinguished from the hen by his white throat and head marking, his throat is sometimes a buffy yellow and it is easy to confuse him with the buffy-throated hen at such times. The cock has several other color varieties, one of the most frequent of them being a black streak along the middle of the throat. The bobwhite resembles the meadow lark in flight and often only the white tail feathers of the lark identify the two species. The plumage of the bobwhite becomes worn and dulled at the end of the breeding season, but after the fall moult, the brighter, full winter coloring is renewed.

The average bobwhite weighs 5 to 6 ounces, and ranges from 8½ to 10½ inches in length, with a 14- to 16-inch wingspread.

The eastern bobwhite *(C. v. virginianus)* is the typical bobwhite, but the other sub-species are very similar to it. The southern variety *(C. v. floridanus)* is smaller and darker, while the western type *(C. v. texanus)* is paler. The western bobwhite is commonly known as "Texas bobwhite" or "Mexican quail." These birds have been imported from Mexico for restocking since 1910, and shipments have continued to the present date. There has been extensive hybridizing of this western sub-species and the typical eastern bird in the South, as well as in the New England states, Pennsylvania, and Illinois. As with all hybridized birds, the cross produces more males than females, but the ratio balances itself after several generations.

The masked bobwhite *(C. ridgwayi)* is the closest relative of the bobwhite, and is commonly known as Arizona bobwhite, hooded quail, and Ridgeway's quail in various localities. Although the two birds are very similar in habits, they differ in appearance. The masked bobwhite looks reddish in a bright light, and the cock's face and throat are black, while the face and throat markings of the female are a tawny brown.

The bobwhite has a large repertoire of call notes which vary in type, range, and emotion from belligerency to tenderness according to the mood of the bird. The most famous of them is the whistling "bob-white" call which changes in volume from "whispered" to loud. It is primarily a love song; when heard throughout the summer it usually indicates that an unmated cock is still hoping to attract a hen. Though a clear call carries as far as a mile, the modified *"ah-bob-white"* often is softer, audible 100 feet or less. Since the cock often calls before and after rain, farmers interpret the cheery call as sounding like "more wet" and a prognostication of rain. The cocks also use a rasping call which is particularly frequent during the breeding season to indicate their fighting spirit toward each other. The ringing "scatter," or "covey" call is one of the most important calls, and is uttered by both sexes at all seasons to keep the scattered birds of the covey from wandering from the protection of the group, and the musical *"ka-loi-kee"* or *"hurlee-he"* frequently is answered by *"whoil-kee."* The alarm call is a sharp *"toil-ick, ick, ick"* which is repeated until the threat of harm has passed. The calls of the masked bobwhite are similar.

**Characteristics.** The bobwhite is a wary bird, but not a timid one, and it becomes exceedingly suspicious where hunted extensively. Since the small bird is essentially terrestrial in habit, it has numerous enemies besides man. The behavior of the bobwhite when pursued is very much like that of its famous relative, the pheasant, which also is largely a ground bird. The quail normally will run rapidly for cover on its powerful legs, and despite its relatively colorful markings is capable of concealing itself in the scantiest coverage. When caught by surprise in the open, and running or flying to cover is impractical, the bird characteristically freezes in place and by remaining motionless often escapes notice by even its most sharp-eyed and dreaded enemies of the air—the Cooper's and sharp-shinned hawks.

Though escape on foot is preferred, brief flights to safety are sometimes necessary. When a bird is flushed by an enemy, it voluntarily makes a noisy "whirrrr" with its wings, and a covey of birds frequently completes a successful getaway by confusing the enemy with noise and speed. The rise of the feathered bombshells averages about 30 miles an hour, but sometimes is over 40 miles per hour. Once suitable altitude is gained and the terrain is scanned, a landing place is chosen and by intermittent gliding and rapid wing-beating, the bird alights. Usually the spot is on the ground, but occasionally a startled bird flushes to a near-by tree. Although quail can swim, birds which are exhausted by long, hard-pressed flights occasionally drop into the water and drown. To exercise its wings the bird rises on its toes several times a day and rapidly "whirrs" them.

The quail is a gregarious bird and habitually is found with others of its kind in a covey or bevy. The number of birds in a covey varies with the season. In the spring and summer the parents with their offspring form a family group, but the mortality rate is high among quails and the young survivors of one brood often are taken in by another pair. By the end of summer several coveys band together and in late winter the remnants of more broods and parent birds merge into larger numbers. In the spring they pair off for the breeding season. Quail are capable of breeding in their first year.

Quail normally roost on the ground in a characteristic circular formation with heads out, and, in cold weather, bodies pressed close together so that the tails are forced upward. This position is for mutual protection and warmth. The roosting spot varies, but the preferred site is among low ground vegetation which serves as camouflage; the birds are, however, exposed from above. A quick take-off is possible when they are uncovered, and they depend on their motionless position as protection from predatory birds. The number of times the covey uses the same roosting spot depends on the availability of suitable roosting sites and the amount of disturbance in the neighborhood. In some regions, they roost off the ground in bushes, grapevines, etc.

Birds in the wild average a three-year life-cycle, although specimens kept in captivity live about three times as long. Stray dogs and the common house cat rank among the most serious predators. Studies of the bobwhite in the north central states show that the great horned owl takes a high toll in that region. Fatalities are few from parasites (such as tapeworms and roundworms), but infected birds are weakened. Frequent dust baths keep the quails relatively free of external parasites, for the mites, lice, ticks, etc., are choked to death. Where pen-raised birds are in contact with domestic poultry, they are susceptible to their diseases. Phosphorus used for rodent poisoning is highly toxic to quail, but there is little negative effect from strychnine used for the same purpose.

**Breeding.** This begins in the spring, but because of the high nesting loss and a strong nesting urge, many nests often are built before one brood is hatched. The prolonged season extends from April to October, on both the northern and southern ranges, but occasional nests are made before and after that date. The "bobwhite" call culminates the pre-mating signs of the pugnacious cocks. Because of an unbalanced ratio of cocks to hens in the wild, there is spirited rivalry among the handsome males for the demure females. The frequent fighting seldom is fatal, but usually is vigorous the few seconds that it lasts. In captivity, when the vanquished bird cannot run away from the pursuing conqueror, he sometimes is pecked to death.

In a typical courtship display, the puffed-out cock turns his head to show his white markings, and spreads his wings so that the tips drag on the ground. If neither beauty of plumage nor prowess in battle wins a mate for the cock, he will continue his search throughout the summer, his repeated love call becoming even more frequent with sultry, warm spells of weather. There is little evidence, however, that the bachelors regularly lure hens away from their mates, for the paired birds are singularly faithful, and sometimes re-mate the next season. Strangely enough, however, unmated cocks eager to raise a family have been captured and successfully used as "foster-mothers" to raise pen-hatched chicks.

The cock is most attentive to the hen, not only during the two-week "honeymoon" period preceding nesting, but also doing his share, and often more, of nesting and raising the offspring. The cock normally builds the nest, which is made in a variety of places. In all seasons the quail is a lover of open woodlands, fields, and clearings—of areas which provide running space yet offer cover and a near-by food supply. Many nests are built among bushes or weeds on the edge of woods or by a roadway. In the Southeast they are commonly hidden among broom sedge, a tall grass which abounds in much of that section. Since the bird characteristically is adaptable and resourceful, nesting sites vary with availability. If the spot chosen ultimately is found to be unsafe because of predators or other unfavorable circumstances, the nest is made again. The cock first forms a hollow in the ground by scratching with his feet and loosening the earth with his bill. Into the hole goes the material immediately at hand, which consequently varies with, and is dependent on, the nesting site. Leaves, weeds, pine needles, and mosses frequently are used in the construction. The nest often has a roof formed by slanting up the lining or by building under vegetation. Nest building sometimes takes but one day to complete.

The number of pure white eggs dropped ranges from 7 to 28, but the average set is from 12 to 16. Very large sets of eggs usually are the product of several laying hens sharing the same nest, and an excessive, unwieldy number usually is abandoned. The 23-day incubation period regularly is performed by the hen, but under extreme, and often dangerous, conditions the cock will take over and sit close on the nest. Regardless of which bird is sitting, the mate stays about 25 feet away from the nest. The pair contact each other by calling and meet for the resting and feeding period. When flushed from the nest, the bird often skillfully and determinedly uses the broken-wing trick to distract the enemy. The hatching bird uses its horn or "tooth," a temporary hard growth on the soft bill, to cut its way out of the shell. Once the egg is "pipped," about 48 hours before the bird actually emerges, the audible peeping noises of the enclosed chick sometimes draw the attention of animal predators. After the hard shell is cracked, the chick also is vulnerable to "thief ants" which eat through the membrane and destroy the helpless bird. Many chicks are lost during this time. If the eggs survive long droughts (which rot the eggs), floods, fire, forced desertion, predation—by skunks, raccoons, rats, weasels, snakes, crows, house cats, and stray dogs, as well as robbing by man—the delicate chick emerges, weighing less than a quarter of an ounce.

The chicks are brooded for the greatest part of the day during their first two weeks of existence. Though they are able to walk, run, and feed themselves the first day they are hatched, their natal down is scant protection from the elements, and they are particularly susceptible to chilling. The mother hen knows that a wet chick is often a dead chick. The young mature rapidly, however, and in two weeks can make weak flights. In a month they weigh about an ounce, and after four months of intensive, usually all day, feeding on seeds and insects which they pick up and jump for, they are nearly full grown. Although their first true plumage begins to develop when they are about two weeks old, the process is not completed until about the second month, and by that time they are able to roost alongside of the adults.

Either cock or hen will raise the brood alone if the mate is killed, but in spite of the solicitude and alertness of both loving parents for their young (and usually strict adherence of the offspring in turn to the "scatter call" and alarm note), the mortality rate among the young birds is very high. Among their worst enemies are snakes and hawks.

The plumage coloring and markings of the young birds begin to segregate the sexes when they are about eight weeks old, and when 15 weeks of age their plumage resembles that of the adults. They are nearly mature in appearance after their first fall moult, but are not fully adult until the completion of the second fall moult after the breeding season, and the full winter plumage of each sex is assumed.

**Feeding.** The bobwhite has a widely variable diet, but since most of its time is spent on the ground, the food eaten usually is that which is found on or near to the ground. Because they prefer to live near a food supply, especially by agricultural areas, they do not have to roam any distance during an average day in order to search for food. If a supply is abundant, they wander about 300 yards or less, and a half mile is far, under ordinary circumstances. During the fall season when seeds, their highest percentage of food, are plentiful, they are virtually stationary, given to spending most of the day resting and taking baths in the dust. Under any conditions they normally feed near to cover and are very alert. The covey habitually leaves the roost in early morning, but since they are loath, at all ages, to get wet, they usually drink of the dew and sometimes eat a little food before returning to the roost to wait until the sun dries and warms the ground and plants. The full meal is taken in the late afternoon, about three hours before dusk or up until roosting time.

The diet is about 86 per cent of vegetable matter, and the bulk of this is seeds, one of the main items being the pod-bearing legumes. The quail aids the farmer by eating a great quantity of harmful weed and grass seeds, such as ragweed, beggarweed, pigweed, and watergrass. The grain (corn, wheat, and rye) consumed is largely waste, and the birds do little damage to other cultivated crops, such as cow beans and soy beans, since they are not given to gathering in large flocks to feed. Some cherries and strawberries are eaten, but most of the fruit consumed grows wild, being mulberries, blackberries, dewberries, persimmons, sassafras, and sumac. They are fond of mast, especially acorns which they can crack with their heavy bills. They eat the tender leaves of plants (sorrels, clover, etc.), and there is some intake of bulbs and tubers. Seeds and other ground food are scratched up in the manner of the domestic chicken, but those fruits which are elevated are reached by jumping or in some instances by flying into the bush or tree and eating from the branch.

The 14 per cent animal matter is composed primarily of insects. As an active feeder on grasshoppers, locusts, beetles, bugs, snails, ants, caterpillars, and slugs, which are serious pests to the farmer where they occur in numbers, the quail does a great deal of good. To a lesser extent they take bees, mollusks, earthworms, rodents, and reptiles.

Dew and succulence are sufficient liquid to sustain the quail, and drinking water is unnecessary. Grit is taken daily into the gizzard.

**Range and Distribution.** The eastern bobwhite is found over an extensive range which includes most of eastern North America from southern Ontario south through the New England states to northern Florida and the Gulf coast, then west to Texas, Colorado, and Wyoming. The southern bobwhite is confined to Florida and the Keys, while the western bobwhite is native to southeastern New Mexico and distributed south through Texas to Mexico, as well as having been introduced to the South and several eastern states where it has hybridized with the eastern variety.

The masked bobwhite formerly resided in Arizona and New Mexico in fair numbers, but now is found in only the northwestern section of Mexico. Attempts have been made to re-establish the bird upon its previous range.

The bobwhite is not a true migratory bird, but some will leave an unfavorable area to settle in a more suitable place. Winter weather and snow force some to move, since even a fat quail is unable to exist longer than four to six days without food if it is in a cold climate.

# DESERT QUAIL

*Lophortyx gambeli*

**History.** The desert quail is one of several species of western upland quail. Though this bird is not as famous as its close relative, the valley quail, it is equally handsome, good eating, and has its own sizable following of sportsmen.

**Identification.** (See color plate on page 483.) The two sub-species are similar in habits, but distinguishable by variations in color and a slight difference in size. The better-known Gambel quail *(Lophortyx gambeli gambeli)* is the typical variety. It is about 9 inches long and appears chestnut and blue in plumage coloring. The adult male is bluish-gray above and gray on his breast, but the belly is marked with patches of buff and black. The chestnut-brown sides have white streaks along them, and the head and throat are strikingly marked with an encircling white stripe. Above the rusty-brown crown curves a handsome, black crest. The mature female looks very much like the male but lacks the markings on the head and abdomen.

The larger Olathe variety *(L. g. sanus)* measures about 10 inches long. The upper parts of the male are gray, and the under parts are buffy in coloration. The female closely resembles the male but has a crown of darker brown. Both sexes have the black crest.

These birds of the desert are very talkative, especially while feeding. Their most common call, a shrill *"chu-chaaa, chu-chaaa"* is uttered by the cock and audible at a considerable distance. Both sexes use the scatter call, *"quirrt, quirrt."*

**Characteristics.** When startled, these ground birds usually take off at a rapid run to hide among the mesquites, creosotes, and cactus, although they sometimes make a short, fast flight to escape to another place of concealment.

Typical of the quails, this bird lives with others of its kind in a covey. In the fall the family groups merge into flocks, ranging in number from 40 to 100 birds. Although these large flocks are inclined to disperse while feeding, they roost together at night in clumps of mesquite or among thick growths of ironwoods and greasewoods. In the last part of the winter, one flock joins another until "packs" as large as 300 are formed. These larger flocks, or packs, are temporary, however, and break up within two weeks or a month, for during that time of intermingling the birds court and mate. The pair goes to the covey-range of either bird, or in some cases starts a new range.

**Breeding.** In a long breeding period the birds raise one and sometimes two broods. The initial laying period is in early spring, while the second nesting comes after the summer rains, about July, when the vegetation is abundant again. The very high mortality rate from shooting, nesting, and predator loss, as well as unexplained, periodic rises and falls in the population, is offset by a fast breeding rate. The birds have a strong nesting urge and are careful guardians of the 10 to 12 white eggs which are incubated in 21 to 24 days. The young chicks need protection by the parents for the first couple of weeks, but grow rapidly.

**Feeding.** The desert quail eats a wide variety of food, the greatest part of it being vegetable—about 91 per cent including mesquite beans, several types of berries, and the grain from barley, corn, wheat, and rye fields. Of the large quantity of insects, beetles and grasshoppers are probably taken in the greatest bulk. The staff of life for many of these quail is the evergreen hackberry bush which not only supplies food, but the other necessities of cover and a roosting spot. Although this desert bird is capable of existing on the moisture contained in its food alone, it normally makes a daily flight to a watering place in most localities.

**Range and Distribution.** The desert quail is distributed in the western United States, from Utah and California south to Mexico. The range of the Gambel quail extends from the southeastern part of California and southern Utah through New Mexico to Mexico. They are numerous in the valleys of the lower Colorado River and Gila River. Some birds have been transplanted to Washington and Idaho. The Olathe desert quail inhabits southwestern Colorado.

## MASSENA QUAIL (Mearns' Quail) *Cyrtonyx montezuma*

Common Names: Black Quail, Fool Hen, Fool Quail, Mearns' Quail, Messena Partridge, Montezuma Quail.

**History.** The Massena quail, named in honor of the French marshal, André Masséna, is found from southern Arizona to Central America. Perhaps the species is best known by a pale variety, Mearns' quail *(Cyrtonyx montezuma mearnsi)*, though the bird is far from familiar to the average North American sportsman and is least hunted of all the quails. Though it is probably more numerous in the mountains of western Texas than in other parts of its American range, it is not abundant anywhere. Six birds form an average covey, while 12 birds in a bunch would be a fairly large number; their flocks are the smallest of all the quail group. It is called "fool quail" because of the ease with which it is killed in some localities.

**Identification.** (See color plate on page 483.) The Mearns' quail is classed with the spotted quails of genus *Cyrtonyx* and the adult male is readily identified by distinctive plumage markings, especially on the side where the white spots show clearly against a slaty-gray or near-black background. The upper parts are pale brown with streaks of black, reddish, and cinnamon along the back, while the under parts are dark brown. The squared-off tail folds well below the short wings which are about half the bird's length. The head is black and brown with white stripes and the depressed crown feathers form an elongated brown crest.

The mature female has mottled brown plumage on the back, barred with black and lavender, and the under parts are a pale lavender-brown or yellowish-brown. The female differs from the male by lacking the white head markings. The average length for both sexes is about 9 inches.

The most common call-note is a soft, but rapid *"cherr-r-r."*

**Characteristics.** The nature and habits of this quail are dependent on the particular locality which the bird inhabits. In a section that is comparatively remote, the birds are very unsuspicious. When living near cultivated land they are more alert, but, if unmolested, are still far from wary. Their habits are much like those of other quail, such as the Gambel's and scaled quail, which live in the arid and semi-arid regions of the Southwest. Adequate coverage is needed from the sun, for they are unable to endure its constant heat any more than is the bobwhite chick which must be brooded until its protective juvenile plumage begins to replace the sparse natal down. In the desert, they require water during the hottest and driest spells when succulence from fruits and insects is insufficient. Like all quail, they habitually remain in a confined range throughout the year, and a proper balance between concealing cover and open spaces is necessary, with nearness to an adequate food supply.

From 8 to 12 eggs are laid on the ground in a comparatively well-built nest, and one set is hatched in the breeding season.

**Feeding.** The food varies according to the range, specifically, according to the nearness of the bird to cultivated lands. The greatest percentage of food is seeds of weeds and grasses and some wild berries. They also feed on a wide variety of insects.

**Range and Distribution.** The Mearns' quail is found from western Texas, southern New Mexico, and southern Arizona south to the mountains of northern Coahuila and Chihuahua, and eastern Sonora. They frequently live among mountainous areas where there are tall grasses and low-growing bushes, and also in rocky ravines.

# MOUNTAIN QUAIL

*Oreortyx picta*

**History.** The handsome plumed quails, also known as mountain partridges, are the largest of the quail group, weighing from one-half to three-quarters of a pound, and measuring 12 inches in length in comparison to the average 9 inches of a bobwhite. They inhabit the mountains of the Pacific coast, from Washington to Lower California, and the names of the sub-species—northern, central, and southern mountain quail—identify the section of the range inhabited by each type. Attempts to transplant this species have been unsuccessful on the whole. Those imported to Massachusetts, Alabama, Nebraska, and Montana left the area without reproducing themselves. They are most numerous in California where they live in either humid or semi-arid regions, and are hunted with dogs at altitudes between 5000 and 10,000 feet.

**Identification.** (See color plate on page 483.) The primary difference among the three types of mountain quail is in minor variation of coloration, for they all range between 11 and 12 inches in length, and are very similar in habits. The central mountain quail, popularly known as "mountain quail" *(Oreortyx picta plumifera)*, is colored an olive-brown on its upper parts, and slatish-gray on the lower parts. The sides are distinctively marked with wide bands of black and white. The 2-inch plume normally is composed of two black feathers which stand erect, in contrast to the curved topknot of the valley quail. quail.

The northern or plumed race *(O.p. picta)* has more olive on its back and is somewhat paler than the bird of the central regions.

The southern or San Pedro mountain quail *(O.p. confinis)* resembles the northern bird more closely than the central one, but its upper parts are grayer.

One of the call notes of the male resembles the common call of the bobwhite, and its clear *"quit, quit, quit, queah"* is familiar. Aside from these, the cock utters a crowlike sound which resembles that of a young bantam rooster.

**Characteristics.** This quail has not proved itself as adaptable as the bobwhite in some respects, for where civilization has advanced the mountain quail usually has retreated or been exterminated. Like the bobwhite, it is a sturdy ground bird, but it is probably fastest on the wing of all the quails, though it flies the shortest distances. The average flock includes up to 25 birds under favorable conditions, and a larger number is unusual.

**Breeding.** The typical mountain quail nest is built in the midst of ground vegetation, in this case low bushes or tufts of grass. Between 6 and 12 creamy-white eggs are dropped each season on the soft nest lining of leaves or grasses. The young birds are alert and shy, and exceptionally quick at dispersing and hiding when warned of danger.

**Feeding.** Where the birds live near agricultural lands, they feed on grain, especially wheat, corn and barley, but the major part of the 97% vegetable food is weed seeds. Some fruit is taken. The 3% animal food is composed primarily of insects.

Unlike the other birds of this group (with the exception of the California quail), the mountain quail is unable to live on succulence alone, and requires drinking water, a fact which automatically limits the habitable sections of the range as a whole.

**Range and Distribution.** Though this quail is mostly a bird of the mountain slopes, it is found in a widely diversified range along the Pacific Coast, and lives from the humid valleys of the California coast to the plains of Oregon, from chaparral thickets to the banks of rushing, mountain streams.

The northern bird is found on the Cascade and Sierra Nevada Mountains from Oregon south to Nevada and west to California. The central race inhabits the high coastal mountains as well as the semi-arid sections of Oregon south to California, including bushy hillsides near small streams. The southern quail is distributed along the San Pedro Martir Mountains of Lower California.

The ways of the northern and central races are very nearly alike because of the similarity of habitat. In the colder parts of their range, both birds leave the snow-covered mountains for the more sheltered valleys during the winter season. If the winter is mild, there is little or no movement, and the bird is not a true migrator. When journeying down the mountain on foot, there is some intermingling among the flocks.

# SCALED QUAIL

*Callipepla squamata*

**History.** The scaled quail or partridge is a bird of the arid southwestern regions of the United States and Mexico. Its two sub-species in the United States are indistinguishable in habits, but readily identified by appearance. As the name indicates, the chestnut-bellied scaled quail *(Callipepla squamata castonagastris)* has a chestnut patch on its belly which is lacking on the more somber blue scaled quail *(C. s. pallida)*. The blue variety is commonly known as Arizona scaled quail, cottontop, blue quail, and white topknot.

The population of this game bird fluctuates violently from abundance to scarcity, but ornithologists do not so far know the reason for the rise and fall or whether it is a cycle. Since the greatest portion of this quail's range is filled with thorns, dogs are not used in hunting it, and most sportsmen consider the hunting of bobwhite quail more enjoyable.

**Identification.** The blue scaled quail, *Callipepla squamata pallida*, has pale-slate and drab-brownish body coloring. The feathers of the pale brown to buff under parts are edged with black, giving a "scaled" effect. The short, brown crest is erect and tipped with pure white, and marks them as belonging to the crested genus.

The chestnut-bellied variety has a chestnut-colored lower abdomen whereas that of the blue is buff. The duller-colored females of the two specimens look more alike than the males. Both birds average about 10 inches in length.

**Characteristics.** The behavior pattern of the scaled quail and bobwhite is similar, since the quail is characteristically a bird of habit. When undisturbed, it is given to repeating its feeding time and place, roosting hours, etc., in the same routine manner each day. It does not lie well to dogs and escapes the enemy by running rather than by flying. When living near pastures and cultivated fields, it sometimes becomes tame around adjoining farm and ranch houses.

**Breeding.** The season is long, but only one brood is raised. The nest usually is a shallow depression or hollow dug out of the sand, and carefully concealed by low-growing vegetation. It is lined with leaves, grasses, or other soft material in the immediate vicinity of the nest. The 8 to 16 cream-colored eggs are marked with buff or brown specks, regularly distributed over the surface. The incubation period lasts 21 days. The percentage of nesting losses is high among this desert variety, as it is among all quail. Of 68 bobwhite nests examined in Wisconsin, one-half survived, but of 10 scaled quail nests studied in Arizona, only one-fifth were hatched successfully.

**Feeding.** The types of food taken by these quails are highly diversified, with little accent on any particular variety. About 50% of the 75% vegetable diet is seeds—weed seeds (such as amaranth, alfilaria, croton, and buffalo burr) and, in agricultural areas, grain (e.g., oats, kafir corn, wheat). They feed on the seeds of mesquite, cactus, sage, etc., and eat miscellaneous green leaves, sprouts, and other herbage. The most important fruits consumed (totaling about 4%) are from the juniper, desert hackberry, mistletoe, barrel cactus, and tomatilla.

The animal food (around 25%) is mostly insects, primarily grasshoppers, beetles, weevils, sawfly larvae, scale insects, and ants. The scaled quail normally consumes a higher percentage of animal food than the bobwhite. The young birds of this species eat an even larger quantity of insects than the adults (about 71%), chiefly grasshoppers, locusts, beetles, and plant bugs. The bulk of the vegetable food of the young, as of the adults, is seeds.

These birds are capable of living on the succulence of their food alone, but dew is desirable, and, where the land is especially hot and dry, they need drinking water.

**Range and Distribution.** The blue scaled quail is found from central Arizona, north to southern Colorado, south through New Mexico to western Texas to the Valley of Mexico. They prefer to live near water, and are found among chaparral and mesquite and in dry gulches. Coverage can be neither too scant nor too dense for its survival, and vegetation growing close to the ground with many open spaces is ideal.

The chestnut-bellied quail is distributed from the northwest section of Texas to the lower Rio Grande Valley, south to Mexico.

The scaled quail *(C. s. squamata)* is the typical sub-species form and is confined to central and southern Mexico.

The preferred habitat for all varieties is dry, open country in valleys, plains, or foothills that have a mixture of bare ground, low herbaceous growth, and such brush cover as mesquite, acacias, mimosas, scrub oak, cacti, greasewood, broomweed, chamisa, and desert hackberry. In the foothills they are lovers of juniper and piñon pine.

# VALLEY QUAIL

*Lophortyx californica*

COMMON NAMES: California Partridge, Helmet Quail, Top-Knot Quail.

**History.** The valley quail is not only the most popular game bird of its genus, but a worthy competitor against the celebrated bobwhite in regard to sport appeal. Contrary to rumor, this quail will lie well to a dog, and some experts say the bird of the valley is more alert and better shooting.

Although the flocks are larger than those formed by any other quail, they are far smaller today than they were at one time. As many as several thousand birds would gather together, but the population decrease was rapid about the 1860's, and a good-sized flock today is 100. The decline was attributed in part to the extensive gunning by market hunters as well as grape growers. An average seasonal shipment by an individual market hunter was 10,000 quail. The birds did serious damage to the vineyards when they pecked at the fruit for its juice. Besides these attacks, extensive cultivation of valley land took place in California, where the birds were most abundant. Much of the bird's natural habitat was destroyed when taken over to raise grain. A decided increase occurred, however, where irrigation activities extended over the land, such as in the Sacramento and San Joaquin Valley areas. Necessary drinking water was provided and different kinds of crops were raised which provided an extensive food supply of not only grass and weed seeds, but other types of food for which the birds acquired a taste. Like most of the quails, its adaptable, resourceful nature has made it at home among lands and ways formerly unknown. It is seen in good-sized numbers among cotton, potato, and asparagus fields. It is not strictly a bird of the valley, however, and its common name does not tell the whole story, for some of its range extends up foothills and mountain slopes to an altitude of 4000 feet. However, it is best known as a lover of the lower foothills and valleys, and is more of a "cousin" than a "brother" of the mountain quail.

Some experiments with artificial propagation have shown the advantages of raising the birds in captivity. One hen can produce as many as 70 eggs during the breeding season.

**Identification.** (See color plate on page 483.) The sub-species of the north *(Lophortyx californica californica)* is popularly known as California quail. The upper parts of the mature male are a deep ashy-brown, and the sides of the back are marked with rusty-brown stripes. The olive-brown sides are streaked with white, and the bird is slate-gray below while the middle of the scaled belly has a distinct chestnut-colored patch. The black crest is curved and rises from a head strikingly marked with black and white lines.

The grayish-brown female is similar to the male but lacks the head and body markings, although she has the white streaks on the side of the body. Her plume usually is shorter than that of the male. Both sexes average about 9 inches in length.

The southern valley quail *(L.c. vallicola)* is commonly called "valley quail." It closely resembles the sub-species of the north, but has lighter plumage coloring.

The Catalina valley quail *(L.c. catalina)* is the largest of the three types, but differs slightly in plumage coloring, though it is just as handsome. It is darker than the southern valley quail but lighter than the bird of the north.

Next to the common call of the bobwhite, the familiar *"cha-qua-qua"* of these quails is perhaps best known. They have a wide range of calls and use them often.

**Characteristics.** Where these birds are intensively hunted, they have been forced to change some of their ways to survive. The preferred method for a wary covey to seek escape cover is to run fast if there is sufficient ground cover to conceal it. If the cover is too sparse, scattered birds often lie close, but a covey usually will rise into fast flight. Although many flights end on near-by low bushes, these birds are inclined to fly farther than any of the other quails, and will head for a fairly distant refuge if necessary. They often disappear into wooded areas of oaks and willows and sometimes fly to the top of the tree. Since the feet of these birds are so constructed that they are unable to encircle an object with the hind toe, they cannot maintain their balance on a perch, so they run along the large branches of a tree.

It is not unusual for a flock of birds to live and die in a very confined area if the food and cover are favorable. The radius for a day or a year usually is the same for these sedentary birds, and averages about one-quarter of a mile. A study in San Mateo showed that 75 coveys, or some 2000 birds, inhabited one 22,000-acre tract.

**Breeding.** Sometimes two broods are raised during one season. Many nests are built in shallow holes dug under low-growing vegetation or alongside of shrubs, a rock, or some like protection. The 13 to 17 creamy-white eggs, covered with brown specks, are dropped into the nest lined with grass and leaves. The incubation period lasts from 21 to 23 days.

A study of the high nesting losses found that ground squirrels were the most serious predators, destroying as many eggs as all other native predators combined. Other predators are the house cat, jay, spotted skunk, bobcat, and gray fox. Apparently squirrel predation is a more important factor in nesting losses than drought.

**Feeding.** This quail feeds on insects and weed plants as well as waste grain, grape juice, and many different kinds of berries, fruits, and seeds provided by the nearness of its habitat to agriculture. The California quail eats more vegetable matter (98 per cent) than the scaled quail, bobwhite, or Gambel's quail, and is a more pronounced fruit eater. Important valley quail food is bur-clover and alfilaria. Though it can live on dew, most parts of the range necessitate daily flights to a drinking place.

**Range and Distribution.** The hereditary range of the northern valley quail is along the narrow, humid coast belt of the Pacific coast, from southern Oregon to central California. Transplantations of this bird have been successful in British Columbia, Washington, and sections of Nevada, Idaho, Oregon, and Utah.

The southern valley quail is found in drier country than that inhabited by the northern variety, and it ranges from Oregon through California, east to western Nevada and down to Lower California. Its population varies from abundance to scarcity.

The Catalina valley quail lives on Catalina Island, off the California coast.

## HUNTING METHODS

**Bobwhite.** Call him "quail," "partridge," or just plain "bird" (his most common colloquial name throughout much of his natural range), bobwhite has two characteristics which account for his high rating on the list of American game birds: He lies well to a pointing dog, and he is an exceedingly sporty target for the shotgun.

Approximately 22,000,000 quail annually grace the game pockets of upland hunters, and this figure is indicative not only of the bird's relative plenty, but of the number of sportsmen whose favorite quarry he is.

"Clean" farming methods of today are possibly more responsible than any other single factor for a dearth of birds in formerly productive cover. In those days when the rail fence was an integral part of every southern farm, bobwhite found ready sanctuary in the tangled vegetation which always bordered it. He must have available sufficient cover not only to escape his natural enemies—cotton rats, coyotes, foxes, hawks, and house cats—but to afford protected nesting sites, and he will abandon land which does not provide either sufficient cover or food.

In far too many localities today, such cover is to be found only along the banks of ditches and irrigation canals, and heavy rains, with resultant high waters, mean that the current quail crop is drowned out before hatching is completed. Quail are in no sense creatures of the wilderness. They prefer settled country, provided their habitat is not totally denuded in the settling; and if food is available in reasonably protected spots, bobwhite proves himself fully capable of holding his own in the face of encroaching agriculture.

It has long been a moot question with conservationists as to whether or not hunting is essential for the good of the quail population. The "ayes" hold that unless the birds are thinned down periodically, inter-breeding, predators, and disease will take a heavy toll. In support of this contention, Ohio's move in naming the quail a songbird and placing him on the protected list seems to have resulted in no marked increase in that state's game birds.

Most conservationists will admit that when the total number of birds which can be supported on the food and cover available on their somewhat restricted range has reached the saturation point, nature will maintain the balance. Whether the excess is disposed of through disease, migration, predation, or the hunter's gun matters little in the general scheme of things. The preponderance of evidence would tend to prove that controlled shooting in territory which supports normal numbers of birds definitely means sturdier and stronger birds, more immune to disease, with no diminishment in the total population.

Next to the young prairie chickens of the Canadian provinces, bobwhite lies more readily to a pointing dog than any other game bird, and is the finest bird on which to train pointing dogs, The reasons for any bird's failure to flush when located by a dog must, necessarily, always remain a subject for conjecture, but it is in all probability an atavistic urge to rely on nature's camouflage, and to escape notice through the bird's inherent understanding of his ability to blend with his wild background when there is no movement to betray him.

Be that as it may, bobwhite lies well to a point, and is much less inclined to flush wild than the ruffed grouse. And it is surprising how invisible a covey of quail can remain to the gunner, even when found in the more open cover they habitually frequent, so different from the hardwood ranges the grouse calls home.

A tremendous part of the appeal of quail hunting comes from the dog work involved, and no pointing dog can reach those heights of performance he is capable of attaining on any bird too wary or nervous to permit his approach, or any bird, like the ring-necked pheasant, for instance, inclined to trust to his legs rather than his wings to escape pursuit.

In any discussion of bobwhite's readiness to lie to a point, however, cognizance must be taken of the fact that in many parts of his home ranges the quail has begun to show an increasing tendency to flush well ahead of dogs. The most plausible theory to account for this change in habit lays the blame squarely on the increasing number of predators, especially coyotes and foxes, in much of our quail cover.

In the West, Southwest, and Midwest, coyotes are almost as numerous as in those days when civilization first pushed westward beyond the Ohio, and foxes have multiplied to an alarming extent in the South and East. It could easily be that bobwhite has come to fear the ever-present threat of four-footed predators, and a fox, coyote, or dog could look the same to him. He is no fool, and cannot be blamed for seeking immediate safety in flight when any canine looms on his horizon.

Since early in the nineteenth century when the first importations of the fine smooth-bored art of British gunsmiths first made wing-shooting practical, bobwhite has been, in point of numbers, the favorite target of the scattergun man. He is by no means the easy target he may sometimes appear. He can be as quick to take advantage of what cover offers, and to put obstacles between himself and the gun, as any grouse, and he possesses an instinct for tricky twistings and changes of plane in flight that can baffle the most accomplished wing shot. Many a hunter will confidently level down on what looks like an easy straightaway shot at a quail in open country, only to have his shot-patterns pass harmlessly under the target because he had failed to consider that the bird was steadily, though imperceptibly, rising in flight.

Too, the nerve-shattering roar with which quail take to the air can add materially to the difficulty of the shot. "Bird fever" can be as disconcerting as buck fever, that result of the hypertension of over-eagerness which takes such strange forms with the hunters of deer. More than one tyro at the game has been known to stand in open-mouthed surprise, completely forgetting that he held a loaded gun, when a covey of birds burst almost from underfoot, even though he was aware that they were directly ahead of the pointing dogs.

A cool head, combined with smooth gun handling, is required to select an individual target from the mass on a covey rise, and most misses on quail come from a tendency to shoot too quickly, and at the covey rather than an individual. Quail attain a top flight speed of possibly 50 miles per hour, but go at a considerably slower pace when they first get under way. Yet the noise of their flight can make their speed seem much greater, and gunners can easily lead the birds by too wide a margin.

It frequently happens that the dogs will point a covey of birds when they are in a more or less scattered formation, and the intervals at which such loosely grouped birds will flush presents another problem to the shooter. Nothing is more disconcerting than to advance ahead of the pointing dogs, only to have birds get up by ones, twos, and half-dozens, some of them close in, some at acute angles, and some even behind the gun. The natural inclination is to change targets, switching from the first bird selected to another offering a closer shot. This generally means that most of the birds will be well beyond effective shotgun range before any shots are fired. This is another of bobwhite's favorite tricks to befuddle the marksman.

Still another common reason for misses lies in bobwhite's predilection for choosing a certain line of flight when flushed, and in sticking to that line in spite of all efforts to deflect him. Hunters, on coming up to pointing dogs, may attempt to place themselves between the birds and the nearest protective cover. Bobwhite, however, will take the shortest route to that cover, no matter how many men stand in his way. This, of course, presents the gunner with the most difficult of all shots; the birds are coming directly head-on, and passing overhead. Experience will show that a going-away or even a quartering shot is a much easier target, and attempts to prevent the birds from flying their chosen line will result only in an added handicap when it comes to hitting them.

Shooting on single birds, after the covey has been flushed and dispersed, is the favorite part of bird hunting to many; and locating singles can be greatly simplified if they are marked down with a fair amount of accuracy. This marking down, however, is an aptitude that can be developed only through experience. It is surprising how far a bird may be from the spot where it apparently pitched to earth. Quail usually cover most of their line of flight in extended glides, once inertia has been overcome and sufficient velocity attained. At the end of the glide, when close to the ground, the bird will frequently turn at a sharp angle before actually alighting, and this switch in direction can easily be missed by the watcher. And a bird can cover relatively long distances at the end of its glide, even when apparently already skimming the grass tops.

Although stories of kills at 40, 45, and 50 yards are numerous among bird hunters, it is amazing how those distances shrink under measurement. Most quail are killed at around that many feet.

But no matter where you find him—on the open plains of the Texas Panhandle, the blackjack growth of Arkansas' Ozarks, the palmetto scrub of Florida, or the tawny broom-sedge fields of Georgia and the Carolinas—bobwhite can be a challenging test of shotgun skill.

Normally, quail are on the move, feeding, during the hours from dawn until almost midday, and from 3 or 4 o'clock in the afternoon until dusk, when they seek a roosting site. During the midday hours the birds find heavy cover in which to rest and digest the crops full of seeds taken during the hours of morning feeding. A dog's chances of finding such sequestered coveys are slim, for the birds must be on the move to spread sufficient scent.

The quail's feeding habits, however, are also subject to change under changing conditions on his range; and the increasing popularity of a new crop has definitely changed those habits in some sectors. This crop is the soybean, the cultivation of which has become popular throughout much of the South. Bobwhite has found the Chinese importation a welcome addition to his customary diet of grain, weed seeds, lespedeza (Japanese clover), occasional acorns, and insects, for the soybean gives him his quota of nourishment in bulk form, and simplifies the feeding problem. The birds can satisfy their appetites in much less time, and seek cover affording more protection than the open fields for their dust baths and rest. They are, therefore, likely to be found away from the feeding ground at a much earlier hour in the forenoon and afternoon than was formerly the case, even where they are plentiful.

The old saying holds that pheasants are, like gold, where you find them, but quail are inclined to range within well-defined and restricted areas, and a knowledge of the habitat of local coveys is of great advantage when hunting any particular district. The characteristic of sticking closely to the home range is so universal with them that it is common to give coveys names descriptive of their own particular range. Throughout bird territory one hears of the "pea-patch covey," the "cotton-patch covey," the "cornfield covey," the "graveyard covey," etc. When the range of a specific covey is more or less definitely known, the problem of locating those birds is, naturally, greatly simplified for both dogs and men, and the hunt is bound to be much more successful than when conducted with any hit-or-miss selection of cover that looks promising from the food and protection viewpoint.

Bird hunters, fortunately, are inclined to regard themselves as a sort of closely knit fraternity, and the stranger in bird country, lacking the services of a native guide, will do well to visit the gathering points of local sportsmen and ask for information on productive cover. Local men are usually generous with information of this kind.

Especially in the Deep South, where climate and scarcity of water must be considered as strongly affecting the stamina of the dogs and the time they can be expected to hunt, a method of locating coveys in unfamiliar territory is coming into more and more widespread usage. The hunter "prospects" the country before ever putting his dogs down, stopping at frequent intervals to give the two-toned "lost whistle" of the quail.

Several birds in the covey will almost invariably respond to the call of the apparently strayed bird, and when he receives an answer, the hunter marks the spot and goes on to look for other coveys. He can then bring his dogs to those marked spots, assured that the coveys located will be found not too far from their answering points, with a resultant saving in the ground the dogs are forced to hunt to find them. The relocating must of course be done while the birds are still feeding, and before they have left the feeding grounds either for their midday rest or to go to roost.

The veteran bird hunter insists on his dogs' hunting for him, rather than hunting for his dogs, and a knowledge of the range of the different coveys, together with the ability accurately to mark down the single birds after the flush, will permit him to direct his dogs to hunt where the birds might logically be expected to be found, rather than calling on them to expend time and energy on barren cover.

**Dogs.** The choice of a quail dog should by all means be limited to one of the pointing varieties. Although both spaniels and retrievers have been used to hunt quail, pointing dogs and the chunky little gentlemen in the barred waistcoats are as concomitant in the minds of bird hunters as are retrievers and ducks to the man who hunts waterfowl.

English pointers and English setters lead in popularity, though the Irish setter, the Gordon setter, and the German short-haired pointer all have their fanciers.

The Gordon setter has two chief drawbacks when bobwhite is the game. He is a rather slow hunter, which is a decided handicap when hunting on horseback, and his mahogany-trimmed black coat makes him difficult to find on point in much of the cover quail prefer.

The Irish setter, rightly or wrongly, has in recent years earned a reputation for wildness and lack of obedience in the field. His good looks have been against him as a gun dog, for he has been taken up to such a great extent by the bench-show enthusiasts that specimens of the breed having an ancestry of hunting dogs are rather rare. Too, like the Gordon setter, his coat does not stand out against neutral-colored backgrounds, and he is easily lost on point.

The German short-haired pointer has attained his popularity in the field mainly through his reputation as an all-purpose dog, suitable for hunting both feather and fur. Grant him all his fanciers claim for him, and he would still be inferior as a quail dog to those breeds which have for many generations been specialists at the game. And the German shorthair can by no means match the speed of the English pointers and setters.

In choosing the most promising prospects in quail dogs, two questions will always remain controversial: Pointer versus setter, and the relative merits of dog versus bitch in the field. But most dog men will acknowledge that neither breed nor sex is of paramount importance in the final analysis. Dogs are as individualistic as people, and ability depends altogether on the individual.

It does hold true, of course, that the pointer will possibly be more satisfactory in open country and in milder climates, simply because his short-haired coat is less heating and tiring for the wide going and warmer weather involved. On the other hand, the long coat of the setter affords more protection in briars and similar punishing cover.

Any pointing dog worth his salt will learn to handle all varieties of game birds, given ample experience on each of them. But there is no gainsaying the fact that any dog used as a specialist on any one particular kind of game can be expected to show more ability and bird sense than the jack-of-all-trades.

This, added to the quail's outstanding excellence as a game for dog training, would certainly seem to indicate the advisability of training quail dogs in quail country. A dog owner living outside the quail's range would do well to send his dogs south for training, rather than to rely on some local professional trainer who trains on pen-raised pheasants. Moreover, any dog hunts better in familiar territory, and will develop his natural bird sense to a greater extent if trained in country at least similar to that which he is called on to hunt.

Some dogs show the pointing instinct at an early age, and some show no indication of it until well along in life. Many of them will point grasshoppers, sparrows, and chickens while still in puppyhood; and you will, sensibly, be avoiding a risk if you pick a candidate that seems to have the pointing instinct firmly ingrained in his make-up. Many a real "meat-dog" has practically trained himself, needing little guidance to direct the choke-bored nose and bird sense he has inherited from his forbears.

Both pointers and setters can show a decided difference in ability to handle coveys and single birds. One dog may find two coveys to one located by his brace-mate, point and hold them perfectly, and then be completely baffled by the singles, which his brace-mate will unerringly pin.

This is another mystery of dog psychology which mere man will never solve. In quail dogs, as in all the other gun-dog breeds, it is impossible to fit square pegs in round holes, and all that can be done is to make the best of it. The man who owns a brace of pointing dogs, one a specialist on coveys and the other a singles-dog supreme, should accept his blessings as they come without inquiring too closely into the reasons for the difference.

A great many of our best quail dogs show little or no natural retrieving instinct, although most of them, with added experience, will at least locate downed birds, even though they make no attempt to bring them in. There is no reason why pointing dogs should not be forced-trained to retrieve, using exactly the same methods as are employed with spaniels and the retrieving breeds.

Some trainers go a step farther than this, and teach their dogs to retrieve birds by the head. With game the size of quail, practically the entire bird may be inside the dog's mouth on the retrieve; so if the added nicety of head-retrieving is desired, it is easily accomplished. It is simply a question of using a special "dummy" in the retrieving lessons, one made by connecting a small bundle of rags by means of a short length of cord to a stoppered 8-ounce bottle. The dog does not like to take the bottle in his mouth, for the hard glass is painful to his teeth, and he will form the habit of picking up the dummy by the rag bundle. The habit will carry over when he is used on real birds, and he will retrieve by the head alone.

Because of the mediocrity of some pointing dogs as retrievers, bird hunters may use a cocker spaniel to supplement their pointers or setters in the field. The spaniel is kept at heel throughout the hunt, being sent out to retrieve only after the birds are downed.

Steadiness to wing and shot is of not too much importance in the pointing dogs used on quail. As a matter of fact, some hunters look on such steadiness as a refinement to be desired only in field-trial contenders, and even consider it undesirable in their bird dogs. Their contention is that a dog who breaks point and goes out immediately after the shots are fired will lose fewer wounded birds than the paragon who dutifully awaits the word of command.

While grouse hunters may prefer a slow, exceedingly painstaking dog, the exact opposite is generally true of quail hunters. The fast, wide-going dog not only covers a great deal more ground in much less time, but the birds apparently lie better to a dog that comes up at top speed and slams into his point. In addition, in country where the terrain and scarcity of fences permit, **bird hunting on horseback** is a favorite form of the sport, and big-going dogs are essential here. In this form of hunting it is necessary to have a handler along to hold the horses when the hunters dismount to shoot, after the dogs have pointed. Guns are carried, always unloaded, in **saddle scabbards.**

**Guns.** There is more room for argument in connection with guns and loads than in any other phase of the sporting picture. "Gun cranks" are notoriously contentious, and widely varying preferences in gauges or calibers, barrel length, correct shot sizes or bullet weights, and powder loads are freely expressed. Quail hunters, however, come closer to accord on these subjects than any other shooters. Their guns and loads are almost standardized.

Number 8 is the generally accepted shot size, though some use even 9's or 10's for shooting in particularly thick cover. While many sportsmen profess to like the old soft shot, claiming greater shocking power and quicker kills for them, modern chilled shot are almost universally used. The harder chilled pellets guarantee fewer deformed shot, with a consequently more uniform pattern in the shot load. Penetration is also greater; and their superiority is pretty well demonstrated by the fact that most ammunition manufacturers now load with them exclusively.

Just as in any other hunting, the gun one shoots best will be the most practical for quail, but the 12-gauge is the gun most widely used. It should have a fairly open bore, for a close-choked barrel gives too tight a pattern for any but the most expert marksmen, and a tightly choked gun also results in too many mangled birds at the comparatively close ranges at which most quail are killed. If a double-barreled gun is the choice, a left barrel of modified choke and a right barrel of improved cylinder is best. For shooters who prefer the pump-gun, the autoloader, or the single-barrel, without the addition of a device offering a choice in degree of choke such as the Cutts compensator of the Poly-Choke, modified choke would be the most practical boring. (See under "Patent Chokes.")

Quail hunters usually prefer shorter barrels on their bird guns, for they lend themselves to faster gun handling. The experienced bird shot shoots more or less by instinct, and has little need for any extended sighting plane, as is given with the longer barrels. And modern smokeless powders attain complete combustion in the shorter barrels, with little loss in the velocity of the shot. A barrel length of 26 inches, or even less, is perfectly satisfactory in the quail gun.

**General.** Proper footwear is a consideration for any sportsman, and in quail hunting afoot it assumes even greater importance. Granted that quail do not habitually frequent the difficult swamps and sloughs the pheasant so often ranges, wide-going dogs can demand a great deal of footwork from their followers, and that is manifestly impossible unless foot comfort is assured. Too, much quail hunting is done in snake country, and boots of leather heavy enough to give protection will add to the hunter's peace of mind. Nine- or 10-inch boots of the moccasin "bird-shooters" types are excellent. Their leather is heavy enough to turn the fangs of most snakes, and few snakes strike higher than 10 inches. Their gristle or composition soles afford sure footing; and liberal applications of neatsfoot oil will keep the leather soft and pliable, and make the boots waterproof against any but prolonged soakings.

If pants are worn loose, outside the boots, additional protection against snake-bite is obtained. Hunting breeches having knitted cuffs for wearing inside the boots are also good, and give full protection. But let your chosen style be briarproof.

As much bird hunting is in milder climates, the skeletonized shooting jacket, supported by web straps and having ample pockets for shells, game, and incidentals, is a favorite with sportsmen. The weight of its contents is evenly distributed, and it has less neck-drag than hunting coats of conventional pattern. A shooting jacket of this type can be worn over wool shirts of varying weights, or even a leather windbreaker when necessary.

A snake-bite kit of the suction type is a wise addition to the outfit if the hunting is done in Florida or southern Georgia, for snakes do represent a threat to dogs, especially those not raised in snake country.

The man fortunate enough to have good dogs, who has chosen his gun and outfit with wisdom, and who, lacking knowledge of local conditions, is not too proud to seek advice from the men who do know, will soon understand fully why the mere mention of bobwhite can arouse so much enthusiasm in those who love our upland coverts.

**Mountain Quail.** The mountain quail, largest member of America's quail family, is distinctly game for the athletic sportsman. Both the terrain he inhabits and his ways of eluding pursuers make him a bird demanding a high order of endurance in those who hunt him. None but the most experienced dogs can relieve the sportsman of much of the footwork involved if these birds are to be forced into the air for a shot. His most thickly inhabited home range, lying as it does at altitudes of 2000 feet and over in the High Sierras of the Pacific Coast Range, is rugged country, and certainly no proper setting for the hunter not in tiptop physical condition.

These birds, unlike bobwhite quail, have no determined local range. They generally feed close to dense cover, their favorite foods being mountain rye and timothy, sage, huckleberries, waxberries, wintergreen berries, clover, and wild oats. They will sometimes seek out a particular kind of lichen, indigenous to the high country, and feed on it exclusively for long periods. They are, moreover, migratory to some extent, and will occasionally be found at much lower altitudes, depending on the prevalence of food as local weather conditions change.

Obviously, territory offering a profusion of their favorite foods, with heavy cover not too far distant from the feeding grounds, should prove most productive for the hunter. The most favorable hunting is to be had on mesa tops, where chaparral, sage, scattered piñon trees, and a rocky, boulder-strewn terrain afford them the kind of cover they prefer.

Pointing dogs capable of handling this bird are few and far between, and if one insists on shooting his birds over points, a pointer or setter with years of experience on the ring-necked pheasant will be the best bet. Experienced pheasant dogs have learned to circle their game when it moves ahead of them. This is the only successful method on birds as prone to run as the mountain quail.

A springer spaniel, or a retriever trained to hunt upland game as the spaniel does, will give the hunter more shots, and a resultantly heavier bag, than any of the pointing breeds. A dog is almost indispensable for finding the birds, and a spaniel or retriever that covers his field intelligently, quartering his ground thoroughly within practical shotgun range, will locate more of the tight-lying birds than will a pointing dog. Also, as in any other form of bird shooting, the use of a good retrieving dog will materially cut down the losses of grassed birds.

The country in which mountain quail are hunted can be extremely hard on the pads of dogs' feet, and some protection is frequently required. Field boots for the dog are the obvious answer, but some dogs, unaccustomed to them, will refuse to hunt when the boots are taped on.

A satisfactory substitute in such cases is a mixture of one-third pine tar, one-third tannic acid, and one-third fine sand. The tar is warmed, and the other ingredients well mixed in. After cooling, the mixture is painted on the dog's feet, and acts not only as a healing agent to already worn pads, but affords good protection on abrasive footing.

Mountain quail are so loosely grouped when feeding that it is erroneous to speak of "coveys" of them. In reality, they range in large "bands" or "droves," and when a band is found the birds almost invariably try to escape by running uphill. They are hard to flush, and the hunter must make every effort to head them off from the uphill side. Cutting off their customary line of retreat apparently bewilders the birds to some extent, and they are apt to flush wildly in all directions, offering a profusion of angling shots at long range. They have a distinctive, curving flight which makes them difficult targets. However, they are more inclined to lie to a point after the drove has been scattered.

The birds always run for quite a distance after alighting, and this makes it almost impossible to mark them down with any degree of accuracy. Here, again, a dog is almost a necessity, if the scattered birds are to be found.

The gun used on mountain quail should be light in weight, for the hunter is handicapped enough by the altitude and terrain, without adding the burden of a heavy gun. By all means let it be a gun throwing a close pattern, full-choked if a single barrel, and with the left full-choked and the right modified if a double gun. Mountain quail are generally killed at much longer ranges than are bobwhite, and an open-bored gun is ineffective on them. Barrels of a length of 28 or 30 inches are practical.

Number 7½ chilled shot is a good choice, although if a double gun or repeater is used, it is a good plan to have the first shell loaded with these, and the succeeding shells loaded with No. 6.

The hunter must always be prepared for quick and marked changes in both temperature and weather conditions. All-wool clothing is best, for the sportsman is not faced with the tangled growth and briars he encounters in the lowlands.

In spite of his restricted range, and the rigors hunting him entails, the mountain quail is the favorite game of numerous upland hunters. No trophy is valued when it is obtained too easily, and the sportsman who puts one of these handsome, sporty birds in his game pocket has fully earned it.

**Valley Quail.** The California valley quail, like his mountain cousin, is found only in a small section of the West. He is a wanderer within the limits of his range, and does not restrict his feeding to any particular area; although, as his name implies, he favors valleys, canyons, and gulches rather than the heights. While these birds sometimes move to the higher altitudes in their search for food, their usual habitat lies in the lower stretches of the Coast Ranges. They are not adaptable to civilization, and, as a general rule, seek more primitive surroundings.

Valley quail are even more confirmed runners than mountain quail, and will refuse to fly as long as any other avenue of escape is open. There, however, the resemblance ends, for after being flushed they will lie very well to a pointing dog. In fact, they lie so closely, and for such long periods after being disturbed, that it takes an exceptionally keen-nosed dog to find the scattered singles. If thoroughly frightened, birds have been known to stay frozen until actually picked up by hand. And these periods of immobility will sometimes last as long as two hours, or more. This trait makes the use of a dog almost imperative; the birds blend well against their native

N. C. Dept. of Conservation & Development.

PLATE I. The Covey Rise.

background, and cannot be seen until almost stepped on.

When found on fairly level ground, valley quail, on finally being put into the air, fly close to the ground, and their curving flight is similar to that of the mountain quail. Their line of flight frequently takes a downhill course, and it is necessary to hold well under the bird when he is thus steadily dropping.

The birds gather in huge flocks during the fall months, as many as 1500 to 2000 being found in a single band. Normally, they need little if any water, so that water holes are by no means always productive of birds. Their favorite food is sage, and the best hunting is to be had in sage patches. Other favored foods are wild oats, weeds, ferns, lupine, and bunch grass. These foods are found in profusion in cattle country, and grazing lands are good hunting cover. Sheep, however, because they browse so closely and destroy the roots of grass and other grazing plants with their sharp hooves, will soon cause birds to abandon any particular section.

Especially sporty pass-shooting can sometimes be had when the terrain is favorable. One gunner takes position in a shallow ditch running between good patches of cover, while his partner and the dogs put up the birds. They offer good targets as they pass overhead, due to their habit of flying low.

A pointing dog is much more practical on these birds than on the mountain variety, and will work the singles well. An experienced dog can sometimes even anchor the flock by circling them when they start to run. A special or spaniel-trained retriever would be the second choice, but by all means use a dog of one breed or the other.

It is a good plan for the hunter to shoot into the air, no matter how far he may be from the birds when they flush; the more frightened and confused they are, the better will they subsequently lie to points.

Since most of the shots will be had at single birds, and at fairly close ranges, a light bobwhite gun is best for valley quail. Many hunters prefer the 20-gauge, and some use even the .410. It should be open-bored—left barrel modified-choke, and right barrel improved-cylinder if a double gun, and with modified choke if a repeater.

Number 8 shot are a good all-round choice, for the closer patterns possible with the finer shot will give cleaner kills than the larger sizes.

The valley quail is another trophy well worth the effort it takes to bag him, but here again is a bird that demands the utmost in stamina from both men and dogs.

**Mearns' Quail.** The Mearns', or Massena, quail really does not deserve the name "fool quail" by which he is sometimes called. He is by far the rarest of our quail, and it is his unfamiliarity with man and his lack of fear that make him so slow to flush. He can frequently be approached within 2 or 3 feet before taking wing, and this trait makes him game par excellence for pointing dogs.

This bird is found only in scattered sections of the highest and most rugged sections of desert ranges along the Mexican border in Arizona, New Mexico, and Texas.

Pointing dogs used on bobwhite are successful on Mearns' quail, and are, in fact, almost indispensable to the success of the hunt. A comparatively slow dog is desirable; the Gordon setter is especially good on these birds. A dogless hunter can pass within a few feet of the hidden birds without either seeing or flushing them.

When flushed, the birds fly only short distances, and are easily marked down and relocated. They rarely run after alighting.

The gun used on bobwhite quail is best for the Mearns', open-bored, and loaded with No. 8 shot. The lighter the gun, the better.

His very rarity and the inaccessibility of his habitat make the Mearns' quail worth-while game; but his lack of fear makes it improbable that he will ever attain sufficient numbers to make him a big favorite with upland hunters.

**Scaled Quail.** Many sportsmen scorn the scaled quail, also called "cottontop" and "Mexican blue quail," and compare hunting him to shooting rabbits due to the difficulty of putting him into the air. There is no doubt that many of these quail brought to bag are killed on the ground.

They are possibly the fastest runners of all birds, excepting the ostrich and the chaparral cock, and often reach a speed afoot in excess of 15 miles per hour. Covey-shooting on them is nonexistent, as it takes an exceptionally fast dog or a man on horseback to run them down and make them flush. Until the practice was outlawed in some localities, they were often hunted by automobile, the gunners riding the fenders and shooting the birds as they ran.

A pointing dog is of little or no use on scaled quail, and they can easily prove the ruination of a stanch pointer or setter. Spaniels or retrievers are little better, for no dog can long continue hunting in the arid country they range. Grassed birds are much more easily found than are mountain or valley quail, but a cocker spaniel, working solely as a retriever, might prove worth while in this hunting.

The home range of the scaled quail extends from central Arizona across New Mexico to central Texas, and north to southern Colorado and south to Mexico, with the most birds inhabiting stretches of New Mexico, where a profusion of their chosen cover of chaparral and mesquite is to be found.

These quail must have water, and the cover around water holes is the most productive hunting country. They feed to a great extent on grass seed, always feeding and watering on a fixed schedule, and usually roosting in the same area at the same hour. Once a band of the birds has been located, they will be found in the same neighborhood, time after time, at the same time of day.

Their feeding habits restrict their range to the more open country, and they show little fear of man. When flushed, they rarely fly over 100 yards; but they begin to run again as soon as they pitch down, and it is impossible to mark down the scattered members of the flock.

Even cattle clean off grazing lands too closely to leave sufficient food and cover for the birds, and they will quickly abandon land where sheep are run. Plenty of grass is necessary for both food and cover; when sufficient cover is lacking, they fall ready prey to sharp-shinned hawks, coyotes, skunks, and other predators.

A closely choked light gun is best on these birds, and No. 8 shot are large enough.

The most confirmed wing shot will admit that any hunting is better than none at all, and will find the scaled quail a not-too-easy mark, even on the ground. Though you may damn him with faint praise, and side with those critics who hold the scaled quail in little esteem as a game bird, a trial will convince any sportsman that the very difficulty of bringing him to bag makes the cottontop an acceptable quarry.

**Gambel's Quail.** To pun upon his name, the Gambel's quail can be a real gamble for the hunter. Throughout most of his range he is a terrific runner, loath to flush, and can drive a pointing dog to distraction by his failure to hold to points. But occasionally, when found in grass, these birds will behave almost exactly like bobwhite, flushing in covey formation, and pitching down within a couple of hundred yards. In such cases, the single birds lie tightly, and a pointing dog can work them satisfactorily. But it is only when the Gambel's is found in cover of this kind that a pointing dog is at all practical for hunting him; and in most of his habitat any breed of dog is useless.

When feeding in the open desert, as they most frequently do, the quail emulate that wise bird, the crow, and post sentinels. This makes it impossible to flush the guarded flock, for the birds will unobtrusively vanish at a fast pace when warned by the lookouts. Locating a flock under these conditions, the hunter's only recourse is to try to run them down and scatter the birds. Singles can find hiding places in what looks like absolutely barren ground, and they will stick tight even when approached within a foot or two. Noise will frighten them into flight quicker than anything else; and some hunters claim that an imitation of the w-h-i-r-r-r-r! of a quail's flight will get them up when all else fails.

The Gambel's chosen range can hold very real dangers for both man and dog. Not only do the trackless and waterless wastes of the desert make getting lost an ever-present threat, but they are the home of the sidewinder, that deadly, small rattlesnake which can so easily be overlooked. Too, cactus and other desert growths make difficult and punishing cover for a dog to face.

Few water tanks and small streams, when located in desert country, fail to attract a quota of birds, and they represent far and away the most promising cover in which to hunt them. Any desert watering places are usually bordered with the kind of cover in which the birds may be hunted to best advantage.

The Gambel's flies strongly, and is hard to kill, for he can carry almost as much lead as a cock pheasant. Wounded birds will find impenetrable hiding places, even seeking refuge in gopher holes.

When shooting over points, the hunter will find No. $7\frac{1}{2}$ shot large enough; but if he hunts in grassless cover, No. 6 would be better.

A full-shoked gun is the most practical, and, if a double, the right barrel should be modified choke.

The Gambel's is one of the handsomest of our

Lee Wulff, Shushan, N. Y.

PLATE II. The Florida "palmetto jumper," a combination dog-lunch-shooter wagon for use on the wide palmetto barrens. Two shooters ride on top while the dogs range ahead. When the dogs point the wagon halts about a hundred yards from the point and the shooters move up on foot.

quail, but he is certainly game for the younger and more athletically inclined sportsman. And if you have the hardihood and stamina to seek him in his forbidding homeland, he is game well worth the effort.

**General.** In the bobwhite's southern range, where the hunter often is mounted—on a horse, mule, or one of the various shooting cars—a fast, wide-ranging dog is preferred, but in the northern range a slower, close-working dog is essential. The quail is not so important in this northern range, where normally he is less plentiful than the pheasant and less popular than the ruffed grouse. The man on foot does not want a fast dog that in many instances will flush or move birds before he can come up to the point.

Another factor enters the picture in the northern range. Most of the farms are mechanized and horses and mules are not used nearly so much as in the South. Also, most of the good shooting areas are more restricted in size, and the man who hunted at a rapid pace might find himself out of good covers well before noon. In the southern range it is the opposite. To find a satisfactory number of coveys the hunter must cover a territory that would be impossible if he depended on "shank's mare."

Many of the southern shooting camps and preserves provide just about everything for the visitor other than clothing, guns, and ammunition—the list includes dogs, horses, guides and accommodations. Many of the operators of such preserves insist that their horses or mules are "broken to shot" and will not react to the explosions of the guns only a few yards away. The man sitting on a horse while his companion or companions move up on foot to the point would be advised to keep a tight rein, however, and not loosen the grip of his knees.

Florida has one of the strangest hunting vehicles the shooter will encounter, but for the type of terrain hunted it is all that could be desired. This vehicle, known as the "palmetto jumper," "palmetto buggy," or "dog car" usually has its origin as a Model A Ford, preferably of the type known as a "pick-up." First a reduction gear is installed; then the ignition, all wiring, and the carburetor are moved to a point *over* the motor. Then a double-size radiator is installed. Larger wheels, with over-size tires, are the next change, thus raising the axles several inches higher, to insure clearance over the "lightwood" stumps. Attention is now given to the box back. The final design depends upon the ingenuity of the converter and the sum he wants to spend.

The driver rides in the cab, and the shooters on the roof, usually in a couple of bucket seats. The accompanying photograph shows one of the typical "jumpers," owned by Judge Harry Dyer of Stuart, Fla. This vehicle is somewhat more elaborate than the average, for the Judge has a place for everything and everything is kept in its place.

Normally from two to four dogs are carried in the cage behind the driver, two of them put down at a time. The dogs range ahead and on either side, and the driver moves the vehicle ahead, to the left or right, as directed by one of the shooters in the bucket seat on the roof. Signals usually consist of a series of thumps on the roof of the cab.

Despite the rumors regarding the seriousness of the rattlesnake and cottonmouth menace, the average shooter in this area does not bother with snake-guards, nor does he even take the normal precaution of wearing high leather boots. "Look where you step before you step," is their advice, "and don't walk through any palmetto clumps." Snakebite kits are included in the equipment, but are rarely used except on the dogs.

# WILD TURKEY

*Meleagris gallopavo*

COMMON NAMES: American Turkey, American Wild Turkey, Bronze Turkey, Eastern Turkey, Florida Turkey, Northern Turkey, Rio Grande Turkey, Wood Turkey.

**History.** The wild turkey is a native American bird, but its scientific and common names have suffered some confusion with a foreign import, the guinea-fowl. The guinea-fowl was brought into Europe from Africa via Turkey, and inherited the names "turkey cock" or "turkey hen," but some 16th- and 17th-century writers confused this species with the dissimilar American bird, and for a time both were known by the same name. Once the species were properly separated, however, the native bird, with a call note of *"turc, turc, turc,"* retained the controversial appelation. There is still a mix-up in the scientific terms. Both birds have the generic name *Meleagris,* although this assuredly is more distinctive of the guinea-fowl since the reference is to Meleager, of Greek legend, whose sisters were turned into guinea-fowl. Formerly, zoologists classed the turkey in a separate family, but today the bird of the order *Gallinae* is included in the family *Phasianidae,* which makes it the exclusive American representative of the pheasant group, and the largest member of that family in the world. The sub-family *Meleagrinae* is peculiar to North and Central America.

There are two turkey varieties in North America. The ocellated turkey, *Agrocharis ocellata,* is the more beautiful and graceful. It is found in southern Mexico, but is more numerous in Central America (Honduras and Guatemala). The familiar, larger genus is *Meleagris gallopavo* and its five sub-species: Eastern turkey *(M.g. silvestris),* Florida turkey *(M.g. osceola),* Rio Grande turkey *(M.g. intermedia),* Merriam turkey *(M.g. merriami),* and Mexican turkey *(M.g. gallopavo).* The Eastern and the Mexican are the most important types, but they are all very much alike, differing primarily in minor color variations. The largest type, the Eastern turkey, is best known because it was most abundant and most widely distributed.

When Francisco Fernandez, and later Cortez, came to Mexico in the early 16th century, they found the turkey under domestication by the Aztec Indians. The Conquistadores transplanted these fine table birds from New Spain (Mexico) to the motherland,

and from Spain they were distributed to other parts of Europe by 1530 and eventually brought back to America by the early immigrants. The Mexican turkey was the first type of turkey placed in domestication and the progenitor of all our present stock. They have since been bred in buff, black, white, slate, and reddish-brown. The Indians of the north did not propagate the turkey, but it was actively hunted and relied on as a favored food, and its plumage was used to make blankets and robes. The first settlers also depended on the turkey for food, from the time of the first Thanksgiving to subsequent bitter winters when food was scarce. Neither the first colonists nor later settlers domesticated the bird in any appreciable numbers for the first 100 years.

The original range of the wild turkey in North America was from southern Mexico through New England to Canada and west, to include 39 out of the 48 states. The Eastern turkey was abundant in New England, especially in Massachusetts. The turkey, primarily a bird of the forest, was unable to withstand the advance of civilization. When its hereditary range was destroyed for lumber or agricultural reasons, the bird moved or was exterminated. Unlimited shooting was allowed and market hunters killed off large numbers of the unsuspecting fowl on their roosts. In the early 1800's they sold for as little as six cents apiece in the New England states, but by 1840 they were rare in that section. The last recorded kill in Massachusetts was in 1850. In the late 19th century, they seldom were seen in the central part of the United States. In the last 100 years they have vanished from 18 of the 39 states. Today, the wild turkey is considered a southern game bird, for there are comparatively few found north of Maryland, Pennsylvania, and Virginia. The fact that the turkey has been reduced to two-thirds of its original range in Virginia, however, shows the relative position of the bird to its present-day environment.

Severe game restrictions have been put on the increasing number of turkey hunters to preserve the decreasing number of turkeys, but in some states illegal poaching sets back the numbers. Conservation and management of the forest regions (the natural habitat of the bird), in addition to artificial stocking, have been backed generously by Federal-State co-operation. Where adequate coverage and food is provided, the birds thrive, and, even where hunted, are able to survive because their present-day fear of man has changed them from a naturally alert specimen of the wilds into one of the wariest game birds. Modern sportsmen consider the turkey "the king of the game birds." Connoisseurs toast him as "king of the table birds." Benjamin Franklin wanted this handsome, noble bird selected for the national emblem.

**Identification.** (See color plate on page 485.) The wild Eastern turkey is a large, trim, and beautiful specimen. The general appearance of the plumage coloring is copper-bronze, margined with black, but the iridescent quality of the feathers reflect green, cocoa-brown, gold, and deep reddish. The female is of duller coloring than the male with less luster and metallic gloss. The wild turkey is more slender and sleek of body than the common barnyard bird, and has deep chestnut tips on the tail feathers in contrast to the white ones of the domesticated bird. Since there frequently is hybridizing between the wild and domesticated, there often is confusion in segregation.

The four other sub-species are similar to the Eastern turkey, varying slightly in coloring. The darker Florida turkey has less white on the wings. The Rio Grande turkey has tail feathers tipped with a light rusty-brown, while the Merriam's are tipped with buff. The upper tail coverts and tail tip of the Mexican turkey are white. (The Mexican variety is the ancestor of the common barnyard turkey, both having the same white markings.)

The small, naked head and long neck are reddish in color with blue and purplish protuberances. The long, powerful legs and large feet are pinkish-gray to a silvery-gray. The wide tail is composed of 14 to 18 blunt-edged feathers which the gobbler is capable of erecting and fanning out when he struts, usually for the admiration of the hen during the courting season. The mature gobbler is distinguished from the hen by his distinctive "beard." It is a tassel-like adornment of feathers which are as stiff and thin as bristles and hangs from the upper breast. The length varies according to the age. The beard grows rapidly for the first three or four years, and thereafter grows a little each year. Many old gobblers have beards of 14 inches and over which sweep the ground when they feed and fascinate the hens when they court.

The Eastern turkey is the largest of all the turkeys and the largest upland game bird in North America. When adult, at three years or over, male birds weigh between 8 and 20 pounds, but average 14 pounds. Some have reached as high as 40 pounds. The females are smaller and lighter, ranging from 6 to 10 pounds. Both sexes are heaviest in the fall. The gobblers are about 4 feet in over-all length, with hens a foot less.

The talkative nature of the turkey is a logical result of a characteristic sociability. The birds habitually feed and travel in flocks and the cock is polygamous, so there is a more or less continual attempt to keep together, and if scattered to contact one another by calling. These numerous call notes have proved to be one of the turkey's most vulnerable traits, for hunters, from the aboriginal Indians to present-day sportsmen, have imitated the calls to lure the bird into shooting range. The wise old gobblers, which have observed the tricks of man from season to season, are most suspicious and cautious in answering any call, and often will approach silently to observe the source of the call before betraying their presence or will lead younger, less wary birds away, giving the alarm call, *"kut, kut."* Perhaps one of his least-heard calls is a harsh *"curek,"* but the most famous is the throaty, courting note, *"gil-obble-obble-obble,"* which has given him his identifying name since the time of the Indians, when he was known as Old Chief Galagina or "the gobbling one." The hen answers the courting call with a plaintive *'keow, keow, keow,"* and the seductive quality of this note is imitated most frequently by the hopeful hunter. The alarm call of the hen is a drawn-out *"kwa-a-a-ah,"* and she also clucks to gather her brood. The distress call of the young is a whining *"kee, kee, kee."* The yelp or *"heoh, heoh, heoh,"* is repeated as the flock leaves the roost in early morning, and on the way to look for food and while feeding they keep up a noisy *"yedle, yedle, yedle."*

**Characteristics.** The attempt to elude man and his gun has intensified the turkey's naturally shy and alert disposition. It rarely relaxes its guard or its use of extraordinarily keen hearing and eyesight, and, being most adept at moving quietly through the woods, is able to avoid most enemies by coming upon them first and slipping off unseen. A man unaccustomed to or uninterested in the ways of the forest turkey could pass near one regularly without being aware of its presence. Since the bird usually shares its forested habitat with the deer, the shooting season on that animal makes the turkey more sharp and suspicious than ever.

The gregarious turkey habitually gathers into flocks which vary in composition and number according to the season. At the end of the nesting season, the hens which were unsuccessful in rearing their own young join up with a family group, so that two or more hens often are seen accompanying one brood. In late summer or early fall several family groups merge into large flocks of 25 to 50, and then generally divide up according to sex, forming smaller flocks of 9 to 12. The segregation of the sexes during the winter is not complete, but the gobblers have a more definite tendency to band together than do the hens. Three or four old gobblers often range together until spring or live a solitary existence during the winter. Throughout the winter season there is a repeated disbanding and merging of smaller flocks with large flocks or "droves" of as many as 40 birds.

The turkey is strong, swift, and forceful on foot, standing erect and capable of walking long distances and running at an average speed of 15 to 18 miles an hour. In short spurts it will do 30 miles an hour. Because of its adeptness on the ground, it often will run rather than fly when flushed if there is adequate coverage. When taking to the air, the turkey leaves the ground with a vertical bound like the pheasant, and its broad, stiffened tail acts as a rudder. If startled, the flight often is no further than a nearby treetop. The normal flight of a turkey is rapid, but not maintained for any prolonged distance—a mile being more than average. The small, rounded wings beat rapidly when the bird is in the air and often give a blurred impression of the wing outline.

Turkeys roost at night, and since they generally are methodical in their habits, they start for their roosts at approximately the same time every day. The objective is to be on the roost by dusk, and they will run at full speed if necessary to make it in time. The flock usually makes a leisurely, pleasurable pastime out of the approach to the roost, scratching and looking for food along the way. The roosting area is checked for enemies or any suspicious noises or changes since they left the neighborhood at dawn to feed. After they are satisfied that all is well, they fly up into the trees. Each is careful to keep a good distance apart from any other, for they never bunch together, and rarely share the same branch. Sometimes they try several spots or different trees before settling down. In wooded areas which provide numerous roosting choices, they rotate among several trees, spending several nights in each one. A preferred roost is one which provides the greatest degree of cover. If the flock is flushed or alarmed at night, they will not fly to the ground but to another tree. Not being nocturnal by habit, they can not see well at night and know they are not safe on the ground where they would become prey to their natural enemies.

The influence of predators on the turkey population is variable with each particular range, but a mature bird has a reputation for being tough and capable of taking good care of itself in the wild, though eggs are eaten by skunks, crows, snakes, and opossums. A relatively small proportion of adult turkeys is taken each year by bobcats, foxes, coyotes, red wolves, and stray dogs, but the turkey's chief enemy is man. As a rule the highest percentage of nest failures is due to man's habit of frightening setting hens into leaving their nests and to illegal nest robbing by those who attempt to gather the eggs in order to raise wild turkeys in captivity, a job which is virtually impossible for an amateur without special equipment and special knowledge.

The wild turkey is prone to the diseases of the domesticated fowl and other barnyard fowl. The diseases are passed when they are in association with one another on the same range or in the same pens.

Before the breeding season begins the large winter flocks begin to break up into small groups, about two to five birds of one sex in each group. The gobblers are ready for breeding at two years of age, the hens at one. The yearling "toms" band together during this time, and usually remain aloof from the breeding grounds. The mating period is variable according to range, but it is roughly from April to June. Up to mating time the gobblers call and strut, but during the breeding season those efforts, which are primarily for the sake of attracting a hen, are intensified. Sometimes the gobbler begins his loud love call from his roost, at other times from a grassy bald or abandoned field. Generally he begins before dawn, repeating until daylight or until a hen answers. As the hen watches, he puts on a show of voice, plumage, and strut which are all in prime condition. The strut is perhaps his most important courtship display. He takes a lungful of air, pulls back his head to accentuate the jutting chest, and then lifts and spreads his broad tail into a fan. While in this position he takes a few high, pacing steps, usually pivoting the wing-tips touching the ground and "strumming." At the climax, the air is exhaled sharply with a *"shuff,"* and the denouement is a reversion to normal. Since the gobbler is polygamous, the attempt to collect four to five hens in a harem often is strenuous, sometimes impossible, as the large "bachelor clubs" at the end of the season verify. The polygamy is of the true harem type, for the hens are herded together by the gobbler and are maintained with jealous care on his territory. Once the gobbler's territory is selected, any challenger seeking access to his hens or his territory is fought off the land. The gobbler seldom takes time to feed during the mating season, but nature supplies him with a "breast sponge" which holds excess fats and oils and upon which he draws when in need of nourishment, much as a camel does with his hump. The older gobblers usually have the largest harems, and the young bachelors sometimes go through an entire season without one mate. Their frantic running around in search of a hen leaves them little time for eating, and though the hunter often is successful in calling up unmated ones he will find them tough and thin.

**Breeding.** After a hen has mated, she leaves the gobbler to look for a nesting site, builds a nest and drops an egg, and then returns to the gobbler's call each morning or every other morning. The nest must be carefully hidden from the gobbler as well as from natural enemies, for he is totally possessive of the love of his hens and will destroy eggs and poults if he comes upon them. Once the incubation is under way, the hens cease returning to the gobblers and the males band together at the end of the season, leaving the nesting area and not returning to the flocks until the young are almost grown.

The nest is built on the ground in a variety of different places, but is always well hidden, often by low vegetation or a fallen treetop, or in a heavy growth of shrubs or thickets. It is rarely placed in the deep woods, and usually is about 200 yards from water. On some ranges the site is an elevated area in a swamp. The hen often flies to and from the nest in order to conceal its whereabouts, but sometimes a crow persistently follows her in the air and on foot as the frantic bird tries to return to her nest. The nest is constructed in a slight depression in the ground among the leaves or other vegetable debris, and usually lined with leaves or suitable material in the immediate vicinity.

From 10 to 18 eggs are laid. They vary in color from old ivory to a pinkish buff and are uniformly speckled with brown. Though only one brood is raised a year, the hen will re-nest if her eggs are destroyed. However, it is sometimes difficult to find a gobbler at the close of the season, and the eggs of a second series often are infertile. The eggs are hatched in 28 days. As is true of most game birds, the turkey hen will desert her nest if disturbed in the early stage of incubation, but as the period lengthens, she sits closer, and when the young are near hatching time, she will even fight to protect them.

Newly hatched poults are far from hardy yiung. They are susceptible to pneumonia if badly wet or chilled and the mortality is high from this cause. Soon after they emerge from the shells, the mother hen leads them to an abandoned field or clearing in the forest and they live on this edge or fringe for two to three weeks while growing stronger, since there normally is an abundant supply of food (insects, seeds, and berries) in such areas. At the end of that fattening time, they can fly to bushes and low tree branches to roost.

When a year old, the young of the Eastern turkey weigh about 7 pounds. The down of the young is a dusky-gray with a black stripe running along the back from head to tail. The first feather plumage is worn until late summer or early fall when their first plumage moult produces their full plumage coloring. Yearling gobblers do not have the beard distinctive of mature gobblers, and though the young males average larger in size than the young females they are most readily identified by a feather marking which is consistent at all ages. The breast and back feathers of the male are tipped with black, and the contour feathers of the female are tipped with buff.

**Feeding.** The turkey enjoys a wide variety of vegetables (about 84%) and animal matter (about 16%). Turkeys rely most heavily upon forest mast (hazelnuts, beechnuts, chestnuts, and acorns) in their diet, but also favor fruit, mountain rice, sedge, poa grass, mesquite beans, peanuts, wild grapes, and wild seeds. They eat numerous kinds of insects, including grasshoppers, beetles, flies, caterpillars, spiders, and snails. Since the whitetail deer and turkey often are found on the same range, and many of the preferred foods of the turkey also are eaten by the deer, an excessive number of deer in a particular area threatens the food supply of the turkey. Overbrowsing by the deer also strips away coverage for the turkey. It has been observed by ornithologists that as the deer increases, the turkey often decreases.

Fall is the best season for feeding, largely because of the abundance of mast. At that time the bird is plumpest and best eating. As winter sets in and the supply of mast, seeds, and hibernating insects begins to get scarce, the turkey begins a more active search for food, and the normal feeding range of one to two miles is increased to about five miles. During severe winters, they will approach cultivated fields to eat corn, but they are so wary of man that they will not eat corn or wheat if it is placed out for them in a suspicious, artificial fashion, even if they are near starvation. In late winter and early spring they turn to green shoots of plants.

Eastern turkeys require drinking water, but the Merriam turkey and other turkeys which inhabit arid or semi-arid regions can survive for an indefinite time on dew and succulence or succulence alone.

**Range and Distribution.** Beside overshooting and clearing of the forests for agriculture and lumber, the turkey's hereditary range was destroyed by forest fires, severe winters, and food shortages. Since the bird is not migratory, it still inhabits original sections of the range which were left intact through the centuries, or partially intact by selective logging or slashing. Fortunately, cutting away of the forest land was a progressive action, and birds of one range were able to join those in another section which was extant. They could survive if the range was not overcrowded and reasonably protected. If lumbering activities start up in an area, they are wont to leave for the length of the operation and return when it is completed—sometimes four to five years later. Their love of the deep woods has been sharpened by the fear of man, but they still visit the lowlands, mountains, and swamps, as well as ridges and borders of rivers and creeks. They thrive in all climates from the cold of Canada to the heat of Mexico. The theory that animals and birds often are controlled in their distribution by nutritional requirements produced by certain soils is suggested by some biologists to apply to the wild turkey. In Pennsylvania, for instance, the greatest part of the wild turkey range is formed from a special sandstone covered by limestone soils. Studies of the soil in Missouri indicate a more definite relationship between turkey and soil (of stony loam and residual limestone) than turkey to woodland itself.

Today, the range of *Meleagris gallopavo* is from Pennsylvania to Florida, west to Colorado and Arizona, then south to central Mexico. The five subspecies are distributed by regions, but all show a preference for the woods, whether the pin oaks of Pennsylvania or the great pines, cypress, and tupelos of the southern swamps. The eastern turkey inhabits Pennsylvania and eastern Kentucky, and as far south as the Mississippi Valley. The Florida turkey is primarily confined to Florida, but is also found in Pennsylvania. The Rio Grande turkey is found from the north central part of Texas, south to Mexico. The Merriam turkey ranges from southern Colorado, New Mexico, Arizona, and eastern Texas south to Chihuahua and nothern Sonora in Mexico. The Mexican turkey is localized in central Mexico.

The mobility of the turkey is influenced by the abundance or scarcity of food, the amount of predation, and the activities of man. If they are unmolested, they remain near to the food supply, but as food becomes less abundant, the range widens, and they will wander several miles while foraging. The average daily radius is one mile, as compared with the whitetail deer's two miles per day. The normal yearly range of the bird is four miles.

In recent years several states have made a great effort to restore the turkey to its original range and rightful place in American tradition, out of objective respect for the lordly bird, and for the sake of excellent shooting. In some states conditions are still favorable to the bird, and in those sections plans are under way to revive the turkey population by providing a suitable habitat, limiting the kill, and stocking the area. Expensive failures by pioneer states, such as Missouri, Virginia, and Pennsylvania, have demonstrated the difficulties of artificial propagation.

The wild turkey is not only expensive and difficult to rear in captivity, because of their susceptibility to the diseases of barnyard fowls and their willingness to hybridize with the domestic turkeys, but also their readiness to become completely domesticated is carried to the extreme and they will not "go wild" when released. It is the inherent wildness of the pheasant which makes it such a fine game bird to raise and release for shooting. Formerly, when the wild turkey was released in a shooting area, it usually forsook the wild life and wandered into the nearest barnyard, if it had not fallen prey to natural enemies before then. The new technique to raise and release wild turkeys for sporty shooting is known as the "wild turkey way." Choice wild hens are kept as brooding stock, and wild gobblers are lured into breeding pens to mate with them for the season. The young birds are conditioned in special pens for several weeks before being released, and are prepared for life in the wild.

The emphasis in rearing wild turkeys, however, is not for the purpose of restocking game areas, as such, but to plant them or re-establish them in suitable locations when the brood stock is inadequate and allow the birds to reproduce themselves. Largely because of the disastrous chestnut tree blight, which destroyed an important source of food, Pennsylvania began expenditures to strengthen the population by artificial propagation. This state has spent considerable money during the last 20 years, with very good results in the last few years, primarily because of the improved method of rearing and releasing them. Pennsylvania is now one of the few states with a shooting season, and has 650,000 licensed hunters who bag between 6000 and 7000 birds annually. Missouri and Virginia have done much propagation and as a result of having a closed season on hunting in past years, have had an average annual kill of 6800 birds in a 60-day season for the last few years.

The wild turkey population is on the increase, and six states are working on turkey projects at present. Individuals in other southeastern states are following the example of Pennsylvania, Missouri, and Virginia and are exerting controls on predation and poaching as well as bettering the natural habitat. Michigan has started a reintroduction of turkeys into a range from which the birds were exterminated over 50 years ago. The "gobbler law," which limits hunting to those gobblers with beards, has restricted over-shooting in some states, and saved the hens to increase the stock. Ten years after this law was enforced in Alabama, where the turkeys had been rapidly decreasing in number, that state had an open season.

Propagation and re-establishment of the turkey is dependent on a complete knowledge of the bird's requirements in regard to food, cover, and breeding areas. Such an extensive study requires a considerable amount of money. Money has recently been made available through the Pittman-Robertson Funds, and the hopes for a greatly increased number of the bird may eventually be realized.

**Hunting Methods.** So exacting is the technique in the hunting of the wild turkey that hunters may usually be classified as ordinary hunters and turkey hunters. This premier American game bird, certainly in size, and perhaps in other respects as well, is so endowed by nature to take care of himself that a hunter has to be unusually qualified to deal with him successfully. This bird is excessively wild, wary, and sagacious. Its rise, though at times rather slow and awkward, is followed by a flight that is graceful and swift, a flight that at times takes it great distances, as over broad rivers. It has been known to fly more than a mile. A fast runner, it can distance a race horse. Apparently, like other game birds, it does not use its sense of smell for protection; but this defect is fully compensated for by its truly marvelous senses of sight and hearing. If a hunter remains motionless, and a buck does not wind him, the man may be in some danger of literally being run over. But the wild turkey will recognize a man at a considerable distance, even though he does not move. All wild creatures are quick to detect motion; but a turkey will not, like many other wild things, mistake a man for a stump. His sense of hearing is acute, and he hates noise. In country in which both deer and turkeys are found, when the former are being driven, the latter invariably come out of the drive first. To cope with a bird of this kind the hunter has to know his game, and he has to have infinite caution and tireless patience.

At times almost or completely exterminated from many of the eastern states, the wild turkey, by wise protecting laws and careful propagation, has now been brought back in considerable numbers, even in so industrialized a state as Pennsylvania. There, of course, it is found only in the wild mountains. In fact, we have no other game bird that is so essentially a bird of the wilderness. It finds its natural habitat in primeval forests, in deep swamps, in regions farthest from the abodes of men. As is well known, thc quail feeds close to the houses and barns of the rural dweller, and the whitetail deer takes rather kindly to civilization. But the wild turkey will thrive only in those regions that are, in a large degree, similar to the beautiful wilderness of pioneer America.

Perhaps the first thing to do in hunting wild turkeys is to make sure that the birds are in the area hunted. No other bird leaves so much "sign." This is because of the turkey's habit of prodigious scratching, throwing up the leaves and trash in whole windrows. Its washes in sunny, sandy, sheltered places can be found. And of course, on clear ground, the tracks are unmistakable. For birds so shy, turkeys are rather noisy—far more so than grouse. Solitary birds may be silent, but flocks make a lot of noise as they move through the woods, especially if they are scratching and talking to one another. At the least alarm, however, they will slip away in swift and ghostly silence.

Suppose the hunter has found turkey signs in a certain area. He should then turn his attention to the flock's daily routine; for this noble bird, like almost every other living thing, is a victim of habit. If undisturbed for a considerable period of time, if the food supply is adequate, a flock of turkeys will roost in the same locality, will follow a certain course, usually in a big circle, every day. Because of this regularity of procedure, the birds can be expected to be at a certain place at a certain time. A familiarity with this routine enables the hunter to waylay a flock. If unmolested on their daily round, turkeys may confidently be expected to arrive at a given point almost on the minute. The hunter who has made himself thoroughly acquainted with the line of their progress has a good chance if he lies in wait for them. A flock, for example, has been known to cross a road at two o'clock daily, at approximately the same place, over a period of nearly two weeks.

But the hunter must be prepared for turkeys to change their range suddenly, and sometimes unexplainably. They appear to get notions that are not easily understood. Sometimes, with food abundant and with nothing to disturb them, they just go trooping off to another range; and as they travel great distances, this idiosyncrasy may upset the best-laid plans.

In the course of their daily rounds, it is rather natural that they should be scared by foxes, wildcats, or other predators; yet such frights appear to be temporary, and may not interfere much with their regular routine. However, the sight of a man usually makes a turkey, especially an old one, abandon his range. Strangely, the sound of a gun does not appear greatly to frighten a wild turkey, though in some cases it may. But there are so many sounds in a wild forest, such as the falling of limbs and dead trees, that the wild turkey does not always associate the blare of a gun with danger. Hunters who have shot a gobbler out of a ranging flock have often been amazed to see the rest of the flock standing around, "*putting*" in some surprise or temporary alarm, but not taking flight. In shooting a wild turkey where others are present, the hunter should be most careful not to disclose himself until the flock has withdrawn out of sight. If the birds once see him, they are likely to leave the range.

When we speak of a flock of turkeys, we ought to remember that this as a rule means an old hen with her grown brood, though sometimes two old hens and their flocks will range together; occasionally old hens that have not hatched that season will join such a group. In such a flock will naturally be some young gobblers, easily identified by their greater size and their less graceful contours. Old wild turkey gobblers, except in the mating season, live a bachelor's existence. Sometimes one will be solitary; oftener two or more will be together; as many as 21 old gobblers have at times been seen ranging together. The usual number of such a flock is, however, more likely to average four or five. There are, therefore, two kinds of flocks of wild turkeys: One is the old hen with this season's brood, which should be full grown by the time the hunting season opens; the other is the group of old males. While each kind of flock has the same daily routine, the old gobblers are the more difficult to locate as they do less scratching than the younger birds, and are much warier.

Although both quail and grouse are regularly hunted with bird dogs, the same is not true of the wild turkey. Though he leaves a powerful scent, that is often readily taken even by a hound, the wild turkey will very rarely lie to a bird dog. He will either run or take flight. A very cautious dog will occasionally point one in a dense covert, in which the turkey feels that he is concealed. Bird dogs can be used in hunting wild turkeys, but not in the same way in which they are used in hunting other game birds. The ordinary purpose of using a bird dog to hunt turkeys is to find and to flush the flock; then the hunter, concealing himself at the place where the birds were flushed (for that is where they will naturally call together), and making his dog lie motionless beside him, will wait a half-hour or even an hour, and then begin to call. This is a sportsmanlike and a thrilling method of killing a wild turkey. Of course, the hunter must know the art of calling, for a false note will undo all his planning. (The art of calling will be discussed a little later.)

As has been said, fox or deer hounds will readily run the trail of a wild turkey; and it is both comic and tragic to watch a really good hound when he comes to the spot whence the turkey has taken wing. The old sagacious master will cast about this way and that, working in concentric circles, going back to pick up the trail, and trying his maneuvers again. Completely baffled, he will apologetically approach his owner, trying hard to tell him that he thinks he has been pursuing a ghost.

Perhaps the best dog on wild turkeys is not a setter or a pointer but a cocker spaniel. This intelligent busybody has a splendid nose; he is small; he investigates every possibility; and he is easily held under control after he has flushed turkeys. Many expert turkey hunters will use no other kind of dog. Moreover, a cocker is so smart that he very quickly learns the whole game: He must find the great birds and flush them, usually barking a good deal at them. Then he returns immediately to his master and lies still for an hour or more until a turkey can be called up. It is useless to try to hunt turkeys with a dog that cannot be taught to keep perfectly still and close to the ground for a long period of time.

It might be thought that turkeys would be badly scared by a dog—so much so that they would not call together near the same place from which they had been flushed. But the wild turkey evidently takes a dog for a fox, by which he has often been flushed before. He will not run far, and if he flies, he will probably alight in a tree in the vicinity. The hunter who has had a flock flushed for him has to be very careful not to disturb any turkeys that may be in trees within sight of him. There is great truth in the remark of an old woodsman: "If a wild turkey ever sees a man, he will quit the country—he will quit the world."

It is generally supposed, even by some men who have hunted wild turkeys a good deal, that a call is effective only if flock is scattered, or in the mating season. Only on rare occasions will a flock that has not become separated answer to a call—that is, in the sense of coming to the call. It is not hard to get answers from individuals in a flock, but they seem to be telling the lone yelper to come to them. But turkeys are naturally gregarious; and if in promising country the hunter will call occasionally he is more likely to get an answer. If it affords nothing more for the moment, it affords the assurance that the great bird is near. One technique about calling that is very important is the matter of stationing oneself in a favorable situation—that is, taking up a position in line with the course that the bird would be likely to travel. It is a mistake to try to call one downhill or through a dense thicket. These birds love big timber and open ground. Where the country is hilly, they work up gullies and ridges. Turkeys of the mountains often fly from the crests clear down to the level of the valley, whence they slowly make their way up again. Turkeys in a love mood or a lonely one will respond to a call; and it is no great feat for an expert caller to lure one across a broad river. Exceedingly curious by nature, wild turkeys probably at times come to a call neither because they are in love or lonely, but just to find out what is going on. On rare occasions a hunter may have the good fortune to hear one wild turkey calling another, and can station himself on a line between them. That is a perfect arrangement, as he is almost sure to have one bird or the other walk up to him.

There are various turkey-calls used for luring the birds. Some hunters call with their mouths, some with an artificial membrane in their mouths. A right in half of a coconut shell; across the top of wing-bone of a turkey. The chief objection to such lures is that, with a bird answering, the hunter's natural excitement may prevent his calling naturally. A normal call is made by affixing a wooden peg upright in half of a coconut shell; across the top of the peg a piece of slate is scraped. This caller, however, is awkward to carry in the woods. Box calls are perhaps the best. They are of two types. In the first, a piece of chalked slate is scraped across the edge of the box. In the second, there is a cover attached which has a bevel on the underside. In calling, this bevel engages the lips of the box. When made of the proper wood and with the right dimensions, this last call is superior to any other.

Many hunters make box calls out of cedar. This gives too shrill and squeaky a tone. The premier wood for the box is basswood or yellow willow, well seasoned. The finest cover is made of locust, though mahogany makes a good top. The lips of the box and the bevel under the cover should be kept well chalked. At all times the box call, to be effective, must be kept dry.

A well-made call can be guaranteed, but no man can guarantee the caller. In some states there is a law against calling wild turkeys; but as expert calling is a real art, and as most calling really warns the birds away from the lure, such a law need hardly be considered a measure of conservation.

In luring this bird to you by artificial notes, you must be familiar with the character of the wild turkey and with the various calls it makes. The hunter's greatest and most common mistake is to call too much. If he gets any intimation of an answer, he must pique the bird's curiosity by silence, or by long pauses between flirtations subdued calls. Continual calling will either make the bird suspicious or else will lessen the allure that always attends shadowy avoidance. For every wild turkey that is killed by an expert caller there will perhaps be five or six that will be warned away from danger by the inexpert calling of his brother hunter.

Against the law in most states, baiting wild turkeys to a blind is the least sportsmanlike way of killing them, and the certainest method of their extermination; for, despite this splendid bird's native sagacity, if a hunter in a blind does not show himself after shooting, the birds will return day after day. A whole flock can be, and some are, killed in this way. But this is a method that should be totally outlawed, for there can be no sport where game has no chance.

Although swift, wild, and crafty, turkeys can at times appear very foolish. This bird is not so uniformly wise as the ruffed grouse. If, for example, a wild turkey comes to a wire fence, he will try for hours to get through it, apparently never thinking of flying over it, though it may be only 3 or 4 feet high. A turkey will sometimes underestimate the amount of cover necessary to hide it. One hunter reports seeing an old gobbler squat under a little bush, actually in plain sight, while the hunter walked right up to it and flushed it. Another hunter shot at a big gobbler in a tree over his head. The bird simply sat there, permitting him to kill it with the second barrel. Still another woodsman reports having shot one gobbler of a pair, when the two were some distance apart. Instead of taking flight or taking to his heels at the sound of the gun, the second bird ran over and began to fight the first one, which was flapping around on the ground. However, such mistakes in acumen are rare, and no man who hunts the wild turkey should count on finding him stupid.

A very old and a standard way to hunt the wild turkey is to roost one, and then to stalk him in the dusk. This method has been condemned by some hunters as unsportsmanlike; yet the difficulties are such that it takes a real woodsman to bag his bird in this way. Turkeys fly to roost about sundown or a little later. If they roost in pines or other evergreens, or in moss-shrouded trees, they are exceedingly difficult to see. More than one hunter has shot at a bunch of mistletoe or at a squirrel nest in mistake for a turkey. After turkeys are up for the night, they move a good deal on limbs, crane their necks, and now and then fly from one limb to a more comfortable one. If the object supposed to be a turkey does not move, yet is clearly visible against the fading sky, identity can nearly always be established by observing its tail, which will be hanging down, shaped about like a shingle. The hunter, having located his bird, must make certain of the tree it is on, and he must keep his eye on the turkey. He must let the light fade so that the woods beneath the trees are in deep shadow. But if he lets the light fade too much, he cannot get his sight on the bird. A wary stalk through the semi-darkness, made preferably with a tree between him and the bird, should bring him within range. Anyone acquainted with the difficulties of these maneuvers will hardly condemn this method of shooting a wild turkey. However, it is outlawed in some states.

Turkeys are often killed by chance. Sometimes they are shot by deer hunters on deer drives, especially in those states where the shotgun is used on deer instead of the rifle. Sometimes regular turkey drives are made, similar to deer drives; and as the great birds will nearly always come out flying, this is an exciting method of hunting them. However, this is hardly possible anywhere except on large preserves, where the birds are abundant.

On the plains of the old Southwest wild turkeys were sometimes ridden to stand; that is, a horseman would flush one, follow him fast, and keep on flushing him in the open country until the bird could be brought, literally by exhaustion, into range. This method was especially successful in dealing with old, heavy gobblers. In Texas, today, they are sometimes hunted in the more open ranges from automobiles. This method need not be considered unsportsmanlike, for the hunter has to shoot at a flying target from a moving car. Any kind of hunting is sportsmanlike which affords the game a fair chance of escape.

In many of the more mountainous states shooting wild turkeys with a rifle in the snow used to be a standard method of getting them. The white background made them plainly visible; a successful shot from a great distance was possible; and if the bird were struck, there was little possibility of its getting away. Today, the wild turkey season in those states which have a good deal of snow rarely corresponds with the periods of snowfall. However, a good many mountaineers still prefer the rifle to the shotgun on a wary gobbler. If a turkey is on a tree, even in broad daylight, it is easily possibly to maneuver oneself into rifle-range of him; but it would be most unusual for the hunter to be able under such circumstances to get within shotgun range. However, there is one exception to this latter statement. If a turkey is in an evergreen, and considers himself well hidden, he may, like a ruffed grouse, let a hunter walk right under him. Occasionally one of these birds will alight on the very crest of a dense tree, rendering himself invisible from the ground.

It is not possible to recommend dogmatically the best gun and the best kind of ammunition for hunting the wild turkey. Much depends on conditions and circumstances. Some hunters prefer a 16-gauge; some prefer a 12. A 28- or a 30-inch barrel affords the best carrying power. The right barrel should be open; the left, modified choke. These suggestions are intended to be merely of a general nature. As to the size of shot, most turkey hunters use 4's in the right-hand barrel and 2's in the left. The wild gobbler is a heavy and powerful bird, and it takes a heavy charge to break him down. If he is in flight, the hunter has to take him as best he can. If he is on the ground, and within 30 yards, he can be shot in the head. This bird is peculiarly vulnerable in the head or the neck. A shot in the back is often more effective than one in the breast. If a turkey's wing is broken, the chances are that he will make good his escape, especially in brush. However, if his leg is broken, he will stay where he comes to ground; and a good bird dog can find him without much trouble. A hen can rise readily from the ground, but a big gobbler always has to make a short run for a takeoff. If one leg is injured, he cannot do this. If a hunter breaks a turkey's leg, he should make a patient search for him; for if the bird spends one or two nights on the ground, a fox or a wildcat is almost certain to pick him up. So heavy is the scent of this game bird that often, especially if he has been severely shot, a man can locate him by smell, if conditions be right.

The successful turkey hunter will study untiringly the habits of this grand game bird, and especially will he familiarize himself with its favorite foods. In the colder months, which naturally correspond with the season for hunting him, he feeds chiefly on acorns, beechnuts, mast, gallberries, sparkleberries, various grains gleaned along the edges of fields, dogwood berries, and those of the sumac, gum, and green briar. He is also very fond of anything green or tender. Gobblers have been killed that have nothing in their crops but fresh blades of marshgrass.

The wild turkey at times is almost semi-aquatic. He wades through watery swamps, and is a good swimmer. As a rule, he is shy of dry thickets, where his worst enemies are likely to lurk; but he goes quite readily into dense canebrakes and marshes if they are wet. If a hunter ever sees the birds go into such a place, he can make sure they will either stop as soon as they are hidden, or will travel very slowly. If he runs into them in such cover, some of the birds will flush and afford him some shots. Under all ordinary circumstances, the best way not to get a shot at a wild turkey is to run at it.

The hunter of the wild turkey should know that this bird, while readily surviving below-zero temperatures, hates rain and fog and general dampness. On dark rainy days turkeys may stay on the roost for hours after sunrise; and even if they come to ground, they move about very little, moping under whatever bushes or beside whatever trees give them shelter. If they travel, they will follow trails, log-roads, or any open ground that takes them away from the wet bushes that they dislike so much. Indeed, in any kind of weather wild turkeys like old roads. In former days when grain was hauled to market along forest roads, a certain amount of wheat and corn used to be spilled. Wild turkeys soon found out about this, and haunted the roads. Backwoodsmen soon found out about the turkeys, and used to waylay them along these woodland highways.

It is difficult to say whether the hunting of wild turkeys is more arduous in the mountains or in the swamps of the low flat lands. Each locality has its objections. At times, in the mountains, turkeys will make a marathon flight that they will never make in level country. Taking off from the crest of a lofty ridge, they may fly across a valley a mile wide, and far up on the slope of the mountain opposite. The hunter of the moununtains has to contend with these long flights and with the roughness of the terrain; the hunter of the swamps has to contend with thickets and morasses. While turkeys love to roam along the banks of wooded rivers, it is often disappointing to hunt them close to an impassable stream, for at the first sign of danger they will betake them to the opposite bank. It is not, however, a difficult matter for a skillful caller to lure scattered birds across a river, however wide. It is one of the grandest sights in nature to see an old gobbler flying across a broad river.

At such a time the turkey's flight is likely to be low; and as this bird has a most remarkable sense of direction, and can locate, at a considerable distance, the exact position of a caller, the hunter who persuades one to fly across water to him is almost sure to be afforded a chance for a wing shot. The chief difficulty will probably be that the great bird will come straight for him. When any kind of game comes too directly for the hunter, especially if he is coming at 30 miles an hour, a real problem of marksmanship is created.

While both the whitetail deer and the bobwhite apparently become used to the peaceful noises of farms, and even to the uproar of a sawmill, the wild turkey hates noise, especially the noise man makes. He appears to be more sensitive to it than any other game bird we have in America. He is a lover of solitude and of silence, so that as man advances, he retreats farther and farther into the wilderness, where all sounds are the sounds of nature, not of civilization.

The hunter of the wild turkey must therefore expect to pursue his game into rough country, often far from home; and he has to be skilled as a patient and a silent hunter. He should be a keen listener, content to wait for hours if necessary until he hears those characteristic sounds that betray the presence of the birds near him. He need not expect them to call unless they are scattered; but a flock will do a good deal of subdued talking while feeding through the forest. The scratching of a flock can be heard for a considerable distance; and if a flock is busily feeding, it is often possible, if there is sufficient cover to hide him, and he creeps up noiselessly, for the hunter to get within sight of the birds, but very rarely within range, unless he is using a rifle. If it is impossible for him to get close enough for a shot, he will have to do some careful and strategic maneuvering. To achieve success under such circumstances calls for dextrous and sagacious woodcraft. The hunter must try to figure the general direction in which the turkeys are feeding. Then he must make a long detour, crafty and silent, and take up a position to waylay them on their approach.

Various methods of hunting wild turkeys have been mentioned, and different types of calls have been described. There is one type of call that demands some daring on the part of the hunter, but at times it is highly effective. It may seem fantastic, yet is not more so than the "rattling of horns" that deer hunters in Texas and Arkansas are accustomed to using for the luring of a buck.

If a gobbler is just out of range of the hunter, and will not come any nearer, the hunter should take his hat and beat sharply on his coat or the leg of his trousers, making a noise that imitates two gobblers fighting. If he does this, he must be very alert; for if the great bird decides to come, he will probably come running fast to the very spot where the hunter is. And, as has been said, he is an expert at locating the exact place whence a sound emanates.

In waiting for wild turkeys, a man has to be a good deal more cautious than he is in waiting for a deer. If a hunter does not move, and the wind is in his favor, he may reasonably expect a deer to come within easy range, even if he is just standing against a tree or rock. But the wild turkey's eyes are among the keenest in all nature; and when one is expected to approach, the hunter should hide himself as completely as possible. So ready is the wild turkey to detect in the woods what does not belong there that in the old days, when turkeys used to be shot from blinds, these blinds had to be built with extreme caution. They had to be constructed a little at a time. If a blind were built in a day, a wild turkey would never come near it. It had to be made with such a degree of deliberation that it had the semblance of growing.

Of all the watches set by wild game, that of the wild turkey is one of the very best. As sensitive to sound as he is to sight, his wariness is of the hair-trigger variety. Woodsmen who have often observed them feeding, always notice that a flock is never without a sentinel—trim, alert, his serpentine head and neck almost rigid. This same guard or outpost is usaully to be seen with a flock of turkeys traveling through the woods, sometimes two or three taking it upon themselves to act as warders. One hunter reports once watching an old gobbler taking a dust-bath; beside him stood another, doubtless his partner in many adventures and escapes. Finally the first gobbler arose, shaking clouds of dust and little feathers from him. Thereupon he took up the sentry business, while his companion relaxed in the sand for his bath.

The hunter of these bronzed monarchs of the hills and the swamps need have no misgiving about killing one. According to the present law in most states, only gobblers may be shot. They have for some years been on the increase. At the close of every season, at least in most parts of the country, there are plenty of gobblers left for breeding. But the main reason why the hunter can justify his pastime is that this bird is just about the most difficult in the whole world to hunt. Of course, even an amateur may stumble on one; but as a rule this sport exacts from the woodsman the maximum of patience, endurance, intelligence, and woodcraft. And it is certain that any sport that lays down these exactions is a splendid and manly type of recreation to have in these days when too many men expect to get their game with no more effort on their part than to pull a trigger with a lazy and effete finger.

# AMERICAN WOODCOCK *Philohela minor*

COMMON NAMES: Bar-Capped Snipe, Big-Eyes, Big-Eyed John, Big-Headed Snipe, Big Mudsnipe, Big Snipe, Blind Snipe, Bog Bird, Bogsucker (Canada), Briar Snipe, Hill Partridge, Hokumpake, John Timberdoodle, Labrador Twister, Little Whistler, Marsh Plover, Mudsnipe, Night Becasse, Night Flit, Night Peck (North Carolina), Owl Snipe, Red-Breasted Snipe, Swamp Partridge, Whistling Snipe, Wall-Eyed Snipe, Woodcock, Woodhen, Woodsnipe.

**History.** The American woodcock, although generally classed as an upland game bird, is in reality a member of the snipe clan. He belongs to the family *Scolopacidae,* and is thus a close relative of the sandpipers, snipe, godwits, yellow-legs, curlews, and willets. Forsaking the usual habitat of his family group, he took to the uplands and a more solitary existence. He retained, however, the same general structure as the jacksnipe and the sandsnipers but developed an aldermanic belly which makes him heavier than either of them. He was not so much disturbed by the encroachments of agriculture as some other species; in fact, he thrives near cultivated land. Drainage and deforestation, however, have destroyed many of his former feeding grounds.

The scientific name *Philohela* means, literally, "swamp lover," while the *minor* indicates that he is smaller than the European variety which he resembles. The name woodcock was derived from the old English name, "wude-cocc," or "wudu-coc," but so far as is known the American woodcock was always native to North America. There is but one species in this country although occasional stragglers from Europe do reach the Atlantic coast. The European woodcock, *Scolopax rusticola rusticola,* is similar in habits and appearance but much larger. His wings are barred with reddish-brown and the under parts have barrings of black.

A glance at the common names listed above will show a profusion of colloquial and local terms by which this bird is known. It has been said that he has a different name or names in every locality where he occurs. Sportsmen and ornithologists have known *of* him since the earliest days of settlement in America, but all too little is known *about* him.

To this day his presence in a community is often unsuspected or unrecognized except by sportsmen and students of birdlife. Small wonder, then, that few references to woodcock appear in the early writings about game birds. He was not an easy bird to shoot with ancient flintlocks and was difficult to snare or trap. When taken he provided little food in comparison with birds much easier to obtain, and hence he escaped general notice. He was known to a few epicures as a delicacy and was eaten by the Indians, although how they managed to kill the little brown ghost is not recorded.

The "timberdoodle" was among the first game birds to be granted legal protection in America. In the late 1700's a game law was enacted prohibiting the killing of woodcock, heath-hen, quail, or partridge within the City of New York. Unfortunately the law was too limited in scope.

Judging from what records are available, the woodcock were abundant in the early 1800's. Game books of that period carry notations of daily bags averaging 50 to 60 birds. The sport of woodcock shooting did not become popular before 1830, or possibly later. As better and more efficient guns were developed more and more attention was centered on this delicious morsel of game.

Gradually it became the pernicious practice of gunners to do most of their cock shooting during the summer. During July the young birds were slaughtered by the thousands. This wanton killing was carried on by market gunners who found ready sale at one to two dollars a pair for all the birds they could deliver. As late as 1874 it was estimated that the New York markets alone took nearly 2000 birds weekly. Early sportsmen and conservationists deplored this summer shooting but for many years their protests were of no avail. By the time they succeeded in getting protective laws against the evils of indiscriminate killing the woodcock population had been sadly depleted.

It is impossible to protect the woodcock against the many hazards which menace his existence. The Federal Migratory Bird Act limits the open season in each zone, usually to two weeks, but John Timberdoodle is a restless bird and is apt to fly from one zone to another and thus be legal game from four to six weeks each year.

His worst enemy, the weather, cannot be regulated. Other causes which take a regular annual toll cannot be controlled. The woodcock flies at low altitude and during migration many are killed by striking electric wires, cables, buildings, lighthouses, radio towers, and other objects. It is suggested that the birds may be nearsighted, which would account for the number of fatalities caused in this manner.

Forest fires claim many birds and nests each year. The hen is reluctant to leave her nest for any reason and is often trapped by the flames.

Natural enemies account for some deaths although not for as many as might be expected. The common house cat is the worst offender and kills more woodcock annually than any other predator.

To offset the rather gloomy picture given above the woodcock has certain advantages over other game birds. His highly secretive ways and nocturnal habits afford him better protection than either the quail or the grouse. Nesting results are almost 100 per cent successful because the eggs are rarely infertile. Mortality among the young is comparatively low; so it is not unlikely that each pair of adult woodcock contributes an average of two or three birds which reach maturity annually. It is fortunate that this is so because the birds do not breed in captivity, nor can their eggs be hatched by artificial incubation like those of the pheasant.

Owing to the migratory habits and the difficulty of determining the number of birds in a given area at any one time, it is next to impossible to compile an accurate census of the present population. Efforts at banding have not been particularly successful so far. Then, too, the woodcock population is likely to fluctuate from year to year depending on the weather. Efforts are being made to obtain a better estimate of their present numbers. From the figures available it appears that, while far from plentiful, the timberdoodle is holding his own and with proper management may be expected to increase in numbers.

**Identification.** In general appearance the woodcock is a compact brown, black, and cinnamon ball with scarcely any tail and an uncommonly long nose and bill. The crown and forehead slope sharply downward and give the head a pointed appearance which is further accentuated by the prominent shoebutton eyes set high and to the rear of the skull. In some respects he resembles his close relative the snipe but is heavier and stockier. Despite his unusual physical characteristics he escapes being grotesque and is really a good-looking bird. (See color plate on page 482.

In detail the coloration is as follows: The forehead and crown are a light bluish-gray washed with buff. An indistinct dark line divides the forehead in the center and another dusky line runs from the bill to the eye. The eye is very dark, prominent, and lustrous. It is encircled by a narrow line of white and a dusky line continues from behind the eye down the side of the head. Three nearly square patches of black extend from the crown down the back of the neck, each being separated from the other by a narrow band of bluish-gray. The sides of the head are a buffy-brown with a dusky streak where the head joins the neck. The chin is whitish and generally the sides of the neck are grayish, tinged with light reddish-brown.

The back, rump, and wing coverts are finely blended in a sort of dead-leaf pattern with black, russet, and warm brown, the brown being the dominant color. Two gray streaks appear above and below the shoulders running laterally along the body. The upper streaks almost meet across the lower back. The upper sides of the breast at the shoulders are marked with dusky crescents. All the feathers on the upper body are margined and tipped with slate-gray, buff, or ochre and create an irregular mottled design which results in perfect camouflage when the bird is on the ground.

The tail is black with gray tipping above. The under tail coverts are a paler cinnamon to orange and the tail feathers end in silvery-white below.

The breast is reddish-brown or cinnamon. The under parts are pale reddish-brown and buff ochre, as are the thighs.

The long, grooved bill is a dull flesh color, dark along the upper ridge and at the tip. The legs and feet are a dull pinkish flesh color.

All the wing coverts are finely mottled with light and dark brown. A narrow grayish band separates the middle from the greater coverts. The first three primaries are little more than quills, being very narrow and stiff. The rest of the primaries are plain dusky but the secondaries are marked along the front edge with brownish-gray.

Both sexes are similar in appearance but the males are generally darker in coloration. The females are almost invariably larger and heavier than the males, and also have longer bills. A rule of thumb followed by most gunners is that if the upper mandible measures 2¾ inches from tip to base the bird is a female; if less than 2½ inches the bird is a male. It is well to remember, however, that only averages can be given and there are exceptions in every case. Positive determination of sex can be made only by dissection.

**Characteristics.** Few American game birds are shrouded in more mystery than the woodcock. A shy, secretive fellow, he sits quietly in some shadowed retreat during the day and waits until twilight to begin foraging for food. His nocturnal wanderings offer little chance to study his ways but from what has been learned he is one of the most interesting of birds.

He is gentle, mild mannered, not so gregarious as some species but willing to live at peace with his own kind and others. In his natural state he could hardly be called tame but his reliance on protective coloration and habit of "freezing" until almost stepped on only makes him appear less wild than the grouse and some other birds. He does become tame in captivity, however, and will then accept food that is handed to him. He walks proudly erect with his bill pointed downward except when he uses it to push some slight obstacle out of his way. When scared or cornered he raises and spreads his tail. Occasionally he bobs up and down while walking, but this is accomplished by bending the legs rather than tilting the body like a sandpiper. This bobbing trait, which is especially noticeable in the hen bird and young, is probably a reaction to unrest and concern for their safety.

Generally speaking, the woodcock is either on the ground or in the air. Isolated reports credit him with perching in a tree or elsewhere on occasion but it is certainly not a common habit.

He is a hardy bird and can endure a great deal of cold providing his food supply is not frozen under. Many birds have been known to remain all winter in the northern latitudes although as a rule they prefer a moderate clime. They are free from disease, as far as can be determined, and do not seem to suffer from infectious epidemics. Early observers of the woodcock held the belief that the birds fed by "suction." They noted the long bill thrust into the ground in a series of "borings," as the holes are called, and assumed that the birds drew up some form of nourishment from the earth. It is quite possible that the term "bogsucker" originated from this belief. Later it was learned that the long flexible bill was both a probe and forceps with which the timberdoodle extracted his food from the soft earth. The upper mandible is unique in that it can be moved independently of the lower like a finger. The lower end of the bill is well supplied with nerves and is so sensitive that with it the woodcock can distinguish food which is edible from that which is not, even when well below the surface.

As an adjunct to his sensitive bill the woodcock possesses very acute hearing. His ears are located directly below his eyes rather than behind them as commonly among most other birds. While feeding he walks along with his head cocked to one side like a robin until he hears a stirring in the earth beneath him. Guided by this sound he thrusts his bill up to its base, or even slightly beyond, into the moist earth. From then on it is a question whether he relies on the sense of touch or hearing to locate his quarry. Probably it is a little of both. Feeding birds have been observed to remain motionless with the bill in the ground as though listening.

but it is equally possible that they were trying to detect further movement through vibration. The theory has been advanced that worms in motion send out vibratory waves which register on the bill as though it were an antenna.

If the first probe fails to locate his prey, the woodcock withdraws his bill and plunges it in again a short distance away. Once found, the forcep-like upper mandible grasps the worm and holds it as the bill is withdrawn, and then the worm or grub is eaten with apparent relish.

As might be expected with so valuable an instrument, the woodcock takes great care of his bill. When through feeding he cleans it with his toes and wipes it on leaves or moss.

It is estimated that the average bird consumes nearly twice his weight in food nightly. His digestive tract is geared to keep pace with this inordinate appetite, and this explains the copious white droppings found wherever there are "borings"—a sure sign of woodcock.

The timberdoodle cannot get along on short rations as can some other creatures of the wild. For this reason the weather plays a very important part in the rise and fall of the woodcock population. These birds are among the first to leave the feeding grounds in the South and many of them arrive on the northern breeding grounds in March or early April. Sometimes late snows and freeze-ups cut off their food supply in these localities and the birds die of starvation. Often, too, nesting has begun by this time and untimely snow storms cause high nesting losses. Unseasonable freeze-ups in the southern feeding range likewise produce starvation. During protracted droughts, when the ground becomes hard and dry, the young birds cannot find their quota of worms and this often results in untimely death for many of them.

The woodcock's fondness for earthworms leads him to frequent low, wooded bottomlands. The banks of a small stream or creek bordered with alders or birches are much to his liking. A wooded bog where the black muck holds his favorite food is also likely to attract him. These are his haunts by night, but during the day he is as likely to be found on a dry, sunny hillside.

During the August moult he loses the power of flight and is virtually helpless. Well aware that his short legs cannot carry his fat body out of danger, he retires to the thickest brush or deep into a large cornfield and hides until his plumage is restored.

The fact that he gives off little scent in comparison to other game doubtless aids him in concealing his whereabouts at this time as well as throughout the rest of the year.

Generally his voice is of no help in locating him because he is, for the most part, silent. Only during the breeding season does he give vent to his feelings vocally. At that time both sexes utter a subdued cackling sound suggestive of the quacks of a female mallard much reduced in volume. The cock has a few special notes which he reserves for courtship, and his only other sound comes when he is frightened and flushed.

Several attempts have been made to prove that the peculiar twittering whistle of a flushed bird is vocal instead of being caused by a rush of air through the stiff, curved primaries. Heated arguments on the subject have led nowhere and opinion is fairly well divided. Much evidence can be advanced to support either theory, but one point, at least, has been established. The woodcock can and does utter a vocal sound almost identical to that made by the rapid wing-beat, and so it is difficult to decide which is which.

Unless flushed from his resting place the woodcock seldom, if ever, flies during the daytime. When forced to take wing he does so with a twisting, dodging flight that is deceptive as to speed. Perhaps the most frequent tactic is to fly straight up until he clears the treetops and then level off on a fairly straight line above the cover for from 50 to 200 yards. The distance which a bird will fly after being flushed is governed somewhat by how high he rises. If he flushes from tall cover his horizontal flight is usually longer than if he pitches up from low bushes.

Generally at the end of his flight he zig-zags into the next cover with a twisting, erratic motion to avoid striking trees or branches. This pitch into the trees or cover is often so sudden that it appears as though the bird had been hurt.

Despite the wide range of vision furnished by his peculiarly set eyes, the woodcock is generally credited with poor eyesight, at least in certain lights. He frequently flies into objects which other birds avoid and he sometimes becomes entangled in the branches when flushed. It is doubtless for this reason that he prefers to fly through the largest opening in the cover, although at times he may flit away through fairly dense growth.

The speed of flight varies with conditions and the ability of the bird. Large hens usually get up more slowly and fly more deliberately, while the males coming down from Nova Scotia and other breeding grounds in the late fall have earned the name "Labrador twisters" because of their rapid, dodging flight.

The woodcock's most outstanding demonstration of his flight powers occurs during the mating season when he puts on an aerial exhibition that is both unique and remarkable.

The male selects the breeding and nesting area, and, being somewhat a creature of habit, it is not uncommon for him to return to the same area year after year. The site chosen nearly always provides a feeding area, some cover for protection, and cleared spots for singing grounds. The latter may be any bare space such as a pasture, plowed land, meadow, or even an old road. Sometimes the breeding site may contain two or more singing grounds fairly close together. These are for the exclusive use of one male, however, and other males respect his title to the area. Rarely will another cock set up a breeding area within a distance less than 100 yards.

Having selected his breeding site, the cock then attempts to attract a mate by a combination of aerial maneuvers and "song." Just after dawn and again at dusk he goes to one of his singing grounds and performs a regular routine. While strutting about he keeps up a subdued whimpering broken at few-second intervals by a nasal "*peent.*"

Suddenly he takes off on a spiral ascent accompanied by the usual twittering sound that he makes when flushed. As he soars in a widening spiral this note changes to a clear, tremulous call until he reaches a height somewhere between 100 and 300 feet directly over the point of take-off. He then pitches abruptly toward the ground in a series of zigzag dives and twists and his song changes to a sharp *"chip, chip."* As he nears the ground he slows his dive and flutters in for a gentle landing. As soon as he lands he resumes his strutting and begins to *"peent"* again. His exhibition flight lasts about one minute and is repeated about every four or five minutes.

When a hen is attracted by these antics she sits on the ground in apparent admiration and between spasmodic flights the male struts pompously before her, tail erect, and wings fanning as they both give utterance to the peculiar whimpering or whining sound. Once the female has been attracted the male usually stops "peenting," or calls it less frequently, and takes up a new note, a pigeonlike *"tuk-oo."*

During the early stages of his courtship the male is so engrossed with the affairs at hand that he loses much of his usual caution. He may be approached at close range and sometimes displays an utter disregard for intrusion on his privacy. If flushed he returns as close as possible to the original spot and continues his routine.

Males are generally believed to be monogamous although they often use more than one singing ground to attract a female. Since they arrive on the breeding grounds early in April the birds have usually mated by May and the courtship flights gradually give way to nesting. By mid-May the breeding grounds are virtually silent and the cock resumes his shy, retiring habits.

**Breeding.** One nesting a season is general, but if a second one becomes necessary it is usual for the same courtship routine to be repeated.

The nest is always on the ground and usually in a swamp thicket or on a dry spot near a small stream. In any case it is well hidden, generally by brush or under protecting roots. It is made of dead leaves, dried grass, and small twigs fashioned in a rather haphazard manner, perhaps purposely so in order to blend with its surroundings. Occasionally nests have been found in quite open terrain but one of the most favored sites is along the edges of a wooded tract.

The eggs, in common with those of other shore birds, are larger at one end than the other. They are a light pinkish-brown sprinkled with deep brown and pale gray on the larger end. Invariably four in number, they are usually deposited about the first of May but may be laid earlier if conditions are favorable. As a rule the hens are sitting before May is far advanced.

The period of incubation is 20 to 21 days, and during that time the hen rarely leaves the nest except for brief intervals to feed. She will permit approach close enough to take pictures and often will submit to being touched by the hand rather than desert her eggs. When she does take flight it is seldom for any great distance and she returns to the nest as soon as possible. If annoyed too often she may abandon the nest permanently and begin another, but this rarely happens. Occasionally she resorts to the "broken-wing" trick and flutters from the nest as though badly injured in an attempt to draw the intruder away. At such times she frequently utters a low squealing or squeaking sound to attract attention to herself.

Robie W. Tufts.

PLATE I. The Woodcock depends on camouflage.

Whether or not the male aids in incubation is another controversial point. Some naturalists contend that the male covers the eggs while the hen is feeding, others believe he has nothing to do with raising the family. There seems to be no proof for either side of the argument.

The downy young are a pale yellowish-buff with markings of deep warm brown on the upper parts. Except for the long bill and the characteristic placement of the eyes, they resemble young bantam chicks but are somewhat smaller.

The young leave the nest soon after hatching but the mother broods, or shelters them under her feathers for a few days. Another subject always good for a spirited debate is: Does the woodhen transport her young from place to place? Those who hold to the affirmative in this case claim to have witnessed the act. Apparently the method of carrying was not fully determined but it appeared that the young chick was held securely between her thighs. It is claimed that the hen does this to remove her brood to a place of safety or to take them to a distant feeding ground. Opposed to this statement are competent ornithologists who have studied woodcock habits for a considerable time. Naturally it is difficult to prove conclusively that she does or does not. It would seem that one would have to see her do it in order to be sure.

The young mature rapidly and in about two weeks are capable of short flights. At one month they are self-reliant and at the end of six months are not only identical to their parents but sometimes weigh more. The flight of immature birds is not so strong as that of the more vigorous adult.

Generally the young birds and their parents remain together from hatching time until early autumn.

**Range and Distribution.** The woodcock is found chiefly in the Atlantic seaboard states but occurs spottily from northern Manitoba, northern Saskatchewan, Alberta, Washington, California, Idaho, Montana, eastward through all the states. It is probable that breeding takes place in every state east of the Mississippi River. The most important nesting areas are Nova Scotia, New Brunswick, Maine, Ontario, and Pennsylvania.

A great many birds winter in Louisiana and Alabama, and some travel as far south as Bermuda and Jamaica. A few remain as far north as New Jersey and the Ohio Valley.

The southern migration usually begins in September, after the first frost, and the flights are most frequent on moonlight nights. The main southern flight is generally in October and the birds seem to pause in the same cover year after year.

**Hunting Methods.** The American woodcock is rapidly becoming one of our important game birds. Ten years ago, the woodcock hunters in this country were relatively few. Today, men who would not have recognized a woodcock two or three years ago are active woodcock hunters. This increased interest tends to work a double hardship on the old-timers who used to have the alder thickets pretty much to themselves. Not only has gunning pressure increased greatly; overcrowded—by gunners, not birds—covers have made it necessary for the seasoned gunners to go farther afield in search of new and unfrequented shooting grounds.

Strangely enough, increased gunning pressure seems not to have affected the woodcock population adversely. Today their numbers have increased to the point where the total estimated figures compare quite favorably with those of 1936 or 1937—the years immediately preceding the big winter freeze-up of the southern wintering areas during which uncounted millions of woodcock were lost.

**Guns.** The choice of a gun is a matter which can be left quite safely to individual tastes. A woodcock is an easy bird to kill and the annual cripple loss is very low. Thus, density of pattern is not such a critical factor as it is with grouse or pheasant. This reduces the choice to a matter of ability. The small-bore fans, who use the 28 gauge and the .410, obviously must be good shots in order to score. They maintain that they prefer a clean miss or a clean kill, with few or no birds "scratched down."

The opposing 12-gauge school of thought is of the opinion that a gun is pointed at something which the man who holds it wishes to kill. The wider pattern and the larger number of pellets in a 12 gauge gives the hunter a greater factor of safety and, as a consequence, fewer misses. To be sure, the 12 gauge weighs more and is comparatively cumbersome to handle in close cover, but it is a more effective weapon.

While an open bore unquestionably gives the widest of patterns for a brush gun, the pellet distribution is apt to be ragged. It is better, perhaps, to use an improved cylinder for the right barrel which throws a pattern of about 35% and a modified barrel for the left, giving about a 45% distribution. These two chokes are open enough so that birds shot at close range will not be mutilated, and they are close and uniform enough to prevent having a bird filter through the pattern at longer ranges.

For a number of years, the single trigger was quite popular on double guns. Now the trend is away from single triggers and back to double triggers again, as the instant selectivity of the latter makes them preferable to a great many gunners. If the gun is stocked with a straight grip, there need be no change of hand position when shifting from one trigger to the other and accuracy is not affected.

Although many gunners use autoloaders in the woodcock thickets, there is no question that this type of gun is unsuited to the woodcock covers. The ideal gun is the double with barrels either parallel or over-under, 26 to 28 inches in length. Double guns are shorter, more easily handled, lighter, and, unless the individual is an outstanding performer, appreciably faster for snap shooting.

While some men use shot as large as No. 7½ or 8 for woodcock, the ideal load is the field load with No. 9 or No. 10 shot. This load is fast and the smaller shot increases pattern density with the resultant build-up in multiple-pellet shock. High-speed loads, with, in the 12 gauge, 3¾ drams of powder or its equivalent, have no place in the woodcock covers.

**Dogs.** While non-pointing dogs, such as cocker and springer spaniels and the retrievers, can be used on woodcock, pointing dogs are by far the more practical. With the non-pointing varieties many shots are apt to be lost in close cover through the inability of the gunner to keep within range of the dog. With a dependable pointing dog, the gunner can take his time. Usually a woodcock is a close sitter and few shots are lost because the gunner is not directly behind his dog, provided, of course, that the dog is stanch and well broken. Avoid wide-ranging "skyline busters" for woodcock. Get a good pointer or English setter that hunts to the gun and stays always within easy reach. A bell on the dog's collar enables the gunner to know at all times the exact location of his dog. Also, the dog should be taught to retrieve, as many times a bird will fall in swamp water or a briar tangle where the gunner will have an uncomfortable time of it if he must do his own retrieving.

A great many men prefer to hunt without dogs and to "walk up" and "brush out" their own birds. While this makes sporty shooting, unquestionably it makes woodcock hunting a pretty strenuous piece of business. No doubt about it—a hunting dog is a great saver of steps. In country that is overrun with briars, a great many birds will be bypassed purely because no sane gunner is willing to have the clothes literally torn off him while he is brushing out a thick briar patch. In briar country, a dog really is a necessity.

**Clothing.** Thought should be given to the matter of clothing if a man is to be comfortable while he is hunting woodcock. In October the weather usually is warm enough for cotton shirts or, at most, lightweight flannel. These, with a selection of three weights of woolen overshirts, will take care of the above-the-waist requirements. Hunting shirts are loose, full-cut, and have large patch pockets. They do not snag seriously on brush or briars and they allow plenty of variation in weight. *Don't* wear a sweater or a close-fitting garment of any kind.

Underwear should be, preferably, of light-weight wool and as loose as possible. Woodcock hunting is likely to be strenuous if the going is heavy and this means that the gunner is going to perspire. It is all too easy to catch cold in damp cotton underwear, whereas wool will keep a man warm and reasonably dry.

A great deal of woodcock shooting is done over wet ground. Thus, waterproof footwear should be worn. The best compromise is rubber foot-leather top boots, not over 10 inches high. These keep the feet dry and do not bind the calves of the legs. For sure foot comfort, wear a light pair of socks next the skin and fill out the shoe with a pair of heavy wool oversocks. These latter cushion the feet and take up condensation so that the undersocks come out dry at the end of the day.

Suitable shooting pants are a problem. Avoid as you would the plague the heavy drill shooting pants that are offered by most of the sporting goods stores. You know the sort—"plywood pants." After much experimentation many hunters have decided that about the best woodcock pants are the Army-reject "fatigue" pants that are available at any of the army surplus stores. It is quite possible to wear out a pair of these in a season but they are inexpensive, light, and flexible, and the two latter factors are the ones that count most.

For headgear, a baseball cap with the button removed from the top (to avoid complications with brush) is about the most satisfying. Once on, it will stay on, and the visor provides shade and protection from brush and twigs.

By all means wear shooting glasses. Far too many eye injuries are the direct result of failure to take this simple and elementary precaution.

Although shooting gloves of light leather may be somewhat warm in October, they will save your hands from a great many scratches and cuts during the course of a season.

Do not afflict yourself with a shooting coat. All that you need is a skeleton shooting vest to carry your shells and your birds. Better still for warm days is one of the new shooting belts that come equipped with a shell pocket and nylon loops to carry birds.

**General.** Time was when much of the woodcock shooting each season was done in bottom lands, along streams, and among stands of black alder, sycamore, and willow. This sort of cover produces woodcock, no doubt about that. But the job of forcing your way through the endless tangles of low brush is a back-breaking chore at best. Often you will find days when the birds seem to prefer that type of cover to any other and, if you want birds, you must endure the heavy tangles of the bottom lands, but that sort of hunting is tiresome in the extreme and not very much fun.

Better by far are the hillsides and the top covers. To be sure, the birds are more scattered in these covers, but the ease with which they can be hunted makes up for the extra walking. Throughout most of the northern woodcock range, there are many deserted farms. You will find many of these in the highlands. Unsound farming methods, with resultant loss of rich top soil, wear out a highland farm in a matter of 25 or 30 years. After the fertility of the soil is reduced to the point where the operation of the farm is no longer profitable, the farmer closes up his home, moves to other territory, and the fallow fields soon take on a scattered growth of weed trees such as birch, aspen, hawthorn, and wild crab. While these trees are growing, the untended land covers itself with a yearly crop of matted grass and weed which holds moisture and makes ideal feeding territory for woodcock. When the saplings are 10 or 15 feet tall, that is when the birds claim such cover for their own.

It is not difficult to find. Just drive about along the old roads of the back country, preferably on the higher ground. You should have little trouble locating deserted farms where the saplings have sprung up in the old fields. For some reason, not all of these will hold birds, but a great many of them will. Devote some time to cover searches before the woodcock season arrives. Often you will get some pleasant surprises, as the resident birds of your area will use these high covers, flying from the bottom lands, evidently for a change of diet in the type of worms to be found in such places.

There is one bad feature about such covers. All too soon the fast-growing trees become too high. Gradually, the woodcock leave them for new feeding grounds and, eventually, these areas become grouse cover. Thus, it is wise to keep an eye open for stands of young growth that may be good two, three, five, or ten years hence. For example, one high cover in central Pennsylvania, which once gave excellent shooting, in five years grew up to the point where only a few scattered woodcock used it.

When you are looking over new hillside and top covers, pay particular attention to ground growth. If the ground is covered with a mat of ground pine, forget it. Never yet has this sort of ground coverage produced consistently good woodcock shooting. The creeper types of dewberry and "black cap" briars also should be avoided. Better by far is grass—poverty grass, crab grass, and, best of all, Canada blue grass that grows lush and green well into the winter. If you can find a deserted farm with its abandoned fields sprinkled with aspen and birch saplings and ground coverage of lush, green grass, there, too, you probably will find birds.

As a general rule, all of the deserted farms that you will find had their own apple orchards. These are rugged trees which manage to hold their own against the encroachments of sapling growth, and their dense summer shade makes an ideal spot for a ground coverage of lush, green grass. It may be, also, that the many yearly crops of ungathered, rotted fruit builds up a soil condition that is attractive to earthworms. Be that as it may, you will almost always find birds in these old orchards. Search them out, hunt them carefully, and cherish them for the gems that they are. Year after year they will give you good shooting.

Strangely enough, not all hillside and top covers hold birds. It is quite possible to find beautiful covers, grown to the proper height, paved with lush underfooting—perfect, all save one thing. Year after year they will be empty of birds. Why this should be so is difficult to determine, but the birds show a marked preference for some covers while others continue to remain empty. To the eye of the hunter they may be as like as two peas in a pod but to the eye of a woodcock they must present a radically different appearance.

You must remember, when looking for woodcock cover, that more than 85 per cent of a woodcock's diet consists of angleworms. Thus, the ground under any stand of likely-looking saplings must be such that angleworms can live in it. While most varieties of angleworms make their homes in the ground, there are some that live in matted grass roots and leaf mold. There is one tiny black breed which takes up its residence in the fall between the matted grass and the overlay of freshly fallen leaves. Next time you shoot a stand of aspen saplings, take time to turn over the leaves on the ground. Usually you will find an ample supply of these little black worms lying between the leaves and the bed of grass. The woodcock know about this and generally avail themselves of this easily found meal.

When you are looking at new cover in anticipation of the coming shooting season, it is not vital that you actually find birds therein. Look the ground over carefully for telltale woodcock "signs"—borings and, more easily seen, woodcock droppings, which whitewash anything they touch. In case you are not familiar with the appearance of markings it will not take you long to recognize them at a glance. Even though the birds have gone, they always leave their calling cards.

Although it is not of absolute, critical importance, it is always best to keep in mind, when searching for woodcock cover, the fact that woodcock are migratory birds, moving from north to south. The north-south valleys generally hold more birds than the east-west valleys. Frequently a range of mountains will influence the direction of the flights. Take, for illustration, the Bald Eagle range which extends, roughly, from Williamsport to Tyrone in central Pennsylvania. The general trend of this mountain range is from northeast to southwest. From late August until mid-December of each year this range of mountains has a decided influence on the flight of birds coming from the north. Woodcock, in their migration flights, fly comparatively close to the ground. Thus, when a mountain range of considerable proportions bars their way, they will, if the deviation be not too extreme, bend their flight lanes to conform to the topography. Generally you will find abandoned farms and overgrown fallow fields in such a valley, as the slope of the land tends to erode away its top soil in relatively few years of farming. In the Bald Eagle valley, it has been estimated that there is a transient woodcock population, when the flights are on, of from 80,000 to 100,000 birds. Throughout the 80-odd miles between Tyrone and Lock Haven, Pa., there extends along the lower slope of Bald Eagle Mountain a bench formation that varies from 100 yards to a quarter of a mile in width. This bench land originally was cleared and made into farms. Over the years soil erosion took its inevitable toll and gradually reduced this bench land to a state of unproductivity. Crop farming no longer being profitable, the land was then used as pasturage. Eventually sapling growth established itself and, in due course, an almost continuous strip of woodcock cover developed. Today a great deal of this land has matured into second-growth woodland, but here and there excellent woodcock covers are spotted. These covers, being handy to ideal feeding grounds along the creek bottom, make ideal resting stations for transient birds. All that is needful to find good shooting is to locate the areas which have good ground coverage and the right stage of sapling growth.

One of the hazards—at least, to the woodcock hunter—is the danger of overgrazing. Too many cattle in any one area can ruin a cover completely. There is a large cover near the village of Ogdensburg, Pa., which, year after year, produced excellent shooting. Recently the farmer who owns this land surrounded it with an electric fence and turned it over to the ministrations of a considerable herd of cattle. In the short space of three months the entire cover was rendered untenable for birds. To be sure, this overgrazed pasturage soon will be useless for cattle also. Then, when the animals are pastured elsewhere, the ground coverage will come back and with it the birds. Temporarily, however, it is useless for hunting.

Here and there about the country experiments have been conducted to manage and control the growth of certain areas so that they will continue to attract woodcock. There is one such area in Maine. This extensive cover is shot each year by wealthy men who can afford to spend some money to keep their shooting uniformly good. Each winter, all trees that have grown to 25 or 30 feet are cut down and removed. The balance of the cover is thinned out so that it does not become too dense. In addition, clearings are made here and there to serve as singing grounds in the spring of the year so that the area is used annually by many nesting birds. This area has been hunted each year for the past 20 years, and it produces just as good shooting today as it did 20 years ago. Fortunately, a great deal of this area is alder cover which grows so slowly that it makes management methods of this sort practical. To attempt like control of the birch-aspen covers would indeed be a major operation.

A woodcock, nine times out of ten, is a very close sitter. It is not uncommon to find a bird crouching almost under the nose of a pointing dog. The tenth time, however, he is quite apt to lead dog and gunner a merry chase. He will flush wild, far ahead of the dog, run like a pheasant, and behave himself generally in a most unwoodcocklike manner. Because of his tendency to sit tight in close cover, it is an excellent plan to hunt slowly and carefully. It is difficult for a dog to cover the ground thoroughly in front of a fast walker. If you walk slowly, hunting out every foot of the cover, not only will you jump quite a few birds that you might otherwise bypass; also, the dog will have time to do a more workmanlike job for you.

When hunting without a dog, there is a trick that will serve you in good stead. That is change of pace. A bird that is hidden feels secure so long as you walk past him at a constant rate of speed. However, if you stop walking and stand for a moment or so, his sense of security leaves him. Often, merely stopping near his hiding place will cause him to flush, whereas, if you had continued at a set rate of speed, he would have been content to stay hidden.

Have you ever noticed how often a bird will flush while you are climbing a fence? He will stay put until you are in the most awkward position possible for shooting. Then out he goes, leaving you to finish your fence climbing with trimmings of caustic comment. There is a way to avoid such contingencies. When you approach a fence, stop about 10 feet short of it and stand perfectly still for a moment or so. Then walk up to the fence and kick around in the brush, enough to cause a disturbance. Then wait quietly for another minute or two. If no bird has flushed by that time, you are safe to climb your fence in peace.

In every good woodcock cover there are certain spots that seem to be favored by the birds in preference to all others. Thus, when you flush a woodcock, mark the spot in your memory for future reference. The chances are that the next time you hunt that cover you will flush a bird from that identical spot. Usually these places—the "hot spots"—give a woodcock two things that he wants: good protective cover and productive feeding grounds. There is one such place in one of the "top covers" in central Pennsylvania which has not failed to produce either one or two birds each time it has been hunted during the past three seasons. In all, 14 woodcock have been flushed and killed from this little woodland growth during the past three years—and it cannot be more than 6 feet square at most.

For reasons best known to themselves, woodcock show marked cover preferences every now and again. Most of the time you will find them just about where you would expect them to be but now and then they do strange things. For illustration, consider the behavior of the birds in Bald Eagle Valley. Usually they are content to stay either in the alder swales along the creek bottom or in the sapling growth of the overgrown fields on the bench land. Once in a while, however, they desert these two cover types and move into the rocky slopes of the mountain proper which are covered with typical hardwood second-growth trees. Why they do this nobody knows. This type of cover has little, if anything, to offer a woodcock in the nature of food. If the hunter knows of this confusing and contradicting variation in cover selection, all well and good. His not to reason why. He must hunt his birds where they are, not where he would like them to be.

When deciding where to go and what cover types to search, it is advantageous to consider not only the existing conditions but also the sort of weather that has gone before. For that reason, it is an excellent idea to scout your covers during August and September. Equinoctial rains may bring dry covers into perfect condition immediately before the woodcock season, but if those same covers have been bone-dry all summer, the chances are that they will not produce well in the fall.

When hunting the bottom covers, keep in mind that a woodcock does not like to have his feet wet. A cover that is too wet is just about as bad as one that is too dry. Moist ground, in which earthworms can live with comfort, is good. Wet ground, with surface water here and there, makes a bad feeding area.

When the dog goes on point and you or one of your party walks in to flush the bird, it is well to have the guns so placed that one of them is sure to get the shot. Generally speaking, when a woodcock is flushed in heavy cover he "flies to the light." In other words, he is apt to make for the nearest unobstructed opening. Keep that in mind and place the guns accordingly. Of course, a bird will fly contrary to the rules now and then, banging his way through the thickest of the underbrush, but most of them choose the easier course. When you are hunting the edges that fringe the forest proper, you can depend upon it that a flushed bird will, eventually, lose himself among the big trees. Thus, it is well to have a gun spotted between the point of flush and the big woods.

A great many of the writings on woodcock tell us that a flushed bird will tower until he clears the tops of the trees. Then he will level off, fly for a hundred yards or so, and pitch in again. That is all very well as far as it goes. Some of them—a few of them—actually do fly that way, particularly those which are flushed from the thick tangles of the bottom swales. But what of the birds that live on the hillsides and in the top covers? No towering birds there. Their flight varies from a leisurely fluttering pace to a twisting, erratic, bulletlike speed that would make a scared jacksnipe envious. A woodcock has an unusually advantageous power-to-weight ratio. The great bulk of his 8 to 10 ounces is made up of huge pectoral muscles that are capable of driving him at astonishing speeds. A bird that has not been badly frightened loiters along in such a fashion that he makes an easy target. But miss him once or twice, and let him hear the pellets whistling past him, and his next take-off is apt to have the power and drive of a ruffed grouse. A frightened woodcock not only turns on full steam ahead; he will take full advantage of any cover, flying erratically, dodging his way behind screening branches and zig-zagging *through* the weed tops, not over them.

Frequently the question arises about how far a gunner should lead a woodcock in quartering flight. That makes as much sense as asking how long is a piece of string. A ruffed grouse takes off and flies at one speed, high gear. But no two woodcock fly exactly alike. Some of them fly so slowly that literally no lead is required. Others, the smart ones and the scared ones, get away at incredible speeds. Some fly in a straight line. Others change course every 10 or 15 feet. How far must you lead a woodcock? As far as is necessary to get him into your shot pattern.

While that sort of information is not in the least helpful, it does at least furnish a clue in the determination of woodcock leads. Let us look into the matter of leads a bit more closely.

There are two separate and distinct schools of thought in the matter of leads—the "pointing out" school and the "swinging through" or "swinging past" school. "Pointing out" means this: From the estimated speed at which that particular bird is traveling, the gunner places an imaginary 30-inch circle ahead of the bird at the correct distance so that shot charge and bird will meet. Then he points his gun at that imaginary spot, swings his gun so that it continues to point at that spot, and presses the trigger. If his estimates are correct, if he does not check the swing of his gun just as it is discharged, and if the bird continues in that same line of flight, he has got for himself one dead woodcock. That is pointing out.

"Swinging through" is something else again. This consists of pointing the gun at a spot somewhere behind the bird in flight. Then swing the gun along the line of flight until it overtakes and passes the bird. As the gun passes the bird, press the trigger. All very good—now let us see what actually has happened. First off, the speed of the bird determines the *overtaking* speed of the swing of the gun. A slow bird means a slow swing or, in extreme cases, no swing at all. A fast bird means a fast swing. As the gun overtakes the bird and passes it, there is a lapse of about one-fifth of a second while the reflexes of the average gunner execute the command of the brain and cause the trigger finger to depress the trigger. During this interval the gun has passed the bird and has built up, automatically, the approximate lead necessary to kill that bird. That is swinging through.

By far the great majority of upland wing shots are "pointers." However, if you can school yourself to the swinging-through method, you probably will have fewer missed birds at the close of the season. Not only does this method virtually eliminate the tendency to check the swing of the gun at the moment it is fired; in addition, it just about eliminates guesswork from the estimation of leads.

Depend upon it, however—you will not get them all. But that is as it should be. Nobody shoots 100 per cent in the woodcock covers. Certainly you will get the easy shots, but they do not teach you much wing shooting. After you have missed a few of the tougher shots, you will begin to wonder what is wrong. That marks the point at which you will begin to learn something about wing shooting. When you come right down to it, the tough shots and the missed birds of each day in the alder swales and the hillside and top covers teach you the lessons that will do your shooting real, lasting good.

North Carolina Conservation & Development Department.

# SHORE BIRDS

## ESKIMO CURLEW

*Numenius borealis*

Common Names: Doe-Bird, Dough-Bird, Fute, Little Curlew, Prairie Pigeon.

**History.** This member of the curlew family is no more than a memory in the minds of old-time gunners. It is possible that a scattered few birds still survive, but scarcely a dozen have been observed in the past 30 years. Early records make note of the fact that these birds were once so plentiful as to "darken the sky," and frequent references comment on the enormous flocks that passed annually down the Atlantic coast. Today these birds are virtually extinct, and it is doubtful that they will again be known to gunners.

**Identification.** In general, these birds resemble the Hudsonian curlew but are much smaller, being only about 14 inches long.

The coloring of the upper parts is similar to that of the Hudsonian curlew but the basic tone is more reddish-brown. There is no white streak through the crown; the under parts are buffy to whitish and profusely marked with dusky bars, streaks, and arrowhead spottings.

**Characteristics.** In general, their habits are similar to those of such shorebirds as the sandpipers, the snipe, and some plovers. They frequent pools and marshes along the coast, and the shallow ponds and sloughs of the interior.

During the fall migrations these birds are especially plump, a condition which earned them the name of "dough-bird" among the old-time hunters.

The nesting grounds were on the Barren Grounds, and not much is known about the actual nesting habits. It is reasonable to assume that they were much the same as those of the other curlews and the various shorebirds.

**Range and Distribution.** No present range can be named because these birds are practically non-existent in North America.

## HUDSONIAN CURLEW

*Numenius hudsonicus*

Common Names: American Whimbrel, Crooked-Billed Marlin, Jack, Jack-Curlew, Short-Billed Curlew, Striped-Head.

**History.** The Hudsonian curlew, a smaller relative of the long-billed curlew, still migrates from the Arctic breeding grounds each autumn. This bird was best known to gunners as the jack curlew and in former years was a welcome addition to any game bag. At one time these birds were abundant along both the Atlantic and Pacific coasts but their numbers have decreased with the years. They now enjoy complete protection and every effort is being made to preserve the remaining flocks in the hope that they may gradually increase.

**Identification.** Adult Hudsonians closely resemble the young of the long-billed curlew. They are about 18 inches in length and somewhat snipelike in contour. The bill curves downward but is much shorter than that of the long-billed species.

The upper parts are dusky-brown heavily mottled with white, buff, and pale chestnut in much the same manner as the long-billed curlew. The crown is dusky-brown with a streak of white down the center, and there is a white stripe above the eye on each side of the head. A prominent dusky streak runs from the bill to the eye and thence beyond the eye toward the back of the head.

The under parts are brownish-white. The upper breast is flecked with blackish-brown streaks which become more arrowhead-shaped on the lower breast and abdomen. On the sides of the body these arrowhead markings are well defined and appear as dark, broken bars.

The bill is dark above and yellowish for less than one-half its length below. The legs and feet are ashy-blue.

**Characteristics.** The Hudsonian seeks out the more remote and inaccessible places to feed and rest. These birds are extremely shy and wary, and have learned to avoid the more obvious danger areas on their long migration from the Arctic. They are sometimes seen with various other shorebirds along the beaches and mud flats where they pick up sand spiders, small crabs, and other forms of marine life. Farther inshore they feed on grasshoppers, grubs, and berries.

They may fly singly, in pairs, or during migration in small flocks like ducks and geese. When moving along the feeding grounds they seldom fly higher than 25 or 30 yards, but at other times they may gain a much greater altitude. On the ground they walk about slowly and with great dignity unless they are chasing some lively insect.

Their common name of curlew comes from their

spring mating call of *"ker-lew, ker-lew, ker-lew."* When alarmed they utter a shrill *"pip, pip, pip, pip."*

**Range and Distribution.** These curlews breed in the far Arctic regions and begin their southern trek as soon as the young are capable of flight. The flight southward follows both the Atlantic and Pacific coasts, and scattered flocks pass over the interior. The main flight comes from Hudson Bay down the coast of New England. They usually reach the Gulf of St. Lawrence about August and proceed in a leisurely fashion to the salt marshes of the Carolinas. In former years they were common along the New England shores but now they usually remain well out at sea until they reach their winter feeding grounds. The west coast flight rarely pauses north of Lower California, and the winter range extends from there to central South America.

## LONG-BILLED CURLEW

*Numenius americanus americanus*

Common Names: Big Curlew, Hen Curlew, Old Hen Curlew, Saber-Bill, Sickle-Bill, Sickle-Billed Curlew, Smoker.

**History.** The curlews, along with the snipes, sandpipers, and various other shore birds, belong to the order *Limicolae* and the family *Scolopacidae.* Unlike some members of the family, the curlews do not seem to have been able to cope with civilization and are fast disappearing.

About 100 years ago they were abundant along the Atlantic and Pacific coasts, where the great wedge-shaped flocks came to the marshes by the thousands. Being fairly large birds and of fine flavor, they were

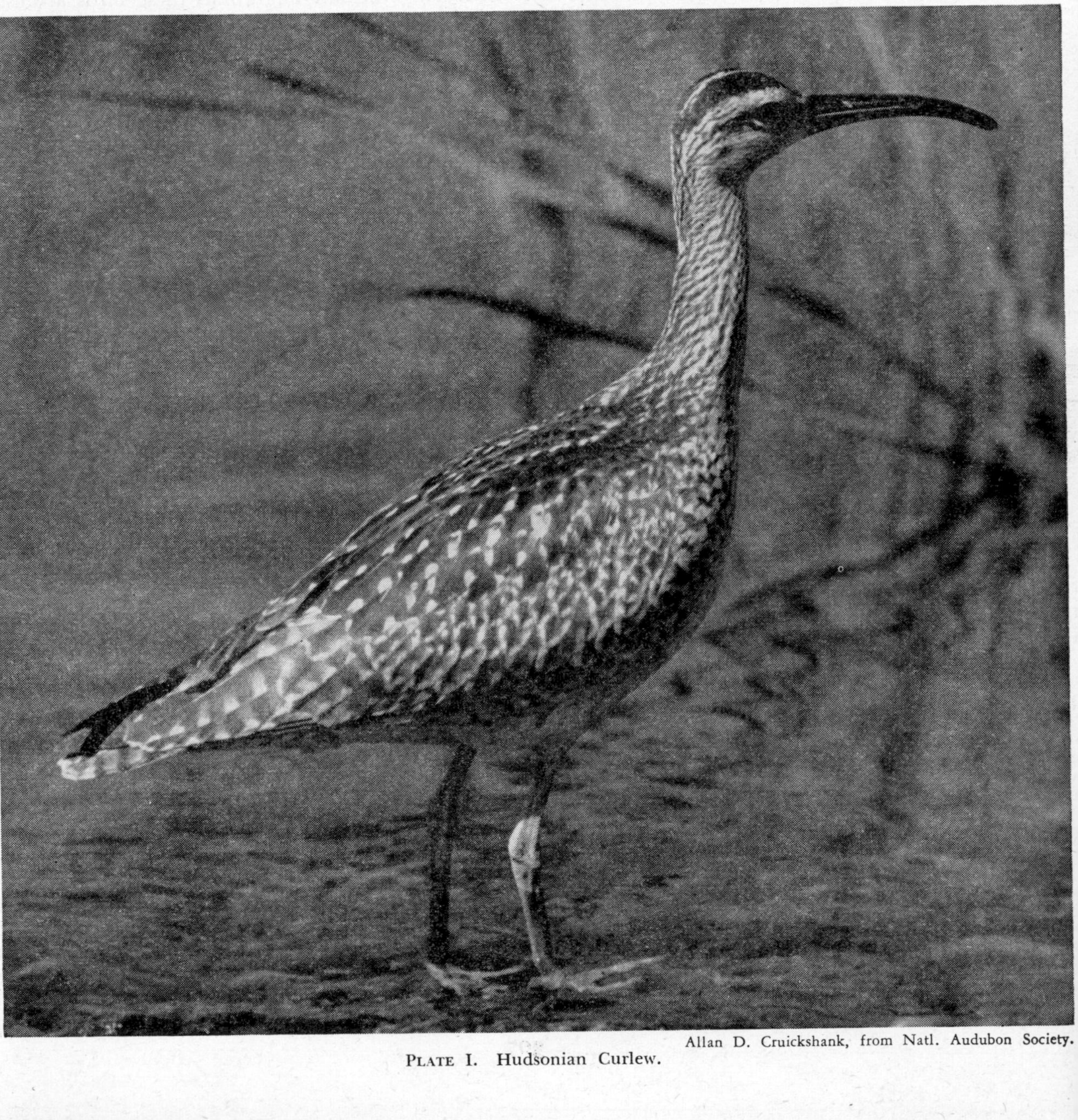

Allan D. Cruickshank, from Natl. Audubon Society.

Plate I. Hudsonian Curlew.

eagerly sought by the gunners of that era. The partial loss of their former breeding grounds to agriculture plus the pressure of hunting reduced their numbers to a mere fraction of the earlier total.

Eventually the Federal Migratory Bird Act placed them on the fully protected list. Whether this will save the remainder from extinction remains to be seen, but it is certain to be many years, if ever, before they will again become legal game.

**Identification.** These birds average about 24 inches in length. They resemble plovers in form, have long legs, a fairly long neck, and a 6 inch bill which curves downward for about two-thirds of its length.

The basic color of the plumage is reddish-brown, but this is broken by fine streakings of black on the crown and by brownish-black, whitish, and tawny markings on the back and shoulders. The wings and tail are pale brownish or reddish-brown with transverse barrings of dusky brown. The under parts vary from ochraceous-brown to pale rust, being generally deeper in tone on the sides of the body, and more or less whitish on the throat and sides of the head. The breast is marked with arrowhead streaks of dusky brown. The upper bill is blackish-brown and the lower mandible is light pinkish-white. The legs and feet are bluish-slate color.

**Characteristics.** During their stay along the Atlantic coast the curlews frequent marshes, grassy areas near the shore, and mud flats, where they find the crustaceans and other small marine creatures that are their chief source of food. They probe in the mud and soil with their long bills and extract grubs, beetles, and other insects. On their breeding grounds they feed on locusts, grasshoppers, and other noxious insects.

When migrating, they form in groups and fly in a triangular formation at considerable altitude. While thus in flight they frequently utter a long, loud whistle.

Their main breeding grounds are in the western provinces of Canada and the prairie lands of the northwestern United States. They seem to prefer those areas where the soil is somewhat alkaline, and nest around sloughs that are practically bare alkaline flats.

The nest is no more than a grass-lined depression in the ground and is usually out in the open with little attempt at concealment other than a natural blending with the surrounding terrain. The eggs usually number three or four and vary from light buff to grayish, spotted with brown and pale purple.

During the nesting season the male guards the sitting female and warns of approaching danger with loud, piercing cries. Both birds then fly or run at some distance from the nest in an effort to distract the intruder.

**Range and Distribution.** In the summer these birds range from the Carolinas to Florida on the east coast, and on the west coast from central California, southern Arizona, and the Gulf states southward to Guatemala. The winter breeding grounds include most of the western provinces, northeastern California, northern New Mexico, and northwestern Texas.

## FLORIDA GALLINULE

*Gallinula galeata*

Common Names: American Gallinule, Common Gallinule, Red-Billed Mud Hen, Water Chicken, Water Hen.

**History.** The name water hen is aptly descriptive of both the Florida and purple gallinules. Their European cousin is commonly called a "moor hen" because it too is like a barnyard chicken which took to the marshes to live. The Florida gallinule is the more numerous of the two and enjoys a wider range. The two species resemble each other in most respects and what affects one is likely to have a similar effect upon the other. Drainage and cultivation have done much to destroy their feeding and nesting areas and they are now found only in those sections where boggy marshlands defy the plow.

**Identification.** This bird is about 14 inches long and of a general dark bluish-slate color. The back and scapulars are washed with olive-brown and the sides of the body are broadly streaked with white. The belly is white or nearly so, and the under tail coverts form a white patch on that area. The crown-plate is a bare patch of bright crimson. The bill is bright red with a tip of yellow. The upper parts of the legs—the tibia—are also bright red and the rest of the legs and feet are greenish.

**Characteristics.** Like its purple cousin, the Florida gallinule is at home in the swamps and marshy shores of lakes, ponds, and sloughs where it picks its way daintily through the reeds and mire. It resembles a chicken not only in voice but in the way it runs with head and body extended, and when an extra burst of speed is needed the wings are raised, chickenlike, for balance. Its long toes permit walking over lily pads and other vegetation and it is equally at ease while swimming. The gallinule might well be termed an amphibious hen and, like the barnyard variety, it flies poorly and with reluctance.

There is never much doubt as to the presence of gallinules for loud *"clucks,"* gurgles, and sundry other noises fill the marsh even when the birds are hidden from sight. Most of the calls are henlike in character but they have a few special notes for certain occasions. Perhaps the most common is the call which sounds like *"ticket, ticket, ticket."* Some naturalists claim this comes from the lovelorn male. Another call sounds like *"tuka, tuka, tuka,"* and at times they utter a peculiar purring noise like a hen with chickens. Any disturbance in their vicinity will draw forth a vehement and inquiring *"chuck."*

During the nesting season their noise decreases markedly and they become even more secretive than usual. Unlike the rails, they are more active during the day and it is unusual to hear them call at night. At times they appear to be singularly stupid—or trusting—and will sometimes permit close approach by boat before they spatter off across the water.

The nest is made of dried reeds or rushes on a bed of the same, or on some elevation, and is usually a platform raised a foot or two above the water. The number of eggs varies from 6 to 13 and they are a buff or creamy white spotted with reddish-brown.

Incubation begins as soon as the first egg is laid and the young begin to appear in sequence, so that there is a difference of as many days in age as there are eggs in the nest.

The downy young, like those of the purple gallinule, are glossy black but the under parts appear somewhat sooty along the central line and the throat and cheeks are interspersed with silvery-white hair-like feathers.

Immature birds are similar to adults except that the under parts are grayish-white, the bill is brownish, the crown-plate is smaller, and there is no red on the legs.

**Range and Distribution.** The Florida gallinule comes farther north than its purple congener, sometimes reaching Maine. It breeds locally from the New England states through Wisconsin and Minnesota southward. The winter range extends south from the Gulf states; it is especially plentiful in the marshes of Alabama, Mississippi, and Louisiana.

Samuel A. Grimes, from Natl. Audubon Society.

**PLATE I. Purple Gallinule.**

## PURPLE GALLINULE

*Ionornis martinica*

Common Names: None so far as known, but possibly a few strictly local terms. In Jamaica it is called Sultana.

**History.** Although limited numbers find their way northward each year, the purple gallinule is primarily a southern bird, being much better known below the Mason-Dixon line than above it. With the possible exception of the wood duck it is easily the most colorful of all the southern water-birds. Numbers of these birds may be found around the rice plantations of South Carolina and in parts of Florida they are still numerous, but in general they show marked decrease in population over the entire range.

**Identification.** The gallinules are the largest of the rail family. The bill is shorter and more henlike than the rail's and there is a hard shield or plate extending from the base of the bill over the forehead to the top of the head. On the purple gallinule this plate is a bluish-lead color. The bill is a rich crimson with a greenish tip. The rest of the head and the under parts are a rich, dark purplish-blue. The back is a shining olive-green and the wings are light blue tinged with greenish overtones. The under tail coverts form a white patch beneath the tail. The legs and feet are chrome yellow.

**Characteristics.** Both the gallinules are somewhat like chickens who have been forced to adopt aquatic ways. They walk gracefully through dense vegetation and their large feet with the long toes permit them to walk or run over lily pads and slimy surfaces where other birds would have difficulty in gaining a foothold. Their feet are not webbed but they swim readily and resemble a coot on the water. While swimming the head bobs back and forth in unison with each stroke of the feet. Like the rails and the coot, they do not take wing if they can avoid doing so and the flight is weak. Their legs dangle during flight and they drop awkwardly to the ground after a short trip through the air.

In general their habits are similar to those of the Florida gallinule with whom they commonly associate. They are extremely noisy birds and have a large variety of calls for different occasions. Most of these are suggestive of barnyard fowls when disturbed. They are particularly loquacious during the nesting season, and like their less colorful relative the Florida gallinule, they give vent to a loud, explosive *"chuck"* when surprised.

The nest is usually a platform of reed-grass and rushes built at varying heights above the water. The eggs, generally eight to ten, are a buffy or creamy white finely speckled with reddish-brown.

The downy young are a glossy black. The head is sprinkled with numerous white, hairlike feathers and the bill is yellowish with a black tip.

The immature birds have upper parts more or less washed with a brownish tone and the lower parts somewhat mottled with white.

**Range and Distribution.** The purple gallinule ranges throughout the lowland swamps and sloughs from Florida to Texas and north to South Carolina and Tennessee. Only occasional stragglers reach farther north. In the winter its range is from Florida and southern Texas southward to subtropical and tropical America.

## BLACK-BELLIED PLOVER

*Squatarola squatarola*

Common Names: Beetle-Head, Black Breast, Black-Breasted Plover, Bottle-Head, Bull-Head, Bull-Head Plover, Four-Toed Plover, Gray Plover (in autumn), Gump, Mud Plover, Ox-Eye Plover, Swiss Plover, Whistling Field Plover.

**History.** The story of the black-bellied plover is essentially the same as that of many other game birds —formerly abundant, now few in numbers. Great flocks of these handsome birds once congregated on the sandbars and tidal flats along the coast and on the western prairies. From all available reports they were never as numerous as the golden plover, with which they are often confused because of the resemblance, and they did not fly in such huge flocks. Nevertheless they were extremely plentiful during the spring and autumn migrations and held in high esteem as a game bird. Like all the plovers, they are now fully protected by law and it is believed that their numbers are on the increase.

**Identification.** In the spring the forehead, crown, sides of the head above the eye, and back and sides of the neck well down to the shoulders are white. The crown and the nape of the neck are spotted with black. The face, fore-neck, breast, and under parts are a solid brownish-black. The back and wing coverts, including the inner secondaries, are white but each feather has an exposed black area which forms a distinct pattern of markings over these areas. The tail and upper tail coverts are also white barred with dark markings. The long, black axillary feathers (under the wing) are a distinguishing mark. The feet, like those of the golden plover, are dark gray but have an additional small hind toe. The brown eye is unusually large and lustrous.

In winter the entire plumage is more inclined to brownish and the distinct markings are more subdued. At this time the birds are commonly mistaken for the golden plover but the black axillary feathers and the white rump and tail determine their identity.

**Characteristics.** Black-bellied plovers are more coastal birds than the golden or upland plovers. They prefer mud flats and sandbars exposed by the falling tide, where they are often seen in company with snipe, sandpipers, ringed plovers, and turnstones. As the tide rises they retire to near-by meadows, uplands, or more exposed sandbars.

Although the largest of the plover family, they seem to have no difficulty in running over soft, muddy flats where less agile creatures would bog down. Like the golden and others, their movements are quick and energetic, but they do not bob up and down. They have the same habit of running swiftly for a few yards and then pausing with raised head before another run.

They are the shyest of all the plovers and it is impossible to approach them. Out on their favorite sandbars and flats they command an excellent view from all sides and at the first sign of danger they sound their peculiar melodious whistle and take wing.

In flight they are swift and steady. During migration they often fly in ranks or in line like ducks and geese.

They commonly utter two calls. One is a clear, mellow, and far-reaching *"whee-u-*REEE" (accent on the third syllable) similar to the call of a bluebird but more drawn out and of a more plaintive quality. The second call is a low-pitched note uttered when they are at ease and contented.

The nest and eggs are very similar to those of the golden plover and the adults employ the same tactics to divert attention from the nest or young.

The immature birds are lighter colored above and the yellow markings on their feathers more closely resemble those of the golden plover. The under parts are white and the breast and sides are streaked with brownish-gray. These juveniles are much less wary than the older birds and are known to gunners as "beetle-heads."

**Range and Distribution.** The black-bellied plover breeds over the same Arctic regions as the golden plover but migrates through eastern North America. The birds winter along the coast from North Carolina southward as far as Brazil.

## GOLDEN PLOVER

*Pluvialis dominicus dominicus*

COMMON NAMES: Brass Back, Bull Head, Common Plover, Field Bird, Frost Bird, Golden Back, Green Back, Green Plover, Hawk's Eye, Muddy Belly, Pale Breast, Pasture Bird, Prairie Bird, Prairie Pigeon, Spotted Plover, Squealer, Three-Toed Plover, Toad Head, Trout Bird, Whistling Plover.

**History.** The plovers belong to the family *Charadriiae,* of the order *Limicolae,* or shorebirds, although some members of the family, notably the upland plover and the mountain plover, are more at home in the fields and pastures than along the shore. There are about 75 species scattered throughout the world, only eight of which were found in North America. Of these, most are now rare or bordering on extinction.

The same conditions which affect the northern breeding grounds of many ducks also affect the plovers who nest in the same areas. It may be assumed, therefore, that much of the decrease in their numbers is due to the same factors that apply to the

Allan D. Cruickshank, from Natl. Audubon Society.

PLATE I. Black-Bellied Plover.

ducks. Actual figures seem difficult to obtain, but there is no doubt that there has been an alarming decrease in plovers for more than two decades. There is no open season on plovers at the present time and it is hoped that at least two species, the golden plover and the upland plover, will show favorable gains in a few years.

The term "frost bird" refers to the time in the old days, about the first frost, when the birds began to appear from the north. Along the New England coast a rousing northeaster would drive the birds several hundred miles off their course and there would be wonderful gunning as the great flocks were blown in from the sea. Old-time gunners had a saying that the golden maple leaves, the goldenrod, the golden grain, and the golden plovers all arrived at the same time.

Except for storms which made them accidental visitors to the Atlantic coast, golden plovers were seldom seen during the fall migration. Throughout the Mississippi Valley region, however, which the birds used as a spring flyway, they were once so plentiful and tame that they could be killed by a plowman with his whip. At one time they sold in the streets of Chicago for 50 cents a hundred.

**Identification.** The golden plover, like others of the same family, somewhat resembles a snipe or sandpiper except for being more squat in appearance and having a shorter neck. The bill is also short, stout, and like a pigeon's it is a trifle enlarged at the tip. The legs are relatively long and the wings are long and pointed. The over-all body length is 10 or 11 inches—a little larger than the more common killdeer.

Like the geese, both sexes are identical in appearance, but the plovers wear brighter plumage during the spring and summer than they do in the winter. The summer markings are as follows: The top of the head, back of the neck, back, and shoulders are a sooty black spangled and margined with golden-yellow (hence the bird's most common name). The wing coverts and secondaries are more inclined to brown but bear the same streaks and markings of golden-yellow. The forehead is white, and a broad stripe of white extends down the sides of the neck and becomes a white patch on the sides of the breast. The tail is short, brownish-gray faintly barred with white and yellow, and is composed of 12 feathers. The lores, sides of head in front of the white stripe, throat, breast, and under parts are a solid black. The bill is dusky. The feet are dull gray and have no hind toe. (The black-bellied plover, which is similar in appearance, has a hind toe.) The brown eyes are large and bright.

In winter the plumage is less striking. The black areas become more brownish and the markings less distinct. The birds appear darker above than below, the under parts being mottled with dark grayish-brown. The white stripe down the sides of the neck becomes narrower and more grayish and there is a faint dark stripe behind the eye. The bill, legs, and eyes remain the same as in the summer.

**Characteristics.** The golden plover is one of the largest and most beautiful of all the plovers. Their habits in a general way resemble those of snipe but their shorter bills are not suitable for probing in the mud and they live chiefly on insects. For this reason

American Museum of Natural History.
PLATE I. Golden Plover.

they are as often found on the uplands as on the shore. Occasionally they frequent marshes and are sometimes, but not often, seen above the high-tide mark along beaches. They seem to prefer sandy hills, plowed fields, old pastures, golf courses, or burned-over areas free from trees or bushes. Since grasshoppers form a large part of their diet, they are likely to be seen wherever the hoppers are most abundant.

All their movements are quick. One of the most characteristic is a frequent bobbing of the head. When running, their legs move so rapidly that they appear to twinkle. They commonly run a few yards, and then stop and hold up their heads for a look around them.

In flight their long narrow wings carry them swiftly with fast vigorous strokes. If there are several in the flight they scatter immediately as soon as they reach the earth.

They gather their food with a quick striking motion of the head and neck.

At one time confident and unmindful of danger, they have since become shy, but adult golden plovers come quite readily to either wooden or tin decoys. The young birds, however, unlike those of the black-bellied plover, are more wary and difficult to bring to the blind. When a flock is approaching the decoys there is a regular whistling chorus of what sound like *"coodle, coodle, coodle,"* or *"queddle, queddle, queddle."*

At other times they utter a strange but melodious *"queep,"* or a more drawn-out *"quee-lee-leep."*

The nest of the golden plover is little more than a depression in the ground or tundra and often merely a hollow among the rocks or pebbles. The eggs, usually four in number, are creamy white blotched with chocolate-brown and black. They blend so perfectly with their surroundings that they are difficult to detect.

The downy young also furnish an excellent example of camouflage. The little bodies of sooty black are mottled with grayish white blending to yellow on the rump. The under parts are pale gray, deeper in tone on the lower neck and breast. Seemingly aware that their coloration renders them invisible among the pebbles and sand on which they lie, the young birds "freeze" when danger approaches.

The parents, after the manner of all plovers, snipe, and some other birds, attempt the broken-wing trick and flutter along the ground in apparent helplessness in hopes of luring the intruder away from the nest or young. If the ruse is successful the older birds allow themselves to be pursued, always just managing to elude the grasp, until a safe distance from the nest. They then take wing and remain aloft until the unwelcome visitor goes away. A second approach to the nest, however, will bring a repeat performance by one or both of the anxious parents.

**Range and Distribution.** The golden plover is especially noted for its remarkable migration flights. Leaving the Arctic breeding grounds in late summer, these birds travel eastward to Labrador and thence down the coast to Nova Scotia, from which they strike out due south over the open Atlantic to South America. Unless blown inland by strong east or northeast gales the fall migration passes far off the Atlantic coast. A few birds go south along the Mississippi Valley and all the return flights from the pampas of Brazil and Argentina use this flyway in the spring. Their annual migrations are the longest of any species, totaling a distance of about 8000 miles.

## UPLAND PLOVER

*Bartramia longicauda*

COMMON NAMES: Bartramian Sandpiper, Bartram's Plover, Bartram's Snipe, Field Plover, Grass Plover, Highland Plover, Hill-Bird, Papabotte, Pasture Plover, Prairie Pigeon, Prairie Plover, Prairie Snipe, Quaily, Uplander, Upland Sandpiper.

**History.** The upland plover, known equally well by the name Bartramian sandpiper, belongs to the order *Limicolae* and the family *Scolopacidae*. For this reason, as well as general structure, it is classed as a shorebird. Actually, there are few birds less fond of water than the upland plover and they are generally found far from any shore.

The upland plover is an outstanding example of a fine game bird brought almost to extinction by the loss of breeding grounds and the destruction of nests by cultivation. Once abundant throughout North America and as common in the eastern fields as the meadow lark, these birds were gradually pushed westward until the last remaining breeding grounds are on the prairies of the Northwest. Even

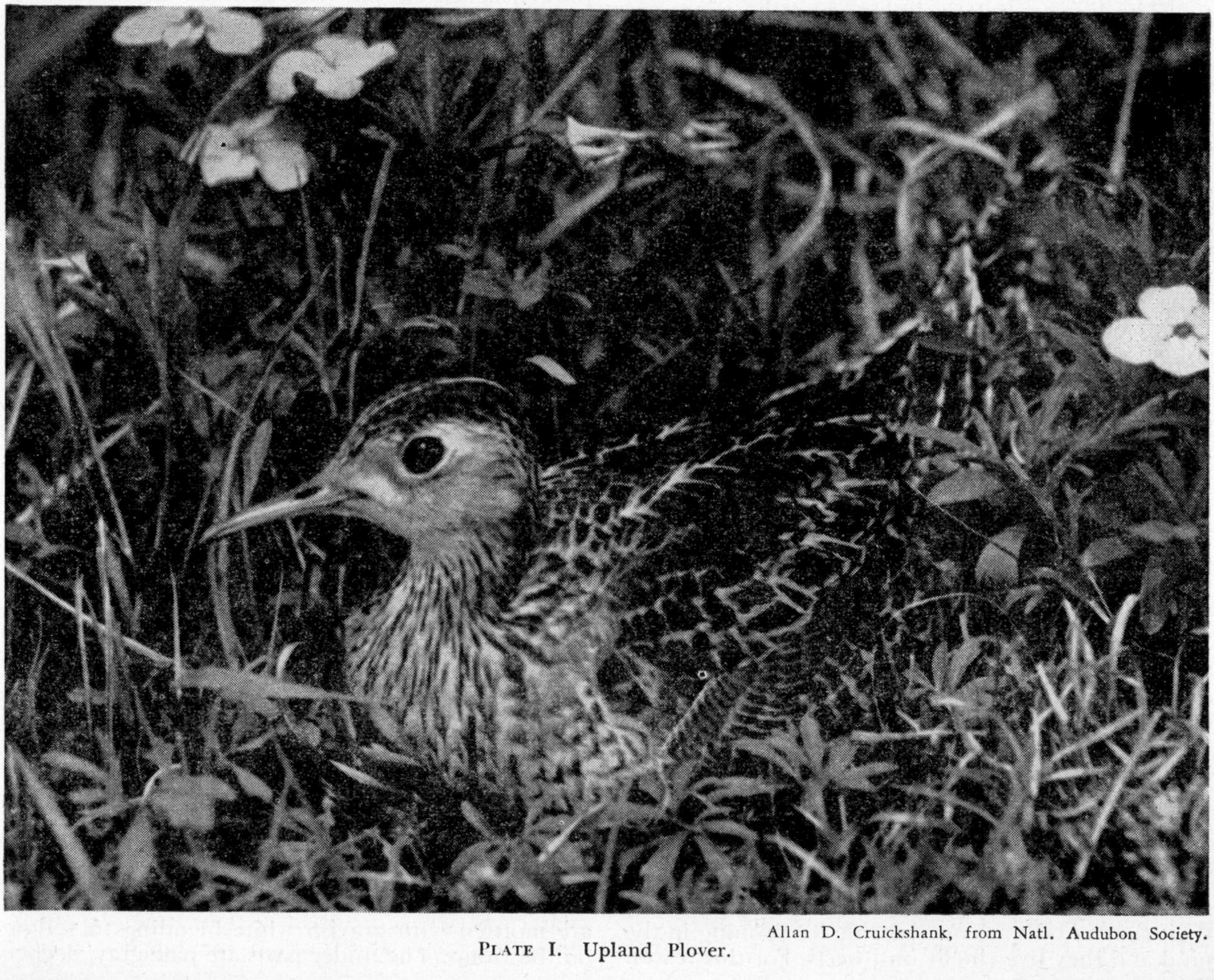

Allan D. Cruickshank, from Natl. Audubon Society.

PLATE I. Upland Plover.

in this region their available range is being drastically reduced by agricultural activities.

Under Federal law these birds are now fully protected, but the only hope for their return to abundance is a restoration of their nesting area. Since these areas are likely to remain under cultivation the future of these birds looks very dark indeed. It will require great care from the states and provinces and the co-operation of public sentiment to preserve this valuable species from extinction.

**Identification.** This plover is large (11 to 12 inches) with no really distinctive markings. The upper parts are streaked with buff-brown and black. The breast is buff-gray streaked with black. The under parts are white or grayish-white. The tail is long, reaching beyond the wings, and the outer tail feathers are barred with white, black, and reddish-brown. The sides of the breast and flanks are light buff streaked with black. The bill is short and pigeonlike, the head small, and the neck long and thin. The legs are yellowish-green and the outer and middle toes are webbed at the base.

The brown coloring, the long neck and tail, and the bird's habit of holding its wings erect when alighting make identification of this species fairly easy.

**Characteristics.** The upland plover, as the common name implies, is definitely a bird of the dry grassy hillsides, prairies, and open fields. Although extremely shy and difficult to approach on foot, they often display little concern over a vehicle or a man on horseback. The few remaining eastern birds are more wary than those of the western plains.

Unlike the majority of plovers and other shorebirds, they frequently perch on fence posts or poles. At other times they assume an alert attitude on the ground with only their heads projecting above the short grass.

Because of their coloration they are difficult to see while on the ground and when they spring into the air they utter a wild, shrill, rolling whistle composed of two drawn-out, windlike notes: *"Whooooleeeeeee, wheeeelooooooo."* The first note ascends the scale to a high pitch, the second descends to a low range. Occasionally this somewhat mournful call may be heard over open fields on moonlight nights. A second call frequently heard is a crisp *"Kip-ip-ip-ip."*

Efforts to restore the upland plover to something of its former abundance would be well rewarded. A study of their food habits by Government biologists determined that they feed almost exclusively on noxious insects. Chief among their food items are the destructive locust, bill-bugs (corn destroyers), clover-root curculios, grasshoppers, grubs, cutworms, and various beetles.

Their nests are constructed of dry grass in a thick tuft of prairie grass and well concealed. The female sits closely, her dead-grass coloration blending perfectly with her surroundings, and she will not flush from the nest unless in danger of being stepped on. The eggs usually number four and are a pale cream spotted with dark brown and light violet.

The birds nest in late May or around the first part of June and the young are ready for flight about mid-July. By early August all the birds begin the southern migration.

In flight, the wings appear to be held in a rather stiff bowed position. The short wing beats are below the horizontal and unlike the deeper strokes of other plovers and most shorebirds.

Upon alighting (as mentioned under "Identification") these birds have a unique habit of stretching their wings upright over their backs before folding them.

**Range and Distribution.** The upland plover in North America lives chiefly in the interior. It breeds principally in the prairie provinces of Manitoba and Saskatchewan, although scattered flocks breed in the Dakotas, Wisconsin, southern Illinois, southern Missouri, and Oklahoma. It migrates through the eastern United States and winters in South America.

## SORA (Carolina Rail) — *Porzana carolina*

COMMON NAMES: Carolina Crake, Carolina Rail, Chicken-Billed Rail, Meadow Chicken, Mud Hen, Ortolan, Rail-Bird, Soree.

**History.** The sora is a member of the rail family whose habitat like that of the coot has earned it the title of "mud hen." Although fairly common throughout the United States it is more often heard than seen, and because of its secretive nature its presence is often unsuspected. Never as numerous or as popular as its larger cousin, the Virginia rail, the sora has nevertheless long been ranked as a game bird and it is to be hoped that it will continue to furnish as much sport in the future as it has in the past. During the breeding season the birds fit the description "thin as a rail" but by fall they become quite plump and ready for the table.

**Identification.** The sora is a bird suggesting a tiny, dark bantam hen. The short, yellow bill is tipped with black. The area about the base of the bill, the center of the crown, and a line running down the foreneck is black. There is no crown plate, the entire head being feathered down to the base of the bill. The remainder of the throat, the sides of the head, the front part of the crown, and the breast are a light bluish-gray. The upper parts are an olive-brown, most of the feathers having black centers, and those on the back and scapulars being streaked with white. The wing coverts are a light brownish-gray and the outer edge of the first primaries are streaked with white. The sides, which are more olive than the under parts, are barred with white and the gray belly is also marked with transverse barrings of white. The tail coverts are whitish, tinged with rust-brown. The legs and feet are green.

**Characteristics.** Soras prefer the larger fresh-water marshes where a heavy growth of vegetation offers shelter and seclusion. Most of their time is spent in threading their way through the tangles of such

Olin Sewall Pettingill, Jr., from Natl. Audubon Society.

PLATE I. Carolina Rail (Sora).

bogs in the never-ending search for something to eat. In the autumn they gather in the wild rice and wild oat marshes where their flesh becomes a delicacy.

The sora swims well and dives expertly but walking is the favored means of locomotion. The long toes support it over the soggy ground and it can run and dodge through the long grass and reeds with considerable speed. While feeding the birds usually walk sedately with tails erect. Like all rails and gallinules, the sora is an indifferent flyer. The flight is slow, straight, and of short duration, and the bird offers an easy target for the gun.

In common with other members of the rail family the sora is nocturnal in habits and feeds mostly at night. Unless disturbed they pass most of the day in hiding and asleep and do not venture forth until dusk. If they were less loquacious they might remain in a locality for some time without detection but their insistent calls betray them. Late in a spring afternoon a clear whistled note, *"ker-*WEE" (accent on the second syllable), is begun by one bird and taken up by the others until about dark the notes become a regular chorus. In the autumn a stone tossed into an apparently deserted marsh will draw forth a series of protesting *"keeks"* from invisible birds.

The sora goes to some trouble to conceal its nest from natural enemies but this very concealment often makes it more obvious to the experienced human eye. The favorite nesting site is just outside the bog or marsh on comparatively firm ground where the shorter grass grows from very shallow water. Here the nest is built up like a little island and the tops of the grasses surrounding it are twisted and fastened by the birds to form a kind of roof or canopy. After one has seen one or two such nests it becomes easy to spot them from their surroundings.

The usual clutch is 8 to 10 eggs but 12 or 13 are not uncommon. The eggs are a buff or creamy white, speckled and spotted with reddish brown.

The downy youngsters are a glossy black with a tuft of bristly, orange-colored feathers on the breast. The immature birds are similar to the adults but lack the black patch around the base of the bill and on the throat. The upper parts are usually darker and the breast more light brown in tone.

**Range and Distribution.** The sora breeds from the fresh-water marshes of Nova Scotia across to British Columbia and south from Maryland through southern Ohio, northern Missouri, and Kansas to southern California. The birds commonly winter in the southern United States although rare individuals may remain in the North.

The population of these birds, especially on the coastal marshes from Connecticut to Virginia, varies considerably during the early fall. There has been considerable conjecture about the factors which influence the movement of the birds during the fall migration. Some observers claim that the mass flights are stimulated by the moon's phases, others by food scarcity, and still others, by sudden temperature drops which cause a mass exodus from a marsh, regardless of moon phase or food. Records of some shooting clubs indicate that temperature does have a definite effect on the movements of the birds, for a sudden cold wave in an area 100 miles to the north usually brings hundreds of flight birds into a marsh within 24 hours. Often, however, a marsh haboring several hundred birds one day will be almost barren of life the next day, for reasons that still remain obscure.

# VIRGINIA RAIL

*Rallus virginianus*

COMMON NAMES: Fresh-Water Marsh Hen, Little Red-Breasted Rail, Long-Billed Rail, Small Mud Hen.

**History.** The Virginia rail is by far the most widely distributed and therefore the best known of the entire rail family. Of course, the term best known is only relative, for, like all the rails, the Virginia is secretive in habits and is difficult to flush. It is this bird, more than other members of the *Rallidae,* who has furnished most of the rail shooting in the past and will likely continue to do so. Although not so numerous as in the early days they are far from rare and if sufficient breeding areas are left to them there is reason to believe that they will remain on the list of American game birds.

**Identification.** The Virginia rail is slightly larger than the sora, or Carolina rail, and unlike that bird has a fairly long, reddish bill slightly curved at the end. There is a tough feather structure on the forehead and crown which serves the same purpose as the plate on the coots and gallinules, namely, to protect the head while running through the tough grass

Allan D. Cruickshank, from Natl. Audubon Society.

PLATE I. Virginia Rail.

and reeds. The upper parts, including the top of the head and the back of the neck, are a dark brown. The feathers on the back have black centers and are edged with light grayish-brown. The wings and tail are a dark gray-brown and the wing coverts are more inclined to reddish-brown. The sides of the head are ashy-gray and there is a white patch on the throat. The breast is an orange-brown or cinnamon and the flanks and under parts are barred with black and white. The legs and feet are a dull red and the iris of the eye is red.

The female varies slightly in being a trifle smaller than the male with a paler tone of cinnamon on the breast and having more white on the throat and chin.

**Characteristics.** In common with all rails, the Virginia displays a marked ability for running through dense vegetation and has a particular aversion to flying unless it is absolutely necessary. The flight is seldom of long duration and is performed with the legs dangling awkwardly. Immediately upon alighting the birds run off with great speed. The legs are placed well to the rear of the long body for better locomotion. The birds walk or run with the head and neck extended, tail erect and frequently jerked upward, and as they move forward turn the head rapidly from side to side as though looking for a safe refuge.

The Virginia rail will often be found sharing the same fresh-water marshes with the sora and other marsh birds. In the West it is commonly associated with the coot and some of the ducks. Along the east coast it frequents the brackish marshes and tidal flats and will most often be found where there is a good stand of wild rice.

In general habits the Virginia rail and the sora are much alike but the former is less gregarious and singles or pairs are more common than groups. The birds announce their presence by a series of peculiar grunting noises not unlike those of little pigs. During the breeding season, especially at night or before a threatened storm, the male utters a low guttural sound which may possibly be his love song. It sounds somewhat like *"cut, cutta, cutta, cutta, cut-ee,"* and is repeated at frequent intervals for hours at a time. The call has a peculiar ventriloquial quality which often makes it seem to come from close at hand when actually the bird is some distance away.

The female is attentive to her young and ruffles her feathers and calls to them like a hen. When particularly anxious over their welfare she voices a low *"ki, ki, ki,"* or *"kiu."* When startled both sexes utter a loud *"kik,"* or *"kep."*

The nest is located on the ground or in a clump of reeds and is rather crudely fashioned of dead grass and rushes. The eggs, usually numbering from six to ten, are a creamy-white speckled with brown.

The female is seldom detected on the nest because she slips silently away at the slightest approach of danger. Some naturalists claim that she will destroy the eggs if they have been handled, but this is a fact not fully established.

The young have a white spot on the bill and are covered with a fine black down. Like all the rails they leave the nest almost as soon as they are hatched.

The Virginia rail feeds more on animal and less on vegetable food than others of the same order. Small snails, slugs, and minute aquatic life form a large part of their diet but, as has been mentioned, they also have a fondness for wild rice. Their food habits seldom impair their flesh, however, and gunners esteem them as a table delicacy.

**Range and Distribution.** The breeding range covers the northern half of the United States and southern Canada from coast to coast. Virginia rails are distinctly migratory, and only rare individuals remain north in the winter. The winter grounds are from the southern limit of the breeding range southward to the Gulf of Mexico.

# RAIL SHOOTING

Rail shooting is one of the few forms of gunning that has not been associated with market shooters. Anyone who has shot a sora for the first time and picked the feathers from it, wondering all the time if it will provide a mouthful of food, can understand why the market gunner would not waste his powder on one. As far back as the early 1800's shooters were being "pushed" through rice flats for the pleasure they got out of shooting them and afterward enjoying the delicately flavored, rice-fattened flesh on their tables in the early fall.

Today a small group of sportsmen, scattered along the tidal rivers and marshes of the Atlantic seaboard, still look forward to early September days when their favorite "pusher" will shove their rail boat through the tall, tasseled, long-leafed, and ripening wild rice which is still pale green in color. Although the gunner seated on his stool in the boat may have boated many rail, he will watch eagerly for the first sora rail to rise almost painfully from the tangle of stalks they are moving through on the top of the tide.

Some species of rail are found in almost every state. There are only eight states that do not have an open season on rail. The rail belongs to the family *Rallidae* of the order *Paludicolae,* and there are 180 species of this family, which include gallinules and coots, distributed throughout the greater part of the world. The six species of rail found in the United States are the king rail, clapper rail, Virginia rail, sora rail, yellow rail, and black rail. The sora and the clapper are the two rails that provide the largest part of the sportsman's bag, and when one of the others is downed it is an occasion.

**Sora Rail.** The sora or Carolina rail *(Porzana carolina)* is found in the greatest numbers and hunted the most. He is a small bird with a short yellow bill, and has long greenish legs which dangle beneath him when he flies. The wings are short and move at a moderate beat when the bird is in flight. The part near the base of his bill, center of crown, and a line down the middle of the neck is black. The rest of the breast and throat, sides of the head, and front of crown are pale blue-gray. The rest of the upper parts are olive-brown; most of the feathers have black centers; the scapulars and back are streaked on either side wilth white; the lower belly

Curtis Marshall, Fairfield, Conn.

**Plate I. Pushing into the Wild Rice to Flush Rail.**

is white, the flanks barred with black and white. The immature bird is similar only there is no black at base of bill and throat, and the black and white hatching on the flanks does not show as pronounced.

This rail breeds from Kansas, Illinois, and Long Island northward to Hudson Bay and Labrador. The nest is made of grass on the ground above the high-water mark in a fresh-water marsh, and they lay 8 to 15 eggs, buffy-white, spotted and freckled with rufous-brown. Although most soras migrate north in the spring to nest, there are many that will nest near their wintering grounds. The sora's summer home is in the fresh-water marshes where it is hard to find them in the tangle of vegetation, as they will run instead of fly when alarmed, and many times the only way you can tell they are in the marsh is to sit quietly after you have made a sharp noise and listen for their clear whistled *"Ker-weee."* They feed on small insects and the seeds of various marsh plants. In the fall when there is a big concentration on their way south, it is possible to observe rail on a moonlight night feeding in the open spots of the marsh when the tide is low. They will also migrate on the full moon or before a storm. During migration they may be plentiful in the marsh one day, and the next tide may find most of them gone until another flight passes through.

When the rail is flushed on the top of a tide his flight is short and he usually drops down into the nearest cover, but records kept of banded rail over large bodies of water show they are capable of flights of several hundred miles. In the fall the soras start migrating southward. They seem to follow routes that keep them near marsh and water, particularly fresh and brackish stretches of tidal rivers and marshes where the wild rice or wild oats *(Zizania aquatica)* grows. This favorite food of the rail is found in most of the Atlantic coastal states from Maine to Louisiana, and in a few of the North Central states. When Père Marquette first came into the Fox River country of Wisconsin he mentioned the fact the rivers were covered with *"folle avoine,"* meaning "wild oats"; even today on the Connecticut River rail shooters call this plant "oats." The plant is an annual, and in early June, after the slate-gray seed has germinated in the shallow-water-covered mud, a floating pale green leaf will rise out of the water. At the end of the month greenish-yellow flowers will bloom at the top of the stalk. After this the plant will begin to grow tall, anywhere from 2 to 12 feet, and in some places so thick that it is difficult to shove a rail boat through it. The ripening seeds are found in a tassel on the top of the stalk and are encased in long-bearded husks, loosely attached to their stalks. The seeds ripen in rotation from the stalk's top downward from the middle of August to the middle of September. Some years, if the summer has been cool and the fall late, it will take longer for the rice to ripen, and the gunners will be partially right in blaming the lack of ripened rice for a scarcity of rail.

It is always possible to distinguish the "oats" from the other marsh growth such as sedge grass, bulrushes, and "redtop" because of its pale green color; it is one of the last of the marsh plants to take on the dry, dull brown hue of the late fall duck marsh. The first part of the rail season finds the "oats" upright and feathery, in many places as thick as a bamboo grove and looking something like one. After a few days, when the wind, rain, and push boats have knocked sections of the heavy growth down, there will be open spots where the stalks lie crisscrossed, and it is easier for the rail to feed in these broken down areas than on the remaining upright stalks whose seeds are probably not ripe.

**Rail-Shooting Areas.** Starting in Maine, the great flyway for rail follows the tidal marshes and rivers southward. There are many fresh-water ponds in Maine where wild rice is found, as well as on that great duck-shooting area, Merrymeeting Bay, and there is a continual stream of both sora and Virginia rail moving through their marshes in the early fall, though no great concentration of rail is found in any particular spots. An occasional duck shooter will kill a few rail, but there is no place in the state where it is worth while to push for rail.

Rail are not hunted seriously in either Massachusetts or Rhode Island. Connecticut offers good rail shooting. It is better in some years than in others; a good crop of "oats" assures wonderful shooting and a poor crop reduces the number of rail to be found on the tidal river marshes. The Connecticut River near the town of Essex offers some of the best sora rail shooting in the country. There are several splendid guides available for pushing in this area, who know in which coves the rail are most plentiful, and they have their own rail boats and power boats for getting out to the sora marshes. Most of the marshes are open to the public. The Connecticut has always been famous for its sora rail, and in the early 1920's one could always find at least a dozen large oceangoing yachts anchored in the river off the town of Essex, whose owners were there for the second week of the rail shooting. In addition to the large marshes of wild rice, the river itself acts as an additional feeder into the main coastal flyway, as it starts near the Canadian border and funnels the migratory sora right into the Essex area.

The next largest river in Connecticut provides sora shooting on a smaller scale, but there are no guides available on this river, which is the Housatonic. Most of the rail are found in the Oronoque section with some Virginia rail found in Nell's Island. The late Charles H. Johnson of Stratford, Conn., who was the last professional shover to push on the Housatonic, kept a log of the rail shooting in this particular area from 1876 to 1925 inclusive; this showed that as far back as 1876 they had their off years when the "oat" crop was skimpy and the rail kill was poor. It is of interest to look at one of these years and note the September log.

| 1880 | | No. of rail | |
|---|---|---|---|
| Sept. 1. | Wm. D. Bishop | 9 | |
| Sept. 6. | Dr. Walker | 17 | |
| Sept. 7. | Morris Ketcham | 12 | |
| Sept. 8. | Morris Ketcham | 88 | |
| Sept. 9. | Morris Ketcham | 145 | |
| Sept. 10. | Morris Ketcham | 181 | |
| Sept. 11. | New York man (no good) | 3 | |
| Sept. 14. | Mr. Leigh | 3 | (2 ducks) |
| Sept. 14. | George Wells | 28 | |
| Sept. 16. | Morris Ketcham | 31 | |
| Sept. 18. | George B. Grinnell | 21 | (1 king rail) |

It is remarkable to think of the action packed into the short two hours of high tide which limited the time in which one man was able to wing-shoot 181 small birds, every one of which got up at a different angle, with the added distraction of high, thick rice stalks stopping the swing of the gun barrel or obstructing the view of the bird. It is hard to tell whether the New York man was no good, or the shooting was poor for lack of birds. There is no doubt there was a large flight on for the three days of the large bags, and the tide must have been extra high.

New Jersey has good rail shooting on most of its tidal river marshes. Most of the good rail shooting is in South Jersey near Atlantic City, Millville, Tuckerton, and Cape May Town. Most of the coastal areas and tidal marshes in Atlantic County and Cumberland County provide both sora and clapper.

Delaware has some rail shooting on the eastern side of the state, between Delaware City and Blackbird. There are no guides in this area who specialize in railing.

Maryland provides excellent rail shooting, which varies from year to year. The Patuxent marshes occasionally are black with them in September. The marshes along the Patapsco River also provide good rail shooting. Information on guides can be obtained from the Game and Fish Commission, Baltimore 2, Md. This state also owns an excellent colored motion picture, with sound, on rail shooting, which is well worth seeing.

Virginia offers sora rail shooting in the freshwater marshes and clapper rail shooting in the saltwater areas. Practically all the sora marshes are in the hands of the private duck clubs, and it would be necessary to be a guest of one of these clubs to enjoy any sora shooting in this state. Clapper rail shooting can be arranged for by writing the postmaster at Chincoteague, Wachapreague, or Oyster, who will be able to put one in touch with guides equipped to push for clappers.

Clapper rail are killed in North Carolina. There is good rail shooting along the coast of the counties of Charlestown, Beaufort, and Georgetown in South Carolina. There is excellent clapper rail shooting around St. Simon's Sound in Georgia. The marshes around Fernandina, Fla., provide good clapper rail shooting, and many clappers are also killed around St. Augustine and Tampa. This state is also a good place in which to observe the rarer black rail and yellow rail. There are probably out-of-the-way marshes in other states where rail may be killed in small quantities; in Wisconsin and Minnesota an occasional sora or Virginia rail will fly across the front of a duck blind, but your best sora shooting, which is the sportiest type, will be found on the Connecticut River, the Patuxent River in Maryland, and the Mullica or Maurice in New Jersey.

**Equipment.** A rail boat that floats level and does not draw much water is a necessity, whether you hire a guide or there are two going who are willing to take turns pushing. The boat can vary from 14 feet in length to 16, and may be low sided. The width of the boat should be kept to a minimum in order to allow an easy entrance into the "oats." However, it can be too narrow, which would make the boat unsteady to shoot from, or allow it to sink so deep that it would not float in shallow water. Some rail boats have a moderately wide stern which will allow the pusher to carry a retriever with him without sinking the rear end of the boat too much. Cedar is suitable for a wood to build with. Bottom planking should be lengthwise of the boat to reduce to a minimum the friction between the bottom and the reeds it passes over. Waterproof plywood 1/8 inch thick has been used with success. Some of the old-timers used a slightly curved bottom instead of a flat one to reduce the friction and make the boat easier to turn in the rice tangle. Others have successfully used copper on the bottom. Grease may be applied to the bottom to make easier pushing.

The old-time rail boats which are still found on

the Housatonic River are double ended and among the easiest-pushing boats in use. When pushing up into a pocket, the pusher and gunner may exchange positions instead of reversing the boat in order to get out into the main marsh again. This maneuver saves time and extra work for the pusher. This type of boat is the best except when you carry a dog or have to work on a moderate tide where the water on the marsh is shallow. A stool firmly fastened slightly forward of the middle section of the boat is useful for the gunner to sit on or steady himself against. This should be about 30 inches high. A platform should be built across the stern end of the boat at the height of the gunwale to provide a place for the pusher to stand. A strip of wood on the platform for the pusher to brace one foot against when the shoving is hard is a necessity.

The push pole is just as important as the boat. Every pusher has his own idea of a pole. A good one can be made from straight-grained ash, free from knots, 17 feet long. A length 2 inches square can be planed down to a 1½-inch cylinder with one end tapered for 3 feet to finish it off. The other end should be provided with a wedge-shaped shoe to prevent the pole from sinking in the mud when it is set, or with a commercially made metal-jointed end. These metal ends spread out when set on the bottom and collapse when withdrawn for another set with the pole so that they do not offer so much resistance in the water or catch on the rice stalks. Most of these types of ends are weak and should be reinforced if you are going to push through heavy cover, but a strong one is much better for shoving where the bottom is soft than a wooden-wedge type. If it is difficult to find good ash, West Coast spruce is suitable for the pole.

Old-timers used the glass balls (painted white) that were made for clay-bird shooting to throw for marking the dead rail that were down. Some throw bottles, or a 4 x 4 piece of wood 12 inches long, turned at one end to provide a good grip for the hand, painted several bright colors so that it will show up in the marsh and mark a dead rail. It is necessary to use something to mark, as you may have three rail down and drop another on your way in to pick up the first one down, and it is almost impossible to remember more than one fall because the cover all looks alike. Unless the rail is floating belly up, his coloration blends into the marsh and you can be on top of him without seeing him unless you throw a marker to guide you near the fall.

A well-trained Irish water spaniel or other retriever that has had experience with rail is very valuable in recovering down birds. In fact, it is almost impossible to find a wing-tipped bird without a good dog, and even then the dog has his work cut out for him, as the sora provides very little scent and will run, dive, and swim to get away. Irish water spaniels have been used successfully on the Housatonic River on rail, and have been particularly useful in working out ahead of the gunner and flushing rail when it was impossible to shove a boat in the marsh because the tide was not high enough. Anyone using a dog for this type of hunting should wait until the dog is grown and fully developed, as the cover provides the hardest kind of going and can injure a growing dog. Short-legged dogs are almost useless on the Connecticut and many other sora rivers, as they literally get stuck in the heavy, matted cover and cannot move. In many places a dog cannot swim or walk, but just seems to pull himself through the morass by his elbows and will power. The Irish spaniel will usually remember two falls, and you can send him for the birds he marks while you pick up the others. This saves much shooting time, which is definitely limited by the two hours the tide is high.

When the dog has a cripple down you will see very little of the dog as he will spend most of his time under the water; but with a dog, very few cripples will get away and he will mark some birds you fail to mark. Some dogs dislike retrieving a rail as much as a woodcock, but if they have been force broken and they are worked enough on rail they will soon get over their dislike and the patience you have shown will be well rewarded. The rail boats are so low sided that it is not difficult to get the dog back in the boat. Many dogs can get in by themselves, and others can be helped by the pusher's holding his hand firmly against the back of the dog's head so he may brace himself against it and get a firm push against the side of the boat with his hind legs to boost himself into the boat. It is wise to have a rail built along the front edge of the pushing platform so the water the dog brings in will run back into the marsh and not into the bottom of the boat.

There is one other accessory worth mentioning; that is a rack to hold a gun, which is fastened to the pusher's platform in such a way as to provide a place for the gun close enough to the pusher, so that he may shove and drop the pole when a rail rises and pick up his gun and shoot before the rail drops down in the cover again. This rack, of course, is used only when a man is alone and has no one to shoot for him. Some men recommend tying a line to the pole so it may be recovered easily from where it has been dropped in the marsh; in many cases, however, the line is a nuisance. High tides and open covers provide the best conditions for this type of rail shooting, as here the rail will stay in the air longer. It is possible for a single shooter-pusher to boat five out of eight rail that rise from the marsh.

A strong back and arms are necessary for a good pusher, but he also must have done plenty of it in order to have acquired the knack of pushing, which is necessary to keep the boat moving steadily on a line or turn it quickly to try a likely-looking cover to one side or the other. A beginner usually finds it difficult to keep the boat straight in light cover. It is necessary to use the pole almost like a canoe paddle at the end of the stroke. Most pushers shove from the right side of the stern of the boat, first setting the pole firmly on the mud bottom. When resetting the pole for another stroke, start raising the top end of the pole hand over hand until you can swing the pushing end of the pole forward over the water by lowering the top end of the pole to a horizontal position. Avoid whacking the head of your gunning companion, who is on the stool ahead of you. This happens once in a while, and is as unpardonable as hooking your guide in the ear on the backcast while salmon fishing from a canoe.

It is wise to wear white, and you can dress lightly as the weather is mild when most rail are killed. If there are many rail boats out, white will show up, and neither you nor your pusher will receive a charge of shot in face or neck. This was not uncommon in the old days when the cover was heavy and the rail parties plentiful but careless. It is also wise in heavy cover for the pusher to cry out as he moves his boat forward.

**Guns and Loads.** Twelve-gauge guns may be used, but a 20- or 28-gauge gun that is bored very open is more suitable. Seven-eighths of an ounce of No. 11 shot with two drams of powder makes the best rail load for a 12-gauge gun, and No. 11 shot with the loads proportionally reduced in the smaller bores will kill your rail cleanly without spoiling the flesh. At the present time Winchester is the only company loading with this size shot. The next best load is a light "skeet" load using No. 9 shot. The .410 shotgun is not recommended as it does not carry enough shot and most of them shoot too close. The drop of the gun is not important as long as the gun fits the shooter.

**Open Seasons and Limits.** The rail season starts in most states on September 1 and runs to November 30. The month of September and the first part of October provide the best part of the shooting in the northern states; it lasts later farther south. The season and bag limits are set by the Federal government, as the rail is a migratory bird; they do not vary much from year to year, but it is best to check with your state warden to be sure.

**Hunting Methods.** The birds found in the first part of the season are usually local sora; they are found deeper in the marshes, and there is more fat on them than on the flight birds. Places where the "oats" have been broken and matted down usually hold more rail than the areas where the stalks are still upright. Rice that has ripened and is dark in color will harbor more rail than the "oats" whose seed is still green in color. There will be plenty of long, thin, husk-covered seed floating on the water in the areas where the seed has ripened enough to attract the rail. Sometimes it will be ripe on one side of the river and not on the other. Small stands of cattails or heavier growths of other marsh plants scattered in the "oats" or along the edge of the "oats" are worth pushing into, as the rail will invariably move into this type of cover if they are hunted hard. Many times the tide is not high enough to allow pushing through this type of heavy cover easily, so you are limited to striking at it with the push pole in the hope that a rail will jump; or, if you have a dog, he can be sent through it. The best way to find where the rail are is to explore and remember the spots where you found them until the next time or next year, as the rail usually stay in the same areas year after year unless the feed is killed off.

The boat should be shoved through the "oats" as rapidly as possible in order to flush the rail. If you move too slowly the rail will just run ahead of the boat, or off to one side, and will not rise for a shot. Many times you will see a young, immature rail running along the matted-down stalks with his head out and his tail up in the air. You will shout and strike at him with your pole, and the little bird will just keep on running and disappear into the "oats."

The shover who is standing on a platform has his feet higher up on the boat than the gunner, and so he will usually see the sora flush from the cover before the gunner who is sitting on his stool, and should shout "Mark ahead"—or left or right as the case may be. Many amateur pushers get so excited when a rail rises that all they can do is shout "Shoot! Shoot!" The gunner invariably looks in the opposite direction from which the rail rose and does not turn the right way until the rail is down in the cover again, and so the shot is missed.

The sora will provide all types of shots. He is not a fast flier, although on a windy day he can really move and change direction quickly. A rail can get up right beside the boat or away ahead of it, and in many cases he will get up behind the boat. Practically every shot offered during a tide is different. The rail is such a small target that the shooting is sporty, and during the hour before the top of the tide and the hour after it starts to ebb there are more opportunities to fire than on most of the other game birds during a similar period. One gunner who was a good bird shot, but had not done much rail shooting, reported they were an easy, slow-moving target, but they did not stay long enough in the air to let him get his gun on them. The rail is anxious to get back into cover, and the inexperienced rail shooter does have trouble getting onto them; this makes railing all the more exciting.

Many times four or five rail will flush at the same time, all within gunshot, but rising from different parts of the marsh and moving in different directions. An old rail shooter will invariably make a double, but the newcomer has difficulty in making up his mind which rail to shoot at. The commonest fault of the beginner is overshooting. During most of the time a rail is in flight he is dropping, and at the end of his flight he just points his two wings to the sky and lets himself drop into the tangle of "oats" just as the gunner shoots and thinks he has him. However, the pusher knows better, even if he does shove over to where the bird dropped in and show the gunner there is no rail lying there. Occasionally a rail will be killed too close to the boat and the bird spoiled for the table. Close birds should be waited out, even if it means missing the shot when they drop into cover before you expect them to pass from your sights. Rail will fly much stronger on sunny and windy days than they will on rainy and dull days. Where the area is large and the cover does not rise above the side of the boat, the rail will make a longer flight before he drops into cover. Black grass, onion grass, and redtop provide this type of cover where both Virginia and sora rail are found, but they are never so plentiful as in wild rice which towers above the gunner and in many cases above the pusher.

Mr. Fred Sturges of Fairfield, Conn., is listed on Johnson's old records as killing nine sora on Sept. 8, 1893, and at the age of 73, on the same September date in 1947, he killed rail on the same Housatonic River where he killed his first rail at 19; obviously, rail shooting is a real sport that can provide pleasure throughout most of one's life. It is a nice way to start youngsters shooting as well as the womenfolk in the family, as the two hours on the sora marsh will provide enough shots so that mistakes can be corrected and another chance to improve the shot can be offered on the same day. The country where rail

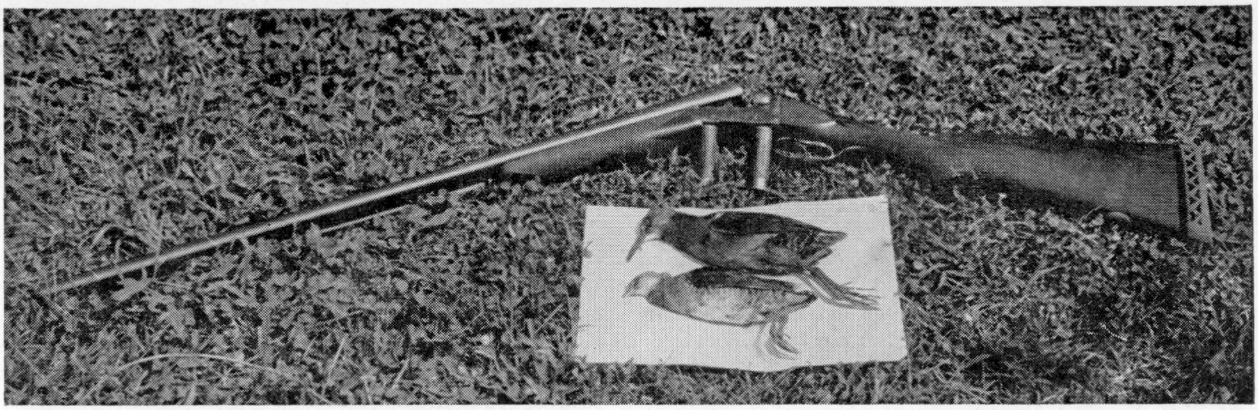

PLATE II. Comparison in Size Between the Virginia Rail (upper) and Carolina Rail.

are found is beautiful in the fall, and the weather is so mild that no one has to bundle up in heavy clothing. Father can be right there on the pusher's platform and observe the misses and correct them, or applaud the hits. Curtis Marshall, living in the same town as Mr. Sturges, killed five rail his first time out at the age of nine, using a .410; this was worth-while shooting, even if he fired 23 other shots at birds he missed on the same day.

It is fun for two men who have shot together to be pushed side by side by separate guides in a large marsh area where the rail are plentiful. The gunner on the right shoots at the birds rising on that side, and the man on the left takes those on his side. If the right-hand man is a right-handed shot he is shooting under a little handicap, and so it is more even if there is a left-handed gunner on the right. Regardless of any handicap, there is always an opportunity for one or the other to "wipe his companion's eye" by knocking down a bird that was missed by the first one to shoot. This type of shooting is one of the most enjoyable forms of rail shooting, and in the old days quite a bit of money would change hands before the end of the tide was reached —shooting for a quarter a bird. Many a good shot could have his morale lowered by the pusher's rocking the boat slightly just as he made his shot; this would be hard to blame on the pusher, as there were many times when the going was hard, and the pusher had sometimes to rock the boat in order to force it over or through a particularly heavy cover. Sometimes, for a little fun, a gunner would persuade the pusher of his companion's boat to throw his shooting off a bit by unnecessary movement of the boat. Today's guides, however, can be depended upon to become motionless when the rail flushes and the gunner swings for his shot. The older a man gets, the slower he swings on a bird, and the smaller the arc in which he can swing, so there is many a time when a guide can turn the boat enough with the bird so that the older man can catch up with a bird he would otherwise miss as it quarters. Some of the younger shots are so agile there seeems to be no limit to their swing or vision, and they will swing so vigorously on a rail, getting up amidship of the boat and passing toward the stern, that it will cause the pusher to drop face down on the platform of the boat.

**Virginia Rail.** The Virginia rail or corncrake *(Rallus virginianus)* is a larger bird than the sora, about the size of an English snipe. As his bill is longer, he is better fitted for probing in the mud for his food like a woodcock. On some sora marshes he is found in the same kind of cover as the sora, but on the Housatonic and many other rivers he is found on the marshes nearer the sea where the water is saltier and the marsh growth is not so high. His flight appears a little stronger than the sora's, he stays in the air for a greater distance, and he looks darker all over when flying.

The Virginias breed from northern Illinois, Pennsylvania, and Long Island to Manitoba and Labrador. They winter from the southern edge of their breeding ground southward. Upper parts of the Virginia are fuscous or black, the feathers bordered by pale grayish-brown; wings and tail are dark grayish-brown; wing coverts are rufous, lores whitish, cheeks gray, throat white, rest of the under parts cinnamon-rufous; flanks and under-tail coverts are barred with black and white. They build their nests of grass in the marsh and lay 6 to 12 eggs. Their blood-red eyes are deeply sunk in their narrow heads. Their legs are long and four-toed, with the hind toe smaller and higher on their leg. The legs dangle below the body when they fly.

This species of rail has the same habits as the sora in skulking in fresh or brackish marshes, and preferring to skitter over the floating leaves of marsh plants rather than rise on wings over the cover when frightened. The Virginia, when startled in the fall, gives a short, abrupt *"kep"* similar to the sora's cry.

Hunt the Virginia the same way as you do the sora, but in the fall look for him in quantities nearer the salt water than the sora. They are not so plentiful as the sora, so it is always a novelty and a pleasure to have one in your bag. Once you have located an area where they are found, remember it and you will find them back there the following fall.

**Clapper Rail.** The clapper rail or marsh hen *(Rallus longirostris crepitans)* is one of our largest rail, about the size of an American coot, but with a very long bill. The clapper flies with the same labored wing-beat as the smaller rail show, and dangles its leg when in flight. He lives in the grassy salt-water marshes, and in the southern part of the range, in mangrove swamps. One of the breeding places in Connecticut is in the marsh back of the beach in the town of Fairfield, and although summer cottages are crowding in on the marsh, and cars run up and down the roads cutting across the marsh, you can hear the clappers calling if you walk quietly along a road. It is difficult to flush a clapper unless the tide is high enough to force a boat across the marsh. They will skulk and move about over well-traveled paths in the marsh grass.

The clapper can generally be told from the king rail by its grayish instead of brownish or blackish upper parts. Its breasts and flanks are paler, as are also the wing coverts. The clapper's upper parts are pale greenish-olive, the feathers widely margined with gray; wings and tail are grayish-brown, wing-coverts pale cinnamon, much washed with gray; the throat is white, neck and breast are pale, between ochraceous and cream-buff, more or less washed with grayish; belly and sides are gray or brownish-gray barred with white. They breed in the salt marshes of the Atlantic coast from Connecticut to the Gulf of Mexico, and winter in small numbers from near the northern limit of the range southward. They live in colonies although they are not strictly gregarious.

They are hunted more in the South, where they are known as marsh hens, and certain marshes that are saltier than the marshes found farther up the tidal rivers are the best places to hunt them. Most of the southern marshes have a very small rise and fall of tides. In many places the rise is not much over 6 inches, and so it is necessary to wait for an exceptional high tide brought on by the moon or wind to provide enough water for a boat to be pushed through the marsh. Without a good tide it is difficult to flush the clapper. However, with only a few inches of water on the marsh, a man with a good pair of retrievers or springers can have a few hours of good sport and see some nice dog work. It is much easier on the legs if a pair of sneakers are worn instead of boots, as the walking is heavy through the shallow water. Most of the marshes have a reasonably hard surface, but there will be soft places and holes where a man can go down and get wet all over. Georgia, as well as Virginia, provides clapper rail shooting. As the clapper is a larger target, he is not quite so sporty to shoot as a sora. He is a good table bird, but the sora is a tastier dish.

**General Notes.** The other smaller rail, which are the black rail and the yellow rail, are not hunted in great quantities, and although they are seen often in Florida and other parts of the South, it is rare when anyone sees or kills one in the North. King rail are not plentiful in any one spot, but may form part of a bag on a sora or clapper marsh.

The rail pass through cycles of plenty and scarcity just the same as other game birds. Too high water will drown out their nests. A drought will deprive the young of feed, and a fire on the breeding areas will kill young rail that cannot fly as well as many adults that can fly. Agriculture and marsh reclamation have reduced the number of available resting and feeding places on their migratory routes as well as their wintering grounds, but occasional reports of marshes black with rail in these modern times show that civilization has not made too serious inroads into their number. Many states where there are rail report that their gunners make no real attempt to gun for rail. It is hard work to shove for rail when it is necessary to do this yourself where no guides are available, and most of the old pushers have died off and there are no young ones to take their places. All these facts are favorable for rail to at least hold their own. However, the states where wild rice or oats is growing should take steps to increase the growth of rice and replant where it has died out, and make a real survey to discover why it has died out. In many states, when the rice disappears the rail will go with it.

It is possible for two amateurs taking turns pushing a properly made rail boat to have some fun on a good tide, but their shooting would be more fun and more certain if they hire a good local guide who knows his marsh. This man has probably been pushing for years and knows just where the rail are to be found. He is cheerful and never complains when you miss a bird, although it can be most discouraging to a pusher to see his gunner continually miss the rail he puts up. Most guides now have power boats to move the gunner up to the rail marsh and tow the rail boats. On many of the good tidal rail rivers there are all kinds of wild life to see. The graceful white American egret is always seen in the fall along the Housatonic. A least bittern may jump before your boat and almost fool you into thinking he is a large rail. You will denounce the large flocks of blackbirds, chattering and stealing the "oats" you feel should be saved for your rail; your trigger finger may itch when a mallard or pintail jumps in front of you; and you can watch the blue-wing teal that are plentiful on this river in September, but will be on their way south long before the duck season opens. The tide may not be such that a lunch is needed. It is always good, however, to have a couple of sandwiches and a jug of milk or a bottle of beer and pull into the bank after the tide has dropped so the boat can no longer be shoved through the oats, and at least satisfy the pusher's hunger and thirst, as he is always thirsty even though he has stopped for an occasional swig at his water bottle. This is the time to talk over the shots missed, the difficult ones made, or laugh again at the thought of the pusher walking himself off the platform into the water.

Everyone has different ideas about cooking a rail. They are tasty whether broiled a short time over an open flame or casseroled in the French manner as long as they are not overcooked and dried out. Pick them but never skin them, although it means more work, or you will lose all the good juices. Avoid much seasoning, or the delicate flavor of the sora will be lost. (See under "Game Cookery.")

Our forefathers knew the rail for what he is, a sporty target and a rare table delicacy that was well worth the time, powder, and shot spent on him, and they probably blessed the fact he was no bigger and that he lacked the habits of the black duck and broadbill which kept the market shooters' big guns booming in the 19th century.

Probably no form of wing shooting is more suitable for the training of the youngster than that of rail shooting, for this bird, although not a difficult target for the expert, trains the novice in alertness and quick shooting. Also, because of the tall wild rice cover, the pusher usually is able to tell his pupil whether he was holding high, low, behind, or ahead of the bird. Even a poor rail shot usually is able to bag a few birds, and for the novice even a small success is encouraging.

## GREATER YELLOW-LEGS *Totanus melanoleucus*

COMMON NAMES: Big Cucu, Big Tell-Tale, Big Yellow-Legged Plover, Cucu, Greater Tell-Tale, Long-Legged Tattler, Stone Bird, Stone Snipe, Tell-Tale Godwit, Winter Yellow-Legs, Yellow-Shins, Yelper.

**History.** Although their flesh was never held in as much esteem as that of some other members of the sandpiper family, notably the upland plover and the woodcock, both greater and lesser yellow-legs have long ranked high as game birds.

The colloquial name "cucu," often applied to the greater yellow-legs, actually refers to the call of the lesser. They are extremely vociferous birds and many of their common names stem from this trait. They are commonly found in company with curlews, plovers, and other shorebirds on the tidal flats and beach ponds. In these groups the greater yellow-legs always act as sentinels and are the first to sound the alarm. Their shrill cries arouse the less wary birds into taking wing also, and for this reason old-time gunners dubbed them "tell-tales" and "tattlers."

**Identification.** The greater yellow-legs attains a length of 14 or 15 inches, making it second in size only to the Hudsonian curlew, which is the largest of the sandpipers. The head, neck, breast, and under parts are white streaked with dark brown. These dusky markings appear as dark, broken lines on the forehead, crown, and back of the neck. The sides of the head and throat are finely lined with the same color. The front of the neck, the breast, and sides of the body are more or less regularly streaked with brownish-gray markings which resemble tiny arrowheads. A conspicuous white ring encircles the eye and there is a small dusky mark in front of it. The bill is long and slender and greenish-brown in color. In some specimens the bill has a tendency to curve slightly upward at the tip.

The back—from the base of the neck—and the wing coverts are a blackish-brown but each feather is edged and tipped with a lighter tone which creates a sort of mottled appearance. The rump and the tail are white, the latter having narrow bars of brownish-gray. The legs and feet are bright yellow.

In flight, the greater yellow-legs appears as a dark-winged bird without wing stripes and with a conspicuously white rump and tail.

**Characteristics.** The greater yellow-legs are extremely watchful and wary birds, very difficult to approach, yet they are often readily duped by decoys and an imitation of their call. When coming in to the artificials, or to other birds at rest, they sail slowly on extended wings and offer an easy target. Their flight is deliberate, in contrast to the twisting, rapid wing-beats of the snipe.

When alarmed they repeatedly voice a loud, clear, whistled *"whew, whew, whew"* and are well known for another distinctive cry which sounds like *"dear, dear, dear."* During the mating season another call is added to their repertoire, an oft-repeated *"whee-oodle, whee-oodle, whee-oodle."*

Their food consists largely of minnows and various forms of aquatic life which they obtain from the

Allan D. Cruikshank, from Natl. Audubon Society.

PLATE I. Greater Yellow-legs.

water or along the shore. Their favorite feeding grounds are on the bare mud flats exposed by the falling tide, where they find a variety of small marine life.

The nest is sometimes in the open but more often is hidden under a clump of grass or low bushes. Generally it is no more than a depression in the ground and often not lined. The usual four eggs are greenish-gray marked boldly with splotches of chocolate-brown, blackish-brown, and lavender.

The juveniles are similar to the adults except for being lighter on the upper parts and having dark streaks only on the neck and chest.

**Range and Distribution.** This bird breeds from western Alaska to Labrador and Anticosti Island, as far south as Minnesota and northern Illinois. It winters from southern California across Texas, Louisiana, and Georgia southward.

The migration is erratic because not all the birds are mated at any one season and the unpaired birds often remain south for the entire year. Waves of migrating flocks seem to come and go along the coast at indefinite periods.

The greater yellow-legs is making a definite come-back in many areas, but most shooters are agreed that the time has not yet come to repeal the regulations protecting it.

## LESSER YELLOW-LEGS

*Totanus flavipes*

Common Names: Common Yellow-Legs, Lesser Long-Legged Tattler, Lesser Tell-Tale, Lesser Yellow-Shanks, Little Stone Bird, Little Stone Snipe, Little Tell-Tale, Small Cucu, Summer Yellow-Legs, Yellow-Legged Plover.

**History.** Formerly one of the most numerous of the shorebirds, the lesser yellow-legs has shown less decline than any other species. The great flocks of the early days are probably gone forever but the remaining birds hold their numbers and in some localities even show some increase.

**Identification.** The lesser yellow-legs is exactly the same as the greater except for size.

**Characteristics.** This miniature of the greater yellow-legs possesses the same traits and habits as his larger relative. A glance at the common names above will show that he too has thwarted many a gunner by his timely warning to the other birds. Despite their watchfulness, however, the lesser decoy as readily as the greater and if one is shot from the flock the others are likely to hover about uttering shrill cries and presenting easy targets.

The food of the lesser yellow-legs consists chiefly of insects and minute aquatic larvae.

Their call notes are flatter and less penetrating than those of the greater. The usual call is a single or double note, *"cu"* or *"cu-cu."*

**Range and Distribution.** The lesser yellow-legs breeds from northern Quebec across to Alaska, south to Manitoba. The migration is mainly east of the Rocky Mountains. They are seldom seen along the eastern coast in the spring because the main flight northward follows the Mississippi Valley route. The birds come down the Atlantic coast from July to the first of October and winter in South America.

W. V. Crich, from Natl. Audubon Society.

Plate I. Lesser Yellow-legs.

Allan D. Cruickshank, from Natl. Audubon Society.

PLATE I. Wilson's Snipe.

# WILSON'S SNIPE

*Capella delicata*

COMMON NAMES: Alewife, American Snipe, Bog Snipe, Common Snipe, English Snipe, Gutter Snipe, Jacksnipe, Marsh Snipe, Meadow Snipe, Shad Bird, Shad Spirit.

**History.** Although generally known as jacksnipe, this bird is often referred to along the coastal areas as the shad bird or shad spirit because it is said to appear when the shad bush blooms and the first run of shad start up the rivers to spawn. The scientific name, *"Delicata,"* is well chosen, for the Wilson's snipe is indeed a delicacy. Long a favorite with sportsmen, this grand shorebird continues to furnish both excellent shooting and fine eating. Although it is less numerous now than in the palmy days of gunning, there is reason to believe that the present numbers will continue and may show a gratifying increase.

**Identification.** In general appearance, this snipe is a brownish bird with a long slender bill, light under parts, and short orange-brown tail. Both sexes are alike in coloration.

In detail the basic color of the head, neck, throat, and breast is a pale brownish-white. This is broken, however, by two brownish-black stripes extending from the base of the bill over the crown of the head to the back of the neck. Another dusky streak extends from the bill to the eye and a little beyond. The prominent brown eye is surrounded by a white ring except at the front and back. There is a small dusky patch on each cheek. The throat is plain but the back of the head, nape of the neck, chest, and breast are regularly streaked with dusky brown. The back and shoulders are brownish-black mixed with chestnut and buff. The feathers on the shoulders have white edging which appears as a lateral white stripe on each side of the bird. The wings are a mixture of reddish-brown, black, and white. The upper tail coverts are brown with narrow black barring. The tail feathers are dusky at their base, blending to bright orange-brown and ending in a sub-terminal bar of black with a white tip. The belly is white and the sides of the body are pale brownish with numerous narrow streaks of dusky brown. The bill is long and slender and the upper mandible extends over the lower. The color is dull flesh except at the tip and along the ridge of the upper mandible. The feet are greenish-gray.

**Characteristics.** Wilson's snipe prefers the fresh-water marshes and the low, boggy meadowlands, but is often found in the brackish marshes along the coast. In spring they sometimes frequent swales and mowing fields, and in the winter or early spring may occasionally linger in the same springy runs of birch, maples, or alders as the woodcock. Usually, however, they show a decided preference for open spaces.

Two things are essential to their well-being: a soft, spongy ground which will offer little resistance to their probing bills, and tufts or long grass, or hummocks which provide concealment. The snipe, unlike most members of its family, seldom ventures out on the bare mud flats in the daytime.

Their food, which is four-fifths animal, consists chiefly of various insects. Crane flies, beetles, dragonfly nymphs, and numerous other larvae form the bulk of their diet; crustaceans and earthworms are also eaten readily and locusts and grasshoppers help to round out the menu. Most of this food is taken by probing in the soft mud with their slender, flexible bills. Although less nocturnal than its close relative the woodcock, the jacksnipe feeds and migrates mostly at night or in thick weather.

Hidden in the long grass these birds are seldom seen until they spring suddenly into the air as if propelled. It is possible that this Jack-in-the-box trait has earned them their popular name. As they spring upward they utter harsh, rasping cries of *"scaipe, scaipe, scaipe"* and immediately dart off in twisting, erratic flight.

At the beginning of the mating season, usually mid-May or early June, the male stages a unique aerial display to win his mate. Soaring to a considerable height he swiftly describes wide circles in the air and suddenly plummets earthward with great velocity. During the descent the rush of air through the extended wings makes a low, tremulous, humming sound. This performance, which is usually reserved for early morning, or for evening twilight, sometimes takes place on moonlight nights or during the day if the weather is lowering. It is often repeated for hours at a time.

As a variation to this drumming, or "bleating," as it is called, the male sometimes flies low to the ground uttering a peculiarly penetrating and continuous cry of *"kuk, kuk, kuk, kuk, kuk"* for several minutes. Occasionally he alights briefly on a tree or stump but continues to call incessantly.

The nest is a grass-lined hollow on marshy ground. Three to four gray-green eggs, splotched and streaked with light and dark brown and black, are deposited and the female sits closely during incubation. The young birds closely resemble the adults and mature rapidly.

**Range and Distribution.** The Wilson's snipe breeds from northwestern Alaska east to Newfoundland, as far south as California, southern Colorado, northern Illinois, Pennsylvania, and New Jersey. It migrates southward from mid-September to freeze-up. The migratory movements are erratic. The birds may suddenly appear in a place one day and be gone the next.

The winter range extends from the southern tier of states southward to northern South America. The birds are usually fairly plentiful in the Louisiana marshes during the winter season.

# SHOREBIRD SHOOTING

Shorebird shooting, except in a few areas in Canada where these birds are present in sufficient numbers to make the sport interesting as well as productive, is a thing of the past. The snipe and plover, once so plentiful on our coastal marshes, have been reduced to a small fraction of their numbers, and it is generally recognized that nothing short of a miracle will ever remove these birds from the protected list.

In a few of the Atlantic coastal areas, primarily in the more isolated sections, the birds are reported to be staging a recognizable comeback, but this condition is far from general. In other areas, equally isolated, where the wildfowler of 30 years ago would see several hundreds in the course of a day's duck shooting, it is an event when a single jacksnipe or plover is seen. The decline of these birds is attributed not to hunting pressure, but to the encroachment of civilization on their breeding and feeding grounds.

In the "old days," several hunting methods were practiced, including that of shooting them over decoys. Today, even on the majority of the good snipe-hunting sections of Canada, one rarely comes across a snipe decoy; when one does, it is a good idea to buy it as a collector's item. Occasionally, while visiting one of the old guides at Chesapeake Bay, Barnegat Bay, Great South Bay, or Merrymeeting Bay, one discovers a snipe or plover decoy, or even a curlew decoy. Then comes a half-hour tale of the days when the hunter could "fill a tow sack with snipe in an hour's shooting."

Normally, the hunter would set out his decoys on a mud flat or sandspit, preferably near the mouth of a tidal river adjacent to a marsh. Shorebirds, as their name implies, are inclined to trade along the fringe of waterways or coastal beaches, and the average shooter found he had as much sport pass shooting as he did decoy shooting. On many of the inland rivers, decoys were rigged out on the open points of low marshy islands, or on the bare points that often protruded at a bend in the river.

This was the sport in which the quick, *snap* shooter did most of the execution. Those who have seen a flight of snipe (or "whisp," as it was termed in older times) swerve in and out along a beach at high speed—now almost sweeping the sand with their wings, an instant later 60 feet high—realize that the man in a blind had to do some quick shooting to score. The man with an open-bored shotgun who could shoot quickly and with reasonable accuracy was the man who took top honors on snipe and plover.

Market hunters often rigged out their stilt decoys on a beach and sought a rough blind in the dune grass. They were interested not so much in sport as in birds for the market, and normally they would wait until a large flight or "whisp" settled among the decoys. Old bay records indicate that often as many as 80 to 130 birds would be clustered among the decoys. Then the hunter would rise up and the birds would jump to a bunched flight, on which he would fire. One old Barnegat bayman reported killing as many as 54 snipe by firing both barrels of his

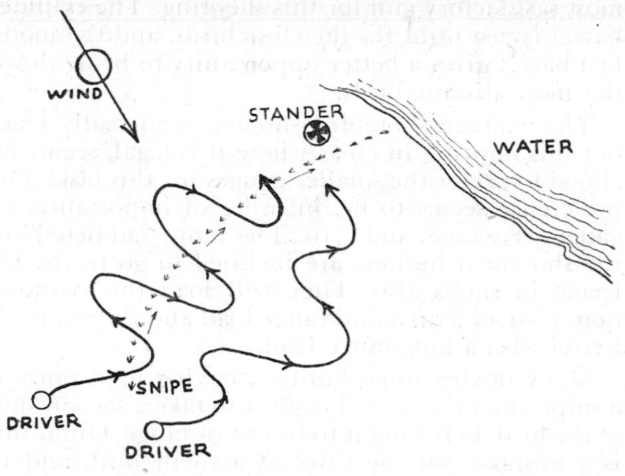


PLATE I. Drivers normally would follow the course shown in pushing snipe past a stander.

8-gauge gun into the bunched birds. Other market hunters would fire one barrel while the birds were among the decoys, the other just as they took flight. This accounts for the fact that so many of the old snipe decoys are badly pockmarked with shot.

Today there are but two methods generally practiced. One can be followed by the merest novice, provided he can shoot quickly and hold true, but the second requires one or two companions and calls for some knowledge of snipe habits.

The first method, with or without the aid of a dog, merely requires legs stout enough to stand up under a few hours of tramping the marsh—which can be heavy going. These birds avoid dry ground, and seem to prefer a terrain that causes the hunter to sink halfway to his knees at every step. Their ideal cover seems to be a salt meadow with an inch or two of water covering it, but with an occasional hummock that is barely moist.

Unless you can mark your birds down better than the average, a retriever is a *must,* for snipe seem to blend perfectly with their habitat. Some hunters mark a bird down, remove the empty shell from their gun and, without removing their gaze from the spot marked, throw the shell as near as they can to that spot. Even this method is not always successful, and the real answer is a good retriever. A spaniel that remains at heel until after the bird is down is preferred by many. The man who gets a double often fails to recover one of the birds unless he has a dog. It must be admitted, however, that doubles on snipe are not common, as any shorebird hunter will testify.

The other method, and one calling for more experience, is that of *driving* the birds. Several factors which affect the success of this procedure, namely, the wind and its direction, the terrain, and the location of the near-by body of water. It also calls for experience and co-operation on the part of the driver or drivers.

When disturbed, these birds normally will fly into the wind, then make a climbing turn across the wind, and in many instances seem to favor a turn toward the nearest body of water.

Successful driving depends entirely upon the knowledge and experience of the drivers, for they can shift the angle of their approach if they see the birds are passing short or over the stander. In some instances, the stander finds it necessary to move 30 or 40 yards in order to bring the passing birds within range. Usually the first few birds flushed will indicate the route the majority will follow.

If there happens to be a line of trees with a gap in them, between the field and the adjacent body of water, the snipe seem to select this gap as a route, although the reason for it is obscure, as usually they pass over higher than the trees.

In driving, noise is to be avoided. Merely enough movement to insure the flushing of the birds is the primary requirement. The drivers must cover the ground thoroughly, however, and work as a team, each overlapping the other's course in criss-crossing the field. Also, the drivers should attempt no shooting, regardless of the opportunities offered. Their turn will come when the others drive.

Often it is possible to drive a field in the morning and again in the afternoon, and by watching the destination of the birds after they have been flushed from the first field, their general location can be determined for the next drive. Often it is possible to spend an entire morning alternately driving two fields, for snipe and other shorebirds of the same family are inclined to select one area for feeding during a certain period, and unless badgered by hunters day after day, will not change their feeding grounds.

Once he has located a good snipe area, the hunter is assured of getting some of the most difficult and at the same time most interesting shooting. The man who can score on three shots out of five on driven snipe, especially in a high wind, need not fear for his laurels as a wing shot in almost any company.

Most of the Canadian coastal marshes, especially those on the Atlantic coast from Nova Scotia southward, have their population of snipe, and they are rarely hunted. The majority of the local hunters prefer woodcock, grouse, or waterfowl shooting, and exhibit little interest in tramping the low ground for a bird that is a difficult target and requires a large bag to constitute a meal. Visiting Americans, except for occasional waterfowl hunters who are confronted with "bluebird weather," are inclined to pass up the snipe in favor of almost any other game bird that happens to be available. Older sportsmen, however, remember the joys of shorebird shooting from the "old days," and often they pass up good opportunities in the duck blind to get a morning of snipe shooting.

The Canadian shore of the St. Lawrence is another haven for these birds, as are the marshes and meadows bordering many of the larger rivers that feed the St. Lawrence. The marshes of Lac St. Pierre, which is nothing more than a wide bulge of the St. Lawrence, were once famous shorebird grounds, but today the visiting hunter might spend a week on these broad meadows without encountering another shorebird hunter.

In some areas on the Pacific coast of Canada the birds are hunted, but here also the sport seems secondary to other forms of hunting. This is fortunate, in one sense, for it insures the future of the shorebird on this continent.

It should not be believed that the shorebirds are confined entirely to the coastal regions, although they were always more plentiful there. Many of the large inland lakes and rivers have large shorebird populations, and the central Canadian marshes provide excellent shooting. Before the law was initiated protecting these birds, Michigan snipe shooting attracted considerable attention.

There are two definite schools of thought regarding the best actual shooting practice on snipe. One holds that the hunter should be constantly alert and shoot as quickly as possible, before the bird begins its erratic flight. The other contends that the bird is still well within range after it has discontinued the zigging and zagging, and that the man who will follow the bird, hold his fire, and wait until the steady course is resumed, will do best.

**Guns and Ammunition.** The average upland game hunter has his own idea as to the best shot size for the various species of birds hunted, but the average shorebird hunter will agree that No. 10 shot is the most satisfactory for this shooting. Regardless of gauge, the double gun, with one barrel bored improved cylinder and the other modified choke, is the most satisfactory gun for this shooting. The cylinder barrel is just right for the close birds, and the modified barrel gives a better opportunity to bring down the more distant birds.

The average shorebird shooter, who really seeks out this hunting in areas where it is legal, seems inclined to prefer the smaller gauges for this task. The preference seems to be, in order of importance, 20 gauge, 28 gauge, and .410. The more "addicted" of the shorebird hunters are inclined to go to the extreme in shells also. They will load the cylinder-bored barrel with a mid-range load and the modified barrel with a long-range load.

Many novice snipe hunters, having fired once at a snipe and missed, will neglect to take a second shot at the bird, believing it to be out of range. Often this is a mistake, for the snipe is a small bird, and in flight seems smaller and therefore more distant. If No. 10 shot is used, the pattern will be much more dense than the larger shot to which the average shooter is accustomed. The longer second shot, if reasonably accurate, often will bring down the bird.

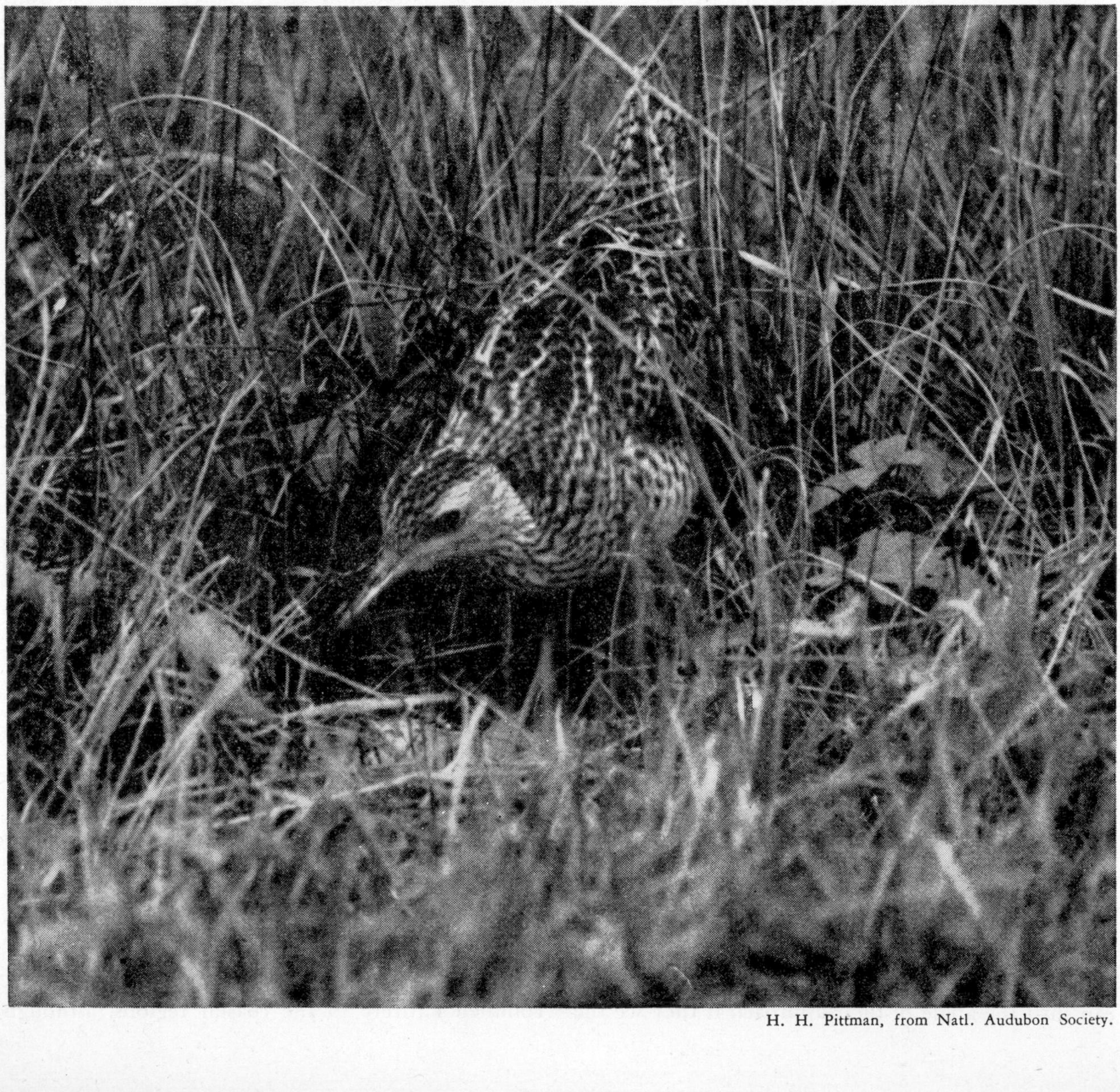

H. H. Pittman, from Natl. Audubon Society.

# WATERFOWL

The ducks and geese of North America, which play such an important part in the sporting scene, are members of a large family, known to the biologist as *Anatidae*. Throughout the world there are approximately 230 different members of this family, of which there are 61 on this continent, including the swans. In addition to the 61 species which are native here, wind, tide, and flight error bring approximately 20 other species to this continent on occasion.

Although the finer points of identification are important to the biologist, the hunter is concerned only with the more important features of the birds, features which identify them as members of the family. They are marked by the following general characteristics: a foot with four toes, three toes joined by webs, the fourth higher and not joined; a broad, flat bill (except in the case of mergansers or geese) that has *lamellae* or small serrations on the edges of the mandibles; a short leg (except in tree ducks); a flat body and (except for the ruddy ducks) a short tail, long neck, and long wing; an oil gland at the base of the tail providing an oil with which the bird dresses its plumage; flightlessness during the moulting period; a tendency to nest on the ground (with few exceptions); the ability of the young to walk and swim almost immediately after being hatched.

In waterfowl, as in other forms, the scientific nomenclature follows a definite pattern, indicating the connection between the genus, species, and sub-species. The first term employed indicates the genus, the second the species, and the third the sub-species: for example, *Branta canadensis minima*. The use of the common names of many species of waterfowl can result in considerable confusion, for many of the common names are of local origin, and the duck that is known as a bluebill in one section will be called a baldpate in another, and the bird called a bluebill there will be termed a broadbill in still another section.

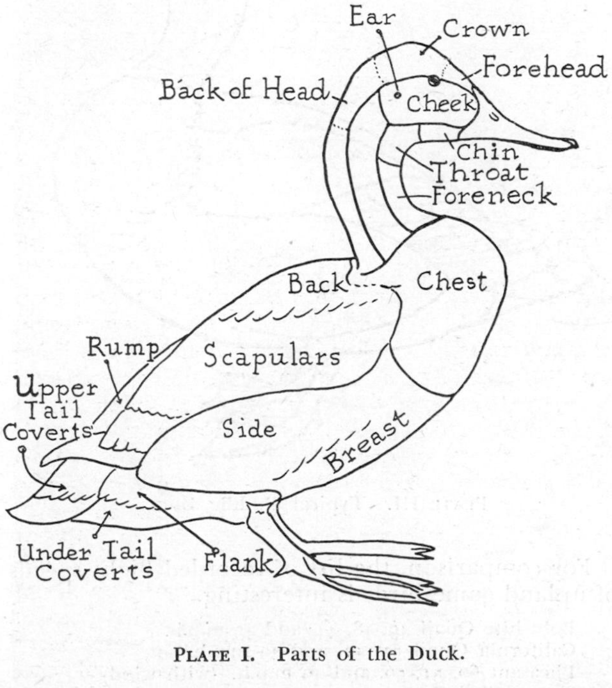


PLATE I. Parts of the Duck.

Most hunters are inclined to break ducks down into two general classifications; *puddle* ducks (river and pond ducks) and *divers* (bay, sea, or diving ducks). Under the puddle *(Antinae)* ducks come the following:

| | |
|---|---|
| Baldpate | *Mareca americana* |
| Black Duck (common) | *Anas fulvigula maculosa* |
| Black Duck (red-legged) | *Anas rubripes rubripes* |
| Florida Duck | *Anas fulvigula fulvigula* |
| Gadwall | *Chaulelasmus streperus* |
| Mallard (common) | *Anas platyrhynchos platyrhynchos* |
| Mottled Duck | *Anas fulvigula maculosa* |
| New Mexican Duck | *Anas diazi novimexicana* |
| Pintail (American) | *Dafila acuta tzitzihoa* |
| Shoveller | *Spatula clypeata* |
| Teal, Blue-winged | *Querquedula discors* |
| Teal, Cinnamon | *Querquedula cyanoptera* |
| Teal, European | *Nettion crecca* |
| Teal, Green-winged | *Nettion carolinene* |
| Widgeon, European | *Mareca penelope* |
| Wood Duck | *Aix sponsa* |

Under diving ducks *(Nyrocinae)* come the following:

| | |
|---|---|
| Bufflehead | *Glaucionetta clangula americana* |
| Canvasback | *Nyroca marila* |
| Eider, American | *Somateria molissima dresseri* |
| Eider, King | *Somateria spectabilis* |
| Eider, Northern | *Somateria molissımi borealis* |
| Eider, Pacific | *Somateria v-nigra* |
| Eider, Spectacled | *Arctonetta fischeri* |
| Eider, Steller's | *Polysticta stelleri* |
| Golden-eye, American | *Charitonette clangula americana* |
| Golden-eye Barrow's | *Glaucionetta islandica* |
| Harlequin, Eastern | *Histrionicus histrionicus histrionicus* |
| Harlequin, Western | *Histrionicus histrionicus pacificus* |
| Labrador Duck (now extinct) | *Camptorhynchus labradorius* |
| Old Squaw | *Clangula hyemalis* |
| Redhead | *Nyroca americana* |
| Ring-necked Duck | *Nyroca collaris* |
| Scaup, Greater | *Nyroca marila* |
| Scaup, Lesser | *Nyroca affinis* |
| Scoter, American | *Oidemia americana* |
| Scoter, Surf | *Melanitta perspicillata* |
| Scoter, White-winged | *Melanitta deglandi* |

The less important members of the family, so far as the hunter is concerned, are the mergansers, the tree ducks, the ruddy ducks, and the masked ducks. These include the following:

| | |
|---|---|
| American Merganser | *Mergus merganser americanus* |
| Hooded Merganser | *Lophodytes cucullatus* |
| Red-breasted Merganser | *Mergus serrator* |
| Ruddy Duck | *Erismatura jamaicensis rubida* |
| Masked Duck | *Nomonyx dominicus* |
| Black-bellied Tree Duck | *Dendrocygna autumnalis autumnalis* |
| Fulvous Tree Duck | *Dendrocygna bicolor helva* |

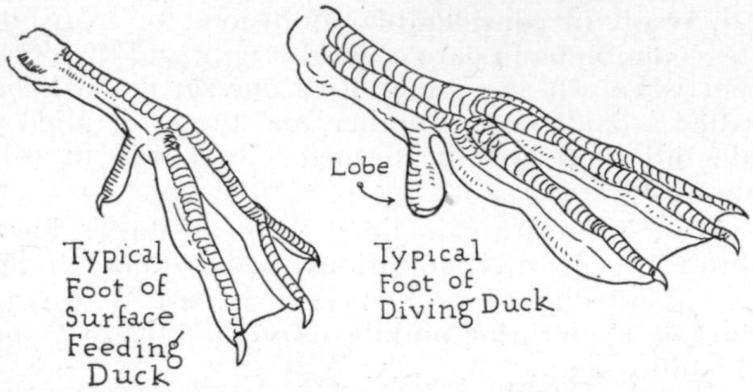


PLATE II.

The hunter is but one of the many enemies with which the waterfowl must contend, and he is responsible for but a small percentage of the annual mortality. Starvation, drought, and disease take the really large tolls, especially on the nesting and wintering grounds, and on the nesting grounds flood also claims a high percentage. Disease, however, is the worst enemy, and while much has been done to eliminate the form of *botulism* which once claimed hundreds of thousands of ducks, this disease still appears in some areas.

This disease, when first discovered, was thought to be the result of a poison peculiar to certain salts, for the areas where the greatest losses were sustained were in the West and Midwest on lakes and marshes of high alkaline content. Careful study, however, revealed that the disease was the result of bacteria, which flourished on marshes where there was considerable decayed organic material. Stagnant waters seemed to be perfect cultures for the disease, and conservation agencies took action to remedy the matter by creating dams to preserve a water level. The situation has not been fully corrected, but conditions are improving each year.

In some of the wintering areas of waterfowl lead poisoning also takes a toll, although this loss was reduced somewhat when the law made baiting illegal. Like other birds of the same family, ducks require a certain amount of grit in their gizzard in order to grind the food for digestion. In areas where the shooting was rather heavy, the ducks picked up some shot when feeding on corn and when taking small stones into the gizzard. In some instances, death resulted from one or two shot in the gizzard, and it was determined that four or five No. 4 shot were definitely a fatal dose. In these baited areas many of the ducks killed late in the season were found to be in poor condition, and gunners often remarked on the numbers of birds that seemed either crippled or sick. This could quite definitely be attributed to lead poisoning, and examination of stomach contents often revealed from 10 to 30 shot pellets.

This section would not be complete without some discussion on the flight speeds of waterfowl. This subject is one of considerable interest and no little debate among shooters, the majority of whom are inclined to attribute a higher speed to some species than they could possibly attain, and fail to recognize the speed of other species which, because of their larger size, seem to be moving more slowly.

The canvasback, which does not appear to be moving rapidly, often escapes the gunner by his deceptive speed, whereas the teals are often overled. The Canada goose, or honker, which seems to be flapping along at a leisurely pace, often is moving almost twice as fast as the shooter believes.

Since the advent of the airplane it is much easier to check the flight speed of various waterfowl, and the maximum speeds attained by some of these birds is rather surprising. Below are listed some of the ducks and geese and the speeds at which they have been clocked by both automobile and plane.

Canvasback 72, 68, 70, and 71 m.p.h.
Pintail 66, 64, 55, and 65 m.p.h.
Canada Goose 61, 60, 52, and 58 m.p.h.
Mallard 60, 58, 57, and 51 m.p.h.
Shoveller 52, 51, 46, and 45 m.p.h.
Whistling Swan 51, 48, 47, and 43 m.p.h.
Snow Goose 50, 48, 46, and 45 m.p.h.
Cackling Goose 49, 48, 43, and 42 m.p.h.
American Brant 45, 44, 43, and 41 m.p.h.
Redhead 43, 42, 41, and 40 m.p.h.
European Teal (English record) 68 m.p.h.
Cinnamon Teal (California) 59 m.p.h.
Golden-eye 50 m.p.h.
Green-wing Teal 44, 43, and 40 m.p.h. (short distance)

PLATE III. Typical Puddle Duck.

For comparison, the list of recorded flight speeds of upland game birds is interesting.

Bobwhite Quail 49, 48, 44, and 43 m.p.h.
California Quail 51, 42, and 39 m.p.h.
Pheasant 60, 51, 50, and 49 m.p.h. (with wind)
Sharp-tailed Grouse 33, 30, 29, and 28 m.p.h.
Ruffed Grouse 24, 23, and 22 m.p.h.

Undoubtedly the fastest bird on this continent is the duck hawk, or peregrine falcon, which has been clocked at speeds as high as 180 m.p.h.

Another point which causes considerable argument among the wildfowlers is that of waterfowl longevity. Average ages, compiled from several sources, indicate that the following ages might be considered to be the "life expectancy" of waterfowl.

Swans, 40 years
Geese, 30 years
Ducks, 20 to 24 years

PLATE IV. Typical Diving Duck.

One point which is the source of great debate concerns the myth that the Canada goose mates but once, and that in the event of the death of that mate it will not mate with another and will live out its days alone. This has often been proved fallacious, and there are few recorded instances where it is known to be a fact. One farmer at Lake Mattamuskeet, N. C., has stated that a gander which he had kept on the farm for 12 years lost its mate as a result of an accident. Three weeks later the gander mated with a goose on the lake and has since remained mated.

The flyways or migration routes followed by waterfowl are mysterious to humans. Although these routes cannot be accurately defined, it has been established that waterfowl and other migratory birds follow certain routes to and from their nesting and wintering grounds. While there is a certain amount of deviation, there are some species which follow a common pathway, and in many instances deviate but slightly from their course year after year. Occasional individuals may stray, but even these individuals rarely move any great distance to the right or left of their accustomed flyway.

As a result of many years of study, banding, and checking, it has been established that there are but four major flyways on this continent. These are known, merely as a means of identification, as the Atlantic, Mississippi, Central, and Pacific flyways. The maps showing the outlines of these flyways

PLATE V. Typical Tree Duck.

bring out one point quite clearly—that is, that the funnel mouth is in the north. For breeding and nesting, the birds move northward and spread out widely, but when driven southward by the cold, they move in a narrower path along a natural terrain feature. Many of the waterfowl which winter on coastal waters travel far inland to nest, as the individual flight maps shown with the various species will show. Some of the ducks that winter in the extreme southern tip of Louisiana travel all the way to northern Alaska to nest, and some of those that

PLATE VI. Typical Ruddy Duck.

winter in Florida go west and north as far as Mackenzie Bay.

Wildfowlers who kill banded birds would do much to aid the biologists, and would contribute to a greater understanding of waterfowl, if they would take the time to send these bands to the agency whose name is on the band. Do not keep the bands as souvenirs; send them in, and do your part in carrying on the study.

The following table gives the average weight of North American ducks and geese (in pounds, except where stated in ounces):

| *Species* | *Male* | *Female* |
|---|---|---|
| Blue Goose | 5¼ | 4¾ |
| Canada Goose | 9 | 8 |
| Western Canada Goose | 9 | 7¾ |
| Richardson's Goose | 5 | 4 |
| Cackling Goose | 3½ | 3 |
| Lesser Canada Goose | 5 | 4½ |
| Emperor Goose | 6 | 6¼ |
| Ross's Goose | 3 | 2¾ |
| Snow Goose | 7½ | 6 |
| Lesser Snow Goose | 5 | 4½ |
| Tule Goose | 6½ | 5½ |
| White-Fronted Goose | 5¼ | 4¾ |
| American Brant | 3¼ | 2¾ |
| Black Brant | 3¼ | 3 |
| Baldpate | 1¾ | 1½ |
| Black Duck | 2¾ | 2½ |
| Black-Bellied Tree Duck | 1¾ | 1½ |
| Bufflehead | 15 oz. | 12 oz. |
| Canvasback | 3 | 2¾ |
| American Eider | 4¼ | 3½ |
| King Eider | 4 | 3½ |
| Pacific Eider | 5¾ | 5¼ |
| Spectacled Eider | 3½ | 3½ |
| Steller's Eider | 2 | 2 |
| Florida Duck | 2¼ | 2 |
| Fulvous Tree Duck | 1¾ | 1½ |
| Gadwall | 2 | 1¾ |
| American Golden-eye | 2¼ | 1¾ |
| Barrow's Golden-eye | 2¼ | 1¾ |
| Harlequin | 1½ | 1¼ |
| Mallard | 2½ | 2¼ |
| Masked Duck | 1½ | 1¼ |
| American Merganser | 2¾ | 2¼ |
| Hooded Merganser | 1¼ | 1 |
| Red-Breasted Merganser | 2¼ | 1¾ |
| Mottled Duck | 2 | 1¾ |
| New Mexican Duck | 2 | 1¾ |
| Old Squaw | 1½ | 1¼ |
| Pintail | 2 | 1¾ |
| Redhead | 2 | 1¾ |
| Ring-Necked Duck | 1½ | 1¼ |
| Ruddy Duck | 1¼ | 1 |
| Greater Scaup | 1¾ | 1¾ |
| Lesser Scaup | 1½ | 1¼ |
| American Scoter | 2¼ | 2 |
| Surf Scoter | 2 | 1¾ |
| White-Winged Scoter | 3 | 3 |
| Shoveller | 1¼ | 1 |
| Blue-winged Teal | 13 oz. | 11 oz. |
| Cinnamon Teal | 12 oz. | 11 oz. |
| Green-winged Teal | 11 oz. | 10 oz. |
| European Teal | 10 oz. | 9 oz. |
| Widgeon (European) | 1¼ | 1¼ |
| Wood Duck | 1¼ | 1 |

# GEESE

**History.** Geese, in the terminology of the scientists, belong in the order *Anseres* (waterfowl), the family of *Anatidae* (gooselike swimmers), and the sub-family *Anserinae*. The group are close relatives of the swans, from which they differ chiefly by having a neck shorter than the body and the "lores," or space between the eye and bill, covered with feathers. They are also related to the ducks, from whom, apart from size, they differ by the sexes' being similar in color and by lacking the cere, or soft raised surface at the base of the upper bill, and having a more rounded body than most ducks.

There are about 40 species but only ten or 12 are found in this country. Of these not more than two or three are actual residents, while the others must be classed as migrant visitors from Canada and Alaska.

Of all the wildfowl on the North American continent the geese are the most highly prized from the gunner's standpoint. Their extreme wariness and the difficulties of decoying them within range of the gun are a challenge to the sportsman's skill, and the delicious flavor of their flesh ranks them as one of the outstanding game birds.

# BARNACLE GOOSE

*Branta leucopsis*

Common Names: None so far as known on the American continent. In the British Isles: Clakis, or Bar Goose. In France: Oie Bernache (barnacle goose) or Oie Nonnette (nun goose).

**History.** The barnacle goose is a European species but occasionally visits the eastern American seacoast in the fall. The name is derived from old legends and beliefs that the young came from the barnacle shells found clinging to ships, pilings, or pieces of driftwood. One fourteenth-century writer actually gave an account of *seeing* young birds emerge from these shells. The legend flourished because until comparatively recent times the breeding places of this goose were unknown and their habits obscure. So few of these birds are killed on this continent that the Fish and Wildlife Service, Washington, D. C., and the Canadian National Museum at Ottawa, Canada, ask that all specimens shot be reported to either of those offices.

**Identification.** (See color plate on p. 469.) In appearance this bird is not unlike the American or black brant. The chief difference is in the head. On the barnacle goose the head is entirely white except for a narrow streak or patch running from the bill to the eye, and a continuation of the black from the neck which extends over the crown to the forehead like a narrow hood (whence the name "nun goose" is derived.)

All other markings are similar to those of the brant except that the sides are a more silvery-gray with barred markings of white.

Both afloat and in the air the barnacle goose closely resembles the brant but the white face and throat are distinguishable from some distance.

**Characteristics.** It is not uncommon for geese to quarrel briefly while feeding but this trait is more pronounced in the barnacle goose. They seldom mix with any other species. They are the least wary of all the geese, and in direct contrast to the wily Canada goose, they sometimes fail to become alarmed even at the approach of man. This is due much more to stupidity than to tameness.

Barnacle geese are less seagoing in their feeding habits than the brant. They do some feeding on the bare tidal flats but prefer the firmer turf behind the dunes and sandhills.

**Breeding.** During the nesting season the gander keeps the usual faithful watch while the goose is sitting on four or five eggs.

The nests, usually formed of small twigs and mosses, are located in the most inaccessible places to escape foxes and other natural enemies. In some instances nests have been observed on narrow ledges with a sheer drop of more than 30 feet beneath them. Naturalists have frequently speculated as to how the young reach the water but no definite conclusion has been reached. So far as is known the parents do not assist them, but newly-hatched birds do descend the almost perpendicular cliff faces apparently unharmed.

Immature birds generally have more brown in the dark areas and the white on the head is mottled by dark feathers. They attain adult plumage after their first summer.

**Range and Distribution.** The breeding grounds are chiefly in the eastern part of Greenland and in Spitzbergen. The winter feeding areas are scattered over Europe and the British Isles but the birds are particularly numerous along the west coast of Scotland. They leave their winter feeding grounds about the first of May and migrate from the north in late Autumn.

## BLUE GOOSE

*Chen caerulescens*

COMMON NAMES: Alaska Goose, Bald Brant, Bald-Headed Brant, Blue Brant, Blue Snow Goose, Blue Wavey, Blue-Winged Goose, Brant, Eagle-Headed Brant, Oie Aigle (eagle goose), Oie Bleue (blue goose) (French), Silver Brant, Skillet Head.

**History.** The blue goose, despite its vast numbers, is comparatively unknown beyond the limits of its restricted range. Unlike most other members of the goose family, its summer and winter homes are far removed from each other and the blue goose does not pause for long on its flights between the two places.

In common with many other geese it is often known locally as "brant." As the scientific name *caerulescens* (bluish) denotes, the body coloring is more bluish-gray than other varieties and the local names for this species frequently refer to the distinct coloration.

At one time is was supposed that the blue goose was a color phase of the lesser snow goose but it has since been established that they are two distinct species.

**Identification.** (See color plate on p. 469.) This is a goose of medium size possessing certain characteristic markings which, once recognized, cannot be confused with those of any other species. At first glance, the all-white head and neck contrast sharply with the dark body and puts this bird in a class by itself. Among all the other geese, only the emperor also has a white head, but his black foreneck as well as other markings distinguish him from the blue goose.

In detail, the coloration of the blue goose is as follows:

The bill is pinkish, sometimes deepening to reddish, and has a light pink or whitish nail. The cutting edges of the mandibles are black and form a "grinning patch" which is lacking on the emperor.

The entire head and neck are white. The forepart of the head, particularly at the base of the bill, is commonly stained rust color. The eye is brown.

The body is a dusky gray, often blackish, and the back and sides are marked with regular wavy lines varying from pale brown to ashy-gray. The under parts are always lighter than the upper parts. The rump may be white, or nearly so, but is often bluish-gray. The tail varies from slate-gray to gray-brown and is generally edged and tipped with a lighter tone. The tail coverts, upper and lower, are pale gray or white speckled with bluish-gray or grayish tan.

All wing coverts are grayish-blue, some of the lesser and middle coverts being streaked with black. The greater coverts nearest to the body are black with wide white edgings varying from light buff to white. These feathers are long and flexible and form a distinctive marking on the bird.

The breast and belly markings are more variable on the blue goose than on any other species. On some the breast is similar to the back only lighter in tone, on others it may be ashy-gray to almost whitish, and on still others it may be pure white.

Some naturalists believe that cross-breeding with the snow geese produces this lighter coloration. Although there seems to be no direct proof that one species mates with the other, there is a general belief that hybridism does occur. It has been pointed out, in support of this theory, that the main flights of blue geese retain their normal markings but on the western fringes of the flight where they mingle with the lesser snow geese variations are extremely common.

The dark birds in a flock of lesser snow geese almost invariably prove to be blue geese and these latter usually bear lighter markings on the breast than the average blue.

The feet are identical with those of the lesser snow goose and, like those of that species, generally change from pinkish to a more orange tone in the winter.

**Characteristics.** The blue goose is gregarious by nature and readily associates with other species whenever the flight lanes or feeding grounds converge. They are most often found with the lesser snow geese but on migration may mingle with lesser Canadas and brant.

They are noisy both in flight and while feeding and give voice to several different calls. The "honking" note is rather deep and hoarse, a raucous "*quack*" is commonly heard, and while feeding there is an incessant chorus of gabbling which sounds something like the excited barking of a small dog. When large numbers of birds are gathered together the monotone of sound is usually broken at intervals by shrill cries from individuals.

Blue geese are gluttonous feeders. Even the young birds gorge themselves and so develop more rapidly than is the general rule. Like the snow geese, they root out most of their food, consuming the entire plant and leaving no trace of vegetation where they have fed. In the north their chief food is the common tundra grass which they devour in such quantities that they become exceedingly plump, and birds have been known to burst open upon striking the earth when shot. On the winter feeding grounds the food consists of various grasses but the method of feeding is the same.

**Breeding.** So far as is known, the courtship proceeds in the usual manner with much bowing and waving of necks, and the birds are generally mated upon arrival at the breeding grounds.

The nests are often rather bulky affairs constructed of grass, moss, and other vegetation and lined with down. They are built on hummocks or slight elevations amid the soggy marshlands of the tundra. The eggs usually number from three to five and the period of incubation is about 24 days. The gander remains close to the nest during the hatching period. Some authorities believe that he takes his turn at sitting on the eggs, while others maintain that he takes no part in the incubation. The breeding grounds are so inaccessible that we have no complete and definite knowledge of the bird's habits.

The more wary females leave the nest at the first approach of possible danger, but others lie close until discovery is certain. Both parents usually fly off about 100 yards and protest loudly over the invasion of their domain. If there is time the female generally covers the eggs with down before leaving the nest. This not only aids in keeping them warm until her return but also hides them from the herring gulls who would otherwise raid the nest.

The young are able to leave the nest soon after birth and become strong and active within a few

**PLATE I.** Distribution of Blue Goose.

days. They are able to fly about five or six weeks after hatching and are nearly full grown at the end of two months. The immature birds resemble the adults except that the head and neck are a pale brownish-gray and only the chin is white. The bill and feet are darker and the greater wing coverts are neither as long nor as well-defined as on the older birds.

**Range and Distribution.** The main breeding ground lies in the tundra country along the western section of Baffin Island in the vicinity of Foxe Basin. Other nesting areas are located on Southampton Island, Hudson Bay, and near the Perry River, Northwest Territories.

The winter home is in the coastal marshes of Louisiana. The bulk of the flocks are found there from the Mississippi delta to just west of Vermillion Bay. Only occasional birds reach farther east and few if any go as far west as Texas.

The autumn migration begins early in September and follows a course down the east side of Hudson Bay and thence directly southwest to the winter grounds in Louisiana. The spring exodus to the breeding grounds begins late in March or early in April and follows a course west of the Mississippi River straight north to Manitoba. There the flights pause to rest before turning eastward to James Bay, whence they follow the autumn route north to the nesting areas. The spring migration thus travels a route about 600 miles longer than the autumn flight. The migration of these geese is more nearly non-stop than that of the other varieties although they do pause to rest at certain favored spots along the flyway.

# COMMON CANADA GOOSE

*Branta canadensis canadensis*

Common Names: Bay Goose, Bernache (French), Big Gray Goose, Big Mexican Goose, Black-Headed Goose, Black-Necked Goose, Canada Brant, Common Wild Goose, Cravat Goose, French Goose, Honker, Long-Necked Goose, Northern Goose, Reef Goose, Wavey, Wild Goose.

**History.** Probably no other game bird enjoys the distinction of being called by so many different names as the ever-popular "honker." While some of these names are widely known, most of them are local terms used in the various localities where *Canadensis* is hunted. By any name, the big Canada has always been eagerly sought by gunners and it is remarkable that the birds remained as plentiful as they have. Under the present-day laws there is every prospect that their numbers will increase.

**Identification.** (See color plate on p. 470.) The group *Branta canadensis* is divided into five varieties or sub-species all bearing the same general markings and differing mainly in size and color shading. The various members of the group are listed as follows:

Common Canada Goose: *Branta canadensis*

Western Canada Goose: *Branta canadensis occidentalis*

Lesser Canada Goose: *Branta canadensis leucopareia*

Cackling Goose: *Branta canadensis minima*

Richardson's Goose: *Branta canadensis hutchinsi*

The Canada goose is a large brownish-gray bird with a long neck and definite characteristic markings. The adult males (ganders) vary in weight from over 8 pounds to 14 pounds and specimens up to 20 pounds are not uncommon. The average weight is about 9 to 9½ pounds. The body may be from 35 to 40 inches in length and the wingspread is often more than 6 feet. The goose averages slightly smaller than the gander both in size and wing span and is apt to be one or 2 pounds lighter.

Both sexes have the same coloration and markings and in those respects are indistinguishable from each other.

The head and neck (commonly called a "stocking") are a rich, shiny black broken only by an oval patch of white extending from the upper sides of the head down each cheek and under the throat. The stocking ends cleanly at the base of the neck in sharp contrast to the pale chest.

The upper body and wings are a gray-brown and each feather is tipped with a paler edge which produces a barred effect. The underside of the wings is a uniformly light gray.

The chest and breast are a pale ash-gray with white-tipped feathers which also give a barred appearance. The flanks and belly are white and the under parts often appear rust-stained. The tail coverts, both upper and lower, are white and the rump is black.

The bill, which is shorter than the head and has a broad "nail," or tip, is black. The feet are also black and the eye is brown.

Afloat or on land the Canada is readily recognized by his big brownish-gray body and the long black neck. The watchers or sentinels hold their necks rigidly upright and the white cheek patches are easily discernible for some distance.

A flight of Canadas, whether in the familiar "V" pattern of long journeys or the irregular groupings of short flights, could hardly be mistaken for any other birds. The large bodies, which appear gray from below, and the long outstretched necks would be sufficient identification even without the frequent telltale honking note which often heralds their approach before they are visible. (The cormorant also flies in "V" or oblique line formation and might be confused, at a distance, with the flying Canada except that cormorants are black in color and silent in flight.)

**Characteristics.** The term wary may be applied to many game birds, but the honker combines with his wariness a cunning and sagacity that has won him the respect of all who come in contact with him. Possessed of a keen sight and excellent hearing, these birds are quick to detect danger and intelligent enough to avoid it.

The "V" formation mentioned above is most commonly used for long flights. A wise old gander usually heads this flying wedge, but the leadership may change several times during the flight. Occasionally the "V" pattern is altered to a long oblique line, but it is unusual to see geese flying one behind the other in Indian file. The wing-beats of the individual are not always in unison with those of his companions and the flight often appears to have a wavy, undulating motion. It is during these flights that the familiar honking is heard so frequently: a deep, resonant "*he*-HONK" or "*ka*-RONK," with the accent on the second syllable.

The flight speed of the Canada goose ranges from 45 to 60 miles an hour but his great size makes him appear deceptively slow.

Like the diving ducks, Canadas ordinarily run a few steps on the surface of the water before taking off, but when alarmed, if in full plumage, they can spring into flight with a single bound like a mallard. However, they do not always depend on flight to escape their enemies. When circumstances warrant they "freeze" and lie absolutely motionless with their long necks stretched out in front of the body. They frequently assume this position while on their nests and sometimes resort to it on beaches and sandbars, or in marsh grass. At such times their coloring so blends with their surroundings that it is almost impossible to detect their presence. They do not move a feather until the danger has passed or is at least some distance away, and then they move only with great caution and are likely to sneak to better cover rather than break into flight.

They are powerful swimmers and if necessary can move quite rapidly through the water. However, they spend more time ashore than other wildfowl and will often walk long distances when it would seem that flight would be easier. They are better equipped for walking than most ducks because their legs are set farther forward on the body.

While feeding, whether on land or water, one or more sentinels are always on guard, their long necks held straight up and ready to give the alarm at the first hint of danger. The feeding geese also raise their heads frequently, so that there is little chance for a surprise attack on the flock.

The food of Canada geese is almost wholly vegetable although they do eat some insects, mollusks, and small crustaceans at times. In shallow water they obtain seeds, roots of aquatic plants, eel grass, and

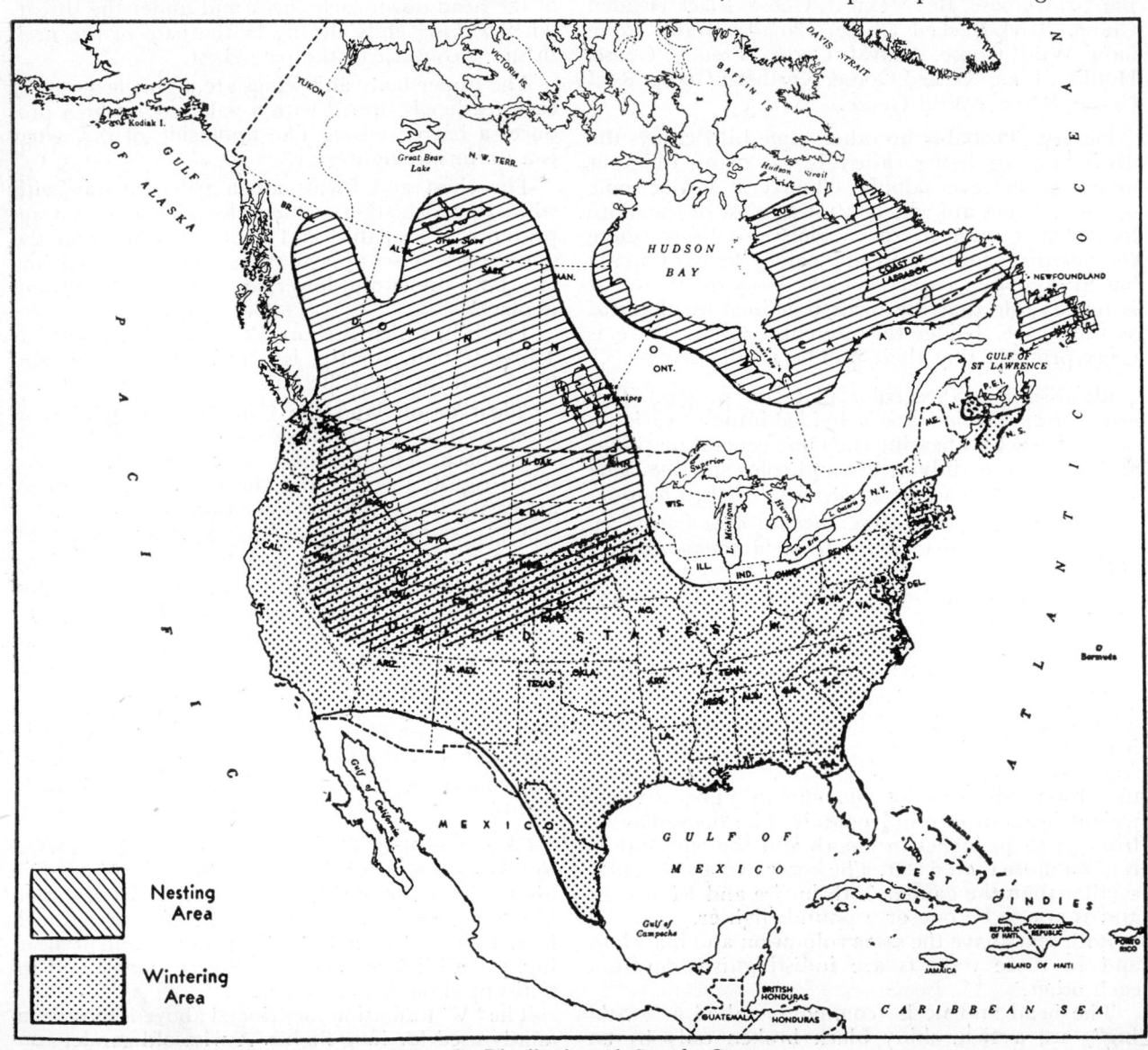

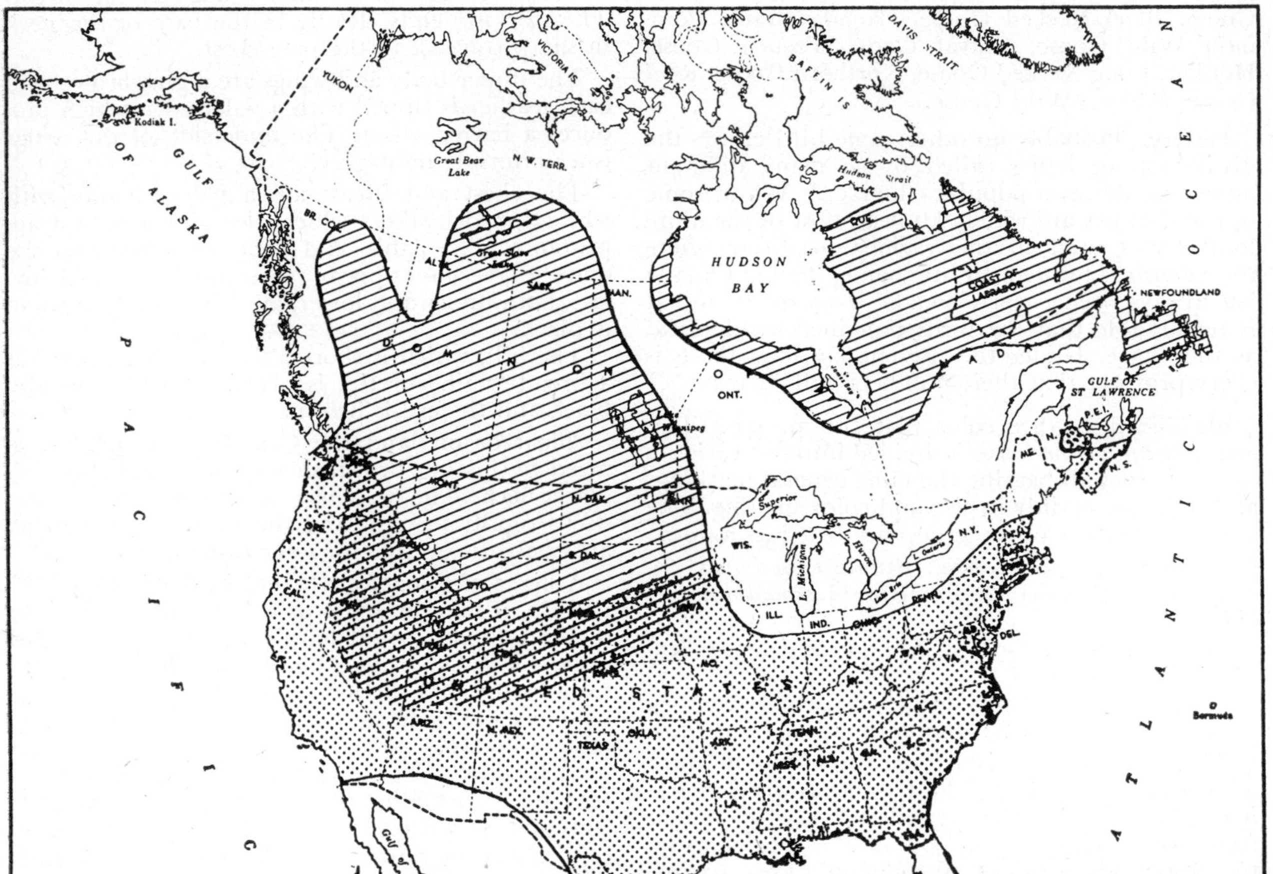


PLATE I. Distribution of Canada Goose.

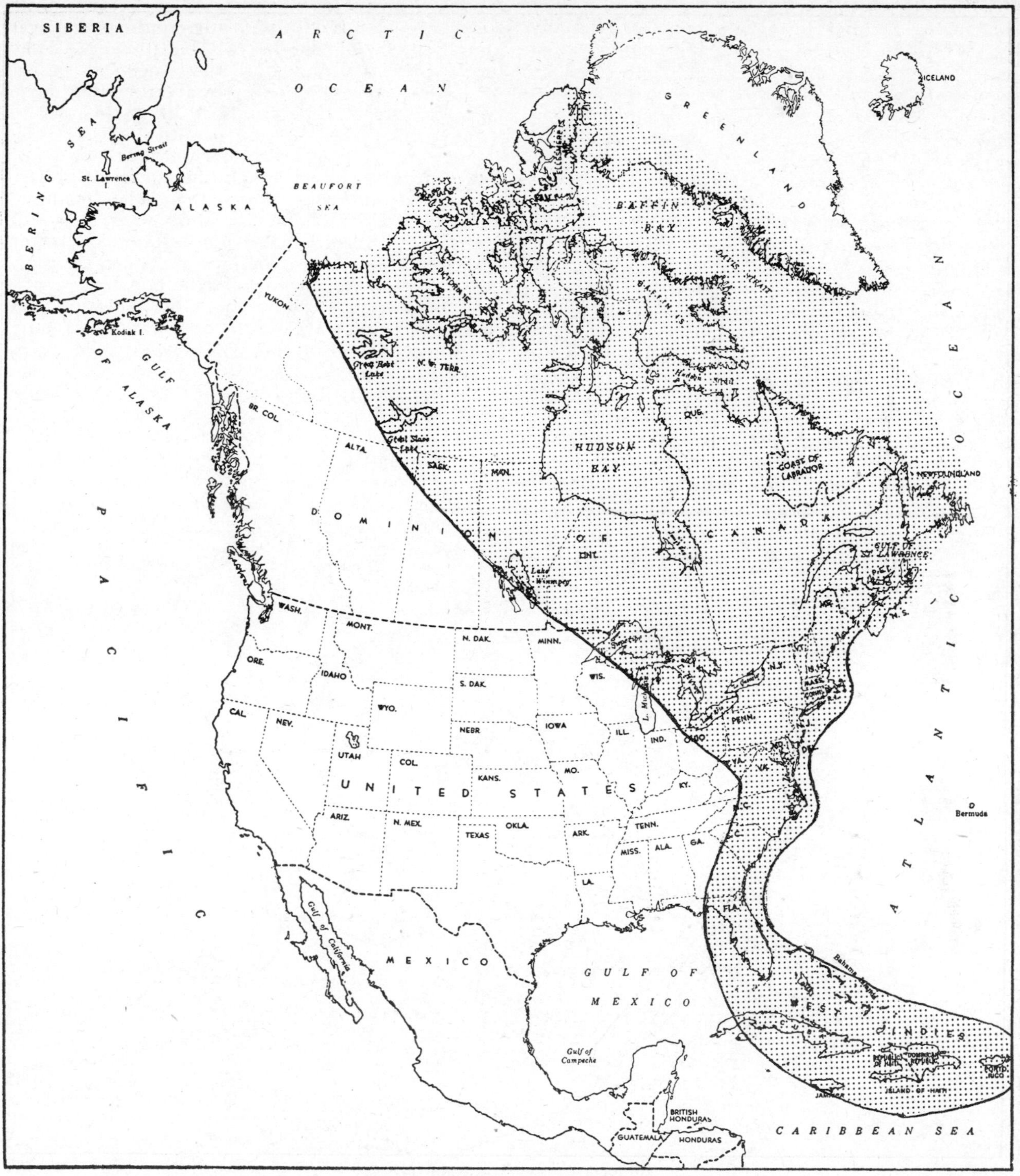


PLATE II. The Atlantic Flyway.

other foods by thrusting the head and neck below the surface in a scooping motion. In slightly deeper water they "tip" like some of the ducks. The head and neck are completely immersed and the tail points straight up, while they maintain their balance by moving their feet. In the course of feeding they swallow quantities of sand and grit as an aid to digestion.

They often feed in pastures, and no sheep could crop the grass any closer. They are fond of barley, wheat, oats, and corn and sometimes do considerable damage to young crops. In the fall they gather in stubble fields and glean whatever has been left from the harvest. Once a feeding ground has been established they return to it regularly if not molested.

The favorite feeding times are early morning and just before sunset, although they may often be seen in stubble fields at noon. Other species may share the same feeding grounds but the Canadas remain in their own group and do not allow the others to mingle with them.

**Breeding.** The early courtship is not without the usual battles between rival ganders. Such battles may last more than half an hour and the antagon-

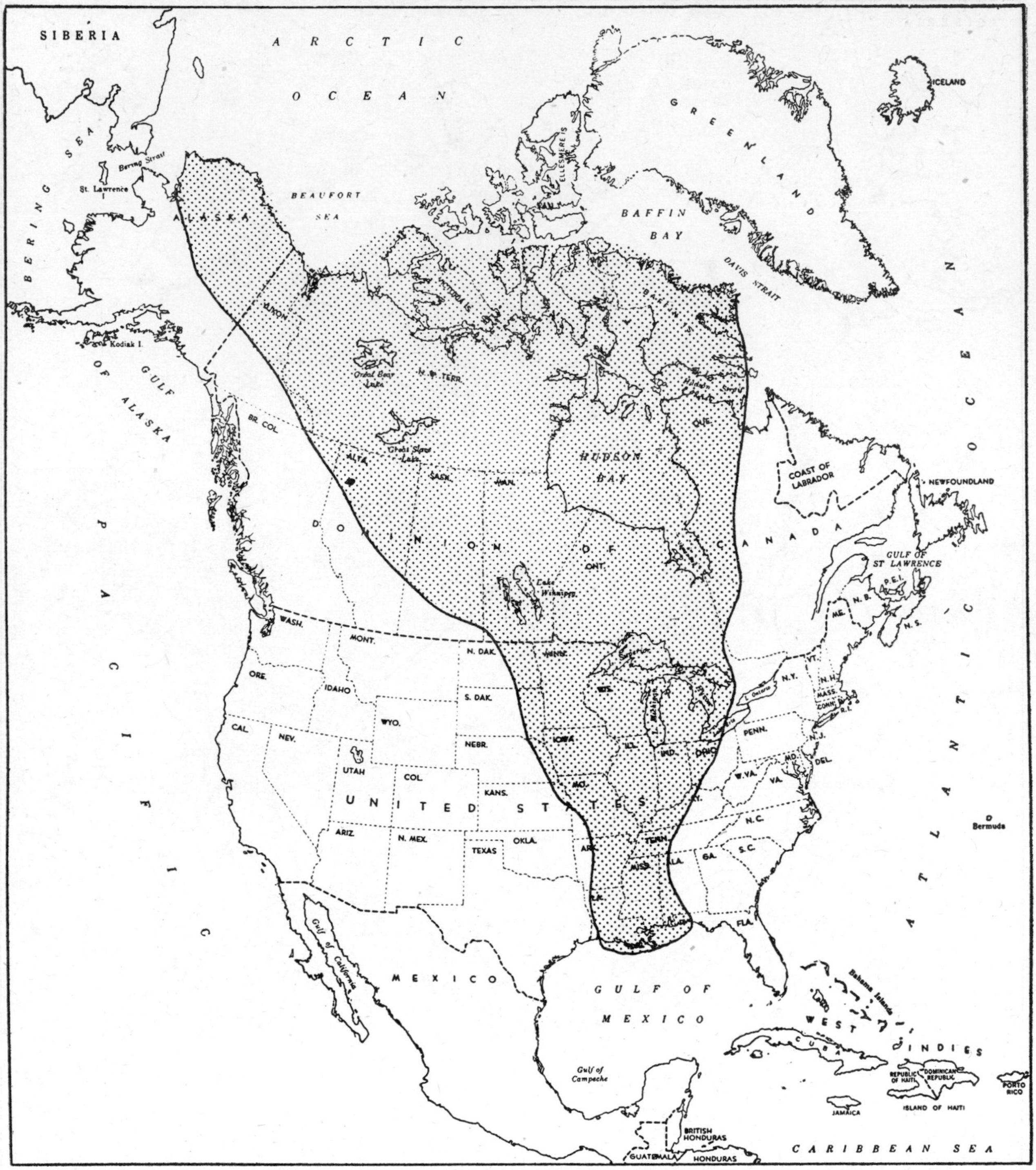


PLATE III. The Mississippi Flyway.

ists give and take considerable punishment from the powerful wing-strokes and stout bills. Even after the victor has been accepted by the goose he may have to defend his position against some persistent suitor.

Between struggles and after having driven off his competitors, the gander applies himself to wooing the goose he has chosen for a mate. He approaches her with his head lowered almost to the ground, his bill wide open, and emitting loud hisses. His feathers are distended until they make a rustling sound and the larger quills fairly rattle. When he reaches the female his neck curves gracefully over and around her in a caressing motion, sometimes brushing her body lightly. She, in turn, moves her neck in various directions in response to his attentions.

With a permanent relationship thus established the pair turn to nest building. The nest may vary in character in different localities but it is almost invariably on the ground. A natural depression is lined with whatever material is available, such as small sticks, grass, moss, or leaves, and topped off with down from the breast of the female. If the original depression is suitable it may only be lined thinly with down, but where large nests are constructed they often reach a width of 2 feet or more. In certain sections the nests may be located in trees and sometimes the abandoned nests of large birds such as hawks are made over. However, this is not common practice, for geese prefer ground nests near the water.

The eggs, generally five or six in number, are a creamy-white color when newly laid. The incubation

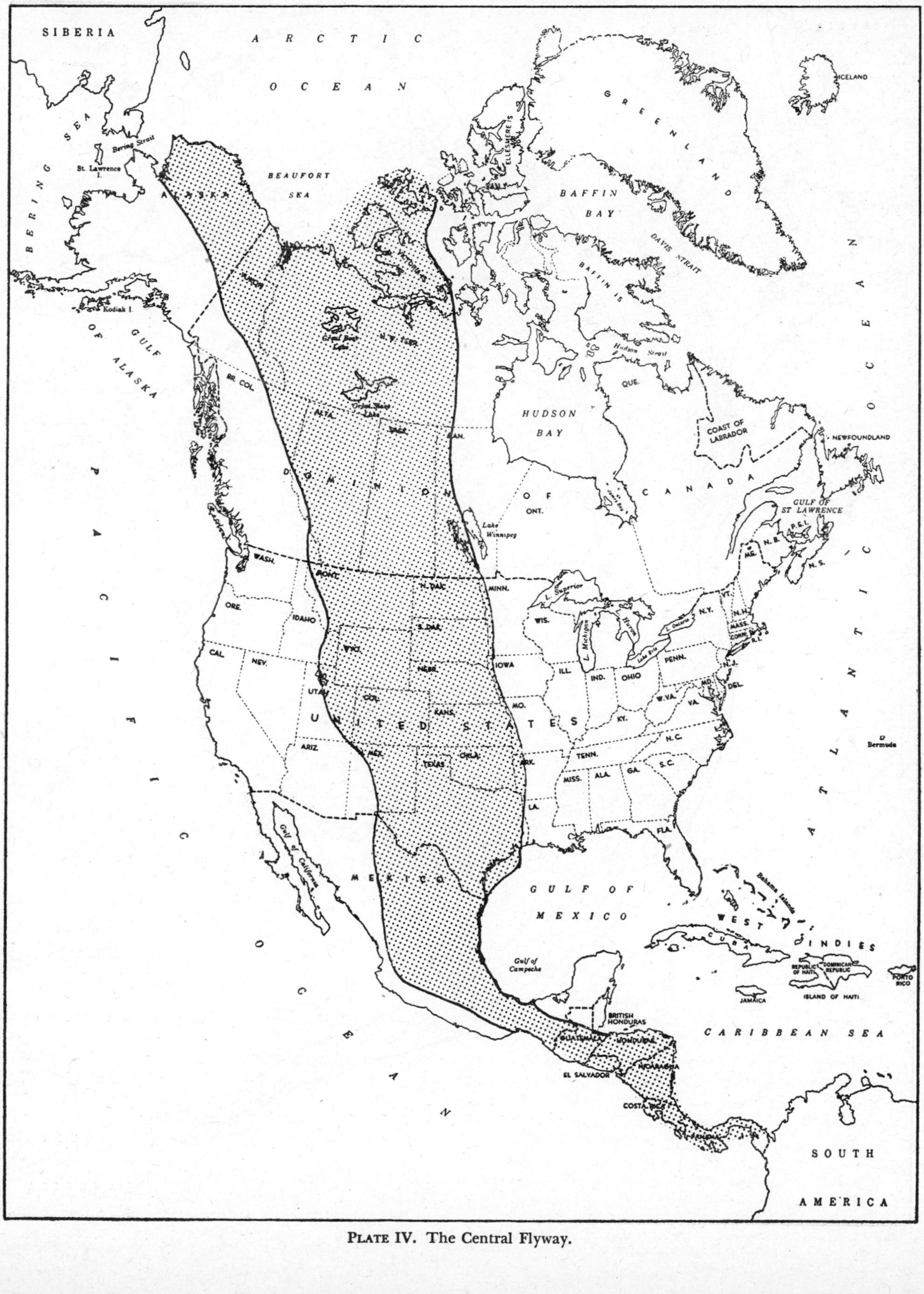


**Plate IV.** The Central Flyway.

time is from 28 to 30 days. Only the goose sits on the eggs, but the gander remains on guard close to the nest all during the hatching period.

Once the goslings leave the nest, which is soon after they are born, both gander and goose guard the young vigilantly. The parents will brave even man to protect their brood and are willing to sacrifice their lives if necessary.

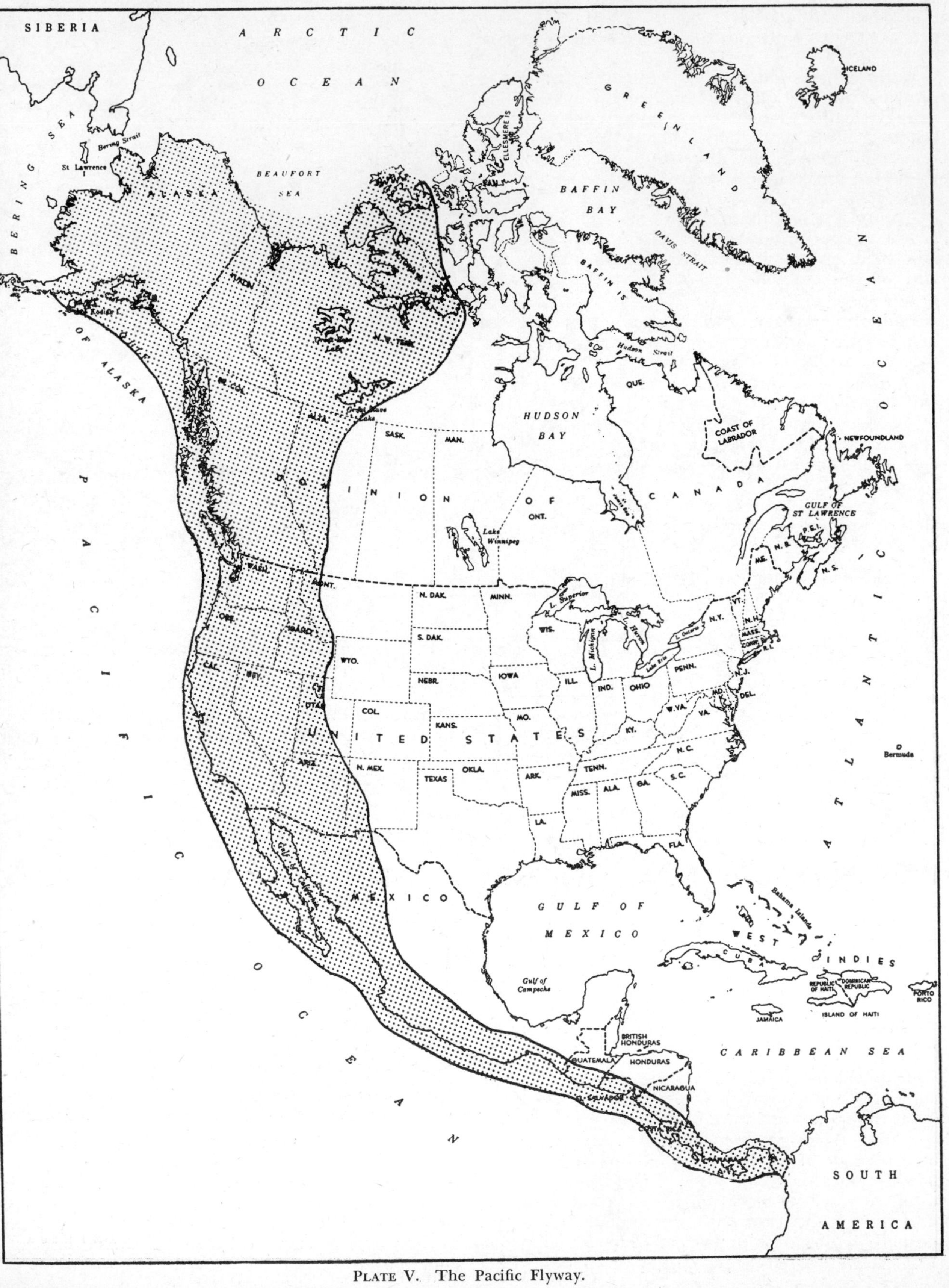


PLATE V. The Pacific Flyway.

The goslings need protection at this stage of their lives, for their enemies are numerous. Hawks, eagles, and gulls prey on them from the air. Foxes, coyotes, and other predators menace them along the shore, and turtles and pike await a meal beneath the water. The gander usually leads the flock while the goose acts as a rear guard and their keen eyes are always on the alert.

A little past midsummer, while the young are growing up, the adult birds begin to moult. The primary feathers loosen and drop out and the birds are then incapable of flight. During this period they remain hidden in the reeds and marshes close to the water, for their only means of escape is by swimming.

Around the middle of August the old birds have grown new plumage and both old and young are able to fly. About two weeks later they are strong and fit for the long journey to their wintering grounds.

Immature birds resemble the adults except for being generally duller in appearance, with the barred markings less pronounced. The head and neck is often a brownish-black and the cheek patch may be flecked or barred with dusky markings. The black edges surrounding the patch are not so clearly defined. The breast is usually darker on young birds and all normally white areas are apt to be marked with brownish tints.

The juveniles remain with the family group for at least one or two seasons and may continue with the group even after mating in their third year.

**Range and Distribution.** The common Canada is more generally distributed and consequently better known than almost any other wild fowl. The summer range extends from the lower Yukon Valley of Alaska to Labrador and the winter range covers a major portion of the United States. The main summer (breeding) grounds lie in the great marshes of the Canadian provinces and extend nearly to the Arctic coast. In the West many birds summer in South Dakota, Colorado, Oregon, and northern California. In this region the summer and winter ranges overlap to a considerable degree.

In common with other migratory birds the geese follow four main flyways as follows (see maps): The Pacific coast flyway, Central flyway, Mississippi flyway, and Atlantic flyway. Since there is some overlapping in each of these it is impossible to draw a clearly defined line for each one, but in the main the same birds follow the same route year after year.

Pacific coast birds from Alaska, British Columbia, and the northwestern states go as far south as the Mexican border. Those on the Central flyway, coming from the Yukon Flats, the Canadian provinces, and the northern tier of states, winter along the western shore of the Gulf of Mexico. The great Mississippi flyway is used by geese from the same general area as those on the Central flyway but the birds separate during the migration and are seldom, if ever, diverted to another flyway. These birds winter along the Gulf of Mexico from eastern Texas to Florida. The Atlantic flyway draws birds from Hudson Bay, Labrador, the Canadian Maritime Provinces, the Gulf of St. Lawrence, and even New England. This flight extends to Florida but the favorite winter grounds for great numbers of these birds are Chesapeake Bay and in the sounds along the North Carolina coast. Many of them winter on inland waters and may be found as far north as there are large bodies of open water and sufficient food.

In the spring the geese are among the first of the waterfowl to migrate to the north. Flocks which have wintered farthest south are the first to begin this migration, others following as the weather becomes milder. The month of March witnesses the greatest general movement, but some birds may start in late February.

This great American bird holds, in addition to the conspicuous esteem in which it is held by the hunter, an important position in the affection of Americans generally. As his honking flight southward marks the close of autumn, so does his appearance in the blue skies of March signal the approach of spring. Those who have witnessed the V-shaped formation of the flock's northern journey welcome the sight as a true harbinger of the season.

# WESTERN CANADA GOOSE

*Branta canadensis occidentalis*

Common Names: In certain localities this bird is erroneously referred to as Brant. It is commonly called the White-Cheeked Goose and probably known by some of the same names as those applied to the Common Canada.

**History.** See that given for the common Canada goose.

**Identification.** In size these birds compare with the common Canada, and their plumage markings are about the same, with the following exceptions. The Western commonly has a white, or nearly white, collar at the base of the "stocking." (The Canada infrequently has this collar also.) The cheek patch is usually divided by black under the throat, which is more rarely the case with the Canada, and the normally white areas of the patch are sometimes a rusty-brown barred with darker markings. The feathers of the Western birds are darker than the Canada, especially the under parts, which are slate-brown.

It is believed that the dampness of the climate on the West Coast tends to produce darker birds. The Western Canada and its smaller counterpart, the cackling goose, which shares somewhat the same range, furnish examples of this theory.

**Characteristics.** In general, this bird shares the same characteristics as those of the common Canada.

**Range and Distribution.** This sub-species, although common and often plentiful in certain areas, occupies such a restricted range that it is not so well known as the Canada. Westerns are found along the coast from Vancouver Island to Prince William Sound, Alaska. They do not go far inland and seldom migrate.

PLATE I. Distribution of Western Canada Goose.

# LESSER CANADA GOOSE *Branta canadensis leucoparia*

COMMON NAMES: Bernache, Black Brant, Black-Leg, Brant, Eastern Brant, Eskimo Goose, Goose Brant, Gray Mud Goose, Little Honker, Short-Necked Goose, Southern Goose.

**History.** It will be noted that the term "brant" in various forms is erroneously applied to this subspecies also. Formerly it was referred to as "Hutchins'" goose—an error which has caused confusion because the Richardson's goose is the true *Hutchinsi,* an entirely different bird. Further confusion is added by the fact that the scientific name *leucoparia* means white-cheeked, but this name is colloquially applied to the Western Canada goose.

**Identification.** The lesser Canada goose is identical in appearance to the common Canada, except for size; this smaller goose has a relatively shorter neck or "stocking," from which comes one of its common names, "short-necked goose."

**Characteristics.** What has been written regarding the common Canada applies also to this lesser species. The mating and breeding habits are similar and the flight pattern usually follows the familiar "V" formation. The honking note is of a higher pitch, which often aids in identification.

**Range and Distribution.** The lesser Canada is the most abundant of all the western species. They range from their breeding grounds along the northern Arctic coasts to the inland valleys of California and as far south as the western shore of the Gulf of Mexico. Great numbers of them join with other species in the stubble fields and grass lands. At one time they were so numerous that ranchers employed gunners to keep the birds away from the sprouting crops. Although the lesser Canada is seldom seen on the Atlantic coast, wildfowlers usually report having killed a few each fall. In some instances a small Canada is mistaken for the "lesser," and undoubtedly many of those reported by wildfowlers represent an error in identification.

# CACKLING GOOSE *Branta canadensis minima*

COMMON NAMES: Brown Brant, Bullneck Goose, Cackler, Crow Goose, Greaser, Little Squeaking Goose, Yelper.

**History.** Cackling geese were once extremely numerous over their western range, but market hunting is said to have decreased their numbers alarmingly since the early days of their abundance. Under the protective laws of the present day, however, there is evidence that they will again be plentiful.

**Identification.** (See color plate on p. 470.) The cackling goose is the smallest of the sub-species, and in appearance is a miniature Western. The only variance in coloration from its larger neighbor is that the upper chest feathers are much darker at the base of the neck. The black "stocking" blends into this darker area and is less sharply defined in front than other members of the *Canadensis* group.

**Characteristics.** The cackling goose, as the name implies, is a garrulous bird and the shrill *"luk-luk,"* repeated over and over, marks it unmistakably. In habits, both as to feeding and breeding, it follows closely those of its larger relative, the Western Canada.

**Range and Distribution.** The breeding grounds are on the western Aleutians. In the winter the birds range from British Columbia to San Diego County, California. Occasionally this variety is reported as far east as Illinois but they are mainly confined to the West Coast area.

PLATE I. Distribution of Lesser Canada Goose.

## RICHARDSON'S GOOSE (Hutchins' Goose) *Branta canadensis hutchinsi*

Common Names: Little Canada Goose, Little Gray Goose, Little Wild Goose, Small Gray Goose.

**History.** This sub-species of the common Canada goose was for many years confused with the lesser Canada. It was originally discovered by Sir John Richardson on Melville Peninsula, north of Hudson Bay, and named after a Mr. Hutchins, a factor of the Hudson Bay Company in that area.

**Identification.** (See color plate on p. 469.) Hutchins' goose is precisely like the common Canada in everything except size and voice. They rarely exceed 6 pounds in weight and the honking note is replaced by a kind of trilling *"k-r-r-r-."*

**Characteristics.** Are essentially the same as those given for the common Canada.

**Range and Distribution.** The breeding grounds are in the far northeastern Arctic, particularly in the region of Baffin Island, and the migration route follows down Hudson Bay through the western United States and the Mississippi Valley. Iowa and Dakota get some of the flight, and the majority of the birds winter on the northern shores of the Gulf of Mexico.

## EMPEROR GOOSE *Philacte canagica*

Common Names: Beach Goose, Painted Goose, White-Headed Goose.

**History.** This most beautiful of all North American geese is much too infrequently seen to be well known. The home grounds are in the most inaccessible country and few but the Eskimo natives have ever laid eyes on these birds. In the earliest reports they were described as plentiful. Later the numbers decreased alarmingly and it was thought that the

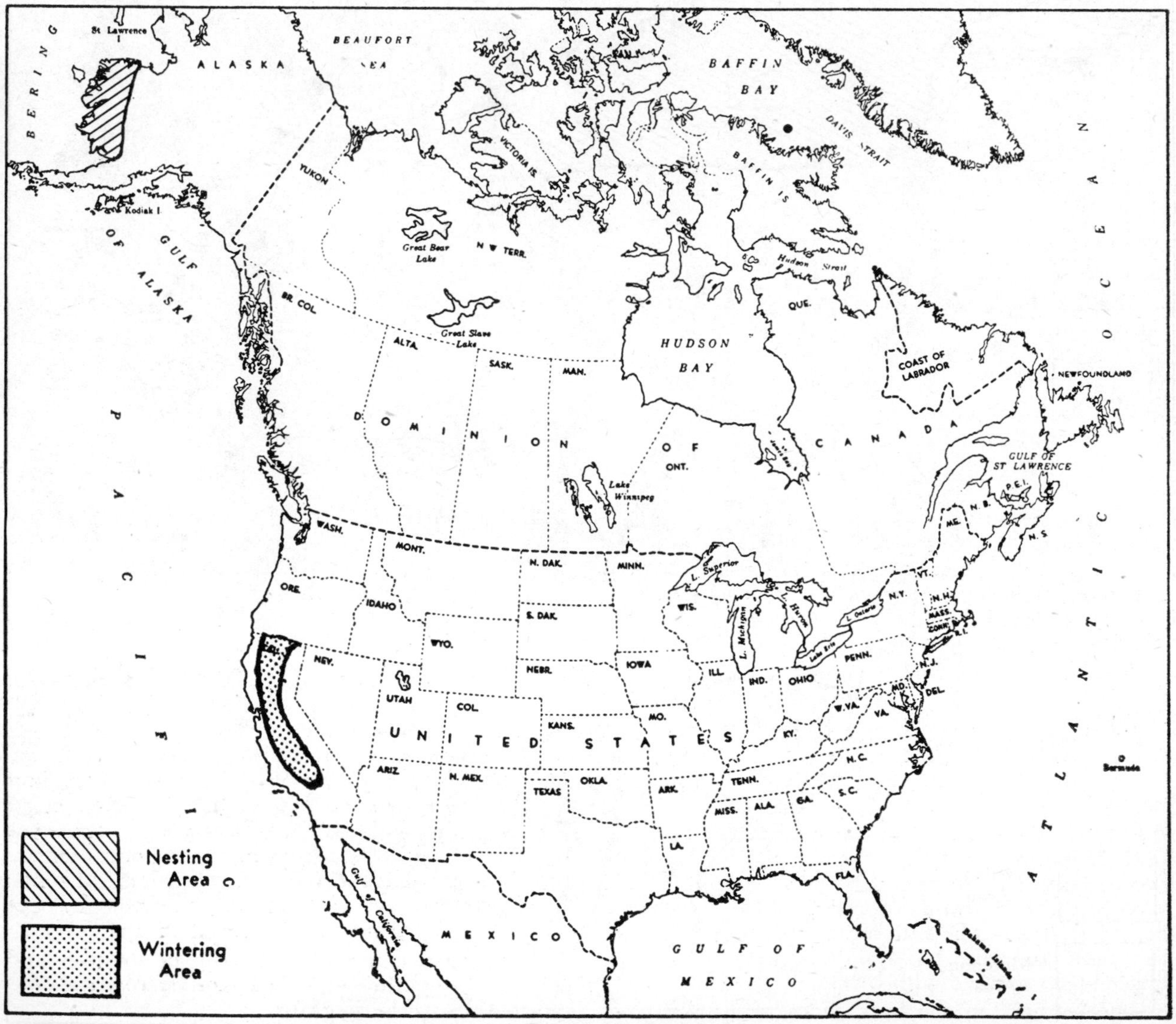


Plate I. Distribution of Cackling Goose.

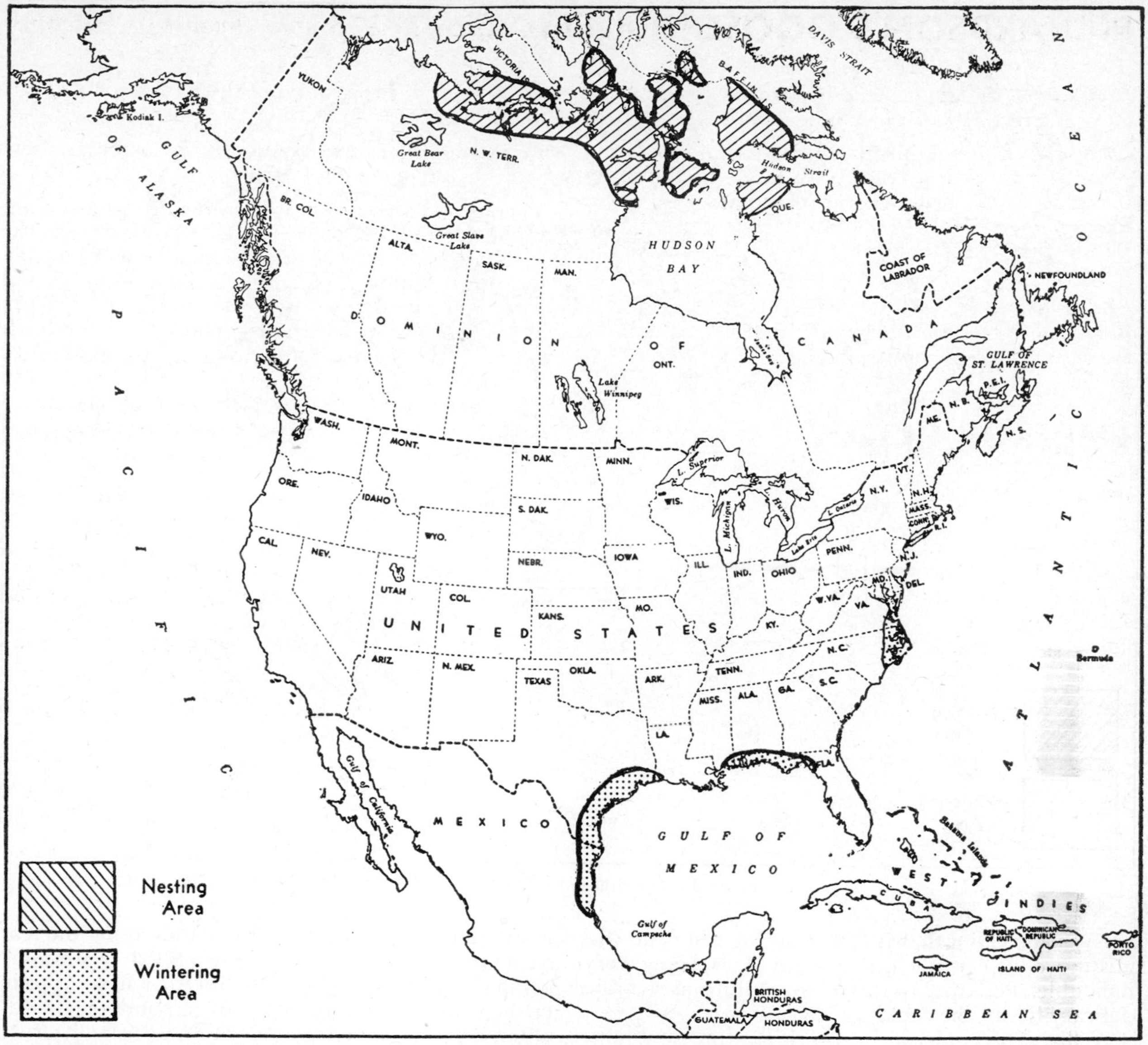


PLATE I. Distribution of Richardson's Goose.

native meat-hunters—who killed them during the moult when they could not fly—were destroying the birds and their eggs to the point of extinction. It is true that prior to the Migratory Bird Act these geese were caught in traps made from fish nets and slaughtered in great numbers. However, a credible authority reports them as abundant in their limited habitat.

**Identification.** (See color plate on p. 469.) The emperor is a medium-sized goose, soft French-gray in color with the head and back of the neck white and the throat a rich, deep brown. On some specimens the white of the head and the sides of the neck appear tinged with rust, or amber-yellow, but the dark brown chin, throat, and front neck marking is always in sharp contrast to the light areas. The eye is brown or hazel. The bill varies from a pale purple to a flesh color and has a white tip or "nail." The lower bill is marked with black.

The feathers on the back, sides, and chest have black crescent-shaped markings near the end with white tips which appear as a scale finish on the silver gray body.

The feet are orange-yellow, a feature shared by only two other geese.

**Characteristics.** What has been said about the common Canada applies in the superlative to the emperor. He is generally acclaimed the wariest of all wild fowl by the few who have been privileged to hunt him. Like the Canadas, they post sentinels while feeding, but whereas the Canada is often content with one or two watchful guards, the emperor is seldom satisfied with less than three or more. Flocks invariably alight in a spot with a clear view on all sides, which makes stalking extremely difficult. One observer concludes that their extreme alertness is due to the fact that one of their enemies, the Arctic fox, is abundant in their environment.

Their food consists principally of shellfish and eelgrass along the tidal flats, and cranberries and mossberries in the foothills.

The quality of their flesh is a matter of contro-

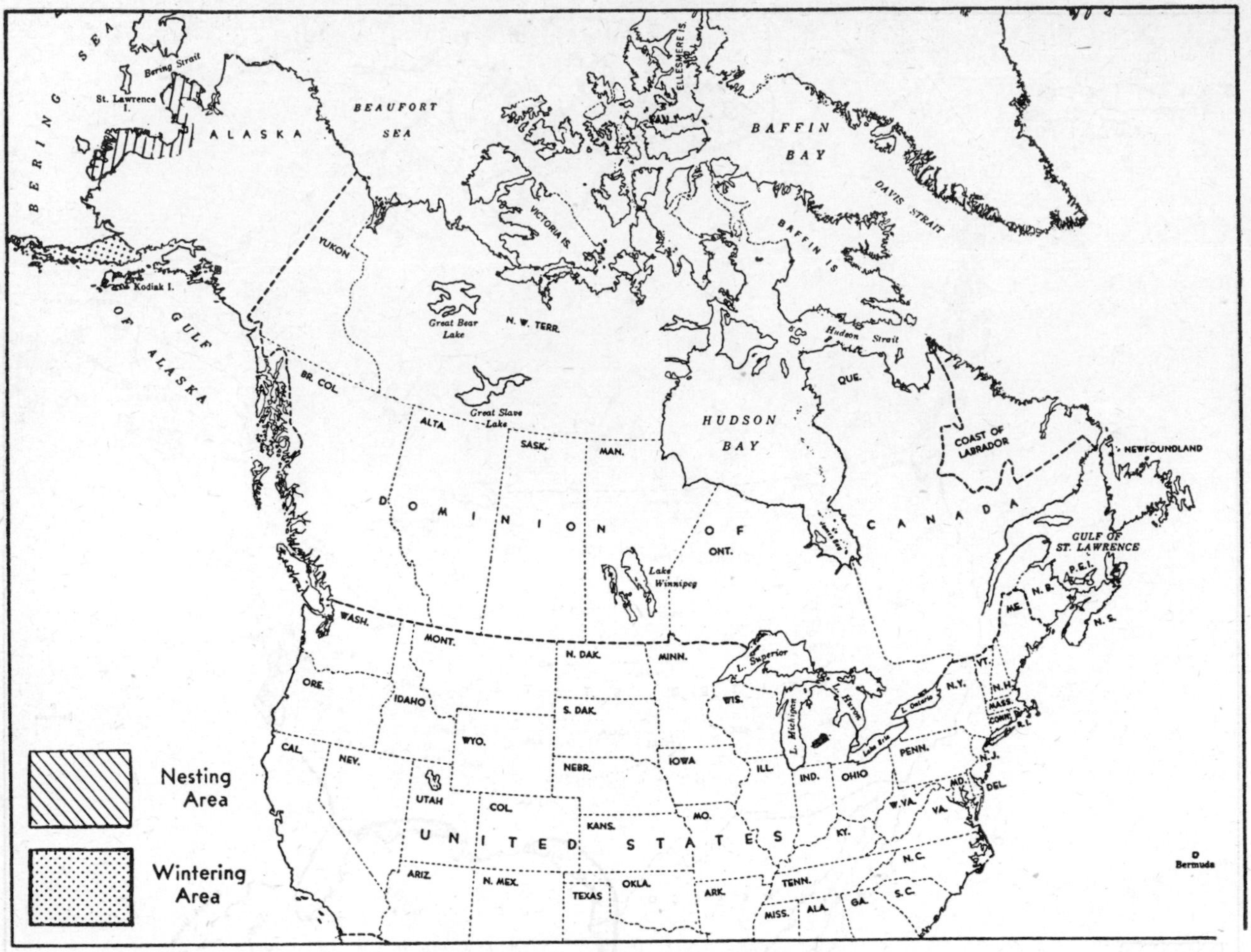


PLATE I. Distribution of Emperor Goose.

versy; some claim that it has a "strong taste and disgusting odor," while others laud it as being very palatable. Perhaps its success or failure as a table delicacy lies in the cooking.

A flight of emperors resembles a line of brant. Like the latter, their wing-beats are short and rapid but their heavy bodies make them less maneuverable. They often fly so close to the ground that their wing-tips barely miss the surface on the down-beat. During flight they utter a shrill, strident, two-syllable call, *"kla-ha, kla-ha, kla-ha,"* unlike that of any other goose. They are less garrulous than the cackling or white-fronted geese, but when in flocks on the ground they have several conversational notes. Another two-syllable call which seems to be reserved for occasions of alarm is a deep, resonant *"u-lugh, u-lugh."*

**Breeding.** Little seems to be known about the actual courtship of the emperor but most accounts agree that the pairs are mated upon their arrival at the breeding grounds, or soon thereafter. The gander parades around the goose, moving his head and neck gracefully as he voices soft "love notes." He guards his spouse jealously against all comers, even those of another species, and will instantly attack any possible rival.

The migrating flocks split up into pairs and these pairs begin the business of nesting at once. The nests vary in character with particular localities. Some nests are found on flat, marshy islands along the seacoast; such nests are merely down-filled depressions among the rocks and driftwood. Other nests appear farther inland on the shore of a pond or island. Often a grass-covered hummock on an island serves as a nesting site, but in almost every case the nest is near water. Seldom if ever are such inland nests more than about ten miles from the coast line.

The eggs, usually five or six, are laid early in June and the period of incubation is approximately 24 days. The female does the hatching and, quite unlike other geese, the gander is seldom seen around the nest. It is possible that he remains hidden close by, but he does not mount guard as does the Canada. The females are reluctant to leave their nests and resort to hiding by stretching out over the nest and remaining motionless. When discovered, however, they fly some distance away and exhibit little concern over the nest. If there are young the female will call to them, but neither parent attempts to give battle like the common Canada.

The gander does assume partial responsibility for the young and shares in their care until both parents moult—generally early in August. Both young and old are then earthbound until the new flight feathers grow in. It is during this period that the greatest toll of lives is taken by the natives and predators.

The immature birds somewhat resemble the adults except that the head and neck often appear more dusky than white, the barred effect is subdued, and the feet are lighter in color.

**Range and Distribution.** Breeding grounds are restricted to a vicinity around the mouths of the Yukon and Kuskokwim Rivers. The winter migration is short compared to other geese, for the feeding grounds are along the western end of the Alaskan Peninsula and the Aleutian Islands. Emperors rarely go south of Sitka, Alaska, and only an occasional straggler is found in British Columbia and northern California.

## ROSS'S GOOSE

*Chen rossi*

COMMON NAMES: China Goose, Galoot, Horned-Wavey, Little Wavey, Wart-Nosed Wavey.

**History.** The name *rossi* is in honor of Bernard R. Ross, a correspondent of the Smithsonian Institution and a factor with the Hudson Bay Company, who sent out the first specimens from the Great Slave Lake region. This smallest of all the geese baffled ornithologists for many years. As a migrant visitor to California during the short winter season it offered little opportunity for close study of its habits. Where it traveled after leaving the winter feeding grounds long remained a mystery. Subsequently it was discovered to nest on a lake in one of the tributaries of the Perry River, some miles north of the Arctic Circle. The breeding area is so small in comparison to that of most geese that it was difficult to locate and many attempts were made before one was successful.

These geese were eagerly sought by the market hunters because of the excellence of their flesh. Before protective laws guarded the remaining flocks from wholesale slaughter they had been seriously reduced in numbers. Under the present laws they seem to be holding their own or even increasing in abundance.

**Identification.** In size the Ross's goose compares

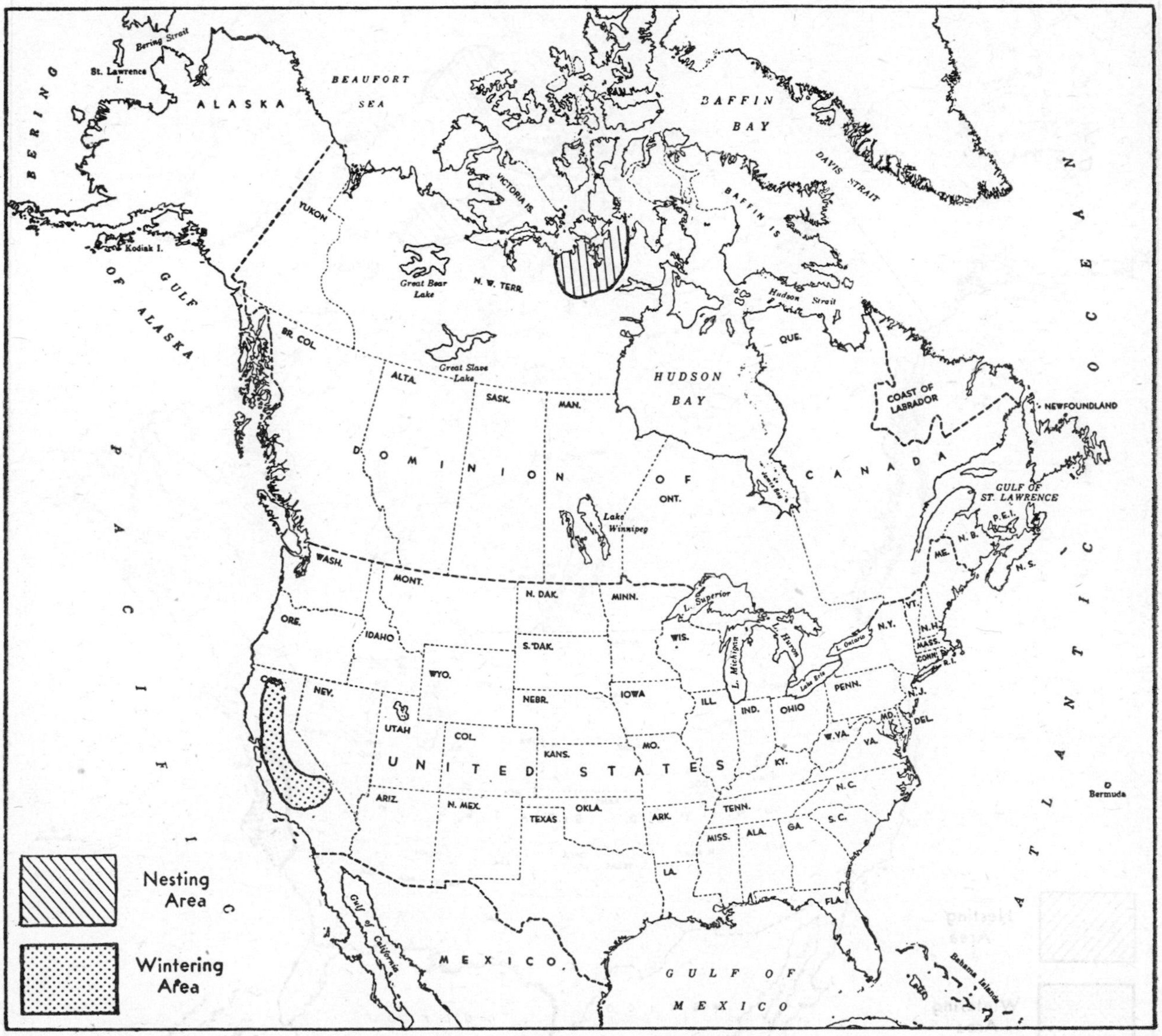


PLATE I. Distribution of Ross's Goose.

with a mallard duck and in appearance is simply a miniature of the lesser snow goose. Like that bird, its entire plumage is a dazzling white except for the black primaries which are more noticeable when in flight than at rest.

In detailed examination the bill color varies from rich red to light purple, often with a salmon-pink tone, and has black edges. The upper bill is furrowed and has well-developed bumps or warts at the base. The feet are usually more dully red than those of the lesser snow goose. Wherever the two species come together size would be the most determining factor in identification.

**Characteristics.** *Rossi* is very similar to the lesser snow goose in both feeding and nesting habits. The nests are relatively small and usually found in colonies at varying distances apart—in many cases only a few feet. The average setting is four eggs and they require about three weeks to hatch.

Like the cackling goose, the Ross's goose is very loquacious and its call sounds like the familiar *"luk-luk"* of that species.

They are fond of short green grass and may often be found in company with other species on the grazing grounds.

**Range and Distribution.** The summer breeding range, as noted above, encompasses a relatively small area in the lakes around the mouth of the Perry River, Canadian Northwest Territories, a section also chosen by the tule geese as a nesting ground. The migration lane differs somewhat from that of the other geese. The main route would seem to be from the breeding grounds to Great Slave Lake, to Lake Athabasca, thence south to the boundary of Canada and the United States at Montana. From here they part company with the eastern geese and cross the Rockies in a southwesterly direction to winter in central and southern California. It is presumed that the spring flight northward follows the same route in reverse.

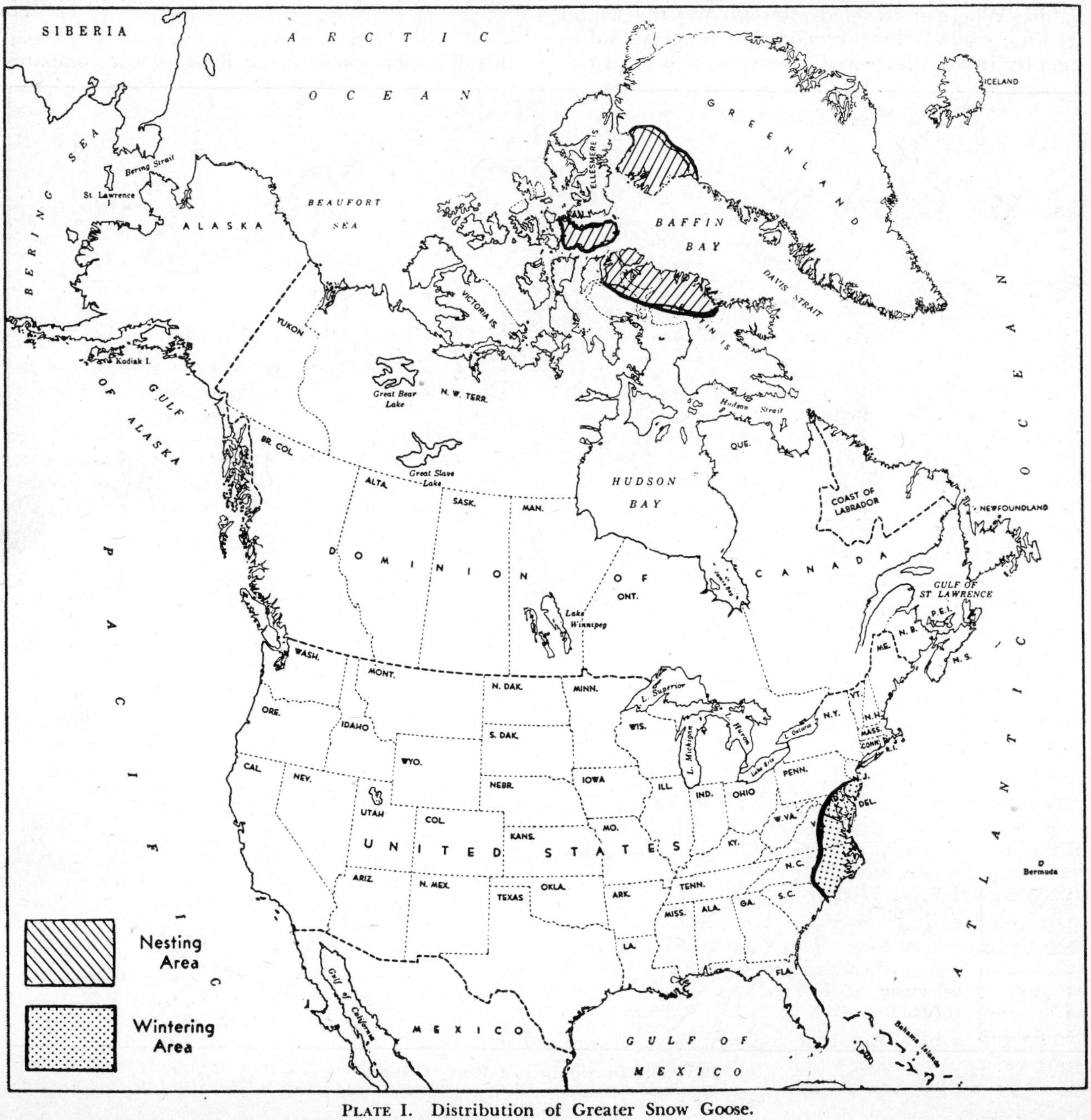


PLATE I. Distribution of Greater Snow Goose.

## GREATER SNOW GOOSE *Chen hyperborea atlantica*

Common Names: Same as given for lesser snow goose.

**History.** The greater snow goose is simply a larger counterpart of the lesser snow goose but is considered by some ornithologists to be a distinct species. The smaller variety seldom if ever find their way to the Atlantic coast, whereas the greater snow goose is strictly an eastern migrant as the latinized *atlantica* implies.

Twice each year during the migration all of these birds pause on the lower St. Lawrence River in the vicinity of St. Joachim, making it possible to estimate a fairly accurate census of their numbers. From the counts in recent years it is evident that they are on the increase and there is every indication that their numbers will multiply. Although a large and beautiful goose, the greater snow goose does not rank very high as a game bird, for the flesh is far from being an epicurean delight.

**Identification.** Except for being somewhat larger the greater snow goose is identical in appearance to the lesser snow goose. (See description of latter.)

**Characteristics.** What has been written regarding the lesser snow goose also applies in a general way to the greater snow. The larger birds do not graze, however, but seem to prefer feeding areas where the grass grows in shallow salt or brackish water. They plunge their powerful bills deep into the mud or sand and tear the grass out by the roots. In a short time a feeding area is completely denuded of vegetation and becomes a bare, muddy flat. On some of the islands along the Atlantic coast former feeding grounds are now merely barren wastes on which even after many years no sign of plant life has returned.

**Range and Distribution.** The breeding grounds range along the northern shores of Baffin Island, north to include Devon and many smaller islands in the Canadian group, and the northwestern portion of Greenland known as Prudhoe Land. The spring and autumn flights pause temporarily on the Lower Gulf of St. Lawrence on their way to and from the winter feeding grounds along the Atlantic coast from Maryland to North Carolina.

## LESSER SNOW GOOSE *Chen hyperborea hyperborea*

Common Names: Alaska Goose, Arctic Goose, Bald Brant, Common Wavey, Little Wavey, Mexican Goose, Oie Blanche (white goose), Oie Sauvage (wild goose) (French), Snow Goose, Wavey, White Brant, White Goose.

**History.** The lesser snow goose, although now not so numerous as in former years, when great flocks appeared like snowbanks on the western plains, is still plentiful over a wide range west of the Great Lakes. The name *hyperborea* (literally, "beyond the North Wind") is an allusion to the breeding grounds beyond the Arctic circle. Only one species, the American brant, nests farther north than the lesser snow goose.

Together with some other varieties the snow goose is often called brant, or white brant, in many localities and in certain sections is known only as a "wavey"—from the Indian *"wa-wa"* (goose). This term is also loosely applied to the white-front and several other geese and only local usage determines to which bird it refers.

**Identification.** (See color plate on p. 469.) Regardless of what names are applied to the lesser snow goose there is no likelihood of confusing it with any other species. There are but two other white varieties, each so distinctive in either size or range as to separate them clearly from each other.

In general appearance the lesser snow goose is entirely white. The ten primaries are black and show as black wing tips when the bird is in flight but are not very obvious otherwise. Often the head is tinged with light reddish brown.

The bill, which is rather high at the rear and narrow, varies in color from a pale pink to a rich red. It has a white tip, or "nail," and a black cutting edge which creates what is referred to as the "grinning patch."

The legs and feet are pinkish-red with black claws. The eye may be various tones of dark brown.

**Characteristics.** The lesser snow goose lacks the intelligence and sagacity of the common Canada goose and is readily duped by calling and decoys. Although normally high flyers, on the feeding grounds they often pass overhead at no more than 30 or 40 yards when vehicles and people are plainly visible. They often return to the same place shortly after being frightened away.

They are quite gregarious and sociably inclined, often mingling with other species. Like the blue geese, with whom they most frequently associate in large numbers, they gabble continuously in a variety of tones punctuated now and then with high, falsetto cries. They sometimes fly silently but often they call and respond to each other with high-pitched *"we-honk, we-honk, we-honk,"* repeated again and again.

The usual flight formation is composed of many birds either in an oblique line or a bluntly curving "V." On long flights, such as during migration, they climb to considerable altitude and seem to skim along with scarcely any wing motion. The flight is sometimes swift and steady when aloft but they are more given to aerial acrobatics than any other goose. Their descent is made in a zig-zagging motion with the wings held rigidly in a down-bent position. They seem to glide softly and easily from great heights, and when they are nearly ready to alight a few swift flaps of the wings bring them to rest on land or water.

Their food is chiefly of a vegetable nature and they are inveterate "grazers." In the fall they invade the stubble fields by the thousands and in the spring they settle on the sprouting grain. Grass ranks high on their menu and they crop or pluck it after the manner of tame geese. They literally mow a field and often pull up and eat roots and all. This fondness for pasture grass often leads them to fields which are a considerable distance from water. They are daytime feeders, and the greatest movements occur after sunrise when they head for the fields and about sundown when they return to the resting areas.

**Breeding.** As with many of the far northern breeders, complete facts regarding courtship and mating habits are lacking, but it is assumed that they are similar to those of the common Canada goose. They have been reported as pairing infrequently with the blue goose, whose range they share.

Nesting as they do in almost inaccessible regions, few but the Eskimo have any opportunity to study their habits in this respect. From what has been learned the nest resembles that of geese previously described—merely a hollow, thinly lined with dry vegetation and the usual down.

The number of eggs may vary from four to eight, with six being about average. The female does the hatching and the gander remains on guard close by. The female seldom leaves the nest because the eggs are sought by crows, foxes, gulls, and jaegers. Again like the common Canada, the pair seem to be

PLATE I. Distribution of Lesser Snow Goose.

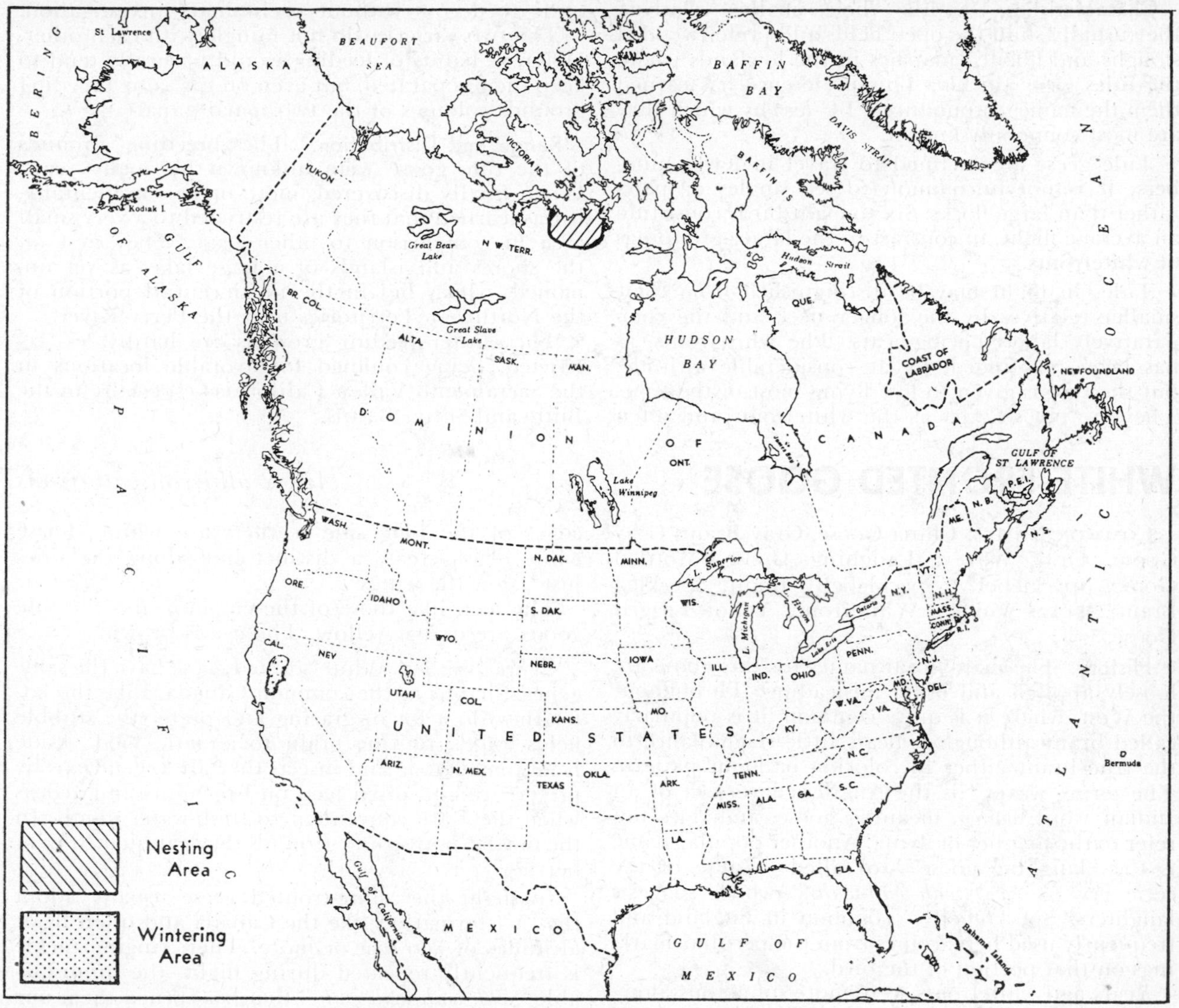


PLATE I. Distribution of Tule Goose.

devoted and it is thought that they mate for life.

Incubation takes from 22 to 24 days. The young goslings are subject to attack from gulls and various birds of prey as well as the Arctic foxes. At the end of their first summer the juveniles are an all-over gray color, slightly darker above than below. The head, and sometimes the neck, is faintly streaked with darker markings. The bill and feet are darker. During the winter and the following spring there is a gradual change in the plumage and after the first complete summer moult it becomes like that of the adult.

**Range and Distribution.** The lesser snow goose breeds along the Arctic coast from around Point Barrow to Southampton Island and the southern portion of Baffin Island and on numerous islands, including Victoria, to the north.

The winter grounds cover a wide range from the west coast to the Mississippi Valley and from southern British Columbia down through Oregon, Colorado, Nevada, Utah, and southern Illinois to the Gulf coast from Florida to Texas. Casual birds find their way east of the Mississippi but are extremely rare on the Atlantic coast.

# TULE GOOSE

*Anser albifrons gambelli*

COMMON NAMES: Timber Goose, Tule Goose, and most of the names given for the White-Fronted-Goose.

**History.** Marked differences in habits and characteristics have caused this goose to be classified as a sub-species of the white-fronted goose, although except for size and slightly darker coloration it is practically identical with the latter.

**Identification.** The variance in size between the tule and whitefront is of the same ratio as the difference between the honker and the lesser Canada goose. The description given for the whitefront may also be applied to the tule with the above-mentioned exception, that the tule is generally darker of plumage, and normally from 20 to 30 per cent larger.

**Characteristics.** Unlike their smaller relatives, they usually shun the open fields and prefer wooded sloughs and flooded marshes in the lowlands where the tules grow thickly. This preference has earned them the name (pronounced TU-*lee*) by which they are most commonly known.

Tule geese are inclined to travel in fewer numbers; it is not uncommon to see singles or pairs rather than large flocks. Six to eight birds constitute an average flight, in contrast to the larger groupings of whitefronts.

Tules in flight may be distinguished from their smaller relatives by the longer neck and the comparatively labored wing-beats. The whitefronts, as has been mentioned, fly at considerable altitude, but the tule is given to low flying most of the time. They are not so wary as the whitefronts and often come to decoys without preliminary investigation.

The two varieties do not mingle with each other. Different habits of feeding would naturally tend to keep them separated, but even on the same breeding grounds colonies of the two remain apart.

**Range and Distribution.** The breeding grounds of the tule goose were unknown for many years. When finally discovered, more or less accidentally, it was learned that they are restricted to a very small area in comparison to other geese. They nest on the shores and islands of a large lake—as yet unnamed—which lies in the north-central portion of the Northwest Territories near the Perry River.

The winter feeding grounds are hardly less restricted, being confined to favorable locations in the Sacramento Valley, California—especially in the Butte and Sutter Basins.

## WHITE-FRONTED GOOSE

*Anser albifrons albifrons*

COMMON NAMES: China Goose, Gray Brant, Gray Goose, Gray Wavey, Laughing Goose, Mottled Goose, Specklebelly, Specklebelly Brant, Speckled Brant, Texas Goose, Whitefront, Yellow-Legged Goose.

**History.** The many local names for this goose are loosely applied and often misleading. Throughout the West, where it is quite common, it is popularly called brant although it bears little resemblance to the true brant either in coloring or flight pattern. The term "wavey" is the Anglicized version of an Indian word *wa-wa,* meaning goose, and does not refer to the manner of flying. Another popular name is the "laughing goose"—so called because of the eerie cry of *"wah-wah-wah-wah-,"* which suggests laughter. "Specklebelly," common in England and frequently used here, comes from the peculiar markings on that portion of the bird.

Years ago whitefronts were more numerous along the Atlantic coast but are now typically western and only an occasional straggler visits the eastern shore.

**Identification.** (See color plate on p. 469.) Slightly smaller than the common Canada, which it resembles in flight, the whitefront's most distinguishing feature is the "white front" from which that name is derived. This "front," or face, is a narrow band of white running entirely around the forepart of the head. It begins immediately behind the bill and extends about halfway to the eye. The rear edge is margined with sooty-black.

The bill, which is shorter than the head, has a rather heavy base and tapers to the "nail," or tip. The forepart is pinkish blending to light blue at the base and the nostrils are outlined with pale orange. The bill changes to yellow in the breeding season.

Except for the white face with its black edging, the entire head, neck, and chest are a dark grayish-brown. The back is of the same color but the feathers have lighter edgings which form regular and distinct transverse bars across the back. The lower back, rump, and tail are a mousy-brown; the tail feathers are tipped with white. The underside of the tail is gray and both upper and lower tail coverts are white.

The sides are of the same general tone as the back but the feathers have wider light tips and the top edges of the long side feathers are white. These white edges create a distinct line along the sides just below the wings.

The feet, like those of the emperor and the tule goose, are orange-yellow. The eye is brown.

**Characteristics.** White-fronted geese have the same general habits as the common Canada. Like the latter they do a lot of grazing and prefer the stubble fields and sprouting grain to aquatic food. Aside from some larvae and insects they are vegetarians by preference and often feed on beechnuts and acorns when these are convenient to fresh-water ponds. In the northern breeding grounds they eat quantities of berries.

In flight the white-fronted geese usually adopt the "V" formation like the Canada and often fly at altitudes of 500 feet or more. Their ringing cackle is frequently repeated during flight—the unmistakable *"wah-wah-wah-wah-"* that has earned them one of their many names.

**Breeding.** These geese arrive early at the nesting grounds, often before the ice is completely gone from the lakes and while there is still snow on the ground. During the mating season the males are particularly noisy and behave much like the ganders of other varieties.

The nests, generally around the ponds in the tundra rather than directly on the seacoast, are often no more than a depression scooped out of the sand. In almost every case the nests are sparingly lined with grass, lichens, and/or moss, and before the last of the usual five or six eggs has been deposited the female supplements the lining with down.

The nesting habits are similar to those of the Canada. The gander does not leave the goose during the hatching period and aids in caring for the young.

Incubation takes about four weeks. A day or two after emerging from the shell the goslings can travel rapidly over the rough ground. Young birds do not have the white face marking or splotches on breast. They acquire adult plumage after moulting in their second summer.

As with all members of the goose family, there is a period while the young are growing when a summer moult deprives the adults of the power of flight, and during this time they suffer heavy casualties from the native hunters.

**Range and Distribution.** The breeding grounds are on or near the Arctic coast from northeastern Siberia to northeastern Mackenzie and south to the lower valley of the Yukon. The main winter range extends from southern British Columbia through Lower California and includes a wide area on the west-central coast of Mexico.

Whitefronts begin the spring migration in March but the big flocks wing northward in April and are on the breeding grounds about May 15.

The southbound flights begin in September, with most of the birds reaching the winter feeding grounds by late October.

# AMERICAN BRANT

*Branta bernicla hrota*

COMMON NAMES: Brant-Goose, Burnt Goose, Clatter Goose, Common Brant, Crocker, Eastern Brant, Light-Bellied Goose, Quink.

**History.** The American brant is closely related to the European or brant goose and is only a winter visitor to the Atlantic coast of the United States. It is the only truly maritime member of the goose family, rarely being found any distance from salt water.

**Identification.** (See color plate on p. 470.) With the exception of the Ross's goose, the American

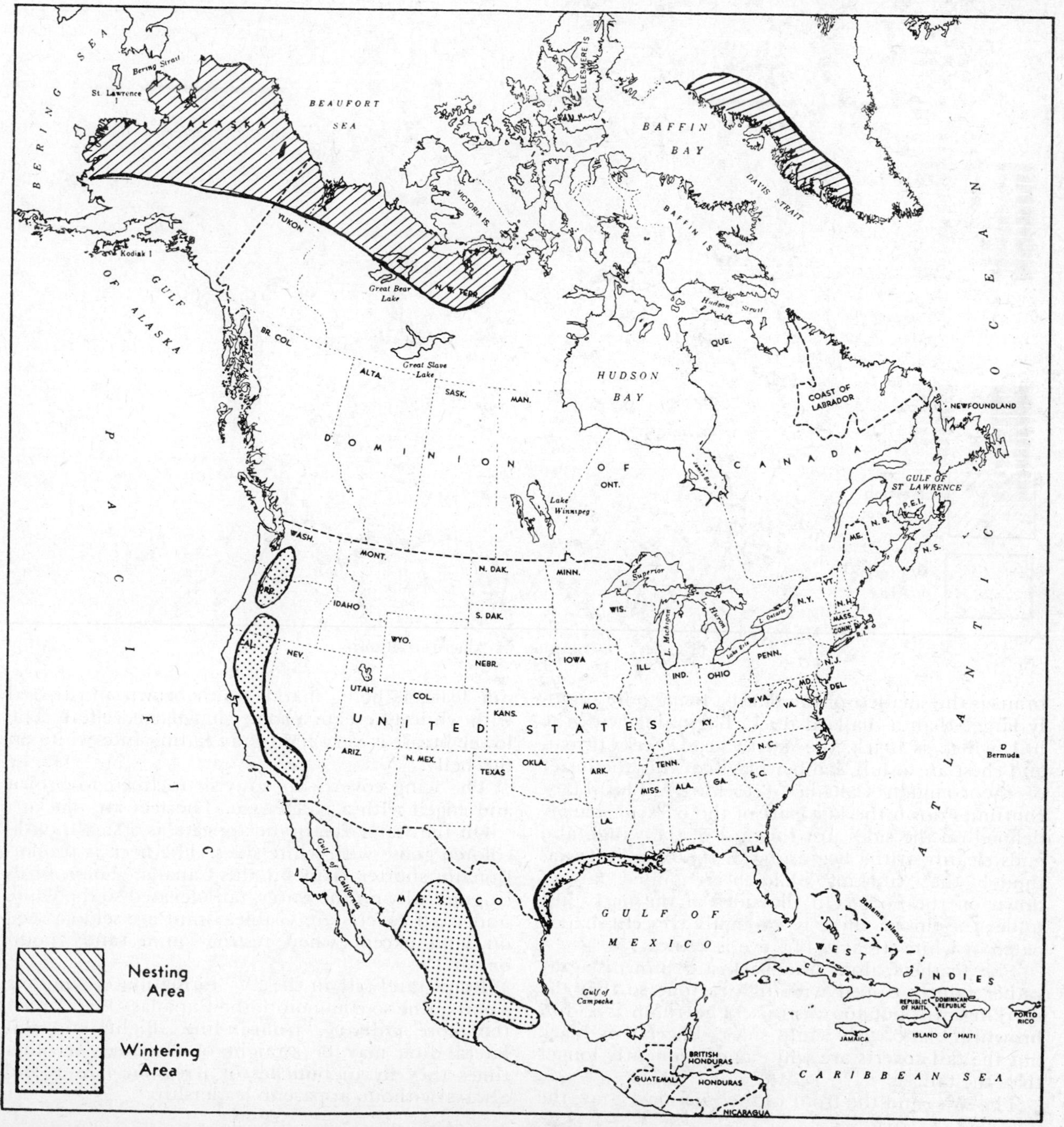


PLATE I. Distribution of White-fronted Goose.

PLATE I. Distribution of American Brant.

brant is the smallest of the family, being only slightly larger than a mallard duck. Beginning with the bill, which is black, the entire head, neck, throat, and chest are a dull, somber black lacking the luster of the common Canada's "stocking." This black continues down the first part of the back, is sharply defined on the sides just forward of the wings, and ends cleanly at the beginning of the breast. It is as though the "stocking" had been pulled farther down on the body. On the sides of the neck, just under the throat, there is a roughly crescent-shaped patch of white streaks. The eye is brown.

The feathers along the back are brownish-gray rather faintly tipped with lighter tone so that the markings are not too distinct. The rump is a dull brownish-black with white sides. The tail is black but the tail coverts are white and frequently longer than the tail.

The sides and the front of the breast are gray, the side feathers being marked with brown and tipped with white to create a somewhat barred effect. The lower breast is very light gray fading into white on the belly.

The wing coverts are grayish inclined to brown and edged with a paler tone. The feet are black.

On the water the brant appears as a small, dark-colored goose with white sides. The neck is proportionally shorter than on the Canada. These birds sit gracefully on the water, tail elevated so the white under-tail coverts are visible. Brant are seldom seen on land except when resting on a sandy point or bar.

Brant rarely fly in the "V" formation or the long sloping line so common to the Canadas. They prefer the more military "front-in-line" flight, and this lateral line may be straight or curving. At other times they fly in bunches or irregular masses and always without apparent leadership.

A flight of brant is easily recognizable even from a distance. They first appear as a long waving line of heavy dark birds which soon begin to show contrast between the dark head and neck and the white under parts. The long, pointed wings move rapidly in short, powerful strokes and the flight speed is greater than that of most other geese. As they fly, a jumbled, gabbling call goes up and down the line.

### BLACK BRANT *Branta nigricans*

COMMON NAMES: China Goose, Eskimo Goose, Sea Brant.

The black brant is found only along the Pacific coast. particularly in California, and like its eastern cousin, the American brant, it is only a winter visitor to that area. Occasionally a straggler is found on the Atlantic coast, just as an occasional American brant appears along the Pacific. Their habits and characteristics are similar to those of the American with few exceptions. They are wild, shy birds but will often come readily to well-set decoys.

**Identification.** In appearance they resemble the American variety except for being darker. On the American brant the black area in front is well defined but on the black brant, whose breast is a dull brownish-gray, this black front unites with the dark breast and is not so distinct. The markings on the neck, which are merely patches on the American, on the black become almost like a collar which does not meet in the back.

When sitting on the water the black brant closely resembles the American variety, but in flight the whole bird appears dark with very little white over and under the tail. They move in groups of varying numbers but almost always in one line, side by side.

The line of flight is not straight and level but is subject to frequent vertical changes. For no apparent reason, the right or left end bird changes altitude, either dropping or rising from a matter of inches to a few feet and this maneuver is followed in unison by every bird in the line until the whole flight is at a new level. The change is so smoothly executed that the interval between birds appears to remain the same at all times.

Unlike most other geese, the black brant prefers to fly comparatively close to the ground. He considers about 30 yards as maximum altitude and usually flies much below that. When passing over hilly country flocks will almost invariably go out of their way to skirt around the hills rather than pass over them.

While flying, and sometimes while at rest, the black brant utters a rather harsh *"g-r-r-r-, g-r-r-r-."* Other notes are a soft *"kronk, kronk,"* and a throaty *"wa-hook."*

**Characteristics.** The flight patterns of both the American and black brant are properly a characteristic but they have been given here under "Identification" for obvious reasons.

Although naturally timid, the brant lacks the caution and sagacity which characterizes the Canada goose. They are much less wary while on their feeding grounds and decoy more readily than most other geese. They also respond to calling more readily than their more suspicious cousins and at times their curiosity may be aroused by raising and lowering some object from the blind.

The American brant, like the Canada goose, fly high while on overland migration but when flying over water they usually skim close to the surface. They have the Canada's habit of hiding inconspicuously by stretching out their necks in the grass or on the water. They are splendid swimmers but do not dive unless forced to do so.

Brant are truly aquatic in habits and do not graze in fields like so many of the other geese. Their favorite food is eelgrass and they gather in large flocks to feed on this at low tide. When feeding they "tip" like the surface-feeding ducks. They are especially fond of the roots and lower portions of the eelgrass and often when "tipping" only the rear end is visible above the surface. Since they can reach the eelgrass only at low tide, they generally pull up more than they can consume immediately and let it float. When the rising tide covers the grass beds they eat this floating food. They devour great quantities of grass, which they have a unique habit of rolling into small balls before swallowing.

The disappearance of eelgrass along the North Atlantic coast has for many years affected the brant. This plant is their main food supply south of their breeding grounds, and as the eelgrass became more and more scarce, so too did the brant. There is some evidence, notably along Long Island, that the eelgrass is coming back, and with its return it is to be hoped that the brant will again become numerous.

**Breeding.** The brant utilize a natural depression in the ground as a base for a well-built nest of grasses, moss, and other local material. This is lined copiously with a blanket of down from the breast of the female.

The eggs may number as many as eight, but from three to five is the usual setting. The period of incubation is approximately four weeks and only the female sits on the eggs. As with all geese, the gander remains on guard close by. Among the chief enemies at nesting time are the gulls, and the gander fights valiantly to keep them away from the eggs which the female is covering

Both parents join in rearing the brood and often several broods band together for greater protection. The young grow rapidly and are ready for migration in about three months.

**Range and Distribution.** The American brant is the most northerly of all the geese. Their main breeding ground is on Ellesmere Island and extends well within the Polar circle. Because of the short summer season in that latitude brant begin their migration earlier than others of the species. Many of the birds are on their way south before the end of August. The bulk of the flight arrives in the Gulf of St. Lawrence region before the end of September. About the middle of October to the first part of November they reach their winter feeding grounds, which range from New Jersey to North Carolina, with some birds remaining as far north as Massachusetts and a few as far south as Florida.

The birds farthest south begin the spring migration as early as March but April finds the main flights headed for their breeding grounds.

Unlike its eastern counterpart, the breeding

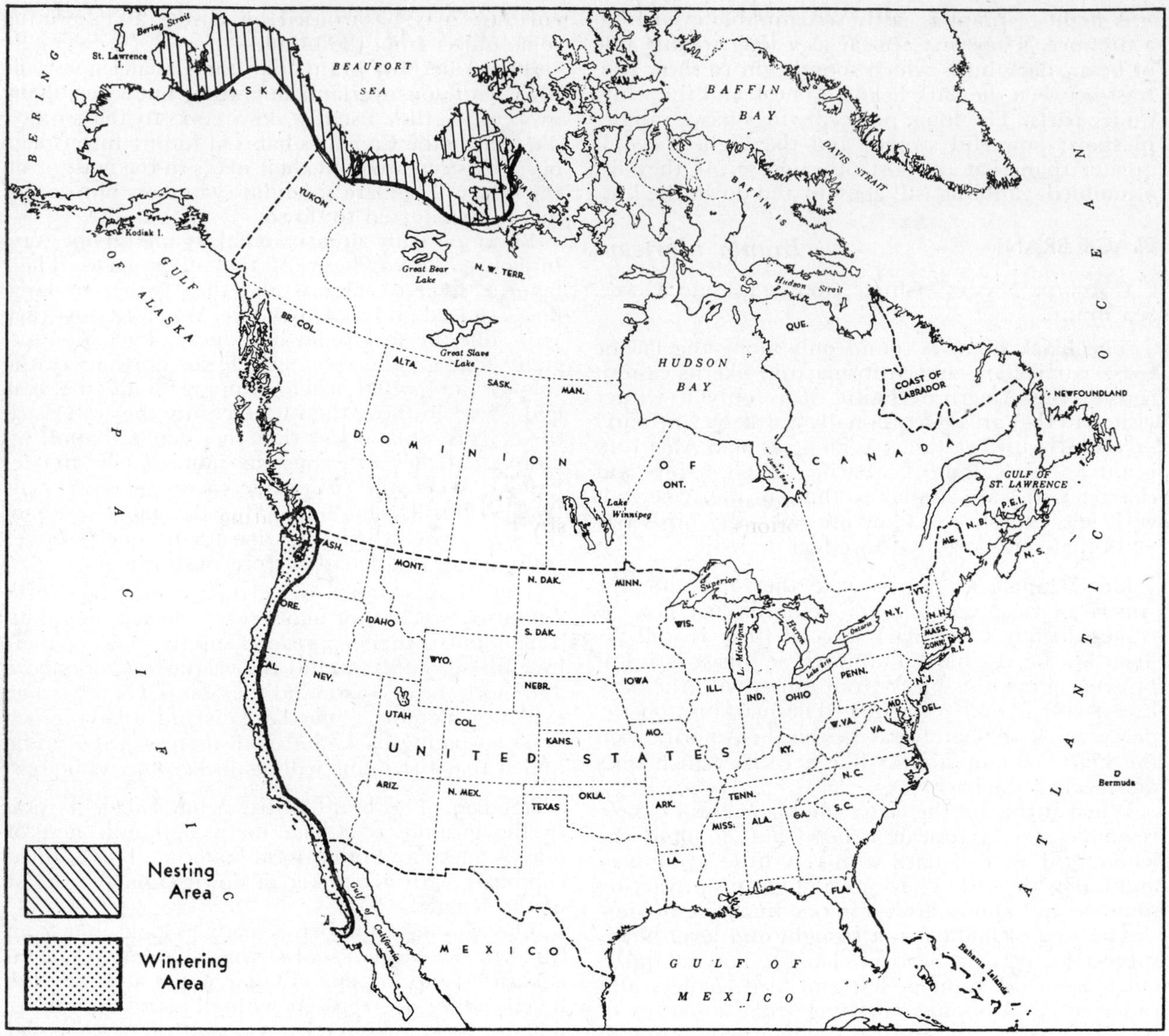


Plate II. Distribution of Black Brant.

grounds of the black brant do not extend to the Polar cap. The chief breeding area is along the northern coast of Alaska from Point Barrow nearly to the mouth of the Anderson River and the eastern Siberian coast.

The main flights pass over the Bering Sea in late September and travel down both sides of the Pacific to Japan and California. The winter feeding grounds are restricted on this continent to the Pacific Coast from British Columbia to Lower California.

The birds head north again in March or the first part of April and reach their breeding grounds about June.

Immature birds are inclined to be more grayish than the adults. The white feathers on the neck are lacking or barely discernible and the tail feathers are often tipped with white. A progressive moult during the winter and spring causes a gradual change in plumage and following the summer moult the young birds appear as adults.

# DUCKS

## BALDPATE

*Mareca americana*

Common Names: American Widgeon, Baldpate, Bald Widgeon, Baldpate Widgeon, Baldcrown, Baldface, Baldfaced Widgeon, Baldhead, Bluebill Widgeon, California Widgeon, Canvasback, Diamond Duck, French Teal, Green-Headed Widgeon, Grey Duck, L-Wing, Norwegian Poacher, Poacher, Southern Widgeon, Specklehead, Wheatduck, Whistler, Whistling-Dick, Whistling Duck, Whitebelly, Whiteface, Zin-Zin.

**History.** The baldpate is a wide ranger and a favorite test to the skilled gunner because of its nervous desultory flight. This duck is commonly and correctly known as "American widgeon" since it is closely related to the European widgeon of the same genus (*Mareca*). The baldpate breeds only on this continent and, in contrast to the Old World species, is larger in size and has more showy head markings.

**Identification.** (See color plate on p. 475.) The adult drake in full winter plumage is handsomely colored, his markings being especially apparent in flight. The drake begins to moult in June and at the peak, about July, is flightless because of the loss of his wing feathers. By August there is little difference in appearance between the two sexes, except for the full-plumaged wing of the male. There are many variations in the color change from the eclipse to winter dress, but, typically, the moult takes from a month to six weeks, ending in December when the dark chest feathers are replaced by the reddish-purple ones of winter.

All the year long the adult duck keeps her plumage of dull yellowish-brown, with whitish breast, giving her a superficial likeness to the female gadwall and pintail. Her feathers are renewed gradually during the "pre-nuptial" moult, so that the shedding is not noticeable, but she becomes flightless during the "post-nuptial" moult when the wing feathers are lost.

Both the drake and duck quack noisily when frightened, but the drake normally repeats a melodious *"Whew, whew, whew"* when in flight or resting on the water.

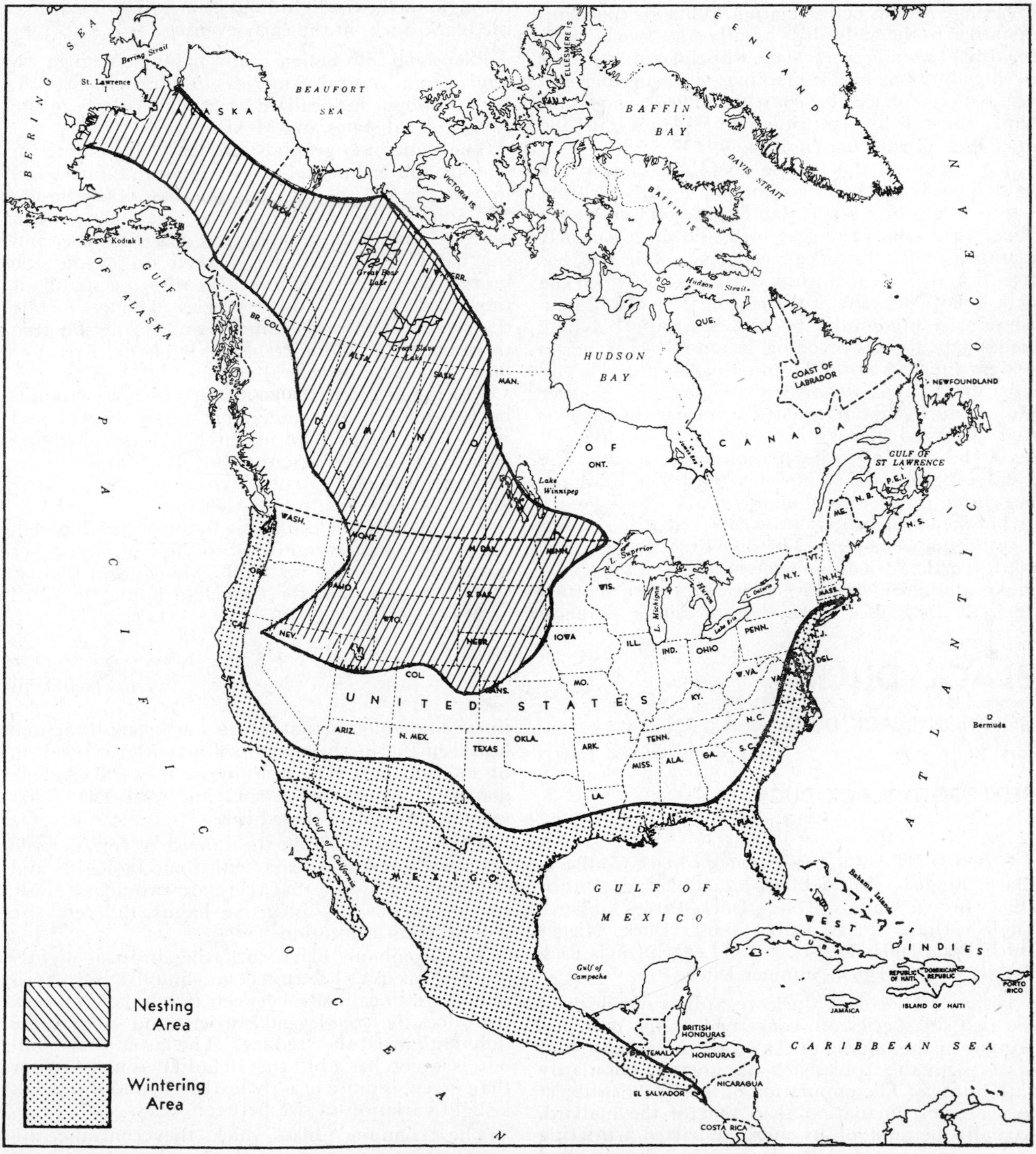


PLATE I. Distribution of Baldpate.

The drake and duck both average two pounds in weight, and 19 inches in length, about 4 inches smaller than the mallard.

**Characteristics.** The baldpate is an astute, shy bird, wary of decoys, and its nervousness and quick flight when frightened are warnings to other ducks with which it associates. It is capable of rising from the water in almost elevator-like straightness and speed, and goes into swift but irregular flight, bending and weaving in tight, excited groups, quacking loudly in alarm. The unruffled flight of the baldpate in mid-air is graceful, however, and is swift and steady, about 40 to 50 miles an hour.

**Breeding.** Often the baldpate waits to reach the breeding grounds before mating. While its courtship is similar to the gadwall's—usually with two advancing drakes wooing one female, whistling and twisting to show off their bright markings—it is speedier and more spectacular. The courting drakes swing low, bank, and roll like stunting fighter planes until the duck flies off with her choice.

Typical of all the puddle ducks, the nest of the baldpate is built on dry ground and usually far from water. Made in a slight depression and lined with grass, weed stems, and gray breast down, it is nearly identical to the European widgeon's. The hen has from six to 12 creamy-white eggs, some of which she occasionally deposits in the nest of the gadwall hen, whose eggs are similar to hers. Since the baldpate comes late to the breeding grounds, egg-laying is seldom finished until the middle of June. The incubation period is shorter than most of the other puddle ducks—about 24 days, or nearly the same as that of the European widgeon. The drake does not leave the duck after incubation starts, as does the average puddle duck, but stays with her until the beginning of the eclipse moult.

The hen is a jealous protector and will risk her own life for her brood. The ducklings resemble the adult female until about September when the young drake assumes identifying wing feathers of mottled gray. By December the first adult winter plumage develops, and becomes fully matured the second winter.

**Feeding.** Since the diet of the baldpate is largely vegetable, it rates as one of the prime table birds. Only seven per cent of its food is animal, normally mollusks and insects, and the other 93 per cent is largely seeds, grasses, and the stems and bulbs of aquatic plants. It often feeds with diving ducks, especially canvasbacks and redheads, and has the common habit of snatching away plant stems which they bring up to the surface of the water. For this thieving habit they are often known by the name "poacher." Normally, the baldpate feeds during the day, but where actively hunted, it often remains inland throughout the daylight hours, emerging to eat, like the black duck, in the early evening.

**Range and Distribution.** The baldpate's range extends from central America to northern Alaska. It is abundant in localized areas, particularly in the south central states and Mexico.

The breeding grounds are vast, beginning in Nevada and Nebraska and ranging into Canada and up into the Yukon and along the coast of the Bering Sea. Since much of this breeding area is far enough north to escape the competition of agriculture, and the baldpate is particularly keen in sensing the hunter, the numbers of this duck are more abundant than those of many other species. Though at one time, extensive market hunting and spring shooting threatened the existence of the baldpate, it is now on the increase in several areas.

The migration to the southern wintering grounds begins early in September, far ahead of cold and frost. They travel in an unhurried fashion, arriving about October in the States, spreading out along the Pacific, Gulf, and Atlantic states, with the majority alighting in the South and Mexico.

The migration in the spring to the northern breeding range is late as compared to those of most other ducks, since it waits for the breaking-up of the ice. It usually arrives at the Canadian border in April or May.

# BLACK DUCK

*Anas rubripes*

## COMMON BLACK DUCK

*Anas rubripes tristis*

## RED-LEGGED BLACK DUCK

*Anas rubripes rubripes*

Common Names: Black Duck, Black Mallard, Black English Duck, Black-Jack, Blackie, Brown Duck, Brown Mallard, Dusky Duck, Dusky Mallard, English Duck, Ledge Duck, Marsh Duck, Nigger Duck, Pond Duck, Red-Leg, Red-Legged Duck, Red-Paddle, Spring Duck, Summer Duck.

**History.** The black duck, regardless of which of the two sub-species are concerned, is the most important of the puddle ducks on the East Coast, and shares with the canvasback the greatest popularity with hunters. The population of this duck is subject to a greater fluctuation than that of the mallard, partially because of its more restricted wintering and nesting area. Another factor which has resulted in considerable fluctuation, in the wrong direction, has been the mosquito-control activities carried on by several states. The draining of many black-duck marshes, plus excessive spraying with DDT, has taken a large toll of these birds.

The species has been the subject of considerable argument for many years, with some biologists and wildfowlers arguing that there are two definite subspecies, each with distinctive habits, different size and different coloration.

The "common" black duck, they insist, is slightly smaller, has olive-brown feet and an olive bill, shows more variation in size between the drake and duck than does the "red-legged" variety, and "acts" quite differently from the "red-leg." The latter, they point out, is larger, has a bill that definitely is more yellow than green, is more heavily feathered, and shows but a slight variation in size between sexes.

The "common" black duck, they continue, migrates earlier and moves farther south for the winter, is inclined to decoy more readily, has a louder voice and uses it more, feeds more during the day than the night, and prefers fresh-water ponds to the open sea. The "red-legged" member of the family, however, migrates southward much later, is very easily frightened, does not decoy well, and is inclined to spend most of the day well out from the shore in salt water; it goes to fresh-water lakes and ponds primarily to drink rather than to feed, and prefers salt-water mollusks to fresh-water vegetation.

The opponents of this argument (and they are many) claim that the differences between the two birds are primarily the differences which separate the old ducks from the young ducks. On the matter of coloration, they insist this is merely a matter of age, pointing out that the juvenile "red-leg" has dark bills and feet, with the latter turning red later in the fall when the full winter plumage has been assumed.

**Identification.** (See color plate on p. 470). The drake, in his winter finery, which is far from gaudy, cannot readily be distinguished from the duck except on rather close comparison. The most apparent point of difference is found in the side of the chest, where the feathers of the male show a U-shaped buff marking and those of the female show a V-shaped buff marking. The drake begins to moult early in May, but with the exception of losing the U-shaped buff markings on the feathers on the chest shows little change from winter plumage. The new wing feathers usually have grown in sufficiently to permit flight by midsummer, and in September the fall moult begins and the winter plumage is complete by late October.

The duck closely resembles the drake, except that the bill is slightly shorter and more yellowish than that of the male and the feet are a pale brown. The color of the feet of the female is not an accurate means of determining sex, however, as there is considerable variation.

The voice of the duck and drake black duck is greatly similar to that of the duck and drake mallard, and, like the latter, black ducks are talkative.

The black duck is somewhat similar to the mallard in size, although the red-leg is inclined to be somewhat heavier, running a trifle over three pounds in weight.

**Characteristics and Breeding.** This is one of the most wary of waterfowl, fast in flight, and able to jump from the water even more rapidly than the mallard. Often, when frightened, they will jump almost straight upward for about 10 feet and then angle away at an extremely fast speed.

The courtship of the drake can only be described as a mad pursuit, whether in the air or on the water, or both. Like the mallard, the duck may have two or three suitors, and at the conclusion of the wild chase she will make her selection.

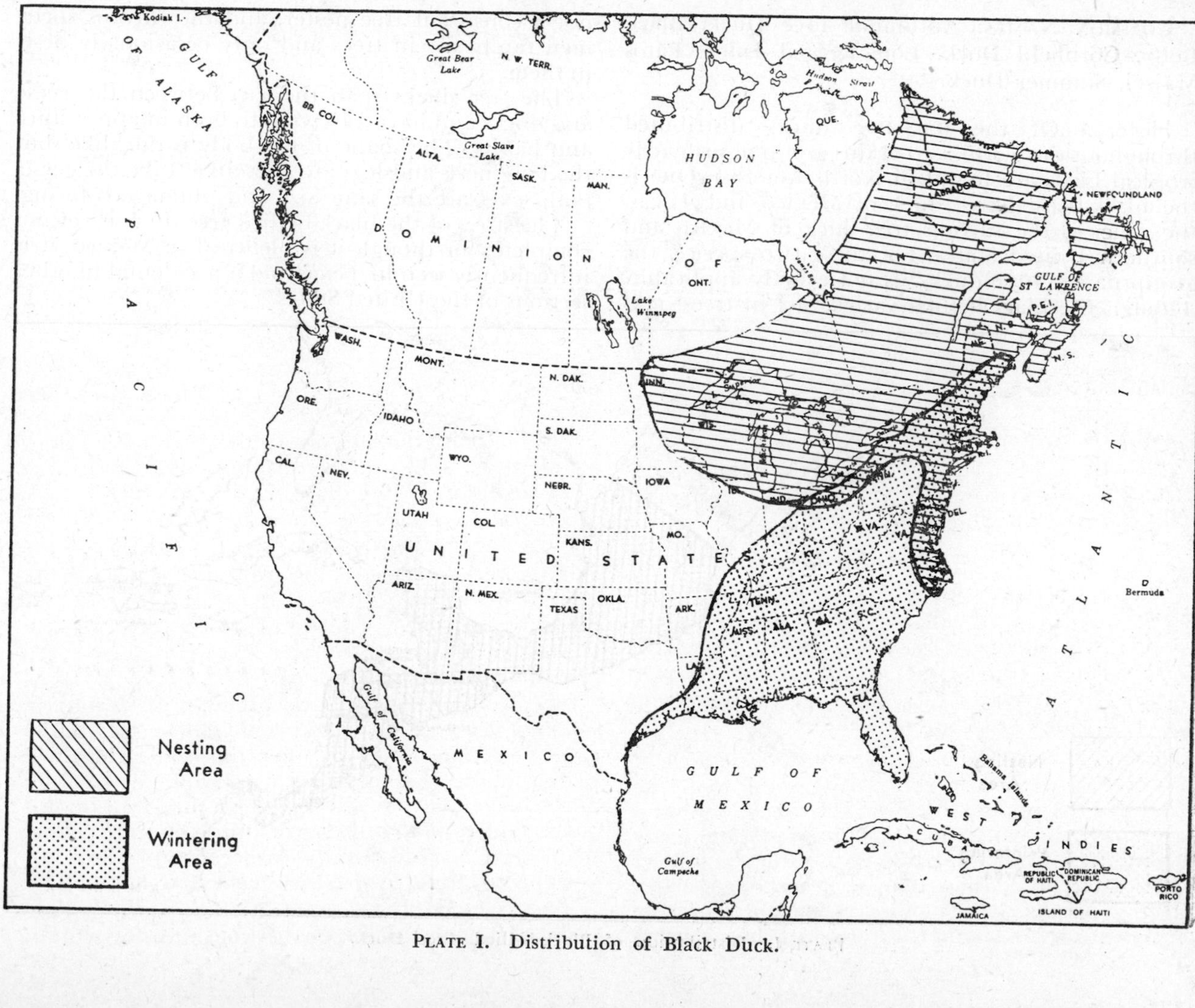


**PLATE I.** Distribution of Black Duck.

The black duck is a nonconformist when it comes to selecting a nest, and almost any location seems acceptable provided it is concealed and is not too far from water. The nest normally is lined with grass and a small amount of down, and the clutch may be from six to 12 eggs similar in size and coloration to those of the mallard. On several occasions black ducks have taken over the nests of other large birds, high up in a tree. Like the mallard, the black duck drake abandons the duck when the incubation begins, and seeks out the company of his own sex.

The duckling, a few minutes after emerging from the shell, fluffs out to twice the size it was on emerging. The hen is a devoted mother, and devotes her entire time to the instruction and feeding of the brood. The young birds are able to take flight by the time they are ten or 11 weeks old.

**Feeding.** The food preferences of the black duck are somewhat similar to those of the mallard, except that the black is inclined to be less of a vegetarian, with mollusks and crustaceans forming a good part of the diet. The normal diet is approximately 75 per cent vegetable and 25 per cent animal.

The black duck not only has excellent vision, but acute hearing. Their constant alertness makes it extremely difficult to approach within 50 yards of a flock, even though they are apparently busy feeding. Many hunters have claimed that the black duck can scent as well as see or hear an enemy, but biologists discount this theory.

**Range and Distribution.** It has a long but rather narrow range extending from eastern Texas to Dakota, and from Florida to northernmost Quebec. There is quite an overlap between the breeding and wintering ranges, extending from Maine to Delaware. The young birds normally begin moving southward around the first of September, the older birds often remaining in the north until late October and November, with the size of the flocks increasing as the season grows older. Often hundreds of birds are caught by a sudden freeze-up, and perish from hunger and thirst or as a result of being frozen in the ice.

Almost every year sporting and conservation groups between Massachusetts and Long Island spend considerable sums on grain to feed large flocks of black ducks that misjudge the weather and temperature.

The spring migration northward usually starts early in April, and the tendency seems to be to follow the coastline until a point opposite the summer breeding grounds is reached.

## BLACK-BELLIED TREE DUCK

*Dendrocygna autumnalis autumnalis*

Common Names: Autumnal Tree Duck, Black Belly, Cornfield Duck, Long-Legged Duck, Patos Maizel, Summer Duck.

**History.** Of the ten tree ducks distributed throughout the world, two of this group of primarily tropical birds are found in North America. One is the black-bellied tree duck of Mexico and Texas, the other is the fulvous tree duck of Mexico and southern United States. For these two species, the group name, "tree duck," is not exactly applicable. Though the black-bellied variety sits in trees, it is not a consistent tree nester, and the fulvous specimen rarely sits in trees and only occasionally nests in them.

The tree ducks span the gap between the geese and ducks and have a likeness to both in appearance and habits. The shape of the body is ducklike, but the long neck and legs are gooselike. Like the geese, both sexes are the same size and plumage coloring.

The story of the black-bellied tree duck is yet not complete, for though it is plentiful in Mexico, it is infrequently seen in Texas and is accidental in other sections of the United States.

Plate I. Distribution of Black-bellied Tree Duck.

**Identification.** This duck is readily identified by its black belly and breast. Both male and female look alike, but the species is difficult to confuse with any other duck except the fulvous tree duck. Beside its distinctive plumage markings, the long legs are pastel pink and the bill is a bizarre arrangement of pink, blue, and yellow. The dark underparts, bill, and feet coloring distinguish these ducks from the fulvous tree duck.

In Mexico one of its popular names is *"pe-che-che-ne,"* after its whistling call note.

Both sexes are small. Exact measurements are not sufficiently numerous to permit an accurate average to be made, but they are of the approximate size of the fulvous tree duck, or weigh slightly over 1½ pounds, with an oversized wingspread of 36 inches.

**Characteristics.** By nature, black-bellies are unsuspicious and may be readily approached by day, but at night their shrill whistle warns of every danger; the most usual danger is their natural enemy, the alligator. When pursued, they fly up into the trees, for they are at home on the land, and also walk with ease. They seldom alight directly on the water, and would rather approach it from the land. The normal flight pattern is a small flock flying low over the water or land in a straight line. They are not active birds; large flocks spend most of the day resting in the trees or along the edge of a river or pond.

**Breeding.** The duck is variable in her choice of a nesting site, but the preference seems to be to build in a stump or tree hollow in a wooded area whether it be near or far from the water. Nests also are placed on the ground in the midst of concealing reeds and rushes. The average clutch is from 12 to 14 whitish eggs. Since their range is southerly, the breeding season is a long one and some naturalists believe that two broods are raised in one season. The plumage development of the young is completed by their second summer.

**Feeding.** Because of a particular fondness for corn, this duck has taken a heavy toll of yearly crops in some parts of Mexico. Although they habitually fly in small flocks, they are most gregarious at feeding time and collect in large numbers in a concentrated area, usually to the detriment of the cornfields. They sometimes feed by "tipping" as do the puddle ducks, but usually graze like geese. Normally they feed at night. Most of their diet is vegetable matter, and they are prized as table food. They are easily adapted to domestication and mingle freely with other barnyard fowl.

**Range and Distribution.** The distribution map shows the range of this duck in North America. As indicated, the summer and winter are spent in one region. It also frequents northern South America. The preferred areas are the fresh-water lagoons of the interior.

## BUFFLEHEAD

*Charitonetta albeola*

Common Names: Buffalo-Headed Duck, Buffle Duck, Bumblebee Dipper, Butterback, Butterball, Butter-Bowl, Butterbox, Butter Duck, Cock-Dipper, Conjuring Duck, Dapper, Didapper, Die-Dipper, Dipper, Dipper Duck, Diver, Hell-Diver, King Butterball, Little Black and White Duck, Marionette, Robin Dipper, Scotch Dipper, Scotch Duck, Scotchman, Scotch Teal, Shotbag, Spirit, Spirit Dipper, Spirit Duck, Widgeon, Woolhead,

**History.** The bufflehead has a wide distribution, comes unsuspiciously to decoy, and though about the size of a teal, often becomes as fat as its popular name, "butterball." In spite of these advantages to the wildfowler, the duck is infrequently hunted, for its normally fishy taste makes it undesirable table food.

This duck is exclusively American, and allied to the American golden-eye and the Barrow's golden-eye. The bufflehead is generally recognized as being in a distinct genus, but some ornithologists classify this triumvirate together, under the genus *Bucephala.*

**Identification.** (See color plate on p. 472.) Though the bufflehead drake in full winter plumage resembles the male golden-eye, he is more white in appearance with a distinctive, large head which looks even larger because of the puffy crest feathers. The large white patch on the head is a chief means of identification from all other ducks. The moult into eclipse plumage begins about August, and, though the color change is incomplete, most of the purple and green reflections on the black head are lost. Soon after the winter flight feathers are renewed, the autumn moult begins and by early winter the drake resumes his most striking plumage.

The adult female is dull in coloring; a patch of white on the side of her puffy brown head is her outstanding identifying feature. She is similar to the female golden-eye, but smaller.

The bufflehead is among the smallest of ducks, averaging a few ounces larger than the teal, smallest of all North American wildfowl. The weight averages about one pound or a little under, and the length is around 4 inches, with an approximate wingspread of 22 inches.

Like the golden-eye, neither the duck nor drake is talkative. Their notes are low and harsh, of little carrying power.

**Characteristics and Breeding.** Unlike the average diving duck, the bufflehead springs vertically from the water (as do the golden-eyes). This short, upward bound is a modified version of a puddle-duck characteristic, but the bufflehead adds another feature to its ascent by being able to sweep into immediate flight after coming from beneath the water. It is fast on the wing, but when pursued sometimes relies on steep dives to escape, plummeting like a stone into the water from great heights. In migration they travel rapidly in small flocks.

The courtship proceedings of the bufflehead are not unusual, but the drake seems to show more indecision in choosing a mate than is common among the ducks. Though he has violent fights with rivals, he showers his attentions on one duck and then another, stretching his neck, puffing out his head feathers, and diving.

After the ducks are paired off, the search for a nesting site begins. The buffleheads are tree nesters, and since they prefer the same natural cavities, deserted woodpecker holes, or crevices as do the golden-eyes, there is sometimes a shortage of suitable places in one locale. The nests normally are near the water. The incubation of the ivory to pale-olive eggs takes about 22 days.

The ducklings descend from their high nests in the manner of the golden-eye and wood duck young. Encouraged by the mother, they tumble to the ground, breaking their fall somewhat by fluttering their wings. Young buffleheads of both sexes look alike and resemble the adult female the first fall, but by the second fall usually are fully developed.

**Feeding.** Primarily a seacoast duck, the bufflehead usually feeds in small flocks by diving for animal food, leaving at least one duck on the surface as a sentinel. Insects, crustaceans, and mollusks are taken in the greatest proportion. The remainder of the 79% animal food is fish; along the Pacific coast, a preference is shown for rotting salmon. The 21% vegetable matter is composed of pondweeds and other aquatic plants.

**Range and Distribution.** The distribution of this duck is comparatively sparse over one of the largest duck ranges in North America. The bufflehead is found from the Arctic to southern Mexico, from the Pacific across to the Atlantic coast. There is an overlapping of summer and winter ranges along the Pacific coast, from northern California to British Columbia.

It is a hardy duck, migrating late (about November) and often remaining north during the winter. The winter range extends from British Columbia on the west and New Hampshire on the east, south to the Gulf of Mexico.

Despite its ability to survive cold weather, the main migration northward is late. Though the summer breeding grounds extend over a wide area, from California and the northern states north to Canada and Alaska, the chief nesting grounds are in western Canada.

It is one of the last of the ducks to leave the wintering grounds, and the only diving duck that follows it in moving northward is the ruddy duck. It is not so plentiful now along the Atlantic coast as it was 20 years ago, although observers have reported that the population in this area is subject to considerable local fluctuation. Some observers report that local feeding conditions seem to have a marked effect on the number of birds wintering in the area.

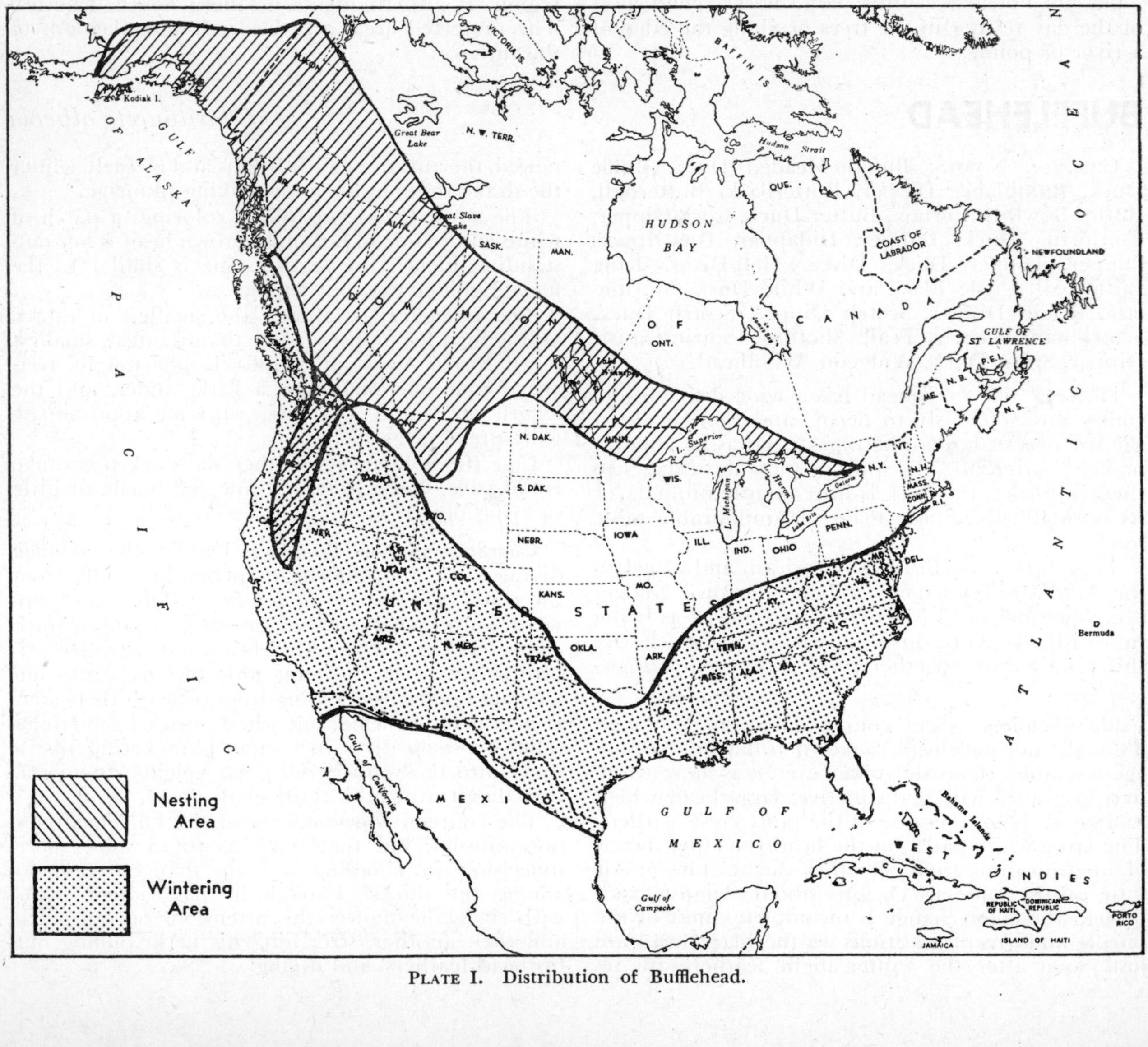


PLATE I. Distribution of Bufflehead.

# CANVASBACK *Nyroca valisineria*

Common Names: Bullneck, Can, Canard Cheval, Canny, Canvas, Gray Duck, Hickory-Quacker, Horse-Duck, Red-Headed Bullneck, Sheldrake, Whiteback.

**History.** The canvasback is known as "king of the ducks" by many North American sportsmen. It is a large, handsome duck of prime table quality and is eagerly hunted from coast to coast by wildfowlers with discriminating palates. Some epicures, however, have particular preferences among the duck family, and hotly contend that a rice- or acorn-fed mallard, wood duck, or teal is on a par with the canvasback. The succulent redhead is a relative of the canvasback, and so closely resembles it that many a host has inadvertently or prankishly substituted the one for the other. Regardless of individual tastes, however, the enviable reputation of this exclusively American duck is known the world over. One of the reasons for its popularity makes up a part of its scientific name *Nyroca valisineria. Valisineria* is a contraction of *Valisineria speralis,* the Latin name for the wild celery plant. Upon the root of this aquatic plant the canvasback purportedly waxes sweet and fat. However, this duck has been found to be equally desirable in locales where this plant is not present.

Market hunters have taken their heavy toll of this duck, firing broadsides into flocks sleeping on the water—using big guns, batteries and sink boxes. The fact that these ducks brought several dollars a pair in some areas offered the necessary provocation for their slaughter.

As with several other duck species, drainage and drought in southerly Midwest breeding grounds of the prairies are two major reasons for the decrease in duck numbers. Much of the nesting range of the canvasback has been drained or destroyed in the interests of agriculture, settlement, mosquito control, and flood control.

**Identification.** The canvasback drake in bright winter plumage is rather similar to the male redhead. The more obvious points of difference between the two ducks are in the head and bill. The canvasback has a deeper bill, a black one, nearly the length of its head; coupled with the sloping forehead this gives the duck an elongated profile. The comparative profiles of the two species readily distinguish them at a distance. The head and neck coloring of the canvasback is a duller red and the distinctive vermiculations of gray and white on its back give the duck its name. (See color plate on p. 470.)

The incomplete moult into the eclipse plumage commences in late June and some of the brighter feathers become drabber. In September the wing feathers are lost and the males, incapable of flight, remain together, apart from the females. After the autumn moult, which takes from late September to early November, the male plumage deepens to its full winter grandeur.

The adult female is gray-brown in color throughout the year. During the post-nuptial moult, when she becomes flightless, the duck does not band together with others of her own sex, but separates from the others and stays under cover of the grasses and reeds as much as possible. The duck resembles the females of the redhead, ringnecks, and scaups.

The drake makes a variety of noises, croaking, peeping, and screaming. His mating call is *"ick, ick coooo,"* which the female answers with *"cuk-cuk."*

Both sexes are about the same size, averaging 3 pounds, but some weigh between 2 and 3 pounds. The length of both sexes ranges between 20 and 24 inches, with a wingspread from 34 to 36 inches.

**Characteristics.** The canvasbacks have the dual, and often conflicting, characteristics of being both wary and curious. Their take-off from the water is slow, a noisy, skipping action, but their flight speed rates is generally considered to be the fastest of all the ducks. Paced by an airplane, it has been clocked at 72 miles per hour. The canvasback often gives an illusion of slower flight than its kinsman, the redhead, because of a slower wing-beat. The "cans" habitually travel in large flocks, in V-formation, but for shorter hops sometimes fly in a straight line.

**Breeding.** The courtship of this duck is vigorous and spectacular. Normally, the mortality rate among the females is higher than for the males and consequently several unattached drakes usually are available to pursue one duck. The drakes compete with each other in displaying their markings, throwing their heads back toward their tails, stretching their necks, and calling softly all the while. Besides these maneuvers and obvious rushes, the drakes try sneak-runs on the duck, flattening themselves out on the water, moving quietly up to her. The duck can successfully evade or postpone the attentions of any one drake, and often it is the rivals who keep each other from the female, but if several drakes crowd her at once, she takes to quick and twisting flight with the group of males in close pursuit. Whether on the water or in the air, the courtship tempo is kept at a pitch by the female who gives the provocative call note if the ardor of the drakes shows signs of slackening. This love-making may continue for several days before the duck chooses a mate. Once the couple has paired off, it is common to see the drake grab at the duck's tail feathers while in nuptial flight and hang on until she shakes him loose by quick snaps and dives.

The duck is haphazard in her choice of a nesting site, but often is found hidden among cattails and bulrushes. It is well constructed of plant material found in the immediate locale and lined with down. Usually built in shallow water, it lies on the swamp, pond, or slough bottom with its rim above the water level. Occasionally, it is made in deeper water and would float free but for the retaining reeds among which it is placed. Sometimes redheads and ruddy ducks drop their eggs in the nest of the canvasback, but the number of her own clutch is beween seven and nine. The incubation of the large greenish-gray eggs takes from 24 to 28 days.

The ducklings are born to a regal manner and show an arrogant attitude toward other ducklings when observed in captivity. Normally, they are able to fly about the tenth week. Their plumage development is fast. As in most duck species, the young resemble the mature female, but in September the drake begins to assume his identifying markings and by November they are distinct. It is not until the next spring, however, that they attain adult plumage and are ready for their first mating season.

**Feeding.** The canvasback is an expert diving duck, and, like the redhead, is often plagued by the poaching baldpate which waits for the ducks to rise from a depth of 10 to 20 feet to try to snatch the succulent roots from its bill. The large canvasback is an indiscriminate feeder compared with many other duck species. Its liking for rotting fish and salmon eggs often has made it distasteful or unpalatable to the duck eaters of the Pacific coast. The greatest portion of its diet is habitually vegetable matter, however, with 81% mostly pondweeds, wild celery, delta duck potato, grasses, and sedges. The remaining 19% is animal food: mollusks, insects, and fishes.

**Range and Distribution.** Canvasbacks are distributed over a wide range from Alaska to southern Mexico, from the Atlantic coast to the Pacific.

The fall migration to the lakes, bays, and brackish coastal waters of the Atlantic, Pacific, and Gulf states starts late in the season for these sturdy ducks. Wintering in New York State in the vicinity of the Finger Lakes sometimes proves fatal for them, however, when the lakes freeze over, leaving the ducks to die of hunger, thirst, and cold. By October the ducks are on their way to warmer climes; their best-known direction is via the Atlantic flyway through Ontario, Pennsylvania, and Virginia, down to the

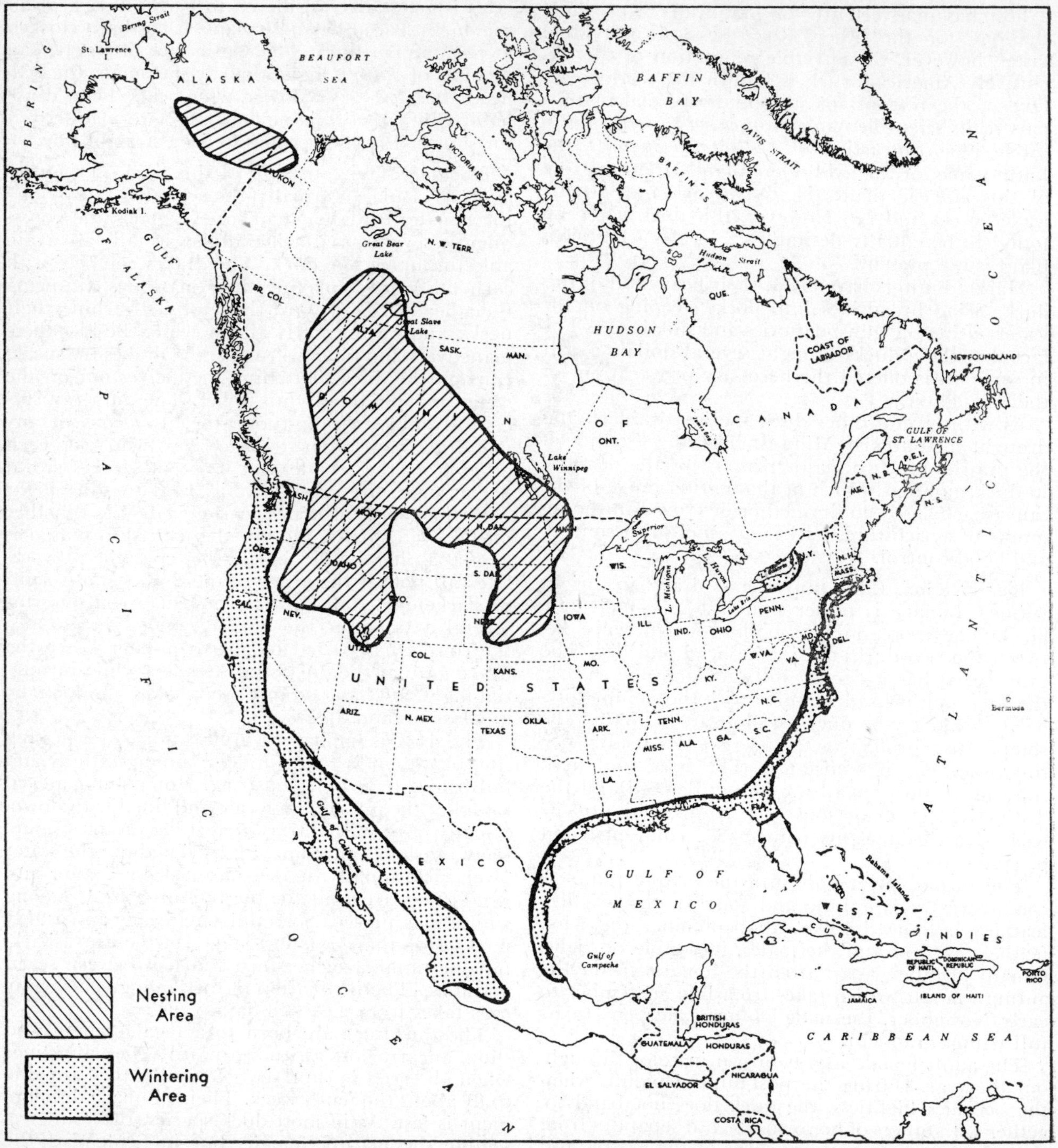


PLATE I. Distribution of Canvasback.

Chesapeake Bay-Currituck Sound region, where the canvasback first became world famous. They also are abundant on the Pacific coast.

In the return spring flight to the breeding grounds the canvasbacks are impatient to be off and are among the first to leave the wintering range. It is common for groups of ducks, or individuals, to use the same migrating route each season, frequenting the same feeding and resting places. Soon after the ice has broken in late February, they begin the migration to the great nesting grounds in the western part of the continent, from central Oregon, east to Nebraska and Minnesota, and north to Canada and Alaska. Normally, the migrants wait until reaching the breeding grounds to pair up, though some of the earliest ducks to arrive are already mated.

## AMERICAN COOT

*Fulica americana americana*

Common Names: Blue Peter, Coot, Crow Duck, Ivory-Billed Coot, Marsh Hen, Meadow Hen, Moor-Head, Mud-Hen, Pond Crow, Pull-Doo, Sea Crow, Shuffler, Splatter, White-Bill.

**History.** The term coot, or sea coot, is often applied to that variety of sea ducks properly known as scoters. The true coot is not a duck at all but belongs to the family *Rallidae,* along with the rails and gallinules. It is the most ducklike member of the group and is sometimes found in company with true ducks. These traits, coupled with the fact that it is most often seen while swimming, have frequently caused it to be thought of as a duck.

"Crazy as a coot" or "silly as a coot" is a common phrase not without foundation, for the coot is a clown among his kind and his antics are often amusing. Coots readily become tame and may be reared in captivity. During the breeding season, however, they do not hesitate to use their sharp bills freely and can hardly be classed as pets.

In common with all the gallinules and rails, coots are popularly dubbed "mud-hens" because of their chickenlike appearance and their preference for shallow ponds and muddy bogs.

**Identification.** The American coot is the only member of the family *Rallidae* having a white or whitish bill. Like nearly all the birds who make their homes in thick reeds and marsh grasses, the coot is equipped with a tough crown-plate extending from the base of the bill up the forehead to the crown. This plate is believed to protect the head from the cutting edges of the grass as the bird runs about in the marsh. The crown-plate on the coot is brownish and two brownish spots occur near the tip of the bill.

The head and neck are of a blackish hue in contrast to the rest of the body which is a slaty-gray color paler below than above. The tips of the secondary wing feathers are white and show as a white border on the trailing edge of the wing in flight. The under tail coverts form a white patch beneath the tail.

The legs and feet are greenish and the long toes are provided with scalloped flaps or lobes in lieu of webbing. The gallinules, which the coot resembles except for color, do not have these scalloped lobes in the toes.

**Characteristics.** Coots are much more aquatically inclined than the gallinules and are better swimmers. They dive readily and have an advantage over their close relatives in being able to swim long distances under water. Like all of the "skittering" tribe, coots swim with a peculiar bobbing motion of the head and neck. They take wing only when forced to do so and they splatter along over the surface of the water with great rapidity using both wings and feet for propulsion.

Although generally shy and retiring, the coot is not very bright and will venture into many places which the more wary ducks would avoid. In many instances the ducks with whom they associate, notably the lesser scaup ducks, permit the coots to investigate a place first and then follow them if the coast seems clear.

They are noisy birds and when disturbed break into a loud chorus of high-pitched cackling notes which are audible for some distance. The most common call is a low *"kuk, kuk, kuk, kuk,"* but they have a variety of notes ranging from a quack not unlike that of the ducks to a heavy, guttural, croaking noise.

Coots prefer reedy pools along creeks and sluggish streams where a dense growth of reeds and marsh grasses offers them protection. Like the rails and gallinules they thread their way through these boggy morasses with ease and feed on the aquatic plants which they pull up from the shallow depths. In Florida they are often found in considerable numbers on lakes which are covered with a species of yellow lilies known as "bonnets," and along some of the larger, shallow rivers, such as Indian River, they may be seen in large groups in company with the lesser scaup ducks.

**Breeding.** They breed in the fresh-water marshes where they make their home in the summer. Several pairs may breed in the same slough or marsh. During the migration they travel in small groups or singly, but when they reach their winter home they seem to become more gregarious and it is then common to see them in large groups.

The nest is a deeply hollowed, basketlike affair made of dead grass and rushes. It is built up from the bottom of the marsh or pond and generally fastened securely to the surrounding vegetation. The number of eggs varies from 8 to 15, with 12 being about average. They are a pale buffy-white in color "peppered" with chocolate-brown or black. Incubation begins as soon as the first egg is laid, so that the young hatch one by one rather than in a brood. The young birds leave the nest as soon as they are born and swim away to be cared for by the other parent. So far as is known the female sits on the eggs, and so it may be presumed that the male takes care of the babies until they are all hatched.

The downy young are a sooty black with just a touch of white under the throat. The head and neck show scattered hairlike feathers of bright orange. The head is bald on top and the bill is bright red tipped with black.

The immature birds resemble their parents but are lighter below and washed with brown above. The crown-plate is smaller than on the adult.

**Feeding.** Their food is chiefly vegetable, and when they feed on plant life exclusively their flesh makes fine eating, but in some localities they feed on quantities of small fish and the flesh then becomes unfit for the table.

**Range and Distribution.** The American coot is found generally, if not in numbers, throughout North America. They breed from New Brunswick west to British Columbia, with some birds reaching Alaska and a few casuals in Greenland. They nest throughout their entire range and except for the most northern portions some birds remain all winter. The winter range covers most of the southern states with the heaviest concentration along the Gulf of Mexico.

# EUROPEAN COOT

*Fulica atra atra*

This species closely resembles the American coot but lacks the white markings on the wings and the white patch under the tail. It is an inhabitant of the northern portions of Europe and only occasionally is found in Greenland, Labrador, or Newfoundland, and rarely seen below Nova Scotia.

# AMERICAN EIDER

*Somateria mollissima dresseri*

Common Names: Big Sea-Duck, Black-and-White Coot, Canvasback, Common Eider, Eskimo Duck, Isle-of-Shoals Duck, Laying Duck, Looby, Metik, Moyac, Moyak, Passing Birds, Pied Wamp, Sea-Coot, Sea Duck, Shoal Duck, Shoreyer, Squam Duck, Squaw Duck, Wamp.

**History.** The American eider, like the northern eider, is a sub-species of the common eider *(Somateria mollissima)*, which has long been protected in European countries and Iceland for the commercial value of its down. The valuable breast down, which is a natural insulator, is world-famous for its use in coverlets and quilts. The Eskimos, and other natives of this duck's northerly range, habitually made blankets and garments from the breasts of eiders.

The people of the North American continent did not have the long-range view of the Europeans in their treatment of their natural wealth, and the eiders here naturally suffered as a result. They were slaughtered by thousands for their down. Killing the bird was more in line with the impatient system of mass production, rather than the Europeans' slower method of protecting the tame ducks on farms and two or three times during an incubation period removing the down from the nest without injury to the eggs. Forty nests normally supplied only one pound of down.

Besides the excessive killing of mature ducks, Indians upset the possibility of replacement since they relied on the eggs for food. They collected as many as several thousand from one small nesting area, placing the majority in winter food caches. In addition to this duck's great losses to man, they were preyed on by numerous natural enemies. This combination of destructive forces was a serious threat to its survival potential, but, in the interest of commerce, eider farms were set up in Canada in 1933, and the duck was protected.

**Identification.** The full winter plumage of the adult drake is a striking black and white, very similar to the northern eider's. The two sub-species are distinguishable by the American eider's having more green on the head and a dip in the bill. He also somewhat resembles the Pacific eider, but lacks the V-shaped marking on the throat. Differences between this duck and the Steller's, king, and spectacled eiders are more distinct. In the eclipse moult, which begins about late June or early July and ends around late August, the plumage of the male resembles the drab coloring of the female. Soon after the duck is able to fly again, the second, or autumn, moult begins, and the full winter plumage is resumed by December.

The mature female is a dark brown with black bars, and her drab coloration is a natural camouflage throughout the year. Her uniformly dull wing easily distinguishes her from the male during the height of the eclipse. Except for a slight difference in the shape and feathering on the bill, she is identical with the female northern and Pacific eiders, and bears a close resemblance to the other female eiders.

Like all the other eiders, except for the Steller's eider, this duck is chunky of build and large. Of all the North American ducks it ranks second only to the Pacific eider in size. The female averages smaller than the male by about 1 pound; approximate weight for the male is about 4 pounds 6 ounces. The length ranges between 22 and 24 inches and the wingspread between 38 and 40 inches.

Both sexes have a wide range of call notes; most of them are loud and strident in quality. The male has a dovelike courting call, *"ah-oo."* The quack of the female is similar to the *"wak-wak-wak"* of a mallard.

**Characteristics.** This duck is unsuspicious by nature and usually is tame even near settlements, as demonstrated by its inclination to thrive on duck farms. It is a true maritime species, diving for food along the shoreline, and resting and sleeping on the sea. It normally flies close to the water, rarely going over land. Its distinctive fashion of flight is different from those of all other ducks. The wing-beat of the average duck is rapid in order to support so large a body, but the eider, though a deceptively swift flier, has a slow wing-beat and looks sluggish and slow as it proceeds with head held low. Its flight usually is steady, in a straight line, with the small flocks in Indian file or abreast. Sometimes, however, they break the steady beat by soaring.

**Breeding.** The courtship call of the drake is clear, loud, and a distinctive herald of the mating

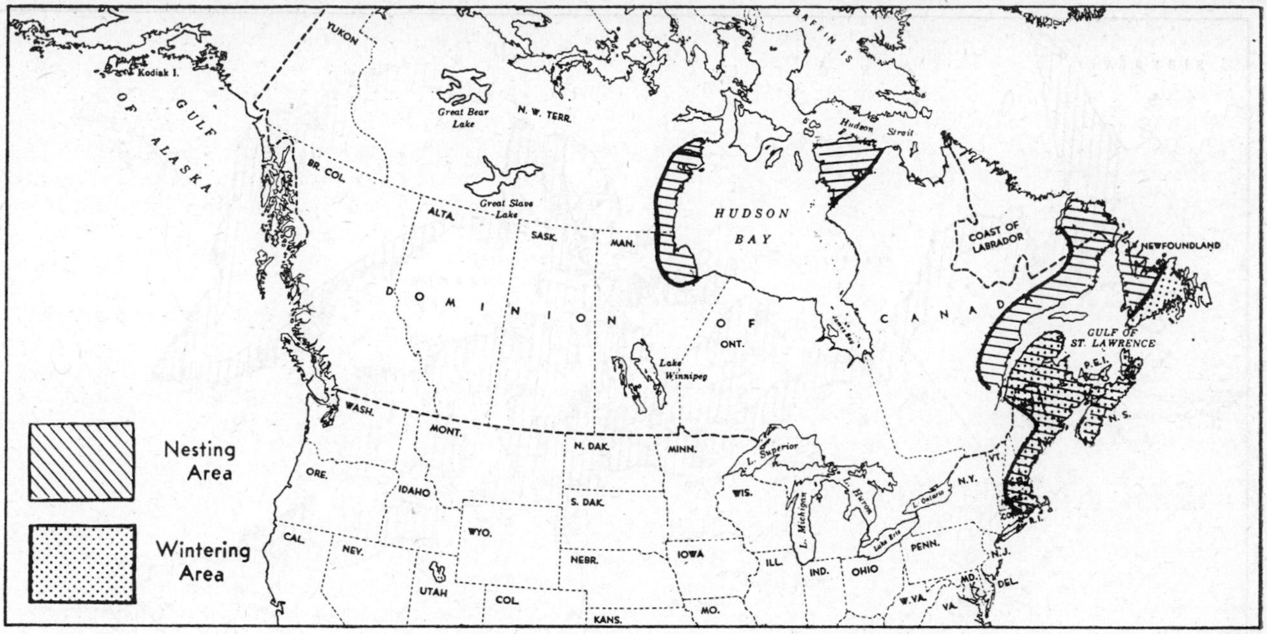


PLATE I. Distribution of American Eider Ducks.

season. It usually is heard when the drake is on the water, facing the duck with his head and neck stretched upward. In his effort to show his plumage to best advantage, especially his black belly, he sometimes raises himself to a near-vertical position and almost rises from the water.

The eider's fondness for nesting near to each other has stimulated man's custom of taking the nest down for his own use. The nests, built on dry ground or in rock hollows, normally are placed near to the water and well hidden by bushes and tall reeds. Into the nest, constructed from seaweed, mosses, grasses, etc., twined together, the duck drops about four to six olive-colored eggs which she is able to conceal with a "blanket" of down. If the eggs survive predation, they hatch in about 28 days.

The devoted mother duck carefully guards her brood, often simulating injury to distract the attention of the enemy. As soon as the young are dry, she leads them to the water to instruct them in feeding and hiding from men, foxes, falcons, skuas, seals, and glaucous gulls. Though the ducklings resemble each other by fall, they do not look like the mature female as is the common appearance of developing juveniles. In early winter the young drake shows more distinctive markings which deepen by his second spring, but his plumage is not fully adult until his third spring. The female's plumage changes are faster, and she is in mature coloring by her second autumn. Normally, the young are not ready for breeding until three years of age.

**Feeding.** Despite the awkward look of the duck, the eider is an expert diver and underwater swimmer. Since most of its food is marine animal life, it is distasteful eating to the wildfowler, and usually is bagged accidentally. Of the 96% animal food, mollusks, crustaceans, and echinoderms are highest in preference. Unidentifiable vegetable matter composes the remaining 4% of the diet. They are especially fond of blue mussels, and in order to crush them and other hard-shelled sea life, the intake of gravel is 14%.

**Range and Distribution.** This hardy duck lives in a northerly climate in all seasons. Though the American eider tends to more northerly coastal areas than its extremist relative, the northern eider, it is nonetheless a lover of cold regions. The chief requirement for the habitat is open water. The distribution map shows a partial overlapping of the summering and wintering ranges.

The main migration to the wintering grounds starts around November and in December the duck is distributed from Newfoundland to the New England states, sometimes south to Long Island.

The migration to the breeding grounds in the north starts in early spring and is unusual because the adult drakes leave ahead of the mature females and young. However, the adults of both sexes end the flight together, coming to the nesting grounds in mixed flocks. The majority breed along the coast of Hudson Bay and Hudson Strait, and also along the eastern coast of Canada.

## KING EIDER

*Somateria spectabilis*

COMMON NAMES: Canvasback, Cousin, Isle-of-Shoals Duck, King-Bird, Mongrel Drake, Passing Duck, Pistrik, Sea Duck, Wamp's Cousin, Warnecootai.

**History.** The king eider is, as its scientific name denotes, "spectacular." Its beautiful plumage pattern distinguishes it from all other ducks.

Though its chief areas of distribution are in the northerly parts of the Northern Hemisphere, it is found in more southerly locales than any of the other eiders. It frequently winters around the Great Lakes and even south to North Carolina.

**Identification.** Though the adult female is very similar to the other large, female eiders (see "Amer-

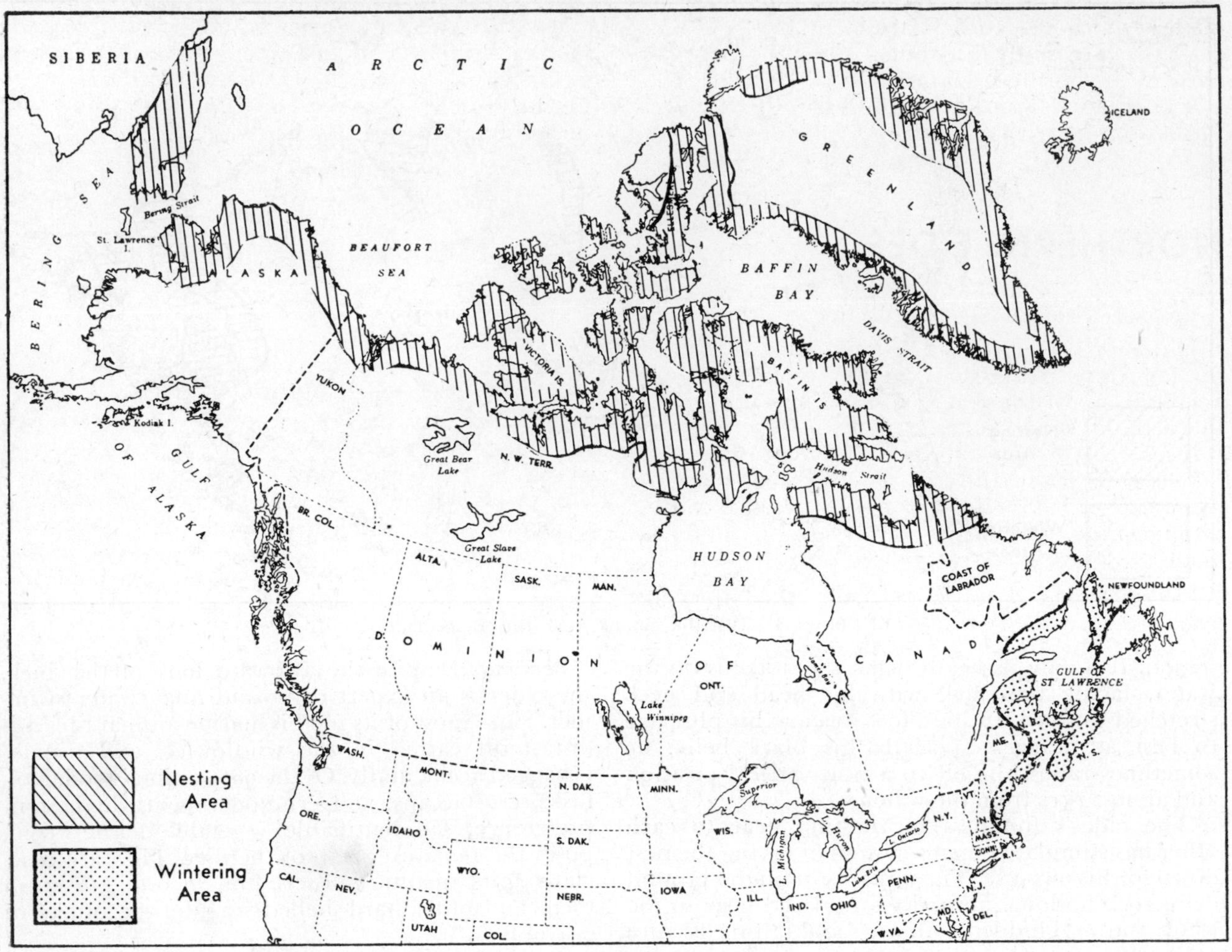


PLATE I. Distribution of King Eider.

ican Eider"), the male king eider has a distinctive appearance. The general effect at a distance is white in the fore parts and black in the rear parts. At close range the head and bill coloring and bill construction readily distinguish it. The plumage moults of both sexes resemble those of the American eider. (See color plate on p. 484.)

The king eider is large and bulky and about the size of the American eider. It is a heavy duck weighing from 3½ to 4 pounds, with a length of about 21 to 22 inches and a wingspread of a little over 36 inches.

The drake habitually uses a guttural, courting note, *"urr,"* which he repeats while in flight or on the water. The duck has been known to utter hissing and growling noises when disturbed during incubation.

**Characteristics and Breeding.** Although the king eiders frequently fly over land as well as water, their characteristic flight habits resemble those of the American eider. The general courting procedure is similar, but the nesting habits differ. The other eiders normally place their nests on small islands in the sea, but this duck usually builds on the coast of the mainland or near large bodies of fresh water. The nest is constructed like the American eider's and liberally supplied with down. The duck drops about five olive-buff eggs and during the incubation period is a close sitter while the drake joins others of his sex on the open sea to begin the flightless eclipse moult.

The upbringing and development of the ducklings are similar to the growth of the American eider's young. The males have mature plumage when about 2½ years old and the females usually are adult by the second fall, but both sexes are ready for mating when three years of age.

**Feeding.** The feeding habits of this duck are the same as the other eiders, but the king eider is capable of diving to greater depths for food. Except for 5% vegetable matter, the diet is animal food, and the tough, fishy flesh is almost inedible. Eskimos consider the soft, fatty lump which grows at the base of the drake's bill a luxury food item.

**Range and Distribution.** The king eider is a northerly duck and its chief areas of abundance are in the sub-Arctic, especially in the Aleutian Islands.

The fall migration commences about August when the ducks move down from the Arctic coasts to more southerly locales, though some remain as far north as Greenland if there is open sea. Usually, they migrate in large flocks, sometimes numbering several hundred, and follow the coastline at a low altitude about a mile off shore. The destination for the winter often is the Aleutians, though they are also found around the Great Lakes and along the Atlantic coast to Long Island and sometimes farther south to North Carolina. On the Pacific coast they are thinly distributed along the Canadian coast to the northern United States.

The breeding grounds are in the sub-Arctic, along the coast of the mainland and inland. When the young birds become fully matured, they join the adults on the nesting grounds, but until that time (normally their third year) they remain in separate flocks. They do not fly far north until ready to breed themselves, and tend to spend both seasons in the warmest parts of the ranges.

## NORTHERN EIDER

*Somateria mollissima borealis*

COMMON NAMES: Same as for the American eider.

**History.** The northern eider is an inhabitant of the far Arctic coasts. This North American duck is a sub-species of the common eider of Europe and, like its Old World relative, is famous for its down which is used commercially for "eiderdown."

It is closely allied to the better-known American eider *(Somateria mollissima dresseri)* and so similar in appearance and habits that reference should be made to that duck. (See p. 368.)

**Identification.** The adult male is a strikingly marked bird in full winter plumage but is barely distinguishable from the American eider drake. The differences are unrecognizable unless the bird is close at hand, and since the two types often are found on the same range, much confusion results. The most distinctive variations are that the northern eider has less green on the head and sometimes it has a prominent black "V" on the throat. During the eclipse moult, when he is flightless, he is well camouflaged by a subdued plumage of mottled brown. The change takes place between early July and mid-August; with the autumn moult, extending from November to late December, the drake resumes his handsome winter dress.

A slight difference in bill construction is the chief means of separating the females of the northern and American eiders. The duck retains her dark-brown coloration following two seasonal moults, and in the pre-nuptial moult adds her special breast down which is particularly sought after by hunters for commercial usage.

These birds are the same size as the American eider.

Both sexes usually are silent, but the drake has a harsh flight call and a cooing courtship note.

**Characteristics, Breeding, and Feeding.** Flight characteristics, courtship behavior, nesting habits,

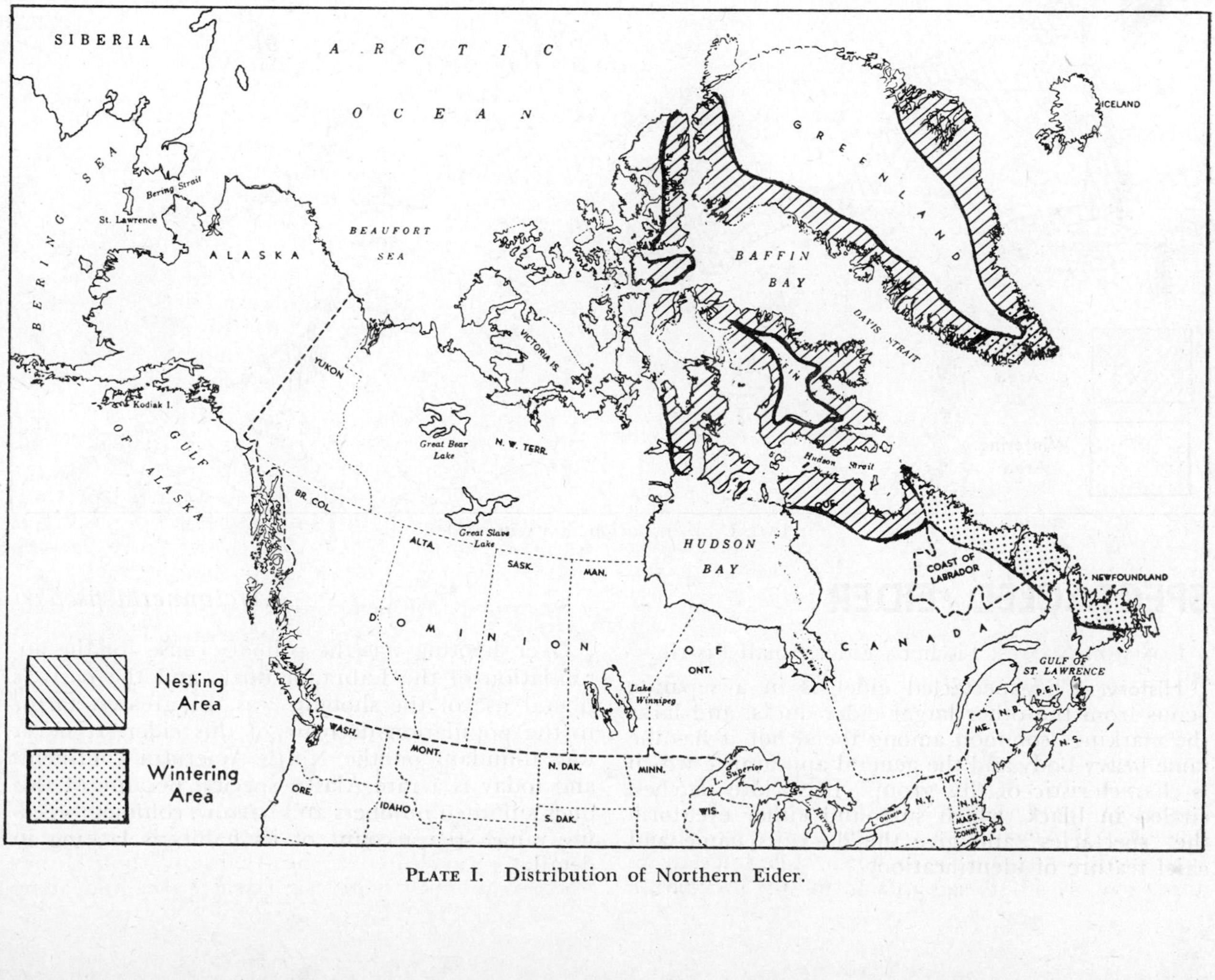


PLATE I. Distribution of Northern Eider.

growth of the ducklings, and feeding habits are similar to those of the American eider (*q.v.*).

**Range and Distribution.** The range of this eider is far north, extending along the coast from Iceland to Newfoundland. The duck can live in the coldest weather as long as the water is free of ice. Since the Arctic salt water is usually far warmer than the air, these oceanic ducks often live comfortably in the Far North during all seasons. The distribution map shows that in some areas the wintering grounds are more northerly than the summering range.

Many migrate southward for the winter, living along the coast of Labrador and Newfoundland, sometimes as far south as Maine. They are not abundant in any region during any season, but are most numerous on the breeding grounds of Baffin Island.

## PACIFIC EIDER

*Somateria V-nigra*

COMMON NAMES: Canvasback, Eider, Eiderduck, Large Pistrik, Sea Duck.

**Identification and Range.** The Pacific eider ***(Somateria V-nigra)*** is very similar to the American *(Somateria mollisima dresseri)* and northern eiders *(Somateria mollisima borealis),* but its scientific name, *V-nigra,* meaning "black V," explains the identifying feature of the species. The male has a V-shaped marking on the throat, with the two branches converging in a point at the base of the bill. Though the king eider has the same throat marking, the plumage patterns of the two species readily distinguish them. Both sexes of the Pacific eider have a characteristic bill construction and feathering which separates them from the other eiders. The Pacific eider averages 5½ pounds and is the largest of all the ducks on the North American continent.

The range of the Pacific eider is an additional difference between this duck and the American and northern eiders. It is distributed in the Far North, but along the western part of the continent, from the Pacific coast of Alaska to Victoria Island. The chief breeding grounds are in the Aleutian Islands and some ducks remain there for the winter, but the majority fly back to the open waters of the sub-Arctic coasts.

These differences in appearance and range are the outstanding points of distinction between the Pacific eider and American eider. (For a detailed account of the American eider, see p. 368.)

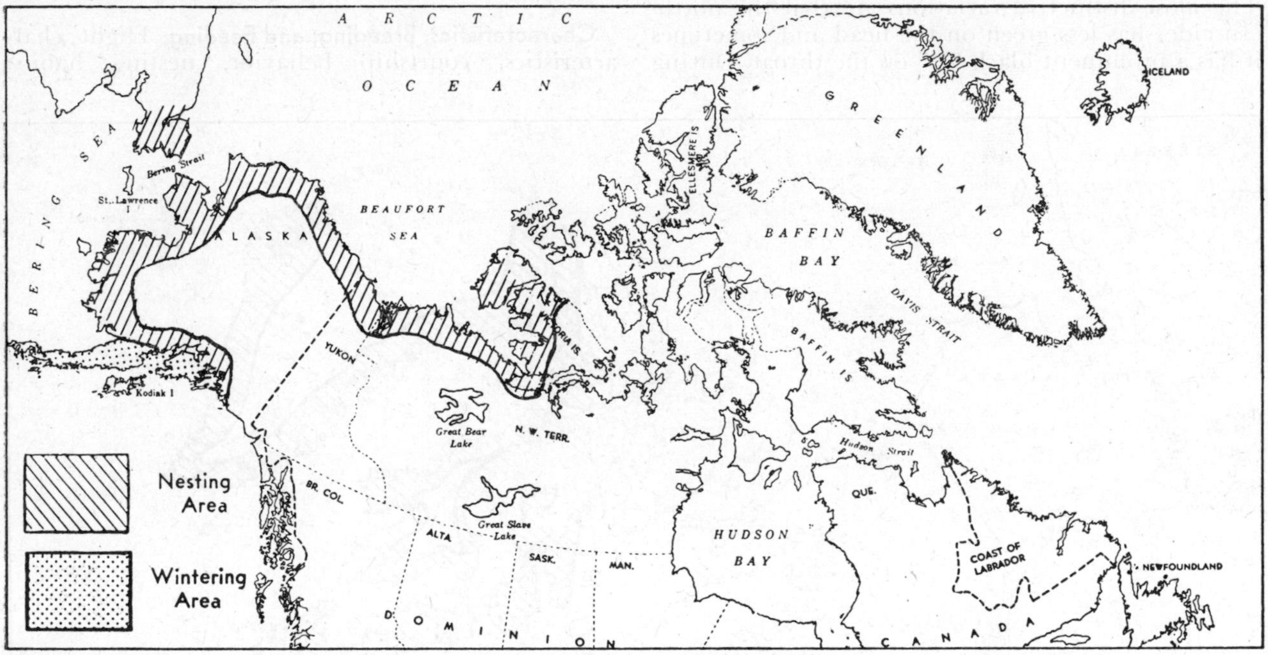


PLATE I. Distribution of Pacific Eider.

## SPECTACLED EIDER

*Arctonnetta fischeri*

COMMON NAMES: Fischer's Eider, Small Pistrik.

**History.** The spectacled eider is in a separate genus from the other larger eider ducks, and lacks the markings common among them, but it has the same heavy body and the general appearance which is characteristic of this group. The white patches, circled in black, which surround either eye form the "spectacles" and give the duck its name and chief feature of identification.

Over-shooting was the primary cause for the annihilation of the Labrador duck, and the native's liberal use of the shotgun was the greatest factor in the population decrease of this eider. It never was abundant on the North American continent, and today is a rare Alaska species. Because of this duck's limited numbers and narrow, confined breeding range, the account of its habits is lacking in detail.

PLATE I. Distribution of Spectacled Eider.

**Identification.** The drake is a beautiful bird in winter plumage. From his "spectacles" down over his nostrils there is an odd feathering which distinguishes him. The general effect of light upper portions and darker undersides resembles the coloring of the northern, American, or Pacific eiders. Though the eclipse moult (which begins in June) is incomplete, the bright head feathering is lost and the over-all body tone is a drab gray-brown. The flightless period in August is followed by the autumn moult, and the second moult reverses the process of plumage change, for by December the drake is once again in resplendent dress. (See color plate, p. 484.)

Like the male, the mature female has the feathering on the bill which is on upper and lower mandible but grown down over the nostrils on the upper mandible. The duck also has a light-brown, modified version of the "spectacled" look. These two aspects distinguish her from other large female eiders.

The spectacled eider is known as a silent duck, seldom calling even during the courting season.

Both sexes are very large, averaging over 3½ pounds in weight, between 21 and 22 inches in length, and about 36 inches in wingspread.

**Characteristics and Breeding.** The fashion of flight resembles that of the American eider, but the courting habits are not known. The nesting site usually is on a small island off the coast or near ponds and marshes of either fresh or brackish water. The nests are placed in hollows in concealing grassy hummocks and are constructed of grasses and lined with down. The incubation period for the five to seven olive-buffy eggs probably is about 28 days.

As in the case of other eiders which have many natural enemies, a single brood sometimes is seen under the protection of two ducks. Ornithologists are not certain of the explanation for this behavior, and do not know whether it is planned or accidental. The two ducks may purposely have merged their broods or just happened to be near together when an enemy approached. At all times the duck is one of the most devoted mothers and one of the most courageous defenders of her young. The male and female ducklings are similar in appearance in the fall, but do not closely resemble the adult female as is usual among juveniles of most of the duck species. Both sexes have mature plumage when about two years of age.

**Feeding.** Since so few specimens of the spectacled eider have been studied, the picture of its feeding habits is not a finished one. The ducks examined showed a higher vegetable content (23%) than usual among the other eiders, but they live largely on animal food (77%). Mollusks, insects, and crustaceans are the outstanding food preferences. Pondweeds, crowberry, sedges, and other plants make up the rest of the food intake. They are fond of feeding in shallow water.

**Range and Distribution.** The range of this duck includes northeastern Siberia (where it is numerous), but on the North American continent it is thinly distributed in the Aleutians during the winter and breeds along the coast of Alaska during the summer, sharing the grounds with the Steller's eider.

About 1900, ornithologists expressed concern over the future of this duck, which was suffering greatly at the hands of Eskimos and natural predators. Eskimos were robbing nests and killing many adult birds. Although many species might have withstood this onslaught, the spectacled eider's limited numbers and extremely limited range made its survival questionable. Its population has remained reasonably stable, however, for the last decade, and it is now generally considered to be out of danger.

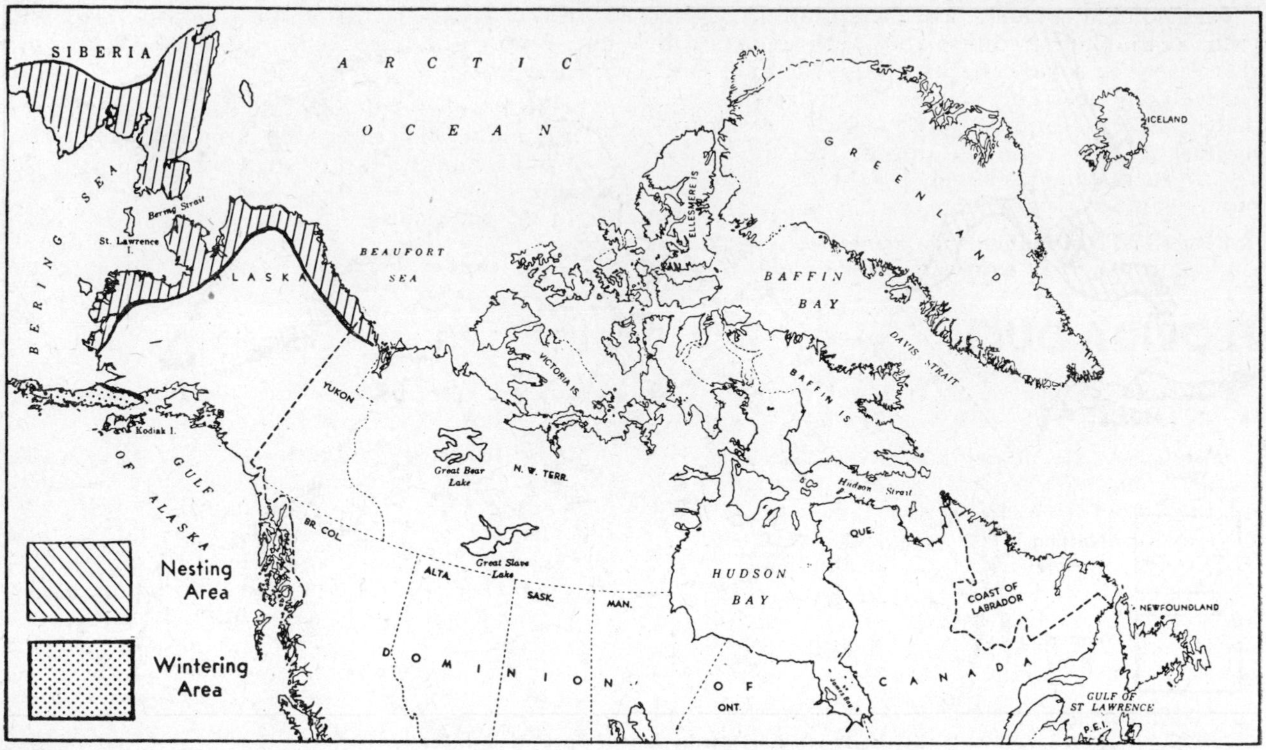


PLATE I. Distribution of Steller's Eider.

# STELLER'S EIDER *Polysticta stelleri*

COMMON NAMES: None known.

**History.** The Steller's eider is little known to the wildfowlers of America because of its thin distribution on a remote range which extends along the most northerly coasts of Alaska and eastern Asia. Because of the inaccessibility of the habitat, comparatively few specimens have been studied and the history of the duck is not complete.

This duck does not have the typical appearance of the other members of the eider group, being smaller and more graceful in build. Though it is poor table food, it is killed during the winter season by natives when the ducks are forced in from the sea by severe storms.

**Identification.** The adult drake is a handsome bird in his full winter plumage, and his bizarre markings distinguish him from other ducks. Particularly striking are the black collar, black throat, and black ring circling the eye as contrasted with a white head. During the eclipse moult, which begins about July, the drake assumes a browner plumage resembling that of the duck. As with most other ducks, the coloring of the winter wing feathers is replaced, but in the Steller's eider, the chestnut under parts are also renewed in one complete moult. With the second autumn moult, the general brownish tone of the drake is lost, and between early fall and December he changes back to striking winter distinctiveness. (See color plate on p. 484.)

The mature female has deep brown plumage throughout the year. Her wing resembles a mallard's and lacks the white coverts of the male, but is brighter than the wing of the typical male diving duck. She is smaller but similar to the females of the eider group.

Both duck and drake are medium in size, averaging slightly less than 2 pounds. The length varies between 17 and 18 inches, and the wingspread between 28 and 29 inches.

**Characteristics and Breeding.** The eiders are tame ducks, probably because they are infrequently hunted, feeding and resting a good distance off shore. They habitually fly in small flocks and are fast on the wing, and, like the golden-eyes, their wings make a whistling noise when in flight. Though they are much swifter than the other eiders, their more streamlined build gives an unfair illusion of excess speed in comparison to their clumsy-looking relatives.

Little has been observed of the courtship habits of the Steller's eider, but since it is known that the adult drake is jealous of the immature, juvenile drakes, it can be assumed the courtship and pairing probably have most of the usual male rivalry in displaying, bobbing, and bowing.

The nest usually is built in a ground hollow near the water, preferably a pond. It is well lined with breast down which the setting duck freely adds as the incubation period continues. The time it takes to hatch the seven to ten olive-buff eggs is not known for certain, but it is assuredly within the 28-day span allowed for all ducks.

The ducklings mature slowly. By the first fall they are a mottled brown but similar to the adult female. They do not develop adult plumage until the second fall, and are ready to breed by the third spring.

**Feeding.** These ducks are expert at diving for their food. Their feeding habits vary slightly with the season; in some cases in winter, the food is exclusively animal. The average diet is roughly estimated at 87% animal food, mostly crustaceans, mollusks, insects, annelid worms, and fishes. The 13% vegetable food is largely pondweeds, algae, and other plants.

**Range and Distribution.** The range of this eider is confined to the Far North. It inhabits the coasts of northern Alaska on the North American continent, but is more abundant across the Bering Sea to the Siberian coast.

Because of a preference for cold weather, there is no noteworthy migration between summering and wintering grounds. Rough weather drives the feeding flocks off the seas, and some travel as far south as the Aleutians for the winter season. During spring breeding they prefer the inland tundra country.

# FLORIDA DUCK

*Anas fulvigula fulvigula*

COMMON NAMES: Same as those given for the mottled duck.

**History.** As its name implies this duck is confined to the State of Florida. Because it does not migrate from this restricted range, it is not a familiar bird to the hunters of the continent as a whole.

Though the Florida duck *(Anas fulvigula fulvigula)*, mottled duck *(Anas fulvigula maculosa)*, and black duck *(Anas rubripes)* are closely related, with similarities in appearance and habits, they are not known to hybridize.

**Identification.** The Florida duck is very like the mottled duck; one of the most distinct differences is a darker streaking on the head and throat. Both the drake and duck have the same mottled-brown coloring when in full winter plumage, though the female is sometimes slightly paler, but, like the mottled duck, they are usually identified by characteristic chest feather markings, U-shaped in the case of the male, centrally-streaked on the female. The black-spotted bill of the duck is also a duller orange in color. For detailed differentiations between the Florida duck and the black duck, as well as other mottled brown ducks, see "Mottled Duck" (p. 392). The Florida duck is about the same size as the mottled duck.

**Characteristics and Breeding.** The flight speed of this duck is equal to that of the black duck, but it is tamer, probably because it is plentiful within its range and not over-hunted.

Its courtship is similar to the black duck's, and the nesting site is chosen with the same variation, either by the water or as much as 200 yards away, but always on dry ground. The nests, formed in a hollow, are exceptionally well hidden under bushes or tall grasses. They are lined with grass and breast-down, added in increasing amounts as the incubation continues. The eggs, ranging from eight to ten in number, are colored creamy-white to pale olive.

The duck protects her wary young with infinite care, noisily and laboriously pretending injuries and generally distracting the enemy while the ducklings hide. The moults and plumage phases are the same as those of the mottled duck.

**Feeding.** The Florida duck feeds like the mottled duck, but on a larger percentage of animal food than the average member of the puddle-duck group. The diet is 41% mollusks, insects, crustaceans, and fishes, and 59% vegetable food, mostly pondweeds, seeds, grasses, and other aquatic plants.

**Range and Distribution.** The Florida duck is numerous in its name state, with specific areas of abundance in the southern and central parts. In April it is often found breeding along the Indian River and the St. Johns River. It is sometimes found in other Gulf states.

# FULVOUS TREE DUCK

*Dendrocygna bicolor helva*

COMMON NAMES: Cornfield Duck, Long-Legged Duck, Mexican Duck, Mexican Squealer, Mexican Wood-Duck, Squealer, Summer Duck, Tee-Kee, Wood Duck, Yankee Duck, Yellow-Bellied Fiddler Duck.

**History.** The fulvous tree duck is named for its coloring, which is brownish to reddish-yellow. Timid and elusive by nature, it is also a night feeder, so that its behavior and habits are not well known to the naturalist or wildfowler, who rarely see it. Though it is found in some of the southern states during the wintering season, its range on the North American continent is primarily in Mexico. Being more northerly in distribution, it is found in the United States more often than its relative, the black-bellied tree duck *(q.v.)*, which it closely resembles.

**Identification.** The full-plumaged adult male and female look alike. Their un-ducklike appearance of long legs and long neck distinguish them from all other North American duck species except the black-bellied tree duck, which is the only other duck of this group found on the continent. The fulvous variety is distinctive for its pale-cinnamon under parts, blue-gray legs and feet, and dark blue bill, whereas the black-belly has a black breast with pinkish legs, feet, and bill.

This duck has several whistling calls, used at various times as a warning or when taking to the air or on the wing.

The fulvous duck is small and averages about 1¾ pounds in weight and 19 inches in length. The large wings reach to more than 36 inches when extended.

**Characteristics.** These ducks habitually lead a secluded life among the ponds, marshes, and lagoons. If surprised on a home site, they often will stand taut and still in an effort to blend with the rushes and reeds. They dive to escape pursuit and sometimes fly into the tops of trees, though they are not consistently found sitting on the branches of trees

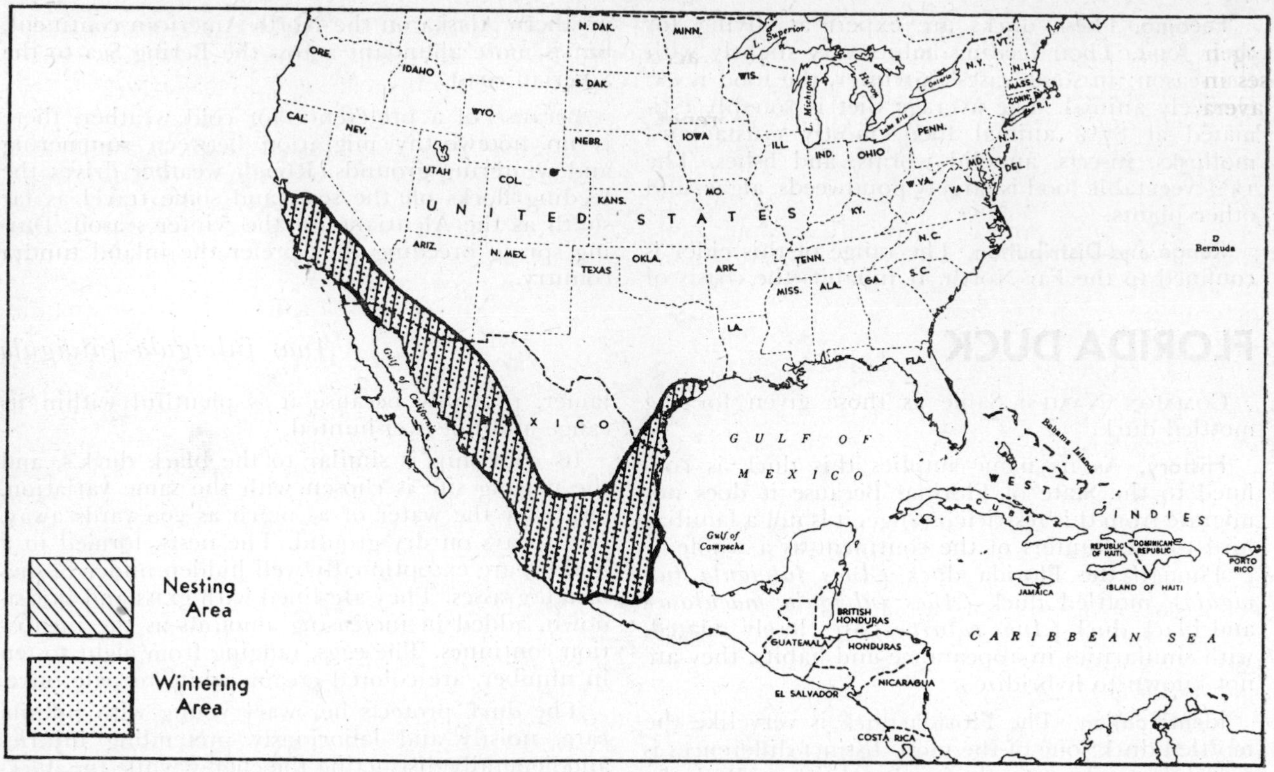


PLATE I. Distribution of Fulvous Tree Duck.

as are the black-bellied tree ducks. A gunner usually finds difficulty in retrieving a slightly wounded bird, for besides their stamina in staying under water, they are adept at walking or running on land. Their flight habits are like those of the black-belly, being strong and steady, with the large wings beating slowly in comparison to the other ducks, which on the average have small wings for a large body.

**Breeding.** This species normally is a ground nester, though the nest sometimes is placed in a tree hollow. The nest, well woven of grass and lined with down, usually is built near water and hidden by low-hanging tree branches, tufts of grass, or tules. Since the duck often drops her whitish eggs in nests other than her own, the number of eggs found in a nest are not necessarily her own. Thirty eggs, piled in layers, is not an unusual find. About 12 to 17 form the average clutch, however, for an individual duck. When this indifferent nesting is practiced, the numerous eggs often are crushed and the hatching rate is low. The first fall plumage of the ducklings is a pale version of the adult's, and the development is not completed until the second fall when the colors deepen.

**Feeding.** The fulvous duck feeds at night or at dusk. Because of its habit of gathering in large flocks to feed and its fondness for corn, crops in Mexico and Texas have been damaged. The diet is primarily vegetable food which the ducks usually obtain by wading in the shallow water of marshes, ponds, and lakes and scooping up the vegetation from the mud bottoms, rejecting the inedibles from the flattened, serrated bill. Since they walk easily on land, they often wander into the woods in search of acorns, or to look for grains and seeds, or graze on grass. They are highly regarded as extremely palatable table ducks.

**Range and Distribution.** The range of this duck, being more northerly than that of the black-bellied tree duck, extends into Texas and up to California, but the main distribution is in Mexico where the duck is abundant. There is little migration, because the one range for this tropical duck includes both summer and wintering grounds. Most of the ducks, however, leave the southern part of the United States and journey south to Mexico for the winter, and return north to breed. They usually travel by night.

# GADWALL

*Chaulelasmus streperus*

COMMON NAMES: Blaten Duck, Canard Gris, Chickacock, Creek Duck, German Duck, Glissom Duck, Gray Duck, Gray Widgeon, Prairie Mallard, Redwing, Shuttlecock, Specklebelly, Widgeon, Welsh Duck.

**History.** The gadwall, never considered numerous as compared with other ducks, is noticeably decreasing. The reasons for this decrease are thought to be the same as those which affect all ducks. Drought and predation in the breeding range take a heavy yearly toll, and "duck sickness," which has been defined as a food poisoning, a form of botulism, is active in the West, one of the areas most populated by the gadwall. The survival potential of the gadwall is at a further disadvantage since its comparatively southerly breeding grounds suffer from encroachment by agriculture. However, the scarcity of the gadwall has often been erroneously reported in some areas because of its confusion with the female and young of the pintail which it resembles.

**Identification.** (See color plate on p. 472.) The winter plumage of the drake is not so markedly different from the female's as in some species. The general appearance of the drake is grayish with a brown wing patch, while the duck is a mottled brown and duller in coloring. Both have the white in speculum (secondary wing features) which distinguishes them from all other puddle ducks, and yellow feet, though those of the female are duller.

The drake begins to moult into the eclipse in early summer, about June, and at the height of the moult, about August, the body, tail, and wing feathers are lost. At this time the drake is virtually indistinguishable from the duck, except for the clear crossbars on his chest and the fact that his bill is not spotted. Shortly after the wing feathers have been renewed, the second moult or pre-nuptial plumage begins and by November the drake is in his full nuptial or winter plumage. There are many arguments as to why the duck, unlike other birds, has a complete moult. Two of the most acceptable suggestions are, that it is (1) a reversal to an early, elemental plumage, or (2) a development to conceal the flightless male.

The gadwall is medium in size, smaller than a mallard, weighing about two pounds.

The voice of the male is a loud *"kack-kack"* which varies with a throaty *"whack"* and a shrill whistle. The far-carrying *"quack"* of the female is somewhat similar to the call of the female mallard, but with less volume.

**Characteristics.** The gadwall is less wary than the mallard and pintail, but can make a quick getaway from either land or water by its ability to jump directly to flight, winging off at a speed which is swifter than the mallard's.

The usual courtship proceedings, like those of the mallard and black duck, include the competition of two or more drakes for the attention of one duck. The drakes usually begin the pursuit on the water. The duck flies off, followed by the males which periodically tilt their bodies before her, showing off their more striking plumage. The most attentive drake, and usually the ultimate favorite, flies close enough at intervals to touch her wings with his. The duck finally drops to the marshes or reeds with the chosen mate.

The nest is usually built on an island, but if in a meadow, or some other area, is always on dry ground. Normally, it is away from the water, hidden among bushes or grasses in a ground hollow. The lining of the nest is made of sticks or reeds, or any other usable material the particular locale provides. This lining is covered, or mixed, with feathers and the soft, strong "nest down" with which the female is especially equipped after her pre-nuptial moult and which

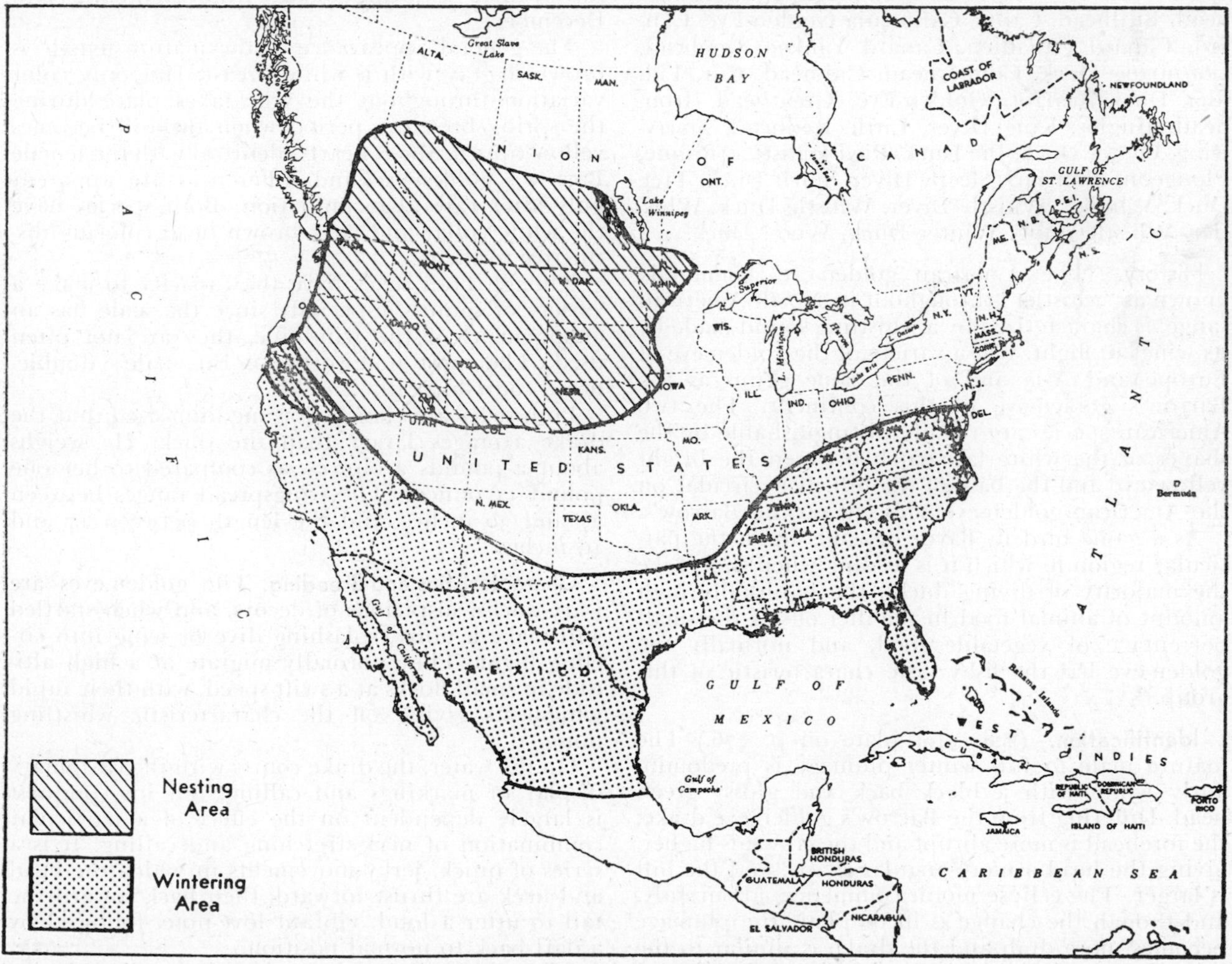


PLATE I. Distribution of Gadwall.

she plucks from her breast. Besides the seven to 13 creamy-white eggs of her own, the nest of the gadwall duck sometimes holds the barely distinguishable eggs of the baldpate and lesser scaup. The gadwall, however, is not known to deposit her eggs in any alien nest. Once the incubation, which lasts about 28 days, is well on its way, the drake flies off to join the other males. They usually fly in a small flock of about 12.

The ducklings, protected by a devoted mother, grow rapidly. The young male and female look much alike until fall when they begin to take on their adult plumage. The drake retains some spotted feathers the first year, but by the following November is in full winter plumage.

**Feeding.** Like other surface-feeding or puddle ducks typically, the gadwall feeds by scooping floating vegetation off the surface of rivers and ponds, or by tipping. The gadwall not only eats from the surface and tips, primarily for leaves and aquatic plants among the marshes and sloughs, but also, when necessary, dives for food.

As is common among the puddle ducks, the gadwall walks easily on land and is often seen searching for food, far inland among the desirable fields of wheat, barley and other grains, or in the woods looking for nuts and acorns. Normally the gadwall diet is vegetable, making the bird fine eating, but the summer diet, largely animal matter such as tadpoles, worms, and fishes, makes the flesh too strong, and inedible to the average hunter.

**Range and Distribution.** The range of the gadwall is wide, as indicated on the map. Though more plentiful along the Pacific flyway, in no section is this duck abundant. The winter migration to the south is exceptionally early. They leave in September for the winter range which extends from North Carolina to the Gulf states and Texas, on across north to Mexico and the Pacific coast states. Lovers of the warmer climates, they are among the last of the ducks to leave the Southern states in the spring.

Great numbers of gadwall follow a somewhat devious route in reaching the Atlantic flyway. From the great nesting grounds of British Columbia, Manitoba, Alberta, and Saskatchewan, they cut diagonally south to reach the Atlantic flyway, passing through Missouri, Tennessee, and South Carolina.

## AMERICAN GOLDEN-EYE

*Glaucionetta clangula americana*

Common Names: Brass-Eye, Bright-Eye, Bronzehead, Bullhead, Caille, California Golden-Eye, Canard, Canard Canadien, Canard Yankee, Cobhead, Conjuring Duck, Copperhead, Cubhead, Cur, Fiddler Duck, Garrot, Golden-Eye, Greathead, Ironhead, Jingler, King Diver, Little Redhead, Merrywing, Oyster Duck, Pie Duck, Pied Whistler, Pisque, Plongeon, Plongeur, Sleepy Diver, Spirit Duck, Tree Duck, Whiffler, Whistle Diver, Whistle Duck, Whistler, Whistle-Wing, Winter Duck, Wood Duck.

**History.** The American golden-eye, commonly known as "whistler" throughout its North American range, is characterized by a whistling sound made by its wings in flight. It is a variety of the golden-eye of Europe and Asia and of the same genus as the Barrow's golden-eye of this continent. The two American species are readily distinguishable by the shapes of the white face-patch between the bright yellow eye and the base of the bill. It is circular on the American golden-eye, crescent on the Barrow's.

As a game bird its flavor depends upon the particular region in which it is feeding when shot. Like the majority of diving ducks, the habitually high amount of animal food in the diet offsets the small percentage of vegetable food, and normally the golden-eye has the fishy taste characteristic of this group.

**Identification.** (See color plate on p. 476.) The mature male in full winter plumage is predominantly white with a black back and glossy green head. Differing from the Barrow's golden-eye drake, the forehead is more abrupt and the crown is higher, giving the head a more angular shape, and the bill is larger. The eclipse moult commences about July, and though the change is incomplete, the plumage becomes more drab and the drake is similar to the duck in appearance. The autumn moult back to full winter coloring takes from September to December.

The general appearance of the mature female is brownish-gray with a white breast. Her only color variation throughout the year takes place during the spring breeding period when the bill becomes yellow-tipped. She is nearly identical with the female Barrow's golden-eye and differences are apparent only after careful examination. Both species have the white collar and dark brown head coloring distinctive to them.

Though both sexes have the capacity to make a variety of sounds, especially since the male has an enlargement of the windpipe, they are not often used. The most noteworthy is the male's double-noted courtship call, *"zzee-at."*

Both sexes are classified as medium-sized, but the drake averages larger than the duck. He weighs about 2 pounds 2 ounces, as compared to her one pound 11 ounces. The wingspread ranges between 27 and 30 inches, and the length between 17 and 19 inches.

**Characteristics and Breeding.** The golden-eyes are wary ducks, suspicious of decoys, and when startled will make a noisy, splashing dive or wing into circling flight. They normally migrate at a high altitude in small flocks at a swift speed, with their rapid wing-beats giving off the characteristic whistling noise.

On the water, the drake courts with the customary display of markings and calling, but his conquest is largely dependent on the effect of a particular combination of neck-stretching and calling. It is a series of quick, jerky movements in which the head and neck are thrust forward, then back toward the tail to utter a loud, vibrant love-note, followed by a dart back to normal position.

The typical diving duck prefers a nesting site on

the ground, but the golden-eye, like the wood duck, habitually nests in a tree hollow or any other natural cavity placed high, usually near or above water. The nests are well constructed and well hidden. The average clutch is 8 to 12, but individual hens have dropped 30 eggs in nesting boxes in Finland, where the duck eggs are gathered as they are laid, as on chicken farms. Incubation is brief as compared with other duck species; the young are hatched from their pale greenish-blue shells in about 20 days.

Since the nest is sometimes 60 feet from the ground, accounts of the untried fledglings' descent to the ground and water have frequently been most imaginative. However, the usual method observed and recorded, is for the hen to check the locale carefully for danger, then cluck from the ground to her two-day-old brood. One immediately following the other, they drop unhesitatingly from their nest, breaking their fall somewhat with their fluttering wings, but landing unhurt. The plumage of the ducklings develops slowly. In the second spring both sexes still resemble each other and the adult female, and not until the second winter do they have the mature markings of their distinct sexes. They do not breed until they are two years old.

**Feeding.** The golden-eye is a graceful and powerful diver, pressing its wings tight against the body in the best diving-duck fashion. When pursued, it has been known to dive to considerable depths. The primary use of the dive, however, is not for escape but for feeding. While feeding they dive and rest intermittently, remaining under water less than a minute at a time. With their bills they pull up aquatic plants or move stones for the insects underneath. Food is not necessarily brought to the surface; most animal food is eaten while submerged. The highest percentage of the duck's normal diet is animal food (74%), with a preference for crustaceans and insects, followed by mollusks and fishes. Since the largest portion of the food intake is hard-shelled sea life, the gravel content of the gizzard is necessarily high. The 26% vegetable food is primarily pondweeds and wild celery.

**Range and Distribution.** The range of the golden-eye is large, and the duck is widely, but thinly, distributed from northern Alaska to the southern United States.

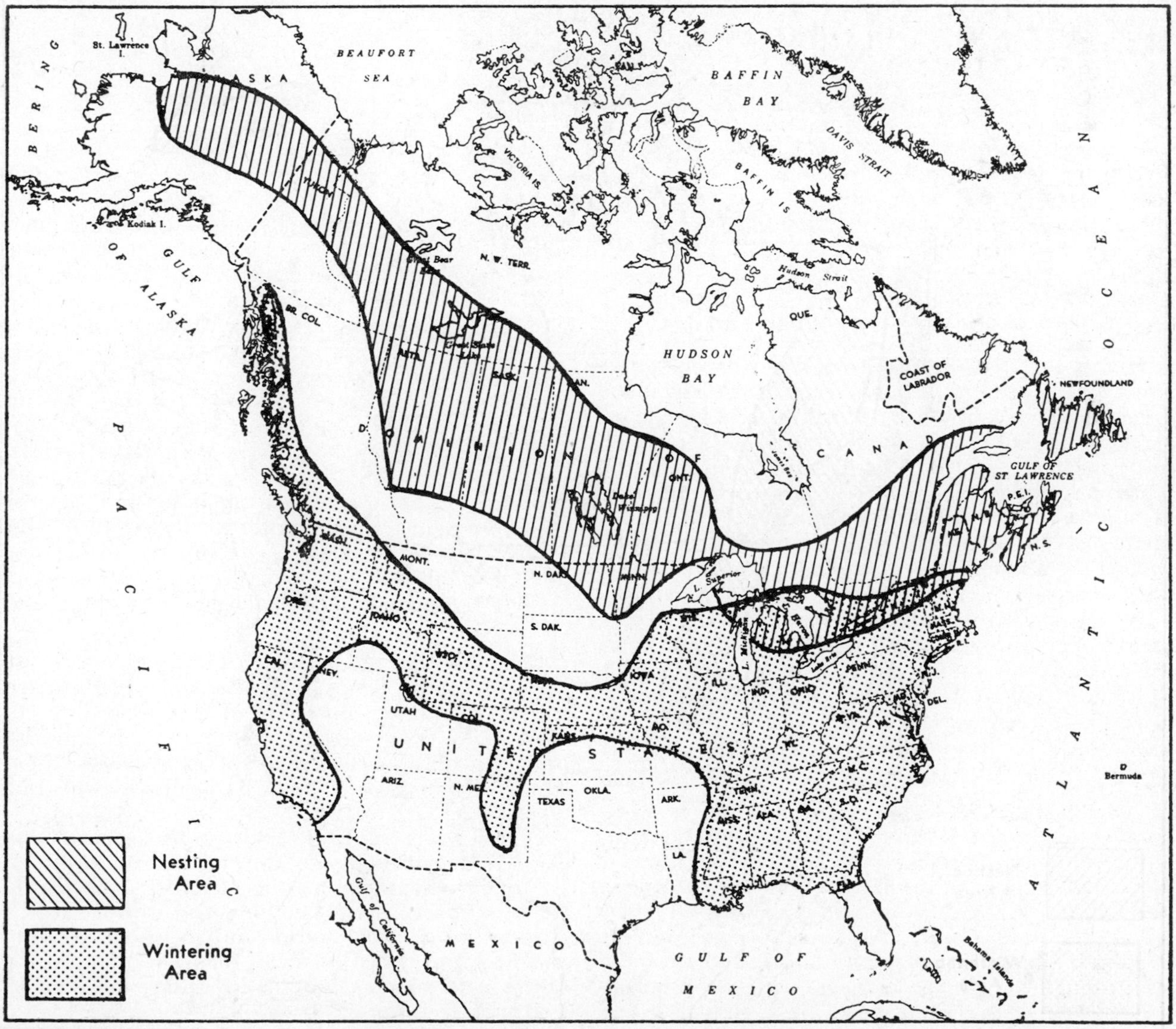


PLATE I. Distribution of American Golden-Eye.

The fall migration southward begins about October, but the older drakes usually do not leave until driven out by the ice and snow. The main wintering grounds are along the Atlantic coast south to North Carolina, and along the Pacific coast from the Aleutians down to Southern California. In the winter season this duck prefers the coastal salt water of ponds and marshes. Hardier than the greater scaup and canvasback, fewer golden-eyes die when the water freezes over around the Great Lakes region.

The spring flight is early, and the main migration starts about April, sometimes March. Though the great nesting grounds are north of the Canadian border, the summer breeding range extends south from Newfoundland and Alaska to New York State and Wisconsin, overlapping the winter range. During the summer season the golden-eye frequents inland ponds, bays and lakes.

## BARROW'S GOLDEN-EYE *Glaucionetta islandica*

Common Names: Cock Pie-Duck, Golden-Eye, Rocky Mountain Golden-Eye, Whistler, Whistle Wing, Wood Duck.

**History.** The Barrow's golden-eye is native to this continent, but rarer than the American golden-eye which it so closely resembles in appearance and habits. Because of confusion between the two species, however, the Barrow's golden-eye has been declared more rare than it actually is.

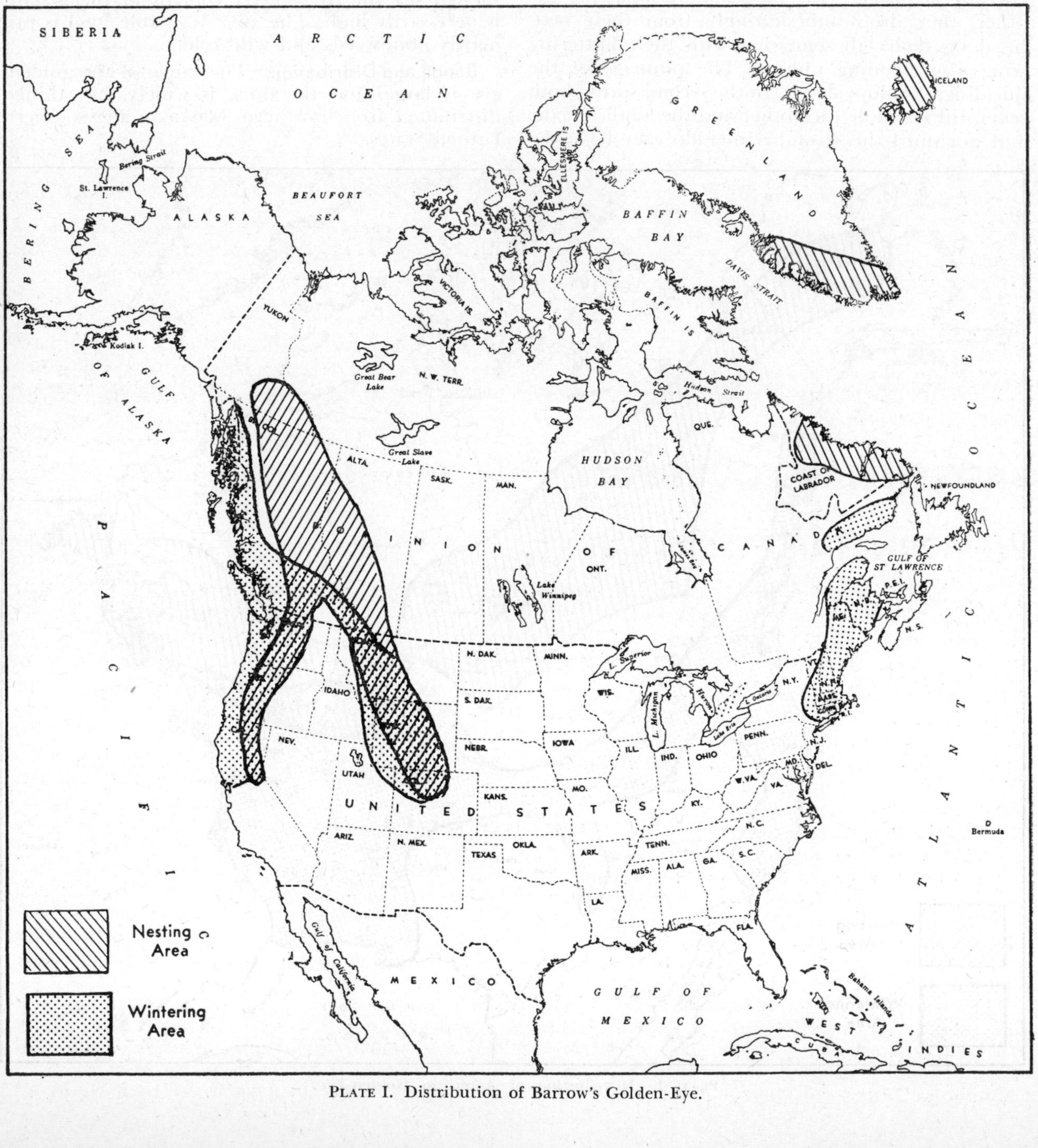


Plate I. Distribution of Barrow's Golden-Eye.

An outstanding difference between the two ducks is the nature of each species. Whereas the American golden-eye is exceptionally wary, the infrequently-hunted Barrow's golden-eye is unsuspicious and tame, often actually or apparently indifferent to the presence of men.

**Identification.** (See color plate on p. 476.) The full winter plumage of the adult male is black and white with a glossy purple-black head marked with a crescent face-patch of white. (See p. 378 for detailed comparison with the American golden-eye.) The plumage moults are similar to those of the American golden-eye.

The mature duck is nearly impossible to distinguish from the female American golden-eye. The bill is the chief identifying mark. It is shorter and more pointed than that of the American golden-eye and is entirely yellow, rather than yellow-tipped, in the breeding season.

Both sexes are comparatively silent, and the male lacks the enlargement of the windpipe which is a distinction of the male American golden-eye. The dominant note is a low, croaking sound.

Measurements for both sexes are about the same as those of the American golden-eye *(q.v.)*.

**Characteristics and Breeding.** Like its close kinsman, it is popularly called "whistler" because of the identifying sound of the whistling wing-beat. Active, but not nervous, they fly in orthodox fashion. In migration they travel at a rapid pace (timed at 50 miles an hour) and keep to a direct course.

During the courtship the drake puffs out his loose head feathers, the better to display his brilliance before the drab duck. He stretches his neck and kicks his orange feet up out of the water behind him, bowing and calling. After pairing, the male sometimes engages in a brief jealous fracas with another male.

Nesting habits, eggs, and incubation period are like those of the American golden-eye.

The ducklings closely resemble those of the American golden-eye. Their plumage development is equally slow, and they do not breed until two years of age.

**Feeding.** Their feeding habits are much like those of the American golden-eye, but their percentage of animal food is higher, making them a less desirable game duck. The smaller types of animal food such as insects, oysters, and mussels are eaten where they are found on the mud bottom, but larger catches, like crawfish, are brought up to the surface to eat. The 78% animal food is largely insects, mollusks, and crustaceans; the 12% vegetable food is mostly pondweeds and wild celery.

**Range and Distribution.** Like the cinnamon teal and harlequin duck, the Barrow's golden-eye has two distinct ranges between which there is no migration. As shown in the distribution map, one is located in eastern North America, the other in the western section. Both the breeding and wintering ranges of the duck are farther north than those of the American golden-eye.

The fall migration in October and November is more a shift than a journey, for the summering and wintering ranges overlap to a large extent. The trip is toward the southern part of the range, to their winter preference of brackish, coastal waters.

The spring migration is northerly and to inland, fresh water. Though they breed as far north as Iceland, the chief area of abundance in any season is the Rocky Mountain region.

## EASTERN HARLEQUIN DUCK

*Histrionicus histrionicus histrionicus*

## WESTERN HARLEQUIN DUCK

*Histrionicus histrionicus pacificus*

Common Names: Blue-Streak, Canard à Collier, Canne de Roche, Circus Duck, Lord and Lady, Mountain Duck, Painted Duck, Rock Duck, Sea Mouse, Squealer, Totem-Pole Duck, Wood Duck.

**History.** Because the most striking difference between the eastern and western harlequin ducks is the range (one being on each side of the continent, without migration between them) they will be discussed here under one heading. Their appearance and habits are to be considered the same unless specifically pointed out as being distinct.

The eastern harlequin is rarely found as far south as the United States, but the western harlequin is well known on the Pacific coast. On either range they are almost exclusively animal feeders, and their tangy flesh is considered poor fare for the wildfowler. The natives of the Far North, however, hunt them for food.

The harlequins are so named because the males' odd plumage, colorfully marked with splotches, streaks, and patches, suggests the particolored tights of the fictional Harlequin, the buffoonlike lover of Columbine. Other nicknames, such as "circus duck," "totem-pole," and "painted duck" describe the strange and striking plumage pattern of these ducks.

**Identification.** Most beautiful of all the diving ducks, the harlequins are not easily confused with any other diving species. The eastern and western harlequin drakes are distinguishable when the birds are in hand. In both species a chestnut striping appears on either side of the crown, but on the eastern harlequin the stripe is deeper in tone and runs farther along to a point approximately above the eye. Also, its bill is lighter. The bright plumage of the males is modified during the eclipse moult when, except for the wings, it is a more subdued, grayish coloring. The change to this female-like dress begins about June; by early fall the moult back to full winter plumage commences and is normally completed by October.

The mature females of both species are identical in appearance. Their dusky-brown plumage coloring is resumed after their pre-nuptial and post-nuptial moults. Differing from the males at all seasons, they have no wing patch and their white face markings are distinct in shape and location. They resemble the female bufflehead, surf scoter, and ruddy duck.

The harlequins are small ducks, averaging slightly under 1½ pounds. The length is about 16 inches and the wingspread about 25 inches.

They are comparatively voluble ducks and one of their calls is a squeaky note which has earned them the name "sea mouse."

**Characteristics and Breeding.** The harlequins are very fast in flight and use a rapid wing-beat as they twist and turn. They habitually move in compact flocks and fly near to the water. A flock often drops as one duck into a plummeting dive, swims submerged, and then rises in flight. True lovers of marine living, they have been known to follow a watercourse so exactly that they have circled or doubled back in their direction if there is such a curvature in the water line.

The drakes court the ducks with much bobbing and bowing and nudging, gestures which the ducks return if they are interested in the suitors. The drakes' most distinctive action is a love-call which is given with neck stretched, bill elevated, and a slight wing-flap—similar to the gestures accompanying a rooster's crow.

The nest site is normally on the ground near to water, but environment sometimes forces the western harlequins to build in tree hollows or other natural cavities, or crevices in cliffs, etc., but usually close to the ground. The western harlequins, therefore, are not true tree nesters, though they have been likened to the wood duck in this habit. The six or seven creamy-buff eggs hatch in about 25 days. During the incubation period, the drakes desert the ducks to begin the eclipse moult.

The harlequins are lovers of swift currents and torrential waters, and since the majority of nests are constructed beside some mountain streams, the ducklings learn to adapt themselves to the tough and hardy ways of their parents at an early age. The hen is a careful mother and passes on to her young the art of skilled diving and swimming. Until November the young resemble each other and the adult female, but at that time the young male commences a distinct plumage change which is nearly developed by January. By the second fall both male and female juvenile are matured. The following spring they breed.

**Feeding.** Like the puddle ducks, the harlequins walk gracefully on land, even run with ease. They combine this unusual walking ability with their exceptional swimming and diving powers and are capable of moving upstream in deep, fast water. They are adaptable in their feeding habits, scooping, tipping, or diving for their food, according to

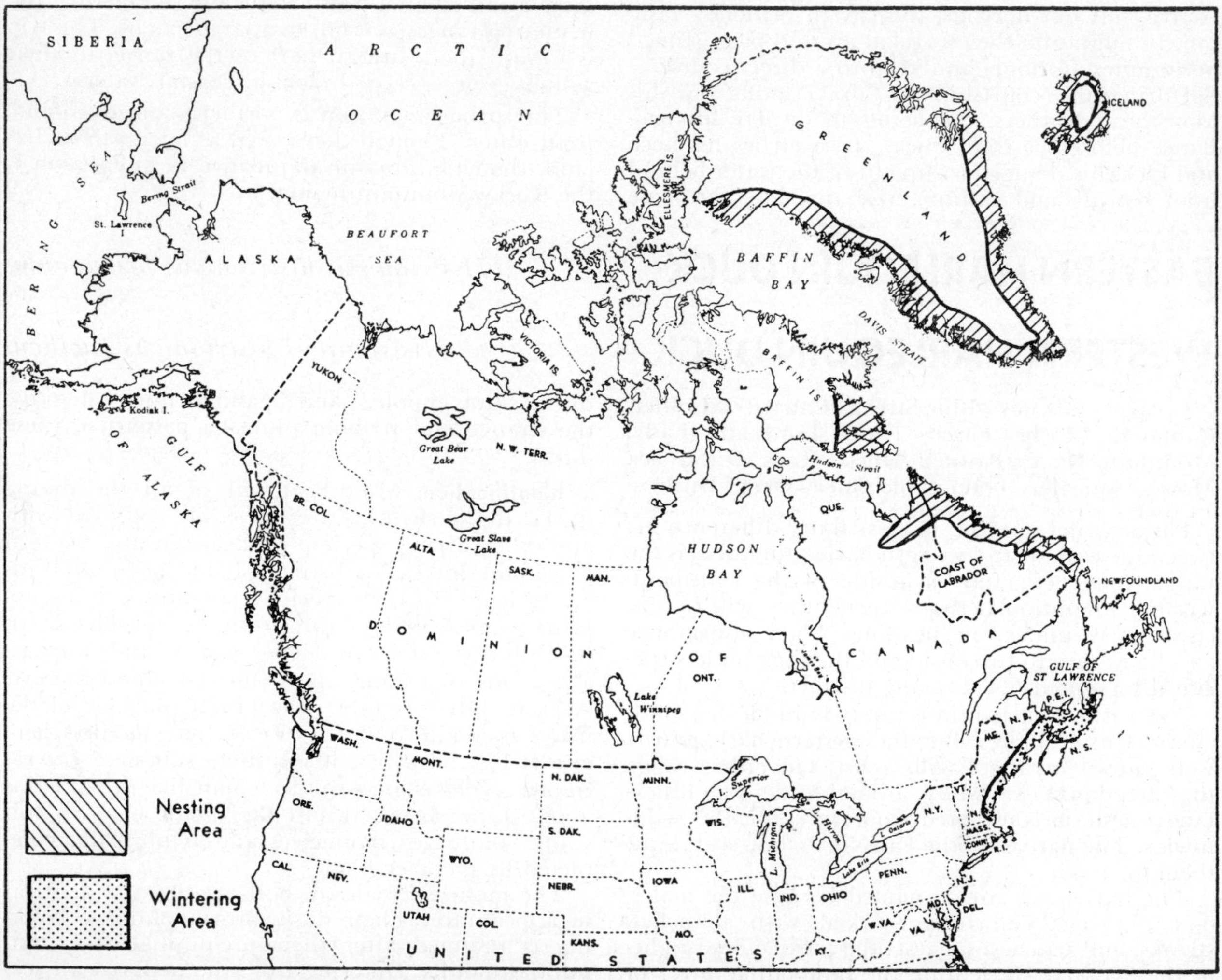


PLATE I. Distribution of Eastern Harlequin Duck.

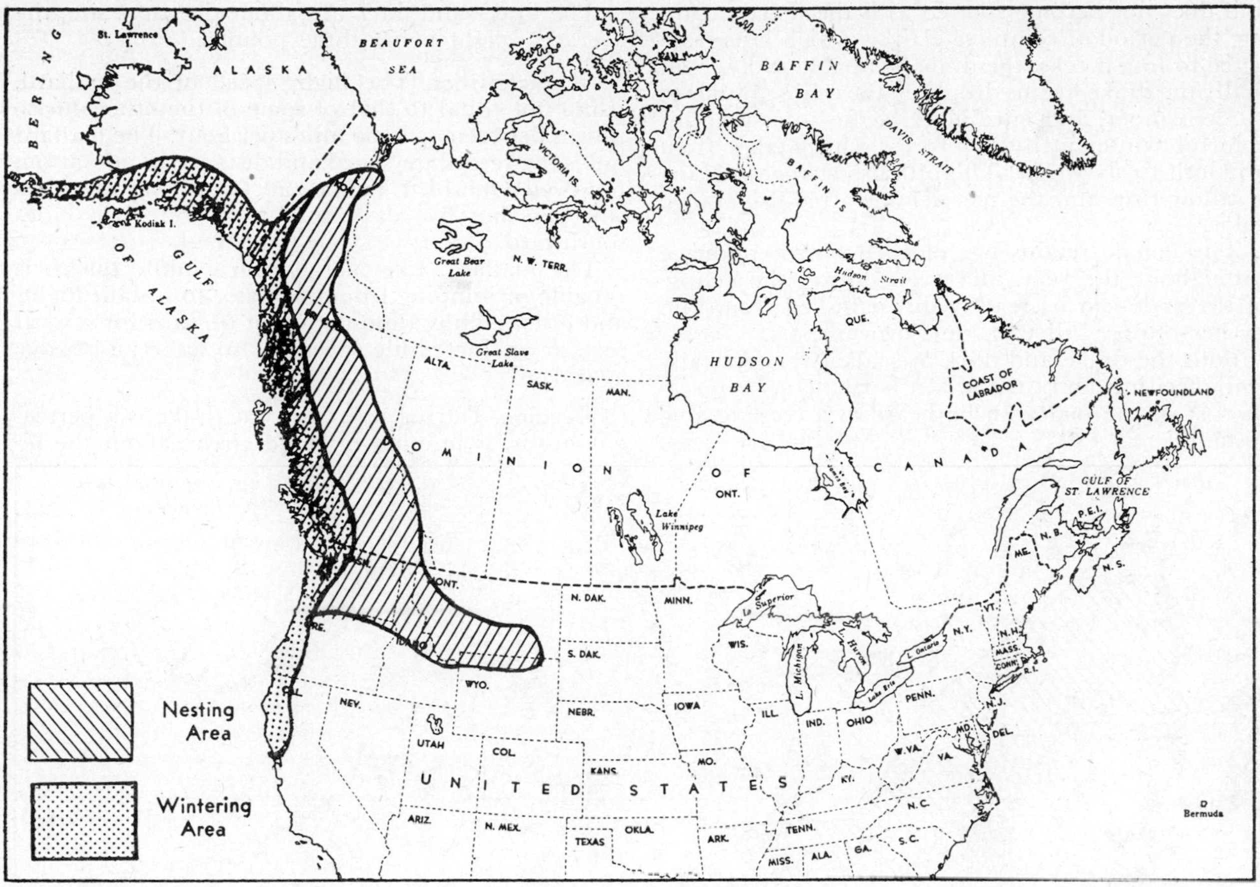


PLATE I. Distribution of Western Harlequin Duck.

the depth of the water. Regardless of the means of reaching it, the food preferences are the same—over 98% animal food. They are particularly fond of crustaceans, mollusks, and insects. They are adept in removing coat-of-mail shells from their clinging holds on rocks, where human collectors find it difficult even with special equipment and knowledge. The remaining 2% of the diet is a confusion of vegetable waste.

Infrequently hunted because of their tough, fishy flesh, they are nonetheless difficult to bag, primarily because of the natural advantages of their habitat. Also these "lords and ladies" of the waters appear to know every trick of eluding a pursuer. Eskimo hunters count on one weak characteristic. With complete lack of foresight an entire flock dives at once, without leaving a guard, and as they surface one by one, they are shot.

**Range and Distribution.** As previously mentioned, the ranges of these sub-species are separate.

The eastern harlequin is found along the sub-Arctic coasts on rocks and ledges southward to Massachusetts, but rarely farther down the coast. The fall migration southward begins about November and the majority spend the winter along the eastern coast of Canada. The trip to the breeding grounds in the spring starts in February and, as the distribution map shows, they breed as far north as Iceland, but the main nesting grounds of this thinly distributed duck are in northern Labrador and Newfoundland.

The western harlequin is distributed from Alaska to central California. The migration between summering and wintering ranges is primarily a move from coastal wintering grounds to the inland breeding range.

# MALLARD

*Anas platyrhyncha*

COMMON NAMES: English Duck, French Duck, Gray Duck, Gray Mallard, Greenhead, Green Mallard, Ice Duck, Ice Mallard, Prairie Mallard, Red-Legged Mallard, Ringneck, Snow Mallard, Stock Duck, Yellow-Legged Mallard.

**History.** The mallard, most commonly known in the United States as "greenhead," is the best known and most plentiful of all North American waterfowl and has the widest distribution. It is the ancestor of most of our domestic ducks and is easily domesticated. It is known on every continent, but probably is most abundant in Asia, and is valued highly as an important item of food in China.

**Identification.** (See color plate on p. 471.) The mature male in its full winter plumage is one of our most colorful ducks, and once seen never is mistaken for another species. The drake begins to moult in June or July and by August has lost most of its bright plumage and is easily mistaken for the female. The bill of the male, however, retains its olive color and does not become spotted as is the female. During the period of complete eclipse, which lasts from three to four weeks, the drake is unable to fly. Normally the drake begins dropping the eclipse plumage by September, and once more begins to assume his colorful winter attire, a process which takes from a month to six weeks. The bill also changes, taking a yellow tint, and the feet assume a reddish-orange color.

The female retains her mottled brown plumage throughout the year, and even during the eclipse of the male can be readily distinguished from him by her orange bill with dull brown spots.

Both the drake and duck are talkative, especially while feeding, and the low but harsh *"Queck-queck-queck"* of the male can be heard at a considerable distance.

The drake and duck are about the same size, the average weight being three pounds.

**Characteristics.** The flight speed of the mallard, while not equal to that of some of the other ducks, ranges between 40 to 60 miles per hour. The mallard holds the record for speed and distance in migration, however. One bird, banded in Green Bay, Wisconsin, was shot five days later at a point 900 miles southward.

The mallard, like many other puddle ducks, is capable of jumping from the water to instant flight, and often climbs almost straight upward for several feet, at an incredible speed for so large and heavy a bird.

**Breeding.** During courtship the drake is a persistent suitor, swimming in rapid circles about the fe-

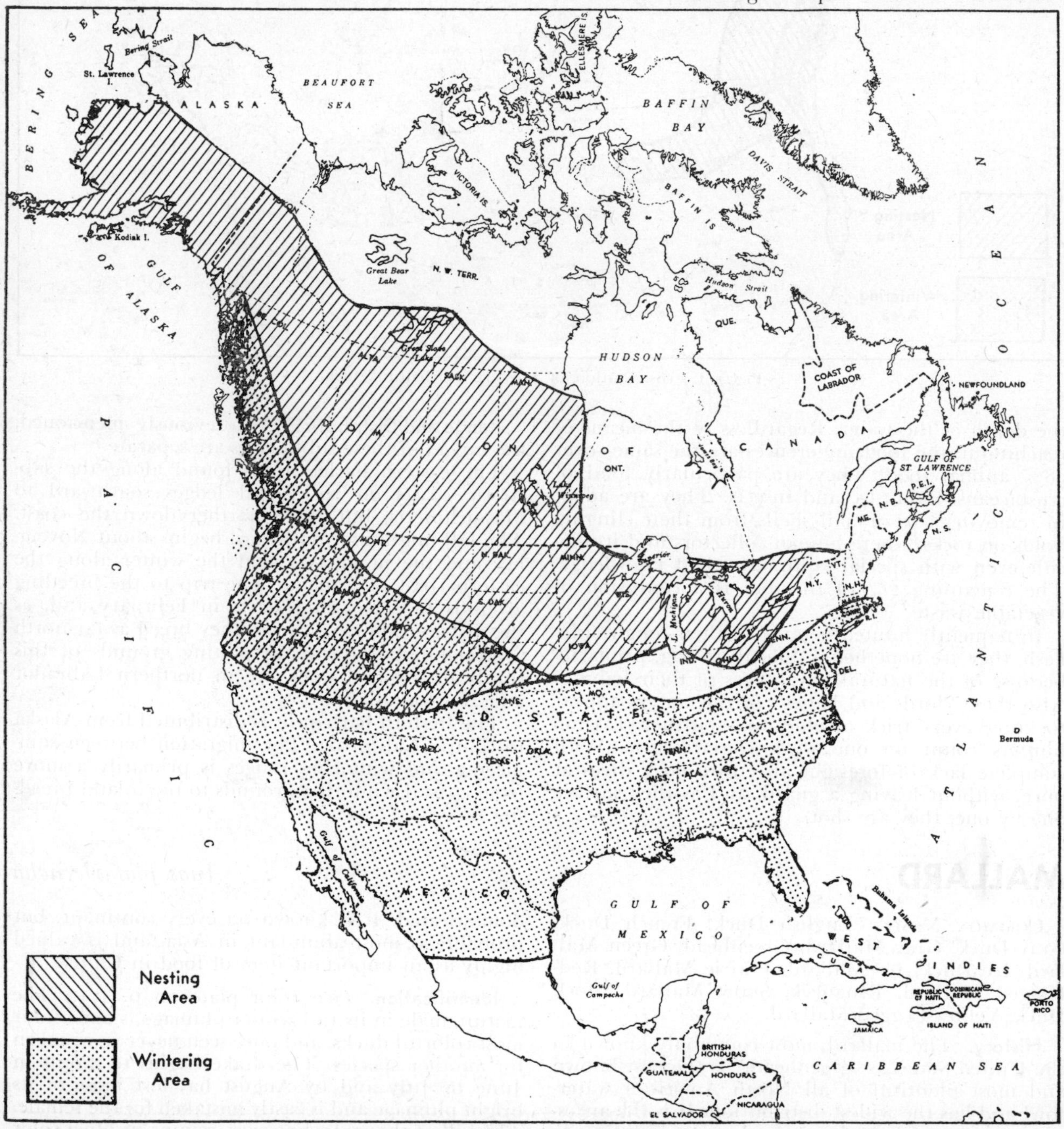


PLATE I. Distribution of Mallard Duck.

male, nudging her and bobbing his head rapidly, and occasionally rising almost clear of the water. When the duck decides to accept these advances she begins bobbing her head in answer. Often several drakes will pursue one duck in the air, diving, circling and making as much noise as possible. The duck will then fly near the drake she has decided upon and depart with him.

The mallard's nest, a slight depression lined with dry grass, down, and reeds, usually is located on the margin of a lake or slough, and normally contains from eight to 12 eggs, ranging in color from greenish-blue to buff. Although they have been known to nest in trees, this is unusual. The incubation period is from 26 to 28 days. Once incubation has started the drake leaves the female and seeks the company of other drakes before the eclipse begins.

The ducklings are voracious feeders, and normally are capable of flight when about ten weeks old. Their first September finds the young ducks and drakes much alike in appearance, but the drakes then begin to take on their first colorful winter plumage which, though bright, is not fully developed until the second year.

Although it is not normal procedure, mallards are known to mate with several other species, and although the cross is more often with the black duck, many instances of breeding with baldpate, gadwall, green-winged teal, and pintail are known.

**Feeding.** The normal diet of the mallard is about 90 per cent vegetable and 10 per cent insect, with a preference for a variety of fresh-water plants, including grasses, aquatic plants, pondweed, sedge, smartweed, and, in the fall and winter, acorns and nuts. The mallard is an avid destroyer of insects, especially mosquitoes, and on occasion will eat small snails and tiny minnows. On the West Coast the mallard's inclination to eat the flesh of dead salmon after the spawning has brought the bird into disrepute in several sections, for the salmon-eating duck is a strong dish for the epicure.

**Range and Distribution.** The mallard's wide range, plus its adaptability to civilization, has enabled this duck to escape the extremes of scarcity and abundance that have affected several other species. As the distribution map shows, the mallard is plentiful from southern Alaska to a point well below the Rio Grande, and while it is found in greater numbers in the West and the lower Mississippi Valley, it is present in fair numbers in several Atlantic coast states.

The main southern migration does not start until late in September, and many mallards delay their departure for a warm climate until late in November, when ice and snow force them southward. Although the major wintering grounds are located in the lower Mississippi Valley, some remain all year on the Oregon, Washington, British Columbia, and Alaskan coasts.

The northward migration begins about the first of March, although some birds begin moving toward their nesting grounds in mid-February. The majority of mallards do not arrive at their northern Canadian and Alaskan breeding grounds until May.

With the elimination of market hunting and the assumption of control over migratory waterfowl by the Federal government, the great threat to the mallard was abolished. Fifty years ago it was not unusual for a market hunter to kill from 6000 to 8000 mallards during the fall and winter. Government records show that one small area in Arkansas contributed no less than 120,000 mallards to the market in one season. It is not difficult to realize what the outcome would have been had such practices not been halted by law.

## MASKED DUCK

*Nomonyx dominicus*

COMMON NAMES: None used in North America.

**History.** The masked duck is little known to the wildfowler of North America. It is a rare visitor to this continent, being native to South America and the West Indies. The ruddy duck, widely distributed and exclusive to North America, is the only other member of the sub-family, and the two species are very similar in habits, though readily distinguishable in appearance. (See "Ruddy Duck," p. 401.)

**Identification.** The male in the winter season is a most handsome and colorful bird. The appearance is heightened by his "mask," the black patch which covers his face and sets off his blue bill and cinnamon-red head. Unlike typical duck species, the drake does not have an eclipse moult, but some ornithologists suggest that, like the ruddy duck, the drabber plumage is assumed in the fall at the completion of the breeding season.

The gray-brown female is very similar to the female ruddy duck, but the masked duck has two brown streaks across her whitish cheeks and a white wing patch, whereas the allied species has a dark crown above mottled cheeks and a solid brown wing. Both male and female have long, pointed tails, but only the male can lift it up into the striking wedge shape.

Both sexes of the masked duck are very small; over-all measurements are slightly smaller than those of the ruddy duck. The length is about 14 inches, and the wingspread approximately 20 inches.

**Characteristics and Breeding.** Its flight, swimming, and diving habits are the same as the ruddy duck's, but its manner of courting is not known. The nesting habits and eggs also are like the ruddy duck's. The ducklings resemble each other and the adult female in their first fall, and by spring they are nearly mature in plumage coloring.

**Feeding.** Presumably, the feeding habits of this essentially fresh-water duck are very similar to the ruddy duck's since this plump little specimen is considered delicious table food by the gourmets of its natural habitat. The ruddy duck is primarily a vegetable eater. Since the legs and powerful feet are set far back on the body, the masked duck is one of the best divers and swimmers, but consequently is incapable of walking more than a few awkward steps on land before falling forward on its breast. The diving ability, it is assumed, is used to feed on aquatic plants, as does the ruddy duck. The average diving duck, such as the sea ducks and mergansers, feeds on marine life or fish.

**Range and Distribution.** The masked duck is a tropical bird, preferring fresh-water lagoons. It is found in the northern section of South America and in the West Indies. It is seldom seen in the United States, but perhaps visits the eastern part of the country more often than any other region. It has been encountered in Louisiana, Maryland, Massachusetts, Vermont, and Wisconsin.

## AMERICAN MERGANSER

*Mergus merganser americanus*

Common Names: Bec-Scie, Big Fish-Duck, Big Pond-Sheldrake, Big Sawbill, Big Sheldrake, Bracket, Bracket Sheldrake, Breakhorn, Canadian Canvasback, Diver, Dun-Diver, Fis, Fish Duck, Fisher, Fisher Duck, Fisherman, Fisherman Duck, Fishing Duck, Fresh-Water Sheldrake, Gony, Goosander, Great Lake Sheldrake, Harle, Irish Canvasback, Morocco-Head, North Carolina Sheldrake, Pheasant, Pied Fisherman, Pond Sheldrake, River Sheldrake, Sawbill, Sawbuck, Sheldrake, Shelduck, Shellbird, Sparling Fowl, Swamp Sheldrake, Spike, Stud, Tweezer, Velvet Breast, Weaser, Weaser Sheldrake, Wheezer, Winter Sheldrake, Wood Duck, Woozer.

**History.** The American merganser is well distributed throughout the North American continent, but perhaps is best known in the United States

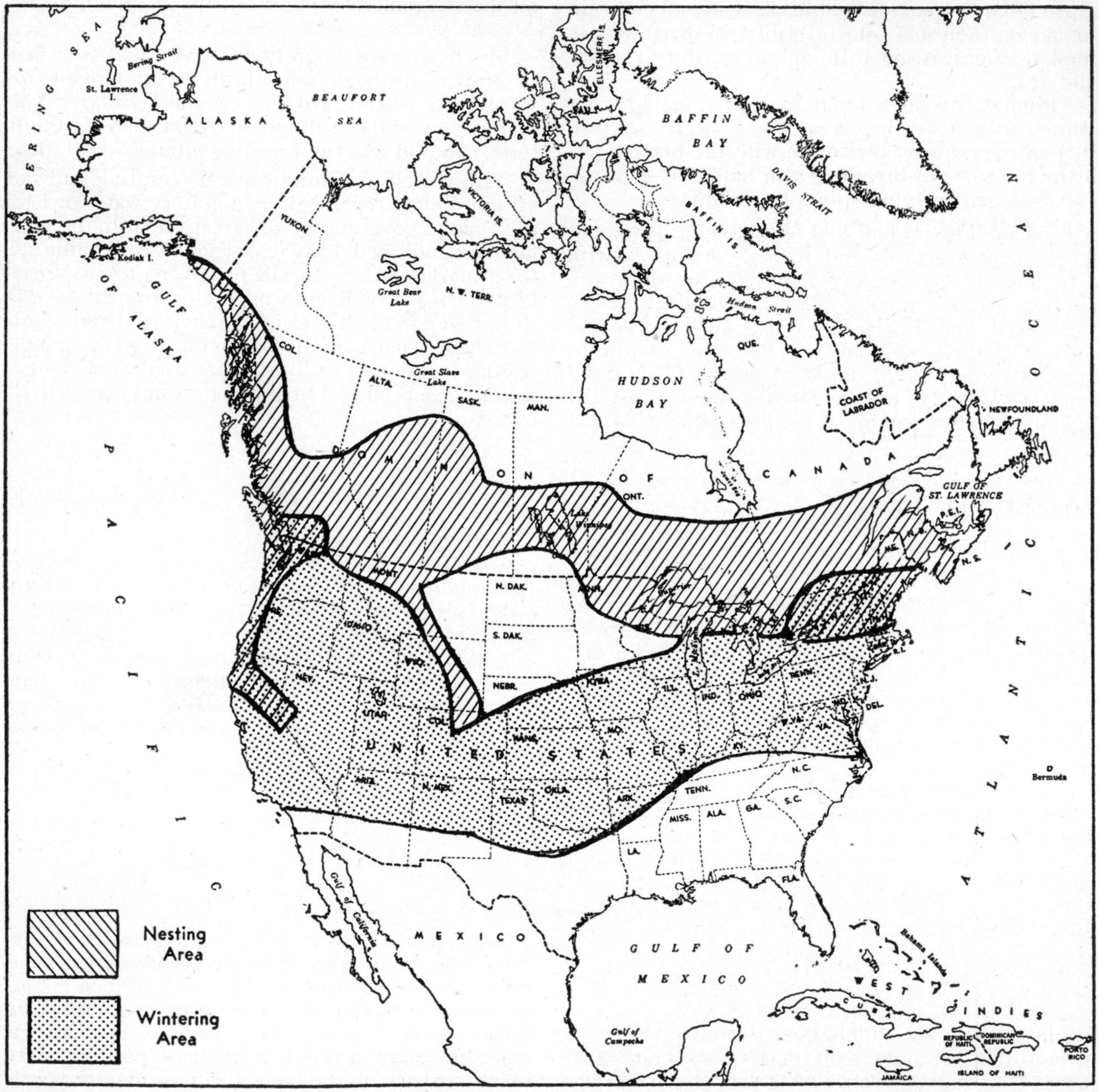

Plate I. Distribution of American Merganser.

where it is most common. Of the same genus as the red-breasted merganser, it is very similar to it. The species is readily identifiable by the distinctive feature of the female American merganser: a crest which the male of this species does not possess.

In spite of the fact that the American merganser is one of the most beautiful ducks in North America, there is some controversy as to the justification for its existence. Most fishermen regard any competition with fish-catching as a detrimental force to be controlled if not eliminated, and in the case of this predatory duck they adhere to the belief that "handsome is as handsome does." They are partially justified, for the mergansers consume millions of game fish each year, and in some localized areas enough fish have been destroyed to affect the interests of commercial fishermen as well as sportsmen. In other cases their feeding on predatory fish and undersized fish in an overcrowded spot has contributed to the balance of nature and the welfare of game fish. Because of their highly specialized diet, their flesh is unpalatable, although they are eaten in more remote, northerly regions.

**Identification.** (See color plate on p. 478.) In the winter season the full-plumaged male is a bird of striking coloration, resembling the red-breasted merganser drake but distinguishable from him by the lack of the breast coloring, white collar, and crest. During the eclipse moult from May to about September, the plumage of the male is similar to that of the female, and at this time the drake assumes a crest. In early fall, the second moult starts; when this is completed in December, the crest is lost and the brighter plumage restored.

The adult female is not so colorful as the male, but is attractive in her own right. She has a chestnut head, on which is raised her distinctive crest of the same coloring, a gray back, and a white breast. Her bill, like the male's, is red, and though the coloring is identical with the red-breasted merganser's, the slight variations in bill feathering and the location of the nostril are often important means of distinguishing between the two species if the plumage is not in mature or prime condition. The shape of the bill is peculiar to the merganser group, and differentiates them from any other type of duck.

This duck is the largest of the merganser group. The female is about a pound lighter than the male; the average weight for the species is about 2½ to 3½ pounds. The length of both sexes is between 25 and 26 inches, and the wingspread runs from 34 to 36 inches.

Neither male nor female is voluble; besides a harsh croak which they both utter, the male emits a low, courting call.

**Characteristics.** Like the others of its kind, these ducks have an elongated appearance in flight because the bill, head, and neck are held on a line with the body. They are swift on the wing; except during migration, they fly habitually close to the water, one behind the other in a straight line. The American merganser is heavy-bodied and resembles a loon as it sits on the water. Though a powerful diver, a strong, fast swimmer above the water, even faster beneath it, and a graceful, swift flier, the duck often has difficulty in clearing the water to take to the air. It usually makes a long, noisy run, using its feet to gain additional momentum.

**Breeding.** Most of the courtship proceedings take place on the water—above and below it. Five to seven males are active rivals for one apparently indifferent duck, and compete for her with a display of swimming speed, diving agility, calling, and the distance water can be kicked back with vigorously-churning red feet. Fights among the suitors are noisy and violent until one bowing and bobbing male is accepted.

The American merganser is midway between its two relatives in nesting habits. The red-breasted merganser is a ground nester and the hooded merganser is a true nester. The American nests in trees by preference, but will build a nest on the ground if the site is more suitable in comparison with available hollows or holes in trees, stumps, or cliffs. The average clutch of 9 to 12 light buff to ivory-colored eggs hatches in about 28 days.

Like the young of the wood duck, the ducklings normally leave their high nests by jumping to the ground as the mother calls to them. The offspring are quick to learn from the mother, and they become adept in the art of maintaining existence, the primary feature of which is diving—for food and to escape danger. The mother shows them the diving duck's style of leaping up before going forward in a fast, deep dive, or, like a grebe, she sinks beneath the surface. The male and female juveniles are similar in appearance and resemble the adult female until the first winter, but they do not have mature plumage until the second fall.

**Feeding.** These "fish ducks" usually seek their favorite food beneath the water, but sometimes they follow a school of small fish by swimming on the surface above them and then diving. If a flock feeds together, it is a noisy procedure accompanied by much splashing and activity. Fish make up the bulk of their diet, but the mergansers also eat mollusks, crustaceans, insects, and larvae as well as a very small percentage of aquatic plants.

**Range and Distribution.** The range of this merganser is large; it is distributed across the continent from the Atlantic to the Pacific and from Alaska to the southern United States. The breeding grounds are mostly in the northerly part of the range, and the wintering grounds are in the southerly section, but there is considerable overlapping as shown by the cross-hatching on the distribution map.

These ducks are hardy and stay north as long as open water will allow. Around October and November the main migration leaves on a leisurely trip southward, traveling just ahead of the ice. The wintering grounds are in the United States, from the Canadian border to the southern states. They usually live near large bodies of water, and one of their areas of abundance is in the vicinity of the Great Lakes, but they also are fond of living by fresh-water ponds and rivers.

The main spring migration is very early, and the ducks leave in March and April for the northerly breeding grounds, which for the most part are in the north, across Canada, and north to the sub-Arctic areas.

# HOODED MERGANSER

*Lophodytes cucullatus*

COMMON NAMES: Bastard Teal, Bec-Scie, California Fish-Duck, Cock-Robin, Cock-Robin Duck, Cottonhead, Crow-Duck, Didapper, Diver, Fan-Crested Duck, Fish Duck, Fisher, Fisher Duck, Fisherman, Fisherman Duck, Fishing-Duck, Frog-Duck, Fuzzhead, Hairycrown, Hairyhead, Hairy-Crowned Teal, Hell-Diver, Hooded Sheldrake, Hooder, Hootamaganzy, Little-Duck, Little Sheldrake, Little Spikebill, Morning-Glory, Mosshead, Mud Sheldrake, Oyster Duck, Peaked Bill, Petit Harle, Pheasant, Pheasant Duck, Pickaxe, Pickaxe Sheldrake, Pied Sheldrake, Plongeon, Pond Fisher, Pond Sawbill, Pond Sheldrake, Round-Crested Robin, Sawbill, Sawbill Diver, Shagpoll, Sharpy, Sheldrake, Smew, Snowl, Spike, Spikebill, Spiky, Strawbill, Summer Duck, Summer Sheldrake, Swamp Sheldrake, Tadpole, Topknot, Tree-Duck, Tuffle-Headed Duck, Water Pheasant, Whistler, Wirecrown, Wood Duck, Wood Sawbill, Wood Sheldrake, Zin-Zin.

**History.** The hooded merganser, exclusive to North America, is one of three species of fish-eating ducks of the sub-family *Merginae*. It is the smallest of the "fish ducks," a group which also includes the American and red-breasted merganser. A handsome bird, it is almost comparable to the wood duck in beauty and plumage.

Because of its small size and normally strong flesh, it is far from being one of the best table ducks and usually is bagged accidentally by wildfowlers. A wounded duck often escapes, for this species is famous for its swift and complete disappearance under water, giving it the name "hell-diver."

**Identification.** (See color plate on p. 478.) It is the male in his full winter plumage which gives this duck its reputation for beauty. Perhaps the most striking feature is a white, fan-shaped crest on a shiny black head. He opens and closes this repeatedly while on the water. The hooded merganser and the wood duck are often found in the same locale since they are both tree nesters and prefer wooded areas near water. The males of each species resemble each other and are sometimes confused at a distance. During the eclipse moult of summer, the male is similar to the female when much of his brighter plumage is replaced by more somber colors. Around September the change back to the winter plumage begins and is completed by October.

The adult female is a grayish-brown duck with a white breast. She has a more modified crest than the male, and it is a more inconspicuous coloring of cinnamon-brown. Though the bill of both sexes is of the same type as that of the other mergansers, it is shorter, narrower, and darker. In addition to the distinct color pattern of male and female, the bill is used as a method of distinguishing it from the others of its kind.

The drake is about 5 ounces heavier than the duck, but the species averages less than 1½ pounds. The length is between 17 and 18 inches, and the wingspread is 24 to 25 inches.

It has never been known as a voluble duck. The odd call note is of a low, harsh tone and usually emitted on the water.

**Characteristics.** This shy duck is very agile on water and in flight. It dives, swims submerged, or rises directly from the water with equal ease and celerity. Using wings as well as feet, its movement under water is rapid. The chief means of escape is not in the air, though they are among the fastest fliers. Rather, they depend on diving or submerging, either by dropping from a height, by diving from the surface of the water, or slowly and quietly sinking so that only the neck and head are visible. Because the birds fly in small flocks or in pairs and are very silent on the wing, catapulting ducks often have startled a dozing gunner. Their flight is strong and direct and they normally keep to the course through rough weather. When on the wing, this merganser, like its kinsmen, has a distinctive appearance from other ducks because the bill, neck, and head are held on a straight line with the body.

**Breeding.** The courtship display of the drake is mostly neck-stretching and exhibition of his striking crest. He pursues the duck on the water and in the air. The ducks often are mated before or during the spring migration, and upon reaching the nesting range the pair immediately sets about looking for a nesting site. Since the mergansers are habitual tree nesters, and often frequent the same areas as the wood duck, which seeks out the combination of wooded land near fresh-water ponds or streams, the two species compete for suitable nesting places. Unlike the American merganser, which readily adapts itself to ground nesting if a tree or stump hollow is not available, the hooded merganser is a true tree nester and will fight the wood duck for possession of a site. Compromises sometimes are reached in friendly fashion, however, and the two species have been known to share the same nest, each duck dropping in her eggs and taking turns sitting on the nest. The nest is made from material found in the hole or cavity, and is lined with down. The 10 to 12 pure white eggs hatch in about 31 days.

Like the wood duck's young, the ducklings jump from their high nests, and their light, downy bodies break the fall. The mother is active and bold in defense of her young. If the enemy is sighted in time, she gives the harsh, alarm call, *"croo, croo."* Gathering her young to her, they skulk off into the concealing grasses and reeds of the bank. If it is impossible to escape unseen, she will throw herself before the predator, flopping about and pretending injury for the sake of diversion until the brood is safely off, and then she flies away. At the end of their first year, the plumage of both male and female young is similar to that of the mature female. By their second fall, however, they show definite changes and the young male's plumage development of moults and color phases resembles the adult drake's moult from the eclipse plumage. Both sexes normally are adult when 2½ years of age.

**Feeding.** Though fish are eaten by all duck species, the mergansers are primarily fish-eaters, and the bills are particularly adapted to catching them. The narrow, "toothy" bill characterizes the group and has given it the popular, identifying names of "sawbill" and "spikebill." It is a specialized tool and

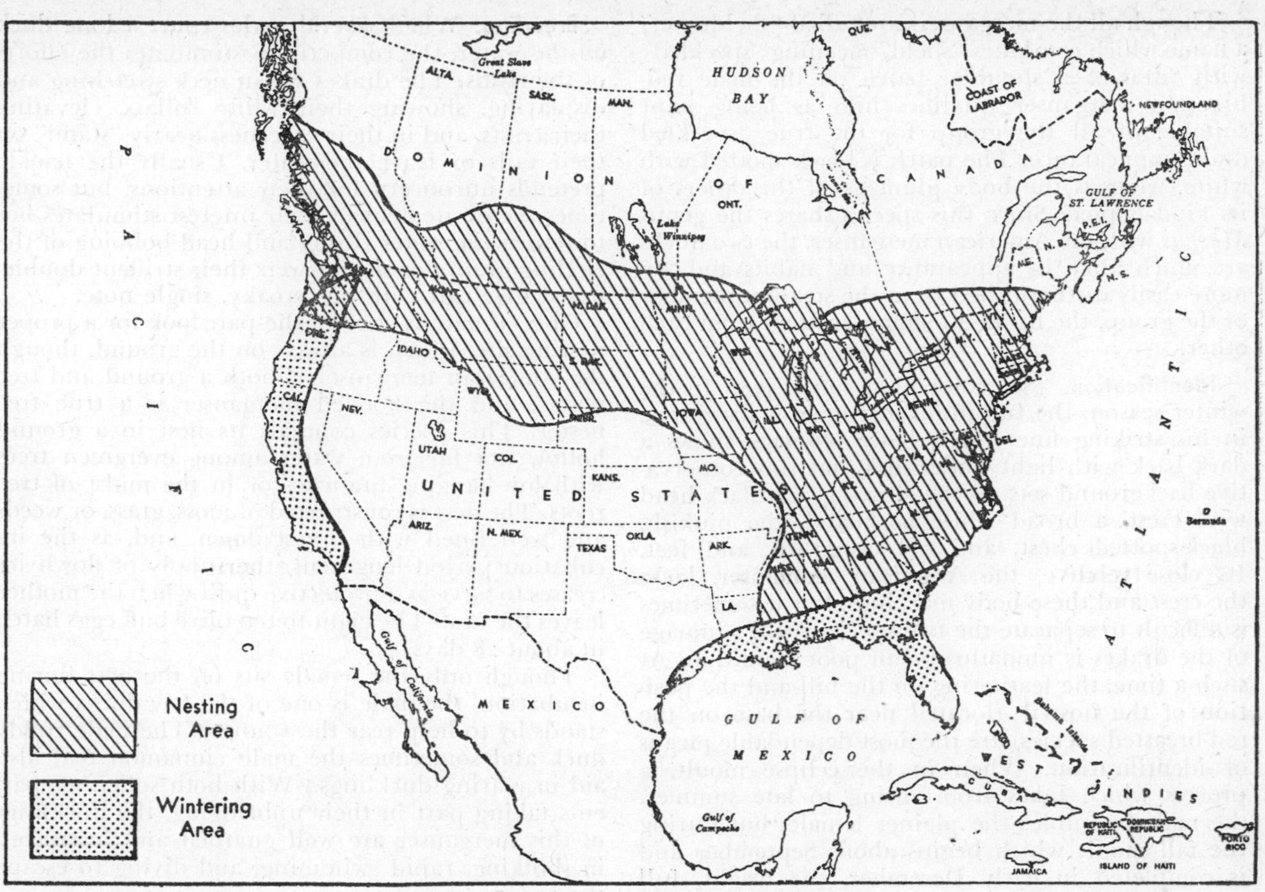


PLATE I. Distribution of Hooded Merganser.

very different from the broad, flattened bill of most ducks; it acts as a sieve, holding back large substances and draining out the water. The mergansers dive and chase small fish under water, sometimes herding them into shallow water. The hooded merganser feeds on a variety of small aquatic animals such as eels, beetles, frogs, tadpoles, and crawfish. The percentage of vegetable matter in its diet is small, and consists mostly of grains and seeds.

**Range and Distribution.** This species prefers the fresh-water ponds and streams of the interior and is seldom seen along the coast. Its range is large, but there is considerable overlapping of summer and winter grounds, and the times and routes of the migrations are not known for certain. The general tendency is to move to a warmer climate in the winter and a more northerly region for the breeding season in the summer.

The distribution map indicates that the ducks winter along the Pacific coast states as well as through the Gulf and Atlantic states, north to the southern part of New England. They breed across the North American continent from the southern states north to Maine and west to British Columbia.

## RED-BREASTED MERGANSER *Mergus serrator*

COMMON NAMES: Bec-Scie, Bec-Scie de Mer, Common Sawbill, Common Sheldrake, Diver, Fis, Fish Duck, Fisher, Fisher Duck, Fisherman, Fisherman Duck, Fishing Duck, Fuzzyhead, Garbill Duck, Hairycrown, Hairy-Crowned Fisherman, Hairyhead, Harle Duck, Herald, Herald Duck, Indian Sheldrake, Jack, Land Harlan, Long Island Sheldrake, Mississippi Buck, Pheasant, Pheasant Sheldrake, Pied Sheldrake, Popping Widgeon, Red-Breasted Fish-Duck, Red-Breasted Goosander, Robin, Salt-Water Sheldrake, Sawbill, Scale Duck, Sea Bec-Scie, Sea Diver, Sea Sawbill, Sea-Robin, Sheldrake, Shelduck, Shellbird, Spanish Drake, Spring Duck, Spring Sheldrake, Stud-Duck, Whistler.

**History.** The red-breasted merganser is common to both the Old and New Worlds. Though it formerly was more abundant in North America than it is now, largely due to unrestrained shooting, it is still numerous on this continent. Since the flesh of the merganser is so tough and of such strong flavor, it usually is accidental to the bag of the wildfowler. In New England, however, some gunners shoot these "fish ducks" with the same zeal enjoyed by those of the same area who follow the sport of scoter or "coot" shooting.

Though most gunners by-pass the merganser as being merely beautiful and ornamental, the fisherman is more violent in his reaction and considers it a vicious scavenger on his rightful domain and wrathfully points to the millions of fish which are destroyed yearly to the detriment of commercial fishermen and sportsmen. (See "History" under "American Merganser.")

Though all the mergansers are called "sheldrake," a name which combines "sheld" meaning "speckled" with "drake," a shoulder patch on the male red-breasted merganser qualifies him as being most suitable of all the group for the true "speckled drake" appearance. The patch is black spotted with white, whereas the body plumage of the others of its kind is pied. Since this species shares the genus *Mergus* with the American merganser, the two ducks are much alike in appearance and habits and are more easily distinguished from the smallest member of the group, the hooded merganser, than from each other.

**Identification.** (See color plate on p. 478.) In the winter season, the full-plumaged male is handsome in his striking finery. His body plumage shows a dark back with light undersides, but this conservative background sets off the glossy, green-black head with crest, a broad white neckband, the pinkish, black-spotted chest, and red eyes, bill, and feet. Its close relative, the American merganser, lacks the crest and these body markings, but it sometimes is difficult to separate the two species if the plumage of the drakes is immature or in poor condition. At such a time, the feathering on the bill and the position of the nostril (located near the base on the red-breasted species) are the most dependable means of identification. When in the eclipse moult, a process which takes from spring to late summer, the male resembles the plainer female, but during the fall moult which begins about September and is completed in early December, the bright, full plumage is renewed.

The mature female is nearly identical with the female American merganser and the subtle differences must be studied carefully. The line that divides the white breast from the rufous neck and head is blended in the red-breasted merganser, but sharply defined in the American merganser. The bill feathering and nostril placing are the most consistent features by which to identify the two species.

The large drake outweighs the duck by about a pound, and averages about 2 pounds 10 ounces to her one pound 13 ounces. The length ranges between 20 and 23 inches and the wingspread from 30 to 33 inches.

Like the other mergansers, this duck is very silent. The calls of both sexes are low and harsh, with little carrying power.

**Characteristics.** Like the American merganser, this duck often has difficulty clearing the water or ground to take to the air and makes a prolonged, laborious run. Once on the wing, however, the silent flight is graceful and swift, being high in migration but close to the water when settled and living on a seasonal range. Typical of the mergansers, it spends most of its time on the water, even when rough, rarely going more than a few awkward steps on land. Since a good part of its time is spent chasing fish, it is necessarily a rapid swimmer above and below the surface of the water. Normally, only the feet are used when the duck is swimming under water and the wings are held close to the sides. Powerful dives are made from a considerable height in the air or from the surface, and the crest is depressed when submerging. Like the other mergansers, it can sink like a grebe.

**Breeding.** When several males court a lone duck on the water, the competition stimulates the efforts of the rivals. The drakes vie in neck stretching and displaying, showing their white collars, elevating their crests, and in their eagerness nearly "stand" on their tails or leave the water. Usually the female pretends unconcern for their attentions, but sometimes the excitement of their interest stimulates her to return the water rushes and head bobbing of the circling group, or she answers their strident double-noted love call with her croaky, single note.

Once a mate is chosen, the pair look for a proper nesting site, which is always on the ground, though the American merganser is both a ground and tree nester, and the hooded merganser is a true tree nester. This species conceals its nest in a ground hollow not far from water among evergreen trees with low-hanging branches or in the midst of tree roots. The nest is constructed of moss, grass, or weeds and well lined with breast down, and, as the incubation period lengthens, the supply of down increases to serve as a protective quilt when the mother leaves the nest. The eight to ten olive-buff eggs hatch in about 28 days.

Though only the female sits on the nest during incubation, the male is one of the few ducks which stands by to help rear the young. (The male ruddy duck and sometimes the male cinnamon teal also aid in rearing ducklings.) With both solicitous parents taking part in their upbringing, the ducklings of this merganser are well guarded and instructed in skulking, rapid swimming, and diving to escape the enemy.

In their first fall the male and female both look like the mature female. Though each sex becomes more distinct by December, the plumage is not mature until their second fall, about November. Since the wing feathers are among the last parts of the feathering to come in, the ducklings are nearly adult before they are capable of flight. The plumage of these juveniles is identical with the offspring of the American merganser, but the species are recognizable by the bill feathering and the more basally located nostril.

**Feeding.** The red-breasted merganser frequents the oceanic areas more often than the American merganser, which is primarily a fresh-water duck. The feeding habits of the two species are much alike. They both feed chiefly on fish, and both are often seen pursuing schools of fish in a noisy, splashing flock. The red-breasted merganser, however, is inclined toward a more maritime diet, since it follows the spawning of herring almost immediately after the discovery of the event by the gulls. This specimen also eats a small amount of mollusks, crustaceans, and insects.

**Range and Distribution.** The large range of the red-breasted merganser extends from Iceland to southern Florida and across the North American continent, from Atlantic to Pacific coasts. Its summering and wintering ranges are more distinct than in the case of the other mergansers. It lives along the seacoasts as well as by clear, fresh-water streams or muddy pools.

The autumn migration to the warmer wintering grounds takes place mainly in October and November. The greater part of the wintering range is in

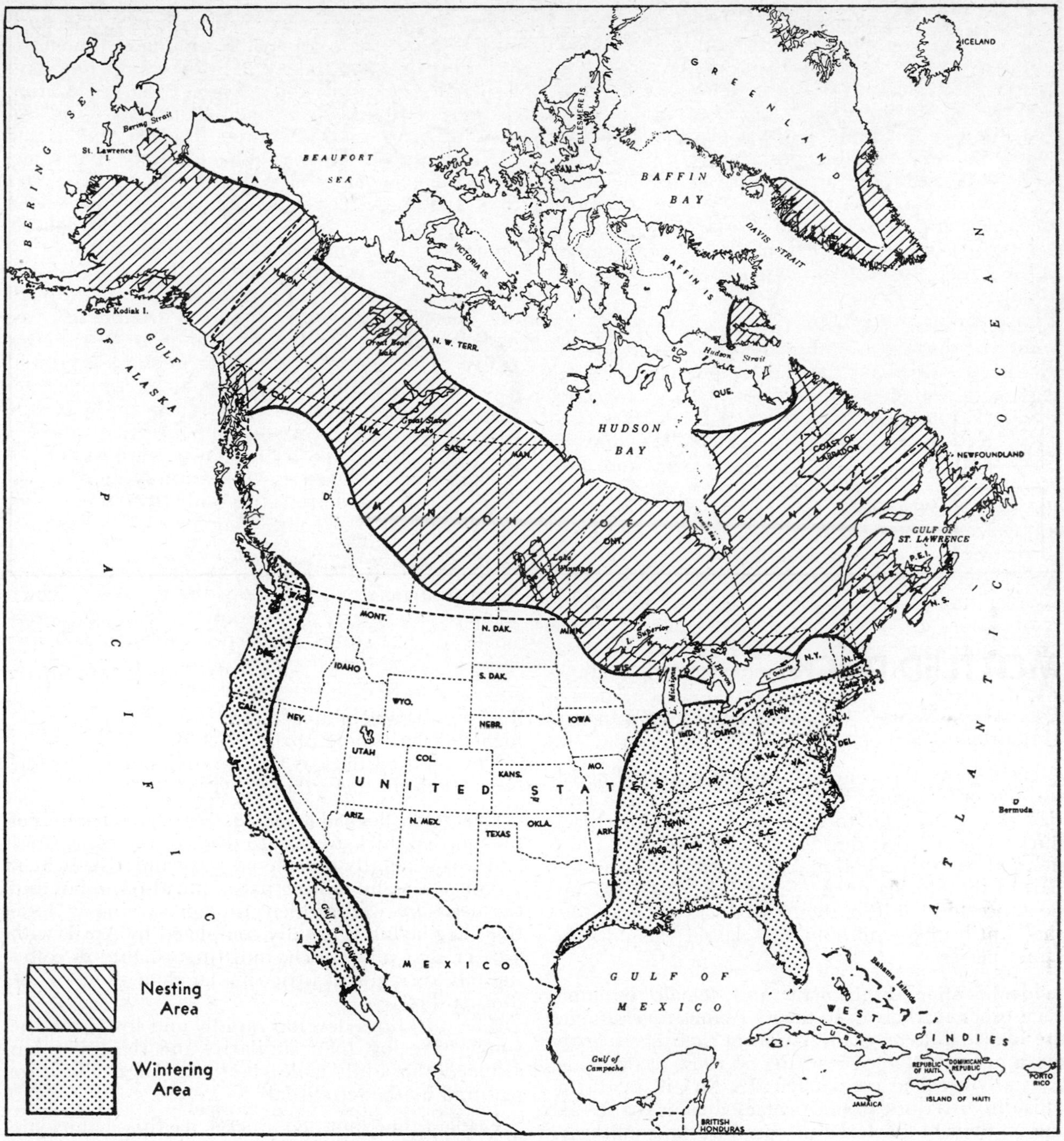


PLATE I. Distribution of Red-Breasted Merganser.

the United States, in the eastern section and along the Pacific coastal states to Lower California. In many regions this merganser shares the wintering range with the American merganser, and both species sometimes are found on the same bodies of water, such as the Great Lakes.

The time for the spring migration is less concentrated; the journey may be made any time between March and May. Since the drakes' autumn moult is not completed until December and the juveniles do not have matured feathering until their second fall, the appearance of a migrating flock of ducks is a variation of female plumage. The vast nesting grounds range from the Arctic south to the northeastern parts of the United States.

In several of the New England states the red-breasted merganser is classed as a pest by anglers, for a few pairs are able to do considerable damage to a small trout pond, especially in midsummer when dry weather has reduced the level of the water. Although only a relatively small number of these birds nest in New England, they are voracious eaters and are fast, skilled divers. Operators of trout hatcheries consider these ducks as the most important predator, and one operator has stated that he would prefer having an entire family of otters on his waters rather than one pair of mergansers.

Most wildfowlers are inclined to shoot these birds only as a last resort, because their flesh is stringy and extremely strong and unpalatable.

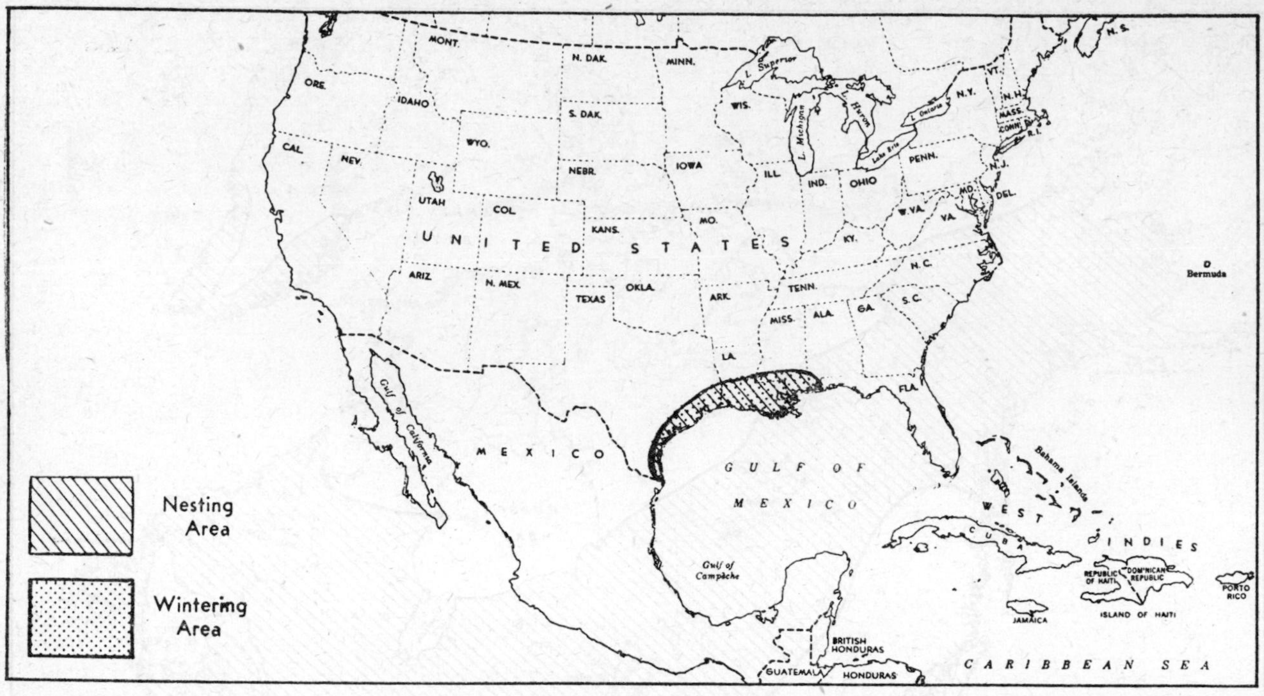


PLATE I. Distribution of Mottled Duck.

## MOTTLED DUCK

*Anas fulvigula maculosa*

COMMON NAMES: Canard Noir d'Été, Southern Mallard.

**History.** As the common French name (English translation: summer black duck) denotes, the mottled duck is similar to its close relation, the black duck. The mottled duck is a lighter version, more mottled than streaked, making it a nearer counterpart of the Florida duck (genus *fulvigula*). The appearance and habits of these two ducks are so similar that until 1889 ornithologists classed them in the same species.

**Identification.** Both male and female resemble each other in their dull, tawny plumage. The sexes are identifiable by examination of their chest feathers, a buffy, U-shaped marking on those of the male, centrally-streaked on the female. An aid in distinguishing this duck from the black duck is the streaking on their buff-colored throats, but these markings are less pronounced on the paler Florida duck. The yellowish bill of the mottled duck is distinct from the greenish one of the black duck, the yellow-green one of the New Mexican drake, and the dark-splotched one of the female mallard. The mottled duck and Florida duck have a single white bar bordering the blue speculum which differentiates them from the New Mexican duck and the black duck. The moults and plumage changes of both sexes are identical with those of the black duck.

The mottled duck is the approximate size of the New Mexican duck. (See p. 393.)

**Characteristics and Breeding.** The characteristics of the mottled duck are like to those of the black duck and it is generally considered wary and a swift flier. Its courtship and nesting habits are also similar, and the nests are well hidden, though varying in location. Egg-laying is usually completed by April, with 8 to 11 eggs in a clutch, indistinguishable in coloring but averaging a little smaller than those of the Florida duck.

The ducklings develop rapidly and by spring the young have lost their similarity and the drake has assumed the adult male chest markings. They are matured by the second fall.

**Feeding.** The mottled duck's feeding habits are similar to those of the Florida duck. (See p. 375.)

**Range and Distribution.** The breeding and wintering ranges of this duck are interchangeable, since it inhabits a limited range in Louisiana and Texas during both seasons. The preferred range is on the coast of these two southern states, but sometimes it lives inland. In Louisiana, where many black ducks spend the winter, it is called "summer black duck."

## NEW MEXICAN DUCK

*Anas diazi novimexicana*

COMMON NAMES: No common names are known.

**History.** The wary New Mexican duck is not well known to the average sportsman of North America. It is localized in distribution to Texas and New Mexico in the United States, and is rarely found outside of this limited range.

**Identification.** Both the drake and duck are barely distinguishable from the female mallard, and the mature male in full winter plumage is one of the drabbest of North American waterfowl. The drake averages larger than the female mallard with a yellowish bill as contrasted with her more orange one marked with black, and his undersides are more definitely striped with distinctive U-shaped markings on his breast feathers. The changes in plumage during the eclipse and autumn moults resemble those of the black duck. (See page 361.)

The orange-ish, black-nailed bill of the duck separates her from the drake and the female mallard. Also, the duck's breast feathers have a definite dusky marking. The New Mexican drake and duck resemble the black duck, Florida duck, mottled duck, and female pintail, but are distinguishable from them by having a white stripe on either side of the blue speculum.

Both sexes are talkative when in flight and courting, quacking volubly back and forth to each other.

The New Mexican duck is large, about the size of a mallard, averaging 2¾ pounds. The length varies roughly from 21 to 26 inches, with a wingspread between 33 and 40 inches.

**Characteristics.** Many of the habits and characteristics of the New Mexican duck are similar to those of the mallard, with which it often associates, and the manner of flight also is similar. It jumps directly from the water with a neat, swift bound. It is a sturdy flier and maintains a steady flight, considered more rapid and unwavering than the mallard's.

**Breeding.** The courtship is a graceful performance, taking place in the water and the air, often near other duck flocks but not mixing with them. On some pond, mud flat, or other likely site, the drake bobs and bows to the female of his choice, affectionately nudging her and pulling at her wing feathers while keeping other males and females at a distance. The aerial flights are leisurely, with the pair flying slowly and gliding effortlessly, returning to the water to mate.

It is assumed that their nesting habits are the same as those of other surface-feeding ducks, but always on dry ground. The clutch and incubation period are apparently comparable to the mallard's. The birds presumably mate in May, for the ducklings are evident in June and July.

The ducklings are as shy and alert as the adults and there is a comparatively scant amount of information on their appearance. The development of their plumage is compared to that of the black young duck.

**Feeding.** The New Mexican duck often flies with the mallard and alights on the same feeding grounds along the river banks, ponds, swamps, and drainage canal. Though their feeding habits are alike, the New Mexican duck normally feeds at a distance from the mallard and all other ducks frequenting the same locale. They are more wary and alert to man and danger than the average duck, and often feed near settlements because of their particular fondness for flooded alfalfa fields. It is a typical surface-feeder, not known to dive but often "tipping" for its food. The largest percentage of its diet is vegetable—roots, corn, wheat, seeds, grasses, and cattail shoots. The small percentage of animal food is mostly fresh-water shellfish.

**Range and Distribution.** The range of the New Mexican duck is minute, confined to the Rio Grande River Valley. From the Rio Grande River west to El Paso, Texas, a short swathe is cut north to Albuquerque, N. M. The wintering and breeding grounds are both within this one range.

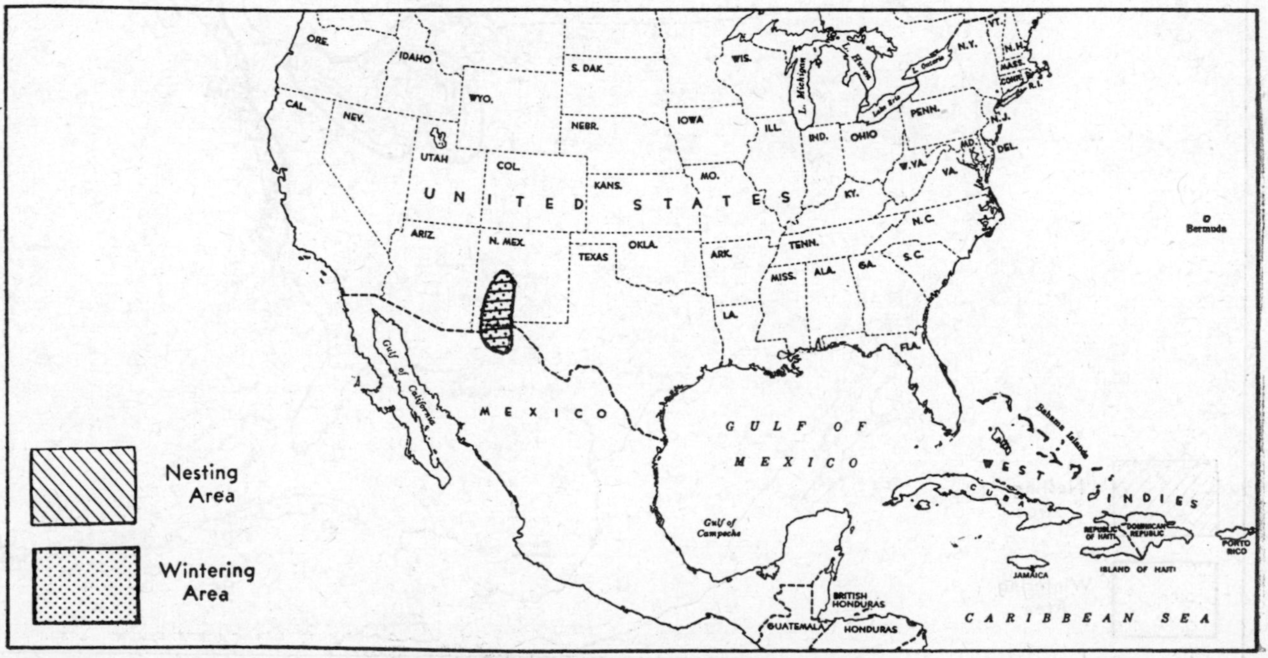


PLATE I. Distribution of New Mexican Duck.

# OLD SQUAW

*Clangula hyemalis*

COMMON NAMES: Caccawee, Callithumpian Duck, Coween, Granny, Ha-Ha-Way, Hell's Chicken, Hound, Jack-Owly, Jay-Eye-See, Kla-How-Yah, Knockmolly, Longtail, Long-Tailed Duck, Mammy Duck, Mommy, O-I, Old-Wife, Organ Duck, Pintail, Quandy, Scolder, Singing Duck, Siwash, Son-Son-Sally Duck, South-Southerly, Swallow-Tailed Duck, Winter Duck.

**History.** The Cree Indians have had the strongest influence in naming the old squaw, a duck which indulges in incessant chattering. They gave this duck distinct nicknames in imitation of particular call notes, and later the traders summed up the quantity and quality of its musical range with "organ duck."

The old squaw is circumpolar in distribution, but confined to the northerly sections of the Northern Hemisphere. It is good hunting for the skilled sportsman who strives to outwit swift, erratic flight habits and elusive diving form.

**Identification.** (See color plate on p. 476.) Both

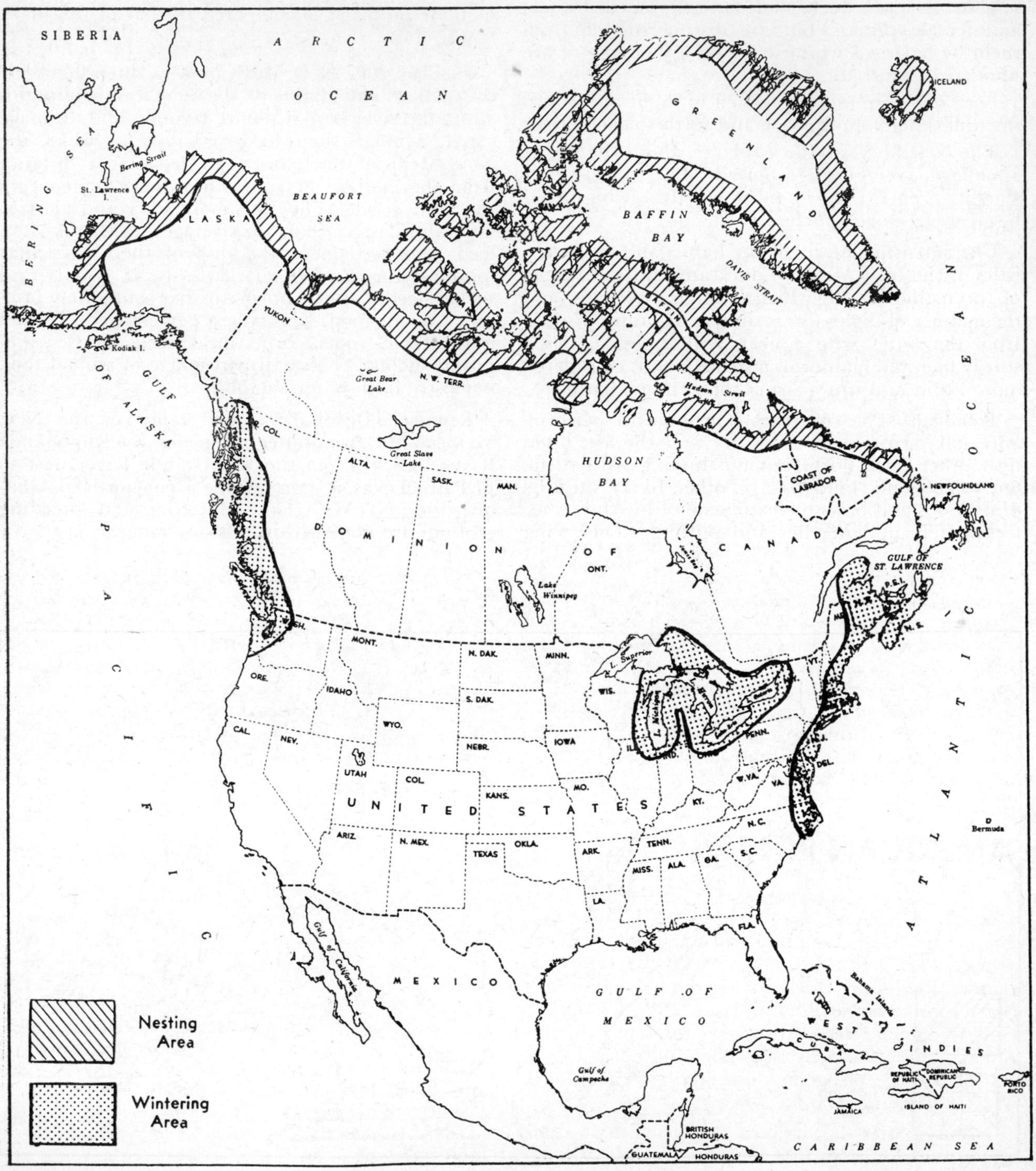


PLATE I. Distribution of Old Squaw.

sexes of the old squaw have distinct winter and summer plumages as a result of two complete moults, one in the spring and another in late summer. It is questionable, however, whether the summer coloring is a true plumage following a complete moult, or a lengthened eclipse moult.

In either season the adult drake is a striking dark brown and white with a graceful elongation of middle tail feathers, much like the male pintail's. The black bill is marked with a pink patch.

The mature female is more brownish than the male, and she lacks the long tail and bill marking. The winter plumage of both sexes is whiter than the summer one.

Reference has been made to the talkative, noisy ways of this duck. There is rarely a let-up in chattering, whether they are on rough water or resting, feeding or in flight, courting or fighting. The explanation for such active communication lies partly in their gay, gregarious manner, partly in a specially tuned voice box.

The old squaw is a small duck, averaging between 1½ and 1¾ pounds in weight, about 15 inches to 20 inches in length, and 27 inches to 29 inches in wingspread.

**Characteristics.** Though the appearance of this duck is not easily confused with any other's, the flight habits of the old squaw are an additional identifying factor. They are restless the year around, and the small flocks rise to great heights and then suddenly swoop to close-to-water flying or splash to a stop. For all their twisting and turning, they are unwary, coming readily to decoy, and are particularly vulnerable when "bunched." Like other diving ducks, they are famous for their alacrity in dropping into a straight dive if startled or pursued when in flight, swimming under water to emerge into full flight without stopping on the surface. Like a few other species of diving ducks, they can rise vertically from the water.

**Breeding.** The regularity of breeding urge is apparently more consistent with the drakes than with the ducks, for a group of males (numbering as many as 15) is usually at hand to vie and fight for one duck. During this season, the drakes rely on a particular call. With necks stretched and heads erected their posturing resembles that of a howling dog, and their repeated notes have been described as sounding like a baying hound.

The nests are habitually built in a hollow on dry ground, well hidden among reeds and grasses. The dark down lining the nest and raised along the edges is carefully pulled over the eggs for heat, protection, and camouflage when the duck leaves to feed, or to visit the drake who remains near by until the end of the incubation. The hen is a careful guardian of her five to seven pale-olive eggs which hatch in about 25 days.

Despite the care and concern of the hen, nests are pillaged for food by the Eskimos and predators, and the ducklings are often attacked by their many natural enemies. As a result of this constant depredation, the "brood" frequently is one lone duckling. As with most other duck species, the plumage of the male and female ducklings at about three months of age is similar to that of the mature female. During the fall and winter, the plumage of the young drake takes on adult coloring and by the second fall, both sexes are matured.

**Feeding.** Though the old squaws rarely fly in a straight line, they usually feed that way. Leaving one or more on guard, they dive rapidly, usually about three dives every two minutes. Unlike some of the best divers, the old squaw uses its wings as well as its feet when swimming under water. Fishermen have hauled in nets, set several fathoms deep, in which many of these ducks were caught. Since 88% of their diet is animal food—crustaceans, mollusks, insects, fishes, etc.—these ducks are mediocre table fare, their flesh being fishy as well as tough. The balance of the diet is 12% vegetable food, mostly grasses and pondweeds.

**Range and Distribution.** The range of the old squaw is northerly in all seasons, and is most heavily distributed along the far Arctic coasts. The most southerly part of its range is North Carolina, but between that point and Delaware they are infrequent.

The fall migration is late, fortunately for the offspring hatched from a second or third clutch. The majority of the ducks leave in October and November for their warmer wintering grounds along the Pacific and Atlantic coasts. They also winter around the Great Lakes.

The spring migration to the breeding grounds starts about April. The breeding range along the Arctic coasts is extensive, as indicated on the distribution map.

## AMERICAN PINTAIL

*Dafila acuta tzitzihoa*

COMMON NAMES: Canard Gris, Cracker, Fall Duck, Gray Duck, Gray Widgeon, Harlan, Kitetailed Widgeon, Lady Bird, Longneck, Necktwister, Paille-En-Queue, Pent-Tail, Pheasant, Pheasant Duck, Picket-Tailed, Pied Gray Duck, Pigeon-Tail, Piketail, Pile-Start, Pinnie, Pintail, Pintail Duck, Pintail Widgeon, Sea Widgeon, Sharptail, Smee, Smethe, Smoker, Spike, Spike-Tail, Spindletail, Split-Tail, Sprig, Spring-Tailed Widgeon, Springtail, Trilby Duck, Water Pheasant, Winter Duck.

**History.** After the mallard and black duck comes the pintail, third in line regarding width of range, abundance of population and table quality. The American pintail, a sub-species of the European and Asiatic pintail (*Dafila acuta*), is well known throughout North America largely because of the easily identifiable appearance of the long-tailed, long-necked drake in flight.

The pintail received a temporary setback during the droughts of the 1930's, but its usually steady abundance is attributable to its natural wariness, and its far northern breeding grounds.

The pintail is easily domesticated, and, like the mallard, is beautiful to behold as well as being a table delicacy.

**Identification.** (See color plate on p. 471.) The majesty of the streamlined pintail drake, with his slender body and pointed tail, is enhanced by his full winter plumage. Particularly striking is the rich brown head contrasted against the white neck. The drake begins to lose his winter grandeur in June, strongly resembling the duck during this complete moult. He can readily be distinguished from the female by the wing feathers which, though lost during the peak of the moult, grow back with the same distinctive winter markings. Shortly after the eclipse moult is completed in August, the autumn moult

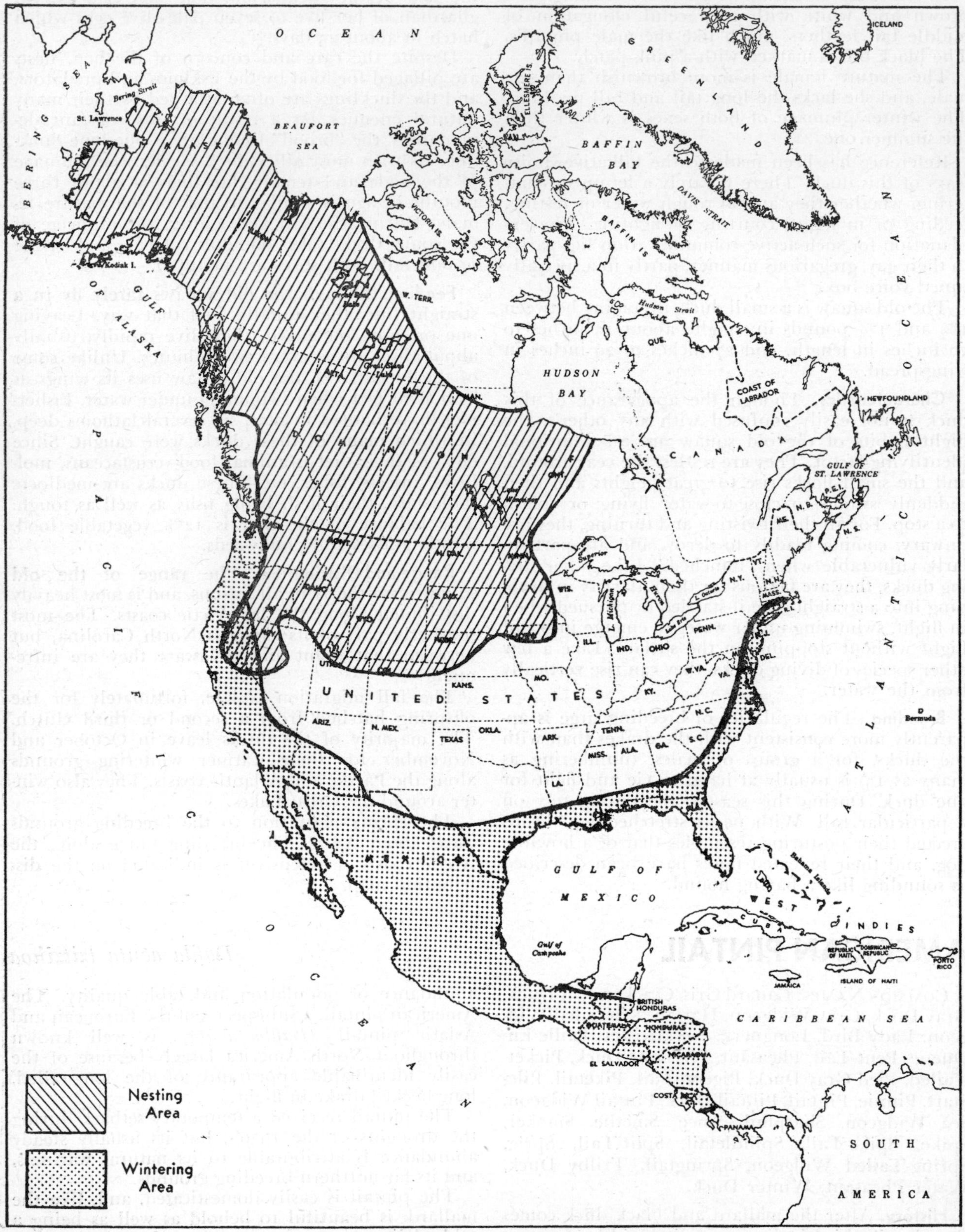


**PLATE I.** Distribution of American Pintail.

begins, usually about September, and by December the drake is in his full winter dress.

The mature female is a consistent mottled brown, and during her two moulting seasons in late winter and early fall the exchange of old feathers for new is barely noticeable. The female pintail and gadwall are very similar, and are differentiated largely by the feet, which are blue-gray in the pintail, yellow in the gadwall. The distinctive white speculum of the gadwall is conspicuous only in flight.

In all seasons, the pintail duck can be identified by her size, which is smaller than the male's. The duck weighs about 1¾ pounds, with the drake averaging a little over 2 pounds. Pintails vary in weight but are typically smaller than the mallard and black duck.

The duck rarely speaks, but the drake whistles and mews when courting and emits a full-throated *"Qua qua"* when in flight.

**Characteristics.** The pintail is one of the most wary of the waterfowl, taking instantly to flight at the first suspicion of danger—remaining alert and aloof while the possibility of danger exists.

The flight speed of waterfowl is often exaggerated because many recorders neglect to take wind speed into account. Forty to 50 miles an hour is considered an average speed for the fast-moving ducks. The pintail is rated among the speediest and sturdiest fliers, with flocks reported making over 60 miles an hour and occasionally spurting up to 90 miles an hour. The sleek body lines of the pintail give the duck an illusion of even faster flight.

**Breeding.** The aerial courtship of this duck is comparatively violent, involving as many as six pursuing drakes. The duck leads the group in an endurance contest of plummeting glides, abrupt turns, and steep climbs, apparently flying off with the survivor. A milder fashion of courtship takes place on the water with the advancing males folding back their slender white necks and the female bobbing an answer to the chosen mate.

The nest of the pintail is more carefully prepared than that of some of the other puddle ducks, since it is hollowed out to a more concealing depth than is the usual ground depression of this group. It is scantily lined, however, with grasses or straw and down. In typical duck manner, it is always built on dry ground, but is located either inland or near water. The eggs are dropped on consecutive days forming a clutch of six to 12, varying in color from olive-green to olive-buff. The drake stands by during part of the 23-day incubation period, leaving with the beginning of his eclipse moult.

The ducklings emerge early in July and are flying by mid-September. Sometimes the drake will return to help raise the offspring, but the young are well cared for by one of the most courageous mothers among the waterfowl. The pintail hen will feign injury, thrash about violently, or try any trick or extreme to distract a trespasser from her ducklings. Both male and female duckling look alike in mid-September, but by December the young drakes begin to assume their adult winter plumage, which is not matured, however, until the second fall.

**Feeding.** The pintail feeds, like the mallard, largely on vegetable food, such as pondweeds, sedges, grasses, and smartweeds which form 87 per cent of its diet, as compared with 13 per cent animal food of mollusks, crustaceans, and insects. The pintail is a skilled surface feeder, capable of tipping in deeper water than other puddle ducks because of its longer-reaching neck.

**Range and Distribution.** The pintail's range includes an abundance of this popular duck from the northernmost to the southernmost extremes of the North American continent. It is also found in Cuba, Puerto Rico, and the Bahamas.

The southern migration starts early—often in August. The first signs of cold send them to the warm wintering grounds along with the blue-winged teals. Their main wintering grounds are along the seacoasts of the Gulf states, but they also favor the Pacific and South Atlantic coast states, preferably inland swamp areas, and Mexico south to Panama.

The pintail is one of the first to flee the cold and head south, but also one of the first migrants north to the great breeding grounds of the sub-arctic. They leave as early as January, but more commonly in February and March, arriving in Alaska by April or May long before the ice has thawed. The great nesting grounds are in Alaska and the Yukon, but the pintail also breeds as far south as Utah.

## REDHEAD

*Nyroca americana*

Common Names: American Pochard, Canard Mulet, Canard Tête Rouge, Canard Violon, Fall Duck, Fiddler, Fiddler Duck, Fool Duck, Gray-Back, Pochard, Red-Headed Broadbill, Red-Headed Raft-Duck, Redneck, Violon, Washington Canvasback.

**History.** The redhead, also known as the American pochard, is the New World relation to the familiar Old World duck, the common pochard. The redhead is widely distributed on this continent, though in some areas the population changes rapidly, varying between extremes of abundance and scarcity. Like the canvasback to which it is allied, the redhead is prized by wildfowlers as prime table food. The duck is curious and trusting and decoys readily.

Excessive market hunting had a dangerous effect on its numbers, as in the case of many North American ducks, but the unsuspicious redhead was plundered more easily than some species because of its characteristic habit of settling in large rafts. This trait has given it the dual names of "raft duck" and "fool duck." Even after market hunting was outlawed, however, its numbers still decreased. During the last 20 years it has been losing ground to droughts, and southerly sections of its breeding range, near to civilization, have disappeared with the drainage of swamps for agriculture.

**Identification.** (See color plate on p. 474.) The adult drake in full winter plumage somewhat resembles the male canvasback, and the outstanding differences are the redhead's smaller size, darker back, higher forehead, and shorter bill. The distinctive profiles of the two ducks readily distinguish them at a good distance. When the typical male diving duck emerges from the eclipse moult, he keeps some of his winter coloring and markings. His plumage is not so drab and female-like as that of the average puddle-duck drake which has a complete moult, except for the winter wing markings. The eclipse moult of the redhead, which starts in June, is an incomplete plumage change, since the bright winter coloring becomes subdued but does not disappear altogether. In early fall, soon after the drake is able to fly again, he begins losing his eclipse feathers and, usually by November, is once again in contrasting full winter plumage.

The female has an unchanging brown back and white breast coloration which gives her a resemblance to the female canvasback, ringneck, and greater scaup. The scaup duck does not have the redhead's wide gray striping on the wing.

Both sexes make a variety of noisy sounds—calls for flight and courtship. The drake has a special call for spring and a peculiar, catlike repertoire of deep, repeated *"me-ows"* and purrs. The raucous *"squeak"* of the female resembles the mallard duck's tone.

The drake is a little larger than the duck, and weights for the species range between 1¾ to 3 pounds. Lengths vary from 17 to 23 inches and wingspread from 30 to 33 inches.

**Characteristics.** The habits of the inquisitive, gregarious redhead are much like those of the canvasback. Rising from the water with the usual, noisy plattering of the diving ducks, the redhead often gives a hoarse cry and wings off into erratic flight. It is commonly warned of danger by the alert baldpate with which it frequently associates, yet, when in an unmixed flock, often "boils up" without cause. Migrating flocks fly swiftly in V-formation, and a normal traveling pace has been clocked at 42 miles per hour for 50 miles.

**Breeding.** The female is sometimes the aggressor during the courtship period on the water, but the four or five males in a group are jealous of her attentions as she moves from one to another, bowing and calling. Once the couple is mated, however, the drake assumes a more forceful role, and the duck is often compelled to dive to avoid him. In aerial courtship the role of pursuer usually reverts to the drakes.

The nest usually is built over water among concealing cattails, bulrushes, or tall reeds of a lake, marsh, or swamp. It is constructed of reeds, or other suitable material found near the nesting site, and is lined with down. The duck freely plucks her breast-down for the nest, and as the incubation period advances, the amount of down increases, serving both for camouflage and to retain body heat when the duck leaves the nest. The number of eggs found in a nest varies from 6 to 27, but since the redhead

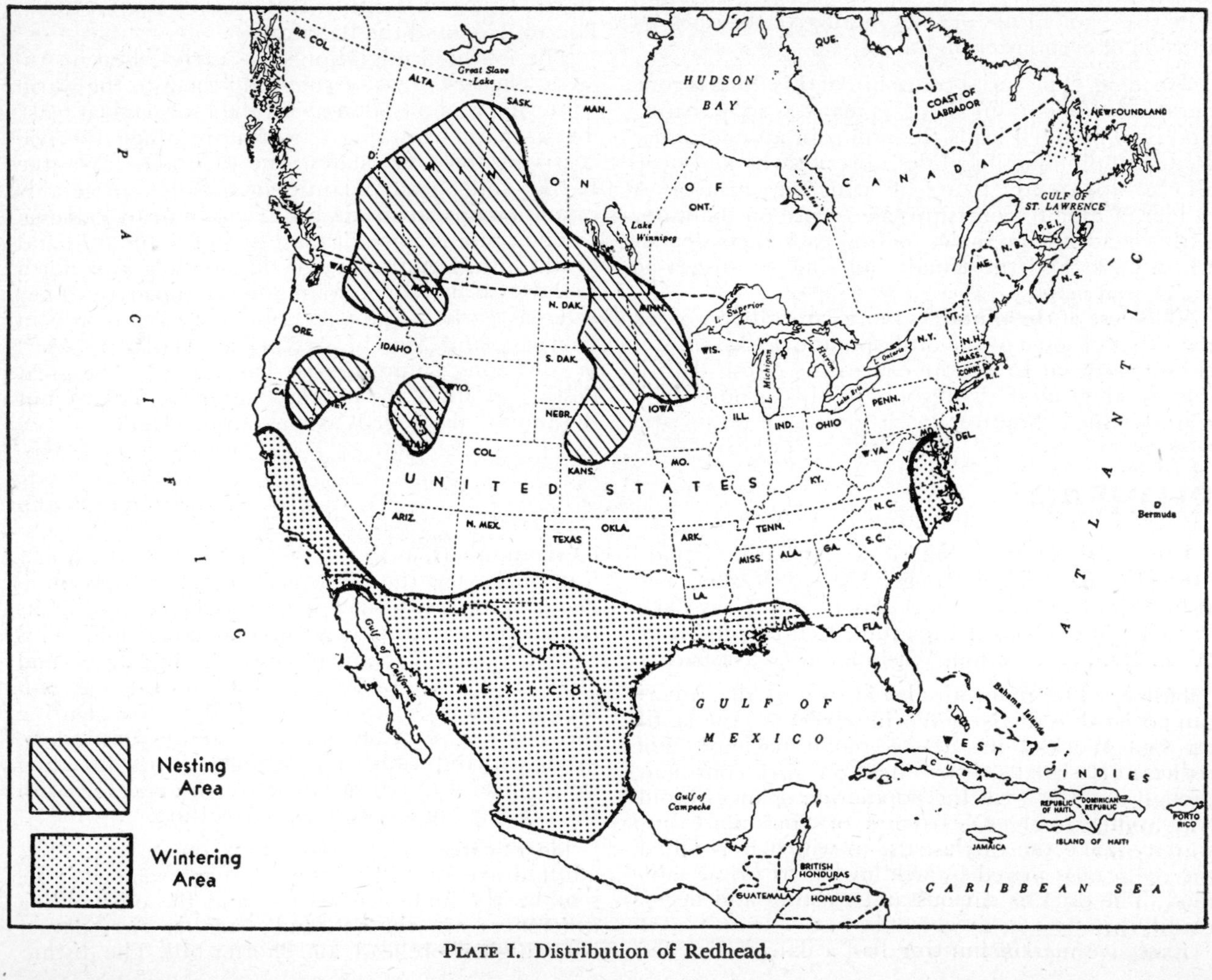


**PLATE I.** Distribution of Redhead.

is inclined to drop eggs in a strange duck's nest (including the canvasback's and ruddy duck's) all the eggs do not necessarily belong to one hen. The typical clutch runs from 10 to 15 and incubation of the very hardshelled, light-blue to cream-buff eggs takes from 24 to 28 days.

At about two months of age, the ducklings resemble the mature female, though the young male is somewhat darker than the female duckling. In early winter, the plumage of both sexes begins to mature, with the male taking on his distinctive red head and neck coloring. By February the young are barely distinguishable in plumage from their parents.

**Feeding.** Some duck connoisseurs consider the redhead a more desirable dish than the much-praised, larger canvas-back. The canvasback prefers a higher percentage of animal food (19% as compared with the redhead's 10%), and in some areas is comparatively less desirable because of its fish-eating habit. The major part of the redhead's 90% vegetable food is composed of the leaves and stems of aquatic plants: pondweeds, muskgrass, sedges, grasses, wild celery, weeds, and water lilies. The duck dives expertly in deep water for these plants, especially craving the wild celery, but the thieving baldpates and American coots, which mix among the redhead flocks, often seize the food from the duck's bill as soon as it surfaces. In the winter, the redhead usually feeds with the puddle ducks for the insects and mollusks which make up the greatest portion of the 10% animal food on its diet.

**Range and Distribution.** The range of the redhead is wide; this duck is well distributed from Canada to Mexico, from the Atlantic to the Pacific. Redheads on the wing usually are unmixed with other ducks, but sometimes they travel with the canvasback or the scaups. By September the young are matured in body and flying skill and ready for the fall migration which begins shortly after the canvasbacks have left. Flying to warmer climates in central and southern California, Mexico, the Gulf States, and the South Atlantic coast states, the redhead takes several flyways. The majority take one of two versions of the Pacific flyway. One route traverses Idaho and Oregon and then goes down the length of California; the other is almost parallel to it, running through Nevada, then cutting into Lower California. Other flocks migrate down the central flyway and cross over to the Atlantic flyway, passing over the New England states on the way down south, but some more robust or foolhardy ones stop as far north as Wisconsin and New York, where they often starve to death when the open inland lakes and bays, chosen as a winter home, freeze over.

The redheads are hardy, and their spring migration is early, again following the lead of the canvasback; they sometimes leave before the ice has broken, but usually around March as the sun is melting the ice on the marshes and sloughs. The great nesting grounds are in Canada, the interior sections of British Columbia, Alberta, Saskatchewan, and Manitoba. The duck is common in Manitoba and has shown a population increase in recent years. The breeding range in British Columbia is virtually intact, unlike the more southerly one in the United States, where 80 per cent of the breeding grounds in the semi-arid regions have been destroyed by drainage and drought. Unfortunately for the greater portion of American wildfowlers, however, the ducks of the Canadian province apparently winter in the same temperature locale around Puget Sound and some migrate either a short distance to the state of Washington or not at all. As shown by the distribution map, the summering range in this country is broken and comparatively limited. This duck is seldom found east of Michigan in the summer season.

## RING-NECKED DUCK

*Nyroca collaris*

COMMON NAMES: Bastard Broadbill, Bastard Redhead, Black Duck, Blackhead, Blackie, Blackjack, Blackneck, Bluebill, Buckeye, Bullneck, Bunty, Butterball, Canard Noir, Creek Redhead, Dogy, Fall Duck, Golden-eyes, Marsh Bluebill, Moonbill, Mud Duck, Pond Bluebill, Raft Duck, Ringbill, Ringbill Bluegill, Ring-Billed Blackhead, Ring-Billed Duck, Ring-Billed Shuffler, Ringneck, Ring-Necked Blackhead, Ring-Necked Scaup, Tufted Duck.

**History.** The common name of "ringbill" is perhaps that most suitable for the ring-necked duck. Both sexes are readily distinguishable by the white band on the bill, but only the male, in deep winter plumage, shows his narrow, chestnut collar when studied at close range.

The ring-necked duck is an American scaup, but so similar to the Old World tufted duck (also of the genus *Nyroca*) that the two species were considered one and the same by ornithologists until about 1840. The American duck does not have the head tufts, but its head feathers grow loosely, giving the deceiving effect of a crest.

**Identification.** (See color plate on p. 475.) In the winter season the adult ring-necked drake has sharply contrasting plumage. He is black on his chest, head, and back, white on his breast and gray on his sides. The black head, with purple reflections, forms a striking backdrop for his yellow eyes—giving him the name "golden-eyes" in some locales. Beside the distinctive bill and neck markings, he is separated from the scaups by his black, not gray, back. The post-nuptial moult begins in July or August. At its height in September the male is a flightless, darker version of the female. The drake starts emerging from his eclipse plumage around late September, and is in full breeding dress by November.

The female is consistently brown with a white breast throughout the year. She is similar to the female canvasback, redhead, and scaups. The duck can be distinguished from the drake during the eclipse by the white ring around her eye.

The duck is slightly smaller than the drake, averaging one pound 8 ounces to his one pound 11 ounces. The length is between 16 to 17 inches, and the wingspread 26 to 27 inches.

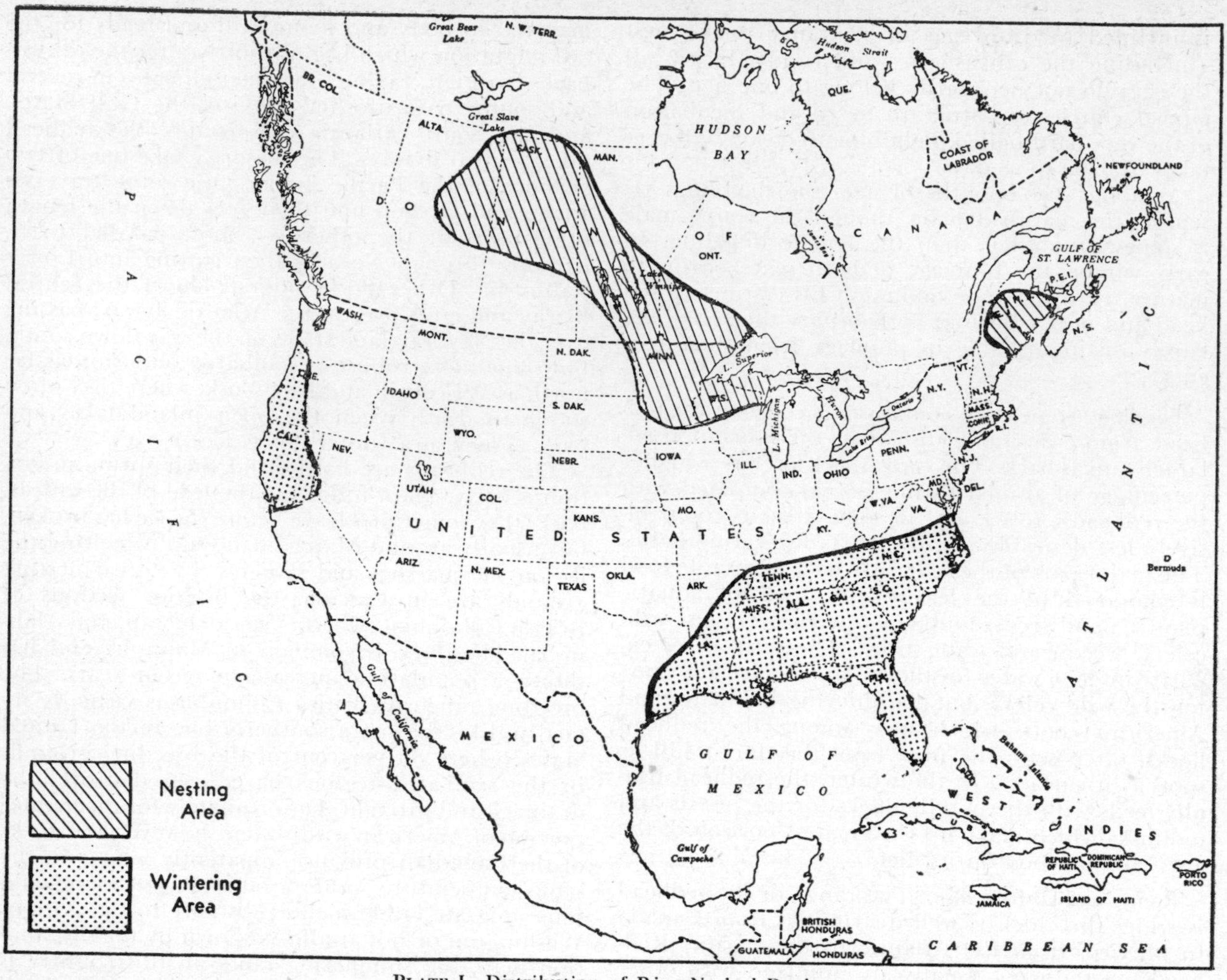


PLATE I. Distribution of Ring-Necked Duck.

Both the duck and drake are comparatively silent. Like the lesser scaup, the drake has soft-toned flight and courtship calls, and a more strident cry when startled.

**Characteristics and Breeding.** Ringnecks are trusting birds, usually decoying readily. Their flight is fast and erratic, but in migration the small flocks travel in a steady and direct course.

The courtship of the drakes is much like that of other ducks. They display their markings by stretching and twisting and repeat their love calls.

The nesting site is usually among the reeds and grasses fringing a fresh-water swamp or slough. The nest is constructed on the ground from grasses and other material at hand, with the edge built about two inches above the water level. Into the down-lined nest the hen drops from 9 to 12 cream-olive to buff eggs which normally hatch in about 23 to 26 days.

The ducklings are lighter counterparts of the young canvasbacks and redheads. Both males and females resemble the adult duck, but are identifiable in September, and around late December the young drake has fully developed plumage.

**Feeding.** Because of its smaller size the ringneck is not generally considered on a par with the redhead and canvasback, though it makes tender table food. The vegetable-food content of the ringneck's diet is as high as the canvasback's. The greater portion of its diet is composed of water lilies, pondweeds, sedges, grasses, smartweeds, muskgrass, and delta duck potato—roughly totaling 81%. The 19% animal food consists largely of insects and mollusks.

**Range and Distribution.** The greatest part of the ringneck's North American range is in the United States, but the breeding grounds extend into northern Canada and the wintering grounds into Mexico.

The fall migration starts in October, and the majority of the ducks use the Mississippi Valley flyway down to the southern states, though some winter in northern California, north along the coast to Washington, and still others remain in New York State.

Many ringnecks spend both winter and summer in the southern states, but the main spring migration takes place in March and April. The ducks usually travel inland along a path of fresh-water ponds, bays, and swamps to more northerly nesting grounds from Minnesota and the Dakotas north to Canada. They also breed in Maine and north to New Brunswick. Until affected by drainage and drought, the great nesting grounds were in northern Wisconsin and Minnesota.

# RUDDY DUCK *Erismatura jamaicensis rubida*

Common Names: Biddy, Blackjack, Blatherskite, Bluebill, Bobber, Booby, Booby Coot, Bristletail, Broadbill, Broadbill Dipper, Brown Duck, Brown Teal, Buck-Ruddy, Bullneck, Bumblebee-Buzzer, Bumblebee Coot, Butterball, Butterbowl, Butterduck, Canard Roux, Chunk Duck, Coot, Creek Coot, Dapper, Daub Duck, Deaf Duck, Dicky, Dinky, Dipper, Dipper Duck, Dip-Tail Diver, Dopper, Dumb-Bird, Dumpling Duck, Dummy Duck, Dun-Bird, Fool Duck, God-Damn, Goose Teal, Goose Widgeon, Greaser, Hard Head, Hard-Headed Broadbill, Hard Tack, Heavy-Tailed Duck, Hickory Head, Johnny Bull, Leatherback, Leather-Breeches, Light-Wood-Knot, Little Soldier, Marteau, Mud Dipper, Murre, Muskrat Duck, Noddy Paddy, Paddywack, Pintail, Quilltail Coot, Rook, Rudder Bird, Rudder Duck, Ruddy, Salt-Water Teal, Shot Pouch, Shanty Duck, Sinker, Sleeper, Sleeping Booby, Sleepy Broadbill, Sleepy Brother, Sleepy Coot, Sleepy Duck, Sleepy-Head, Sleepy-Jay, Soldier Duck, Spatter, Spatterer, Spiketail, Spinetail, Spoonbill, Spoon-Billed Butterball, Steelhead, Sticktail, Stifftail, Stiff-Tailed Widgeon, Stiffy, Stub-and-Twist, Stub-Tail, Tough-Head, Water Partridge, Widgeon, Widgeon Coot, Wiretail.

**History.** The ruddy duck is of the sub-family *Erismaturinae,* a combination of two Greek words roughly translated "propped tail," a name suitable for this stiff-tailed group. Its normal behavior, in many instances, is unlike the ways of other ducks, and the numerous nicknames fail to describe every phase of its appearance and habits. Though the masked duck is a member of the same sub-family, it is an infrequent visitor to the North American continent and therefore is little known to the wild fowler. The ruddy duck, on the other hand, is native and exclusive to the New World and well distributed throughout the continent.

Since this duck has a southerly breeding range, it is one of several duck species which has suffered a serious decrease in population because of drainage and drought on the prairies of the western part of the United States. It never was abundant in the true sense, and is less common now. Because its diet is mostly vegetable matter, it is considered good eating by the discriminating gunner, and though it is small, it is fat.

**Identification.** (See color plate on p. 475.) The adult has two distinct, seasonal plumages. In the summer breeding season he is a handsome ruddy-colored duck with bright markings and a sky-blue bill, but in the winter (October to April) he adopts a duller plumage, similar to the female's. Even the bill coloring, which is peculiar to the ruddy duck drake alone, changes to a dark slate-gray. Except for the old squaw, no other duck species in North

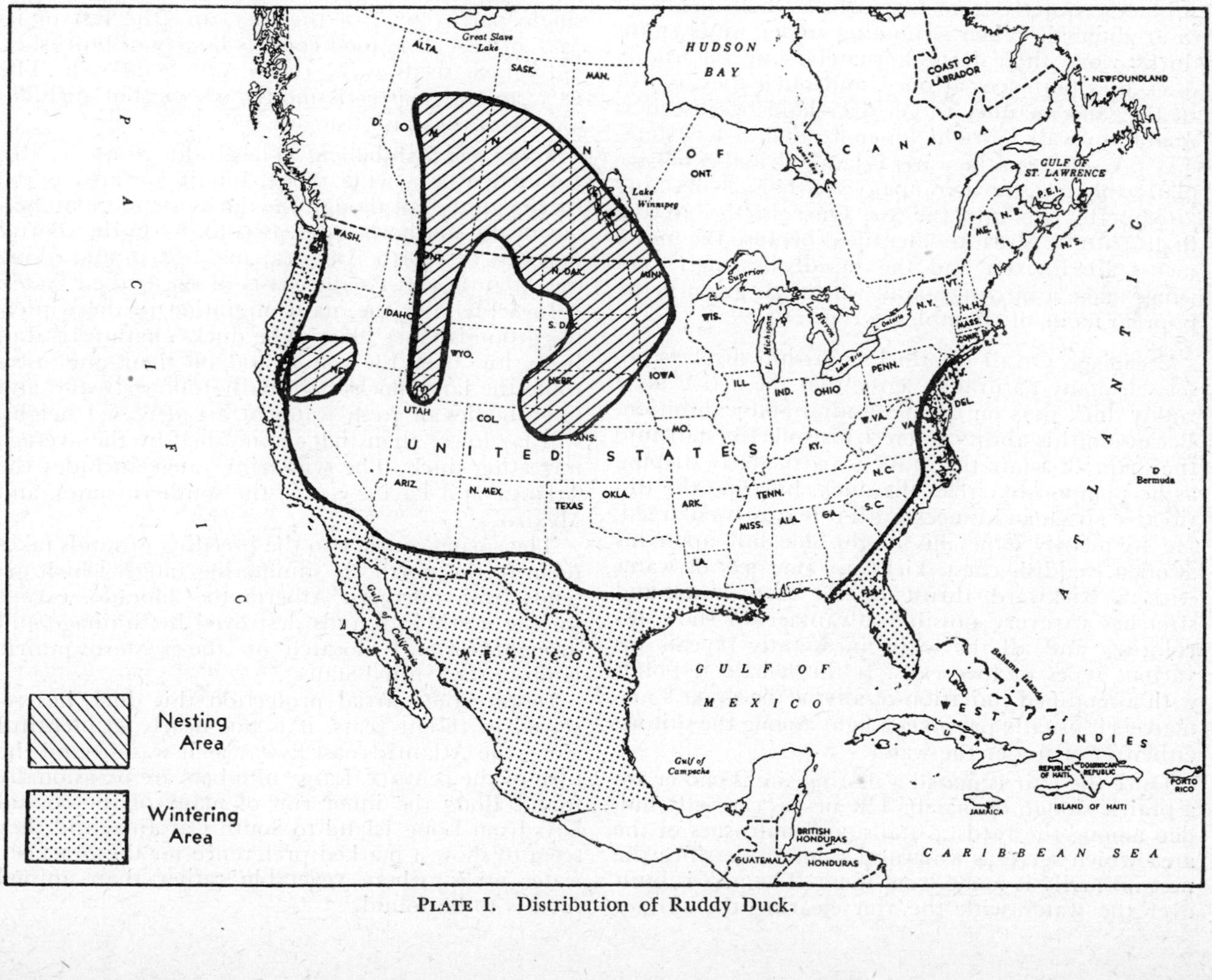


Plate I. Distribution of Ruddy Duck.

America has two separate plumages; but some ornithologists maintain that the drab, female-like plumage of both ducks is an incompleted eclipse moult. The summer plumage is a result of the spring moult in April and May, and the winter plumage is produced by the autumn moult of August and September. In either plumage he resembles the masked duck, but is difficult to confuse with any other species.

The brownish-gray female retains the same plumage throughout the year. Like the male, she has no color pattern except for the cheeks, which, in the male's winter plumage are white whereas the female's are light crossed by dark lines or mottled in appearance. During this winter season the male and female resemble each other more than any other type of duck, but are similar to the female masked duck and female American scoter.

The male is a few ounces heavier than the female, with weight ranging between 1 pound 2 ounces and 1 pound 5 ounces for the specimen. The length (15 inches) and wingspread (22 inches) are about the same for both sexes.

The female is silent, but the male has several courting calls.

**Characteristics.** Wildfowlers find this species tame or stupid, and the bird shows little fear of man. It is more at home in the water than in the air and has several features of the grebe in its agility in aquatic habits but a bewildered, powerless manner on land. It is a swift swimmer, powerful diver, and able to submerge quietly from the surface when disturbed or frightened. When swimming under water, most ducks work their feet alternately, but the ruddy duck uses both feet at once, and often uses its feet in the same manner to get over land because it is unable to walk upright for more than a few steps. The take-off from the water is labored, and extensive plattering usually accompanies a noisy, splashing attempt to rise into the air. Once in the air the flight pattern is readily identified because the movements are uneven and the rapidly-beating, small wings make a buzzing sound which has given it the popular name of "bumblebee coot."

**Breeding.** Of all the duck courtship displays observed, many naturalists agree that the active male ruddy duck puts on the most admirable exhibition. Because of his ability to erect his spikelike tail into the shape of a fan, the drake is particularly striking as he pompously circles the duck, inflating the distinctive air-sac in his neck until it is greatly enlarged. He frequently wipes his bright-blue bill upon his swollen, reddish chest, kicks up long jets of water with a backward thrust of the feet, bows and stretches to every possible advantage to show his coloring, and all the while incessantly repeats his various types of love calls. If the female responds with a modified imitation of any of the drake's maneuvers it usually provokes a fight among the suitors, either on or under the water.

Once the pair is mated a nesting site is chosen on a prairie slough or marsh. The nest is carefully hidden among the reeds, cattails, and bulrushes of the area which serve as a natural camouflage since the nest normally is made from them. The nest is built over the water with the rim clearing the surface by about 8 inches, and is held in place by the restraining reeds. The amount of breast down provided by the mother, when provided at all, is usually sparse. The six to ten creamy-white eggs are large compared to those of most duck species, but immense compared to the size of the small female. A large clutch of eggs weighs three times, and more, as much as the duck herself. The duck sometimes drops eggs in the nests of the redhead and canvasback. Though the incubation time is not known, 28 days is the approximate time for all ducks. The female performs the incubation alone, but unlike most male ducks, the drake stays near by, and once the young are hatched he aids in their rearing. The normal procedure is for the male to lead his brood of large ducklings with the female following in the rear of the group. The young are of notoriously bad disposition and are precocious—capable of diving for food soon after hatching. They mature rapidly, but normally do not leave the protection of their parents until half-grown. In the more southerly sections of the breeding range, this species is known to raise two broods in one season. Like other ducks, both sexes have the same plumage coloring their first fall, and are much like the adult female. By winter they are similar to the adult drake in his femalelike winter dress, but change into full plumage by spring.

**Feeding.** Along with the sea ducks and mergansers, the ruddy ruck is primarily a diving duck when it comes to escaping an enemy or feeding. Different types of pondweeds make up the largest single part (30%) of the diet, and the rest of its 72% of vegetable food consists largely of bulrushes, muskgrass, seeds, wild celery, and wild rice. The 28% animal matter is mostly insects, but includes some mollusks and fish.

**Range and Distribution.** The ruddy duck is distributed over a wide range, but in no area is the species abundant though the ducks are more numerous in the southern states. It is found in the central portions of North America, in Mexico, and along the Atlantic and Pacific coasts of the United States.

In September the main migration to the wintering grounds takes place. The ducks characteristically fly low over the water, and on their migration route the large flocks habitually follow streams and large bodies of fresh water at an increased height, still far lower than that maintained by the average migrating duck. The wintering range includes the Atlantic and Pacific coasts, the southern states, and Mexico.

The spring journey to the breeding grounds takes them to the northerly summering range, which extends from northern Alberta to Colorado, except for the nesting grounds destroyed by drainage and drought formerly located on the western prairie lands in the United States.

Despite the partial protection this duck has received in recent years, it is not nearly so plentiful along the Atlantic coast flyway as it was around the turn of the century. Large numbers are occasionally found along the inner rim of many of the coastal bays from Long Island to South Carolina, and they seem to show a marked preference for the brackish-water areas, where vegetable rather than animal food is to be found.

# GREATER SCAUP

*Nyroca marila*

COMMON NAMES: American Scaup Duck, American Widgeon, Bay Blackhead, Bay Broadbill, Bay Shuffler, Big Bay Bluebill, Big Blackhead, Big Bluebill, Big Broadbill, Big Fall-Duck, Black Duck, Blackhead, Black-Headed Broadbill, Black-Headed Duck, Black-Headed Raft Duck, Blackjack, Blackneck, Bluebill, Blue-Billed Widgeon, Broadbill, Broadbill Bluebill, Bullhead, Bullneck, Butterball, Canvasback Bluebill, Deep-Water Broadbill, Dos Gris, Dos Gris de Mer, Fall Duck, Flock Duck, Grayback, Greenhead, Lake Bluebill, Laker, Mussel-Duck, Raft Duck, Salt-Water Broadbill, Sea Dos Gris, Sea Duck, Shuffler, Troop Duck, Troop Fowl, Widgeon, Winter Broadbill.

**History.** The greater scaup is represented in Europe and Asia, where the name of the duck is believed to have originated. It is fond of feeding in the scaup (oyster or mussel) beds of Europe. Added to this habit is the duck's identifying call of *"scaup."* The characteristic bill of the species has given it the popular names of "bluebill" and "broadbill." It is indistinguishable from the lesser scaup unless carefully examined, and it is sometimes impossible definitely to separate the greater and lesser. As the name indicates, the lesser scaup is usually slightly smaller in size, but habits, rather than appearance, are the real determining factors.

The greater scaup is primarily a marine duck, preferring coastal areas along the Atlantic, Pacific, and Great Lakes. Because its diet is about half animal food, it does not rate so high in table quality as its diving duck relatives, the redhead, ringneck, and canvasback, all of which have a diet of higher vegetable content.

**Identification.** (See color plate on p. 474.) The full winter plumage of the adult male gives the general impression of being black and white, though the back is grayish and the glossy head is high-

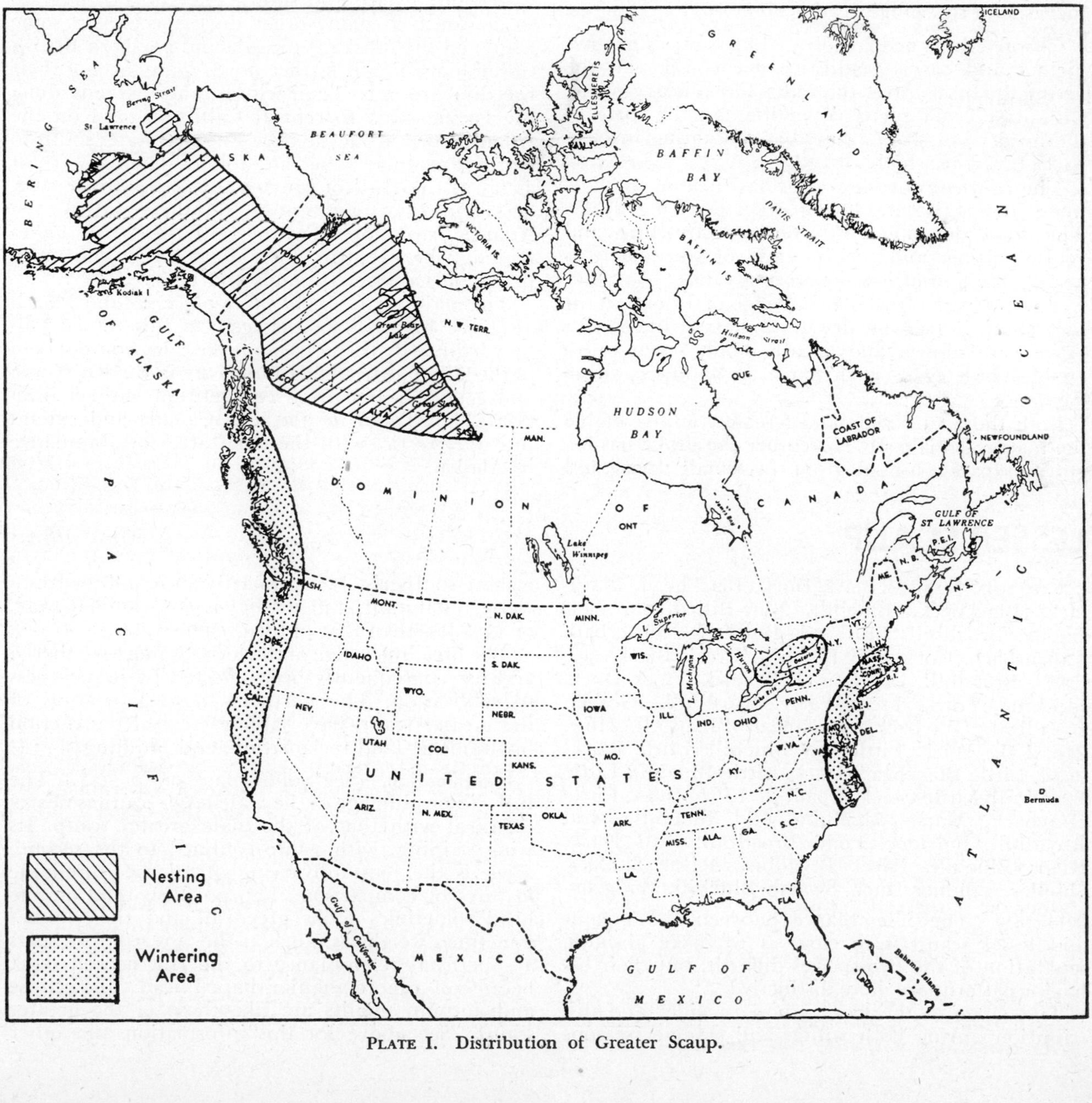


PLATE I. Distribution of Greater Scaup.

lighted with green. (The lesser scaup is glossed with purple.) The eclipse moult is a slow, incomplete plumage change which begins around June and is at its peak in September when the drake is flightless and similar in appearance to the duck. Soon after the drake has regained his power of flight, the autumn moult starts, and by December he usually has reverted to full dress.

The mature female is dark brown except for a white breast and white face marking which extends from the base of the bill midway up to the eyes like a mask. The wing, which is like that of the drake, is the chief means of distinguishing her from the female lesser scaup. The white striping on the secondary wing feathers is distinctive to both species, but on the wing of the lesser scaup the white extends about half the length of the primaries.

Except for the raucous *"scaup, scaup,"* the courtship and flight calls of both duck and drake are soft and low, inaudible unless listened for at close range.

The scaups are medium in size, both sexes averaging about 2 pounds. The length is about 17 to 18 inches, and the wingspread is about 30 to 31 inches.

**Characteristics and Breeding.** The scaup is not suspicious and comes readily to decoy. Like all the diving ducks, it leaves the water like a heavy plane, with its take-off speed depending on the force of the head wind. It is a fast flier, migrating in compact groups at a high altitude.

The courtship of the scaups has little of the liveliness and active display of other courting ducks. The drake depends mostly on neck-stretching and gentle calling, and the response of the female is head-bobbing and low, answering calls.

The nest site often is at the edge of a pond, built in a slight hollow on dry ground. It is lined with grasses and down, and usually holds seven to 10 greenish-buff eggs which hatch in about 25 to 28 days.

Both the young male and female scaup resemble the mature female. By November the drake has begun to separate himself from the female young and adult ducks, and by spring both juveniles have the plumage distinctive of their sex.

**Feeding.** The greater scaup is one of the most powerful swimmers and expert divers of the diving ducks. Typical of its group, in contrast to the surface-feeders, the hind toe has a skin flap, and the larger feet are placed farther to the rear make deep-water diving for the roots of aquatic plants easier, and swimming under water or on the surface faster, but walking to grain fields difficult and therefore unlikely. The food ratio is almost equally animal and vegetable. The 47% vegetable food is largely composed of pondweeds, muskgrass, sedges, and water milfoils, with a liking for wild celery and rice when it is at hand. The 53% animal food is mostly insects and crustaceans, with a special emphasis on oysters and mussels.

**Range and Distribution.** The first-flight juveniles of the southerly parts of the breeding range begin in fall migration. The scaups are hardy ducks, however, and the majority leave late, waiting until forced out by ice and snow. They do not migrate so far south as many other duck species, for some winter on the Alaska Peninsula and northern British Columbia which is farther north than parts of their breeding grounds. Their winter range extends along the Pacific coast to central California and on the Atlantic coast from the New England states south to North Carolina; some are found down the coast as far as the Gulf of Mexico. Like the sturdy ring-necked ducks, some scaups, on their way to the Atlantic, stop for the winter in the Great Lakes region, where entire flocks have been known to perish on ice-covered ponds and bays.

The main spring flight takes place around March after the break-up of the ice. On this return trip they habitually travel back on the same routes taken in the fall. The nesting grounds are in the Far North and generally free from competition with civilization. They begin in northern Canada and extend into the Arctic, with the chief areas of abundance in Alaska.

## LESSER SCAUP

*Nyroca affinis*

Common Names: Black Duck, Blackhead, Blackjack, Blackneck, Bluebill, Blue-Billed Shoveler, Booby, Broadbill, Bullhead, Bullneck, Butterball, Canvasback, Cottontail Bluebill, Creek Blackhead, Creek Broadbill, Dos Gris, Fall Duck, Flock Duck, Flocking Fowl, Fresh-Water Broadbill, Goshen Broadbill, Grayback, Greenhead Broadbill, Howden, Lake Duck, Little Bay Bluebill, Little Blackhead, Little Blackhead, Duck, Little Bluebill, Little Broadbill, Little Creek Broadbill, Little Duck, Little Grayback, Marsh Bluebill, Mud Bluebill, Mud Broadbill, Polridge, Pond Broadbill, Raft Duck, River Bluebill, River Broadbill, River Shuffler, Shuffler, Summer Duck, Swamp Bluebill, Widgeon.

**History.** The resemblance between the greater and lesser scaup is so close as to make absolute separation of the two species difficult, but their behavior patterns are more distinctive.

The range of the lesser scaup is wider and distribution during both winter and summer seasons is more southerly. It is primarily an inland or fresh-water inhabitant, and its diet is 40% animal food, or 13% less than that of the greater scaup.

The breeding range of the lesser is more southerly, and has consequently been affected by its nearness to civilization. The northerly nesting grounds of the greater scaup have largely escaped destruction by drainage, land reclamation, and building.

**Identification.** (See color plate on p. 474.) The full winter plumage of the male lesser scaup is nearly identical with that of the male greater scaup. Its wing striping, with white confined to the secondaries, is the most unvarying of all the unreliable features of comparison. The purplish tone on the head sometimes looks greenish, and the "lesser" sometimes weighs as much as the "greater." It bears a superficial resemblance to the ring-necked duck because of a more angular-shaped head. The eclipse and autumn moults are like those of the greater scaup. (See above for this information and other comparisons on appearance and habits of these two species.)

The wing and bill of the female lesser scaup separate her from the female greater scaup, from which she is indistinguishable in body plumage coloring. She resembles the female ringneck.

Averaging slightly smaller than the greater scaup, the lesser scaup weighs about one pound 13 ounces, and is around 16 inches long. The wingspread averages 27 inches.

Like its kinsman, the lesser scaup is not very talkative. Except for their loud *"scaup,"* the calls and whistles are low.

**Characteristics and Breeding.** The erratic twisting and turning of the swift-flying scaups indicate their nervous nature. Under normal conditions the group flies high in close formation on a steady course, but when startled, specifically by a gunshot, they scatter.

The drake usually begins the courtship by bowing

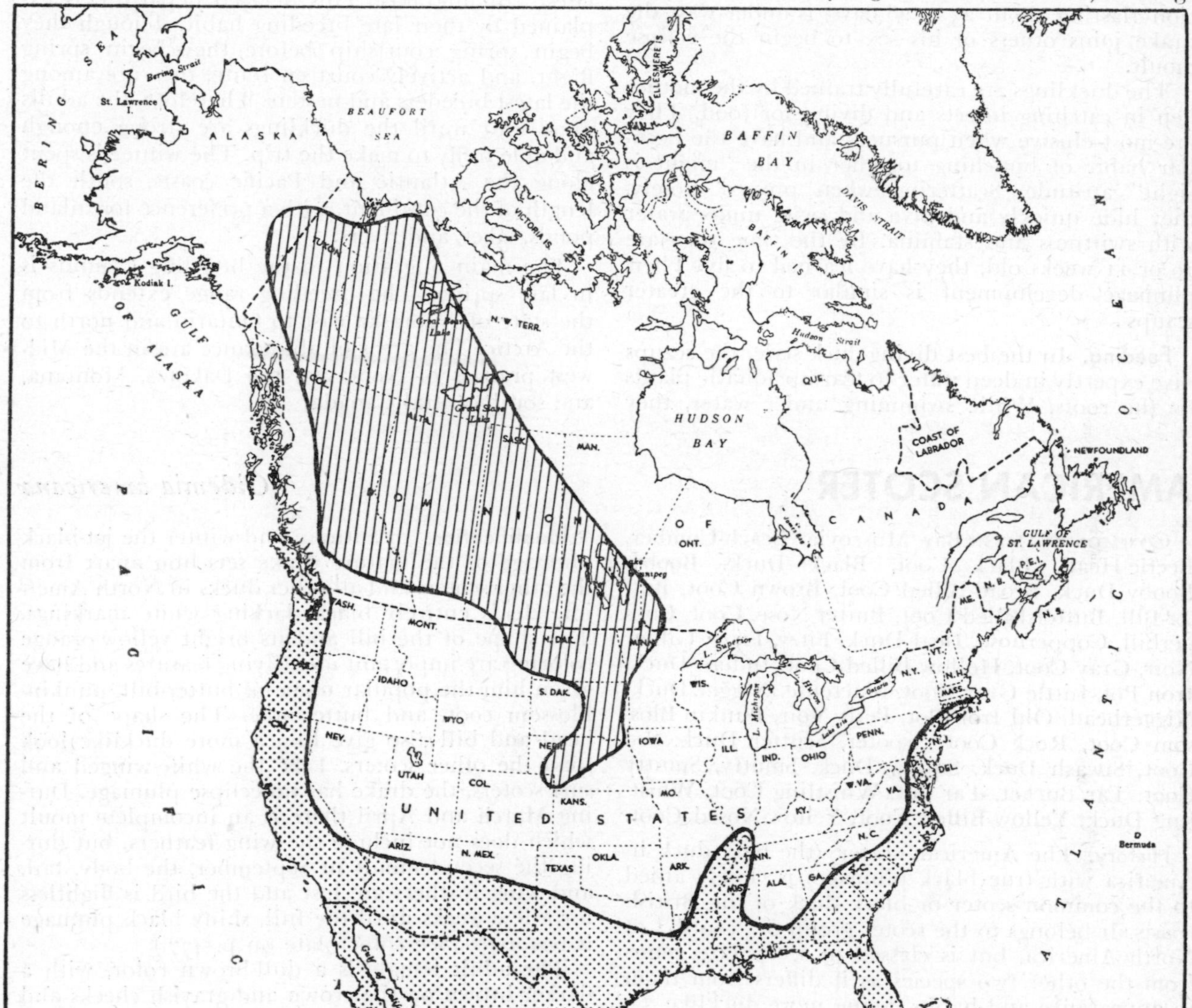

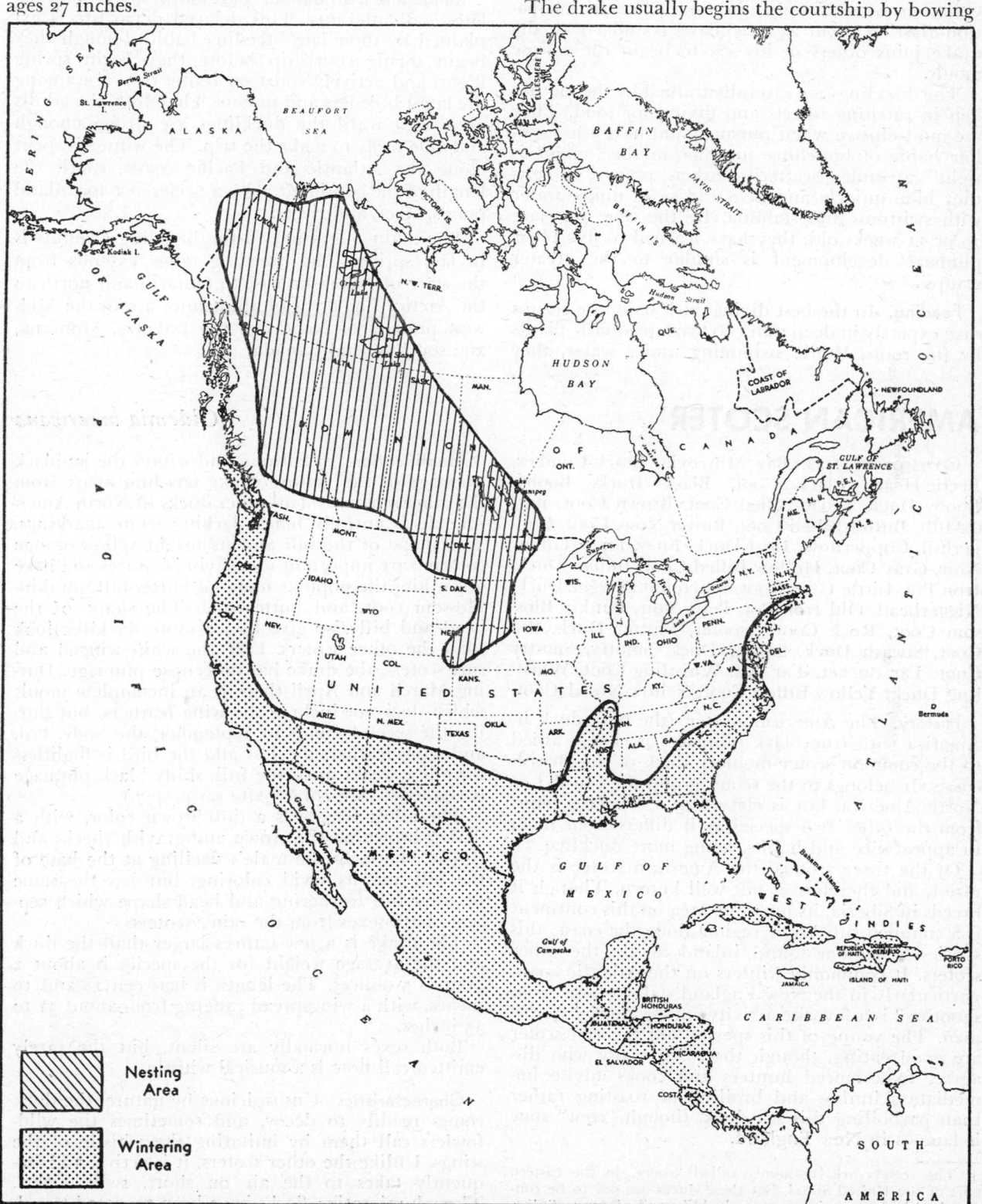

PLATE I. Distribution of Lesser Scaup

and calling to an unattached female. If she selects him after a sufficient display of his plumage, she usually returns his pecks and takes short dives under him or with him.

The nest often is placed among tall grasses by a swamp or pond, either by the water, in a hollow on dry ground, or over the water, with the nest edge built high. Into the grass-lined nest, amply softened by down, the hen lays from nine to 12 eggs, variations of creamy-olive in color. Once the incubation (lasting about 23 to 26 days) is under way, the drake joins others of his sex to begin the eclipse moult.

The ducklings are carefully trained by the mother hen in catching insects and diving for food. They are most elusive when pursued, and have the peculiar habit of bunching together in the "might is right" attitude. Scattering when pressed closely, they hide quickly and dive and swim under water with swiftness and stamina. By the time they are 10 or 11 weeks old, they have learned to fly. Their plumage development is similar to the greater scaups'.

**Feeding.** In the best diving-duck style, the scaups dive expertly in deep water to tear up aquatic plants by the roots. While swimming under water, they use only their feet for propulsion; their wings lie motionless and pressed close against their bodies. Of their 60% vegetable food pondweeds form the largest single item consumed, followed by grasses, sedges, and wild celery. They are exceptionally fond of wild rice and are most palatable eating when fed on it. The 40% animal food is normally made up of mollusks, insects and crustaceans.

**Range and Distribution.** The scaups are among the latest fall migrants. This delayed departure is explained by their late breeding habit. Though they begin spring courtship before they begin spring flight, and actively court en route, they are among the latest breeders and nesters. Therefore, the adults must wait until the ducklings are strong enough and able to fly to make the trip. The winter is spent along the Atlantic and Pacific coasts, south the length of the continent, with a preference for inland ponds, lakes, and rivers.

The main migration to the breeding grounds is in late spring. The breeding range extends from the state of Nebraska east to Ontario and north to the Arctic. The areas of abundance are in the Midwest prairies of Nebraska, the Dakotas, Montana, and south-central Canada.

## AMERICAN SCOTER[1]

*Oidemia americana*

COMMON NAMES: Bay Muscovie, Beach-Comber, Beetle-Head, Black Coot, Black Duck, Booby, Booby Duck, Broad-Billed Coot, Brown Coot, Butter-Bill, Butter-Billed Coot, Butter-Nose, Coot, Copperbill, Coppernose, Deaf Duck, Fitzy, Fizzy, Gibier Noir, Gray Coot, Hollow-Billed Coot, Indian Duck, Iron Pot, Little Gray Coot, Macreuse, Nigger Duck, Niggerhead, Old Iron Pot, Petit Noir, Punkin-Blossom Coot, Rock Coot, Scooter, Scutter Duck, Sea Coot, Siwash Duck, Squaw Duck, Smutty, Smutty Coot, Tar Bucket, Tar Pot, Whistling Coot, Whistling Duck, Yellow-Billed Coot, Yellow-Nosed Coot.

**History.** The American scoter (the only duck in America with true black plumage) is closely allied to the common scoter or black duck of the British coasts. It belongs to the scoter group or "coots" [1] of North America, but is classed in a separate genus from the other two species as it differs from them in appearance and habits, being more ducklike.

Of the three scoters, the American scoter is the rarest, and therefore is not well known. Though it breeds in Siberia, its breeding area on this continent is a confined sub-Arctic region along the coast; this species is seldom found inland as are the other scoters. It commonly winters on the Atlantic coast, particularly in the New England states where "coot shooting" is a favorite activity among rugged sportsmen. The young of this species and the surf scoter are good eating, though there are many who disagree. Experienced hunters and cooks advise immediate skinning and broiling or roasting rather than parboiling this sea duck, though "coot" stew is famous in New England.

[1] The scoters are commonly called "coots" in the eastern part of the United States, but these ducks are not to be confused with the genuine coot, a ducklike rail of genus *Fulica*.

**Identification.** In autumn and winter the jet-black plumage of the mature drake sets him apart from the other scoters and all other ducks in North America. He is entirely black, lacking white markings. The shape of the bill and its bright yellow-orange coloring are important identifying features and have given him the popular name of butter-bill, punkin-blossom coot, and butter-nose. The shape of the head and bill also give him a more ducklike look than the other scoters. Like the white-winged and surf scoters, the drake has no eclipse plumage. During March and April there is an incomplete moult which does not include the wing feathers, but during the second moult in September, the body, tail, and wing feathers are lost and the bird is flightless for a few weeks until the full, shiny black plumage is restored. (See color plate on p. 477.)

The adult female is a dull-brown color, with a darker brown on the crown and grayish cheeks and throat. She lacks the male's swelling at the base of the bill and its vivid coloring, but has the same peculiar bill feathering and head shape which separate both sexes from the other scoters.

The drake is a few ounces larger than the duck and the average weight for the species is about 2 pounds 5 ounces. The length is between 18 and 19 inches, with a wingspread ranging from about 31 to 33 inches.

Both sexes normally are silent, but the rarely emitted call note is a musical whistle.

**Characteristics.** Unsuspicious by nature, the duck comes readily to decoy, and sometimes the wildfowlers call them by imitating the whistle of the wings. Unlike the other scoters, it is active, and frequently takes to the air on short, swift flights. Though migrating flocks have been reported traveling at 200 miles an hour, authoritative sources claim that 60 miles per hour is a more likely speed. The flocks, varying in size, have no set flight pattern. They move in V- or U-shaped formation, bunch in irregular groups, or proceed in single file. In clear weather they fly high, but storms drive them down, close to the water.

**Breeding.** Because of the remoteness of the breeding range, little is known of the behavior of this scoter during courtship and nesting time. The nests are carefully hidden, but from the few examined, six to ten seems to be the usual clutch of pinkish to pale-buff eggs. The female performs the incubation alone. Though the male deserts her during this time, he does not begin the flightless, eclipse plumage that is typical in most duck species.

The duck is a solicitous mother, and she trains her offspring thoroughly in hiding and feeding, though, like all ducklings of sea ducks, they are inclined toward insects and a wide range of foods. The mother sometimes carries them on her back from the water to the shore if they become exhausted from diving. Typical of most duck species, the young look alike when about three months old. They resemble the mature female but are lighter with a more grayish breast, hence the name "gray coots." By their first winter each sex begins to assume identification by its plumage coloring; the male becomes blacker and the female browner. They attain adult plumage by their second fall. The juveniles of all three scoter species are very similar, but the bill feathering and the shape of the head separate the young of this duck from the other scoters.

**Feeding.** The American scoter is a lover of the seacoasts. However, it habitually feeds in protected bays and sounds where there is a greater concentration of mussels in the comparatively undisturbed tidal flats. They are capable of making deep dives but usually feed in water under 25 feet in depth. Like the others of its kind, it feeds almost entirely on animal food. Along with the large eider species, the preferred food of these ducks is bivalved mollusks upon which they feed while submerged. Because of this specialized feeding, they have done some dam-

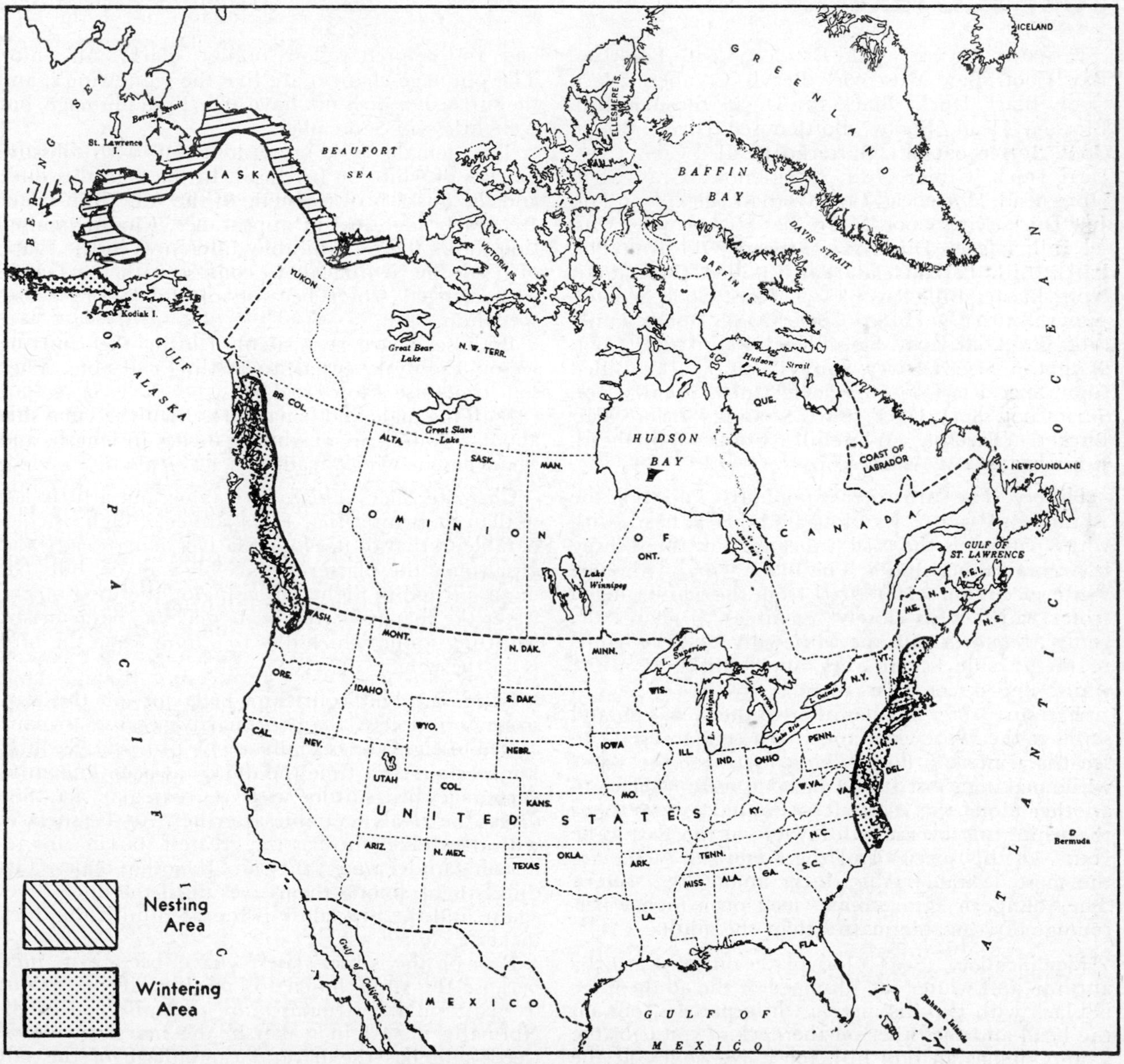


PLATE I. Distribution of American Scoter.

age in localized areas to commercial shellfish beds. Beside the mollusks, which form 65% of the diet, the 90% animal food is composed of crustaceans, insects, and fishes. The 10% vegetable matter is mostly pondweeds and muskgrass.

**Range and Distribution.** The range of the American scoter extends from the sub-Arctic to Florida, but, differing from the other scoters, it is confined to coastal areas and is rarely found inland.

The main fall migration to the southerly wintering grounds takes place around mid-September. The American scoter leaves before the other two scoter species, and the adults (like those of the surf scoter and the drakes of the whitewing) take off from the nesting grounds ahead of the young. The juveniles migrate during October. They winter on the Atlantic from Maine to South Carolina and sometimes to Florida, but the areas of abundance are off Massachusetts, around the islands of Martha's Vineyard and Nantucket and smaller islands and reefs in the area. Since the distribution of this duck is largely controlled by the amount of available food, the American scoter is numerous about these islands, where their preferred foods of mussels, scallops, and clams are plentiful. Where they have fed over commercial beds of shellfish, almost 50 per cent of their food was taken from those localized areas. The percentage is lower, however, than that of the white-winged scoter. On the Pacific coast, the wintering range is more northerly than on the Atlantic side, and extends less than half the distance southward as compared to the range of the other scoters. It begins in the Aleutians and goes along the coast from northern British Columbia to Washington. A few ducks are found as far south as California.

The spring migration is between April and May when the birds travel north to the nesting grounds which extend around the greater part of Alaska's coasts, along to the Arctic coast.

## SURF SCOTER

*Melanitta perspicillata*

Common Names: Bald-Headed Coot, Baldpate, Bay Coot, Bay Muscovie, Beach Comber, Black Coot, Black Duck, Black Sea-Duck, Blossom Bill, Blossom Head, Booby, Bottlenosed Diver, Brown Coot, Butterboat-Bill, Butterboat-Billed Coot, Coot, Deaf Duck, Gibier Noir, Gogglenose, Gray Coot, Horsehead, Horsehead Coot, Indian Duck, Iron Pot, Jew Duck, King Coot, Macreuse, Morrocojaw, Mussel Bill, Nigger Duck, Niggerhead, Old Iron Pot, Patch Bill, Patch-Head, Patch-Polled Coot, Petit Noir, Plaster Bill, River Coot, Rock Coot, Scooter, 'Scovy, Scutter Duck, Sea Coot, Siwash Duck, Skunkbill, Skunkbill Coot, Skunkhead, Skunkhead Coot, Skunktop, Sleepy Diver, Snuff-Taker, Speckle-Billed Coot, Spectacle Coot, Spectacle Duck, Squaw Coot, Surf Coot, Surf Duck, Surf Scooter, Surfer, Tar-Bucket, Tar-Pot, Whitebill Coot, Whitehead, Whitehead Coot, Whitescop.

**History.** The surf scoter is popularly known as the "skunkhead coot." Its elongated black head with white patches is the easiest means of distinguishing it from all other ducks. The black wing, without a white speculum, sets it apart from the white-winged scoter which it so closely resembles. It shares the genus *Melanitta* with the whitewing, and the habits of the two ducks are very much alike. (For the white-winged scoter see p. 410.)

The surf scoter is as familiar to the New England states as the whitewing, and it is a common sight to see the wintering flocks flying low over the water while making short trips from one feeding place to another along the coast. It is hunted as eagerly as the whitewing by the wildfowlers of the East. The young of this species and the American scoter are the most desirable table ducks among the scoters. The young, or "gray coots," feed on a higher percentage of vegetable matter than the adults.

**Identification.** (See color plate on p. 477.) In autumn and winter the plumage of the adult drake is black with two distinctive white patches, one on the head and the other on the neck. Typical of the scoters, it has an odd bill, for it is swollen at the base and colored yellow, orange, black, and white. The plumage changes are like the whitewing's, and the surf scoter does not have an eclipse plumage, but is flightless in September.

The female is a grayish-brown with obscure patches of white on her head. In the field this duck and the dusky-brown female of the American scoter are nearly identical in appearance. Close examination shows the recognizable differences in the shape of head. She is difficult to confuse with the female white-winged scoter because of the latter's white speculum.

Both sexes are very silent. During the courting season, the drake utters a whistling call note. They sometimes use a low croak.

Both the male and female are about the same size, about 2 pounds in weight, 19 inches in length, and 31 inches in wingspread.

**Characteristics.** This coot is tame, but a little less so than the whitewing. The manner of flight is comparable to that of its close relative, being steady and rapid once the plattering take-off is made, but it is more spirited in flight. On rising or alighting on the water the first few wing beats make a characteristic whistling sound which dies to a hum when the bird is on the wing.

**Breeding.** The courtship behavior of the surf scoter is a violent affair, primarily because as many as five to eight drakes pursue one provocative duck. For an hour at a time the duck has been known to encourage her suitors with a particular act. She dives—the rivals scramble after her. As she surfaces with the drake who has the greatest stamina for remaining under water, they face the other males. The drakes fight among themselves until the duck dives again, and the procedure is repeated until the duck makes a choice.

Few of the scoter's nests have been examined because the sites chosen for nesting are precarious to man and the structures are carefully concealed. Normally placed in a marsh, the nest is made of weeds and has the natural camouflage of the tall

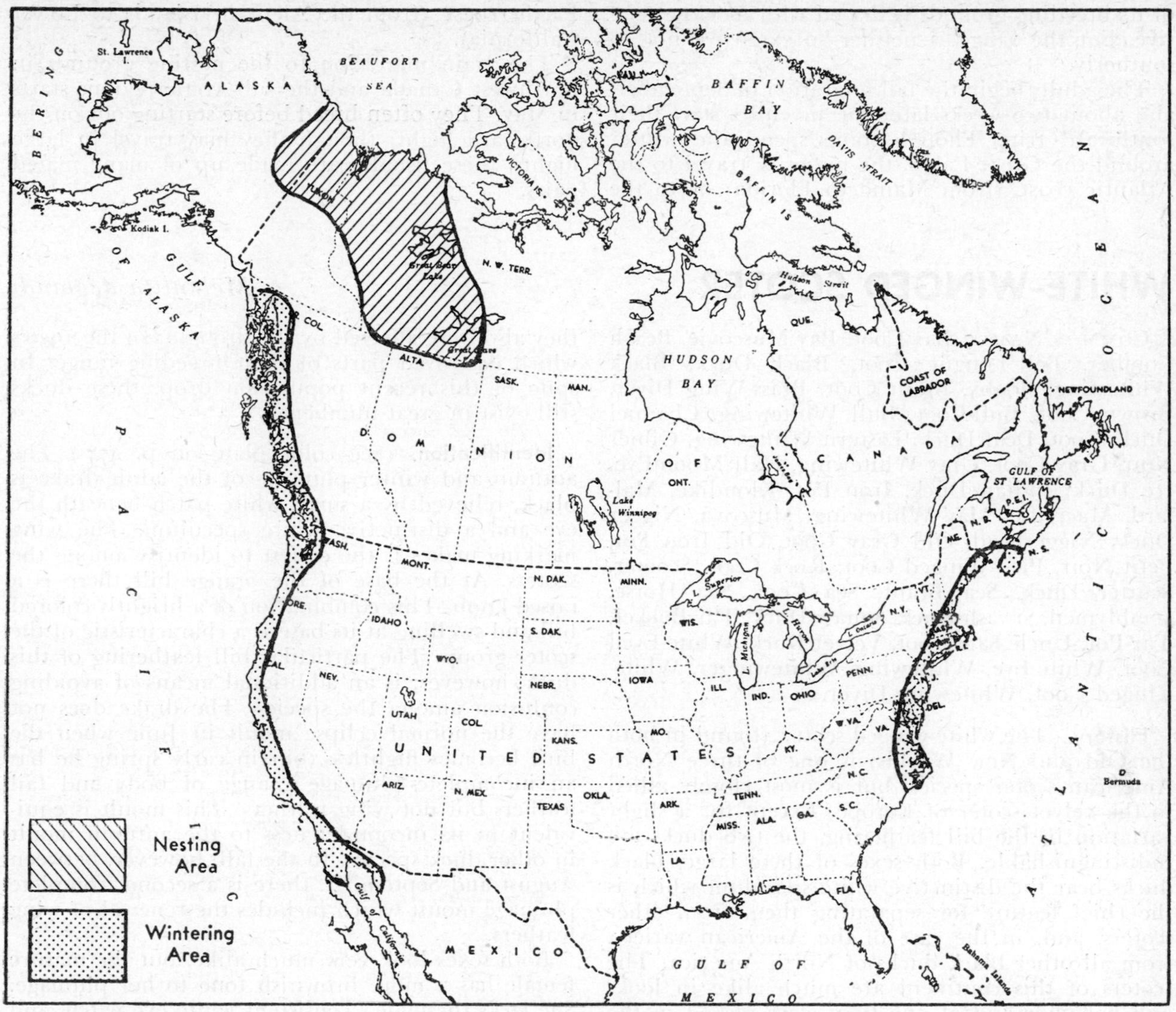


PLATE I. Distribution of Surf Scoter.

grasses which surround it. Into the nest, lined with down, the duck drops from five to nine pinkish or pale-buff eggs.

Both sexes of the scoter offspring look alike and resemble the mature female, though patches on the side of the head are more distinct, usually white without mottling. In their first winter, the plumage changes distinguish the sex of the ducklings, but it is not until the third fall, when they are over 2½ years old, that they have adult coloring and markings. They closely resemble the young of the other scoters, but are without the white speculum of the whitewing. When in hand, the shape of the head and bill, and the peculiar bill feathering, separate the three species.

**Feeding.** The surf scoter is inclined to feed more in shallow water than the other scoters, but it is capable of making powerful dives in deep water. The initial plunge beneath the surface gives an awkward appearance as the duck spreads its wings and departs with a splash, using both wings and feet for propulsion. As its name explains, it is frequently seen "scooting" through the surf, diving beneath breaking waves. Eighty-eight per cent of this scoter's diet is animal food, mostly mollusks, crustaceans, insects, and fishes. Though over one-half of this duck's food consumption is composed of bivalved mollusks, the percentage is smaller than the other scoters'. The surf scoter does no appreciable damage to commercial scallop and oyster beds as the white-winger and American species sometimes do.

When mollusks are consumed by a duck, the hard shells become powerful crushing and grinding material in the duck's gizzard. Ornithologists suggest that the amount of gravel taken is in proportion to the percentage of hard-shelled foods consumed. Though the gizzard of the whitewing has been found to contain unusually large pebbles, they feed on a greater percentage of hard-shelled mollusks (i. e., rock clams and quahogs) than is common among sea ducks, and consequently the gravel content found in the average whitewing is as low as 7% as compared to the surf scoter's average of 18%. The surf scoter feeds more on vegetable food than does the whitewing. Of the 12% plant food eaten, pondweeds make up the highest identifiable percentage. As is the habit with true marine ducks, the scoter feeds by day.

**Range and Distribution.** The wintering range of the surf scoter is about the same as the whitewing's, but is more northerly on the Atlantic coast. A part of its breeding grounds is shared with its close relative, but the range is neither so extensive nor so southerly.

The adults begin the fall migration in September, and about two weeks later the juveniles start their southward trip. Though some spend the winter around the Great Lakes, the majority travel to the Atlantic coast (from Maine to Florida) or to the Pacific coast (from the Aleutian Islands to Lower California).

The main migration to the nesting grounds in northwest Canada and the sub-Arctic regions starts in May. They often breed before starting out on the northward flight; though they may travel in large flights, these usually are made up of many mated pairs.

## WHITE-WINGED SCOTER

*Melanitta deglandi*

COMMON NAMES: Bay Coot, Bay Muscovie, Beach Comber, Bell-Tongue Coot, Black Duck, Black Whitewing, Booby, Brant Coot, Brass-Wing Diver, Brown Coot, Bull-Coot, Bull Whitewing, Channel Duck, Coot, Deaf Duck, Eastern Whitewing, Gibier Noir, Gray Coot, Gray Whitewing, Half Moon-Eye, Ice Duck, Indian Duck, Iron Pot, Klondike, Mallard, Macreuse, May Whitewing, Muscova, Nigger Duck, Niggerhead, Old Gray Coot, Old Iron Pot, Petit Noir, Pied-Winged Coot, Rock Coot, Scooter, Scutter Duck, Sea Brant, Sea Coot, Sea Horse, Semblymen, Siwash Duck, Squaw Duck, Tar Bucket, Tar Pot, Uncle Sam Coot, Velvet Duck, White-Eyed Coot, White-Eye, Whitewing, Whitewinger, White-winged Coot, Whitewing Diver.

**History.** The white-winged scoter (found in both the Old and New Worlds) is one of three North American scoter species, but is most closely allied to the velvet scoter of Europe. Except for a slight variation in the bill feathering, the two ducks are indistinguishable. Both sexes of these large, black ducks bear the distinctive white speculum which is the chief feature for separating them from other scoters, and, in the case of the American variety, from all other black ducks of North America. The scoters of this continent are much alike in looks and behavior and at one time were placed in the same genus, but today ornithologists classify them into two distinct genera.

The scoters share many characteristics with the eiders, which also are large, hardy surf ducks, but the scoters are better known because of their wide distribution and more southerly range. The white-winged scoter is one of the commonest of our sea ducks and the most abundant of the scoters. Though found in the interior of North America and along the Atlantic and Pacific coasts its abundance is perhaps most appreciated in the New England states where wildfowlers have long enjoyed the virile sport of "coot" shooting.

There are violently conflicting opinions on the table appeal of the scoters. Some consider the dark flesh tough, strong, and fishy and unfit food for man. Other hunters, with most sensitive palates, declare that there is no finer table duck than a coot if it is correctly prepared. Broiling and roasting are among the best ways to cook it, but perhaps the most practiced method is stewing. The young of the American surf scoters are the most desirable.

Like many other duck species which breed in southerly latitudes, the white-winged scoter has decreased sharply in numbers. Civilization has advanced on their hereditary nesting grounds, and they also were affected by the droughts of the 1930's which destroyed parts of their breeding range. In spite of this recent population drop, these ducks still exist in great numbers.

**Identification.** (See color plate on p. 477.) The autumn and winter plumage of the adult drake is black, relieved by a small white patch beneath the eye and a distinctive white speculum. The wing marking makes it the easiest to identify among the scoters. At the base of the orange bill there is a raised knob. This combination of a brightly-colored bill and swelling at its base is a characteristic of the scoter group. The particular bill feathering of this duck, however, is an additional means of avoiding confusion among the species. The drake does not have the normal eclipse moult in June when the bird becomes flightless, but in early spring he has an incomplete plumage change of body and tail feathers but not wing feathers. This moult is equivalent in its incompleteness to the autumn moult in other duck species. In the fall, however, between August and September, there is a second, complete plumage moult which includes the renewal of wing feathers.

Both sexes look very much alike, but the mature female has a more brownish tone to her plumage. She lacks the male's consistent white eye patch, and sometimes has two light splotches on the side of her head. When the wings are flapped, the distinctive white wing marking is obvious.

The white-winged scoter is larger than the surf or American scoter. The female whitewing is about one pound smaller than the male and the weight for the species ranges from 2½ to 3 pounds. The length is between 20 and 21 inches and the wingspread averages 37 inches.

The whitewing is not a chattering duck, and normally it rests and feeds silently in large rafts on the water. It is more inclined to use its voice when in flight, emitting a low, repeated whistle which is bell-like in tone.

**Characteristics.** Each duck species usually has a habit peculiar to it. One of the whitewing's pastimes is an odd game which resembles the children's game of tag. The whitewing is considered a stupid duck by most hunters, for it has come readily to the crudest decoys and a high-flying flock can be whistled or shouted down without much skill involved. A wounded duck is nearly impossible to retrieve, however, for the scoters are thick-skinned, are powerful divers, and swim under water with great speed and stamina. At the bottom they sometimes clasp a weed with their bill in order to stay submerged, and hang on until drowned. When migrating, they habitually fly high, in irregular formations, but they are more commonly seen flying low over the water, as close as a few feet when looking for food. This large, heavily-built duck has more trouble getting off the water than any of the other sea ducks. Its take-off into the wind is labored, and, unless there is a stiff wind, the clumsy run is prolonged with excessive plattering even though the feet are used in an attempt to increase the speed. Once it has has slowly risen and leveled off, the flight is swift and direct.

**Breeding.** The whitewing is a true sea duck, but its habit of breeding so far inland is unusual among this oceanic group. Its nest is placed in a ground hollow near a small body of fresh water, and carefully hidden by shrubs. Normally, the nest is made of leaves, sticks, and other suitable material from near by, and is lined with down. The usual clutch is from 6 to 14 eggs, which are pink-coral in coloring. The immature male and female resemble each other in their first fall season, but are more grayish than the mature female. They are popularly known as "gray coots" to distinguish them from their elders. Their white wing patch separates them from the other juvenile scoters which they closely resemble. By the first winter the young whitewings begin to take on body plumage coloration distinctive of their sex, and by the second fall are nearly adult. Not until the third fall, however, are they fully matured.

**Feeding.** The feeding habits of these ducks are much the same as the eiders', and, like them, they take most of their food from the animal kingdom. They normally feed by day, diving to an average depth of 15 feet for the preferred mollusks (which make up 75% of their diet) and crustaceans. Insects and fishes also are a part of their diet, and the total amount of animal food is 94%. Sometimes the open valve of a mollusk claps shut on the tongue of a feeding duck; such a trapped bird usually drowns, chokes, or starves to death. The scoter's excessive feeding in planted beds of oysters, scallops, and clams has occasionally affected the commercial production of these mollusks, but such cases are isolated and unusual and are susceptible to control. Eelgrass and burr reed are the identifiable types of the 6% plant food consumed. When on the inland breeding range, however, the diet of the scoter con-

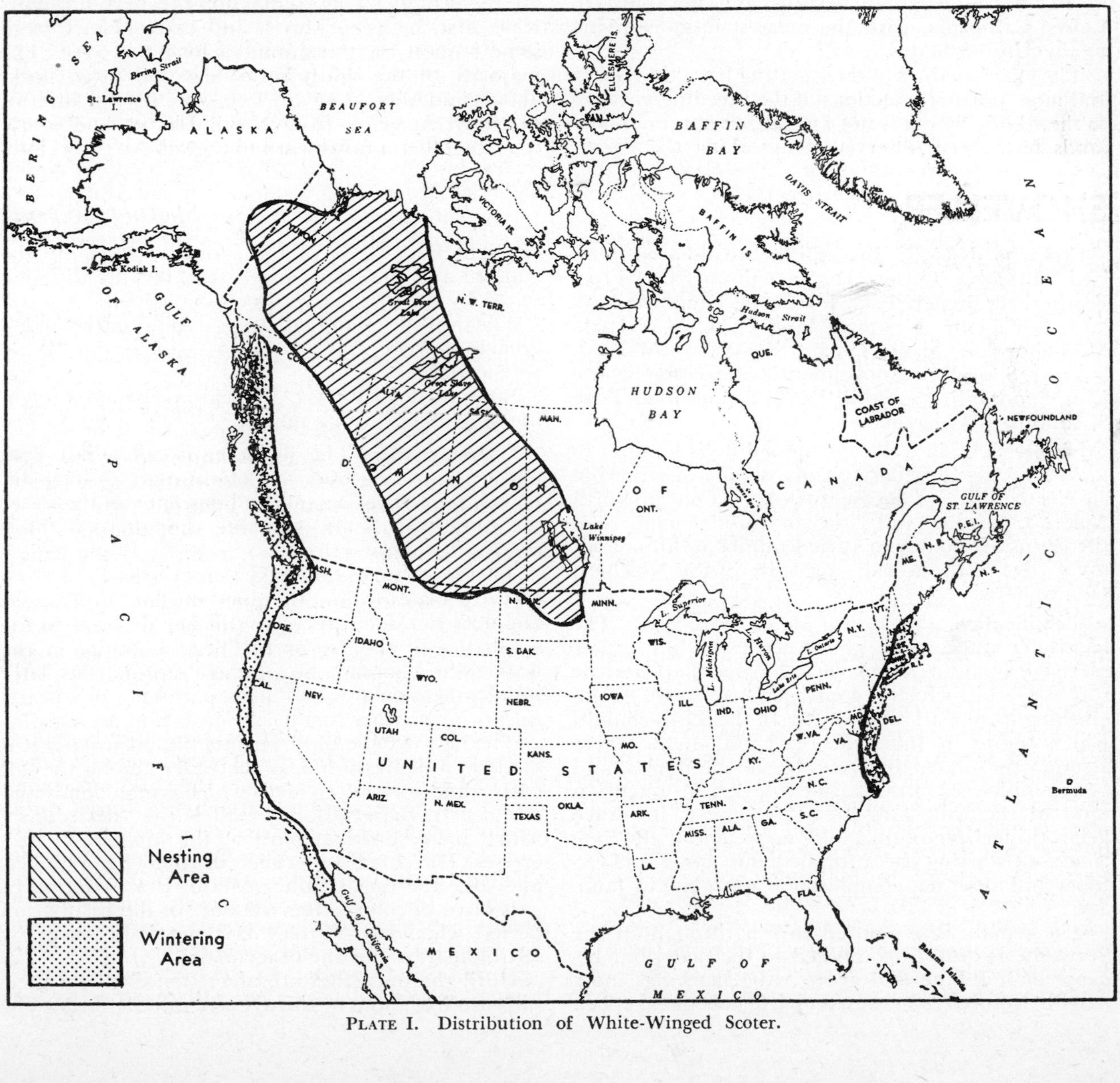


PLATE I. Distribution of White-Winged Scoter.

tains a higher percentage of vegetable matter than when the duck lives on the coastal wintering range.

**Range and Distribution.** The range of the whitewing is far-flung, reaching from the Arctic coast south to Lower California. The breeding grounds are extensive, and this duck is distributed with comparative evenness over it, but on the more confined wintering grounds along both coasts of North America there are more definite areas of abundance.

Though some flocks leave as early as August, the main migration southward is around October. The scoters are all late nesters, and the young of the whitewing presumably are not strong enough on the wing to make the long flight when the adult birds are ready to leave. Some authorities offer this reason for the adult drakes' taking off about a month ahead of the young and mature females. The wintering range of the Atlantic coast extends from New Brunswick to South Carolina, but the ducks are most plentiful near Long Island and Vineyard Sounds. The migration route to the eastern coast is almost a direct line from the nesting grounds of the interior to the coast of Labrador and then southward. The wintering grounds of the Pacific coast begin in the Aleutian Islands and go south to Lower California, with the greatest number living in the United States.

The exact method of their getting from the Alaska and more northerly sections of the breeding grounds to the Pacific flyway is not known for certain. Thousands have been observed flying along the Pacific coast, hugging the shore line, but occasionally crossing over land to shorten the trip. The large flocks usually fly at great altitude, but strong head winds and rough weather drive them down low to the water. Each species of scoter—white-winged, American, and surf—normally migrates in distinct flocks, but once the wintering grounds are reached they are often seen in large, mixed flocks. The ducks spend most of their time on the water, on the open sea or in more sheltered bays and estuaries where food is easier to find. A few winter around the Great Lakes.

As sometimes occurs among other diving ducks, which habitually dive and remain submerged when pursued, the whitewing is one of the few duck species which flies at night as well as by day when in migration. The night flying usually is done over land; they remaining over water during the daytime. In some cases, they make non-stop journeys from one range to another without eating on the way.

The migration from the coastal, salt-water range where the ducks live during the winter to the fresh-water nesting areas of the summer season is late for all the scoters. The young non-breeders normally leave first, between March and early May, though some remain for the summer along the coast. The majority of the adult birds leave in large flocks about mid-May. The duck breeds in the interior of North America, from North Dakota and southwestern Alberta northward to the sub-Arctic regions.

## SHOVELLER

*Spatula clypeata*

Common Names: Broadbill, Broad-Faced Mallard, Broady, Butler Duck, Cowan, Cow-Frog, Featherbed, French Teal, Jew Duck, Laughing Mallard, Loffel-ente, Mesquin, Mud Duck, Mud Lark, Mud-Shoveler, Mule Duck, Salt-Water Mallard, Scooper, Shovelbill, Shovelmouth, Shovelnose, Soup-Lips, Spoonbill, Spoonbill Duck, Spoonbilled Teal, Spoonbilled Widgeon.

**History.** The shoveller, or spoonbill, is familiar to most duck hunters because of its wide distribution and its readiness to decoy. It is conspicuous in North America, Europe, and Asia, and other members of the genus are found in varied numbers throughout every part of the world, especially in the Northern Hemisphere.

**Identification.** (See color plate on p. 471.) The handsome appearance of the drake in full winter plumage is marred somewhat by the characteristic shoveller's bill which is longer than its head, distinguishing it from all other ducks. In the eclipse moult, which begins in June, the black bill of the drake assumes the orange-brown color of the duck's, and he resembles her in plumage except for his retention most of the wing and breast feathers. The drake keeps this eclipse plumage for an exceptionally long time, not starting the autumn moult until mid-October and often not completing it until late in January.

The female is a mottled brown throughout the year. She is drab as compared to the male, but because of her blue and green wing markings more brightly colored than the average female duck. When in flight both sexes of the shoveller resemble the mallard and the blue-winged teal, but are differentiated by the distinctive spoon-shaped bill.

The shoveller is not talkative, except for the male's homely courtship calls and an occasional, low *"Woh-woh-woh."*

Both the duck and the drake are very small, weighing only a little over a pound.

**Characteristics.** The shoveller is not a fast flier, but a persevering one, and often migrates long distances. Its vertical ascents and descents on the water are equally swift and graceful, though its flight is awkward when startled.

The courtship of the drake is not the flashiest. Two or three males follow the duck on land and water. She does not delay very long in her reaction to the acrobatics in the air or the head bobbing in the water. She chooses one of these suitors, but later usually takes on a second mate, partaking in a peaceful polyandry rare among all birds and animals.

The nest may be built far inland, but usually it is made in a depression near the water among the tall grasses and concealing reeds which fringe ponds and sloughs. In the grass-lined nest is the "nest down" which increases in amount as the incubation progresses. The clutch is between six and 14 in number, and, like the eggs of the mallard, is a variation of pale-olive in color. After the start of the incubation period, which lasts 21 to 23 days, the drake leaves the setting hen to join the other males.

Until the ducklings are about ten days old their bills are like those of the average puddle duck. The bills grow rapidly, however, apparently more quickly than the body, and extend ahead of them in a top-heavy manner, giving them their distinctive spoon-billed feature when very young.

The ducklings look like the adult females until January when the drake begins to assume the adult male plumage. Though the second fall season finds the drake more colorful and mature, the bright winter plumage is not completed until the second spring. The young drakes mate the first year, usually being taken on as second husbands, but the females flock together, not pairing up until the second year.

**Feeding.** In most areas the shoveller is considered one of the least desirable table ducks because of its small size and its tangy flesh. Its diet has a high percentage of animal matter—34 per cent—which is mostly mollusks, crustaceans, insects, and fishes. The 66 per cent vegetable matter is composed of seeds, grasses, water lilies and other plant matter dug from the mud bottoms of marshes, ponds, and creeks. The bill of the shoveller is more highly developed than that of any other duck for scooping food off the water's surface or mud probing. The long, closely-placed "teeth" act as a sieve to let out the water and hold back whichever edibles the sensitive tongue has selected.

**Range and Distribution.** They range over a wide area on the North American continent, but are not

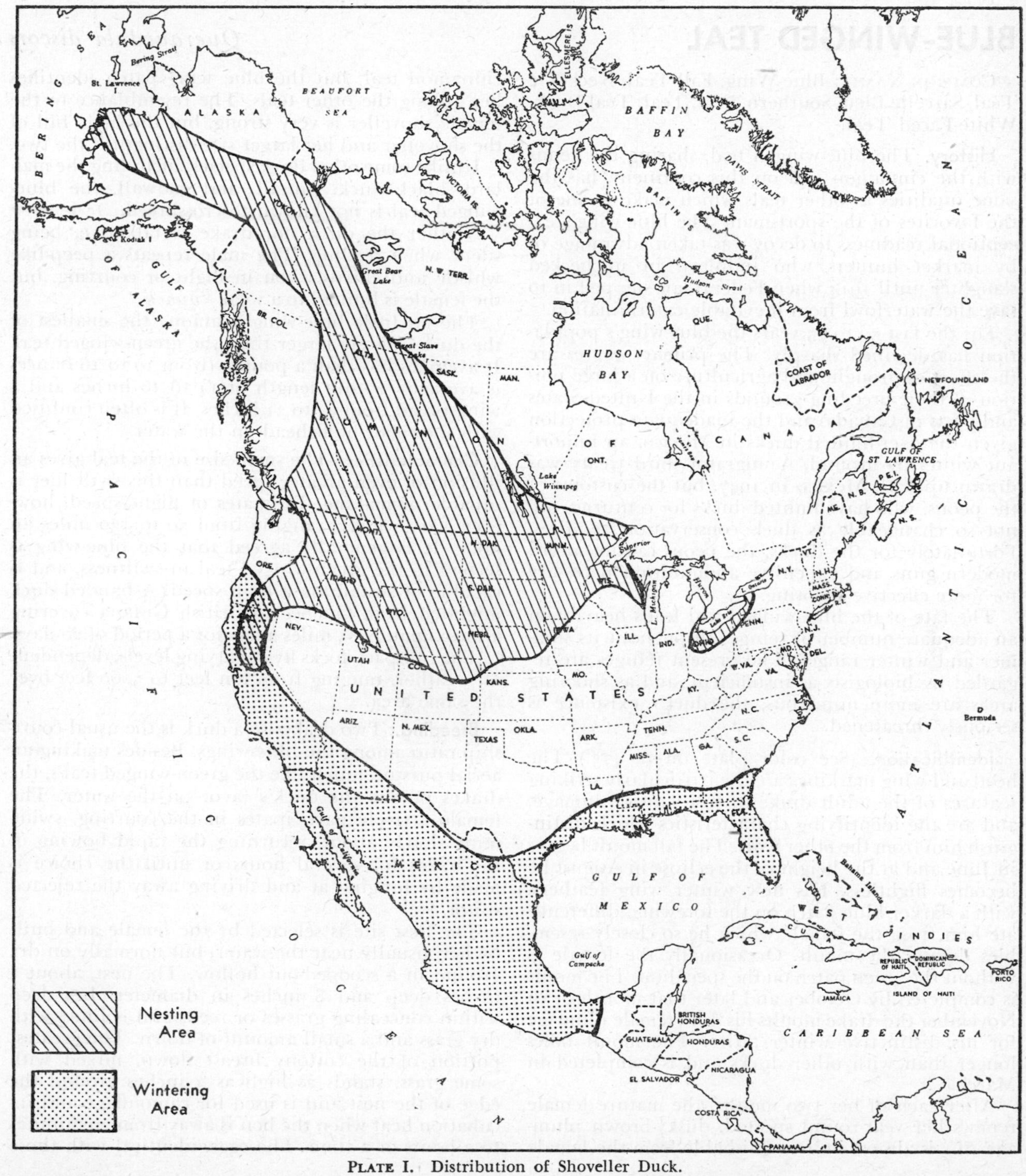


**PLATE I.** Distribution of Shoveller Duck.

abundant in any one region. They prefer the warmer climates, and are more numerous along the Pacific Coast states, through Mexico and the Southern states, than they are along the Atlantic seaboard; they are far from plentiful in the New England states.

They start an early winter migration from the great nesting grounds in Canada. They leave the northern breeding range with the frosts, completing their migration south by October. They characteristically fly in small groups along the Pacific flyway down through Oregon, California, Arizona, and Mexico, and also use the Mississippi flyway to the Gulf states.

The migration north to the extensive breeding grounds in north central United States, British Columbia, Alberta, Saskatchewan, Manitoba, and Alaska begins in spring. Unlike the winter migration, when they are often seen with the blue-winged teal, in the spring migration they travel alone, aloof from other ducks. Normally, they leave as early as March from Central America and southern Mexico to reach Canada and Alaska by May or June, but some of the shovellers stay within the Central and South Central states to breed. The percentage of pairs nesting on the Atlantic coast has decreased in the past 20 years.

## BLUE-WINGED TEAL

*Querquedula discors*

Common Names: Blue-Wing, Fall Teal, Neck-Tie Teal, Sarcelle Bleu, Southern Teal, Teal, Teal Duck, White-Faced Teal.

**History.** The blue-winged teal, sharing the genus with the cinnamon teal on this continent, has the same qualities as other teals which make it one of the favorites of the sportsman. The blue-wing's exceptional readiness to decoy was taken advantage of by market hunters who indulged in unchecked slaughter until 1914 when Federal law stepped in to save the waterfowl from inevitable extermination.

For the last 50 to 75 years the blue-wing's population has declined sharply. The primary causes are the effect of drought and agriculture on a large portion of their breeding grounds in the United States and parts of Canada, and the inadequate protection given the over-hunted ducks in Mexico, an important wintering ground. A migratory-bird treaty was drawn up with Mexico in 1937, but the customs of the peons, who have hunted ducks for centuries, are not so changeable as duck conservation requires. Fortunately for the ducks, the peons cannot afford modern guns and expensive ammunition necessary for more effective shooting.

The fate of the blue-winged teal leans heavily on an adequate number of refuges throughout its summer and winter ranges. The present refuges are regarded by biologists as insufficient, and as shooting areas are more numerous, the duck's existence is seriously threatened.

**Identification.** (See color plate on p. 473.) The head and wing markings are the particularly striking features of the adult drake in full winter plumage, and are the identifying characteristics which distinguish him from the other teals. The fall moult begins in June and at the height of the eclipse in August he becomes flightless. His new winter wing feathers, with a darker blue patch on the forewing, differentiate him from the female which he so closely resembles during the moult. Occasionally the female is without the green patch on the speculum. The moult is completed by October and later that month or in November the drake moults his dull, female plumage for his distinctive winter attire. The moult takes longer than with other ducks and is completed in March.

After each of her two moults, the mature female renews her year-round spotted, dusky-brown plumage. She is almost indistinguishable from the female cinnamon teal, but the blue wing patch identifies her among the other teals. The resemblance to the female shoveller is very strong, but the huge bill of the shoveller and her larger size distinguish the two.

Unlike some other duck species, including the mallard, black duck, pintail, and gadwall, the blue-winged teal is not known to crossbreed.

Neither the duck nor drake is talkative, being silent when feeding. The male repeats a peep-like whistle and chirps when in flight or courting, but the female is limited to a weak *"quack."*

The fat little blue-wing is among the smallest of the ducks, barely larger than the green-winged teal. It averages less than a pound (from 10 to 16 ounces is average) with a length of 14 to 16 inches and a wingspread from 24 to 31 inches. It is often confused with the small bufflehead on the water.

**Characteristics.** The small size of the teal gives an illusion of even greater speed than this swift flier is capable of making. Estimates of flight speed, however, vary widely, ranging from 50 to 130 miles an hour. It is generally agreed that the blue-wing is second to the green-winged teal in swiftness, and is capable of sustaining a high speed. A banded duck migrated from Quebec to British Guiana covering approximately 85 miles a day for a period of 28 days.

The compact flocks fly at varying levels, dependent on weather, ranging from ten feet to 5000 feet over the same area.

**Breeding.** Two drakes to a duck is the usual courtship ratio among the blue-wings. Besides making an aerial pursuit, much like the green-winged teal's, the drakes pursue the duck's favor on the water. The female actively participates in the courting, swimming slowly about, returning the rapid bowing of the males for several hours or until the choice is made by lunging at and driving away the rejected suitor.

The nest site is selected by the female and built by her, usually near the water, but normally on dry ground in a scooped-out hollow. The nest, about 5 inches deep and 8 inches in diameter, lies deep within concealing grasses or reeds and is lined with dry grass and a small amount of down. The greatest portion of the cottony breast down, mixed with some grass, stands as high as 3 inches around the edge of the nest and is used for camouflage and incubation heat when the hen is away from 20 minutes to 2 hours at a time. The eggs, identical with those of the green-winged teal, are usually deposited in the early morning. The clutch of ten to 12 varies from creamy-white to pale olive in coloring. The duck is most cautious in her approach to the nest, quietly sneaking along the ground to it, often from a distance of 200 yards, and rarely dropping down near it. While the egg-laying continues, the amorous drake waits for the duck near by at special spots, such as muskrat houses or logs in a marsh or pothole. Once the incubation is well on its way, however, the drake leaves. The incubation period of 21 to 23 days starts about 24 hours after the last egg is laid, and the duck shows increasing concern for her unhatched brood as the time for their arrival nears.

Twelve hours after being hatched the ducklings are in the water learning about swimming and feed-

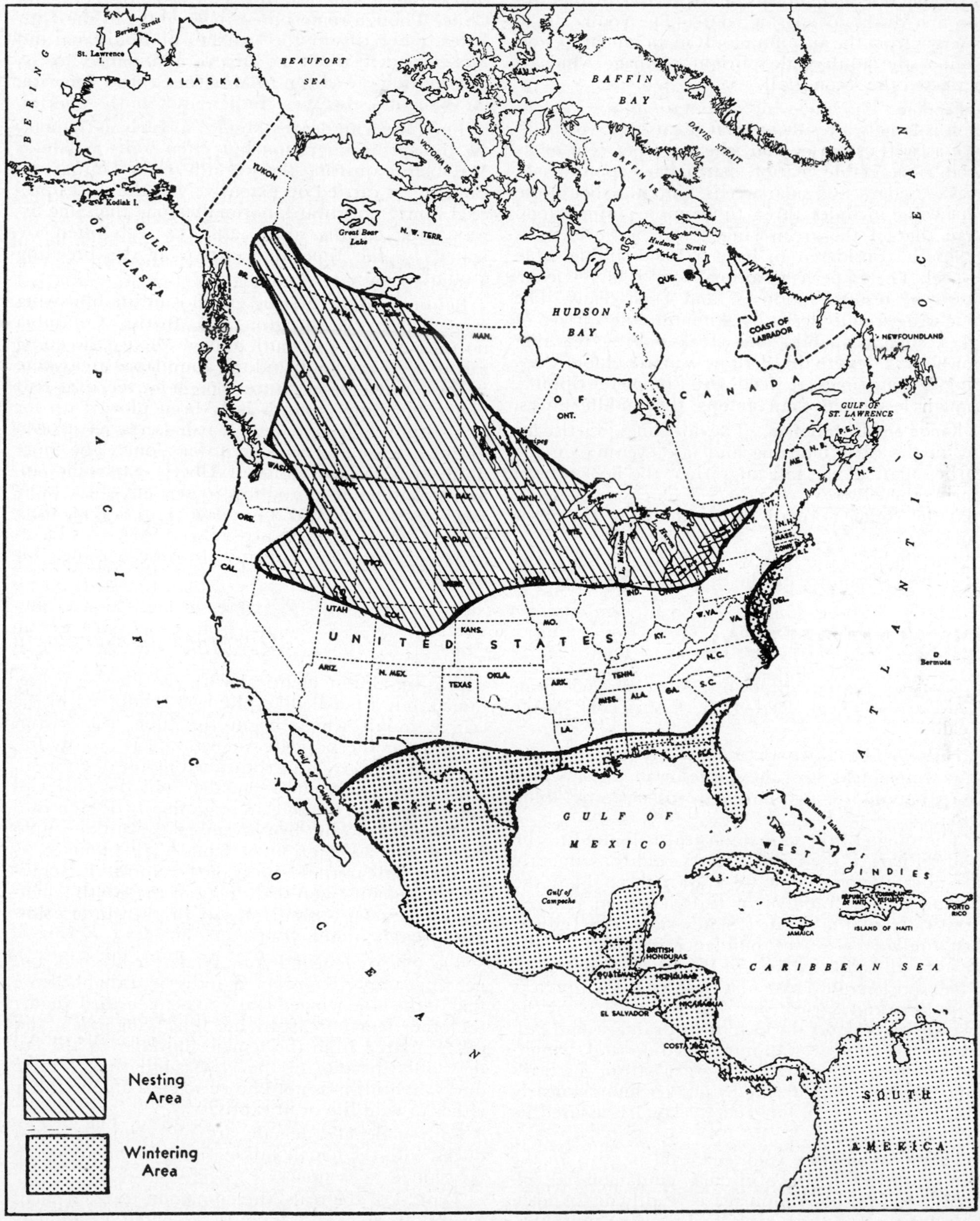


**PLATE I.** Distribution of Blue-Winged Teal.

ing and hiding expertly according to the warning notes of an ever-watchful mother. The blue-wing hen is among the most courageous and loving mothers, ready to give her life for her young. The ducklings, which look alike and resemble the adult female, are able to fly when about six weeks old. Their growth is necessarily rapid because they are late in arriving at the nesting grounds, and late in breeding, but, being lovers of warm climate, they are the first ducks to migrate south. The young drake emerges from the autumn moult in an immature version of the adult male's bright plumage which is perfected the second fall.

**Feeding.** The blue-wing's reputation for succulent flesh is largely a result of what it eats. It favors wild rice as well as barley and wheat; 71 per cent of its food is vegetable matter, particularly pondweeds, grasses, sedges, and smartweeds. Since the diet of the blue-wing includes three times more animal food than that of the green-winged teal, however, it is generally considered to have a less-desirable table appeal. The 29 per cent animal food is largely composed of insects, mollusks, and crustaceans. The blue-wing usually feeds by skimming the surface of lakes, sloughs, ponds, and creeks, or by reaching down neck length in shallow water, seldom "tipping." Sometimes it feeds by complete tipping, though less often than among the puddle ducks.

**Range and Distribution.** The ducklings practice flying in the early morning and late evening; in the earliest part of the fall migration, the flocks travel during these two extreme times. There is no evidence that the young normally fly on ahead of the adult ducks.

The flight of the blue-wings in August starts the migration season for all the ducks, and the majority of the teals set off on a trip farther south than any other North American duck. They fly at a leisurely rate, about 90 per cent using the Central and Mississippi Valley flyways, following the main waterways and arriving at the wintering grounds in the Southern states in six to eight weeks. The wintering range extends from Texas, Mexico, and the Gulf states far south through Central America to the northern section of South America, to Brazil, Ecuador, Peru, and Chile. Though some blue-wings winter in the Gulf states, especially in the marshes of Louisiana and Mississippi, it is not an area of abundance, for 95 per cent migrate down to Mexico, Central America, the Bahamas, the West Indies, and South America.

The blue-wing leaves Mexico as early as January for the spring migration but often waits as late as May before quitting the warmth of the Gulf states. Courting is carried on extensively as the ducks proceed slowly northward, normally along the same flyways used coming south, and the teals often are mated by the time they arrive at the breeding grounds.

Before 1900 the nesting grounds of the blue-wing ranged from Washington and British Columbia north to Alaska, and south to New Mexico, sweeping east to New England, and the abundance areas were in the United States. Since 1900, however, over half of the breeding grounds have been plowed up for agricultural purposes and marsh lands have been drained, 6,000,000 acres in Iowa alone. The more northerly Canadian range of Alberta, Saskatchewan, and Manitoba now produces 80 per cent of the blue-wing population, and the scattered areas remaining in the United States, mostly around the Great Lakes and northern New England, provide a refuge for the rest.

## CINNAMON TEAL

*Querquedula cyanoptera*

Common Names: Bluewing, Blue-Winged Teal, Red-Breasted Teal, Red Teal, River Teal, Silver Teal.

**History.** The cinnamon teal, closely related to the blue-winged teal, is of the species *cyanoptera,* which is a composite of two Greek words meaning "blue wing."

The range of the cinnamon teal is limited to the western part of the United States, and consequently the duck is not commonly known throughout the continent. The number of teals has been reduced drastically in the United States since the Indians first told of excessive abundance of ducks on the swamps and prairies west of the Rocky Mountains. The Louisiana Purchase first exposed the wild ducks to settlers and agriculture; but particularly in the last 50 years or so the extensive drainage and cultivation of the overlapping breeding and wintering grounds have destroyed a great part of the teal's range. Spring slaughtering by market hunters nearly obliterated the teal, but Federal law has assured its existence.

**Identification.** (See color plate on p. 473.) In the winter, the adult drake in dark, cinnamon-red colored head and body plumage is readily distinguishable from other duck species. The wing markings, which are almost identical with the duck's, are retained, but a female-like plumage is adopted in the eclipse moult which begins in June, leaves him flightless at the peak in August, and is rapidly followed by the second or continued moult of autumn. The moult begins in September and the pale cinnamon feathers of the eclipse gradually deepen into full winter coloring by November. Since the eclipse moult, and assumption of female-like plumage, is peculiar only to those ducks of the Northern Hemisphere, the cinnamon teal drake of the South American range retains his distinctive bright winter coloring throughout the year.

The mature female is a buffy, mottled-brown, and her appearance, considered indistinguishable from that of the blue-winged teal, can be identified among the other female teals by her blue wing-patch, and differentiated from the female shoveller by the latter's bill. In spite of the close similarity of these ducks, hybridism is not known to exist among them, either in wild life or in captivity.

Both male and female are exceptionally silent ducks, with the female talking more often, giving an occasional, weak quack.

Typical of the teals, the cinnamon teal is a small bird; both duck and drake weigh about a pound.

**Characteristics.** The characteristics of the cinnamon teal are similar to those of the blue-winged teal. Its table appeal, readiness to decoy (showing an unwary tameness), and vertical springing from the water into unorthodox, twisting flight are features common to the teals. Like its relations, the cinnamon teal is a fast flier, too, but is seldom found in a flock; more often just a duck and a drake fly together, or parents along with their young.

**Breeding.** The female is much courted during the season; six to eight jealous males fight for her attention, usually on the water. She chooses among them by bobbing her head in answer to the selected mate and together they scatter the interlopers.

The site and construction of the nest are dependent upon the efforts of the individual duck, but usually the nest is a carefully-scooped hollow, well-built on dry ground and near the water. Into the grass- and down-lined enclosure the duck drops a clutch of ten to 12 white buffish-colored eggs. Like many of the puddle ducks, the cinnamon teal drake sometimes stays with the duck during the incubation (about 23 days) and on into the hatching and rearing. He guards his young with belligerent care.

The ducklings are trained by the parents to heed their warning call. The young rapidly become skilled in the art of concealment and quick escape, camouflaging themselves rapidly and quietly in tall grasses and reeds, or, if caught in the clear, by diving and swimming under water. The ducklings resemble the female until the winter season when the young drake begins to assume mature color markings which are further developed by spring and fully adult in the second autumn.

**Feeding.** The cinnamon teal is exclusively a surface-feeder. The rough percentages of its diet are: 60% vegetable food (primarily sedges, pondweeds, smartweeds, and mallows), 20% animal food (largely insects and mollusks), and 20% miscellaneous food.

**Range and Distribution.** The long, narrow range of this duck, on the North American continent, extends from Canada southward to southern Mexico, chiefly west of the Rocky Mountains. Sometimes this teal is found east to the Prairie States, but rarely east of the Mississippi River. It has a second, separate range in southern South America, but there is no migration between the two areas 2000 miles apart. The wintering and breeding ranges overlap to a great degree, as shown on the distribution map, and the migrations in fall and spring are primarily a shifting of population, especially in southern California, southern Arizona, and northwestern Mexico. The flight southward toward Mexico takes place in September and October.

The southern breeding grounds, exclusively west of the Rockies, are unique among the ducks. It is the greatest section of teal abundance. The spring trip to the nesting grounds takes place in March and April.

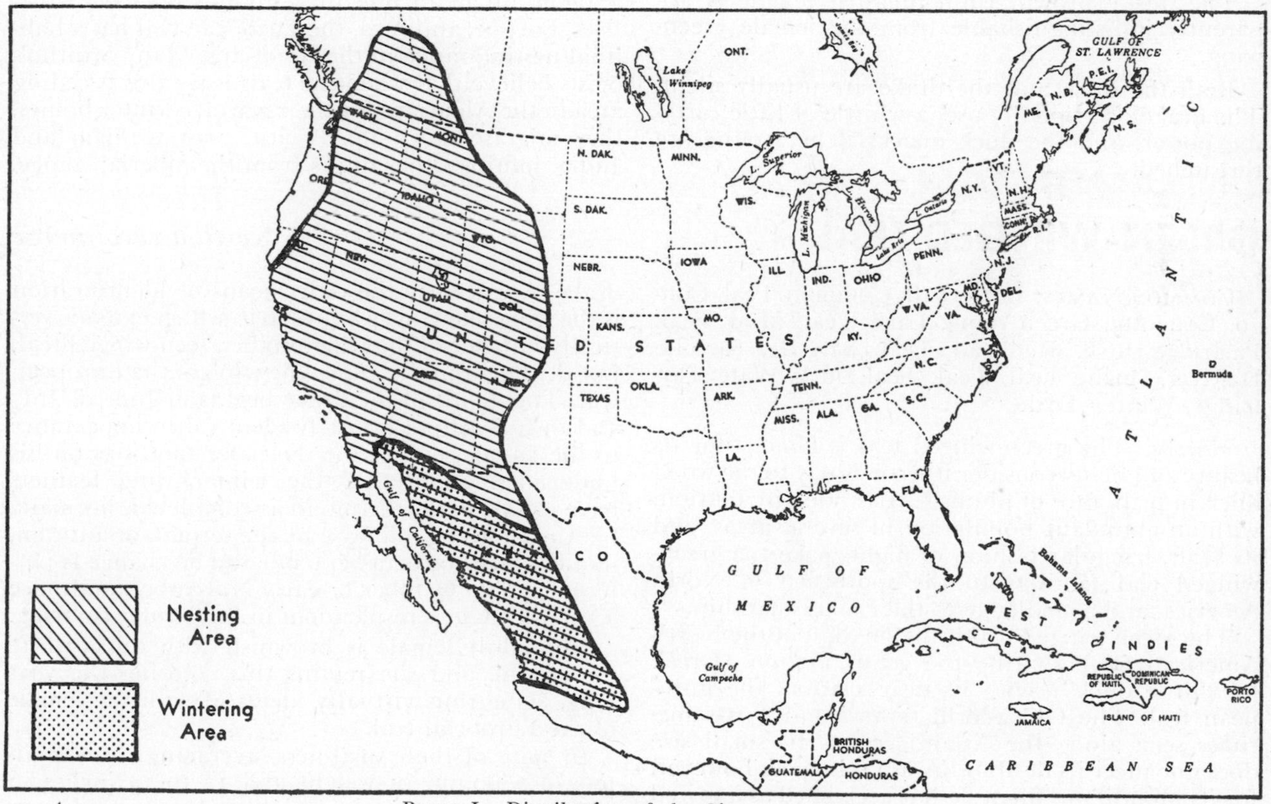


PLATE I. Distribution of the Cinnamon Teal.

## EUROPEAN TEAL

*Nettion crecca*

Common Names: This Old World species is not known to have any common names in North America.

**History.** The European teal is a common game bird in Europe and Asia but a comparatively rare duck on the North American continent. It is so similar in appearance and habits to the green-winged teal (the New World representative of the genus) that the two ducks are often confused. An important clarification of recent date concerned the breeding range. Until about 50 years ago, the European teal was not known to breed on this continent, but a study of the Aleutian breeding grounds identified many nesting ducks as being European teals. Because of repeated mix-ups in species identification, the visits of the European duck to this continent were thought to be less frequent than in actuality.

**Identification.** The adult male has the same bright winter plumage as the green-winged teal. The striking resemblance between the males of the two species is distinguishable primarily by a white body marking. The European teal has a white *horizontal* stripe *above* the wing, as contrasted to the green-wing's white *vertical* bar *in front of* the wing. The marking is readily observed under all normal conditions, whether the ducks are near or far, in flight or on the water. The eclipse moult is identical with that of the green-winged teal (See below).

The dusky brown, white-breasted female is apparently indistinguishable from the female greenwing.

Both the duck and the drake are usually silent. The drake occasionally uses a whistle of little carrying power, and the duck quacks if her young are threatened.

Like the other teals, the European teal is small. The average weight is nine ounces, with a length of about 19 inches and wingspread of 31 to 33 inches.

**Characteristics and Breeding.** The manner, altitude, and speed of the European teal's flight are the same as its green-winged kinsman's.

Much of the courtship takes place on the water. Several drakes circle the duck, twisting, turning, doubling back their necks and nearly rising from the water in an effort to show off as much of their handsome markings as possible. When the duck has made her selection, she either drives off the other suitors, or they voluntarily leave when they see their causes are lost.

The site and construction of the nest, the size of the clutch, egg coloring, and the incubation period are identical with those of the green-winged teal.

The behavior of the ducklings and their juvenile moults and plumage developments are the same as those of the green-winged teal.

**Feeding.** The European teal has the same feeding habits as the green-winged teal, with a like percentage of vegetable matter and animal food, qualifying as a top table delicacy.

**Range and Distribution.** This teal is generally considered a visitor, with a liking for the northern Atlantic coast, from North Carolina to Greenland. They are found also along the Pacific coast.

Beside its main breeding grounds on the British Isles, Europe, and Asia, the European teal has a habitual nesting range in the Aleutians. Many ornithologists believe that when the teals leave this breeding area in the Aleutians for their warmer winter homes, they migrate down the Asiatic coast to Siam and India, joining other ducks from the Siberian range.

## GREEN-WINGED TEAL

*Nettion carolinense*

Common Names: Butterball, Common Teal, Congo, Congotte, Green-Wing, Lake Teal, Mud Teal, Partridge-Duck, Redhead Teal, Sarcelle, Sarcelle D'Hiver, Spring Teal, Teal, Teal Duck, Water-Partridge, Winter Teal.

**History.** The green-winged teal is famous for its beauty and many consider it second only to the wood duck in brilliance of plumage. Its wide distribution, with an abundant population in several areas, and its swift, irregular fashion of flight make the green-winged teal familiar to the sportsmen of North America, and a challenge to their marksmanship.

The green-winged teal is the smallest of the North American fowl, sharing the genus *nettion* (Greek for "little duck") with its near-relation, the European teal. The Old World representative is sometimes seen along the Atlantic coast. Its small size does not affect its desirability as table food, however, for its plump, succulent flesh is acclaimed as a prized dish by the gourmet.

**Identification.** (See color plate on p. 473.) The bright winter plumage of the adult male is nearly indistinguishable from that of the European teal drake. Apparently the only means of identification is the wing marking, a white strip which extends vertically *in front of* the wing on the green-winged teal, but lies horizontally *above* the wing of the European teal. The moult of the drake begins in June or July and in full eclipse is nearly identical in appearance to the female, except for the paler spottings on his undersides. Soon after the winter wing feathers have grown back, the moult is completed, normally by August, to be followed by the second, or autumn, moult which starts in September. The change is perfected in late October or early November, and once again the male is resplendent in full winter coloring.

The adult female is brownish with dusky-white undersides, and she retains this coloring the year long, being thus virtually identical with the female of the European teal.

In spite of their smallness, averaging three-quarters of a pound in weight and 12 to 15 inches in length, size is an undependable identifying factor, since the green-winged teal resembles the other teals and other smaller ducks in size. Color is a more reliable means.

The drake has a fair range of musical notes, calling

with whistles and chirps, and courting with a *"pheep pheep."* The duck's voice is largely confined to a high quack.

**Characteristics.** This sturdy little teal ranks as one of the swiftest fliers. It is capable of springing neatly, rapidly, and vertically from land or water, speeding off into an erratic, unpredictable flight, typical of all the teals. Their great speed, estimated to be as much as 60 miles per hour, often enables them to elude the hunter, but their normal manner of flying in large tight flocks, and their habit of "bunching" when startled, often nets the sportsman several ducks to a shot.

**Breeding.** The drakes do not show the competitive sense common to most other duck species. Usually two males woo a female on the water, and the performance is like a chorus routine. Their movements are identical and precisely timed as they circle, bob, and call softly in unison until the duck selects one of them.

The nest, lined with grasses, weeds, leaves, and breast down, is built in a slight hollow on dry ground. It is found both at the edge of ponds or lakes and far from water, among bushes and willow trees. The typical clutch of ten to 12 is a variation of pale-olive buff in color and resembles that of the blue-winged teal. The male leaves as soon as the eggs are laid, and the duck begins the incubation which lasts from 21 to 23 days.

The ducklings are brought up carefully by the hen, but it is believed the enemies are many, since the clutch is large but the brood is small. The young

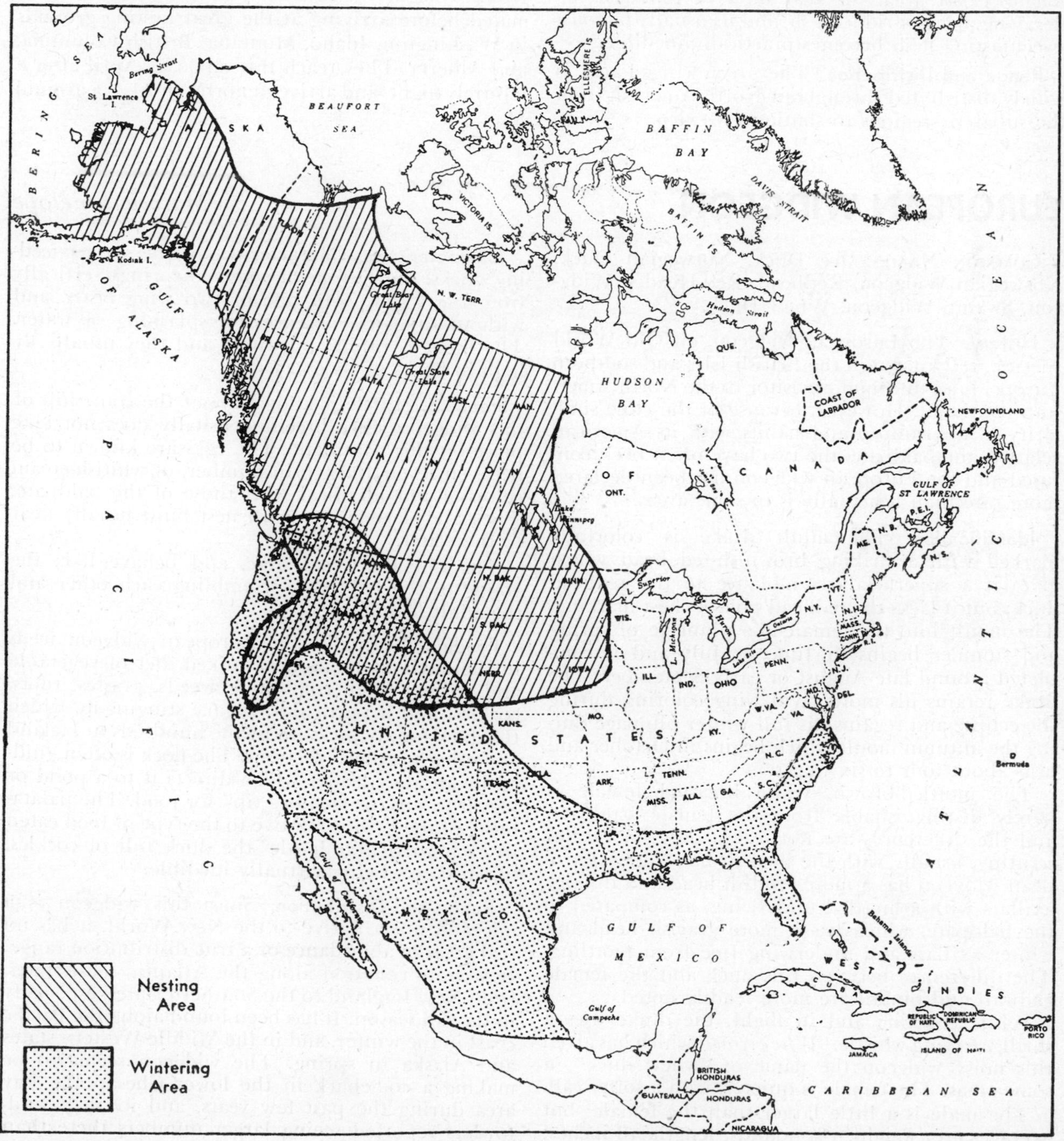


**PLATE I.** Distribution of Green-Winged Teal.

duplicate each other in plumage, and resemble the adult female until September when the drake shows his early maturity. Except for the wing markings, which are completed in December, full winter plumage is assumed by October.

**Feeding.** The teal is primarily a surface feeder, often tipping by kicking its feet for steadiness in so upright a position, while it probes the mud bottom. Occasionally, it dives for food or submerges to escape pursuit, but more often it is seen walking well inland to the rich rice, corn, and wheat fields. The greatest portion of its diet is vegetable (91 per cent), mostly sedges, pondweeds, grasses, and smartweeds, but it also feeds on animal food (9 per cent), usually insects and mollusks. Along the salmon rivers of the Pacific Coast area, the teal shows a fondness for decaying, maggot-ridden fish, and its usually famous, sweet-tasting flesh becomes practically inedible.

**Range and Distribution.** The green-winged teal is widely distributed throughout North America, from the subarctic regions to southern Mexico.

The journey to the south begins with the first cold frosts of fall, but the main migration is later; the majority wait for real winter weather of ice and snow before leaving with the last of the puddle duck migrants. The wintering grounds and breeding grounds overlap in some areas, and teals may be found wintering in British Columbia and Alberta as well as other northerly sections. The main wintering grounds, however, are in the Gulf states and Mexico. The distribution map shows the inclusive winter range extending from the Pacific coast states and Lower California west to Kansas and south to the Gulf states, then north along the Atlantic coast in diminishing numbers.

The early northward migration to the breeding grounds begins in February. Most of the teals are mated before arriving at the great nesting grounds in Washington, Idaho, Montana, British Columbia, and Alberta. They reach this range by April after a leisurely flight, and arrive in northern Alaska around May.

## EUROPEAN WIDGEON

*Mareca penelope*

COMMON NAMES: Ice Duck, Norwegian Duck, Norwegian Widgeon, Redhead, Red-Headed Widgeon, Swamp Widgeon, Whew Duck.

**History.** The European widgeon, an Old World species, well known in the British Isles and southern Europe, is an uncommon visitor to the North American continent. However, because of the close similarity in appearance and habits with its American relative, the baldpate, the two have often been confused and the European widgeon has been declared more rare than it actually is in some areas.

**Identification.** The adult drake is colorfully marked with a striking brownish-red head which gives it a superficial resemblance to the redhead duck; but it lacks the redhead's black chest marking. The moult into the female-like plumage of spring and summer begins in June or July and is completed around late August or early September. The drake retains his more vivid wing coloring during the eclipse and regains his full winter plumage during the autumn moult which begins in October and lasts about four to six weeks.

The mottled-brown, white breasted female is barely distinguishable from the female baldpate, and the differences are noticeable only on careful scrutiny, usually with the bird in hand. The European widgeon has a more reddish head and duskier axillars with a mottled underwing, as compared to the baldpate, which has a more grayish head and whiter axillars and underwing free from mottling. The differences between this duck and the female gadwall and pintail are more readily noted.

While courting and in flight, the drake uses a shrill, carrying whistle, *"Whe'e-you,"* which has given this noisy widgeon the name of "whew duck" in some areas. The female is quieter, with a softer call.

The male is a little larger than the female; but averages are: weight, 1½ pounds; length, 18 inches; and wing spread, 31 inches.

**Characteristics.** Characteristic of the surface-feeding ducks, the European widgeon springs vertically from the water, with one or two wing beats, and without dragging or excessive splashing of water. The flight is rapid and direct and they usually fly high in flocks of about 25.

**Breeding.** Little is known about the courtship of this widgeon since breeding usually does not take place on this continent. The eggs are known to be between seven and ten in number, of whitish-cream coloring and identical with those of the baldpate. They are placed in a small nest built usually near to the water.

The ducklings look like, and behave like, the young of the baldpate, resembling each other and the adult female.

**Feeding.** Normally, the European widgeon feeds in the daylight hours on a mixed diet of vegetable and animal food, combining weeds, grasses, roots, cockles, and a particular, sugary stinging-fly which the duck fondly picks up by the hundreds in Iceland and other northerly sections. The flock is often guided by an alert leader which directs it to a pond or marsh to surface feed or "tip" for food. The palatability of the flesh is relative to the type of food eaten in each particular locale—the duck full of cockles, for instance, being virtually inedible.

**Range and Distribution.** Since this widgeon is a migrant, not a native to the New World, it has no real areas of abundance or a true distribution range. It is more common along the Atlantic coast states, from New England to the Southern states, especially in the fall season. It has been found along the Pacific coast in the winter, and in the Middle Western states and Alaska in spring. The widgeon seems to be making a comeback in the lower Chesapeake Bay area during the past few years, and in 1947 wildfowlers reported seeing larger numbers there than for many years.

## WOOD DUCK *Aix sponsa*

Common Names: Acorn Duck, Black, Branchier, The Bride, Canard du Bois, Canard d'Eté, Crested Wood Duck, Gray Duck, Plumer, Squealer, Summer Duck, Swamp Duck, Tree Duck, Widgeon, Wood Duck, Wood Widgeon, Woody.

**History.** The wood duck, generally considered the most beautifully plumaged of any North American duck, is named from the Greek (*aix*) and Latin (*sponsa*), a combination of words meaning, roughly translated, a waterfowl in wedding dress. The buffle-head and golden-eye, prairie ducks which also nest in trees, are also called wood duck.

The wood duck, found exclusively on this continent, was formerly very abundant, but, being a tender table bird, it was killed in great numbers by market hunters and was extensively sought by milliners for its valuable, iridescent plumage. The greatest threat to its survival, however, was the destruction of a large part of its range. The first Swamp Act of 1849 started the drainage of about 70,000,000 acres of water and marsh regions in this country, and the wood duck fed in these acres. Its natural habitat was cut down for lumber, and it was easily accessible to near-by civilization. In 1918, legislation in Canada and the United States saved this duck from extermination by declaring a closed season. This law was relaxed somewhat in 1941, allowing a limit of one duck in some states where the wood duck had shown signs of actively reviving its population status. In Canada, however, since the duck is rare there, the law is rigidly maintained.

**Identification.** (See color plate on p. 472.) Many naturalists find words inadequate to describe the adult drake in resplendent winter plumage. The color range is large and the combination and contrasts of shades are a work of art, making the drake readily distinguishable from other ducks. Much of his brilliance is lost during the eclipse moult which starts in June or July. At the height of the eclipse in August the drake resembles the duck, which is distinguishable by the white patch circling her eye, but retains his white face and neck markings and red and white bill. He is more similar to the juvenile male. After the flightless period, the full winter wing is renewed. The autumn moult is rapid, starting in August or September and generally completed by early October when the drake is in radiant dress again.

Though the female is dull compared to the male, she is more strikingly marked than most female ducks. She resembles the female baldpate, European widgeon, and teal, but her showy wings and distinctive crest identify her. The duck is also confused with the female gadwall, especially on the water when the characteristic white speculum of that species is not obvious.

Both the duck and drake are talkative while feeding, repeating a series of squealing and clucking

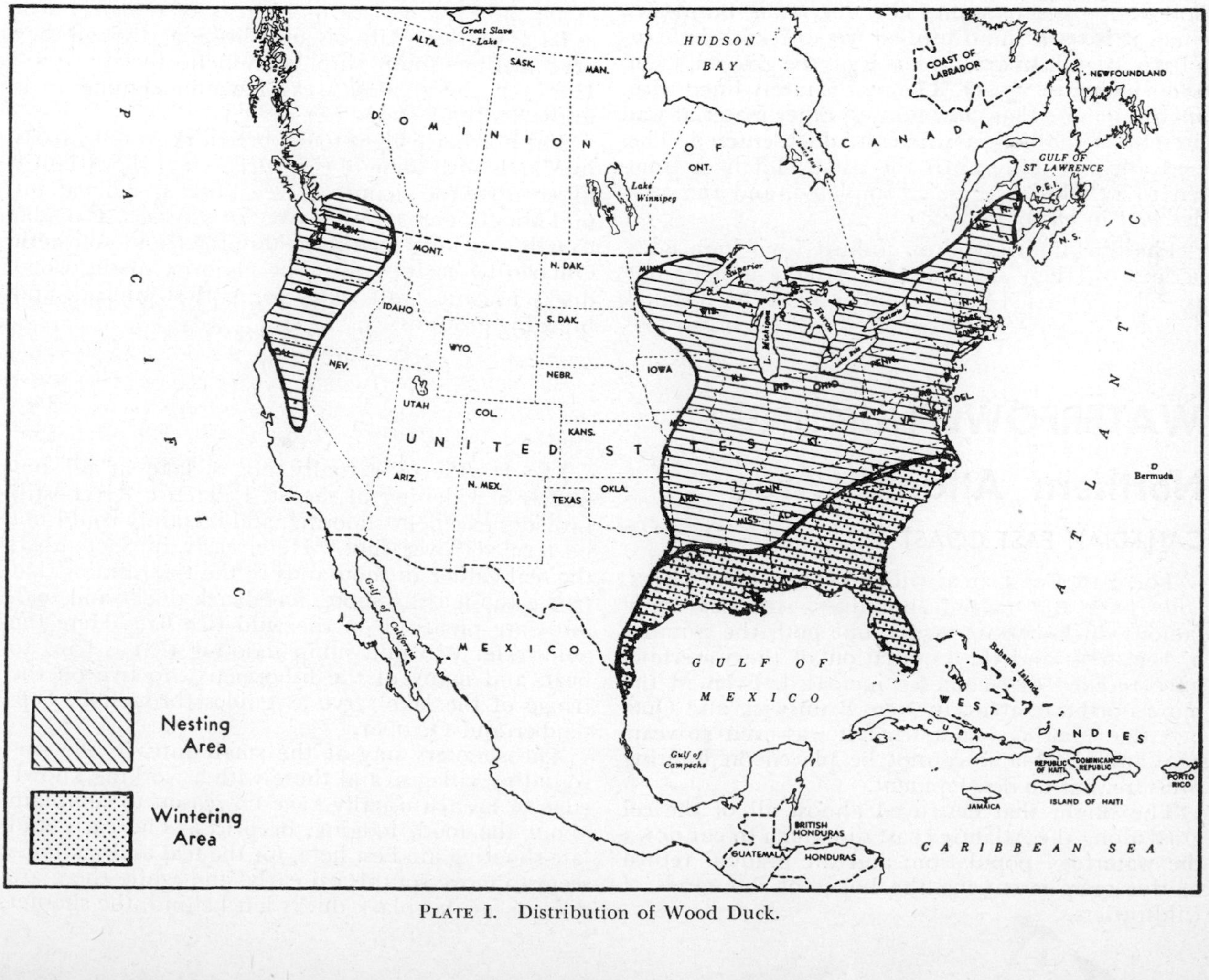


Plate I. Distribution of Wood Duck.

noises, and the hen and ducklings peep back and forth to each other. The male has a penetrating mellow whistle and, when frightened, prolongs a *"Jeeeee,"* while the female utters a shrill *"Whoo-eek"* when alarmed.

The wood duck is small but averages larger than the teals, weighing from one to 1½ pounds with a length usually between 17 and 20½ inches. It has a wingspread of about 29 inches.

**Characteristics.** Though it is comparatively tame, coming readily to decoy, the wood duck sits alertly on the water, ready to spring into swift and steady flight. He is an expert at twisting gracefully through the branches of his habitat.

The courtship of the wood duck normally takes place on the water, usually on an inland pool where the whole flock is gathered. The males are anxious in their rivalry for a mate and occasionally indulge in a brief, bloodless fight. The duck encourages one of the drakes without definitely committing herself. She gracefully returns his bows, admires his lifted crest, answers his guttural calls, and caresses him with her bill. Finally, she makes her choice known, and after mating, the pair fly off together to look for a suitable nesting site.

**Breeding.** Unique among puddle ducks, the wood duck normally nests in trees. The site is selected by the female, though the male often comes along. She looks for a roomy cavity even though she is capable of entering a hole 4 inches in diameter. By preference, the nest is placed in the natural or rotten hollow of a tree or stump near the water, but sometimes it is built in an unused woodpecker's hole or a barn inland. In any case, it is off the ground, from a few inches to 50 feet. The nest is rarely lined with anything more than down unless other material was present in the hollow when the duck entered. The eggs are laid daily until the usual clutch of from ten to 15 whitish eggs is completed, and they are hatched in 28 to 30 days.

The ducklings can drop unhurt from high nests because of their soft down and light weight, but are seldom carried by the mother as has been stated by some writers. The juvenile drake begins to lose his resemblance to both the young and adult female in September and October and by November his markings are complete. Not until the second spring, however, does his plumage have the deep radiance of the adult drake.

**Feeding.** The feeding habits of the wood duck include the ease and nimbleness with which it lives in all parts of its wooded habitat, whether running or diving or moving gracefully among and along stretching tree branches. This duck feeds largely on land, along woodland streams and ponds, but also looks to the marshes and streams for rice and insects and water plants. The strong gizzard of this duck crushes and grinds the hardest-shelled nuts with particular ease, and acorns, beechnuts, chestnuts, and pecan nuts are among its food preferences. Ninety per cent of its diet is vegetable matter—duckweeds, cypress cones, sedges, grasses, pondweeds, etc.—and the other ten per cent is animal food—dragon flies, bugs, beetles, and grasshoppers.

**Range and Distribution.** This duck's main range is in the United States, east of the Mississippi River to the Atlantic coast. A second, smaller concentration extends from southern Canada along the Pacific coast states to southern California. The summer and breeding ranges overlap extensively, and seasonal migrations are often difficult to follow. Cross-hatching on the distribution map designates these areas.

In the early fall, around September or early October, some of the warmth-loving ducks travel from a more northern summering range, going south along the eastern coast of Mexico, or remain north as far as southern Illinois and Virginia (though they are sometimes found through more northerly states). However, the greatest area of winter abundance is in the Southern states.

The northerly flight to the breeding grounds starts in March with some of the ducks using the Atlantic flyway up to the vicinity of New York, arriving about mid-March, and crossing over to southern Canada, usually reaching southern Manitoba and southern Ontario by early April. The majority of the wood ducks use the Gulf states for both wintering and breeding grounds.

# WATERFOWL HUNTING

## Northern Atlantic Area

### CANADIAN EAST COAST

The East Coast area, with its many great rivers, wide bays and ragged shorelines, still has many famous duck-shooting areas, but both the number of the areas and the population of the waterfowl have receded as commerce increased. Even in the more northerly areas, in New Brunswick and Quebec, the shooting is not what it was even 20 years ago, and the blame cannot be placed on hunting pressure, but on development.

The blight that destroyed almost all of the eel grass along the Atlantic coast did much to cut down the waterfowl population, and the gradual return of this grass is stirring the hopes of thousands of wildfowlers.

Lac St. Pierre—actually not a lake at all but merely a widening of the St. Lawrence River—still provides excellent shooting, and certainly could not be termed "over shot." Here, early in September, the teal gather in thousands in the tidal drains that fringe the marshy shore, and black ducks and mallards are plentiful on the wild rice flats. Here the wildfowler will find jump shooting that is hard to beat, and many of the fishermen who live on the fringe of the lake serve as guides throughout September and October.

The shooters stay at the small inns in the surrounding villages, and those with a working knowledge of French usually have no reason to complain about the food, lodging, or prices. The early and late shooting are best here, for the teal and mallards seem to move southward early, and while there are quite a few fat black ducks left behind, the shooter

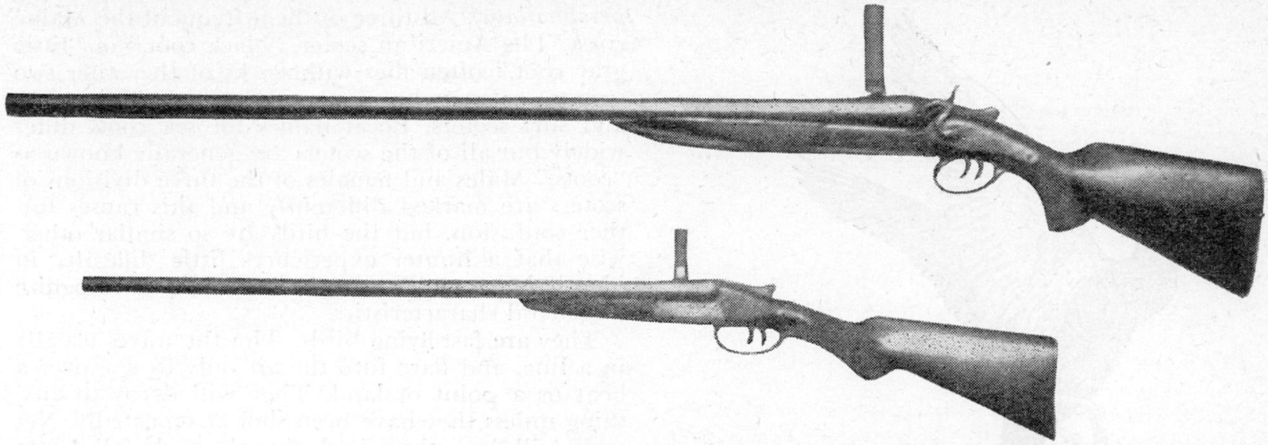

PLATE I. The Old and the New—the old 4-gauge (upper) and the modern 12-gauge duck gun. The market hunter took a heavy toll with the big gun.

must wait for cold weather to bring the great flights of diving ducks. The divers are primarily canvasbacks and scaup, but some years find redheads quite plentiful.

Early in the season, the shooting is regulated by the tides. The normal procedure is to get an hour or two of early morning shooting from one of the brush blinds. These are merely stakes, laced with cedar and spruce, and the only reason they are at all effective probably is that they are permanent structures and the local birds are accustomed to them. After an hour or two in the blind, the average guide suggests poling the rice flats for jump shooting. This is where the full-choked gun comes in handy, for the birds are rather wild, and normally get up about 30 yards or more ahead of the boat. When the tide drops too low for the boat to be poled, the shooter returns to the blind for the late afternoon shooting.

Many of the really ardent American shooters who make this trip every year bring their own decoys, and some of those who come for the diving duck shooting late in the season bring their own duckboats. The local duckboat is a cross between a Cape Cod dory and a woodbox, and those who want really good shooting bring a scooter or a sneakbox with them. With this boat they can rig out well off shore, and improve their shooting about 100 per cent. The local decoys must be seen to be believed, and the majority of them bear more resemblance to a dying seagull than to any member of the duck family. The guides are enthusiastic, however, and do their best to provide the visitors with the best shooting possible.

Moving southward to the St. John River valley, in New Brunswick, offers almost similar shooting conditions, but this type of sport appeals to many duck hunters who like to do some of the work themselves. As on the St. Lawrence, the local shooters burn up all of their ammunition during the first few days of the season. After that they go back to work and leave most of the shooting to visitors from the other side of the line. No Yankee would be advised to try the shooting at many of the good areas until the third day of the season, for the primary purpose of many of the local duck hunters seems to be to shoot their guns as often as possible, regardless of the range. They blaze away at a duck that is 20 yards distant with no more enthusiasm than that with which they greet one that is 200 yards from the gun. The second day finds the shooting more desultory, and by the third day the waterfowl have partially calmed down.

The average guide along the St. John might better be described as a porter. He will carry the shells, the lunch, and any other equipment, and he will handle the boat. Any definite program is left in the hands of the shooter, and the man who comes prepared with his own rig of decoys and a duckboat on a trailer will unquestionably find better sport.

Black ducks are the major incentive, and they are fat and tender. During the early part of the season the teal are reasonably plentiful, and later there are whistlers and scaup with an occasional redhead. The blind usually is a makeshift affair on a point or an island, although there are a few stake and brush blinds. Many shooters bring a boat of their own that can be grassed up to serve as a floating blind.

The river threads its way through broad marshes on part of its journey, and these marshes are the best shooting areas. During a year waterfowl are plentiful the shooting on these marshes is unexcelled, and even during a poor year it is fair so far as the black duck is concerned. Later in the season the big red-legs appear, and the broadbill show up in great flights.

## MAINE COAST

Waterfowl shooting is practiced off the Maine seacoast from Kittery on the New Hampshire line to Calais on the border of New Brunswick. From an ocean shooter's viewpoint, two species of birds, with their sub-species, are more important than any others, simply because these species are more abundant than the mallard, black duck, and other puddle ducks which "come" only occasionally to an ocean set of decoys. The abundant seafowl are eiders and scoters, with the latter having precedence in southeastern Maine.

The first part of this section, therefore, will concern itself with these sea ducks. A later section will consider bay shooting and the birds that use Maine's

PLATE II. Black Ducks Jumping.

coastal bays most frequently. Sea coots, or scoters, visit the bays but in smaller numbers than in the heavy flights seen offshore, while eiders seem to prefer the vicinity of the ocean ledges.

Maine has a direct coast line of 250 miles, so notched with bays and inlets that the tidal line measures more than 2400 miles. Equal in length to one-half the Atlantic coast line of the United States, the Maine shore provides a continuous and natural flyway for hundreds of thousands of scoters. The eiders are found from Calais to Boothbay Harbor in appreciable numbers, although a few of them visit the Atlantic coast as far south as Massachusetts, where gunners call them sea ducks. In the Cape Porpoise section, hunters know them as "ducks" and "drakes."

One spot particularly favored by eiders is Egg Rock off Winter Harbor. Flanders Bay at Sorrento, in the same section, affords scoter shooting that rivals the offshore gunning for this latter species.

There are three scoters: the common scoter *(Oidemia americana),* the white-winged scoter *(Melanitta deglandi),* and the surf scoter *(Melanitta perspicillata).* All three of them frequent the Maine coast. The American scoter, "black coot," or "little gray coot," often flies with flocks of the other two scoters, or may be seen without the white-wings and surf scoters. Local names for sea coots differ widely but all of the scoters are generally known as "coots." Males and females of the three divisions of scoters are marked differently and this causes further confusion, but the birds are so similar otherwise that a hunter experiences little difficulty in identifying a scoter once he has come to recognize its general characteristics.

They are fast-flying birds, skim the waves usually in a line, and flare into the air only to rise over a boat or a point of land. They will decoy to anything unless they have been shot at repeatedly. Net corks will draw them in during the early fall. Later on, they may become more wary, but a hunter can sit upright without motion in a dory or gunning float with his decoys 20 yards astern and the scoters will "toll" all around his head. There are days when they may be more cautious, but if conditions are right it is customary to allow the birds to pass when they are flying wide and to sit quietly, knowing that they will turn and come dropping right back into the set. Some old-time hunters actually wait for them to alight. Frequently they will draw together after hitting the water and these old-timers "give them a barrel of fine shot" (6's or 7½'s) and "let them have the other barrel when they jump." (In a double, the second tube usually is full choked and the shot size would be No. 4 or 5.)

There are certain days when scoters fly best. Maine hunters seem to feel that a southerly wind will keep them on the move. When the wind is off the land shooting seems to be poorest. Blowing toward shore the wind appears to drive the scoters in where they can see a set of decoys, but if it blows off-shore it seems to take the birds off with it and they skirt by well out of range, paying scant attention to a set.

Experienced seafowlers pick a headland that juts out into the ocean, particularly if there is a bay near by. If several "cooters" are to hunt, boats form a line straight out from the headland and make their sets about 100 yards apart. By this strategy, scoters are enticed to fly from one set of decoys to the next, instead of passing between the boats and continuing on their way.

As many as a dozen or 15 boats may form a line of this kind, although the formation idea seems to run out as one progresses east from Kennebunk or Cape Porpoise. Down-Easters are prone to hunt singly to a large degree.

In southeastern Maine the average coot hunter has a lap-streak gunning float with a raised platform in the bottom that is used as a seat. This seat has a back rest that may be lowered to permit the shooter to duck down when a flock of scoters is sighted. There is a gun rack on the side of the float. Not to be confused with sneak floats used in bays, these sea-type gunning floats are from 14 to 16 feet long but are low and light. Long oars are nicely balanced and are secured by means of a ring around each oar which holds an iron pin that in turn fits into an iron receiver on the rail. Using this type of float, the decoys are anchored; the shooter sits to windward in his float and keeps it a little more than a gunshot away from his tollers. When he sights birds winging his way, he drops his oars, picks up his gun and ducks as low as possible into the float. With his head raised just high enough to watch his decoys, he does not move until he is all set to shoot. Meanwhile, the wind has moved his float down toward his decoys and he arrives within close shooting distance at the approximate time the birds drop into his set. It is surprising how closely experienced hunters can estimate these factors.

A few of the hunters in southeastern Maine and most of them farther east use dories in preference to floats. Such hunters usually anchor their dories to a lobster-pot buoy or drop a small anchor with a buoy attached. The decoys may be attached by a long line to the same buoy. When birds scale in these shooters fire away. If they drop any coots they cast off the dory and leave the decoys attached to the buoy, picking it up again after they have retrieved their dead birds.

Two hunters frequently shoot from one dory. In this case, they often sit back to back, one hunter watching each way for birds, warning the other of their approach and shooting in turn according to position, the stern gunner getting first shots as the coots decoy, his partner taking them on the way out.

There is considerable variance in the arrangement of decoys along the coast. The gunning-float clan are pretty apt to use two or three strings of shadow tollers with half a dozen block decoys on the end of their strings. Moreover, they space each pair of their shadows several feet apart. Down-Easters use a long line of blocks and a set of 12 or 18 pairs of shadows that are strung rather closely together. The fact that both sets seem to attract scoters is an indication of their inclination to decoy.

These shadow tollers or profiles are just that. They are cut from half-inch or seven-eighths inch pine or cedar boards in pairs and the pairs are fastened together by means of two cross pieces on the bottom edge—one under the breast, the other under the tail. The cross sticks are about the width of common laths. Lobster fishermen who like to hunt usually use surplus laths from their pot material, but most decoy makers employ a heavier stock.

Again, there is some variance in the way these sets are put together. Most Maine hunters have the widest pair at the head of the string (nearest the dory). Near the New Hampshire line, the narrowest set of profiles is nearest the gunning float. The idea is to nest them together in pairs, whichever way they are strung up. Starting with one set about 14 inches apart, the next pair is made just the thickness of two boards wider and so on. This makes it easy to pick them up, keeps them in order and allows a larger number of them to be used, as they can be laid across the stern of a small float or dory, whereas blocks in such numbers would be bulky.

Some hunters nail their decoys at exact right angles to the cross pieces; others turn the tails of each pair slightly toward each other.

Pieces of cod-line are used to string up the pairs, two lines being used between each two sets of shadows to keep them from twisting in tide or wind. Light line is used because with this they can be more easily nested and because the line does not show from above, as a heavier cord would be likely to do. In stringing up the pairs of tollers, some gunners space them as much as 4 or 5 feet apart; others place them as close as 18 inches to a foot apart. The idea of wide spacing is based on the thought that they will show up as a larger, longer flock and can be spotted by scoters from a greater distance. Those who bring their sets together maintain that "coots" tend to bunch up on the water.

Shadows are painted black. A dull paint is considered best, as sun-glint may cause the birds to avoid a set. Some of the tollers have a white patch on the side to look like a wing; some have orange or yellow bills; only a few of them have painted eyes, but occasional birds are struck with white on the side of the head to attract "skunk-heads" or "patch-heads," as certain of the sea coots are called.

Most gunners believe that larger tollers work best, but because of the additional weight few are cut from boards more than a foot wide.

It is apparent that scoters can see only the sides of these shadows. Because they fly so close to the swells, however, this does not make much difference in the way they decoy. There are some days when block decoys seem to have much advantage over a string of shadows and even two or three blocks used with the shadow set seem to toll more coots than otherwise would be the case.

At spots where long points make out into the sea or where ledges are exposed at half tide, many shooters prefer to hunt from the land. They use a skiff or dory to set decoys and, after concealing the boat a short distance from their set, they hide behind a large rock, with a smaller rock or a piece of driftwood as a seat. Almost every locality on the Maine coast has such a favored spot, locally termed "gunner's rock" or "the laidge."

When lobster fishermen are active they break up rafting birds and good shooting may be had as long as they are hauling traps. Again, birds may leave a bay and skim along the coast for an hour or so just previous to and following sunrise. If the wind is right they may keep coming along all day. Early October in Maine is an ideal time, under normal conditions, for scoter shooting. Later the little gray coots or brown coots are largely replaced by white-wings.

Scoters are not easy birds to kill. The early fall coots come to decoys so well that a reasonably open gun may be used, but most hunters like a full-choke bore. The 12-gauge magnum is popular, both in a double and in the pump and autoloading models. Maine gunners use No. 4, 5, and 6 for shot size; some hunters even drop down to 2's, particularly if they are shooting a double on the larger coots. In this case, they have one barrel loaded with 4's or 5's, the other with 2's. Probably 6's are the most widely used, with a maximum load of powder. Ten-gauge guns used to be more popular in the days of black powder, but 12-gauge magnums have largely replaced these "old Betseys," and unusually fine shots sometimes go scoter shooting with 16's and 20's, picking single birds and carefully estimating lead.

Few hunters go offshore with less than two boxes of shells, even with the limit down to seven scoters. Gunners who can kill a bird with one shot are rare and cripples are prone to dive repeatedly.

While dress is not so important as it is for inland waterfowling, coot shooters prefer to wear brown and to avoid making themselves too conspicuous. They would not use a white skiff or dory; green, gray, or brown are common colors, with lead-gray leading in popularity because it blends into the ocean scene.

Coot shooters who go offshore usually can pick up a tow from a lobster boat. Some men use outboards, in which case the motor must be taken completely off the stern and laid in the bottom of the skiff or float, according to Federal regulations. Actually, most shooting is done within a few hundred yards of the shore, however, and if the boats are kept on a beach or in a near-by harbor the rowing may not be too arduous. Point hunting is popular in foul weather, as the birds are apt to swing in closer and hunters can get in under a lee.

Eider ducks have increased in a surprising manner within recent years along the Maine coast. From Rockland to the New Brunswick border they are particularly numerous. Local hunters maintain that eiders have become so abundant they are seeking new feeding grounds and that they have worked inshore as their supply of mussels has decreased from over-feeding. Whether or not this is true, it is a fact that 200 to 300 birds at a time occasionally will come to a set at such spots as Egg Rock, offshore from Winter Harbor. On favorable shooting days, large numbers of eiders fly by ocean ledges and come well to decoys. Flocks of from half a dozen to 300 afford hunting from the rocks, and pass shooting is possible if a hunter does not care to take the eiders as they drop into the decoys.

Inasmuch as these birds use an area quite definitely offshore, however, hunting is done safely only when a powerboat is available to make the trip outside and to stand by to take hunters aboard quickly if the weather turns foul. Usually shooters establish contact with a lobsterman or a coastal resident who owns a seaworthy boat in the cabin cruiser class. Dories or skiffs are taken in tow and hunters use them to row to the ledges from the larger boat at half tide.

Eiders are big ducks, measuring about 24 inches long and having a particularly heavy coat of feathers and an unusually thick skin. They must be hit hard to be killed. Therefore, as in the case of scoters, guns of the magnum type or full-choke bores and heavy loads are favored by hunters.

Seafowlers seem to be assured of the perpetuity of their sport for two reasons: First, the North Atlantic brews too much foul weather to permit continual shooting and, secondly, the flesh of neither eiders nor scoters is palatable to all tastes. It has been said that a person born on the seacoast has a natural palate for "coot" while an inlander does not.

However, the preparation of these birds for the oven has more to do with their edibility than the fact of an individual's birthplace, in the opinion of most authorities. Only the breasts should be cut out, skinned, and cooked, unless an epicure has acquired a liking for the strong, fishy taste of the rest of the meat, they maintain. If a whole scoter is to be cooked, it should be soaked overnight in fresh soda water. The bird should then be steamed for a little while next morning and an onion or an apple placed in the bird when it is roasted, with

N. C. Dept. of Conservation & Development.

PLATE III. Brush blind with a platform, and a big rig of goose decoys out.

strips of salt pork on its breast. When they have more birds than they can use immediately, Hancock County hunters cut out and steam the breast of eiders and scoters, place this meat in glass jars, and allow it to stand until they need it. Often they fry the fresh or canned breasts in butter and say they find them to be delicious when served with brown gravy.

Bay shooting is practiced all along the Maine coast, but high spots probably are Casco Bay from Portland to Bath and Merrymeeting Bay, up-river from Bath where five streams join the Kennebec; the Androscoggin, the Abagadasset, the Cathance, the Eastern, and Muddy rivers. In Casco Bay hunting is done from point blinds or from rather elaborate floating blinds. In Merrymeeting Bay, where it is not legal to leave a blind overnight or to have decoys set permanently, hunting is done by sculling to birds in sneak floats or by pass shooting from points, old breakwaters, or the land edging the bay.

In Casco Bay waterfowl feed on eelgrass, mussels, and other animal food. In Merrymeeting Bay, wild rice attracts the birds. Within recent years shooting has been so heavy at Merrymeeting during open seasons that it is quite likely Casco Bay gets some of the waterfowl driven out by this barrage, especially since Back Bay in Portland is a waterfowl sanctuary.

Merrymeeting long has been and still is a favorite spot for Canada geese. Black ducks are probably the most numerous birds, with wood ducks, bluewing and greenwing teal, and bluebills (scaup), crowding the bay in early fall. Whistlers (golden-eye), a few mallards, and other species come along later.

Comparatively few geese are shot at Casco Bay, although these birds visit the area occasionally. Black ducks that are native to Maine, and Canadian red-legs, are numerous. Bluebills and whistlers also are plentiful and scoters raft in Casco Bay. Other species of waterfowl are less numerous. Occasional Barrows' golden-eyes are shot by hunters, but the American golden-eye is the common bird, as it is at other bays along Maine's shore.

Sculling sneak floats on Merrymeeting Bay, Montsweag Bay, Brookings' Bay, and other inlets near Bath has been developed into something of an art by local waterfowlers. The boats themselves are usually strip-(carvel-) built, which means that the strips meet flush at the seams. However, some of them are clinker-built (the edges of planking overlapping downward like clapboards). They are very low on the water and are decked in forward with an opening part-way back for the bow gunner to shoot from; then a middle section, decked over, separates the bow hunter from the one in the stern, who sculls the float. (This middle partition is used to store shells.)

The stern gunner lies down and sculls with a light paddle that is inserted through a round hole in the stern transom. The bow hunter also keeps down so low in the float that very little of his body shows. The float is covered with chicken wire and dressed down carefully with marsh grass. When sculled properly, it resembles a drifting log, certainly not a boat. The bow is long to receive the legs of the forward hunter; it is pointed for easy sculling. These floats can be hazardous but are safely handled if hunters do not move too abruptly. Skilled men can scull them right up to a flock of birds and at the right moment one or both occupants sit erect and shoot as the birds jump.

In order to get a "scull," decoys are set at the edge of the wild rice or swale—sometimes right in the middle of the grass, especially if the tide is rising and it will be comparatively easy to reach birds as the water flows in. Hunting pressure is so great early in the season that birds move about constantly on Merrymeeting Bay, and temporary blinds or gunners stationed on points take a fair toll. Later, birds are more apt to fly according to weather, wind, and tide.

At Casco Bay the blacks feed on extensive mussel beds and when native flocks are augmented by red-legs late in the fall hunters have a picnic as these beds become exposed. Usually a section of the bay is selected that is known to harbor ducks frequently. A floating blind is anchored in the middle of this area and decoys are set at half ebb-tide. This allows several hours of shooting. The blacks will start moving in as the tide drops, will continue to fly during low water, and will keep coming until the flats are well covered again by the rising tide. Occasional bunches of other birds may happen along, but whistler shooting is more widely enjoyed on the high water.

Again, native hunters know the sections used by the golden-eyes and they gun them either from floating blinds or from a rocky point that has a background of gravel bank and trees. Casco Bay is dotted with scores of small islands and ideal conditions exist from throwing up a temporary blind or for constructing a de luxe hiding place.

Block decoys are used for both blacks and whistlers, and a few bluebill tollers also are included in most sets. The blocks used in this part of Maine usually are made from cork with wooden heads and most of them are oversize. Equipped with cords and individual anchors around floating blinds, they sometimes are set by snapping them to an endless line running on iron pulleys from the better-equipped point blinds. They prove very effective.

A floating blind is made of heavy stock with two doors that open on one end to permit a skiff to be floated right into the blind. These blinds are lined with canvas to keep out the wind. (See "Blinds.") Spruce trees a few feet high form a thick cover outside the canvas on all four sides and these floating blinds resemble nothing more or less than a tiny island. Entering the blind an hour or two before high water, the hunters anticipate a steady flow of whistlers until the tide has begun to slacken considerably.

Whistlers decoy so well that hunters on the land often sit tight against a rising bank, with a skiff hidden out of sight a hundred yards beyond their point and decoys set below, a short distance from the shore. If there are two gunners, it is often customary to allow the birds to alight, then to shout at them and take them as they jump. This gives both gunners a chance to get in shots. The whistlers do not always alight, however, and some gunners prefer to take them when they offer the best target. It is not often that blacks will come to a set of this kind but they do fly well to point blinds if hunters

PLATE IV. Floating brush blind of Maine, with everyone ready for the "blacks" to come in.

keep well hidden until they set their wings to scale in. Doubtless, nothing can compare to strategically located floating blinds on Casco Bay but nowadays they are few in number.

November and early December afford best shooting in normal years on Casco Bay. The big red-legs have had an opportunity to come along by that time. Cold weather and strong winds keep birds moving.

Merrymeeting Bay shooting for teal and native blacks is good early in October, if seasons are open then. Bluebills also are probably more numerous on both bays early in the fall. Whistlers, geese, and both native blacks and Canadians, as well as mallards, seem to fly better later on.

Sturdy skiffs that are tended by larger boats or are equipped with removable outboard motors are standard equipment on Casco Bay, for rough seas can prove dangerous at times.

There are many miles of salt-water bays all along the coast "Down East" from the two more popular shooting grounds (Casco and Merrymeeting Bays). Some of these bays perhaps are as widely used by waterfowl as those named but they have been so little exploited that only local gunners and a few others hunt them. Large flocks of whistlers use the entire coast and rafts of black ducks numbering in the hundreds can be observed at scores of places from Portland to Calais. Like scoters, thousands of the "fresh-water" ducks migrate along this flyway at a time of year when non-resident hunters either are too busy deer hunting to take note of the ducks or else have left the state for the winter.

A glance at a map of Maine will show the shoreline to be a maze of bays, fed by fresh-water streams or rivers and dotted with wooded islands that themselves often contain small ponds to attract ducks. The Penobscot, Blue Hill, and Frenchmen's Bay areas are far greater in extent than Casco and Merrymeeting, yet still other bays (Pleasant Bay, Englishman Bay, and Machias Bay) lie to the northeast of the Penobscot River mouth.

As hundreds of lakes freeze over inland from the coast, waterfowl move seaward and afford excellent shooting, provided that open seasons occur in time for these migrations.

Southwest of Portland to the New Hampshire line small creeks, harbors and river mouths also offer hunting for black ducks, whistlers, and other species. Great Bay lies inside New Hampshire but it is upriver from the Piscataqua which divides the two states. Therefore, Maine residents gun the bay to some extent by buying non-resident licenses. Geese often winter at Great Bay, and not only the big, white-fronted Canadas but blue geese find the area attractive. Black ducks, whistlers, and other freshwater species use the bay as well.

In hunting geese, most Maine waterfowlers employ heavy loads of No. 2 or 4 shot. If a double is used the load may be 4's in a modified tube, with 2's in the full-choked barrel. More often, perhaps, both barrels are full-choke in duck and goose guns. Repeaters and autoloaders are popular with barrels full-choked, and magnum 12-gauges are coming into favor more every year.

Geese profiles or big, barrel-like bodies with long necks and heads are set at strategic locations. (Sometimes a few geese tollers are included in a set for ducks, if geese are known to be in the vicinity.) Often the profiles are set on a beach or a sandbar. When bays freeze over before the season ends the decoys are even placed on the ice, but this has not occurred at many spots in this area within recent years.

A majority of bay hunters favor heavy, close-bored shotguns for whistlers and black ducks, too. Sixes are a popular load in long-range shells, with 4's and even 2's being used by some hunters.

While not all waterfowlers along the coast of Maine gun for oceangoing and bay birds, the guns used for one species are acceptable for all ducks and geese, provided they are adequate in size.

Boats, too, can be interchanged, with the exception of sneak floats, which should not be used "outside."

Hunting clothes that are suitable to bay gunning can be worn by scoter shooters, but late-season hunters figure it is easier to take off garments than to add them and they dress unusually warm in either case.

Wind, tide, and weather can "make" a day of hunting on the sea or inland bay.

Late November on is the best time for bay shooting. Early October is ideal for scoters, but they also come along throughout the rest of the fall, if a hunter can "take" the conditions.

There are many unexploited areas for waterfowl shooting along Maine's 2400 miles of tidal water.

The proof of a sea duck's flavor is in the eating, and cooking is important even on fresh-water birds that have fed on mussels or other bay foods.

## Central Atlantic Area

### LONG ISLAND SOUND—GREAT SOUTH BAY—BARNEGAT BAY

Long Island Sound, both the wide water and the marshy river mouths that feed it, still provides food and some shelter for countless waterfowl, but it must be admitted that the population is made up for the most part of scoters. Teal and mallards are fairly plentiful at the mouths and for some miles up most of the large rivers, but usually they have moved on by the time the shooting season opens.

The scoter season opens early, however, and from the opening of the season until its end there is hardly a breakwater or reef that extends beyond the outer harbor lines that does not have a group of shooters, and many of the small rocky islands just off the shore have their quota also.

When the season opens early there is fair native black-duck shooting, but as this calls for a more elaborate shooting rig than is possessed by the average shooter, and the guides are few in number, the majority of the shooting is done along the shore rather than on the rivers. The blacks are not slow to become gun-shy, and after the first few days they seem inclined to move well out into the sound at

PLATE V. A "Fancy" Setup. This is a permanent blind. Underwater slats hold the decoys in formations of 12 or more. They are hauled out by means of a mooring-pulley arrangement.

daybreak and not return to the rivers and marshes until sundown.

Broadbill supply the real sport, and in good years the broadbill shooting along the fringe of the Sound is second to none.

It is not at all unusual, in December, to cruise along the rim of the Sound, keeping about 2 miles offshore, and count several thousand broadbill on a 10-mile trip. Today, however, it is extremely difficult to find guides with offshore rigs. The Connecticut duck boat is perfect for offshore broadbill shooting, for it is low in the water and does not show up enough to frighten the birds. It has much in common with the Great South Bay scooter, and like this craft, is not a rough-water duckboat. The shooter who plans to go well offshore to rig out is taking quite a chance unless he has someone else along in a seaworthy skiff or dory. Long Island Sound can jump from flat calm to whitecaps in much less time than a man could row 2 miles to shore.

During the late shooting, these boats ice up considerably, and the average gunner is ready to give way to his companion after an hour of shooting. There are few more frigid sports than that of shooting from one of these boats during a really cold day when there is enough chop to send an occasional gust of spray into the boat. In many instances the shooter, as well as the boat, has a coating of ice.

The man gunning from one of these boats rests flat on his back and tries to keep an eye to both sides and ahead without poking his head above the leaded rim of the cockpit. When the birds come in to the rig he waits until they are about to settle, then sits up and does what damage he can from a boat that is moving from side to side as well as up and down. After a dozen or so such exercises, in which he pulls himself from the supine to the sitting position by the use of his stomach muscles, the novice shooter becomes convinced he has acquired a hernia.

Many of the ponds a few miles inland provide unusually fine shooting, but the days of "open" ponds have passed. Most of them have been bought up or leased by individuals or small groups, and the visiting shooter and the native alike have little chance of trying their luck.

The reef and breakwater shooting along the fringe of the Sound has one feature that is far from satisfactory. Many of the shooters, being without boats, wait until low tide to reach their shooting point. They are limited to pass shooting, and when they kill a bird down-wind from the reef or breakwater they have no means of recovering it unless the tide happens to be right and brings it in. In some instances, other shooters with boats will recover the bird for them, but as this imposes on the man with the boat, many dead birds are never recovered. A few have retrievers, which solve the problem, but the situation is far from a satisfactory one to the real sportsman.

Good shooting on Great South Bay, as well as on Barnegat Bay 100 miles to the southward, depends on the dates of the season as much as on the weather. There have been great changes on both of these historic shooting grounds during the past generation. In the "old days," of which you hear less as the old baymen disappear from the scene, the ponds and marshes on their margins harbored thousands of teal, widgeon, pintails, and mallards. These species were the advance guard of the diving ducks which came later with the lower temperatures. There are still a few areas where these species make an appearance, but in a mere fraction of their former numbers. Here again, the blame may be placed not on over-shooting, but on the encroachment of civilization. Also, the teal and mallards normally arrive before the season opens and have moved southward by opening day.

Black ducks continue to be reasonably plentiful on the marshes and ponds that are not fringed by summer cottages, but as most of these areas are owned or leased by private shooting clubs, the "open" shooting has been greatly reduced.

Broadbills and scoters are still plentiful on both bays, but with baiting and battery shooting forbidden, neither black duck nor broadbill shooting is what it was. The late season shooting for broadbill on some of the eastern area of the Great South Bay is often as fine as any shooter could want. This is open-water gunning, for the most part, and though it is cold sport it has its compensations.

Both bays have suffered from the eelgrass blight, but the grass is gradually coming back, and baymen insist that the waterfowl population will increase with it.

"The shooters who come down here can't seem to figure out why the gunning isn't what it was," one old Barnegat guide complained. "I never went to school, but I can understand it. There's more hunters less ducks, more towns, less feed, and to top it off the law won't let you shoot a full day and kill as many ducks. It appears to be simple enough for me."

On Barnegat, also, the best ponds, sloughs, and islands are privately owned and leased, and most of them are well guarded. Because of the many small islands, the majority of which are barely dry at high tide, there is less open-water broadbill shooting here than on Great South Bay. This results in equally good shooting for these ducks, and at the same time, more comfortable shooting. Sunken box blinds dot most of the good islands, and sneakbox coves can be seen inside most points. Both of these methods are warmer and drier than shooting on the open water in a scooter, but perhaps the sport is just a trifle less exciting.

There are still good brant years on Barnegat, but the goose shooting does not compare to that of the "old days." The big Canadas still follow this flyway, but they seem to pause but briefly on their way to Currituck, Pamlico, Albemarle, and Mattamuskeet on the North Carolina coast.

The picture of Barnegat would not be complete without the inclusion of one of its familiar tales:

Two gunners, guided by an old bayman and his "not too bright" son, were spending a week on one of the isolated reaches of the bay. They lived in a shantyboat which the guide had moored in the lee of one of the outer islands. The shooting had been fair, with enough mallards and broadbill moving to make it interesting.

Late one afternoon it began to blow from the northeast, and as the wind increased long lines of

N. C. Dept. of Conservation & Development.

PLATE VI. Getting rigged out by sun-up on Currituck Sound. On the other side of the dunes in the background is the Atlantic.

brant began moving in to the shelter of the islands. The old guide groaned as he watched them.

"Here we are, brant comin' like chickens, an' every last one of my brant decoys is at the shantyboat 10 miles up the Bay." Then he was inspired. He called to his son and laid down explicit directions as to where the shantyboat was moored, where the decoys were, and where the key would be found.

"Take a sneakbox and row up to the shantyboat. Bring back about 20 of the brant stool. Remember now, the key to the door is under the stern thwart."

This was before the motorboat was common on the bay, and the son, despite his retarded intelligence, protested at the long row, but finally pulled away in the dusk. Late that night he returned, but without a single decoy.

His father, aroused from a deep sleep, listened to his explanation of failure with resignation. "I told you three times that the key was under the stern thwart," he emphasized. "Can't see why you couldn't find it."

His son shook his head. "Not a thing under the stern thwart save a hatchet," he insisted.

His father looked at him with sad eyes, then shook his head. "That was the key, you idjit!"

## Southern Area

### CURRITUCK AND PAMLICO SOUNDS

From Currituck to Pamlico, several hundred square miles of shallow, brackish water offer a haven and feeding ground for great concentrations of ducks and geese. Separated from the ocean by narrow strips of duned sand, ranging in width from a few hundred yards to 2 or 3 miles, these sounds send a myriad of fingers and coves into the mainland, and are dotted by small islands. Along the western fringes the marshes and ponds offer additional havens for waterfowl, and although the ducks and geese are not so plentiful as they were 20 years ago, they are still present in sufficient numbers to attract hunters from points more than a thousand miles distant.

Currituck is shallow and almost tideless, and offers a variety of succulent water plants that not only find favor with the waterfowl but give them a flavor that finds favor with the hunters. The great curse of this sound, to waterfowl as well as hunters, is the host of swans that "infest" it. They manage to eat more than their share of food, and do more to spoil the shooting than any other single factor.

Puddle ducks as well as several species of divers, including canvasbacks, redheads, and scaup, grow fat on the wild celery and other aquatic growths, and the Canada geese that winter here serve as the major attraction. Many visiting hunters find it no problem to get a goose limit daily, but unless they come late in the season it is not always possible to complete the duck bag. After two weeks on Currituck even the thinnest Canada fills out and begins to fatten. Old guides who once made a living as market gunners claim that a Currituck canvasback or redhead brought exactly twice as much at the market as one killed at Pamlico, where the birds feed more on fish and mussels than they do on vegetable matter.

Many famous gun clubs, some of which have changed hands many times during recent years, are strung out along Currituck and through Pamlico Sound. The Currituck Gun Club, the Corolla Club, Gooseville Gun Club, Bodie Island Club, and Green Island Club are well-known names to the active wildfowler of 30 years ago. Those were the days when waterfowl were really plentiful there, when hunters were few and land cheap.

N. C. State News Bureau.

PLATE VII. A nice "double" from a grass blind on Pamlico Sound.

Duck shooting is still a poor man's sport in this area, however, for guide fees are reasonable and the man who knows something of the waters can go out without a guide and expect a good day's sport. While some of the shooting is done from shore blinds, the brush blind and reef blind are more popular here than at any other point along the Atlantic coast. (See "Blinds.")

Many duck hunters who travel from Canada to Mexico and from the Atlantic to the Pacific, insist that Pamlico Sound has one of the greatest winter concentrations of pintails anywhere on the continent, and certainly few can dispute that Currituck and Pamlico, with Lake Mattamuskeet thrown in for good measure, offer Canada goose shooting that is excelled by no other place in the country.

Before World War II, the Coast Guard air base at Elizabeth City contributed considerably to the goose shooters' sport, for at that time the geese were frightened of airplanes, and the Coast Guard air traffic along the beach kept them moving. On "bluebird" days the geese would move from the Sound to the fringe of the ocean, and only the planes could stir them up. During the war the airplane traffic in this area was so great that the waterfowl became accustomed to them, and they no longer take to the air when they pass.

### FLORIDA

Florida duck shooting, like that of the Southwest, offers a variety of birds as well as types of hunting. Shooters in the North who find that the local seasons open too late for some species and too early for others can run the gamut of species in the sloughs, potholes, lakes, rivers, and marshes of this area. Geese are not too plentiful, but the teal, scaup, pintails, blacks, ringnecks, and Florida ducks are present in sufficient numbers to atone for this loss, and there are a few northern mallards, shovellers, and broadbill to add to the variety.

Civilization has spoiled the shooting on parts of the St. Lucie and Indian Rivers, especially in the coastal area, but the Ten Thousand Islands and the Banana River areas offer excellent wildfowling. The myriad of small ponds provide excellent shooting, although some of them are rather difficult to reach, and call for considerable tramping on foot. A dozen decoys, of almost any kind, will answer the requirement on these ponds; lack of transportation facilities makes balsa decoys highly favored. The larger inland lakes also provide fair shooting, and although guides are far from numerous in any of the east coast or central areas, the gunner with a few decoys and a hatchet can throw up a temporary blind and have no trouble in finding ducks.

The west coast and lower Everglades shooting calls for a guide, however, unless the gunner is really familiar with the area and can find his way home through the maze of tiny sloughs, coves, guzzles, and waterways. Low water provides the best shooting in these sections, for the ducks come in to feed on the flats when the tide has dropped. Because of the multiplicity of bars and flats, the shooter normally must travel to his shooting area at high water and wait for the next high tide to make the return trip. After a man has dragged a powerboat over a few dozen bars and shallow spots, he never departs thereafter without a knowledge of the tides. The mangroves offer natural blinds, and all that is needed is a hatchet or machete to hack an opening. The gunner who has no great love for snakes usually flails the area he intends using for a blind with an oar; this normally sends the cottonmouths on their way.

There are times when the Florida hunting can be both wet and cold, and it pays to take along a heavy sweater and a waterproof despite the protestations of the Chambers of Commerce. On other occasions it is a good idea to take along some form of temporary icebox, in which the dead birds can be placed. Meat can spoil rapidly in that climate.

## Southwestern Area

### GULF COAST—TEXAS—PLAINS—MEXICO

Sweeping down from the prairies of Saskatchewan, Manitoba, and Alberta, ducks and geese cross the Great Plains on their southern migration. Inside, to the east of the Rockies, they plow along. The Dakotas are left. The sandhill lakes of Nebraska—the potholes of Oklahoma and Texas—then the Gulf Coast and the country below the Rio Grande are invaded.

Of special interest, ducks of many species make this flight. Geese of at least five varieties honk their way southward over a terrain much to their liking. Open bald prairies and low elevations make this a flyway that is geographically ideal. Small grains, corn, maize, and sorghum cause these birds gradually to infiltrate the Southland and hold them along their route of migration offering shooting over a long period of time.

Rolling prairies of stubble, interspersed with shallow open lakes free of heavy vegetation, offer food and safe sanctuary to the web-footed clan. Human population is low. Even close to large towns, such as Amarillo, Liberal, or Garden City, a hunter may build his blind and feel reasonably sure that he may be able to use it most of the time without the need of an argument with another occupant.

Severe northers may sweep the plains, driving birds before their sleety gale; or blue skies may send shimmering heat waves dancing along the horizon that can hardly be told from wavering lines of waterfowl. Bright days and clear air call for decoys that do not glisten, and blinds must be good to conceal the occupants.

Along the Rockies, in Colorado, New Mexico, and Arizona, high plateau lakes offer early shooting on locally raised ducks. Shallow rivers devoid of feed often attract birds passing through the country and produce some good gunning. Irrigation reservoirs and flooded fields are frequently fine locations for hunters to complete a respectable bag of quackers. Many a rancher has a meal or two each year from birds that alight on his stock tank, or a small artificial lake that is produced by making an earth fill across a small draw or arroyo.

Shooting in the Southwest is as varied as to procedure as the many types of habitat and geographic environments that are present. On the plains, blinds are often thrown up composed of tumbleweeds, or shocks of maize. These are especially common around lakes closely adjacent to the growing crops, and as a rule are more for the taking of ducks than geese. Many honkers in this land do fall before the duck blinds. However, the better goose shooter goes in for digging a pit in fields that geese frequent, or, in some cases, on the shores of shallow open lakes.

A pit blind for ducks or geese is about the ideal concealment devised by man to date. The soil as a rule lends itself to easy digging, and a hole is excavated almost as large as a grave—deep enough to hide completely a seated hunter. Around the edge of the pit small soapweeds, Spanish daggers, or bunches of bear grass are stuck in the sand. A wily goose will alight within 10 feet of such a blind without seeing it—if allowed to come that close.

Decoy spreads for prairie lakes usually consist of a dozen or more mallard blocks, depending upon the size of the water area. Small holes need few decoys. Large lakes need more. Just apart from the duck spread, a few goose decoys, a bit aloof, often turn an ordinary duck shoot into something to be remembered on Thanksgiving or Christmas when the fowl is served.

Calling is with the usual quacking devices as found in the Mississippi Valley. However, birds here are not so violently urged by the hunters, nor is calling so necessary. Possibly the clear air makes decoys more easily visible and open shore lines give fowl a sense of security. As in all duck shooting, poor calling is worse than none. In case geese are in the air a good call, used sparingly, will often turn the flock to the hunter's blind.

Such rivers as the Arkansas, Cimarron, Canadian,

PLATE VIII. Cold sport in the Midwest, with Robert Taylor heading for the blind.

Pecos, Rio Grande, and others frequently furnish sites for sandbar blinds. Here, large numbers of decoys may often be employed and usually shadows, silhouette figures, are used in conjunction with regular blocks. Blinds may be of the pit variety or, in some instances, drift logs work well toward making a concealment.

In the mountain states blinds are more casual. Sometimes rocky shore lines conceal rock-built blinds. These are most excellent; usually diving ducks are more frequently killed from them than are birds of the tipper class. Because of the rougher terrain, often good pass shooting may be had between lakes.

Desert rivers are often so narrow that a shotgun will kill a bird completely across them. Here shooting is often to be had at cruising fowl flying up or down the river. Decoys are not so often used in such locales, but the real duck hunter will enjoy good shooting with a blind made on the point of a bar and a few decoys in the shallow alkaline water.

Frequently desert rivers are not as unproductive as they appear at first glance. Often old cutoff channels have been dammed by industrious beaver and small sloughs formed. These are widely used by both local and transient birds as roosting places, or loafing spots, while their feeding may be carried on in the irrigated fields miles away.

Gun clubs recognizing the feed value of flooded alfalfa fields or of inundated maize patches have created winter shooting places in the irrigated country. The fields are not taken out of production, and a plow is sufficient to form a dam high enough to impound all the water necessary for attracting ducks and making the decoys visible on the open water. In the field borders barrels are sunk to protrude but a few inches above the high-water mark. These form excellent blinds and if properly taken care of are dry and warm.

A few isolated areas have large impoundments of water that form storage facilities for irrigation. These are often deep, without a vestige of waterfowl feed in them. In some instances they have margins that form shallows and waterfowl by the millions use them for both rest and feed areas. If demands by farmers for irrigation waters are not too severe, and the lakes are consequently not lowered too rapidly, both marginal and aquatic vegetation is often produced in large quantities. Such oases, when they do exist, offer shooting as good as any in the country.

Along the Gulf coast open, sandy shore lines may have thousands of resting ducks and geese. Pintails especially like this salt-water isolation. Along Laguna Madre, from Corpus Christi to the Mexican border, these birds may be seen during the winter months by the thousands. They are required to fly inland to fields for food in any quantity. Off Port Isabel, redheads gather in the open salt water in rafts numbering into multiple thousands. The water here is far too deep for the puddle species to feed, but a plant much to redhead liking grows on the bottom of the bay. This food is pulled up and the

PLATE IX. This shows why a good retriever is worth his weight in gold.

root eaten. After feeding, the redheads fly inland to fresh-water lakes. Here shooting is ideal and one needs only to get in the line of flight from the salt water. Pintails also use this same area, and a mixed bag of divers and puddle ducks is very common.

Bordering the coast are lagoons usually fringed with mesquite trees. These are not wide, as a rule, and often shallow enough for wading. Puddle ducks furnish fine shooting in such places. Here the Florida black ducks join their green-headed cousins. Widgeons and gadwalls, shovellers, pintails, and often three species of teal may be taken.

Deeper water, off Copano Bay in the Rockport and Aransas Pass area, furnishes the redhead and canvasback shooting of the Gulf coast. Blinds are often elaborate and house the hunter's boat. Decoy spreads, as in the case of all diving-duck shooting on large waters, are big. Shallow-water ducks are taken from these same blinds, pintails being most common.

Texas, like Louisiana, furnishes rice-field shooting on the tipper ducks. In the eastern coastal marshes blue and snow geese, as well as honkers and specklebellies, are taken. Blinds and decoy setups are similar to those of western Louisiana. The Cajun influence on hunting is noted also in the boats used and the small, homemade reed calls.

Great variation throughout the Southwest is also noted in equipment used in waterfowl shooting. Boats on the plains may be portable affairs one can carry on top of the car. This gives the hunter a chance to use some selection in the area he is to hunt. Because of the field feeding of ducks and geese, their flight may vary considerably from day to day as they change around, eating in different localities. It is an advantage to be on the line of flight, and the smart hunter studies this, also shifting from day to day to small lakes located in such strategic places. A portable boat is the only answer, as the lakes, though not deep, are often too deep to wade. Some shooters also use a portable blind of woven wire with grass laced through this material. This may be rolled up and hauled along inside the boat.

Clothing demands for Southwest shooting also are subject to wide variation. On the Texas plains a single day may begin with an 80-degree temperature and end in a howling sub-zero blizzard. Light wool underwear is never amiss during waterfowl season, and a down jacket is fine extra equipment to carry along. In the mountain states, clear, sharp air of early morning demands clothing as warm as that needed in the Arctic, but as soon as the sun comes out, the hunter can almost be comfortable in shirt sleeves.

If wading must be done, rubber hip boots are, of course, necessary in any climate. If shooting is such that boots can be avoided, shoe-pacs and wool socks, or common leather hunting boots, are much warmer and more comfortable. In all Southwest shooting, with the possible exception of the rice fields and coastal marshes, one can often supplement his waterfowl shooting with upland shooting. In many places desert, or bobwhite, quail form a midday diversion. Rabbits, pheasants, and even wild turkeys are not infrequently added to the waterfowl hunter's bag. Big game may be common in the same area where the duck blind is located. Be sure to have footgear other than hip boots if any side excursions from the blind are to be taken.

Choice of weapons for duck hunting is a matter of preference. However, it has been noted that the farther westward one goes, the smaller are the shotguns used. Maybe the mountain states duck shooting is more of a casual nature, or possibly the smaller lakes and ponds, the jump shooting along irrigation ditches, or the narrow rivers do not demand the long-range guns. The fact remains that the outdoorsman of the Southwest is more of a small-gauge addict than his eastern relatives.

The Plains states do need shotguns that shoot a dense pattern for open, clear-sky shooting. Also geese are plentiful, and they take a bit of killing. Any standard 12-bore full-choke gun is not out of line for the plains where big ducks and tough geese are not unusual. Shooting over decoys in marsh or timber is another matter. Any hunter who handicaps himself with a full-choked gun for short-range shooting is making a mistake.

Probably fewer double-barreled shotguns are to be found in the Southwest than farther to the east. The country is new. Pumps and autoloaders belong to the twentieth century. There was not much population in a great part of this area only a few years back. Pioneers go for new things. History does not need be scanned deeply to find how readily the West adopted six-shooters and Winchester carbines. The West has always gone in for firepower.

Shot sizes should be mentioned. Near Cairo, Illinois, geese are seldom shot with anything smaller than No. 2's. Buckshot are not uncommon, and these missiles can be heard whistling overhead like rocket planes on many and frequent occasions. Sometimes a goose is hit, and at yardages completely out of reason one may be observed plummeting down to the earth. Heavy shooting competition seems to breed long-range shooters. It seems that one is afraid his fellow shooter about 30 corn rows down the line will get ahead of him and take the shot on an incoming duck or goose. To counteract this evil, shot size is stepped up. To aid this, magnum guns are bored to shoot a pattern of shot of a bit more weight. This competition seems an endless process.

In the Southwest gunning competition is not so keen. A most successful goose shooter was observed who always used No. 6 shot. He never shot a bird beyond 35 yards. The head and neck was hit. The goose was more cleanly killed than was possible with any of the big stuff. The cripple loss was zero.

Retriever dogs are just as valuable in the Southwest as anywhere else. It might be remarked that cripple losses are usually less in this area because of the lack of vegetation that a bird can use for concealment after being shot down. Shallow lakes and open shores free of vegetation, give the cripple little opportunity to get away, yet there is always some loss. A retriever will prevent almost all escape of wounded birds and give the hunter a good feeling at the end of the day. Saving cripples is good conservation.

Mention has not been made of shooting in Mexico. Probably the land south of the border should receive some consideration, for many Americans are going down there yearly to shoot. Close to the U.S.-Mexican line, local hunters flock across to shoot a

PLATE X. Blue Geese and Snow Geese on the Louisiana Marshes.

later season than opportunity gives them at home. A few elaborate rigs have been noticed for this work. High-wheeled autos to negotiate severe roads or cross flooded areas have been built. Outboards and portable boats invade some of the less remote country.

Interior Mexico has a few very fine waterfowl lakes. Some are in the highlands and winter thousands of birds. Shooting is seldom as exacting as in the States. Frequently a barefooted peon will push the hunter about in a dugout, and jump shooting is the practice. Birds are much tamer, due to lack of shooting pressure, and many Americans make kills that should give them unpleasant dreams. It is to be remembered that if we are to have shooting in the United States for years to come, we must see that more birds return to northern nesting grounds. There is no short cut on production that might increase waterfowl. Brood stock in large numbers is essential. A hen bird is just as unproductive if killed lawfully in the United States as in Mexico, contrary to law or legally; in either instance she is dead.

We deplore the shooting in Mexico by the natives. We talk of the "Armadas," big-bored cannons that shoot a pound of shot—of birds killed with these howitzers even by night and then sold in the market places—of a country where laws are not enforced and a big bag limit may be killed at any time of the year the ducks are down there. All of this is at least partly true, but the thing should be analyzed a bit further.

In the first place, the big kills are chiefly made by Americans who want more shooting than they can get at home and who can afford the Mexico trip. Secondly, the market selling is but a drop in the bucket so far as numbers are concerned as compared to our own legal kill. Thirdly, a duck is dead only once. The method, time, or place has little to do with the results during nesting season. The thing that counts is how many waterfowl are allowed to get back north.

Far down on the Central American line, natives have been observed hunting ducks with three-pronged bamboo spears. It takes a good hunter to bag four birds a day. In far northern Arctic lands, Eskimos have been noted throwing a very similar weapon with bone-tipped points, also three in number. One could almost imagine that the same mechanic fashioned both the weapons, yet the hunters were the length of the continent apart.

The natives are not the ones accountable for our duck and goose shortage, though they kill at every opportunity. This meat supply is important to them. We who love to gun the marsh and streams are the guilty. There are just too many of us in the field trying to enjoy this recreation. Possibly the Southwestern states are a bit kinder to the waterfowl. They have good shooting and enjoy it, yet they do not go at it quite so hard, maybe because there are other things to hunt. Also, one seldom hears a gun boom beyond the noonday in much of this whole area.

Duck and goose shooting, after all, is not a serious business competition. Our future is not dependent upon whether we get the limit or not. Glorious days afield beneath blue skies and crisp tangy air are the usual rule in much of the Southwest. A keen appreciation of other things out of doors goes far toward making a small bag take on larger proportions.

# Interior United States

## MIDWESTERN AREA

Many a coastal wildfowler labors under the illusion that there is no duck shooting that can compare to that found on the salt marshes, sounds, and bays, but one short trip up the Illinois River in the autumn would convince him of his error.

"You can have your broadbills and blacks," one White River duck hunter announced. "I'll take the mallards on the flooded bottoms."

Probably there is no place in the world where there is better or sportier mallard shooting than the flooded timberlands along the margins of the Illinois and White Rivers. The birds begin piling in around mid-October, and usually the rivers begin flooding the lowlands about that time. Unhappily for the average shooter, much of the really good shooting area is posted by clubs, and by organizations that lease the shooting rights. This means that John Duckhunter is able to get in only an occasional day as a guest of a club member, unless he can afford from $40 to $60 a day at one of the commercial shooting clubs. There are scattered sections where anyone with a license and duck stamp can get quite good shooting, but such spots are rather isolated and require considerable advance reconnaissance to locate.

This is the country where duck calling is reduced to a fine art, and while decoys are rigged out by those shooting the open potholes or ponds, it is in most instances, the caller who gets the birds down. To understand the real importance of a duck call, walk down the main street of a town such as Stuttgart, Ark., in the fall. Almost every male, from the age of ten on up, will have a call strung around his neck or bulging his pocket. And, regardless of age, they know how to use them. Until they have mastered the art, they very wisely leave the calls at home.

Elaborate blinds are not necessary, and while many of the clubs have them, most of the shooting is done from a punt or from a seat on a shell box in the high grass. The normal procedure is to travel up one of the swales until the pushing gets too difficult,

PLATE XI. A mallard rig "set" in an opening, taken from the blind in the Arkansas pin-oak flats.

then get out and walk. Almost every flooded clearing will have a large population of ducks. When you approach they leap to flight, but no one shoots into the big bunches. Stand with your back to a tree and within a few minutes the fat mallards will begin coming back, in twos, sixes, and dozens. If the wind is strong you are due to get some of the most sporting duck shooting to be found anywhere.

Some shooters merely take up a stand along a slough and lure passing birds within range by means of the call. It is amazing to hear and see these callers work. One will spot a high-passing pair and send out an urgent call. The birds will swing their long necks in curiosity, and then the calling begins in earnest. Pleading, coaxing, demanding, with the pair circling closer all the time. Then, almost inevitably, they will pitch past within range. The rest is up to the shooter, his gun, and his estimate of the range and lead.

## MISSISSIPPI RIVER AREA

The largest waterfowl flyway in America is clearly defined in that it follows the Mississippi River. This ancient highway of the birds extends in its northern dimensions from the Canadian Rockies on the west to the regions of Hudson Bay to the easward. From well beyond the Arctic Circle migrating fowl follow this level land, bottlenecking in the vicinity of St. Louis, then flaring a bit to invade the wintering grounds of Louisiana, Arkansas, and East Texas.

From such a tremendous nesting area comes waterfowl of many species. As this flight extends from our northern borders to the Gulf coast, shooting methods vary to a marked degree. The wild-rice lakes of Minnesota, with their businessmen hunters from St. Paul and Minneapolis, contrast to a marked degree with the Cajun hunters of the Evangeline country of the Louisiana rat marshes.

All forms of waterfowl are most easily taken in their nesting grounds. In their wintering areas, by virtue of their abundance, they are usually not too difficult to bring to bag. Along their flyway, where they are bombarded by an overabundance of hunters in restricted small shooting areas, the competition is keen. Blinds, decoys, and equipment must be good. Waterfowling in such areas has reached near perfection.

In Minnesota, Wisconsin, Iowa, Illinois, and much of Missouri two main forms of duck shooting are most common. They are:

(1) On ponds, lakes, and sloughs from permanent blinds.

(2) On rivers, from sandbars, points, or overflow timberland of willows and hardwoods. Here, too, permanent blinds are usually employed.

PLATE XII. Small lakes need few decoys. Here in a small lake in Texas the decoy spread will be about a dozen blocks. Shooting in such a plpace will be on mallards, pintails, widegons, and other puddle ducks.

In a few instances, particularly in northern lake regions, excellent pass shooting may be had. Usually in this event the hunter merely conceals himself in the line of flight used by the birds between two lakes and drops his game on hard ground. Full choke-bored guns are the best for this work because the fowl, as a rule, fly high.

In some reedy lakes or overflow timberland jump shooting is practiced. The hunter either wades or propels a boat as noiselessly as possible through the lanes of tules or flooded timber. Rising fowl offer fair chances as they flare away from the gunner. Here again full choked boring is essential in the shotgun, as most jump shooting is at longer yardage than shooting over decoys. Small winding creeks and ditches often common in the corn belt also furnish jump shooting of considerable merit. In this hunting the shooter will do well to approach such streams only in the bends. Ducks invariably alight in such places in order to keep watch both up and down stream. Old hands at creek shooting cut from one bend to another and pay little attention to any possible fowl between such points.

Lake, pond, and slough hunting in the northern states of the Mississippi River region usually is from permanent blinds. In such habitat the waterfowl are mostly the tipper or shallow-water feeding birds. Mallards, pintails, wigeon, gadwalls, blue and green-winged teal, and shovellers are the most common. On large lakes in particular, and especially in the northern states, many of the diving ducks are taken from blinds designed for shallow-water birds. Canvasbacks, redheads, and scaups do on occasion swing to the lifeless mallard or pintail stools. They frequently make up a large part of the hunter's bag.

Blinds are often works of art. (See "Blinds.") In shallow marshy lakes the hunter may wade to them and step up on a solid floored structure. In deep water he may anchor his duckboat within the device, or, in some instances, park his craft beneath his shooting platform and step up high and dry to the solid footing above. Well-made blinds usually are covered with vegetation that matches the surrounding terrain. This may be over a framework of willows or boards. Many are plywood boxes, made wind-tight, and then carefully camouflaged with native tules, grasses, willows, or whatever the surrounding foliage affords. Some structures are lined with tar paper. Many have heating devices ranging from charcoal burners to gasoline or coal-oil stoves. Seats may be plush-lined and padded or they may be rude boards or empty shell cases.

Of importance in all blind structure is that the coverage is natural and blends in with the native cover of the region. Blinds should be sufficiently dense that waterfowl will not detect the hunter's movement behind the camouflage. They must offer protection against visibility from above. This latter feature may be accomplished by making the blind much wider in the bottom than in the top. Also, quite often the top, or open part of the blind, is covered between the two gunners. That is, it contains open cockpits of sorts, one for each shooter. It should be stressed that more than two hunters to a blind is definitely poor business. One man is much easier to conceal than two, and two are the limit. Interference in shooting, hazards of gun handling, and shooting on the same birds is the inevitable result of more than two gunners in a blind.

Lake and marsh blinds are usually so situated that they look out over an open hole of water where artificial decoys are placed. The concealment should be so situated that the prevailing wind is to the shooter's back, or at least to his right or left. Often two blinds are built, one on either side of an open hole, so that regardless of wind direction the hunters may select a blind where they will not have wildfowl stooling over their position from the rear.

Making sets of artificial decoys is important. (See "Decoys.") In small openings of water the number of decoys may be few. A dozen or even less may suffice. On large, open bodies of water the set should be larger. Frequently 50 to 100 decoys are used. Care should be taken to arrange the decoys so that decoying birds breasting the wind will be brought directly before the front of the blind. If the wind is blowing sharply from one's left, for example, the decoys would be set well into the wind, considerably to the left of the front of the blind. Birds invariably come in against the wind. Experimentation will show you where to place the stool. For effective shooting the birds must be brought in directly before you. Decoying ducks from the rear or the extreme ends of your blind will give but one hunter a chance to shoot. Even then he will either be caught unawares or, at best, off balance for his shots.

Shallow-water ducks, or puddle ducks, usually do not sit in as tight formation as the diving species. For this reason, in shallow-lake shooting spread your decoys out a bit. For divers, mass them in a more compact group. A tight, close set of decoys for mallards, for example, would indicate to decoying fowl that they were a new flock, just arrived, and were still in the process of looking things over to see if all was well. Spread out the decoys; they then fool their living brethren into thinking that this spot is satisfactory and there is something in these parts to eat.

Ever remember that the greatest device in the world for luring waterfowl is food. It is against the law to scatter such an inducement for hungry birds, so the next best thing is to lead them to believe that the artificial decoys are sitting in a land of plenty, with the napkins tucked up under their chins.

With a good blind and a proper set of decoys, the last act in a duck shooter's procedure before the actual shooting is the calling of the birds. Here, again, geographic location, the size of the body of water where one is shooting, the strength of the wind, and dozens of other factors enter into the picture. No matter what is stated herein as to methods of duck calling, many duck shooters are going to disagree. Each man to his opinion is an old American right. But, anyway, take this or leave it, as one man's observation and opinion.

A Cajun with a half-dozen homemade decoys parks his pirogue in waist-high sawgrass, or three-cornered bulrush. With a little anemic homemade call from native bamboo he squeaks an invitation to hardy red-legged mallards from the north country, and the idiots swing in. On Reelfoot Lake, Tennessee guides pump up the bellows and sound forth on calls a foot long, the most terrific high-tuned blast ever heard in ducking places. Believe it or not, the birds swarm in, though everyone knows a mallard never was guilty of such a noise. Along the Mississippi River a rubber duck call, which sold for 50 cents prewar and is as harsh as a horseshoe rasp on the edge of a shovel, blares forth. It lifts the duck cap from your head and curls your graying sideburns. Nevertheless the birds breast the wind and settle, some of them not 10 feet away from you as you crouch awaiting the word to rise and fire.

This all adds up to something—but it is hard to define. If birds flare when you call, you had better remain silent. Also on the larger, more open bodies of water, or on Old Man River himself, you may blast loud and long. The birds seem to like it. In the confines of small timbered potholes, or little sloughs, the loud notes bounce around a bit too much. A well-modulated form of calling would be in better taste, for the auditorium is not too large and the acoustics might lead the birds to believe that superman duck was sounding forth. Few of the webfeet care to meet him.

Careful analysis of duck calling leads us to these conclusions. First, be sparing with the chatter. Wildfowl do not call a great deal to their fellows. Why should they attempt to get someone to come in and join the party when the feed is free? It is not duck nature; they are a bit hoggish.

It has been observed, secondly, that the pitch of the duck call has little to do with results. Some people sing tenor, others bass. Ducks probably have as much variation in their vocal cords. More important, it has been noted that a call should be tuned to a certain vibration, or *timbre,* of sound. If this vibration level is maintained—if you stay on the beam of this—you can almost feel the call vibrate. Then you can call ducks. The 50-cent job will go right along with the silver reeds if you are artist enough to do this. Duck-calling records and treatises are informative. Play or read them, then try them out. They are still informative.

Duckboats in the northern lakes and marshes will be briefly mentioned. For sneak-shooting activities they need to be pointed, inconspicuous as to color, and easy to propel. For blind shooting, they must be sufficient in size so that they will get you there and back and of such proportions that they can be concealed beneath the blind, or in it, or in the vegetation closely adjacent. A boat painted dead-grass color and dotted or spotted with camouflaged dabs of black or dark brown paint is good. Make the thing as mottled as a mallard hen. Birds will not easily be alarmed when they see it.

In a like manner treat your duck coat to the same process as camouflaging your boat. Our Pacific fighters wore jungle suits. Imitate them in decorating your shooting garb. You may not need go so far as our fighting men in painting your face, but it is well to remember that the smart duck shooter does not twist and turn, peering at decoying fowl and letting the white of his face reveal his whereabouts.

Rivers, sandbars, points, and overflow timberland of willows and hardwoods will be discussed next. Much of the previously written matter is applicable here. A few differences are to be noted.

On the rivers you are more apt to get into the shooting of the diving ducks. Canvasbacks, redheads, and scaup loathe the marshes as a rule and keep the majority of their flight along the big streams. Puddle ducks, particularly the mallards, pintails, and teals, will often give you a swing. A set of decoys for them in sheltered water, close to your blind, often brings surprising results. Large stools of decoys for the divers is the rule. Remember that few of these creatures can utter a single quack. You need to appeal to them by sheer numbers. If you can get a burr in your tongue like a Scotchman, a guttural sort of a croak, calling helps. How to spell it, or depict it on paper, is beyond us.

Your blocks or decoys should be many. If the water is large, about 200 will at least give you proper exercise in setting them before you can wilt down in your blind and await results. Divers are most clannish, and for them the decoys must be in tighter formation. Be careful that you are not too far from the stool. You are better off in the middle of it, for the big number of your decoys may put you a "fur piece" from the decoying birds. Also divers are tough and rugged and you need to center your shots to kill them. Divers and deep water are a bad combination. If not riddled in the air, canvasback, redheads, and scaups can dive to China and are hard to retrieve. Even a good dog gets a tough workout in flowing water. However, good dogs are the best investment one ever made and wise conservation decrees their wider use.

River blinds on points may be brushed-up affairs coinciding with the surrounding vegetation. On sandbars, pits are often employed. Here you may spread your goose decoys—stuffed ones or profiles. Often they bring results. In marshes and on lakes, goose spreads are a waste of time unless you hunt one of those rare areas where migrating geese do fly over your territory. Sandbars are a different proposition. Geese love them and a few decoys for them go along well with the duck stool in the waters close by.

Overflow timberland is part of Old Man River. Illinois has a bit of it, Missouri more of it, and in Arkansas this form of shooting reaches its zenith. Blinds are built in the margins of timbered potholes or sloughs. Usually they are heavily brushed with willows from the back side and all shooting is done out in front over the decoys. This, by the way, is where it should be done. Some open areas in the St. Louis vicinity have sunken barrels where gunners squat and shoot as if in a revolving turret. These spots, however, are rare.

Timber shooting is definitely of the puddle-duck variety. A few wayward scaup do wander in these areas, but the divers taken in such surroundings are rare. Decoys are usually used grudgingly. The water area of visibility does not warrant large spreads. A dozen to 18 blocks in such places usually is sufficient. Some hunters are loath to use these exacting numbers, maintaining that the ducks can count and immediately recognize the spread as a dozen, or a dozen and a half, "deeks" purchased in a local sporting-goods store.

Arkansas blinds deserve special mention. They are usually as big as boxcars and placed in the wooded overflow timber. The tops are wide open and an ordinary orchestra might be seated on the benches in them and in accompaniment to their music tap their feet on the wooden floors. The blinds are covered with a poor concealment of brush. But they get results. Maybe the abundance of the birds trading

PLATE XIII. Blue and Snow Geese in East Texas. As one progresses eastward toward Louisiana, blue geese become more abundant than the snows. In Texas snows are the most abundant.

over the area accounts for the shooting success. Possibly the heavy timber conceals the structures so well that the birds are upon them before they are noticed.

Calling in Arkansas is the Reelfoot Lake variety, or a chatter that is used only by mating ducks in the spring of the year. Some interpret this gabbling as a feed call. Maybe it is, an invitation to come roll the acorns as they are so numerous that help is solicited in eating them up. Anyway, the Stuttgart blinds and calling are effective. Several thousands of acres of domestic rice may have something to do with the worthwhileness of this area.

Before leaving this vicinity, mention might be made of the geese in the Cairo, Illinois, district. Baited into a small area by the Illinois Department of Conservation, some 35,000 Canada honkers spend a leisurely winter gobbling man-raised corn or making sojourns to the gravel and sand on the bars in the Mississippi. In this area pits are dug, profile and stuffed geese are placed in cornfields closely adjacent to the refuge, and every precaution is taken which seems in keeping with goose-shooting tactics. For $10 or $15 a hunter may crawl into a pit and kill his two birds. He could do equally well, as has often been observed, by standing in the back barn door of some of the farms catering to the hunters.

En route to the Delta country where Old Man River spews into the Gulf, one other form of duck shooting deserves mention. This is in the Cadahoula Lake vicinity. Here blinds are built with the same care as those made by the Yankees in Minnesota and Wisconsin. Spreads of decoys are put out in the same manner and ducks are called with a combination of the Reelfoot call and the Illinois River chatter. In low-water years one may wade knee deep a mile out in this large lake and get shooting on the milion fowl that frequent it. High water offers some boat shooting, and birds feeding in the margins on acorns offer something similar to Arkansas conditions.

Below New Orleans the Mississippi spreads out into a delta. These low mud flats are frequented by an abundance of blue geese. Snow geese are common, and the ringneck, or Canada goose, may be taken in some numbers by the initiated and the fortunate.

Blinds are generally built along the line of flight utilized by the birds. This flight is subject to change, and so it is studiously observed. A pirogue usually is towed behind a speedboat and furnishes a seat and blind to the hunter when he determines just where the place is to be. A bundle of roseau-cane is cut and poked down alongside the boat in the shallow waters. Duck decoys are placed for the puddle ducks. Often lumps of mud are kicked up in the bog with boots and decorated with bits of paper to decoy snow and blue geese.

The geese are called by Cajun guides with the voice. Puddle ducks are squeaked in with small, slender cane calls. Decoys are usually homemade from cypress knees by Cajun craftsmen. They are the most perfect imitation of a duck ever constructed. Often eager hunters pay as much as $75 per dozen for them. There definitely is no supply on the market. Cypress is practically waterlog-proof and will last for an eternity; also, it is almost as light as balsa wood.

Westward from New Orleans one shoots in the coastal marsh or directly north of it in the rice fields. This same terrain extends into East Texas. Of the rice-field shooting, there is little to tell. Birds swarm into this area of abundant food and are popped off in the canals surrounding the fields. Either that, or they are flight-shot as they trade back and forth toward the coastal region.

In the coastal marsh, duck and goose shooting again resembles a science. As previously mentioned, waterfowl are gullible in the wintering grounds. Seldom do the gunners have definite blinds where they go. Usually the Cajun guide poles out into the boggy, reedy country. He infrequently has over a dozen decoys. A small opening of water in the reeds usually answers admirably. The decoys are set close into the fringe of tules, bulrush, or whatever the cover is. The pirogue is backed into the vegetation and the ever-present slender cane duck call is brought into view.

Mallards and, more commonly, pintails respond eagerly. The latter is probably the finest eating bird of all the duck clan in the vicinity of the rice fields. A gadwall or widgeon readily decoys, teal sweep past, and often a stupid diver will give a shot. Over the coastal marsh blue and snow geese drift aimlessly. Generally they are in small numbers. The Cajun whoops and hollers with his voice and the silly fowl turn about. Squawking and answering excitedly, they more often than not fly directly over the concealed gunners. Less often Canadas are called by the voice and in for a kill. It is not unusual by any means. The white-fronted geese, while not abundant, present a more difficult problem. Few of the marsh men can call them and no artificial call was ever developed to entice this most wary of the geese.

**Plate XIV.** Gene Howe, Amarillo, Texas, and Nash Buckingham, Memphis, Tenn., begin digging a pit blind on the South Canadian River in West Texas. Both geese and ducks are commonly taken along Southwestern rivers from such a blind. The hunters have their quail-shooting togs on. Hunting is divided between bobwhite and the ducks and geese.

Testimony to the effectiveness of this hit-and-miss hunting is borne out by data taken in a day shooting place south of Lake Charles, in 1942. Over 10,000 ducks were killed and over 5,000 geese were taken. There was not a blind on the whole property. The guides were Cajuns and the calling was done by voice. Duck decoys were never more than a dozen and goose decoys were never used.

Inland from the coast in the vicinity of Abbeville a blind frequented by a former governor of Louisiana is now used by one of the clubs. It was a sunken concrete structure 6 feet square in a lake over 4 feet in depth. The shooter could pick his birds and kill a limit of mallards, pintails, or canvasbacks. Calling was not necessary and possibly two dozen decoys were used.

In shooting waterfowl along the Mississippi it should be remembered that gunning on this webfoot thoroughfare is as old as our white civilization. Conditions are ever changing. If you are a casual hunter and go out once a season, avail yourself of guides and place your shooting destiny in their hands. If you are a dyed-in-the-wool duck pursuer your observations and experiments will keep you abreast of the times. Ten years from now you may be using decoys 3 feet long. You may be using radio short waves for your calling and resorting to radar to locate your quarry. The mallard may be a new American upland game bird and the limit may be one fowl per season.

Whatever the score, your shooting success will be measured by your persistence. As in training a dog, the same thing is applicable in outwitting a duck or a goose. You must know more than they do.

## CENTRAL-WEST AREA

The great shooting area in the central section of the United States is the famous Bear River marshes in Utah, which most shooters claim has more species of waterfowl and a greater abundance of them than any single place in this country. Many shooters, when the daily limit permitted, vied to see how many species rather than how many ducks they could bag in one day's shooting. Though no one is recorded as having killed one each of all 16 of the species found there in a single day's shooting, a few shooters have come close to this mark. Pintails, teal, mallards, redheads, gadwall, shovellers, widgeon, greater and lesser scaup all are plentiful, and quite a few Canada and lesser snow geese are found.

The greatest problem encountered by the shooters on these marshes is that of transportation. The marsh is too soft for a vehicle and too shallow for a boat, except along the fringes. To overcome this some shooters have turned inventors and the contraptions called "marsh gliders," "mud gliders," "mud boats," and varied other names, have resulted. These have much in common with both a boat and a tractor, and they provide a means of getting through the broad marshes. The average shooter uses reed mats and temporary makeshift blinds.

Although large tracts of the marsh are taken up by private duck clubs, the individual shooter does not have any trouble finding plenty of sport. There are few great human population centers in that area, as there are in other and less populous waterfowl marshes, which may be one reason why there is plenty of shooting for everyone.

The Colorado River and the Platte River both supply good duck shooting, and many of the man-made reservoirs in the central area attract large concentrations during the migration period.

Both North and South Dakota are among the best waterfowl shooting states, especially the former. Birds from thousands of square miles of Canadian marshes funnel through North Dakota, beginning early in the fall and continuing all through the season. Here also the shooting is varied, with good sport found in the wide stubble fields and marshes, as well as on the lakes and rivers.

## PACIFIC COAST

The Pacific coast wildfowler of today not only has a wider variety of waterfowl, but a greater abundance than that of the Atlantic coast shooter. A number of species of geese winter along the coastal area west of the Sierra and the Cascade ranges, including the cackling, Canada, western Canada, lesser Canada, tule, Ross's, lesser snow and white-fronted geese as well as the black brant. The ducks found there include the mallard, gadwall, baldpate, pintail, green-wing and cinnamon teal, shoveller, wood duck, redhead, ring-necked duck, canvasback, greater scaup, lesser scaup, golden-eye, bufflehead, old squaw, western harlequin, white-winged scoter, surf scoter and American scoter, all of the mergansers, and in Southern California the fulvous tree duck. With this variety, and with an abundance of some of these species wintering along the coastal area from Georgia Strait to the Gulf of California, it is not surprising that duck shooting is a popular sport in this area.

In California the wide river valleys, stubble fields, rice flats, and marshes offer opportunities for nearly every type of duck shooting. Here occur almost every kind of blind, from the sunken barrel, sunken box, stake blind, tule blind, brush blind, and boat blind to the various floating types.

In the southern part of the state the tules *(tooleys)*, which grow in rank profusion in many areas, make the shooter's task somewhat easier. While some shooters build platforms in the tules, many follow the simpler method of merely pushing into them with a boat after scattering a few decoys on the open water. This is one area where a good retriever really pays his way, for nose as well as eyes is required to find a dead bird in the tules. Teal and pintails are fairly plentiful early in the season and the canvasbacks and mallards appear later.

Along the coast there are large number of various species of diving ducks, and the black brant are reported to be making a comeback in some areas. The geese are more plentiful inland, on the lakes and through the river valleys, where they find rich gleaning in the fields and plenty of food in the marshes. Areas such as the Suisun marshes, Salton Sea, and Butte Creek have no scarcity of waterfowl, and with the many private and commercial duck clubs there is no difficulty in finding a good shooting spot. The commercial clubs which have sprung up in recent years have increased the problem faced by the shooter of moderate means, however, and they have also been accused of doing their share in reducing waterfowl abundance. But California is a big state, and there still is good open shooting to be found by the man willing to seek it out.

In the willows area the lesser snow goose and the white-front offers plenty of sport, and they are still reasonably plentiful. The San Joaquin Valley is the gathering place for myriads of waterfowl, but many of the really good areas are privately owned, most of them by private clubs. The private clubs, however, are seldom charged with overshooting, for most of them follow self-imposed regulations which tend to conserve waterfowl.

California has probably the only duck club, the Bolsa Chica Club, which paid a cash dividend to its original members, for oil was located on the club property and the members have been getting royalty checks as well as unusually fine waterfowl shooting.

The lesser snow geese, or *waveys*, are not so plentiful as they were shortly after the turn of the century, but they still provide plenty of sport. The favorite method of hunting is from sunken barrels in the open fields and marsh fringes, and profile decoys are widely used. Many shooters insist they would rather shoot waveys than any other goose, but would rather have one of any other species than ten waveys for eating. In the early days these geese were so plentiful in California that they were killed by the thousands by men with clubs. Today, however, it takes a full-choked 12 to get a limit.

The duck shooting in Washington is not what it was, but conditions are improving in most areas. The large bays, lakes, and rivers have an assortment of ducks and geese, and the coastal area provides fair shooting on diving ducks.

Oregon has excellent shooting in the central and coastal areas, with Klamath Lake one of the concentration ploints for both waterfowl and shooters. Some of the ducks, including the lordly canvasback, are not highly prized for the table at some periods, for those that are taken on the big salmon rivers of both Washington and Oregon eat a lot of salmon eggs. This gives the duck the flavor of a mackerel that has rested too long in the sun. Tule Lake Refuge harbors a tremendous variety of both ducks and geese, and while this is sanctuary, there is excellent shooting outside the refuge borders.

## Canada

From the edge of spruce in eastern Manitoba to the foothills of the Rocky Mountains in Alberta lies a vast region of prairie and parkland. This is where Canada raises her tremendous crop of wheat, barley, and other cereals; wherever land is tilled there are grainfields. Scattered throughout most of this great expanse of agricultural land are countless sloughs and potholes, marshlands and rush-bordered lakes, the home and breeding grounds for many of our waterfowl resources from April through October. When the dark-green tules turn to brown and the reeds to golden yellow, this land of wheat and ducks becomes one of the finest wildfowling regions in the world, for it holds not only the birds that were bred and born there, but it is the early-autumn rendezvous and travel lane for waterfowl that breed beyond in the unsettled North. Any discussion of wildfowling in Canada, then, naturally is built around this region of the Prairie Provinces.

**Kinds of Waterfowl Hunted.** The mallard leads the list as the most abundant and popular duck on the prairies. Whether encountered in small numbers in slough or pothole, or in its many thousands on the stubble fields, the mallard is, over all, the chief Canadian sporting duck. The pintail, although a common breeder both on the prairies and farther north, is not so abundant in autumn as the mallard, probably because of an earlier shift of its population southward. Nor is it so highly favored as a table bird. Occasionally the black duck is taken in the west; it is usually, however, a single bird traveling with mallards. These do not breed on the prairies, but in late summer there is a westward movement of "blackies," mostly adult males, which join up with the mallards. In eastern Canada, of course, the black duck takes the place of the mallard as the most popular of wildfowl.

The blue-winged teal is well along in its migration when the Canadian season opens, and at best there is seldom more than a week of good teal shooting before all but a few stragglers have moved out of the country. Some hunters favor this teal during early-season "shirtsleeve" weather, but because of its size and early departure it is of secondary importance as a game species.

All other river ducks—the gadwall, baldpate, green-winged teal, and shoveller—individually make up a small portion of the total bag. While frequently taken in the mixed bags of early season, they seldom are especially sought-after as is the mallard. In market days these birds were known as "rough ducks," and this term still is applied to the bag of indiscriminately-plumaged birds of these kinds which, except for the shoveller, the gunner often is unable to identify as to species.

Of the diving ducks, the canvasback is the most favored; and in some regions where it is particularly abundant in fall flight, it replaces the mallard in popularity. The redhead, though not so well liked as the canvasback, is shot heavily. Most of the redheads shot are late-hatched young, poor in flesh and plumage. Its abundance in the bag is not due to the redhead's popularity, but because in the mild early season these young, unwary birds often are the only ducks coming to the decoys. Both the canvasback and the redhead have suffered severe reductions in number.

Canvasback shooting is largely an early-October affair, this being the period when the birds rendezvous on the larger marshes before their southward departure. In most years their main passage takes place in the middle of October and, even though open water may persist for several more weeks, the species is uncommon the remainder of the season.

The lesser scaup, or bluebill, is the most common diving duck on Canadian waters. In old times it was shot only when other kinds were scarce or lacking, but now it is taken regularly wherever it gathers, although it is by no means so popular as the canvasback. The bluebill is the *fall duck* of western shooters. During the early part of the season there is only a thin scattering of scaup over the prairies,

PLATE XV. Eskimo calling cackling geese by waving his cap and shouting *"L-u-u-k, L-u-u-k."*

its greatest concentrations being attained after the middle of October. The mass exodus of bluebills with the freeze-up is the most spectacular event of the Canadian season, and on a clear, quiet evening of the first hard frost the sky east and west as far as the eye can see is strewn with darts of bluebills heading southward.

The greater scaup, the "broadbill" of eastern shooters, is uncommon in the west and is shot only rarely. Nor is the ring-necked duck a common game species. The scoters, the golden-eyes, the bufflehead, and the harlequin duck are only of local importance as game ducks and generally are not especially sought after. Likewise, the coot, although present almost everywhere ducks are found, is not considered a sporting bird. Thus, studying species composition of hunters' bags, biologists of the Detla Waterfowl Research Station, in Manitoba, examined 11,000 ducks without recording a single bagged coot.

The Canada goose, frequently called "gray goose" or "honker," is the most popular and abundant of the larger waterfowl. Although the systematic ornithologists are somewhat uncertain regarding the racial subdivisions of this group, Canadian hunters recognize the bird in three sizes: big, medium, and small. The big honker, the common Canada goose, ranges from 7½ to 14 pounds, with reports of larger birds, up to 18 pounds. The middle-sized bird is the lesser Canada goose, ranging from 3½ to 7 pounds. The tiny bird is the Richardson's goose, 3 to 6 pounds. Farther west the largest and smallest of the geese are represented by darker birds, the western Canada goose and the cackling goose.

In Saskatchewan and in Alberta the white-fronted goose is an important game species; and recently its numbers have shifted eastward into Manitoba. The lesser snow goose and the blue goose are common spring migrants through western Canada, but are rare there in autumn. The best-known shooting ground for these species is the south shore of James Bay, in Ontario. The greater snow goose is concentrated only on the lower St. Lawrence River where it stops a while each autumn on its way to its Carolina wintering grounds. The brant are coastal species only, the American brant being shot on the east coast and the black brant along the British Columbia shoreline.

**Types of Shooting.** Shooting practices fall under two broadly-defined types: dry-land shooting and over-water gunning. In the west, there are many old-timers who have shot ducks all their lives without ever having stepped in a canoe or donned a pair of hip boots. This, of course, is where stubble or pass shooting is at its best, and where the finest kind of wildfowling may be had with one's feet firmly set on dry ground. Elsewhere, in marshland, or lake or coastal waters, most of the gunning is done over water with decoys.

**Stubble Shooting.** In late July and early August, mallards begin to gather in small crowds on the western marshes or lake shores. Many of these are adult males which have been skulking flightless in the tules for the last few weeks. Now, with their new wing feathers fully grown, they are on the move again. Their numbers are increased as the new-flying young-of-the-year join their company, until by late August or early September individual bands have grown from a few hundred to several thousand. Sometimes a single group will hold from 20,000 to 30,000 ducks. By and large, the old females still are moulting in the marshland during this early gathering period.

At this same time the grain harvest is in full swing, and the gleanings left behind by the harvest crews are the main source of food for these birds. They fly to the stubble morning and evening to feed on the fields, loafing and preening on their mudbars or beaches between flights. During the early season there may be shuttles back and forth between loafing bars and stubble field all day long; the mass of birds, however, generally hold to the early and late hours. As the season advances, and particularly as the hunter comes afield, there is little or no movement during the middle hours of the day.

These stubble gatherings are made up mostly of mallards, although a few pintails are found with them and an occasional black duck. Usually solid flocks of pintails are not found on the stubble until late in the season.

In September most of the males are in drab, female-like plumage, the adults in their eclipse, and the young in their juvenile dress. Many hunters mistake these for hens. As the season advances into October, however, the drakes, old and young alike, assume the bright green head and ruddy breast of the breeding plumage. It is then that stubble shooting is best of all; the birds dress firm and yellow, with hardly a pinfeather.

Before the hunting season, large groups of several thousand may feed together on one field, but as hunting gets under way they quickly break into smaller bands, and reach farther afield for their food. Sometimes they fly 50 or 60 miles to favored

PLATE XVI. Eskimo Hunter and Emperor Geese.

fields, particularly when some distant region has suffered late-summer or early-autumn rains to delay the harvest. At such times the birds leave the home marsh with the first hint of dawn, arriving on the stubble at sun-up. After the morning feed, they loaf on some wet field, feed again at twilight, and then fly the long way back to their loafing bars for grit and night's rest.

The hunter who would take these stubble birds must count on two days afield for every good hunt. First he locates a field the birds are using; then he returns the next morning or afternoon, well ahead of the flight, to take his position. He may dig a pit to hide himself, or take a position in a grassy fence-row, or pull a few woods and straws together. If he uses decoys he sets them up-wind of his hiding place in a spot where droppings are fresh or where he saw the birds yesterday. If it is a dawn shoot he must arrive in the dark of night and be settled at the first hint of light; if an evening shoot, he must arrive while the sun is still well up over the horizon. Shortly after he has arranged his decoys and hidden himself, the flight begins; everywhere the sky is broken by strings of mallards moving out to the fields. Most of the ducks are going to other destinations, but some of these will cross the gunner's field and he may have some excellent shooting of birds passing overhead. If he has chosen his field well, however, most of his shooting will be at birds coming in to feed. A band will come straight from the marsh or lake, swing low over the field, circling again and again, more like doves than ducks, the light flashing golden on their white under-wing coverts. As the band circles, it is joined by stray twos and threes until suddenly a host of mallards is upon the gunner, who must be clear of head and steady of hand to take his double. Often, particularly if he has taken his birds from the rear of the flock, they will swing over at least once more for another shot before departing for a more peaceful feeding spot. Seldom does the stubble hunter take his limit, and the shoot invariably is "short and sweet." Hardly has it begun before the shades of evening or the bright morning light has ended the shooting. The chances are that this field will be abandoned following the shoot, and will yield small return the next day; then the stubble-hunter must go elsewhere.

With the careful sportsman stubble hunting is the least wasteful of all wildfowling, for the birds are downed on dry land in very light cover. They must be retrieved as shot, however, for the crippled mallard is almost as quick of foot and can hide in as scant a cover as the ring-necked pheasant. Thus, in the fading light of evening shoots, the careless gunner may bring heavy waste.

Geese, like mallards, generally are shot on stubble fields. They likewise fly from the marsh or lake morning and evening to partake of the gleanings. They come to the prairies in late September and reach peak numbers by mid-October; a few flocks remain each year for a short while after the marshes and lake shores are frozen over. The technique for hunting is much the same as with mallards, a using field being located and the hunters returning the next day to dig pits and set decoys before the flight begins. When heavily shot, the Canada geese become extremely wary, seldom feeding more than a day or so in the same field and shying away from the very best of decoy set-ups.

**Pass Shooting.** Although ducks move freely in the unbounded sky, their local travels are dictated by the pattern of the terrain below them. Thus, when traveling from one water area to another they follow the shortest overland route, such as the "narrows" separating two lakes. Or they will follow creek beds, even when dry, or take their flight line along a chain of potholes. For this reason, patchwork of small and large water areas in western Canada gives the finest of all pass shooting; often the hunter in a new region may find his stand by merely studying a map.

In slough and pothole country where many small water areas sit one close to another, there is a regular back-and-forth traffic of ducks, offering first-rate pass shooting. Sometimes hunters help the flight along by taking separate stands and forcing the birds, in turn, from one pothole to the next. Such hunting is at its best during the early season before the birds have moved from their local marshes to the larger concentration centers. Mixed bags are the rule and young birds, probably native to the region, are taken in greatest number. On some of the larger lake systems, such "narrows" are famous the land over for the pass shooting, both in the early season and later in the fall when the migration is in full swing.

Larger marshes often are patterned in intricate mazes by the growths of bulrush, cattail, and cane-reed; and, naturally, there is movement of birds from one portion to another. In these travels, very definite air trails are followed across the marsh growth in passage from one bay to the next. If he is lucky, a gunner may place himself at a stand over which passes a seemingly endless flight of birds, usually swinging low and often crossing over a lane hardly a gunshot wide. The word "lucky" is used advisedly for, even though the hunter knows the marsh well, certain passes are used only in certain winds; where one evening he may spot a heavy flight, a slight shift in wind is followed by a change in passage. When he returns the following day, not a single bird crosses at this stand. Marsh passes are at their very best in early October when the canvas-backs are making ready to move south; or in late October when the bluebills are down in their many thousands.

Mallards flighting to stubble regularly follow lanes of travel when leaving or coming to their loafing bars. They may cross a lake-shore ridge at a creek mouth, or follow a stream-bed, or a chain of sloughs—not only day after day, but year after year. Indeed, the recorded history of some mallard passes goes back half a century or more. The gunner who takes his stand at one of these crossings must be skilled and careful, for those birds passing just out of range invariably outnumber the fair shots; if thoughtless or eager, he is tempted to "reach out" farther than he should. Most of the birds he takes are passing straight overhead.

Even though the passage of mallards is regular, the shooting is by no means a routine affair. Success depends upon wind and weather. In a blow, particularly if there is light snow, the finest kind of gunning may be enjoyed if the birds are moving against the wind. On the other hand, most of the birds moving with a tail wind may pass out of range. Then, again, the movement of mallards is higher on fair days when, even with a heavy flight, the entire passage is out of range.

Such mallard passes usually are many yards wide, so that only a small part of the total flight is covered by one gun.

Some old-time goose shooters do most of their gunning at passes. As with mallards, the history of many goose passes predates the experience of modern hunters, and the shooting stands are traditions for man and bird alike. Some passes function for both geese and ducks. The passes may be near marshes or lakes where the birds cross the shore line near the same place day after day, year after year. Others are far from the resting waters where the travel to and from the fields follows old creek beds or strips of marsh. When shooting at such passes the gunner tries to take a stand behind cover where he can spot the advancing geese far away. Should their course bear to the left or right he moves breathlessly as best he can in half-crouch to intercept the birds. But if it is a windy day the honkers may take a new bearing before they are in range, crossing over the place the hunter has just left! Hence the rule is "stay put" regardless of the temptation to move.

**Marsh Shooting.** On the larger marshes, hunting with decoys is the most popular type of wildfowling. Marsh shooters may be considered in three categories: those seeking a bag of ducks regardless of species, those seeking mallards, and those who seek canvasback. Most gunners fall into the first class and, by force of circumstances, most early-season bags are mixed, regardless of the hunter's desire. This is because of the heterogeneous make-up of the early-fall population, when young of all species ply the marsh edge, when the solid bands of mallards move only to stubble, and when the canvasback either will not decoy or are not yet down from the north in any number. A typical prairie marsh bag during the early season holds a teal or two, a baldpate or a shoveller, a brace of young mallards full of pinfeathers, a couple of young redheads, and perhaps a gadwall or young canvasback.

As the season advances, the mallard and canvasback hunters find good shooting and, if they are as wise as the birds, they may take solid bags of the kinds they seek. Some old-timers seek to take a limit of males only in canvasback or mallard when the birds are working well. Good mallard shooting depends upon time and weather. During the early season—that is, during late September and the first days of October—mallards do not decoy well in the marsh. The stubble birds move to and from their fields, offering only the chance shot to the gunner in his marsh hide. The advent of good shooting coincides with the rough autumn weather that comes when the drakes have changed into their bright nuptial dress. When winds blow hard and heads are bright green, mallard shooting is good in the marsh. The setup for mallards is a protected lee shore or a small marsh slough. The birds make their regular morning flight to the fields, and then return to their usual loafing places on the open bars. In the face of the rough winds, however, they do not wait long in the open and, after taking grit, they begin to move in to the protected marsh edges. Thus there is a steady passage of birds seeking cover, the makings of a first-rate shoot. Generally a small set of decoys is best. Such shooting is to be had for only a few days each autumn, for the rough winds and the bright plumage are advance notices of winter weather shortly to follow.

In some regions where all marshes are small and scattered, these waters are the only areas used by stubble birds in the absence of lake beaches or marsh mudflats. Often such small waters are immediately adjacent to stubble fields; morning and evening the birds merely take a "hop and a jump" over to the grain and back. Such sloughs may hold from 3 or 4 to 75 or 100 mallards plus a few other kinds. They are best hunted at twilight when suddenly in the fading light there is a rain of plump, thick-necked birds, full of barley, seeking their night roost.

Canvasbacks, like mallards, do not stool well until the season has moved along toward its middle. When the gunning opens, the man after canvasback hardly can hope for a setup that will lure the birds in, wings set, feet wide-spread. Instead, his best chance is to place decoys where there is a regular movement of canvasbacks—at a point of reeds or at the mouth of a heavily-used lead. Birds swinging by may be drawn over within range of such decoys, even if they have no intentions of joining the blocks. Once the birds are stooling, however, the gunner can set up for the finest of all marsh shooting. His successful hunt depends upon adherence to two rules: (1) He must place his decoys where canvasbacks are feeding; (2) he must arrange his decoys and hide so that the birds can swing in easily.

In regard to the first point, the canvasback on the prairies feeds mostly upon the tubers of sago pondweed *(Potamogeton pectinatus)*, and decoys regularly only where beds of this grow. Evidence of feeding activity is found along the bulrush edge where the long stems and leaves of the pondweed, cast aside by the ducks, collect in heavy windrows. The best indication, of course, is to surprise the feeding birds themselves, put them off without a shot, and then quickly set up to await their return. This is one reason for the canvasback's inability to stand up under heavy gun pressure. The best canvasback shooting is on a heavily-shot marsh, for then the birds are pushed from one feed bed to the next, to be greeted almost everywhere by a set of decoys and a couple of guns.

The special arrangement of the decoys and hide is highly important because the canvasback is a heavy-bodied bird with relatively small wing area. Even when dropping into decoys it comes at a terrific speed. Plainly speaking, it needs a long landing strip. Should the hunter place his hide directly upwind of the decoys, the birds find it awkward to come in to the stool. The result is equally awkward for the hunter whose gunning is poor and crippling heavy. Thus, the successful canvasback hunter sits with the wind hitting his shoulder, letting the birds come in for crossing shots, with plenty of water up- and down-wind of the stool.

Many Canadian hunters favor the last marsh shoot of the year when the bays are frozen over except for here and there a few open holes. In these a few mallard and lesser scaup remain until the bitter end. Dressed in white clothes, or with a sheet to cover their togs, the hunters sit beside holes and may take their limit within an hour. These hunters drag a canoe over the ice to slip into the hole when they pick up their bag. Or they may carry a pole and fishline with a hooked wire tip for snagging birds from the icy water. Some of these late shooters wear ice skates to travel from one hole to the next. One or two days of this and wildfowling for the year is over, regardless of how many more days the record has set for the season. Ice usually ends the Canadian shooting season before the legal closing arrives.

Jump shooting on the prairie marshes is largely the sport for youths, novices, or the few old-timers who particularly favor jumping. For the most part, the old marsh shooter seldom jumps his birds. Indeed, in some circles it is the code that no shot is fired in the marsh while going to or from the hide. The exception, of course, is in "bluebird" weather when the decoys promise little more than the stray teal or redhead. This comparative unpopularity of jump shooting on the prairies undoubtedly has its roots in the make-up of the early marsh population. In late September and early October the birds skulking in edge cover, lingering until the jumper's canoe is quite upon them, are mostly late-hatched young or old females, both still in moult and poor of flesh. Hence, even though the sport may be good and the bag large, the quality of birds taken is poor. It is a different story with the blue-winged teal, of course; and if the hunter is early enough to catch the last of the blue-wings, he may take a fine bag.

In the east, particularly in rice country, jumping is something else again. Often this is the only way a bag is to be had in any weather, and the birds, seldom locally reared, may be in excellent condition.

**Wildfowling in Eastern Canada.** Those in the west think of the "east" as all of Canada lying between the Lake of the Woods and the Atlantic, a parcel of terrain some 2000 miles wide. Although the abundance and variety of ducks through much of this region seldom is as great as on the prairies, there are some localities with fine waterfowling. And in almost any part of this land one will find a representative of that special breed of man, the black duck hunter. His bird is the finest and the wariest of all wildfowl. A brace of northern redlegs taken from a beaver pond or tidal marsh to him is worth a couple of limits of western pothole ducks, particularly (as is often the case) if there are a ruffed grouse and a woodcock or two to fill out the other game pocket. Black ducks are jumped from rice in Ontario, or over decoys on the coastal marshes, or on the bottom lands of the big river valleys. Where there are farms they sometimes flight to the fields like mallards, and make twilight flights from open-water loafing grounds to marshland feeding areas.

Eastern shooters have long held that there are two kinds of black duck: the common black duck of early season and the big red-legged black duck which comes out of the north in late fall. Ornithologists likewise divided this bird into two species until a young Toronto biologist, Terry Shortt, carefully demonstrated the fact that all were one and the same kind, those with the bright red legs being adult males. These old drakes separate from the young and females during the summer and come down from the north later, so that this second shift of big, red-legged birds was easily mistaken for another species.

On the shores of the larger lakes there is excellent point shooting of diving ducks; and there are some good marshes as well. In many regions the blue-winged teal provides fair early-season hunting and

PLATE XVII. Eskimo hunter in kayak reaching for gun as eiders approach.

the green-winged teal comes down in mid-autumn. Along the rivers and lakes, golden-eyes are in some places top ducks, although mostly because they are the most common species. On coastal waters there is "coot" shooting of scoters, and some of the finest brant hunting in the world.

Although eastern gunners do not have as much wildfowling as in the west, they take it just as seriously, and a program for the study of eastern waterfowl problems has been estabished in the University of New Brunswick, at Fredericton.

**Wildfowling in British Columbia.** British Columbia is the mountain province, hence wildfowling is limited to a relatively small part of the province. But it is a big area (bigger than Texas) of widely differing terrain, so that actually it offers the widest range of duck hunting of any Canadian province. In the Peace River country of the northwest is the finest stubble shooting in the world. There are prairie marshes, sloughs and potholes, mountain lakes and rivers, wide river valleys with rich bottomland. And the coast line, including the island coast, reaches more than 1000 miles between the State of Washington and Alaska.

**Guns and Ammunition.** Wildfowling in Canada is largely a 12-gauge affair. This is so much the case that in many towns and outlying districts dealers handle only 12-gauge shells. Since the war, however, new hunters have picked up any gun they could obtain and, in some makes, new arms have been available only in small gauges. Of the lesser guns, the 20 gauge is more popular than the 16 gauge. Only novices and a few experts use the .410, which nowhere is considered a fowling piece. Oldtimers, particularly the goose hunters, frequently carry 10 gauges, but this is not a common gun in marsh shooting. American-made guns outnumber the foreign makes.

The double-barreled gun and the pump are about equal in popularity. The auto-loading gun is nowhere as common in the United States because of special regulations covering the use of automatic arms. In the Prairie Provinces the automatic is outlawed for wildfowling, while in the other provinces it must be permanently plugged to hold not more than one shell in the magazine, thus placing it on par with the double.

Number 6 shot is the favorite for ducks, but stubble shooters often carry No. 4's; No. 2's and No. 4's are standard for geese. Number 7½ shot is not popular, and is therefore unobtainable in some regions. So close is the adherence to No. 6 shot that many small dealers carry nothing else, and it is used for pheasant and chicken as well as for duck. The standard load of 3¼ drams of powder and 1⅛ drams

PLATE XVIII. Eskimo and White-Fronted Geese.

of shot is used mostly in marsh shooting, although many of the younger hunters go all-out for the heaviest load they can get for all shooting. For stubble, pass, and goose shooting the 3¾-1¼ load is generally used. Three-inch hulls scattered about is the record left behind by American visitors, for this big load is not currently popular with Canadian shooters.

**Working Dogs.** The Labrador retriever is the most popular duck dog throughout the west. The black phase is most commonly seen, and there is hardly a community between Winnipeg and the Peace River which does not have at least one of these dogs. The golden Labrador, however, is growing in popularity, particularly since the end of the war, after which time new golden stock was shipped in from overseas. All other water retrievers are far behind the "lab" in most regions, but the Chesapeake still is a local favorite and there are scattered golden retrievers, Irish water spaniels, and curly-coated retrievers. The springer spaniel is a popular upland dog in Canada, often used for ducks. It is not generally considered hardy enough, however, for late-season and cold-water shooting.

The new interest in the golden Labrador is due, in some measure at least, to the feeling that it is much the less conspicuous both in marsh and stubble, and hence a more efficient color for wildfowling. Even with the best-trained beast it is not always possible to keep the jet coat of the black "lab" a secret. Strangely, however, the conspicuous coat of the black Labrador does not unduly disturb waterfowl. Indeed, it often happens that when the dog is in action, as when making a retrieve, passing ducks actually are attracted toward the dog, "tolled," as it were; and many hunters have seen their dog attract birds within range that otherwise might have passed by well out of gunshot. This, of course, brings to the discussion the dog which was especially bred to toll ducks on the Atlantic coast, and which now is found only in certain parts of Nova Scotia. With these small collie- or foxlike dogs the wildfowler sits hidden on shore where he can watch birds sitting out in open water. He tosses sticks or stones up and down the beach where his dog races back and forth after them in mad excitement. The ducks, unable to contain their curiosity, swim to see what all the commotion is about, and suddenly find themselves within gun range of the dog's owner.

As in the United States, the number of duck hunters who work dogs is relatively small. In many areas not more than one or two out of every 100 gunners takes a dog into the marsh. With the ever-greater need for more careful shooting, and with the proved value of the good retriever, it is expected that the next few years will see a marked increase in the number of retrieving dogs used by Canadian wildfowlers.

**Decoys.** The decoy is used in all types of Canadian shooting except pass or jump shooting, and so the stool has an important place in hunting techniques. Since much of Canada still lies at the edge of the frontier, the improvising of decoys with materials immediately at hand still is common practice. This is followed in many settled regions by modern hunters who cling to old techniques for "the good of the sport," or who do not wish to carry heavy blocks around. Most commonly, the dead bird itself is used as the decoy, particularly in stubble shooting; and it is considered a test of skill to start from scratch, hunt the hard way for three or four decoy birds, and then settle down for a steady shoot.

When a bird is taken it is arranged in lifelike position with a sharp willow stake thrust up through the chin. Or, as on sandbars, the bird is placed in a loafing position with the bill tucked under the wing. Some marsh shooters carry floating slabs with wire arrangements to hold the bird. Present-day shooters use such decoys mostly when mallards are sought, and on some bright days when the wary green-heads will not be fooled by the best of wooden blocks, they will swing in steady and true to three or four of their dead brethren. This steadying effect of the carefully arranged dead bird is so pronounced that some mallard hunters always set up two or three, even when using blocks.

James Bay Indians lure geese to their guns by setting out white paper, or wings, or cloth. When they used to shoot these waveys on the prairies in spring, hunters sometimes lured them to the guns by scattering pages from a mail-order catalogue over a field. In some parts of the west, black paper or cloth held on stakes is used by mallard hunters on stubble.

On sandbars or mudbars a common practice is to work up a "flock" of duck-shaped mounds, using one or two dead ducks as well to improve the illusion. This magic often works, particularly when the bar is one regularly used by local birds. A variation of this trick is accomplished by the hunter who carries a pocketfull of dried duck or goose wings, planting these, ducklike, on the sides of the mudpiles. This setup is rendered well-nigh perfect by silhouette heads on sticks arranged in proper position.

Stubble hunters sometimes use the duck head alone. Silhouette tin heads are tacked to short lath stakes. Since the head is the most conspicuous part of the duck standing in stubble, this idea is very effective. In snowstorms (the best of all stubble shooting) some hunters claim that passing ducks will come over to take a look at the dark depressions made by foot tracks deliberately spaced about the pit.

Silhouette decoys are the most popular for geese. They are effective, and a dozen or more can be carried in a small parcel. Many of these are fashioned by the hunter himself, who cuts them from tin. But the commercial type—the photo mounted on heavy waxed cardboard—is everywhere in common use. Duck silhouettes are not so common, and are used mostly on the stubble.

Wooden block decoys are used in marsh or lake shooting, 12 to 25 birds being the usual set. Larger sets are favored for diving ducks, while smaller sets are considered best for mallard in many circles. The species most commonly represented in blocks are mallard, canvasback, and lesser scaup. By and large, decoys in use today are but slightly over-size and the huge out-sized blocks are not popular. In some regions most of the blocks are carved by native guides during off season; and there still are many hunters who make their own decoys. Since most

Canadian shooting is of birds still in drab immature or eclipse plumage, it is not considered important to have the breeding plumages clearly and brightly portrayed. For instance, canvasback hunters would rather have mostly gray decoys, to match the most abundant juveniles, than the bright white and brick-red adult males.

**Blinds.** Permanent blinds are so uncommon over much of western Canada that the term "blind" seldom enters the wildfowler's vocabulary. Instead, he speaks of his "hide." He hides in whatever growth is available. If marsh shooting, he pulls his canoe into the reeds or bulrushes, ties it down firmly and rearranges the cover to hide himself and his craft. If the cover is poor he cuts some to cover his canoe. The lake-shore or river hunter may gather branches or driftwood or boulders together for his hide. The pass shooter generally finds enough cover to stand in without preparing a special hide. In the stubble field the "stooks" of sheaves used to be the universal hide, the hunter piling the sheaves around him. With the advent of the new swathing technique, however, these piles of sheaves are fast disappearing in many regions. In such open fields a pit is the rule unless there is enough weed growth or loose straw to gather together.

For goose and mallard shooting the very best of hiding cover is essential for a good shoot; the slightest movement or exposure of face or body reveals the hunter's secret before a fair shot is to be had. Diving ducks, on the other hand, often are less wary, and good shoots may be had sometimes from cover too scant to hide the hunter or his canoe, providing he does not move. With all species, the conditions of light and weather govern the hide. In many instances a good hunt may be had by merely sitting low and still. In twilight shooting some excellent bags may be taken by the man who merely lies down with enough wisps of weeds or straw over him to break his contour.

**Seasons and Regulations.** Canada regulates the pattern of its shooting under the same over-all plan as the United States under the Migratory Bird Treaty. This leaves room, however, for certain modifications so that the Canadian waterfowling rules are not necessarily the same as in the United States.

A. Protected Species. As in the United States, all cranes, swans, and shorebirds excepting woodcock and Wilson's snipe are protected. The Ross's goose is protected in Alberta, which is on its travel lane south from the Arctic. The wood duck is protected in all provinces except Ontario where not more than one wood duck may be taken in the daily bag.

B. Bag Limits. In all provinces the 1947 daily bag limit for ducks was seven birds, with a possession limit of 14. The annual legal kill of ducks was 100 in all provinces except Alberta and Saskatchewan, where it was 56, and Manitoba where it was 35.

For geese, including brant, the daily bag for all provinces was five for 1947, except in Manitoba where is was three. The possession limit for geese was 15, excepting in Alberta and Saskatchewan where it was ten, and in Manitoba where it was six. Season goose limits were 25 except in the Prairie Provinces, where it was 20 in Alberta and Saskatchewan, nine in Manitoba.

C. Shooting Restrictions. Live decoys and baiting are outlawed. Guns larger than 10-gauge are banned, and so is bow-and-arrow hunting. Nor can waterfowl be hunted from power-driven vehicles. Automatic guns must be permanently plugged to hold not more than one shell in the magazine, excepting in the Prairie Provinces where they are banned altogether. There are various provincial rules governing the plugging of pump guns. In British Columbia and Prince Edward Island pumps can hold one shell in the chamber; in Manitoba they may not hold more than two shells in the chamber. Elsewhere there are no special restrictions listed for the plugging of pumps.

Hours and Seasons. In all provinces except British Columbia, shooting hours are from one-half hour before sunrise until one-half hour after sunset. In British Columbia the shooting begins at sunrise and may continue for an hour after sunset except in certain areas where there are "clock hours." As in the United States, Canadian duck shooting is divided into zones from north to south. Thus in 1947 the shooting opened September 1 in the Yukon and Northwest Territories, and the last shooting ended December 15 in Nova Scotia. Most Canadian duck shooting is in the southern zone, where it begins in late September or early October. Length of season varies from province to province, but almost everywhere frost usually puts an end to duck hunting well in advance of the legal closing. Thus over a period of ten years, the average duck season in Manitoba was less than 40 days.

The Canadian Department of Mines and Resources, Ottawa, Ontario, will supply a full outline of Canadian waterfowl regulations upon request.

**The Future of Wildfowling in Canada.** The conservation of migratory waterfowl is an international problem facing both Canadian and United States wildfowlers. The largest part of our continental duck population now breeds in Canada, yet most ducks and geese winter south of its border. Just as United States hunters look toward Canada for a large part of their fall flight, so Canadians look southward in spring for the breeding stock which must return in sufficient numbers each year to produce a shootable surplus. For several years there have been shortages in both spring and fall flights.

A fair portion of the Canadian breeding grounds lies within the agricultural region, particularly in the three Prairie Provinces. And here, with Dominion, provincial, and private funds (which have been advanced by sportsmen themselves), there has been a program of breeding-habitat improvement matching similar conservation measures in the United States. Despite such improvement and management of habitat, there are now vast regions of breeding grounds which are underpopulated with breeding stock. In other words, the physical management of the land is ahead of the management of the population itself. However great the need may be for more marshland in the over-all plan for ducks, the main requirement in the late 1940's is more ducks to fill the existing marshes. In 1947 the lack of breeding stock was so apparent in Manitoba that sportsmen

PLATE XIX. Eskimos and Blind on Kayak on the Edge of Ice.

voted their support for a closed season should that be necessary.

The middle 1940's reduction concerns almost all kinds of ducks, with the decline most noticeable in the blue-winged teal and black duck in eastern Canada, and in the mallard, redhead, canvasback, and lesser scaup in the west. So far these reductions have been detected only regionally. For instance, in the Prairie Provinces the 1947 decline was severe in Manitoba but only locally apparent elsewhere. Since its smaller population shoots a relatively smaller number of the ducks it raises, Canadian hunters look toward the United States for management of the breeding flock during the fall—just as United States hunters looked northward for the improvement of breeding conditions. But Canadians themselves have taken a hand in conserving the stock through regulation. Manitoba, whose breeding stock has been most seriously depleted, accepted a duck season of 25 days, with further restrictions on special shooting-breeding areas.

The species which are in greatest need of special attention and study are those whose main breeding grounds are centered largely in southern Canada. For these species, such as the redhead, the international boundary merely bisected the breeding range which, in early times, included vast areas in the United States. Now their breeding stronghold is within Canada, breeding numbers have been greatly reduced south of the boundary. For these kinds, the need is for a general build-up in numbers sufficient to fill the breeding marshes already available. Since they often suffer their heaviest losses where shooting grounds overlap breeding areas, and when seasons open before local stock has dispersed, protection and upbuilding may depend upon special date or place regulation which prevents shooting of these kinds until after they have spread out from the home range. In other words, all of the stock of a given locality are "eggs in one basket" during the early season; later openings would give them a chance to spread.

Some Canadian wildfowlers are greatly concerned over the increasing movement of United States hunters into Canadian marshes, particularly during the early part of the season. While the total number of such tourist-shooters is relatively small, their total man-hours of hunting bid fair to match or exceed those of natives in some localities. The problem is partly economic. Canadian provinces, like many of of the states in the United States, are anxious to "cash in" on their natural resources; and immediately following the war, many United States hunters suddenly found themselves in possession of the wherewithal to make their hunting dreams come true. On the other hand, it is a conservation problem as well, for the shift northward only reflects the diminishing returns at home. This emphasizes the international nature of the waterfowl conservation problem. A duck is just as dead whether shot in Manitoba or Wisconsin. If there are enough ducks to provide shooting for everyone, any place, any time, then such expansion of the hunter's range of activity is quite in order. However, in a period of diminishing supplies it is just as natural to expect shooting to be practiced on a home-locality basis.

Sportsman organizations are strong in Canada, particularly in the Prairie Provinces, and work closely with the Game and Fish Branches of the provincial governments.

## Alaska

Primitive man left his marks on the walls of caverns, inscribed papyrus scrolls, and painted his methods and results of the chase on various media. They all were pretty crude. We of the atomic age wonder at such records—evidently game was abundant and stupid.

**Southeast Alaska.** Today, in Alaska, waterfowl are still in enough abundance that blinds, decoys, and calling equipment are, for the most part, wholly disregarded. Even the white men, sport shooters in every sense of the word, resort to the more primitive form of hunting. Concealment may well be behind a drift log or a block of ice. Duck calls are Cheechako (tenderfoot) implements employed by "dude" hunters who live "outside" in the States. Decoys and well-built blinds are only things one sees pictured in the shooting magazines.

To say that in Alaska waterfowling is a hit-or-miss proposition is hardly correct. Pass shooting of one form or another is standard practice. The Wrangell news publisher and the Territorial Judge know pretty well which stump to hide behind when the ducks and geese start working in from the Stikine Flats at high tide. Their bag limit is often realized. In a like manner, the Eskimo knows the cutoffs taken by ducks, geese, and brants on their southern migration. Such cutoffs may be concealed behind a rock pile a mile from the Bering Sea or the Arctic Ocean. However, previous hunting success, generations back, selected this particular spot as a place the web-footed clan might make a by-pass and cut off many miles.

Waterfowl under their first baptism of fire from their northern nesting grounds to the States are a bit slow-witted. As they progress southward, running the gauntlet of gunners, their wits are sharpened. To survive in any appreciable numbers they become cagey by the time they arrive at Tule Lake, Stuttgart, or the Maryland coast.

Because Alaska waterfowl have not lost their nesting-ground stupidity or simplicity, hunters are not required to go into all the methods of concealment, enticement, and smart tactics employed by the gunners in the States. Opening day in Southeast Alaska is anticipated and entered into with the same zeal as in the States. The majority of the birds in the vicinity of Juneau, Wrangell, Petersburg, or Cordova are local fowl. One day of shooting makes them fully aware of all the passes, stumps, and rock concealments. Small sloughs, lakes, and tidal creeks do offer jump shooting, and this method of hunting ranks second only to pass shooting.

As the season progresses new migrants arrive. Snow geese usually are abundant in the Stikine Flats by October 14. The local residents keep close watch for the new arrivals. An aviator en route from Petersburg to Wrangell usually reports the first flocks. In a few days the white fowl are abundant and remain the greater part of the shooting season.

Not to be discounted are the "yellow feet," or white-fronted geese, that arrive in the Copper River flats early in the season. Cordova residents almost proclaim a holiday when these most toothsome of all the geese arrive. Unfortunately they often beat the season by several days and Alaskans are hard-headed when their rights to waterfowl are questioned. A platoon of game wardens is necessary to protect these birds. Even then violators often take a chance to bag a white-front.

Alaska is regarded as an iceberg country. Few gunners in the States realize that in the southern coastal regions waterfowl winter in great abundance. Mallards, pintails, wigeon, scaups, shovellers, gadwalls, and green-winged teal are the so-called shooting ducks. White-winged scoters and harlequins, and many of the inedible sea ducks, are numerous but are seldom shot for food.

Of the geese, the white snow geese are most abundant. Locally raised, a large Canada goose frequently weighing as much as 10 pounds is a year-round resident. His cousin, the lesser Canada, and the diminutive little honker, known as the cackling goose, make up the species. White-fronted geese report only in very limited numbers at any place south of the Copper River Flats. Rarely an emperor goose finds his way down coast below the Aleutian Islands.

Rare ducks reported in the Stikine country are blue-winged teal, cinnamon teal, and canvasbacks. The golden-eyes, both the Barrow's and the American species, are also found in some numbers.

Wearing apparel is a problem for the Alaska shooter. To date no garment has ever been devised to combat the inclement weather of that rainy, windswept coast. Hunting coats as a rule are avoided. Something heavily rubberized worn over as many layers of wool garments as one can squeeze into is the best bet.

A parka hood keeps rain from going down the back of the neck but obscures vision. The tail of the outside garment should be at least knee length, coming well below the tops of hip boots. Such length also offers some protection when riding bouncing speedboats to the shooting grounds. That part of the anatomy that usually gets wet first, either from squatting on a soggy log or sitting on wet boat seats, needs extra protection. When one has the seat of his pants soaking wet he is miserable all over. (This feeling is inherent, dating back to the days of swaddling clothes.)

Gloves are a problem. They are always wet. Many hunters prefer the cheapest kind of canvas or jersey and at periodic intervals wring the water out of them and put them back on. Rubberized trousers worn over the hip boots are commonly noted. They do shed water but, like all rubber garments—and this goes for the knee-length parka—they are usually too hot or too cold. Perspiring from wading muck, the hunter steams up his rubber raiment and is soaking anyway.

Shot size for the shooting of waterfowl varies considerably, even in Alaska. A tendency toward smaller sizes seems to rule in the white settlements. In the Arctic, the natives go in for big stuff. Snow geese are easily killed and a good mallard load of No. 6 shot will suffice. Honkers are more heavily feathered and often one will observe No. 2 shot in use. Possibly the shorter shooting ranges for Alaska birds have some influence on shot size, though magnum guns are beginning to appear all over the Territory.

A brief mention of retrievers might be in order. A few Labradors, Rat-tails, Chesapeakes, and Goldens are cropping up. Alaska today is serviced largely from the air. It is but a small problem for a good puppy to leave Seattle in the morning and become a resident of Anchorage before the sun sets. Fliers are often hunters and many of the retriever breeds belong to the airmen. Also Army personnel are bringing these dogs into the Territory.

Anywhere in the world a duck is taken, the hunting of it can be better and more pleasurably done with the aid of retriever. The saving in cripple losses would go far toward restoring our diminishing birds were it unlawful to hunt them without the aid of a dog.

Before leaving the coast of Southeast Alaska and examining waterfowl hunting procedure in the Arctic, let us recapitulate. Ducks and geese are eagerly sought by sportsmen of this region, men as keen as any of those found in the United States. Their methods of hunting are simple, pass and jump shooting being the rule. There are two good reasons for this: (1) Waterfowl are still fairly abundant and uneducated this far north; (2) The high tides of the Alaska coast make the building of blinds and the use of decoys a decided chore. One can quickly picture the inconvenience and hazards in building a blind at low-water mark that will, in the matter of minutes, be flooded at high tide with 18 feet of water, rushing in with the velocity of a tidal wave.

Waterfowl automatically adjust themselves to the high tides of Southeast Alaska. Feeding along the water margin of small river deltas, they often find weed seeds in abundance. Succulent roots of sedges provide geese with a fine fattening diet. As inrushing waters inundate the grassy areas, both ducks and geese turn tail and head toward higher ground. Often they are backed up almost to the very foot of the many mountainous islands that dot the area. As the tide recedes, birds follow the water out again. A hunter would almost need wings to keep pace with them. Hence the system of no blinds, no decoys, and no duck call.

**Arctic.** Waterfowling in the Arctic is done chiefly by the Eskimos, though the few white residents also participate in this activity. Sport hunting is at a minimum, and shooting is chiefly for food. Waterfowl to the Eskimo are often a necessity. To the whites it is at least a diversion in diet from canned meats or the only other fresh meat, reindeer.

Again, as in the settled part of Alaska to the southward, blinds are merely some natural concealment on the line of flight. Often along the Bering Sea ice cakes are piled up, not only for concealment, but to break the cruel icy winds blowing in from the ice pack. Decoys are unknown and the only calling is done with the voice.

Some of the species of waterfowl eagerly sought in the States are commonly taken by the Eskimos. Outstanding among these are the cackling geese, the lesser Canada geese, and the white-fronted geese. On the other hand, few of our "eating" ducks are taken by the Eskimos. Their main ducks are the various species of the eiders. These fowl are not relished by white palates. Also the emperor goose, a beautiful fast bird weighing up to 7 pounds, has a seafood diet that makes it anything but a delectable table bird to the white man. However, few of these are ever available to the sport hunter's gun.

Few of the emperor geese winter south of the Aleutian Islands. This geographic distribution makes

PLATE XX. Reef Shooting for Scoters. Count the shooters. Some birds are about to pass over, which calls for a series of deep knee bends by the shooters. (Long Island Sound).

them chiefly a bird for the Eskimo. Though white hunters seldom bag them, they nevertheless play an important part in the waterfowl picture. Like the lowly mud hen, or coot, that is prized on the same plane with a duck by Indians and Mexicans, the emperor furnishes food to a destitute people who might just as easily replace it with a fine Canada or white-fronted goose.

The only blinds ever used by the Eskimos other than natural hiding places behind boulders or ice cakes are their camouflaged kayaks. Frequently one may see the tiny sealskin-covered boats pulled up on the edge of an ice pan with a windbreak of worn sailcloth propped up before them. The canvas does conceal any movement of the hunter, but, more important, it breaks the wind. Often one sees grass mats used in lieu of the sailcloth.

Eider ducks, and often the various species of geese, do fly within range of these blinds. Why they do is a mystery. They can be seen for miles. The motionless hunter crouched behind his windbreak gets sufficient opportunity for shooting to make the thing pay off.

Shot shells are often hand-loaded brass affairs from 20 gauge to 12 gauge. The most popular shot size is No. 3. The top wadding is usually a shaved-up mass of driftwood resembling excelsior packing. This is the Eskimo version of the crimp load. The stuff blasts away from the muzzle of the shotgun, giving the shot an unobstructed path of flight. It might be remarked that the Eskimo is an excellent wing shot and rarely does he waste ammunition.

Clothing for waterfowl shooting may be any color except red. The Northern natives recognize that red is bad medicine and that waterfowl notice it and shun such color. White, green, black, tan, yellow, or blue might be confused with snow, drift logs, tundra vegetation, or with water colorations—but never red.

Decoys are never employed by the Alaska Eskimo hunter of today. In the Hudson Bay region mud decorated with bits of feathers or papers is often employed to decoy geese. Calling is never practiced to any extent except in hunting cackling geese. These half-pint Canadas in the springtime seem almost devoid of brains. Frequently the Eskimo hunter will post himself on a prominent knoll in the tundra, wave his cap at these silly birds and call *"L-u-uk, l-u-uk"* in a loud voice. Invariably they will gabble an answer and come from a half-mile distance to circle over the Eskimo hunter. Cacklers have been observed that were called in this manner and shot into and then were called back again within easy range for another barrage.

Probably there is little application a hunter of the United States might make to his local shooting problems from observing Eskimos hunting in Alaska. The outstanding lesson to be learned from such a hungry and primitive people is as old as the world itself. It is the key to success of the various predators that hunt to live; it made possible our ascendancy from the cave man of the earliest times. This one thing is applicable in the finest duck club in America. It is a *must* and far overshadows the element called luck. This quality is *patience*. All primitive people have this to a marked degree. If they did not, they would not be here.

Few birds one can eat are ever bagged in the clubhouse. The bluebird days are the ones to try men's souls. In our geared-up civilization we want action. We have not the patience to hang on when there is not a duck or goose in the sky—yet when the chips are down, hunt as does the Eskimo. Stay in there and pitch. It is the only possibility. Some of the time you will be rewarded.

A word as to the native kill might not be amiss here. Let no one mislead you that because Eskimos will eat goose or duck eggs, or kill the fowl in the spring, they are the reason for the present waterfowl shortage. Bear in mind, first, that there are not many Eskimos. Secondly, their villages are few and far between. Only areas within a few miles of their settlements are ever hunted. Even in such places one can see little difference in the abundance of waterfowl when the hatch comes off. Lastly, because the Eskimos occupy the land other enterprise has not come in. No place has ever yet been observed where the activity and presence of white men ever increased the supply of ducks and geese in their nesting grounds.

Alaska has waterfowl by virtue of her isolation. The shooters on the Pacific coast get the majority of their ducks and geese from the Territory. Let old duck hunters rejoice, in their sunshiny security of Washington, Oregon, and California, in having their good neighbor to the north to send them the web-footed migrators in such quantities. Without Alaska there would be no waterfowl shooting whatever in the Pacific states.

In a like manner rejoice, duck hunters, at the methods of taking waterfowl in the Territory of Alaska. Alaskan hunters reduce the ranks of ducks and geese but a small fraction of one per cent. Their primitive methods of hunting use only natural blinds. Their decoys do not exist and they do not seduce the fowl with calling devices. They are conservationists—possibly because they do not need to resort to more vigorous methods in order to fill the pot.

## Goose Shooting

The wildfowler is inclined to ignore the scientific nomenclatures favored by the biologist, and roughly divide the geese of North American into three groups: the gray, the white, and the blue.

Under the gray classification, he includes the Canadas and their numerous subdivisions, such as the cackling, Hutchins, lesser Canada, and western Canada, all of which sub-species are still in a rather confused and uncertain state. The white-fronted geese, or speckle-bellies, which also are known to European hunters, and occur in such unbelievable numbers on the plains of Hungary, also are included in this grouping.

The white geese comprise the greater snow goose, which is confined to the Atlantic coast and is greatly reduced in numbers today, hence protected, and the lesser snow goose, or wavey, which occurs throughout most of our western states and is found in Mexico in large numbers. There is one other white goose, the Ross's goose, which is slightly larger than a mallard duck, and which confines its wintering ground almost entirely to the Sacramento Valley in California.

Another of the rare geese, which some hunters place in the gray category and others in the blue, is the emperor, which winters in the Aleutians, and seldom is found in the States. Occasionally, of course, an East Coast wildfowler will come across one or two members of the Old World species, such as barnacle geese, pinkfeet, and bean geese.

The blues probably are the most plentiful of all, but as they make practically a nonstop flight from Hudson Bay to the coastal marshes of Louisiana they are seldom if ever seen by sportsmen outside the Mississippi flyway. Yet in winter in the Vermillion marshes of Louisiana at least 6,000,000 of these geese concentrate in areas so inaccessible that they are hunted only with the utmost difficulty.

There are also the brant or brant geese, a coastal salt-water bird occurring on both the Atlantic and Pacific coasts.

The Canada, or honker, is our most widely distributed and best-known goose from the Arctic to Mexico. They are the harbingers of autumn and spring, and normally come south in October and move north in March. It has been established that they move north in the spring directly behind the isotherm (a line drawn on the weather map with the same temperature at all points) of 30 degrees. They are hunted in a variety of ways, depending a great deal on the locality.

In the Canadian Northwest they are hunted from wheat stooks, on the Mississippi from pits dug in sandbars. On the great sand barrier reefs of the outer Carolina coast they are hunted from pits also, and form bush, stake, and rolling blinds.

A *bush blind* is one into which you shove your boat, constructed of wood with bushes thatched around it. A *stake blind* is merely a large box on stilts stuck up on some sand reef far from land. The whole trick to a stake blind is to have it out and in position early in the season before the geese arrive so they become accustomed to it.

A *rolling blind*—which is rarely seen anywhere except on the Hatteras and Ocracoke Banks in North Carolina, consists of a burlap-covered framework on wheels. The blind is left for several days on some great sand flat or bar which the geese are using in order to give them time to get used to it.

The hunter conceals himself in the blind and then, when the geese alight on the flat or bar, slowly, foot by foot, pushes the blind until he is within range of the geese, when he jumps up and fires.

Although the Canada goose is the most widely distributed of our geese, the great concentration grounds are near Cairo, Ill., in California, and on the outer coast of North Carolina. At Lake Mattamuskeet the Government maintains a refuge where thousands of geese congregate every winter.

Honkers are extremely difficult to approach, as they always post a sentinel or "watch gander" who is constantly on the alert and never stops to feed until another watch gander has taken his place. This is true of nearly all the geese, but the Canadians, bein gsuch large birds and having such long necks, can see farther than the other geese and seem to be more on the alert.

There are authentic records of 16- and 17-pound honkers, but as a rule they run from 8 to 10 pounds. The largest seen at Hatteras weighed 13½ pounds.

A member of the Gooseville Gun Club at Hatteras was once struck on the head by a falling goose and knocked out. He had hit one goose out of a flock, and, turning to fire at another, did not see the first one falling directly at him. Being struck on the head by an 8- to 10-pound goose falling from a considerable height is nothing to laugh at.

Live decoys, of course, are the best, but since their prohibition, wooden decoys, profiles, or stuffed geese must suffice. With wooden decoys the geese are apt to alight out of range and swim in; profiles sometimes disappear (to the geese, that is) when the geese are right over them; in general, the full-bodied stick-ups seem the best.

In Massachusetts, before the ban on live decoys, flyers were used. These were young birds, released from the top of a cliff when a flock of wild geese were sighted, which would immediately circle and settle down in front of the blind where their parents were staked out close by. This was a very effective way of luring geese within range, although on one occasion 14 pens of flyers—a total of some 40-odd geese—were flown at a large flock which refused to come closer, probably because it was on migration.

To many hunters there is nothing more thrilling in wildfowling than the long waving line of honkers etched against the sky and the bell-like cries floating down from above. In the wheat and stubble of the Northwest, the sandbars of the Mississippi, the lonely "banks" of North Carolina, the effect is the same.

**Cackling and Hutchins Geese.** These lovely little geese, miniatures of their larger relative, the Canada, can be found in great numbers in the Sacramento Valley of California, especially in the vicinity of Gridley and Willows.

The Government maintains a wildlife refuge near Willows and here these geese, along with snows and Ross geese and speckle-bellies, congregate in huge flocks. They fly out into the rice fields to feed but rise high in the air after leaving the refuge and may go for miles before alighting to feed.

The best way to hunt them is to locate, if possible, the field they are using and get there before they do, so as to greet them when they come.

Many hunters locate the line of flight—which with all geese, once it starts, generally follows the same direction—and get under it at some point. In this way, particularly in a heavy wind, some excellent pass shooting may be had.

The Hutchins goose, whose habits are similar to the "cacks," may be found in the same territory.

It is fairly safe to say that any miniature Canada goose east of the Rocky Mountains is a Hutchins.

**White-Fronts or Speckle-Bellies.** These geese are found mostly in the western states and Mexico, rarely east to the Mississippi Valley. At Willows and Gridley in the Sacramento Valley they are found with the "cacks" and snow geese with whom they mingle freely.

There is a large form of this goose, called a tule goose, whose center of abundance seems to be in the Butte and Sutter basins in the Sacramento Valley, but there is some dispute among ornithologists as to whether these may not be just large examples of the white-front.

PLATE XXI. "Shang" Wheeler's Impression of "Skunkheads Coming In."

One of the greatest concentrations of wild geese probably is on the plains of eastern Hungary during the migration periods, where flocks frequently contain 50,000 or more birds. These are the European white-fronts, similar in every way to our speckle-bellies.

The next greatest concentration is the blue goose wintering ground on the Vermillion marshes in Louisiana, and another is the Sacramento Valley. Here, and in Mexico, is the best place for the white-fronts that will be found on this continent.

**White Geese.** The greater snow goose, a bird confined entirely to the Atlantic coast, is so reduced in numbers that hunting it is prohibited in the United States.

These birds winter mainly on the Pea Island Government Refuge on the Outer Banks of North Carolina south of Oregon Inlet. A few flocks winter in Currituck, but the main body is concentrated at Pea Island. From the air one may see practically the whole species in one gigantic flock on the water offshore, looking like a great patch of snow.

In Canada, at Cap Tourment on the St. Lawrence, a few are shot on migration, but this species exists in such limited numbers that it might better be protected in both countries.

On the other hand, the lesser snow goose, white brant, or wavey, is extremely abundant from the Mississippi westward. With the great flocks of blue geese in Louisiana there are always many snows. One curious fact is that as you go farther west on the Gulf coast toward Texas, the proportion of snows in the flocks increases and the proportion of blues decreases until you have flocks of snows with an occasional blue, the exact reverse of conditions in the Vermillion Marshes.

These snow geese are hunted quite extensively in Utah, also in Texas, California, and Mexico. With a proper "set" they decoy readily. When short of profile decoys, hunters frequently use paper picnic plates and pieces of cleaning tissue stuck on bunches of grass. In fact, Van Campen Heilner, who has traveled almost all over the world hunting waterfowl, reports that he once used a man as a decoy in hunting these geese.

He was shooting with Lynn Bogue Hunt, the wildlife artist, and as Hunt has snow-white hair, Heilner prevailed upon him to sit in the blind without his cap. From a distance his white head looked just like the top of an old gander, and Heilner insists the geese decoyed perfectly to him.

In California, the gathering of the white geese is a marvelous sight—like acres of snow in the clear blue air of the Sierras. There they are hunted from pits and from blinds in the rice fields, but they are such a beautiful bird, with the bold black markings on the under surface of their wings, that many hunters feel it is a shame to kill them.

The Ross's goose, a small white goose, also is found in fair numbers in the Sacramento Valley. It was fully protected for many years, and its breeding ground was one of the ornithological mysteries until recent years, when it was discovered on the Mackenzie Delta, near the Arctic.

**Emperor Geese.** This is one of the most beautiful of all the geese. It is found in one of the wildest and most desolate regions in the world, and deserves mention if only because of its extreme rarity. Very few ornithologists have ever seen this goose, and extremely few hunters, except those who hunt the Alaska brown bear.

They breed at the mouths of the Yukon and the Kuskokwim Rivers, and winter in the Aleutians. They are extremely shy, perhaps more so than any other waterfowl, not because of man, who is seldom seen in that area, but because of the foxes which are so plentiful on these islands.

They have some resemblance to a blue goose and a pintail duck, in the long white streak that reaches from the head down the back of the neck. They are called "beach geese" because they frequent the tidal flats and estuaries, as opposed to "land geese," which are the Canadas.

The best shooting area seems to be in a place

called China Lagoon, near Pavlov Bay on the Peninsula, not far from Unimak. It is one of the world's loneliest spots.

**Blue Geese.** One hundred and forty miles west of New Orleans lie the Vermillion Marshes, the wintering grounds of the third greatest concentration of wild geese in the world. The late T. Gilbert Pearson, head of the Audubon Society in his time, estimated *six million* blue geese wintering on these marshes. It is not unusual to see over 50,000 geese at one time.

These geese make a practically nonstop flight from the James Bay area of Canada directly to their wintering grounds on the Vermillion Marshes. A few stop off in the Saginaw Bay area of Michigan and an occasional flock may be seen along the Mississippi flyway, but the main body goes right on through, arriving in the latter part of October.

These marshes are so swampy and inaccessible that the only way to approach the geese is by means of "marsh buggies"—specially designed machines made out of old cars with wide cleated wheels which can traverse these swamps without sinking in.

Some of the flocks are extremely tame, never having seen man, and can be approached to within very short distances.

The old birds have white heads and necks like those of the pintail drake and are very beautiful. The younger birds have dark heads and are more uniform in color. With every flock of blue geese, several snow geese will generally be found, and as one goes farther west toward the Sabine River in Texas the proportion of snows increases until the flocks are practically all snows with very few blues.

The main body of blues lies between the delta of the Mississippi and the Rockefeller-Sage Refuge, with the greatest concentration on the Vermillion Marshes.

They decoy readily to any white object and can be killed easily with No. 4 shot. A good goose call is an asset, and if one can imitate the high-pitched double note of these birds his task is far easier.

The wintering grounds of the blue goose are difficult to reach, but just to see these birds rise in vast clouds that literally obscure the sun is well worth the trip.

**Brant—Atlantic and Pacific.** These very wild and strange little geese which come from Greenland and the fringes of Baffin Bay have a primitive air about them which is hard to describe.

In the early days when eelgrass, their natural food, was present in abundance everywhere, they were extremely common and quite plentiful. On the main wintering grounds of these birds, near Cape Hatteras, N. C., it was not unusual to see 20,000 brant at one time.

With the disappearance of the eelgrass, the brant seemed to disappear also, with the result that today the main body of wintering birds seems to be in the vicinity of Great Egg Harbor Bay on the New Jersey coast. There are many birds at Hatteras, but not so many as in the old days.

Brant fly in long, undulating lines, occasionally balling up in great masses at the head of the flock, and it is not at all unusual to see six or eight of these birds fall to one shot. Occasionally they are very wary, but at other times seem absolutely stupid, especially if there are many young birds in the flock. On occasions a hunter may stand upright in the middle of his decoys and brant will continue to sail right in without hesitation.

The black brant of the Pacific coast is similar to the Atlantic species, except for a darker breast.

These birds are found from Vancouver Island southward to San Diego, with the best spots being Tufino on Vancouver Island, the Puget Sound area, Humboldt Bay and Tomales Bay. The eelgrass blight did not strike the Pacific coast as it did the Atlantic, and consequently the birds were not so badly affected.

"Branting," whether on the Atlantic or Pacific coast or elsewhere where these birds occur, is a fascinating sport under any conditions.

The wild geese of the world are a lifetime study in themselves, and when he gets too old to hunt them, the goose hunter will get almost as great a thrill reading about and studying them.

## Duck Shooting

**General.** Duck shooting was almost a necessity during the winter months in the days of our forefathers, and though the kill was not tremendously large it constituted a valuable addition to the food supply of the early settlers along the Atlantic Coast.

History tells us of the vast numbers of wildfowl that visited the shores and marshes annually but records but little about the toll taken by Indians and the settlers, and less about their methods of hunting.

In the case of the Indians, their method of hunting ducks was, for the most part, stalking with bow and arrow, although there is a tale of an Indian, with the skin of a duck pulled over his head like a cap, wading or swimming to a flock of ducks, catching one by the legs and pulling it quickly under water, then another and another until his hands were full. While the story seems rather fantastic, it probably is true and even the skeptics of today will say "could be."

Indians were known to lie in ambush along the shores or beside a creek waiting for ducks to swim within arrow range. Many were taken in this way—and many missed, as is evidenced by the number of arrow points found in some of the shore and marsh areas today.

With the white man, the blunderbuss and later the scattergun was the means of killing, and both stalking and ambushing were the methods used. As a matter of fact, the white man learned his duck hunting from the Indian.

Both resorted to the use of decoys of various types. While "necessity was the mother of invention" in those early days, some of these same makeshift decoys have been used quite successfully within the memory of some old-timers of today.

Duck hunting for food gradually broadened out to include hunting for sport and then to include hunting for market. For many of the hunters this last was "duck soup." Not very busy on their farms in the winter, they had plenty of time to hunt, it was good fun, and there was an ever-increasing demand for fowl. It naturally followed that market hunting grew and new ways of hunting developed, such as the use of scull-boats, sink boxes, batteries, bush-blinds, and shooting boxes sunk in sandbars.

As fast as market gunners found new ways of increasing their kill, just so fast did the sporting gunners adopt them as a means of increasing their sport, which in most cases consisted of taking larger bags. And so the program of killing went on, unrestricted, for years until finally the decrease in the number of both native and visiting wildfowl suggested that something should be done to regulate this wanton slaughter of a valuable natural resource.

There were several schools of thought on this subject. There were those who, prompted by selfish motives, argued that theirs was a "God-given right" to take the "beasts of the field, the birds of the air, and the fishes of the sea" as they chose; there were those who claimed that if men in the North did not kill them, they would be killed in the South; there were those who abhorred all killing; there were those who advanced the idea that all of these things belonged to all of the people and not to a few who sought to kill all of them; and there were those who suggested a compromise of restricted killing plus limited periods for hunting plus protection for brood stock during breeding periods. Out of it all came legislation, local, state, and Federal, which did limit the slaughter to some extent.

The development and use of new equipment followed, and several types of blinds and boats were designed. A brief description of these may prove interesting both to the hunter of today and to the young folks coming on who will be the hunters of tomorrow.

**Blinds.** In the North, during the winter, temporary blinds were made by piling ice cakes on the shore high enough to conceal the hunter, and stone blinds were made in a similar way when ice was not available. In general the problem of a blind was usually solved by the gunner who built the type best suited to the area to be gunned, some temporary, some permanent.

**Decoys.** Decoys are a subject presenting a wide divergence of opinion. Some gunners claim that anything is good enough that even suggests a duck while others are quite fussy about their decoys and insist that the better the decoys, the more apt an oncoming bird is to be decoyed. Experiences over a long term of years have proved that, in the case of early fall shooting, before the young birds have become sophisticated and before they have taken on their adult coloration, almost anything will answer to decoy them within range. But later in the season when the broods of young have been separated from their mothers, when they have taken on the distinctive colors of the male and female and are definitely on their own, then it is a different story. There have been instances in which several "shoots" in the Carolinas just could not coax the ducks to within range after the first few days of shooting. One fellow laid it partly to the nondescript lots of decoys being used and went to the trouble of getting a setting of well-made, nicely painted decoys, with the result that he had better shooting than did any of his neighbors in that entire local area.

Then there was a similar case in which the early shooting had been done over a bunch of motley blocks and the ducks had become afraid to approach the shore or near a setting of these ill-shaped, poorly painted decoys. Here again the placing of a new setting of high-grade devoys proved to be the determinating factor between days of disappointments and days of good sport.

It stands to reason that if anything will decoy a bird from its line of flight, it is either a bunch of its own kind, in the flesh, or a bunch of imitations that resemble the live ducks so closely that the difference is not noticeable until it is too late. There have been innumerable instances where the best decoys have been the most successful in the stiffest kind of competition.

Of course, even the best of decoys must be properly set in order to be most effective. They sho look natural, in a place where ducks are wont to go and under conditions when ducks will naturally use that area.

A knowledge of how, when, and where to set decoys comes after long years of experience in local areas. However, there are a few fundamentals that apply in all places. It is always a good plan to set decoys so that birds can get to them easily by stemming along slowly up-wind, and this provides them a way to a quick getaway when they jeer and turn, right or left, and down-wind. Another help is to set one or two extra-nice, oversize decoys just outside the main setting, as tollers. Incoming birds see these first, make their approach, are reassured by these two fine specimens, then stiffen their wings and plane in to a desirable place to alight. And the smart gunner always prepares just such a place for them to see and choose. In the case of a right-handed shooter, this open space should be a little to his left, as you look from the blind, and a little to the right for a "left-winger."

The number of decoys to be used depends, first, on the kind of duck to be hunted, and second on the amount and quantity of competition. In the case of broadbill, redhead, or canvasback settings it is desirable to have a fairly large flock and have these set rather closely together, simply because the birds usually travel in sizable groups and when on their feeding grounds usually sit rather closely together. A good setting for marsh-feeding ducks, such as mallards, black ducks, pintails, gadwalls, shovellers, or teal, could be from a pair up to a dozen, according to conditions and competition. These birds are more apt to be found in smaller groups on their feeding grounds, but in the event of a bad storm they do gather in large bunches for shelter. A few decoys at the right place, at the right time, will answer when ducks are coming in to feed. If you know that a gunner is rigged out in an adjoining creek with eight or ten decoys, it might be well to use a larger group so as to attract attention a little farther away and thus get the birds started toward your flock first.

In the case of rigging out in a blow it is well known that ducks coming in for shelter usually swing well down to leeward and then stem along easily up-wind, reducing their altitude as they come. Under these conditions it is well to have sizeable setting and have it so set as to be quickly seen when the birds haul up-wind. A large group of nondescript decoys may swing a bunch of birds toward a blind, but to have them come in gently and unafraid, a setting of really good decoys seems to do the trick better when the gunning is tough. And so the problem of decoying ducks sums up to having a knowledge of where and when the ducks are to be found.

**Successful Shooting.** Success comes with years of experience, observation, and ability to profit by other people's mistakes.

Many a boy is actually brought up with a gun in his hands by a father who is a shooter and who believes that his boy will get into less mischief over in the marsh hunting ducks and learning something of the great outdoors than he would hanging around street corners, doing nothing. On the other hand, a great number of boys never think of duck hunting until they happen to hear one of their schoolmates tell of the fun he had last Saturday hunting ducks, so they think they'll try it. Some like it and some do not. Those who do, just lay plans for another trip as soon as possible and even go so far as to commence getting a rig of their own together. The boy with the hunting father has a distinct advantage over the other one, and soon learns the fundamentals and later on the finesse of duck shooting. But the lad who learns the hard way, in many instances, has to work and earn his own equipment, really gets all there is in the game. His gun, his boat, his decoys may not be of the best but they mean a lot to him, especially his decoys; he made them himself, and while they are not prize winners, they look good to him and he gets now and then a duck over them. Both boys have much to learn and have a lot of fun learning it, as experience is always the best teacher.

There are a few fundamentals that every duck hunter should know, to wit: how to handle a gun, both ashore and in a boat; how to handle a boat in smooth or rough water; how to rig and set his decoys; and last but not least, how to hide his boat and himself properly and be able to keep absolutely still during the approach of ducks.

Hiding a boat consists of tucking her away in the natural surroundings and dressing her up with materials such as grass, rockweed, or snow and ice so that she blends with the environs and is almost unnoticeable. Then comes the trick of hiding oneself. Lying down in the boat or squatting down in the grass or rocks does most of the hiding, but not all. One's clothing should blend with the surrounding colors. Then, as a part of hiding oneself, comes the most important and hardest thing to accomplish,

PLATE XXII. A Rock Blind Setup on an Island. With rock behind, no cover is needed in front if the shooters sit still.

that of keeping motionless until ready to rise and shoot. Many gunners spoil a majority of their shots by being unable to "freeze" while the game is approaching. A duck may see you perfectly and yet pay no attention to you until you make the slightest move. An instance of this is nicely illustrated by the experience of a gunner who was all rigged out on a rocky point, with a good setting of decoys off the shore and himself hidden behind a big rock. Ducks would lead up to within a "gunshot and a half" and then turn away. Every duck did the same thing. Something was wrong. The gunner came out from behind the rock and looked the decoys over; they were O.K. He looked at his boat hauled up on the shore 100 yards away; she was O.K. He looked at his hiding place; that was O.K. What he did not see was a man behind that rock, poking his head up and down while he watched the ducks coming in. But reasoned that the trouble must be with him, so he moved from behind the rock and sat down in front of it, where he did not have to move a muscle while watching the approach. That was the answer. From then on the ducks came in as gently as chickens. It doesn't seem possible that a little thing like that would make such a difference, does it? Just ask an old duck hunter and see what he says.

Ducks will notice instantly anything that moves. An old trick among battery shooters, when ducks were flying past quite a distance away, was to stick an arm or leg up out of the box, *just once,* to attract their attention so they would notice the decoys. This was especially effective when the birds were flying low and would invariably cause them to take a little altitude so they could see better. Then, seeing the decoys, they would usually swing toward them and sometimes come in. Some gunners used a small red flag for the same purpose, in the belief that ducks were curious and attracted by anything red. One old-timer used to toss his cap into the air to give the impression that a duck was alighting.

Hunting wildfowl divides itself into two methods, one of having the game come to the hunter and the other of having the hunter go to the game. By the first method the hunter lies in ambush, hidden either in the marsh grass, reefs, breakwater rocks, shore blind, floating blind, sink-box, battery, or gunning boat and, with or without decoys, awaits the approach of flying or swimming ducks to within range. By the second method the hunter undertakes to stalk the game on their feeding or resting grounds by making a quiet, cautious approach, either by boat or afoot, partially hidden by surrounding cover, or by a rapid approach from upwind in a fast-moving sail- or powerboat. Scull boats and sneak boats also are used in stalking and are camouflaged with ice or marsh grass so as to resemble such floating materials. There is still another method of stalking used in the Middle and Far West, in which the hunter makes his approach by walking closely alongside of his pony or trained ox, using the body of the animal to shield him from view. In any or all of these methods the idea is to get the target within range of the gun or the gun within range of the target.

Back in the early 80's there was in vogue a style of duck shooting known as "line shooting," which was exactly what the name implies: to form a line across the mouth of a river, from an island to the mainland, from one point to another across the line of flight of low-flying ducks such as coots and old squaws. A group of men, from three or four up to a dozen, would organize the shoot for a certain day at a certain time. They would draw lots for position in the line, No. 1, No. 2, No. 3, etc., extending, say, from a breakwater across to a near-by point. Each man in his boat anchored about two gunshots from his neighbor for safety's sake. Birds coming around either the breakwater or the point, intent upon going to their feeding grounds in the harbor, have to cross this line, either over or between the boats. Often an old coot would approach one end of the line, turn, and go almost the whole length of the line before seeing a place that looked good for crossing. All the while he was running the gantlet past the several boats amid a cannonade of shots and shouts, all of which tended to bewilder the bird and resulted finally in his trying to cross at imminent risk of his life. Shouts of derision such as "Give 'im the other barrel," "Get a cannon," "Throw the gun at 'im," and other equally taunting jibes passed between the gunners as the shoot went on. Each man retrieved his own kill and chased his own cripples. At the end of the shoot all hands rowed up the river together and the good-natured jokes flung from one to another were really worth hearing.

With the building of breakwaters at harbor entrances came a new sort of blind that was patronized by a great many gunners, especially in rough weather. With a setting of decoys out in the lee of the rocks, the gunners would sit among the rocks or in a boat alongside of the rocks and often enjoy very good shooting. Competition was usually pretty stiff, but as a rule everybody got a little shooting. The growth of mussels, barnacles, and other duck foods along the rocks makes breakwaters real feeding grounds for a great many ducks, especially in the winter when the inland streams and marshes are frozen over. Breakwaters continue to be popular gunning places all along our eastern seaboard today.

Different varieties of ducks frequent different sorts of places, primarily in search of food and secondarily for rest or shelter. The observing gunner soon learns when and where the ducks "use" and plans his hunts accordingly.

In general, the "tip-up" ducks, such as mallards, black ducks, gadwalls, spoonbills, pintails, baldpates, and teal, frequent the marshes and the creeks and sloughs adjacent thereto, in either fresh- or salt-water areas where they find wild grain kernels, grass seeds, insects, tender grasses, roots, and various forms of crustacea. They are averse to visiting grain fields either when the young shoots are just coming up or when the grain has ripened. Farmers have been known to hire hands to patrol their grain fields and shoot blank cartridges, at intervals, day and night, just to keep the fowl from doing damage to their crops.

The diving ducks might well be divided into three classes: (1) the sea ducks, eiders and scoters (coots); (2) bay ducks, canvasbacks, redheads, ruddy ducks, scaup (broadbill), golden-eye (whistler), buffleheads (dippers); and (3) the saw-billed, fish-eating mergansers (sheldrakes). All of these feed under

PLATE XXIII. This Chesapeake earns his board and keep, and he is interested in the ingredients for the "coot stew" which his master is holding.

water, for the most part, gathering small shellfish, crab life, crustacea, and water grasses from the bay bottoms for food; the mergansers feed principally on small finny fish, shrimp, and other small swimming forms found in both fresh and salt water.

To gun any of these birds successfully the hunter should study their habits and habitats and "beat them to the punch." When baiting was permitted it was no trick to attract hundreds of either marsh or diving ducks to an area by distributing food regularly around a blind. Large kills were made from these baited blinds, but now that baiting has been prohibited by law the gunners have to make a much more careful study of flyways and feeding grounds in order to be at the right place, at the right time, with legal equipment.

The several Federal laws and regulations which were aimed chiefly at the market hunter and game hogs have made an excellent score to date, and while a clean-up of all violations cannot be hoped for, a great good has been and is being done by way of regulating wildfowl hunting, and both conservation and restoration are well under way.

Another group of web-footed wildfowl that has contributed largely to the sport of shooters and to the profits of market hunters is the brant and geese group. These birds are prairie, marsh, and shoreline feeders. They have in the past been mercilessly slaughtered from large battery rigs, over baited areas, and from palatial "goose blinds" over live decoys and callers, on well-baited grounds. But this is all history now, and brant and geese have to be hunted the hard way, with the kill severely restricted, *as it should be*. Both brant and geese are a large, slow-moving, easy target for the sharpshooters of today with their modern guns and hard-hitting ammunition. Methods and equipment for hunting these birds are practically the same as those used in duck hunting. Here, too, a knowledge of feeding and resting grounds is very essential. They differ in one respect from ducks in that they travel, almost daily, to a gravel bar or beach to replenish the gravel content of their gizzards, and many a gunner has hidden himself in a beach or blind to take his toll of birds from those visiting there for gravel. Usually the birds pitch and alight some distance from the shore and swim in slowly. In such instances the gunner never bats an eyelash but just rolls his eyes to watch the old couple lead their brood within range. Then he takes the gander with the first barrel and the goose with the second, after which a few honks will call the youngsters back again and again until nearly all have paid the penalty for their filial loyalty. They are easy to kill, not as they come in, head on, but as they turn to swing away when their necks and under-wing parts are vulnerable.

As with all other sports, there is something to duck hunting besides killing. As the fox hunter loves to hear his dog giving tongue on the trail, as the quail and partridge hunter enthuses as his dog straightens out and says "Here he is," and as the angler gets a great thrill out of taking a grand fish on light tackle, under ideal conditions, so it is with the duck hunter, who gets a lot of pleasure out of having and using a good rig. His boat, his decoys, his gun, and his dog are all a part of the game. What better reward or greater satisfaction can a gunner have than to be well hidden in a comfortable boat or blind, have a fine cock mallard come scaling in on stiff wings to a setting of really good-looking decoys, look along the barrel of an "old trusty" that never misses (if you hold it right), see "his duckship" crumple up to a clean kill, and last but not least, to have "Old Bog" make a perfect fetch with the best of manners? A brace or two taken like that means a perfect day; and they actually taste better for Sunday dinner.

Modern-day duck shooting has developed a plan of commercial shooting under which thousands of mallards are raised in captivity and during the shoots are taken to a point adjacent to their home feeding grounds. Then on a signal that the shooters are properly stationed, they are released in pairs or trios to fly back down to their home pool. This provides both pass shooting and shooting over decoys as well as an opportunity to work the retrievers. A charge is made for the sport, based on the kill, and the shooter is guaranteed a legal bag.

This sort of shooting is getting to be quite popular with the older men who have been through the rough, tough days of old and are now delighted with the plan that lets them leave their office in town, ride an hour or so, slip into some gunning togs, and have an hour's shooting de luxe. One good thing about this kind of shooting is that it does lessen in a small degree the toll taken of wild birds.

It is not necessary to kill a pile of game in order to have a good hunt. Nothing illustrates that better than the ancient story about the Irishman who, when his friend asked him where he had been on Saturday, replied, "I was duck huntin' and I had the time of me life." "And did ye get any ducks?" asked his friend. "No, but I gave 'em one terrible serenadin'!"

There is a great deal to hunting and fishing beyond taking a big bag. No essay on either of these sports would be complete without a word of warning from the old-timers of yesterday, who took more than their share, either because they were greedy or did not know any better, to the youngsters coming on who will enjoy these outdoor sports tomorrow.

It was just too bad that the old-timers could not look beyond the end of their noses and realize that "You never miss the water till the well runs dry" and that "You can't have your cake and eat it too." These old sayings are being brought more forcibly to mind as our fish and game population becomes alarmingly smaller. Oldsters who have enjoyed the "taking" from these natural resources, far beyond their right, can do little now but acknowledge their guilt and support those reconstruction programs which are already well under way, and preach and practice the principles of sound restoration. These natural resources belong to all of our citizens. The present generation are simply custodians, entitled to a reasonable toll, but morally obligated to turn these properties over to the next generation in equally good condition, if not better than that in which we received them. The simple gospel must be preached that suitable and ample breeding grounds should be set aside and maintained, that sufficient breeding stock should be returned each year to these areas and protected while there, that the offspring must be protected from their natural enemies, and that their natural food supply must be maintained (and in some instances supplemented by added plantings). These simple principles apply equally as well to migratory fish as to migratory birds and also to the several species peculiarly native to our several states. In all situations we are brought face to face with the need for controls having to do with such factors as reproduction, predators, pollution, closed seasons, bag limits, sanctuaries, and food supply.

We must help Nature restore and maintain a balance, progressively better each year. This involves a curtailment of the killings by all natural enemies and also the killings by several unnatural enemies, among which are the market hunter and the game hog.

**Legislation.** Duck hunting, till 1900, was a decidedly one-sided game in which the cards were stacked against the ducks and the gunners killed all they could with no thought of leaving some for seed. The supply was decreased to an alarming low and many of the sportsmen and conservationists who looked into the future saw the inevitable end if killings were to be continued, uncontrolled, and nothing were done to replenish stocks.

After much talk and a great deal of writing on the subject, a great many people became actually alarmed at the conditions surrounding the hunting of web-footed wildfowl and demanded some sort of action that would check the slaughter.

In answer to this call, the State of Connecticut took the first definite step in behalf of our wildfowl by enacting a law in 1901 that put a stop to spring shooting in that state and protected the brood stock from January 1 to September 1. This move struck a responsive chord in other states and several passed similar legislation. Then, in 1913, the Congress passed the Weeks-McLean act, prohibiting duck shooting during the spring and summer months. More and more influential people became interested in this conservation movement and gave it their active support, with the result that in 1916 an act was passed by the Congress providing for a group of delegates from the United States to meet in convention with a similar group from Great Britain, to draw up a treaty having to do with the protection of migratory birds in the United States and the Dominion of Canada.

The conclusions of this Convention were later ratified and in 1918 the Migratory Bird Treaty Act was passed and the treaty ratified. This really launched the rebuilding of a great natural resource on an international basis.

Then came the treaty with Mexico in 1937, followed by the passage of such acts as the Migratory Bird Hunting Stamp Act, the Lacey Act, the Coordination of Wildfowl Conservation Activities Act, the Federal Aid to Wildlife Restoration Act, the establishment of several state and Federal sanctuaries, and many regulations having to do with the taking, sale, and transportation of wildfowl. All were aimed at the job of conserving and rebuilding our wildfowl population.

As a nation, we are everlastingly indebted to the late John W. Weeks, from Massachusetts, Secretary of War, and to the late George P. McLean, United States Senator from Connecticut, for their tireless joint and individual efforts in support of this great international movement for co-operative conservation.

## Scoter Shooting

The scoter, like many other game birds and animals, is more familiarly known under an erroneous name. In the areas of his greatest abundance he is called a "coot," despite the fact that not even the most unlettered biologist would confuse him with a true coot. He is likewise scorned by many (equally ignorant) as a table bird. Those who have tasted a properly prepared "coot stew" along the fringe of Cape Cod, or who have tried coot breast sautéed in butter, will never again consider this duck as a bird to be passed off on an undesirable neighbor.

During periods when puddle ducks and diving ducks, due to population decreases, were protected by drastic bag limits, thousands of ardent duck hunters turned to the scoter as a means of supplying a full day of shooting. From Maine to Long Island, the scoter was hunted well in advance of the opening of the regular waterfowl season, and despite the rather heavy bags that were taken the population of the bird seemed to suffer no noticeable setback.

One veteran waterfowler once remarked that there seemed to be as many methods of hunting coots as there were coots, but in several areas the hunting follows a set though rather simple routine.

Up in Maine there seem to be two general methods in practice. One entails the use of a boat to reach the small rocky islets outside harbor lines. The hunter merely pulls his boat up on a shelving rock to prevent it from bobbing around, then seeks a place to sit that offers a good view of passing birds. If he avoids wearing any bright-colored or white clothing, the birds will pass within easy gunshot. Some, feeling they must have decoys out, will rig eight or ten profile or standard scoter decoys 30 or 40 feet to the leeward of their position.

The second method practiced up there is equally simple. The hunter, equipped with a dozen scoter decoys, will move offshore for several hundred yards to an area where the birds are passing. Normally the last two hours of the flood and the first two hours of the ebb tide provide the best shooting. If he has used an outboard motor as a propelling agent, the first move is to unship it from the stern and place it inside the boat. He is then legally prepared to shoot any coot that may pass along. Putting out the decoys, usually one or two trawls (see Plate V), he merely sits back in the boat and waits for the scoters to pass his way. Often they will not come in to the decoys, for the scoter seems to prefer a lot of company rather than dropping in on a small group. However, they are curious birds, and will cut over or behind the decoys to look them over. Often, when a flight of scoters appears to be passing the rig out of gunshot, one or two waves of the arm or a couple of kicks of a boot will attract their attention and they will turn in, passing within easy range.

Too many novice scoter shooters are inclined to underestimate the flight speed of the lowly coot, especially when he is moving down-wind. Being a large bird, his speed is deceptive, and for every one that is over-led, about a thousand are under-led. Also, if there happens to be any kind of sea running, the movement of the boat adds to the sporting qualities of the situation.

Another mistake made by many scoter shooters is that of being *over* gunned, that is, of taking along a gun that would be more suitable for pass shooting at blacks or mallards. While the magnum with 32-inch barrels will reach an occasional wide bird, under normal conditions plenty of scoters will pass within 30 yards or less, and the man with the full choke will find it necessary to do some very careful shooting.

Many scoter shooters prefer their regular upland game gun for this shooting, finding that it gives them a more desirable pattern at ranges at which they will get most of their shots. Others prefer a gun with one barrel improved cylinder and the other modified choke.

Occasionally, Maine scoter shooters will follow the method which is practiced quite consistently along the Massachusetts and Long Island shores as well as along the rim of Long Island Sound. Having located a "line," an area offshore where the scoters "trade" back and forth, several boats will line up across this area, anchoring a gunshot apart. This could quite properly be termed pass shooting, and normally it proves as successful as any other method, provided there are enough scoters feeding in that area.

Many broadbill (scaup) shooters gather in a few scoters in addition to the diving ducks for which they are gunning, for in many areas as many as 80 to 100 decoys will be rigged out for broadbill. To the passing scoter this rig constitutes a crowd, and he joins it. Under these conditions the scoter sets his wings and glides in toward the head of the rig in a manner which the British are inclined to term "money for old rope."

Along the fringe of Cape Cod the individual hunter merely rows out to a line area, anchors his boat, tosses over a half-dozen or so decoys (not necessarily scoter decoys), and waits for the birds to pass. When a boat is used, the hunter will find it advisable to tie a light buoy or a few net corks to his anchor line. Then when he wants to pick up a dead bird it is merely necessary to throw off the anchor line and pick up the buoy on his return. Some hunters use a spare decoy as a buoy.

The Federal law on scoter shooting, in areas where the season opens in advance of the regular waterfowl season, specifies that all shooting will be done "outside harbor lines." In a few areas this term is rather shrouded in mystery, and what constitutes the harbor line to the hunter may not be in accord with the local warden's view on the same line. It is best to obtain a chart of the local waters or else pay a visit to the harbor master and check the extremes of the harbor line.

There is one long, fingerlike reef on the Connecticut shore which is certain to be occupied by anywhere from 30 to 50 scoter shooters during the early part of the season. The reef is bare at low tide, but covered at the flood, so the hunters seldom get more than four hours' shooting on a tide. One morning, with the reef crowded, a newly appointed game warden appeared and put some 40-odd hunters under arrest for shooting "inside" the harbor lines. How he planned to transport his victims to the nearest judge was a problem, but he was adamant. Fortunately, a member of the game commission happened to be passing. He had been one of a committee appointed to determine the harbor lines, and convinced the warden that the hunters were well within their rights. During the course of the discussion, scoters literally poured over the reef, and when the matter had been settled, the birds had stopped flying and were feeding. The warden escaped with his life, but a shattered reputation.

Scoter shooting with more than one person in the boat can be dangerous as well as unsatisfactory. In many instances it more than cuts the shooting in half, for the careful hunter will pass up many shots because of the proximity of his companion. Also, when more than one boat is used, it pays to overestimate the range of the shotgun.

Almost any offshore reef, within a mile of shore, as well as any rock capable of supplying a dry seat for the shooter, will provide reasonably good shooting in an area where there are scoters. So far as is known, no one ever tried to make even an approximate estimate of the numbers of these birds living along the shore line from Maine to Long Island. That the number would be well along in the millions is certain, for in 1940 it was estimated that there were roughly 2,000,000 of these waterfowl between Westport and New London, Connecticut. If anything, this number seems to have increased rather than decreased.

When you get a shot at a scoter moving briskly down-wind, and he appears to be passing at about 35 yards' range, just pretend he is a black duck or pintail, and give him the same *lead,* always bearing in mind that your shot string is longer than you think. Do this and you will stand a good chance of bringing him down, and less chance of having to chase him in your boat and spend a few more shells getting in shots between his dives.

Very few scoter shooters use retrievers, although many train their dogs before the opening of the regular waterfowl season by taking them along on "coot" shoots. By concentrating on shooting birds that will drop outside the decoys, the retriever gets excellent training.

In the event you have never found the scoter to be palatable, try a few of the recipes given undeɪ "Recipes" and the chances are you will change your mind.

Those responsible for drawing up the shooting-hour regulations which have done so much to destroy pass-shooting prospects were not swayed by a desire to spoil the sport for the wildfowler. It was done, primarily, to avoid the waste of waterfowl. A high percentage of the shots made after sunset resulted in dead or fatally wounded ducks that never were recovered. Rather than stop shooting to hunt up and finish off a cripple, many hunters shrug and wait for another duck to come within range. "If I stop to pick up that cripple it will be dark before I can return, and I won't get another shot," is the normal thought process.

A good retriever, of course, would make a tremendous difference in the percentage of dead and wounded birds recovered, but only a small fraction of the duck shooters have retrievers and a small percentage of those retrievers are "good" ones.

While many wildflowlers, especially those in areas which "could" offer fair pass shooting, agree that a late closing hour would not be beneficial to the waterfowl population, they profess themselves puzzled as to where this argument would apply to an early opening hour. The result of the delayed opening hour has been illegal shooting by men who in all other respects are law-abiding citizens. It requires considerable strength of character to stand in a marsh or sit in a duck boat or blind and let ducks pass within easy range because the regulations state that you cannot shoot for another six minutes. It is especially difficult for the hunter who realizes that the best shooting he will be offered is during the period when he cannot shoot. Normally, the good sportsman is the only sufferer, for others shoot as soon as they can see, knowing that the wardens are few and far between.

## Pass Shooting

Good pass shooting is almost a thing of the past, because of the regulations which govern the shooting hours, for the best pass shooting is over and done an hour after daybreak and does not begin again until an hour before dark. This statement is not intended as a criticism of those individuals responsible for the drafting of the waterfowl regulations; it is merely a statement of fact.

There are a few marshes in Alberta, Manitoba, and Ontario, as well as some in Mexico and Southern California, and scattered sections along the Mississippi flyway, where pass shooting continues to be fair. But the old-timers moan that it is not "what it used to be." The hunter who has the time, money, and inclination to go up to James Bay, in Ontario, can find pass shooting that is second to none on this continent, but most of those who travel there today find it a difficult sport.

Most wildfowlers of today are spoiled—not by the range and pattern of their gun, which is far superior to those of yesterday, but by habit. The modern duck shooter is accustomed to shooting over decoys, and while many of them are unaware of it, the greater portion of their birds are killed at a range of under 40 yards. They have learned to wait a duck out, rather than to estimate the range accurately and allow for angle and speed. Also they are doing most of their shooting at anything from zero to 20 degrees off the horizontal.

In pass shooting the ranges are greater, normally the birds are moving faster, and the angle of the shot ranges from 20 to 45 degrees off the horizontal. The man who does most of his shooting over decoys has a lot to learn when he tries pass shooting for the first time.

It is a much simpler form of duck shooting, in that much less equipment is required. Essentially, a gun and plenty of shells constitute the basic requirements, but a good retriever is a distinct asset. The methods followed are very simple. It is merely necessary to locate a "pass," or flyway, followed by the waterfowl each day, locate some natural cover as near the middle of the pass as possible, and wait for the birds to begin moving. A narrow neck of land between two bodies of water, a point at a sharp bend in a river, or even the fringe of a narrow waterway between two marshes, often proves to be a good flyway. If the area is heavily gunned, however, the waterfowl seem to get gun-shy quite rapidly, and normally will move out before the legal shooting hour arrives and not return until the curfew has rung.

In some areas, especially if there happens to be a period of high winds and bad weather, the birds are inclined to do more "trading," which will offer an opportunity for pass shooting that normally would not exist in that section. Along the coastal areas the pass shooting for scoters, scaup, and occasionally for black ducks is especially good when a good blow drives the birds in from the open water. On such occasions hunters shooting on reefs and breakwaters are offered excellent sport. The same conditions exist on many of the large inland lakes. In Southern California, where there is a reasonable amount of movement by waterfowl between lakes and rivers, even during the day, fairly good pass shooting can be found.

Regardless of where it is practiced, this form of shooting calls for a gun that will offer an effective pattern at long range. This is where the 10-gauge and 12-gauge magnums pay their way. The man with a gun that will not deliver a good pattern at 60 and even 70 yards, is due to pass up many shots and miss even more.

Another factor enters the problem with the additional range, for it takes considerable experience to do consistently good shooting at 60 yards, especially when you are accustomed to shooting ducks at about half that range. After a certain number of misses you awaken to the fact that you are underleading the birds. This will be brought home more sharply after you have pulled well ahead of a line of six or eight birds and seen the fourth bird fall instead of the leader. Just as you get the groove ironed out on the overhead shots, the birds will begin passing at an angle, and you start school all over again.

Maine Development Commission.

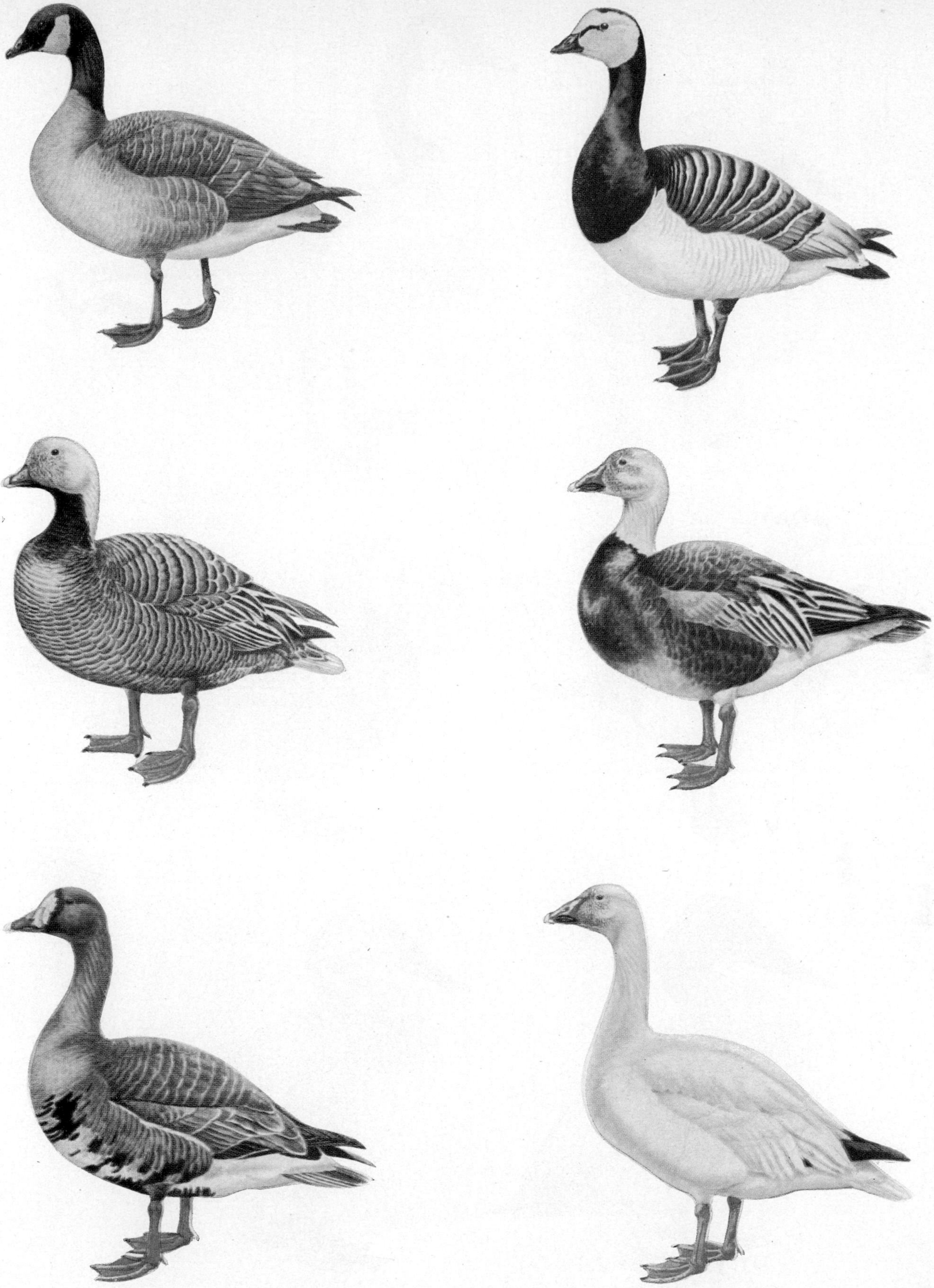

Upper left: Richardson's Goose. Upper right: Barnacle Goose.
Center left: Emperor Goose. Center right: Blue Goose.
Lower left: White-fronted Goose. Lower right: Snow Goose.

Upper left: Cackling Goose. Upper right: Canada Goose.
Center left: American Brant. Center right: Black Duck, male.
Lower: Canvasback. Left, male; right, female.

Upper: Mallard. Left, male; right, female.
Center: Shoveller. Left, male; right, female.
Lower: Pintail. Left, male; right, female.

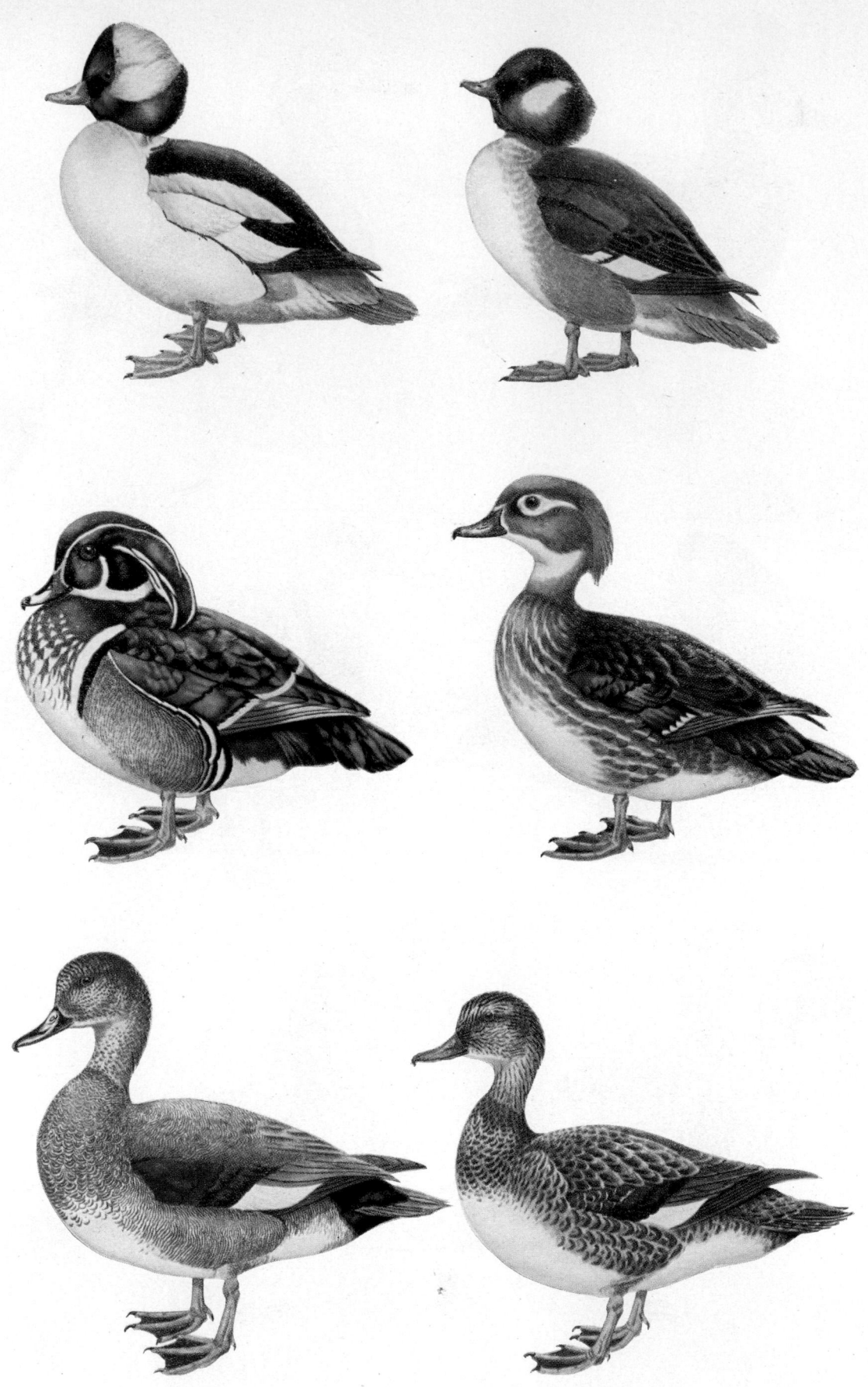

Upper: Bufflehead. Left, male; right, female.
Center: Wood Duck. Left, male; right, female.
Lower: Gadwall. Left, male; right, female.

**Upper:** Blue-Winged Teal. Left, male; right, female.
Center: Green-Winged Teal. Left, male; right, female.
Lower: Cinnamon Teal. Left, male; right, female.

Upper: Greater Scaup. Left, male; right, female.
Center: Lesser Scaup. Left, male; right, female.
Lower: Redhead. Left, male; right, female.

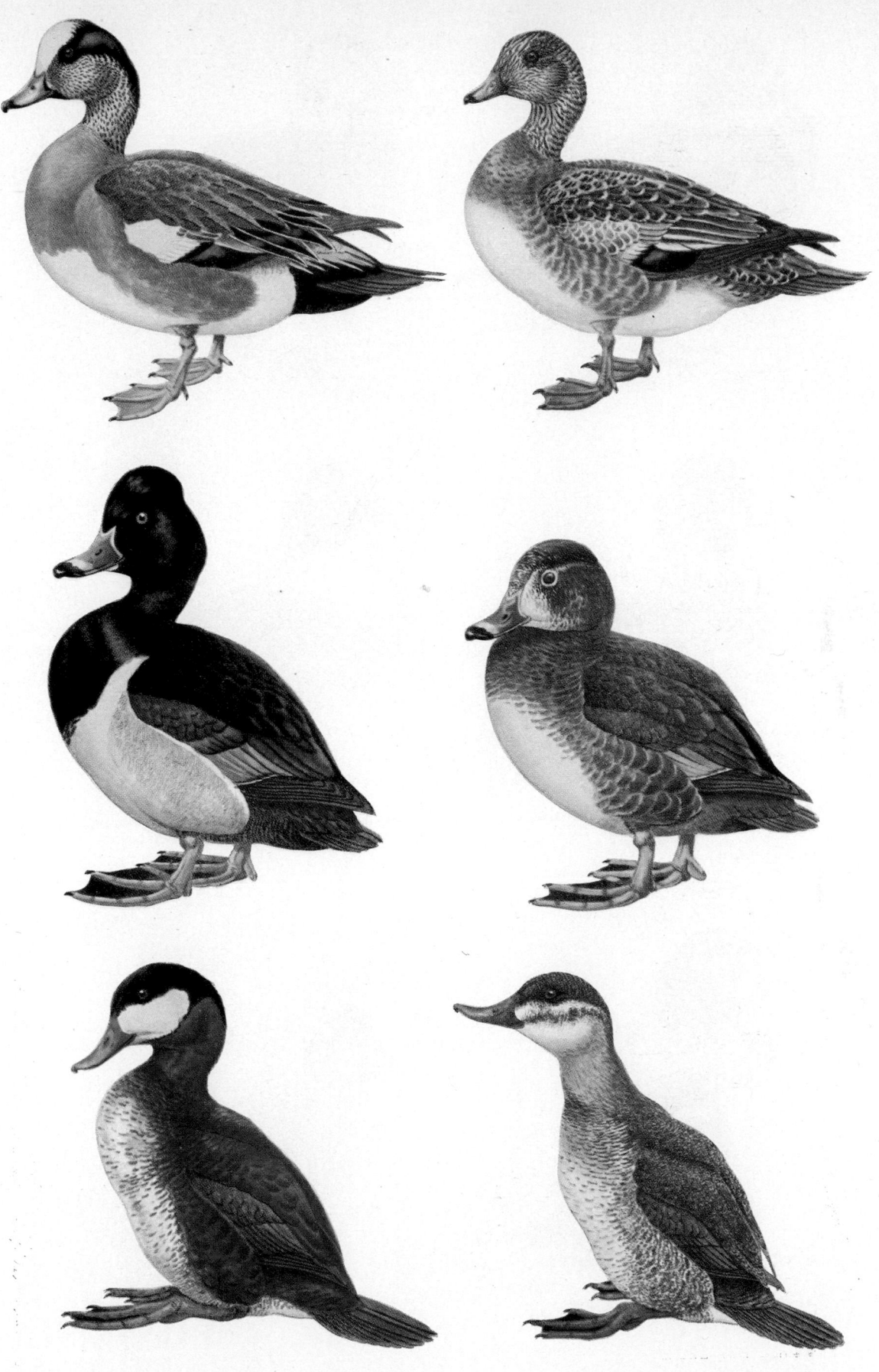

Upper: Baldpate. Left, male; right, female.
Center: Ring-Necked Duck. Left, male; right, female.
Lower: Ruddy Duck. Left, male; right, female.

Upper: Old Squaw. Left, male; right, female.
Center: Common (American) Goldeneye. Left, male; right, female.
Lower: Barrow's Goldeneye. Left, male; right, female.

Upper: American Scoter. Left, male; right, female.
Center: Surf Scoter. Left, male; right, female.
Lower: White-Winged Scoter. Left, male; right, female.

Upper: Goosander (American Merganser). Left, male; right, female.
Center: Red-Breasted Merganser. Left, male; right, female.
Lower: Hooded Merganser. Left, male; right, female.

DECOYS

Mallard. Left, male; right, female.
Pintail. Left, male; right, female.
Black Duck. Left, standard; right, oversize.
Green-Winged Teal. Left, male; right, female.
Blue-Winged Teal. Left, male; right, female.

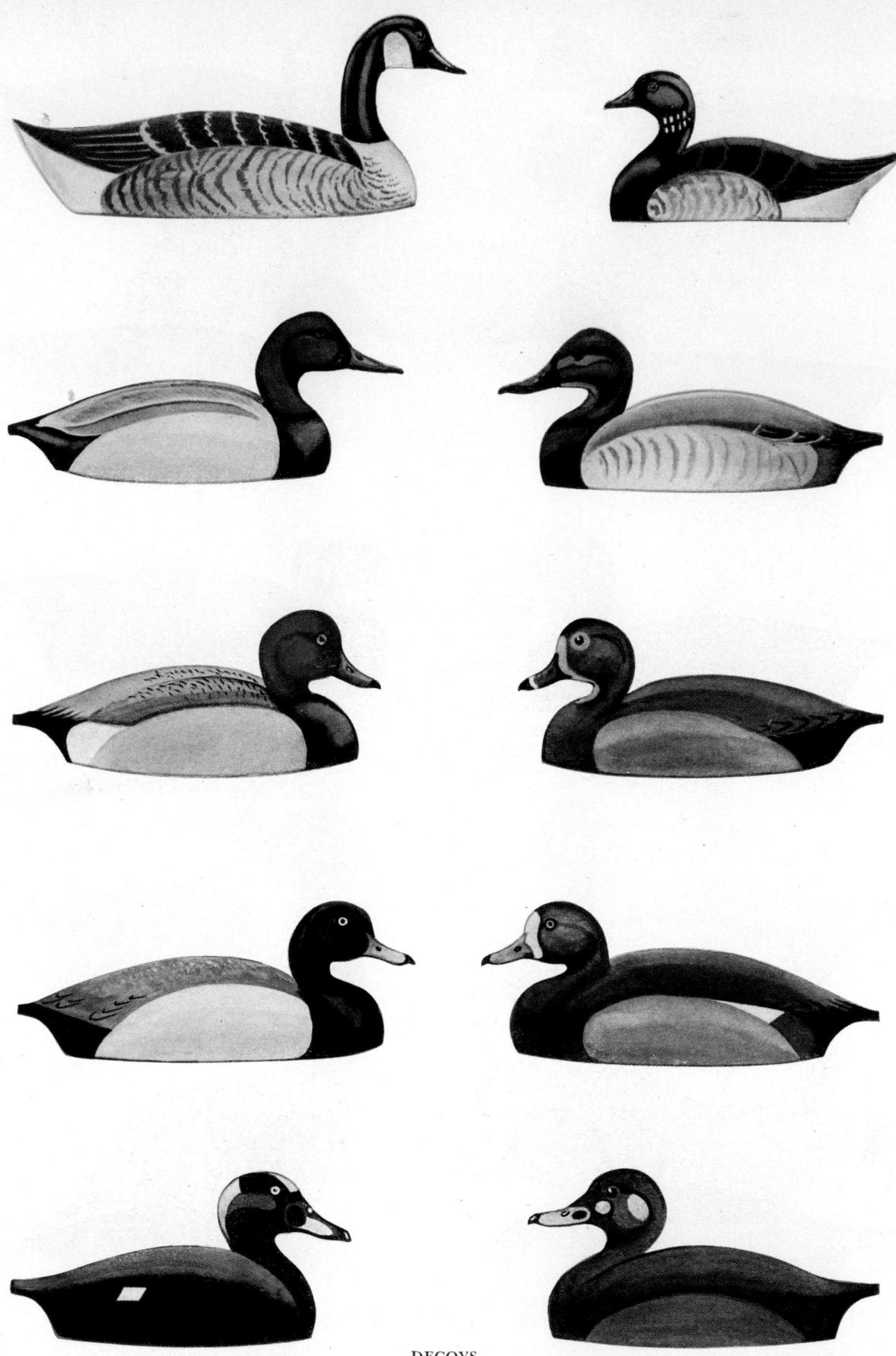

DECOYS

Left: Canada Goose. Right: Brant.
Canvasback. Left, male; right, female.
Redhead. Left, male; right, female.
Scaup. Left, male; right, female.
Scoter. Left, male; right, female.

Upper: Willow Ptarmigan. Left, male; right, female.
Center: Sage Grouse. Left, male; right, female.
Lower: Prairie Chicken. Left, male; right, female.

Upper: Left, Ruffed Grouse. Right, Sharp-Tailed Grouse.
Center: Left, Dusky Grouse, male. Right, Hungarian Partridge.
Lower: Left, Woodcock, male or female. Right, Chukar Partridge, male.

Upper: Left, Bobwhite Quail. Right, Mountain Quail.
Center: Left, California Quail. Right, Scaled Quail.
Lower: Left, Mearns's Quail. Right, Gambel's Quail.
Males are shown to the front, females to the rear.

Upper: Steller's Eider. Left, male; right, female.
Center: King Eider. Left, male; right, female.
Lower: Spectacled Eider. Left, male; right, female.

Upper: Ringneck Pheasant. Left, male; right, female.
Lower: Wild Turkey, male.

# FIREARMS

## RIFLES

## RIFLE DEVELOPMENT

**History.** Although it is termed a *rifle,* mainly for convenience, the early firearm might as aptly be termed a *musket* or a *gun,* for the early examples of the gunsmith's art did not have rifled barrels. One of the first of these firearms designed to be discharged from the shoulder, and bearing some resemblance to the modern rifle or shotgun, was the famous Tannenburg Gun. No definite date has been established for the origin of this gun, but it is believed to have been made just prior to 1400.

The modern shooter who is unfamiliar with firearm history is inclined to believe that the rifled barrel did not come into being until some time during the middle of the 18th century. Actually, the rifled barrel was employed by a number of 15th-century shooters, and "rifled" guns are mentioned in several books written before 1550. It was not until late in the 18th century, however, that the value of the rifled barrel was generally recognized.

From the muzzle-loading matchlock to the breech-loading cartridge there stretched a 350-year period of almost constant experimentation. No historian has ever been able to trace the authenticity of the claims and counterclaims which would establish one individual as having filled the greatest gap in this bridge.

The matchlock was the earliest and most elementary form of the rifle. The ignition of the powder was simplicity itself. An arm, curving over the breech, held a "match," in reality a glowing or burning cord or wick. When the arm was depressed the glowing end of the cord was brought in contact with a hole at the breech, igniting the powder.

Then came the wheellock, which was not widely used until about 1550, and evidenced an advance in mechanics. Before firing each shot, the shooter wound up a small wheel at the breech. Upon pressing a trigger this wheel was spun against pyrites. causing sparks to fly into a breech-hole, thus igniting the powder charge.

The flintlock came next, and was instantly popular. The flintlock undoubtedly attained the peak of its perfection, so far as balance and accuracy were concerned, in the so-called "Kentucky rifle," a development of the flintlock that was typically American. (See "Kentucky Rifle.") This method of ignition was in general use for approximately two centuries, until the ignition of the charge through "percussion" was developed. The first patent on the percussion method was issued in 1807, and thus the first real step toward the creation of a practical breech-loading rifle was taken. The copper percussion cap was developed about ten years later, but was not widely used for another 30 years. For example, the first U. S. Government rifles employing percussion caps were turned out in 1844 at the Springfield Armory, although a few flintlocks had been converted to percussion arms just prior to that date.

Scores of volumes have been written on the experiments conducted and the rifles invented and discarded during the past 550 years, and space permits us only to list the significant changes which took place from time to time and resulted in the modern rifle. In this country alone, the Government turned out a dozen models of the flintlock, each but slightly different from the one which preceded it, during the period which ended with the development of the famous John H. Hall rifle in 1835.

Hall's rifle, the first important step in breech-loading, was invented in 1811, but was not fully developed for approximately 25 years. This rifle embodied several features which aided in the development of the modern rifle.

Although a flintlock, the Hall rifle was hinged at the breech. This eliminated the need for a ramrod, simplified and speeded up the reloading process, and made it possible for the shooter to reload from any position. It is interesting to note that Hall received $1000 from the Government for permission to turn out 1000 of his rifles, and was paid $60 a month for supervising their manufacture at the Harper's Ferry Armory. Even before the full development of this rifle, tests conducted by the Army indicated the Hall rifle to be superior to the Government musket then in use.

Hall, in addition to supervising the manufacture of his rifle, aided in the development of machinery for producing it, with the result that by 1835 the rifle cost approximately $15 to produce. The specifications of the arm also are interesting. It was of .52 caliber, fired a ball weighing about 220 grains, and weighed 10¼ pounds without the bayonet. The sights were offset because of the hammer design. In another feature this rifle led the current field: an adjusting screw was inserted through the sear, permitting the trigger pull to be adjusted to a "hair" if desired.

Although the majority of the Halls turned out were rifles, a smoothbore musket and carbine also were manufactured, both in .64 caliber. As the parts of all Hall rifles were fully interchangeable, the value of the rifle for Army use was greatly enhanced.

Although the records are badly confused by several claimants, it is reasonably certain that the copper percussion cap was not developed until 1816.

PLATE I. A Matchlock Musketoon, Austrian, about 1608.

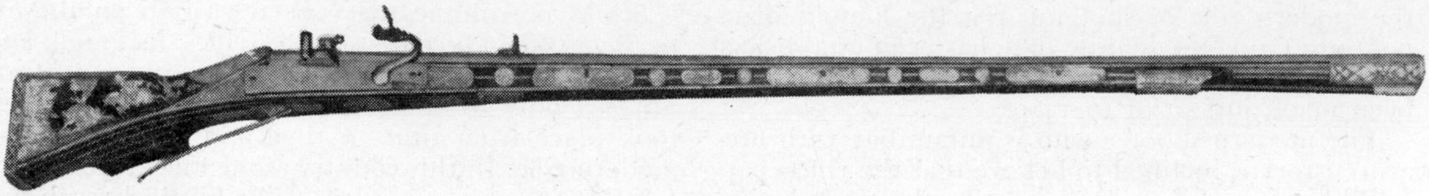

PLATE II. A Matchlock Musketoon, Austrian, about 1608.

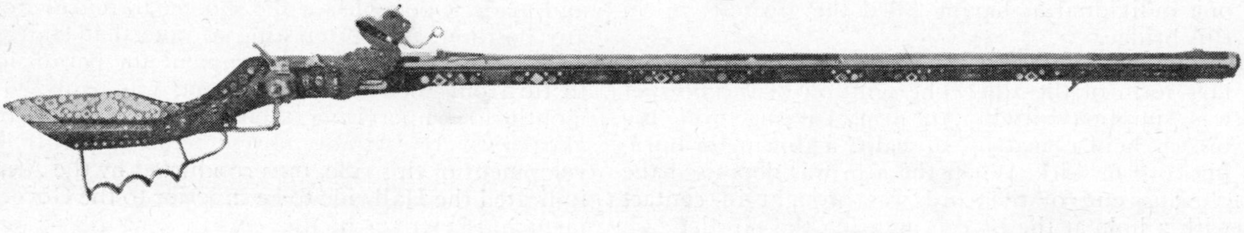

PLATE III. An Arquebus Wheellock, German, about 1571—rifled barrel.

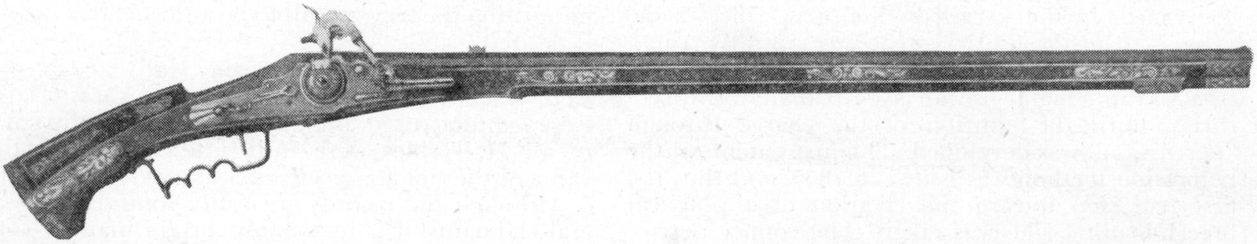

These pictures by courtesy of Metropolitan Museum of Art.

PLATE IV. A Wheellock Gun, German, 16th Century.

PLATE V. An Arquebus Wheellock, with Rifled Barrel—early 17th century, Brescian.

PLATE VI. Wheellock Gun—Austrian, mid-17th century.

PLATE VII. Wheellock Rifle—Saxon, about 1700; caliber .62.

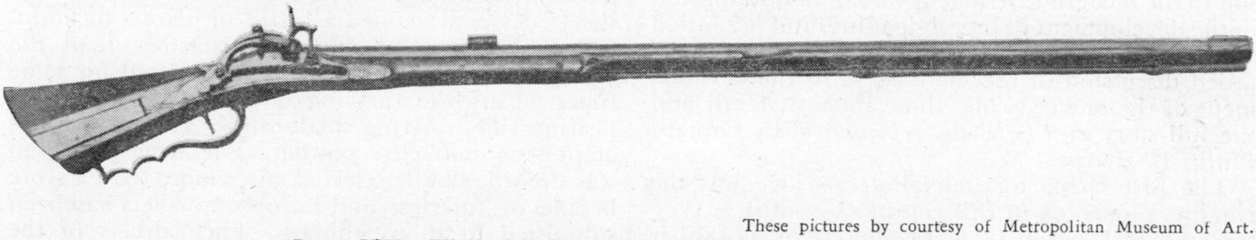

These pictures by courtesy of Metropolitan Museum of Art.

PLATE VIII. Flintlock Rifle, snaphaunce—German, late 17th century.

This opened the way for a variety of detonating caps, including tape primers similar to those used in the "repeating" cap pistols of today.

The U. S. Government began manufacturing percussion rifles in 1844, and for the next 20 years a wide variety of models were turned out in rapid succession, all muzzle-loaders. The last of the muzzle-loaders made for the Army was the Model 1864, for the Battle of Gettysburg in 1863 offered easily decipherable handwriting on the wall. War Department records show that more than 35,000 muskets were picked up on this battlefield, of which more than 20,000 were loaded. Approximately 6000 of these loaded rifles had single loads, twice that number had two loads, and the rest had from three to ten loads in the single barrel. It became very clear that in the excitement of battle the average soldier required a foolproof rifle. Just how much these multi-loaded rifles cost the Union Army in effectiveness will never be known.

Several years before the Civil War American gunsmiths had been engaged in experimenting with breech-loading rifles, employing a cartridge, and similar experiments were being carried on in France and England. It would be difficult to say whether the evolution of the modern breechloader was delayed due to the lack of a satisfactory cartridge or the lack of an adequate breech mechanism.

Bullet design also entered the picture, for several experiments were being conducted with a conical bullet. One of the earliest samples of this new bullet was the one designed by Captain C. A. Delvigne, a French officer, who also had designed a rifle with a new powder chamber. This chamber was smaller in diameter than the bore, and made it possible for the bullet to be flattened at the base by a sharp blow of the ramrod. This resulted in greatly improved gas sealing and resultant increases in velocity. Captain Minié, another French officer, came forward with a cylindrical-conical bullet with a solid base, and later one with a conical base which was expanded on firing and offered better gas sealing than previous bullets.

The development of the paper cartridge, used in Sweden 200 years before, undoubtedly contributed the first move toward the solid cartridge case. The next important step was the Sharps waterproof linen cartridge, merely a small linen spill containing powder and ball. This was used in the early Sharps breechloader. When the breech was open, the cartridge was thrust, bullet first, into the chamber, and the rising breechblock sheared the base off the cartridge. It was necessary to point the muzzle toward the ground in order to avoid spilling much of the powder when the breech was closed.

The first of the satisfactory metallic cartridges appeared in 1850, and while it was crude in comparison to the modern cartridge it was an important step in the development of breech-loading, and permitted more rapid firing. Space here does not permit detailed discussion of the many steps in the development of the modern rifle; those interested will find the full story in *The Rifle in America,* by Captain Philip B. Sharpe.

The first satisfactory metallic cartridge was the rim-fire, pioneered in this country by Smith & Wesson and marketed in 1858. These were in .22 caliber only, but the next step was the Henry .44, and the center-fire cartridge followed quite rapidly. All of these were "rimmed" cartridges, and neither the date nor the maker of the first "rimless" center-fire cartridge can be given with certainty. The Winchester Arms Company claims the distinction of being the first company to turn out these cartridges in this country (1895).

The development of the breechloader in this country moved hand-in-hand with cartridge development, but any accurate chronological listing of this development is impossible because of the number of gunsmiths involved and their varying claims and counterclaims. Several breechloaders, including a few capable of firing more than one round, were used during the Civil War, and their value in this conflict did much to stimulate the Government and private gunsmiths to greater effort. Among the many gunsmiths and many small-arms companies who contributed to the development are the following, whose names will be listed to aid shooters who may have one of the old rifles in their gun collections:

Ethan Allen & Co., Worcester, Mass.
Allen & Thurber, Worcester, Mass.
Allen & Wheelock, Worcester, Mass.
R. M. Berdan, Hartford, Conn. (Colt Patent Fire Arms Mfg. Co.)
Brown Manufacturing Co., Newburyport, Mass.
J. Brown, Fremont, N. H.
H. A. Buck & Co., Stafford, Conn.
Bullard Repeating Arms Co., Springfield, Mass.
Connecticut Arms and Mfg. Co., Naubuc, Conn.
Empire Breech-Loading Rifle Co., New York City
Warren R. Evans, Thomaston, Maine
Farrow Arms Co. (Target Rifles)
Folks Gun Works, Bryan, Ohio
Forehand Arms Co.
Greene Rifle Works, Worcester, Mass.
J. E. Harder, Clearfield, Pa.
Cyrus B. Holden, Worcester, Mass.
Hopkins and Allen, Norwich, Conn.
Howard Brothers, Whitneyville, Conn.
B. S. Joslyn, Worcester, Mass.
E. G. Lamson & Co., Windsor, Vt.
Lee Arms Co., Milwaukee, Wis.
Maynard Arms, Co., Washington, D. C.
J. Meigs, Lowell, Mass.
Morse Arms Mfg. Co.
National Arms Co., Brooklyn, N. Y.
H. L. Peabody, Boston, Mass.
H. M. Quackenbush, Herkimer, N. Y.
Richardson & Overman, Philadelphia, Pa.
Smith & Wesson, Springfield, Mass.
S. M. Spencer, South Manchester, Conn.
Standard Arms Co., Wilmington, Del.
Starr Arms Co., New York City
Triplett and Scott, Columbia, Ky.
Ward-Burton
Frank Wesson, Worcester, Mass. (B. Kitredge & Co.)
Nathaniel Whitmore, Mansfield, Mass.
Whitney Arms Co., New Haven, Conn.
William Wurfflein, Philadelphia, Pa.

The development of the modern rifle in this country did not gather any real impetus until 1890 when the U. S. Army named a board of officers to find a rifle which would be more satisfactory than the .45/70 Springfield. The board deliberated for some time, meanwhile carrying out tests of various repeating rifles offering small-caliber jacketed bullets employing smokeless powder. The Krag-Jorgensen was the rifle finally selected, after more than a score of rifles of American and European makers had been submitted to thorough tests. The calibers of the various rifles tested ranged from .25 to .45, although the majority were in the .30-caliber class.

The first Krag was a five-shot, bolt-action rifle, in .30 caliber employing a rimmed cartridge. The round-nosed, metal-jacketed bullet weighed 220 grains, and had a muzzle velocity of approximately 2000 foot-seconds. This model was turned out in two types, one weighing about 9½ pounds, having a 30-inch barrel; and a carbine with a 22-inch barrel, for use by the cavalry. In 1896 a new model was turned out which was a considerable improvement on the original. In 1898 another model was produced, with a few minor changes, which became the

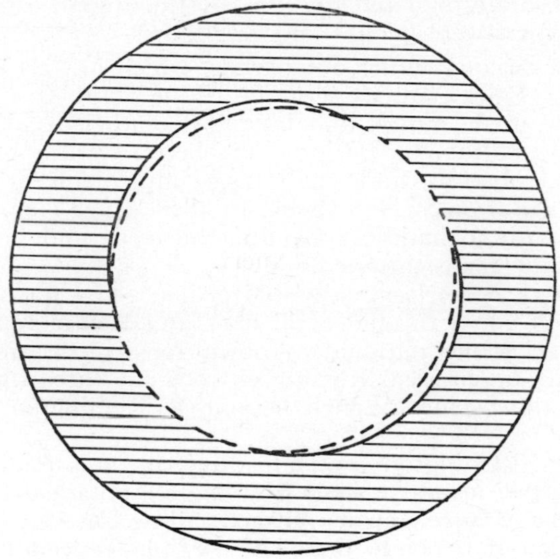

PLATE IX. The Newton Oval Bore Rifling. Dotted line shows bore prior to rifling; solid line shows cut made for oval rifling.

Krag known to most modern shooters. Shortly after the turn of the century, this rifle was replaced by the Springfield, upon which the 150,000 Krags were released by the Government for sale to civilians. Members of the National Rifle Association were able to obtain these rifles for $1.50 each.

Among the rifles submitted by American gunsmiths, after the adoption of the Krag, was the Blake bolt-action repeater, a seven-shot rifle in .30/40 caliber, but having a much greater muzzle velocity than the Krag. When the Blake was turned down by the Army board, despite many features which were definitely improvements over the Krag, the inventor began production of the rifle as a sporting arm, and it was turned out in four grades, ranging in price from $100 to $50. The materials and workmanship embodied in this rifle were excellent, and both accuracy and barrel-life were guaranteed. Shortly after 1900 Blake began turning out special grades, some costing as much as $1000. The best grades of this rifle were guaranteed to shoot a one-inch group at 220 yards, which even today is asking quite a lot from a rifle. Such guarantees, according to Captain Philip Sharpe, "contributed to the failure of the firm."

The American rifle which has since become world famous, and is conceded to be one of the finest military or sporting arms ever designed, the "Springfield .30 '06" made its appearance in 1903, under the official designation of "U. S. Magazine Rifle Caliber .30 Model 1903."

An entire volume was written on this rifle by Captain E. C. Crossman, *The Book of the Springfield,* and the library of no "gun crank" is complete without it. The action of the Springfield is a modification of the Mauser action. The original rifle was chambered for a rimless .30/03 cartridge, with a longer neck than the cartridge developed later, and had a muzzle velocity of about 2200 foot-seconds with the .220-grain Krag bullet. In 1906 a new bullet, with a shorter neck and using a 150-grain spitzer bullet, with a muzzle velocity of about 2700 foot-seconds, was developed, and the 1903 model rifles were rechambered for this cartridge.

One of the most prized rifles found anywhere was the so-called "star-gauge Springfield," but few people who acquired one knew exactly how it obtained the "star-gauge" distinction. When barrels were finished at the armory, a special gauge was employed to measure the uniformity of the grooves and lands. This gauge, terminated by tiny metal fingers, was inserted in the barrel and a reading was taken every inch. If the variation between the grooves and lands was less than .0001 inch from breech to muzzle, the rifle barrel received a star-gauge stamp. The star is stamped on the muzzle.

During the first 14 years, approximately 1,000,000 of these Springfields were made. The first 800,000 of these rifles had case-hardened receivers, but succeeding receivers were turned out by a special double heat-treated process, which gave additional strength. In 1927 a nickel-steel receiver and bolt replaced the heat-treated receiver, and resulted in a further increase in strength. The serial numbers indicate the type of receiver on this rifle. Those with a serial number lower than 800,000 have the case-hardened receivers. Those from 800,000 to 1,275,767 have the heat-treated receivers, and those with higher numbers have the nickel-steel receivers.

The Enfield, a British Army rifle, entered the United States picture during World War I, when we turned out large numbers of these rifles for the British. The rifle was originally chambered for a .276 cartridge, but this gave way to the .303 British cartridge. Upon our entry into the war, several American plants were tooled up to make the Enfield, and it was decided to equip some of our troops with this rifle, but chambered for the .30 '06 cartridge. Originally the parts for this rifle were not interchangeable, but when turned out for the U. S. Army they were standardized.

**Repeating Rifle Development.** During the period of experimentation before and after the Civil War, several American firearms manufacturers had been turning out various models of rifles employing metallic cartridges, and several repeating arms were developed, the majority of which were short-lived.

Samuel Colt, founder of the Colt Patent Firearms Manufacturing Company, was one of the pioneers in this field, and his company turned out a number of repeating models, some of the earlier models percussion types, and those developed later employing metallic cartridges. Most of these early models employed a revolving cylinder magazine of six-shot capacity. Later in the 19th century, slide-action and lever-action rifles were turned out by this company in varied calibers. The Colt "New Lightning," first marketed in 1885, was an extremely popular rifle, and was made in several calibers. Another model, employing a center-fire cartridge, was developed the same year.

The Sharps rifles, turned out by Christian Sharps, who obtained his first patent in 1848, was a definite contribution to the evolution of the modern rifle, and were widely used. More than two-score models, each showing some improvement over its predecessor, were turned out by the Sharps Company, including sporting as well as military models, and several fine target models.

Winchester, which entered the firearms picture as the New Haven Arms Co. in 1860, was the real pioneer of the repeating rifle, and Oliver Winchester was its founder. It was not until the entry of B. Tyler Henry into the firm, however, that the Winchester rifles began to assume real importance. The Henry "mark" is still to be found on every Winchester rim-fire cartridge, which has an "H" on its base.

The Henry lever-action repeating rifle is only slightly altered in appearance today, as a glance at the Winchester Model 94 will show. The 1860 rifle is known as the .44 rim-fire, although measurements indicate that it was actually of .43 caliber. The rifle was bored .42 caliber, and rifled with six grooves, each one approximately .005 inch in depth. The rifling had what is known as a "gain" twist, increasing from one turn in 120 inches to one turn in 33 inches. The bullet weighed 216 grains. The magazine was tubular, under the barrel, and had a 15-cartridge capacity. The rifle weighed approximately 10 pounds.

In 1866 the New Haven Arms Co. became the Winchester Repeating Arms Co., operating as such in Bridgeport, Conn., until 1870, when the new plant in New Haven was completed. In 1885 Winchester absorbed the business of the Browning Brothers, a western arms company operated by John, Edward, and Matthew Browning, and the following year came out with the Model 1886, a modified lever-action rifle invented by John Browning, who later attained fame as the greatest inventor and designer of firearms in the world. At the time of his death in 1926, John Browning held patents on more than 125 firearms, and several additional patents had been applied for. The majority of the earlier Winchester models were invented and designed by him. At the time of his death he was completing the design of the popular Browning over-and-under shotgun, in Liège, Belgium.

In 1910 Browning, still with Winchester, designed a recoil-operated shotgun. Disputes as to the royalty basis on which this gun was to be handled resulted in the severance of Browning's connection with Winchester, and the manufacture of the new shotgun by Remington. In 1911 Winchester developed a recoil-operated autoloading shotgun of its own, and although it had an excellent sale it could not compete with the performance of the Browning patent.

In 1932 Winchester was absorbed into the Western Cartridge Co., and in 1940 the two companies came under the control of Olin Industries, Inc. Since its inception, Winchester has turned out more than 50 rifle models, of which the modern examples are shown and described in the "Rifle" section.

The Remington history started in 1816, which gives this company first place in the "oldest existing firearms manufacturers" list. Eliphalet Remington, like Harry Pope, the precision barrel maker, had to make his own rifle because he could not afford to buy one. Remington turned out his first rifle at his small forge in Ilion, N. Y. The barrel was made by welding bands of iron around a rod, but as Remington had no means of rifling it, he walked to Utica, 15 miles distant, and had the work done by a Utica gunsmith. The gunsmith supplied him with a lock, and Remington made his own stock. The rifle was an accurate one, and like Pope's, Remington's first customers were friends and neighbors.

He began turning out barrels, which he carried to the Utica gunsmith for the rifling work. In the fall of 1816 Young Eliphalet and his father decided to go into the gun business, and began turning out rifles, shotguns, and small farm implements at a water mill on Steele's Creek. In 1828 a new factory was built to handle expanding business, and new machinery was installed.

By 1850 the lap-welded barrel had given way to barrels bored through steel bars, and Remington's plant became nationally known for its precision work, and in 1856 Remington took his three sons into the business, which became E. Remington & Sons.

The Remington breech-loading rifle was finally perfected in 1863, when Remington obtained its first large Government contract, calling for the production of 10,000 of these rifles. Eliphalet Remington died in 1861, but his sons carried on the business, and by the end of the Civil War they had so prospered that the plant had an estimated value of $1,500,000. In 1866 John Rider, an inventor and designer, entered the employ of the company and revolutionized the breech designs. Orders began pouring in for Remington rifles from several foreign countries and for many years the major output of the Remington plant went abroad.

In 1886, due to the expansion of the company and its entry into fields far removed from firearms, the corporation went into receivership. In 1889 control of the corporation passed to Marcellus Hartley, a master of business organization and organizer of the Union Metallic Cartridge Co. This accounts for the marking found on all Remington ammunition, "REM-UMC," an abbreviation of Remington and Union Metallic Cartridge. At this time Alfred C. Hobbs became associated with the company, and to his inventive genius is attributed the development of many of the metallic center-fire cartridges. In 1934 E. I. du Pont de Nemours & Co. obtained complete control of both Remington and UMC, at which time the Parker Shotgun Co. was absorbed, as well as the Peters Cartridge Co.

Since its inception, almost 100 models of rifles have been designed and manufactured by Remington, of which the modern examples will be found in the photographic section which follows.

The Savage Repeating Arms Co. was founded in 1894 by Arthur W. Savage, whose famous lever-action rifle formed the backbone of the Savage business. The company entered the arms-manufacturing business at a time when the black-powder cartridge was giving way to smokeless powder, with resulting increases in power, and the company began turning out small-caliber, high-velocity rifles without delay. In 1915 the company was purchased by the Driggs-Seabury Ordnance Co., of Pennsylvania, and in 1917 became known as the Savage Arms Co. In 1920 it absorbed the J. Stevens Arms Co., and in 1930 the A. H. Fox Gun Co.

Several of the small-caliber, high-velocity loads in modern use were developed by Savage, including the .250/3000, the .22 High Power and the .300 Savage. Almost 50 rifle models have been designed by Savage, of which the modern examples will be found in the photographic section.

The Stevens Arms and Tool Co., though it originated with J. Stevens in 1864, was not incorporated until 1886, and prospered because of the fine rifles it turned out. Shortly after 1900 the Stevens firm, which meanwhile had absorbed an optical company and was turning out telescope sights as well as arms, claimed to be the largest manufacturers of sporting arms in the world. While they turned out a few heavy-caliber models, the company specialized in small-caliber match rifles, and the famous Walnut Hill match rifle has long been the most popular single-shot match rifle turned out by any factory.

One of the great advantages enjoyed by Stevens was the advice of Harry M. Pope, whose precision .22-caliber match rifle barrels are the treasured items in any shooter's gun cabinet.

In addition to rifles and shotguns, Stevens turned out a score or more of various telescope sights, for pistols as well as rifles. They turned out almost 100 different rifle models since their inception, of which the modern examples are shown in the photographic section.

The Marlin Firearms Co. was first organized in 1870 by John H. Marlin, and during the first few years limited its production to a few pistols, revolvers, and single-shot rifles. The Ballard single-shot, rifle, in great demand at the time, was made by this company. The company was operated by the Marlin family until 1914, when it was sold to the Marlin Arms Corp. Almost 50 rifle models were turned out by the company, including several models of the very popular Marlin lever-action rifles in varied calibers. Modern examples of Marlin models will be found in the photographic section.

This volume would not be complete without some discussion of the contributions made by the late Charles Newton, whose designs and experiments in high-velocity arms made an important contribution to firearms development in this country. To him must go the credit for the first high-velocity rifle in .22 caliber, which later was manufactured by the Savage firm. Newton produced this rifle in 1905, but it was not until 1911 that it was produced in quantity. This rifle employed a bullet weighing 70 grains, and had a velocity of about 2800 foot-seconds.

While this proved popular for vermin, and was used to some extent for deer, it did not satisfy Newton, who began experimenting with heavier bullets, larger loads, and later larger calibers. The next step in the .22-caliber field was his 90-grain bullet, with a muzzle velocity of 3100 foot-seconds, and from this he moved to a .25-caliber bullet with a muzzle velocity of about 3100 foot-seconds. The bullet weighed 123 grains. This became known as the Newton .256, and is still favored by many vermin shooters because of its flat trajectory.

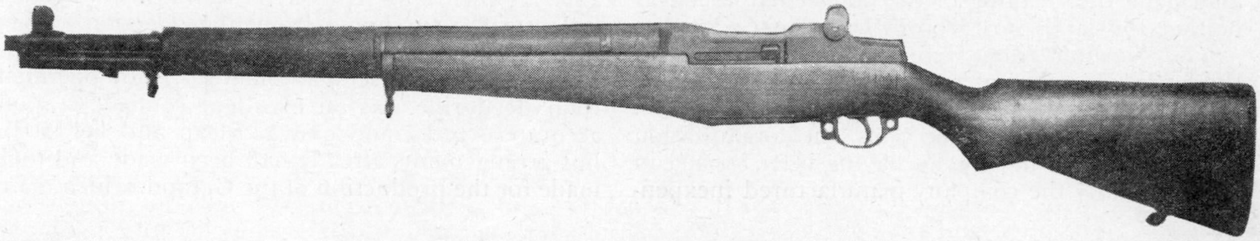

PLATE X. U. S. Rifle, Cal. .30 M-1 (Garand).

The Newton .280 was the next in line, but it did not prove popular. Until the development of the .300 magnum cartridge, however, Newton's .30 was one of the top favorites of the big-game hunters who took their hunting seriously. This cartridge was somewhat larger than the .30 '06, and the case was built much stronger to permit reloading and to withstand the heavy pressures. With this, Newton used bullets ranging in weight from 150 to 225 grains, with a muzzle velocity of about 2600 foot-seconds. The cartridge was first known as the Adolph Express, as the rifles in which it was used were tested by Fred Adolph of Genoa, N. Y.

For those who were not satisfied with the .30 caliber cartridge, Newton produced the .33 caliber, which had a muzzle velocity of about 3000 foot-seconds. The barrels for these rifles were custom made, and very few of them were turned out in this country. The .35 caliber, the most powerful of the Newton loads, held its popularity longer than the other large-caliber loads developed by him. This cartridge employed a 250-grain bullet, and had a muzzle velocity of almost 3000 foot-seconds. Later a 270-grain and a 300-grain bullet was developed for this cartridge, which developed more punch than the bullets of larger caliber that were favored by many of the African hunters.

Newton's game bullets, employing a pointed (spitzer) design with a special point, which minimized air resistance in flight but opened up on penetration, were popular with many hunters who demanded a bullet with extreme accuracy as well as good shocking power.

Newton's rifling experiments also caused considerable discussion and no little argument among the "gun cranks" of yesterday. He was indefatigable in his experiments, and one of his tests included the use of the "oval" rifling, which though not new, had never been developed since its origin more than 75 years before. This method eliminated lands and grooves, and called for boring the barrel oval rather than round and spiraling the bore from breech to muzzle. The bore originally is cut round, and the barrel reamed and lapped to the proper diameter. A tool then cuts two shallow, flattened grooves from each side of the circle of the bore approximately .005 inch in depth, these grooves spiraling up the barrel. Tests made by the Army indicated that this method of rifling was satisfactory, meeting all requirements of accuracy and velocity, but the boring was not adopted. Newton later experimented with other types of rifling, including the "segmental" rifling, employing five shallow, rounded grooves. This rifling was a modification of a boring used by a few British gunsmiths, and gave extreme accuracy and made the cleaning of the bore much easier, as neither the lands nor grooves had sharp edges.

The Newton rifles were never successful, and there are a number of recorded instances in which they were not only very poorly made but dangerous.

The O. F. Mossberg and Sons, Inc., organization is a comparative newcomer, having been formed in 1919. Initially the company manufactured inexpensive four-shot pistols, and it was not until 1920 that they began turning out inexpensive .22-caliber rifles, and in 1935 the company added telescope sights and spotting scopes to the line. Since its inception, the company has turned out more than 75 models of rifles and shotguns, all in the low-price field, but of excellent design. Examples of their current models will be found in the photographic section which follows.

Johnson Automatics, Inc., formed by Melvin M. Johnson, Jr., owes its inception to the inventive and designing genius of its founder, whose automatic and semi-automatic rifle caused considerable stir in Ordnance circles just before our entry into World War II. The arguments that arose regarding the comparative merits of the Garand and the Johnson never have been settled, and the chances are they never will be. Changing the basic infantry weapon from a manually operated rifle to a semi-automatic rifle would have been sufficient to stir up considerable argument in Army circles, but with two excellent rifles to choose from, the selection of one was certain to result in heated arguments.

The Johnson semi-automatic, recoil-operated, rotary-feed rifle was an excellent combat weapon, accurate, sturdy, and easy to clean and field-strip, but arrangements already had been made and tools made for the production of the Garand, which many

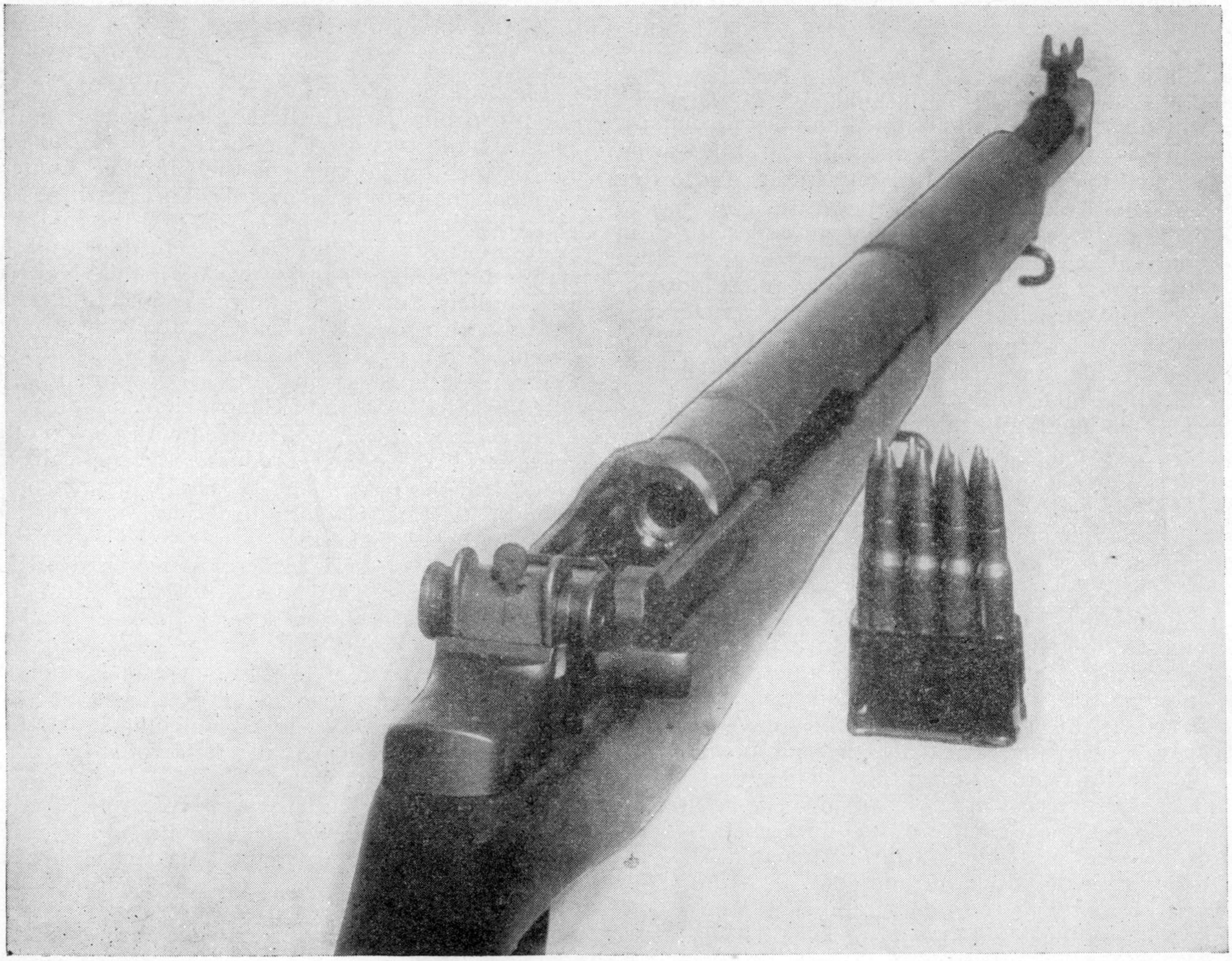

PLATE XI. Showing the U. S. Rifle, Cal. .30 M-1 (Garand) with action open, and showing the 8-round clip.

PLATE XII. U. S. Carbine, Cal. .30 (Winchester).

experts claimed to be a completely satisfactory arm. A number of the Johnson semi-automatic rifles were used by special combat units during the war, and proved to be satisfactory in every respect. The Johnson light machine gun also was used, and was favored by Marine Corps parachute units.

The Garand, officially known as the U. S. Rifle Caliber .30 M1, was the design of John C. Garand, chief civilian engineer at the Springfield Armory. Garand had been working on the design for more than 20 years, and in 1919 had submitted drawings for a light machine gun operated on a new principle, which had possibilities as a semi-automatic rifle. He was employed at a salary to experiment with modifications of his principle with the view of eventually producing such a rifle. Several other designers were employed during this period, each working on his own designs, and in 1934 the Ordnance Department conducted tests on five rifles which resulted from their experiments. The Garand proved to be the most satisfactory to the Ordnance experts, but it was not until 1936 that formal approval was made and manufacturing began. During the two-year period mentioned, several minor changes were made in the design, and as late as 1939 additional changes were made. The finished rifle, a gas-operated, semi-automatic, clip-loaded arm, weighed slightly more than 9 pounds.

The value of the Garand as a sporting arm can hardly be settled for some years. Until these rifles are made available to civilians in sufficient numbers, any discussion on this matter would be premature. There are several features of the rifle, however, which would operate against the Garand as a sporting arm, including its weight and the fact that the mounting of a telescope sight would be difficult if not impossible.

The companion piece to the Garand, known officially as U. S. Semi-Automatic Carbine Caliber .30 M1, believed by many to be merely a small edition of the Garand, was developed by the engineers of the Winchester Arms Company, and was designed to replace the .45-caliber pistol by offering greater accuracy, more fire power, and longer range. It was designed just before our entry into World War II.

The Winchester engineers had developed a .30-caliber semi-automatic rifle weighing about 7½ pounds, and this rifle had proved so satisfactory in tests that the company decided to alter it to produce a 5-pound carbine for entry in the competition for the selection of a standard carbine. The complete alteration and change in design was accomplished by the Winchester engineers in 14 days, and their carbine was selected. After a few minor changes were made the carbine was produced in large numbers, and proved to be an unusually satisfactory arm. The carbine is a gas-operated rifle, weighing 5 pounds, with a barrel length of 17¾ inches and a magazine capacity of 15 rounds, employing a .30-caliber bullet weighing 110 grains and having a muzzle velocity of about 1800 foot-seconds.

Many sportsmen who used the carbine on game during the war found it to be a satisfactory rifle for taking game as large as deer, at ranges up to 150 yards. With a few alterations to the stock, different sights, and the use of a five-round magazine, and perhaps a change in bullet design and velocity, most sportsmen who have used the carbine insist that it would make an excellent brush gun for the deer hunter.

# TYPICAL MODERN RIFLES

PLATE I. WINCHESTER Model 70 (Standard). Available in the following calibers: .22 Hornet, .250 Savage, .270 Winchester, .30 '06 Springfield, 7 mm., .257 Roberts, .35 Remington, all these available in either 20- or 24-inch barrel. Also, .375 H. & H. Magnum with 25-inch barrel; .220 Swift and .300 H. & H. Magnum with 26-inch barrel. Action, Mauser-type bolt, firing pin cocks on opening lift of bolt, bolt immediately removable, speed lock, three-position safety, box magazine with hinged floor-plate, capacity 5 rounds except for .300 and .375 H. & H. Magnum which take 4 rounds. Weight, as shown, about 8 pounds, 4 ounces.

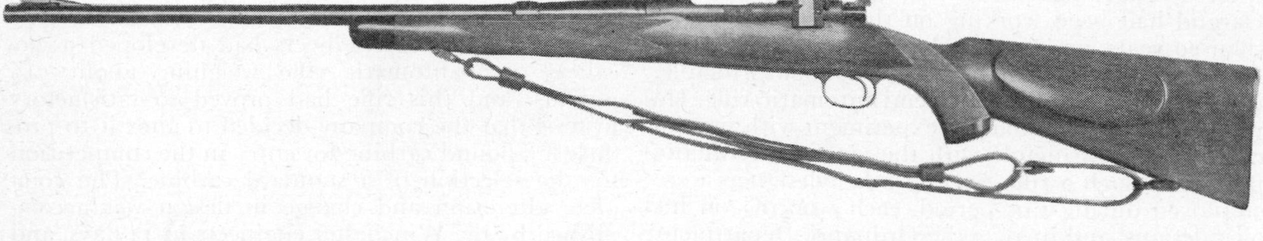

PLATE II. WINCHESTER Model 70 (Super Grade). Available in the same calibers as the Standard Grade shown above. Stock of special design selected American walnut, with cheekpiece, and fancy checkering. Black plastic fore-end tip. Barrel bored, rifled, chambered, and lap finished to highest standards.

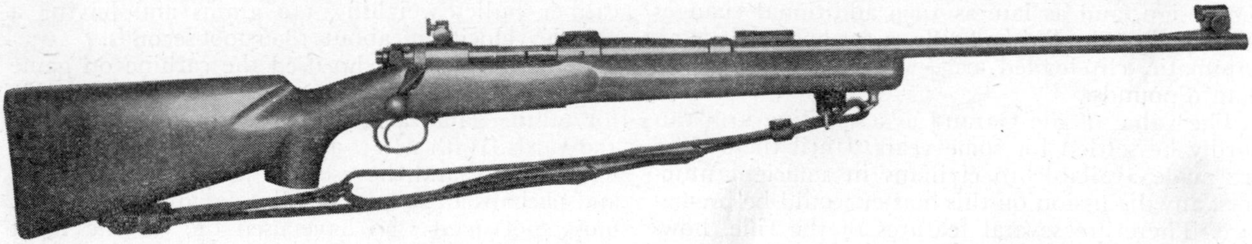

PLATE III. WINCHESTER Model 70 (National Match). Available only in .30 '06 Springfield, with 24-inch tapered barrel, bored, rifled, chambered, and lap finished to highest standards. Equipped with Lyman 77 detachable hooded target front sight with interchangeable inserts on forged ramp base and Lyman 48 receiver sight. Telescope mount bases attached. Weight, about 9 pounds, 8 ounces.

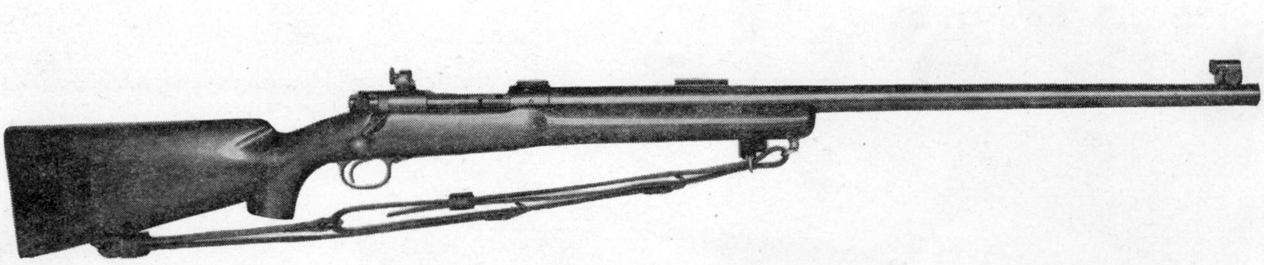

PLATE IV. WINCHESTER Model 70 (Target). Available in the following calibers with 24-inch *medium*-weight barrel: .22 Hornet, .250 Savage, .270 Winchester, .30 '06 Springfield, 7 mm., .257 Roberts, .35 Remington. With 26-inch *medium*-weight barrel, .220 Swift and .300 H. & H. Magnum. Same stock and sights as the Model 70 Bull Gun. Weight, about 10 pounds, 8 ounces.

PLATE V. WINCHESTER Model 70 (Bull Gun). Available in 28-inch barrel, in two calibers: .30 '06 Springfield and .300 H. & H. Magnum. Bored, rifled, chambered, and lap finished to highest standards. Other specifications similar except for heavy barrel and semi-beavertail fore-end. Weight, about 13 pounds, 4 ounces.

PLATE VI. WINCHESTER Model 94 (Carbine). Available in the following calibers: .25-35, .30-30, .32 Winchester Special. Magazine capacity, 6 cartridges; barrel length, 20 inches. Weight, 6 pounds, 4 ounces.

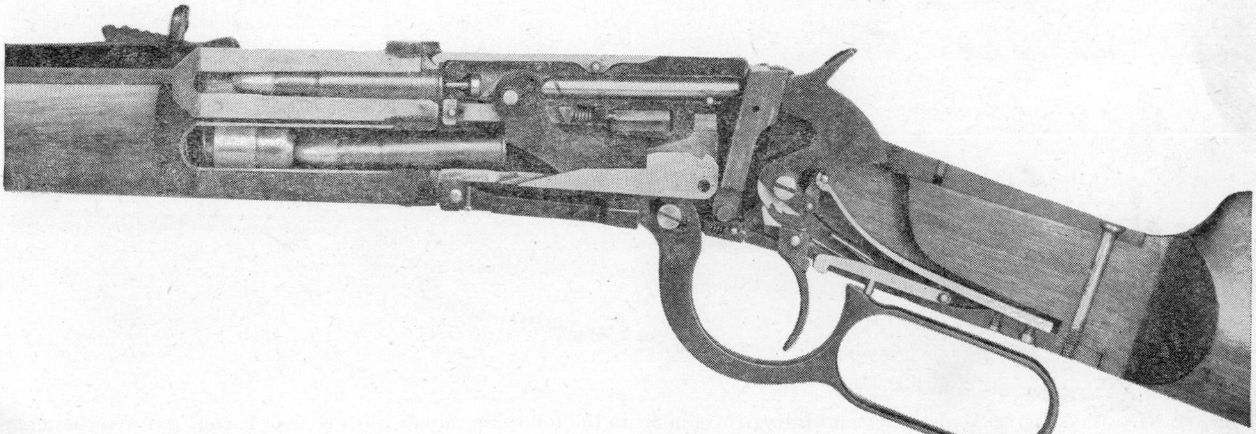

PLATE VII. Sectional View of Model 94 Winchester.

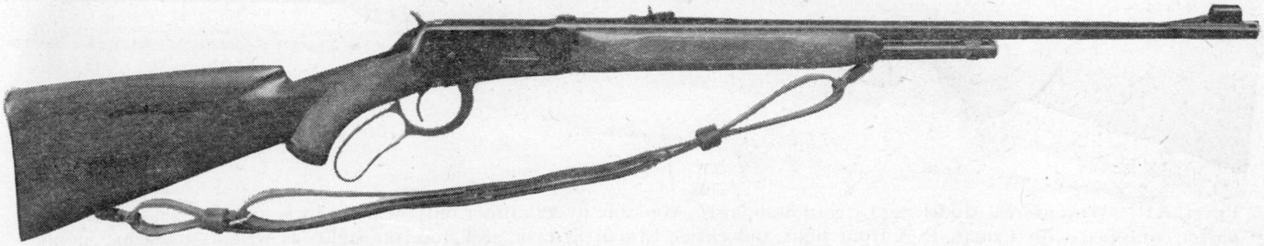

PLATE VIII. WINCHESTER Model 64 (Deer). Available in the following calibers, with 20- or 24-inch barrel: .30-30, .32 Winchester Special. Magazine capacity, 5 cartridges. Weight, about 7 pounds.

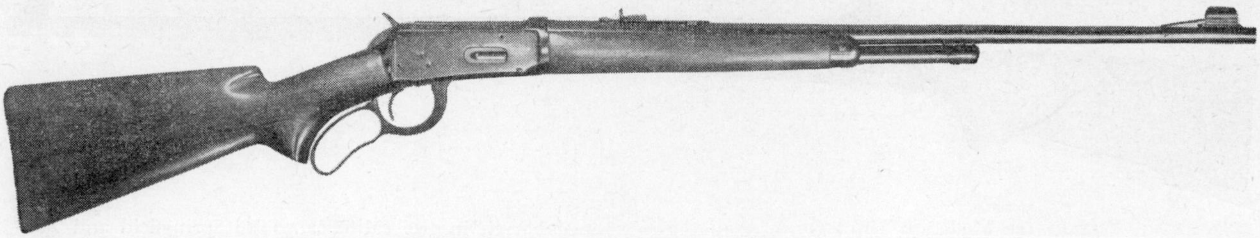

Plate IX. Winchester Model 64 (Standard). Available in the following calibers, with 20- or 24-inch barrel: .25-35, .30-30, .32 Winchester Special. With 26-inch barrel, .219 Zipper. Weight, about 7 pounds.

The Model 65, similar in appearance, is available with 24-inch barrel, in .218 Bee. Magazine capacity, 6 cartridges. Weight, about 6 pounds, 12 ounces.

Plate X. Winchester Model 71. Available in the following calibers, with 20- or 24-inch barrel: .348 Winchester. Magazine capacity, 4 cartridges. Weight, about 8 pounds.

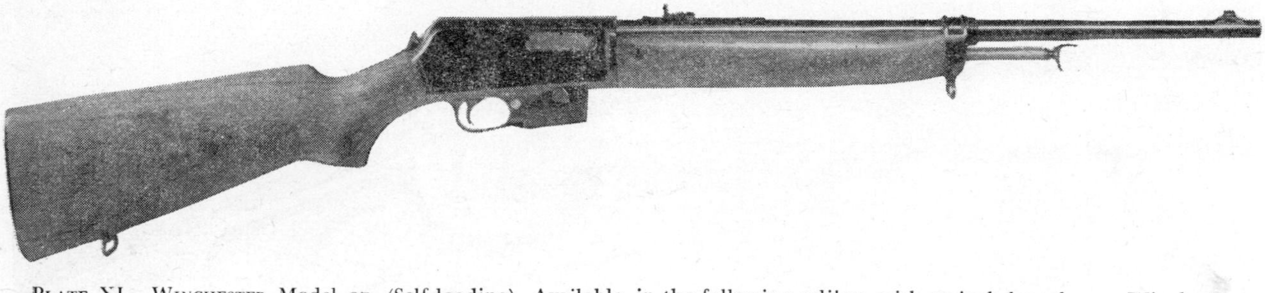

Plate XI. Winchester Model 07 (Self-loading). Available in the following caliber, with 20-inch barrel: .351 Winchester. Magazines hold either 5 or 10 cartridges. Weight, about 7 pounds, 12 ounces.

Plate XII. Winchester Model 52 Target (Standard). Available in .22 caliber only, with 28-inch standard-weight, tapered barrel equipped with Lyman 17-A front sight and either Lyman 57-F or 48-F receiver sight, as well as telescope mount bases. Several additional Redfield or Lyman sight combinations optional. Standard trigger pull of 3½ pounds. Special bolt action with speed lock. Detachable box magazine of 5 .22-caliber long rifle capacity and single-shot adapter. Weight, about 10 pounds.

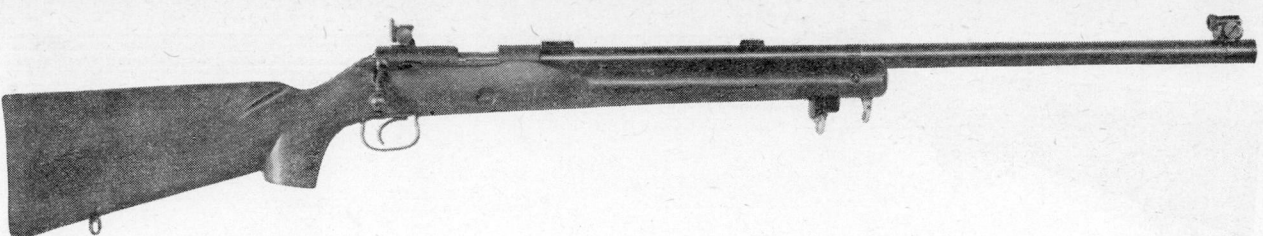

PLATE XIII. WINCHESTER Model 52 Target (Heavy Barrel). Similar to Standard Model except for heavy-weight barrel. Approximate weight, 12 pounds. Also available is a Model 52 Bull Gun, with extra-heavy barrel. Weight, approximately 11 pounds, 12 ounces without sights or sling.

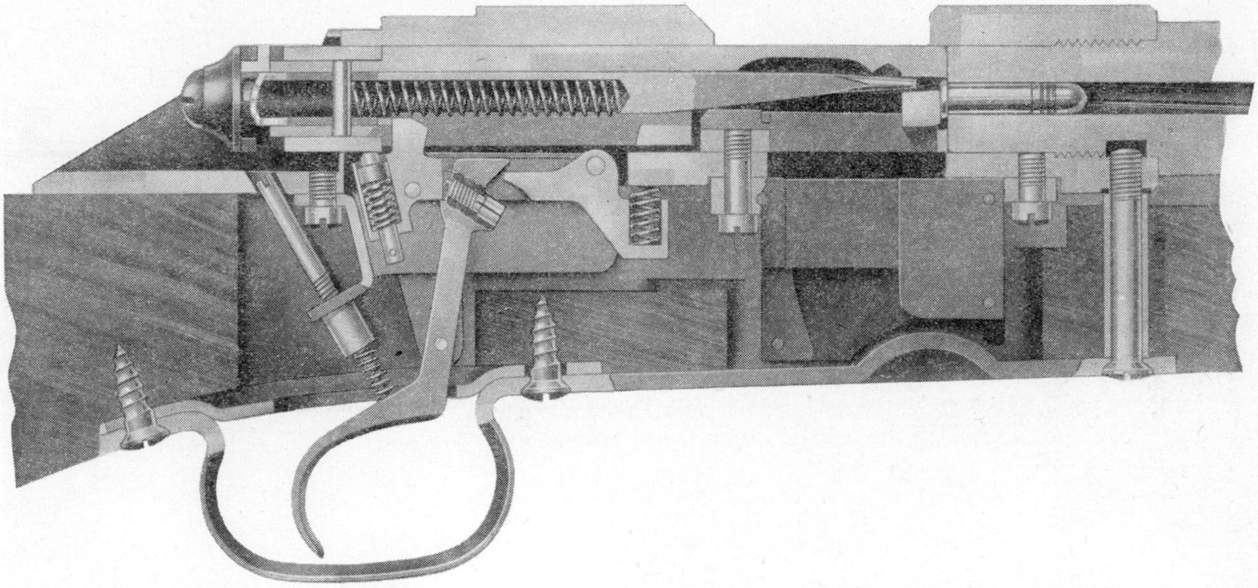

PLATE XIV. Sectional View of Model 52 Winchester.

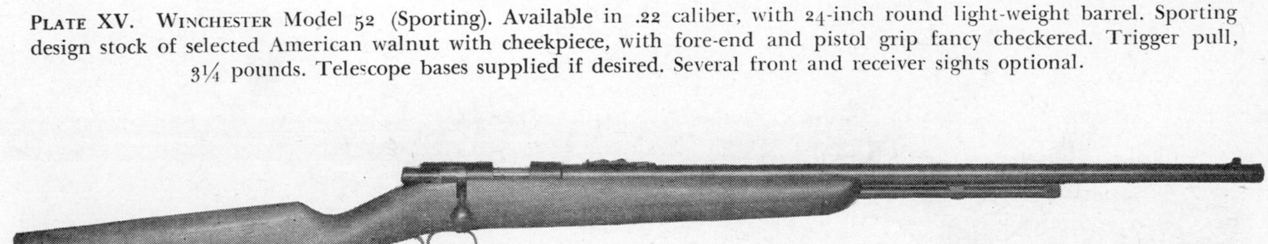

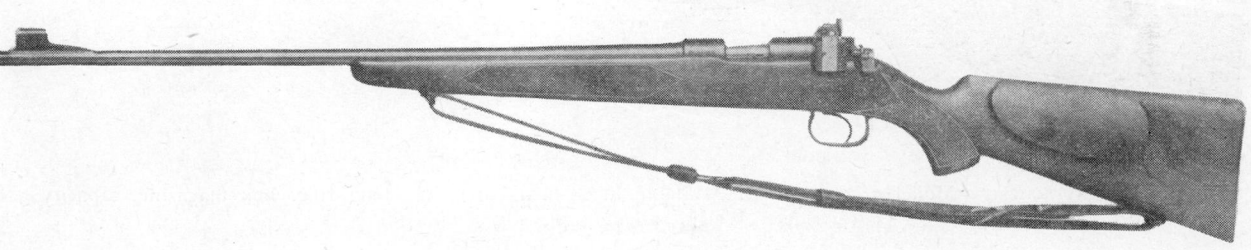

PLATE XV. WINCHESTER Model 52 (Sporting). Available in .22 caliber, with 24-inch round light-weight barrel. Sporting design stock of selected American walnut with cheekpiece, with fore-end and pistol grip fancy checkered. Trigger pull, 3¼ pounds. Telescope bases supplied if desired. Several front and receiver sights optional.

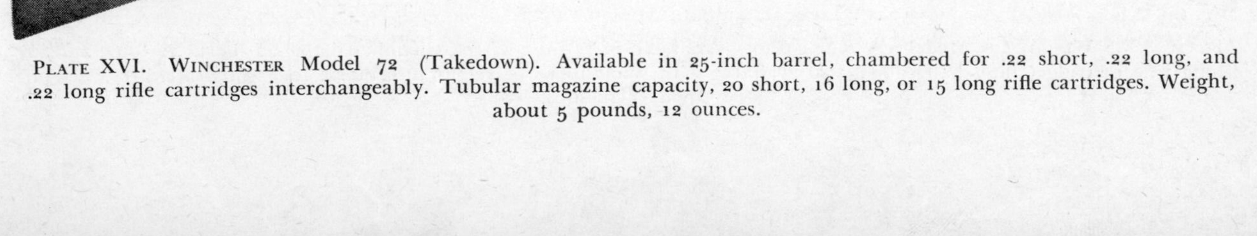

PLATE XVI. WINCHESTER Model 72 (Takedown). Available in 25-inch barrel, chambered for .22 short, .22 long, and .22 long rifle cartridges interchangeably. Tubular magazine capacity, 20 short, 16 long, or 15 long rifle cartridges. Weight, about 5 pounds, 12 ounces.

Plate XVII. Winchester Model 69 (Takedown). Available in 25-inch barrel, chambered for .22 short, .22 long, and .22 long rifle cartridges interchangeably. Box magazine of 5-cartridge capacity. Separate magazine supplied for .22 short cartridges. Weight, about 5 pounds, 8 ounces.

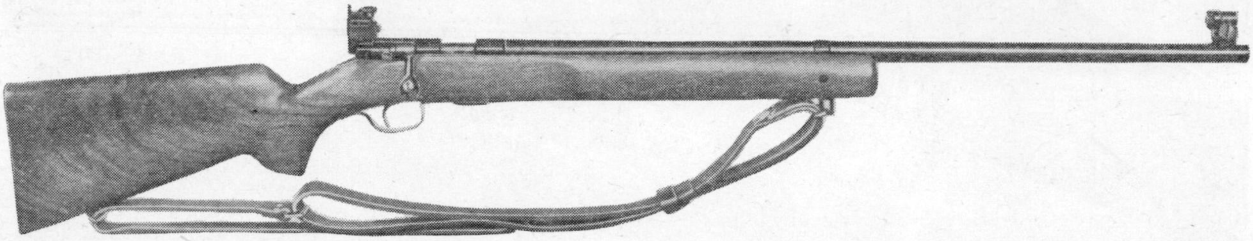

Plate XVIII. Winchester Model 75 (Standard Target). Available in 28-inch barrel, .22 long rifle. Magazine capacity, 5 cartridges. Several sight combinations optional. Weight, about 8 pounds, 10 ounces.

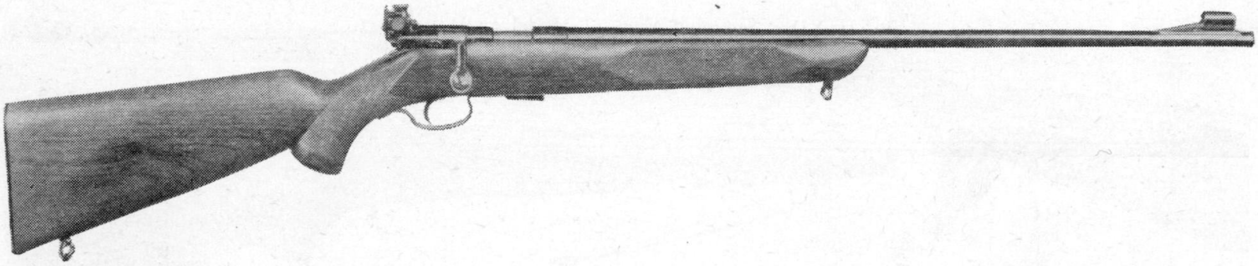

Plate XIX. Winchester Model 75 (Sporting). Available in 24-inch barrel, .22 long rifle. Box magazine, capacity 5 cartridges. Weight, about 5 pounds, 8 ounces.

Plate XX. Winchester Model 67 (Single Shot). Available in 27-inch barrel. Chambered for .22 short, .22 long, and .22 long rifle cartridges interchangeably. Also available with smoothbore barrel for use of .22 long shot cartridges. Weight, about 5 pounds.

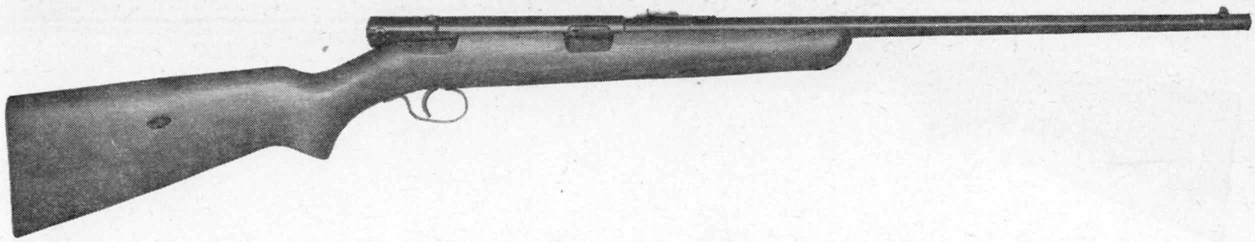

Plate XXI. Winchester Model 74 (Self-loading). Available in 24-inch barrel. Chambered for *either* .22 short or .22 long rifle cartridges, not interchangeable. Tubular magazine (in stock), capacity, 20 short cartridges or 14 long rifle cartridges. Weight, about 6 pounds, 4 ounces.

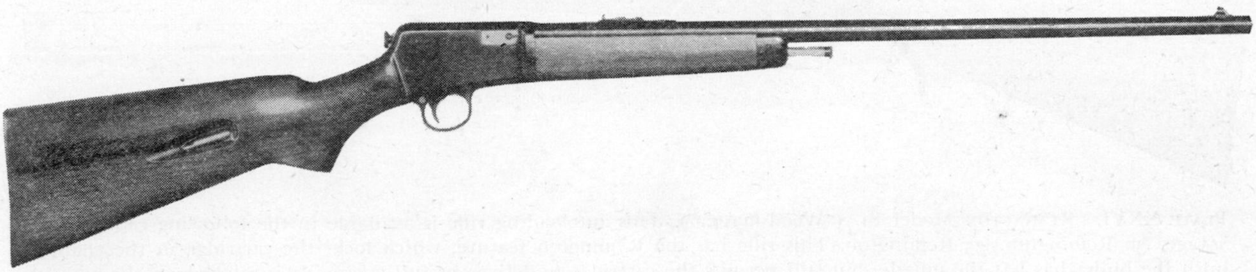

Plate XXII. Winchester Model 63 (Self-loading). Available in 23-inch barrel for .22 long rifle cartridge. Tubular magazine of 10-shot capacity. Weight, about 5 pounds, 8 ounces.

Plate XXIII. Winchester Model 61 (Takedown). Available in 24-inch round tapered barrel or 24-inch octagon barrel, chambered for .22 short, .22 long, and .22 long rifle cartridges interchangeably. Tubular magazine, capacity 20 short, 16 long, or 14 long rifle cartridges. Weight, about 5 pounds, 8 ounces.

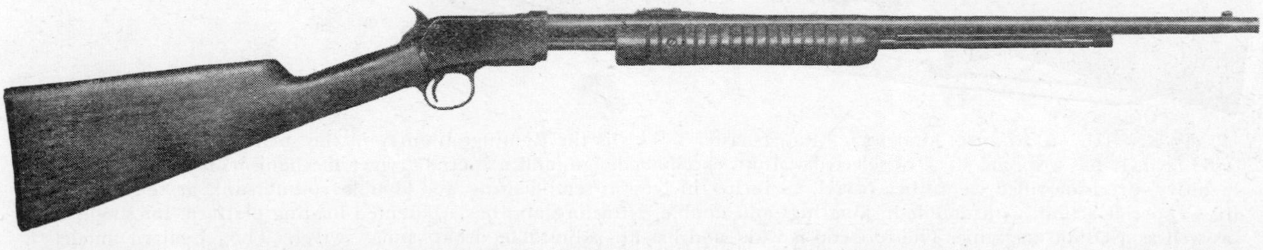

Plate XXIV. Winchester Model 62 (Takedown). Available in 23-inch barrel, chambered for .22 short, .22 long, and .22 long rifle cartridges interchangeably. Tubular magazine, capacity same as Model 61, Weight, about 5 pounds, 8 ounces.

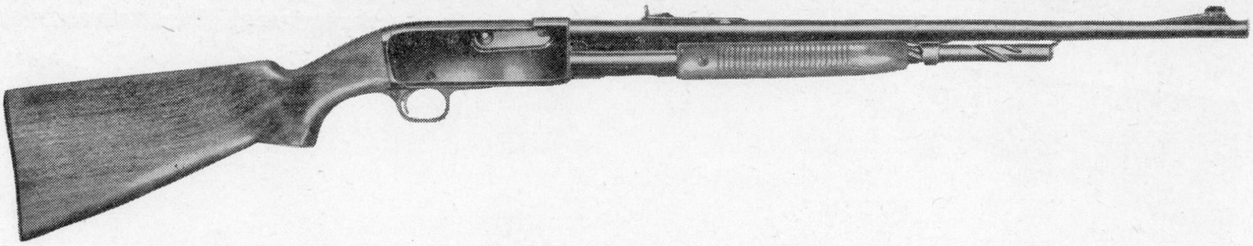

PLATE XXV. REMINGTON Model 141 ("Gamemaster"). This slide-action rifle is available in the following calibers: .30 Remington, .32 Remington, .35 Remington. It is the only high-power rifle made with the slide action. (Replaces Model 14.) It is a takedown rifle, hammerless, with solid breech, and 24-inch barrel. Standard model is equipped with step-adjustable rear sight and white metal bead front sight, with the receiver tapped for a tang peep sight. Magazine capacity, 5 cartridges. Stock of American walnut, with half pistol grip and steel butt plate. Over-all length, 42¾ inches; taken down, 29½ inches. Weight, about 7½ pounds. This model is available in "Special," "Peerless," and "Premier" grades.

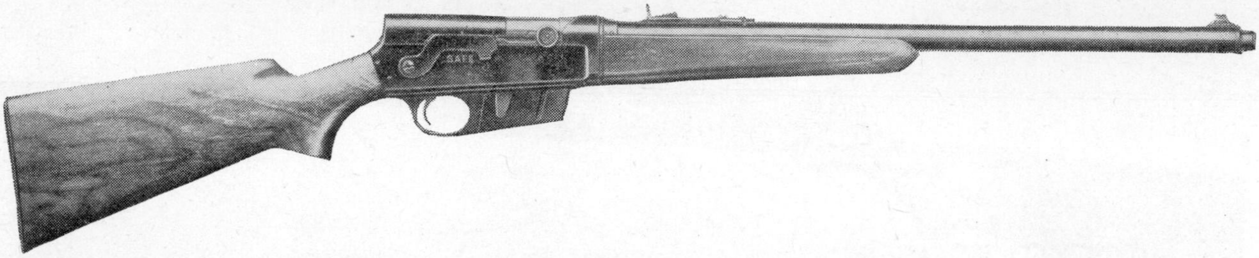

PLATE XXVI. REMINGTON Model 81 ("Woodsmaster"). This autoloading rifle is available in the following calibers: .300 Savage, .30 Remington, .35 Remington. This rifle has the Remington feature, which locks the cartridge in the chamber until the bullet has left the muzzle, but still permits the cartridge to deliver its full energy. It is a takedown, hammerless rifle, with a solid breech. The standard model is equipped with a step adjustable rear sight and white metal bead front sight. The receiver is tapped for a tang peep sight. Magazine capacity, 5 cartridges. Stock and fore-end of American walnut, half pistol grip, steel butt plate. Over-all length, 41½ inches; taken down, 23 inches. Weight, about 8½ pounds. This model is available in "Special," "Peerless," "Expert," and "Premier" grades.

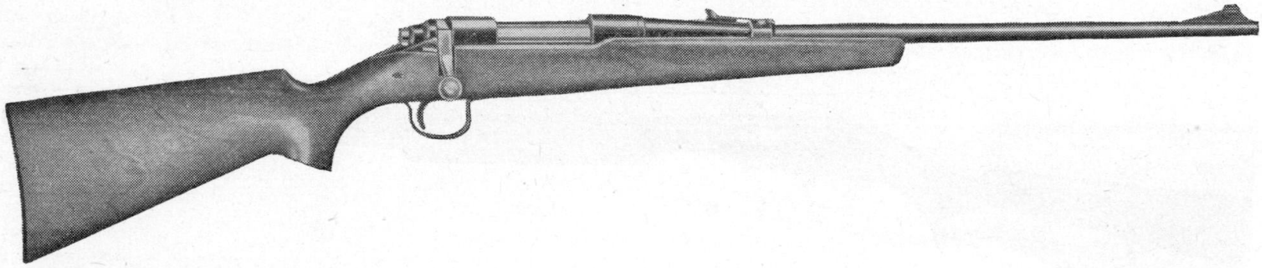

PLATE XXVII. REMINGTON Model 721 and 722. This bolt-action rifle is available in the following calibers: Model 721, .30 '06, .270, and .300 magnum; Model 722, .300 Savage and 257 Roberts. Both models are identical except for the shorter action and receiver of the Model 722. Both models have a 24-inch round, tapered barrel, carefully bored and rifled for extreme accuracy. Sporting stock of American walnut, pistol grip, semi-beavertail fore-end. Rifle cocks on opening movement of the bolt. Magazine capacity, 4 rounds. Receiver drilled and tapped for telescope mount and standard micrometer receiver sights. Sharp, crisp pull, positive ejection, thumb-operated safety. Sights: white metal front sight, with matted ramp; step adjustable rear sight. Low upturn of bolt handle permits low mounting of telescope sight. Over-all length: Model 721, 44¼ inches; Model 722, 43¼ inches. Weight: Model 721, 7¼ pounds; Model 722, 7 pounds.

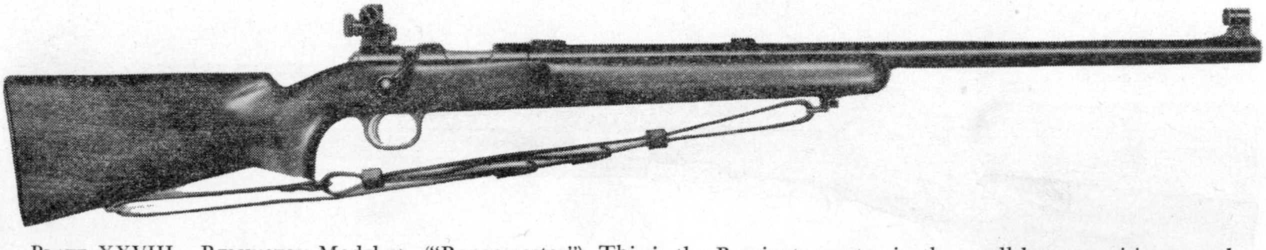

PLATE XXVIII. REMINGTON Model 37 ("Rangemaster"). This is the Remington entry in the small-bore, precision, match rifle field. It has a special stock of selected walnut, excellent design, and a special trigger mechanism. It is equipped with a heavy, precision-rifled .22-caliber barrel, 28 inches in length, semi-floating and double countersunk at the muzzle. It has a special action, with double-locking lugs and double extractors, and has a patented loading platform for single shots as well as a 5-shot magazine. The fore-end is wide, and has an adjustable front sling swivel. The standard model is equipped with the Remington micrometer target rear sight, with six-hole eyepiece, and ¼-minute clicks. It has a Redfield globe front sight with seven interchangeable inserts. It also is equipped with standard telescope blocks. Weight, approximately 12 pounds. Over-all length, 46½ inches. This model may be had with the following modifications: without rear sight, without rear and front sights, with rear sight adapter for Redfield, Lyman, Marble-Goss, Pacific, or Merit disks.

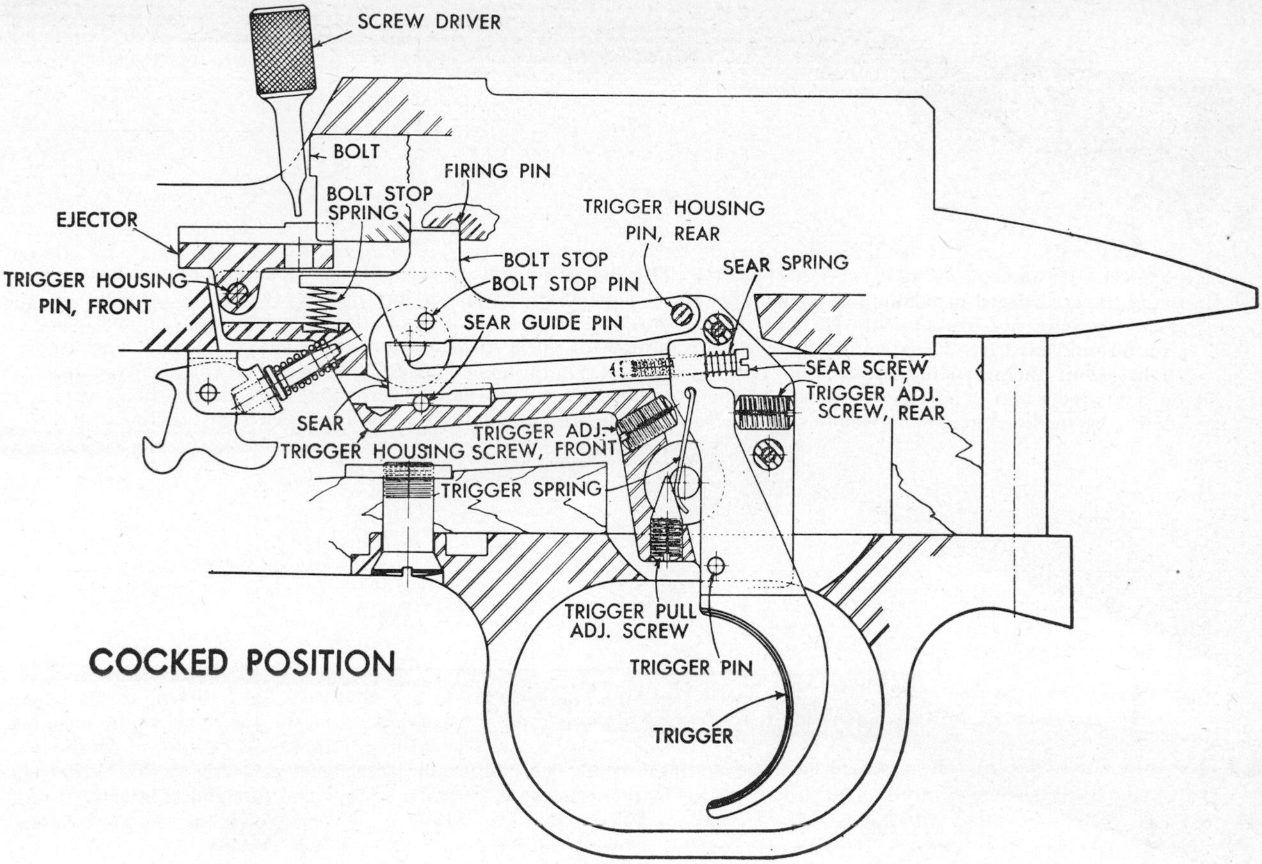


PLATE XXIX. Sectional View of Model 37 Remington, showing action and parts.

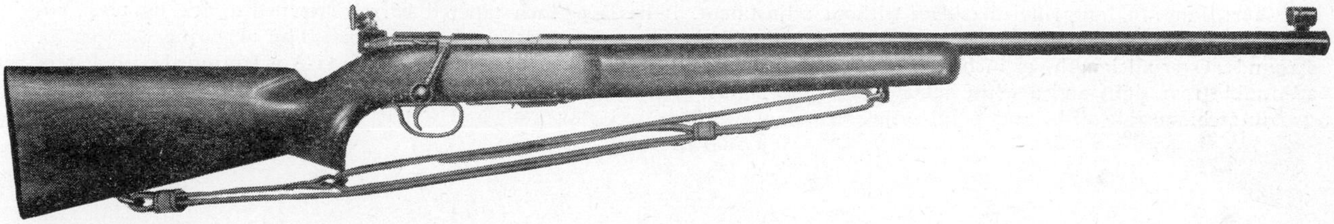

PLATE XXX. REMINGTON Model 513 ("Matchmaster"). This rifle is available in .22 caliber only. It is a medium-weight target rifle, specially designed, and with fine accuracy. It has a tailored walnut stock of good design, a medium-weight 27-inch barrel, adjustable trigger pull, box magazine of 6-round capacity, and is equipped with double locking lugs and a double extractor. The barrel is carefully bored and rifled and is double countersunk at the muzzle. It is equipped with a Redfield No. 75 micrometer rear sight with ¼-minute clicks, a Redfield globe front sight with seven interchangeable inserts, and the barrel is drilled and tapped for telescope blocks. The front swivel is adjustable. Over-all length, 45 inches; taken down, 33 inches. Weight, including sling strap, 9 pounds. This model is available with the following modifications: without sights, with interchangeable 10-round magazine.

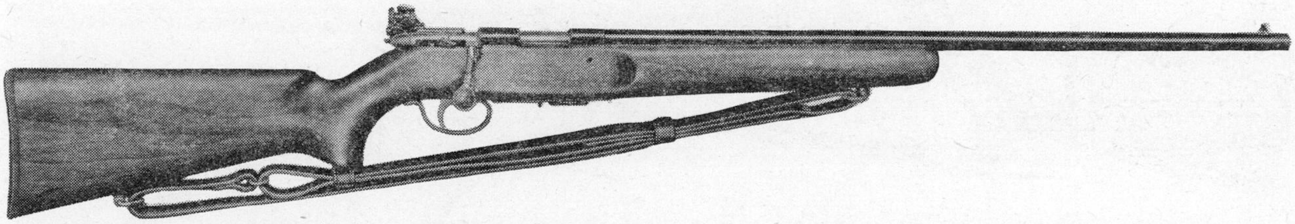

PLATE XXXI. REMINGTON Model 521-T ("Junior Special"). This rifle is available in .22 caliber only, and was specially designed for the boy interested in target shooting. It has a match-type stock of walnut, double locking lugs, double extractors, and an excellent trigger pull. It has a 25-inch, round, tapered barrel, crowned at the muzzle, and a 6-round box magazine. It has a Patridge-type blade front sight, with a Lyman No. 57 RS rear sight with ¼-minute clicks. The front sling swivel is adjustable, and it is equipped with a one-inch leather sling. Over-all length, 43 inches; taken down, 31 inches. Weight, 7 pounds.

PLATE XXXII. REMINGTON Model 513-S ("Sporter"). This bolt-action rifle is available in .22 caliber only. It has a 27-inch, round, tapered barrel of medium-heavy weight, carefully bored and rifled for fine accuracy. It has an excellent trigger pull and a short, fast firing-pin travel. It is equipped with double locking lugs and double extractors. The box magazine has a 6-round capacity. The stock is of American walnut, with pistol grip and fore-end checkered, and a steel butt plate. It has front and rear sling swivels. The rear sight is a step adjustable Marble No. 63 and a Patridge-type front sight on a matted ramp. The receiver is tapped for a Redfield No. 75 micrometer rear sight. Over-all length, 45 inches; taken down, 33 inches. Weight, 6¾ pounds. It is also available with a Remington receiver peep sight, and with a 10-round magazine.

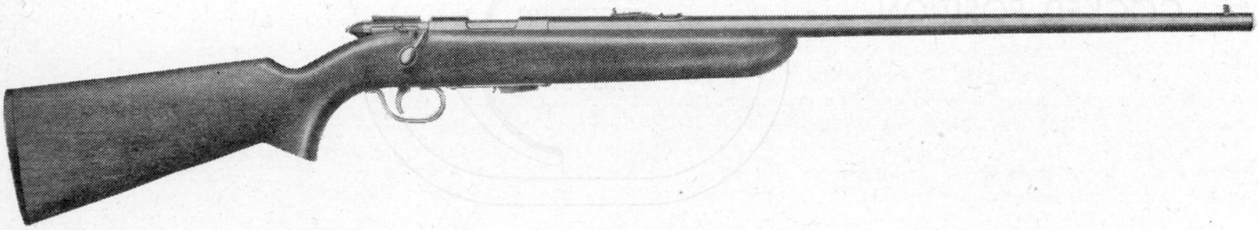

PLATE XXXIII. REMINGTON Models 511-A and 511-P. This model is available in .22 caliber only, and is adaptable to the short, long, or long rifle cartridges without adjustment. It has a 25-inch tapered barrel, crowned at the muzzle, and cocks on the opening movement of the bolt. It has double locking lugs and double extractors. The magazine capacity is 6 rounds. Over-all length, 43 inches; taken down, 31 inches. Weight, about 5½ pounds. The 511-A is equipped with a step adjustable rear sight and a white metal bead front sight. The 511-P has a Remington "Point-crometer" rear sight with two interchangeable disks and point adjustments for windage and elevation, and a Patridge-type blade front sight on a matted ramp.

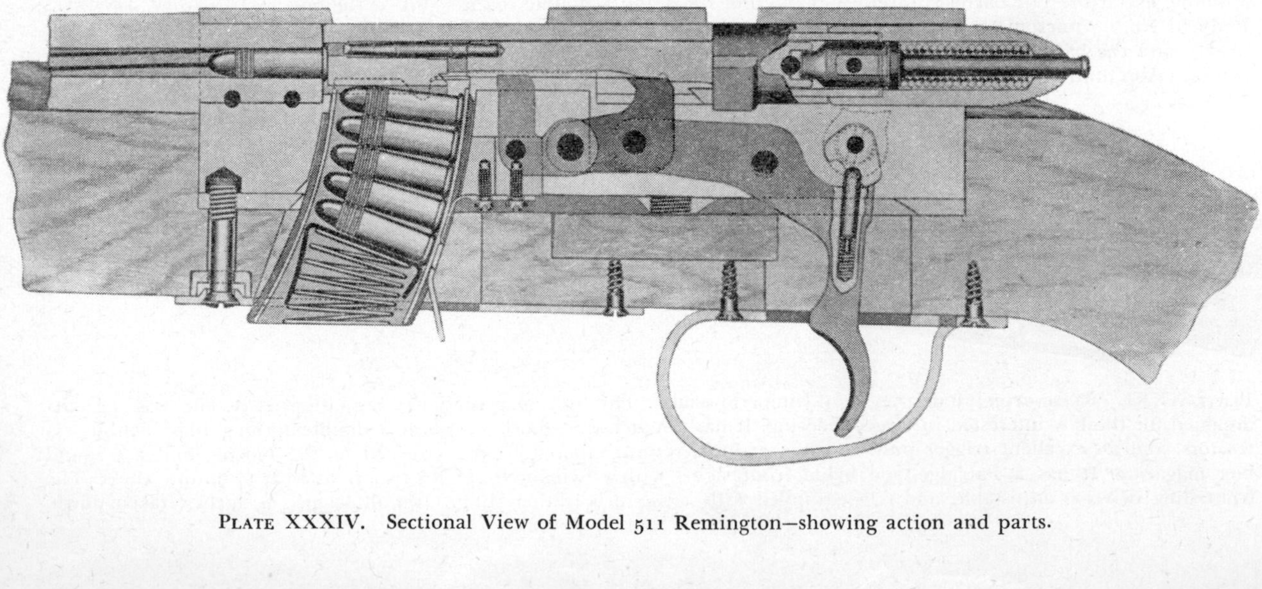

PLATE XXXIV. Sectional View of Model 511 Remington—showing action and parts.

PLATE XXXV. REMINGTON Model 512 ("Sportmaster"). This bolt-action rifle is available in .22 caliber only, and is adaptable to the short, long, or long rifle cartridge without adjustment. It has a 25-inch tapered barrel, crowned at the muzzle, and has double locking lugs and double extractors. The stock is of American walnut with a semi-beavertail fore-end. The tubular magazine has the following capacity: 22 short, 17 long, or 15 long rifle cartridges. Over-all length, 43 inches; taken down, 31 inches. It has a step adjustable rear sight with a white metal bead front sight. Model 512-P is equipped with the Remington "Point-crometer" rear sight and a Patridge-type front sight on a matted ramp. Weight, 5¾ pounds.

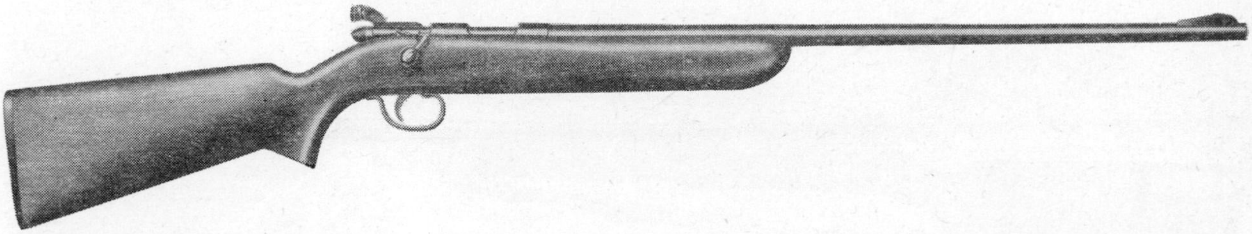

PLATE XXXVI. REMINGTON Model 510-A and 510-P. This is a bolt-action, single-shot rifle, available in .22 caliber only, adaptable for the short, long, or long rifle cartridge without adjustment. It has a 25-inch tapered barrel, crowned at the muzzle. The stock is of American walnut with semi-beavertail fore-end. It has double locking lugs and double extractors. The safety goes on automatically when cocking. Over-all length, 43 inches; taken down, 31 inches. Weight, about 5½ pounds. The 510-A is equipped with the step adjustable rear sight and white metal bead front sight. The 510-P is equipped with the Remington "Point-crometer" rear sight with Patridge-type blade front sight on matted ramp. This model is also available with smoothbore barrel for use with the .22-caliber shot cartridges, with a bead front sight and no rear sight.

PLATE XXXVII. REMINGTON Model 121 ("Fieldmaster"). This rifle is available in .22 caliber only, and the short, long, or long rifle cartridges may be used without adjustment. It is a slide action, with tubular magazine of the following capacity: 20 short, 15 long, or 14 long rifle cartridges. The stock and fore-end are of American walnut, with a half pistol grip and steel butt plate. It has a step adjustable rear sight and white metal bead front sight. The receiver is tapped for a tang peep sight. It has a 24-inch, round, tapered barrel. Over-all length, 41 inches; taken down, 27½ inches. Weight, 6 pounds. This model is available in the following grades: "Standard," "Special," "Remington Special," "Standard Smoothbore," "Peerless," "Expert," and "Premier."

PLATE XXXVIII. REMINGTON Model 550 ("Autoloading"). This autoloading rifle is available only in .22 caliber, and can use short, long, or long rifle cartridges without adjustment. It has a tubular magazine with the following capacity: 22 short, 17 long, or 15 long rifle cartridges. It has a 24-inch, round, tapered barrel. The standard model is equipped with a step adjustable rear sight and a white metal bead front sight. The stock is of American walnut, with a semi-beavertail fore-end. Over-all length, 43½ inches; taken down, 31½ inches. Weight, 6¼ pounds. Model 550-P is equipped with a "Point-crometer" rear sight with two interchangeable disks, and a Patridge-type blade front sight with a matted ramp.

PLATE XXXIX. REMINGTON Model 241 ("Speedmaster"). This autoloading rifle is available in .22 caliber only, and is chambered for either the short or long rifle cartridge. The tubular stock magazine has a capacity of 15 short or 10 long rifle cartridges (regular or high speed). It has a solid breech and a 24-inch tapered, round barrel. The stock is of American walnut with a semi-beavertail fore-end. It is equipped with a step adjustable rear sight and a white metal bead front sight. Over-all length, 41½ inches; taken down, 24 inches. Weight, 6 pounds. The model is available in the following grades: "Standard," "Special," "Peerless," "Expert," and "Premier."

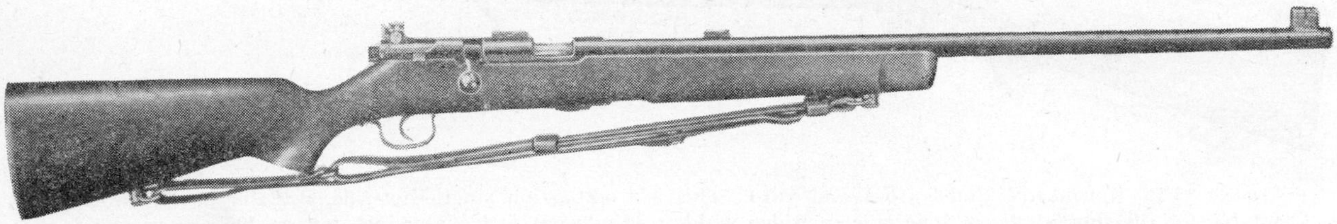

PLATE XL. STEVENS Model 416-2. This bolt-action rifle is available in .22 caliber only. It is the only heavy-barrel, well-stocked, accurate match rifle available in the low-price field. Barrel, 26 inches, heavy, tapered. Magazine, 5-round capacity. Speed lock. Adjustable trigger pull. Telescope sight blocks. Bolt handle designed to permit low mounting of telescope sight. Stock, American walnut, oil finish. Adjustable front sling swivel. Sling, 1¼-inch treated leather. Sights, new Stevens No. 25 hooded front sight with 5 removable inserts, and No. 106 peep sight. Weight, about 9½ pounds.

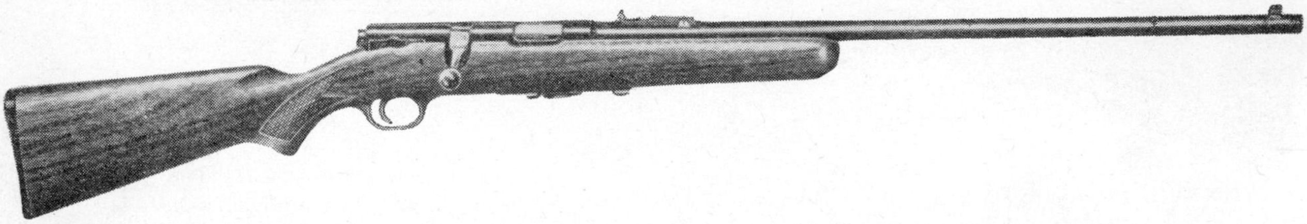

PLATE XLI. STEVENS Model 87. This bolt-action rifle is available in .22 caliber only. It has a 5-shot magazine and is chambered for the .22 long rifle cartridge, regular or high speed. Barrel length, 24 inches. Crowned muzzle. Stock, walnut, with full pistol grip. Hooded ramp front sight with 3 interchangeable inserts, step adjustment rear, and peep receiver sight, with 3-aperture sighting disk. Weight, about 6½ pounds.

PLATE XLII. STEVENS Model 053. This bolt-action, single-shot rifle is available in .22 caliber only. It is chambered for the .22 long rifle cartridge, regular or high speed. Barrel length, 24 inches. Crowned muzzle. Takedown. Stock, American walnut. Same sights as those on Model 87. Weight, about 5½ pounds.

PLATE XLIII. SAVAGE Model 99-EG. This rifle is available in the following calibers: .250/3000 and .300 Savage. It is a lever-action rifle made on a solid frame, embodying the hammerless Savage action with a positive safety, and has a rotary magazine with 5-round capacity. The stock is of American walnut and has a full pistol grip. Weight, 7¼ pounds.

PLATE XLIV. SAVAGE Model 23-D. This rifle is available in the following calibers: .22 Hornet and .32/20. It is a bolt action rifle, with a 25-inch barrel, and features the new Savage high-speed lock (about 2/1000 of one second). The stock is of selected American walnut and has a full pistol grip. The detachable magazine is of 5-round capacity. Weight, about 6½ pounds.

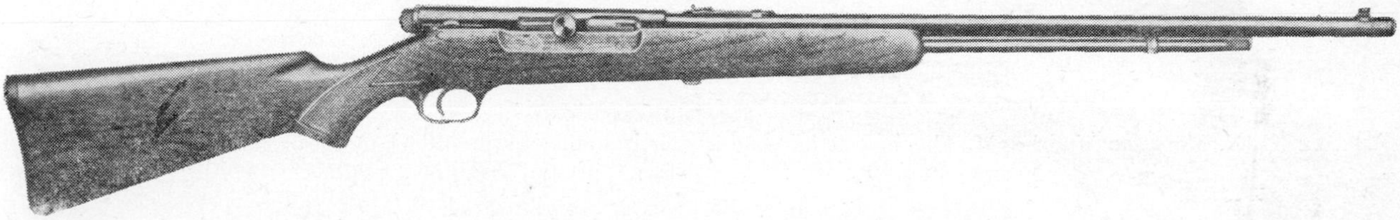

PLATE XLV. SAVAGE Model 6. This model is available only in .22 caliber, and is a takedown model, with 24-inch barrel. It is autoloading, chambered for the .22 long rifle cartridge, and has a tubular magazine of 15-round capacity. When employed as a manually operated (or single-shot) repeater, the .22-caliber long or .22-caliber short cartridges may be used. The stock is of selected walnut. When used as semi-automatic or autoloading, it is recoil operated. Weight, about 6 pounds.

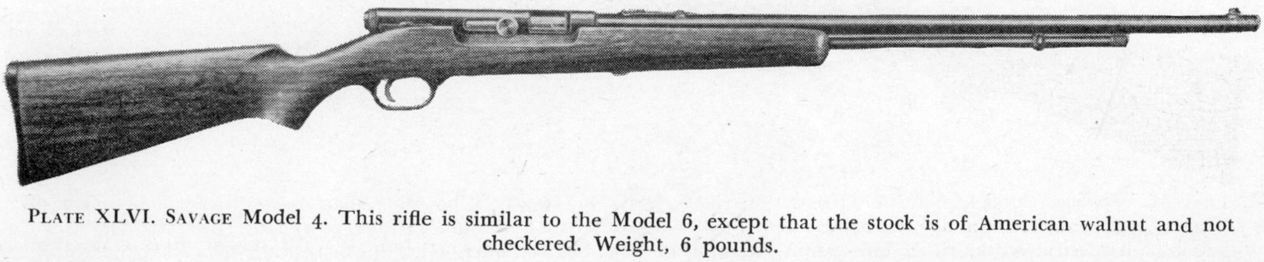

PLATE XLVI. SAVAGE Model 4. This rifle is similar to the Model 6, except that the stock is of American walnut and not checkered. Weight, 6 pounds.

PLATE XLVII. SAVAGE Model 3. This rifle is available only in .22 caliber and is a single-shot, bolt-action model. It has a 26-inch tapered barrel and is chambered for the .22-caliber short, long, and long rifle cartridge. The receiver is drilled and tapped for a telescope sight. Stock is of selected walnut. Weight, 5 pounds.

PLATE XLVIII. MOSSBERG Model 44US. This bolt-action rifle is available in .22 caliber only. It has a box-type magazine with a 7-cartridge capacity. Stock, oil-treated walnut, with detachable sling swivels. Mossberg No. S106 ramp front sight with four selective inserts, with the Mossberg No. S130 receiver peep sight with ½-minute micrometer click adjustments for windage and elevation. Receiver drilled and tapped for any Mossberg side-mount telescope sight. Barrel, extra heavy, 26 inches long, with crowned muzzle. Over-all length, 43 inches. Weight, 8½ pounds.

PLATE XLIX. MOSSBERG Model 42M. This bolt-action rifle is exactly similar to the Model 46M, except that it has a detachable box magazine with a 7-cartridge capacity. Weight, 6¾ pounds.

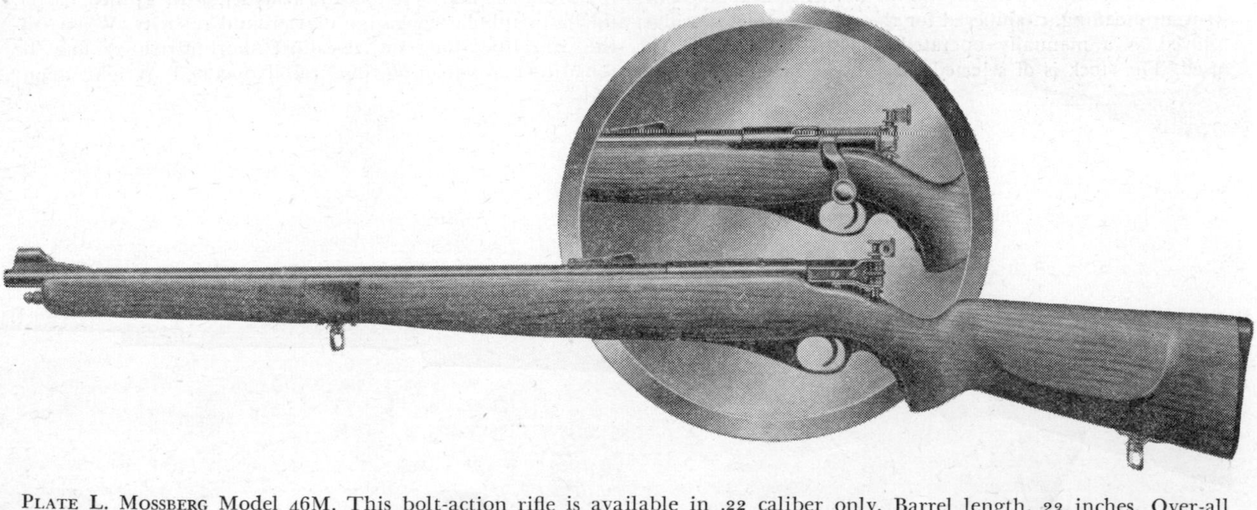

PLATE L. MOSSBERG Model 46M. This bolt-action rifle is available in .22 caliber only. Barrel length, 23 inches. Over-all length, 42 inches. The tubular magazine has the following capacities: 22 short, 18 long, or 15 long rifle cartridges (regular or high speed). Stock, oil-treated walnut, Mannlicher type. Sights, "micro-click" peep rear sight, hooded blade front sight. Receiver drilled and tapped to take any Mossberg side-mount telescope sight. Weight, 7 pounds.

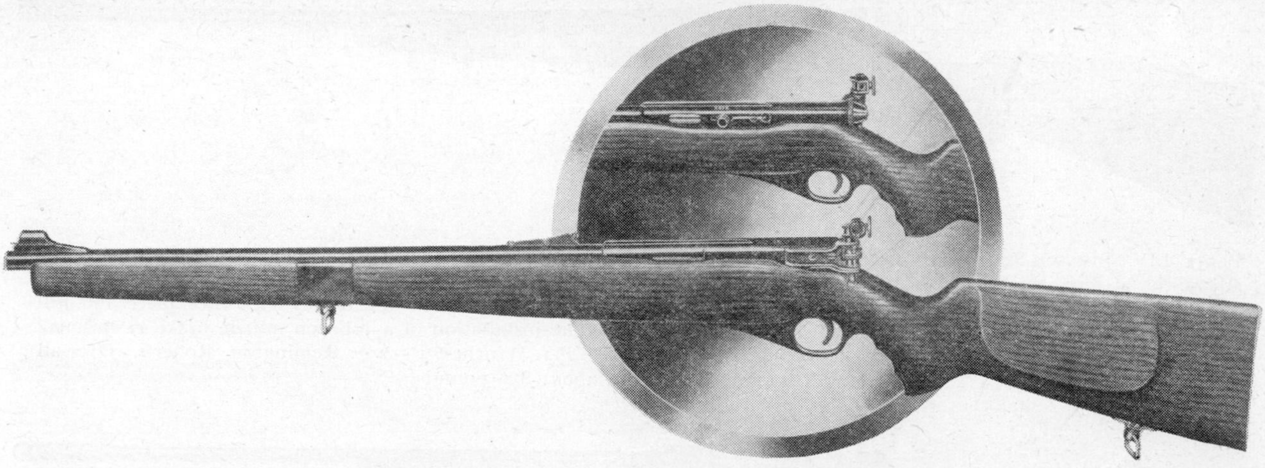

Plate LI. Mossberg Model 151M. This autoloading rifle is available in .22 caliber only, and will handle only the .22-caliber long rifle cartridge (regular or high speed). The tubular magazine, in the stock, holds 15 rounds. New type safety locks both trigger and sear and holds action open. American walnut Mannlicher-type stock with cheekpiece, and detachable sling swivels. Barrel length, 20 inches. Over-all length, 40 inches. Weight, 7 pounds.

Plate LII. Mossberg Model 46B. This rifle is available in .22 caliber, and will handle short, long, or long rifle cartridges (regular or high speed). The tapered barrel is 26 inches long. The stock is of walnut, oil treated. The tubular magazine has the following capacities: 30 short, 23 long, or 20 long rifle cartridges. The barrel is drilled and tapped for any of the Mossberg side-mount telescope sights. It is fitted with an S130 "micro-click" peep rear sight and a hooded blade front sight. Over-all length, 43¼ inches; taken down 31½ inches. Weight, 7 pounds.

Plate LIII. Springfield, Caliber .30, Model of 1903. This rifle, best known as the Springfield, was initially turned out at the Springfield Armory, although it has been manufactured at Rock Island Arsenal and by the Remington Arms Co. Considered one of the finest bolt-action rifles in the world, it was first developed during the Spanish-American War. Several models were made and tested before this one was developed.

This is a five-shot, bolt-action rifle, and has a staggered magazine into which the cartridges are stripped by the pressure of a thumb on the clip. It was originally issued in 1905, and the first models employed a 220-grain cartridge which developed a muzzle velocity of about 2000 foot-seconds. Later a 150-grain Spitzer-type bullet with a muzzle velocity of 2650 feet per second was used. This called for a cartridge with a shorter neck, and the majority of the rifles issued were called in and re-chambered. The new cartridge became known as the .30 1906. This was the rifle with which our troops were supplied during World War I, with the addition of the Model 1917 Enfield.

The receiver steel of the first rifle has been altered twice since the first rifles were issued; in each case the receiver was hardened. Rifles numbered from 1 to 800,000 have the softer steel receivers, those from 800,000 to 1,257,767 have better steel. All those with numbers higher than 1,257,767 have nickel steel receivers. The latter are safer for use with modern high-power loads.

This rifle was the standard service rifle of the Army until 1936, when the caliber .30 M1 (Garand) was adopted. This rifle is an excellent one, and is readily adapted to sporting use.

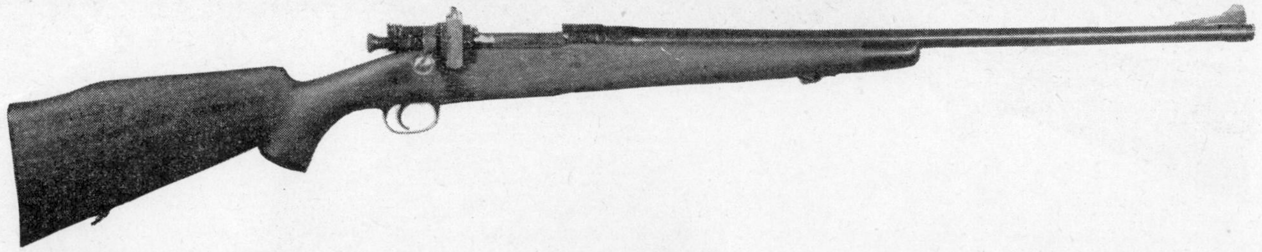

PLATE LIV. JOHNSON-SPRINGFIELD Conversion (Target Sporter). In this conversion the following is done: Inspect and adjust the action; install 24-inch Johnson custom barrel; install Lyman 48 micrometer peep rear and open ramp front sight with 1/16-inch ivory bead; fit an oil-finished walnut sporter stock of standard dimensions with cheekpiece and full pistol grip; attach sling swivels; polish and blue all metal parts. The installation of a Johnson muzzle brake is optional. This rifle will be fitted with any of the following barrels: .30 '06, .270 Winchester, .257 Remington Roberts. Over-all length, 44 inches. Weight, about 8½ pounds.

PLATE LV. JOHNSON-SPRINGFIELD Conversion (Featherweight Sporter). In this conversion the following is done: Inspect and adjust the action; install Johnson custom barrel of 22-inch length; install Lyman micrometer peep rear and open band front sight with 1/16-inch ivory bead; fit featherweight oil-finished walnut stock with full pistol grip; install Johnson muzzle brake; polish and blue all metal parts. Approximate weight, 7 pounds. Over-all length, 44 inches. This is available in the following calibers: .30 '06, .270 Winchester, .257 Remington Roberts.

PLATE LVI. ENFIELD Model 1917. This rifle, .30 caliber, commonly called the Enfield, was of British origin, and was manufactured in this country during World War I by several American arms companies, including Winchester, Remington Ilion, and Remington Eddystone. It was originally chambered for the British .303 rimmed cartridge, but upon the entry of the U. S. into the war the design was slightly altered and the bolt and chamber were altered to take the .30-caliber rimless cartridge (.30 '06). Approximately two million of these rifles were turned out by our arms companies during the war, and afterward they were held as reserve weapons. Civilians were able to obtain these rifles through the Director of Civilian Marksmanship and the National Rifle Assn., at a cost as low as $7.50. The Enfield action is an excellent one, and is extremely adaptable to sporter conversion.

The Johnson Automatic Manufacturing Co. has tooled up to handle such conversions, and they offer several types of very fine conversions; ultimate cost depends upon the extent of the work and the quality of the wood and additional equipment.

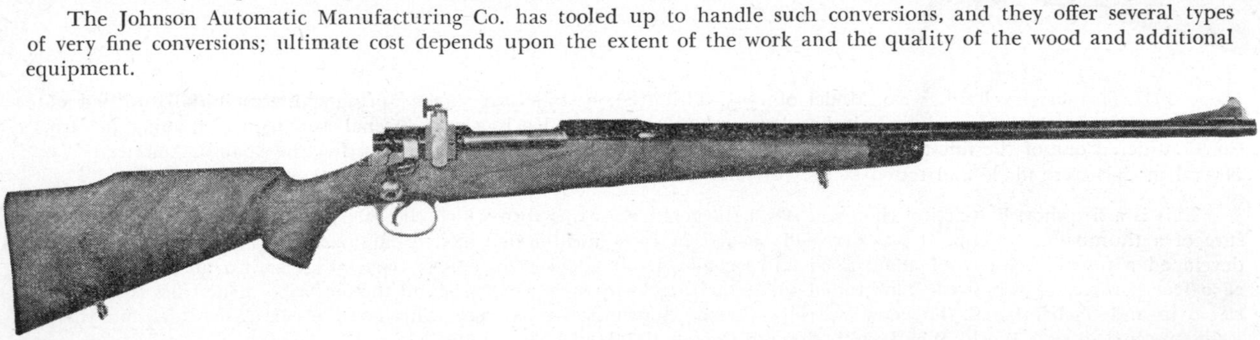

PLATE LVII. JOHNSON-ENFIELD Conversion No. 2. This is the "Target-Sporter" conversion. The old stock is discarded and the action is inspected and adjusted. The owner may have a choice of the following calibers: .30 '06, .270, or .257 Remington Roberts. The magazine is reduced to 5-round capacity, the trigger guard is straightened, rear sight ears are removed, and a Lyman 48 micrometer peep rear and open ramp front sight with 1/16-inch ivory bead is installed. The 24-inch barrel, of the caliber chosen, is installed. The stock is of selected walnut, oil finished, with a cheekpiece, full pistol grip, Monte Carlo comb and non-detachable sling swivels. All metal parts are blued and polished. Johnson muzzle brake optional. Weight, 8½ pounds.

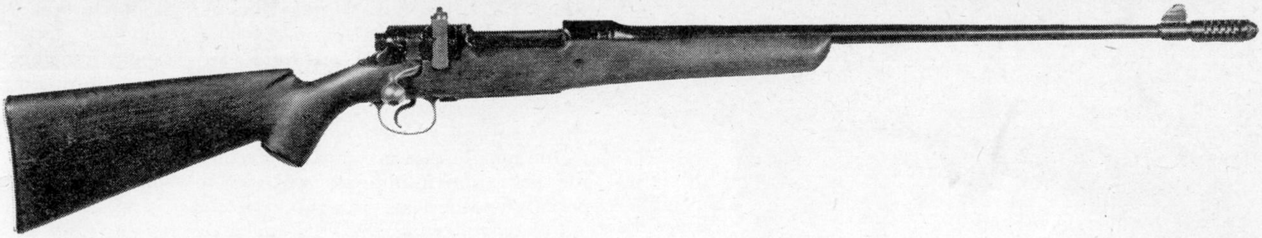

PLATE LVIII. JOHNSON-ENFIELD Conversion No. 3. This is the "Featherweight Sporter" conversion, available in .30 '06, .270, or .257 Remington Roberts. This conversion entails the following: Inspect and adjust action; reduce magazine to 5-round capacity; straighten trigger guard; remove rear sight ears and install Lyman 48 micrometer peep rear and open band front sight with 1/16-inch ivory bead; install Johnson featherweight barrel in 22-inch length; fit lightweight, walnut, oil-finished stock, with full pistol grip; install rubber recoil pad and Johnson muzzle brake; polish and blue all metal parts. Over-all length, 44 inches. Weight, 7 pounds.

PLATE LIX. MAUSER (German) Model 1898. This is a bolt-action, repeating sporting and military rifle, originated by Paul Mauser in 1888. This rifle employed the 7.92-mm. (7.92x57) (8 mm.), but had a Mannlicher-type magazine, loaded by a clip which formed part of the magazine.

The rifle was modified a few years later, and in 1898 the 8-mm. cartridge was settled upon. The original model had a much longer barrel, and while this long barrel was employed in the rifles used during World War I, the short barrel was used during World War II. Twenty other countries took up this rifle, with some variations in the caliber. Our own Springfield 1903 was patterned after the Mauser, which has one of the finest bolt actions in the world. It is very easily converted into a sporting arm.

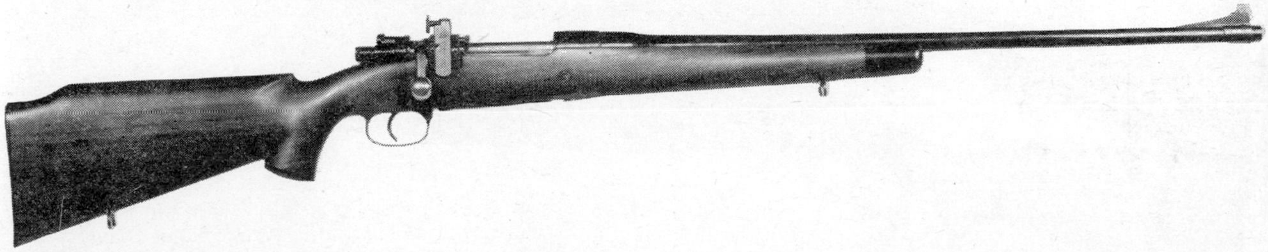

PLATE LX. JOHNSON-MAUSER Conversion (Target Sporter). In this conversion the following is done: Inspect and adjust the action, turning down the bolt handle; alter the magazine and extractor to handle the cartridge selected; install Johnson custom barrel 24 inches in length; install Lyman 48 micrometer peep rear and 1/16-inch ivory bead ramp front sight; install oil-finished walnut sporter stock of standard dimensions, with cheekpiece, full pistol grip, Monte Carlo comb, and non-detachable sling swivels; polish and blue all metal parts. Over-all length, 43½ inches. Approximate weight, 8½ pounds. Available in the following calibers: .30 '06, .270 Winchester, .257 Remington Roberts.

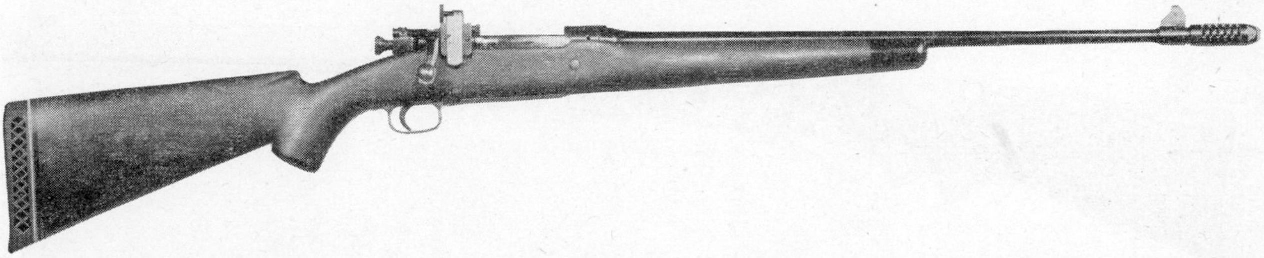

PLATE LXI. JOHNSON-MAUSER Conversion (Featherweight Sporter). In this conversion the following is done: Inspect and adjust action, turning down bolt handle; alter magazine and extractor to handle the cartridge selected; install Johnson custom featherweight barrel in 22-inch length; install Lyman 48 micrometer peep rear and open band front sight with 1/16-inch ivory bead; install and fit featherweight oil-finished walnut stock with full pistol grip; install Johnson muzzle brake; polish and blue all metal parts. Over-all length, 43½ inches. Approximate weight, 7 pounds. This rifle is available in the following calibers: .30 '06, .270 Winchester, .257 Remington Roberts.

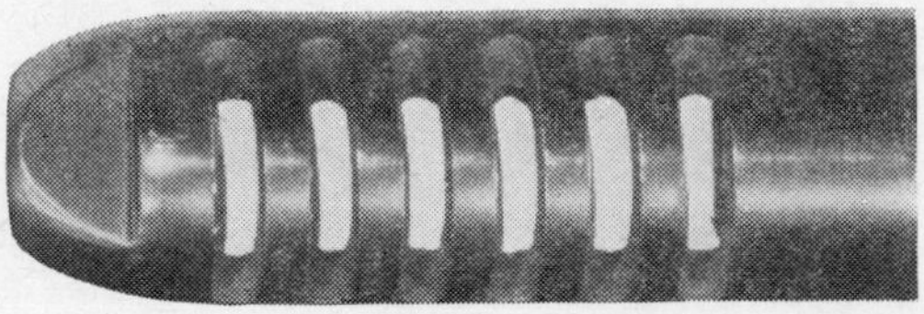

PLATE LXII. JOHNSON MUZZLE BRAKE. This muzzle brake is a development of recoil-reducing appliances used during World War II on European weapons ranging from automatic rifles to antiaircraft artillery. Its purpose and functions are threefold: It reduces the recoil between 40 and 50 per cent; it greatly reduces the jump of the muzzle that accompanies recoil; and by "dampening" vibration it improves accuracy to some degree, especially on the featherweight barrel.

In accomplishing this, the brake diverts the gases at the muzzle in a sidewise direction and there is an apparent increase and higher pitch in the noise of the shot. The brake is 2 7/16 inches long, ¾ inch in diameter, and weighs two ounces. It can be fitted to the muzzle of most rifles from .25 to .32 caliber; it should be left on the rifle at all times and does not prevent the proper cleaning of the weapon.

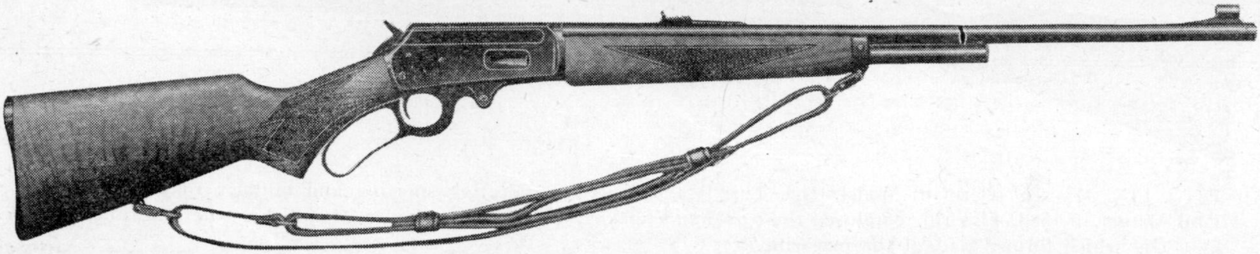

PLATE LXIII. MARLIN Model 36A DL. This lever-action rifle is available in .30/30 and .32 Special calibers. The tubular magazine has a 5-round capacity. Barrel length, 24 inches. Crowned muzzle. Equipped with "Huntsman" non-glare ramp front sight, detachable hood, and step adjustment rear sight. Stock and fore-end of American black walnut, full pistol grip, checkered. Receiver drilled and tapped for Lyman and other receiver sights and for tang peep sight. Low hammer spur permits the low mounting of telescope sight, equipped with detachable swivels for 1-inch sling. Over-all length, 42 inches. Weight, 6½ pounds.

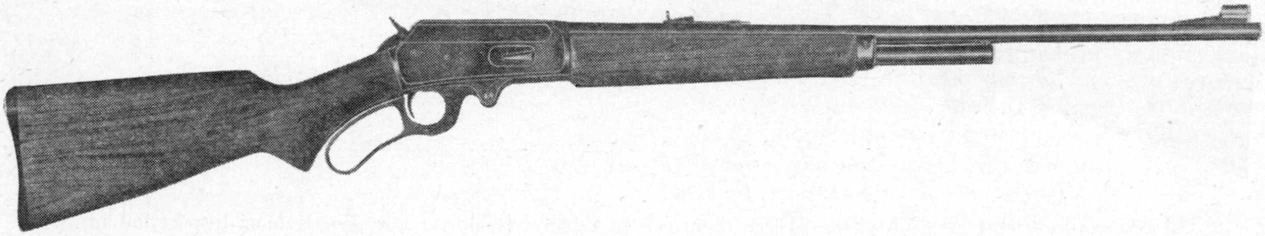

PLATE LXIV. MARLIN Model 36A. This rifle is similar to Model 36A DL except that it has no sling swivels or sling and is without checkering.

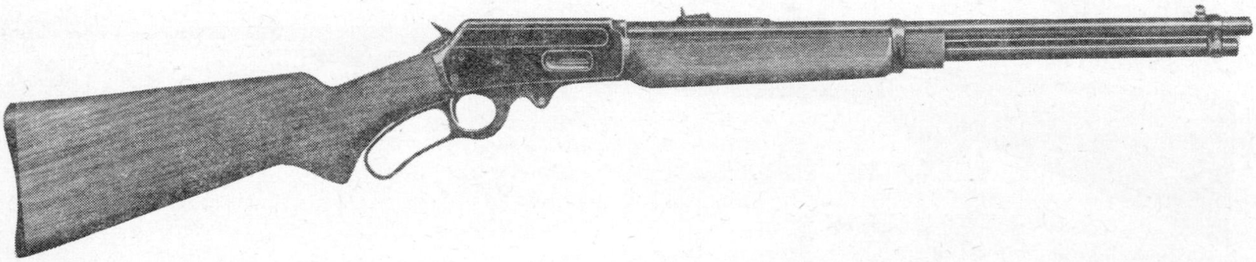

PLATE LXV. MARLIN Model 36 Carbine. This lever-action rifle is available in .30/30 and .32 Special calibers. It has a tubular magazine of 6-round capacity. Solid top receiver, crowned muzzle, 20-inch tapered barrel. American black walnut stock and fore-end. Flat top, step adjustment rear sight, bead front sight. Receiver drilled and tapped for Lyman No. 56 and other receiver sights and for tang peep sight. Low hammer spur for low mounting of telescope sight. Weight, 6½ pounds.

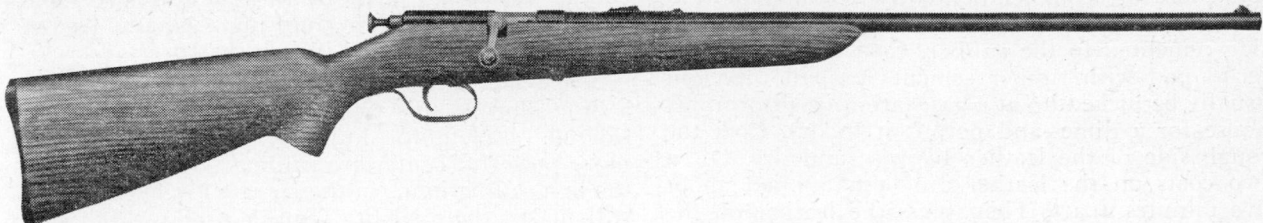

PLATE LXVI. MARLIN Model 100. This is a low-priced, single-shot, .22-caliber rifle, chambered for short, long, and long rifle cartridges, regular or high speed. The tapered barrel is 24 inches in length. Walnut finish with full pistol grip, Patridge-type front sight, step adjustment rear sight. Over-all length, 40½ inches. Weight, 4½ pounds.

# ACTION TYPES

Every sporting magazine maintains a Firearms and Ammunition Department. A special writer called a "firearms editor" runs this department and is always at the service of readers in answering mail inquiries requesting the solution of an individual problem. His biggest headache is the simple inquiry: "I'd like to buy a rifle for hunting, this fall. What type and caliber should I get?"

No one can give an intelligent answer to such an inquiry. The firearms editors want to help, but it is obvious that no suitable information is given to guide them. They should know: (1) what type of action you prefer; (2) what type of game you plan to hunt; (3) where; (4) the size of your pocketbook. The above information is basic; *you* may know what you want, but unless you tell them, you cannot expect them to give you proper answers.

First of all—action types. These will be discussed in detail later, but there are several basic designs—the single shot, the lever action, bolt action, slide or pump action, and finally the semi-automatic, often miscalled the "automatic." To the old-time lever fan, recommending a bolt action is like suggesting to an ardent Republican that he vote the straight Democratic ticket. The firearms editor has wasted his time and failed to make a friend.

The second item covers type of game you wish to hunt. You may be thinking of small-game rifles when you write; you may have in mind deer or bear. You may even have planned a real trip after moose, elk, or mountain sheep, or even grizzly. Obviously the same type and caliber of gun would be inadequate for all forms of game. Keep this in mind.

Item three—that simple "where" is important. Your address tells little. You may live in Florida and may want a rifle to hunt deer in Florida swamps—or you may have planned a trip to Wyoming for bigger game. The same gun would be improper—what would be satisfactory for Florida deer hunting might be worthless at the long ranges of western and mountain hunting.

Item four is another thing. You may desire to spend little on your gun, or you may be splurging after years of saving and planning. You may be planning a new car—possibly in the Ford price class. So you ask about new cars. Your reply covers the new model Rolls-Royce—at prices starting around $18,000. It may be interesting but not very practical assistance.

The choice of a gun type involves study on *your* part. Some states even bar the use of rifles in hunting deer and permit you to use only a shotgun. Possession of a rifle in the woods means confiscation, arrest, and a heavy fine. Study your state laws. Other states bar certain calibers in hunting deer and larger game. Still others bar the use of "automatics," either in rifle or shotgun, for all types of hunting.

**Design.** Many hunters object to recoil—yet demand the lightest gun they can find. With any given cartridge, the lighter the gun, the more actual "free recoil." If your rifle weighs 7 pounds, that is translated into 49,000 grains at 7000 grains to the pound. Assume the bullet to weigh 170 grains. The same amount of energy in a rearward direction is applied to the 49,000 grains of rifle as to the 170 grains of bullet. Some of it is absorbed by the inertia of the gun's mass, but this is not a discussion of ballistics—you will find that elsewhere. It just briefly explains "free recoil."

It is not "free recoil" that bothers a shooter, but the actual recoil he feels on his shoulder. You may recall in the old days of a quarter-century ago that rifles were fitted with a well-curved steel buttplate with very sharp toe and heel, called "rifle butt." Gradually this shifted to a "carbine butt"—somewhat similar but with rounded toe and heel. Then came the practical change—the "shotgun butt"—almost flat with only a slight curve, and much wider than the old style. Such a butt distributes the recoil over the shoulder and while you may have the same actual "free recoil," what you feel is much less. A well-fitting gun is less punishing to fire than a poor one, and many of the standard makes of rifles still on the market after as much as a half-century have been modernized by their makers with better-shaped and wider butt stocks.

Of course, should you still feel that recoil is too great, this can be reduced through the addition of a rubber recoil pad on the butt or through the use of a muzzle brake.

For hunting, recoil pads often are a nuisance. Rubber does not slip well, and many a shooter in tossing his gun to his shoulder for a quick shot has "flubbed" it, with the recoil pad grabbing a wad of loosely-fitting hunting jacket. No experienced hunter who has ever used a recoil pad in the woods can or will claim that he has never had this happen. If you must use a recoil pad, "doctor" it. A discarded ladies' purse or handbag will often yield a good piece of very soft, pliable calfskin leather. This can easily be attached to the shoulder area of the recoil pad and does not detract from its appearance. Cut this piece of scrap leather oversize and mount it with the smooth side against the shoulder—rough side cemented to the rubber. Coat the face of the recoil pad with rubber cement—a small tube can usually be picked up at a gas station or auto supply house for a dime—and permit it to dry. Coat the rough side of the leather likewise and dry. Often two coats on the leather are best, applied about five minutes apart. Then press the leather on the butt with the hand. Surplus is quickly trimmed with a discarded razor blade, making a neat job. One such job made 15 years ago is still in service—the leather has never torn loose.

The alternative to the recoil pad is the muzzle brake, widely used on artillery and certain foreign military rifles. The only type available in the United States is the Johnson, made by Johnson Automatics, Inc., of Providence, R. I. It can be fitted at the custom gun department of that firm to any modern rifle and is reasonably inexpensive.

The muzzle brake is a short metal cylinder a couple of inches long having scientifically designed slots to permit the escape of the powder gas when it blasts out of the muzzle. (See p. 512.) It adds little weight and to some people does not look unattractive. In principle, the escaping blast of gas expands into this cylinder as the bullet passes through an opening at its muzzle. The gas, moving forward and sidewise in expansion, strikes the walls and bursts forth through the angled slots, dragging the muzzle of the rifle forward and thus counteracting much of the recoil. It actually reduces recoil 40 per cent, but on some rifles it *seems* to reduce it still further.

Drawbacks to the use of a muzzle brake are not many—some may object to the looks of that ¾-inch diameter slotted attachment. The added 2 ounces' weight does not disturb balance—and it can quickly be removed when desired.

The muzzle brake must not be confused with a silencer. Silencers are illegal on all firearms under Federal law, and have been off the market for many years. A muzzle brake does not act as a silencer—in fact, it works just the opposite. It seems to increase the blast and sound of the report when the gun is fired, but this does not disturb the shooter. Anyone standing too close to the muzzle would probably have unkind remarks to make. But it *does* reduce recoil better than any other known means. Recoil while hunting rarely bothers a shooter. When he tries the same rifle at inanimate targets, the deliberate shooting causes him to notice recoil which would be overlooked in the excitement of the hunt.

Many a 200-pound husky has declared that his little "thutty-thutty" kicks him painfully. It is not easy to gush words of sympathy when one recalls seeing 100-pound women shooting all day on a target-range firing line with the Springfield Model 1903. The brutal answer is that either (1) the 200-pounder is a "sissy," or (2) he has not learned to hold his rifle properly. The chances are strong that the latter is the case. This can be overcome with proper practice with an experienced instructor to help him correct his gun-handling errors. Try this if recoil bothers you.

Another thing in selecting a hunting rifle is to consider its fit to you with proper clothing. Many a shooter picks his rifle while dressed in business clothes. It handles just the way he requires it. Then he bundles up in bulky hunting togs and has an "entirely different gun." Think that over.

**Single-Shot Rifle.** Little space need be given to a discussion of this type since it is generally considered obsolete for hunting, particularly in the more powerful center-fire calibers. It is still one of the best selling items in the .22 rim-fire field. Savage still makes their Utility Gun—a single-barrel shotgun with an interchangeable .30/30 barrel. Naturally this is a low-priced number, but it has proved popular since its introduction in 1938.

Generally speaking, the single-shot rifle belongs to the target shooter. It should be borne in mind that in the early days of America, *all* hunting rifles were single shots—and muzzle-loaders, at that! There is one advantage to such an arm. It teaches a hunter to shoot properly, because he gets one chance only. Today, with rapid repeating-action types, many a tyro enters the woods determined to spray the quarry with bullets—and he rarely hits. Only the shots that hit, count. The single-shot rifle teaches careful aim and proper trigger control.

It is surprising to find how many ancient single-shot rifles are still doing duty in the woods. Many of these are 75 years old, and still getting meat. But it is the man behind the gun who really scores.

**Lever-Action Repeaters.** Among the first of the successful repeating rifles was the Spencer of pre-Civil War days. Patented in 1860 by C. M. Spencer of South Manchester, Conn., this rifle saw service in the Civil War as an unofficial military rifle—the Army's first repeater. It was made in several calibers, all large and stubby rim-fire cartridges. It held seven cartridges in a magazine tube in the butt, loaded through the butt plate.

New ideas were presented in such short-lived rifles as the Jennings, Volcanic, and Henry. Then Winchester was born. Oliver Winchester, a former lieutenant governor of Connecticut, became interested in these early experimental repeaters about 1855. The most interesting was the invention of B. Tyler Henry—a lever-action repeater for a .44 Henry rim-fire cartridge.

The major features of Henry's development were a tubular magazine below the barrel to hold cartridges, and a carrier, operated by a finger-lever-trigger-guard which lifted a fresh cartridge into position when the lever was pulled downward to open the breech. On closing the lever, the cartridge was scooped into the chamber of the barrel; the carrier dropped out of the way; and the breech bolt moved in to closed position.

Henry had been associated with both the Jennings and the Volcanic. Winchester took over, and Henry rifles began a busy but short life. The first of Henry's developments to bear the Winchester name was the Model 1866, and the Henry was promptly discontinued. This Model 1866 was chambered for the original .44 Henry rim-fire cartridge. (To perpetuate his memory, you will find the Winchester general offices on Henry Street in New Haven, and on every Winchester commercial rim-fire cartridge made you will find the trademark "H".)

John M. Browning designed most of the actions of the lever-action rifle models produced by Winchester from 1886 on. They operate on the basic principle of the Henry, with refinements. Models produced in the current century are merely refinements of the earlier type, which has been proved in worth with more than two million made for the hunter. (See Model 94, p. 497.)

A somewhat different design of lever action repeater is the famous Savage Model 1899 (see p. 507), still a popular number in its current refined version. Designed by Arthur W. Savage as a military rifle, it was so produced as early as 1895 for state militia units. The sporting model was first manufactured in 1899, hence the name.

The Savage differed greatly from the Winchester in design and cartridge feed. This has always been a hammerless rifle with a solid breech, closed in around the shooter's face in the days when a burst cartridge was not infrequent. Actually, "hammerless" is a misnomer—it was a concealed-hammer type, with all operation of the hammer taking place inside the receiver. Position of the hammer was determined by a "horn" or small indicator projecting through the top rear of the breech. A touch of the thumb would show position of the hammer—up indicated cocked; if it was flush with the receiver, the gun was uncocked.

The second major difference was in the magazine. The Savage type was rotary—a spool unit with notched compartments held the cartridges. Operation of the finger lever operated the bolt—no carrier was necessary to lift the bullet. To load, you forced the cartridges through the port in the right side of the receiver—the finger lever down, and the bolt to the rear. The spring-loaded spool magazine would feed a live round at each operation of the finger lever. Savage claimed that such a magazine "did not cause the gun to change balance as it became empty." This is undoubtedly an indictment against tubular magazines, but is actually of little importance.

A third popular number was the Marlin lever-action repeater which made its appearance in 1881. After several models with refinements, it took its place as a member of the popular lever-action family. The basic design is much like the Winchester as far as magazine and cartridge feeding are concerned; the major difference is in the receiver. In the Marlin, the semi-solid breech is used, with a closed top and left side. (See p. 512.) The bolt slides to the rear in an opening in the right side.

Numerous other rifles of the lever-action type appeared and disappeared. The Winchester, Marlin, and Savage are still on the market. Advantages of each are as follows:

*Winchester and Marlin.* Exposed hammer. May be carried at half-cock for safety and easily cocked with the thumb. This is not possible with the Savage. Tubular magazine may be refilled with the weapon loaded and the gun ready for action. On the Savage, it is necessary to open the breech.

*Marlin and Savage.* Closed breech top means side ejection of fired shell cases. This permits the mounting of a modern hunting telescope sight if desired. On the Winchester, ejection is straight up through the open top, and a telescope must be mounted offset and in an awkward position or it will be struck by the fired and ejected case—usually causing the case to drop back into the action and jam the gun.

*Savage.* Strongest action in the lever field. Completely enclosed to protect mechanism from rain, snow, and dirt in the field.

In choosing a lever-action rifle, all three should be studied carefully since there are many minor features to each. There is nothing "new-fangled" in the lever tribe—all features have been time-tested. These rifles are compact, light for the power they pack, and make excellent saddle guns. They are not generally built for the more powerful military and sporting cartridges, and because of this, are losing popularity with the present generation of shooters.

**Bolt-Action Rifles.** For nearly three-quarters of a century the bolt-action rifle has ranked high in favor as a military weapon. Its major advantage over rifles of the lever type is greater strength, fewer working parts, and a one-piece wood stock. Many claim that it is not so rapid in operation as the lever type, and thus not well adapted to hunting. Those individuals should witness some well-trained riflemen on a target range during a rapid-fire match—or a skilled bolt-action hunter in the field.

Give two equally trained riflemen weapons with which they are familiar, and the lever man will probably fire five shots faster than the bolt man where it is only a test of speed. However, speed without hits is worthless. At the instant of discharge comes recoil. The sights completely leave the target and the shooter takes a sudden jolt. It takes a second or two to recover and realign the sights on the target. The well-trained bolt rifleman uses this recoil time to operate the action, the same as the lever man, and his *practical* speed will be the same. It is not necessary to remove the rifle from the shoulder or get out of shooting position to operate the bolt; only a beginner will do that.

It was not until Stewart Edward White, noted international big-game hunter and explorer, had a custom-built sporting rifle made for him in 1910 that hunters really began to notice the bolt action. Shortly thereafter, Theodore Roosevelt had one made for his African expedition. Germany began to develop sporting-model Mausers and shipped a few to the American market.

At the time of our entrance into World War I, the lever action was still *the* hunter's type. But many thousands of hunters, war trained, returned to the fields in 1918 and began the job of converting captured German military rifles into sporters. (See pp. 559 ff.) The new generation wanted the bolt action.

In 1921 Remington brought out their now-famous Model 30. They had been producing the Model 1917 Enfield (see p. 510) for the Army, and surplus parts and machinery were easily converted to sporting type. Meanwhile, in 1920, Savage had brought out their Model 20. Finally in 1925, Winchester released their Model 54. (See p. 496.) The high-power bolt action was here to stay.

Curiously enough, the three above-mentioned guns have been off the market for years. Out of the Savage Model 20 grew their Models 40 and 45. Out of the Winchester 54 came their Model 70. Remington developed the Model 30 into the 30S and finally into their current Model 720.

Some of the advantages of the bolt action have been mentioned above. Others include rugged simplicity. The hunter caught in a wet snow or rain can clean his gun completely, disassembling most action parts without tools. The greater strength of design and materials, heavier and fewer parts, and many other features, permit the use of more powerful ammunition. The camming action of the opening stroke of the bolt gives powerful primary extraction to pry stuck cases from the chamber. The sturdy design and one-piece stock makes the average bolt-action sporter much more accurate at the longer ranges than the lever gun. Most types permit the use of telescope hunting sights when desired.

The bolt-action hunting rifle is here to stay, and sales figures show that while some models of lever guns are selling well, they are not showing a sales gain while the bolt type has shown steady growth throughout the years.

**Slide-Action Rifle.** For some reason, slide-action rifles, sometimes called "pump-action" or "trombone action"—have never been too popular with the American hunter. A few were introduced but fell by the wayside. Only one ever enjoyed much of a sale, although pump-action .22 rim-fires have long been popular.

In this type of action, operation of the repeating mechanism is a function of the forearm. A quick movement of the left arm backward and forward and the gun is reloaded.

In 1912 Remington introduced the Model 14 (see p. 502), which when sold today in modern dress is called the Model 141 Gamemaster. With the rifle came a new series of rimless cartridges—actually rimless counterparts of the Winchester .25/35 which they called the .25 Remington; the .30 Remington—a version of the .30/30; the .32 Remington, a version of the .32 Winchester Special; and later, a more powerful cartridge known as the .35 Remington.

This Remington slide-action rifle uses a tubular "half" magazine below the barrel and within the forearm. This pressed-steel tube has a peculiar spiral formed into it. Few owners have ever figured it out. This design was planned to tip the cartridges slightly to keep the nose of the bullet from direct contact with the primer of the live cartridge in front of it. With today's ammunition this is of little importance—super-sensitive primers in those early days sometimes fired a cartridge in the magazine tube during recoil. The destruction was great, and often the shooter was seriously injured. Today it serves only to protect the noses of soft-point and other expanding bullet types.

The action is of the "hammerless" type with a completely enclosed solid top and breech receiver. It thus permits use of a well-mounted hunting telescope. It balances well and is today's only slide-action high-power rifle.

**Autoloading or Semi-Automatic Action.** There is no fully automatic rifle, shotgun, or pistol on the American market. Such a gun would actually be a machine gun, the possession and use of which is barred by Federal, not state law. The "automatic" rifles, pistols, and shotguns are actually, as Winchester calls them, "self-loading" and as Remington prefers, "autoloading." The difference between the automatic and the autoloader is that in the "automatic" the gun continues to repeat as long as the trigger is held back until the magazine is empty. In the latter, or sporting type, the trigger must be *released* to operate a "disconnector," whereupon it may be again pulled to operate the firing mechanism. The full automatic action is strictly military and will not be discussed here.

There are three types of operation of autoloading actions. The simple type of straight blowback does not have a securely locked breech. Such guns are chiefly in the .22 rim-fire class. To balance the tiny .22 cartridge, a heavy mass of metal in the breechblock is necessary—in a high-power type it would, of necessity, weigh several pounds. The only practical center-fire rifles of this type are today classed as "medium power." In 1905 Winchester introduced their Model 1905 Self-Loading for the .32 and .35 Self-Loading cartridges—scarcely more powerful than heavy revolver loads. They solved the required mass of breechblock in a unique manner. A sliding weight in the forearm was connected to the breech block as a sort of "drag anchor." Since a tubular magazine could not be used, Winchester developed the box magazine type within the receiver.

Since these cartridges were in the same power class as the Model 1873 rifles, the .32/20, and the .38/40, they never achieved great popularity. On the market for 15 years, only 29,113 were ever built.

In 1907 Winchester improved slightly on the gun and thus was born their .351 Self-Loading—a cartridge fitting no other gun. This was made even more powerful in 1910 with the development of the .401 Self-Loading.

Today all that is left of the Winchester Self-Loaders is the .351 (see p. 498), called the Model 07 Police Rifle. It is unique in design, but the cartridge is not considered adequate for most American big game. But the rifle itself is neat and well balanced. After loading the magazine the weapon is cocked and a cartridge is fed into the chamber by pressing rearward on a button-tipped plunger protruding from the forearm. This pushes the forearm weight and attached breech bolt to the rear. Let go of the plunger and the action closes, feeding a live round to the barrel. After that initial operation the gun functions as an autoloader, the plunger being used only to open the bolt to remove a cartridge from the chamber when not needed.

Two other types of semi-automatic mechanisms are in general use—the gas-operated and the recoil-operated locked breech. One or two gas-operated types have appeared on the market for a short time, but they fell by the wayside. Only the Army's Garand or M1 rifle, the little .30 Carbine, and the full or semi-automatic Browning, all military types, remain.

It remained for John M. Browning, again, to design a practical sporter in the autoloading family. Remington put this on the market in 1906 as their Model 8. Although this rifle, and its current version, the Remington Model 81 Woodsmaster (see p. 502), has survived in the test of time, it is probably the ugliest sporting weapon ever designed. One user habitually called it his "piano leg" but swore by it because despite its clumsiness, it had always produced meat for him.

Originally this was produced for the .25, .30, and .32 Remington rimless cartridges. Later the .35 Remington was added. In 1946, Remington announced that it would be produced for a still more modern and powerful cartridge, the popular .300

Savage. Today it is available only in .30 and .35 Remington and the .300 Savage calibers.

This action is extremely sturdy but complicated. A rotating bolt locks into an extension of the barrel. What appears at first glance to be the barrel is actually a tube surrounding the barrel and containing a recoil spring. Upon discharge, the barrel slides through bushings in its jacket, compressing this heavy spring as it moves to the rear with the barrel extension and bolt locked to it. At the rear of the stroke, with most of the recoil expended, the bolt rotates slightly, unlocking from the barrel extension.

At this point the released barrel flies forward, impelled by the compressed spring within the jacket, the bolt continuing slightly to the rear against a buffer or shock-absorber spring. As this returns the bolt to closed and locked position, the forward-moving bolt picks a new cartridge from the box magazine and feeds it into the chamber. Clumsy or not, many people love this gun, and if your state permits self-loading rifles, and you must have one—you have no other choice.

The former soldier of World War II became accustomed to self-loading rifles with his Garand and his carbine. He wants them. He wants the government to release some carbines for hunting. The military powers object—but even if they decided to release carbines, few realize that Federal laws would have to be changed. Barrels less than 18 inches long are illegal—and the carbine barrel is 17¾ inches. Furthermore, that cartridge does not have sufficient power for deer—as hundreds of GI's found in Europe when they tried it on even the 50-pound German roe deer. State legislators object to self-loading guns in the woods, and almost every year a new state joins in the ban. The ban is on hunting. You can use an autoloading shotgun for skeet and traps in many states—but not in the field during hunting season.

Selecting your hunting rifle involves many things—choice of action types, and choice of cartridge. First comes the action type you desire; you must then be content with one of the calibers in which the manufacturers make it. The more modern cartridges are used in the bolt-action rifles—today's biggest sellers.

# CALIBER CONFUSION

The men who like guns always ask questions. Those who write about them in the magazines receive thousands of letters indicating confusion in the field. It has always been thus.

Among these questions are such simple ones as: "Is the .38 Special revolver cartridge a .38 caliber?" *(No.)*

"I just had an argument with Bill. I insist that the .218 Bee, the .219 Zipper, and the .220 Swift are all .22 caliber. Am I right?" *(Yes.)*

"Does the name of a cartridge indicate the true caliber of the bullet?" *(No.)*

"Where do cartridges get their names?" (A complicated question to answer.)

"What is bore diameter?" "What is caliber?" "Why is the period or decimal point in front of the caliber figures?" "Why do foreign countries use different caliber designations from ours?" "Why don't ammunition makers call cartridges by their true calibers?"

Let us look at this confusion in an analytical way.

Perhaps the last question comes first. Cartridges have frequently been misnamed as to caliber due to a long-standing habit—so old that it is perhaps too late to now correct it. It dates back more than 100 years. It invoves bore diameter; bullet diameter; caliber with decimal point; calibers long. Yet the the rules are simple.

*Actual* caliber under the American and British system is in decimal fractions of an inch. In most other European and South American countries, it is expressed under the metric system in millimeters and decimal fractions. Thus a true .30 caliber has a bore diameter of .3000 inch. In the United States we write it as .30. In England they call it .300. It amounts to the same.

Among sportsmen, the term *bore diameter* is greatly misunderstood. It has nothing to do with *bullet* diameter.

In a rifle barrel, the solid bar of metal is first drilled lengthwise, and then carefully reamed. In modern manufacture it is possible to hold the final diameter almost to .0001 inch. In the case of the Springfield Model 1903 service rifle for the Model 1906 cartridge, this reamed diameter is held to about .3000 inch. *This is bore diameter.*

Since the bore is smooth, it is necessary to cut rifling into it. The grooves are usually individually cut in a spiral to spin the bullet, holding them to a depth of only .004 inch. Since four opposite grooves are cut, this makes the groove diameter .3080 inch, while the land or bore diameter remains at .3000. The Government bullet to fit this barrel tightly is slightly oversize, with the standard running .3085 inch. This tight fit prevents escape of the powder gas past the bullet during its passage through the barrel.

It will thus be seen that in this case a true .30 caliber uses a bullet having a diameter of .0085 inch greater than the land or bore diameter. The handloader knows this, and regardless of the name of his cartridge, measures the groove diameter of his barrel by pushing a soft lead bullet through it with a cleaning rod, and then measuring the land marks on his "slug." These lands on the bullet naturally represent the groove diameter of the barrel, since they are reproduced in reverse. He can thus choose any bullet which fits his barrel properly.

In the American system of cartridge designation, there are many contradictions and different names for the same cartridge. For instance, our service military cartridge, available commercially with both military-type target bullets and the expanding type used for hunting, goes under many names. Originally developed as the Model 1903 cartridge for the Model 1903 rifle, it had the same round-nose 220-grain bullet used in its predecessor, the Krag rifle. In 1906 the 150-grain pointed bullet was adopted. The neck of the old cartridge was too long for the shorter bullet, so it was cut off about 1/10 inch. Thus was born the Model 1906 cartridge.

This cartridge was officially called "U. S. Cartridge, Caliber .30, Model of 1906, for U. S. Rifle, Caliber .30, Model of 1903." The Army always liked long and complicated names. Commercially it became known as ".30 Gov. 1906," but various ammunition makers have called it ".30/06," ".30-06," and ".30 U.S.G."—regardless of the bullet used.

Shortly after World War I, the Army wanted a heavy boattail bullet for use in both rifles and

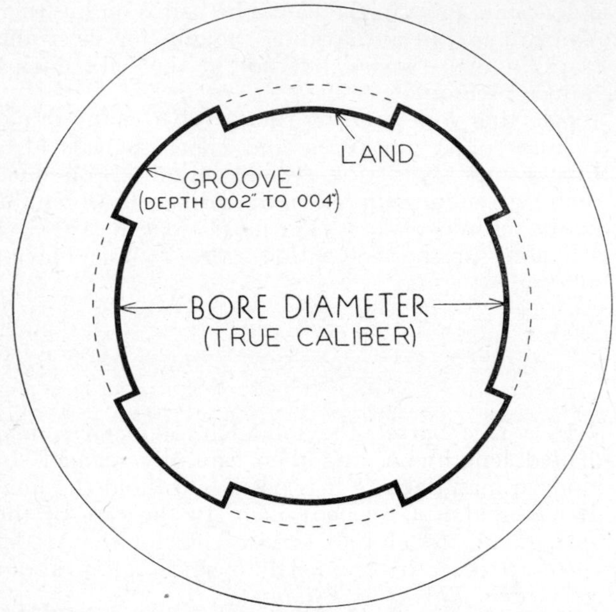


PLATE I. Caliber Measurement.

machine guns—the Germans had developed and used such a bullet during the war with great effectiveness. Thus was born a 173-grain pointed bullet with a 9° boattail. When Remington made them, they called it "taper heel." The Government abandoned the Model 1906 designation and called the cartridge the "Caliber .30 M1" meaning "Modification One."

By the mid-1930's, arms progress had indicated that for most military work the heavy .50-caliber machine gun would be far superior to the .30. Thus long-range use of the .30 machine gun was abandoned, and it was decided to use a lighter bullet and load, giving less recoil to the rifleman. The original Model 1906 bullet used a jacket of heavy cupro-nickel—an alloy of 85% copper and 15% nickel—about the same as the material used in the standard five-cent piece. This fouled barrels, and by the time the M1 bullet was developed, the Army adopted gliding metal for jackets—90% copper and 10% zinc.

The "new" cartridge was a reversion to the old Model 1906 bullet but with gilding jacket. Thus the old 150-grain bullet came back, but the Army never backtracks. The new name was "Caliber .30 M2." It is still called by the same old names by commercial ammunition makers.

The above example is chosen to illustrate a true .30-caliber rifle *and* its cartridge.

Now let us look at England and their quaint mix-ups. The English generally express caliber with three figures—hence their current service cartridge, the .303 Mark VII. They also maintain a system of *six* figures which can be quite confusing.

In 1853, England used a muzzle-loader, the .577 Snider. This was about .58 caliber, or better, since most of those early black-powder muzzle-loading rifles were oversize. In 1886, the action was modified to use a metallic cartridge, also called the .577 Snider. The rifle was officially called the Model 1853-66.

Since the military trend was toward smaller-bore weapons to save lead and cartridge weight, as well as to increase velocity, range, and accuracy, England adopted the new Martini-Henry rifle in 1871. The caliber designation was ".577/450." What was this, a .45 or a .58 caliber? It was a .45, but they had taken the large-diameter, straight-sidewall brass case and bottlenecked it to .45. It should have been called the .450/577, but . . . .

This same multiple designation was applied to various big-bore sporting cartridges, as they were necked down to smaller caliber. The first set of figures refers to the *original* cartridge—the last set is the new caliber.

On the Continent, the most practical system was used, but here, again, there is confusion. Most Europeans use the metric system; thus in Germany a new cartridge cropped up, the 8-mm. Mauser. Translated to the inch system, 8 millimeters is .31496 inch. Again the caliber was a misnomer. Bullet diameter (remember that it is greater than *bore* diameter) was .3177 inch. This was a 236-grain round-nose bullet, first used in the German Military Mannlicher-type action, and later in the Mauser.

In the early part of the century, Germany adopted a 154-grain pointed bullet—and changed caliber designation. The new cartridge became the 7.92 mm. This would indicate a *smaller* bore diameter—but actually diameter of both bore and bullet was increased. The new bullet diameter ran .3228 to .325 inch. The sporting version of the same cartridge continued to be known as the 8 mm., even when designed for the current barrels.

Herr Wilhelm Kalb, manager and custodian of the big Dynamit, A.G., plant in Nürnberg (formerly the Rheinische Westfälische Sprengstoff Aktiengesellschaft, largest prewar maker of sporting ammunition on the European continent) explained the mixup in 1947. Bullets for sporting ammunition, he wrote, are made in two diameters:

(1) Cartridges for the old German normal barrel, used both in sporting and military service have a diameter of 7.80 to 8.07 mm. land and groove diameter, translating into .3071 to .3177 inch. Such cartridges are called the 8×57 Normal, and are usually head-marked 8×57 Norm.

(2) Cartridges for the current barrels have larger bullets and are usually headstamped 8×57J, the *J* representing *infanterie* or infantry cartridge. Such bullets, Herr Kalb explained, were for barrels having minimum gauges of 7.89 to 8.20 mm. (.3107-.3228).

Generally the German system of designation is informative and better than the American and British type. Thus the 7×64-mm. cartridge uses a 7-mm. bullet with a cartridge case 64-mm. in length. In addition, many European cartridges are made in both rim and rimless types. Rimmed types are made for single-shot rifles, or these combination rifle-and-shotgun forms. Thus the 8×57 is the rimless cartridge, while the same cartridge with a rim is called and headstamped "8×57R."

A practice common with both German and English-speaking countries is to use names with cartridges. In England they have the .300 H. & H. Magnum (Holland & Holland)—also made in this country. We have the .257 Roberts, named after the cartridge designer, Major N. H. Roberts. In Germany they have the 11.2×72 Schüler, the .500 Schüler, the 7-mm. Vom Hofe Super Express, and the 8×64 Brenneke. Again, these are named for their designers. Note the interesting use of the .500 Schüler—the inch system instead of the metric.

In all countries, certain names are standard. Some American cartridges are standard throughout the world. In the United States, one of the most common of the old-timers is the .44/40 Winchester. Winchester calls this the .44 Winchester Center Fire, marking cases .44 W.C.F. in standard velocity, and .44 W.H.V. in the high-velocity loading. Remington calls the cartridge the .44/40 Winchester.

England makes the same cartridge and calls it the same as Remington. Germany calls it the .44 C.F. Model 1873 *and* the .44 Winchester. Special American cartridges have two German names—one for home consumption and the other for export. Thus the .22 Savage Hi-Power is exported under that name and sold to Germans as the 5.6×52R.

It was previously stated that American bore diameters are frequently different from the caliber name. Why?

No one knows the answer to this. In the old days of muzzle-loading percussion revolvers, the .36 Navy Colt was actually .38 to .39 caliber. Misnomers occurred regularly after that.

Take the current American line of cartridges:

In the rifle class, we have numerous .22 center-fire cartridges, all different, and ranging from small to large. Only one is called a .22 in the commercial line. A half-century ago we had the .22 Winchester Center Fire or .22 W.C.F. This became obsolete, and was revived after many years in a modern cartridge using a jacketed bullet and smokeless powder instead of the old lead bullet-black powder combination. This became the .22 Hornet.

In addition we have the .218 Bee, a .25/20 Winchester necked down to .22 caliber; the .218 Zipper, a .25/35 Winchester necked down to .22; and the .220 Swift, a still more powerful and especially designed cartridge. Add to that, an entire series of special .22 Wildcats (cartridges made by handloaders by re-forming various commercial cases, and not commercially made as such) running through Varminters, Lovells, R2's, Arrows, and many others named by and for their designers.

In the current commercial sporting cartridges we have no assortment of names. The .22 Savage Hi-Power was the first of the small-caliber, high-velocity cartridges, designed in the late 1890's by the late Charles Newton. He sold the cartridge to Savage, who brought it out with their own name for their Model 1899 rifle in 1912. Another Newton development was the .250/3000 Savage. In this case a light 87-grain .25-caliber bullet was driven at the then-unheard-of- velocity of 3000 feet per second. When this was released in 1913, Savage adopted a new designation—the British three-figures for caliber, and the last group of figures for *velocity*. Today the cartridge is known under its original name and also as the .250 Savage.

In 1920, Savage designed a cartridge in .30 caliber to compete with the popular .30/06. Since the design of their short action would not permit the full .30/06 length, they shortened the case and changed its shape, giving it the new name of .300 Savage.

Such cartridges as the .25/20, .32/20, .38/40, and so forth, were originally black-powder cartridges. The first group of figures represents the *caliber*, the second indicates the weight of the powder charge *in black powder*. When they were modernized to smokeless powder, the name continued although the figures no longer represent the powder weight.

Then, along the same lines, came the .32/40. Originally designed by Ballard for the famous single-shot target rifles, it was made into a sporting cartridge, variously known as the plain .32/40 and the .32/40 Winchester, Marlin, and Ballard. Ballard's name followed those of the repeating-rifle makers.

Three or four other black-powder cartridges in various sizes and shapes came out. There was the .25/20 Single Shot, the .25/20 Repeater, the .25/21 Stevens, the .25/25 Stevens, the .25/35 Winchester, and the .25/36 Marlin. These are all different sizes and shapes and none will interchange. The first four were black-powder and lead-bullet types; of these, only the .25/20 remains in repeater version with smokeless-powder and metal-jacketed bullets. The latter two were *never* black-powder cartridges, so their names are incorrect.

Winchester developed the .25/35 which they called the .25/35 Winchester. Remington brought out a rimless cartridge for their slide or pump action and for their autoloading rifle. They called the rimless version the .25 Remington. Both cartridges are still made, but in higher velocity loadings than originally. Winchester calls their products the .25/35 Super Speed; Western, the .25/35 Super-X; and Remington and Peters the .25/35 Express and .25/35 High Velocity.

Major N. H. Roberts designed a cartridge known as the .25 Roberts before 1906. With modifications, many of these guns appeared as custom-built rifles, the cases being made by re-forming brass cases for the .30/06 and 7-mm. Mauser. When Remington introduced it as a standard number for their Model 30 rifle, they altered the shape of the bottleneck slightly and called it the .257 Roberts.

Another interesting cartridge—probably the most popular American deer cartridge ever made—is the famous .30/30. Winchester introduced this in 1894 with a metal-jacketed bullet and smokeless powder. It was never a black-powder cartridge. Why the last "30" has never been officially answered; some years ago Phil Sharpe made an interesting test—he found that the case would *hold* 30 grains of black powder of Fg rifle size. The Army cartridge, then in use, was the .30 Krag, often called the .30/40 although this was never loaded with black powder. The "40" in this case was comparative—it was the Government's first smokeless-powder rifle cartridge, and would hold 40 grains of black powder.

To settle arguments, we should state that the .30/30 was never used by the Army, although military versions of rifles handling it were sold to foreign countries as auxiliary weapons, even as late as World War II. However, Remington once made a quantity of their old single-shot rolling-block military rifles for this, selling them to the New York State Militia in the first decade of the century. There is no other record of military use in this country.

Let us look at a few of the misnomers of true caliber. Remember the definition of true caliber—*bore diameter.*

The .22 Savage Hi-Power is .221.
The .303 Savage is .300.
The .22 Hornet and Bee are .217.
The .219 Zipper and .220 Swift are .219.
The .32/20 Winchester is .3045.
The .32 Winchester Special is .315.
The .351 Winchester Self-Loading is .345.
The .401 Winchester Self-Loading is .400.
The .38/40 Winchester is .395.
The .44/40 Winchester is .4225.
The .32 rim-fire Marlin is .302.
The .32/40 Winchester and Marlin is .313.
The .38/55 is .370.
The .32 Remington Rimless is .312.

In the rim-fire line, the actual bore diameter depends on make and model of rifle. Marlin .22-caliber barrels run .216 in some models and .217 in others. But then, they use five and six grooves to make more "space" for the bullet. Savage barrels run .217 with four grooves; Stevens runs .2175 with six grooves; Remington runs .217 with five and six grooves; Winchester uses .219 with four and six grooves. All of these diameters are for the .22 long rifle rim-fire cartridge.

Pistols and revolvers often have great deviation from true caliber. Bore diameter of most .22 rim-fire revolvers and pistols runs about .214.

The .25 Colt auto pistol cartridge is made and used throughout the world. In Europe and South America it is known as the 6.35-mm. Browning. Bore diameter is usually .243.

Two foreign automatic cartridges, made in this country for 40 years, are the .30 Mauser and .30 Luger, both bottleneck cartridges of different size and power for pistols of the same names. The European (and American) designation of the Mauser is 7.63-mm. Mauser; of the Luger, the 7.65-mm. Luger. Both have a bore diameter of .300, despite the different metric designation.

In the revolver famly in .32 caliber we have a general mix-up. There is the .32 S. & W., the .32 S. & W. Long, the .32 Colt New Police, and the .32 Colt Police Positive. The .32 S. & W. is a short cartridge; all others have the same cartridge case and bullet weight—the Colt numbers having a flat-nose bullet as the only difference.

Then we have the .32 Colt Automatic—called the .32 A.C. and .32 CAPH (Colt Automatic Pistol Hammerless). This, too, like the .25 automatic, is a Browning development, and throughout the world is called the 7.65-mm. Browning. Again we have a misnomer in the American caliber designation—bore diameter is .304. The European metric designation is correct.

Two identical cartridges are the .38 S. & W. and the .38 Colt New Police or Police Positive. Again the only difference is in a flat nose section on the Colt-type bullet. Bore diameter is .359, again indicating a misnomer.

The most popular cartridge for police and target shooters in the center-fire family is the .38 Special. Originally there were two names—the .38 S. & W. Special and the .38 Colt Special. Again the only difference is in the Colt flat-nose bullet, and cartridge manufacturers have discontinued the Colt. Before that, they discontinued the two types of head marks, merely stamping the cartridge ".38 Special." Such guns will handle the old .38 Short and Long Colt cartridges and the .38 Army, now all obsolete, but they will not chamber the .38 Smith & Wesson or the .38 Colt Police Positive since the shorter cartridges are larger in diameter. Bore diameter on the Colt barrel is .356 and on the Smith & Wesson .358.

Due to its popularity, many variations of this cartridge are found—including the .38/44 and the .38 Special Super Police. In the latter, a very heavy 200-grain bullet is used. In the former, standard bullets are loaded to higher-than-normal velocity. The name of .38/44 came from its introduction by Smith & Wesson—the heavy-frame .44 revolver was chambered to handle this more powerful cartridge. Most guns are safe with this, but it is inadvisable to use it in light-frame revolvers.

The .38/40 rifle cartridge is used in some Colt revolvers chambered for it, but here the bore diameter is .392. It is very dangerous to use the high-velocity cartridge in any revolver; the powder was designed to produce rifle pressures and has blown up thousands of revolvers.

The .38 Colt automatic is another misnomer—bore diameter is .348. The same applies to the .380 automatic, another Browning design known in other parts of the world as the 9-mm. Browning Short to distinguish it from the special European 9-mm. Browning Long and the 9-mm. Luger or Parabellum.

The .44 Smith & Wesson Special has a bore diameter of .423—again a misnomer, whereas the .45 Automatic is true caliber.

Finally, bear in mind that most rifles are designed to handle but one type of cartridge. Substitution should not be made. Foreign rifles are difficult to feed; for most of them the ammunition has never been made in America. There are a few exceptions—the 8-mm. French Lebel is standard here with sporting bullets; the 8-mm. Mauser as made here is intended for the 7.92 German and other makes of military and sporting rifles if chambered for the $7.92 \times 57$ or $8 \times 57$; the 7.62-mm. Russian is intended for Russian arms and for rifles made in this country for Russia; and the .303 British (differing from the .303 Savage) is also an American standard.

Most other foreign rifle calibers are not made here, and the owner of such an arm must never try a cartridge in it to see if it will fit. For instance, many a Springfield rifle—one of the world's strongest—has been blown up through the use of the somewhat shorter 7.92 Mauser cartridge. The short case does not fill the chamber and bursts on firing. That .325-inch bullet just refuses to squeeze through a .308-inch barrel.

In many cases, odd foreign calibers can be fed

by having custom-made ammunition with the case formed from some other cartridge. At other times, barrels may be rechambered for American cartridges only by a competent gunsmith. Rechambering means removing metal. Only a good gunsmith can tell you if it is practical and safe in your gun.

Remember the American standard practice—every rifle or revolver barrel is marked with the correct name of the cartridge for which it is chambered. Ask for it only by that name. Do not let anyone tell you that some different cartridge "can be used." That is the way accidents happen.

# CARE OF FIREARMS

Among the most common questions are those which concern the care of firearms before and after use and in storage. Is gun care complicated? Offhand, the answer is an emphatic "No!" but a visit to the repair department of any firearms manufacturer, and a study of the weapons coming in, clearly reveals that more than 95 per cent of all firearms are destroyed through abuse and neglect—*not wear!*

A visitor once was admiring one of the custom sporting rifles in Phil Sharpe's fine collection. "Beautiful," he sighed, "but you'd never dare to take such a fine gun into the woods."

The gun in question was then more than ten years old—today it is 17 years old. Yet it looks new and perfect despite the facts that: (1) It has been shot about 2500 times. (2) It has killed much game. (3) It has made 12 week-long trips into the Big Woods of five states. (4) It has been rained on and snowed on. (5) It has been exposed to summer's heat and subzero winter cold. The answer is that it has been given proper care.

Suppose you have a new gun and want to keep it that way. First, remove the stock if there is excessive grease. If not, remove all grease from barrel and action, using clean cotton rags—canton flannel preferred. Use gasoline sparingly to remove grease—or cigarette lighter fluid. The later is best—it costs more and you will not be so careless with it.

How about oiling it? More trouble is caused by over-oiling than by under-oiling. For cleaning and oiling, the most useful gadget is a pack of ordinary pipe cleaners. These twisted-wire fuzz-covered swabs help to get dirt out of inaccessible corners. Snip off the dirty end with a pair of scissors occasionally, giving you a new surface to work with. A pipe cleaner, with a faint drop of oil on it, will lubricate hard-to-reach moving parts. Use as little as possible.

What kind of oil to use? There are numerous special gun oils on the market, but few are any better than a standard motor oil of SAE 10-W body, costing 35 cents per quart. Never use combination oils and powder solvents for lubrication.

With .22 rim-fire guns, gas and powder smoke frequently come back through the action. This mixes with excess oil to form a black and abrasive paste. Dust and dirt also gum up oil and make the mechanism hard to operate.

Cold weather, during the hunting season, requires that a gun be free from oil. Commander Richard E. Byrd, noted Arctic and Antarctic explorer, who has carried firearms into 50-below temperatures, once explained: "We always clean all guns with benzine and see that there are no traces of oil in the mechanism. They may not work as smoothly, but they never freeze solid. A small amount of oil would freeze an action so thoroughly that it could not be made to function."

It was interesting to watch certain tests that were conducted by one of the Winchester technicians. A gun, normally oiled, was refrigerated for two hours at 40° below zero. When the trigger was pulled, nothing happened for two or three seconds; then the hammer slowly arced forward, failing to put the slightest mark on the primer of a cartridge in the chamber.

In the woods on a hunting trip, if temperatures are below freezing, do not bring your rifle into a warm cabin at night. Leave it in the woodshed. A cold piece of metal, brought into a warm room, will sweat. Moisture collects in all parts of the action and the barrel. If it does not rust immediately, it can freeze the gun mechanism the next day.

How about cleaning? Do modern non-corrosive primers prevent rust? They do not *prevent* rust—they just do not leave salts in the barrel which *cause* rust. There is an exception to this rule: If you do not clean often, stick with the same brand of ammunition. The fouling of all brands of non-corrosive ammunition is harmless in itself, but if the different mixtures of two brands are left in the barrel, the residue can cause a rusting action through chemical reaction.

There are numerous "powder solvents" on the market. Most of these are unnecessary, but they speed up the cleaning process. And you should always clean and protect your guns before placing them in storage, even for only a week or two.

The best cleaning equipment is a solid steel rod—not the jointed type. A button tip and proper-fitting cotton flannel patches, a cleaning solution or just plain water, and a rust inhibitor are necessary. Clean from the breech if you can; this protects the rifling at the critical point—the muzzle. First use a dry patch, snugly fitting over your button tip so that it can be pushed through the bore with little effort. Place the muzzle on the floor and scrub the patch full length several times. Pull it out and discard it.

If you wish to use solvent, then put a few drops on a clean patch and repeat, following this with a dry patch. If you use the water-cleaning process, use a small funnel to pour boiling water through the barrel, permitting it to escape through the muzzle into the bathtub. Immediately wipe with a dry patch, and the water-heated barrel will finish drying itself inside.

Normally, with water or solvent, it takes little effort to clean a smooth barrel. You are then ready for protection.

An oil of ordinary character will not protect against rust. Two proven rust inhibitors have been on the market for years—RIG, or Rust Inhibiting Grease, and SHEATH, the latter a light oil base. Both are available through better sporting goods stores.

A 35-cent tube of Rig will last the one- or two-gun shooter for years—and will protect bright tools, fishing tackle, etc.

With a clean and dry barrel, put a small quantity of your Rig or Sheath on a clean patch, scrub it well into the bore, and then use the soaked patch to wipe lightly all exposed metal parts. On .22 rifles, particularly wipe the breech block or bolt around the firing-pin hole. This thin coating will really protect—if the gun is first cleaned.

There are many other anti-rust compounds on the market, and new ones are appearing. Make your own tests in a simple way. Use clean discarded but unrusted safety-razor blades. Boil a moment to free them of oil and grease, then wipe dry. Use a grease or wax pencil to mark a code number on each.

To use these for tests, take one clean blade and stick a corner in a block of wood. Lightly wipe others with a clean patch coated with the oils or greases you are testing. Stick these in the block. Set this aside where moisture and all changes of atmosphere can get at them, keeping notes of the numbers on your blades and the material used to coat them. Observe them daily and note rust forming or protection given.

If you want a more complete test, mix a wide-mouth jar of saturated brine from table salt. Suspend coated and uncoated blades in this by strings. Watch them daily. Pick the material that gives you best protection. It is cheap insurance.

Should you use brass, steel, and bristle brushes?

They can do no harm—even steel brushes are soft and will not injure rifling. Their main use is in the removal of lead or copper jacket fouling, and they should be used with a good solvent.

Looking sidewise into the muzzle of a high-power rifle, you may see a faint trace of copper coloring in the bore. It is not necessary to remove this unless it becomes patchy. Usually powder solvents remove most of it, but the jacket of the next bullet passing through will replate the bore.

What makes the blue wear from guns where you handle them? Perspiration on the hands of some people is very acid. Many a gun owner has found fingerprints clearly etched on the finish after friends have handled his pets. A rust inhibitor will completely prevent this. A small patch of sheepskin with Rig rubbed into the wool is a handy thing to have around to wipe all guns after handling. In fact, one firm markets a patch made in this fashion—and has sold countless thousands in the past ten years. This sheepskin pad is cleaner to keep around if you make yourself a cellophane or pliofilm envelope to hold it and to keep it free from dirt. When it becomes too dirty, wash it with mild soap, dry slowly, and recoat with Rig. Do not use too much.

The stocks or woodwork on firearms of yesteryear had an easy-scratching varnish finish. Today most stocks are oiled, although a few lacquer finishes are found. It will do no harm to spill a few drops of oil on them. Scratches of minor nature can be eliminated by applying a drop of oil and rubbing briskly with the palm of the hand.

Never store your guns in wet places. And do not keep them in leather or canvas cases. These draw moisture from the air and can cause bad rusting. Rifles and shotguns can be stored in closets if gun cabinets are not available. If you hang a gun on the wall, see that it is wiped and cleaned regularly.

Proper care insures long life to your guns. A match .22 rifle is good for from 30,000 to 50,000 shots. The lead in front of the chamber is then slightly eroded and many a shooter salvages a good barrel by having an inch cut from the breech with new fitting and chambering.

High-power match rifles usually require a match barrel after 3000 to 5000 shots, although such barrels are still more accurate than the average hunting barrel.

The average rifle, shotgun, pistol, or revolver, if properly cared for, will outlast its owner. It is all up to you.

## CUSTOM-BUILT RIFLES

Among the phrases we hear these days is a sadly overworked one—"custom built." The generally recognized definition of a "custom-built" rifle is one that is made to order. The degree of special work on the customer's order cannot be defined. It may be a minor job, or a major one.

These preliminary words, we hope, are not being wasted. The arms enthusiast who purchases an advertised custom-built weapon will do well to understand the many meanings of the term, so that he may ask the proper questions before making the purchase. You will see for example, an advertisement listing a "custom-built Mauser Sporter." To be absolutely correct, this would mean a hand- or machine-manufactured rifle with a Mauser-type action, also built to order, with hand-tailored barrel, stock, and accessories. The seller may take a different view. The action may be a cheap-production military Mauser with its original barrel, polished and refinished and with a sporter stock made by discarding parts of the old military one, polishing, rounding corners a bit, and smoothing up in general the original military stock. The military sights may have been discarded and sporting types fitted in their stead.

Such alteration work falls in the "custom" class, but the finished weapon would never fall in the truly custom classification.

Suppose you are having a custom-built rifle manufactured. Let us analyze the work to be done, that a true understanding of what is meant by custom work may be had.

Suppose, for example, a choice Polish Mauser military rifle is the foundation. Its barrel, stock, and all accessories are removed and scrapped. This leaves only the action—the receiver, bolt, and trigger and magazine mechanism. This was forwarded to a custom gunmaker such as Roy E. Weatherby of South Gate, California. With it go the necessary instructions for alterations because, since it is custom work, the gunmaker would prefer to have the customer express his desires rather than leave that up to the maker.

Fifteen points of work are ordered:

PLATE I. A custom-built rifle intended for the heaviest of game on the North American continent—a .300 Weatherby Magnum on a Mauser action. Note the Weatherby-made stock of exotic California mesquite wood.

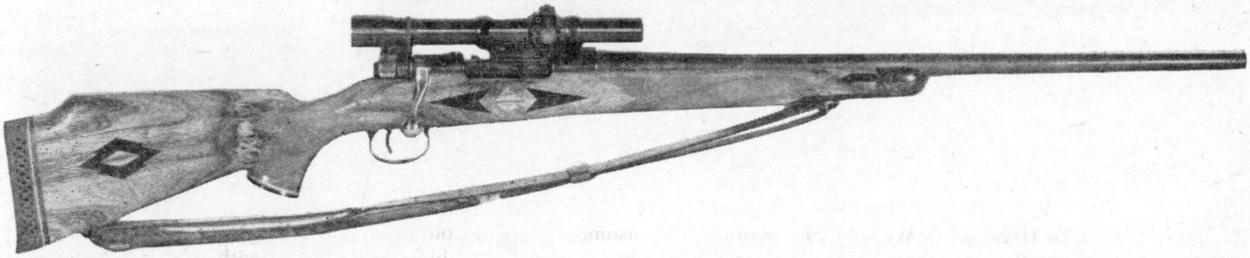

PLATE II. Another custom-built super varmint rifle for the Weatherby .220 Rocket—a modification of the .220 Swift. This is built on an altered Model 1917 Enfield action and is Weatherby-stocked from curly Oregon maple.

(1) Grind lip from front of receiver ring.

(2) Polish, but do not remove arsenal marks on receiver.

(3) Hand checker back of spur on bolt release gate for easy operation. Checking to be fine and unobstructive, yet sharp for firm gripping.

(4) Bend down bolt handle, angled to center over trigger.

(5) Polish and engine-turn (fancy finish like inside of a good watchcase) bolt body and extractor.

(6) Polish bolt handle. Do not blue bolt body or handle.

(7) Round all sharp edges and humps of receiver to streamline action and add beauty. No sharp corners or angles to remain, yet no excess metal to be removed.

(8) Round edges of bolt-release lock or gate.

(9) Round all sharp edges on sleeve.

(10) Streamline trigger guard, removing surplus metal, finish to width of 0.4 inch and polish.

(11) Groove trigger. Check about 1/8-inch tip, using cross or square checking.

(12) Alter magazine follower to permit bolt to function with empty magazine.

(13) Alter bolt face to take .270 Weatherby Magnum cartridge.

(14) Alter magazine to take same cartridge.

(15) Polish magazine floorplate. Smooth up lock parts to permit of easy removal.

Note the concise list. The customer did not ask to have the action reblued—that is naturally assumed. The list of known wants makes it possible for the gunmaker to turn out a job which must satisfy the customer—if he is a good workman and can follow directions.

Next comes a custom-built barrel to be fitted to this action. In this case, the barrel was to be made by the gunmaker and nothing but a work data sheet was furnished. Again, the specifications were listed:

Barrel: .270 Weatherby Magnum caliber. Fit to Polish Mauser action dated 1929, Serial Number 3804K.

(1) Material, Timken Roller Bearing Co. Graph-Mo steel. Finished length 28 inches, bolt face to muzzle.

(2) Diameter in front of receiver first 2 inches, straight cylinder 1.30 (same diameter as receiver ring). Where barrel joins receiver, turn twin hairline cannelures 1/16th inch apart to conceal joint.

(3) Straight taper from 2 inches in front of receiver ring to muzzle, diameter 1.125 inches at muzzle.

(4) Engrave on right side of barrel near receiver in three lines: ".270 Weatherby Magnum . . . Made for *(customer's name)* . . ." and on third line, date barrel completed.

(5) No sights to be fitted.

(6) Do not freebore throat. Sample bullet submitted to fit barrel throat by contact when loaded to over-all length of magazine. Do not counterbore muzzle.

(7) Crown muzzle slightly over lands and round edge sufficiently to remove sharp surfaces. Muzzle to be retained flat.

(8) Polish muzzle of barrel to mirror bright—muzzle face not to be blued.

(9) Telescope sight blocks furnished herewith to be mounted on barrel, rear mount just in front of receiver ring, with distance between centers 7.2 inches.

That takes care of the metal parts. Next to come was the stock. For this the customer also had ideas. He bought a special heavy and thick Oregon myrtlewood blank with grain and measurements to meet his ideas. If you know your stock blanks, this is an excellent way to get the wood and figure which appeals. On one occasion, seeking a certain figure for a different special rifle stock, this same man obtained, on approval, nine different blanks from various sources, picking the best grain and figure. Eight blanks returned cost approximately $1.50 each for two-way postage alone—but he found what he wanted.

Here, again, a suitable data sheet should be prepared for the benefit of the stock maker—whether he supplies the blank or you do. Make sketches if you can, illustrating shape of cheekpiece, shape of comb, heel, grip, etc. Give exact measurements on everything. Indicate the location and type of decoration, such as inlays, carving, checking, etc. If you cannot do this yourself, you had better ask the stock maker to submit designs before he starts. He does not like to guess at your ideas.

When you receive the product of such an order, you have a true custom rifle.

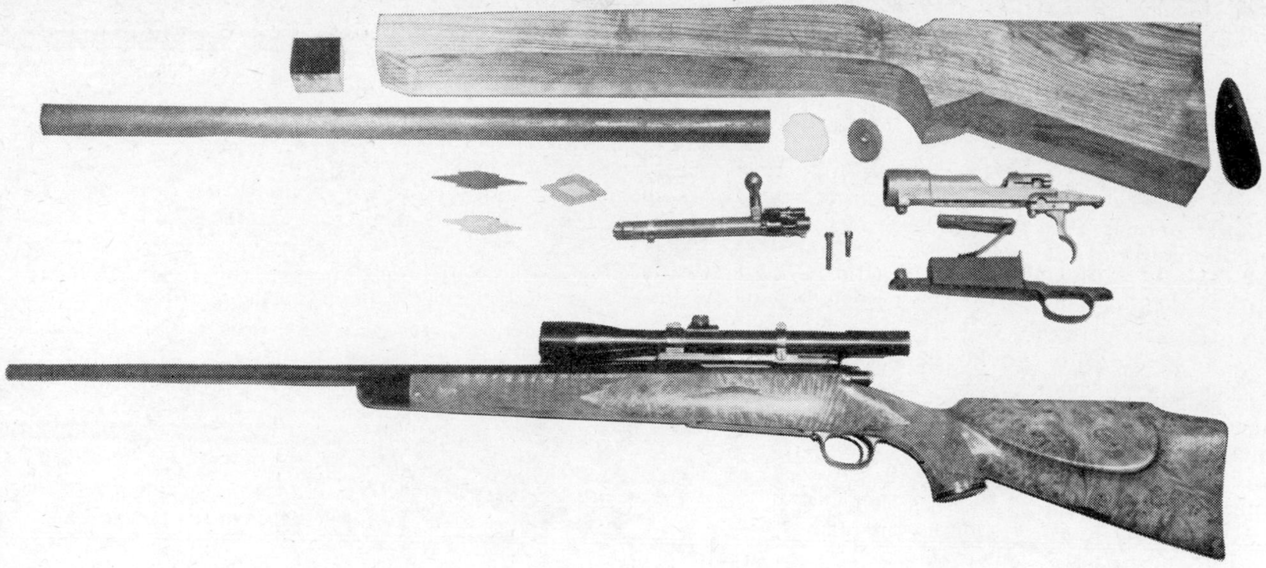

PLATE III. Roy Weatherby planning a custom rifle lays out the components of the new rifle above a completed job of approximately the same general stock design. The rough blank is shown with black plastic block to be used as the fore-arm tip plus the heavy barrel blank for the Weatherby .270 Magnum cartridge. Plastic inlays are shown—the white patch is a plastic layer to go under the pistol grip cap. This rifle is being made on a military Polish Mauser action.

One of the biggest rackets in this country is the "custom" game. Many small shops turn out rifles on a small production line in several "grades" and at fixed prices. While they like to call these "custom built," they are really stock models, costing more than regular factory-made rifles chiefly because of small production. A made-to-order gun will, of necessity, cost you more—but you will have an individual rifle, built your way, and meeting your ideas.

Colonel Townsend Whelen, an authoritative writer for over a half-century, states:

> "I have just made a careful count and so far as I can determine, there are today in the United States approximately 198 small rifle-making firms, rifle makers, barrel makers, stockers, reloading tool makers, custom handloaders, and other specialists, firms and individuals advertising to build rifles to order and to prepare special ammunition for those rifles."

It is doubtful if all of these firms and individuals are properly qualified to do custom work. The Winchester, Remington, Savage, and Marlin plants make rifles—*good rifles.* But these firms produce rifles as a business. They produce in quantity at a small individual profit.

The custom rifle maker does not compete with these firms. To a true rifle maker or barrel maker or stock maker, his work is an art—a creative task with every job an individual one. His work is a headache in many ways. Often his customers do not know what they want and he spends valuable time writing suggestions. They expect to pay but little more than for a production-line factory job.

A fancy piece of wood in a stock is not luck. This begins with a skilled lumberman who often picks his tree. He personally cuts the log to take advantage of crotch or butt grain. He cuts his slabs at an angle, wasting much wood to get one piece grained properly.

Properly grained? The fancy figures must be in the butt. The grain must curve with the grip, and be fairly straight in the forearm. Improper grain in the grip means a weak stock, easily broken. Twisted and fancy grain in the forearm can mean warpage in damp weather, destroying accuracy.

Good stock wood is expensive. In the prewar days of normal prices, shooters paid as high as $35 for a blank piece of wood for a stock. Figured American walnut is probably the most popular, but imported Circassian walnut from Russia is also popular for light sporters. The trouble with Circassian is that one can rarely find a blank of sufficient size and thickness to make a heavy stock for a target-weight rifle. Exotic woods are also popular. In the early days of the Kentucky muzzle loader, flame grain and curly maple were often used. Today these woods are again in demand. Apple is sometimes used. Oregon myrtle and California mesquite are two beautiful woods, light in color, but of excellent figure.

Stock blanks after cutting must be carefully seasoned to prevent warping, splitting, and cracking. This is of special importance in fancy figured woods. Blanks thus take years to prepare—and this adds to the cost.

What should you pay for a custom rifle built to your order?

First, you plan to supply the action. Alterations and refinishing will cost from $8 to $30, depending on the work ordered. Rechambering a standard barrel costs about $15. If you are to have a special barrel, the rough blank will cost from $20 to $35, bored and rifled. Charges for turning it to dimensions outside, fitting to the action, chambering and adjusting headspace, and finishing will run from $25 to $50.

Then comes the matter of sights. These will cost you the standard retail price for what you pick, plus a small installation charge.

Finally comes the stock with its accessories. One stock maker lists his custom stocks starting at $50 and running by $25 stages up to $200, depending on the kind and quality of the wood and the work involved.

All of this is not intended to frighten the reader away from custom work. It does point out that one should never expect too much for too little. It takes a good man to build a rifle that is better than a factory-production model. Most so-called custom rifles by gunmakers who try to approach a factory price are almost worthless, and to a person who appreciates quality, this quickly becomes evident.

**Gunsmithing vs. Custom Guns.** It would be unjust to state that gunsmithing work is different from custom gun work. All custom gun work is gunsmithing, but not all gunsmithing is custom building.

Webster's Dictionary defines the term thus: *"Gunsmith:* one whose occupation is to make or repair small firearms; an armorer." Note that "or repair."

At the beginning of this section a typical modern gunsmith, Roy Weatherby, the proprietor and manager of a small gunsmithing firm, was mentioned. This firm makes custom guns except for the actions. His staff includes a couple of gunsmiths who have long specialized in the art of barrel making. They handle this type of work only. Two skilled woodworkers who have specialized for many years in making stocks handle only that work. Other skilled workers handle miscellaneous jobs such as the fitting of sights, altering, smoothing, polishing of actions, and such other jobs required to complete a rifle.

Many one-man gunsmith shops are in existence. Some of these do only one special kind of work. They classify themselves accordingly. One man, for instance, does not claim to be a gunsmith—he is a *barrel maker*. Another may also refuse the gunsmith title—he is a *stock maker*. It is not unusual for a firearms enthusiast to have his custom rifle built in several parts of the country. He may have one man or firm alter and smooth his action; he then sends it to a barrel maker who builds the barrel to his order. Sometimes this specialist may install the required standard or special sights. The gun may then be sent elsewhere to a stock maker who completes the job.

Most repair work to metal parts is done by the general type of worker just called a gunsmith. He may

PLATE IV. John Barnett, a Weatherby gunsmith, altering the straight Mauser bolt handle on a rifle to achieve proper sporter turn-down angle.

rebuild, replace parts with handmade ones or install factory parts, or he may rebarrel with standard factory barrels or with special handmade ones obtained elsewhere. The latter is unusual; most barrel makers prefer to do their own installation, since the best-made barrel, not properly installed, may be worthless from the start.

Many gunsmiths have specialties of their own. They may have developed a certain type of alteration on a particular model of action. Many have designed a special type of safety intended for easier operation with a telescope sight. Many go in for the installation and/or design of hunting telescope mounts. Some of these general gunsmiths may be good; some are definitely very poor.

The choice of your gunsmith is a delicate, yet

PLATE V. The Mauser trigger guard of a rifle being streamlined to desired sporter dimensions. Note that a good custom gunsmith does much of the work by machine rather than by hand filing.

PLATE VI. Joe Doutra, another Weatherby gunsmith, starting to cut off and crown the barrel.

highly important task. Every war produces a crop of "gunsmiths" with little experience who are ready to tackle work beyond their particular skills. The results are usually far from satisfactory to the customer—and some products can be very dangerous. For your assistance, every sporting magazine usually has a staff writer called their "firearms editor." He can frequently aid you by recommending a gunsmith, if you are careful to indicate the type of work you wish done.

**Remodeling Military Rifles.** Most of the special rifles often called "custom built" are actually altered military rifles. In the rifle example previously mentioned, the basis of his custom rifle was a military action. In this respect, it is well to offer a few suggestions which might well be interpreted as a warning of impending danger.

Most American custom rifles and "alteration jobs" are based on Mauser-type actions. The famous Model 98 Mauser and its variations is undoubtedly the most widely used action type in the world. The famous Springfield rifle, the Model 1903, used by millions of American troops in two world wars, is a Mauser type, and for years after its adoption the United States paid royalties to Paul Mauser. These actions are the strongest yet designed for a bolt-action shoulder rifle.

Today, with hundreds of thousands of "genuine Mausers" in this country as war trophies, many of the actions are widely sought for rebuilding. Not all of these actions are either good or safe.

Recently made foreign weapons are recognized as poor, but many an American picked up a Mauser marked "Erfurt 1914" or "Danzig 1915." He thus feels that he has an action which is perfect. It is of "prewar quality." It is much better than anything the Germans made at later dates.

That same enthusiast would refuse to have his rifle built on the Springfield action of the same date, "because it bears serial number 500,000, and all Springfields below 800,000 are dangerous." The latter generally accepted theory is incorrect. It should be modified by the claim that "all Springfields over number 800,000 are much stronger than earlier actions due to the improved double-heat treatment." The science of gunmaking is progressive.

Put another way, can you believe that the rifle with which the United States entered and completed World War I was inferior to the German rifle in quality? Those Mauser actions mentioned were good, but they were still made with metals and manufacturing practice of a third of a century ago.

Coming to World War II actions, we find something different. Germany set up a new system of production. She girded for war, built many new factories, and staffed them with slave labor. The idea may have been practical, but Germany forgot a very important detail. Slave labor is usually unskilled and also generally is *unwilling* labor. Slaves work for an existence, not for love. They take no pride in their work.

Yet these slaves, through the process of constant supervision by the Gestapo and by S.S. men secretly working with them in factories, did a good job, if unwillingly. The quality of their product was frequently excellent.

Then came "D-Day." The underground spread the word to the slaves, and the picture changed. Not only did quality of workmanship fall, but sabotage entered the picture. There is insufficient space here to describe this in detail, but in Army Intelligence files there are millions of words of reports on these subjects. Workers were executed by the thousands when caught in the act. This, as actual reports reveal, did not check deliberate sabotage—it only made workers *more careful about getting caught!*

There were other contributing factors to low quality of late manufacture. Our technical intelligence men overseas knew the effect of bombing raids

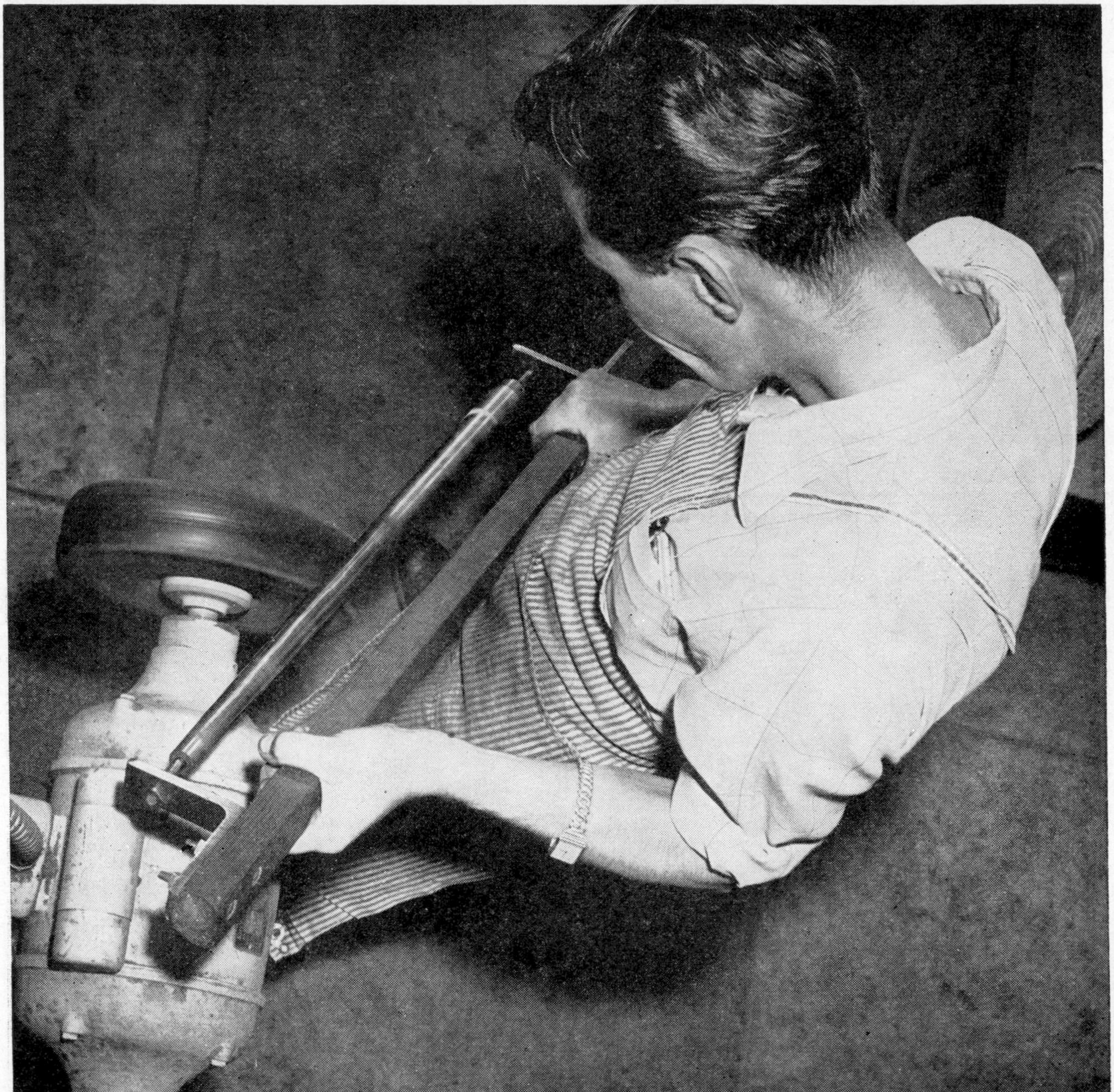

PLATE VII. Gunsmith Wallington of the Weatherby shop polishing a rifle barrel in a special fixture that permits the barrel to revolve against the polishing wheel. Note angle of polishing. This prevents "waves" in the precision-ground barrel surface. Little details like this make the difference between a good and a "fair" custom job.

PLATE VIII. Barrel and action assembled, Gunsmith John Barnett starts altering the Mauser magazine to handle the big Magnum cartridge cases. The complicated gadget projecting to the rear of the receiver is a special jig for holding the finished action securly without marring. Note that the finish has been applied.

on Axis industry. Small and badly damaged factories with totally inadequate manufacturing equipment produced materials and parts to the best of their shattered abilities. Yes, the quality *had* to be poor.

Ordnance Technical Intelligence in Paris used the facilities of a large physical, chemical, and metallurgical laboratory. The laboratory analyzed materials; the intelligence men analyzed workmanship. From 1943 on, there was a steady decline in material quality, so that by early 1945, rifles were being built of steels that the United States would have prohibited for the manufacture of anything other than stove bolts.

The same downward trend of quality was found in the products of other enemy powers. They were fighting a losing war, but doing the best they could. Germany, for instance, by mid-1944, officially abandoned the proof-testing of all small arms, since too many weapons were being blown up by this operation.

After the surrender of Germany, a high-ranking German officer who had for years served as chief of German small-arms research and development, worked in confinement in Paris under Ordnance Intelligence, preparing detailed reports on German research over a long period of weeks. One of the things he readily admitted was the poor quality and danger in weapons of late manufacture.

"Certainly they were unsafe, according to our earlier standards," he admitted with typical German unconcern, "but we didn't care much about that. Military rifles have a short life. If they last through one battle they have served their purpose. Suppose they did blow up? Rarely was it on the first shot. And if the soldier was able to fire some shots at the enemy, what matters his life? Some very poor and very dangerous weapons did not blow up. Most of them served their purpose. That was sufficient."

This admision is worthy of more than passing thought. These delayed-action booby traps are scattered throughout the country by the hundreds of thousands today. Your custom-made rifle can be no stronger than the action. Pick carefully, and avoid all actions that are dated later than 1943, or that are undated. Many 1945 actions bore no date. Thousands of recently made actions were captured and sent home by souvenir hunters as new trophies.

PLATE IX. Weatherby's stockmaker laying out the blank for a rifle. Wood is Oregon myrtle. Note heavy barrel with blocks for target telescope.

Many were low-grade spare parts, intended as replacements.

Of all Mauser actions encountered, those produced in Czechoslovakia proved on analysis to be the best. Polish makes ran a close second. Belgian actions made at *Fabrique Nationale* at Herstal ran a close third. German actions made during the 1920's and 1930's, *if composed of original parts,* are all excellent. But late actions are not worth spending money on.

If you want a custom rifle, plan it carefully. Do not attempt to decide everything overnight. Search for an action until you find what you need. Study books on gunsmithing—their cost is little in comparison with the cost of your rifle. Although you will do none of the work yourself, you will learn much and know what to demand of your gunmaker. You will learn about stock design, and why a rifle which fits your friend does not "feel right" to you.

The custom rifle is not the gun for the beginner. Until he learns just what he wants, he is not qualified to order, and will not be satisfied with his purchase.

Experience comes slowly.

# HANDLOADING

The art of handloading ammunition is as old as the problem of loading firearms. Today two terms are used more or less interchangeably—handloading and reloading. Technically handloading is the assembly of a complete cartridge using new components; reloading is the same, but indicates re-use of the once-fired brass cartridge case.

When firearms were in their youth, a weapon was loaded by pouring a charge of black powder into the muzzle, tamping in a wad of cloth, paper, leaves, moss, or other material, and adding a charge of small stones or a lead ball, frequently with an additional wad to hold it in place. Discharge was created by applying ignition through a touch-hole at the breech of the barrel.

Later came lock mechanisms—the matchlock, in which a slow-burning wick when pressed forward applied the "light"; the wheellock, in which a revolving wheel sent a shower of sparks into the touchhole, much like a modern cigarette lighter;

then the flintlock, and finally the percussion gun.

All of these weapons were handloaded, and in later days of muzzle-loaders, the complete materials to fire a gun once—bullet, powder, and percussion cap—became known as a *round.* Today, a complete modern metallic cartridge, with all of these units assembled in a brass case, is also known as a round.

Today there are two methods of obtaining ammunition: buying it factory-manufactured by the box, or handloading it at home. Which is best?

Of the two types of modern ammunition, the rimfire and the center-fire cartridges, only the latter is practical to handload, and only the latter can be *re*loaded. But the science of handloading is not for the careless individual. It is not for the man who looks only for "cheap" ammunition. Handloaded ammunition means better ammunition, and what is most important, individual "diets" for favorite weapons.

The most misunderstood word in the shooters' language is "accuracy." This is just a synonym for "uniformity." If every shot from a weapon goes consistently to the same spot when human and mechanical errors are eliminated, the load is accurate. Manufacturers of ammunition constantly strive to reach this goal, and today's cartridges are truly accurate. Why, then, bother to handload one's cartridges?

If ten consecutively manufactured Winchester Model 70 rifles, apparently identical, were mechanically test-fired with the same lot of ammunition, there would be a slight variation of group size on the targets. What is odd is that one rifle might shoot a smaller group at 100 yards than another. The difference would probably be slight, but the test would clearly show that weapons, like human beings, have slight variations.

Take, for example, a single caliber. Probably the most thoroughly developed cartridge in the United States is the ".30/06" or, under its other names, the "Caliber .30, Model of 1906," "Caliber .30, M1," "Caliber .30, M2," ".30 U. S. Government," and ".30-1906 U. S. Government." Today Winchester makes their Model 70 rifle, bolt action, in several grades, weights, types, of stocks, barrels, and other important variations. Remington makes their Models 30 and 720. In addition there are plenty of others in service—the Model 1895 Winchester lever action, the Newton, various Mausers, the old and the World War II version of the Springfield Model 1903, the Model 1917, the current Army M1 (Garand), plus various old single-shots and a host of assorted custom-built rifles.

If you find variations in "identical" rifles, what variations would be found in this wide group? Thus it is readily understood that a manufacturer must build ammunition that is: (1) reasonably safe in all guns, and (2) of best possible accuracy in all.

The handloader has no such problem. He may tailor his custom loadings to fit an individual gun. Thus, if he uses due care, plus good components, plus skill, plus careful testing of loadings, he can easily assemble ammunition that is more accurate in his individual gun.

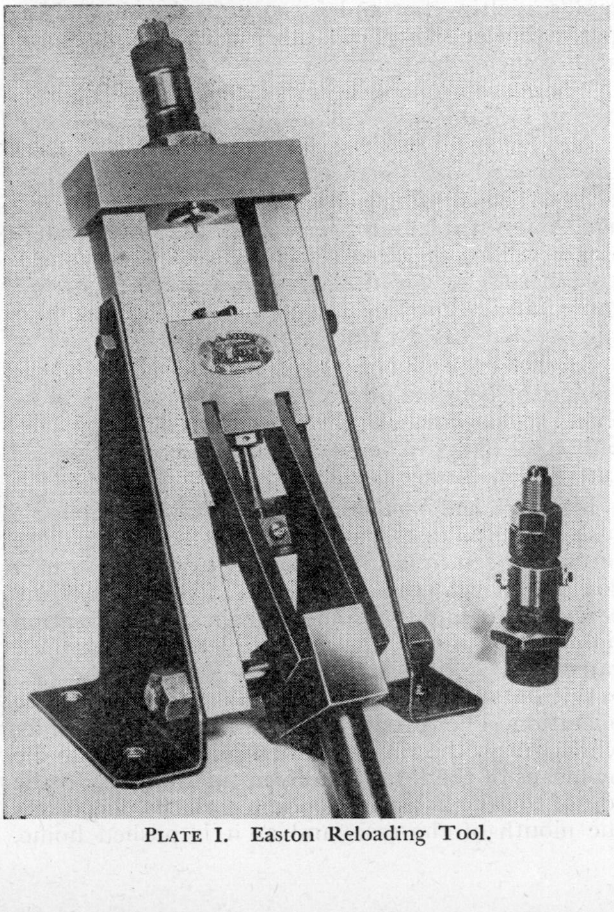

PLATE I. Easton Reloading Tool.

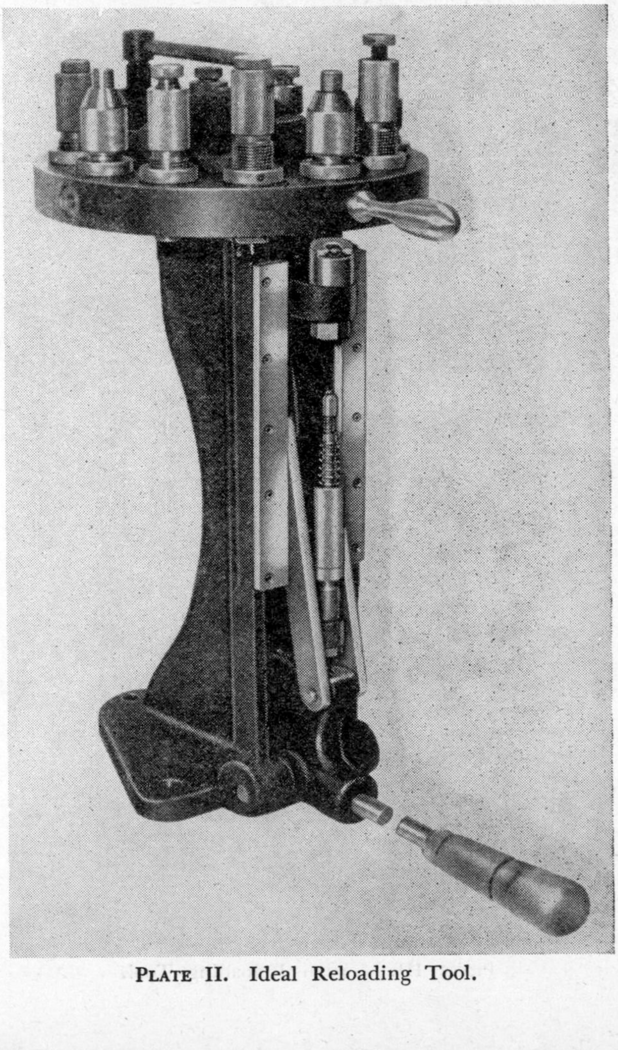

PLATE II. Ideal Reloading Tool.

There is still another angle—if he purchases factory .30/06 ammunition, he is limited to a few standard loads. If he assembles his own, he is unlimited. He may load his powerful .30/06 with a load as low in power as a little .22 short rim-fire using round lead balls or buckshot. He may load light cast bullets suitable for target or squirrel hunting; and if he has a good gun, he may load ammunition more powerful than standard factory loads. In *The Complete Guide to Handloading* (Funk & Wagnalls Co.) there are listed, for instance, over 700 different handloads in this one caliber! With new bullets appearing constantly, this list could be expanded indefinitely by serious experimenters.

Unfortunately, a beginner in the art of handloading seems to feel that making perfect ammunition is both cheap and simple. If he reloads his fired cases, there is definite economy—the most expensive single part of a cartridge is the brass case, discarded by the non-handloader. But the preparation for handloading requires study plus a reasonable investment for suitable tools.

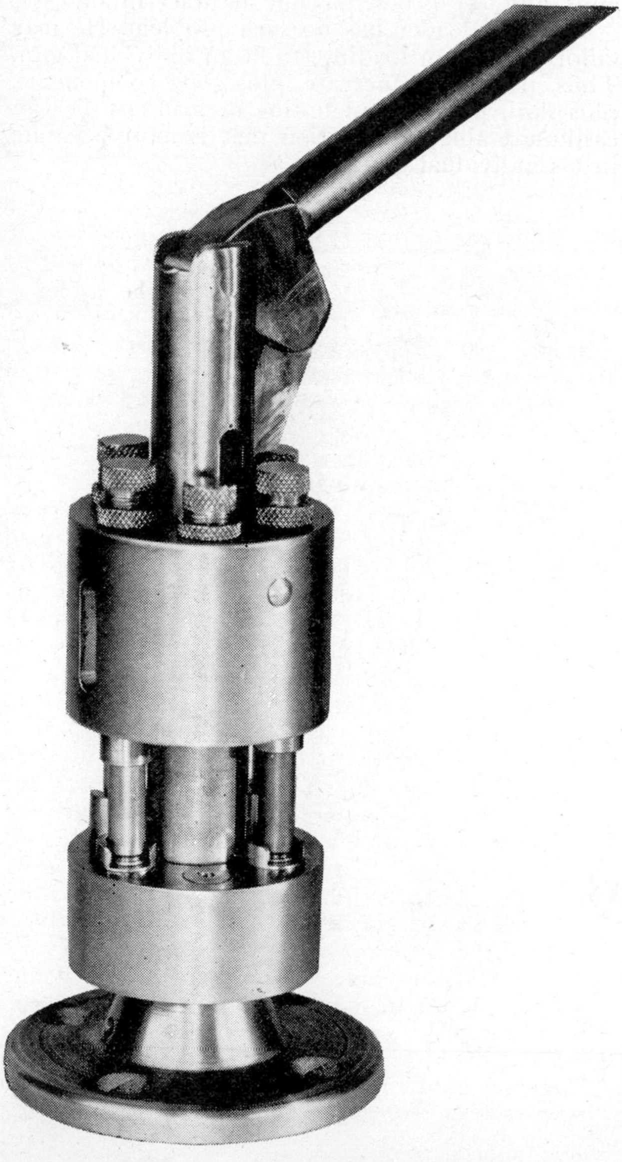

PLATE III. Jordan Reloading Tool.

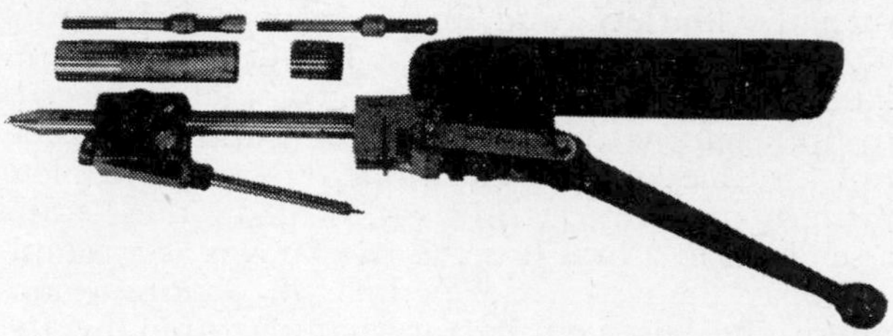

PLATE IV. Belding & Mull Reloading Tool. This can be mounted in vertical or horizontal position on loading bench.

**Tools.** Fifty years ago the handloader had only the hand or tong-type tools, sometimes called "nutcrackers." The modern handloader uses the heavier and better precision instruments known as "bench type." Early tong tools were made for an individual cartridge *and* a single weight and shape of bullet. Later the tong type was improved to permit the use of adjustable dies, to a certain extent interchangeable as to caliber. Modern bench tools are all fitted with interchangeable dies, permitting the handloader to change calibers at will; some types handle two set-ups so that two different cartridges may be loaded without changing dies.

The serious handloader requires the following equipment:

(1) Basic loading tool complete with dies for full-length and neck resizing of the cartridge case, decapper for removing the fired primer, primer seating unit, neck expander, bullet seater.
(2) A good powder measure.
(3) A small balance with a set of weights. Balance must be sensitive to less than 1/10th grain, avoirdupois.

If he desires to make his own bullets of the lead-alloy variety, he must add to his list: proper bullet molds, melting pot and furnace or electric melting pot, a bullet sizing and lubricating machine, and a micrometer caliper.

There are numerous other gadgets he will add as he gets into the game—many of which may be homemade. He may purchase factory-made bullets from the standard manufacturers, or custom-made bullets. He will keep adding to his collection, since the average American handloader loads for more than a single caliber of cartridge. This should be considered, that the additional equipment may be obtained at a minimum of expense *and* without making obsolete his existing equipment.

Several entire books have been written on the subject of handloading—one of them running more than 450,000 words. In the limitations of these pages, only basic data can be given, and this popular .30/06 cartridge is chosen as an example.

**Materials and Methods.** Assume that you have a supply of fired cases from various sources. They have probably been fired in an assortment of guns, and if you carefully try these fired cases in your own chamber, you may find that some of them stick. Operation number one is to decap and full-length resize these cases.

With modern bench tools this is done in a single operation. The cartridge case is inserted in a holder which grasps the rim. It is then pushed into the die by means of the lever-type operating handle. In the top of the die is a needle-pointed rod which enters the mouth of the case, and as it is pushed home, lines up with the flash-hole in the primer pocket, pushing the fired primer out. As the case is forced into the die, it is squeezed down toward its original size. It will thus fit your rifle chamber, but since all *new* cartridges are made smaller than chambers because of manufacturing variations, the fully resized case will be slightly larger than a new and unfired specimen. This is an advantage.

Should you clean these cases? Generally speaking, it is unnecessary. However, the primer contains a quantity of harsh abrasives, including powdered glass. The by-product of combustion leaves a slight cake in the bottom of the primer pocket. For precision ammunition, many handloaders remove this, using a small rotary steel brush, or a hand scraper. This operation leaves a clean pocket, and permits the selection of perfect flash holes for precision ammunition. This "dirt" is highly abrasive—test it. Shake a small amount on a piece of broken window glass, and rub the two together for a moment. Note the scratches and you will see what wear can be caused by it on barrels and loading-tool dies.

Chemical cleaning of tarnished brass is not necessary and is not advisable.

A new primer is seated in the case pocket after all resized cases have been inspected and defective ones have been discarded. In this operation, reasonable care must be taken. The primer should fit the pocket properly, and the seating punch used must fit the primer. Different makes have different shapes of faces—some are convex and others are flat. A good handloader has seating punches to fit each make and size of primer.

After primer seating, the cases should once again be carefully inspected. If any primers are "marked"

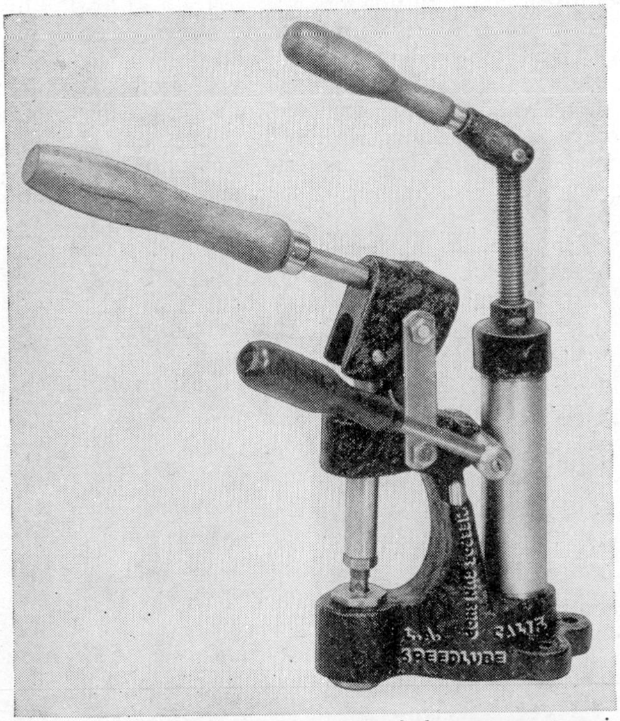


PLATE V. A good bullet lubricator of the pressure type is almost a "must" for quantity precision bullet casting. The Meepos is typical of the many types available. Levers maintain pressure on the grease supply, force the bullet through the die, and apply the required amount of grease without making a "messy" job or wasting lubricant.

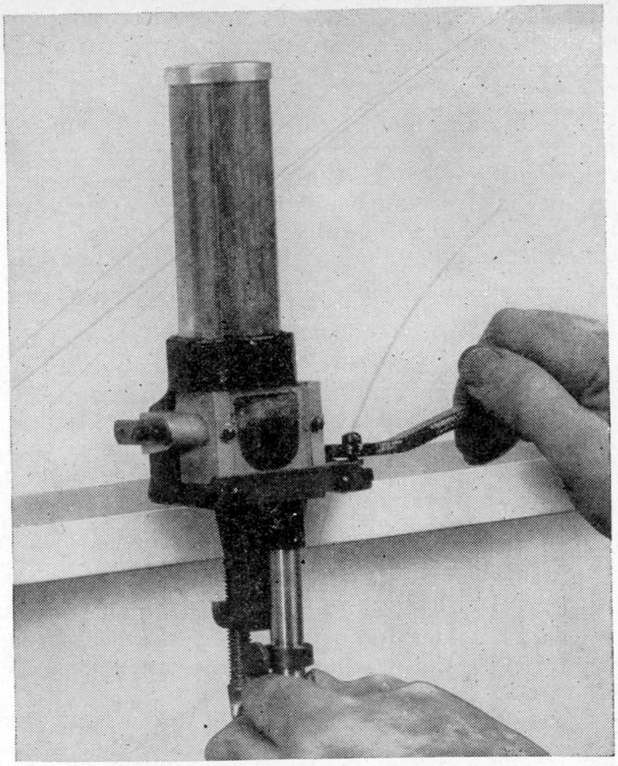

PLATE VI. Belding & Mull Powder Measure.

by the seating punch, they should be weeded out, decapped, the primers discarded and new ones seated. With proper tools and care, it is rare that one needs to discard, but the inspection should be included. Note that high and low primers must be watched. If they are high, reseat—if they will not enter, perhaps old primer dirt is in the bottom of the pocket. If low, decap and try another primer. If that is still low, the pocket is defective and the case should be discarded.

The discarding of cases is important. Make it a habit to ruin that case with a hammer or pair of pliers before throwing it in your scrap box. You will then never be tempted to "salvage" it.

Next comes the insertion of the powder charge. There are literally more than a dozen powders suitable for this one cartridge. One should first choose a type suited to the desired velocity, pressure, and bullet weight. Only two makes of powders are available—DuPont and Hercules. Of these two makes, there are many "obsolete" powders, but they keep turning up, and all of them are usually as good as the day they were released. Few powders made in the last 25 years actually spoil. The shooter is not handicapped with the older powders, and in many cases he may even get better performance with his combination of components.

There are only two basic types of powders—single and double base. The single-base type is mostly nitrocellulose, gelatinized, and with a coating of DNT to slow its initial rate of burning. Double-base powders include varying percentages of nitroglycerin added to the nitrocellulose before it is colloided or gelatinized.

Since the beginning of modern smokeless powders, there has been a never-ending argument as to which type is best. Nitroglycerin powders create a higher temperature on burning. Therefore let us assume that they are more destructive to barrels. Straight nitrocellulose powders burn at lower temperature, *but* at higher pressure for a given velocity of bullet. Therefore the temperature advantage is canceled out by the pressure disadvantage when straight nitrocellulose is used. While nitrocellulose powders are in the greatest demand, there are many accuracy records in the .30/06 caliber that cannot be duplicated with any other than double-base powders. With either type and normal loadings up to full charge, barrel life is entirely satisfactory.

With the proper powder chosen, next comes the preparation of the charges. Weighed or measured?

The precision handloader weighs his charges. If he is working with heavy loads, he must weigh them in the interests of safety. Normal full-charge loads in the .30/06 develop about 50,000 pounds per square inch in chamber pressure. A little more than this can be dangerous, and heavy charges should be avoided unless all facts of the load are fully known.

Bench-type powder measures are satisfactory and useful, but it has long been established that best results are obtained when the powder charges do not vary by more than 1/10 grain. This writer has used about every measure on the market, and has yet to find one which, despite claims of advertisers, can be depended upon to run that close. Therefore maximum and all precision charges should be weighed.

The chief criticism of weighing charges is that it is necessarily slow. The skilled handloader saves time by using both balance and measure. If a 45.6 grain charge is desired, he sets his measure to throw about 45.1 or 45.2. This charge is dropped into the balance pan, and the tiny additional quantity can then be quickly added.

A loading block and powder funnel are necessary for easily charging the case. The powder funnel should fit inside the case neck. Good funnels can be obtained from a drugstore or other place selling small plastic funnels for filling baby bottles. These funnels can be shaped to fit the neck with a file.

A loading block is simply a block of wood with holes of uniform depth bored into it of proper size to hold the head of the case and prevent upsetting. One way to make these is to use a soft pine board about one inch thick, bore the holes through, and glue or nail a layer of ¼-inch plywood to the bottom. For convenience in handling, rifle blocks should hold no more than 20 cases.

The operation of a powder measure requires skill and care. Generally these consist of a hopper to hold the powder and a rotary or sliding drum with an adjustable cavity. Powder feeds from the hopper supply into the drum cavity. This is then rotated or slid to "cut off the charge," which is then dropped into the waiting case. Unless a steady, uniform operation is conducted, the cutting off will shear some grains and settle others into the cavity, permitting additional powder to fall into the newly created space, varying the charge. Smoothness of operation is therefore essential.

Since much of the powder flow is regulated by pressure of the column remaining in the hopper, it is wise to see that this does not fall below the halfway mark.

One of the most important inspections must always follow. The loading block is held to the light and the eye quickly inspects the level of the powder within the case. High or low levels should be quickly dumped back. In some light loads the case will accidentally accommodate a double charge. Or there may be a missed charge. No honest handloader of experience will claim that he has never missed a charge or thrown a double charge. Inspection at this point shows that it can happen.

Next comes bullet seating. With modern tools this is a simple operation. With some it is not even necessary to hand-start the bullets in the case neck. Bullets are dropped into a guide above the charged cartridge case and the lever is closed, forcing the bullet into the case neck or the case neck over the bullet, depending on the tool design. The cartridge is then complete, except for a visual inspection to determine that all bullets are seated uniformly and properly.

The above applies to all bullets—cast or jacketed. If you make your own bullets, these should always be prepared in advance.

The home manufacture of bullets was once a dirty and messy job, usually accomplished during the absence of the feminine members of the family. Today it can be done in any room with proper equipment, and without dirt or mess.

First comes the choice of bullet metal. Pure lead is never used—it is too soft to stand the strain of being driven through rifling, and will strip or slide straight through without rotation. This will mean very poor accuracy and a seriously fouled barrel.

Tin, antimony, and copper are usually added to lead to give the bullet sufficient hardness. A favorite alloy of rifle handloaders is 1:10, tin and lead. This means that for 10 pounds of pure lead, 1 pound of tin is added, giving 11 pounds of bullet metal. 1-to-20 is also used for light and medium velocities. Bullet metal can be prepared without tin, using much cheaper antimony, which, however, has a much higher melting point and is more difficult to use. A good alloy for rifle bullets consists of 1 pound of antimony to each 25 or 30 pounds of lead.

Handloaders may find it difficult to locate pure block tin for their bullet metal. A readily available source is bar solder, usually cheaper than the wire type. If "50-50" solder is used, 2 pounds of solder will contain one pound each of lead and tin. To make the 1:20 bullet metal, add 2 pounds of this solder to 19 pounds of pure lead.

Bullet metal should always be prepared in a large quantity for uniformity. Never let it harden in your melting pot—it will take too much heat to bring it to fluid state again. Once the metal is mixed, if it will not be used immediately in casting, it may be poured in small puddles on a concrete floor. These small lumps melt quickly when desired.

An electric bullet caster is of great help. These consist of a small electric melting pot holding from one to two pounds of metal. A side lever controls a valve in a pouring spout which fits the sprue cutter of all standard bullet molds. In use the mold is gripped by its handles with the sprue cutter held tightly against the pouring spout. The valve lever is lifted for an instant, then dropped. The mold is then filled, a blow on the sprue cutter cleanly shears the surplus, the mold is opened, and the completed bullet is dropped.

There are many tricks to bullet casting. First, the mold must always be hot, or the bullet will not completely fill, and will have seams and flaws. Until the mold is at proper temperature, all castings from it will be scrap, to be thrown back into the pot.

Hot bullets mutilate easily. They should always be dropped on a wool blanket or turkish towel from a distance of not more than 12 inches. They are not hot enough to burn or scorch this material, although they are too hot to handle. Keep an old spoon handy—defective bullets are thus easily scooped back into the pot, along with surplus sprue. Always drop bullets on the cloth—never on each other. As they cool, they may be scooped aside into a pile, again using that spoon.

In using an electric caster, never permit the pot to become more than half empty. Add new metal or discarded bullets. With the average caster used in this manner, the metal stays at proper temperature and there is no waiting for the new metal to melt.

Bullet molds come in single- or multiple-cavity types. Unless you make enormous quantities of bullets, not more than a two-cavity mold should be used. The big gang molds are too heavy to handle and require skill to keep them at operating temperature.

With both single- and double-cavity molds, one can sometimes cast too fast and get the mold too hot. If your castings look frosty instead of shiny silver, let the mold cool slightly. Those frosted bullets will shoot poorly and may shrink too much on cooling.

With bullets cast, they should be air-cooled and then individually inspected. Bullets with the slightest flaws should be tossed into your bullet-metal box for recasting. To use them is a waste of time, powder, and primers. To recast them is to save good metal.

Cast bullets must be lubricated. You can make special bullet lubricants, but this is a messy job and prepared bullet lubricants cost very little.

Bullets of the cast variety must always be resized or you will have trouble properly seating them in case necks. Cast bullets are best stored "dry" and lubricated and sized at loading time. A modern bench machine that sizes and lubricates in one operation is most convenient. Bullets are individually fed into a sizing die, then a lever is operated, forcing the casting into the die to reduce it to a uniform diameter, and hard stick lubricant is forced into the grooves of the bullet through orifices in the die. The bullet is then either pushed out, or another bullet is started, forcing the sized and lubricated one through the bottom, depending on the make and design of the sizer.

For high-speed loads, cast bullets are usually fitted with a copper cup on the bullet base to prevent fusing of the base from the hot powder flame. These cups, known as gas checks, are purchased ready-formed, applied lightly by hand to the bullet base, and the sizing die locks them in position.

**Storage.** Components will keep indefinitely if given proper storage. A few simple rules will cover this subject.

Cases. Brass cartridge cases need very little special attention. Keep them in boxes where they are free from dust, dirt, and excessive moisture which might cause corrosion.

Bullets. Jacketed bullets are best stored in the cartons in which they are received from manufacturers. If of the expanding variety, they should not be bulk packed, or damage to soft or unprotected points may occur. Cast bullets are best stored in small boxes of wood or paper, and unlubricated. Messy lubricant must be wiped from the base to

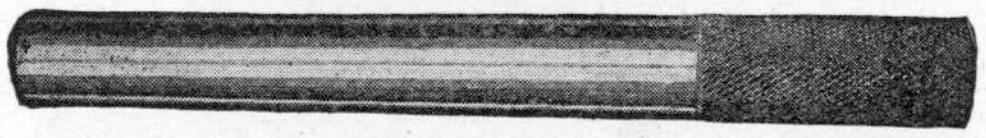

Plate VII. A full-length shell resizer is necessary for the reloader who uses the same cartridge in several guns. This Bond type is of the most simple design—the shell is forced in and punched out by hand. Caution: do not use a hammer to insert and remove shell. If an arbor press or large vise is not available, use a heavy block of hardwood to prevent battering of the case.

keep it out of the powder when loading, and from the nose of the finished cartridges to make them clean handling.

Primers. These should be stored carefully. They are sensitive, and dangerous for such a small item. Excessive moisture can ruin them. They may be stored in the original cartons in which they are received if kept in a dry place free from excessive heat, but many handloaders prefer to keep them in small screw-cover glass mayonnaise jars. Do not mix primer lots! Regardless of manufacturing claims,

Plate VIII. A good powder scale or balance, capable of sensitivity to 1/10 grain, is necessary for precision hand-loading.

each lot shows different performance and often a slightly varying formula.

Powders. These must be kept away from excessive heat and moisture. They may be kept in the original cans in normal room temperatures, but be certain that the cork seal in the cover is present and forms a moisture-proof seal. Never shake cans or other powder containers. Shaking can build a dangerous charge of static electricity.

**Cost of Handloading.** Good tools for handloading are like good tools for the practice of any other hobby such as woodworking, metalworking, and so forth. They cost money. But here is a great difference—the upkeep is nil if they are used properly and purchased wisely. A careful study of the features of each make of tool will save you money. Get the type meeting your requirements and remember that you must always allow room for expansion. A new set of dies in a different caliber is far less expensive than a new tool.

Phil Sharpe's *The Complete Guide to Handloading* is on file in hundreds of public libraries and in most Army libraries. This book also gives the greatest collection of individual loads ever assembled between one set of covers. Some ten dozen

PLATE IX. This Bond Model C tool is a simple, low-priced bench unit. The special reamer on the top is used to chamfer the rough edges on the mouth of a fired case.

American cartridges are covered with more than 7000 tested handloads. Since the powder companies have discontinued the release of loading data, this volume is the primary source of data for handloading.

**"Wildcat" Cartridges.** A "wildcat" is any cartridge which is not and never has been commercially manufactured. Wildcats have been with us since the beginning of the metallic cartridge. In fact, many of the standard cartridges of today were developed as wildcats by private experimenters. Among this list are the .22 Hornet, .220 Swift, .22 Savage Hi-Power, .250-3000 Savage, .257 Roberts, .357 Magnum revolver, and many others. A wildcat becomes a "standard" when commercial ammunition makers add it to their line.

Many of the wildcats of today are in the ultra-velocity brackets, developed by private experimenters and small gunsmiths. Generally they are formed by using a standard brass cartridge case and reshaping it. The handloading fan usually *must* load his own ammunition for such guns, since he will probably have no other source of ammunition. There is just one weak point to this field: dangerous pressures.

It is very doubtful if there are many of the dozens of wildcats on the market which have ever been tested for pressure. This should be thoroughly understood. Why? Because pressure equipment is not

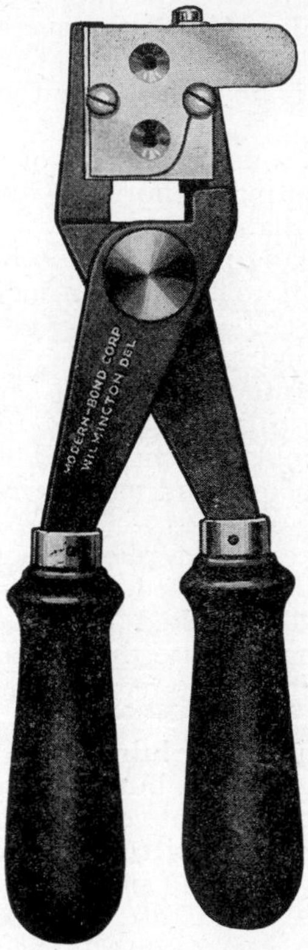

PLATE X. Bullet molds are available in a number of makes and types. Generally the double-cavity type is adequate for most handloading, since two bullets can be made at one time. More cavities make the mold too slow and heavy to handle.

available. Any cartridge may be easily tested for velocity—one merely fires it on a chronograph range which instantly measures the time it takes a bullet to pass between two points. This is translated into speed through a prepared table.

Taking cartridge pressures requires a special gun. This is handmade with a precision hole through the top of the chamber carefully fitted with a hardened steel bushing. Into this a tool-steel piston is carefully lapped for an airtight fit. An arbor is mounted around the barrel over this assembly. A copper crusher cylinder is used to record the pressure.

In operation, a cartridge is chambered, the piston is fitted with an oiled copper gas-check cup, inserted in the piston hole, pushed down to contact the case. On this is placed the crusher, a cylinder of copper .500 x .225 inch, of precision dimensions, purity, and hardness. An "anvil" in the arbor is screwed downward to contact the crusher, and the gun is then fired.

On firing, the high-pressure powder gas bursts the case, driving the piston upward, crushing the cylinder slightly. This is measured with micrometers and reference to a previously prepared table for that lot of crushers translates this shortening into pressure in pounds-per-square-inch.

All of this sounds simple, but a pressure gun is very expensive—only the most skilled of toolmakers can alter a gun. Factory records show that fitting labor on a pressure barrel usually costs well over $100, plus the price of the gun. Life is short because of wear on the piston and erosion of the piston hole. Factory technicians estimate that with standard calibers, the wear and tear alone on a pressure barrel amounts to more than 75 cents per shot.

**Special Note to the Handloader.** Never load a heavier charge than you need for the purpose for which it is intended. Light loads are more economical in powder, in barrel life, and in wear and tear on the shooter through reduced recoil.

High pressures can be dangerous, and there is no method of calculating pressures with pencil and paper. As you increase the charge of powder with a given bullet in a given cartridge case, the velocity and pressure both increase. At a certain point the increase in velocity is slight, while pressure goes up in an alarming manner.

What pressure is safe? That question can never be answered. Many a shooter has been living on borrowed time because he has been shooting ammunition which *should* blow up his gun. It only happens once.

There is no positive way of telling when pressures approach the danger mark. A study of "flattened primers" is useless. Very low pressures will flatten primers more than high pressures. If, however, there are signs of gas leaks around the primer, or you get pierced primers, it would be wise to reduce the load.

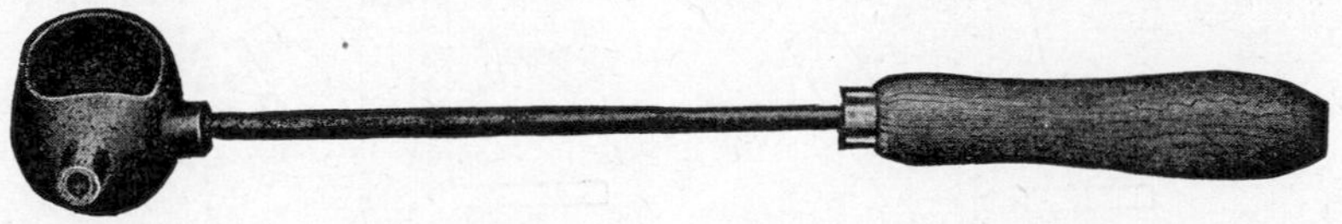

PLATE XI. Bullet metal is poured more readily with these dippers. The nozzle fits the cavity in the sprue cutter.

Non-corrosive primers create higher pressures than the old corrosive types containing potassium chlorate. There is no mystery about this "non-corrosive" primer, despite the fact that manufacturers will not give you their "secret" formula. The corrosive primer, in use until the middle 1920's, contained potassium chlorate. After discharge, the products of combustion left a deposit of potassium chloride in the bore. This is almost identical in action to sodium chloride—ordinary table salt. It gathers moisture from the air and causes corrosion —*rust*. Demonstrate this with razor blades. Clean two of them, put a pinch of table salt on one, and expose both to ordinary atmosphere. In a day or so wipe the salt away and note the rust beneath it.

Thus, when primer improvements came, *any* primer not containing potassium chlorate became

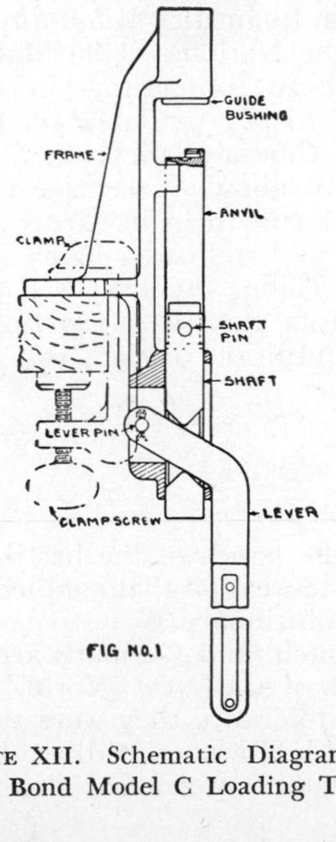


PLATE XII. Schematic Diagram of the Bond Model C Loading Tool.

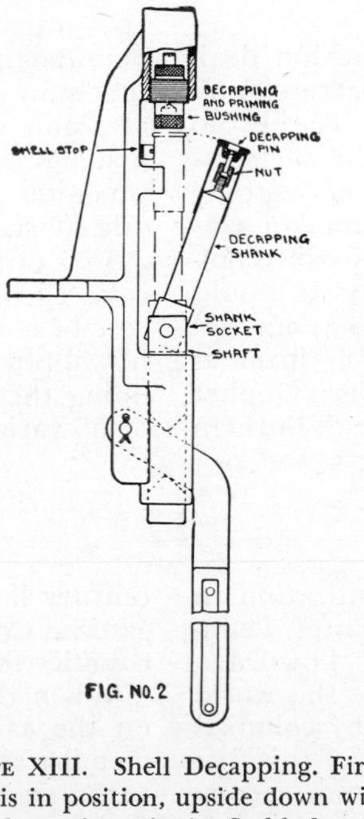


PLATE XIII. Shell Decapping. Fired case is in position, upside down with decapping pin in flashhole.

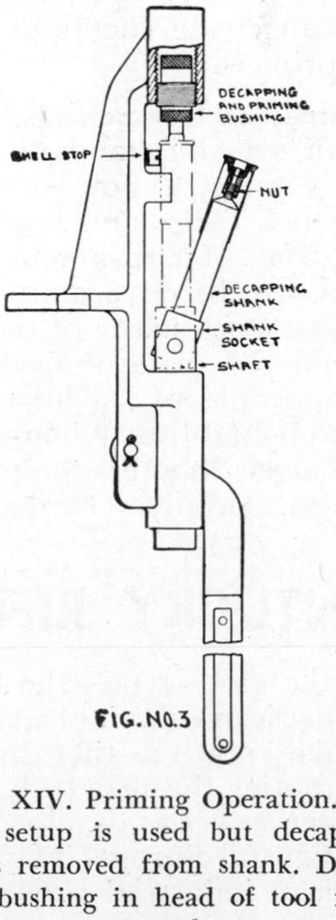


PLATE XIV. Priming Operation. The same setup is used but decapping pin is removed from shank. Decapping bushing in head of tool is reversed.

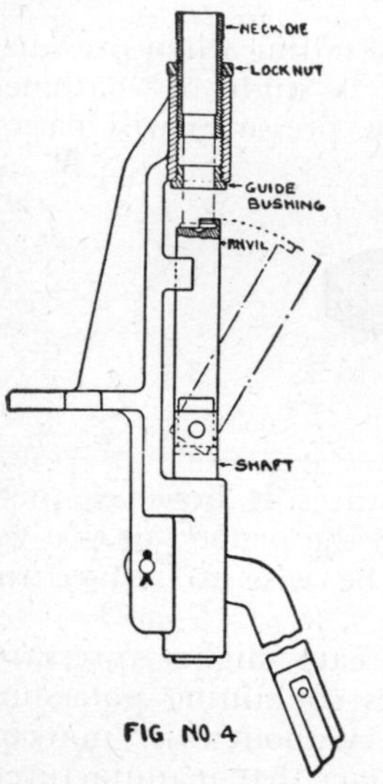


FIG NO. 4

PLATE XV. Resizing die is used in head and shell holder replaces decapping and priming pin.

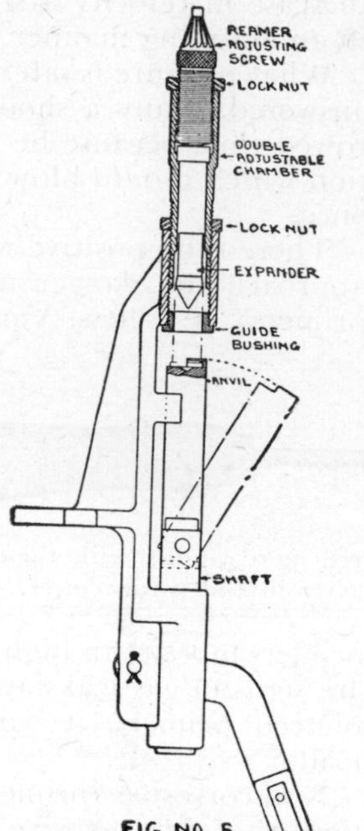


FIG. NO. 5

PLATE XVI. Resizing die in head is replaced with expander die to bring inside of case neck to proper diameter to hold the bullet.

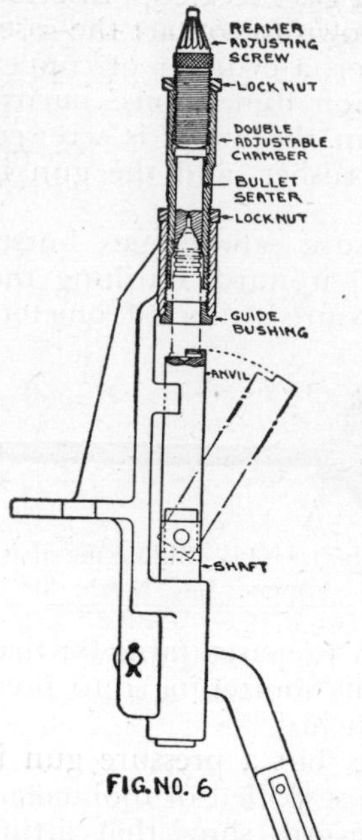


FIG. NO. 6

PLATE XVII. Expander is removed from head and bullet-seating die replaces it. This completes the loading operation.

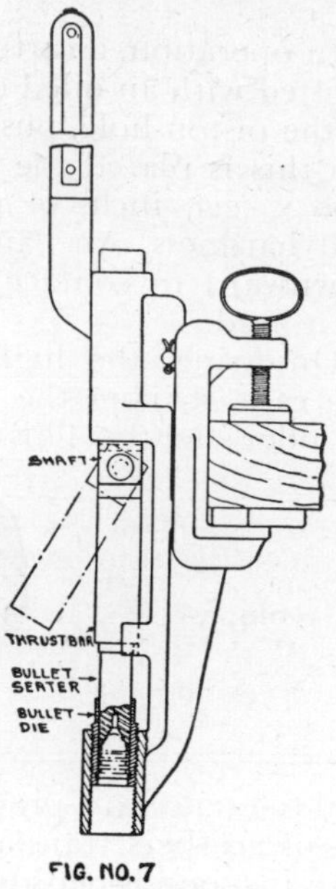


FIG. NO. 7

PLATE XVIII. Resizing alloy bullets with the Bond Model C is possible with a bullet-die attachment. They should be lubricated before sizing. This is one of the lower-priced bench tools and has been widely used for several years.

known as "non-corrosive." There are two basic formulas in use today—the Remington-Peters containing a basis of lead styphnate, and the Winchester-Western founded on the use of diazol. There is just one important warning: The by-products of these two primer mixtures are in themselves non-corrosive. May a good barrel has been ruined because a shooter fired *both* and left the barrel uncleaned. Mixed, they can create chemicals as corrosive as the old-style primers.

**Sources of Components.** Most ammunition dealers can get you standard new cartridge cases and various primers, powders, and bullets. Rarely do they stock them, and "on order" usually means a long delay. There are numerous shooters' supply houses which, on acount of their volume of this business, stock many of these components in quantity and can make immediate shipment. It would be impossible to list all of these sources, but old and well-established houses include such firms as the Badger Shooters Supply, Owen, Wis.; Gopher Shooters Supply, Faribault, Minn.; Thurman Randle & Co., 208 N. Akard St., Dallas 1, Texas; Lindahl Gun Company, Central City, Nebr.; Al Freeland, 3737 14th Ave., Rock Island, Ill.; The Hollywood Gun Shop, 6032 Hollywood Blvd., Hollywood, Calif.; Kerr's, 9582 Wilshire Blvd., Beverly Hills, Calif.; and Belding & Mull, Box 428, Philipsburg, Pa.

The handloading of ammunition is entirely practical and to the experienced shooter it is both an economy and a definite part of the sport of shooting. It is interesting to recall that in recent years many manufacturers have taken quantities of *handloaded* precision cartridges to the National Rifle Matches at Camp Perry for sale to competitors in these matches. Since they had to pay for labor on these precision loads, the few thousand they offered for sale at standard prices of about 10 cents each in .30/06 caliber, frequently cost them in excess of 40 cents each to produce. The handloader figures only cost of components. The labor involved is part of his hobby. And there is a certain satisfaction in doing the job with ammunition of the "roll-your-own" variety.

# KENTUCKY RIFLE

In the early 1700's the border of civilization in the American colonies had reached Lancaster, Pennsylvania, known at that time as Hickory Town. On this frontier the first truly accurate rifle the world had ever seen was developed and built by colonists from Central Europe. The development of this first American industrial product resulted from a combination of circumstances, which more than half a century later, put into the hands of the hastily organized Colonial Army the weapon that enabled the colonies to win the Revolutionary War.

When these Swiss, French, and Germans arrived on the eastern seaboard of the New World, they met the same kind of intolerance they were trying to escape in the Old World. However, William Penn and his peace-loving Quakers welcomed the new-

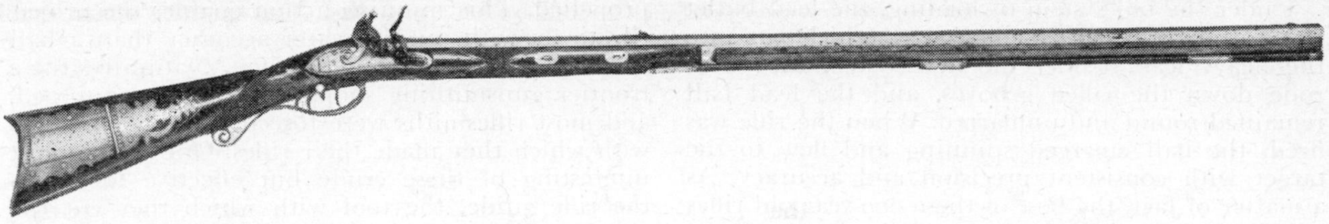

Courtesy Metropolitan Museum of Art.

PLATE I. Kentucky Rifle—lock by W. Allport, barrel by S. Aller; made about 1810.

comers who found themselves unwelcome in Virginia and New England, and they settled in what became the state of Pennsylvania.

**Development.** Most of these settlers were farmers. They knew they were going to a wild, unexplored continent, and they brought with them whatever firearms were available. In most cases these were cumbersome Jaeger rifles which had been in use in the German and Austrian armies. They were shorter than smoothbore muskets and were equipped with heavy barrels that shot big .75-caliber balls. These big bullets required heavy powder charges to propel them. Further, the Jaeger rifles were difficult to load, inaccurate, and unreliable. They were designed to be used by massed soldiers firing into ranks of enemy soldiers at fairly close range, and they were completely inadequate for the problems of the colonial frontier.

Odd as it may seem today, the abundance of wild animals in early days in this country was a hindrance to the westward movement of civilization, and the frontier-colonists held tremendous game drives to get rid of the wild life. They would gather at an appointed spot and form a tremendous circle of hunters who would converge on the wild life encircled, killing as many animals as possible. In one drive in 1760, near Pomfret Castle, a Pennsylvania fort for defense against the Indians, 198 deer, 111 buffalo, 109 wolves, 112 foxes, 114 mountain cats, 41 panthers, and more than 500 other animals were slaughtered.

Quite naturally, the Indians resented this wholesale and wasteful killing of the game they counted on for food, shelter, and clothing, and they took their resentment out on any white men they could find alone in the woods. Moreover, their bows and arrows were almost as effective against the European firearms as these firearms had been against the encircled animals. Indians could actually stand out in the open, beyond the effective range of the cumbersome firearms, and be fairly certain of hitting a man with an arrow.

Although the hostile Indian was probably the most important firearm problem the Pennsylvania frontiersman confronted, he was faced with others. He wanted to explore the vast country to the west, and when traveling through the woods, he wanted to feel certain that he could kill the game he needed for food with a single shot. Therefore, in thinking about a new kind of rifle, he put accuracy—both for protection against Indians and for the procurement of food—at the top of the list. The size of the bullet was an important consideration, especially to those who traveled as far as the Allegheny Mountains and had a look at the almost endless wilderness beyond. They wanted to explore that wilderness. To do so meant they had to travel great distances on foot, and when traveling on foot, the weight they had to carry became of vital importance. Therefore, they wanted rifles that used small bullets so that they could get more shots from every pound of lead and powder they could carry.

Although most of the Swiss, German, and French settlers came prepared to live on the land, enterprising gunsmiths came along, too, believing that the opening of a new continent would call for the constant use of firearms and afford excellent business opportunities. Between 1720 and 1730 Leman, Ferree, Stenzel, Albright, Le Fevre, and many other gunsmiths were setting up crude rifle shops in the rolling country beyond the Delaware River. The frontiersmen presented their firearm problems to these gunsmiths, and before long many were devoting more time to the development of new rifles than to the repairing of old ones. The short, thick Jaeger barrels were replaced by long, comparatively thin barrels. The heavy, chunky, walnut stocks were replaced by slim, curly maple and cherry wood stocks.

In spite of their length, these experimental rifles were easier to carry than the heavy military arms. They shot smaller balls with less powder, and although their accuracy was considerably improved, it fell short of the needs of the frontier, and the loading process was unavoidably slow. They were loaded from the muzzle, the lead ball being forced into the grooves in the barrel and then pushed down the barrel with the loading rod. It was usually a tight fit, and a great deal of pressure was required to accomplish the loading. The bullet would usually be distorted by the rod which was sometimes hammered and often slammed down the barrel with great force. Because it was pressed or hammered out of shape, the bullet would usually be inaccurate in flight.

History seems to have forgotten exactly who it was who solved the problem—or when it was solved. Some forgotten gunsmith, perhaps by accident, developed what is known as the patched ball. He simply made a round-ball bullet that was somewhat smaller than the inside bore of the rifle—loose enough, in fact, so that it would roll down the barrel without any pressure whatsoever. When the rifle was loaded, the powder charge was poured down the barrel. Then a piece of greased buckskin or linen was placed over the muzzle. The ball was placed on top of the buckskin or linen patch and pressed down into the muzzle so that it was flush with the end of the barrel. Then the buckskin or linen that still protruded was cut away, and the bullet was quickly and easily pressed down the barrel to the powder charge.

Under the old system of loading, the lead bullet was forced into the rifled grooves which cut into the heavy lead. Under the new system the patch rode down the rifled grooves, and the lead ball remained round and unmarred. When the rifle was fired, the ball emerged spinning and flew to the target with consistent precision and accuracy. As a matter of fact, the best of these 200-year old rifles will perform, today, more accurately than many of the modern hunting arms now being used.

The new long, thin, remarkably accurate rifle gave the frontiersman an immediate advantage over the arrow-shooting Indian and enabled him to move through the forest with confidence, for he knew that he could shoot a hostile Indian far beyond the range of the red man's arrows. Because this new kind of rifle enabled Daniel Boone and his followers to cross the Alleghenies and open the wilderness, it became known as the Kentucky rifle, even though it was created, developed, and manufactured in Pennsylvania.

**How They Were Made.** Early American flintlock rifles were the products of frontier shops and, in most cases, each arm was turned out by an individual craftsman. The men who made these weapons had to be able to make everything: barrels, locks, stocks, and hardware.

First came the barrel. Since there were no boring machines on the frontier, the early riflesmith was forced to develop some other method of getting a straight hole through a bar of iron that varied in length from 30 inches to 54 inches or more. He would select a bar of iron which would be just about as heavy as the desired weight of the finished barrel. He would then place the long flat bar in a charcoal fire, hammer it around a core, overlap the edges, and weld them together. He would than loosen the rod around which the weld had been made and hammer the edges of the bar together again for another inch or so. Working from the center of the bar toward both ends, and loosening the rod around which the iron was bent, he would hammer and weld until the barrel was welded its full length.

Once the barrel was welded its full length, the riflesmith would insert a hard metal core which was slightly smaller than the final caliber. He would then hammer the barrel until it was as nearly perfect as possible, remove the core, and smooth out the bore.

The next problem was to straighten the barrel. He would take a fine thread, drop it through the barrel, and attach it to a light hickory bow to hold it taut. By holding the barrel up to the daylight, he could see the shadow of the thread inside the bore. If the shadow seemed to break at any spot, he knew that the barrel was crooked at that spot and would tap it lightly with a hammer until every bend was out of the barrel. He would then grind eight flat sides on the outside of the barrel, giving it an octagon shape on the outside.

In most cases one man made the complete rifle, lock, stock, and soft-iron barrel. And although he had only crude tools at his disposal, he was able to rifle the barrels with such precision that they performed with truly astounding accuracy.

To rifle the barrel is to cut grooves inside the bore, grooves that force the bullet to spin as it is propelled. This spinning action enables the projectile to fly with much greater accuracy than a ball fired from a smoothbore weapon. Naturally, these frontier gunsmithing shops were poorly equipped, and most riflesmiths were forced to make the tools with which they made their rifles. One of the most interesting of these crude but effective tools was the rifle guide, the tool with which they cut the rifling grooves inside the bore of the barrel. It consisted of a cylinder of wood, approximately 54 inches long, which was held in a wooden framework. It revolved when the frame was moved backward and forward on the bench. Spiral grooves on the outside of the cylinder guided the cutting tool. A rifling rod was fastened to the end of the spiral-grooved cylinder. A short hickory rod was fastened to the end of the rifling rod, and the saw for cutting the grooves in the barrel was set in the hickory rod.

The riflesmith would align the barrel with the rifle guide on his bench, and run the rifling rod through the barrel until the hickory rod extended out the other end. He would then set the saw and make a cut by pulling the guide along the bench while the spiral-cut cylinder revolved, guided by an index which fitted the grooves. As the spiral-cut cylinder revolved, the rod and cutting saw inside the barrel also revolved, cutting thinly into the bore of the barrel. The riflesmith could cut a groove in the barrel with approximately 100 cuts. It took him approximately 800 cuts to complete a barrel with eight grooves. After the gunsmith completed rifling of the barrel, he would forge out trigger guards and other fittings. He would then select a stock blank from his supply of curly maple, walnut, or cherry stock material, which he usually seasoned for three or four years. After completing the stock and lock and mounting the barrel, he would put on the sights and target the rifle.

Many riflesmiths took pride in decorating stocks and even barrels with inlaid scrollwork of German silver, brass, and other material. Although a great variety of decoration and hardware developed through the years with elaborate results, some smiths preferred to keep their rifles simple, and the style and amount of decoration on a rifle is frequently a key to the period of its manufacture. Even the simplest rifles, however, usually had a brass star inlaid in the cheekpiece and a patch box on the right-hand side of the stock. In this box, the rifleman carried his greased patches, one of which he needed every time he loaded his rifle. Frequently, the patch boxes were ornate as well as practical and extended from the butt plate halfway to the trigger.

Actual targets and tests have proved that the best of these handmade frontier rifles could keep shots on a quarter at 100 yards, which is considerably straighter shooting than hunters can count on from 85 per cent of hunting rifles in use today.

Once word spread through the backwoods that the Lancaster riflesmiths were making accurate-shooting, small-bore rifles, settlers and pioneers came to order and remained to watch their rifles being made, Pennsylvanians got to know Virginians and Marylanders, and when they lifted their finished rifles to their shoulders and sighted down their long barrels, shooting matches were inevitable.

Beef and turkey shoots became popular, rivalry was keen, and the hunters and inland settlers learned to shoot with amazing skill. While the seaboard colonists and the British politicians were motivating the causes of the Revolution, the frontiersmen were sharpening their skill in shooting matches.

**The Rifle in the Revolution.** General Washington knew that the colonists in Pennsylvania, Virginia, Maryland, and points west were armed with Kentucky rifles and skilled in their use. He knew, too, that these bold, freedom-loving frontiersmen had lost contact with the Old World, unlike many of the seaboard colonists who were doing business with English merchants and financiers, and, since they had no interests at stake, would probably make better soldiers if a break came.

Therefore, when the British, in the spring of 1775, provoked skirmishes at Lexington, Concord, and Bunker Hill Washington influenced the Continental Congress to take a very intelligent step on June 14, 1775. Tension between the colonists and the British was increasing. The Continental Congress needed troops, and although there were plenty of men in Massachusetts, Connecticut, and New York who were eager to enlist and take up arms against the British in Boston, the resolution the Continental Congress passed on June 14, one day before George Washington was made Commander-in-Chief, stated: "Resolved: That six companies of expert riflemen be immediately raised in Pennsylvania, two in Maryland, and two in Virginia . . . and march and join the Army near Boston."

Instead of calling up men near the scene of military activity and depending on their imported European arms and smoothbore muskets, the Continental Congress called on the hunters, Indian fighters, and pioneers of the Alleghenies. Washington knew that the rifles these men used in their daily lives were superior in accuracy to the finest products of the European arms makers and vastly superior to the smoothbore muskets of the British Army. The original call for six companies from Pennsylvania resulted in enough volunteers for nine. The Southern colonies responded with equal enthusiasm, and within a month the newly organized companies were moving toward Cambridge.

Michael Cresap, a famous frontiersman, organized his company in Maryland and started north. Here is an eyewitness account of the rifle practice his men indulged in on the way:

". . . I have had the happiness of seeing Captain Michael Cresap marching at the head of a formidable company of upwards of 130 men, from the mountains and backwoods, painted like Indians, armed with tomahawks and rifles, dressed in hunting shirts and moccasins, and though some of them had traveled near 800 miles, from the banks of the Ohio, they seemed to walk light and easy, and not with less spirit than at the first hour of their march. Health and vigor, after what they had undergone, declared them to be intimate with hardship, and familiar with danger. . . .

"Yesterday the company were supplied with a small quantity of powder from the magazine, which wanted airing, and was not in good order for rifles; in the evening, however, they were drawn out to show the gentlemen of the Town their dexterity of shooting. A clapboard, with a mark the size of a dollar, was put up; they began to fire offhand, and the bystanders were surprised, few shots being made that were not close to or in the paper. When they had shot for a time in this way, some lay on their backs, some on their breast or side, others ran 20 or 30 steps, and firing, appeared to be equally certain of the mark. With this performance the company were more than satisfied, when a young man took up the board in his hand, not by the end, but by the side, and holding it up, his brother walked to the distance, and very coolly shot into the white; laying down his rifle, he took the board, and holding it at it was held before, the second brother shot as the former had done. By this exercise, I was more astonished than pleased. But will you believe me when I tell you that one of the men took the board, and placing it between his legs, stood with his back to the tree while another drove the center. What would a regular army of considerable strength in the forests of America do with one thousand of these men, who want nothing to preserve their health and courage but water from the spring, with a little parched corn, with what they can easily procure in hunting; and who, wrapped in their blankets, in the damp of night, would choose the shade of a tree for their covering, and the earth for their bed?"

It did not take long for word to cross the Atlantic. In August 1775, the London *Chronicle* published an excerpt from a letter from a Philadelphia printer named Bradford:

"This province has raised 1000 riflemen, the worst of whom will put a ball into a man's head at the distance of 150 or 200 yards, therefore advise your officers who shall hereafter come out to America to settle their affairs in England before their departure."

"Maryland, December 20, 1775. . . . Rifles, infinitely better than those imported, are daily made in many places in Pennsylvania, and all the gunsmiths everywhere constantly employed. In this country, my lord, the boys, as soon as they can discharge a gun, frequently exercise themselves therewith, some a-fowling and others a-hunting. The great quantities of game, the many kinds and the great privileges of killing, making the best markmen in the world, and thousands support their families principally by the same, particularly riflemen on the frontiers, whose objects are deer and turkeys. In marching through woods, 1000 of these riflemen would cut to pieces 10,000 of your best troops."

When the riflemen arrived in Cambridge, they caused considerable excitement among the Americans and casualties among the British, according to Dr. James Thatcher's diary:

"August . . . Several companies of riflemen, amounting, it is said, to more than 1400 men, have arrived here from Philadelphia and Maryland, a distance of from 500 to 700 miles. They are remarkably stout and hardy men; many of them exceeding 6 feet in height. They are dressed in white frocks, or rifle shirts, and round hats. These men are remarkable for the accuracy of their aim; striking a mark with great certainty at 200 yards distance. At a review, a company of them, while on a quick advance, fired their balls into objects of 7 inches diameter, at the distance of 250 yards. They are now stationed on our lines, and their shot have frequently proved fatal to British officers and soldiers who expose themselves to view, even at more than double the distance of common musket shot."

The following newspaper clippings covering the action around Boston give a good indication of the effectiveness of long-range sniping activities with the rifles the British referred to as "cursed twisted guns, the most fatal widow-and-orphan makers in the world."

"The express, who was sent by the Congress, is returned here from the Eastward, and says he left the Camp last Saturday; that the riflemen picked off ten men in one day, three of whom were Field-Officers, that were reconnoitering; one of them was killed at the distance of 250 yards, when only half his head was seen." (Dunlap's *Pennsylvania Packet,* Aug. 14.)

"A gentleman from the American camp says—Last Wednesday, some riflemen on Charlestown side, shot an officer of note in the ministerial service, supposed to be Major Small, or Bruce, and killed three men on board a ship at Charlestown ferry, at the distance of full half a mile." (*Pennsylvania Gazette,* Aug. 21.)

The boys got so that they would take pot shots at red targets as far as they could see them, and their eyesight was exceedingly sharp. Officialdom reacted in the customary negative way, restricting the riflemen too much. Here is General Lee's order to Colonel Thompson:

"It is a certain truth, that the enemy entertain a most fortunate apprehension of American riflemen. It is equally certain, that nothing can contribute to diminish this apprehension so infallibly as a frequent ineffectual fire. It is with some concern, therefore, that I am informed that your men have been suffered to fire at a most preposterous distance. Upon this principle I must entreat and insist that you consider it as a standing order, that not a man under your command is to fire at a greater distance than 150 yards, at the utmost; in short, that they never fire without almost a moral certainty of hitting their object." (*Correspondence of the Revolution,* ed. Sparks, XI, 501-2.)

The British decided the thing to do was to get some expert riflemen for their side, and they made a deal with certain German princes for the hire of their Hessian mercenaries, stipulating that as many as possible be *chasseurs,* i.e., sharpshooters.

Once independence was declared on July 4, 1776, and war got under way in earnest, the superiority of the Kentucky rifle and American riflemen decided important engagements, which decided important campaigns, which made possible the final success at Yorktown.

**Characteristics.** Once the Kentucky rifle had achieved its characteristic form—long, slender fore stock, usually extending to the end of the octagon barrel, short, sharply dropped stock, low, graceful trigger guard—it changed very little. However, the carving that was frequently found on some of the early rifles began to disappear in the 1770's and is seldom found on flintlock stocks made after 1780.

On the other hand, the early rifles had few metal decorations. A brass star in the cheekpiece and a small silver setting on the upper small of the stock were characteristic right from the start, but the highly decorated rifle came after the Revolution, growing in popularity as the carved stock disappeared.

Following the opening of the wilderness by Daniel Boone and others, rifle manufacturing spread to the South and West, and noticeable differences between rifles manufactured in the different areas became obvious. For example, in the later period, the Northern rifle was often highly decorated while the Southern rifles were frequently beautifully made but devoid of decoration. Some were made without patch boxes in the stocks.

The early stocks were usually made with straight butts, similar to our present-day shotgun butt plates and with only a trace of the crescent that became popular after 1800.

Several explanations for the rather steep drop of the stock have been advanced, but the most logical theory is this: The steep stock enabled the rifleman to sight his rifle with his head raised, his face and hair a safe distance from the flash and flame that spurted from the pan when the arm was fired.

The early makers almost without exception colored their stocks very dark, using a solution of soot and oil, and rubbing to a high polish. The light varnished stock came later.

The American flintlock varied in length from 51 inches to 77 inches, probably because almost every rifle was custom made to fill the needs of the individual buyer.

**Triggers.** Kentucky rifles were equipped with both plain and set triggers. Although set triggers were used on crossbows and arms made in Europe in the 1500's, most of the Kentucky rifles built before the Revolution were equipped with plain triggers. After the Revolution, nearly 40 per cent of the flintlocks made in this country were equipped with set triggers. Although the evidence is not conclusive, the fact that a flintlock is equipped with a set trigger is a fairly good indication that it was made after the Revolution.

**Trigger Guards.** The huge trigger guards of the Central European rifles were completely inadequate on the rough American frontier, and the pioneer riflesmiths were quick to replace them with low, strong, graceful iron guards.

**Sights.** When a rifle was primarily used for hunting, the sights were plain, open sights. Front and rear sights were fixed to the barrel by grooved slides which could be moved sideways. They were usually made so that the rifle shot a few inches high at 50 yards and a few inches low at 100, the ball reaching the top of its trajectory between 50 and 75 yards.

Target rifles were usually equipped with pinhead front sights and some kind of an aperture rear sight, adjustable for elevation. Some had sunshades for both front and rear sights. There is no convincing evidence that telescope sights were used on the early flintlocks. The Continental Congress did in 1776 authorize the purchase of telescopes for rifles, but this authorization probably referred to tube sights, for many of the early target rifles were equipped with tube sights, many of which extended the full length of the barrel.

## MATCH RIFLE SHOOTING

Back in 1856 Messrs. Smith and Wesson blossomed into the revolver field. Differing from their competitor, Colt, they came out with a completely self-contained metallic cartridge, the first on the American market. One Rollin White had patented the idea of boring a revolver cylinder straight through, but in the days of muzzle-loading percussion pistols, nothing could be done with it, so he sold the patent to Smith & Wesson.

About the same time, Flobert of France brought out a tiny 6-mm. rim-fire cartridge and a smoothbore salon or parlor rifle to handle it. The rim-fire priming idea was there, the primer serving as a propellant for a .236-caliber round lead ball crimped into the mouth of the stubby copper case.

From this, Smith & Wesson evolved the .22 rimfire Short cartridge, a cartridge which has been improved somewhat, but is almost identical today with the 1856 version. Instead of just a primer as a propellant, the new cartridge had a longer case contain-

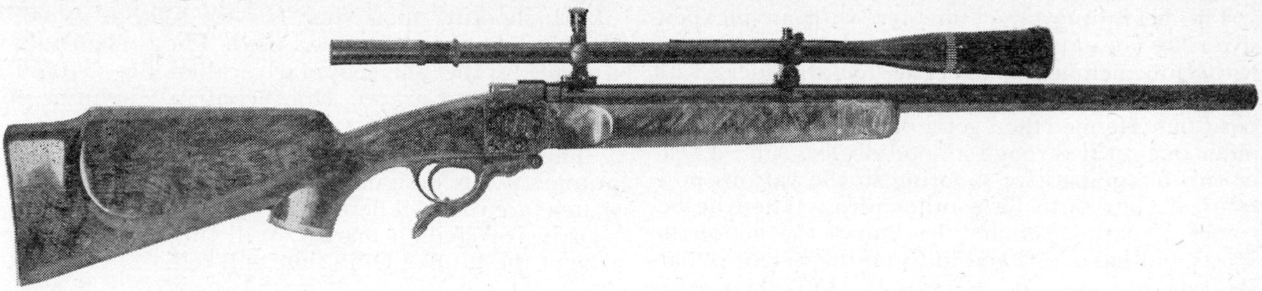

PLATE I. This is one of the fine custom-built match rifles, also used as "varmint" rifles, turned out by Mashburn. The action is an English "Farquharsen." The stock is selected crotch burl walnut. Equipped with Lyman super target spot.

ing a charge of black powder and a round-nose 29-grain bullet. This is the oldest cartridge on the American market, although the 6-mm. Flobert cap is still popular in other parts of the world.

About 1870 (exact date unknown), rifle makers developed a new cartridge—the .22 Long. This used the bullet of the .22 Short, but the case length and charge of powder were increased. The result was a bastard cartridge not popular despite its increased power.

In 1887, the Peters Cartridge Company, working with the J. Stevens Arms Company, developed another newcomer, using the .22 Long case, but changing the bullet to a heavier 40-grain number, and increasing the rate of twist from 1 turn in 26 inches to 1 turn in 16. They also introduced this in the then new King's Semi-Smokeless powder. This cartridge really proved popular, and in 1900, Peters produced the first of these with the case mouth crimped to the bullet instead of friction tight. Oddly, this new crimped load was first called the *.22 Smith & Wesson Long,* since it was designed to give best performance in their single-shot target pistols. The new name was soon dropped as confusing.

The short cartridge did not die. It was still the most popular number with indoor riflemen, and as late as 1920, special match rifles for the .22 Short were establishing range records which completely stopped the .22 Long Rifle—on indoor ranges. It was not until the now-defunct United States Cartridge Company of Lowell, Mass., brought out their famous .22 U. S. R. A. Lesmok (semi-smokeless) cartridge, that the .22 Long Rifle stepped into the field to win matches. Other companies soon developed match-grade ammunition, and today the .22 Long Rifle cartridge is standard the world over—and throughout the world is known as the "Small-bore Match Cartridge."

In the United States, there are today two types of match shooting, distinctly classified as "small bore" and "big bore." Small-bore match rifles are invariably chambered for the .22 Long Rifle rim-fire—and other cartridges are ruled out in such matches. Big-bore shooting may be anything. Generally the most popular caliber is the military cartridge for the country. In the United States, most such matches are shot with the .30 Model 1906 cartridge. In England and Canada, it is the .303 British. In Germany and many other countries, it has always been the 7.92-mm. Mauser.

There are exceptions in this. Some matches permit "any rifle." In this the shooters take their favorite calibers, some of them heavily loaded long-range numbers, and some of the shooters prefer their favorite "wildcats" (non-standard).

**Small-Bore Match Rifles.** In shooting competitive matches, styles change. Up to World War I, single-shot match rifles were the recognized type. Repeating rifles were given no serious consideration. In the early 1920's, returning soldiers demanded good bolt-action repeating target rifles, despite the fact that practically all of their shooting was "slow fire" and even with the repeaters they fed cartridges into the chambers singly.

The style trend then changed. Today, most of the rifles used in competition are bolt-action repeaters, although one still finds many of the other types.

To analyze this trend, the National Rifle Association investigated the equipment used at the 1946 National Championship Matches, held as usual at Camp Perry, Ohio. The top 38 winners were chosen for equipment analysis. Sixteen shooters were lined up for the Remington Model 37. Another 16 used the Winchester 52. Of the remaining six, five used Ballard single-shot actions, and one used a custom-built special single-shot action.

Of the 32 using the 37 and 52 rifles, 17 had special bedding jobs on the stock (carefully refitted by hand) and 15 used the guns as they came from the factory. These 38 shooters had a total of 40 match rifles with them. Only 16 were custom-made stocks. Average weight of the 40 rifles was 12.7 pounds, with a variation of from 11 to 17 pounds.

Fourteen of those shooters used custom-built barrels, with eight of these made by Erik Johnson. Six other custom barrel makers each had one representative.

One nationally known firearms expert, who has instructed and advised many a beginning rifleman—some of them today grown up and in the "hot" competitive brackets—has discouraged the beginner from buying an expensive match rifle. It is a good idea to buy any rifle you can find, preferably used and in excellent condition. Even though it is a low-priced unit, it will shoot well. The beginner learns to handle his rifle and himself.

There is another reason: Small-bore shooters are about the crankiest group one can find. They get certain ideas. Many a match rifle appears with everything except built-in radio and running water. In the 1947 National Matches one shooter had a rifle with a peculiar dent hollowed out in the stock. When asked the reason, he pointed to a wart on his cheek—the cavity fitted.

The beginning target shooter, with an inexpensive rifle, not only learns to shoot; he also associates with club members and begins to form ideas with regard to actions, trigger types, sights, and sling positions. He may then get a better rifle, trading his older one on it through a good dealer. After a year or two of competitive shooting in the various positions, he begins to form other ideas. When he becomes a mature shooter, he knows the action he wants, but has additional ideas on the weight of barrel, type of stock, and accessories. He is then ready to get what he believes to be the best.

In earlier days the Stevens, Ballard, Winchester, and English Martini actions in the single-shot field were the most popular. Today, most of the top shooters use Winchester Model 52's (introduced in 1919, redesigned in 1937) and the Remington Model 37, introduced in 1937. Yet both Remington and Winchester, as well as Savage and Stevens, turn out excellent target rifles of a lighter weight at about half the "big gun" price. The man who suggests too much in this field is, to be colloquial, "sticking his neck out."

**Big-Bore Match Rifles.** Since most of the big National Matches are more or less fired on military ranges, running through the various shooting positions and at 200, 300, 500 600, 800, and 1000 yards, the standard rifle is usually the service or military rifle of the country in which those matches are shot. In the United States, the Model 1903 Springfield has been "it" for more than a quarter-century.

The Springfield is a bolt-action magazine repeater. Many of the matches, to prevent undue handicap through the use of special equipment, specify "service rifle, as issued." This means no heavy barrels, no heavy stocks, no special sights. In prewar days, the Springfield Armory always produced a batch of special rifles called "National Match" which differed from standard guns only in fancy-quality barrels, actions, and sights, with most of the parts hand fitted and the final gun tested to prove its superior accuracy.

The Model 1903 Springfield is probably the most "rebuilt" rifle in the country. Countless thousands have been custom-altered to sporter; others have been doctored up into special match rifles and "bull guns." A bull gun means a very heavy barrel—and a heavy barrel means a matching stock and accessories. These are the guns that were popular in the "any rifle" matches. Then Winchester came along with their Model 54, superseded by their Model 70 action, first as a sporter and later with various match or target stocks, barrels, and sights. Since the Model 1917 American Enfield action was also widely used on custom-built match rifles, and since Remington built many during 1917-18, it was only natural for them to enter the new field with their Model 30, first as a sporter, and later in target grades. The two guns are today the biggest sellers in the field. But the custom guns are being built for match shooting on the Springfield Model 1917, Winchester 70, Remington 30, and foreign Mauser actions.

Since most match shooting calls for certain rapid-fire stages, it is well to recall that this necessitates bolt-action types. Hence the above actions. Yet a stickler is before the house at present. In National Match shooting specifying "service rifle, as issued" the Model 1903 always was used. The present service rifle is the M1, popularly called the Garand, for John C. Garand, chief civilian engineer of Springfield Armory, its inventor.

This poses a new problem—the Garand is a semi-automatic. Its designer claims that it is capable of match accuracy. There is no competition in the sporting or civilian market. Will this be the match rifle of the future? Only time will tell.

**Match Shooting Accessories.** This category of goods applies to both small-bore and big-bore shooting. It covers both accessories and *equipment.* A competitive shooter needs additional equipment—clothes, special sights, telescopes for sighting and others for range spotting, slings, trigger shoes, special butt plates, shooting gloves, shooting glasses, sling cuffs—on and on, *ad infinitum.*

Many of these are important. Since this match game admits both sexes, it is well to recall that the female of the species asks—and gets—no quarter. There is no "handicap." She shoots the same guns, the same ammunition. She uses the same accessories. She draws a competitor number in her match registration, and her scores are handled without regard to sex—just another competitor number to be processed.

Most shooters wear trousers or slacks, roomy enough to prevent binding in any position and capable of permitting the shooter to assume that position quickly. Breeches are rarely seen. Hip fullness is a must.

Shooting jackets are usually worn—and most competitors decorate them with sewn-on insignia of their clubs and matches they have attended. They must be roomy without being bulky. Frequently the shoulders are padded and covered with a leather patch for protection against recoil and to prevent slippage of the butt of the rifle in shooting position —fatal to scores. Elbows are padded, as most firing points are hard. Here again leather usually covers the padding. Gussets allow free arm movement and stretch as the shoulders are rounded.

Eyeshades are frequently worn and may vary from "pith" helmets to long-visored caps.

Shooting glasses are a "must." These are a form of "sun glass," built larger, more fully curved, and permitting complete vision, unobstructed, at all angles. The most popular shade is Bausch & Lomb's "Ray-Ban" and American Optical's "Calobar," both in a pale green tint. These glasses protect the vision through eliminating both ends of the spectrum—the infra-red on one side and the ultra-violet on the other. Another color commonly called "kalichrome" is a light yellow. On bright days these are unsatisfactory for many people, but they sharpen the vision under dull or hazy conditions.

Another, and equally important, use for shooting glasses is the eye protection they offer in case of accidents. In any gun the danger of pierced or punctured primers or ruptured shells can occur. At such times a small portion of the gas under high pressure can escape backward through the action. With the naked eye such an accident can cause—and has caused—loss of vision. Any well-designed shooting glass gives complete eye protection.

No successful small-bore or big-bore match shooter would enter competition—or even serious practice—without his ever-present spotting scope. This unit, mounted on a low stand or tripod beside him on the firing line, serves as an observation unit and weather recorder. With it the shooter spots the exact position of his bullet holes in the black bull's-eye at 100 yards; he may then correct his sights. By a study of waving blades of grass on the range, the drifting heat waves or mirage, he can analyze shooting conditions and make the necessary corrections in sights or holding. Without his scope, shooting is more or less luck.

The better of these range spotting scopes are of the prismatic variety, with about 20-power magnification the most popular. Lower-priced instruments are of the simple draw-tube telescope design.

Target telescope sights are generally used, since many matches permit them. Telescope sights are never used in competition with "iron" sights. Such sights are usually detachable. The most popular power is 10, although target telescopes in 6, 8, 12, 12½, 14, 15, and 20-power are found. The higher magnifications are used chiefly for indoor shooting.

Almost every competitive shooter has a "kit" or trunk to hold all of his accessories when not in use. These are generally long trunk-type units with a carrying handle, with space for the spotting scope, cleaning equipment, small tools, ammunition, and all other equipment.

Shooting gloves and sling cuffs are optional, but are widely used. A "glove" is usually a fingerless, heavily-padded mitten used on the left hand to protect the forearm against the pressure of a tight sling. A "cuff" is usually of very stiff leather, fitting over the upper left arm, for similar protection.

Match shooting is a serious business. At many of the bigger matches, various accessory makers frequently have sales booths. They are always well attended. Shooters buy everything that looks good—and useful—to them.

Here is a list of custom rifle makers specializing in match rifles:

Custom Barrel Makers

Joe Pfeifer, 7837 Sancola, Roscoe 3, Calif.
Johnson Automatics, Inc., Providence 1, R. I.
Paul Clark, 481 Finley, Dubuque, Iowa.
Bennett Gun Works, 517 Delaware Ave., Delmar, N. Y.
G. R. Douglas, Route 3, Box 297A, Nitro, W. Va.
O. H. Elliott, Williamsburg, Mich.
La Crosse Gun Shop, 1932 Loomis St., La Crosse, Wis.
Eric Johnson, New Haven, Conn.
C. R. Pederson & Son, Ludington, Mich.
L. E. Wilson, Cashmere, Wash.
Griffin & Howe, Inc., 202 East 44th St., New York 17, N. Y.
Roy Cradle, 205 W. Islay, Santa Barbara, Calif.
J. R. Buhmiller, Eureka, Montana.
James D. Adair, Route 1, Box 161, Roseburg, Ore.
The Gun Rack, Menlo Park, Calif.
Kenneth L. Hopper, Box A, Eureka, Mont.
I. O. Stone Co., 23540 West Eleven-Mile Road, Route 3, Birmingham, Mich.
Niedner Rifle Corp., Dowagiac, Mich.
Thurman Randle & Co., 208 N. Akard St., Dallas 1, Tex.
M. L. Smith, Route 3, Bryan, Tex.
Kellaby Co. 1103 North Bristol St., Santa Ana, Calif.
Kess Arms Co., 1004 West Center St., Milwaukee, Wis.
Winchester Repeating Arms Co., New Haven, Conn.
Remington Arms Company, Ilion, N. Y.

Rifle Makers

Kess Arms Co., 1004 West Center St., Milwaukee 6, Wis.
Parker-Whelen Co., Inc., 827 14th St., Washington 5, D. C.
Weatherby's Custom Sporting Goods, 8823 Long Beach Blvd., South Gate, Calif.
Gartman Custom Gunworks, 12 Richfield Ave., Cranston 10, R. I.
Brown & Edgar, 10320 Stagg St., Roscoe 3, Calif.
L. E. Wilson, Cashmere, Wash.
Kenneth Clark, Route 1, Box 95, Madera, Calif.
Thurman Randle & Co., 208 N. Akard St., Dallas 1, Tex.
I. O. Stone Co., 23540 West Eleven-Mile Rd., Route 3, Birmingham, Mich.
Frank Pugliese, 2829 So. Broad St., Trenton 10, N. J.
Griffin & Howe, Inc., 202 E. 44th St., New York 17, N. Y.
C. R. Pederson & Son, Ludington, Mich.
Al Biesen, La Crosse Gun Shop, 1932 Loomis St., La Crosse, Wis.
Johnson Automatics, Inc., Providence 1, R. I.
Paul Mack, 50945 Ann Arbor Rd., Plymouth, Mich.
Columbia Gun Co., N2220 Division St., Spokane 13, Wash.
Paul Clark, 481 Finley, Dubuque, Iowa.
Robert U. Milhoan, Elizabeth, W. Va.

# MUZZLE-LOADER SHOOTING

Even though obsolete for three-quarters of a century, the muzzle-loading rifle of the early frontiers still has a tremendous romantic appeal to nearly all gun-loving Americans. Convincing proof is the fact that there are today many thousands of the old flintlock and percussion rifles in active use on the target ranges and hunting fields of this country. Although the use of these weapons had never really died out completely, yet their proper management and capabilities were known to relatively few persons. Among these were the thinning ranks of gunsmiths, who had worked on the muzzle-loaders in their youth—men who still possessed the tools and ability to restore a rusty rifle bore to something approaching its original accuracy. They also knew the secret of correct loading for this style of firearm—the charge of powder required for a given caliber, the thickness of materials used for patching the pure lead ball, and all the important details that were necessary to get the ultimate performance from the weapons up to the limit of its effective range.

The revival of target matches for these muzzle-loading rifles in Ohio and Indiana, some 20 years ago, aroused such a degree of interest and enthusiasm among those who were at first merely curious, that within a few years many hundreds of persons were attending these colorful events. It seems fortunate that this revival came when it did, for a few years later might have been too late. The gunsmiths were without exception very old men, and the knowledge which they possessed would almost certainly have died with them. Those who today enjoy the sport of competitive shooting with muzzle-loading rifles should be everlastingly grateful to such men as E. M. Farris, Oscar Seth, Walter M. Cline, "Boss" Johnston, C. R. Ramsey, and others who pioneered the modern sport of shooting the old rifles.

This section has been written to enable the man who knows little or nothing about these weapons to recondition and safely use one which he may already own, or may acquire. The selection of necessary equipment for loading and shooting the rifle will be discussed in detail. Powder, patching material, casting of lead balls, cleaning of the rifle bores, sights, and the accuracy of the round ball will be treated as completely as space permits.

**Types.** Until the perfection of breech-loading and the metallic cartridge, firearms were loaded from the muzzle end, and the projectile was seated onto the charge of powder by means of a loading rod, or ramrod, as it was commonly called. Some breech-loading flintlock and percussion rifles were made long before the development of the metallic cartridge, but because of the excessive leakage of powder gases at the loading mechanism, rapid fouling soon rendered these arms temporarily unserviceable. Consequently, they never achieved popularity for military or sporting purposes.

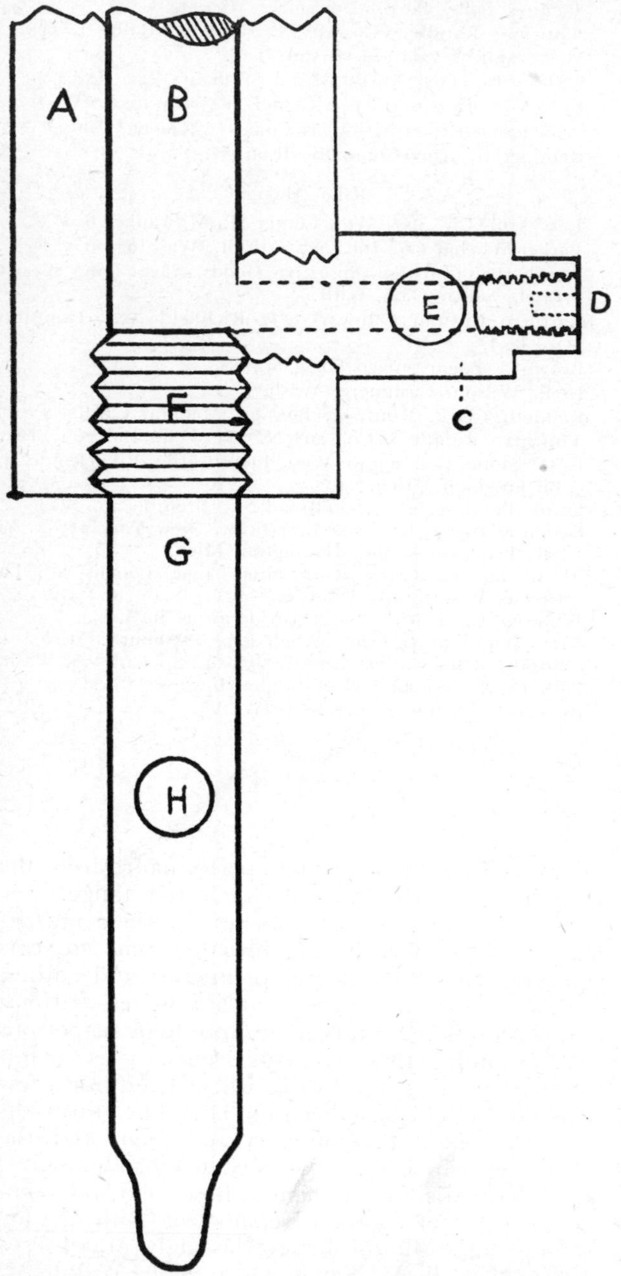


Plate I. Breech Plug and Tang Detail: (*A*) Barrel. (*B*) Bore. (*C*) Cylinder. (*D*) Takeout screw. (*E*) Nipple. (*F*) Breech plug. (*G*) Tang. (*H*) Screw hole.

The rifled musket with which the infantry of both the North and South were armed in the Civil War was muzzle-loading, but at the end of the war the breech-loader was adopted by the Northern Army. Production of repeating rifles soon rendered the muzzle-loader obsolete, and it is doubtful if many

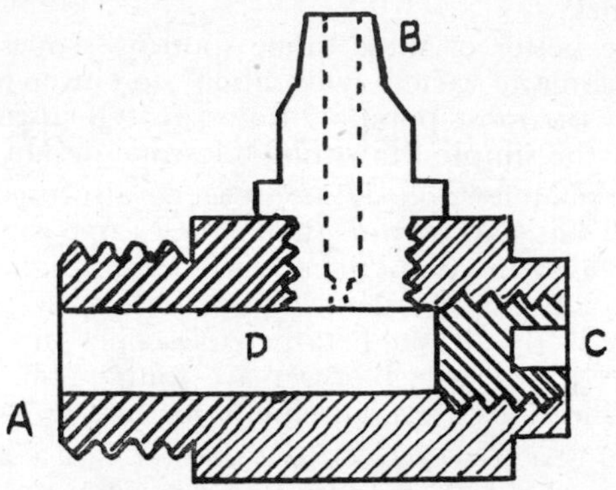


Plate II. Cylinder Detail: (*A*) Cylinder. (*B*) Nipple. (*C*) Hollow-head set screw. (*D*) Powder passage.

were produced from then on, except in the backwoods areas of the nation.

The American flintlock rifle was the product of eastern Pennsylvania gunsmiths. From the European rifle of large bore was developed a weapon which was particularly suited to the needs of the pioneer frontiersman. Smaller in caliber, longer in barrel, graceful in design, it filled the demand for a practical arm.

It might be mentioned that in those early days the ball was forced into the barrel "unpatched," being deformed in loading so that the lead filled the grooves sufficiently to give the ball a spinning motion when fired. Fouling and leading of the bore must have been extremely annoying under these circumstances. Then someone, by accident or a brilliant stroke of reasoning, discovered that a ball of bore diameter or even slightly less than bore size could be loaded into the barrel encased in a greased or saliva-moistened cloth patch. This method gave far less fouling, no leading of the bore whatever, and speeded up the loading process immensely. Flintlocks were made in this country for about 100 years, being supplanted by the percussion system about 1825. In the years following, many flintlock rifles were converted to use the percussion cap.

Original, unaltered flintlock rifles are becoming increasingly rare, and their great value has placed most of them in private collections or museums.

Most of the muzzle-loaders available today are percussion locks. These are of many different types, depending on the purpose for which they were made, or the locality and period of their manufacture. Most common through the eastern and southern states are the full-stock hunting rifles, with barrels averaging about 40 inches in length, weight close to nine pounds, and of an average caliber of .42. Through the Middle West the hunting rifles were generally half-stock, of somewhat shorter barrel length and smaller caliber. On the western plains a very sturdy weapon was developed, of large caliber —above .50—generally half-stock, and built to withstand the rough usage of the plainsman. The most famous maker of these rifles was Hawken of St. Louis.

Though single-barrel rifles were most common, double-barrel flintlock and percussion rifles were by no means rare. In nearly all of the earlier specimens the over-under barrels revolved so that one lock fired both barrels. During the percussion period many of these guns were made, the upper barrel rifled, the lower barrel smooth bored for shot. Two locks were often fitted to these guns, the left hammer generally having an extension welded to its face to reach the nipple on the lower barrel.

In some sections of the country especially heavy rifles were made for target shooting from a rest, either prone with the muzzle supported on some object, or from a low bench or table. These rifles weighed, on an average, about 20 pounds, were generally from .45 to .55 caliber, and were made in both the flintlock and percussion periods. The customary ranges at which they were fired were 60 and 100 yards. These rifles attained the greatest accuracy possible with patched round balls. It might be timely to mention here that these heavy bench-rest rifles are most widely used in today's muzzle-loader contests, since the majority of events are fired from rest. It is apparent, however, that they are far too heavy for offhand shooting, where the lighter hunting type is the rifle used.

Since the supply of these heavy rifles was not sufficient to provide all the modern muzzle-loader devotees with a practical bench-rest rifle, quite a number have been made by the shooters themselves in recent years. Others have been produced in the gunshops of men who have since died or been forced by age to retire. D. C. Addicks of Rome, Georgia, who died in 1941, made in 1940 a 22-pound barrel, 45 inches in length, of .53 caliber. The rate of pitch in the rifling is one turn in 52 inches. There are eight grooves, the lands and grooves being of equal width. The complete rifle weighs 26½ pounds, and is still as accurate as when it was made in 1940. Many thousands of shots have been fired from it, with no loss of superior performance.

**Renovation.** Before such a rifle is fired, it should be thoroughly checked for safety of operation. The first step in this respect is to make certain that screw joints are strong and tight. The bores of muzzle-loaders are closed at the breech end with a heavy screw, which, in flintlocks and most percussion round-ball rifles, is forged in one piece with the tang. In some cases this part will have become loose and worn, but in most instances it will be found amply safe. If it should be judged unsafe by a gunsmith, a new one will be required.

Practically all percussion round-ball rifles are fitted with a cylinder (or drum). This is a hollow plug which screws into the barrel, just forward of the breech plug. Into this cylinder is fitted the nipple. It is often found advisable to have the original cylinder replaced with a new one, as in most cases the old one will be found to have suffered a great deal of abuse and damage through the years. Incidentally, the cylinder should always be removed from a barrel first, as it generally fits tightly against the breech plug at its forward part. Heat will often be found necessary to loosen the band of rust in these screw joints, but be certain that there is not an old load in the barrel before resorting to this method.

In fitting a new cylinder, it is sometimes necessary to drill out the old threads in the barrel wall and

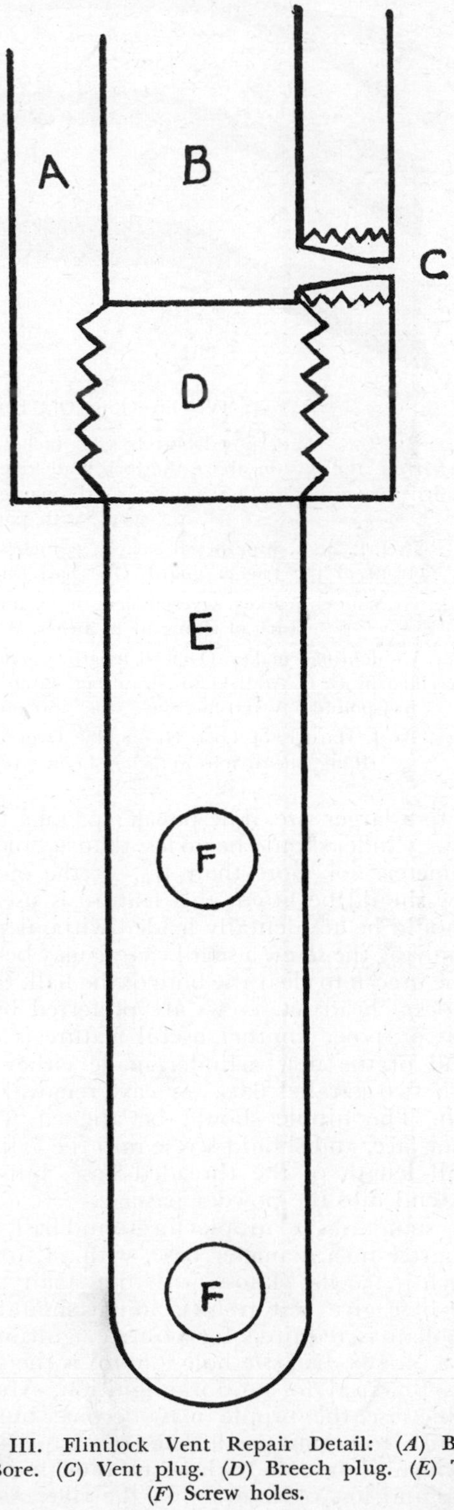


PLATE III. Flintlock Vent Repair Detail: (*A*) Barrel. (*B*) Bore. (*C*) Vent plug. (*D*) Breech plug. (*E*) Tang. (*F*) Screw holes.

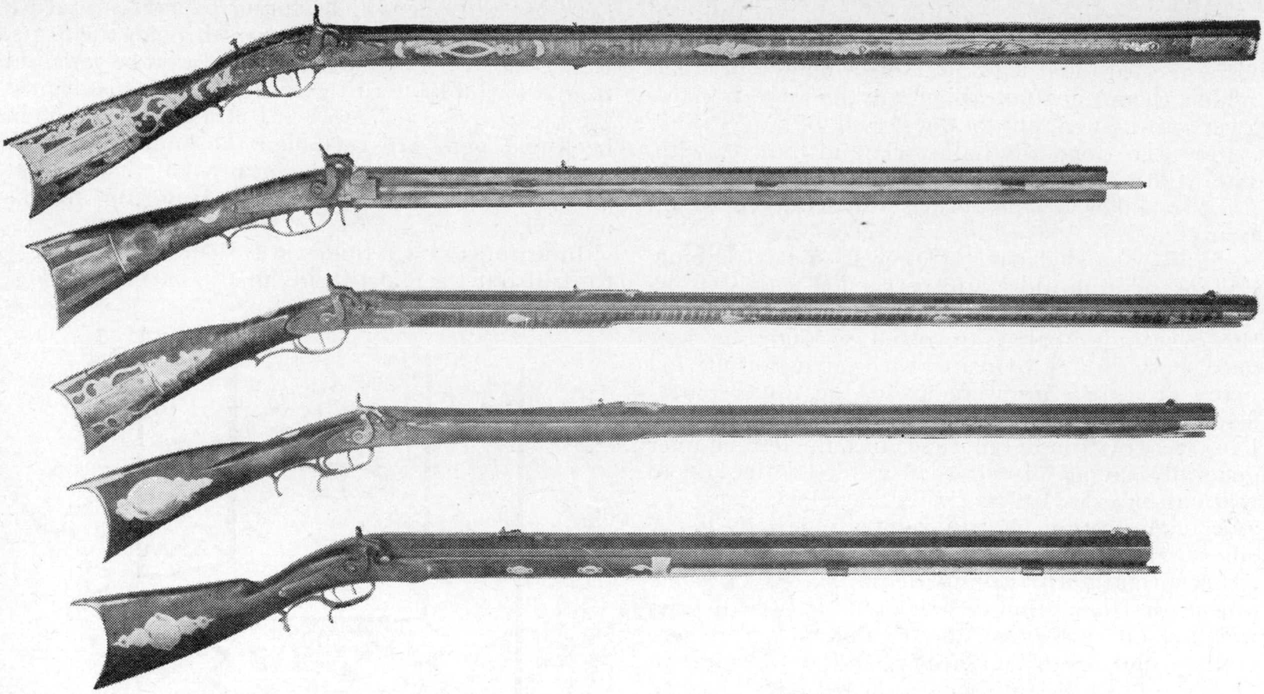

PLATE IV. Five Fine Old Pennsylvania Percussion Rifles. From top to bottom:

(1) By "C.D." Superposed barrels, 38½ inches in length. Over-all length, 54 inches. Weight, 11 pounds. One lock fires both barrels; the button above the lock plate releases a catch; the barrels then must be turned manually. Both barrels are rifled, .42 caliber, with 8 grooves. Curly maple stock, with full-length barrel panels. Exceptionally fine silver inlay work, with patch box and other fittings of brass.

(2) By I. L. Beck. Superposed barrels, 33 inches in length. Over-all length, 48½ inches. The barrel catch is located in front of the trigger guard. One barrel rifled, the other smooth. Weight, 10¾ pounds. Caliber .44.

(3) By Samuel Walkey. Over-all length, 55 inches, Barrel length, 40 inches. Has been relined to .37 caliber, with one turn of rifling in 42 inches. Weight, 9¾ pounds. Full-length stock of curly maple.

(4) Unidentified maker. Over-all length, 53 inches. Barrel length, 37 inches. Originally a .36-caliber rifle, but rebored and rerifled by D. C. Addicks to .45 caliber. Pitch of rifling, 1 turn in 42 inches. Eight grooves of .006 inch depth. Weight, 9¼ pounds. A very accurate rifle, and one used in offhand shooting at ranges of from 25 to 100 yards.

(5) By J. Harder, of Lock Haven, Pa. Over-all length, 51½ inches. Barrel length, 35¾ inches. Caliber .51. Pitch of rifling, one turn in 50 inches. Eight grooves of .007 inch depth. Weight, 16½ pounds. A walnut stock.

re-tap to a larger size. The powder passage through the new cylinder should be no less than 5/32 of an inch in diameter, nor more than 3/16. At the outer end a screw should be fitted; this feature is useful if a ball should be accidentally loaded without powder. By removing the screw a small charge may be poured into the breech to clear the bore of the ball. Quarter-inch socket head set screws are preferred by many for this purpose. Another useful feature is to have the end of the new cylinder made either square or with two parallel flats, for easy removal with a wrench. The nipple should be aligned with the hammer face, and should screw into the cylinder to the full length of the threaded base, but should not extend into the powder passage.

The standard-size nipple for round-ball rifles is one-quarter inch diameter base, with 28 threads to the inch (.250-28). Those with the small opening at the base give best results, and it should be no larger than is required for positive ignition. Generally a No. 68 drill-size hole (.0310) is the smallest that is practical for uniform ignition. After considerable use the nipple may become burnt out sufficiently to permit gas leakage and cap fragmenting, which is bound to lead to flinching by the shooter and loss of accuracy in the rifle. A pair of shooting glasses should be worn while firing these rifles if the shooter does not wear ordinary spectacles. Most of the unpleasant experiences with muzzle-loaders are caused by excessive gas leakage from worn-out nipples.

The vents in flintlock rifles are often enlarged by rust and erosion, with consequent loss of efficiency and performance. An effective method of correcting this fault is to drill out and tap the vent to 3/16 inch. A piece of tool steel is then threaded, and a cone-shaped recess cut into the end to a depth less 1/16 inch the thickness of the barrel wall. The threaded portion is then screwed into the barrel and cut flush with the outside. The plug is then centered, and drilled with a No. 53 drill. This new vent will give the fastest possible ignition, with gas leakage reduced to the minimum.

Rifle locks should be in first-class working order, and repairs should be made where necessary. The mainspring should be of such strength that a pull of from 6 to 8 pounds is required on the hammer spur to begin moving the hammer face from the nipple. A weak mainspring cannot be expected to give uniform ignition in the percussion-cap system, or in a flintlock to throw a generous shower of sparks.

The double-set triggers found on nearly all flintlock and percussion rifles may need some attention to make them safe and reliable. Adjustment of pull is regulated by means of the small screw located between the triggers on the outside of the trigger plate; if this is missing, a new one should be made.

The bore of the rifle is sometimes found in perfect shooting condition, although this is rare. Nearly always it will need some attention to be restored to its original accuracy. In some barrels all that is necessary is to lap out the bore with a lead plug coated with fine abrasive such as valve-grinding compound. This method will be satisfactory only in barrels that have not been pitted deeply through rust and neglect. Generally, one of three methods of restoring will be found necessary: (1) Recutting, commonly called "freshing-out"; (2) reboring and rerifling; or (3) relining.

In "freshing-out" an old barrel, the original rifling serves as a guide for the cutting tool, and the grooves and lands are cut down to a uniformly clean surface from the muzzle to the breech. Years ago, this "freshing-out" was believed necessary for continued accuracy, and before an important match it was common to "sharpen up" the lands by a few passes of the cutting tool.

In the second method, all trace of the original rifling is removed by boring to a larger size, and new grooves are cut in the barrel. Another barrel may be used as a guide, or the gunsmith may use an indexed rifling machine for the purpose. This method of barrel rejuvenation is preferable to "freshing-out," but is possible only in barrels where the caliber is sufficiently small to warrant the enlargement of the bore in the process of boring and rifling. In some specimens the bores have been recut and enlarged so greatly beyond their original size that only the third method, relining, is advisable.

In relining, the barrel is bored out to the size of the steel tubing to be used, which is soldered in place and then rifled. There are many relined muzzle-loaders in use, and they are as accurate as any others.

The replacing of breech-plugs and cylinders is a job that a good machinist can usually be trusted to do with confidence, but the barrel work lies in the

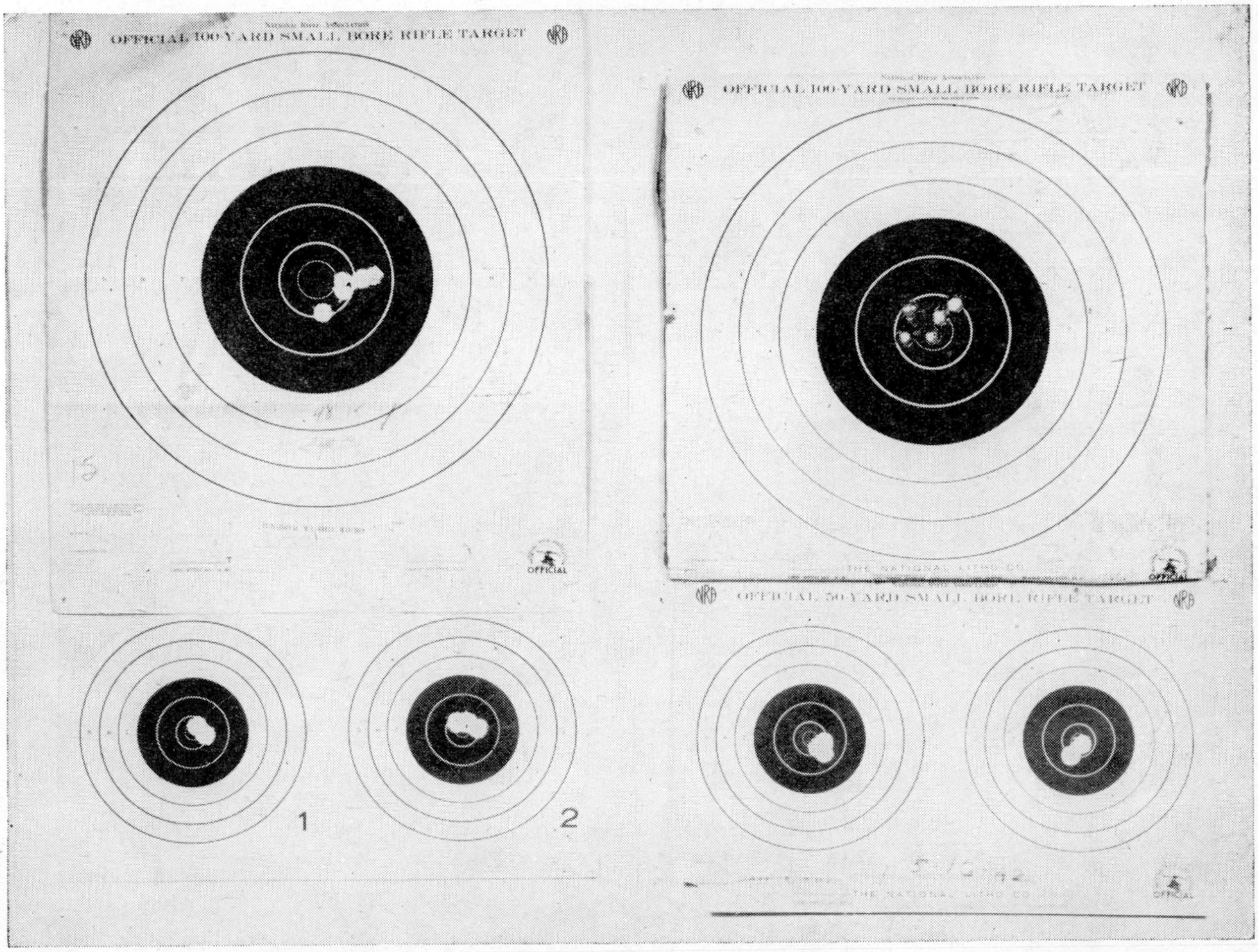


PLATE V. Those who doubt the accuracy of the old muzzle-loader may be convinced of their mistake by the four targets shown.

Upper left: Range 100 yards, open sights, score 48 out of 50. (Fired with the Addicks rifle shown in Plate XIII.)
Upper right: Range 100 yards, peep sights, score 50 out of 50. (Fired with the same rifle.)
Lower left: Range 50 yards, open sights. (Fired with the .53-caliber flintlock shown in Plate XIII.)
Lower right: Range 50 yards, open sights, score 49 out of 50. (Fired with the Addicks rifle.)

experience and skill of the gunsmith. There are today a few of these old-time riflesmiths who are still doing this work.

Good, sound muzzle-loading rifles in perfect shooting order are offered for sale quite often in *Muzzle-Blasts,* the official magazine of the National Muzzle-Loading Rifle Association. This organization numbers about 6000 members; its headquarters are at Portsmouth, Ohio, where the revival of the modern muzzle-gun movement was begun. E. M. Farris, who as former secretary of the Association guided it through many years of steady growth, now runs one of the most up-to-date supply houses for muzzle-loader equipment in the country. Powder, caps, ramrods, nipples, cylinders, powder measures, pouring spouts for powder cans, molds, hammers, locks, flints, and other articles are available from him. His business address is Farris & Son, Portsmouth, Ohio.

**Bullet Molds.** If a barrel has been recut or relined by a gunsmith, he has probably made a mold of the proper size. If not, the bore must be accurately measured so that a mold may be made to order, or else bought to the nearest dimensions. The Lyman Company manufactures round-ball molds from .244 to .760. To determine the bore size of a barrel, remove the cylinder and breech-plug, and then run an oiled patch through the bore. Upset a lead slug in the breech end so that it is a tight fit. Push through to the muzzle, and then measure across the

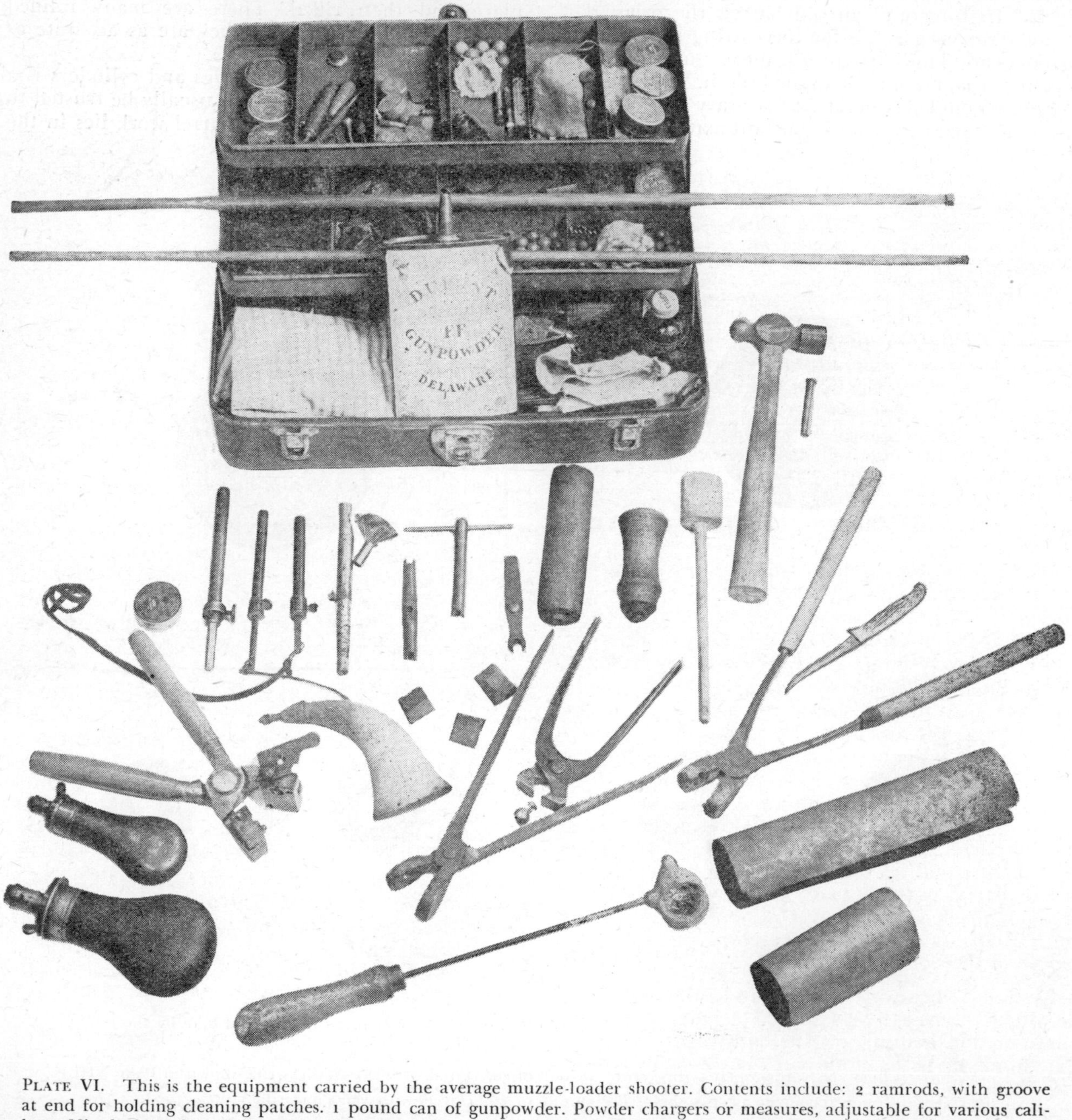


PLATE VI. This is the equipment carried by the average muzzle-loader shooter. Contents include: 2 ramrods, with groove at end for holding cleaning patches. 1 pound can of gunpowder. Powder chargers or measures, adjustable for various calibers. Nipple wrenches. Ball seaters. Straight starter. Molds, pincers, priming horn, flints, pouring ladle, sight shades, and powder flasks.

diameter of the slug on the land marks with calipers. This will give the bore diameter. If the rifle is to be used for target shooting, a mold .001 to .002 larger than bore diameter will be required, as very tight-fitting balls are necessary for the finest accuracy. If the rifle is to be used for hunting and "plinking" purposes where target accuracy is not essential, the mold should be of exactly bore diameter. The difference is that in target work the cloth patch is lubricated with saliva, which softens the fibers of the material so that no damage occurs to the patch in loading. With a hunting rifle, where the patch is commonly lubricated with tallow, vaseline, or sperm oil, the ball must not be oversize because of the difficulty of loading when the patches have been made stiff by cold. Also, a tight ball cannot be loaded as rapidly as one of bore size, and there is less danger of a broken ramrod with the smaller ball.

The Lyman round-ball molds are very accurately made, with heavy blocks, a sprue cutter, and comfortable handles. They are very popular among muzzle-loader riflemen. However, any mold that is cherried out true, of heavy construction to hold heat in casting, may be depended on to produce good balls. If the mold is not equipped with a sprue cutter, this function must be performed after the balls have cooled. A pair of pincers ground flat on top of the jaws will make a clean cut nearly as well as a sprue cutter.

Additional equipment for casting balls should consist of a pouring ladle with a spout, a melting pot, and a source of contant heat to keep the molten lead at an even temperature. A gasoline plumbers' furnace may be satisfactorily used for this purpose.

The lead used should *not* contain tin or antimony, but should be as pure as possible. The beginner may experience some difficulty in using molds with heavy blocks and small pouring holes, but if he knows that pre-heating the mold will help a great deal, he will save himself much time and loss of patience.

It might be well to discuss here the barrel of the round-ball rifle, both the target and hunting types. In length they may vary from 36 to 48 inches. The caliber of the hunting rifle will seldom be over .45, while the heavy target rifles are generally from .45 to .55. Pitch of rifling may vary in different barrels, from one turn in 40 inches to one turn in 72 inches. The average pitch is about 52 inches. The number of grooves may be anywhere from five to eight, the latter being the average. Best accuracy seems to be in barrels in which the lands and grooves are nearly equal in width. The depth of grooves may be .006 in one barrel, and .010 in another, and both guns will shoot equally well. Most barrels are cut somewhere between these two extremes. No choke or taper is needed in a barrel designed for patched round balls; it should be a true cylinder the entire length of the bore.

**Patches.** The bore of a round-ball rifle must be slightly beveled or crowned at the muzzle, to facilitate the loading of the tightly patched ball. The function of the cloth patch is primarily to provide a gas check for the ball. Since the ball is but slightly over bore diameter, it is imperative that the patch fill into the grooves to create a gas-tight seal, and also be compressed into the soft lead ball to grip it securely in its passage out through the barrel. Accuracy is impossible if for any reason the patch is torn or mutilated in loading or firing.

PLATE VII. Pouring the powder into a Demport adjustable measure. The funnel is then placed in the bore and the measure tilted to a vertical position.

A number of conditions may cause torn or burned patches. Using a ball too large for the bore, even though the muzzle is properly beveled to a 45° angle, will crowd the patch so tight that the fibers of the cloth will be sheared on the lands at the muzzle. With the proper size ball, too-thick patching could cause the same trouble. Too-thin material might not have sufficient strength, and might also tear in loading. Using a ball too small for the bore even though loaded in a thick patch might cause gas leakage through the grooves. A rough, pitted barrel may abrade the material through to the lead surface of the ball in seating. Grooves cut too deep (over .010) may be the fault.

A condition exists in some old barrels at the breech called "breech-burn." This is a noticeable enlargement of the powder chamber and the bore just ahead of it, due to the corrosive action of the percussion caps used in the old days, improper care in cleaning, and leaving the rifle loaded over periods of time. This enlargement is very noticeable when seating the ball, and it is easily understood why the patches will be burned and torn when fired from such a barrel.

Patching cloth should be new material, washed in soap and water before using. It needs to be of a uniform thickness, and preferably of tight weave. In thickness it may vary from .007 to .017, depending on the caliber and the depth of the grooves in the barrel in which it is to be used. Shallow-grooved barrels will use the thinner patching, while the ones with deep grooves will need the thick material.

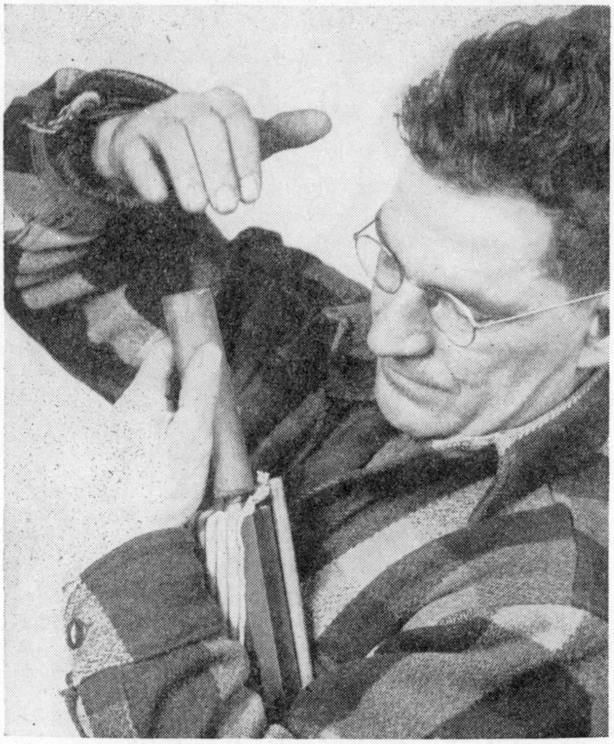

PLATE VIII. The saliva-moistened side of the patching cloth is laid over the muzzle, the ball placed over the bore (sprue cut up), and the ball seater given a sharp blow. The top of the seated ball should be at least 1/16 inch below the muzzle.

In barrels of .007 groove depth the cloth needs to be .014 in thickness for best accuracy. It is evident that there is no chance for gas leakage past a patch that is compressed to half its thickness in the grooves. Bed ticking, either striped or flowered, makes good patch material, and is widely used for the purpose. Pocket drill, muslin, linen, and even light canvas might be needed for a particular rifle. The beginner must do some testing and experimenting to learn which is best.

**Powder.** No powder should be used in muzzle-loaders except black rifle powder. To experiment with any smokeless powder in these firearms is to be risking certain injury to oneself, and destruction to the rifle. Black powder is a mechanical combination of charcoal, saltpeter, and sulphur. It is highly inflammable, and should be handled with respect and caution. It is inadvisable to smoke or strike matches near open cans or horns of the stuff, and in storing it is best to put it where, in case of fire, it would do the least damage. If children or inquisitive adults have access to black powder, it is best to keep it in a locked place. The granulation of black powder is designated by the symbol FG, which is the coarsest size, to FFFFG, which is the finest. FFG and FFFG are the sizes generally used for muzzle-loading rifles, the FFFFG size being used by some flintlock shooters for priming, for which purpose it gives very rapid ignition.

In choosing the granulation of powder for a given caliber it will be found that for most rifles up to .45, FFFG is generally used. Above .45, FFG is the accepted size. As to the weight in grains of black powder for the various calibers of round-ball rifles, best results will be obtained in accuracy if the maximum charge of powder is used. The following table was arrived at from observations conducted over a period of ten years, from the experience and conclusions of many different users of round-ball rifles:

| | | |
|---|---|---|
| .32 caliber, | 25 grains | FFFG. |
| .34 " | 30 " | FFFG. |
| .36 " | 38 " | FFFG. |
| .38 " | 40 " | FFFG. |
| .40 " | 45 " | FFFG. |
| .42 " | 50 " | FFFG. |
| .44 " | 60 " | FFFG. |
| .46 " | 68 " | FFG. |
| .48 " | 80 " | FFG. |
| .50 " | 90 " | FFG. |
| .52 " | 100 " | FFG. |
| .54 " | 115 " | FFG. |
| .56 " | 125 " | FFG. |

These charges are for rifles loaded only with round ball. The use of long, conical bullets in these rifles will create heavy pressure beyond the safety limits of iron barrels.

If your rifle does not shoot as accurately as you think it should, vary the powder charge as much as five grains either way. This may discover the precise powder charge best suited to your rifle.

The three best-known makes of black powder available at the present are DuPont, Hercules, and Kings. It is packed in one-pound cans, 6¼-pound kegs, and 25-pound kegs. It may be shipped only by freight, and the rates for one pound and 100 pounds are the same.

Percussion caps are manufactured in both rifle and musket sizes, the No. 11 size being the accepted standard for rifles. Percussion caps are not mailable, but must be shipped by express.

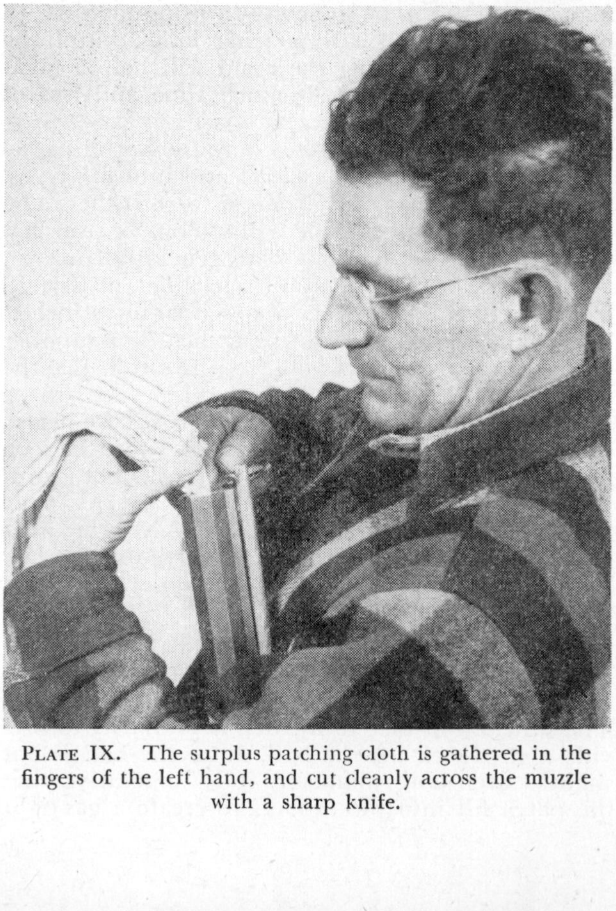

PLATE IX. The surplus patching cloth is gathered in the fingers of the left hand, and cut cleanly across the muzzle with a sharp knife.

PLATE X. The straight starter is used to seat the ball about 6 inches down the bore.

**Equipment.** Gun rods should be of straight-grain hickory, well seasoned, and of sufficient diameter that they will not easily be broken. The cleaning rod should have a groove at one end for gripping the cleaning patches. For this purpose the rod should not be more than 3/32 inch smaller than the bore, else the patch may slip off the rod. It is convenient to have these rods perhaps 6 inches or more longer than the barrel, to provide a good hand grip in cleaning. The loading rod should be concave on the end used to seat the ball.

A ball seater is needed to seat the tightly patched balls in the muzzle of the barrel when loading. This can be easily made from a piece of hickory hammer handle about 5 inches in length. At one end is a projecting stub somewhat smaller than the caliber of the bore, and about 5/32 inch long. The end of the stub is also concave.

A third loading tool is the straight starter, this being a rod of the same diameter as the ramrod, and about 6 inches in length. A wood knob is fitted at one end, and the rod end is made with a concave face. The use of these tools will be discussed later.

The traditional powder horn and hunting bag are used for carrying the hunter's ammunition, but for target purposes this equipment is more conveniently carried in metal boxes with tray compartments. A well-stocked shooting box will contain these items:

1 metal screw spout for pouring powders from 1-lb. cans.
1 sharp knife for trimming patches.
1 adjustable powder measure, with hinged funnel.
1 nipple wrench.
2 screwdrivers—one large, one small.
1 light hammer.
1 length of four-inch brass rod of 1/4-inch diameter for driving open sights to secure windage.
A quantity of ready-cut canton flannel cleaning patches.
Patching material for loading.
A generous supply of rifle balls.
Percussion caps.
Black rifle powder in 1-lb. cans.
Extra nipples, or flints if the rifle used is a flintlock.
Gun oil or grease. "Rig" is a favorite among many muzzle-loader shooters.
A pair of shooting glasses.

Fifty yards is the ideal distance at which to sight in your rifle. The standard N.R.A. small-bore 50-yard bull's-eye target should be used. It is a good idea to fasten this to a large piece of cardboard, so that if the sights are out of adjustment the balls will strike where they may be seen. You will want to do your first shooting from a rest, so if a bench rest is not available it will have to be prone with the muzzle of your rifle resting on a sand-bag, or a tightly folded coat or blanket. Make certain that the rifle rests at the same place for each shot, as this is important for best results. A spotting telescope will save many trips to and from the target.

**Loading.** Before loading the muzzle-loader you should wipe out the oil and grease from the bore. Then point the muzzle downward, and snap several caps to clear the nipple and cylinder passages. Cock the hammer before loading, but never under any circumstances place a cap on the nipple, as this is the last step in loading. The reason for cocking the hammer is to permit the air in the bore to escape ahead of the patched ball in seating. Now hold the rifle as nearly erect as possible, with the butt plate resting on the ground and the barrel held under the left arm against the body. Pour the powder from the can or horn into the measure, level full, and then empty it carefully into the bore. Wet the patching material thoroughly with saliva, over an area about the diameter of the barrel, then lay the wet

PLATE XI. The loading rod is gripped firmly with both hands and the ball seated with a uniform pressure until it reaches the powder charge.

surface over the bore. Place the ball on the patch, sprue up and central to the bore, and seat it with thumb pressure as far as it will go.

Next, place the concave stub of the ball seater on the sprue cut of the ball, and strike the seater a sharp blow with the heel of the hand or with the hammer. This will seat the ball in its patch about 1/16 inch below the muzzle. Gather the surplus patching in the left hand, and cut the patching flush with the muzzle. Now use the straight starter to force the ball to its length in the bore, after which use the loading rod to seat the ball on the powder. Do not use more force at one time than another in seating the ball, but use a uniform pressure for each operation, seating the ball firmly but gently on the powder.

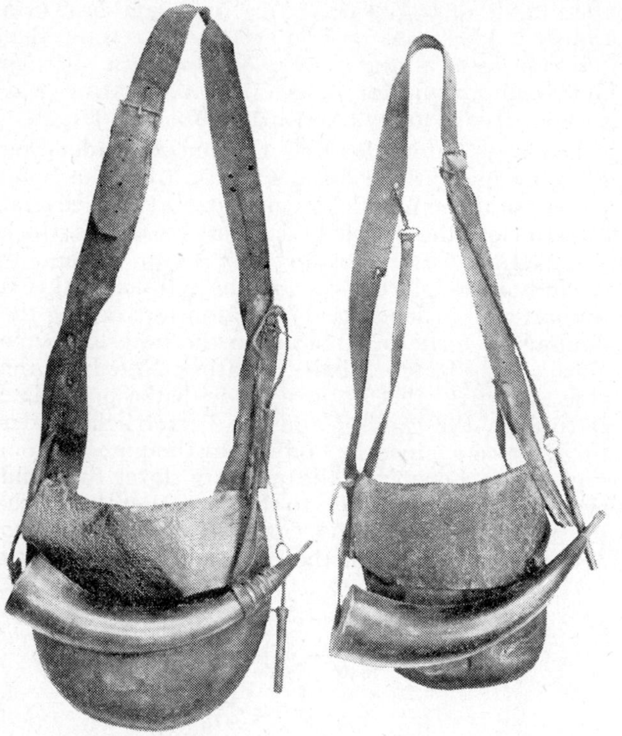

PLATE XII. Two hunting bags and powder horns from the mountains of central Pennsylvania; very old specimens.

Place the rifle in position for firing. Only then should the cap be placed on the nipple. Align the sights on the bottom of the bull's-eye and squeeze the shot off. Do not be discouraged if your shot strikes wide of the bull's-eye, as the fault may be in the sights.

Before reloading, it is a good practice to clean the bore. Despite claims made by some writers that one of these rifles could be fired for dozens or even hundreds of shots without cleaning, the experience of many users of these rifles is this: The finest accuracy can be attained only by cleaning after each shot. The bore itself does not become badly fouled, but the fouling builds up rapidly in the powder chamber at the breech, so that each ball will be seated just a bit farther up the barrel as the fouling reduces the size of the bore at the powder chamber. This will cause variation in pressure and consequent loss of accuracy.

The accepted method of cleaning after each shot is to run a water-dampened patch to the bottom of the bore, letting it remain for perhaps five or ten seconds to dissolve the powder residue. Then use a dry patch to absorb any moisture in the bore. This cleaning between shots, although a lot of extra work, pays off in better scores.

After firing a group of five shots, you should have some evidence as to the accuracy of your rifle. If the day is calm and the light constant, and you have had a background of experience with modern rifles, your shots should be grouped fairly well, say within 2 or 3 inches (measuring from the centers of the widest shots). If the group is larger, and you are certain that it is through no fault of your own, examine the fired patches. They will be found within 20 or 30 feet of the muzzle. If they are torn or gas-burned, you will never get the accuracy needed to win matches.

**Ranges and Sights.** We have here assumed that these first tests have been made with the rifle's original open sights. Open sights, as found on practically all flintlock and percussion round-ball rifles, are seated low on the barrel, the front sight being of brass, German silver, or perhaps bone. The iron rear sight has no provision for windage or elevation. These rifles were sighted so that at ranges up to 50 yards just the tip of the front sight was seen through the rear-sight notch, while at 100 yards the entire front sight would have to be taken in the notch. Beyond that range the necessary elevation was secured by aiming above the target.

A round ball loses velocity rapidly, and a rifle sighted for point of impact at 50 yards will shoot about 6 inches low at 100 yards, and about 42 inches low at 200 yards.

It is evident to the beginner that better open sights for target shooting must be fitted on his rifle if he is to compete on equal terms with the other fellow. Since open-sight shooting is very popular in present-day muzzle-loader contests, he will want his rifle equipped with the type of sights that will give him every possible advantage.

The square post front and square notch rear are in universal use by modern muzzle-gun target shooters. Globe front sights, either Lyman or Redfield, are widely used. For open-sight shooting the post inserts are just right, and if the rifle is equipped with peep sights an aperture of the desired size may be used.

Match rules of the National Muzzle-Loading Rifle Association require that a rear open sight must have a notch no narrower at the top than at any other point in the opening. These open sights may be the usual type found on hunting rifles, where windage is corrected by driving the sight to left or right in the barrel slot, or they may be constructed with screw adjustments for windage and elevation. The latter type is obviously the most practical and desirable.

The width of a front post or square-top blade is proportional to the barrel length. One good bench-rest rifle has a barrel 45 inches long. It has a Redfield globe sight, and for open-sight work the broad post of .100-inch width is used. The rear open sight, located 11 inches from the breech, has a rec-

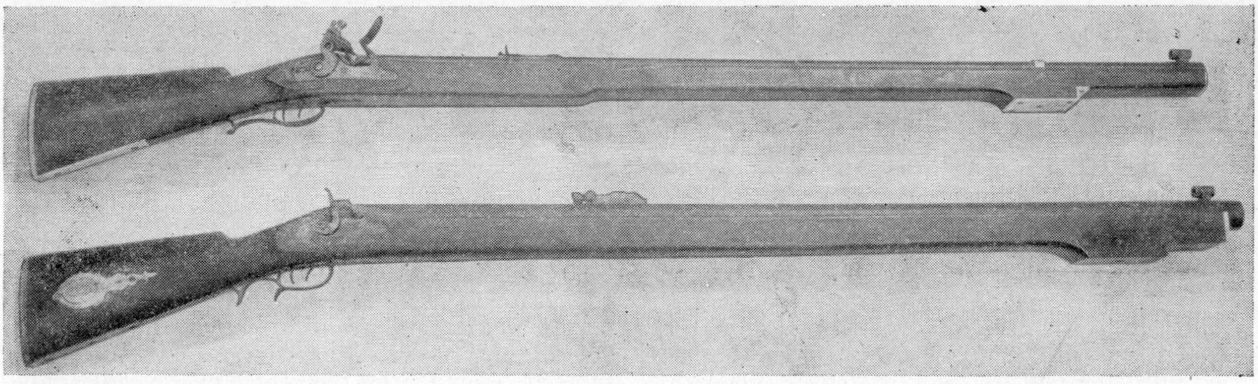

PLATE XIII. These two muzzle-loading rifles are modern.

Top: A flintlock, bench-rest rifle. Over-all length, 59 inches. Barrel length, 44 inches. Caliber .53. Eight grooves, .007 inch in depth. Grooves and lands of equal width. Pitch of rifling, one turn in 52 inches. Barrel bored and rifled by D. C. Addicks. Weight, 13½ pounds. The lock is a Tower, made in 1835, with inside frizzen spring. It is very reliable in ignition, and is well adapted to the heavy bench-rest rifle.

Bottom: A percussion bench-rest rifle. Over-all length, 60 inches. Barrel length, 45 inches. Caliber .53. Eight grooves. .007 inch in depth. Grooves and lands of equal width. Pitch of rifling, one turn in 52 inches. Barrel bored and rifled by D. C. Addicks. Weight, 26½ pounds. Both of these rifles are extremely accurate, the flintlock being fully up to the performance of the percussion lock.

tangular notch 3/64 inch in width and 1/32 inch in height. On a certain particularly good offhand Kentucky percussion rifle, the barrel is 37 inches long. The square-blade front sight is 1/16 inch wide, and 1/8 inch high. The rear open-sight notch is of identical dimensions as that on the bench-rest gun. Individual eyesight requirements will govern the dimensions of open sights best suited for various persons. This can be determined solely by trial and experiment.

The muzzle-loader shooter will find it necessary to correct his sights for windage and elevation on nearly every trip he makes to the rifle range. If the rear open sight on his weapon is fitted in a dovetail slot, the brass rod and hammer will be used to correct windage. Elevation with this sight may be secured by means of a notched wedge, preferably with a screw through its top for fine adjustment. The drift of the round ball in even a moderate wind is so pronounced that the user of these rifles must learn very early to set his sights accordingly. To make the balls strike to the right on the target, the rear sight must be moved to the right, and to make them hit to the left, the rear sight must be moved to the left. Adjustments for windage on the front sight are just the opposite to those for the rear sight.

Sight shades are no recent innovation for open-sight equipped rifles. They were developed long ago, and serve a useful purpose in shutting out sun glare and heat waves while aiming. Sometimes they are made full barrel length, but the majority are perhaps 6-inches long. Two of this type are needed, one for the front sight and one for the rear. They may be made by splitting a length of auto radiator hose, or formed from a piece of sheet metal. They need only to arch about an inch above the barrel.

Any metallic sights are permitted in many matches, and the popular makes of receiver and extension sights are often fitted to these rifles. It is obvious that only with the best available sighting equipment will the utmost accuracy be realized from any rifle, whether a hundred years old or one year old.

If the beginner has had his rifle fitted with the square-type open sights, he should notice a great improvement in his shooting. The size of his five-shot group at 50 yards should be under 2 inches and often close to one inch. It must be stressed that groups such as this will be possible only in calm weather, or in a wind that is constant in velocity. With good peep sights fitted to a target rifle, he will reduce the size of his groups, so that some will measure less than an inch. These figures are not over-optimistic; they are an accurate statement of what is possible with the round-ball rifle.

One-hundred-yard shooting is popular in the modern muzzle-loader matches, and at this distance the large calibers of from .45 to .55 will be more dependable than the smaller ones, as the bigger ball can be trusted to buck wind better. Under ideal weather conditions it is *possible* to fire five-shot scores and have all balls strike inside the 2-inch 10-ring. However, these "possible" scores are not the general rule, as any round-ball rifle that will group within 3 inches at this distance is a good one. At 200 yards a good rifle will keep its shots inside a 10-inch spread, but hardly a breath of air must be stirring, so sensitive is the round ball at this range.

This seems to be the basic fascination of shooting these old rifles—the exacting degree of judgment necessary in wind doping, and the personal element attending the proper loading and management of one's weapon. The muzzle-gun shooter realizes that he is engaged in a game where good scores are secured only by a maximum of attention to details that are not encountered in any other form of shooting.

**Cleaning.** Even with proper cleaning after each shot the percussion rifle will eventually build up an accumulation of hard fouling in the cylinder passage. This causes hang-fires, and will, in time, completely close the passage so that the percussion cap cannot ignite the powder charge. Users of these rifles should guard against such conditions by removing the cylinder after firing 100 or more shots, and clean out the fouling by immersing the cylinder in cold water for a few minutes. Water is the most effective solvent for black-powder residue. Dry the cylinder thoroughly before screwing it back in the barrel.

After each day's shooting the bore should be swabbed out with wet patches and then carefully dried until the patches come out clean. Then coat the bore liberally with a good gun grease. Also give the same attention to the lock plate, hammer, and nipple. Iron and cast-steel barrels will rust very quickly in warm, humid temperatures unless adequately protected.

**Matches.** Muzzle-loader matches have, in recent years, been given considerable publicity by nationally known magazines and newspapers, so it is possible that nearly everyone has heard or read of them at some time or other. They are common only in those sections of the country where sufficient shooters of the old rifles exist to make such events possible. In the eastern United States the larger shoots are held at Shartlesville, Pa.; Cos Cob, Conn.; and Fort Ticonderoga, N. Y. The Middle West is represented by the Canal Fulton, Marietta, Mansfield, Salem, and Dayton shoots in Ohio; in Indiana by the National Muzzle-loading Rifle Association championships at Friendship, and the state competitions at Marion. Shoots are held in other states in the Southwest, Northwest, and on the Pacific coast. Announcmeent dates of the various matches are made in the pages of *Muzzle-Blasts,* and in a later issue the scores that have been fired in the events are recorded.

Tournament programs list open-sight matches at 50 and 100 yards, peep-sight matches at the same distances, and offhand events at 30, 50, and 100 yards. Official N.R.A. small-bore targets are used, and shots are scored from the center of the bullet hole, and not the break. Because of the variety of calibers used by contestants, obviously this is the only fair manner of scoring. A contestant enters and fires any event which he desires, at any time, as there is no squadding, due to the difficulty of holding to a set schedule in case of rain. Registration and match fees correspond to those charged at small-bore tournaments, and prizes may be medals, trophies, merchandise, or cash.

Targets are hung each hour, and this gives the shooter plenty of time for his sighting and record shots. There is an atmosphere of friendly informality at these shooting matches, and everyone has a grand time.

# PRINCIPAL FOREIGN PROOF MARKS

The interest in foreign guns has been enormously increased as a result of the tens of thousands of these arms brought back by servicemen. Practically all of these guns carry certain proof marks which indicate not only that the particular piece has been tested, but also serve as a guide to the country of origin, the caliber, and the type of tests carried out. The proper understanding of a proof mark is not only interesting and instructive, but sometimes very necessary in determining the safety of both gun and shooter. Because more than 90 per cent of the guns in question are of German origin, this article has been written with special emphasis on German guns and their testing.

In most civilized countries, there are laws which require every firearm which is offered to the trade to be submitted to a proof-testing institute for the necessary tests for strength and safety. If the gun stands up under these tests, then those sections which are important for the safety of the gun—such as, for example, the action and barrel—are marked with the necessary proof or testing mark. If, however, in testing any type of irremediable damage is shown, then the principal parts are rendered useless either by sawing them up or breaking them completely. The government proof, therefore, has nothing to do with "shooting in" the rifle or determining its accuracy, but is concerned only with its safety.

For carrying out these tests, there are government institutes, which in Germany were called Testing Institutes. These institutes were found in Suhl, Zella Mehlis, Frankfurt, and Berlin. In Austria, they were located in Ferlach, Vienna, and Steyr.

The method of testing the barrels and finished weapons has been precisely formulated through an international agreement, the "Brussels Convention," of June 15, 1914. The proof marks of Germany, Austria-Hungary, Belgium, France, Italy, and Spain were recognized as being equally valid. Germany and Austria recognized the proof marks of Great Britain, although Britain does not belong to the Convention. Firearms of other countries may be sold in countries abiding by the Convention only upon condition that they be proved anew according to the requirements of the country importing them.

The first proof, for rifles or shotguns, is a proof test of the unfinished barrels which are bored smooth inside, turned on the outside, and delivered to the institute with a testing screw. Assembled barrels which are connected by soldering and have been finished to their proper size, are then given a second temporary proof. Before this test, however, they are examined at vital spots and checked for thickness of material; barrels which are thinner than the allowable minimum are returned to the manufacturer as unsuitable. For shotgun barrels in 12, 16, and 20 gauge, manufactured of ordinary good steel, the thickness of the barrel wall at the end of the chamber, is measured, according to the length of the cartridge case in question, whether it be 2¼", 3", or 3½" from the face of the breech; minimum thickness here has been determined upon at 2.3 mm.; where special steel has been used, a diminution of only .2 mm. is permitted. The barrel wall of calibers .24 and .28 with their higher pressure may not be less than 2.4 mm. Likewise the minimum outside measurements of the shotgun barrels is exactly determined. They are 24.9 mm. in 12 gauge, 23.2 mm. in 16 gauge, 22 mm. in 20 gauge, 21.3 mm. in 24 gauge, 20.4 mm. in 28 gauge. Examination of the thickness of the wall are continued into the front third of the barrels, where there must be an evenly distributed thickness of at least .6 mm.

The final test is made in shotguns and rifles when the finished barrel has been fitted into the action or is completely finished. In this test, shotgun barrels which are designed only for black powder must stand a certain gas pressure, and those designed for smokeless powder in 12, 16, or 20 gauge must withstand greater pressures. In order that the front section of the barrel may stand the required pressures, all guns tested for smokeless powder are likewise given a black-powder proof with a heavy load of shot, which at a distance of 170 mm. from the face of the breech still develops a certain pressure. In Austria, the smokeless-powder test has been declared a government requirement. In Germany as well as in Austria, Rottweil Testing Powder for shotguns, Type 1817, is used.

The final testing of the rifle barrel is always preceded by an exact examination of land and groove diameter, and the precise measurements have been determined for each caliber and type of cartridge.

Barrels which develop too much pressure with too

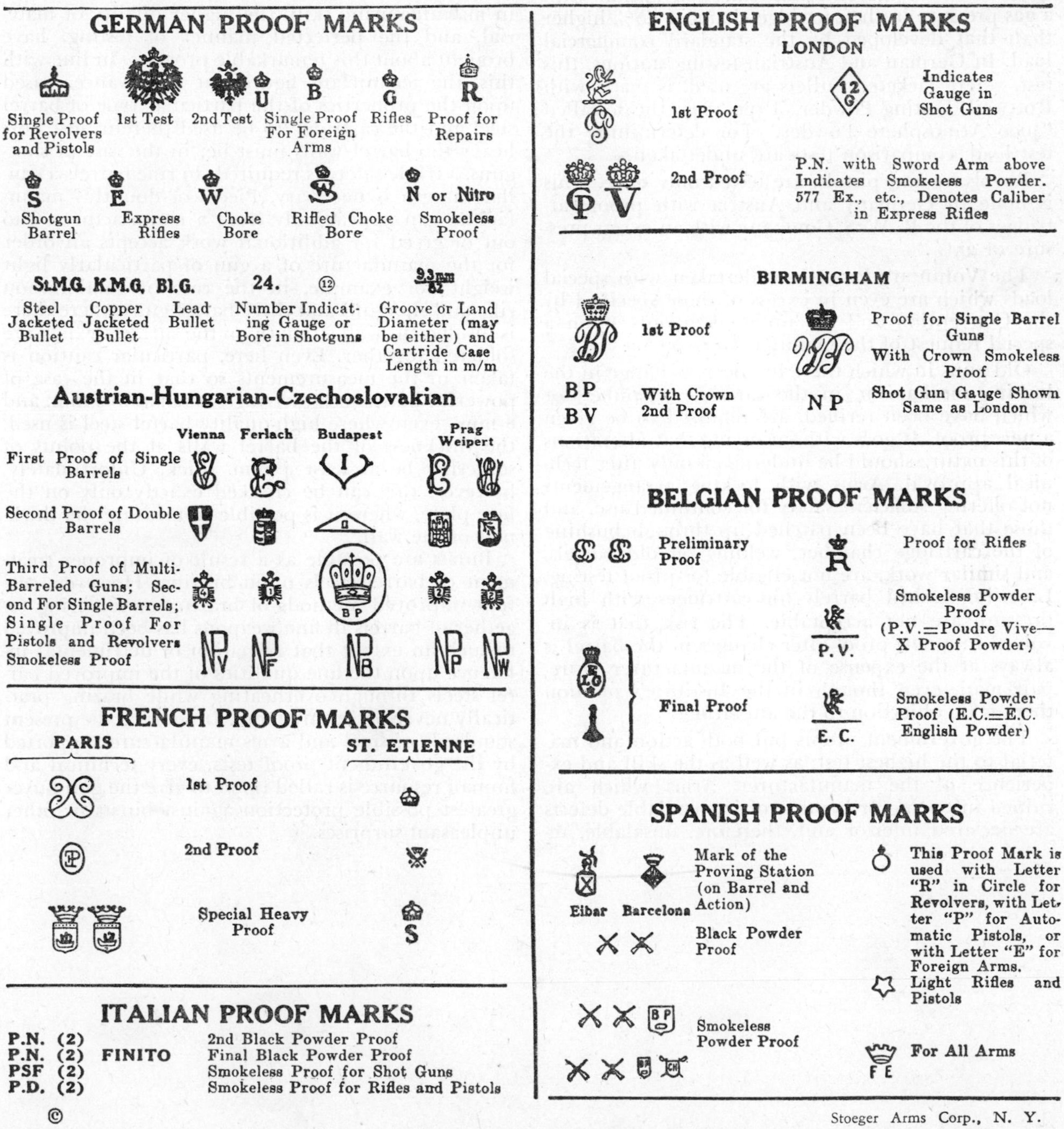


PLATE I. While there are a great variety of proof marks not listed here, those not shown are for the most part obsolete. Those shown are in common use today.

small a bore are returned to the manufacturer for alteration, because even a slight difference may set up a considerable increase of gas pressure in the cartridge chamber and endanger the gun. The diameter of the groove should be equal to the maximum diameter of the standard jacketed bullet. In 7 mm., for example, this size is 7.24 mm. and for this the land diameter should be 7 mm. Tests made with a gas-pressure instrument, using a groove diameter of only 7.15 mm. and a land diameter of 6.8 mm., increases the gas pressure with ordinary loads, which causes erosion to an extent which no barrel can long stand.

The testing of rifle barrels is according to the requirements of the International Convention with a gas pressure in the cartridge chamber 30% higher than that developed by the standard commercial load. In German and Austrian testing stations, this test, where jacketed bullets are used, is made with Rottweil Testing Powder, Type 1847, the so-called "4000 Atmosphere Powder." For determining the test load, comparison tests are undertaken.

Revolvers and pistols, are tested only once. This is done in Germany and Austria with proof cartridges of the R. W. S. Company with an excess pressure of 25%.

The Voluntary Proof is undertaken with special loads which are even in excess of those specified by the Convention and are undertaken only upon a special request of the manufacturer.

Old guns in which there has been a change in the locking mechanism, in the cartridge chamber, or which have been rerifled, are required to be given a new proof. It goes without saying that alterations of this nature should be undertaken only after technical approval. Arms with locking arrangements not offering sufficient safety for continued use, and those that have been patched up through bushing of the cartridge chamber, welding on old barrels, and similar work, are not eligible for proof testing. Likewise bushed barrels for cartridges with high pressure are not acceptable. The risk that is involved in a new proof after changes in the barrel is always at the expense of the manufacturer or repair man, even though in the Institute's opinion there is no objection to the alteration.

The government proofs put both action and material to the highest test, as well as the skill and experience of the manufacturer. Arms which are ruined in testing or because of irremediable defects are declared inferior and, therefore, unsalable, represent lost work and effort on the part of the manufacturer, a loss which may in some circumstances strike him very hard. For his own good, he will, therefore, make an effort to put into every piece the care which every buyer expects. In this manner, the rigid proof tests have had a very educational effect in the course of years, so that barrel bursts or other causes of rejection in the government proofhouse now seldom occur.

In former years in Suhl, approximately .3% to .4%—i.e., three or four in a thousand—barrels would burst. Today, this has been cut down to only .01 to .02—i.e., at most two in ten thousand—and this percentage will no doubt be further reduced. Not only the rigid proof test, but likewise the improvements in manufacturing skill, the higher quality of material, and the perfected manner of testing, have brought about this remarkable progress. In line with this, the technicians figure out in advance, based upon the properties of the particular type of barrel steel and the cartridge to be used therein, just how heavy the barrel walls must be; in the case of shotguns, a triple safety is required; in rifle barrels a similar margin is necessary. Pieces of doubtful manufacture can appear only from a manufacturer who out of greed for additional work accepts an order for the manufacture of a gun of particularly light weight—for example, in the case of combination rifle and shotguns and three-barrel guns where there is insufficient wall strength on the surfaces which are soldered together. Even here, particular caution is taken in the measurements so that in the case of powerful bottleneck cartridges, such as 6½ mm. and 8 mm., even where high-quality barrel steel is used, the thickness of the barrel walls at the points of soldering be at least 4 mm. thick. Unfortunately, however, this can be checked exactly only on the face plate, where it is possible to measure the thickness of the wall.

Bursts are possible as a result of improper treatment of barrel steels upon brazing. However, current improved methods of brazing or soldering together of barrels in fine weapons has been improved to such an extent that ruination or detrimental influence upon the fine qualities of the improved barrel steels through overheating while brazing practically never occur any more. In view of the present standards of steel and arms manufacture supported by the government proof tests, every technical and human resource is called upon to give the gun buyer greatest possible protection against bursts or other unpleasant surprises.

# REBUILDING A MILITARY RIFLE

How can I learn the art of gunsmithing? Is it possible to do the work at home without expensive tool equipment? What is the best way for a beginner to learn? Is it possible to make good sporting rifles from foreign military rifles? Is this work expensive if you do most of it yourself?

These questions, and many others, are asked of the country's various firearms editors in every mail. The answers, summed up, indicate that the best way to learn is by doing. It may be done at home without expensive equipment, and the conversion of military rifles to sporters can be done with very little expense.

None of this work is for the careless man. While skill is acquired only through experience, the brain should be used as frequently as the hands in gunsmithing. Various operations should be carefully thought out *before you touch a tool*. Never hurry. Do not try to do a job in one sitting—it is best to spread your work over a lengthy period, using spare hours while you relax.

Since volumes can be—and have been—written on the subject of gunsmithing, the many thousands of topics cannot be covered here. Instead, an effort will be made to give all of the facts and information necessary to convert one model of military rifle into a good, attractive, and practical big-game sporting rifle. If you learn such a basic art, you are capable of tackling minor gunsmithing jobs on your weapons.

Of all military conversions, the Mauser Model 1898 rifle, or its slightly refined version, the Model 1924, are perhaps the world's most popular rifles for this work. They have been converted in every civilized country for more than a half-century. Early conversions were very simple; later ones resulted in a factory-built Mauser sporter, which is identical with the mechanics of the military weapon—but in full dress.

A quarter-century ago, following World War I, thousands of 98's came into this country as souvenirs—the product of sweat and blood of our early doughboys. After their souvenir value faded, with a few years, their owners either converted them to sporters, or sold them to someone who was willing to tackle the work. Most of our current crop of elder gunsmiths got their start in business in Model 98 conversion work.

Unless you are willing to work slowly and carefully, you should give up all thoughts of this work. If you believe you can do this, and are handy with tools, tackle the job as you would any other hobby, and enjoy each step in the work.

**Tools.** First, you will need tools. The basic tool of the gunsmith is the screwdriver—yet just *any* screwdriver will not work. And strangely enough, you will have to *make these tools for yourself!* You begin with good screwdrivers, and reshape and often reheat-treat them.

How many will you need for the various home jobs you will want to do? This question cannot be answered—but ten or so will be a minimum. You will want big ones, medium ones, and little ones. You will want long-shank and short-shank types. And the blade, or working edge, will have to be altered. Above everything, *do not* use your gunsmithing screwdrivers for general household work—once you have those screwdrivers correct, guard them carefully. A skilled gunsmith would about as soon lend his wife to a stranger—or his friends—as his pet screwdrivers.

Why are these screwdrivers "special"? Because few screws used in gun manufacture are made to normal screwhead standards. It will pay you to look up an assortment of wood and machine screws and study the heads. Compare them with some of the visible screws in various firearms. Note the difference in slot shape, width, and depth.

Never use a screwdriver to remove or tighten any screw unless it fits the slot full width and depth. Always maintain it clean and with square edges—otherwise mutilated screws will result. If you take pride in your handiwork, you will never be happy with an otherwise good job if screwheads have been mutilated.

Few screwdrivers as purchased are of proper hardness for gunsmithing work. If too soft, the blade will twist and edges roll over. If too hard, the tip of the blade will break. Either accident results in a damaged screwhead, and can seriously damage surrounding parts—and injure the worker.

Build your collection of screwdrivers as you need them, first getting a half-dozen *good* ones. Do not buy cheap, unbranded makes. Even the best makes will require a little reheating. In one custom gun plant a high-grade tool broke while a smith was using it on an expensive, engraved custom gun. The jagged edge ruined a $50 (prewar price) engraving job; the expert engraver who had done the work could find no way to retouch it to make it inconspicuous.

One of the best known gunsmiths supplied the following data many years ago:

"The handle should be of octagon walnut, at least one inch across the flats for proper grip, and about 9 inches long, with a brass ferrule to prevent splitting. If you prefer the best, make your own, using high-quality tool steel rods. Heat and hammer forge to a square rather than round. For a screwdriver 3/16 inch wide at the bit, use 1/4-to 5/16-inch rod and after forging, file and dress the soft metal by hand to a square.

"Before filing, reheat and forge the bit to rough shape so that the flat of the bit will be at a 45-degree angle to the square. This gives added strength. Then file to finished shape while still soft.

"To harden it properly, heat it to a dull cherry red, which is approximately 1600 degrees F. Temper by quenching in linseed oil. Remove from the oil and polish with fine abrasive cloth until you get bright bare metal. Then reheat to a dark purple or blue color. Remove from heat and permit it to cool slowly *without* quenching—this will avoid a brittle blade. You are then ready to grind the bit carefully to the exact shape to fit a particular type of screw. Use a very fine grinding wheel, and never let your blade become hot—or it will burn and ruin it. Keep it cool by quenching."

[One practical way of keeping a blade cool is to place a guiding finger on the opposite side of the bit as you grind. You will feel heat as it starts.]

"Mount it carefully in the handle. You have a square blade and a solid handle with a brass ferrule on its lower end. Drill a hole in your handle 3½ inches deep and slightly under size. Lock the blade in a vise, tang up. Drive the wood handle on this tang, using a mallet in preference to a hammer."

For most work, 2 to 4 inches of blade is sufficient, and decreases the possibility of slippage and damage to work. For many other screws, longer blades, up to 8 inches, give better leverage for starting tight, heavy receiver and tang screws.

Once you get your screwdriver made, *test it!* Never use it on work until you are sure of it. If it must break, let it happen now. Use an ordinary woodscrew with a head about 1/4 inch wide, or to fit the bit. Lock this tightly in your vise close up to the head. Use extreme care to prevent slippage. If the screwdriver is satisfactory, you will split the head of the screw, or twist it from its shank. A good gunsmith will test on several screws and split them all before he will trust the tool on a gun.

If your screwdriver bends slightly without breaking, it is too soft. If it breaks, it is too hard. Either way it should be retempered and redrawn. Just remember—if you cannot turn hard enough to split a woodscrew, do not assume that your tool is perfect. Hold it firmly in the screw slot, and use a tight wrench on the flats of the shank.

This lengthly discussion of screwdrivers is important because more beginners become discouraged in their work because of improper basic tools than anything else. *Start right.*

**Conversion.** You should now be ready to begin on your rifle. If you do not have one, consider what you want. The German Model 98 Mauser, and that of many other foreign nations, uses the 7.92-mm. Mauser cartridge. That is an excellent hunting cartridge for use here, since it has long been made by American manufacturers. There should be no necessity for discarding the original barrel—thus you want one which is in good condition inside. Wear and tool marks on the outside are of no importance, since you will take care of those.

The proper cartridge as made in this country is the 8-mm. Mauser or 8-mm. Special, as it is called by one maker. Remington and Peters load this with a 170-grain soft point at a muzzle velocity of 2530 f.s. At 100 yards it is traveling at 2210 f.s., at 200 yards it has dropped to 1920 f.s., and at 300 yards it is still going at 1660 f.s. Compared with the old reliable .30-30 with the same weight bullet starting at 2200 f.s., the remaining velocity at 100, 200, and 300 yards in 1930, 1680, and 1460 f.s.

Before you start to rebuild that Mauser, look it over carefully. If it is of Polish, Czech, or Belgian manufacture, it is probably an excellent gun. If of Belgian make, be certain that it is not chambered for the Belgian 7.65-mm. Mauser cartridge, a type no longer made in this country. But the big Belgian factory of *Fabrique Nationale* has made the Mauser 98, and the slightly altered version, the Model 24, for dozens of other nations in the caliber used by the buyer, so many came over here as souvenirs in the German caliber.

German-made Model 98 rifles dated 1943, 1944, and 1945, are of progressively lower quality in both materials and workmanship than earlier dates. Many thousand of others dated 1914 to 1917 turn up in this country. These are good rifles, but not so strong as those made in the 1930's, because of improvements in metals and heat-treatment of parts.

SIGHTS. If you have a good action and barrel, except for wear on the outside, you are ready to start your work. Study it carefully for design. For-

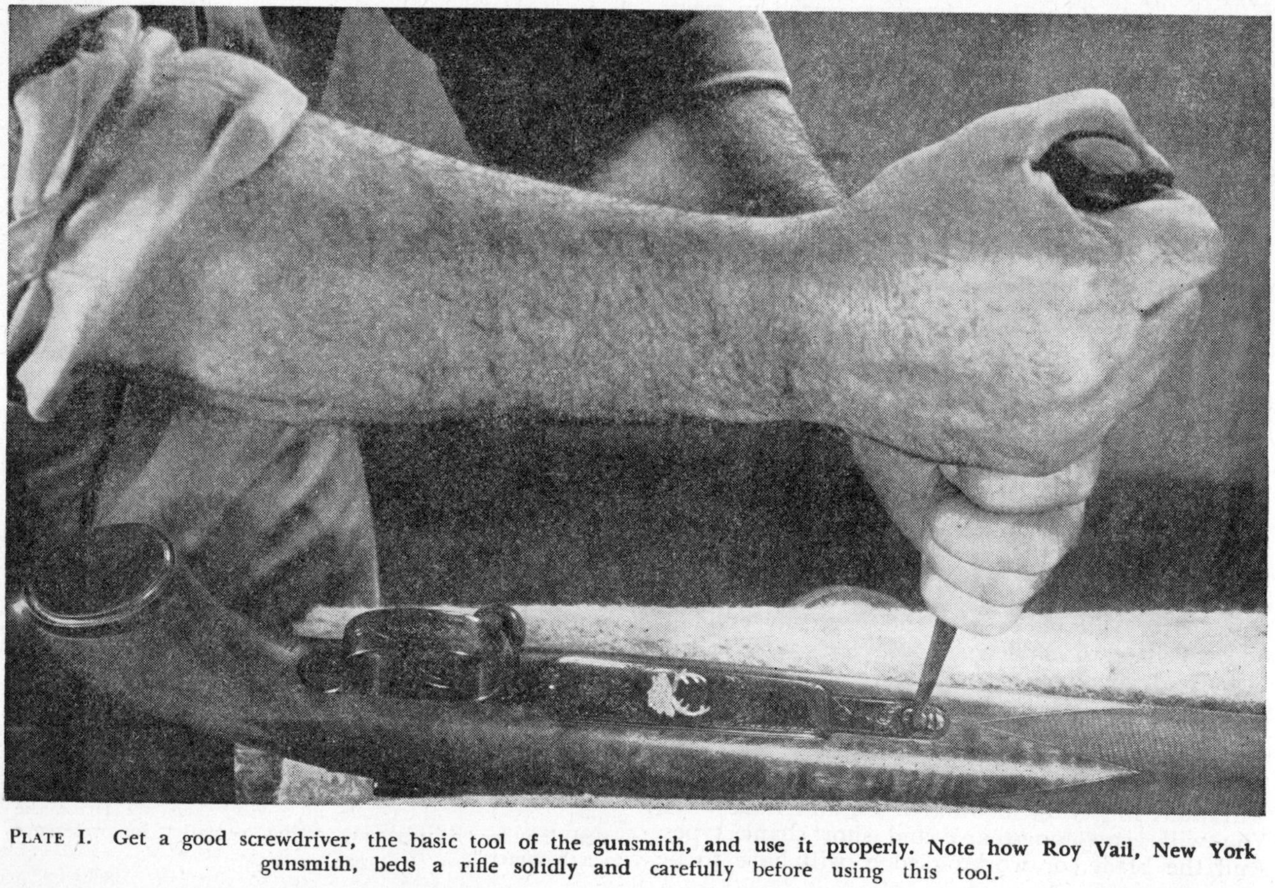

PLATE I. Get a good screwdriver, the basic tool of the gunsmith, and use it properly. Note how Roy Vail, New York gunsmith, beds a rifle solidly and carefully before using this tool.

PLATE II. This is the "basic" Mauser, Model 98, ready for the home conversion job.

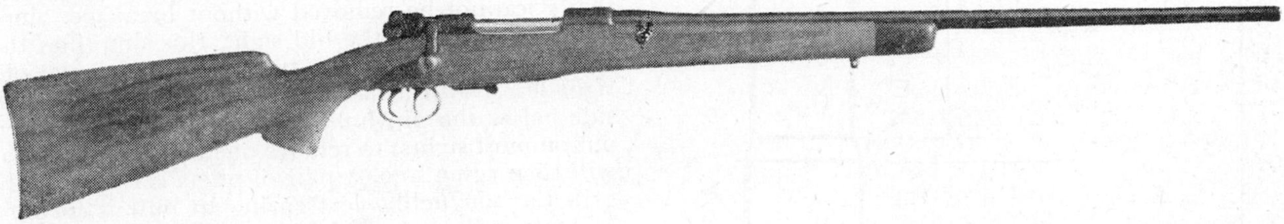

Both pictures from Pete Barrett.

PLATE III. This is the same Mauser, fitted with a .270 barrel, a fine walnut stock, and careful checkering.

eign military sights are crude, have no windage, and are unsatisfactory for hunting. The rear sight will have a V-notch. The front is a "barleycorn" or inverted "V" or pyramid. For accurate shooting, they fit together like a square peg in a round hole.

You will decide to remove that ugly rear sight, and its equally ugly base. Lyman, Redfield, Pacific, and other sight makers have low, medium, and expensive receiver sights to fit the Mauser action. Their installation is simple. Get all catalogs and choose your sights before you do any work—otherwise your alterations will be such that the new sights will not fit. These sight makers also produce good hunting front sights with gold, silver, ivory, or red beads, either square or round, and in various sizes.

Look over the Mauser front sight. You will see that the "barleycorn" is on a tiny dovetail base fitting into the sight base. You will find some hunting front sights listed to fit this base. If you plan to spend more money, you will note that you may remove the base and replace it with a good ramp-type sight. Do not get this until you are ready to use it—when most of your work has been finished, as you must have the exact diameter of the barrel in ordering. But make your plans and figure your costs. Many sight makers will mount these for you—at a charge—and it is a good idea to have them tackle this job if you are not confident of your own abilities.

STOCK. With your sights planned, look at the stock. Most German 98's are marked "K 98" meaning *Karbiner* 98. A few older ones will have a longer barrel and may be marked "G 98" *(Gewehr* 98) meaning Rifle Model 98. Most of the German rifles used in World War II have the carbine stock. Made of laminated wood, this consists of 1-mm. (.039-inch) layers of hard, light-colored wood, bonded together with a bakelite type of plastic. Laminated wood differs from plywood in that in the former the grain all runs in one direction. The plastic bonding of these thin sheets makes the wood very difficult to cut, and scraping and filing will be necessary. You will most likely decide to "make your own stock," since there will probably be an ugly hole through the butt in back of the grip for the German type of side sling, plus an even more homely projecting metal escutcheon behind this. Added to these problems is a stock too short for the average hunter, no pistol grip, and a poorly shaped butt and forearm.

After completing this study, you are ready to take the rifle apart for additional examination.

At the lower front of the stock, near the bayonet lug, you will find a long spring lock on the right side. Depress this and tap the forward barrel band from the stock, moving it to the front of the barrel. It will slip off over the front sight. Pick the spring lock out of its slot in the wood with the fingers, and tap the rear band toward the front. This also slips off easily. The handguard, or wood section on top of the barrel, may then be lifted free of its lip in the front of the rear sight base.

Once again you study the rifle as it now stands. If you plan to use the same stock for your sporter, note that the barrel must be polished and reblued to remove rough tool marks. You will want to discard the military rear sight, but how to do it without leaving an ugly base in the way? If you remove the base, there will be a bad cut in the stock to disfigure the gun. If you do not remove the base, but remove the sight leaf only, you will find that the top of the base does not cover the barrel—and things will look worse. You will then probably decide to remove both the sight and sight base.

You are now ready to remove the stock for further examination. At the front and rear of the trigger guard are two heavy screws, locked in by retaining screws in front of each main screw. Some retaining screws have a small arc cut into one edge to permit removal of the main screw when the retainer is turned to proper position. To avoid mutilation, remove the retainers completely. Discarded envelopes or small boxes will hold your parts—and each should be labeled as to location at the time of removal, so that they may be returned to their proper position.

Those main stock screws will probably be hard to start. Be careful. They must always be as tight as you can get them when shooting a gun. When these are removed, the trigger-guard assembly and maga-

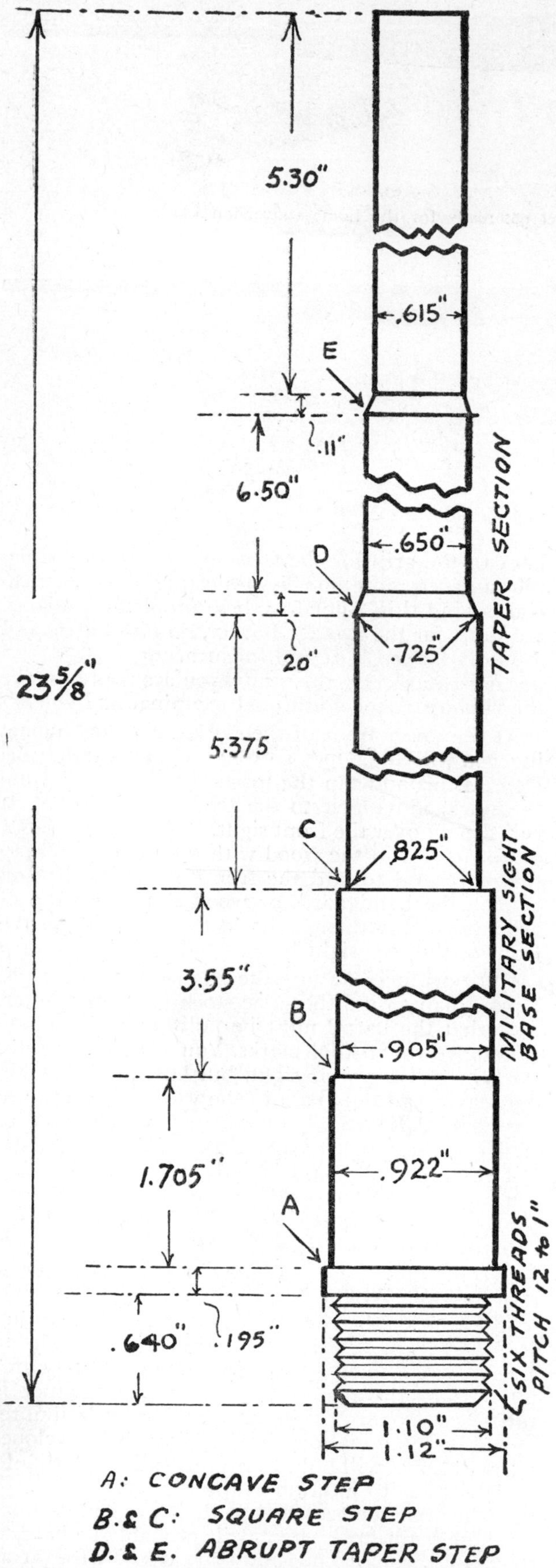


PLATE IV. **This shows the diameter and taper of the Mauser barrel.**

zine may be lifted out of the stock from the bottom, the barrel and receiver assembly from the top.

Study the sight base and note its thinness. Its removal will mean a space of about 1/16 inch at that point in the stock, but careful use of plastic wood can easily fill such gaps if you insist in rebuilding the old stock. If you plan to make a new one, save the old—you will need it for many examinations later.

You are now ready to start the actual work. Most recent Mausers have this sight base fitted so tightly that it cannot be removed without breakage. Since you will not need the old sight, this simplifies the matter. At the front are two ears holding the old sight leaf. With a hacksaw, carefully cut along the side below the pin hole (the pin cannot be driven out on most sights) to remove one lip. The sight leaf will then come free. A pair of pliers is then used to grip the tonguelike leaf spring to pull it forward and out of the rear of the base groove.

Cut off the remaining lip. The sight assembly can then be knocked free of its thin base. Hacksaw through the handguard lip on the front of the base, being careful not to cut into and damage the barrel. Do the same with the rear lug after first removing the locking screw. Careful and slow use of a hammer, chisel (metal), and a few drifts will then peel this from the barrel.

BARREL. You may then study the odd construction of the Mauser barrel. You will note that it is outside-shaped by stepping down the diameter abruptly. Only one short section is tapered. The diameter of the barrel in front of the receiver ring is .992 inch and runs forward this diameter for 1.90 inches (including the shoulder of larger diameter). At this point it steps down with a square cut to the first step formerly filled by the rear sight base to a diameter of .905 inch and runs straight for 3.55 inches.

Again here you have an additional square step to a diameter of .825. This runs forward for 5.375 inches for the only taper in the barrel, reducing to a diameter of .725 inch. The next step-down occurs in .20 inch to a diameter of .650, running straight for 6.5 inches. An additional and final step reduces the diameter in .11 inch to .615 inch, the barrel continuing straight in this diameter for 5.3 inches to the muzzle.

Many attractive sporters have been made from these barrels without removing these steps; only the square steps have been rounded over. This, however, is a delicate job for the man who does not own a big lathe which will permit handling both barrel and receiver assembly. It can be rounded by hand, but filing will be slow—as the slightest slip can damage the barrel—and such a mark always seems to occur on top where it shows.

The man who demands a neater job may require the aid of a gunsmith to taper the barrel slightly. This rarely is too satisfactory as the straight cuts mean the removal of too much metal, and a "featherweight" barrel is neither strong nor does it give satisfactory accuracy. In its new condition, the K-98 barrel without sights weighs only 2 pounds 7 ounces, less than most 24-inch sporter barrels—and it only runs 23⅝ inches.

To finish the barrel properly, you will need an assortment of flat, triangular, and half-round files.

PLATE V. These various types of sporting stocks are inletted for the Springfield, Mauser, and Enfield rifles, and are available in varied grades of walnut. Those shown are made by Stoeger Arms Corp. of New York. Top to bottom: (1) for Springfield, Mauser, or Enfield; (2) for Springfield, Mauser, or Enfield; (3) for Springfield, Mauser, or Enfield; (4) for Enfield only; (5) for Springfield only; (6) for Mauser only.

These should be fine-cut machinists' files—the standard bastard cut is too coarse. Always remember to work slowly. You can easily cut off a little more, but you can't put any of the metal back. If you are lucky, you may have a barrel with a ground surface. If not, it will have been lathe-turned, and many tool marks will be evident. Use a wide file, very fine cut, not less than an inch wide. Use very light pressure on the barrel, rotating the barrel as you push the file forward. *Do not rock the file.* Clean the file teeth with a stiff brush after almost every cut—or you will scratch the surface badly. Cut only in a forward motion of the file—never drag it back over the work. Practice this operation on a short piece of scrap water pipe or steel rod to get the feel of it before you start work on your barrel—and save yourself much grief.

You are now ready to polish it when the rough tool marks have been removed. This is a slow process and should not be rushed or you will have much hard labor to do over. Progress slowly, take pride in your work, and learn while you are at it.

For polishing metal, you will need several grits of the finest abrasive cloth—do not use paper. Grit sizes of the "aloxite" and similar cloths should never be coarser than 4/0, and you will need 6/0, 8/0, and finer.

One thing to remember is to never discard worn polishing cloth, even when "worn out completely." New cloth *cuts.* Used cloth *polishes without cutting.*

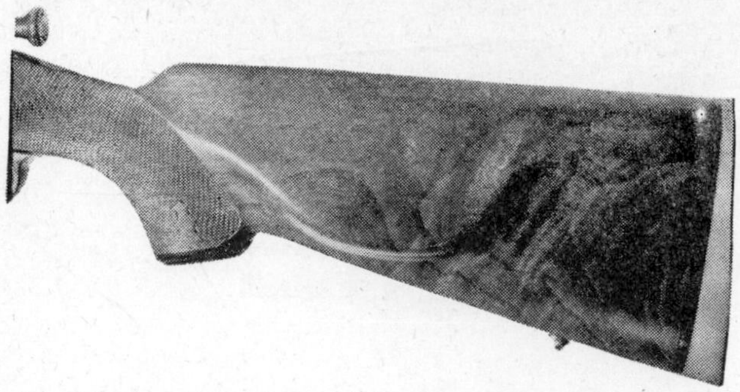

PLATE VI. Careful checkering and a lot of hand rubbing made this stock what it is.

The cutting effect can be slowed with a small amount of oil on the cloth. Tear your cloth into one-inch strips for most surfaces—narrower as needed. Use small flat blocks of hardwood about one by 3 inches to support the cloth and to prevent cutting a wavy surface.

Use progessively finer polishing cloth to remove all tool marks. Finish with crocus cloth. Unless you polish that barrel mirror bright without a trace of a scratch or tool mark, it will not look well when blued. Blueing does not cover scratches.

This polishing is best done in easy stages. It is slow and tiring. But when you set the job aside for another spare evening, be certain that you scrub it with a slightly oily rag—or you may find etched fingerprints to polish out when you return to the job.

When that barrel is polished the way you want it, oil it and coat it with strips of waxed paper wrapped spirally to keep it clean. After you have done the work, you will appreciate this protection.

RECEIVER. Now polish the receiver carefully. DO NOT attempt to file out the maker's markings, date, or serial number. Possession of a gun without serial numbers and maker's markings is against Federal law, subject to gun confiscation plus fine or imprisonment.

Put that barrel and receiver back in position in your old stock and note the parts that show. Polish only this section to remove tool marks. Small polishing stones or "slip stones" available at a gunsmith supply house or from many hardware stores are very useful if you get different shapes and grades of fineness. They cost but a few cents each.

Polish the runway where the bolt operates, but be careful: You can't afford to remove much metal here—just enough to get smooth operation.

The machined "corners" of the top side and the rear section of the receiver can be rounded with a file before polishing. This will greatly improve the looks and "streamline" the action. Otherwise it will never look like a completely finished job.

Before you work on the rear of the receiver, it would be well to fit your sight. Many types of these Mauser receiver sights mount on the bolt stop. They require no skill to fit, and no drilling. By thus installing the sight before rounding sharp metal edges, you avoid working on a point where removal of metal will create improper fit in the sight. However, remove the sight before attempting to file receiver metal.

Do no work on the bottom of the receiver. This is important. This must be flat and as originally shaped to insure proper bedding in the stock. Slip your barrel and action back in the old wood stock frequently to see that metal is not removed in the wrong places.

Polish again to mirror brightness, removing all tool marks on the receiver. On the bolt, use only polishing materials, and keep away from the bolt-locking lugs—or you will destroy head space.

With the above metal work done, there remains only a minor task of reshaping and polishing the trigger guard and magazine floor plate.

Slip this guard back into the military stock and notice how wide it is, with semi-sharp edges. Streamline this with a file. Using half-round and flat files, work on the sides of the guard, tapering them slightly from the base to the bottom. Width of this guard at the bottom is .635 inch. Thinning this to about .50 inch will greatly improve the beauty. Round the edges well and polish. Do not remove much metal from the floor plate and tangs—just enough to eliminate tool marks and add a good polish. Oil these parts when you have finished to maintain their brightness. Now you are ready for your stock. Up to this point you have done no serious alteration—you have just smoothed up and polished the metal parts.

**Stock Work.** Many a man has made a good-looking sporter by redressing his military stock. Some "gun cranks" will insist that while this can be done with early Mausers having solid walnut stocks, "nothing can be done with laminated wood to make it beautiful." This statement is wrong—definitely so. The telescope-sighted K-43—the German semi-automatic—was designed to rival our Garand. The stock does not look like walnut—but neither do some of the fancy woods we use—Oregon myrtle, California mesquite, apple, cherry, maple, and so on. It is beautiful, if properly polished. If your stock is not filled with dents and deep scratches, you can rebuild it with little effort. A recoil pad fitted to the butt will lengthen the stock to normal. By proper use of coarse files, sandpaper, polishing cloth, and steel wool, you can thin slightly on the over-thick grip, reshape the comb and thin this a little, and smooth up the forearm. The latter should be cut off and rounded at the step where the rear barrel band was placed. It is not necessary to attach that forearm to the barrel in any way.

So you don't care for those gaps in the stock around the barrel? Use plastic wood. Clean the barrel groove in the forearm with gasoline on a rag to remove traces of oil. Insert the barrel and action into this stock after you have coated the "loose spots" with plastic wood; on a laminated stock, natural color is best. Lay a sheet of waxed household paper over the groove before you insert barrel and action. Then press together. Replace the trigger guard and tighten the guard screws, pulling everything together as tightly as possible while the plastic wood is soft. Surplus will flow out around the sides of the barrel.

Permit the rifle to remain this way for at least 24 hours at room temperature. A little longer would be better since plastic wood dries slowly without air. A week will do no harm. Then remove the barrel and receiver and you will find that the thin waxed paper has prevented the plastic wood from adhering to the polished barrel. The paper will probably stick to the wood, but may be removed with a little gasoline or lighter fluid and a small pad of steel wool. The surplus which flowed at the edges is filed away—do not cut—and polished to match the remainder of the stock. You will then have a hairline of clearance around the barrel, preferred by many.

You still have unsightly holes in the butt. One is the rough-cut sling slot, the other that metal escutcheon. Most of the latter are riveted in position, but a small pipe reamer in a brace, working on one side, will cut through and permit easy removal without further disfiguring the stock. The countersunk hole may then be filled in many ways.

Hobbyists are familiar with tne art of cementing plastic inlays into wood. Thinning the stock will eliminate part of the countersunk cavity, but if you plan to inlay, do not thin the wood to desired dimensions until your inlay has been cemented into position and properly hardened. You may then round the wood and inlay to make a neat job.

The left side has a bad machined slot. This can be filled with a plate of stainless steel, highly polished, as one shooter did. When the gun was completed, the owner had his name engraved thereon. The escutcheon hole may be reshaped to a diamond, if desired, for a plastic inlay—or if you have any foreign souvenir coins of proper diameter, they make unique decorations.

When your stock is polished, oil it lightly with pure linseed oil. This laminated wood will not take oil because of the plastic impregnation, so don't waste too much time trying to make it soak in. Let it dry, and polish. If the oil becomes gummy, scrub with a cotton flannel cloth using a small amount of light machine oil. Then apply any hard rubbing wax and polish this dry. Such a waxed stock sheds water, does not scratch easily, and can easily be retreated as it dulls with time.

Perhaps you prefer to make a good walnut stock, complete with pistol grip and better sporting dimensions. The first thing is to determine the dimensions. If you have a friend with a rifle which fits you, use it as a pattern. Use brown wrapping paper and make a full-size scale drawing. Project a cleaning rod through the breech of the barrel carefully to measure the amount of drop from line of bore to the heel of the butt. Sketch the shape of the action outline as well as the stock, that you may visualize your proposed shape in the butt, the grip, and the forearm. If you have your military stock, superimpose a sketch of this on your other drawing, that you may more readily note changes. Planning is important—after you start shaping it will be too late.

Many dealers handle semi-inletted walnut gunstock blanks for the Mauser action. These range in price at from $7.50 to $15, depending on the grade and figure of the wood. By all means get a semi-inletted blank. In these, much of the space for the receiver and action has been cut away by machinery, saving countless hours of difficult labor. There will still be much work on the inletting, as this must be cut away to fit your action.

Semi-inletted blanks are supplied either rough turned to shape, or in slab form. You will be better satisfied with the slab form, as the outside shaping is not difficult and you have more wood to work with to get the dimensions you require. The cost is usually a dollar or two less.

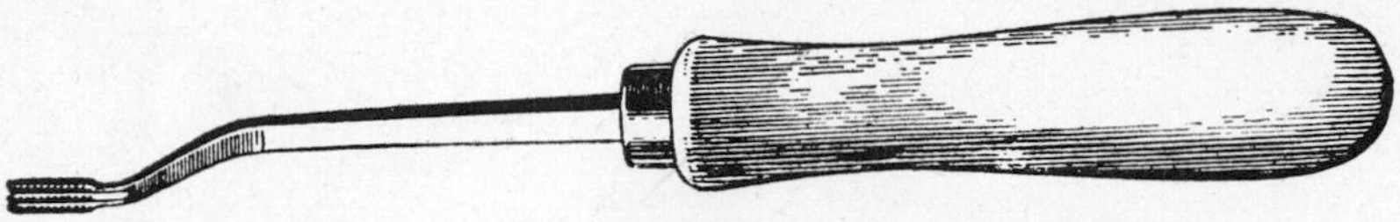

PLATE VII. Stoeger special checkering tool, with two rows of teeth for checkering narrow patterns and reaching corners and angles. This tool is made in three sizes: 16, 18, or 20 lines to the inch.

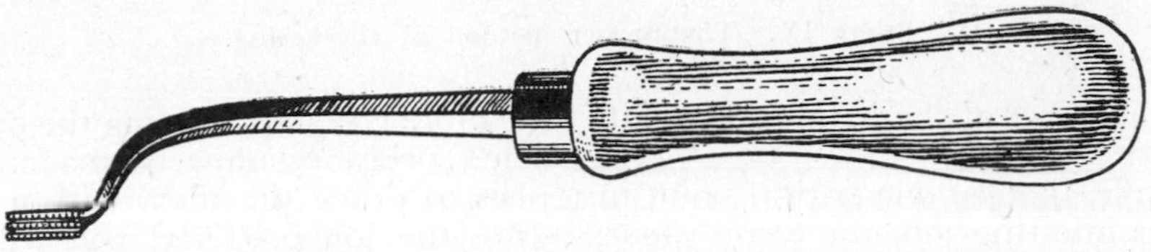

PLATE VIII. Three-tooth Stoeger checkering tool. This is easier for the novice to operate than the two-tooth tool, and makes more rapid work possible. Available in three sizes: 16, 18, or 20 lines to the inch.

Never shape the outside of your blank until the barrel, receiver, and trigger guard assembly have been properly fitted. Certain measurements for these can be taken from the military stock you are discarding. Note carefully what parts of the metal fit tightly, and where there is clearance. Such clearance is planned and is necessary to prevent splitting on firing. Slight clearance on the receiver tang is important—not as much as on the military stock, but enough to permit insertion of a calling card.

Inletting cannot be done without proper tools. Special chisels and gouges can be purchased from gunsmithing supply houses at a reasonable price, usually in sets. Keep them stoned to razor edge constantly.

Barrel inletting rasps, circular files with an offset handle, are extremely useful. They remove wood rapidly where required, and on fancy wood with crooked grain are far better than gouges and chisels. Sometimes, at the final stage of inletting the action, so little wood need be removed that scraping with a sharp cutting edge is more practical than cutting and filing.

A good job of inletting cannot be done without a color marker. A thinly wiped smear of artists' oil paint, prussian blue, or even lampblack and oil is an easy way to check. The latter mixture, however,

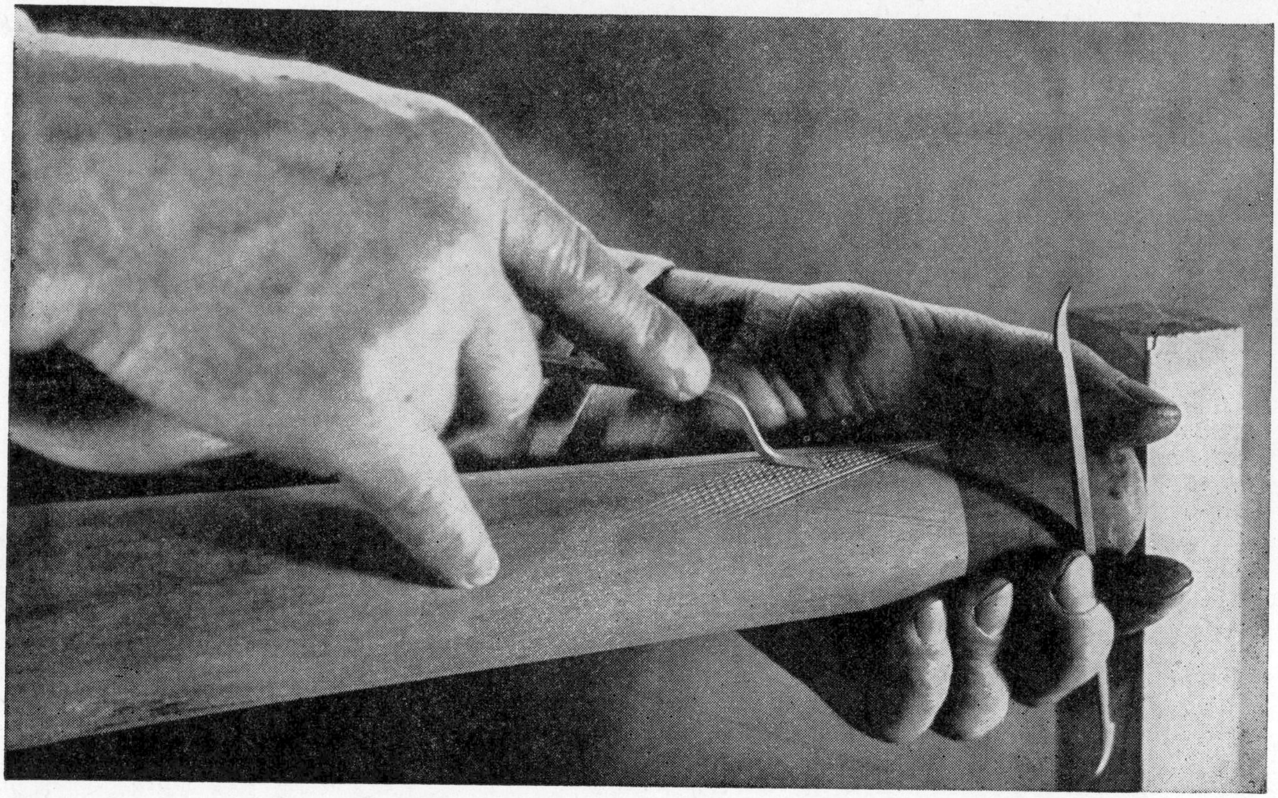

PLATE IX. The proper method of checkering.

is messy; it enters the pores of the hands and is difficult to wash away.

In a bolt-action rifle, there is one critical point in the task of a proper inletting job—the recoil shoulder. Study your action again. Note the lug with its square face on the bottom of the receiver ring, just below the breech end of the barrel. The rear face of this must bear evenly and solidly on the wood of the stock. The bottom face must seat firmly, that the forward guard screw may pull it tight at all points. Now look inside your discarded military stock and you will see how the problem was solved in the production line—through the insertion of a through-the-stock square-face strain bolt, the metal taking the recoil strain in place of the wood you will use. If the fit is perfect, wood is adequate.

As you gradually chisel and gouge and file away the wood in your inletting operation, you must constantly fit the barrel and action into your cavity. A thin smear of oil paint on the wood will show the points of contact. Cut these away—*and only* these colored points. Then rewipe the metal parts with oil paint and try again. Slowly the job will near completion. But be very careful to get a perfect fit on the recoil shoulder—otherwise the action will set back in the stock on firing and split the wood.

Once the action is completely inletted, it is advisable to test-fire it before spending the time on shaping and finishing. One very skilled gunsmith takes the gun with its rough slab stock out into the open. Placing the rough-sawn butt solidly against a telephone pole, he fires a shot. If the inletting job is not proper, the stock will crack or split under this rigid punishment. But then is the time to find out. If it appears to hold, he cleans the barrel and is ready to shape the outside to dimensions.

Before you start shaping the outside of your stock, a few decisions must be made. You will probably plan to shape the stock with a pistol grip, and to dress the job properly, you will need a grip cap. These may be made from metals or plastics, but it is best to purchase one already made. Gunsmith supply houses have a variety of sizes and shapes in steel and plastics. They usually sell at from 50 to 75 cents, complete with screw for attaching.

A butt plate should also be obtained. Recoil pads may be installed if you prefer; these usually cost about $3.50. Butt plates of steel or plastics can be purchased in a variety of sizes for about $1. Here, again, you will find that size and shape are important, that the finished stock may be exactly as you desire it. Study of a borrowed sporting rifle that fits you, and measurements taken from this, should be recorded on your pattern as a guide.

Finally comes the choice of cheekpiece. Semi-inletted blanks, both of the rough-turned variety and the slab type, usually have ample wood for this. Plan its shape carefully, and in roughing it to your dimensions, slip the barrel and receiver, with your sporting sights fitted, into the wood. Try tossing it into offhand aiming position—the butt plate must be fitted for this work. Check carefully by throwing it into position with the eyes closed. Then open them. If the sights are in proper position, the cheekpiece fits your face. If you are looking at the left side of the sight and have to "crowd" into your gun, the cheek rest is too thick. Continuous trial is necessary to prevent removing too much wood.

Shaping this also requires an analysis of its contact with the face—it should come to the same point and bear evenly to prevent bruising the cheekbone with recoil in snap shooting. Since individual faces vary, you must custom-fit it to yourself. The lower edge should be rounded, not undercut as is often found in European rifles. Proper shaping here dresses up the stock and adds streamline beauty. At the top, if the cheekpiece "flows" into the wood of the butt, you will not achieve the "stuck-on-pancake" look.

The choice of a forearm cap is optional. Some like these, others prefer natural wood. If you insist on a tip of contrasting material, you may obtain a blank of buffalo horn at from $5 to $10, or of black plastic at about $1. Fitting this cap should be attempted when the forearm has been roughed to shape. Plan the finished tip to be from 1½ to 2¼ inches long; see that one face is perfectly square; then cut the blank end of the forearm wood perfectly square and smooth. Fit the two together so that there is a surplus of tip to shape up. Drill two holes in the end of the forearm side by side and at least ½ inch apart and about 9/32 inch in diameter. These holes should enter the forearm straight to a depth of at least an inch. Repeat this operation on the plastic tip, and insert 1⅞-inch sections of ¼-inch cold rolled steel rod. This will prevent the tip from breaking loose when finished.

Using a tube of Duco cement, insert some cement into each hole, coat the rods or dowels with cement, and the faces of both the wood and the tip. Press tightly together, forcing surplus cement to escape at the edges. Clamping this in place to dry or "set" is difficult, but the stock may be propped up on its tip and carefully weighted. It should set at least 24 hours—the longer the better. Then rough-saw the top surplus, file it slightly oversize, and inlet this to fit the barrel.

The surplus wood on the outside can be more quickly hogged away through the use of a coarse wood rasp—not a file—than with any cutting instrument. A half-round rasp is excellent for this roughing. If you have a fancy grain, do not rasp too closely to final dimensions, or there may be tearing of the wood. Coarse double-cut files should next be used, and kept clean constantly through use of a stiff brush or file card. Final shaping is done with finer files, but when used on wood the double-cuts work better than single and do not fill as quickly. Sandpaper, in various fine grades, then removes file marks and hollow spots. Various-shaped sanding blocks can be made from small pieces of softwoods as needed to eliminate hollows.

When you get the wood ready, perfectly smooth, and meeting your critical requirements, the final polishing is started. Some use steel wool for this work, but fine emery cloth is better on some places. If steel wool is used, very fine is the only type to use. And polish only with the grain—never across it.

When the wood is as smooth as you can get it, raise the grain. For this, the kitchen gas range is convenient. Wipe the stock with a slightly wet rag so that some water soaks in. Then remove surplus with a dry rag and hold it over the gas flame, turning it constantly to distribute the heat and prevent scorching. This steams the surface. Dry it completely with the gas heat—it takes but a few minutes—and run your hand over the once-polished surface. The grain will then be raised or "feathered." The stock will feel rough. Using fine steel wool or polishing grade of emery paper, again polish smooth, removing the feathers. This takes but a few moments for the entire stock. Wet and repeat. Again the feathers will raise. From three to five of these treatments will be necessary—or until you fail to raise feathers when you heat-dry it. Now the wood will not feather with dampness and you are ready to apply the oil finish.

Inspection of the surface of the wood under a magnifying glass will reveal the condition of the pores. If these are large, a filler will help to build and protect the finish of your stock. It is usually most practical to take your stock to a paint supply house and ask them for a small quantity of filler. What you will need will cost but a few cents, but be sure to indicate that you will use an oil instead of varnish filler. The reason for taking your stock along is that you may need a colored filler to match the wood—your paint man can quickly pick the correct shade.

Most stocks of good dense walnut require no filler. The hand rubbing of the oil into the wood does a good job of filling. Many craftsmen make their own filler by using scrap walnut. Use a medium file to create walnut dust on a small sheet of glass. A few drops of linseed oil stirred into this dust with the fingers will make a thick paste. Rub this paste into the pores of the wood by smearing it on with a finger and burning it in by rubbing with the heel of the hand. Rub until dry, with most strokes in the direction of the grain. This will make the hand hot. Too much rubbing will not hurt the wood but can create blisters on the hand. It would be best to rest a few moments when the hand becomes hot. Rags may be used, but the results will never be as satisfactory.

After filling, and initial polishing of the filler, permit the stock to stand for a day or two. This hardens the filler, the oil soaking into the wood. This makes the final finish easier to apply.

A discussion of stock finishes would require half a book. In the oil-finish family alone, there are dozens of formulas, and all work well. You may purchase numerous finishes—or make your own: Ingredients, plain, raw linseed oil only. These are several wood finishes on the market. Some are faster than others, but it is interesting to note that most of the "quick" finishes do not wear as well as a slow finish, do not offer the moisture and abrasion protection, and require attention to keep them looking well.

Back a century ago, the most expensive pianos had a "dull London oil finish." It was anything but "dull" and it lasted generations. This finish is still the most popular among the gunsmiths who make expensive guns; cheap stocks are given a quick finish.

The famous oil finish required nothing but linseed oil and elbow grease—little oil and much rubbing. Raw linseed will work, but boiled oil is better because of its thicker body. If your stock is well filled, repolish with very fine steel wool—the finest you can get, *working only with the grain.* This will take care of slight traces of dried-on excess filler. A small 3-inch-square patch of clean washed cotton cloth is used to apply a light smear of oil. Do not try to coat the entire stock at once—it will be too messy to handle and will become sticky.

With the stock across the knees, coat a patch about 3 by 6 inches with the oil; then rub until dry with the palm and heel of the hand. Coat a near-by patch, and repeat. Keep at this until the entire stock is coated and rubbed. If it is rubbed dry all over, it may then be set aside. If it is left wet, the next day will present you with a very sticky mess that cannot be rubbed. *Do not rub with a cloth!* Do not forget the inside of the stock. Coat it with oil and permit it to soak in, then wipe dry with a clean rag before it becomes sticky. This will keep moisture out and prevent warping. Several coats to the inside over a period of days will help. Polishing is not necessary.

Should your stock become sticky through the application of too much oil, use a little *raw* linseed on a clean cloth. Smear it over the sticky area, let it soak a few moments to soften, and then scrub the sticky mess away with the cloth.

*Never use steel wool to remove this!* The result will be a rough, abrasive goo, impossible to remove without turpentine of other solvents—plus much hard repolishing with oil and the bare hand.

An hour or so of rubbing each evening with additional oil will continue to add polish and darken the stock. At the end of a week or so, you will have a finely polished stock. After that, additional oil and rubbing, as the spirit moves, will continue to improve the finish. Slight scratches occurring through service are quickly removed through application of a drop of oil and a few minutes of rubbing it dry.

**Checking.** We have not yet mentioned checking. It is much better to check the stock after finishing than before. The checkered area may then be oiled with the fingers and lightly polished dry with a discarded toothbrush. Note this latter. All surplus oil must be polished away or it will "fill" your checking. In using your toothbrush to polish, wipe it frequently on a cloth to remove excessive oil.

The subject of checking your stock has been left to this point, since this calls for skill. By now, you have put little money into your stock, but a great deal of hard labor. Do not spoil it. If you insist on checking, plan it carefully, and practice a lot before you start work—otherwise you will spoil the stock.

A set of checking tools—special file-like cutters on handles—is not expensive, and can be obtained from various gunsmith supply houses. Note that there are two points generally checked—the pistol grip and the forearm. Practice your checking on scrap lumber—it need not be walnut. On the forearm, remember that you will be checking on a taper curve. Make a dummy forearm of birch, beech, oak, or some other wood, to the same shape as that of your stock. Sketch an exact-size pattern of your planned checking on ordinary letter-paper—then cut it out. Fold it around the rifle stock forearm and hold in place with short pieces of cellophane tape. Note its size and appearance—you may have to make several patterns to get what you want.

Determine the size of your diamonds from the assortment of checking tools you have. Usually these sets are equipped for fine, medium, and coarse checking. Practice on scrap wood, and when you have chosen the size you desire, use a good scale rule and rule up one of your paper patterns to see if your design will come out properly. You may have to alter the pattern slightly. Diamonds may be long, medium, and short. Try all types on scrap wood before making your decision.

When the pattern is complete, make several cutouts of identical size; this will save you trouble if one becomes damaged.

Use one of these cutouts on your dummy forearm. Wrap and tape it in position—the dummy need only be smooth, not finished—and outline it carefully, using a thin flexible steel rule as a guide, and a scriber or heavy needle to scratch an outline. On your naked wood dummy, this might be done with a pencil, but when you get to the finished stock, pencil marks will not show and a scratched line will be the answer. Then remove your pattern and go to work with your tools, using your flexible straight edge as a guide. If one sample pattern has been ruled in pencil, it will show you how the job will look

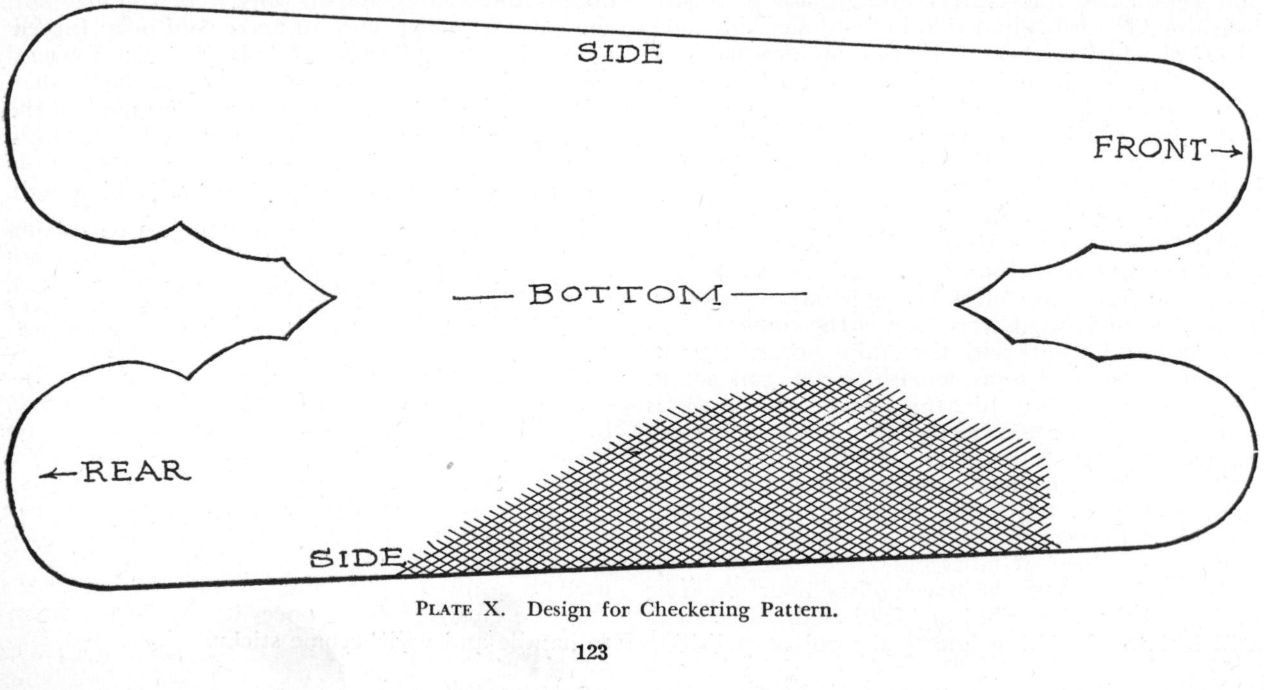


PLATE X. Design for Checkering Pattern.

and help you to start your checking job correctly.

Measure the pattern to locate the exact center of the design, and transfer this to the wood. Scratch a guide line on the wood in a straight direction, then start your cut. You should use the single cutting edge for this starter line, and work slowly to prevent tearing of the wood, which will ruin your diamonds. A light cut with sharp tools produces the best result. Dull tools can be saved for polishing the finished diamonds. Use your flexible steel rule as a tool guide and work from the center to the edge of your planned pattern. Then reverse the work and do the other half. The result will be a series of straight "inverted-V" ridges. In your set of checking tools you will find that multiple tools, after you have used the original single groove-starter, will follow the previous groove so that all are parallel.

The important point is to *half-cut* your grooves so that the ridges have a flat top—otherwise tearing will spoil your work.

Next comes the cross-cutting to form the diamonds. A few scraps of practice wood, with grooves cut halfway and to a full "V" will show you the problems of tearing. When you feel ready to tackle your work on your dummy, again start at the center. When the pattern is completed with half-finished flat-top diamonds, go over these carefully to complete the cutting, working a little in each direction instead of trying to finish one direction first. The deeper the cut, the more delicate the diamond points become, and the greater tendency to tear. *Be careful!*

Another point requiring care is at the edge of the pattern. Do not overrun your outline, or the finished job will not look neat. Slight touching-up at these edges will be necessary, plus cutting the outline with your bordering tool from the set.

Do not start work on your stock until you are certain that you can work slowly and carefully.

Checking on your stock requires, first, a good vise to hold it securely, and in a position where you can work comfortably. Next is suitable light. If bright daylight is not available, use a flexible gooseneck desk lamp with a shade which puts light where you want it. Poor light is to blame for more "slips" than lack of skill.

Checking of the forearm will not be so difficult as work on the pistol grip. A dummy grip for practice will reveal that working around the reverse curves is not easy—your straight lines may not come out properly. Try some practice work on your discarded military stock. Make patterns as desired.

When the checking has been finished, polish the diamonds dry with your finest cutter or with a special tool you may make. An inexpensive small triangular file with a tip section to fit those grooves may be heated red hot in a gas flame and air-cooled to soften it. It may then be bent in your vise to about a 30-degree angle at the tip. Rehardening is not necessary. This tool works soft on wood for final polishing. If it fills in the teeth from oil-soaked wood, soak the tip in gasoline or turpentine and remove debris with a stiff brush.

**Reblueing.** The application of the blued finish has been purposely left until this stage. You may do it at any time, but finished metal parts invite the assembly of the gun before the stock is completed. No woodwork should be done with the metal parts in place.

There are more solutions for reblueing than one could list here. Jim Howe, in his two-volume book, *The Modern Gunsmith,* devotes 15 pages to 49 different formulas, and there are several others. Most solutions can be prepared by yourself or your druggist, or you can purchase prepared solutions. WARNING: Most formulas include poisons. You can obtain rich blue, dull blue, blacks—dull, shiny, and medium—in fact, many odd results. Generally the gun-lover prefers a rich, deep blue.

One of the best is the quick process with hot solutions, and can be used to apply a finish to your metal parts in one evening. First, prepare your solutions.

Have your druggist mix 750 grains corrosive sublimate, 1000 grains potassium chlorate, 1200 grains potassium nitrate, 300 grains ferric chloride, 150 grains cupric chloride, and 300 grains sodium nitrate. These chemicals should be placed in a glass receptacle or jug. Use 1700 cc. of distilled water heated to 130° F. Pour this slowly into the glass containing the chemicals, and stir with a glass rod until all are dissolved. Let this cool and set for at least ten hours. At that time—and not until then—add 175 cc. of sweet spirits of niter and place the solution in a blue or brown bottle—never clear glass.

Copy the above paragraph carefully and take it to your druggist. After he gives you the solution, do not use it for at least 24 hours.

You should have tanks for proper blueing. Any tinsmith can make these of sheet galvanized iron. They should be about 5 inches wide and deep, and long enough to hold your barrel and receiver plus room for handling. A minimum length of 36 inches is advisable. Three tanks should be used and should be labeled for convenience. Tank No. 1 holds a caustic soda solution, tank No. 2 holds lime, and tank No. 3 holds hot water. Lime can be eliminated to simplify the work. Before you start blueing, you must clean all metals completely free from the slightest trace of oil or grease—otherwise the finish will take in a spotty manner. Fill tank No. 1 with 3 inches of water; when hot, add caustic soda or ordinary household lye to make a strong solution. Bring this to a boil.

Lightly oil the inside of the bore and make two plugs of soft wood to fit into the chamber and muzzle. If these project through the receiver and from the muzzle, they serve as handles. Hooks should be made of about ⅛-inch iron wire for handling, because once started, the bare hands must never touch metal or spotting will be the result. Practice with the hooks on the cold dry metal, handling the barrel and receiver by the wood plugs. Use clean, recently washed cotton work gloves for further protection. In addition, have on hand a quantity of 3/0 steel wool, and a few swabs made by wrapping clean cotton cloth around wood sticks, securely tied with heavy white cotton thread.

You are now ready to start the work. It would be best to practice on small parts first, a trigger guard or floor plate. If you spot the work it will have to be repolished and done over, so you may learn a great deal from small parts.

First boil the bright metal for at least ten minutes in the lye solution to remove all grease. If tank No.

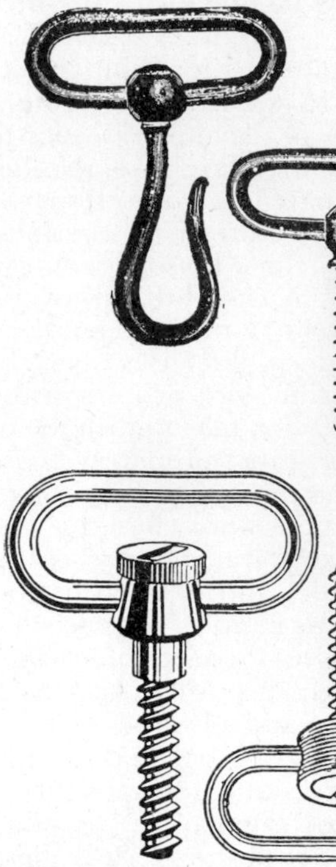

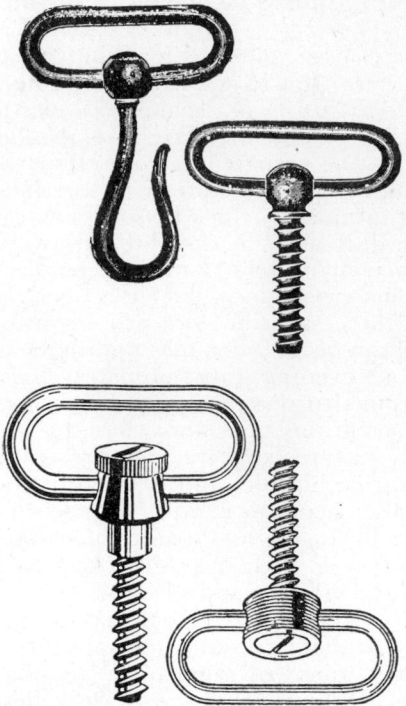

PLATE XI. These are stock swivels and bases available through the Stoeger Arms Corp. of New York. *Upper left:* Swivel snap hook, made for 1-inch or 1¼-inch sling. *Upper right:* Stock screw-eye swivel, available for 1-inch or 1¼-inch sling. *Lower left:* Detachable swivel and base with screw, available for 1¼-inch sling; this can be instantly removed by unlocking the nut. *Lower right:* Stock swivel, not detachable, for 1¼-inch strap only.

2 is filled with boiling water, soak it immediately in that, or rinse in very hot water in a sink or bathtub to remove traces of lye. The heat of the water will permit it to dry itself.

Your tank No. 3 will contain water, brought to a boil. In one corner out of the way, suspend a small wide-mouth jar such as a vaseline jar, thoroughly washed. Fill this half-full of the blueing solution. An iron-wire framework hooked to the tank will properly suspend this below the surface but away from the bottom. Do not permit water to enter this. The idea is to keep it hot at the same temperature as the boiling water.

Use a 4-foot board about 6 inches wide with a couple of short wooden uprights nailed to it in proper position. In these cut simple V-notches to support the ends of the dowels so that you may use both hands on the work after taking it from tanks.

After your work has been rinsed, place it in tank No. 3 to boil for about five minutes. It must be hot. Be careful not to upset the jar of solution. Here is where the wire hooks come in handy. Use those hooks to remove the barrel-receiver, and rest it on the notched board supports, using only the dowel plugs. Wipe water away with a dry cotton cloth, and with your swab apply a coat of solution quickly and evenly in a lengthwise direction, using steady strokes. Do not let it run. It should start to dry from the metal heat almost immediately, and also start to rust. As soon as it is dry, put it back in the boiling water for another five minutes.

Once again remove and place it in the rest. Use a large handful of steel wool and *gently* wipe away some of the rust—not too much—just surplus. Then quickly apply another coat of the solution and permit it to dry; then place it back in the water. Repeat this from five to ten times, depending on the steel, until an even coat of rust is obtained. Do not let the metal parts remain out of water too long. Card off rust with steel wool at each operation, so that an even coating is obtained.

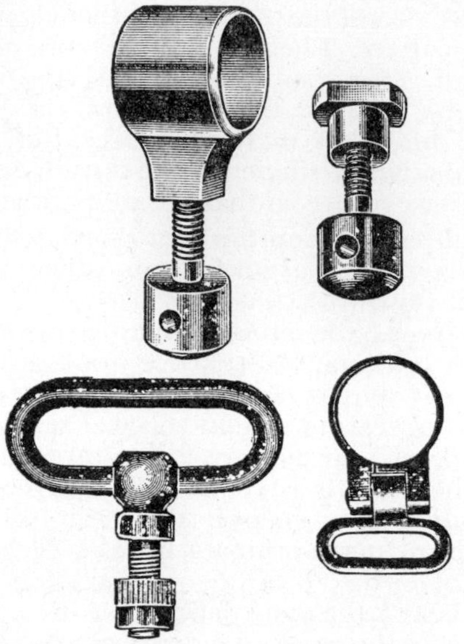

PLATE XII. These are various types of barrel and forearm swivels available through the Stoeger Arms Corp. of New York. *Upper left:* Barrel band, with screw to take detachable swivel. Screw passes through fore-arm. Available in following band diameters: .85 inch, .78 inch, .74 inch. *Upper right:* Fore-arm swivel base, complete with screw for detachable swivel. This must be countersunk inside fore-arm. *Lower left:* Fore-arm screw-eye swivel and base. This must be countersunk inside fore-arm. *Lower right:* Detachable barrel band and swivel. Comes with inside ring diameters of: 9/16, 5/8, 45/64, 25/32, and 55/64 inch. Swivels for 3/4, 7/8, or 1¼-inch sling.

When you think the job is complete, card off rust for the final time and inspect to see that there are no streaks. Then swab the barrel lightly with raw linseed oil or light gun oil. Linseed is best. Permit this to set not over five minutes; you can now handle it with bare hands. Wipe it dry, and rub with beeswax or a little turpentine. Rub with a soft cloth, and you will quickly achieve a high polish. The job is finished. Not until then should you remove the barrel plugs. Save them; you may need them again. Remove the muzzle plug first, and then use a cleaning rod to poke out the chamber plug.

If you are satisfied with your finish, you may now assemble the gun after a good cleaning and oiling.

If you do not have room for three tanks, you can get by with a single tank, first using it to clean with lye, and then washing it carefully and filling it with water. Three tanks are more useful.

Whether you have a beautiful sporter or a crude job depends on careful work. It will be seen that materials cost little; most of the work is labor. You can enjoy both the work and the finished job. If you do well, you will always keep that gun to show friends with a remark, "This is the first rifle I ever rebuilt. Not bad, is it?"

# RIFLE SHOOTING

**Marksmanship.** A good rifle shot is never born such, although he may inherit that perfect co-ordination of brain, eye, nerve, and muscle which will make it easy for him to excel in shooting if he started right. But good shooting is possible with every person who has a fairly good physique, good habits, and good eyesight, either with or without glasses. The trouble is that many people start wrong in shooting a rifle, and they learn bad habits which they then have to break if they are ever to shoot well; particularly they learn bad habits as to trigger squeeze. It seems to be instinctive to jerk the trigger, which is fatal to good shooting. The fine rifle shot is not a man with iron nerves and keen eyesight, as popularly supposed; but rather, if it can be described in a few words, he is a man who has learned how to squeeze the trigger.

There are three primary essentials in rifle shooting which must be thoroughly learned before one can even start on the road toward good shooting. These are AIMING, HOLDING, and TRIGGER SQUEEZE, and the most important of these is *trigger squeeze.* These three essentials must be learned together, as their co-ordination plays an important part. If one aims his rifle accurately, if he holds it steadily, and then if he squeezes the trigger so as not to spoil the aim and hold, he will always strike the bull—provided his rifle and ammunition are accurate and his sights are correctly adjusted. Here is where co-ordination comes in—that is, the teamwork between eye, brain, and muscle to hold the rifle and send the bullet on its way.

In addition to these primary essentials, the beginner should learn the mechanical operation of his rifle, how to adjust the sights, how to allow for wind, and how to take care of his weapon. This is really all there is to rifle shooting, and once the beginner has mastered these things he becomes a good shot, and soon progresses to an excellent shot. Real expertness, as in every other sport, requires experience that comes only with much practice and time.

The bugbear of the beginner is *inability to hold the rifle steady.* Using the usual antiquated methods, it takes a very long time, and tedious and often discouraging practice to learn to hold the rifle steady. Before the average shooter becomes proficient in holding by these old and obsolete methods, he is usually completely discouraged, loses all interest, and quits the game. Until he can hold steadily he cannot see if he is aiming right or not, and likewise he cannot apply the correct trigger squeeze. Before the development of our present system of shooting, and instruction in shooting, not one beginner in a thousand developed into a good rifle shot.

But in about five days' practice of half an hour a day, a beginner, following the instructions detailed below, can teach himself to hold the rifle almost absolutely steady *in the prone position with the gunsling.* In this position, not being bothered with holding difficulties, he can apply himself to accurate aiming, to proper control of the trigger, and to their co-ordination. Then, having learned to make a small group of shots anywhere on the target, he can teach himself sight adjustment, learning to move this group promptly into the center of the bull's-eye. Thus he learns to hit small objects. Therefore the beginner should always *start shooting in the prone position with the gunsling,* and should perfect his holding, aiming, trigger squeeze, and sight adjustment in this position before he proceeds further. Learn to shoot well prone with the gunsling before taking up other positions.

The next step is to take up the sitting position with the gunsling, which will be found to be but little more difficult than the prone position. Success is thus attained from almost the start.

Shooting in the standing or offhand position takes much longer to learn before one can become really proficient at it. But the advantage of learning with the .22-caliber rifle is that ammunition is so inexpensive that one can afford that large amount of careful practice that is necessary to become a good offhand shot.

It is necessary, therefore, that one's rifle be provided with a shooting gunsling. It is also essential that it be equipped with an aperture rear sight that has ready, accurate, and recordable adjustments for both elevation and windage, preferably reading to half minutes. As will be seen later, good rifle shooting is almost a continuous process of sight adjustment, and if one would shoot accurately he must be able to adjust his sight accurately. No good shooting can be done day in and day out, nor can any great interest in the game be sustained, with cheap, poorly equipped rifles.

The purpose of the next few sections is to start the novice right in what has been found to be "the one best way," so that he will progress steadily and will not develop the bad habits which might limit his ultimate perfection in the art of shooting.

**Aiming.** The greatest pains and precision must be taken about the aim, because any inaccuracy in aiming results in the bullet's hitting wide of the mark. A rifle is aimed by first getting the front and rear sights into correct alignment, and then holding them thus aligned, moving or directing the rifle so that this line of aim is brought into line with the bull's-eye or other object to be struck.

Plate I shows how to aim with the various forms of front sights and aperture or peep rear sights. *A* in Plate I shows the manner of aligning the sights and bull's-eye when the cup disk is used in the rear sight, and when a flat-top post front sight is used. This is the usual combination of target sights, and the best for general shooting. The top of the front sight is aligned in the center of the peephole in the disk, and then the rifle is directed at the target so that the top of the front sight appears almost to touch the bottom of the bull's-eye. Both sights are dead black in color, the front sight being kept so by smoking it in the flame of burning camphor or a candle. The reason why we align the front sight below the bull's-eye is to have it appear as a black silhouette against the white surface of the target, so that its exact position is seen distinctly. If we were to attempt to aim at the center of the bull's-eye the black front sight would blend with the black bull's-eye and you could not tell if you were aiming at the center, top, or bottom of the bull. With this form of front sight the sights are adjusted so that when aiming at the bottom of the bull, the bullets will strike in the center of the bull's-eye.

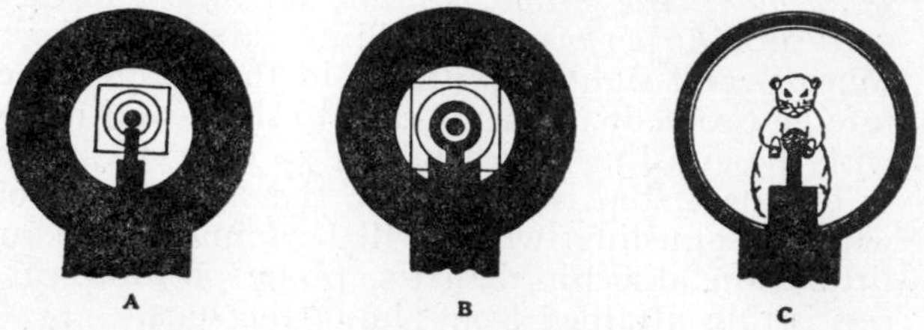


PLATE I. The Sight Picture.

Use the right eye only to aim with, partially closing the left eye. If the right eye is the master eye (see p. 648 for a simple test) you may be able to keep both eyes open when aiming, and this may be a slight advantage in giving you clearer vision. Always focus your eye so as to get the best combination vision of the front sight and target. Do not focus on, or look at, the rear peep sight, but look through it, letting it blur all it wants to, and center the top of the front sight in this round blur.

Take particular pains to aim precisely the same every time you fire. That is, always try to align the two sights exactly the same every time, and direct this alignment at the same point below the bull's-eye. Gradually your eye will form a memory "picture" of the sights and target correctly aligned, and you will be able to reproduce the picture with great accuracy every time you aim. If the bullet does not strike the bull's-eye when you aim this way, then the sights should be adjusted. You should never aim high or low, or to one side or the other, in order to strike the bull's-eye in target shooting. To do so would mean inaccurate aim, because you would not be reproducing the "picture," but would be estimating how much to aim off in a given direction, and we do not want any "estimation" in our aiming.

In all aiming it is *absolutely necessary* that you lay your right cheek firmly against the left side of the comb of the butt-stock in such a position that the eye comes naturally and accurately into the correct line of aim. The firing positions illustrated on page 574 show the cheek thus pressed against the stock. This position of the cheek against the comb will be learned quickly and should be assumed the same each time. Only thus can you hold your eye steady in the line of aim and see the sights aligned with precision. If your eye were unsupported, and not held steady as if it were a part of the rifle, then the eye would tremble and "bob" around with respect to the rifle, and you could never see the two sights and bull's-eye aligned alike for more than a very small instant of time. For this reason, for accurate aim, you should use a rifle having a modern stock with a rather high, thick comb.

For bull's-eye shooting only, if you have keen eyesight, you will gain a slight advantage by using the hooded-aperture type of front sight, which is like a little peep sight with a cover or hood to keep it always in the shade and consequently always lighted the same. *B* in Plate I shows the manner of aligning this type of front sight on the target. The aperture front sight is made to "ring" the bull's-eye, the bull's-eye appearing in its center; the front sight is, of course, aligned in the middle of the peep rear sight as before. If the bull's-eye does not appear distinct and black through the aperture of the front sight it indicates that either the aperture is too small, or else your eyesight is not quite equal to the task. Hooded-aperture sights are provided with a number of aperture disks having various sizes of apertures, and considerable experiment is sometimes necessary to find the particular disk which will give the clearest aim with the particular diameter of bull's-eye you are shooting at.

Most modern rear sights have two apertures. There is a type of aperture with large peep and small disk which is a permanent part of the sight, and in addition there is provided a large cup disk with small aperture which may be screwed into the peephole. This large disk with small peep is intended only for bull's-eye target shooting, and is best for such shooting. It may sometimes be used for other slow-fire shooting where the light is very good and the target well defined, but it is very slow to catch aim with in snap shooting or rapid fire. The large aperture should always be used for all firing at natural targets, for hunting, for rapid-fire or snap shooting, and for field shooting. This aperture is usually used in conjunction with a gold, ivory, or red bead front sight.

*C* in Plate I shows how to aim with such a combination of sights on game. Center the top of the front sight in the center of the aperture, and align the top of the front sight on the exact spot on the target that you wish your bullet to hit. Focus your eye on target and front sight, look through the rear sight, letting it blur all it wants to, and center the blur. Do not object to the fact that you can see a great deal of country through this large peephole, as this is what enables you to catch aim so quickly with this type of rear peep, and to keep moving or running objects continually in view. Take great pains in aiming very accurately in this way for the first week or two, until your eye forms an indelible memory of the picture. Then begin to disregard the rear sight entirely when aiming, merely looking through it but paying no attention to it, letting the eye center the front sight in the peep naturally. This it will do after you have aimed enough carefully to get the "picture" firmly impressed, because the eye has a natural aptitude for centering objects. When this method of aiming with the front sight only is learned, the peep-sight becomes the most accurate and rapid of all iron rear sights.

Bright bead sights are not nearly as good as dead black front sights for target shooting, but for all shooting at natural objects or game they are much better because they show up more distinctly against natural backgrounds. Ivory beads are best for deep woods, but are not good over snow. Gold beads are strongest, and can be smoked black for target shooting without injuring them. The surface of the bead toward the eye should always be flat and perpendicular, never rounded. It will then be illuminated evenly all over by sunlight, and the aim will be constant. If the bead were rounded toward the eye, only that portion toward the sun would be illuminated, you would favor that bright spot in aiming, particularly when aiming quickly, and your bullet would strike wide of the mark in the direction away from the sun or light.

Remember to *aim exactly the same each time.* If your rifle does not shoot where you aim it, then your sights should be adjusted—never alter the method of aiming.

**Firing Positions.** If you are a beginner in rifle shooting your greatest difficulty at the start will be to hold the rifle steady. In fact, for the first three or four days you will not be able to hold steadily enough to aim accurately or to squeeze the trigger properly. You should not attempt to do any shooting at this stage, because you will get no results at all, you will simply waste time and ammunition, and you may become discouraged.

It will take you quite a long time to learn to hold fairly steadily in the standing and kneeling positions, and you should never attempt to shoot in those positions until you have become a really good shot in the prone and sitting positions. You should start to shoot in the prone position with gunsling only. The proper way to learn this position is to practice it first in your home, without cartridges, until you become perfect, steady, and comfortable in it. Not until then should you take your rifle out to the range to do any shooting. In just a few days of practice in this position you can hold the rifle with absolute steadiness, and then you will be able to concentrate on aiming accurately, and squeezing the trigger carefully, a thing you absolutely could not do while your rifle was wobbling all over the landscape.

Practice the prone position in your home for ten minutes, twice a day, until you learn it. Then, when you have become a good shot in this position, similarly practice each of the other positions at home for a few days until you learn them before you start shooting in them. These are the positions used by every rifle shot who has had any success whatsoever.

**Adjusting the Gunsling.** The gunsling is of tremendous assistance to steady holding in the prone, sitting, and kneeling positions. We do not mean to say that you cannot shoot in these positions without the gunsling, but we do say that it will take you weeks and months to hold and shoot fairly well without it, and with it you can learn to hold steadily and shoot very well in just a few days. Every expert rifleman uses the gunsling in these positions. Without it he would be hopelessly handicapped when competing against those who use it. But it must be used correctly to get the benefit from it.

The upper or forward half of the sling is called the "loop." When you stretch the sling along the bottom of the stock the loop should be adjusted to

PLATE II. Putting the arm through the loop of the sling. Note twist.

PLATE III. Left hand, arm and loop in proper position for holding.

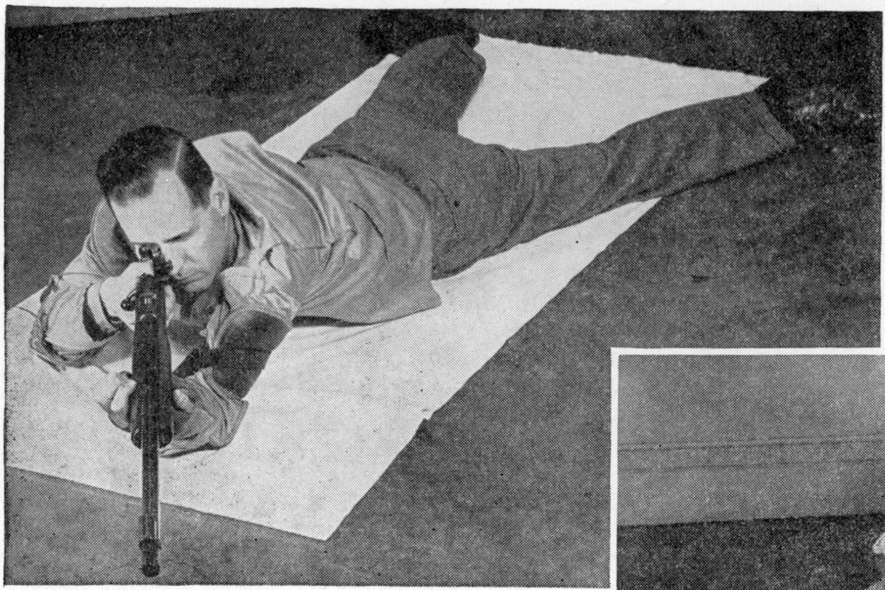

PLATE IV. Prone position.

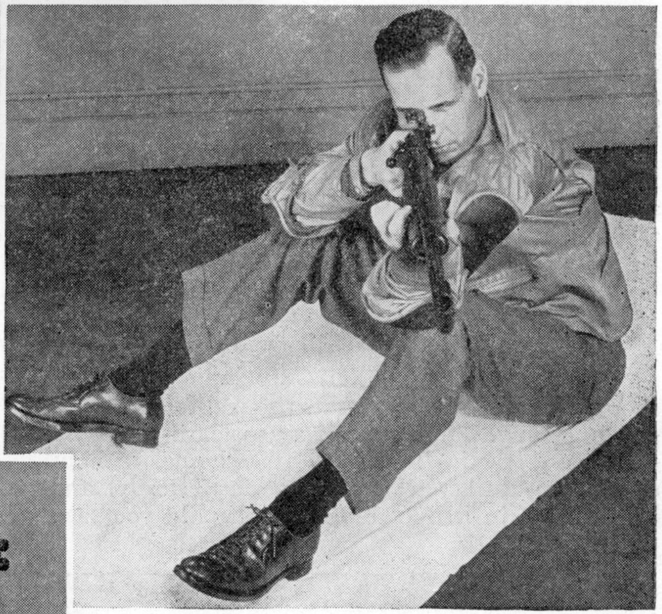

PLATE V. Sitting position.

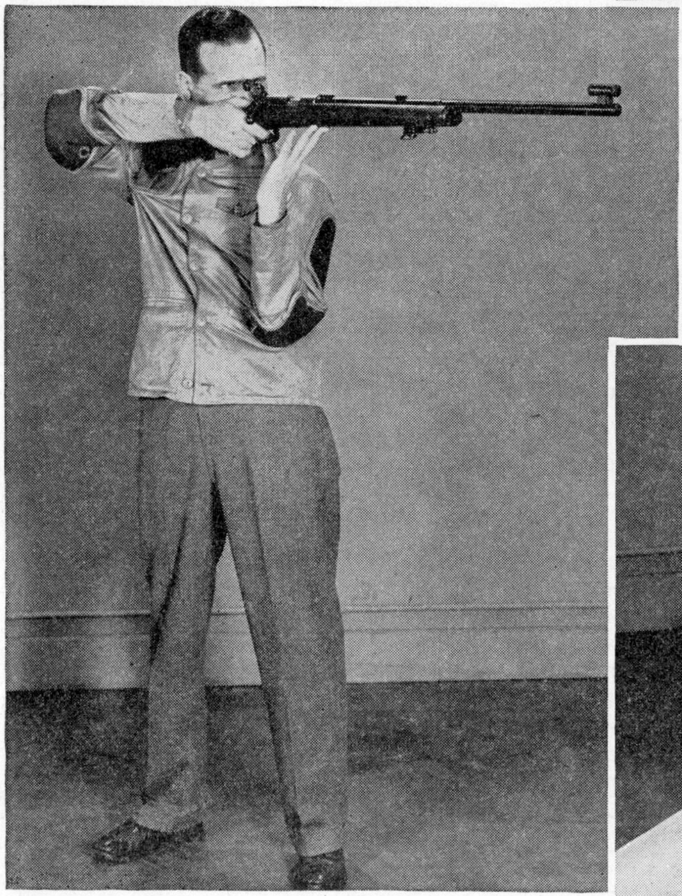

PLATE VI. N. R. A. standing position. (Offhand)

PLATE VII. Kneeling position.

such a length that it will come to within about 2 inches of the butt-swivel. Exact lengths will differ with different lengths of arms, and can only be tested by experience. If the loop is too short you cannot get the rifle to your shoulder; if too loose the sling will not be tight on the arm. The rear portion of the sling, called the "tail," should always be so loose that it will never be stretched tight when you are in the firing position.

To place the sling on your arm, move the hand between the entire sling and the stock just in front of the trigger guard, and then bring the hand and arm back through the loop. That is, your arm should pass through the loop from its right to its left. This twists the upper portion of the sling so that its flat rests against your wrist. Then carry the left hand, in a circular motion, high and left, over the forward part of the sling, and grasp the forearm just in rear of the front sling swivel. With the right hand, then pull the loop as high up on the left upper arm as it will go, and slip down the keeper to hold it there. Notice that the loop passes from the forearm swivel, to the right of the left wrist, and then around the left upper arm high up, near the armpit. The faults of the beginner are (1) placing the hand through the loop from left to right instead of right to left so that the edge instead of the flat of sling rests against the right side of the left wrist, and (2) having the rear of the loop around the upper arm near the elbow instead of high up, almost to the armpit.

**Prone Position.** To assume the prone position, having adjusted the sling on the arm as described above, you should first half face to the right of the target, then lie down on your stomach, elbows on the ground, taking particular care that you lie at an angle of 45 degrees to the right of the target, never head on to the target. Place the butt of the rifle to your shoulder and aim at the target. If you cannot get the butt of the rifle to your shoulder, the sling is too tight. When the sling is just the right length it takes a little effort, but not much, to place the butt to the shoulder. The left elbow must be on the ground at a point almost under, never more than an inch or two to the left of the rifle. The right elbow should be sloped outward more. The elbows should be neither too far apart nor too close together. Regard the upper arms and the chest as the legs of a tripod: if the legs are set too far apart the tripod will be unsteady; so also if they are too close together. The forearm should now rest well down in the palm of the hand, fingers curling up over the forearm and fingers and thumb almost but not quite meeting over the top of the barrel. Do not grasp the forearm with the fingers and hold palm away from the bottom of the forearm, but let that forearm press down hard well into the palm of the hand. The sling loop should now be quite tight, binding the forearm down hard in the palm of the hand, and binding the butt quite tight against the shoulder. The sling loop should feel as though it had about 10 to 15 pounds' tension on it.

The legs should be spread wide apart and should hug the ground closely, feet turned outward, and inside of shoes resting on the ground.

Now read all these instructions over again to see that you have got them right. Every word is important. Also, carefully study Plate IV, which shows the details of the prone position. Copy this as nearly as you can. At the beginning, this position will probably be intensely uncomfortable. Persist in it. Practice it ten minutes at a time. Try first to get it precisely right. About the third day it will begin to seem more natural and comfortable. The fourth day you will find that you are beginning to hold quite steady. Before the week is out you will find that you can place the sights on the target and hold them aligned there steadily.

The principal faults of the beginner are: (1) lying head on to the target instead of faced 45 degrees to the right; (2) left elbow too far to the left of a point directly under the rifle; (3) forearm of rifle not well down in the palm of the hand; (4) sling loop too loose or too tight; and (5) loop around arm down near the elbow instead of high up near armpit.

It is well to have some kind of soft padding on the elbows of your shooting coat, otherwise your elbows may get sore from contact with the ground.

**Holding the Breath.** When you have got the position correctly, and have practiced it enough so that it is no longer uncomfortable and you are beginning to hold steadily, then you can begin to practice aiming at a small target while attempting to hold steady. When you aim you must hold your breath. Take a deep breath, then let it out until the lungs become normal, and then start to aim. Hold the breath while aiming, and then attempt to squeeze the trigger exactly as described hereafter (pp. 576-578). If it becomes difficult, or you become shaky, bring the rifle down, rest a minute, then try again.

**Sitting Position.** Do not practice this position until you have become a good shot in the prone position. Adjust the gunsling as before. The sling, arms, hands, and rifle are in the same relative position as when shooting prone. Half face to the right of the target and sit down. Rest the elbows on the knees, or just a little bit below the knees, the left elbow and left knee almost under the rifle. If possible, stamp small holes in the ground for the heels to rest in to keep them from slipping. It is also permissible to cross the legs below the knees if you desire and if it gives added steadiness. Gradually you will find that there is just one spot on the kneecaps, or slightly below them, where the elbows will tend to rest firmly. Study Plate V (page 574) and imitate this as closely as possible.

As before, practice this position, and holding, aiming, and squeezing the trigger in it for several days at home, before attempting to use it on the range.

**Kneeling Position.** Do not practice this position until you have become a good shot in the prone and sitting positions. Adjust the gunsling on the left arm as before. Half face to the right of the target. Sit on the right heel, resting the weight of the body on it. If your ankle is limber enough you may sit on the side of the foot instead of on the heel. The left knee should point toward the target, with the left elbow resting on or a trifle in front of the kneecap. The sling, hands, arms, and the rifle are in the same relative position as when shooting prone, except that the right elbow is not rested. The left elbow should be a little more under the rifle than in the preceding positions. Lean a little forward to get a good balance, then train yourself to control the slight tendency to sway from side to side. Study Plate VII (page 574) and endeavor to duplicate the position shown as closely as possible.

**Standing Position.** Do not practice this position until you have become a good shot in the prone and sitting positions. After that, practice it at home almost daily, and on the range whenever you can do so. It is much more difficult to shoot well standing than in the other positions, and it takes longer to learn it. But as in practical shooting you often cannot assume other positions because there is not time, or because ground or vegetation interfere with a view of the target from lower positions, you should endeavor to perfect yourself in shooting standing. No one is a finished rifleman until he can shoot at least fairly well in the standing position in both slow and rapid fire.

Face almost directly to the right of the target. The left side should be toward the target, the feet from 12 to 18 inches apart (whatever distance seems steadiest). The left elbow should be well under the rifle. With long-armed shooters the left hand should grasp the forearm well out toward its tip. Short-armed shooters will have to grasp slightly closer to the trigger guard. The right elbow may be held high or low as seems steadiest. Hold the rifle medium hard to the shoulder with the right hand, using the left hand mostly to direct and steady the rifle. The right cheek should be pressed hard against the left side of the butt-stock. Let the forearm rest well down in the palm of the hand. Slight variations in this position are permissible, and after considerable experience you may find that you can vary the position with advantage; at the start, however, you should endeavor to duplicate the position as we have here described it as closely as possible.

It is important that you get a good balance on both feet and the hips. If your body is out of balance you will sway and tremble. Assume an erect, well-balanced standing position without the rifle in the hands. Now when you take up the rifle and aim with it, the weight of the rifle stretched out in front will tend to pull you forward. You should now lean back just a trifle, perhaps an inch or two, just enough to counteract the tendency of the rifle to pull you forward, thus getting in perfect balance. Do not lean forward at all as the beginner and poor shot usually do.

It takes a great deal of practice to learn to hold steadily and shoot well standing. Practice daily in your room, assuming the position, aiming most carefully, and then practicing the trigger squeeze, all at a little target on the wall. Every good offhand shot practices daily in this way the whole year, besides getting all the regular shooting on the rifle range that he can find time for.

The position described is known as the "Army Standing" position, and is prescribed in military matches and many matches in R.O.T.C. units. In N.R.A. Club competitions, the "N.R.A. Standing" position may be used; in this it is permissible to use the gunsling, and the elbow of the arm supporting the rifle may be placed against the body or rested on the hip.

The gunsling is of little or no advantage in standing positions, but often the resting of the left upper arm against the body, or wedging the left elbow into the hip, does give a slightly steadier position, although the "N.R.A. Standing" position is not a quickly assumed one for rapid-fire or snap shooting. (See Plate VI.)

For slow-fire shooting the position that one finally assumes as his best position will depend much upon his physical conformation. The beginner should experiment a little with slight changes in position before selecting one in which to perfect himself. As one aims and endeavors to hold steadily, the sights will drift and tremble around the bull. It is never possible to hold with such absolute steadiness in the standing position as one can in the prone position, or as often can be done in the sitting position. But with considerable practice one does hold steadier, and he must try to control and time his trigger squeeze so that the last ounce of pressure which discharges the rifle is squeezed or "wished" on just as the front sight drifts under the bull.

**The Secret of Steady Holding.** Holding must never be a physical exercise. Do not try to hold by brute strength. Contract your muscles only enough to place your bones in such position that the bones will hold the rifle up. Then relax every other muscle. Particularly, have the comb of the stock high enough so that you can lay or rest (not press) your cheek down on it so as to relax the large muscle at the back of the neck and between the shoulder blades (trapezius). Relax all the other muscles also that are not needed to hold the bones in the position. Try to make the bones hold the rifle. Relax, be lazy, be quiet, be slow, be uniform, and thus you will gradually learn to hold steady. He who fusses, frets, screws himself into an uncomfortable position, changes his position, tries to hold by brute strength, never learns to hold steady.

**Trigger Squeeze.** After you have learned to aim your rifle uniformly, and to hold the rifle steadily in the prone position with the gunsling, the next essential you must master is the trigger squeeze so you can discharge the rifle without disturbing the accurate aim and steady hold. This is one of the most important things in rifle shooting. A very natural tendency is to jerk the trigger when the aim is right, and to set the muscles and flinch against the recoil and report which you know are coming; you will have to train yourself out of these natural tendencies. The difference between the poor and good shots, and between the good and excellent shots, all lies in the relative excellence of their control of the trigger.

Long years of experience in the training of hundreds of thousands of men to shoot the rifle have shown that there is one best way for a beginner to train himself to squeeze the trigger so that he will not jerk or flinch. You should squeeze or press it so gradually that you will not know when the rifle is going to fire. Not knowing exactly when the rifle will be discharged, you will not know when to set your muscles against the kick; that is, you will not flinch. Therefore, during the beginning of your practice you should invariably squeeze the trigger in the following manner until it becomes a fixed habit, so that you will do it naturally in this way even when you do not think particularly about it.

Assume a correct and steady prone position with the gunsling. You must be able to hold steady in this position before you start to learn trigger squeeze. Aim roughly at the bottom edge of the bull's-eye, forefinger applying a slight pressure on the trigger, enough to take up the slack on the trigger if your trigger has a slack or preliminary pull, but not nearly enough pressure to discharge the rifle. It is best to press or squeeze the trigger with the first joint of the forefinger, because this is the most sensitive and delicately trained portion of the human body. Some marksmen, however, prefer to use the second joint. It really does not make much difference which you use. As soon as you become well set in the position, take a deep breath, let the lungs become normal, and then start your effort to hold steadily and aim accurately. When the aim appears to be correct, the front sight having steadied down under and almost touching the bottom of the bull's-eye, very gradually and carefully increase the pressure of your forefinger on the trigger. Increase the pressure ounce by ounce, but *increase it only when the front sight is aligned properly on the bottom of the bull's-eye. If, through difficulty in holding, or in seeing the sights, your front sight drifts away from the bottom of the bull, stop increasing the pressure, hold what pressure you have already applied to the trigger by keeping the forefinger immobile, and go on with the increase of pressure, ounce by ounce, only when the front sight is aligned correctly again.* During one of the moments when the squeeze or pressure is being increased, and when the sights are correctly aligned, the rifle will be discharged more or less unexpectedly. Now, not knowing exactly when it was going off, you did not set your muscles against the kick, did not flinch, and the rifle was not disturbed in its alignment at the critical instant just before the discharge. Then, if the sights were correctly adjusted for range and wind, the bull's-eye will surely be struck.

**Trigger-Squeeze Exercise.** You should practice this trigger squeeze and its co-ordination with holding and aiming in your home for a few days before you begin to shoot on the range with ammunition. To be specific: When you get your first rifle, do not rush right out on the range to try it out. Instead, first teach yourself to hold it steadily in the standard prone position with the gunsling. Then study the sights and aiming. Then start in to practice the trigger-squeeze exercise described below for three or four days before you begin to shoot with ammunition. This is the quickest and safest way to learn. Any other way is almost certain to cause you to develop bad habits which must be broken before you can succeed.

Every rifle shot of note practices trigger-squeeze exercises. Most really fine shots practice them for 15 minutes at a time, at least two or three times a week. The exercise may be done in your home, with a small bull's-eye target tacked or taped on the wall ten feet or more away. Place the target in a good light where it can be seen distinctly, at about the same height above the floor that your rifle is when you aim it. Pad your elbows, or else place a thick mat on the floor to rest them on to keep them from getting sore. It does no harm to a good rifle to snap it, but it is desirable to insert a fired case and rotate it from time to time. The following are the details of this exercise when it is done in the prone position:

(1) Adjust the gunsling properly, tight enough to give firm support, loop high up on upper arm.

(2) Lie down, assume the correct prone position with gunsling, rifle aimed roughly at the target.

(3) Place forefinger on trigger with very light pressure, just enough to take up the slack or preliminary pull if the trigger has such a pull, but not nearly enough to discharge the rifle.

(4) Take a deep breath, let out about half of it, and then hold the breath.

(5) Aim accurately at the bottom edge of the bull's-eye, at the same time holding as steadily as you can.

(6) Squeeze or press the trigger slowly, increasing pressure only when the aim is right, holding what pressure you have already applied when the front sight drifts off the bull, and go ahead with the increase of pressure only when the front sight drifts back to the bull again.

(7) Just at the instant, or the instant before, the rifle "snaps," try to call your shot—that is, catch with the eye the exact point where the sights were aligned the instant before the trigger gave way, which is the spot where you would expect your bullet to strike the target had the rifle been loaded and the sights correctly adjusted for range and wind.

Take the rifle down from the shoulder and wait a few seconds after each shot. Do not attempt to fire more than ten shots at a time in these exercises at the start or you will get tired and shaky. Get up, rest a few minutes, then go at it again. Ten to 15 minutes at a time, twice a day, is as much as you should do.

This exercise teaches you not only trigger squeeze, but the proper co-ordination of holding and aiming with the squeeze. Remember that it is absolutely necessary that you learn this by home practice before you start to shoot on the range with ammunition, otherwise you will be merely wasting your ammunition and time, and your complete lack of results will discourage you. It will also be very helpful if you practice this exercise regularly even after you have become a good shot.

After two or three weeks of this exercise, combined with range shooting, you will be able to place all but about a couple of ounces of the pressure on the trigger necessary to discharge the rifle as you place your rifle to the shoulder. This greatly quickens the trigger squeeze, and makes it simpler. But you must be careful to squeeze these last ounces on very carefully, and only when the aim is right. After still further practice you seem to be able to often "wish" this last ounce of pressure on the trigger just as the aim is most perfect. Then you

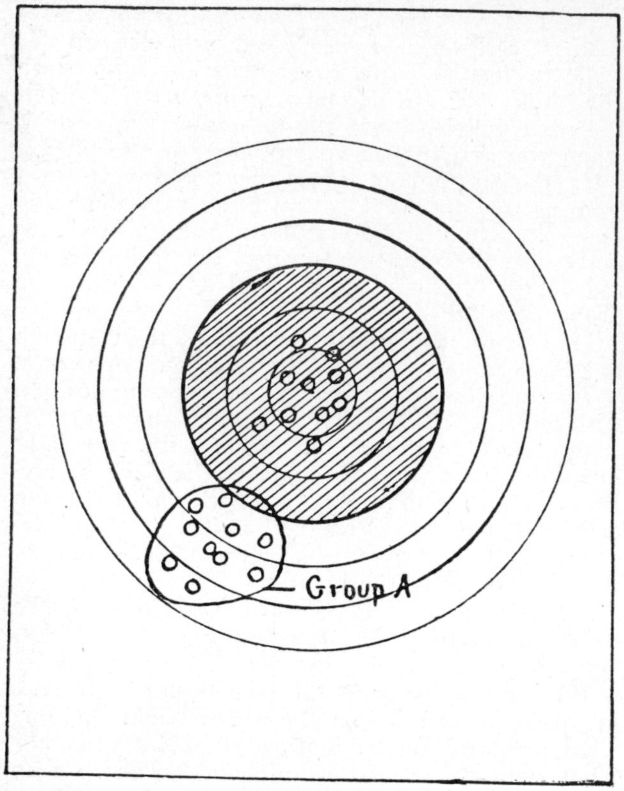


Plate VIII.

have arrived. After reaching this point, see that you continue with these trigger-squeeze exercises so that you retain this highly desirable skill.

**Sight Adjustment and Range Practice.** After you have become fairly proficient in the co-ordination of holding, aiming, and squeezing by practicing the trigger-squeeze exercise in your home for a few days, you can then profitably proceed to range practice. At the outset this should be conducted similarly to the trigger-squeeze exercise. Start firing at a range of only 25 yards. At this distance it will be easy for you to hit the target. If you do not have a regular spotting telescope, any field glasses or cheap telescope will enable you to see the bullet holes as you shoot, and thus you will not have to leave the firing point and go down to the target to see where you are hitting it until after you have completed firing on all targets you have placed on the butt.

Rifle sights are adjusted at the factory, but they may not suit the individual or the sights may have been damaged or misaligned in shipment. Thus it sometimes happens that with normal aim a new rifle will not even hit the entire target at 25 yards when you first start to shoot it. In that case you should lie down at only 10 yards from the target, and fire, say, three shots at it. At this short range these bullets should almost surely strike the target somewhere, no matter how far the sights are from normal adjustment. Now adjust your sights as described below so that when you fire again the bullets will group close to the bottom edge of the bull's-eye. When you go back to the 25-yard firing point, your shots fired from there with this adjustment of the sights should surely strike somewhere on the 25-yard target. An improvised target with a black aiming bull's-eye about 2 inches in diameter may be used for this practice, but it will be much more convenient and instructive if you use the standard N.R.A. 75-foot (25-yard) small-bore target.

At the start, do not endeavor to hit the bull's-eye, but rather try to make a small group of ten shots. Let this group center anywhere on the target. You are really testing out your ability to co-ordinate hold, aim, and squeeze, and do it uniformly. Keep at this group shooting until you can do these things so well and so uniformly that you can group ten consecutive shots in about a 2-inch circle as shown in group *A* on Plate VIII. When you can get your group this small it indicates that you are co-ordinating very well for this stage of your practice, and you are ready for your first lesson in sight adjustment, which consists of learning how to move your group into the center of the bull's-eye. You should always adjust your sights to do this. Never change your aiming point.

The *point of aim* is the spot on the target where the front sight is aligned, usually the bottom edge of the bull's-eye. The *center of impact* is the center of the group on the target where the bullets from an aligned rifle strike. The object of sight adjustment is to make the center of impact come to a certain position with reference to the point of aim. If you aim at the bottom of the bull's-eye (see p. 572) you want your center of impact to be a little above the point of aim so that the bullets will strike in the center of the bull's-eye. In hunting it is usually best to have the point of aim and center of impact coincide.

To make your rifle center its shots higher with respect to the point of aim, raise the rear sight. To lower the center of impact, lower the rear sight. To make the rifle shoot to the right, move the rear sight to the right, or to move the center of impact to the left, move the rear sight to the left. In other words the general rule is: *"Move your rear sight in the direction in which you wish to move your center of impact."* Memorize this rule.

Let us now introduce you to a measurement or graduation which is in general use among all modern, well-informed rifle shooters. A *minute of angle,* or a *minute,* as it is called for short, is that graduation or dimension on the rear sight which has an adjusting value of *one inch per hundred yards.* That is, raising your rear sight one minute will raise your center of impact one inch on a target 100 yards away, or 1/4 inch at 25 yards, or 1/2 inch at 50 yards, or 2 inches at 200 yards. Similarly, one minute in windage adjustment will move your center of impact horizontally a like amount. Memorize this rule: *"One minute equals one inch per hundred yards,"* and all will be easy.

Now look again at Plate VIII, the target there illustrated being the standard N.R.A. small-bore target. On these targets the scoring rings are always one minute apart. Thus on the 25-yard target the rings are 1/4 inch apart, 50 yards, 1/2 inch, and 100 yards, one inch apart. Notice group *A* in this plate. The center of the group is four rings (i.e., minutes) below the center of the bull's-eye, and three rings or minutes to the left of the center of the bull. Therefore, if you had been shooting for a small group only, and had just made group *A*, then if you were to raise your elevation 4 minutes, and move your windage to the right 3 minutes, and then shoot another group of shots, that group would be located something like the group shown in the center of the bull's-eye, and your score would total about 97 points.

Let us now look at the sights themselves. Modern sights with minute of angle adjustment operate on the same principle as the machinist's micrometer. Plate IX shows the elevation scales on such a sight. The lower graduated scale on the slide has lines for each 5 minutes. The graduations around the head of the screw above are for single minutes, with short lines between them for half-minutes. There are 5 graduations of minutes, or 10 half-minutes, around the circumference of this screw. Turning this screw one complete revolution will raise or lower the elevation 5 minutes, moving the scale past the pointer on the slide from one graduation to the next 5-minute graduation above or below it, depending on which way you turn the screw.

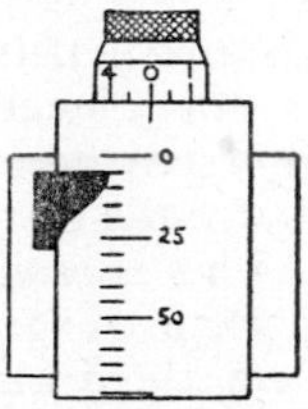


PLATE IX. Elevation Scales.

As you turn the screw around you will notice that it "clicks" as it passes each half-minute graduation. This is so that you can feel the graduations as well as see them in case you should have to adjust the sight in too dim or glaring light to see the graduations. If you turn the sight four clicks you know you have adjusted it just 2 minutes.

Plate IX shows the sight adjusted to 5 minutes in elevation—that is, 5 minutes on the lower scale—and zero on the screw. Suppose your sight was set at this elevation when you fired the group shown in Plate VIII. Then to raise the sight 4 minutes to bring the center of impact up to a level with the center of the bull, you would turn the screw to the right, clockwise, until the figure 4 on the screw came to the index line, or turn the screw in the same direction eight clicks. Then the index pointer on the lower scale should be just slightly above the 10-minute line, and the sight would read 9 minutes—that is, considerably over 5 minutes on the slide, and 4 minutes on the screw. If you will take this particular example we have been describing and move the sight on your rifle accordingly, you will get onto the whole theory and process in a few minutes. The system is exceedingly simple, despite this long description, and once you have become familiar with it all uncertainty as to sight adjustment will disappear. You can move your sight and place your center of impact wherever you want it on the target with absolute certainty.

The windage adjustment works on the same micrometer principle, but the scale is sometimes a little different. Plate X shows the usual windage scale. The graduated lines on this scale are 4 minutes apart instead of 5 minutes on the elevation slide. The screw to the left has eight graduations around its head, each of which clicks. A complete turn of the screw moves the scale one graduation of 4 minutes; therefore, each click on the screw is for a half-minute, the same as each click on the elevation screw. Plate X shows an adjustment of 2 minutes right windage. If your windage was set at this adjustment when you made group *A* on Plate VIII, then you would simply turn the windage screw six clicks, moving the sight 3 minutes to the right, to shift the center of impact to a vertical line passing through the center of the bull's-eye.

The reason why these sights are provided with half-minute graduations and clicks in addition to those for minutes, is that the accurate rifles and ammunition now provided by our manufacturers will respond to a more accurate adjustment than an inch per hundred yards, and for the finest competitive target shooting we need the refinement of the half-minute. Indeed, some sights are now being graduated in quarter-minutes. The matter of half- or quarter-minute graduations need not confuse you because they change the point of impact just a half- or a quarter-inch per hundred yards.

You will need not only to adjust your sight at the beginning of a score to bring your group into the center of the 10-ring, but also you will frequently have to make minor adjustments during the shooting of a string of ten or 20 shots to keep the shots well into the 10-ring. While a good rifle and ammunition ought to shoot quite consistently to the same spot once the rifle has been warmed up, they do not invariably do so. Also, temperature and wind conditions may change while you are firing this string of ten or 20 shots, making a change in sight adjustment desirable.

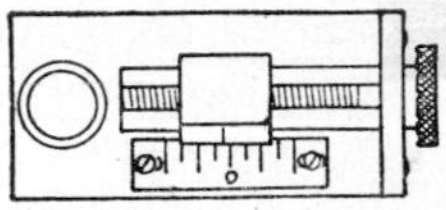


PLATE X. Windage Scale.

Thus, suppose your first three or four shots strike in the 10-ring, but on looking at the bullet holes through your spotting scope you notice that they are all above the center of the ring. At this point it is advisable to reduce your elevation a half-minute, as you might pull a shot a trifle high, and if so it would probably strike above the 10-ring. This same thing may occur in windage due to a slight increase or decrease in the wind.

As you proceed from shooting at a short range to a longer one you will have to raise the adjustment of the rear sight to compensate for the drop of the bullet. For example, the bullet of the .22 long rifle regular-velocity cartridge drops, by the force of gravity, about 8 inches in its flight from 50 to 100 yards, and if you were to fire at 100 yards with the elevation you found correct for 50 yards your bullet would strike the 100-yard target about 8 inches below the center of the bull's-eye. Therefore, you must add about 8 minutes to your 50-yard elevation when shooting at 100 yards, because

8 minutes will raise your center of impact 8 inches at 100 yards.

When you use a rear sight adjusting to minutes you gain another advantage. The angles of elevation for different ranges have been determined for all cartridges with a table of these angles for the cartridge you are using, and having determined your elevation for a given range by shooting at that range, you at once know your approximate elevation for all other distances. For example, here is the table for the .22 long rifle cartridges, both regular-velocity and the high-speed variety.

**ANGLES OF ELEVATION**
**.22 Long Rifle Cartridges**

| Range | .22 L. R. Regular M.V. 1100 f.s. | | .22 L. R. High Speed M.V. 1400 f.s. | |
|---|---|---|---|---|
| Yards | Minutes | Half Minutes or Clicks | Minutes | Half Minutes or Clicks |
| 25 | 3.4 | 6.8 | 2.3 | 4.6 |
| 50 | 7.1 | 14.2 | 4.7 | 9.4 |
| 75 | 10.9 | 21.8 | 7.5 | 15.0 |
| 100 | 15.1 | 30.2 | 10.5 | 21.0 |
| 125 | 19.2 | 38.4 | 13.7 | 27.4 |
| 150 | 23.8 | 47.6 | 17.2 | 34.4 |
| 175 | 28.3 | 56.6 | 20.7 | 41.4 |
| 200 | 33.0 | 66.0 | 24.6 | 49.2 |
| 225 | 37.9 | 75.8 | 28.4 | 56.8 |
| 250 | 43.2 | 86.4 | 32.6 | 65.2 |
| 275 | 48.5 | 97.0 | 37.0 | 74.0 |
| 300 | 53.7 | 107.4 | 41.3 | 82.6 |

PLATE XI.

To use this table: Suppose you had shot at 50 yards with regular-velocity ammunition and found your normal elevation to be 9 minutes. Then for 100 yards your elevation should be about 17 minutes, because the table shows that the 100-yard elevation is 8 minutes higher than the 50-yard elevation. Or, as the table shows an angle of 7.1 minutes for 50 yards, and the correct angle determined for you and your rifle is 9 minutes, you could simply add 1.9 minutes to all the figures above, and you would have approximately the elevations on your sight for the various distances.

We say "approximately the elevation" because this table will seldom be absolutely correct for every man and rifle. But it will usually be so close that you can set your sights by it and the first shot at the new range will hit in the aiming bull or close to it.

This table has been prepared on the assumption that aim is taken at the center of the bull's-eye. If, however, you aim at six o'clock on the bull's-eye of the standard small-bore targets, then allowance must be made for the varying radii of the aiming bull's-eyes. Thus in changing from the 3-inch aiming bull at 50 yards to the 6-inch aiming bull's-eye at 100 yards, you must add 1½ minutes (or 3 clicks) to the difference between the two figures shown in the table to allow for actually aiming 1½ inches farther below the center of the bull's-eye on the 100-yard target than you did on the 50-yard target.

Although this table is very useful and convenient, the really good shot does not depend much on it. He records all his elevations and windages, together with wind and weather conditions, in his score book. Soon he has records therein for every distance and condition, and from them he can set his sights so accurately that he gets a large percentage of his first shots in the 10-ring. It is impossible to keep all such records in one's head, and the score book is a very necessary help to good shooting.

**Adjustment with Crude Sights.** Unfortunately many shooters buy rifles with crude sights because they are cheaper, not realizing that such sights handicap them so much that really interesting or successful shooting cannot be done with them. Nevertheless, we give you here what rules we can for adjusting such sights, if only to show their shortcomings.

The only rule we can give you for adjusting an open rear sight is the general one: *"Move your rear sight the way you want your shot to go."* You will have to guess, more or less, at how much to move it in elevation by means of the little step elevator, and by driving it to the right or left through the barrel slot for windage. Then shoot to see if you have moved it enough, and if not, try again. Also, the influence of the intensity and direction of light shining on open rear sights is enough to upset all calculations completely. It is not possible to do consistently good shooting, day after day, with such sights.

If your rear sight is an aperture sight with rather crude sliding scales for elevation and windage, then proceed as follows to determine the rule for its adjustments: Measure the distance between graduations on the scale. This is easiest done by placing a ruler on the scale. If, for example, you find that there are five lines on the scale to every quarter-inch on the rule, then the lines are 0.05 inch apart. Then measure the distance between the front and rear sights. Say you find this to be 28 inches. In 100 yards there are 3600 inches, which divided by 28 equals 128. Therefore, every move on the rear sight will move the center of impact 128 times that amount on the 100-yard target. The distance between lines on the scale having been found to be 0.05 inch, multiply this by 128, and we get 6.4 inches. Therefore, for the scale on this sight we have determined the rule: Moving the sight one graduation on the scale moves the center of impact 6.4 inches at 100 yards—or, of course, 3.2 inches at 50 yards.

To see these rough scales clearly enough to set the sights with any pretense of accuracy you will usually have to get up from the firing point, hold the sight in a good light close to the eye, and, looking carefully at it, count the number of lines from the top of the scale to the index pointer, then loosen the clamping screw, and carefully shove the slide up or down the desired amount, guessing at adjustment between lines. A screwdriver is necessary with some sights to loosen and tighten the windage adjustment. After moving the sight approximately the desired amount, you will then have to fire a few shots at the target to see if the adjustment is correct. Of course none of this can be done within the time limit of one minute per shot allowed in target shooting. Such sights are very unsatisfactory for such shooting, or any shooting where any great degree of accuracy is desired.

**Wind Allowance.** Wind deflects the bullet from its straight course from muzzle to target, carrying or blowing the bullet with it. Thus a wind from the right will carry a bullet to the left, causing it to strike on the left side of the target. Wind from the rear may very slightly decrease the air resistance, causing a bullet fired over a long distance to strike slightly higher on the target, and a head wind has the opposite effect.

Wind force is measured in miles per hour of its travel. The higher the wind force or velocity the greater the deflection. If the wind velocity is under three miles per hour the wind can hardly be felt, and only smoke drift will show it. A wind of five miles per hour can be felt on the face, and leaves begin to rustle; this is called a gentle breeze. At ten miles per hour leaves and small twigs are in constant motion and light flags are extended; this wind is called "fresh." At 15 miles per hour, wind begins to raise dust and loose paper, and move small branches; this wind is called "strong." At 20 miles per hour, small trees in leaf begin to sway, and you jam your hat tighter on your head; this wind is called "very strong." At wind velocities over 20 miles per hour it does not pay to shoot with small-bore rifles. (See Plate XII, p. 583.)

Wind direction is indicated by the hours of the clock, assuming that the clock is laid on the range, face up, with 12 o'clock at the target and 6 o'clock at the firing point. Thus a wind blowing directly from the right is a 3-o'clock wind. Winds from 3 and 9 o'clock give the greatest lateral deviation. Those from 2, 4, 8, and 10 o'clock have about seven-eighths of the deflecting force of 3- and 9-o'clock winds of the same velocity, while those from 1, 5, 7, and 11 o'clock have about one-half the 3- or 9-o'clock deflection.

When you shoot at a certain distance on a very calm day—no appreciable wind—you find that you have to set your wind gauge at a certain reading to strike the center of the bull's-eye. This sight setting then becomes your "zero" windage for that range. It is from this zero that you have to calculate and set your sights for wind allowance.

Wind correction will always be an estimate, as force and direction can never be told exactly and, as a matter of fact, both change slightly every second or so. Set your sights as nearly as you can calculate by the table, and then make the necessary sight correction. Afterward make elaborate notes in your score book, as to the force and direction of the wind, and the amount of wind correction found necessary. With a month or more of such estimating, correcting, and recording you should become a very fair wind calculator. Your entries in your score book, if rather elaborately and understandingly kept, will help a lot.

**Telescopic Sights.** Practically every rifle tournament now carries several events in which telescope sights are permitted. Many riflemen whose eyes are no longer sufficiently keen to compete with the younger generation of shooters, using iron sights, find that with a good telescope sight their ability to score well has diminished little if any. Telescopic sights at their best are slightly more accurate than iron sights as they practically eliminate the errors of aim. A good telescopic sight score will usually have more shots in the X-ring than will an iron sight score.

Several splendid American-made telescope sights are available. (See "Sights.") They are made with various powers of magnification from 2½ to 20. The 10-power glass is the one most generally used for small-bore target shooting. Glasses can be had with objective lenses from ¾ inch to 1½ inches. Those with the smaller diameters are entirely satisfactory, but the larger the objective the brighter is the view through the scope, and the more effectively it can be used for spotting shots in the target. The reticule should be the "medium" or "medium fine" cross hair.

All the above telescopes are equipped with double micrometer mounts, adjustable for both elevation and windage. Screwing out (counterclockwise—up) on the top micrometer screw results in taking higher elevation. Screwing out (counterclockwise—left) on the right-hand micrometer screw results in taking windage to the right, and vice versa. The stems of the screws are graduated with lines 25 minutes apart, and the barrels of the screws are graduated with lines half-minutes apart. In addition, the best mounts have quarter-minute clicks, the barrel clicking for each half-minute and also between the half-minutes. To read a telescope sight mount, if, for example, two graduations are in sight on the stem (50 half-minutes), and the barrel reads halfway between 15 and 16, the reading is 65½ half-minutes. The value of these adjustments is as stated only when the distance between the centers of the base blocks on the barrel of the rifle is 7.2 inches. Bases are so located on most of the best small-bore target rifles.

In order that the mountings can be set at the location of these bases, and also that the eyepiece can be adjusted about 2 inches in front of one's eye when one assumes the standard firing positions, it is necessary that the tube of the telescope sight be at least about 18 inches long. A collar encircles the tube just in front of the front mount, and can be clamped in position with a screw. Each time the rifle is fired the scope tube recoils slightly forward, and it should be pulled back before the next shot until this collar abuts against the front of the front mount to insure that the scope will be the proper and uniform distance from the eye.

Proper focusing of the telescope sight is essential for accurate results and to avoid eyestrain, and the instructions furnished by the manufacturers should be carefully read and followed.

Telescope sights can be readily removed from the rifle by merely unscrewing the clamping screws and sliding the mounts off their bases, when the iron sights can be used. The telescopes can then be replaced again in about a minute in perfect adjustment.

Usually a higher comb is desirable on the stock when telescope sights are used. This can be easily accomplished by lacing a Monte Carlo cheek pad on the stock when the scope is used, and removing it when iron sights are used.

**Slow Firing.** In slow-fire target shooting we have ample opportunity to train ourselves in all those things that are necessary for accurate shooting. We know the exact distance to the target, we have a well-defined black bull's-eye on a white background to aim at, we see where each bullet strikes the target, and we have plenty of time to correct our errors and to perfect ourselves in the execution of each detail. This is what slow fire is for—the perfection of each detail, so that practical shooting, which we will take up later, will be more accurate and effective. Thus our constant endeavor in slow fire is to do everything so perfectly and so uniformly that a high score will result—to place every bullet in the 10-ring in the center of the aiming bull's-eye.

In the United States, slow-fire shooting with .22 caliber rifles is conducted in accordance with rules prescribed by the National Rifle Association. The distances are usually 50 and 75 feet indoors, and 50 meters, 50, 100, and 200 yards on outdoor ranges. The targets used are the standard National Rifle Association small-bore targets; there is a different target for each distance. Such shooting is usually conducted by rifle clubs that are affiliated with the National Rifle Association on their home ranges. Competitions are held among their own members or with other clubs. There are also regional and state competitions, and the National Rifle Association holds indoor and outdoor mail matches and stages large regional and national competitions at various rifle ranges throughout the country. It is a great advantage to the shooter to join a club affiliated with the National Rifle Association and shoot with it, because he is then able to use their well-equipped range, and he learns a lot by association with the good shots in the club. But if a shooter is so situated that he cannot join a club it is not difficult to build quickly a small-bore range almost anywhere in farming country, and to practice alone on such a range. The present discussion and the advanced works on marksmanship are an aid to one who has to train himself without the aid of a coach. Although such a lone shooter cannot compete shoulder to shoulder with others, he can compete with world's record scores, and it is entirely possible for him to develop his shooting ability in this manner, alone on his own range, so that he can visit the big national competitions with as good a chance of winning as anyone.

Thus, if you want to excel with the rifle, get a range, even if you have to build it yourself, study this volume and indulge in home practice until you know the theoretical side, and then get all the practical shooting you can on the range, preferably one morning or afternoon a week if you can afford that much time. About two months of careful weekly practice should make you into a very fair shot, but to reach and stay in the expert class requires much longer. Indeed, progress is very analogous to that in learning to play golf—no harder, and no easier, but containing a little simple mechanics and science which make a particular appeal to the majority of our boys and men.

We shall assume that you have a suitable rifle range available. Before you leave your home for the range, wipe all the oil out of the bore and chamber of your rifle, because the first few shots from a clean, oily bore are likely to fly a little wild. Also check over and see that you have the following material—nothing forgotten:

Rifle with bolt in it and sights on it

| | |
|---|---|
| Score book and pencil | Spotting scope and stand |
| Ammunition | Cartridge block |
| Forked rifle rest | Shooting coat and glove |

The following material may also be necessary, depending on conditions:

- Paper targets, tacks, and small hammer
- Canvas sheet to lie on (damp or dirty ground)
- Telescope sight
- Shooting spectacles
- Tool kit

Advanced shooters usually carry all these articles, except rifle and shooting coat, in a small satchel or metal box termed a "dope bag."

On arriving at the range, the first thing to do is to look at the wind and weather conditions and set your sights. If you have done considerable shooting with your rifle and ammunition, then you should turn to your score book, see if you can find in it a sheet where you fired at this same distance under the same weather and wind conditions as now prevail, and set your sights at the elevation and windage that proved correct on that occasion. Then record the sight setting, together with the distance you are shooting at, wind and weather conditions, and details of rifle and ammunition on a blank page in your score book. Then smoke your sights black so they will not glisten. This may be done in the flame of burning camphor, a small acetylene lantern, a candle, or even a match; wipe all oil off the sights before attempting to blacken them. *Do not* blacken ivory or red bead sights.

**Slow Fire, Prone.** When the range officer tells you that a certain target is available for you to fire on, go to that firing point, set up your spotting scope trained and focused on your target, and place your forked rifle rest, cartridge block with the required number of cartridges in it, score book and pencil in position. Adjust the gunsling on your arm, and then lie down ready to fire. In this position everything should be arranged in a convenient and methodical manner. Set up the spotting scope so that it is just to the right or left of the barrel of your aimed rifle, but not so close as to interfere with free holding. The forked rifle rest should be in the ground a little to the right of where your left hand is when aiming, and the score book and cartridge block should be convenient to your right hand. Thus, when you fire a shot you can lower your rifle into the rifle rest, and leaning your head a little to one side, bring your eye over to the spotting scope without disturbing your position on the ground.

Get everything arranged systematically and your position correct before you start to fire. This is very important. Place your rifle to your shoulder, sling correct, aim at the target, and see if your position is correct and comfortable. If not, shift the position a little until it is right. Note where your elbows rest on the ground and make little holes there for them so they will not slip out of position. Then do not get out of this position or vary it a particle while you are firing your string of ten or twenty rounds. It is necessary, of course, to bring your rifle down into the rest after each shot, and to lean over to see through the spotting scope, but any other movements should be avoided, so that each time you put the butt of the rifle to your shoulder to aim it comes to as identically the same position as you can make it—same lie on the ground, same tension on gunsling, elbows at same spot on the ground. Uniform and accurate shooting requires uniform holding. The shooter who fidgets around on the firing point, or who gets up and lies down again after he has started his string, gets a miserable score, and at once publishes the fact that he is a tyro.

Everything about your position being correct, place the rifle to your shoulder, looking for and aiming at your own targets, steady down, perfect your aim, and squeeze off as carefully and correctly as you can. Call your shot. Then methodically lower your rifle into the forked rifle rest which takes its weight off your arms and prevents fatigue, lean over to the spotting scope, look at your target, note where the bullet has struck, then place a figure 1 on the target diagram on your score sheet to indicate where the first shot struck.

If this first shot did not strike where you called it, then you should make the necessary correction in sight adjustment. Assume now that you are firing the score shown on Plate XIII at 100 yards. It is a sunny spring day with an 8-mile wind from 3 o'clock, and for your first shot you have set your elevation at 24 half-minutes or clicks, and your wind gauge at 3 half-minutes or clicks left. You call your first shot a bull, and you therefore place a small dot in the center of the square in the "Call" column. When you look through your spotting scope you see that the bullet has struck in the 9-ring at one o'clock and you place a figure 1 on the target diagram. Now you change your sight adjustment to elevation 21 and windage 5 left, because this lowering of 3 half-minutes or clicks will lower your next shot 1½ inches, or 1½ rings, which is just how much too high your first shot struck; and moving the wind gauge 2 half-minutes left will bring your next shot just one inch or one ring to the left, which is just how much your first shot struck to the right of the center of the bull's-eye. You now fire your second, third, fourth, and fifth shots under identical conditions, and all strike in the 10-ring, but you note that your group is forming in the upper left-hand section of the 10-ring. It is not safe to let it form so far from the center, because there is danger of a shot going out. So you lower your elevation a half-minute, or half-inch, to 20, and also move your wind gauge a half-minute right. Your sixth, seventh, and eighth shots, all of which are called bulls, center well in toward the center of the 10-ring. On the ninth shot you get a bad pull when the front sight appears a little to the right of directly under the bull, and, sure enough, when you look through your spotting scope you see your bullet hole in the 9-ring over at 3 o'clock. Of course, this is just where you pulled it, and no change in sight setting is indicated, so you are more careful how you pull your last shot, get it off perfectly, and it lands well into the 10-ring. Afterward, when you have time, you add up your score which totals 98, a fine average score for a very good shot.

**TABLE OF WIND ALLOWANCE**

.22 Long Rifle Cartridge, 40-Grain Bullet. M.V. 1100 f.s.

| Distance | Miles per Hour | Inches and Minutes Bullet Is Deflected | | | | | |
|---|---|---|---|---|---|---|---|
| | | By 1, 5, 7 and 11 o'Clock Winds | | By 2, 4, 8 and 10 o'Clock Winds | | By 3 and 9 o'Clock Winds | |
| | | Inches | Min. | Inches | Min. | Inches | Min. |
| 50 Yards 1 Minute=½ Inch | 5 | .22 | .45 | .38 | .77 | .45 | .9 |
| | 10 | .45 | .90 | .78 | 1.57 | .90 | 1.8 |
| | 15 | .67 | 1.35 | 1.19 | 2.38 | 1.35 | 2.7 |
| | 20 | .90 | 1.80 | 1.57 | 3.15 | 1.80 | 3.6 |
| 100 Yards 1 Minute=1 Inch | 5 | .90 | .90 | 1.57 | 1.57 | 1.80 | 1.8 |
| | 10 | 1.80 | 1.80 | 3.15 | 3.15 | 3.60 | 3.6 |
| | 15 | 2.70 | 2.70 | 4.82 | 4.82 | 5.40 | 5.4 |
| | 20 | 3.60 | 3.60 | 6.30 | 6.30 | 7.20 | 7.2 |
| 200 Yards 1 Minute=2 Inches | 5 | 3.60 | 1.80 | 6.30 | 3.15 | 7.20 | 3.6 |
| | 10 | 7.20 | 3.60 | 12.60 | 6.30 | 14.40 | 7.2 |
| | 15 | 10.80 | 5.40 | 18.90 | 9.45 | 21.60 | 10.8 |
| | 20 | 14.40 | 7.20 | 25.20 | 12.60 | 28.80 | 14.4 |

Table is approximately correct for .22 L. R. High-Speed Cartridges also.

PLATE XII.

It is a great advantage to record every score you fire in this perfect manner. You can get to know your rifle thoroughly in no other way. There are too many of these data for any man to remember. The shooter who trusts to memory is continually making mistakes which lower his scores and his season's average, and particularly he does not know his rifle well enough to often get a "10" for the first shot. If you keep your score book conscientiously you will win out in the end. This score sheet now gives you a most perfect guide for the next time that you come to shoot this rifle and ammunition at 100 yards.

**Slow Fire, Sitting.** Here the procedure is almost exactly the same as when shooting prone. Set up the spotting scope to the right so that you can lean over and look through it when necessary. The forked rifle rest is seldom needed, as it is easy to rest the rifle in the lap between shots. Select your ground so that if possible you sit on a spot a little higher than the spots where your heels rest, as this gives you a steadier position. You cannot hold sitting quite as steadily as you can prone, and detailed concentration and co-ordination are necessary to get the trigger squeezed off during one of the periods when the front sight has drifted or is lingering just right under the bull. Call every shot, and note the calls in the proper column on your score sheet.

It is usual to shoot sitting only at the shorter distances, and it is not customary to spot each shot on the score sheet. You usually start out knowing your sight adjustment pretty well from having previously fired at this distance in the prone position. Every two or three shots, however, you should lean over and look through the spotting scope. If your shots are not going where you call them, make the necessary correction in sight adjustment. Then when you finish your score, get up and go back of the firing point, sit down, and complete all necessary entries in the score book. Particularly put down just what sight adjustment proved best, and the wind and weather conditions, rifle and ammunition used, and the fact that the score was shot sitting. Sometimes in shooting sitting a shooter will find that he requires one or two half-minutes' sight adjustment higher than is correct when he fires prone at the same distance. This is because, not being quite so steady, he does not aim with the top of his front sight quite so close to the bottom of the bull, and he has to take a little more elevation to compensate for it—that is, he aims lower, and has to increase his elevation slightly to make the bullet hit high enough.

**Slow Fire, Kneeling.** In general the same instructions pertain as for shooting sitting. There is usually a tendency to swing from side to side when aiming, and one must try to overcome this, and also to time his squeeze carefully to get off when the front sight is drifting under the bull. Much practice kneeling is necessary to limber up the right knee so that one does not get cramped in the position. At first it may be necessary to stand up once or twice during the string to relieve the pain in the knee. Some shooters with limber knee joints do not have this trouble at all.

You should start this shooting in a slow, almost phlegmatic manner. Do not exert yourself, or hurry, or get in the least excited. Some of the best rifle shots have a camp stool at the firing point and sit down between shots. It is a great advantage to call and spot each shot. For this purpose either have your spotting scope on a high tripod, or else have a friend at the scope, call your shot to him, and let him note your call and the location of your hit in your score book. When you get to the point where your bullets are striking close to where you call them you are making real progress, and incidentally you know that your sight adjustment is absolutely correct.

Now look again at *B* in Plate XIV. You are making an effort to get the final squeeze on the trigger when your front sight is in those parts of its tremors represented by the heavier portions of the line, that is, while the front sight is hugging around the bottom of the bull. At first you cannot do this, but don't get discouraged, keep on trying. Gradually your rifle will swing or tremble more slowly. Before long you will have co-ordinated so that you are putting your increase of squeeze on the trigger as the front sight swings under the bull. Soon you can do it two or three times in ten shots, and then a greater number, and the first thing you know you are getting good scores, and you have arrived.

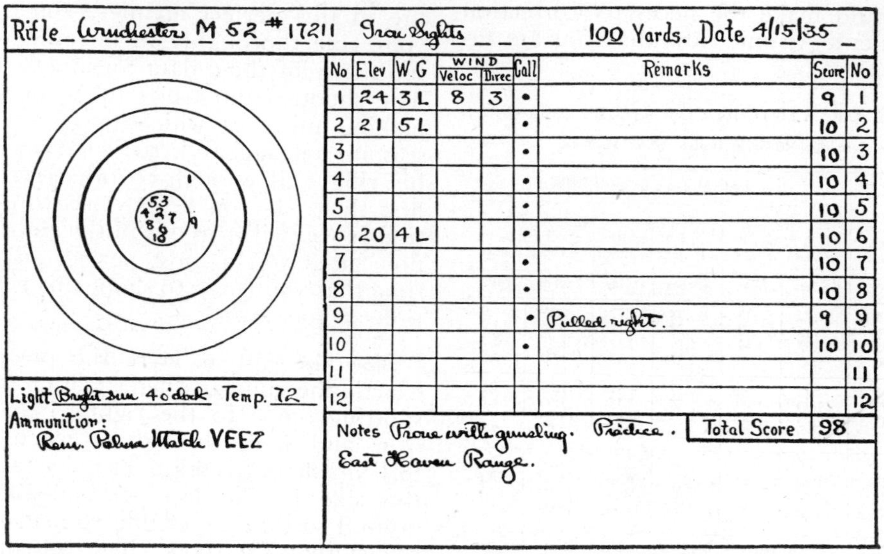


PLATE XIII. Score Sheet, Slow Fire, Prone.

**Slow Fire, Standing.** This is the most difficult of all manners of firing the rifle, and the one taking the longest practice in which to become proficient; and yet it is always the position first attempted by the beginner who has no coach or manual to start him off right. His total lack of results too often discourages him so that he soon quits the game. And yet no other form of shooting gives quite so much satisfaction to the shooter once he has learned to excel in it.

It is best not to start shooting standing on the range until you have done several weeks of conscientious trigger-squeeze exercises in this position at home, because at the start your inability to hold the rifle with anything that approaches steadiness will be very discouraging. When you first start these standing exercises in all probability your front sight will wander all around the target like the thin line in *A* of Plate XIV. But two weeks of these exercises will narrow your tremors to something like that shown in *B*, and then you can profitably start your range shooting.

As you attempt to hold and squeeze you will find that it often takes a long time to get the shot off. In such cases your hold may become shaky before you manage to get the final squeeze. If so, don't fire, but bring the rifle down, sit down, and wait a minute or so before starting again. Gradually, however, try to get your shot off within 10 to 15 seconds of the moment when you begin to aim. The slow, poky shooter seldom becomes a really good offhand shot. Keep cool, don't hurry, but don't poke too much either. If you shoot on the range once a week, then at least two other periods of 20 minutes of trigger-squeeze exercises at home will help your progress a lot. Don't expect to get scores up in the 80's in your first season's practice; very few can do that.

All of the above description is for shooting in the "Army Standing" position as previously described (p. 576), with the left upper arm and elbow free from the body. There is another standing position known as the "N.R.A. Standing" position in which the left elbow is rested on the advanced hip, and the rifle is either balanced on the finger tips, or held by a palm rest. This position is permitted in "Free Rifle Shooting" and in many N.R.A. competitions. It is steadier than the standard offhand position, but it is not suited to practical shooting—rapid fire and snap shooting.

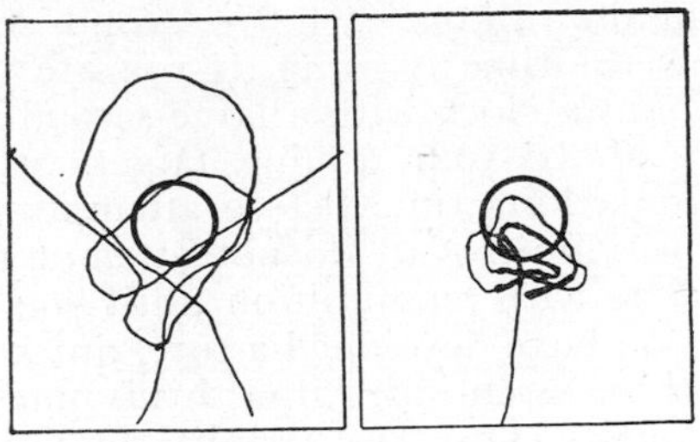


PLATE XIV. Typical Waverings of Front Sight.

**What to Expect.** If you are a beginner you will naturally want to know how well you are progressing at various stages of your practice. If you scan the scores made in the big matches you will note that the winners usually get possible scores of 100 at all ranges when shooting prone, about 96 to 97 when sitting, and about 80 to 85 standing. Don't expect to average anywhere near this in your first season. The shooters who win matches with such scores have been playing the game for all they are worth for several years at least. Moreover, they don't win or make scores like these every time. The winners in a match are the topnotchers who are particularly lucky on that day, and their high scores do not represent their regular average, which is slightly lower.

Shooting prone, if you have carefully studied all the fine points outlined above and have done your best to apply them, in about a month you should be averaging scores around 90 to 95. A month more and you should be running around 93 to 96 in good weather. Toward the end of your first season you ought to be making around 95 to 99. Perhaps a few of you will average 97 to 99, and get an occasional possible. If so, you are getting close to competition form for prone shooting.

In the sitting position, scores around 85 are excellent for the first two or three months, and anything over 92 is splendid toward the end of the first season. Kneeling scores normally run about five points lower.

Your progress will probably be much slower standing. At the start you will do well to keep all ten shots on the target. After two months you should be running scores somewhere around 75. Perhaps if you are specially gifted you may get up almost to an average of 80 toward the end of your first season. A shooter who averages much over 80 points standing has not only been doing a lot of conscientious work, but he is more or less gifted in his ability to co-ordinate. There are not many such men.

**Rapid Fire.** Although we have made a sport of it, theoretically at least, slow fire is instructional fire in which the shooter learns to fire accurately and consistently, and to hit the object he aims for at known distances. All practical firing in sport is more or less rapid fire. Therefore, as soon as you have become skilled in slow fire, you should take up rapid fire and make yourself proficient in it as well. Rapid fire is not different from slow fire except that it is performed more rapidly. The usual requirement is that the five shots contained in the magazine be fired within 30 seconds or less, instead of the time limit of one minute per shot in slow fire. Thus rapid fire involves a faster, but if possible no less accurate, performance of assuming the firing position, aiming, squeezing, and then a rapid but sure manipulation of the breech action of the rifle for the next shot.

It is very desirable that you practice the following rapid-fire exercises in your home with empty rifle until you have acquired the skill to perform rapid fire quickly, surely, without fumbling, and in a more or less subconscious manner. While it is possible to quicken considerably the operation of loading a single-shot rifle, yet, in general, rapid fire can be executed only with a repeating or magazine rifle. Most bolt-action magazine rifles have magazines which contain five cartridges. Therefore, in small-bore shooting rapid fire consists of firing two strings of five shots each within a time limit of 30 seconds per string. Sufficient time is given between the two strings to permit you to refill your magazine. When you are at the firing point, magazine filled, one cartridge loaded into the chamber, safety lock turned to "Safe" and rifle in the position of "Ready" (butt below the shoulder), the range officer gives the command "Commence firing," and 30 or 20 seconds later the command "Cease firing." At the command "Commence firing" you turn your safety to "Ready," assume the firing position, aim at your target, and endeavor to fire five shots within the time limit. For every shot you fire before or after the commands, ten points will be deducted from your score. The regular slow-fire target is usually used. Rapid fire may be held in the standing, kneeling, sitting, or prone positions, as prescribed. This, in general, is the procedure, although it may differ a little on various ranges and in certain matches.

Rapid fire should always start with the safety of the rifle turned to "Safe" because skill and speed in unlocking the rifle is an essential part of rapid fire. The rifle should always be operated without removing it from the shoulder, or from the firing position. Relinquish the grip of the right hand on the stock, grasp the knob of the bolt handle with the thumb and two fingers, lift and pull back the bolt smartly, quickly, but surely, doing this seemingly all in one motion rather than first a lift up and then a pull back. Then at once shove the bolt forward and turn it down, also all in one motion. Make these movements complete, quick, and smooth, with enough force to insure their positiveness. Then regrasp the stock, finger on the trigger, and enough pressure on the trigger to take up surely any slack in the trigger. The rifle will now be swaying from side to side as a result of this operation. Stop this swinging at once so that you can aim by pressing the cheek against the left side of the comb of the stock, and the ball of the thumb against the right, lower, front side of the comb. This pressure from two sides is merely a part of assuming the firing position again; no alteration of position need be made to exercise this squeeze which stops the swinging.

In operating the mechanism in the prone and sitting positions, turn or cant the rifle a little to the right as you open your bolt, and straighten the rifle up as you close the bolt. Also carry the left hand slightly down and to the right as you open the bolt, and bring it up and to the left into aiming position as you close the bolt. Keep both elbows in their holes in the ground, or on your knees, and the sling in proper position on the arm all the time.

In the kneeling and standing positions, as the right hand lets go of the stock to operate the bolt, pull back hard on the rifle with the left hand to keep the butt of the rifle in position on the shoulder. Operate the bolt without canting the rifle, or lowering the left hand, keeping the rifle fairly well aimed toward the target while operating. Of course you must always carry your head a trifle to the left when opening the bolt to prevent your cheek from being struck by the bolt as it is withdrawn.

Always keep your eye on your target *(your own target)* while operating the rifle. Never look at the rifle to see the bolt operate and the cartridge go in. This is most important. If you do not keep your eye on the target your rapid fire will be very slow, and you will lose your target, or fire on the wrong target continually.

Now practice this operation of the bolt for a few minutes, doing it exactly as described above, slowly at first, reading the instructions over a number of times to be sure you get it exactly as described in every detail. When you have learned the movement, begin to practice the rapid-fire exercise as described below, learning it first in the prone position, then sitting, kneeling, and finally standing. Continue practicing the exercise until you have become proficient, sure, and quick before finally taking up rapid fire on the range with ammunition.

**Rapid-Fire Exercise.** Start with rifle locked, sling on the arm (except standing position), rifle in ready position, butt below the shoulder, eyes on the target.

(1) Assume the firing position, unlocking rifle at the same time, place enough pressure on the trigger to take up any slack, aim at the target, steady down, and then squeeze the trigger as soon as your aim appears correct. Hasten these operations, but without sacrificing accurate aim and careful squeeze. It is usually best to swing the front sight from one side to its alignment under the bull, and to try to time the squeeze so that the rifle goes off as the front sight gets squarely below the bull. Usually this will result in a larger proportion of hits than were you to try to raise the front sight from below and fire as it almost touches the bull.

(2) At once let go with the right hand and operate the bolt quickly and surely as described above. Regrasp the small of the stock and stop the swing of the rifle by pressure between the cheek and ball of the thumb. Take up any slack on the trigger, start aim, and continue as in Paragraph 1 until you have fired five shots. Then rest a couple of minutes before repeating.

Do not time yourself at first. Do not attempt to do the operations so quickly that you fumble. Make every operation correctly, and gain speed slowly. Never hasten the aim and trigger squeeze, but get these as perfect as possible every time. When you think you are beginning to get fair rapidity, with perfection in all details, have someone time you, giving the commands for commencing and ceasing firing, and also call out each five seconds so you will know how the time is going. If you are practicing alone, mount a clock with a large second hand immediately above your aiming target. Stick to 30 seconds for a long time before attempting the 20-second time limit. And do not attempt rapid fire on the range with ammunition until you are satisfied that you have developed a sure, quick performance of all the essentials. All of this is much simpler than it sounds. Very fair rapidity and surety can be acquired in about five practice periods of about 15 minutes each.

The one big stumbling block in rapid fire is the tendency to snatch or jerk at the trigger just as soon as the sights appear aimed with anything near to correctness. You must constantly fight against this tendency at first. Strive for a correct trigger squeeze, try to put all the pressure on the trigger you dare, and then carefully squeeze on the last ounce as the front sight drifts below the bull's-eye. This is not very difficult either. You soon learn it, but learn it you must if you would do well at rapid fire.

**Tournaments and Competitions.** After you have become proficient in slow fire and have mastered the instructions given up to this point, you will, no doubt, be taking part in the shoots at your local club and enjoying the pleasures of shoulder-to-shoulder competition. Use the first opportunity to go to some larger competition or tournament, and though you may not win a prize the first time, you need to take part in such tournaments to overcome the "buck fever" which afflicts all beginners at such shoots.

At these larger tournaments you will have a chance to meet the topnotchers of the shooting game and to observe the way they do things. You will see all sorts of strange gadgets for which great claims are made, but above all you will have a chance to mingle with and make the acquaintance of other sportsmen with a common interest.

You may hesitate to go to such a tournament for fear of doing the wrong thing or of making yourself conspicuous because of your ignorance of the customs and manners of such affairs. Do not let this deter you. As you read on, we will try to point out some of the things you should do, and besides, you will find the staff and the competitors most considerate to the beginner and very willing to explain and assist.

The National Rifle Association through its system of "Registered Tournaments" and nation-wide classification of shooters makes it possible for you to find a small-bore tournament within easy driving distance of your home almost any week-end. Registered Tournaments are all conducted under identical rules and each one is umpired by an N.R.A. Official Referee. All scores are immediately reported to the Association and shooters from Maine to Hawaii are classified under a uniform system based on their scores in actual competition. The N.R.A. will be glad to furnish you with complete information on how the classification system works. *The American Rifleman* each month tells you where and when Registered Tournaments are going to be held during the two months ahead.

Small-bore rifle shooting, through the organization provided by the National Rifle Association, boasts as complete a list of championship events as any sport in America. At the top are the International Rifle Teams, next the annual National Championships, then Regional Championships, below them come District and State Championships, and finally the local registered tournaments for city and county titles.

Suppose you decide to attend the Eastern Regional Small-Bore Tournament over the Fourth of July. You find that the shoot is to run from July 1 to 5, inclusive, and that you will be able to go on July 2. Of course, you will want to shoot the first day you arrive, so read the program carefully and either mail your entry for your first day's matches or be prepared to pay post entry fees for that day.

When you arrive in camp you should first register, giving full information as to name, address, rifle club, the type and make of the gun and ammunition you will use. You will then be assigned a competitor number by which you will be known at this tournament. You will also be assigned tent or quarters if available and told where you may draw bedding, etc. You will be charged a registration fee, usually one dollar. After you have located your place in camp and got your bedding arranged, it is well to go next to the Entry Office and make entries in all the single-entry matches you wish to enter. At the large tournaments there are two types of competition: single-entry matches, in which you shoot a prescribed course once, and re-entry matches in which you may shoot the same course a number of times and in which the aggregates of your best two or three or five targets count. Matches may be either squadded or unsquadded. If squadded, this means that you will be expected to fire your score on a designated target at some specified time. This target and time are given to you on what is called a squadding ticket. These are usually distributed by the Entry Office on the evening before a match is fired or at least two hours before the scheduled time of starting the match. Unsquadded matches are those which may be fired at any time that targets are available during the tournament.

When you have made your entries in the various single-entry matches you will get a receipt showing the matches entered. Save it for your own information and as a check to prove your entry, should it get misplaced.

When the time arrives for your first match, look at the squadding ticket which you have previously obtained at the Entry Office; you will generally find on it a target number, a relay number, and a time. Let us say it reads, "Target 27, Relay 2, time 8.40/a." This means that one relay of shooters will fire before you do. Go to a point back of firing point 27 about 8:15 A.M. after checking to see that you have all of your equipment. When you have located your place on the line as shown by a numbered stake on the firing point, there are two or three things to do. See that your sights are set properly for elevation and windage and that your spotting scope is mounted on the tripod and adjusted. Also see that you have the bolt in your rifle; it is amazing how many bolts get lost or misplaced at a tournament. Count out the number of cartridges you will need for this stage of the match and put them in your loading block. When the order is given for the second relay to get on the line, move up and take your place on the firing line.

These preliminary preparations will give you more time to select a satisfactory position and get set to go before you hear the command "Commence firing." After the targets have been changed and your targets put up, the Range Officer will give the command "Commence firing." It is common practice to allow some interval of time before record fire starts in which you will be permitted to fire fouling shots and in most matches five sighting shots. Fouling shots are not aimed but are fired rapidly into the ground in front of the firing point or into the backstop and serve to warm up the gun and to deposit a uniform fouling in the barrel. It has been found that unless five or more fouling shots are so fired through a barrel it will tend to show gradual change of elevation on the first few shots for record and thus spoil what would otherwise be a good score.

In small-bore matches it is customary to permit five sighting shots, on a target placed above the record targets, to check sight setting and to facilitate adjustments for effect of wind and light conditions.

Be careful to avoid hitting the record targets with either the fouling or sighting shots. If this happens, have the Range Officer inspect and note it before you start your record string. When you have fired the required number of shots—you should use a loading block to insure this, and be sure to fire at your own target—do not get up and leave the line until the shooters on either side of you have completed their scores, as you may disturb them. When they are done, or on command, move off the firing line quietly after cleaning up for the next man.

If you are firing at long ranges where targets are operated from a pit, each shot will be marked from the pit and signaled to the scorer, who announces the number of the shot and its value and posts it on a scoreboard. It is your job to see that he announces and posts the value correctly. If he makes a mistake, call the Range Officer and get it corrected before firing again. No correction will be made after you fire the next shot.

**The Bulletin Board.** At every tournament shoot

you will find a Bulletin Board on which are posted scores and other official notices. It is the duty of the competitor to consult the Bulletin Board at least twice a day, since changes in the program and rules will be posted here and the management have officially given full notice of changes, etc., if they are posted on the board. After you complete your scores in the match the targets are taken in and scored and the Statistical Office will post them as quickly as feasible. There are three kinds of bulletins: Reveille, Preliminary, and Official bulletins. The Reveille Bulletin will usually show no names except the name and number of the match and will be posted by relays in target order. You will look at the sheet for Relay 2, target 27, and see that the score posted agrees with the score you recorded in your score book. If it does not agree and you had no doubtful shots, you should question it by indicating the mistake to the Statistical Office.

Shortly after all targets are scored the Statistical Office will post a Preliminary Bulletin showing the scores ranked according to the rules. If the score you make would entitle you a listing on the Preliminary Bulletin and your name does not appear, you should file a protest in the manner provided for in the program and in Official Rules.

The Preliminary Bulletin will carry a notation of the hour of posting and fix some time, from 4 to 12 hours later, after which no protests will be received. If there is a mistake, make your protest known at once or you may forfeit your right to make one.

After the period noted on the Preliminary Bulletin has expired, an Official Bulletin will be posted showing winners, their scores and prizes, medals, etc. Medals and trophies are generally distributed at a meeting at the end of the shoot, though custom varies on this and they may be available as soon as the Official Bulletins are posted.

When the time comes to go home, clean up your quarters and turn in any equipment you have drawn and go on home. You will have made new acquaintances and friends, and when the next opportunity arises you will be back again to enjoy the thrill of competition with the best of the shooters in the territory, the chance to improve your ability and knowledge of the game on the firing line.

**Field Shooting.** All of the shooting we have considered so far has been what is known as "known distance shooting"—that is, the distance to the target is known exactly, and the sights can be set in advance for that distance so that with correct aim the bull's-eye will be struck somewhere near its center. In practical field shooting, however, the distance to the target is seldom known exactly, but must be estimated, and either the sights must be set quickly for that estimated distance, or else they must be set in advance for some certain distance over which the trajectory is known intimately, and allowance must then be made for the rise or fall of the bullet above or below the line of aim at the estimated distance. Here we depart from our previous rule that aim is always taken with the front sight almost touching the bottom of the bull's-eye, and we often aim a little high or low to allow for the trajectory.

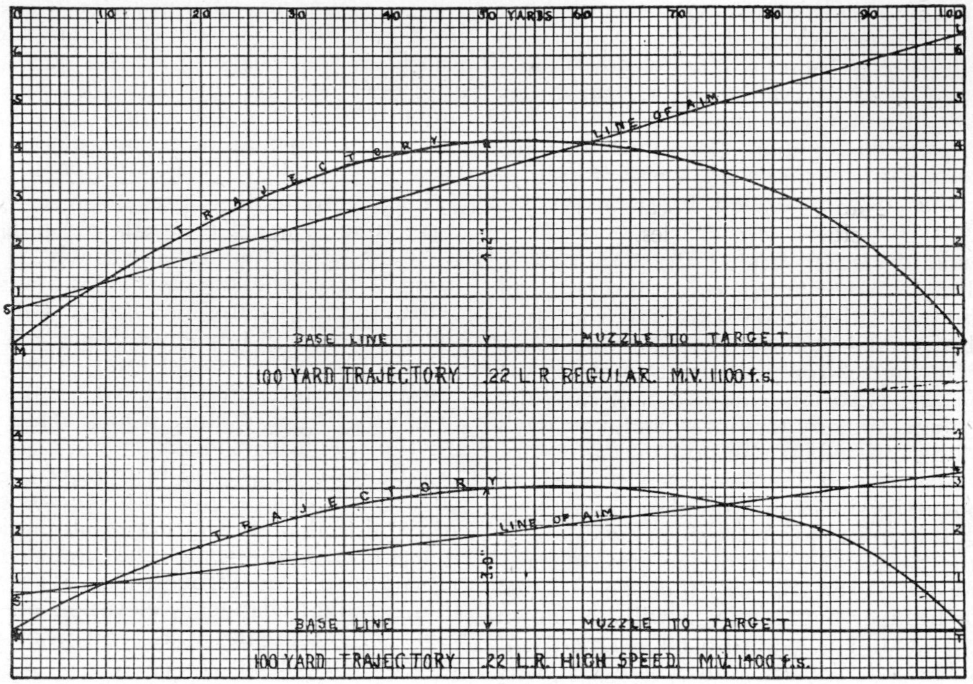


PLATE XV.

At this stage, therefore, it is desirable for you to know the trajectory of the .22 long rifle cartridge, both the regular and the high-speed varieties. These trajectories are the same in all rifles; the cartridge, not the rifle, determines the trajectory. The trajectory or path of the bullet through the air is always curved like that of any object thrown through the air. The amount of the curve over a certain distance is designated by the number of inches the bullet rises above a straight line joining the muzzle of the rifle and the bullet hole in the target, this distance being usually called the "mid-range height of trajectory." For example, in shooting at 100 yards with the cartridge of regular velocity the bullet rises to a height of 4.2 inches above an imaginary line connecting muzzle and target, and for the high-speed cartridge this height is 3 inches.

The sights, however, stand above the barrel, and the line of aim is considerably above the axis of the bore from which this trajectory given in the usual table is figured. This makes considerable difference in the practical trajectory above the line of aim, which is the trajectory we want to know for practical purposes. Let us say that the height of the front sight above the axis of the bore on your rifle is $\frac{3}{4}$ inch. In Plate XV the heavy cross-section lines indicate 5 yards horizontally and one inch vertically. *M* is the muzzle of the rifle and *T* is the target. The line *M-T* is the base line from muzzle to target above which the trajectory curve is determined and plotted as shown.

Now take a point $\frac{3}{4}$ inch above *M;* that is where your line of aim starts if your front sight is $\frac{3}{4}$ inch above the axis of the bore. Suppose you sight in your rifle to strike the exact point of aim at 60 yards. Then a line drawn from the $\frac{3}{4}$-inch high point, which we will call *S,* through the 60-yard point on the trajectory curve will be your line of aim for figuring your practical trajectory. From this line you can then measure how far above or below the line of aim your bullets will strike at all distances, merely measuring vertically from the line of aim to the trajectory curve on the chart.

For example, with the regular velocity cartridge we see from Plate XV that if we set our sights for 60 yards so as to strike the point of aim at that distance (strike the bull's-eye at 6 o'clock when aiming at 6 o'clock), then at 35 yards our bullet will strike one inch above the line of aim, at 71 yards it will strike one inch below the line of aim, at 80 yards 2 inches low, at 90 yards 4 inches low, and at 100 yards it drops about 6$\frac{1}{2}$ inches low. Thus, if your sights were set for 60 yards, and you suddenly had to fire on a target that you estimated to be 90 yards away, you would need to aim 4 inches above it to strike it. Also with your sights set for 60 yards you can aim directly at an object, and you will not miss it by more than an inch all the way from the muzzle to 71 yards.

Similarly, for the high-speed cartridge, if you set your sights for 75 yards your bullet will strike one inch high at 40 yards, drop about one inch low at 85 yards, 1$\frac{1}{3}$ inches low at 90 yards, and 3$\frac{1}{3}$ inches low at 100 yards. Aiming directly at an object, you will not miss your point of aim by more than an inch from the muzzle to 85 yards.

In field shooting it is usually much more practical to set the sights in some such manner, and then allow for the rise or fall of the bullet, than to set the sights for the estimated distance, because you very often have to estimate the distance quickly and fire at once, and you have no time to set sights. You see a target appear, you estimate it to be 80 yards, you are using regular-velocity ammunition, and so you hold 2 inches high to allow for the drop of the bullet. The reason why we set our sights for 60 and 75 yards in the two foregoing examples is because these settings give us the longest distance with regular and high-speed ammunition at which our bullets will not miss the point of aim by more than an inch.

**Estimating Distance.** You should practice estimating distances until you become skilled at it. Measure off 100 yards over a piece of ground. Set up a natural target of known size. Note how it appears at various distances on your 100-yard course. Aim at it at various distances and see how much of it is covered by the width of your front sight.

Set up a standard 100-yard target at 100 yards, with 6-inch aiming bull's-eye, and aim at it steadily. How much in width on the target does the top of your front sight cover? If it seems to be exactly as wide as the bull's-eye, then you can say your front sight subtends 6 inches at 100 yards, or 3 inches at 50 yards. If you then were to aim at a 3-inch target, and it appeared just the width of your front sight, it would then be approximately 50 yards away —say, between 40 and 60 yards, because you cannot measure accurately enough with your eye to see the small difference that 10 yards would make in the subtended angle.

Such practice, together with regular shooting on the 50- and 100-yard small-bore range, will soon accustom you to how things look at various dis-
hit small, rather indistinct targets at long, unknown
tances, to how they compare with the width of your front sight, and to the extent of ground between you and the object, so that soon you can estimate the distance to any object quite closely. It is also profitable to continue this practice beyond 100 yards, although this distance is about the limit of effective field shooting at small objects with the small-bore rifle.

**Rules.** There are no established rules for field shooting, except that safety precautions must be observed. Every shooter or club makes rules to suit the occasion. It is usually best to make no rules restricting the shooter or his rifle, but to make the game more difficult or interesting, as skill is acquired, rules are applied to vary the target or the time, to require shooting at more difficult targets or in a shorter time limit. The object is to learn to distances with the greatest speed. Competitions can be arranged in any way desired. Who can make the greatest number of hits in the fewest shots? Who can hit all the targets in the fewest shots? Who can break all the targets in the shortest time?

**Safety.** Field firing targets should be set up only in front of a hill or other backstop which will stop the bullets. They can be set up on a regular small-bore rifle range, although this would have the disadvantage of permitting the shooters to know the distance to the targets. Stony ground should be avoided as bullets may glance from it and possibly fly over the bullet stop. Bullets do not glance from dry sand, and seldom from loam covered with grass. Remember that the extreme range of the .22 long rifle cartridge is 1700 yards with barrel elevated at an angle of 33 degrees. A ricochet may fly as far as

500 yards from the spot from which it glances. Bullets are dangerous even at these extreme ranges.

**Care of the Rifle.** A rifle needs daily cleaning and attention when in use, and proper storage when not in use, or its accuracy and effectiveness will deteriorate rapidly; but, if properly taken care of, a good rifle will last you a lifetime, as it practically never wears out from firing alone.

You should understand clearly the effect of rust. Many people think that rust can be removed. Red rust is evidence of the eating away of the surface of the metal. Even if you remove the red evidence you can never repair the damage the rusting has caused. Rust is always the result of neglect or ignorance. A clean steel surface oiled to protect from moisture does not rust. Never allow even a suspicion of rust to appear on or in your rifle. It will not appear if you will care for your rifle as described below.

Many shooters complain that their barrel "leads" —that it gets full of lead and will not shoot accurately. A rifle barrel that is properly used will not lead if rightly cared for; no lead will be deposited in the bore that cannot be pushed out at once with a snug-fitting flannel cleaning patch. But a barrel that has been permitted to rust slightly will have a rough, pitted barrel instead of the smooth one you have ruined by neglect. An automatic rifle may lead or "copper" if fired very rapidly for a large number of rounds. Instructions for removing such leading or coppering are given below.

You should understand the action of the fouling of the various types of cartridges. The particular priming powder and kind of bullets with which a cartridge is loaded are always named on the carton in which the cartridges are packed.

Cartridges loaded with non-corrosive priming, smokeless powder, and lubricated or film-coated lead bullets leave a fouling in the bore which is both non-corrosive and rust preventative. It is very easy to keep the bore in condition when such ammunition is used. Ordinarily, if this type of cartridge is used exclusively the bore need not be cleaned from day to day while the rifle is in continued use, although, of course, there is no objection to cleaning it. But the bore should be cleaned before you put the rifle away for a long period, or in localities where the air is excessively damp.

Cartridges loaded with non-corrosive priming, smokeless powder, and copper or cadmium-plated bullets give a non-corrosive but not a rust-preventing fouling. On rare occasions after such cartridges have been fired the bore might rust from moisture in the air, particularly damp night air. It is therefore safest to clean the bore not later than the evening of the day on which it was fired.

Some target varieties of cartridges are loaded with Lesmok or Semi-smokeless powder. The fouling of these powders will cause rust if the bore is not properly cared for. When such ammunition is used the bore should *always* be cleaned as described below not later than the evening of the day on which the rifle was fired; then no deterioration of the bore will occur. If the rifle be left overnight without cleaning rust will start.

Ordinarily, fouling does not accumulate in a good barrel during a day's firing to an extent that would interfere with accuracy unless the atmosphere is very hot and devoid of moisture, when cleaning between strings is recommended. Therefore, there is no advantage in cleaning in the middle of the day's firing or between scores. Clean before evening when the air becomes damp.

For cleaning you need a steel cleaning rod with a tip like that shown in Plate XVI, a supply of canton flannel cleaning patches, and a can of gun oil. Patches should be cut from a medium-weight canton flannel, about ¾ inch square, so that when centered with the tip of the cleaning rod and pushed into the bore, they will make a snug fit in the bore, but not so tight that the patch might be

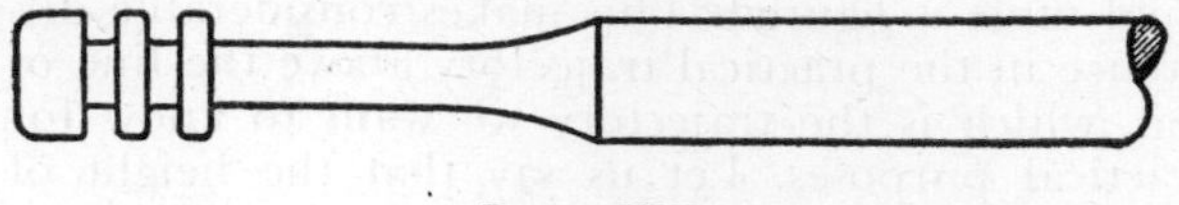

PLATE XVI.

punctured by the rod, or that the rod and patch might get stuck in the bore. Clean from the breech of the barrel if possible, but if the mechanism of the rifle will not permit this, then clean from the muzzle and use the fingers as a guide to prevent the cleaning rod from rubbing and wearing the muzzle.

(1) Wet a flannel patch with water, powder solvent, or light oil, lay it over the breech or muzzle, center it with the tip of the cleaning rod, and push it straight through the bore and out the other end. This pushes out the bulk of the fouling.

(2) Swab the bore with two or three patches wet with water, powder solvent, or light oil. To swab: Place a piece of paper on the floor, rest the muzzle on it, push the patch down to the paper, and pull it back to the chamber a dozen times, thus swabbing the bore thoroughly from end to end with each patch.

(3) Dry the rod. Then swab again with about half a dozen clean, dry patches so that the bore is thoroughly dried and cleaned out, and becomes slightly warm from friction.

(4) Saturate a patch with gun oil and swab the bore with it, and leave the bore in this condition. The bore is now clean and protected and will not rust. If you are putting the rifle away for over a week, the next day wipe out the oil and swab with a patch heavily coated with gun grease. Do not use "powder solvent" for this last swabbing. It is a cleaner only, and not a good rust preventative.

(5) Wipe the exterior of the rifle and all parts of the mechanism that can be reached with a dry rag and then with an oily one.

(6) Before starting to fire always push a clean, dry patch through the bore to wipe out the film of oil or grease. Oil in the bore and chamber will cause the first few shots to fly slightly wild until the oil is shot out. Grease in the bore may cause serious injury to the barrel if the rifle be fired without removing it. Gasoline on a patch will facilitate the removal of grease.

Sometimes an automatic rifle that is fired very rapidly for some time, so that the barrel gets very hot, will have lead or copper deposited in the bore. To remove this, screw a brass bristle brush on the rod, dip the brush in kerosene, and swab the bore with it, pushing the brush all the way through the bore, and then pulling it all the way back, without reversing it in the bore.

The above cleaning is all that is necessary to preserve the rifle in first-class condition indefinitely. It is the one best way. Other methods may or may not be efficient. *Note also* the following:

The bolt, particularly its interior mechanism, should merely be wiped dry and then wiped with a slightly oily rag. Any quantity of oil or grease on the interior mechanism of a bolt may cause poor accuracy by interfering with perfect ignition.

On a sandy or dusty range, pay particular attention to keeping the action clean during the use. The cutting effect of sand or dust on the moving parts may cause wear which would eventually result in the rifle's not breeching up tight enough for accuracy or safety.

Perspiration is a great promoter of rust. After use, therefore, wipe the exterior of the rifle with a dry rag and then with an oily one. Occasionally rub raw linseed oil into the stock, and neatsfoot oil into the gunsling. Do not lay the rifle on damp ground or grass, as dampness might warp the stock; use your forked rifle rest. After a rifle has been wet from rain wipe it off dry, oil the metal parts, and apply linseed oil to the stock. Constantly guard the rifle and its sights against blows and falls.

**Small-Bore Targets.** The official targets used in small-bore rifle shooting are printed on unfinished tag board for shooting at 50 and 75 feet indoors and 50, 100, and 200 yards and 50 meters outdoors.

The targets used at 50 and 75 feet indoors, and dimensions, are shown in Plate XVII. The 6- to 10-rings are blackened to give the black aiming bull's-eye. These indoor targets are usually printed with either five or ten targets on one cardboard sheet measuring approximately 10¾ x 13 inches. Where ten bull's-eyes are shown, the shooter fires only one shot at each of them; where five bull's-eyes are used, he fires two shots in succession at each of the five bull's-eyes. Accurate scoring makes it necessary to fire no more than two shots at any one target because at these ranges a group of ten shots fired on one target would probably cut one large hole through the center of the bull's-eye and it would be impossible to tell which of the shots were 8's, 9's or 10's.

The targets used at 50 and 100 yards outdoors have dimensions as shown in Plate XVIII. The 8-9-, and 10-rings are blackened to give the black aiming bull's-eye. Sometimes in important matches two targets are set up alongside of each other, or two targets are printed on one cardboard, five shots being fired at each target to facilitate accurate scoring of each shot. More recently in registered N.R.A. matches, it has been customary to print two or four full's-eyes on one target card; these bull's-eyes are numbered to establish the order of fire in the ranking of tied scores.

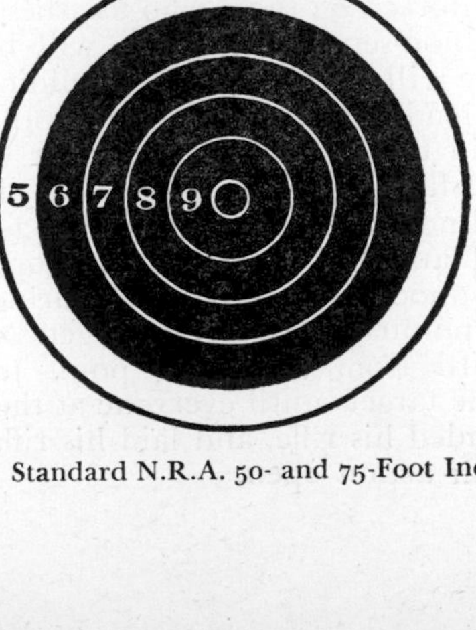


PLATE XVII. Standard N.R.A. 50- and 75-Foot Indoor Target.

For some years, the official target for 200-yard shooting has been one known as the "Decimal" target (Plate XIX). The 8-, 9-, and 10-rings are blackened to give the black aiming bull's-eye. This target is printed on thin cardboard sheets and is used exclusively at 200 yards. The dimensions are:

| | | | |
|---|---|---|---|
| X-ring | 2 inches | 8-ring | 12 inches |
| 10 " | 4 " | 7 " | 16 " |
| 9 " | 8 " | 6 " | 20 " |

Size of cardboard 21″ x 24″

In addition to the 200-yard decimal targets, there is another target which is sometimes used for long-range small-bore shooting at 150, 175, and 200 yards, generally known as the "C-5" target. It gets its name from the fact that it is a reduction of the Army Target "C," used at 800, 900, and 1000 yards with the .30 caliber Springfield military rifle, but is reduced to one-fifth size. It is printed on a thin cardboard sheet 15 x 24½ inches. The black bull's-eye counting 5 is 7.2 inches in diameter with a V-ring of 4 inches. The 4-ring is 10.6 inches in diameter. The space counting 3 is a square in the center of the target 14.4 inches on each side. The spaces counting 2 at each end of the target are 4.8 x 14.4 inches, which makes the entire counting target 14.4 x 24 inches.

PLATE XVIII. Standard N.R.A. 50- and 100-Yard Outdoor Target.

Small-bore matches are often shot at 50 meters (54.6 yards) under International Shooting Union and Olympic conditions. The 50-meter target is similar to the 300-meter International Free-Rifle target, reduced to one-sixth size and has the dimensions as shown in the table below Plate XX. The 4- to 10-rings are blackened to form a sighting bull.

Matches at 50 meters have become very popular in recent years, since this target rewards very close holding, and it is the target which is used in several of the International team matches.

**Small-Bore Rifle Ranges.** It is, of course, apparent that if a shooter or a newly organized rifle club is to undertake small-bore rifle shooting, a suitable indoor or outdoor rifle range is necessary. Often great difficulty is experienced in obtaining such a range, although usually one can be had if some energy and ingenuity are exercised to obtain it. Once a location has been found the matter of proper equipment is comparatively easy, and not necessarily expensive.

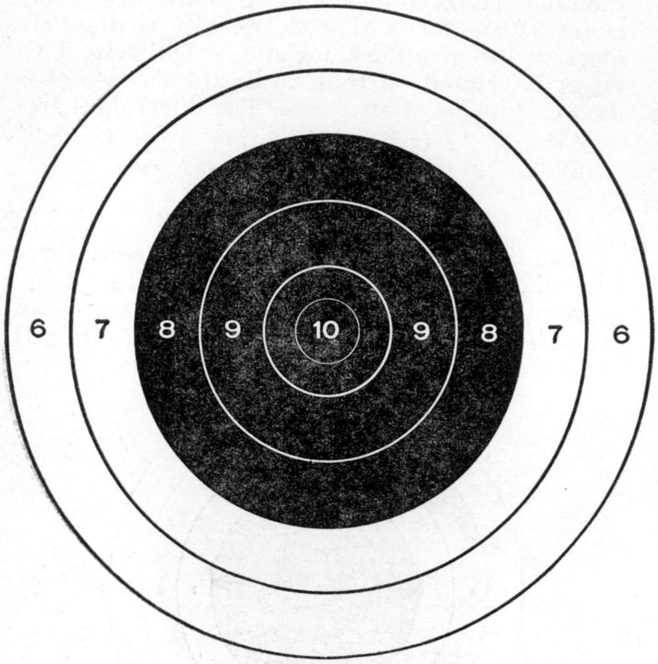


PLATE XIX. Decimal Target.

Often a range is already in existence in your locality. A letter addressed to The Secretary, National Rifle Association, 1600 Rhode Island Ave., Washington, D. C., will bring information as to the nearest civilian rifle clubs to your locality, and these clubs usually have ranges. National Guard armories sometimes open their ranges for use by civilian shooters on certain evenings or days. Similar shooting arrangements can sometimes be made at the nearest Army post.

In towns and small cities a suitable location for an outdoor range can almost always be found on a near-by farm. Farmers are usually willing to rent the necessary ground for a reasonable figure, as very little ground is needed—merely enough for the firing points and butts, with paths leading thereto, the remainder of the ground shot over being planted in low crops. Also, a farmer may even donate the ground because of ability to sell some of the produce of his farm to members of a rifle club, or he may become interested in rifle shooting himself. Of course the ground must be suitable and safe. Instructions for selecting suitable and safe ground are given hereafter (p. 595).

Even in large cities the obtaining of a range is not always as difficult as it would seem. On a recent afternoon's survey in a large city one club representative found a vacant lot with a high brick wall on its north side, two basements, and the flat roof of a garage, all of which could be obtained for a reasonable rental. With safe backstops and bulkheads any of these localities could have been made into a suitable small-bore range. When a club is organized among the employees of a large industrial organization that organization can often find a suitable location on its premises.

Small-bore rifle ranges, because of differences in construction, surroundings, and location, may be divided into Indoor Gallery Ranges at 50 and 75 feet, Outdoor Ranges at 50 feet, 50 and 100 yards, and 50 meters, and Long Ranges at 200 yards. The exact distances are important because these are the ranges at which all small-bore shooting competitions are held in the United States. England, Canada, and all British Colonies also use the 50- and 100-yard ranges with targets exactly similar to ours. The great advantage of these ranges is that they can almost always be conveniently located in or very close to towns or cities where they are easily accessible to all who desire to shoot on them. It is easy and relatively cheap to build them so that they are perfectly safe. The members of a club, or even an individual rifleman, can build perfectly satisfactory ranges in their spare time, sometimes at practically no cost. Indoor gallery ranges can be located in cellars, basements, gymnasiums, or any place indoors where there is sufficient room. Outdoor ranges for 50 and 100 yards can be constructed so that they can be safely located in a city park or in a vacant lot. The report of a small-bore rifle is so slight that no objection by the surrounding residents will be encountered if proper safety precautions are taken.

**Junior Rifle Ranges.** Small-bore rifle shooting has become popular in all types of educational institutions from grammar school up to and including the high schools and colleges, also among the Boy Scouts and in boys' and girls' summer camps. It is a simple matter to set up a satisfactory and safe indoor and outdoor range by following the rules laid down elsewhere in this book. The standard distance for junior shooting is 50 feet, and on account of this short range a suitable location with a natural hillside backstop may be easily obtained. The National Rifle Association conducts a Junior Department of Shooting for boys and girls below the age of 19 years and will gladly furnish complete information on application covering formation of rifle clubs, building of ranges, rules and regulations regarding competitions, as well as how to become an N.R.A. Junior Marksman.

**Safety Precautions.** The designs for small-bore ranges which follow are predicated on the assumption that a certain amount of necessary discipline will be enforced on those who use these ranges, and that common-sense precautions will be taken. No rifle range will ever be safe for the idiot who points his rifle, loaded or unloaded, at another; who fires his rifle in the air or to the rear; or who proceeds to fire without being familiar with the operation and loading of his weapon. Rifles must be kept unloaded and the breech actions open until the firer is in shooting position at the firing point, with his rifle pointed toward the target. No man may go forward from the firing point to inspect or change the targets until everyone at the firing point has unloaded his rifle, and laid his rifle down with the breech action open.

Small-bore rifles using the .22 caliber long rifle cartridge have an extreme range of about 1700 yards when the barrel is elevated at an angle of about 33 degrees. Even at this extreme range the little bullet has remaining energy and penetration sufficient to wound seriously a human being. At short ranges the following thickness of material have been found to be proof against occasional direct hits:

12 inches of earth or sand
3 inches of gravel between planks
4½ inches concrete or good brickwork
5 inches of hard timber, such as railroad ties, etc.
6 inches of fine gravel
⅛-inch steel plate

Where continuous direct hits are to be expected, as immediately behind the paper targets, double the above protection is necessary, but as the bullets will gradually wear away most of the above materials and thus gradually drive through, it is most economical and convenient to use a ¼-inch steel plate or similar thickness of boiler iron, preferably set at an angle of 45 degrees so the bullets will be deflected downward into a box of sand. In positions where only occasional glancing hits may be expected, such as side walls, floors, or ceilings, the following thickness may be considered to be safe:

| | |
|---|---|
| 1 inch planking | Galvanized iron roofing |
| Ordinary plaster | Tile or slate roof |

**Indoor Gallery Ranges.** Such ranges can be constructed in almost any cellar, basement, gymnasium, or other large room where there is sufficient space. The range is measured from the firing point to the target; the room, therefore, should be at least 15 feet longer than the range to give room for targets, backstop, men lying at the firing point, and room to move back and forth behind the firing point. The room should be capable of ventilation, should have electric-light wiring installed, and, if there are any doors or windows in the line of fire, they should be blocked off, closed, and protected by material impervious to bullets, as noted above.

A very simple combined backstop, target carrier, and light may be made. It consists of a box backed by a ¼-inch steel plate set at an angle of 45 degrees. The back is a steel plate which deflects the bullets downward, the bottom of the box being filled with about 3 inches of sand to catch the bullets. The front boards, on which the paper gallery target is fastened with thumb-tacks, slide in slots at the front corners of the box, and are removable so that they can be replaced as they are shot away. The framework of the box should be made of 2 x 4-inch lumber, with ⅞-inch boards for the remainder. A 2 x 6-inch board faced with white paper to reflect light is used with a 60-watt Mazda globe, the board being placed at an angle to reflect light effectively over the surface of the target.

Modern design has shown the desirability of good average illumination over the entire shooting space, desirably at a level of at least ten foot-candles. The box is placed on the floor for prone shooting, or on a pair of wooden horses for standing. This arrangement works very well if one to three fairly skilled and careful riflemen only are using the gallery. But, if a club is to use this arrangement, there should be some sort of a backstop immediately behind the target box to catch the occasional wild shots. This backstop should be at least 5 feet high 6 feet wide for each target. It may consist of ⅛-inch steel plate, or a pile of railroad ties, or a bulkhead of double board 4 inches apart with fine gravel filled in behind the boards. It may also be desirable to face the lamp board with ⅛-inch steel plate or boiler iron to prevent a stray shot from damaging the light. In a club gallery there should be some kind of a fence just in front of the firing point to prevent anyone from straying into the danger zone in front of the rifles. This fence should have a gate with an electric switch so that, when anyone opens the gate and goes forward to tack up a fresh target, the light at the target will go out automatically. When the light goes out, everyone at the firing point should at once open the breech of his rifle and leave it open until the light goes on. Telescopes or field glasses at the firing point permit the shooter to see where each of his shots strikes.

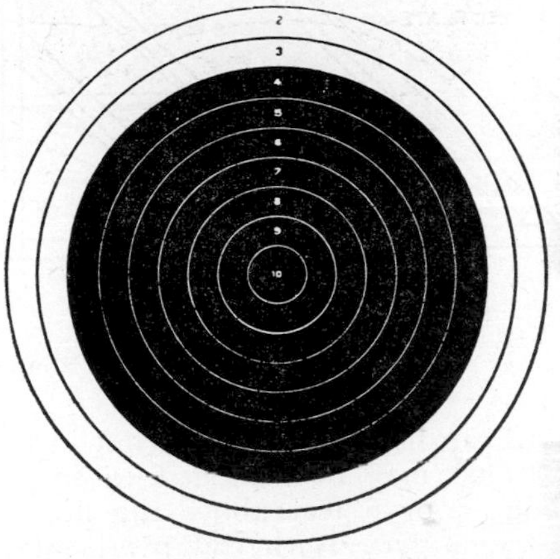

PLATE XX. Standard N.R.A. 50-Meter Target..

| | | | | | |
|---|---|---|---|---|---|
| 10 ring | .787 inches | (.02 meters) | 5 ring | 4.723 inches | (.12 meters) |
| 9 " | 1.574 " | (.04 " ) | 4 " | 5.510 " | (.14 " ) |
| 8 " | 2.361 " | (.06 " ) | 3 " | 6.297 " | (.16 " ) |
| 7 " | 3.148 " | (.08 " ) | 2 " | 7.084 " | (.18 " ) |
| 6 " | 3.936 " | (.10 " ) | 1 " | 7.872 " | (.20 " ) |

Plate XXI shows a similar arrangement, but much larger, and more suitable for a large club gallery or for use in a gymnasium or armory. The unit permits of four men firing at one time, each man having his own target. It consists of a framework of 2 x 4 inch lumber, faced with a sheet of beaver board, and backed by a ¼-inch steel plate set at an angle of 45 degrees to deflect the bullets downward into a sand box. The front of the framework should be about 5 feet high by 9 feet long. The beaver-board front is replaced when large holes have been shot in it. One unit is placed opposite the center of four firing points, and as many units as required may be used. In an armory or gymnasium the units may be raised with crowbars, rollers may be slipped under them, and they can then be run off to one side when not in use; or they may be constructed on wheels. To lighten them for moving around, the sand box may be made as a separate tray and slipped under them. Racks containing four targets, as described below for the 50- and 100-yard outdoor ranges, are hung in front of the beaver board on pins, the targets being tacked to the racks about a foot apart. Two racks are provided, and, while one rack is being fired upon, the other one is having fresh targets tacked on it for the next relay of shooters. After a relay completes its scores, rifles are unloaded and breech actions opened by command, the lights at the targets are turned off, and a man takes down the new rack of targets, hangs it up and brings back the old rack for scoring. For prone shooting the rack is hung about two feet from the floor, and, for standing shooting, about four feet from the floor.

Lights may be arranged for as shown in Plate XXI by placing a board on the floor about 5 feet in front of the targets, with white paper tacked on its face, and carrying strong Mazda lamps. This

low, for the protected outdoor range, to catch effectively any bullets which would not strike the steel plate of the unit.

One-quarter-inch steel plates, or similar boiler iron, inclined at an angle of 45 degrees to deflect the bullets downward into a sand box, are by far the best and most durable arrangement to catch the bullets behind the targets. The objection to placing this plate vertically is that the bullets splash backward objectionably. If steel plate cannot be obtained, some arrangement such as railroad ties, or frames filled with fine gravel, may be used instead, but these must be inspected frequently and replaced when necessary, as the bullets will gradually drill holes through them immediately behind each target.

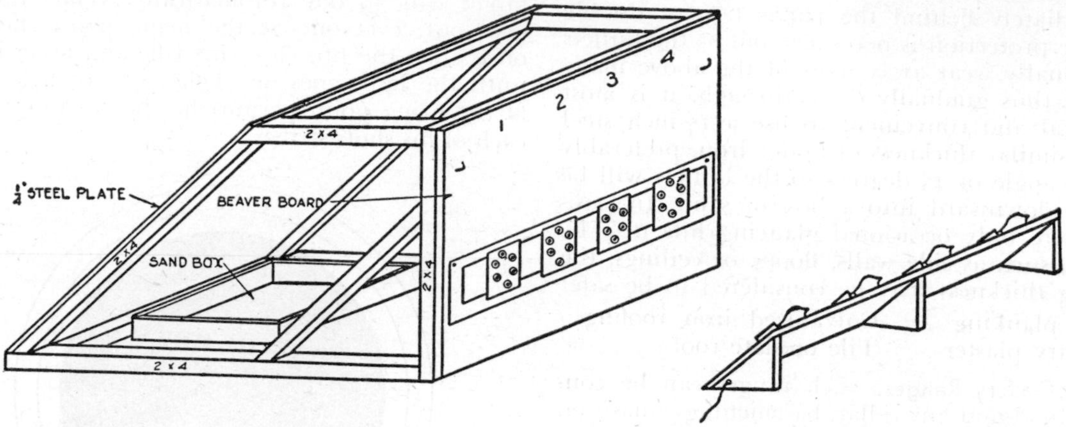

PLATE XXI. A Simple Setup of Lights, Targets, and Backstop.

lamp board can be removed when not in use. Or a hanging frame may be arranged to suspend the lights about 5 or 6 feet above the floor and in front of the targets. With this overhead lighting a very satisfactory light can be secured by using two General Electric Co. Type L-9, 500-watt flood lights with stippled lenses, or PAR-38 lights, placing the lights about 15 feet in front of the targets and directing the lamps at a mid-point between the upper and the lower positions of the targets.

Suitable gallery units are made by several companies. The "X-Ring" model of trap is illustrated in Plate XXII. It consists of a steel, funnel-shaped box, the funnel guiding the bullets into an inner scroll where their energy is dissipated by friction and centrifugal action. The box is supported in position by a standard. The paper target is secured by convenient clamps at the opening of the funnel, and suitable electric-light fixtures are provided. An individual can set one up in the basement of his home and have a very satisfactory range in a few minutes, or any number of units may be set up side by side in a larger range.

The above units are all that are necessary if only fairly good, careful shots are to use the gallery; but, if uninstructed or careless shooters are to use it, some backstop must be placed in rear of the units as described above, or it may even be necessary to place a bulletproof bulkhead a short distance in front of the firing points, as described be-

At the firing point the positions from which each shooter fires should be arranged at least 4 feet apart, 5 feet if possible. They should be marked by a plain number painted on the floor, or a short stake bearing the number, and a similar plain number should be painted above the corresponding target's position on the backstop. Firing points should also be provided with some sort of mat which will cushion the elbows from the hard floor. Gymnasium mats are the best, but expensive; ordinary doormats will do.

Much more elaborate and convenient gallery ranges may be constructed, if desired. In these, permanently constructed steel bullet stops and flood lights are installed. The targets are suspended from carriers which run on wires suspended from the ceiling and running from the firing point to the bullet stop. The shooter at the firing point affixes a target in the carrier, and turns a wheel which runs the target down to the firing position, thus making it unnecessary for anyone to go forward of the firing point, and also permitting any one shooter to change his target at any time he desires, or reel it back to the firing point for inspection without the other shooters having to stop firing. Complete plans and blueprints for the construction of permanent ranges of this kind may be obtained from The Secretary, National Rifle Association, 1600 Rhode Island Ave., Washington, D.C.

**Outdoor Ranges.** Outdoor shooting with small-bore rifles is, as a rule, more interesting than gallery shooting, and one learns more. Outdoor shooting can be carried on at all periods during the year when the weather is not too cold. Indeed it can be carried on all year if a warm shooting house with ports to shoot from can be afforded. Even moderate rain need not deter the enthusiast if there is a cheap roof shelter over the firing point. They may even be used at night by illuminating the targets with electric flood lights, as described for the gallery range. The only problem of the outdoor range is to obtain a suitable location. It is sometimes possible to obtain a large vacant lot in a town or city which will be very convenient and easily reached, and ranges have often been built in out-of-the-way corners in city parks. Usually, however, one will have to go a short distance out into the country to build the range, preferably to a location that can easily be reached by trolley or automobile.

The discussion of outdoor ranges from this point on will be divided into two classes: (1) Ranges in not too well built-up areas where there is either a large, adequate, natural backstop such as a hill 40 to 50 feet high and of a slope not less than three to two, or a clear area approximately 50 yards wide and 1700 yards deep from the firing point, that can be adequately observed, into which the bullet may fall; and (2) Safety ranges for use in public parks and closely built-up areas where safety facilities are provided to prevent bullets fired in the direction of the target from missing the backstop.

In any case, the site should be fairly level, or at least the firing point and the targets should be level. The lot should be at least 110 yards long, and wide enough to accommodate the number of firing points desired, with preferably at least 25 yards to spare on each side of the range proper. If a piece of ground can be obtained which is at least 220 yards long, that is ideal, as this permits installing a 200-yard range, but the 200-yard range is by no means essential for the thorough enjoyment of small-bore shooting. The range should face preferably north, northeast, or east, so that the sun will not be in the eyes of the shooters at the time of day when they use the range most, and so that the targets will not be in the shade.

It is necessary that there be some sort of a backstop to catch the bullets and that this be sufficiently large to stop the occasional slightly wild shot that goes wide of the targets. No range is safe with the careless man who discharges his rifle to the rear or pointed upward, and we must always depend on a certain discipline being exercised on a rifle range and certain safety precautions being rigidly enforced. If possible, there should be a steep hill behind the targets, extending at least 15 to 20 feet above the line of fire. If the hill be not steep, it should be kept plowed up to prevent bullets from glancing and carrying on to places where they would be dangerous. Beware particularly of a hill composed largely of rock or gravel. If there be no hill, then an artificial backstop should be built in the rear of the targets extending, if possible, 6 feet above the line of targets and 6 feet beyond the flank targets. On a city lot a brick wall or stone building might sometimes provide a sufficient backstop for the very wild shots, but in such case there should also be a built-up backstop immediately behind the targets which will catch 99 per cent of the shots and keep them from gradually drilling into the wall. Such built-up backstops can consist of piles of logs or railroad ties, or two rough board walls filled in with a 12-inch thickness of earth between, or, if fine gravel can be had, 6 inches thickness will suffice.

The National Rifle Association has prepared excellent working drawings for indoor and outdoor ranges and range houses and has available on its staff competent consultants who can assist in suitable safe range designs.

Targets are easily arranged for outdoor ranges of 50 feet, and 50 and 100 yards. A rough board fence should be erected in front of the backstop and the correct distance (50 feet, 50 and 100 yards) in front of the firing point. This fence should be about 6 feet high and built with 2 x 4-inch uprights faced with rough boards. It is most convenient and economical to build the fence in sections about 15 feet long for the various distances. These sections should be placed opposite the center of each five firing points, the targets for five men (three targets for each man may sometimes be needed) being tacked on racks and the racks hung on these fences. The slight convergence of the fire of five men on such a butt does no harm. Such a fence or butt is shown in Platc XXIII. There

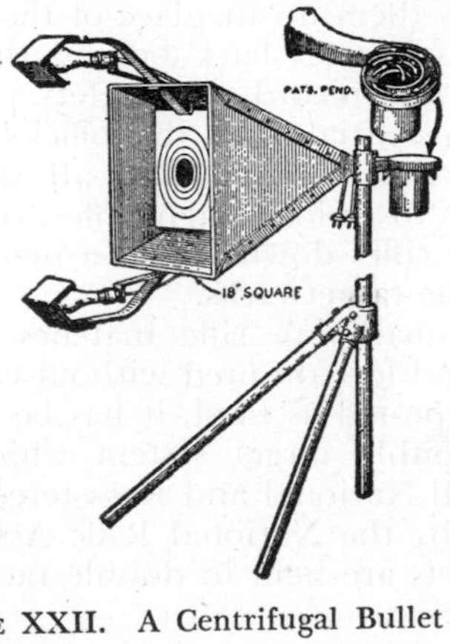


PLATE XXII. A Centrifugal Bullet Trap.

should be an open gap in the fence immediately behind the bull's-eyes of the targets as they hang in the racks, this gap being obtained by leaving one board out of the fence. This gap is to permit light to shine through the targets from the rear, thus making the bullet holes in the black bull's-eye plainly visible when viewed from the firing point through the shooter's spotting telescope. At the top of the fence, above each target or series of three targets, should be painted a large white number corresponding to the number of the firing point, and showing the shooter which are his targets. The remainder of the fence should be painted dark green.

The targets are tacked on rectangular racks of boards made of wood strips about 3 inches wide, as shown in Plate XXIV, long enough to hold five to nine targets tacked alongside of one another, with about one inch between targets. Two sets of

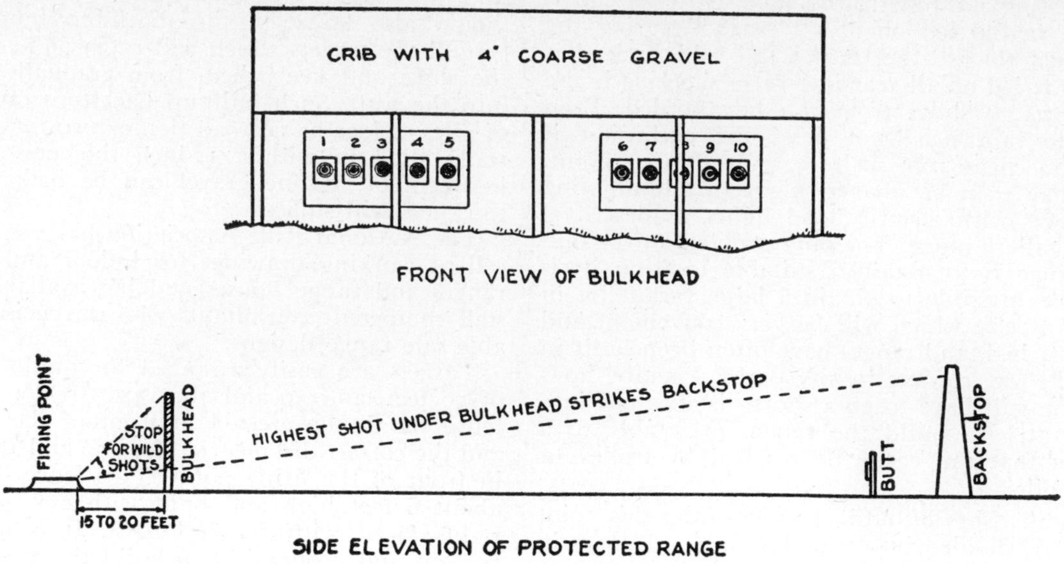


PLATE XXIII. Design for a Protected Range.

racks are provided for each butt. One set, with the targets tacked on, is taken down and hung up in position on the butt or fence, as shown in Plate XXIII, and five men at the firing point fire their scores on these targets. When these shooters complete their firing, a man takes down a set of new racks, hangs them up in place of the old ones, and brings the old ones back behind the firing point for scoring and record. As a safety precaution it is absolutely essential that the official at the firing point give the command for all shooters at the firing point to unload their rifles, open chambers, and lay the rifles down before a man goes forward to change the target racks.

Because small-bore rifle matches are ranges of 100 yards and less are fired without each shot being scored and posted as fired, it has been necessary to devise a double target system which is now required in all National and Registered competitions recognized by the National Rifle Association.

The targets are held in double racks constructed similarly to those shown in Plate XXV. The "record target," carrying the bull's-eyes, is placed in the front and the "backing target," which is a plain card without bull's-eyes, is placed on the rear. The proper spacing interval is indicated in Plate XXV. In competition the target card carries one bull's-eye for sighting shots and two or more bull's-eyes (depending on the conditions of the match) for the record shots. The target cards are usually tacked or clipped onto a piece of composition board with holes properly spaced behind each bull's-eye so that the light may come through from the rear and assist in spotting the shots. The composition board is fastened to the frames with turnbuttons or in some other quickly detachable manner.

All of the shots fired by a competitor on his own target will make a group on the backing card which will be an exact duplicate of his group on the record target. But should a shooter at the firing point to the right of the competitor fire a shot on the competitor's target, the bullet hole made by that shot in the backing card will be 1/4 inch to the left of its corresponding hole in the record target; shots fired from the second firing point to the right would be 1/2 inch to the left on the backing card, etc. Thus the shots from the shooters on either side can be eliminated from the competitor's target, and the competitor be given full value for all the shots he has fired on his target. Also the shooters who fired on the wrong target can be identified and penalized. To make this system work each competitor must fire with his rifle close to his number stake at his firing point.

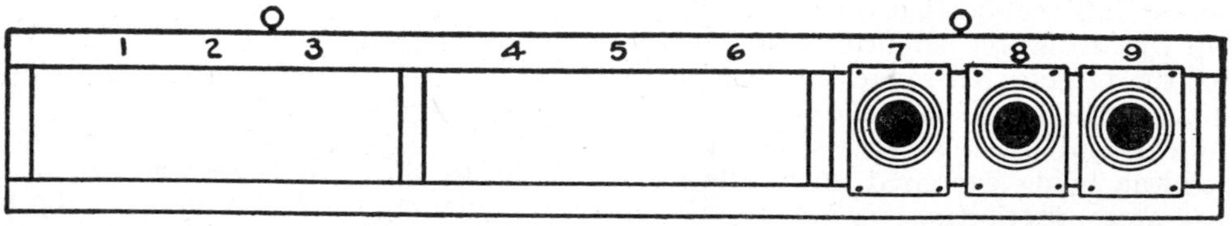


PLATE XXIV. A Good Type of Rack for Outdoor Targets.

The double target rack, one for each competitor, is usually set up permanently at the butt, the upright supports being planted in the ground. A range assistant takes the record targets and backing cards of a relay down to the racks, the signal "Cease firing" having previously been given. The assistant takes out the record targets and backing cards of the previous relay (taking care to keep each backing card behind its record target) and then fastens the record targets and backing cards of the new relay in their proper place. Each record target and backing card is numbered with the number of the firing point and the number of the relay.

It is best, where sufficient land is available, to have separate butts and separate firing points for the various distances to be used, but it is possible to get along with a butt at 100 yards only, and between the firing point and the butt to place posts only on which the racks of targets for either 50 feet or 50 yards can be hung. In fact, the fence is not absolutely necessary at the butt, but it costs little or nothing, as it can be made of scrap materials, and it makes the target stand out plain and distinct, and gives something on which to place the large numbers designating which target belongs to which firing point.

The firing point ought to be raised a little above the surrounding ground, both to keep it dry and to permit view of the targets when firing prone without having to cut the grass so often. The mound ought to be at least 7 feet from the front to rear on top, and should slope very slightly to the rear. At the front of each individual firing point there should be a stake with a number painted on it corresponding to the number painted on the butt above the corresponding target position. There should be at least 5, preferably 6, feet between the individual firing points. It adds to convenience and comfort if a simple roof can be erected over the firing point. This roof should be about 8 feet from front to rear and should slope about a foot toward the front, being 6½ to 7 feet high in the clear at the rear. It can be made of scrap lumber covered with tar paper. The shooter takes his position or lies down just behind the stake bearing his number, and fires on the target or targets at the butt corresponding to the number of his stake. In order to see where each bullet strikes his target, he must be provided with a spotting telescope which he sets up on a holder to one side so that, by moving his head slightly to one side when in firing position, he can view his target through the glass and see the bullet holes. This and the cheap construction cost are the great advantages of the short-distance small-bore outdoor ranges. No hired markers are necessary, as the telescopes take their places.

All of the above is not necessary where only two or three shooters wish to fire together. Many shooters have been known to get along very well for years with nothing more elaborate than a measured range in a field, and a large packing box filled with earth for a butt, on the front of which the targets were tacked. But shooters using this type of range must, of course, be good and careful shots and keep all their bullets on the box.

**200-Yard Butts.** If an individual or club wishes to shoot at 200 yards and has that distance available on the outdoor range, a little more elaborate butt and target carrier are necessary. It is only in the most perfect light, and when no mirage or heat waves are present, that the best spotting telescopes will show .22-caliber bullet holes at 200 yards. Therefore, when shooting at this range, it is necessary to have a man or boy as a marker at the butt to indicate the value and location of each shot on the target. The butt must be so constructed that it will shelter the marker from any possibility of being struck by a bullet. This butt may be a boxlike shelter about 3 feet thick filled with earth, or it may be a pit in the ground, or a combination of the two. The targets are fastened to frames, which are best made about 4 feet square, covered with cotton cloth over which heavy paper has been pasted, the targets being pinned in the center of the frame. The larger paper backing shows most of the shots which miss the target; this is quite desirable, as the C-5 target is not very high vertically and many shots miss it and are hard to locate. These frames are arranged on sliding carriers so that they slide behind the butt where the marker puts in the spotter and pastes the old bullet hole and then slides into firing position, either above or to one side of the butt.

A backstop to catch the bullets is, of course, very necessary. If this is not provided by a hill or other obstacle, a large one must be built, boxlike, and filled with earth or gravel.

Plate XXVI shows the construction of a simple type of 200-yard small-bore butt, comprising a target house, marker's shelter, target carriers, and artificial backstop, that is relatively simple and inexpensive to build and yet answers every purpose. It permits four shooters to fire at one time, there being two targets at each side of the shelter. All boxes shown are filled to the top with sand or fine gravel. The markers are fully protected by the box connected to the house and by chicken wire fastened securely over both ends of the house so that no part of the body can be exposed or be directly in the line of fire. The artificial backstops behind the targets are necessary only when there is no natural bullet stop. The boxes will, of course, gradually get shot away immediately behind the targets, and to avoid having to repair them constantly that portion of the backstop immediately behind the targets, where 90 per cent of the bullets strike, may be covered with a steel plate set at an angle of 45 degrees to deflect the bullets downward, or railroad ties or logs may be piled up.

The target frames are arranged to slide as shown in a wooden framework. The marker slides the frame out into the exposed position. When it is fired on he pulls it into the shelter, places a target spotter in the new bullet hole, pastes up the old bullet hole with a paster, and slides the target into position again for another shot. The spotters are 2-inch-round cardboard disks, white on one side (for hits in the bull's-eye) and black on the other, with a wire or .22-caliber peg stuck through them and projecting to each side. This spotter, stuck through the last bullet hole, is visible from the firing point through the shooter's spotting telescope, and shows him exactly where his last shot struck. For shots in the bull's-eye the spotter is stuck through the bullet hole with the white side showing and can be seen easily through the telescope.

Markers must be very careful how they leave the shelter at such a butt. The targets must first be withdrawn, and a red flag displayed in their place.

Instead of having the targets arranged to slide

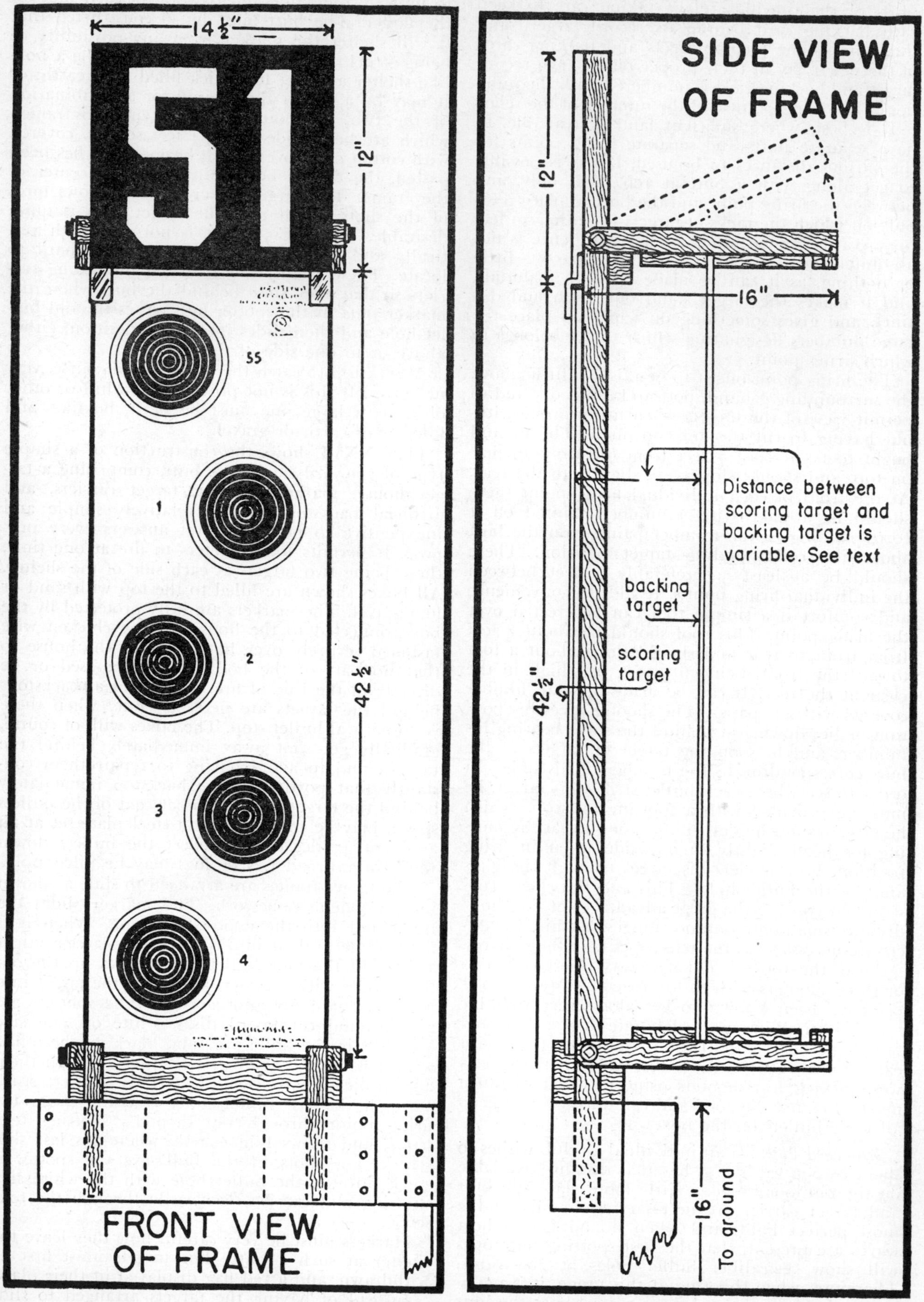


PLATE XXV. Double Target Rack.

out at each side of a short shelter as shown, the shelter may be made continuous, as in a large military rifle range, and the carriers built so that the target frames will slide vertically to an exposed position above the shelter. This is the best arrangement where there are to be more than four shooters firing at the same time. Or, if desired, a regular military target carrier may be used, the standard small-bore target being pinned on the frame in lieu of the regular military target.

**Safety Regulations.** On any rifle range the following safety regulations must be strictly enforced. Anyone who disregards these regulations should be subject to dismissal from the range.

(1) *A rifle must never,* under any circumstances, *be pointed at or in the direction of any person,* whether it be loaded or not.

(2) *All rifles must habitually be carried with the breech action open* until the shooter takes his place at the firing point with the rifle pointed in the direction of the target.

(3) *No rifle shall be loaded unless the shooter is in position* at the firing point with the rifle pointed at the target, and then not until the range officer shall have given the command "Commence firing," or "Load."

(4) *At the command "Cease firing,"* or when a shooter is through firing, *he shall at once unload his rifle,* and lay it down, muzzle to the front, breech open.

(5) On ranges where it is necessary for a person to walk out in front of the firing point to change targets, *no person shall do so without permission of the range officer* who shall first command "Cease firing" and then watch to see that all shooters have unloaded and laid down their rifles. On gallery ranges the target lights shall also be turned off.

(6) When there are markers at the butt, the *markers shall not leave their shelter nor expose themselves until they have withdrawn all targets* from the firing position, *have exposed the red danger flags,* and *have received* from the firing point *the signal that all is safe.* In the absence of a telephone connecting butts and firing point, this "All clear" signal may be given by horn or bugle.

For further information relative to rifle ranges, write to The Secretary, National Rifle Association, 1600 Rhode Island Ave., Washington 6, D.C., stating the information desired.

**The Rifle Club and the National Rifle Association.** In any community where a number of individuals are interested in rifle or pistol shooting it is to the advantage of all of them to organize a rifle and pistol club. Such a club helps each shooter by introducing the element of competition and sport, which adds considerably to the enjoyment of any pastime by establishing contact with other shooters and providing for an exchange of ideas and experiments and by enlisting the interest of the community at large through the medium of the rifle and pistol matches which the club can hold and the resulting newspaper publicity. There is the further consideration that the construction of a range by an individual is frequently out of the question, due to the cost, but, where a group of men get together into a club and pool their funds through initiation fees and club dues, the matter of acquiring a range becomes comparatively simple.

Although a club may be loosely organized among a group of congenial spirits, it is far better to have the group properly organized along the officially recognized lines and to affiliate the local club with the National Rifle Association of America. Clubs so organized and affiliated enjoy numerous advantages, among which may be mentioned the holding of a nationally recognized charter; the privilege of qualifying for the Regular Army marksmanship decorations—Marksman, Sharpshooter, and Expert Rifleman, and Marksman, Sharpshooter, and Expert Pistol Shot; the privilege of competing in nationwide inter-club matches sanctioned by the National Rifle Association; the privilege of purchasing ammunition, paper targets, spare parts for rifles, etc., direct from the War Department; the receipt of programs, bulletins, and other publications issued by the National Rifle Association, including *The American Rifleman* each month. Up until June 30, 1927, civilian rifle clubs were entitled to draw under bond from the War Department a limited number of rifles, some ammunition, targets and target carriers, and similar supplies without cost to themselves. The economy program of the administration induced Congress, however, to appropriate only enough money to continue this aid to clubs already in existence and did not provide for assistance to newly organized clubs. For this reason, rifle clubs now organizing cannot obtain assistance from the War Department without cost to themselves. They may, however, if they so desire, place a requisition on file with the Director of Civilian Marksmanship to be filled when supplies again become available.

The affiliation of a rifle and pistol club with the National Rifle Association requires a minimum of ten citizens of the United States, 16 years of age or older for a senior club, or not over 19 years of age for a junior club. Clubs may be organized in schools, colleges, fraternal organizations, industrial plants, athletic clubs, fish and game protective associations, or just among groups of interested citizens who have no other affiliations. At least ten men must pay their initiation fees and dues into the club before it can be recognized by the National Rifle Association. There is no maximum, however, to the number of men who may be enrolled under one club charter. The club dues are not fixed by the National Rifle Association, but may be placed at any figure which is deemed advisable by the club itself. A senior club pays ten dollars per year dues, while junior and college clubs pay five dollars per year dues to the National Rifle Association. This fee is the same, regardless of how many members there are in the club.

The necessary application blanks and more detailed information may be obtained by writing to the National Rifle Association, 1600 Rhode Island Ave., Washington 6 D.C. It is required that application for club affiliations be made on the regular application blanks which are furnished by the Association.

There are at the present time about 3000 rifle and pistol clubs in the United States operating under National Rifle Association charters, so that

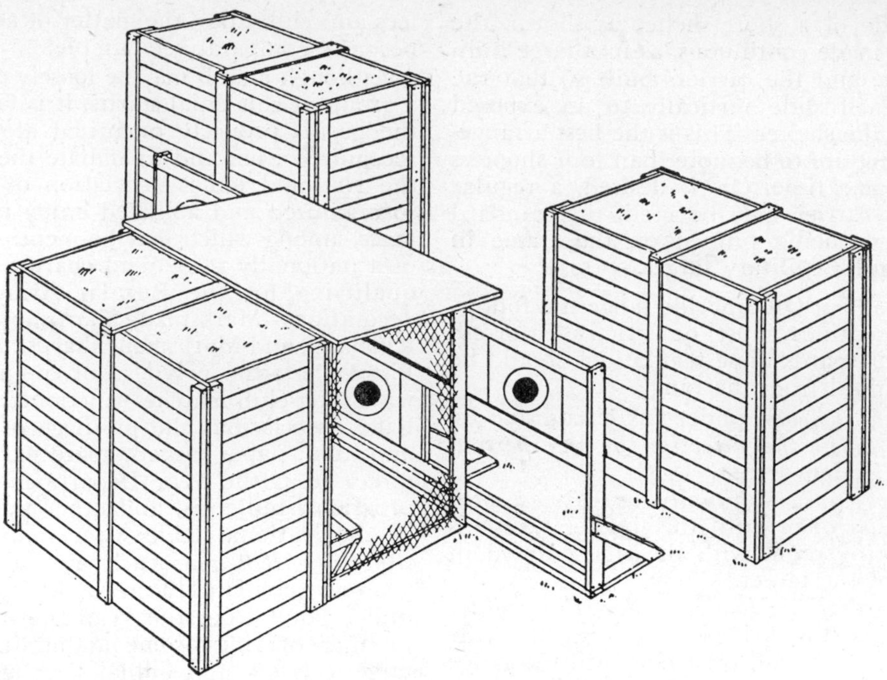

PLATE XXVI. A Homemade 200-Yard Butt and Target Carrier.

there is ample opportunity for the local club to arrange a wide variety of matches with other organizations, in addition to the local matches which should be arranged between club members and the National Matches under the sanction of the National Rifle Association.

**Individual N.R.A. Membership.** In order that a satisfactory check-up may be made and a record kept of arms sold by the War Department, it is required that an individual be an individual member of the National Rifle Association, rather than a club member, before he can purchase a rifle or revolver. These individual members are required to be indorsed by someone who is already a member of the Association or by some of their local police or National Guard authorities.

There are several types of individual membership open to men who desire to support the rifle and pistol shooting game without being members of clubs, or in addition to their club membership. The two most popular types of individual membership are known as Annual Membership, which, as the name implies, is a membership for 12 months, and Life Membership, which gives the holder the privileges of membership for life. Annual Membership costs $3.00 per year, and Life Membership $50.00. These individual members may, under normal conditions, buy military arms and ammunition direct from the War Department; they may compete in the numerous Individual Matches which are conducted by the Association throughout the year; they receive *The American Rifleman* magazine regularly every month; they receive direct all programs, bulletins, and other materials issued by National Headquarters; they are entitled to the personal advice and suggestions of the experts retained by the National Rifle Association to advise its members in regard to their shooting problems; and they, also, of course, receive the golden-bronze membership button and the membership card of the Association. In addition to these general privileges, life members have the privilege of voting at the annual election of directors of the Association and they may occupy directors' chairs and be elected to the executive committee of the Association.

**The American Rifleman.** *The American Rifleman* magazine is the official publication of the National Rifle Association. It is the only magazine published in America devoted exclusively to shooting subjects. Among the shooters who have known this magazine for years you will find the general impression prevailing that if *The American Rifleman* says so, it is so. Among other unique features of the shooters' magazine may be mentioned the fact that it maintains a "Question and Answer Department" in charge of a nationally recognized expert in the technique of arms, ammunition, and rifle and pistol shooting who will solve as far as possible by mail the problems which confront members.

*The American Rifleman* is sent to all club secretaries without charge and to all life members and annual members without additional charge. Club members may subscribe for the magazine through their club secretaries.

# SHOOTING AT ACUTE ANGLES

One of the most confounding mysteries encountered by the average hunter, especially the one who hunts in the mountains, is why he makes so many misses when shooting at game that is at an acute angle *above* or *below* him.

You will hear many explanations of this phenomenon, and most of them are incorrect. One old-timer will tell you to be "sure to hold high when you shoot at game at an acute angle upward, and hold low when you shoot at game at an acute angle downward." Another veteran hunter will advise just the opposite. Neither of them will tell you *how much* to hold high or low at a given range and a given angle.

Thousands of letters reach the desks of rod and gun editors each year, asking for the answer to this problem. Usually such inquiries are made as a result of a wager, and the rod and gun editor, unless he is a graduate ballistician and a mathematician, is unable to supply the answer. To answer the question, and at the same time supply an answer that is not clouded with complicated mathematical theorems is not a simple task, but it can be done.

The answer is relatively simple, for those willing to accept simple facts without argument. However, there are some with a scientific bent who insist on having the matter presented with all the formulas and figures. First we shall present the simple explanation. Then we shall present the scientific explanation as prepared by one of the foremost ballisticians in the country.

**Simple Explanation.** When a target is at a considerable angle *above* or *below* the level of the shooter, it is sometimes observed that the shot will be *high*. That is, the shooter will *over*-shoot the target. This can be explained by saying that the "slant range" (the distance along the slope from the gun to the target) is greater than the "horizontal range," even though the sight setting of the gun is correct for the distance between the muzzle of the gun and the target.

To illustrate this, see diagram (Plate I) below, which shows a shooter 350 yards from a target which is on the same horizontal plane. As you know, the sight setting at this range would elevate the angle of the bore of the rifle to compensate for the curving trajectory of the bullet. In other words, the line of sight between the shooter and the target is a straight line, but the angle of the bore of the rifle is (for the purpose of illustration) at a 10-degree angle upward, to allow for the curving flight of the bullet.

Now turn to Plate II (page 602). You will note that the range is the same, 350 yards, but the target is at a 30-degree angle upward, a situation not unusual in mountain sheep or goat hunting. With the sights still set at 350 yards, the shooter now has the rifle bore elevated *not* at a 30-degree angle off the horizontal, but at a 40-degree angle off the horizontal. Therefore, the trajectory of the bullet would pass *over* the target and the point of impact, X, would be some distance *beyond* the target.

The effect described previously is predicted by ballistic theory. On the basis of this theory a table can be set up which will give, but only approximately, of course, the ratio of "slant range" to "horizontal range." The table which follows is valid for either *uphill* or *downhill* shooting and for all of the angles of elevation (sight setting) up to about 30 minutes.

TABLE

| Angle of Slope (Up or down) | Divide Estimated Range by |
|---|---|
| 0° | 1.0 |
| 5° | 1.0 |
| 10° | 1.02 |
| 15° | 1.04 |
| 20° | 1.06 |
| 25° | 1.10 |
| 30° | 1.15 |
| 35° | 1.22 |
| 40° | 1.31 |
| 45° | 1.41 |

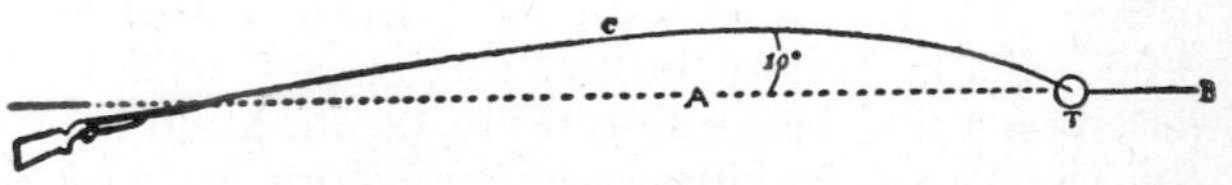


PLATE I. Targets Above or Below.
A. Line of sight to target.
B. Horizontal line (same as line of sight).
C. Trajectory of bullet.
T. Target.

NOTE: The trajectory and the angle of the rifle are exaggerated for the purpose of illustration.

To use this table you first decide upon the range to the target. You then estimate the angle of the target off the horizontal. A glance at the chart will show a listing of angles from 0 to 45 degrees. When you have estimated the angle of the shot, find that angle on the chart. Opposite this angle you will find another number on the chart. Divide the estimated range by this number. The result will be a number smaller than the estimated range. This figure is the *correct* sight setting for your rifle.

For purposes of illustration, let us take a hunter who has spotted a sheep. He happens to be adept at figuring the range, and has estimated the sheep to be 350 yards distant. The hunter is armed with a .30 '06 rifle and is using the 180-grain bullet. Being familiar with the zero of the rifle with this bullet, he is ready to set his sights. The angle above the horizontal he determines to be about 30 degrees. A glance at the angle chart tells him that for a shot at a 30-degree angle he should divide the estimated range by 1.15. He does this and finds he has the figure 304. This means that if he were to set his sights at 350 yards the point of impact would be as though he were shooting at the same target at a range of about 395 yards. (In other words, the bullet would pass *above* the target.) Therefore, he sets his sights at 304 yards, which is the correct setting for a shot at 350 yards at a 30-degree angle.

Actually the hunter would set his sights at 300 yards and not 304, as sights are not calibrated for such minor variations. The variation would amount to a fraction of an inch, which is quite readily absorbed by that ever-present factor known as "human error."

Were the angle to be reversed—that is, if the hunter were on high ground and the sheep at a 30-degree angle below him—the same process would be followed, the same sight setting made. Whether the shot is at an acutely high angle or acutely low angle, the course of the bullet is the same—that is, *high.*

Consideration of the above discussion would show that the seriousness of the tendency to overshoot is much less with the modern high-velocity, flat-trajectory bullets than it would be with the older low-velocity bullets, such as those requiring an acute angle of departure due to their high, looping trajectories.

The table of corrections given previously is only approximate, for, like most ballistic calculations, it is based on simplifying assumptions. In view of the relatively large errors introduced in estimating ranges and angles, however, it should be sufficiently accurate to act as a guide.

**Scientific Explanation.** The derivation of the correction table is not difficult, and provides an interesting example of a normal ballistic calculation. The calculation of bullet trajectories usually is based on a number of simplifying assumptions, since the rigorous calculation of a trajectory is a task of considerable difficulty and labor. One of these simplifying assumptions is that a trajectory is "rigid"—that is, that, having computed a single trajectory, it

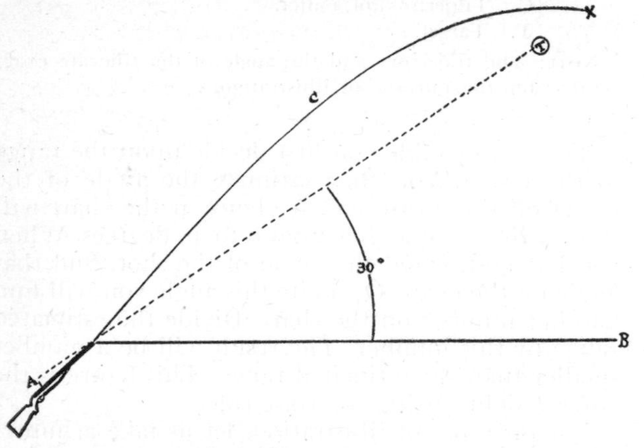


PLATE II. Targets Above or Below.
A. Line of sight to target.
B. Horizontal line.
C. Trajectory of bullet.
T. Target.
X. Point of impact of bullet.

NOTE: The trajectory and the angle of the rifle are exaggerated.

can then in imagination be rotated about the firing point and will be a true representation of the path of the bullet for these various other angles of elevation. For angles up to 5 or 10 degrees the approximation is sufficiently accurate in most cases to outweigh any justification for laboriously calculating the individual trajectories by the more precise methods. For the situations of interest in this section, however, this assumption is no longer valid.

Even here we must depart from actuality in order to obtain a simple solution to our problem. In order to present a rigorous and at the same time simple demonstration it will be necessary to consider our problem as applying to trajectories in a vacuum. Although the trajectory in a vacuum is not even a good approximation to a trajectory in air, it is not unreasonable to assume that tilting the trajectory will have the same relative effect on trajectories in air as on trajectories in a vacuum. In other words, it is assumed that, although the actual trajectories are quite different, the ratio of the slant range to the horizontal range for bullets fired in air will be the same as that for bullets fired in a vacuum under the same initial conditions with regard to muzzle velocity, angle of elevation, and angle of slope.

For a given muzzle velocity $V$ and a given angle of departure $A$, the horizontal range in feet of a projectile fired in a vacuum is given by the equation

$$R = (V^2/32.2) \sin 2A \qquad (1)$$

Consider now a projectile fired with the same initial velocity $V$, but with the angle of departure

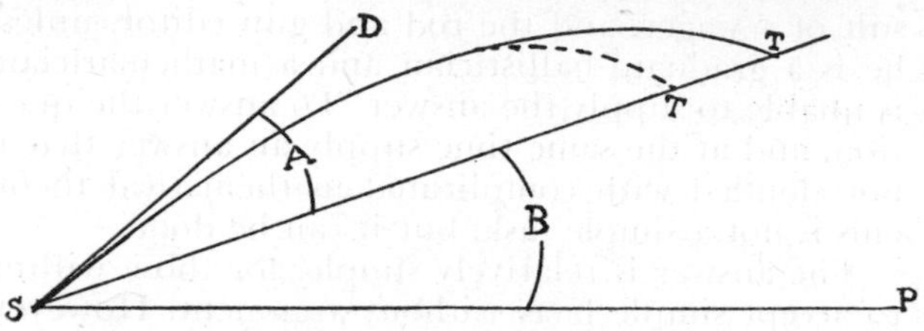


PLATE III. Targets Above or Below.
Angle TSD equals *A.*
Angle PST equals *B.*

$A$ relative to a slope which makes an angle $B$ with the horizontal (see Plate III). it can be shown that the slant range (i.e., the horizontal distance $ST'$) is given by the equation

$$R' = \frac{2V^2 \sin A \cos (A+B)}{32.2 \cos^2 B} \qquad (2)$$

To get an expression for the ratio of the slant range to the horizontal range for the same sight setting we divide Equation (2) by Equation (1) and obtain

$$\frac{\text{Slant Range}}{\text{Horizontal Range}} = \frac{R'}{R} = \frac{2 \sin A \cos (A+B)}{\sin 2A \cos^2 B} \qquad (3)$$

This expression can be simplified to give

$$R'/R = \sec B\ (1 - \tan A \tan B) \qquad (4)$$

It is obvious from this equation that the relationship between the slant range and the horizontal range for various sight settings and slopes is not a simple one. However, with Equation (4) and a table of trigonometric functions, the ratio can be computed for any combination of slope $B$ and angle of elevation $A$. It was from this equation that the table given in the first part of this discussion was derived. Of interest is the fact that for values of $A$ greater than 16° 43′ the slant range is *less* than the horizontal range for positive values of the ground slope $B$ and greater than the horizontal range for negative values of the ground slope. It is only for very small values of $A$ (such as are encountered in normal shooting with a rifle) that the correction can be considered the same for both positive and negative values of the ground slope.

References: *Handbook of Ballistics,* by C. Cranz and K. Becker, English Translation, Vol. I, pp. 12-17, 238-239; *Exterior Ballistics,* by E. E. Herrmann (1935), pp. 15-16.

# USED GUNS

Generally speaking, every gun is "used" by the time you receive it. The chap who offers that gun as "new" and insists that it has never been fired is not technically correct. Every American rifle, pistol, revolver, or shotgun of standard make, has been fired, proof tested, function tested, and sighted before it leaves the factory.

What is generally clasified as a used gun is one which has been fired by one of its original owners. Few items made today change hands as many times as firearms. One would be safe to claim that the *average* gun may change hands a dozen times before it is scrapped.

Used guns have always been on the market. The recent war forced many thousands out of hiding. New guns were not available, and prices on all used equipment soared frequently to double their original new cost. Thousands of men who were about to enter the armed forces decided to cash in on the high market and dispose of their weapons—they could be replaced after the war.

Even by 1948, all standard models of firearms were not easily obtainable in the "new" market. Many a hunter and target shooter must still depend on used equipment. If you buy right, you may get an excellent bargain. If you buy unwisely, you may end up with an item which may be dangerous or useless, or one needing costly major repairs—some of which cannot be obtained.

**Rules.** The wise shooter has ten commandments for the addition of a new gun to his growing collection. Study them carefully and be so guided when you are about to make a purchase.

(1) Be certain that the manufacturer is still in business if you plan to use the weapon. If he is not, don't buy it.

(2) Get a currently popular model. Repairs may not be available on some discontinued types—and if they are, they will be costly.

(3) Do not purchase a gun for an obsolete or rare cartridge unless you are buying it as a collection piece.

(4) Do not buy a gun which requires repairs. Factory parts and labor are expensive—and if parts are handmade by a gunsmith, the price may astonish you.

(5) Do not purchase a gun "sight-unseen." Always inspect carefully before you close the deal.

(6) Do not buy a gun which shows excessive wear or "play" in the action.

(7) Do not buy a gun with a barrel that is rough, rusted, or pitted inside.

(8) Do not buy a gun if the outside shows signs of abuse. Internal parts may be worse.

(9) Do not become a victim of "sales talk." Study your proposed purchase and make your decision on the basis of your own examination—and needs.

(10) Do not buy a gun if the seller will not permit you to try it before you decide. There may be a reason for his refusal.

Let us study these Ten Commandments individually.

(1) Is the manufacturer still in business? Every firearms writer is constantly flooded with sad letters asking, "Where can I get parts for . . ." If the original maker is not in business, you can usually count on having any and all repairs made *by hand* by a gunsmith. Let us take a prewar example.

An active sportsman had a nearly-new Winchester lever-action rifle. On a hunting trip a canoe upset. The rifle was recovered, taken apart, and cleaned and dried. But he lost the firing pin. When he returned and checked the Winchester parts list he found that his dealer could obtain a new one for about 60 cents. The following year he turned up with a sad story—he had forgotten to obtain the firing pin and was leaving with a party in two days on another hunting trip. Where could he get a firing pin? Because of the urgency, a local gunsmith made one by hand, a complicated little unit. The price was about $8. Excessive? No! That gunsmith had a similar model in stock. He took it apart—which takes valuable time—and used the firing pin as a pattern to hand-file a piece of metal to proper shape, and then installed it—at $2 per hour.

If you buy a model for which the original maker is not available, or a model no longer produced, you will meet with repair problems like the above. Unless you have proper machine facilities plus plenty of skill, you will have to *buy* these repair services. It would be better to make a small deposit to hold the gun while you investigate—and then lose your deposit—than to invest unwisely.

(2) Comments on models not currently popular are also covered in the above. Manufacturers frequently maintain a parts list on obsolete models, but do not always have all parts available.

(3) Many guns are available for obsolete and rare cartridges. New barrels are expensive, and may not be the answer. To change to different cartridges often means replacement of magazine parts, bolt, and feed mechanisms. Many factories will refuse such alteration work on the ground that "your old action does not have sufficient strength to handle this new cartridge."

(4) Observe how the ten rules are hinged together. We have already covered the problem of repairs and their costs.

(5) When you buy a gun "sight-unseen" you always take a chance. Even an honest seller can be mistaken in describing the condition—or he may have been himself stuck with it and be trying to unload it to recover his unwise investment.

(6) "Excessive play in the action" may indicate more than one thing. Older guns, even of current models, were not made to the same quality standards of their current counterparts. The quality of the many kinds of steels—you may frequently get from 8 to 12 kinds of steel in one gun, each alloy designed for its particular job—has been improved throughout the years. The machine methods have changed, permitting close-fitting parts. Heat-treatment has been improved to strengthen and prevent wear. If there is excessive play in the parts, it may result from wear, abuse, poor quality, or a little of all three.

(7) Rough, rusted, and pitted barrels are a definite indication of neglect. If the rest of the gun is perfect, this situation may mean new barrels. Cur-

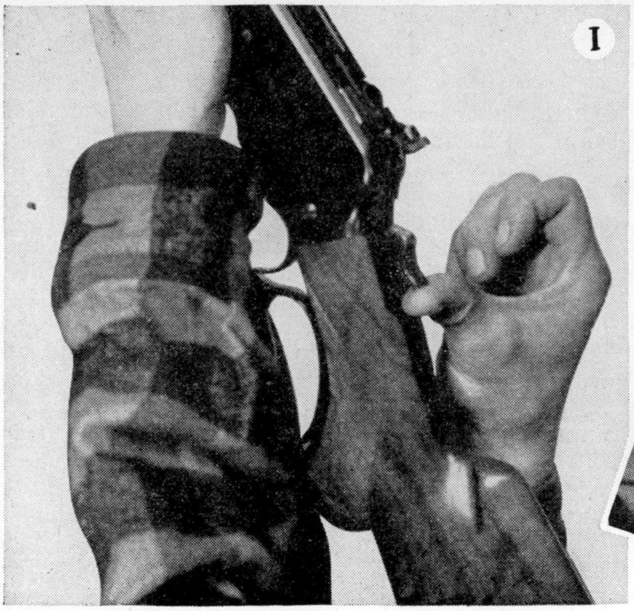


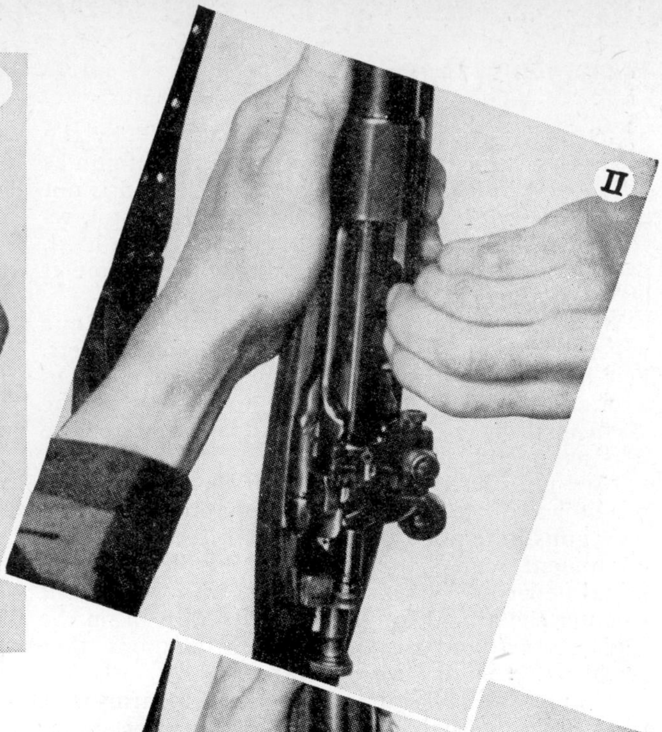


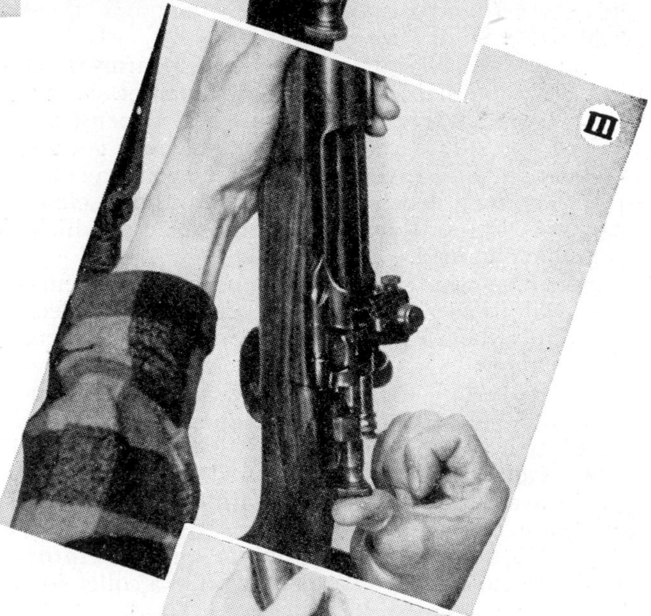

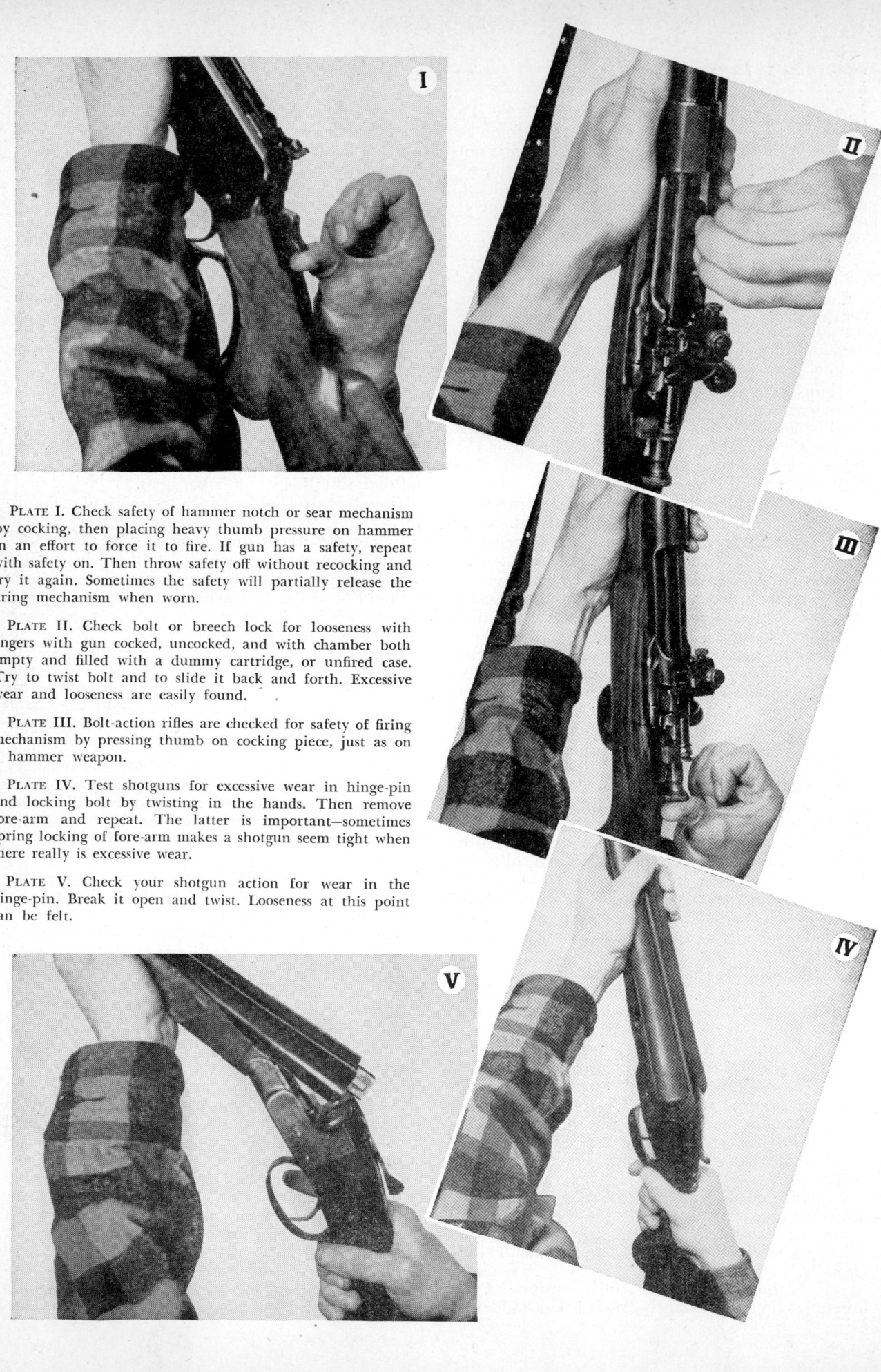

PLATE I. Check safety of hammer notch or sear mechanism by cocking, then placing heavy thumb pressure on hammer in an effort to force it to fire. If gun has a safety, repeat with safety on. Then throw safety off without recocking and try it again. Sometimes the safety will partially release the firing mechanism when worn.

PLATE II. Check bolt or breech lock for looseness with fingers with gun cocked, uncocked, and with chamber both empty and filled with a dummy cartridge, or unfired case. Try to twist bolt and to slide it back and forth. Excessive wear and looseness are easily found.

PLATE III. Bolt-action rifles are checked for safety of firing mechanism by pressing thumb on cocking piece, just as on a hammer weapon.

PLATE IV. Test shotguns for excessive wear in hinge-pin and locking bolt by twisting in the hands. Then remove fore-arm and repeat. The latter is important—sometimes spring locking of fore-arm makes a shotgun seem tight when there really is excessive wear.

PLATE V. Check your shotgun action for wear in the hinge-pin. Break it open and twist. Looseness at this point can be felt.

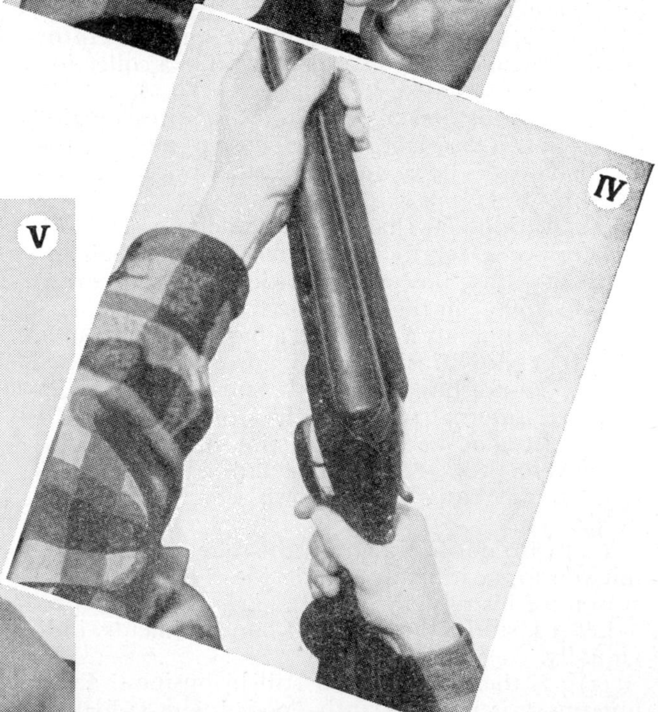


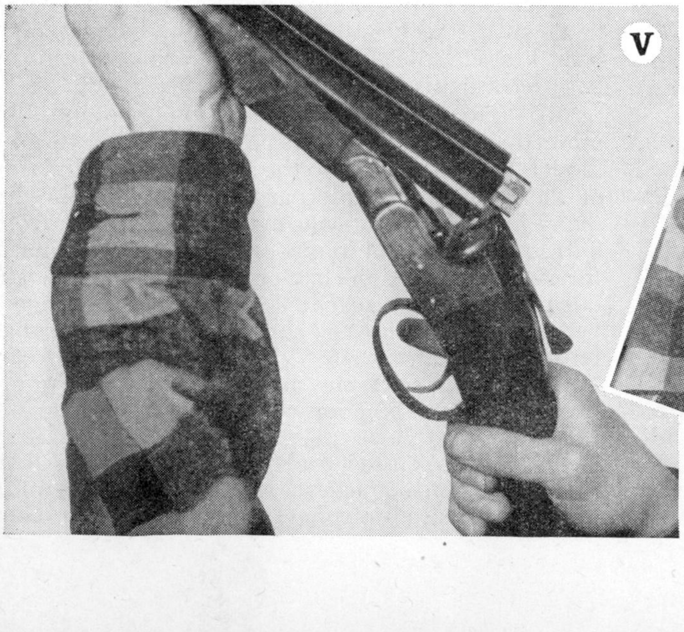

rent prices for factory barrels are high—custom barrels are higher. Revolver barrels, fitted, may cost $10. Standard rifle barrels run about $20 to $25. Shotgun barrels run about the same for singles, and up to $50 for *field grade* doubles.

Don't expect to remove rust and pits. A *rough* barrel is usually one which has had rust and pits "removed." When a barrel rusts within the bore or outside, a chemical action takes place, forming iron oxide, a mixture of iron and oxygen from the air. This is all that "rust" actually is. Remove the rust from a small spot and you have a cavity or pit. You cannot remove the pit, because the metal is no longer there. Removing rust means removing what was originally barrel steel.

(8) Is comment necessary on this?

(9) This, also, should be obvious.

(10) It is always good policy to try a gun before buying, but this is not always possible. Do your best to get the seller to permit this.

All of these Ten Commandments are basic. But there is much more detail to be considered in buying used guns.

**Tests.** Checking guns for wear requires some amount of skill and a little patient examination. Head space is very important in rifles and shotguns. It may seem strange, but this is little understood by the average hunter and even many target shooters. In simple language, it means merely the distance between the face of the cartridge in the chamber and the face of the breech-bolt. This clearance takes care of minor variations in cartridges, and is usually only two or three thousandths of an inch.

Head space is measured with precision gauges, an entire set of three to six being required for any given caliber. Such gauges cost about $6 each in larger calibers and few individuals own them. An easy test is accomplished by using an *unfired* cartridge case and shims. *Do not use a fired case or a live cartridge!* The former will have expanded and stretched to fit the gun, and the latter is dangerous.

If you do not have a new case available, unload a cartridge. To remove the bullet without damaging the case, place the neck on a hard surface and with a very light hammer, *gently* tap it many times while rotating the cartridge with your fingers. Gentle tapping expands the brass slightly, and the bullet may then be picked free with the fingers. Pour out and discard the powder.

Sheet brass shim stock may be obtained from any garage in thicknesses of from .0005-inch up. For all practical purposes, .003 or .004 (three or four thousandths) does not mean excess head space. Most standard double-edge safety razor blades run .006, while the Gillette "Veri-Thin" is .004. To make a shim of this hard blade stock requires two pair of pliers. Hold your blade tightly with one pair, and gently chip a disk to a size slightly smaller than the head of your cartridge case.

With the muzzle of the rifle on the floor, balance the disk on the head of the cartridge case and gently insert into the chamber. Then close the breech-bolt gently. *Do not force.* If it will not close on .004, you have a tight head space and it is all right. If it will close on *two* of these .004 shims, better pass up that bargain.

There is only one way to correct head space: reseat the barrel closer to the breech-block or bolt. This usually means cutting off, rethreading, and rechambering—an expensive job which only a few skilled gunsmiths will tackle. Excessive head space usually indicates much use—wear on the bolt-locking lugs and the wells into which they lock.

Check trigger pulls for smooth operation. If they are rough, work is usually necessary. To test for roughness or "creeps," make certain that the gun is empty, cock, and rest it solidly across the knees. Take a firm grip and tighten the trigger-finger slowly but steadily. "Creeps" can be felt. Try this several times to check your count. If any are present, hand work in stoning or burnishing certain trigger-action parts will be necessary—not a job for the unskilled.

Weigh the trigger pull. If it is too light, the gun will be dangerous and accidental discharge may occur. Accept no weapon with a pull less than 3 pounds.

Pulls are weighed by hanging definitely known weights on the trigger of a cocked piece. On a rifle, the butt usually rests on the floor with the weights. The gun is then very gently lifted, with the weight drag in the direction of normal trigger pull. If the weight does not trip the trigger mechanism, you know that the pull is greater than the weight you are lifting. Always recheck three or four times.

Another method of weighing a trigger pull is with an ordinary household scale reading in ounces up to about 20 pounds. Cock the weapon and rest the muzzle on the scale to get the weight. Steady it with one hand to prevent falling or false reading. Use an assistant to help you read. Pick up the gun gently and very slowly by the trigger, the lifting being done in the direction of normal trigger pull. As you lift, the scale will show a decreasing weight. At some point, the trigger will release. An assistant can read this point. Thus, if the gun weighs 7 pounds, 2 ounces, and the trigger was released at 3 pounds, 2 ounces, the trigger pull is an even 4 pounds.

Regardless of the weight of the pull, the gun may still be unsafe. If it has an exposed hammer or cocking piece, cock the gun and with your finger away from the trigger, press as hard as possible with the thumbs on the hammer. If you can make it fall, the gun is dangerous. If the gun has a safety, repeat the test with the safety on, and *again* after you have thrown the safety to the "off" position. Safeties sometimes are dangerous. This test does not hurt a gun.

Test parts for excessive looseness by cocking with your unfired case in the chamber. Do not touch the trigger, but try twisting the breech-block or bolt with the fingers. See if you can slide it back and forth. Repeat the test with the chamber empty. Then uncock and try it again—chamber empty. Looseness can be felt.

If it is a breakdown shotgun, single or double, grasp it by the grip and forearm and twist firmly. Note looseness between barrel and frame. Now break it open and repeat the twisting. If you find play, the hinge-pin is probably worn. Remove the wood forearm and replace the barrel. Close. Again check for twist and other play or looseness. Sometimes the locking device of the forearm is spring-loaded, and covers excessive play.

All of the above tests require care and attention to detail, but little skill. If you don't know much about firearms, *have a friend who does know* aid you in these tests.

**Foreign Guns.** At no time in the history of the United States have so many and varied foreign firearms been within the borders of this country. Servicemen "liberated" them by the hundreds of thousands. In most cases the liberation was legal and proper. Germany liberated all weapons—military and sporting—from the countries she had occupied. When we occupied Germany, military orders required every German civilian to turn in all weapons.

Countless thousands of these weapons went to waste and destruction. Hundreds of truckloads were dumped in open fields—rain and sun quickly ruined them completely. An Army order authorized men and women in service to send home rifles, shotguns, and pistols as souvenirs. Each had to be certified, and officers signed these certificates for their men, the proper papers to accompany the guns through the mails, whereupon they passed customs "free of duty."

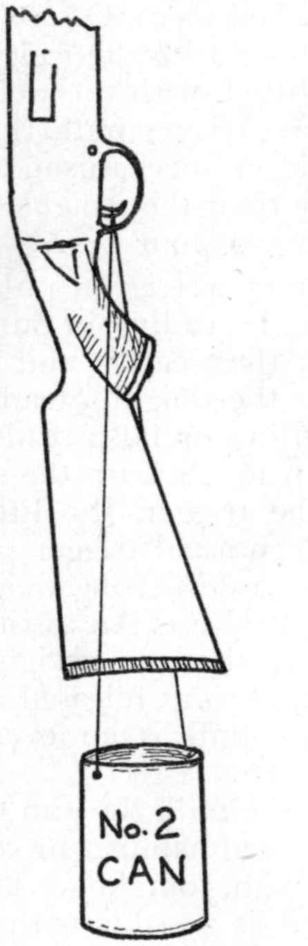


PLATE VI. To determine the amount of the trigger pull, affix string to can as shown, rest heel of gun on chair or table, then pour sand into can until the hammer falls. Weigh the can and you know the exact amount of pull.

Unfortunately many a souvenir hunter knew little about guns, and while he picked unique or beautiful specimens, many of these are practically worthless. On returning home, thousands of the boys discovered this—and quickly dumped them on the used market, where they have been changing hands and will continue to do so for many years.

Speaking now of military arms, we know the quality of materials and workmanship were deteriorating during the war. German-made Mauser Models 98 or 24 rifles made in 1943, 1944, and 1945 were progressively worse—many were dangerous. Bombings had badly hampered manufacturing. Quality steels and proper heat-treatment were impossible to obtain. Most German factories employed from 40 to 85 per cent slave labor—and with the war running against Germany, those slaves undertook a successful campaign of concealed sabotage. It got so bad that by the middle of 1944, the German High Command ordered the abandonment of all proof-testing of small arms—too many were being blown up.

It would be well to avoid German-made rifles bearing the dates mentioned—or no date. Many final 1945 rifles bore no date. What is even worse, when the Americans captured factories, they found huge stocks of parts. They assembled many of these inferior-quality components into souvenir rifles, and pistol parts were not neglected.

Older Mausers, as well as those made by Belgium, Poland, Czechoslovakia, and a few other countries, seemed to maintain a quality standard. But remember that many of the old Mausers of World War I date were no better than the Model 1903 Springfield we used in that war. It is difficult to sell one of our own rifles of that period—"not strong enough," the boys claim.

Regarding ammunition—the cartridge used by the Germans, Czechs, Poles, and many other European countries, is the 7.92 Mauser, made in this country as the 8-mm. Remington Special. Many other foreign souvenir military rifles use a cartridge not made here. This includes the latest French 7.5-mm., the Italian 6.5-mm. and 7.35-mm., the rifles of Hungary, Austria, The Netherlands, Greece, Turkey, Norway, Sweden, Denmark, Belgium, Japan, and a few others. Such rifles are of value chiefly as souvenirs.

Russian rifles used the 7.62-mm. Russian—a cartridge made here. Many British rifles were our own; others were for the .303 British cartridge, also made here. Some foreign pistols used the 9-mm. Parabellum, made here as the 9-mm. Luger. Pocket types usually handle the 6.35-mm. (.25 Colt automatic), the 7.65-mm. (.32 Colt Automatic), or the 9-mm. Browning Short, Kurz, or Corto (.380 Colt automatic). This ammunition is available. A few of the foreign revolvers handle the American Smith & Wesson line of cartridges; others are distinctly special and unobtainable numbers.

European shotguns are standard. They will handle American shells, but these guns are lighter than the American type. The average 16-gauge double is lighter than our average 20-gauge. And there is a reason for it. European loadings are much lighter than ours. If the gun bears nitro-powder proof marks it is safe with *standard* loads, but DO NOT use the high-velocity loadings in any foreign gun.

Many of those interesting two-, three-, and four-barrel rifles or combination rifle and shotgun designs were built for low-velocity, low-pressure smokeless-powder cartridges not available here. Many were built for black powder only. It would be wise to consider such guns strictly as souvenirs.

Sporting rifls are sometimes found for standard Mauser cartridges. If they are built for the 7x57 or 8x57, they will handle the American 7-mm. and 8-mm. Mausers. But it would be wise to drive a lead slug through that 8-mm. barrel to see if it measures less than .320. If so, it is for the obsolete 8-mm. Mauser, not made here. Standard ammunition will chamber, and can be discharged, but the oversize bullet will create dangerous pressures and will probably wreck the gun.

Summed up, if you are a gun collector and can buy these foreign weapons at a price you think is right, go ahead. If you want to buy a gun to use, *leave them alone*. They will keep on changing hands as their owners learn the folly of their purchase. It need not be you.

Buying a used gun requires more old-fashioned horse sense than buying a new one. Most of us learn the hard way.

# SHOTGUN DEVELOPMENT

The modern shotgun has a long history, as the smoothbore was the first type of gun to be produced and was in existence a great many years before rifling was attempted. The Swiss are credited with having made the earliest attempts at rifling, but their guns were extremely difficult to load and were practical only in match shooting where all the loading facilities and plenty of time were readily available. It was not until the advent of the Kentucky rifle, the product of central Pennsylvania gunmakers (see p. 538), and the discovery of new methods of loading that rifled arms became at all practical. Smoothbore guns were used interchangeably to throw charges of shot or a single ball, but the inaccuracy of the weapon with the single ball was notorious and is possibly best summarized by quoting from official British reports concerning the accuracy of the King's Musket.

In 1814 Colonel Hanger of the British Army reported as follows:

"A soldier's musket, if not exceedingly ill-bored (as many are), will strike the figure of a man at 80 yards; it may even at 100; but a soldier must be very unfortunate indeed who shall be wounded by a common musket at 150 yards, provided his antagonist aims at him; and, as to firing at a man at 200 yards with a common musket, you may just as well fire at the moon and have the same hopes of hitting your object. I do maintain and will prove, whenever called on, that no man was ever killed at 200 yards, by a common soldier's musket, by the person who aimed at him."

In 1841 a Board of Royal Engineers reported:

"It was discovered that as to the distance a regulation musket would carry nothing more certain could be inferred than that it might be 100 yards, or it might be 700 yards, according to the elevation of the piece. At no elevation, however, was there less than 100 yards' variation in its possible range, and at some elevations this difference exceeded 300 yards. So much for this primary point. Then came the point of accuracy, on which the revelations were still more astounding. At a distance of 150 yards, a target, about twice as high and twice as broad as a man, could, with very careful shooting, be hit three times out of four; beyond that distance, notwithstanding that the musket was fired from a stand and every precaution employed to ensure steadiness and success, the result was nil. Nothing could be learnt at all, except that the target could never be hit and the balls could never be found. The mark was made twice as wide as before, but of ten shots at 250 yards not one struck."

The smoothbore musket, however, was highly prized by the early settlers because with a shot charge it could be used for small-game shooting and with a single ball for defense at close range as well as on big game.

No sooner was the first gun built than efforts were started to provide two things: first, breech loading, and secondly, a second and third shot. Breechloaders, the multi-barrel gun, and crude types of revolvers were early attempted. Without following these attempts in detail, the first reduction to practice that is recognizable to the modern shooter apparently came from Spain, as some very usable, light, double-barrel fowling pieces were produced there in the late 17th century. England, France, Belgium, and some of the German provinces followed with ever-increasing refinements until the great English family of Mantons produced double-barrel guns in flintlock that cannot be bettered today in balance and weight. The all-hand workmanship on these pieces was superb and spoke highly for the craftsmanship of these artisans who had to work without the aid of modern machine tools.

During this long span of years breech loading and repeating principles were tried in innumerable ways but always failed and consequently were forced to await the invention of the cartridge case, which, in addition to forming a handy package to hold the various ingredients of the charge, plays a much greater role in acting as a temporary gas seal at the breech. Not until this principle was discovered just before the American Civil War were such arms practical.

The designation of the size of our shotguns was directly inherited from the smoothbore musket, as the diameter of the bore was given by the size of the ball it would accept, and these balls were sized by the number that could be produced from a pound of lead. If a pound of lead were poured into 12 balls, the individual balls were said to be 12 gauge. If the pound was split into 20 parts, the individual ball was smaller and designated as 20 gauge. This nomenclature applies to all modern shotgun loads except the .410, .36 and 9 mm., which are diameters of the bore, hence calibers.

The diameters of the various gauges have been approximately standardized to the following sizes:

| | | | |
|---|---|---|---|
| 4 | gauge | | .935 inch |
| 8 | " | | .835 " |
| 10 | " | | .775 " |
| 12 | " | | .729 " |
| 14 | " | | .693 " |
| 16 | " | | .670 " |
| 20 | " | | .615 " |
| 24 | " | or 12 mm. | .579 " |
| 28 | " | | .550 " |
| 32 | " | or 14 mm. | .502 " |
| 36 | bore or 9 mm. | | .360 " |
| 410 | bore | | .410 " |

When the Reverend Alexander Forsyth discovered the fulminating salts of mercury, among other things he touched off a controversy between the advocates of the new percussion system and the diehards who were fighting a losing battle to preserve the flintlock that had served so well for the preceding 200 years.

By the time of our Civil War the percussion system was thoroughly established and with the invention of the pin-fire cartridge by Lefaucheux in the late '40's breechloaders were coming in. Many and weird breech mechanisms were tried, but the conventional breakdown system prevailed. By the end of the Civil War the cartridge was well understood and in the early '70's paper shot shells appeared.

With the advent of this new form of cartridge, making it possible to load through the breech, a new idea was born, namely, the choking of shotgun barrels, whereby the muzzle is constricted to a slight degree. This constriction was not practical in the muzzle-loader, for you could not force a wad through the choke and have it tight at the breech where it was needed but also where the barrel diameter was greater. The records are not plain

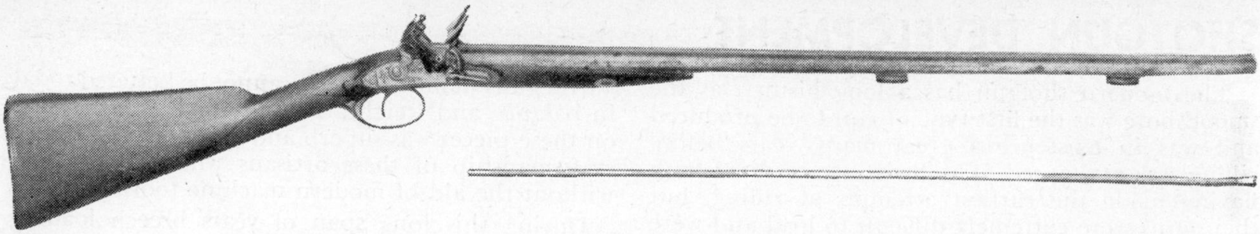

Courtesy Metropolitan Museum of Art, N. Y.

PLATE I. This is one of the famous Manton shotguns, a double-barrel flintlock made by Joseph Manton of London in 1795. The butt and stock are of mahogany, the barrel of watered steel.

as to who actually invented the idea of choking a barrel, but F. W. Olin of the Western Cartridge Company was one of the very early experimenters with this new and startling discovery.

The fabulous amounts of game of all sorts available on the American continent, such as the pigeon flights in Pennsylvania, the migratory ducks and geese, and the abundant quail and turkey put a great urge before the American gunmakers, a demand that had to be reckoned with.

By the late '80's the first successful repeating shotgun had appeared in the form of the Winchester lever-action repeater made in 10 and 12 gauge. Several sturdy doubles appeared, among which the Remington, Parker, L. C. Smith, and Lefever were perhaps the outstanding ones. By the turn of the century, however, Winchester had produced another milestone in a long line of "firsts" with the production of the famous Model 97 slide-action repeater. This gun soon became so well known for its reliability and hard-shooting qualities that it became the standard by which all other guns were measured. It also had other qualities that were destined to make a lasting impression on the gun art of America. It was advertised as machine made, a bold step when gun users had been taught that only handmade firearms were safe and reliable. It was made on the interchangeable system so that even if parts broke they could be easily replaced by the ordinary tinker. Lastly, the company boldly proclaimed that the cheapest model was made from the best steel obtainable and paying more only procured greater ornamentation. This latter idea was seized upon and further popularized by Henry Ford when he began his successful rise in motordom.

In a day and generation when this principle has become common in practically all quality items, and when we accept the fact that the only way to make a mechanically perfect surface is to keep all hand work off, it is impossible to realize the degree of pioneering represented.

However, the demand persisted and the doubtful public gradually began to realize the truth of the claims, with the result that the quality level of all shotguns was forced higher. By 1912 alloy steel had been developed so that lighter-weight parts could be made, and the second famous repeating shotgun appeared in the Winchester Model 12. This gun was so popular that it has been copied by several makers.

The year 1911 saw the advent of the third type of shotgun, namely, the self-loader. In this field the Remington Browning gun became the leader and it, too, was widely copied. This was such a game killer, however, that it invoked legislation in many states governing its use.

There had been many attempts by the double-gun makers to improve their product and equal the high-grade and correspondingly high-priced English doubles equipped with Damascus steel barrels, single triggers, and selective automatic ejection. American manufacturers were greatly aided in the first instance by the steelmakers of America, for by the time of World War I the American steel industry had demonstrated that it was making the finest steels obtainable anywhere or at any time. Barrels made from American heat-treated alloy steels so far surpassed the finest Damascus barrels that there was no comparison. Damascus barrels were made by wrapping a string of iron around an iron mandrel and welding it the entire length of its spiral. The strength of the barrel, therefore, was only that of the weakest weld. With a barrel drilled from a solid bar of American alloy steel properly heat treated, no such risk was encountered, with the result that American barrel makers were able to produce the finest barrels that the world had ever seen. Modern smokeless powder completed the death knell of Damascus barrels; its sustained pressure made it no longer safe to shoot a Damascus barrel regardless of how expensive the arm had originally been.

About 1925 Winchester again came out with an announcement that made shotgun news and marked a new era in shotgun progress. This was the placing on the market of their now famous Model 21. This gun was made from alloy steel throughout, taking full advantage of the American superiority in this field, and, further, it was made on the interchangeable system, so far never before accomplished in double-gun manufacture. The barrels were mechanically dovetailed together, no longer relying on the hitherto conventional brazing with the accompanying variation in the center distances between the barrels.

Another innovation was an entirely new and for the first time unbalkable single trigger. Many attempts at a satisfactory single trigger had been made and put on the market but none of these had been free from trouble. The parts were delicate, requiring close adjustment, and in spite of the greatest care would occasionally "double" (fire both barrels when only one was wanted), a quite disconcerting occurrence from the shooter's standpoint. They were also expensive. The Winchester Company developed a single trigger which carries its shift button in the trigger itself, and Winchester has never heard of a single instance of this trigger doubling or going out of commission.

With these innovations a new standard of performance was set, with the result that the Model 21

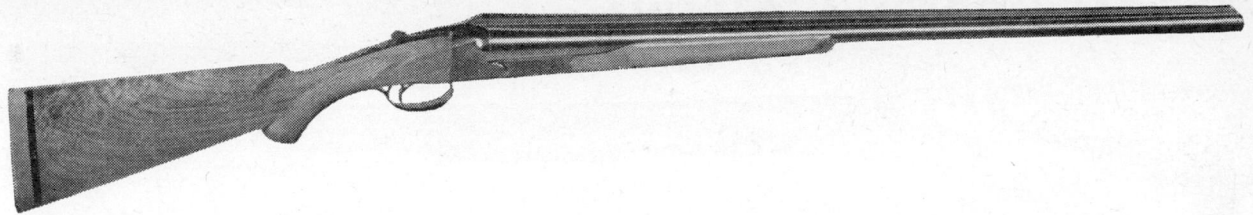

PLATE II. This is one of the modern counterparts of the fowling piece, a Winchester Model 21 duck gun, 12 gauge, 32-inch barrels, stock and fore-end of selected walnut.

is today regarded as one of the finest shotguns made anywhere in the world.

Of these, the single barrel is characterized by low price, with the exception of the small number of high-grade single-barrel trap guns. This latter was a single-purpose gun made especially for standard trap-shooting and is no longer made by many companies except on special order.

The double gun has been conventionally made since the late 16th century with migulet, flint, percussion, and breech-loading hammer and hammerless mechanisms, and is the generally accepted "gentleman's" gun.

Repeating shotguns are made to operate by finger lever, right- or left-hand slide actions. This is distinctly an American product and numerically by far the most popular.

The self-loading gun is as yet an undeveloped class as to date only one mechanism has survived. Because of its killing efficiency many laws have been passed limiting its use. Its popularity was on the decline until the invention of the new trapshooting game—Skeet—whereupon the gun regained its popularity to a large extent. The principle of a self-loading gun still has many undeveloped possibilities and these undoubtedly will be developed as time goes on.

# TYPICAL MODERN SHOTGUNS

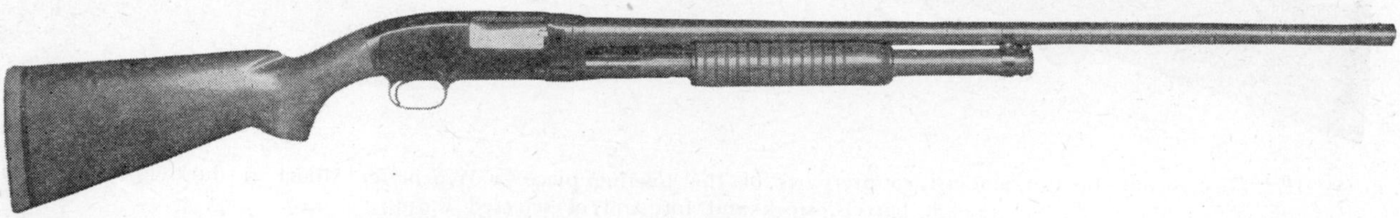

PLATE I. WINCHESTER Model 12 (Standard). Available in the following gauges: 12, 16, 20, and 28. Barrel length, weight, and bore as follows:

*12 gauge*—26-inch barrel; 7 pounds, 3 ounces; cylinder, improved cylinder, or modified choke.—28-inch barrel; 7 pounds, 5 ounces; cylinder, improved cylinder, modified choke or full choke.—30-inch barrel; 7 pounds, 7 ounces; modified choke or full choke.—32-inch barrel; 7 pounds, 9 ounces; modified choke or full choke.

*16 gauge*—26-inch barrel; 6 pounds, 5 ounces; cylinder, improved cylinder, modified choke, or full choke.—28-inch barrel; 6 pounds, 6 ounces; cylinder, improved cylinder, modified choke, or full choke.—30-inch barrel; 6 pounds, 8 ounces; modified choke or full choke.

*20 gauge*—26-inch barrel; 6 pounds, 5 ounces; cylinder, improved cylinder, modified choke, improved modified choke, full choke.—28-inch barrel; 6 pounds, 7 ounces; cylinder, modified choke, or full choke.—30-inch barrel; 6 pounds, 10 ounces; modified choke or full choke.

*28 gauge*—26-inch barrel; 6 pounds, 8 ounces; cylinder, modified choke, or full choke.—28-inch barrel; 6 pounds, 10 ounces; cylinder, modified choke, or full choke.

The Model 12 (Standard) is an extremely popular shotgun, with excellent balance, smooth operation, side ejection of empty shell, and positive safety features. Tubular magazine capacity, 5 shells, furnished with magazine plug to reduce magazine capacity to 2 shells. Stock and fore-end of American walnut. Chambered for 2¾-inch shells in 12, 16, and 20 gauge, and for 2⅞-inch shells for 28 gauge. Also available with raised matted rib. Extra barrels of standard lengths and bores are obtainable in any gauge. The Model 12 also is available in a "heavy duck gun," with 30- or 32-inch barrels, 12 gauge, full choke, chambered for the 3-inch (magnum) shell. Extra 12-gauge barrels of any standard length or bore are available to fit this model.

PLATE II. Sectional View of Model 12.

PLATE III. WINCHESTER Model 12 (Skeet). Available in 12, 16, 20, and 28 gauge, chambered for 2¾-inch shell, and with 26-inch barrel, with special skeet bore. Stock and slide handle of selected American walnut, finely checkered. Also available with ventilated rib, and with Cutts Compensator. Variations from standard stock dimensions furnished at extra cost.

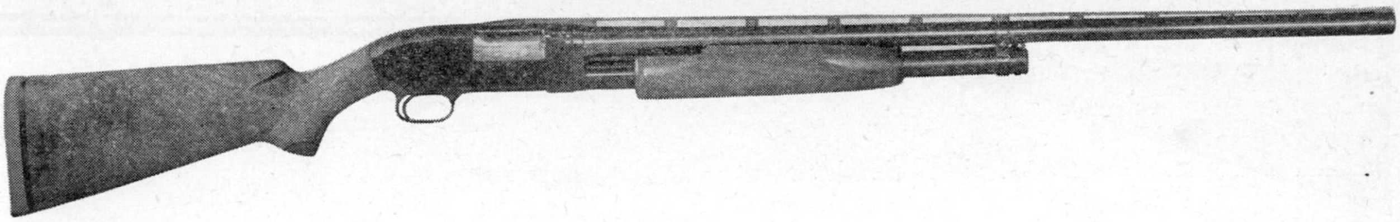

PLATE IV. WINCHESTER Model 12 (Trap). Available in 30-inch barrel for 12 gauge, 28-inch barrel for 16 or 20 gauge, or 26-inch barrel for 16 gauge. Straight or pistol grip stock of selected American walnut, finely checkered. Varied stock dimensions available at no added cost.

PLATE V. WINCHESTER Model 42. Available in .410 bore, with 26- or 28-inch barrels, chambered for 2½- or 3-inch shell and with the following boring: cylinder, modified choke, skeet choke, full choke. Standard model in American walnut, without checkering. Also available in selected American walnut, finely checkered, with matted rib. Variations from standard stock dimensions furnished at extra cost.

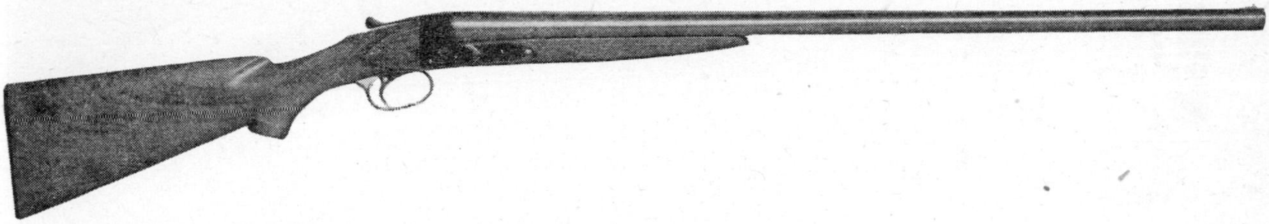

PLATE VI. WINCHESTER Model 21 (Standard). Available in 12, 16, or 20 gauge, all chambered for the 2¾-inch shell. Stock and fore-arm of selected American walnut, finely checkered. Raised matted rib. Barrels of proof steel, precision made. Stocks, with straight or pistol grip, supplied to customer's dimensions at no additional cost. Available with raised, ventilated rib at additional cost. The 12 gauge is available in 26-, 28-, 30-, or 32-inch barrels, with barrels bored with any combinations desired. The 16 gauge is available in 26-, 28-, or 30-inch barrels, bored in any combination desired, with the exception of the 28-inch barrels which cannot be supplied with right barrel full or improved modified choke. The 20 gauge is available in 26-, 28-, or 30-inch barrels, bored as desired. Single selective trigger, selective ejector. Weight, about 7½ pounds, varying with varied barrel lengths.

This model also available in a "Heavy Duck Gun," with 30- or 32-inch barrels, both full choke, and chambered for the 3-inch (magnum) shell.

Also available in special "Skeet Gun," with 26-inch barrels, bored right barrel skeet choke No. 1 and left barrel skeet choke No. 2, in 12, 16, or 20 gauge.

Also available in "Special Trap Gun," in 12 gauge only, with 30-inch barrels.

Extra barrels, of any standard length and bore desired, may be obtained for the Model 21, and the beavertail forearm also is available. In addition, there is a "De Luxe" grade, with specially smoothed working parts and fancy American walnut stock and fore-arm.

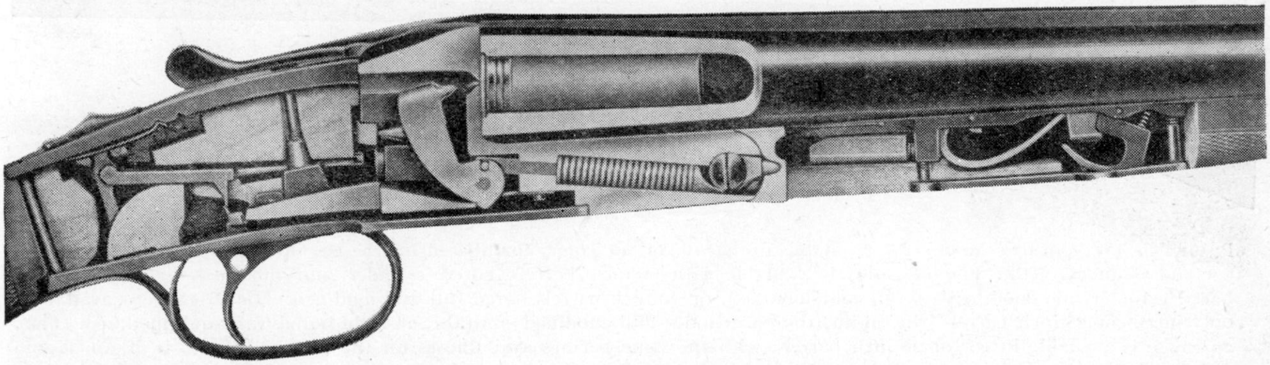

PLATE VII. Sectional View of Model 21 Winchester.

PLATE VIII. WINCHESTER Model 97 (Takedown). Available in 12 and 16 gauge, both chambered for the 2¾-inch shell. The 12-gauge model is available in 26-, 28-, 30-, or 32-inch barrel, and in cylinder, improved modified choke, modified choke, or full choke. The 16-gauge model is available in 26-, 28-, or 30-inch barrel, and in cylinder, modified choke, or full choke. The tubular magazine capacity is 5 shells. Extra barrels, in any standard length and boring, may be obtained on order. Weight: 12 gauge, about 7 pounds, 12 ounces; 16 gauge, about 7 pounds, 8 ounces.

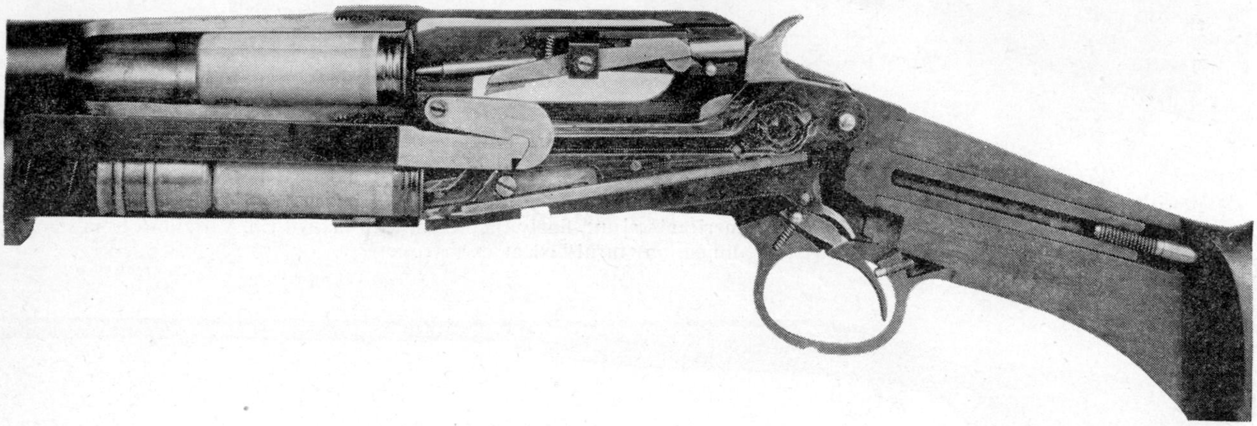

PLATE IX. Sectional View of Model 97 Winchester.

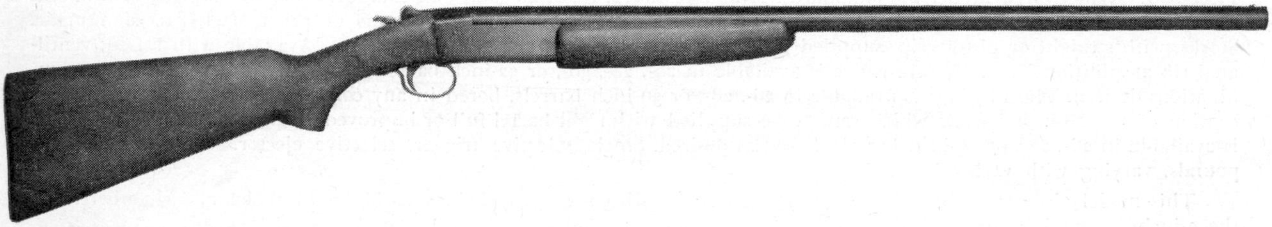

PLATE X. WINCHESTER Model 37 (Single Shot). Available in 12, 16, 20, 28, or .410 gauges. This gun is available only in full choke boring. The 12, 16, and 20 gauges are chambered for the 2¾-inch shell, the 28 gauge for the 2⅞-inch shell, the .410 for the 3-inch shell. Stock of American walnut. Automatic ejection. Standard stock dimensions. Semi-hammerless. Weight, about 6 pounds, 8 ounces.

PLATE XI. WINCHESTER Model 24. Available in 12, 16, or 20 gauge, chambered for the 2¾-inch shell, with double trigger and plain extractor. The 12 gauge is available with 26-inch barrels bored cylinder and modified, 28-inch barrels bored cylinder and modified or full and modified, or 30-inch barrels bored full and modified. The 16 gauge is available only in 26- or 28-inch barrels, the 26-inch bored cylinder and modified and the 28-inch bored full and modified. The 20 gauge is available in 26- or 28-inch barrels, with the same borings available as for the 16 gauge. Stock is of American walnut, available only in standard size, with 14½-inch pull, 1½-inch drop at comb, and 2½-inch drop at heel. Weight, about 7 pounds, 8 ounces.

PLATE XII. REMINGTON Model 31 (Improved). This gun is available in 12, 16, and 20 gauges, with a variety of barrel lengths and borings. In 12 gauge, the following: full choke in 28-, 30-, or 32-inch barrel; cylinder or improved cylinder in 26-inch barrel; skeet choke in 26-inch barrel. In 16 gauge, the following: full choke in 28- or 30-inch barrel; modified choke in 26- or 28-inch barrel; cylinder, improved cylinder, or skeet in 26-inch barrel. In 20 gauge: full choke in 26-, 28-, or 30-inch barrel; modified choke in 26- or 28-inch barrel; cylinder, improved cylinder, or skeet in 26-inch barrel. The standard grade is of American walnut and is without a raised rib. All grades have a 4-shell magazine. Standard grade has 14-inch pull, 2½-inch drop at the heel, and 1⅝-inch drop at comb. Weight: 12 gauge, 7¼ pounds; 16 gauge, 6¾ pounds; 20 gauge, 6½ pounds. This model also is available in "Lightweight" grade, with each gauge weighing about 1 pound less. Available also in "Special" grade, with selected, figured American walnut stock and fore-end, finely checkered; and with raised solid matted rib, or variations in stock dimension, at extra cost. Extra barrels are available.

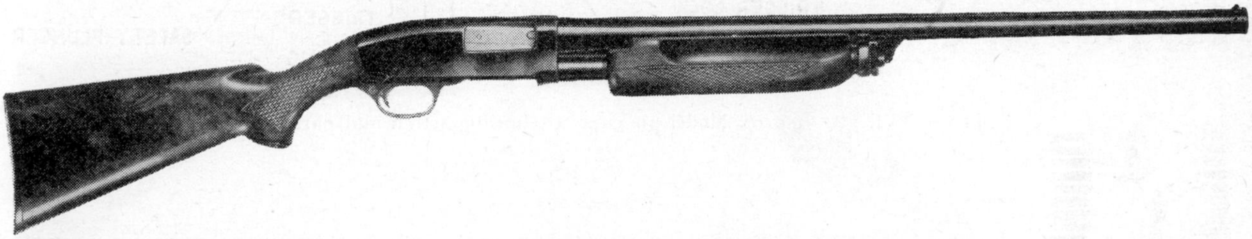

PLATE XIII. REMINGTON Model 31. This gun is available in 12, 16, and 20 gauges, with 26-inch barrel and "skeet" boring only. The stock and beavertail fore-end are of American walnut, finely checkered, and barrel has a raised, solid rib with ivory bead front sight. Magazine holds 4 shells. Weight: 20 gauge, 7 pounds; 16 gauge, 7¼ pounds; 12 gauge, 8 pounds. Available also in "Skeet" grade, with raised ventilated rib (12 gauge only) and with Cutts Compensator. Regular model in standard stock dimensions: 14-inch pull, 2½-inch drop at heel, 1⅝-inch drop at comb. Variations in stock dimensions at extra cost.

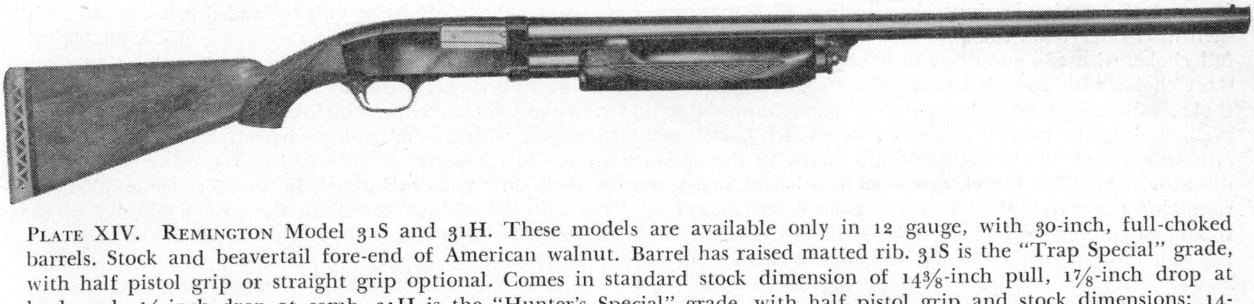

PLATE XIV. REMINGTON Model 31S and 31H. These models are available only in 12 gauge, with 30-inch, full-choked barrels. Stock and beavertail fore-end of American walnut. Barrel has raised matted rib. 31S is the "Trap Special" grade, with half pistol grip or straight grip optional. Comes in standard stock dimension of 14⅜-inch pull, 1⅞-inch drop at heel, and 1½-inch drop at comb. 31H is the "Hunter's Special" grade, with half pistol grip and stock dimensions: 14-inch pull, 2½-inch drop at heel, and 1⅝-inch drop at comb. An extra barrel may be had for the 31H. Variations in stock dimensions may be had at extra price. Weight, 8 pounds.

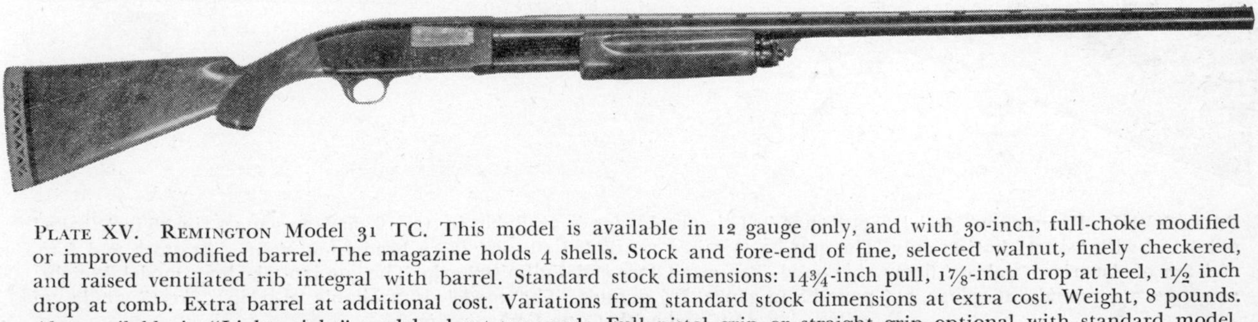

PLATE XV. REMINGTON Model 31 TC. This model is available in 12 gauge only, and with 30-inch, full-choke modified or improved modified barrel. The magazine holds 4 shells. Stock and fore-end of fine, selected walnut, finely checkered, and raised ventilated rib integral with barrel. Standard stock dimensions: 14¾-inch pull, 1⅞-inch drop at heel, 1½ inch drop at comb. Extra barrel at additional cost. Variations from standard stock dimensions at extra cost. Weight, 8 pounds. Also available in "Lightweight" model, about 7 pounds. Full pistol grip or straight grip optional with standard model.

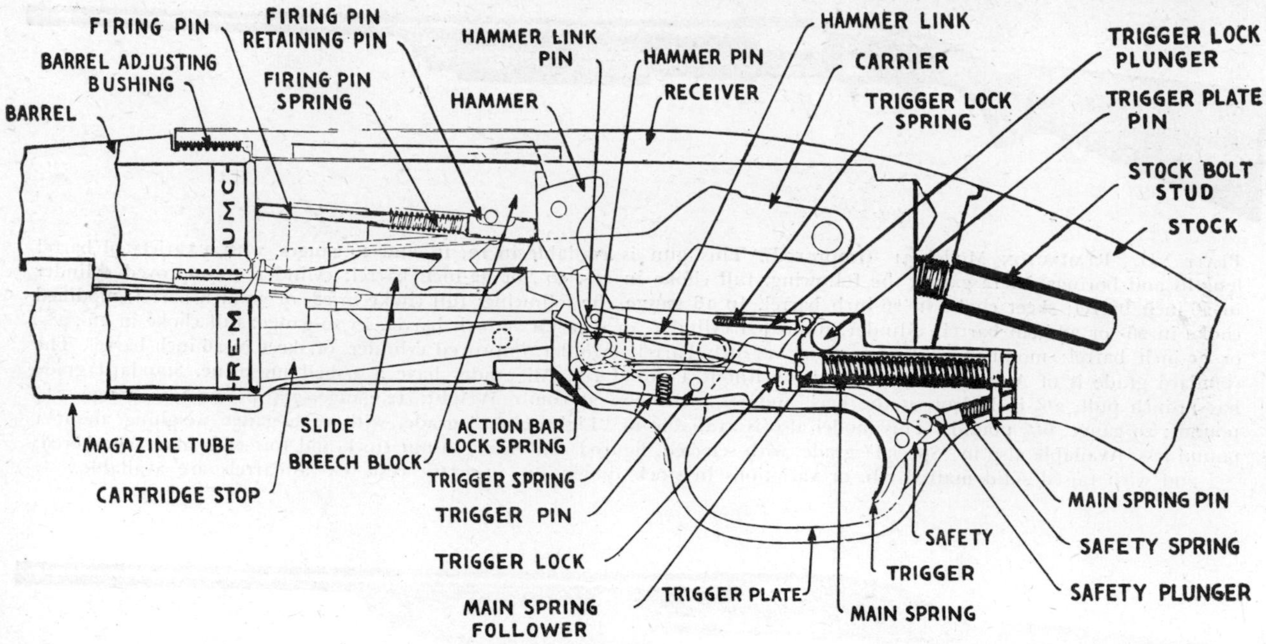


PLATE XVI. REMINGTON Model 31—cutaway showing action and parts.

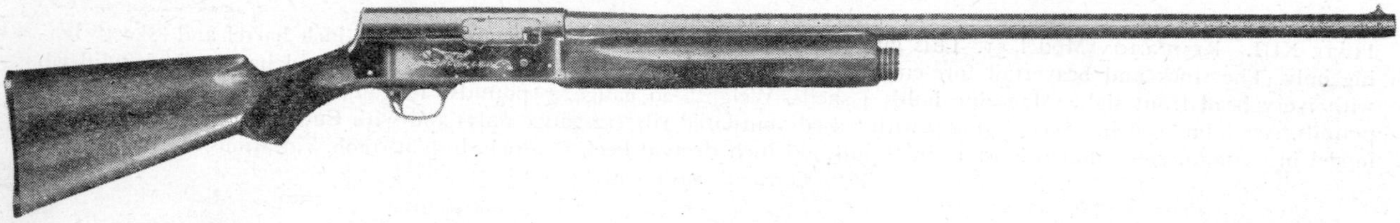

PLATE XVII. REMINGTON Model 11 available in 12, 16, and 20 gauges, with a varied choice in barrel lengths. Stock and fore-end of American walnut. Autoloading, with magazine capacity of 4 shells. Magazine may be loaded or unloaded with shell in chamber, and chamber may be unloaded without disturbing shells in magazines. The 12-gauge gun is available in: full choke, with 28-, 30-, or 32-inch barrel; modified choke, with 28- or 30-inch barrel; cylinder, improved cylinder, or skeet choke, with 26-inch barrel. The 16-gauge gun is available in: full choke, with 28- or 30-inch barrel; modified choke, with 26- or 28-inch barrel; cylinder, improved cylinder, or skeet choke, with 26-inch barrel. The 20-gauge gun is available in: full choke, with 26-, 28-, or 30-inch barrel; modified choke, with 26- or 28-inch barrel; cylinder, improved cylinder, or skeet choke, with 26-inch barrel. In the 12-gauge gun, solid rib barrel may be had in the full-choke barrel, the 28-inch modified barrel, or the 26-inch barrel, and a ventilated rib on the 30-inch barrel. In the 16 gauge, solid rib or ventilated rib may be had with the 28-inch barrel, and solid rib with the 26-inch barrel. In the 20 gauge, solid rib or ventilated rib may be had with the 28-inch barrel. The standard grade has a 14-inch pull, 2½-inch drop at the heel, and 1⅝-inch drop at comb. Weight, 12 gauge, 8 pounds; 16 gauge, 7½ pounds; 20 gauge, 7¼ pounds. This model is available in several grades, with the following extras: raised or ventilated ribs, variations from standard stock dimensions, selected figured American walnut, extra barrel.

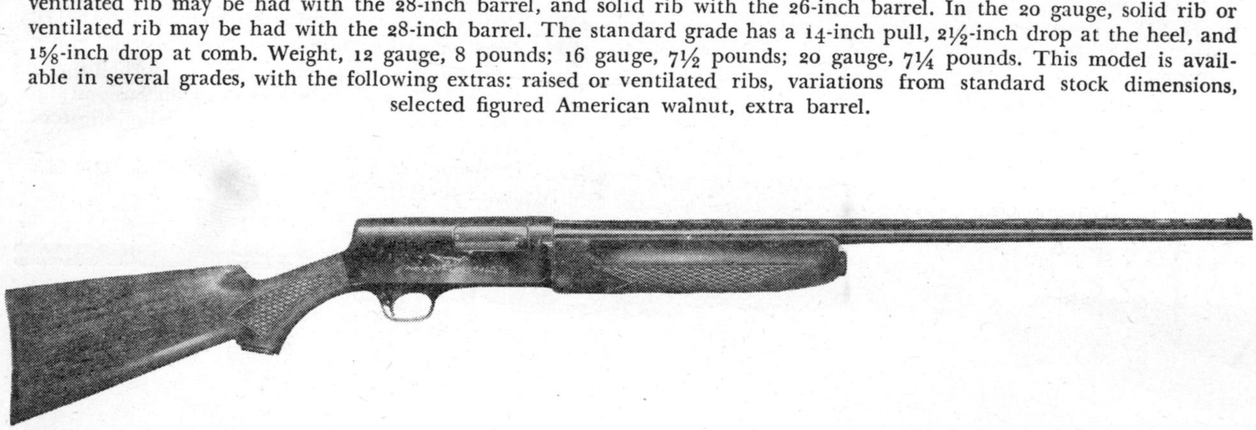

PLATE XVIII. REMINGTON Model "Sportsman." This autoloader is available in 12, 16, and 20 gauges, in 26-inch barrel only, and with "skeet" boring only. The gun has a raised ventilated rib and ivory bead front sight. The stock and fore-end are of American walnut, finely checkered. Beavertail fore-end. Full pistol grip. The gun is a takedown model. Weight: 20 gauge, 7¼ pounds; 16 gauge, 7½ pounds; 12 gauge, 8¼ pounds. The model is available also in "Skeet" grade, of selected walnut and with Cutts Compensator.

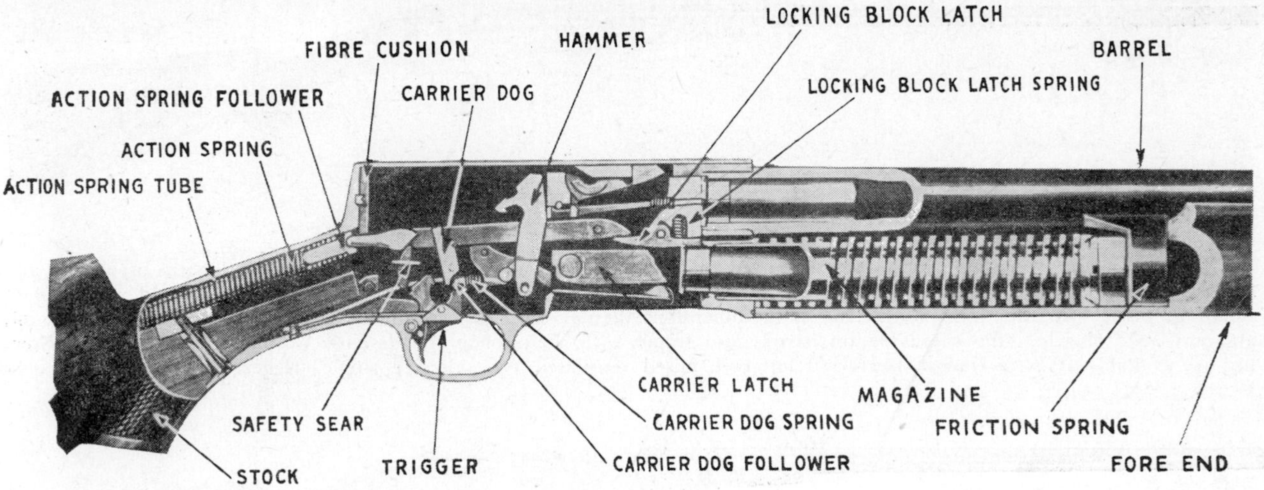


Plate XIX. Remington Model 11—cutaway showing action and parts.

Plate XX. Remington (Model 32A Standard).

This over-and-under gun is available in 12 gauge only, and is chambered for the 2¾-inch shell. Barrels are available in 26-, 28-, 30-, or 32-inch lengths. Option of full choke, modified choke, improved cylinder, or cylinder borings, or any combination. Selective three-way safety. Front trigger fires lower barrel. American walnut stock and fore-end, both finely checkered. Regular stock dimensions, 14-inch pull, 2½-inch drop at heel, 1⅝-inch drop at comb. Half pistol grip. Weight, about 7½ pounds. Can be furnished with Remington selective single trigger, beavertail fore-end, rubber recoil pad, 3-inch chamber for magnum shells, raised solid matted rib, raised ventilated rib, or special stock dimensions, all at extra cost.

Plate XXI. Parker (V.H.E. Grade).

This double gun is available in 12, 16, 20, 28, and .410 gauges, all bored for "Skeet" and with 26-inch barrels, unless otherwise specified. Option of any other barrel length or degree of boring. Automatic ejectors, option of non-automatic safety, single selective trigger, beavertail fore-end. Stock dimensions, unless otherwise specified: 14-inch pull, 2¼-inch drop at heel, 1½-inch drop at comb. Option of straight, full or half pistol grip. Special stock available. Quality of walnut, type of engraving, and other features depend upon grade selected. Also available with raised, ventilated rib.

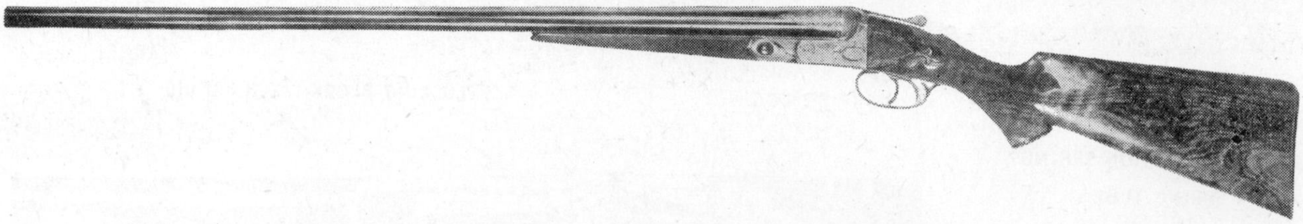

Plate XXII. Parker (A.A.H.E. Grade).

This double gun is available in 10, 12, 16, 20, 28, and .410 gauges, and in any selection of barrel lengths as well as any degree, or combination, of borings. The stock is of fine Circassian walnut, expertly checkered. Solid gold name plate inlaid in pistol grip cap or in stock. Any stock dimensions desired, with or without cheekpiece, Monte Carlo or cast off, and any style of grip. Fine engraving on barrels and frame, with choice of several designs. Automatic ejectors. The following are available at extra charge: Beavertail fore-end, raised ventilated rib, selective single trigger, extra interchangeable barrels.

Plate XXIII. Parker (D.H.E. Trap Grade).

This double trap gun is available in 12 gauge only and chambered for the 2¾-inch shell, with 30-, or 32-inch barrels. both bored full choke. It is equipped with automatic ejectors and non-automatic safety. Selective single trigger, beavertail fore-end, and raised, ventilated rib. Stock dimensions, unless otherwise specified, 14⅜-inch pull, 1⅞-inch drop at heel, 1½-inch drop at comb. Straight, or half pistol grip optional. Cheekpiece, Monte Carlo or cast off, available at additional charge. Weight, with 32-inch barrels, 8 to 8¼ pounds. Stock and fore-end of fine, selected walnut.

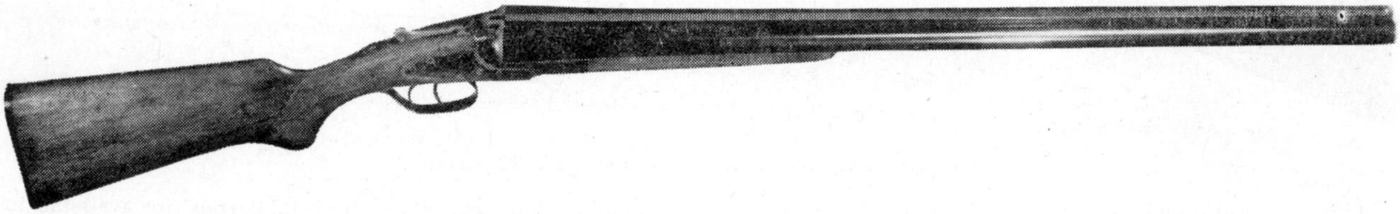

Plate XXIV. L. C. Smith "Improved Field Grade."

This double gun is available in 12, 16, and 20 gauge. One of the features of the Smith gun is the rotary bolt which locks the action and barrels. The barrels have the new Smith "single sighting plane rib," a raised, broad rib extending to the rear of the standing breech. It is available in the following barrel lengths: 12 gauge, 26, 28, or 30 inch; 16 and 20 gauge, 26 or 28 inch. Borings: 26-inch barrels, right barrel improved cylinder, left barrel modified choke; 28- or 30-inch barrels, right barrel modified choke, left barrel full choke. Weight: 12 gauge, 6⅞ pounds; 16 gauge, 6⅝ pounds; 20 gauge, 6¼ pounds. The stock is of seasoned black walnut, checkered. Standard stock dimensions only: 14-inch pull, 1½-inch drop at comb, 2½-inch drop at heel.

Plate XXV. L. C. Smith Model "Ideal."

This custom-built double is available in 12, 16, or 20 gauge. It has the "single sighting plane rib," selected walnut stock and fore-end with fine checkering, engraved lock-plates and frames. It is available in 26-, 28-, or 30-inch barrels (30-inch barrels in 12 gauge only). In the 26-inch barrels, the following boring: Right barrel improved cylinder, left modified choke. In the 28- or 30-inch barrels, right modified choke, left full choke. Weights, 12 gauge, 6⅞ pounds; 16 gauge 6⅝ pounds; 20 gauge, 6¼ pounds. Stock dimensions: 14-inch pull, 1½-inch drop at comb, 2½-inch drop at heel. Full pistol grip.

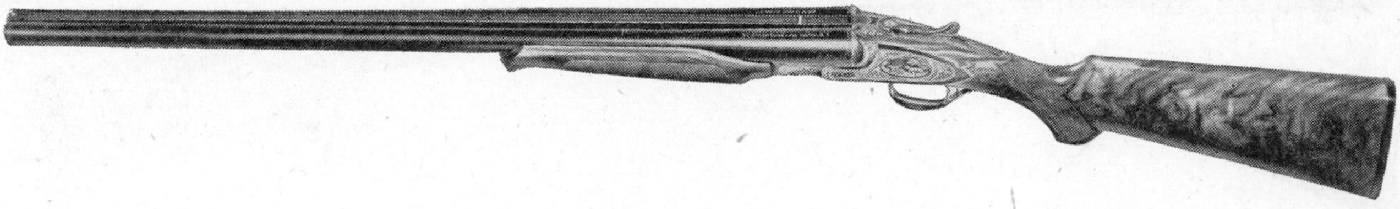

PLATE XXVI. L. C. SMITH MODEL "CROWN."

This is a custom-built double gun, available in 12, 16, and 20 gauge. Beautifully engraved, all parts precision made and hand honed. The barrels are available in any degree of boring and any standard length. Automatic ejectors, single trigger. Stock of selected fine-grain walnut, finely checked. Beavertail fore-end optional. Stock made to customer's dimensions.

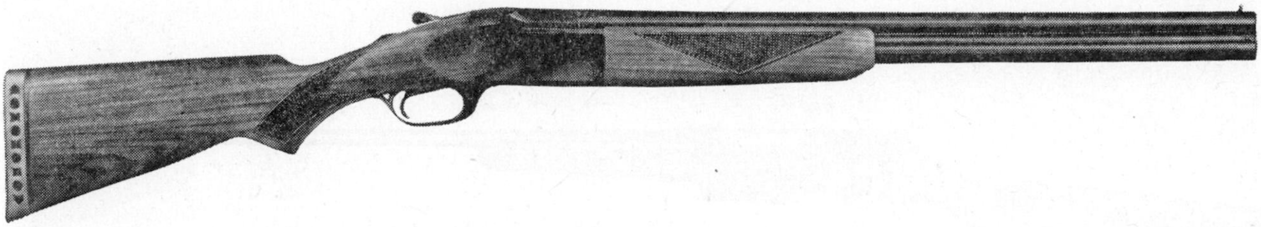

PLATE XXVII. MARLIN MODEL 90.

This over-and-under shotgun is available in 12, 16, or 20 gauge. The upper barrel is matted. It is available in the following barrel lengths: 12 gauge, 26, 28, or 30 inches: 16 and 20 gauge, 26 or 28 inches. Borings: 26-inch barrels are bored with top barrel modified choke, lower barrel improved cylinder; 28-, or 30-inch barrels are bored with top barrel full choke, lower barrel modified choke. This gun cocks on opening. Front trigger fires lower barrel. Stock and fore-end of American black walnut, with full pistol grip. Standard stock dimensions: 14¼-inch pull, 1⅝-inch drop at comb, 2¼-inch drop at heel. Weight: 12 gauge, 7½ pounds, 16 and 20 gauge, 6¼ pounds.

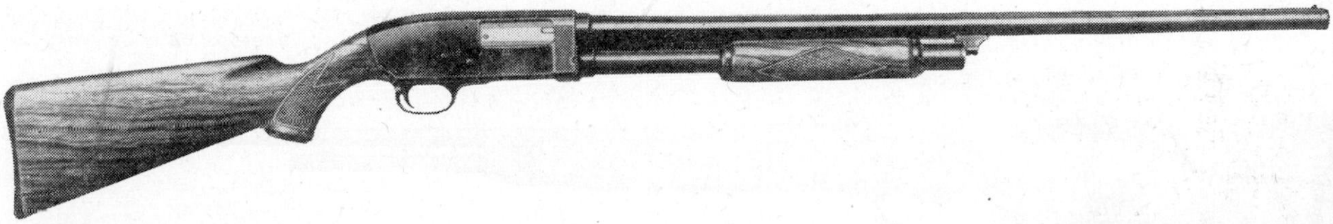

PLATE XXVIII. STEVENS MODEL 620.

This slide-action shotgun is available in 12, 16, and 20 gauge. Barrel lengths and borings: 12 gauge, 28, 30, or 32 inch, with 30- and 32-inch barrels bored full choke, 28- and 30-inch barrels bored modified, and 26- or 28-inch barrels cylinder bored; 16 gauge, 26- or 28-inch barrels, with 28-inch barrel bored full choke, modified choke, or cylinder, and 26-inch barrel bored cylinder; 20 gauge, 26- or 28-inch barrels, bored modified or full choke. Action: hammerless, visible locking bolt, safety ring pin, side ejection, take down. Stock of American walnut with checkered full pistol grip. Standard stock dimensions: 13¾-inch pull, drop at heel 2¼ inches, drop at comb 1½ inches. Weight, 12 gauge, 7¾ pounds; 16 gauge, 7¼ pounds; 20 gauge, 6 pounds. Magazine capacity, 5 shells. Plug supplied to reduce magazine capacity to two shells. Model 620P, same as above, but equipped with Poly Choke. Model 620C, same as above, but equipped with Cutts Compensator.

PLATE XXIX. STEVENS MODEL 311.

This double gun is available in 12, 16, 20, or .410 gauge. The stock and fore-end are of "Tenite," a plastic developed by this company with the strength, appearance, and weight of fine walnut. Barrel lengths: 12 gauge, 26, 28, 30, and 32 inches; 16 gauge, 26, 28, and 30 inches; 20 gauge, 26 and 28 inches; .410 gauge, 26 inches. All 12-gauge 32-inch and .410 gauge guns are bored full choke in both barrels; all others are bored right barrel modified choke, left barrel full choke. Weight: 12 gauge, 7½ to 8 pounds; 16 gauge, 7 to 7½ pounds; 20 gauge, 6½ to 6¾ pounds; .410 gauge, 5¾ to 6 pounds. Model 530ST is the same as above, but fitted with single trigger. These guns do not have automatic ejectors.

PLATE XXX. STEVENS MODEL 94.

This single-barrel shotgun is available in 12, 16, 20, and 28 gauge. It is available in the following barrel lengths: 12 gauge, 28, 30, or 32 inches; 16 gauge, 28, 30, or 32 inches; 20 gauge, 26, 28, 30, or 32 inches; .410 gauge, 26 or 8 inches. All barrels are bored full choke. The stock and fore-end are of "Tenite." This hammer gun is equipped with an automatic ejector. Weight, about 6 pounds.

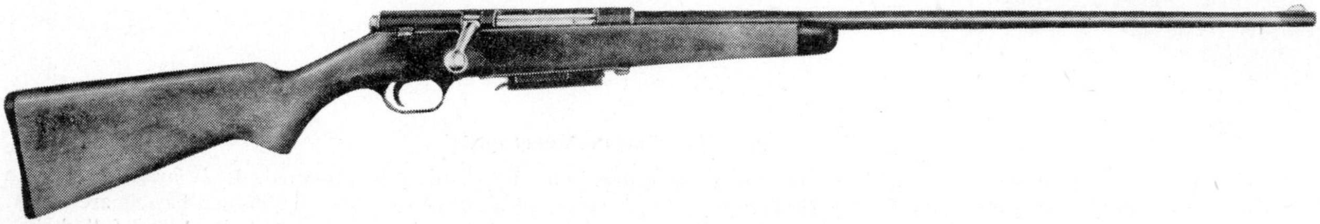

PLATE XXXI. STEVENS MODEL 258.

This shotgun, bolt action, is available in 20 gauge only. It has a box-type magazine with a 2-shell capacity. The stock is of American walnut. Barrel length, 26 inches. Boring, full choke. Weight, 6¼ pounds.

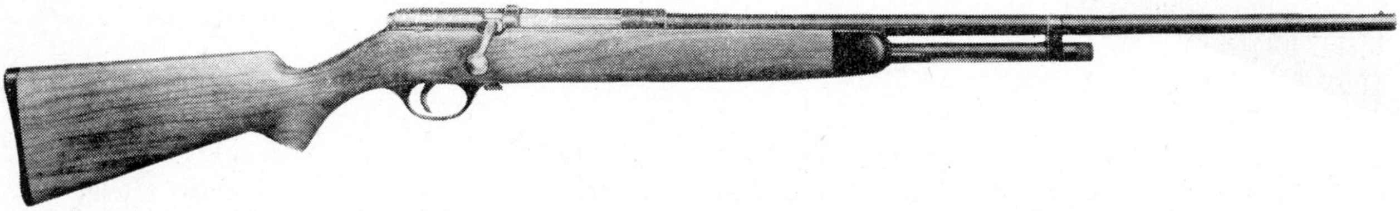

PLATE XXXII. STEVENS MODEL 59.

This shotgun, bolt action, is available in .410 gauge only. It has a tubular magazine of 5-shot capacity. It will handle the 2½- or the 3-inch shell. Barrel length, 24 inches. Boring, full choke. Weight, about 6 pounds.

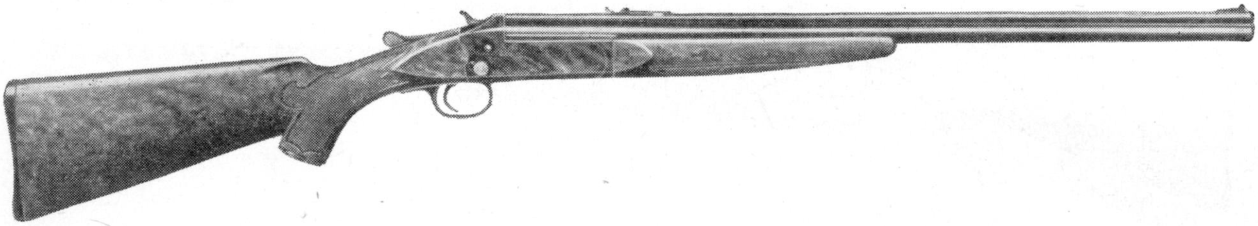

PLATE XXXIII. STEVENS MODEL 22-410.

This over-and-under rifle-shotgun combination is available only in the .22 caliber-.410 gauge combination. The .22-caliber rifle, chambered for the long rifle cartridge, is over the .410 shotgun barrel. Barrel length, 24 inches. Button on right side of frame selects barrel to be fired. Stock and fore-end are of "Tenite." Single trigger. Separate extractors. Top lever operates left or right to open action. Regular or high-speed .22-caliber ammunition may be used. .410 barrel bored full choke and chambered for the 3-inch shell. Weight, 6 pounds.

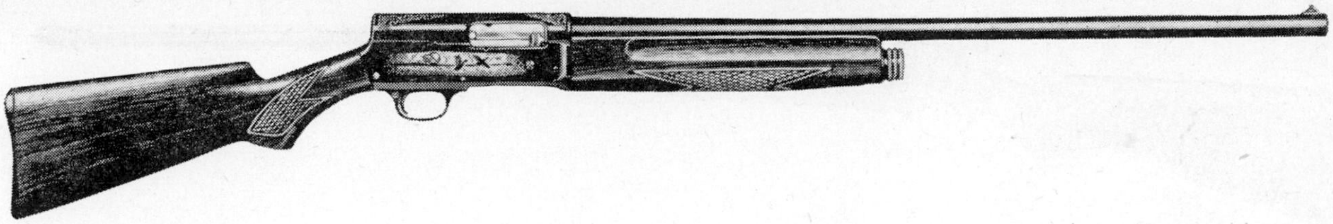

PLATE XXXIV. SAVAGE MODEL 720.

MODEL 720. This shotgun is available in 12 or 16 gauge, and is semi-automatic, or autoloading. It is made in two grades: "Standard," with a magazine capacity of 4 shells, and "Upland Sporter," with a magazine capacity of 2 shells. It is available in barrel lengths of 26, 28, or 30 inches, with the option of full choke, modified choke, or cylinder boring. The stock is of selected American walnut, checkered, and with full pistol grip. Weight: 16 gauge, 7½ pounds; 12 gauge, 8 pounds.

MODEL 720-P. The same as Model 720, except that it is equipped with a Poly Choke and has a 28-inch over-all barrel. Magazine capacity, 2 or 4 shells, optional.

MODEL 720-C. The same as Model 720, except that it is equipped with a Cutts Compensator and has a 28-inch over-all barrel when fitted with No. 705 full-choke tube, and 27-inch over-all barrel when fitted with spreader tube. Magazine capacity, 2 or 4 shells, optional.

MODEL 745. The same as Model 720 in appearance, but by the use of a new metal, the weight has been reduced approximately 1 pound. This model is available in 12 gauge only, but will be equipped with Cutts Compensator if desired. Otherwise available only in 28-inch barrel, bored full choke, modified choke, or improved cylinder.

All of the above models have standard specifications, 14-inch pull, and 2¾-inch drop at heel. Extra barrels of 26-, 28-, or 30-inch lengths may be obtained with any gun, and can be supplied with raised matted rib or raised ventilated rib at extra cost.

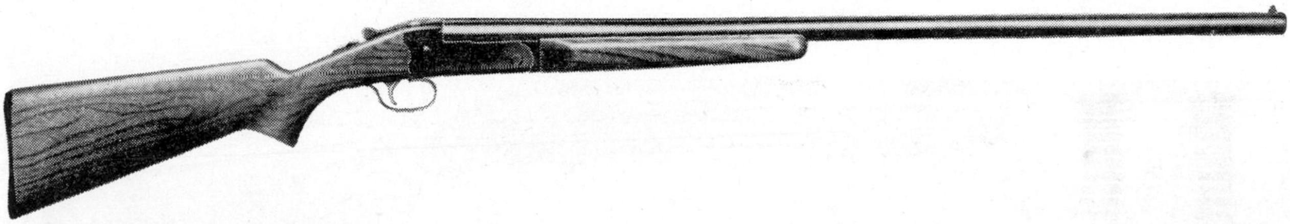

PLATE XXXV. SAVAGE MODEL 220.

This single-barrel shotgun, available in 12 gauge, 16 gauge, 20 gauge, and .410, is a hammerless takedown model equipped with an automatic ejector. It has a stock of American walnut, with full pistol grip and wide fore-end. The 12 gauge is available in 28-, 30-, and 32-inch barrels, the 16 gauge in 28-, and 30-inch barrels, the 20 gauge in 26- and 28-inch barrels, the .410 only in 26-inch barrel. The .410 is chambered only for the 3-inch shell. Weight, about 6 pounds.

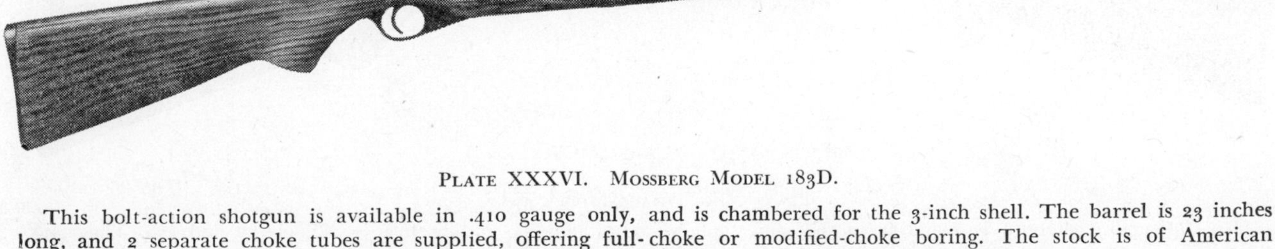

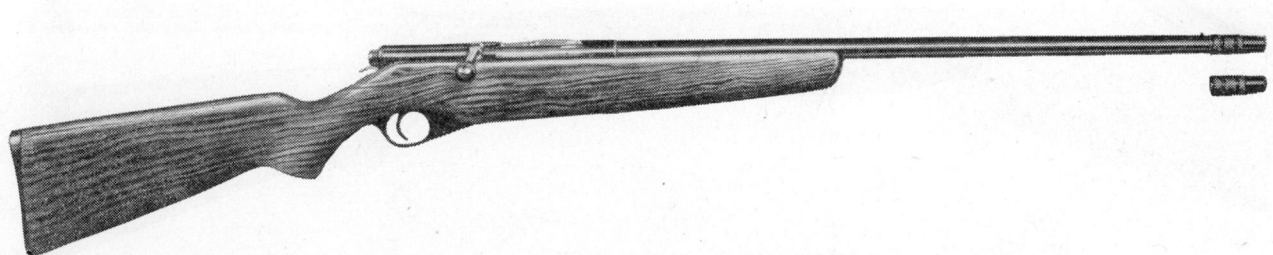

PLATE XXXVI. MOSSBERG MODEL 183D.

This bolt-action shotgun is available in .410 gauge only, and is chambered for the 3-inch shell. The barrel is 23 inches long, and 2 separate choke tubes are supplied, offering full-choke or modified-choke boring. The stock is of American walnut. The box-type magazine has a 3-shell capacity. Length over-all, 44½ inches. Weight, 5½ pounds.

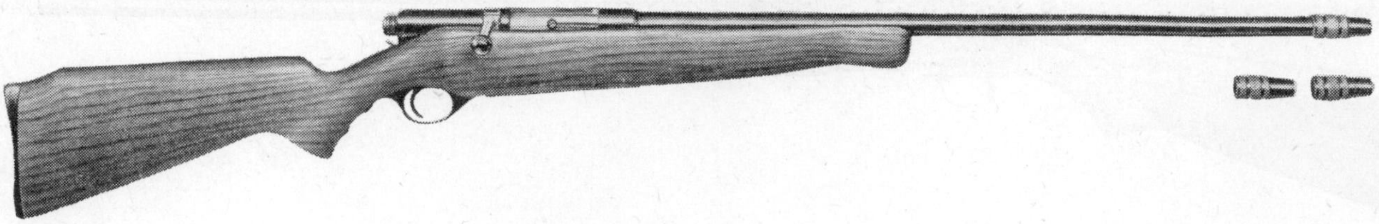

PLATE XXXVII. MOSSBERG MODEL 185D.

This bolt-action shotgun is available in 20 gauge only. It has a 25-inch barrel, proof tested, and is accompanied by 3 separate choke tubes, improved cylinder, modified and full choke. The stock is of American walnut. Hammer is cocked on the up stroke of the bolt. The detachable box magazine has a 2-shell capacity. Length over-all, 45½ inches. Weight, 6¼ pounds.

PLATE XXXVIII. ITHACA MODEL 37 (FEATHERLIGHT).

This slide-action shotgun is available in 12, 16, and 20 gauge. The 12 gauge is available in 26-, 28-, or 30-inch barrels, the 16 and 20 gauges in 26- or 28-inch barrels. Barrels may be bored for any degree of choke. The tubular magazine has 4-shell capacity. Standard stock dimensions: 14-inch pull, 2¾-inch drop at heel, 1⅝-inch drop at comb. Full pistol grip. Hand-checkered walnut stock. Weight: 12 gauge, 6½ pounds; 16 gauge, 6 pounds; 20 gauge, 5¾ pounds.

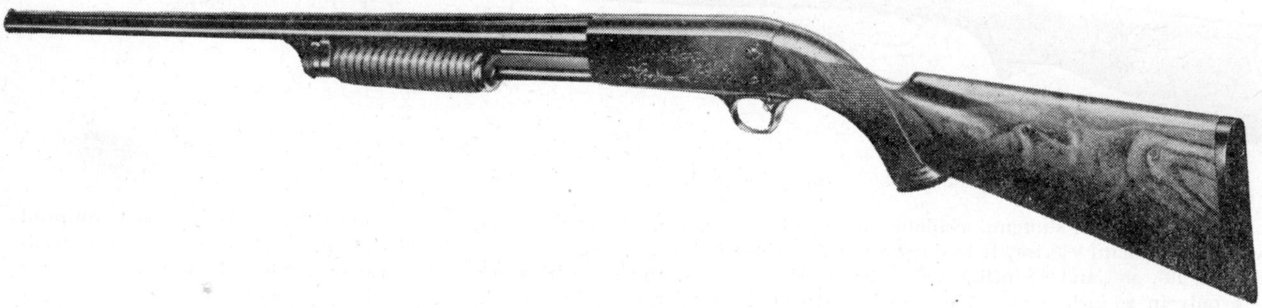

PLATE XXXIX. ITHACA MODEL 37R.

This slide-action shotgun is available in 12, 16, and 20 gauges. Barrel lengths, borings, and other specifications similar to Model 37, with the exception that the barrel has a raised, matted rib. Weight: 12 gauge, 6¾ pounds; 16 gauge, 6¼ pounds; 20 gauge, 6 pounds.

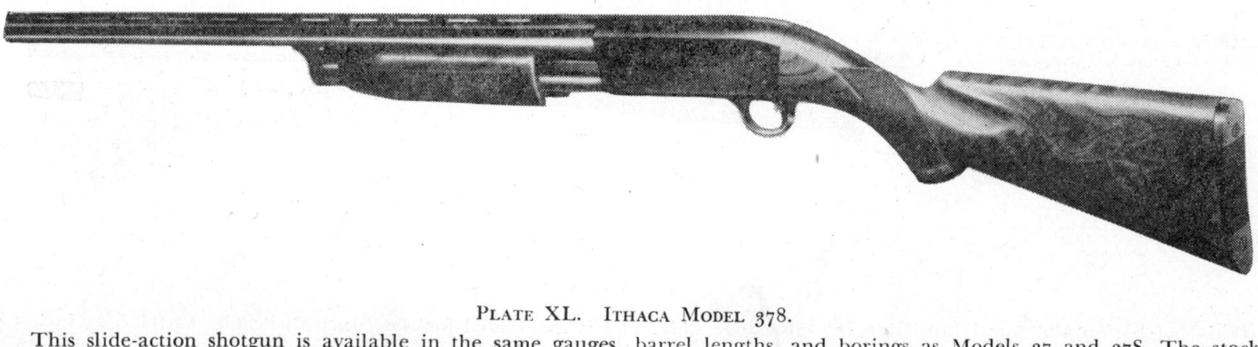

PLATE XL. ITHACA MODEL 378.

This slide-action shotgun is available in the same gauges, barrel lengths, and borings as Models 37 and 37S. The stock dimensions are: 14-inch pull, 1½-inch drop at comb, 2½-inch drop at heel. This model has a raised, ventilated rib, and a large fore-end. Weight: 12 gauge, 7 pounds; 16 gauge, 6¾ pounds; 20 gauge, 6½ pounds.

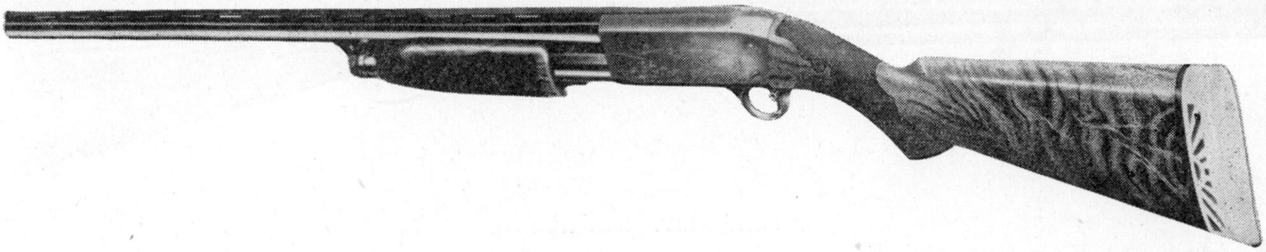

PLATE XLI. ITHACA MODEL 37T.

This slide-action shotgun is available in 12, 16, and 20 gauge. Barrel lengths: 12 gauge, 30 inches; 16 gauge, 26 and 28 inches; 20 gauge, 26 and 28 inches. Full choke is standard, but any boring is optional. Raised ventilated rib. Stock dimensions: 14½-inch pull, 1½-inch drop at comb, 1⅞-inch drop at heel. Rubber recoil pad. Weight: 12 gauge, 7½ to 7¾ pounds; 16 gauge 6¾ to 7 pounds; 20 gauge, 6½ to 6¾ pounds.

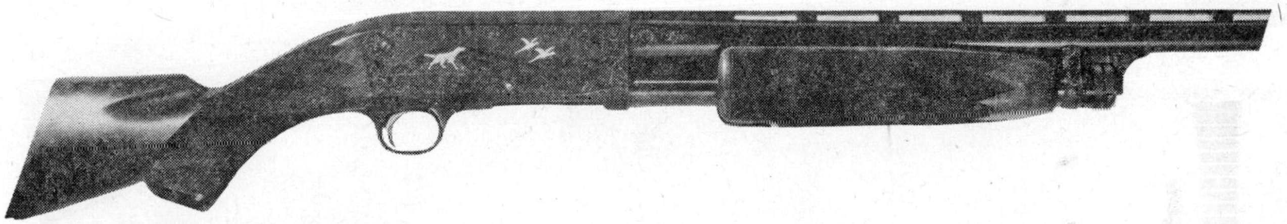

PLATE XLII. ITHACA S-5A AND ITHACA S-5B.

All four models of Ithaca slide-action shotguns are quick takedown, and have a short, smooth fore-end stroke. Shells are fed into the magazine from the bottom, and ejection is from the bottom. The safety is a cross-bolt, built into the trigger guard. Plug is provided to conform with various state and Federal regulations restricting shotguns to 3-shell capacity. Any change in stock specifications may be had at additional cost. Extras include: rubber recoil pad, extra barrel.

In addition to the standard models, Ithaca slide-action shotguns are turned out in custom grades. The balance, quality of material, and fine hard work, as well as the engraving, inlay, and beautiful wood of these custom-built guns places them on a plane with the finest guns in the world. Two examples of these custom guns are shown here.

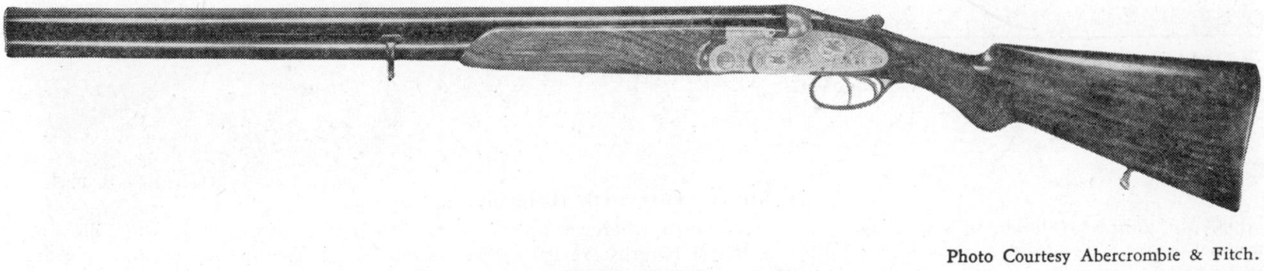

Photo Courtesy Abercrombie & Fitch.

PLATE XLIII. BERETTA (Italian)

This shotgun, from an Italian arms company that has turned out fine arms for two and a half centuries, is available in 2 gauge only, but with 26-, 28-, 30-, or 32-inch barrels. The buyer has an option of borings: improved cylinder, modified choke, full choke. Weight, 6¼ to 8 pounds, depending upon gauge and barrel length. The stock is of the finest-grade European walnut, specially treated, hand rubbed and finely checkered.

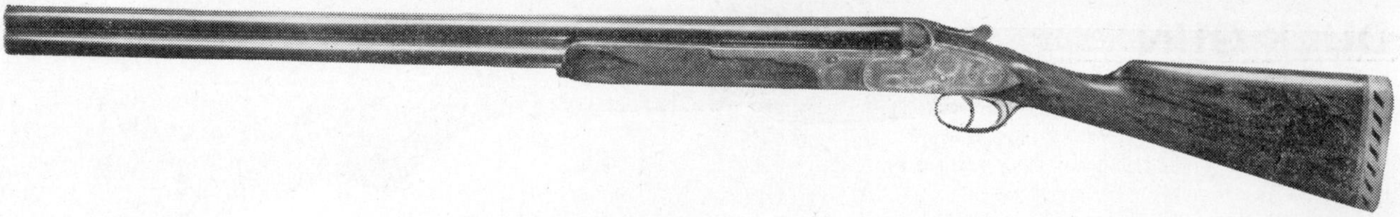

Photo Courtesy Abercrombie & Fitch.

PLATE XLIV. BOSS (British).

This shotgun is one of the finest made in the world, and needs no introduction to any shooter familiar with fine arms. Boss has pioneered many changes and improvements in shotgun and rifle construction during the past century. This model is available in the following gauges: 12, 16, 20, 28, and .410, and in 26-, 28-, 30-, and 32-inch barrels. It is available in any standard boring or combination. The stock and fore-end are of the finest European walnut, specially treated, hand rubbed and finely checkered.

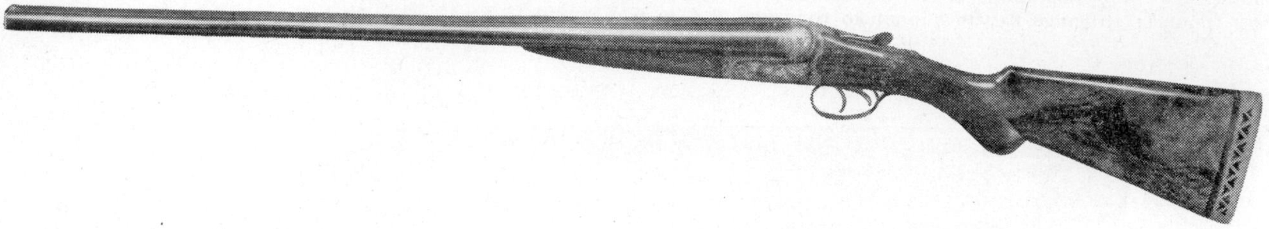

Photo Courtesy Abercrombie & Fitch.

PLATE XLV. GREENER (British).

This gun also is made in several grades, and is the favorite of many shooters who demand fine guns. It is available in the following gauges: 12, 16, 20, 28, and .410; and with barrel lengths of 26, 28, or 30 inches. The stock and fore-end are of the finest European walnut, hand rubbed and specially treated. It may be had with straight, half or full pistol grip. Any degree of boring, or any combination, may be ordered. It also is available with single trigger, single-selective trigger, or double triggers. Weights: 12 gauge, 6 to 8 pounds; 16 gauge, 5¾ to 6¼ pounds; 20 gauge, 5¼ to 6 pounds; 28 gauge, 5 to 6 pounds; .410, from 4¾ to 5¾ pounds.

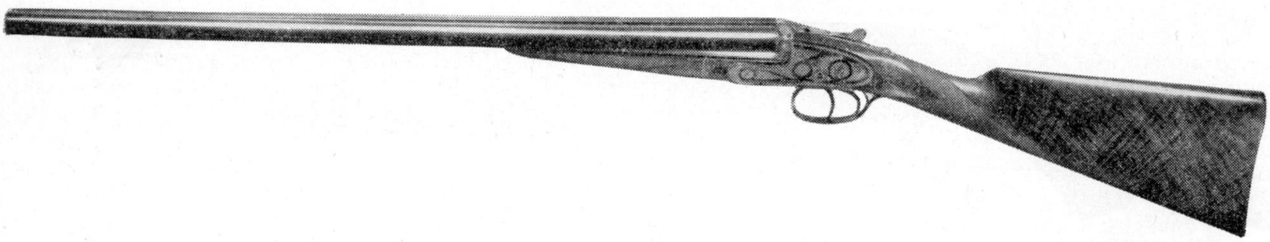

Photo Courtesy Abercrombie & Fitch.

PLATE XLVI. PURDY (British).

Purdy guns are known for their quality of material and workmanship, and while they are made in more than one grade and type, the emphasis is on fit, balance, and quality of materials rather than on ornamentation. The guns are available in the following gauges: 12, 16, 20, 28 and .410, and with barrel lengths of 26, 28, 30, and 32 inches. Any degree of boring, or combination of borings, is optional. Purdy also makes an over-and-under. The "Hammerless Ejector" grade is chambered for the British 2-inch shell, and weighs but 5¼ to 5½ pounds in 12 gauge. All grades are available with matted rib, ventilated rib, semi-beavertail fore-end, single or double trigger, straight, half or full pistol grip stock, and extra barrels may be obtained.

Photo Courtesy Abercrombie & Fitch.

PLATE XLVII. FRANCOTTE (Belgian).

This shotgun is available in several grades, and is known wherever fine guns are used. It is available in the following gauges: 12, 16, 20, 28, and .410; with the following barrel lengths: 12 gauge, 26, 28, 30, or 32; the 16, 20, 28, and .410 are available in either 26- or 28-inch barrels. Any degree of boring from cylinder to full choke, in any combination, may be had. The ejecting mechanism is a Francotte patent, and is contained almost entirely in the fore-end. In the higher grades all locks and actions are finished by hand. It is available with straight, half or full pistol grip. The stock and fore-end are of fine selected European walnut, the quality and finish depending upon the grade selected. The gun is available with single-selective or double triggers. Weight: 12 gauge, 6¼ to 8 pounds; 16 gauge, 6, to 6¼ pounds; 20 gauge, 5¼ to 6 pounds; 28 gauge, 5 to 6 pounds; .410, 4¾ to 5¾ pounds.

# DUCK GUN

The all-around duck gun is as much of a myth as the all-around upland game gun, for the shotgun that is bored just right for shooting black ducks and high mallards will not turn in as satisfactory a performance when used on broadbill or scoters.

For many years there has been an erroneous belief to the effect that "a good duck gun must be choked down to the limit." This belief has crippled more ducks that are never recovered, and has caused more wildfowlers to score clean misses, than any other single factor in duck shooting. One day on a popular duck marsh will convince the most profound skeptic of one thing—namely, that the majority of duck shooters have not the faintest conception of range.

You will see scores of shots sent after birds that are fully 200 yards, and often as much as 300 yards, from the muzzle of the gun. If you could visit the various blinds you would see ducks killed at 30 and 35 yards, and hear the shooters proclaim that range to be 55 to 60 yards. A survey would reveal that at least 75 per cent of the duck hunters have a greatly exaggerated idea as to how far their guns will reach, and an equally exaggerated idea of the range at which they are killing their birds. While this is true, to a certain degree, even in upland game shooting, it approaches the "phobia" stage in duck shooting.

**Borings.** The choice of a duck gun depends on several factors, and unless all are considered and properly weighed, the most satisfactory results cannot be expected. The man who does most of his shooting in one area usually gets one kind of shooting. If this is open-water shooting for diving ducks he will want one boring; if it is river or lake shooting for puddle ducks, the chances are he will want a different boring. The factors to be considered are not directly influenced by the ducks themselves, or even by the type of blind or boat, but by the range at which most of this shooting will be done.

Assume, for example, that the shooter is going to do almost all of his shooting on Great South Bay, in New York, which offers something of an extreme. The waterfowl most abundant there are broadbill, (excepting scoters, of course) and the popular method of gunning there is an open-water rig. As a rule, the broadbill come in to the decoys like chickens, and it is safe to assume that the majority of the hunter's shots will be at a range of from 25 to 40 yards. However, there is a good chance that he will get an occasional shot at a black duck. As this is a more wary bird, and does not normally come in to the decoys on open water, the assumption here is that most of his shots at blacks will be from 40 to 55 yards.

The boring that is most satisfactory for the majority of shots at broadbill will prove unsatisfactory for the occasional black duck. Under these circumstances a double gun, either standard or over-and-under, with one barrel bored modified choke or even improved cylinder and the other full choke, undoubtedly would be the most satisfactory gun for this shooting. This would give the average shooter a chance of scoring twice on incoming ducks: using the open barrel on the first bird and, allowing for normal reaction, permit the shooter to get in a shot with the choked barrel before the ducks are out of range. The normal reaction time is sufficient to permit the average duck to increase the range by at least 15 yards. Also, the choke barrel will give the shooter a chance to rake down a passing black duck at 50 yards.

It should be pointed out, however, that not every shooter is going to kill a duck at 50 yards, even though he has a gun with both barrels bored full choke. Consistent accuracy at 50 yards is most unusual, and the shooter who can drop half the birds at which he shoots at this range is in the top bracket. It is therefore quite apparent that shooting ability, as well as the average range, is a matter that should be taken into consideration.

Long-range killing power, despite the too-common belief, is not the most important factor in a duck gun. The Great South Bay shooter who goes out to his "scooter" with a double gun, both barrels bored full choke, is taking on a handicap that his ability may not warrant. He is reducing the size of his shot pattern at ranges where he will get most of his shots, and he not only must hold extremely "close" on his birds, but is apt to find them pretty well torn up by the dense pattern at close range.

Now, move to another area, and another extreme. Take the man who will do most of his shooting in the flooded woodlands of Arkansas, where he will be shooting among the tall oaks. Here the shooting calls for a gun that will give a proper pattern of heavier shot at a range of from 35 to 50 yards, at mallards. Move northwest, to the potholes and lakes of the flat country, where the decoys must be well out in front of the blind, and the ducks whistle past at extreme ranges. The man with the gun that performed so well on Great South Bay might as well not bother loading the barrel bored improved cylinder.

From these examples alone, it is not difficult to understand that the selection of a duck gun is a matter for considerable study.

While it is true that many duck hunters are over-gunned, there are many instances where the man who is over-gunned in one area is undergunned in another. For goose shooting, or pass shooting, often the full-choked 12 must give way to the magnum 12, chambered for the 3-inch shell, and with 32-inch barrels.

Before ordering the duck gun, spend a little time questioning the old-timers in the area in which you plan to do most of your shooting. Get some idea of the average ranges at which you will do your duck shooting. Once you have worked this out to your own satisfaction, select the boring that will give you the best patterns at three ranges.

The diagrams that follow will give you some idea of the patterns you will get at ranges from 30 to 50 yards, with the 12-gauge gun bored from improved cylinder to full choke. It must be understood that these are average patterns, and that the patterns shown are best at the point where they coincide with the extreme of the circle.

In Plate I, for example, with the full-choked gun, the pattern is extremely narrow at 30 yards, which

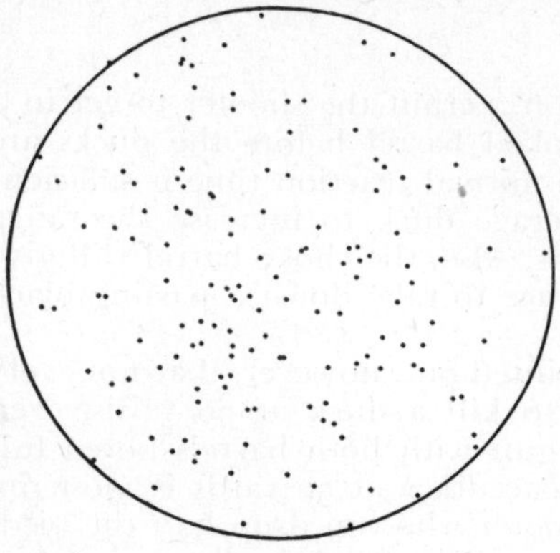

PLATE I. 10 ga. Super-X Magnum—2 oz. No. 2. Full choke at 40 yards. Average pattern: 70-75%.

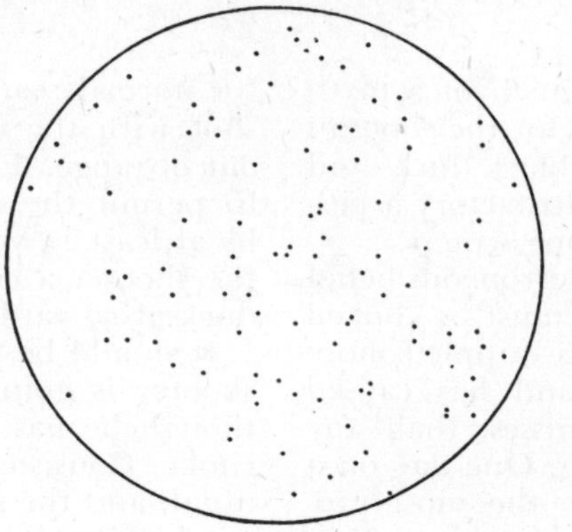

PLATE II. 10 ga. Super-X Magnum—2 oz. No. 2. Full choke at 50 yards. Average pattern: 56-61%.

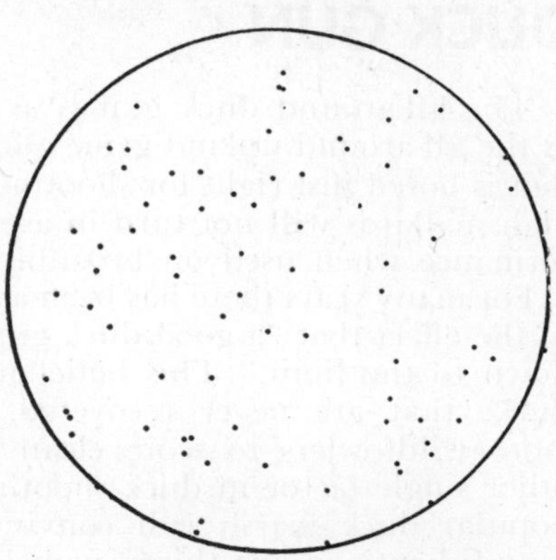

PLATE III. 10 ga. Super-X Magnum—2 oz. No. 2. Full choke at 60 yards. Average pattern: 47-52%.

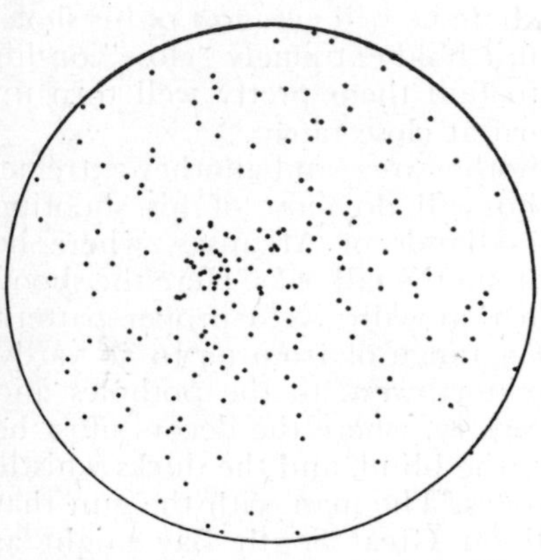

PLATE IV. 12 ga. Super-X Magnum—1⅝ oz. No. 4. Full choke at 30 yards. Average pattern: 93-98%.

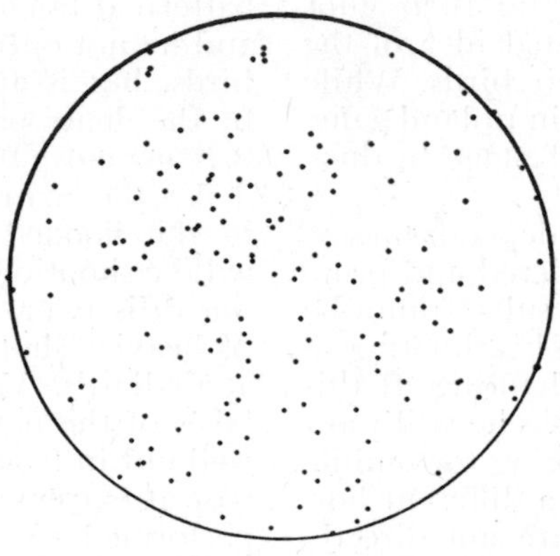

PLATE V. 12 ga. Super-X Magnum—1⅝ oz. No. 4. Full choke at 40 yards. Average pattern: 70-75%.

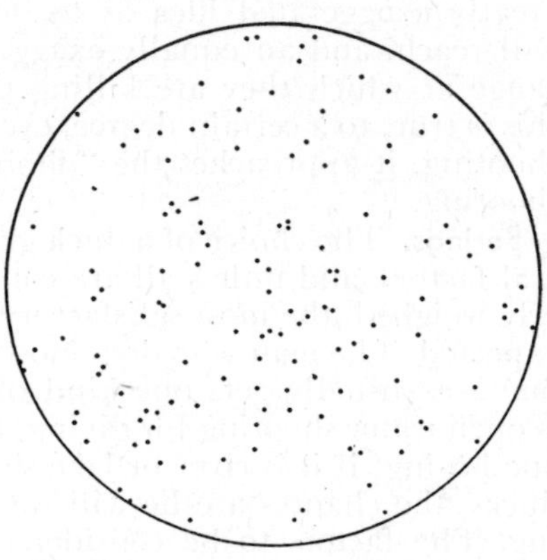

PLATE VI. 12 ga. Super-X Magnum—1⅝ oz. No. 4. Full choke at 50 yards. Average pattern: 56-61%.

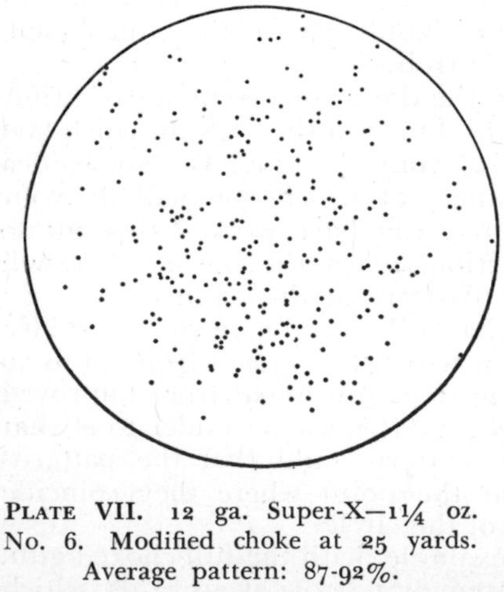

PLATE VII. 12 ga. Super-X—1¼ oz. No. 6. Modified choke at 25 yards. Average pattern: 87-92%.

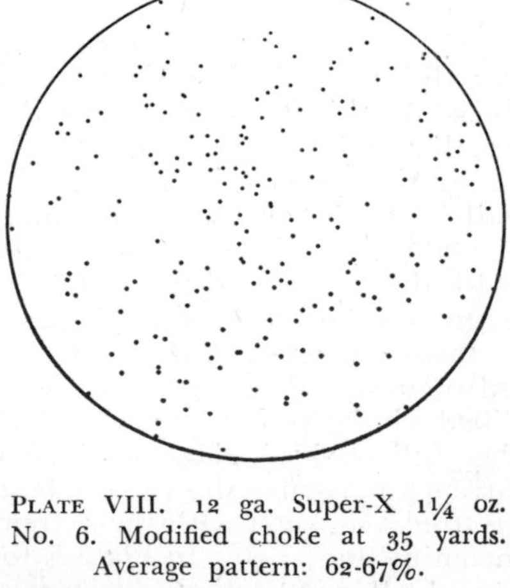

PLATE VIII. 12 ga. Super-X 1¼ oz. No. 6. Modified choke at 35 yards. Average pattern: 62-67%.

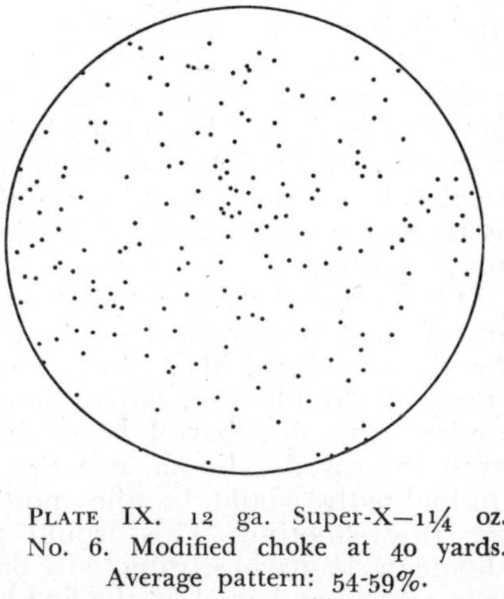

PLATE IX. 12 ga. Super-X—1¼ oz. No. 6. Modified choke at 40 yards. Average pattern: 54-59%.

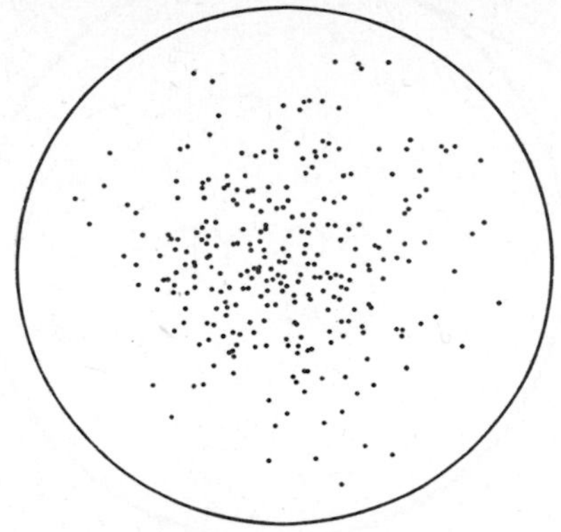

PLATE X. 12 ga. Super-X—1¼ oz. No. 6. Full choke at 25 yards. Average pattern: 100%.

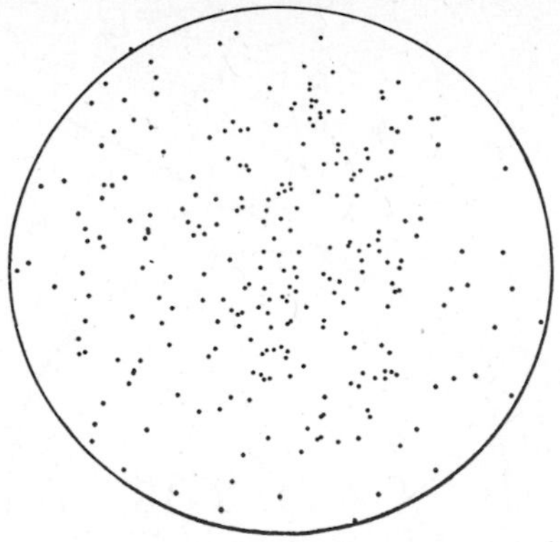

PLATE XI. 12 ga. Super-X—1¼ oz. No. 6. Full choke at 35 yards. Average pattern: 80-85%.

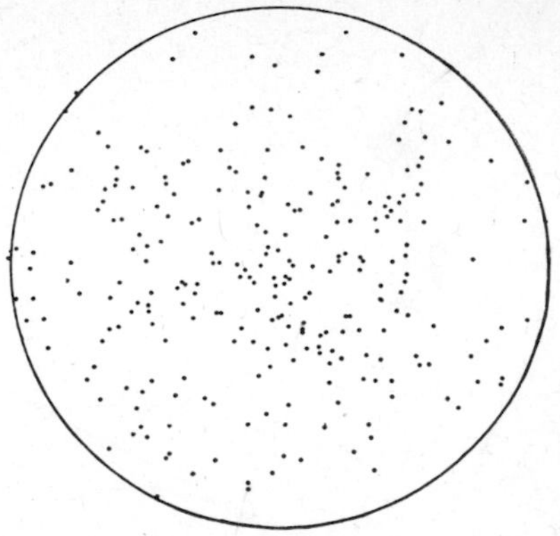

PLATE XII. 12 ga. Super-X—1¼ oz. No. 6. Full choke at 40 yards. Average pattern: 70-75¼.

demands more accurate shooting, is better at 40 yards, still better at 50, and just right at 60.

In Plate II, with improved cylinder, the pattern is about right at 30 yards, is too thin at 40, and very thin at 50.

**Gauges.** There is one thing concerning duck guns in which the great majority agree, and that is gauge.

The 12-gauge gun is by far the most satisfactory for almost all duck shooting. The feight as well as the recoil operates against the 10-gauge gun. While a few wildfowlers use the 16 and an even smaller number use the 20, there are very few areas where the smaller gauges can equal the performance of the 12. Also, there are very few shooters who can shoot the smaller gauges in competition with those using the 12. For this shooting the small-gauge gun presents a definite handicap.

This section would not be complete without a more detailed discussion of the magnum 12, which is increasing in popularity every year. There are relatively few areas where the use of this magnum is either justified or necessary. It quite definitely is not every shooter's gun, and for several reasons.

For pass shooting at high birds, or for shooting in areas where the average shot is at extreme range, or for areas where geese are plentiful, the magnum is an extremely valuable gun. But even in such areas, it will not prove to be the best gun for every shooter. For example, the shooter who is fairly consistent at moderate ranges with a gun properly bored for shooting at such ranges, probably will miss just as consistently with the magnum at extreme ranges, despite the fact that the magnum gives a proper pattern at those ranges. The man who begins shooting at extreme ranges must learn to judge speed and lead all over, and in most instances he will find he is shooting well behind his birds.

There are other features of the magnum which rule it out for some shooters. These include the added weight, which may tend to slow up the shooter, as well as increased recoil, which often results in a tendency to flinch. Until he has become accustomed to the greater recoil, many a shooter will brace his muscles just as he pulls the trigger, in anticipation of the jolt he is about to receive. It does not require much imagination to understand what this does to his accuracy. Another habit which may emerge from the use of the magnum is overconfidence in the range of the gun combined with an underestimation of the range.

Until he has learned to tell when a duck is within range, the novice to the magnum often begins sending shots at birds 80 and 90 yards distant. This will frighten off a duck that might have passed within range on his next circle.

They still tell the story at Hatteras of the wildfowler who appeared there with a 10-gauge magnum, and spent several days shooting from a reef blind. This shooter weighed about 120 pounds, and was attempting to handle a shotgun that tipped the scales at 12 pounds and had a recoil that would have rattled the teeth of a man 50 pounds heavier. The big gun was new to the shooter, who was an excellent duck shot with the standard 12-gauge gun. After two shots with the magnum his procedure was interesting to watch. He would heave the gun to his shoulder, swing it in the general direction of the passing bird, close both eyes, hunch his shoulders, and touch off the trigger. The recoil slapped him back against the boards of the blind so hard that it was necessary to tighten them up with 20-penny nails. He gave the gun to his host on the third day.

**Shot Patterns.** One picture is said to be better than 10,000 words, so let us offer a picture of just what you may expect from the various borings previously discussed. The patterns in Plates I-XII were made expressly for *The Hunter's Encyclopedia* by the Western Cartridge Company, and are indicative of what might be expected from the gauge, boring, and shot size specified. All patterns are shown in a 30-inch circle.

First, let us take the 10-gauge gun with 32-inch barrels, bored full choke and chambered for the magnum shell. In making this test the load used employed 2 ounces of No. 2 shot. At 40 yards the pattern was quite dense in the center, at 50 yards it was normal, and at 60 yards it was rather thin, but still adequate.

Now look at the patterns made by the 12-gauge gun with 32-inch barrels, bored full choke and chambered for the magnum shell. In making this test the load used employed 1⅝ ounces of No. 4 shot. At 30 yards the pattern was extremely dense in the center This indicates that the shooter would have to hold quite "close" and then would do con-

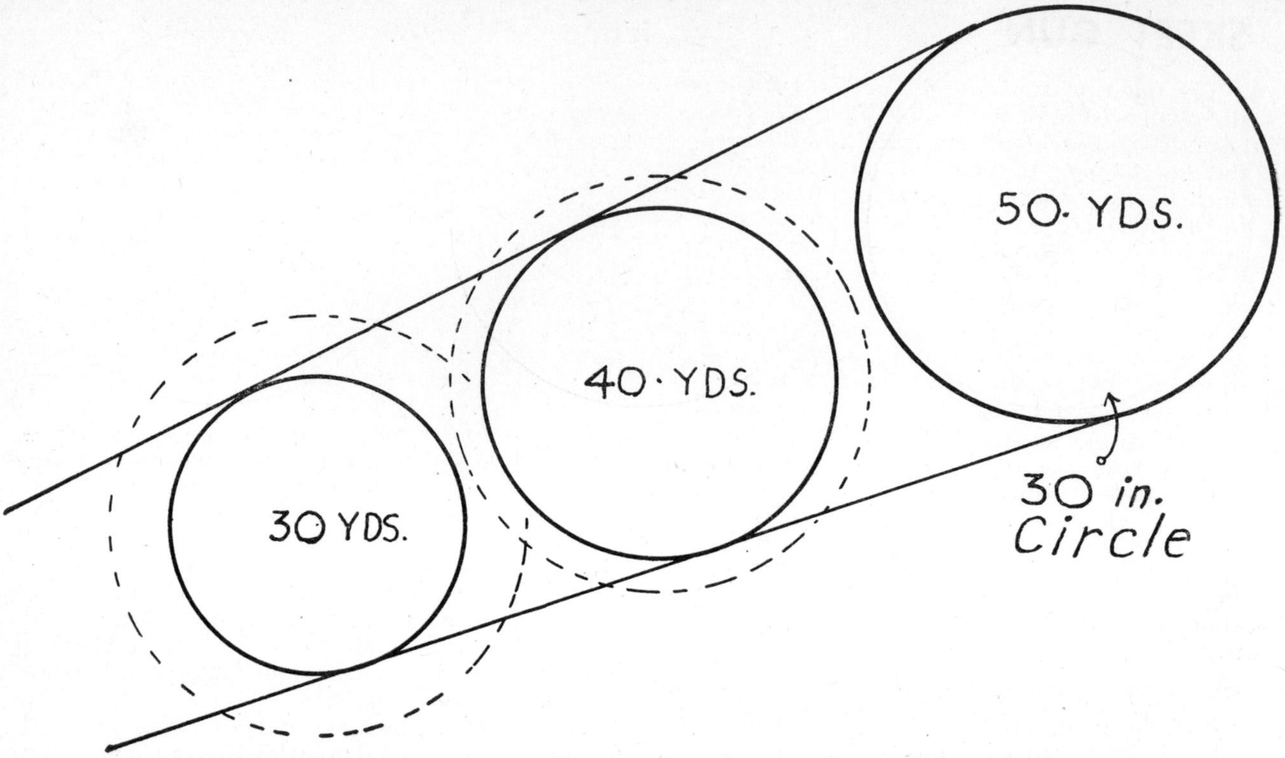


PLATE XIII. This diagram illustrates the handicap assumed by the shooter using a full-choked, 32-inch barrel duck gun for shooting at normal ranges. The two lines indicate the ever-increasing width of the usable pattern of shot. At 30 yards, it will be seen that the usable pattern is well inside the 30-inch circle (broken line). At 40 yards the pattern is wider, and at 50 yards just right.

siderable damage to the bird. The pattern is excellent at 40 yards, although rather dense in the center, and is all that could be asked at 50 yards.

Now see the pattern made by the 12-gauge gun with a 30-inch barrel, bored full choke and chambered for the standard shell. In making this test the load used employed 1¼ ounces of No. 6 shot. One look at the pattern made at 25 yards indicates how close the shooter would have to hold at that range, and also gives some idea of what this dense pattern would do to the duck at that range. The pattern at 35 yards is good, but still somewhat dense at the center, and is all that could be asked at 40 yards, as well as indicating that another 10 yards would give an adequate pattern.

Now look at the pattern made with the 12-gauge gun with a 30-inch barrel, bored modified choke, chambered for the standard shell. In making this test the load used employed 1¼ ounces of No. 6 shot. The pattern at 25 yards is dense, but not nearly so heavy in the center as with the full choke barrel, at the same range, and is more widely distributed over the 30-inch circle. The pattern at 35 yards is excellent and at 40 yards shows an excellent distribution over the circle.

After you have analyzed the matter of the average range for the type of shooting which you normally anticipate, you can give the pattern diagrams more careful study and then make your decision on the boring or borings you want for the new gun. In doing this, however, do not ignore the shot size, for this is important. The shot pattern will vary not only because of the range factor, but with various shot sizes. The larger shot have a higher velocity at the extreme ranges and also tend to shoot a closer pattern at such ranges. The shot used in the pattern diagrams just given vary from 2 to 6 in size, and few waterfowl shooters employ shot larger or smaller than are included in this range. (For a table showing the number of pellets of various size shot in both the standard and the express load see p. 757.)

Those who prefer the autoloader or slide-action shotgun are more fortunate, in one sense, than those who favor the double gun, whether regulation or over-and-under. The gun with the single barrel can be equipped with one of the patent compensators or chokes (see p. 781) which will give the shooter a range of borings from improved cylinder to full choke. In the instance of the Poly Choke, the gun can be converted from one boring to another in about two seconds. If the Cutts attachment is used, one merely inserts another tube to change boring.

Even in those instances where the conversion requires only a couple of seconds, there often is not enough time to get in a shot at one duck and make the change in time for a second shot. But this can be overcome by using a shell with heavier shot for the second round. Many duck hunters load the chamber with a shell carrying No. 6 shot, and back it with either one or two shells carrying No. 4 shot.

For the man who shoots in several areas during the course of a season, thus encountering different types of shooting, the patent choke is a great advantage, for he can readily adapt his gun to the type of shooting he will be doing. While the slide-action guns are turned out by two of the companies chambered for the magnum shell, in either 10 or 12 gauge, there is no point in equipping such guns with compensators or chokes, for the magnum is intended only for long-range shooting.

# SKEET GUN

The question as to whether or not skeet improves the score or skill of the bird shooter is one that has been debated ever since the game was invented, and the pros and cons of the matter will not be discussed in this volume. Many shooters are inclined to refer to the old saw concerning the country doctor who prescribed a certain medicine for a patient believed to be suffering from an incurable disease: "It may not do him any good, but it certainly can't do him any harm." While many shooters are willing to admit that the game of skeet will teach a novice how to handle his gun and give him an idea of the rudiments of *lead,* most of them are unwilling to concede much more than this.

The above argument is carried on with about the same amount of heat as is the debate concerning the best *type* of gun for skeet. If a shooter is a novice, and is primarily interested in skeet and has field shooting as a secondary interest, he should be concerned as to the best type of gun for the primary interest. If a shooter intends to take up skeet merely as a sideline, or as a means of getting in some shooting during a period when hunting is out of season, the same type of gun used in his field shooting is the one he should use.

The best means of determining the proper gun for skeet is to check on the type most popular with those shooters who take the game seriously and attain the highest scores. To make such a check, the national matches certainly provide the best proving ground, coupled with the preferences shown by shooters at the large regional matches. The results, after going through the necessary addition, multiplication, and division, indicate that the autoloader towers over the other types. A rough average would be as follows: the autoloader, 50%; pump or slide action, 25%; and the double and over-and-under splitting the other 25% almost evenly.

In other words, about half of those who take skeet seriously shoot autoloaders, and the overwhelming majority of those who shoot autoloaders use the Cutts Compensator. This device, with the skeet attachment, is used not only as a means of obtaining an even pattern of the diameter desired, but to reduce the recoil. The shooter who is planning to burn up from 100 to 200 shells a day is interested in using any device which will give him less of a jolt when he pulls the trigger. Of those who favor the pump or slide-action gun, the great majority also equip their guns with the compensator. So popular is this device that the majority of the manufacturers who turn out a skeet gun equip the standard grade with the compensator.

The most popular skeet gun, therefore, is the 12-gauge autoloader, with a 26-inch barrel (including compensator) and bored either cylinder or skeet boring. Except for the difference in type, the same specifications apply to the pump or slide-action gun.

Experienced skeet shooters insist that the single sighting plane of the autoloader or pump offers an opportunity for greater precision as well as greater speed in aiming, all of which means nothing when opposed to habit or preference.

The loudest complainant about the compensator is not the shooter, but the man standing near him, for while this device cuts down the recoil it does nothing to reduce muzzle blast, and this accounts for the fact that most skeet shooters plug their ears with cotton while engaged in the sport. The shorter the barrel, the greater the blast, and as a gun equipped with a compensator has 4 inches less barrel length, the individual behind and to one side of the shooter is the one who suffers.

Although in many sections the regulation double gun and the over-and-under share the low popularity bracket, the over-and-under gun quite definitely is becoming more popular, and when all of the manufacturers of this type are able to reduce the percentage of malfunctions of the gun the chances are that it will jump far ahead of the regulation double on the skeet field. The majority of skeet shooters prefer their double guns to be equipped with the single trigger, and this complication, added to the already complicated and crowded mechanism of the over-and-under, proved the last straw in many instances.

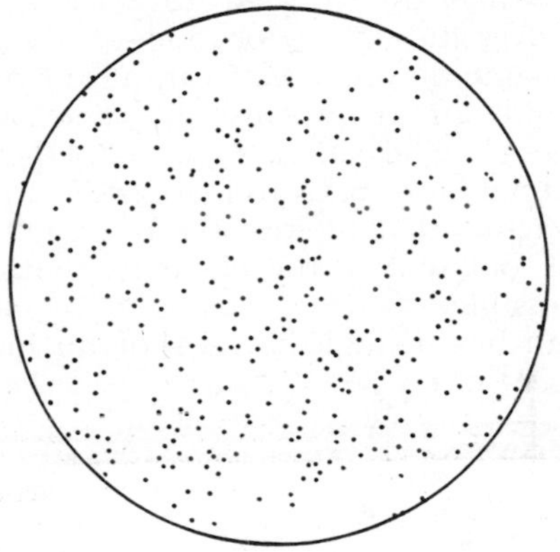

PLATE I. This is an "average" pattern, produced by the use of the compensator with the "spreader tube," at 25 yards.

There are many reasons why the single trigger, selective or otherwise, is preferred by the shooter who burns up 100 or more shells a day: first, the speed and ease of shooting without changing the conformation of the grip in the slightest; second, the freedom from bruising the finger when the rear trigger is used. It takes very little to develop a "flinch," and the shooter who anticipates a sharp rap on the index finger each time he uses the rear trigger can very readily fall into this fault.

In either of the double-gun types, the 26-inch barrel, bored either cylinder or skeet boring, is preferable.

With reference to stock length, the average skeet shooter will find that a stock slightly short of fit is better than one that is long. The opposite is true of trap shooting, where the target is rising and where the position prior to "pull" is different. The short stock usually results in a "low" shot, and in skeet the target is dropping, not rising. Many skeet shooters who are equally interested in field shooting, have their skeet guns cut from ½ to ¾ inch shorter than their field guns.

# TRAP GUN

Many shooters who are willing to take almost any type of gun into the field evidence extreme care in the selection of a trap gun, and demand perfect fit, precise balance, and other features that are not embodied in the standard 12-gauge shotgun.

Although many shooters buy a trap gun that is expected to perform both on waterfowl and at the traps, many others demand a special gun for this shooting, and having settled the matters of fit, balanct, trigger pull, and boring, they turn their attention to ornamentation. The field gun, which normally is brought into close contact with the elements and with rough usage, does not lend itself to the elaborate inlay and tooling that is found on many trap guns.

Those who demand a trap gun also suitable for field shooting are inclined to select a standard double, over-and-under, or one of the magazine shotguns, but the man who can afford one gun to be used only at the traps usually selects one with a single barrel. The single sighting plane normally permits finer accuracy, and accuracy and pattern are the factors that interest the trapshooter. Fit, of course, is but one of the elements that makes accuracy possible.

You can buy a single-barrel shotgun for $20, but the really fine, custom-built trap gun with a single barrel costs from $300 up, and at some of the old-established trap clubs you will see guns that cost as much as $2000. Much of the money involved goes into ornamentation, of course, but a good portion of it is represented by fine workmanship, balance, and smooth-working parts.

Any gun that will give you a fine pattern at ranges between 30 and 45 yards with No. 7½ or 8 shot will make a satisfactory trap gun, *provided* it flows to your shoulder and presents a sighting plane that seems to move *naturally* out from the eye. The gun that offers a perfect fit at the traps does not always promise an equally fine fit in the duck blind, for the average hunter in the blind needs a shorter stock to compensate for the layers of clothing he is wearing. Some who demand that the long-barreled, full-choke gun answer both needs add a laced recoil boot to the stock when at the traps.

Exacting trapshooters seem to prefer a 30- or 32-inch barrel, bored full choke, and most of them demand a single sighting plane; to provide a really flat plane, the raised, ventilated rib is used on most guns. While some use No. 8 shot at the 16- and 18-yard lines, the majority go to the heavier No. 7½ or even 7 at longer ranges.

PLATE I. The Parker single-barrel trap gun typifies the gun required by many trapshooters. This model is available in 12 gauge only, in 30-, 32-, and 34-inch barrels, all with full-choke boring.

# UPLAND GAME GUN

Rod and gun editors the country over are besieged with letters, primarily from novice shooters, but some from men with sufficient experience to know their own minds, requesting information on "the best all-around gun" for the hunting of small game, upland game birds, and waterfowl. The answer is very simple: There is no such shotgun in existence.

Many experienced hunters contend that they possess an "all-around gun" which is every bit as satisfactory for quail as it is for geese. The man who consistently engages in both of these forms of shooting will insist that no gun can fulfill all the requirements of these two quite different forms. The slide-action or autoloading shotgun, to which has been fitted a Poly Choke or a Cutts Compensator, probably comes nearest to answering the needs of both upland game and waterfowl shooting. With either of these devices, a shotgun may be converted in a few seconds from a gun with a cylinder-bored barrel to one with a full-choke barrel. However, there are a few points which prevent such guns from attaining the goal of "all-around" perfection, such as: weight, barrel length, range, and pattern.

Several factors enter into the hunter's requirements in the selection of an upland game gun. First, he wants a gun that is light enough to permit it to be carried through a long day afield without becoming a burden. Secondly, he wants a gun that will be heavy enough to eliminate excessive recoil. Thirdly, he wants one that will give him a good pattern at ranges between 20 and 40 yards. On top of all this, he may have a definite preference as to gauge, and in this matter he should be guided by his ability as a wing shot. Finally, he is confronted by the problem of type: whether to select a regulation double, an over-and-under, a pump or slide action, or an autoloader.

In a few states, and in some Canadian provinces, the autoloader is ruled out by law, so on this question the novice may not be faced with the problem of making a decision. Some hunters rule them out on the basis of balance. Many, who in addition to spending much time in the field are skeet enthusiasts, prefer to use the same shotgun for both pursuits, and many of them are inclined to favor the autoloader.

Where it is possible, the novice should arrange to try all four types, for many who shoot very well with the double are unable to shoot a single-barreled gun with equal ease and skill. There are enough handicaps lurking around the corner for the novice shooter without risking the possibility of adding another.

**Borings.** The double gun, regular or over-and-under, has many advantages to the upland game hunter, although the sensible shooter of the single barrel may overcome some of the things which at first seem to make the gun inferior to the double. The majority of those whose primary interest is in upland game shooting prefer the double gun, with the right barrel bored improved cylinder and the left barrel modified choke. Those whose preference runs to the over-and-under seem to prefer the same boring. On the matter of weight, preference varies between 6½ and 7½ pounds, depending upon gauge. The 28-inch barrel is the odds-on favorite, and the great majority favor 12 gauge over the others.

Fit is more important in the upland game gun than in the duck gun for the simple reason that the average upland game shooter must shoot more quickly than the waterfowler, who normally is able to see the duck or goose well in advance, and can be prepared to shoot. The upland game bird hunter, even when shooting over a dog, does not know just when the bird will flush and what line it will take when it does. If his gun does not *come up* properly and line up naturally, he is definitely handicapped. The majority of shooters are able to adapt themselves an dtheir shooting to the standard stock, which can be very easily altered and at little cost to the owner. By changing the angle of the butt, lengthening the stock by the addition of a recoil pad or cutting it down, the standard stock may quite easily be fitted to the average shooter. For those who require a higher comb, leather comb pads are available which are fully adequate. (See Plate II, p. 636.)

Here are a few of the advantages of the double gun which many insist make it tower over the other types.

The design makes it possible to attain a finer balance, and at the same time to offer a fairly wide range of weights. Very few hunters will find a 7-pound shotgun a burden, and a 12-gauge gun of this weight does not have an excessive recoil when the standard load of 3 drams of powder and 1⅛ ounces of shot are used. The recoil is felt more if the long-range or express loads, with 3¾ drams of powder and 1¼ ounces of shot, are used. Many upland game shooters with guns of this weight use a standard load in the cylinder-bored barrel and an express load in the modified-choke-bored barrel. This permits them to get in a shot at 20 to 30 yards with the open barrel and stretches the possibilities of the choked barrel. Normally, the hunter will use the choked barrel only about one-third as often as the open barrel, so the occasional heavier recoil is not too disturbing.

The double shotgun is limited to two shots, of course, but the shooter who can get in more than two aimed shots before the birds are out of range is an unusual one. Also, the modern hammerless shotgun with automatic ejectors can be reloaded with ease and speed. In many states the hunter is limited to a shotgun with a three-shell capacity, and in a few the law limits the capacity to two shells. Except for waterfowl shooting, it is only on rare occasions that a third round would be of real value, although many quail shooters who hunt in the open country prefer a pump or autoloader primarily because of this third shell. For shooting in any kind of cover, however, it is rare indeed that a shooter would be able to get in a third shot before the bird disappeared in the foliage.

The over-and-under double has all the advantages of the standard double, plus the added feature of a single sighting plane, which is not a point to be ignored. Many novices find this gun easier to handle and it is claimed that the "learning" period can be cut down as much as 20 per cent merely because of the single sighting plane which makes it easier to align. In some makes, however, the over-and-under is a bit heavier, due to the necessity for strengthening certain parts, and as the action is more complex than the standard double this gun is likely to require more frequent trips to the gunsmith or factory for repairs.

The adherents of the pump gun and autoloader seem to be gaining in number every year, and under certain conditions these types have greater value to the shooter. Normally, their weight is slightly greater than the two doubles, although the Ithaca pump is comparable in weight to almost any double of the same barrel length. The autoloader in the standard grades is somewhat heavier, but great strides have been made in improving the balance.

The advantage of both the pump and autoloader is that the gun with the 28-inch barrel may be fitted with a Poly Choke or Cutts Compensator and thus be changed from an upland game gun to a duck gun in a few seconds or a minute, depending upon the attachment used. The increased weight, however, seems to turn many upland game hunters toward the doubles.

It is claimed by those who favor the double that the big disadvantage of the single-barrel repeaters is the fact that the bore cannot be instantly changed from cylinder to some degree of choke. You have an equal chance on the first bird that gets up within easy range, they insist, but the pattern is too thin when it comes to the second shot at a more distant bird. This is not necessarily the case, for the fault can be partially overcome by a very simple expedient. When the magazine is loaded, it can be topped by a long-range or express load, with ¾ of a dram more powder and ⅛ ounce more shot. Thus the upland game shooter would have a standard load in the chamber, but a maximum load, or two maximum loads, in the magazine.

While this expedient is satisfactory in most instances, because the additional powder and shot will give a closer pattern at greater range, the double-gun adherent is not to be defeated that easily.

"Suppose a bird flushes wild, say 30 yards or more out. By the time you are ready to pull he would be at a range where the pattern is too thin to be practical. We can merely pull the rear trigger and get him with the choked barrel. To reach him you would be forced to eject the standard load from the chamber and throw in an express load. By the time you have done this there is no point in shooting."

The pump-gun shooter will insist that he can

eject a shell in less time than it takes the double-gun shooter to blink one eye, and thus be ready to get in a shot while the bird is in range of his heavier load. The autoloader shooter says that he does not have to eject the light load; he can shoot it at the departing bird, even though vainly, and be ready instantly with the heavy load or two.

Any and all of these arguments will be heard at most rod and gun clubs throughout the country, or in any country where there is much hunting. They are endless, and prove little. The matter narrows down to personal preference, which statistics can never change.

The novice who is not concerned with price, and is influenced by the old theory that "imported shotguns are the finest made," may be influenced by the propaganda concerning the ultra-light shotguns of German, Austrian, or Belgian manufacture. Before buying one, however, he would be well advised to take one out and fire 25 rounds. Such guns are a delight to carry in the field, for they weigh just a shade over nothing. But most shooters—and this takes in big, heavy men—find the recoil of the very light gun too excessive for pleasure. Twenty-five quick, snap shots with one of these guns usually will provide the shooter with a bruised shoulder and possibly a swollen cheek or jaw. A rubber recoil pad and a cheek pad do little to reduce the jar the shooter will receive.

**Gauges.** If you must reduce weight, change to a 16-gauge or 20-gauge gun, and spend more time in practice to compensate for the thinner, smaller patterns they offer.

The trend toward smaller gauge is very definite, and a great increase can be noted in the number of 16- and 20-gauge guns seen in the field. The 20 gauge is rapidly approaching the 12 in popularity, at least on upland game birds, but probably never will crowd the 12 gauge when it comes to waterfowl shooting.

As to just what you lose in pattern, if you favor the 16- or 20-gauge gun over the 12, the following should be informative.

Let us take No. 8 shot, which is the most popular for most upland game shooting.

The 12-gauge standard load has about 460 shot pellets, and at a range of 40 yards approximately 230 pellets would be inside a 30-inch circle if the barrel is bored improved cylinder.

The 16-gauge standard load has about 405 shot pellets, and at a range of 40 yards approximately 200 would be inside a 30-inch circle if the barrel is bored improved cylinder.

The 20-gauge standard load has about 350 shot pellets, and at a range of 40 yards approximately 140 would be inside a 30-inch circle if the barrel is bored improved cylinder.

Therefore, the 12-gauge gun will give a closer pattern, with 30 more pellets spread over the 30-inch circle than the 16 gauge and 90 more pellets than the 20 gauge.

The above figures are approximate and are compiled from tests made by various arms companies using standard shot shells, and while they will vary with various barrels and loads, the percentages will remain almost unchanged.

**Shot Size.** Although the "best shot size" for upland game birds is the basis for many violent debates among shooters, experienced shooters agree that a variation of one or even two sizes often has very little effect on the results. The following list of sizes is generally recognized as most satisfactory for upland game birds.

| | |
|---|---|
| 8 or 9 for: | Jack snipe, quail, rail, sora, woodcock. |
| 7, 7½, or 8 for: | Doves and pigeons. |
| 5, 6, or 7 for: | Chukars, grouse, Hungarians, pheasants, prairie chickens, ptarmigans, rabbits, sage hens, squirrels, varying hares. |
| 1, 2, or BB for: | Turkey. |

The type of shell to be used, whether standard load or the express load, depends upon the type of game sought as well as the type of cover. For open shooting, where most of the shots will be taken at ranges or from 20 to 35 yards, the standard load will prove just as effective, will cost less, and will be less likely to tear up the game. Where the range normally is between 25 and 40 yards the heavy load will prove more satisfactory. The heavy load also gives better results in thick cover, and this load is preferred by almost every experienced turkey hunter.

**Shot Patterns.** A large volume, devoted entirely to a dissertation on the best gauge and boring for upland game, would be inadequate, for no writer could determine just what gauge and boring would be most satisfactory for each individual reader. However, there is one method of showing the reader what the various gauges and borings will produce—in the way of shot patterns—and letting him decide for himself just what combination would best suit his purpose.

Through the cooperation of the Western Cartridge Company, the following patterns were prepared for *The Hunter's Encyclopedia*. Each individual pattern was developed, not by firing one round at a pattern sheet with a certain gauge and certain boring, but by firing enough rounds to insure that the pattern was "typical" or "average." In each instance, regardless of the range, a 30-inch circle was used. In addition to the explanatory text, the gauge, boring, range and the percentage of the load within the circle is given.

A few readers may ask: "Why show patterns made with a full-choke gun for upland game shooting?" The answer is quite simple. In many areas a hunter encounters several types of shooting, and in an effort to find an "all-around" gun it may be necessary to use the standard double or over-and-under, with the two barrels bored at extremes of "open" and "choke." By showing what each boring and gauge will produce, the man who is contemplating the purchase of a new gun will be able to decide which combination would best suit his requirements. Also, the matter of loads enters the picture. Some of the patterns shown were made with standard loads (mid-range load) and others with long-range (express) loads. The load used is clearly indicated. The "Xpert" load is the standard load produced by Western; the others, "Super Trap," "Super Skeet," and "Super-X," are heavier loads.

The following patterns were made with a 12-gauge gun, chambered for the standard shell, with a full-choke boring. The load used was the "Super Trap," comprising 3 drams of powder and 1⅛ ounces of No. 7½ shot. The first pattern, made at 25 yards, indicates how closely a shooter would have to hold if this gun were used at 25 yards, and also gives some idea of how this dense pattern would tear up a bird at that range. The next pattern, at 35 yards, is well distributed, but still somewhat dense in the center. The last pattern, at 40 yards, is just about what would be desired at that range, and indicates that the gun could stretch its effective range another 10 yards and still produce quite a satisfactory pattern.

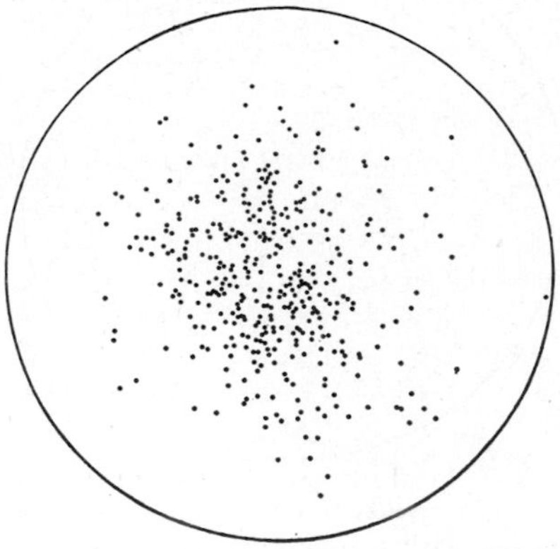

PLATE I. 12 ga. Super Trap—3 dr.—1⅛ oz. No. 7½. Full choke at 25 yards. Average pattern: 100%.

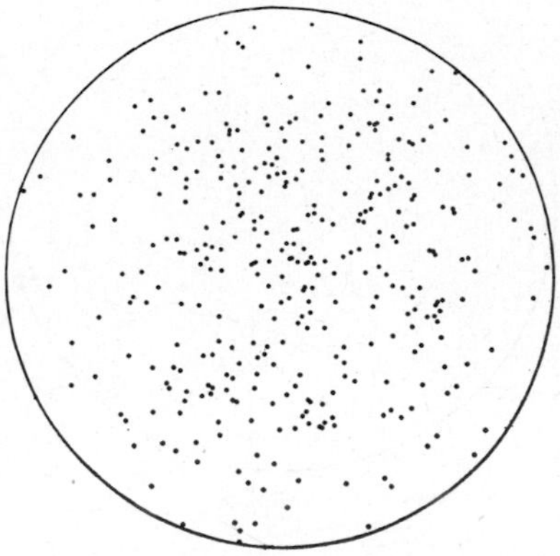

PLATE II. 12 ga. Super Trap—3 dr.—1⅛ oz. No. 7½. Full choke at 35 yards. Average pattern: 80-85%.

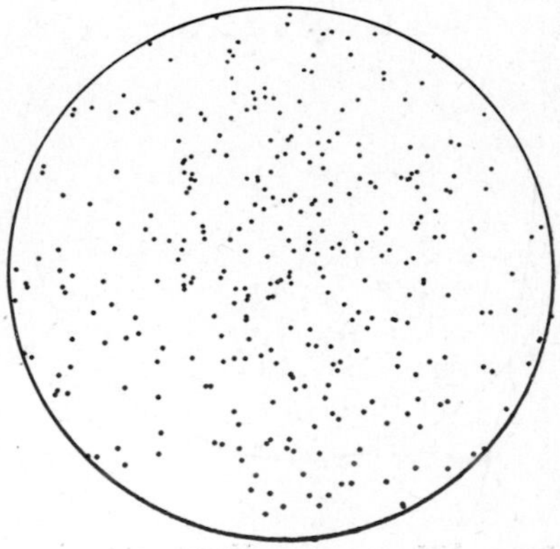

PLATE III. 12 ga. Super Trap—3 dr.—1⅛ oz. No. 7½. Full choke at 40 yards. Average pattern: 70-75%.

The following patterns were made with a 12-gauge gun, chambered for the standard shell, with a "skeet No. 1" boring. The load used was the "Super Skeet," comprising 3 drams of powder and 1⅛ ounces of No. 9 shot. The first pattern, made at 25 yards, shows an excellent distribution of shot, with some density at the center. The next pattern, made at 35 yards, is excellent. The third pattern, at 40 yards, is thinner. In these patterns it should be kept in mind that a very small shot pellet is used, and that such shot is not intended for long-range execution.

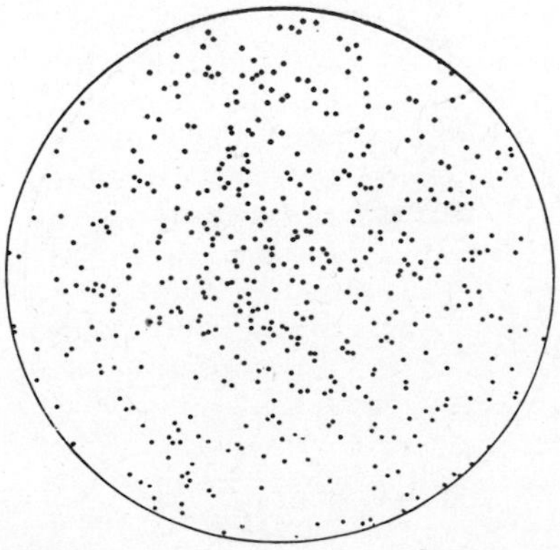

PLATE IV. 12 ga. Super Skeet—3 dr.—1⅛ oz. No. 9. Skeet No. 1 at 25 yards. Average pattern: 62-67%.

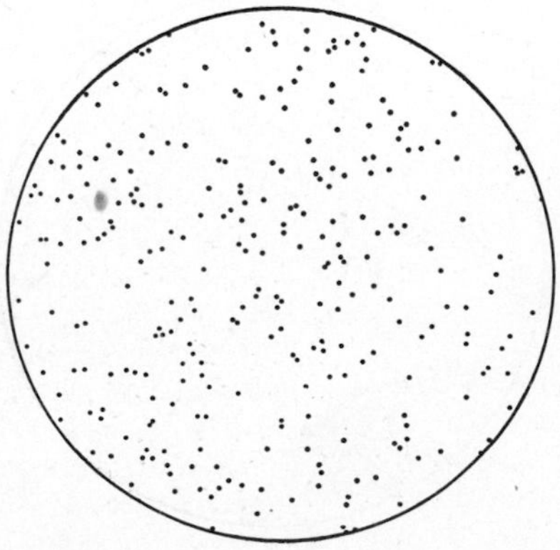

PLATE V. 12 ga. Super Skeet—3 dr.—1⅛ oz. No. 9. Skeet No. 1 at 35 yards. Average pattern: 40-45%.

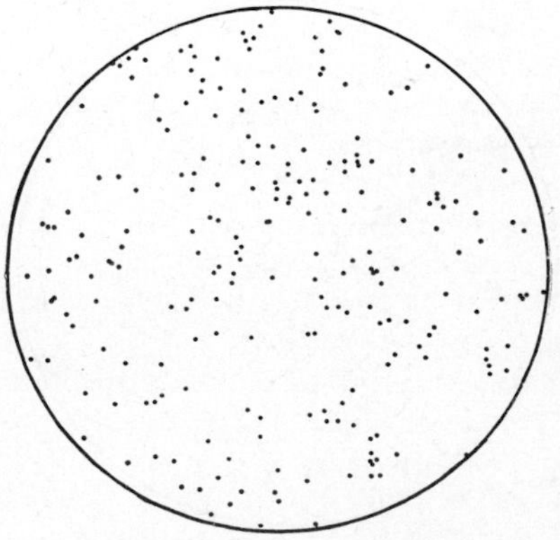

PLATE VI. 12 ga. Super Skeet—3 dr.—1⅛ oz. No. 9. Skeet No. 1 at 40 yards. Average pattern: 35-40%.

The following patterns were made with a 12-gauge gun, chambered for the standard shell, with a cylinder boring. The load used was "Xpert" (medium range) with $3\frac{1}{4}$ drams of powder and $1\frac{1}{8}$ ounces of No. 8 shot. Any quail or woodcock shooter will not be slow to realize the excellence of this pattern made at 25 yards. The pattern made at 35 yards is adequate, but this boring and shot size is not at its best for shooting at 40 yards, as the pattern made at that range indicates.

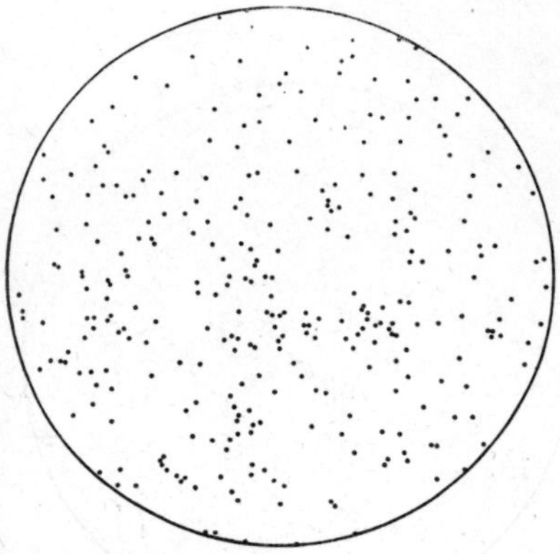

PLATE VII. 12 ga. Xpert—$3\frac{1}{4}$ dr.—$1\frac{1}{8}$ oz. No. 8. Cylinder bore at 25 yards. Average pattern: 65-75%.

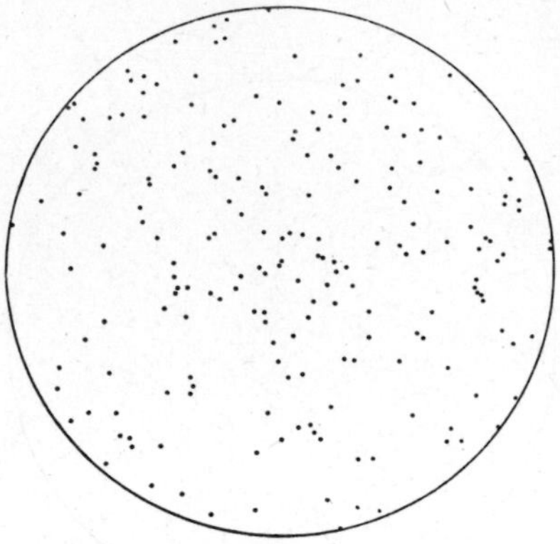

PLATE VIII. 12 ga. Xpert—$3\frac{1}{4}$ dr.—$1\frac{1}{8}$ oz. No. 8. Cylinder bore at 35 yards. Average pattern: 40-50%.

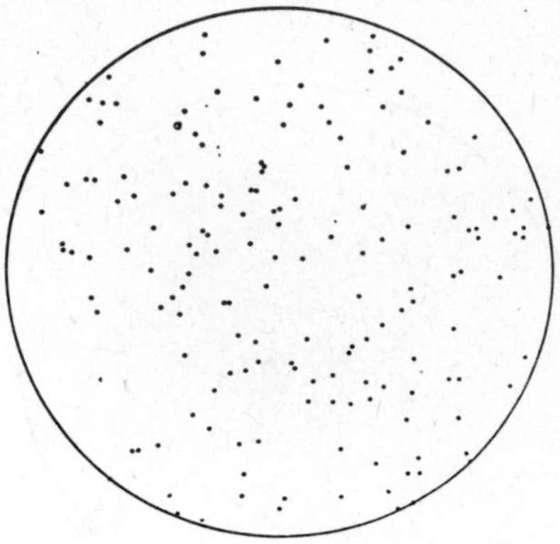

PLATE IX. 12 ga. Xpert—$3\frac{1}{4}$dr.—$1\frac{1}{8}$ oz. No. 8. Cylinder bore at 40 yards. Average pattern: 25-35%.

The following patterns were made with a 16-gauge gun, with an improved cylinder boring. The load used was the "Xpert" (mid-range) comprising $2\frac{3}{4}$ drams of powder and $1\frac{1}{8}$ ounces of No. 8 shot. The pattern made at 25 yards is good, but somewhat dense in the center. The pattern at 35 yards, however, is just about perfect. The 40-yard pattern, although thinner, is satisfactory, but undoubtedly at that range would be more satisfactory for quail, doves, or woodcock than for one of the larger birds capable of carrying away more small shot.

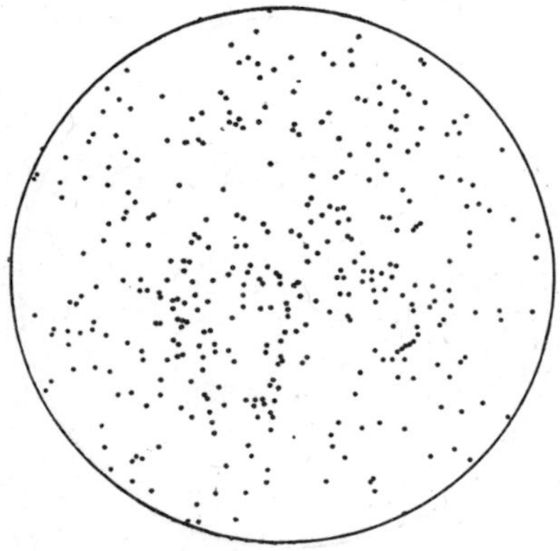

PLATE X. 16 ga. Xpert—$2\frac{3}{4}$ dr.—$1\frac{1}{8}$ oz. No. 8 Improved cylinder bore at 25 yards. Average pattern: 70-75%.

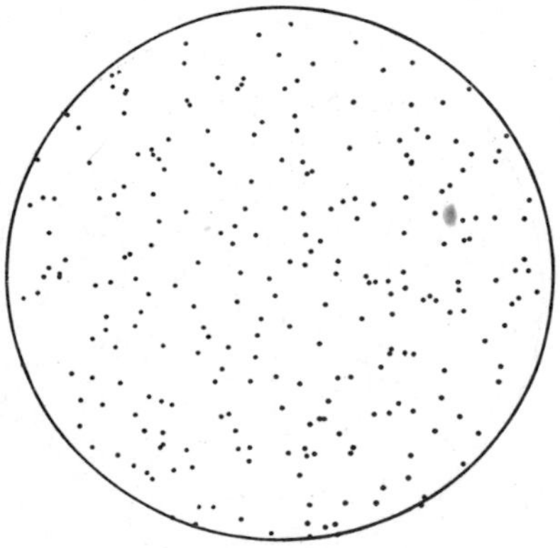

PLATE XI. 16 ga. Xpert—$2\frac{3}{4}$ dr.—$1\frac{1}{8}$ oz. No. 8. Improved cylinder bore at 35 yards. Average pattern: 50-55%.

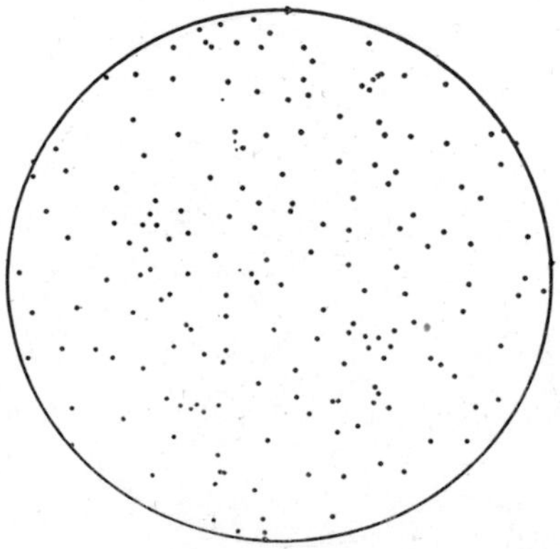

PLATE XII. 16 ga. Xpert—$2\frac{3}{4}$ dr.—$1\frac{1}{8}$ oz. No. 8. Improved cylinder bore at 40 yards. Average pattern: 40-45%.

The following patterns were made with a 20-gauge gun, with a full-choke boring. The load used was "Super-X" (long-range) employing one ounce of No. 7½ shot. As the first pattern indicates, this boring and load was not intended for shooting at upland game at 25 yards, and the shooter who uses it is taking on quite a handicap. At 35 yards, however, the pattern is excellent, and at 40 yards is unusually well distributed. A pattern such as this, at 40 yards, undoubtedly is one reason why so many shooters have switched to the 20-gauge double for upland game shooting, and have one barrel bored improved cylinder and the other full choke.

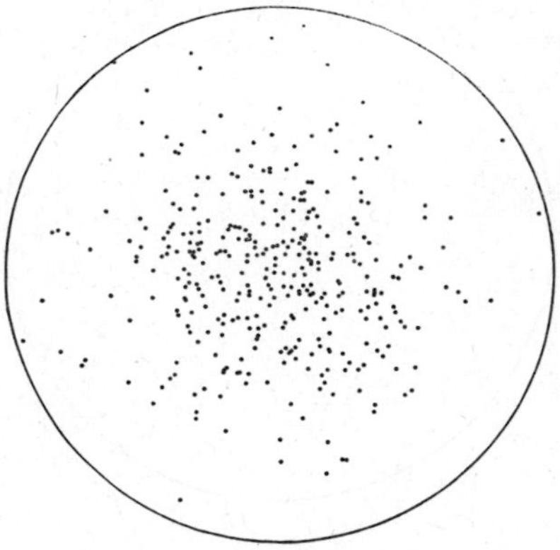

PLATE XIII. 20 ga. Super-X—1 oz. No. 7½. Full choke at 25 yards. Average pattern: 100%.

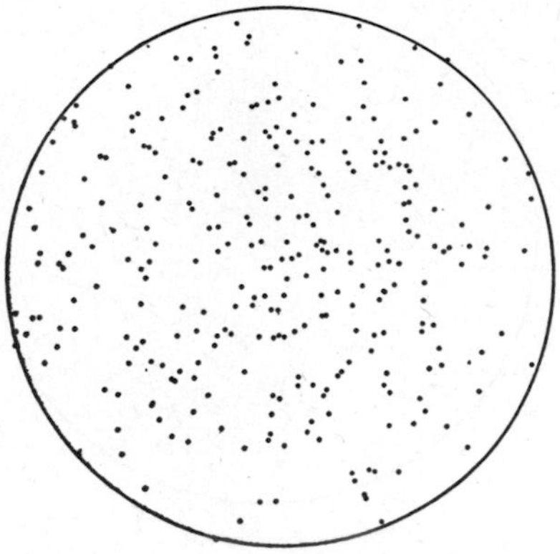

PLATE XIV. 20 ga. Super-X—1 oz. No. 7½. Full choke at 35 yards. Average pattern: 75-85%.

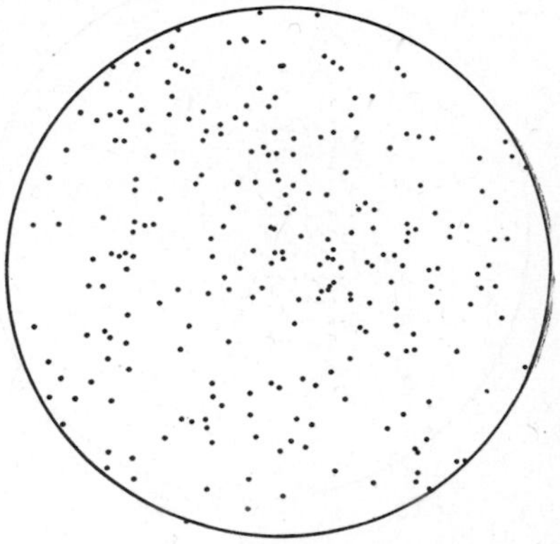

PLATE XV. 20 ga. Super-X—1 oz. No. 7½. Full choke at 40 yards. Average pattern: 68-73%.

The following patterns were made with a 20-gauge gun with an improved cylinder boring. The load used was "Xpert" (mid-range) comprising 2½ drams of powder and one ounce of No. 8 shot. As the first pattern indicates, the distribution is rather thin on the extreme edge of the 30-inch circle, and excellent otherwise. This pattern would indicate that the perfect range for this boring and load would be about 30 yards, although the 35-yard pattern is satisfactory. The 40-yard pattern shows an extremely even distribution, but at that range No. 8 shot would be more adequate for the smaller rather than the larger upland game birds.

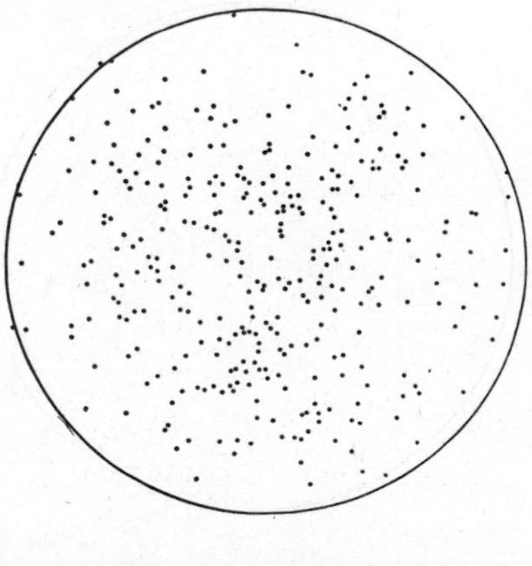

PLATE XVI. 20 ga. Xpert—2½ dr.—1 oz. No. 8. Improved cylinder bore at 25 yards. Average pattern: 70-75%.

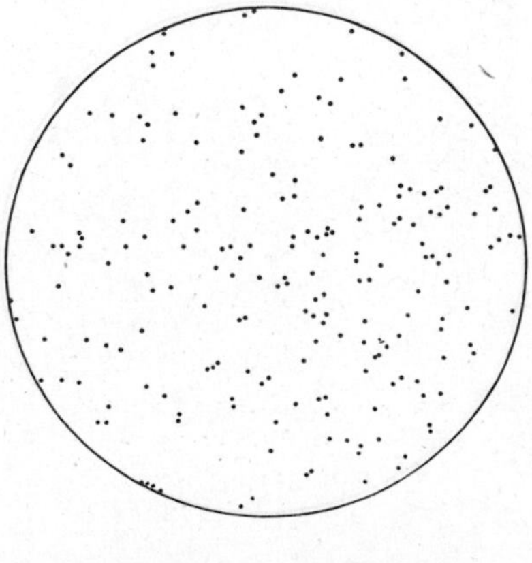

PLATE XVII. 20 ga. Xpert—2½ dr.—1 oz. No. 8. Improved cylinder bore at 35 yards. Average pattern: 50-55%.

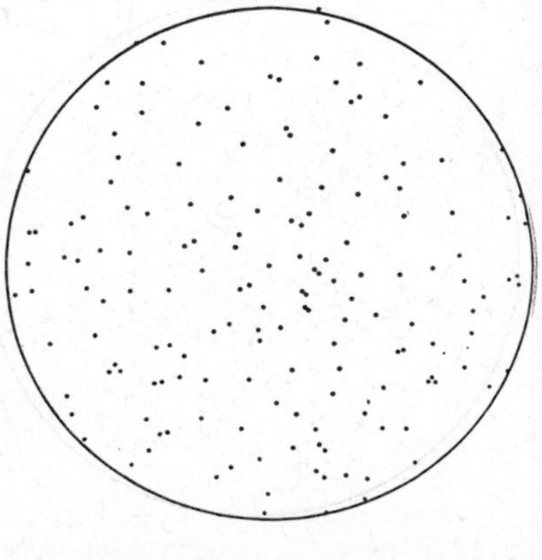

PLATE XVIII. 20 ga. Xpert—2½ dr.—1 oz. No. 8. Improved cylinder bore at 40 yards. Average pattern: 40-45%.

The following patterns were made with the .410 gun, chambered for the 3-inch shell, and bored full choke. The load used was "Super-X" (long range), employing 3/4 ounce of No. 7½ shot. These patterns will come as something of a surprise to those who are inclined to scoff at the sub-small-gauge shotgun. The first pattern, made at 20 yards, indicates how close this gun will shoot, and also indicates the need for "close" holding on the part of the shooter. The pattern at 30 yards, however, is excellent, and at 40 yards the pattern is surprisingly good for a gun this small.

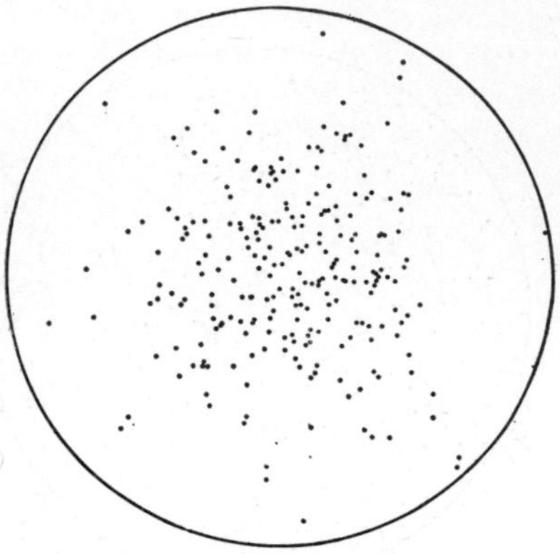

PLATE XIX. 410 ga. 3" Super-X—3/4 oz. No. 7½. Full choke at 20 yards. Average pattern: 93-97%.

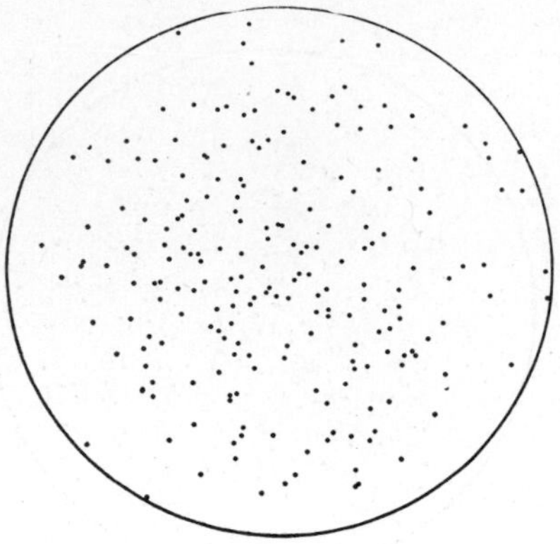

PLATE XX. 410 ga. 3" Super-X—3/4 oz. No. 7½. Full choke at 35 yards. Average pattern: 80-85%.

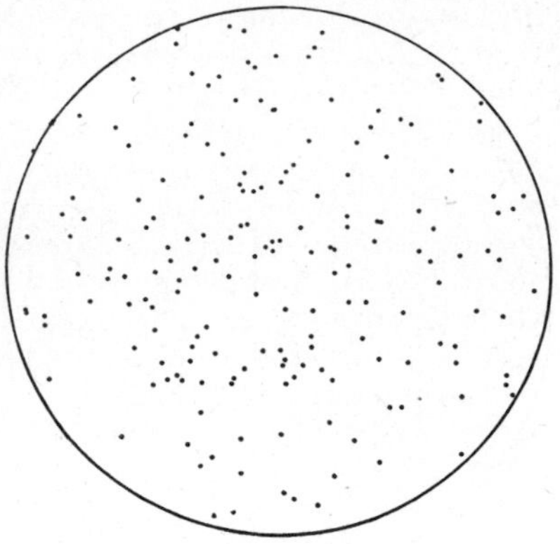

PLATE XXI. 410 ga. 3" Super-X—3/4 oz. No. 7½. Full choke at 40 yards. Average pattern: 68-73%.

The following patterns were made with the .410 gun, chambered for the 2½ inch shell, bored "Skeet No. 1." The load used was "Super-X," employing ½ ounce of No. 9 shot. The first pattern, at 20 yards, is excellent, and the 30-yard pattern is far from thin. At 40 yards, however, the pattern falls somewhat short of "satisfactory" for the average shooter.

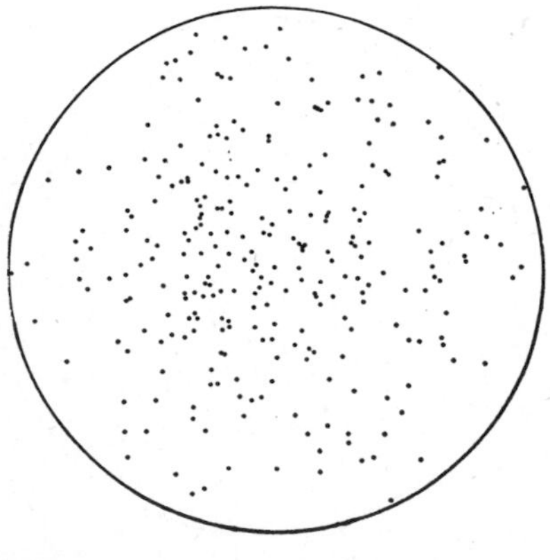

PLATE XXII. 410 ga. 2½" Super-X—½ oz. No. 9. Skeet No. 1 at 20 yards. Average pattern: 80-90%.

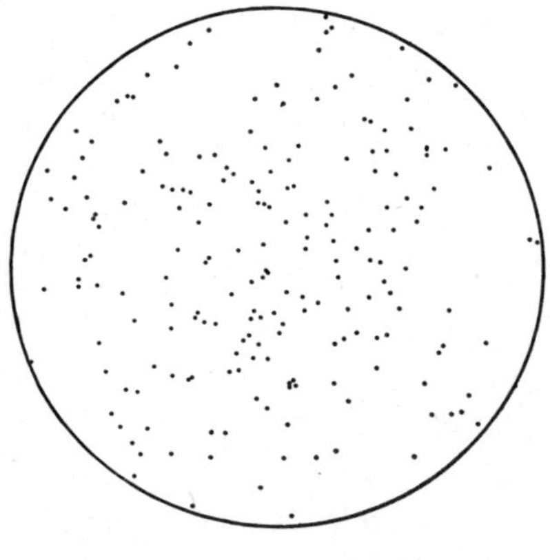

PLATE XXIII. 410 ga. 2½" Super-X—½ oz. No. 9. Skeet No. 1 at 30 yards. Average pattern: 53-60%.

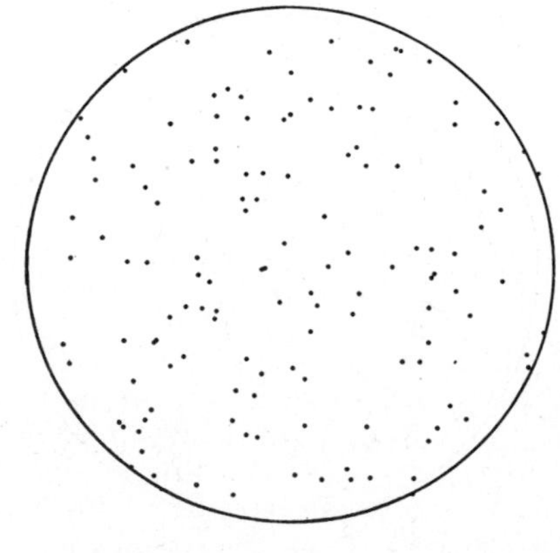

PLATE XXIV. 410 ga. 2½" Super-X—½ oz. No. 9. Skeet No. 1 at 40 yards. Average pattern: 40-45%.

# SHOTGUN FIT

**Stock Fit.** The shotgun that *fits* pays for itself in two or three seasons of shooting. This statement is based entirely on a financial computation, and does not take into consideration the matter of personal pride and satisfaction that accompanies accurate shooting.

The man who is going to spend several hundred dollars on a shotgun normally makes his purchase from a shop that has at least one experienced clerk who will insure that the expensive gun will fit the buyer. However, not every American sportsman can afford to spend such a sum on his sport. The expensive gun will be turned out to the buyer's exact specifications, but the standard-grade shotgun is designed to fit the *average* shooter, and, regardless of the maker, conforms to a *standard* of pull, drop at comb, pitch, and drop at heel. This gun could not be turned out by the manufacturer at its present price if turned out on special order. The manufacturers have done the next best thing: They have produced a gun of stock dimensions that permit alterations to be made at slight cost to the buyer.

A survey by one large gun shop indicated that of those who bought standard-grade shotguns, fewer than 30 per cent were properly fitted. You may be one of that lucky percentage, but if you are not, the few dollars you spend with a good gunsmith in having the stock altered will not only save you money but will add immeasurably to the pleasure you get in the use of the gun.

If your arm is an inch shorter or longer than the average, if your neck is longer or shorter, if the distance from your shoulder to your eye varies from the average, the chances are that a few minor alterations to the stock of your shotgun will pay dividends. Instead of running an average of one kill to five shots fired, there is a possibility of bringing your average up to one kill for three shots fired, and this alone would cut your ammunition costs down 40 per cent, to say nothing of the personal satisfaction you receive as a result of more accurate shooting.

Plate I shows the various terms employed in shotgun measurement. The standard-grade shotgun is made according to the following dimensions: length of pull, 14 inches; drop at comb, 1½ inches; at heel, 2½ inches; and the pitch normally is 2 inches down.

So far as pitch is concerned, the average shooter can ignore it, for stock alterations can be made to compensate for the change required off standard.

Suppose, for example, you have followed the rule-of-thumb method of buying a standard shotgun, having never owned one and being unfamiliar with the importance of fit. Having arrived home, unwrapped the gun, and moved out to the back yard, you decide to see how it "comes up."

You hold the gun at "ready" as you have seen others do, and try to snap it to your shoulder. Much to your surprise, the heel catches your coat. Or perhaps, having brought it up, you find it is necessary to pull it back to your shoulder. In the first instance, it is too long in the stock, or pull. In the second instance, it is too short. If it is too long, the normal tendency, in snap shooting, will be to shoot to the left. If it is too short, the tendency will be to shoot to the right.

When you drop your cheek to the comb, you find you are not looking along the barrel, but down upon it, which will result in your shooting high, which means the comb is too high for you. If the comb is too low, it will result in your shooting under the target, and also will result in slowing down your speed. Most shooters prefer a comb to err on the high rather than the low side.

**Alterations.** You now have discovered that the gun does not fit you properly, but you do not know just what changes must be made or the extent of these changes.

If the stock is too short, the problem is simple. You can select a rubber recoil pad that not only will bring the stock length out but will absorb some of the punch of the gun (see Plate IV). If it is too long, any good cabinetmaker will cut it down for you at a nominal cost.

But as yet you do not know just how much alteration is necessary, and you cannot determine this without the expenditure of a few shells. There is always the possibility that the alterations should include a change of the angle of the heel and toe. The comb may be just right, but the pitch may be wrong. A numer of shots at a patterning sheet will give the answer. If you are shooting low consistently, despite the fact that the comb seems just right and the stock length or pull is correct, a slight change in the angle at the heel may be the only alteration

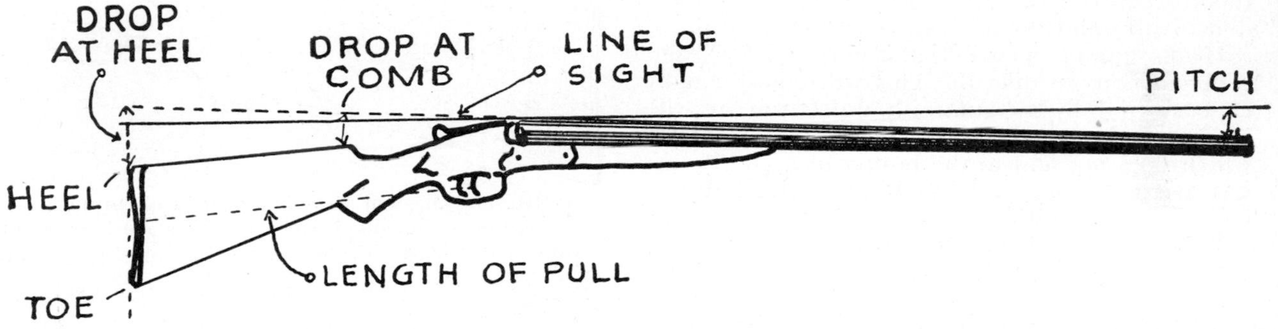


PLATE I. This diagram illustrates the method of determining the various measurements to insure shotgun "fit."

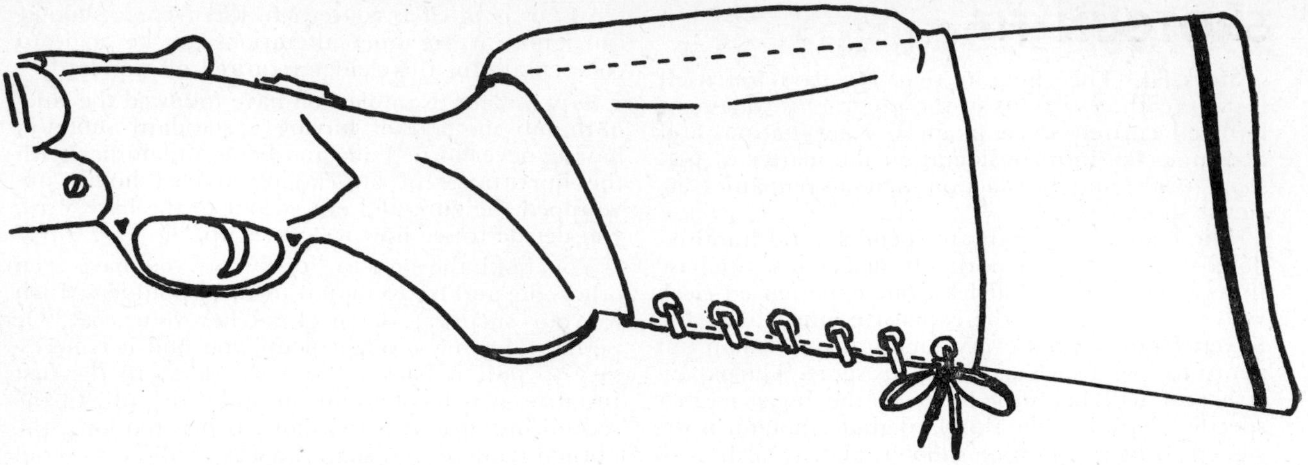

PLATE II. This diagram shows the laced sleeve which may be used to raise the comb. The shooter with the "glass jaw" who suffers as a result of recoil often prefers the sleeve to a high wooden comb.

necessary. Have the gunsmith or cabinetmaker take from 3/8 to 1/2 inch off at the heel (see Plate III). It is better to take off too little than too much on the first cut. It is easy to cut a stock down, but more difficult to build it up.

If your gun has a comb that is much too low, your problem is more difficult. This will entail a more expensive job by the gunsmith, unless you are willing to put up with a comb sleeve (see Plate II), which does not add to the beauty of a gun, but is just as satisfactory as the more expensive build-up job by the gunsmith.

Before you have any alterations done, it would be best to seek the advice of an experienced shooter or a good gunsmith. An experienced gunsmith, after watching you throw the gun to your shoulder a few times, can just about determine the changes that will be necessary to insure a proper fit.

Some gunsmiths have "try guns," which will eliminate much of the guesswork in the fitting. These guns are equipped with a variety of hinges and extensions, and can be adjusted to fit any shooter. When the correct adjustment has been made, measurements are taken of the pitch, pull, drop at comb and drop at heel, and the variations from standard are easily determined.

The cost of altering the standard shotgun to fit the shooter normally will range from about $2 to $15, depending entirely upon the extent of the alterations and the prices charged by the local gunsmith. Many shooters have home workshops, and if they have even normal skill with tools many of the alterations can be done without cost.

Regardless of the cost, however, a shotgun that fits is worth the price. If you can go in a shop, pick up a shotgun from the rack, raise it to your shoulder, drop your cheek to the comb as it comes up and look straight down the barrel, you are fortunate. The manufacturers of the American shotgun offer you a sound, well-balanced, well-stocked, safe and sturdy gun at about one-quarter the price you would pay for a similar product in any other country in the world. If you are able and willing to pay more for a gun stocked to your specifications they can provide it, but the average shooter will find it much cheaper to have his "standard"-grade gun altered to fit.

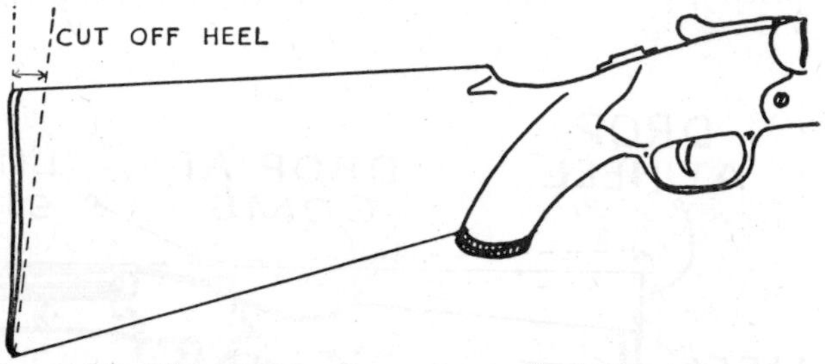


PLATE III. This diagram shows the method of cutting down the "heel" of a shotgun. Do not take this much of a cut initially, but take a little at a time to insure proper fit.

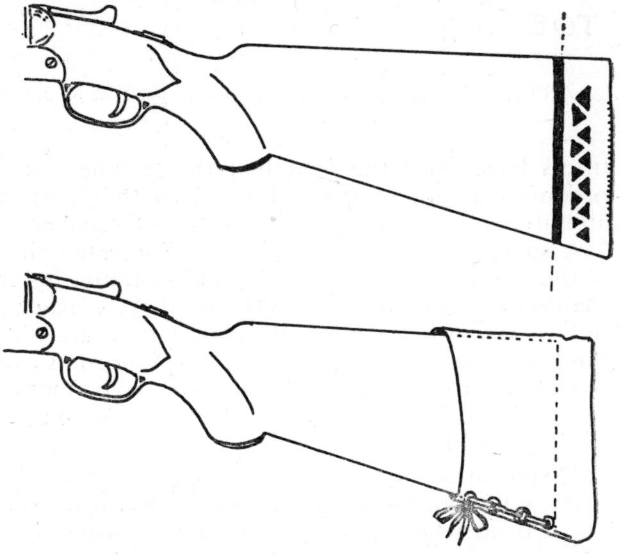

PLATE IV. This diagram shows a method of increasing the length of the stock by the use of a rubber recoil pad (*upper*) and by a "sleeve" or "boot."

Many shooters, having decided to buy an extra gun just for waterfowl shooting, measure their upland gun and have the new gun altered to conform with it, or else they order a gun to those specifications. In doing this, they forget that in the normal course of events they wear much heavier clothing when duck shooting, and that this extra padding calls for a shorter stock and pull. This difference may amount to only a half-inch, but it is an important half-inch.

# SHOTGUN SHOOTING

## I. ENGINEERING YOUR SHOOTING

**1. The Snap Shot.** Shotgun shooting is a sport of controlled relaxation, remarkably like golf in its mental and physical requirements.

It is not necessary to be a mental or physical giant in order to shoot well. You need merely to exercise normal control over both mind and body in order to master the fundamentals of wing shooting. Wing shooting demands co-ordination of feet, legs, hips, shoulders, arms, hands, head, and eyes, all to the end of doing one specific thing with a mechanical appliance at a definite split-second of time.

It has been proved that a good instructor can make an excellent "businessman golfer" out of any normal individual who is willing to engineer his golf—who will devote the necessary thought to the mastery of the fundamentals of golf, and thereafter apply a reasonable expenditure of time and energy toward continued improvement in the mechanics of the game.

The same thing may be accomplished in wing shooting with the shotgun. The proper way to begin is with pencil and paper. By means of simple diagrams, ordinary shooting situations can be dramatized, with each mental and physical process definitely assigned to its proper place in the continuity. Proceeding in this manner, the importance of each step can be evaluated, lost motion eliminated, the number of variables reduced to the minimum—in short, your shooting will be engineered.

The fundamentals of good wing shooting were mastered years ago when muzzle-loading shotguns had been improved to the point of reasonable reliability. Through the past half-century, many excellent works on the art of wing shooting have been circulated widely. Yet, within the current decade, the practice of applying cold analysis to business and personal problems has become so widespread as to be almost universal. The analytical approach to any problem now is regarded as the only proper treatment to insure a satisfactory solution. Hence, the short cut to better shooting presented herein does represent something new in technique. After all, it is somewhat revolutionary to enter upon a shooting career armed only with pencil and paper.

Even the "natural" shooter, endowed with good eyes, a fine physique, and healthy nerves may be able to find something helpful on these pages. Fallacies bearing upon shooting technique are being dispelled almost every day on some skeet field or trapshooting ground. Perhaps in the release of the mind from some minor detail, heretofore considered important, lies that additional fraction of a percentage point in competitive shooting that has separated some shooter from a winning average.

Conversely, perhaps a merely average shooter suddenly will become a star through stumbling upon some point which previously had seemed inconsequential, but which, when properly evaluated, furnished the spark leading to the heights of stellar performance. One young trapshooter, for example, became a star at handicap trapshooting, merely because it occurred to him over night that he might improve his long-range handicap by "pointing them out."

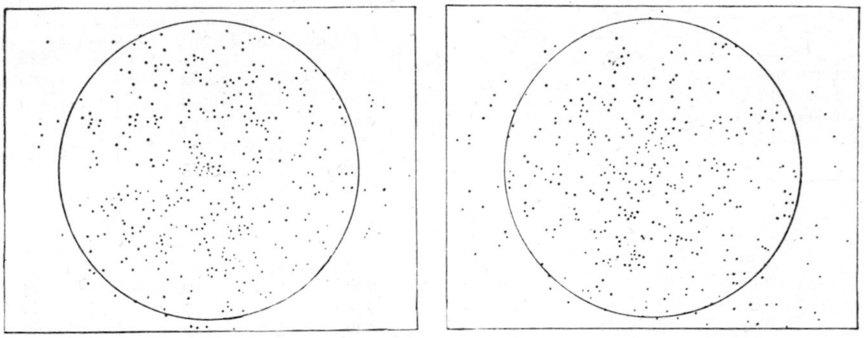

PLATE I. This figure shows how the boring of a shotgun barrel controls the pattern spread at a given distance from the muzzle of the gun. The pattern on the left was fired with an improved cylinder barrel at 20 yards. The pattern on the right was fired with a full-choke barrel at 40 yards. Without counting the pellets or computing pattern percentages, casual inspection shows that each pattern completely filled a 30-inch circle with no open or blank spots through which a target might escape.

As a start toward engineering your problem, get a clear picture of the basic mechanics of wing shooting. Reduced to the simplest terms, wing shooting consists of releasing one moving object with the purpose of intercepting in flight another moving object, within the effective range of your shotgun. Do not, for the present, concern yourself with further details.

Now visualize the easiest shot possible in wing shooting. Suppose you mounted a crossbow on the top of your shotgun, attaching the release to the trigger of the gun so that the bow would release a clay target a fraction of a second before the gun fired. The charge from the gun, moving more rapidly than the target, would overtake the mark before the force of gravity had begun to pull down the target from its horizontal flight. The nature of the target and the method of its release remove any and all variables from the shooting problem involved. There simply is not any problem, because there are no variables involved. You could stand up all day, pull the trigger, break the target, and repeat—no variation, no misses, no fun. There is no work for the brain, no job for the eye, nothing for the feet and legs and hips—just a mere routine of the hands and arms, reduced to ridiculous simplicity because there is no possible chance for human error.

Now contrast the simplest possible shot in wing shooting to one supposedly the hardest—and don't forget to do your contrasting with pencil and paper. Suppose you are standing in a field with a gun in your hands. Suddenly a target appears, moving from left to right across your front at a speed of 60 miles an hour or 88 feet per second. The first glimpse of the flying object tells your mind it is going places. You remember your definition of wing shooting, and you want to hit that target by releasing the object which you control—the shot-charge—upon such a line of flight that the target will be intercepted. Lacking an acquired technique—or shooting form—you would have to make certain mental calculations and put into effect certain physical reactions to these calculations. What would you do?

First, you would estimate the distance from your position to the approximate line of flight of the target—say 20 yards as about comparable to the mid-field shots at skeet. Your reason would tell you that in order to direct the shot-charge at some point far enough ahead to intercept the target, you would have to face in that direction. You shift your feet so as to be able to point the gun.

Second, having shifted your feet, you would point

TABLE SHOWING TIME OF FLIGHT VALUES FOR VARIOUS GAME BIRDS, SHOT SHELL LOADS, AND CLAY TARGETS

| | 20 yds. 60 ft. | 30 yds. 90 ft. | 40 yds 120 ft. | 50 yds. 150 ft. | 60 yds. 180 ft. |
|---|---|---|---|---|---|
| GAME BIRDS | Time of Flight in Seconds | | | | |
| Duck @ 95 ft. per second.............. | .632 | .948 | 1.262 | 1.580 | 1.895 |
| Goose @ 80 ft. per second.............. | .750 | 1.125 | 1.500 | 1.880 | 2.250 |
| Mallard @ 70 ft. per second.............. | .857 | 1.289 | 1.714 | 2.143 | 2.571 |
| Grouse @ 48 ft. per second.............. | 1.250 | 1.872 | 2.50 | 3.13 | 3.750 |
| Quail @ 72 ft. per second.............. | .834 | 1.250 | 1.675 | 2.085 | 2.50 |
| Shot Shell Loads | | | | | |
| 12 Gauge — Inst. Velocity | | | | | |
| 3 —1⅛—9C ............940 over 25 yds. | .058 | .101 | .154 | .221 | .300 |
| 3 —1¼—7½C ..........850 " 40 " | .059 | .096 | .140 | .194 | .259 |
| Max.—1¼—4C ...........1015 " 40 " | .052 | .082 | .117 | .160 | .205 |
| Max.—1¼—6C ............975 " 40 " | .053 | .086 | .123 | .166 | .214 |
| Max.—1¼—7½C ..........940 " 40 " | .054 | .087 | .129 | .175 | .230 |
| 16 Gauge | | | | | |
| 2½—1 —9C ............900 over 25 yds. | .062 | .106 | .160 | .229 | .318 |
| Max.—1⅛—4C ............965 " 40 " | .052 | .087 | .121 | .164 | .209 |
| Max.—1⅛—6C ............925 " 40 " | .053 | .089 | .129 | .172 | .227 |
| Max.—1⅛—7½C ..........890 " 40 " | .055 | .090 | .135 | .182 | .240 |
| 20 Gauge | | | | | |
| 2¼—⅞—9C .............890 over 25 yds. | .064 | .109 | .164 | .233 | .322 |
| Max.1 oz.—4C ...........940 " 40 " | .052 | .089 | .127 | .172 | .217 |
| Max.—1 oz.—6C .........900 " 40 " | .054 | .092 | .133 | .178 | .231 |
| Max.—1 oz.—7½C .........865 " 40 " | .057 | .094 | .138 | .188 | .248 |

(Skeet velocities are for cylinder bore guns over 25 yards. All other velocities are over 40 yards in full choke guns.)

CLAY TARGETS

| | Distance of Clay Bird from Trap | Velocity in Foot Seconds | Time of Flight in Seconds |
|---|---|---|---|
| Slow Bird—35 Yards ............ | at 0 yards | 70 | 0.0 |
| | " 20 " | 34 | 1.3 |
| | " 25 " | 30 | 1.8 |
| | " 30 " | 28 | 2.3 |
| | " 34 " | 26 | 2.8 |
| Regulation Clay Bird—50 Yards .. | " 0 " | 85 | 0.0 |
| | " 20 " | 47 | 1.0 |
| | " 25 " | 43 | 1.3 |
| | " 30 " | 40 | 1.7 |
| | " 50 " | 31 | 3.4 |
| Fast Bird—56 Yards ............ | " 0 " | 96 | 0.0 |
| | " 20 " | 52 | 0.9 |
| | " 25 " | 47 | 1.2 |
| | " 30 " | 43 | 1.5 |
| | " 50 " | 35 | 3.1 |
| | " 56 " | 34 | 3.6 |

PLATE II.

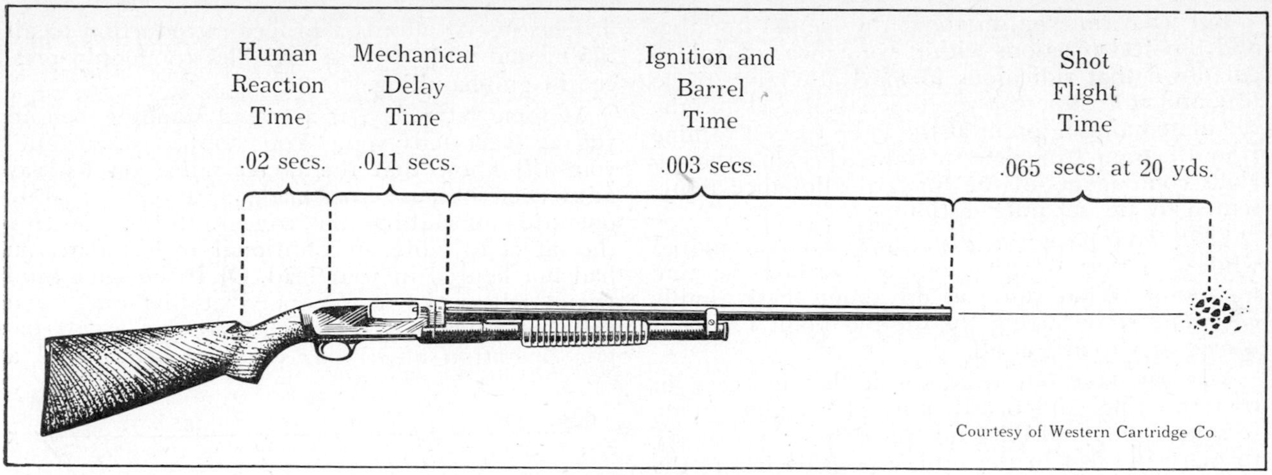


PLATE III.

your gun—or "mount" it, if you prefer to be technically correct. You are careful to see that the gun is pointing at the exact spot you have selected for the coincidence of the line of flight of the two moving objects.

Third, you would pull the trigger, releasing the shot-charge.

Fourth, you would hold your position, looking intently at that mathematical crossing point in mid-air, waiting to see the target crash into bits upon impact with the shot-charge.

Now, having thought out what you would have to do to put the charge on the target by mere mathematics, take your pencil and draw a diagram like that in Plate IV. Sketch by successive steps just what the target was doing while you were getting all set to end its meteoric flight.

First—corresponding to your initial movement in facing the direction of fire—you compute by mathematics that the target was moving approximately 18 feet while you were getting set. You remember from some former personal efficiency test that it requires approximately one-fifth of a second in reaction time to do most of the things we try to do in the biggest hurry. Mark a section of 18 feet long in the path of the target in the direction of its flight, which is how far the target will move in one-fifth second.

Next, mark off another section 18 feet long, adjoining the first section, and representing the distance the target moved while you were pointing the gun.

Again, mark off a third section 18 feet long, adjoining the second section you have just sketched in, to represent the distance the target moved while you were pressing the trigger. As you mark off with your pencil, you will have the consolation of knowing you are right in this calculation, because repeated tests with an electrical timer have demonstrated the average reaction time of shooters—the "lag" between the willing of the shot and the actual release of the trigger—to be approximately $\frac{1}{5}$ (0.20) second. Actually, the time ranges between 0.16 and 0.25 second for normal persons of all ages.

Finally, you compute that the shot-charge will require approximately $\frac{1}{15}$ second to reach the crossing point with the path of the target. You make this calculation on the basis of an average shot-charge velocity of 900 feet per second over your original estimated range of 20 yards. In this period of time, the target has moved up approximately 6 feet to the crossing point.

Now, add up the four figures representing the travel of the target while you were doing the things necessary to put the shot-charge in the proper place to intercept it.

You will find the target has moved a total distance of 60 feet—and then you realize that you couldn't hit it, after all. The target moved as far along its path as your original estimate of the range. It would be impossible, you reason, to pick out a spot in the air 60 feet ahead of a rapidly moving object at such close range—or any other range, for that matter. You actually would have to turn your back to the target while you were getting in position. Unless you were blessed with eyes in back of your head, you couldn't see the target and the point of aim at the same time.

Yet, a shooting problem such as this is being solved correctly thousands of times every day in the year. You have only to go out to some skeet field and watch the boys break the high-house target from Number 5 position to know that it can be done, and is being done right along. If they can do it, so can you.

With your diagram before you, check each mental impulse and its corresponding physical reaction in the entire sequence represented on your chart. You find that the target was sailing merrily along for a distance of 54 feet while you were willing and accomplishing three specific actions necessary to discharge the gun along a definite line of sight. The target moved 6 feet more while the shot was getting out where the target was supposed to be.

It occurs to you right here that time of flight of the shot-charge is one factor you can't do anything about. Arms and ammunition manufacturers have done their best, but until it is possible to load a shotgun with light rays capable of disintegrating a target, there will always be a time-of-flight factor to be reckoned with. The 6 feet the target moves while the shot-charge is getting out to it must stay in the diagram, at least for the present.

But what can you do about the mental impulses and physical reactions within your own control, to cut down that ridiculous forward allowance of 60 feet, and at least permit you to see the target and the calculated aiming point at the same time? Examine your diagram from left to right, checking the various components of the forward allowance represented by the separate sections.

First, you have the distance the target moved while you were shifting your feet to face the aiming point. What can you do about that? Simply *eliminate it* by facing the aiming point before it is necessary to aim at all.

You can take our word for it that in skeet, in trap shooting, and in all other clay target games, it is not only possible but ABSOLUTELY NECESSARY to place the feet in the proper position before the target is trapped. Secure in this knowledge, cross out the 18 feet representing target travel while you were getting set. Then on to the next operation.

The target moved another 18 feet while you were mounting your gun. Here you have a different type of problem, not only from the mechanical standpoint, but according to the rules of the various shooting games. In skeet and field shooting, you will have your gun down, with the stock below your forearm. In trapshooting, it will be up—in the mounted position. But assuming that you go into action with your gun down, what can you do about that 18 feet of target travel while you are pointing the gun?

There doesn't seem to be anything you can do about it until you consider the act of pointing the gun in connection with the next and most important step in the sequence—pressing the trigger.

Why not combine the two mental processes into a decision *to shoot,* rather than make a decision to point the gun, followed by a second decision to press the trigger?

It sounds complicated at first, but it isn't: You may have read somewhere that experts with the revolver can draw from a holster and deliver an aimed shot in one-fifth of a second. Your reason tells you that if they willed the movements of drawing and firing as separate impulses, their minds could not work fast enough to bring about the actual result in the required time.

Common sense thus dictates that these handgun artists must combine the two mental processes into one. If they can do this, you can, simply and easily. In any type of shooting with your gun in the down position, you must learn to hold it at the ready always, and mount it only when you have determined to shoot. This trains your mind in willing the shot as a single impulse.

When you can do that—and you have our word for it that you can, within reasonable limitations—you have cut down the forward allowance necessary to hit that same target to a mere 24 feet. You have also done something else: You have worked out for yourself the most difficult of all shotgun-pointing techniques—the so-called *snap shot.*

Snap shooting is the approved method of bagging fast-flying upland game where rapid gun-handling follows the unexpected appearance of a target. You were asked to analyze snap shooting first because it affords a proper introduction to all the mental and physical variables commonly present in gun-handling.

At some later day, if a friend standing behind you at skeet tells you, "You stopped your gun!" you will know that the target sailed on its way untouched because you made a second, separate operation of pulling the trigger, thus permitting the target to move an additional 18 feet that you had not figured in your lead. Or if the same kind friend tells you, "You popped at that one!" you will know that you mounted your gun as a separate operation after your eye had determined a

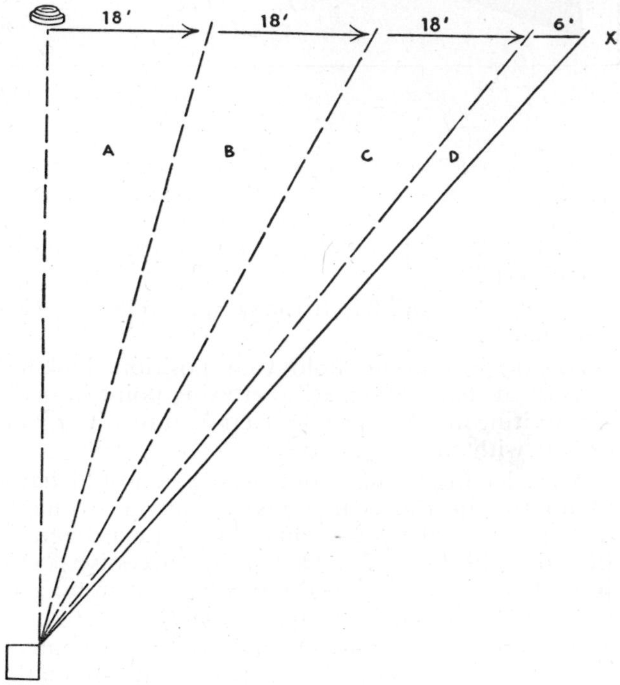


PLATE IV.

line of aim, again permitting the target to get 18 feet of jump on you.

So ends the first lesson. Yet you have not done a thorough job of analyzing shotgun shooting—even with pencil and paper—if you stop here.

**II. Pointing Out.** No thinking person who has started to whittle down a theoretical lead of 60 feet is going to be content with a reduction to 24 feet. You can see much daylight through an orifice 24 feet wide only 60 feet away. You realize it must be something of a feat to place an approximate 24-inch or 2-foot circle—representing the approximate diameter of the shot pattern at 20 yards—on the target in exactly the right place, if you have to deal in forward allowances equivalent to one-third or more of the actual range. So you begin to look about for a method of further reducing forward allowance, and you find it in "pointing out."

You feel that if you can reduce your forward allowance to the mere time of flight of the shot-charge, you can hit more consistently. You are now on the high road to becoming a pointer-outer of the first degree. You can do the trick merely by adding one more impulse to that mental command to fire which is already controlling two other physical reactions. Here is what you must do:

(1) Mount the gun to your shoulder.

(2) Press the trigger to release the shot-charge.

(3) Swing the gun muzzle in a horizontal arc, at exactly the same apparent speed as the movement of the target, and maintaining a forward allowance in advance of the target which you have mentally calculated to be equal to the forward movement of the target during the time of flight of the shot-charge.

If this sounds a bit complicated, just remember that a single mental process controls the three physical reactions required to produce a definite result. Once having received the go-ahead signal

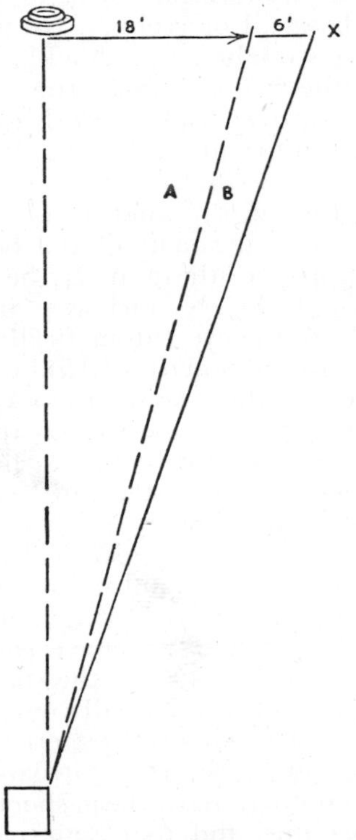


PLATE V.

from the brain, every member of the body concerned in the business of pointing and discharging the gun becomes automatically subservient to the eye. In effect, the brain tells the eye, "Get that gun muzzle out ahead of the target, and keep it there until the charge lets go!"

Once having received these general instructions from the brain, the feet, legs, hips, shoulders, arms, hands, and head can proceed with their respective jobs *at the same time,* all co-ordinated by the eye.

Now look at a diagram of the "pointing out" system, as shown in Plate V. You know that the target is going to move 16 feet while the gun is being mounted. Therefore, it will be easier to catch up with the target and move the gun the required distance out in front if you begin to swing the gun in the direction of target movement at the very instant you begin to mount it. Merging the two operations of mounting and swinging into one smooth, rhythmic movement will remove any danger of a mental balk or block in changing from one operation to the other.

The ideal swing-and-mount motion will bring the gun muzzle to the line of flight of the target at exactly the proper forward allowance. At this point, the arc described by the gun muzzle levels off slightly to conform to the anticipated path of the target.

Further, the movement can be accomplished at one standard pace or rate of swing—the same rate of pace as the apparent speed of the target—if the gun is mounted while swinging. Otherwise, the rate of swing would have to be accelerated to catch up with the target and to pass it to the required lead. Then the speed of the swing would have to be retarded to the exact speed of the target in order to hold the proper lead. It follows that to swing the gun in a prescribed arc at one standard rate of pace will be easier to learn—and infinitely easier to remember—than to attempt to introduce two separate and distinct speeds into the operation. Accordingly, on the basis of your own analysis, you rewrite the three rules for "pointing out," as follows:

(1) Begin swinging the gun muzzle to the right at exactly the same rate or pace as the apparent speed of the target; *at the same time . . .*

(2) Begin mounting the gun without checking or altering the swing in any manner, with the object of bringing the line of sight to the path of the target at the proper forward allowance; *now:*

(3) Initiate the pressure on the trigger, by squeeze, slap, or whatever may be your preferred method, which will cause the gun to be discharged while in full motion, maintaining its proper forward allowance ahead of the target.

Now that you have progressed from a snap shooter to a pointer-outer, you will realize why the swing's the thing—in shooting as well as in golf. The two sports even have the same name for it—*timing.* If the golfer is getting his hands into the stroke ahead of his body, his timing is faulty. If the shooter is lagging too much in releasing the trigger, his timing also is off, and he is "riding out" his birds too far. All of this implies that "pointing out" is not an infallible system for producing perfect results. It is merely the next thing to it. No man ever lived who could hit them all But day in and day out, the system of "pointing out" will produce a better score or a bigger bag than any other. Another inspection of your diagram will show you why this is true.

So far, you have concerned yourself only with one possible shooting situation—a target crossing from left to right directly across your front. On your diagram, without changing the direction of the target, move the point representing your own position to the left and upward, so that the target, instead of crossing in front, moves away diagonally to the right front—a "right quartering" bird.

The same 6-foot line will indicate the movement of the target while the shot is getting out of it—but the line will be shortened to the eye by reason of the changed perspective, or the "obliquity." If you have drawn your diagram to scale, you will note that the proper forward allowance is reduced by the obliquity to approximately one-half at the shooter's eye.

At the same time, the apparent speed of the target decreases as the obliquity increases. It is a well-known principle of photography that it requires much greater speed in the lens to "stop" moving objects at right angles than when the movement is away from or toward the camera.

Taking your diagram corresponding to Plate V as the basis, now use several sheets of transparent paper, one to each supposed shooting position, and plot the lead necessary for various shots at different angles. In every case, let the 6-foot forward allowance remain constant, drawing a line from each end of this 6-foot section to the proposed new shooting position. The measure of the angle will then be the required lead *at the gun muzzle* to put the charge on the target.

It is not necessary or even advisable to measure the angles in degrees—merely compare the width of the angles at some given distance from the shooting position.

Figure out for yourself, why, if the target flying directly across your front requires the full lead of 6 feet, the target quartering away will require only approximately one-half the forward allowance necessary when the line of fire is perpendicular to the line of flight of the target.

Gradually work around to the point where the line of fire and the line of flight of the target coincide—the shooting position from which no forward allowance is necessary. Do NOT start at this point and work around to the position of full forward allowance, because then you will have no tangible value as a basis for your computations.

For all practical purposes, you can develop in your own mind a system of leading targets consisting of a series of tangible values based on unity and fractions thereof—full-lead, half-lead, quarter-lead, no lead. Remember that you have the spread of the shot-charge working for you to take care of any minor errors in computing the forward allowance. Usually you can err one-quarter of full-lead in computing the forward allowance and yet the pattern will take care of you.

Always, of course, play safe by estimating leads on the *long* side. The charge of shot from your gun will proceed through the air in an elongated cone, into which the target probably will fly if the lead is too great. However, a lead estimated too short invariably results in a miss. The target has no mathematical chance to fly into the shot-charge because the entire charge will pass behind it.

Work out these probabilities for yourself, still using transparent paper on your Plate V diagram. Assign to the shot-charge an arbitrary length of 10 feet, and, if you care to go to that trouble, figure out for yourself how much you can overestimate your lead and still hit the target. For practical purposes, it is necessary only to know that a lead overestimated by one-quarter of a full lead usually will hit the target, whereas a lead underestimated by the same amount may cause the shot-charge to pass behind the target, resulting in a complete miss.

After you have worked over your diagram several times, it will occur to you that you have not yet taken into consideration a lead over or under a target which is not maintaining level flight. Again common sense will come to your rescue in prompting you to lead rising or incoming overhead targets ABOVE, falling or outgoing overhead targets BELOW.

How will you know whether a target is rising or falling? Simply by the *apparent direction* of the flight of the target. In succeeding sections (p. 643 and p. 648) vertical as well as forward allowances will be treated in detail. It is enough to say here that the system of "pointing out" is the only system of gun-pointing that permits correction of both vertical and forward allowances. The gun swings along just ahead of the target. If the target dips, the gun can dip—and keep on swinging. If the target starts to fall, the gun can be lowered—and keep on swinging.

Don't forget that every shot in "pointing out" is a true swing—a physical movement on a pivot, just as in golf or baseball or croquet. No matter if the target is going straight away shoulder high—there will be a definite *swing* as you bring the gun into position. If the proper lead—as in this case—is zero, then the gun steadies and stops, rather than swinging on in its arc.

The whole theory of "pointing out" is PERFECT CONTROL of every movement of the body, and its mechanical appliance, the gun. If the target—as a startled grouse—suddenly increases its speed or changes direction, the eye automatically follows the target and the gun automatically follows the eye.

If the target—as a duck poised to look over the decoys—suddenly stops in midair, then the eye stops, the gun stops to maintain the proper line of sight—and the trigger is pulled just as automatically as in an orthodox swinging shot.

You have now gone to a great deal of trouble to build up a system of gun-pointing based on the necessary mathematical lead to bring the shot-charge upon the moving target. You have considered the distance the target moves until the shot-charge can reach it as a constant factor in all your calculations. You will learn, as your shooting experience develops, that "pointing out" is the most satisfactory method to use in trapshooting; in overhead shooting at ducks or driven pheasants, and its counterpart in target shooting, called "tower shooting."

**III. Swinging Past.** You can progress now to another system which is applicable to skeet shooting, to certain types of upland shooting (such as quail in open country), and to a lesser degree to hand trap shooting. This is the method of "swinging past."

The "swinging past" method is at its best in all types of shooting at close or medium range where the flight of the target is fixed along a definite path—in skeet shooting, for example. Skeet targets follow the same track, one after another, and do very little bobbing or ducking while the full power of the trap still urges them forward. About midway of their flight, they lose momentum, and consequently slow down to the point where air resistance, wind pressure, and gravity begin to affect them.

If your eyesight is normal and your physical reactions reasonably prompt, you can actually eliminate calculation of the forward allowance—merely by increasing the speed of the swing to a pace faster than the rate of progress of the target. Then, as the gun muzzle swings past the target, you press the trigger, sighting on the target itself. What happens is this:

The gun, moving in its own arc at a faster pace than the target, overtakes and passes it. The brain wills the command to pull the trigger at the exact instant the gun muzzle passes the target. In the one-fifth second required for the shooter to react to the mental command to fire, the gun continues to swing at its faster pace, and automatically builds up a forward allowance which is sufficiently exact for targets in stable flight.

Draw a diagram illustrating the "swinging past" method, as shown in Plate VI. Note that the time of

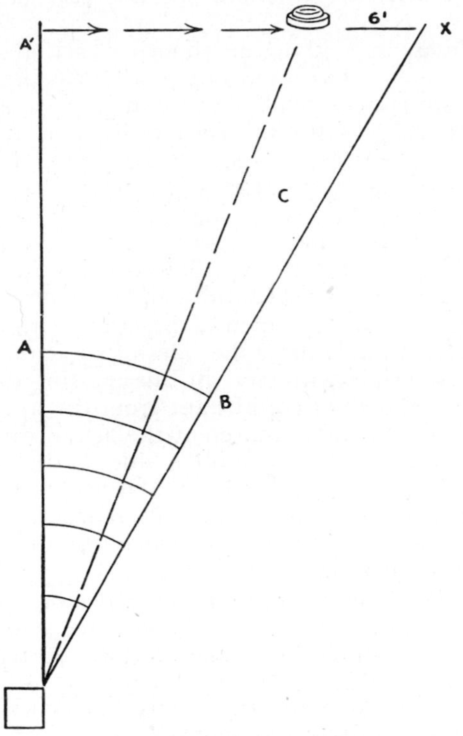


Plate VI.

flight of the shot-charge is definitely a factor; it has not been ignored or pushed out of the picture, by any means. Rather, the same mathematical lead representing target movement during the time of flight of the shot-charge is still the basis for the forward allowance, but the correction for trigger time—you recall it was *plus* in the case of snap shooting—becomes *minus* because the gun is swinging faster than the target. Trigger time is thus converted into forward allowance—just the reverse of your snap-shooting method.

The ideal timing under the "swinging past" system is achieved when the *minus* correction for faster gun swing exactly equals the *plus* correction of the estimated mathematical lead.

You have figured out for yourself that the mathematical lead changes with each change in direction of the target from your own position. Therefore, it will be necessary to change the pace of your swing under the "swinging past" system with each change in shooting position with respect to the path of the target, since speed of swing alone regulated lead under this system.

The big advantage claimed for "swinging past" is the fact that the trigger is pulled when the line of sight is exactly upon the target—a definite object—rather than a visualized aiming point a fixed relative distance away from the target. A big disadvantage, however, is the lack of a definite rule for regulating the speed of the gun swing. Again, sudden changes of direction of the target are difficult to detect with the faster swing required when "swinging past."

As your experience increases, you will be able to analyze your own shooting problems and definitely assign each type of shot to the proper system. Eventually the time will come—if you devote enough thought to your shooting—when you will be able to execute any shot by the most appropriate method of gun pointing—and without the slightest preparation! Just like pulling rabbits out of a hat!

**IV. The Vertical Clock.** One of the best plans for applying the proper pointing method is to visualize the old army method of the vertical clock. Imagine that the exact center of the clock face is the point in space immediately over your gun muzzle as you "face the shot." Then the *apparent* direction of the target can be flashed to the brain by the eye as a "2 o'clock" shot or a "5 o'clock" shot.

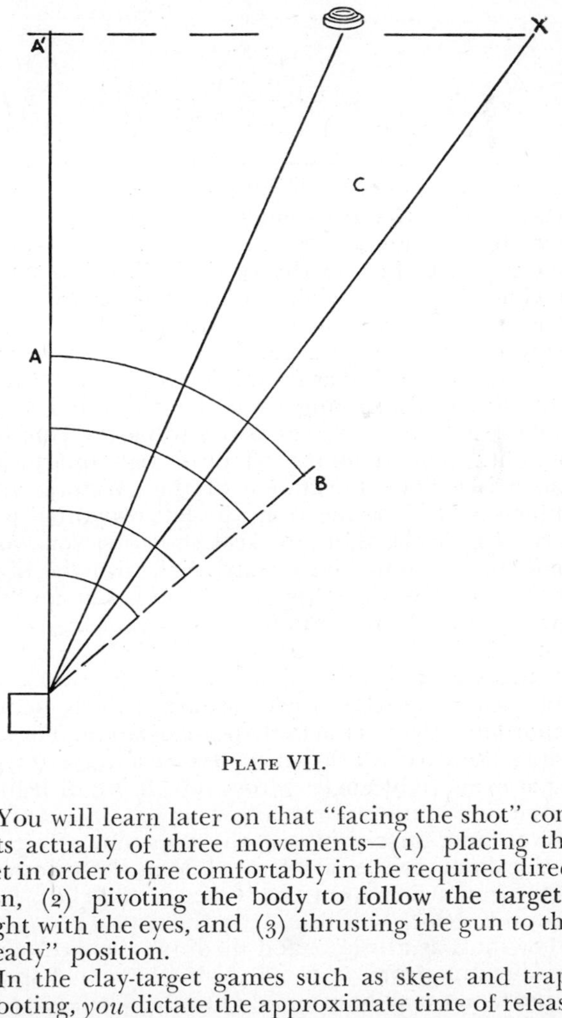


Plate VII.

You will learn later on that "facing the shot" consists actually of three movements—(1) placing the feet in order to fire comfortably in the required direction, (2) pivoting the body to follow the target's flight with the eyes, and (3) thrusting the gun to the "ready" position.

In the clay-target games such as skeet and trapshooting, *you* dictate the approximate time of release of the target. The fixed location of the trap regulates the point of beginning of the target's flight. Accordingly, your clock-face zero will be the point in space where you can expect the target to appear.

In game shooting, the time of appearance of the target and the direction of its flight will be beyond your control. You will merely snap into the ready position as the target appears suddenly before you. Your clock-face zero then will be a point on or near the line of flight of the target, usually the point—as in upland game shooting—where the fleeing bird or animal is recognized as a target. Thus, the eye must register the direction of the shot from this point onward along the path of the target.

In any kind of shooting, the zero of the clock face will be that point in space on or near the path of the target which serves as a beginning point for the eye

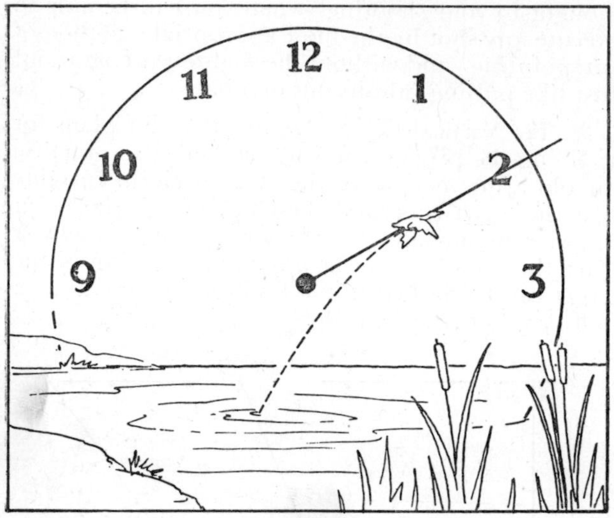


PLATE VIII.

in estimating the apparent direction and apparent speed of the target.

A 2-o'clock shot on the vertical clock is a target moving from left to right, and rising at an angle of about 30 degrees from the horizontal. The proper swing to produce the right forward allowance will move upward as well as from left to right. A 5-o'clock shot will be descending from the horizontal at an angle of about 60 degrees as it also moves from left to right. A quail taking off on a right-quartering course is a perfect example of the 2-o'clock shot, while a duck decoying from the left rear often produces a 5-o'clock shot. In skeet shooting, you work completely around the vertical dial, with the high-house bird at Station One as a 6-o'clock shot, and the low-house bird from Station Seven as a 12-o'clock shot.

Always bear in mind that the *apparent* direction and *apparent* speed of the target are of vastly greater importance than its actual speed of flight. For example, the 2-o'clock shot may involve a target traveling at exact right angles across your front, or it may be the right-quartering quail serving as the example above. Since in either case the apparent direction at the shooter's eye is the same, then the *direction* of the gun swing from the center of the clock face toward 2 o'clock will be exactly the same.

For shots at all short and medium distances with the shotgun—from 20 to 40 yards—the actual speed of the target may be ignored entirely. The *apparent* speed only need concern you, because at short and medium ranges, the velocity of the shot-charge is reasonably constant, and the relationship between the actual speed of the target and the velocity of the shot-charge remains—for all practical purposes—definite and fixed.

The eye quickly learns to estimate *apparent* speed along with *apparent* direction, and to combine both factors in its flash to the brain. After all, it is merely necessary for the eye to warn the brain that the swing of the gun must be fast, or slow, or in between, in order to overtake the target. The muscles of the body, responding to the urge of the brain, then go into action at somewhere near the proper speed to overtake and pass the target, using either the "pointing out" or "swinging past" methods. The speed of the swing is accelerated or retarded as the movement progresses, as a correction of the original estimate of the eye, with the apparent speed of the target as pacemaker.

In long-range shotgun shooting, actual target speed assumes vital importance. Whereas the speed of the target will remain constant, the velocity of the shot-charge will diminish rapidly with distance. The between-target and shot-charge speed will not be the same as 60 yards as at 40 yards. If the ratio remained the same, "swinging past" would be just as effective at the longer range as at the shorter, because the actual forward allowance at the target would increase in exact ratio with the range.

Prove this to your own satisfaction with pencil and paper. Merely draw the sides of an acute angle, and cut the sides with straight lines passing through points on the sides equidistant from the apex. Let one side of the angle represent the actual direction of the target in space, the other side the line of the shot-charge. Thus, while the angular lead or forward allowance at the gun remains the same, the actual lead in advance of the target increases in direct proportion to the range.

Much of the efficiency of high-speed shotgun loads is derived from their higher remaining velocity at long ranges, which thus make possible shorter leads than would be necessary with loads of ordinary velocity, such as skeet and trap loads. For many shooters, high-speed or long-range loads produce excellent results with the "swinging past" system, even at the extreme ranges of modern wildfowl shooting.

For the average shooter, however, "pointing out" is far more satisfactory at long and extreme ranges. "Pointing out," being essentially slower in pace than "swinging past," permits more exact correction of swing direction and swing speed, based upon the visible relationship between line-to-target and line-of-flight of the shot-charge. The eye actually estimates this distance in "pointing out." In "swinging past," there is no such estimation, the lead being entirely dependent upon speed of swing.

An excellent example of the difference between the two systems is afforded by the practice of many top-notch trapshooters in changing the method when changing from 16-yard to handicap targets. Although the difference between the 16-yard position and the longest handicap position—at 25 yards—is only 9 yards, many fine shots habitually use the "swinging past" method for 16-yard targets, but change to "pointing out" for handicap targets.

A good rule is to observe the distance at which you take your shots, in comparison with your shooting companions. If you are slower in "getting on" your targets, no doubt "pointing out" will be best for you until you learn to speed up your timing to deliver the shot in reasonably fast time. Then, and then only, will "swinging past" produce the best results.

## II. APPLYING YOUR KNOWLEDGE

**1. The Gun and the Target.** In the preceding section you have learned *what* you must do in order to hit flying targets successfully. It is necessary to know *what* to do in order to do it. *How* to do *what* you must do is now the order of business.

Changing over from a pencil to a shotgun may seem like a large order, particularly to beginners in the art of wing shooting. Many men who never learned to use a pencil can do things with a shotgun. However, if we cultivate the "feel" of a shotgun to the point where we are as familiar with its weight and balance as we are with the pencil's, then wing shooting need hold no mysteries for us.

Modern shotguns are built to inspire confidence. Their slim, streamlined beauty puts to shame the old fowling pieces with which Bogardus, Kimble, and many other famous wing shots achieved undying fame. One has only to "heft" a truly modern gun in his two hands to realize that it is a marvelous precision instrument, quite different from the crooked-stocked, sway-barreled implements which Bogardus and Kimble used. Yet Bogardus and Kimble developed a skill with their ancient weapons scarcely less phenomenal than that of many modern gunners.

The reason: practice, constant practice! The old masters had uncounted targets upon which to train their minds and bodies, ultimately achieving such perfect co-ordination that even their clumsy weapons appeared as feathers in their hands. Their shooting was principally at flying game, of which there was no lack before the opening of the twentieth century. On the other hand, the modern clay target and practical, efficient target traps were practically unknown in their day. They could not get in an automobile and drive in five minutes to a skeet field or trapshooting ground. They had to take the shooting game the hard way. It is really easy for us moderns, if we take it in our stride, don't worry about details, and persevere in practice until we achieve the same dexterity in gun handling that characterized the good shots of grandfather's day.

Summing up the problem of applying the knowledge of wing shooting you have already gained from the preceding pages, it must occur to you that modern arms and ammunition will assist you tremendously in becoming a good wing shot. You may even tell yourself, truthfully enough, that you have a big advantage over the old masters in the perfection of present-day guns and shot shells. Also, you have just as much opportunity to shoot as the old-timers, utilizing clay targets which an obliging attendant will throw for you in the same track until you conquer a difficult post at skeet or a sharp angle at the traps. Could any arrangement be more ideal—particularly when so many kindred spirits in the ranks of clay-target shooters stand ever ready to give you a lift with your shooting problems?

Your tendency at first will be to overdo—and this applies both to the novice and to the veteran fighting a new handicap. You will want to shoot too much at a time; you will over-control your gun, putting too much effort into the job to acquire a smooth, easy rhythm; and, perhaps, you will over-control mentally as well, fighting the game instead of playing it. After a few sessions, remembering never to keep on shooting until you grow tired, it will come a little easier. Finally, you will slip into the groove some day, perhaps unexpectedly.

If you continue on for any length of time without showing visible improvement, consult the arms or ammunition company representative in your community. He will be glad to devote just as much time to your problems as you do yourself—sometimes more. He will prove an invaluable aid in acquiring that smooth, easy swing, that is just as essential to success in shooting as in golf, swimming, or any other personalized sport. He will point out the lost motion, the overexertion, the fixed tensity that intrude to prevent perfect co-ordination between brain, eye, and body.

After all, you *know* that shooting is a game of controlled relaxation. The obvious purpose of relaxation is to assist co-ordination. A blocked brain, fixed eyes, and frozen muscles defeat co-ordination by preventing relaxation. From the instant you take your stance, and until the shot is delivered, smoothness must characterize your every mental process and physical reaction. Thus the proper way to approach your shooting is to resolve, first of all, not to do anything that will interfere with smoothness of swing.

One way to acquire smoothness of swing—and an excellent bridge for that gap between pencil and shotgun—is to practice a little "dry shooting" with a walking stick or some similar tubular object 3 or 4 feet long. If you or your neighbor own a playful terrier, draw him into the game. Try sighting the stick at the terrier as he plays around you, being careful to keep the end of the stick pointed exactly at your unwitting assistant. Notice how easy it is actually to see the tip of the stick and the terrier at the same time—how easily the tip of the stick follows every movement of the "target." If no terrier is available, simply sight the stick quickly at objects on the wall, shifting from one to the other as rapidly as your brain can will the movement and your eyes and hands can obey the command of the brain.

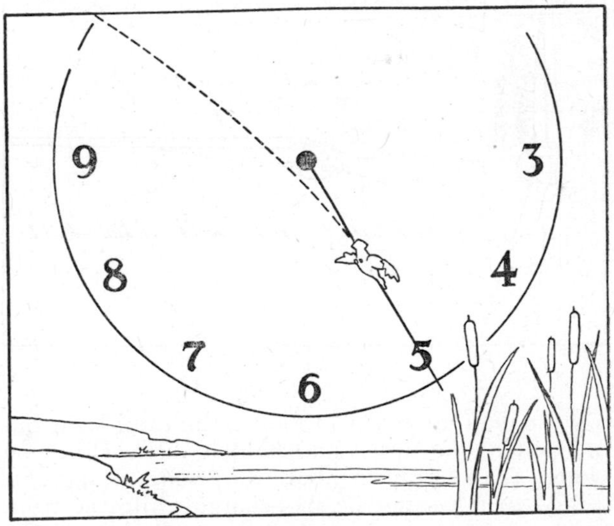


PLATE IX.

If, later on, you experience difficulty in lining up your shotgun on a moving target, remember your experience with the stick. *Then* there was no difficulty whatever in keeping both the target and the point of the stick in perfect alignment. You knew the end of the stick was right there where you wanted it. You were not worrying about releasing a trigger at the proper moment. No thought of "pointing out" or "swinging past" intruded upon your mental or physical processes. All you had to do was follow the target with the end of the stick, no matter how the target leaped or changed direction.

The smooth, easy following of a moving target with the muzzle of your shotgun is exactly the same thing as following the terrier with the stick. If you do not strain mentally or physically, it is really even easier. Your shotgun has a crook in it to make it line up easily with your eye. It has a straight edge in the form of a rib down the top of the barrel—or between the barrels if it is a double gun—that automatically guides your eye to the front sight. If you never learn anything else about wing shooting beyond following the target with the front sight, you will still break a lot of targets and bag a lot of game.

Remember, you have already learned that you must not stop following the target while you trip the trigger. That will give the target 18 feet, more or less, head start on the shot-charge. You will *not* be following the target if you stop your swing while you release the shot-charge. Call it "follow through," "calling your shot," or whatever you will—if the muzzle of your gun remains in smooth motion, following the target, until the shot-charge leaves the barrel, then in truth you will have mastered the one great problem in wing shooting.

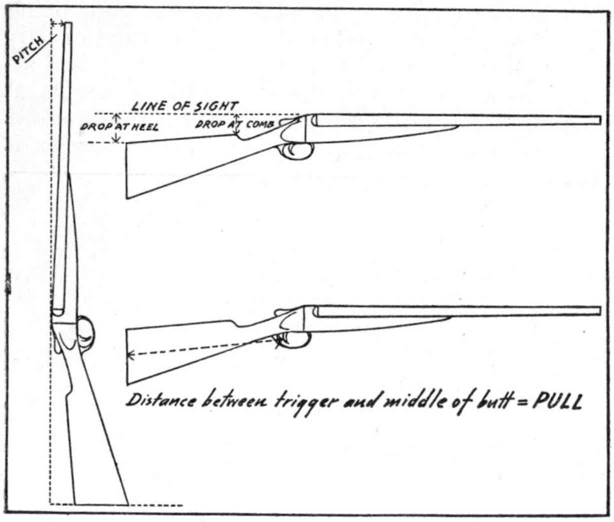


PLATE X.

True, you must learn to move the front sight out in front of the target and hold it there while you swing—as in "pointing out." Or, you will become skilled in releasing the shot-charge while the front sight is passing the target—as in "swinging past"—and in performing changes of *both* speed and direction of swing at the same time. These maneuvers will not bother you if you have learned to follow the target—just as the good golfer learns to keep his eye on the ball. Every golf pro knows that unless his pupil actually *sees* the club-head take the ball, he has merely hit it from memory while the eye was roving down the fairway. The same thing holds true in wing shooting. Unless you actually *see* the front sight—or at least the tip of the barrel or barrels—in juxtaposition with the target at the instant of release of the shot-charge, the shot was fired from memory, not by gun pointing.

If this be treason, make the most of it—and be wise. Listen patiently to those shooters who claim never to see—or even be conscious of—the front sight or gun muzzle when they release the shot-charge. They are absolutely honest in their statements. No doubt they have acquired such perfect co-ordination of mind, eyes, and body that they point their shotguns instinctively—like pointing the forefinger at an object without ever bringing the finger within range of the eye. They are the blessed of the shooting fraternity—but they win few championships. Listen to their theory, yes—but then sneak out and watch a trap or skeet champion in action.

If you watch a trapshooter, you will see him press his cheek on the stock just so, actually sight along the rib of his shotgun, and call for the target. Watch his head carefully. You will see him swing for the widest angle without ever disturbing the perfect alignment of the eye and front sight. When the front sight covers or precedes the target by exactly the right distance, he pulls the trigger.

The champion skeet shooter does exactly the same thing, except that he does it all after the target is in motion. Note carefully how quickly his cheek finds the stock, which was held below the elbow until the target appeared in the air. You suspect that he had no time to sight along the rib—but that he knew, during every inch of the swing, the exact position of his front sight or gun muzzle.

Your own observation of high-class shooters will thus convince you of the necessity of maintaining that perfect alignment of eye with front sight. You will note, too, that the eye finds its place above the rib by the sense of *feel* in the cheek—there is no such thing as looking at the stock to see where to put the cheek. Some shooters exaggerate this motion so that they resemble sandpipers in their dipping. Others merely slide the head forward quickly and smoothly—and find the stock waiting there. Whatever the motion, the effect is the same—to insure proper alignment of eye and gun muzzle.

This brings up the question of the proper fitting of your gun to permit your cheek to fall into exactly the same position each time you fire. Proper gun fit is the best way—if not the only way—to insure proper alignment of eye and gun muzzle. If you still see the front sight in the proper place, and yet miss the target, you can wager your chance at Paradise that you popped that one off "from memory"—with your head up and your cheek away from the stock. Just as "looking up" is the most common fault in golf, so is the lifting of the head the most common fault in shooting. There are many other ways to miss a target, some of them beyond your own control—but head-lifting has ruined more good scores than all other faults combined.

Be sure, above all else, that proper gun fit includes the shaping of the stock so that it will not hurt you when the gun is discharged. Such proper shaping depends upon the contour of your face, particularly the location and prominence of your jaw and cheek bones. If your face is a perfect "long oval" and your cheekbones not too prominent, perhaps a high "comb"—the portion of the stock coming in contact with the cheek—will serve you well. High, thin combs are of the English style—but they bang the cheekbones of many men. Low, rounded combs that fit under the cheekbone and line up against the fatty portion of the cheek are more in the American tradition—and serve just as well to line up the eye and front sight. Finally, a Monte Carlo comb may be needed to provide a fuller, rounder comb than either of the other types—with the added advantage of holding the eye at an exact level, whether the gun swing goes to left or right.

"Drop" and "pitch" are important elements in gun fitting, since they have an important bearing on the point of impact of the shot-charge out where the target is winging its way. Drop merely regulates the height at which the head is held in pointing the gun at the target. Persons with long necks and sloping shoulders require more drop to put the comb up against the cheek and the butt down against the shoulder. Normally-built persons should get along with as little drop as possible, since excessive drop may cause under-shooting if the butt happens to slide too far up on the shoulder.

No amount of drop—too much or too little—affects the point of impact at the target as does the pitch of the butt. The proper amount of pitch in a gun varies with the purpose for which it is intended. Field guns and skeet guns usually have more "pitch down" than trap and wildfowl guns, since the latter usually are used on rising targets, and a high point of impact is desirable. Proper points of impact for different kinds of shooting will be checked in succeeding paragraphs. It will serve here to say that height and shape of comb, drop, pitch, and length of stock—or "pull"—all have a definite bearing on the perfect alignment of eye and gun muzzle.

Be sure to consult an arms or ammunition trade representative or an experienced dealer at the outset

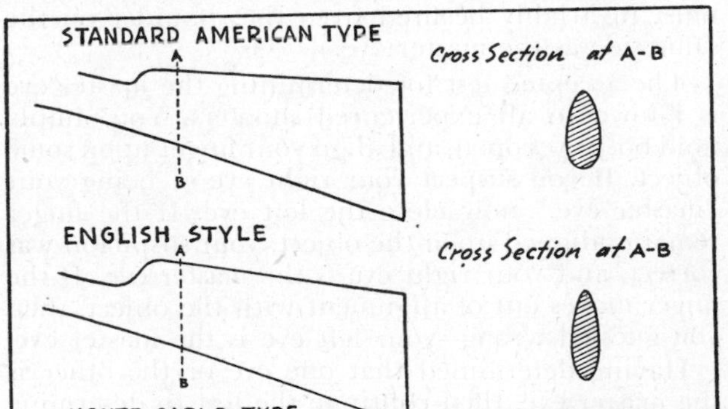

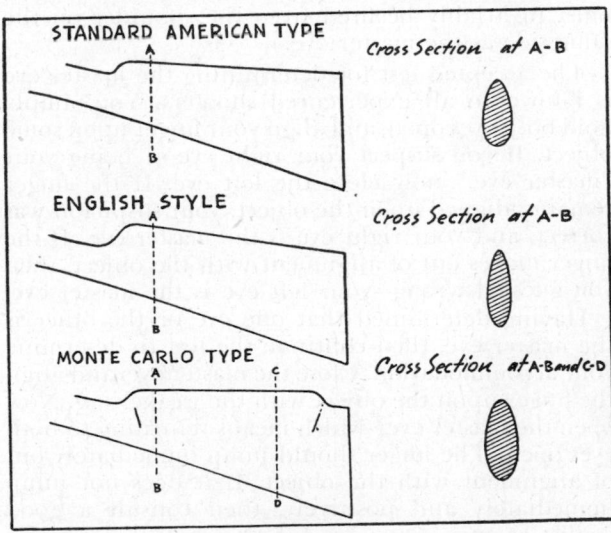

PLATE XI.

of your shooting career—likewise if you are an old-timer with a jinx. It is seldom necessary to order a specially-built stock. Usually, simple alterations will fit a standard stock to a normal person. Standard stocks are designed specifically to fit the greatest possible number of people. But if you are in doubt, seek counsel. Do not let yourself be hurt. Above all, do not attempt to shoot with a stock which does not permit accurate alignment of eye and front sight every time the gun is mounted.

Proper gun fit is discussed in detail on pp. 635-636. The human eye, after all, is merely a lens. When in universal focus—"infinity," to the camera-wise—it sees distant objects clearly, but cannot distinguish near-by objects without a definite change of focus to provide short-range vision.

The eye at universal focus can, however, see the front sight clearly—and the middle sight, if one is provided (as on many trap guns). Or the eye can see the forward two-thirds of the rib clearly, at the same time that the target is sharply in focus. The inference is plain—that the eye should be elevated slightly above the rear of the rib to give the straight-edge effect of viewing the rib from slightly behind and above—just like sighting along a yardstick. This relationship of eye to rib presupposes a point of impact higher than dead center—but is not our goal the following of the target with the front sight? How can we follow it if we blot it out with the muzzle?

It follows that no shotgun should shoot exactly point-blank, which means that the center of the shot pattern would correspond exactly to an extension of the rib. Rather, the pattern should be centered above the rib—how far above depending on the type of shooting for which the gun is intended.

**II. The Brain and the Eyes.** The brain has only one function in advance of that all-important flash from the eyes—"There's the target!" That function is to create the proper state of mind to permit the body to perform its functions easily and smoothly.

All good shooting is a result of proper direction of the conscious mind. All poor shooting results from combined errors of the mind and the body, which may be induced either by conscious or subconscious interference with a normal relationship between the mind and its servants—the eyes, the hands, and all the rest of us.

The most common fault of the conscious mind is an improper approach to the shot. If the mind prepares itself for the shot with a "Get this bird! Get this bird!" fixation, the same fixation is transmitted to the muscles of the body. Bound muscles destroy smoothness of swing. A bodily as well as a mental fixation exists. Even the eyes become fixed with a glassy stare, and are physically incapable of performing the work assigned to them.

The proper mental preparation, as you get ready to fire each shot, is a "Watch for the target!" attitude. This induces an alert, watchful consciousness of the work to be done by both mind and body. The eyes, in their primary function of agents of the brain, do not become fixed. Rather, they are held at universal focus, ready to change direction instantly upon the appearance of the target. This thing called determination is all right in its place, and it even has a place in shooting, if properly applied. If determination—to you—means a set jaw and a fixed stare, dispense with it at once. You will break more targets or bag more game if you take your shooting less seriously.

The most common fault of the subconscious mind is flinching. Anticipation of recoil, muzzle blast, a bump on the jaw, or some other physical discomfort, blocks the normal mental process so necessary to proper functioning of the body. Again, intrusion of some extraneous thought as the mind concentrates on the job of the moment may interpose a mental block just as disastrous to good shooting as a physical manifestation. Inability to keep the mind on the job of the moment is a common fault, even with good shooters. The remedy for this state of affairs is to keep your mind on your business.

Physical manifestations of flinching may be classified as downright gun-shyness. The conscious mind is not afraid of the discharge of the gun. The subconscious mind, however, resents something about the procedure. If ever there was an excuse for the ancient platitude, "An ounce of prevention is worth a pound of cure," that excuse applies to the fault of flinching. Continued use of an ill-fitting gun, heavy loads in a light gun, a gun with too short barrels, or any one of a hundred ill-advised errors of judgment, may cause flinching. Plain, everyday horse sense would have prevented 99 per cent of all cases of flinching since the beginning of the sport.

Do not get the idea that actual physical pain always is associated with flinching. The most common fault in golf—the lifting of the head—is exactly the same thing as flinching in shooting. It has no association with pain. The mind simply rebels at doing something that calm reason insists must be done, if the shot is to be executed properly. In shooting, the mind may rebel against departure from the normal sequence, in "willing the shot," instead of following the natural sequence of lining up the gun, and then willing the shot. All this has been explained in the section on "Pointing Out" (p. 640). Cases of mental flinching, however, yield quickly and rapidly to treatment—and the best treatment is practice.

Physical flinching may be cured by exactly the same methods that should be applied in the case of a gun-shy dog. Any person with sensitive ears should plug them with cotton or the little rubber devices known as ear-stops, thus deadening the effect on the ears of the report of the gun. If physical flinching persists, abandon temporarily all attempts at game or target shooting with the larger bores, and take up "plinking" with a .410 and "short shells"—the lightest efficient gun and charge combination possible to procure. Then work up gradually to the larger bores again. Sometimes, laying off all shooting for a few months will effect a cure. Finally, have a friend assist you by standing behind you and handing you the gun before each shot, loading it or leaving it empty without your knowledge. Few men can endure the self-ridicule of flinching with an empty gun. In extreme cases, consult your local arms or ammunition company representative as you would consult your doctor.

Since the primary function of the eyes is to act as agents of the brain, they may be expected to conform to mental processes more nearly than any other member of the body. In the section on "Pointing Out," it was shown by diagram that the eyes can and must combine two definite assignments in delivering the shot, these being:

(1) To serve as agents of the brain in setting off the mental processes necessary to the delivery of the shot.

(2) To operate as a range-finder to determine the location of the target, and its *apparent direction* and *apparent speed*.

The third important function of the eyes—that of aiming or pointing the gun—comes into play *after* the brain has been set to functioning, and *after* the target has been located and its apparent direction and apparent speed reported to the brain. As explained in "The Gun and the Target" (p. 645), this third function of the eyes should become as nearly mechanical as possible. Shooting skill will improve in direct proportion to the achievement of this ideal.

Mankind has never been able to improve upon the number and arrangement of the eyes in performing any task involving the *apparent* direction and *apparent* speed of an object. Mechanical range-finders, binoculars, ordinary field glasses, all employ two lenses set some distance from each other. The old-fashioned parlor stereopticon is perhaps the best example of them all.

At the same time, monocular instruments are used universally in the process of lining up one object on another, or placing an object in a definite position with respect to another. The telescope, the surveyor's transit, and the mariner's sextant are examples of devices of this type.

From the foregoing, you will deduce that binocular action of the eyes best performs the functions of setting off the mental process and acting as range and direction finder. Monocular action is best for alignment of the gun upon or in front of the target.

Therefore, shoot with both eyes open! After the eyes have performed their two binocular functions, that something which oculists call "accommodation" will cause the action of the eyes to become monocular. In shooting parlance, your "master eye" will take command, and the gun will be aligned upon the target by the master eye, assuming that the gun must invariably be fired from the shoulder on the same side as the master eye.

The accepted test for determining the master eye is known to all experienced shooters. You simply hold both eyes open, and align your finger upon some object. If you suspect your right eye of being your "master eye," now close the left eye. If the finger remains aligned upon the object, your suspicion was correct, and your right eye *is* the master eye. If the finger moves out of alignment with the object, then you guessed wrong—your left eye is the master eye.

Having determined that one eye or the other is the master eye, then continue the test to determine your accommodation. Close the master eye, and align the finger upon the object with the weaker eye. Now open the master eye—which means returning to both eyes open. The finger should jump immediately out of alignment with the object. If it does not jump immediately and positively, then consult a good oculist at once.

No person should engage in any form of clay-target shooting without some form of shooting glasses. If your oculist tells you an optical correction is necessary to restore normal vision, then your shooting glasses by all means should carry this correction. If your eyes are normal, plain glasses of a proper tint should be worn to shield the eyes from glare, to protect them from chipped pieces of the target, to protect them from wind-blown dust and dirt which would cause blinking—and flinching—at the instant of delivering the shot.

The practice of closing one eye now is discouraged in pistol and rifle shooting as well as in shotgun shooting. Closing one eye has a decidedly adverse muscular effect upon the other, since our eyes were designed to be used as a team. If you are a beginner at shotgun shooting, you will learn to shoot just as quickly with both eyes open. If you are a confirmed one-eyed gunner, and are dissatisfied with your scores, begin immediately to make yourself a two-eyed shooter.

In the beginning, you may cross-fire because your training in monocular gun-pointing has destroyed the accommodation of your eyes as far as shooting is concerned. Your eyes will not work together as a team. The master eye will not take control when, other duties having been performed, your eyes concern themselves only with the alignment of gun upon target. You may have a hard time overcoming this self-imposed handicap, but, in the end, improved scores will justify your efforts.

Do not assume from this, however, that all good shots are binocular shooters. Many of the nation's foremost trapshooters swear by one-eyed shooting as the best method, and can point to a long list of champions to prove it. From long habit, monocular shooters have reduced the first two functions of the eyes to mere mechanical routine, concentrating upon gun alignment as the only conscious effort of the open eye. And—a monocular instrument is ideal for aligning one object upon another.

In trapshooting, however, the target always appears instantaneously at the same place at the command of the shooter. In all other forms of shooting, the target appears at different places—or at least has that appearance. One-eyed shooting, therefore, will be more successful at the 16-yard traps than at skeet or in game shooting. If you intend to devote your shooting career to straight trapshooting, there is much to be said for the monocular system. If you intend to do any other kind of shooting along with trapshooting, by all means shoot with both eyes open.

Remember your experience in keeping the stick aligned upon the playful dog. If the accommodation of your eyes is normal, there is no reason why you should not align a shotgun upon a moving object just as easily as you aligned the stick. This means simply that binocular shooting is the natural, easy way to point a shotgun. You never have time to *aim* it in the sense that an engineer aligns an alidade upon a place-mark. Approximate alignment is sufficient, since shotguns are loaded with hundreds of shot pellets instead of one ball in order to permit approximate aiming.

Take your shooting the natural, easy way. Remember, it's a sport, designed for enjoyment. Any departure from this principle may lead to complete dissatisfaction with your sport because it becomes just too much work.

**III. Grooving the Swing.** Since the brain is the master engineer of your shooting, and the eyes are the chief assistants of the brain, all other muscular action may be combined into one physical function—grooving the swing of the gun to keep it aligned on the target until the shot-charge is unleashed.

Practically every muscle of the body is brought into play in grooving the swing. The lower part of the body, from feet up to and including the hips, regulates lateral movement. The upper part of the body controls vertical movement. Co-ordination of all these muscles must be insured by a proper shooting position, which in itself must combine the factors of torsion and balance. Torsion initiates and controls lateral movement. Balance controls and regulates vertical movement, at the same time permitting final minor adjustment of the swing by the arms and shoulders.

Thus we arrive at a fixed relationship between torsion and the lower part of the body, and between balance and the upper part of the body. The feet, legs, and hips must be so placed as to provide proper torsion to insure lateral movement. The upper part of the body must be so balanced as to permit vertical adjustment of the arc of the gun swing. The normal placement of the weight of the body, as well as the weight of the gun, the distribution of that weight, and the method of swinging it, must all be considered in assuming a proper shooting position.

First of all, the shooter must so place his feet "to face the shot"—to deliver the shot-charge at the point where he expects to hit the target. In skeet, trapshooting, and upland game shooting, targets will be slightly above the horizontal plane of the gun muzzle—not far enough above that plane to require overhead shots, except in the case of Number 8 shots at skeet. Since modern shotguns are designed to point naturally just above horizontal, when held with the butt flat to the shoulder, it follows that an upright, natural shooting position will serve best to keep the axis of the body's center of gravity perpendicular to the horizontal plane.

Just as in golf, a natural pivot, not a sway, will produce the smoothest swing. Wide-spread legs, hips held askew, abnormally bent knees—all these affectations merely serve to destroy torsion and balance. While it is true that the weight of the gun in front of the body will displace the center of gravity toward the front, this displacement is not so great in a normal person as to require abnormal measures of control. At most, the weight of the gun in shooting position merely shifts the center of gravity to the left leg—in the case of a right-handed shooter—and thus, the left leg becomes the pivot leg and the right leg the balance or "steering" leg. The feet are the twin platforms of the body, and so all discussion of shooting position must begin with the feet.

In "facing the shot," the gun normally crosses the left toe—of a right-handed shooter. This means that the left toe will point a little to the right of the exact spot where the shot-charge is to be placed. Since the feet give a firmer foundation to the body if they are separated at an angle, the right foot will be a few inches back of the left, and with the right toe turned still farther to the right. Conformation of the shooter will regulate the exact distance between the feet and the exact angle between the toes of the two feet. Generally speaking, turning the right toe too far to the right restricts ease of movement to the left. A good rule is to assume a position that is perfectly comfortable and without muscular strain through any possible arc of lateral swing. Try it a few times, and you will find that the feet find their natural position and their natural angle without any conscious attention on your part, provided you face the shot.

Most of the weight of the body will be upon the left foot, evenly distributed as between toe and heel. That part of the body's weight borne by the right foot will be principally upon the toe. The heel of the left foot thus can never leave the ground without upsetting the balance of the upper part of the body. The heel of the right foot may leave the ground in the process of "steering," if it seems more comfortable to swing in this manner. However, if the feet are held reasonably close together under the body, it will not be necessary to raise the right heel to obtain a smooth, easy swing.

Having faced the shot, pivot the lower part of

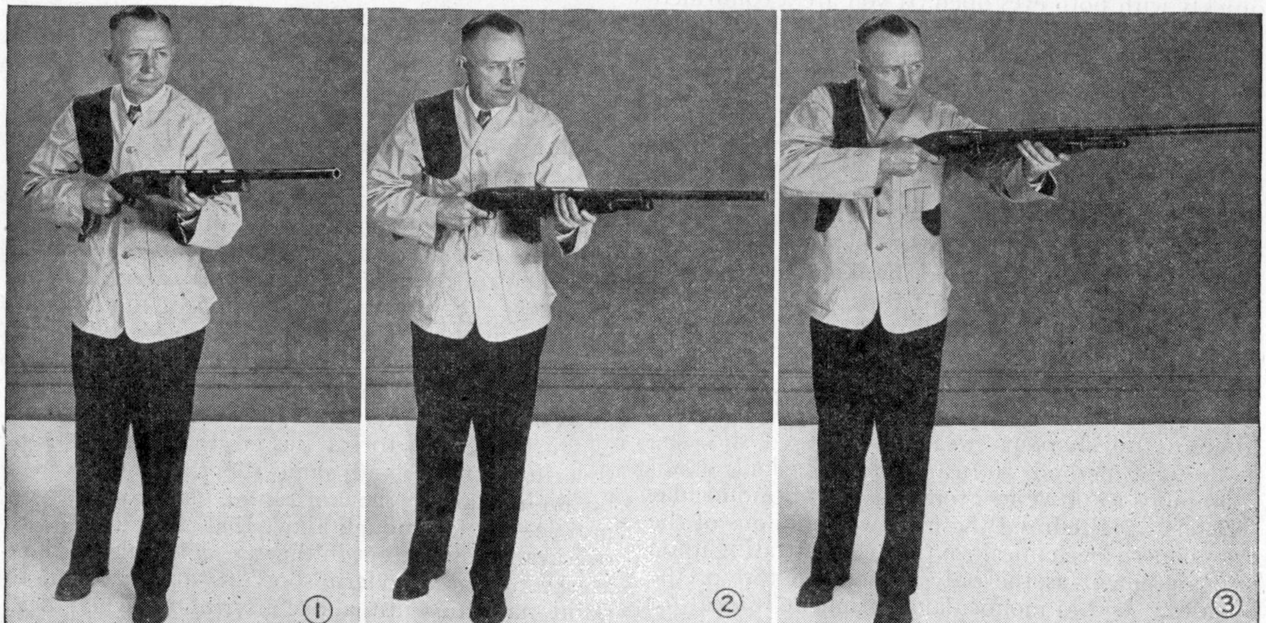

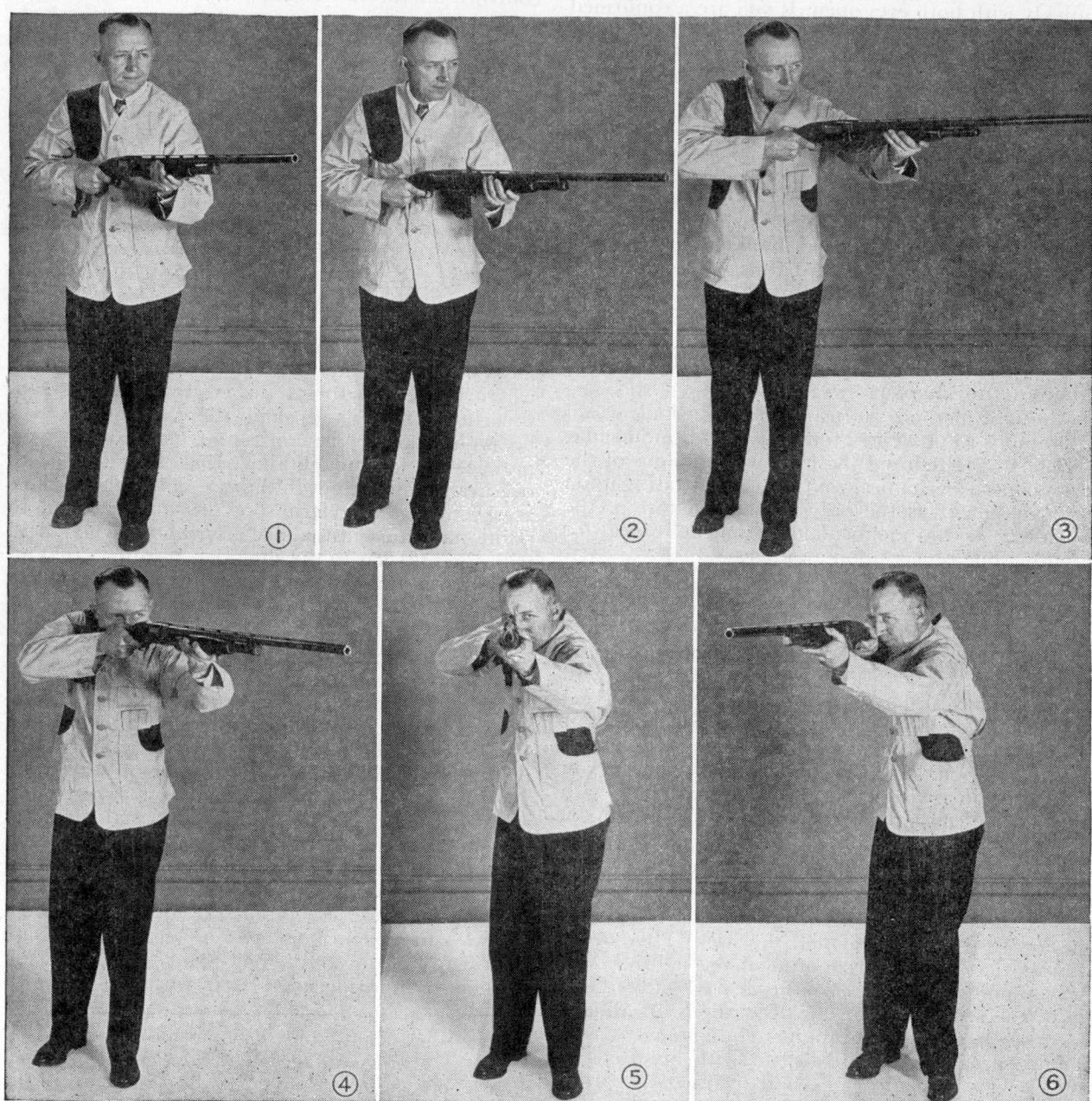

PLATE XII—SHOTGUN SHOOTING. The series of photographs above illustrates in slow motion the complete gun swing of a shooter firing at a target crossing in front at right angles from the shooter's left to his right. (1) The shooter sees the target while holding gun at ready position and begins swing to the left to pick it up with the sighting plane of his gun. (2) As the swing to the left to intercept the target progresses, the gun comes upward and forward, being under perfect control of co-ordinated movement between the two hands of the shooter. (3) The shooter has now reached the extreme limit of his swing to the left to intercept the target, reverses the direction of his body pivot, now moving to the right in the wake of the flying target. (4) The gun is brought to the shoulder by the co-ordinated action of *both* hands, the shooter's cheek moves forward upon the stock, and the pivot to the right in the wake of the target continues. (5) The pivot of the shooter overtakes the target, since the movement of the muzzle of the gun to the right is faster than the movement of the target, and the shot is fired with the tubes pointing exactly at the target. (6) The pivot continues to the right after the shot is fired, in order that the speed of gun swing will not be diminished as the gun passes out to the right to establish an automatic lead ahead of the target. This series of photographs is a perfect illustration of any crossing shots taken with the "swinging past" method.

the body—without moving the feet—to face the spot where the target will appear—the zero of the vertical clock. The muscles of the feet, legs, and hips will then be under torsion—ready to swing back to the position at which the shot is to be delivered. This torsion, it has been explained, is best achieved by a pivot—not a sway. If the knees are bent abnormally, pivoting becomes impossible. A shift of weight to one side is inevitable, and weight does not always shift back to its original position. Thus, after the feet, the knees become the next important consideration in the swing.

Straight legs twist, or take on torsion, much easier than crooked ones. At the same time, the knees must not be locked, which makes pivoting impossible. Just enough "break" or bend in the knees to permit free pivoting is the ideal position for these members. At first this position may be assumed consciously, and tried out tentatively in your bedroom or anywhere else. It is not necessary to stand upon a shooting ground in order to cultivate a proper shooting position.

The hips should be level, permitting their pivoting—and that of the upper part of the body—in a horizontal plane. If the hips are not level, balance of the upper part of the body is destroyed, and the resulting swing will be upset by th edisplacement of the center of gravity. In other words, the swing will be low at one end, high on the other. Or it may start in the proper arc, only to become high or low as the shifting of balance interferes with the smooth continuity of the swing. Too much stress cannot be placed upon this point of the smooth, even, *level* pivoting of the hips upon the foundation of the feet and legs.

One of the primary reasons for a smooth, level swing is to prevent "canting" the gun—rotating the sighting plane on its long axis, so that the front sight is not exactly on top at the moment of firing. Canting is not the serious fault in shotgun pointing that it is in rifle and pistol shooting, since the sighting plane will place some part of the pattern on the target, even with the gun canted, provided you sight along the rib. The big difficulty is trying to sight along the sighting plane with the gun canted. The head is displaced from its normal position, and thus the result of excessive canting will be improper pointing—and a missed target.

It has already been pointed out that if the hips are level and the body upright, the upper part of the body will retain that perfect balance so necessary to produce the vertical component of the gun swing. In a natural, upright position, the torso, shoulders, and arms point the gun naturally and normally at a point in the foreground just above horizontal. Thus, the gun may be lowered by bending forward at the waist and continuing the movement through the arms and shoulders—which moves the balance of the body forward. Conversely, the gun muzzle may be elevated by bending upward or backward at the waist and continuing the movement through the shoulders and arms—which has the effect of shifting the balance backward.

In the movement of depressing the gun muzzle, the left foot takes more of the weight of the body, checking the transfer of weight to the left foot when the gun muzzle has been sufficiently depressed. Conversely, more weight is transferred back to the right toe by the movement of elevating the gun muzzle—the shifting of balance being checked by the right toe when sufficient weight has been transferred. All of this shifting must be accomplished without the slightest disturbance of the torsion factor—and this is impossible if the body is bent too far forward, or is held rigid in a too-upright position.

The transfer of weight from one foot to the other is so slight, with a good shooting position, as to be imperceptible. It is mentioned here merely as a check point in determining whether or not you have achieved proper balance. If you are conscious of the shifting of the weight, your feet are too far apart, your knees are bent too much, or abnormal placement of some other member of the body is serving to destroy balance—and probably torsion as well. Check yourself thoroughly. Make sure you are swinging from side to side, and up and down, with the least possible shifting of weight, and with the smallest practical displacement of feet, knees, and hips.

With the torso held reasonably erect—remember the center of gravity of your body is slightly forward because of the weight of the gun—your shoulders must conform to the job of the arms in holding the gun in the proper position. Since the left hand and arm must be well under the fore-end of the gun to support it properly, your left shoulder will be relatively low. Since the right hand must grasp the gun at the grip, the right shoulder will follow the right elbow. If the right elbow is held high, the right shoulder will be relatively high. If the elbow is held down, hanging relaxed in a natural position, the right shoulder will be little higher than the left.

However, a high right elbow tends to straighten out the shoulder and thus present a flat surface against which to place the butt of the gun. Again, a high right elbow serves to elevate the wrist of the right hand, which is desirable from the standpoint of co-ordination of the hands. A good compromise is to shoot with the right elbow moderately high—not as high as the horizontal position of the rifle shooter, not so low as to permit the upper arm to touch the chest. Midway of the two extreme positions will be just about right. The shooter can judge for himself what is best after studying the functions of the arms and hands.

The arms simply follow the hands—and thus the hands become all-important in regulating the position of the entire upper body. The old school of American shotgun shooting was based upon pivoting the gun with the left hand against the right shoulder, thus leaving nothing for the right hand to do except pull the trigger. The newer school prescribes a much more important duty for the right hand—that of co-operation with the left hand in pointing the gun as a two-handed movement, perfectly co-ordinated as to tensity of grip and ease of movement. This change in technique is responsible for the change of dimensions of the modern shotgun from the old—for the abandonment of the "crooked" gun in favor of the modern, straighter type.

The right hand—in the case of a right-handed shooter—also has the responsibility of releasing the trigger. The index or trigger finger must not be frozen by too tight a grip with the right hand. Likewise, it must not freeze as a manifestation of the fault of flinching. It must be flexible in order to obey the command of the eye instinctively, immediately—not so flexible as to require a general tightening of all the muscles of the hand in order to produce a firmness in the muscles controlling the trigger finger. This general tightening-up will cause the shooter to shove or jam the right hand into the trigger-pull, resulting in canting or even actual displacement of the muzzle.

Volumes might be written on the subject of trigger-pull alone. It is enough to say here that the slow process of "squeezing" the trigger, so necessary in accurate shooting with the rifle and pistol, is too slow for shotgun shooting. Again, in "squeezing" the trigger, the rifleman is not supposed to know when the sear will be released and the gun will be discharged. The shotgun shooter *must* know when the trigger will release in order to estimate his forward allowance properly. Therefore, he will pull or slap the trigger sharply—but not so sharply as to communicate the motion to the gun itself.

"Pulling" a trigger may be described as a contraction of the muscles controlling the index finger, with the index finger already curled around the trigger, and in close contact with it. "Slapping" the trigger consists of bending the index finger from a straight position along the trigger guard, *not* in actual contact with the trigger when the movement is begun.

It may interest the reader to know that a former Clay Target Champion of North America and a Woman's Clay Target Champion of North America were trigger-slappers. Many other expert shots at skeet and the traps subscribe to this method of releasing the shot-charge. They claim for it an almost total absence of contraction of the muscles of the hand not directly concerned with the business of releasing the trigger. Further, there is a tremendous argument for this form of trigger-release in the additional safety factor gained by the absence of contact with the trigger until the shot actually is willed by the brain.

The great majority of shooters, however, are trigger-pullers. They go about the business of letting off the shot-charge with the index finger curled about the trigger, effecting final release by a contraction of the muscles—not by suddenly crooking the finger.

It follows that one method or the other will be better for *you*. The better method will be the one which communicates the least possible movement to the gun, the least possible disturbance of alignment. If you find yourself jamming into the trigger-pull with your whole hand, try the other method. Realize that if either method causes all the muscles of your hand to tighten, with a resultant death grip upon the small of the stock, then your fault lies somewhere else than in mere trigger-release. It will then be time to forget the trigger for the time being, and concentrate on a balanced relationship between the muscles of the two hands.

The whole business of gun pointing may be summed up in this thought: the ideal is to preserve the illusion of pointing a stick, which is obviously a two-handed movement, founded on natural instinct, and assisted tremendously by modern changes in gun design. The new, so-called beaver-tail fore-end is intended to keep the hands at the same level in pointing the gun, just as they would be in pointing a stick. Naturally, the major part of the job of starting and stopping the gun, in swinging, is assigned to the left hand, because its arc represents an outer circle of the swing, while the arc of the right hand represents an inner circle. In the main, however, the two hands work in unison after the left hand has started the swing from its normal position of support under the fore-end.

It follows that your gun will be pointed more accurately the farther you extend your left hand out toward the muzzle. You extend the pointing base, which is the distance between the hands, and thereby obtain more uniform control of the swing. At the same time, you sacrifice speed at the gun muzzle in favor of steadiness. Everything about this shooting business is a compromise somewhere along the line. If you hold your left hand back toward you on the fore-end, it can swing through a shorter arc, thus increasing its speed of travel, and relatively increasing the speed of swing of the gun muzzle.

Work out for yourself the problem of the proper position of the left hand, remembering that an extended left arm makes for steadiness, a retracted left arm for speed. It may help you to know that most crack skeet shooters prefer the extended left arm—and skeet requires the fastest gun handling of any shooting game. If topnotch skeet shooters can gain sufficient speed with an extended left arm, undoubtedly you can do the same. Try it.

There remains only to discuss the position of the head in relation to the gun, and to the other members of the body. This already has been touched upon in the discussion of gun fit. The right cheek is the means of locking the eye to its position slightly above and behind the back end of the rib or barrel. The cheek should be able to find this position merely by a forward inclination of the head—the least dipping and ducking, the better. At the same time, the pressure of the cheek should not be so heavy as to drag upon the hands, the arms, and the rest of the body in aligning the gun.

The cheek must ride the comb of the gun stock, invariably, without the slightest variation in position or pressure. It is easy to show by mathematics just why this rule is axiomatic—and the most important in shooting technique. A far easier method of proof, however, is to visualize what happens in the case of a right-handed shooter swinging to the right. The entire movement of the gun is away from the cheek. If pressure is relaxed, the head lags behind the swing, and when the shot is delivered, the eye is not in its proper position to point the gun. This would not occur in pointing a stick—which can be held by the hands in front of the master eye. But the gun has a stock for the purpose of absorbing recoil against the shoulder, and the master eye must adapt itself to the position defined by the very construction of the gun.

It may be stressed here that the tendency of the head to lag behind the swing in shots crossing from left to right is responsible for making this type of shot the hardest in all gun games, or in game shooting, It is not that a right-handed shooter swings more naturally to the left. If his shooting position is correct, he can swing either way with equal facility. It is merely that a swing from right to left carries the cheek—and the master eye—along with it, and thus insures perfect alignment of the gun muzzle upon the target.

On the same principle, the nearer the comb line of the gun stock approaches parallel with the horizontal, the more accurate the placement of the eye through all parts of the gun swing, either from left to right, or right to left. A swing to the right serves to pull the cheek back along the stock. A swing to the left moves it forward. If there is a big difference between drop at comb and drop at heel, the height of the eye above the sighting plane increases or decreases with movement to the side.

The ideal is approached in the Monte Carlo stock, which has a perfectly level comb line, with the same drop at both ends of the comb. Much the same thing can be accomplished, however, by reducing drop at heel, and bringing drop at comb and drop at heel into a practical relationship.

Whatever the method used to obtain proper gun fit, it is absolutely essential that the cheek ride the comb with unvarying pressure, thus insuring a constant position for the master eye at the rear of the sighting plane. A shot delivered with the eye in any other position means a miss.

# SKEET SHOOTING

The sport of skeet shooting is only a little over 20 years old, but in those 20 years it has grown from a method of informal practice for a few upland gunners to a well-organized, highly competitive sport, indulged in by thousands of shooters from coast to coast. Its development has been little short of phenomenal, and it is still one of the fastest-growing of all outdoor sports.

The reasons for its immediate popularity are numerous. Like trapshooting, skeet appeals to all classes and types of people. Hunters like skeet because it is excellent practice for the field and gives them a chance to use their favorite guns when the hunting season is over. There is no closed season on clay targets. Business and professional men like it for the relaxation it affords them and for the competitive spirit it engenders. Women find it eminently suitable, and at it they can compete on equal terms with men. Size and strength are not important factors at skeet, and the light-weight guns are easy for them to manage. The same reasoning applies to juniors, who often outshine their parents at this versatile sport. Lastly, older people like it because it gets them out of doors and permits them to participate in a sport which is not too arduous. Anyone with normal eyesight can become a proficient skeet shot, after a fair amount of practice.

**Development.** The seed of this sport was planted long before skeet, as known today, was organized. In back lots all over the country, field shots were in the habit of using clay targets to take the place of live birds when practicing up for the hunting season. Such shooting was all of an informal nature, and targets were usually thrown from a hand-trap or from small, portable traps mounted on planks. Practice shooting of this sort dates back to the time when artificial targets and target-throwing devices were first invented.

As early as 1910, one group of gunners, including William H. Foster, the originator of skeet, C. E. Davies, and his son, H. W. Davies, used to shoot in a field behind the Glen Rock Kennels in Ballard Vale, Mass. They were all enthusiastic partridge hunters in the covers of eastern Massachusetts and southern New Hampshire, and like so many others of their kind, found the hunting season all too short. They therefore turned to clay targets as a means of keeping in practice for the hunting season, as well as for the pleasure they derived from the shooting.

Instead of shooting all targets from a straightaway, they used to move away from the trap and shoot at angles similar to those encountered in the field. If one of the group had missed a partridge that was quartering to the left, they would set the trap and stand in such a position as to simulate that particular shot. The clay targets were thrown at much the same speed as the partridge flew, and in this manner they could very closely reconstruct a field situation by mechanical means. Since the targets were shot at much the same range, the same gun and load could be used as was in the field. A long check cord was used to release the trap, as a safety precaution.

Even at that early date, incoming targets were shot at close range, similar to the present-day Station 8 shot. Although such a shot is occasionally encountered in partridge shooting, this particular target was intended primarily to reproduce a snap shot. While angle shots permit a certain amount of swing, situations are often encountered in the brush where the shooter either makes a snap shot or just does not shoot at all.

As time went on, and as the men became more accustomed to shooting from the various angles, they decided to set up a regular sequence of shots which would duplicate all of the angles that might be encountered in the field. As a result, "clock-shooting" was introduced around 1915. In "clock-shooting" a circle with a radius of 25 yards was measured off, and shooting positions were established at each of the hours on the clock. The trap was placed at 12 o'clock and threw targets over 6. Two shots were fired from each of the shooting positions, starting at 12 and making a complete circuit of the clock. This made a total of 24 shots, and the 25th target was shot as an incomer by standing in the center of the circle. Over this course, a score of 15 out of 25 was considered excellent.

During the next ten years very few changes were made in "clock-shooting" as it was originally established. In 1920, Foster entered the employ of the *National Sportsman Magazine* in Boston, Mass., and wrote an article containing a description and diagram of this type of shooting, which was published in the November 1920 issue. Gradually hunters came from surrounding towns to view the new shooting sport, and they usually went away enthusiastic about it.

In 1923 it was decided that a 25-yard circle was a little too large, and the radius was reduced to 20 yards. Field guns proved more effective at this range, and scores were bettered appreciably.

Later that same year, a hen-farm was built in the adjoining field at Ballard Vale, making it necessary to cut out all angle shots which were fired in that direction. This problem was solved by placing a second trap at 6 o'clock which threw targets over 12. By going only halfway around the circle, and shooting one target from each trap, all the angles were preserved and the hen-farm went unpeppered. This semicircle was made the basis for the present-day skeet lay out. It is doubtful if the farmer, when he built his hen-farm, could have been convinced that he was influencing the format of what was to become a great international sport. In any event, the new arrangement worked out admirably, as it happens. Whereas under the old "clock-shooting" system the gallery had to follow the shooters around, to keep out of the line of fire, they could now remain safely behind the shooting positions.

When the second trap was added, the original trap at 12 o'clock was elevated about 10 feet in the air, to the top of a tree trunk, to simulate more truly a bird in full flight. The trap at 6 o'clock was left at ground level to simulate a bird flushed from the ground. In all cases the shooter held his gun in an informal position, down from his shoulder, and did not put it to his shoulder until the target appeared in flight.

During 1925 hunters in several other Massachusetts communities constructed similar layouts. In 1925 it was decided to introduce this form of shooting to sportsmen at large through the *National Sportsman* and *Hunting and Fishing* magazines, and articles with complete information and diagrams were published. A prize contest was also run by the magazines, offering $100 for a name for the new shooting sport. Thousands of names were received from all over the country, ranging from "Bang" to "Bye-Bye Blackbird." The name of "Skeet" was finally selected. It had been submitted by Mrs. Gertrude Hurlbutt, of Dayton, Montana. "Skeet" is an old Scandinavian form of our present word "shoot."

The first report of a skeet event being held outside of Massachusetts was received from Bremerton, Wash., and a picture was published in the May 1926 issue of *National Sportsman*. In the meantime, work was completed on a booklet containing complete information on skeet, together with a diagram of the layout and a set of shooting rules and regulations.

The Everett Gun Club, Everett, Mass., was one of the first large clubs in the country to take up skeet shooting. Henry E. Ahlin, later to become president of the National Skeet Shooting Association, was then manager of the club. Skeet met with immediate acceptance at Everett, and their field was soon hard-pressed to handle all the shooters who came out.

During the early days of the sport, there were no specialized guns or ammunition for skeet, as there are today. In most cases, field guns with fairly close boring were used, with the result that scores were generally low. To Mr. H. M. Jackson, Jr., of Garner, N. C., goes the credit for breaking the first 25 straight. Up to that time such a feat was considered to be practically impossible.

**Competitions.** Probably the first inter-club event in skeet was staged late in 1926 by the Raleigh Skeet Club, Raleigh, N. C. Clubs from Rhode Island, Massachusetts, and Michigan competed by correspondence with the Raleigh club. Raleigh won with a score of 117 out of 125.

By 1925, thousands of shooters had been bitten by the skeet bug, and clubs were being organized all over the country. It soon became apparent that a central organization was necessary, and therefore during that year the National Skeet Shooting Association (N.S.S.A.) was formed. W. H. Foster was the first president, and headquarters were located at Boston, Mass. An official set of skeet rules and regulations were prepared, and membership cards were distributed.

The first Massachusetts State Skeet Championship was held in April 1929, and later that year the Remington Gun Club conducted the first of the famous Great Eastern Skeet Championships, at Lordship, Conn. That marked the beginning of big-time competitive skeet shooting, and ever since then—the Great Eastern has maintained its position as one of the biggest and most popular of all skeet championships.

By 1930 and 1931, the organization of state skeet shooting associations was well under way. Working with the National Skeet Shooting Association, these groups were able to meet local problems and did much to establish skeet on a firm foundation.

In 1936 the official skeet layout was altered to a certain extent, largely as a safety precaution. The lines of fire from the two trap houses were changed to cross at a point 18 feet outside of Station 8, instead of directly above it. This helped to eliminate the danger of a shooter's being struck by the flying pieces of a broken incoming target.

Before a method was devised for releasing targets by electrical or mechanical means from a central pull-house behind Station 4, it was common practice for the trap boys to release them by hand at the command of the shooter. Since the boys were installed inside the trap houses, it was sometimes impossible for them to tell which target the shooter wanted. A solution was found on the Lordship grounds, whereby a shooter called "Pull" for the high-house target and "Mark" for the low house. Although such a distinction is no longer necessary, these calls are still frequently heard on skeet fields all over the country.

In 1935, a national skeet championship was held for the first time. L. S. Pratt, of Indianapolis, was the winner, with a score of 244 out of 250. The second national event took place at St. Louis in 1936, and Dick Shaughnessy, a 14-year-old schoolboy from Boston, won the coveted crown with the remarkable score of 248 out of 250. Over the years Shaughnessy has become one of the most consistently fine shooters in the game. The Nationals moved to Detroit in 1937, and Odis Walding from Hollywood was victorious with 248 out of 250. In 1938 Henry Joy, Jr., of Detroit, turned in the first perfect score of 250 straight ever recorded in this event, to win in

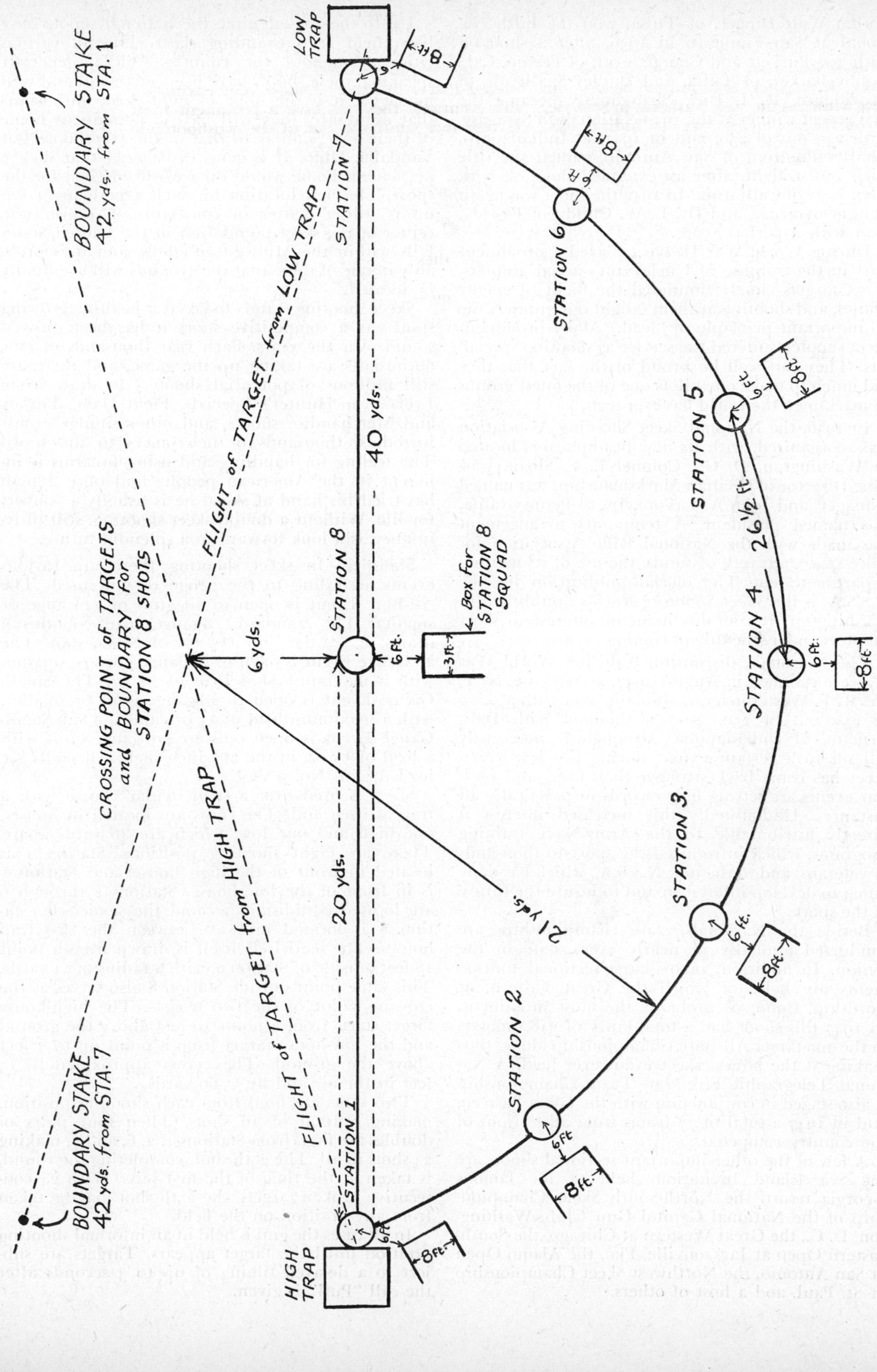


PLATE I. Skeet Shooting.

Tulsa. Walt Dinger, of Tulsa, won the Fifth National at San Francisco in 1939, after a shoot-off with Joe Puckett and George Scott, of Fresno, Cal., Bobby Parker, of Tulsa, and Dudley Shallcross, of Providence, R. I. Dick Shaughnessy became the first repeat winner at the 1940 Nationals in Syracuse, with 249 out of 250, and in 1941, at Indianapolis, Charles Poulton, of San Antonio, gained the title with 250 straight, after an extended shoot-off with Alex Kerr of California. In 1942 the shoot was again held at Syracuse, and Dr. L. W. Childs, of Florida, won with a perfect score.

During World War II, skeet played a prominent part in the training of Uncle Sam's aerial gunners. Skeet targets closely simulated the flight of enemy planes, and shooting at them taught our gunners the all-important principle of "lead." Many prominent skeet shooters entered the service as shooting specialists. They can well be proud of the fact that they did much to make our pilots one of the finest groups of marksmen the world has ever seen.

In 1946, the National Skeet Shooting Association was reorganized, with its new headquarters located in Washington, D. C. Colonel E. F. Sloan, wartime Director of Civilian Marksmanship, was named manager, and John A. LaFore, Jr., of Pennsylvania, was named president. A temporary arrangement was made with the National Rifle Association for office space, advance of funds, the use of its mailing department, etc. The official publication for the N.S.S.A. is the *Skeet Shooting Review,* published in Washington. It contains items of interest to skeet shooters and a schedule of coming events.

The Nationals, discontinued during World War II, were resumed in August 1947, at Syracuse, N. Y. Dr. R. F. Westermeier, of Buffalo, won with a score of 250 out of 250, after a shoot-off with Dave Arnette, of Indianapolis. Although it necessarily fell off to a certain extent during the war years, skeet has come back stronger than ever, and post-war events are setting new records in practically all instances. Undoubtedly this increased interest is directly attributable to the Army-Navy training programs, which introduced the sport to thousands of veterans, and to the new N.S.S.A., which has done much to develop interest in and to insure the future of the sport.

Beside the Nationals, state championships are conducted annually in nearly every state in the Union. In addition, many large sectional tournaments are held, of which the Great Eastern, at Lordship, Conn., is probably the most prominent. In 1947 this shoot had a total entry of 318 shooters in the 100-target All-Bore Championship alone, thus making it the largest skeet event ever held. A National Telegraphic Five-Man Team Championship is also staged in conjunction with the Great Eastern, and in 1947 a total of 77 teams from all sections of the country competed.

A few of the other important sectional shoots are the Sea Island Invitation, held at the famous Georgia resort, the North-South Skeet Championship of the National Capitol Gun Club, Washington, D. C., the Great Western at Chicago, the Southeastern Open at Jacksonville, Fla., the Alamo Open at San Antonio, the Northwest Skeet Championship at St. Paul, and a host of others.

Up to the present time the national shoots have been held at outstanding skeet clubs in various cities throughout the country. While, generally speaking, these shoots have been successful and well managed, it is the hope of most skeet enthusiasts that eventually they will have a permanent home of their own, similar to that of the trapshooters at Vandalia, Ohio. It is generally agreed that such a permanent home would do a world of good for the sport. The best location for such a permanent set-up is still a matter of conjecture. However, the center of the skeet population in the United States falls within the Midwestern states, and it is probably in one of these that the grounds will eventually be located.

Skeet shooting stands today as a healthy, growing sport. As a competitive sport it has been proved sound over the years. Each year thousands of new enthusiasts are taking up the game, and there are still millions of potential shooters to draw from. Every year Hunter's Specials, Field Days, Turkey and Merchandise shoots, and other similar events introduce thousands of newcomers to the sport. The feeling for handling and using firearms is inherent in the American people, and once a man has tried his hand at skeet, he is usually a convert for life. Without a doubt, skeet shooting, still in its infancy, can look forward to a splendid future.

**Statistics.** In skeet shooting there are various events according to the gauge of gun used. The All-Bore Event is open to all guns of 12 gauge or smaller. The standard 12-gauge load contains 3 drams of powder and 1⅛ oz. of No. 9 shot. The 20-Gauge Event is open to 20-gauge guns or smaller, with a maximum shot load of ⅞ oz. The Small-Gauge Event is open to 28-gauge guns or smaller, with a maximum load of ¾ oz., and the Sub-Small-Gauge Event is open only to 410-gauge guns with a load of ½ oz. in the 2½ inch shell. All shells are loaded with No. 9 shot.

Skeet is fired over a semicircular course with a trap at each end. The traps are located in houses, one high and one low, which are 40 yards apart. There are eight shooting positions. Station 1 is located in front of the high house, and Station 7 is in front of the low house. Stations 2 through 6 are located equidistant around the semicircle. Station 8 is located midway between the two trap houses. The semicircle itself is drawn from a point 18 feet outside of Station 8, with a radius of 21 yards. This same point outside Station 8 also serves as the crossing point of the two targets. The high-house target starts from a point 10 feet above the ground and the low-house target from a point up to 3 feet above the ground. They cross approximately 15 feet in the air and fly 55-60 yards.

Two shots are fired from each shooting position, making a total of 16 shots. Then four pairs of doubles are fired from Stations 1, 2, 6, and 7, making 24 shots in all. The 25th shot, completing the round, is taken at the time of the first miss. With 24 consecutive broken targets, the 25th shot may be taken from any position on the field.

In all cases the gun is held in an informal shooting position until the target appears. Targets are subject to a delayed timing of up to 3 seconds after the call "Pull" is given.

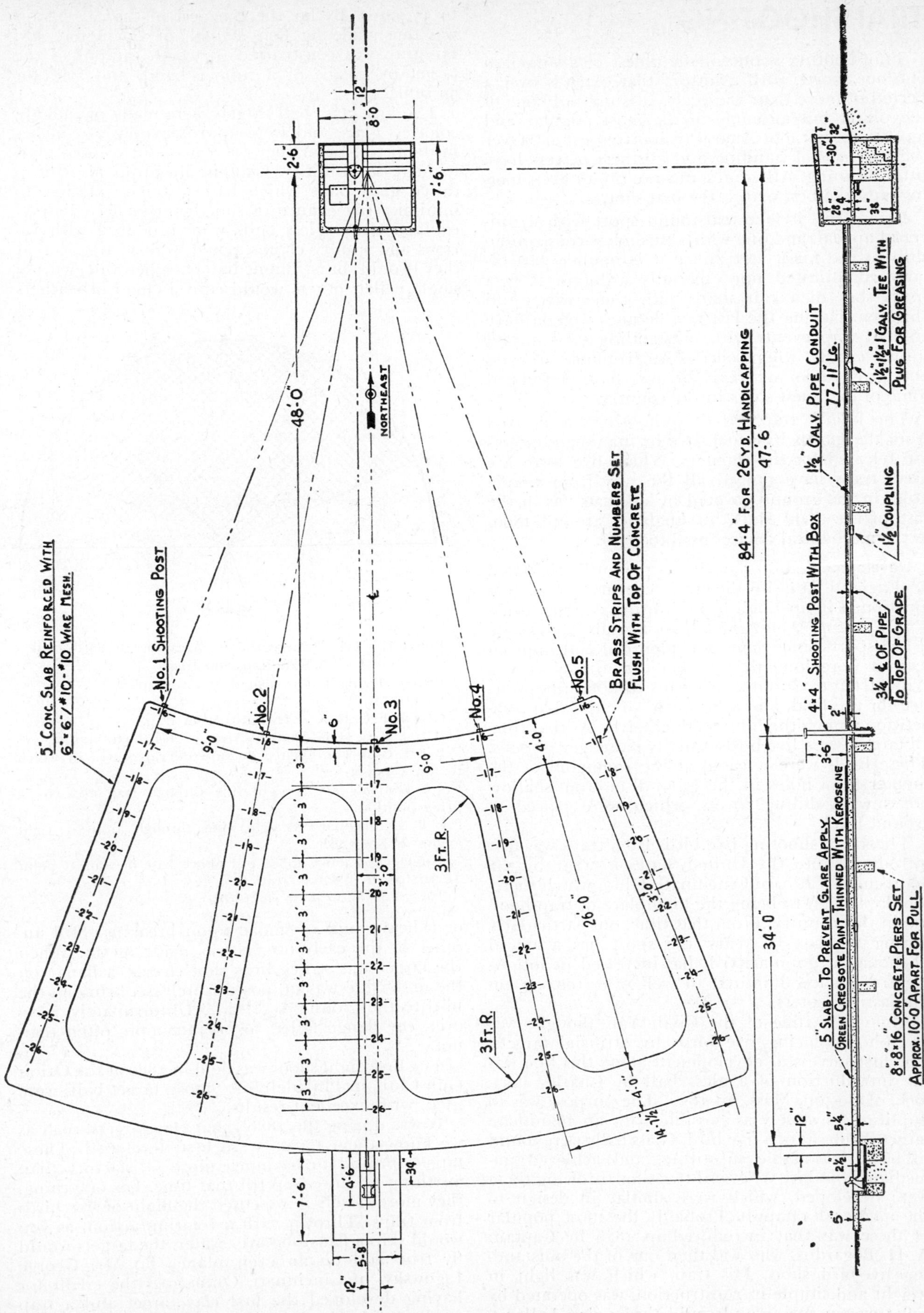


PLATE I. 26-Yard Field Layout with Concrete Shooting Platform.

# TRAPSHOOTING

Trapshooting is one of the oldest of all modern outdoor sports, with a history that extends over a period of more than 150 years. It is not only one of the oldest but also one of the most popular and most democratic of American sporting events. Over the traps social standing and business powers have little meaning. All contestants are on an even footing, and the best man is the best shot.

Like skeet, it is a year-round sport with a universal appeal, and one which engenders companionship of the finest sort. Since it is neither particularly complicated nor especially arduous, it is a sport that men can share with their wives and children. During the last two decades women have entered trap events with outstanding success, and junior events, where entries are confined to boys and girls under 17 years of age, have developed some of the finest shots in the country.

The name "trap" or "trapshooting" is derived from the means by which live or inanimate targets are released for the shooters. Where live birds are used, traps have ranged all the way from simple holes in the ground covered by silk hats (as in the case of the "Old Hats" in England, around 1800) to the mechanical devices used today.

**Development.** Trapshooting apparently originated in England late in the 18th century. It is first mentioned in an English publication of 1793 called *The Sporting Magazine* as an already well-established sport. Since game was plentiful and hunting seasons were long during that era, the sport was evidently introduced as a means of obtaining practice for the field, and as a source of enjoyable competition among the hunters themselves. At that time all targets were live birds, usually passenger pigeons. These birds were released at the command of the shooter from holes in the ground, or from shallow boxes with sliding covers, which were placed at ground level.

The art of shooting live birds from traps was first introduced into the United States in 1831 by the Sportsmen's Club, of Cincinnati, Ohio, which therefore lays claim to being the birthplace of trapshooting in this country. From that time, on, particularly during the last 50 years, the sport has achieved phenomenal popularity. It has increased its following from a few hundred to well over 100,000 enthusiastic shooters.

About the time of the Civil War, thought was given to replacing live birds by artificial targets. The first successful development along this line was the introduction of a glass ball by Charles Portlock, of Boston, Mass., in 1836. The purpose was to duplicate as closely as possible with an inanimate target the flight of a live bird. Glass balls were found to be a reasonable substitute, and achieved immediate popularity. Several traps for throwing them were developed, which were similar in design to the medieval catapult. Probably the most popular of these was that introduced in 1876 by Captain A. H. Bogardus, who was then one of the outstanding live-bird shots. His trap, which was light in weight and simple in construction, was operated by a flat wagon spring and could throw glass balls up to 35 yards. By far the cheapest of the early traps was one made by Ben Teipel, of Covington, Ky. His trap was constructed of wood, catapulted the target by means of a rubber band, and sold for 50 cents.

The first glass ball targets were made of smooth, colorless glass, and were approximately 2½ inches in diameter. Later they were made of colored glass to increase visibility. Captain Bogardus also introduced glass balls which had a rough exterior, to minimize the chance of shot being deflected upon contact. Other glass balls were produced with various and sundry claims. Some were so fragile that they would burst immediately, when hit with a single pellet; others would emit a cloud of feathers or a heavy puff of smoke upon breaking. Still another of the early targets was made of tin. When the target was struck by a shot charge, a flange on the underside was supposed to release, bringing the bird to the ground as "dead." Unfortunately, however, the flange failed to operate more often than not.

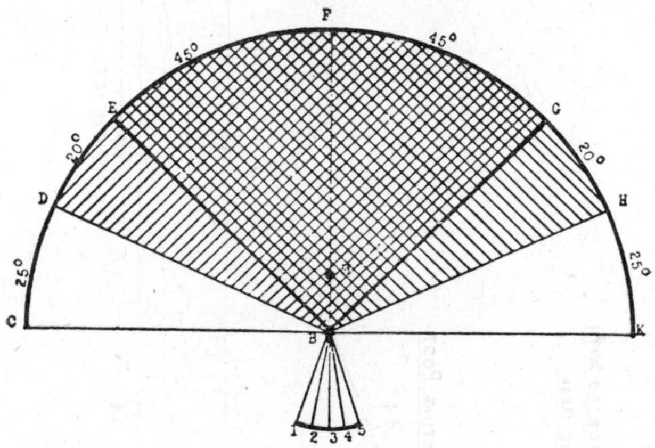


PLATE II. Legal Target Flight Area for 16 Yards and Handicap Shooting.

1 to 5—Firing points spaced 3 yards apart.

B—Trap.

C D E F G H K—Fifty yards from trap.

B D E F G H B—Shaded—Area of legitimate target.

B E F G B—Cross hatched—Most desirable area in which to throw target.

3 B F—Imaginary straight line through trap and No. 3 firing position.

C B K—Imaginary straight line through trap at right angles to No. 3 BF.

Target elevation 6 to 12 feet above base of trap at point M, 30 feet in front of trap.

Target distance 48 to 52 yards.

The first night shoot was held in 1880 at the Orion Gun Club, in Philadelphia. Smoke target balls were used, with excellent results.

It was during the 1880's that clay targets, such as we know them today, were first developed. These targets proved to be much more satisfactory than anything produced up till that time. For one thing, they more closely represented the flight of live birds from traps. Thrown with a rotating action, as you would skip a flat stone over water, the targets would fly true and on an even plane. To Mr. George Ligowsky, of Cincinnati, Ohio, goes the credit for having developed the first clay target and a trap to throw it. The initial demonstration of his new idea was made by Mr. Ligowsky at the close of the New York State Shoot at Coney Island, in 1880. One unsatisfactory factor about the first targets was that they were made entirely of clay, rather than of pitch and clay or pitch and limestone, as they are today. Shaped in molds and hardened in kilns like bricks, when struck with a full charge of shot they would often ring like a bell and jump in the air without losing a single chip.

Although the advent of the clay target produced an increased interest in inanimate shooting, live-bird shooting continued to be extremely popular also—as, indeed, it is today in those states where it

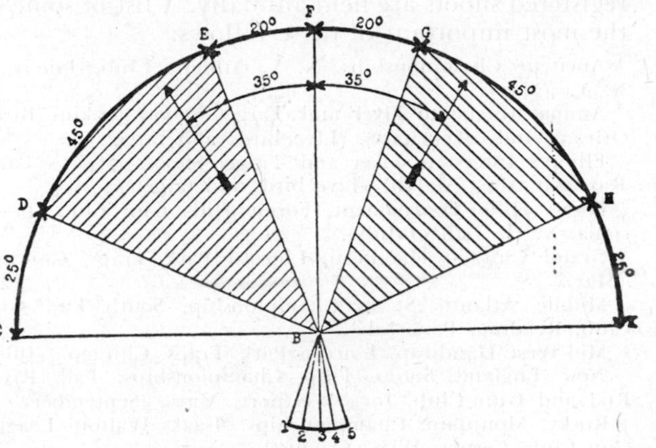


PLATE III. Double Target Shooting.

1 to 5—Firing points spaced 3 yards apart.
B—Trap, 16 yards from firing points.
C D E F G H K—Fifty yards from trap.
B D E B and B H G B—Shaded areas within which targets should be thrown.
3 B F—Imaginary straight line through trap and No. 3 firing position.
C B K—Imaginary straight line through trap at right angles to 3 B F.
Arrows indicate most desirable flight of targets.
Distance of target flight—48 to 52 yards.
Elevation of target 6 to 12 feet above base of trap at a distance of 30 feet in front of the trap.

NOTE: Most clubs set traps to throw maximum left and right angle single and double targets along an imaginary line midway between lines E and F, and F and G, PLATE II.

has not been banned, principally Pennsylvania, Missouri, Indiana, and Wisconsin.

**Competitions.** The first organization was known as the Interstate Manufacturers and Dealers Association. It was established in 1893, and Charles Tatham was the president. While the association operated on a precarious basis at its start, shooters as a whole realized that a national organization with standard rules was necessary if trapshooting was to prosper as a nation-wide sport. The First Grand American Handicap at live birds, which was held at Dexter Park, Long Island, did as much as any one thing to establish the new organization on a firm foundation, although only 21 contestants entered the event. The second tournament was also held at Dexter Park, and drew a total of 54 entries.

In 1895 the name of the association was changed to The Interstate Association. The organization was now well established, and annually received hundreds of applications to hold shoots from clubs all over the country. That year the Third Grand American Handicap at live birds was held at Willard Park, and the entrants reached a total of 61. Each succeeding year brought increased interest and a larger entry to the popular event, until in 1902 it drew 456 shooters. That was the end of it, however, for public sentiment and adverse legislation finally caused the cancellation of the Grand American Handicap at live birds.

In 1900, or thereabouts, an interesting variation in live-bird shooting was introduced at the Limited Gun Club, at Indianapolis, with the substitution of English sparrows for targets, instead of the usual passenger pigeons. They were popular for a few years, but their naturally small size and erratic flight made them very elusive and difficult to shoot, and high scores were few and far between.

It was in 1900, also, that the first Grand American Handicap at inanimate targets was held at Interstate Park, Queens, Long Island. That was the beginning of what was to become the stellar attraction of the trapshooting world.

In 1908 the idea of holding registered tournaments was developed. For the first time, scores were sent in to the national headquarters, and central records were kept of the average scores of all individuals participating in these events. Standard rules for the organization were also prepared and placed in effect.

From the year 1908 on, trapshooting made rapid strides towards its present status. In 1911 the first Double Target Championship was held in conjunction with the Grand American. It was about this time, also, that women began to take up trapshooting in earnest, and the scores they turned in showed clearly that it was a sport for both sexes. The first time that the ladies took a really active part in trap was in 1913, when the first women's trapshooting club in the world was organized in Wilmington, Del., by Miss Harriet D. Hammond, under the name of the Nemours Trapshooting Club. Other women were immediately encouraged by the establishment of that club, and from then on they have played an increasingly important part in the development of the sport. Undoubtedly the most famous of the early women shooters was Annie Oakley (Mrs. Frank E. Butler.) So ardent a shot was she that at one time she even tried trapshooting from a plane. In 1916, the Interstate Association, then the governing body of the trapshooting organization, recognized women shooters and opened all handicap events to them. Special events were also provided for them, and 15 women shooters competed in the Grand American that particular year.

In 1914 all state champions were invited to compete in the National Amateur Championship, held in conjunction with the 15th Annual Grand American, at Dayton, Ohio. By 1915 the Grand could boast a roster of 884 entrants.

It was in 1918 that the Interstate Trapshooting Association changed its name to the American Trapshooting Association, or Amateur Trapshooting Association, as it is known today. The principle reason for changing the name to "American" was to recognize an increasingly large number of Canadian shooters. One of the most important steps taken by the new association was to set up a system by which targets shot at during registered tournaments would count in a season's official average. These averages would then be used as a means of classifying shooters in conjunction with their known ability. That system has remained in effect up to the present day, and each year the Sportsmen's Review Publishing Company, of Cincinnati, issues a booklet containing the averages of all registered shooters.

Another important development was inaugurated by the American Trapshooting Association, or A.T.A., in 1920. At that time the management of trapshooting was divided into five zones, the Eastern, the Southern, the Great Lakes, the Prairie, and the Pacific zones. It was then, also, that they established a clear definition between professional and amateur shooters. Briefly, it was decided that any shooter not dependent upon his skill as a trapshot as a means of livelihood, and who received no compensation or concession therefor, monetary or otherwise, should be classed as an amateur, whether employed in the manufacture or sales of trapshooting equipment or not; and that any shooter who received any salary, or expenses, for use in trapshooting, or discounts on trapshooting equipment as compensation for the promotion of the sale or advertising of such articles, should be classed as a professional.

Between the years 1900, when the first Grand American was held, and 1924, the shoot was shifted from city to city annually. Chicago was host to the Grand nine times, and other cities such as Indianapolis, Columbus, Dayton, Kansas City, Cleveland, Atlantic City, and St. Louis held the shoot on one or more occasions. During that period, considerable thought was given to the establishment of a permanent home for it, where shooters could return year after year to shoot on their own grounds. In 1924 this dream became a reality, and the new permanent home at Vandalia, Ohio, just outside of Dayton, was dedicated. At that shoot the amazing total of 400,000 targets was trapped in the various events throughout the week.

From 1924 up to the present time the Grand has become more and more popular, and each year an ever-increasing number of trap enthusiasts makes the trek to Vandalia. In 1946, 1700 shooters took part in the program, the largest entry up till that time. A total of 1478 shooters entered the Grand American Handicap alone. It was won by Captain Frank Bennett, of Miami, Fla., with a score of 98 out of 100. The 1947 Grand again set a new record for attendance, with Hugh Crossen, of Gardiner, Mont,., leading the field of close to 1800 shooters with a score of 99 out of 100.

In addition to the Grand, hundreds of other registered shoots are held annually. A list of some of the most important of these follows:

Amateur Championships, N. Y. Athletic Club, Travis I., N. Y. (May).

Annual Interstate Flyer and Target Shoot, Jenkins Bros., Orleans, Ind. (February) (Live birds and targets).

Elliott's Interstate Flyer and Target Shoot, Elliott's Park, Raytown, Mo. (March) (Live birds and targets).

Forest Hills Tournament, Forest Hills Gun Club, Franconia, N. H. (4th of July).

Grand Chicago Handicap, Lincoln Park Traps, Chicago. (May).

Middle Atlantic States Championship, South End Gun Club, Reading, Pa. (July).

Mid-West Handicap, Lincoln Park Traps, Chicago. (July).

New England States Trap Championships, Fall River Rod and Gun Club, Inc., Westport, Mass. (September).

Rocky Mountain Championships, Isaak Walton League Gun Club, Casper, Wyo. (August).

Sunny South Little Grand, Etchen's Shooting Country Club, Miami, Fla. (January).

T. Clarence Marshall Tournament, Yorklyn Gun Club, Yorklyn, Del. (Usually the week before the Grand).

Practically every state holds a state championship before the Grand sends it winners, both men and women, to compete in a special event for state champions. Besides their state shoots, many states hold zone and league shoots, which have proved to be very popular.

Over 7000 contestants shot in registered competition during 1946, but this figure represents only a small proportion of the actual number of shooters who follow the sport in this country. Scattered

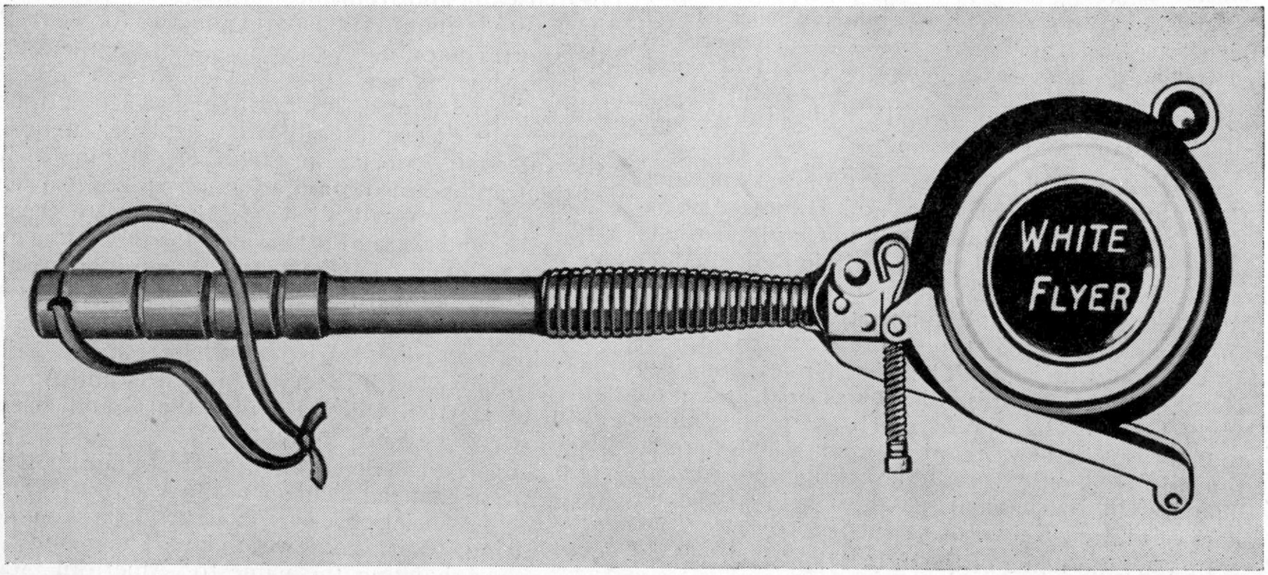


PLATE IV. Hand Trap. With this hand trap, a clay target can be thrown by someone standing behind the shooter, offering shots at varied heights and angles.

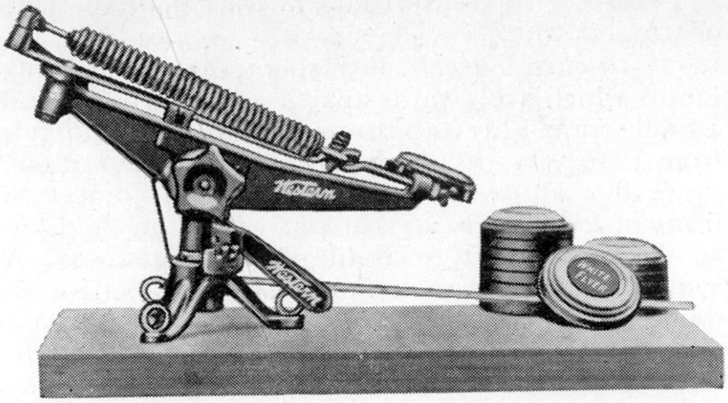

PLATE V. A Good Practice Trap.

through every state in the union are thousands of clubs where members go regularly, just for the pleasure and good fellowship which they derive from the shooting. Each year thousands of new shooters flock out to Hunters' Specials, Turkey Shoots, Merchandise Shoots, Field Days, and other special events which are held for the purpose of interesting field shots and beginners in trap.

Many groups of trapshooters have been organized during the history of the sport, and have done much to enhance its growth and popularity. Among them are the Pacific Indians, on the West Coast, the Westy Hogans, most prominent in the East, the Atlantic Indians, also operating on the East Coast, the Konne Yaut Indians, of Pittsburgh, the Okoboji Indians in the Midwest, the Sioux Indians in Iowa, and many others.

The official publication of the Amateur Trapshooting Association is the *Sportsmen's Review,* issued semi-monthly in Cincinnati. This magazine carries summaries of trapshooting events, items of interest to the trapshooting fraternity, and a complete listing under "Fixtures" of all forthcoming registered shoots.

Besides the A.T.A., a second trapshooting organization operates sucessfully today—the Pacific International Trapshooting Association (P.I.T.A.). It was founded by the famous marksman, Colonel O. N. Ford, and is comprised largely of shooters from the states of Oregon, Washington, California, Idaho,Utah, and Montana. Every year championship shoots are held by each of the states in the organization.

Without a shadow of a doubt, trapshooting has and still is making rapid strides in growth. It has a host of potential followers in the thousands of individuals who take out hunting licenses every year, and the millions of others—men, women, and

PLATE VI. Skeet Trap.

juniors alike—who may never have used firearms but who have become fascinated by the sport of breaking clay targets. It has received added impetus from the thousands of servicemen who first learned to handle firearms during World War II, and who shot at clay targets as a part of their training program. Shoot after shoot during 1946 and 1947 set new records for attendance, and trapshooting looks forward to many prosperous years ahead.

**Statistics.** The following general information will be found useful:

GUNS. The typical gun for trapshooting is 12-gauge with full-choke, ventilated-rib barrel 30 or 32 inches in length.

LOAD. The standard load contains 3 drams of powder and 1⅛ oz. of No. 7½ or No. 8 shot.

TARGETS. According to regulations targets should measure not more than 4$\frac{5}{16}$ inches in diameter and 1⅛ inches in height. Composed of pitch and clay or limestone, they are saucer-shaped, black in color, and usually painted on the crown to increase visibility

TRAPS. Modern artificial target-throwing traps throw single or double targets at a variety of angles. Some are operated electrically; others determine the angle of flight by means of a mechanical auto-angling device.

TYPES OF TRAPSHOOTING. There are three types of trapshooting:

(1) *16-Yard Targets.* Five shooters stand at firing points which are 3 yards apart and 16 yards behind a single trap. This trap throws variable-angle targets from 48 to 52 yards. They reach an elevation of one to 12 feet above the base of the trap, 30 feet in front of it. Targets are thrown within an angle of 45 degrees to left or right of a straightaway. A round of trap for each shooter is composed of 25 shots, five from each of the five shooting positions. The gun is held at the shoulder, and the target is released as soon as the call "Pull" is given. Progression is from left to right, except that upon completion of his five shots at Position 5, the shooter moves behind the other shooters to his next post—Position 1.

(2) *Handicap.* Handicap targets are shot in a similar fashion to 16-yard targets, except that shooters take their positions at distances from 16 to 25 yards in back of the trap, in accordance with their registered average or known shooting ability.

(3) *Double Targets.* These targets are shot from the five 16-yard shooting positions. Whereas in 16-yard and Handicap shooting, targets are released singly, here two targets are thrown at the same time and two shots are fired at each pair. Double targets follow a set course, usually 35 degrees to left and right of a straightaway.

PLATE VII. The White Flyer Trap.

# HANDGUNS—Pistols and Revolvers

The story of the invention and development of pistols, revolvers, and automatic pistols, from their earliest forms to the present day, is a complex one. It is really a part of many other stories: Of *ammunition,* from the crudest black powder to the most modern brass- and steel-cased center-fire rimless cartridges with smokeless propellants. Of *ignition systems,* from the primitive touching of a lighted match to powder over a simple priming hole in the barrel to the most advanced flying firing pins striking swiftly at the metal primer cup to crush the priming mixture and flash fire into the propelling charge. Of *mechanical developments,* from the simple hollow metal tube fastened to a stick which formed the early cannon-locks, to the present finely machined double-action automatic pistols which, once loaded, require only successive pulls on the trigger to discharge their magazines. Of *metallurgy,* from the crude iron which would stand the blast of the weak early powders, to the high-tensile metals which permit the use of today's charges developing pressures in the tens of thousands of pounds.

It is part and parcel, too, of the rise of the common man. The development of firearms as cheap and readily produced instruments of force gradually brought home to the robber barons of early days the necessity for easing social conditions which could stir up armed strife in which the serf was a match for his lord in combat.

Their story reaches deep into the history of art, of sport, and of the military sciences and is indeed complex.

The drawings and photographs, designed to tell what mere words alone cannot tell, have the further feature of being an art form rather than a series of mechanical drawings or blueprints. Understanding them requires no special knowledge.

**History.** Because it is intended to cover, primarily, modern weapons, this article will deal but briefly with the past. Histories must always deal in conjecture, in opinion, and in the finding of earlier writers, researchers, and historians. If we remember that firearms were in general use in Europe for two centuries or so before the introduction of printing there, it becomes immediately apparent that trustworthy accounts of early arms developments are difficult to unearth; the more so when it is realized that inventions very often appear simultaneously in widely separated parts of the world, and that only the Church had adequate facilities for communication in the Middle Ages. Developments in Germany and Italy of those days seem to have followed so closely that it is often impossible to ascribe a new design either to a given year or a given country.

Many histories seek to establish that guns and gunpowder first made their appearance in the Far East and came to Europe through Arabia. Study and research among museums, manuscripts, and contemporary tapestries throughout Europe indicate that such histories have been influenced too much by legends, technically incorrect translations, and ambiguous accounts. Lieutenant Colonel H. W. L. Himes published in London, in 1915, *The Origin of Artillery,* unquestionably the most exhaustive work the world has yet seen dealing with the invention of gunpowder. Weighing all the evidence presented in previous books, showing in detail the misapprehensions which arose when authors dealt with languages, sciences, periods, and customs with which they were not thoroughly familiar, Colonel Himes concluded that true gunpowder (as distinguished from "Greek fire" preparations) should be ascribed to Europe in the Middle Ages.

It advanced through but few elementary stages from its first specific mention by Roger Bacon in 1249, until the 16th century. In 1540 a treatise was published in Venice, Italy, under the title *De la Pirotechnia,* by Vanucchio Biringuccio. In 1546 one of the most remarkable research manuscripts in the long history of explosives made its appearance under the title *Questi e Inventioni Diversi.* This work marks Tartaglia, the author, as one of the true scientists of recorded history, little though his name is known. In an earlier book, *Nuova Scienzia,* published in Venice in 1537, he first applied abstract mathematical reasoning to the use of artillery, establishing, among other things, that no portion of a projectile's flight is ever in a straight line. He was probably the discoverer of the gunner's quadrant.

However, Tartaglia's most amazing sections in the 1540 book are those dealing with actual gunpowder formulas. He gives 25 detailed, specific compositions covering all types of powders from those giving a faint squib action, through priming powders, to types entirely too powerful to be used in ordinary weapons. At this period, when knowledge of chemistry was just developing, Tartaglia employed an inspired combination of deductive reasoning and routine trial-and-error methods to develop these formulas.

While the scientist himself is little known, his formulas are well known because, ironically enough, Niccolo Machiavelli in *The Arte of Warre* (English Whithorne translation, 1588) copies them exactly—and without credit to Tartaglia.

Just when or where originated the idea of loading powder and ball together in a piece of paper or linen so the entire barrel charge could be loaded down the muzzle speedily and easily, again is not clear. However, as early as 1590, Sir John Smythe, in his *Certain Discourses Concerning the Formes and Effects of Divers Sorts of Weapons,* makes specific mention of musketeers loading with a single operation by the use of "cartridges" containing both powder and ball.

Even today, incorrect ideas about weapons reach the public and become records which some future researcher accepts in good faith, only to be entirely in error in his findings.

Writers with a knowledge of foreign languages are unable to analyze foreign arms (or any other) technical developments without a thorough knowledge of the subject itself. The best general translator available cannot make intelligible a handbook on

German or Russian arms unless it happens to be so well illustrated that the drawings fill in the gaps in the word translations. This applies particularly to German arms, which by and large have been the most highly developed during the past 30 years. As they developed new designs and refinements, the Germans coined new words. Hence, even an arms expert might be unable to visualize a new development from a correctly translated description of it. Consider the German term *Scheintot Pistol*. Literally translated, this means "Appearance-of-Death Pistol." This is a variety of pistol intended to shoot gas cartridges. When of standard pistol size, it usually has a barrel constricted enough to prevent the passage of a bullet. The name developed from the fact that the gas it projects will produce unconsciousness—"the appearance of death"—when used at close quarters. Unless one has a very close acquaintance with German arms, or has an opportunity to examine and use both the ammunition and the pistol, it would take a vivid imagination indeed to identify and classify this weapon.

Differences of terminology and unusual conditions of manufacture all through history to the present day have also led to honest but fundamental errors by many writers. In the United States during World War I, the service automatic pistol was made by Colt, Remington, and Springfield Armory. All look alike but have different stampings. In World War II, the very slightly modified version of this pistol may be encountered stamped only US&S; and some future collector might feel he has stumbled on an exceptional weapon, rather than the standard pistol made by the Union Switch & Signal Company. Or he may find it stamped *Ithaca*—or even *Singer*, for the Singer Sewing Machine Company. All these organizations, as well as Colt's, turned out standard .45 automatics for the Army. Meanwhile, imitations of this design, perfect in every exterior detail but bearing no manufacturer's name, have been made of pot metal in Spain and of second-class workmanship in South America. An excellent close imitation has been made in Sweden. The possibilities for a future researcher with limited facilities to make very serious errors are quite apparent.

Yet another factor difficult for any researcher to evaluate except in unusual cases is what constitutes a really "qualified source." Catalogs of the present are not necessarily reliable—if, as has happened, manufacturers and government sources have published and widely distributed data and drawings which are inaccurate, and have failed to check and correct them over the years, it is clear that care must be taken to check even these sources before accepting their material.

**Research in the United States** has not nearly come into its own; and so we find our manufacturers complacently turning out good arms and smugly assuring all and sundry that they are the very best. As a matter of cold fact, no arms manufacturer in the United States in the year 1945 had either a complete collection of foreign types or an adequate weapons library to enable him to do intelligent research!

**Evolution of the One-Hand Gun.** PHASE I — THE CANNON LOCK. Since earliest times the means of firing a weapon has been called the "lock." The earliest one-hand guns were miniature cannon, elementary tubes of wrought iron fastened to a frame or grip with metal bands or leather thongs.

Like the first cannon, they were loaded with powder, wad, and ball from the muzzle. A hole in the top of the tube at the rear or breech end gave access to the powder charge. A small charge of priming powder was placed over this hole. While the weapon was thrust forward with one hand to "aim" it, a lighted match or a hot wire or iron was applied to the priming powder over the "touchhole." The ignited priming powder flashed fire down into the main charge in the barrel to discharge the piece.

These early "cannon-locks" are very rare. In view of the inefficient powders of those early days, as well as the crude method of ignition and aiming, it is obvious that accuracy was out of the question, and that the arm had very little use other than the psychological one of noise-making.

Just when or where the earliest handguns were used is impossible to determine accurately. While W. W. Greener, in *The Gun and Its Development* (London, 1881), cites a number of instances of the reported use of cannon in Spain between 1247 and 1311, the earliest record we can authenticate concerning their introduction is in the chronicles of the city of Ghent, Belgium. Among the records listed for the year 1313 is one which states that in that year the use of cannon was discovered in Germany. In 1314 the same chronicles list shipments of gunpowder and cannon to England. Just how soon after the introduction of cannon the hand versions were used cannot be definitely determined, as recorded items seldom distinguish between heavy portable cannon and small one-hand types which were the forerunners of true pistols.

However, in Grazzini's "Chronicle" in *Archivio Storico Italiano* we have the authenticated record of an order by the town of Perugia, Italy, for 500 portable bombards of only a span's length. It is noted that they are to be fired from the hand. The Roman "span" then in use was equivalent to 7½ inches.

It would appear that such short arms were in common use at the time, as the town order does not indicate that the items are unusual in any respect. In fact, the Chronicles of Modena, Italy, for the year 1364 list "Four little *scioppi* for the hand" as being among the town's possessions. The term *scioppi*, it may be noted, finally emerged as *sclopetum*, the authorized Latin word for pistol.

Possibly these early arms were generally used fastened to pikes or staffs, but they were obviously capable of use from the hand in pistol fashion.

One of the very few authentic illustrations of a very early short handgun is to be found in the fresco in the Palazzo Publico at Sienna, Italy, which pictures the battle of Poggibonzi, where the Duke of Calabria defeated the Florentines in the 15th century.

Auguste Demmin, whose *Die Kriegswaffen* is a monumental if not always too well documented coverage of early arms and armor (an English edition, Black's translation, titled *An Illustrated History of Arms and Armor*, was published in London in 1877) attributes the earliest use of hand firearms to the Flemings. However, his statements that the town of

Liège had made several experiments in manufacturing *knallbüschen* or hand cannon, while probably correct in the face of the known early history of that city, have never been documented.

The first use of the term "handgun" thus far authenticated appears in English records in the year 1386 when one Ralph Hatton sent three to the Chamberlain of Berwick. (See "14th Century Art," in the 1911 *English Historical Review.*)

The first recorded use of the cannon lock as a cavalry weapon is that of the so-called *petronel,* whose barrel was usually about 7 inches long and was attached to a wooden staff or welded to an iron rod. The *Mss. of Marianus Jacobus,* written and illustrated in 1449, shows a mounted soldier ready to fire a *petronel.* The barrel is supported by a forked rest attached to the front of the saddle. The stock is held with the left hand while its tip rests against the man's chest. In his right hand he holds a lighted slow match ready to apply it to the touch-hole. The German Black Knights, the *Reitres* (also known as *Ritters* or *Raitres),* used these guns against French infantrymen, to their great surprise. While the German records list them only as *knallbüschen* (literally, popguns), the French named them *poitrinal,* indicating "fired from the chest" a term probably later corrupted into "petronel." This seems a more logical derivation than that advanced by some writers who have thought petronel was derived from an early Spanish term *pedernal,* meaning a firearm.

Combinations of the one-hand cannon with the war mace and the battleax were common early in the 16th century. Indeed, the most reliable museum specimens of the cannon-lock for one hand use are of this variety.

An English development of which many museum specimens of known authenticity exist is the "Holy Water Sprinkle." This instrument is a heavy mace whose front end or head consists of four or more short barrels resembling an oversized revolver cylinder. These barrels were loaded with powder, ball, and wad. Pushing back a cover to the rear of the barrels exposed a cavity leading to a single touch-hole. Priming powder was placed in the cavity and, when the weapon was pointed with one hand and a lighted match was thrust down into the priming powder, fire was flashed to all barrels, discharging them simultaneously. This is the earliest authenticated attempt at developing a multi-shot one-hand gun.

Phase II—The Matchlock. The first great advance in pistols, as in all small firearms, came with the introduction of the matchlock, which made it possible to fire the weapon with one hand and hence gave some opportunity to aim it. In this type of arm the barrel was still loaded with powder, ball, and wad rammed down the muzzle, and priming powder was placed over the small touch-hole near the breech end of the barrel, or in a shallow pan near the hole.

The very earliest matchlock, as Thierback copied it from the Glockenton manuscript, is merely a curved hook screwed to the right side of the stock. This "serpentine" as it was called (it developed into the "cock" which was roughly equivalent to the "hammer" in a modern revolver) was split at the end to receive a "match," as the prepared slow-burning cord was named. There was no trigger section to this first serpentine. It was merely pushed or pulled to drop the lighted match on the priming powder. The second step appears to have been merely to lengthen the serpentine so that a lower arm acted as a trigger to pivot the upper end down into the priming. This was an adaptation of the string release then in use on crossbows. The third step was to provide a slot in the stock and mount the serpentine on a cross-pin which served as a pivot. The use of springs to retain the head of the serpentine in safety and to withdraw it as the weapon fired were the next developments.

While some writers have ascribed the matchlock development to Liège about 1375, the earliest form of serpentine of which there is satisfactory documentation appears in an early 15th-century illustration (now at Vienna, Codex Manuscript 3069); it is shown attached to a handgun.

While literally scores of variations of the matchlock are recognized, they fall into two general classes: (1) Those in which pressure on the trigger end of the serpentine merely pivots the upper end to bring the lighted match down into the powder pan. This is the pressure type. (2) Those of later date—generally toward the end of the 15th century—in which a trigger and spring-rebound action drop the lighted match quickly into the priming powder, permitting better aiming and ignition. This is the snapping type.

Probably the most exhaustive study of matchlocks ever presented is that published in Dresden in 1899 by Thierback in his work, *Die Geschichtliche Entwickelung der Handfeurwaffen.* No English translation exists.

During the era of the matchlock dependable English records appear. Under Henry VIII, for instance, who reigned from 1509 to 1547, we find that many cavalry were armed with early forms of pistols. It is on record, too, that Henry induced Peter Bawd and Peter Van Collen to move from Flanders, where Henry's earliest firearms were made, to London where he set them up in the business of gunmaking.

In the Ashmolean Museum at Oxford University in England are three pistol barrels of the matchlock era fastened together to form a single unit revolving on a pin attached to the stock. Each barrel has a separate flash-pan fitted with a sliding cover. This unit formed a three-barreled pistol with a single serpentine. The barrels were loaded from the muzzle in regular fashion; then the pan covers were opened and priming powder placed in each pan, over which the cover was then drawn. In firing, a pan cover was slid forward; the trigger end of the serpentine was pulled to drop the lighted match into the primer pan to fire the first barrel. The barrels were turned by hand to bring the second one in line with the serpentine and the process repeated. Here we have the forerunner of the American "pepperbox" of the 19th century!

The pans and covers on these barrels (which, by the way, are usually credited to the 15th century) resemble very closely those employed on the famous four-chambered, single-barreled true-revolver-type arquebus believed to have belonged to Henry VIII, now in the Tower of London.

It has a single brass barrel, a brass cylinder with eight chambers which was revolved by hand to bring each chamber successively in line with the barrel, and individual priming pans and touch-holes for each chamber. While the lock itself is missing, the construction makes it evident that it was fired with a single-serpentine matchlock. A Tudor rose is embossed on the pommel. Another early matchlock revolver, which seems to be of 17th-century origin, is now part of the Pitt-Rivers Collection at Oxford.

The matchlock, as in the case of every other advance, persisted long after more efficient systems had been developed. In quite recent years it has been encountered in Mongolia and in Korea.

The matchlock, of course, suffered from the major defect that it required a lighted slow-match to fire it, thus rendering it practically useless in surprise attack or for hunting, and making its use in damp or rainy weather impracticable. It was not until the turn of the 16th century that human ingenuity found a partial answer in the next evolutionary step.

Phase III—The Wheellock. This development completely revolutionized the art of war. It resulted in new tactics which for a time made cavalry supreme on the field of battle. It made ambush with firearms possible for the first time, since it did away with the necessity for the lighted match; and this same feature also made practicable the use of firearms in hunting. Both directly and indirectly it produced economic and military advances of epochal stature.

What was this startling development? Just a complicated forerunner of our modern pocket lighter!

In its simplest forms it consists of a steel wheel mounted on the side of the weapon at the rear of the barrel. The circumference of this wheel is grooved, roughened, or notched. An axle protrudes from the side of the wheel and a spanner or wrench is provided to fit over this protrusion. Inside the lockplate a chain is attached to the inner axle of the wheel at its forward end and to a spring at its rear on the principle of a watch drum. Thus when the wheel is turned with the spanner, the chain is wound around the inner axle and the spring is tensioned. A bar in the lockwork drops into a notch in the wheel, acting as a sear to keep the wheel from revolving and thereby relieving the spring.

Part of the wheel edge projects into the flash pan which communicates with the touch-hole in the breech of the barrel. The pan is usually covered, and the cover must be pushed forward when the arm is made ready for firing. The serpentine is pivoted on the side of the lockplate just ahead of the flash pan, where it is held by a powerful spring. The jaws of the serpentine open to the rear and are really a small vise. A piece of pyrites (originally used instead of flint because it would not wear the wheel rapidly) is clamped securely in the jaws and the serpentine is pulled down until the pyrites is in contact with the wheel. Pressing the trigger pulls the stop pin out of the notch in the wheel and frees the spring to unwind the chain. This action, of course, spins the wheel rapidly on its axle. The edge of the steel wheel strikes sparks from the pyrites and showers them down into the priming powder, igniting it to flash through the touch-hole into the barrel charge.

Where did the wheellock originate? While some writers have ascribed it to Italy, there is weighty evidence to indicate that it originated in Nuremberg, Germany, in 1515 or 1517. Records of Germany and of the Low Countries, which even then were hives of activity as arms centers, link the names of Kaspar Rechmagel and Georg Kuhfuss to improvements of the system. But another Nuremberg gunmaker, Johann Kiefuss, is generally credited as the direct inventor.

It is an interesting sidelight that about this same time in Nuremberg, which was a noted mechanical center, the clock operating on the same spring system as the wheellock first appears. Whether the invention was first applied to clocks or firearms has never been decided.

The wheellock made possible the first reasonably satisfactory pistol—more particularly the military cavalry pistol. The Germans, whose Black Knights had already shocked the French by the surprise use of the petronel in cannonlock days, speedily applied the wheellock to long-barreled all-steel pistols carried in holsters swung across the pommels of their saddles, each man carrying two or four.

The *Century Dictionary and Encyclopedia* states that the Ritters made common use of pistols in 1520. Whether they were armed widely with wheellocks at that time is not certain; but in 1544, at the battle of Renty, they introduced against the French King Henry II an entirely new maneuver using pistols as their main arm. While the French waited in formation for the charge, the Ritters galloped in rank formation almost to the French lines, discharged their pistols into the massed men, then wheeled their horses out of line to reload while their next rank rode up to continue pouring demoralizing fire from their pistols. This maneuver, afterwards named *caracole,* was adopted by the French. Henry shortly afterward hired the Ritters (who were paid mercenaries, the Hessians of those early days) to join his army. Henry of France called these troops "pistoleers."

And here develops one of the puzzles of firearms history: *Why is a pistol called a pistol?*

Most dictionaries and encyclopedias repeat the early explanation that the pistol was invented by one Camillio Vettelli in Pistoia, Italy, about 1540. So far as recent research has been able to determine, no satisfactory documentation exists for that statement. Vettelli as a gunmaker may have lived, though even that has not been clearly established.

As indicated above, short guns of the pistol type existed long before the date ascribed to Vettelli; and in view of the development and use of wheellock pistols in Germany, France, Belgium, Holland, and even England—records of the time of King Henry VIII of England show that some of his cavalry were armed with clumsy wheellock pistols by 1545—it is difficult to believe that all Europe, in less than five years, in those days of slow travel and poor communication, would have evolved the term "pistol" or "pistole" from the name of the town of Pistoia.

Could "pistol" have evolved from the fact that the general caliber of the arm was about that of a coin called *pistole,* which has also been offered as a derivation? It is rather far fetched, particularly in view of the fact that no two guns were of the same caliber in those days.

Why, then, did Henry II of France name his pistol-carrying troopers "pistoleers"?

There is a third solution, already suggested by Demmin and other researchers whose backgrounds in languages, knowledge of arms, and opportunity to check early European records qualify them as expert witnesses. It seems most likely that the term derived from the fact that those original pistols, commonly associated with the cavalry, were invariably *carried in holsters swung across the pistallo* (or pommel) of the saddle.

The French assigned the name *petronel* quite evidently to a hand weapon hung across the *poitrine*—the chest—and rested against it when firing. What is more logical, then, that a later French king and army should link the name with the method of carrying? Certainly, *pistole* would represent a closer approach to *pistallo,* a word any French cavalryman of the day would associate with the pommel of the saddle, than it would to the name of a distant city in Italy which by no stretch of the imagination could have been the source of the surprise mass of weapons the Ritters used against the French at Renty!

The wheellocks which have come down to us in original condition, and there are thousands of them, are nearly all rich man's weapons. Very few are plain and unornamented. Even the cheapest were far too expensive for the average citizen or for general issue to all soldiers. Another drawback was that it took considerable time to wind the spring. If kept wound ready for action, it soon lost its strength, since the steels of those days were not suited for spring purposes. In the heat of battle or the hunting chase the all-important spanner might be lost. A cheaper and simpler ignition system was needed.

While the wheellock pistol reached an advanced stage of evolution in Germany, Belgium, France, and Italy toward the close of the 16th century, it was not widely manufactured in England. The English showed little interest in pistols until the introduction of the flintlock.

One development of the era which has a most important bearing on the use of pistols and all firearms is unfortunately shrouded in mystery. It is the employment of rifling to give better accuracy. The earliest English patent records dealing with rifling are dated 1635. It was employed on the Continent long before that date, Augustin Kutter of Nuremberg being known for star-shaped rifling as early as 1520. Yet in a novel, *Jewel House,* written by Sir Hugh Plat and first published in 1594, there is an account of a *rifled pistol!*

While the wheellock was widely manufactured as late as 1640, by the turn of the 17th century it was gradually making way for its successor.

Phase IV—The Flintlock. The elementary principle of the flintlock is that of fastening a piece of flint in the head of the "cock" or hammer, so that when the trigger is pulled the hammer spring will drive the flint down to strike a glancing blow against a piece of case-hardened steel so placed that the resulting sparks shower down into the priming pan.

The evolution of the true flintlock was long. Just when or just where it first appeared, no man can say positively. The standard way of lighting fires in the day of the early matchlock was to strike flint against steel. Why, then, the long use of the complicated wheellock? Even in our own day we find cheap and simple forms of weapons failing to get attention or acceptance because the military or the manufacturers, for reasons peculiar to themselves, resist change and simplification. Such conservatism may have had something to do with the delayed general appearance of the flintlock. Then, too, the flintlock made possible the arming of the common man with cheap, dependable weapons, an undesirable factor to those who controlled the policies of those early days.

While isolated examples of the use of some form of flintlock may be traced, with necessarily foggy documentation, to the early 16th century, its first wide use cannot be established with acceptable proof until the beginning of the 17th century.

Writers in the 17th century listed all flint-and-steel ignition weapons generally as "snaphaunces." It should be noted that this type of ignition differed in the various countries of its manufacture. In an early form in Germany it actually was a steel-and-pyrites system of the type found in the "Monk's Gun" in the Dresden Museum. Pyrites was not satisfactory, however, because it was highly friable. A lock using it had to provide a scraping, rasping effect to produce sparks. This type of lock, though authenticated, is little known.

Modern writers generally distinguish the varieties of flintlocks about as follows:

*The Snaphaunce.* Mechanism and mainspring covered by lockplate. Cock (hammer) has a miniature vise in its head to hold the flint. Flash-pan opposite touch-hole holds priming powder. A pan-cover, which *must be manually pushed back* before the weapon can be fired, protects the priming. The steel against which the flint is struck, usually works on a hinged arm and was variously called "frizzen," "battery," "hen," or "hammer".

The derivation of the word *snaphaunce* has been argued about for centuries. It may be from the Dutch *schnapp-hahn,* indicating a pecking cock (the "cock" or hammer falling and pecking at the "hen" or steel); it may be from the Dutch *snaap-haans,* meaning chicken thieves. (Some of the earliest reported uses of cheap flint-type weapons indicate their employment by poachers.) It has been corrupted in both English and French usage and spelling in many ways.

*The Miquelet Lock.* Mainspring on outside of lockplate. Steel "frizzens" and pan-cover are *in one piece.* Thus when the cock is driven forward by the mainspring, it strikes the flint against the upright steel piece and, as the sparks shower down, the frizzen is rocked back so its pan-cover section exposes the powder in the priming pan to be ignited by the sparks.

*Miquelet* is said to derive from the Spanish or Portuguese raiders, called *miguelitos,* who first achieved attention for their use of this form of arm. This form of lock is common to all types and qualities of small arms made in Spain at the flintlock period. Its manufacture was continued well into the 18th century.

*The True Flintlock.* Essentially the same as the snaphaunce except that it uses the Miquelet principle of a combined pan-cover and frizzen. This unit is mounted on a pivot and is spring-supported. The weapon being loaded both in the barrel and in the priming pan, and cocked, pressure on the trigger releases the cock to strike the flint a glancing blow at the upright steel piece. The frizzen, thus rocked back on its pivot as sparks are produced, carries the pan-cover section away from the priming, permitting ignition. These weapons have a half-cock position which serves as a safety. England, Holland, Sweden, and Scotland all produced variations with individual characteristics.

The flintlock, which survived for over 200 years and is even today made and used in some far corners of the world, appeared at various times in practically every form of one-hand weapon known today, with the sole exception of the automatic pistol. A revolver dating from the period of King Charles I (1625-1647) is in the Tower Collection in London. It is unusual in early revolver types in that the cylinder is automatically revolved as the hammer is raised. A patent was granted the Marquis of Worcester for a revolver in 1661. In Pepys' *Diary* for July 3, 1662, mention is made of a "gun to discharge seven times," which Mr. Pepys found reliable. On March 3, 1664, patent office specifications were filed by Abraham Hill for a gun or pistol to carry seven or eight charges in the stock. Hill was also granted a patent for a breech-loading gun or pistol "which hath a hole at the upper end of the breech to receive the charge, which hole is opened or stopped by a piece of iron or steel that lies alongside the side of the piece which is movable."

Magnificent flintlock pistols, with hinged-frame, drop-down barrels very similar to those of the present day, were manufactured in Italy. Many of these were supplied with steel inserts which were carried loaded and were dropped into the breech end of the barrel for quick loading. Side loader, screw-plug breeches, three- and four-barreled pistols, magazine pistols of the "Cookson" type, seven-barreled pistols revolving around a spindle in the manner of the later "pepperbox" pistols, over-and-under pistols, removable-barrel types—these are but a few of the varieties known and authenticated. (J. N. George's classic work, *English Pistols and Revolvers* [Small-Arms Technical Publishing Co., 1938], dealing specifically with English weapons, gives a general idea of the enormous scope and the fertility of early arms development.)

What about America during the flintlock period? Of the period before 1680, not much is known. Some very fine examples of pocket-type snaphaunces now in the Smithsonian Institution have come down from the families of early Dutch settlers. Some few gunsmiths came to New England with the twenty-odd thousand souls who came between 1630 and 1640. However, there is no early record of their making pistols. Later, when it was customary to import the locks (which were difficult to make), pistols with those locks were made by numerous gunsmiths.

The records of the Massachusetts Bay Company show the importation of snaphaunce weapons for their soldiers in 1628 and 1629; while early records of the same Company also indicate that about that same time Indians residing near the villages were well supplied with both pistols and bullet molds. The Dutch in those early years did a tremendous business with the Indians in firearms—a business which led to the eventual loss of their American colony. The *bosch-lopers,* or woods runners, dealing with the Indians as agents of the wealthy patroons, found arms and powder the best trading units for fine furs.

Pistols are seldom mentioned in the first half of the 17th century in America. The Rev. William Hubbard, of Ipswich, Mass., in his story of the Pequot Wars written in 1677, tells of "pieces laden with 10 or 12 pistol bullets" being fired at close range into the Pequots. Bodge, in his *Soldiers in King Philip's War,* tells how Captain John Gallup, of Boston Harbor, attacked a boat the Indians had stolen. "Gallup," he writes, "was armed with two guns and two pistols and with buckshot for bullets."

With the start of the French and Indian Wars, however, the picture grows clearer. Pistols by then were, for the most part, those manufactured in England or whose locks were made there. But, by 1720, John Kim was advertising in the *Boston News Letter* that, at his shop near the drawbridge, at the sign of the crossed guns, he would manufacture to order. The extent to which pistols were in use in the Colonies as the day of the American Revolution drew near may be grasped from the account in Frothingham's contemporaneous *Siege of Boston,* wherein he lists 634 pistols as having been turned in by Boston householders when the British General Gage assured them they might leave the city if the arms were surrendered. (As a matter of further record, General Gage broke his promise.)

Here we reach another milestone in the always-too-obscure history of firearms: Was "the shot heard around the world" fired from a pistol?

Paul Revere, in his *Letter,* states that a pistol was fired to start the Battle of Lexington. The *Essex Gazette,* Vol. III, No. 353, dated April 25, 1775, makes the same statement. Parson Stiles, an eyewitness, states in his *Diary* that British Major Pitcairn, after cursing the colonists and ordering them to lay down their arms and retreat, when they did not obey, "rushed forward and discharged his pistol."

If, as might well have been the case, Major Pitcairn did fire that world-shattering shot, it came from one of two Highlander flintlock pistols now reposing in the battered little old Hancock Clark House which serves as a museum at Lexington, Mass. In common with many officers of his day, Pitcairn took great pride in his pair of beautiful all-metal Scotch-made pistols whose distinctive grips, magnificent workmanship and quality are still a wonder to every lover of fine handguns. These pistols—lineal descendants of the all-metal wheellock pistols and of the long-dead German Ritters—were carried like their earlier counterparts in holsters swung across the pommel of the saddle, the "pistallo" of an earlier day. As the British retreated from the Common, shots fired from ambush hit Pitcairn's horse, throwing the rider. The wounded horse bolted and was captured, with the pistols hung from the pommel, by Minutemen. The pistols were offered to General Washington, who declined to accept them. It is an interesting sidelight on Washington that, except for presentation pistols, all weapons we can trace definitely to him have been plain, unornamented arms intended strictly for field use.

Pitcairn's pistols were carried throughout the War by Captain Parker, and were later donated to the little museum where they now rest, little known and less seen—a strange commentary on the interest the average man has in the people and the things which paved the way for his present liberties.

As an evidence of the extent to which the flintlock pistol contributed to later American history, consider the fact that some 70,000 men shipped out of New England ports alone aboard privateersmen during the War of 1812, and that it was customary for such men to carry at least two heavy belt pistols, as close-quarter arms for boarding ships. Yet today only a handful of pistols of this type are in the hands of collectors. Such is the way with weapons of use—as opposed to ornamented weapons—at the close of each war.

As the 18th century drew to a close, experience had shown that, with flintlock ignition, only the single and the double-barreled pistols were truly practical. In 1763, the British for the first time adopted an official pistol for the army—a single-shot weapon with an over-all length of about 15 inches, firing a ball of about .69 caliber. While authorized pistols were made in America during the Revolutionary period by the Committee of Safety's orders, the first official pistol contract let by the United States Government was not until 1813, when Simeon North furnished 500 "North's Berlin Model" pistols.

Early in the 19th century attempts were again made to apply the multi-shot ideas to the flintlock. "Pepperbox" flintlocks similar to the somewhat earlier Twigg and Ketland types; "volley guns" of the Nock type in which several barrels are fired simultaneously by a single flint; magazine weapons of the Mortimer type in which two motions of a lever loaded the barrel, primed the pistol, and cocked the arm for firing—these and scores of other types were tried.

In 1818, Elisha H. Collier, of Boston, Mass., was granted an English patent on a flintlock revolver of unusual design. The first of Collier's revolvers was developed in the United States about 1809, but the inventor had to go to England to obtain financing. Specimens of this revolver exist with 4-inch barrels and an over-all length of about 11½ inches; also with 6⅛-inch barrel, longer (1⅞-inch) cylinders, and over-all length of about 14 inches. It is doubtful that more than a few hundred were made.

An automatic primer holding enough priming powder for about ten charges was mounted on top of the pan cover. The cylinder, which contained five chambers, was rotated by hand to bring each chamber in line with the barrel for firing. The truly original feature of the Collier, however, was the gas-check cylinder which today is used in principle in the Russian Nagant service revolver, and which may possibly be further developed. The rear or breech end of the barrel was cone-shaped, and the chambers in the cylinder had countersunk mouths. The cylinder was normally thrust forward by a spiral flat spring working on a center pivot, and was supported when firing by a trigger-actuated sliding bolt. In its forward position the chamber ready for firing was thrust over the tapered end of the barrel, thus assuring positive alignment of barrel and cylinder (the most important feature in revolver design), and also holding to a minimum the escape of gas between cylinder and barrel, thereby assuring the utmost use of the power of the discharge and reducing the danger of fire from one chamber setting off the charges in the other chambers. The cylinder had to be drawn back about one-eighth of an inch against spring tension before it could be revolved on its center pin. While a few samples of the Collier were known later for use with percussion powder, the patent granted covered use of the flintlock system of ignition.

By now the era of the flintlock was drawing to a close. Whereas all major evolutionary steps had heretofore been the result of mechanical changes in ignition systems, chemistry now entered the field.

Phase V—The Percussion Lock. "I do make use of some one of the compounds of combustible matter, such as sulphur or sulphur and charcoal, with an oxymuriatic salt; . . . or of fulminating metallic compounds, as fulminate of mercury. . . . Instead of permitting the touch-hole, or vent, of the species of artillery, firearms, mines, etc., to communicate with the open air, and instead of giving fire by lighted match, or flint and steel, or by any other matter in a state of actual combustion applied to a priming in an open pan, I do so close the touch-hole, or vent, by means of a plug or sliding piece so as to exclude the open air . . . and, as much as possible to force the said priming to go in the direction of the charge and to set fire to the same. . . ."

Those direct quotations from the letters patent of the Rev. Alexander John Forsyth, LL.D. (for 52 years minister of Belhelvie, Scotland), dated April 11, 1807, mark the accepted legal proof of the application of a revolutionary principle for exploding gunpowder—the percussion principle. Heretofore it had been necessary to produce fire to explode the charge. Now the priming could be done by a blow delivered directly by the hammer. With the development of this principle, the successful revolver was at last to become an actuality.

Forsyth did not discover the fulminating mixtures. Even before 1700 a French scientist, Peter Bolduc, is known to have conducted inquiries into this field. Nicholas Lemery gives notices in the reports of the Royal Academy of Sciences of experiments in 1712 and again in 1714. The first important authenticated discovery, however, is that of Louis XV's Chief Army Physician, Dr. Bayen, who reported fulminate of mercury and told of its explosive properties. As in the case of Roger Bacon, who, in 1249, described gunpowder without apparent thought to its application to firearms, Bayen overlooked the application of mercuric fulminate to weapons. Berthollet, in 1788, was injured doing experimental work which resulted in the ultra-sensitive silver fulminate. In 1800, "Howard's powder," a mixture of mercuric fulminate and saltpeter, was developed in England as an outgrowth of the inventor's study of earlier French researches. But first official *application* of the principle is credited to the Rev. Forsyth.

From 1807 to 1845 a tremendous range of systems for applying the percussion principle were developed, as well as of weapons to use these systems. In 1808, a Swiss gunmaker, Pauly, then working in Paris, developed a paper cap in which fulminate was enclosed. This was fired by a needle driven through the paper when the trigger was pulled. Somewhat later, the priming mixture came in pellets and resulted in the development of "pill-lock" pistols, many of most ingenious design. Egg, Manton, and other famous gunmakers, as well as dozens of less-known figures, claimed to have invented the most successful percussion system—that of the metal cap in which the fulminate was housed so that the cap could be placed over the nipple of the touchhole and fired when the falling hammer crushed the cap.

However, the earliest instance of use duly credited seems to be that of an Englishman, Joshua Shaw, then working in Philadelphia, Pa. In 1814, he employed a steel cap, which could be reloaded. In 1815, he used pewter and, in 1816, developed the copper cap used through the American Civil War period.

The Maynard tape primer was invented in the United States in 1845. It fed fulminate, held between strips of paper as in children's cap pistols into position to be struck by the hammer. Variations were copper strip primers on the general principle of the tape, and disk primers. All met with some temporary success.

Of all systems, that of the copper cup which could be placed over the nipple was by far the best. Although its application was made to both breech- and muzzle-loading arms, it was truly successful only in the latter, since escape of gas at the breech was not fully controllable in early breechloaders.

In the United States, Derringer of Philadelphia was the first to develop a pistol to use the new percussion cap. The first models were very small, compact muzzle loaders of .52 caliber shooting a half-ounce ball. These arms were widely used during the great American era of the Ohio and Mississippi steamboats. It was with one of them that John Wilkes Booth killed President Lincoln; and it is a strange comment on mankind that the publicity given the Derringer as a result of Lincoln's assassination resulted in such a huge demand for the arm that imitators of the pistol sprang up overnight and plagued the original manufacturer for years by unfair competition.

In 1845, Ethan Allen patented the arm which was one of the principal weapons of the Forty-niners —the Allen & Thurber pepperbox. At the age of 21, Allen, then living at North Grafton, Mass., had manufactured cane guns for a Dr. Lambert. At 23 he was turning out rifled pistols with saw-handle grips. It is possible that he was the real inventor of the "double-action lock," in which simple pressure on the trigger acts both to cock and drop the hammer. In England, pepperboxes are thought to have been introduced some time before the Allen. However, the record is not clear, and it is probable that the invention had parallel development in several countries.

In the case of the Allen, both patents and weapons definitely establish that Ethan Allen actually manufactured them for general sale. The pepperbox is essentially a series of barrels—usually six—either gathered together around a central axis pin or bored from a single block of metal. This design, obviously, results in a very heavy weapon for any caliber employed. The weapon was loaded from the muzzle and percussion caps were placed over the individual nipples at the breech. They were held on by an enclosing metal band at the breech. The lockwork is timed so that, as the trigger is pressed, it raises the hammer and turns the barrel assembly. At each fall of the hammer a barrel is in line to have its percussion cap crushed to fire that barrel, the entire barrel assembly being momentarily locked by mechanical action.

The pepperbox cannot be fired with any degree of accuracy because of the heavy trigger pull required. However, as a dependable, close-quarters weapon—both as a firearm and as a club in emergency—it was quite successful in its day.

One other specimen of pepperbox is worthy of American note: the almost unknown Blunt & Syms. Unlike the Allen, which had a top hammer, this arm had an underhammer. Blunt & Syms, of 44 Chatham St., New York City, were among the largest gun dealers in the country in the 1830's and for the following two decades. One of their employees, John Zettler, who came to the United States from Marburg, Germany, in 1837, manufactured a model of a pepperbox for an inventor whose name is lost to record. He never made an appearance to claim his model, and Blunt & Syms took out patents on it and put it into manufacture. Naturally, they sold their own arm wherever possible, and large quantities went to California in the period of 1849. These pistols usually had six barrels, each about 5½ inches long. The bullets used were distinctive, being .368 in diameter and .430 inch long. These egg-shaped bullets would turn end-on-end at 10 yards; but what they lacked in accuracy they made up in close-quarters stopping power.

The Mariette pepperbox used on the Continent was patented in Belgium in 1837. This was an under-hammer weapon operated by trigger pull. The barrels had to be unscrewed from the frame to permit the priming powder to be loaded in. The nipples were in line with the axis of the barrels, thus varying from the standard vertical type.

All these were merely transitional arms, however; for, with the coming of percussion caps, Samuel Colt had found the way to provide a rifled, multishot arm in which a single action would cock the hammer and revolve and lock the cylinder—an arm which would combine accuracy, sturdiness, simplicity, and dependability.

**The First Successful Revolver.** In the long history of pistols and revolvers, no name stands out as clearly as that of Samuel Colt. "Colt" has become synonymous with revolver. Yet Colt did not invent the revolver as such, and never claimed he did.

As we have seen, the principle of the true "revolver"—a weapon with a revolving cylinder containing a number of firing chambers which may be successively lined up with and discharged through a single barrel—was known in very early times. Perhaps the most famous early revolver is that mentioned in General Norton's *American Breech Loading Small Arms,* published in 1872. This is a snaphaunce revolver of the days of King Charles I of England, and is still to be seen in the Royal United Service Museum in Whitehall. The date of manufacture is prior to 1650.

This early revolver, astonishingly enough, is

practically identical with the action covered in Colt's first patents and still used in that most famous of all Colts, the Single-Action Army or "Frontier" Model. A ratchet with six teeth is cut into the head of the cylinder. As the hammer is thumbed back, a metal hand attached to the front of the hammer thrusts up against the ratchet to turn the cylinder the distance of one chamber. A spring catch engages in a notch in the cylinder to lock it at that point. This early revolver is a brass-barreled, brass-cylindered giant of .500 caliber with a 9½-inch barrel. It is nearly 22 inches long and weighs about 6¼ pounds. The barrel is badly worn, but seems to have the remains of rifling in it. Ignition and metallurgy were not far enough advanced when it was designed to make it a success, but it is strange indeed that its revolving system should have been overlooked for centuries.

Samuel Colt's original patent was granted in England—then the world seat of small-arms manufacture—in 1835. While it dealt with the revolving of the cylinder by action of the hammer-attached hand acting on the cylinder ratchet when the hammer was cocked, it specified in great detail the feature of center-fire ignition through horizontal nipples which were separated by partitions to prevent the accidental firing of chambers adjoining the one in line with the barrel. It also dealt specifically with the lockwork. It was first patented in the United States on February 25, 1836.

The first model Colt had made for him by Anson Chase of East Hartford, Connecticut, blew up because it lacked partitions between the nipples. The discharge of the first chamber set off the others. His next one, now in the Colt Museum at Hartford and known as the "Anson Chase Model," from the name of the gunsmith who made it, bears in general appearance and in weights and measurements an astonishingly close resemblance to the Single-Action Army model still in manufacture.

Colt's patents were so ironclad, and he fought so hard to protect them, that nothing but freak revolvers were developed from 1840 to 1850, either in the United States or in Europe. Colt's first revolvers were made at Paterson, N. J. That company went bankrupt. Six years later, at the outbreak of the Mexican War, Colt—with the help of Eli Whitney, one of the earliest of the assembly-line-production geniuses, and with suggestions from Captain Walker of the Texas Rangers—was back in production at Whitneyville. Shortly afterward, Colt was able to finance his own orders, and he started at Hartford the plant which was to become the best-known revolver manufactory in history.

By 1850, Colt was exporting to Europe. In 1853, he opened a plant in London, using trained men brought from the United States as foremen.

The only British competition Colt received during these years was from the Deane-Adams revolver patented in 1851. This was the first successful solid-frame revolver. The barrel and the frame were a single forging, providing a weapon which was actually stronger than the Colt of that period. This was a double-action revolver in which a pull on the trigger rotated the cylinder and cocked and dropped the hammer. While others were made—notably the Lang and the Witton & Daw—they were too expensive to compete with the mass-production Colts.

In February 1855, the Beaumont selective double-action system was patented in England. This was a real advance in lockwork, as it permitted the revolver to be thumb cocked, then fired by trigger pressure—or fired double action by pulling through on the trigger to raise and drop the hammer. This Beaumont action was incorporated in the Adams revolver. Later, when Adams sold out to the London Armoury Company and that company was awarded a government contract for the double-action Adams as the British service revolver, Colt saw the writing on the wall and, in 1857, shut down the London factory. Tranter, Webley, Kerr, Daw, and Westley Richards all made percussion revolvers in England, none of which had the success of the Adams. In Europe, Comblain of Liège, Belgium, developed a single-action weapon in 1854, Amangeot of Brussels developed a double-action system; but in general nothing of particular merit emerged.

In the United States, when the Colt patents expired, a wide variety of revolvers flooded the market. Of those used during the Civil War, the best was the Remington—a standard design percussion-cap revolver. Another type, the Starr, had a double trigger. Pressure on the first trigger raised the hammer and revolved the cylinder. Continued rearward pressure forced the second trigger to trip the hammer. The Pettingill was a massive .44-caliber hammerless (enclosed hammer design) and had a quick-removable cylinder. The Savage, patented by H. S. North in 1865, was double action and had a ring trigger. Like the earlier Collier flintlock revolver, the Savage employed the principle of the chambered cylinder. Action of the trigger-guard lever forced the mouth of the cut-back chamber forward over the breech end of the barrel to make a gas-seal.

But again a new phase was under way, a new era beginning. In France, experiments with breech-loading arms were underway, and the end of muzzle-loading revolvers was in sight.

Phase VI—The Metallic Cartridge. *Pin-fire.* The Pauly cartridge already mentioned paved the way for the Lefaucheux pin-fire cartridge, which in its original form closely resembled the modern shotgun cartridge. Its base was a brass cap, its body a pasteboard tube carrying the powder, ball, and percussion cap. A pin through the side of the case rested on the percussion cap. This system made it possible to confine the gases in the chamber at the instant of firing, as the brass expanded momentarily and provided a positive breech seal.

Lefaucheux pin-fire revolvers in various types of 5 mm., 7 mm., 9 mm., 12 mm., and 15 mm. calibers are still widely used in Europe and South America, the cartridges being standard manufacture there before the outbreak of World War II. In this type of revolver the cylinder is notched at the side of each chamber at the breech end. The cylinder, instead of being solid except for the touch-hole, as required in percussion types, is bored through with chambers so that the complete cartridge can be inserted in the chamber through the breech. The pin projecting from the side of the cartridge case (which is now made of copper or brass) drops into the notch prepared for it. It will be seen that this requires the cartridge to be loaded in the chamber in just one way. That is, if the pin is not opposite its notch, the cartridge cannot enter the chamber fully.

In a pin-fire revolver, when the trigger is pressed and the hammer falls, the hammer strikes the projecting pin and drives it down inside the case to explode the primer which sets off the powder charge. The expansion of the gas inside the cartridge case swells the case to grip momentarily against the chamber wall as the bullet is driven out of the chamber. Thus any rearward escape of gas is impossible—unless, as happens on occasion, the head of the case is weak. Even then, little harm can result. The projecting pin can be used to lift the empty case out of its chamber.

*Rim-Fire.* With the introduction of rim-fire cartridges, the story of the modern revolver really begins. The honor of its initial development belongs to a Paris gunsmith, Flobert, who produced it as early as 1847, and who exhibited it at the Great International Exhibition in London in 1851. How Colt, whose revolvers achieved great attention and renown at that same Exhibition, ever missed the potentialities of the metallic cartridges, is another of the mysteries of the history of revolvers. Flobert's invention is in use today. We know it as the "BB cap" —the bulleted-breech cap. As originally issued it contained no powder. It was designed for indoor target service, and the fulminate under the rim porvided all the power necessary to drive the bullet out. The rim-fire cartridge has a relatively soft copper case with a hollow rim in which is the priming mixture. The rim rests on the cylinder metal around the chamber. When the hammer falls, its nose (or a special firing pin, as the revolver design requires) hits the rim of the cartridge case, crushing it and thus detonating the priming mixture.

In 1855, Smith & Wesson patented the first revolver to fire rim-fire cartridges—a hinged-frame revolver of .22 caliber in which the barrel was tipped up on a hinge at the top of the standing breech. This permitted the cylinder to be removed for loading and unloading. Smith & Wesson had previously patented a center-fire cartridge and had worked on the idea of a revolver to use it. They found that a patent for the necessary type of cylinder, bored through to permit insertion of cartridges through the breech end, had been granted to Rollin White on April 3, 1855. Their purchase of those patents gave them a monopoly on the device needed to use metallic cartridges until 1869. Where Colt had formerly strangled development, Smith & Wesson now were able to do the same.

Colt introduced the "Thuer Alteration" which made possible the use of either percussion or a special metallic ammunition inserted from the front of the cylinder. This and dozens of other hybrids were produced while the arms makers sat back and waited for the S. & W. patents to expire, just as previously they had to wait for Colt's to expire.

The Civil War was fought almost entirely with percussion-lock revolvers, but the arms most highly prized by the few who could get them were Smith & Wesson's of .22 and .32 rim-fire caliber. The Colt model of 1860, a .44-caliber six-shooter, was the most widely used revolver in that war, over 200,000 having been made.

In 1871 and 1872 Colt's purchased patents covering an alteration which permitted loading rimmed cartridges from the rear. In 1872 an open-top .44 was introduced, which paved the way for the most famous revolver in all history—the solid-frame Single-Action Army, which was issued in 1873.

With the passing of the Smith & Wesson patents, a flood of breech-loading arms in calibers from .22 to .50 were marketed. This era saw the introduction of the counterbored or recessed-head cylinder, where the entire cartridge head is below the outer circumference of the cylinder to prevent injury from a blown-out cartridge case head—a feature used also in Europe about the same time, and which appeared in the 20th century as a "modern" development. The Colt House Pistol, the Remington Elliot, and the Italian Glisenti were just a few to employ it.

General Norton, writing in 1872, states that the Union Metallic Cartridge Company at Bridgeport, Connecticut, was then the largest and best known cartridge company in the United States. He lists the sale of .22 Smith & Wesson (the .22 short) cartridges as being then 30,000,000 per year. Truly the era of the revolver had arrived.

In Europe and in England numerous experiments were under way, though few were put into general production, and fewer had any real merit. Except for the beginning of the Webley firm as arms manufacturers of quality in England, there were few developments of interest.

The day of the rim-fire, except for the super-accurate .22, was on the way out, as was the copper cartridge case associated with the rim-fires. They continued to be manufactured until well into the present century; but today only the .22 remains—a monument to the original cartridge design Smith & Wesson developed from the Flobert cap.

*Center-Fire.* With the development of the center-fire cartridge another great milestone was reached. Only the primer cup needed to be made soft enough to be crushed by the firing pin. The cartridge case could be made of heavy metal which would act as a safe gas seal for pressures much higher than were permissible with the soft copper rim-fire case. The fired primer cups could be punched out and a new primer inserted so that the sturdy brass case could be reloaded many times. "Rimless" cases could be designed for better functioning through the magazines of repeating arms. Through the years, the center-fire cartridge has undergone hundreds of modifications which cannot be recounted here. But with its coming the reliability of the revolver was greatly enhanced.

The various types of weapons using these cartridges are so numerous that only a few observations on types are required here.

The Colt S.A. Army Model 1873, which required but few alterations in the basic Colt heavy-frame design, introduced the sliding-rod ejector below the barrel with its spring to return it to place after ejecting a cartridge. While the principle of the self-extracting or automatic-ejecting revolver has been often credited to the Belgian Galand revolver, the weight of evidence seems to show that it was really developed in the United States. From 1860 to 1871, over 500 patents for breech-loading firearms were recorded in the U. S. Patent Office. When it is known that fewer than 200 had been filed in all the history of the Office prior to 1860, the interest in development is obvious.

Apparently W. W. Greener was the first person to ascribe (without any attempt at documentation) the honor to Galand, whose principle was that of sliding forward the barrel and cylinder while the cartridge cases were held by the extractor until clear of the chambers. W. C. Dodge, an examiner in the U. S. Patent Office, conceived the idea of a hinged-frame weapon in which the act of bending down the barrel and cylinder assemblies on the hinge would automatically raise the extractor and eject the empty cartridge cases. The law did not permit a Patent Office employee to acquire an interest in a patent, and not until he retired did Dodge seek patents. They were granted on January 17 and 24, 1865, and were assigned to Smith & Wesson, who proceeded to use the system in their revolvers. On May 1, 1872, Dodge wrote a bitter letter, later published by General Norton, the outstanding arms writer of that day, complaining about Greener's statement. He claimed to have invented his principle three years before the appearance of the Galand. Dodge also complained, and with a good deal of grounds, of treatment he had received at the hands of the British Patent Office. Under a technicality (the boat carrying a check for the patent fee was a few days late in arriving) his British patent was invalidated, resulting in like action to his applications in France and Belgium. The Liège Small Arms Company soon after went into manufacture on the Dodge principle. Oddly enough, British manufacturers in Birmingham were marketing revolvers using his principle within six weeks of the time of the invalidation of his patents! Dodge believed they had been "tipped off" as to the action the British Patent Office planned to take in invalidating his patent.

To add to the plausibility of Dodge's charges, it might be said in passing that the very earliest English manufactured cartridge breechloader was an *exact copy* of the original Smith & Wesson .22. This weapon was made and sold without identifying marks, though many researchers of the caliber of J. N. George indicate they were probably made by Webley.

During this period multi-barreled pistols such as the Lancaster were introduced in England and also on the Continent. They were usually hinged weapons with drop-down barrels and suffered from the defects of inaccuracy and great weight that had marked the earlier pepperboxes. English Adams and Tranter revolvers of this period and the Webley Royal Irish Constabulary revolvers were solid-frame types with hand-operated ejectors for ramming the cartridge cases individually from the chambers. Calibers ran as high as .577, the largest revolver caliber ever generally produced; and one which, except for the pinfire equivalent, the 15 mm., is no longer made.

In 1876 C. Pryse was granted a patent in England on a revolver of the general Smith & Wesson type, but using a cam-functioned ejector and a dual-bolt lock operated from spring catches on either side of the standing breech. Webley introduced this weapon in calibers as high as the now obsolete .476. This system still exists in Belgian-manufactured revolvers of the "Montenegrin" type, using an extra-long .45-caliber cartridge. This was the first English revolver to use the principle of the "rebounding hammer" in which spring tension automatically pulls the hammer back out of possible contact with the cartridge case when the trigger is released; and in which a metal bar rises between hammer and frame to positively prevent accidental discharge. Only a pull on the trigger can discharge the piece.

This rebound-and-steel-wedge safety principle had appeared earlier in solid-frame revolvers made in Austria and Italy. It is the principle later made famous as the "Colt Positive Lock," variations of which are in general revolver use.

The English Thomas and the Belgian and French Galand types of extraction systems in which the barrel and cylinder slide ahead for extraction were passing developments. In this class the American Merwin & Hulbert, in which the barrel assembly could be unlocked to swing away from the standing breech, and then be slid ahead while the cartridge cases were held by extracting surfaces on the face of the standing breech, was a finely made weapon but one too complicated to achieve lasting success. The Enfield .476, designed and manufactured at the Government Enfield Small Arms Factory in England and adopted there as a service revolver in 1882, was a remarkable example of how not to develop a weapon. In this monstrosity, releasing the catch on the standing breech permits the barrel to be tipped down and the cylinder to slide *straight ahead* to eject. The design was impracticable, and it was supplanted by revolvers of hinged-frame Webley manufacture, also introduced about 1882. In 1889 a slightly modified version of this "Mark I" Webley, under the designation "Mark II W. G." (Webley Government) was officially adopted as the British Service Revolver. This used the Webley stirrup-type breech lock, which is mounted on the standing breech and locks over the barrel strap. This, the strongest hinged-frame locking system ever devised, has been in use ever since by the British.

In 1899 the U. S. Government adopted officially a Colt .38 revolver using a new locking system—the now familiar swing-out cylinder type in which the great strength of the solid frame design is combined with a cylinder mounted on a crane which permits it to be swung away from the frame for quick loading and unloading. This design was modified and adopted by the French in 1892. It was further modified in Europe by Pieper to permit use of a forward-sliding chambered cylinder to use the Russian gas-check cartridge (which up to this time had been used only in solid-frame hand-ejector models). It was later adopted in principle, with modifications which included front as well as rear cylinder locking devices, by Smith & Wesson.

A multitude of types and makes which were little but variations of the Colt and Smith & Wesson systems—the swing-out cylinder and the hinged-frame with lock-on barrel strap—have since flooded world markets. The Webley design, curiously, has never been imitated on a production basis. Smith & Wesson's "hammerless" (enclosed hammer) pocket revolvers have also been widely copied with only minor variations.

The Webley-Fosbery "Automatic Revolver," in which recoil serves to turn the cylinder and cock the hammer in the place of the customary spring action, first appeared in England in 1901. It had only one imitator, the Union Arms Company .32 and .38 made in Toledo, Ohio, for a short period.

With the introduction of smokeless powder, more powerful cartridges have been developed but no real changes have been made in the basic revolver designs. Aside from developing improved metals, sights, and grips, it would seem that little can be done to improve their efficiency. Automatic ejecting systems which throw the empty cases out as adjoining chambers are fired—either by gas operation as done experimentally in Spain or by mechanical leverage as introduced by Stieger of Thun—have more bad features than good.

PHASE VII—THE AUTOMATIC PISTOL. The *principle* of the automatic or self-loading pistol was grasped centuries before the necessary combination of fixed ammunition, solid-drawn cartridge case, slow-fouling smokeless powder, and metallurgical advances made it possible to *utilize* that principle.

In Birch's *History of the Royal Society* we find that on March 2, 1664, Sir Robert Moray reported that a mechanic had approached Prince Rupert with the claim that he could "make a pistol shooting as fast as it could be presented and yet be stopped at pleasure; and wherein the motion of the fire and bullet within was made to charge the piece with powder and bullet, to prime it and to bend the cock."

When we see the difficulties the successful inventors of automatic pistols encountered in the late 19th century trying to interest governments and arms manufacturers, it is astonishing to find that the academic scientists of 1664 should even have gone so far as to record the idea of the nameless inventor who suffered from being more than 200 years ahead of his time.

While patent office records from 1863 on show numerous instances of attempts to develop various forms of gas- or recoil-operated arms, historically the first successful automatic pistol marketed was the Austrian Schonberger. This was a weapon in which the primer was set deeply in the head of the cartridge case. At the instant of firing the breech was securely locked and was solidly supporting the entire head of the cartridge case *except the center* where the primer, being countersunk, could be blown back by gas reaching it through the small touch-hole. The metal primer, striking the breechblock sharply, started the unlocking action. This system of operation, long discarded, has in recent years again received considerable attention in arms development circles. It should be noted that this arm was made possiblbe primarily because of ammunition developments. The strong rimless brass cartridge case which would stand the violent strain of automatic extraction, which permitted firm seating of the bullet, and which permitted cartridges to be easily stacked on top of each other in the magazine; the smokeless powder which burned rapidly and with a minimum of fouling; and the jacketed bullet which assured proper feeding—all these had evolved in the '80's. Together they were combined to make a type of successful automatic-pistol cartridge which allowed new arms developments.

One of the great designers of automatic arms, the Austrian Andrea Schwarzlose, produced a model pistol operated by barrel recoil in 1893. This arm was never in production, but was the beginning of a long line of Schwarzlose designs.

The first *commercially successful* automatic pistol was an American design. Hugo Borchardt, a Connecticut Yankee, invented the clumsy pistol (also intended to be used with a stock as a carbine) which really started the era of military automatic pistols. Unable to finance his pistol in his own country, Borchardt took it to Germany. The great arms factory of Ludwig Loewe & Company undertook production and engaged Borchardt as an engineer. Borchardt's pistol was marketed in 1893. This was the first arm to use the detachable box magazine inserted in the handle which has come to be the most successful of all automatic-pistol loading systems. It was the forerunner of the famous Luger, employing a locked breech in which the barrel recoiled a short distance locked to the breechblock, then was unlocked as the barrel travel was halted and a toggle was buckled to draw the breechblock away from the barrel to extract and eject the empty case. Quite as important as the pistol design was the cartridge design. The cartridge Borchardt developed was later made famous as the 7.63-mm. Mauser, a cartridge so correct in conception that today, more than 50 years later, it is one of the world's outstanding pistol cartridges.

In 1893 Theodore Bergmann patented the first of his series of unique automatic pistols. During the succeeding ten years he developed various pistols of both locked and unlocked types, all with exposed hammers and with readily accessible lockwork and with magazines placed in front of the trigger. In the period between 1894 and 1897 he made a series of pocket pistols, all unlocked blowback types, at Gaggenau, in calibers 5-mm., 6-5-mm., and 8-mm. German export and ammunition catalogs included ammunition for these arms as late as 1930, though the weapons themselves have not been manufactured since late in the last century. This is certainly a tribute to the original design and manufacture. A Bergmann cheaply manufactured in Belgium in 1897 and marketed under the name "Simplex" is of interest because the 8-mm. cartridge it uses developed into the 7.65-mm. Browning or .32 Colt Automatic Pistol cartridge, as we know it—the most widely distributed pocket automatic caliber in existence. In the same year another Bergmann was manufactured in Spain as the "Charola-Anitua."

In 1896 the great American inventor Hiram Maxim—who also had to go to England to have his new arms manufactured—patented an unusually simple automatic pistol of unlocked blowback design. Samples only were made; and it is a most interesting commentary that some were chambered for the *rimmed* .455 British Service cartridge. Except for a few experimental freaks and the American Reifgraber which used the rimmed .32 S. & W. cartridge, no later automatic pistol in production used rimmed cartridges until the Colt .22 Woodsman appeared. Recently automatic pistols to shoot the .38 S. & W. Special rimmed cartridges have been made by Hi-Standard in Connecticut. It has been assumed that proper feed could not be achieved in an automatic with rimmed ammunition—though an examination of an early Maxim would have shown the feasibility of it. Only recently, too, have modern designers and manufacturers rediscovered what Maxim demonstrated nearly 60 years ago—that heavy calibers can be safely made in cheap blowback-design weapons.

The story of the truly successful automatic pistol in the light of modern experience begins in 1898 with the introduction of the 7.63-mm. Military Mauser which had been patented in 1896. This used the cartridge developed by Hugo Borchardt for his own pistol. The published history of the Deutsche Waffen und Munitionsfabriken (DWM), the greatest of the European ammunition manufacturers from the turn of the century to the end of World War II, credits Borchardt with having done much of the engineering work on the Mauser pistol.

The Mauser was so fundamentally right that it is today changed only in comparatively minor details. Winston Churchill in his history of the Sudan campaign of 1898 tells in great detail how he purchased one of the first Mauser pistols to reach England, and credits it with saving his life because of its efficiency and magazine capacity when he shot his way out of a native trap, killing several Fuzzy Wuzzies.

Also in 1898 appeared a new pistol by Andrea Schwarzlose in Austria. Shooting the 7.63-mm. Mauser cartridge from a detachable magazine in the handle, this pistol had a number of features which have since become standard on military pistols of the best type. In this weapon for the first time we find the device to hold the action open when the last cartridge has been fired, thereby warning that the arm is empty and also speeding up the reloading. In the unique locking system in this pistol, the barrel and bolt recoil a short distance locked together, then by cam action after the barrel is stopped the bolt is revolved out of locking recesses in the barrel extension. This principle has reappeared in the past ten years as the locking principle of the German Machine Gun 34 and the American Johnson Light Machine Gun. This pistol was not very successful. Some were marketed in the United States by Bannerman of New York under the name "Standard."

John Browning, the greatest of all American small-arms designers, introduced his first pistol in 1889. Browning, too, had to go to Europe to obtain backing for the manufacture of his pistol, which he had patented in 1898. It was manufactured by the Fabrique Nationale d'Armes de Guerre (world famous as "FN") at Herstal, Liège, Belgium. Again the success of this entirely new form of blowback pocket automatic pistol rested partly on the cartridge which, as we have already seen, Browning and FN developed from the 8-mm. Simplex. Over 1,000,000 of these pistols were sold. On April 19, 1900, the magazine *Shooting and Fishing* (the direct ancestor of the *American Rifleman,* the official magazine of the National Rifle Association) carried the first public announcement of the first Colt Automatic pistol—the .38 Automatic invented by Browning. The editor of that day wrote that the Colt company had presented him with the Number One pistol for inspection and test. The report is of historical interest in many ways. It states that the *first* Browning pistol was *a hammerless full automatic*—a single pull on the trigger emptied the magazine. Browning found at once that a pistol so designed was both useless and dangerous: it was practically impossible to hit anything with it, and the rapid successions of recoil kicked the muzzle up so fast that spectators or the firer might be accidentally shot. The magazine would empty in 1⅖ seconds. They found on testing the new pistol that the velocity, then given as 1260 feet per second, actually registered as high as 1350. This compared with the velocity of 750 feet per second then being obtained from the regular .38 Army revolver with its black-powder load. They found further that the arm would not function at a lower velocity than 850 f.s. Penetration was 11 inches in pine.

In June of that year Browning wrote to the editor explaining that he had tried many varieties of safeties, some being released by gripping the handle and some being turned down by the thumb and held while firing. He also explained that in designing the .38 Automatic with a hammer (his earlier FN pistol was striker fired) he intended the firer to cock the hammer first, then pull back the slide thereby lessening the amount of pull necessary for the first manual-loading stroke. This arm was later improved by Browning; full data on the later models will be found in the section dealing with the Colt .38 Automatic.

In 1901 the Austrian Mannlicher still in wide use in Europe and in some sections of South America was introduced. It uses a special cartridge of considerable power whose case is straight sided in appearance, though measurement shows it to be actually slightly conical to help easy extraction.

DWM brought out the Luger in 1902. This arm, which except for minor refinements is the same arm today, was developed by George Luger from the original Borchardt. Its cartridge, the 7.65-mm. Parabellum, remained in general use through the years. The German service caliber, 9-mm. Parabellum, was adopted in 1908. These are the only calibers in which this famous arm has ever been commercially manufactured. A few experimental models were made for the .45 Colt Automatic pistol cartridge.

In 1903 the Colt Hammerless .32 Automatic Pistol, an enclosed hammer blowback designed by John Browning, was introduced. From this developed the Browning Model 1910 manufactured by FN. It is one of the most widely imitated, copied, and modified designs ever developed. Literally hundreds of variants of Belgian, German, and Spanish manufacture exist.

A new Mannlicher lock-breech pistol was introduced also in 1903, but it was never very successful. In this year also Bergmann produced the locked-breech designs which were later manufactured in Belgium and met with considerable success under the name of Bergmann-Bayard and Bayard 1908 and 1910.

In England the first Webley Automatic Pistol, one of .455 caliber with the typical Webley V-recoil spring, was introduced in 1904. It was not a success and should not be confused with the official .455

Mark I adopted the the British Royal Navy in 1913.

The 1905 Model Colt in .45 caliber and its later modification in 1908 were based on the general slide design of the earlier .38 Colt Automatics, and were, of course, designed by John Browning.

Webley brought out their first blowback automatic, a .32 pocket model in 1906; while in the United States in the same year the Savage .45 was introduced at U. S. Government trials. This arm later appeared in a modified form in .32 caliber in 1910. The last model of this make was introduced in 1917. Also in 1906 the Italian Glisenti was first seen, though it was not adopted by the Italian Army until 1910. Austria-Hungary officially adopted the Roth-Steyr 8-mm. for cavalry use in 1907, marking the first large-scale production of an arm which had been patented seven or eight years earlier.

The year 1908 marked the introduction of the .25 Colt Vest Pocket Model, a Browning striker-fired design which was also manufactured in the same year by FN in Belgium under the name of the Baby Browning. Like its enclosed-hammer type big brother the .32 Colt Automatic, this arm has been copied, imitated, and modified under a fantastic number of trade names.

Webley launched an automatic in 1910 to shoot the .38 Colt Automatic pistol cartridge, using the breech lock of the type found in the more widely distributed .455 Mark I. This must not be confused with the blowback pistol of similar appearance called the 9-mm. High Velocity, which did not appear until two years later and which shoots the weaker 9-mm. Browning Long cartridge.

The Browning-designed .45 Colt Government Model was introduced in 1911. This is one of the finest military pistols ever made and is still, with a few modifications, the official pistol of the U. S. forces. Also in 1911 another basic type, the powerful 9-mm. Steyr-Hahn, appeared in Austria. This was slightly modified in 1915 and 1916, and converted to German service caliber in 1940.

The Hungarian long-recoil .32 Frommer-Stop was marketed in 1912, an unusual locked type to shoot the low-powered .32 automatic cartridge. Also in this year S. & W. launched their .35 Automatic based on the Belgian Pieper. As we have seen, the Webley & Scott .455 Mark I was produced in 1913; and except for the Italian Beretta of 1915 and a tremendous variety of pocket-pistol types, nothing further of consequence was developed until 1918 when the Remington .380 Automatic Pistol with a hesitation-locked breech was made.

For the next ten years development was confined for the most part to Spain, where dozens of makes under hundreds of brand names were made for export trade. Practically every known variety was imitated or modified. The one real development of this area and this period was in the field of cheap blowback pistols to shoot powerful cartridges which were generally believed to require an expensive locked-breech pistol. There is something to be learned from the Spanish development of blowbacks to shoot such cartridges as the 9-mm. Bayard and the 9-mm. Parabellum.

By 1926 the Czechs had developed arms plants which seemed to show marked German trends in their designs. In that year Ceska Zbrojovka produced a Steyr-type revolving barrel locked pistol of .380 caliber which possessed a lockwork of general Mauser design. This arm was later adopted as the official side-arm of the Czech army. A later version, popularly called the Strakonitz from the location of the government plant making it, incorporated a double-action trigger feature. A .32 automatic of the same general design but of blowback type with a rigid barrel was manufactured and marketed as the 1928 Model by Bohmischerwaffen at Prague.

In 1928 a military model of the Le Français blowback was first sold in France, a weapon embodying several interesting features, including a simple double-action firing mechanism and several novel safety features.

For the succeeding years until the present a quick résumé tells the story of development as follows:

*U. S.:* Only .22 target automatic pistols received any real attention.

*Great Britain:* Practically none.

*Belgium:* Important modifications by FN in 1935 of the basic Colt-Browning locked-breech design.

*Poland:* Same as Belgium—the F. B. Radom.

*Russia:* Same as Belgium—the Tokarev.

*Japan:* Introduction of a highly efficient design, the 1925 Nambu, of inadequate caliber. Later further simplified for manufacture.

*France:* Modification of the Browning system—the MAS 1935.

*Italy:* Modifications and improvements of Beretta pistols—the 1923 to 1934.

*Austria:* Introduction of several advanced forms of double-action automatic systems, notably the "Little Tom," Wiener Waffenfabrik.

*Hungary:* Modification of the Browning system—the M 1937.

*Argentina and Chile:* New factories making excellent copies and imitations of standard Colt and Smith & Wesson designs —the Criolla and FAG.

*Germany:* Widespread development of new and highly improved forms including the famous Walther PP and PPK Pocket Automatics with double-action trigger systems, simplified takedown, new safety features, improved metals. The Mauser and the Sauer & Sohn streamlined pistols competing with the Walthers. Minor modifications of the Luger and lockwork improvement in the Military Mauser. The Walther Heeres Pistol, the double-action new lock-breech pistol, was adopted in 1938 to replace the Luger. Shooting the Luger (Parabellum) 9-mm. cartridge, it is the pistol every veteran of the African and European campaigns knows as the P-38.

*Czechoslovakia:* Improved Strakovitz double-Action automatic pistols whose barrels hinge at the muzzle to permit ease of cleaning.

*Spain:* Further modifications of Mauser Military (Astra, Royal, Azul) and of the Colt-Browning (Astra, Llama).

*Finland:* The Lahti.

*Norway:* Colt-Browning modifications.

**Pistol and Revolver Types.** PISTOLS. The term pistol, signifying the smallest general type of firearm—a type intended to be fired from one hand, wherein the cartridge or cartridges must be inserted directly into the chamber *which is an integral part of the barrel itself*—embraces the following types:

*Single-Shot Pistols.* Originally made with short barrels in calibers .22, .32, .38, and .41 rim-fire as pocket pistols. Later manufactured in calibers as high as .50 as Army and Navy issue. Still later, as target pistols in calibers from .22 rim-fire to .44 Russian center-fire.

Modern *production model* single-shot pistols are almost entirely .22 Long Rifle. Special models, of course, may be any caliber or description. Practically all are intended for target use. Since single-shot target pistols represent the only class of true pistols (as distinguished from revolvers and automatic pistols) which have any present or predictable future value, the characteristics of the outstanding types are given herewith, with particular reference to the outstanding types are given herewith, with particular reference to the tested systems of locking the breech. Successful pistol designs fall into the following classifications:

*Breech Locking Systems.* (1) *Hinge frame, standing breech.* In this type, the barrel is hinged to a forward extension of the receiver and is fastened with a spring-controlled latch to the upright section of the receiver forming the standing breech which supports the head of the cartridge case as the weapon is fired. When the latch is released, the muzzle of the barrel is tipped down to expose the cartridge chamber and to operate the extractor to lift the empty case up or to eject it completely from the pistol. This is the commonest form of successful single-shot pistol.

The outstanding examples are listed here. *The .22 Long Rifle Smith & Wesson tipup pistols:* In these, the latch is on the breech end of the barrel and snaps down over the standing breech to lock. The firing pin is attached to the hammer. Opening the pistol ejects the empty cartridge case from the pistol. *The British .22 Long Rifle Webley & Scott Single Shot:* In this pistol, the breech latch is operated by pushing forward the front of the trigger guard. The firing pin is attached to the hammer. Opening the action ejects the cartridge case. *The .22 Long Rifle Harrington & Richardson U.S.R.A. Model:* This is similar to the S. & W. *The Stevens No. 10:* The latch is on the left side of the receiver. A knob-type striker of the rifle type is used; there is no hammer. Opening the pistol extracts the case far enough to permit it to be withdrawn, but does not eject it from the pistol. *The Stevens, Conlin, Diamond, Gould, and Offhand Models:* Calibers .22 and .22 Long Rifle. These models vary only in weights, trigger designs, sights, and grips. Mechanically they function alike. Latches in these pistols are push buttons mounted on the left side of the receiver. *The U. S. Wurfflein and Hopkins & Allen .22 Long Rifle:* Similar to the S. & W. but with different types of latches. *The German Arminius,* operated by right- or left-side latches on the receiver, and the *Stoeger Challenger* operated by pushing forward the trigger guard tang.

(2) *Crane frame, standing breech.* The barrel is assembled to a forward extension of the receiver on a swinging crane, and is fastened with a pull-type spring-controlled latch to the standing breech. When the latch on the left side of the receiver is pulled back, the barrel assembly can be swung out to the left on the crane, as in the case of a swing-out-cylinder revolver. Pressure on the base of the ejector rod ejects the empty case. This is a manual rod-ejector, as opposed to the automatic-lever type found in hinge-frame types. In exterior appearance this pistol closely resembles a regular Colt revolver.

The .22 Long Rifle Colt Camp Perry Model is the only modern pistol to use this system. The basic principle is derived from the old National and Colt Derringer .41 rim-fire pocket pistols. In those old pistols, however, it is necessary to half-cock the pistol, then press a spring button to swing the barrel on its crane and push up the side ejector latch to eject. The Camp Perry has an ultra-fast double-action lockwork.

(3) *Pivot frame, standing breech.* In this type, the barrel is fastened by a pivot to a forward extension of the receiver, permitting it to be swung away from the standing breech when the spring latch is released. The act of swinging the breech end of the barrel away (usually to the right) operates a lever arrangement to extract the empty case.

The .22 Long Rifle Smith & Wesson Straightline model uses this system. Instead of the regulation pivot-type hammer, this pistol has a striker which moves forward in a straight line to fire the cartridge. The basic principle is derived from the .22 Short pistol of Frank Wesson and from several early types of Derringer pocket pistols. In exterior appearance and in balance this type of pistol suggests an automatic pistol.

(4) *Rigid frame, rolling breechblock.* In this type, the barrel is fastened securely to the receiver, and the cartridge in the chamber is supported by a breech piece containing a firing pin and extractor which is rolled forward on a heavy center pin after the cartridge has been inserted. The hammer is also the breech bolt and is mounted on the same center pin as the breech piece. A spring holds the breech piece against the cartridge head until the hammer falls. The fall of the hammer not only drives the firing pin ahead to discharge the cartridge, but also rolls the hammer ahead to positively lock the breech. Recocking the hammer, then drawing back the breech piece, extracts the cartridge case far enough to permit it to be withdrawn with the fingers.

The .22 Long Rifle Remington pistol on the Army model .50-caliber frame exemplifies this type. This pistol is extremely heavy for its type, weighing about 2¾ pounds. It is an extremely accurate pistol, not so subject to wear as is the hinge-frame type. It is no longer manufactured in this country.

(5) *Rigid frame, falling breechblock.* In this type the barrel is screwed securely to the receiver, and the cartridge in the chamber is supported by a heavy Martini-type falling block. When a lever, often the trigger guard, is depressed it lowers a hinged block containing the firing pin. The bottom of the block strikes an arm of the extractor and ejects the empty cartridge case. Lowering the block may also automatically recock the pistol. A cartridge is inserted in the firing chamber. Returning the lever to its closed position raises the block and presses it securely against the head of the cartridge case.

Examples of this type are the German Udo Anschutz .22 Long Rifle Record Match and similar pistols. The blocks in these pistols are usually actuated by pulling an extension of the back strap on the grip. Triggers are usually set on these models by a lever on the left side of the receiver. When the breechblock is down, the chamber is entirely exposed. Literally scores of pistols of this general type were made in Germany and Switzerland prior to 1945.

(6) *Rigid frame, turning bolt.* In this type, the action is that of the familiar bolt-action rifle. Lifting

the bolt handle and pulling it straight back ejects the empty cartridge case and cocks the striker. A cartridge is inserted, the bolt is pushed forward, and the handle is turned down to locked position exactly as in the case of the common door bolt. *Examples:* German .22 Long Rifle Mauser target pistols and French M.A.S. Buffalo-Stand .22 Long Rifle target pistols.

*Double-Barreled Pistols.* These were originally made early in the metallic-cartridge era as pocket pistols and Derringers. Barrels might *(a)* swing out on a pivot, as in the National Derringer; *(b)* hinge down, as in double-barreled shotguns; *(c)* hinge up on the standing breech; *(d)* pivot to right or left away from the standing breech; *(e)* slide forward on the receiver extension over the trigger guard.

Modern *production models* of double-barreled pistols are made only in Europe. Usually they are parallel-barrel types intended for shot cartridges or for heavy Continental cartridges which are obsolete in the United States or which were never manufactured here. It should be noted that while barrels in the early pocket types were usually mounted one on top of the other, or superposed, saddle pistols of the same era were generally of the parallel-barrel type. In England these were often made for the British .577 Boxer cartridge.

Double-barreled pistols have outlived their usefulness, and have been replaced by more accurate revolvers. Early in the present century several European weapons of the .25-caliber BAR type were introduced having two superposed barrels. These do not class as straight pistols inasmuch as the cartridges were inserted in a swinging block, and the bullets have to jump a gap exactly as in the revolver before entering the barrel.

*Multiple-Barreled Pistols.* These fall into two general classes, both of which are now obsolete because of great weight, unwieldiness, and bulk, as well as lack of accuracy. *(a)* Those in which several barrels are fastened together or bored from a solid cylinder like the old pepperbox pistols of the percussion cap era. These are freaks. *(b)* The obsolete Remington-Elliot .22 is a true revolving pistol. Barrels are bored the full length of the cylindrical block. Pressure on the trigger revolves a striker to fire them successively. *(c)* Four- and six-barreled pistols with parallel barrels superposed on lower barrels. These weapons are usually British and many will shoot current ammunition. They have a single trigger and are of hinge-frame construction. As many of these weapons were brought into use by the British after Dunkirk in World War II, and as they will handle the British .455 Service cartridges, these weapons may be classed as obsolescent only. In the Mitrailleuse pistol of Braendlin Armoury, each barrel has a separate striker and spring. The trigger is hooked to a vertical spindle on which are projecting studs which, when the trigger is pulled, pull back and release the strikers to fire the barrels in rotation. In the .455 Lancaster four-barreled pistol, which resembles the Mitrailleuse closely in exterior appearance, the lockwork operates like that of the obsolete United States .22 Remington-Elliot pistol. The striker is in the form of a sleeve which has a projecting arm. Pressure on the trigger turns a ratchet to rotate the striker to permit its arm to hit the four firing pins in succession as the trigger is pulled four times.

Four-barreled pistols with the barrels *mounted on top of the other* were manufactured early in the century as transition arms in Europe. Some of these were exposed-hammer and some the enclosed hammer type. The four barrels formed a single unit which, when loaded, was inserted in guides in the standing breech section of the receiver or was hinged to the forward extension of the receiver. The American Marston was a popular arm of this type.

*Examples:* (1) *The Reform Pistol.* This was made in Germany, Belgium, and Austria. It is usually chambered for the .25 Colt Auto Pistol cartridge. The barrel block is removed for loading. The block is inserted and the trigger pulled to fire the first shot. Pulling the trigger the second time lifts the barrel block to bring the second barrel in line with the firing pin and, as the second cartridge is fired, gas from it escapes through a breech hole into barrel No. 1 to blow the empty case out of that barrel. The third pull fires No. 3 and ejects No. 2 barrel. The fourth pull fires No. 4 barrel and clears No. 3. The barrel block is then removed for reloading, and the fourth barrel must be cleared with a stick or cleaning rod. This ingenious pistol is widely distributed in Europe and South America, and, as it uses current cartridges, may be classed as obsolescent but not obsolete.

(2) *The Regnum Pistol.* This European pistol also has four barrels bored one on top of the other from a solid block, but the barrel block is tipped down when the release catch on the left side of the receiver is depressed, to load and unload. The four barrels are loaded with .25 Colt Auto Pistol cartridges. Four pulls on the trigger will fire the four barrels in succession. The arm is then hinged open to unload. This is the enclosed-hammer type, which is flat and readily concealed. It is purely a close-quarters arm, of course, and is deficient in both accuracy and striking energy.

The only *production models* of multiple-parallel-barreled pistols in the present century were freak four-barreled pistols like the U. S. Brownie made by Mossberg Arms as a cheap .22-caliber arm; and several European imitations of the U. S. Shattuck Unique, a short four-barreled pistol intended to be concealed in the palm of the hand.

*Repeating Pistols.* These are weapons in which a number of cartridges (usually five) are inserted in the handle of the pistol, and in which the barrel is loaded and the cartridge fired and case ejected by mechanical spring action, usually brought about by squeezing levers in the grip against spring tension, then releasing the grip and repeating the motion to fire successive cartridges.

These are transition arms which were an attempt to provide the gas-seal feature of the pistol (where no gas can escape because the bullet does not have to jump a gap in the revolver when going from the cylinder to the barrel) together with the mechanical sureness of action possessed by the revolver which, unlike the automatic pistol, is not dependent on the cartridge (which may be defective) for reloading.

The French Gaulois and Merveilleux are examples of this type. The Gaulois held its special 8-mm. cartridges in the handle of the pistol. The Merveilleux closely resembled the Gaulois, but used a special 6-mm. cartridge. With the magazine loaded, pressure of the hand around the grip squeezed in a section which forced a cartridge into the chamber of the single barrel, cocked and tripped the striker to fire the cartridge. Releasing the pressure permitted springs to force back the grip, open the breech, and eject the empty cartridge case. The magazine spring forced the next cartridge in.

These weapons are still widely distributed in Europe, but no ammunition for them has ever been made in the United States. These are overly complicated and inaccurate.

*Magazine Pistols.* These differ from automatic pistols in that some manual operation by the *free* hand is necessary to prepare them for successive shots. They usually require the employment of both hands. They resemble automatics in that they carry extra cartridges—often in the handle—ready for mechanical feeding into the chamber of the single barrel.

*Example:* The .22 Long Rifle Fiala pistol. This weapon is no longer manufactured. While in exterior appearance it very closely resembles a regular .22 target automatic pistol and houses its cartridges in a removable magazine in a grip, it differs in that the sliding breechblock is mechanically locked whenever it is in forward position. When a .22 automatic pistol is fired, the slide is blown back to eject the empty cartridge case, cock the hammer, and compress the recoil spring, which then moves forward to reload the firing chamber from the magazine. In the magazine pistol of Fiala type, when the cartridge has been fired, it is necessary to press in and release the slide lock at the breech, then pull the slide back by hand to eject the empty, recock the hammer, and clear the top of the magazine so the slide may go home to pick up a loaded cartridge.

Bittner, Schwarzlose, and similar repeating pistols were merely transition arms which do not merit attention here.

*Semi-Automatic Pistols.* While this specific term is applied by Webley & Scott to their British-made self-ejecting pistol, it is not properly applied. Actually this weapon resembles an automatic target pistol, but in reality is a single-shot *automatic-ejecting-cocking* pistol. Each cartridge must be inserted in the firing chamber by hand. The breechblock slide must be pulled back by hand before the first cartridge can be loaded, then pushed forward by hand to close the breech.

As the cartridge fires, the pressure of gas in the cartridge case forces the head of the case back against the face of the breechblock. As the bullet leaves the barrel, backward pressure blows the slide back to cock the hammer while the residual pressure in the chamber blows the empty case out of the pistol—sometimes. A hand ejector is provided for use when ejection does not occur automatically. When a loaded cartridge is inserted, the slide must again be pushed forward manually.

Automatic Pistols. The term automatic pistol by accepted usage signifies a weapon intended to be fired normally with one hand in which pressing the trigger when the chamber and magazine are loaded *(a)* fires the cartridge in the chamber; *(b)* ejects the fired cartridge case; *(c)* cocks the firing mechanism ready for the next shot; and *(d)* loads a cartridge from the magazine into the chamber in position for firing. Strictly speaking, of course, automatic pistols should really be classed as "semi-automatic"; but popular usage makes it necessary to class them by the term under which they are generally known.

During the rearward movement of the breech mechanism, which is normally accomplished by recoil, a disconnecting unit is automatically forced down to break the connection between the sear which holds the hammer or striker at full cock and the trigger bar. This principle (which may vary greatly in mechanical application in different arms and is considered in detail in discussing specific designs) prevents the firing of more than one shot for each pull of the trigger, since the trigger must be released to permit springs to force the connecting trigger bar into position to release the sear for the next shot.

Full-automatic pistols in which a single pressure on the trigger will fire the full contents of the magazine are useless and generally dangerous. Such types are not made in the United States and they have no practical value for defense or target work.

Pistols of the Le Français type (for example, .32 ACP, 9-mm. Browning Long, and 8-mm. Roth-Steyr) are more correctly classed as "self-loading" pistols in that the rearward motion of the breechblock does not cock the firing mechanism but merely ejects and reloads the firing chamber. In these types pressure on the trigger cocks and releases the striker.

Commercially successful automatic pistols fall into the following classes:

*Simple Blowbacks.* The vast majority of all .22, .25, .32, and .380 automatic pistols operate on this system. A powerful spring holds the breechblock against the head of the cartridge in the firing chamber at the instant of discharge. Theoretically the expanding gases inside the cartridge case force the bullet down the barrel and simultaneously force the head of the case back against the face of the breechblock. In actual practice the light bullet is out of the barrel before the breech opens appreciably. This system works most efficiently when the weight of the bullet is 110 grains or less, the case is parallel sided, and the chamber pressure is under 5000 pounds per square inch. However, it must be noted that in Spain blowbacks are made with very heavy springs to shoot the most powerful pistol cartridges made; and the true mechanics of this system warrant much more scientific study by arms manufacturers.

(1) *Barrels.* Since blowback pistols are operated by recoil (or projection of the fired case as it imparts momentum to the breechblock) the barrels are stationary, and may be easily removable as in the Colt .32 ACP or may be pinned into their mounting as in the case of the Walthers using the .32 ACP cartridge.

(2) *Magazines* are normally removable and positioned in the handle (similar to that of the Colt Government .45), but in the Bergmann 6.5-mm. are not removable and are positioned ahead of the trigger guard.

(3) *Breechblocks* may be integral parts of the slide forging (Browning, Colt, Sauer, Walther, and

Webley under .25 ACP, .32 ACP, and .380 ACP), or may be separate units of lesser weight requiring more powerful recoil springs (S.&W. and Steyr .32 ACP and .35 S.&W. Auto).

(4) *Firing mechanisms* may be the striker-type in which trigger pressure releases the firing (striker) pin and permits its spring to drive it ahead to discharge the cartridge (Colt and Mauser .25 ACP); the concealed hammer (hammerless) type such as the Colt .32 ACP, Sauer Model 38 for the .32 ACP cartridge, and the Browning 9-mm. Long in which the slide completely encloses the hammer to provide a smooth exterior which will not catch on clothing when being drawn rapidly; and the exposed-hammer type such as the Czech and Star automatic pistols for the .32 ACP cartridge.

In general, strikers in pistols require fewer parts than hammer mechanisms but are not so reliable. Concealed hammers (and strikers also) have the disadvantage commonly encountered (Colt type) that they are always fully cocked when the firing chamber is loaded, which weakens the mainspring by too long compression if the arm is carried constantly ready for action. In European types such as the Sauer Model 38 where an exterior lever permits the hammer to be safely lowered on a loaded chamber and a double-action trigger permits bringing the arm into immediate action, this defect has been overcome. Exposed hammers have the advantage that they can be lowered to ease the mainspring, but have the disadvantage that they must then be thumb-cocked before the arm can be fired.

Triggers may have trigger bars passing stirrup-fashion across the magazine well to transmit finger pressure and push the sear out of engagement with the hammer (.32 Colt Auto); connector bars to push the sear out of engagement with the striker (.25 Colt Auto); a trigger nose to transmit pressure through an interceptor block to the sear to release it (Mauser .32 ACP); a pivoted trigger whose bar is pulled forward as the trigger is pressed and draws the sear out of engagement with the hammer (Walther PPK .380 ACP); and other operating differences which are covered under the descriptions of individual pistols where necessary.

(5) *Cocking systems* of the double-action type have been highly developed in Europe (Walther PPK, Sauer Model 38, and Little Tom, .32 ACP). In these pistols, as in all standard types, the slide must be drawn to the rear and released manually to load the firing chamber; this action also cocks the hammer. If the hammer is then lowered, the weapon may be carried in complete safety and without the mainspring being compressed. Instead of thumb-cocking the hammer or pulling the slide back as is normally required to fire an automatic pistol under these condtiions, in the double-action types it is necessary only to press the trigger to raise and drop the hammer. If the cartridge should misfire, a second pull on the trigger will again raise and drop the hammer, usually discharging the average defective cartridge.

(6) *Disconnectors* are an essential design factor in all good automatic pistols, since they prevent firing more than one shot for each pull of the trigger. The most common design is that developed by Browning and used in the Colt .32 Auto. In this type a bar mounted with the sear rises so that when the slide is fully home the top of the disconnector seats in a cut in the underside of the slide; and when it is so seated the sear is in contact with the trigger bar. Any opening movement of the slide causes it to ride over the projecting head of the disconnector, thrusting it down against its spring pressure and breaking the connection between trigger bar and sear. Thus when the slide returns to full forward position, it is necessary to momentarily release trigger pressure to permit the spring to force the disconnector up into its slide slot to complete the trigger connection. The various types of disconnectors are discussed where necessary under the individual automatic pistols described. All types require that the trigger must be deliberately released between shots, and that the slide or breechblock must be fully home before trigger pressure will release the hammer or striker.

(7) *Magazine disconnectors* are spring-controlled levers or bars projecting into the magazine well or so mounted in the grips that when the magazine is withdrawn their springs force them out or down to break connection between trigger and sear; when the magazine is in place the firing contact is maintained. These are designed as a safety measure to prevent discharge of a round in the chamber which is often overlooked when the magazine is extracted. The various types are discussed under the arms employing them (see Beretta, Colt, Mauser, and Sauer under .32 ACP).

(8) *Safeties* fall into two general classes, manual and automatic. Manual safeties are generally thumb-pieces so mounted on the receiver or slide that pushing the exposed lever turns a cutaway pin to lock the hammer or striker and sometimes the sear also, though some types lock the trigger. Automatic grip safeties are movable pieces so mounted in the grip that in general they are held out by springs when at rest, and in that position they prevent connection between trigger and sear; but when the pistol is held firmly in the hand ready for shooting, the grip is squeezed in and completes the firing hookup. The manual and grip safeties used in the Colt .25 and .32 Auto are the basis for most of the variations, but the important types are all considered under descriptions of specific weapons where necessary. One unusual type of automatic safety is that employed in double-action Walther pistols, where the firing pin is securely locked by a floating cutaway pin at all times except when the sear, as it is pushed to full cock, lifts a hammer lever which raises the lock pin out of the path of the firing pin. Cutaways of the Colt .45 (Plate II) and of the Walther "P-38" (Plate XXXV) show two types employed.

(9) *Mainsprings* may be flat springs (Colt and Mauser .32 Auto) or coil springs (Beretta and Webley) mounted in the grip section of the receiver.

(10) *Recoil springs* are generally coil springs. They may be mounted with guides below the barrel (all Colt Auto Pistols except the .22); above the barrel (S.&W. .32 Auto); around the barrel (Walther PPK); in the front of the grip (Le Français); or in the side (Colt .22 Woodsman). The Webley .32 Auto uses a powerful V-spring mounted under the right-hand grip.

*Blow Forward.* This is essentially the same as the

blowback except that the breech is solid and the barrel and other recoiling units slide forward to eject and reload the chamber on the return stroke. The Schwarzlose .32 ACP is one of the few examples of this type.

*Delayed Blowback—Hesitation System.* This system mechanically delays the breech opening on the general principle of the common door-check. As in the standard blowback design, the breech opening starts simultaneously with the movement of the bullet, but in the case of the 7.65-mm. Mannlicher a cam supported by the mainspring is held in contact with the breechblock providing additional resistance to rapid breech opening; while in the Remington for the .32 and .380 ACP cartridge the forward member of a two-piece movable breechblock supports the cartridge-case head and transmits the momentum imparted to it to the rear member, causing it to unlock the forward unit which has engaged with the receiver after short opening travel. In a recoil-operated arm, when as in the case of the pistols just listed the barrel is rigid, it is obvious that the breechblock begins its opening action with the discharge of the cartridge, hence the action is not truly locked but is actually merely checked or delayed.

*Locked-Breech Design.* When powerful loads or heavy bullets are used in an automatic pistol it is desirable to have the breech firmly locked until the bullet has left the barrel. Without exception all the successful automatic pistols ever put into production are recoil operated. (Primer- and gas-operated pistols have been made or produced experimentally but have never achieved commercial success and are only of interest to the collector.) In locked-breech actions the barrel is secured to the breechblock by a variety of mechanical means at the instant of firing. The rearward thrust of the expanding powder gases pushes the head of the cartridge case back against the face of the breechblock exactly as in the common blowback design; but unlike the blowback the breech does not begin to open immediately. The breechblock, which is held forward by the recoil spring, starts back but is compelled to draw with it the barrel and lock. After the bullet has left the barrel, the motion of the barrel is halted and unlocked from the breechblock, and at that point the momentum imparted to the face of the breechblock can continue to carry the breech mechanism still further to the rear to carry out the cycle of ejecting, cocking, and compressing the recoil spring to provide the power for the forward loading stroke of the action.

(1) *Browning-Colt Locked-Breech System.* This is the most widely imitated locking system ever designed for an automatic pistol. When the breechblock (which is part of the slide in this design) is fully forward the recoil spring holds it thrust forward against the face of the barrel, in which position the rear of the barrel is raised up on a swinging link so that ribs on its top surface lock securely into corresponding grooves in the ceiling of the slide. During recoil the slide and barrel travel locked together until the rear of the barrel swinging down on its link is disengaged from the slide and its travel halted, permitting the breechblock-slide to continue rearward travel to function the action. (Under .45 ACP see U. S. Govt. Model 1911-1911A1 for an example of this system. There are a number of modifications of this system of breech-locking, some of which are employed in the official side-arms of several nations. The French 7.65-mm. and the Russian Tokarev 7.62-mm. are examples.

(2) *Browning Hi-Power Locked-Breech System.* While this is essentially the system developed by John M. Browning for the Colt listed above, it uses a barrel nose forged as part of the barrel unit in place of the earlier swinging link to cam the barrel down and up to unlock and lock into the slide ceiling. The over-all design is simpler than that of the earlier type. The 9-mm. Luger and the Belgian and Canadian Browning Hi-Power 13-shot pistols are examples of this type, of which there are also some modifications.

(3) *Mauser Military Locked-Breech System.* This is one of the oldest and most successful systems in use. Instead of the conventional slide this design utilizes a separate breechblock traveling in an extension of the barrel. A separate prop-up locking piece on the receiver is forced up engaging in recesses in the bottom of the breechblock when the action is closed. After short rearward travel locked together, the barrel is halted and the bolt lock forced down to free the breechblock (or bolt) to let it travel back to eject and cock. The 7.63-mm. Mauser is a perfect example, of which there are several modifications.

(4) *Steyr Hammer Military Locked-Breech System.* This type uses a conventional breechblock slide which recoils locked to the barrel for a short distance. As the barrel moves it is revolved by cam action. Locking lugs on the barrel are rotated out of locking recesses in the slide freeing the slide to continue to the rear as the barrel travel is halted.

The 9-mm. Steyr, shown in Plate XLI, is an example of this system, which involves a barrel rotation of 60 degrees. Several modifications of this system are in existence, some of which involve a barrel rotation of 30 degrees; and the 8-mm. Roth-Steyr has a similar system which involves a barrel rotation of 90 degrees. Savage pistols, since they employ revolving barrels, are true locked-breech design; however, the degree of rotation is so slight and the weight of the reciprocating parts is so light that they represent a comparatively inefficient lock. They open practically as fast as an ordinary blowback and have heavy recoil for the cartridges employed. However, it is not strictly correct to class them as anything but locked-breech types in view of their construction.

(5) *Luger Parabellum Locked-Breech System.* This design has never been imitated, probably due to the cost of manufacture. Instead of the familiar slide this pistol utilizes a breechblock unit mounted in arms extending back from the barrel. When the breechblock is fully forward it is securely locked to the face of the barrel by a toggle joint behind it which lies below the horizontal. After short locked recoil the barrel is halted and at that point the gripping surfaces on the toggle strike ramps on the receiver breaking the toggle joint, causing it to buckle and draw the breechblock straight back to eject and

cock. (See 9-mm. Luger at Plate XXXVII for example of this system.)

(6) *Glisenti Locked-Breech System.* This is a design employing a vertical swinging block which locks in the underside of the breechblock. It is not a strong design; it is employed only in the 9-mm. Italian Glisenti and has never been imitated.

(7) *Japanese Nambu and Pattern 14 Locked-Breech System.* Unlike the other Japanese service pistols, this weapon uses a slide which covers the barrel and comprises the breechblock. It is locked by a rising wedge cammed up from the receiver ahead of the trigger. (See under 8-mm. Nambu for complete description.)

(9) *Webley & Scott Locked-Breech System.* After short recoil during which the barrel and breechblock are securely locked together by a locking shoulder on top of the barrel engaging in a corresponding shoulder in the breechblock slide, the barrel moves down diagonal grooves in the slide and is halted while the freed slide continues on to the rear in its tracks in the receiver. (Under .455 Automatic see Webley & Scott.)

(10) *Bergmann-Bayard Locked-Breech System.* This arm does not employ the slide principle but utilizes instead a falling block through which the separate breechblock can pass. Barrel and breechblock recoil locked together for a short distance until the block is forced down, the barrel is halted, and the breechblock completes its rearward travel. The 9-mm. Bayard Military is an example of this system.

(11) *Walther P-38 Locked-Breech System.* This is the latest and one of the strongest designs. A locking block is hinged in a specially shaped lug which is an integral part of the barrel forging and is positioned below the chamber. The lock has projections on either side at the top which engage in recesses machined into the slide. The barrel and breechblock-slide recoil together about one-half inch. Then a plunger mounted in the forward face of the barrel lug strikes against the receiver and is forced back to push the hinged locking block down out of engagement with the slide. The barrel is halted and the slide travels alone to the rear for ejection and cocking functions.

While this ingenious design is one of the strongest known it has the serious defect that when the arm is dismounted the locking block may be easily removed, and the pistol can be assembled without replacing the block. The pistol can be operated by hand in this condition without the defect being noted. If it is fired the slide will be jammed and may ruin the pistol, as the cartridge used develops an extremely high breech pressure. (Under 9-mm. Luger see Walther P-38 for complete description.)

(12) *Frommer Locked-Breech System—Long Recoil.* This arm differs radically not only in its method of locking the breech but also in its type of operation.

Under the short-recoil system used in all other successful automatic pistols (the term is relative and indicates a barrel travel of one-eighth to one-half the length of the cartridge in different arms) the breechblock members continue rearward travel after the barrel has been halted. In the long-recoil system the bolt and barrel travel back locked together for the full distance of the recoil stroke, which is necessarily longer than the length of the cartridge used. The bolt (or breechblock) is then mechanically caught and held while a barrel-return spring pushes the barrel ahead for extraction and ejection of the empty case, after which a second spring drives the bolt forward to chamber a new cartridge. The locking action consists of locking lugs on a revolving bolt head which engage in corresponding recesses in the barrel extension. When the action recoils and the bolt is held back by its catch, forward motion of the barrel pulls on the bolt head causing it to revolve out of locking engagement. The Frommer .32 ACP is an example of this system.

(13) *Schwarzlose Locked-Breech System.* In this unique short-recoil system the continued rearward movement of the bolt (or breechblock) after the barrel travel is halted results in a cam action which revolves the bolt to turn its locking lugs out of recesses in the barrel extension. The 7.63-mm. Schwarzlose is an example, but is unsafe if regular Mauser 7.63-mm. cartridges are employed.

*Other Characteristics of Locked-Breech Pistols.* The mechanical features covered under blowback designs are utilized in locked-breech automatic pistols. In addition it should be noted that most military (and a few blowback type) pistols utilize a stop generally operated by the rising magazine platform (follower) to hold the action open when the last shot has been fired.

(1) *Slide Stops.* For types which remain open when the magazine is withdrawn and are used to speed reloading see Colt under .45 ACP; Luger under 9-mm.; Luger and Mauser under 7.63-mm. Mauser. For types which close when the magazine is withdrawn, and so are intended only to warn that the pistol is empty, see Nambu under 8-mm. Japanese.

(2) *Magazines.* For description of removable-magazine-in-the-handle systems see Colt Auto under .45 ACP. For non-removable magazine in the handle see Steyr under 9-mm. Steyr. The Mauser 7.63-mm. has a non-removable magazine ahead of the trigger, and the 9-mm. Bayard has a removable magazine ahead of the trigger.

Revolvers. The term revolver, signifying a weapon intended to be fired normally with one hand, and in which the cartridges are inserted in individual chambers in a cylinder so mounted behind the barrel that it can revolve to bring cartridge chambers successively in line with the firing pin at the rear and the barrel at its front end, and *in which the bullet must jump a gap from the chamber in the cylinder to the barrel,* embraces the following types:

(1) *Solid-Frame, Swing-Out Cylinder, Hand-Ejector Revolvers.* All modern revolvers intended to shoot powerful cartridges (with the sole exception of the British hinge-frame .455) are of this type. In this type of revolver, the frame is the structure to which the barrel is fastened and into which the revolving cylinder assembly is fitted, and which provides the standing breech, the grip, and the receiver for the lockwork. When this is a single-quality forging, it assures maximum strength. By mounting the

cylinder on a crane assembled to the front of the frame, it is possible to swing the assembly out by releasing a latch, thus permitting speedy unloading and reloading without removing any part from the revolver, and without sacrificing the inherent strength of the solid-frame design. Pressure on the ejector rod, which passes down the center of the cylinder, forces the head of the ejector out the rear of the cylinder, bringing with it all the cartridge cases in the chambers, since their rims are resting partly on the ejector head. Releasing pressure permits the compressed ejector spring to force the ejector back into place in the cylinder ready for reloading.

While experimental models have been made (notably in Belgium and Germany) of solid-frame, swing-out-cylinder revolvers in which the act of swinging out the cylinder affected a series of levers which automatically worked the ejector, these models were too cumbrous or too complicated to stand the test of time.

*(a) United States Examples.* All recent Colt and Smith & Wesson revolvers, including pocket, police, army, and target models. These are the finest in the world from the standpoint of manufacture, accuracy, and dependability. (See pp. 690, 691, and 692.) All these weapons swing their cylinders out to the left. All are exposed-hammer, selective-double-action types; that is to say, either the hammer may be cocked by the thumb so that the only function of the trigger when pressed is the single one of releasing the hammer to fire the cartridge, or the hammer may be cocked and dropped by simple continuous pull on the trigger itself, which thus performs the double action of cocking and releasing. All of these revolvers have built-in mechanical devices to prevent the weapon from being fired except by deliberate pull on the trigger. None are provided with manually operated safeties, as they are not deemed necessary.

*(b) French Example.* The official French Army revolver, Model 1892, is in principle the same as the U. S. types. However, its cylinder swings out to the *right,* and its latch operates on a pivot. It is provided with a hinged side plate which may be swung open to afford access to the lockwork. This differs from U. S. types in which the side plates are fastened by screws. While this is a good revolver in its class, it is not to be compared to the Colt and Smith & Wesson. It is, however, well made of good materials.

*(c) Belgian Examples.* Literally scores of types of solid-frame, swing-out-cylinder, rod-ejector revolvers have been manufactured in Belgium. The quality of any of these has never been better than fair by U. S., British, and German standards. Those made by Pieper are the most reliable. These revolvers in general are imitations of the Colt and are usually classed in Europe as "Colt ejector" types. The most common calibers are 5.5-mm. Velodog (a cartridge manufactured in this country before the war to a limited extent), the 7.62-mm. Russian Nagant, and the 8-mm. French Lebel cartridges. Neither of the latter cartridges is generally known here.

Belgian revolvers of this type are made with cylinders swinging to the right, with cylinders swinging to the left, with exposed hammers, with enclosed hammers (the so-called "hammerless" type), with and without trigger guards, with and without manually operated safety catches such as are common to automatic pistols in this country, and in an endless variety of barrel lengths and shapes, cylinder flutings, and grip designs. Complete coverage of this group of freaks would require hundreds of pages of discussion which would be of little value since ammunition is not generally available for them in the United States and since they are all of inferior workmanship or design. Normally they bear proof marks, but no manufacturer's name.

*(d) Spanish Examples.* All Spanish revolvers of this type are imitations or modifications of Colt or Smith & Wesson designs. The best of them are fair; the worst are positively dangerous. In those which are made of fair-quality forgings, the fitting and tolerances are poor. Many are made from castings which frequently blow up when used with standard U. S. ammunition. While there are some Spanish automatic pistols of reasonably reliable quality, at the time of this writing there are few Spanish revolvers worthy of American ownership.

*(e) South American Examples.* Recently there have appeared numerous swing-out-cylinder weapons made in Argentina which are letter-perfect copies of Colt revolvers in exterior appearance. Usually these arms do not bear any identifying marks to show their point of origin, and are intended to be sold in South America as genuine Colts. All specimens of such weapons so far examined have been of good-quality forgings, very well finished on the outside and fairly well finished inside. Most of them, curiously, have the S.&W. type of rifling. However, any weapons whose origin cannot be determined at a glance should not be listed as reliable, since only the products of an established organization can be depended upon to maintain quality.

*(f) Other Nations.* No nations other than those listed manufacture revolvers of this type on a production basis.

(2) *Solid-Frame, Swing-Out-Cylinder, Hand Ejector, "Gas-Check" Revolvers.* This type of revolver corresponds generally to those already described, but differs in the mechanical arrangement by which the cylinder is revolved. It has the added feature of a block which *thrusts the cylinder forward* as the hammer is cocked, so that the cut-back (or chamfered) chamber is pushed over the tapered mouth of the barrel. A specially designed Russian cartridge is used with this type of action, and the escape of gas between cartridge chamber and barrel is minimized.

While United States manufacturing tolerances are so close that comparatively little gas escapes between the chamber in the cylinder and the barrel, this design is capable of considerable development.

The Belgian Pieper, as made for the Russians, exemplifies this type. It shoots the 7.62-mm. Russian Nagant gas-check cartridge, and has been widely sold commercially throughout Europe. The cylinder swings to the left.

(3) *Solid-Frame, Fixed-Cylinder, Rod-Ejector Revolvers.* The good types on this system fall into two classes: single action and double action.

*(a) Single Action.* In the Colt Single-Action Army Frontier Model the frame is solid as in the swing-out-cylinder types, but the cylinder is mounted on

a bushing and retained in place by a cylinder pin inserted through a hole in the frame below the barrel, which passes through the bushing and locks its head in the standing-breech section of the frame. A hinged "loading gate" covers the head of the cylinder on the right side of the revolver. When the hammer is half cocked to permit the cylinder to be turned by hand, the loading gate is swung out and a cartridge chamber lined up with the loading slot. A cartridge is inserted and the cylinder turned by hand the distance of the next chamber. The hammer must be drawn back manually. Pressure on the trigger has no function except to drop the hammer to fire the cartridge.

Since the cylinder is fixed, the weapon is normally unloaded by half cocking the hammer, opening the loading gate, lining up a chamber with the loading slot, then pushing back the rod ejector mounted in a tube below the barrel. The tip of the rod will enter the chamber and eject the cartridge. When pressure is released, a spring around the rod will move it back to its original position. Turning the cylinder the distance of a chamber and pushing the rod will eject the next case. As an alternative method, the fixing pin may be removed and the cylinder withdrawn to the left to permit the cartridge cases to be forced out of their chambers in the cylinder. However, this is not standard procedure.

While this is one of the oldest and most widely known systems, and is noted for its grip, balance, and strength, of frame, in actual practice it is not so dependable as the Colt and S.&W. swing-out-cylinder types.

*(b) Double Action.* In the .455 British Royal Irish Constabulary revolver the frame is solid and the cylinder is free to revolve on a fixed pin; but the ejector rod normally must be pulled forward out of its seating in the front of the frame, then turned on a pivot or collar before it can be thrust up into the cartridge chamber. The cylinder, of course, must be revolved by hand to bring the chambers in line for ejection. This type normally is not provided with an ejector return spring; hence the ejector must be pulled out of the chamber manually and must be returned manually to its seat in the frame.

*(c) Italian Types.* Numerous varieties of this type were developed in Italy from 1870 on, and were in use with practically no design changes as official Army weapons in World War II. They are usually classed as Bodeo or Bodego revolvers. If made by Glisenti of Brescia, they are of good material and fair workmanship.

They are most often encountered in Italian 10.35-mm. caliber. Barrel lengths and styles, as well as finishes and trigger styles, vary greatly. It must be noted that these revolvers *when designed* were ahead of their time. They employed rebounding hammers, counter-bored chambers, positive mechanical locks, and loose hammer noses years before such developments were thought of in the United States. Usually they have quick-detachable side plates which permit cleaning the lockwork without removing any parts.

*(d) Austrian Types.* Like the Italians, the Austrians in the 1870's developed double action and other mechanical features far ahead of their general acceptance. Austrian Gasser revolvers in particular are made of good materials and are of good design, of their type. Gasser 8-mm. revolvers used by the Italians and by some Austrian contingents in World War II had been in service since 1880!

*(e) European Imitations.* Imitations of the Colt S. A. Army have been made in Spain with a double-action lockwork, but otherwise resembling the Colt in exterior appearance. All such revolvers are uniformly inferior and are often dangerous.

*(f) Belgian and German imitations,* particularly of the Webley design, are numerous. If German-made by Pickert, they are good cheap revolvers. Belgian makes are fair or poor. None are as good as the United States low-priced Harrington & Richardson or Iver Johnson arms.

Like the swing-out cylinder imitations made in Europe, this design appears with exposed and enclosed hammers, with and without trigger guards, with and without manual safeties, with folding triggers, and in a tremendous range of lengths, weights, grip styles, etc.

The range of calibers, too, is tremendous. It includes the following:

*Pin-Fire:* 5 mm., 7 mm., 9 mm., 12 mm., and 15 mm.

*Rim-Fire:* .22 Short, Long, Long Rifle, and Longue Portée; .297 (7.5 mm.), .30 (7.8 mm.), .320 Extra Short, .320 Short and .320 Long (8.05 mm.), .340 (8.75 mm.), .380 Short and Long (9.6 mm.), .410 (10.2 mm.), .442 (11.3 mm.), .440 (11.1 mm.), and .44 (11.2 mm.).

*Center-Fire:* .230 (5.7 mm.), .320 Short and Long, .340, .380 Short and Long, .442 (11.3 mm.), .450 (12.05 mm.), several types of 11.5 mm. and 11.55 mm., the entire line of U. S. and British cartridges, the 7.5 mm. Swedish Velodog, 7.7 mm. Swiss, 8 mm. Austrian Gasser, 8 mm. French Lebel, 9.6 mm. Dutch, .430 Short and Long (11.35 mm.), 11.75 mm. Long Montenegrin Gasser, 12 mm. Rand, .500 (13.15 mm.) and .577 (15 mm.) Eley.

To add to the confusion, these revolvers are also made to take *rimless and semi-rim automatic pistol cartridges,* including the .25 and .32 Colt Automatic Pistol cartridges.

(4) *Solid-Frame, Fixed-Cylinder, Non-Ejector.* This is the cheapest form of revolver ever manufactured. In recent years it has been manufactured in the United States only by Harrington & Richardson and Iver Johnson. The frames are uniformly solid, and the cylinders are securely mounted on a fixing pin inserted through the frame below the barrel and passing back through the axis hole in the cylinder to the standing breech face of the frame. Revolvers of this type may or may not have a hinged loading gate on the right side of the frame to cover the loading slot when the weapon is ready for firing. They are uniformly double action with exposed hammers, though the type and shape of hammer may differ in various models. While the regular spur hammer is the standard one, and is intended to permit thumb cocking, special models intended for quick drawing have a cut-down hammer without spur.

The line of baby revolvers of this type made by Sedgley in .22 caliber differ from all others in being hammerless—that is, having the hammer inside the frame and concealed by side plates. This type also has a folding trigger to make the weapon more compact.

Since the turn of the century, revolvers of this type have been produced in quantity for the American market in short—and long-barreled, pocket, and target types only, in calibers .22 Short, .22 Long Rifle, .32 Smith & Wesson, .32 Smith & Wesson Long, and .38 Smith & Wesson. Some for European use have been made, notably by Harrington & Richardson, in caliber .455 British.

The characteristic difference of this basic type is that *no provision is made for mechanical extraction.* The cartridge cases must be pried or punched individually out of their chambers through the loading slot if the cylinder is in place, or from the cylinder if it is removed from the frame.

Examples of this type are .22 Iver Johnson Solid Frame and .32 H. & R. Solid Frame.

*(a) Obsolescent American Types.* Revolvers of this type were manufactured in the late 1890's and early 1900's under dozens of brand names for mail-order houses. Some were well made of forged steel but many were made with cast frames. Hopkins & Allen revolvers were the best of these, and thousands are still in use. Early Colt and Webleys, of course, were outstanding.

*(b) European Types.* All the data under solid-frame, fixed-cylinder, rod-ejector as to makes, styles, and calibers apply to this classification also.

(5) *Hinged-Frame, Tip-Down Barrel, Barrel Latch.* This is the American type of hinged-frame revolver originally introduced by Smith & Wesson. The barrel is forged with a mounting for the cylinder and extractor assembly, and with an extension or strap which passes over the top of the cylinder and is provided with a latch which can be snapped down over the standing breech to lock the arm in firing position. The form of latch varies with the manufacturer and also with the date of manufacture; but always it is attached to the barrel strap.

The barrel is fastened to an extension of the frame or receiver ahead of the trigger guard at its locking point forward of the cylinder. Raising (or pressing) the latch permits the barrel and cylinder assemblies to be tipped down. This action automatically forces the extractor up from its seat in the center of the cylinder to extract and eject the cartridge cases in all the chambers, and to compress the extractor spring which snaps the extractor back into its seating in the cylinder at the end of the tip-down motion.

Except when manufactured by Smith & Wesson, this type was never produced as a quality revolver. As manufactured by Harrington & Richardson, Hopkins & Allen, and Iver Johnson, it was a substantial pocket revolver worth its selling price but not to be rated with Colt, S. & W., or Webley. Recent target models of this type in .22 caliber by H. & R. and Iver Johnson are good revolvers in their class.

*(a) United States Examples.* Smith & Wesson hinged-frame .32 and .38 S. & W.; Harrington & Richardson and Iver Johnson .22, .32, and .38 hinged-frame. Hopkins & Allen (no longer manufactured but still widely distributed) are also a representative type.

*(b) Lockwork Variations.* This type of revolver as made in the United States varies in lockwork with manufacturer and also with date of manufacture. The following, however, are the principal successful types:

1. Smith & Wesson: Double action, exposed hammer. Can be thumb cocked for accurate firing.
2. Smith & Wesson: Double action only, enclosed hammer. Can be fired only by continuous trigger pull. This is the so-called "hammerless" type, and is fitted with automatic grip safety.
3. Harrington & Richardson: Double action, exposed spur or cutdown hammer.
4. Harrington & Richardson: Enclosed hammer (called hammerless). Rebounding hammer safety but no grip safety.
5. Iver Johnson: Double action, exposed hammer. Unique automatic safety and special coil mainspring.
6. Iver Johnson: Enclosed hammer. Otherwise like hammer model. In IJ safety system, hammer never touches firing pin or cartridge, but when brought to full cock it can strike an intermediate lifter which in turn strikes the firing pin.
7. Hopkins & Allen: Manufacture discontinued, but was made in hammer and hammerless models with a special safety which worked on an eccentric to bring the hammer in line with the firing pin *only* at the full-cock position and when the trigger was pulled.

*(c) Calibers.* While early Smith & Wesson revolvers on this system were made in large calibers, in the present century this type has been confined to low calibers (.22 Short, .22 Long Rifle, .22 Winchester; .32 S. & W. Short, .32 S. & W. Long, and .38 S. & W.) because of the comparative weakness of the system of frame locking.

*(d) Obsolescent American Types.* Dozens of makes of this type were turned out for the mail-order trade by factories no longer in business. Some were sold under as many as 50 different trade names. None should be used with today's ammunition.

*(e) European Imitations and Variations.* In general, all that has been said about European solid-frame revolvers applies here also, with the further warning that because of the hinge (instead of a solid frame) this variety is potentially much more dangerous to the user.

German weapons of this class are the best; Belgian when proof-marked (as they customarily are) rate next; while Spanish types foot the list. All these countries made nearly exact copies of Smith & Wesson revolvers at one time or another. Many of these copies were made to shoot very powerful cartridges which no American manufacturer would countenance using in a barrel-latched hinged-frame design. When chambered for the .38-40, .44-40, .45 Colt, and similar cartridges, these European makes are almost without exception dangerous. Only those made in Germany by Ludwig Loewe are reasonably safe. These European makes may be chambered for any American, British, or European cartridge already listed. They may be hammer or hammerless. They may have grip safeties, thumb safeties, folding triggers, barrel lengths from 1½ to 12 inches or more, all types of finishes or engraving. A thousand variations could easily be identified. The one thing they have in common by United States standards is unreliability.

*(f) Japanese Variation.* The Japanese, in 1892, adopted and still use as a cavalry revolver a variant of the Smith & Wesson hinged frame. The latch is the same, being on the barrel strap. The lockwork is quite different, however, employing a hinged side plate adapted from Italian and Austrian designs which can be swung out on a hinge to give quick access to all the working parts for immediate cleaning and easy replacement. The hammer is of peculiar design and cannot be thumb cocked.

(6) *Hinged-Frame, Tip-Down Barrel, Barrel Latch, and Thumb Latch.* This is identical with the hinged-frame S. & W. in the previous section, *with*

*the addition* of a thumb latch of the type used in solid-frame swing-out-cylinder revolvers. Not only must the barrel latch be lifted, but the thumb latch on the left side must be simultaneously pushed to unlock the barrel for tip-down. While this is an improved form and gives a much stronger lock, it has been discarded for the solid-frame type in American manufacture.

(g) *European Imitations.* As in all other categories, poor European imitations of this system are known. None can be recommended.

(9) *Hinged-Frame, Tip-Down Barrel, Stirrup Breech Latch.* This is the British type of hinged-frame revolver originally introduced by Webley & Scott. Its principal difference from the American variety lies in the ultra-strong breech fastening, consisting of a stirrup-shaped lock *pivoted to the standing breech* under spring tension. When the lower thumbpiece end of the lock on the left side of the frame is pushed forward, the upper locking stirrup is drawn back from over the top of the barrel strap (or extension), permitting the barrel and cylinder assemblies to be tipped down for automatic ejection and for loading. (For detailed description and drawings of this as a basic type, see .455 Webley Revolver on pp. 700-701.)

(a) *British Types.* This system has never been used in United States manufacture, but has stood up under the most rigid service conditions wherever British troops have fought. While not a strong theoretically as the American swingout-cylinder design, in field practice it has proved strong enough for any loads used in it, and for general sturdiness is usually rated ahead of the solid-frame varieties. It is the official British service revolver in the original .455 caliber and in the more recent official .380 caliber. The two differ in lockwork as relates to firing gear and cylinder indexing, but are identical in frame locking.

Such Webley pocket revolvers as do not require such a positive stirrup lock use a modification of it in the form of a thumb latch mounted on the standing breech and locking over the barrel strap.

(b) *European Types.* European imitations of this design are uniformly poor, with the notable exception of some Belgian types originally made for Montenegro.

(c) *Montenegrin Stirrup.* This is a variant of the Webley stirrup based on an early Webley once made for the Chinese Navy in caliber .476. It consists of two separate thumbpieces pivoted on either side of the standing breech. When the lower ends are pressed, the upper locking ends are drawn to right and left away from the barrel strap in some types, while in others, where the strap fits down into a cut in the standing breech, they are drawn out of locking holes in the barrel strap. As made to shoot the tremendous .45 Montenegrin (a cartridge unknown in the United States, but much longer than the .45 Colt) this is a formidable arm of excessive weight for a revolver. Much of the strength of its locking device derives from the weight of the parts rather than the efficiency of the system.

(8) *"Automatic" Revolvers.* Actually these are a *self-cocking variant* of the Webley hinged-frame, tip-down barrel, stirrup-breech-latch type. The barrel lock is identical. In this type the barrel and cylinder assemblies are free to ride backward and forward a short distance in the receiver or frame, being driven back by the force of recoil, then thrust forward by the compressed return spring. During this travel the hammer is automatically cocked and the cylinder revolved one chamber. Loading and unloading require the same manual pressure on the stirrup end and tipping down of the barrel as in the regular type. The .455 Webley-Fosbery Automatic Revolver is an example of this type.

(a) *Imitations.* The only imitation of this design put into limited manufacture was by the American Union Arms Company, of Toledo. This design might be capable of further development.

(9) *Miscellaneous Revolver Types.* Among the frame types which did not stand the test of time may be listed the strong but complicated pivot frame of the Mervin Hulbert, an American revolver in which the barrel and its strap turn out of engagement with the standing breech on a pivot in the frame ahead of the cylinder. Many of these finely constructed revolvers are still in use. The design, however, is inferior to the current types. The design was imitated in England by Kynoch.

Very early Smith & Wesson revolvers and their imitators had frames in which the barrel strap was hinged to the standing breech and the release catch was on the frame ahead of the cylinder. In these, the barrel hinged and was tipped up to remove the cylinder for loading and unloading. This design was imitated in Europe. In some European types, the barrel and barrel strap could be moved straight ahead when the catch was released.

(10) *Automatic Revolver Ejecting Systems.* Attempts to provide for automatic ejection of empty cartridge cases from revolvers take two forms; use of gas, and mechanical action in connection with the fall of the hammer.

In the first class, numerous experimental revolvers have been designed in which gas escaped through a small hole in the barrel as the bullet passed over it, to drive back a short piston much in the manner of the Winchester Carbine M1. This piston had an arm extending to the right ahead of the cylinder, with an attached short ejecting rod. The unit with a return spring was mounted in a tube below the barrel. As a shot was fired and the piston was driven back, the ejector rod was driven up into the chamber *to the right* of the one just fired, hurling the contents of that chamber out of the weapon, whether the contents was a loaded cartridge or an empty case. As this missile came straight back at the shooter, a deflecting shield was sometimes employed.

In the second class, which was widely developed and to some degree produced in Germany and Switzerland, the mainspring was made unusually powerful. When the trigger was pressed, as the hammer fell it hit a pivoted lever in the standing breech to the right of the firing-pin hole at the same time that the hammer nose struck the cartridge in the chamber ahead of it. The tip of this pivoted lever was engaged under the rim of the cartridge to the right of the one being fired, which it hurled out the loading slot on the right side. This system was even a worse failure than the gas system because of over-complication.

In passing it should be noted that much experimental work along this line was also done in Italy, and that the Italian Ricci gas-operated revolver—now unknown—was at the turn of the century given some attention by U. S. Navy authorities.

(11) *Quick-Loading Systems for Revolvers.* Some European revolvers have been issued with quickly removable cylinders and with extra loaded cylinders intended to be inserted in the manner of extra magazines in automatic pistols. These all suffer from the facts that the cylinders are bulky and that the cartridges will fall out of the spare unless they are protected by a cover which must be removed.

Special metal clips and disks perforated to receive cartridges and to drop over the head and ratchet of the ejector rod have been used, notably in the Webley-Fosbery Automatic Revolver in caliber .38 ACP. Besides being bulky and easily deformed, these are impractical because the cartridges take too long to line up with the chambers. Linked chargers suffer from this failing, also.

The only practical quick loader yet produced is that intended to permit the use of rimless cartridges in a revolver intended to be used with rimmed ammunition.

# TYPICAL MODERN HANDGUNS

PLATE I. COLT (Government Model .45). This pistol is the famous "Government" model, the official side arm of the Army, Navy, and Marine Corps. Caliber .45; magazine capacity, 7 rounds; barrel length, 5 inches; Over-all length, 8½ inches; weight, 39 ounces, Trigger and hammer spur checked; arched housing checked. Stock, plastic. Finish, dual-tone.

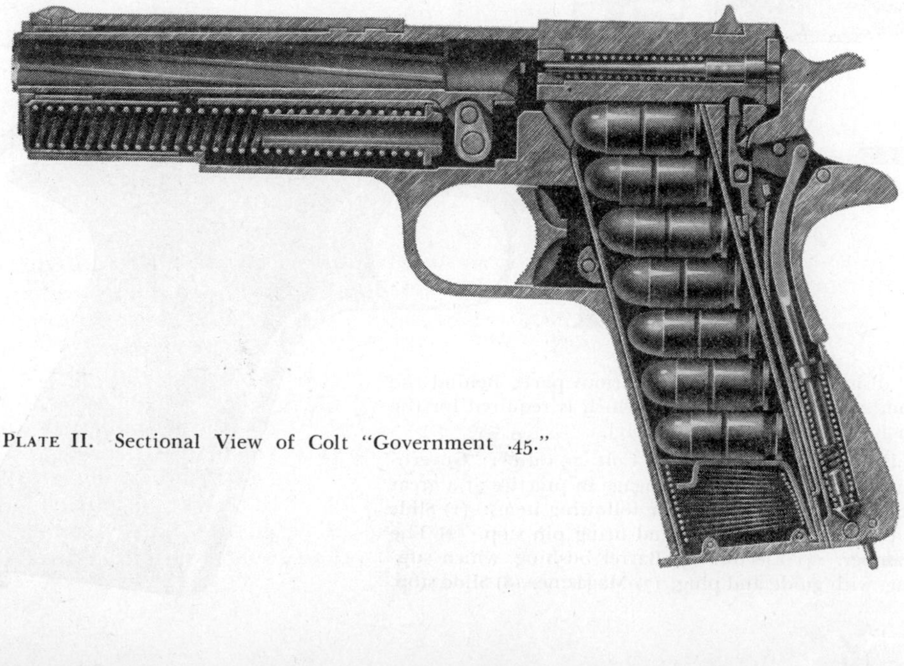

PLATE II. Sectional View of Colt "Government .45."

PLATE III. COLT (.38 Auto). This model is in .38 caliber, but built on the same frame as the famous "Government .45." Magazine capacity, 9 rounds; barrel length, 5 inches; over-all length, 8½ inches; weight, 39 ounces. Sights, fixed Patridge type. Trigger and hammer spur checked; arched housing checked. Stock, checked walnut. Finish, dual-tone. This pistol will handle the Super .38 cartridge, with a muzzle velocity of 1300 foot-seconds.

PLATE IV. COLT "Service Ace," dismounted to show the various parts. Behind the barrel is shown the floating chamber. The special ejector which is required for the conversion is shown beneath the barrel.

With the complete unit it is possible to convert the Colt .45-caliber "Government" into a .22-caliber pistol, permitting the owner to engage in practice at a great saving in ammunition cost. The entire unit comprises the following items: (1) Slide assembly, with extractor, firing pin, firing pin spring, and firing pin stop. (2) The .22 barrel. (3) The floating chamber. (4) Ejector. (5) Barrel bushing, which supports the barrel. (6) Recoil spring, with guide and plug. (7) Magazine. (8) Slide stop.

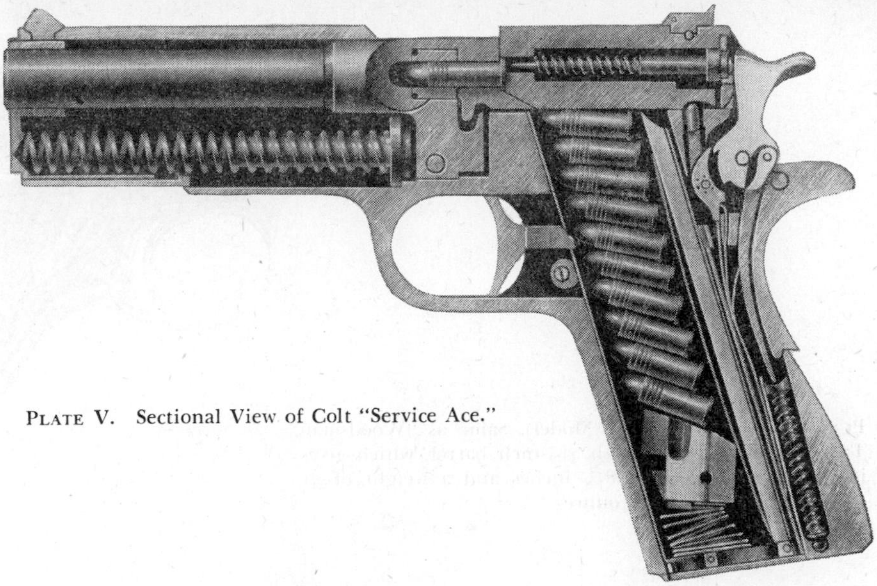

PLATE V. Sectional View of Colt "Service Ace."

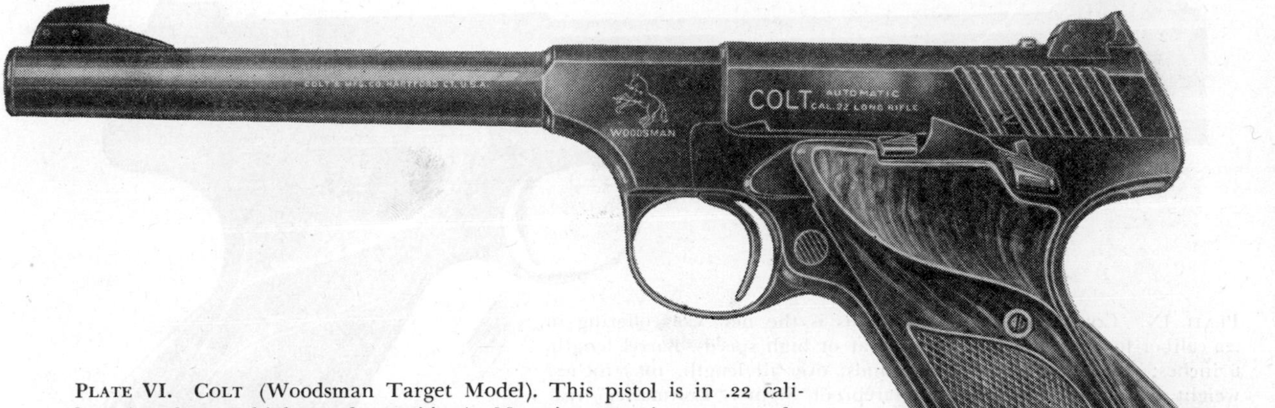

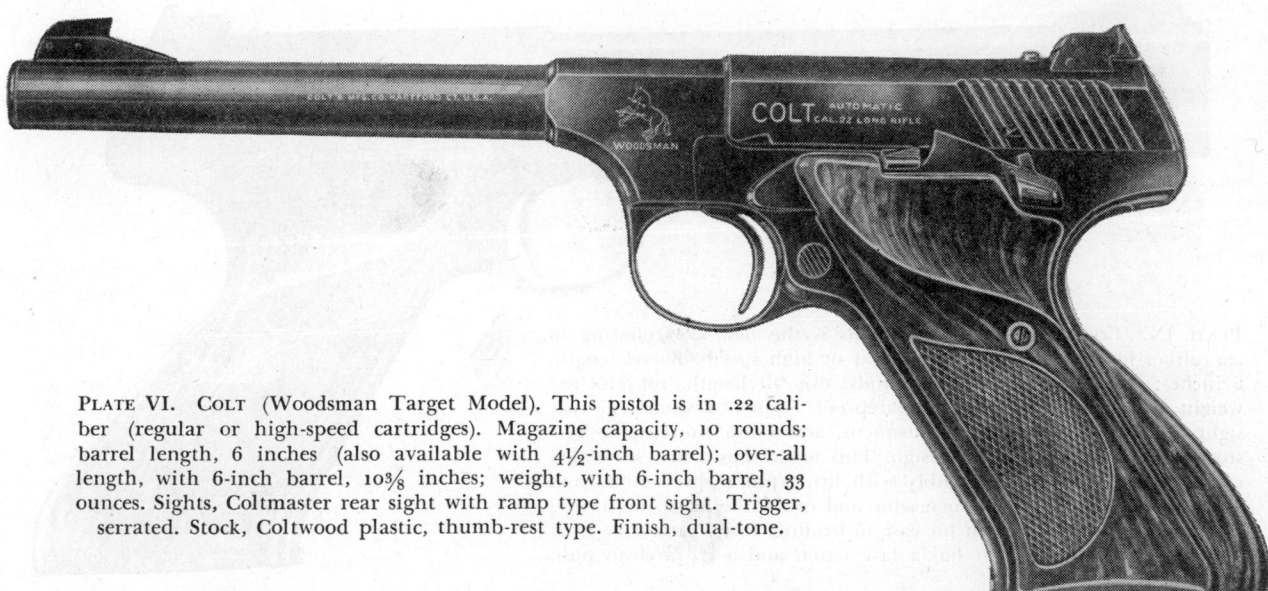

PLATE VI. COLT (Woodsman Target Model). This pistol is in .22 caliber (regular or high-speed cartridges). Magazine capacity, 10 rounds; barrel length, 6 inches (also available with 4½-inch barrel); over-all length, with 6-inch barrel, 10⅜ inches; weight, with 6-inch barrel, 33 ounces. Sights, Coltmaster rear sight with ramp type front sight. Trigger, serrated. Stock, Coltwood plastic, thumb-rest type. Finish, dual-tone.

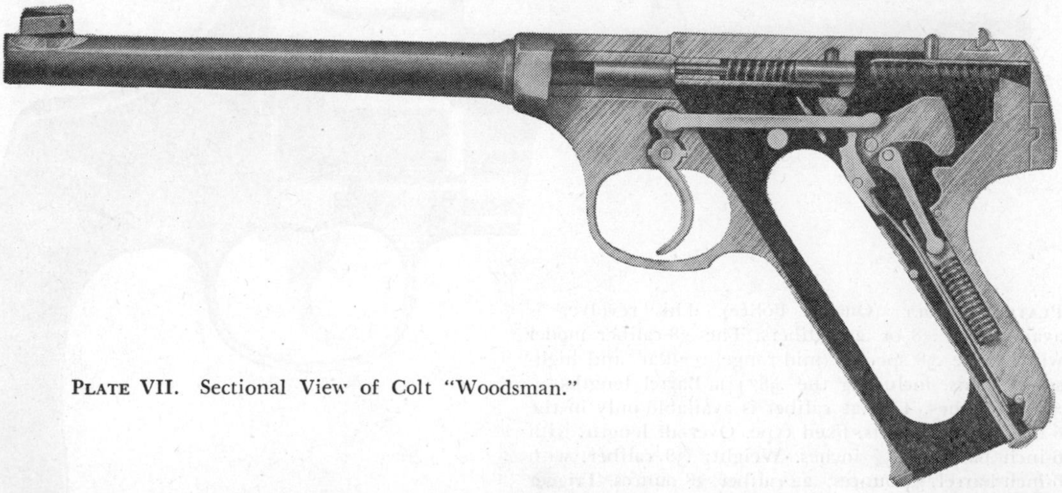

PLATE VII. Sectional View of Colt "Woodsman."

PLATE VIII. COLT (Sport Model). Same as "Woodsman Target Model," except with 4½-inch barrel, which gives it an over-all length of 8⅞ inches and a weight of 31 ounces.

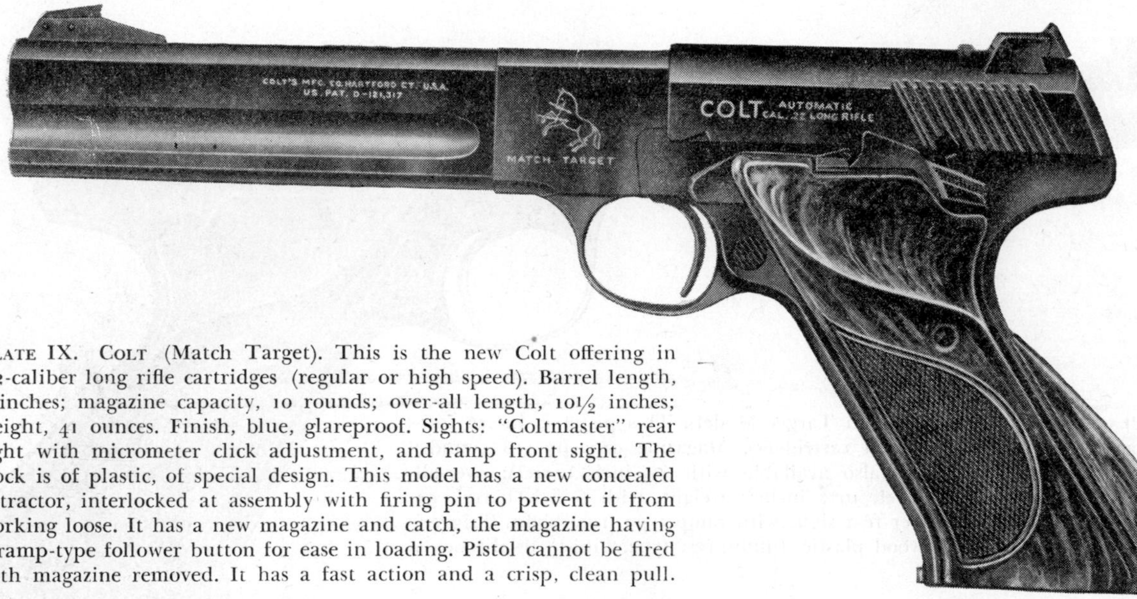


PLATE IX. COLT (Match Target). This is the new Colt offering in .22-caliber long rifle cartridges (regular or high speed). Barrel length, 6 inches; magazine capacity, 10 rounds; over-all length, 10½ inches; weight, 41 ounces. Finish, blue, glareproof. Sights: "Coltmaster" rear sight with micrometer click adjustment, and ramp front sight. The stock is of plastic, of special design. This model has a new concealed extractor, interlocked at assembly with firing pin to prevent it from working loose. It has a new magazine and catch, the magazine having a ramp-type follower button for ease in loading. Pistol cannot be fired with magazine removed. It has a fast action and a crisp, clean pull.

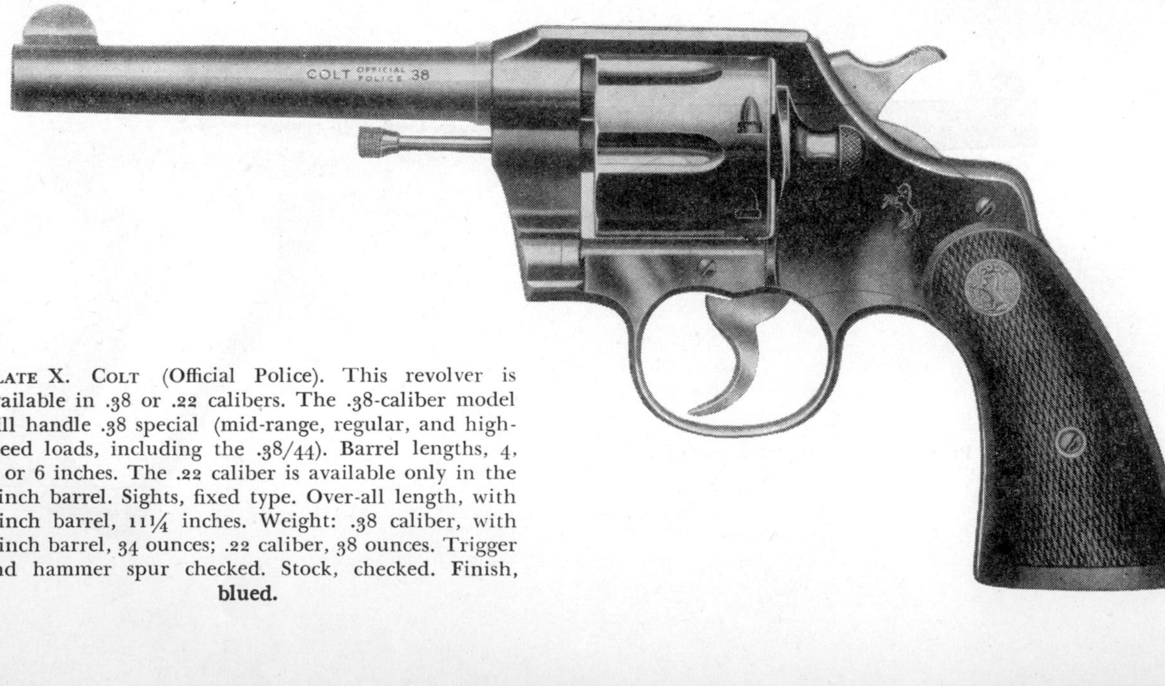


PLATE X. COLT (Official Police). This revolver is available in .38 or .22 calibers. The .38-caliber model will handle .38 special (mid-range, regular, and high-speed loads, including the .38/44). Barrel lengths, 4, 5, or 6 inches. The .22 caliber is available only in the 6-inch barrel. Sights, fixed type. Over-all length, with 6-inch barrel, 11¼ inches. Weight: .38 caliber, with 6-inch barrel, 34 ounces; .22 caliber, 38 ounces. Trigger and hammer spur checked. Stock, checked. Finish, blued.

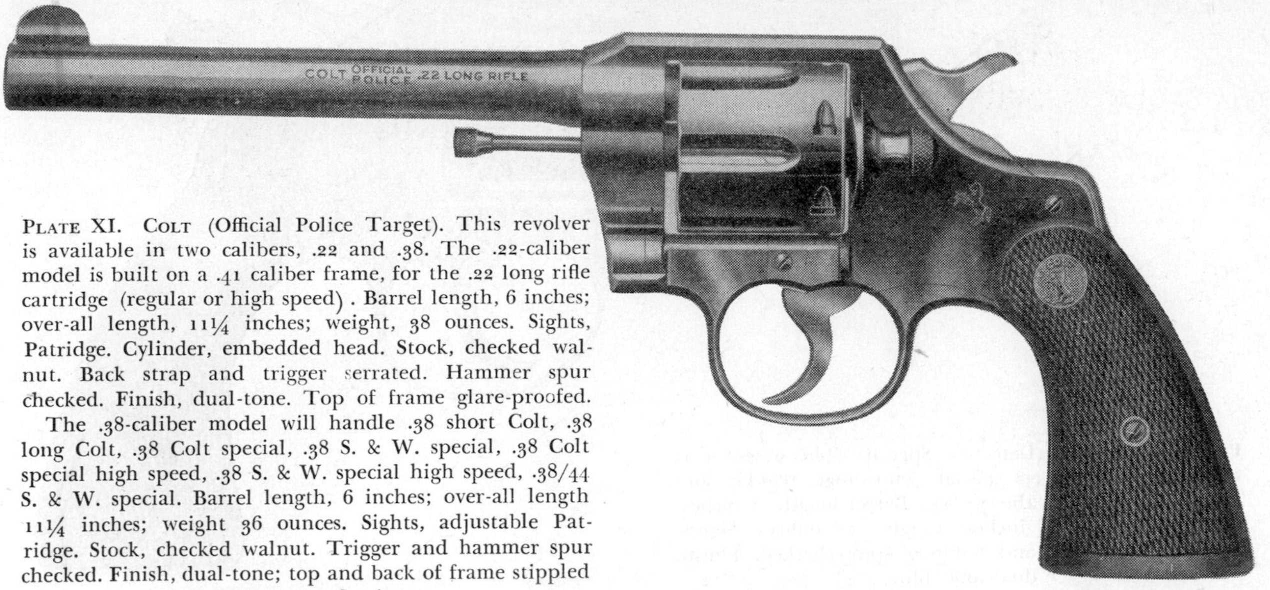


PLATE XI. COLT (Official Police Target). This revolver is available in two calibers, .22 and .38. The .22-caliber model is built on a .41 caliber frame, for the .22 long rifle cartridge (regular or high speed). Barrel length, 6 inches; over-all length, 11¼ inches; weight, 38 ounces. Sights, Patridge. Cylinder, embedded head. Stock, checked walnut. Back strap and trigger serrated. Hammer spur checked. Finish, dual-tone. Top of frame glare-proofed.

The .38-caliber model will handle .38 short Colt, .38 long Colt, .38 Colt special, .38 S. & W. special, .38 Colt special high speed, .38 S. & W. special high speed, .38/44 S. & W. special. Barrel length, 6 inches; over-all length 11¼ inches; weight 36 ounces. Sights, adjustable Patridge. Stock, checked walnut. Trigger and hammer spur checked. Finish, dual-tone; top and back of frame stippled to prevent reflection.

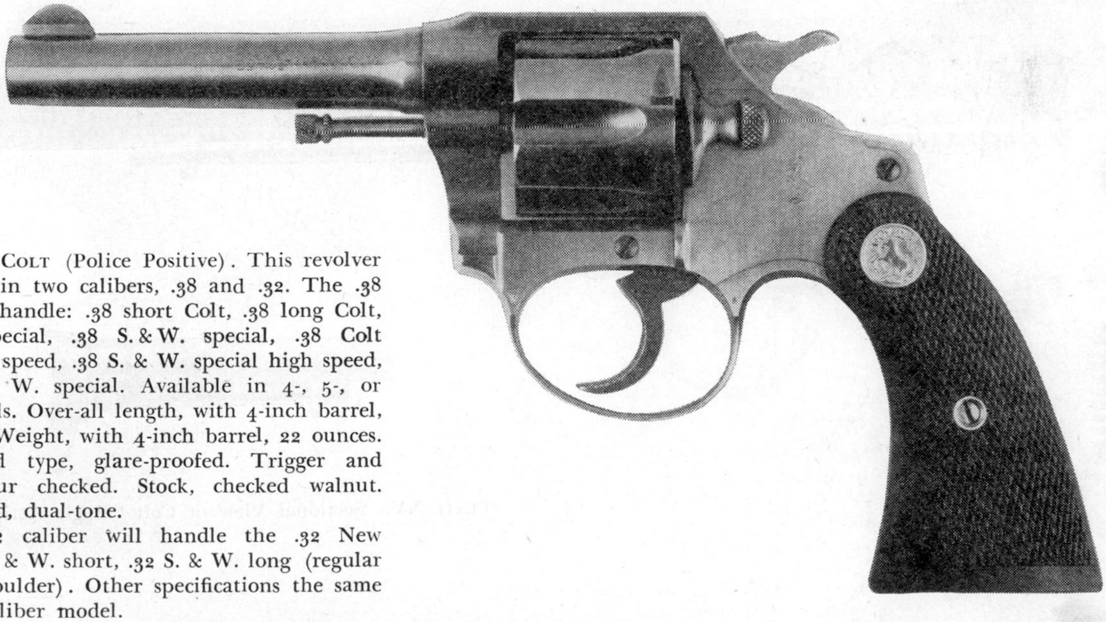

PLATE XII. COLT (Police Positive). This revolver is available in two calibers, .38 and .32. The .38 caliber will handle: .38 short Colt, .38 long Colt, .38 Colt special, .38 S. & W. special, .38 Colt special high speed, .38 S. & W. special high speed, .38/44 S. & W. special. Available in 4-, 5-, or 6-inch barrels. Over-all length, with 4-inch barrel, 8¾ inches. Weight, with 4-inch barrel, 22 ounces. Sights, fixed type, glare-proofed. Trigger and hammer spur checked. Stock, checked walnut. Finish, blued, dual-tone.

The .32 caliber will handle the .32 New Police .32 S. & W. short, .32 S. & W. long (regular or sharp shoulder). Other specifications the same as for .38-caliber model.

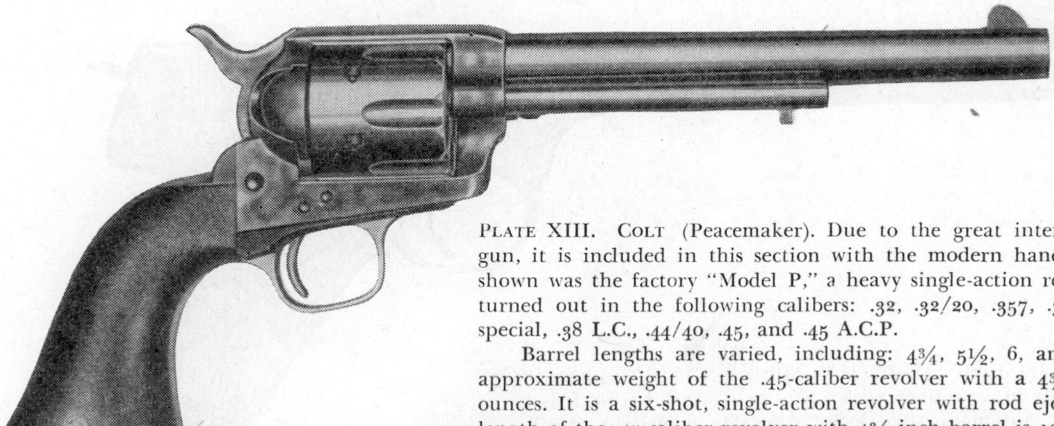

PLATE XIII. COLT (Peacemaker). Due to the great interest in this famous gun, it is included in this section with the modern hand guns. The model shown was the factory "Model P," a heavy single-action revolver. It has been turned out in the following calibers: .32, .32/20, .357, .38/40, .41 L.C., .44 special, .38 L.C., .44/40, .45, and .45 A.C.P.

Barrel lengths are varied, including: 4¾, 5½, 6, and 7½ inches. The approximate weight of the .45-caliber revolver with a 4¾-inch barrel is 36 ounces. It is a six-shot, single-action revolver with rod ejection. The over-all length of the .45-caliber revolver with 4¾ inch barrel is 10¼ inches. To load, it is necessary to swing out the loading gate as far as possible and draw the hammer back to half-cock then the cylinder must be turned sufficiently to bring the chamber in line with the loading slot.

Plate XIV. Colt (Detective Special). This revolver is chambered for the .38 special (mid-range, regular, and high-speed loads, or the .38/44). Barrel length, 2 inches; over-all length, 6¾ inches; weight, 21 ounces. Sights, fixed type. Trigger and hammer spur checked. Finish, dual-tone blue.

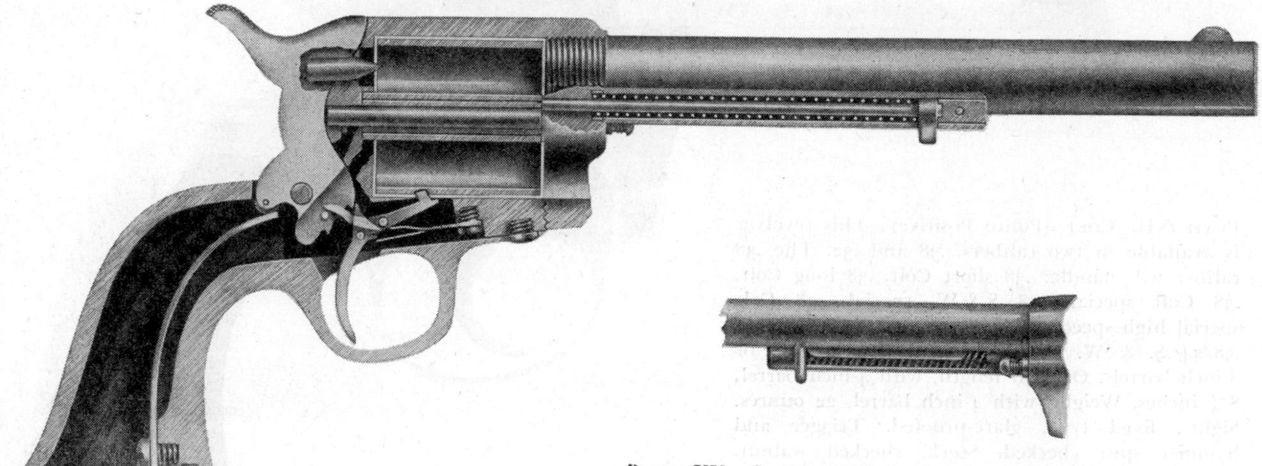

Plate XV. Sectional View of Colt "Single Action .45."

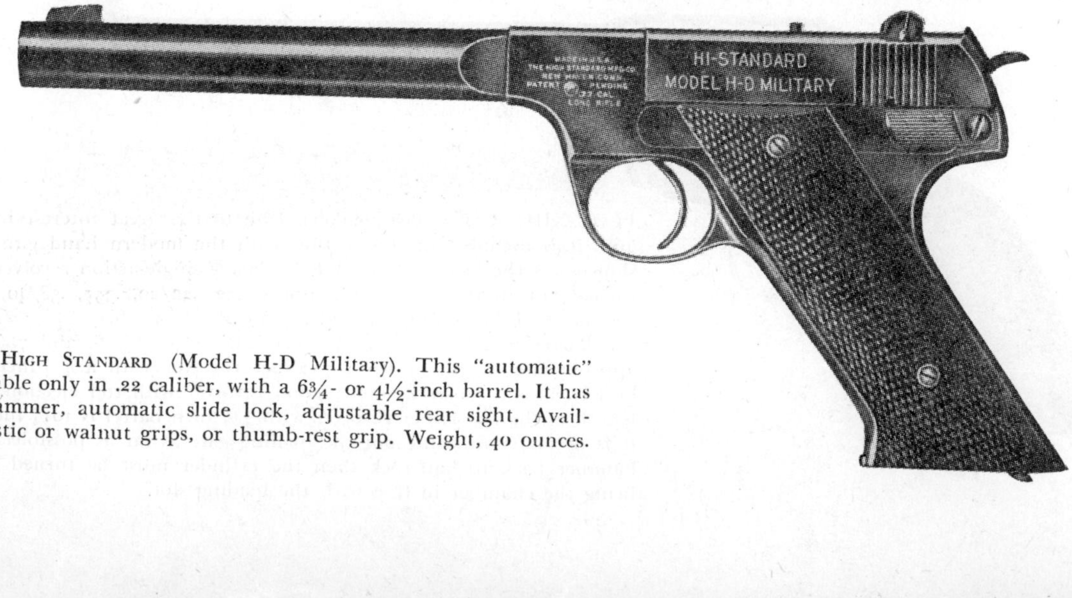


Plate XVI. High Standard (Model H-D Military). This "automatic" pistol is available only in .22 caliber, with a 6¾- or 4½-inch barrel. It has an outside hammer, automatic slide lock, adjustable rear sight. Available with plastic or walnut grips, or thumb-rest grip. Weight, 40 ounces.

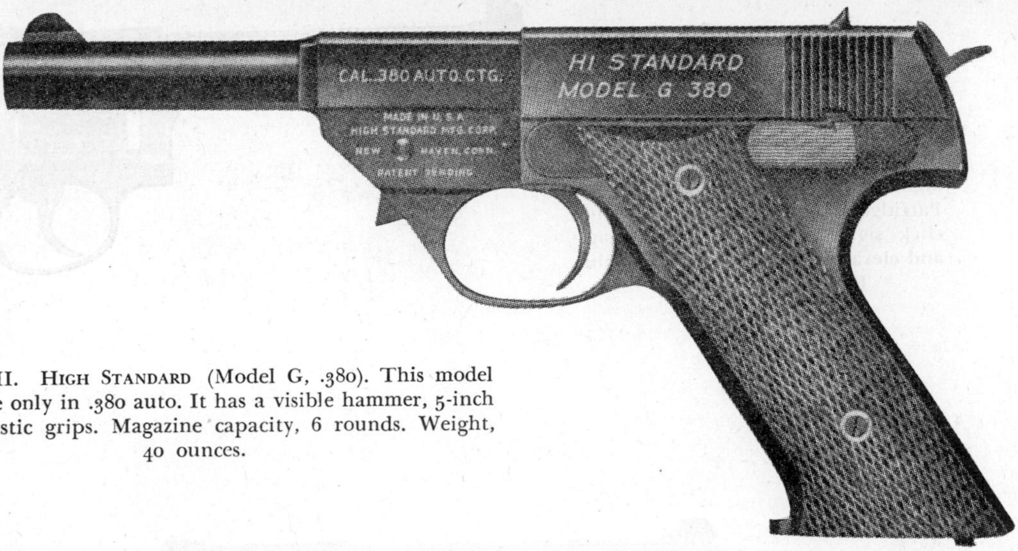


PLATE XVII. HIGH STANDARD (Model G, .380). This model is available only in .380 auto. It has a visible hammer, 5-inch barrel, plastic grips. Magazine capacity, 6 rounds. Weight, 40 ounces.

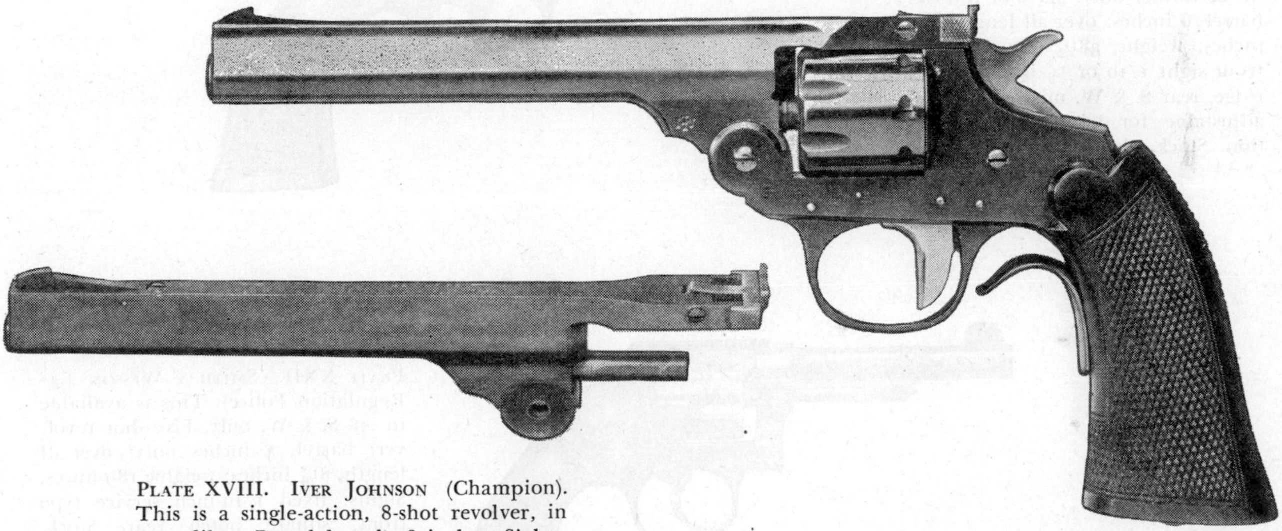

PLATE XVIII. IVER JOHNSON (Champion). This is a single-action, 8-shot revolver, in .22 caliber. Barrel length, 6 inches. Sights, adjustable Patridge type. Hammer spur and trigger scored. Stock, walnut. Over-all length, 10¾ inches. Weight, 28 ounces.

PLATE XIX. SMITH & WESSON (K-38 Masterpiece). This is available in .38 S. & W. only. Six-shot revolver; barrel, 6 inches; weight, 36 ounces. Over-all length, 11⅛ inches. Sights: front sight 1/10 or ⅛ plain Patridge, rear sight S. & W. micrometer click, adjustable for windage and elevation. Stock, checked walnut. Finish, S. & W. blue.

PLATE. XX. SMITH & WESSON (K-32 Masterpiece). This is available in .32 S. & W. only. Six-shot revolver; barrel, 6 inches; over-all length, 11⅛ inches; weight, 36¾ ounces loaded. Sights: front sight 1/10 or ⅛ plain Patridge, rear S. & W. micrometer click sight, adjustable for windage and elevation. Stock, checked walnut. Finish, S. & W. blue.

PLATE XXI. SMITH & WESSON (New K-22 Masterpiece). This is available in .22 caliber only. Six-shot revolver; barrel, 6 inches; over-all length, 11⅛ inches; weight, 38½ ounces. Sights: front sight 1/10 or ⅛ inch plain Patridge, rear S. & W. micrometer click, adjustable for windage and elevation. Stock, checked walnut. Finish, S. & W. blue.

PLATE XXII. SMITH & WESSON (.38 Regulation Police). This is available in .38 S. & W. only. Five-shot revolver; barrel, 4 inches only; over-all length, 8¼ inches; weight, 18 ounces. Sights: fixed 1/10-inch service type front, square notch rear. Stock, checked walnut. Finish, S. & W. blue or nickel.

PLATE XXIII. SMITH & WESSON (.32 Regulation Police). This is available in .32 S. & W. only. Barrel lengths, 3¼, 4¼, or 6 inches; over-all length, with 4¼ inch barrel, 8½ inches; weight, 4¼-inch barrel, 19 ounces. Sights: fixed 1/10-inch service type front sight, square notch rear. Stock, checked walnut. Finish, S. & W. blue or nickel.

PLATE XXIV. SMITH & WESSON (.22/32 Target). This is available in .22 caliber only. Six-shot revolver; barrel, 6 inches; over-all length, 10½ inches. Sights: 1/10- or ⅛-inch Patridge front sight, with square notch rear adjustable for windage and elevation. Finish, S. & W. blue.

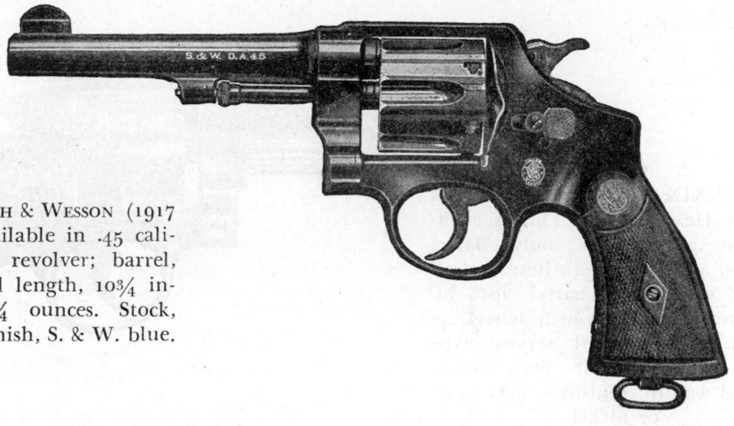

PLATE XXV. SMITH & WESSON (1917 Army). This is available in .45 caliber only. Six-shot revolver; barrel, 5½ inches; over-all length, 10¾ inches; weight, 36¼ ounces. Stock, checked walnut. Finish, S. & W. blue.

PLATE XXVI. SMITH & WESSON (Model .44 Target). This is available in .44 S. & W. Special only. Six-shot revolver; barrel, 6½ inches only; over-all length, 11¾ inches; weight, 39½ ounces. Sights: 1/10- or ⅛-inch Patridge front, square notch rear, adjustable for windage and elevation. Stock, checked walnut. Finish, S. & W. blue.

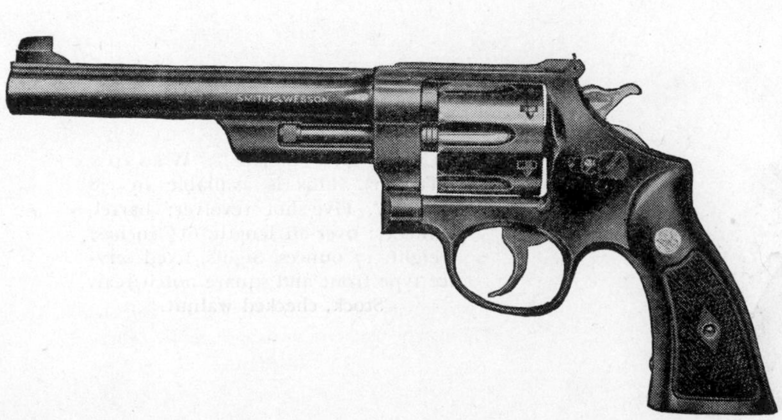

PLATE XXVII. SMITH & WESSON (.38/44 Outdoorsman). This is available in .38 S. & W. Special. Six-shot revolver; barrel, 6½ inches only; over-all length, 11¾ inches; weight, 41¾ ounces. Sights: 1/10- or ⅛-inch Patridge front, square notch rear, adjustable for windage and elevation. Stock, checked walnut. Finish, S. & W. blue.

Plate XXVIII. Smith & Wesson (.38 Military and Police). This is available in .38 S. & W. Special only. Barrel length, 2, 4, 5, or 6 inches; weight, with 6-inch barrel, 31 ounces. Sights: fixed service type front, square notched rear. Finish, S. & W. blue or nickel. Stock, checked walnut. Overall length, with 6-inch barrel, 11⅛ inches.

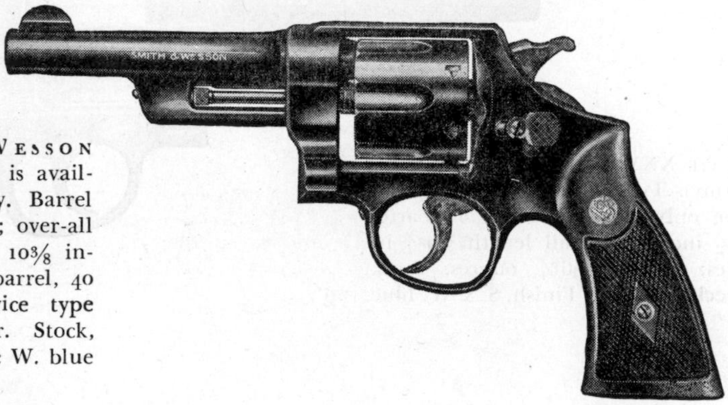


Plate XXIX. Smiih & Wesson (.38/44 Heavy Duty). This is available in .38 S. & W. only. Barrel lengths, 4, 5, or 6½ inches; over-all length, with 5-inch barrel, 10⅜ inches; weight, with 5-inch barrel, 40 ounces. Sights: fixed service type front, square notch rear. Stock, checked walnut. Finish, S. & W. blue or nickel.

Plate XXX. Smith & Wesson (.357 Magnum). This is available in .357 Magnum caliber only. (Bullet diameter .38 S. & W. Special.) Barrel lengths, 3½, 5, 6, 6½ or 8¾ inches. Choice of any standard target sights. Checkered walnut stock. Finish, S. & W. blue or nickel. Hammer thumbpiece checkered, trigger grooved. Trigger pull: single action 3 to 4 pounds, double action 10 pounds. This bullet has tremendous shocking power.

Plate XXXI. Smith & Wesson (Terrier). This is available in .38 S. & W. Five-shot revolver; barrel, 2 inches; over-all length, 6¼ inches; weight, 17 ounces. Sights, fixed service type front and square notch rear. Stock, checked walnut.

PLATE XXXII. SMITH & WESSON (.38 Military and Police Round Butt). This is available in .38 S. & W. only. Six-shot revolver; barrel, 2, 4, 5, or 6 inches; over-all length, with 2-inch barrel, 6⅞ inches; weight, with 2-inch barrel, 26 ounces. Sights; fixed service type front, square notch rear. Stock, checked walnut. Finish, S. & W. blue or nickel.

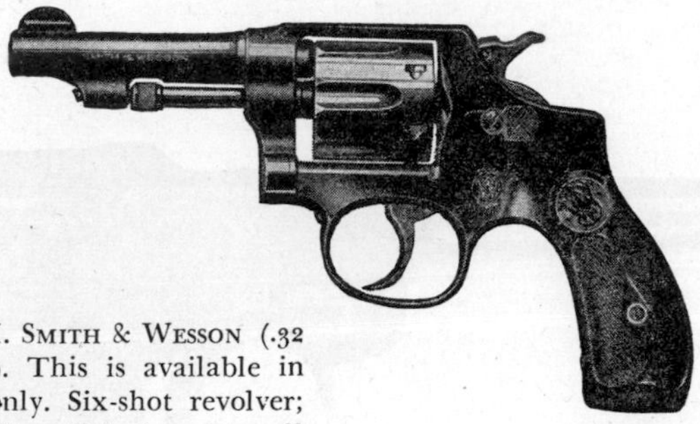

PLATE XXXIII. SMITH & WESSON (.32 Hand Ejector). This is available in .32 S. & W. only. Six-shot revolver; barrel, 3¼, 4¼, or 6 inches; over-all length, with 4¼-inch barrel, 8¼ inches; weight, with 3½-inch barrel, 18 ounces. Sights, fixed service type front, square notch rear. Stock, checked walnut. Finish, S. & W. blue or nickel.

PLATE XXXIV. WALTHER "P-38" (German). This pistol was one of the prized souvenirs of those who served in the European Theater during World War II, and many were brought back to this country. The pistol is unusual in that it is a "double-action" pistol, with an external hammer. After the first shot, the hammer is forced backward to the "cocked" position. It has several special features other than the "double action," including the "loading indicator." A small pin protrudes from a hole directly behind the rear sight and in front of the hammer when there is a round in the chamber. This pin recedes in the hole when the chamber is empty. It is recoil operated. Barrel, 4¾ inches; caliber, 9 mm. Luger; over-all length, 8½ inches; weight, 34 ounces.

PLATE XXXV. Sectional View of Walther "P-38."

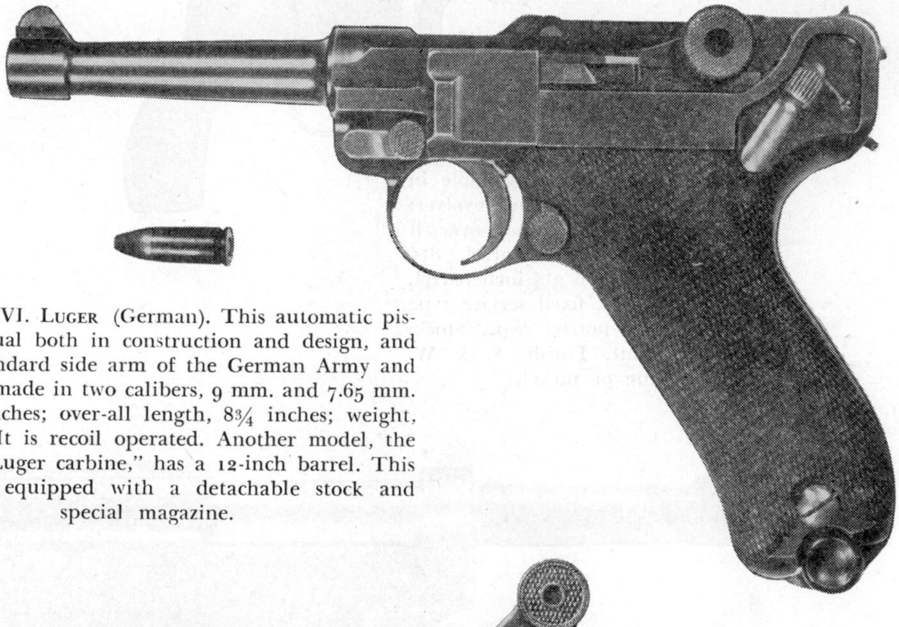

PLATE XXXVI. LUGER (German). This automatic pistol is unusual both in construction and design, and was the standard side arm of the German Army and Navy. It is made in two calibers, 9 mm. and 7.65 mm. Barrel, 4 inches; over-all length, 8¾ inches; weight, 30 ounces. It is recoil operated. Another model, the "7.65-mm. Luger carbine," has a 12-inch barrel. This model was equipped with a detachable stock and special magazine.

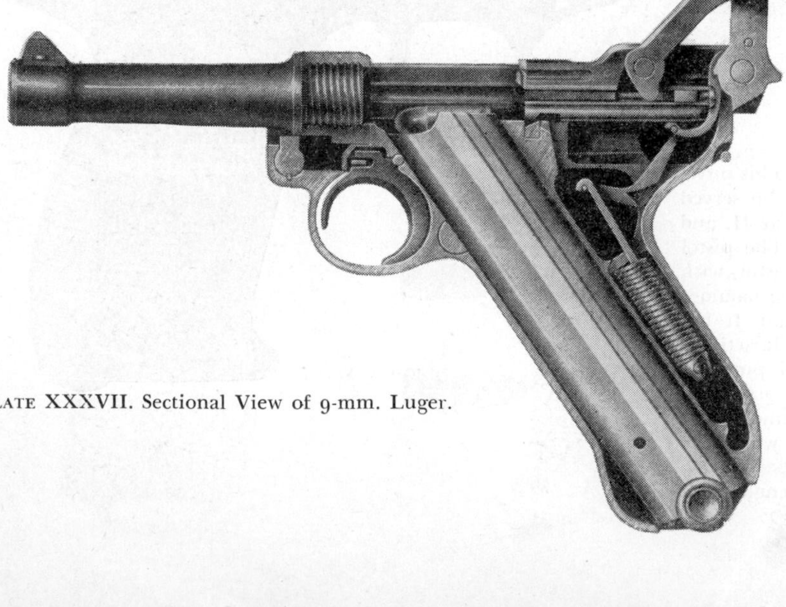

PLATE XXXVII. Sectional View of 9-mm. Luger.

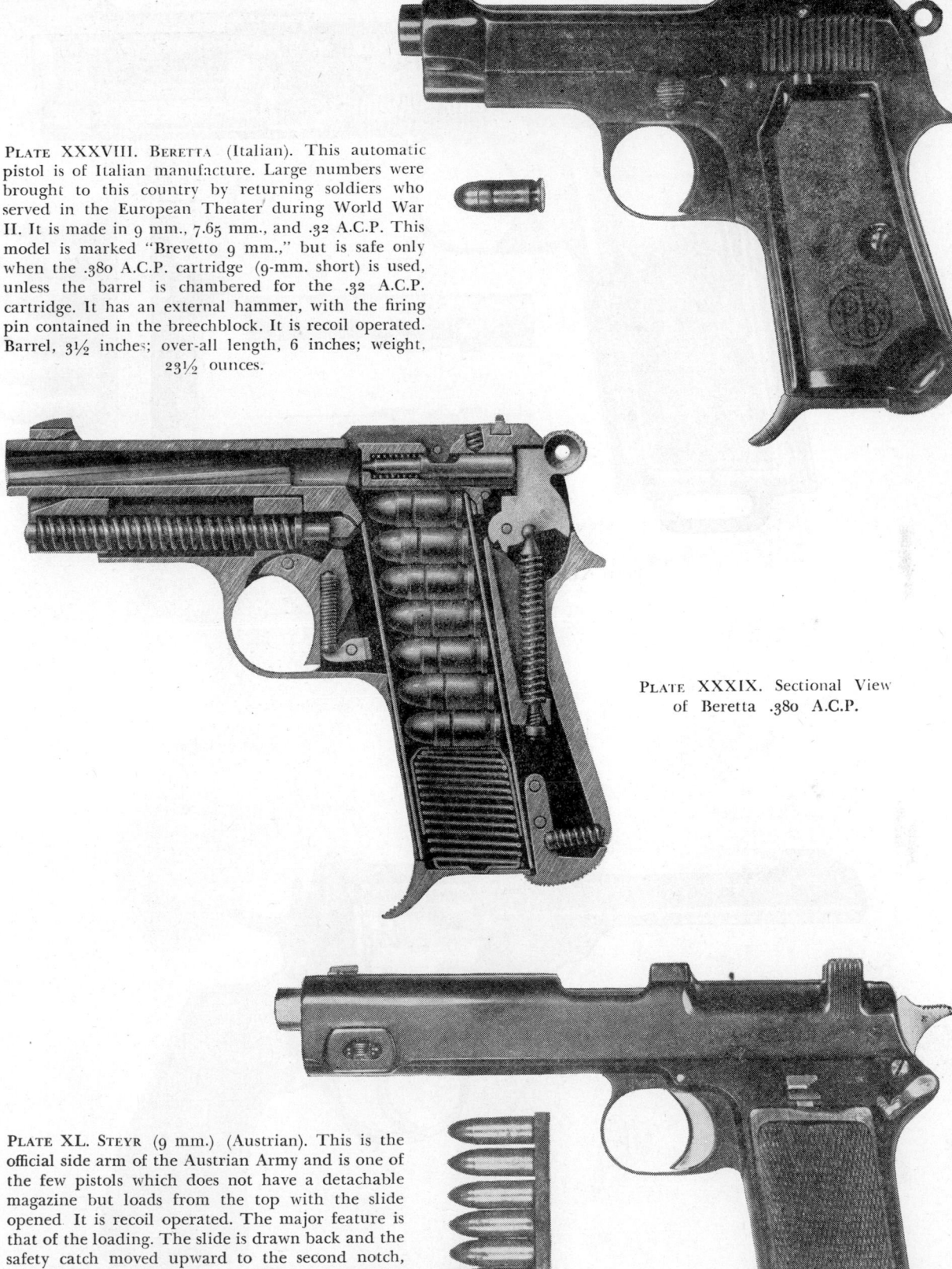

PLATE XXXVIII. BERETTA (Italian). This automatic pistol is of Italian manufacture. Large numbers were brought to this country by returning soldiers who served in the European Theater during World War II. It is made in 9 mm., 7.65 mm., and .32 A.C.P. This model is marked "Brevetto 9 mm.," but is safe only when the .380 A.C.P. cartridge (9-mm. short) is used, unless the barrel is chambered for the .32 A.C.P. cartridge. It has an external hammer, with the firing pin contained in the breechblock. It is recoil operated. Barrel, 3½ inches; over-all length, 6 inches; weight, 23½ ounces.

PLATE XXXIX. Sectional View of Beretta .380 A.C.P.

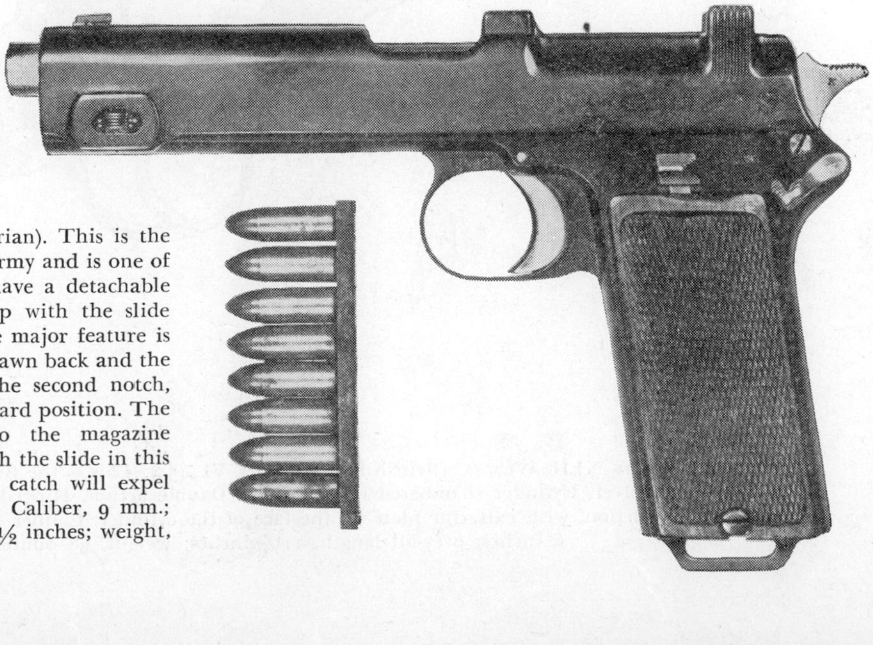

PLATE XL. STEYR (9 mm.) (Austrian). This is the official side arm of the Austrian Army and is one of the few pistols which does not have a detachable magazine but loads from the top with the slide opened It is recoil operated. The major feature is that of the loading. The slide is drawn back and the safety catch moved upward to the second notch, which holds the slide in the rearward position. The cartridges are then thrust into the magazine through the top of the action. With the slide in this position, pressure on a magazine catch will expel all cartridges from the magazine. Caliber, 9 mm.; barrel, 5 inches; over-all length, 8½ inches; weight, 18½ ounces.

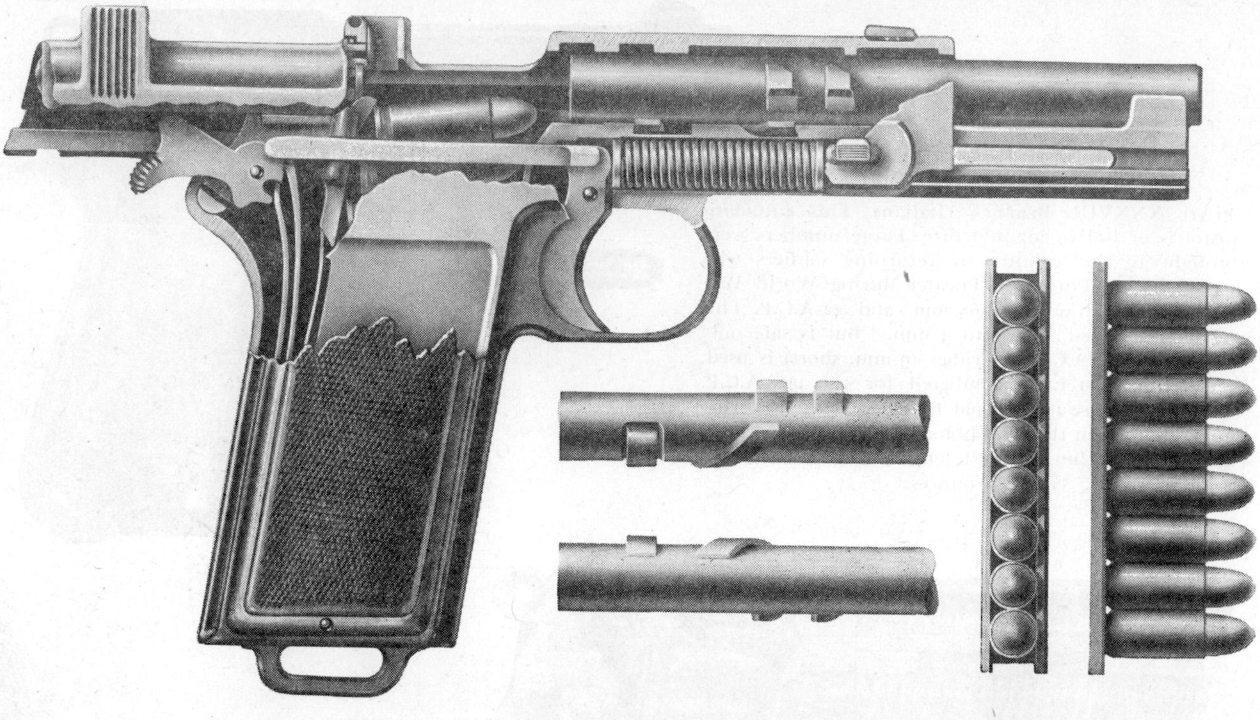

PLATE XLI. Sectional View of Steyr 9 mm.

PLATE XLII. WEBLEY (British Service, Mark VI .455). This is the British service revolver. Cylinder chambered for 6 rounds. Double action. Hinged frame construction, with extractor plate on the face of the cylinder. Caliber, .455; barrel, 6 inches; over-all length, 11¼ inches; weight, 38 ounces.

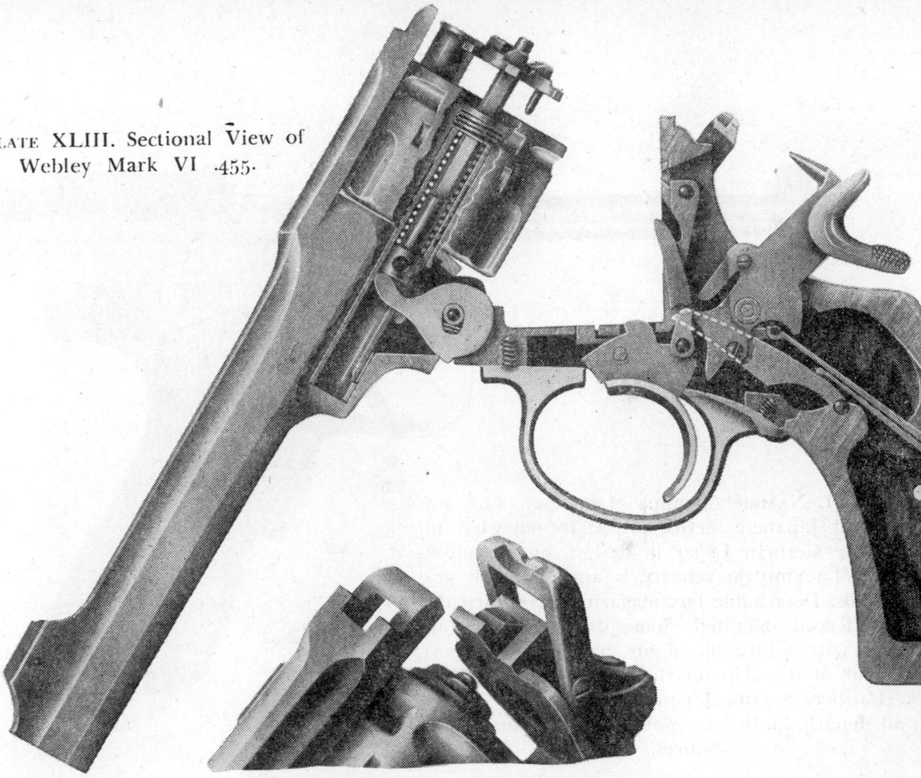

Plate XLIII. Sectional View of Webley Mark VI .455.

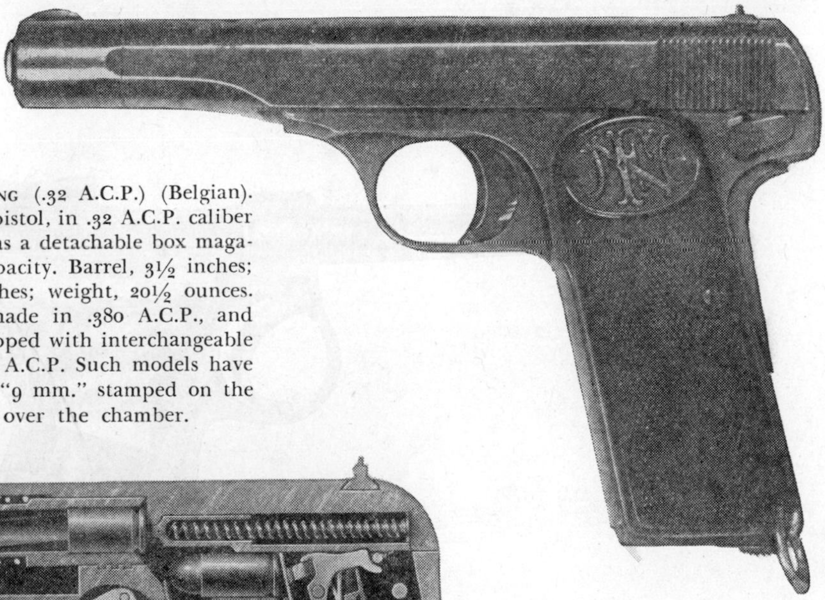

Plate XLIV. Browning (.32 A.C.P.) (Belgian). This is an automatic pistol, in .32 A.C.P. caliber (7.65 Browning). It has a detachable box magazine of 7-cartridge capacity. Barrel, 3½ inches; over-all length, 6 inches; weight, 20½ ounces. This pistol also is made in .380 A.C.P., and some models are equipped with interchangeable barrels in .32 or .380 A.C.P. Such models have "Cal. 7.65 mm." and "9 mm." stamped on the barrel directly over the chamber.

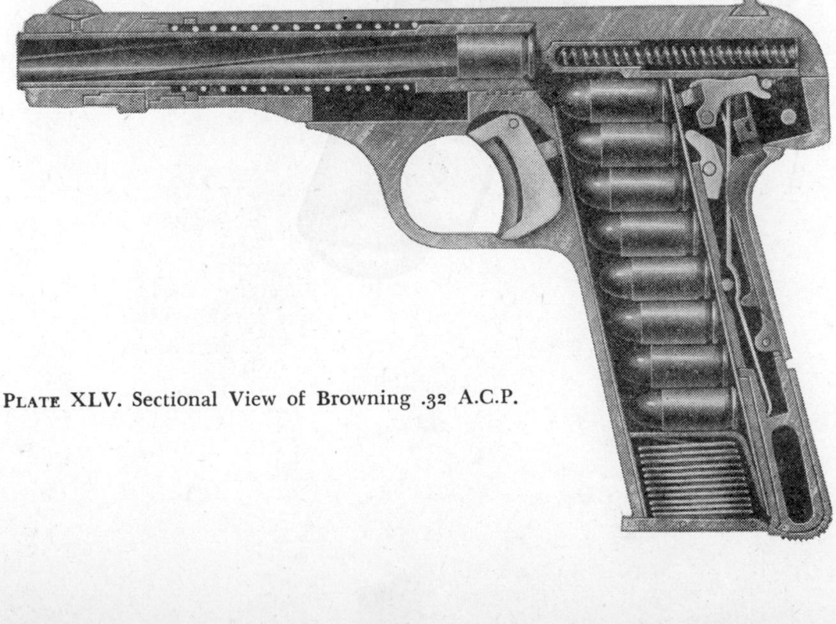

Plate XLV. Sectional View of Browning .32 A.C.P.

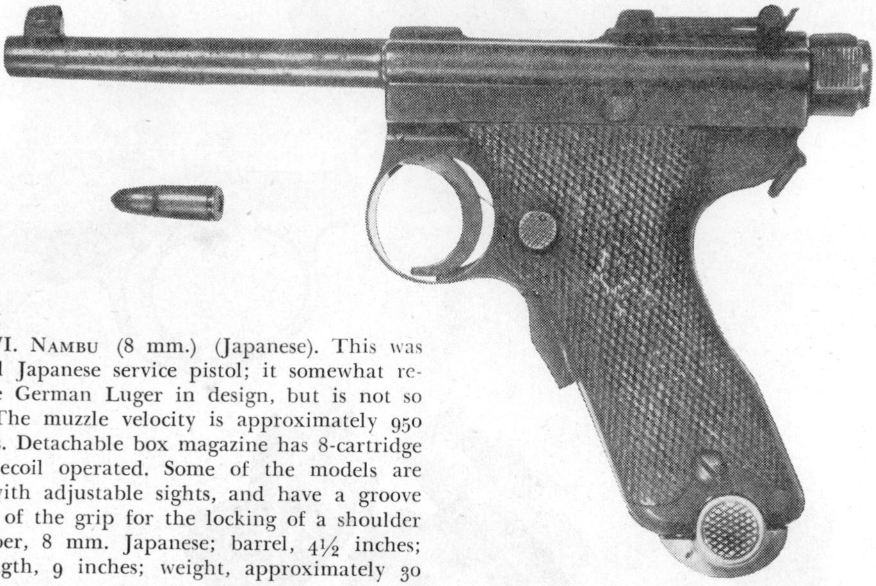

Plate XLVI. Nambu (8 mm.) (Japanese). This was the original Japanese service pistol; it somewhat resembles the German Luger in design, but is not so powerful. The muzzle velocity is approximately 950 foot-seconds. Detachable box magazine has 8-cartridge capacity. Recoil operated. Some of the models are equipped with adjustable sights, and have a groove at the rear of the grip for the locking of a shoulder stock. Caliber, 8 mm. Japanese; barrel, 4½ inches; over-all length, 9 inches; weight, approximately 30 ounces.

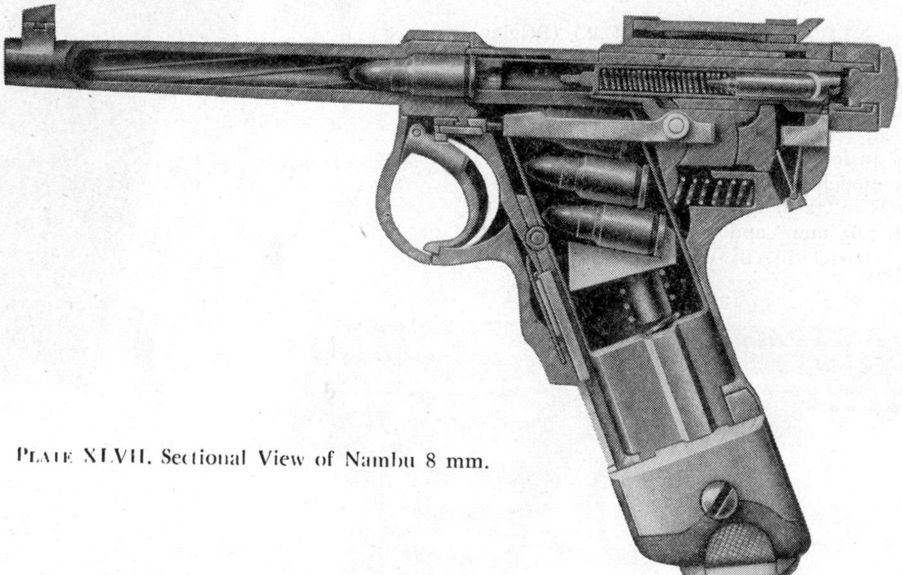

Plate XLVII. Sectional View of Nambu 8 mm.

# HANDGUN SHOOTING

There is but one secret to good handgun shooting, once the fundamentals of stance, grip, sighting, and trigger-squeeze have been mastered, and that is —*practice.* In every type of shooting, including that of the handgun, a factor known as "form" has been developed. This form is not followed because a shooter *looks better* in a certain position, but because he *shoots better.* Those who follow the form consistently find that it makes their shooting easier, reduces tension, and prevents fatigue, and even the novice shooter knows what tension and fatigue can do to his score.

**Stance.** First things come first. The initial instruction of a handgun shooter, therefore, should be concerned with *stance.* No one can tell you, with any degree of accuracy, the exact position you should assume in relation to the target, for to some extent this position is influenced by your physical proportions. The easiest angle of your body in relation to the target is the best one. The best method

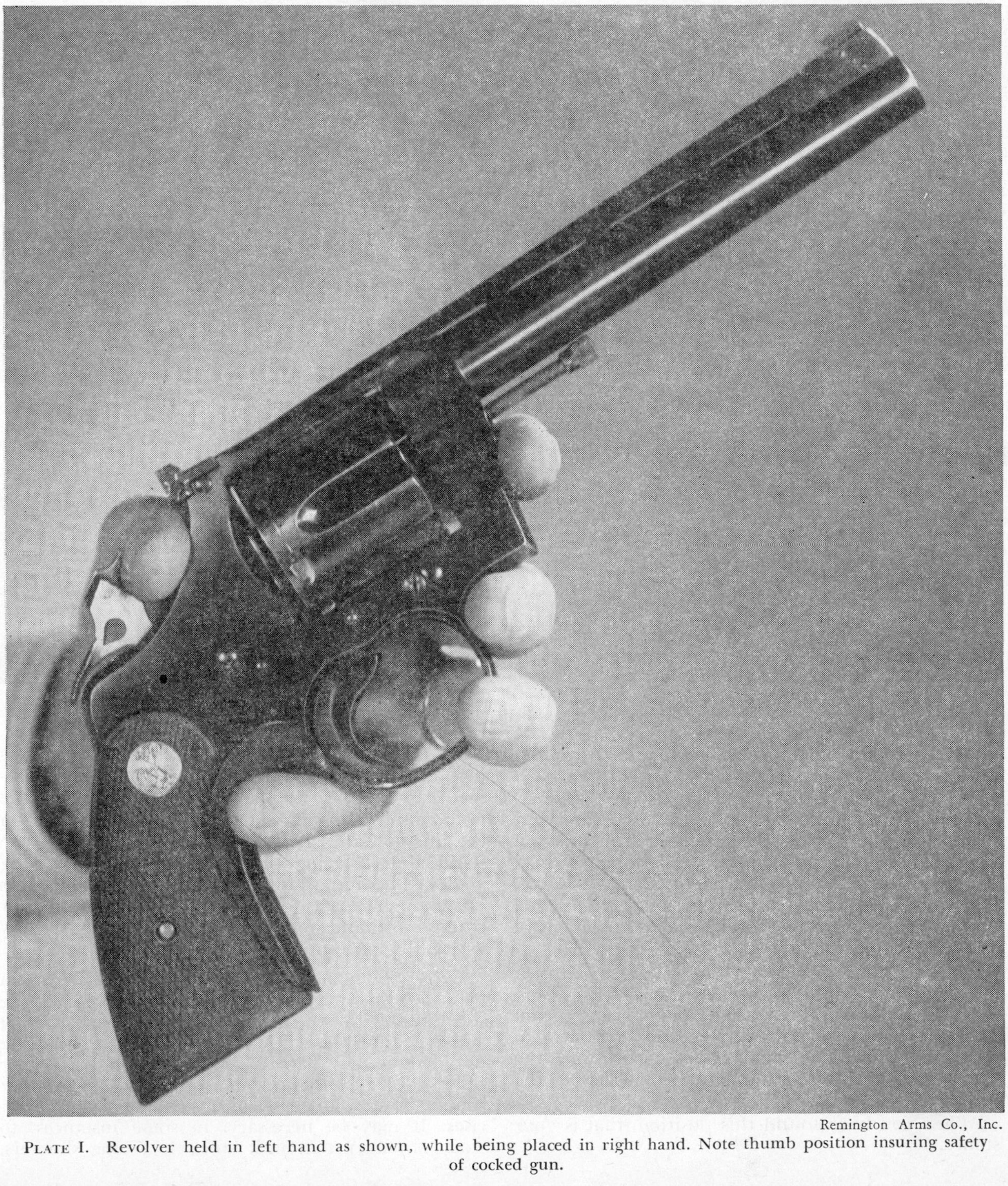

Remington Arms Co., Inc.

PLATE I. Revolver held in left hand as shown, while being placed in right hand. Note thumb position insuring safety of cocked gun.

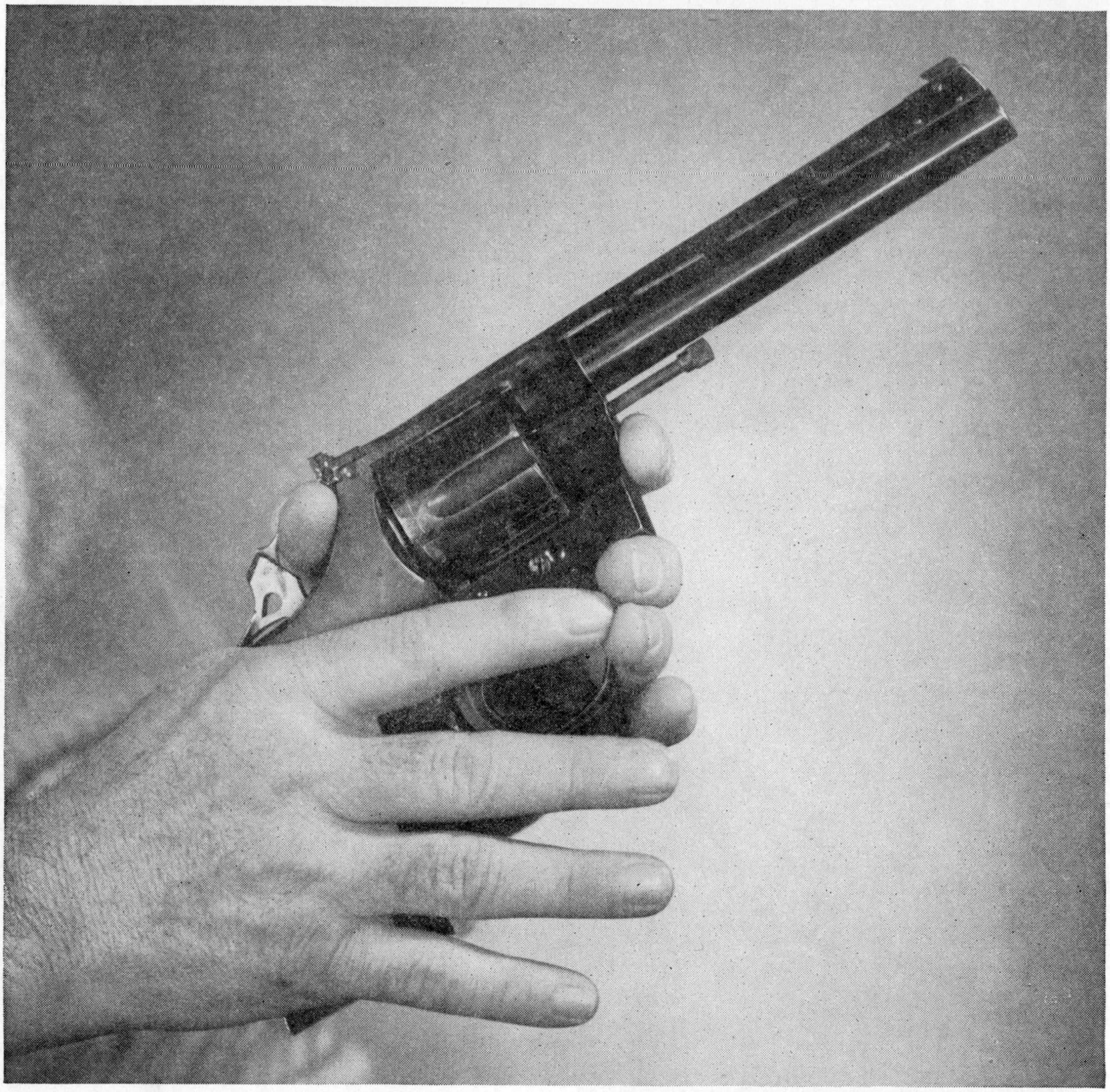

Remington Arms Co., Inc.

PLATE II. Revolver Being Placed in Right Hand.

of determining your stance is to stand, feet together, arms relaxed at your sides. Move your left foot from 13 to 15 inches to the left. The distance is determined by two things: ease and firmness. Raise your pistol arm and aim at the target in front of you. The chances are that you will find your arm in a strained position. Using the right foot as a pivot, move the left foot backward (for right-handed shooter) a few inches. Once more raise the pistol and take aim at the target.

Continue to move the left foot to the rear an inch at a time until you have found a stance that is comfortable and unstrained, that does not cause you to twist your neck, and that permits your arm to come up naturally and remain extended toward the target with the least strain on the muscles of the shoulder and neck.

When you have found this position, that is *your* stance.

Do not be influenced by the photographs, drawings, or paintings you have seen of shooters presenting their side to the target. Rather, look at the photographs showing some of the top shooters on the line at Camp Perry. You will notice that some stand almost facing the target, others at varying angles. The important thing is to have your legs far enough apart for ease and stanchness, your trunk erect and relaxed, your head turned only within the limitation of ease.

**Grip.** The next thing to learn is *grip*. The way in which you grip a pistol or revolver determines the steadiness with which you can hold it in sighting and squeezing the trigger. There are hands that are not designed by nature and habit for the proper holding of a handgun, but no one has hands that cannot be developed by means of the proper exercises. It may be necessary, in some instances, to work out a custom-built stock for some shooters, because of their short fingers or small palms, but these difficulties can be overcome. This is not a matter that can be worked out by any textbook, but one that calls for experiment and the personal advice of experts.

The individual with normal hands of average size, strength, and development will have little trouble in learning the proper grip. The most important factor is to learn this grip and *never* vary it under *any* circumstances, regardless of whether you are shooting rapid fire or slow fire, at a target that is high or one that is low. The following illustrations will do more to explain the proper grip than a million words. Insure that your palm is flat against the side of the stock of the pistol or revolver. The gun should be held firmly in a position that would permit a line to pass straight through the bore of the pistol, the wrist, and the forearm. If this position is held, the pull of the trigger finger will be in a straight line rearward, and not to either side, or up or down. The fingers themselves should be curled *naturally* around the stock, with the middle finger close against the junction of the trigger guard and the frame and the two lower fingers supporting it. Do not attempt to grasp the stock too tightly, for a firm grip is all that is necessary. A tight, strained grip will inevitably result in undesirable movement when the trigger is being pulled. Nor is it necessary to grip the stock tightly with the little finger. If each finger grasps the stock with equal tension, the desirable steadiness will result.

Now, the trigger finger. That part of the finger exactly midway between the first joint and the tip of the finger should rest on the trigger. The rest of the trigger finger should be *away* from the gun. In this position, the squeezing of the trigger will result

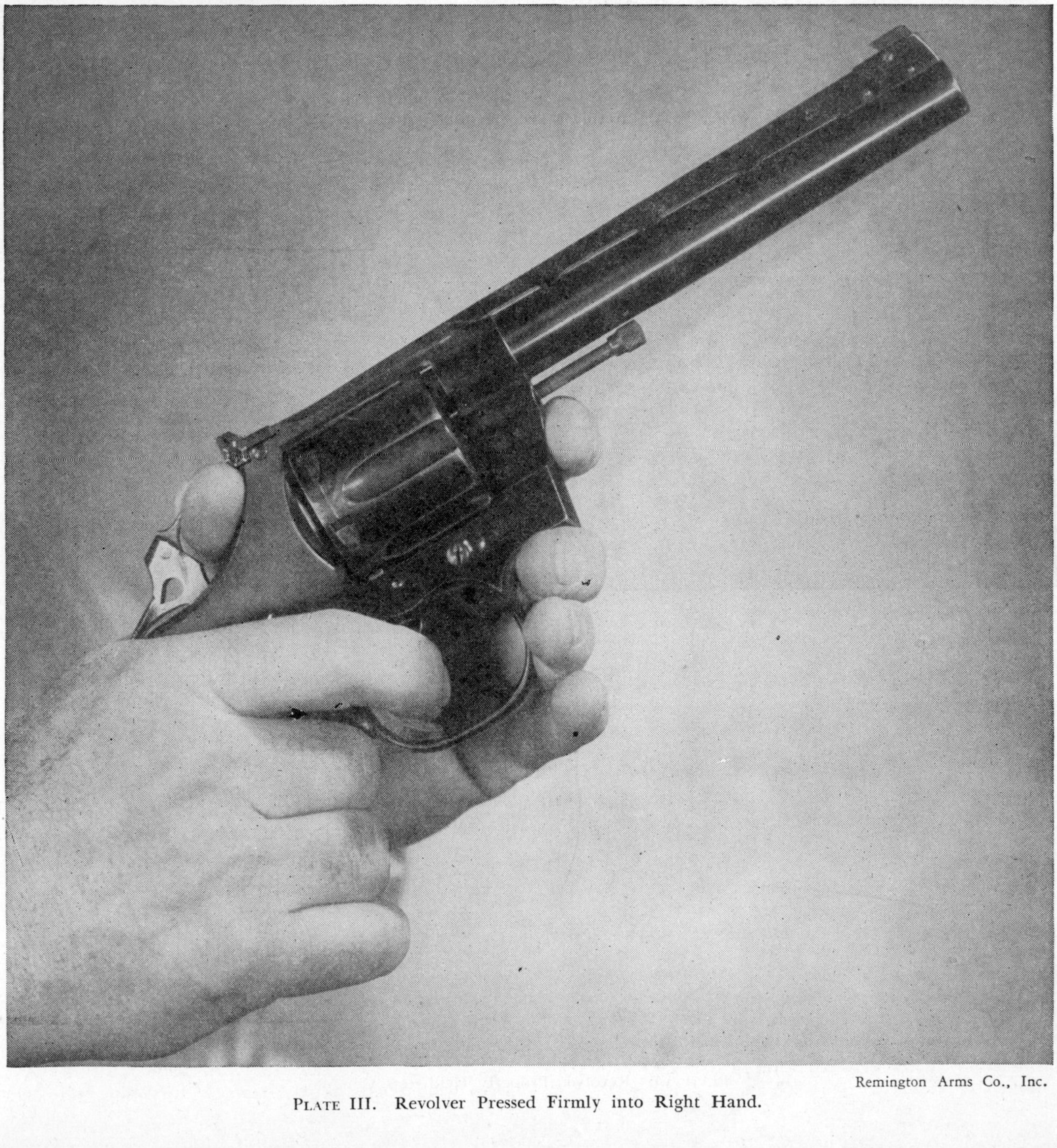

Remington Arms Co., Inc.

PLATE III. Revolver Pressed Firmly into Right Hand.

Remington Arms Co., Inc.

PLATE IV. Revolver Properly Held—side view.

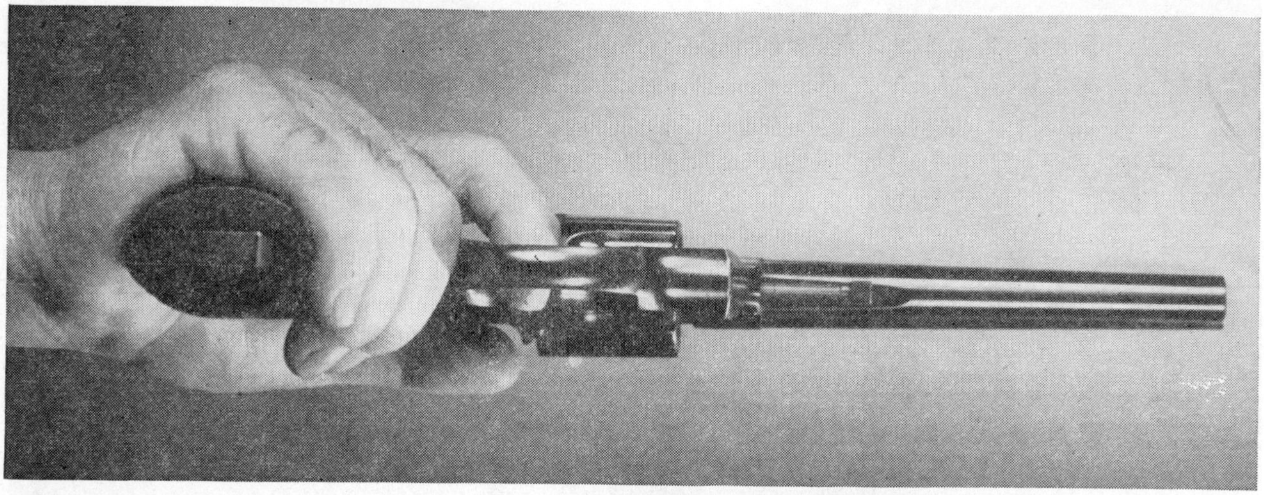

Remington Arms Co., Inc.

PLATE V. Revolver Properly Held—underneath view.

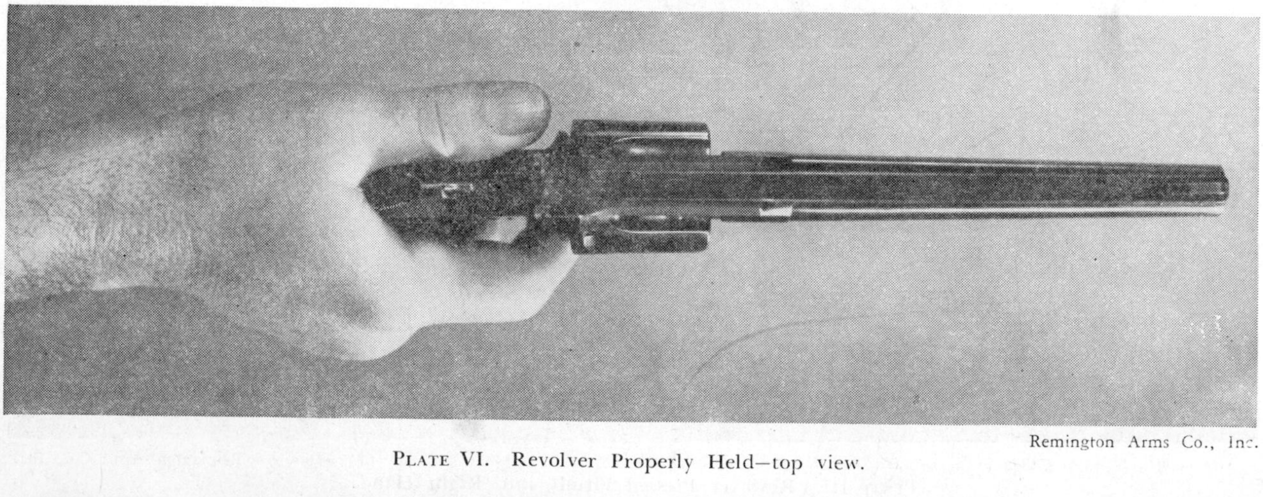

Remington Arms Co., Inc.

PLATE VI. Revolver Properly Held—top view.

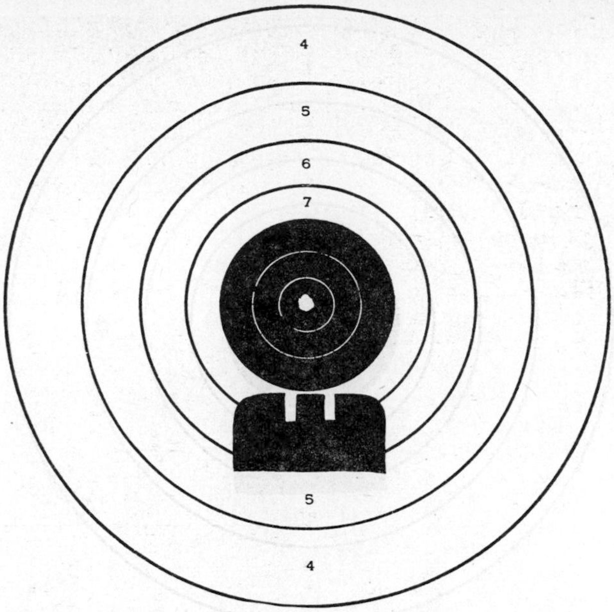


PLATE VII. This is the correct sight picture to put the bullet in the center of the bull, provided your pistol or revolver is sighted-in for "6 o'clock."

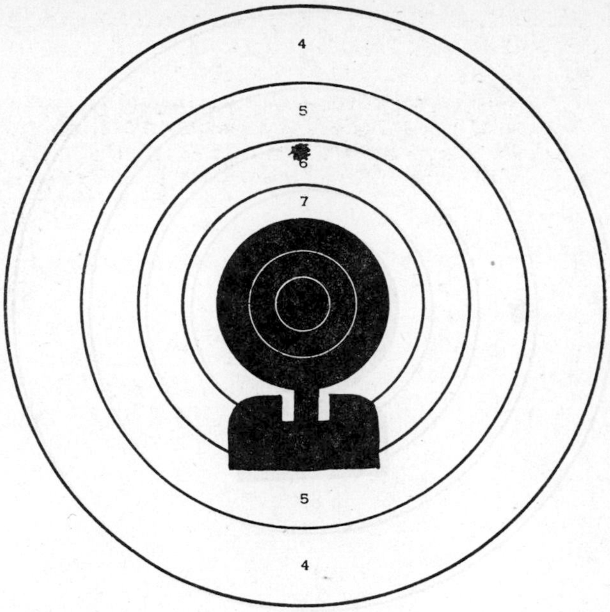


PLATE VIII. If you "squeeze off" with this sight picture you will get a "12 o'clock six"; front sight is too high.

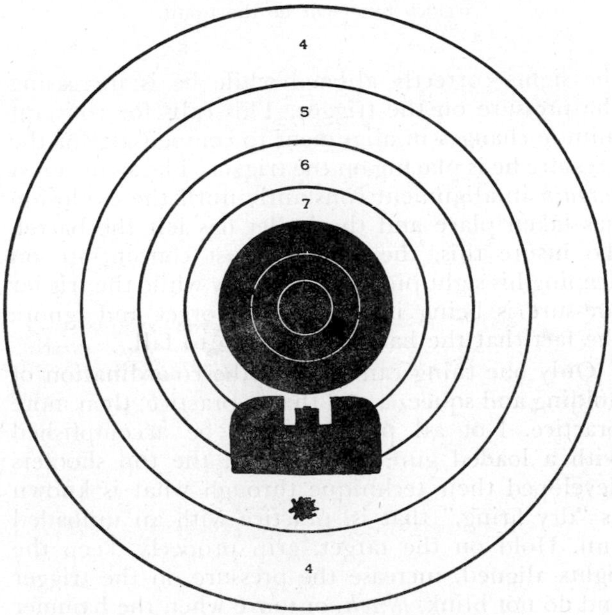


PLATE IX. Raise that front sight, otherwise the best you can get will be a "12 o'clock five."

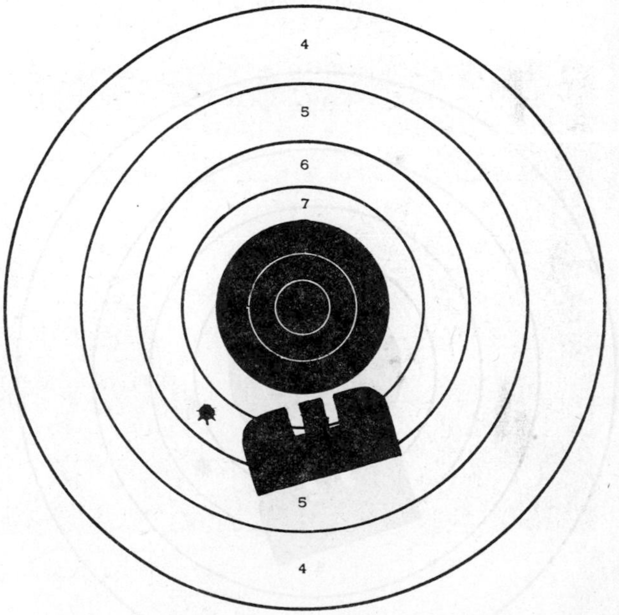


PLATE X. Here you are "canting" to the left. This will give you a "7 o'clock six."

in a pull that is straight backward. If you think this to be unimportant, try allowing your trigger finger to press against the side of the frame when you shoot, and you will find your shot group well to the left. It may be necessary to experiment with stocks of various sizes in order to determine which is best for your hand in order to permit the proper grip.

The thumb is *not* used in handgun shooting, except as a means of cradling the stock in the palm, and for the function of cocking the gun. The thumb should rest, relaxed, on the side of the frame or on the cylinder latch, and should exert no pressure in *any* direction.

One thing is very important. The grip should be *constant*. If you grip tightly on one shot and loosely on another, this variation will show very clearly on your target. The grip should be firm enough to insure steady holding. At the time of the explosion and while the bullet is passing through the barrel, there is a slight but definite movement of the gun upward and to the left. Photographs taken while the bullet was still passing through the barrel have proved this conclusively. You cannot hope to control this movement, but by holding the handgun in the same grip and with the same tension or firmness each time, you can compensate for it by sight adjustment. Not completely, of course, but enough to insure that the slight variation will not put your shots out of the black.

**Squeeze.** Trigger pull, in any shooting, is important, but with handguns it is *all*-important. There

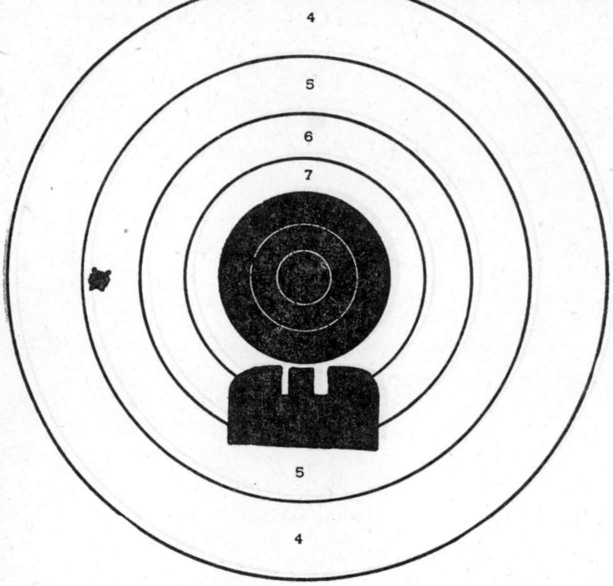


PLATE XI. Move the front sight more to the right and center it in the rear sight, otherwise a "9 o'clock five" is your reward.

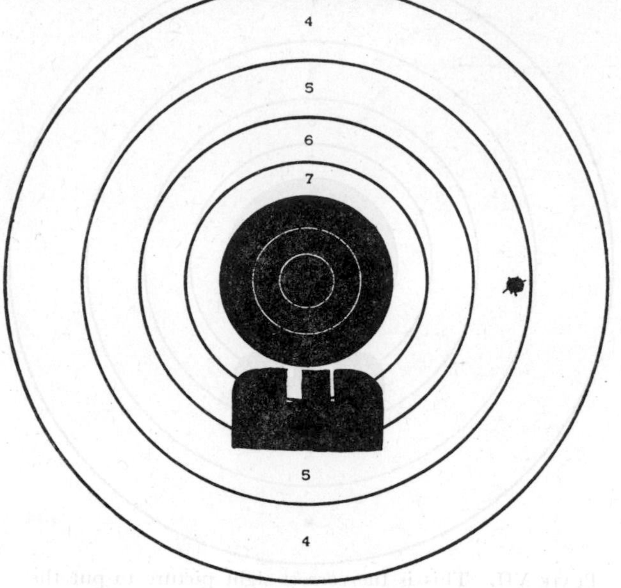


PLATE XII. Here you have a poor sight picture. Move the front sight to the left and center it, otherwise a "3 o'clock five" will be the result.

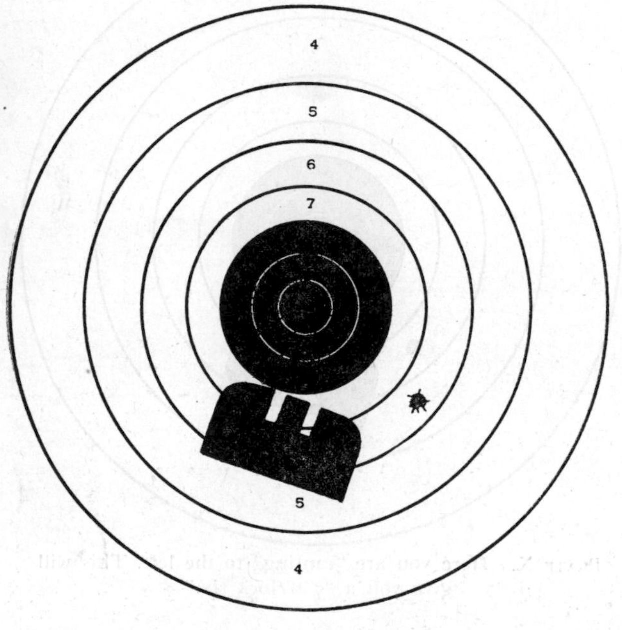


PLATE XIII. Now you are "canting" again, this time to the right. Everything is right but the "cant," which will give you a "4 o'clock six."

are thousands of handgun shooters who can grip properly, hold steadily, and sight properly, but to do these things and maintain them while the trigger is being pulled is another matter.

Accurate shooting is very easy to explain. The shooter merely raises the pistol or revolver and aligns the sights properly on the bull. Many can do this, and keep the alignment perfectly for several seconds. But then comes the pressure of the forefinger. Immediately the sight alignment goes *off,* and as the pressure is increased on the trigger it continues to go off. The champion learns to keep the sights correctly aligned while he is increasing the pressure on the trigger. This calls for constant minute changes in alignment to compensate for the pressure he is placing on the trigger. The sights must *remain* in alignment constantly until the explosion has taken place and the bullet has left the barrel. To insure this, the shooter must concentrate on keeping his sight picture constantly while the trigger pressure is being increased and forget and ignore the fact that the hammer is going to fall.

Only one thing can develop the co-ordination of holding and squeeze, and that is practice, then more practice. Not all practice need be accomplished with a loaded gun, for many of the top shooters developed their technique through what is known as "dry firing," that is, practice with an unloaded gun. Hold on the target, grip properly, keep the sights aligned, increase the pressure on the trigger and do not blink, *flinch,* or move when the hammer falls. When the hammer has fallen insure that the sights are still aligned.

The first step in the development of the shooter should be slow fire—that is, slow, deliberate, and unhurried shooting. Until the shooter has learned to control his gun and can shoot good groups consistently, no attempt should be made at rapid-fire shooting. Also, the novice would do well to begin his actual shooting at short range, preferably at 15 yards. When he has had sufficient practice and has overcome at least a few of the initial faults, he can move back another 5 yards. He should continue to practice at this range until he is satisfied that he has attained reasonably good co-ordination, and then move back to the 25-yard line.

The shooter who has a contact with a good coach should take advantage of this—not after he has developed a number of faults that will require cor-

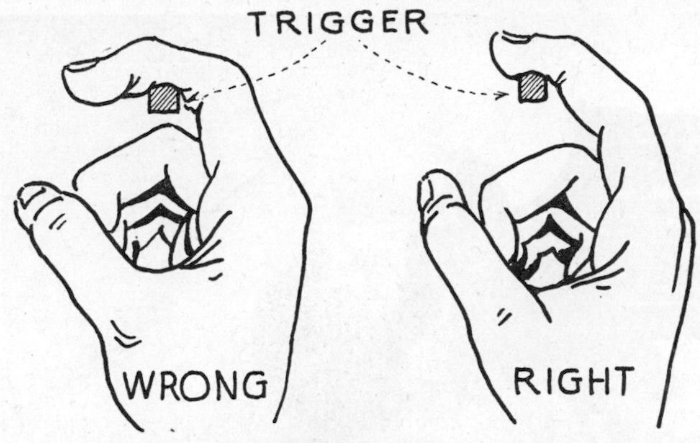


PLATE XIV. Proper Position of Finger on Revolver or Pistol Trigger.

recting, but right at the beginning. Most pistol and revolver clubs have good shooters who are willing to correct the errors of novice members, and membership in such an organization often does a lot to hasten the progress as well as smooth the path for the beginner. It is very easy to fall into bad practices, but it is extremely difficult to climb out of them. Any offer of instruction should be accepted without delay, for the man who said "you must creep before you walk" might very well have been thinking of the handgun shooter.

One important point to be remembered is this: Never fire a shot that you know is going to be a bad one. If your arm is tired and you cannot hold steadily, rest until you can. Do not continue the squeeze while your sights are wobbling all over the target. Be slow and take the utmost pains. The novice is going to find that his arm tires very quickly, and his hand and fingers become cramped and shaky. Do not attempt to empty the pistol or revolver without allowing the arm to drop. It will take several months of frequent and regular practice before you are ready to fire five shots without a rest. If you ignore this advice your progress will be slowed to a marked degree. When your arm grows tired, allow it to rest, but if you can do so, do not relax your grip. Then raise your arm for another shot. Fire the five shots before changing the position of the fingers.

If you are not convinced that this is good advice, try laying the gun down between shots; then when you have fired five, look at your group. Then try resting after each shot without changing the position of the fingers. See if you do not get a better group.

When you can shoot in the 90's consistently at slow fire, the time has come to begin rehearsing for rapid fire. The best coaches insist that no man should attempt rapid fire until he has practiced it for many hours with an empty gun. Learn how to thumb the hammer easily and rapidly. Time yourself accurately, and make sure you get five *aimed* shots off in the ten seconds allotted.

Many novices, having bought an expensive match pistol or revolver, may hesitate at using it for dry firing. Actually, snapping the modern pistol or revolver will not harm it in the least.

If you can obtain the services of a good instructor or coach for your first actual firing at rapid fire there is a chance that your progress will be more rapid and your scores much better than if you merely practice alone.

It is impossible for the rapid-fire shooter to get in too much practice, for he must learn to aim, shoot, thumb the hammer, and aim with as little lost motion and time as is possible. He should practice going from "raised pistol" to sight alignment until

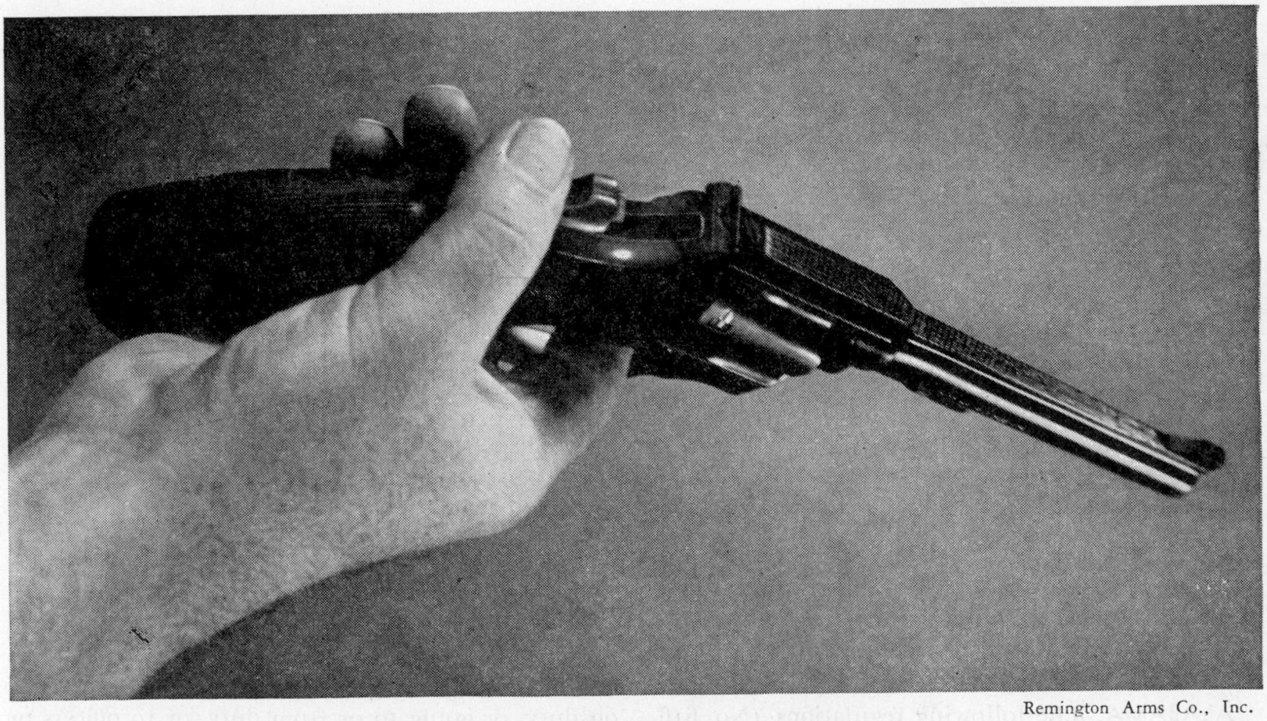

Remington Arms Co., Inc.

PLATE XV. The Wrong Way to Cock the Hammer.

Remington Arms Co., Inc.

PLATE XVI. The Right Way to Cock the Hammer.

his speed in this alone has developed sufficiently to permit him to get "on" the target and have one aimed shot off before the two seconds allotted to a single shot are up. The shooter who loses time in getting off the first shot is inclined to hurry the rest of his shots and fight tension during the time they are being fired.

Even the grip used by the rapid-fire shooter is somewhat different, for he must grasp the stock tighter. If he fails to do this, the recoil of the first shot will result in a change in his grip, and he will not have time to correct his grip after each shot—not if he hopes to get off five shots before the whistle sounds. Also, the squeeze must be accomplished more rapidly than in slow firing and a loose grip will result in serious dis-alignment as a result of the faster squeeze.

Considerable practice in thumbing the hammer also is necessary, for the thumb must draw the hammer straight backward without forcing the barrel up or down or twisting the gun. Until you can do this, continue with your dry firing.

# HANDGUN REGULATIONS

The following is a summary, by states (including Canada), of the pistol and/or revolver regulations in effect as of January 1, 1948.

It must be recognized that such laws are subject to change from time to time, and while the current trend is toward a more rigid code regulating the sale, transportation, and possession of pistols and revolvers, there are few legislative amendments now contemplated which would materially change the methods for obtaining a permit or license as outlined below. Bills are now pending in a few states which have no provision for the granting of permits or licenses, to amend the law to embody such provisions.

The information below should be extremely valuable to the person who desires to apply for a permit to purchase, transport, or possess a pistol or revolver, as well as to those who travel to pistol or revolver matches in other states and wish to comply with the laws concerning the transportation of firearms in the states through which they travel.

**ALABAMA.** The following regulations (No. 616, S. 276 Mize) were enacted by the legislature of Alabama relating to pistols and/or revolvers. This act, summarized below, amends Sections 172, 174, 175, 176, 177, 179, 181, 182, 185, and 186 of Title 14 of the 1940 Code.

The term pistol or revolver refers to any firearms with a barrel less than 12 inches in length.

The following persons are forbidden to *possess* pistols or revolvers:

*A.* Those who have been convicted, in this state or elsewhere, of committing or attempting to commit a crime of violence.

*B.* Any person who is a drug addict or an habitual drunkard.

No person shall carry a pistol or revolver either openly or concealed in any vehicle, or on or about his person, *except* on his own land, in his own abode or fixed place of business, without a license. This does not apply to any marshal, sheriff, prison or jail warden or their regularly employed deputies, policemen or other law-enforcement officers of this state or any other state, or to members of the National Guard or Organized Reserve or State Guard when on duty, or going to or from duty, or to officers or employees of the United States duly authorized to carry a pistol or revolver, or to any person engaged in manufacturing, repairing or dealing in pistols, or the agent or representative of such person, or to any common carrier, or to any person permitted by law to possess a pistol or revolver, while carrying it unloaded in a secure wrapper from place of purchase to his home or place of business, or to or from a place of repair, or in moving from one place of abode or business to another.

LICENSING OFFICIAL. The sheriff of a county may, upon the application of any person residing in that county, issue a qualified or unlimited license to such person to carry a pistol in a vehicle or concealed on or about his person within this state, for a period of not more than one year from the date of issue, if it appears that the applicant has good reason to fear injury to his person, or property, or has any other proper reason for carrying a pistol or revolver, and if he is a suitable person to be licensed. The fee for issuing such license shall be $1, which shall be paid into the county treasury. The sheriff shall, at the county's expense, publish on or before the 15th day of each January, the names of all persons to whom licenses have been issued by him during the preceding year and the reason for issuing the license. The sheriff may revoke a license upon proof that the licensee is not a proper person to be licensed.

SALE REGULATIONS. No seller shall deliver a pistol or revolver to a purchaser until 48 hours shall have elapsed from the time of the application for the purchase thereof, and, when delivered, the pistol shall be securely wrapped and unloaded. The purchaser shall sign a statement giving his full name, address, occupation, color, place of birth, date and hour of application, the caliber, make, model, and manufacturer's number of the pistol or revolver, and a statement that he has never been convicted in this state or elsewhere of a crime of violence. The seller shall, within 6 hours of such application, forward by registered mail one copy of such statement to the chief of police of the municipality or the sheriff of the county.

The above does *not* apply to the purchase, possession, or sale of antique firearms or such firearms sold as curiosities or ornaments.

The above act was approved October 9, 1947.

**ARKANSAS.** The law of Arkansas forbids the transportation of any pistol and/or revolver, except the type employed by the Army or Navy, which must be "uncovered and in the hand." No provision is made in the law for the sale of pistols or revolvers, nor is there any provision made for the granting of permits or licenses, nor for honoring the permit or license granted by any other state. The statute does not forbid the possession of a pistol or revolver in the home or place of business. Various municipalities have local ordinances concerning the transportation and possession of pistols or revolvers, which may be obtained from the local police department.

**ARIZONA.** The state law has no provision for the licensing or granting of permits for the possession of pistols or revolvers. A law is in effect which prohibits the carrying of a pistol or revolver concealed on the person. Municipalities within the state have laws or ordinances concerning the possession and transportation of pistols or revolvers, which information may be obtained from the chief of police of the municipality. While there is no legal statute covering the honoring of licenses or permits granted by other states, persons having such permits or licenses encounter no difficulties.

**CALIFORNIA.** The following regulations (Dangerous Weapons Control Law, as amended in 1947) cover the possession, transportation, and sale of pistols and/or revolvers in California. The term refers to any firearms with barrel length of less than 12 inches.

Any person over the age of 18 years, who is a citizen of the United States, may possess or keep within his place of residence or place of business any revolver or pistol or other concealed weapon without the necessity of obtaining a license or permit. Such firearms also may be carried openly in belt holsters.

The carrying of pistols and/or revolvers concealed upon the person or within any vehicle is unlawful unless the driver or bearer has upon his person a license or permit issued for the carrying of such pistol or revolver. This law does not apply to local, county, state, or Federal officials or other persons properly authorized to carry concealed weapons, nor does it apply to "members of any club or organization now existing or hereafter organized, for the purpose of practicing shooting at targets upon established target ranges, whether public or private, while such members are using any of the firearms referred to upon such target ranges, or while going to and from such ranges, nor to licensed hunters or fishermen while engaged in hunting or fishing, or while going to or returning from such hunting and fishing expeditions."

LICENSING OFFICIALS. The following officials may issue a license for the carrying of a revolver and/or pistol: sheriffs, board of police commissioners, police chiefs, city or town marshals or other head of the police department of any city, county, town, or other municipal corporation. The official shall insure that the applicant is of good moral character and has a good cause for the possession of such license.

The applicant shall state his name, occupation, residence and business address, age, height, weight, color of eyes and hair, and reason for application. The license when issued shall give the caliber, make, and serial number of the pistol and/or revolver, and shall be valid for one year from the date of issuance.

SALE REGULATIONS. The seller of any pistol and/or revolver, whether such firearm be new or used, shall keep a register in which shall be entered the following: time and date of sale, name of salesman, place where sold, make, model, manufacturer's number and caliber of firearm, signature, name and address of the purchaser.

The act does not apply to antique pistols or revolvers incapable of use.

**COLORADO.** This state has made no definite provision for the licensing or granting of permits for the possession, transportation, or sale of pistols and/or revolvers, and does not forbid the carrying of such firearms openly. The statute provides that no person may "carry a concealed weapon without a permit from the local authorities." While no provision is made for honoring the licenses or permits issued by other states, persons bearing such authorizations encounter no difficulties. Some municipalities have local ordinances concerning the carrying of concealed weapons, and permits are granted upon application to local police officials. The only regulations covering the sale of firearms are local ordinances in the various municipalities.

**CONNECTICUT.** The regulations which follow (Laws relating to Fire Arms and Dangerous Weapons, Secs. 2664, 2665, 2666, 2667, 2668, 2669, 2670, 2671, 2672, 2673, and 2679, as amended by Secs. 1443*e*, 812, 813) relate to the possession, transportation, and sale of pistols and/or revolvers in Connecticut.

The regulations may be summarized as follows:

The term pistol and/or revolver refers to any firearm with a barrel length less than 12 inches.

No permit is necessary for the possession of a pistol or revolver in the dwelling house or place of business by a citizen of the United States, nor is a permit required for the carrying of such a firearm concealed upon the person of any individual authorized by the municipality, county, state, or Federal government, nor is a permit required to transport such a firearm properly wrapped and unloaded from the place of purchase to the home or place of business of the purchaser, or to and from a place of repair, nor is a license required by any person removing his household effects from one place to another.

Licensing Official. The chief of police, warden of the borough, or the first selectman of the town, may issue to any citizen of the United States a permit to carry a pistol or revolver openly or concealed within the jurisdiction of the issuing authority provided the issuing authority is satisfied that the applicant is a suitable person to receive such permit. The fee for this permit shall be $1, and for each annual renewal thereof 25 cents.

Sale Regulations. No person, firm, or corporation shall sell at retail or otherwise transfer any pistol or revolver except upon written application by the purchaser and no delivery shall be made upon the date of the filing of the application, and when delivery is made the firearm shall be enclosed in a package, securely fastened, and the firearm shall be unloaded. The purchaser shall sign a receipt which shall contain his name, address, and occupation, the date of sale, caliber, make, model, and manufacturer's number, and a general description of the pistol and/or revolver. The purchaser must present a purchase permit issued by the chief of police, warden of the borough, or first selectman of the town in which he resides.

**DELAWARE.** The following regulations (Article 22, Deadly Weapons, Secs. 197, 198, 199, 200, 202) are effective as of November 12, 1947, governing the sale, possession, and transportation of pistols and/or revolvers in Delaware.

Any person of full age and good moral character may apply to be licensed to carry a pistol or revolver concealed on his person. No permit or license is required to possess a pistol or revolver in the home or place of business, but no pistol or revolver may be carried in a vehicle without a license. The law does not provide for the honoring of permits or licenses issued by other states, but persons bearing such authorization encounter no difficulties.

Licensing Official. Any person desiring a license to carry a concealed revolver and/or pistol must apply in writing, and file this application with the clerk of the peace of his county not less than 15 days before the next session of the court of general sessions, stating that he is of full age, stating his reasons for desiring the license, and giving his residence and occupation. He shall accompany this application with a certificate, signed by five respectable citizens of the election district within which he resides, stating that the applicant is of full age, sobriety, and good moral character. Both documents must be verified by the applicant's oath or affirmation in writing, taken before an officer authorized by the laws of the State of Delaware to administer same. At this time he shall pay to the clerk of the peace the full tax for the said license, and a fee of $1 to the clerk of the peace for issuing the same, together with his proportionate share of the cost of advertising his said notice of making application.

The clerk of the peace shall cause notice of such application to be published once, in any newspaper of the applicant's county, at least 10 days prior to the then next session of the court of general sessions. The clerk of the peace shall lay before the court of general sessions all necessary papers pertaining to the application. In the event the application is approved, the clerk of the peace shall issue a proper license upon the payment of a fee of $2 by the applicant. The license shall expire on the first day of June next succeeding the date of approval.

Sales Regulations. The person, firm, or corporation engaged in the selling of revolvers and/or pistols shall, in a book supplied by the clerk of the peace, keep a record of the date of sale, name, address, and occupation of the purchaser, and the caliber, type, make, and serial number of the revolver and/or pistol purchased, as well as the names and addresses of at least two freeholders resident in the county who shall positively identify the purchaser. No clerk, employee, or other person associated with the seller shall act as one of the identifying freeholders.

No license is required for the carrying of a pistol or revolver by any official of the municipality, county, state, or Federal government who is otherwise authorized to carry a concealed weapon.

**FLORIDA.** The following regulations (Florida Statutes, Chapter 790, Secs. 05, 06, 17, 18) relate to the carrying of concealed weapons, revolver and/or pistol in Florida.

The Florida law concerns not only the carrying of a pistol and/or revolver, but the possession of such firearms, except by licensed persons, or by officials of the municipal, county, state, or Federal government otherwise authorized to carry or possess such firearms. The law does not provide for the honoring of pistol and/or revolver permits or licenses issued by other states, but persons bearing such authorization encounter no difficulties.

Licensing Official. Application for a license to carry a pistol and/or revolver may be made to the county commissioner of the county in which the applicant is a resident, provided the applicant is over 21 years of age and of good moral character. In the event the application is approved, the licensee must give a bond payable to the governor in the sum of $100, which is forfeited in the event the firearm is put to improper use.

SALES REGULATIONS. Any dealer offering for sale any rifle, pistol, or revolver must possess a state license to engage in this trade, and is forbidden by law to hire, barter, lend, give, or sell any such firearm to an unlicensed person.

**GEORGIA.** The following regulations (Statute 26-5101, 347 P.C. Also 26-5103, 26-5104, 26-5105, 26-5106) pertain to the carrying on the person of any concealed weapon, pistol and/or revolver in Georgia.

All persons, even persons licensed by law, are forbidden to carry any concealed weapon, pistol or revolver, except in an open manner and fully exposed to view. No license is required to possess a revolver and/or pistol in the home or place of business, but a license is required to carry such a firearm in any vehicle.

LICENSING OFFICIAL. The applicant for a license to carry a pistol or revolver must make application to the ordinary of the county in which he resides. The applicant must be at least 18 years of age, and in making application must give his name, age, residence, occupation, and reason for making application. If the application is approved the licensee must pay a license fee of 50 cents and shall give a bond payable to the governor in the sum of $100, which shall be forfeited in the event of improper use of the firearm. The license is effective for a period of three years from the date of approval. The ordinary shall keep a record of the caliber, make, and serial number of the firearm for which the license was granted.

SALES REGULATIONS. No sales regulations are included in the statute.

OTHER REGULATIONS. No provision is made in the statute to cover the honoring of permits or licenses of other states, but no difficulties are encountered by persons so authorized, provided the pistol or revolver is carried unloaded and securely wrapped. The statute specifically states: "It shall be unlawful for *any person* to have or carry about his person or to have in his manual possession outside of his own home or place of business any pistol or revolver without first taking out a license."

**IDAHO.** There is no specific statute covering the issuing of a license for the purchase, transportation, or possession of a pistol and/or revolver in this state, although there are county and municipal regulations, details of which may be obtained from the sheriff of the county in which the person resides. There is a statute covering the carrying of a concealed revolver and/or pistol.

To obtain a permit for the carrying of a revolver or pistol concealed on the person, application must be made to the sheriff of the county of residence. This permit must be removed in the event another sheriff takes office. The form and content of the application vary in various counties.

Permits or licenses of other states are honored, provided the pistol and/or revolver is carried openly. If carried concealed on the person, the visitor possessing a permit or license from another state must obtain a written order from the sheriff of the county, which is issued for a specified period.

There is no statute covering the purchase of such firearms.

**ILLINOIS.** The Illinois Statute forbids the carrying of a pistol and/or revolver concealed on the person, but there is no provision for the granting of a permit or license to carry such firearms. While the state law does not forbid the carrying of a pistol or revolver openly there are local regulations and ordinances in effect in various municipalities concerning the above.

No provision is made for the honoring of permits or licenses isued by other states, but those so authorized encounter no difficulties. The statute does, however, prohibit any person from carrying a pistol or revolver in a vehicle if that person has been convicted of a crime of violence less than ten years prior to the date.

SALES REGULATIONS. All persons dealing in pistols or revolvers shall keep a register of all such weapons sold or given away by them. Such register shall contain the date of sale or gift, the name, address, age, and occupation of the person to whom the pistol or revolver is sold or given, the kind, description, make, and serial number of the firearm, and the purpose for which it is to be employed. No person, firm, or corporation shall sell or give to any alien or to any minor under the age of 18 any firearm of a size or type which might be concealed upon the person.

**INDIANA.** The following regulations (Burns Indiana Statutes, Secs. 10-4740, 10-4741, 10-4742) pertain to the sale, transportation, and possession of pistols and/or revolvers in Indiana.

No person shall carry a pistol or revolver in any vehicle or on or about his person, *except* in his place of abode or fixed place of business, without a license to carry such a firearm. These regulations do not prohibit the carrying of such firearms by local, county, state, or Federal officials otherwise authorized, or to common carriers, nor to any person who may be carrying a pistol or revolver in a secure wrapper and unloaded from the place of purchase to the home or place of business, or to a place of repair, nor do they apply when an individual is moving from one place of abode or business to another.

LICENSING OFFICIAL. An individual desiring a license to carry a pistol on his person shall apply to the chief of police or corresponding police officer of the municipality in which he resides, and if that municipality has no such officer he shall apply to the sheriff of the county in which he resides. The officer to whom the application is made shall ascertain of the applicant, his name, address, length of residence in the community, citizenship, race, age, criminal record if any, occupation, place of business, character, reputation, experience with firearms, and his reason for desiring a license. *The desire to engage in target practice is a proper reason.* The officer to whom applications is made shall forward this information together with his recommendation to the superintendent of the state police, who may make whatever further investigation he deems necessary and shall issue to the applicant a qualified or unlimited license to carry a pistol or revolver for not more than one year from the date of issue, if it appears that he has a proper reason for carrying a pistol and is of good character and reputation and a suitable person to be licensed. The fee for this license shall be $1.

Sales Regulations. No dealer, shall sell or give a pistol or revolver to a person under 18 years of age, or to a person he has reasonable cause to believe has been convicted of a crime of violence, or a drug addict, an habitual drunkard, or a person of unsound mind. No dealer shall deliver a pistol or revolver to a purchaser until 48 hours have elapsed from the time of application for the purchase. At the time of delivery the pistol or revolver shall be unloaded and securely wrapped. In making application the purchaser must state in writing his full name, address, occupation, color, place of birth, date and hour of application, the caliber, make, model, and manufacturer's number of the pistol or revolver, and a statement that he has never, in this state or elsewhere, been convicted of a crime of violence. The dealer shall forward, by registered mail, a copy of this statement to the chief of police of the municipality or the sheriff of the county, and another copy shall be sent to the superintendent of the state police.

**IOWA.** The law of Iowa forbids the transportation or possession of a pistol and/or revolver without a permit, except for local, county, state, or Federal officials otherwise authorized. No permit or license is required to purchase, but a permit to carry and possess must be obtained.

Licensing Official. Any person of legal age who has not been convicted of a crime of violence may apply for a permit to carry and possess a pistol or revolver. Application is made to the Commissioner of Public Safety, Des Moines, who, when investigation reveals the applicant to be a proper person to be so licensed, may issue free of charge a permit to possess, and carry concealed on the person or in a vehicle, a pistol or revolver.

The state recognizes the permits or licenses issued by other states, and those so authorized encounter no difficulties.

**KANSAS.** This state has made no provision for the licensing or granting of permits for the possession, sale, or transportation of pistols and/or revolvers, but there is a law prohibiting the carrying of a weapon concealed on the person. A "Uniform Pistol Act" is expected to be passed by the state legislature in the near future.

Pending the passage of this law there is no provision for the honoring of permits or licenses issued by other states; but persons so authorized encounter no difficulties.

Several municipalities of the state have local ordinances and regulations concerning the sale and transportation of pistols or revolvers, details of which may be obtained from the chiefs of police of the municipalities.

**KENTUCKY.** The following regulation (Revised Statute 435.230) pertains to the transportation, possession, and sale of pistols and/or revolvers in Kentucky.

It is forbidden for any person, not expressly authorized by law, to carry *concealed* a deadly weapon. This does not apply to local, county, state, or Federal officials otherwise authorized to carry a concealed weapon. A pistol or revolver, concealed in a vehicle in such a position as to be readily accessible to the occupant or occupants, is considered to be "concealed about the person" and is in violation of the law.

There is no law prohibiting the possession of a pistol or revolver in the abode or place of business.

There is no provision for the granting of a license or permit for the carrying of a pistol or revolver, nor is there any provision for honoring the license or permit issued by another state, but persons so authorized encounter no difficulty.

Sales Regulations. There are no state laws covering the sale of pistols and/or revolvers other than a section of the statute which forbids the sale of a deadly weapon to a minor.

Some municipalities have local ordinances concerning the transportation of pistols and/or revolvers, details of which may be obtained from the local chiefs of police.

**LOUISIANA.** The following regulations (Firearms Registration Act 1277.1 to 1277.20) cover the possession, sale, and transportation of firearms, including pistols and/or revolvers in Louisiana. The term "firearm" as defined by the above act refers to "any rifle or shotgun with a barrel of less than 20 inches in length, or pistol and/or revolver."

Legally to possess such a firearm, or to transfer a firearm from one person to another, the purchaser or person in possession must obtain the written approval of the Superintendent of the Bureau of Criminal Identification and Investigation of the state. (Approval forms may be obtained from the superintendent, or from local, county, or state police officials.) Approval to carry a firearm on the person (concealed or otherwise) must be obtained by submission of the above form.

Although there is no provision for honoring the permit or license issued by another state, the Act (1277.16) states that "Under regulations prescribed by the Superintendent of the Bureau of Criminal Identification and Investigation, any firearm may be imported or brought into this State, possessed or transferred, when the purpose thereof is shown to be lawful." Visitors desiring to transport a pistol or revolver through the state should direct a letter to the Superintendent, State House, Baton Rouge, giving the number and date of their license (or a photostat copy of the license), as well as their own name, address, occupation, and race, and also their reason for desiring to transport the firearm into or through the state.

**MAINE.** The following regulations (1944 Revised Statutes, Chapter 124, Sec. 18) pertain to the possession, sale, and transportation of pistols and/or revolvers in Maine.

Although the statute does not prohibit the carrying of pistols or revolvers openly, the open carrying of a pistol or revolver might constitute a violation of the section which states: "No person shall in a threatening manner display" such firearms.

Any citizen of good moral character may obtain from the chief of police, city marshal, or a selectman of his town or city of legal residence, a certificate granting him the right to carry, concealed, a pistol or revolver. Such certificate shall state that he has been duly licensed to carry the weapon or weapons mentioned, and shall continue in effect to the end of the calendar year in which it is issued and for one year thereafter, unless sooner revoked.

No provision is made in the statute for honoring the license or permit issued by another state, but those so authorized encounter no difficulties.

SALES REGULATIONS. The sales regulations prohibit the sale of pistols or revolvers to any person under 16 years of age, unless the parents, guardians, teachers, or instructors of such minors may furnish them with such weapons for hunting or target shooting. Dealers shall keep a record of all firearms sold, rented, loaned, or given. This record shall be kept in a book and shall include the name, address, occupation of the person to whom the firearm has been transferred, with the purpose for which it is to be employed, and the make, caliber, and type of the firearm, as well as the manufacturer's number.

**MARYLAND.** The following regulations (Chapter 622 of the Acts of 1941, codified as Secs. 531*B* and 531*H* of Article 27, Annotated Code of Maryland, 1943 Supplement) concerns the sale or transfer of pistols and/or revolvers in Maryland. The statute has no provisions for the granting of a permit or license to an individual for the carrying of a concealed pistol or revolver.

The matter of the carrying of pistols or revolvers has been placed under the direction of the Department of Legislative Reference. Ordinance No. 853 (Dec. 2, 1942) makes it unlawful for any person to carry a pistol or revolver in any vehicle or concealed on or about his person, except in his place of abode or fixed place of business (except local, county, state, or Federal officials otherwise authorized). "Nothing in this ordinance shall be construed to prevent the carrying of a pistol by any person as a reasonable precaution against apprehended danger, but the tribunal before which any case arising under the ordinance may be tried shall have the right to judge of the reasonableness of carrying such a pistol or revolver." The police commissioner of Baltimore City is authorized to issue certificates good for one year to persons whom he believes have reasonable cause to carry a pistol or revolver as precaution against apprehended danger.

"Nothing in the ordinance shall be construed to prevent a target shooter from carrying, within the city, one or more target pistols or revolvers, with barrels at least 4 inches long, unloaded but not concealed on his person."

No provision is made to honor the license or permit issued by another state, but a person so authorized encounters no difficulties.

SALES REGULATIONS. Dealers are required to keep a record of all pistols or revolvers sold, transferred, or otherwise disposed of, the individual record to contain the date of sale, the caliber, make, model, and manufacturer's number of the firearm and the name and address of the purchaser. The dealer will immediately supply a copy of the record to the clerk of the court of the county wherein the sale or transfer is made, or the Police Commissioner of Baltimore City, if the sale is made in the city. It is the duty of the above to transmit promptly such copies to the superintendent of Maryland State Police for file. It is unlawful for any dealer or person to sell or transfer a pistol to a person he knows, or has reasonable cause to believe, has been convicted of a crime of violence or who is a fugitive from justice.

**MASSACHUSETTS.** The following regulations (Chapter 140, Secs. 121 to 131*C*; Chapter 269, Secs. 10, 10*A*, 10*B*, 11*A*, 11*B*, 11*C*, 11*D*) pertain to the sale, transportation, and possession of pistols and/or revolvers in Massachusetts.

The statute does not require an individual to be licensed to possess a pistol or revolver in his abode or place of business, but a license is required to carry on the person or transport in a vehicle any such weapon.

LICENSING OFFICIAL. The justice of a court or a trial justice, the board of police, the mayor of a city, the selectmen of a town, or the commisioner of public safety, or persons so authorized by them, may, upon the application of any resident or person having a place of business within their jurisdiction (except an alien, a person who has been convicted of a felony, or a minor under 15 years of age), issue a license to carry a pistol or revolver. The applicant must be a suitable person to be so licensed. *The carrying of a pistol or revolver for use for target practice only shall be held to be a proper purpose.* The license shall be upon a proper form, to be filled in with the following information: name, residence and place of business, commencement and expiration date of license, reason for issuing said license, license number, date of issue, and place of birth, height, weight, color of hair, color of eyes, and signature of licensee. The fee for this license is 50 cents.

No provision is made for the honoring of the license or permit issued by another state, but persons so authorized encounter no difficulties.

No person carrying a pistol or revolver under a license shall carry the firearm in a vehicle unless such pistol or revolver is under the direct control of the person while so carried.

SALES REGULATIONS. Dealers in pistols or revolvers must be licensed, and must keep a record of all sales, rentals, or transfers of such weapons, the record to include the name, address, occupation, and sex of the purchaser, as well as the make, description, manufacturer's number, caliber, and type of the firearm. A copy of this record shall be forwarded to the licensing authorities and the commissioner of public safety within seven days of the date of the sale. The firearms shall be delivered to the purchaser unloaded and securely wrapped. No delivery of a pistol or revolver shall be made on the day of application for purchase, rental, or lease, except to a person having a license to carry the firearm. No pistol or revolver may be transferred to a person who does not possess a permit to purchase, rent, or lease such a firearm. Permits to purchase a pistol or revolver may be obtained from the same officials authorized to grant licenses for the carrying of such firearms.

**MICHIGAN.** The following regulations (Concealed Weapons License Act, Act No. 372 of 1927 as amended by Act No. 333 of 1931, No. 86 of 1939, No. 112 of 1941, No. 51 of 1943, and No. 113 of 1943) pertain to the sale, transportation, and possession of pistols and/or revolvers in Michigan.

The law requires all individuals to register all

pistols or revolvers in their possession, whether in their place of abode or place of business. The registration is accomplished without the payment of a fee, and a certificate of registration may be granted by the commisioner or chief of police or their duly authorized deputies, or by the sheriff or his authorized deputy.

Prior to the purchase of a pistol and/or revolver, the purchaser must obtain from the commissioner or chief of police, or their deputies, or from the sheriff or his authorized deputy, an application for a purchasing permit. The permit or license to purchase may be issued to any resident who is 21 years of age or over, a citizen of the United States, and has resided in the state not less than 6 months. No license may be issued to a person who has been convicted of a felony or has been adjudged insane in this state or elsewhere. The license is void unless used within 10 days after the date of issue. Two copies of the license are issued to the licensee, both to be presented to the dealer at the completion of the purchase.

A license is required to carry any pistol or revolver, concealed or in the open, but only a certificate of registration is required to possess a pistol or revolver in the abode or place of business. A certificate of registration only is required by a person transporting a pistol or revolver to or from his abode or place of business, provided the weapon is unloaded and securely wrapped.

The law exempts the following from the requirement to possess a permit to carry, concealed, a pistol or revolver: local, county, or state peace officers otherwise authorized, members of the armed forces, duly authorized military organizations when on duty or drill or going to or returning from customary places of assembly or practice, and *any person issued a license by another state permitting him to carry a pistol concealed on his person.*

Licensing Official. Each applicant for a license to carry a concealed weapon (pistol or revolver) shall apply to the sheriff of the county in which he resides, if he lives outside the corporate limits of any town or city, otherwise application is made to the commisioner or chief of police, or marshal or his authorized representative. The application is made on a form supplied by the commissioner of the Michigan State Police, and shall contain the fingerprints of the applicant, as well as his name, address, occupation, and reasons for desiring the license. The application must be favorably passed by a board comprising the Prosecuting Attorney, the Sheriff, and the Commisioner of the Michigan State Police, which board shall convene once in each calendar month. The license will be approved only upon the approval of the majority of the said board. A fee of $1 shall be charged for the license, which shall be issued for not more than one year and no renewal shall be granted except upon the filing of a new application. Every license issued shall bear the imprint of the right thumb of the licensee, or, if that be not possible, of the left thumb or other finger.

Sales Regulations. Any person engaged in selling at retail any pistols or revolvers shall require the purchaser to sign both copies of the purchasing license, giving his name, address, the make, style, caliber, and manufacturer's number of the pistol or revolver. The dealer shall retain one copy of the purchasing license and shall forward the other copy by registered mail to the Commissioner of the Michigan State Police within 48 hours.

**MINNESOTA.** This state has made no provision for the granting of a license or permit for the possession or transportation of pistols or revolvers. A law is in effect which prohibits the carrying of a pistol or revolver concealed on the person or in a vehicle. Several municipalities have ordinances concerning the sale and transportation of pistols and revolvers, details of which may be obtained from the local chiefs of police.

While the statutes do not specifically prohibit the transportation of pistols or revolvers openly, or the possession of such firearms in the abode or place of business, certain municipalities have ordinances covering both transportation and sale. Some municipalities require that prospective purchasers register with the police department all pistols or revolvers, the registration to be carried out prior to the delivery of the firearm by the dealer.

The state law does not cover the honoring of licenses or permits issued by other states, but those so authorized encounter no difficulties.

A statute provides that no firearms may be sold to a minor without the written consent of the parents or guardian.

**MISSISSIPPI.** This state has made no provision for the granting of a license or permit for the possession or transportation of pistols and/or revolvers, nor is a license or permit required to carry such firearms openly, except in certain municipalities where ordinances regulate this matter, and within two miles of any school or college.

The transportation of a pistol or revolver in a vehicle, openly or concealed, is prohibited, except in the instance of travelers or persons fearing attack, and no minor under the age of 16 years may possess a pistol or revolver.

The law provides for the honoring of permits or licenses issued by other states.

A dealer is required to keep a record of the name, address, and occupation of the purchaser of a pistol or revolver, as well as the type, make, and manufacturer's number of the firearm sold.

**MISSOURI.** The following regulations (Carrying Concealed Weapons, Secs. 4423, 4424, 4426, 4825, 4826, 4827, 4828, 4829) pertain to the possession, sale, and transportation of pistols and/or revolvers in Missouri.

Provision is made for the obtaining of a permit to purchase a pistol or revolver, but persons traveling through the state on a "continuous peaceable journey" may carry a pistol or revolver on their person or in their vehicle. Permits or licenses to carry concealed weapons issued by other states are not required of those traveling through the state. The law, as it reads, does not prohibit any resident of the state from carrying openly a pistol or revolver, provided he does not transport such a weapon, openly or concealed, in any church or place of assemblage, schoolroom, or any other place where people are assembled for educational, political, literary, or social purposes, or to any election precinct, or court room.

Sales Regulations. No dealer may sell, lend, give, or transfer a pistol or revolver to any person until that person shall present a permit to purchase. The permit may be obtained from the circuit clerk of the county in which the applicant is a resident. The clerk shall issue the permit upon approval of the sheriff, but it shall be invalid if the purchase is not completed within 30 days of the date of issuance. The cost of the permit is 50 cents. The permit shall state the name of the dealer from whom the pistol or revolver is to be purchased, the type, caliber, and manufacturer's number of the firearm, and the name, address, and occupation of the applicant. Upon completion of the delivery of the pistol or revolver the dealer shall forward the permit to the county clerk by whom it was issued, with a notation regarding the details and date of the sale.

**MONTANA.** With the exception of local ordinances in a few large municipalities, the only regulatory law in Montana is one which forbids the carrying of a pistol or revolver concealed on or about the person. Those desiring to carry a pistol or revolver concealed on or about their person must obtain a permit.

Licensing Official. An applicant for a permit to carry a pistol or revolver concealed on or about the person may apply to a district judge, giving his name, address, occupation, and reason for desiring the permit.

The law does not require a purchaser of a pistol or revolver to obtain a purchasing license or permit; but the dealer must keep a record of the name and address of the purchaser, as well as the date of purchase and the type, caliber, and manufacturer's number of the pistol or revolver purchased.

There is no provision in the law for the honoring of a permit or license issued by another state, but no difficulties are encountered provided the visitor or traveler complies with the Montana regulations.

**NEBRASKA.** The statutes pertaining to the transportation, sale, possession, and use of pistols and/or revolvers in Nebraska have no provisions for the issuing of a license or permit to carry such firearms concealed on the person, but do not specifically prohibit the carrying of such firearms openly. Some of the large municipalities have local ordinances concerning the carrying of pistols or revolvers, whether openly or concealed, and the cities of Omaha and Lincoln have regulations which require that such firearms be registered with the chief of police.

With the exception of certain municipalities, no permit is required to purchase a pistol or revolver, although all dealers are required to keep a record of the name, address, and occupation of the purchaser, as well as the type, caliber, and manufacturer's number of the pistol or revolver purchased. There is no law prohibiting the possession of such firearms in the abode or place of business.

The law prohibits the possession of pistols or revolvers by aliens or those who have been convicted of a felony, and also forbids any person to sell, offer for sale, give, or lend such firearms to any Indian not a citizen.

While there is no definite provision for the honoring of the permits or licenses issued by other states, those having such permits or licenses encounter no difficulties provided they comply with Nebraska regulations. There is no law prohibiting the transportation of a pistol or revolver in a vehicle.

**NEVADA.** The following regulations (Act Concerning the Carrying of Weapons, Secs. 2300, 2301-NCL 1929, Act Concerning the Sale and Possession of Weapons, Secs. 2302, 2303, 2304-NCL 1929, Crimes and Punishment Act of 1911-NCL 1929, Sec. 10251) apply in Nevada.

The law does not specifically prohibit the carrying of pistols and/or revolvers openly, but prohibits the carrying of such firearms concealed on or about the person. Any person desiring to transport a pistol or revolver concealed on his person may apply to the board of county commissioners, which is empowered to grant such a permit free of charge. There is no law prohibiting the transportation of such firearms in a vehicle, or upon trains or buses by a traveler.

There is no provision in the law for the honoring of permits or licenses issued by another state, but those possession such authority encounter no difficulties.

**NEW HAMPSHIRE.** The following regulations (Sale, etc., of Pistols and Revolvers, Chapter 179) pertain to the transportation, sale, and possession of pistols and/or revolvers in New Hampshire.

The law specifically prohibits the carrying of a pistol or revolver concealed in any vehicle or on the person, except in a dwelling house or place of business, without the possession of a license. It is also prohibited for any alien or person who has been convicted of a felony to own or have such firearms in his possession or under his control. These laws do not apply to local, county, state, or Federal officials otherwise authorized, or to members of duly authorized military or civil organizations when parading or when going to or from customary places of assembly.

Licensing Official. The selectmen of a town, or the mayor or chief of police of a city, may, upon application by any resident, or the superintendent of the state police or some person designated by him, upon application by a non-resident, issue a license to an applicant authorizing him to carry a pistol or revolver for not more than one year from the date of issue. The individual issuing the license must insure that the applicant has good reason to receive such a license and that he is a suitable person to be so licensed. The fee for resident licenses shall be 50 cents, the sum to be allocated to the use of the law enforcement department of the town or city granting the license, and the fee for a non-resident license shall be $1, which fee shall be for the use of the state.

Sales Regulations. No permit is required to purchase a pistol or revolver, but no such firearm shall be delivered to a purchaser not personally known to the seller, or who does not present clear evidence of his identity. A true record shall be made of every pistol or revolver sold in a book kept for that purpose, in the form prescribed by the Secretary of State, and shall be signed by the purchaser and include the date of the sale, the caliber, make, model, and manufacturer's number of the firearm, as well as the address of the purchaser. A copy of this record shall be forwarded by registered mail to the selectmen or police chief of the town or city. No such firearm shall be sold, bartered, rented, or given to any minor.

No provision is made in the law to honor the license or permit granted by another state.

**NEW JERSEY.** The following regulations (Weapons and Explosives, Chapter 176, Articles 1 to 7 inclusive) pertain to the sale, possession, and transportation of a pistol and/or revolver in New Jersey.

The laws of this state do *not* prohibit a person from possessing a pistol or revolver in his abode or in his place of business, or from carrying such firearms on premises or land possessed by him, or from carrying such firearms from any place of purchase or place of repair to the place of abode or business, nor do they prevent any person from carrying a gun, rifle, or knife in the woods or fields or upon the waters of the state for the purpose of hunting or target practice.

The law does require that a permit be obtained to purchase a pistol or revolver, and that a license be obtained to carry a pistol or revolver on the person, concealed or openly, or in a vehicle.

Licensing Official. In order to purchase a pistol or revolver in this state the purchaser must first obtain a permit by applying to one of the following persons: the chief of police of a municipality, the sheriff of the county, or the judge of any court within the state, except justices of the peace. Any person of good character, who is of good repute in the community in which he resides, and who is 18 years of age or over and a citizen of the United States, may, upon the endorsement of two reputable citizens, apply for a purchase permit. The application blank may be obtained from the Secretary of State or from a licensed retail dealer, and upon being properly filled out shall be presented to the licensing authority, together with the fee of 50 cents. The licensing authority shall investigate the application and unless good cause for the denial thereof shall appear, shall grant the permit within 7 days of the receipt of the application. If the permit is not granted the fee shall be returned to the applicant, and if granted shall be paid into the general fund of the state if issued by the Secretary of State, to the general fund of the municipality if issued by a municipal officer, and to the general fund of the county if issued by any other official. The permit shall be issued to the purchaser in triplicate, and upon completion of the purchase the seller shall fill out the form, one copy of which shall be retained by the purchaser, one copy forwarded by registered mail to the Secretary of State, and the third copy retained by the seller as part of his permanent record. The form shall contain the make, model, caliber, and serial number of the pistol or revolver sold under the permit. A person shall not be restricted as to the number of pistols or revolvers he may purchase, but only one pistol or revolver shall be purchased or delivered on each individual permit.

Any person desiring to carry a pistol or revolver on his person or in his vehicle may apply for a permit to any of the officials listed in the above paragraph. If the application is approved by the official to whom it is submitted, the applicant shall then present the application to the justice of the supreme court presiding in the county in which he resides, or to a common pleas judge of that county, who, after investigation, shall include the name and address of the manufacturer, the manufacturer's serial number, and a list of the calibers and types of all pistols and revolvers owned by the applicant. The applicant must agree to be fingerprinted in order that the fingerprints may be compared with those in the files of the local, county, state, and Federal agencies. At the time of the granting of the permit the applicant shall pay to the clerk of the county a fee of $3. All permits shall expire on the 31st day of December subsequent to the date of issue, and may thereafter be renewed annually in the same manner.

The following do *not* require a permit for the carrying of a pistol or revolver on or about their person: local, county, state, or Federal officials otherwise authorized; members of the armed forces or National Guard on duty; a person having a hunting license in going to or from places of hunting; members of duly organized shooting clubs in going to and from their places of target practice.

Sales Regulations. Any retail dealer in pistols or revolvers must be so licensed by the state. He shall deliver to a purchaser no pistol or revolver until the purchaser shall have obtained a permit to purchase, until 7 days shall have elapsed after the date of the application for the permit, and unless the purchaser is personally known to the seller or shall present evidence of his identity. When delivered the pistol or revolver shall be securely wrapped and unloaded. A true record of every pistol or revolver sold shall be kept by the dealer, this record to include the name, address, age, color, nationality, occupation, and residence of the purchaser, the name of the salesman making the sale, the place where sold, the make, model, caliber, and manufacturer's number. The purchaser shall be required to sign his name in duplicate to this record, one copy of which shall be forwarded, before midnight of the day of the sale, to the office of the chief of police of the municipality, or to the office of the captain of the precinct of the city, or to the clerk of the county in the event the municipality has no chief of police.

There is no provision for the honoring of permits or licenses of other states, but persons so licensed encounter no difficulties.

**NEW MEXICO.** The following regulations (New Mexico Statutes Annotated, 1941 Compilation, 41-1701 to 41-1711, and Sec. 42-234) pertain to the transportation, sale, and possession of pistols and/or revolvers in New Mexico.

There is no provision in the law for the granting of a license or permit to carry a pistol or revolver, concealed or otherwise, in or about the settlements of this state, "except it be in his or her residence or his or her landed estate," unless such carrying be done by legal authority. The law does not specifically prohibit the carrying of pistols or revolvers "outside" the "settlements," but does specify that "no firearms shall be carried at any cattle roundup in the State."

While there is no provision for honoring the permits or licenses issued by other states, there is a specific provision which permits persons "traveling to carry arms for their own protection, while actually prosecuting their journey, and they may pass through settlements on their road without disarming, but if such travelers shall stop at any settlement for a longer time than 15 minutes they shall remove all arms from their person or persons, and not resume the same until upon eve of departure."

Municipalities throughout the state have local ordinances with reference to the transportation, possession, use, and sale of pistols and revolvers, details of which may be obtained from the local chiefs of police.

The state has no provision with reference to regulations on the sale or purchase of pistols or revolvers, although some municipalities have local ordinances regulating their sale or purchase.

**NEW YORK.** The following regulations (Article 172, Public Safety, of the New York State Penal Law, Secs. 1896, 1897, 1897*a,* 1897*b,* 1898, 1898*a,* 1906, and 1914. Amendments, Chapter 112, 532, 533, 436, 442) pertain to the possession, sale, and transportation of pistols and/or revolvers in New York.

No person may possess, purchase, or transport a pistol and/or revolver in the state without a license, and the state does *not* recognize the permit or license issued by any other state which would permit an individual to possess, purchase, sell, or transport any pistol and/or revolver within the boundaries of New York State. Further, the City of New York does *not* recognize the license or permit issued by any licensing authority *outside* of the City of New York, until such licenses or permits have been validated by the Police Commissioner of the City of New York.

LICENSING OFFICIAL. In order to be eligible for a license to carry, possess, or purchase a pistol or revolver in New York State, a person must be an actual resident of the state, principally employed therein, or maintain a principal place of business within the boundaries of the state. To obtain a license the applicant must obtain an application form from his local or county police official and after properly filling out this application, present it to a Court of Record (supreme court, county court, or surrogate court) of the county in which he is a resident. In the City of New York applications are obtained from the local precinct and are isued, upon approval, by the police commissioner. In Nassau County applications may be obtained from the local police official and are issued, if approved, by the county police commissioner.

The expense of providing a judge, justice, or officer with blank applications, licenses, and record books for carrying out the provisions of this section are a charge against the county, or the City of New York in the case of the police commissioner of such city. Such judge, justice, or officer shall collect a fee for each license issued of not less than 50 cents or more than $1.50 as may be determined by the board of supervisors where such license is issued or, in the case of the City of New York, as may be determined by the City Council, and shall pay the same into the treasury of the county or of such city, as the case may be. Every such license shall specify the weapon or weapons for which the license is issued, and whether it is to be carried on the person or possessed on the premises.

Elsewhere than in the City of New York a person licensed to possess or carry a weapon as prescribed by this section, may apply at any time to the judge or justice by whom his license was issued, or his successor in office, for an amendment to this license, so as to include one or more additional weapons or one or more different weapons, and upon payment of a fee of 25 cents, payable to the county, such judge or justice may issue an amended license to cover such additional or different weapons. Elsewhere than in the City of New York such license shall be in force and effect until revoked. In the City of New York every such license shall expire on the ensuing first day of January unless limited to expire prior to that date.

Each original application for a license to carry a pistol and/or revolver on the person shall be accompanied by a photograph of the applicant in duplicate, which photograph shall have been taken within 30 days prior to the filing of application. One copy shall be attached to the license and the other remain with the application. The fingerprints of each applicant shall be taken in triplicate, and one copy shall be forwarded to the Division of Criminal Identification in Albany, and shall be searched and retained in the files of said division. Of the remaining two copies, one shall be filed in the office of the Executive Department, Division of State Police, the other shall remain on file in the office of the officer taking the fingerprints. No fingerprints shall be inspected by any person other than a peace officer, except on order of a judge or justice of a court of record. No person who has been convicted of a felony in New York or elsewhere is eligible to be licensed.

SALES REGULATIONS. No pistol, revolver, or other firearm of a size which may be concealed upon the person, shall be sold, or given away, or otherwise disposed of, except to a person expressly authorized to possess and have such firearm. Every person licensed to sell firearms shall keep a record book in which shall be entered, at the time of every sale or transfer, the date, name, occupation, and residence of the purchaser, who must produce a license for possessing or carrying the firearm. The record shall also include the date of such permit, the number thereon, and the name of the magistrate or other officer by whom it is issued.

**NORTH CAROLINA.** This state has made no provision for the licensing or granting of permits for the possession of pistols and/or revolvers, or for carrying such firearms concealed on the person, but it is necessary to obtain a permit to purchase a pistol or revolver.

It is permissible to carry a pistol in North Carolina, provided it is carried openly and can be seen at all times. The law prohibits the carrying of a pistol or revolver concealed on or about the person or in a vehicle, but such a firearm may be carried concealed by any person in his own abode.

Any person may apply to the clerk of the superior court for a permit to purchase a pistol or revolver, which shall be granted upon payment of a fee of 50 cents to any person of good moral character who is a resident of the state, is of age, and who has not been convicted of a felony.

The statute does not cover the honoring of licenses or permits issued by other states, but visitors having such permits or licenses encounter no difficulties.

**NORTH DAKOTA.** The law of this state prohibits the carrying of a pistol and/or revolver, whether openly, concealed, or in a vehicle, except by those who have been granted a permit, but such firearms may be possessed in the abode or place of business, by any resident of the state who is of legal age and has not been convicted of a felony.

Any person desiring to purchase a pistol or revolver must apply to the dealer from whom the purchase is to be made in writing, prior to the date of purchase, the application to contain the name, address, occupation, business address, age, and reason for the purchase.

Licensing Official. Any person of legal age who has never been convicted of a felony may make application to the local chief of police, the county sheriff, or the judge of any court of record, who shall, after investigation and approval, issue a permit to carry, concealed on the person or in a vehicle, a revolver or pistol. Such permit shall be issued without cost and shall be effective for one year.

There is no provision in the law for honoring a license or permit issued by another state, but the possession of such a license or permit will enable the holder to obtain a North Dakota permit without difficulty.

The law does not prohibit the transportation of a pistol or revolver, if unloaded and securely wrapped, from the place of abode to the place of business, or to and from a place of repair.

**OHIO.** This state has a law which prohibits the carrying of pistols or revolvers "concealed on or about the person," but another section of the same statute directs a trial jury in a concealed weapon case to return a verdict of "not guilty" if the defendant has shown a valid reason for carrying a pistol or revolver. In practical application of the statutes, the police customarily make arrests only when suspicious circumstances enter into the case.

The application of the law is thus explained by Colonel George Mingle, Superintendent of the State Highway Patrol; "Shooters from all parts of the continent gather annually in this state for the National Matches with their target arms, and without police hindrance."

The law makes no definite provision for the granting of a license or permit to carry a pistol or revolver concealed on or about the person or in a vehicle, nor does it provide for the honoring of a permit or license issued by another state. In application, no person carrying a pistol or revolver unloaded and properly wrapped or enclosed, or having such a firearm in his abode or place of business, will be prosecuted. The law further states that "upon the trial of an indictment or information for carrying a concealed weapon, the jury shall acquit the defendant if it appear that he was at the time engaged in a lawful calling or employment, and that the circumstances in which he was placed justified a prudent man in carrying such a weapon for the defense of his person, property, or family."

Various municipalities have local ordinances regulating the sale, transportation, and possession of pistols or revolvers, details of which may be obtained from the local chiefs of police.

**OKLAHOMA.** This state has a law which prohibits the carrying of a pistol and/or revolver "concealed on or about the person," and no provision is made for the granting of a license or permit to carry such firearms concealed on the person, nor is there a provision for honoring the permits or license issued by another state. There is no specific statute which forbids the transportation of a pistol or revolver in a vehicle, nor is there a state law which forbids the possession of a pistol or revolver in the abode or place of business.

Various municipalities have local ordinances regulating the sale, transportation, and possession of pistols and revolvers, details of which may be obtained from the local chiefs of police.

**OREGON.** The following regulations (Firearms Regulatory Act, Secs. 25-11 to 25-124; Secs. 25-201 to 25-209; Secs. 25-301 to 25-303) pertain to the sale, possession, and transportation of pistols and/or revolvers in Oregon.

The laws of this state specifically prohibit the carrying of a pistol or revolver concealed on or about the person or within the vehicle of any person who does not possess a license so to carry such firearms. "Pistols or revolvers carried openly in belt holsters shall not be deemed to be concealed within the meaning of this section." The law does not prohibit any citizen of the United States over the age of 18 years who resides in or is temporarily sojourning within this state, and who has not been convicted of a felony, from owning, possessing, or keeping within his place of residence or place of business, any pistol, revolver, or other firearm capable of being concealed.

Licensing Official. It shall be lawful for the sheriff of a county, the board of police commissioners, the chief of police, city marshal, town marshal, or other head of the police department of any city, county town, or other municipal corporation, upon proof before said official that the person applying therefor is of good moral character, and that good cause exists for the issuance thereof, to issue to such person a license to carry concealed a pistol or revolver for a period of one year from the date of such license. All applications for such licenses shall be filed in writing, signed by the applicant, and shall state the name, occupation, residence and business address, age, height, weight, color of eyes and hair, and reason for desiring a license to carry concealed such a weapon. Any license issued upon such application shall set forth the foregoing data and shall, in addition, contain a description of the weapon authorized to be carried, giving the name of the manufacturer, the serial number, and the caliber thereof.

Sales Regulations. Each person engaged in selling, leasing, or otherwise transferring a pistol or revolver, shall keep a register in which shall be entered the time of sale, date of sale, name of the salesman, place where sold, the make, model, manufacturer's number, caliber, or other marks of identification on such pistol or revolver, in addition to which the salesman shall require the purchaser to sign his name and affix his address in duplicate and the salesman shall affix his signature in duplicate as a witness to the purchaser's signature. No sale shall be made to any alien, any minor, or to any person who has been convicted of a felony. In no instance shall any such firearm be delivered to the purchaser upon the day of the application for the purchase, and when delivered the firearm shall be unloaded and securely wrapped.

OTHER REGULATIONS. The law requiring the possession of a license for the carrying of a pistol or revolver concealed on the person or in a vehicle does not apply to the following individuals: local, county, state, or Federal officers; or summoned deputies and individuals otherwise authorized; members of the armed forces or National Guard when on duty; duly authorized military or civil organizations while parading, nor to the members thereof when going to and from places of meeting; nor to members of any club or organization now existing, or hereafter organized, for the purpose of practicing shooting at targets upon established target ranges, whether public or private, while such members are using any of the firearms referred to in this act upon such target ranges, or while going to and from such ranges; nor to licensed hunters or fishermen while engaged in hunting or fishing, or while going to or returning from such hunting or fishing expeditions.

**PENNSYLVANIA.** The following regulations (No. 216, amending Sec. 628 "An Act to consolidate, amend, and revise the penal laws of the Commonwealth") pertain to the sale, transportation and possession of pistols and/or revolvers in Pennsylvania.

The law forbids the carrying of a pistol or revolver, concealed on the person or in a vehicle, without a license. The law does not apply to local, county, state, or Federal officials otherwise authorized; or to any person while carrying such a firearm securely wrapped and unloaded from the place of purchase to his home or place of business, or to a place of repair, or in moving from one place of abode or business to another; or to any person licensed to hunt or fish in the state, provided that such persons are actually hunting or fishing or going to the places where they desire to hunt or fish, or returning from such places, or to persons training dogs (provided that before any such exemption shall be granted to any person licensed to hunt or fish or who desires to train dogs, such person shall at the time of obtaining his hunting or fishing license or at any time after such license has been issued, register with the county treasurer the make of the firearm he desires to carry, and the caliber and manufacturer's number, for which the county treasurer shall collect a fee of 15 cents, and the registration shall be good only for the year for which the hunting or fishing license is issued).

No license or registration is required to possess a pistol or revolver in the abode or place of business.

LICENSING OFFICIAL. Any person 18 years of age or over, who is a citizen of the United States, has not been convicted of a crime of violence, and is not a drug addict, an habitual drunkard, or of unsound mind, may obtain a license to carry a pistol or revolver concealed on the person or in the vehicle in which he or she is riding. The chief or head of any police department of any city or village, or the sheriff of any county, may upon application of any person, issue a license to carry a pistol or revolver, the license to be granted for not more than one year from date of issue, provided the applicant has a proper reason for carrying such a firearm and that he is a suitable person to be so licensed. The original of this license shall be delivered to the person so licensed, one copy shall be forwarded by registered mail to the commissioner of the state police, and the second copy shall be preserved by the authority issuing the license. The fee shall be 50 cents, *except that if the applicant exhibits a resident hunter's license for the current year the fee shall not be charged.* Any such license may be revoked by the person issuing it at any time upon written notice to the holder thereof.

SALES REGULATIONS. No dealer shall deliver to a purchaser any pistol or revolver until 48 hours shall have elapsed from the time of the application for the purchase thereof, and when delivered the firearms shall be unloaded and securely wrapped. At the time of application the purchaser shall sign in triplicate a statement containing his full name, address, occupation, color, place of birth, date and hour of application, as well as the caliber, type, length of barrel, make, and manufacturer's number of the pistol or revolver, and a statement that he has never been convicted of a crime of violence. The seller shall, within 6 hours of such application, forward by registered mail one copy of such application to the chief or head of the police department, or the sheriff of the county in which the applicant is a resident. Another copy shall be sent to the commissioner of the state police, and the third shall be retained by the seller for not less than 6 years.

No provision is made in the law for honoring the permit or license issued by another state, but those so authorized encounter no difficulties.

**RHODE ISLAND.** The following regulations (Chapter 404, Public Laws, 1927; Chapter 404, General Laws of 1938; Chapter 405, General Laws of 1938) pertain to the sale, transportation and possession of pistols and/or revolvers in Rhode Island.

No person shall, unless properly licensed, carry a pistol or revolver in any vehicle or concealed on or about his person, save in his dwelling house or place of business or on land possessed by him, nor shall any such firearm be sold or given away or otherwise disposed of except to a person expressly authorized under the law to possess and have such a firearm. This law does not apply to local, county, state, or Federal officials otherwise authorized, nor to any person while carrying a pistol or revolver unloaded and securely wrapped, from the place of purchase to his home or place of business, or to a place of repair, or in moving goods from one place of abode or business to another.

LICENSING OFFICIAL. The licensing authorities of any city or town shall upon application of any person having a bona fide residence or place of business within such city or town, or of any person having a bona fide residence or place of business within the United States, and a license to carry a pistol concealed upon his person issued by the authorities of any other state or subdivision of the United States, issue a license to such person to carry concealed upon his person a pistol within this state for not more than one year from date of issue, if it appears that the applicant has good reason to fear an injury to his person or property, or has any other proper reason for carrying a pistol, and that he is a suitable person to be so licensed. The license shall be in triplicate, in form to be prescribed by the attorney general and shall bear the fingerprint, name, address, description, and signature of the licensee and the reason given for desiring a license. The original thereof shall be delivered to the licensee, the duplicate shall within 7 days be sent to the attorney general, and the triplicate shall be preserved for 6 years by the licensing authorities issuing said license. A fee of $2 may be charged and shall be paid for each license, to the officer issuing the same. Before issuing any such permit the applicant for the same shall be required to give bond to the city or town treasurer in the penal sum of $300 with surety satisfactory to the authority issuing such permit, to keep the peace and be of good behavior. Every such permit shall be valid for one year from the date when issued unless sooner revoked. The fee charged for the issuing of such license or permit shall be applied for the use and benefit of the city or town. Any such permit may be revoked at any time by the authority granting it, and upon such revocation such authority shall give immediate notice thereof to the attorney general, who shall immediately note such revocation, with the date thereof, upon the copy of such permit on file in his office.

No provision has been made to honor the license or permit issued by another state. The previous paragraph clearly states that the same law that applies to a resident applies to "a person licensed to carry a pistol concealed upon his person issued by the authorities of any other state or subdivision of the United States."

**SOUTH CAROLINA.** The law of this state does not contain any provision for the licensing of any individual to carry, concealed or openly on his person, any pistol and/or revolver, but the law specifically forbids the carrying of a pistol or revolver on the person, concealed or otherwise, but does not prohibit the possession of such weapons in the home or place of business. In application, precedent has established the right of an individual to carry, in his luggage or securely wrapped and unloaded, a pistol or revolver. No provision is made for honoring the permit or license issued by another state, but the traveler who transports a pistol or revolver through the state in his luggage, or securely wrapped, unloaded, will encounter no difficulties. Some municipalities have regulations covering the sale of pistols and revolvers, details of which may be obtained from the local police officials.

**SOUTH DAKOTA.** The law forbids the carrying of a pistol and/or revolver on the person unless by the possessor of a permit, nor can such a firearm be carried in any vehicle without a permit. The law makes no provision for honoring the permits or licenses issued by another state, and the visitor is subject to the same law as the resident. In application, the visitor so authorized who carries in his luggage a pistol or revolver, unloaded and securely wrapped, will encounter no difficulties. No license or permit is required to possess a pistol or revolver in the abode or place of business, nor for carrying such a firearm, unloaded and securely wrapped, from the place of purchase to the abode or place of business, or in moving from one abode or place of business to another.

Licensing Official. The chief or head of the police department of any city or town, the sheriff of any county, or the judge of any court of record may issue a permit, which must be renewed annually, to any person who has a proper reason for carrying a pistol or revolver, provided that person is a resident of the state, of legal age, has never been convicted of a crime of violence, and is not addicted to the use of drugs or is an habitual drunkard. The cost of this permit is 50 cents.

Sales Regulations. No dealer in firearms or other individual may sell, rent, give, or otherwise dispose of a pistol or revolver to any person until an application has been made in writing at least 48 hours in advance of the delivery, and the dealer must keep a complete record of the transaction, including the signature, name, address, occupation, and color of the purchaser, and the caliber, type, make, and manufacturer's number of the pistol or revolver sold.

**TENNESSEE.** The law of this state prohibits the sale, importation for sale, or other disposition of pistols and/or revolvers, and the statute makes no provision for the transportation, possession, or sale of such firearms, nor is there any provision to honor the license or permit issued by any other state.

The law reads as follows: "Any person who shall carry in any manner whatever, with the intent to go armed, any pistol or revolver of any kind whatever, except the Army or Navy pistol, which shall be carried openly in the hand, shall be guilty of a misdemeanor."

Application of the law, however, indicates that any visitor in possession of a permit or license issued by another state, will encounter no difficulties provided the firearm is unloaded and is enclosed in the luggage or securely wrapped.

The law does not specifically prohibit the possession of a pistol or revolver in the abode or place of business.

**TEXAS.** The law of this state, while it requires the possession of a permit to purchase a pistol and/or revolver, does not specifically prohibit the carrying of a pistol or revolver openly, nor does it prohibit the possession of such a weapon in the home or place of business. Certain municipalities have local ordinances regulating the sale, transportation, and possession of pistols or revolvers, details of which may be obtained from local police officials. No provision is made to honor the permit or license issued by another state, but in application any person so authorized encounters no difficulties if the weapon is carried in a vehicle, or is unloaded and securely wrapped. The law also provides that a pistol or revolver may be carried to and from the home and place of business and when moving from one abode or place of business to another.

Sales Regulations. No person may sell, lend, or otherwise transfer a pistol or revolver unless the person to whom it is delivered or sold has in his possession a certificate of good character issued by a justice of the peace, district judge, or county judge in the county of his or her residence. Upon delivery, the person transferring the pistol or revolver shall require the person receiving it to sign his name, and give his address, occupation, and color, as well as list the caliber, type, and manufacturer's number of the firearm. One copy of this record shall be forwarded by registered mail to the state adjutant general for file and another copy shall be kept as a permanent record of the dealer.

**UTAH.** The law of this state does not specifically prohibit the carrying of a pistol or revolver openly, but certain municipalities have local ordinances regulating the sale, transportation, and possession of such firearms. The statute prohibits the carrying of a pistol or revolver concealed on or about the person unless the individual is in possession of a permit in writing issued by a local police official. The state law does not require the possession of a permit or license to purchase a pistol or revolver, but most municipalities have such regulations.

It is forbidden for minors, or persons under 14 years of age, as well as aliens, to possess a pistol or revolver.

The state recognizes the permit or license issued by another state.

**VERMONT.** The law of this state does not prohibit the carrying or possession of a pistol and/or revolver, except by a minor under the age of 16 years who shall do so without the consent of the parent or guardian. (This regulation does not apply to an instructor or teacher who furnishes a military weapon to pupils for instruction or drill.) The constitution of the state provides that "the people have a right to bear arms for the defense of themselves and the state," and no infringement of this "right" has been enacted.

The law makes no provision for honoring the permit or license issued by another state, but those so authorized encounter no difficulties.

Sales Regulations, Any person dealing in pistols or revolvers must keep a record book in which shall be recorded the sale of all pistols and revolvers, with the name, age, height, birthplace, color of hair and eyes, address, and occupation of the purchaser, and the date of the transaction, as well as the caliber, type, maker, and manufacturer's number of the firearm sold. This record shall be preserved for not less than 6 years after the date of the purchase.

**VIRGINIA.** The following regulations (Michie's Code of 1942, Sec. 4535-*a*) pertain to the sale, transportation, and possession of pistols and/or revolvers in Virginia.

The law provides that the judge of a circuit or corporation court, upon written application and satisfactory proof of character and necessity, may grant permisison to any resident of the state 18 years of age or over, to carry a pistol or revolver concealed on or about the person for a period of one year.

There is no provision in the law for the honoring of the license or permit issued by another state, but in application no person so authorized will encounter difficulties. As written, the law does not specifically prohibit the carrying of a pistol or revolver openly, nor does it prohibit the possession of such a weapon in the abode or place of business.

A section of the Code of Virginia (2728-*b*, 1946) requires any dealer in pistols or revolvers to keep a record of the name, address, and occupation of any purchaser of such a firearm, as well as the caliber, type, make, and manufacturer's number of the pistol or revolver sold. A copy of this record shall be forwarded by registered mail to the clerk of the circuit court of that county within 10 days of the date of the sale.

**WASHINGTON.** The following regulations (Short Firearms, Chapter 172 S.B. 147) pertain to the sale, transportation and possession of pistols and/or revolvers in Washington.

The statute provides that no person shall carry a pistol or revolver in any vehicle or concealed on or about his person, except in his fixed abode or place of business, without a license. This law does not apply to any local, county, state, or Federal official otherwise authorized, *or to regularly enrolled members of clubs organized for the purpose of target shooting and affiliated with a national shooting organization,* provided such members are at or are going to or from their places of assembly or target practice, or to any person while carrying a pistol or revolver unloaded and securely wrapped from the place of purchase to his home or place of business or to and from a place of repair or in moving in one place of abode or business to another.

Licensing Official. The judge of a court of record, the chief of police, the sheriff of a county, shall, upon application by any person (other than a minor under the age of 21, or a person convicted of a crime of violence, a drug addict, an habitual drunkard, or a person of unsound mind) issue a license to carry a pistol in a vehicle or concealed on or about the person for a period of not more than one year from the date of issue, provided the applicant has a proper reason for desiring such a license. The fee for such license shall be $1, and shall be paid into the state treasury.

Sales Regulations. No dealer shall deliver a pistol or revolver to a purchaser until at least 48 hours shall have elapsed from the time of application, and when delivered the firearm shall be unloaded and securely wrapped. At the time of application, the purchaser shall sign in triplicate a statement containing his full name, signature, address, occupation, color, place of birth, date and hour of application, the caliber, make, model, and manufacturer's number of the firearm to be purchased, and a statement that he has never been convicted of a crime of violence. The dealer shall, within 6 hours after the receipt of this application, forward by registered mail one copy of the statement to the chief of police of the municipality or the sheriff of the county, and another copy shall be forwarded, within 7 days of the date of purchase, to the director of licenses of the state. The third copy shall be retained by the seller as a part of his records for a period of 6 years. No license is required to purchase, but no pistol or revolver shall be sold to any person who is not personally known to the dealer or who fails to present clear evidence of his identity.

No provision is made in the law to honor the permit or license issued by another state.

**WEST VIRGINIA.** The following regulations (West Virginia Code, Chapter 61, Article 7, Sec. 9) pertain to the sale, transportation and possession of pistols and/or revolvers in West Virginia.

The law forbids any person, without a license therefor, to carry about his person openly or concealed any pistol or revolver. The law does not prohibit the possession of a pistol or revolver in the home, nor does it prohibit the sale of such firearms provided the sale is in conformity with the law.

LICENSING OFFICIAL. Any *resident* may obtain a license to carry, concealed on or about the person, from the judge of the circuit court, provided the applicant can offer proper reason for being so licensed. The license fee is $20 for one year, and in addition the licensee must provide a $3500 bond, which is forfeit in the event of the misuse of the pistol or revolver.

No provision is made to honor the license or permit issued by another state, nor is there any provision in the law for a non-resident to obtain a license in the state.

**WISCONSIN.** The law of this state specifically provides that no person shall carry a pistol and/or revolver concealed on his person, nor shall such a firearm be carried by any minor or person in a state of intoxication, but there is no specific law prohibiting the carrying of such firearms openly. There is no provision in the law for the granting of a permit or license to carry a pistol or revolver concealed on the person, nor does the law provide for honoring the permit or license issued by any other state. The law does not prohibit the possession of such firearms in the abode or place of business. Various municipalities have local ordinances regulating the sale and transportation of pistols or revolvers, details of which may be obtained from local police officials.

**WYOMING.** The law of this state forbids the carrying of a pistol and/or revolver concealed on the person, but does not specifically prohibit the carrying of such firearms openly. There is no provision in the law for the granting of a permit or license to carry a pistol or revolver concealed on the person. Certain municipalities have local ordinances regulating the sale and transportation of pistols and revolvers, but the state recognizes the licenses and permits issued by other states.

No permit is required to purchase a pistol or revolver, but the dealer in such firearms is required to keep a register, to contain the name, signature, occupation, birthplace, and address of the purchaser, as well as the make, model, caliber, and manufacturer's number of the pistol or revolver sold.

**CANADA.** The importation of pistols and/or revolvers is banned in Canada, except by permit from the Department of National Revenue, Ottawa, Canada.

No pistol or revolver may be purchased in Canada except by persons in possession of a permit. Individuals requesting such a permit may apply for "Form 76E," which may be obtained from the agents of the attorneys general of the various provinces. No person may sell a pistol or revolver without first obtaining a permit to do so, which may be obtained by applying for "Form 76C." A permit to carry a pistol or revolver may be obtained by application to the attorney general of the province in which the permit is desired, but such permits are granted only after a thorough examination of the reasons leading to the application and to individuals of unquestionable character.

The various provinces have special regulations concerning the sale, transportation, and possession of pistols and revolvers, details of which may be obtained by writing the attorney general of the province or the head of the provincial police. Such information may be obtained from the following:

The Commissioner
Quebec Provincial Police
Place Vauquelin, Montreal, P. Q.

The Commissioner
Ontario Provincial Police
13 Queens Park Crescent
Toronto, Ont.

The Commissioner
British Columbia Provincial Police
Victoria, B. C.

The Officer Commanding
R.C.M.P.
Charlottetown, P.E.I.

The Officer Commanding
R.C.M.P.
Halifax, N.S.

The Officer Commanding
R.C.M.P.
Fredericton, N.B.

The Officer Commanding
R.C.M.P.
Winnipeg, Man.

The Officer Commanding
R.C.M.P.
Regina, Sask.

The Officer Commanding
R.C.M.P.
Edmonton, Alta.

# AMMUNITION

## RIFLE AMMUNITION

The detailed and complete story of the development of ammunition from the discovery of gunpowder to the present time would require years of concentrated research and no one could estimate how many volumes the finished work would comprise. The history of the various types of firearms, and the ammunition they employed, has been covered in other sections of this book. This section will, therefore, be concerned only with modern rifle cartridges.

Thirty years ago the cartridges and shells turned out by the various ammunition companies not only showed great variations in type and power, but conformed to the standards set up by the individual companies. (See p. 744.) But that was before the initiation of the Sporting Arms and Ammunition Manufacturers' Institute. Today, as a result of the self-imposed standards (for the Institute is formed of representatives from the various companies), the great majority of the cartridges you buy are standard—except, of course, handloads. In other words, the cartridge of a certain caliber, bullet type and load that is turned out by one company will give you just about the same result as a similar cartridge produced by another company.

The cartridge itself is of tremendous importance. It is what happens after the firing pin has fallen, the powder has exploded, and the bullet has departed on its course that is of concern to the average shooter, who is unaware of the tremendous amount of time that has been spent in research and experiment before that cartridge is sold over a counter. There are several factors to be decided before a cartridge is ready for production, and each of these factors has a definite effect on the value of the finished product.

First, there is the matter of the cartridge case itself: its type, diameter, length, and shape must be decided upon. These measurements depend upon the diameter, shape, and weight of the bullet as well as the amount of powder that will be required to give the bullet the velocity desired. It is necessary that there be a perfect balance between the velocity generated and the ability of the bullet to travel at that velocity without tending toward an erratic flight.

Many shooters are inclined toward the belief that high muzzle velocity insures long range, flat trajectory, and accuracy. This is far from the true fact. The mere presence of high muzzle velocity does not

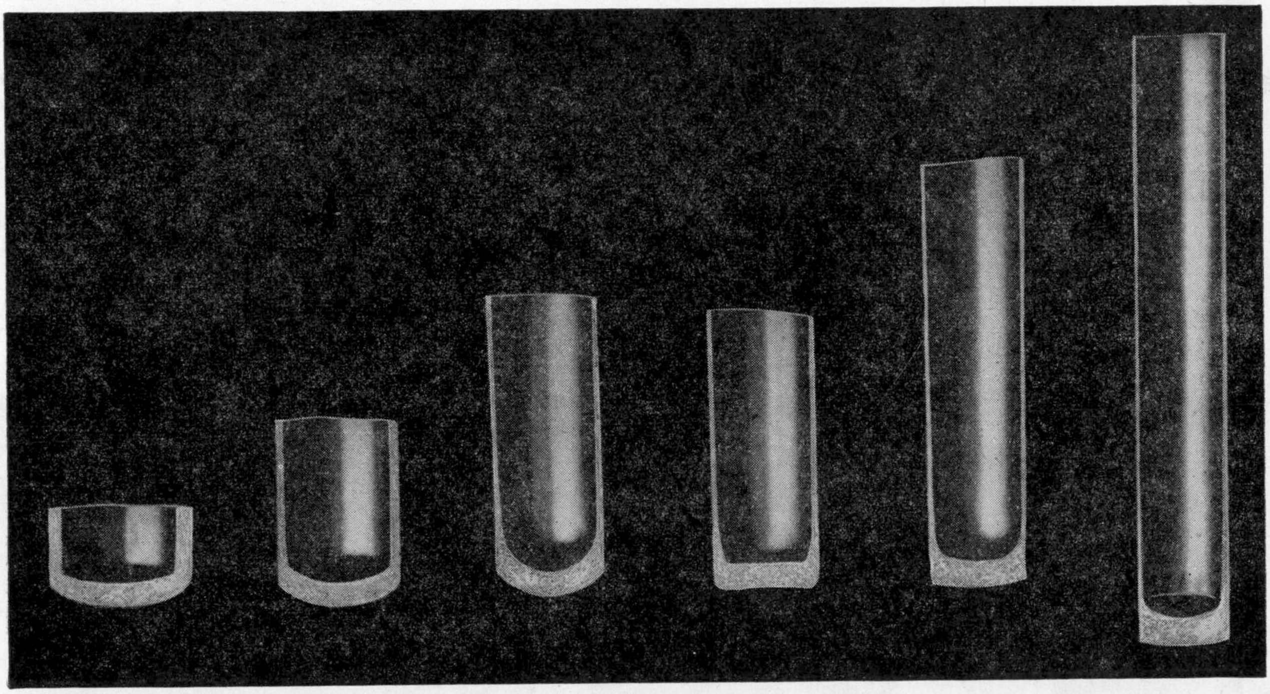

**PLATE I.** Steps in the Drawing of a Cartridge Case. *Left to right:* First draw. Second draw. Bunted. Third draw. Finish draw.

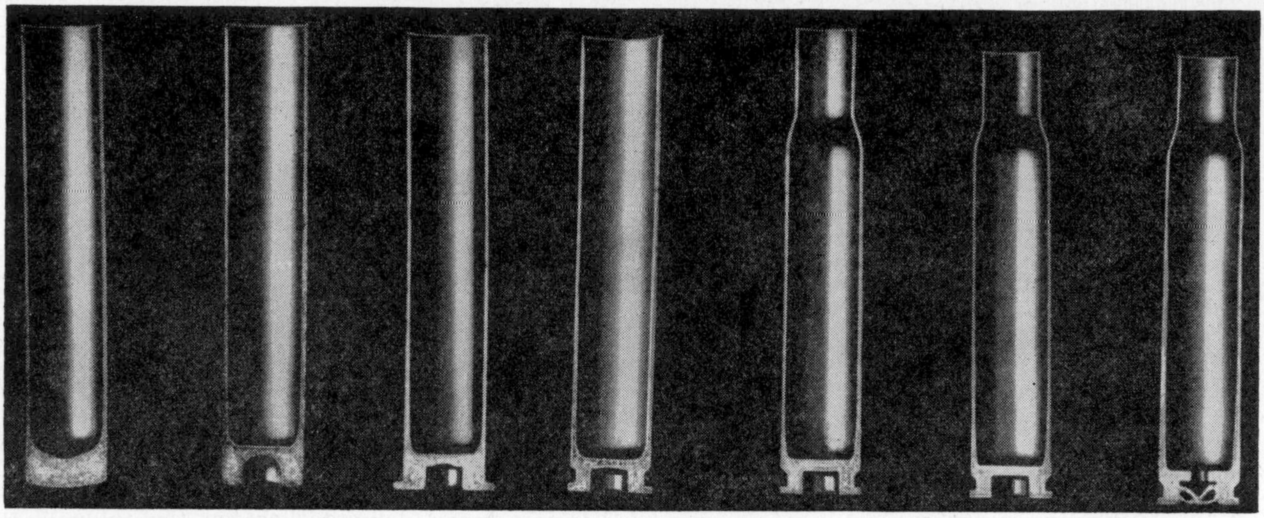

PLATE II. Steps in the Drawing of a Cartridge Case (continued). *Left to right:* Trim. Pocketed. Headed. First head trim. Reduced. Second Head Trim. Cap.

insure any one of these three, *unless* the weight and design of the bullet is in balance with this velocity.

Take, for example, the .220 Swift which has a muzzle velocity of 4140 foot-seconds at the muzzle, and the .45-70 Government, which has a muzzle velocity of 1310 foot-seconds at the muzzle. At 300 yards, the .220 Swift has lost almost 50 per cent of its initial velocity, whereas the .45-70 has lost only approximately 25 per cent of its initial velocity. The .220 Swift bullet weighs only 46 grains and the .45-70 bullet weighs 405 grains. While this example gives an extreme case, it is merely cited to prove that the mere fact of initial velocity has little to do with ballistic values. The trajectories of the two bullets (see chart on pp. 783-786) are quite another story.

Bullet velocity, and the many arguments that arise on the subject, is the basis for thousands of letters to rod and gun editors and ammunition manufacturers. One of the strangest, yet most common, inquiries concerns the relative speed of a bullet and sound.

**Bullet Speed and Sound.** "Should I *lead* a deer, even though it is standing still, to compensate for his forward movement when he hears the sound of the shot?"

It is quite apparent that such inquiries are from individuals who are unaware of the speed of bullet flight and its relation to the speed of sound. The bullet employed in the regulation .30 '06 Springfield, which is not a fast load compared to many others now used, might serve as an example. This bullet will travel 300 yards in .365 seconds (just a hair more than a third of a second). The sound of the rifle shot would take .803 seconds (about four-fifths of a second) to reach a point 300 yards distant.

Another favorite query is this one: "Suppose I am in an airplane flying at 500 miles per hour and I fire a bullet directly to the rear, and this bullet has a velocity of 500 miles per hour. What happens to the bullet?"

The scientific answer to this question is very simple. The bullet will drop vertically to the ground, but with some irregularity of movement due to its spin. Dr. C. S. Cummings, Remington's ballistic expert, explains that what those propounding this question seem unable to understand is the fact that there is no such thing as "motion by itself." Motion must always be relative to some other object.

"The question, if properly phrased, almost answers itself," Dr. Cummings states. "Suppose we phrase it this way: What is the motion, relative to the earth, of a bullet which is

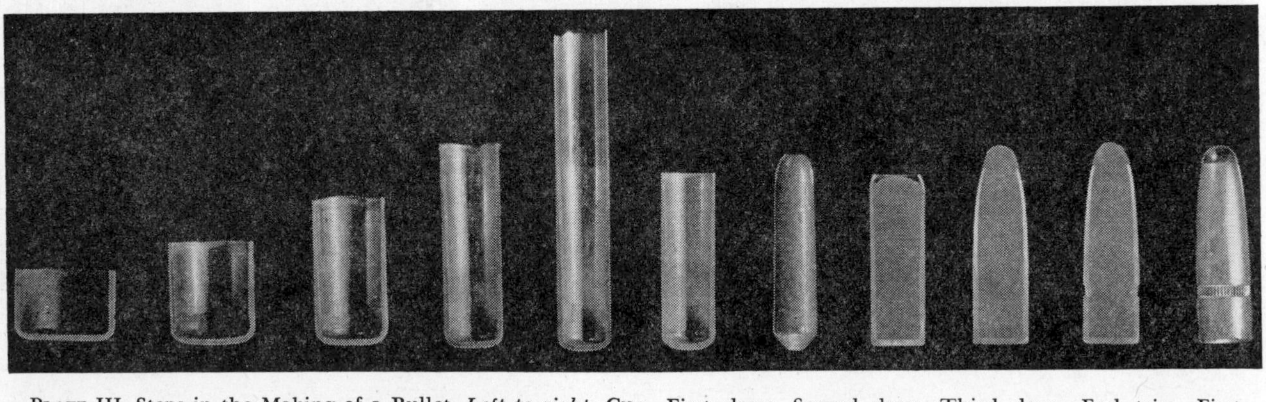

PLATE III. Steps in the Making of a Bullet. *Left to right:* Cup. First draw. Second draw. Third draw. End trim. First assembly. Second assembly. Knurl and size. Finished bullet.

fired in a rearward direction from a plane whose forward velocity, relative to the earth, is equal to the velocity with which the bullet leaves the gun?

"To be specific, let us imagine that we are in a plane traveling 800 feet per second due north. The bullet is one which, when fired, will leave the gun at a speed of 800 feet per second relative to the gun. Picture now the situation just before the shot is fired. The plane, gun, and gunner are all moving due north at the speed of 800 feet per second relative to the earth. The gunner pulls the trigger. The bullet starts to move down the gun barrel—that is, changes its position relative to the gun. Since the gun is presumed fixed, relative to the plane, the bullet is not moving north quite as rapidly now as is the plane and gun. By the time the bullet reaches the muzzle of the gun, it is traveling with its full velocity of 800 feet per second away from the gun in a direction due south. Relative to an observer on the ground, the velocity of the bullet is zero. Hence, the bullet will drop vertically to the ground."

**Bullet Shape.** The shape of a bullet plays an important part in all rifle shooting, whether it be for game or score. Unfortunately, the best bullet for game and the best bullet for accuracy do not follow the same design.

The sharp-pointed bullet will retain its velocity for a greater distance than the blunt or round-nosed bullet, but the latter is much more effective in knock-

PLATE IV. Finished Bullet.

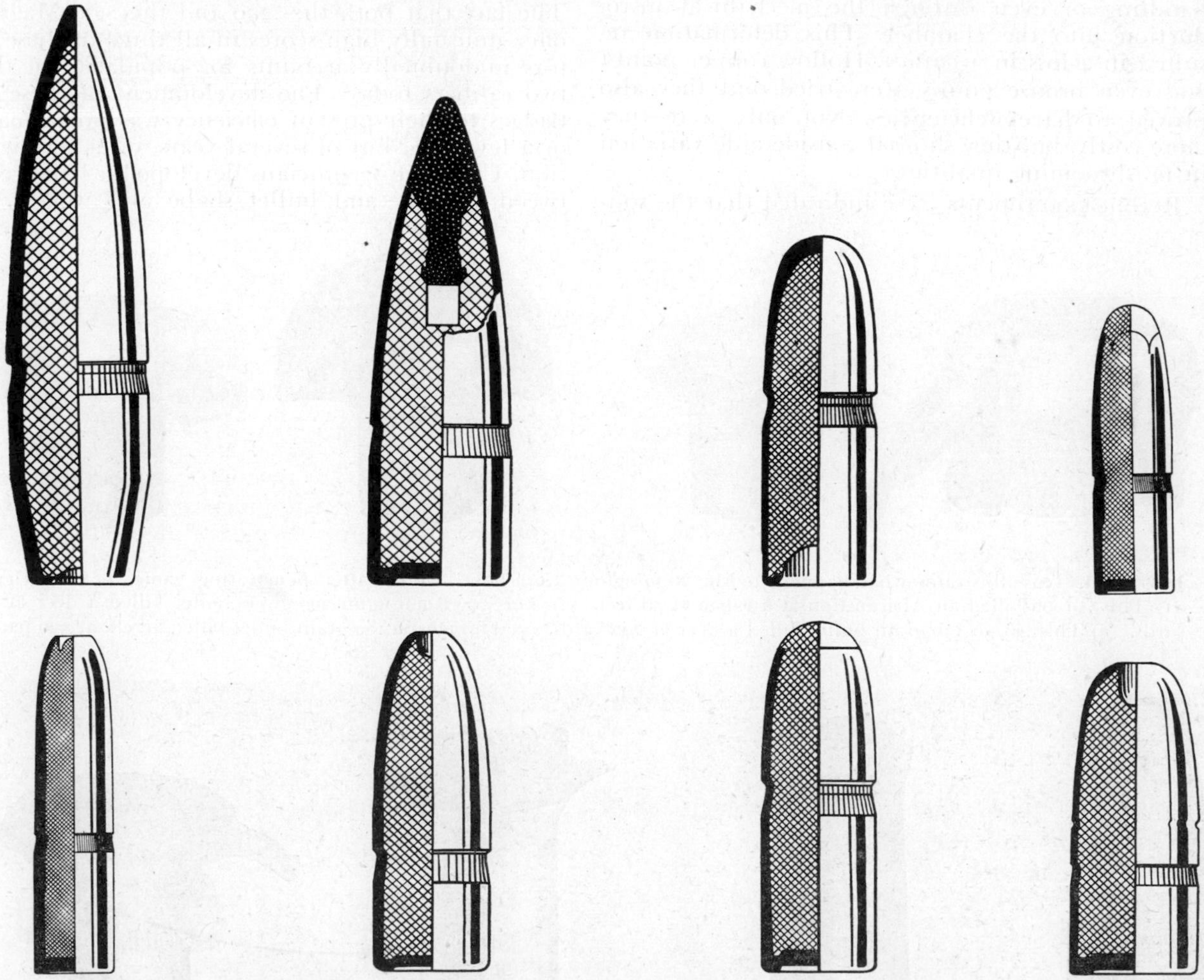

PLATE V. These illustrate some of the bullet designs of the Remington Arms Co. The cross-hatch section indicates the lead core, the heavy black line indicates the metal jacket. (1) Metal jacket boat-tail. (2) Bronze point expanding. (3) Metal jacket, solid point. (4) Inner belted or "core-lokt" soft point. (5) Inner belted or "core-lokt" hollow point. (6) Metal jacket hollow point. (7) Soft point. (8) Metal jacket hollow point.

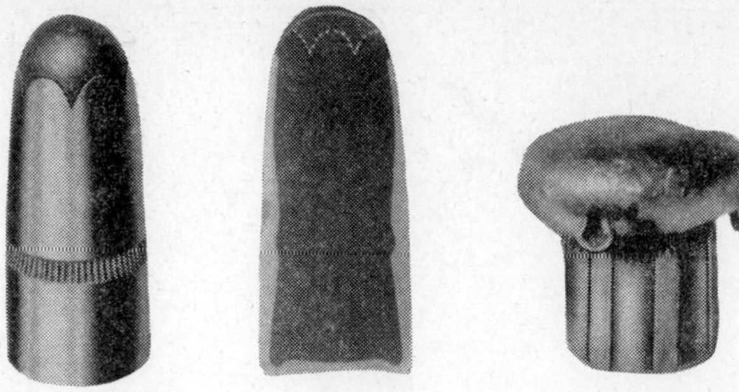

PLATE VI. Remington "Core-Lokt" Bullet—showing cross section and mushrooming effect.

ing down the game. The reason for this is simple: the round-nosed bullet offers greater air resistance than a bullet of similar weight and diameter with a pointed nose.

In an effort to overcome the loss in velocity occasioned by the shape of the good game bullet, manufacturers have tried several expedients. One of the first was to turn out a bullet with a sharp lead point. This was abandoned when it was discovered that the softness of the lead resulted in deformities due to handling or even through the mechanical introduction into the chamber. This deformation resulted in a loss in accuracy. Hollow copper points, and even bronze points, were tried, but they also proved to have deficiencies. Not only were they more costly, but they showed considerable variation in mushrooming qualities.

Recent experiments have indicated that the soft-nosed bullet, pointed as much as possible and with a thinner jacket near the nose, may be the best answer to the problem.

**Ballistic Research.** Ballisticians still are confronted by many knowns, and in some instances they are able to prophesy the *end* without fully understanding all the factors which constitute the *means.* Certain bullets of certain weight and design with certain velocities give a certain result. Yet if you double the velocity anything can—and often does—happen. A bullet of a given weight, shape, and muzzle velocity will prove to be much more satisfactory at 200 yards than another of a different weight, shape, and muzzle velocity. Yet the second bullet will prove much more satisfactory at 500 yards.

By far the most satisfactory bullet for range, accuracy, and penetration is the sharp-pointed (Spitzer) boat-tail, yet it is far from the most satisfactory bullet for big-game hunting. The hunter normally prefers to sacrifice these virtues to shocking power, for the bullet that leaves a nice clean hole too often fails to halt the game.

The hunter is interested in the bullet that will give him the highest over-all score in the following factors: flat trajectory, accuracy, and shocking power. The fact that both the .270 and the .300 Magnum offer unusually high scores in all three of these factors undoubtedly accounts for popularity of these two calibers today. The development of these cartridges to their present efficiency was not a matter of a few days, but of several years, of experimentation. Until the technicians developed a balance between velocity and bullet shape and weight, the

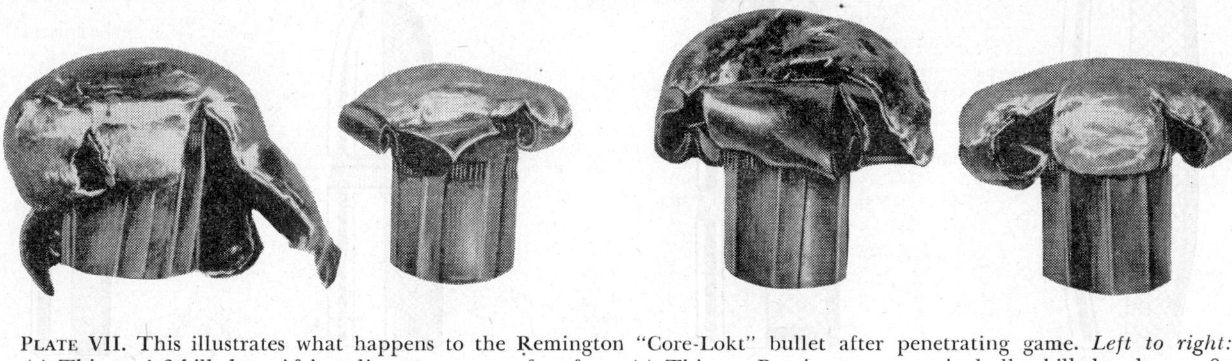

PLATE VII. This illustrates what happens to the Remington "Core-Lokt" bullet after penetrating game. *Left to right:* (1) This .30 '06 killed an African lion at a range of 50 feet. (2) This .35 Remington 200-grain bullet killed a deer at 80 yards. (3) This .30/30 170-grain bullet killed a deer at 200 yards. (4) This .30 '06 180-grain bullet killed an elk at 390 paces.

PLATE VIII. This is what happens to the Remington "Core-Lokt" bullet under vise pressure.

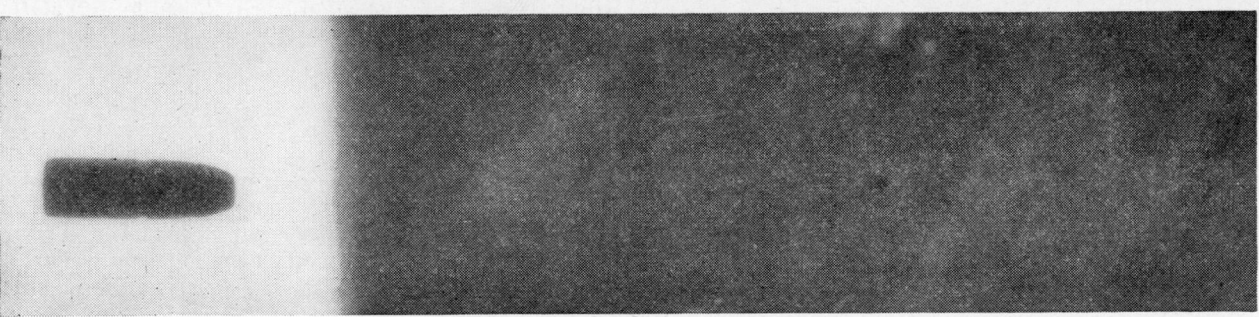

PLATE IX. Bullet About to Enter Block of Gelatine.

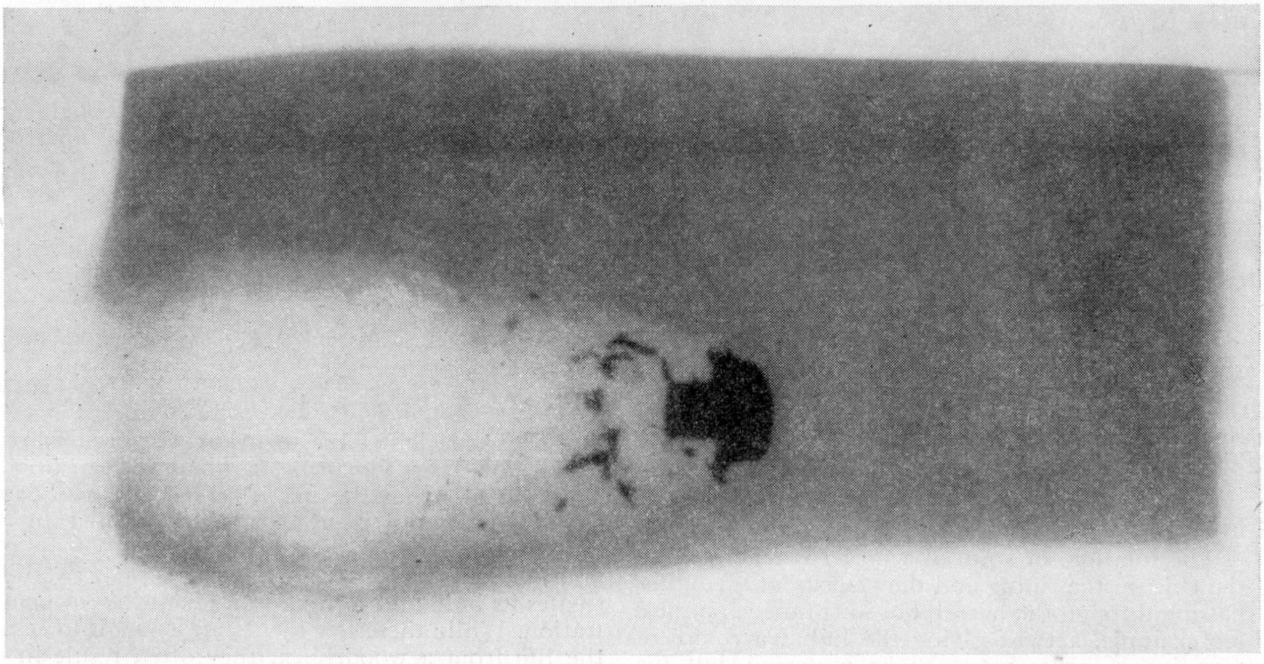

PLATE X. Bullet Halfway Through Block of Gelatine. Note mushrooming and partial break-up of bullet.

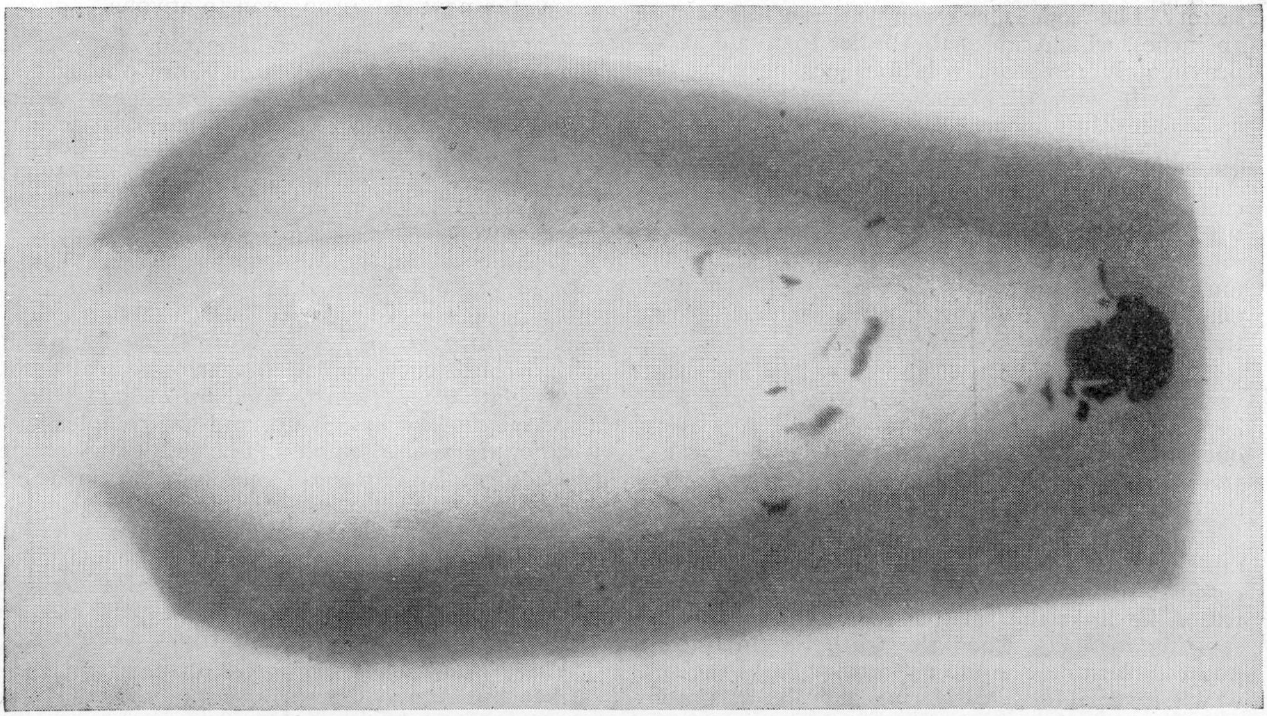

PLATE XI. Bullet Almost Through Block of Gelatine. Note expansion of gelatine due to shock.

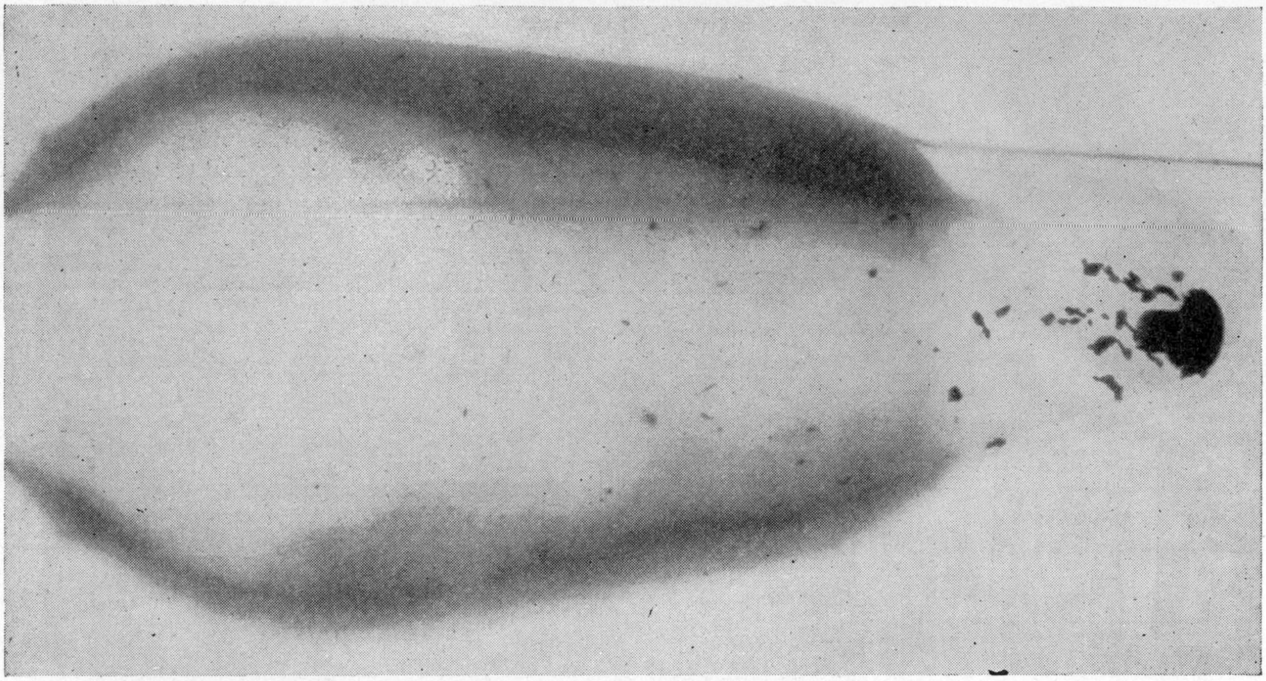

PLATE XII. Bullet Through Block of Gelatine. Note expansion due to shock, and that the shock is not completed until bullet has passed through.

three important factors did not exist. The balance itself depended upon the amount of "twist" in the rifling of the barrel itself, which was another of the hidden factors.

The rotation, or spin, of a bullet is regulated by the twist in the rifling and the velocity of the bullet passing through the barrel. For long-range accuracy, for example, a twist giving the bullet a complete turn in 10 inches seems to be preferred, but for ranges under 400 yards a twist giving the bullet a complete turn in 15 or 16 inches seems more satisfactory. The .30 '06, for example, has a full twist in 10 inches, which causes the bullet to rotate at approximately 180,000 revolutions per minute. The .220 Swift with the same twist rotates at about 280,000 revolutions per minute, which is too great a spin for full stability. For this reason many shooters who have special .220 Swift barrels turned out by custom barrel makers, specify that the twist be one turn in 14 or even 15 inches, and others specify as much as one turn in 18 inches. Many of the old muzzle loaders, extremely accurate at short ranges, employed a very *slow* twist, often as much as one turn in 40 inches.

The demands of rifle shooters are many and varied, which accounts for the fact that many calibers and loads are necessary in order to keep everyone happy. The man who wants a rifle for long-range vermin shooting does not need a bullet that would stop a bear in his tracks at 200 yards.

Unhappily, the novice vermin shooter often attains a distorted set of values, and too often he confuses caliber with sportsmanship. For some reason he links the small-caliber bullet with high sporting instincts, when the truth lies in the opposite direction. The most sporting rifle is the rifle which is capable of delivering a bullet accurately and with sufficient force to insure the most merciful death. The .220 Swift, a fine rifle for woodchucks or other small game, is far from an adequate rifle for whitetail deer, except when used by a shooter of exceptional talent. The light 46- or 48-grain bullet, traveling at very high velocity, dissipates its bulk and force after a few inches of penetration. While these few inches are enough to blast the life from a woodchuck, they often result in a bad wound in a deer, but not necessarily a wound that is immediately fatal. The deer that dies in the woods the next day is no good to anyone.

**Photography and Ballistics.** The modern development of high-speed spark and X-ray photography has done much to extend the knowledge of technicians experimenting in ballistic matters. In developing a bullet for the hunter, it is necessary to know just what will happen when that bullet penetrates the game. To determine this, many materials are called into use.

Technicians in the Winchester research laboratory, for example, wanted to know the extent of the shocking power of certain bullets. They experimented with various gelatines until they found one with a consistency similar to that of animal tissue. This gelatine was then molded into a large block. a special camera was set up, and the complex electrical equipment assembled. The result was a series of photographs showing a bullet in various stages during its passage through the block of gelatine.

Another point which comes up for considerable discussion among shooters concerns the matter of recoil, and when it takes place. This also has been settled beyond dispute by the high-speed camera, as Plates XVI and XVII will testify.

Those who scoff at the power of the popular .22-caliber bullet may be surprised to see what this

PLATE XIII. A .22 Long Rifle Hollow-Point Bullet About to Enter a Block of Soap.

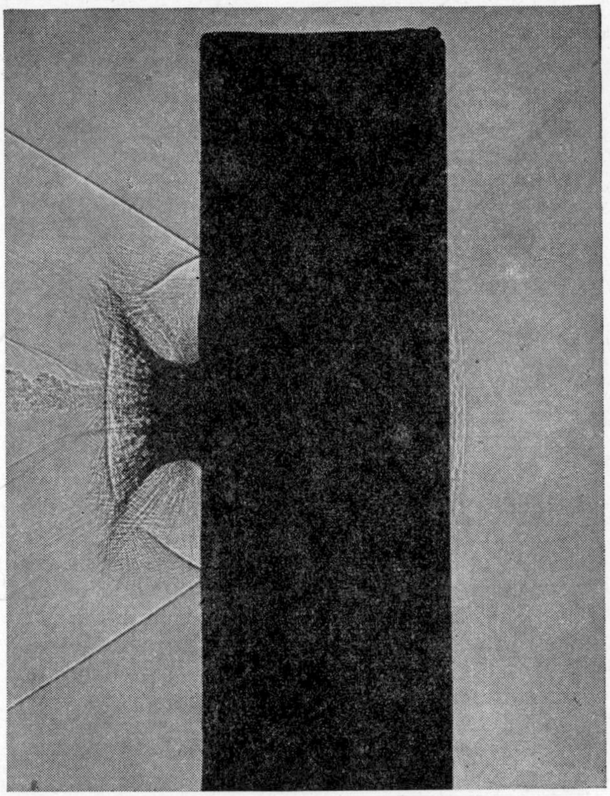

PLATE XIV. Same Bullet Entering Soap Block.

bullet can do to a bar of ordinary laundry soap. Anyone can make this experiment, but to stop the bullet in flight at several points, as did the high-speed camera, is possible only when you have a special laboratory.

**Pendulum Gun.** A good ballistician, with his accumulated knowledge, and with a pencil, some tables, and enough paper, can come up with a really sound theory as to what a certain cartridge would produce under given conditions. But before they begin the expensive process of making dies and tools to produce that cartridge the arms companies want to know *exactly* what characteristics this cartridge possesses. To determine this they developed what is known in the Winchester plant as the "pendulum gun." The one shown here in Plate XVIII

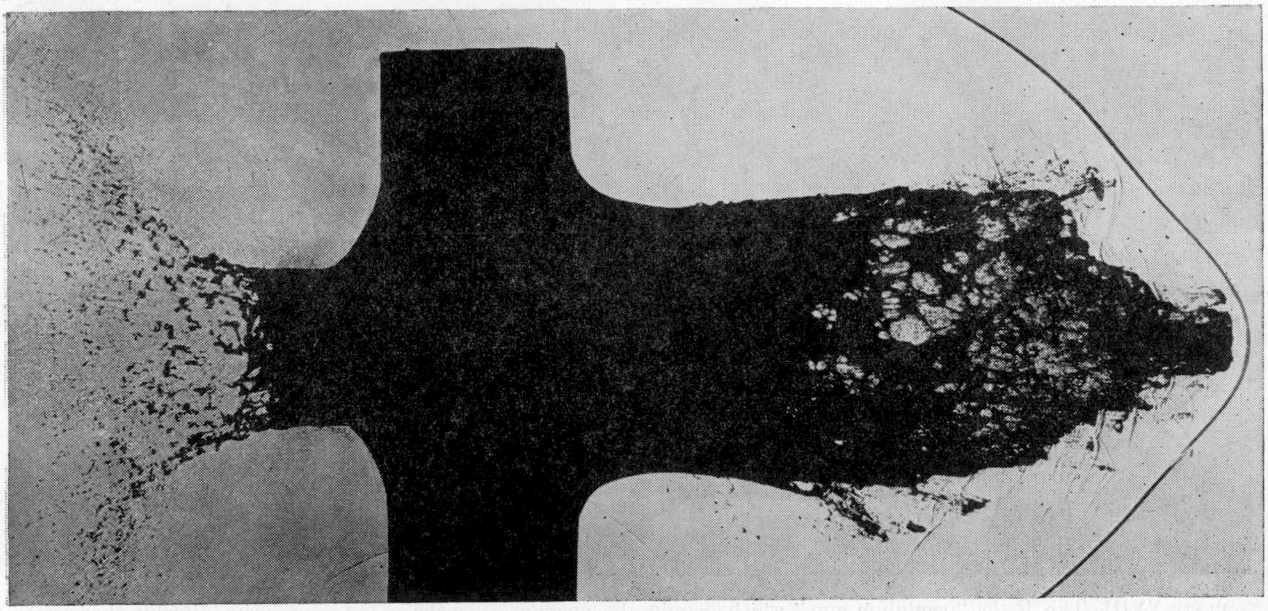

PLATE XV. Same Bullet Emerging from Soap Block. The shape of the bullet can be seen at extreme right.

PLATE XVI. This is a spark photograph of a bullet a few inches from the muzzle of a Winchester Model 94 rifle. The barrel of the rifle is resting on two pegs, showing that no recoil is apparent at this point.

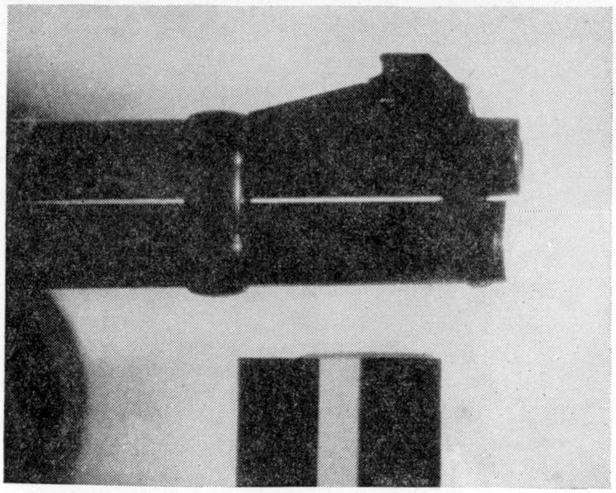

PLATE XVII. This is the same rifle shown in Plate XVI. The bullet is now approximately 30 feet distant. Note that the recoil has begun, as the barrel is now more than a half-inch above the pegs.

is used for testing shotgun shells, but a similar device is employed for rifle cartridges.

This gun, that swings almost like the pendulum of a clock when it is fired, uses but one instead of five shotshells to test velocity, "time-up-the-barrel," chamber pressure, recoil, and shot pattern.

It determines velocity by measuring the time it takes the tiny shot pellets to cover a distance of 120 feet. A slender copper wire, .003 inch in diameter, is stretched in the path of the shot, 6 inches from the muzzle of the barrel. The operator who fires the pendulum gun is connected by telephone with a Boulenge chronograph operator, from whom

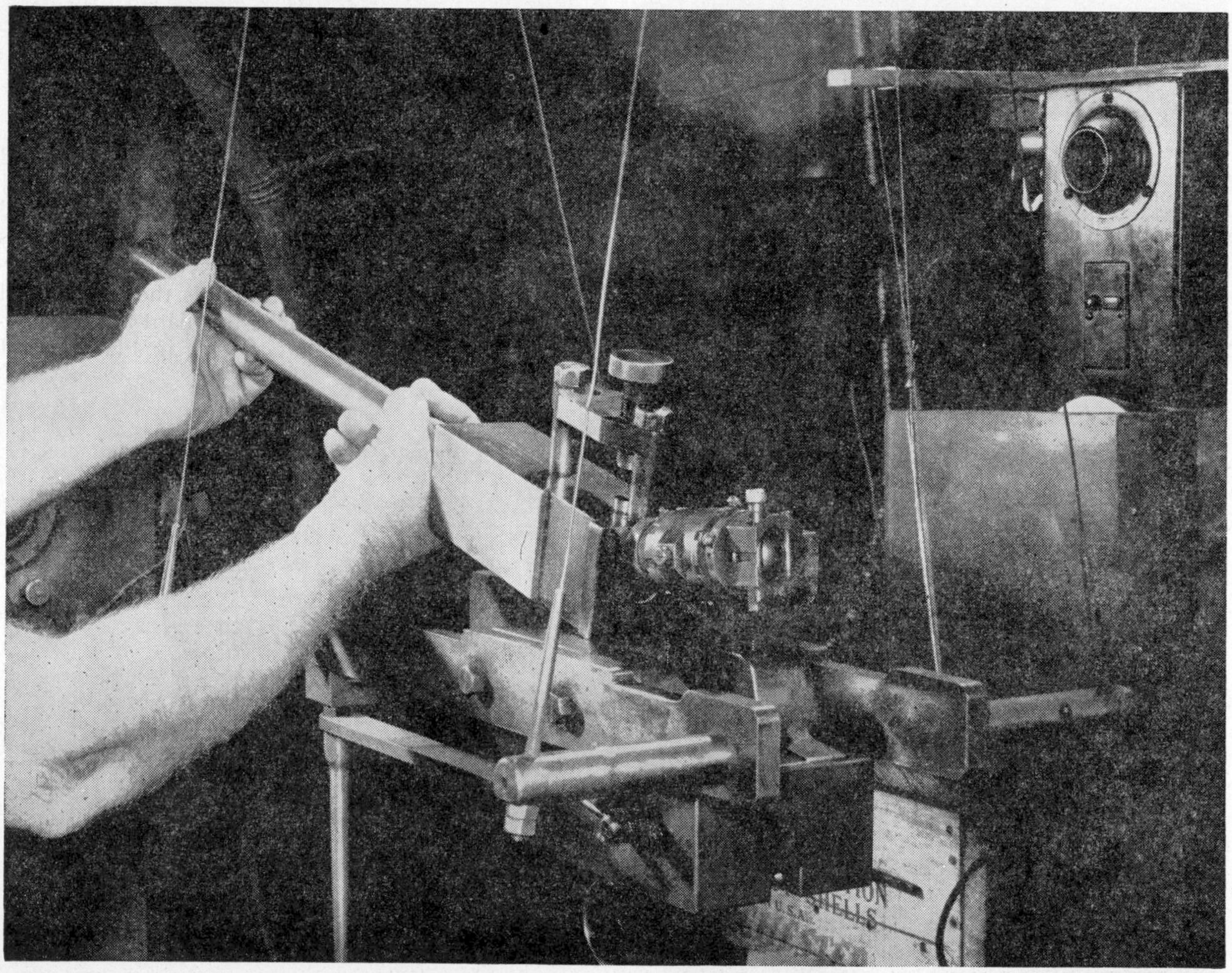

PLATE XVIII. This is the "pendulum gun," which permits the operator to make a test of velocity, time-up-the-barrel, chamber pressure, recoil, and shot pattern.

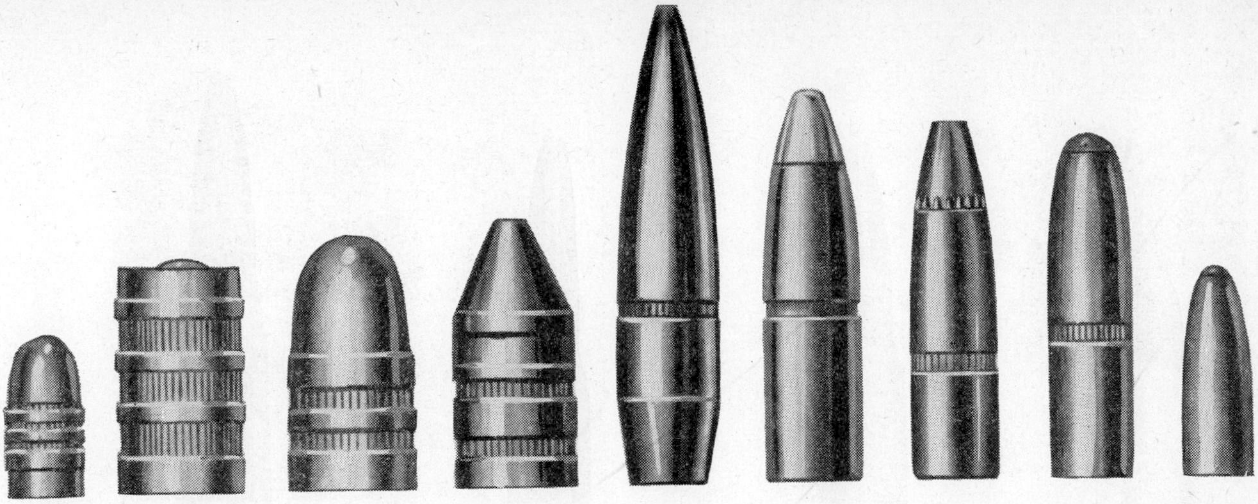

PLATE XIX. Bullet types turned out by the Western Cartridge Co. are shown here. *Left to right:* .22-caliber 40-grain lead bullet; .38 Special (revolver) clean-cutting, 148-grain lead bullet; .38 Special (pistol) 158-grain Lubaloy bullet; .357 Magnum 158-grain metal-piercing bullet; .30 '06 180-grain full metal case bullet; .30 '06 180-grain silvertip expanding bullet; .270 130-grain open-point expanding bullet; .257 Roberts 117-grain soft-point bullet; .220 Swift 48-grain soft-point bullet.

he receives the order to fire. As the pellets break the wire, the chronograph, which is an electric time-recording instrument, is set in motion. This device is halted automatically when the pellets strike the target, which is also connected electrically with the chronograph. Translating the elapsed time into feet-per-second gives the velocity of the shot.

The "time-up-the-barrel" test, to determine the speed and uniformity of the primer, is a variation of the velocity test, but is confined to the time it takes the shot to pass through the barrel. When the gun is fired, the hammer raises a ball bearing in its socket, setting a second chronograph into operation. When the pellets strike a second copper wire stretched in front of the muzzle of the barrel, the chronograph is automatically halted, and the elapsed "time-up-the-barrel" is recorded in ten-thousandths of a second. Average "time--up-the-barrel" for a 12-gauge skeet shell is .0030 seconds.

The amount of gas or breech pressure generated by the burning of smokeless powder must be carefully controlled in shotshells. The pressure is determined by directing the expanding gases to shorten or compress a clear lead cylinder.

A hole, exactly 1/25 of a square inch, is drilled through the gun barrel one inch from the breech. Into this hole is placed a piston upon which rests the lead cylinder which "records" the pressure. When the shell is fired, the upward movement of the piston compresses the cylinder. The amount of com-

PLATE XX. Super Speed .22 Hornet with 45-grain Soft-Point Bullet. Approximate Size.

PLATE XXI. Super Speed .22 Savage with 70-grain Pointed Soft-Point Bullet. Approximate Size.

PLATE XXII. Super Speed .250 Savage with 100-grain Silvertip Bullet. Approximate Size.

PLATE XXIII. .257 Roberts with 100-grain Silvertip Bullet. Approximate Size.

Plate XXIV. .30-30 Winchester with 170-grain Silvertip Bullet. Approximate Size.

Plate XXV. .30 '06 (Springfield) with 180-grain Silvertip Bullet. Approximate Size.

Plate XXVI. .270 Winchester with 130-grain Silvertip Bullet. Approximate Size.

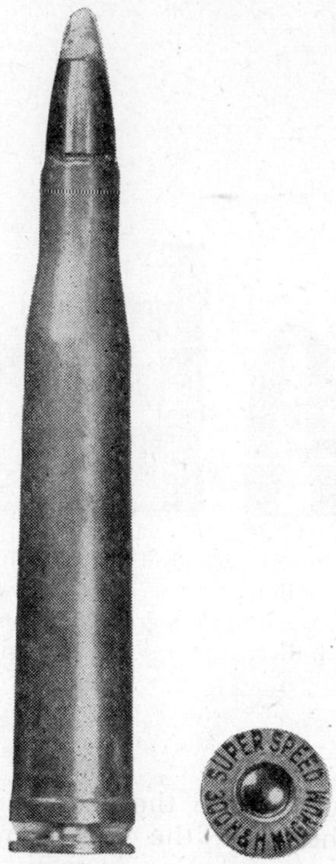


Plate XXVII. .300 H. & H. Magnum with 180-grain Silvertip Bullet. Approximate Size.

pression, in thousandths of an inch, is translated into pounds per square inch of pressure.

The pendulum gun hangs from four wires primarily to enable it to test recoil. The gun is suspended directly above a double-trace gauge, one side of which is calibrated in tenths of an inch. A "pointer" connected with the gun carriage moves back between the double-track when the gun is fired, and carries before it a sliding marker. The marker stops at the farthest point reached by the pointer. A 12-gauge skeet shell has a recoil of approximately 20 foot-pounds.

Pattern-testing consists of shooting at a paper-covered target, and counting the number of perforations in the paper within a circle that has a diameter of 30 inches. The 12-gauge skeet loads used for training aerial gunners are loaded with 1⅛ ounces of No. 8 shot, or a total of approximately 460 pellets, each about .09 inch in diameter. The effective spread of pattern is 30 inches when fired in a full-choke barrel at 40 yards.

Although there are many other tests made in the production of shotshells, the pendulum gun does the biggest job of all, in the most economical way—making one test shell serve the purpose of five.

Plate XXVIII. .300 Savage with 180-grain Silvertip Bullet. Approximate Size.

# Modern Loads and Velocities

NOTE: The data presented in these tables are standards adopted by the Sporting Arms and Ammunition Manufacturers Institute, June 21, 1940.

## *BALLISTICS OF PETERS CARTRIDGES*

### Rim-fire, with "Rustless" priming

#### High Velocity

| *Index No.* | *Cartridge* | *Bullet Weight Grains* | *Bullet Type* | *Velocity—Feet per Second Muzzle* | *Velocity—Feet per Second 100 Yards* | *Energy—Foot-Pounds Muzzle* | *Energy—Foot-Pounds 100 Yards* | *Mid-Range Trajectory Inches—100 Yards* |
|---|---|---|---|---|---|---|---|---|
| 2267 | 22 Short High Velocity | 29 | Lead | 1125 | 920 | 81 | 54 | 4.3 |
| 2268 | 22 Short Hollow Point, High Velocity | 27 | Lead | 1155 | 920 | 80 | 51 | 4.2 |
| 2269 | 22 Long High Velocity | 29 | Lead | 1240 | 965 | 99 | 60 | 3.8 |
| 2283 | 22 Long Rifle High Velocity | 40 | Lead | 1335 | 1045 | 158 | 97 | 3.3 |
| 2284 | 22 Long Rifle Hollow Point, High Velocity | 36 | Lead | 1365 | 1040 | 149 | 86 | 3.3 |
| 2291 | 22 W.R.F. (Rem. Spl.) High Velocity | 45 | Lead | 1450 | 1110 | 210 | 123 | 2.7 |

#### Target—Intermediate Velocity

| *Index No.* | *Cartridge* | *Bullet Weight Grains* | *Bullet Type* | *Velocity—Feet per Second Muzzle* | *Velocity—Feet per Second 100 Yards* | *Energy—Foot-Pounds Muzzle* | *Energy—Foot-Pounds 100 Yards* | *Mid-Range Trajectory Inches—100 Yards* |
|---|---|---|---|---|---|---|---|---|
| 2214 | 22 Short Target | 29 | Lead | 1015 | 850 | 66 | 46 | 5.0 |
| 2224 | 22 Long Rifle Target | 40 | Lead | 1230 | 1010 | 134 | 91 | 3.6 |

#### Standard Velocity

| *Index No.* | *Cartridge* | *Bullet Weight Grains* | *Bullet Type* | *Velocity—Feet per Second Muzzle* | *Velocity—Feet per Second 100 Yards* | *Energy—Foot-Pounds Muzzle* | *Energy—Foot-Pounds 100 Yards* | *Mid-Range Trajectory Inches—100 Yards* |
|---|---|---|---|---|---|---|---|---|
| 2212 | 22 B.B. Cap | 20 | Lead | 780 | .... | 24 | ... | ... |
| 2241 | 22 C.B. Cap | 29 | Lead | 720 | 605 | 33 | 24 | ... |
| 2204 | 22 Short Gallery, Krumble Ball, Lubricated | 29 | Lead | 995 | .... | 57 | ... | ... |
| 2206 | 22 Short Gallery, Krumble Ball, Lubricated | 29 | Lead | 995 | .... | 57 | ... | ... |
| 2295 | 22 Short Gallery, Krumble Ball, Filmkote | 29 | Lead | 995 | .... | 57 | ... | ... |
| 2279 | 22 Long Rifle | 40 | Lead | 1145 | 975 | 116 | 84 | 4.0 |
| 2237 | 22 Winchester Automatic | 45 | Lead | 1055 | 930 | 111 | 86 | 4.6 |
| 2239 | 22 Remington Autoloading | 45 | Lead | 920 | .... | 84 | ... | 5.5 |
| 2505 | 25 Stevens | 67 | Lead | 1130 | 985 | 184 | 140 | 3.8 |
| 3203 | 32 Short | 80 | Lead | 945 | 840 | 158 | 125 | 5.3 |
| 3206 | 32 Long | 90 | Lead | 945 | 850 | 178 | 144 | 5.3 |

#### Match Cartridges

| *Index No.* | *Cartridge* | *Bullet Weight Grains* | *Bullet Type* | *Velocity—Feet per Second Muzzle* | *Velocity—Feet per Second 100 Yards* | *Energy—Foot-Pounds Muzzle* | *Energy—Foot-Pounds 100 Yards* | *Mid-Range Trajectory Inches—100 Yards* |
|---|---|---|---|---|---|---|---|---|
| 2296 | 22 Long Rifle Dewar Match | 40 | Lead | 1145 | 975 | 116 | 84 | 4.0 |
| 2223 | 22 Long Rifle Police Match (Rifle) | 40 | Lead | 1145 | 975 | 116 | 84 | 4.0 |
| 2223 | 22 Long Rifle Police Match (Pistol) | 40 | Lead | 970 | .... | 83 | ... | ... |

## *BALLISTICS OF REMINGTON CARTRIDGES*

### "Kleanbore" Rim-fire Cartridges

| *Index No.* | *Cartridge* | *Bullet Weight Grains* | *Bullet Type* | *Velocity—Feet per Second Muzzle* | *Velocity—Feet per Second 100 Yards* | *Energy—Foot-Pounds Muzzle* | *Energy—Foot-Pounds 100 Yards* | *Mid-Range Trajectory Inches—100 Yards* |
|---|---|---|---|---|---|---|---|---|
| R11 | .22 Short | 29 | Lead | 1130 | 925 | 82 | 55 | 4.1 |
| R13 | .22 Short | 27 | H.P. | 1155 | 925 | 80 | 51 | 4.1 |
| R16 | .22 Long | 29 | Lead | 1375 | 1020 | 122 | 67 | 3.2 |
| R18 | .22 Long | 27 | H.P. | 1395 | 1010 | 117 | 61 | 3.3 |
| R21 | .22 Long Rifle | 40 | Lead | 1375 | 1080 | 168 | 104 | 2.9 |
| R23 | .22 Long Rifle | 36 | H.P. | 1400 | 1075 | 157 | 92 | 3.0 |
| R28S | .22 W.R.F. (Remington Special) | 45 | Lead | 1450 | 1110 | 210 | 123 | 2.7 |
| R28AS | .22 W.R.F. (Remington Special) | 40 | H.P. | 1475 | 1095 | 193 | 107 | 2.7 |

### New and Improved "Kleanbore"—Intermediate Velocity

| *Index No.* | *Cartridge* | *Bullet Weight Grains* | *Bullet Type* | *Velocity—Feet per Second Muzzle* | *Velocity—Feet per Second 100 Yards* | *Energy—Foot-Pounds Muzzle* | *Energy—Foot-Pounds 100 Yards* | *Mid-Range Trajectory Inches—100 Yards* |
|---|---|---|---|---|---|---|---|---|
| R12 | .22 Short | 29 | Lead | 1030 | 860 | 68 | 48 | 5.1 |
| R15 | .22 Long | 29 | Lead | 1080 | 900 | 75 | 52 | 4.3 |
| R19 | .22 Long Rifle | 40 | Lead | 1230 | 1030 | 135 | 94 | 3.8 |

## "Kleanbore"—Standard Velocity

| Index No. | Cartridge | Bullet Weight Grains | Bullet Type | Velocity—Feet per Second Muzzle | Velocity—Feet per Second 100 Yards | Energy-Foot-Pounds Muzzle | Energy-Foot-Pounds 100 Yards | Mid-Range Trajectory Inches-100 Yards |
|---|---|---|---|---|---|---|---|---|
| R2 | .22 (B.B.) Bullet Breech Caps | 20 | Lead | 780 | .... | 24 | ... | ... |
| R6 | .22 (C.B.) Conical Bullet Caps | 29 | Lead | 720 | 605 | 33 | 24 | ... |
| R326 | .22 Short Gallery Special Spatterless | 28 | Lead | 995 | .... | 57 | ... | ... |
| R17L | .22 Long Rifle | 40 | Lead | 1130 | 970 | 111 | 84 | 4.0 |
| R25 | .22 Extra Long | 40 | Lead | 1030 | 900 | 94 | 72 | 4.9 |
| R31B | .22 Remington Autoloading | 45 | Lead | 920 | .... | 85 | ... | 5.5 |
| R28 | .22 W.R.F. (Remington Special) | 45 | Lead | 1105 | 955 | 122 | 91 | 4.0 |
| R31 | .22 Winchester Automatic | 45 | Lead | 1055 | 930 | 111 | 86 | 4.6 |
| R31A | .22 Winchester Automatic | 45 | H.P. | 1055 | 930 | 111 | 86 | 4.6 |
| R57 | .25 Short Stevens | 67 | Lead | 945 | 845 | 129 | 103 | 5.6 |
| R56A | .25 Stevens | 67 | Lead | 1130 | 985 | 184 | 140 | 3.8 |
| R140 | .32 Short | 80 | Lead | 945 | 840 | 159 | 125 | 5.3 |
| R142 | .32 Long | 90 | Lead | 945 | 850 | 179 | 144 | 5.3 |
| R318 | .41 Short | 129 | Lead | 520 | .... | 78 | ... | ... |
| R326 | .41 Swiss | 300 | Lead | 1325 | 1165 | 1170 | 905 | 2.9 |

## Special Match Cartridges *

| Index No. | Cartridge | Bullet Weight Grains | Bullet Type | Velocity Muzzle | Velocity 100 Yards | Energy Muzzle | Energy 100 Yards | Mid-Range Trajectory |
|---|---|---|---|---|---|---|---|---|
| R54P | .22 Long Rifle ......Palma | 40 | Lead | 1100 | 950 | 108 | 80 | 4.3 |
| R22T | .22 Long Rifle ......Police Targetmaster | 40 | Lead | 1155 | 940 | 119 | 79 | 4.0 rifle |
| R22T | .22 Long Rifle ......Police Targetmaster | 40 | Lead | 970 | .... | 84 | ... | pistol |

* "Lesmok" Powder—*Not* "Kleanbore."

## BALLISTICS OF WESTERN CARTRIDGES *

| Primer No. | Cartridge | Weight Grains | Bullet Type | Velocity—Feet per Second Muzzle | Velocity—Feet per Second 100 Yards | Energy—Foot-Pounds Muzzle | Energy—Foot-Pounds 100 Yards | Mid-Range Trajectory Inches—100 Yards |
|---|---|---|---|---|---|---|---|---|
| ... | 22BB | 19 | Lubaloy C'd | 780 | 570 | 24 | 13 | ... |
| ... | 22CB Greased | 29 | Lubaloy C'd | 720 | 605 | 33 | 24 | ... |
| ... | 22 Short KANT-SPLASH Greased | 24 | Synthetic | 970 | ..... | ..... | ..... | ... |
| ... | 22 Short SUPER-X Wax Coated | 29 | Lubaloy C'd | 1,130 | 925 | 85 | 55 | 4.1 |
| ... | 22 Short H. P. SUPER-X Wax Coated | 27 | Lubaloy C'd | 1,155 | 925 | 80 | 51 | 4.1 |
| ... | 22 Short XPERT Greased | 29 | Lead | 1,030 | 860 | 68 | 48 | 5.1 |
| ... | 22 Long SUPER-X Wax Coated | 29 | Lubaloy C'd | 1,375 | 1,020 | 122 | 67 | 3.2 |
| ... | 22 Long Rifle SUPER-X Wax Coated | 40 | Lubaloy C'd | 1,375 | 1,080 | 168 | 104 | 2.9 |
| ... | 22 Long Rifle H. P. SUPER-X Wax Coated | 37 | Lubaloy C'd | 1,400 | 1,075 | 161 | 95 | 3.0 |
| ... | 22 Long Rifle Shot SUPER-X Clay Target | .. | No. 12 Shot | ..... | ..... | ..... | ..... | .. |
| ... | 22 Long Rifle XPERT Greased | 40 | Lead | 1,180 | 995 | 124 | 88 | 3.8 |
| ... | 22 Long Rifle SUPER-MATCH Mark II Greased | 40 | Lead | 1,160 | 985 | 120 | 86 | 3.8 |
| ... | 22 W. R. F. (22 Rem. Spec.) SUPER-X Inside Lub | 45 | Lubaloy C'd | 1,450 | 1,110 | 210 | 123 | 2.7 |
| ... | 22 W. R. F., H. P. SUPER-X Inside Lubricated | 45 | Lubaloy C'd | 1,450 | 1,110 | 210 | 123 | 2.7 |
| ... | 22 Win. Auto. Inside Lubricated | 45 | Lubaloy C'd | 1,055 | 930 | 111 | 86 | 4.6 |
| ... | 22 Win. Auto. H. P. Inside Lubricated | 45 | Lubaloy C'd | 1,055 | 930 | 111 | 86 | 4.6 |
| ... | 22 Rem. Auto. Inside Lubricated | 45 | Lubaloy C'd | 920 | ..... | 84 | ..... | 5.5 |
| ... | 25 Short Stevens Inside Lubricated | 65 | Lubaloy C'd | 945 | 845 | 129 | 103 | 5.6 |
| ... | 25 Stevens Inside Lubricated | 65 | Lubaloy C'd | 1,130 | 985 | 184 | 140 | 3.8 |
| ... | 32 Short Greased | 80 | Lubaloy C'd | 945 | 840 | 159 | 125 | 5.3 |
| ... | 32 Long Greased | 90 | Lubaloy C'd | 945 | 850 | 179 | 144 | 5.3 |
| 6½ | 218 Bee SUPER-X | 46 | Op. Pt. Exp. | 2,860 | 2,260 | 835 | 520 | 0.7 |
| 8½ | 219 Zipper SUPER-X | 56 | Op. Pt. Exp. | 3,050 | 2,530 | 1,155 | 795 | 0.6 |
| 6½ | 22 Hornet SUPER-X | 46 | Op. Pt. Exp. | 2,650 | 2,090 | 715 | 445 | 0.8 |
| 6½ | 22 Hornet SUPER-X | 45 | Soft Point | 2,650 | 2,080 | 700 | 430 | 0.8 |
| 8½ | 220 Swift SUPER-X | 48 | Soft Point | 4,140 | 3,490 | 1,825 | 1,300 | 0.3 |
| 8½ | 22 Savage SUPER-X | 70 | Soft Point | 2,780 | 2,480 | 1,200 | 955 | 0.6 |
| 6½ | 25-20 Winchester Inside Lubricated | 86 | Lubaloy C'd | 1,450 | 1,190 | 400 | 270 | 2.6 |
| 6½ | 25-20 Winchester | 86 | Metal Case | 1,450 | 1,190 | 400 | 270 | 2.6 |
| 6½ | 25-20 Winchester | 86 | Soft Point | 1,450 | 1,190 | 400 | 270 | 2.6 |
| 6½ | 25-20 Winchester High Velocity SUPER-X | 60 | Op. Pt. Exp. | 2,210 | 1,700 | 650 | 385 | 1.1 |
| 8½ | 25 Remington-Auto. Load SUPER-X | 117 | S. P. B. T. | 2,300 | 2,020 | 1,375 | 1,000 | 0.9 |
| 8½ | 25-35 Winchester SUPER-X | 117 | Metal Case | 2,280 | 1,970 | 1,350 | 1,010 | 1.5 |
| 8½ | 25-35 Winchester SUPER-X | 117 | S. P. B. T. | 2,280 | 1,970 | 1,350 | 1,010 | 1.0 |
| 8½ | 250 Savage SUPER-X | 87 | Soft Point | 3,000 | 2,710 | 1,740 | 1,420 | 0.5 |
| 8½ | 250 Savage SUPER-X | 100 | Op. Pt. Exp. | 2,810 | 2,490 | 1,755 | 1,375 | 0.6 |
| 8½ | 6.5m/m Mannlicher-Schoenauer | 160 | Soft Point | 2,160 | 1,950 | 1,660 | 1,350 | 1.0 |
| 8½ | 257 Roberts SUPER-X | 100 | Op. Pt. Exp. | 2,900 | 2,570 | 1,870 | 1,465 | 0.6 |
| 8½ | 257 Roberts SUPER-X | 117 | Soft Point | 2,630 | 2,330 | 1,800 | 1,410 | 0.7 |
| 8½ | 270 Winchester SUPER-X | 130 | O.P.E. B.T. | 3,140 | 2,820 | 2,850 | 2,295 | 0.5 |
| 8½ | 270 Winchester SUPER-X | 150 | Soft Point | 2,770 | 2,490 | 2,560 | 2,065 | 0.6 |

* All cartridges loaded with smokeless powder.

## Western Rifle Cartridges—Specifications and Ballistics—Continued

| | | Weight Grains | Bullet Type | Velocity—Feet per Second Muzzle | 100 Yards | Energy—Foot-Pounds Muzzle | 100 Yards | Mid-Range Trajectory Inches—100 Yards |
|---|---|---|---|---|---|---|---|---|
| 8½ | 7m/m Mauser SUPER-X | 175 | S. P. B. T. | 2,460 | 2,220 | 2,350 | 1,915 | 0.8 |
| 8½ | 30-30 Winchester SUPER-X | 170 | M.C. B.T. | 2,200 | 1,930 | 1,830 | 1,405 | 1.0 |
| 8½ | 30-30 Winchester SUPER-X | 170 | S. P. B. T. | 2,200 | 1,930 | 1,830 | 1,405 | 1.0 |
| 8½ | 30-30 Winchester SUPER-X | 150 | Op. Pt. Exp. | 2,380 | 2,060 | 1,890 | 1,415 | 0.9 |
| 8½ | 30 Remington SUPER-X | 170 | S. P. B. T. | 2,200 | 1,930 | 1,830 | 1,405 | 1.0 |
| 8½ | 30 Remington SUPER-X | 165 | O.P.E. B.T. | 2,200 | 1,920 | 1,770 | 1,350 | 1.0 |
| 8½ | 30-60 Springfield SUPER-X | 150 | Op. Pt. Exp. | 2,980 | 2,650 | 2,960 | 2,340 | 0.6 |
| 8½ | 30-06 Springfield SUPER-X | 180 | M.C. B.T. | 2,720 | 2,400 | 2,960 | 2,300 | 0.7 |
| 8½ | 30-06 Springfield SUPER-X | 180 | Soft Point | 2,710 | 2,420 | 2,940 | 2,340 | 0.7 |
| 8½ | 30-06 Springfield SUPER-X | 180 | O.P.E. B.T. | 2,710 | 2,420 | 2,940 | 2,340 | 0.7 |
| 8½ | 30-06 Springfield SUPER-match | 180 | M.C. B.T. | 2,690 | 2,500 | 2,895 | 2,500 | 0.6 |
| 8½ | 30-06 Springfield SUPER-X | 220 | S. P. B. T. | 2,410 | 2,190 | 2,840 | 2,345 | 0.8 |
| 8½ | 30-40 Krag SUPER-X | 180 | Soft Point | 2,480 | 2,210 | 2,460 | 1,955 | 0.8 |
| 8½ | 30-40 Krag SUPER-X | 180 | O.P.E. B.T. | 2,480 | 2,210 | 2,460 | 1,955 | 0.7 |
| 8½ | 30-40 Krag Blank | ... | Paper Bullet | ..... | ..... | ..... | ..... | ... |
| 8½ | 300 H. & H. Magnum SUPER-X | 220 | S. P. B. T. | 2,610 | 2,380 | 3,330 | 2,770 | 0.7 |
| 8½ | 300 H. & H. Magnum SUPER-Match | 180 | M.C. B.T. | 3,030 | 2,820 | 3,670 | 3,180 | 0.5 |
| 8½ | 300 Savage SUPER-X | 150 | Op. Pt. Exp. | 2,680 | 2,380 | 2,390 | 1,890 | 0.7 |
| 8½ | 300 Savage SUPER-X | 180 | Soft Point | 2,380 | 2,140 | 2,265 | 1,830 | 0.8 |
| 8½ | 303 Savage SUPER-X | 190 | Soft Point | 1,960 | 1,740 | 1,620 | 1,280 | 1.3 |
| 8½ | 303 British SUPER-X | 215 | S. P. B. T. | 2,160 | 1,940 | 2,230 | 1,795 | 1.0 |
| 8½ | 32 Winchester Special SUPER-X | 170 | S. P. B. T. | 2,260 | 1,960 | 1,930 | 1,450 | 1.0 |
| 8½ | 32 Winchester Special SUPER-X | 165 | O.P.E. B.T. | 2,260 | 1,950 | 1,870 | 1,395 | 1.0 |
| 6½ | 32 Winchester Self-Loading (Oilproof) | 165 | Soft Point | 1,390 | 1,190 | 710 | 520 | 2.6 |
| 8½ | 32 Remington SUPER-X | 170 | S. P. B. T. | 2,200 | 1,910 | 1,830 | 1,380 | 1.0 |
| 8½ | 32 Remington SUPER-X | 165 | O.P.E. B.T. | 2,200 | 1,900 | 1,775 | 1,325 | 1.0 |
| 6½ | 32-20 Winchester (Oilproof) Inside Lubricated | 115 | Lubaloy C'd | 1,280 | 1,080 | 420 | 300 | 3.1 |
| 6½ | 32-20 Winchester (Oilproof) | 115 | Metal Case | 1,280 | 1,080 | 420 | 300 | 3.1 |
| ... | 32-20 Winchester (Oilproof) | 115 | Soft Point | 1,280 | 1,180 | 420 | 300 | 3.1 |
| 6½ | 32-20 Winchester High-Velocity SUPER-X | 80 | Op. Pt. Exp. | 2,050 | 1,520 | 745 | 410 | 1.4 |
| 8½ | 32-40 Winchester | 165 | S. P. B. T. | 1,440 | 1,230 | 760 | 555 | 2.6 |
| 8½ | 33 Winchester | 200 | Soft Point | 2,180 | 1,870 | 2,110 | 1,555 | 1.1 |
| 8½ | 8m/m Mannlicher-Schoenauer | 200 | Soft Point | 2,150 | 1,940 | 2,055 | 1,670 | 1.1 |
| 8½ | 348 Winchester SUPER-X | 150 | Soft Point | 2,880 | 2,380 | 2,765 | 1,890 | 0.6 |
| 8½ | 348 Winchester SUPER-X | 200 | Soft Point | 2,520 | 2,160 | 2,820 | 2,075 | 0.8 |
| 8½ | 35 Winchester | 250 | Soft Point | 2,160 | 1,910 | 2,590 | 2,025 | 1.1 |
| 6½ | 35 Winchester Self-Loading Rifle (Oilproof) | 180 | Soft Point | 1,390 | 1,170 | 775 | 545 | 2.5 |
| 8½ | Remington Auto. Load SUPER-X | 200 | Soft Point | 2,180 | 1,870 | 2,110 | 1,555 | 1.0 |
| 8½ | 35 Remington Auto. Load SUPER-X | 200 | Op. Pt. Exp. | 2,180 | 1,870 | 2,110 | 1,555 | 1.0 |
| 6½ | 351 Winchester Self-Loading Rifle (Oilproof) | 180 | Metal Case | 1,850 | 1,560 | 1,370 | 975 | 1.5 |
| 6½ | 351 Winchester Self-Loading Rifle (Oilproof) | 180 | Soft Point | 1,850 | 1,560 | 1,370 | 975 | 1. |
| 8½ | 375 H. & H. Magnum (Rm'l B'td.) SUPER-X | 235 | Op. Pt. Exp. | 2,860 | 2,520 | 4,270 | 3,315 | 0.6 |
| 8½ | 375 H. & H. Magnum (Rm'l B'td.) SUPER-X | 270 | Soft Point | 2,720 | 2,460 | 4,440 | 3,630 | 0.7 |
| 7 | 38-40 Winchester (Oilproof) | 180 | Soft Point | 1,310 | 1,090 | 685 | 475 | 3.2 |
| 8½ | 38-55 Winchester | 255 | Soft Point | 1,320 | 1,150 | 985 | 750 | 3.0 |
| 8½ | 401 Winchester Self-Loading Rifle (Oilproof) | 200 | Soft Point | 2,140 | 1,750 | 2,035 | 1,360 | 1.1 |
| 8½ | 405 Winchester | 300 | Soft Point | 2,220 | 1,940 | 3,285 | 2,510 | 1.0 |
| 7 | 44-40 Winchester (Oilproof) | 200 | Soft Point | 1,300 | 1,070 | 750 | 510 | 3.3 |
| 8½ | 45-70 Government | 405 | Soft Point | 1,310 | 1,160 | 1,545 | 1,210 | 2.8 |

## Center-fire, with "Rustless" Priming

| Index No. | Cartridge | Bullet Wgt. Grs. | Type | Velocity—Feet per Second Muzzle | 100 Yds. | 200 Yds. | 300 Yds. | Energy—Foot-Pounds Muzzle | 100 Yds. | 200 Yds. | 300 Yds. | Mid-Range Trajectory Inches—100 Yds. |
|---|---|---|---|---|---|---|---|---|---|---|---|---|
| 2274 | 22 Hornet High Velocity | 45 | M.C.H.P. | 2650 | 2080 | 1580 | 1220 | 700 | 430 | 250 | 150 | 0.8 |
| 2276 | 22 Hornet High Velocity | 45 | S.P. | 2650 | 2080 | 1580 | 1220 | 700 | 430 | 250 | 150 | 0.8 |
| 2271 | 22 Savage H.V. Inner-Belted | 70 | I.B.S.P. | 2780 | 2480 | 2200 | 1940 | 1200 | 955 | 755 | 585 | 0.6 |
| 2552 | 25-20 Winchester | 86 | Lead | 1450 | 1190 | 1050 | 950 | 400 | 270 | 210 | 175 | 2.6 |
| 2553 | 25-20 Winchester | 86 | S.P. | 1450 | 1190 | 1050 | 950 | 400 | 270 | 210 | 175 | 2.6 |
| 2554 | 25-20 Winchester | 86 | M.C. | 1450 | 1190 | 1050 | 950 | 400 | 270 | 210 | 175 | 2.6 |
| 2555 | 25-20 Winchester High Velocity | 60 | M.C.H.P. | 2210 | 1700 | 1300 | 1060 | 650 | 385 | 225 | 150 | 1.1 |
| 2569 | 250 Savage H.V. Inner-Belted | 100 | I.B.H.P. | 2810 | 2490 | 2180 | 1900 | 1755 | 1375 | 1055 | 800 | 0.6 |
| 2568 | 250 Savage H.V. Inner-Belted | 100 | I.B.S.P. | 2810 | 2490 | 2180 | 1900 | 1755 | 1375 | 1055 | 800 | 0.6 |
| 2572 | 250 Savage High Velocity | 87 | S.P. | 3000 | 2710 | 2430 | 2170 | 1740 | 1420 | 1140 | 910 | 0.5 |
| 2575 | 25-35 Winchester | 117 | M.C. | 2280 | 1970 | 1690 | 1440 | 1350 | 1010 | 740 | 540 | 1.0 |
| 2582 | 25-35 Winchester H.V. Inner-Belted | 117 | I.B.S.P. | 2280 | 1970 | 1690 | 1440 | 1350 | 1010 | 740 | 540 | 1.0 |
| 2584 | 257 Roberts H.V. Inner-Belted | 117 | I.B.S.P. | 2630 | 2330 | 2050 | 1790 | 1800 | 1410 | 1095 | 835 | 0.7 |
| 2579 | 25 Remington H.V. Inner-Belted | 117 | I.B.S.P. | 2300 | 2020 | 1760 | 1530 | 1375 | 1060 | 805 | 610 | 0.9 |
| 2702 | 270 Winchester H.V. Inner Belted | 150 | I.B.S.P. | 2770 | 2490 | 2220 | 1970 | 2560 | 2065 | 1645 | 1295 | 0.6 |
| 2703 | 270 Winchester H.V. Inner-Belted | 130 | I.B.H.P. | 3140 | 2820 | 2530 | 2260 | 2850 | 2295 | 1850 | 1470 | 0.5 |
| 2801 | 7 m/m Mauser | 175 | S.P. | 2460 | 2220 | 1990 | 1780 | 2350 | 1915 | 1540 | 1230 | 0.8 |
| 3064 | 30-30 Winchester High Velocity | 160 | M.C. | 2200 | 1910 | 1650 | 1420 | 1720 | 1295 | 970 | 720 | 1.0 |
| 3043 | 30-30 Winchester H.V. Inner-Belted | 170 | I.B.H.P. | 2200 | 1930 | 1680 | 1460 | 1830 | 1405 | 1065 | 805 | 1.0 |
| 3044 | 30-30 Winchester H.V. Inner-Belted | 150 | I.B.S.P. | 2380 | 2060 | 1770 | 1510 | 1890 | 1415 | 1045 | 760 | 0.9 |
| 3058 | 30-30 Winchester H.V. Inner-Belted | 170 | I.B.S.P. | 2200 | 1930 | 1680 | 1460 | 1830 | 1405 | 1065 | 805 | 1.0 |

## Center-fire, with "Rustless" Priming—Continued

| Index No. | Cartridge | Bullet Wgt. Grs. | Bullet Type | Velocity—Feet per Second Muzzle | 100 Yds. | 200 Yds. | 300 Yds. | Energy—Foot-Pounds Muzzle | 100 Yds. | 200 Yds. | 300 Yds. | Mid-Range Trajectory Inches—100 Yds. |
|---|---|---|---|---|---|---|---|---|---|---|---|---|
| 3066 | 30 Remington | 160 | M.C. | 2200 | 1910 | 1650 | 1420 | 1720 | 1295 | 970 | 720 | 1.0 |
| 3048 | 30 Remington H.V. Inner-Belted | 170 | I.B.H.P. | 2200 | 1930 | 1680 | 1460 | 1830 | 1405 | 1065 | 805 | 1.0 |
| 3054 | 30 Remington H.V. Inner-Belted | 170 | I.B.S.P. | 2200 | 1930 | 1680 | 1460 | 1830 | 1405 | 1065 | 805 | 1.0 |
| 3046 | 30-40 Krag H.V. Inner-Belted | 180 | I.B.S.P. | 2480 | 2210 | 1950 | 1710 | 2460 | 1955 | 1520 | 1170 | 0.8 |
| 3049 | 30-40 Krag H.V. Inner-Belted | 220 | I.B.H.P. | 2190 | 1980 | 1780 | 1600 | 2345 | 1915 | 1550 | 1250 | 1.0 |
| 3047 | 30 40 Krag H.V. Inner-Belted | 220 | I.B.S.P. | 2190 | 1980 | 1780 | 1600 | 2345 | 1915 | 1550 | 1250 | 1.0 |
| 3045 | 30-40 Krag H.V. Inner-Belted | 180 | I.B.H.P. | 2480 | 2210 | 1950 | 1710 | 2460 | 1955 | 1520 | 1170 | 0.8 |
| 3077 | 30-06 Springfield | 150 | P.P.Exp. | 2960 | 2720 | 2480 | 2260 | 2920 | 2465 | 2050 | 1700 | 0.5 |
| 3079 | 30-06 Springfield Pointed Taper Heel | 180 | M.C. | 2730 | 2540 | 2350 | 2170 | 2975 | 2575 | 2205 | 1880 | 0.6 |
| 3080 | 30-06 Springfield High Velocity | 180 | P.P.Exp. | 2690 | 2500 | 2310 | 2130 | 2895 | 2500 | 2135 | 1815 | 0.6 |
| 3031 | 30-06 Springfield | 150 | M.C. | 2800 | 2560 | 2340 | 2120 | 2610 | 2185 | 1825 | 1500 | 0.6 |
| 3037 | 30-06 Springfield H.V. Inner-Belted | 180 | I.B.H.P. | 2710 | 2420 | 2150 | 1900 | 2940 | 2340 | 1850 | 1445 | 0.7 |
| 3036 | 30-06 Springfield H.V. Inner-Belted | 220 | I.B.H.P. | 2410 | 2190 | 1970 | 1780 | 2840 | 2345 | 1900 | 1550 | 0.8 |
| 3038 | 30-06 Springfield H.V. Inner-Belted | 220 | I.B.S.P. | 2410 | 2190 | 1970 | 1780 | 2840 | 2345 | 1900 | 1550 | 0.8 |
| 3056 | 30-06 Springfield H.V. Inner-Belted | 180 | I.B.S.P. | 2710 | 2420 | 2150 | 1900 | 2940 | 2340 | 1850 | 1445 | 0.7 |
| 3027 | 300 H.&H. Magnum H.V. Inner-Belted | 220 | I.B.H.P. | 2610 | 2380 | 2160 | 1950 | 3330 | 2770 | 2280 | 1860 | 0.7 |
| 3084 | 300 Savage High Velocity | 150 | P.P.Exp. | 2660 | 2430 | 2210 | 2000 | 2360 | 1970 | 1625 | 1325 | 0.7 |
| 3022 | Savage H.V. Inner-Belted | 180 | I.B.H.P. | 2380 | 2140 | 1910 | 1700 | 2265 | 1830 | 1460 | 1155 | 0.8 |
| 3019 | Savage H.V. Inner-Belted | 150 | I.B.S.P. | 2660 | 2430 | 2210 | 2000 | 2360 | 1970 | 1625 | 1325 | 0.7 |
| 3021 | Savage H.V. Inner-Belted | 180 | I.B.S.P. | 2380 | 2140 | 1910 | 1700 | 2265 | 1830 | 1460 | 1155 | 0.8 |
| 3085 | 303 British | 215 | S.P. | 2160 | 1940 | 1740 | 1550 | 2230 | 1795 | 1445 | 1145 | 1.0 |
| 3032 | 303 Savage H.V. Inner-Belted | 180 | I.B.H.P. | 2120 | 1840 | 1590 | 1370 | 1800 | 1360 | 1010 | 750 | 1.0 |
| 3035 | 303 Savage H.V. Inner-Belted | 180 | I.B.S.P. | 2120 | 1840 | 1590 | 1370 | 1800 | 1360 | 1010 | 750 | 1.0 |
| 3101 | 8 m/m Mauser | 170 | S.P. | 2530 | 2210 | 1920 | 1660 | 2415 | 1845 | 1390 | 1040 | 0.8 |
| 3269 | 32-20 Winchester | 100 | Lead | 1280 | 1060 | 940 | 850 | 365 | 250 | 195 | 160 | 3.1 |
| 3270 | 32-20 Winchester | 100 | S.P. | 1280 | 1060 | 940 | 850 | 365 | 250 | 195 | 160 | 3.1 |
| 3271 | 32-20 Winchester | 100 | M.C. | 1280 | 1060 | 940 | 850 | 365 | 250 | 195 | 160 | 3.1 |
| 3272 | 32-20 Winchester High Velocity | 80 | M.C.H.P. | 2050 | 1520 | 1150 | 980 | 745 | 410 | 235 | 170 | 1.4 |
| 3278 | 32 Winchester Spl. H.V. Inner-Belted | 170 | I.B.H.P. | 2260 | 1960 | 1690 | 1450 | 1930 | 1450 | 1080 | 795 | 1.0 |
| 3279 | 32 Winchester Spl. H.V. Inner-Belted | 170 | I.B.S.P. | 2260 | 1960 | 1690 | 1450 | 1930 | 1450 | 1080 | 795 | 1.0 |
| 3283 | 32 Winchester Self-Loading | 165 | S.P. | 1390 | 1190 | 1060 | 980 | 710 | 520 | 410 | 350 | 2.6 |
| 3295 | 32 Remington H.V. Inner-Belted | 170 | I.B.H.P. | 2200 | 1910 | 1640 | 1400 | 1830 | 1380 | 1015 | 740 | 1.0 |
| 3292 | 32 Remington H.V. Inner-Belted | 170 | I.B.S.P. | 2200 | 1910 | 1640 | 1400 | 1830 | 1380 | 1015 | 740 | 1.0 |
| 3288 | 32-40 Winchester | 165 | S.P. | 1440 | 1230 | 1080 | 1000 | 760 | 555 | 430 | 365 | 2.6 |
| 3391 | 33 Winchester | 200 | S.P. | 2180 | 1870 | 1600 | 1360 | 2110 | 1555 | 1135 | 820 | 1.1 |
| 3481 | 348 Winchester High Velocity | 150 | S.P. | 2880 | 2380 | 1930 | 1550 | 2765 | 1890 | 1240 | 800 | 0.6 |
| 3483 | 348 Winchester H.V. Inner-Belted | 200 | I.B.H.P. | 2520 | 2160 | 1840 | 1560 | 2820 | 2075 | 1505 | 1080 | 0.8 |
| 3484 | 348 Winchester H.V. Inner-Belted | 200 | I.B.S.P. | 2520 | 2160 | 1840 | 1560 | 2820 | 2075 | 1505 | 1080 | 0.8 |
| 3581 | 35 Winchester Self-loading | 180 | S.P. | 1390 | 1170 | 1040 | 960 | 775 | 545 | 430 | 370 | 2.5 |
| 3584 | 35 Remington High Velocity | 200 | M.C. | 2180 | 1870 | 1590 | 1360 | 2110 | 1555 | 1125 | 820 | 1.0 |
| 3594 | 35 Remington H.V. Inner-Belted | 200 | I.B.H.P. | 2180 | 1870 | 1590 | 1360 | 2110 | 1555 | 1125 | 820 | 1.0 |
| 3589 | 35 Remington H.V. Inner-Belted | 200 | I.B.S.P. | 2180 | 1870 | 1590 | 1360 | 2110 | 1555 | 1125 | 820 | 1.0 |
| 3585 | 351 Winchester Self-Loading | 180 | S.P. | 1850 | 1560 | 1310 | 1140 | 1370 | 975 | 685 | 520 | 1.5 |
| 3586 | 351 Winchester Self-Loading | 177 | M.C. | 1850 | 1560 | 1310 | 1140 | 1370 | 975 | 685 | 520 | 1.5 |
| 3856 | 38-40 Winchester | 180 | S.P. | 1310 | 1090 | 960 | 870 | 685 | 475 | 370 | 305 | 3.2 |
| 3872 | 38-55 Winchester | 255 | S.P. | 1320 | 1150 | 1050 | 980 | 985 | 750 | 625 | 545 | 3.0 |
| 4409 | 44-40 Winchester | 200 | S.P. | 1300 | 1070 | 940 | 860 | 750 | 510 | 390 | 330 | 3.3 |
| 4553 | 45-70 Government | 405 | S.P. | 1310 | 1160 | 1060 | 990 | 1545 | 1210 | 1010 | 880 | 2.8 |

Velocities when fired in revolvers are 300 f.p.s. to 400 f.p.s. lower than when fired in rifles.

Abbreviations: S. P.—Soft Point; H. P.—Hollow Point; M. P.—Metal Point; M. C.—Metal Cased; M. C. H. P.—Metal Cased, Hollow Point; H.V.—High Velocity; P. P. Exp.—Protected Point Expanding; Spl.—Special; I.B.—Inner-Belted

## GAME CARTRIDGES WITH "CORE-LOKT" BULLETS

### With "Kleanbore" Priming

| Index No. | Cartridge | Bullet Wgt. Grs. | Bullet Type | Velocity Muzzle | 100 Yds. | 200 Yds. | 300 Yds. | Energy Muzzle | 100 Yds. | 200 Yds. | 300 Yds. | Mid-Range Trajectory 100 Yds. |
|---|---|---|---|---|---|---|---|---|---|---|---|---|
| R432 | .22 Savage Hi-Power | 70 | S.P. | 2780 | 2480 | 2200 | 1940 | 1200 | 955 | 755 | 585 | 0.6 |
| R435 | .25 Remington Express | 117 | S.P. | 2300 | 2020 | 1760 | 1530 | 1375 | 1060 | 805 | 610 | 0.9 |
| R84 | .25 Remington Express | 117 | Mush. | 2300 | 2020 | 1760 | 1530 | 1375 | 1060 | 805 | 610 | 0.9 |
| R85 | .257 Rem.-Rob. Hi-Speed | 100 | Mush. | 2900 | 2530 | 2190 | 1870 | 1870 | 1420 | 1065 | 775 | 0.6 |
| R431 | .257 Rem.-Rob. Express | 117 | S.P. | 2630 | 2330 | 2050 | 1790 | 1800 | 1410 | 1095 | 835 | 0.7 |
| R439 | .25-35 Winchester Express | 117 | S.P. | 2280 | 1970 | 1690 | 1440 | 1350 | 1010 | 740 | 540 | 1.0 |
| R72 | .25-35 Winchester Express | 117 | Mush. | 2280 | 1970 | 1690 | 1440 | 1350 | 1010 | 740 | 540 | 1.0 |
| R472 | .250 Savage Hi-Speed | 100 | Mush. | 2810 | 2490 | 2180 | 1900 | 1755 | 1375 | 1055 | 800 | 0.6 |
| R433 | .250 Savage Hi-Speed | 100 | S.P. | 2810 | 2490 | 2180 | 1900 | 1755 | 1375 | 1055 | 800 | 0.6 |
| R494 | .270 Winchester Hi-Speed | 130 | Mush. | 3140 | 2820 | 2530 | 2260 | 2850 | 2295 | 1850 | 1470 | 0.5 |
| R130 | .30-30 Winchester Express | 170 | Mush. | 2200 | 1930 | 1680 | 1460 | 1830 | 1405 | 1065 | 805 | 1.0 |
| R440 | .30-30 Winchester Express | 170 | S.P. | 2200 | 1930 | 1680 | 1460 | 1830 | 1405 | 1065 | 805 | 1.0 |
| R450 | .30-30 Winchester Express | 150 | S.P. | 2380 | 2060 | 1770 | 1510 | 1890 | 1415 | 1045 | 760 | 0.9 |
| R130 | .30 Remington Express | 170 | Mush. | 2200 | 1930 | 1680 | 1460 | 1830 | 1405 | 1065 | 805 | 1.0 |
| R436 | .30 Remington Express | 170 | S.P. | 2200 | 1930 | 1680 | 1460 | 1830 | 1405 | 1065 | 805 | 1.0 |
| R100 | .30-40 Krag Express | 220 | Mush. | 2190 | 1980 | 1780 | 1600 | 2345 | 1915 | 1550 | 1250 | 1.0 |
| R442 | .30-40 Krag Express | 220 | S.P. | 2190 | 1980 | 1780 | 1600 | 2345 | 1915 | 1550 | 1250 | 1.0 |
| R101 | .30-40 Krag Hi-Speed | 180 | Mush. | 2480 | 2210 | 1950 | 1710 | 2460 | 1955 | 1520 | 1170 | 0.8 |
| R441 | .30-40 Krag Hi-Speed | 180 | S.P. | 2480 | 2210 | 1950 | 1710 | 2460 | 1955 | 1520 | 1170 | 0.8 |
| R135 | .30-06 Springfield Hi-Speed | 180 | Mush. | 2710 | 2420 | 2150 | 1900 | 2940 | 2340 | 1850 | 1445 | 0.7 |
| R443 | .30-06 Springfield Hi-Speed | 180 | S.P. | 2710 | 2420 | 2150 | 1900 | 2940 | 2340 | 1850 | 1445 | 0.7 |
| R138 | .30-06 Springfield Express | 220 | Mush. | 2410 | 2190 | 1970 | 1780 | 2840 | 2345 | 1900 | 1550 | 0.8 |
| R444 | .30-06 Springfield Express | 220 | S.P. | 2410 | 2190 | 1970 | 1780 | 2840 | 2345 | 1900 | 1550 | 0.8 |
| R464 | .300 Savage Hi-Speed | 150 | S.P. | 2660 | 2430 | 2210 | 2000 | 2360 | 1970 | 1625 | 1325 | 0.7 |
| R465 | .300 Savage Express | 180 | Mush. | 2380 | 2140 | 1910 | 1700 | 2265 | 1830 | 1460 | 1155 | 0.8 |
| R445 | .300 Savage Express | 180 | S.P. | 2380 | 2140 | 1910 | 1700 | 2265 | 1830 | 1460 | 1155 | 0.8 |
| R466 | .300 Magnum Express | 220 | Mush. | 2730 | 2490 | 2270 | 2050 | 3640 | 3030 | 2520 | 2055 | 0.6 |
| R475 | .303 Savage Express | 180 | Mush. | 2120 | 1870 | 1640 | 1430 | 1800 | 1400 | 1075 | 820 | 1.0 |
| R446 | .303 Savage Express | 180 | S.P. | 2120 | 1870 | 1640 | 1430 | 1800 | 1400 | 1075 | 820 | 1.0 |
| R191 | .32 Win. Special Express | 170 | Mush. | 2260 | 1960 | 1690 | 1450 | 1930 | 1450 | 1080 | 795 | 1.0 |
| R447 | .32 Win. Special Express | 170 | S.P. | 2260 | 1960 | 1690 | 1450 | 1930 | 1450 | 1080 | 795 | 1.0 |
| R199 | .32 Remington Express | 170 | Mush. | 2200 | 1910 | 1640 | 1400 | 1830 | 1380 | 1015 | 740 | 1.0 |
| R437 | .32 Remington Express | 170 | S.P. | 2200 | 1910 | 1640 | 1400 | 1830 | 1380 | 1015 | 740 | 1.0 |
| R217 | .348 Winchester Express | 200 | Mush. | 2520 | 2160 | 1840 | 1560 | 2820 | 2075 | 1505 | 1080 | 0.8 |
| R213 | .35 Remington Express | 200 | Mush. | 2180 | 1870 | 1590 | 1360 | 2110 | 1555 | 1125 | 820 | 1.0 |
| R438 | .35 Remington Express | 200 | S.P. | 2180 | 1870 | 1590 | 1360 | 2110 | 1555 | 1125 | 820 | 1.0 |
| R67 | .218 Bee Hi-Speed | 46 | Mush. | 2860 | 2260 | 1740 | 1330 | 835 | 520 | 310 | 180 | 0.8 |
| R65 | .219 Zipper Hi-Speed | 46 | Mush. | 3390 | 2720 | 2140 | 1640 | 1175 | 755 | 470 | 280 | 0.4 |

## Center-fire, with "Kleanbore" Priming—Continued

| Index No. | Cartridge | Bullet Wgt. Grs. | Bullet Type | Velocity—Feet per Second Muzzle | Velocity 100 Yds. | Velocity 200 Yds. | Velocity 300 Yds. | Energy—Foot-Pounds Muzzle | Energy 100 Yds. | Energy 200 Yds. | Energy 300 Yds. | Mid-Range Trajectory Inches—100 Yds. |
|---|---|---|---|---|---|---|---|---|---|---|---|---|
| R66 | .219 Zipper Hi-Speed | 56 | Mush. | 3050 | 2530 | 2070 | 1660 | 1155 | 795 | 535 | 345 | 0.6 |
| R29H | .22 Hornet Hi-Speed | 45 | Mush. | 2650 | 2080 | 1580 | 1220 | 700 | 430 | 250 | 150 | 0.8 |
| R295 | .22 Hornet Hi-Speed | 45 | Ptd. S.P. | 2600 | 2210 | 1860 | 1550 | 675 | 490 | 345 | 240 | 0.8 |
| R50C | .22 Savage high power Hi-Speed | 70 | Mush. | 2810 | 2400 | 2030 | 1700 | 1230 | 900 | 640 | 450 | 0.7 |
| R51 | .220 Swift Hi-Speed | 46 | Mush. | 4140 | 3370 | 2710 | 2130 | 1750 | 1160 | 750 | 465 | 0.3 |
| R52 | .220 Swift Hi-Speed | 48 | Ptd. S.P. | 4140 | 3490 | 3040 | 2570 | 1825 | 1300 | 985 | 705 | 0.3 |
| R505 | 6.5 m/m Mann-Schoen | 150 | S.P. | 2260 | 2030 | 1810 | 1610 | 1700 | 1375 | 1090 | 865 | 0.9 |
| R64 | .25-20 Single Shot | 86 | S.P. | 1380 | 1150 | 1020 | 930 | 365 | 255 | 200 | 165 | 2.6 |
| R80H | .25-20 Winchester Hi-Speed | 60 | Mush. | 2210 | 1700 | 1300 | 1060 | 650 | 385 | 225 | 150 | 1.1 |
| R78 | .25-20 Winchester | 86 | M.C. | 1450 | 1190 | 1050 | 950 | 400 | 270 | 210 | 175 | 2.6 |
| R79 | .25-20 Winchester | 86 | S.P. | 1450 | 1190 | 1050 | 950 | 400 | 270 | 210 | 175 | 2.6 |
| LR77 | .25-20 Winchester | 86 | Lead | 1450 | 1190 | 1050 | 950 | 400 | 270 | 210 | 175 | 2.6 |
| R83H | .25 Remington Hi-Speed | 87 | Mush. | 2710 | 2300 | 1930 | 1600 | 1420 | 1020 | 720 | 495 | 0.7 |
| R82XK | .25 Remington Express | 117 | Mush. | 2300 | 2020 | 1760 | 1530 | 1375 | 1060 | 805 | 610 | 0.9 |
| R83 | .25 Remington Express | 117 | S.P. | 2300 | 2020 | 1760 | 1530 | 1375 | 1060 | 805 | 610 | 0.9 |
| R86H | .257 Rem.-Rob. Hi-Speed | 87 | Mush. | 3220 | 2770 | 2350 | 1980 | 2005 | 1485 | 1070 | 760 | 0.5 |
| R74H | .25-35 Winchester Hi-Speed | 87 | Mush. | 2650 | 2250 | 1880 | 1560 | 1355 | 980 | 685 | 470 | 0.7 |
| R73 | .25-35 Winchester Express | 117 | M.C. | 2280 | 1970 | 1690 | 1440 | 1350 | 1010 | 740 | 540 | 1.0 |
| R73XK | .25-35 Winchester Express | 117 | Mush. | 2280 | 1970 | 1690 | 1440 | 1350 | 1010 | 740 | 540 | 1.0 |
| R74 | .25-35 Winchester Express | 117 | S.P. | 2280 | 1970 | 1690 | 1440 | 1350 | 1010 | 740 | 540 | 1.0 |
| R477 | .250 Savage Hi-Speed | 87 | Mush. | 3040 | 2600 | 2210 | 1840 | 1785 | 1305 | 945 | 655 | 0.6 |
| R476XK | .250 Savage Hi-Speed | 100 | Mush. | 2810 | 2490 | 2180 | 1900 | 1755 | 1375 | 1055 | 800 | 0.6 |
| R493 | .270 Winchester Hi-Speed | 150 | S.P. | 2770 | 2490 | 2220 | 1970 | 2560 | 2065 | 1645 | 1295 | 0.6 |
| R516 | 7 m/m Mauser Express | 175 | S.P. | 2460 | 2220 | 1990 | 1780 | 2350 | 1915 | 1540 | 1230 | 0.8 |
| R125H | .30-30 Winchester Hi-Speed | 110 | Mush. | 2720 | 2260 | 1840 | 1480 | 1810 | 1250 | 825 | 535 | 0.7 |
| R124 | .30-30 Winchester Express | 160 | M.C. | 2200 | 1910 | 1650 | 1420 | 1720 | 1295 | 970 | 720 | 1.0 |
| R124XK | .30-30 Winchester Express | 165 | Mush. | 2200 | 1920 | 1670 | 1440 | 1770 | 1350 | 1020 | 760 | 1.0 |
| R129H | .30 Remington Hi-Speed | 110 | Mush. | 2720 | 2260 | 1840 | 1480 | 1810 | 1250 | 825 | 535 | 0.7 |
| R128 | .30 Remington Express | 160 | M.C. | 2200 | 1910 | 1650 | 1420 | 1720 | 1295 | 970 | 720 | 1.0 |
| R99H | .30-40 Krag Hi-Speed Expdg. | 180 | Br.P. | 2460 | 2250 | 2100 | 1930 | 2420 | 2020 | 1765 | 1490 | 0.7 |
| R98XM | .30-40 Krag Express | 220 | M.C. | 2190 | 1980 | 1780 | 1600 | 2345 | 1915 | 1550 | 1250 | 1.0 |
| R131H | .30-06 Springfield Hi-Speed | 110 | Mush. | 3380 | 2850 | 2370 | 1940 | 2790 | 1980 | 1370 | 920 | 0.4 |
| R136H | .30-06 Spfd. Hi-Speed Expdg. | 150 | Br.P. | 2960 | 2720 | 2480 | 2260 | 2920 | 2465 | 2050 | 1700 | 0.5 |
| R120 | .30-06 Springfield | 172 | M.C.T.H. | 2700 | 2500 | 2260 | 2070 | 2785 | 2385 | 1950 | 1640 | 0.6 |
| R126 | .30-06 Spfd. Palma Match | 180 | M.C.T.H. | 2730 | 2540 | 2350 | 2170 | 2980 | 2580 | 2210 | 1890 | 0.6 |
| R137H | .30-06 Spfd. Hi-Speed Expdg. | 180 | Br.P. | 2690 | 2500 | 2310 | 2130 | 2895 | 2500 | 2135 | 1815 | 0.6 |
| R522 | 7.62 m/m Russian Hi-Speed | 150 | Br.P. | 2810 | 2570 | 2330 | 2110 | 2635 | 2205 | 1750 | 1435 | 0.6 |
| R467 | .300 Magnum Match (Rimless) | 180 | M.C.T.H. | 3030 | 2820 | 2620 | 2430 | 3670 | 3180 | 2745 | 2360 | 0.5 |
| R469 | .300 Savage Hi-Speed Expdg. | 150 | Br.P. | 2660 | 2430 | 2210 | 2000 | 2360 | 1970 | 1625 | 1325 | 0.7 |
| R471 | .303 British Express | 215 | S.P. | 2160 | 1940 | 1740 | 1550 | 2230 | 1795 | 1445 | 1145 | 1.0 |
| R529 | 8 m/m Mauser Express | 236 | S.P. | 2100 | 1890 | 1700 | 1530 | 2310 | 1875 | 1515 | 1230 | 1.1 |
| R523 | 8 m/m Special Hi-Speed | 170 | S.P. | 2530 | 2210 | 1920 | 1660 | 2415 | 1845 | 1390 | 1040 | 0.8 |
| R549 | 8 m/m Lebel Hi-Speed | 170 | S.P. | 2610 | 2320 | 2040 | 1780 | 2575 | 2030 | 1570 | 1195 | 0.7 |
| R190H | .32-20 Winchester Hi-Speed | 80 | Mush. | 2050 | 1520 | 1150 | 980 | 745 | 410 | 235 | 170 | 1.4 |
| R185 | .32-20 Winchester | 100 | Lead | 1280 | 1060 | 940 | 850 | 365 | 250 | 195 | 160 | 3.1 |
| R186 | .32-20 Winchester | 100 | M.C. | 1280 | 1060 | 940 | 850 | 365 | 250 | 195 | 160 | 3.1 |
| R187 | .32-20 Winchester | 100 | S.P. | 1280 | 1060 | 940 | 850 | 365 | 250 | 195 | 160 | 3.1 |
| R189H | .32 Win. Special Hi-Speed | 110 | Mush. | 2630 | 2140 | 1700 | 1340 | 1690 | 1120 | 705 | 440 | 0.7 |
| R196 | .32 Winchester Self Loading | 165 | S.P. | 1390 | 1190 | 1060 | 980 | 710 | 520 | 410 | 350 | 2.6 |
| R205H | .32 Remington Hi-Speed | 110 | Mush. | 2630 | 2140 | 1700 | 1350 | 1690 | 1120 | 705 | 445 | 0.8 |
| R204XK | .32 Remington Express | 165 | Mush. | 2200 | 1900 | 1630 | 1390 | 1775 | 1325 | 970 | 710 | 1.0 |
| R205 | .32 Remingtotn Express | 170 | S.P. | 2200 | 1910 | 1640 | 1400 | 1830 | 1380 | 1015 | 740 | 1.0 |
| R201 | .32-40 Winchester | 165 | S.P. | 1440 | 1230 | 1080 | 1000 | 760 | 555 | 430 | 365 | 2.6 |
| R214 | .33 Winchester | 200 | S.P. | 2180 | 1870 | 1600 | 1360 | 2110 | 1555 | 1135 | 820 | 1.1 |
| R218 | .348 Winchester Hi-Speed | 150 | S.P. | 2880 | 2380 | 1930 | 1550 | 2765 | 1890 | 1240 | 800 | 0.6 |
| R219 | .348 Winchester Express | 200 | S.P. | 2520 | 2160 | 1840 | 1560 | 2820 | 2075 | 1505 | 1080 | 0.8 |
| R222 | .35 Winchester Self Loading | 180 | S.P. | 1390 | 1170 | 1040 | 960 | 775 | 545 | 430 | 370 | 2.5 |
| R481 | .351 Winchester Self Loading | 180 | S.P. | 1850 | 1560 | 1310 | 1140 | 1370 | 975 | 685 | 520 | 1.5 |
| R480 | .351 Winchester Self Loading | 177 | M.C. | 1850 | 1560 | 1310 | 1140 | 1370 | 975 | 685 | 520 | 1.5 |
| R220 | .35 Winchester | 250 | S.P. | 2160 | 1910 | 1680 | 1480 | 2590 | 2025 | 1565 | 1215 | 1.1 |
| R216H | .35 Remington Hi-Speed | 150 | Mush. | 2360 | 1930 | 1560 | 1270 | 1860 | 1240 | 810 | 535 | 1.0 |
| R215XK | .35 Remington Express | 200 | Mush. | 2180 | 1870 | 1590 | 1360 | 2110 | 1555 | 1125 | 820 | 1.0 |
| R215 | .35 Remington | 200 | M.C. | 2180 | 1870 | 1590 | 1360 | 2110 | 1555 | 1125 | 820 | 1.0 |
| R276H | .38-40 Winchester Hi-Speed | 145 | Mush. | 2060 | 1520 | 1140 | 980 | 1365 | 745 | 420 | 310 | 1.3 |
| R276 | .38-40 Winchester | 180 | S.P. | 1310 | 1090 | 960 | 870 | 685 | 475 | 370 | 305 | 3.2 |
| R282 | .38-55 Winchester | 255 | S.P. | 1320 | 1150 | 1050 | 980 | 985 | 750 | 625 | 545 | 3.0 |
| R269 | .38-56 Winchester | 255 | S.P. | 1400 | 1210 | 1090 | 1010 | 1110 | 830 | 675 | 580 | 2.7 |
| R306 | .40-65 Winchester | 260 | S.P. | 1360 | 1170 | 1050 | 970 | 1070 | 790 | 635 | 545 | 2.9 |
| R312 | .40-82 Winchester | 260 | S.P. | 1500 | 1260 | 1100 | 1010 | 1300 | 915 | 700 | 590 | 2.3 |
| R488 | .401 Winchester Self Loading | 200 | S.P. | 2140 | 1750 | 1420 | 1170 | 2035 | 1360 | 895 | 610 | 1.1 |
| R491 | .405 Winchester | 300 | S.P. | 2220 | 1940 | 1690 | 1460 | 3285 | 2510 | 1905 | 1420 | 1.0 |
| R379H | .44-40 Winchester Hi-Speed | 160 | Mush. | 1980 | 1430 | 1100 | 940 | 1395 | 730 | 430 | 315 | 1.6 |
| R379 | .44-40 Winchester | 200 | S.P. | 1300 | 1070 | 940 | 860 | 750 | 510 | 390 | 330 | 3.3 |
| R407 | .45-70 Government | 405 | S.P. | 1310 | 1160 | 1060 | 990 | 1545 | 1210 | 1010 | 880 | 2.8 |
| R428 | .45-90 Winchester | 300 | S.P. | 1530 | 1270 | 1090 | 1000 | 1560 | 1075 | 790 | 665 | 2.2 |

Abbreviations:
S. P.—Soft Point
H. P.—Hollow Point
M. P.—Metal Point
M. C.—Metal Cased
M. C. H. P.—Metal Cased, Hollow Point
H.V.—High Velocity
P. P. Exp.—Protected Point Expanding
Spl.—Special
I.B.—Inner-Belted

# WILDCAT CARTRIDGES

**Development.** Books have been written on "wildcat" cartridges. The subject is vast—and complicated. But first, just what is that type of cartridge today known as a "wildcat"? This name is applied to all special cartridges and guns chambered for them which are not produced by the recognized firearms manufacturers. Explained in another way, a wildcat is a cartridge developed by some home experimenter which has "not yet" become standardized and produced by commercial ammunition makers.

Wildcats can be dangerous—perhaps that is how they acquired that name—but it is the wildcatters who have developed most of the interesting cartridges on the market today. The home development of ammunition is almost as old as the cartridge gun—it applies to both rifles and shotguns. Back in the 1880's when the world's greatest rifle-barrel maker, the one and only Harry M. Pope, started to produce the barrels for target riflemen, all of his guns were for wildcat cartridges.

Why? Riflemen of that day were handicapped in their factory ammunition. They lived in the black-powder era, and brass center-fire cartridges were not too old. Most were being made with what is known as a folded head case construction. The brass case was drawn thin with a hollow rim similar to a rimfire cartridge. This was squeezed together to make a "folded head" rim. It would stand little reloading; cases frequently burst at that weak rim fold.

The serious target rifleman was not satisfied. He designed slight variations of existing cartridges, had his barrels chambered to fit, and paid heavily to get a few Ideal "Everlasting" solid brass cases turned from brass rod on a lathe. These cost several times as much as the thin drawn cases, but with care would last indefinitely. Pope claimed to have one case he had reloaded 30,000 times.

With the coming of smokeless powder, the home experimenter went to work with even greater enthusiasm. The goal of these rifle enthusiasts was: (1) Small bore, (2) high velocity, (3) flat trajectory, and (4) extreme accuracy. Probably thousands of cartridges were developed with no commercial interest. Some had names; others were known only to their makers and a few intimate friends.

During the first decade of this century, one of these gun enthusiasts, a noted designer of arms and ammunition, worked out a new centerfire .22 cartridge with a 70-grain pointed soft-point bullet. Considering the powders available in 1906-1908, it was an amazing number. It showed tremendous possibilities, so Charles Newton, the designer, sold the idea to the Savage Arms Company. Savage first produced it in 1912 as the .22 Savage Hi-Power. It became known to the public as "The Imp."

Newton had a better idea in mind as early as 1908. He developed a rimless .25-caliber cartridge using an 87-grain bullet at the then unheard-of velocity of 3000 feet per second. He also improved this with a 100-grain bullet at 2800 f.s. Savage also bought this idea, and in 1913 introduced it as the now-famous .250-3000 Savage.

In 1930, a group of top gun enthusiasts—Colonel Townsend Whelen, Captains G. L. Wotkyns and A. A. Woody, and A. L. Woodworth—decided that they wanted a cartridge which would be of sufficient power and accuracy at 200 yards to insure positive hits and kills on woodchucks. Thus was born the .22 Hornet. This cartridge established a new record—the designers engineered it. They had full equipment in the form of the laboratories of Springfield Armory to test for velocity and pressure. They standardized all cartridge case and chamber dimensions. Soon custom gunsmiths were making guns to handle the new cartridge, which had to be handmade by a few small ammunition handloaders or by the shooter.

Then the ammunition makers started to produce it—with no factory-made rifle available for it. This is an outstanding record. For several years all ammunition makers produced the cartridge, and then the inevitable happened; they began to produce the guns for it.

Another "wildcat" was the .25-caliber development of Major N. H. Roberts, noted New England author. Ned Roberts took the 7-mm. Mauser cartridge and changed the case slightly, reducing it to .25 caliber in 1905. For 25 years Roberts changed, altered, experimented, and finally developed it into the .25 Roberts. Custom gunmakers took it up, and Roberts once estimated that some 600 rifles had been built for it. Then in 1934 Remington introduced this cartridge with slight alterations, and brought out a rifle to handle it, calling the development the .257 Roberts. A year afterward Winchester followed suit.

A little later, some of the home experimenters wanted an improvement on the Hornet. One of the Hornet designers, the late Captain Grosvenor L. Wotkyns, developed a new .22 made by reforming the .250 Savage case. Winchester became interested in it, because for the first time on record a velocity in excess of 4000 feet per second was achieved. They took over development work, but were forced to make a premature announcement of the number they called the .220 Swift. This cartridge came out on April 23, 1935.

But all wildcats are not in the rifle field. There have been few automatic pistol wildcats, but in the revolver field many of the developments in the commercial field can be traced to the private experimenters. One of the most interesting of these is the now popular "wadcutter" target bullet. Depending on the ammunition maker, this is called "Clean-Cutting" and "Sharp-Shoulder." It punches a clean hole in the target, full bullet diameter, and makes scoring a simple task.

Handloaders are familiar with two popular "Keith" and "Sharpe" bullets, with a sharp wadcutting shoulder and truncated cone nose in the popular .38 Special and other calibers. Few realize that although these bullets date back only to post-World War I days, the idea is much older. Famous shooter-experimenters of yesteryear, men such as B. F. Wilder, used similar types in 1904-1905, and Ideal included their designs in their standard bullet-mold catalog. Pope used the same idea prior to 1890, and admitted that he had "copied ideas of some fellows before him."

The point is that revolver target shooters developed the wad-cutting bullet. It became a standard in the line of commercial ammunition makers because of popular demand.

Few new revolver cartridges have appeared on the market during the past 50 years. Perhaps the most interesting is the .357 Magnum. This began life as an idea for a high-velocity load and Philip B. Sharpe went at the development. In 1933 his good friend, Colonel Douglas B. Wesson, then of Smith & Wesson, became interested, and that fall, armed with a couple of special heavy experimental revolvers they went into the Maine woods on a vacation-hunting trip for deer and small game. The ammunition was handloaded by Sharpe, but all kinds of factory ammunition went along to be actually tested on game.

One day, deep in the quiet of the forest, two dirty, tired, and bewhiskered hunters sat on a fallen tree and worked out the idea of the Magnum revolver—something better than was on the market, and capable of handling the power of the experimental loads they had used. Even the name, ".357 Magnum," was born that afternoon. Winchester worked with them, helping to develop the ammunition. The first two revolvers out of the factory went to Sharpe and to J. Edgar Hoover of the F. B. I., that department later adopting this gun and cartridge as the world's most powerful revolver.

Most wildcatters have concentrated on the rifle. Today custom gunsmiths offer two-score super cartridges. Although they are used it would be premature to recommend any because they are not properly developed. Development work in this field is costly—and dangerous.

The chief criticisms of the wildcats may be listed as follows: (1) Short barrel life, (2) high and dangerous pressures, and (3) critical accuracy—many loads fail to perform well.

It is very difficult to explain these reasons for failure. Many wildcats are developed by persons without proper technical background. Too many theories have been developed. Improper understanding of powder characteristics and ignition problems creates multiple development headaches. Many of the wildcats now being sold by custom gunsmiths, regardless of the claims of their designers, are developing pressures in the 70,000 pound-per-square-inch class—positively dangerous.

**Velocities.** Few cartridge developers have access to chronographs for measuring velocity—they "estimate" the speed of their brain-children. None of them have pressure-taking equipment. The inventor who can develop accurate and fast-performing equipment within the reach of enthusiasts will have an unlimited market.

First, let us briefly review the present methods of taking velocities and pressures.

Velocity is the easiest to record, yet the only successful method available until recently was the 60-year-old standby, the Boulenge Chronograph. The word *chronograph* means "record of time." The chronograph records the time it takes a bullet to cover a certain distance, and this is then translated into average or *instrumental* velocity.

The simple basic principle of the Boulenge is that of the falling rod. Two carefully balanced electric circuits are used, known as the *muzzle* and *disjunctor* circuits. On firing the gun being tested, the bullet cuts a fine wire, breaking the muzzle circuit; a few thousandths of a second later, it arrives at the target, breaking the disjunctor circuit. Time between the breaking of the circuits is measured accurately.

Each circuit passes an electric current through an electromagnet. The muzzle circuit energizes a magnet to which is attached a long non-metallic rod with a ball nose of steel. When that circuit is broken the rod starts to fall instantly, at the normal rate of gravity. As the bullet strikes the target the second circuit breaks. From this magnet is suspended a short weighted rod. It falls on a trigger, releasing a knife blade which swings sideways, striking the long falling rod and leaving a mark. The operator measures the distance between a zero mark and this knife mark, quickly translates inches of free fall into time, and this in turn, into "velocity."

Since there is air in a rifle barrel, and this is expelled violently in front of the bullet, it could break the very fine wire if that were stretched directly across the muzzle. For elimination of false reading, therefore, that wire is usually located 3 feet from the muzzle. For low and medium velocities, an accurate reading can be obtained with the two circuits 100 feet apart. Since velocity is *average* over this distance, the recording is given as "instrumental velocity at 53 feet." High velocities are usually checked on a 150-foot range and listed as "instrumental velocity at 78 feet."

The trouble with the Boulenge is its complication, the fact that it becomes a permanent installation, and takes skilled individuals to operate and maintain it. The average installation costs several thousands of dollars—out of reach and totally unadapted to the home experimenter's requirements.

During World War II a new electronic instrument known as the "Potter Counter" made its appearance, and is being used in many large laboratories. A bullet is shot over a pair of photoelectric cells on the range. Either the natural illumination of the sky or light from special spotlights shining on the cells keeps a bank of special neon lights on a small table-radio-size cabinet "dancing." As the bullet passes over the cells, its shadow on the muzzle-circuit cell stops the "dancing" and starts the instrument counting. The shadow on the second cell stops the counting and leaves certain of the tiny lamps lighted. A direct reading in milliseconds (thousandths of a second) can thus be made.

Translated into simple language, if the bullet is traveling 4000 feet per second, and the photocells are 40 feet apart, this distance will be covered in .010 second or 10 milliseconds.

The trouble with this outfit is that the complication and delicate assembly of the counter, photocells, and their amplifiers make the price run about $1000. If you are a student of electronics, see if you can't develop something to do this work with the following "must" requirements: It must be capable of operation by one man. It must be sufficiently portable to be taken to a range and set up for operation in a short time. Finally, it must not cost the buyer more than $150—preferably about $100. There is nothing in sight yet.

**Pressure Testing.** In this field nothing new has been developed for a half-century. This is the basic idea of recording pressures. A "pressure gun" is a converted weapon fit for no other use. It is a precision job, expensive to make and operate. Only a skilled toolmaker can build one.

The alteration consists of a hole drilled through the barrel of the gun into the chamber. This is fitted with a carefully hardened bushing, and a tiny piston is lapped to a smooth airtight fit. A yoke is fitted around the chamber end of the barrel over the hole, and into this a precision-finished anvil is fitted.

To take pressures a copper crusher cylinder is used—carefully ground to length, of special pure copper of predetermined hardness. A live cartridge is inserted in the chamber of this gun. A tiny copper cup is oiled and placed over the head of the piston to act as a seal and prevent piston burning. The assembly is then pushed into the bushed barrel hole until it contacts the cartridge. On this piston the copper cylinder is balanced, and the threaded anvil is screwed down solidly.

When the gun is fired, the high-pressure gas within the cartridge case bursts that case at the piston hole, the force of the gas driving the piston upward and crushing the cylinder against the anvil. This cylinder is then carefully measured and the amount of shortening or compression is read and translated from a special tarrage table prepared for that lot of crushers into "pounds-per-square-inch pressure." The system is fast enough, but its faults are many.

A pressure gun is expensive—besides the price of the gun and barrel, alterations to make the conversion cost about $300. Its life, in some calibers, is less than 100 shots, due to wear of the piston and piston hole. Wear and tear expense costs from 75 cents to $1 *per shot.* For the experimenter, the cost would be more.

Something new in the basic method of recording pressures must be designed. Possibly some inventor can solve this problem through electronics. The ideal would be the "impossible"—an attachment that would not mar or alter the standard gun and which could be changed from one gun to another at will. Again the cost must be considered—something at from $100 to $150 would readily sell. Here are two ideas for inventors to work on.

Why is pressure important? Besides guaranteeing the safety of the gun and shooter, problems in ballistics cannot be solved without knowledge of pressure. With a given set of components and one lot of powder, slight increases in amount of powder used show an increase in velocity and a corresponding increase in pressure. At some point, with that group of components, increasing the powder charge gives practically *no* increase in velocity *but the pressure goes up dangerously!* That point is the useful limit of that powder.

Wildcatters have no way of determining the pressure developed by their concoctions. Pressure also means *heat.* The very hot powder gases burn out the rifling in the barrel—*erosion.* This destroys the accuracy of the cartridge—which is the primary goal of the wildcatter. When some cartridges burn out a $50 heavy barrel in less than 200 rounds, something is wrong.

Lest this be considered as a criticism of all wildcat high-velocity cartridges, it should be pointed out that were it not for these enthusiasts who constantly develop the ultra-velocity cartridges, there would be little progress in the firearms field. These men alone, not arms manufacturers, are the real experimenters and to them should go credit for progress. They create the demand for improvements, and eventually that demand builds itself to the point where commercial manufacturers can afford to enter the picture.

The wildcatter is critical. He wants accuracy better than is possible. He insists that his weapon is not "accurate" unless it will shoot to "a minute of angle." That fancy term merely means that all shots must group in a circle one inch in diameter at 100 yards, or 2 inches at 200 yards. Few commercial hunting rifles and ammunition will do this. But such accuracy with wildcats is common. Many developments record groups as small as a half-inch at 100 yards.

The vice-president of one of our largest commercial arms plants once said:

> ". . . They ask the impossible—then they do it. They wanted inch-groups—they got them; then they asked for three-quarter inch. Soon they will be demanding that all .22-caliber bullets go through the same hole—and will not be satisfied until that hole never exceeds .23 caliber. Then, I suppose, they will demand such performance at 300 and 500 yards. I don't think they will make it, but they'll keep trying . . . and as long as they keep at it, we'll make and sell guns."

# DEVELOPMENT OF THE .220 SWIFT

In the early 1930's, Captain Grosvenor L. Wotkyns evolved the bright idea of reducing the neck of the Savage .250 shell to accommodate a .22 metal-jacketed bullet. He hoped to obtain a muzzle velocity of at least 4000 feet per second with the Hornet 46-grain bullet. Captain Wotkyns named this new cartridge the .220 Swift.

At this time, Winchester was invited to enter the picture in order to perfect the development. The purpose of this development was to produce a cartridge with reduced time of flight, flat trajectory, and satisfactory accuracy.

With any combination of cartridge and rifle, it is necessary to control the breech pressures within safe limits. These limits must be sufficiently low to assure freedom from shell defects, such as pierced or blanked primers, expanded or burst heads. The strength of rifle intended to be used must also be taken into consideration.

Since 1908, all Winchester rifles, center-fire and rim-fire, as well as shotguns, have been definitely proved with a cartridge loaded to produce pressures of at least 25% and not more than 40% above the service pressure limits. In the year 1925, these proof limits were raised to a minimum of 30% and maximum of 45% above the service cartridge.

These proof loads serve a double purpose. They not only prove the safety of barrel and action of the weapons, but also indicate the strength and safety of the service shell. Obviously a rifle that shows an increase in breech space or an expanded chamber as a result of firing therein proof loads cannot be considered to have a sufficient factor of safety. Likewise, fired proof shells showing expanded heads or other serious defects indicate a faulty design and lack of strength.

The first Winchester tests were with the .250 Savage shell. Satisfactory accuracy was obtained with this combination when loaded to the 4000-foot velocity level, but breech pressures were found to be beyond what was considered a safe limit.

Further trials were made with the .30 Springfield case and later with the 7-mm. Mauser in order to take advantage of the increased volume. At each step, new chambering tools, pressure, velocity, and accuracy barrels were necessary.

A 48-grain pointed soft-point bullet was developed as a substitute for the 46-grain hollow-point type. This produced a better ballistic form with improved ranging qualities.

In the initial experiments DuPont IMR 3031 powder was used. This powder was found to be unsatisfactory for the larger-volume shells because of a too-low density of loading. With a low density of loading, the powder is free to move from one position to another depending upon the position of rifle before and at time of firing. If, when loading, the muzzle of the rifle is depressed and brought to the horizontal when fired, the powder charge will be located near the bullet and air space at the primer end. In the reverse, if the muzzle is pointed upward during loading and brought to the horizontal when fired, the powder is located next to the primer with air space at the bullet end.

The location of powder within the case when fired has a very material effect on velocities and pressure, and this difference is exaggerated with progressive-burning powders. This condition makes it imperative to load this cartridge to a density of at least 90 per cent in order to secure uniform ballistics.

With these larger-volume shells, they switched to a slower, more progressive powder such as DuPont IMR 4064. This change in powder was made in order to secure increased velocity with moderate pressures. The slower powder also permitted a higher loading density. The slower powder did permit increased velocities with moderate pressure, but the uniformity was not satisfactory, indicating poor burning qualities with the slow powder and light bullet.

In this development, they had originally set as their goal a velocity level of 4000 feet per second with the Hornet 46-grain bullet. As the development progressed, they raised their sights for the purpose of reaching the ultimate speed at which a compound bullet can be pushed through a rifled barrel satisfactorily and still obtain uniform ballistics and accuracy.

The next step was to experiment with the 6-mm. Lee case. The volume of this case lent itself admirably to the loading of the faster DuPont IMR 3031 powder with satisfactory density of loading and a

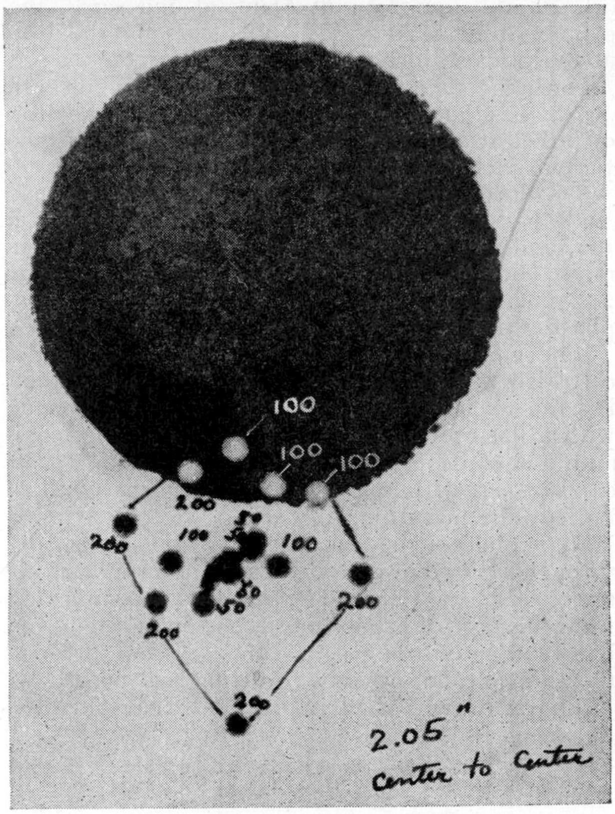


PLATE I. This group of 15 shots was made with a .220 Swift which was sighted in at 100 yards. The 48-grain "pointed soft point" bullet was used, and 5 shots each were fired at 50 yards, 100 yards, and 200 yards. This is an unusually fine group, under such conditions, but the .220 Swift is an unusual rifle.

safe pressure level. Changes in case design were made in order to increase strength. These included a thicker web, a steeper cannelure cut under the rim, and improved shape of head bunter.

There is a limit to how fast a compound bullet, forced through a rifle barrel, can hold together at the muzzle and fly true to the target.

If the bullet jacket is too thin, excessive fusing of the core will result even though reasonable target accuracy is obtained. When the bullet jacket is increased in thickness, the tendency toward fusing is reduced; but this may mean a loss in target accuracy. They are confined, therefore, between the too-thin cover with its excessive fusing and the heavy cover with its poor accuracy.

This problem was solved by copper plating the bullet core, thus placing a high-melting-point metal between the cover and core. The melting or fusing of the core was reduced even with the thinner jacket and permitted uniform ballistics, flat trajectory, and fine target accuracy.

The trajectory of any bullet is of utmost importance to the sportsman. If the range is not carefully estimated, a miss may occur with a cartridge producing a high trajectory and a hit still be obtained with a cartridge producing a flat trajectory.

A comparison of the trajectory or range table of the Winchester .30/30 and the .220 Swift is of interest.

With the sights of a Winchester M/64 deer rifle

cal. .30/30 aligned point blank at 100 yards, the drop of bullet at 200 yards is 7.5 inches and the drop at 300 yards 28 inches.

With the sights of a Winchester M/70 rifle cal. .220 Swift aligned point blank at 100 yards, the drop of bullet at 200 yards is only 2.5 inches and at 300 yards 9 inches.

To illustrate the flatness of trajectory for the .220 Swift, five shots were fired each on one target at 50, 100, and 200 yards without change in sight alignment. The extreme spread of the 15 shots was only 2.05 inches from center to center. This target emphasizes the advantage of a flat trajectory.

The 25/35 Winchester full metal patch bullet cartridge was an extremely popular one for shooting fish in Southern waters. This bullet was made with a flat nose, a type which results in the maximum penetration in water with less deflection than experienced with a pointed or even round-nosed bullet. The main difficulty was occasional stripped jackets due to the increased friction of passing through a pitted or corroded barrel as a result of the use of chlorate primers. The products of combustion from this type of primer must be promptly removed by swabbing out the barrel with a solution in which they are soluble; otherwise, rusting will occur.

The .220 Swift shell is primed with a Staynless non-corrosive type of priming. The potassium chlorate is entirely eliminated in this type of priming and the products of combustion in both powder and priming mixture actually serve as a rust preventive. This makes unnecessary the prompt cleaning after firing with the assurance of freedom from rust or corrosion. If the barrel is cleaned at any time, it must be promptly oiled to preserve the interior surface.

The ultimate in ballistics and accuracy can be obtained only by exercising the greatest care in uniformity of components and assembling into the completed cartridge.

The same care must be followed in the manufacture of the rifle. Barrels conform to a standard throughout the industry and interior dimensions of chamber and bore are held to the closest tolerances possible.

With the final version of the 220 Swift cartridge loaded with a 48-grain pointed soft-point bullet, a muzzle velocity of 4140 feet per second is produced with uniform ballistics, safe pressures, short time of flight, extreme flatness of trajectory, and excellent accuracy. This is the highest velocity practical commercial cartridge ever produced.

Its surpassing ballistics and ranging qualities are the reason for the popularity of the .220 Swift cartridge.

# SHOTGUN AMMUNITION

**Development.** Few shooters realize that only 30 years ago the six companies producing shotshells turned out a total of 14,383 *different* kinds of loads. This figure seems almost incredible today.

In 1916, the ammunition companies gave shooters a latitude of loads so wide that a large percentage of these loads produced almost identical results, even though they were made up of a wide range of different types and quantities of powder and shot. At this time shotshells were made up of the following unnecessary components:

- 8 different kinds of smokeless powder
- 3 different kinds of black powder
- 11 variations of powder quantity by dram
- 11 variations of powder quantity by grain
- 13 sizes of chilled shot
- 20 sizes of dropped shot
- 11 sizes of buck shot
- 7 variations in weight of chilled shot
- 7 variations of weight of dropped shot.

In 1921, the various companies voluntarily eliminated 5200 different loads. During this same year, the Division of Simplified Practice was established in the National Bureau of Standards of the Department of Commerce. Its purpose was to aid industry in the reduction of needless variety of products. In 1923, this agency was called into action on behalf of shot shells. A survey revealed that a total of 4067 different loads were still being produced.

Then, in January 1924, 2320 loads were dropped, leaving a total of 1747 loads still being turned out. Since then, the line has been cut down each year, and in 1947 the number of different loads was reduced to 137. This includes the number of varieties required for all normal shooting purposes.

The simplification of center-fire and rim-fire ammunition came under the knife in 1926. Neither of these cartridge types offered the tremendous variety involved in shotshells, however. During the past 20 years, the types of center-fire ammunition have been reduced by 35 per cent, and the number of rim-fire items by 40 per cent.

The most complicated example of mechanical perfection in the field of low-priced manufactured articles undoubtedly is the shotgun shell. No other article in this price field requires such a high degree of technical perfection or such infinite care in the completion of the multitude of processes necessary to its production.

A shotgun shell contains 14 separate component parts. All of these, with the exception of the powder, which comes to the loading company in its finished form, must be processed from raw material to finished product by manufacturer.

The number of operations involved in the production of each component part that goes to make up the finished shell vary, but the total, including inspections, amounts to over 200. For example, more than 30 separate operations are required to produce one shot pellet.

There are more than 100 different chemicals employed in the making of a single shotgun shell. Manufacturers make constant checks to insure the maintenance of shell quality. In the Remington plant, for example, more than a million shells are fired each year in tests to insure the maintenance of standards.

In addition to testing their current product, all of the ammunition companies have large staffs of trained experts engaged in constant research in an effort to improve the various loads by making some change in the component parts.

An interesting example of the experimentation is

| Shot Size | No. of chilled shot in ounce | No. of dropped shot in ounce | Diameter in inches |
|---|---|---|---|
| Dust | .... | 4565 | .04 |
| 12 | 2385 | 2326 | .05 |
| 11 | 1380 | 1346 | .06 |
| 10 | 868 | 848 | .07 |
| 9 | 585 | 568 | .08 |
| 8 | 409 | 399 | .09 |
| 7½ | 345 | 338 | .09½ |
| 7 | 299 | 291 | .10 |
| 6 | 223 | 218 | .11 |
| 5 | 172 | 168 | .12 |
| 4 | 136 | 132 | .13 |
| 3 | 109 | 106 | .14 |
| 2 | 88 | 86 | .15 |
| 1 | 73 | 71 | .16 |
| B | .... | 59 | .17 |
| BB | .... | 50 | .18 |
| BBB | .... | 42 | .19 |
| T | .... | 36 | .20 |
| TT | .... | 31 | .21 |
| F | .... | 27 | .22 |
| FF | .... | 24 | .23 |

*BUCKSHOT*

| Shot size | Balls in pound | Diameter in inches | No. of balls in standard load |
|---|---|---|---|
| 4C | 341 | .24 | 27 |
| 3C | 299 | .26 | (20 gauge only) |
| 2C | 238 | .28 | Not Standard |
| 1C | 175 | .30 | 12 or 16 |
| 0 | 144 | .32 | 12 or 16 |
| 00 | 122 | .34 | 9 |
| 000 | 103 | .36 | Not Standard |

Courtesy Abercrombie & Fitch, N. Y.

PLATE I.

the recent research carried out by Remington-Peters concerning the effectiveness of *wads*. Wads, as the X-ray and spark photographs show, have a definite effect on the pattern offered by the shell. The spark photographs in Plates III and IV, made about one foot from the muzzle of the gun, show exactly what a wad can do to a load, and its tendency to produce a "blown" pattern.

There always has been considerable argument among shotgun shooters as to the importance of "blown" patterns. One shooter will insist that only one shell in 50 will produce a blown pattern, and that it is merely a matter of luck (bad luck) if the pattern happens to be blown in the section of the pattern taken up by the bird. Others insist that even though a blown pattern occurs once in a thousand rounds, it should be eliminated if possible.

"If there is a hole in the pattern," one shooter will insist, "that hole will be exactly where my target is at that instant. I have that kind of luck."

How many skeet and trap matches have been lost because of blown patterns will never be known, but it is an excellent alibi.

For those unfamiliar with exactly what constitutes a "blown" pattern, Plates V and VI will give an excellent example.

Extended research convinced Remington-Peters technicians that there was less chance of there being a blown pattern and a better opportunity to obtain the full velocity of the powder charge if a new type of wad could be employed. The wad desired was one which would compress following the explosion and seal the powder gas behind the shot column as it passed through the bore of the gun.

To find the material which would fill all the requirements called for additional research and experimentation, and finally a new material, known as "Du Pont Strux cellular cellulose acetate," was selected for the "cushion wad." Upon firing, this cushion wad is compressed to ⅛ its original length, and serves as a piston behind the powder wad. With this new wad, the pellets press into its foamy surface and are not distorted, but immediately part from the wad when the load leaves the bore, with no evidence of sticking. It was proved, by test, that the new cushion wad improved the ballistic balance of the shot shell from a pressure and velocity standpoint. It not only eliminated much of the power loss, thus adding to the velocity of the load, but improved the pattern. Plate VII shows the cushion wad before and after firing.

The spark photographs in Plates VIII and IX prove quite conclusively that the new wad has a definite effect on power loss.

**The Shotshell and "Choke."** The effect of choke on the shot column is another matter of great interest to shotgun shooters, who engage in many arguments as to the effect of choke on the shot column while it is in the barrel as well as after it has left. Some of the experiments carried out by the Winchester Arms Company offer visual examples of just what happens to the load from the time of the explosion to the arrival at the target.

Plates X and XI show the progress of the shot column for the last six inches of their course through a shotgun barrel. It will be noted that in the *cylinder*-bored barrel the shot column was compressed following the explosion, and maintained an almost constant depth and diameter during its passage through the barrel. In the *choke*-bored barrel, however, the shot column was initially compressed, but upon reaching the portion of the barrel where the choke began, the column became elongated.

"What happens to a shot column when it has passed a few feet from the muzzle?" is a query that thousands of shooters put to any ballistician they meet.

Plates XII to XX show very graphically just what happens, and how the difference in the boring of the gun affects the spread of the shot.

Plate XII shows the shot column as it is 6 feet from the muzzle, having passed through a barrel bored *full choke*. Note that even at this distance the shot column has strung out to several times its original depth, but has widened very little.

Now look at a similar load 6 feet from the muzzle, after it has passed through the barrel bored *modified choke* (Plate XIII). The shot column has

# WHAT IT TAKES TO MAKE A SHOTSHELL

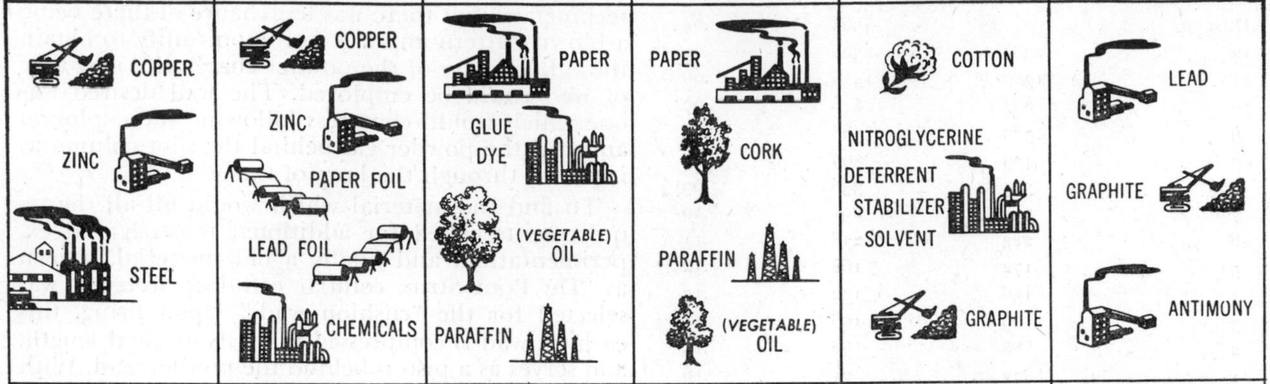

| HEAD | PRIMER | TUBE | WADS | POWDER | SHOT |
|---|---|---|---|---|---|
| COPPER<br>ZINC<br>STEEL | COPPER<br>ZINC<br>PAPER FOIL<br>LEAD FOIL<br>CHEMICALS | PAPER<br>GLUE<br>DYE<br>(VEGETABLE) OIL<br>PARAFFIN | PAPER<br>CORK<br>PARAFFIN<br>(VEGETABLE) OIL | COTTON<br>NITROGLYCERINE<br>DETERRENT<br>STABILIZER<br>SOLVENT<br>GRAPHITE | LEAD<br>GRAPHITE<br>ANTIMONY |
| MINE METALS<br>SMELT<br>ROLL STEEL | MINE METALS<br>MAKE PAPER<br>ROLL LEAD<br>MAKE CHEMICALS | MAKE PAPER<br>MAKE GLUE<br>PRESS OIL<br>SEPARATE PARAFFIN | MAKE PAPER<br>GRIND CORK<br>SEPARATE PARAFFIN<br>PRESS OIL | PURIFY COTTON<br>NITRATE COTTON<br>MAKE CHEMICALS<br>PREPARE GRAPHITE | MINE METALS<br>SMELT<br>ALLOY METALS<br>PREPARE GRAPHITE |
| CAST BRASS<br>ROLL SHEET<br>BLANK DISC<br>SHAPE CUP<br>EXPAND BASE<br>IMPRINT<br>PIERCE POCKET<br>KNURL<br>REINFORCE (STEEL)<br>ASSEMBLE | CAST BRASS<br>ROLL SHEET<br>MAKE CUPS<br>MAKE ANVIL<br>MAKE EXPLOSIVES<br>PREPARE MIX<br>CHARGE MIX<br>FOIL AND PRESS<br>ASSEMBLE<br>DRY | ROLL TUBE<br>APPLY PASTE<br>APPLY OIL<br>DRY<br>SIZE<br>CUT TO LENGTH<br>WATERPROOF | BASE WAD<br>ROLL AND PRESS<br>SEAL-TITE WAD<br>MIX AND MOLD<br>HEAT TREAT<br>NITRO WAD<br>BLANK<br>SUPER SEAL CUP WAD<br>BLANK<br>WATERPROOF<br>CUP<br>LOAD | DISSOLVE GUN COTTON<br>ADD NITROGLYCERINE<br>EMULSIFY<br>REMOVE SOLVENT<br>SCREEN TO SIZES<br>APPLY DETERRENT<br>DRY<br>APPLY GRAPHITE<br>BLEND<br>MEASURE<br>LOAD | MELT<br>DROP<br>SCREEN TO SIZES<br>CULL, (ROUNDNESS)<br>MEASURE<br>LOAD |

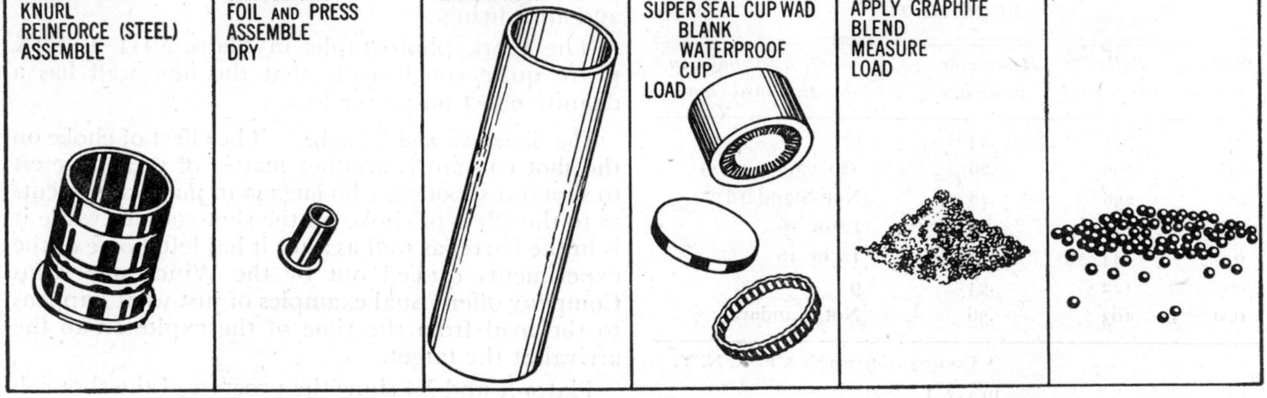

Courtesy Western Cartridge Co.

PLATE II.

about doubled its depth and more than doubled in width.

Now examine the column that passed through a *cylinder bore,* at the same 6-foot distance (Plate XIV). Here the shot column has compressed in depth, but spread out greatly in width.

Now look at the shot column shown 9 feet from the muzzle (Plate XV). This was fired through a *full-choked* barrel. Note that the column has extended still more in depth, but not greatly in width.

Here is the shot column at 9 feet, as fired from a gun bored *modified choke* (Plate XVI). Compare it with the modified-choke photograph taken at 6 feet (Plate XIII); there is little increase in depth, but quite an increase in width.

Plate XVII shows the shot column from the *cylinder*-bored gun at 9 feet. This, compared to the cylinder-bore photograph made at 6 feet (Plate XIV), shows that the shot column has increased considerably, both in depth and width, but much more in the latter.

The test is now carried on to 12 feet. At this distance the shot column has pulled well ahead of the wads, and while the column shows a great increase in depth, with the *choke*-bored barrel, it has not increased greatly in width (Plate XVIII).

Plate XIX shows the shot column that passed through the *modified-choke* bore, as it was at 12 feet. Note that it has expanded both in depth and width, but not nearly as much as has the *cylinder*-bored load at the same distance.

Plate XX shows the shot column after it has passed 12 feet from the muzzle of a *cylinder*-bored gun. Note the increased spread of the column in width.

This series of photographs, made at the Winchester laboratories, were taken at a speed of four millionths of a second. The shells used were all "Super-Trap," with 3 drams of powder, 1⅛ ounces of shot, and No. 8 pellets.

One point which undoubtedly will catch the attention of those studying these photographs is the length of the shot column or "shot string" of the

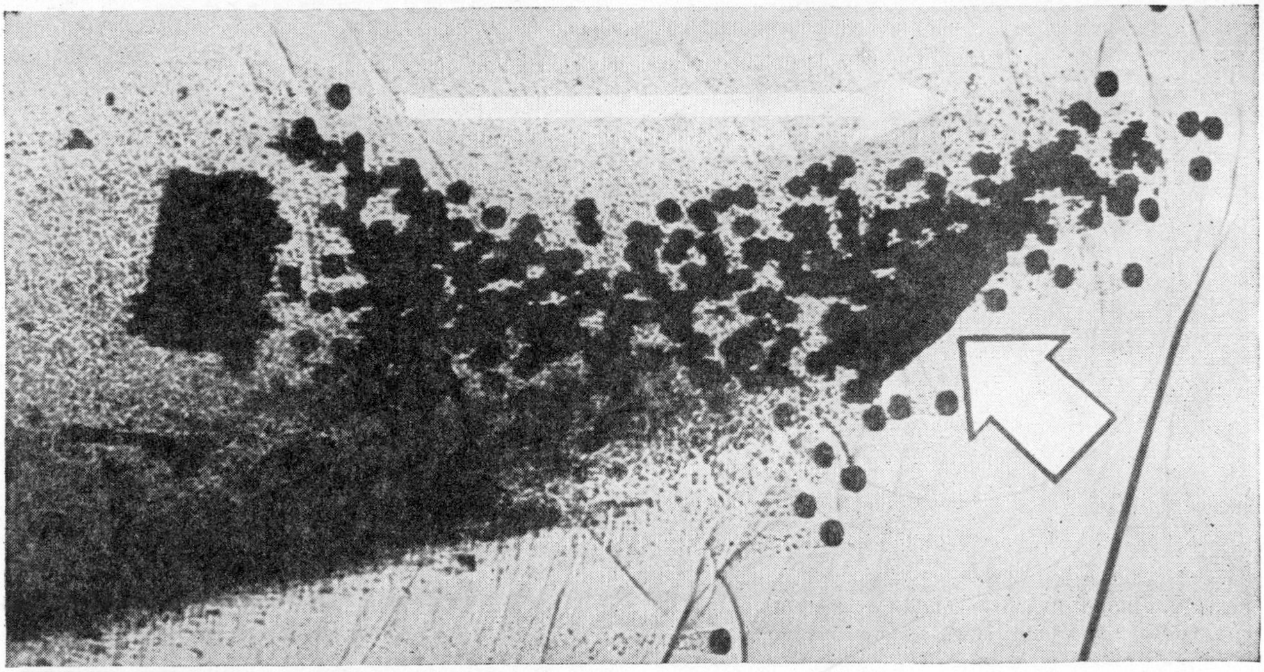

PLATE III. A Blown Pattern in the Making. Note shot wad interfering with shot column.

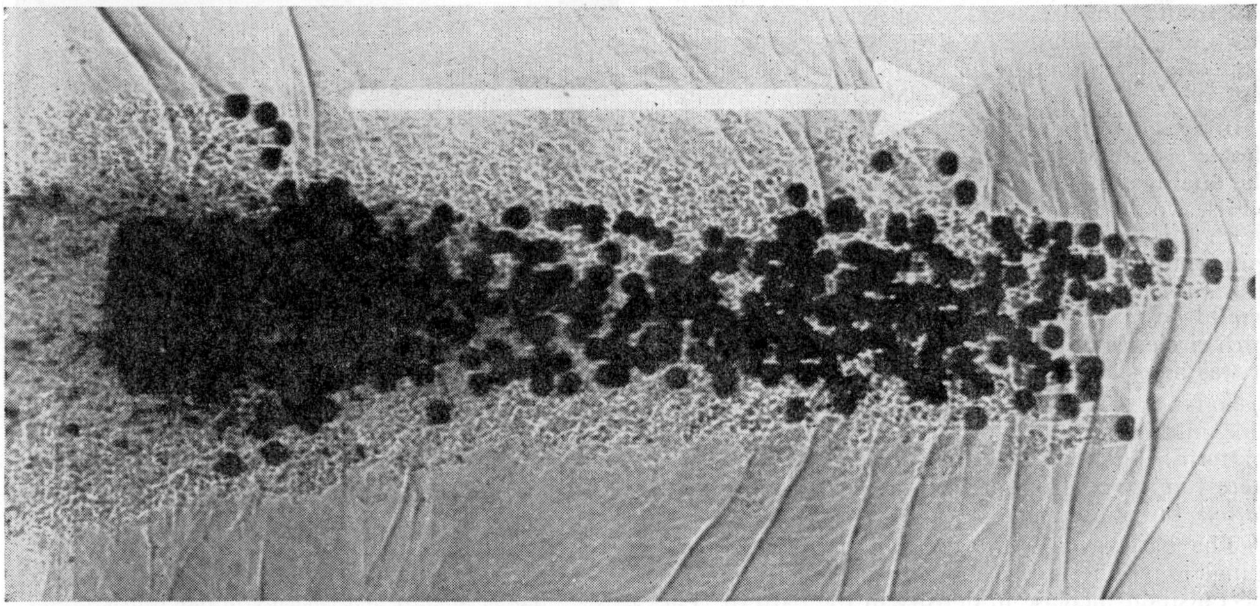

PLATE IV. A Perfect Shot Pattern in the Making—from a Remington New Crimp shell. There is no top shot wad to interfere with shot columns.

choke-bored gun at 12 feet. There is considerable discussion, not only among shooters, but among ammunition manufacturers, concerning short shot strings. In actuality, the shot strings of the modern shotgun shell are not "extremely" short, but they are much shorter than those of the fabulous "good old days."

Another sequence of photographs, which give a better illustration of the actual spread and distribution of shot than could be accomplished by many thousand words, is that which follows. This sequence shows the passage of a shot column to the point where it reaches a clay target. The trap or skeet shooter who can powder a "clay bird" in this manner usually has quite a row of trophies on his mantel.

Any shooter who sees these photographs will realize that he stands a much better chance of killing game (or breaking clay targets) if he *over*-leads than he does if he *under*-leads. Despite this fact, which many shooters recognize as true but continue to ignore when shooting, the greatest number of misses are scored through failing to allow for sufficient lead.

**Loads and Patterns.** Another question which interests thousands of shooters, concerns the pattern

PLATE V. Blown Pattern—made with shell of conventional roll crimp, caused by over-shot wad.

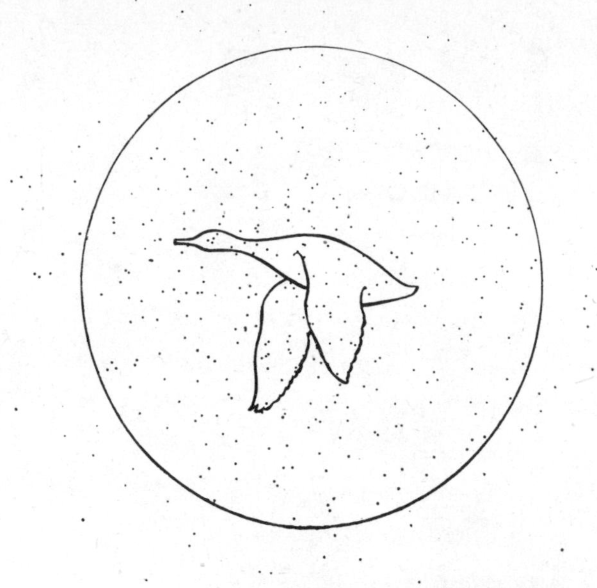

PLATE VI. Perfect Pattern—in which the over-powder wad is eliminated.

they will get from a given gun, of certain boring, with certain shot, at the normal extreme range. To answer this in every detail, for every load, boring, gauge, and shot size, would require several volumes. However, the technicians of the Western Cartridge Company have prepared for this Encyclopedia, exclusively, a set of patterns which will offer a "mean."

In arriving at a decision as to the gauge, boring, shot size, and range, the following factors influenced the final result. The most satisfactory "mean" is one which would be of value to the greatest number. With this in view, it was decided that a 12-gauge gun would be used; that the gun used would have a *modified-choke* boring; and that the patterns would be made at a range of 40 yards, using a 30-inch circle. In order to obtain an "average" pattern, it was necessary to fire several thousand rounds.

So far as is known, this is the first book to present this information by means of the actual average patterns. The value of this must be apparent, for here you are confronted with no *theory,* no *computation,* but simple *fact.*

The patterns shown were produced with a 12-gauge gun. The man using a 10-gauge gun may expect a slight increase in density in the pattern. The man using a 16-or 20-gauge gun will get a somewhat thinner pattern, but not much thinner, for the difference in pellet count is not so great as the difference in gauge. (Plates XXVII to XXXV.)

However, let the actual patterns tell their own story. Each pattern was made with a different size shot. This shot ranged from No. 9 to No. 00 buckshot. Under each pattern is given the type of shell used, the load, and the percentage of the shot load that is inside the 30-inch circle.

**Recoil.** The argument as to which gun "kicks the most, and how much" is one that has waged for more than a century, but modern instruments are able to measure just about anything, including recoil. Recoil tables prepared by cartridge technicians take

PLATE VII. Cushion Wad—before and after firing.

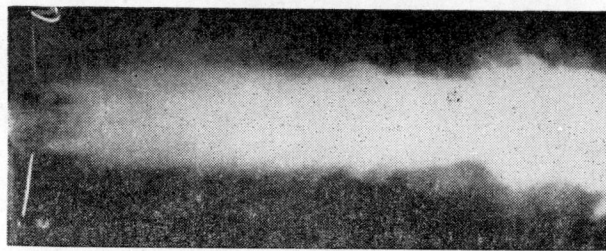

PLATE VIII. This photo shows the gas-sealing ability of the average, conventional wads. Notice the blast of escaping gas ahead of the shot charge, resulting in inefficient use of pressure and tendency to fuse pellets.

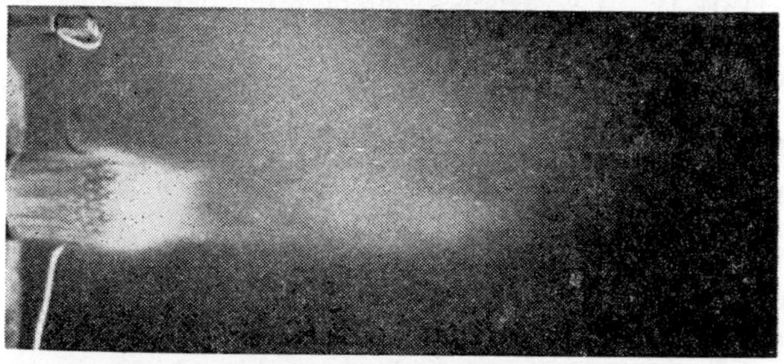

PLATE IX. This shows the excellent gas sealing of the power wad as the shot charge emerges from barrel. Wad seals powder gas from shot and provides an effective piston against which pressure may act without dissipation of energy through gas leakage.

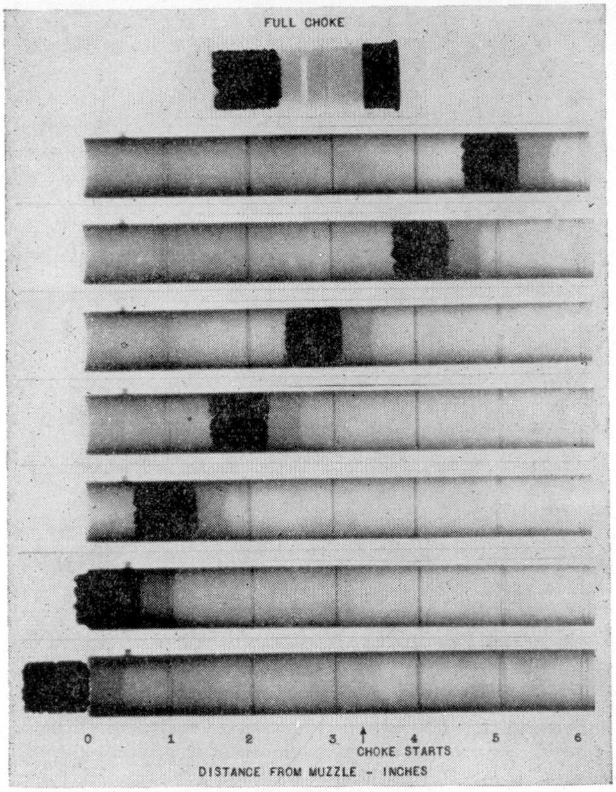


Plates X-XX—Courtesy Winchester Arms Co.

PLATE X.

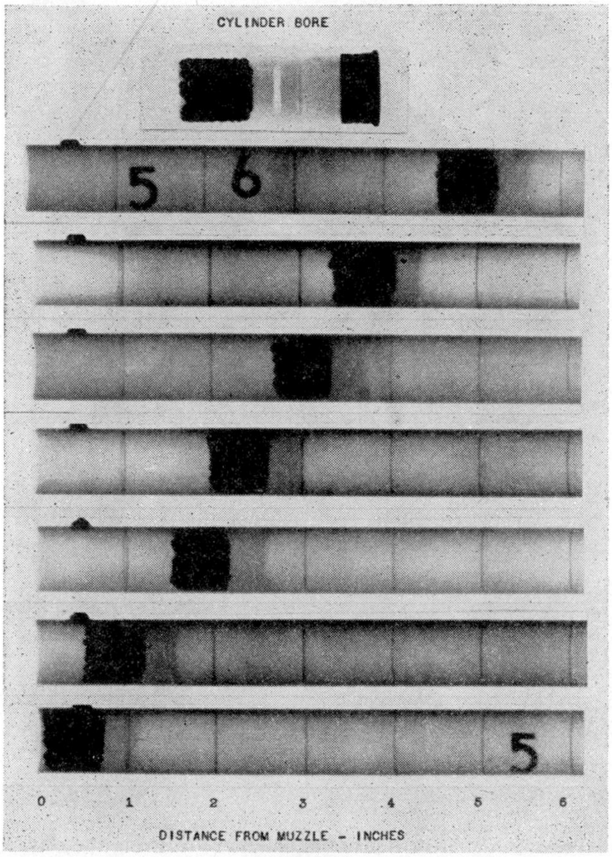


**PLATE XI.**

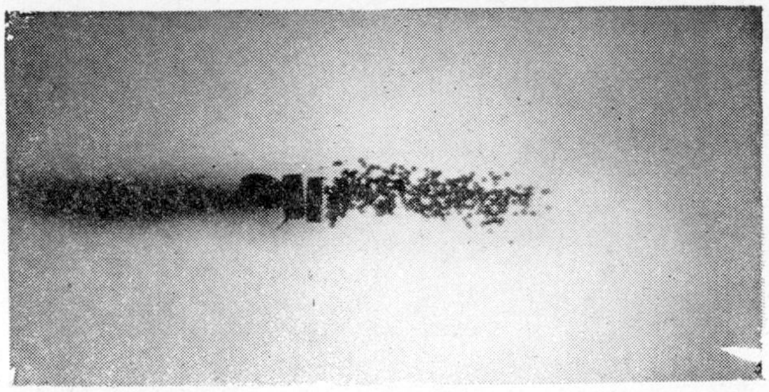

PLATE XII.

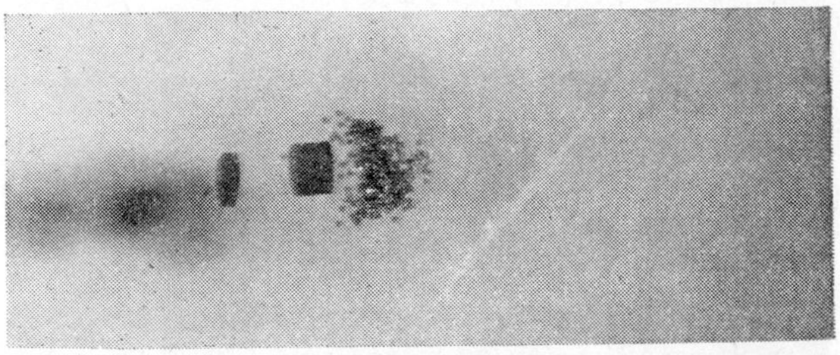

PLATE XIII.

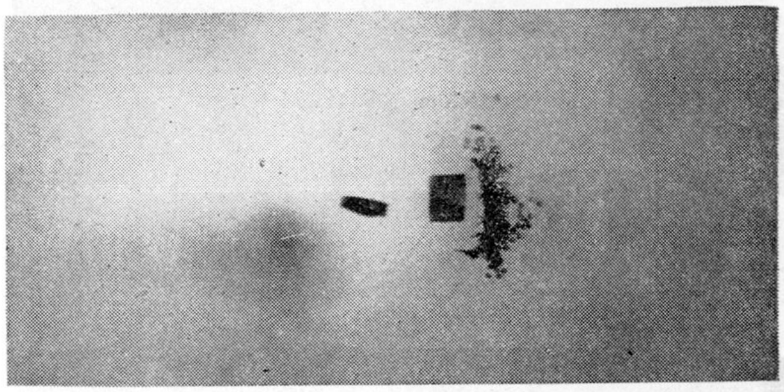

PLATE XIV.

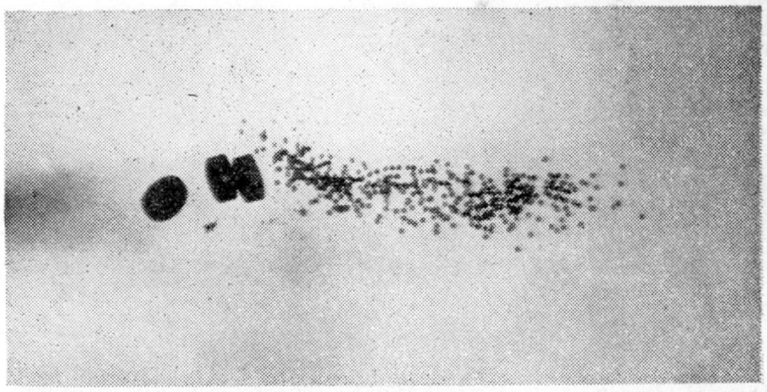

PLATE XV.

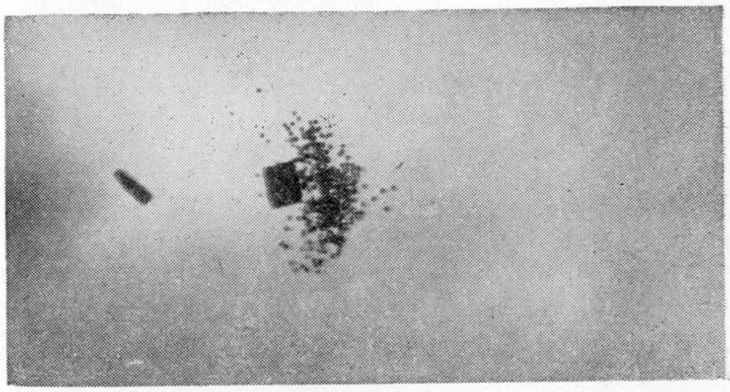

PLATE XVI.

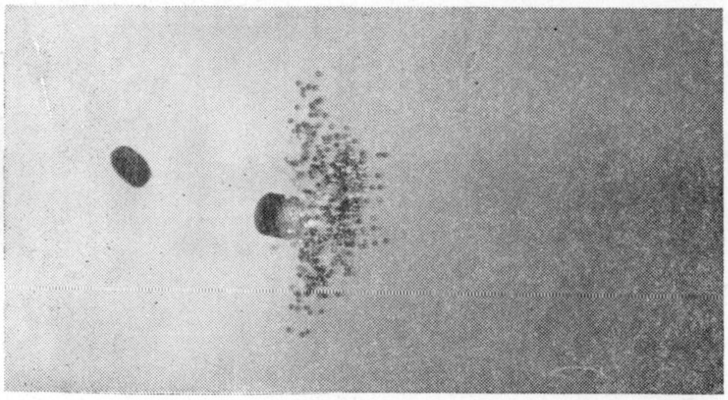

PLATE XVII.

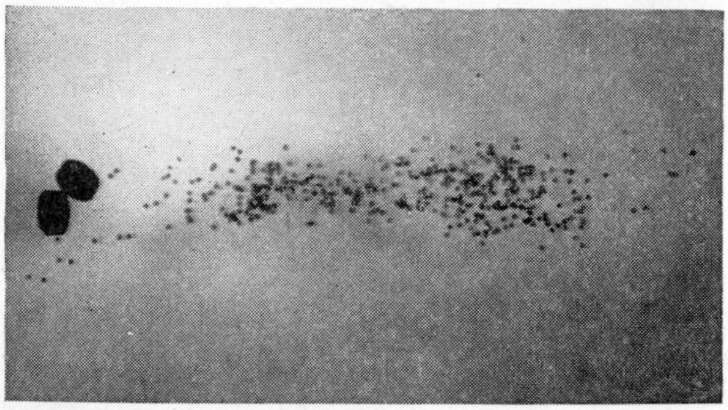

PLATE XVIII.

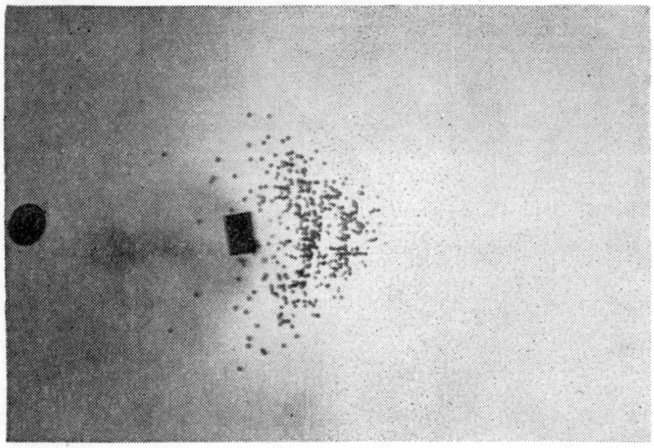

PLATE XIX.

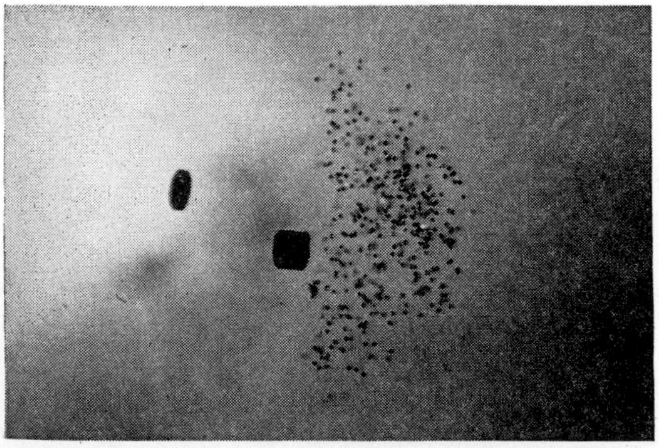

PLATE XX.

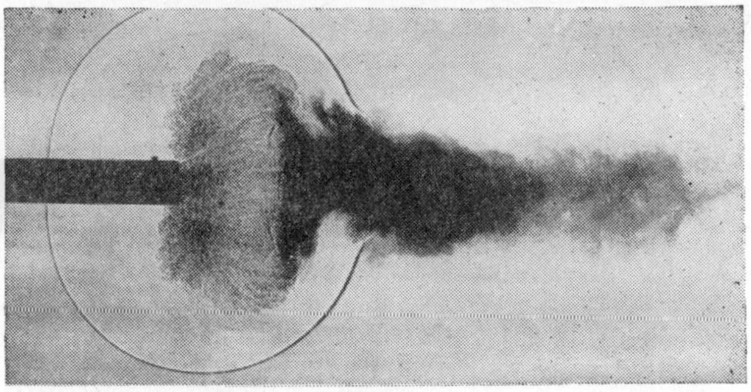

PLATE XXI. This shows the shot just emerging from the muzzle, a choked bore.

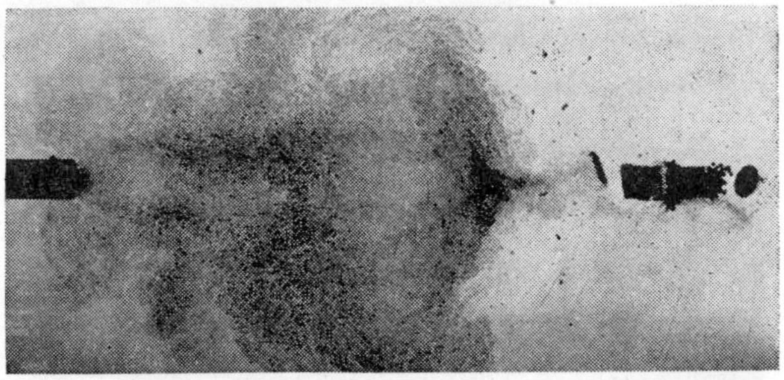

PLATE XXII. This shows the charge about 15 inches from the muzzle. At this point the front wad is still ahead of the shot column.

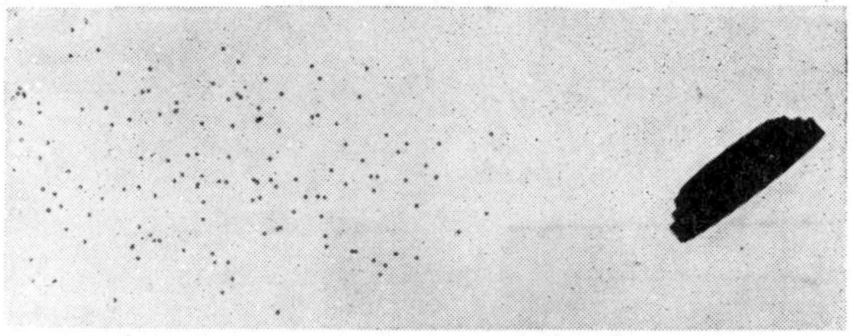

PLATE XXIII. Here the shot column, rather spread out now, is approaching the clay target.

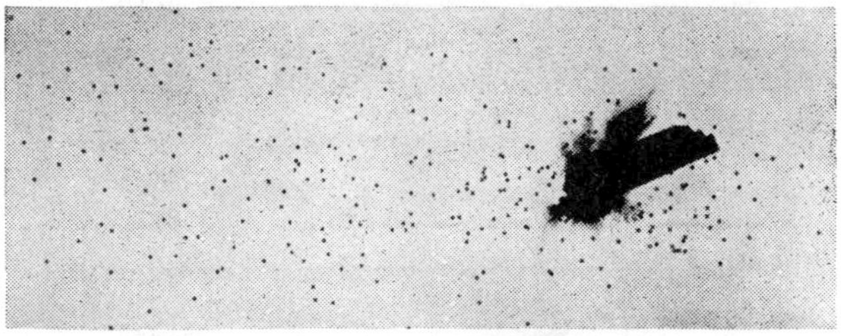

PLATE XXIV. The first of the pellets have now struck the clay target, but a good part of the shot column is still on its way.

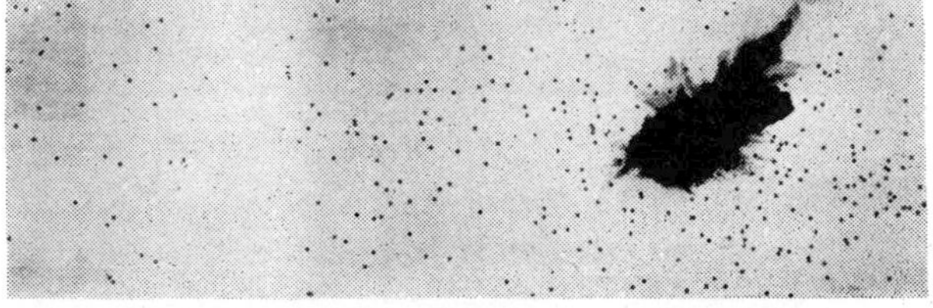

PLATE XXV. Here still more pellets are reaching the clay target, but the shot string has not "run out" as yet.

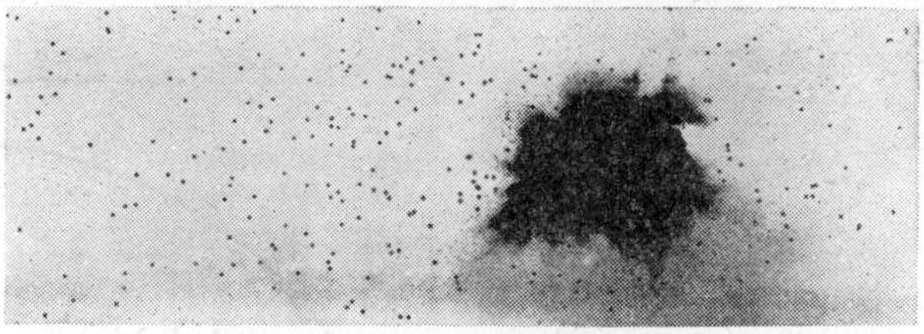

PLATE XXVI. In this final photograph the clay bird is almost completely powdered, but the shot string is still coming.

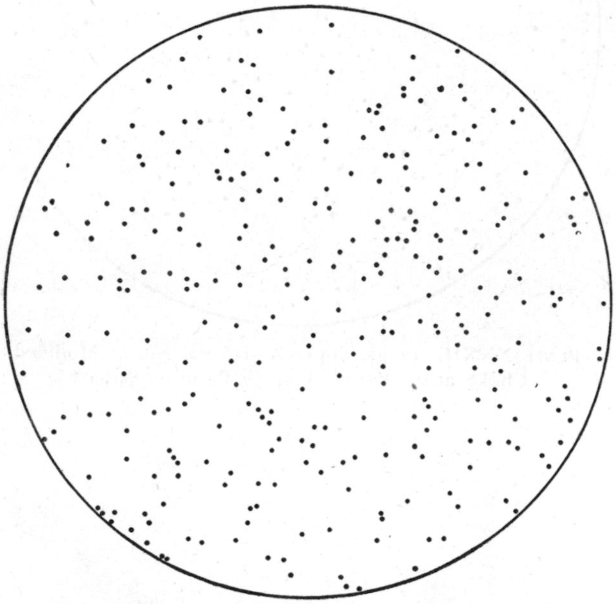

PLATE XXVII. 12 ga. Xpert Super Skeet—3 dr.—1⅛ oz. No. 9. Modified Choke at 40 Yards. Average Pattern: 40-45%

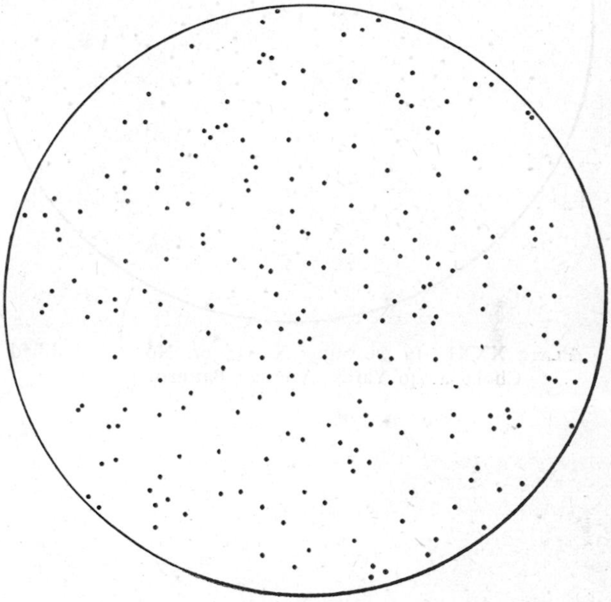

PLATE XXVIII. 12 ga. Xpert Super Trap—3 dr.—1⅛ oz. No. 8. Modified Choke at 40 Yards. Average Pattern: 45-50%

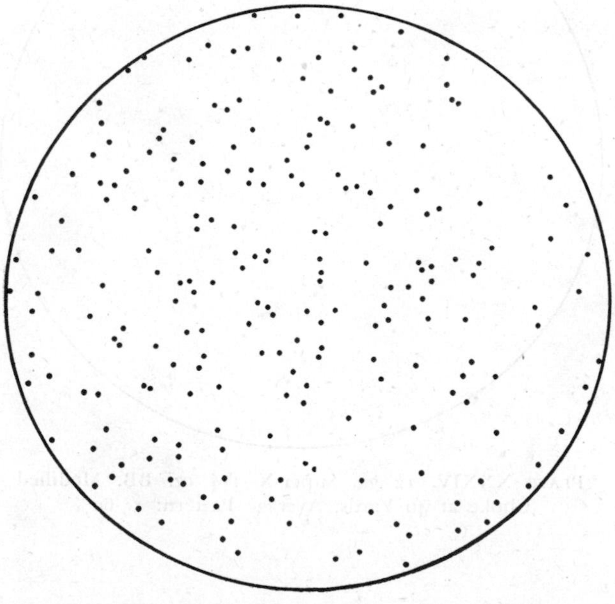

PLATE XXIX. 12 ga. Xpert Super Trap—3 dr. 1⅛ oz. No. 7½. Modified Choke at 40 Yards. Average Pattern: 50-55%

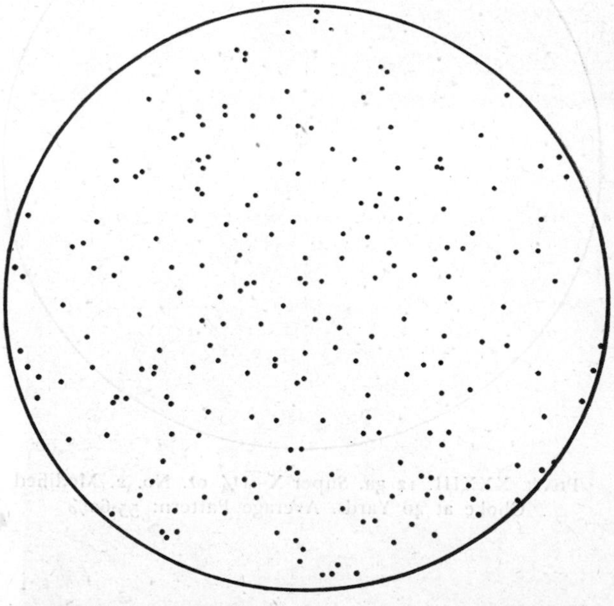

PLATE XXX. 12 ga. Xpert Super Trap—3¼ dr.—1¼ oz. No. 7. Modified Choke at 40 Yards. Average Pattern: 50-55%

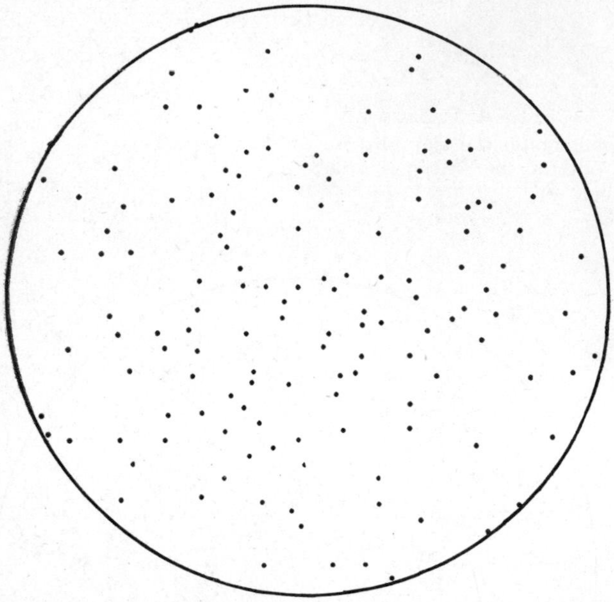

PLATE XXXI. 12 ga. Super-X—1¼ oz. No. 5. Modified Choke at 40 Yards. Average Pattern: 55-60%

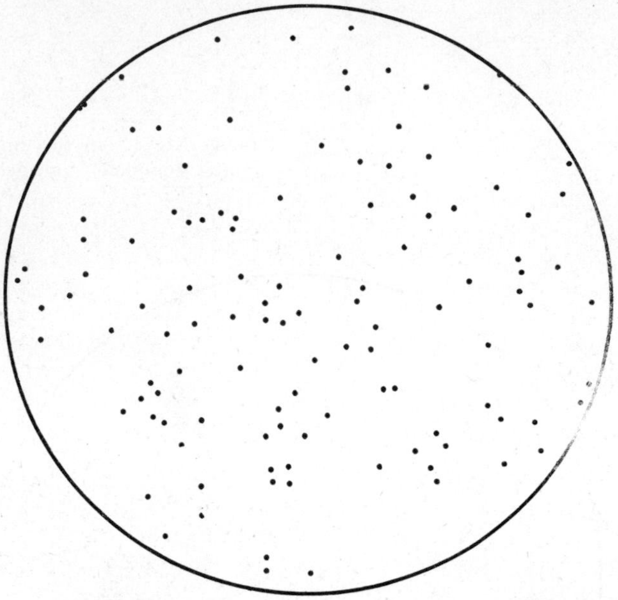

PLATE XXXII. 12 ga. Super-X—1¼ oz. No. 4. Modified Choke at 40 Yards. Average Pattern: 55-60%

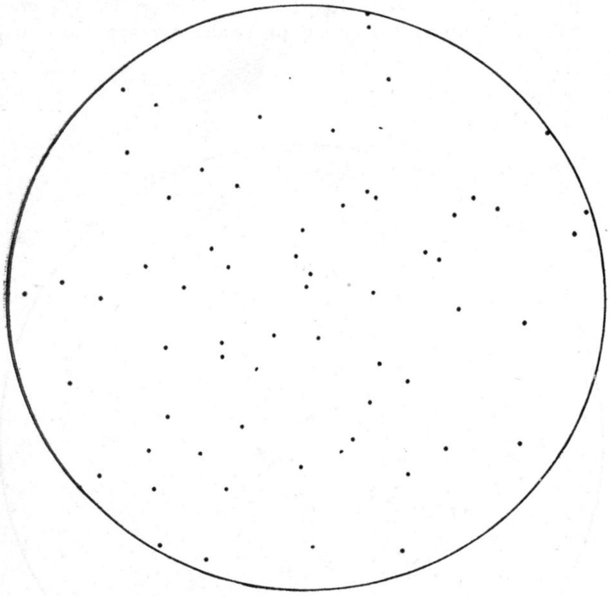

PLATE XXXIII. 12 ga. Super-X—1¼ oz. No. 2. Modified Choke at 40 Yards. Average Pattern: 55-60%

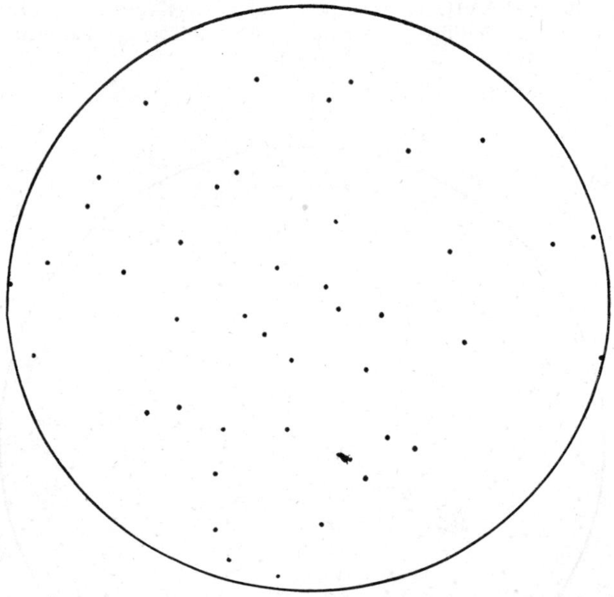

PLATE XXXIV. 12 ga. Super-X—1¼ oz. BB. Modified Choke at 40 Yards. Average Pattern: 55-60%

the guesswork out of recoil, for if you shoot a certain load in a certain gauge gun with a certain weight, you can compare it with any other gun of any gauge or weight. The following tables will tell you just how much more recoil you will get with the express loads, and how little you will get with the light loads.

These tests were made with an instrument known as a "ballistic pendulum," which gives the most reliable determinations of recoil that exist. As everyone knows, the recoil increases as the velocity or the weight of the shot-charge is increased. It is impossible to increase the velocity and weight of the shot-charge and not increase the recoil, *if the same gun is used*. Decreasing the weight of the wads and powder will help to a very limited extent, but the total of these items is a small percentage of the shot-charge weight, and undesirable effects on the load are produced by decreasing the weight of these items. To decrease the recoil of any given load, use a heavier gun.

In the tables two sets of values are given. One is the "velocity of recoil," and represents the velocity that the gun would have if unrestrained in its motion as the shell is fired. This velocity is expressed in feet per second.

The other value, designated as the "kinetic energy of recoil," represents the energy imparted to the gun as the charge is driven out through the barrel. This value is expressed in foot-pounds.

It will be noted that no shot sizes are given in the tables. *The recoil value is the same for all sizes of shot*. This is true because the muzzle velocities of all of the shot sizes are the same for the nominal powder and shot load. For this reason, the recoil values are the same whether No. 8 or No. 2 shot are used.

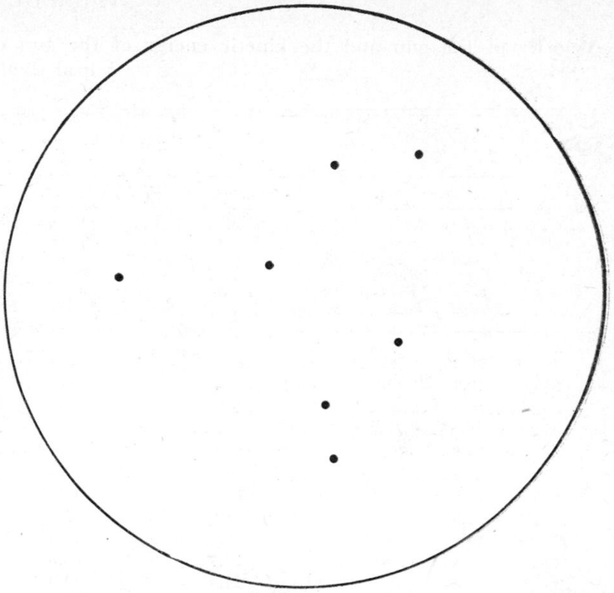

PLATE XXXV. 12 ga. Super-X—1¼ oz. No. 00 Buck. Modified Choke at 40 Yards. Average Pattern: 65-70%.

Note that the energy of recoil of the same nominal load in different gauges will, in general be different. For example, a 2¼—1 load in a 20-gauge gun will show a higher recoil value than a 2½—1 load in a 16-gauge gun. The reason for this is that a 2½—1 load in a 20-gauge gun has a higher velocity than the same nominal load in a 16-gauge gun.

But here are the tables. You can see for yourself.

### 10 GAUGE RECOIL TABLE

Velocity of the gun and the kinetic energy of the gun during recoil when guns of various weights are used to fire the load combinations listed.

| *Weight of Gun (Pounds)* | *LOAD* | | | |
|---|---|---|---|---|
| | *4¼ dr.—1¼ oz.* | | *4¾ dr.—1⅝ oz.* | |
| | *Velocity of Recoil Feet per Second* | *Kinetic Energy of Recoil Foot-Pounds* | *Velocity of Recoil Feet per Second* | *Kinetic Energy of Recoil Foot-Pounds* |
| 7 | 22.9 | 57.1 | 27.6 | 82.6 |
| 7¼ | 22.1 | 55.2 | 26.6 | 79.8 |
| 7½ | 21.4 | 53.0 | 25.7 | 77.2 |
| 7¾ | 20.6 | 51.6 | 24.9 | 74.6 |
| 8 | 20.0 | 49.8 | 24.1 | 72.4 |
| 8¼ | 19.4 | 48.2 | 23.4 | 70.4 |
| 8½ | 18.8 | 46.9 | 22.7 | 68.4 |
| 8¾ | 18.3 | 45.5 | 22.0 | 66.1 |
| 9 | 17.8 | 44.3 | 21.4 | 64.2 |
| 9¼ | 17.3 | 42.9 | 20.9 | 62.8 |
| 9½ | 16.9 | 41.9 | 20.3 | 61.2 |
| 9¾ | 16.4 | 40.8 | 19.8 | 59.4 |
| 10 | 16.0 | 39.8 | 19.3 | 57.9 |
| 10¼ | 15.6 | 38.9 | 18.8 | 56.4 |
| 10½ | 15.2 | 37.9 | 18.4 | 55.2 |
| 10¾ | 14.9 | 37.1 | 17.9 | 53.8 |
| 11 | 14.6 | 36.2 | 17.6 | 52.6 |

## 12 GAUGE RECOIL TABLE

Velocity of the gun and the kinetic energy of the gun during recoil when guns of various weights are used to fire the load combinations listed.

| Weight of Gun (Pounds) | LOAD: 3 dr.—1 oz. | | 3 dr.—1¼ oz. | | 3¼ dr.—1⅛ oz. | | 3½ dr.—1⅛ oz. | | 3¼ dr.—1¼ oz. | | 3½ dr.—1¼ oz. | | 3¾ dr.—1¼ oz. | |
|---|---|---|---|---|---|---|---|---|---|---|---|---|---|---|
| | *Velocity of Recoil Feet per Second* | *Kinetic Energy of Recoil Foot-Pounds* | *Velocity of Recoil Feet per Second* | *Kinetic Energy of Recoil Foot-Pounds* | *Velocity of Recoil Feet per Second* | *Kinetic Energy of Recoil Foot-Pounds* | *Velocity of Recoil Feet per Second* | *Kinetic Energy of Recoil Foot-Pounds* | *Velocity of Recoil Feet per Second* | *Kinetic Energy of Recoil Foot-Pounds* | *Velocity of Recoil Feet per Second* | *Kinetic Energy of Recoil Foot-Pounds* | *Velocity of Recoil Feet per Second* | *Kinetic Energy of Recoil Foot-Pounds* |
| 5 | 20.1 | 31.2 | 21.9 | 37.3 | 23.2 | 42.0 | 24.6 | 47.1 | 24.7 | 47.4 | 27.0 | 56.7 | 28.2 | 62.2 |
| 5¼ | 19.1 | 29.9 | 20.8 | 35.6 | 22.1 | 40.0 | 23.4 | 44.8 | 23.6 | 45.1 | 25.7 | 54.0 | 26.8 | 58.8 |
| 5½ | 18.3 | 28.5 | 19.9 | 33.7 | 21.0 | 37.8 | 22.3 | 42.7 | 22.5 | 43.4 | 24.6 | 51.2 | 25.6 | 56.2 |
| 5¾ | 17.5 | 27.2 | 19.0 | 32.3 | 20.2 | 36.4 | 21.4 | 41.0 | 21.5 | 41.4 | 23.5 | 49.4 | 24.5 | 53.5 |
| 6 | 16.8 | 26.2 | 18.2 | 31.0 | 19.3 | 34.8 | 20.5 | 39.2 | 20.6 | 39.2 | 22.5 | 47.4 | 23.5 | 51.4 |
| 6¼ | 16.1 | 25.2 | 17.5 | 29.7 | 18.6 | 33.4 | 19.7 | 37.7 | 19.8 | 37.9 | 21.6 | 45.4 | 22.6 | 49.4 |
| 6½ | 15.4 | 24.2 | 16.8 | 28.6 | 17.8 | 32.2 | 19.0 | 36.3 | 19.0 | 36.4 | 20.8 | 43.8 | 21.7 | 47.5 |
| 6¾ | 14.9 | 23.3 | 16.2 | 27.6 | 17.2 | 30.9 | 18.2 | 35.0 | 18.3 | 35.2 | 20.0 | 42.0 | 20.8 | 45.5 |
| 7 | 14.4 | 22.4 | 15.6 | 26.5 | 16.6 | 29.8 | 17.6 | 33.6 | 17.7 | 33.9 | 19.3 | 40.5 | 20.1 | 44.0 |
| 7¼ | 13.9 | 21.6 | 15.1 | 25.7 | 16.0 | 28.8 | 17.0 | 32.6 | 17.0 | 32.7 | 18.6 | 39.2 | 19.4 | 42.6 |
| 7½ | 13.4 | 20.9 | 14.6 | 24.8 | 15.5 | 27.9 | 16.4 | 31.4 | 16.5 | 31.6 | 18.0 | 37.8 | 18.8 | 41.2 |
| 7¾ | 13.0 | 20.3 | 14.1 | 24.0 | 15.0 | 26.9 | 15.9 | 30.4 | 16.0 | 30.7 | 17.4 | 36.6 | 18.2 | 40.0 |
| 8 | 12.6 | 19.6 | 13.7 | 23.3 | 14.5 | 26.1 | 15.4 | 29.5 | 15.5 | 29.7 | 16.9 | 35.4 | 17.6 | 38.4 |
| 8¼ | 12.2 | 19.0 | 13.3 | 22.5 | 14.0 | 25.3 | 14.9 | 28.6 | 15.0 | 28.8 | 16.4 | 34.4 | 17.1 | 37.3 |
| 8½ | 11.8 | 18.4 | 12.9 | 21.9 | 13.6 | 24.6 | 14.5 | 27.7 | 14.5 | 27.9 | 15.9 | 33.4 | 16.6 | 36.3 |
| 8¾ | 11.5 | 17.9 | 12.5 | 21.2 | 13.3 | 23.9 | 14.1 | 27.0 | 14.1 | 27.2 | 15.4 | 32.4 | 16.1 | 35.2 |
| 9 | 11.2 | 17.2 | 12.2 | 20.6 | 12.9 | 23.2 | 13.7 | 26.2 | 13.8 | 26.5 | 15.0 | 31.5 | 15.6 | 34.2 |

## 16 GAUGE RECOIL TABLE

Velocity of the gun and the kinetic energy of the gun during recoil when guns of various weights are used to fire the load combinations listed.

| Weight of Gun (Pounds) | LOAD: 2½ dr.–1 oz. | | 2¾ dr.–1 oz. | | 3 dr.–1 oz. | | 3 dr.–1⅛ oz. | |
|---|---|---|---|---|---|---|---|---|
| | *Velocity of Recoil Feet per Second* | *Kinetic Energy of Recoil Foot-Pounds* | *Velocity of Recoil Feet per Second* | *Kinetic Energy of Recoil Foot-Pounds* | *Velocity of Recoil Feet per Second* | *Kinetic Energy of Recoil Foot-Pounds* | *Velocity of Recoil Feet per Second* | *Kinetic Energy of Recoil Foot-Pounds* |
| 5 | 18.8 | 27.4 | 21.2 | 34.9 | 22.1 | 37.9 | 23.8 | 44.0 |
| 5¼ | 17.9 | 26.1 | 20.2 | 33.6 | 21.0 | 36.1 | 22.7 | 42.0 |
| 5½ | 17.1 | 25.0 | 19.3 | 31.7 | 20.1 | 34.5 | 21.6 | 39.9 |
| 5¾ | 16.3 | 23.8 | 18.4 | 30.3 | 19.2 | 33.0 | 20.7 | 38.3 |
| 6 | 15.6 | 22.8 | 17.6 | 29.0 | 18.4 | 31.8 | 19.8 | 36.7 |
| 6¼ | 15.0 | 21.9 | 17.0 | 27.8 | 17.7 | 30.4 | 19.0 | 35.2 |
| 6½ | 14.5 | 21.1 | 16.3 | 26.8 | 17.0 | 29.2 | 18.3 | 33.9 |
| 6¾ | 13.9 | 20.3 | 15.7 | 25.8 | 16.4 | 28.2 | 17.6 | 32.6 |
| 7 | 13.4 | 19.6 | 15.1 | 24.9 | 15.8 | 27.1 | 17.0 | 31.4 |
| 7¼ | 13.0 | 18.9 | 14.6 | 24.0 | 15.2 | 26.2 | 16.4 | 30.5 |
| 7½ | 12.5 | 18.3 | 14.1 | 23.2 | 14.8 | 25.3 | 15.9 | 29.4 |
| 7¾ | 12.1 | 17.7 | 13.7 | 22.5 | 14.3 | 24.5 | 15.4 | 28.4 |
| 8 | 11.8 | 17.1 | 13.2 | 21.8 | 13.8 | 23.7 | 14.9 | 27.5 |
| 8¼ | 11.4 | 16.6 | 12.8 | 21.2 | 13.4 | 23.0 | 14.4 | 26.7 |
| 8½ | 11.1 | 16.2 | 12.5 | 20.5 | 13.0 | 22.3 | 14.0 | 25.9 |
| 8¾ | 10.7 | 15.7 | 12.1 | 19.9 | 12.6 | 21.7 | 13.6 | 25.2 |
| 9 | 10.4 | 15.3 | 11.8 | 19.5 | 12.3 | 21.1 | 13.2 | 24.6 |

20 GAUGE RECOIL TABLE

Velocity of the gun and the kinetic energy of the gun during recoil when guns of various weights are used to fire the load combinations listed.

| *Weight of Gun (Pounds)* | LOAD *2¼ dr.—⅞ oz.* *Velocity of Recoil Feet per Second* | *Kinetic Energy of Recoil Foot-Pounds* | *2½ dr.—1 oz.* *Velocity of Recoil Feet per Second* | *Kinetic Energy of Recoil Foot-Pounds* | *2¾ dr.—1 oz.* *Velocity of Recoil Feet per Second* | *Kinetic Energy of Recoil Foot-Pounds* |
|---|---|---|---|---|---|---|
| 5 | 16.8 | 22.0 | 19.7 | 30.1 | 21.8 | 36.9 |
| 5¼ | 16.0 | 20.9 | 18.8 | 28.7 | 20.8 | 35.3 |
| 5½ | 15.3 | 20.0 | 17.9 | 27.4 | 19.8 | 33.6 |
| 5¾ | 14.6 | 19.1 | 17.1 | 26.2 | 19.0 | 32.1 |
| 6 | 14.0 | 18.3 | 16.4 | 25.1 | 18.2 | 30.9 |
| 6¼ | 13.5 | 17.6 | 15.8 | 24.1 | 17.4 | 29.6 |
| 6½ | 13.0 | 16.9 | 15.2 | 23.2 | 16.8 | 28.4 |
| 6¾ | 12.5 | 16.3 | 14.6 | 22.3 | 16.2 | 27.4 |
| 7 | 12.0 | 15.7 | 14.1 | 21.5 | 15.6 | 26.4 |
| 7¼ | 11.6 | 15.2 | 13.6 | 20.8 | 15.0 | 25.5 |
| 7½ | 11.2 | 14.7 | 13.1 | 20.1 | 14.5 | 24.6 |
| 7¾ | 10.9 | 14.2 | 12.7 | 19.4 | 14.1 | 23.9 |
| 8 | 10.5 | 13.8 | 12.3 | 18.8 | 13.6 | 23.1 |
| 8¼ | 10.2 | 13.3 | 11.9 | 18.3 | 13.2 | 22.4 |
| 8½ | 9.9 | 12.9 | 11.6 | 17.7 | 12.8 | 21.7 |
| 8¾ | 9.6 | 12.6 | 11.3 | 17.2 | 12.5 | 21.1 |
| 9 | 9.4 | 12.2 | 10.9 | 16.7 | 12.1 | 20.5 |

**Barrel Length and Velocities.** Although there is considerable argument as to the relative merits of the long barrel and the short barrel in a shotgun, and the resulting lowering or increasing of velocities, the effect this difference in velocity has in field shooting is negligible.

It is a known fact that a load of shot fired through a 30-inch barrel has a greater velocity than a similar load fired through a 22-inch barrel, but few shooters realize the extent of this difference. Tests made several years ago, during which guns were cut down an inch at a time and the velocities measured, indicated that the reduction in velocity amounted to about 7½ feet per second per inch of barrel length.

More recent tests, made with 12-gauge trap loads, gave more accurate figures. The original barrel length of the gun used in the test was 30 inches. This barrel was reduced, 2 inches at a time, to a final length of 22 inches. This test indicated that the average loss in velocity was about 6½ foot-seconds per inch.

The field shooter is interested in what effect such reductions in velocity would have on his *lead* for various game birds. The answer is "almost none." For example, at 20 yards, which is something of an average for quail shooting, the difference in the speed of flight of the charge between a 30-inch barrel and a 22-inch barrel is only .004 second. On a crossing bird flying at a speed of 60 miles per hour, the man shooting the gun with 22-inch barrels would have to increase his *lead* approximately 5 inches, and at 30 yards his lead would have to be increased about 11 inches. Thus, at 20 yards the bird would still be well within the pattern. At 30 yards it would be somewhat out of the center of the pattern but still inside it. At 40 yards, however, the difference in lead would amount to 16 inches. However, a gun with 22-inch barrels would not be too effective at 40 yards in any case, because of the great enlargement of the shot pattern.

Tables I and II show the instrumental velocities of various shotshells of varied gauge, length, load, and pellet size.

**Pellet Counts.** Tables III and IV show the pellet count of the shot loads of various gauges of shotshells, of various lengths, loads and shot sizes.

Table VI shows the average percentage of shot and average number of pellets that are placed in a 30-inch circle at 40 yards, using varying charges of all standard sizes of chilled shot.

**Shot Sizes and Weights.** Plate I (p. 745) shows the diameter of the various sizes of chilled and dropped shot as well as the number of shot in the ounce or in the pound.

TABLE I. INSTRUMENTAL VELOCITIES OVER 40 YARDS EXCEPT 410 AT 50 FEET.*
WESTERN—WINCHESTER

| *Ga.* | *Length Inches* | *Load Ounces* | *BB* | *2* | *4* | *5* | *6* | *7½* | *8* |
|---|---|---|---|---|---|---|---|---|---|
| | | | | | *Super Speed Loads* | | | | |
| 10 | 2⅞ | 1⅝ | 1065 | 1035 | 1005 | 985 | 965 | .... | .... |
| 12 | 2¾ | 1¼ | 1075 | 1045 | 1015 | 995 | 975 | 940 | .... |
| 12 | 3 | 1⅜ | 1065 | 1035 | 1005 | 985 | 965 | .... | .... |
| 12 | 3 | 1⅝ | 1065 | 1035 | 1005 | 985 | 965 | .... | .... |
| 16 | 2¾ | 1⅛ | .... | 1025 | 995 | 975 | 955 | 920 | .... |
| 20 | 2¾ | 1 | .... | 970 | 940 | 920 | 900 | 865 | .... |
| 28 | 2⅞ | ¾ | .... | .... | 990 | .... | 950 | 915 | .... |
| *410 | 2½ | ½ | .... | .... | 1020 | 1000 | 980 | 950 | .... |
| *410 | 3 | ¾ | .... | .... | 1020 | 1000 | 980 | 950 | .... |
| | | | | | *Field Loads* | | | | |
| 12 | 2¾ | 3-1 | .... | .... | 965 | 945 | 925 | .... | 875 |
| 12 | 2¾ | 3-1⅛ | .... | .... | 945 | 925 | 905 | 870 | 855 |
| 12 | 2¾ | 3¼-1⅛ | .... | .... | 975 | 955 | 935 | .... | 885 |
| *16 | 2 9/16 | 2½-1 | .... | .... | 925 | 905 | 885 | .... | 835 |
| 16 | 2¾ | 2¾-1⅛ | .... | .... | 935 | .... | 895 | .... | 845 |
| 20 | 2¾ | 2¼-⅞ | .... | .... | 925 | 905 | 885 | .... | 835 |
| 20 | 2¾ | 2½-1 | .... | .... | 930 | .... | 890 | .... | 840 |

* Rolled Crimp—Other Super Seal.

TABLE II. REMINGTON-PETERS

| *Ga.* | *Shell* | *Shell Length —Inches* | *Drams Equiv.* | *Shot Wt. Ozs.* | *Average Velocity—over 40 yard Range—Feet per Second* | | | | | | | | |
|---|---|---|---|---|---|---|---|---|---|---|---|---|---|
| | | | | | *BB* | *2* | *4* | *5* | *6* | *7* | *7½* | *8* | *9* |
| 10 | S.S. & V. | 2⅞ | 4¼ | 1¼ | .... | .... | 1025 | 1005 | 985 | .... | .... | .... | .... |
| 10 | RX & PHV | 2⅞ | 4¾ | 1⅝ | 1065 | 1035 | 1005 | 985 | 965 | .... | .... | .... | .... |
| 10 | RX & PHV (Magnum) | 3½ | 5 | 2 | 1065 | 1035 | 1005 | 985 | 965 | .... | .... | .... | .... |
| 12 | S.S. & V. | 2¾ | 2¾ | 1⅛ | .... | .... | .... | .... | .... | .... | 840 | 825 | .... |
| 12 | S.S. & V. | 2¾ | 3 | 1 | .... | .... | 965 | 945 | 925 | .... | .... | 875 | .... |
| 12 | S.S. & V. | 2¾ | 3 | 1⅛ | .... | .... | 945 | 925 | 905 | .... | 870 | 855 | †920 |
| 12 | S.S. & V. | 2¾ | 3¼ | 1⅛ | .... | .... | 975 | 955 | 935 | .... | .... | 885 | .... |
| 12 | S.S. & V. | 2¾ | 3¼ | 1¼ | .... | .... | .... | .... | .... | 890 | 880 | .... | .... |
| 12 | RX & PHV | 2¾ | 3¾ | 1¼ | 1075 | 1045 | 1015 | 995 | 975 | .... | 940 | .... | .... |
| 12 | RX & PHV | 3 | 3¾ | 1¼ | .... | .... | .... | .... | .... | 950 | 940 | .... | .... |
| 12 | RX & PHV | 3 | 4 | 1⅜ | 1065 | 1035 | 1005 | 985 | 965 | .... | .... | .... | .... |
| 12 | RX & PHV (Magnum) | 3 | 4¼ | 1⅝ | 1065 | 1035 | 1005 | 985 | 965 | .... | .... | .... | .... |
| 16* | S.S. & V. | 2 9/16 | 2½ | 1 | .... | .... | 925 | 905 | 885 | .... | .... | 835 | †920 |
| 16 | S.S. & V. | 2¾ | 2¾ | 1⅛ | .... | .... | 935 | .... | 895 | .... | .... | 845 | .... |
| 16 | RX & PHV | 2¾ | 3 | 1⅛ | .... | 995 | 965 | 945 | 925 | .... | 890 | .... | .... |
| 16 | RX & PHV | 2¾ | 3¼ | 1⅛ | .... | 1025 | 995 | 975 | 955 | .... | 920 | .... | .... |
| 20 | S.S. & V | 2¾ | 2¼ | ⅞ | .... | .... | 925 | 905 | 885 | .... | .... | 835 | †920 |
| 20 | S.S. & V. | 2¾ | 2½ | 1 | .... | .... | 930 | .... | 890 | .... | .... | 840 | .... |
| 20 | RX & PHV | 2¾ | 2¾ | 1 | .... | 970 | 940 | 920 | 900 | .... | 865 | .... | .... |
| 28 | RX & PHV | 2⅞ | 2¼ | ¾ | .... | .... | 990 | .... | 950 | .... | 915 | .... | †920 |
| 410 | RX & PHV | 2½ | .... | ½ | .... | .... | †1020 | †1000 | †980 | .... | †950 | .... | †920 |
| 410 | RX & PHV | 3 | .... | ¾ | .... | .... | †1020 | †1000 | †980 | .... | †950 | .... | †880 |

* Supplied in Rolled Crimp.
† Instrumental velocity over 25 yards.

Index—S.S. Means Shur Shot (Remington)
V. means Peters Victor
RX means Remington Express
PHV means Peters Hi-Velocity

## TABLE III. PELLET COUNT VARIOUS GAGES

Western-Winchester

| *Ga.* | *Length Inches* | *Load Ounces* | *BB* | *2* | *4* | *5* | *6* | *7½* | *8* |
|---|---|---|---|---|---|---|---|---|---|
| | | | | | *Super Speed Loads* | | | | |
| 10 | 2⅞ | 1⅝ | 80 | 143 | 221 | 276 | 355 | .... | .... |
| 12 | 2¾ | 1¼ | 62 | 112 | 169 | 212 | 281 | 437 | .... |
| 12 | 3 | 1⅜ | 74 | 124 | 187 | 234 | 303 | .... | .... |
| 12 | 3 | 1⅝ | 80 | 146 | 221 | 276 | 355 | .... | .... |
| 16 | 2¾ | 1⅛ | .... | 101 | 151 | 191 | 251 | 394 | .... |
| 20 | 2¾ | 1 | .... | 90 | 135 | 170 | 225 | 350 | .... |
| 28 | 2⅞ | ¾ | .... | .... | 101 | .... | 169 | 263 | .... |
| 410 | 2½ | ½ | .... | .... | 68 | 85 | 112 | 175 | .... |
| 410 | 3 | ¾ | .... | .... | 102 | 136 | 169 | 263 | .... |
| | | | | | *Field Loads* | | | | |
| 12 | 2¾ | 3-1 | .... | .... | 132 | 168 | 218 | .... | 399 |
| 12 | 2¾ | 3-1⅛ | .... | .... | 148 | 189 | 245 | .... | 449 |
| 12 | 2¾ | 3¼-1⅛ | .... | .... | 148 | 189 | 245 | .... | 449 |
| *16 | 2 9/16 | 2½-1 | .... | .... | 132 | 168 | 218 | .... | 399 |
| 16 | 2¾ | 2¾-1⅛ | .... | .... | 153 | .... | 251 | .... | 461 |
| 20 | 2¾ | 2¼-⅞ | .... | .... | 116 | 147 | 191 | .... | 349 |
| 20 | 2¾ | 2½-1 | .... | .... | 136 | .... | 225 | .... | 410 |

* Rolled Crimp

## TABLE IV. REMINGTON-PETERS STANDARD SHOT

| *Shot Size* | *Approximate Average Number of Pellets in Load* | | | | | | | | |
|---|---|---|---|---|---|---|---|---|---|
| | *½ oz.* | *¾ oz.* | *⅞ oz.* | *1 oz.* | *1⅛ oz.* | *1¼ oz.* | *1⅜ oz.* | *1⅝ oz.* | *2 oz.* |
| BB | .... | .... | .... | 50 | .... | 63 | 69 | 81 | 100 |
| 2 | .... | .... | .... | 90 | 101 | 112 | 124 | 146 | 180 |
| 4 | 68 | 101 | 118 | 135 | 152 | 169 | 186 | 219 | 270 |
| 5 | 85 | 128 | 150 | 170 | 191 | 212 | 234 | 276 | 340 |
| 6 | 113 | 169 | 197 | 225 | 253 | 281 | 309 | 366 | 450 |
| 7 | .... | .... | .... | 300 | .... | 375 | .... | .... | .... |
| 7½ | 175 | 263 | .... | 350 | 394 | 438 | .... | .... | .... |
| 8 | .... | .... | 359 | 410 | 461 | .... | .... | .... | .... |
| 9 | 293 | 439 | 512 | 585 | 658 | .... | .... | .... | .... |

## TABLE V.

| Chilled Shot | *⅞ oz.* | | | | | | *1 oz.* | | | | | |
|---|---|---|---|---|---|---|---|---|---|---|---|---|
| | Number of Pellets in Charge | Cyl. Bore | Imp. Cyl. | Modified | Imp. Mod. | Full Choke | Number of Pellets in Charge | Cyl. Bore | Imp. Cyl. | Modified | Imp. Mod. | Full Choke |
| Size of Shot | | 40 per cent | 50 per cent | 60 per cent | 67½ per cent | 75 per cent | | 40 per cent | 50 per cent | 60 per cent | 67½ per cent | 75 per cent |
| 1 | 64 | 26 | 32 | 38 | 43 | 48 | 73 | 29 | 36 | 44 | 49 | 55 |
| 2 | 77 | 31 | 39 | 46 | 52 | 58 | 88 | 35 | 44 | 53 | 59 | 66 |
| 3 | 95 | 38 | 48 | 57 | 64 | 71 | 109 | 44 | 54 | 65 | 74 | 82 |
| 4 | 119 | 48 | 60 | 71 | 80 | 89 | 136 | 54 | 68 | 82 | 92 | 102 |
| 5 | 150 | 60 | 75 | 90 | 101 | 112 | 172 | 69 | 86 | 103 | 116 | 129 |
| 6 | 195 | 78 | 98 | 117 | 132 | 146 | 223 | 89 | 112 | 134 | 151 | 167 |
| 7 | 262 | 105 | 131 | 157 | 177 | 197 | 299 | 120 | 150 | 179 | 202 | 224 |
| 7½ | 302 | 121 | 151 | 181 | 204 | 226 | 345 | 138 | 172 | 207 | 233 | 259 |
| 8 | 358 | 143 | 179 | 215 | 242 | 268 | 409 | 164 | 204 | 245 | 276 | 307 |
| 9 | 512 | 205 | 256 | 307 | 346 | 384 | 585 | 234 | 292 | 351 | 395 | 439 |
| 10 | 760 | 304 | 380 | 456 | 513 | 570 | 868 | 347 | 434 | 521 | 586 | 651 |

| Chilled Shot | *1⅛ oz.* | | | | | | *1¼ oz.* | | | | | |
|---|---|---|---|---|---|---|---|---|---|---|---|---|
| | Number of Pellets in Charge | Cyl. Bore | Imp. Cyl. | Modified | Imp. Mod. | Full Choke | Number of Pellets in Charge | Cyl. Bore | Imp. Cyl. | Modified | Imp. Mod. | Full Choke |
| Size of Shot | | 40 per cent | 50 per cent | 60 per cent | 67½ per cent | 75 per cent | | 40 per cent | 50 per cent | 60 per cent | 67½ per cent | 75 per cent |
| 1 | 82 | 33 | 41 | 49 | 55 | 62 | 91 | 36 | 45 | 55 | 61 | 68 |
| 2 | 99 | 40 | 50 | 59 | 67 | 74 | 110 | 44 | 55 | 66 | 74 | 83 |
| 3 | 122 | 49 | 61 | 73 | 82 | 92 | 136 | 54 | 68 | 82 | 92 | 102 |
| 4 | 153 | 61 | 77 | 92 | 103 | 115 | 170 | 68 | 85 | 102 | 115 | 128 |
| 5 | 193 | 77 | 97 | 116 | 130 | 145 | 215 | 86 | 108 | 129 | 145 | 161 |
| 6 | 251 | 100 | 126 | 151 | 169 | 188 | 279 | 112 | 140 | 167 | 188 | 209 |
| 7 | 336 | 134 | 168 | 202 | 227 | 252 | 374 | 150 | 187 | 224 | 252 | 281 |
| 7½ | 388 | 155 | 194 | 233 | 262 | 291 | 431 | 172 | 215 | 259 | 291 | 323 |
| 8 | 460 | 184 | 230 | 276 | 310 | 345 | 514 | 206 | 257 | 308 | 347 | 385 |
| 9 | 658 | 263 | 329 | 395 | 444 | 494 | 731 | 292 | 365 | 439 | 493 | 548 |
| 10 | 976 | 380 | 488 | 586 | 659 | 732 | 1085 | 434 | 542 | 651 | 732 | 814 |

Courtesy Abercrombie & Fitch, N. Y.

## MODERN LOADS

### WINCHESTER SHOTGUN SHELLS

LEADER SUPER SPEED STAYNLESS

| Ga. | Powder Drams | Shot Oz. | Shell Length | Shot Sizes |
|---|---|---|---|---|
| 12 | 4 | 1⅜ | 3 | BB 2 4 5 6 |
| 12 | 4¼ | 1⅝ | 3 Mag. | BB 2 4 5 6 |

SUPER SPEED STAYNLESS

*Loaded with Progressive Burning Smokeless Powder*

| Ga. | Powder Drams | Shot Oz. | Shell Length | Shot Sizes |
|---|---|---|---|---|
| 10 | 4¾ | 1⅝ | 2⅞ | BB 2 4 5 6 |
| 12 | 3¾ | 1¼ | 2¾ | BB 2 4 5 6 7½ |
| 16 | 3¼ | 1⅛ | 2¾ | 4 5 6 7½ |
| 20 | 2¾ | 1 | 2¾ | 2 4 5 6 7½ |
| 28 | 2¼ | ¾ | 2⅞ | 4 6 7½ |
| 410 | Max. | ½ | 2½ | 4 5 6 7½ |
| 410 | Max. | ¾ | 3 | 4 5 6 7½ |
| 410 | Max. | ½ | 2½ | 9 (Skeet) |
| 410 | Max. | ¾ | 3 | 9 (Skeet) |
| 28 | 2¼ | ¾ | 2⅞ | 9 (Skeet) |

*Buckshot Loads*

| Ga. | Pellets | Size Eastern | Layers | Shell Length |
|---|---|---|---|---|
| 10 | 16 | 0 | 4 | 2⅞ |
| 12 | 9 | 00 | 3 | 2¾ |
| 12 | 12 | 0 | 4 | 2¾ |
| 12 | 16 | 1 | 4 | 2¾ |
| 12 | 27 | 4 | 4 | 2¾ |
| 16 | 12 | 1 | 4 | 2¾ |
| 20 | 20 | 3 | 5 | 2¾ |

*Riot Buckshot Loads—(With Protected Crimp)*

| | | | | |
|---|---|---|---|---|
| 12 | 9 | 00 | 3 | 2¾ |
| 12 | 12 | 0 | 4 | 2¾ |

*Rifled Slug Loads*

| Ga. | Shell Length | Powder Charge | Weight of Ball |
|---|---|---|---|
| 12 | 2¾ | Max. | 1 Oz. |
| 16 | 2¾ | Max. | ⅞ Oz. |
| 20 | 2¾ | Max. | ⅝ Oz. |
| 410 | 2½ | Max. | ⅕ Oz. |

RANGER STAYNLESS—FIELD LOADS

| Ga. | Powder Drams | Shot Oz. | Shell Length | Shot Sizes |
|---|---|---|---|---|
| 10 | 4¼ | 1¼ | 2⅞ | 4 5 6 |
| 12 | 3 | 1 | 2¾ | 4 5 6 8 |
| 12 | 3 | 1⅛ | 2¾ | 4 5 6 8 |
| 12 | 3¼ | 1⅛ | 2¾ | 4 5 6 8 |
| 16 | 2½ | 1 | 2 9/16 | 4 5 6 8 |
| 16 | 2¾ | 1⅛ | 2¾ | 4 6 8 |
| 20 | 2¼ | ⅞ | 2¾ | 4 5 6 8 |
| 20 | 2½ | 1 | 2¾ | 4 6 8 |

*Ranger Super Skeet—Super Seal Crimp*

| Ga. | Powder Drams | Shot Oz. | Shell Length | Shot Sizes |
|---|---|---|---|---|
| 12 | 3 | 1⅛ | 2¾ | 9 |
| 16 | 2½ | 1 | 2¾ | 9 |
| 20 | 2¼ | ⅞ | 2¾ | 9 |

*Ranger Super Trap—Super Seal Crimp*

| | | | | |
|---|---|---|---|---|
| 12 | 2¾ | 1⅛ | 2¾ | 7½ 8 |
| 12 | 3 | 1⅛ | 2¾ | 7½ 8 |
| 12 | 3¼ | 1¼ | 2¾ | 7 7½ |

*Blank Loads—(Black Powder)*

| | | | |
|---|---|---|---|
| 10 | 8 | Blank | 2⅞ |
| 12 | 6 | Blank | 2¾ |

RANGER BRUSH LOADS

| | | | | |
|---|---|---|---|---|
| 12 | 3 | 1⅛ | 2¾ | 6 8 |
| 16 | 2½ | 1 | 2¾ | 8 |
| 20 | 2¼ | ⅞ | 2¾ | 8 |

SUPER-X

*The Original Long-Range Load*

| Gauge | Length Shell | Ounces Shot | Size, Chilled Shot | Wt. Case |
|---|---|---|---|---|
| 10 | 2⅞ in. | 1⅝ | BB, 2, 4, 5, 6 | 76 |
| †*10 | 3½ Mag. | 2 | BB, 2, 4, 5, 6 | 98 |
| 12 | 2¾ in. | 1¼ | BB, 2, 4, 5, 6, 7½ | 63 |
| *12 | 3 in. | 1⅜ | BB, 2, 4, 5, 6 | 71 |
| *12 | 3 Mag. | 1⅝ | BB, 2, 4, 5, 6 | 78 |
| 16 | 2¾ Mag. | 1⅛ | 2, 4, 5, 6, 7½ | 56 |
| 20 | 2¾ | 1 | 2, 4, 5, 6, 7½, 8 | 49 |
| 28 | 2⅞ | ¾ | 4, 6, 7½ | 39 |
| 410 | 2½ | ½ | 4, 5, 6, 7½, 9 | 24 |
| 410 | 3 | ¾ | 4, 5, 6, 7½, 9 | 33 |

*Loaded in high brass shell.

†Adapted only to guns weighing 10½ lbs. or more, with 3½ inch chambers and modern steel barrels. Specify Super-X Magnum.

*Buckshot—Rifled Slugs*

| Gauge | Length Shell | Size and Kind of Shot | Pellets Layer | Wt. Case |
|---|---|---|---|---|
| 10 | 2⅞ in. | 0 Buck-16 Pellets | 4 | 83 |
| 12 | 2¾ in. | 00 Buck- 9 Pellets (Riot) | 3 | 66 |
| 12 | 2¾ in. | 0 Buck-12 Pellets | 3 | 66 |
| 12 | 2¾ in. | 0 Buck-12 Pellets (Riot) | 3 | 66 |
| 12 | 2¾ in. | 1 Buck-16 Pellets | 4 | 66 |
| 12 | 2¾ in. | 4 Buck-27 Pellets (6* Pellets in top layer) | 7* | 66 |
| 16 | 2¾ in. | 1 Buck-12 Pellets | 3 | 54 |
| 20 | 2¾ in. | 3 Buck-20 Pellets | 3 | 49 |
| 12 | 2¾ in. | Rifled Slugs-1 oz. | | 58 |
| 16 | 2¾ in. | Rifled Slugs-⅞ " | | 50 |
| 20 | 2¾ in. | Rifled Slugs-⅝ " | | 42 |
| 410 | 2½ in. | Rifled Slugs-⅕ " | | 19 |

*With Lubaloy (Copperized) Shot*

Supplied in High Brass Shell with Progressive Burning Powder.

| Gauge | Length Shell | Ounces Shot | Size Shot | Wt. Case |
|---|---|---|---|---|
| *10 | 3½ Mag. | 2 | BB, 2, 4, 5, 6 | 98 |
| 12 | 2¾ in. | 1¼ | 2, 4, 5, 6, 7½ | 65 |
| 12 | 3 in. | 1¼ | 7, 7½ | 67 |
| 12 | 3 in. | 1⅜ | BB, 2, 4, 5, 6 | 71 |
| 12 | 3 Mag. | 1⅝ | BB, 2, 4, 5, 6 | 78 |
| 16 | 2¾ in. | 1⅛ | 4, 5, 6, 7½ | 56 |
| 20 | 2¾ in. | 1 | 4, 5, 6, 7½ | 50 |

* Adapted only to guns weighing 10½ lbs. or more, with 3½ inch chambers and modern steel barrels. Specify Super-X Magnum Lubaloy.

## XPERT

| Gauge | Length Shell | Dram Equiv. Powder | Ounces Shot | Size of Shot | Wt. of Case |
|---|---|---|---|---|---|
| 10 | 2⅞ in. | 4¼ | 1¼ | 4, 5, 6 | 65 |
| 12 | 2¾ in. | 3 | 1 | 4, 5, 6, 8 | 54 |
| 12 | 2¾ in. | 3 | 1⅛ | 4, 5, 6, 8 | 57 |
| 12 | 2¾ in. | 3¼ | 1⅛ | 4, 5, 6, 8 | 57 |
| 16 | 2⁹⁄₁₆ in. | 2½ | 1 | 4, 5, 6, 8 | 50 |
| 16 | 2¾ in. | 2¾ | 1⅛ | 4, 6, 8 | 50 |
| 20 | 2¾ in. | 2¼ | ⅞ | 4, 5, 6, 8 | 45 |
| 20 | 2¾ in. | 2½ | 1 | 4, 6, 8 | 45 |

*XPERT (Brush Loads)*

| | | | | | |
|---|---|---|---|---|---|
| 12 | 2¾ | 3 | 1⅛ | 6, 8 | 57 |
| 16 | 2¾ | 2½ | 1 | 8 | 50 |
| 20 | 2¾ | 2¼ | ⅞ | 8 | 45 |

*XPERT Super Skeet Loads with Super Sealed Crimp*

| | | | | | |
|---|---|---|---|---|---|
| 12 | 2¾ in. | 2¾ | 1⅛ | 7½, 8 | 57 |
| 12 | 2¾ in. | 3 | 1⅛ | 7½, 8 | 57 |
| 12 | 2¾ in. | 3¼ | 1¼ | 7, 7½ | 63 |

*XPERT Super Skeet Loads with Super Sealed Crimp*

| | | | | | |
|---|---|---|---|---|---|
| 12 | 2¾ in. | 3 | 1⅛ | 9 | 57 |
| 16 | 2¾ in. | 2½ | 1 | 9 | 50 |
| 20 | 2¾ in. | 2¼ | ⅞ | 9 | 45 |
| 10 | 2⅞ in. | 8 | | Blank | |
| 12 | 2¾ in. | 6 | | Blank | |

*Other Skeet Loads*

28 ga. SuperX 2⅞ in.—¾ oz. shot No. 9—
410 ga. SuperX 2½ in.—½ oz. shot No. 9—
410 ga. SuperX 3 in.—¾ oz. shot No. 9—

PLATE I. Shotgun Ammunition Charts.

## PETERS SHOTGUN SHELLS

"HIGH VELOCITY"

*With "Rustless" Non-Corrosive Priming*

| Gauge | Length Shell Inches | Powder Equiv. Drams | Ozs. Shot | Standard Size Shot |
|---|---|---|---|---|
| 10 Ga. | 2⅞ | 4¾ | 1⅝ | BB, 2, 4, 5, 6 |
| 12 Ga. | 2¾ | 3¾ | 1¼ | BB, 2, 4, 5, 6, 7½ |
| 16 Ga. | 2¾ | 3 | 1⅛ | 2, 4, 5, 6, 7½ |
| 16 Ga. | 2¾ | 3¼ | 1⅛ | 2, 4, 5, 6, 7½ |
| 20 Ga. | 2¾ | 2¾ | 1 | 2, 4, 5, 6, 7½ |
| 28 Ga. | 2⅞ | 2¼ | ¾ | 4, 6, 7½, 9* |
| 410 Ga. | 2½ | ... | ½ | 4, 5, 6, 7½, 9* |
| 410 Ga. | 3 | ... | ¾ | 4, 5, 6, 7½, 9* |

* 410 Ga. and 28 Ga. 9 Shot marked "Skeet Load."

*Rifled Slug Loads*

| | | | | |
|---|---|---|---|---|
| 12 Ga. | 2¾ | 3¾ | 1 | Rifled Slug |
| 16 Ga. | 2 9/16 | 3 | ⅞ | Rifled Slug |
| 20 Ga. | 2½ | 2¾ | ⅝ | Rifled Slug |
| 410 Ga. | 2½ | ... | 1/5 | Rifled Slug |

Rifled Slugs packed: 5 to box.

*Buckshot Loads*

| | | | | |
|---|---|---|---|---|
| 10 Ga. | 2⅞ | 4¾ | ... | 0 Buck—16 Pellets |
| 12 Ga. | 2¾ | 3¾ | ... | 0 Buck—12 Pellets |
| 12 Ga. | 2¾ | 3¾ | ... | 00 Buck— 9 Pellets |
| 12 Ga. | 2¾ | 3¾ | ... | 1 Buck—16 Pellets |
| 12 Ga. | 2¾ | 3¾ | ... | 4 Buck—27 Pellets |
| 16 Ga. | 2 9/16 | 3 | ... | 1 Buck—12 Pellets |
| 20 Ga. | 2½ | 2¾ | ... | 3 Buck—20 Pellets |

"DE LUXE TARGET"

*With "Rustless" Non-Corrosive Priming*

| | | | | | |
|---|---|---|---|---|---|
| 9150 | 12 Ga. | 3 | 3¾ | 1¼ | 7, 7½ |
| 9160 | 12 Ga. | 3 | 4 | 1⅜ | BB, 2, 4, 5, 6 |
| 9170 | 12 Ga. | 3 | 4¼ | 1⅝ | BB, 2, 4, 5, 6 magnum |

All loaded shells packed 25 to a carton.

"VICTOR"

*"Victor"—Field Loads*

| Gauge Shell | Length Shell Inches | Powder Equiv. Drams | Ozs. Shot | Standard Size Shot |
|---|---|---|---|---|
| 10 Ga. | 2⅞ | 4¼ | 1¼ | 4, 5, 6 |
| 12 Ga. | 2¾ | 3 | 1 | 4, 5, 6, 8 |
| 12 Ga. | 2¾ | 3 | 1⅛ | 4, 5, 6, 8 |
| 12 Ga. | 2¾ | 3¼ | 1⅛ | 4, 5, 6, 8 |
| 16 Ga. | 2 9/16 | 2½ | 1 | 4, 5, 6, 8 |
| 16 Ga. | 2¾ | 2¾ | 1⅛ | 4, 6, 8 |
| 20 Ga. | 2¾ | 2¼ | ⅞ | 4, 5, 6, 8 |
| 20 Ga. | 2¾ | 2½ | 1 | 4, 6, 8 |

*"Victor"—Spreader Loads*

| | | | | |
|---|---|---|---|---|
| 12 Ga. | 2¾ | 3 | 1⅛ | 6, 8 |
| 16 Ga. | 2¾ | 2½ | 1 | 8 |
| 20 Ga. | 2¾ | 2¼ | ⅞ | 8 |

*"Victor"—Blanks*

| | | | | |
|---|---|---|---|---|
| 10 Ga. | 2⅞ | 8 | ... | |
| 12 Ga. | 2⅝ | 6 | ... | |

FLAT-TOP CRIMP

*"Victor Trap Loads—With New Peters Flat-Top Crimp*

* Choice of Dupont M. X. or Hercules Red Dot Smokeless Powder

| | | | | |
|---|---|---|---|---|
| 12 Ga. | 2¾ | 2¾ | 1⅛ | 7½, 8 |
| 12 Ga. | 2¾ | 3 | 1⅛ | 7½, 8 |
| 12 Ga. | 2¾ | 3¼ | 1¼ | 7, 7½ |

Maximum Load for Registered Shoots is 3 drs.—1⅛ oz. shot.

*Skeet Loads—With New Peters Flat-Top Crimp*

| | | | | |
|---|---|---|---|---|
| 12 Ga. | 2¾ | 3 | 1⅛ | 9 |
| 16 Ga. | 2¾ | 2½ | 1 | 9 |
| 20 Ga. | 2¾ | 2¼ | ⅞ | 9 |
| 28 Ga. | 2⅞ | 2¼ | ¾ | 9 |

*Skeet Loads—Rolled Crimp*

| | | | | |
|---|---|---|---|---|
| 410 Ga. | 2½ | ... | ½ | 9 |
| 410 Ga. | 3 | ... | ¾ | 9 |

All loaded shells packed 25 to a carton—500 to the case.

## REMINGTON SHOTGUN SHELLS

EXPRESS

*Extra Long Range Shot Shells*

| *Gauge* | *Length Shell Ins.* | *Powder Equiv. Drams* | *Shot Ozs.* | *Size Shot* |
|---|---|---|---|---|
| 10 | 2⅞ | 4¾ | 1⅝ | BB, 2, 4, 5, 6 |
| 12 | 2¾ | 3¾ | 1¼ | BB, 2, 4, 5, 6, 7½ |
| 16 | 2¾ | 3 | 1⅛ | 2, 4, 5, 6, 7½ |
| 16 | 2¾ | 3¼ | 1⅛ | 2, 4, 5, 6, 7½ |
| 20 | 2¾ | 2¾ | 1 | 2, 4, 5, 6, 7½ |
| 28 | 2⅞ | 2¼ | ¾ | 4, 6, 7½, 9* |
| 410 | 2½ | ... | ½ | 4, 5, 6, 7½, 9* |
| 410 | 3 | ... | ¾ | 4, 5, 6, 7½, 9* |

* 28 Ga. and 410 Ga. 9 Shot marked "Skeet Load."

"EXPRESS" BUCKSHOT

| | | | | |
|---|---|---|---|---|
| 10 | 2⅞ | 4¾ | ... | 0 Buck—16 Pellets |
| 12 | 2¾ | 3¾ | ... | 0 Buck—12 Pellets |
| 12 | 2¾ | 3¾ | ... | 00 Buck— 9 pellets |
| 12 | 2¾ | 3¾ | ... | 1 Buck—16 Pellets |
| 12 | 2¾ | 3¾ | ... | 4 Buck—27 Pellets |
| 16 | 2 9/16 | 3 | ... | 1 Buck—12 Pellets |
| 20 | 2½ | 2¾ | ... | 3 Buck—20 Pellets |

"EXPRESS" RIFLED SLUG

| | | | | |
|---|---|---|---|---|
| 12 | 2¾ | 3¾ | 1 | Rifled Slug |
| 16 | 2 9/16 | 3 | ⅞ | Rifled Slug |
| 20 | 2½ | 2¾ | ⅝ | Rifled Slug |
| 410 | 2½ | ... | 1/5 | Rifled Slug |

"ARROW EXPRESS"

| | | | | |
|---|---|---|---|---|
| 10 | 3½ | 5 | 2 | BB, 2, 4, 5, 6 (Mag) |
| 12 | 3 | 3¾ | 1¼ | 7, 7½ |
| 12 | 3 | 4 | 1⅜ | BB, 2, 4, 5, 6 |
| 12 | 3 | 4¼ | 1⅝ | BB, 2, 4, 5, 6 (Mag) |

"SHUR SHOT" FIELD LOADS

| | | | | |
|---|---|---|---|---|
| 10 | 2⅞ | 4¼ | 1¼ | 4, 5, 6 |
| 12 | 2¾ | 3 | 1 | 4, 5, 6, 8 |
| 12 | 2¾ | 3 | 1⅛ | 4, 5, 6, 8 |
| 12 | 2¾ | 3¼ | 1⅛ | 4, 5, 6, 8 |
| 16 | 2 9/16 | 2½ | 1 | 4, 5, 6, 8 |
| 16 | 2¾ | 2¾ | 1⅛ | 4, 6, 8 |
| 20 | 2¾ | 2¼ | ⅞ | 4, 5, 6, 8 |
| 20 | 2¾ | 2½ | 1 | 4, 6, 8 |

"SHUR SHOT" SCATTER LOADS

| | | | | |
|---|---|---|---|---|
| 12 | 2¾ | 3 | 1⅛ | 6, 8 |
| 16 | 2¾ | 2½ | 1 | 8 |
| 20 | 2¾ | 2¼ | ⅞ | 8 |

Remington Express Buckshot, Rifled Slug, BB, and 410 gauge; Remington Shur Shot 16 gauge—2 9/16 inch length and all Remington Arrow Express shells have roll crimp.

# HANDGUN AMMUNITION

Complete details on the development of pistol and revolver ammunition will be found in the section on "Handguns—Pistols and Revolvers." This section, except for the discussion of certain bullet types and designs, will be limited to the listing of factory pistol and revolver cartridges of various calibers, with their bullet velocities and energies and penetration.

With the exception of the .357 magnum, developed by Smith & Wesson, which is nothing more than a high-velocity .38 special, American firearms designers have done little to bring out handguns for high-velocity loads. The reasons for this apparent neglect are quite understandable: The handgun is a short-range weapon and is not intended for long-range shooting. The overwhelming majority of handgun shooters are target shooters, and a high-velocity load offers no advantage in increased accuracy, whereas its increased recoil creates a disadvantage by stimulating fatigue. Most of the American handguns are designed to handle cartridges offering velocities under 1000 foot-seconds, and for accuracy at moderate ranges no greater velocity is required.

Some European military weapons, such as the Mauser and Luger, are designed to handle cartridges offering 1200 or 1400 foot-seconds, but with the exception of the .357 Magnum, which has 1510 foot-seconds, only a half-dozen American handguns are designed for loads giving velocities over 1000 foot-seconds.

During the last two decades there have been few changes in American cartridge or bullet design. The most outstanding of the changes is the so-called "wadcutter" bullet. This bullet, intended primarily for target shooting, is almost a true cylinder, and is designed to cut a clean hole in the target, thus aiding materially in marking the target. Most wadcutter cartridges are loaded for mid-range shooting, although some are given full powder loads.

## BALLISTICS OF PETERS PISTOL AND REVOLVER CARTRIDGES
### "Oil-Tite," with "Rustless" Priming

| *Index No.* | *Cartridge* | *Bullet Wgt. Grs.* | *Bullet Type* | *Muzzle Velocity Feet per Second* | *Muzzle Energy Ft. Lbs.* | *Barrel Length, Inches* | *Pen. 7/8" Pine Boards* |
|---|---|---|---|---|---|---|---|
| 2562 | .25 (6.35 m/m) Automatic | 50 | M.C. | 820 | 75 | 2 | 3 |
| 3052 | .30 Luger (7.65 m/m) | 93 | M.C. | 1250 | 323 | 4½ | 11 |
| 3252 | .32 Short Colt | 80 | Lead | 800 | 114 | 4 | 3 |
| 3254 | .32 Long Colt | 82 | Lead | 800 | 117 | 4 | 3 |
| 3256 | .32 Colt New Police | 100 | Lead | 795 | 138 | 4 | 3 |
| 3260 | .32 Automatic (7.65 m/m) | 71 | M.C. | 980 | 152 | 4 | 5 |
| 3262 | .32 Smith & Wesson | 88 | Lead | 720 | 98 | 3 | 3 |
| 3265 | .32 S. & W. Long | 98 | Lead | 795 | 138 | 4 | 4 |
| 3250 | .32 S. & W. Long Police Match Wadcutter | 98 | Lead | 770 | 129 | 4 | .... |
| 3575 | .357 Magnum High Velocity | 158 | Lead | 1450 | 690 | 8⅜ | 12½ |
| 3651 | 9 m/m Luger | 124 | M.C. | 1150 | 365 | 4 | 10 |
| 3822 | .38 Smith & Wesson | 146 | Lead | 745 | 179 | 4 | 4 |
| 3820 | .38 Smith & Wesson | 200 | Lead | 630 | 176 | 4 | 5 |
| 3846 | .38 Special Police Match Round Nose | 158 | Lead | 870 | 266 | 6 | 6½ |
| 3844 | .38 Special | 158 | Lead | 870 | 266 | 6 | 6½ |
| 3841 | .38 Special | 200 | Lead | 745 | 247 | 6 | 7½ |
| 3826 | .38 Special Metal Point | 158 | M.P. | 870 | 266 | 6 | 6½ |
| 3847 | .38 Special Police Match Wadcutter | 146 | Lead | 770 | 193 | 6 | .... |
| 3828 | .38 Special Target Wadcutter | 146 | Lead | 770 | 193 | 6 | .... |
| 3810 | .38 Spl. Highway Patrol Metal Penetrating H.V. | 110 | Special | 1330 | 433 | 5 | .... |
| 3842 | .38 Special High Velocity | 158 | Lead | 1115 | 436 | 5 | 7½ |
| 3839 | .38 Special Flat Point (Colt Spl.) | 158 | Lead | 870 | 266 | 6 | 6½ |
| 3831 | .38 Colt New Police | 150 | Lead | 695 | 161 | 4 | 4 |
| 3833 | .38 Short Colt | 125 | Lead | 770 | 165 | 6 | 4 |
| 3835 | .38 Long Colt | 150 | Lead | 785 | 205 | 6 | 6 |
| 3849 | .38 Super Automatic | 130 | M.C. | 1300 | 488 | 5 | 10 |
| 3851 | .38 Automatic | 130 | M.C. | 1070 | 331 | 4½ | 9 |
| 3853 | .380 Automatic (9 m/m) | 95 | M.C. | 970 | 199 | 3¾ | 5½ |
| 4154 | .41 Long Colt | 195 | Lead | 745 | 241 | 6 | 3 |
| 4403 | .44 Smith & Wesson Russian | 246 | Lead | 770 | 324 | 6½ | 7½ |
| 4405 | .44 Smith & Wesson Special | 246 | Lead | 770 | 324 | 6½ | 7½ |
| 4502 | .45 Colt | 250 | Lead | 870 | 421 | 5½ | 6 |
| 4504 | .45 Automatic | 230 | M.C. | 860 | 378 | 5 | 6 |
| 4510 | .45 Automatic Police Match | 230 | M.C. | 750 | 288 | 5 | .... |
| 4512 | .45 Auto. H'way Patrol Metal Penetrating H.V. | 173 | Special | 1140 | 500 | 5 | .... |
| 4505 | .45 Automatic Rim | 230 | M.C. | 820 | 343 | 5½ | 6 |
| 4506 | .45 Automatic Rim | 230 | Lead | 820 | 343 | 5½ | 6 |

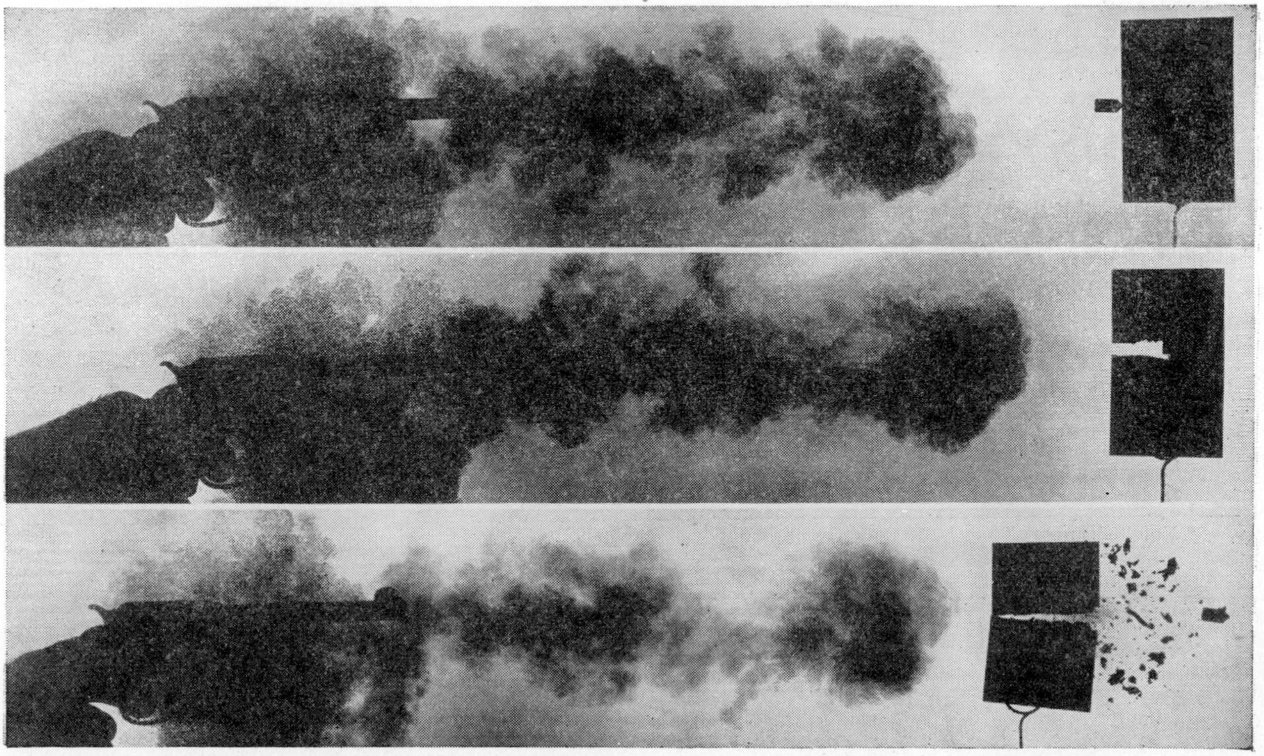

PLATE I. The Peters "wadcutter" .38-caliber bullet shown in the process of cutting a thin strip of cardboard in half.

### Match Cartridges—Pistol and Revolver

| | | | | | | | |
|---|---|---|---|---|---|---|---|
| 2223 | .22 Long Rifle Police Match (Rim Fire) | 40 | Lead | 970 | 83 | 6 | .... |
| 3250 | .32 S. & W. Long Police Match Wadcutter | 98 | Lead | 770 | 129 | 4 | .... |
| 3846 | .38 Special Police Match Round Nose | 158 | Lead | 870 | 266 | 6 | 6½ |
| 3847 | .38 Special Police Match Wadcutter | 146 | Lead | 770 | 193 | 6 | .... |
| 4510 | .45 Automatic Police Match | 230 | M.C. | 750 | 288 | 5 | .... |

## BALLISTICS OF REMINGTON OIL PROOF PISTOL AND REVOLVER CARTRIDGES

| *Caliber* | *Bullet Type* | *Wgt. Grs.* | *Muzzle Velocity Feet per Second* | *Approx. Muzzle Energy Ft. Lbs.* | *Barrel Length, Inches* | *Penetration 7/8" Pine Boards* |
|---|---|---|---|---|---|---|
| .25 (6.35 m/m) Automatic Pistol | M. C. | 50 | 820 | 75 | 2 | 3 |
| .30 (7.63 m/m) Mauser Automatic Pistol | M. C. | 85 | 1420 | 380 | 5½ | 11 |
| .30 (7.63 m/m) Mauser Automatic Pistol | S. P. | 90 | 1420 | 400 | 5½ | 11 |
| .30 (7.65 m/m) Luger Automatic Pistol | M. C. | 93 | 1250 | 325 | 4½ | 11 |
| .30 (7.65 m/m) Luger Automatic Pistol | S. P. | 93 | 1250 | 325 | 4½ | 11 |
| .30 (7.65 m/m) Luger Automatic Pistol | H. Pt. | 93 | 1250 | 325 | 4½ | 11 |
| .32 Smith & Wesson* | Lead | 88 | 720 | 100 | 3 | 3 |
| .32 Smith & Wesson | Lead | 88 | 720 | 100 | 3 | 3 |
| .32 Smith & Wesson, Long* | Lead | 98 | 820 | 146 | 4½ | 4 |
| .32 Smith & Wesson, Long | Lead | 98 | 820 | 146 | 4½ | 4 |
| .32 Smith & Wesson, Long | M. Pt. | 95 | 820 | 142 | 4½ | 4½ |
| .32 Short Colt | Lead | 80 | 800 | 114 | 4 | 3 |
| .32 Long Colt | Lead | 82 | 800 | 117 | 4 | 3 |
| .32 Colt New Police (Police Positive) | Lead | 100 | 795 | 139 | 4 | 3 |
| .32 (7.65 m/m) Automatic Pistol | M. C. | 71 | 980 | 152 | 4 | 5 |
| 9 m/m Luger Automatic Pistol | M. C. | 124 | 1150 | 365 | 4 | 10 |
| .357 Magnum | M. Pt. | 158 | 1510 | 800 | 8¾ | 12½ |
| 9 m/m Luger Automatic Pistol | H. Pt. | 124 | 1150 | 365 | 4 | 10 |
| .380 (9 m/m) Automatic Pistol | M. C. | 95 | 970 | 199 | 3¾ | 5½ |
| .38 Super Automatic Colt Pistol | M. C. | 130 | 1300 | 488 | 5 | 10 |
| .38 Super Automatic Colt Pistol | H. Pt. | 130 | 1300 | 488 | 5 | 10 |
| .38 Colt Automatic Pistol | M. C. | 130 | 1070 | 331 | 4½ | 9 |
| .38 Smith & Wesson* | Lead | 146 | 745 | 180 | 4 | 4 |
| .38 Smith & Wesson | Lead | 146 | 745 | 180 | 4 | 4 |
| .38 Smith & Wesson | M. Pt. | 143 | 745 | 177 | 4 | 4½ |
| .38 Smith & Wesson—Special* | Lead | 158 | 870 | 266 | 6 | 7 |
| .38 Smith & Wesson—Special | Lead | 158 | 870 | 266 | 6 | 7 |
| .38 Smith & Wesson—Special | Lead | 200 | 745 | 247 | 6 | 5 |
| .38 Smith & Wesson—Special | M. Pt. | 158 | 870 | 266 | 6 | 7½ |
| .38 Smith & Wesson Special Sharp Shoulder Bullet | Lead | 146 | 770 | 193 | 6 | .... |
| .38 Smith & Wesson Special Targetmaster | Lead | 146 | 770 | 193 | 6 | .... |
| .38 Smith & Wesson Special Targetmaster | Lead | 158 | 870 | 266 | 6 | 7 |
| .38/44 Smith & Wesson—Special Hi-Speed | M. Pt. | 158 | 1115 | 436 | 5 | 10 |
| .38/44 Smith & Wesson—Special Hi-Speed | Lead | 158 | 1115 | 436 | 5 | 7½ |
| .38 Colt New Police (Police Positive) | Lead | 150 | 695 | 161 | 4 | 4 |
| .38 Short Colt | Lead | 125 | 770 | 165 | 6 | 4 |
| .38 Long Colt | Lead | 150 | 785 | 205 | 6 | 6 |
| .38 Colt Special | Lead | 158 | 870 | 266 | 6 | 6½ |
| .38 Colt Special Hi-Speed | M. Pt. | 158 | 1125 | 445 | 6 | 10 |
| .38 Colt Special Hi-Speed | Lead | 158 | 1115 | 436 | 5 | 7½ |
| .41 Short Colt | Lead | 163 | 720 | 186 | 6 | 4 |
| .41 Long Colt | Lead | 195 | 745 | 241 | 6 | 5 |
| .44 Smith & Wesson—American | Lead | 218 | 695 | 235 | 6½ | 4 |
| .44 Smith & Wesson—Russian | Lead | 246 | 770 | 324 | 6½ | 4 |
| .44 Smith & Wesson—Special | Lead | 246 | 770 | 324 | 6½ | .... |
| .44 Smith & Wesson—Special | M. Pt. | 246 | 770 | 324 | 6½ | .... |
| .45 Colt | Lead | 250 | 870 | 421 | 5½ | 6 |
| .45 Colt Automatic Pistol | M. C. | 230 | 860 | 378 | 5 | 6 |
| .45 Colt Automatic Targetmaster | M. C. | 230 | 750 | 288 | 5 | .... |
| .45 Automatic Rim | M. C. | 230 | 820 | 343 | 5½ | 6 |
| .45 Automatic Rim | Lead | 230 | 820 | 343 | 5½ | 6 |
| .455 Webley Mark II | Lead | 265 | 600 | 210 | 6½ | ... |

* Not "Kleanbore."

## BALLISTICS OF WESTERN PISTOL and REVOLVER CARTRIDGES*

| Cartridge | Bullet Wgt. Grs. | Bullet Type | Barrel Length | Muzzle Velocity Feet per Second | Muzzle Energy Foot Lbs. | Penetration 7/8" Soft Pine Boards at 15 Ft. |
|---|---|---|---|---|---|---|
| .22 Short SUPER-X Wax Coated | 29 | Lubaloy C'd | 6" | 1,035 | 69 | .... |
| .22 Short XPERT Greased | 29 | Lead | 6" | 925 | 55 | .... |
| .22 Long SUPER-X Wax Coated | 29 | Lubaloy C'd | 6" | 1,125 | 81 | .... |
| .22 Long Rifle SUPER-X Wax Coated | 40 | Lubaloy C'd | 6" | 1,160 | 120 | .... |
| .22 Long Rifle XPERT Greased | 40 | Lead | 6" | 980 | 85 | .... |
| .22 Long Rifle SUPER-MATCH Greased | 40 | Lead | 6" | 975 | 84 | .... |
| .41 Short Greased | 130 | Lubaloy C'd | 3" | 520 | 78 | 2 |
| .25 Automatic (6.35 m/m) (Oilproof) | 50 | Metal Case | 2" | 820 | 75 | 3 |
| .30 Mauser (7.63 m/m) (Oilproof) | 86 | Metal Case | 5½" | 1,420 | 385 | 11 |
| .30 Luger (7.65 m/m) (Oilproof) | 93 | Metal Case | 4½" | 1,250 | 323 | 11 |
| .32 Automatic (7.65 m/m) (Oilproof) | 74 | Metal Case | 4" | 980 | 158 | 5 |
| .32 S. & W. (Oilproof) Inside Lubricated | 85 | Lubaloy C'd | 3" | 720 | 98 | 3 |
| .32 S. & W. Long (Oilproof) Inside Lubricated | 98 | Lubaloy C'd | 4¼" | 820 | 146 | 4 |
| .32 S. & W. Long Clean Cutting Super-Match Inside Lubricated (Oilproof) | 98 | Lead | 6" | 770 | 129 | .... |
| .32 Short Colt (Oilproof) Greased | 80 | Lubaloy C'd | 4" | 800 | 114 | 3 |
| .32 Long Colt (Oilproof) Inside Lubricated | 82 | Lubaloy C'd | 4" | 800 | 117 | 3 |
| .32 Colt New Police (Oilproof) Inside Lubricated | 98 | Lubaloy C'd | 4" | 795 | 138 | 3 |
| .32-20 Winchester (Oilproof) Inside Lubricated | 115 | Lubaloy C'd | 6" | 1,030 | 271 | 6 |
| .32-20 Winchester (Oilproof) | 115 | Metal Case | 6" | 1,030 | 271 | 6 |
| .32-20 Winchester (Oilproof) | 115 | Soft Point | 6" | 1,030 | 271 | 6 |
| .357 Magnum (Oilproof) SUPER-X Inside Lubricated | 158 | Lubaloy C'D | 8¾" | 1,510 | 800 | 12.5 |
| .357 Magnum Met. Pier. (Oilproof) SUPER-X In. Lub. Lead Bear | 158 | Metal Point | 8¾" | 1,510 | 800 | 12.5 |
| 9 m/m Luger (Oilproof) | 125 | Metal Case | 4" | 1,150 | 365 | 10 |
| .38 Smith & Wesson (Oilproof) Inside Lubricated | 145 | Lubaloy C'd | 4" | 745 | 179 | .... |
| .38 S. & W. Super Police (Oilproof) Inside Lubricated | 200 | Lubaloy C'd | 4" | 630 | 176 | 5 |
| .38 Spec. Met. Pier. (Oilproof) SUPER-X In. Lub. Lead Bearing | 150 | Metal Point | 5" | 1,175 | 460 | 11 |
| .38 Special (Oilproof) SUPER-X Inside Lubricated | 150 | Lubaloy C'd | 5" | 1,175 | 460 | 9 |
| .38 Special (Oilproof) Inside Lubricated | 158 | Lubaloy C'd | 6" | 870 | 266 | 7 |
| .38 Special SUPER Match (Oilproof) Inside Lubricated | 158 | Lead | 6" | 845 | 251 | 7 |
| .38 Special (Oilproof) Inside Lubricated, Lead Bearing | 158 | Metal Point | 6" | 870 | 266 | 7.5 |
| .38 Spec. Clean Cutting Mid-Range (Oilproof) In. Lub. SUPER-MATCH | 148 | Lead | 6" | 770 | 195 | .... |
| .38 Special Super-Police (Oilproof) Inside Lubricated | 200 | Lubaloy C'd | 6" | 745 | 247 | 7.5 |
| .38 Short Colt (Oilproof) Greased | 130 | Lubaloy C'd | 6" | 770 | 171 | 4 |
| .38 Long Colt (Oilproof) Inside Lubricated | 150 | Lubaloy C'd | 6" | 785 | 205 | 6 |
| .38 Colt New Police (Oilproof) Inside Lubricated | 150 | Lubaloy C'd | 4" | 695 | 161 | 4 |
| .38 Automatic (Oilproof) SUPER-X | 130 | Metal Case | 5" | 1,300 | 488 | 10 |
| .380 Automatic (Oilproof) | 95 | Metal Case | 3¾" | 975 | 199 | 5.5 |
| .38-40 Winchester (Oilproof) | 180 | Soft Point | 5" | 975 | 380 | 6 |
| .41 Long Colt (Oilproof) Inside Lubricated | 200 | Lubaloy C'd | 6" | 745 | 247 | 3 |
| .44 Smith & Wesson Russian (Oilproof) Inside Lubricated | 246 | Lubaloy C'd | 6½" | 770 | 324 | 4 |
| .44 Smith & Wesson Special (Oilproof) Inside Lubricated | 246 | Lubaloy C'd | 6½" | 770 | 324 | 7.5 |
| .44-40 Winchester (Oilproof) | 200 | Soft Point | 7½" | 975 | 422 | 6 |
| .45 Colt (Oilproof) Inside Lubricated | 255 | Lubaloy C'd | 5½" | 870 | 429 | 6 |
| .45 Automatic (Oilproof) | 230 | Metal Case | 5" | 860 | 378 | 6 |
| .45 Automatic SUPER-MATCH | 230 | Metal Case | 5" | 710 | 257 | 5 |
| .45 Automatic Met. Pier (Oilproof) SUPER-X | 230 | Metal Case | 5" | 940 | 450 | 11 |
| .45 Automatic Rim (Oilproof) | 230 | Metal Case | 5½" | 820 | 343 | 6 |

* All Cartridges Loaded with Smokeless Powder.

| Cartridge | Bullet Wt. | Muz. Vel. | Muz. Energy | Cartridge | Bullet Wt. | Muz. Vel. | Muz. Energy |
|---|---|---|---|---|---|---|---|
| Super Speed .22 Short | 29 | 1,035 | 69 | Leader .22 Long Rifle | 40 | 980 | 85 |
| Leader .22 Short | 29 | 925 | 55 | Super Speed .22 W.R.F. | 45 | 1,170 | 137 |
| Super Speed .22 Long Rifle | 40 | 1,160 | 120 | | | | |

## BALLISTICS OF WINCHESTER CENTER-FIRE PISTOL and REVOLVER CARTRIDGES *

| Symbol | Primer No. | Cartridge | Bullet Type | Bullet Wgt. Grs. | Muzzle Velocity Feet Per Second | Muzzle Energy Foot Lbs. | Penetration 7/8" Soft Pine Boards at 15 ft. | Barrel Length Inches |
|---|---|---|---|---|---|---|---|---|
| K2541T | 108 | .25 Auto Colt (6.35 m/m) | F.P. | 50 | 820 | 75 | 3 | 2 |
| K3272T | 108 | .32 S. & W. Staynless | Lead | 85 | 720 | 98 | 3 | 3 |
| K3278T | 108 | .32 S. & W. Long, Staynless | Lead | 98 | 820 | 146 | 4 | 4¼ |
| K7631T | 108 | 7.63 m/m Mauser (.30 Mauser) | F.P. | 86 | 1,420 | 385 | 11 | 5½ |
| K7653T | 108 | 7.65 m/m Luger (.30 Luger) | F.P. | 93 | 1,250 | 323 | 11 | 4½ |
| K7654T | 108 | 7.65 m/m Luger (.30 Luger) | H.S.P. | 93 | 1,250 | 323 | 11 | 4½ |
| K3256T | 108 | .32 Short Colt | Lead | 80 | 800 | 114 | 3 | 4 |
| K3254T | 108 | .32 Long Colt | Lead | 82 | 800 | 117 | 3 | 4 |
| K3241T | 108 | .32 Automatic Colt (7.65 m/m) | F.P. | 74 | 980 | 158 | 5 | 4 |
| K3289T | 108 | .32 S. & W. Long, Sharp Corner Match | Lead | 98 | 770 | 129 | .... | 6 |
| K3208T | 112 | .32 Winchester Staynless | Lead | 100 | 1,030 | 235 | 6 | 6 |
| K3249T | 108 | .32 Colt New Police | Lead | 98 | 795 | 138 | 3 | 4 |
| K3570T | 111 | Super Speed S. & W. .357 Magnum | Lead | 158 | 1,510 | 800 | 12.5 | 8¾ |
| K9001T | 108 | 9 m/m Luger | F.P. | 125 | 1,150 | 367 | 10 | 4 |
| K9002T | 108 | 9 m/m Luger | H.S.P. | 125 | 1,150 | 367 | 10 | 4 |
| K3849T | 108 | .38 Colt New Police | Lead | 150 | 695 | 161 | 4 | 4 |
| K3856T | 108 | .38 Short Colt | Lead | 130 | 770 | 171 | 4 | 6 |
| K3872T | 108 | .38 S. & W. Staynless | Lead | 145 | 745 | 179 | 4 | 4 |
| K3867T | 108 | .38 S. & W. | Lead | 200 | 630 | 176 | 5 | 4 |
| K3862T | 111 | Super Speed .38 Special | Lead | 158 | 1,115 | 436 | 7.5 | 5 |
| K3863T | 111 | Super Speed .38 Special, lead bearing | Metal Point | 158 | 1,115 | 436 | 10 | 5 |
| K3898T | 111 | Super Speed .38 Special, metal piercing | Metal Piercing | 150 | 1,175 | 460 | 11 | 5 |
| K3859T | 108 | .38 Colt Special | Lead | 158 | 870 | 266 | 6.5 | 6 |
| K3884T | 108 | .38 S. & W. Special, Staynless | Lead | 158 | 870 | 266 | 7 | 6 |
| K3866T | 108 | .38 S. & W. Special Match | Lead | 158 | 870 | 266 | 7 | 6 |
| K3885T | 108 | .38 S. & W. Special, lead bearing | M.P. | 158 | 870 | 266 | 8 | 6 |
| K3868T | 108 | .38 S. & W. Special | Lead | 200 | 745 | 247 | 7.5 | 6 |
| K3877T | 108 | .38 S. & W. Special, Mid Range Sharp Corner | Lead | 148 | 770 | 195 | .... | 6 |
| K3897T | 108 | .38 S. & W. Special, Full Charge, Sharp Corner | Lead | 148 | 870 | 249 | .... | 6 |
| K3844T | 112 | .38 Automatic Colt | F.P. | 130 | 1,070 | 331 | 9 | 4½ |
| K3841T | 112 | Super Speed .38 Automatic Colt | F.P. | 130 | 1,300 | 488 | 10 | 5 |
| K3840T | 112 | Super Speed .38 Automatic Colt | H.S.P. | 130 | 1,300 | 488 | 10 | 5 |
| K3854T | 108 | .38 Long Colt | Lead | 150 | 785 | 205 | 6 | 6 |
| K3851T | 108 | .380 Automatic Colt | F.P. | 95 | 970 | 199 | 5.5 | 3¾ |
| K4154T | 108 | .41 Long Colt | Lead | 196 | 745 | 242 | 5 | 6 |
| K4474T | 111 | .44 S. & W. Russian | Lead | 246 | 770 | 324 | 4 | 6½ |
| K4484T | 111 | .44 S. & W. Special | Lead | 246 | 770 | 324 | 7.5 | 6½ |
| K4544T | 111 | .45 Colt | Lead | 255 | 870 | 429 | 6 | 5½ |
| K4556T | 111 | .45 Automatic Colt | F.P. | 230 | 860 | 378 | 6 | 5 |
| K4553T | 111 | .45 Auto Rim | Lead | 230 | 820 | 343 | 6 | 5½ |
| K4554T | 111 | .45 Auto Rim | F.P. | 230 | 820 | 343 | 6 | 5½ |
| K4555T | 111 | .45 Auto Colt Match | F.P. | 230 | 750 | 287 | .... | 5 |

* All these Cartridges are Staynless (Smokeless Powder) except those marked Black powder.

S.P.=Soft Point H.P.=Hollow Point F.P.=Full Patch P.E.=Pointed Expanding H.C.P.=Hollow Copper Point

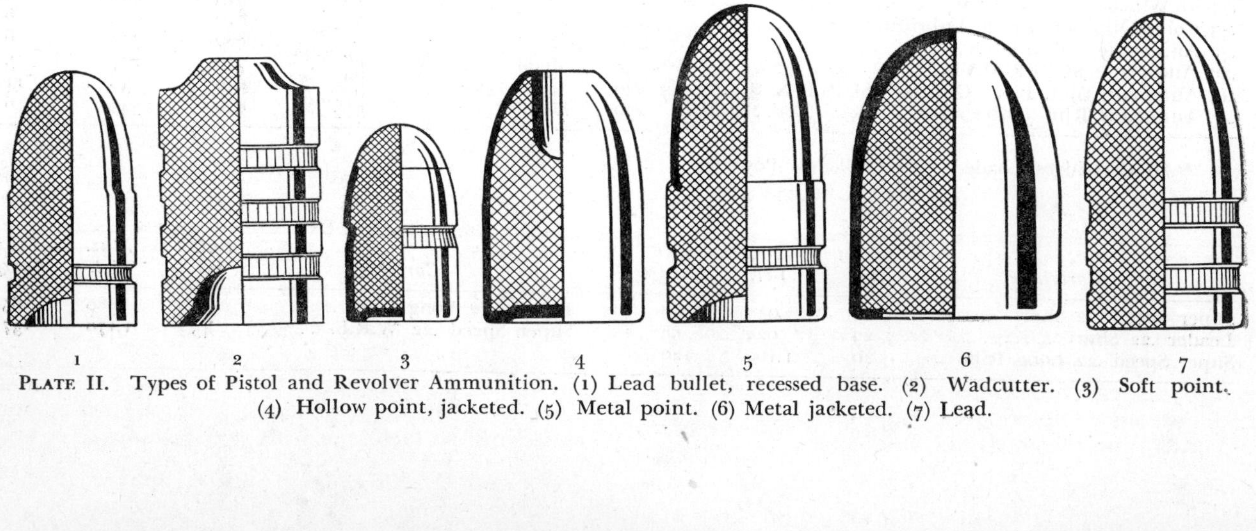

1 2 3 4 5 6 7

PLATE II. Types of Pistol and Revolver Ammunition. (1) Lead bullet, recessed base. (2) Wadcutter. (3) Soft point. (4) Hollow point, jacketed. (5) Metal point. (6) Metal jacketed. (7) Lead.

# BALL POWDER

Every round of ammunition has at least two explosive systems—a primer and a propellant. The primer, which is a sensitive material, is ignited when struck by the firing pin of the gun. The burning primer spits flame and incandescent particles into the propellant charge causing the latter to burn and develop a large volume of gas which, in an effort to escape, drives the bullet forward at a high velocity.

The velocity developed by the projectile and the pressure attained in the gun barrel depend upon the rate at which the gas is developed. If the gas were produced instantaneously, excessive pressure would be produced in the gun barrel before the projectile could move any appreciable distance. If, on the other hand, the gas were generated at a slower, controlled rate, the projectile would have time to move down the barrel and thus allow a larger quantity of gas to be generated without attaining objectionably high pressures.

**Development of Propellants.** The history of guns and propellant explosives dates back to the 13th and 14th centuries. The propellant developed at that time was a black-powder mixture; the composition (15 parts charcoal, 10 parts sulphur, and 75 parts saltpeter) was virtually the same as the most modern formulas.

In the middle of the last century, investigators began to seek more efficient explosives to replace black powder, and nitrocellulose was discovered. From the time of this discovery in 1846 until the turn of the century investigators sought ways of stabilizing the nitrocellulose so that it would not spontaneously explode in storage and also for means of controlling the burning rate.

The processes that evolved consisted of a stabilization treatment requiring days of treatments and large volumes of boiling water. The control of the burning rate was accomplished by dissolving the nitrocellulose in a mixture of ether and alcohol, and after a number of preparatory operations, this colloidal solution was extruded from a press to form strands of powder that were cut to special lengths.

No major changes in smokeless-powder manufacturing procedures were introduced after that until 1936 when the Western Cartridge Company, in U. S. Patent No. 2,027,114, made available a propellant which they called Ball powder.

The developers of Ball powder make certain claims as to its superiority over extruded powder and also as to the superiority of the manufacturing process over the extrusion process. These claims concern chemical and ballistic stability features and improved uniformity and cleanliness of burning. The process is claimed to be safer and quicker. These advantages are described below.

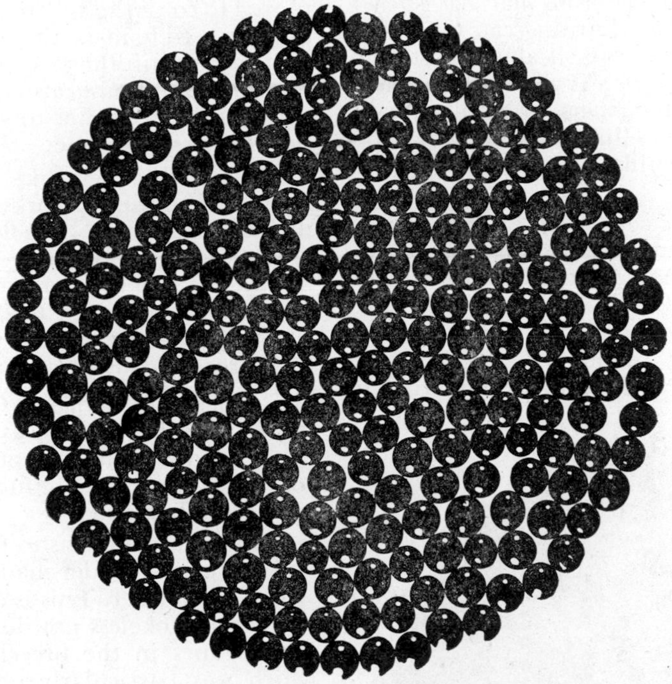

PLATE I. Ball Powder Grains Magnified 20 Times.

**Chemical Stability.** Nitrocellulose is inherently an unstable chemical; that is, in time it tends to decompose into the chemicals from which it was made. If conditions of confinement exist which prevent the rapid radiation of this heat of decomposition, it is quite likely that fires or explosions may result. In the extrusion process, the purity of the nitrocellulose, which is what affects the stability, is increased by boiling the nitrocellulose for many hours to extract the unwanted impurities. A new principle is used in the Ball powder process where the nitrocellulose is dissolved in a solvent to form a "lacquer" that is then agitated in a vat of water. The impurities are released by the lacquer to the water where they are neutralized and made harmless. The purification is complete, and powder having outstandingly good chemical stabilities results whether the base nitrocellulose to be made into Ball powder has been purified by the conventional process or not.

This improved chemical stability is gauged by the ability of the powder to remain in storage at high temperatures without decomposing. The most reliable of the heat stability tests is the 65.5° C. (150° F.) surveillance test, in which samples are placed at this temperature and the number of days required to evolve red gases of decomposition is noted. In this test, it appears that the Ball powder stabilization is more complete than the hot-water boiling stabilization. Tests made by the manufacturer show that Ball powder has surveillance life of over twice that of extruded powder.

**Ballistic Characteristics.** In its natural state, nitrocellulose is a cottonlike material that has such a huge surface area on which burning can take place that, when ignited, it is consumed almost instantly. In general smokeless powder is made from nitrocellulose by dissolving the fibers in a solvent and forming the paste of nitrocellulose into dense shapes which are hard and hornlike after the solvent has been evaporated.

The rate of burning is controlled by forming the powder grains into definite shapes of closely controlled sizes. Chemicals are sometimes added to reduce the rate of burning. Slower burning is a desirable characteristic because this allows the gas pressure to be developed gradually as the projectile moves, allowing greater energy to be imparted to

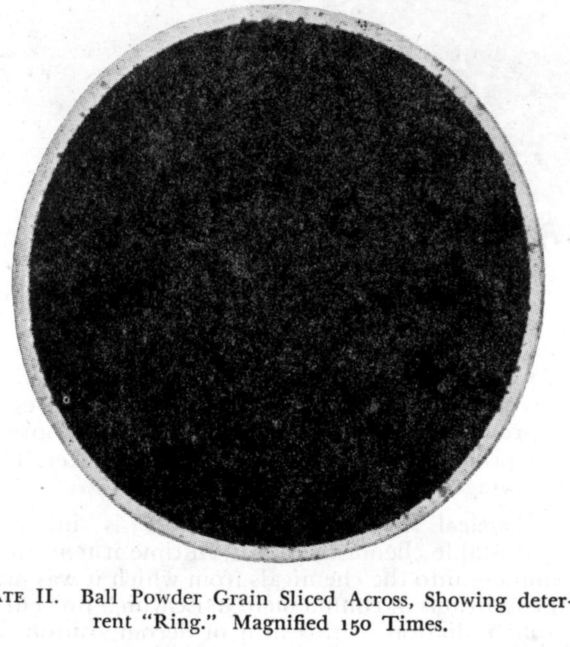

PLATE II. Ball Powder Grain Sliced Across, Showing deterrent "Ring." Magnified 150 Times.

the projectile without attaining objectionably high gas pressures.

The burning rate of Ball powder is controlled chemically by a process called the "molten emulsion method" which applies the material on the outside of the grain to give a slow initial gas production followed by an increased gas production as the projectile moves down the barrel. The burning rate is so definitely fixed by this process that there is little tendency for the powder to change in storage. Of course, changing ballistic properties must be minimized because the safety and accuracy of ammunition depend upon the ability of the powder to remain unchanged by heat or age.

Data gathered by the manufacturer show that Ball powder ballistically modified by the "molten emulsion" chemical process can be stored for years at elevated temperatures without changing its ballistic properties.

**Uniformity.** Ball powder is produced in the form of tiny spheres. It is used in this form for some loads of ammunition; for others, the balls are passed between revolving rolls to flatten the grain to effect improved ballistic uniformity.

The forces of nature—i. e., surface tension acting to form droplets of nitrocellulose lacquer—are employed to form the spheres, instead of machines such as those used to make the extruded grains. This leads to a more uniform product which, combined with the chemical modification, produces powder which varies little from shot to shot, thus allowing exceptionally strict accuracy specifications to be met.

Ball powder flows like ball bearings, the grains rolling freely. This works to the advantage of the shooter, since the free-flowing properties insure greater accuracy of charge weight in loading. It is not uncommon for the variations in powder charge from round to round to be less than one-half that encountered with regular powder. This contributes to improved ballistic uniformity and better accuracy.

**Cleanliness of Burning.** One of the greatest objections of black powder was that, when fired, it produced great volumes of smoke. The smoke was, of course, solid particles of fuel that were not consumed by the combustion.

Nitrocellulose burns to form all gaseous products, and therefore powder made from it has been called smokeless powder. This is essentially true, of course, but early smokeless powders nevertheless sometimes left residues in the breech and barrel of the gun which was particularly objectionable to trap and skeet shooters. One of the claims for Ball powder is that it was designed to be clean burning.

**Manufacturing Process.** Contrasted with the conventional hazardous manufacturing procedures for smokeless powder, the Ball powder process is a straightforward chemical operation. The purification, grain forming, and solvent removal are all conducted in the same tank while the nitrocellulose is submerged in water. The water practically eliminates fire or explosion hazard while further safety is introduced by the elimination of the many transfers.

The molten emulsion deterrent coating is also applied to the powder while it is submerged in water. This not only makes a more stable deterrent coating, but is safer than the conventional processes where the deterrent material is applied in a hot tumbling barrel to the dry powder.

Completed powder can be made by the Ball powder process in an elapsed time of less than 100 hours, whereas it requires 300 hours or more to make extruded powder.

# SIGHTS AND OPTICAL AIDS

This section deals with the new as well as the time-tested types of sights, iron and telescopic, and the various optical and mechanical aids devised to improve the shooter's score on the range and in the field.

The telescope sight is playing an increasingly important part in hunting as well as match shooting. During the past few years several newcomers have appeared in this field, some of them turning out fine, precision scopes, others producing inexpensive but unsatisfactory products. The sights which have been selected for discussion here are a cross section, so far as price range is concerned, but each one is a dependable, precise instrument.

## TELESCOPE SIGHTS

PLATE I. LYMAN "Alaskan."

Power—2½
Length—10½ inches
Diameter—19 mm. (¾ inch)
Weight—11 ounces

This is one of the most popular big-game scopes made, and is used on high-power rifles of every caliber. It has excellent optics, and like other modern scopes is designed to make low mounting possible. Changes in elevation and windage are made internally by manipulation of the external adjusting knobs, graduated for visual adjustment as well as by click. One click represents one inch of vertical or horizontal movement at 100 yards. The eye relief is about 5 inches. This scope gives a 40-foot field of view at 100 yards. The ocular lens is adjustable for individual vision. Reticules: Blunt picket post and cross-wire; blunt picket post, sharp picket post, and cross-wire, sharp picket post, tapered post and cross-wire, tapered post, cross-wire.

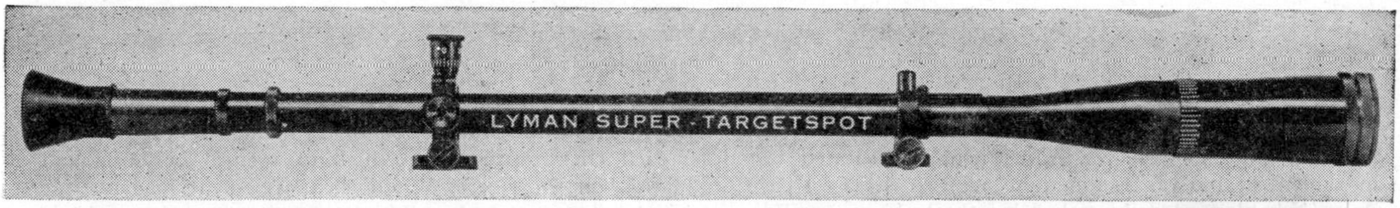


PLATE II. LYMAN "Targetspot."

Power—8, 10, 12, 15, and 20
Length—22 inches and 24 inches
Diameter—1⅛ and 1 11/32 inches
Weight—24 ounces and 25 ounces

This target scope is one of the finest made. It is a precise optical instrument, and was designed for the target shooter who demands not only optical excellence but mechanical precision. It permits the shooter to take full advantage of the accuracy of his rifle. This instrument is made in three sizes, as follows:

"Super-Targetspot," available in 10, 12, 15 or 20 power. The lens diameter is 1 11/32, providing twice the field of view of scopes of equal magnification. The ocular lens can be adjusted for individual vision. Its large objective provides increased light-gathering power. Under normal light conditions shots may be spotted in the black at 100 yards. Field of view: 10 power, 12 feet at 100 yards; 12 power, 9 feet 3 inches at 100 yards; 15 power, 8 feet 9 inches at 100 yards; 20 power, 5 feet 6 inches at 100 yards. Ranges of 50 feet, 25, 50, 100, and 200 yards are indicated by graduations on front sleeve and tube.

The rear mount has three-point suspension, with ¼-minute clicks for both windage and elevation. Available in the following reticules: Extra-fine cross-wire (.0007 inch diameter), super-fine, cross-wire (.0005 inch diameter); also any one of 5 other reticules. Eye relief for 10, 12, and 15 power, 2 inches; for 20 power, 1 15/16 inch. Over-all length, 24 inches; weight, 25 ounces. Comes with rubber eye cup, bases, and wooden carrying case.

"Targetspot," available in 8 and 10 power only. It has a lens diameter of 1⅛ inch, offering an extremely wide field of view. It has the other features embodied in the "Super-Targetspot" model. The 8-power scope has a field of view of 14 feet at 100 yards, the 10 power a field of view of 12 feet at 100 yards. Front and rear mounts are the same as in the "Super-Targetspot," and same reticules are optional. Normal eye relief is 2 inches. Over-all length, 22 inches; weight, 24 ounces. Furnished with rubber eye cup, bases, and wooden carrying case.

"Junior Targetspot," designed to serve not only as a target scope, but for vermin shooting. It is available in the following power; 6, 8, or 10. The objective lens has a diameter of 19 mm. (¾ inch). The other features are similar to those found on the "Super-Targetspot." The scope has the following fields of view at 100 yards: 6 power, 16 feet; 8 power, 14 feet; 10 power, 12 feet. Over-all length, 21½ inches; weight, 22 ounces. Option of one of five reticules.

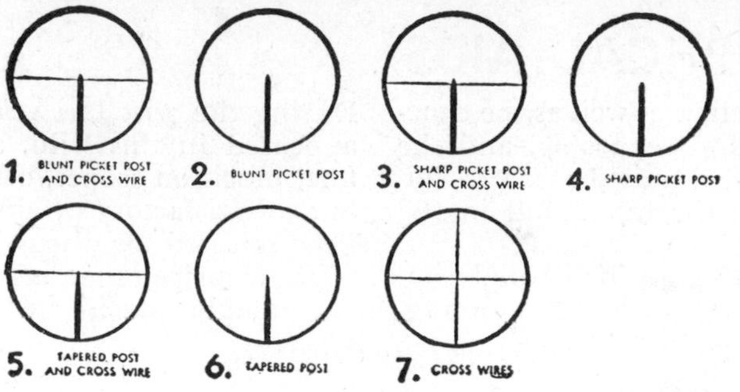


PLATE III. Scope Reticules.

PLATE IV. NORMAN-FORD "Texan." This 2½-power hunting scope is a precision instrument, and is designed to permit low mounting on any high-power rifle. It is an internal adjustment scope, with external knobs for adjusting windage and elevation. The eye relief is 4½ inches, and it has a field of view of about 40 feet at 100 yards. The lenses are coated. The ocular lens is adjustable for focus to the individual vision.

PLATE V. LEUPOLD.

Power—2¼
Length—10 inches
Diameter—⅞ inch
Weight—7 ounces

This is an excellent internal-adjustment sight. The changes in elevation and windage are made by turning the knurled, graduated sleeves. Adjustment is indicated by clicks; each click represents ½ inch of vertical or horizontal movement at 100 yards, and there are two clicks for each graduation on the sleeve. When the adjustment is made the sleeve is held in place by tightening the locking ring. The eye relief is 2¼ to 5 inches. This scope gives a 40-foot field of view at 100 yards. Lenses are fluoride coated. It is available with the following reticules: medium cross hairs, tapered post and lateral hair, and tapered post.

PLATE VI. LEUPOLD Scope Mounted on a Conversion Sporter.

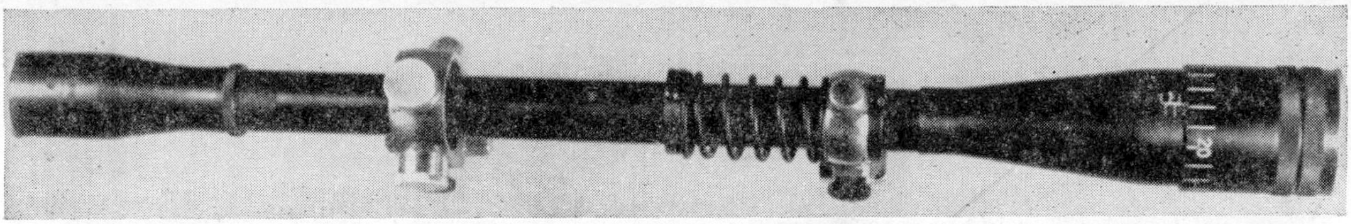

PLATE VII. EDWARDS Model "V."

Power—6, 8, or 10
Diameter—1¼ inches
Length—15 inches
Weight—12 ounces

These scopes come in three models: V-6, in 6 power; V-8, in 8 power; V-10, in 10 power. They have been designed principally for the varmint shooter. There are exterior adjustments for windage and elevation contained in the mounts. The field of view is excellent in all three models. The mounts are designed to bridge across the receiver of the rifle on bolt-action rifles, falling block actions, or lever actions. It cannot be mounted on bolt-action rifles which are split at the rear of the receiver. The reticule is supplied with fine cross hairs. The scope is focused from the objective end with a graduated focusing scale. The adjustment moves the lens forward or back, but does not rotate the lens, which would require re-sighting of the rifle. Adjusting screws for windage aand elevation are notched to fit a coin. Caps cover adjustment screws to prevent accidental movement. The 6-power scope has a 20-foot field of view at 100 yards, the 8 power a 15-foot field of view, and the 10 power a 12-foot field of view.

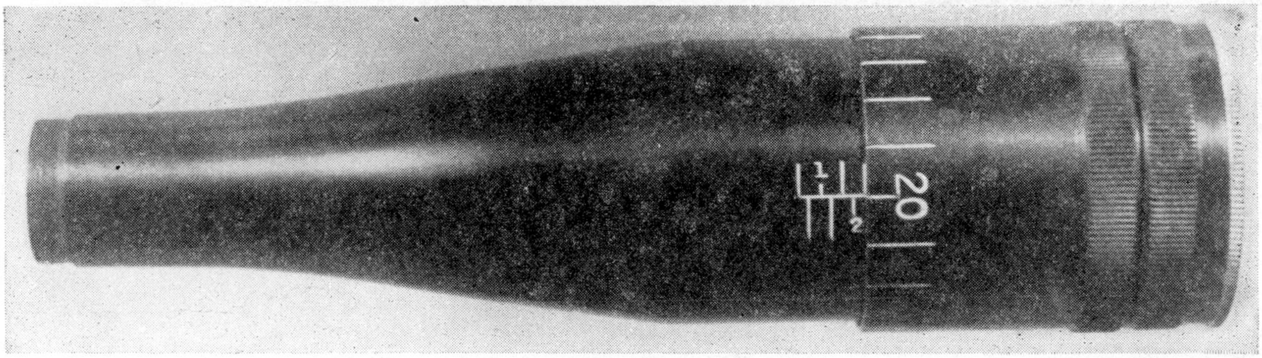

PLATE VIII. EDWARDS Attachment.

Power—6, 8, or 10
Weight—4½, 5, and 5½ ounces
Length—3¾, 4½, and 4⅝ inches
Diameter—1¼ and 1⅜ inches

These attachments are designed to increase the power of the low-power hunting scope, thus making it adaptable for use on the target range or for vermin hunting. The attachment fits flush to the end of the scope and is the same diameter as the scope tube at that point. It does not have to be threaded, as it screws into the front end of the scope. The attachment gives a finer adjustment to the low-power scopes, as it changes the ¼-minute clicks to approximately ⅛-minute clicks. It does not alter the cross hairs and the eye relief remains the same. The rifle must be re-sighted after the attachment has been installed. The field of view of the low-power scope is cut down in relation to the power increase. For example, a 4-power scope with a 30-foot field of view at 100 yards would have the field of view reduced to approximately 16 feet with the attachment. It can be fitted to the following scopes in the power given: Weaver 29S, 6 power; Weaver 330, 6 or 8 power; Weaver 440, 8 or 10 power; Weaver K-2.5, 6 power; Weaver K-4, 8 power; Lyman Alaskan, 6 power; Texan, 6 power; Leupold, 6 power.

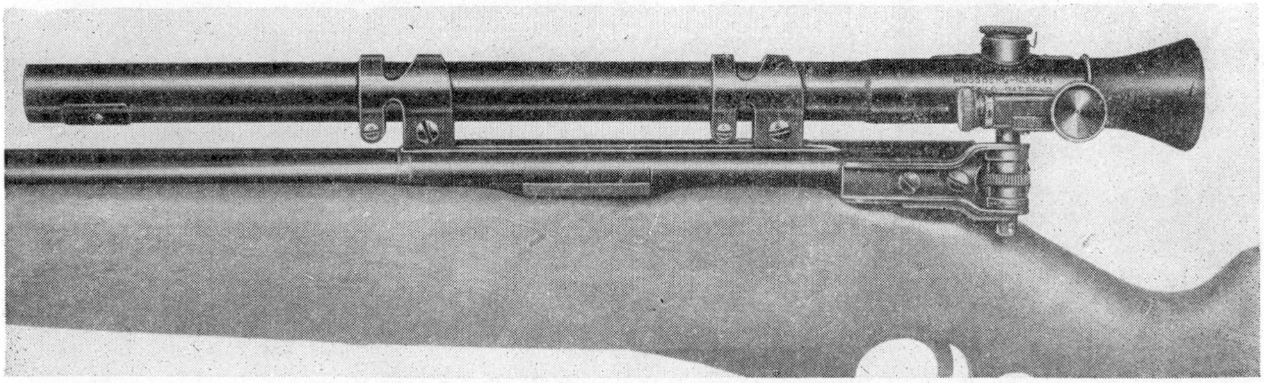

PLATE IX. MOSSBERG Model 4M4 (B). This is an inexpensive 4-power scope, with a field of view of 20 feet at 100 yards. It is not made to stand the jar and recoil of high-power rifles, but was designed for use with the .22-caliber rifle. It has an internal adjustment, by means of external knobs, for both windage and elevation, in ¼-minute clicks. It is equipped with medium-fine cross hairs. The five-lens optical system gives the scope reasonably good illumination and clear definition. The mount (included with scope) is rigidly mounted on the side of the receiver. Eye relief, 2 inches.

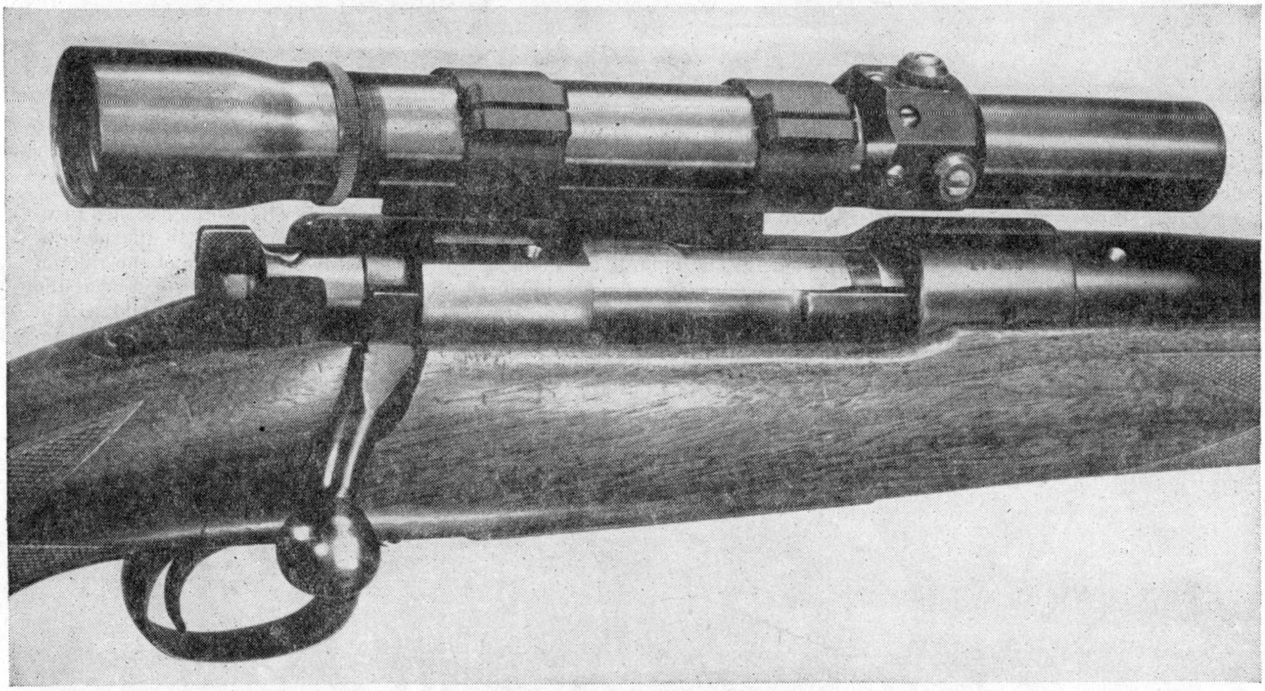

PLATE X. WEAVER K-2.5 Scope, with Weaver "U" Side Mount.

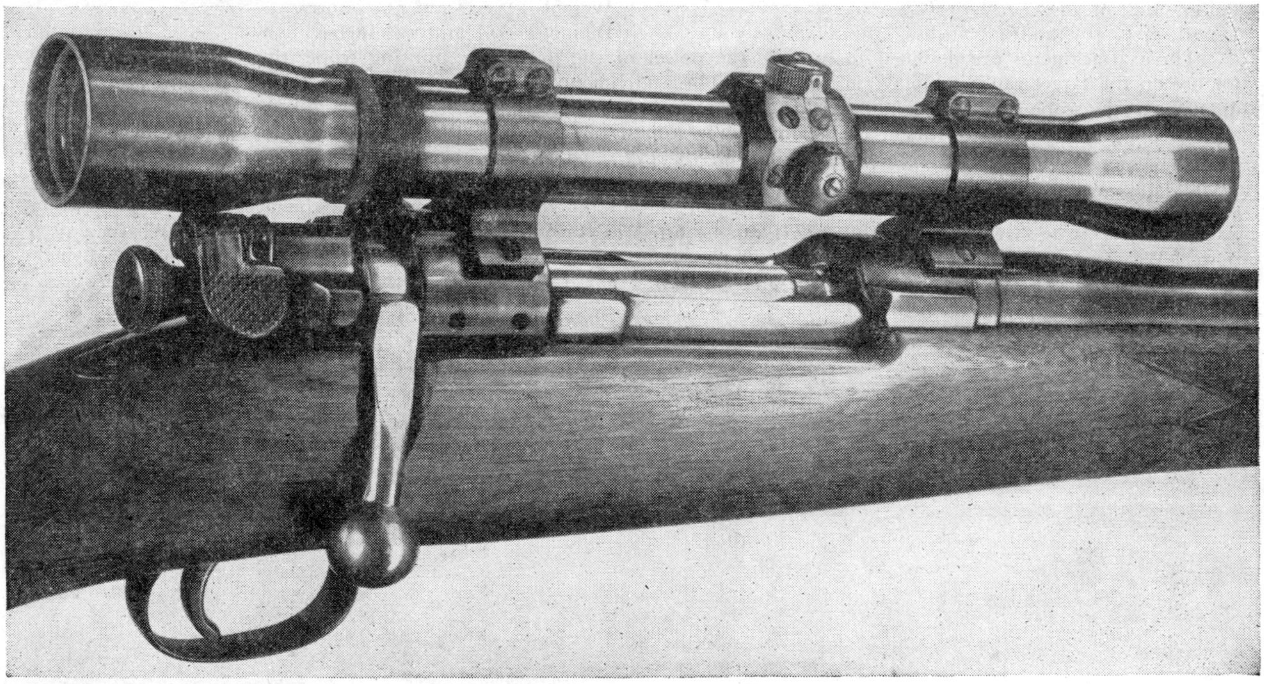

PLATE XI. WEAVER K-4 Scope, with Weaver "U" Bridge-Type Mount.

PLATE XII. GRIFFIN & HOWE. This is one of the time-tested low mounts, designed primarily for the bolt action, and is mounted on the left of the receiver. It is easily detachable, and can be removed and replaced without affecting the zero of the rifle. It is precision made, extremely sturdy, and completely reliable. Despite the advent of a number of new mounts, some of which are lighter in construction, these mounts continue to hold their popularity with big-game hunters.

PLATE XIII. Scope, with Griffin & Howe Mount, on Sporter.

PLATE XIV. MASHBURN Mount, Assembled and Disassembled. This is a quick-detachable, precision mount, and although of the bridge type, is so made that it is possible to use iron sights when the scope has been dismounted. It is extremely sturdy, and is popular with big-game hunters.

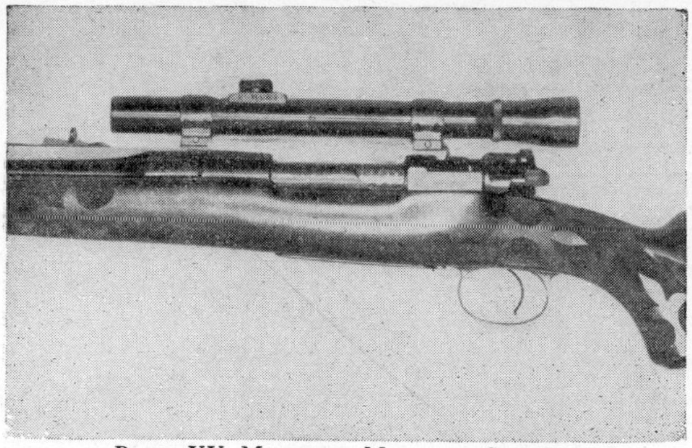

PLATE XV. MASHBURN Mount on Sporter.

PLATE XVI. "ECHO" Mount. This scope mount is extremely popular among big-game hunters due to its ease of affixing to the rifle, precision construction, and light weight. Wih this mount, the scope can be removed and replaced wihout any change in the zero of the sight. Being a side mount, it has one important advantage over the bridge-type mount. It can be removed in a few seconds, permitting the shooter to use iron sights. (E. C. Herkner Co., Littleton, Colo.)

## Other excellent target and hunting scopes are made by the following companies:

FECKER (J. W. Fecker, Pittsburgh, Pa.). *Target.* Available in 8, 10, 12.5, and 16 power. This scope has 1½-inch objective lens, and can be used also to spot a shot in the black at 100 yards. Cross-wire reticules available in five different degrees of fineness. Length, 25 inches; weight, 19 ounces.

*Sporting.* Available in 4.5, 6, 8, and 10 power. This scope has a ¾-inch objective lens, and may be fitted with an auxiliary lens which brings 4.5-power scope to 8 power. Available with precision click or micrometer mount.

*Small Game.* Available in 2¼, 3, or 4 power. Over-all length, 16 or 18 inches; weight, 14 ounces. Field of view of 3 power, 26 feet at 100 yards. Available with cross-wire or flat top post reticule.

STITH (M. L. & M. J. Stith, San Antonio, Tex.). *Sporting.* Available in 2½ power. This scope is ⅞-inch in diameter, individual focus, coated lens, internal adjustment, and capable of low mounting. Field of view at 100 yards is 35 feet. Weight, 9 ounces.

MAXWELL SMITH. *Sporting.* Available in 2½, 4½ and 6 power. Precision made, with internal adjustments for windage and elevation. Eye relief, 3 to 5 inches. Over-all length, 10¾ inches. Weight, 11 ounces. Coated lens. Individual focus. Field of view at 100 yards about 40 feet. Reticule, tapered post, cross-wires, or tapered post with cross-wire.

Made by Maxwell Smith Co., Los Angeles 25, Calif.

UNERTL (John Unertl Optical Co., Pittsburgh, Pa.). *Target.* Available in 10, 15, 18, 20, and 24 power. Objective lens, 1¾ inch, tube 1 inch in diameter. Over-all length, 24 inches; weight, 34 ounces. Eye relief, 3 inches. Equipped with ¼-minute click mounts. Individual focus. Cross-wire reticule.

*Target.* Available in 10, 12, 14, 16, 18, and 20 power. Over-all length 24 inches; weight, 24 ounces. Objective lens, 1½ inch. Interchangeable eyepieces raise or lower original magnification 35 per cent.

*Target and Varmint.* Available in 6, 8, or 10 power. Over-all length, 21⅝ inches; weight, 17 ounces. Field of view at 100 yards, 16 feet in 6 power. Mounts, ¼-minute click. Interchangeable eyepieces available to raise or lower magnification by 25 per cent.

*Falcon.* Available in 2½ power only. Over-all length, 10½ inches; weight, 7 ounces. Coated lenses. Internal adjustments for windage and elevation made by external click knobs. Eye relief, 3 to 4 inches. Objective lens and eye lens, ¾ inch.

WEAVER (W. R. Weaver Co., El Paso, Tex.). *G-4.* An inexpensive scope designed for use with the .22-caliber rifle. Available in 4 power. Over-all length, 11½ inches; weight, 7 ounces. Reticule, cross hairs. Eyepiece adjustable for individual focus. Internal adjustment for windage and elevation. Eye relief, 2½ inches. Field of view, 30 feet at 100 yards. Tube diameter, ¾ inch.

*K-2.5.* Available in 2½ power. Eyepiece diameter, about 1¼ inch; objective lens, .807 inch. Field of view at 100 yards, 43 feet. Over-all length, 10⅜ inches; weight, 8½ ounces. Individual focus. Internal adjustment for windage and elevation, with external knobs graduated, ½-minute click. Eye relief, 3 to 6 inches. Reticules, cross hairs or post and cross hairs.

*K-4.* Available in 4 power. Over-all length, 11¼ inches; weight, 9½ ounces. Eyepiece diameter, 1.355 inch; objective lens, 1.130. Individual focus. Internal adjustment for windage and elevation, with external knobs graduated, ¼-minute click. Eye relief, 3 to 5½ inches. Reticule, cross hairs or post and cross hair.

## Other excellent scope mounts for sporting rifles are manufactured by the following companies:

ALLEN (R. E. Allen, Highland Park, Mich.). This mount is a bridge type, but has one excellent feature found in only one other precision mount. The scope clamps are hinged, permitting the scope to be swung to the left for the use of iron sights. The hinges are on a tapered pin, so designed that any looseness will be taken up by a powerful spring washer, causing the scope to be held in a set position.

PACHMAYR (Pachmayr Gun Works, Los Angeles, Calif.). This also is a "swing-out" mount. It is a bridge-type mount, precision made, and extremely sturdy. Like the Allen mount, it is hinged, permitting the scope to be swung to the left for the use of iron sights.

REDFIELD (Redfield Gunsight Co., Denver, Colo.). This is a bridge-type mount, quickly detachable. It can be removed or attached without changing the zero of the sight. This is a light-weight, precision-made, and inexpensive mount, and is very popular.

STITH (M. L. & M. J. Stith, San Antonio, Tex.). This is an extremely popular mount with those who demand precision and lightness of weight. It permits the scope to be mounted low, and is extremely simple to attach to the rifle. It is extremely valuable to those who carry a rifle in a saddle scabbard as it has no obstructions to prevent smooth withdrawal.

WILLIAMS (Williams Gun Shop, Davison, Mich.). This is a sturdy, precision-made, and quickly detachable mount. It permits low mounting of the scope, and can be removed and replaced without changing the zero of the sight.

PLATE XVII. "ECHO" Mount on Sporter.

PLATE XVIII. NYDAR Shotgun Sight (Nydar G nsight Division, Swain Nelson Co., Glenview, Ill.)

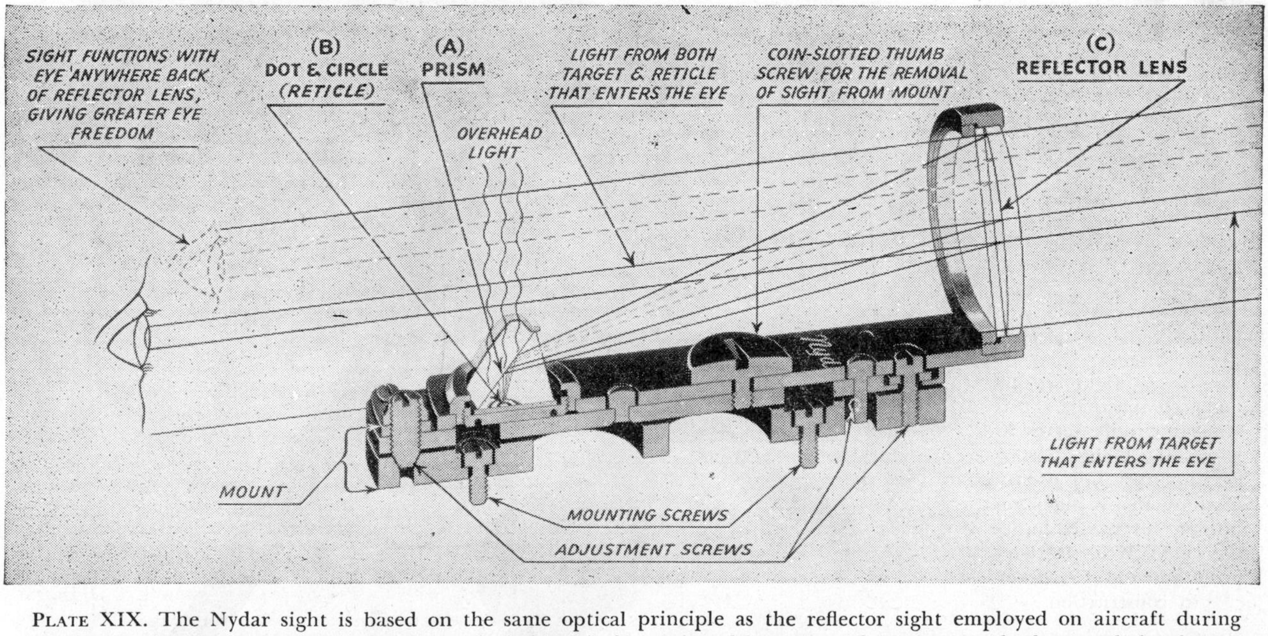


PLATE XIX. The Nydar sight is based on the same optical principle as the reflector sight employed on aircraft during World War II. As shown here, the dot and circle reticule, projected by means of a prism on the lens, and the shooter merely looks through the large lens (reflector plate), using the dot as a sight. This dot indicates the center of impact of the shot load. At 50 yards the projected (transparent) dot is approximately 1 foot in diameter, which aids the shooter in computing the necessary lead. At 50 yards the projected (transparent) ring is approximately 4 feet in diameter.

PLATE XX. The installation of the Nydar sight is accomplished by drilling and tapping two holes on the top of the receiver of the auto-loading or slide-action shotgun, and in the breech end of the rib on the double or over-and-under shot-gun. After the sight has been mounted and assembled, adjust-ments are made to align the sight with the bore of the gun. Adjust-ment screws, for both windage and elevation, are provided. Bore-sight-ing is a simple means of lining up the sight. The final adjustment is made after patterning the gun on a target, insuring that the center of the pattern coincides with the center of the dot. Once the adjust-ment has been made, the sight may be removed or replaced without changing the adjustment.

PLATE XXI. ARGUS Spotting Scope. This model, a recent development, is one of the finest spotting scopes made. It has the following specifications:
Power—20
Diameter—2.165 inches (55 mm.)
Field of View—11.5 feet at 100 yards, 23 feet at 200 yards
Over-all length—14 inches.
Weight—32 ounces.
Lens—coated.
Range of focus—40 feet to infinity.
Focus—eyepiece adjustment.
Due to its light weight and compactness, this scope not only serves as a spotting scope for target shooting, but is favored by many big-game hunters for use in locating game. It is weather-proof and water-resistant in construction.

## BINOCULARS

There are several types of optical aids which are invaluable to the hunter, but the modern binocular, light in weight and small in bulk, has pushed the old telescope and field glass to the background.

The mechanical function, if it may be so termed, of the binocular is mathematical, and unlike the telescope or field glass, the viewer employing a 6-power binocular, for example, not only views a distant object as though it were one-sixth as far away, but views it with greater perception of depth. How this is made possible is shown in Plate XXIII.

No big-game hunter needs to be "sold" on the importance of good binoculars, for too often he has been confronted with circumstances in which binoculars decided the success or failure of a hunt.

There are several factors to be considered before deciding upon the purchase of binoculars, and these factors do not concern the decision as to the power, size, and weight. First, when you have decided upon the power you require, you want to be certain that you get what you pay for. Any of the well-known makers is fully dependable, but if you buy a glass that is turned out by some obscure company it is important to check the magnification.

This check is not as difficult as it may seem. For example, suppose you have bought a pair of 8× glasses (× equals power or the multiple of magnification). If you want to be certain that they are really 8×, set up an object (a two-foot length of stove-wood will do) 100 feet away. Rest your binoculars on something firm and adjust them to focus on this object. Then look at the object with one eye exposed and the other through one tube of the binoculars. The result will be two images side by side. Move the binocular until the two images overlap. If the smaller object is one-eighth the size of the larger, you have eight-power magnification.

Another important factor in binoculars is the "field of view." It is important to have as wide a field of view as possible, but unhappily, the greater the magnification of the binocular, the smaller the field of view. In making your selection, if you are interested in having a glass with a wide field of view you must sacrifice some magnification. For example, the 6× binocular has a greater field of view than the 8×, which means that less movement of the binocular is required to cover an area.

The layman is sometimes confused by the numbers employed in designating the various binoculars. One pair of binoculars may be marked "6×30" and another "7×35." The first figure always means the power, or magnification; the second refers to the diameter of the "objective" or front lens. The larger the diameter of the objective lens, the greater the light-gathering quality of the binocular. Under some circumstances brightness of the image is more important than magnification. You may determine the relative brightness quite readily by simple arithmetic.

For example, if your binoculars are 7×35 you follow the rule of dividing the diameter by the magnification and squaring the result. To work this out:

$$7\overline{)35}\ \ 5 \qquad 5^2 \quad (5\times5)=25$$

Therefore, the relative brightness is 25.

Now take a pair of 7×50 binoculars:

$$7\overline{)50}\ \ 7.1 \qquad 7.1^2 \quad (7.1\times7.1)=50.4$$

Therefore, the relative brightness is 50.4.

Formerly the best glasses came from Europe; nowadays, however, several American optical companies turn out notably high-quality products.

One large American optical company has prepared a chart to guide sportsmen in their selection

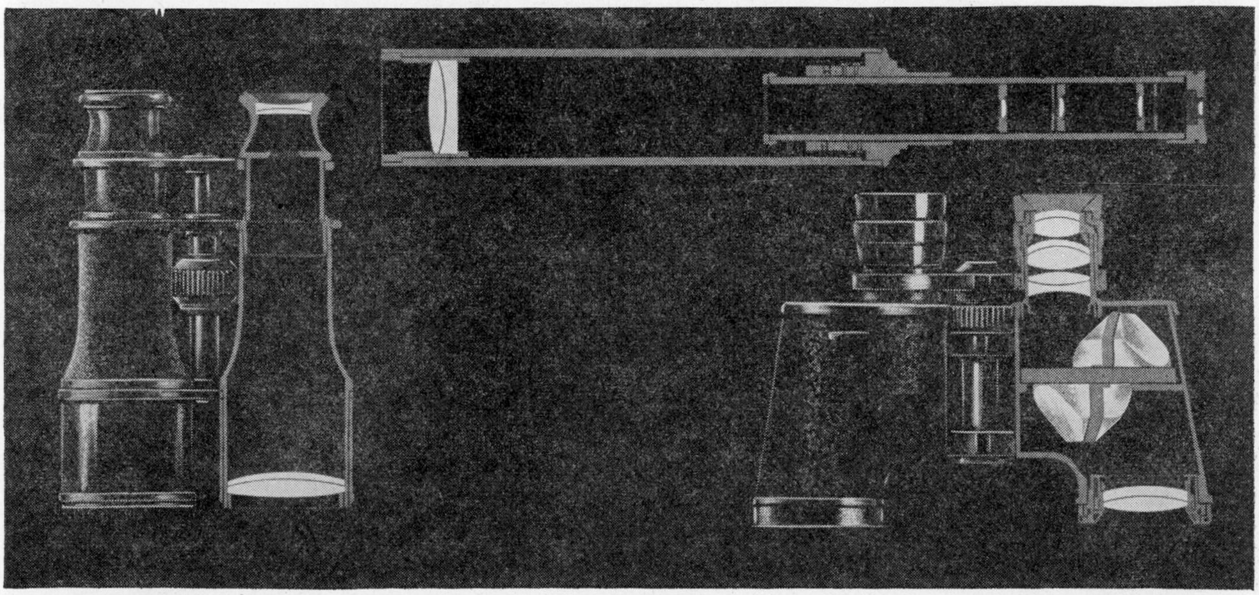

PLATE XXII. The Three Types of Glasses. *Left:* the old Galilean field glasses; *upper:* the telescope; *right:* the prism binocular.

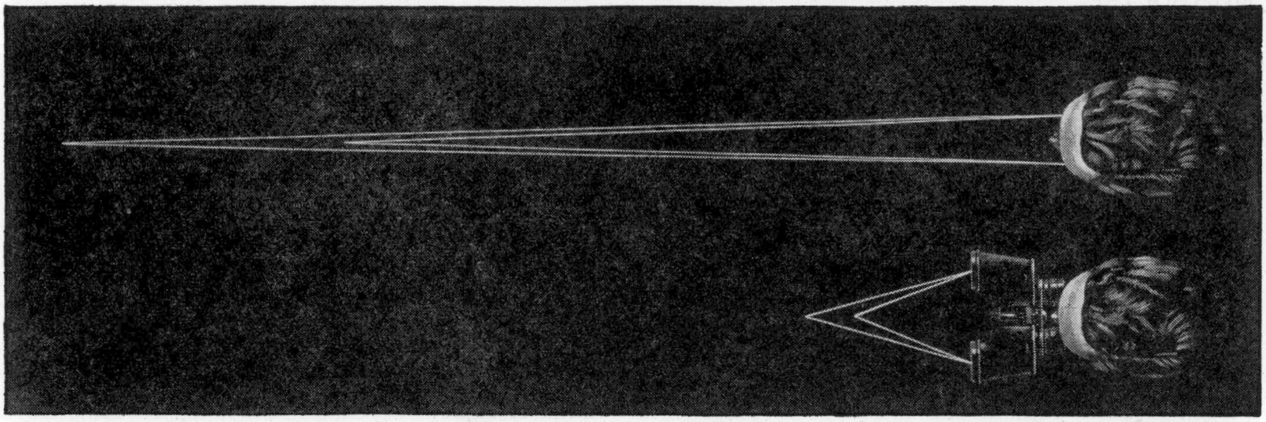

Plates XXIII-XXVII courtesy Bausch & Lomb.

**Plate XXIII.** Depth perception (stereoscopic effect) is achieved by the fact that the two eyes see slightly different views due to the slight difference in angle at which they look. In the diagram above a man looks at two points. One is 600 feet distant, the other 840 feet distant. In the lower diagram a man looks at the same objects through a 6-power binocular, the objective lenses of which are twice as far apart as the eyepieces. The effect is to bring up the objects to an apparent one-sixth of their actual distance. The increase in stereoscopic effect is 12 times, indicated here by the increase in the angle made by the lines from the binoculars to each point, and in the angle made by the lines from each point to each side of the binoculars.

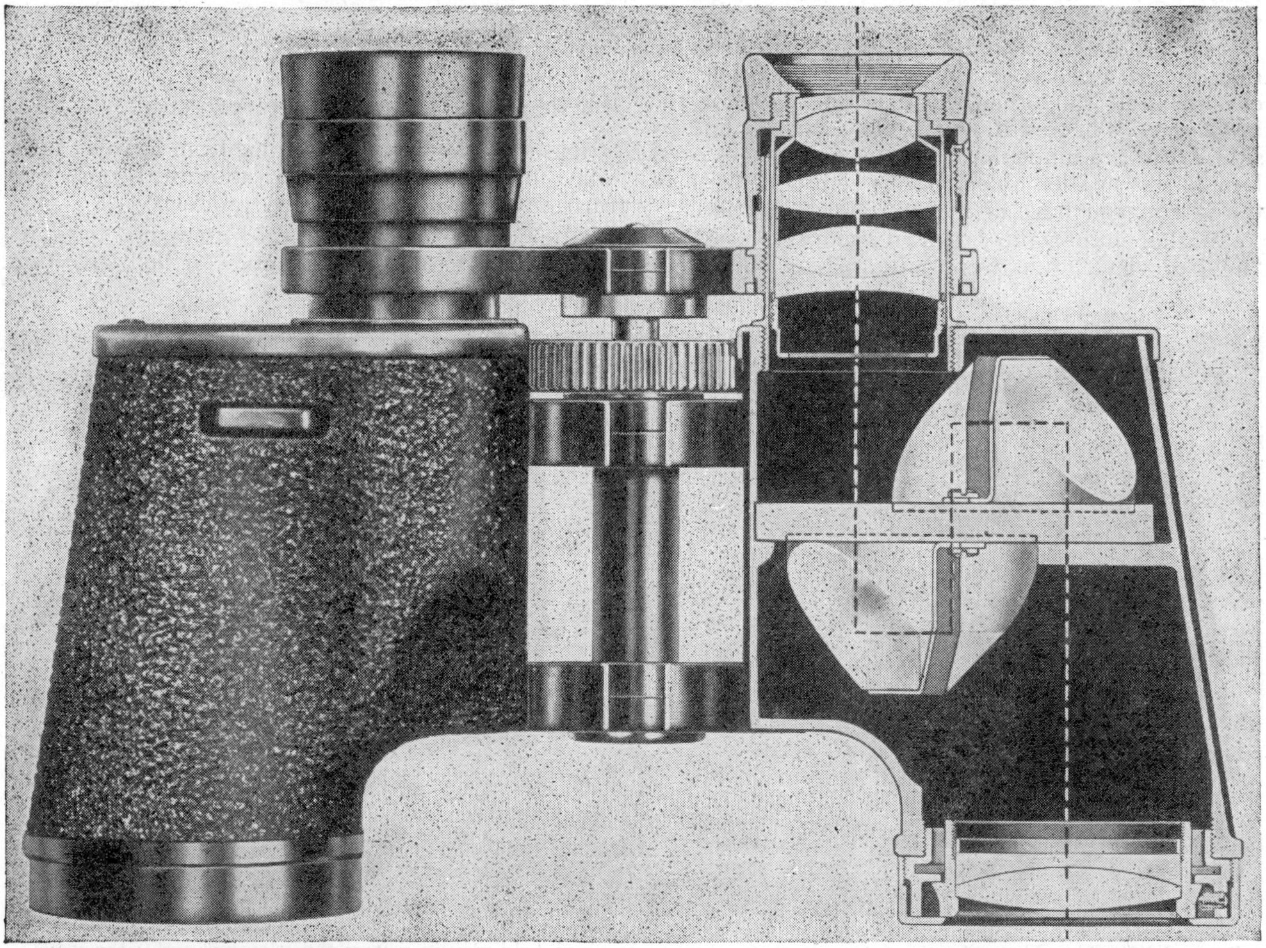

**Plate XXIV.** Cross Section Showing Path of Light through a Modern Prism Binocular.

of binoculars to suit their needs, which advises the following models and magnification:

| | |
|---|---|
| Bird Study 7×35 | Mountain Goat 9×35 |
| Mountain Hunting 9×35 | Coyote 9×35 |
| Prairie Hunting 9×35 | Big Game 8×30 |
| Woodland Hunting 6×30 | Vermin 7×35 |
| Deer 7×35 | Field Trials 7×35 |

Although binoculars are available in several models, the types shown here are those in which the hunter will be interested. The selection of the individual model depends upon the requirements.

PLATE XXV. Bausch & Lomb 6×30 "Zephyr-Light." These are the lightest and most compact of the binoculars. Field of view, 445 feet at 1000 yards. Power, 6. Objective lens diameter, 30 mm. Relative brightness, 25. Length, 4¾ inches; weight, 15¾ ounces. Coated lens. Central focusing.

PLATE XXVI. Bausch & Lomb 7× 35 "Zephyr-Light." This type is popular for all-around use. Field of view, 381 feet at 1000 yards. Power, 7. Objective lens diameter, 35 mm. Relative brightness, 25. Length, 5⅝ inches; weight, 18 ounces. Coated lens. Central focusing.

PLATE XXVII. Bausch & Lomb 8×30. This is a general-purpose glass, preferred by those who want higher power and extreme compactness, even at the expense of image brightness. Power, 8. Field of view, 445 feet at 1000 yards. Objective lens, 30 mm. Length, 4 9/16 inches; weight, 16¾ ounces. Relative brightness, 14.3. Coated lens. Central focusing.

PLATE XXVIII. Bausch & Lomb 9×35. These are good binoculars for the man planning a trip to the "wide open spaces," where the clarity of the atmosphere permits the use of such powerful binoculars. Power, 9. Field of view, 381 feet at 1000 yards. Length, 5 7/16 inches; weight, 20 ounces. Relative brightness, 14.4. Objective lens diameter, 35 mm. Coated lens. Central focusing.

## IRON SIGHTS

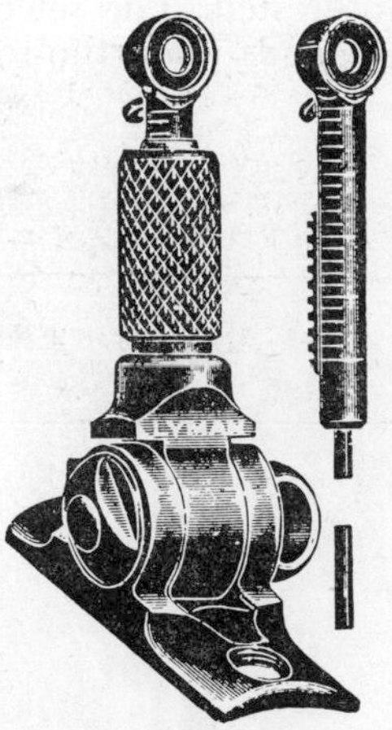

*Folded Down*

Plate XXIX. Lyman Tang (Rear) No. 1. This sight is a "veteran" among peep sights, and is still popular with many hunters. It has the Lyman turn-down feature, assembled in the stem, offering two aperture diameters. The knurled sleeve elevates or lowers the stem. The stem is clearly graduated. When not in use it can be turned down to the rear of the tang, where it is out of the way.

There are several models, designed to fit various makes and models of rifles. Also, it is available with a larger aperture disk, with a .052-inch aperture. These sights are made to fit the following rifles: Remington models 12, 121, 14, 141, 24, 25, 8, 81; Savage Model 1899; Springfield, Krag, Mannlicher-Haenel, Mannlicher-Schoenauer, Newton, and Mauser.

Plate XXX. Lyman No. 48 Series. This famous sight, long the popular favorite with both hunters and match shooters, comes in a number of models. The change in design of the various models is made primarily to permit the sight to be mounted on varied types of rifles. It is a micrometer peep sight, with both graduations and click for both windage and elevation. Each click and graduation changes the center of impact 1/4 inch at 100 yards.

This sight is made in the following models: 48S, for Springfield .30 Government '06; 48C, for Springfield M-1 and M-2 .22-caliber rifles; 48WJS, for Winchester Models 70 and 54; 48RS, for Remington models 720, 30A, 30S, and Enfield; 48M, for Mauser; 48K, for Krag-Jorgensen; 48L, for Stevens Model 417; 48J, 48JH, 48F, 48FH, for Winchester Model 52.

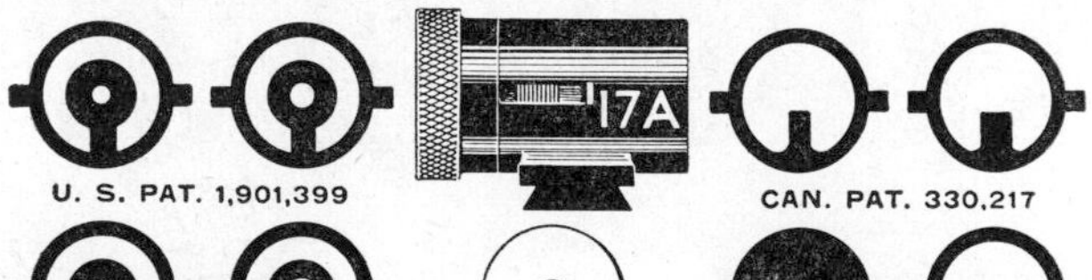


Plate XXXI. Lyman No. 17A (Front) Sight. This globe target front sight is easily adapted to the majority of the match rifles, and is widely used. It comes with 9 inserts, which may be quickly changed without the aid of tools. The four apertures among the inserts have holes with diameters of .140, .120, .110, and .093 inch. Transparent inserts, amber or clear, are available on order. The inserts are precision made, and are positively positioned in exactly the same place in relation to the line of sight, so no change in the rear sight is necessary regardless of which insert is used.

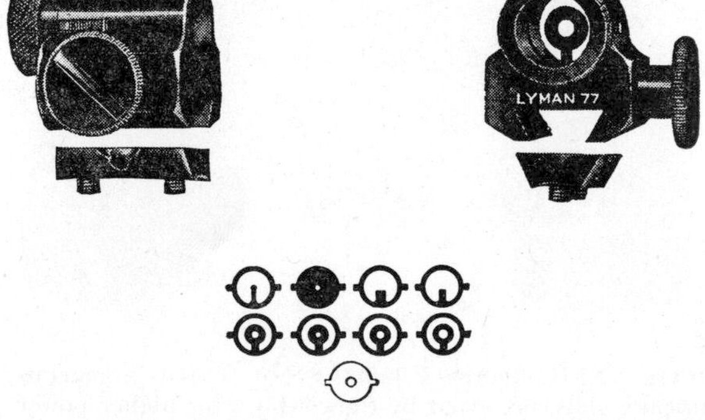


Plate XXXII. Another Lyman front sight the No. 77, similar to the No. 17A in design, is equipped with a locking knob and dovetail, permitting it to be removed and replaced without changing the zero. This model is favored by shooters who change from telescope sight to iron sights in the course of a match. Furnished with nine inserts, circular beveled mill cut vase and two screws.

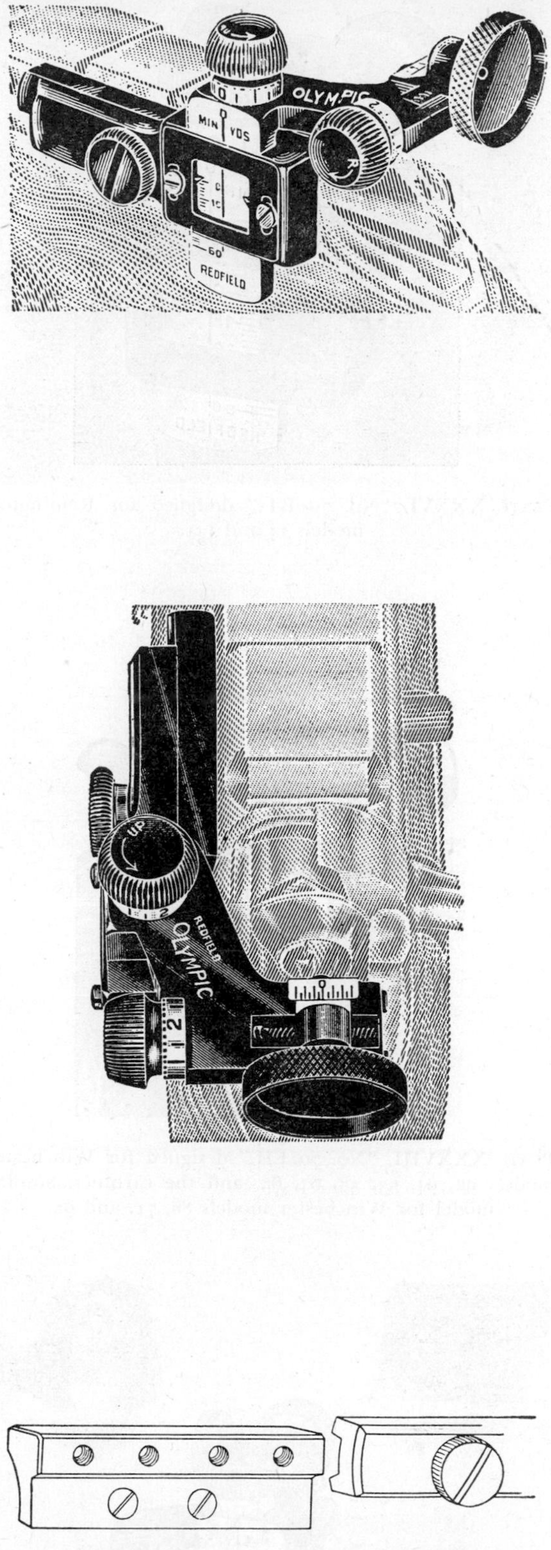


Plate XXXIII. Redfield "Olympic" (Rear). This is a precision sight, popular with many match shooters. It has the following features: Streamline design, full 60-minute elevation adjustment, full 36-minute windage, extension adjustment permits 2-inch movement forward or to the rear, quick removal without any change in zero adjustment, clear graduation marks for elevation and windage, positive 1/4-minute adjustments by click and graduation.

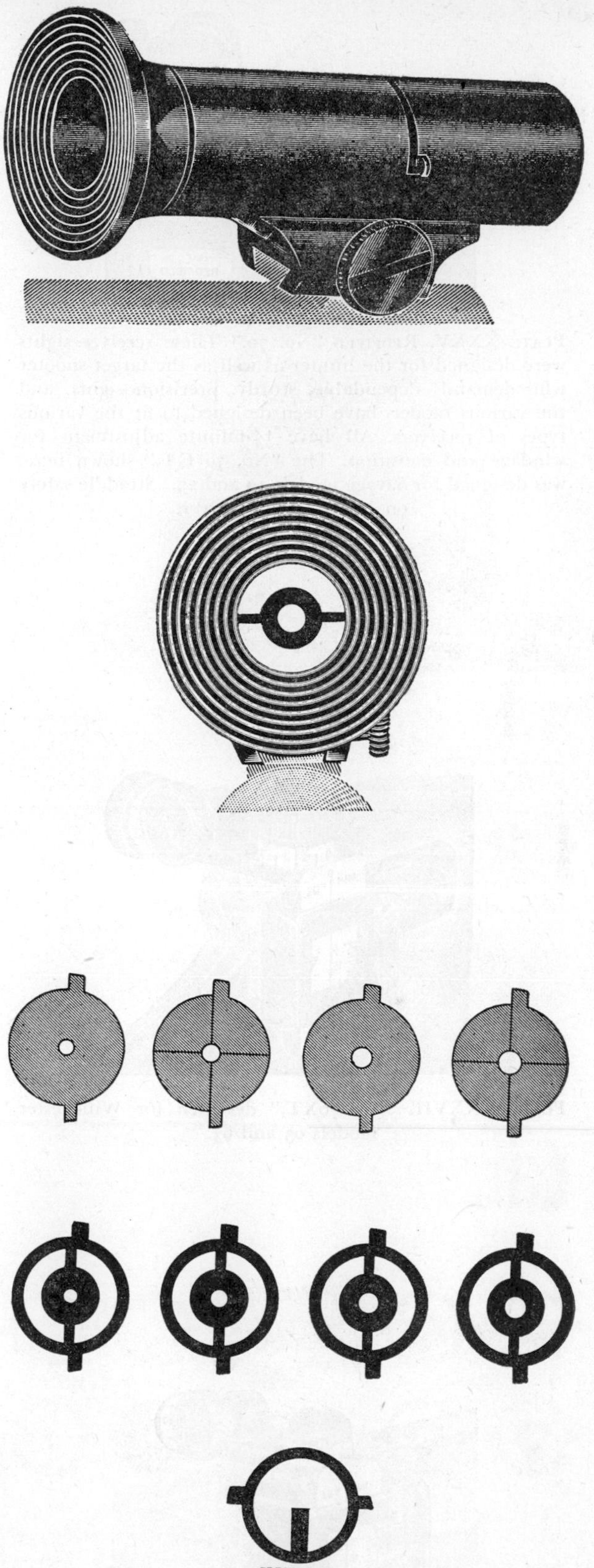


Plate XXXIV. Redfield "Olympic" (Front). This sight, with ten inserts, will fit any standard Redfield, Lyman, or Fecker scope block. The corrugated face of the enlarged eyepiece tends to obscure the under part of the sight and concentrates the vision on the bull. Inserts are quickly and easily changed.

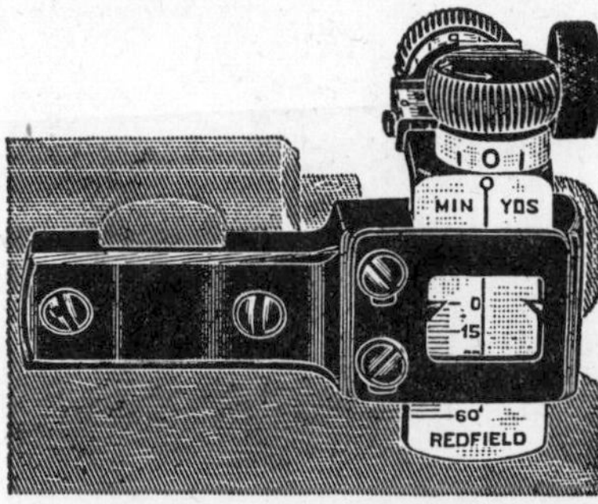


**Plate XXXV.** Redfield "No. 70." These receiver sights were designed for the hunter as well as the target shooter who demands dependable, sturdy, precision sights, and the various models have been designed to fit the various types of receivers. All have ¼-minute adjustment for windage and elevation. The "No. 70 GT," shown here, was designed for Savage models 19 and 23. Straddle safety on left side of receiver.

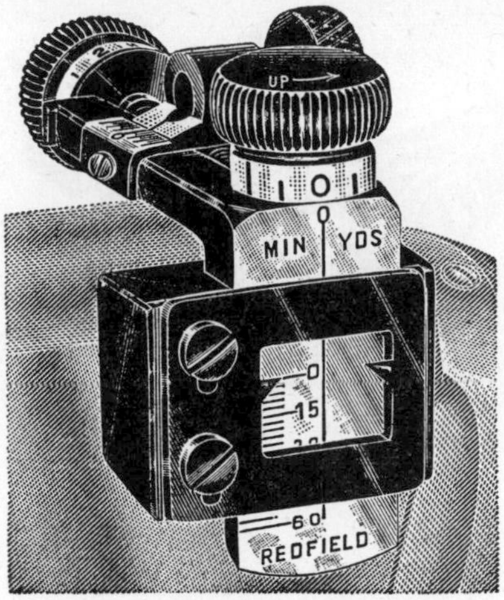


**Plate XXXVI.** "No. 70 BT," designed for Remington models 14 and 141.

**Plate XXXVII.** "No. 70XT," designed for Winchester models 03 and 63.

**Plate XXXVIII.** "No. 70 EH," designed for Winchester models 92, 94, 53, 55, 64, 65, and the carbines. Similar model for Winchester models 86, 71, and 95.

**Plate XXXIX.** "No. 70 KH," designed for Krag rifles. No drilling, tapping, or cutting of stock is necessary.

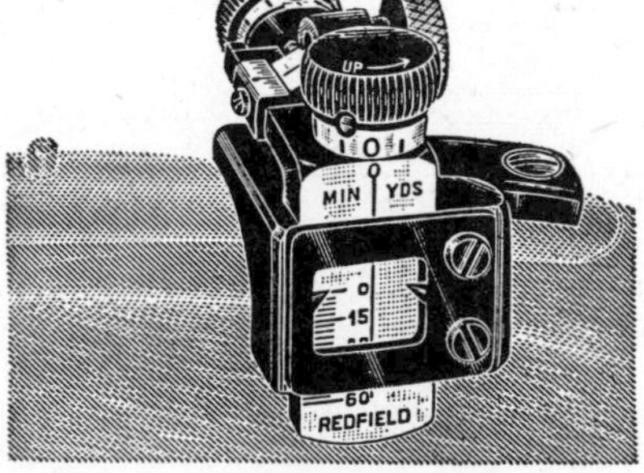


**Plate XL.** "No. 70 LT," designed for Savage model 99. Attaches to rifle by screw holes already provided in the tang.

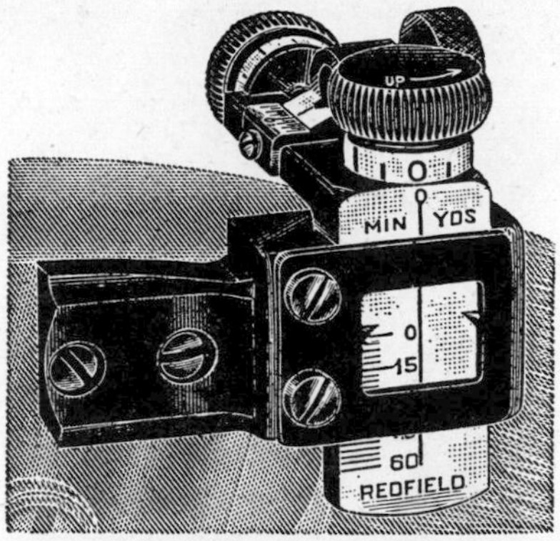


PLATE XLI. "No. 70 TT," designed for Remington rifles models 12, 121, 241, 24 and 25. Two holes must be drilled in the left side of receiver. Also designed for Winchester model 61 for attachment to right side of receiver.

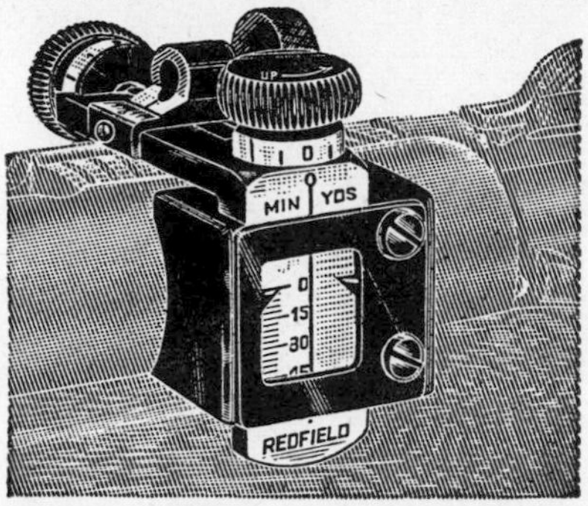


PLATE XLII. "No. 70 WT," designed for Winchester model 70 and most bolt-action high-power rifles. This is simple to install and requires no cutting of the stock. If mounted on Springfield, Enfield, Newton, or Mauser rifles, receiver must be drilled and tapped.

# PATENT CHOKES

Courtesy Lyman Gunsight Corp.

PLATE I. CUTTS Compensator. This patent choke and recoil-reduction device is very widely used and has proved highly satisfactory. It is a standard fixture on many single-barrel skeet guns, and is widely used by field shooters who prefer to use one gun for all types of shooting. It is equipped with six separate inserts, or "tubes," each with a different degree of choke. In addition to its value as a means of regulating pattern, the compensator reduces recoil by approximately 30 per cent. It is available for the following gauges: 12, 16, 20, 28, and .410. Only the 12-gauge gun may be fitted with all six tubes; the other gauges are limited to three tubes each. The compensator is made of special alloy steel. Less than a minute is needed to change the tube.

The following tubes are available for the 12-gauge gun:

No. 680: Long-range tube, designed for use with heavy loads and large-size shot. Extreme choke.
No. 690: Long-range tube, but giving a more open pattern than No. 680.
No. 705. Comparable to full-choke boring.
No. 725: Comparable to modified-choke boring.
No. 755: Comparable to improved cylinder.
Spreader. Comparable to "skeet" boring. Gives an even pattern over a 30-inch circle at 25 yards.

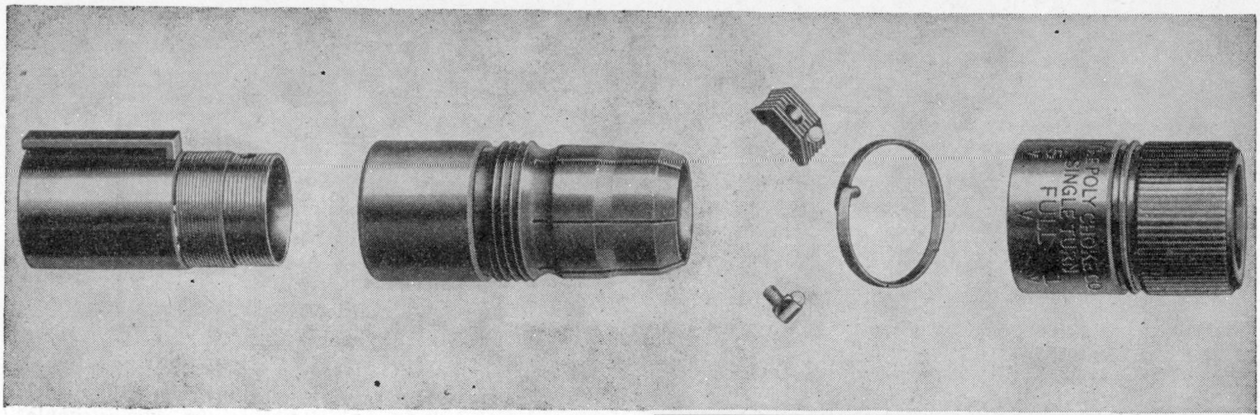

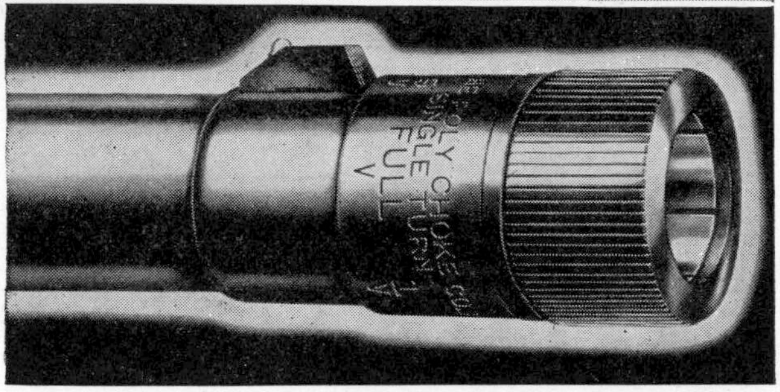


Courtesy Poly Choke Co.

PLATE II. POLY CHOKE. This patent choke device may be fitted to the muzzle of any single-barrel 12-, 16-, or 20-gauge shotgun that is bored "cylinder." It offers a choice of 9 degrees of choke, ranging from cylinder to full choke. The change from one degree to another can be made instantly by a mere twist of the wrist. Each degree of choke is indicated on the device by a graduation line. This choke permits the shooter to regulate the pattern of shot for extremely close or distant targets. It will handle any size shot, as well as rifled slugs, and performs equally well with mid-range or express loads.

The choke weighs only 2½ ounces and is 2¼ inches long. It is approximately ⅛ inch larger in diameter than the outside diameter of the average barrel. In the event the same length of barrel is desired, to include the choke, about 1 ounce of weight is eliminated, which would increase the weight of a gun with the choke by but 1½ ounces. The price of the choke includes the installation charge.

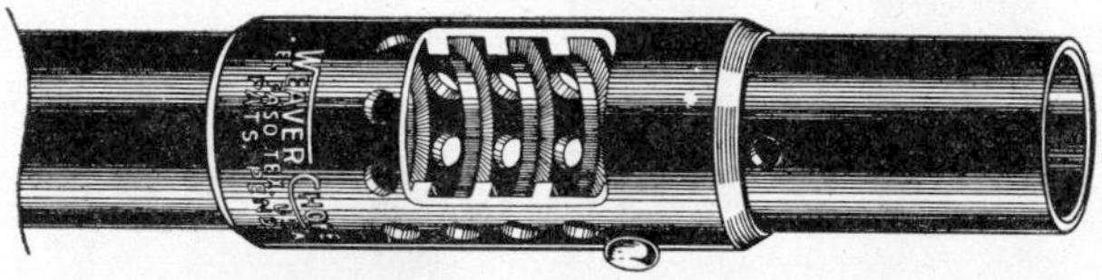

PLATE III. WEAVER Choke. This choke is somewhat similar in function to the Cutts Compensator, and is available for all single-barrel shotguns in 12-, 16-, or 20- gauge. Like the compensator it has a series of baffles designed to divert the gas through a series of vents, thus reducing the recoil. The choke is available with six inserts, each with a different degree of choke. Inserts are available for 12-, 16-, and 20- gauge. As with the compensator, less than one minute is required to change the tubes.

The following inserts are available:

XFC Extra full choke. For extreme long range shooting.
FC Full choke.
¾ Comparable to modified choke.
½ Comparable to improved cylinder.
¼ Comparable to cylinder.
S Comparable to "skeet" boring. Gives even distribution of shot over a 30-inch circle at 25 yards.

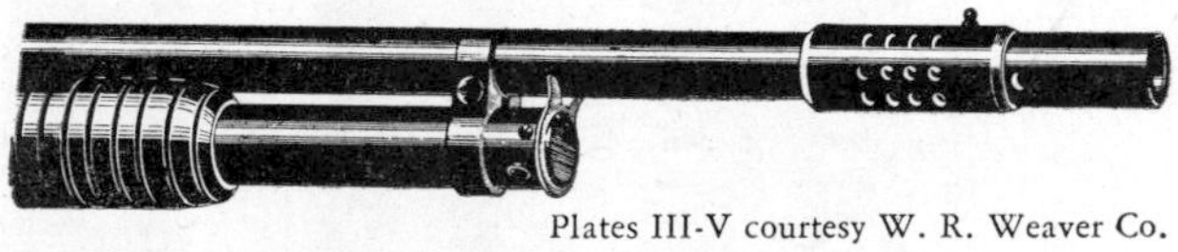

Plates III-V courtesy W. R. Weaver Co.

PLATE IV. Weaver Choke on Slide-Action Shotgun.

PLATE V. Inserts or "Tubes" for the Various Patterns.

# TRAJECTORY CHART

## Computed Sighting—In Table for Western and Winchester Center-Fire Cartridges

NOTE: The computations in this table have been prepared especially for THE HUNTER'S ENCYCLOPEDIA by competent ballisticians as an aid to shooters in sighting in sporting and target rifles of standard center-fire calibers. The data as presented differ from standard ballistic tables in the line of sight, rather than the initial line of flight of the bullet, is the basis for the computations. As a further aid to riflemen using this table, maximum figures have been taken in most cases for drop of bullet below line of sight at long ranges, thus assisting the rifleman in getting his first shot on the target.

HEIGHT ABOVE OR BELOW LINE OF SIGHT

+ = Above line of sight. — = Below line of sight.

| *Cartridge* | *Bullet Weight Grains* | *Bullet Type* | *Sighted In At* | *Range in Yards* 50 | 100 | 200 | 250 | 300 | 350 | 400 | 450 | 500 |
|---|---|---|---|---|---|---|---|---|---|---|---|---|
| .218 Bee. | 46 | OPE | 100 | + 0.7 | 0 | — 6.0 | —16.0 | —26.5 | | | | |
| | | | 200 | + 2.5 | + 3.5 | 0 | — 7.5 | —19.0 | | | | |
| .219 Zipper | 56 | OPE | 100 | + 0.6 | 0 | — 4.5 | —11.0 | —18.0 | | | | |
| | | | 200 | + 1.7 | + 3.5 | 0 | — 4.5 | —13.0 | | | | |
| .22 Hornet | 45 | S. P. | 100 | + 0.8 | 0 | — 7.5 | —19.5 | —32.0 | | | | |
| | | | 200 | + 2.5 | + 4.0 | 0 | — 9.0 | —22.5 | | | | |
| | 46 | OPE | 100 | + 0.8 | 0 | — 6.5 | —17.0 | —31.5 | | | | |
| | | | 200 | + 2.5 | + 3.5 | 0 | — 9.0 | —22.5 | | | | |
| .220 Swift | 48 | S. P. | 100 | + 0.3 | 0 | — 2.5 | — 5.0 | — 9.0 | | | | |
| | | | 200 | + 0.7 | + 1.5 | 0 | — 2.0 | — 6.0 | | | | |
| | | | 300 | + 1.5 | + 2.8 | + 3.5 | + 2.5 | 0 | | | | |
| .22 Savage | 70 | S. P. | 100 | + 0.6 | 0 | — 4.5 | —10.0 | —17.0 | | | | |
| | | | 200 | + 1.7 | + 3.0 | 0 | — 4.0 | —11.0 | | | | |
| .25/20 Win. | 60 | OPE | 100 | + 1.2 | 0 | —11.0 | —26.0 | —48.0 | | | | |
| | 86 | SP, FP, Lub. | 100 | + 2.6 | 0 | —18.5 | —41.5 | —76.0 | | | | |
| .25/35 Win. | 117 | SP, FP | 100 | + 1.0 | 0 | — 8.0 | —17.0 | —29.5 | | | | |
| | | | 200 | + 2.5 | + 4.0 | 0 | — 7.0 | —18.0 | | | | |
| .25 Rem. | 117 | SP | 100 | + 0.9 | 0 | — 6.5 | —15.0 | —26.0 | | | | |
| | | | 200 | + 2.5 | + 4.0 | 0 | — 6.5 | —17.0 | | | | |
| .250 Sav. | 87 | SP | 100 | + 0.5 | 0 | — 3.5 | — 7.5 | —14.5 | | | | |
| | | | 200 | + 1.2 | + 2.5 | 0 | — 3.5 | — 9.0 | | | | |
| | 100 | OPE, ST | 100 | + 0.6 | 0 | — 4.5 | —12.0 | —15.0 | | | | |
| | | | 200 | + 1.7 | + 2.5 | 0 | — 4.5 | —10.0 | | | | |
| .257 Roberts | 100 | OPE, ST | 100 | + 0.6 | 0 | — 3.5 | —10.5 | —16.0 | | | | |
| | | | 200 | + 1.5 | + 2.5 | 0 | — 4.0 | — 9.5 | | | | |
| | | | 300 | + 3.0 | + 6.0 | + 6.5 | + 4.5 | 0 | | | | |
| | 117 | SP | 100 | + 0.8 | 0 | — 5.5 | —13.0 | —22.5 | | | | |

## HEIGHT ABOVE OR BELOW LINE OF SIGHT

| Cartridge | Bullet Weight Grains | Bullet Type | Sighted In At | Range in Yards 50 | 100 | 200 | 250 | 300 | 350 | 400 | 450 | 500 |
|---|---|---|---|---|---|---|---|---|---|---|---|---|
| .257 Roberts—*Continued.* | | | 200 | + 2.0 | + 3.0 | 0 | — 5.0 | —13.5 | | | | |
| | | | 300 | + 3.5 | + 7.0 | + 8.0 | + 5.5 | 0 | | | | |
| .270 Win. | 100 | SP | 100 | + 0.4 | 0 | — 3.0 | — 6.0 | —10.5 | | | | |
| | | | 200 | + 1.0 | + 1.5 | 0 | — 2.5 | — 6.5 | | | | |
| | | | 300 | + 2.0 | + 3.5 | + 4.0 | + 2.5 | 0 | | | | |
| .270 Win. | 130 | OPE, ST | 100 | + 0.5 | 0 | — 3.5 | — 7.0 | —12.5 | | | | |
| | | | 200 | + 1.0 | + 2.0 | 0 | — 3.0 | — 7.5 | —15.0 | —23.0 | —34.0 | —48.0 |
| | | | 300 | + 2.5 | + 6.5 | + 6.5 | + 3.5 | 0 | — 5.0 | — 7.5 | —22.5 | —38.0 |
| | 150 | SP | 100 | + 0.6 | 0 | — 4.5 | —10.5 | —18.0 | | | | |
| | | | 200 | + 1.5 | + 2.5 | 0 | — 4.0 | —11.0 | —19.5 | —33.5 | —43.0 | —70.0 |
| | | | 300 | + 3.0 | + 6.0 | + 6.5 | + 4.5 | 0 | — 7.0 | —17.0 | —30.0 | —48.0 |
| 7 MM Mauser | 175 | SP | 100 | + 0.8 | 0 | — 5.5 | —13.0 | —22.0 | | | | |
| | | | 200 | + 2.0 | + 3.0 | 0 | — 5.0 | —14.0 | | | | |
| 7.62 Russ | 145 | HCD | 100 | + 0.6 | 0 | — 3.5 | — 7.5 | —14.0 | | | | |
| | | | 200 | + 1.5 | + 2.0 | 0 | — 3.5 | — 9.0 | | | | |
| 30/30 Win. | 150 | OPE | 100 | + 0.9 | 0 | — 6.5 | —17.0 | —26.0 | | | | |
| | | | 200 | + 2.5 | + 4.0 | 0 | — 6.0 | —16.0 | | | | |
| | 170 | SP, MC, ST | 100 | + 1.0 | 0 | — 8.0 | —18.0 | —28.0 | | | | |
| | | | 200 | + 3.0 | + 4.5 | 0 | — 7.0 | —19.0 | | | | |
| .30 Rem. | 170 | SP, ST | 100 | + 1.1 | 0 | — 7.5 | —18.0 | —29.5 | | | | |
| | | | 200 | + 3.0 | + 4.5 | 0 | — 7.0 | —19.0 | | | | |
| .30/40 Krag | 180 | OPE, ST | 100 | + 0.8 | 0 | — 4.5 | —12.0 | —19.5 | | | | |
| | | | 200 | + 1.5 | + 3.5 | 0 | — 4.5 | —11.5 | | | | |
| | | | 300 | + 3.5 | + 6.5 | + 7.5 | + 5.0 | 0 | | | | |
| | 180 | SP | 100 | + 0.8 | 0 | — 5.5 | —13.0 | —22.5 | | | | |
| | | | 200 | + 2.0 | + 3.5 | 0 | — 5.0 | —14.0 | | | | |
| | | | 300 | + 3.5 | + 7.0 | + 8.0 | + 5.5 | 0 | | | | |
| | 220 | ST | 100 | + 1.0 | 0 | — 7.0 | —16.0 | —27.0 | | | | |
| | | | 200 | + 2.5 | + 4.0 | 0 | — 6.0 | —16.0 | | | | |
| .30/06 Sprg. | 150 | OPE | 100 | + 0.5 | 0 | — 4.5 | — 9.0 | —16.0 | | | | |
| | | | 200 | + 1.5 | + 2.0 | 0 | — 3.5 | — 9.5 | —18.0 | —29.5 | —44.5 | —64.0 |
| | | | 300 | + 3.0 | + 5.0 | + 6.0 | + 4.0 | 0 | — 6.5 | —16.0 | —28.0 | —46.0 |
| | 180 | OPE, ST | 100 | + 0.6 | 0 | — 4.5 | —11.0 | —18.0 | | | | |
| | | | 200 | + 1.3 | + 2.0 | 0 | — 4.0 | — 9.5 | —17.5 | —28.0 | —38.0 | —55.0 |

| | | | | | | | | | | | | | |
|---|---|---|---|---|---|---|---|---|---|---|---|---|---|
| | | | 300 | + 2.5 | + 4.5 | + 5.5 | + 3.0 | 0 | — 5.5 | —12.0 | —19.0 | —32.0 |
| | 180 | SP | 100 | + 0.7 | 0 | — 4.5 | —12.0 | —21.0 | | | | |
| | | | 200 | + 1.8 | + 3.0 | 0 | — 4.5 | — 9.5 | —22.0 | —35.0 | —53.0 | —76.0 |
| | | | 300 | + 3.5 | + 6.0 | + 7.0 | + 4.5 | 0 | — 8.5 | —18.5 | —33.0 | —54.0 |
| | 180 | MCBT | 100 | + 0.6 | 0 | — 4.5 | —10.5 | —16.5 | | | | |
| | | | 200 | + 1.3 | + 3.0 | 0 | — 3.5 | — 8.5 | —15.5 | —24.5 | —34.5 | —49.0 |
| | | | 300 | + 2.0 | + 4.5 | + 5.0 | + 3.0 | 0 | — 5.0 | —12.0 | —19.0 | —30.0 |
| | 220 | SP, ST | 100 | + 0.8 | 0 | — 5.5 | —13.0 | —22.0 | | | | |
| | | | 200 | + 2.0 | + 3.5 | 0 | — 5.0 | —13.5 | | | | |
| | | | 300 | + 3.5 | + 7.0 | + 8.0 | + 5.5 | 0 | | | | |
| .300 H. & H. Mag. | 180 | ST | 100 | + 0.6 | 0 | — 4.5 | — 9.5 | —15.0 | | | | |
| | | | 200 | + 1.5 | + 2.5 | 0 | — 3.5 | — 9.5 | —18.0 | —29.5 | —44.5 | —65.0 |
| | | | 300 | + 3.0 | + 5.0 | + 6.0 | + 4.0 | 0 | — 6.5 | —16.0 | —28.0 | —46.0 |
| | 180 | MCBT | 100 | + 0.5 | 0 | — 3.5 | — 9.0 | —13.0 | | | | |
| | | | 200 | + 1.0 | + 2.0 | 0 | — 3.5 | — 8.0 | —15.0 | —22.0 | —31.0 | —45.5 |
| | | | 300 | + 2.5 | + 4.0 | + 5.0 | + 3.0 | 0 | — 4.5 | — 9.5 | —15.5 | —23.0 |
| | 220 | ST | 100 | + 0.7 | 0 | — 4.5 | —10.5 | —18.0 | | | | |
| | | | 200 | + 1.5 | + 3.0 | 0 | — 4.0 | —11.0 | —20.0 | —34.5 | —44.0 | —73.0 |
| | | | 300 | + 3.0 | + 6.0 | + 6.5 | + 4.5 | 0 | — 7.0 | —17.0 | —30.0 | —48.0 |
| .300 Sav. | 150 | OPE | 100 | + 0.7 | 0 | — 4.5 | —12.0 | —19.0 | | | | |
| | | | 200 | + 1.8 | + 3.0 | 0 | — 4.5 | —11.0 | | | | |
| | 180 | ST | 100 | + 0.9 | 0 | — 7.0 | —13.5 | —23.5 | | | | |
| | | | 200 | + 2.0 | + 3.0 | 0 | — 6.0 | —14.5 | | | | |
| | | SP | 100 | + 0.9 | 0 | — 7.5 | —15.0 | —26.5 | | | | |
| | | | 200 | + 2.0 | + 3.5 | 0 | — 6.0 | —15.5 | | | | |
| .303 Sav. | 190 | SP, ST | 100 | + 1.5 | 0 | — 7.5 | —20.0 | —35.0 | | | | |
| | | | 200 | + 3.0 | + 4.5 | 0 | — 8.0 | —21.0 | | | | |
| .303 British | 215 | SP | 100 | + 1.0 | 0 | — 7.0 | —18.0 | —28.5 | | | | |
| | | | 200 | + 3.0 | + 4.5 | 0 | — 7.0 | —19.0 | | | | |
| .32 Win. Spl. | 165 | OPE | 100 | + 1.0 | 0 | — 7.5 | —18.0 | —28.5 | | | | |
| | | | 200 | + 3.0 | + 4.5 | 0 | — 7.0 | —19.0 | | | | |
| .32 Win. Spl. | 170 | SP, ST | 100 | + 1.0 | 0 | — 7.5 | —18.0 | —28.5 | | | | |
| | | | 200 | + 3.0 | + 4.5 | 0 | — 7.0 | —19.0 | | | | |
| .32 Win. S. L. | 165 | SP | 100 | + 2.6 | 0 | —21.0 | —41.5 | —74.0 | | | | |
| .32 Rem. | 170 | SP, ST | 100 | + 1.0 | 0 | — 7.5 | —18.5 | —31.0 | | | | |
| | | | 200 | + 3.0 | + 4.5 | 0 | — 7.5 | —20.0 | | | | |
| **.32/20 Win.** | **80** | **OPE** | **100** | **+ 1.3** | **0** | **—13.5** | **—31.5** | **—59.0** | | | | |
| | **100** | **SP, FP, Lub.** | **100** | **+ 3.0** | **0** | **—24.5** | **—49.5** | **—98.0** | | | | |

## HEIGHT ABOVE OR BELOW LINE OF SIGHT

| Cartridge | Bullet Weight Grains | Bullet Type | Sighted In At | Range in Yards 50 | 100 | 200 | 250 | 300 | 350 | 400 | 450 | 500 |
|---|---|---|---|---|---|---|---|---|---|---|---|---|
| .32/40 Win. | 165 | SP | 100 | + 2.6 | 0 | —19.5 | —38.0 | —66.0 | | | | |
| .33 Win. | 200 | SP | 100 | + 1.1 | 0 | — 8.0 | —20.0 | —32.5 | | | | |
| | | | 200 | + 3.0 | + 4.5 | 0 | — 8.0 | —21.0 | | | | |
| 8 MM Mann. Schoen | 200 | SP | 100 | + 1.0 | 0 | — 7.5 | —17.0 | —29.0 | | | | |
| | | | 200 | + 2.5 | + 4.0 | 0 | — 7.0 | —18.0 | | | | |
| 8 MM Mauser | 170 | SP | 100 | + 0.8 | 0 | — 5.5 | —13.0 | —23.0 | | | | |
| | | | 200 | + 2.0 | + 3.0 | 0 | — 5.0 | —14.0 | | | | |
| .348 Win. | 150 | SP | 100 | + 0.6 | 0 | — 5.5 | —13.0 | —22.5 | | | | |
| | | | 200 | + 1.8 | + 3.0 | 0 | — 4.5 | —14.5 | | | | |
| | 200 | SP | 100 | + 0.8 | 0 | — 6.5 | —16.0 | —28.0 | | | | |
| | | | 200 | + 2.5 | + 4.0 | 0 | — 6.0 | —16.0 | | | | |
| | 250 | ST | 100 | + 0.9 | 0 | — 7.5 | —16.5 | —30.0 | | | | |
| | | | 200 | + 2.5 | + 4.0 | 0 | — 6.5 | —19.0 | | | | |
| .35 Win. S. L. | 180 | SP | 100 | + 2.5 | 0 | —22.0 | —43.0 | —74.0 | | | | |
| .351 Win. S. L. | 180 | SP, MC | 100 | + 1.5 | 0 | —12.5 | —25.5 | —45.5 | | | | |
| .35 Rem. | 200 | SP, OPE, ST | 100 | + 1.1 | 0 | — 8.5 | —20.0 | —32.0 | | | | |
| | | | 200 | + 3.0 | + 4.5 | 0 | — 8.0 | —21.0 | | | | |
| .375 H. & H. Mag. | 270 | SP | 100 | + 0.7 | 0 | — 4.5 | —10.0 | —17.5 | | | | |
| | | | 200 | + 1.5 | + 3.0 | 0 | — 4.0 | —10.5 | | | | |
| | | | 300 | + 3.0 | + 6.0 | + 6.5 | + 4.5 | 0 | | | | |
| | 300 | ST, MC | 100 | + 0.7 | 0 | — 5.5 | —12.0 | —21.0 | | | | |
| | | | 200 | + 1.8 | + 3.0 | 0. | — 4.5 | — 9.5 | | | | |
| .38/40 | 180 | SP | 100 | + 3.3 | 0 | —26.0 | —52.0 | —90.5 | | | | |
| .38/55 | 255 | SP | 100 | + 3.0 | 0 | —22.0 | —44.0 | —76.0 | | | | |
| .401 Win. S. L. | 200 | SP | 100 | + 1.2 | 0 | — 9.5 | —22.0 | —41.0 | | | | |
| .405 Win. | 300 | SP | 100 | + 1.0 | 0 | — 7.0 | —16.5 | —31.0 | | | | |
| .44/40 Win. | 200 | SP | 100 | + 3.3 | 0 | —31.0 | —55.0 | —91.0 | | | | |
| .45/70 | 405 | SP | 100 | + 2.8 | 0 | —21.0 | —43.0 | —76.0 | | | | |

Legend:
ST=Silvertip
SP=Soft Point
OPE=Open Point Expanding
MC=Metal Case

FP=Full Patch (Same as MC)
Lub.=Lubaloy
BT=Boat-tail
HCP=Hollow Copper Point

# DOGS

Someone once said that "the dog is the only hunting companion who pays his way," which is merely another way of pointing out that the upland game hunter without a dog cannot hope to get the full measure of enjoyment from his sport.

A good hunting dog, whether setter, pointer, spaniel, or hound, not only insures better sport in the material sense, by providing a heavier game bag with less effort on the part of the hunter, but increases the hunter's pleasure in his days afield. The hunting, not the shooting, occupies the greater portion of the hunter's day, and many hunters find more pleasure in watching the work of the dog than they do in making the kill.

Today, with game populations unable to keep pace with the hunting pressure, the hunter without a dog is at a distinct disadvantage. He must cover the ground that otherwise would be covered more adequately by the dog, and as he hunts without the aid of a "nose," he sees but a small fraction of the game within gunshot. When he does make an occasional kill he is faced with the problem of retrieving it, which in heavy cover often proves a difficult if not impossible task. An appalling percentage of wounded and dead game birds and animals never are recovered by the hunter, and in this era of relative scarcity, such a situation is deplorable. The man without a good dog cannot hope to recover more than a small percentage of the cripples he brings down, and the average shooter seldom obtains clean kills on more than 50 per cent of his shots.

These are the material arguments in favor of the hunting dog, but to the majority of hunters with dogs, the spiritual values are of greater importance. Many men who make hunting their primary interest would not think of taking to the field without a dog, except for big game—not because they would return with an empty game bag, but because hunting without the dog would rob the sport of too much pleasure. You will never find a better example of pride of ownership than that exhibited by the man with a good dog, and even the man with a poorly trained dog will endow the animal with qualities it does not possess—except in the owner's mind.

The man with a dog never hunts alone, and only those who couple the sport with the dog can realize the extent of the companionship offered by a dog. Divorce sentiment from dog ownership, if you can; consider the animal merely as a means to an end, and that ownership still will give a return far in excess of the initial cost and upkeep.

The breed of dog you select is not important, and you have a wide choice which covers every phase of hunting. You do not even have to limit your selection to the registered breeds, for atavism is a dominant trait in almost every member of the dog family, and the hunting instinct can be stimulated through training. In Connecticut there was a Pekinese that proved to be a satisfactory rabbit dog, and in Maryland a grotesquely clipped French poodle retrieved ducks with a style that was beyond reproach. The South is full of "droppers," offspring of a hunting breed and a "plain" dog, whose owners loudly announce their willingness to match them "with anything that comes along" as far as finding and retrieving quail is concerned.

The important thing is to use a dog—not only to increase your own pleasure in the field, but as a means of conserving game for the future. In the following pages you will find detailed information on all of the popular breeds employed in the field today, some one among which should certainly suit any purpose you might choose.

## BASSET HOUND

The most distinguished looking member of the hound family is, undoubtedly, the basset. In appearance, he is somewhat of a conglomerate, having the coloring of a fox hound, the head of a bloodhound, the running gear of an extraboned dachshund, and a long, heavy body. In action he belies his looks to some extent, being considerably more agile than his appearance would indicate.

**History.** The breed, an ancient one, flourished chiefly in Belgium and France, and also in some sections of Russia. The basset originated in France and was developed through crossing the old French bloodhound on the white hounds of the Abbots of St. Hubert. The hounds of St. Hubert were used for hunting in very heavy cover, and a dog which held its nose close to the ground, because of its short legs, was to be preferred to one which could not easily put its nose close to the ground. Through selective breeding the shorter leg was intensified and the crooked foreleg of the basset developed.

The first bassets came to England in 1866, when the Comte de Tournow sent Lord Galway a pair of hounds, which were named Basset and Belle. Some of their offspring were sold to Lord Onslow, who supplemented his pack from the kennels of Comte Canteleu le Contealx. Some of the descendants of these hounds were imported into America and were crossed upon earlier importations from Russia.

From this breeding has come the American basset, a bit sounder in limb than the lighter French type and more compact and not so bulky as the English type, which was considered too large.

**Characteristics.** In height the basset runs from 10 to 15 inches; 13 inches is about right. Weight runs

PLATE I. Basset: Ch. Hartshead Pepper.

from 25 to 50 pounds, although some dogs weigh as much as 60 pounds in show condition. This dog is exceedingly heavy in bone and weighs more than he appears to.

The basset has never been very popular in this country. Perhaps his rather grotesque appearance militates against him to some degree, but he makes a good gunning companion for one who likes a slow, painstaking hunter. He is used on rabbits and hares but is beginning to find favor as a pheasant dog. In some sections of the country he is used on grouse also and is taught to retrieve. He can be easily taught to tree and makes a good dog for coon, opossum, and squirrel hunting. Of excellent disposition, the basset readily takes to training, and if worked by a single person soon becomes a one-man dog.

One of his outstanding characteristics is the basset's voice. Deep and resonant, his bell-like note makes fine "music" and carries well. The "cry" is fairly heavy in quality and the tonguing of a pack of bassets will set the welkin a-ring.

Another outstanding characteristic is the keenness of his nose. The basset possesses what is generally conceded to be the best nose in the hound group with the exception of the bloodhound's.

For rabbit hunting, or even fox hunting where the fox is shot, many prefer the basset to all other hounds. They maintain that his slowness will keep the game on the move without frightening it too much, will cause it to make smaller circles, and hence will give the gunner a better chance for a shot.

In recent years, breeders of bassets have emphasized the dog's value as a pheasant hunter. It is best to hunt the basset by himself or with one or more of his own breed. His main value is lost when he is hunted with dogs of greater speed.

**Description and Standards.** HEAD: Head should be large, the skull narrow and of good length, the peak being very fully developed, a very characteristic point of the head, which should be free from any appearance of, or inclination to, cheek bumps. It is more perfect when it most closely resembles the head of a bloodhound, with heavy flews and forehead wrinkled to the eyes. The expression when sitting or when still should be very sad, full of reposeful dignity. The whole of the head should be covered with loose skin, so loose, in fact, that when the hound brings its nose to the ground the skin over the head and cheeks should fall forward and wrinkle perceptibly.

JAWS: The nose itself should be strong and free from snipiness, while the teeth of the upper and lower jaws should meet, a pig-jawed hound, or one that is underhung, being distinctly objectionable.

EARS: The ears are very long, and when drawn forward fold well over the nose. They are set on the head as low as possible and hang loose in folds like drapery, the ends curling inward, in texture thin and velvety.

EYES: The eyes should be deeply sunken, showing a prominent haw, and in color they should be a deep brown.

NECK AND SHOULDER: The neck should be powerful with heavy dewlaps set on sloping shoulders.

FORELEGS: The forelegs should be short, very powerful, very heavy in bone, close fitting to the chest with a crooked knee and wrinkled ankle, ending in a massive paw. A hound must *not* be "out at elbows," which is a bad fault.

FEET: He must stand perfectly sound and true on his feet, which should be thick and massive, and the weight of the forepart of the body should be borne equally by each toe of the fore feet as far as compatible with the crook of the legs. Unsoundness in legs and feet should absolutely disqualify a hound from taking a prize.

CHEST AND BODY: The chest should be deep and full. The body should be long and low and well ribbed up. Slackness of loin, flatsidedness, and a roach or razor back are all bad faults.

HOCKS: A hound should not be straight on his hocks nor should he measure more over his quarters than he does at his shoulders. Cowhocks, straight hocks, or weak hocks are all bad faults.

QUARTERS: The quarters should be full of muscle, which stand out so that when one looks at the dog from behind it gives him a round, barrel-like effect, with quarters "round as an apple." He should be what is known as "a good dog to follow," and when trotting away from you his hocks should bend well and he should move true all around.

STERN: The stern is coarse underneath and carried "gaily" in hound fashion.

COAT: The coat should be similar to that of a foxhound, not too fine and not too coarse, but yet of sufficient strength to be of use in bad weather. The skin should be loose and elastic.

COLOR: No good hound is a bad color, so that any recognized foxhound color should be acceptable to the judge's eye, and only in the very closest competition should the color of a hound have any weight with a judge's decision.

SCALE OF POINTS:

| | |
|---|---|
| Head, Skull, Eyes, Muzzle, Flews | 14 |
| Ears | 10 |
| Neck, Dewlap, Chest and Shoulders | 18 |
| Forelegs and Feet | 18 |
| Back, Loin, Hocks, and Hindquarters | 18 |
| Stern | 5 |
| Coat and Skin | 5 |
| Color and Markings | 5 |
| Basset hound character and symmetry | 7 |
| TOTAL | 100 |

In all-around appearance the basset hound is a docile, somewhat awkward dog of great dignity. In action he is every inch the workman.

# BEAGLE HOUND

**History.** Probably the most popular of the hound breeds is the beagle. There are several reasons for this likelihood. First, the beagle is essentially a gun dog. Second, he is a specialist on the cottontail rabbit, the most prolific of all species of American upland game animals and the most widely hunted. Third, his merry and affectionate disposition make him a favorite as a pet and companion for children, a loyal and ornamental house dog. And fourth, his great versatility allows his use on almost any type of upland game. He is particularly effective on squirrels and pheasants.

PLATE II. Beagle: Ch. Newman's Toney.

As with practically all hound breeds, the exact origin of the beagle is not definitely known. It is established, however, that the little fellow was in favor in the days of King Henry VIII and came into even greater vogue during the reign of that monarch's daughter, Elizabeth. It was the custom in those days for the hunting gentry to take their beagles to the fields in the panniers of the saddles. From this we may judge that the beagles of those days were very small—from 8 to 12 inches high.

It has been said that the beagle resulted from experiments in crossing the harrier with the old South of England or Southern hound. In some instances they were called "little harriers." The claim is that selective breeding, using only the smallest specimens, brought the beagle down to the diminutive size known in the days of good Queen Bess. This miniature hound, however, did not enjoy sustained popularity; they were too small for use.

Early beagles were classified as "shallow-flewed" or "deep-flewed" in proportion to the deepness of the upper lip. The shallow-flewed were said to be the fastest and the deep-flewed the surest and more musical. The wire-haired beagle was considered the stronger and better dog.

Though most of our information concerning the early beagles came from England, it is known that the name originated from the corrupted French word *beigle,* meaning small.

The present-day beagle gets his keen nose probably from the Kerry beagle, in color and general appearance a miniature bloodhound. Except for that, however, it is doubtful that the Kerry beagle exerted any influence over the beagle of today, and his contribution was more likely made to the foxhound and coonhound breeds.

General Richard Rowett, of Carlinville, Ohio, is generally credited with bringing the first beagles to America, in the early 1870's; among them were Rosey and Dolly. At about the same time, Mr. C. H. Turner brought over Sam and Warrior, and Mr. Norman Elmore of Granby, Conn., imported Ringwood, a dog of exceptional ability, and others.

From the matings of Warrior and Rosey a number of excellent dogs were produced. Among them was Dodge's Rattler, a dog which had a profound influence in developing what was known as the Rowett strain. This blood has carried on through many generations and the Rowetts are recognized as the fountainheads of the present-day beagles. These early importations found immediate favor among American sportsmen who wanted a small hound of excellent type, large enough to cope with the cover in this country and small enough to be "handy."

**Development.** Along in the eighties there was much discussion as to what constituted the ideal beagle. These controversies resulted in the formation of the American-English Beagle Club in 1884. General Rowett, Mr. Elmore, and Dr. L. H. Twadell, of Philadelphia, were appointed as a committee to draft the standard for the breed. That they were men of foresight and wrote well is demonstrated in a comparison of the standard adopted by the American-English Beagle Club and the present standard of the National Beagle Club of America, for few changes have been necessary.

General Rowett was not a commercial breeder and the dogs from his kennel were not distributed indiscriminately. However, he did let some of the more enthusiastic fanciers, who were seriously interested in breeding better beagles, have some of his stock. The progeny of these dogs added to the prestige of the Rowett strain and these bloodlines became justly famous.

Upon the noted Carlinville sportsman's death most of his stock was acquired by Mr. Pottinger Dorsey of New Market, Md., and Mr. C. Staley Doub of Frederick, Md. These gentlemen carried on in the Rowett manner, without thought of profit to themselves, and beagle fanciers of today owe much to their breeding operations. Their efforts produced Lee, Triumph, Wanderer, Welcome, Harker, Hooker, and many other of the outstanding performers of their day. Dogs from the Dorsey and Doub kennels were field performers, backed by generations of practical dogs, and while neither cared to commercialize his dogs they did dispose of some top-flight individuals to thoughtful breeders who carried on to the further fame of the Rowetts.

Another famous strain is the Blue Cap, developed largely by Mr. Hiram Card, a Canadian breeder. The foundation stock of this strain were the imported blueticks, Blue Cap and Blue Bell, brought over by Captain William Assheton of Virginia from the kennels of Sir Arthur Ashburnham of England. A mating of these two produced Card's Blue Cap, a dog which when crossed on the Rowetts and bitches of Champion Bannerman blood exerted a startling influence on the dogs of his time.

Champion Bannerman was imported by Dr. L. H. Twadell for Mr. Lewis Sloan, of Philadelphia, about 1884 and proved a great sire. One of his sons, Jack Bannerman, was used extensively by Mr. Card in the development of the Blue Cap strain. Mr. Card always preferred the blue-ticked or mottled color, with black markings and tan trimmed and bred for that color, producing some very handsome beagles which were excellent workers in the field.

Another imported dog of the early days which proved a prepotent sire was Chimer, imported by Mr. Diffendoeffer of Pennsylvania.

The outstanding dog of the early nineties was Frank Forest, a line-bred Rowett on his sire's side, and out of Skip, which stemmed from the blood of the kennels of Sir Arthur Ashburnham. Mated with Sue Forest, Frank Forest, owned by Mr. H. L. Kreuder of Nanuet, N. Y., produced Champion Clyde, Sunday, and Gypsy Forest and through them established a well-nigh unbeatable family. Clyde was the sire of many excellent hunters and his son, Champion Trick, also produced many rabbiters of exceptional ability.

Soon after the turn of the century beagles and beagling in America began gaining rapidly in popularity. Quite a number of organized or privately owned packs were established and in some sections the sport took on a more formal flavor. Among some of the well-known packs of yesteryear are the Hempstead Beagles, the Round Hill, the Thornfield, the Rockridge, the Dungannon, the Somerset, the Wolver, the Piedmont, the Sir Sister, the Belray, the Old Westbury, the Ragdale, the Fairfield, the Mt. Brilliant, and the Windholme.

The first beagle field trials in this country were those held at Hyannis, Mass., November 4, and Salem, N. H., November 7, 1890. The change of venue was necessitated by conditions. These trials were held under the auspices of the newly formed National Beagle Club. The noted Frank Forest was the winner of the all-age stake for dogs 15 inches and under. Second was Don and third was Sunday, a son of Frank Forest out of Sue Forest. Tone, owned by the Glenrose Kennels, won the stake for bitches 15 inches and under, while Gypsy Forest, another member of the Frank Forest-Sue Forest litter, was second. Belle Ross, owned by B. S. Turpin, was the winner of the stake for bitches 13 inches and under.

A larger entry was noted in the trials of 1891, and the sport of beagle field trials has enjoyed a steady growth ever since. Hundreds of these contests are held every season and there is hardly a section of the country where the bugle mouth of the merry little beagle is not heard in competition with members of his breed.

Training beagles for work in the field is now a recognized profession and many professional trainers take their charges over a regular circuit of field trials, beginning in early fall and running into late spring. Field trial clubs set their dates so they will not conflict and will allow time enough for the competitors to travel from one event to the other and also give their charges the needed rest or tune-up workouts in between events.

Professional trainers map out their campaigns months in advance, planning to enter their charges in trials that are easily accessible, that are of greatest importance, or where they consider they have the best chances of winning. As a general rule a set fee and half the winnings are charged for handling each beagle in a trial. A typical itinerary for one of the prominent professional beagle handlers includes the following trials: Belmont-Jefferson, Old Town, Northern West Virginia, Summit, Keystone, Pucketos, Northern Ohio, Central West Virginia, Muskingum Valley, Highland, Monon Valley, Huntington, Ohio Valley, Bluegrass, Miami Valley, Carolina, Coastal Plains, Black Jack, Peach State, Square Deal, Dixieland, Yazoo, and Pelican State. Such a route will keep him and his hound on the move.

At bench shows and field trials, beagles are divided into two classes, those of 15 inches in height or under, and those of 13 inches or under. Beagles over 15 inches in height are automatically disqualified for competition.

At beagle trials, the dogs are run in braces or pairs. The names of individual hounds are placed on single slips of paper and drawn from a receptacle, the first dog drawn running with the second dog drawn, and so on. After all braces have been run, the judges may call back any competing hounds they may desire to see again and brace them in any manner they desire, running them a second time, a third, or even more until they have found the best performers on that particular occasion. The cottontail rabbit is the game used although occasionally in some sections hares are employed.

Not all beagles have field trial qualifications. Some do not perform so well in strange country or with a gallery of enthusiastic beaglers following as they do when they are hunting in familiar territory with their masters. Others seem to have a highly developed competitive spirit and do their best work when urged on by the incentive of competition.

The ideal beagle is a dog of great determination. He should possess the desire to hunt in a marked degree, a keen nose which will allow him to work out a comparatively cold trail and rout out his quarry, and stick to the line until that quarry has gone to earth or has been caught. He should be able and willing to work in rough, heavy, briar-infested cover as well as in the easy going of the open, and in any kind of weather. A major requisite is a good mouth, not too freely used, but freely and happily given when the rabbit is up and going. Beagles are truly the music-makers of the meadows and the rippling cry of a well-balanced pack will thrill the most sophisticated.

**Characteristics.** The beagle is a hardy dog, easy to keep in condition. He does not need much kennel room and adapts himself quickly to all climates. Like all hounds, he thrives on work and the more he is hunted the better he likes it.

While not a particularly sensitive dog, the beagle likes attention and readily responds to kindness and affection. He is quick to learn and about all the training he needs is work. The more hunting his owner can give him the closer the bond between them will become, and the more finished performer he will be.

Bred and developed primarily for rabbit hunting, the beagle is a very useful dog on practically every species of upland game. He makes a master squirrel dog, is extremely valuable on the trap line, and as a pheasant dog doffs his hat only to the pointing breeds and spaniels. Though he is not fast enough to be used to best advantage on fox, there have been instances when the beagle proved himself proficient on this species, even running an occasional fox to the death.

Carrying himself with the cocky air of the sportsman he is, the beagle attracts attention wherever he goes. He has the quality of combining ruggedness with daintiness which is possessed by no other dog in such degree and as an ideal dog around farm or home he is hard to excel. His dignity is not akin to aloofness and he is willing to meet any friendly advances more than halfway.

**Description and Standards.** Beagles come in all hound colors, and any hound color is good. However, the most popular color is white, black, and tan.

The standard adopted by the National Beagle Club of America follows:

HEAD: The skull should be fairly long, slightly domed at occiput, with cranium broad and full.

EARS: Ears should be set on moderately low, long, reaching when drawn out nearly, if not quite, to the end of the nose; fine in texture, fairly broad—with almost entire absence of erectile power—setting close to the head, with the forward edge slightly inturning to the cheek—rounded at tip.

EYES: Eyes large, set well apart, soft and houndlike, expression gentle and pleading; of a brown or hazel color.

MUZZLE: Muzzle of medium length, straight and square cut, the stop moderately defined.

JAWS: Level. Lips free from flews; nostrils large and open.

DEFECTS: A very flat skull, narrow across the top; excess of dome, eyes small, sharp, and terrier-like, or prominent and protruding; muzzle long, snipy, or cut away decidedly below the eyes, or very short. Roman nosed, or upturned, giving a dish-face expression. Ears short, set on high or with a tendency to rise above the point of origin.

BODY: NECK AND THROAT: Neck rising free and light from the shoulders, strong in substance yet not loaded, of medium length. The throat clean and free from folds of skin; a slight wrinkle below the angle of the jaw, however, may be allowable.

DEFECT: A thick, short, cloddy neck carried on a line with the top of the shoulders. Throat showing dewlap and folds of skin to a degree termed "throatiness."

SHOULDERS AND CHEST: Shoulders sloping, clean, muscular, not heavy or loaded, conveying the idea of freedom of action with activity and strength. Chest deep and broad, but not broad enough to interfere with the free play of the shoulders.

DEFECTS: Straight, upright shoulders. Chest disproportionately wide or with lack of depth.

BACK, LOINS, AND RIBS: Back short, muscular, and strong. Loin broad and slightly arched, and the ribs well sprung, giving abundance of lung room.

DEFECTS: Very long or swayed or roached back. Flat, narrow loin. Flat ribs.

FORELEGS AND FEET: FORELEGS: Straight, with plenty of bone in proportion to the size of the hound. Pasterns short and straight.

FEET: Close, round, and firm; pad full and hard.

DEFECTS: Out at elbows. Knees knuckled over forward, or bent backward. Forelegs crooked or dachshundlike. Feet long, open, or spreading.

HIPS, THIGHS, HINDLEGS, AND FEET: HIPS AND THIGHS: Strong and well muscled, giving abundance of propelling power. Stifles strong and well let down. Hocks firm, symmetrical, and moderately bent. Feet close and firm.

DEFECTS: Cowhocks, or straight hocks. Lack of muscle and propelling power. Open feet.

TAIL: Set moderately high; carried gaily, but not turned forward over the back; with slight curve; short as compared with size of hound; with brush.

DEFECTS: A long tail. Teapot curve or inclined forward from the root. Rat-tail with absence of brush.

COAT: A close, hard hound coat of medium length.

DEFECTS: A short, thin coat, or of a soft quality.

HEIGHT: Height not to exceed 15 inches, measured across the shoulders at the highest point, the hound standing in a natural position with his feet well under him.

COLOR: Any true hound color.

GENERAL APPEARANCE: A miniature foxhound, solid and big for his inches, with the wear-and-tear look of the hound that can last in the chase and follow his quarry to the death.

SCALE OF POINTS:

| | | |
|---|---|---|
| *Head* | | |
| Skull | 5 | |
| Ears | 10 | |
| Eyes | 5 | |
| Muzzle | 5 | |
| | | 25 |
| *Body* | | |
| Neck | 5 | |
| Chest and Shoulders | 15 | |
| Back, Loin, and Ribs | 15 | |
| | | 35 |
| *Running Gear* | | |
| Forelegs | 10 | |
| Hips, Thighs, and Hindlegs | 10 | |
| Feet | 10 | |
| | | 30 |
| Coat | 5 | |
| Stern | 5 | |
| | | 10 |
| TOTAL | | 100 |

**Breeders.** Beagles are bred and run wherever Miss Molly Cottontail Rabbit makes her home. And that is in a great portion of this country. We can list only a few of the prominent American breeders of beagles here, but some of them are: I. W. Carrel, editor of *Hounds and Hunting Magazine,* Greenfield, Ohio; Manitou Beagles, Hanrock, Mich.; Beryl Bishop, Snow Hill, N. C.; Lee S. Wade, Cleveland, Ohio; Frank Patton, San Antonio, Texas; Chickamauga Beagles, Cleveland, Tenn.; Condoro Kennels, Kenmore, N. Y.; Pine Hollow Beagles, McKees Rocks, Pa.; Frank L. Dearman, Jr., Madison, Tenn.; Stilglass Beagles, Closter, N. J.; Octorara Beagles, Quarryville, Pa.; Francis D. Dougherty, Wilmington, Del.; E. W. Briggs, Jr., Auburn, Me.; Eberle's Beagles, Kewaskum, Wis.; Carlton E. Kay, Belton, S. C.

# BLACK AND TAN COONHOUND

**History.** The latest addition to the "official" circle of American sporting dogs is the Black and Tan Coonhound. By "official" is meant that the breed has at last received the stamp of approval of the American Kennel Club, governing body of dog shows in this country, and has been recognized by that organization as a separate and distinct breed.

Although a newcomer to official limelight, there is nothing really *new* about the old-fashioned, long-eared "cooner." The very word "old-fashioned," in his description, stamps him as an old-timer. For many years, night hunters in almost every section of the country where the raccoon is the object of the chase have used black-and-tans and preferred them to all other breeds. Generations of intensive use in coon and possum country have developed the black-and-tan into a specialist on these two species of furred game. His super-bored nose, keenness on trail, and great determination to force his quarry to take to a tree or log for safety have made him the choice of many coon hunters and his popularity is growing.

There are other breeds of hounds which are known as "coonhounds" and are used almost exclusively on small furred game. Notable among these are the Redbone and Blue-ticked. There are many packs of these dogs which have been bred from the same foundation stock for many generations and whose blood might well be considered pure.

It remained, however, for a group of far-sighted fanciers of the black-and-tan strain to practice careful selective breeding, to keep detailed breeding records and pedigrees, and to adopt programs pointed to the improvement of their favorite breed. Through such progressive activities and aggressive promotion work, the black-and-tan became the first breed to be officially recognized as worthy of the name coonhound.

Of course, there are many who contend that any hound which will run and tree a coon is entitled to the appellation "coonhound," and this argument has merit. But that brings up the question as to whether the ancestors of that particular hound were proved coonhounds and whether his progeny will instinctively take to the trail of a coon. Breeders of the old-fashioned black-and-tan will not dispute the point and are willing to admit that many types of hounds coming from foxhound breeding can be trained and developed into proficient cooners—and many are. But, through generations of careful breeding, using only dogs of undisputed ability as trailers and honest treers, the black-and-tan exponents have developed a dog which, as a breed, has a natural instinct for night hunting on coons and possums.

**Development.** Comparatively little has been written about the origin of the old-fashioned black-and-tan. The first ancestor is said to have been the now extinct Talbot hound, which came to England with William the Conqueror. It is generally conceded that the foundation stock came from the old Virginia foxhound known locally as the "black-and-tan," many of which were used in coon hunting. Most of the old Virginia foxhounds were black and tan in color, although among them were also reds, white-spotteds, and fawns. Some of these black-and-tans were selected for breeding purposes, not only for their proficiency as coon hunters, but the color factor also played a part. This was not a common practice among foxhound breeders, as color has counted but little with them. These hounds, however, were developed particularly for coon-hunting and trained in this sport for years.

The general appearance of the black and tan coonhound is proof positive that considerable bloodhound blood was introduced years ago, exactly how many seems unknown. Nevertheless, the blood of the bloodhound is most obvious, and though the characteristic wrinkles are not present, the flews are not so heavy, and the expression is more alert, the low-hung, somewhat ponderous ears and the general make-up of the dog are indicative of that cross. In fact, the black-and-tan is frequently mistaken for a bloodhound by those unfamiliar with both breeds. Closer inspection, however, or a side-by-side comparison, will quickly reveal the differences.

**Characteristics.** The bloodhound influence is also seen the manner in which the black-and-tan works his trail. The black-and-tan works entirely by scent and keeps his nose close to the trail. The "breast-high" scent frequently so important to a good fox race is apparently not so interesting to the black-and-tan, who sticks to foot-scent. The bloodhound has undoubtedly contributed the the coonhound's nose. At the same time he has caused him to work his trail at a somewhat slower pace than that of the foxhound, although he is fast enough for the type of game in which he specializes.

Although a specialist on raccoons, the black-and-tan does excellent work in hunting bear, deer, bobcat, mountain lion, and other big game, and many of

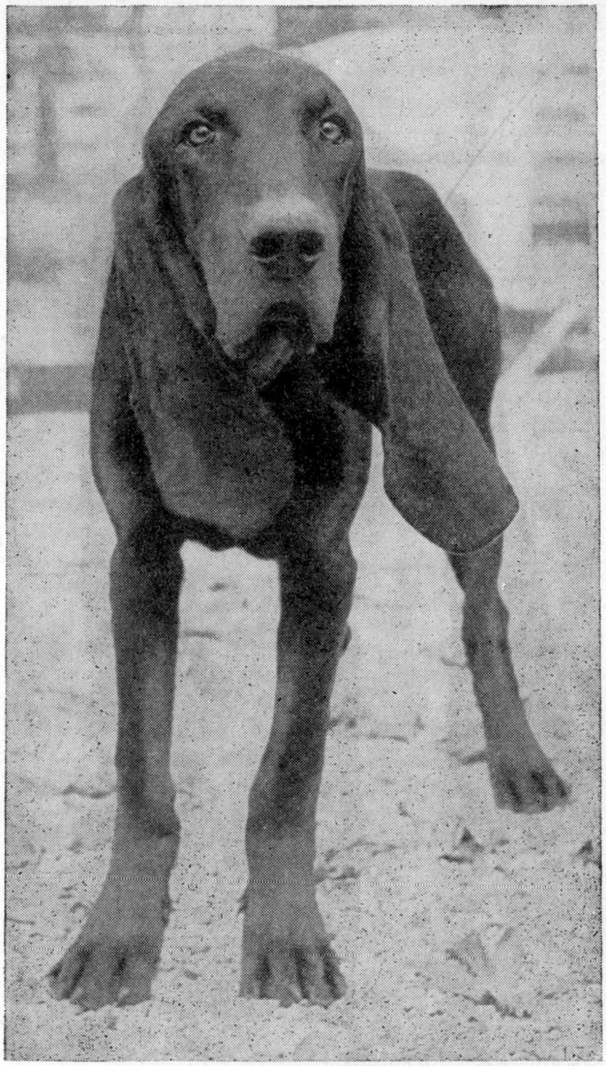

Courtesy D. H. Stringer, Mundelein, Ill.
PLATE III. Black and Tan Coonhound.

the "lion" hunters of the west find him of particular value in helping control these cats and other predators in the stock country.

The big hound is a hardy animal and is capable of standing the rigors of winter and the heat of summer and is able to negotiate the rough and difficult terrain over which he is called upon to work.

The black and tan coonhound is easily trained. He is a dog of great determination, his keen nose allows him to pick up and stick to the trail, his deep, musical voice is thrilling, and when he points his handsome nose skyward and lets go with his roaring "tree bark" it generally means the end for Mr. Coon.

**Description and Standards.** A "Standard of Excellence" has been set up for the black and tan coonhound. It is outlined below:

General Characteristics: The coonhound possesses in a most marked degree the points and characteristics of the dog which hunts by scent. The general impression should be that of power, agility, alertness, and ability to cover the ground with powerful, rhythmic strides. He stands over more ground than is usual with hounds of other breeds.

Temperament: In temperament the coonhound

is extremely affectionate, not quarrelsome with companions or other dogs. His nature is somewhat shy and he is equally sensitive to kindness or correction.

HEAD: The head should be cleanly modeled and narrow in proportion to its length, with medium stop occuring midway between the occiput bone and the nose. The head should measure from 9 to 10 inches in males and 8 to 9 inches in females. Viewed from the profile, the line of the skull is on a practically parallel plane to the foreface or muzzle. The skin is thin to the touch, loose, but devoid of folds or excess dewlap. The flews should be well developed with typical hound appearance. Nostrils should be well back and always black. Eyes should be dark hazel to dark brown, the darker preferred; almost round and not too deeply set.

The ears should be set low on a high domed head and hang in graceful folds, the lower parts curling inward and backwards. In length they should extend well beyond the tip of the nose. Teeth should fit evenly with a slight scissors bite.

BODY: NECK, SHOULDER, AND CHEST: The neck is medium long, the shoulders muscular and well sloped backward, the ribs well sprung, avoiding flatsidedness. The chest should be well let down between the forelegs to form a deep keel.

BACK AND STERN: The back should be nearly level, powerful and strong. The stern is long and tapering and set on rather high. The tail should be strong with the base slightly below the level of the back line and carried free.

LEGS AND FEET: The forelegs are large in bone with elbows squarely set, the feet strong and well knuckled up, the pasterns strong and erect. Unsoundness in legs or feet should disqualify a hound from winning a prize.

HINDQUARTERS: Well boned and muscled, from hip to hock long and sinewy, hock to pad short and strong—the hocks well bent and let down and squarely set. The stride should be easy and graceful, with plenty of reach in front and drive behind.

COAT AND COLOR: The coat should be short but dense to withstand rough going. As the name implies, the color should be jet black with rich tan markings above the eyes, on the sides of the muzzle, chest, legs, and breeching, and with black pencil markings on the toes.

SIZE: Measured at the withers, males 24 to 26 inches, females 22 to 24 inches. Height should be in proportion to general conformation so that the dog appears neither leggy nor close to the ground. Dogs oversized should be penalized unless general soundness and proportion are in favor.

The following defects should be penalized: Splay feet, snip nose, flatsidedness, light eyes, short neck, oversize, lack of angulation in hind quarters, angulation of back. White spots on chest or other parts of body are highly undesirable and should disqualify.

Torn ears, broken or worn teeth, scars, or other evidence of work afield should not disqualify. As a field dog the coonhound is not mature until three years of age.

**Breeders.** Among the prominent breeders of the black and tan coonhound are Don H. Stringer, Ten Oaks Kennel, Mundelein, Ill., and Hermosa Vista Farm, Bannock, Ohio.

# BRITTANY SPANIEL

Unique among all the spaniels is the Brittany, for a number of reasons: (1) He is the only spaniel with a highly developed pointing instinct; (2) He looks and acts much like a setter; (3) Many are born without tails. The standard calls for a tail no longer than 4 inches or no tail at all.

**History.** Although he has been here for only ten years or so, the Brittany has already made remarkable progress toward a prominent place in the American sporting scene, and interest in the breed shows a healthy growth. He is also beginning to make himself known in field trial circles; 19 Brittanies won places in American field trials in 1946, several placing more than once. There are several breed trials for these dogs but a number of Brittany fanciers do not hesitate to enter them against pointers and setters, particularly in shooting-dog stakes where excessive range is not desirable.

The Brittany spaniel boasts an ancient lineage. These dogs have been popular on the continent of Europe for centuries, although the first important importations to this country were made in 1934-1936 by the late Louis Thebaud and his friends. The American Brittany Club, now affiliated with the American Kennel Club, is working along sound lines for the improvement of the breed, being definitely in favor of keeping the Brittany a "dual" dog and opposed to the establishment of separate "bench" and "field" types.

Some believe that the Brittany is distantly related to the red and white setter, the original ancestor of the Irish setter of today. It is possible that early Irish warriors invading that portion of France brought along their setters and these dogs played a part in the development of the Brittany.

Pontou, a little town in the valley of Douron, is the birthplace of the first tailless ancestor of the Brittany. This dog was the surviving member of two tailless specimens in a litter which resulted from the crossing of a white and lemon dog, brought to Brittany by an English sportsman for woodcock shooting, on a white and mahogany bitch owned by a native hunter. The puppy developed into an exceptionally fine hunting dog and was much in demand as a stud. All litters sired by him contained puppies without tails or with mere stubs as appendages.

A French sportsman named Arthur Enaud is largely responsible for the early development of the breed. M. Enaud greatly favored white and orange dogs and bred for that color. In order to intensify the color fixation possibilities and increase the scenting ability, he used two breeds as outcrosses, the Italian *Bracco,* or pointer, and the *Braque de Bourbonnais,* also a pointer. In the latter breed, he found a cross to his liking for another reason. This breed had a very short tail as a characteristic. After improving the blood lines to some extent, selective breeding practices were adhered to and the use of outcrosses was discontinued. The characteristics and quality of the breed have long been firmly established.

**Characteristics.** For the "one-dog" man, the Brittany makes a fine companion. He has the temp-

Courtesy E. W. Averill, Birmingham, Mich.

PLATE IV. Brittany Spaniel: Ch. Patrice of Sharvogue.

erament and somewhat the size of the spaniel, possesses a natural instinct to retrieve and, in addition, points his game in the manner of the setter and pointer. This is not to say that all Brittanies are natural pointing dogs, for this instinct must be developed just as in the setter and pointer. But it is there and can be easily brought out and put to work.

The Brittany, although not exactly timid, is a rather sensitive dog and will be spoiled by rough handling. He can take correction but it had best be administered in mild doses; in fact, that is all that is generally necessary. This does not mean that "the spaniel that looks like a setter," as he is frequently called, is super-thin-skinned and must be handled with kid gloves, but kind treatment and mild, yet positive, correction will get results where harsh treatment may ruin the prospect.

The Brittany is the widest ranger of all the spaniels. Although not, as a rule, so wide as the setter or pointer, his range frequently compares favorably with these breeds in open country. He adapts his range to the cover, hunting close in the brush yet with greater range than the average springer spaniel. He is at his best in heavy cover and likes to keep in contact with his master.

Interest in the Brittany spaniel will probably continue to grow in this country. For the sportsman who hunts on foot (and most of us do), and is not sensitive to the absence of a merry tail (but, frankly, most of us are), the Brittany makes an ideal gunning companion. He has a definite place in the American kennel of gun-dogs.

**Description and Standards.** The description and standard of points follow:

HEIGHT: 17 inches minimum, 19¾ maximum, with toleration of ¾ inch more for males. Back short; head rounded; muzzle rather pointed; with lips close fitting; ears rather short than long and placed high, relatively but little fringed; hair close to body; fringes wavy, never curly, a compact cob type; tail always naturally short, about 4 inches (unless tailless or exceedingly short).

NOSE: Nostrils well open; color brown or rose according to whether the dog is white and liver or white and orange.

MUZZLE: Medium length narrowing toward nose; straight or very slightly curved.

LIPS: Fine, close fitting, the upper lip overlapping the under lip by very little.

CROWN OF HEAD: Medium length, rounded; each side of the depression well marked and rounded; well-defined stop though sloping gently and not too abrupt.

EYES: Deep amber, bright and expressive.

EARS: Placed high, short rather than long slightly rounded, but little fringe, though the ear should be well covered with wavy hair.

NECK: Medium length, well placed on shoulders; without dewlap.

SHOULDERS: Slightly oblique and muscular.

ARM: Muscular and bony.

CHEST: Deep, reaching quite to level of elbow; sides rounded enough and quite large.

BACK: Short, withers well marked; never hollow or saddle-backed.

LOIN: Short and strong.

FLANKS: Well tucked up but not to excess.

HIND QUARTERS: Broad, strong, and muscular.

TAIL: Straight and carried low; always short naturally; about 4 inches long, often screw tail ending in a mesh of hair, or "anoure."

FRONT LEGS: Very straight; forearm slightly oblique; fine and muscular; fringes not heavy but wavy.

HIND LEGS: Thighs large, well muscled, well fringed and wavy half down thigh, cannon well set with hock and not too angular.

FEET: Toes close with little hair between them.

SKIN: Fine and fairly loose.

COAT: Hair flat on body, fine but not to excess, and quite smooth or slightly wavy.

COLOR: Liver and white preferably with roan ticking, or orange and white preferably with roan ticking.

AS A WHOLE: A small dog, closely knit and strong though elegant, very vigorous; energetic of movement; intelligent expression; presenting the aspect of a thoroughbred cob.

No numerical standard of points has yet been formulated.

# CHESAPEAKE BAY RETRIEVER

It is said of the Chesapeake Bay dog that he is the superior of any breed on earth in his ability to stand punishment in heavy seas and zero weather. This claim was made as far back as 1827, and it is still being made wherever duck-hunting conditions demand the ultimate courage and endurance in a dog.

The Chesapeake weighs from 65 to 75 pounds, with an occasional male weighing up to 80. Shoulder height is 23 to 26 inches. The most distinctive features of the Chesapeake are his very dense, oily coat, a yellow eye, strong, rather long tail, and his color, which ranges from brown to faded dead grass, and even to straw.

He has a broad skull, powerful muzzle, and high set ears. A thick and muscular neck has the appearance of being too short for his body, and his feet appear abnormally large for his size. A small spot of white is sometimes found on the chest.

The Chesapeake is not, therefore, a beautiful dog. Chesapeake breeders fiercely resent any effort to beautify him, or to make of him a bench show competitor. Thus, the breed has not gone through the style stages which have so changed most other breeds. The Chesapeake remains a peerless ducking dog, but a homely one.

**History.** There are many stories about the Chesapeake's origin. All agree, however, that he is at least partly descended from the Newfoundland dog of 150 years ago. Despite their great differences, it is assumed that the Labrador descends from the same Newfoundland stock as the Chesapeake.

Two stories agree that an English brig was wrecked off the coast of Maryland in 1807. Aboard, and rescued, were two Newfoundland puppies. From that point the stories vary.

According to George W. Kierstead, an authority who wrote about 1885, the two puppies were Sailor, a dingy red dog who was given to John Mercer of West River, and Canton, a black bitch, who became the property of Dr. James Stuart of Sparrows Point. However, Joseph A. Graham, in *The Sporting Dog* (1904), quotes a letter from General Ferdinand Latrobe, former mayor of Baltimore, who gives a different version. General Latrobe was a member of the Carroll Island Club for 30 years, and had personal supervision of the Chesapeakes. According to him, the dogs were given to George Law, who had showed hospitality to the wrecked crew. He added that they were crossed with yellow and tan coon hounds, getting from them their great nose and stamina, dead-grass color, yellow eye, and long tail.

Both accounts credit the two Newfoundland dogs with extraordinary powers as retrievers. And both credit the Newfoundlands with supplying the new breed with its aptitude for water going. General Latrobe said breeding records had been kept by the Carroll Island Club for many years.

A third story is that a Chesapeake bitch was tied in a swamp, and there was mated to an otter. This is obviously absurd. However, there are a number of references to the dogs as Chesapeake otter hounds.

A fourth story is now given little credit, though it may be the most accurate of all. This is to the effect that the Newfoundland dogs were crossed with English water poodles. The story is given by O. D. Foulks, writing in the *American Sportsman* shortly after the Civil War. Foulks called the dogs "Brown Winchester," or "Red Chester." His account of their performance is one of the best in literature on fowling dogs:

> "He does not shiver like a setter, or raise and drop his fore-feet like a wet spaniel; the shaking he has given his coarse, oily coat, has freed it entirely from ice and water; he cannot be enticed into a kennel, but must sit out on the frozen shore, rain or shine, and watch as well as the gunner.
>
> "If one of the fallen birds chance to be only crippled, he swims past dead ones, keeping the wounded in sight; when it dives he swims to the spot, and there continues turning round and round, now and then throwing himself high in the water, especially if the waves are heavy. . . . If the duck falls too far out for the dog to see, he takes his direction from the motion of the hand."

There is one more very early reference to the breed, but here it was called the Newfoundland breed of duck dog. It appears in the *American Shooting Manual,* written in 1827, by a "Gentleman of Philadelphia": "The Newfoundland breed makes the best water dogs, and will plunge into the most rapid stream, or break through the ice in the coldest weather, to bring out the ducks."

**Development.** There were a number of early clubs which sponsored the Chesapeake Bay dog, but the first really successful club of national scope was the American Chesapeake Club, which was founded in 1918. The first president was Earl Henry of Albert Lea, Minn. He was president until 1923, when Matt Barron of Mason City, Iowa, became president.

This shows rather clearly that the Chesapeake had

PLATE V. Chesapeake Bay Retriever at Work.

become a nationally known duck dog. Probably a majority of sporting specialty clubs were organized on the Atlantic seaboard. Members and officers were chiefly from this area. But the Chesapeake had become the supreme duck dog for the Minnesota and Manitoba swamps and lakes, and the Mississippi flyway.

After a time, the club languished. It had not been able to give trials for the breed. The dogs never have been popular as show dogs, and the breed's sponsors have feared shows might beautify the dog at the expense of his working ability. Perhaps the modern history of the club should begin in 1935 when Anthony Bliss became president. He edited the club booklet. His great Dual Champion Sodak's Gypsy Prince was one of the great competitors of all time, both bench and field, and has become the greatest of all Chesapeake sires. Sodak's Gypsy Prince competed from 1932 to 1938. The 1947 officers were W. D. Hoard, president, of Fort Acheson, Wis., and Oleva Groulx, secretary to Ferdinand Bunte of the Cocoa King Kennels, secretary. The club is actively promoting the breed by giving trials and similar activities.

**Characteristics.** The quoted references to the Chesapeake show that early writers considered him a peerless dog in zero weather and heavy seas. This is still true today. The Chesapeake is a compound of four qualities which make him ideal for work under these conditions.

The first is water-going aptitude. Almost all Chesapeakes exhibit an astonishing love for water. They do not walk or run into water, but leap far out into it. Many of them will completely submerge, either in play or when looking for a duck. Coldness of water and weather do not diminish the dog's desire to enter the water.

The second is the dog's coat. The typical Chesapeake has a dense under coat, covered by a rather heavy, wavy coat of guard hairs. The coat is quite oily, so that if one scratches his fingers through it, there will be a coating of oil on them. This coat prevents the Chesapeake from getting wet through, as other dogs always do eventually. As Foulks pointed out, a couple of shakes free the coat entirely of ice and water.

The third of the Chesapeake's distinguishing qualities is his endurance. This is a compound of his protecting coat, great strength, and unusual aggressiveness for a sporting dog. There are well-authenticated stories of Chesapeakes retrieving as many as 200 ducks in a single day under punishing weather conditions, and of swims a mile or more in length for a single duck.

The fourth quality is his memory. On the average, Chesapeakes appear to have extraordinary memories. Once experienced in duck hunting, they learn to mark down six or more ducks at a time. They never forget the location of these ducks. Even though the current may carry the duck around a river bend, the dog remembers and will follow out of sight around the bend, to appear a long time later with the duck.

It must be admitted that the Chesapeake has not prospered in field trial work according to his obvious abilities. Chesapeake enthusiasts say this is because the trials are too simple to bring out the Chesapeake's true abilities. There are necessarily limits to what can be done in a trial, and Chesapeake trainers say the limits are set for lesser dogs than theirs.

A second reason is that there are fewer Chesapeakes competing. The dog has not "caught on" with the field trialers, partly because of his homeliness, and partly because of a factor which even the earliest writers spoke guardedly of as "rugged individualism."

The plain facts are that the Chesapeake is inclined to like to fight. That limitless courage, aggressiveness, and endurance in heavy seas is translated in the kennel into kennel fights. Those top sportsmen who have understood the breed have been able to handle this problem. Lesser ones have given the breed up for dogs which they could handle without much trouble.

Nevertheless, the last 15 to 20 years have produced at least a good half-dozen field dogs which have ranked with the best trial dogs in America, and which have, at one time or another, given unforgettable performances.

Running during the same years as Dual Champion Sodak's Gypsy Prince, was Field Trial Champion Skipper Bob. This dog made the greatest competitive record of any Chesapeake. He was the greatest marker of his time, an unbeatable dog in the water, if less good on land, and he certainly ranks with the best of all time in any retriever breed, Skipper Bob was owned, trained, and handled by Harry T. Conklin.

Among other great winners of this period were Field Trial Champion Shagwong Gypsy, a consistent dog who seldom made a mistake; and Field Trial Champions Chesacroft Baron, Chesabob, and Gunnar II.

Two present-day competitors are Field Trial Champions Bayle and Tiger of Clipper City. Both rank with the best retrievers of any breed, and both have a chance to place among the all-time Chesapeake greats before their trial days are over.

**Description and Standards.** These standards were adopted by the American Chesapeake Club, July 1, 1933, and approved by the American Kennel Club, Sept. 12, 1933.

General Disqualifications:

(1) Black or liver colored.

(2) White on any part of body, except breast, belly, or spots on feet.

(3) Feathering on tail or legs over 1¾ inches long.

(4) Dewclaws, undershot, overshot, or any deformity.

(5) Coat curly or tendency to curl all over body.

(6) Specimens unworthy or lacking in breed characteristics.

Head: Skull broad and round with medium stop, nose medium short—muzzle pointed but not sharp. Lips thin, not pendulous. Ears small, set well up on head, hanging loosely and of medium leather. Eyes medium large, very clear of yellowish color and wide apart.

Neck: Of medium length with a strong muscular appearance, tapering to shoulders.

Shoulders, Chest, and Body: Shoulders, sloping and should have full liberty of action with plenty of power without any restrictions of movement. Chest strong, deep, and wide. Barrel round and deep. Body of medium length, neither cobby nor roached, but rather approaching hollowness, flanks well tucked up.

Back Quarters and Stifles: Back quarters should be as high as or a trifle higher than the shoulders. They should show fully as much power as the forequarters. There should be no tendency to weakness in either fore or hind quarters. Hind quarters should be especially powerful to supply the driving power for swimming. Back should be short, well-coupled, and powerful. Good hind quarters are essential.

Legs, Elbows, Hocks, and Feet: Legs should be medium length and straight, showing good bone and muscle, with well-webbed hare feet of good size. The toes well rounded and close pasterns slightly bent and both pasterns and hocks medium length—the straighter the legs the better.

Stern: Tail should be medium length—varying from: Males 12 to 15 inches, and females, 11 to 14 inches medium heavy at base, moderate feathering on stern and tail permissible.

Coat and Texture: Coat should be thick and short, nowhere over 1½ inches long, with a dense fine woolly undercoat. Hair on face and legs should be very short and straight with tendency to wave on the shoulders, neck, back, and loins only. Curly coat or coat with a tendency to curl not permissible.

Color: Any color varying from a dark brown to a faded tan or dead grass. Dead grass takes in any shade of dead grass, varying from a tan to a dull straw color. White spot on breast and toes permissible, but the smaller the spot the better, solid color being preferred.

Weight: Males, 65 to 75 lbs.; females 55 to 65 lbs.

Height: Males, 23 inches to 26 inches; females, 21 inches to 24 inches.

Symmetry and Quality: The Chesapeake dog should show a bright and happy disposition and an intelligent expression, with general outlines impressive and denoting a good worker. The dog should be well proportioned, a dog with a good coat and well balanced in other points being preferable to the dog excelling in some but weak in others.

The texture of the dog's coat is very important as the dog is used for hunting under all sorts of adverse weather conditions, often working in ice and snow. The oil in the harsh outer coat and woolly undercoat is of extreme value in preventing the cold water from reaching the dog's skin and aids in quick drying. A Chesapeake's coat should resist the water in the same way that a duck's feathers do. When he leaves the water and shakes himself, his coat should not hold the water at all, being merely moist.

Color and coat are extremely important as the dog is used for duck hunting. The color must be as nearly that of his surroundings as possible, and together with the fact that dogs are exposed to all kinds of adverse weather conditions, often working in ice and snow, the color of coat and its texture must be given every consideration when judging on the bench or in the ring.

Courage, willingness to work, alertness, nose, intelligence, love of water, general quality, and, most of all, disposition should be given primary consideration in the selection and breeding of the Chesapeake Bay dog.

Positive Scale of Points:

| | |
|---|---|
| Head, including lips, ears and eyes | 16 |
| Neck | 4 |
| Shoulders and body | 12 |
| Back quarters and stifles | 12 |
| Elbows, legs, and feet | 12 |
| Color | 4 |
| Stern and tail | 10 |
| Coat and texture | 18 |
| General conformation | 12 |
| Total | 100 |

*Note:* The question of coat and general type of balance takes precedence over any scoring table which could be drawn up.

Approximate Measurements:

| | Inches |
|---|---|
| Length head, nose to occiput | 9½ to 10 |
| Girth at ears | 20 to 21 |
| Muzzle below eyes | 10 to 10½ |
| Length of ears | 4½ to 5 |
| Width between eyes | 2½ to 2¾ |
| Girth neck close to shoulder | 20 to 22 |
| Girth of chest to elbows | 35 to 36 |
| Girth at flank | 24 to 25 |
| Length from occiput to tail base | 34 to 35 |
| Girth forearms at shoulders | 10 to 10½ |
| Girth upper thigh | 19 to 20 |
| From root to root of ear, over skull | 5 to 6 |
| Occiput to top shoulder blades | 9 to 9½ |
| From elbow to elbow over the shoulders | 25 to 26 |

# CLUMBER SPANIEL

The Clumber spaniel was once described as the "retired gentleman's shooting dog." This was because retired British military men and civil servants found the Clumber ideal for shooting in the turnip patches and other truck garden areas close to the city. The fields were small, the pace leisurely, and the dogs were easily handled.

**History.** The story of the origin of the Clumber is based entirely on an article which appeared in *Sporting Magazine* in 1807. A British writer misquoted from this article, and most authors have continued the error ever since. The original article showed part of a dog painting. Part of this article is given here:

". . . The annexed engraving is the portrait of William Mansell, game keeper to His Grace, Henry Clinton, Duke of Newcastle, and painted by F. Wheatly, Esq., R. A., now in the Duke's possession at Clumber House, Nottinghamshire.

"The group of springers, or cock-flushers, by which the game keeper is so tastefully surrounded in the picture, was a gift to Duke Henry when in France, from the Duke of Noailles; and William Mansell, during a uniform attention to the duties of his office (near 30 years) has, above other things, studied to increase, unmixed, this peculiar race of flushers."

Since this Duke of Noailles died about 1766, it is supposed that the dogs may have been given to the Duke of Newcastle about 1760. However, no other kennel of dogs of similar type was ever found in France, though many British sporting authorities tried to trace dogs of that type there.

The dogs pictured were obviously Clumbers, about as we know them today. Early writers ascribed the long, low body to basset crosses, and the heavy head to St. Bernard or "Alpine" spaniel crosses. Probably neither is correct, since most spaniels tend to short legs and heavy heads.

A good description of the Clumber of 100 years ago was given by Colonel Hamilton in his *Recollections,* published in 1860.

"This spaniel is red and white, is larger than the usual spaniel, strong made, an intelligent countenance, dark eyes, and the ears not very long.

"These dogs have excellent noses and display great spirit in beating strong covert, and after having been shot over two or three seasons, become very valuable for pheasant and cock shooting. They are naturally ill tempered, and rarely form any attachment but to their master or game keeper."

A dog of that period, Mr. Holford's Jock, is described by Stonehenge (1859) as being 2 feet 10 inches long from the tip of the nose to the root of the tail. He had an 11-inch tail, and he was 17 inches tall.

James Watson, the American dog authority, was something of a Clumber enthusiast, having taken part in drawing the American standard for the breed. But his opinion of the dogs in the field was not too high. In 1906, he wrote:

"One dog was of little use, so slow are they in their movements, and it called for a team of several braces, as many as could be obtained, in fact, to be of use for a shooting party. This entailed special training, and looking after by a man who could handle them, for they would not work for every person, or any person."

Despite Watson's uncomplimentary opinion, Clumbers almost monopolized the early spaniel trials, and at the very time Watson was writing. The first spaniel trials were held in 1899, and all spaniel breeds competed together in them. Mr. J. Sharpe's Stylish Pride, a cocker, won both the puppy and open stakes. But Clumbers took all other placings. In the open stake, Mr. Watt's Hoar Cross Shortly was second, and Mr. Cockburn's Carry One was third. Second in the puppy stake went to F. Winton Smith's Beachgrove Toy, and Mr. Warwick's Compton Roger was third.

At the second trial, held the same year, Mr. Smith's Clumber, Beachgrove Bee, won both puppy and open stakes. This dog dominated the trials for years, and became the first field trial champion spaniel of record. Here is a description given of him at this trial: ". . . A dog with a narrow face, but good body, and well ahead of anything in competition. Way he worked coverts and hedgegrows was a treat, and he retrieved capitally; sensible but did not show great excellence of nose."

In those days it was said: "In almost any litter of spaniel puppies, there will be three kinds, cockers, springers or field spaniels, and Sussex." Clumbers were not included because it was felt they were of a radical type, with little relationship to the others. Yet the pedigrees of all these breeds were mixed up. Thus, Beachgrove Teal, a Clumber, was the dam of

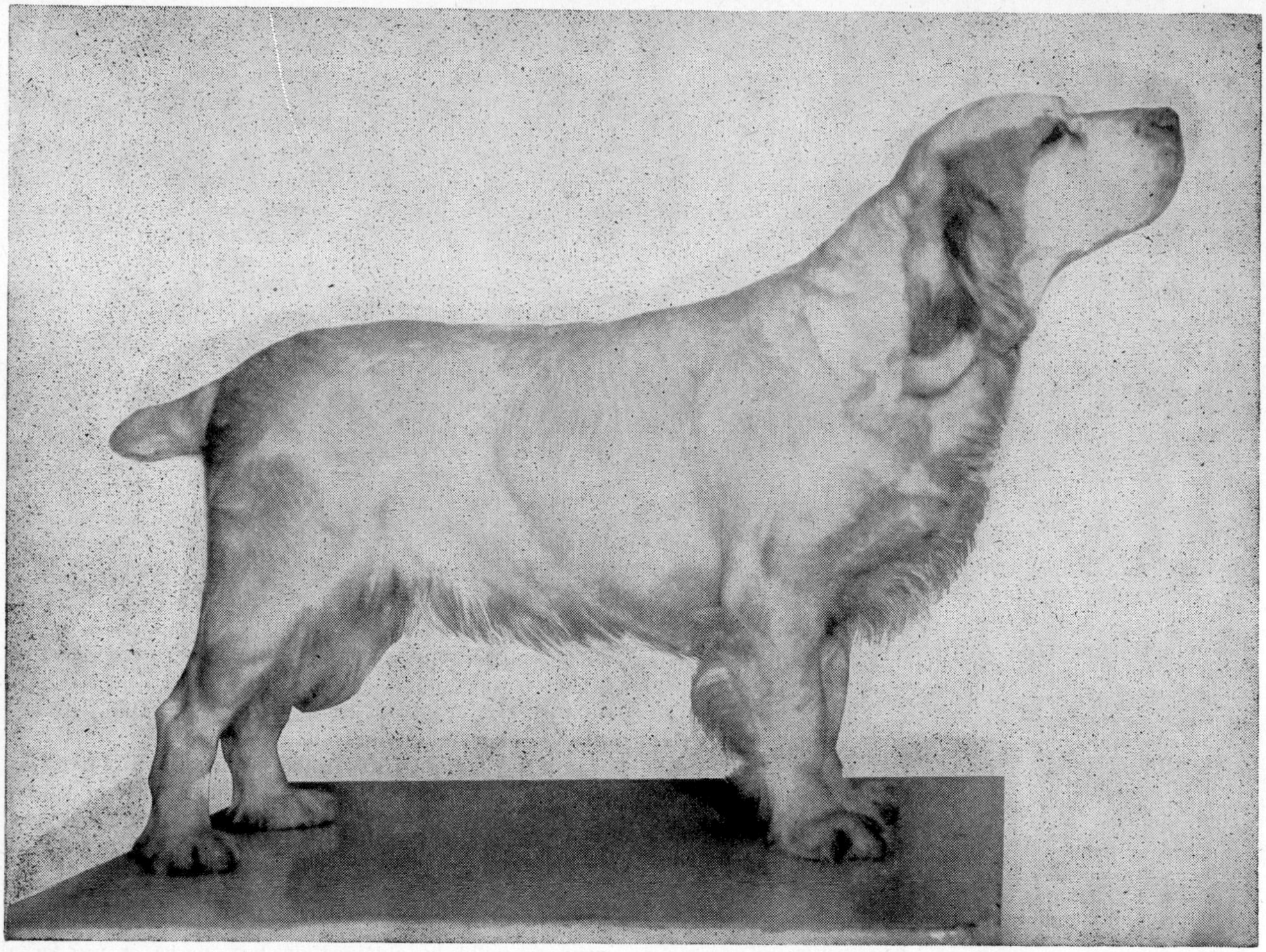

Courtesy of Evelyn M. Shafer.

PLATE VI. Clumber Spaniel.

Longbranch Teal, one of the first springers ever to be shown in Canada.

Primarily, it was the field trials which changed this. With Clumbers taking the honors, breeds began to be separated, and trials were held for the separate breeds. The Clumbers then gradually lost out because the cockers and springers became faster, and gained in favor as all-around dogs.

Among the great English Clumbers were Beachgrove Minette, Beachgrove Maud, Rivington Honey, Ch. Hempstead Toby, and Ch. Tramp of St. Mary's. All these dogs won in the field and on the bench.

In America, the Clumbers never have had a specialty or "parent" club to back them. Thus there have been no trials for the breed, and no way in which the dogs could bring their abilities before the sportsmen. Moreover, our hunting conditions have not been such as would show the dogs to advantage.

This does not necessarily doom the Clumber forever in America. For our population is building up rapidly, and game is growing more scarce. Game-farm shooting may become more common, and conditions may come around to the point where the Clumber will fit into the American shooting scene.

When that time comes, these claims will be made for the breed. The Clumber is perhaps the most easily trained of any of the spaniel family. He is not headstrong. Once he has learned his lessons, he remembers them and does not have to be re-trained twice a year. Perhaps because of his white coat and his "sedate" pace, he is said to be the finest of all hot-weather hunting dogs.

**Characteristics.** The Clumber is to the spaniel family what the basset is to the hounds—a slow-moving, short-legged, large-bodied dog. He does not, however, give tongue when on a hot scent as the basset does, and as does also the Sussex spaniel.

The modern Clumber spaniel is 17 to 18 inches tall at the shoulder, and males will weigh 55 to 65 pounds. This may be compared to the springer which, at 18.5 inches at the shoulder, will average 45 pounds in weight.

The Clumber is orange and white, or lemon and white, with almost no orange or lemon on the body. The head somewhat resembles that of a St. Bernard, both in type and in markings. Considering the size of the dog, the head is very heavy, the lips are pendulous, and the eyes often show haw (the lid droops to show the red membrane).

**Description and Standards.** GENERAL APPEARANCE AND SIZE: A long, low, heavy-looking dog, of a very thoughtful expression, betokening great intelligence. Should have the appearance of great power. Sedate in all movements, but not clumsy. Weight of dogs averages between 55 and 65 pounds; bitches from 35 to 50 pounds.

HEAD: Head large and massive in all its dimensions; round above eyes, flat on top, with a furrow running from between the eyes upon the center. A marked stop and large occipital protuberance. Jaw long, broad, and deep. Lips of upper jaw overhung. Muzzle not square, but at the same time powerful looking. Nostrils large, open, and flesh-colored, sometimes cherry-colored.

EYES: Eyes large, soft, deep set and showing haw. Hazel in color, not too pale, with dignified and intelligent expression.

EARS: Ears long and broad at the top, turned over on the front edge; vine-shaped; close to the head; set on low and feathered only on the front edge, and there but slightly. Hair short and silky, without the slightest approach to wave or curl.

NECK AND SHOULDERS: Neck long, thick, and powerful, free from dewlap, with a large ruff. Shoulders immensely strong and muscular, giving a heavy appearance in front.

BODY AND QUARTERS: Body very long and low, well ribbed up and long in the coupling. Chest of great depth and volume. Loin powerful and not too much arched. Back long, broad, and straight, free from droop or bow. Length an important characteristic; the nearer the dog is in length to being 2½ times his height at shoulder the better. Quarters shapely and very muscular, neither drooping nor stilty.

LEGS AND FEET: Forelegs short, straight, and immensely heavy in bone. Well in at elbows. Hindlegs heavy in bone, but not so heavy as forelegs. No feather above hocks, but thick hair on back of legs just above foot. Feet large, compact, and plentifully filled with hair between toes.

COAT AND FEATHERS: Coat silky and straight, not too long, extremely dense; feather long and abundant.

COLOR AND MARKINGS: Color, lemon and white, and orange and white. Fewer markings on body the better. Perfection of markings, solid lemon or orange ears, evenly marked head and eyes, muzzle and legs ticked.

STERN: Stern set on a level and carried low.

SCALE OF POINTS:

| | *Points* |
|---|---|
| General appearance and size | 10 |
| Head | 15 |
| Eyes | 5 |
| Ears | 10 |
| Neck and shoulders | 15 |
| Body and quarters | 20 |
| Legs and feet | 10 |
| Coat and feather | 10 |
| Color and marking | 5 |
| TOTAL | 100 |

# COCKER SPANIEL

**History.** The cocker spaniel probably is the world's most popular dog. It leads other breeds in almost every country where dogs are registered. In the United States, the lead is overwhelming, being as much as five times greater than some of the nearest rivals, such as the beagle and the Boston terrier. During 1946, almost 75,000 American-type cockers alone were registered.

Yet the cocker's popularity does not carry over into the field, where only the bitterest kind of struggle has kept intact any of the cocker's former reputation as a great sporting companion. This has been due not so much to the cocker's lack of ability in the field as to his extraordinary beauty and quality as a pet and show dog.

The modern cocker spaniel is divided into two main types, the English cocker and the American. Until quite recently, the two were very much the same. Many had common ancestors, and differed chiefly in size. At present, the two are divided both as to size and type.

The English cocker is the larger of the two, and somewhat resembles a small springer. Males run from 28 to 34 pounds. The muzzle is slightly longer than that of the American dog, and there is not the excess of hair of the American black type. Self colors, such as all black, liver, and red are seen, as well as parti-colors, and roan colors of blue, red, orange, liver, and lemon. Several hundred are registered annually in America.

The American type is perhaps the most beautiful of all the spaniels. He has a pronounced stop, rounded skull, large, rather prominent eyes, and long ears. The ears are set on at eye level, or lower, and the leather reaches to the muzzle.

The body is short, with a much broader chest than is true in other spaniels. The top line slopes from the withers to the croup. The stifle angulation is pronounced, sometimes excessively so in blacks. A serious fault in many is a weak, spreading foot, with thin pads.

The American cocker is divided into three varieties, based primarily on color. These are black; any other solid color, but including black and tan; and parti-colors. The blacks, generally, have a much more profuse coat and feathering than the others. Weight limits for all American types are 22 to 28 pounds.

Good cockers have a merry, effervescent disposition which is a distinct mark of the breed. But, in recent years, shyness and hysteria have appeared to a serious degree. Responsible cocker breeders, however, are now waging an apparently successful battle to eliminate these character faults.

**Development.** The early history of the spaniel family is outlined under the section on springer spaniels (p. 839). The history of the cocker as a breed starts with the birth of Mr. Farrow's Obo, June 14, 1879. Obo is generally considered to have been the first modern cocker. He was by Fred, out of Betty, weighed 22 pounds, and was 10 inches tall.

Four years after Obo's birth, cockers were granted a separate classification of British dog shows, and in 1893, separate cocker registrations were made in the English stud book. The first field trial was given in 1899, and these have continued to grow in popularity in England ever since.

On the whole, the great English cocker families of the early days played an equal role in the United States and Canada. For instance, many of Obo's descendants were sent to America. Braeside Bob, one of these, is sometimes called the father of the American cocker.

Both the Ware and Rivington kennels in England bred both springers and cockers. Both sent great dogs to America. Among the famous Rivington cockers were Rivington Signal, Rivington Red Coat, Rivington Blue Gown, and Rivington Sam. The latter,

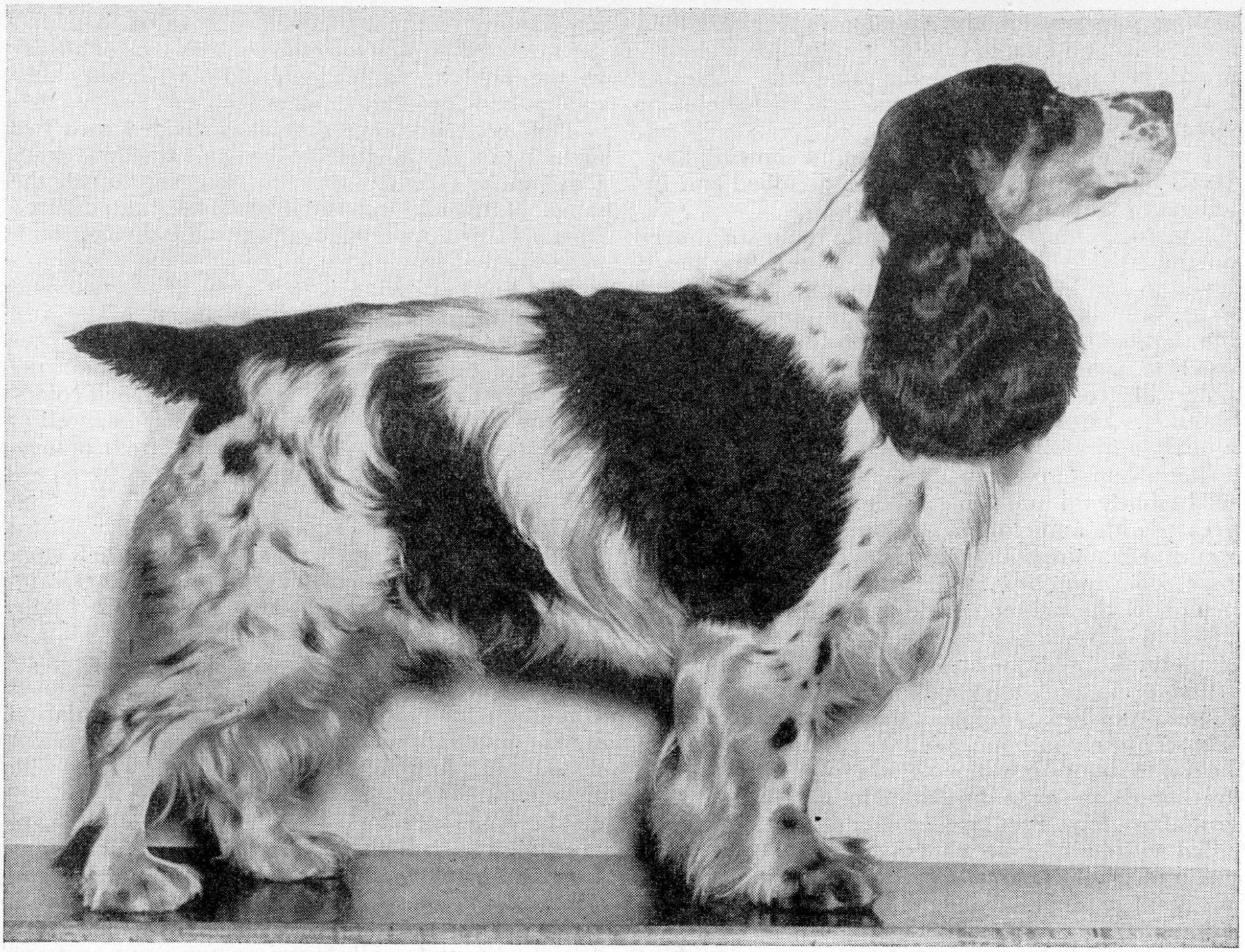

Courtesy M. E. Litchfield.

**PLATE VII. Cocker Spaniel: Ch. Belfield Bolivar.**

though a cocker, founded one of the strongest springer lines.

From 1850 to 1900 in America, hunting with spaniels went out of favor. After the organization of the American Spaniel Club in 1881, some efforts were made to bring hunting cockers into favor again. But these efforts failed, and for many years cockers remained merely pets and bench dogs.

Among the early bench champions can be mentioned Hornell Dandy, 1881; Hornell Silk (by Obo), (1882); Black Pete (by Obo, Jr.), 1885; and Bambo (by Bob Obo), 1890.

The first championship field trial given in the United States was sponsored by the Cocker Spaniel Field Trial Club of America at Verbank, N. Y., in 1924. The judges were William Hutchinson and A. Clinton Wilmerding, the latter one of the founders of the American Spaniel Club.

Because of the backing of such people as Colonel H. S. Nielson, Elias Vail, Ralph Craig, Herman Mellenthin, Leonard Buck, and Ella B. Moffitt, cocker trials began to prosper. These people selected top stock for training, with the result that many dual champions were made. The first dual, or bench and field, champion was My Own High Time. Others include such noted performers as Live Oak Spring Storm, Miller's Esquire, Don Pablo from Jourdains, and Rowcliffe Hill Billy.

At first, the trials were mainly in the East. This section produced such great field dogs as Latch Up George, Rowcliffe Blue Streak, Rowcliffe Bangaway, High Time Elcova, Horsford Delight Em, and the famous Blue Waters Magnificent. All were field champions.

The Midwest produced Jimmie, a field champion of extraordinary class but of unknown pedigree, and field champions Ravine Top Freckles, Stipe's Cricket, and Miller's Esquire.

On the Pacific Coast a great many top performers have been produced. Two of these, field champions Nugget and Bunny, could not be registered. Nugget, however, ran for seven years and won five open all-age stakes. Other noted field champions from this section include Roanfeather Argonaut, Isleton Boy, Rex of Windsor, Camino Boy, Aubrey Squib, and Chequamegen Laddie. The last three are English champions.

Just before World War II, a number of English cockers were imported. Many of them made field championships here or produced them. In this group are Rivington Bean, Cinar's Chuck, Cinar's Dash, Cinar's Ring, and Cinar's Spot of Earlsmoor.

The war almost mortally injured cocker trials. Only a couple of trials were held. The old dogs died off, and the dilemma of the modern cockerites is that they no longer can buy field trial strains. However, Mr. Ralph Craig, as head of the American Spaniel

Club, is leading that organization in an aggressive policy of rebuilding.

Arguments as to the value of field trials are never ending. But there can be no doubt that, so far as cockers are concerned, they are of tremendous value. They prove performance, set standards for performance, help to identify blood lines which will produce top field dogs and generally stimulate the breeding for character.

An argument against field trials is that, because of the competitive angle, performance standards are set far above the reach of the amateur trainer-owner, and even above the requirements for top hunters. There is considerable truth to these points as far as field trials in general are concerned. But, probably because of the overshadowing of field cockers by their bench brothers, this has never been true in cocker trials. There simply have not been enough performers to make it true. Even if true, however, the great advantages conferred by the trials would outweigh the disadvantages.

**Characteristics.** All the spaniels—including the springer, cocker, clumber, Sussex, Welsh springer, and Brittany—are called bird dogs. This assumes that they search the air currents for the body scents of birds, in contrast to the hounds which search out and follow trail scents. The majority do hunt by locating body scents in the air. But because hounds, or dogs with hound trailing proclivities, were sometimes bred with the spaniels, many do have a trailing, rather than a body scent, nose. This explains why a good flusher is not always a good finder.

The dog who hunts by body scent is at an advantage when working into the wind, or when game is "setting." If the wind is right, he may have equal chances of locating and flushing moving game. The dog with the trailing nose is, however, at a heavy disadvantage except when game is moving and he can pick up a trail. He has a distinct advantage when he is after the "runner," as, for instance, the pheasant which has been knocked down but can still run.

The best performers are those dogs which learn by experience to use their noses both ways. Many of the better cockers and springers have this ability. But the truly observing spaniel owner will note which dogs have the desired body scenting nose, and will breed for this quality.

It is the tendency among sportsmen to buy from a pedigree. This is excellent as far as it goes, since, if the parents were field winners, most of the offspring may be expected to have some field ability. But the puppy buyer does not want to be the one to get the non-performer in the litter.

In general, spaniels inherit certain aptitudes which are necessary for high-class workmanship in the field. By aptitude is meant an innate or inherited proficiency in doing a certain thing. These appear in varying numbers in cockers and springers. Here are some of them: Water going, briar hitting, retrieving, proper carry of the retrieve, soft mouth, capacity for training, bird hunting, and fence crashing.

It is easily observable that some spaniels will dive into water no matter how rough or cold. Others enter grudgingly, and some refuse entirely. Puppies of six to eight weeks of age can be tested for this as easily as older dogs. The tester merely walks out into the water and calls the pups to follow. Some walk out and swim without hesitation. Others will not enter.

Spaniels, or at any rate the good ones, are supreme workers in briars. Many of them will smash through a briar patch at top speed, come out bleeding, and hit the next patch just as hard. While few want their dogs torn up in this way, the briar-shy dog is nearly useless, particularly in the Midwest.

Many dogs seem to retrieve naturally. The only training they require is to be taught "must." Others resent retrieving and are taught only with difficulty. Most spaniels belong to the former class. Some of the better ones also appear to have a very definite aptitude for carrying. They never seem to be able to pick up a bird incorrectly, while others always have to lay the bird down several times in order to get a better grip.

Capacity for training is an important feature in the spaniel. Most of them are highly alert, give you their complete attention, and take correction in stride.

Most spaniels are primarily interested in flying things. If spaniel pups and beagle pups are placed in the same run, the spaniels will show interest in every flying thing, whereas the beagles will pay little attention. Their interests are on the ground.

Many spaniel pups are hard to contain behind a fence. They crawl through, or over, or under. In the field, you need never worry about them. They will always find a way to get through the fence, or up the creek bank, even when very young and inexperienced.

The prospective purchaser of a cocker field dog, having little to go on in pedigree research, can make simple tests to prove almost all of these aptitudes before he buys. He can test the pups for water, briars, fences, curiosity, and courage in going out and away into cover, simply by taking them for a walk before he buys.

**Description and Standards.** SKULL: Not so heavy as in other sporting spaniels, with smooth forehead and clearly defined eyebrows and stop, the median line distinctly marked and gradually disappearing until lost rather more than halfway up, a well-developed, rounded, and comparatively wide skull showing no prominence in the cheeks, which, like the side of the muzzle, should present a smooth, clean-cut appearance.

MUZZLE: Proportionately shorter and lighter than in the field spaniel, showing no fullness under the eyes, the haws even and approaching squareness. Teeth sound and regular, the front ones meeting. Lips cut off square, preventing any appearance of snipiness. Nose well developed in all directions and black in color excepting in the reds, livers, particolors of these shades and in the roans of the lighter lines, when it may be brown or black.

EYES: Comparatively large, round, rather full, yet never goggled nor weak, as in the toy spaniel kind. They should be dark in the blacks, black and tans, the darker shades of parti-colors and roans. In the reds and livers and in the parti-colors and roans of these colors they should be brown, but of a shade not lighter than hazel.

EARS: Lobular, set low, leather fine and not extending beyond the nose; well clothed with long, silky hair, which should be straight or wavy.

NECK AND SHOULDERS: Neck sufficiently long to allow the nose to reach the ground easily, muscular, free from throatiness and running into clean-cut, sloping shoulders, not wide at the points.

BODY: Comparatively short, compact and firmly knit together, giving the impression of a concentration of power and untiring activity. Chest deep rather than wide, not narrow fronted nor yet so wide as to interfere with free action of the forelegs. Ribs well sprung, deep and carried far back, short in the couplings and flank, free from any tucked appearance. Back and loin, immensely strong and compact in proportion to the size of the dog, the former level and the latter slightly arched. Hips wide, with quarters considerably rounded and very muscular.

LEGS AND FEET: Forelegs short and straight, though proportionately longer than in any of the other breeds of short-legged spaniels; strongly boned and muscled, with elbows well let down and straight, short, strong pasterns. Hindlegs proportionately short. Stifles well bent, strong thighs, clearly defined. Hocks clean, strong, well let down, presenting an impressive combination of propelling power. Feet neither small nor large, round, firm, not spreading, and with deep, strong, horny pads and plenty of hair between toes. They should turn neither in nor out.

STERN: Should be set on and carried level with the back, and when at work its action should be incessant in this, the brightest and merriest of the whole spaniel family.

COAT: Flat or slightly waved, silky and very dense, with ample setter-like feather.

COLOR AND MARKINGS: Blacks should be jet black, and reds, livers, etc., should never be faded or "washy" shades, but of good, sound colors. White on the chest of self-colors, while objectionable, should not disqualify.

WEIGHT: Not under 18 or exceeding 24 pounds.

GENERAL DESCRIPTION: Embodying the foregoing, i.e., a neat-headed, wide-awake, serviceable-looking little dog, with an expression of great intelligence; short in body when viewed from above, yet standing over considerable ground for one of his inches upon strong, straight front legs, with wide, muscular quarters suggestive of immense power, especially when viewed from behind. A downward tendency in front he ought not to possess, but should stand well up at the shoulders, like the clever little sporting dog that he is. Massive in appearance by reason of his sturdy body, powerful quarters and strong, well-boned limbs, he should, nevertheless, impress one as being a dog capable of considerable speed combined with great powers of endurance and in all his movements he should be quick and merry, with an air of alertness and a carriage of head and stern suggestive of an inclination to work.

SCALE OF POINTS:

| | |
|---|---|
| Skull | 8 |
| Muzzle | 10 |
| Eyes | 7 |
| Ears | 4 |
| Neck and shoulders | 15 |
| Body | 18 |
| Legs and feet | 18 |
| Stern | 5 |
| Coat | 10 |
| Color and marking | 5 |
| TOTAL | 100 |

# CURLY-COATED RETRIEVER

The curly-coated retriever is a living proof that quality of performance and good looks do not always bring popularity. This is a dog of great beauty, and there never has been any question as to his water ability. Yet the breed has never reached great prominence, either on the bench or in the duck marshes. Perhaps the only exception to this is the great popularity of the breed in New Zealand. There he is used both for wildfowling and quail shooting. Apparently the New Zealanders greatly prefer him.

**History.** Perhaps the first allusion to them occurs in the *Sportsmen's Cabinet* (1803): "These dogs are exceedingly singular in their appearance, and most probably derive their origin from the Greenland dog, blended with some particular race of our own."

"Stonehenge," in 1859, guessed that this cross was the Irish water spaniel. ". . . This variety of retriever is always a cross between the St. John's Newfoundland and the water spaniel, which is generally Irish." Stonehenge may have been right, but other writers disputed this, pointing out that in crosses with the Irish water spaniel, the peculiar topknot of the Irish usually showed up, but it is absent in the curly-coated retriever.

Other suggested crosses were the English water spaniel, the poodle, and perhaps the Gordon setter. These crosses undoubtedly were tried, but their final influence on the curly coat is not known.

The curly-coated retriever was first shown on the bench in 1859. At the Islington International show in 1864, he was given a separate classification from other retrievers. Mr. Gorse's Jet was the victor. Jet and Jet II dominated the show picture for several years. Later William Arkwright's Sweep and Mr. Salter's King Koffie gained fame.

The Curly-Coated Retriever Club was formed in England in 1896. In February 1933, the Curly Retriever Club was formed. Since that day, it has sponsored the breed, and has given trials for curly coats.

Perhaps the best known English field dogs in recent years have been Calgary Grizzly and Pycombe Sable. Both dogs, and others later, have shown up well enough in competition with other breeds.

Writing in 1905 and 1906, the great American dog authority, James Watson, predicted that retrievers would never gain a foothold in the United States. He could not foresee modern hunting conditions, with duck flights dangerously reduced. Yet Watson felt that if any retriever breed was destined for popularity here, it was the curly coat. He thought the breed a beautiful one, compared its coat favorably with that of the Chesapeake, and thought the dog's coat was superior to that of the Irish water spaniel.

Still, the curly coat has not gained popularity here, even though he was perhaps the first in the field so far as English retriever breeds are concerned. There were a scattered few of the curly coats in America from pre-Civil War days on. Two are mentioned in 1907 as having created a very favorable opinion by their working ability.

J. Gould Remick tried to popularize the breed just before World War II. During this period there were at least three curly coats who proved themselves in field trial competition with Chesapeakes,

Courtesy of Evelyn M. Shafer.

PLATE VIII. Curly-Coated Retriever.

Labradors, goldens, and Irish water spaniels. These were Sarona Sam of Marvadel, Sarona Jacob of Marvadel, both owned by Mr. Remick, and Carbon of Marvadel, owned by F. Royal Gammon.

**Characteristics.** This dog is a square-built dog standing about 24 inches tall at the shoulder. He is a mass of tight curls from the occiputal crest of the head to the end of his tail.

The curly-coated retriever is either black or dark liver. There are occasional white hairs on the chest, but a patch of white is severely penalized. Actual size and weight are not important, and the standard for the breed gives neither maximum nor minimum height or weight qualifications.

The outstanding characteristics of the breed are water-going eagerness and stamina in cold water. The dogs will dive continuously after crippled ducks. They are good markers and have excellent memories. Most of them are good land workers, and are said to stand out in locating "runners."

An early criticism of them, which is not generally true today, was that they were hard mouthed. Most authorities consider them easy to train, and all are agreed as to the sweetness of their temper. Most Americans criticize them as being too slow in field trial work, while admitting their competence. In England, they are considered very fast, particularly in the water.

**Description and Standards.** HEAD: Long and well proportioned, skull not too flat, jaws long and strong but not inclined to snipiness, nose black, in the black coated variety, with wide nostrils. Teeth strong and level.

EYES: Black or brown, but not yellow, rather large but not too prominent.

EARS: Rather small, set on low, lying close to the head, and covered with short curls.

COAT: Should be one mass of crisp curls all over. A slightly more open coat not to be severely penalized, but a saddle back or patch of uncurled hair behind the shoulder should be penalized, and a prominent white patch on breast is undesirable, but a few white hairs allowed in an otherwise good dog. Color, black or liver.

SHOULDERS, CHEST, BODY, AND LOINS: Shoulders should be very deep, muscular, and obliquely placed. Chest not too wide, but decidedly deep. Body, rather short, muscular, and well ribbed up. Loins, powerful, deep and firm to the grasp.

LEGS AND FEET: Legs should be of moderate length, forelegs straight and set well under the body. Quarters strong and muscular, hocks low to the ground with moderate bend to stifle and hock. Feet round and compact with well-arched toes.

TAIL: Should be moderately short, carried fairly straight and covered with curls, slightly tapering toward the point.

GENERAL APPEARANCE: Strong, smart, upstanding, showing activity, endurance, and intelligence.

No numerical scale of points has been set up.

# ENGLISH SETTER

**History.** The English setter is America's oldest gun-dog. Long before his short-haired rival, the pointer, came into popularity the English setter was proving a prime asset to the gun wherever American upland game birds were found. His firm entrenchment in the affections of the American gunner made it doubly hard for the pointer to gain a foothold.

Concerning the origin of the setter, the old-time writers agreed upon one thing. He was called "A spaniel improved," and most of the early writers maintained that the setting spaniel is an older breed than the pointer. Some others, including "Stonehenge," intimate that there might have been an introduction of pointer blood in the early setting spaniels, but no proof of this has ever been offered.

**Strains.** England has long had a number of varieties or strains of setters. Among them were the Featherstone, Southesk, Lovat, Naworth Castle, Seafield, and Ossulton. Later came the Laveracks, established by Edward Laverack. Wales also had setters, the strain of that section being known as Llandidloes, chalk white in color. Ireland had the Irish setters of solid red or red and white in color. Scotland had the black and tans, later known as the Gordons.

Specimens of most of these breeds came to America in the early days. Occasionally a Russian setter came over. These strains were frequently intermingled and the offspring became known as "natives." This designation was, of course, erroneous but the name "native" served as well as any.

One of the earliest and most popular strains of "natives" was the Gildersleeve, held in high esteem particularly by the gunners of Maryland, Delaware, and eastern Pennsylvania. Most of these medium-sized dogs were orange and white and were said to possess excellent noses and splendid action.

Another orange and white strain was the Morford, established by Theodore Morford of Newton, N. J. The Morfords enjoyed considerable popularity and bred true to type.

The Ethan Allens, founded by a sportsman of that name who lived at Pomfret, Conn., came in a variety of colors and were not level in conformation. These dogs were especially good on grouse, woodcock, and snipe.

Another breed of so-called "natives" which bred true to type and characteristics was that established by Asa Sherwood of Skaneateles, N. Y., and William Vie of St. Louis, Mo. These dogs probably bred as true to type as any strain established before or since.

The Campbell setter, a strain established by M. C. and George M. Campbell of Springhill, Tenn., was the most popular and noted of the "natives." The Messrs. Campbell entered their dogs fearlessly in Southern field trials where they acquired an enviable reputation. The strain was, like many others, a mixture of many lines, with the Gordon probably, and the Irish setter certainly, contributing most. The original fountainheads of the strain were Mason's Jeff, a black dog, and Fan or Old Fannie, a white and lemon bitch. It has been said that every puppy from this mating developed into an exceptional bird dog.

One of the first of these offspring was Old Buck, which produced Buck, Jr., when bred to Old Joe, a son of Otto and Fannie. Buck, Jr., when bred to Elcho, probably the best, and certainly the most famous, Irish setter of all time, produced Joe, Jr., the greatest of all the Campbells. The first dog to win a field trial in America was a black setter named Night, the property of H. C. Pritchett of Nashville, Tenn. Night was a native-bred dog but his dam was a Campbell setter, being by Otto and out of Fan. He won the free-for-all stake of the first American field trial, sponsored by the Tennessee Sportsman's Association and held near Memphis, Tenn., Oct. 8, 1874.

Mr. Edward Laverack, whose Laverack strain was attracting much attention on both sides of the water, began to experiment with the Duke-Rhoebe-Laverack cross and these dogs quickly came to the forefront. They attracted the attention of Mr. R. Purcell-Llewellin, at that time an extensive breeder, and it was from this stock that the strain now known as the Llewellin setter was established.

One of Mr. Llewellin's early exportations to North America was Petrel, who was bred to Dan and then sold to L. H. Smith of Strathroy, Ontario. Petrel whelped after her arrival and one of her puppies was Gladstone, later to become one of the greatest of the early American-Llewellins. Mr. Smith gave Gladstone, as a very young puppy, to P. H. Bryson of Memphis, Tenn. The dog developed rapidly and soon became famous, both as a field performer and as a sire. He had much to do with the great popularity of the so-called Llewellin strain in this country.

Interest in the setters increased rapidly and it was only natural that there was much difference of opinion concerning the merits of the Campbell "natives" and the vaunted "blue-blooded" Llewellins. These discussions reached a climax in the great match race between Joe, Jr., the greatest of the Campbells, and Gladstone, the chief of the American-Llewellin tribe, and the greatest exponent of the Duke-Rhoebe-Laveracks.

The race was scheduled as a three-day endurance test, but shortly before the date set Gladstone had the misfortune to fracture the tip of his tail and came to the mark with the tip wrapped in bandages of canvas glued together. At the request of his owner the race was limited to two days, $500 a side, with the number of actual points on quail to be the only determining factor. Style, speed, range, and other field trial qualifications to be disregarded.

At the end of the first day Joe, Jr. was four points up on the "blueblood," having 34 to Gladstone's 30. Early the next day Gladstone passed his rival, and the Campbell, which had gone lame, looked like a sure loser. Joe, Jr., recovered, however, and at noontime was one point in the lead. He worked out of his lameness in the afternoon and began scoring rapidly, winning at sundown with the decisive score of 61 points to Gladstone's 52.

The Llewellins, however, continued to gain popularity, due to general excellence in field performance coupled with a well-planned advertising campaign. So great did the Llewellin vogue become that, with some American breeders, it amounted to almost a fetish. For more years than were good for the strain, the owner who could not boast that his dog's pedigree traced back in an unbroken line to the Duke-

PLATE IX. English Setter: Sam L's Skygo, All-Age Winner.

Rhoebe-Laveracks was looked upon as one who could not recognize the best. Too many Llewellin breeders began to pay more attention to pedigrees than to proved field qualities and the popularity of the strain began to decline. The *Field Dog Stud Book* recognizes the "Llewellin" as a separate and distinct strain, but no dog is designated as a "Llewellin" whose pedigree does not trace back to the original fountainheads without an outcross.

At the present time there are comparatively few 100 per cent Llewellins in the country, although the majority of our English setters have a preponderance of that blood. Color had nothing to do with the strain, but many novices today erroneously classify any lightly-marked blue-ticked English setter as a "Llewellin."

Mr. Laverack's breed of dogs stemmed from Ponto and Old Moll, a brace of dogs he obtained from the Reverend Mr. Harrison of Carlisle in 1825. Mr. Laverack stated that the Rev. Mr. Harrison had kept the strain pure for 35 years before he acquired Ponto and Old Moll.

Duke, the property of Barclay Field, was a black and white dog which came to be known as Field's Duke. His dam was descended from the North of England Border breed which was favored by Sir Vincent Corbett. His sire was Sir F. Graham's Duke. According to early writers, he had quite a reputation but was never able to display his good qualities in public, appearing, on these occasions, to be deficient in nose.

Rhoebe was a heavily marked black, white, and tan with little quality of conformation. Neither was she considered a field performer, but this cross produced excellent dogs, which continued to produce exceptional performers when bred to Laverack bitches. Rhoebe was owned by Mr. Statter.

In 1871, while attending the field trials at Shrewsbury, Mr. Llewellin purchased Dan and Dick, sons of Field's Duke and Statter's Rhoebe, for breeding to his Laverack bitches. Thus was the foundation of the "Llewellin" strain laid. Much has been written about the origin of this strain, and some authorities claim that the Duke-Rhoebe-Laveracks were bred by Mr. Laverack some time before Mr. Llewellin became interested in the cross. It was the latter, and his kennel manager, G. Teasdale Buckell, who popularized the "Llewellin breed" and gave it its accepted name.

Llewellin's Dan was a dog of great prepotency and when he was crossed with the flighty Laverack bitches he seemed to add just what was needed and his offspring were dogs of sterling qualities. Foremost of these, of course, was the great Gladstone. This handsome white, black, and tan dog possessed unusual stamina, great hunting intelligence, an unusual nose, and the right amount of highstrung nervous energy. In addition he was a great sire.

Count Noble, imported by David Sanborn of Baltimore, was another early Llewellin who had a great influence on the setters of America. He came over at just the right time, for there were many daughters of Gladstone to come to his court and this cross was very successful. He was also a fine field performer and won several times in trials. He was especially good on prairie chickens. He sired 30 winners, five more than Gladstone. Another successful cross with Count Noble were the daughters of Dashing Rover. Count Noble made a great impression and his name is found in the pedigrees of many present-day setters.

Leicester, also imported by Mr. L. H. Smith, enjoyed considerable patronage and is generally considered one of the pillars of American field trial setters, but he produced to Dart alone. His daughters, however, were good producers.

Druid, imported by Arnold Burgess of Hillsdale, Mich., in 1877 is another which exerted considerable influence on the setter in this country.

Space will not permit a tabulation of anything like all the setters which helped make the field-type English setter as we know him today. Among them, however, were Dan Gladstone, Ruby's Dan, Sportsman, Gath, Roderigo, Count Gladstone IV, and Eugene T. Also not to be overlooked were Antonio, Rodfield, Tony Boy, Mohawk II, Prince Rodney, and Connell's Gleam. Later came Candy Kid, Eugene M, Fairy Beau, Marse Ben, Eugene's Ghost, Phil Essig, and still later Sport's Peerless and Florendale Lou's Beau.

Lamberton's Mack was a great grouse dog which produced a good number of grand gun-dogs in the East. But the setter which is more responsible than any other single setter sire for the excellence of the grouse and woodcock dogs in this country is Nugym, the son of Eugym Mohawk and Bridge's Bonnie Lassie. Nugym produced 93 winners which ran up a total of 400 wins. Sam L's Skyrocket is another noted producer of excellent grouse dogs, and his sons seem to be carrying on his prepotency.

The setter sire producing the greatest number of winners to date is Sport's Peerless, with 132 winners to his credit. Next to him is Florendale Lou's Beau with 109. Both are now dead but their sons are carrying on.

Time was when the English setter had things pretty much his own way in American field trials. In fact, so superior was his performance to that of the pointer that competition between the two breeds was considered not very sporting, and the pointer had separate stakes in which to display his wares. This is certainly no longer true today, for, in annexing field trial laurels, the pointer has surpassed his long-haired rival, who finds himself hard put to hold his own.

**Development.** The argument concerning the merits of setters of the early days and setters of the present is always in evidence where "old-timers" gather. It will, of course, never be settled, for hunting conditions have changed, game supplies have diminished, and modern requirements are a bit different. There are those who contend, and with sound argument, too, that the setter has not gone backward but, rather, the pointer has improved. Be that as it may, it is a fact that the period when preference for the "Llewellin" strain bordered on the fanatic and many setter breeders paid far more attention to pedigrees than to the field performance and qualities of prospective sires, was concurrent with the pointer's rise in field trials. Breeders of the short-hair have always flocked to the sire that could and did prove his ability in the hunting field. Regardless of the fact that the pointer is now winning more places in field trials than the setter, the prime favorite of the early days will always remain a favorite wherever upland game birds are hunted, for his handsome appearance and lovable disposition win friends everywhere.

The first National Bird Dog Championship was won by the setter, Count Gladstone IV, in 1896. Each succeeding year found a setter at the top of the class (the diminutive setter bitch, Sioux, proclaimed by many as the greatest bird dog of all times, having won the title twice, 1901 and 1902) until 1909, when the pointer, Manitoba Rap, gained the crown.

Setters held forth for the next four years, with Monora, Eugene M, Commissioner, and Phillipides winning the title, until the pointer Comanche Frank was crowned in 1914. From 1918, when Joe Muncie won it, until 1926, when Feagin's Mohawk Pal won it, the pointers held the stage. Feagin's Mohawk Pal is the only setter to have won the title three times (1926, 1928, and 1930). It was not until 1939 that another setter, Sport's Peerless Pride, could gain the honors; and then began another period of pointer supremacy until 1946, when the sensational little setter, Mississippi Zev, won the stake outstandingly. In addition, Zev won the National Amateur Championship, the Texas Open Championship, and the Regional Amateur title.

The history of upland game bird hunting in this country is heavily dotted with the names of famous English setters. For every one which, through opportunities, gained national or sectional acclaim there are literally thousands of no less proficient setter performers who will be long remembered in the small circle of their local activities.

**Characteristics.** The English setter thrives on attention and affection. He loves to be in the company of a kind master, to hunt for him and to worship him. His performance is at its best when his training has not been hurried or forced. Once the setter learns a lesson he learns it well and is not so apt to forget or disregard it as the pointer. He is also much more prone to become a "one-man" dog than his short-haired rival.

**Field Qualities.** The first American Field Quail Futurity was won by the setter Tonopaugh, in 1905. For many years setters dominated this stake—until 1947—but no setter won it since 1929 when Outacite topped the field and only four setters have even placed in this classic since 1935. In 1947, however, the sensational Tennessee Zev, son of the illustrious four-times champion, Mississippi Zev, won the stake with a brilliant performance, defeating 93 other entrants. It is a rather significant fact that no setter has even won a place in the American Field Pheasant Futurity established in 1934. No setter has ever won the National Derby Championship, and only five have gained runner-up honors since the inaugural stake in 1920. This is interpreted by some authorities as proof that the setter does not mature as early or reach the peak of his capabilities as soon as the pointer.

Field trials, however, while serving as an indicator of breed performance and popularity, do not tell the whole story. The many splendid qualities of the English setter will always endear him to the sportsman who prefers gunning success to field trial wins. And for the sportsman who fully appreciates the pleasures of a day afield with a willing, industrious, loyal, and affectionate gun-dog companion that is also a thing of beauty in action and repose, the English setter knows no peer.

**Selection and Training.** In choosing a young setter gun-dog prospect one should look for boldness, grace of carriage, and sturdy, yet not bulky, conformation. Setters come in a variety of colors: white and black; white, black, and tan; white and orange; blue belton, orange belton, and, occasionally white and chestnut. Color makes no difference in field performance or a dog's general abilities, yet, all other factors being equal, it is best to choose one on which white predominates. A heavily marked dog or one of the belton types is sometimes rather difficult to see in the field, particularly on a cloudy, hazy, or rainy day.

Be sure that he comes from ancestors that have proved their worth as hunting dogs. If his parents are good field performers the chances are high that he will also, under proper training, develop into a good gun-dog.

Do not try to rush his education or crowd him in his training. Allow his natural instincts to develop and direct them in the proper channels. Be extremely careful in the use of force. Many good young setters have been ruined by too much correction or punishment when they did not know why it was being administered. Be sure that your dog knows *why* before you punish him. A sharp scolding or a bit of shaming can often accomplish much more than painful force. Never take a chance on cowing the young dog. The setter, while sensitive, is not generally a timid fellow, but his reaction to kind treatment and his aversion to punishment that he does not understand are parts of his nature. He can be led into doing great deeds, but he hates to be forced, and once he begins to sulk you have a problem on your hands.

Other than the above words of caution, there are no specific training instructions which pertain only to the setter. Standard procedures are generally readily effective, but one should always bear in mind that in training a young dog of any breed or strain each individual should be treated as such and his distinctive characteristics should be carefully studied in order that one may build the training program around them. It is not as hard as it may sound, if one will only be patient and not expect too much too soon.

Above all, make a companion of your setter. Spend as much time with him as possible. You will grow to understand each other better and more quickly. It is safe to prophesy that your setter will meet you more than halfway.

"Once a setter-man, always a setter-man," is an old saying which is by no means a half-truth. The man who owns one English setter shouts the praises of the breed to the housetops. The one who owns two English setters does the same thing—only louder!

**Description and Standards.** The physical standards of the breed follow:

HEAD: Long and lean, with a well-defined stop. The skull oval from ear to ear, of medium width, giving brain room but with no suggestion of coarseness, with but little difference between the width at base of skull and at brows and with a moderately defined occipital protuberance. Brows should be at a sharp angle from the muzzle. Muzzle should be long and square, of width in harmony with the skull, without any fullness under the eyes and straight from eyes to tip of nose. A dishface or Roman nose is objectionable. The lips should be square and fairly pendant. Nose should be black or dark liver in color, except in white, lemon and white, orange and white, or liver and white dogs, when it may be of lighter color. Nostrils should be wide apart and large in the openings. Jaws should be of equal length. An overshot or undershot jaw is objectionable. Ears should be placed close to head, well back and set low, of moderate length, slightly rounded at the ends, and covered with silky hair. Eyes should be bright, intelligent, mild, and dark brown in color.

NECK: The neck should be long and lean, arched at the chest, and not too throaty.

SHOULDERS: Shoulders should be formed to permit perfect freedom of action to the forelegs. Shoulder blades should be long, wide, sloping moderately well back and standing fairly close together at the top.

CHEST: Chest between shoulder blades should be of good depth but not of excessive width.

RIBS: Ribs, back of the shoulders, should spring gradually to the middle of the body and then taper to the back ribs, which should be of good depth.

BACK: Back should be strong at the junction with the loin and should be straight or sloping upward very slightly to the top of the shoulder, the whole forming a graceful outline of medium length, without sway or drop. Loins should be strong, moderate in length, slightly arched, but not to the extent of being roached or wheel backed. Hip bones should be wide apart without too sudden drop to the root of the tail.

FORELEGS: The arms should be flat and muscular, with bone fully developed and muscles hard and devoid of flabbiness; of good length from the point of shoulder to the elbow, and set at such an angle as will bring the legs fairly under the dog. Elbows should have no tendency to turn either in or out. The pastern should be short, strong, and nearly round, with the slope from the pastern joint to the foot deviating very slightly forward from the perpendicular.

HINDLEGS: The hindlegs should have wide, muscular thighs with well-developed lower thighs. Stifles should be well bent and strong. Hocks should be wide and flat. The pastern should be short, strong, and nearly round, with the slope from the pastern joint to the foot deviating very slightly forward from the perpendicular.

FEET: Feet should be closely set and strong, pads well developed and tough, toes well arched and protected with short thick hair.

TAIL: Tail should be straight, set low, and taper to a fine point, with only sufficient length to meet the hocks, or less. The feather must be straight and silky, falling loosely in a fringe and tapering to the point when the tail is raised. There must be no bushiness. The tail should not curve sideways or above the level of the back.

COAT: Coat should be flat and of good length, without curl; not soft or woolly. The feather on the legs should be moderately thin and regular.

WEIGHT: Dogs about 55 to 70 pounds; bitches, 50 to 65 pounds.

HEIGHT: Dogs, about 23 to 25 inches; bitches, 22 to 24 inches.

COLORS: Black, white, and tan; black and white; blue belton; lemon and white; lemon belton; orange and white; orange belton; liver and white; liver belton; solid white.

MARKINGS: Dogs without heavy patches of color on the body, but flecked all over preferred.

SYMMETRY: The harmony of all parts to be considered. Symmetrical dogs will have level back or be very slightly higher at the shoulders than at the hips. Balance, harmony of proportion, and an appearance of breeding and quality to be looked for, and coarseness avoided.

MOVEMENT AND CARRIAGE: An easy, free and graceful movement, suggesting rapidity and endurance. A lively tail and a high carriage of head. Stiltiness, cumbersome and lumbering gaits are objectionable.

SCALE OF POINTS:

| | | |
|---|---|---|
| *Head* | | |
| Skull | 5 | |
| Ears | 5 | |
| Eyes | 5 | |
| Muzzle | 5 | 20 |
| *Body* | | |
| Neck | 5 | |
| Chest and Shoulders | 12 | |
| Back, Loin, and Ribs | 10 | 27 |
| *Running Gear* | | |
| Forelegs | 5 | |
| Hips, Thighs, and Hindlegs | 12 | |
| Feet | 6 | 23 |
| *Coat* | | |
| Length and Texture | 5 | |
| Color and Marking | 3 | 8 |
| *Tail* | | |
| Length and Carriage | 5 | 5 |
| *General Appearance and Action* | | |
| Symmetry, Style and Movement | 12 | |
| Weight and Size | 5 | 17 |
| TOTAL | 100 | 100 |

**Breeders.** A complete roster of the breeders of English setters in this country would fill a sizable volume itself and, of course, is impracticable here. There is no section of the country where this grand bird dog cannot be found and there is no type of upland game bird which he cannot or will not handle successfully. His versatility and his ability to adapt himself to almost any type of hunting make him popular wherever the shotgun is used in hunting.

Some well-known setter breeders are: Virgil P. Hawse, Staunton, Va.; Harold Shaw, Spokane, Wash.; Sam Light, Punxsutawney, Pa.; F. H. Farnsworth, Chicago, Ill.; W. Lee White, Norwalk, Conn.; Carl E. Duffield, Tyler, Texas; and Edward Soph, Tulsa, Okla.

# FOXHOUND

**History.** The foxhound is our oldest sporting dog. When he first reached the shores of this country is uncertain, although it is known that hounds roamed American woods more than 200 years before the Declaration of Independence. These were the dogs said to be hounds, which Hernando De Soto, the Spanish explorer, had with him when he discovered the Mississippi River in 1541. De Soto, of course, was not a fox hunter; he is said to have used these hounds in hunting Indians.

Lord Baltimore, in his plans for the settlement of Maryland, recognized the value of "dogs" in colonization efforts and made it a definite requirement that each family should bring at least one "dog" to the new country. Although these dogs, or hounds, very likely ran foxes on occasion, it was not for sport alone that their presence was desired; hunting then generally was a necessity, not a sport.

Perhaps the father of American fox hunting was one of Lord Baltimore's friends, one Robert Brooke, whom Baltimore appointed as a member of the "Privy Council of State within our said Province of Maryland." Mr. Brooke, his wife, eight sons, two daughters, 28 servants, his household goods, supplies —and *hounds* arrived from England on June 30, 1650. Mr. Brooke lived only five years after coming to America, but he is recognized as the first Master of a pack of hounds in this country. His early activities mark the beginning of a sport which spread rapidly and widely and is now enjoyed by practically every state of the Union, American fox hunting.

Mr. Brooke's sons, and their sons and their son's sons, kept, bred, and hunted hounds descended from the original pack. True, they did not confine their hunting to foxes alone, but Reynard provided the greatest share of their sport. The Brooke hounds still live on, and descendants from the original family still breed them and hunt them. New blood was brought in occasionally; that was only to be expected. But enough resemblance to the original stock still exists in the present-day Brooke hound to stamp him as a definite entity.

The establishment of the first pack in England used exclusively for fox hunting has been given numerous dates, 1666, 1690, and 1698 being named most often, and Viscount Lowther, Lord Arundel, and Thomas Boothby being separately credited with ownership. For this reason, perhaps, there are those who maintain that fox packs have existed in this country almost as long as they have in England. This is probably erroneous, for the early American fox packs were almost certainly used to hunt other game as well as fox. The American foxhound is a versatile creature and can be trained to hunt almost any animal which leaves a scented trail on the ground.

One of the most interesting fox packs of the early days was the Castle Hill Hounds, established by Dr. Thomas Walker, of Albemarle County, Va., in 1742. Dr. Walker was a man of magnificent physique, marvelous endurance, and superb horsemanship. He was a "hell-to-breakfast" sportsman and his many feats in the field gave birth to the expression "the Devil and Tom Walker."

Considerably over 100 years from the establishment of the Castle Hill Hounds, Mrs. Allan Potts, a lineal descendant of Dr. Walker, became its Master and the pack gained the distinction of being the first of record to be owned and hunted by an American woman.

Many of the founders of this nation were foxhunters. Foremost among these was George Washington, who learned much of the sport, while still in his teens, from Thomas, Lord Fairfax. Many of the entries in Washington's diaries recount his foxhunting activities and he took great pride in his hounds, carefully selecting them for speed, endurance, and hunting intelligence. During the period from 1759 to 1774, Washington devoted almost all of his spare time to foxhunting, and when he rode across his acres on inspection trips he was generally accompanied by hounds in the hopes of a chance chase.

The Marquis de Lafayette sent Washington seven "stag-hounds" which arrived late in August 1785. These large French hounds did not take well to fox and Washington was disappointed in them. Washington, however, continued to hunt fox until the late 1780's. Thomas Jefferson, though not quite so closely identified with the sport as Washington, was an ardent fox hunter, as were also Alexander Hamilton and John Marshall.

The early history of American fox hunting was written across the broad reaches of Maryland and Virginia; the sport soon spread to other sections. In 1766, 27 Philadelphia and New Jersey sportsmen gathered at the Philadelphia Coffee House and formed the Gloucester Fox Hunting Club, the first fox-hunting club to be organized in this country. The New Jersey members were residents of Gloucester County, from which the club took its name. Before this time, however, the sport had already gained a foothold in Pennsylvania. One of the rules of the club, to the effect that "The sportsman who first touches the fox after the dogs have caught him, or who first touches the tree on which the fox may have taken shelter, if he does not make his escape therefrom, shall be entitled to the brush," is indicative that the game was the gray fox, as his red cousin seldom takes to trees.

Even in those days there was much heated debate, in print, among the farmers of New Jersey regarding the sport of fox hunting, some denouncing the practice and others defending it with equal vigor.

Interest in the sport continued to grow and spread to other localities. The formalities of the chase became more pronounced as the sport grew, and through this common bond the sportsmen of the colonies were brought into closer understanding.

Fox hunting was enjoyed in New York as early as the 1760's, the gentry and farmers of "the English settlements of Oyster Bay, Hempstead, Long Island, and Westchester County" banding their individual hounds together in a common pack to hunt, on stated days, the hare or an outlying fox or deer. In fact, Manhattan Island was the scene of many fox hunts in the early days.

Sportsmen loved and were sentimental about their hounds even as they are now. In Volume I of J. Blan Van Urk's masterful work, *The Story of American Fox Hunting,* appears the following tribute to one of the hounds of the Washington Hunt, written by "A Member":

"Died, on the 25th ult. in Fairfax county, old June, for many seasons the favorite leader of the Washington pack of fox hounds.

"If the deceased was not the best to *find,* she was amongst the best *chasing* hounds that ever was followed; whether at *hits, heels,* or *close running,* she had few equals. Her voice was truth itself, and whenever she *gave tongue,* her companions always *hark'd* with attention. But after being herself *in at the death* of so many, grim death has *run into* her, Alas! nor the woods of Arlington, nor Chapman's fields, will ever more re-echo her voice . . . neither, by one of *her* infallible *hits,* shall we again be reminded of the poet's lines . . .

"See where they spread
"And range around, and dash the glittering dew.
"If some staunch hound with her *authentic* voice
"Avow the recent tail, the justling tribe
"Attend her call; then with one mutual cry
"The welcome news confirm, and echoing hills
"Repeat the pleasing tale."

Even then the subject of hound speed was a matter for much discussion, even in print, several well-known sportsmen contending that the breeding tendency was wrongly in the direction of placing too much emphasis on fleetness to the detriment of nose and tongue. They warned that if the practice continued, many hounds would become practically worthless from a sporting standpoint because they were "too fast for their noses."

It was only natural that such a rare sport should gain a place in the scheme of things in other communities. The first record of foxes in the Carolinas was contained in a legislative act in the State of Franklin (North Carolina) in 1785 which determined the legal currency for the state. This act provided that the skin of a raccoon or fox represented the value of a shilling and three pence.

In the 1820's the Raleigh Hunt was formed; club records show that the red fox had not yet come to that section and the gray fox provided the sport.

Also in existence about the same time was the Smithfield Hunt, which apparently enjoyed the sport in a less formal manner than the Raleigh. Considerable rivalry existed between the two.

The Byron strain of hounds, established by Colonel Thomas Goode Tucker, of Gaston, N. C., and named for his famous stallion hound Byron, enjoyed great popularity in that state for a long time.

It is said that the red fox was first introduced into South Carolina in 1783 by an English captain, William Rapilir, who hade the planting in the Abbeville district.

The sport in that area was not followed in the English manner, but rather with the friendly informality which has characterized Southern fox hunting since its inception.

There is little authentic early history of fox hunting in Georgia. Deer hunting seems to have been the field sport of the gentry in early times. Possibly the first red foxes ever to come to Georgia were those shipped by W. T. Porter, then editor of *The Spirit of the Times,* to Colonel George F. L. Birdsong in 1849. Some of these were "planted" on Pine Mountain, in Talbot County, and took to their new home well, multiplying rapidly.

There are records of fox hunting in Alabama as early as 1838 and in Louisiana before that. Mississippi and Arkansas planters were devotees of fox hunting and many maintained packs in the early 1800's. Tennessee sportsmen also played their part in the early development of the breed.

What was most likely the first American military hunt club was organized at Fort Gibson, Okla., in 1835.

Fox hunting had become a favorite pastime of the sporting gentry in almost every section of settled country in the early 1800's, and as time passed it was only natural that more interest should be shown in improving the foxhound.

Different conditions, such as type of terrain, scope of country, preference in hunting methods, called for different kinds of hunting. In the East and in parts of Maryland, Virginia, and Kentucky where organized hunt clubs held scheduled meets at stated intervals, in the formal English manner, it was necessary that the pack be amenable to discipline if the field were to get the most enjoyment out of the chase. In the South, and in other parts of Maryland, Virginia, and Kentucky and in the Middle West, where the hunting was of an informal nature and the pack was made up of individual hounds owned by neighboring planters or businessmen, conditions required that hounds, while willing to hark in immediately and run as a pack, should be possessed of great independence and cast at greater ranges. In the North, where the fox was and is shot for his pelt, a somewhat slow, painstaking, and steady hound was desired.

When the red fox—faster, more cunning, and with more stamina than his gray cousin—came drifting across the borders of the southerly states, the comparatively slow hounds of the early days, which had given such royal sport on the gray fox, were simply unable to meet the challenge of the quarry from the North and serious-minded fox hunters set to work to meet that challenge by developing faster hounds.

Breeding experiments were conducted in many quarters, and soon practically every section had its own "strain," which—to the originators, at least—had no superiors—until they were defeated by the hounds of another section. Then, most likely, new blood was brought in and the experimenting started all over again. A number of the strains, however, were kept "pure" and are still in existence today. Some are still growing in popularity.

**Development.** The two most popular strains of foxhounds in the country today, with the exception of those used in formal hunt club packs, are the Walker and the Trigg. These two now officially recognized strains, although started on different foundations, are related not too distantly. The origin and the development of each will be discussed at greater length later.

The Buckfield hound has long been a favorite in New England. These rather large, heavy-boned dogs have great power to enable them to negotiate the rugged covers and terrain of the northeastern states. They have keen noses, good mouths, and seem specially well equipped for hunting in New England.

This breed is said to have started in about 1858 when a Canadian peddler came to the town of Buckfield, Maine. With him he brought a red and blue-mottled bitch named Skip. The unusual-looking dog is described as looking like a cross between a foxhound and an Irish setter. At about that time an American, described as a "tramp," came to the Maine village and had with him a black, stump-tailed hound named Tige, which his master claimed was of English ancestry. From the mating of these two dogs came Bose, a compact, red bitch, somewhat shaggy in coat with considerable flag on her tail and hindquarters. Bose, an exceptional fox dog, is credited with being the mother of the Buckfields.

B. F. Robinson, of Mount Sterling, Ky., bred a strain of hounds which bore his name and had many admirers. He developed them by breeding the Irish hounds to hounds which came from some of the older Maryland packs.

W. C. Goodman obtained some of the Robinsons and crossed them with his own dogs, which were of the Maupin-Walker blood. In this manner he produced the Goodman hound; most of this breed were splendid individuals.

The Wild Goose hounds of Tennessee were developed in 1835 by C. S. Lewis and John Fuquay of Virginia and brought to Tennessee by Mr. Lewis. They were successfully bred by William Lewis, Walter Crawford, and Robert Gates.

The Redbone was a strain of Southern hound which was used in fox hunting for a number of years. These dogs have good noses and are painstaking trailers, but they do not possess the speed necessary for top-flight fox hunting, particularly on red fox. They were generally discarded for fox hunting purposes in the early 1900's, although here and there some of this blood is still used. The Redbone, however, has not passed into limbo. He has become a specialist after coon and possum, and there is no section of the South where he cannot be found—or, rather, some hound or pack whose owner boasts of their Redbone lineage. Almost any solid red hound of the smallish order, or red with black saddle, is generally called a "Redbone" by those who are not intimately acquainted with his immediate ancestry. But there is no denying the fact that many of the best tree dogs in the country are Redbones who make the swamplands ring with their musical cry after raccoon.

In Arkansas, Judge C. Floyd Huff, of Hot Springs, set a fast pace with his Arkansas Travelers, which were very popular throughout that state and Louisiana. Judge Huff's original stock were "Missouri" hounds. To prevent inbreeding to an injurious extent and also to give his hounds a bit more size and bone, Judge Huff imported a couple of hounds from England. Later he secured La Tosca, a celebrated hound by Big Strive out of Lygia, from Norvin T. Harris of Kentucky. These crosses brought to the pack the qualities the Arkansas jurist wanted.

Mr. J. M. Avent, of Hickory Valley, Tenn., whose fame is almost legendary wherever hound and bird-dog men gather, developed a strain which carried his colors and name to hunting fame. These dogs were a mixture of the Ferguson Virginia Black and Tans, "Bachelors," and the "native" hounds which had been used for years with great success around Hickory Valley. Mr. Thomas Hitchcock obtained a number of these dogs and hunted them in South Carolina, running them separately from his other pack. Mr. Paul Rainey purchased quite a number of these dogs and took them on his big-game hunts in Africa, running lion and other beasts of prey. He also hunted wolves and coyotes throughout the West with them.

Although Mr. Avent achieved his greatest fame as a developer and handler of field trial bird dogs, he was almost as equally well known as a huntsman and woodsman. Many prominent sportsmen, including Theodore Roosevelt, hunted bear with his pack in the Mississippi Delta country.

One of Mr. Avent's famous hounds was Ringgold, which he had trained to trail up lost or bolting bird dogs. When a dog refused to handle to the course and went self-hunting, Ringgold was placed on his track; he could be generally depended upon to round up the miscreant or bring him to bay. For a good many years Mr. Avent kept such a hound as part of his bird-dog training equipment; this hound was always known as Ringgold. Other well-known strains were the Whitlocks, Wash Rheas, Poolers, Greenbackers, Longfellows, and Williams.

In 1893 a group of foxhunting enthusiasts gathered at Waverly, Miss., as the guests of Captain Billy and Val Young. There the National Fox Hunters Association was organized.

Beginning November 20, 1894 and lasting for three days, the organization held its first annual field trials at Olympia, Ky. After hunting for three days without any decisive work, on account of extremely dry weather, the meet was called off with no awards made.

The second meet was held at Owingsville, Ky., beginning December 2, 1895. First in the Derby (for dogs under 18 months of age) went to Jay Bird (by Sam out of Lou), owned by Walker and Hagan. Second place went to the Bourbon Kennels' Red Blaze (by Rare out of Rill), while third was annexed by A. Ware's Speed (by Ranger out of Old Speed).

The All-Age stake went to Spencer Brother's Kit (by Gamester out of Lou), with E. H. Walker's Lewis (by Brewer out of Mag) second. Third place was won by Strodes Valley Kennel Club's Bird (by Kale out of Hett).

At the third annual meet, held at Bardstown, Ky., beginning Nov. 17, 1896, Gamester Kennels' Prudy (by Gamester out of Queen) won the Derby, with E. H. Walker's Rock (by Joe Carr out of Alice) second and H. C. Trigg's Longfellow (by Rattler out of Dove) third.

Osie (by Sam out of Mag), owned by Walker and Hagan, won the All-Age stake. Second place went to a litter brother, Blackbird, owned by R. J. Fincks, and J. B. Park's Fan (by Boston out of Cricket) won third.

These, however, were not the first organized field trials to be held in America. Perhaps that distinction goes to the Brunswick Fur Club, which staged a meet at Albany Hills, Maine, November 11-15, 1889. On this occasion, the Derby was won by E. L. Toothaker's Bugle, with Gerry and Emmon's Hunter second and E. L. Toothaker's Modest Girl third. The Open Hound Class went to L. O. Dennison's Ben Butler.

Less than a month later, December 2, 1889, the Interstate Fox Hunters Club held its first recorded trials at Waverly, Miss. The Puppy stake went to the Wild Goose Pack's Mounter, with the Avent Pack's Flora second and the Wild Goose Pack's Boston third. The Avent Pack's Rock won the Speed class, with the Wild Goose Pack's Callie Gates second and the Waverly Pack's Stonewall third. In the Hunting and Trailing class, Callie Gates took first honors, with Wild Goose Pack's Stonewall Jackson second, and the Waverly Pack's Truman third. High interest was centered in the Pack stake, won by the Wild Goose Pack with the Avent Pack second and the Willis Pack third. The Wild Goose Pack's Callie Gates was declared the best all-around foxhound.

Volume I of the National Fox Hunter's Association Stud Book, issued in 1898, shows that the first hound to be registered was Mack, a red hound (by Scott out of Minnie), owned by E. H. Walker, Hammack, Ky. Mack was whelped in 1883. Second registration honors went to Lizzie, a white, black, and tan, (by Abelard out of Patsy), whelped November 24, 1893, and owned by Strodes Valley Kennel Club, Winchester, Va.

More than 35,000 hounds have been individually registered in the International Fox Hunters' Stud Book since then, which represents only a minute portion of the foxhounds in this country. The vast majority of American foxhounds, while of pure hound blood and ancestry traceable for many generations, are, unfortunately, unregistered simply because the owners, keeping and hunting hounds for pleasure and with no thought of breeding them for profit, will not take the trouble to do so. There are, however, enough thoughtful breeders who want to improve and perpetuate the various strains that there is little danger of their separate identities becoming lost. Fortunately for the welfare of foxhound strains, this type of hunter is becoming more numerous. One has only to glance through a copy of *The Chase,* the "official" magazine of the breeder, to see the great amount of intense breeding interest existing today.

**Hunting.** There are three types of fox hunting in this country. First, in New England and in a few other sections, the fox is hunted with the gun and valued for his pelt probably more than for the sport he provides. Here, as in a great many other sections, the fox is considered vermin and whenever one falls before the hunter's gun, the gunner considers that he has done the upland game bird hunter a favor by exterminating a menace to feathered-game resources. True, the fox does occasionally catch a pheasant and can do real damage to poultry but lovers of the chase are quick to argue, and with good evidence, too, that Reynard is not so black as he is painted.

The New England fox hunter generally uses a single hound, comparatively slow and not too mouthy, but true-trailing and of great determination. It is his purpose to drive the fox around to his master's gun, the gunner taking his stand in known fox runs and choosing his hiding place by the direction of the chase. Such a hound should not press his quarry too closely for fear of causing him to leave his usual range. For this same reason a single hound is often better than a pair or a pack, for much noise will cause the fox to become too wary and the gunner may lose his chance for a shot. State-paid bounties on fox, as well as the value of his pelt, make fox hunting a profitable pastime in some sections, and good foxhounds, broken to the gun, are highly prized.

In the eastern states, and in some sections of Virginia, Maryland, and Kentucky, organized hunt clubs still ride to hounds in the orthodox English fashion. Good fox-hunting grounds are hard to find and expensive to maintain, as they must be properly paneled, gated, and gapped. Hunting fixtures are set for the season by the clubs at regular intervals and, in most instances, the customs and traditions of field etiquette are strictly observed. The packs are composed mainly of English hounds, or hounds heavy in English blood. These dogs must be amenable to discipline, as it is often necessary to "lift" them from one covert and "cast" them into another. The development of agriculture and dairying and the encroachment of the wire fence have restricted the grounds of many organized clubs, although there are quite a number who carry on in country where a good race is almost always assured. Others depend largely upon "drag" races for their sport.

Besides the two classes of fox hunters enumerated previously (pp. 153-154), there is a third class of fox hunter who far outnumbers the other two classes combined. He is found in greatest numbers in the southern states; his ranks are filled with planters, farmers, small-town businessmen, city dwellers, professional men, all drawn together by a common bond, the love of the chase. There are those who own one hound, or a couple or even a kennel full, but they all speak the same language and any person, of good deportment, who likes hounds and fox hunting is welcome at their meets, whether it be an informal gathering on a moonlit country hillside, or a hotly contested field trial with a state championship title at stake.

Most of the hunting of this group is done at night, for these are busy folk and many cannot afford to take off too much time from their daily pursuits. Then, too, in the South scenting conditions are generally better during the coolness of the night.

These sportsmen generally have no regular hunting dates, but go afield when the spirit moves them —and the spirit moves them often. To them the shooting of a fox is nothing short of an unpardonable sin and he who dares to commit such an act is certain to find himself quite unpopular among his neighbors.

Sometimes called "hilltoppers," these "hell-or-high-water" fox hunters gather in some rural section where foxes are known to range and cast their hounds in a common pack. Should some be latecomers, it is quite all right to put their dogs in the race even after the fox is up and going. The meet is strictly informal and the spirit of friendliness runs high. While there are no stated hunting dates, it is not uncommon for the same groups to gather at different locations as many as three nights a week during the autumn months. It does not take long for word to get around that so-and-so plans to hunt on such-and-such a night. Generally the farmers of the district have hounds of their own which they put in the pack, and those who are not owners join the hunt for the sport of it.

Night hunting across country from horseback is rather dangerous business, but in some sections where the wire fence does not present a problem to the hunters it is sometimes done when the moon is high. Most sections now have too many fences to afford satisfactory horseback hunting and the group generally goes to the meeting place in automobiles. When the chase is on they drive from vantage point to vantage point in order better to hear the music of the hounds and occasionally catch a glimpse of the hounds and, sometimes, the fox.

The conversation on these hunts is sometimes almost as enjoyable as the hunt itself, for every hunter is loyal to his own hounds and tall tales are told and wide exaggerations made during checks in the race. The sensitive hunter who cannot take good-natured, but sometimes irritating, banter, is out of place on these hunts.

From the ranks of these hunters comes the membership of the county, state, sectional, and national fox hunters' associations, and from these informal packs come many of the hounds which compete in the multitude of field trials held annually throughout the fox-hunting sections.

That fox hunting is a popular sport wherever Reynard, red or gray, is found is evidenced by the number of state organizations holding annual championship events. Some of these states are Missouri, Kentucky, Alabama, Ohio, Texas, Georgia, West Virginia, Maryland, Pennsylvania, New York, South Carolina, Connecticut, Arkansas, Florida, and Minnesota.

The recently formed Fox and Foxhound Protective Association, with headquarters at Rushville, Mo., is dedicated to the combating of propaganda which brands the fox as an important enemy to upland game-bird resources and seeks to exterminate him, thereby threatening the future of the sport of fox hunting. The fox, however, is not so easy to exterminate. He is a wary, cunning creature, well able to take care of himself, and wherever field mice and rabbits, his main diet, exist, he will very likely eke out an existence for generations to come.

**Characteristics.** The versatility of the foxhound is something at which to marvel. His accomplishments are so many that one might ask "When is a foxhound a foxhound?" The answer would be "When he is used for hunting foxes."

The foxhound can be trained to run almost anything which walks or runs and gives off scent. In the South, and in other sections, too, for that matter, foxhounds are probably used for hunting rabbits more than for any other species of game. The reason is that the rabbit is by far the most popular species of game in the South.

But the foxhound comes in for his share of praise as a tree-dog, also, and there are few good night-hunting sections where the foxhound does not prove his ability on raccoons and opossums. One should not expect a young foxhound, whose forbears have been used for fox hunting exclusively for generations, to develop into as proficient a tree-dog or take to coon and possum hunting as well as the old-fashioned black and tan, bluetick, or the redbone, which are specialists at this sport, but it has been done, many times.

Foxhounds are easily trained to run deer, and in the West they are extensively used in coyote and mountain lion hunting. Many trappers find them indispensable on the trapline and they have been used occasionally as sled dogs and beasts of burden.

One lover of foxhounds summed up this dog's versatility by saying, "A hound can do anything any other dog can do . . . if he just sets his mind to it."

A truly good foxhound possesses more qualities than any other domestic animal used for sport. He must have an amazing amount of endurance, more than the quarry he seeks. He must have a better nose than any other sporting dog, exceptional speed, good, free cry, strength to carry him through heavy coverts and over rugged country, the agility to negotiate any sort of terrain quickly, and remarkable intelligence. In addition he must possess determination in a high degree, a high desire to reach his quarry, and the gameness and stamina to match his determination. He must be willing to "pack up" or run with the pack, "harking in" immediately when another casting member of the pack "speaks" the trail. And he must possess that mysterious quality which has brought so many wandering hounds home, a homing instinct.

This is, indeed, a large package, yet it is wrapped up in countless blocks of hound hide wherever hounds are bred and hunted.

To possess strength, speed, and stamina a hound must be physically "right." He must have sufficient bone on which to hang muscle, but not so much that it will become burdensome. His legs must be free and swing like pendulums, his shoulders and pastern joints not so straight as to give any jar, and feet which are strong and closely knit, but sufficiently flexible to withstand long and hard travel without lameness. His pads should be strong and cushiony. In other words, a foxhound's build should lend itself to the utmost physical ease in action.

No other sporting dog possesses anything like the great endurance of the foxhound. Many bird dogs are practically exhausted after a 3-hour field trial heat. True, they were running at top speed most of the time. But a 3-hour race over rough country is nothing unusual for a pack of foxhounds.

There have been many instances of unusual gameness and stamina among foxhounds. One which bears repeating here, is that of Scout, a Trigg hound owned by Mr. Robert Rodes of Bowling Green, Ky. Scout was entered in the First Chase Futurity, held at Crab Orchard, Ky., in 1921. The event was scheduled for three days but lasted five. Two days before the field trials, Scout was caught in a steel trap and, despite earnest ministrations, went to the field trials lame. Scout won the event over a large field of splendid hounds, surpassing in every department, although he ran practically on three legs during the five days of continuous competition.

The homing instinct of a foxhound is something at which to marvel. Practically every hound owner has seen remarkable demonstrations of this quality among his own hounds. Years ago Judge C. Floyd Huff, of Hot Springs, Ark., was attending a field trial in Kentucky. On the last day of the running, Seminole, an Arkansas Traveler bitch, which had been high scorer throughout the event, disappeared in a race. Judge Huff hunted for her several days unsuccessfully and returned home. Six months later, Seminole, reduced almost to skin and bones, staggered into his kennel yard.

Some of the common faults of foxhounds are jealousy, babbling, skirting or cutting, and dwelling. Occasionally a hound, finding himself consistently outpaced by other members of the pack, will become jealous to the point of surliness and start "cutting" or refuse to hunt. Skirting or cutting is a form of jealousy. In his desire to run at the head of the pack, a hound of this habit will run wide of the line, gambling on picking it up on a turn ahead of the pack. There is no cure for this fault. "Babbling" is giving cry through nervousness or exuberance when not on trail. "Dwelling" is lingering on the scent after the pack has gone ahead.

Foxhounds come in a variety of colors. It has been said, with great truth, too, that a good hound cannot have a bad color. A pack of hounds matched for color is a beautiful sight, but the breeder who places much stress of color makes a serious mistake. Most common colors are black, white and tan, black and tan, red, white and lemon, blue-mottled with black and tan, fawn, and light red.

For versatility, stamina, nose, natural hunting intelligence, and gameness the foxhound knows no superior in the American sporting dog scene. Running the trail hour after hour, with seldom or never a glimpse of his quarry, the foxhound gives his best in the sheer joy of the chase.

For description and standards, see "Walker Hound."

**Breeders.** Foxhounds are bred and raised in almost every state in the Union, not necessarily for fox hunting exclusively, for the versatility of the hound is great. It is not possible to list many of the breeders of the various strains in this article but a few of the well-known fanciers and authorities deserve mention:

*Walker strain:* Woods Walker, Paint Lick, Ky., Ed Power, Frankfort, Ky.; Roger Stone, Lexington, Ky.; S. L. Wooldridge, Jr., Versailles, Ky.; Robert Goode, Gastonburg, Ala.; J. Wade Walker, Paint Lick, Ky.; Jack Malone, Portersville, Ala.; and Alex Parrish, Richmond, Ky. *Trigg strain:* Robert Rodes, Bowling Green, Ky.; J. S. Kriby, Bowling Green, Ky.; L. S. McMillian, Laurens, S. C.; and Paul Greer, Glasgow, Ky. *Spalding-Norris strain:* Ralph Wingo, Monroe City, Mo. *Goodman strain:* John H. Allen, Iuka, Miss.; Tom Davis, Hazelwood, N. C.; and Hughes Atkinson, Owingsville, Ky. *July strain:* E. Burton Cooke, Asheville, N. C. *Trumbo strain:* Glenn Sutton, Hurley, N. M.; and John W. Scott, Shelbyville, Ind.

# GERMAN SHORT-HAIRED POINTER

In the American gun-dog kennel there is a dog to fit the individual tastes and requirements of every upland game bird gunner. Whether his desires run to a wide-ranging, high-stepping, swashbuckling ground-coverer or to a close-working, careful plodder that is amenable to his owner's every command, there is a dog to fill the bill if the gunner will only take the time to look for it.

**History.** A comparative newcomer to America, the German short-haired pointer is fairly made to order for the sportsman who prefers to take his hunting in a somewhat leisurely manner and needs a pointing dog with a choke-bore nose, medium range, and moderate speed. If the gunner wants to combine a bit of waterfowling along with his upland game shooting, he will do well to give the German serious consideration. For a combined job of pointing game and retrieving from land and water, the German short-haired pointer takes a back seat for no dog. But if he wants great speed and high style on point along with the rest he must look elsewhere, for this dog goes about his job in the fashion of the true workman he is—all business, with no fancy frills.

As his name implies, the German short-haired pointer originated in Germany. The basic stock of the breed was the old Spanish pointer. A cross with the bloodhound brought more nose, greater intelligence, and better trailing ability. The cross also brought bigger bone, greater size, and less speed. This dog was not entirely satisfactory, and so a cross on the foxhound was used, which added the speed but probably diminished the pointing instinct. So again new blood was brought in, this time the English pointer providing it. After several generations of careful selective breeding, the patient and thorough German breeders had the dog they were seeking—a dog of great versatility, able and willing to track down ground game with the gameness and keen nose of the hound, to point instinctively his feathered game with the sure location and stanchness of the pointer and setter and, in addition, with the strength and fortitude to brave rough and icy water in retrieving wildfowl. The German short-haired pointer possesses all three traits.

**Characteristics.** The versatility of this dog is attracting considerable attention among American sportsmen and he is growing in popularity. In Minnesota, Michigan, and near-by states where a varied game supply allows full use of this capabilities, he is in great demand. The average German short-haired pointer owner is generally unwilling to admit that the big fellow has any superior as an all-around gundog. Generally the jack-of-all-trades is a master of none, and so it might be with this dog—but you should be sure of your own dog before you challenge the owner of a German short-hair to a rough-and-tumble, catch-as-catch-can game-getting contest on feather and fur, with retrieving ability to count.

The short-hair is not a fast dog. His rugged, somewhat bulky make-up prevents him from being as speedy as his smaller, more wiry rivals. And, too, he is not intended for speed, for it is the nature of this dog to work his ground carefully and pick up, with his keen nose, the faintest scent, working it out to a contract with game. His excellent nose causes him to carry a rather low head generally, although when scenting conditions are good he travels with it held high. On point he is intense enough, though many are inclined to crouch to some extent, apparently in an endeavor to make their bulk as inconspicuous to game as possible.

The German short-hair is a dog of an exceedingly kind and mild disposition, seldom quarrelsome but more than capable of holding his own with a more pugnacious opponent.

In open field trial competitions the German short-hair seldom appears, due largely to the fact that he is outclassed in speed and range by the better pointers and setters. He does show up occasionally in shooting-dog stakes and generally gives a good account of himself.

There are, however, several breed trials in the country and exponents of the breed are growing more interested in this form of breed display and promotion. Several German short-haired pointer field trials have been held here sponsored by the mother club, the German Short-haired Pointer Club of America, with headquarters in Minneapolis, and those sponsored by the German Short-haired Pointer Club of Michigan, at Detroit. All trials are conducted under the rules of the American Kennel Club and field trial championship points are awarded the winners.

These trials are one-course affairs, and unlike the usual bird dog field trials, are conducted under a point-awarding system. For instance, to place first in an Open All-Age stake a dog must be awarded at least a total of 75 points in four categories by the judges. The number of points may be reduced at the discretion of the judges and are awarded on the following basis: run a good ground heat and hunt the cover where birds are likely to be found, 40; locate and point a game bird during the time allotted to him, 25; be steady to points, shot, and wing, 45; back, 15; general handling, 15.

Another feature of German short-hair field trials which is not seen in other pointing dog contests is the presence of a "center line" in the field where birds are planted. On entering the bird field, the handler must keep on the center line until his dog comes on point. After he has flushed the bird, shot, and sent his dog on, the handler must return to the center line. This is to prevent handlers from guiding their dogs up to places where birds are likely to be planted. Thus the dog must show independence in his hunting.

To get a good idea of how the German short-haired pointer performs in the field, with the exception of retrieving, one has only to attend one of these trials, held in the spring and fall. They have done very fine work at these events and perform equally well in the field. The man who hunts on foot and wants a tractable dog of medium range for combination shooting will do well to consider the short-hair. He might need to look no further.

**Description and Standards.** HEAD: Skull long and broad, slightly rounded, with well-defined stop. Slight furrow between eyes, not so deep as on the English pointer, nor is the occiput and the start of the neck so distinct as in the English. Muzzle sufficiently long to enable the dog to pick up and carry game for a long distance. Muzzle should not be snipy, but should be square. Jaws should be of equal length, teeth evenly matched. Nose solid brown. Ears placed rather high, have short soft coat, medium long, and not too thin or too thick in leather; hung close to the cheeks, slightly folded, and should somewhat resemble the hound's in appearance. Eyes, soft and of medium size, varying in shades of brown or olive to harmonize with coat, neither protruding nor too deep set. Lips well developed and slightly pendulous.

NECK: Moderately long, muscular, and slightly arched, and larger toward the shoulders. Moderate houndlike throatiness permitted.

SHOULDERS AND CHEST: Shoulders should be muscular, oblique, moderately wide, with top of blades close. Chest deep and wide. Ribs deep and well sprung.

BODY: Back should be short and strong with slight rise to top of shoulders. Loin of moderate length, slightly arched. Body well tucked. Hips rather wide,

PLATE X. German Short-haired Pointer: Int. Ch. Searching Wind Bob.

which should fall slightly toward tail in graceful curve. Tail should be docked, leaving two-fifths of length. Quarters should denote strength and field stamina with agility.

LEGS AND FEET: Legs should be straight in front, muscular and well boned. Elbows well let down and should turn neither in nor out. Hind legs strongly muscled with stifles well bent. Hocks square with the body and slightly bent. Both front and back pasterns should be strong and nearly upright. Feet should be round, turn neither in nor out, close, deep, well padded, and toes well arched and heavily nailed.

COAT: Should be short, flat, and firm.

WEIGHT AND HEIGHT: Dogs 55 to 70 pounds and bitches 45 to 60 pounds. Height: dogs 23 to 25 inches and bitches 21 to 23 inches at the shoulders. Symmetry and field quality are most essential. A dog well balanced in all points is preferable to one with outstanding good qualities and defects. A smooth, lithe gait is most desirable.

COLOR: Solid liver, liver and white spotted, liver and white spotted and ticked, liver and white ticked. Any colors other than liver and white not permitted.

FAULTS: Bone structure too clumsy or too light. Head too large. Too many wrinkles in forehead. Dish-faced. Snipy muzzle. Ears too long, pointy, or fleshy. Flesh-colored nose. Eyes too light, too round, or too closely set together. Cowhocks. Feet or elbows turned inward or outward. Down on pasterns. Loose shoulders, swayback. Black coat or tri-colored. Any colors except liver or some combination of liver and white.

No numerical scale of points has yet been adopted.

**Breeders.** A few of the well known breeders are:

Schwarenberg Kennels (Jack Shattuck), Minneapolis, Minn.; Searching Wind Kennels (Dr. and Mrs. Zahala), Minneapolis, Minn.; Mr. William Olson, Minneapolis, Minn.; Dr. Clarke Lemley, Detroit, Mich.; William Ehrler, Mt. Clemens, Mich.; Dr. Lewis Kline, Detroit, Mich.; Leland Kennels, Aurora, Ill.; and Quality Lane Kennels, Augusta, Wis.

# GOLDEN RETRIEVER

**History.** The Golden Retriever enjoys a rather unique introduction to the shooting field. In the year 1860 Sir Dudley Majoribanks visited a circus at Brighton, England, and saw the immediate ancestors of the Golden. The circus was featuring a troupe of Russian performing dogs. The feats accomplished by these dogs so impressed Sir Dudley that after the show he made an effort to purchase a pair of them, and approached the Russian trainer. The trainer, however, refused to sell a pair, on the grounds that it would spoil his act. Sir Dudley, however, had been so impressed by the performance of these dogs and their intelligence that he made an offer for the entire troupe of eight. The trainer accepted and the deal was accomplished. This proved a fortunate purchase, for he now had enough stock and variety of blood lines to try some extensive breeding.

These dogs were called Russian Trackers, and came from a very old breed that had served the usual variety of purposes in its original home in Asiatic Russia. One of the chief uses of the Russian Tracker was as a guardian for flocks of sheep, and he was admirably suited to withstand the rigors of the severe winters in the Caucasus Mountains where he made his home.

The Russian Tracker was a much larger dog than his descendant, the Golden Retriever. The original breed measured 30 inches at the shoulder and often weighed as much as 100 pounds. Today, the males weigh from 65 to 68 pounds, the bitches from 55 to 60 pounds. Sir Dudley established these dogs at his Scottish seat in the Guisachan deer forest in Ivernessshire, Scotland. He bred these dogs without outcrossing for ten years. As the original eight dogs were much larger than what is now known as the Golden Retriever, many sportsmen considered them too cumbersome, and so around 1870 Sir Dudley decided to try an outcross. It is on record that he did cross them in 1870 with the bloodhound. As far as is known, this is the only cross perpetuated, and this only once. This reduced the breed to its present size, increased the scenting powers, and developed a more refined texture of coat, slightly darker in color.

**Development.** It was not until 1911 that these dogs were recognized by the English Kennel Club as a separate breed. At that time, Mrs. W. M. Charlesworth formed the Golden Retriever Club of England, and through this body, official recognition was obtained from the Kennel Club to register them as a separate breed.

According to W. M. Charlesworth's *The Golden Retriever; History, Breeding, and Management,* the first time a Golden was exhibited at a show was around 1908 or 1909 by the late Lord Harcourt of Nuneham. The first Goldens to compete in open field trials were owned by Captain H. F. H. Hardy and W. M. Charlesworth. This was in the year 1912. Captain Hardy was the first to gain honors with his Golden Vizie.

There is no doubt that the first purebred Golden Retrievers imported to this continent were brought out by retired British army officers about 1900, to Vancouver Island and Victoria, B. C. This fact has been verified by various old settlers there, although there is no Kennel Registration proof as neither the Canadian Kennel Club nor the American Kennel Club had recognized them as a separate breed at that time. These Vancouver Island Golden Retrievers spread up and down the coast, some of them reaching Alaska.

The first serious breeder of Goldens that we know of on this continent was the late Bart Armstrong, of Winnipeg, Manitoba. Solely through Mr. Armstrong's efforts, the Golden Retriever was finally recognized in Canada as a separate breed in 1927, and the Secretary-Treasurer of the Canadian Kennel Club, the late Mr. J. D. Strachen, was instructed to have Goldens separately classified in the list of breeds. The American Kennel Club did not follow suit until some time in 1932. Mr. Armstrong, at this time, owned the Gilnockie Kennels, registered both in the Canadian and American Kennel Clubs. He was not, however, very successful in popularizing Golden Retrievers, as they were a new breed, and there is very little of his original bloodlines in the winning dogs of today.

Shortly after World War I, Mr. S. S. Magoffin, of the Rockhaven Kennels, North Vancouver, B. C., and Englewood, Colo., became interested in Golden Retrievers. His first importation was Speedwell Pluto, who developed into a first-class gun-dog and proved a tremendous influence at stud in transmitting his qualities to his progeny. He later imported Saffron Chipmonk, Chiltington Light, and Wilderness Tangerine from England. It was such dogs as these that laid the foundation from which our present-day Goldens are built. In the East, the late Dr. Charles H. Large of New York City started breeding at the same time as did Mr. Magoffin. His kennel prefix was known as Frantelle, now owned by Mr. M. A. Clemens.

The first Golden Retriever to obtain the title of Field Trial Champion in this country was Rip, owned by Paul Bakewell III of St. Louis, Mo. Rip came into the title in December 1939. Rip, who has now gone to his last resting place, will always be remembered as a great dog. Rip was not only the first Golden to win his Field Trial Championship, but he also won the Field and Stream Trophy in 1939 and 1940 for the outstanding Retriever of the year—the only Golden to duplicate this award.

The first Golden Retriever bitch to win her Field Trial Championship was Banty of Woodend, owned by W. J. Nickerson of Wayzata, Minn. Banty was another who worked hard for this title and deserved it.

The first Dual Champion was Stilrovin Rips Pride, owned by Kingswere Kennels, Winona, Minn. Rips Pride did not live long to enjoy this honor, as he passed away shortly afterward while undergoing an operation.

The next to become a Dual Champion was Tonkahof Esther Belle, also owned by Kingswere Kennels.

Field Trial Champion Stilrovin Nitro Express, owned by Mr. Ben Boalt, Milwaukee, Wis., added Dual to his name a short time ago, which makes him the only living Dual Champion Golden Retriever male in America today.

Four Goldens enjoy the honor of Best in Show awards in this country. The first to gain this distinction was Canadian and American Champion

Courtesy Kingswere Kennels, Winona, Minn.

PLATE XI. Golden Retriever: Dual Ch. Rips Pride.

Speedwell Pluto, owned by Mr. S. S. Magoffin. Pluto won his award at the Puget Sound Kennel Club Show, December 2-3, 1933. Next came Champion Toby of Willow Loch, owned by J. S. Thompson, Jr. He went Best in Show at the St. Paul Kennel Club, April 16-17, 1938. On April 7, 1945, Champion Tonkahof Bang, owned by J. MacGaheran and H. W. Norton, went Best in Show at the St. Paul Kennel Club. The only Golden ever to duplicate this honor is Ch. Czar of Wildwood, owned by Eric S. Johnson. Czar won his first Best in Show at the Golden Gate Kennel Club, Feb. 2-3, 1946. He repeated this at the King County Kennel Club show, August 11, 1946, and again at the San Gabriel Kennel Club Show on August 10, 1947.

At the present time, the Golden Retrievers' record stands at 16 Field Trial Champions, 55 Bench Champions, and 3 Dual Champions. There were 994 Goldens registered by the A.K.C. in 1946 against 20 in 1932. The Golden Retriever has not gained this high position without stiff competition from the other two most popular Retriever breeds, namely, the Chesapeake Bay and Labrador.

There were 1736 Labradors registered in 1946, giving the Labrador numerical strength over the Golden. However, with these heavy odds against him, he has more than held his own on the bench and in the field. He is a great favorite all through the West. This is easily understood in view of the fact that the West is the hunter's paradise. He has proved to the hunter since 1932 that he has everything that a good Retriever should have. First of all, his great love for his work endears him to his master. His stamina, nose, tender mouth, and sagacity are only a few of the fine qualities that go to distinguish the Golden Retriever as an outstanding sportsman. As a companion he has few equals. He is not aggressive—yet he is not a coward; he is most loyal and trustworthy. His intelligence goes without question. This fact, coupled with his love for his work, makes him an easy dog to train. There is still another field in which the Golden has proved his intelligence and amiability, namely, obedience classes. This is a large field today, and is one of the most popular attractions at most shows. The two outstanding Goldens in this division are Goldwood Toby CDX and Goldwood Michael CDX.

The foregoing record shows that the Golden is a utility dog and not just a figurehead in the sporting world. The high position that he holds in the sporting world today, he has won on his merit.

**Description and Standards.**[1] GENERAL APPEARANCE: Should be a symmetrical, active, powerful dog, a good level mover, sound and well put together, with a kindly expression, not clumsy or long in the leg.

HEAD: Broad in skull, well set on a clean and mus-

[1] By courtesy of The Golden Retriever Club of America.

cular neck, muzzle powerful and wide, not weak jawed, good stop. *Eyes:* Dark and set well apart, very kindly in expression with dark rims. *Teeth:* Even, neither under nor overshot.

COLOR: Rich golden, must not be as dark as an Irish red setter or cream color. The presence of a few white hairs on chest permissible, but white collar, feet, toes, or blaze to be penalized.

COAT: Must be flat or wavy, good undercoat, dense and water resisting.

EARS: Small and well set on.

FEET: Round and catlike, must not open or splay.

FORELEGS: Straight, with good bone.

HINDLEGS: Strong and muscular, well-bent stifles.

HOCKS: Well let down, not cowhocked.

NOSE: Should be black, but a light-colored nose should not debar from honors a dog who is good in all other respects.

TAIL: Should be straight, not curled at tip or carried over the back.

BODY: Well balanced, short coupled, and deep through the heart. Loins must be strong, back ribs must be deep and strong with good second thighs; shoulders must be well laid back and long in the blade.

WEIGHT AND SIZE: The ideal weights for adult dogs and bitches in good, hard condition should be: Dogs, 65-68 lbs.; bitches, 55-60 lbs.; and heights at shoulder: Dogs, 23-24 inches; bitches 20½-22 inches.

SCALE OF POINTS:

| | |
|---|---|
| Head | 20 |
| Color | 10 |
| Coat | 5 |
| Ears | 5 |
| Feet | 10 |
| Forelegs | 10 |
| Hindlegs | 10 |
| Hocks | 10 |
| Nose | 5 |
| Tail | 5 |
| Body | 25 |
| TOTAL | 115 |

# GORDON SETTER

"What has become of the Gordon setter?" This is a question frequently asked of every writer on canine topics, and a rather difficult one to answer to the inquirer's satisfaction. Yet there is a definite reason for the comparative scarcity of the Gordon and his somewhat dubious standing as a field dog.

The wearer of the tan-trimmed ebony-hued coat, once the darling of the ruffed grouse and woodcock covers and a fair favorite in the quail fields, has lost little of his imposing appearance, but many, probably the majority, of the breed members in this country today go through life without ever having enjoyed the intoxicating thrill of upland game bird scent or heard the cracking report of a fowling-piece. Yet there was a time when the Gordon setter knew no peer as a cover-working gun-dog.

"Frank Forester" wrote thrillingly about the outstanding field abilities of a brace of Gordons which hunted to his gun in his favorite New York-New Jersey covers and on the marshy snipe flats of the Eastern Shore. He fairly sang their praises to the housetops, and many other sportsmen of his day preferred the Black and Tans to all other pointing dogs.

It is indeed a rare day now when one comes across a fellow-gunner depending upon a Gordon setter to find his game. True, the dog will hunt, has a good nose, and will point. But his English cousin and his Irish neighbor so far surpass him in dash, ambition, determination, and all-around "class" that the field merits of his breed are hardly to be compared with those of the other long-haired clans.

**Characteristics.** The Gordon today might be called a "collection piece" in the dog world. Like collectors of antique furniture, unusual objects of art, ancient armor, etc., there are always certain people who like to own "something different." Dog fanciers are no exception to this rule, and some people have "taken on" the Gordon setter simply because he is now a rather rare animal of great beauty—forgetting, overlooking, or caring little about his utilitarian capabilities. Those owners seldom take him afield except for casual walks or to give him the exercise necessary to round him into what is called "show condition." Such breeders are largely responsible for the Gordon setter's decline in popularity as a gun-dog, for they have bred for a type which could hardly do an acceptable day's work in the field under present conditions. While the present accepted standard calls for a rather racily built, medium-sized dog of clean setter type, comparatively few of the specimens of today could approach that ideal.

There are, however, serious-minded breeders among the Gordon setter fanciers who are earnestly trying to promote more interest in the dog as he was originally intended, an asset to the hunt and an adjunct to the sportsman's gun. In these days of short game supplies they are having added difficulties, for the Gordon is not a fast dog but a rather slow one, as a rule, and his range is generally restricted. With game as scarce as it is the modern top-flight gun-dog must be a hustler from the word "go"; not only must he work his ground thoroughly, but he must cover a lot of it at a fast clip if he is to give his owner a fair number of shooting chances.

There are other reasons why the Gordon setter does not enjoy high favor among the gunning public. As stated above, he is a rather slow dog and somewhat methodical, even to the point of being phlegmatic, in his work. He is, however, thorough and goes about his work in a businesslike manner.

His black and tan color, strikingly handsome as it is in the show-ring, works against him to some extent in the field. It makes him rather hard to see in heavy cover—and it is in heavy cover that the Gordon does his best work.

Even his splendidly loyal disposition may handicap him at times. The Gordon is generally very much a one-man dog. He is exceedingly loyal to his owner or trainer and when professionally trained often finds it difficult to adjust himself to a new "boss" when returned to his owner. His loyalty is indeed an admirable trait, but his desire for his master's companionship should not interfere with his ambition to hunt.

These characteristics, however, should not weigh too heavily against the dog, for he has many other good qualities. His handsome and shiny coat of black, set off with its trimmings of mahogany tan,

Courtesy W. Brown, Forest Hills, N. Y.

PLATE XII. Gordon Setter: Ch. Blakeen Saegryte.

makes a pretty picture in the field or before the fireside. While the dog is not particularly lofty in action he is attractive enough to catch the eye. He possesses a splendid nose, and, given the opportunity to use it, can prove his worth in this respect. He is quite a tractable dog and takes to training quickly and kindly. He makes a good retriever from land or water.

There are some specimens which show dash and verve comparable to the English setter. It is to these individuals that Gordon setter fanciers should turn if they are to improve the breed's hunting qualities and restore him to gunning favor. Unfortunately for the breed, however, too many fanciers are more interested in the Gordon's ornamental features and prefer to keep him as a pet and show dog. It has been a good many years since the Gordon played any considerable part in field trials. The Gordons of today just do not, as a rule, have that snap and dash so necessary in the makeup of a successful field trial contender.

The Gordon setter gets his name from the Duke of Gordon, at whose castle kennels the breed is supposed, by some, to have originated. This is a disputed question, for it is known that quite a few wealthy Scottish sportsmen were breeding black-and-tan setters at about the same time, and even before, the Duke of Gordon showed his preference for setters of that color.

The Duke of Gordon is said to have used a collie bitch named Maddy in his breeding operations. Maddy is reported to have been an exceptionally intelligent dog of extreme "birdiness." She did not actually "point" her game but stopped upon some game scent and "watched," as writers of that day described her actions. Whatever influence Maddy might have exercised upon the breed has long since been dissipated, and the Gordon can now claim as much "legitimacy" as any other of the sporting breeds.

The Gordon setter is an old-established member of bird-dogdom's aristocracy. In the eyes of many of us who admire and value bird dogs for their field qualities above all else the Gordon is not getting a fair deal from present exponents of the breed in this country. He deserves a much better break and, given it, will take his rightful place among American gun-dogs.

**Description and Standards.** GENERAL IMPRESSION: A stylish, rather racy built, medium size, muscular dog of clean setter type, usual length legs and of symmetrical conformation throughout. Strong fairly short back and short tail, a fine head, clearly lined, intelligent expression, clear colors and straight or slightly waved coat.

SIZE: Shoulder height for males 22 to 25 inches; females, 21 to 24 inches.

HEAD: Deep rather than broad with plenty of brain room, nicely rounded, good-sized skull, broadest between the ears. The head should have a clearly indicated stop. Below and above the eyes should be lean and the cheek as narrow as the leanness of the head allows. The muzzle fairly long with almost parallel lines and not pointed either as seen from above or from the side. Flews not pendulous but with clearly indicated lips. The nose big, broad, with open nostrils and of black color.

Eyes: Of fair size, neither too deep set nor too bulging, dark brown, bright and wise.

Ears: Set low on the head, fairly large and thin.

Neck: Long, lean, arched to the head and without throatiness.

Shoulders: Long shoulder blades, lying close to the chest and not going above the back line of the neck.

Chest: Deep and not too broad in front; the ribs well sprung, leaving plenty of lung room.

Forelegs: Big boned, straight, not bowed either in or out, with elbows free, well let down, and not inclined either in or out.

Hindlegs: The hindlegs from hip to hock should be long, flat, and muscular, from hock to heel short and strong. The stifle and hock joints well bent, and not inclined either in or out.

Feet: Both fore and hind feet should have close-knit, well-arched toes with plenty of hair between with full toe pads and deep heel cushions.

Tail: Short; should not reach below the hocks, carried horizontal or nearly so, thick at the root and finishing in a fine point. The feather, which starts near the root of tail, should be straight, have a three-square appearance, growing shorter uniformly toward the end.

Coat: Should be soft and shining, resembling silk, straight or slightly waved but not curly, with long hair on ears, under the stomach and on chest, on back of the fore and hindlegs down to the feet.

Color and Markings: Deep, shining, coal black with tan markings, either of rich chestnut or mahogany red color. The tan should be shining and not dull, yellowish, or straw color, and not mixed with black hairs. Black penciling allowed on toes. The border lines between black and tan colors should be clearly defined. There should be no tan hairs mixed in the black.

Tan Markings: (1) Two clear spots over the eyes not over ¾ inch in diameter. (2) On the sides of the muzzle, the tan should not reach above the base of nose resembling a stripe around the end of the muzzle from one side to the other. (3) On the throat. (4) Two large, clear spots on the chest. (5) On the inside of the hindlegs and inside of thighs showing down the front of the stifle and broadening out to the outside of the hindlegs from the hock to the toes. It must, however, not completely eliminate the black on the back of hindlegs. (6) On the forelegs from the knees or a little above downward to the toes. (7) Around the vent.—A white spot on chest is allowed, but the smaller the better.

Faults. *General Impression:* Unintelligent appearance. The bloodhound type with heavy and big head and ears and clumsy body; also the collie type with its pointed muzzle and curved tail. *Head:* Pointed, snipy, dropping or upturned muzzle, too small or large mouth. *Eyes:* Too light in color, too deep set, or too prominent. *Ears:* Set too high or unusually broad or heavy. *Neck:* Thick and short. *Shoulders and Back:* Irregularly formed. *Chest:* Too broad. *Legs and Feet:* Crooked legs. Outturned elbows. Toes scattered; flat footed. *Tail:* Too long, badly carried, or hooked at the end. *Coat:* Curly like wool, not shining. *Color:* Yellow or straw-colored tan or without clearly defined lines between the different colors. White feet. Too much white on the chest. In the black there must be no tan hairs.

No numerical point standard has yet been set up.

# IRISH SETTER

If one took the time to canvass almost any group of bird-dog fanciers, he would find that a goodly percentage would say, "The first gun-dog I ever owned was an Irish setter." This will be hardly true of the sportsmen of the next generation, but that is not the Irish setter's fault. It is, rather, because the beauty of this breed has caused it to become the darling of the bench show sporting-dog world—so much so that its sterling field qualities have been sadly neglected by too many people, who have grown to love the red dog for his beauty alone.

His great popularity on the bench has caused many newcomers to the sport of upland game shooting to labor under the misconception that the Irish setter is a thing of beauty only and a second-rate gun-dog at best. Fortunately for the breed, there are a few breeders who know that this is not true and through their own breeding programs are proving that this dog can still take his place alongside the English setter and the pointer in the niches set aside for pleasant and efficient gunning companions.

Recent showings of some of these dogs in field trial competitions, running on even terms with their English cousins and the short-hairs, offer fairly potent evidence that the standing of the Irish setter is definitely improving in the eyes of sportsmen. It is true that the number of Irish setters competing in present-day field trials is comparatively small, but if present breeding tendencies continue his position in this sport is likely to be improved in the next few years.

Although this dog does not shine with consistent brilliancy in field trials he takes his place in the winner's circle often enough to prove that, despite his bench show popularity, he is definitely *in* the gun-dog picture and is certainly not *out* of the field trial scene. In thousands of towns and communities will be found a red dog or two which, perhaps without benefit of extended pedigree, uphold the traditions of field excellence left him by his ancestors.

**History.** Now hailed as the most beautiful sporting dog, the Irish setter was not always the solid-red-coated animal we know today. Most of the original Irish setters were red and white, with red predominating, and even today a bit of white on the breast or toes is not exactly uncommon.

In earlier days he was a great favorite because he was a general-purpose dog. Rough and rugged, he did a good job for the gunner, whether pointing quail, grouse or woodcock, or retrieving ducks from icy waters. The flashy Llewellin setters came into

Courtesy E. M. Berolzheimer, Tarrytown, N. Y.

**Plate XIII.** Irish Setter: Rufus McTybe O'Cloisters.

vogue along in the eighties and became quite the fashion. With this, and the rise of the pointer, the Irish setter was placed somewhat in the gun-dog background and most of the breeding stock fell into the hands of men who cared for their dogs more for their private shooting or bench shows rather than for engaging in field competitions.

In the early days of field trials, however, Irish setters played an important part. In 1876 an imported dog, Erin, won the Greenwood Stake of the Tennessee State Sportsmen's Association trials, which were held near Memphis. These were the third trials in the history of the sport.

A year later, Berkely, the son of Elcho and Lou II, won second in the puppy stake and Carrie, a bitch owned by the late Jesse Sherwood, was third. In the next trials of the Tennessee State Sportsmen's Association, Champ was second and Ida, Jr., a daughter of Erin and Ida, was third. First in the Championship Stake went to Joe, Jr., the son of Elcho and the Campbell bitch, Buck, Jr. In a match endurance race between Joe, Jr., and Gladstone, most prominent English setter of his day and one of the fountainheads of the field trial strain, Joe, Jr., emerged the winner. The race was for $1000 and lasted from sunrise to sunset for two days. It was judged on the number of actual points scored on game birds. Joe, Jr., had 61 points to Gladstone's 52.

Space will not permit a recounting of Irish setter achievements in early field trials; suffice it to say that the breed garnered a surprising number of places, considering the limited number of representatives competing.

Elcho might properly be considered the fountainhead of the breed in this country. He probably had more influence than any of the earlier importations and there are few pedigrees of the present day which do not contain the name of this great individual. Elcho, a second-place winner in the Irish setter class at the Dublin show, was brought to this country by Charles H. Turner of St. Louis. His bench show career in this country was a succession of victories.

No account of the Irish setter would be complete without mention of the late Otto Pohl of Fremont, Nebr. During his career in the early part of the century, Mr. Pohl gathered together a remarkable kennel of red dogs which, for a combination of bench and field quality, were not to be equaled. Some of his well-known dogs were Drug Law, Pat-A-Belle, Rheola Clanderrick, and Morty Oge. His famous field trial winning bitch, Donegal's Alizon, won the cup offered to the best setter with a field trial record awarded by Bob Weil, owner of National Champion Joe Muncie, an English setter. This was at the Dayton show in 1918. Her victory at Dayton the following year was even greater than that, for she won the "Master Benson" trophy, offered by the noted sportsman, Harry D. Kirkover, to the best pointer, English, Irish, or Gordon setter with a field trial record.

Another sportsman who did much for the Irish setter was Elias C. Vail, of Ridgefield, Conn. Mr. Vail's Modoc Bedelia won a number of places in field trials, the most important of which was a place in the trials of the English Setter Club of America, at Medford, N. J., in 1924. Competition at this club is usually exceedingly keen, many famous field trial dogs having started their careers on these grounds, and not until 22 years later did another Irish setter place in these events. This, appropriately enough, was Rufus McTybe O'Cloisters, a great grandson of Bedelia, owned by Edwin M. Berolzheimer.

Mr. Vail also had good success with Elcova's Kinkie, Elcova's Admiration and Elcova's Terence McSwimey, running them against pointers and English setters.

Among other prominent breeders, some of them now deceased, were:

Dr. G. G. Davis, of Philadelphia; Walter Arnold, Westfield, N. J.; William Cary Duncan, North Brookfield, Mass.; Dr. W. C. Ellis, Orange, N. J.; John Cuneo, Boston, Mass.; Dr. G. S. Currier, New York; John Neff, executive director of the American Kennel Club; F. J. Lefferdink, Hickman, Nebr.; Ben M. Curtis, Tulsa, Okla.; H. A. Simms, New Britain, Conn.; Patrick Hehir, Worcester, Mass.; E. D. Levering, Ruxton, Md.; Judge T. M. Marshall, Pittsburgh; A. Bush, Williamsport, Pa.; R. B. Wheeler, Bridgewater, Mass.; William Monan, Blasdell, N. Y.; and R. J. Branstetter, Seattle, Wash.

The outstanding breeder of field-working Irish setters in the country today is Edwin M. Berolzheimer, Tarrytown, N. Y., and Ridgeland, S. C. Mr. Berolzheimer maintains a considerable breeding establishment at his New York home, The Cloisters, and his "O'Cloisters" suffix is familiar to every Irish setter fancier. He hunts over his dogs on his southern plantation each season and campaigns them fearlessly on the eastern field trial circuit. His famous performer, Rufus McTybe O'Cloisters, considered by authorities as the best field trial Irish setter in the country today, has won in the hot competition of the South.

Mr. Berolzheimer has had his share of bench show wins, but is more concerned with the development of the field qualities of the breed. If the breed had a few more champions of the same caliber as Mr. Berolzheimer, who would strive as earnestly for breed improvement, the Irish setter would soon become a more serious contender for field trial and field honors.

Among Mr. Berolzheimer's more prominent field trial winners are Elcova McTybe, the only dog to win first place in the All-Age stake of the trials of the Irish Setter Club of America three times, Shaun McTybe O'Cloisters, a 14-times winner, Clodagh McTybe O'Cloisters, Tyron McTybe O'Cloisters, Brian McTybe O'Cloisters, Wheeler's Kildare Rusty, Wheeler's Red Boy, and the well-known Rufus, mentioned above.

The Irish Setter Club of America has done much to keep the flame of interest in the breed ablaze and its annual field trials mark the debut of many prospects which later prove their worthiness in the hunting field.

**Characteristics.** The reputation given the Irish setter—headstrong, hard to handle, etc.—is not well deserved. This bad name was given him by several of the Irish setters brought over in the early eighties from Ireland and England; to those who really know him, he has long since lived this down. The average Irish setter of today is as easily broken as his English cousin.

True, as in any other breed, some individuals develop more slowly than others and consequently more time and patience are required to bring them to the fulfillment of their capabilities. This dog is not one to be forced or abused. He responds to kindness with apparent gratefulness and once he realizes what his master expects of him, his desire to please is quickly apparent.

It is true that the Irish setter is somewhat lacking in "style," as the term is interpreted today. Few possess the rather exaggerated loftiness on point which characterizes some of our English setters and pointers, but most of them show a decided intensity on point. Many Irish setters—in fact, most of them—point with a rather low tail which detracts somewhat from the beauty of the pointing posture. Efforts are being made by seriously interested breeders to correct this fault through selective breeding and progress is being made, although at present a low-stationed point seems characteristic of the breed.

The Irish setter may not possess the excessive dash on the breakaway which field trialers fancy, but he goes about his work in a businesslike manner which generally produces results. He seldom shows the extreme range of the English setter or the pointer, but generally is more restricted in his course, although he covers his territory thoroughly. Above all, he works to the gun, and whether for horseback hunting in the South or searching the close coverts of the ruffed-grouse country he has his master's gun constantly in mind. His dark coat, although beautiful, works against him to some extent by making him rather hard to see in heavy cover. This is one reason why some gunners lost interest in him and chose lighter-colored gun-dogs.

There is no particular age at which to start field education of the Irish setter. A year or a year and a half is early enough, for the youngster should be allowed to develop naturally. He should never be crowded and if correction becomes necessary it should be administered in mild doses at first and only when he knows why he is being punished. The young dog should never be punished severely. He is generally quite sensitive and needs careful handling. If treated harshly he will probably not understand why, and there is great danger of thus breaking his spirit and diminishing his desire to hunt. This should be avoided by all means.

The Irish setter is decidedly an individual. The accepted training methods work well with this breed, but they must be modified or intensified to fit each individual case. He is no more timid than any other breed, but he definitely does not take kindly to harsh treatment.

Of all the pointing breeds, the Irish setter is most likely to become a "one-man" dog. He forms a great attachment for his master and no matter how keen he is to hunt he is not prone to follow the first man who comes along with a shotgun over his shoulder.

By nature he is a very affectionate dog, and though he has a good sense of property rights, he seldom becomes vicious. The best advice to any prospective Irish setter owner is to make a companion of the dog. Treat him like one of the family. Lavish affection on him, but not to the extent of coddling him. He will meet you more than halfway and be anxious to please. By making a close friend of him, your job of bringing him under control is almost finished.

His nose is equal to that of any pointing dog. He is strong, sturdy, can stand any kind of weather, and makes an ideal companion afield or in the home. As an ornament he knows no equal in the realm of dogdom.

**Description and Standards.** HEAD: Should be long and lean. The skull oval (from ear to ear), having plenty of brain room and with well-defined occipital protuberance. Brows raised, showing stop. The muzzle moderately deep and fairly square at end. From the stop to the point of the nose should be long, the nostrils wide, and the jaws of nearly equal length, flews not to be pendulous. The color of the nose dark mahogany or dark chocolate, and that of the eyes (which ought not to be too large) rich hazel or brown. The ears to be of moderate size, fine in texture, set low, well back and hanging in a neat fold close to the head.

NECK: Should be moderately long, very muscular but not too thick, slightly arched, free from all tendency to throatiness.

BODY: Should be proportionately long, shoulders fine at the points, deep and sloping well back. The chest deep, rather narrow in front. The ribs well sprung, leaving plenty of lung room. The loins muscular and slightly arched. The hind-quarter wide and powerful.

LEGS AND FEET: The hindlegs from hip to hock should be long and muscular, from hock to heel short and strong. The stifle and hock joints well bent, and not inclined either in or out. The forelegs should be strong and sinewy, having plenty of bone, with elbows free, well let down and, like the hock, not inclined either out or in. The feet rather small, very firm, toes strong, close together and arched.

TAIL: Should be of moderate length, set on rather low, strong at root and tapering to a fine point; to be carried in a slight scimitar-like curve or straight, nearly level with the back.

COAT: On the head, front of legs, and tips of ears should be short and fine, but on all other parts of the body it should be of moderate length, flat and as free as possible from curl or wave.

FEATHERING: The feather on the upper portion of the ears should be long and silky, on the back of fore and hindlegs long and fine, a fair amount of hair on belly, forming a nice fringe which may extend on chest and throat. Feet to be well feathered between the toes. Tail to have a nice fringe of moderately long hair, decreasing in length as it approaches the point. All feather to be as straight and flat as possible.

COLOR AND MARKINGS: The color should be a rich golden chestnut or mahogany red, with no trace whatever of black; white on chest, throat, or toes, or a small star on the forehead, or a narrow streak, or blaze on the nose or face not to disqualify.

| SCALE OF POINTS: | *Points* |
|---|---|
| Head | 10 |
| Eyes | 5 |
| Ears | 5 |
| Neck | 5 |
| Body | 15 |
| Shoulders, forelegs, and feet | 12 |
| Hindlegs | 10 |
| Tail | 8 |
| Coat and feather | 8 |
| Color | 8 |
| Size, style, and general appearance | 14 |
| TOTAL | 100 |

# IRISH WATER SPANIEL

**History.** The Irish water spaniel was one of the first retrievers to be imported into this country. Many old books mention this breed as used in the 1860's, but the first accurate record we have is in the first volume of the American Kennel Club published in 1878. Richard Tuttle of Chicago registered a male Irish water spaniel named Bob as number 1352 in the stud book of the National American Kennel Club, which later became the American Kennel Club. This dog was bred by J. H. Whitman, another Midwesterner, and was out of Queen by Sinbad.

There were 12 dogs and 11 bitches of this Irish breed registered in 1878. The only other retrievers registered on this date were two Chesapeakes. There were no Labradors or Golden retrievers. The majority of Irish water spaniels registered in the next 20 years were owned by sportsmen living around Milwaukee, St. Louis, Chicago, and Cleveland. At the time there were no restrictions on shooting waterfowl, which were plentiful; thousands were killed for market and sport from early fall to spring. The Irish water spaniel was imported from Ireland to provide a rugged water dog that could work in heavy cover and icy water day after day when the flight was on. Ducks and geese that had been shot formed a large part of the nation's food supply at the time and the market shooter could not afford to waste powder and shot on crippled birds if he were going to compete successfully in the market, but every cripple brought in was a quarter-dollar saved.

Gradually the breed's popularity spread to the East and sportsmen on Long Island and Cape Cod began to use and register Irish water spaniels. There is no way of determining the number of Irish water spaniels in the country in this period when American waterfowl shooting was at its peak, as many of the owners did not register their dogs in the stud books, but between 1880 and 1920 it was one of the popular retrievers because it could really do a day's work when large bags were common. In the Field Dog Stud Book of 1922 the Irish water spaniel outregistered the other popular retriever breeds.

In Ireland, where this breed originated, it is easy to trace their history back to Justin McCarthy who lived there and was actively breeding Irish water spaniels in 1850 as we know them today. His most famous dog was Boatswain, who lived to an old age and was found in the pedigree of one of the early dogs registered in our American Stud Book. Before McCarthy started his breeding experiments there were two distinct breeds of water spaniels in Ireland. The one in the north was small, particolored with a wavy coat, and very similar to the English water spaniel. A larger water spaniel with a curly coat was found in the South of Ireland around the bogs of the River Shannon, and this water spaniel is believed to be an ancestor of the modern dog. Many theories have been advanced on the ancient origin of the Irish water spaniel. One authority claims that they are a cross between an Irish setter and a poodle. This is unlikely, because both breeds have long hair on the tail and the Irish water spaniel, except for a few inches at its base, has a tail like a pointer. The poodle has long hair on his face and comes in a variety of colors, whereas the Irish water spaniel has a smooth face covered with short hair and shows only one color, solid liver.

There is no doubt about the Irish water spaniel being the largest member of the spaniel family. His face, ears, and disposition are typical of the spaniel family which originated in Spain. So, somewhere in the background is an ancestor from the Iberian Peninsula where so many of our good sporting dogs originated. The Irish water spaniel has bred true to type for the last 70 years in this country and except for size, looks no different from the dogs of McCarthy's breeding. Whether this Irishman developed our modern Irish water spaniel by selective breeding of the South of Ireland water spaniels or cross-breeding with a liver-colored Spanish pointer no one will ever know because McCarthy left no records of his breeding experiments. Regardless of lack of records, however, we know that his breeding theories were sound, as we have a dog today that looks entirely different from any other breed. The Irish water spaniel is always solid liver in color, curly coated, with short straight hairs on face and tail. Never seen is a particolor or the range in coat shades found in other retriever breeds.

About the same time the eastern American gunners began to find the Irish water spaniel useful, West Coast duck hunters started to use them. Although American gunners originally imported these dogs from Ireland because the conditions and cover in the Irish rough shoots were similar to those found in this country, they soon began to breed larger dogs that were heavier and longer legged and even better suited to working in western sloughs and tidal rivers. Although flat-coated retrievers were imported from England where the cover was more open and the shooting of driven game was more in vogue, the Irish water spaniel maintained his popularity for years because of his background of experience in the heavy Irish covers where he was used on upland game as well as waterfowl.

Today the Irish water spaniel is still popular among a group of sportsmen and guides who are confirmed duck shooters and consider their Irishman as essential a piece of equipment as their gun or decoys. These dogs originated in the Irish marshes and the love of working in water is bred into them to the point where a real duck hunter, who really kills a lot of birds under natural conditions, realizes their value as a meat dog. In the 1930's, registrations of Irish water spaniels dropped as the popularity of the newer imports of other retrieving breeds increased, but today the number of these dogs being registered is starting to increase again. Unfortunately registration in a recognized stud book is the only real record of a breed's popularity as compared with other breeds, but there are many good Irish water spaniels of pure breeding scattered all over this country that are never registered because their owners are typical of old-time gunners who appreciate the dog for the honest day's work he will give but cannot be bothered to fill out a form.

It is doubtful if the Irish water spaniel will ever reach the popularity of other retrievers unless a moneyed group makes an effort to popularize the breed with the modern sales tactics that have been used to help other breeds. The small group of gunners who really love and share their hunting with this grand Irish dog are not over-anxious to see him become popular because too much popularity will raise the breed's value to the point where he will be beyond the pocketbook of the average hunter.

**Characteristics.** This is a large sporting dog classified as a retriever and used mainly for retrieving upland game and waterfowl; many owners use him to spring game. The majority of these Irish dogs have excellent noses which they must inherit from their spaniel ancestors. They have sufficient length of leg so that they move fast on the land and can go through broken-down sedge and rice in marshland that slows shorter-legged breeds almost to a standstill. A 65-pounder is large enough for rough going.

One of the few remaining good sora rail rivers in the East, the Housatonic, will always have at least one pusher with an Irish water spaniel on the stern of his shoving boat. There is nothing harder to find than a dead rail in a tangle of standing and broken-down wild rice, and it is almost impossible to find a crippled bird, but these dogs lose very few birds and save the pusher from throwing markers by their marking ability. The going on this river is particularly difficult as the tangle of vegetation and height of tide are such that the dog can neither swim nor walk most of the time, but must pull himself through the cover almost by his elbows and at the same time keep afloat. The Irishman is a willing worker under these conditions and will retrieve 25 birds in the two hours the tide will allow the shooting. Many times the tide will drop off before the limit is boated and the pusher cannot move his boat through the cover where the rail are, but the Irishman will work through the watery cover and drive the rail out just as nicely as a springer will drive a pheasant out of heavy cover in an upland meadow.

The spaniel will work from a shore blind, a duckboat in open water or one that is surrounded by sedge grass, or will work off of rocks. He is not afraid of mud and will wade into mud that keeps sucking the hunter's boots off if he attempts to wade through it. He soon learns how to pick up fallen birds in a tidal river where the current is strong, and will always cut below the fall of the bird and wait for it to drift down to him. He is a strong swimmer, usually swimming with a level back and the rat tail moving all the time and occasionally coming out of the water. He learns quickly from experience, and it is not long before he knows enough to distinguish the fall of a dead black duck from one that is down crippled, and head for the creek below the fall instead of wasting time going directly to the fall as he would on a stone-dead bird. He soon learns all the tricks of a skulking black duck and before he is many years old he can outsmart a crippled duck of any species found in the marsh.

The Irish water spaniel will retrieve all kinds of upland game as well as he does waterfowl. There is even a record of one retrieving a large red dog fox. These big spaniels are used in many parts of the country to spring pheasants and many of them learn to circle a running bird. They are particularly adapted for country where the going is rough and a shorter-legged dog is slowed down to the point of being handicapped. He will trail rabbits and provide many a shot at a cottontail if the country is not too open. Where the country is very open, the

PLATE XIV. Irish Water Spaniel: Ch. Handsome Mahoney.

dog is so close to the rabbit when he comes past the shooter that he is afraid to shoot, or the rabbit holes up too quickly for a shot with the big spaniel pushing him so closely. Usually the gunner with an Irish water spaniel will get enough rabbits for a pie, however. The beagle is a better rabbit dog, but the Irish spaniel will provide a larger variety of game for the table than many of the specialists.

The Irish Water Spaniel Club of America was founded in 1937 to help this dog, and eight Irish water spaniels ran the first trial at that time. Since then a scattering of Irish spaniels have run against other retrievers in trials all over the country. A number have placed in large trials, but most of their owners have not brought their field trial training to the high perfection found in the other breeds that are winning most of the trials. Probably one out of 20 in any breed of retrievers is suited for successful field trial competition. The majority of the Irish water spaniels that have run in trials, however, have just been good field dogs; although they usually did everything asked of them in a trial, they lacked that extra something that is found only in a retriever which has been selected as outstanding in temperament from a large group of dogs. The Irish water spaniel has a nose, is fast on land and water, marks well, and handles easily yet can think for himself. Some of them would certainly be capable of winning field trials if the same time and money were spent on them as on other breeds who nowadays win field trials. Most Irish water spaniel owners are mainly interested in a dog who will give them a good day's shoot. However, there are people who remember Irish Singer, Bog's Jiggs, Blackwater Bog, Step and Mike—all Irish water spaniels who did well in competitive retriever trials.

The first sporting dog in this country to win his obedience title was an Irish water spaniel; these are willing, happy workers in an obedience test, giving pleasure to anyone watching them. The Irish puppy can start training at four months and, if the water is warm, start swimming at the same time. Although many Irish spaniels are natural retrievers, they all should be force broken, as this type of training makes a more useful dog. Extreme patience must be used at all times, as an Irish water spaniel will not stand abuse. They develop physically only slowly, and do not reach their full growth until they are two years old and in many cases retain many of their playful traits until they are full grown. Trainers who have had experience training other breeds of spaniels usually do the best job in training an Irish water spaniel as well.

Pick out a heavy-boned dog that has a tightly curled coat which is dark rather than light in color. The ear leathers should be hung low and have considerable length. Eyes should be dark brown, although there is no objection to a light eye in the standard. The head should be moderate in size, but with the jaws sizable and well developed so they are capable of carrying a large waterfowl. The tail should be smooth and shaped like a pointer's except

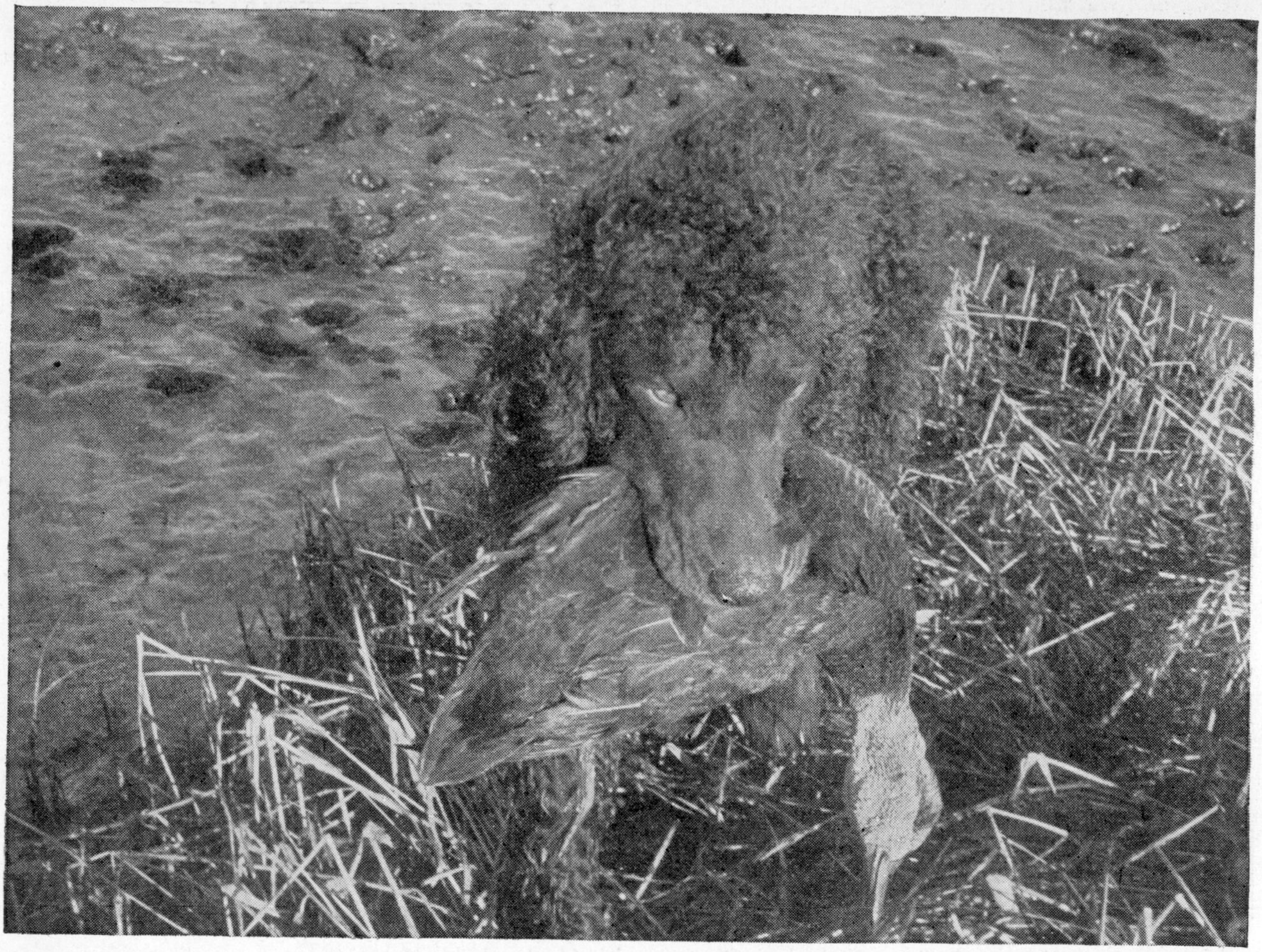

Courtesy Thomas Marshall, Fairfield, Conn.

Plate XV. Irish Water Spaniel at Work.

at the root where the hair abruptly grows heavy and curly for several inches before the tail meets the hind quarters. The tail should not set too low on the body. The dog should stand 24 to 27 inches at the shoulder, but should not give the appearance of legginess but rather the appearance of a close-coupled animal capable of great drive on the land or in the water. The face should be smooth and free from long and curly hair. The hair on the legs should give the appearance of pants rather than the feathering of a setter.

It is difficult to pick a suitable dog when he is a puppy, but the curly, tight, dark coats usually show up as well as the long ears and smooth rat tail. The only other thing you can do is pick a sound one. Treat the Irish water spaniel as a friend, bring him in your house, take him around with you, let him hunt, and by all means give him the opportunity to swim because he is a real water dog and water is his element. The Irish water spaniel will work as a real gunning companion and retrieve anything on land or water, and when a good bird or rabbit dog is not available will do a reasonable job of locating your game as well as retrieving it. All you have to do is give him plenty of experience in live game. There is no substitute for experience in making your water spaniel a finished worker.

**Description and Standards.** Head. Skull is rather large and high in dome with prominent occiput; muzzle square and rather long with deep mouth opening and lips fine in texture. Teeth strong and level. The nose should be large with open nostrils and liver in color. The head should be cleanly chiseled, not "cheeky," and should not present a short, wedge-shaped appearance. Hair on face should be short and smooth.

Topknot: Topknot, a characteristic of the true breed, should consist of long loose curls growing down into a well-defined peak between the eyes and should not be in the form of a wig, i.e., growing straight across.

Eyes: Medium in size and set almost flush, without eyebrows. Color of eyes hazel, preferably of dark shade. Expression of the eyes should be keenly alert, intelligent, direct, and quizzical.

Ears: Long, lobular, set low, with leathers reaching to about the end of the nose when extended forward. The ears should be abundantly covered with curls becoming longer toward the tips and extending 2 or more inches below the ends of the leathers.

Neck: The neck should be long, arching, strong, and muscular, smoothly set into sloping shoulders.

Shoulders and Chest: Shoulders should be sloping and clean; chest deep but not too wide between the legs. The entire front should give the impression of strength without heaviness.

Body, Ribs, and Loins: Body should be of medium length, with ribs well sprung, pear shaped at the brisket, and rounder toward the hindquarters. Ribs should be carried well back. Loins should be short, wide, and muscular. The body should not present a tucked-up appearance.

HINDQUARTERS: The hindquarters should be as high as the shoulders, or a trifle higher, and should be very powerful and muscular with well-developed upper and second thighs. Hips should be wide, stifles should not be too straight, and hocks low set and moderately bent. Tail should be set on low enough to give a rather rounded appearance to the hindquarters and should be carried nearly level with the back. Sound hindquarters are of great importance to provide swimming power and drive.

FORELEGS AND FEET: Forelegs medium in length, well boned, straight and muscular with elbows close set. Both fore and hind feet should be large, thick, and somewhat spreading, well clothed with hair both over and between the toes, but free from superfluous feather.

TAIL: The so-called "rat-tail" is a striking characteristic of the breed. At the root it is thick and covered for 2 or 3 inches with short curls. It tapers to a fine point at the end, and from the root-curls is covered with short, smooth hair so as to look as if the tail had been clipped. The tail should not be long enough to reach the hock joint.

COAT: Proper coat is of vital importance. The neck, back, and sides should be densely covered with tight, crisp ringlets entirely free from wooliness. Underneath the ribs the hair should be longer. The hair on lower throat should be short. The forelegs should be covered all around with abundant hair falling in curls or waves, but shorter in front than behind. The hind legs should also be abundantly covered by hair falling in curls or waves, but the hair should be short on the front of the legs below the hocks.

COLOR: Solid liver; white on chest objectionable.

HEIGHT AND WEIGHT: Dogs 22 to 24 inches at shoulder; bitches 21 to 23 inches. Dogs 55 to 65 pounds; bitches 45 to 58 pounds.

GENERAL APPEARANCE: A smart, upstanding, strongly built but not leggy dog, combining great intelligence and rugged endurance with a bold, dashing eagerness of temperament.

SCALE OF POINTS:

| | | |
|---|---|---|
| *Head* | | |
| Skull and topknot | 6 | |
| Ears | 4 | |
| Eyes | 4 | |
| Muzzle and Nose | 6 | 20 |
| *Body* | | |
| Neck | 5 | |
| Chest, Shoulders, Back, Loin, and Ribs | 12 | 17 |
| *Driving Gear* | | |
| Feet, Hips, Thighs, Stifles, and Continuity of Hindquarter Muscles | 14 | |
| Feet, Legs, Elbows, and Muscles of Forequarters | 9 | 23 |
| *Coat* | | |
| Tightness, denseness of curl, and general texture | 16 | |
| Color | 4 | 20 |
| *Tail* | | |
| General appearance and "set on," length, and carriage | 5 | 5 |
| *General Conformation and Action* | | |
| Symmetry, Style, Gait, Weight, and Size | 15 | 15 |
| TOTAL | 100 | 100 |

# LABRADOR RETRIEVER

There are many theories as to the origin of the Labrador. It is well known that they were introduced into England from Newfoundland, but there is still some doubt as to which species of Newfoundland they stem from. Old documents make it appear that they favor the St. John breed. The earliest record of their introduction into England is around the year 1835, but it is possible that they were known in England before this date.

**History.** The third Earl of Malmesbury was one of the first to own specimens of the original breed, obtaining his dogs from fishermen trading between Poole Harbour, England, and Newfoundland. The pure-bred Labrador of today can be traced to these early importations. By careful breeding, the integrity of the breed has been maintained, but there is little doubt that some breeders crossed their dogs with other retrievers such as the flat-coated and curly-coated varieties. It has also been claimed that some were crossed with pointers and setters, but of this there is no record. It was not, however, until 1903 that the Labrador was recognized by the English Kennel Club as a special breed. In 1906 the Honorable A. Holland Hibbert ran Mundin Single, the first Labrador ever to compete at field trials or on the bench. Up to this time the flat-coat had held undoubted sway over the curly-coat, but from this time onward the Labrador gradually established the extraordinary record of work that he now holds. There are two dogs that did the most to produce the modern Labrador; Mr. A. C. Butters' Peter of Faskally, and Major Portal's Flapper. Their pedigrees go back as far as 1878. It was not long before fanciers of this breed, desiring to stop this interbreeding, drew the standard so as to discourage crossing with other retrievers.

A book published in 1936 entitled *The Labrador Dog: Its Home and History,* written by Lord George Scott and Sir John Middleton, sheds much light on the origin of this splendid breed. In the 16th century the fishermen of Devon, England, first invaded the shores of Newfoundland—Britain's oldest colony—bringing with them dogs from England. This raises the probability that the Labrador is perhaps, after all, of English origin. This book is well worth the attention of all those interested in the origin of the Labrador.

It was not until the late twenties and early thirties that Labradors began to appear on these shores in any appreciable numbers. The first licensed Labrador trial was held in this country in 1931 at Glenmere, Chester, Orange County, N. Y., with 16 dogs in the Open All Age. The winner of this stake was Carl of Boghurst, owned by Mrs. Marshall Field. Since that date the Labrador has increased not only in numbers but in quality in this country, and has endeared himself to countless American sportsmen.

Before the Labrador's American debut, the Chesapeake Bay retriever, with a few curly-coated retrievers, held undoubted sway in the retriever world. The coming of the Labrador changed this picture. He came in as a conqueror, and has held this position ever since, numerically and from the point of

PLATE XVI. Labrador Retriever: Bracken's Sweep (1947 National Retriever Champion).

view of quality. This short-coated dog has found himself popular in practically every state. One reason for this is his hardiness to withstand climatic conditions; another is that many states are unsuited to long-coated dogs because of weeds such as sandburrs and cockleburrs. The Labrador has been condemned in some states because of his black color; he shows up too clearly in dead grass or sand. However, this is easily overcome in view of the fact that the Labrador comes in yellow and black color. This fact, coupled with the Labrador's ability, gives him a firm place in the retriever world.

The first all-breed field trial held in this country—in which all retriever breeds were eligible—was held at Strongs Neck, East Setauket, N. Y., Dec. 29, 1934. The Labrador finished first, second, and third. The late J. F. Carlisle, owner of the Wingan Kennels on Long Island, was one of the early serious importers and breeders of this dog. In 1933 Mr. Carlisle imported from England stock that has done much to place the Labrador where he stands today in this country. Mr. Averill Harriman, owner of the Arden Kennels, is another who has done so much through good breeding to produce some of the finest stock from a utilitarian point of view. The Labrador owner owes a great deal to these early breeders for the position the Labrador holds today in this country.

It is now common knowledge that both Federal and state conservation authorities have long since come to the conclusion that the retriever is one of the greatest assets in game conservation, because the retriever has proved to the authorities and the American sportsmen in general, that less game can be shot, but more taken home, with a well-trained retriever than could ever be done without one.

In 1931, 40 Labradors were registered by the American Kennel Club; in 1946 there were 1736. These figures show very definitely that the Labrador is here to stay. His field trial record is a most enviable one. Between 1931 and 1946 he placed 428 times in Open All-Age stakes, out of which total he won 117. He has also won the National Retriever Field Trial four times since 1941, one dog, Dual Champion Shed of Arden, having taken it three times. The first American Field Trial Champion was Blind of Arden, who gained this title in 1935. The first Dual Champion Labrador was Michael of Glenmere, owned by Mr. Jerry Angle of Lincoln, Neb. Michael gained his title in 1941. Since 1935 the Labrador has developed a long list of both field trial and bench show champions, and the popularity of the breed is continually growing.

**Description and Standards.** GENERAL APPEARANCE. The general appearance of the Labrador should be that of a strongly built, short-coupled, very active dog. Compared with the wavy or flat-coated retriever he should be wider in the head, wider through the chest and ribs, wider and stronger over the loins and hind quarters. The coat should be close, short, dense, and free from feather.

HEAD: The skull should be wide, giving brain room; there should be a slight "stop," i.e., the brow should be slightly pronounced, so that the skull is not absolutely in a straight line with the nose. The head should be clean-cut and free from fleshy cheeks. The jaws should be long and powerful, and quite free from snipiness or exaggeration in length; the nose should be wide and the nostrils well developed.

The ears should hang moderately close to the head, rather far back; should be set somewhat low and not be large and heavy. The eyes should be of a medium size, expressing great intelligence and good temper, and can be brown, yellow or black.

Neck and Chest: The neck should be long and powerful, and the shoulders long and sloping. The chest must be of a good width and depth, the ribs well sprung and the loins wide and strong, stifles well turned, and the hind quarters well developed and of great power.

Legs and Feet: The legs must be straight from the shoulder to ground, and the feet compact with toes well arched and pads well developed; the hocks should be well bent, and the dog must neither be cowhocked nor move too wide behind; in fact, he must stand and move true all round on legs and feet.

Tail: The tail is a distinctive feature of the breed; it should be very thick toward the base, gradually tapering toward the tip, of medium length; should be practically free from any feathering, but should be clothed thickly all round with the Labrador's short, thick, dense coat, thus giving that peculiar "rounded" appearance which has been described as the "otter" tail. The tail may be carried gaily, but should not curl too far over the back.

Coat: The coat is another distinctive feature; it should be short, very dense and without wave, and should give a fairly hard feeling to the hand.

Color: The color is generally black, free from any rustiness and any white marking except possibly a small spot on the chest. Other whole colors are permissible.

No numerical scale of points has yet been formulated.

# PLOTT HOUND

Undoubtedly the breed of sporting dog which, as a breed, has received the widest publicity in the past several years is the Plott hound. Yet this dog is certainly not a newcomer to the American sporting picture. He has, in fact, long been famous in the Great Smoky Mountains of Tennessee and North Carolina. It is only that his light has been hidden under the bushel of his somewhat restricted home venue. His great capabilities have been largely confined to hunting the bears and wild boars which range his native rugged terrain.

The Plott hound has been successfully used on smaller game than bears and boars, and, properly trained, makes a splendid tree dog. But he has come into national prominence only since the annual wild boar hunts were inaugurated and conducted by the state of Tennessee in the Great Smokies. The publicity given the breed through these annual affairs has won for him the recognition he has long deserved and the present demand for Plott hound stock is far in excess of the supply.

**History.** Ancestors of this dog were used for boar hunting in Germany many years ago, but, of course, were not then called Plott hounds. Jonathan Plott left his native Germany and came to this country in 1750, bringing a few wild-boar hounds with him. These dogs had been bred for generations for their stamina and gameness, for it took a great deal of both qualities to cope successfully with the big tuskers of that day. He settled in the mountains of western North Carolina and his dogs soon developed great proficiency in hunting the game of that area—the black bear which abounded in the wilderness.

It was not until many years afterward that a company of European sportsmen introduced the European wild boar into this section; in Plott's time the only "wild boars" in the neighborhood were domesticated hogs which had gone feral through foraging for a living in the wilds. Plott was not interested in hunting these "razorbacks" and used his dogs almost exclusively for bear hunting. Their proficiency on this species soon attracted attention among his neighbors, and it was not long before the hounds of Jonathan Plott had acquired a considerable reputation among the hunters of that section.

Mr. Plott kept his breeding and training secrets strictly to himself for 30 years, selecting his breeding stock carefully and jealously guarding the upbringing of their offspring. His were not the only bear dogs in those mountains, but his strain was kept entirely pure and free from any outcross during all those years. In this manner the breed became firmly established and his strict adherence to a careful program of breeding selectively not only kept the blood pure but improved the quality of his pack, for only the best performers were used for breeding purposes. A Plott hound had to prove its worth in the hunting field before it was allowed to pass along its blood in succeeding generations.

The fame of the Plott pack spread, and word of the exceptional ability of these dogs reached the ears of a North Georgia bear hunter, whose own pack had an enviable local reputation. In fact, the Georgia man was firmly convinced that nowhere in the land were there superior hounds to his own.

His dogs were known as "leopard dogs" originally and later as the "leopard-spotted bear dogs." Authentic information concerning their origin is unavailable, but it is generally believed that they were brought over from Europe in the 1730's. It has been claimed by some that these dogs were from a strain used by English sportsmen in hunting leopards in foreign lands. They are also said to have been of the same strain from which the original Plott hounds stemmed, some of the stud dogs having been shipped to Germany from England to bolster up the boar-hunting packs of that country.

The Plott pack passed into the management of Henry Plott in 1780. The fame of these dogs continued to spread and the curiosity of the Georgia hunter, whose name seems to have been lost, could no longer be denied. He simply had to find out if there were any better bear dogs anywhere than his own. So, with some of his best "leopard" dogs, he started the long trek through the mountains to North Carolina, finally locating the home of Henry Plott. The two hunters apparently had much in common and a staunch friendship developed. They hunted their packs separately and collectively, comparing notes and carefully checking performances.

PLATE XVII. Plott Hounds.

The Plott hounds evidently made quite an impression on the Georgia sportsman, for upon his return to his native state he took with him one of Henry's stud dogs to cross on some of his "leopard" bitches. The dog was only on loan from Plott; a year later he was returned by the Georgian, who presented Plott with a male puppy, sired by the Plott dog and out of one of the "leopard" bitches which had been selected by both men on the occasion of the Georgian's first visit.

The male puppy turned out to be an outstanding individual. So great were his good qualities that Henry Plott added him to his carefully selected pack and bred him to several of his bitches. This single cross is the only known instance of introduction of new blood into the Plott hound since the original dogs were brought to this country in 1750. There have been rumors of numerous crossings with bloodhounds, airedale, black and tan, and common mongrel, but this is strongly denied by members of the Plott clan and their friends. They maintain, in words which leave no doubt as to their sincerity, that, with this single exception, the strain of Jonathan Plott's hounds has been kept pure since 1750.

In 1946, the United Kennel Club recognized the Plott hound as a distinct breed.

Despite the considerable publicity given the breed since its "rediscovery" by enthusiastic writers several years ago, there are probably but few full-blooded Plott hounds in existence today. Certainly their numbers are few when compared with other hound strains. The Plott hound has, for many generations, been a "family" strain. The members of the Plott family have not cared to publicize or commercialize the breed. Only in the past few years has the Plott hound been given any considerable amount of publicity. These dogs had been famous among the bear and boar hunters of the East Tennessee and western North Carolina mountain section for many years, but no attempt had been made to exploit them and but few had passed out of the possession of the Plott family.

When the wild-boar hunting of that section took on a national flavor through "organized" hunts and prominent sportsmen from "outside" were invited to participate, knowledge of the real worth of this strain of hounds began to spread rapidly. A great demand for these dogs sprang up among hound lovers the country over and some were sold "outside." G. P. Ferguson, a neighbor of John and Von Plott, had been taken into their confidence, and these three men, with George Plott (who lost his life in the invasion of Normandy), are largely responsible for the program of careful breeding which has kept the strain intact. They bred their hounds with improved hunting performance as their prime objective, discarding those individuals which did not measure up to their rigid standards of field quality and keeping only the best. Their culls were not sold, but were done away with and, as a result, their packs always had their "best feet forward."

**Description and Standards.** Of medium height, the Plott hound has a rather large and somewhat beefy head, with the jaws of a fighter. His shoulders are muscular, his hind quarters strong, and his body is generally of the right proportions to give a well-balanced appearance.

In weight, the males average close to 60 pounds, and the bitches 8 to 10 pounds lighter.

The color is generally a deep brownish-brindle with a black saddle and often white points. Occasionally a white spot on the chest or a white "shirt-front" is seen. The Plott hound is likely to breed true to type and color, although occasionally a lighter-colored individual is seen. This is attributed by most to the influence of the single cross with the "leopard dogs," as this strain was lighter than the original Plotts.

They are usually free-opening hounds with a bawling cry which often shortens to a chop when the trail is hot.

Although they are particularly good on the game of their native section, Plott hounds have been used successfully on wolf, mountain lion, coyote, wildcat, deer, and various smaller game. They are said to be exceptionally good on game which runs and fights. Accustomed to the rugged terrain of the Great Smokies area, the Plott hound is probably a bit too slow to fit in with a good pack of southern foxhounds, but as an all-purpose hound he merits serious consideration. The demand is still far in excess of the supply.

No numerical scale of points has yet been formulated.

**Breeders.** There are said to be three types or strains of the Plott hound. Von and John Plott make their homes at Waynesville, N. C. Von Plott's hounds are of a long-eared variety which is said to possess exceptionally good noses, enabling them to pick up and unravel colder trails than the other two.

John Plott's hounds have shorter ears and are a little "hot-nosed." They are faster and are particularly hard and courageous fighters. Mr. Ferguson's dogs seem to strike a happy medium between the other two. Mr. Ferguson lives at Cullowhee, N. C.

All three varieties were in the pack of George Plott. After his death, most of his hounds were purchased by H. T. Smithdeal, of Johnson City, Tenn. Mr. Smithdeal proceeded to bolster up his pack by buying selected hounds from the kennels of Von and John Plott and Mr. Ferguson. The Johnson City sportsman is carrying on the Plott tradition of selective breeding.

Among the leading Plott hound breeders today, other than those mentioned above, are Leonard Moffett, Cantrill, Iowa; L. M. Patton, Bloomfield, Iowa; Oscar Seward, Cambridge, Md.; Guy Hamilton, Johnson City, Tenn., and A. F. Stegenga, Ionia, Mich.

# POINTER

**History.** Brockton's Bounce, Statter's Major, Whitehouse's Hamlet, Garth's Drake! What names to conjure up visions of past glory in the game-fields of England! Mention this quartet and you have named the four cornerstones in the foundation of the pointer breed. Add the name of Price's Champion Bang and you have heralded the principal fountainhead of the breed as we know it in this country today.

These were not the first pointers of exceptional quality, for behind each lay many generations of careful breeding, as early-day pointer breeders kept meticulous records of their breeding operations long before bench shows and field trials came into being and before the Kennel Club was organized. But these five dogs, more than any others, exerted a lasting influence on many future generations and many of their individual characteristics and good qualities are seen in the everyday performances of "short-hair" gun-dogs and field trial contenders in every state.

Although many fanciers of the breed are under the impression that the pointer originated in Spain, it is a matter of history that dogs of similar conformation and characteristics were to be found in France, Belgium, and other countries at about the same period when the breed was seen in Spain. The "braques" of France "that stop at scent and hunt with the nose high" may have come from Spain but that is a question which has never been settled. There are seventeenth- and early eighteenth-century paintings by French artists which show the pointer. It may have been that the pointer was brought into England from both France and Spain. Be that as it may, it is the English sportsman to whom we are indebted for the *development* of the pointer.

**Strains.** Among the pioneering English breeders of pointers were Thomas Webb Edge, George John Legh, J. C. Antrobus, Lord Combermere, Sir Vincent Corbet, the Earl of Sefton, Thomas Statter, Lord Derby, Sir Richard Garth, J. W. Whitehouse, R. J. Lloyd Price, J. Lang, and George Moore. These were not all, of course, and many others who contributed much came later.

It is fortunate for the pointer that these men were thoughtful breeders, attaching great importance to field performance and the intermingling of the blood of Bounce, Major, Hamlet, and Drake, the "four aces" of pointerdom, carried on for improvement.

Although Brockton's Bounce was considered a medium-sized dog he would be called a very large specimen today. He was dark liver and white in color, with the white heavily ticked. Most of his progeny were much like him in appearance and many inherited his good field qualities. In the first field trials ever held in England, in April 1865, Brockton's Bounce, along with Whitehouse's Hamlet and J. A. Hanley's Moll, scored 90 out of a possible 100 per cent, while Sir Richard Garth's Jill and Mr. Fleming's Dandy made perfect scores. The judging was done on a point system, an untried method, of course, and the rather crude way in which the conclusions were arrived at did not prove a great deal. Bounce produced many good sons and daughters, one of which was Price's Vesta, the dam of Price's Champion Bang, the most famous pointer of his day.

Statter's Major was an even larger dog than Brockton's Bounce but, despite his size, was of good conformation. He was said to be the greatest stud pointer which had been seen in England in 30 years and his ancestry traced directly back to Spanish origin. He was considered a fast dog of great determination, with excellent range. Major sired a number of dogs which figure far back in present-day pedigrees. Among them was Lord Sefton's Sam, which was the sire of the well-known Faust, imported in the eighties by the St. Louis Kennel Club. Sefton's Sam was the sire of Jane, the dam of Croxteth, a dog which did so much for the pointer on this side of the waters.

Whitehouse's Hamlet was a somewhat different type of dog, both in color and conformation. At the same time the Antrobus, Edge, Sefton, and Moore strains, from which Bounce and Major descended, held sway in England, there was a strain of lemon and white pointers, which, while not generally popular, were in high favor with an enthusiastic few. Leading these fanciers was Mr. H. Gilbert, and with the advent of public competitions his dogs created much favorable comment. Hamlet, a white and lemon son of Gilbert's Bob and Whitehouse's Juno, made a score of 90 per cent in the first English field trial. He soon became exceedingly popular as a sire. Hamlet was a powerfully built dog, a bit short in muzzle, yet representing a clean-limbed lithe type somewhat in contrast to the bulky conformation of Bounce and Major.

Garth's Drake was, according to authorities, the greatest bird dog—pointer or setter—of his day, particularly when it came to the matters of speed and handling of game. His speed was something to marvel at, and he approached his game at such a reckless pace that it became necessary for him to put on all brakes and slide into a dropping point in order to keep from running over his game. It was not until his seventh season that he began to slow down to such an extent that he could really assume a standing position on point. He was a large, rangy dog, clean in the shoulders and particularly good in loin. In action he was a frictionless-moving machine which seemed fairly to glide over the terrain, rough and smooth alike. There are probably many pointers today which are just as fast as Drake was, but in those days excessive speed was unusual and Drake's gait attracted much attention. He was not a beautiful dog in conformation but his splendid style and extreme intensity were qualities much to be desired and he became the most famous pointer stud of his time. He possessed remarkable prepotency and his fame, both as a producer and performer, was justified. Sir Richard Garth, his breeder and owner, disposed of his dogs in 1874 just before going to India. Drake, then seven years old, was purchased by Mr. R. J. Lloyd Price for 150 guineas, considered a very high figure at that time. The dog left his mark on the pointer breed, and even today when a dog of particularly smooth action comes before the field-trial public oldtimers are prone to remark "He has the Drake gait."

Price's Champion Bang was a powerful white and liver pointer considered, in his prime, the handsomest pointer in England. His sire was Coham's Bang, a son of Whitehouse's Hamlet, and his dam was Vesta, the daughter of Brockton's Bounce. In him we see the combining of the blood of two of the "cornerstones," a most happy combination.

Bang was quite different from Drake, not only in conformation but in action. His was not the smooth, gliding stride but rather a reckless, powerful fling marked with fire and dash. His breeder was Sam Price, of Bow, Devonshire, England, one of the most successful breeders of his day. Bang nicked well with the daughters of Drake, Brockton's Bounce, Whitehouse's Hamlet, Statter's Major, Sefton's Sam, and others and it is most fortunate for the pointer fancy that he did, for he was bred to extensively. In addition to his grand manner of going, he was extremely bold and stylish on point. He was not, however, so fast as Drake.

The two sons of Bang which are held in highest regard by American breeders were Croxteth and Priam. The latter never came to the States but he sired King of Kent and Beppo III, both of which were imported to this country in the eighties.

Croxteth was the head of the first important field trial family here, for his sons and daughters were quite successful and their progeny were also frequent winners, carrying on through generations.

King of Kent, the son of Priam, established a family which was not only exceedingly successful in field trials but also in bench shows. Among the field winners he produced were the famous Rip Rap, Maid of Kent, Zig Zag, Tapster, Hal Pointer, Kent Elgin, and Tick Boy. His many sons and daughters were the sires and dams of a long succession of winners and producers.

Beppo III, a son of Priam out of a full sister to the dam of King of Kent, was not so successful but his sons and daughters produced many winners in the field and on the bench.

Probably the best producing son of Price's Champion Bang was Mike, which, like Priam, never left England's shores. Through his son, Mainspring, he established a very important field trial family. Mainspring, brought over to this country, became the sire of Jingo, whose name and deeds are familiar to students of pointer breeding. Jingo's progeny are among the pointer greats. The successful sons of Bang are too numerous to enumerate in detail but Bang-Bang, his litter brother, Bob, Poyneer's Bang, and Vandevort's Don certainly deserve mention.

The so-called "native" pointers of the early days also played their part in the development of the pointer in this country. One of the most famous was Champion Rush, bred and owned by Mr. Edmund Orgill, a very careful and thoughtful breeder who preferred the white and lemons. Rush was a successful bench show winner.

**Development.** The Westminster Kennel Club and the St. Louis Kennel Club, two organizations interested in pointers, imported a number of good ones and some which did not exactly please the American fancy. The St. Louis group imported Sleaford in 1877, but had indifferent success. Undaunted, they continued their importations. In 1877 they secured, through E. C. Stirling, the heavyweight, white and liver Bow, imported by Mr. T. H. Scott. He proved a bench show winner and also placed in field trials. In 1879, Mr. S. A. Kaye, a member of the club, imported Faust, paying $1,350, the largest price to be paid for a pointer in America up to that time. Faust enjoyed a series of bench show victories in this country and was a successful sire. A number of very fine bitches were also imported during this period, among them Jessamine, Lassie, Zeal, Trinket, and Lena.

The families of Rip Rap and Jingo have long been the subject of comparison, both having supporters contending superiority of one over the other. Both were wonderful field dogs and both established families which made pointer history. Both were top-flight field trial winners and both were great producers. As a sire, Jingo perhaps had some advantage as he came before the field trial public some three seasons later than did Rip Rap and consequently had the opportunity of mating with many of Rip Rap's best daughters.

Rip Rap was one of the first white and black pointers to make a big mark in the field trial world. For many years prior to his appearance, black in a pointer was frowned upon with suspicion, but it was not long before this prejudice was dispelled. So prominently did his name become associated with the white and blacks that to this day many of those not so well informed as they consider themselves

Courtesy A. G. C. Sage, N. Y.

PLATE XVIII. Pointer: The famous Ariel, three times National Bird Dog Champion.

refer to every white and black pointer as a "Rip Rap." Rip Rap sired 19 field trial winners, many of them fine producers. His best son was Young Rip Rap, a brilliant performer and a successful sire.

His most neglected son, from a breeding standpoint, was probably Fishel's Rip Rap, owned by the well-known breeder, U. R. Fishel, of Hope, Ind. Fishel's Rip Rap had no field trial record and was used at stud but little because of the availability of more brilliant sires. He sired, however, the famous Fishel's Frank, and that one accomplishment is enough to clinch for him a place in pointer history. Unfortunately he died just about the time Fishel's Frank began his brilliant career, and when pointer breeders wanted to use him it was too late.

Jingo sired 22 field trial winners, eight of them being the result of his matings with Dot's Pearl, a daughter of Rip Rap. Lad of Jingo was Jingo's best producing son, which was the sire of the sensational Hard Cash, one of the few really great prairie-chicken dogs.

What the "four aces" were to the pointers of the early days, what Croxteth and King of Kent were to a later period, and what Rip Rap and Jingo were still later, Alford's John and Fishel's Frank were in the period following the turn of this century. Their advent marked the real rise of the pointer in field trial competitions. The blood of these two great bird dogs, more than that of any others, brought the pointer up to a basis of even competition with his long-haired rival, the English setter.

Alford's John was a "country town dog," about which much has been written. It was by accident that he attracted the attention of W. J. Baughn of Ridgeville, Ind., who recommended his purchase to C. H. Foust of Warren, Ind. Mr. Foust had invited Mr. Baughn to look over a couple of setter puppies he had purchased from Mr. Baughn as field trial prospects. The puppies were a disappointment to the latter, but the young pointer which accompanied them uninvited set such a pace that the Ridgeville sportsman suggested that he be acquired immediately if he wanted a winner. Mr. Foust, primarily a setter fancier, did not take too kindly to the suggestion but did acquire an interest in the pointer from his owner, Mr. Thomas Alford, a druggist of Warren. Later, while he was already successful, he became the property of R. R. Dickey, Jr., of Dayton, Ohio. Winner of the Manitoba chicken championship, along with other victories, Alford's John set a hot pace for the setters of that period and his puppies were in great demand. He did not come from a long line of winners and but few dogs of any prominence appear in his pedigree, but he was a peerless performer and his daughters were the best producers of any family of pointers before or during his time. His sire was Dave Kent and his dam was Cleade. Alford's John is credited with having been one of the smartest of all bird dogs. In 1909, when Alford's John was in his ninth year, he was entered in the National Championship, a three-hour heat event. It was his luck to be drawn to run with the young pointer, Manitoba Rap, then less than three years of age. It was a battle of youth and dash against age and experience, and the race was one which is still talked about. Manitoba Rap won it, but even though he was defeated Alford's John's sensational race won him many friends and proved him to be one of the greatest bird dogs of his time.

In Hope, Ind., there resided a breeder of pointers whose ambition was to produce one possessed of the class, fire, bird sense, and determination necessary to break lances successfully with the setters of that time. Three years after Alford's John made his first appearance, this breeder, Mr. U. R. Fishel, brought out a youngster named Fishel's Frank, and won second with him in the Nebraska Derby. Frank, a son of Fishel's Rip Rap (Rip Rap x Ghay Estill) and Boy's Queen (Jingo's Boy x Nellie Rush), soon attracted much attention by his spectacular performances and it was not long before breeders were flocking to his banner. He was an extremely intense dog in everything he did, putting everything he had into his work; sometimes his extra exuberance or fire and dash caused him to lose stakes he would have won with the exercise of more caution. Win he did, however, and on many occasions, but the race which brought him more fame than any was a race he lost. This was the National Championship of 1908. Frank was drawn in the last brace with the setter Danfield. He had the misfortune to contact a bevy of quail early in his three-hour heat. The birds were on barren ground and the sight of them proved too great a temptation for Frank, for he dashed forward as they went up but stopped promptly at command. After that his exhibition was flawless and many in the gallery thought he had won the stake even with the slight error. The judges felt otherwise, however, and called the setters Count Whitestone II and Danfield back to run for the title. Count Whitestone II won, but for months afterwards the field trial gallery buzzed with the argument that Fishel's Frank should have been the new champion. And the dog's fame continued to spread. After this race he was retired to the stud.

Fishel's Frank sired 58 field trial winners, many of them champions and top-flight performers. The list and their deeds are far too long to enumerate here, but two of his sons made pointer history. They were Comanche Frank and John Proctor, both out of daughters of Alford's John. Close behind them were two more sons, Lewis C. Morris and Desota Frank.

The first pointer to win the National Championship was Manitoba Rap, whose bloodlines combined those of Rip Rap, Jingo, and Rush of Lad. He was retired from competition immediately after winning the championship in 1909, when he was still less than three years of age. Even in that short time he had a brilliant field trial career, and though he had but little chance in the public stud he sired a number of winning and producing sons and daughters.

The two sons of Fishel's Frank which brought the pointer to the pinnacle of success and proved beyond a doubt his worthiness to compete on even terms with the setter were Comanche Frank and John Proctor. Both won the National Championship (Comanche Frank in 1914 and John Proctor in 1916) in addition to other field trial title events. Both established winning and producing families which have made and are continuing to make pointer history. Both occupy enviable positions in the Bird Dog Hall of Fame.

Comanche Frank was a dog of unusual stamina and courage, no matter under what conditions he was called upon to hunt. He was one of the greatest, most consistent, and most intelligent ground-working bird dogs ever known. His nose, particularly in his younger years, was not always at its best and his location was sometimes none too good. But in his more mature seasons he proved that he was an excellent bird finder and handler on both quail and prairie chickens, winning titles on both. His dam was Lady Johns, a daughter of Alford's John. He surpassed his sire as a producer and many of his winning sons and daughters also proved prepotent. He was white and liver in color. In conformation he was a workman all over.

Comanche Frank was the sire of the sensational Mary Montrose, winner of the National Championship when still a derby and the first dog to win this title three times. When she was right, "Peerless Mary," as she was called, was practically unbeatable.

John Proctor, whose dam was Miss Mariutch, another daughter of Alford's John, won four championships, including the National Championship of 1916. In all he had 23 wins, 14 of them being first places, and left a long list of winning progeny, 47 in all. Like Comanche Frank, John Proctor had a magnificent way of going and showed remarkable intelligence in working his ground. But, unlike his illustrious half-brother, he was inclined to loaf occasionally, for he would not hunt on barren ground.

In more recent times, two more families of pointers have been established to the further glory of the breed. These are the families of Triple Champion Muscle Shoals Jake, a son of Ferris Jake and a grandson of John Proctor, and Amateur Champion Seaview Rex, a son of Tarheel John.

Muscle Shoals Jake was not only a most successful sire but also an outstanding field trial performer. He was an extremely bold dog, sometimes bold to a fault and for several seasons had a bad fault which kept him out of the money on occasions. This was the lust to kill which would occasionally assert itself in the dog; when it did he would tackle almost anything which came in his path: goats, sheep, pigs, turkeys, and even colts or calves were not immune from his attacks. In his later years he was broken of this habit, although the trait occasionally cropped up in some of his many sons. The dog was exceedingly prepotent and was bred to extensively. His winning progeny, also, are too numerous to list here. One of his best sons, however, was Champion Air Pilot, which produced, among other good ones, National Champion Air Pilot's Sam. Sam also proved a splendid producer.

Seaview Rex was not a frequent winner in major field trials but he produced a family of great renown. An extreme stylist himself, he possessed the ability to transmit this exceedingly attractive quality to the majority of his get and to such a degree that they were generally easily recognized. He stamped his progeny with other qualities, too, among them being a rather heavily-shouldered gait. Perhaps his most prominent son was the sensational National Pheasant Champion Village Boy, whose son, Champion Spunky Creek Boy, is now the leading pointer sire.

No treatise on the pointer would be complete without prominent mention of the famous pointers of A. G. C. Sage. This New York sportsman has long maintained an extensive hunting preserve near Alberta, Ala., called "Sedgefields," and more pointer breeding history has been made at this establishment than in any other single area.

Mr. Sage has long been a patron of field trials; in fact, his connection with the sport has extended over a longer period than any other man's at the present time. He has never campaigned his dogs extensively, concentrating instead on the more important stakes, but he has been outstandingly successful wherever his dogs have been started. His derbies have won more American Field Futurities than those of any other breeder and he has won more National Championships, National Free-for-All, and National Derby Championships than any other individual.

Space will not permit the mention of all of his winners here but a few of his Futurity winners have been Superlette, Morpheus, Rockaby Baby, Ariel, Astra, Bye Bye, Oration, and Bolero. Some of his National Free-for-All winners have been Superlette, a repeater, Timbuctoo, Ariel, and Saturn. His National Champions have been Rapid Transit, Sulu, Luminary, Ariel (three times), and Saturn.

Three pointers have won the National Championship three times. These were Mary Montrose, Becky Broomhill, and Ariel. Only one setter, Feagin's Mohawk Pal, has ever held that distinction.

Time was when a professional brought a pointer to a field trial with half an apology. In fact, in the early days of public competition the pointer was not considered the equal of the setter and, consequently, separate stakes were run for pointers only. There was a time when the charge of "unjust discrimination" against the pointer was quite prevalent in field trials and owners of pointers would not run them under certain judges. Such a proceeding was an exhibition of poor sportsmanship and would be laughed at now. These charges were probably not justified and the fault very likely lay with the pointers themselves, but nevertheless the feeling did exist.

At the present time there are more pointers being entered in field trials than setters, and more places are won by pointers. Perhaps the numerical force has something to do with it, but it is a fact that, as a breed, the pointer develops faster than the setter and can be brought to the peak of his ability at an earlier age.

**Characteristics.** More force can be used with the average pointer than with the average setter, but too much force, of course, will either ruin the dog entirely or make him into a mechanical performer who does not have his heart in his work. This type of dog is entirely unsuitable for field trials and is not to be desired as a gunning companion.

The pointer, while not unresponsive to kind treatment, does not have the affectionate disposition of the setter and is much less apt to become a one-man dog. In fact, the desire to hunt is so firmly imbedded in many of them that they will hunt for anyone who has a shotgun. Yet there are pointers who are loyal in the extreme. The pointer, because of the shortness of his coat, can generally stand hot weather and arid terrain better than a setter. By the same token, the setter can generally stand cold weather and heavy, briary cover better than the pointer. In both cases, though, much depends on the individual.

As a rule, the pointer is a dog of rugged constitution, in which the desire to hunt and a well-defined pointing instinct are deeply ingrained. As in any breed, some are rather phlegmatic, others are brilliant. But if one will carefully choose from well-known bloodlines of proved merit and give his prospect the proper training he will have a gun-dog second to none on any type of upland game birds. The pointer was developed for a hunting dog—a gun-dog—and a gun-dog he will be as long as present breeding practices continue.

**Description and Standards.** HEAD: Skull long, moderately wide with forehead rising well at brows, showing marked stop. Full development of the occipital protuberance with slight furrow between eyes. Muzzle long, square, and straight with widely opened nostrils, cleanly chiseled under the eyes. Nose black or dark brown except in the white and orange and white and lemon, where deep flesh shades are permissible. The ears should be thin and silky and of such length as to reach just below the throat, that is, when hanging in usual position. They should set on just below the square of the skull and hang flat to the cheeks. Eyes soft and of medium size, color black, in the white and black, hazel in the white and liver, black or deep hazel in the white and orange, brown varying in shade with that of coat in the white and lemon. Regardless of color, dark eyes are to be preferred. Lips should be well developed but not flewlike.

NECK: Long, clean, and firm, arched toward the head without suggestion of dewlap or throatiness.

SHOULDERS AND CHEST: Shoulders should be long, oblique, and free from excessive width with top of blades close. Chest, deep and as wide as a proper shoulder will permit. Ribs deep and well sprung, not narrowing too abruptly at the brisket.

BODY: Back should be strong with slight rise to top of shoulders, Loin of moderate length, slightly arched. Hips wide which should fall slightly to the tail. Tail should be straight, strong, tapered, and carried level with or slightly above the line of the back. Quarters very muscular.

LEGS AND FEET: Stifles moderately bent. Legs should be moderately short rather than long, with plenty of bone. Front legs straight but with no tendency to knuckle. Elbows should be well down and straight. Hocks should be square with the body and well bent. Both front and back pasterns should be short, strong, and nearly upright. Feet should be round, closely set, deep, well padded, and toes well arched. Coat should be short, flat, and firm.

SYMMETRY AND QUALITY: Most essential. A dog well balanced in all points is preferable to one with outstanding good qualities and defects. A smooth frictionless movement with high head carriage is required and will always receive preference.

No scale of points has yet been formulated.

Courtesy Althea M. Howath.

PLATE XIX. Springer Spaniel: Ch. Chaltha's Cordite Son.

# SPRINGER SPANIEL

The English springer spaniel is a medium-sized hunting dog, weighing from 45 to 55 pounds, and standing 18 to 22 inches tall at the shoulder. He has a dense but not curly coat, long ears set on at eye level, and a docked tail. His colors are black and white, liver and white, often with tickings of either color, and blue or liver roan.

The dog is relatively heavy boned. His feet are webbed for swimming and work in swamps, with well-arched toes and deep, horny pads. Viewed from the side, the dog should be square, from the withers to the ground, and from the withers to the set of the tail.

**History.** The term "spaniel" comes from the Roman term for Spain—Hispania. Dr. Caius, an English dog authority who wrote about 1570, says the English took the name of "Hispaniolus." But it could have come to us from the French "Chiens du Espagnol," meaning "dogs of Spain." Early English writers used Spagnell, Spainell, and Spanyell.

Dr. Caius, and others, divided the spaniels into land spaniels and water spaniels. Gradually the former became known as springers, those who flushed game for the greyhounds or the falcon, and setting spaniels, those which pointed out setting game, or kept it setting for the net. Of the springers, Dr. Caius said, "they have no special names but take their names from the birds which they naturally pursue." Hence, the origin of cockers, "cocking spaniels," which were used for woodcock hunting. The setting spaniels became our setters.

Though the early writers said the spaniels came from Spain, this is by no means certain. Indeed, the long-eared spaniel may have been an established type the world over. The Cyriote Collection in the Metropolitan Museum has a figure of a dog which must have been a spaniel, so that the type may be as old as 3000 B.C. And one of the first white men to visit North America remarked that the Indians had spaniel dogs. There is a single reference to spaniels in the Irish laws, about A.D. 17, and later in Welsh law. But we have no means of knowing whether or not these were spaniels as we know them.

Gaston de Foix is the first to tell us of the work of spaniels. Gaston was a French nobleman who kept as many as a thousand hunting dogs in his kennels. About 1387, he wrote one of the most famous hunting books of all time, the *Livre du Chasse*. In it he tells us of "hounds for the hawk and [or] spaniels." He says the dogs quarter about in front of their masters, sometimes becoming so active as to lead the hounds astray. He praised the dogs for their ability in water, and their efficiency at retrieving ducks which had dived under water.

Two hundred years later, Dr. Caius wrote: "Some pursue birds only on land, and start the bird, following it up openly and barking, or simply point it out without noise. . . . All are nearly all over white. If they have spots, these are red and scarce and big. There is a red and also a black variety."

In 1637, another English sporting authority, Aldrovandus, gives a description of a "spaniel dog with floppy ears, the chest, belly, and feet white, picked
From about 1800 on, spaniels were divided about as follows: Those under 14 pounds were called comforter spaniels, or lap spaniels. Spaniels from 14 to 28 pounds were called cockers. Those over 28 pounds, with 35 about average, were called springers, English spaniels, or field spaniels.

At least among the cockers and larger spaniels, bloodlines were not kept separate. Moreover, a dog might be called a cocker until he outgrew the cocker weight limits, after which he would be called a springer, clumber, or field spaniel, depending on his looks. But about 1812, the Boughey family of Aqualate, Shropshire, began to keep a pure line of springer spaniels. Many modern springers trace back to Mop and Frisk, who lived in that early period. In the Norfolk hunting country, a fairly typical springer was developing as the Norfolk spaniel.

**Development.** The modern history of the springer spaniel begins on January 3, 1899, when the sporting Spaniel Club gave its first field trial on the estate of William Arkwright of Sutton Scarsdale. Arkwright and Elias Bishop judged. A second trial was held on December 12, 1899, on the estate of B. J. Warwick. At neither trial did a springer place among the first three. But at succeeding trials, the larger and faster dogs began to whip the clumbers and the cockers, and those loosely called field spaniels. Agitation therefore grew for a separate classification. This came in 1903 when springers were first exhibited at English bench shows. F. Winton Smith's famous field dog, Beechgrove Will, became the first male champion, and Harry Jones' Fansome, the first bitch to win a championship.

Sportsmen now combed the British Isles for dogs which looked like springers. These were registered as springers, though previously they might have run in trials under other breed names. Sometimes, as in the case of Beechgrove Will, they had descendants which were registered as still other breeds. Despite this variable background, it is an extraordinary fact that all modern American and Canadian champions, both bench and field, trace back to six patriarchs. These were Sam, Bruce, Rivington Sam, Horsford Honour, Dash of Hagley, and Velox Powder.

Three great British dogs which set up powerful families in North America were the bench and field (dual) champions, Flint of Avendale and Horsford Hetman, and the field trial champion, Rivington Sam. Other field champions who have had the greatest influence on American field dogs were Dalshangan Dandy Boy, Rex of Avendale, Cally Podge, Spy O'Vara, half a dozen of the famous Banchory dogs, and Bryngarw Firearm.

The old liver and white or black and white "English spaniels" had been popular in America up to the period of the Civil War. After that, the breed disappeared. It seems probable that the reason was the opening up of the great quail-hunting territories of the Midwest. On the Great Plains, long-legged, wide-ranging dogs were required to locate the coveys, and staunch points were necessary to hold the birds until the hunters could come up. Thus the spaniel gave way to the pointer and setter.

The recent upsurge of the springer spaniel in America is due to the rise of the pheasant as the chief game bird of our times in the North. In the Southern quail territories, springers are still few in
out with black, the rest of the body black."

number. Only the very best of the pointers and setters can pin and hold a pheasant, since this bird loves to scurry off. This continued running away from point corrupts many an otherwise satisfactory bird dog, who suddenly begins to break his points and chase.

But the springer is a flushing dog. He quarters his ground, stays within gun range, and flushes the pheasant to his master's gun. Thus the running tactics of the pheasant fit into his natural hunting procedure.

Several other factors are also involved in the springer's growing popularity. It cannot be doubted that sportsmen will turn to another breed simply because they cannot train and handle the dog of their first choice. Such hunters turned to a flushing dog when they could not teach their pointers and setters to point.

It is as hard to teach a springer to drop to flush and shot as it is to teach a pointer to hold a point. But a springer can be a very useful gun-dog even though he does not drop to flush, whereas a ranging pointer who will not hold a point is useless.

It is probable, too, that restricted hunting areas, by reason of the increasing population of the country, have played a part in the advance of the springer. Short hunting fields are an advantage to a dog whose natural hunting range is only the reach of his master's shotgun, whereas they are a disadvantage to a pointer or setter, who is a wide-ranging dog by long usage and nature.

On the whole, the springer is easily trained. He quarters naturally, and is taught to work to a gun without difficulty. The majority inherit an aptitude for retrieving, and learn to mark the fallen bird with great rapidity. They are readily adaptable to other hunting besides pheasant, and are superb workers in briar patches and swamps.

Certainly many springers are kept because of their all around ability. This is particularly true of those hunters who desire a combination duck and pheasant dog. Springers cannot stand icy waters as some of the retrievers do, but they will take all the duck work the average hunter cares to, or can, give them. Many of these dogs inherit as much water-going aptitude as any of the retrievers. Because of this, the 1947 Midwestern field trials included a water series to the extent of two 60-yard retrieves in water.

Purebred springers came to America as early as 1907. But they did not catch on here until Eudore Chevrier of Winnipeg, Manitoba, began to import and train them in huge numbers about 1921. Chevrier is credited with importing more dogs, particularly springers, than any other kennel. He sold these dogs trained, or partly trained, all over North America.

In the United States, Freeman Lloyd interested a group of New York sportsmen in the breed. The English Springer Spaniel Field Trial Association was formed in 1924, and held its first trial at Fisher's Island that year. Aughrim Flash won that year, and the next. The annual Fisher's Island trials are still the "blue riband" of springerdom.

First American field trial champions were Tedwys's Trex and Aughrim Flashing in 1929. Trex was an English field trial champion, and became an American dual champion. Those early years in the East produced three more dual champions, Fast, Bozo's Bar Mate, and Green Valley Punch.

Other noted field champions which were produced on the Eastern circuit were Fleet and Flight of Falcon Hill, Trex and Squire of Chancefield, and Indian, English, and American Field Trial Champion Wake's Wager of Greenfair.

The Midwest developed its own field trial circuit which, at first, was not recognized by the Eastern clubs in national championship competition. However, in the period from 1935 to 1946, they swept everything before them. Perhaps the greatest of these dogs, and perhaps the greatest ever to run in this country, was Solo Event. She was owned by James Simpson, Jr., who imported her; Clifford Wallace trained her.

Other imported dogs who won field championships on the Midwest circuit, and who regularly won at other trials over the country, were Staindrop Patricia. Bryngarw Fireside, Water Splash, and Dalshangan Pomme de Terre. American-bred champions from the Midwest include Cloverdale Zipper, Biff of Riverside, Don of Mendota, and Sudden Sue.

Field trials on the Pacific Coast have grown steadily in importance in recent years. Famous early field dogs in the Far West include Dual Champion King Lion, and field champions Elysian Eric and Elysian Echo. Recent ones include field champions Russet of Middlefield, Pendleton Static, and Pendleton Rocket.

In spaniel trials, dogs are put down in braces. Brace mates work parallel courses each about 50 yards wide. They must not interfere with each other. Live, full-winged pheasants are "planted" ahead of the dogs, and in this manner each dog is given an equal chance to find, flush, and retrieve game.

Dogs are expected to drop to flush and shot, or to the shot of the other dog's flush. Each dog is followed by a handler, gunner, and judge. The gunner gives the bird a long lead and then brings it down. The dog must drop to flush and must stay there until the judge orders the retrieve. The dog is scored on his ability to mark the fall, to follow the bird if it is a runner, and to bring it quickly to hand.

When all dogs have worked, those dogs which have shown merit are called back to work under the other judge on the other course. A third and fourth series may be called when needed. Dogs are thrown out for breaking to flush or shot, for hard mouth, and other errors. Water tests are given, though by no means as difficult as now planned for the Midwest dogs.

A dog becomes a field champion when he has won two stakes at which there were sufficient starters to qualify as a championship trial. At first, six starters were sufficient. The number jumped to ten, but then fell back to eight during the war years.

The majority of springer spaniels are registered in the American Kennel Club Stud Book. A few however, are registered in the *Field Dog Stud Book,* About 3500 are registered annually. In all-breed popularity, the springer ranks about 12th. No figures are available on the number actually used in the field. However, they probably rank behind the pointer, English setter, and beagle.

**Description and Standards.** Foreface: Nostrils well developed, soft, liver color or black, according to color of coat. Muzzle deep, with plenty of upper lip and flew. Jaws good length, straight, fairly square, neither under not overshot. Nicely chiseled below eyes.

Skull: Should rise from foreface without a pronounced stop. Skull of medium length and fairly broad. From the stop the median line, or groove, continues backward to the front of the sagittal crest (forehead) forming two slightly rounded halves above the eyes. Eyebrows and temples well developed, not thick in cheeks. Top of skull flat from forehead to occiput and slightly rounded on sides and back; occiput not domed; the top of occiput bone should be rounded, not pointed or angular in contour.

The resulting appearance is a head of medium length, fairly broad and slightly rounded, with a well defined stop effect—well chiseled under the eyes and free of cheekiness—with a strong, lean, fairly square jaw and well muzzled with plenty of lip, but not too thick or pendulous as in the hound, even set teeth, and well developed nostrils—an impressive head without being heavy. A ponderous head is objectionable.

Faults: Oval skull—cheekiness—too much stop which gives Clumber expression. Too heavy appearing head.

Eyes: Neither too full nor too small—medium size—not prominent or sunken but well set in, not showing haw, of an alert and kindly expression. In color dark hazel, brown or nearly black, harmonizing with the coat. Note: Seldom darker than dark hazel in the liver and white.

Faults: Light yellow eyes, or eyes showing much haw, should be penalized.

Ears: Lobular, long and wide, set on not higher than in line with level of eye, flaps hanging close to cheeks, well covered both inside and outside with fine feather, which should not be curly. The leather should not be longer than to reach to the tip of the nose.

Faults: Ears off line of level of eyes, or set too far back on head.

Neck: Moderately long, strong, and muscular, coming out of shoulders rather full and tapering to the head, slightly arched and free from throatiness. "A Springer grasps with the teeth, but weight is borne by the neck."

Faults: Too short, or ewelike; set into head too heavily, causing throatiness.

Brisket: Not too wide so as to interfere with the free action of the forelegs, but well developed and nicely rounded.

Shoulders: The blades wide, strong, and sloping, well set back forming a strong and powerful upper arm, muscular without being mutton-shouldered.

Faults: Straight shoulders or mutton shoulders, which cause the dog to be paddle gaited.

Body: The chest deep and well developed, with plenty of heart and lung room, but not too round or wide. Walls of chest deep with well-sprung ribs. Back from withers to root of tail equal height at shoulder. Back should be strong, straight—never sway-backed. Strong loins, with hips nicely rounded, slight arch over loin and hip joints, thighs broad, well developed, and muscular. The hind quarters giving the appearance of great driving power. Rump slightly sloping to base of tail, belly nicely curved from chest to flank, but not in any way "tucked up."

Faults: Sway-back. Ribs too round, too flat, or too shallow. Too long body, or loosely coupled body. Too high rump.

Legs: Forelegs—elbows well let down, setting close to the body, with free action from the shoulder. Forearms straight, with the same degree of size to toes, with slightly flattened bone and muscle. Wrist, sometimes called the "knee," straight and almost flat. Pastern short and strong. Feet strong and compact, with good strong round pads, well feathered between toes. Wavy feathering of moderate heaviness down to pastern. Note: When viewed from the front, springer should be straight from shoulder to foot, elbow close to body and knee bending neither in nor out.

Faults: Crooked legs. Too light bones. Splay or hare feet.

Hindlegs: From hip to hock, long and sinewy; hock to heel, short and strong. Stifles and hock moderately bent and not inclining either in or out, firm on feet, feet round and not too small, with strong, thick close pads. Well feathered between toes. Moderately feathered down to hock. Profuse feathering objectionable.

Stern: Set on low, well fringed with wavy feather. Preferably never carried above the level of the back. Of lively motion when dog is excited.

Coat: On head, front of forelegs, and below hock on front of hindlegs, short and fine; on other parts of body, flat or wavy (never curly), of medium length but of sufficient density to be waterproof, weatherproof, and thornproof, glossy and refined in texture. A nice fringe of wavy hair on throat, brisket. chest, and bell. (Close trimming or treatment of coat to give artificial appearance should be severely penalized.)

Height: Dogs—18½ inches at shoulder. Should not vary more than ½-inch either way therefrom. Bitches—18 inches at shoulder. Should not vary more than ½-inch either way therefrom.

Weight: Dogs about 45 lbs.—Should not exceed 50 lbs. Bitches about 42 lbs.—should not exceed 47 lbs. Note: It is desirable that proper balance and proportion shall always be considered more important than mere weight, and the dog or bitch possessing true springer type which is balanced in both vertical and horizontal dimensions and possesses bone and substance in keeping with its size, should, even though under or over the weight and dimension limits set down, always be considered preferable to one which is ill proportioned and attains the weight limit through excess or lack of height, length, width, or substance.

Color: Liver and white; black and white; liver and tan; black and tan; tan and white; black, white, and tan; liver; black; roan, etc.—anything except red and white, and lemon and white, which should be penalized.

Gait: The springer gait is strictly his own. His forelegs should swing straight forward from the shoulder, throwing the foot well forward in an easy and free manner, not a paddle or with a choppy or terrier stride. In the rear his hocks must drive well under his body following on a line with the fore-legs. NOTE: At slow movement many springers have a pacing stride which is also acceptable for springer gait.

GENERAL APPEARANCE AND TYPE: The springer spaniel is a hunting dog of all work. His qualities, stated in this standard, will give him speed, agility, and endurance to cope with the most difficult field trial and hunting conditions. He is a medium-size variety of spaniel, active, symmetrical, upstanding, strong, built for endurance, but not in any way coarse or ponderous. A well-balanced sporting dog of distinct spaniel character, combining beauty and utility. Excessive lowness or length should be penalized as interfering with the dog's activity.

SCALE OF POINTS: The following table of positive and negative points is attached simply as a guide to the relative importance of perfect or defective features. NOTE: The question of "type" and "balance," however, takes precedence over any scoring table which could be drawn up.

| | *Positive Points* |
|---|---|
| Head and Jaw | 15 |
| Eyes | 5 |
| Ears | 5 |
| Neck | 5 |
| Body | 10 |
| Forelegs | 10 |
| Hindlegs | 10 |
| Feet | 10 |
| Stern | 5 |
| Coat and Feather | 10 |
| General Appearance | 15 |
| TOTAL | 100 |

| | *Negative Points* |
|---|---|
| Light Eyes | 5 |
| Light Nose | 10 |
| Poor Ears | 5 |
| Bad Neck | 5 |
| Curly Coat | 10 |
| Weak or Uneven Jaw | 15 |
| Bad Carriage of Tail | 5 |
| Crooked Legs | 15 |
| Poor Gait | 15 |
| Excessive Lowness or Length | 15 |
| TOTAL | 100 |

PLATE XX. Tolling Dog.

# TOLLING DOG

Few American sportsmen have ever heard of the tolling dog, and an even smaller number have ever hunted waterfowl with the aid of one of these animals. Although the tolling dog is occasionally used in parts of Europe, the only reports on their use on this continent come from Nova Scotia.

In France and England these dogs, of no special breed, were used to *toll* or lure waterfowl into large funnel-shaped nets, where they could be taken alive. Usually the net was placed over a small stream which opened out into a larger body of water. The mouth of the funnel faced outward at the point where the stream entered the larger water, and the procedure employed in this method of taking waterfowl was quite simple.

The dog would run up and down the stream bank, from the mouth to a point 50 or 60 yards upstream. The sight of this dog running back and forth would be too much for the curiosity of the ducks, and they would swim toward the mouth of the funnel. As the ducks approached the dog would shorten his runs, always keeping far enough from the ducks to allay their fears and leading them up the net-covered stream to the trap.

The modern method of employing the tolling dog is quite different. In Nova Scotia the dogs are used to lure waterfowl, but not to a net or trap. A hunter will locate a lake with a number of ducks on it. He will hide on the shore, preferably on a small point. The tolling dog then begins running up and down the shore, occasionally emitting a sharp bark. He normally runs back and forth between his master's hiding place and a point 60 or 70 feet distant. This attracts the attention of the ducks, who swim in to see what is causing the dog's excitement. Within a few minutes they come within range of the hunter's gun.

In Nova Scotia these dogs are bred to resemble a red fox in size, coat, and coloration, as local guides claim this method of luring ducks is one that is practiced by foxes, and that the waterfowl do not connect man with the fox. There are very few of these dogs even in Nova Scotia; the principal breeder is Vincent Potier, of Yarmouth.

# TRIGG HOUND

One of the most popular strains of foxhound in this country today is the Trigg hound, which takes its name from its greatest exponent and originator, the late Colonel Haiden C. Trigg, of Glasgow, Ky., who wrote under the pseudonym "Full Cry." The strain may be properly described as the result of Colonel Trigg's carefully planned selective breeding program, using the Birdsong hound as foundation stock, with judicious crosses of July and Maupin or Walker blood. Years of patient experimentation and breeding, with a definite goal in mind, brought Colonel Trigg his reward in the establishment of a strain of foxhound which is noted for its speed, stamina, and gameness.

**History.** Dr. T. Y. Henry, a grandson of Patrick Henry, kept a pack of hounds in Virginia which had an enviable reputation as foxhounds of exceptionally high quality. Dr. Henry called these dogs Irish hounds, as they were descended from Mountain and Muse, imported from Ireland by Bolton Jackson of Maryland, and presented by him to Colonel Sterrett Ridgely. Colonel Ridgely gave them to Governor Samuel Ogle, of Maryland, who gave Mountain to Captain Charles Carroll, Jr., of Carrollton. Captain Carroll presented the dog to Dr. James Buchanan, who presented Captain, a direct descendent of Mountain and Muse, to Dr. Henry. Captain was by Traveler out of Sophy, both by Mountain out of Muse. Thus was laid the foundation of the Henry hounds, later known as the Birdsong hounds.

Early in the 1840's Dr. Henry presented a pair of puppies from his pack to George L. F. Birdsong, of Thomaston, Ga. Mr. Birdsong valued them so highly that he sent a wagon overland for them, there being no rail transportation at that time. These puppies and their progeny proved to be far superior to any hounds the famous Georgia sportsman had ever had before and he set about building a pack which soon was recognized as the best in that section.

Several years later Dr. Henry was threatened with tuberculosis, and his doctor ordered him to go South. Accompanied by several friends and his pack of hounds, Dr. Henry started overland for Florida, traveling by wagon and horseback. The trip was made in leisurely fashion, the party stopping occasionally to enjoy the hunting and fishing offered by the countryside. Knowing of the trip, Mr. Birdsong joined the party en route and spent several days hunting with Dr. Henry.

Although his move to Florida was beneficial to Dr. Henry's health, circumstances threatened to wipe out his famous pack. Deer abounded in the section in which the Virginia sportsman settled, and his dogs could not resist the temptation to chase them. Often the trail carried them across streams and lagoons infested with alligators. A number of the finest individuals in the Henry pack fell victim to alligators. Realizing that his pack would soon be wiped out if he continued to hunt them in his new location and desiring to preserve their good qualities for posterity, Dr. Henry wrote Mr. Birdsong and offered to give him the remnants of this famed kennel if he would come after them. Though saddened by his friend's plight, Mr. Birdsong was delighted to obtain these highly prized hounds and left post-haste for Florida, bringing the dogs back to his Georgia home.

Mr. Miles G. Harris secured a very fine hound from a Mr. Nimrod Gosnell of Maryland and brought him to Georgia. The dog came to him on the first day of July and, for this reason, was named July. It is believed that July came from the same strain as old Captain, the foundation of Dr. Henry's "Irish" hounds.

In 1861, July was crossed on the Birdsong dogs. This cross was successful, although there existed some difference of opinion as to the comparative merits of the Birdsong dogs before and after the July cross. It brought fresh blood into the pack, however, and many considered that it strengthened the bloodlines.

Dr. Henry called his dogs "Irish" hounds. After the pack passed into the possession of Mr. Birdsong,

Courtesy Robert Rodes, Bowling Green, Ky.

**Plate XXI.** Trigg Hound: Jimmie Hill.

he insisted that they be known as "Henry" hounds. However, as their fame spread through Georgia and the surrounding states, they became generally known as "Birdsong" hounds, and after the infusion of July blood, they were called by many "July" hounds. The straightbred Birdsong hound is one whose breeding can be traced back to Captain without showing the July cross. Yet it is generally believed that July descended from Mountain and Muse, the progenitors of Captain.

In the meantime, Colonel Haiden C. Trigg, of Glasgow, Ky., was having good sport hunting gray foxes with his pack of long-eared, deep-toned, rat-tailed black-and-tan Virginia hounds. But in 1860 the red fox made its appearance in Colonel Trigg's territory and began to spoil his sport. His hounds were too slow to cope with the racing red raider. Not to be outdone, he was determined to secure, or develop, a pack of hounds game enough and fast enough to deal with the red fox.

Colonel Trigg bought five hounds from Mr. Birdsong in 1866 and 1867, paying $400 for them, at that time considered a high price. These were Chase and Bee (by Longstreet, a straight-bred Birdsong), George, Rip, and Fannie. Mr. Birdsong gave the colonel a dog named Lee, probably for "good measure."

In 1868, Colonel Trigg visited Mr. Birdsong, who was ill with tuberculosis (he died the following year). He was, however, able to show his guest some excellent hunting. At that time Mr. Birdsong owned July and a number of his progeny. He also had Longstreet, a straight-bred Birdsong, and several promising puppies by this celebrated sire. After much pleading, Mr. Birdsong sold Colonel Trigg two young hounds for the sum of $500. These were Lightfoot, by July, and Delta, by Longstreet out of Echo, a daughter of July.

At about the same time, Colonel Trigg purchased from Colonel R. H. Ward, of Green County, Ga., Forest, by Boston, and Emma, paying $100 each. Rose, a full sister to Echo, and a splendid dog named Hampton were loaned to him. Colonel Trigg raised a litter of puppies from Rose and returned her; Hampton died shortly after he was received.

Shortly before his visit to Mr. Birdsong, Colonel Trigg spent a few days hunting with General George Washington Maupin, of Madison County, Ky., and purchased the young bitch Minnie, a close descendant of General Maupin's celebrated hound Tennessee Lead on one side and the imported English dogs Fox, Rifler, and Marth, on the other. At the same time Colonel C. J. Walker presented Colonel

Trigg with the young bitch Mattie, whose sire and dam both traced back to Tennessee Lead.

In 1869, after hunting with Colonel Trigg, Messrs. W. L. Waddy and Thomas Ford of Shelby County, Ky., who had a pack of Maupin-bred hounds, insisted that the colonel try the qualities of some of their best dogs. Colonel Trigg selected Tip, Waxey, and One-Eyed King, and hunted them, breeding the latter to Delta, and getting the dog later known as Money, noted for his exceptional speed. Returning the courtesy, Colonel Trigg let Messrs. Waddy and Scott take his celebrated Forest for breeding purposes.

After General Maupin's death, W. S. Walker and brothers of Gerrard County, Ky., became the leading breeders of the Maupin or Walker hounds, carefully preserving the bloodline of what is now known as the Walker hound. In 1890 Col. Trigg secured the Walker hound Trooper from Mr. Walker and used him to some extent as a stud dog.

In those days there were plenty of red foxes and plenty of good country in the South to run them in. Each line of breeding had its champions and match races were not unusual.

General Maupin, a pillar in the house of foxhound breeding, and his friends, among whom were the Walkers, Sam Martin, the Gentrys, and the Whites, all famous fox hunters, were convinced beyond all change that the finest foxhounds of that day were Fox, Rifler, Marth, Queen, Tennessee Lead, Tickler, Doc, Kate, Top, Minnie, and others of their packs.

Equally high in the esteem of Mr. Birdsong and others of the Georgia contingent (the Wards, Robinsons, Ridgleys, and Jacksons), were Hodo, July, Longstreet, Flora, Forest, Echo, Hampton, Madcap, Lightfoot, Fannie, and others of their breeding.

Messrs. Waddy and Ford of Shelby County, Ky., also had their own ideas, and were confident that no hounds were better than their One-Eyed King, Tip, Josephine, and Venus.

After years of careful selection, judicious breeding, and crossing lines only for a definite purpose, Colonel Trigg developed the strain of hounds which now bears his name.

The Trigg hound is a combination of blood from the Birdsong, Maupin, and Walker kennels. From 1867 to 1890 he mingled these strains with one end in view—the improvement of his pack. How well he succeeded is reflected in the deserved popularity the Trigg hound enjoys today.

During that period Colonel Trigg had the following dogs in his kennels for breeding purposes, as well as for hunting:

*Birdsongs:* Chase, Bee, George, Lightfoot, Delta, Rip, Fannie, Lee, Forest, Emma, Hampton, Ward, Rose, and Emma Sampson; *Maupins:* Minnie, Mattie, Lead, Couchman, Bob, Dick, Rock, Venus, Mercy, Lee, and Brenda; *Walkers:* Buckner, Scott, and Trooper.

Colonel Trigg never bred his dogs for distinctive color or markings. His original dogs ranged from black and tan to fawn and included white, black and tan, tan with white points, red, red and white, black and white, red with white points, black with white points, light red with white points.

**Description.** The Trigg hound is a handsome, rugged individual in appearance, strong but without coarseness, rangy yet not gaunt. He has abundance of bone but is not considered a heavy-boned dog. He has good length of muzzle, well-set ears and stern, strong shoulders and quarters, and is a workmanlike type of dog.

In height the Triggs run from 23 to 24½ inches, seldom 25 inches, in weight from 45 to 55 pounds. They are generally equipped with splendid noses and are noted for exceptional speed and splendid endurance.

There is no set scale of points.

# WALKER HOUND

**History.** The most popular strain of American foxhound in the country today is the Walker. Wherever fox hunters gather the inevitable argument about strain supremacy provides the conversational sauce which allows the otherwise reticent sportsman to pop out of his shell and soar into forensic heights, often to his own surprise. But, also, wherever fox hunters gather there are sure to be found a number who champion the Walker hound to the utmost of their ability. And, most likely, the exponents of that strain will be largely in the majority. For full-blooded Walker hounds are now found in every section where the fox is chased for sport.

The history of the Walker foxhound is an interesting one. The greatest portion of the credit for the development of the strain properly goes to two Kentucky sportsmen. Close friends and neighbors, George Washington Maupin, later more familiarly known as "Uncle Wash" Maupin, and John W. Walker had more than community interest in common. They were bound together by a mutual love of hounds and hunting, and this bond drew them closer as the years went by. There were others, of course, friends and neighbors, who contributed their share to the metamorphosis of the Walker hounds. These were the Deatherages, Neil Gooch, Anse Martin, the Whites, the Williamses, the Gentrys, the Clays, the Goodmans, and others. But the roles they played were minor compared to that of Maupin and Walker.

Daniel Maupin, the father of George Washington Maupin, and William Williams came to Kentucky from Virginia. John W. Walker was a nephew of Mr. Williams and lived with his uncle until manhood. These gentlemen owned hounds of the native Virginia and Kentucky stock of that day, and bred them carefully and judiciously, selecting the best with which to carry on. Although the hounds of "Uncle Wash" Maupin and John W. Walker were of the same breeding there existed between the two sportsmen that same spirit of friendly rivalry which still characterizes fox hunters the country over. For fifty years they bred from the same stock, taking care to weed out the unworthy and undesirables.

**Development.** Then came the outcross, the influence of which was so profound as to result in the strain now called the Walker. Too much praise, however, cannot be given to the descendants and relatives of both gentlemen, particularly Mr. Walker, whose close adherence to the breeding principles laid down by their forebears was so basically essential to the development of the strain which now bears the Walker family name. Without a strict program of breeding and the keeping of careful records on the results, this strain would probably have passed into the limbo populated by other good strains which enjoyed, for a time, the limelight of popularity but are not now well remembered.

This outcross was furnished, and at about the same time, by the almost legendary hound Tennessee Lead, and the two English importations, Rifler and Marth. It is interesting to note that one of the most, if not really the greatest, fountainheads of the Walker foxhound was a "stolen" dog. Perhaps a kinder and more charitable word would be one made again popular in World War II—"Liberated." From what stock he stemmed, no one knows, and the circumstances of his acquisition probably precluded any serious attempt to find out. But, regardless of his origin, he made a great impression on the packs of "Uncle Wash" Maupin and John Walker, and the introduction of this new blood came at just the right time to effect the needed improvement in performance. This dog was known as Tennessee Lead.

Tom Harriss was one of "Uncle Wash" Maupin's friends and neighbors. He was a dealer in livestock and drove his stock, overland, to the Southern markets. Returning from one of his regular trips, he was passing through the mountains in Tennessee when he heard a pack of hounds running, headed directly toward him. Presently their quarry, a deer, crossed the road, closely followed by the pack. Harriss quickly dismounted and caught one of the hounds, bringing it back to Kentucky, where he presented it to Mr. Maupin.

The hound, later to be given the name Tennessee Lead, was not very prepossessing in appearance. He was a medium-sized black dog with a small tan spot over each eye, a thin coat, and no brush on his tail. He had an exceptional amount of fox-sense, plenty of drive and speed, a clear short mouth, and, though not a standout in any department, was, over-all, a high class, game-to-the-core foxhound.

Mr. Maupin was not particularly impressed with the dog at first glance, but after a few races became enthusiastic about him—so much so, in fact, that he sent two of his sons to the section of Tennessee in which Harriss had picked Lead up, in an endeavor to purchase his duplicate or equals. His sons returned with two or three which resembled Lead in appearance—but in nothing else. Tennessee Lead became the idol of that section of Kentucky in which the Maupins and Walkers resided and was used extensively on Maupin-Walker bitches. His influence was immediately felt, and his blood became highly prized.

About this same time, Mr. Maupin and several of his fox-hunting friends arranged with Billy Fleming, a Philadelphia merchant with whom they transacted business, to purchase for them two foxhounds on his next trip to England. Mr. Fleming contacted the Buccleuch Kennels and secured a dog, Rifler, and a bitch, Marth. Upon arrival in New York, the dogs were sent by rail to Cincinnati and thence by stage to Richmond, Ky. Here they were met by nearly all the fox hunters in that section, who were anxious to see what the "foreigners" could do.

So high did that enthusiasm run that arrangements were made for a hunt that very night, and although he had been confined in a crate for more than two weeks, Rifler was tossed into the pack. This was, indeed, an entirely unfair test, prompted, of course, by impatient enthusiasm, and no doubt his new owners would have given this full consideration had Rifler's efforts not proved up to proper standards. Regardless of his lack of condition, however, the "Englishman" proved himself a real foxdog that night and all those who had contributed toward his purchase felt themselves participants in a splendid investment. Their predictions were justified. This was perhaps the most severe test a foxhound had ever been subjected to. Although the group, of course, would have been charitable and reserved opinion until he could have been tested under more favorable conditions, it was, nevertheless, composed of seasoned hunters who were inclined to be particularly critical of individual hound work. The fact that Rifler was able to satisfy them makes his performance all the more outstanding. Marth, the bitch, had been bred in England before shipping and was showing in whelp. For this reason she was not subjected to the extreme test which faced her kennel-mate.

There were other hounds in the Maupin and Walker packs which are said to have compared favorably with Lead and Rifle, but it was felt that new blood was needed and the three dogs mentioned above were the ones to provide it. This judgment proved to be sound.

Marth whelped a litter and from it four were raised, three males and one female. The three male puppies were called Fox, Bully, and Bragg. All were fine foxhounds and were used extensively at stud. The bitch puppy had the misfortune, when she was nearly grown, to be run over by a wagon which badly injured her foot. This prevented her from being hunted, and she was used for breeding purposes only. She was called Mash Foot. Due to the sketchiness of the early records, not a great deal is known about Mash Foot's progeny, although one of her sons figures quite prominently in the pedigrees of the older Walker hounds. This was Rush, whose sire was Middleton's Eagle. Rush was a grand hound and his blood was prepotent. There may have been some other outcrosses in the early days, but if so they were either discarded or were not persisted in.

In 1892, however, another importation from England brought fresh blood to the Walker hounds. Striver, Relish, and Clara were brought over from England by James Crawford of Chicago. Mr. Crawford presented these dogs to his friend, Colonel Jack Shinn. Colonel Shinn visited the Walkers for a hunt soon afterward and brought the trio of hounds with him, giving Striver to W. S. Walker, Relish to E. H. Walker, and Clara to Arch Walker. None of these hounds proved entirely satisfactory. Striver was an outstanding hound in every department except one: he was weak in mouth. His "open" was a mild squeal which could not be heard at any considerable distance. Otherwise he was an excellent performer. A good hunter, tireless and game, he could generally be found near the front of the pack, but his voice was not one of the kind "heard throughout the countryside." Relish was what is known as an "in-and-outer." She could travel with the best—when she wanted to, which was seldom. Clara is said to have been no good.

PLATE XXII. Walker Hound: Woods Walker.

It has been said that the Walkers and Maupins were too jealous of their own stock to try to improve it by making outcrosses. This is denied. Hounds were brought in from New England, Maryland, and other points and the results of the crosses were carefully nurtured and watched, but none approached the high standard set by the Walkers and Maupins to such an extent that continued use as breeding stock was warranted.

One of the hounds of the 1865-70 period which figures far back in the pedigrees of practically every present-day Walker hound is Top, bred by Neil Gooch, later owned by "Uncle Wash" Maupin, who still later sold him to W. S. Walker for $100. According to Walker records, Top was the first dog to be sold for such a price, considered extremely high in those days. Top was by Maupin's Couchman and out of Gooch's Aggie II. His dam traced back to Tennessee Lead.

Red Mack II, whelped in 1883, was another outstanding hound which left his mark as a performer but unfortunately was not a great success as a sire. Red Scott, a brother, while an excellent fox dog, was not quite so good as Red Mack II but his blood carried on through generations.

Space limits will permit mention here of only a few of the outstanding hounds which, in later days, carried the Walker banner on to new heights and contributed to the well-deserved popularity which the strain enjoys today. Worthy of more than mere mention, however, are Cable, Big Stride, War Cry, White Rowdy, Cork, Mark, and String. Hub Dawson is another which should not be overlooked, as his name is much in evidence in many present-day pedigrees.

Big Stride, whelped in 1916, and bred and owned by S. L. Woodridge, was the most famous Walker hound of his day. An exceptionally fine fox dog, his greatest success came as a sire. It is unlikely that any other Walker hound has been used more extensively for breeding purposes, and his progeny warranted his use. His name very probably appears in more pedigrees of present-day Walker hounds than that of any other dog, with the possible exception of Cable, his sire.

Cork, owned by Woods Walker, was an outstanding hound which left a lasting impression on the strain. He was in great demand as a stud and sired many exceptional foxhounds. An extremely game hound, Cork is known to have been in two hard races in close succession, in fact with hardly a let-up between, the combined time of which totaled about 19½ hours. During all that time Cork was either at the front of the pack or, indeed, leading it.

**Breeders.** Space will not allow mention of more than a few of the prominent modern breeders of

Walker foxhounds, but among them are Walker Kennels, Paint Lick, Ky.; Woodridge Kennels, Versailles, Ky.; M. R. Garris, LaGrange, N. C.; J. H. Cline, Columbia, Pa.; T. C. Wells, Bowling Green, Mo.; W. E. (Bill) Avant, Georgetown, S. C.; Ben Dial, Wellston, Ohio; E. R. Fleming, Clintwood, Va.; W. V. Ward, Dublin, Ga.; J. Percy Flowers, Clayton, N. C.; and Harry Loyd, Germantown, Md.

The Walker foxhound is no longer a "family affair." Lovers of the chase all over the country have recognized the excellent qualities of the strain and it can be truly said that the mighty cry of the Walker hound is a "voice heard throughout the land."

**Description and Standards. (American Foxhounds).** HEAD: SKULL: Should be fairly long, slightly domed at occiput, with cranium broad and full.

EARS: Ears set on moderately low, long, reaching when drawn out nearly, if not quite, to the tip of the nose; fine in texture, fairly broad, with almost entire absence of erectile power—setting close to the head with the forward edge slightly inturning to the cheek—round at tip.

EYES: Eyes large, set well apart—soft and houndlike—expression gentle and pleading; of a brown or hazel color.

MUZZLE: Muzzle of fair length—straight and square cut—the top moderately defined.

DEFECTS: A very flat skull, narrow across the top; excess of dome; eyes small, sharp and terrier like, or prominent and protruding; muzzle long and snipy, cut away decidedly below the eyes, or very short. Roman nosed, or upturned, giving a dishface expression. Ears short, set on high, or with a tendency to rise above the point of origin.

BODY: NECK AND THROAT: Neck rising free and light from the shoulders, strong in substance yet not loaded, of medium length. The throat clean and free from folds of skin, a slight wrinkle below the angle of the jaw, however, is allowable.

DEFECTS: A thick, short, cloddy neck carried on a line with the top of the shoulders. Throat showing dewlap and folds of skin to a degree termed "throatiness."

SHOULDERS, CHEST AND RIBS: Shoulders sloping—clean, muscular, not heavy or loaded—conveying the idea of freedom of action with activity and strength. Chest should be deep for lung space, narrower in proportion to depth than the English hound—28 inches (girth) in a 23-inch hound being good. Well-sprung ribs—back ribs should extend well back—a 3-inch flank allowing springiness.

BACK AND LOINS: Back moderately long, muscular and strong. Loins broad and slightly arched.

DEFECTS: Very long or swayed or roached back. Flat, narrow loins.

FORELEGS AND FEET: FORELEGS: Straight, with fair amount of bone. Pastern short and straight.

FEET: Foxlike. Pad full and hard. Well-arched toes. Strong nails.

DEFECTS: Straight, upright shoulders, chest disproportionately wide or with lack of depth. Flat ribs.

DEFECTS: Out at elbows. Knees buckled over forward, or bent backward. Forelegs crooked. Feet long, open, or spreading.

HIPS, THIGHS, HINDLEGS, AND FEET: HIPS AND THIGHS: Strong and muscled, giving abundance of propelling power. Stifles strong and well let down. Hocks firm, symmetrical, and moderately bent. Feet close and firm.

DEFECTS: Cowhocks, or straight hocks. Lack of muscle and propelling power. Open feet.

TAIL: Set moderately high; carried gaily, but not turned forward over the back; with slight curve; with very slight brush.

DEFECTS: A long tail. Teapot curve or inclined forward from the root. Rat tail, entire absence of brush.

COAT: A close, hard, hound coat of medium length.

DEFECTS: A short thin coat, or of a soft quality.

HEIGHT: Dogs should not be under 22 or over 25 inches. Bitches should not be under 21 or over 24 inches measured across the back at the point of the withers, the hound standing in a natural position with his feet well under him.

COLOR: Any color.

SCALE OF POINTS:

| | | |
|---|---|---|
| *Head* | | |
| Skull | 5 | |
| Ears | 5 | |
| Eyes | 5 | |
| Muzzle | 5 | 20 |
| *Body* | | |
| Neck | 5 | |
| Chest and Shoulders | 15 | |
| Back, Loins, and Ribs | 15 | 35 |
| *Running Gear* | | |
| Forelegs | 10 | |
| Hips, Thighs, and Hindlegs | 10 | |
| Feet | 15 | 35 |
| *Coat and Tail* | | |
| Coat | 5 | |
| Tail | 5 | 10 |
| TOTAL | 100 | 100 |

# WEIMARANER

If you do not like to hear the virtues of another's dog extolled hour after hour, do not engage the owner of a Weimaraner in conservation. The enthusiasm of all the Weimaraner owners is contagious. No breed ever brought to this country has been accorded such an ardent welcome, nor has the possession of any breed been so carefully guarded, for the promoters of the Weimaraner in this country are following the precedent of the Weimaraner Club of Germany, which was extremely careful concerning ownership of surplus stock, breeding practices, and prohibition of the infusion of new blood.

The Weimaraner originated at the German court of Weimar a little more than 125 years ago. The nobles of Weimar wanted an all-around hunting dog which would do everything; point, retrieve, trail, work in all sorts of cover and all kinds of weather —and with it all be a loyal, loving companion and house dog. Probably the heaviest contributor to the Weimaraner's hunting ability was the old red schweisshunde, a sort of super-bloodhound which provided the background for most of Germany's hunting breeds. Just how long it took and what crosses were needed to establish the Weimaraner as a distinct breed is not a matter of exact record.

Courtesy Charles S. Hartung, Chevy Chase, Md.

PLATE XXIII. Weimaraner: Ch. Silver Blue Luke.

But once established, the breed was carefully guarded and no exploitation was allowed. It is said that there have never been more than 1500 of these dogs in all of Germany at one time and none were allowed outside. It was the desire of the Club that the Weimaraner remain Germany's own dog exclusively, and club members were subjected to rigid breeding regulations. This same careful supervision prevails today and is practiced, to a large extent, by members of the Weimaraner Club of America.

Howard Knight of Providence, R. I., succeeded in obtaining and bringing to this country a pair of these dogs in 1929. Several others were imported shortly after and so a foundation stock for the breed in this country was obtained. The Weimaraner is thus the newest addition to America's sporting-dog group.

Naturally, the breed is not numerically strong in this country and, under the careful supervision of the Weimaraner Club of America, it is possible that it will never be. This is as the Club would have it, as the members are determined to keep the quality high, regardless of the excellent opportunity for commercial exploitation. For the "Gray Ghost," as the dog has been dubbed in this country, has had fine publicity and the Club's avowed intention to confine ownership to those who meet certain qualifications has whetted the desire of many to own these dogs. "Make it hard to get" is always good promotion, but backers of the Weimaraner are quick to deny any such purpose and equally ready to declare the breed equal to the extraordinary claims made for it.

So far the Weimaraner has not attracted much attention by his prowess in the hunting field. It is, of course, too early for that. But the high intelligence and tractability of the breed has definitely been demonstrated in many obedience trials. Grafmar's Ador, CD (Companion Dog), won his obedience degree at the age of six months, the youngest dog ever to acquire it. He also proved proficient on game and an excellent producer of quality puppies.

The Weimaraner is a large dog, but free from coarseness. Males weigh from 65 to 85 pounds, females 55 to 75. Despite their size, 24 to 26 inches for males and 22 to 25 inches for females, they are remarkably smooth in gait and their stealthy movements in the field, together with their solid coat, has won for them the nickname "gray ghost."

The solid color ranges from silver-gray to a dark gray called silver taupe. The outer coat is slick and velvety, with a dense woolly undercoat which gives the dog comfort in rigorous weather.

The eyes are blue-gray or amber, changing with light conditions, and adding to the unusualness of the dog's appearance. The tail is always docked to one-half or two-thirds its length.

The Weimaraner learns his lessons early and well. He is exceedingly tractable and willing to obey whenever he understands. He is a striking dog in appearance and never fails to attract attention. No numerical standard of points has yet been set up.

# WIRE-HAIRED POINTING GRIFFON

Regarded as a French breed but originating in Holland, the wire-haired pointing griffon is the only pointing breed with a harsh coat. First brought to this country in 1901, the dog has enjoyed several spasmodic spurts of popularity. None of these periods, however, has been very long, for the dog's unique appearance and lack of speed kept it from being popular with the American sportsman, and its coat and color also failed to appeal. There are still a number of these dogs on this side of the ocean, and occasionally a serious attempt at breeding them is made, but the pointing griffon has never gained a real foothold in American game fields.

**History.** This dog owes its existence to one man, E. K. Korthals, son of a wealthy banker who lived at Schooten, near Haarlem, Holland. Young Korthals desired to develop a new breed of hunting dog which would possess such great utility that it could be used on any type of game. Its characteristics must include keenness of nose, ability to trail, possession of the pointing instinct, and a rugged constitution which would enable it to cope with the toughest of cover and also to retrieve from icy and rough waters.

Korthals bought a gray and brown griffon bitch named Mouche from M. G. Armand of Amsterdam in 1874 as the keystone of his proposed new breed. Five other dogs were purchased during the next three years. These were Janus, a woolly-haired dog, Junon, a short-hair, and Hector, Satan, and Banco, all three rough-coated. Mouche was mated to Janus and this union between rough-coat and woolly-coat produced one puppy, Huzaar. Mouche was mated to Hector, and a bitch puppy from that mating named Madame Augot was bred to the dog Satan, producing Zampa.

The first really productive cross, however, was effected when Huzaar was bred to the short-haired bitch Junon. Here was a combining of the woolly-haired, rough-coated, and short-haired types, and from this mating came a bitch named Trouvée, whose coat was harder than any other of the Korthals dogs. When bred to Banco, another rough-coat, Trouvée produced Moustache I, Querida, and Lina. These three dogs proved the fountainheads of the breed.

Korthals' father did not share his son's enthusiasm for dog breeding and, apparently, they quarreled over the matter, for the young man left Holland, going to Germany where he resumed his breeding operations. It was in France, however, that most of the development work on the breed was done, and in that country the wire-haired pointing griffon is today known as the Korthals griffon.

Just what breeds made up the background of the dogs which formed the foundation of the pointing breed is not known, but authorities claim that in their veins ran spaniel, setter, and otterhound blood. It has also been fairly well established that an infusion of German short-haired pointer blood was used.

The wire-haired pointing griffon is a rather slow, close-working dog who does his best work in the heavy growth of marshy country where his harsh coat provides him much protection. He is intelligent and

Courtesy H. G. Kirkelie, Kalispell, Mont.

**PLATE XXIV.** Wire-haired Pointing Griffon: Stout Hearted Rex.

takes to training readily, but, even though versatile, he is unable to compete on even terms with several other breeds among American pointing dogs. Most of them, in fact, can give him "cards and spades" and still take almost every trick.

**Description and Standards.** The official description and standard of points follow:

GENERAL APPEARANCE. The wire-haired pointing griffon is a dog of medium size, fairly short-backed, rather low on his legs. He is strong-limbed, everything about him indicating strength and vigor.

His coat is harsh like the bristles of a wild boar, and his appearance, notwithstanding his short coat, is as unkempt as that of the long-haired griffon, but, on the other hand, he has a very intelligent air.

HEAD: Long, furnished with a harsh coat, forming a moustache and eyebrows, skull long and narrow, muzzle square.

EYES: Large, open, full of expression, iris yellow or light brown.

EARS: Of medium size, flat or sometimes slightly curled, set rather high, very lightly furnished with hair.

NOSE: Always brown.

NECK: Rather long, no dewlap.

SHOULDERS: Long, sloping.

RIBS: Slightly rounded.

FORELEGS: Very straight, muscular, furnished with rather short wire hairs.

HINDLEGS: Furnished with rather short stiff hair, the thighs long and well developed.

FEET: Round, firm and well formed.

TAIL: Carried straight or gaily, furnished with a hard coat without plume, generally cut to a third of its length.

COAT: Hard, dry, stiff, never curly, the undercoat downy.

COLOR: Steel gray with chestnut splashes, gray-white with chestnut splashes, chestnut, dirty white mixed with chestnut, never black.

HEIGHT: 21½ to 23½ inches for males, and 19½ to 21½ inches for females.

No numerical standard of points has yet been set up.

# LION AND CAT HOUNDS

If you were to ask, "What sporting dog is *really* worth his weight in gold?" many hunters would unhesitatingly answer "An experienced, well-trained lion or cat hound." Lion and cat hunters, wherever found, would readily join in the chorus.

Kennel editors of outdoor magazines receive frequent letters from readers who want to know where they can purchase trained cat and mountain-lion hounds. These inquirers are most likely novices in the sport, for this class of hound is rarely offered for sale. A good mountain-lion dog generally is beyond price, and when you do occasionally see one offered for sale you can almost be certain that the owner is moving to some section not inhabited by mountain lions and that his neighbors cannot afford to pay his "asking" price. *Good* mountain-lion dogs are scarcer than tax reductions and do not often change hands.

Lion hunters seldom stick to one breed of hounds. The main reason for this is that dogs of the proper temperament for this sport are hard to find, and when one is discovered the hunter cares little about his pedigree. He takes them as he finds them—and is glad to get them, regardless of size, color, or blood lines. Some lion hunters try to breed their own dogs to a certain type, but they are seldom averse to the introduction of new blood when it comes from tried and proved performers.

The professional lion hunter probably is more qualified than any other individual to discuss the merits of the various breeds or crossbreeds most suitable for this hunting. Henry P. Davis offers an interesting experience with one of these hunters, Bob Snow, who was in charge of the predatory-animal control work for Texas. On one trip Davis and Snow hunted an area known as the "Big Thickets" on the King Ranch, a tract embracing thousands of acres on which mountain lion or puma were quite common, and where an occasional ocelot and jaguar could be found. In this area the javelina also was found in fairly large numbers.

"Bob kept two packs. One consisted of his 'cat' hounds, the other of 'hog' hounds. The leader of the 'cat' pack was a stout-hearted white-and-tan hound appropriately named Lead. Up to that time Bob and his brother, Luther, had taken 38 mountain lions alive, by treeing them and roping and tying them up. Lead had been in on all 38 catches and many more, too, in which he had proved his ability as a warrior. I tried to place my hand on his rugged body without touching a scar, but found it impossible. Bob said the man from whom he had bought him said he was a Walker, but insisted the breeding or breed was unimportant, for 'no better cat dog ever lived.'

"One night around the campfire I asked the sun-bronzed Texan what he would take for Lead. He wouldn't have jumped higher if I had stuck him with a pin. 'Shucks, you ain't serious!' he snorted. Then, running his hand over his chin-stubble, he said, 'I might take a coupla sections of good bottom land if it laid along a good highway . . . But then—where would I find another one like him?' Next in line was a keen black hound with rich tan points. 'Some say he's a Trigg,' explained Bob. The rest were 'natives' picked up here and there and fashioned by experience into a dead-game, rough-and-tumble efficient pack that would cry nothing but a 'cat,' and would stay with it until the big yellow-eyed fellow came to bay or took to the low trees of that thorn-infested jungle.

"'Some of the best "cat" hounds I've had were Birdsongs,' said Bob. 'On a par with them were a few Hudspeths. I've run out of that blood now, but sure wish I could get some of it to cross on old "Lead."' Some time later I came across a litter of puppies whose ancestry could be traced back to what I was reasonably sure was some of the original Birdsong blood. I bought a dog and a bitch puppy, both black and tan in color, and sent them to Bob. The bitch proved too ambitious in battle and was killed in one of her first contacts with the big cats. The dog made an excellent adjunct to Bob's pack.

"To hunt in the country in which Bob was working a hound had to have courage and stamina above all else. Practically every form of vegetation down there is thorny or prickery and a good rough coat is essential. In other sections similar conditions may not be encountered, but the matter of 'bottom' still holds good. Mountain lions or pumas are generally found in rough and rugged country and to negotiate same a hound must be of the same nature. Boldness is another requisite—boldness tempered with caution."

Perhaps the best lion and cat dogs have a bit of "this and that" blood in their make-up. Bloodhound crosses are frequently made, and a dash of Airedale sometimes proves good. The Airedale adds gameness but diminishes voice to some extent. A good cat dog must have the nose to ferret out the trail in rough or rocky country, sometimes quite arid. He must have the perseverance to stay with the trail for a long stretch and the courage to push his quarry close enough to make him get above ground. A good mouth is very important, for the hunter must keep in touch with his pack.

In some western sections where bounty payments often make lion hunting pay its own way, the bluetick and redtick crosses, with a bit of bloodhound added, make excellent cat dogs. The old-fashioned black and tan, given the right opportunity, can do a good job. Sometimes the black and tan proves a bit too slow, but his speed is stepped up when crossed with the bluetick or redtick.

The Plott hound, originally developed in the Great Smokies of North Carolina and Tennessee for bear and boar hunting, is rapidly gaining the attention of lion and cat hunters. This hound possesses the ruggedness necessary, plenty of courage, and good mouth and pace. He will tackle anything on four feet with enough sagacity to keep it at bay. The dash-in—dash-out tactics are quickly learned by good lion dogs. If a dog does not learn them quickly he does not live long enough to become a *good* lion dog. The big cats are, as a rule, great cowards. They will not fight unless they have to; but then they can cut a pack to pieces unless wariness becomes a hound instinct. A game hound may kill a puma in a fair fight but he will seldom live to take up the trail again.

The good lion dog must have "heart" in plentiful quantity. This is the quality which carries him ever on, no matter how vague the trail or how rough the going. Without it he is not a *good* lion dog. The many qualities which a lion or cat dog must possess make him definitely scarce.

Do not expect to step out and pick up a good lion or cat pack as you would a pair of setters or pointers. Do not start your quest without reasonable amounts of money available. As Bob Snow put it, "Just tell me where I can find one half as good as old Lead. I'll crank up the flivver and we'll head in that direction. You don't need to mention price!"

## SQUIRREL DOGS

The wildfowler and the upland game bird hunter may not realize it, but the squirrel hunter outnumbers either clan. His sport is comparatively unsung, but when one gets back off the main highways and into the rural districts where shotguns and smallbore rifles are almost as much a part of the household equipment as axes and hammers, one is quite likely to find fried squirrel or squirrel and dumplings gracing the dinner table with regularity during the open season. If the roll were called on famous American army snipers in World Wars I and II one would discover that a great many of them learned the fundamentals of marksmanship cheeking the stock of a squirrel rifle.

For hunting almost every species of American game bird and small-game animal, a gun-dog specialist has been developed. As far as individual breeds go, however, this has not happened for the squirrel hunter. This seems strange when one considers the large number of hunters who go agunning for squirrel. Perhaps one reason is that a large portion of these hunters—in fact, probably the majority—prefer to do their squirrel hunting without benefit of dog. They contend that still hunting gets better results. Maybe it does, but those hunting are missing much when they deny themselves the companionship of a dog equally enthusiastic about the sport. If that dog 's properly trained he will put game in the bag for his master when the still-hunter will come home empty-handed.

True, in some sections certain types of small dogs have been developed which breed fairly true to type and seem to inherit the squirrel-hunting instinct. But, as a general rule, the most efficient squirrel dogs seem to have been made up of a bit of this breed, a bit of that, a dash of another breed, and then a little of another and another and no one knows how many others. But these little nondescript fellows knew their business—which is treeing squirrels and jockeying them into such positions as to afford the gunners a shot.

Quietness is essential in squirrel hunting, and so the best squirrel dogs are generally small ones, who work closely and with very little noise. The big blustering dog which goes racing through the woods will make his presence known immediately and every squirrel in the section will promptly take to cover.

Color is also important in the squirrel dog. A white or brightly colored dog is easily seen and instantly arouses suspicion. The brown, tan, gray or even black dog attracts little attention other than to arouse curiosity and he can often have his squirrel properly located without causing extreme wariness on the part of his quarry.

Good squirrel dogs should "tree" without barking too much or making too much noise. If he is working at proper range a low whine at frequent intervals should be enough to attract the attention of his master and also hold the curiosity of the squirrel. When a squirrel dog and his master understand each other thoroughly they make a most efficient team and watching them work is a thrilling pleasure.

Henry P. Davis, the well-known field trial authority, does not always follow the blooded dogs, and occasionally leaves the birds for a day of squirrel shooting. His story of Jumbo is an example of what a squirrel hunter wants, but does not always get, in a good squirrel dog.

"Some of the best squirrel dogs I ever saw were of no definite breed, but of definite squirrel-dog ancestry. One of these was Jumbo. Esau, my old colored mentor and constant companion during boyhood hunting trips, was Jumbo's master. The dog's name fitted him in reverse. No one would have granted him a second glance, for he was self-effacing and quiet, but many a day I have tagged along at Esau's heels and watched Jumbo and his master outwit brace after brace of unsuspecting nut cutters to the businesslike crack of Esau's single-shot .22. The master woodsman seemed not to turn a fallen leaf as he glided along, with an occasional 'Shhhhhhhhhh' to me. Other than to keep in touch with him with an occasional glance, Esau paid but little attention to Jumbo, but concentrated on the upper branches of the hickories. Occasionally we'd sit quietly on a fallen log while the little wraithlike dog cast about and Esau swept the trees with his all-seeing eyes. An accelerated pace was enough to warn Esau that Jumbo was on trail. A faint but eager whine would lead us near the trees under which the efficient Jumbo sat, gazing upward with his tail acting as a whiskbroom among the leaves. Esau would carefully and quietly work himself around to the opposite side of the tree and then, when all set, he'd give a low whistle. At the signal Jumbo would back a short way from the tree, bounce around enthusiastically and set up a rapid yapping. This was generally enough to cause some movement on the part of the squirrel, and once he revealed his whereabouts he was just about the same as in the bag which I was privileged to carry.

"I have said that Jumbo was not without benefit of ancestry. Esau could trace his breeding for several generations. To express it in his words: 'Jumbo's mammy is Unc' Isom Dickens' little blue Nellie. She is de daughter of Tobe Gentry's Bess and her pappy is Mister Ed Hall's proud little black-and-tan, Jet. Jumbo's pappy is ol' man Seab Newton's part fox-terror, part redbone and part pug-dog, named Racket. Now, Mister Hall's Jet is uh fulluhblood dog and Bess she's . . .' etc., etc. Jumbo was a bit of this and that, but it was all squirrel dog!"

Many small farm dogs get to be good squirrel dogs simply because they run loose most of the time and there are usually squirrels to chase in almost every farm woodlot. Once their masters shoot a few squirrels for them, their education is on its way to completion. Thereafter experience is all that is necessary.

It is a good idea to let the young squirrel dog get his mouth on a fallen squirrel now and then to keep up his enthusiasm. But be sure that the animal is past inflicting any punishment, for it can nip a young dog severely.

Practically any hound (beagle or other strain) can be taught to tree squirrels. The hound breeds, however, are often too mouthy for best results, and while hound blood most likely forms the background of most of the little bandy-legged mongrels which seem characteristic of the small farms of the South and Midwest, a mixed breed seems to work out best for this sport. They will not give you much music and the chase will be too short for thrills, but they will let you know where your quarry is—and it is up to you to do the rest.

# DOG HEALTH AND CARE

There are certain fundamentals of dog care and general health which all dog owners must remember to keep dogs through a full life span and have them healthy, good looking, and ready to serve as companion and hunting assistant. For example, knowledge of the danger of distemper, the problem of worms, methods of combating ticks and fleas, skin troubles, ear mites and infections of the inner ear, correct feeding, and similar subjects cannot be ignored by any dog owner who wants to avoid numerous veterinarian bills.

**Distemper.** This disease, like human influenza, is airborne. As young dogs are particularly susceptible to distemper, it pays to have a dog immunized. Your veterinarian can give you some sound advice on procedure. The worst part of distemper is what the "secondary invaders" do to the weakened dog. Dog owners have had too much trouble with pneumonia following distemper to not have a healthy respect for the disease and its after-effects. If you like your dog and want him with you for a long time, do not attempt home doctoring if you suspect the animal has distemper. It is better to hurry the animal to a small-animal hospital for treatment. As one veterinarian points out, any lively young dog that suddenly becomes sluggish and has no appetite may be suspected of coming down with distemper.

**Worms.** Americans are so worm conscious that far too many young dogs are overdosed with worm medicine. It is true that most pups bought for companion dogs or hunting may have roundworms and will require a vermifuge. It is easy to administer a medicine that will get rid of the common roundworm. But the trouble is that many owners think that every time a dog is indisposed worms are the cause. They administer a vermifuge and often make the dog worse instead of better.

Hookworms, heartworms, and whipworms are the types that should give the novice dog owner the most concern. The heartworm is principally a menace in the South although it has recently been appearing also among northern dogs. Some dogs sold today are now subject to an examination and statement showing them free of heartworm. Hookworms, little parasites, can make a dog quite anemic if they are not detected in time. The dog owner should not attempt home diagnosis if there is a suspicion of hookworm, whipworm or heartworm. If your dog is not up to par an examination by a good graduate veterinarian will (with his microscope) detect these dog enemies and he can adminster the correct treatment.

Tapeworms also use dogs as hosts. They can be removed easily by a veterinarian. This type of worm is readily visible, so that it is not so difficult for the amateur owner to detect.

**Care of the Ears.** A healthy dog has clean ears. An owner who does not examine the ears of his dog occasionally and clean the outer part, is usually reminded of his carelessness by the odor from the ears of his pet. Unfortunately cleaning the part of the ear that is visible to the eye and accessible without instruments does not always prevent infections or ear mites.

The ear mite is a very tiny creature that gets into a dog's ears and multiplies. It is not visible to the naked eye. One hunting dog picked up a colony of mites in a kennel. The owner knew that something was wrong with her ears because she worked on them so much. When the veterinarian made his examination (he used a microscope to examine a scraping from the ear) he could see the tiny pinpoint mites scampering around. A drug is needed to kill the mites, and a dog may develop a slight infection as a result of playing host to the parasites. When a dog works on his ears, it is wise to have a veterinarian determine what is wrong and prescribe treatment. So-called ear cankers (deep infections of the ear) are not to be toyed with. Any delay in treatment makes more trouble for both owner and the dog.

In some severe, chronic cases it may be necessary to remove a small piece of the ear cartilage, to give the ear more ventilation.

If you are miles away from a veterinarian the next best thing to calling on him is to treat the dog with some of the excellent preparations which have been brought out recently for ear infections. These are sold by drugstores and pet shops.

**Correct Food.** A sound diet, clean kennel runs, plenty of fresh drinking water, and adequate grooming mean more to the health of the dog than most inexperienced dog owners realize, according to those who have studied canine nutrition and related subjects. Meat, prepared dog foods, cereals in proper proportion, a small amount of fat in the diet, and a few vegetables are basic items in adequate nutrition and good health just as two and two make four. No matter where dog owners have to "cut corners," it does not pay to do the cutting on the dog's diet.

It has been definitely established that a dog needs and digests fat easily. The fatty acids are essential to health. In fact, recent experiments lead to the belief that some dogs which are apt to develop a summer skin trouble on the slightest provocation can be helped considerably when they receive a small amount of fat in their meals daily. The dog's tolerance and assimilation of fat is such that a chunk of lard can be dropped into his food pan and he will eat it and digest it easily. For a hunting dog or a house pet that is down in weight, give plenty of fat in the evening meal. It can be beef suet, fat from mutton, grease from the pan, or anything of that sort as long as it is animal fat. This item in the diet will help a dog put on weight and improve his coat.

One winter in a mountain-lion hunting camp in the Chiricahua Mountains of Arizona, guests noticed and asked about the meals being served to the big hounds. In every pan of food given to a dog were several lumps of fat. The dogs which were running miles every day over the mountains needed this element in their diet.

**Skin Troubles.** Skin troubles are the bane of most dog owners. Some have an obscure origin which makes it difficult for the owner (and the animal). A prominent veterinarian was asked some time ago for the percentages on the different kinds of skin trouble he sees each year. Here they are:

| | | |
|---|---|---|
| Sarcoptic mange | — | 1 per cent |
| Follicular mange | — | 2 " " |
| Ringworm | —about | 5 " " |
| Eczema of obscure origin | — | 10 " " |
| Skin eruptions due to the dog's skin being irritated by a fungus picked up from grass and weeds | — | 75 to 80 " " |

In caring for a dog one has to keep these percentages in mind. Fortunately there is a cure for the so-called "summer-itch" which is caused by a fungus. A specific drug has been found to handle such cases. But obscure eczemas are another thing. As a rule, these eczemas, whether dry or moist, are called "mange," although they are not true mange. It is good to have a veterinarian, with his microscope, make a diagnosis to determine whether or not a dog has true mange (caused by a living organism), eczema, or an "itch" caused by fungus. A veterinarian is definitely needed after which treatment may be continued at home.

**Ticks and Fleas.** In caring for a dog (especially one with a rather dense coat) some work is called for if the animal lives in a tick-infested country. This is one parasite that cannot be ignored in dog care, especially if the dog comes into the home, because ticks will drop from the dog and hatch out a new crop indoors. (One tick can lay up to 3000 eggs.)

An owner has a choice of a powder or a liquid dip for fighting ticks. For years many owners have relied on a dip that is non-irritating to the dog's skin, yet kills the ticks in a short time and makes very short work of fleas and lice. This particular dip has rotenone as the insecticide. The preparation can be bought in almost any pet shop. The dog is put in a cast-iron tub, and then, with a sponge, he is soaked with the dip, which leaves a fresh, fragrant, sassafras odor in his coat.

There are also powders that will kill ticks and help to keep them out of a dog's coat. These can be obtained from most drugstores and pet shops.

An owner has an obligation when he owns a dog—an obligation to give the animal proper care, food, and housing. But all dog owners know that the amount of care given a dog is repaid a thousandfold by the devotion and loyalty that the pets give in return.

# DOG TRAINING

For the man who acquires his first gun-dog, be it pointer, setter, spaniel or retriever, there lie ahead many pleasant problems plus untold satisfaction in the end. There is no better age at which to acquire such a dog than at the age of eight or nine months. At that age a young dog should be getting past the more severe problems of puppyhood, but at the same time should be still too young to have become spoiled by improper previous handling.

If the prospect is brought to his new home in your car, and has not previously had such experience, nine out of ten dogs will show car sickness. This invariably worries most people and they wonder if the dog will ever get over it and how to proceed toward that end. Car sickness is the least of your worries. This because there is but one method to cure it and that method is absolutely certain of results. The cure consists simply of taking the dog for a ride at any and every opportunity. It is not possible to predict how soon a cure will be effected. A complete cure, however, is as certain as sunrise, whether it comes quickly or takes some little time.

**Kennels.** Unless the dog is to be kept in the house, you should previously have arranged for his accommodation. Many persons believe that for a hunting dog to become a house dog will sooner or later affect his value in the field. That idea is as mistaken as are most such ideas in connection with dogs. If the dog is by nature and inheritance imbued with an indefatigable hunting desire, that desire and the ability to fulfill it will in no way be affected by any proper amount of petting or living with the family.

Even so, outside accommodations for the dog are desirable. A dog is better off to have his own outside quarters and to be kept in them except when taken afield or astream. Even for the dog permitted in the house there are many times and circumstances under which having suitable kennel quarters will be necessary. The runway should be as large as space permits—though it may be relatively small if that is the best you can do. The fencing should be heavy and sturdy enough to hold any dog under any circumstances. Many dogs will be able to bite through and escape from any such light fencing material as chicken netting. The fencing should be sunk in the ground to a depth of at least a foot, and there meet cement. This will prevent a dog so inclined from digging under to freedom—which most dogs will try. The runway fencing should be high enough that no dog may climb or jump it. If it is faced inward a couple of feet at the top, supported by angle bars, it need not be so high as straight upright fencing.

The dog house or kennel proper need be no larger than to accommodate the dog or dogs in comfort. It will thus be more snug and warmer in winter. It should be entirely free from dampness or drafts. If the house is neither wet nor windy, any dog accustomed to it can take almost any amount of merely cold weather—and be just as well off for it. The actual bed in the kennel should be raised slightly and/or hinged so that it may be lifted to clean under it. Wheat straw is about as good winter bedding as can be found. For summer bedding red cedar shavings are ideal. These may be obtained from many sources, as advertised in dog magazines or kennel departments. Never use oat straw at any time, as it seems very conducive to skin troubles.

The first thing to consider on bringing any dog to a new home, and especially if kenneled outside, is how to overcome the annoyance of barking. The best answer to that is a simple one: Have *two* dogs instead of one. Whether young or old, any dog gets lonesome when left alone. The only way he has to tell his troubles is by barking. Even with two dogs, one or both may need to be quieted. Punishment with a rolled-up newspaper is the best procedure. This will not do the dog a bit of harm but will make a lot of noise and cause him to feel that more is happening to him than actually is. As the punishment is administered the word "Quiet!" should be constantly repeated. Before very long a dog will learn to obey the spoken command minus the punishment that he knows will follow if he doesn't.

It is many times more difficult—but possible—to keep one dog and train him against barking. Having said that, it should also be stated that there can be exceptions to every rule. If you find yourself with a dog that simply cannot be made to do this or that, then the only answer may be to change dogs and try again. To train a single dog not to bark in the kennel, the procedure is the same as already outlined except that the difficulty of accomplishment will be greatly increased, and take longer. The process, however, is to administer the newspaper punishment in the same way, accompanied by the word "Quiet!"

There is only one other alternative; that is to get an anti-barking bridle. This device is constructed in such a way as not to prevent a dog from lapping water in hot weather and yet at the same time to interfere with his objectionable barking. In connection with barking or any other later training, however, there is one very definite rule that should always apply to yourself. *Never* be unreasonable or unfair to the pupil. In the case of barking prompted by a visiting stray dog that constitutes the provocation for your dog to bark, then the thing you should do is remove that provocation—not just punish your dog. In short, never in any way ask anything unreasonable of your future hunting companion. Always be fair and he is more apt to repay you in kind. More than that, if you are sure in your own mind of your fairness, you will have a better "right" to insist upon whatever you may feel necessary. This is more important than many may imagine.

It should scarcely need saying that kennels should always be clean and the dog's water always be fresh daily. For hot weather it is well to have the largest possible water trough or tub. In winter less water is called for, and when there is ice to contend with a much smaller pan of water should be substituted.

Young dogs should be fed often but less at a time. At eight or nine months of age two meals a day are sufficient. After the dog is a year and a half old most authorities prefer but one meal a day, preferably at night, and then as much at a time as a dog cares to eat or his condition seems to call for. But dogs, like human beings, are as individual as thumb prints. Some are light and others are hearty eaters. The answer lies in what his or her condition shows—or what is suggested in consultation with your veterinarian.

**Health and Care.** Young dogs need worming from time to time. This should be based upon your veterinarian's examination and his finding as to what kind of worms are encountered. Not all worms are the same and proper treatment differs accordingly. This you should not try to determine for yourself. Another important thing in connection with mention of your veterinarian is that at eight or nine months of age every dog should be inoculated against distemper, and the Laidlaw-Duncan treatment is recommended. When you acquire a dog it is essential that you find out just what, if any, distemper treatment he has had. If none, then one of your first jobs is to select your local, licensed, graduate veterinarian with whom to discuss the matter.

It has been stated that eight or nine months of age is the best age for acquisition of your dog. At that age, too, whether pointer, setter, spaniel, or retriever, the dog will be approaching the right age to begin any sort of training. It is not true that you can't teach an old dog new tricks. There are many who will prefer to let a dog reach 16 or 18 months of age before getting very serious with training. It is not recommended to try serious training with a dog younger than eight or nine months. Suffice it to say that the younger the pupil the more judicious the master should be with discipline. There is a different approach as between a high-school pupil and a college student. The same principle applies to dogs. Regardless of breed or what you hope to train the dog to do, the first job is to win his friendship and fullest confidence. Make him your friend. Until you have accomplished that you might as well give no thought whatever to discipline from any standpoint. Always be friendly, always fair, and at the same time always firm. The Three F's of *friendship, fairness,* and *firmness* are the foundation on which all training is laid. Build that foundation well.

**Yard Training.** The first essential is that the dog must come to you promptly when called. Forty-nine times in fifty this will be his natural inclination and you will have no trouble at all. If, however, you have the exceptional pupil who refuses—who tries to insist upon whatever his own inclinations may be—then he has to be circumvented and shown that there is no alternative but to obey your every command. Equip yourself with a long lead (a good length of clothesline is ideal for the purpose). To make the lesson more emphatic and drive it home all the harder, place a pan of milk in the yard and let the dog start to lap it while you walk away to about the end of the lead. By the time you have let him drink some of the milk—but not more than half—call him to come to you: "Here, Bob!" Since you are working with one you know to need discipline, he does not obey you. He sticks to the milk and ignores the command. Call him a second time, somewhat more firmly. Give him a slight jerk to pull him away from the milk but not hurt him, and then bring him to you by taking in the lead hand over hand. Pat him when he has come within reach and say, "Good boy." Soon pat him again and say "All right"—this as permission to return to the pan of milk. Keep this up as long as needed to accomplish your purpose. Most dogs will learn quickly. Some are more stubborn. How long this lesson will take depends entirely upon the individuality of the pupil.

Never make any lesson too long. Regular short lessons daily are many times better than fewer but longer lessons. The idea is never to wear a dog out with discipline. Short lessons, but decisive, are the thing. That way you are not a party to working him to the point of boredom. Reserve punishment for willful disobedience to known rule. Never punish a dog in the process of learning. At that time he does not know any better. Other ways than punishment must be found to get over any idea. Punishment, when used, must be short and severe. The perpetually punished dog will soon be a ruined dog. The dog needing constant punishment has never been properly *reached*. That business of reaching him is your job. Until you have somehow won and reached him you have not done your job. You cannot blame him for that. There are many rules of procedure in discipline. There can be no rule for art in handling. Some are naturally gifted with it. Others are not. Every man must try to teach himself to train his dog.

Every gun-dog must be susceptible to being led. With many you just attach a lead to the collar and they will follow along without any restraint. Just as many, however, will fight the lead before accustomed to it. Do not jerk or roughly handle any such dogs. A dog that does not immediately respond to the lead will either lie down or sit. Without jerking, simply pull the pupil hard enough to move him. Whether on stomach or rear end, he will not want that long. The dog will get up to his feet. One lesson or two at most ought to suffice for full accomplishment. Always reward with praise and a pat for each and every proper response your dog ever makes.

The dog fully under control is taught to walk at heel. You have already taught him to lead, but the eager dog will do so ahead of you. Now you want to teach him to walk behind you in docile compliance. A little switch with leaves on the end is a good aid to teaching. Lacking that, a newspaper will do. You walk along with dog on lead and say, "Heel." He does not know what you mean, so you pull him back, holding the lead in your left hand and extending it behind you until the dog is forced to walk with his nose not ahead of your left knee. As he tries to pull farther ahead, repeat the word "Heel," and at the same time gently switch his nose with the leafy end—or newspaper if that is what you use. This keeps him back. There is nothing else to it except sufficient daily repetition until the pupil will walk in position unrestrained by the lead or anything other than the word "Heel" itself.

An important thing to teach the dog (especially true of retrievers) is to lie down and stay there until given permission to leave. With lead attached, order the dog "Down." He will not know what you mean, and so you gently press him down to give him the idea. If he does not drop, the pressure will have to be increased until he does. It is well to press down the hind quarters first. When the dog is lying flat, release the pressure but repeat the word "Down" the instant he attempts to arise. If saying "Down" in itself is not enough, you will have to reapply the pressure. That will be enough for one lesson, and try not to make it too long.

It is rather essential that you manage the ending of each lesson so that it may terminate with praise and a job well done, rather than unpleasantness. Toward this end, if the results from a particular lesson being taught do not properly permit of a pat, then it is well to go back to something else you know the dog will perform properly, and have him do whatever that is in order that the ending of the training session may be on a happy note.

Having taught the dog to lie down at command, the next step is to assure yourself that he will stay until permission to leave is received. There is no use to attempt this until a number of lessons have given full assurance that there is no misunderstanding on the part of the pupil and no lack of compliance when you say "Down." When such time arrives, the only thing further is that you gradually move farther and farther away from the dog and order him to "Stay" as you do so. At any indication of getting up, you repeat the word "Down." It may be that to get proper compliance you will have to move back closer and then try all over again after ordering "Stay."

It will call for a lot of patience on your part and a lot of practice on the dog's, but practice makes perfect, and if you do your part the day will come when you can order the dog "Down" and he will promptly obey; when you can then order him to "Stay" and be assured that he will, even though you may go out of sight and remain for some little time. Training a dog takes not only patience but often even much ingenuity. If you have a problem pupil you may have to do considerable thinking through to the cause of your difficulties and concoct some inglorious schemes to circumvent them. The average intelligent master should be able to outthink the average dog. Even so, it is a challenge and always an interesting one.

The breeds that point game are the Pointer, Setter, Brittany Spaniel, and German Shorthaired Pointer. There are two other breeds that will point game, both very rare in this country. These are the Wire-haired Pointing Griffon and the Weimaraner. Anyone interested in the pointing dog will be concerned chiefly with the first three breeds named. However, any of the pointing breeds should be handled similarly so far as field training is concerned.

**Field Training.** The first step is to take the dog while young to the field as often as possible and preferably where upland game birds may be encountered. Let the dog run and hunt to his heart's content. If he finds, flushes, and chases birds, so much the better. There is nothing gained by trying to restrain him until he has learned to hunt. If he has not enough natural hunting instinct, the chances are that he may never amount to much. Nevertheless, there are exceptions to all rules. It happens now and then that a dog showing little early heart for the hunt may develop it later, with age and experience. It stands to reason, however, that it is better to work with a good prospect than a poor one. If one is not gifted with abundant patience—or has not yet formed a deep fondness for the dog—it is well to exchange a poor prospect for a good one as soon as possible. Beware of the prospect that does too much piddling around or puts his or her nose to the ground too incessantly. A high-class pointing dog should work for body scent only and seldom or never waste time on foot scent or attempts at trailing. All game birds will lie better to the bold, vigorous dog that dashes up to body scent and learns exactly how close he may approach with impunity.

It is a good idea every time you turn a dog loose to give a short, sharp double note on the whistle. If this is kept up, he associates this signal with the act of going away. The advantage is that if he ever later starts to potter, or you wish him to go wider to some destination, you can give him this signal and send him on. The come-in signal is prolonged whistling. The way to teach this is to practice it when attempting to take your dog up at the end of a workout. Some may respond naturally. Others may be both slower to catch on and to yield. You may have to call the dog by voice as an aid to the whistle. But if the whistle is used in connection with the calling, it will help the dog to get the idea of the signal. Most hunting-dog men prefer an Acme Thunderer whistle, and preferably of bakelite. A metal whistle in zero weather may stick to the lips and take the skin off; a bakelite whistle is suitable for any weather.

It is assumed that in turning any dog loose in the field he will previously have been made proof against young pigs, poultry, sheep, or what not. If the average young dog is subjected to an old hen with a brood of chicks, she will cure him in a hurry. To protect her chicks she will fly directly at the dog with a flapping, pecking, and stabbing that will cure him of poultry. If a dog has killed a chicken, the best cure is to get the dead chicken and wire it firmly up under the dog's neck. Wire it tight to his collar in a manner to make it secure. He may claw at it but he cannot reach it with his teeth. What he does to the chicken by clawing will but aid in sickening him of dead poultry. If the weather is warm for this cure, so much the better. The idea is to leave the chicken attached to the dog until it practically rots away. Then remove the feet or whatever is left, and it is safe to bet that no repeat will be necessary.

For a dog that attacks young pigs no cure is known except to get to him and punish him. If the old sow gets to him first, there may be no dog left to cure. Many dogs have an almost insane desire to tackle sheep. If they ever taste blood, a high percentage may never be trusted again. Beware of the first sheep. Any extremity of punishment is in order and will be but fair to the dog, whether he knows it or not. Otherwise he is sure to be killed some day by an irate farmer.

Do not bother too much at first about a young bird dog chasing rabbits. You may talk to him in a tone of voice to indicate that you do not approve, but in the early stages do not take extreme measures. The idea above all else is that the dog should learn to hunt and learn to love it. Fur is naturally as attractive as feather. Later, after a pointing dog is fully finished on game, and has had every reason in the world to know that you neither expect nor wish him to hunt rabbits—then will be time enough for a cure, if he still persists. Kill a rabbit in front of him some day when he is chasing it, but not close enough to run any danger of his getting even a stray shot. Then take the rabbit firmly by the legs and use it as a whip to flog the dog until he decides to let rabbits alone.

**Steadying.** Any of the pointing breeds should at least "flash" point on first contact with game. That is, they should flash point if the scent is right. If flushing birds catch a young dog by surprise, there will be no flash point. If he winds them first, however, he should stop, if but for an instant. Stanch pointing is simply prolonging that instantaneous pause until the dog will hold such a point for an indefinite time. There are dogs so full of the pointing instinct that they may practically stanch themselves if they have opportunity to find enough game under good scenting conditions. Some of these dogs, having chased a lot of game and finding they cannot catch it, have sense enough to decide that pursuit is no use, and that tends toward a greater willingness to hold the point.

With more pupils than not, however, you will just have to be patient and wait for the day when you can get close enough to get your hands on them. For this the breaks will have to favor you. The scent must be coming so strong as to help stop and hold the dog. You must be close enough so that he doesn't have to wait too long. When you get your hands on the dog, stroke him soothingly and let him know he is doing right. Stroke his tail up so that he will tend to hold it proudly. With your hands on him you can keep him steady for some little time. And here is a trick to be sure to use: Gently place a hand on his hind quarters and exert a little pressure to push him toward the birds. It is surprising how this tends toward steadiness. He might be wishing he could jump in and send the birds out. He does not, however, want to be shoved into them by you. Therefore, he resists the pressure. In the process of doing just that he is learning stanchness as nothing else can teach it. Naturally the dog should not be kept on point long enough to tire him out. Two or three minutes is plenty. Then step in, flush the birds, and let him go with them. Keep this up until he is so surely stanch on point that you can trust him under any and all circumstances to hold point for your arrival.

The next step is steadiness to wing and shot. For this you want a long, stout check cord. It must be really stout—one that will stand plenty of strain. For this lesson it is preferable to have someone with you to do the flushing. If that is impossible, you will just have to manage it yourself. Hold the check cord loose but wrapped firmly around your right hand at the end. When the birds are flushed, the dog will go with them as usual. Speak *"whoa"* to him very severely. He won't listen. Brace yourself. Just as he is about to hit the end of the check cord, speak *"whoa"* again. If he is going fast enough, and you are braced well enough, and if the check cord stands it, and you have a sufficiently good grip on the end of it, that dog will turn a somersault that will surprise him. Two or three times of this—if that many are necessary—and he will stay steady to wing when you say "Whoa." He may even stay steady without the command. Being steady to wing, he will automatically be steady to shot. There is this exception: If a bird is killed, he may want to go in to retrieve without waiting for the command. A good many hunters do not object to this and some even prefer it. There is no question but that the dog will thus recover many a crippled bird that might otherwise be lost.

It is presumed that the dog is already proof against gun shyness. Find out when you buy if he has ever heard gunfire—and to what extent. Even if he has, you should not at once try to test him. It is important first to have made friends with him and won his confidence. Never shoot too close to any dog. Never shoot except in the field and when the dog is flushing, chasing, or pointing game. The point is that he should have his whole heart and soul centered on the game before him. Then if the gun is fired, and not too close—and you have previously won his confidence—he need never be gun shy. If a bird is killed, and he thus sees what the gun can accomplish, it will do much to assure that he will always love and never fear a firearm. Gun shyness is not natural. It is not hereditary. It is always some man's fault. It is never the fault of the dog.

**Spaniel Training.** Spaniels (other than Brittanys, which point their game) should be taken afield in the beginning just as already indicated for the pointing breeds. However, spaniels (which in this country practically means springers and cockers) do not point game, but flush it within gun range. Since this means an average of 30 yards, spaniels should quarter or "beat" their course within that distance. Beyond 40 yards they will be useless so far as delivering game to the gun is concerned. Therefore, the whole job in training a spaniel consists in seeing to it that he responds to whistle or spoken command to confine his cast back and forth in front of the hunter. As this is the natural range of the spaniel, there probably will not be much difficulty. With the individual that proves exceptional there is nothing to do but let him drag a long rope while hunting—which you can run to and step on to make him heed if he fails to obey your command. That command is the sharp single note of the whistle to call his attention—and then a wave of the arm to direct him to swing back and quarter across in front. Until he learns to respond to the signal of the arm, the trainer may turn himself and start to walk in the direction indicated. That may be dispensed with later when the spaniel has got the idea of response to the arm signal.

Since spaniels flush or "spring" game rather than point it, it becomes especially essential that they should be steady to shot and wing. Custom decrees that spaniels sit, rather than drop or simply stand steady. The command used for spaniels to sit is "Hup." There is, of course, no reason why a spaniel might not be taught to drop to flush. You have already learned how to teach a dog to drop—and also stay there. If you want to teach him merely to "hup," the only difference would be that instead of pressing him flat in the early lesson, you simply press his hind quarters to the ground and permit him to sit, using the command "Hup" instead of the command "Down." For its practical application in the field, a spaniel being taught to hup steadily to wing should be worked with a check cord the same as a pointing dog when being made steady to wing. There is no difference except that the one stands and the other sits. Many oldtime hunters used to teach their hunting dogs to drop to wing and shot. There is no question but that a dropped dog can be kept steady more readily than one standing. Perhaps that is a main reason why spaniels are taught to hup rather than allowed to stand at flush.

**Retriever Training.** The retrievers are the following: Chesapeakes, Labradors, Goldens, curly-coated retrievers, flat-coated retrievers, Irish water spaniels, and American water spaniels. All of these are adapted by coat and nature to stand long, hard hours in a duck blind and retrieve wildfowl from icy water. Other breeds might retrieve ducks under moderate conditions, but have no business being subjected to the icy elements on a typical duck day. Individuals of many breeds will take naturally to retrieving. Some mere puppies like to play with a ball and retrieve it. Some dogs will naturally retrieve the first bird ever killed in front of them. Some excellent retrievers have been just naturally developed. The fact remains, however, that these dogs retrieve because they like to. If for any reason one such should ever get it into his head that he has changed his mind about liking it, then the master may well have quite a problem on his hands about how to correct the situation. Therefore, even the naturally inclined retrievers are usually what is called "force" trained.

The word "force" as here used has nothing to do with cruelty in any respect whatever. It simply means that retrieving has been definitely taught and by a system which compels compliance. Since this same system applies equally to the retrievers, pointers, setters, spaniels, or any other breed asked to do the job, the following "force" system is recommended. (All hunting dogs should be taught to retrieve, because a good retriever is a true conservationist by saving game. Few hunters will dispute this; as a matter of fact, many hunters are as much interested in retrieving as in any other phase of performance.)

To go about teaching retrieving, the first thing you need is an object. Make a tiny sawbuck and you will have about as good as any. Another excellent ready-made object is a corncob. An old glove or any sort of pad is an objectionable object because it absorbs saliva and soon becomes soiled and offensive. But a corncob may always be clean; merely substitute a fresh one as often as needed. The only possible objection to a corncob is its softness, which may encourage some dogs to pinch down too hard and develop a tendency to hard mouth; there is, however, a remedy for that which will be mentioned shortly.

Adjust your training collar to the dog's neck, with the running-free end on the upper side, and attach a short piece of stout cord. Grasp this up close to the ring with the right hand and hold the corncob with the left hand in front of the dog's nose where he can easily see it. Give the command "Fetch" in an ordinary tone of voice and accompany this command by a very slight jerk or pressure on the collar. As the dog opens his mouth, instantly and gently place the cob in it, slackening the pressure of the collar at the same moment. Hold your left hand under his mouth and thus keep it closed on the cob. Soothe his fears and induce him to hold the cob steadily, caressing him if he holds it well. The first lesson should not be too prolonged. After one or two repetitions call it a day.

Continue with this first lesson regularly, from day to day, until the dog will open his mouth promptly when you give the command "Fetch." Teach him to hold and carry the cob reliably without mouthing it. These lessons should be given in a well-ventilated room, avoiding any distractions, diversions, or annoyances from spectators. A room has the further advantage of keeping the dog from cherishing ideas of escape, which may be his natural inclination during these early stages of training. In hot weather, the lessons should be given during the cool of early morning or late evening; under no circumstances should they be continued until the dog is manifestly discouraged under the restraint of discipline. Never end a lesson abruptly or with punishment. Lead the dog about for a few moments, praise and reassure him, then take off the training collar, thus concluding the lesson pleasantly.

Should the dog show strong tendencies toward an uncontrollably hard mouth, this fault must be corrected at once. Prepare a device as follows: Through a piece of wood about the size of a corncob drive some wrought nails and clinch the ends around the outside of it. Put in enough so that he cannot grasp the wood without somewhere touching the nails with his teeth. After grasping it once harshly he may afterward refuse to retrieve it. If so, force him to do it just as you began the first lesson with the cob. All dogs have an intense dislike of closing their teeth on a hard substance. This device will enable you, after a bit of constant use, to effect tenderness in retrieving.

Having taught the dog to open his mouth promptly to the order of "Fetch," the next stage is to teach him to step forward and grasp the object. In this lesson you need several feet of stuot cord attached to the training collar so that the dog is free to step forward when he hears the order. Hold the cob a few inches in front of the dog's mouth and on a level with it, where he may both readily see and grasp it. Give the order "Fetch," exerting the necessary pressure on the collar at the same time and in a forward direction toward the cob, thus assisting him to grasp it. The moment the cob is in his mouth the collar pressure must be slackened. Be deliberate, and praise the dog when he has done well. Continue such lessons in this manner until he will, without the pressure of the collar, step forward promptly and grasp the cob at the order of "Fetch."

At this juncture, the dog may continue holding the cob when you wish him to release it, being apprehensive that, if it is not in his mouth, the pressure of the force collar may follow. Reassure him kindly every time he surrenders it to command. If he will not let go promptly upon order, grasp the end of the cob in the left hand, but do not pull strongly on it. It is unwise to take it by *direct* force. When you have grasped the end of the cob with your left hand, command him to "Give." Be prepared, if he refuses, to step on the toes of his forefoot. Use just enough pressure on his foot to force him to open his mouth—and this will require but very little. After a few repetitions, he should surrender the cob instantly upon the order to "Give."

If you twirl the cob temptingly and playfully before the dog's nose, he may attempt to grasp it. It is a distinct gain if he will do so. Then he can be taught in a few lessons to pick up the cob. But too much playfulness should not be encouraged. The lessons must not lose the character of discipline. If too much playfulness is permitted, the force system will have no advantage over natural retrieving.

Having trained the dog so that he will step forward to grasp the cob as ordered, the next stage is to teach him to lower his head to grasp it. This is accomplished simply by the process of gradually lowering the cob, at first only 2 or 3 inches at a time so that the change of position is not too suddenly radical. If you can tempt the dog with the cob, it should be easy to get him to follow it as it is lowered. If the dog takes kindly to this new lesson, he will sometimes even pick up the cob from the floor after a very few attempts, particularly if you are tactful and do not proceed in too much of a hurry. A dog which is really anxious to please requires very little punishment and there may not be any perceptible stages in his progress; but in most instances the successive stages have to be formally and thoroughly observed. The dog requires time and schooling to comprehend his lessons. Hurrying him faster than he can comprehend or remember simply results in loss of time in the end.

At last the dog will pick up the cob when he is ordered to "Fetch," provided it is held on the floor; but if the hand is removed, he may at first make mistakes. He has previously been guided by following the hand. He may still follow the hand, which results in confusion if the hand is not near the cob. By keeping the hand close to the cob, after the latter has been placed on the floor, the dog is induced to pick it up. Finally, after many repetitions, he should gradually forget the hand and learn to concentrate on the cob alone.

It must be admitted that it is sometimes difficult to persuade certain dogs to lower their heads. Some may be exceptionally obstinate in this respect. Force is the only answer in such cases. You must compel obedience. This means that you must be firm. It does not mean that you must be rough.

After the dog will pick up the cob, you may next throw it a foot or two in front of him and give him the order to "Fetch." In this lesson a longer check cord is required. If the dog does not move forward to the order, give him a pull to start him forward and at the same time repeat the order. If the previous stages of the training have been hurried over too rapidly, or imperfectly taught, the effect will be more manifest now than at any previous stage. It may even be necessary to return to some prior stage of development and begin all over again. If the dog has been properly prepared up to this point, it should be easy. This lesson should be thoroughly and regularly given, until the dog is reliably trained to fetch the object promptly without the use of the collar.

Then he should be given practice on a dead bird. If he shows any tendency to be hard-mouthed with this, you may tie some ten-penny nails to the bird, which may be removed after he begins to pick it up and carry it tenderly.

When he will retrieve the dead bird well (which may require a number of special lessons) he may next be taken to the yard or even an open field for practice. Be sure that you have him under perfect control; for if the pupil once learns that he may escape from discipline by using his heels, you will but give yourself a new problem before the training in retrieving can proceed.

No slovenly obedience should ever be accepted. Some men are satisfied if the dog brings the bird in and drops it close by. Do not accept such a performance. Insist that the dog complete his task. If you start slowly to walk away from him, this will often assist in inducing him to bring the bird in a direct line to you.

After your dog will fetch reliably, continue the lessons for many weeks so that the training will be indelibly imprinted upon his memory, and also to the end that perfect and prompt obedience may be established. He will then become so habituated to the work that disobedience or shirking never enters his mind.

In time, you may venture upon variations from the regular formula, with a view to developing the dog's intelligence. The cob may be shown him and then thrown into bushes or tall grass, where he cannot see it, thereby forcing him to use his nose in finding it. The dog should learn to exercise a close watchfulness; this becomes an especially valuable trait later on in marking down game which falls to the gun.

He may even be schooled to carry dead birds steadily to heel. You might drop a bird unobserved by the dog, but do it so that he will pass close and have a chance to smell it. Praise him highly if he picks it up. If he sniffs it but passes on, you should pretend to find it yourself and your manner should give evidence of pleasure at discovering such a prize, so that the dog's interest and desire to emulate may be aroused. Then require the dog to retrieve it. This program should be repeated from time to time until the dog will invariably fetch a bird he runs across accidentally. The result of this should be the bringing in of dead or wounded birds of which even the hunter may not have been aware.

As mentioned before, always insist on a perfect retrieve to hand. If you have adopted the method of giving him rewards, do not permit him to hurry through his work or half do it, in his eagerness to get the reward. Insist on having every detail properly observed. Nothing is more annoying in practical work than the dog's dropping a bird brought halfway in, or dropping the bird on the opposite side of a creek, necessitating a chase and retrieve on the part of the shooter, or another retrieve of the same bird by the dog.

Do not move when you send your dog in to retrieve game in the field. This is important. Tramping and stamping around in the vicinity of where you think the bird should be, you confuse your scent with that of the game you seek—and simply make it that much harder for the dog. If a dog can smell a dead bird, he can also smell your scent—and where there are two such scents, one is bound to have a diminishing effect upon the other. So there is good logic in adopting the practice of standing perfectly still in one place and sending your dog on to do the seeking for dead or wounded game.

**Rules of Training.** There are a number of important *do's* and *dont's* in connection with dogs. Perhaps the *do's* will pretty much take care of themselves—but here are some *dont's.*

Don't ever nag at a dog; when you speak to him, mean it. The dog constantly nagged at will never amount to much—and can't.

Don't ever punish if in doubt. Always give the dog the benefit of any doubt. But if punishment is unconditionally called for, make it severe enough to count. Thus once should suffice for any given infraction. It is a question whether constant punishment is worse than constant nagging; both are bad.

Don't ever tease a dog. Respect him and earn his respect. Don't accept partial or slovenly performance. Insist that the dog perform completely any task, as he has been taught he should.

Don't vary commands. Make them always the same. Thus you preclude any confusion or uncertainty.

Don't work or hunt your dog except with his peers. If you go with men whose dogs will but spoil yours, leave them and hunt alone—or if you go with them, don't take your dog.

Don't ever lend your dog to anyone, not even a best friend—any more than you would your wife. If you lend your dog to a friend the chances are you won't be friends for long.

Don't ever ask anything unreasonable of a dog. Be jealous to guard his respect for you and his desire to perform as you would have him.

Don't give him freedom to roam and find bad company. Dogs can become tramps and get into bad habits the same as people.

Don't let companions who hunt with you spoil the dog by breaking shot or otherwise. If a man breaks shot you can't blame a dog for doing so.

## BIRD DOG FIELD TRIALS

"Are bird dog trials *really* of value in improving bird dog breeds?" This question is frequently asked by novitiates witnessing their first field trial. Those who take an active interest in these events answer the question with an unqualified "Yes!"

Field trials are events wherein individual bird dogs are given the opportunity to display their field qualities in direct competition.

They serve varied purposes. The primary object is the improvement of the bird-dog breeds through a more general dissemination of information concerning producing blood-lines and breeding procedure and a demonstration of the results of various breedings. This knowledge, so essential if future bird-dog generations are to measure up to the highest standards of field performance, can be best obtained through the avenue of public competition provided in field trials. Field trial standards approach the ideal and the history of progress in American bird-dog breeding is found in the annals of the sport.

Field trials provide the weathervane of bird-dog breeding programs.

The social side of a field trial is one of its most attractive features. The friendships formed are lasting. There is always a spirit of good-fellowship and camaraderie and there is no class distinction among the devotees of the sport. Every field trial is a gathering of high-class sportsmen and sportswomen on common ground and in a common interest and no higher degree of sportsmanship is prevalent in any sport.

The sport provides a medium for the interchange of constructive ideas concerning everything pertaining to the gun dog and, while the theories advanced may not always be in accord, the ensuing arguments are in the spirit of friendliness.

Field trials have always been, and are now recognized as, outstanding contributions to game restoration and conservation programs. Many game-management programs, beneficial to the entire countryside, have been launched on field trial grounds, the resulting research proving of great value to wildlife resources in general.

The first public field trial in America was held at Memphis, Tenn., October 8, 1874. The winner was Knight, a black setter dog belonging to H. Clark Pritchett. The stake was sponsored by the Tennessee State Sportsmen's Association and the judges were J. W. Burton and J. H. Acklen. The contest was the result of some rather heated arguments among the members concerning the field merits of their respective dogs.

The Tennessee State Sportsmen's Association sponsored the sport exclusively until 1877, when the Hampton, Iowa, trials were held. Since that time the growth of interest has been steady. From 1880 to 1890, the sport recorded an average of six trials annually, with an average total of 120 dogs competing. After that period the sport rapidly spread to all sections of the country. In the decade from 1920 to 1930 an average of 144 trials, with 369 stakes, was held. During this period an average of 5535 bird dogs of various breeds competed annually in field trials. In more recent years the sport has grown by leaps and bounds until now there are a number of annual events in practically every section of the country. There are now about 250 recognized field trial clubs in the country and it is safe to estimate that well over 15,000 canine competitors appear before the field trial fancy annually.

In the early days the judges reached their decisions through the "point system." The scale of "points" used approximated the following: Nose, 30; pace and style, 20; backing, 10; breaking, 15; retrieving, 5; style and stanchness in pointing, 15; roading, 5; total, 100. ("Breaking" here referred to handling or obeying the handler's commands.)

In 1879 the first "heat" system was adopted. Under this method, each dog that defeated his bracemate or competitor was carried into the next series until the final elimination was made and the winner declared. This system was found unsatisfactory as, in the drawing, it was possible for the two best dogs to be run together in the first heat, thereby penalizing one good dog to the advantage of an inferior one. Soon what is known as the "spotting system" came into being and it prevails today.

Under the "spotting" method, the judges are unhampered by red tape and unnecessary rules and are left free to pick the winners from the performances on that occasion. The contesting dogs are run in braces, the running time of the first series heats being stipulated in the rules of the club. Unless the winners stand out decisively at the end of the first series, the dogs that have performed with the greatest brilliancy are picked as second series contenders, braced in any manner the judges may desire, and put down again, running until the judges are satisfied as to the comparative merits of the contestants on that occasion.

The first series heats in a field trial are all of the same duration, but the time allotted for second series competition is at the discretion of the judges unless otherwise stipulated in the club rules.

With the increase in interest, it is only natural that there should be a number of changes in the *modus operandi* of field trials. Now there are puppy stakes for dogs up to certain age limits; derby events for candidates up to 30 months of age; and all-age stakes open to all ages. There are amateur and professional stakes, winners' events, championship competitions, and shooting-dog stakes.

In the early days field trial dogs were handled on foot. Changes in conditions, the scarcity of game, and difference in standards have brought about almost an abandonment of this practice, and now practically everyone who attends a major field trial follows the running from horseback. Professional handlers train from horseback almost exclusively. This does not, of course, apply to shooting-dog stakes or the cover-dog trials in grouse country, where the handlers and, in some cases, the judges, walk.

The so-called "big circuit" of major trials is composed of a series of clubs holding annual events in the prairie chicken and quail sections. These are inaugurated annually on the Canadian prairies, where prairie chicken, Hungarian partridge and, in recent years, the pheasant furnish the game. They continue through the winter months in the south on quail, generally closing with the National Bird Dog Championship held toward the end of the winter. This event, to the winning of which every professional handler aspires, is held on the famous Hobart Ames plantation near Grand Junction, Tenn. These trials are all run under natural conditions, the courses being laid out across country. The entrance and starting fees are comparatively high and the cash purses correspondingly large. The heats range from 30 minutes to 3 hours.

When the curtain falls on the winter competition, the spring events are ushered in. These are generally held on one-course grounds in the East with liberated pheasants or quail providing the game.

The dogs that compete in the major stakes are considered the cream of the country, and it is upon their performance that the pendulums of breeding activity generally swing. Many of the dogs are developed for field trial and stud purposes only, although a large portion of them are annually used by their owners in the season's shooting. The dogs of A. G. C. Sage, prominent New York sportsman, who has won more National Championships than any one individual owner, are developed along combination lines. Entered only in the fastest company,

Courtesy H. P. Davis, Bridgeport, Conn.

PLATE XXV. The Field Trails Along.

they are always dangerous competitors and are shot over heavily each year by their owner at Sedgefields, his Alabama preserve. Other notable examples of field trial shooting dogs are Sioux, Candy Kid, Feagin's Mohawk Pal, Doughboy, Becky Broomhill, Norias Roy, and Mississippi Zev. These are but a few field trial champions which were excellent shooting dogs.

There has been, and always will be, extensive discussion regarding the ability of the dog developed for field trials to adapt himself to the requirements of shooting. Years ago this question formed the basis of an interesting competition between the famous sportsmen, Herman B. Duryea and Pierre Lorillard. Duryea selected J. M. Avent, the veteran professional handler who had charge of the Duryea string of field trial dogs, as his shooting companion. Lorillard chose Charles Tucker, his handler, and pitted the bird-finding ability of his shooting dogs against the Duryea field trial winners. The contest was to be determined by the number of quail each party bagged on a given day.

Of course, marksmanship was an equation of the competition, but all were expert shots and no handicap was asked or given. The Duryea-Avent combination won by a wide margin, not only in the number of birds bagged but also in the number of coveys and singles found and handled. The great little setter bitch, Double National Champion Sioux, was a member of the Duryea-Avent string. She was hunted in short heats several times during the day and found more birds than any other dog that competed.

There is no reason why the properly trained field trial winner cannot be used to the best advantage as a shooting dog in the type of country in which he has been developed. The winning setter, Phil Essig, was a shooting dog of the finest quality and the noted Eugene's Ghost, always difficult to handle in field trial competition, was shot over heavily after his field trial career was ended. National Champion Mary Blue was used extensively as a shooting dog by her owner, Walter C. Teagle.

The adaptability of really top-flight field trial dogs has long been noted. The pointer, Dr. Blue Willing, won championships on prairie chickens, quail, and pheasants over widely varying terrain, as did the pointer Schoolfield. The setter Travelaire, a well-known winner on the southern quail circuit, was purchased by an Eastern sportsman and hung up an enviable record in the cover dog trials of the East and New England. One of the most versatile dogs in recent history was the pointer bitch, Colonial Lady M, which won more field trial places (62) than any other female, and had a career that embraced cover-dog stakes in the close country of New England, shooting-dog stakes, one-course trials, amateur events in the South, and major circuit competitions. Without special intensive preparation she even made a good showing in the National Championship. Field trial judges fill a volume with examples of bird-dog versatility.

Several of the major clubs hold "owner-handler" stakes, in which the competing dogs must be handled by the owners. To many judges these are most important events, for the owners are often strangers to their own dogs, as many of these dogs have been professionally trained and campaigned by their trainers in major trials.

This brings up the question "Can an amateur develop and successfully campaign a dog against professionals in major trials?" The answer is: "It has been done and is being done." Cecil S. Proctor, Oklahoma City fancier, Carl E. Duffield, Tyler, Texas, sportsman, and the late C. Watt Campbell, of Tulsa, Okla., to mention a few, have won important stakes in open trials with dogs they have trained themselves. Both Proctor and Duffield have handled first-place winners in the American Field Quail Futurity, the annual derby classic. Raymond B. Hoagland, Carterville, Ga., Harry S. Kirkover, Camden, S. C., George M. Rogers, Mt. Holly, N. J., the late Louis M. Bobbitt, Winston-Salem, N. C., the late Dr. T. W. Shore, Booneville, N. C., Virgil P. Hawse, Staunton, Va., and Edwin S. Vale, Merion, Pa., have all been frequent winners in open stakes with dogs they have trained themselves. In the New England cover-dog trials, Dr. James S. Goodwin, Concord, Mass., has been a frequent winner with dogs of his own training.

The amateur, however, is indeed handicapped in competition with professionals. Bird-dog training with him is a hobby, a source of pleasant and healthful recreation. Consequently he cannot devote as much time to his dogs as the professional, who makes bird-dog training a business. The professional is a valuable asset to the general bird-dog fraternity. He makes the sport of field trials or hunting with a bird dog possible for many enthusiasts who do not have the time, the facilities or even the know-how to train their own dogs. He lives a hard life, his work returns comparatively little in a financial way, and he generally adopts his vocation as a life's work because of his love for bird dogs and the outdoors.

The amateur trials really constitute the backbone of the sport. In these events, the entries are generally made up from the ranks of shooting dogs and are handled, in the main, by their fond owners. The trophies given as awards are highly prized, not so much for the intrinsic value but as evidence of accomplishment. These trials are "feeders" for the major circuit, as many patrons of amateur events are ambitious to own and campaign a "big time" contender. The major amateur events of each year are the Regional Amateur Championships, the National Amateur Quail Championship, and the National Amateur Pheasant Championship, sponsored by the Amateur Field Trial Clubs of America.

The *American Field,* a weekly publication with headquarters in Chicago, devotes most of its editorial matter to field trial activities and subjects pertaining to the gun dog. The publication maintains the Field Dog Stud Book and annually sponsors the American Field Futurity (run on quail) and the American Field Pheasant Futurity. Other breeders' stakes are the Grouse Futurity, sponsored by the Grand National Grouse Championship, and the New England Futurity, sponsored by the Association of New England Field Trial Clubs.

The novitiate in the field of bird dog activities should attend a few field trials. Ride the courses, see all the running, ask questions. They will provide an excellent medium for the comparison of the performance of your own dog with that of others. In attending these events you will meet genuine sportsmen always willing to extend a helping hand to a fellow fancier. These contacts will prove of value in developing your own dog. Acquaintanceships formed at field trials often ripen into long and valued friendships.

Most important of all bird dog field trials is, of course, the National Bird Dog Championship. With heats of 3 hours' duration, this is an endurance stake. Its standards are of the highest. Not only must the winner be able to go the long route at rapid pace but he must also handle to the gun. Whenever a dog wins this greatest of all bird-dog titles one can rest assured that here is a dog that is capable of providing a thrilling day of gunning. The National Championship is no place for an aimless runner. It is a stake for the highest type of shooting dog, the gun dog at the very peak of his ability. The dog that will not handle kindly commands little consideration here. This is as it should be, for the bird dog's mission in life is to be an asset to his master's gun. The best field trial dog is nothing more than the shooting dog at his very best. The dog which cannot be gunned over is not deserving of the term "field trial dog."

Next in field trial importance is the National Free-For-All Championship. In this stake the qualifying heats are one hour in length, the finals 3 hours. No dog is out of it until the decision is announced. This stake is quite a difficult one to win. The dog must qualify by turning in a sparkling performance in his one-hour appearance, and then he must go the long 3-hour route in impressive fashion. Some dogs may be quite capable of finishing the 3-hour grind at good pace, but an unlucky draw of courses or the lack of class in the first hour may prevent them from qualifying. On the other hand, a dog may turn in a wonderful performance in the first hour, but not be capable of finishing the long final heat in good form. Hence the winner generally is a dog which is keyed up to go the long heat, showing class and brilliance all the way. There have been instances when all dogs first announced as qualifiers have failed in the 3-hour finals. The winners on those occasions were found in the ranks of those which had not performed so brilliantly in the comparatively short qualifying heat. Thus no dog is considered out of the stake until the decision is announced.

Space limitations will not permit the enumeration of all the important field trials in this country and Canada, but among them are:

The Texas Open Championship, the All-America, the United States, the Saskatchewan, the Manitoba, the Dominion, the Continental, the Great Northern, the National Pheasant Championship, New England Championship, Grand National Grouse Championship, Georgia Arkansas-Oklahoma, United States Chicken Championship, Pacific Coast Championship, English Setter Club of America, Pointer Club of America, Irish Setter Club of America, German Short-Haired Pointer Club of America, Old Hickory, Jockey Hollow, Orange County, and the Catahootchee Valley.

Many of these clubs have had long and colorful histories.

"Which makes the best field trial dog, the setter or the pointer?" is a frequently asked question, but few persons are qualified to give the answer. It all depends upon the individual, of course, for there are field trial winners and champions in both breeds. However, the pointers have held the major portion of the field trial spotlight in recent years, one reason being that more pointers are entered than setters.

This has not always been true—in fact, it is somewhat the reverse of what the situation was in the early days of field trials. Most field trial contenders then were setters; there were few pointers in the first trials. It was generally admitted that early-day pointer performance was not on a par with that of the setter and the long-hairs held full sway. The first winners were "native" setters and then the progeny of imported English setters of the Llewellin strain came into vogue, practically dominating the field for a number of years.

In order not to leave the pointer completely out in the cold, and also to promote more interest in the breed, field trial clubs began to hold separate stakes for two breeds, the winner of the setter stake being pitted against the winner of the pointer stake for the settlement of the "absolute." Seldom was the winner of the "absolute" not a setter.

The first pointer to win an important field trial was Don, owned by R. T. Vandevort. Don won first place ($250 cash) in the Free-For-All stake of the National American Kennel Club's trials, which were run on prairie chickens at Fairmont, Minn., beginning September 4, 1882, eight years after the first field trial was held. In addition to the cash purse, Vandevort's Don won the Pennsylvania State Field Trials Association cup for the best dog in the stake owned in Pennsylvania, and a special prize of $20 for the best pointer in the stake.

Later during the same year the first important pointer derby stake wins were made. This was in the Eastern Field Trial Club derby in which 10 English setters, 2 Irish setters, and 4 pointers started. The black pointer Darkness won first, the liver and white pointer Tick was second, and the lemon and white pointer Lalla Rookh accounted for divided third. One of the judges in this stake was Elliott Smith, who was also a judge in the All-Age stake, except, according to the records of the late Major J. M. Taylor, *when pointers ran!* In which direction he was supposed to be prejudiced the record does not state, but Lalla Rookh also won divided third and the pointer Croxteth was second in the All-Age stake.

Separate stakes for pointers continued to be held until around 1900, when the careful breeding programs of the pointer fanciers began to show results.

The first pointer to win the National Championship was Manitoba Rap. This was in 1909. Three pointers have won it three times each since. These were Mary Montrose, Becky Broomhill, and Ariel. Only one setter, Feagin's Mohawk Pal, has annexed this coveted crown three times. And only two setters, Sport's Peerless Pride (1939) and Mississippi Zev (1946), have been returned the winner since Feagin's Mohawk Pal won it for the third time in 1930.

During the past 25 years there has been much discussion concerning the so-called "rise of the pointer and fall of the setter" in the realm of field trials. To speak of the "rise and fall" is, to place an incorrect evaluation on the situation. The fact that the pointer is now more than holding his own with the setter in field trials does not indicate the deterioration of the setter as much as it does the improvement of the pointer. At the time the pointer fanciers were sticking strictly to their knitting and breeding to characteristics and proved ability rather than to pedigrees, the setter lovers had gone "purist" and frowned upon any dog which could not boast a 100% Llewellin pedigree, regardless of his field qualities. This fad is no longer in vogue and the setter breeders are again back on a sound foundation.

There was a time, too, not long ago, when "class," interpreted by too many as "heels," had its fling in field trials and a number of judges put too much emphasis on extreme range. This brought about the development of some whistle-running pointers and near-bolting setters to the detriment of both breeds. The pendulum has now swung back to proper balance and the field trial contender of these days has to be endowed with a goodly portion of unusual ability in every department if he is to be successful. Not only must he have range which will take him to the limits of his country, but he must also hunt with intelligence and be amenable to his handler's commands. He must possess an excellent nose and use it well, show style and intensity in action and on point, and be perfectly mannered under the gun. When one considers the high degree of excellence in so many phases of field performance that is expected of the field trial dog it is, indeed, surprising that so many make the grade. In the final analysis, the field trial dog is the shooting dog of the highest order.

Most judges insist that the English setter has not deteriorated to any appreciable extent since the time when he was practically supreme in field trials. Rather, they explain, the pointer has improved. The setter wins the majority of places in grouse trials. Here again the main reason may be because he outnumbers the pointers in those events.

The Irish setter, during the early days, played an important part in field trials. He was, however, a real field dog then and not the hothouse product that we see shuffling around in bench shows today. Many believe he would still be a contender had his fanciers been as much interested in the perpetuation of his field abilities as they were concerned about his beauty. Had this breed behind it a number of sportsmen and breeders such as Edwin M. Berolzheimer the hunting status of the breed would very probably be different.

One reason for the enviable field trial position the pointer enjoys today is the fact that the short-hair, as a breed, develops a bit earlier than his long-haired rival. If care is used the pointer can be "pushed along" in his education without damage, but to bring him to his best the setter must be allowed to develop naturally. When all the arguments relative to which is the best breed for field trials are in and the shouting has died down the verdict is written in these words: "It all depends upon the individual." There are good ones and not-so-good ones in both breeds. There is one quality which is seldom mentioned but which is most important. That is the competitive spirit. Some dogs have it, some dogs do not. Without it the field trial contender is greatly handicapped. Any number of dogs seem to catch the spirit of competition and are at their best, often surpassing themselves, when hunting in front of a gallery. Others become too keyed-up, excited, or even a bit too frightened to be at their best in field trials. Dogs of the latter type generally do

Courtesy H. P. Davis, Bridgeport, Conn.

PLATE XXVI. A Brace of Pointers Cast Away at the Pinehurst Field Trials, Pinehurst, N. C.

their best work at home and often their owners and trainers cannot understand why, when brought to field trials, they seem to have left their good races at home. It is simply because they do not have the competitive spirit.

Champion Norias Roy was one of these dogs that seem to sense that he was expected to "wear his Sunday clothes" when brought out before a field trial gallery. Champion Subsidy, noted pointer bitch, did her best work, perhaps, in workouts at home. She was practically unbeatable when she was "right" but needed a lot of work all the time and when she was, of necessity, laid up a few days before her time to run in a field trial was inclined to "take the bit in her teeth" and handle the course in her own way. The setter Belleview Bob was an excellent shooting dog but extremely difficult to handle in field trials, often leaving the course entirely. The pointer bitch Outcast, beautifully mannered on her game and a frequent winner in her early form, had to be retired from competition because she became so upset in front of a crowd that she would sulk. It is that competitive spirit which sometimes carries a no-better-than average field trial contender to the heights. The setter Beau Essig's Don had it in a marked degree.

From a spectator standpoint a field trial is a thrilling thing to watch for anyone interested in bird dogs—or, for that matter, competitions between animals. Not all the races are brilliant, of course, but in every major field trial and in most smaller and amateur events some sparkling performances are registered. To see a high-class bird dog work out his country at good range, with dashing speed and lofty and merry carriage, showing rare judgment in his casts and swinging to the course with every evidence of having his master's gun in mind, is something not soon to be forgotten. And when such a ground-working performance is rewarded by a smashing find of game, stylishly and intensely pointed and perfectly handled no sportsman, no matter how blasé, can fail to get a tingling sensation along his spine. It is not the quantity but the quality of the work that counts in field trials.

One of the most sensational races in the history of field trials was that of the diminutive setter bitch Sioux, in 1902 when she won the National Championship for the second time. There is no one now alive who witnessed that race, but it has been discussed in detail by the late Hobart Ames, president and judge for many years of the National Bird Dog Championship Association, and the late Al F. Hochwalt, the great field trial authority, reporter, and author. Both of these gentlemen considered Sioux the greatest bird dog of all time.

On this occasion there were only two starters in the Championship, Sioux and the setter Clip Wind-'em. The dogs were cast off in the rain and before many minutes had passed it began to sleet and a cold north wind cut over these hills on the Ames preserve near Grand Junction, Tenn. Soon the vegetation was encrusted in ice but Sioux seemed oblivious to this and raced over the rugged terrain as if it was a fair fall day. Her coat became covered with frozen mud and the under parts of her body matted with ice, but the game little setter found birds galore and finished the long 3-hour heat at a pace just as fast as it had been at the start. According to Mr. Ames, one of the judges that race has never been equaled.

Then there was the time when another small setter bitch made lasting history in this famous stake. She was La Besita, the last Llewellin to win the title. This was in 1915. Birds were unusually plentiful that year, but when La Besita was called to run with Brunswick Countess the weather took a drastic turn for the worse. The frozen ground had thawed during the middle of the morning but before the heat was long under way the weather turned colder and the mud on the dogs' bodies turned to dirty icicles. Yet the great heart of the little bitch carried her through and she ran up a bird score of nine coveys and three singles. Most of the gallery thought she had won it then, but the judges ordered her back to run the next day with the pointer Lewis C. Morris in a second series. During the early part of the night the alarming news came that La Besita had pneumonia! Serious consideration was given to withdrawing her, but it was decided to wait until morning. Careful nursing throughout the night seemed to check the ailment but La Besita was far from a well dog when she went to the mark the next afternoon. She crashed through to victory, however, in another demonstration, this time mercifully short, of great courage.

Another outstanding race in National Championship history was that of the pointer Doughboy in 1924. Doughboy's performance not only sensationally surpassed the field but surprised the entire gallery, for the dog was not considered a serious contender. His previous performances that season were far below championship caliber but his trainer, John Willard Martin, had spent many hours in preparing him for this event and he came to the trial in top form. Old-timers still talk about the brilliancy of his performance on that occasion.

Manitoba Rap's race in 1909 when he became the first pointer to win the National Championship made real field trial history. No second series was necessary and the little underestimated pointer topped the field of 15, the largest to that date, by a wide margin.

Few races in the National Championship ever caused more comment than that of the setter Eugene's Ghost, in 1922. "Mike," as he was called, found 17 coveys and 11 singles in his 3-hour heat, more than any other dog before or since—and still did not win the stake! The pointer bitch Becky Broomhill took the honors that year and again in 1923 and 1925. Her exhibition in 1922 was an example of perfect handling and she found birds in sufficient quantities. Many thought Eugene's Ghost lost the title when the high-strung young setter jumped and circled his birds, as a nervous young lady spectator slipped her riding slicker with her riding crop. Some thought the judges charged him with a blink, but such was not the case. The dashing setter was too headstrong on that occasion, as he usually was, and his canny handler, the veteran J. M. Avent, had scouts placed all along the sides of the course to turn him back on it when he got too wide. It is hard to realize that a dog could find and handle that many birds under judgment and still run too wide, but there was no limit to Eugene's Ghost's range.

In recent years perhaps the most sensational performance was that of the pointer Luminary, who won the National Championship in 1942. Here were 3 hours replete with thrills from start to finish, yet the judges could not agree and called him back for a second series with that sterling pointer, Tarheelia's Lucky Strike. Fortunately, Luminary proved his superiority in the second series just as decisively, if not more so, than in his first try.

One of the memorable heats between pointers at the National Championships was that between Doctor Blue Willing and Norias Annie. Between them, this brace found 20 coveys, with the bitch having something of an edge in bird finding honors. She did not run with the dash and verve of her rival but her heat was the more consistent. A number of Dr. Blue Willing's finds were made off to one side or behind. In the last 40 minutes the dog was doing more running than hunting while his less sensational bracemate continued to find coveys up to the last. The judges awarded the title to Norias Annie, but many in the gallery, who did not closely analyze the work, thought that Dr. Blue Willing had won it.

The nearest approach to Luminary's heat in recent years was that of the little setter Mississippi Zev, winner in 1946. Zev scored on nine coveys and his finish was nothing short of sensational.

All brilliant heats, however, are not run in the National Championship. Most judges could name any number which have come under their judgment, such as the heats of Norias Roy and Evergreen Jersey Mack in the Continental; Eagle Ferris' 45 minutes in the All-America; Ariel's one-hour qualifying heat in the 1944 National Free-For-All Championship, which he won, The Texas Ranger in the National Free-For-All; Titan in the National Pheasant Championship; Belle the Devil in the National Amateur Championship; Air Pilot's Sam in the Saskatchewan All-Age; Granite State Mischief in the New England Championship; Shore's Carolina Jack in the Southern New York All-Age; Sun Beau in the Continental Derby; Morpheus in the American Field Futurity; and others too numerous to mention.

One of the most thrilling second series of recent years was that between the pointer bitches, Homewood Flirtatious and Sulu, with the National Championship title of 1935 at stake. Flirtatious literally threw herself into point in less than a minute after being cast away. She had a covey nailed on barren ground, while her bracemate continued her first cast. Flirt scored again before Sulu could be turned, and then again within a few minutes. The judges saw range more than bird work, for each dog had found plenty during the first series. Flirtatious really gave evidence of amazing speed, with Sulu doing her share also. After 38 minutes of brilliant performance the judges were about to order them up when Flirt was seen pointing with exceptionally high head. Bevan, her handler, was unable to produce birds in front of her and the spirits of her backers sank, for they feared that she had marred this spectacular performance with an error. The keen eyes of Mr. Ames, however, spied Sulu on point up ahead. Flirtatious was backing! After a short heat between Sport's Peerless and Dr. Blue Willing, in which the setter flushed a covey and the pointer did nothing startling, Homewood Flirtatious was declared the champion.

Sometimes things happen fast in field trials. Did

you ever hear of an unconscious dog winning a stake? Henry P. Davis, a nationally known judge, reports having seen that happen. It was in the Cotton States derby of 1926. Twice National Champion Mary Blue was the dog. At the close of a brilliant ground-working second-series heat, Mary pointed a covey in fairly heavy sedge. Chesley Harris, her handler, picked up a rather heavy pine-knot as he walked toward her. His apparent intention was to throw the pine-knot into the sedge to flush the birds. Instead, fearful that Mary would break, he "dropped it rather heavily" on her head as he passed her. Mary dropped, knocked out cold. Harris flushed the birds, slowly returned to his dog, and before he could get her to her feet (he took his own time), the judges ordered her up and announced the decision, with Mary as the winner.

Some amusing things happen, too. Often a usually calm businessman will get tremendously excited when handling his own dog in an amateur stake. There is one instance in which an amateur handler was so excited when his dog pointed that he handed his gun to his scout and took his horse in to flush. Another man tried to blow his gun and shoot his whistle!

The sport of field trials is a grand one. Not only does it point the way to better bird dogs and promote the conversation and restoration of wildlife resources, but it is also good, clean, healthful recreation where sportsmanship in the highest degree is manifest. It is the one sport in which the gambling element is conspicuous by its absence. For that reason alone the sport will continue to flourish. Gambling raised its head on one occasion, but the late Dr. T. W. Shore and Henry P. Davis were in position to take prompt action to halt it. The unthinking amateur, would-be "bookmaker" immediately saw the danger of such action and the error of his ways. He would be the first to frown on it now.

The best dog does not always win in field trials. If it did, many dogs would compete only one time. Bird dogs, like human beings, have their off-days when they are not feeling up to par physically or mentally. And the luck of the draw plays a considerable part in field trials. The very uncertainty of the sport makes it all the more fascinating. The field trial sport is no place for a poor loser. As a result, the highest type of sportsmanship will always maintain.

If you want to see how good—or how bad—your dog is, enter him in a field trial.

**How Bird Dog Field Trials Are Judged.** There are no set rules for judging bird-dog field trials. Men who accept invitations to act in a judicial capacity in these events are generally men of considerable field hunting experience. They serve without pay. This fact makes the sport of bird-dog field trials the only field competition known in which the professionals must accept the decisions of amateurs as final.

Field trial judges are charged with the responsibility of interpreting individual bird-dog performances properly, evaluating them correctly, and selecting the winners on the basis of the performances of the occasion, impartially and without any regard for past records or performances.

While field trial standards, though unwritten "officially," are based on the highest concepts of excellence in gun-dog performance, the judges are not hampered by any red tape or bound by any set rules in their interpretation of individual action. This is as it should be, if their decisions are to be well balanced, for attending circumstances often play a considerable role in determining the manner in which a judge will interpret and evaluate a given situation or performance. Field trial judging may well be termed an inexact science. No magically mysterious qualities are required in the make-up of an able arbiter, yet he must possess certain capabilities if he is to be successful. He must know the ideal he seeks and be able to recognize the performances which most nearly approach it. He must be fearless in his opinions and absolutely fair and impartial in his decisions.

Each field trial is different in the situations which arise, and the necessary flexibility which attends their interpretation is sometimes confusing to the uninitiated who finds difficulty in understanding a decision in which the reasoning of the judges would be perfectly obvious to the understandingly observant eye of the experienced spectator.

There are certain guideposts in judging field trials which are known to judges, handlers, and spectators alike. The all-age field trial dog must show "class," which embodies bird sense, speed, range, style, and stamina. He must hunt the course, responding to his handler's commands or directions. He must take advantage of the wind in his quest for game. He must locate and point his quarry accurately and positively. He must be stanch, steady, and back on sight. (See Glossary for definition of terms.) These same requirements hold good for the derby dog, yet to some lesser degree, as allowances are made for his age and inexperience.

The best way the novice may learn what field trial judges are looking for and how they reach their decisions is by attending a number of these events. Follow each brace carefully, watching each contestant closely. Ask experienced spectators questions on the finer points of performance. Judge the trial for yourself and then compare your decision with that of the judges. If you can recognize quality in performance, your own decision is not likely to be far afield. For if the judges go about their work carefully, even painstakingly, and unhurriedly the dogs will generally judge themselves. Occasions will often arise, of course, when fine analysis is called for; herein lies the test of a good field trial judge.

For the benefit of the reader who is not entirely familiar with field trial procedure we here point out a number of situations which arise occasionally and how the experienced field trial judge will meet them. Let us put them in the form of questions and answers.

TRAILING—*Question:* If a dog is interfering with his bracemate's work by trailing in any form, what action should the judges take, if any?

*Answer:* After a warning from the judges, the handler of the offending dog should bring him in and cast him away in a different direction. If he persists in trailing, the judges should order him up, but only after he is given ample opportunity to hunt properly.

BACKING—*Question:* How much should a dog be penalized for refusal to back when it is obvious that he has seen the pointing dog?

*Answer:* An All-Age dog which refuses to back his pointing bracemate should be heavily penalized. Not long ago, some professional field trial handlers did not require their dogs to back, rather hoping that the refusal to back would be out of the sight of the judges and their dogs would be given credit for the find when they were finally discovered pointing closer to the birds. These handlers went on the theory that "A dog can't win a field trial backing." After seeing numerous demonstrations of the fact that "A dog can't win a field trial by refusing to back" these handlers, in the main, abandoned this practice and most all-age dogs are now trained to back. In a championship stake each dog should be given an opportunity to back if possible, and refusal to back should disqualify. Derby dogs should not be required to back, but performance of this nicety reflects with credit on them.

GRABBING—*Question:* To what extent should a dog's standing in an all-age stake be penalized when his handler grabs for his collar either before firing or so soon thereafter as to show lack of confidence in the dog's manners?

*Answer:* It is obvious that one cannot shoot birds while reaching for a dog. Such an action should be taken as evidence that the dog is unsteady until his stanchness is demonstrated on future finds in the same stake.

DELAYED SHOT—*Question:* Should a dog be penalized if his handler waits until the birds are out of gunshot before firing?

*Answer:* Such action on the part of the handler creates the impression that the dog is not a finished performer, and such an impression can be dispelled only by prompt shooting over future flushes. The handler is supposed to shoot before the birds have passed beyond killing range. If the birds have flushed wild, some delay is expected and permissible. A handler should never shoot when the dog is in error. Such action, however, should not penalize the dog.

INTIMIDATING—*Question:* Should a dog be penalized if his handler uses a quirt, leash, or riding crop, ostensibly to flush birds but in such manner as to intimidate the dog?

*Answer:* This practice is abused by some handlers and should be discouraged by the judges. If it is evident that the handler is deliberately intimidating the dog, the dog should be penalized. Judges should warn handlers against this practice.

STOPS TO FLUSH—*Question:* Should a dog be penalized for a stop to flush?

*Answer:* Circumstances determine this. If the conditions are such as to make it improbable that the flush was the fault of the dog he should not be penalized; in fact, his stopping should be treated as additional evidence of good manners. If a dog stops to flush on a number of occasions, faulty nose may be the cause.

BIRD WORK IN ALL-AGE STAKES—*Question:* Should bird work be required by judges before making placements in All-Age stakes?

*Answer:* Every effort should be made to secure bird work of acceptable quality before awards are made in an All-Age stake. This can usually be secured if the judges will take sufficient time and make the effort. In one-course trials there is little excuse for not providing every dog deserving of recognition an opportunity to show on game. On rare occasions in cross-country trials bird work of acceptable quality is at high premium and the judges are forced to make the best of a poor situation. No qualified judge is satisfied to make All-Age placements on "class" alone.

BIRD WORK IN JUNIOR STAKES—*Question:* What degree of bird work should be expected in different age classes?

*Answer:* Puppies, none; fall derbies, flash points; spring derbies, stanchness but steadiness to shot and wing not required.

STYLE—*Question:* To what extent should style be considered?

*Answer:* Joy in hunting is a most desirable characteristic and should always be looked for. It may be indicated by merriness, sometimes by dash and verve, sometimes by other physical attributes of a dog in motion; but it is unmistakable. Loftiness is a desirable characteristic of a dog on point but intensity is the most desirable characteristic of a pointing dog and is far more important than the position of the head or tail.

CHAMPIONSHIPS—*Question:* Should a Championship be judged on a different basis than an ordinary All-Age Stake?

*Answer:* While it is desirable that the winner of a Championship be charged with no errors, it is better practice to award a title to a dog that displays all of the characteristics of style, pace, drive, bird sense, etc., even though such a dog be charged with some minor error or breach of manners, than to award a title to a dog lacking many of these characteristics even though with a high bird score and no errors. Champions should be named for brilliance of performance in spite of trivial errors rather than on the basis of errorless mediocrity.

RANGE—*Question:* How much should extreme range count, particularly if there are plenty of birdy objectives in sight?

*Answer:* Dogs should *hunt* their way out rather than cast in straight lines. A "straight-line" initial cast may be excused on the theory that field trial dogs are at high pitch and may be expected to work off some nervous energy on the first cast. A field trial dog should apply his range intelligently and with due regard to cover and objectives rather than with regard only to the distance from the handler.

"OVERBIRDINESS" IN BIRD FIELD—*Question:* Should a dog be penalized if he shows "overbirdiness" or extreme caution in the bird field or approaching it, as a possible result of being worked often on planted birds?

*Answer:* Dogs should work the bird field naturally and at a fair pace. They are expected to locate birds by testing the air for body scent. Dogs that linger over ground scent, sneak from bush to bush at any unnaturally slow pace, or hunt the bird field in any unnatural manner, are to be regarded as "pottering" and should not be placed except as a last resort.

COMING FROM BEHIND—*Question:* To what extent should coming from behind penalize a dog?

*Answer:* Persistent back-casting should eliminate a dog. A dog that comes in from behind occasionally should not be faulted too much, particularly if the pace of the gallery is fast and the dog is hunting desirable objectives. It may be necessary for him to come up from behind occasionally to take advantage of the wind. It is deliberate or aimless back-casting which should be heavily penalized.

UNPRODUCTIVE POINTS—*Question:* What value should be placed on an unproductive point when the judges are unable to determine whether the game has recently flushed unobserved by dog, handler, or judges?

*Answer:* Dogs should be given the benefit of any doubt. No credit should be given and no penalty imposed unless the dog persists in making unproductive points.

DROPPING ON POINT—*Question:* How much should dropping on point count against the dog (1) when found or dropping when point is made, (2) dropping at approach of handler?

*Answer:* There are only two good reasons for a dog dropping on point; (1) coming on birds too fast, especially down-wind, and dropping to prevent a flush; (2) if cover is very thin and dog tries to make himself as inconspicuous as possible. Persistent dropping on point is poor style and should be considered. Dropping at the approach of handler should incur no penalty unless fear of punishment or gun-shyness is evident.

DIVIDED FINDS—*Question:* When two dogs are found on point which should be given credit for the find?

*Answer:* This calls for keen analysis on the part of the judges. Generally the position of the dogs in relation to the birds, their postures and attitudes will give some clue. When it is impossible definitely to determine, each dog is given credit for a divided find.

The above situations are but a few which are common to field trials. They will serve, however, to give the reader some idea of the task which confronts the judges, who serve for love of the sport alone.

## BEAGLE HOUND FIELD TRIALS

No organized sport which utilizes the talents of hunting dogs has known a faster or healthier growth in this country than that of beagle hound field trials. The National Beagle Club was formed in 1890 and held its first trial in November of that year. Conditions at Hyannis, Mass., the scheduled site of the trial, were so unfavorable that the venue was moved to Salem, N. H., where the event was successfully terminated.

In 1891 and 1892 the National Beagle Club was the only club holding formal or organized competitions for beagles, but the following year the Northeastern Beagle Club and the New England Beagle Club came into being. For several years the sport knew a slow but nevertheless steady growth, but in very recent years it has grown by leaps and bounds. For instance, in 1942, 7548 beagles were entered in licensed field trials. In 1943 the number totaled 8326; in 1944, 11,384; in 1945, 15,887 and in 1946, the amazing total of 20,895 merry little hounds faced the judges in field competitions. This represents the activities of approximately 200 clubs holding beagle trials, located in practically every section of the country.

To the outdoor sportsman whose favorite pastime is hunting of upland game, the growth of interest in beagles and beagle field trials is not surprising; in fact, it is only a natural sequel to the high popularity enjoyed by this great little gun dog throughout this country.

The beagle is universally recognized as a specialist in rabbit hunting. Although he possesses other qualities which endear him to the sporting public, rabbit hunting is his mission in life. He was primarily bred for this purpose and it is in the chase of Molly Hare that he is at his best.

The cottontail rabbit is the most prolific of our upland game animals. He is found in practically all sections of the country and seems to withstand hunting pressure better than any other species. He provides great sport in the field, in hound music and gunning pleasure, and his succulent flesh can be whipped up into delicious dishes capable of tempting the jaded palate of the most blasé gourmet.

Pride of ownership is a human quality which glows in the breast of every beagler and the remark, "My hound is better than any around here," is a challenge which no true beagler can resist. If his own dogs are not "up to snuff" he is sure to have a friend whose pack or kennel can provide proper and instant competition.

The beagle is an easy dog to keep. He requires but little room and his board bill is a minor matter. Unlike bird dogs and retrievers, it is not necessary to give him an extensive and expensive education in field work and manners before he can successfully compete in field trials. No great skill in handling is required of the owner and no specialized training is necessary. Some of the leading winners were taken directly from a farm where they had self-hunted all their lives to win highest honors at trials under the guidance of owners who had never before attended such an affair.

There is no dearth of good beagle trial grounds in this country. Suitable terrains well stocked with rabbits are to be found in almost every section and the application of simple yet sound game-management principles can provide favorable running conditions almost anywhere within a short time. The beagler is not confronted with the problems which beset the bird-dog fancier in this respect. And he has many more opportunities for training over a longer season each year.

The sport of beagle field trials is comparatively inexpensive. The customary fee at licensed trials is $5; at sanctioned trials the fee is usually $2 or $3. If the dog is unregistered, an additional fee of 25 cents is charged. Entry fees in bird dog trials range from $5 to $75. The greatest single item attached to beagle trials is transportation. The sport is the least expensive of any in the gun-dog field.

These are only some of the reasons why beagle hound trials are growing in popularity. There is always a fine spirit of friendliness evident when beaglers get together, competitive yet coöperative. The beagle is primarily a gun dog, an ideal companion for the outdoorsman as well as a decorative friend at the fireside. He makes as much music as the foxhound and is far more tractable, for he keeps his master's gun in mind all the time. And his cocky manner and friendly disposition make him a favorite everywhere. It is no wonder that he is one of the best contenders for American popularity honors.

The avowed purpose of beagle field trials is the improvement of the field qualities of the breed, as well as improvement in type. Proof that the sport has served well in this respect is the fact that field trial winners are frequently also winners of honors on the bench. Good type and conformation are necessary for the best field performance.

All beagle trial stakes, except a Championship stake, are divided by height into two divisions. These are stakes for beagles not exceeding 13 inches in height and stakes for beagles over 13 inches but not exceeding 15 inches in height.

Stakes may also be divided by sex if the field-trial giving club so desires and so states in its premium list or entry forms. The entries in beagle trials have become so large in recent years that the division of stakes by sex has become a general practice.

Practically all beagle trials in America are held under the jurisdiction, license, or sanction of the American Kennel Club. At each trial all entries except those mature beagles 18 months or older in age whose height has been officially determined by the American Kennel Club by its certificate of measurement shall be measured by the standard of the National Beagle Club before starting, and if found to be incorrectly entered as to height shall be transferred to the corresponding stake or stakes of their proper height.

At all field trials run on cottontail rabbits, beagles are run in braces, but when the trial is run on hare all entries in a stake are run together as a pack.

When the dogs have been entered, the names are placed in a receptacle (such as a hat), stirred up, and drawn one at a time. The first dog drawn runs with the second dog drawn, constituting the first brace. The third and fourth dog drawn make up the second brace, and so on until all the dogs are drawn. Should there be an odd number or bye dog, such bye dog shall run with a bracemate selected by the judges. This bracemate shall be under judgment when so running.

After the running of the first series has been completed, the judges may call for whatever dogs they wish to run in the second series, and brace them together in any manner they desire. In determining the final winners, the judges may run the hounds any number of times in any number of additional series they may desire. The idea is to give the competitors full opportunity to display their qualities under judgment When hounds have been laid on a line together, or have been given the opportunity to hark in to one another, this shall be considered as competition. Beagle trials are not elimination affairs, although the *modus operandi* may cause the novice to think otherwise. Judging is done under the "spotting" system and each brace does not constitute a race, with the loser being eliminated from further consideration. In fact, both dogs can be, and frequently are called back into second and subsequent series.

However, one of the rules in beagle trials reads as follows: "Before the judges announce the winners in a class, the placed hounds must have beaten the hound placed directly beneath them." This rule is exclusive to beagle trials and is not in effect in field trials for any of the other sporting breeds.

There are a number of rules of procedure and instructions to the judges in beagle trials. While these rules are good guide-posts for the judges, strict adherence to the letter of their wording sometimes brings about confusing situations which could be eliminated if the judges were allowed full leeway in conducting the competition to a successful conclusion. The less red tape in any gun-dog competition the better. The selection of competent, unbiased, and impartial judges, who know what to look for in a good beagle performance and how to find it, should insure correct decisions.

Beagle judges know that the beagle is primarily a hunting hound. His primary object is to find game; then he must drive it in an energetic and decisive manner and show an animated desire to overtake it. Ability and desire to hunt are of first importance. It is not the quantity but the quality of the performance which should be given first consideration.

To quote from the American Kennel Club's "Instructions to Judges":

> "Undue credit shall not be given for speed and flashy driving if the trail is not clearly followed. Accuracy in trailing, voice, endurance, starting ability, style, and obedience shall be the principal points of merit, but nothing in the foregoing shall excuse a dog from pottering, swinging, skirting, babbling, leaving checks, racing, running in hit or miss style, backtracking, running mute, running a ghost trail, all of which shall be considered demerits."

Handling is taken into consideration in beagle trials. Section 5 of Rule 10 reads:

> "If the competition is close, the judges shall give greater credit to the hound that is obedient to the commands of his handler. A hound will be expected to maintain an efficient range throughout a heat and to show hunting sense in his work. Hunting sense is shown by the desire to hunt for game, the selection of likely places to hunt it, the method of hunting places, the industry in staying out at work and the skill in handling and trailing the game after it is found."

Interference by one hound with his bracemate will be penalized. "Pottering" is remaining too long in one spot and not trying to advance. "Swinging" is making loops by reaching too far at checks or when the scent is lost. "Skirting" is running alongside those on the line and trying to get in front by catching the scent at a turn. "Babbling" is giving tongue when not trailing game. "Leaving checks" occurs when a hound refuses to come back to the place where he lost the scent. "Racing" occurs when a hound depends upon his heels rather than his nose to keep in front. He generally over-runs the track. "Running in hit-or-miss style" might be whipping the line by driving ahead, weaving back and forth trying to get ahead rather than sticking to the trail in an accurate manner. "Backtracking" is self-explanatory.

There is a considerable amount of luck in field trials, yet the worthy hound will generally make his mark eventually. Quality will not be continually denied. Beaglers all know that the vagaries of scent are many, that atmospheric conditions sometimes play havoc with a hound's ability to unravel a trail, that the "luck of the draw" is ever present. They also know "Old Lady Luck" will sometimes smile on them, and this, coupled with sheer love for the sport, keeps them knocking at the door of beagle-trial fame.

PLATE XXVII. Typical Scene at Beagle Field Trial.

Conscientious judges, and most of them are just that, know too that varying conditions may mean varying performances, and they try to equalize chances as nearly as possible.

Rule 15 in "Instructions to Judges" comes in for considerable discussion. It is:

"Hounds running in all series shall be scored by percentages, and hounds for all series may come from same or different braces. Percentages in all series must be considered in awarding places."

The reduction of individual hound performance to a mathematical formula is extremely difficult, calling for an exceedingly analytical mind and probably much splitting of hairs. Each judge probably has his own method of arriving at percentages, if, indeed, he follows this rule strictly, and the figures may not always agree. But experienced men work a stake out to a logical conclusion, generally, particularly if they take the time necessary and do not resort to snap judgment or jump to impulsive conclusions. The top-heavy sizes of some of the more important stakes make rather arduous undertakings of judging assignments and the conscientious fortitude of these officials under such circumstances is to be admired.

Championship points for beagles are awarded only to winners of Open All-Age Stakes. These points are awarded on the following basis: 1 point to the winner of first place for every hound started; ½ point to the winner of second place for each hound started; ⅓ point to the winner of third place for each hound started; and ¼ point to the winner of fourth place for each hound started. At present a hound of either sex must win a total of at least 120 points, which must include three first places in licensed or member trials, to be declared to be a Field Trial Champion of Record by the American Kennel Club.

In the early days of beagle trials, when annual events were few, only ten points were required to win a championship, but at least one win had to be made at a field trial that was rated 3 points or over and only one win of a hound was recognized at any trial. Beagle trials were rated as follows: 50 or more starters, 5 points; 40 starters and under 50, 4 points; 30 starters and under 40, 3 points; 20 starters and under 30, 2 points; under 20 starters, 1 point.

At beagle trials, the gallery walks behind the judges, who are generally mounted, and the handlers. Members of the gallery must remain far enough back not to interfere with the running and when game is raised they must stand fast. However, the gallery, as a general rule, can see a considerable portion of the running, and almost every beagle trial is followed closely by a large and enthusiastic gallery of contestants and spectators. To insure ample opportunities on game for every competing dog, field trial clubs generally release captured or pen-raised rabbits prior to the start of the trials. In many instances these rabbits are released some days before the running in order to allow the animals to become oriented and accustomed to the area.

Not all good beagles make good field trial contenders. Some dogs which do very fine work on their home grounds and when hunting with their kennel-mates become too excited, nervous or timid to make a good showing when in competition. The change of environment, the presence of the gallery, the association with strange hounds and the general air of excitement attendant upon a field trial has an upsetting effect on some dogs and their performance in competition is far below the level of their known ability. Others catch the spirit of the occasion quickly and become what is known as "gallery dogs." They thrive on competition and seem to outdo themselves when braced with a strange dog in front of a gallery.

A good field trial beagle must have more than a good nose, a properly used voice, and the desire to hunt. He must have great determination and independence; and while he must hark in to his bracemate's cry he must not depend upon his competitor to carry the trail. He must show intelligence in hunting the gamey spots, no matter how different the terrain may be to that with which he is accustomed. He must take advantage of every opportunity to display his good qualities and make the most of the limited time accorded him, and he must do it all with energy, enthusiasm, and style.

Space will not permit the listing of more than a portion of the beagle clubs now holding field trials annually or more often, but here are a few:

St. Louis, Pinckneyville, Ill.; Merrimack Valley, Hamilton, Mass.; Bluegrass, Versailles, Ind.; National, Aldie, Va.; Indiana County, Indiana, Pa.; Long Island, Commack, N. Y.; Memphis, Memphis, Tenn.; Yadkin Valley, Ronda, N. C.; Miami Valley, Yellow Spring, Ohio; Oak Hill, Attleboro, Mass.; Pocono, Reading, Pa.; Bunker Hill, Walnutport, Pa.; Garden State, Mt. Laurel, N. J.; Alabama, Gadsen, Ala.; Carolina, Salisbury, N. C.; Nutmeg, Durham, Conn.; Southern Maryland, Brookville, Md.; Tennessee, Jackson, Tenn.; Black Jack, Rembert, S. C.; Wyoming Valley, Falls, Pa.; Columbus, Columbus, Ohio; Peach State, Monroe, Ga.; New Eagle, New Eagle, Pa.; Texas, San Antonio, Tex.; Spring Church, Spring Church, Pa.; Dixieland, New Albany, Miss.; Yazoo, McComb, Miss.; Pelican State, McComb, Miss.; Southern, Dallas, Texas; Southern California, Murietta, Cal.; South Texas, Houston, Texas.

A glance at the locales of these trials will give the reader a good idea of the national interest in beagle hound field trials.

Under the point system and with the large number of trials being held annually, a beagle has a better chance to gain the title of field trial champion than fox hounds and bird dogs which must win title events to annex such honors. But the acquiring of the necessary points, particularly when three first places must be won, is certainly no mean accomplishment, and many fine contenders have amassed far more than the necessary total of points only to miss the title because of failure to meet the first place wins requirement.

Beagle breeders who want to use winning sires have a wide choice of field champions to choose from. A glance at the advertising pages of *Hounds and Hunting*, the beaglers' bible, will reveal many famous field trial champion beagles at stud. Here are a few:

Contentnea Jack II, Contentnea Jackson, Bishop's Meddler, Bishop's Rebel, Chickamauga Button, Smoky Mountain Scrappy, Straight's Squire, Step-a-Head Rusty, Pleasant Run Banker, Amawalk Link, Commando Sam, Hunsicker's Rob Roy, Kiley's Tiny Tim, Sked's Captain, Davidson's Nifty, Little Beaver Chief, Sambally Brandy, Grayline Venture, Karo Lad, Gaysong Doughboy, Concord Sindy, Sam Bright, Happyland Scott, Wildcliff Mistake, Warfield Red, Skylight, Royal Run Red Prince, Congamond Woodman, Shaw's Clipper, Pine Hollow Nifty, Pastime Plowboy, Hillcrest Duster, Watatic Rocket, Truetone Dandy, Liberty Streak, Rolcap Satin, Beaupre's Hunter, Smokey, Bearkill Tim, Tumbleweed Tumble, Valiant Toney, Rippling Run Ringer, Trailaway Linesman, Gray's Linesman, and others.

With over 19,000 beagles registered by the American Kennel Club in 1947 and more than 20,000 running in field trials, it is easy to see that the popularity of the miniature music-makers of the meadows is still on the upswing. And as long as Br'er Rabbit and Molly Cottontail and their family continue to lay down scent-filled trails in America's fields and coverts the beagle will continue to be the favorite gun dog of millions of American sportsmen.

# RETRIEVER FIELD TRIALS

It has long been the conviction of experienced hunters that the most effective contribution any individual sportsman can make to the cause of wildlife conservation is the use of a retrieving dog while hunting. This statement is not limited to the specialists, the retrieving breeds, but includes *any* dog—which is not gun-shy, has a nose, and will hunt!

The annual loss of game birds, both upland and waterfowl, which fall to the gun but are *not* retrieved, mainly through the lack of a retrieving dog, is enough to make the far-thinking sportsman who first used the term "game conservation" turn over in his grave. Yet almost all of this wasted game could be salvaged if a retrieving dog were made a "must" in the necessary equipment of every gunner. Although any sort of dog which will hunt and has a nose will be of value in game salvage, the retrieving breeds are specialists in this department of field performance and their importance in the over-all picture of game conservation is inestimable. Their value cannot be overstated. For example, authorities freely estimate that at least one out of every five wild ducks which fall to the hunter's gun are cripples which get away to be taken by predators or to die lingering deaths, or are dead ducks which fall in such thick or heavy cover that they are extremely difficult to find, so that search for them is only cursory. The recovery of only a considerable portion of this annual waste, some of it needlessly wanton, would be a most effective contribution to the restoration of a priceless, natural, renewable resource which is in great danger today, and would materially assist in the preservation of wildfowling.

Hunting dogs have been taught to retrieve ever since they first became adjuncts to the gun, but until recent years the use of "specialists," retrievers developed solely and used exclusively for retrieving, has been comparatively limited in this country. The publicity given to retriever field trials in America during the past 17 years has, however, given great impetus to interest in the various breeds to which this sport is devoted.

The performances of these dogs, some of which have been nothing short of marvelous, have attracted the attention of many sportsmen who realize that the sport of field shooting loses its zest when the game downed is not retrieved. As a result, breeders of Chesapeakes, Labradors, goldens, flatcoated, and curly-coated retrievers and Irish water spaniels in this country are hard pressed to supply the demand. The sport of retriever field trials is rapidly growing. First fairly well confined to the eastern seaboard, this sport has spread into the Middle West, the Mississippi Valley, and some of the prairie tsates. Thirty retriever trials were held in this country during 1946, 75 dogs being placed or awarded certificates of merit, as compared with 57 dogs receiving like awards in 21 trials during 1945. During 1946 approximately 2500 retrievers were entered in field trials, 1013 of them in All-Age stakes.

Pioneers in the sport are the members of the Labrador Retriever Club, Inc., which held its first annual trial (licensed by the American Kennel Club) on Dec. 21, 1931. The competition was confined to Labrador retrievers only, and two owners,

Mrs. Marshall Field and Robert Goelet, won all places. Mrs. Field's Carl of Boghurst and Odds On accounted for first and second places respectively, while Mr. Goelet's Sab of Tulliallan won third-place honors. Fourth place was divided between Mrs. Field's May Millard and Mr. Goelet's Glenmere Joe. Sixteen Labrador competitors faced the judges, David Wagstaff and Dr. Samuel Milbank.

The American Chesapeake Club held its inaugural trials in 1932, and these two clubs were the sole promoters of the sport until late in 1934 when the Brookhaven Game Protective Association held its first trial at Strong's Neck, East Setauket, N. Y.

The year 1935 saw the spread of the sport to the midwestern section of the country when 11 retrievers started in the first trials of the Midwest Field Trial Club at Barrington, Ill. Since that time the sport has known a healthy growth. Most of the events held in this country are now open to all members of the retriever breeds, although each breed organization, the Labrador Retriever Club, the American Chesapeake Club, the Golden Retriever Club, and occasionally the Irish Water Spaniel Club, hold trials in which the competition is confined to the individual breeds.

The American Kennel Club of New York and the *American Field* of Chicago outlined, in considerable detail, rules and regulations for the holding of retriever trials. These formulas are quite similar; the *American Field* concept gives more latitude, perhaps, to the judges. The great majority of the trials are held under the licensing of the American Kennel Club.

Retriever trials in this country are not only public exhibitions of gun-dog proficiency. They are the best insurance retriever-breed fanciers can have against the relegation of their favorites to the somewhat cloistered confines of the bench-show ring. The retriever is a workman and he reserves the opportunity to demonstrate his peculiarly outstanding capabilities in the wildfowl blind and game field. Retriever field trials are devoted to just that.

It might be well here to quote an extract from the Rules and Regulations governing retriever trials as formulated by the *American Field:*

"The object of retriever trials is the promotion and development of the high-class retriever, to demonstrate by public performance the great intelligence, usefulness and perfection of training attainable by dogs of the breeds named.

"Retriever trials are designed to provide competition of the highest kind among the various retriever breeds, to stimulate enthusiasm among owners and to afford a practical guide to breeders by setting a high standard of performance. The tests in retriever trials should not vary from those encountered in an ordinary day's shooting, except that since the tests principally are artificially conducted they may be somewhat more exacting, but must be as uniform as possible for all contestants in a single stake.

"Retriever trials educate the sportsman to a fuller appreciation of the work of his dogs and are a mighty influence in the significant work of conservation to promote perpetuation of wildlife."

In these trials, as in other gun-dog trials, the competing dogs are judged on natural ability and training. Under natural ability come nose, pace, style, determination, drive, and marking. The refinements of training, which augment the dog's natural ability, include steadiness, obedience to handler, excellence of delivery, and tender mouth.

There are a number of factors which come under consideration by the judges in evaluating a retriever's performance in field trials. The most important quality of a good retriever is the possession of exceptional scenting ability. Without a good "nose" a retriever is practically hamstrung before his education begins. True, his ability to "mark" down his game will serve him in good stead, but his eyes alone are not sufficient to lead him to his quarry. An exceptional "nose" will lead him to the capture of a running cripple, no matter how elusive.

The successful retriever must not only work out the area of the fall quickly and thoroughly, but he must mark it down properly and go to it at command with dash and speed. If he fails to locate the fallen game immediately he will continue his search in determined and enthusiastic fashion, using initiative and independence, but responding promptly to the directions of his handler when they are given. He should quarter his ground thoroughly, taking every advantage of the wind to aid his nose, but conducting his search in accordance with his handler's directions as long as he can see or hear him.

Once the game is found it must be returned with promptness, without dallying, and delivered with tenderness. A slow delivery often mars an otherwise sparkling performance, although pace is not the prime requisite. A fast search, quick pick-up, and swift return make a well-rounded performance which always deserves high praise.

A good retriever must also be "water-wise." He must unhesitatingly enter the water when ordered to do so, no matter how cold or rough, and his ability swiftly to negotiate difficult water conditions is most essential to a successful and satisfactory performance. The "higher" a dog swims the better his chances are to end his quest with the greatest dispatch.

The retriever must be under perfect control at all times. Not only must he show obedience to his handler while actually at work, but he must be completely steady in the duckboat or blind or as a non-slip retriever (retriever working only at heel) in the field, particularly under the gun. Under actual waterfowl shooting conditions, many wildfowlers insist that their retrievers be on their way for the retrieve as soon as they have marked the fall, contending, and sometimes properly so, that the sooner he reaches the spot of the fall the better his chances are for a retrieve. Field trial procedures, however, will not permit such unsteadiness. The dog must remain "steady" until ordered to go. This is as it should be, for "steadiness" demonstrates the high degree of excellence which has been attained in the dog's training. And field trials are exhibitions of gun-dogs in performances approaching perfection as nearly as possible.

The argument concerning "shot-breaking" as an assistance to retrieving chances in "rough-and-tumble" shooting is as old as gun-dog training itself. There is an unnecesary element of danger present in "jump" shooting with a shot-breaking retriever in the boat, and numbers of capsizes have resulted. A shot-breaker can also upset things in a duck blind, although it is granted that the sooner he gets on the job the better. However, if a dog is allowed to break-shot he is more liable to become unsteady in other respects, and a successful and satisfactory retriever *must* be under control.

Proper retrieving performance includes tender retrieving. The "hard-mouthed" dog will be disqualified in field trials.

Much has been said about the speed and style of a retriever. The good retriever will go about his work with enthusiasm and dash, reaching his destination quickly and hunting his quarry at good pace. Pottering should not be tolerated. He should show animation and spirit in his work. Pleasure in his job and merry action are always pleasing to the eye.

Consistency of a high order is demanded in a retriever trial. Often in pointing-dog trials a single outstanding performance is sufficient to obtain a place in the stake, at least, and possibly means a first-honors win. Such is not the case in retriever trials. One spectacular performance is not enough. Those dogs which win are called upon to repeat and repeat again as often as the judges deem necessary for the clear determination of the winner on that occasion.

While the dogs are drawn in braces, as in pointing-dog trials, and run in pairs, there is no definite time limit set on any single series. In this respect retriever trials differ from pointing-dog competitions. In the latter, too, it quite often occurs that a number of the contesting dogs run birdless heats and so have not demonstrated, in the first series, their ability to handle game. This is due to the considerable part the "luck of the draw" plays in bird dog trials. This "luck" is, in a large measure, eliminated in retriever trials, for in these events every competitor is assured of chances to prove his wares as a retriever of game. The shooting of pen-raised game assures this. The "luck" is not entirely eliminated, however, for it is simply impossible to give every dog identically the same retrieving problem to solve, although every effort is made to do so. One dog may draw a couple of kills which fall in fairly easy cover, while to the lot of his bracemate may fall a strong-running wing-tipped cripple which will give him quite a run for his money. The judges, however, have a way of balancing these performances one against the other so that the decisions are arrived at with equal fairness to all.

In the land tests the dogs compete in braces, although each dog performs his own task without aid or interference from his bracemate. The two dogs walk at the heels of their handlers, who are in line with the judges. Each must stand quietly or sit when the "line" comes to a halt. The game-bearers and the guns proceed at fair distance in front of the judges and handlers, and at a signal from the judges game birds are released and the guns go into action.

The dogs must remain, unleashed, quietly on the line and should mark the fall of the game. The judges then will order one handler to send his dog in for the retrieve, the bracemate remaining "steady" until its turn is called. It is indeed quite a temptation for a dog to watch his rival dash out and proudly make an enthusiastic return to be petted by his master when he knows that another bird is down. And it is doubly tempting when the same dog is again sent—to fetch the second bird. Yet control and "steadiness" play an extremely important part in retriever trials. Breaking to shot or retrieving without orders are errors which disqualify. The same applies to chasing rabbits in Open All-Age stakes.

In water tests, the dogs are worked singly, generally remaining in the blind with their handler until ordered to retrieve. Upon making the retrieve they must come around the blind and enter it from the rear or side to make the delivery.

There are no set programs which are required in all retriever trials. The judges and the field trial committee have complete control over the requirements and mechanics of each stake. Difference in conditions which exist in various areas and over different field trial locales makes this latitude necessary. The general idea, however, that dogs are expected to retrieve any type of game bird under any and all conditions always prevails.

As an example of the diversified working procedure of a retriever trial we may cite the tests given the winners of the Open All-Age stake of the Long Island Retriever Club on Oct. 24, 25, and 26, 1947. The first test was a long widespread double mark in water. The second was a double mark in heavy cover on land, one bird 75 yards out and the other 10 to 15 yards farther on in the same line. The third was a combination marked retrieve and blind in water. The fourth was a long double mark in marsh grass. The fifth was a single mark across water and on land.

Another example was the tests given the winners of the Midwest Field Trial Club on Oct. 4 and 5, 1947. First, a short triple-marked retrieve in water; second, a double-marked retrieve on land, both birds shot on the same line, one 40 yards out, the other 80 yards; third, a double land blind, one 40 yards out, the other 80, the dogs being required to return the near bird first; fourth, a short blind requiring water entry and handling in a narrow creek.

Simple problems, these? Most trainers do not think so. Their proper solution requires plenty of nose, brains, strength, and willingness.

Some retriever owners deride retriever trials as being "too artificial." "This is just a show. These are trick dogs," some have said. "You won't get these sort of conditions in actual wildfowling in a month of Sundays." The answer to such charges is: attend a modern retriever trial and see for yourself. True, some of the conditions do have an artificial flavor, for this is necessary to provide equal opportunities for all contestants and also to make the tests properly difficult. When one makes the statement that most of the situations in retriever trials are not encountered in regular wildfowling he has merely admitted that he is not an experienced wildfowler.

"Trick dogs?" Some of the retrieving feats of the competing dogs in practically every retriever field trial are spectacular and sensational, and these dogs *do* know a lot of so-called "tricks" of the retrieving game, but they are "tricks" far different from the parlor variety. Do not forget that practically all the winning retrievers are top gunning companions in rough-and-tumble shooting and have had their share of open-season experience.

For evidence that these dogs get plenty of experience in field trials one should take a glance at the amazing record of Field Trial Champion Rip, a golden retriever which carved his niche in the Retriever Hall of Fame in the seasons of 1939, 1940, and 1941. Rip, according to his owner, Paul Bakewell, retrieved under judgment, from the fall of 1938 until his death in August 1941, the remarkable total of 236 pheasants and ducks without a miss.

The champion Chesapeake retriever, Dilwyne Montauk Pilot, declared the best retriever in 1936, was a marvelous gun dog and was heavily shot over by his owner, R. R. M. Carpenter of Montchanin, Del. A field trial performance of this grand retriever is considered one of the greatest exhibitions of canine sagacity. In the American Chesapeake Club's trials at Benton, Md., in 1937, Pilot was given a blind water retrieve of two ducks; one fell dead, the other was a strong swimming cripple. A sharp cross-wind was blowing and a fairly strong tide was running, making swimming difficult. Pilot picked up the dead duck and started for the blind, when he saw the cripple rapidly swimming away. He dropped the dead duck and started for the cripple. The bird was a strong swimmer, but the high-swimming Pilot was more than his equal. However, the bird was a clever diver and time after time eluded his pursuer. Pilot, too, was a diver and finally caught his quarry, returning the duck alive. He immediately started out after the dead duck, returning to the spot where he had left it. The duck, however, had floated far down the bay and was not in the dog's sight. The clever retriever started swimming in wide circles, caught his handler's direction, and finally made a bee-line for the fallen bird, retrieving it promptly. In all, the dog was in the water many minutes and he was busy every one of them. He won the stake.

Meadow Farm Night, Charles L. Lawrance's handsome black Labrador, is another whose performance is outstanding. This was in the Long Island Retriever Club's trials. Night drew a wing-tipped water retrieve. The duck was barely injured but was unable to fly. The big Labrador could not get his mouth on the bird because of its expert diving. Time after time he dived after the duck, only to see his quarry come up yards away. Finally, the dog drew on his instinctive intelligence and began to swim back and forth by the duck, crowding him just enough to cause the duck to swim toward shore but staying far enough away to keep from causing undue excitement. Once the duck was on land, the pick-up was easy for Night and a news photographer secured an excellent picture of the big fellow racing back to the blind with the live bird in his mouth. Night won that stake.

As demonstrations of gun-dog control, steadiness, willingness to tackle difficult situations, and plain canine intelligence, retriever field trials have no counterpart in this country. They are here to stay. If they do nothing more than demonstrate to the shooting public the extreme value of the retriever breeds in game salvage and conservation, they have more than justified their existence!

A frequent question is, "Which breed is the best retriever?" Discussion of this hotly debated matter has no place in this article. However, a listing of the placings by breeds in Open All-Age or Limited All-Age stakes which were open to all breeds of retrievers and Irish water spaniels from 1931 through 1946 is taken from the 1945-46 Year Book of the Labrador Retriever Club, Inc.

| *Breed* | *First Place* | *Second Place* | *Third Place* | *Fourth Place* | *Total Places* |
|---|---|---|---|---|---|
| Labradors ..... | 117 | 108 | 106 | 97 | 428 |
| Goldens ....... | 38 | 39 | 36 | 30 | 143 |
| Chesapeakes ... | 15 | 14 | 17 | 22 | 68 |
| Curly Coats ... | 0 | 2 | 1 | 2 | 5 |
| Irish .......... | 0 | 0 | 3 | 0 | 3 |

The winner of the 1947 National Retriever Championship was the black Labrador, Bracken's Sweep, owned by Daniel E. Pomeroy, Englewood, N. J.

The sport of retriever field trials is growing every year. Most of the clubs holding one or more retriever trials each year are listed in the following:

American Chesapeake Club; Del. Bay Field Trial Club, Del.; Golden Retriever Club of America; Idaho State Field Trial, Association, Ida.; Irish Water Spaniel Club of America; Labrador Retriever Club; Long Island Retriever Field Trial Club, N. Y.; Midwest Field Trial Club, Ill.; Minnesota Field Trial Association, Minn.; Mississippi Valley Kennel Club, Mo.; Missouri Valley Hunt Club, Nebr.; Nebraska Dog and Hunt Club, Nebr.; North Dakota Retriever Club, N. D.; Northeastern Wisconsin Kennel Club, Wis.; Northern Retriever Field Trial Club, Wis.; Northern State Amateur Field Trial Association, Minn.; Northwest Retriever Club, Wash.; Oregon Retriever Club, Ore.; Wisconsin Amateur Field Trial Club, Wis.; Women's Field Trial Club, N. Y.

Prominent field trial winners among retrievers have been:

The *Labradors* Banchory Night Light of Wingan, Banchory Varnish of Wingan, Black Panther, Blind of Arden, Bracken's Sweep, Firelei's Hornet, Freehaven Jay, Glenairlie Rocket, Glenairlie Rover, Marvadel Black Gum, Black Roland of Koshkonong, Decoy of Arden, Gun of Arden, Little Pierre of Deer Creek, Meadow Farm Night, Nigger of Barrington, Shed of Arden, Black Magic of Audlon, Tar of Arden; the *golden retrievers* Pirate of Golden Valley, Rip, Royal Peter Golden Boy, Stilrovin Rip's Pride, Stilrovin Nitro Express, Stilrovin Superspeed, Sheltercove Beauty, Tonkahoff Esther Belle; the *Chesapeakes* Chesacroft Baron, Chesacroft Bob, Dilwyne Chesabob, Dilwyne Montauk Pilot, Skipper Bob, Sodak's Gypsy Prince, Sodak Rip, Shagwong Gypsy, Tiger of Clipper City, Laddie's Rowdy, Bayle, and the *Irish water spaniel* Step; the *curly-coated retrievers* Sarona Jacob of Marvadel and Sarona Sam of Marvadel.

# MISCELLANY

## THE AIRPLANE AND HUNTING

Airplanes will complete the conquest of the wilderness carried almost to its finish by automobiles and other methods of transportation that preceded them. Each improvement in transportation makes more of the wild country accessible. Where he goes man tames the land and leaves only those animals and fish that can survive contact with people. In our grandfathers' time it took a day or two to travel by team or on foot to reach satisfactory wilderness conditions. Today a similar amount of time will put a hunter down at any desired spot on the entire continent. Within the next decade there will be practically no hunting spot at which another hunter may not conceivably arrive during your time in the field. The days of solitude, of complete isolation from the rest of humanity, are numbered.

There is talk (but too little action) of setting aside suitable wilderness areas still remaining in which all vehicles and airplanes will be banned. We can hope that such preserves will be established, but the chances are that they will not be established in the best game lands and that soon after their establishment it will be possible to reach their boundaries easily by car, rail, or boat. It is doubtful whether they will be so large that a man cannot walk across them in a week or two, at most, and, given easy transportation to their edges and enough ambitious walkers, they will no longer remain truly wild. The forest will be the same but the game and the solitude will not. Our wilderness is passing and there seems no way to save it.

The regulations regarding the use of airplanes in hunting game follow those of the automobile and motorboat. The actual shooting of game from an airplane is forbidden everywhere. The airplane's value to the hunter lies in carrying him to the wild hunting grounds quickly, or making possible trips that were beyond his reach because of time, labor, or difficulty formerly involved.

There are, and will continue to be, objections to the use of airplanes by hunters, just as there used to be similar objections to their use of automobiles. But it will have no real effect on the situation. It will be impossible to prevent a hunter from flying to a given spot to hunt as long as we permit a prospector to fly there to look for uranium or anything else. It would be foolish to forbid prospectors to use airplanes and impossible to prevent the prospector from taking out a hunting license and combining a hunt with his prospecting trip. The bulk of the complaints come, as they did with the automobile, from those who do not have them, are afraid to ride in them, or cannot afford to.

The important thing to realize is that our real wilderness on this continent is at its tail end. A few years will see its passing. Many a living hunter regrets not having lived at the time of Daniel Boone. Many a future hunter will regret that his birth took place after the year 1930. The wiser hunters now living who have a real desire to see wilderness hunting and to hunt game that may never have seen a man will make the necessary arrangements or sacrifices to do so if it lies within the realm of possibility.

Flying in itself is a thrilling business, whether you ride or handle the controls. Most hunters will buy their passage on the planes of bush pilots or regular air services in order to reach the hunting grounds. A few will become pilots and buy or rent their own planes in order to fish and hunt. Many choose boat planes because in the wilderness to the north a seaplane can take you where no rails, roads, or waterways now reach. Floats can be changed to skis for winter bush flying and safe landings on frozen snow-covered lakes and fields. The conventional wheel landing gear can operate in a few wild areas where there is smooth terrain, but flying on wheels in the wilderness is normally a very hazardous business. Airstrips for land planes require a previous approach by one of the standard methods of surface transportation before the field can be built, and a staff on hand to operate them.

Lee Wulff, a nationally known outdoor writer, explains a few of the advantages of the flying sportsman.

"Eight days after my first flying lesson I soloed, and in less than three weeks I obtained my private pilot's license which permitted me to take up passengers (not for hire although they could share expenses on trips) and to fly wherever I wished.

"Once I left the railhead, the road's end, or the last stop of the boat in my seaplane, a minute of time in the air was equal to an hour or more on the ground. An hour of flying would take me as far as I could have packed in a week. My plane also gave me the advantage of mobility. If I failed to find good sport at the first lake selected, I could switch to another at almost a moment's notice. The plane gave me an opportunity to look over the area from above and to get a better knowledge of the terrain when I landed than could possibly have been learned from books or maps, and in some cases it would give me actual sight of the game I was seeking."

How much can you see from a plane? There are a number of factors involved. If the air is clear and the sun is bright you will see the terrain below you with amazing clarity. If the country is open or if the trees are bare and your plane flies at less than 100 miles an hour, you will see considerable game if you know how to look for it. Tracks in the snow give a good account of the game's activity. Ducks and water birds are easily spotted when at rest on the surface,

Photo by Lee Wulff.

**Plate I. Taking Out a Buck by Air.**

and any birds on the wing are easy to see. It is motion rather than size or color that gives most game away. A fox running across a field can be seen easily from altitudes up to 2000 feet. A moose standing motionless out in a bog is reasonably easy to pick out; if he moves, you can hardly miss him. You can fly over salmon pools and count the fish lying in them. You can fly over salt water and spot big bluefin tuna, sharks, and various schools and individuals of many other species.

The airplane has been effectively used in taking a census of game. It is possible to spot herds of antelope, mountain sheep, or other open-country animals and obtain an accurate count of the numbers in a given area. The only things you can shoot from an airplane are those permissible to be shot from a yacht, such as seals and some of the northern sea birds—and predators in some states. Coyotes and wolves in the western country are easily seen from the air. A good pilot can put his gunner in excellent position for a shot at a distance within range of his charge of buckshot. This flying, as you may imagine, is hazardous as well as exciting.

The requirements now in force in South Dakota are interesting. Hunting of predators by airplane is permitted only by permits granted for limited periods. A $250 bond must be posted to be forfeited if there is any law violation during the hunting. The airplane must be licensed and the pilot at least 21 years old with at least 400 hours of logged flying time, of which at least 200 hours shall have been devoted to flying substantially the same type of aircraft to be used in the hunting, and at least 30 hours shall have been logged in the ship to be used within the six months immediately preceding the term of the permit. The aircraft's license number must be painted on both sides of the fuselage so as to be readable from the ground when the plane is in flight. This low-level flying is only for the most skilled pilots and, all things considered, it is a type of hunting which few of us will achieve. It is probable that in the not too distant future even predator hunting by planes will be restricted to conservation department employees in the few states that permit it.

Here are the negative factors affecting the use of airplanes in hunting. With the exceptions just mentioned, they must be used only for transportation to and from the hunting area. If a car is required after the hunting area is reached, the saving of time is important only if the traveler rides a fast plane, and the need to hire a car while on the ground may offset that gain. A car will cover more ground than most light planes during the days of the hunting season when the nights are long. Not all planes are equipped for night flying, and traveling in dark air is always more hazardous than by daylight. Bad weather which grounds your plane seldom stops your car, and surface travel permits you to take more luggage.

Now for the other side of the situation. Once you get into real wilderness on floats or skis you can use your plane just about as you would use your car at home. You fly right to your camp and you fly from there to any other hunting spot you choose from among the many at which you can land your plane safely. There are times when ice may be forming on the lakes to hamper float flying or the snow may melt too much for a takeoff on skis, conditions which require judgment on the part of the pilot in advance as to whether to pull out or to stay. Incidentally, a float plane can land and take off safely in deep snow, or on ice heavy enough to skate on. The hunting pilot must have the viewpoint of an Indian, whose viewpoint was that of the game he hunted. Time did not matter. It went by whether he was here or there, and he was as much at home at one spot as at another. He moved when conditions were right for moving and holed up when they were not. You cannot fly airplanes in wild country on a rigid schedule, and the only safe frame of mind is one that does not worry too much about what time of day it is—or what day.

A light, single-motored airplane can be handled by one man whether it be on floats, wheels, or skis. He can moor it safely, turn it as required, and operate without worry, barring motor failure. Given a motor failure, the chances are about nine out of ten that he can land the plane with little or no damage and about 99 out of 100 that he can walk away from it. Beyond that point everything depends upon how good a woodsman he is. He can build a signal fire and munch away at his supplies in the comfort and warmth of his sleeping bag or he can take the compass out of the airplane and head for the nearest settlement. The hazards are not too great for the experienced woodsman pilot and the rewards are exceptional.

For the hunter lacking that combination of piloting skill and woodsmanship, there is an airfield near him from which he can fly to another airport on civilization's outer fringe. There he and his companions can board a bush plane and be dropped in the heart of the hunting country together with their guides and all the necessary supplies. They can hunt for their allotted time and depend upon being picked up from their camp at the edge of the lake by the same bush plane and whisked back to their homes over the air route. For them the last of the wilderness is still open. All too soon it will be gone.

# ARCHERY

**New Interest in Archery.** During the last ten years interest in archery has grown by leaps and bounds. Although target and flight shooting have made considerable progress, the main trend has been toward field archery and hunting. There are a number of reasons for the recent tremendous strides made by this ancient sport.

A series of some 20 featured short subjects, released by Warner Brothers, depicting true records of hunting big game with the bow, showed conclusively what could be done with that weapon. It was not that the archer had never killed such game as the wary bighorn sheep, the cougar, bear, jaguar, alligator, swordfish, shark, wild boar, and other species, but for the first time millions of people had the opportunity to enjoy the thrill of actually seeing these feats performed. Consequently, many persons who had literally never seen a bow and arrow (other than perhaps a toy) wanted to try shooting one.

New clubs sprang up everywhere in all the states. This time most of the converts were not satisfied with shooting a bale of hay: they had seen big game brought down with the long bow, and nothing less than a chance to try their own skill in the field would satisfy them. Target shooting at the butts seemed too tame.

A lack of proper tackle for such field shooting was soon remedied by the major tackle companies, including Ben Pearson, Fred Bear, Howard Hill, Potter and McQuarrie, and others. However, there was one essential still lacking before the new sportsmen could try their luck, and that was a place to hunt.

Of course archers could hunt in most states of the Union during the regular season in open territory, but hunting under such conditions was, and is, dangerous business. It is necessary to keep under cover as much as possible when hunting with the bow and arrow and to wear clothing as inconspicuous as can be had, because the archer has to get much closer to game than does the rifleman in order to get a shot. Definitely, hunting under cover and wearing clothing that blended with the background of the woods were not conducive to safety from the rifle where the archer was concerned. A considerable number of people were being shot with rifles each year while they were wearing red hats and shirts, and while standing out in the open in plain view of other hunters. How much more unsafe, then, was the archer who did not go in for red clothing and who had to stalk under cover!

Besides the danger to himself, an archer does not have much chance to get within bow range of deer

PLATE I. Proper Method of "Bracing" the Bow.

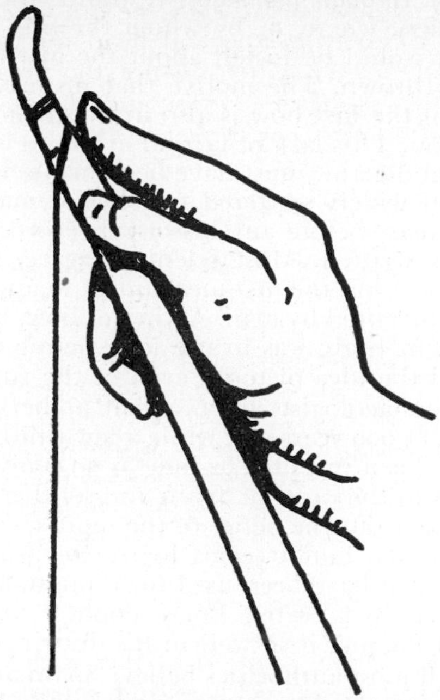

PLATE II. Push bowstring into the groove with the thumb and forefinger.

after the game has smelled gunpowder a few times. The wary creatures are not slow to learn that their old enemy, man, is back of this firestick that roars like thunder.

Most archers understood the facts just enumerated, and they naturally wanted a place where it would be safer for them and where they would have a better chance of getting within bow-shooting range of the game than had been possible in the past. In order to have special areas set aside for shooting the bow only, a great deal of work had to be done.

This new group of bow-and-arrow converts, together with the old archery hunters, went to work on the various state legislatures, and soon a few states—among them Oregon, Michigan, Utah, Tennessee, Pennsylvania, and Arizona—had archery hunting reserves, from which rifle hunters were excluded.

In some of these reserves game was plentiful and a few archers were lucky enough to bag a deer, bear, moose, or wild boar. The various local newspapers were generous in giving the fortunate ones credit by printing pictures of the trophies and writing articles on such feats. This publicity helped to start other archers in hunting, as well as to inspire more people to take up shooting the bow and arrow in general.

The various archery clubs began putting on more field archery shoots, the National Field Archery Association was formed, archery magazines began publication, more articles about hunting with the bow began to appear in the leading national sports magazines, numbers of short subjects on big game hunting with the bow were released by the major moving-picture studios, and gradually the nation realized that a new era in hunting with the long bow had dawned.

As this is written, most states now either have established archery reserves or else have a pre-season for bow-and-arrow hunting exclusively, before the regular season opens. In most of the states that follow the latter method the big-game hunting season for archers is opened 10 or 12 days before the regular season for riflemen begins. The archer is so much less proficient than the gunner and his range of accurate shooting so much less than that of the rifle hunter that it is essential for the former to have a head start. However, there are a few archers who go into the woods during the regular season and get their deer, bear, moose, elk, wild boar, or other game, and ask no special privilege. A few archers have killed almost all the varieties of big game on the North American continent, and yet have never shot an animal in an archery reserve.

Anyone who is a good enough sportsman, however, to go after big game with the long bow should not hesitate to take advantage of all the breaks possible, for even with the breaks it is ten times as hard to get a deer with the bow as it is with the rifle.

The state game commissions and the riflemen have no cause to worry about the slaughtering of game by the archers: the year 1946 was the most successful one the archers ever had, so far as the number of deer bagged was concerned, and the percentage of game killed was less than one deer by every hundred archers. At such a rate, a thousand archers kill less than ten deer annually. When their score is compared with that of the rifle hunters, who killed 80 deer for every 100 hunters in the state of Nevada in 1946, it must be acknowledged that this new crop of Nimrods are not exactly a deadly lot with the bow, but are truly game conservationists.

Even the ratio of hits by the archers was only slightly above one per cent. This percentage will

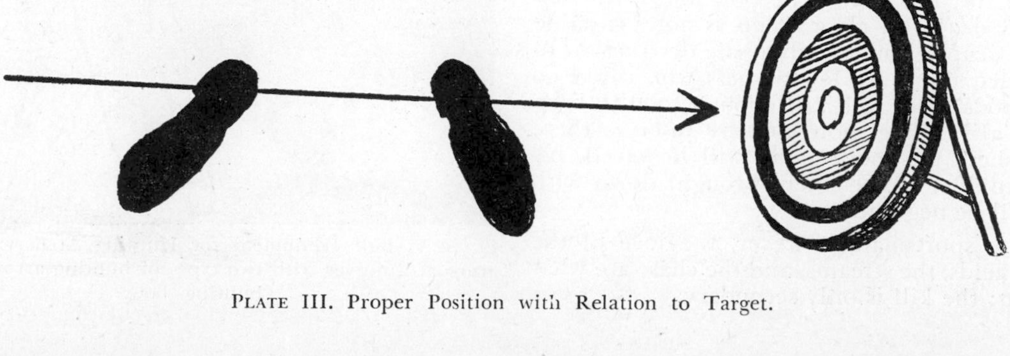

PLATE III. Proper Position with Relation to Target.

PLATE IV. Howard Hill illustrates correct draw for hunting archery.

naturally increase as the bowmen become better stalkers and as their weapons improve, but there is no chance that they will ever inflict any heavy losses on the animal tribes. A real archer, however, is a true sportsman, and he does not have to make a kill in order to enjoy hunting with the bow.

It seems clear that if the game commissions and legislative bodies continue to co-operate, the archery hunters are here to stay; their number will grow, rather than decrease.

Bow hunting requires careful study of the animal to be bagged, his strong and his weak points. The archer must know these traits of the game, so that he can properly respect the one and take advantage of the other. He must also be a good woodsman.

Despite the fact that some individuals will probably always be found to have a tendency toward slaughtering game, most Americans have a love of, and respect for, fair play. The bow and arrow, although very deadly at close range, is not a suitable or efficient weapon for the wholesale destruction of game. In fact, there are few archers who could go into the woods today and kill enough food to keep themselves alive. The more archery reserves there are established, the more game will be saved, because the number of specimens brought down with the bow will be negligible.

To a true sportsman, however, the love of the woods, the fields, the streams, and the chase are what really count; the kill is only secondary.

**Archery Through the Ages.** It would be as difficult to say when, where, or by whom the first bow was shot as it would be to tell about the first rock that was ever thrown. The motive that inspired the invention of the first bow is also in the realm of pure speculation. This lack of factual evidence is because the bow and arrow must have been made by various peoples in widely scattered regions for many thousands of years before any historical record of man's work was written. Most scientists agree, however, that the bow was the first mechanical weapon of any sort ever invented by man. A kind of bow, fashioned from a bent limb, was in use long before man had conceived the idea of tools, even of the rudest sort.

Most archaeologists believe that archery is from 12,000 to 13,000 years old, while a few think the bow may have been invented as long as 30,000 years ago. Drawings in the caves of Spain and southern France seem to bear out the belief of the more conservative archaeologists, but it seems logical to assume that the bow must have been used for thousands of years before the early artist knew enough about this weapon to depict it so well in his drawings.

Though most authorities believe Spain and southern France to have been the locale of the first archery it could have easily been elsewhere. However, if only evidence is to be considered, one must go along with the idea that Paleolithic man was the first to use the bow. At that time man lived out in the open and had no shelter of any kind. Neither did he have smooth tools to finish his weapon with. Consequently, the rough surface of the bow was soon affected by the influences of weather and time, and rotted quickly when not in use. Therefore, no trace of the earlier examples of the bow has ever been found.

Theories as to what motive inspired the first archer to invent the bow and arrow vary widely. Some think there is little doubt that the need for protection from animal foes inspired him to the deep thought

PLATE V. Full Equipment for Hunting Archery: fingertips, armguard, quiver with two types of hunting arrows, bamboo hunting bow.

that resulted in the bow. Others, perhaps of a more romantic turn, are just as sure it was the jealous heart in the bosom of some little man which proved the inspiration. This latter group seem to feel that love and hate are stronger motives than is fear, or even the urge to kill food more readily. Then there is a minority who are of the belief that perhaps the bow was invented by some man of small size who was hounded by an inferiority complex, and who needed this weapon in order to gain equality with, and respect from, his fellow men.

There are still other theories, but no one will ever know the truth about the beginnings of this weapon, which has made more history than any other one invention of man so far. Every country of renown that exists today, with the single exception of the United States, was built by the use of the bow and arrow, and this same weapon delayed the formation of this country almost half a century. Had the Indian flat bow been as efficient as the English long bow it would have taken considerably longer than it did for the white man to subdue the red man on this continent.

It is not only as a weapon, however, that the bow has been used. It was the first musical instrument, and even today there are some tribes in Africa that make music on the bowstring, and have built a little box to amplify the sound. It is entirely possible that the beauty of the design of the drawn bow with the arrow on the string did much to inspire and promote the work of the early artist as he drew his pictures, using a burnt stick as his first crayon. Certainly the curves, the straight lines, and the angles shown in the design of the drawn bow with the arrow holding the string taut were copied by the cave-man artist. At any rate, hardly any other design has been used so often as a model or a motif as has that of the bow and arrow in historic times.

In literature—not only in history, but also in poetry, drama, and sacred writings—the number of references to the bow literally and as a figure of speech, is simply astounding. Some of the bravest, the most romantic, and most lovable characters in literature were famed for their feats of skill with the bow. Such men as Ishmael and Jonathan in Biblical history were noted archers, and the poems called the Psalms are full of references to this weapon.

A whole library might be filled with the volumes it would require to give the authentic history of the bow. Josephus, early Jewish historian, considered it the most efficient weapon of the Jews, yet the Babylonians were more skilled in the use of the bow, as they conquered the Jews and left many sculptured memorials of their prowess with it.

The Persians also cultivated the use of the bow while neighbors of the Babylonians, and in turn the Scythians took a lesson from them and passed what they learned on to the Greeks. When the latter nation lost the empire of the world to the Romans, archery became a strong part of the defense of the Romans. However, that nation fell before the sturdy arms and accurate shooting of the Goths, Vandals, and Huns. In 1066 William the Conqueror won the Battle of Hastings from Harold and the English. The Norman archers of William shot their arrows high into the air and they dropped on the Saxons behind their wall of shields.

PLATE VI. Kneeling Position for Hunting Archer.

There is no authentic proof as to just who introduced archery to the English. Some have believed that because William the Conqueror defeated the English so decisively at Hastings with the bow they then began to use it, but this assumption is incorrect. The English had already learned the use of this weapon from the Scandinavians at a much earlier date, although no doubt the trouncing at Hastings did much to increase the respect of the English for this implement of war. At any rate, for a long time after the battle no other archers in the world were a match for the English long bowmen. This nation did more than merely to shoot the bow: they improved the weapon, itself, and invented a new type of *draw*, or *release*, that gave them more accuracy in shooting. At the same time this new three-fingered draw enabled them to shoot heavier weapons than had been in use until then.

The English long bow, without a doubt the most famous of all bows, was perfected by them. So important were good bows to the English army that the king gave prizes for the best yew trees grown by his subjects. The nation also imported great quantities of yew from Spain.

By the skilled use of the English long bow the yeomen changed the course of history in 1346 at Crecy, in 1356 at Poitiers, and in 1415 at Agincourt. The true story of the skill of the English archers has come to us from many sources, through ballads and other poems and through the very laws of the country. The French, Scotch, and Irish alike ac-

PLATE VII. Correct Form for the Target Archer. Note low draw, to side of chin.

knowledged the superiority of the English long bowmen.

There was an English craftsman named Bodkin, who invented and perfected a point for an arrow that would penetrate armor of the heaviest sort. This point was a triangular affair several inches long, and hollow ground on three sides, leaving an extremely sharp cutting edge. The point had a gradual taper. When it was complete it resembled the end of a modern French bayonet. This secret weapon, named after its inventor, when first used astounded the enemy. Never before had any nation been able to use the hand bow effectively against men in armor. This very effective point all but made obsolete the heavy crossbows that had previously been in use. A bodkin-pointed arrow shot from a long bow was just as effective as the heavy missiles from the crossbow, and the English bowman could discharge three or four arrows from the long bow for every one shot by the crossbowman. It was comparable to the difference between the single-shot rifle and the repeating one.

There are of course many legends, ballads, and poems depicting the skill of famous bowmen. Without a doubt the most famous archer of all the world was Robin Hood. The ballads about him ascribe feats to him that would tax the skill of the best modern rifleman. Robin Hood used, of course, the famed English long bow and shafts fletched with the gray goose feather. He is credited with having shot at the end of a competitor's arrow in the center of the gold (bull's-eye) at 100 yards, and with having hit it so squarely that the arrow of his opponent was split from nock to pile in the very center of the shaft; the arrow of Robin then entered the target, taking the place of the shaft at which he had shot.

Another archer spoken of in Percy's *Reliques* was almost as good a shot as Robin Hood, although considerably less famous. This bowman, shooting befor the king, split a wand in two at 400 yards. It would seem that these English bowmen had eyes which were as far superior to those of modern man as was their skill with the bow and arrow. To test the truth of this statement, an archer of the present day should go out and try to see the end of an arrow at 100 yards, or a wand at 400. Nevertheless, these stories make good reading and have helped to keep interest in archery alive through the ages, and no doubt these bowmen will become even more famous as the years roll on.

The English have no monopoly on these archery legends. For instance, the Swiss had a pretty fair archer in William Tell, even if he was using a crossbow. All other stories pale into insignificance, however, when compared with some of the feats credited to the Turks and what it is claimed their archers did. One of their best stories goes something like this:

There was a very strong and famous archer who shot great distances with powerful bows, and he made a new bow that required much strength to pull. For this bow he fashioned a special arrow. When the bow and arrow were completed, darkness was about to settle down. Not wanting to take a chance of losing his new arrow, yet being most eager to try the new bow, he decided to shoot the arrow straight up so that it would fall near where he stood. With great effort he drew the arrow to the head and loosed the string. The arrow shot skyward, but though he waited until darkness fell, the arrow still had not come down. He retired to his home near by, feeling sure that the arrow would fall soon and that he would be able to locate it the next day. He slept the long night through and early the following morning he hurried out to get his arrow. As he neared the spot where he had stood the night before he failed to see his shaft. However, while he stood scanning the landscape, the arrow came down squarely on top of his head and killed him. The Turks are still wondering what feats this bowman might have accomplished had not this accident cut short his promising career!

So many such stories are told that sometimes one wonders just how much he can believe. Regardless of the amount of truth contained in these legends, the fact remains that among so many thousands of archers as have lived and shot, some of them must have been very skilled indeed. Yet in the opinion of most qualified critics, the best archers of today, with their improved tackle and better technique, are without a doubt better shots than the most famous bowmen of antiquity.

The American Indian, handicapped as he was by shooting a short, unsteady bow and using a bad release, still was able to shoot his weapon with considerable skill. The red men developed the ability to shoot from horseback more successfully than did any other people of any age. They could cling to the bare back of a horse running at full speed and shoot an arrow accurately into the chest cavity of the fleeing bison, which is no easy task.

According to records of some of the most famous American scouts and adventurers, certain of the Plains Indians could ride alongside a herd of fleeing buffalo and shoot from 20 to 30 of them before their horses became winded. What is more surprising, a great many of the flint-tipped arrows passed completely through the huge beasts.

Kit Carson, famous scout for General Frémont, told a story of a Sioux Indian archer whose skill rivaled that of the best of the ancients. He said that once while he was scouting for the general he spotted three Indians cooking supper. They had with them three good horses. Carson was, of course, interested in obtaining those animals, as they were worth $20 each, the price the government had agreed to pay him for all the good Indian horses he could get. The method used to gain possession of them mattered little to Uncle Sam. Carson watched the Indians and after they had eaten they bedded down for the night.

Early morning found Kit well hidden in a cliff of rocks near where the Indians were sleeping. He had decided to wait till the Indians were up and busy about the chores of preparing breakfast, when he would attempt to kill the braves and take the horses. He had noted that they were armed only with bows and arrows. He picked a spot out of bow range and waited. It was barely daybreak when the three Indians roused themselves and started to prepare their meal. When it was light enough for the old scout to see his gun sights, he shot one Indian. The other two dashed for the horses that were tethered near by. Kit killed the second brave before they reached the animals. The third one, however, was on the back of the best horse and was off before the scout could get a good shot at him. This Indian had not forgotten his bow. As the brave sped away, Kit raised his gun and was taking a bead on him when the buck slid out of sight behind his horse. All Carson could see was one foot above the back of the horse, and an arm around the horse's neck. For fear he would kill the $20 horse, he did not shoot. Instead, he quickly mounted his own horse and gave chase to the Sioux.

After a considerable pursuit he came into rifle range, but again the buck was riding so that Kit could not shoot without killing the horse. At this point they came to a hill. The Indian guided his horse around the side of it. Kit decided to go around the other side, hoping to get a shot when they should come to the other end of the hill. Carson was driving his horse for all he was worth, hoping to be close when the buck should come around the far end of the hill.

In the meantime, the Indian had seen what the strategy of Kit was, and instead of going around the hill, he cut up to the top where he could see over. Carson was 40 yards below him. While lying along the horse's side opposite Carson, the Sioux drew and loosed an arrow under the neck of his running horse. The arrow went through the crown of Kit's hat. Before he could get a bead, a second arrow went through the neck of Carson's horse, and the Indian was by then out of sight over the opposite side of the hill. Carson turned his wounded horse toward the top of the hill, but by the time he made the crest, the Sioux was down the hill and crossing the flat a hundred yards or so away. He was still riding on the off side of his horse, and the scout could not shoot the buck without killing the coveted horse. His own mount was bleeding badly and needed attention, so he let the Indian go, rather than kill the horse.

Kit Carson, in relating this story, failed to give any details as to just how the Sioux performed this great archery feat; he merely said that the Indian shot under the horse's neck from the opposite side to the one turned toward Carson himself. There are many such tales told of the prowess of the Indian with the bow, but few that seem so authentic.

In connection with Indian archers, it is extremely interesting to note that different tribes used different techniques; some were expert archers, while others

PLATE VIII. Correct Form for the Hunting Archer. Note that draw is high, to cheekbone.

were very poor ones. This is probably the true reason why critics and historians have varied so much in their estimates as to the ability of the red man with the bow. The fact is that a few Indian tribes, notably the Sioux, Blackfeet, Creeks, and Seminoles, were exceptional archers. There are a few Seminole archers even today who would tax the skill of some of the best white bowmen to defeat them at close-range field shooting.

Among the most noted archers of the United States were the brothers Maurice and Will Thompson, who contracted tuberculosis during the War Between the States, and who, when that war ended, left their home in the state of Georgia and went into the Florida Everglades, where they hunted only with the long bow. For several years they hunted in the famous Okefenokee Swamp in South Georgia and North Florida. There they killed with the bow bear, alligator, deer, and other big game, and, remarkable to say, became so proficient with the weapon that they shot rabbits on the run, and ducks, geese, cranes, and other birds on the wing.

Maurice Thompson kept notes on their experiences and later wrote a book, *The Witchery of Archery,* that gives an account of many of their treks in the swamp. No archer should fail to read this beautifully written and interesting record of the adventures of two of the greatest archers America has produced.

The late Dr. Saxton Pope and Arthur Young also made history by their prowess with the bow, within recent years. They both killed a considerable variety of big-game animals in America, and Art Young not only bagged a polar bear and other species of the North Country, but he even succeeded in getting an Alaskan brown bear with the long bow. On an expedition to Africa these two men killed many species of game, including the leopard and the lion.

At the present time there are any number of bowmen who have killed bear, deer, elk, and moose with the bow and arrow. A few, perhaps, will be as famous by the time they pass on as are the Thompsons and Dr. Pope and Arthur Young. There are also a large number of noted American target and flight archers, but they do not fall within the scope of this article.

As time passes, the skill of the archers of America will continue to grow, and perhaps 500 years from now there will be legends, ballads, and poems singing the praises of some of them, which will compare favorably with those concerning Robin Hood and William Tell. At any rate, as Maurice Thompson once wrote:

"So long as the new moon
Returns to the heavens, a bent silver bow,
So long will archery retain its hold on the heart of man."

**Types of Bows and Arrows.** There are so many different types of bows that it would not be possible within the scope of any one article to discuss them all. A number of types, however, are so similar that for practical purposes it seems best to discuss only a few of the most popular designs. Some characteristics that every good bow must have are: speed of cast, durability, smoothness in the hand when being shot, sturdiness, and penetration.

There are four distinct types of bows with which the archer should be familiar. In discussing these bows each feature will be considered separately and the four types will be compared. Under the heading "Bow Woods," below, an effort is made to emphasize the importance of speed, durability, sturdiness, and sweetness in the hand. It is also pointed out that the kind of wood used to make a bow will have much to do with how any type of bow will perform.

The four distinct classes of bows are as follows:

(1) The English long bow.
(2) The Turkish composite recurved bow.
(3) The Indian flat bow.
(4) The American semi-long bow.

Of the four varieties mentioned the English long bow is perhaps the easiest to learn to shoot. It is durable, very sweet in the hand, and fairly fast. Most of the original long bows were made of yew. The English army developed the most proficient archers in the world (see pp. 881-882). It was the English who developed the three-fingered loose, which gave their yeomen a tremendous advantage over archers of enemy countries. This three-fingered loose is fast, strong, simple, and quite practical, and is used by most good archers today. Most English long bows were from 6 feet to 6 feet 8 inches in length, and some few have been found that were 7 feet long. That was how the English long bow got its name: it *was* long.

The Turkish composite recurved bow was made of horn and wood laminated together. This type was much shorter than the historic English bow just described, and some have been found that are less than 4 feet long. This kind of bow is no longer made, except when occasionally some enthusiast builds one for experimental purposes. The outstanding feature of this type is its speed of cast, especially when light arrows are used. However, this bow has an unsteady feel in the hand, and although it does not kick too badly, it is very sensitive and is extremely hard to shoot accurately. With the exception of the Indian flat bow it is the hardest type to learn to shoot.

Although the Americans have broken all English target records, the Turks set distance marks that are far beyond anything the American archers have yet been able to shoot. It is for flight shots, or distance, that the Turkish bow is famous. The Turks are said to have shot arrows more than 800 yards, and although there seems room for reasonable doubt of these claims, some of the best authorities accept these old records as authentic. So far, no American has been able to shoot an arrow from a hand bow as far as 700 yards, but there have been some practice shots of more than 675 yards. It is entirely possible that before many more years have passed someone will shoot an arrow more than 800 yards, and the feat will be authenticated. Howard Hill was the first modern archer to shoot an arrow more than 400 yards. This feat was accomplished in 1926 in Miami, Florida, with a bow that pulled 172 pounds at 24 inches. This is the heaviest bow that has ever been pulled by any man with his hands, so far as the records show. Curtis Hill, of Dayton, Ohio, and Homer Prouty, of Portland, Oregon, have done more to improve distance or flight shooting than any other two archers of modern times.

The Turkish composite recurved bow, although it has been used for some remarkable flight shooting, does not compare favorably with the English long

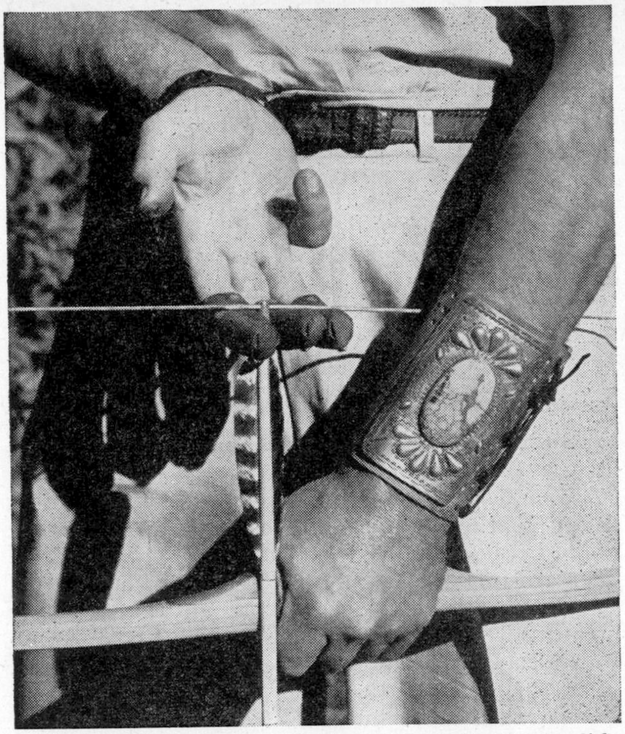

PLATE IX. Correct Position of Fingers on String for English-Type Loose.

bow for all-around shooting. The recurved feature of the Turkish bow has much to offer, and is used by a considerable number of modern archers for both target and hunting bows; and it is a fact that all the flight bows which have set records have been those with recurved ends, with the single exception of that used by Howard Hill to shoot more than 400 yards, in 1926.

The Indian flat bow was often made with ends recurved like those of the Turkish bow, and frequently the Indian bow was backed with animal sinew, the addition of which helped the speed of cast and the durability of that particular type of bow.

Because of the shortness of the Indian bow some support was needed to keep the limbs from breaking, for which reason the backing was necessary. The wide, thin feature of the limbs was also a great help in extending the life of the bow. Some Indian bows were no more than 3 feet long, yet arrows were drawn in them from 25 to 26 inches in length. Some of these weapons were as much as 4 inches wide and less than 1/4 inch thick. The thinner the limb of any bow, the less the expansion and contraction that the wood cells have to undergo in the act of shooting.

Some Indian bows were very fast, so far as cast was concerned, but most of them were extremely unsteady and rough in the hand. The shortness of this weapon caused it to vibrate to an extreme degree.

The Indians were exceptionally good shots at close range, but few developed the skill to shoot well at the longer ranges. After the white man came to America the Indians did a great deal of shooting from horseback, and the short bow was well suited to this type of archery. It was easily handled and shot while the brave rode his pony. The Plains Indians, such as the Blackfeet, Sioux, and Crows, became expert at shooting the flat bow from a running horse. During the wars between white men and Indians, fighters like Frémont, Custer, and other military notables learned to respect the Indians as light-horse cavalrymen.

Probably the most outstanding feature of the Indian flat bow was the sinew backing. No other material has yet been discovered which has so many good features as does animal sinew for backing on bows, especially if it is correctly applied.

The American semi-long bow is like the American-bred five-gaited saddle horse in its adaptability. It can be used for many different kinds of shooting and is by far the best all-around bow of any type yet developed. It is fast, durable, sturdy, and very sweet in the hand. Although it is a trifle harder to learn to shoot than the English long bow, it is so much superior in durability and performance that the gain far overshadows the loss of time experienced in learning to control it.

This modern American bow has most of the good features of the other three types, but with few of their faults. It is not so long as the English long bow, but is longer than either the Turkish or the Indian type. Many of the best target archers use recurved ends on their bows, and a considerable number of hunters prefer this feature to straight-ended weapons; for game shooting, however, the most successful hunting archers prefer a bow with straight ends. The chief reason for this preference is that in the bush one is often forced to shoot quickly, without having time to take the proper stance, or he may have to drop to one knee and hold his bow almost parallel to the ground to get under an overhanging branch or limb. Under such conditions and other unusual ones which sometimes confront the hunting archer, he is more likely than under everyday circumstances to make a mistake in his draw or loose. The recurved ends on a bow exaggerate these slight mistakes and often cause a clean miss, whereas if a straight-ended bow is used a slight mistake will not cause the arrow to deviate so much as if the ends were recurved. One can make a slight mistake and yet get a killing hit. The American semi-long bow has no radical differences from the other bow types, but is rather a combination of them all.

Before anyone fully decides just what type of bow he wants, it would be well to know the kind of shooting he intends to follow, whether target, flight, or strictly hunting. If it be target it is well (though not absolutely essential) to use a recurved type of bow. If flight shooting be the intention, then it is necessary to have recurved ends on one's bow to compete with other distance shots; but if his desire is to hunt, the archer will do well to stick to the straight-limbed bows, using fairly heavy strings and not too light arrows. All three of these features make for sturdiness and accuracy, despite slight mistakes, and no real hunter is going to be able to keep from making plenty of mistakes, because most of the conditions under which he will have to shoot will be difficult. For each shot made under ideal conditions there will be three that entail some obstacle, and in many cases there will be several difficulties connected with making a shot that are not covered by instructions in any book on how to shoot the bow.

Some of the best hunting archers can shoot from

almost any conceivable position and from any angle; the position of the bow matters little to them. It might be well for the new hunting archer to bear this fact in mind, and in practicing, to shoot from every position he can think of, and at various distances from the target.

As with bows, it would require considerable space to discuss all the various designs and types of arrows. However, there are really only a few different duties for arrows to perform.

For target shooting there are three shapes of arrow shafts, which may be chosen on individual preference. They are straight shafts, barreled shafts, and straight-tapered ones. Good arrows that fly well can be made from a shaft of any of these three shapes. The straight type, however, is the most widely used. The length of feathers used on target arrows is also a matter of choice. Opinions differ as to what is preferable, but most target archers like a parabola-shaped feather about 3 or 3½ inches long.

Flight arrows are made much like target arrows, except that thin strips of celluloid are used instead of feathers, and the length of the celluloid strips is less than one inch. The barreled type of shaft is decidedly to be preferred for flight arrows, and is the shape used by all flight archers who have set

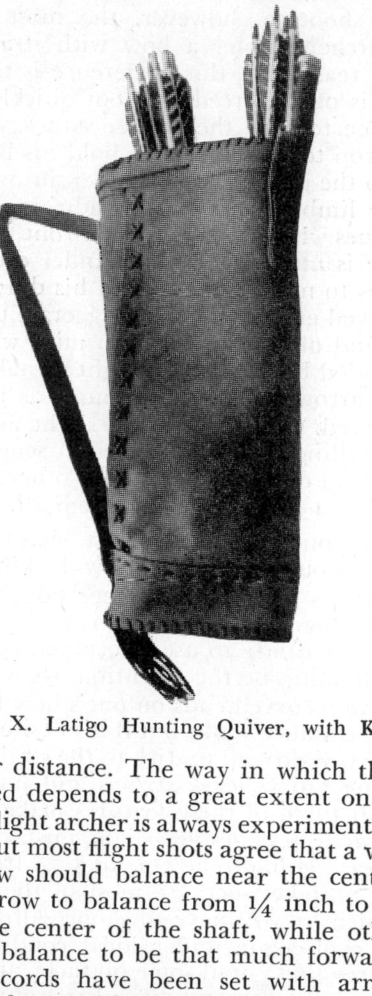

PLATE X. Latigo Hunting Quiver, with Knife.

records for distance. The way in which the arrows are barreled depends to a great extent on the user. Any good flight archer is always experimenting along this line, but most flight shots agree that a well-made flight arrow should balance near the center. Some like the arrow to balance from ¼ inch to one inch back of the center of the shaft, while others may prefer the balance to be that much forward of the center. Records have been set with arrows constructed in both of these ways.

There are almost as many ideas as to what constitutes a good hunting arrow as there are hunting archers. These preferences vary from a small head of from one-half to three-quarters of an inch wide and one inch long, to huge affairs that are 2 or more inches wide and from 3 to 4 inches long. Almost every archer will swear that the type of broadhead he is using is the only one he ever saw that was perfect, but the truth is that there has never been a perfect broadhead made.

However, the heads that will shoot the straightest under all conditions without windplaning, that have the greatest penetrating power, and that are strong enough to cut through bone without bending or breaking, are three times as long as they are wide and have either a straight or a concave cutting edge, and are, in addition, barbed. No broadhead should be more than one inch wide, or less than three-quarters of an inch. To give the blade the proper proportions for penetration it has to be 3 times as long as it is wide.

Game commissions in some states have ruled against barbed heads, but these rulings have come about because the members of the commissions have been misinformed, and as a result believe that a barbless arrow will work out of an animal if the creature is not hit in a vital spot. This is an erroneous idea. The arrow will keep working in deeper, or else will stay in the same place. The barbed arrow is much more humane, for the simple reason that if it is made as described above it will drive clean through any animal in America, even a buffalo, if shot from a bow of 60 pounds pull, or more, and if the arrow shaft is fairly heavy—this despite the fact that the broadhead may hit a bone in its passage.

If the head goes through the animal and protrudes, the first limb, weed, or other obstacle that comes into contact with the blade will catch in the barb and the shaft will be pulled out, leaving a clean wound, whereas if a barbless head is used there is no place for any obstacle to become entangled with it and so the shaft cannot be pulled clear and will stay in the wound. Most experienced hunting archers agree on this. Any hunter with trained powers of observation will realize the truth of these remarks.

A great many theories advanced by supposedly experienced hunters cause a great deal of unnecessary animal suffering. Any broadhead, no matter what shape or design, having a spot which is flat and at the same time more than half an inch wide, will cause the arrow to windplane under certain conditions, no matter how long the feathers may be or how much twist they may have. The beginner will be wise to accept these statements, which have been proved time and time again by many of the nation's most successful game shots. Careful experimentation has been carried out both on the drawing board and in the field over a period of more than 25 years.

There was once a great Indian archer who said to a friend: "Any old stick can be used for bow, but takes dam' good man make arrow." Most archers may not agree with the first part of the brave's statement, but few will deny the latter part. The broadhead on the end of a hunting arrow is the most important piece of archery equipment for the bow and arrow hunter. It would pay the beginner not to guess what to use as a broadhead or to concoct some outlandish design of his own, but to follow the proportions that have already been proved best.

A blunt-ended shaft is about the best type of arrow for shooting birds. An empty .38 cartridge shell makes a good head for both birds and small game. It is cheap and efficient. It is best, if possible, always to use footed shafts for blunt-pointed arrows. In the first place, they will be better balanced, but the chief advantage is that footed arrows are much harder to break, and will prove more economical in the long run.

No archer is any better than the arrows he shoots. If you must economize, get a cheaper bow, but never a cheaper arrow.

**Bow Woods.** There are many varieties of wood that can be made into good bows, but only a few of

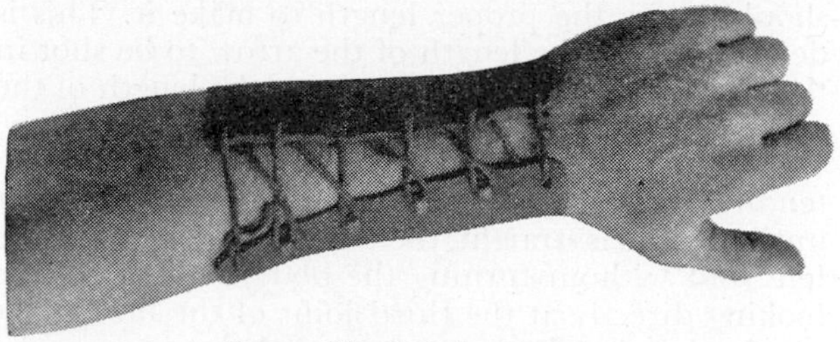

PLATE XI. Cuff Armguard.

these woods are easily obtainable. Others are not practical because they are so hard to work with the usual tools at hand. The four most popular materials for bow-making are lemonwood, yew, osage, and bamboo.

Lemonwood is by far the most widely used of all bow woods, even though it is imported to this country from Cuba and South America. It is easy to work, makes a good serviceable bow and is not expensive. Among top-flight archers yew is the generally preferred wood, and a more desirable bow can be made from it than from lemonwood, but in addition to being expensive, it is very hard to work by inexperienced bowyers. It is easily obtained if one does not mind the cost, and is one of the very best woods for bow-making. Although yew is grown in many countries, that grown in California, Washington, and Oregon cannot be beaten as a bow wood by that imported from other countries.

Osage (also known as beau d'arc, hedgwood, and by other names) is a very tough, hard, and fast wood when made into a bow, but it is not cheap and it also is exceptionally hard to work. This wood grows in many states of the Union, but in no foreign countries. The Plains Indians used it most successfully.

Bamboo makes the fastest and best bow of any material yet discovered and is not prohibitive in price, but can be worked only by expert bowyers. It is necessary to have special tools to work bamboo into a suitable shape for lamination, and three or more layers have to be laminated together to make a proper stave from which to fashion a bow. However, a good bamboo bow will retain its cast longer than any other bow. There are bamboo bows estimated to have been shot more than 200,000 times during a period of ten years, but which are yet as fast at the end of that time as when first made. If properly cared for, a bamboo bow will last indefinitely.

Bamboo is not a true wood, but is considered a grass. It does not have wood cells, but consists of many stringlike fibers which run the whole length of the cane. These fibers stretch and contract after the fashion of rubber, whereas wood has cells and it is necessary for these cells to expand and contract continually while the bow is being shot. After a long time the walls of the wood cells break down, causing a fracture in one of the limbs of a bow. The best bamboo is imported to this country from Japan.

In selecting or determining a good bow wood there are several factors that must be given careful consideration, which may well be classified as follows:

(1) Speed of recoil, known as *cast*.
(2) Toughness or *durability*.
(3) Smoothness or *sweetness in the hand*.

If a bow jars or kicks noticeably when it casts the arrow it will tire the hand and wrist, and may even blister the hand. The kicking is, of course, not desirable, and can be partially eliminated by the proper construction of the bow handle. (More concerning this fault or bad quality in a bow will be found in the section on "How to Make a Bow.") This *kick* is sometimes referred to as excess vibration.

Fast recoil or cast is, of course, essential in order to keep the arrow traveling in as nearly flat a trajectory as possible. The faster the cast, or recovery, of a bow, the more accurately it can be shot, other factors

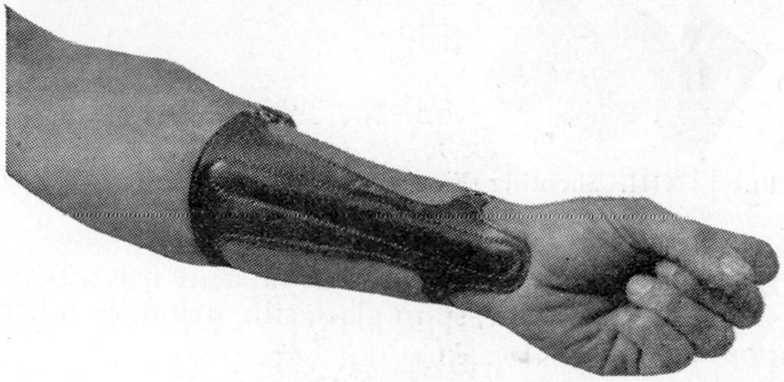

PLATE XII. Strip-Type Armguard.

being equal. Then, too, if a bow is exceptionally fast in cast it is unnecessary to have the bow pull unduly heavily, in order to throw an arrow on an almost flat trajectory. When an archer tries to pull a bow heavier than he can easily and comfortably control, he losses accuracy, as well as most of the pleasure that comes from shooting this weapon.

It is very desirable to have a bow that will last. After one has been hunting a few times with a given bow it seems like an old friend, and to have it break is a real tragedy. Each bow has its own peculiar and individual qualities, and the archer has to learn to shoot successfully each different bow, so besides the cost of obtaining a new one too frequently, there are several other reasons why the archer should seek the qualities of toughness and durability in the stave which is made into his bow.

No material ever tried, so far, will make the perfect bow. Split laminated bamboo comes the closest to perfection, with yew second, osage next, and lemonwood last, in order of their desirability. There are other woods, such as red cedar, juniper, black locust, sassafras, palma brava, and many others, that will make good bows, but most of these varieties have some outstanding poor quality that keeps them out of the first four woods for bowmaking.

The design of a bow has a great deal to do with the speed, durability, and smoothness of any weapon, but this fact has been taken into consideration, and it is assumed that the correct design is to be followed in making a bow from any of the woods just described.

Many readers may wonder why hickory has not been listed as a deisrable bow wood, but the cast of most hickory is so poor that it really cannot be classed as a bow material. True, it can be used for

PLATE XIII. Shooting Fingertips, Shooting Tab, Shooting Glove.

backing a bow, but even in that capacity it is a poor substitute for sinew, spun glass, silk, nylon, or other popular materials.

**How to Make a Bow.** There may be some who would like to try making a bow for themselves. A great many good archers got started by making their own equipment. Although it is almost impossible for anyone to make a really good bow on the first effort, if care is taken and instructions are carefully followed, it is entirely possible for one to make a first bow that will perform sufficiently well to learn to shoot with.

It is not advisable for a person to make his first bow from a wood that is hard to work, such as yew, osage, or bamboo, to mention a few. Although hickory is not a good bow wood, because it is too slow of cast and will soon take such a set that it will shoot poorly, it is one of the best woods to use in learning how to make a bow. It is so tough that it will stand over-drawing without breaking, provided, of course, that the stave used in making the bow is of straight grain and clear of knots.

Another wood which the beginner can use and which makes a much better bow than hickory is lemonwood. This is imported from Cuba and some of the South American countries. Although imported, it is much cheaper than some of the native North American woods. Mulberry, sassafras, ash, and red cedar can be used, but it is really safer for the beginning bowyer to use either hickory or lemonwood.

Whatever material is chosen, it should be properly seasoned. In ordering a stave to make a bow, be sure to specify to the dealer that the stave must be properly dried and seasoned. A bow made from green wood will take a bad set (that is, will *follow the string)* and will have a poor cast.

If one knows the proper tools needed in making a bow, one will not need many. The only ones really essential are: a good jack plane, a drawing knife, a spoke shave (preferably a Stanley 85), a vise, a 14-inch half round bastard file, a 6-inch rat-tail file, and some sandpaper, Nos. 1, 0, and 00. There are other tools that can be used in making bows, but the ones mentioned will suffice.

Before beginning to make a bow, however, one should know the proper length to make it. This is determined by the length of the arrow to be shot in the bow, which in turn depends on the length of the arm of the person who will shoot the bow and arrow. By holding a bow handle in the left hand and extending the left arm straight out from the shoulder until the arm is straight, then turning the head to the left (but without turning the body), so that one is looking directly at the third joint of the first finger on the left hand, the length of the arrow can be found. While holding the position just specified, the distance from a line directly under the right eye to the third joint of the index finger of the left hand should be measured with a yardstick or tape line. Subtract 1½ inches from whatever this distance is found to be, and the correct length for that particular person will be obtained.

As a table to go by in making the correct length bow to fit the arrow, or the right arrow to fit the bow, the following may be used: With a 6-foot bow and a 28-inch arrow as the standard, for every inch or portion thereof taken from the length of the arrow, twice that amount in inches can be taken from the length of the bow. If a person's measurement for an arrow is 27 inches, that is one inch less than the standard length for arrows, which is 28 inches. Therefore, for a 27-inch arrow, a 5 foot 10 inch bow will be the right length. For a 26-inch arrow, a 5 foot 8 inch bow will be correct, and so on.

If a person has an unusually long arm and has a reach, say, of 30 inches when measured as detailed above, again using the same standard, that person should shoot a bow 6 feet 4 inches long, but it has been proved not advisable to make a bow that is longer than 6 feet, or an arrow longer than 28 inches. There is not space to go into detail about the matter here, except to say that a longer bow will be slow and sluggish in cast, and a longer arrow will be found much harder to make with the correct balance in both spine and weight. The archer with the long arm can compensate for the shorter arrow by allowing his left arm to bend a little more at the elbow than he otherwise would, or by foreshortening his draw by not bringing his left shoulder fully forward. Some of the best archers shoot arrows from 2 to 3 inches shorter than their correct measurements call for.

When the arrow length has been determined, the proper stave secured, and the needed tools provided, one is ready to begin making a bow. The correct size of the stave which is to be worked into the weapon is from 1½ to 1¼ inches square, and 6 feet long. The grain of the wood should be checked and the smoothest and best side should be decided on for the back of the bow. The grain of the wood should run at right angles to the back and belly of the bow.

After the back side has been selected, the rough saw marks should be removed from the wood by using the jack plane. If the grain of the wood has a tendency to eat in, the half-round file can be used to smooth it. When this is done, heavy No. 1 sandpaper should be used to smooth the back still further and to remove all file marks and other roughness. This smoothing should be followed by using No. 0 sand paper, and then finished by No. 00. Care should be taken to keep the back of the bow perfectly flat. If the stave has a natural backset, the concave side should be selected for the back of the bow, provided, of course, that the grain position is correct.

If the stave has a side cast (that is, is not straight from side to side), this irregularity can be taken out by getting the wood hot and bending it to take out the cast. Care must be taken not to burn or scorch the wood. However, if a crooked stave is to be properly straightened it must be pretty hot, too hot to hold in the bare hands. It is necessary to heat only that portion of the wood where the curvature occurs.

When the stave is straight from side to side, and the concave side (or back side) is smoothed and finished with No. 00 sandpaper, the bow should be laid out as follows: The center of the bowstave is found and a line is marked across the back. Another mark is made 1¼ inches above the center line and still another 2¾ inches below the center line. The section between these two lines will comprise the bow handle, or grip. Each of these lines is then extended so that the stave will be marked on all four sides.

The stave is then measured on the top and bottom sides of the handle section of the finished back of the stave and the center is found. Two small dots are made; then with a straight edge a line is drawn from end to end along the center of the back, so that each of these two dots will be center cut by the lines thus drawn. Next a distance of ¼ inch is measured on either side of this center line at the extreme ends of the bow, and other dots indicate this distance. Using a straight edge, the bowyer then draws four lines on the back of the bow, taking each of these four dots at each end as one point, and the corner of the back where the bow handle section is marked off as the other. If this is done correctly the bowstave will be ready to work down to the lines thus drawn.

The bowyer next cuts all the wood away down to the four lines along the sides of the bow. After the stave is thus shaped, the bowyer draws two other lines along the sides of the bow from the upper and lower lines of the handle section to ½ inch of the back. He then cuts down to this line, using the jack plane and the file, according to how well or how badly the grain works.

If these instructions are carried out in the proper manner the stave should be flat on the back side, from end to end. It should be tapered gradually from the upper and lower lines of the handle section to the ends, and on the belly from the same two lines to the ends. The stave should be ½ inch square at each end, gradually tapered to the upper and lower handle lines, leaving a 4-inch section for the handle, the same size as when the work started. (See Plates I, IV, VI, XV, and XVII for details of bow shapes.)

The stave should now be caught at the handle section with the back down, and the drawing knife used to round off the two corners. By using the spoke shave, drawing knife, and file, the limb should then be shaped to look as in Plates I and VI, taking care in working each limb so as not to get it too thin. The 6-inch rat-tail file should next be used to make the nocks (or notches) in each end of the bow for the bowstring to fit into (Plate II).

The bow is now ready to be strung for the first time, with only a slight bend in each limb. The stiff spots should be marked with a pencil and worked down so that every inch of both limbs from the handle to the tip is bending in equal proportions. When this is accomplished the bow should be strung up again with the string somewhat shortened.

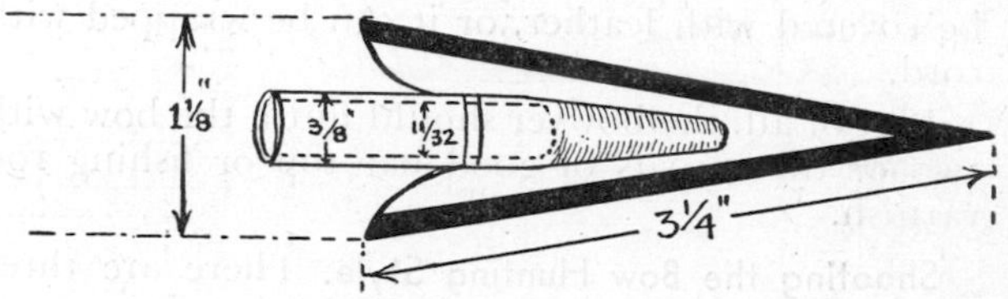


PLATE XIV. Excellent Type of Broadhead Arrow for Big Game.

When the bow is strung this time, the distance from the top of the handle to the bottom of the string should be 5 inches. The bowyer should check the stiff spots in each limb, again marking them. Using the spoke shave and the file, he should then work these spots until all parts of each limb are working in equal proportion.

An arrow should now be placed on the string, and the bow be pulled 8 or 10 inches. The bow should again be checked for stiff spots, and if any are found they should be marked and worked down until they bend correctly. The bow is drawn a few inches farther the next time, and again any stiff spots should be worked out, until the full length of the arrow has been reached, with all parts of both limbs working the same.

It is absolutely essential not to pull the bow more than a few inches at a time until one is sure the limbs bend properly, for the bow will surely break unless all the wood in each limb is doing its part of the bending.

As much wood as possible should be left in each limb, so that the bow will be amply heavy when the limbs have been worked down and the proper bend has been attained. Once the right bend is achieved the bow can be brought down to the proper weight by filing a little off each limb from handle to tip of bow. If too much wood has been taken off, however, and the pull of the bow is too light, there is no way of adding poundage, as no wood once removed can be replaced.

After the bow has been balanced in and the handle shaped to suit the owner, the weapon is ready to be finished, using first the coarse sandpaper, and finish-

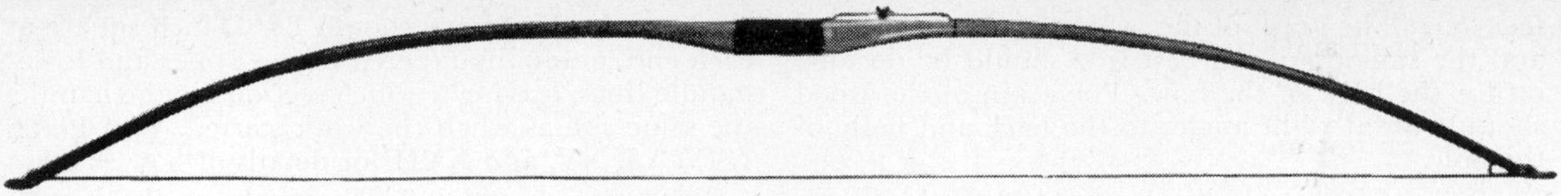

PLATE XV. Yew Target Bow, with Bow Sight; made by "Fleetwood."

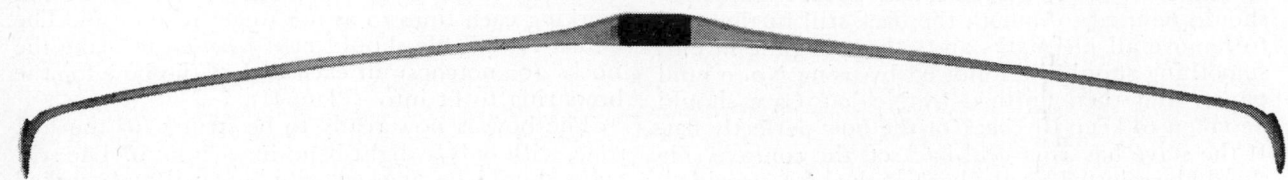

Photo from S. E. Wells, Wayland, N. Y.

PLATE XVI. An Excellent Example of the "Recurve Flareback" or "Setback" Bow.

ing with the very fine oo. If desired, the handle can be covered with leather, or it can be wrapped with cord.

Last of all, the bowyer should finish the bow with two or three coats of good bar top or fishing rod varnish.

**Shooting the Bow Hunting Style.** There are three different methods of *aiming* in field shooting, namely, using sights, instinctive, and imaginary point-of-aim. The *draw* of the archers using these differing ways of aiming may also vary. The sight method of aiming differs greatly from the other two, and some archers have met with fair success in field shooting, using bow sights. Others use what is called the instinctive method, and they too have bagged a goodly number of animals and game birds. However, the indirect, imaginary point-of-aim method is by far the most efficient of the three, and is used exclusively by the most prominent and successful hunting archers.

When the sight method is used, more time is required to calculate distances, adjust sights, and so on. There are various kinds of bow sights; in fact, rarely are two archers found together who use the same kind of sighting device. No really standard type of sight has yet proved successful enough to satisfy the majority of hunters who use bow sights. Although the sight method has some advantages, there is much improvement to be made before this method of aiming an arrow can compete successfully with the other two styles of field shooting.

Some sights are so constructed that the archer has a set point for the various distances, but for moving animals and flying birds the sight method is not practical. The most popular type of bow sight is a simple, inexpensive one. A piece of cork is made secure to the back of the bow above the handle. One milliner's pin, or maybe three or four pins, may be stuck in this cork pad so as to stick out on the left side of the bow. The archer must predetermine the correct spot on the cork to insert each pin for the various distances.

If only one pin is to be used, then the archer may mark lines on the cork pad for the various distances and move the pin in the pad to correspond to the distances at which he desires to shoot. The method of a series of fixed pins is much faster than using only one, but is also more confusing. It is perhaps easier for the beginner to meet with a limited degree of success by using a sight than in any other way, but as yet there are too many detrimental features to this method of aiming.

For instance, suppose one has a series of pins correctly laid out and placed and goes into the brush, hunting. Perhaps the weather was cool when he adjusted his sights the night before. When he starts out in the early morning the chances are that the weather will still be cool, but he may not get a shot until later in the day, after the sun has become hot. The bow will have let down and lost considerable cast, so when the archer uses the 40-yard fixed sight the arrow falls short of the mark, simply because the heat has caused the bow to let down and to weaken in cast. There are other faults, also, in bow sight shooting when hunting, which make this method less practical than the other two methods.

The instinctive type of aiming is very simple and is used by more hunting archers than any other method. It has but one outstanding fault: the archer has no way to know how to compensate for a mistake. If one aims instinctively and shoots the first arrow high, he has no definite way of correcting his mistake on the second shot, because he does not know definitely where the point of the arrow was aimed when he made the first shot. Instinctive shooting is like throwing a rock, shooting a slingshot, or pointing a finger. One merely looks directly at the object he wants to hit, draws his bow and lets go; in fact, he is feeling where he is shooting, rather than actually seeing.

This type of aiming, although it may sound foolish, is fast and fairly accurate. One will be surprised with what accuracy he can learn to shoot a bow by using this method. Some very successful hunting archers have used it. The late Dr. Saxton Pope and Arthur Young were two who definitely proved that this type of aiming had merit. Dr. Pope was a very fine shot, and killed many varieties of big game both on this continent and in Africa. Arthur Young hunted with Dr. Pope a great deal, and was with him in Africa.

The third and last method is without any doubt the most practical and efficient of hunting styles, yet it is the most difficult method to master, and some archers cannot use it. In shooting with an indirect, imaginary point-of-aim, the hunter has to concentrate his thoughts and focus his eyes directly on the object to be hit, but secondarily he must also see the point of his arrow and aim it at an imaginary point, either on the object to be hit, or below or above it, according to the distance he estimates the target to be from him.

As an illustration, a rabbit is sitting at an unknown distance from the hunter. As soon as the latter sees the creature he should be able to start his draw to make a shot. However, there are two or three things to be done first, before the arrow can be loosed. The archer must estimate the distance, pick out an imaginary spot on, above, or below the rabbit, according to how far away the rabbit is, at which to aim the point of the arrow when it is fully drawn. After a little practice, one will be able both to figure the distance the arrow has to travel and to select the point to aim at by the time the arrow can be drawn and in correct shooting position.

When the distance has been calculated and the point selected the eyes are focused on the rabbit primarily, and the mind is also concentrated on the rabbit, but secondarily the eyes must hold the point of the arrow in the field of vision and the mind must also be conscious of the arrow point. When the point of the arrow is in direct line with the imaginary point at which one is aiming, then the string is loosed.

At first glance, this may seem a very complicated method, but if broken down a little further, it is seen to be in reality, quite simple. One knows that the eyes cannot be equally focused on two different spots at the same time if those spots are more than a few inches apart; further, everyone will agree that the mind can actually concentrate on only one thought at one time. Even though the eye cannot shift from one object to another and see them both perfectly, it can concentrate on one and hold the other in the field of vision, while the mind can think of one thing, then of another, and go back to the original, all within a split second. In such case, the original thought will be are dominating one, while the second consideration will be the second one—in this case, the lining up of the point of the arrow with the imaginary point-of-aim.

Following the reasoning just outlined, when the archer sees an object he desires to hit with an arrow, his eyes should be focused directly on that object and kept on it, but his mind must act very fast. It must estimate the distance, select the imaginary point, instruct the muscles to act, and remind the eyes to hold steady on the object. Then, though the eyes are focused on the rabbit, they must also see the point of the arrow (that is, keep the attention on it in the field of vision), follow its line of action; and when the arrow is in line with the imaginary point at which one is going to shoot, the string is loosed. At first, the archer will find himself shifting his eye from the object to be hit (target) to the point of the arrow, to the imaginary aiming point and back again to the object (if the point is above or below the object instead of directly on it), but this tendency will have to be overcome if good results are to be expected.

It is best to begin with the instinctive method and slowly work into the method just described. It can easily be seen, however, how readily the hunter can correct a misjudged first arrow before making the second shot, whereas if the archer does not know where the first arrow was held and was just guessing, then he will still be guessing on the second shot—and on the third and fourth if he is lucky enough to get them. On the other hand, if he knows that he

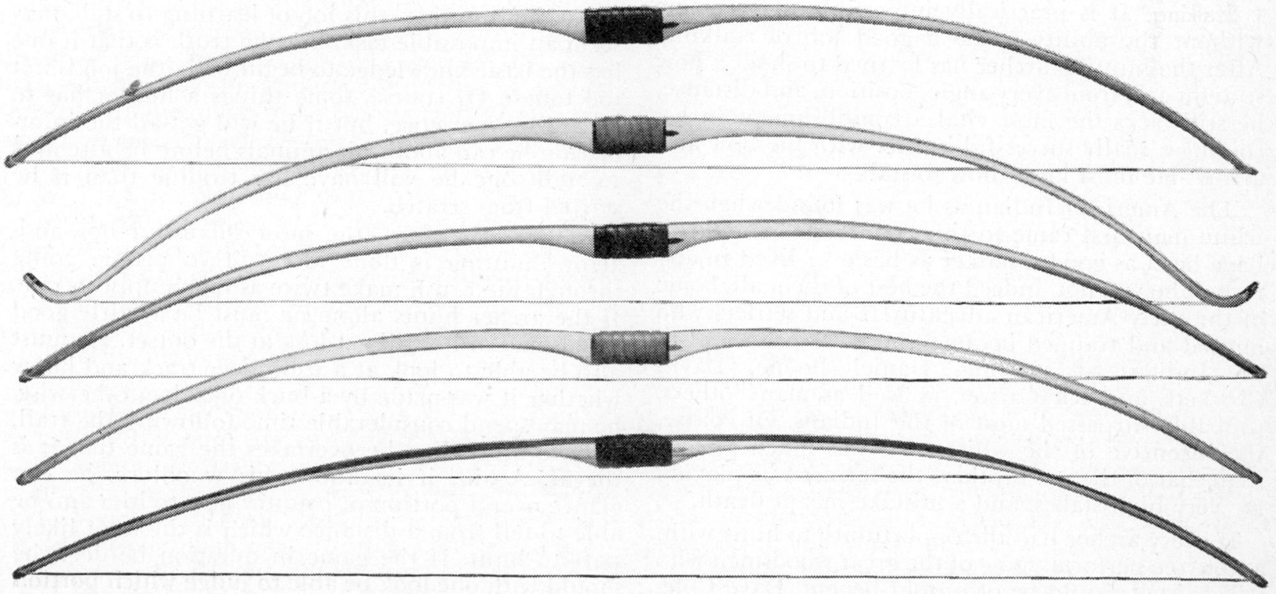

Photo from Ben Pearson, Pine Bluff, Ark.

PLATE XVII. Five Excellent Bows. These bows illustrate the proper bend, showing they are well "tillered." Notice also that the distance between the string and belly of the upper limb of each bow is greater than the distance between the string and belly of the lower limb. Also the upper limbs are from 2½ to 3 inches longer.

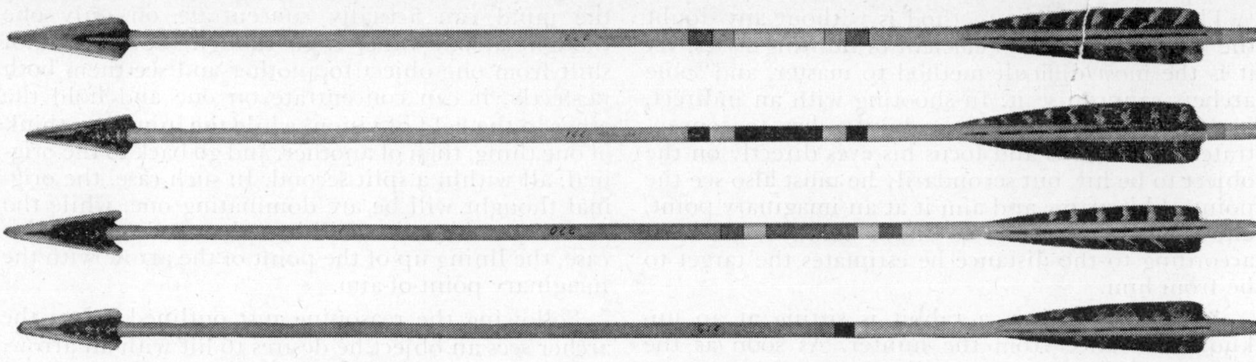

Photo from Ben Pearson, Pine Bluff, Ark.

PLATE XVIII. Four Excellent Types of Inexpensive Hunting Arrows.

pointed the arrow at a spot 6 inches above the object he was shooting at, and the arrow flew 6 inches under the target, he also knows that on his next shot he must hold not 6 inches above, but 12 inches above the target.

There are many good rifle shots who cannot shoot well with a peepsight, because they try to focus the eye on the peep and the front sight both, which naturally confuses the mind, and results in poor shooting. As soon as they forget the peep and concentrate on the front bead, their shooting improves. It is not that the peep is to be ignored, but merely to be used as an opening in which to center the front bead. Indirect, imaginary point-of-aim shooting is done in much the same way as shooting with a peep, except that both the point of the arrow and the point of aim are seen secondarily.

Many good, experienced instinctive-shooting field archers have improved their shooting from 50 to 100 per cent in a very short time by using the indirect, imaginary point-of-aim method, which is still relatively a new one. Even today many hunting archers have never heard of it.

**Stalking.** It is practically impossible to get game without the ability to do a good job of stalking. After the hunting archer has learned to shoot a bow straight and from every angle, position, and distance, he still lacks the most vital accomplishment in becoming a really successful hunter with the bow and arrow: He must know how to stalk.

The American Indian as he was found when the white man first came to this country is believed to have been as good a stalker as has ever lived in any race, if he was not, indeed the best of them all. Some of the early American adventurers and settlers who hunted and trapped became almost as proficient as the Indians at stalking. Daniel Boone, David Crockett, and Kit Carson, as well as many others, probably surpassed most of the Indians. Of course, the incentive of the white man was much greater than that of the red brother; the former was playing for very high stakes, and a mistake meant death.

If every archer had the opportunity to hunt with, and to see perform, some of the great woodsmen who still exist it would be of untold benefit. Dave Coleman, Algonquin Indian of Ontario, Canada, can move through the brush with the smooth grace of a big cat. His keen eye sees every track, every disturbance among the leaves or rocks, and his knowledge of the outdoors is so thorough that he can read these tracks and signs as accurately as the ordinary man can read a newspaper. Charlie Snow, Seminole Indian of the Florida Everglades, Mose Lanier of the same region, Wally Gravett, of northern British Columbia, and many other well-known woodsmen are just as proficient.

No man, however, has the muscle co-ordination or the physical build to reach the stage of perfection that many of the wild animals have attained. All species of the feline family, for instance, are past masters in stalking, and members of the canine group are not far behind.

In its broader sense, stalking includes much more than merely being able to get through the woods quietly, or to make a successful sneak on an individual animal. One must have a fair knowledge of woodlore, must be thoroughly familiar with animal habits, animal senses, and peculiarities that distinguish the various groups, and must also be able to recognize and identify by their tracks the different species of game. A good stalker must also be observant and must have a large store of patience and an equal amount of perseverance.

To the beginner, this job of learning to stalk may seem an impossible task, but the truth is that if one has the basic knowledge to begin with, the job is not too tough. Of course, some things a hunter has to learn by experience, but if he will get all the information he can about his animals before he attempts to stalk one he will have less trouble than if he started from scratch.

In the first place, the most successful bow-and-arrow hunting is done alone. Two people going through the brush make twice as much noise as one. If the archer hunts alone he must be a fairly good woodsman or he will get lost, at the outset. He must also be able to look at a fresh deer track and know whether it was made by a buck or a doe; otherwise, he may spend considerable time following the trail, only to find when he overtakes the game that it is illegal. Again, if he knows his woodlore, he can glance over a portion of country new to him and be able to tell from a distance which is the most likely part to hunt. If the game in question be deer, he should with one look be able to judge which portion is best suited for deer. In order to do this, the hunter must know the deer; knowing him, he will be familiar with what the deer eats, where he likes to sleep, and the most promising place to find that animal at various times of the day. In any case, regardless of what game he is hunting, one should be able to look the country over and know where to begin hunting, or he will waste a great deal of time and energy before he discovers where the game is.

Among the bovines, the deer, elk, and moose all like the forest, rather than the open country, for they all browse a great deal, yet all three families also eat grass. Each of these species, however, has its own favorite food, which the other two eat seldom if at all.

The moose loves water-lily bulbs and some forms of water-cress and other aquatic plants. He also likes to wade and swim in the mud and water.

The favorite tidbits of the deer are alder, bitter brush, and mountain mahogany. He never touches the favorite dishes of the moose, and he cares little for water, except to drink.

The elk, on the other hand, does not care at all for the preferred foods of the moose, nor does he particularly care for what the deer favors: his own taste leans toward bunch grass and buffalo grass.

The moose likes to bed down in deep, dense thickets near water. The deer prefers a hilltop where he can see out, and where the cool breeze is blowing. If the weather is very cold he still wants to bed down where he can see, but is likely to choose a spot on the sunny side of the hill, behind a big rock or under a sheer cliff. The elk likes high country, but he likes it open, and not too rough and rocky. He likes dirt and sod under his feet, rather than mud or rocks.

If the tyro remembers these animal preferences when he looks out over new country he will have a pretty good idea where to look for the various kinds of bovines just discussed.

The animal being hunted might be mountain sheep, wild goat, or antelope. Like the other three, these are bovines, but they differ so much in their food requirements and places of abode that they cannot be grouped with the three already considered. The antelope is a plains animal and does not like heavily timbered country. Though he sometimes ranges in the foothills and is fairly agile in hilly country, he prefers the open flats where he can run without any obstacles to interfere. He depends on speed alone for his safety, and when pushed can run up to nearly 60 miles an hour. For any distance over a hundred yards he is the fastest thing in the world on four legs. His chief food consists of the various grasses, though he does browse to some extent. He likes to sleep on a low knoll, from which he can see in all directions, and where there is no chance of an enemy's approaching him without being seen.

The mountain sheep and goat are the exact opposite of the antelope in many ways. The higher the peak, the steeper the cliffs and the rockier, the better they like it. They eat more grass than anything else, but are fond of moss, too, and during the winter they browse on twigs when most of the grass is covered with snow. Both these animals like to bed down on rock ledges where they can see for miles below. They have few natural enemies. The cougar and the wolf killed a good many of them in former years, but the wolf in this country is almost extinct, and the cougar is certainly on his way out.

The guides and natives of any country are a great help to a hunter in locating likely spots for various kinds of game, but it is well for one not to have to depend entirely on a guide. It is wise for the archer to listen to the advice of the natives, but not to lean too heavily on anyone but himself when hunting.

The bear is an individualist and eats anything from wild honey to a dead horse, but his taste leans toward worms, bugs, lizards, grubs, tender grass roots, berries and fruits in season, and a number of other edibles. He likes both the high and the low country, is at home in the water or on rocky ledges. In the spring and fall he may bed down in a muggy swamp. In the summer he likes the high, rough, cliffy terrain, but he wants plenty of cover, so the more timber the better. Any high, rough, rocky, steep canyon densely covered with pine, spruce, or hemlock is a good place to look for him in daylight. In winter he usually is not to be found, as he is hibernating in a cave or under a heavily protected windfall.

The true American wild hog, or peccary, as well as other wild hogs not native to this country, but rather planted ones, can be hunted on foot, but the hunter is much safer to go after any of this family on horseback and with dogs.

Cougar, bobcat, lynx, ocelot, coyotes, wolves, and jaguar, all night prowlers, are far too alert for archery hunting, except with dogs. These predatory creatures usually hole up in the daytime in places where it is impossible for men to go without first disturbing them. So long as it is necessary to have the help of dogs to hunt these varieties, it is of little benefit to the average hunting archer to go into a study of their particular habits and traits.

The different animals vary in their senses, peculiarities, and traits even more than they do in their diet and habitat. There are but few wild animals that have all their senses acutely developed. Although there are five senses, only three of these need to be considered when stalking wild game. They are sight, hearing, and smell. Even though one particular kind of animal may be lacking in keenness of one or two of these senses, usually the acuteness of the remaining one or two is such that the animal is still well protected from his enemies.

The mountain sheep depends almost entirely on his eyesight to give him warning, and he has the best eyes of any animal alive. It is interesting to notice, too, that whatever dominant senses one kind of animal may have, they are the ones best adapted to the locale of that creature. The sheep who usually stays atop the highest peaks certainly has a view not enjoyed by the animals of the dense swamp, and hence he has a range for his truly binocular eyes.

This creature, however, does not hear well or smell acutely, and there is a reason for these limitations, too. In the high country among the rocky cliffs, the wind is usually blowing and is constantly changing direction, as it whips down a canyon or glances off a towering cliff. For this reason and the fact that there are often snowslides and shale rock sloughing off, a poor sheep would be forever trying to figure out the various noises if he paid them any attention. The changing wind currents might bring to his nose the smell of an enemy from any direction, and if the sheep chose to flee down-wind he might run squarely into this enemy. At any rate, the

PLATE XIX. Set of Hunting Tackle by Potter & Macquarrie. A 60-pound hunting bow with latch handle. Engraved quiver with matching armguard, and shooting glove.

bighorn pays little attention to anything he hears or smells, but for anything or anyone to come upon him without having first been seen is practically impossible.

When the stalker does not need to worry about having the sheep hear or smell him it is decidedly easier to stay out of sight than it would be otherwise, for any hill, rock, or cover of any other kind can be taken advantage of by the hunter after the bighorn. A wise old Indian buck once said: "Sheep no hear thunder, no smell dead horse, but he can see through thin rock." He may have exaggerated a little, but not too much, especially in regard to the eyesight of the sheep. It has been proved that a bighorn sheep sees as well with his natural eye as does man with the aid of eight-power binoculars.

The eagle, wild turkey, hawk, and many other birds have good eyes, and some of them see perhaps almost as well as the sheep.

Both the moose and the bear have very poor eyesight, and the wild boar is another creature that does not see too well. However, all these animals have exceptionally keen ears and acute noses. The damp dark stillness where these animals like to spend much of their time is decidedly conducive to keen smelling and hearing, but not well enough lighted to develop acute vision. No four-legged creature except the sheep and goat is quick to recognize still objects, yet many birds can do this at a glance.

Deer, elk, antelope, caribou, wolves, coyotes, and all the cats see, hear, and smell acutely, and with the single exception of the mountain sheep, these animals just named are the hardest of all the species to approach closely. The mountain goat sees almost as well as the sheep, but has one pecularity that makes him easy to stalk: He always looks down, but never up. Once the hunter gets above the goat without being seen, it is easy to come down on him within bow range.

Almost every animal has some defect in his makeup which, if known to the hunter, may be turned to advantage. A deer has a great deal of curiosity. When he hears an unusual noise, many times he will come closer to see if he can discover the source of the sound. Another thing a deer will often do is to stop and look back just before topping out over a hill. Many times he may be in full flight, but when he comes to the brow of the hill he stops dead still for an instant or two before going on over the hill and out of sight.

A bear also has a great deal of curiosity. His eyesight is so poor that if one stalks a bear in low, bushy country and gets close enough for a shot but finds that the animal is partly hidden by the bush, the hunter can put his handkerchief, hat, or some other object that is unfamiliar to the bear on a stick, raise it above the cover, and move it gently back and forth a few times, and the bruin will often stand up on his hind feet to have a better look. This rising on his hind feet will sometimes give the hunter a shot at the chest, and a well-placed shot will finish the beast off in short order.

Bull elk can be readily lured into close shooting range during the mating season by giving the four-noted bugle or by taking cover in a dense thicket, securing a dry hardwood limb, and beating and scraping it on brush in the fashion of a buck deer or bull elk rubbing his antlers. Although this usually draws the elk, most deer are too clever to fall for such a subterfuge.

In the old days whole herds of antelope used to be lured right up to a hunter by hanging a rag or shirt on the end of a tall stick where it would wave in the wind. However, this trick by now has been worked so many times on antelope that they have become wise, and it is seldom effective any more.

If there are more than two hunters together and an animal is sighted a considerable distance away, one may hide behind the nearest cover while the others keep on going, but they should not go directly toward the game, but rather to one side or the other of him, always keeping in plain sight. As soon as the two (or more) are several hundred yards away from the spot where one of the party hid, that one can slip out under cover and work around behind the game and sneak up on it. The hunters acting as decoys should show no interest whatever in the animal being stalked, but should merely move around in sight to keep the game interested and on the alert. In fact, when any animal is occupied by watching an enemy at one quarter he is much easier to approach, because he is too busy watching the person in plain sight to be alert and watchful in other directions. By using this decoy method Howard Hill once stalked and shot with the bow and arrow a big mountain sheep ram at a distance of only 50 feet. Without a decoy this feat would have been utterly impossible.

In hunting with the bow the idea of making long, fast treks in search of game should be forgotten. A very slow gait should be taken, with occasional stops at short intervals. Often these pauses and the walks between them should not be of equal duration. When any animal is feeding he moves from one spot to another, stops and eats or looks for food, and then moves on. Very seldom does he spend the same amount of time in any two places, nor are the various spots he pauses in equally distant from one another. If the hunter uses the same timing as does a feeding animal he may often be heard by a wild creature and be taken for merely another animal, but if the hunter moves with one steady gait, no matter how slowly he progresses, any animal that hears him will become suspicious and at once on the alert.

Occasionally one should stop for several minutes in one place and look and listen. He can often locate animals by hearing them feeding, or game that has been standing behind cover of some sort may move out into plain sight of the hunter. In no case should the archer cover more than a mile in an hour, and a half-mile is better. Neither should he relax his vigilance for a moment, because invariably if he does relax and become careless, some opportunity will present itself which cannot be taken advantage of. For those who have extraordinary patience, still hunting in country where game is plentiful is a very good method to follow. One must remember that luck plays some part in how many animals one may see in a day's time.

Often one may be able to locate game by observing the action and noises of birds, chipmunks, squirrels, and so on. The hunter should study the various calls of the bluejay, the Canadian Jay (sometimes called the camp robber), chipmunks, red, gray, and ground squirrels, catbirds, flickers, crows, ravens, and so on, and try to identify the meaning of the various calls. In a short time he will find himself able to distinguish whether these creatures are angry, scared, or just talking to one another. Even though

PLATE XX. Howard Hill showing 12-foot alligator taken in the Everglades with bow and arrow.

most animals do not speak each other's language or understand ordinary conversation, they know perfectly well the distress calls and warning signals of each other. Any time a jay or a squirrel goes into a fit of chatter, every animal within hearing becomes alert. They know that these creatures are often excited, but usually for a good reason, so they pay attention. When moving through the woods, if one surprises any small creature and causes it to become excited, it is a good idea to stop and wait 10 or 15 minutes before going farther.

Most of the animals that have hoofs give warning signals by stamping the front feet; this is why most of these animals are so sensitive to ground vibrations. Not often will one deer take immediate flight when he hears another one stamp his feet, but he will stop feeding or whatever he is engaged in and will become alert. He too will usually stamp his own feet to warn any deer that may not have heard the first warning. Many times after such signals have been passed back and forth several times, the creatures will quiet down and begin feeding again, without fleeing. For an immediate flight signal, all these animals use a snort, which is made by forcing air rapidly through the nose. Very seldom does a deer linger after such a signal has been given. Bear, although not of the hoofed family, use the same flight signal. A wild boar also snorts and, on a quiet day, may be heard giving this signal several hundred yards away.

It has been mentioned that most animals are very sensitive to vibrations of the ground. This fact makes it imperative for the stalker to learn to walk in such a manner as to cause no appreciable ground vibration. It takes effort and practice to learn to walk as the Indians did. After one learns to progress in this manner it will be slower than one is accustomed to walking, which slowness is a good point in stalking, anyway. This Indian method of walking when one stalks differs from the white man's ordinary walk, in that when using the Indian walk, the weight of the body is not carried forward over the advancing foot, but is held well back over the rear foot that is still in complete contact with the ground. Because of the high center of gravity in the human body, it is extremely hard for the hunter to move a foot forward while he keeps his whole weight on the leg and foot that are still in contact with the ground, as is necessary.

Also, the construction of the human leg and foot is not conducive to quiet locomotion. One may recognize this fact at a glance by examining the arrangement of one's own leg and foot. The knee and ankle joints are directly in line with the leg bones, and the only possible way one can absorb vibration when placing a foot is by touching the ground first with the ball of the foot, and then lowering the heel into place. If this is done without any bodily weight on the advanced foot and with the knee slightly bent, the maximum amount of vibration is absorbed. For this reason one should never allow any of the weight to be forward when placing an advancing foot.

It is very important for the stalker to select the proper gear and clothing. Mixed colors of soft weaves are the best for garments. The colors should not be too dark, but should contain a good deal of browns and greens. Bits of red, yellow, and white are desirable, but should not be used in areas so big as to be conspicuous. Footgear should be soft-soled—moccasins, tennis shoes, or rubber-soled shoes that are not too heavy. Of course, if one is not accustomed to wearing moccasins or tennis shoes care should be taken at first until the arches of the foot become used to having practically no support. Anyone who makes a long hard hike with either of these kinds of shoes during the first few days they are being worn may injure the arches and soles of the feet. After becoming accustomed to this type of footgear, however, the feet will be strengthened by wearing them.

**Helpful Hints for the Beginner.** In order to become a good shot with the bow and arrow it is necessary for one to decide just what style of draw, aim, and loose he wants to use, and then adhere to that style and practice it, always keeping in mind that it will take time and patience.

A common mistake of most beginners is to select bows that are too heavy for them to pull. One should by all means use one no heavier than can be drawn easily and comfortably. Once the correct technique has been achieved and the proper muscles have been developed, the archer can then increase the pull (or weight) of his bow gradually as much as he desires, without losing efficiency. Many people who would have made good and efficient archers have quit the sport in disgust because they could never derive any pleasure from, or become proficient in, the use of the bow because the first one they owned was too heavy for them to draw. The muscles that are used to pull a bow are seldom used in performing other work, and have to be developed gradually. The fact that a person is strong does not mean that he should start shooting a strong bow to begin with.

It is not advisable for one to shoot too many arrows the first time he tries archery. The result may be a strained ligament or a broken muscle.

Each bow requires a certain spine in the arrow that is to be shot in that particular bow. The arrow can be too weak or too strong. One should be sure that the bow and arrow are fitted to each other. The stronger the bow, the stiffer the spine must be in the arrow that is shot in that bow. The length and diameter of an arrow have a bearing on the spine and must be taken into consideration.

The best archer in the world cannot do good shooting with a bow and arrows that do not match. For the most satisfactory results, arrows should be made or bought in groups of a dozen or more. Wood varies so greatly in its spine, weight, and speed of recovery that it is all but impossible to shoot well with a mixed set of arrows, even if they weigh the same and have the same spine.

It is not advisable to use small feathers on arrows. Some archers claim that large feathers on an arrow slow it down too much. The truth is, if an arrow is feathered correctly the difference in the trajectory of the same arrow fletched with 5-inch and with 3-inch feathers is less than 10 inches at 100 yards. This is by far closer than anyone can shoot, even target archers who use sights, points-of-aim, and other mechanical aids. Long feathers, well spiraled, are definite assurance of a true-flying arrow, if properly applied. A shaft which is under-feathered is tricky and decidedly unsteady.

For the hunting archer a set of fingertips, rather than a shooting tab or a full glove, should be used.

(See Plate XIII.) A set of tips (or stalls) so constructed is less binding and clumsy than either a tab or glove. In making a set of fingertips, one should use firm, tough leather, so the tips will not become grooved or stretch out of shape. However, the leather must be pliable and smooth.

Any armguard that is smooth and will protect the wrist may be used, so long as it is comfortable. It should, in addition, be so made that it can be easily donned and fastened.

The most comfortable and efficient quiver is the type carried on the back, rather than at the side or on the hip. The shoulder type is much more easily handled in the brush, can be used on horseback nicely, and is much more suited to fast shooting than any other type, an important point to consider. Often a split second may decide whether one gets a shot or not.

As soon as the archer learns to shoot well, he should make every effort to improve the speed with which he can draw, nock, aim, and loose an arrow. The shoulder- or back-type quiver should be made of good strong leather, not too thick and stiff, yet not thin and flimsy. By no means should one use rawhide or any other hard, stiff leather which will not allow the quiver to collapse. No hunting quiver should be less than 6 inches in diameter, and 9 inches is better. It should be adjusted so that the arrows stick up 6 or 8 inches above the right shoulder, halfway between the head and the point of the right shoulder. The large quiver will allow the archer to draw the arrows without raising them so high in the air as would otherwise be necessary. Latigo leather of medium thickness makes a fine quiver. A small pocket should be made on the back of the hunting quiver, in which should be carried an extra string, a small cake of beeswax for the string, a good pocket knife, a small pair of pliers, a little whetstone, and a 6-inch flat mill file.

A dozen good broadheads and a half-dozen blunts are about as many arrows as can be carried comfortably in a hunting quiver. Very seldom does one need more than this number of arrows for a day's hunt. In order to be able to get quickly at the kind of arrow he wants, it is well for the archer to have a division between the broadheads and the blunt-pointed arrows. To make this, a short length of string that will reach across the top end can be made secure on each side of the quiver. At least two-thirds of the space should be used for the broadheads, while the other third will be sufficient for the blunts.

When walking around the side of a hill one should carry the bow and arrow in the hand that is on the down-hill side. If one should slip and fall, which

PLATE XXI. Howard Hill with 600-pound black bear, killed in the Tonto Rim country with bow and arrow.

often happens, there is less danger of being hurt by the sharp points of the arrows; besides, this practice leaves the up-hill hand to catch with, if necessary.

When an arrow has been shot in the woods and is found, it should be carefully checked for cracks and crystallization, either of which may cause the arrow to break the next time it is shot, in which case the broken arrow may go through the hand that is holding the bow. In no event should a cracked or crystallized arrow be shot; it is an extremely dangerous practice.

It is wise to carry no other arrows than good ones when hunting, as often when the archer is excited

PLATE XXII. Howard Hill with jaguar killed in Mexico with bow and arrow.

and in a hurry to get a shot at game he will pick the bad arrow, even if there is only one bad one in the quiver.

When an animal is shot with an arrow and gets out of shooting range, the archer should never follow immediately. Rather, he should wait at least three-quarters of an hour before taking up the trail. If one follows at once, the wounded animal will keep going as long as it is possible for him to stay on his feet. However, if given time and not followed closely, wounded game will often stop and lie down within a short distance from the spot where he was shot. He may die there, or else he may become so stiff that he can be finished off before he can get away.

When one has made a successful stalk to within bow range of game, it is wise to shoot from behind cover. The bow makes so little noise that the hunter often gets more than one shot without frightening the quarry if he is not visible. It is a good idea to wait until the animal's head is turned away from the hunter's position, so that the movements of the bow limbs will not be detected.

If hunting arrow whistles when it is traveling through the air, the feathers should be removed and the arrow re-fletched. Often such a noise, caused by a limber feather on an arrow, will make the game move quickly, thus avoiding the shot.

No good bow-and-arrow hunter ever goes hunting with his equipment in poor repair. It should be remembered at all times that no archer can shoot better than the equipment which he has to shoot with.

See the Glossary for archery terms that are often used, and with which the novice archer should become familiar.

**Target Archery.** The target archer can be compared to the hunting archer only as the "gun crank" can be compared to the hunter. He is interested not in the use of this ancient weapon in the field but in the accuracy with which he may deliver a specified number of arrows at a target at a given range.

Many Americans are inclined toward the belief that organized archery is limited to a few girls' colleges, but this indicates little knowledge of the actual facts. Archery clubs are scattered throughout the country, and their members are overwhelmingly male. Although their enthusiasm and interest is second to none, they have little interest in publicizing themselves or their sport.

This country has played an important part in world archery, and has contributed considerably to the sport. Organized archery received its first stimulus here in 1828, when five Philadelphians formed the Club of United Bowmen. Many have heard, perhaps without understanding the term, of the famous "York Round," an event which in rifle or pistol shooting would be termed a "match." To the uninitiated this is the old and traditional "round," yet the first definite target round of any English-speaking nation was the round regularly shot by the United Bowmen. The York Round was not initiated until nine years later.

Membership in the United Bowmen increased, as did the interest in archery, and as a result of the activity of this group even the target standards were changed. At that time the standard target was 40 inches in diameter, with the center gold 8 inches in diameter and the outer rings 4 inches wide. The Bowmen also carried out many experiments with various bow woods, which have since been recognized as important contributions.

The standard target, now used in both English and American competition, is 4 feet in diameter, with all of the rings and the radius of the bull's-eye the same width. The bull's-eye is gold, with the succeeding rings colored red, blue, black, and white. The scoring for the bull and succeeding rings is: 9, 7, 5, 3, and 1.

The United Bowmen Round, although the oldest, is but one of many, and there are a number of English and American rounds that are more universally fired. The York Round calls for a total of 144 arrows: 72 at 100 yards, 48 at 80 yards, and 24 at 60 yards. The American Round calls for 90 arrows, 30 each at 60, 50 and 40 yards. The United Bowmen Round calls for 84 arrows, all fired at 80 yards.

The National Archery Association was formed in 1879, at which time it was decided that the championship of the country would be competed for annually, with the double York Round as the basis of competition. This was continued until 1910, when the Association decided to award two championships, one for the York Round and another for the American Round. In 1914, however, the Association returned to the single championship, awarding it for the combined score attained in both rounds, York and American.

**Dealers in Archery Tackle.**

Archery Tools, 3700 Sumner St., Lincoln 2, Nebr.
Henry A. Bitzenberger, 800 East Fourth St., Los Angeles, Calif.
Easton Archery Shop, 1807 Fifth Ave., Los Angeles, Calif.
Fleetwood Archery Co., 4430 East 8th Ave., Denver 7, Colo.
Earl D. Grubbs, 2437 Alsace St., Los Angeles, Calif.
Stew Hamilton, 4250 Warner Rd., Cleveland 5, Ohio.
Ivanhoe Sporting and Mfg. Co., Box 249, Dept. F, Ludington, Mich.
Madison Archery Supply, Spring Harbor, Madison, Wis.
Monte Vista Archery Co., Box 5, South Tacoma, Wash.
Ben Pearson, Inc., Pine Bluff, Ark.
E. Bud Pearson, 3109 Burnet Ave., Cincinnati 29, Ohio.
Potter and McQuarrie, 3400 Fruitvale Ave., Oakland 2, Calif.
Rose City Archery Co., Powers, Ore.
Stanley Schaeffer, South Lake Shore Rd., Racine, Wis.
John W. Schwenk, 1611 Stanford Ave., St Paul 5, Minn.
L. E. Stemmler, Queens Village, Long Island, N. Y.
Stalker Archery Co., Clintonville, Wis.
Earl L. Ullrich, Roseburg, Ore.
S. E. Wells, Wayland, N. Y.
Whiteman's Craft Shop, Box 27, Oakland, Wash.

# BACK-PACKING TRIPS

From the standpoint of hunting trips there are three kinds of back packing to consider: (1) The packing of the articles that the hunter needs during a day's hunting; (2) the packing of outfit and food over more or less short distances, or over portages on a canoe trip; (3) back-packing trips where the hunter packs his entire outfit and all his food on his back for extended trips into game country. It is necessary to consider the three separately as they are quite different.

**Daily Packs.** The intelligent and modern hunter needs certain things with him on his day's hunt—things required for efficient hunting, comfort, and safety. While these do not bulk or weigh much, yet it is inconvenient and handicapping to endeavor to carry them in the pockets, on the belt, or suspended by straps from the shoulders, where they impede activity and catch in every branch. By far the best method of carrying these is in a light rucksack on the back. This is the method adopted by all experienced wilderness hunters. The articles that it is usually desirable to carry daily when hunting comprise most of the following (question marks indicate optional items):

PLATE I. The light rucksack carries everything the hunter needs for his day's sport and for comfort.

Lunch.
Camera, extra film, exposure meter.
10 to 20 rounds of ammunition.
Skinning knives.
Tape measure.
Waterproof match box, filled.
Drinking cup.
Map of the locality.
Toilet paper.
Notebook and pencil.
Light jacket or extra wool shirt.
Rain coat (?)
Meat bag (?)
Hand ax (?)
Machete (?)
Canteen with water (?)

Only those articles likely to be needed many times during the day, such as watch, compass, jackknife, handkerchief, tobacco, matches, should be carried in the pockets. Five extra cartridges may be carried in a small pouch on the belt, but it is a mistake to load the belt with more than this. When actually hunting, binoculars should be carried on the chest suspended by a short neck-strap.

D. T. Abercrombie, N. Y.

PLATE II. A Convenient Type of Rucksack.

Most of the articles carried in the rucksack are self explanatory. Hunting on foot is a very strenuous exercise. Even in cold weather one will probably be more or less wet with perspiration while in motion. Very heavy clothing is a mistake. But when the hunter stops for even a few minutes it is very desirable that he have something warm to slip on to prevent becoming chilled, hence the high desirability of carrying a light jacket or an extra wool shirt. Wind blows through a sweater too readily, and the sweater is bulky.

For carrying all this impedimenta the rucksack slips on and off easier than a coat, and one can shoot when wearing it. It has one large center compartment with considerable capacity, and two small pockets for camera and small articles. The large center compartment is very desirable. It permits carrying a movie camera (perhaps wrapped in the jacket), or enables the successful hunter to bring back to camp some meat or the liver of an animal he kills, or even the head and scalp of a deer, sheep, or goat. Usually it is best to adjust the shoulder-straps so that the rucksack carries rather low down on the back. The hunter's center of gravity is thus low, he is not top-heavy, and his footing and balance are steadier. The straps pull straight down instead of back on the shoulders, and some of the weight rests on the hips. One does not have to worry about the weight because it will seldom exceed 10 pounds, and after the pack is worn two or three days this small weight is never noticed. It is far preferable to

D. T. Abercrombie, N. Y.

PLATE III. With a pack harness many kinds of bundles can be converted into a shoulder pack.

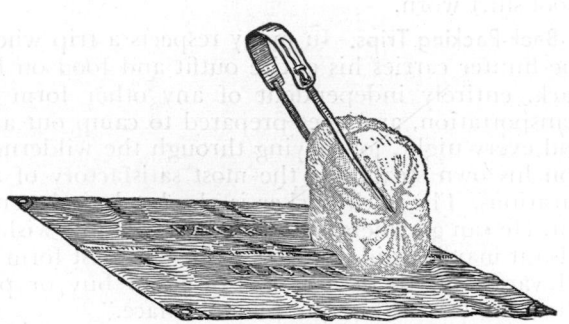

D. T. Abercrombie, N. Y.

PLATE IV. This is the tump line and pack cloth, also an excellent portage pack.

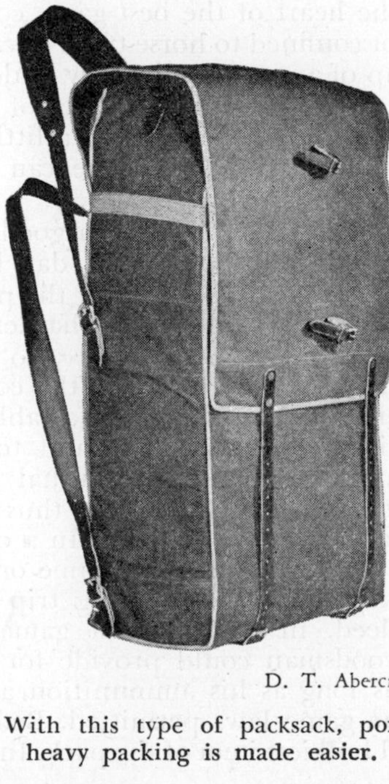

D. T. Abercrombie, N. Y.

PLATE V. With this type of packsack, portaging and heavy packing is made easier.

carrying articles draped all over the person and on the belt.

Carrying a light load every day in this manner also has another advantage. It gets one more or less used to back packing so that if he has to carry heavier loads at any time it comes much easier to him, and he does not "fight his pack."

When hunting with a pack train in the rougher mountain country of the West it sometimes happens than one comes on a stretch of fine game country, but so extremely rough that it is impossible to get horses into it. Then one can pack a little food, a kettle, and a frying pan in the rucksack, tie a light tarp and blanket on the outside, and pack on foot into this rough country, and hunt it successfully for a few days. The hunter should always carry a light rucksack in his outfit.

**Portaging and Heavy Packing.** In portaging, the distance over which the outfit, food, and other articles have to be carried is relatively short. On a portage it is often desirable to carry as heavy a pack as possible in order to shorten the number of trips across. There are many packs more or less suitable for such packing. Almost any strong back-pack with broad shoulder-straps will do. A pack harness consisting of shoulder-straps with other straps to go around duffle bags or bed roll, thus converting them into shoulder packs, is furnished by some city outfitters.

The most commonly used pack throughout all the northeastern portion of America, where most portaging is done in connection with canoeing, is known as the Northwestern, Duluth, Poiter, or Woods packsack, or usually as just "packsack." It consists of a waterproof canvas sack of varying size, usually about 16 inches wide, 22 inches long, and 6 to 8 inches deep, with leather shoulder-straps and tump line attached. It is most convenient for packing a hunter's personal articles and for food. The various articles articles of food, when placed in it, are usually separately packed in small waterproof cotton bags supplied by city outfitters. One advantage of this packsack is that when the tump line is used in addition to the shoulder-straps a heavier load can be carried as the tump line eases the burden on the shoulders. Also a sort of "shelf" is then formed on top of the sack proper on which other articles such as a duffle bag, a small bed roll, or a sack of flour can be carried balanced on top. (See also "Canoe Hunting.")

The tump line is the common device used for heavy packing among Indians and guides in northeastern Canada, and heavier and bulkier loads can be carried with it than in any other way when the packer is used to it, but it is usually intensely uncomfortable for the novice. It consists of a leather strap 2½ inches wide and about 18 inches long, to each end of which a 9-foot leather thong or rope is attached. The articles to be carried are usually wrapped in a pack cloth, and the two thongs are then tied around, leaving the headstrap on a loop. The headstrap goes over the forehead with the bundle carried rather low on the back. Boxes of almost any shape can be carried in this manner provided they are wrapped in a tarp or blanket so that they do not dig into the back. In the old days the Hudson's Bay Company used to make up their packs of furs, food, and pemmican in bundles

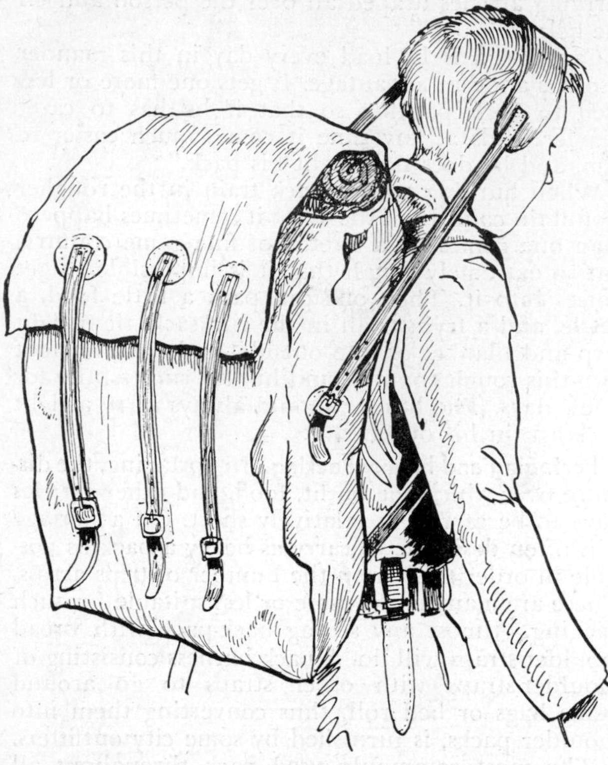

PLATE VI. Portaging a Heavy Load with a Packsack.

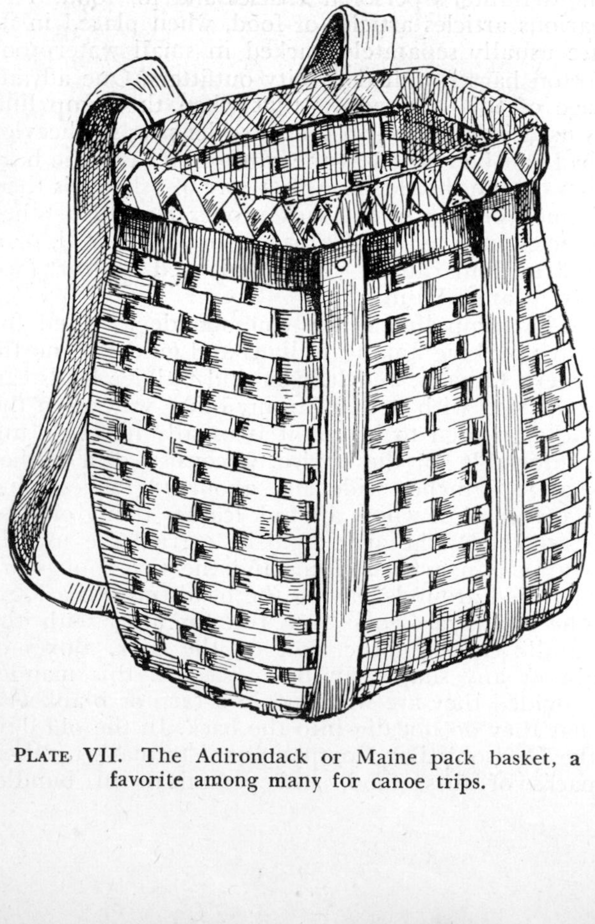

PLATE VII. The Adirondack or Maine pack basket, a favorite among many for canoe trips.

weighing 90 pounds, and it was nothing for a good packer to take two or three of these over a long portage without a rest.

Cooking utensils are most conveniently packed in a small fiber or wood box which can be slipped into a large packsack or carried by the tump line. The Alaskan packboard described under "Back-Packing Trips" below, will carry such hard and sharp-cornered articles as boxes, outboard motors, and cans of gasoline best of all. Two cans of gasoline can be suspended from either end of a stout 6-foot pole, and the pole is then carried on one shoulder as a Chinese carries his load.

A cardinal rule with all packsacks is that the shoulder-straps must be attached to the top of the center of the sack, and close together. If they were attached to the two upper corners, or even the width of the shoulders apart, they would be continually slipping down off the shoulders. The straps should be a full 2 inches wide where they pass over the shoulders, and if they are made of heavy, oil-softened leather no padding will be needed other than the wool shirt worn.

**Back-Packing Trips.** In many respects a trip where the hunter carries his entire outfit and food on his back, entirely independent of any other form of transportation, and goes prepared to camp out any and every night, journeying through the wilderness "on his own steam," is the most satisfactory of all vacations. The back packer is absolutely independent. He can go where he wishes and when he wishes. Also it may be said that this is the cheapest form of all vacations—there is not a thing to buy or pay after one leaves the "jumping-off place."

From the standpoints of hunting and nature study it is also in many ways the most successful. The back packer can enter game country in absolute silence, can make his camps without noise that would disturb the denizens of the forest, and can also take advantage of the wind so that he will not be scented. The wilderness is never met on such intimate terms as when back packing. One can go right into the heart of the best game country, with traveling not confined to horse trails or canoe routes. He can camp of an evening in view of deer runways or moose licks, the upland pastures of sheep, caribou, and goats, or on the shore of a little unknown lake deep in the wilds where he can see all the game undisturbed.

A young, fairly athletic man in good health can easily pack about 35 pounds all day long at the start of such a trip if the pack is of the proper kind. In three or four days, after he is hardened, he can pack 50 pounds and cover from 5 to 15 miles a day, depending on the nature of the country. The necessary outfit to keep him comfortable, dry, well rested at night, cook his food, and to hunt will weigh about 25 pounds for the usual fall climate in the United States, and so he can thus pack about 25 pounds of concentrated foods. In a country that will supply occasional meals of game or fish a man can thus extend his back-packing trip to about a month. Indeed, in an excellent game country a thorough woodsman could provide for himself indefinitely, as long as his ammunition and matches lasted—if the game laws permitted. Bedding is the heaviest and bulkiest item of the pack. In the tropics, where this can be largely dispensed with, and all kinds of small game and fish are plentiful, a back-packing trip may be considerably extended. However, the desirability of making the pack light enough to make one's vacation a real pleasure, and not a hard physical stunt, usually limits the duration of such trips to about two weeks. The physical effort of carrying such a pack of slightly under 40 pounds is not nearly so great as might be imagined. About the only disadvantage is that it is difficult to pack meat and trophies out of the woods.

The types of packs mentioned above under "Portaging" are not well adapted to all-day packing or long trips. They are not comfortable enough, and they all have a tendency to cause one to stoop over with his eyes to the ground so that one does not get much of a view of the scenery, enjoy the country, or see game while traveling. It is difficult to use the rifle with such packs on the back, and they overheat and gall the back if carried for long periods.

In Alaska, the Yukon, and the mountains of the Northwest more all-day back packing is done than anywhere else in the world, and it is done by white men with ingenuity. It is natural, therefore, that the Alaskan sourdough should have devised the best form of pack for all-day packing through a wilderness. The Alaskan packboard there mostly used consists of a light wood frame, about 17 by 22 inches, the frame itself being about 1½ inches thick. Over this a canvas cover is tightly stretched, and shoulder straps are added. The load is lashed to the outside of this canvas-covered frame, and shoulder-straps are added on the side toward the back. Only the canvas touches the back, and there is an air space between the canvas against the back and the load, so that the pack neither overheats nor digs into the back. It feels as though the packer were lying on his back on a canvas cot.

This packboard can seldom be bought, and most packers make their own, but there are several commercial variations of it such as the Trapper Nelson Pack and the Bean Packboard, and the Army has used several variations, all of which are good. The packboard itself weighs about 2½ pounds.

The outfit to be carried must be figured down to the last ounce. Each item should be the lightest and smallest in bulk as is possible for efficiency. Only the absolute essentials should be included, and any article that can be extemporized in the woods should be ruthlessly discarded. For example, a fork can always be cut from a tree, the hunting knife will also serve for eating, and the frying pan for a plate. Two light aluminum kettles are desirable, one for food and the other for a hot drink at the same meal. As food can be packed inside these, they really take up no space.

The most important items are shelter and bedding, as they comprise most of the weight and bulk. When there are no mosquitoes a simple tarp of the lightest waterproof cotton, about 7 feet square with triangular ends, can be pitched as a lean-to; this sheds rain, can be warmed by a fire in front, and weighs but 3 pounds. For mosquito time one city outfitter makes a light "Mountaineer" tent, which weighs only 3¾ pounds and is bugproof. (See "Tents.") Generally speaking, however, the lean-to tarp is best, because with the small tent all one can

PLATE VIII. The Alaskan packboard will carry outfit and food for a month.

do in the rain is to go inside and lie down, while under the lean-to cooking and other work can be done.

In warm weather a light wool blanket weighing about 3 pounds may be all that is needed, but if night temperatures are likely to go below 40° F. the best bedding is light down-filled robes; these are made as light as 3 pounds. With the lean-to and small ax with full-length handle an all-night fire can be kept up, so that one can dispense with bulkier and heavier bedding.

OUTFIT FOR BACK PACKING

| | | |
|---|---|---|
| Alaskan packboard | 2 lbs. | 8 oz. |
| Ax with 28″ handle and sheath | 2 " | 12 " |
| Tarp with triangular ends | 3 " | 0 " |
| Down-filled sleeping robe | 3 " | 0 " |
| Featherweight rain jacket | 0 " | 12 " |
| Underwear, socks | 1 " | 4 " |
| Toilet articles, light towel | 0 " | 12 " |
| Cathartic, antiseptic, and aspirin | 0 " | 2 " |
| Fishing tackle—hooks, line, sinkers | 0 " | 3 " |

| | | |
|---|---|---|
| Carborundum stone | 0 " | 2 " |
| Cleaning rod, can oil, flannel patches | 1 " | 0 " |
| Extra ammunition | 1 " | 0 " |
| Matches in can, toilet paper | 1 " | 0 " |
| Camera and films | 2 " | 0 " |
| 2 aluminum kettles, 1 Army mess pan | 2 " | 8 " |
| Enamel cup, teaspoon, tablespoon | 0 " | 3 " |
| TOTAL WEIGHT | 22 lbs. | 2 oz. |

This outfit, including the food in the list below, is rolled first in the bedding, and then in the tarp or tent, so as to form a bundle about 26 inches long, 16 inches wide, and 10 inches thick, and tied with several short ropes which are afterward used in pitching the lean-to. The bundle is then lashed on the outside of the packboard with the ax, and possibly also the camera, tied outside.

In his pockets the back packer carries watch, compass, handkerchief, hunting knife, pipe, tobacco, and a map. Five extra cartridges can go in a pouch on the belt. The featherweight raincoat serves in cold as well as rainy weather.

Food packed in light waterproof cotton bags, is distributed in the pack to make it shipshape before rolling in the bedding. Every man must make up his own food list according to his likes and what he can prepare properly with two kettles and a small frying pan. It should be largely concentrated food that is not constipating, and should be selected to help out on the game and fish which will be secured. Flour and canned goods are hardly practical. The list for a back-packing trip in a good game and fish country for approximately a month is as follows:

BACH-PACKING FOOD LIST

| | | |
|---|---|---|
| Cereals: oatmeal, cornmeal, hominy | 4 lbs. | 0 oz. |
| Sugar 4 lbs.; Milk powder 2 lbs.; Salt 1 lb. | 7 " | 0 " |
| Bacon 3 lbs.; White navy beans 3 lbs. | 6 " | 0 " |
| Crisco or lard in can 1 lb.; Pepper 4 oz. | 1 " | 4 " |
| Tea and Instant Coffee | 0 " | 12 " |
| Prunes 2 lbs.; Dates and Figs 2 lbs. | 4 " | 0 " |
| Sweet chocolate 1 lb.; Tobacco 1 lb. | 2 " | 0 " |
| TOTAL WEIGHT | 25 lbs. | |

This one-month supply of food for a good game country, together with the outfit, will make a pack of about 50 pounds. A husky, athletic young man, but soft from the city, may have trouble in packing this more than 5 miles a day (with frequent rests) at the start, but in four or five days he will be packing it all day without trouble over average woods trails. Bad and steep going will of course cut down the mileage. Of course each day the pack grows lighter as the food is consumed, unless one adds fresh meat to it. The beginner at back packing should not attempt the wilderness on his first trip, but should test his outfit, his methods, and his strength in the woods near home or civilization, at least for a week-end. This kind of hunting trip needs experience to pull off successfully. The saying, "The less a man carries on his back, the more he must carry in his head," is very true of back packing. But when one becomes adept at it he will find it a fascinating kind of vacation.

PLATE IX. Bivouac of a back-packer, with tarp pitched as a lean-to.

# BLINDS

A good duck or goose blind is something more than a mere hiding place, for whether it is elaborate or simple it has but one essential function; that that of *blinding* the duck to the presence of the hunter, his boat, or his dog. Many wildfowlers are inclined to sacrifice utility to comfort, and too often this is obtained at the cost of good shooting. In many circumstances a blind cannot be both *good* and *comfortable,* although in most instances the hunter who is willing to spend some time and effort prior to the opening of the waterfowl season may strike a satisfactory balance.

A good blind, as many experienced wildfowlers know, does not have to be hidden. It may emerge like the proverbial "sore thumb" and clash completely with its surroundings. At the same time, it *blinds* the waterfowl, for they do not associate it with the presence of danger. The *stilt* or *reef* blind is a perfect example of this, for it rises 12 or 14 feet from the surface of the water, yet produces bags that compare with those taken at blinds in the same areas which merge completely into their surroundings.

In many of the good shooting areas, a large percentage of the waterfowl killed during the course of the season are local or *native* birds, ducks that have bred, nested, and reared their young in that area. In such sections only a blind in the full sense of that term will be consistently successful, and the really interested shooter will keep that blind in condition not only during the season but throughout the entire year.

Before going into detail on the many types of blinds, their construction and maintenance, it might be wise to touch on their proper use. The value of many fine blinds has been destroyed by unthinking carelessness in approaches and departures. For example, many point blinds and pond blinds are surrounded by the very growths of which they are constructed, whether this be broomstraw, tules, meadow grass, cattails, brush, or wild rice. The hunter who uses the same route each time he approaches and leaves the blind soon has a clearly defined path. If this path is permanent all is well; otherwise, it may serve as a red danger signal to native ducks. Take a different route each time, and do as little damage to the vegetation as is possible. Many hunters, with a duck down in front of the blind, will push their way straight through, rather than make a detour behind and around the blind. The damage this practice causes soon will be apparent.

Another shooter will use every precaution to preserve the natural appearance of the blind, yet will leave his duckboat 20 or 30 feet distant, drawn partially into the reeds or grass, with most of the boat's outline visible. The careful wildfowler will have an irregular mat, formed of the natural cover, under which he can hide the boat, or he will carry a bundle of grass (gathered at a point remote from the blind) to scatter over and around the boat and hide its presence.

One of the common faults is that of taking a bright object (perhaps a thermos, lunch box, or white bag) into the blind and failing to cover it with a neutral material. Even the glint of an empty shell case, tossed carelessly outside, often sends waterfowl wide of the blind. Sun glinting on gun-barrels protruding from the blind can bring a similar result.

Another very common error is often made, even by experienced wildfowlers: that is, using the same blind six days a week, or seven—provided Sunday shooting is permitted. The maximum use should be every other day, and every third day is much to be preferred. The man who plans to shoot consistently during the season should prepare for this by having more than one blind, and keeping the blinds as far apart as possible.

Many duck-shooting clubs, especially those where pond shooting for puddle ducks is of primary interest, do not permit the same pond to be used more than twice a week, unless the pond is large enough to make more than one blind practical. In addition, many such clubs have rigid rules concerning the gauge of the gun which may be used and the size of the duck flights which may be shot into. Some permit shooting on these ponds only with shotguns of 20 gauge or under, and prohibit shooting into flights of more than six birds. In the event a large flight comes in, and settles among or near the decoys, the member must rise up and cause the birds to leave without firing at them. This is a sound practice, for it does not frighten the birds to an extent which causes them to shun that pond.

For the purposes of organization, blinds will be divided into two classes, *fixed* and *floating,* and the former will be taken up first.

**Fixed Blinds.** The fixed blind may be on a wooded or grassy point, a reef, a rocky promontory, a sandbar, beach, mudflat, island, or river bank. In most instances its location is based upon several factors. Wind, being an important influence on waterfowl, is equally important on blind location. In some areas a northeast wind produces the best shooting, in others it may be a southwest wind. In almost every instance, however, the best shooting is obtained when the wind is from a certain direction,

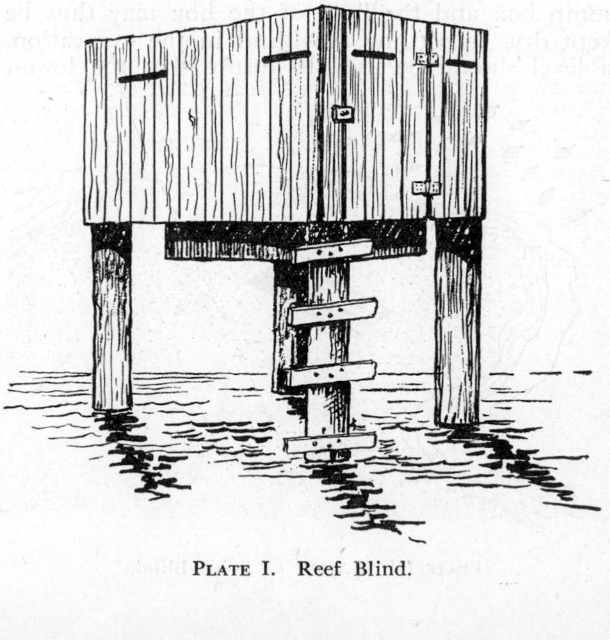

PLATE I. Reef Blind.

and the location of the blind should be based on this factor. There are areas where the terrain makes it impossible to be guided by prevailing winds in locating the blind; under such conditions it generally pays to consider some form of floating blind, or plan on the construction of more than one fixed blind.

PLATE II. Natural Blind with Mud Decoys.

A good blind, and one that is comfortable as well as productive of good shooting, cannot be thrown together in a few minutes by using any materials which happen to be at hand. One of the best types of point blind, and a comfortable one even in zero weather, is the sunken box. This blind should be constructed in the spring for the fall shooting, in order to permit the vegetation to grow up again and to avoid activity that might frighten native waterfowl.

The sunken box will require a full day's work by one man merely to excavate, and another full day to build. In many instances the blind is constructed elsewhere and transported to the site by the shooter and some helpers. It is heavy, however, and at least six men will be required to get it in place.

Upon completion and placing, the earth should be banked up around the rim for 2 or 3 inches, and should stop 3 inches below the lid. In tidewater areas the top of the box should be at least 6 inches higher than the mean high-water mark, as otherwise the box will be filled with water at each high tide. There is almost certain to be a small amount of seepage, so it is advisable to keep a boat pump in the blind. The base of this pump will fit into the sump box and the floor of the box may thus be kept dry. In settling the blind in the excavation, a level should be used to insure that the lowest

PLATE III. Layout of Point Blind.

point, if any, is at the end where the sump box is located.

Upon completion, vegetation similar to that around the blind should be brought *from a distant point* and transplanted around it. If this is done in the spring, the blind will have merged with its surroundings by fall. The cover, or lid, should be constructed in two sections, to permit ease of removal, and should be well hidden in the vicinity of the blind or else removed to a distant point.

On many of the large coastal bays, blinds similar to the sunken box are found on points, on the fringe of small coves, and on small islands. Many of the islands selected as sites for these blinds have very short, sparse vegetation, and are almost awash at high tide. Almost any other type of blind would stand out sharply in profile, and would frighten more birds than the largest rig of decoys could attract. Under such circumstances the shooter usually keeps a supply of grass and weed in the blind and has the cover hinged at the back. When the cover is laid back it is hidden under scattered tufts of grass and weed, which also serves as a background for the shooter's head.

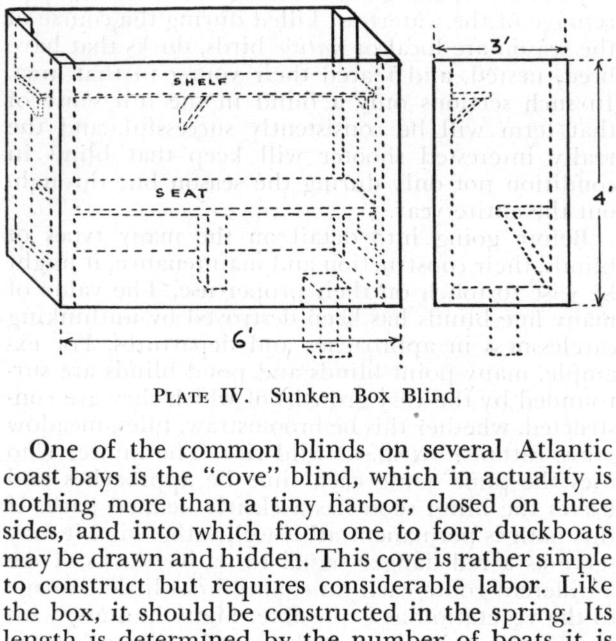


PLATE IV. Sunken Box Blind.

One of the common blinds on several Atlantic coast bays is the "cove" blind, which in actuality is nothing more than a tiny harbor, closed on three sides, and into which from one to four duckboats may be drawn and hidden. This cove is rather simple to construct but requires considerable labor. Like the box, it should be constructed in the spring. Its length is determined by the number of boats it is expected to hide. On Barnegat Bay, where this is an old favorite, the length is normally 12½ feet, which accommodates the Barnegat sneakbox, one of the most practical shallow-water duckboats ever built. The diagram in Plate V explains the construction. The first requirement is about 600 green stakes, cut from the limbs of oak, aspen, alder, poplar, or any tree that will provide straight stakes form ½ to ¾ inch in diameter and from 2 to 2½ feet long. This cove blind is extremely practical in areas where the good points or small islands have insufficient grass or other growth to permit a blind to be constructed above the ground and where the expense and effort of constructing a sunken box blind are to be avoided.

The first step is to outline the cove with the stakes, placing them only about 2 inches apart, and driving them to a depth of at least 18 inches, allow-

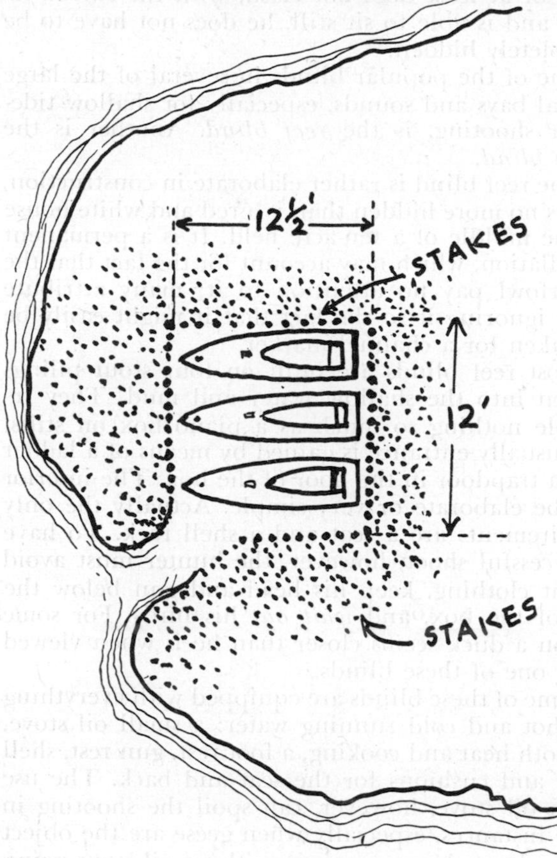


PLATE V. Cove Blind.

ing about 6 inches to protrude. When this has been done, begin driving stakes around the perimeter.

In front of the cove the stakes should be more numerous and closer together. Then comes the spadework, which should be started about two hours before dead low water. The cove must be dug out inside the staked outline, but not too much should be removed close to the outline stakes. The mud and dirt removed should be thrown around the cove until the protruding stakes are covered. This fill should then be tamped around the stakes. The purpose of the stakes, of course, is merely to hold the fill and prevent it from being washed by rain and high tides. A few boatloads of soil containing some grass roots from an adjoining area should be brought to cover the last inch of the fill with this soil, roots and all. If this is done, the chances are the cove will present a natural appearance within two months, and the roots will spread out and serve to hold the soil. The depth of the cove in the center is determined by the amount of water required to float the duckboat at dead low tide. There should be just enough to insure flotation. At high water the top of the duckboat will be almost level with the top of the filled area. The next requirement is a near-by cache of grass and weed that will merge with the color of the island. A stained canvas cover is stretched over the front and rear of the row of duckboats and the grass and weed is scattered over this.

Upon the arrival at the cove, the preparations for shooting require about five minutes.

Another shore blind which is almost universal in popularity, and not at all difficult to construct, is the simple grass, tule, or brush blind, the material depending upon the vegetation in the area in which it is located. Because of the lightness of the construction, this blind can be readily moved from place to place at the cost of about one hour of labor.

The first step is a framework to hold the material to be used. For grasses, tules, or cattails, the requirement is merely about 125 feet of shingle lath, a hammer, and a pocket full of 6-penny nails.

The grasses, tules, or brush (any vegetation growing at the site of the blind) are wedged into the frames to form a screen. The screen should be neither too thick nor level along the top, but should be uneven, with an occasional clump protruding a few inches above the others. A ragged appearance gives the blind a more natural quality. One thing is important. While the material should be gathered some distance from the blind, it *must* be the same color and texture as the vegetation around the blind. If brush is used, such as evergreens, they should be renewed when they begin to lose their natural color. The same is true of the tules or grasses.

Those who build such blinds of brush are prone to make one common error. Brush should be employed *only* when the blind is to be located in *similar* brush. In many instances such locations are near tall trees. This is especially true where evergreens are used. Do not construct the blind in front of a clump or line of trees, for if you do you are certain to spoil your shooting.

In some areas where puddle ducks are plentiful and feed in sloughs or small ponds completely encircled by forest, they are not averse to flying close to trees. Diving ducks, however, prefer more open water. In any event, a blind close to trees will spoil your chances except when you have the wind directly at your back, for the trees immediately behind you will prevent the birds from coming in to your decoys. You may get some long shots, but you can hope for little more. Ducks like to come in for a landing against the wind, and one glance will tell them they cannot do this if your decoys are too close to the trees. They may alight outside and swim

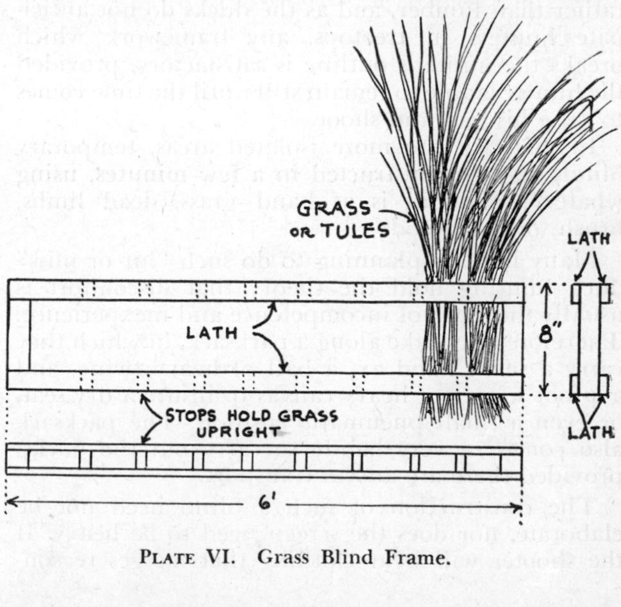


PLATE VI. Grass Blind Frame.

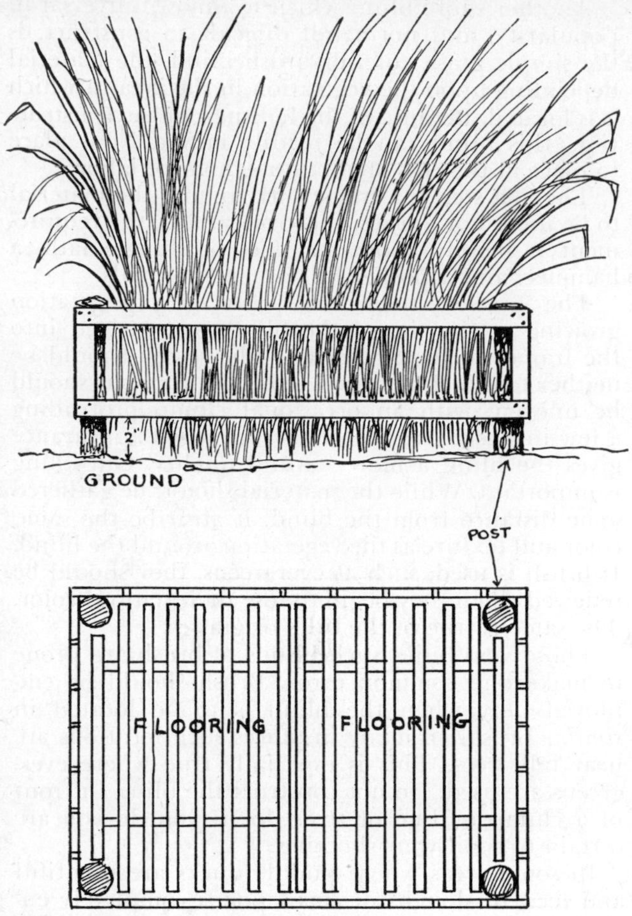


PLATE VII. Grass Blind.

in, but this procedure is not only less interesting but less frequent.

In some areas, especially where the ducks feed in the sloughs and flooded cypress or pin-oak sections, tree blinds are popular. These are usually far from elaborate, and normally are merely a small platform with enough of a framework around it to prevent the shooter from falling out. An effort is made to construct these blinds primarily of natural limbs rather than lumber, and as the ducks do not anticipate hunters in treetops, any framework which breaks the hunter's outline is satisfactory, provided the hunter is able to remain still until the time comes to raise his gun and shoot.

In many of the more isolated areas, temporary blinds may be constructed in a few minutes, using whatever material is at hand—grass, dead limbs, brush, or driftwood.

Many hunters planning to do such "hit or miss" duck hunting hold the theory that discomfort is usually the mark of incompetence and inexperience. Therefore, they take along a packsack, in which they carry a small hand ax, a ball of heavy twine, and a 4-foot square of heavy canvas to insure a dry seat, or even a small pneumatic cushion. The packsack also comes in very handy to carry out the ducks, provided there are any to transport.

The construction of such a blind need not be elaborate, nor does the screen need to be heavy. If the shooter will wear clothing that merges reasonably, or at least does not clash, with the surroundings, and is able to sit still, he does not have to be completely hidden.

One of the popular blinds in several of the large coastal bays and sounds, especially for shallow tidewater shooting, is the *reef blind*. Another is the *stake blind*.

The reef blind is rather elaborate in construction, and is no more hidden than is a red and white house in the middle of a ten-acre field. It is a permanent installation, which may account for the fact that the waterfowl pay no attention to it; many attribute their ignoring it to the fact that it might easily be mistaken for a channel marker.

Most reef blinds are built on four stout pilings driven into the shallow water and mud. They resemble nothing so much as a piano box on stilts, and usually entrance is gained by means of a ladder and a trapdoor in the floor of the box. The interior can be elaborate or very simple. Actually the only requirements are a seat and a shell rack. To have a successful shoot, however, the hunter must avoid bright clothing, keep his head and gun below the top of the box, and *wait out* his birds. For some reason a duck seems closer than he is when viewed from one of these blinds.

Some of these blinds are equipped with everything but hot and cold running water: a small oil stove, for both heat and cooking, a foot rest, gun rest, shell rack, and cushions for the seat and back. The use of an oil stove, however, can spoil the shooting in some instances, especially when geese are the object of the shoot. Many gunners, with an oil stove going full blast, have found to their surprise that geese gliding in for a landing among the decoys suddenly will increase their wing-beats while still out of range and flap off at top speed. When the oil stove is extinguished, the geese come in without hesitation. The answer is oil fumes. The geese, though not knowing what they were smelling, decided that the smell was strange, unpleasant, and to be avoided.

The stake blind, where it is not prohibited by law, is very popular. This blind also is constructed on piling—usually four piles, with a framework around them, a floor high enough off the water to permit a

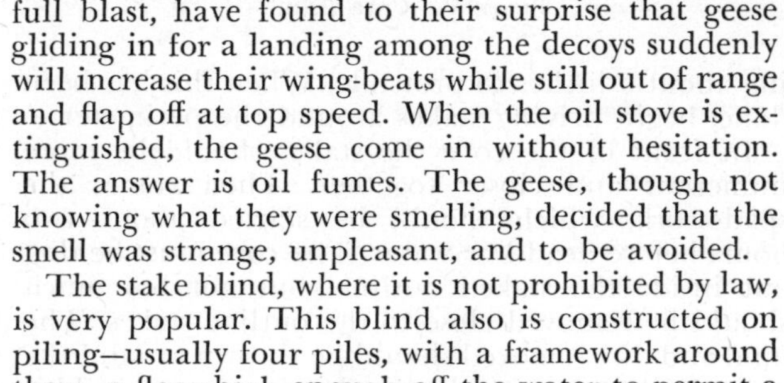

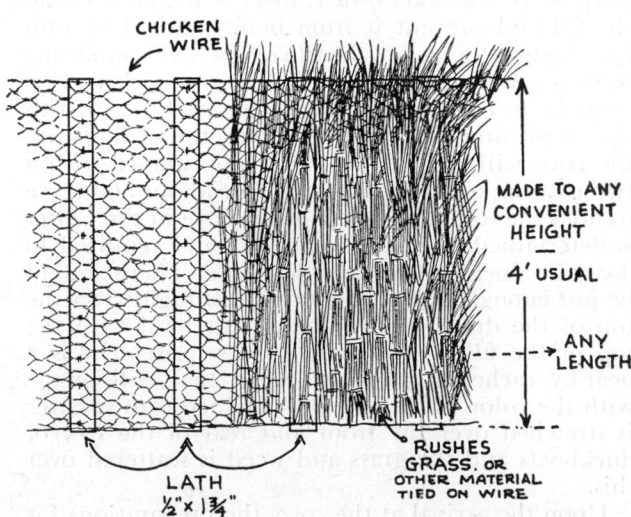

PLATE VIII. Portable Grass Blind.

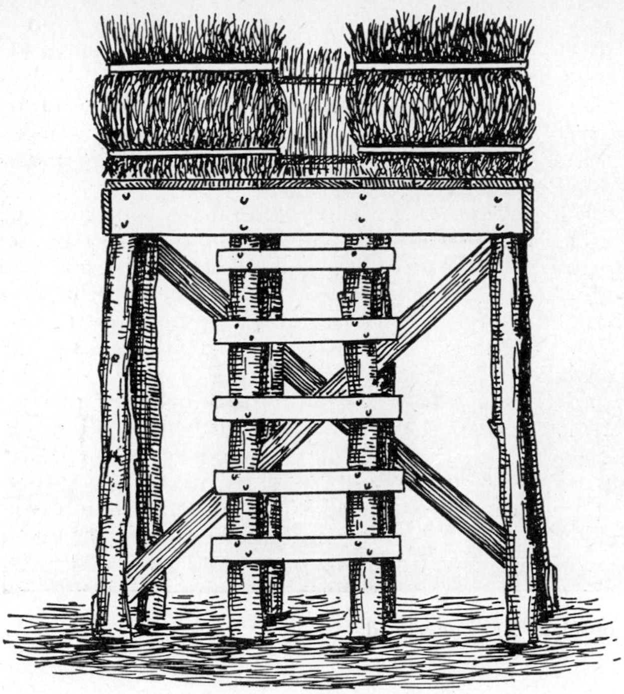

PLATE IX. Another Form of Reef Blind.

As with other blinds employing vegetation, this screening vegetation should be renewed regularly. In many areas, however, stake blinds are screened by evergreens that are renewed only once a year, and despite the fact that the green fades and finally turns a rusty red, the waterfowl do not seem to shun them. Why this should be true in some areas and not in others is a question that can be answered only by the ducks and geese.

*Rock blinds,* popular among coastal shooters, especially in areas where the majority of the waterfowl are diving ducks, normally are cold, wet, and generally uncomfortable, although they are simple to construct and never wear out. As a rule, the shooter merely selects a rocky ledge, reef, or island where

PLATE X. Pit Blind.

boat to be shoved underneath, and a screen of grass or brush around the sides. In some instances the framework is covered with canvas to keep out the wind and the grass or brush is fixed over this windbreak. There is a gate or door at one end which permits the entry of the boat and the hunter. Other stake blinds are simpler in construction, having sides but no floor, and the boat is merely pulled through the gate and the gate closed.

These blinds are not too satisfactory where there are extremes in tide, for this calls for stouter, deeper piling, a stouter framework, and much higher sides. They are seldom used in sections where there is more than a 2-foot rise and fall of tide, and are found in their greatest numbers where there is no tide at all.

he has reason to believe the ducks will pass. With the decoys out, he selects a rock that will be higher than his head when he is seated, piles a few rocks around it and a few in front, and sits back. The shooter who does much of this hunting usually has a coarse, loose smock, dyed to blend as closely as possible with the color of the rocks. If he uses a retriever it is a good plan to have a square of similar cloth to throw over the dog.

Most wildfowlers will testify that this form of

PLATE XI. One Form of Floating Blind—gate open.

PLATE XII. Floating Blind of Plate XI—gate closed.

shooting, especially in northern climates, takes first place in discomfort. Diving ducks normally will raft up on the open water, during the day, unless a cold wind blows so hard that they tire of constant swimming and seek out a lee. The rock blind then proves to be a shooting hot spot but a sitting cold spot.

One blind, if it could be so termed, which is rather universal in use, is the so-called *pit blind.* This blind may be found in almost every type of terrain where waterfowl are hunted, but seems favored in sections where the waterfowl feed in open fields.

The construction is quite simple, and the location depends upon the feeding habits of the birds. The materials required are few, primarily a stout spade and an empty barrel. In some areas a large, watertight olive cask or pork barrel is used, and in sections where water does not constitute a hazard, any barrel large enough to hold a hunter and provide elbow room is satisfactory. In wet areas a lid is provided to prevent the barrel from filling with rainwater. When the lid is not used, the normal procedure is to bore a half-dozen holes in the bottom of the barrel to permit the water to run out, and some large rocks are placed under the bottom to insure drainage.

**Floating Blinds.** Although there are several shapes and types of floating blinds, normally they are based upon a common structural principle. The safest and most comfortable one but not the cheapest to construct, is shown in the outline below. This requires the following material:

Six 5-gallon drums
Two 8 x 8 beams 14 feet long
Four 4 x 4 timbers, 5 feet long
About 100 feet of 2 x 4 timbers

The simplest form of floating blind, but one that is quite widely used, is the *brush float.* To construct this the hunter merely requires two lengths of 15-foot 4 x 4's, and about 60 feet of 2 x 4. The blind merely serves to hide the boat and the hunter, and the material of which it is made depends upon the type of local growth. If it is used off a shore that is grown up in grass, wild rice, cattails, or similar vegetation, this material is used. Otherwise, brush or evergreens are employed.

One of the most popular forms of floating blind, the battery, is forbidden today by Federal law, but despite the fact that this blind is a relic of a by-gone day and probably never will be permitted in the future, this section would be incomplete without some mention of it. (See Plate XVI, page 920, for illustration of this type.)

The battery, which undoubtedly resulted in the bagging of more canvasbacks, redheads and broadbill than any other medium, was of three general types: the sitting, lay-down, and double. In each instance, the general plan was the same. It was formed of a watertight box, weighted until it was almost

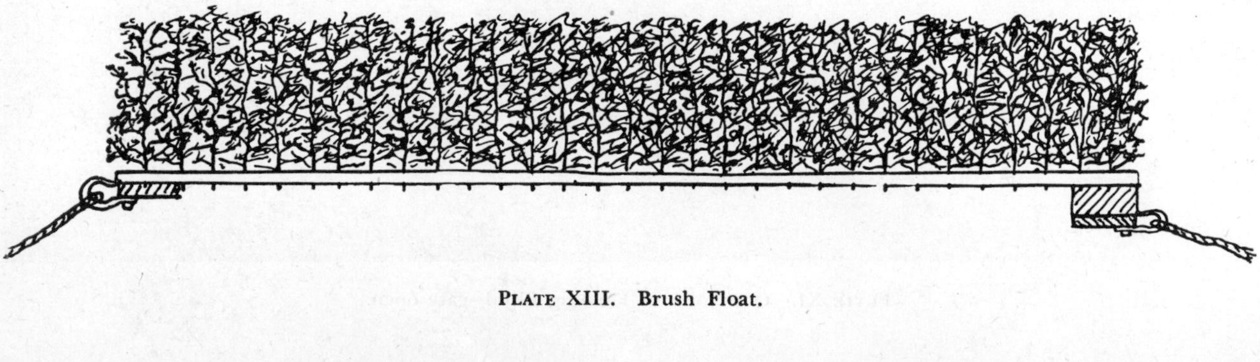

PLATE XIII. Brush Float.

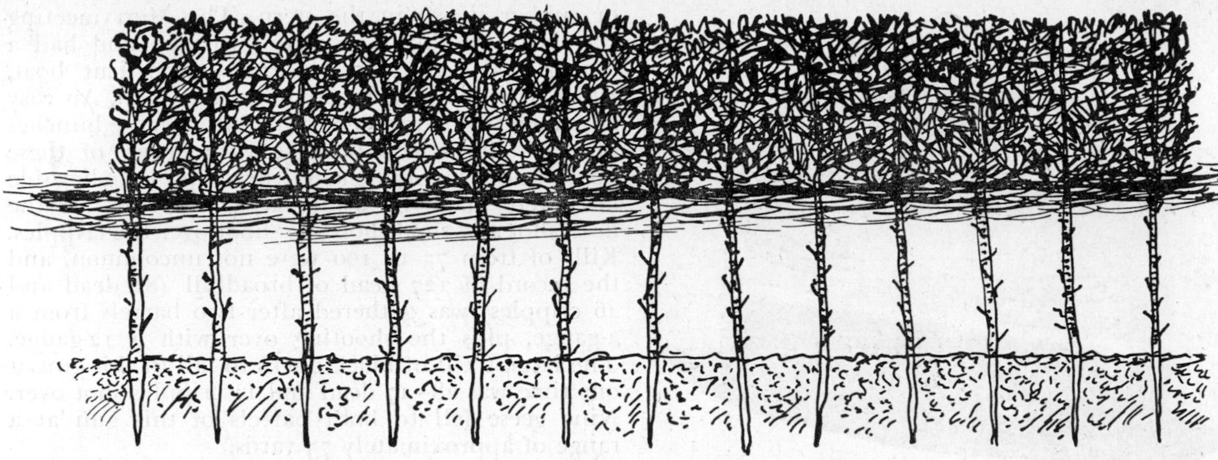

PLATE XIV. Stake Blind.

completely submerged, with flat wings on all four sides. These wings were hinged, as shown in Plate XVI (p. 920), which permitted them to undulate with the water movement and thus eliminate much of the wash which would otherwise soon drown out the gunner in the box. In many instances, a sheet-lead coaming around the rim of the box could be adjusted to compensate for the roughness of the water. In some areas, cast-iron decoys were placed on the wings to keep them barely awash. The battery, once in position and properly anchored and weighted, surrounded by a tremendous raft of decoys, constituted not only the most elaborate but the most deadly of waterfowl blinds.

It had one serious drawback, but this was partially compensated for by the fact that it was used primarily on the bays and not on the broad waters—it was no blind for rough water. When the waves exceeded a few inches in height it was necessary to rig a baffle, formed of lath and canvas, at the head of the battery in order to smooth out the water. Also, it required the presence of a "tender," a man in a boat who stood by at a safe distance ready to rescue the shooter in the event the battery took on too much water.

Many a battery shooter got a cold bath and a narrow escape from drowning, but few ardent wildfowlers would pass up an opportunity for a day of battery shooting merely because of the danger involved.

Without an extremely large rig of decoys, the battery lost much of its value, and in some areas it was not unusual to see a battery surrounded by a flotilla of from 100 to 400 decoys. The average rig, however, was about 200 decoys. The double battery, or "sink box" as it was called in some areas, was never as popular with the shooter as the single, although it was more satisfactory if one of the shooters happened to be left-handed. The sitdown battery was more popular than the lay-down type, as it was more comfortable for the shooter. In the lay-down battery the shooter employed his back and stomach muscles to bring him erect for the shots, and after about 20 such movements the novice shooter became convinced that he had developed a severe hernia.

# BOATS

The best type of duckboat to use under varying conditions has always been a problem, but one that each gunner has to solve for himself. There are innumerable designs and models, some of which are very practical and others extremely impractical.

Most gunning boats were designed to fill a special need, some for marsh shooting, some for point or reef shooting, and some for open-water shooting. The over-all purpose of the majority of these boats was to conceal the hunter and yet be as unnoticeable as possible to the ducks.

Probably the most popular style of duckboat is the light-weight, shoal-draft boat, well decked over, having a cockpit large enough to accommodate one gunner. Among this type of boats are the flat-bottomed gunning skiffs, the Long Island scooter, the Barnegat Bay sneak box, the Merrymeeting Bay grass boat, and the grass boat used on many of the Midwestern and Western waters. Each of these boats is designed for the work to be done, and having proved their worth over a period of years, they are still popular today. All are capable of carrying heavy loads on a light draft, and are very seaworthy for their size.

The flat-bottom skiff is used for marsh shooting, but also for point, reef, or line shooting. The Long Island scooter would do everything that a flat-bottomed skiff would do and in addition would show you a mile a minute under sail on the ice in a good breeze. These boats are fitted with a pair of runners on their bottom, parallel with the keel, and have been made to sail over the ice into open water, across the opening, and out on the ice again. They are very fast on runners, and the scooter races of years ago were both interesting and exciting. The equipment for this type of boat consists of a sprit-sail, a pair of oars, a small grapnel with long line for throwing out on thin ice, and a special "scooter

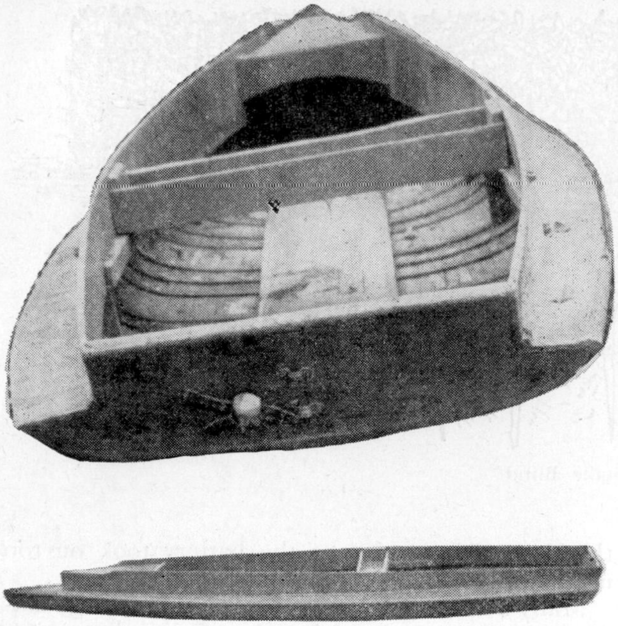

PLATE I. Two Views of the Merrymeeting Bay Scull Boat.

hook" made similar to a boat hook but with a wide palm, like a pointed hoe, for use in pulling the boat up on the ice, where it can be poled easily by using the pike end on the "scooter hook." All of this equipment can be stowed under the deck. This boat is very effective when used alongside of icy shores or rocks.

Scull boats were something different and designed to do a special job. Of these there were two rather different models, one the Merrymeeting Bay boat from down in Maine and the other the Connecticut boat used largely by the market hunters. The Maine boat was an oval-bottom type while the Connecticut boat was a V-bottom model. Both could be camouflaged with either grass or ice and both were operated by a curved oar passing out through a leather or rubber sleeve in the stern. The Merrymeeting Bay boat was built to carry two men and had a longer open cockpit than the Connecticut boat, which was designed to carry but one man. An easy approach to great rafts of broadbill or large bunches of black ducks was possible with either of these boats, under favorable conditions, and unbelievable kills were made by using large-bore guns for the flock shot and small bores to shoot over the cripples. Kills of from 75 to 100 were not uncommon, and the record of 127 head of broadbill (81 dead and 46 cripples) was gathered after two barrels from a 4-gauge, plus the shooting over with a 12-gauge. The largest kill of black ducks to fall to this gun at one time was 28—17 dead and 11 cripples shot over. Nine geese fell to both barrels of this gun at a range of approximately 75 yards.

Scull boats are not outlawed, but the closed winter months render the Connecticut boat useless, so far as ice sculling is concerned, although a few birds are taken by sculling with the boat covered with sedge.

The Connecticut boat is much more seaworthy than the Maine boat and can be used effectively in the outlying rocks and reefs, when painted a dark brown color and camouflaged with rockweed.

The sink-box, so-called, was designed for use in open water where diving ducks were feeding a considerable distance out of range from the shore. The first of these boats were built with water compartments in the ends or in the sides which could be filled by pulling a plug or opening a small valve, thus sinking the hull down nearly level with the water. They were designed to circumvent the law which eliminated the use of batteries by providing that it was unlawful to shoot ducks from any boat propelled otherwise than by oars.

The main purpose of sinking a boat down to a really low level was to make it less noticeable from a short distance. The use of water compartments did not last long, as more than one man has found himself in a tough situation trying to bail or

PLATE II. Merrymeeting Bay Scull Boat "Grassed Up."

pump out the compartments in the face of an approaching violent wind squall. As a substitute for water ballast some of the gunners used pigs of iron or lead, placed in the compartments, each having a short rope and cork float attached. In case of an emergency these weights could be dropped overboard with the float marking the location so that they could be picked up later. Some gunners had lead or iron decoys cast that weighed about 25 pounds each. Several of these were placed on the deck of the sink-box to sink her down to the proper level for shooting. These decoys were nicely painted and each had a small line tied to its neck with a float at the end so that they too could be slid overboard in case of rough weather. The fact that these boats were equipped with oars and oarlocks for rowing made them legal even though in many cases they were attended by a pickup boat, so that the gunner did not have to leave his position to retrieve his kill. Sink-boxes were used largely in the fall for early shooting of coots and broadbill and were put away for the winter when snow and ice came and the white scull boat, scooter, or Barnegat boat could be used for open-bay shooting.

The old-time sink-boxes are about outmoded now because of the risk involved in their use and the number of serious situations into which inexperienced and venturesome gunners got themselves. In their stead today a much more seaworthy boat is used, one that is a sort of all-purpose boat suitable for marsh, point, or reef gunning, large enough to carry a good setting of decoys, the gunner, and often his dog, and bring them all home safely through rather rough water.

Courtesy Olin Brewster, Bayshore, L. I.

PLATE III. Great South Bay scooter rigged as an iceboat. This is the regulation duckboat. During the late winter shooting many shooters carried a short mast and a triangular sail stowed away in the boat. With this "jury" rig they often sailed home on the ice.

Courtesy C. "Shang" Wheeler.

PLATE IV. Connecticut Scull Boat—showing method employed in sculling up on a raft of ducks. The progress of this boat, with a good sculler, is soundless.

Photo from Curtis Marshall, Fairfield, Conn.

PLATE V. Connecticut Scull Boat "Iced Up." These boats, so iced, were used to drift down upon rafts of birds. Often they were iced up in a similar fashion for shooting on the Sound over decoys.

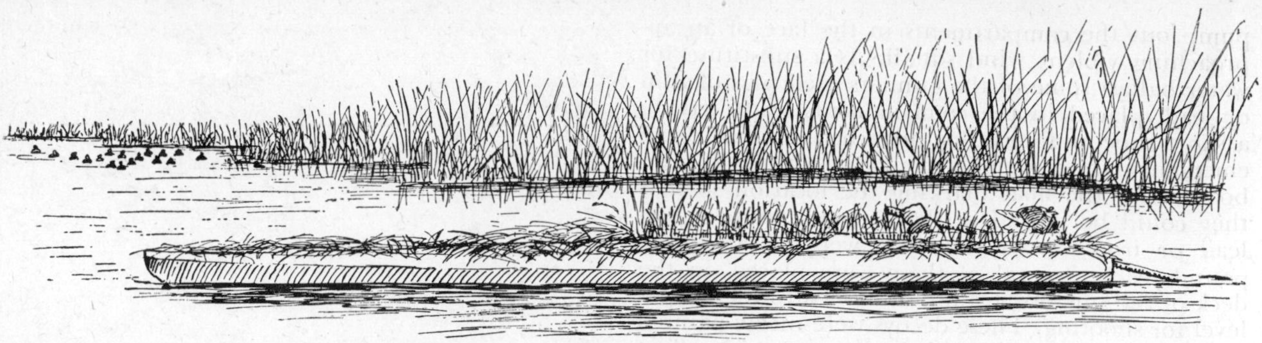

**Plate VI. Sketch of Connecticut Scull Boat Grassed Up.**

**Plate VII. Sink Box. Side view showing lead coaming around cockpit. As the deck is flush with the water, this coaming is all that keeps the "slop" out of the cockpit.**

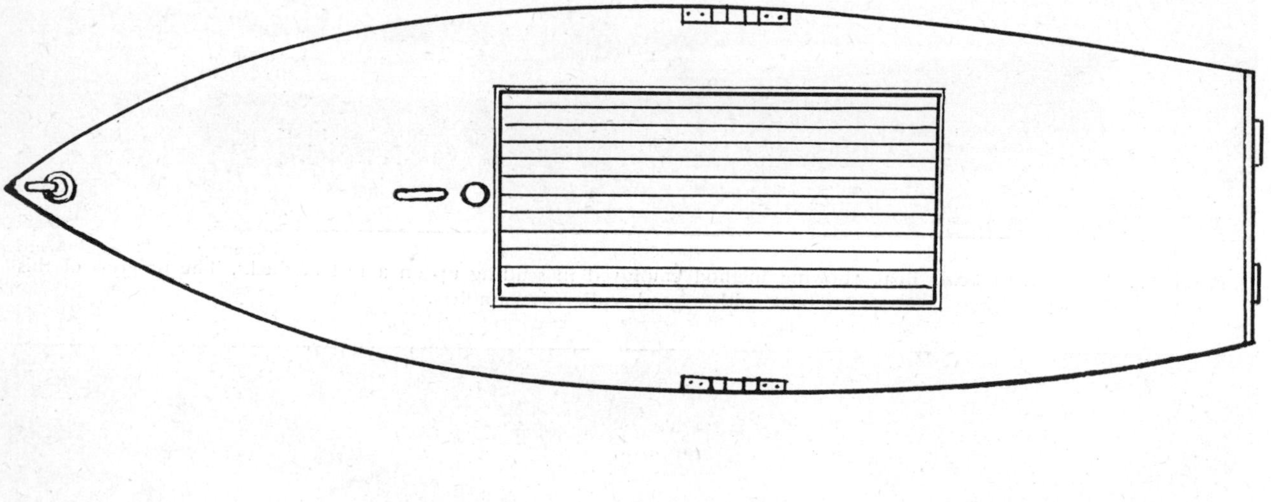

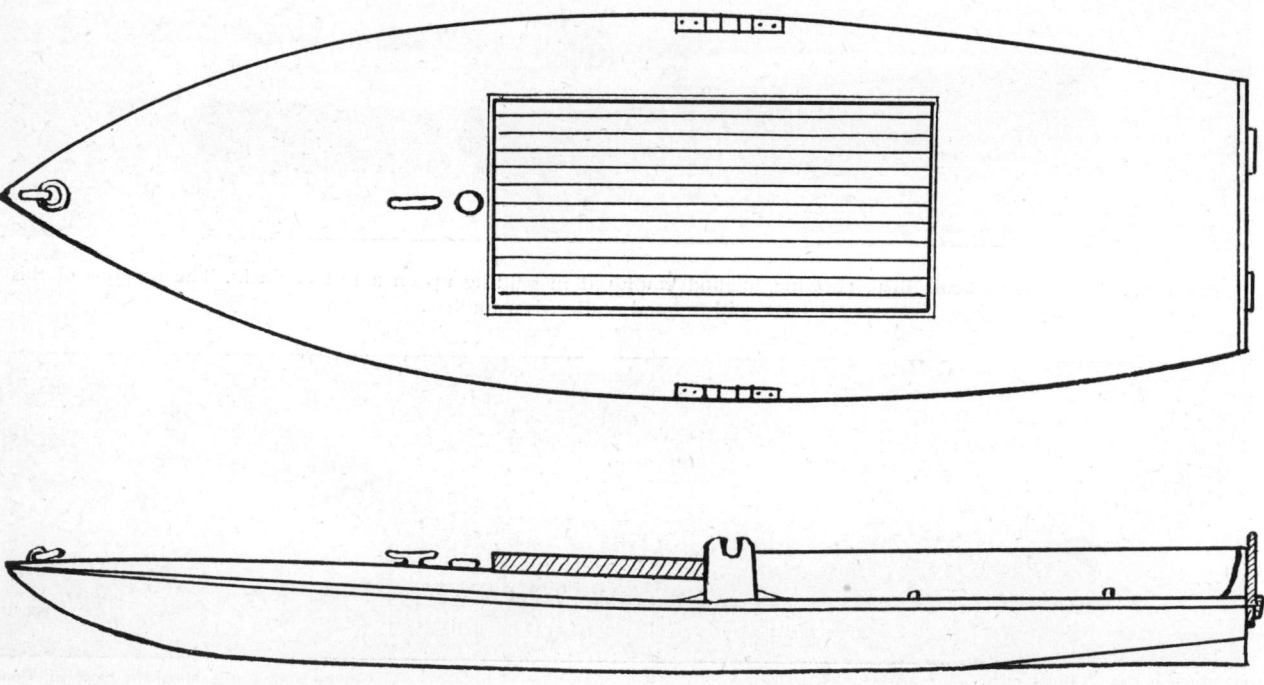

**Plate VIII. Barnegat Sneak Boat or Sneak Box. Some are equipped with a slot well just forward of amidships, through which a slat is thrust to hold the boat in position in shallow water.**

The battery (now forbidden by law) was a floating device made to conceal from one to four gunners and built in various sizes to accommodate them. These were not boats, in the sense that they could not be propelled either by oars, sail, or power, but were floats resting flat on the water with a shooting box in the center, deep enough so that the gunner, when stretched out on his back in the box was down level with the deck of the float. A single battery consisted of a shooting box 7 feet long by 2 feet wide by one foot deep, surrounded by a deck 12 feet long by 6 feet wide, with a canvas head fender 12 feet long by 12 feet wide, made of canvas tacked to 12-foot slats, 1 by 4 inches, spaced about 2 feet apart so that when spread out on the surface ahead of the battery it broke up the rough water very effectively before it slopped into the shooting box. There was also a canvas wing hinged to each

Photo from Kendrick Kemball.

PLATE IX. A popular duckboat in the West and Midwest, used principally on the large lakes.

Photo from Thomas Marshall.

**Plate X.** Rail Boat. Note pushing platform and shooter's stool. Rail cover in the background.

Photo from Kendrick Kemball.

**Plate XI.** Two of the popular duckboats used in the Midwest. The boat with the outboard is normally used when more than one man is shooting. The smaller boat is for a single shooter. Both can be "grassed up."

Photo from Thomas Marshall.

PLATE XII. Connecticut Rail Boat. Note narrow stern, pushing platform, and scull hole.

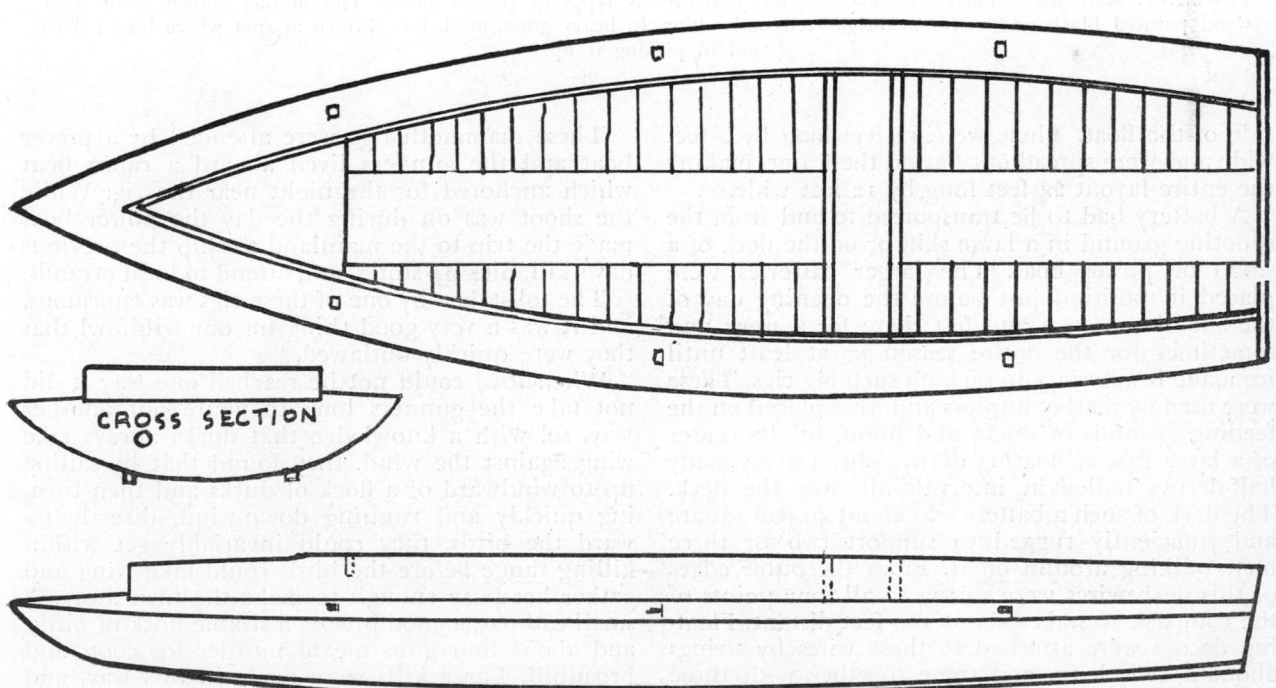

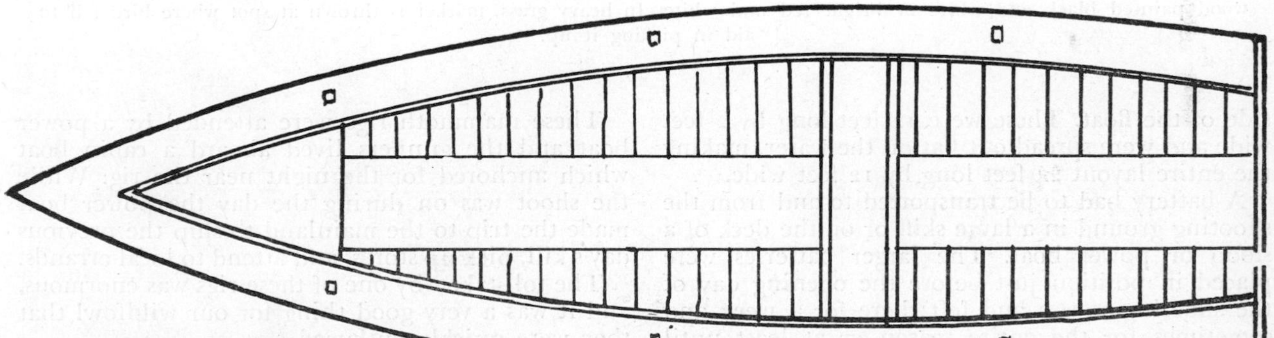


PLATE XIII. Merrymeeting Boat. This boat, grassed up, often is used in sculling up on a raft of ducks. Note scull hole in stern.

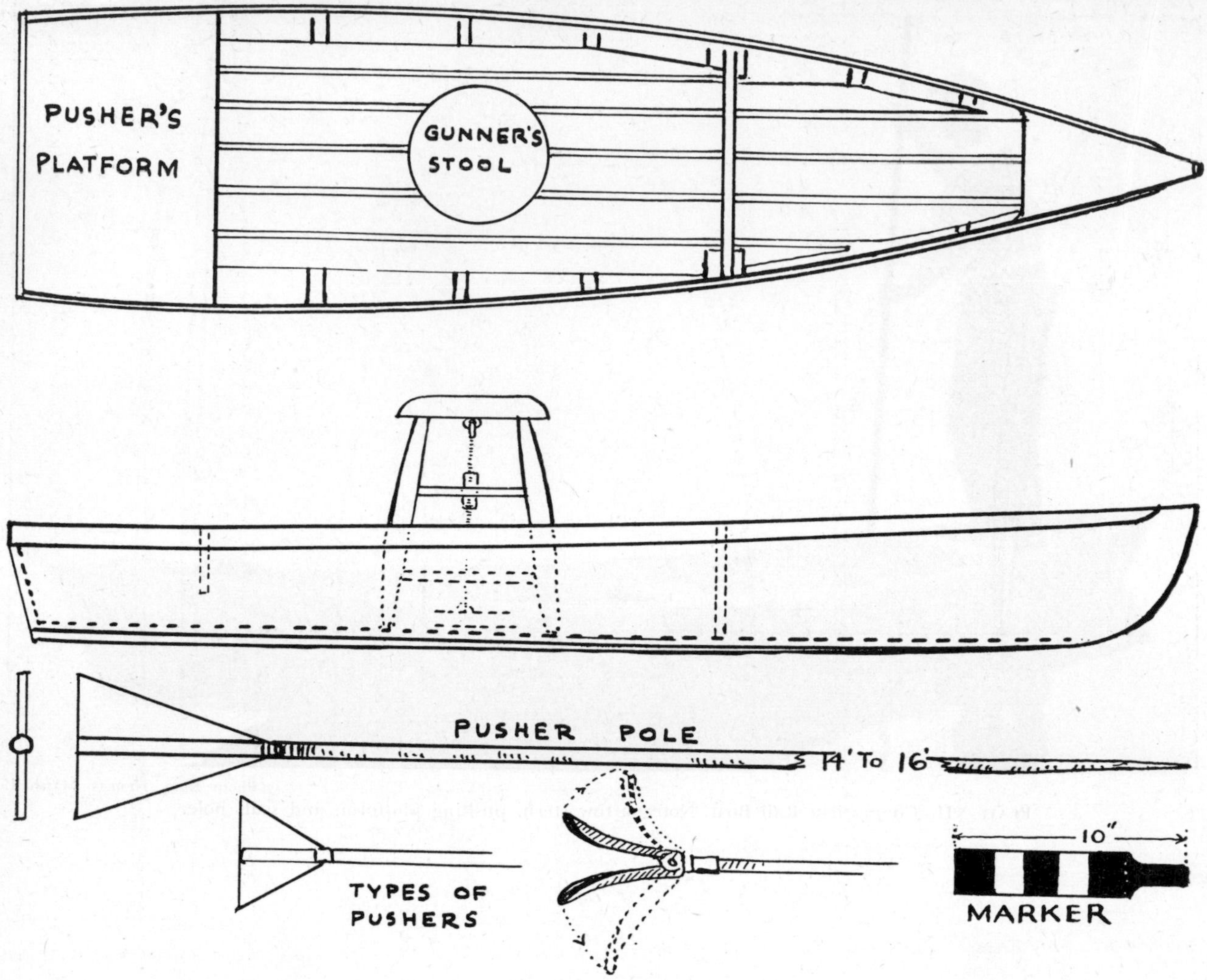


PLATE XIV. Rail Boat—shown with shooter's stool and various types of pusher poles. The marker shown is of light wood painted black and white or bright red and white. In heavy grass, marker is thrown at spot where bird fell to aid in picking it up.

side of the float. These were 12 feet long by 2 feet wide and were spread out flat on the water, making the entire layout 24 feet long by 12 feet wide.

A battery had to be transported to and from the shooting ground in a large skiff or on the deck of a sloop or power boat. The larger batteries were placed in position just before the opening day of the shooting season and left there for a week and sometimes for the entire season or at least until ice made it necessary to pick up such big rigs. These were used by market hunters and were placed on the feeding grounds of ducks and brant, in the center of a large raft of floating decoys plus a great many half-decoys nailed at intervals all over the deck. The deck of such a battery was about 40 feet square and sufficiently rugged to support two or three men walking around on it. From the outer edges of this deck wires were strung to all four points of the compass, to stakes about 100 feet distant. Floating decoys were attached to these wires by strings about a foot long, and these together with those nailed to the deck totaled from 500 to 700. The entire rig, from a distance, looked like an immense raft of fowl.

These mammoth rigs were attended by a power boat and the gunners lived aboard a cabin boat which anchored for the night near the rig. While the shoot was on during the day the power boat made the trip to the mainland to ship the previous day's kill, pick up stores, and attend to local errands.

The toll taken by one of these rigs was enormous, and it was a very good thing for our wildfowl that they were quickly outlawed.

When fowl could not be reached one way it did not take the gunners long to figure out another way, so, with a knowledge that ducks always take wing against the wind, they found that by sailing up to windward of a flock of ducks and then turning quickly and running down-wind, directly toward the birds, they could invariably get within killing range before the birds could take wing and gather headway enough to make the turn away. A small catboat, a good breeze, a sizable flock of birds, and about four guns meant murder for coots and broadbill. Large kills were made in this way, and later, when speedboats came into use, the same method of getting to windward and running down on ducks resulted in shameful kills with scores of

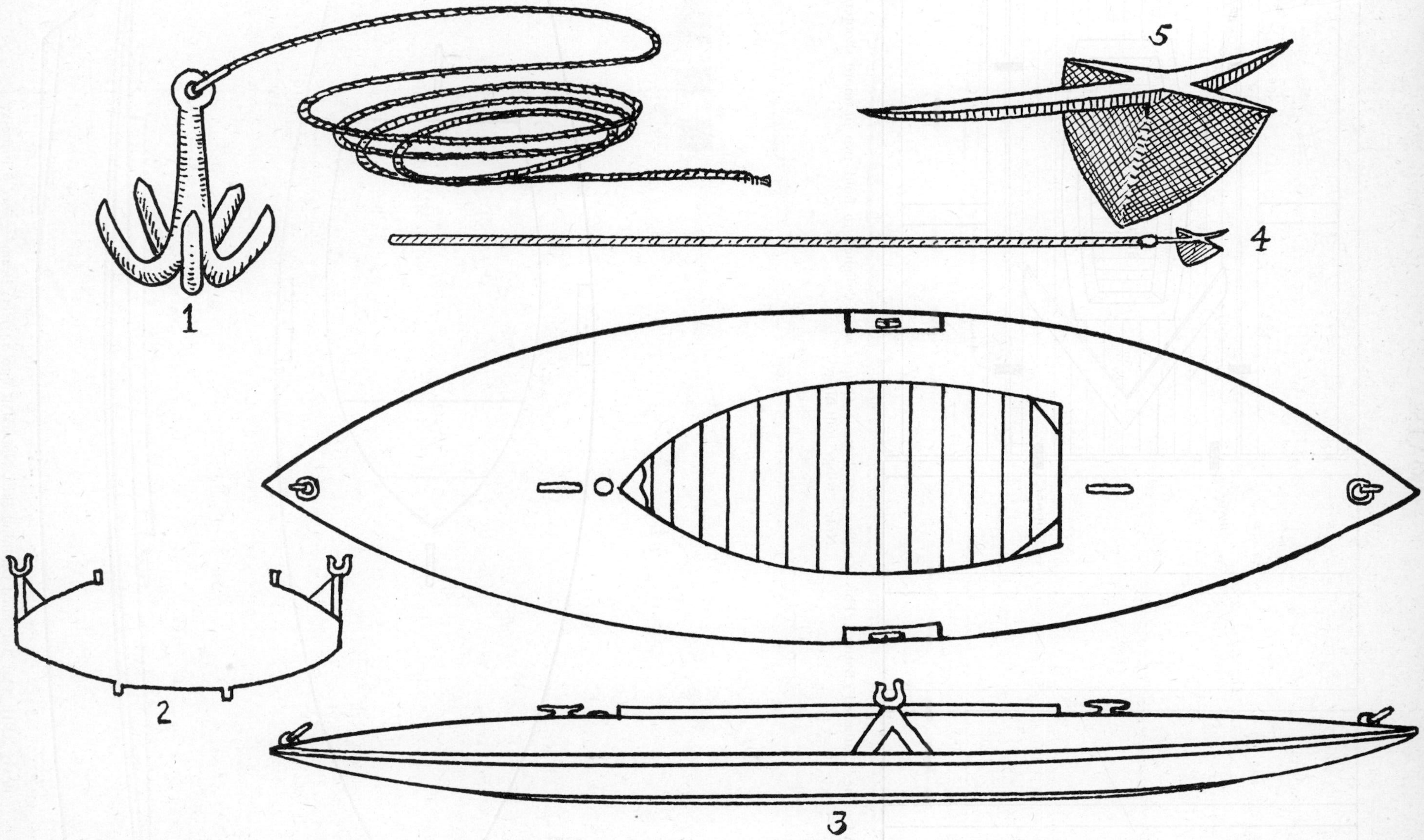


PLATE XV. Long Island (Great South Bay) Scooter. (1) Small grapnel with 100 feet of 3/8″ rope. (2) Cross section of boat, amidships; note runners. (3) Profile, (4) Scooter hook on 10-foot handle. (5) Detail of scooter hook.

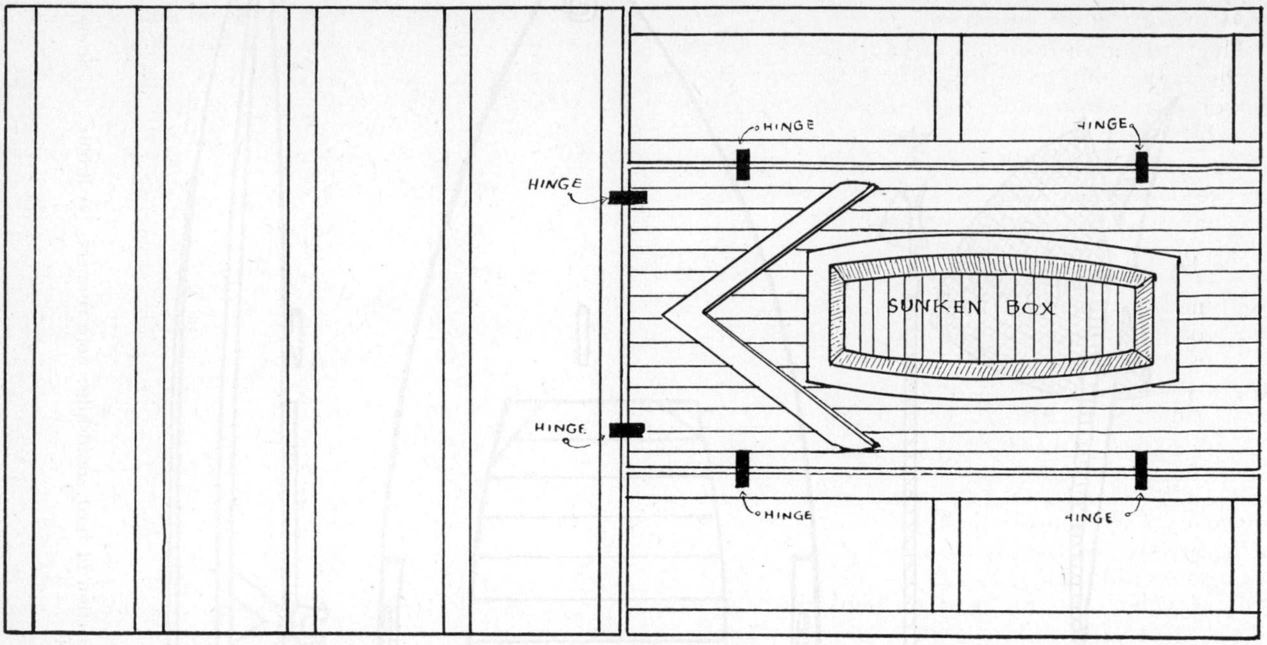


PLATE XVI. The "Outlawed" Battery. This is a "one-man battery. Others were designed to hold two or more shooters. Note "wings" on hinges.

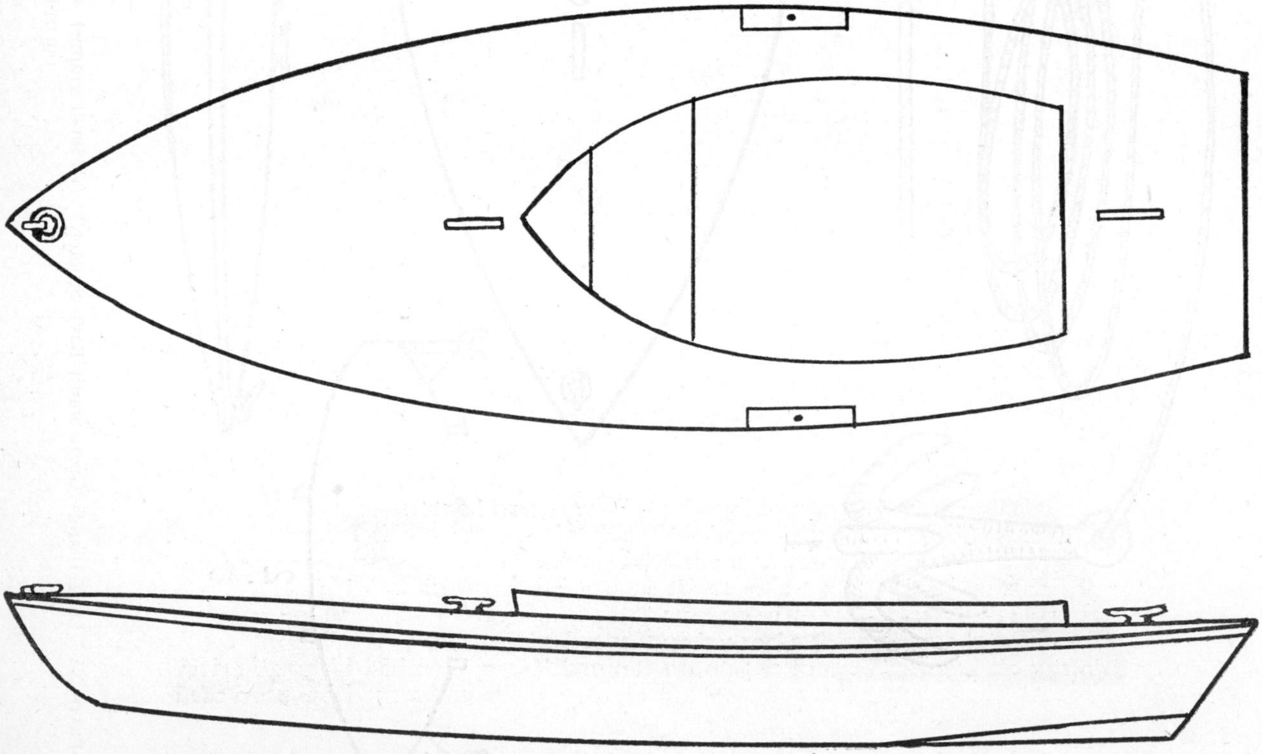

PLATE XVII. Flat-Bottomed Gunning Skiff. Normal length 14 feet; beam, 4 feet 6 inches.

cripples left to die of blood poisoning, or starvation, or as food for gulls and crows.

This method of hunting ducks was also outlawed by the passage of the law which prohibited the shooting of ducks from any boat propelled otherwise than by oars.

On some of the broad waters of the West and Midwest, it is necessary to sacrifice low freeboard and narrow beam to the interests of safety, and as many of the boats used on such waters serve as "stool" boats as well as duck boats, some strange combinations emerge from local boatyards. While the broader beam makes them more difficult to row or pole, these boats provide greater safety on waters where the wind can whip up high waves in a very short time. Some are built with square sterns to permit the use of an outboard while moving to and from the shooting grounds, but others are pointed at both bow and stern. Neither of the two types are made too wide or high to prevent them from being grassed up, but they cannot be used as a substitute for craft such as the "scooter" or "sneakbox," both of which often are used without grass.

The duckboats shown in Plates IX and XI (pp. 915-916) are typical of those found on many of the large lakes throughout the West and Midwest. The square-stern boat on the left often is used where two men plan to shoot from the same boat, and the punt on the right is designed for one man.

The punt shown in Plate IX also is common to this area. While higher and wider of beam than the boats normally used on the rivers and sloughs, they can be poled with ease except through thickly grassed areas.

The "rail" boat, designed primarily for use in very shallow water and thick reeds, grass, or wild rice, is somewhat varied in design in various areas, but has one thing in common—low freeboard. The requisites for this boat are lightness, sharpness, reasonable stability, and a smooth bottom. There are many variations of the two general types, but all show a great similarity in design. The Connecticut rail boat has more freeboard than most of the other types, and comes very close to the "double-ender" classification. It was designed long before the advent of the outboard motor, and as it was necessary to propel the boat by hand to the wild-rice flats the boat was designed to be rowed or sculled without too much effort. The modern tendency is to use an outboard motor to reach the shooting area, then put the motor ashore and use the push-pole. (See Plates X, XII, and XIV, pp. 916-918.)

# CAMP BEDDING

Any way you take it, you are going to spend one-third of your hunting trip or vacation in bed, and the energy you will have to enjoy your waking hours will depend on the quality of your sleep—on the comfort and warmth of your bed. Perhaps it is incorrect to say that a bed should be warm. No bed is warm unless it is made so by an old-fashioned warming pan or one of the new electric blankets. All that a camp bed can do is to retain the warmth that your body generates, preventing that warmth from being carried off quickly to the outside air. This is best accomplished by making the covering above and below so that it contains *dry, dead-air space,* which is the best non-conductor of heat. The body exudes much water vapor during sleep. Cotton would retain this and make the bed damp and cold (we wear cotton in summer to keep cool). But even if the covering contained much dry air, a wind would dissipate that unless there were also some sort of windbreak, which, however, should permit bodily vapor to escape. Thus we derive the principles on which a warm bed should be built.

The best bedding insulators to retain the body warmth without also retaining body vapor are, in the order of their efficiency, feathers, fur, and wool. They contain much dead air. An outside cover of showerproof cotton will absorb the vapor which escapes, hold this moisture where it will be absorbed by the outside air, and at the same time protect the inner covering from wind.

Wool blankets are rather old-fashioned bedding so far as their outdoor use is concerned. They are heavy in weight in proportion to the warmth they retain. Two light blankets are warmer than one heavy one of the same weight because of the layer of dead air between them. Blankets can, however, sometimes be taken from home without expense, and are thus not to be despised. They can readily be pinned into sleeping-bag form with horse blanket safety pins, and any sort of a tarp can be spread below and above them.

Next in order of low cost comes the wool comforter or quilt, which is much warmer than a blanket because of the greater amount of dead air contained.

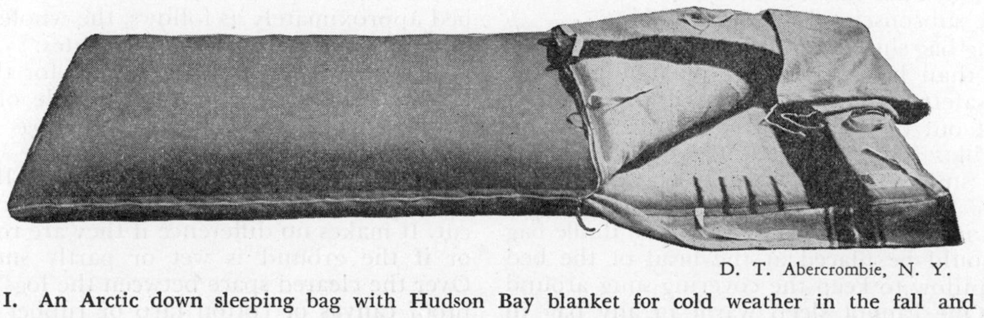

D. T. Abercrombie, N. Y.

**PLATE I.** An Arctic down sleeping bag with Hudson Bay blanket for cold weather in the fall and winter.

These are best when used between two blankets, or lined on both sides with all-wool flannel. They can often be purchased cheaply from mail-order houses.

The warmest of all camp bedding for its weight is the modern down sleeping bag, composed of a comforter or quilt of goose feathers, often called eiderdown, lined with light all-wool flannel, and with an outer covering of cravenetted cotton. These are usually made in bag form by zipper or snap fasteners all around the edge so they can be opened and spread flat for drying in the sun. Many weights and sizes are made, from the heaviest arctic robe or bag intended for temperatures down to 40° below zero, and weighing about 12 pounds, to very light ones weighing only about 4 pounds and intended for back packing and night temperatures down to freezing.

D. T. Abercrombie, N. Y.

PLATE II. A very light down sleeping bag for mountaineers and back packers, weighing only 3 pounds and satisfactory to freezing weather.

Commonly these bags are about 84 inches long by 36 inches wide, about correct size for small and medium-sized men, but a large man would be uncomfortable in a bag less than 40 inches wide inside.

At this point we should mention the best method of sleeping comfortably in a sleeping bag.

Even in sound sleep every man turns over and assumes different positions many times during the night. In bed at home this presents no difficulty because sheets are slippery, they do not cling to him, and so he does not disarrange his bedding when he turns over. But in camp he sleeps in flannel pajamas or wool underwear between wool or flannel covers, all of which cling and stick. Thus when he turns over the entire bag is likely to turn with him, and soon he is all tangled up and most uncomfortable, or else he has rolled completely out of the bag. This is particularly true of the narrow "mummy"-shaped down bags made for the Army during World War II. These are both warm and very comfortable. But if the bag is wide enough the sleeper can, as he turns over, place a hand on either side of the edge inside as he turns, holding the edges down to the ground, and the bag will remain "shipshape" and right side up. This he does drowsily the first couple of nights; thereafter it becomes second nature and is done subconsciously without waking.

A sleeping bag should not be fastened or "zipped" shut more than halfway up the open side in the interest of safety, as one can never tell when he may have to get out of it in a hurry in case of fire or other trouble. The unfastened opening is kept closed and snug subconsciously, just as one keeps the edges of covers down in bed at home. When a bag is used in the open, without a tent, a duffle bag or pack should be placed at the head of the bed above the pillow to keep the covering snug around the neck. One cannot sleep warm in any bag in damp or wet underwear. He should change to flannel pajamas, or clean, dry underwear and, if necessary, dry socks on retiring.

Of course blankets or a sleeping bag would be very uncomfortable if laid on the bare ground, and would get dirty and damp. Some form of mattress is essential. The old-fashioned camp mattress often consisted of a bed-tick filled with grass or leaves gathered on the spot, or—much better—in the north, of the finer branches of balsam, hemlock, or spruce shingled thickly on the ground. Such a browse bed has a fine odor, there is nothing to carry from camp to camp, and if it is laid at least 8 inches thick it will be very comfortable the first night. But it soon packs down and then it is hard. It takes half an hour to make a good browse bed, usually just at the time of day when the camper is tired or busy with other camp chores. Mattresses for camp use are also commercially made of kapok, but they are heavy and bulky.

Decidedly the best for all camp use is the air mattress, which need not weigh over 4½ pounds or occupy more space than a small blanket when deflated. It can be blown up in a minute with a small pump, or in five minutes by lung power. It makes the bed just as comfortable and dry as the finest "four-poster" at home. Do not buy the big, full-sized mattress. The small size, 48 inches long and 26 inches wide, will provide all the cushioned surface the largest man can use. The overhang of the lower legs is never noticed—or if it is, a small bundle of boughs, grass, or leaves will bring the bottom up even with the top. Further, a full-sized air mattress has a tendency to "bounce" the sleeper from side to

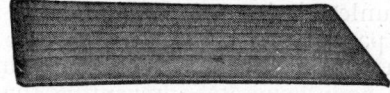

D. T. Abercrombie, N. Y.

PLATE III. An air mattress for campers' use.

side when he rolls over, and finally he rolls or bounces completely off the mattress. This is entirely avoided with the shorter 48-inch length, as the "drag" of the feet on the more stable bottom seems to keep one in control of one's position.

We now come to the best camp bed for cool or cold hunting countries in the fall of the year. The arctic down sleeping bag is entirely too warm when the night temperature is over 40 degrees above zero. An air mattress is cold at temperatures below zero. So the experienced northern hunter makes his camp bed approximately as follows, the whole process not taking more than five or six minutes:

Choose a level piece of ground for the bed, and clear and smooth it. On either side of this space, about 3 feet apart, lay two small logs 6 feet long, and stake them down at the outside of each end or lay rocks there. These logs can usually be picked up on the forest floor, and do not often have to be cut. It makes no difference if they are rotten or wet, or if the ground is wet or partly snow covered. Over the cleared space between the logs lay a waterproof canvas or cotton tarp or rubber poncho. At the top of this bed lay the short air mattress and inflate it so that when kneeling on the ground alongside it, and pressing down in its middle with the full weight on his hand, you can just feel the ground underneath. On top of this lay the arctic down sleeping bag covered with the blanket. In extreme cold, the blanket, folded once, can be placed directly on top of the air mattress thus insulating one from cold below. Also do not neglect some kind of a pillow; an air pillow is the lightest and least bulky. To most of us a comfortable pillow is as essential for a night's rest as a soft mattress.

Camp cots are also often used, and under certain conditions are sometimes essential, particularly in the tropics. The best and most convenient type is about 7 feet by 30 inches in size, which folds to a bundle about 40 by 6 inches, and with canvas bottom a foot above the ground. A cot keeps the bedding clean and up away from ants and other insects. It can be insulated from ants by placing the legs in tin cans filled with water with a film of kerosene on top. The canvas cot is the coolest bed known for hot nights in the South, but it will freeze its occupant out in short order even at 45 degrees above zero, unless a good, thick, and warm mattress is used on top of it. Any sleeping bag or blankets would be very cold in fall weather if used on a cot without a mattress.

In tropical jungle, hammocks are also commonly used, tied between two trees. These are made of canvas, not netting, and are combined with a mosquito bar which stretches above. The top of the mosquito bar is sometimes made of waterproof cotton, or a waterproof tarp is thrown over all to protect from rain.

Coming down to first principles, in the tropical jungle the writer cut a mattress of palm fronds, on which he laid a rubber poncho, and above it erected a mosquito net on sticks, then crawled inside, took off his clothes, and slept comfortably in the raw. In back-packing in the North he has pitched his little lean-to tarp in a spruce thicket, made a browse bed under it, and with a good fire in front has slept fitfully without a blanket, being awakened by the cold every two or three hours to build up the fire. But such roughing it does not pay, even for the young man trying to be tough. It is far better to insure a dry, warm, comfortable bed with proper equipment. One will then have more energy to enjoy the daily sport, and he will successfully resist the many ills to which a tired human body is prone.

# CAMP FOODS AND COOKING UTENSILS

There is a saying that "What is one man's food is another man's poison." By the time a man is old enough to go on hunting trips that involve camping and outdoor cooking he knows pretty well what foods he likes, what agree with him, and what give give enery when working hard in the open air. Within certain limitations there is no reason why he should not make up hi food list from the things he prefers.

These limitations on camp food are about as follows: (1) The various components must not be such as will spoil in hot or freezing weather. (2) They must be those that the hunters or their hired cook know how to prepare. (3) They must not be too heavy or bulky for the means of transportation. (4) Under certain conditions ease of preparation may be a consideration.

For example, canned goods are very heavy in proportion to their food value, soups in particular. Where the hunter cannot count on killing his meat or catching fish, meat of some kind must be taken. Bacon and ham keep well and have the greatest nutriment for their weigh and bulk, but one may tire of them as a steady diet, and some canned meats may be very desirable.

Bread is a little tedious and difficult to bake in camp. Cereals in the form of porridge are a good substitute for bread, contain even more food value, and are the lightest, quickest, and easiest of all foods to prepare. Dry breakfast foods are not appetizing unless one has fresh milk.

There is no reason why campers should deny themselves fresh vegetables. Potatoes and onions carried in a gunny sack keep well. Most other vegetables will keep fresh for a long time if wrapped first in waxed paper, and then in an outside wrapper of brown paper, both tied tight. Fresh butter keeps a long time in brisk fall weather, or canned butter can be had. Fresh eggs will also keep for a month if wrapped in waxed paper, and then in crumpled newspapers to prevent breaking. Any of these foods can be prevented from freezing at night by placing them in a shallow pit within the tent and covering it with a tarp.

Except in a warm and humid climate fresh meat can be kept for a long time, by hanging in the shade and air in a meat safe, which is simply a large cheesecloth bag, suspended bottom up with a hook inside the bottom, and hoops like barrel hoops to extend it. The meat is inserted in the open under end and hung from the hook, the open end being then tied shut. The hoops keep the cheesecloth from touching the meat, and the safe is thoroughly flyproof. Free circulation of cool air keeps the meat fresh for a long time, often as much as a month in the high Northwest. Or meat may be cut up and placed in a covered pot in a cold spring. In canoe travel meat can be kept cold by placing it in the extreme bow or stern close to the keel.

Incidentally, it may be well to mention here something which has been forgotten for a long time, and has only recently been proved again—namely, that men, families, can live their whole lives in excellent health, well nourished, on a diet of meat alone, provided that some of it is eaten very rare, and that as much *fat* meat as the system craves is available. Fresh raw meat is a perfect cure for scurvy. In the absence of fresh meat, those obliged to subsist for long periods on dried and canned foods alone can now avoid scurvy by daily vitamin pills.

When fresh milk cannot be carried or obtained, excellent substitutes are canned evaporated milk or powdered whole milk; the latter is considerably preferable. To prepare powdered milk, place a heaping tablespoonful in a cup of cold water and beat until dissolved.

A great many food lists for campers have been published, all differing considerably in components and amounts, being naturally based on the preferences and experiences of the writers. These will seldom suit the tastes, appetites, and transportation facilities of any particular party of hunters without considerable modification. Broadly speaking, when hunters cannot count on getting much meat and fish from the country, 2 pounds per man per day should be taken of the fairly dry foods such as flour, cereals, beans, and bacon, or 3 pounds per day of the more liquid canned meats and vegetables; so that the total food for one man for a month will run between 60 and 90 pounds. The amount of each particular article depends upon how many portions one wishes to prepare of that article, and how much he eats of it at one meal; these data can be gained only by experience. For example, if you prefer rolled oats each morning, find out at home how many of your usual portions are contained in a 3-pound package.

The following is a very old-fashioned food list such as experienced wilderness hunters preferred years ago for trips where they expected to kill at least some meat, and for canoe and pack-horse transportation. The amounts given are for one healthy, hard-working man for one month—or, of course, for two men for two weeks. It should be used as a general guide only. Note the large amount of sugar and sweets, craved by men exercising hard in the open air. If a city man is to hunt by canoe, and his guide does most of the paddling, he will not need such quantities.

| | |
|---|---|
| Flour | 15 lbs. |
| Baking powder | 1 can |
| Cereals (rolled oats, corn meal, hominy, rice) | 6 lbs. |
| Salt | 2 lbs. |
| Sugar, granulated | 5 lbs. |
| Maple syrup | 1 qt. |
| Black pepper | 1 can |
| Butter, fresh or canned | 3 lbs. |
| Powdered milk | 3 lbs. |
| Eggs, fresh | 2 doz. |
| Eggs, powdered | 1 can |
| Bacon, breakfast | 3 lbs. |
| Ham | 2 lbs. |
| Salt pork (for beans) | 2 lbs. |
| Beans, white navy | 5 lbs. |
| Lard or Crisco, I can | 5 lbs. |
| Potatoes, fresh | 15 lbs. |
| Onions, fresh | 5 lbs. |
| Dried fruits (prunes, apricots, apples, figs, dates) | 5 lbs. |
| Tea | 1 lb. |
| Coffee, powdered, instantaneous | 2 lbs. |
| Sweet chocolate (for lunches) | 20 cakes |
| Kitchen soap | 4 cakes |
| Matches in cans—ample and then some more | |
| TOTAL WEIGHT, about | 90 lbs. |

Fill up to limit of transportation facilities with fresh fruit and fresh vegetables.

This list will not suffice unless at least a small amount of meat or fish can be counted on from the country. If not, go to a good grocery and add about five cans of meat or other foods according to preference. Always consult guides and cooks before finally completing the food list, and take any foods they prefer. Unless they are well fed according to their tastes they cannot be expected to give their best and most enthusiastic services. There is no reason why some luxuries should not be taken. For example, a little fresh lettuce and celery, plus a can of mayonnaise dressing, plus canned lobster, plus hard-boiled eggs, spells lobster salad.

Most of these articles had best be packed in waterproof cotton bags of 5 to 10 pounds' capacity furnished by city outfitters. Bacon, ham, butter, etc., should be wrapped in waxed paper before placing in the bags. Lard, powdered coffee, milk, etc., go in pressed-top cans. Take an extra can into which to pour and salvage bacon grease. All the food can then be packed in panniers, packsacks, or duffle bags.

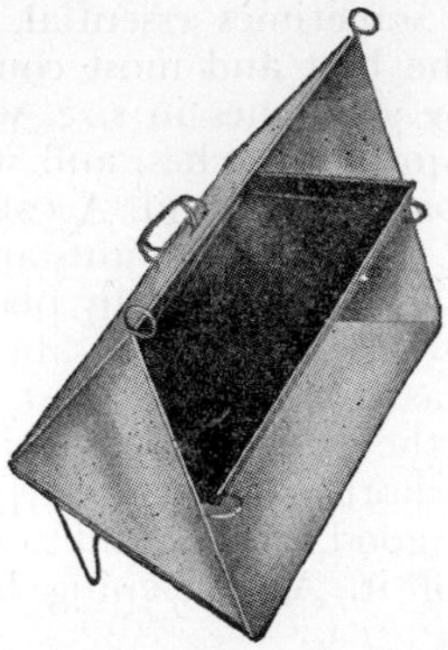

D. T. Abercrombie, N. Y.

PLATE I. A Reflector Oven, an Invaluable Aid.

The place to learn to cook is at home over the kitchen range. There are a number of excellent camp cookery books which will help a lot, but if you have to cook for yourself in camp, *do not count on book knowledge alone—get some home experience.* Cooking in camp is no different from cooking over the home stove, as the campfire can be regulated to give any degree of heat desired. As a rule, however, home cooking utensils are extremely inconvenient for cooking over an open fire.

A hunter who is going to do his own cooking needs a carefully selected outfit of camp cooking utensils. He needs at least three kettles, as potatoes, boiled meat, and coffee may be desired at the same meal. Two frying pans permit bacon and flapjacks to be cooked simultaneously. There should be some sort of oven for baking, and a big pan that will do for both flour mixing and dishwashing. There should be a plate, bowl, cup, knife, fork, teaspoon, and tablespoon for each man, and one or two extras for serving, as well as other miscellaneous articles shown on the following list. The kettles should have covers and bails so they can be suspended over the fire, and they should also nest together. The smallest kettle will probably be used for tea and coffee, but *do not* get one with a spout; spouts are virtually impossible to clean, and unfit the kettles for any other use. A spout with strainer is not needed if you use powdered coffee, which is in any case far preferable for camp use. Frying pans are most conveniently packed if they have folding or detachable

D. T. Abercrombie, N. Y.

PLATE II. A complete camp cooking outfit of aluminum which will nest in a small space.

handles. Most of the utensils are best of fairly thick aluminum, but the cups should be of enamelware or tin, as aluminum burns the lips.

City outfitters sell excellent sets of aluminum cooking utensils, as shown in Plate II, above. All nest in a canvas bag about 12 by 12 inches, except the aluminum reflector baker which goes in a bag of its own. Thus the utensils for a party of three should consist approximately of the following:

3 Camp kettles, to nest.
2 Frying pans, 12", with folding handles.
1 Dishpan, large.
1 Folding alumium reflector baker with pan.
4 each; plates, bowls, cups, forks, knives, teaspoons, tablespoons.
1 Large cooking spoon.
1 Large cooking fork.
1 Butcher knife with sheath.
1 Cake turner.
1 Can opener.
1 each; salt and pepper shakers.
2 Dish towels.
1 Dish mop.
1 Canvas water bucket.
1 Canvas bag to hold the outfit.

For four or five men, add one larger kettle, one more frying pan, and the necessary plates, cups, bowls, and cutlery.

**Cooking Fires.** A word or two about fires may be helpful to those without experience. Place two 4-foot logs about 5 inches apart, raising them an inch or so off the ground with rocks at the ends. Build the fire between these logs, small dry pieces first, then long, split wood. When the small stuff is blazing up high, let the water in the kettles be boiling. As this burns down, add the dry split wood; this will reduce the size of the blaze and soon you will have fine coals between the logs just right for frying and broiling.

At each end of the two logs drive a stout forked stake, with the forks about 4 feet above the ground. Lay a cross-pole of green wood in the forks. From this cross-pole suspend the kettles with reversed forked sticks with notches for the bails. These should be the right length to hold the kettle bottoms the right height above the fire. A kettle hung near the center of the fire boils hard; hung at the side close to the upright forked posts, it will just keep the contained food warm. Frying pans can be balanced on the two logs. Regulate the fire by adding dry, split wood between the logs as needed. For baking, put on another backlog and pile split wood against it so as to make a high wall of flame, and stand the reflector baker in front of the blaze. Have a green-wood poker at hand, and a pair of cheap cotton work gloves to handle hot utensils. After the evening meal remove the cross-pole and pile 4-foot logs high for the friendship fire.

*And before you leave camp put that fire DEAD OUT.*

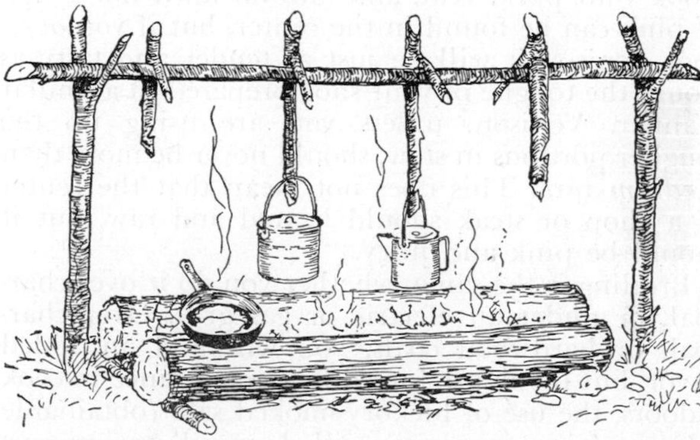

PLATE III. The Best Arrangement for the Cooking Fire.

# CAMP AND HOME GAME COOKERY

Not all of the recipes and cooking methods covered in this section can be followed under all conditions, for some hunters prefer to "rough it" gastronomically as well as physically. The camps of such individuals will have salt, pepper, and sugar, and while these items are important, they are not conducive to an interesting diet. If you are traveling light, limiting yourself to such spartan staples is not only reasonable but in many instances necessary. If, however, you have horses, mules, a canoe, or a boat to aid in carrying the burden, there is no reason why you should not enjoy a more interesting cuisine. Tasteless food and discomfort are the indelible mark of the inexperienced hunter, hiker, camper, or woodsman. If you think fine fare is foreign to the deep woods, drop in on an isolated lumber camp and taste the dishes prepared by the woods cook.

This section will be divided in two parts. One devoted to camp cookery, the other to game cookery at home, where the amateur chef has a greater opportunity to practice his exacting art. Every recipe listed herein can be followed by any individual capable of obeying directions, and no vague cookery terms will be employed to confuse the rank amateur of the skillet.

Many experienced woodsmen would not think of leaving home without what some of them term their "cook box" or "spice bag." The contents of these containers vary, but the following items will serve as a nucleus for yours. You may add or subtract according to your taste and abilities.

| | |
|---|---|
| 14 oz. bottle catsup | 4 oz. bottle concentrated vinegar |
| 5 " bottle Worcestershire sauce | 2 " tin dried parsley |
| 2 " tin dry mustard | 2 " tin red pepper |
| 2 " tin peppercorns | 4 " tin onion flakes |
| 2 " tin dried bay leaves | 8 " bottle pure olive oil |
| Salt (usually included in general supplies) | 1 doz. cloves of garlic |

The weight of this "spice box" is about three pounds, but its value to the man who enjoys good food can never be measured in dollars. There are a number of individuals who, if it became necessary to reduce weight, would put aside a blanket rather than the "box."

The experienced camp cook will see to it that his equipment includes one of three important items: a dutch oven, a portable iron oven, or a reflector oven. Where weight and utility are factors, the dutch oven or reflector oven wins out. The former can and does serve as a stew pot and dishpan as well as an oven, whereas the latter is limited to its primary function.

## RECIPES

### VENISON

Broiled (steaks, chops, cutlets, tenderloin fillets, saddle).

There is one thing to remember in the cooking of venison, whether the method be broiling, frying, or roasting—that is, *cook it as you would prime beef.* Cook your pork, veal, and mutton until not a sign of pink can be found in the center, but if you *over*-cook venison it will be just as tender and tasty as would the tongue of your shoe prepared in a similar manner. Venison, unless you are using up the tougher portions in stew, should never be more than *medium rare.* This does not mean that the center of a chop or steak should be red and raw, but it should be pink and juicy.

Broiling is the same, whether you do it over charcoal, or under an electric or gas grill. Over charcoal, or hardwood coals, you will find an added flavor, but if you are forced by circumstance to cook indoors, the use of hickory-smoked salt (obtainable in most fancy groceries) will do much to improve the flavor.

First, the chop, steak, cutlet or fillet should be at least an inch thick. Split a clove of garlic and pass it lightly over both sides of the meat. Just a bare touch is all that is needed. You will taste no garlic in the cooked chop, but the flavor will be enhanced. Then rub the meat with a little oil or melted butter. Salt and pepper lightly, and place the meat CLOSE to the fire. When seared on both sides (approximately ½ minute per side) reduce the heat (for gas or electric grills) or place the meat farther from the fire, just far enough to prevent burning, but close enough to insure that the portion facing the heat is sizzling. The amount of time required properly to cook it must be determined, either through long practice or by testing. The heat of various types of fires varies, and testing is the best method. Cut to the center of the meat with a sharp knife. If too rare, return the meat to the fire for more broiling. Normally, 6 to 8 minutes of cooking is sufficient.

Broiled Saddle.

Rub the entire saddle thoroughly with a split clove of garlic. Split 1 clove-half into tiny splints as thick as a toothpick. Insert these splints (8 or 10) into knife punctures made along the backbone the length of the saddle. Rub the entire saddle thoroughly with olive oil or vegetable oil. Then prepare the following basting.

Mix the following: ⅔ cup of olive or vegetable oil, ½ of a small onion grated very fine, 2 tablespoons catsup, ½ teaspoon of hot pepper sauce, ⅓ cup lemon juice, ½ teaspoon of salt, ½ teaspoon of prepared mustard.

Take a stick the size of a pencil and tie enough parsley or chives to the end to form a brush the size of an egg.

Place the prepared saddle *very* close to the fire and sear it thoroughly on all sides. This will require from 2 to 3 minutes. Remove to less intense heat, and turn and baste the saddle every 2 or 3 minutes, using the parsley or chives brush to apply basting sauce. The average saddle will require from 70 to 90 minutes, and will require considerable attention on the part of the cook. The results will more than justify the effort. Test to determine when done by a cut to the center.

When carving the saddle for serving, *do not* cut *across* the saddle, but cut *lengthwise.* With a sharp boning knife, make a cut parallel to the backbone and right through to the ribs. Then make another cut ½ inch lower. This will remove a strip as long as the saddle, ½ inch thick, and from 1½ to 2 inches wide. Each portion will be about the same and no one will be favored.

Roast (leg, shoulder, saddle, round).

Rub meat with split clove of garlic, and insert 6 or 8 fine slivers (thin as toothpicks) in fatty portions or in vein openings. Rub thoroughly with olive or vegetable oil, lightly salt and pepper, dust lightly with flour. Place in open roasting pan on a rack. Before placing in oven add 1 cup of water to bottom of roasting pan. Place in *very hot* oven for about 15 minutes to sear the meat thoroughly. Reduce heat, and baste every 5 minutes, using basting given in previous recipe. The roast should be basted with a spoon, and when prepared basting gives out, baste with drippings. The time required to cook depends upon the size of the roast. (Venison is not so thick as beef, hence requires less cooking time.) For a thick roast, allow 12 minutes per pound for rare, 14 minutes per pound for medium. For cooking venison more than medium, no chart is necessary. It will lose most of its flavor and tenderness through over-cooking. Those who wish to avoid steady basting may lay thin strips of fat salt pork over the top of the roast, holding them in place with toothpicks. If this is done, basting will be required only every 20 minutes. The secret of a good roast of venison is frequent and thorough basting and *under* rather than *over*-cooking.

Stew.

Rub about 4 pounds of stew meat (cut in 2-inch cubes) with salt and pepper, rub with flour, sauté in frying pan using any good cooking oil or butter. When brown, place in heavy metal cooking pot with a good cover. Add 1 quart of water, 4 peppercorns, 2 medium bay leaves, and a pinch of marjoram. Simmer very gently for about 2 hours. Meanwhile prepare the following: 8 onions (egg size), 6 carrots (cut in 2-inch sections), 6 medium potatoes (cut as for boiling), 4 medium tomatoes cut in quarters (2 cups of canned tomatoes). Add these vegetables to the pot of simmering meat and continue to simmer lightly until onions are thoroughly cooked. Just before serving test for seasoning and add salt as desired. Some prefer using 1 pint of white wine and ½ pint of water for the original simmering of the meat. This adds slightly to the cost of the stew but much to its ultimate flavor.

VENISON CACCIATORE.

This is better if cooked in a heavy glazed clay pot with a heavy cover. Why this should make a difference is an obscure point, but try it with an ordinary metal pot once, and the next time with a glazed clay pot. If your taste buds are acute the difference will be apparent.

Prepare the following: Dice *very* fine, 6 onions (egg size). Dice *minutely* 1 clove of garlic. Dice into 1-inch squares, 6 medium tomatoes. In a muslin spice bag place 2 crushed bay leaves, a sprig of marjoram, 4 peppercorns, a few sprigs of parsley.

Place the above in a pot in which has been poured 1 pint of white wine and ½ pint of red wine. Add 1 teaspoon of salt.

Take the 2-inch cubes of meat and rub with salt and pepper, dust with flour, and sauté until brown, using ½ cup of olive oil or good vegetable oil. Meanwhile have the contents of the pot simmering on the stove. When meat has been browned, tilt frying pan into the pot, adding both meat and oil in which it was sautéed to the simmering vegetables. Simmer so lightly that the necessity for stirring can be eliminated. The cooking should require from 3 to 3½ hours. Test for seasoning before serving. When cooked in this manner, the diced vegetables have merged and so disintegrated that they form a thick gravy. Remove the spice bag just before serving. This is best served on a mound of well-cooked brown rice.

NOTE: Any game bird, cut into sections, rabbit, squirrel, or, for that matter, veal, beef, or lamb, is excellent prepared as above.

LIVER.

Venison liver can be sliced in ½-inch-thick slices, dusted with salt, pepper, and flour and sautéed in a frying pan; or rubbed with salt, pepper, and oil and grilled; or it can be cut into cubes and broiled. The latter method is not too well known or too often practiced, but it is a dish the epicure will enjoy.

Cut liver into cubes of about 1 inch square. Dip into a sauce prepared as follows:

One-fourth cup of olive or vegetable oil, ½ teaspoon of salt, large pinch of pepper, 1 teaspoon Worcestershire, 1 teaspoon prepared mustard. Blend the above in a cup or small bowl. Dip the cube of liver into this sauce. Wrap the cube in a slice of bacon, and place on a spit or individual skewer. Place over a charcoal fire or under a grill, turning almost constantly to avoid burning, until bacon is thoroughly cooked. When the bacon is done, so is the liver.

HEART.

Too many are inclined to feed deer heart to the dog, which literally is throwing a really tasty tidbit "to the dogs." Properly prepared, the heart is known as a gourmet's delight.

Split the heart in half (top to bottom). With a small, sharp knife remove all the vents and ducts (not so difficult as it sounds). Soak the halves for 1 hour in the following sauce. ("Marinate" is the stylish term for this.)

| | |
|---|---|
| 1 cup red wine | 1 bay leaf |
| 2 tablespoons vinegar | 1 onion (sliced) |
| 1 teaspoon salt | 1 teaspoon prepared mustard |
| 2 peppercorns | |

(Blend wine, vinegar, salt, mustard, then add other ingredients.)

After hearts have soaked in the above sauce for 1 hour, drench them with flour and place in a HOT skillet in which ⅛ of a pound of butter (or similar amount of cooking oil) has been melted. After thoroughly searing, reduce heat slightly and cook for about 5 minutes. (Test with knife cut.)

VENISON PASTY.

This requires the following ingredients: 6 egg-size onions, 6 medium potatoes, 6 small carrots sliced lengthwise, 3 cups of diced tomatoes, 3 cups of diced cold venison.

Cook all vegetables separately. Make a paste of 3 tablespoons of flour and water, and stir into stewed tomatoes until thickened. Drain carrots and onions and add to thickened tomatoes, adding 2 teaspoons of salt and pepper to taste. Simmer this slowly for 2 minutes, then add diced venison. Reduce heat to mere simmer, and mash potatoes, adding 1 cup of hot milk and ⅛ pound of butter. Beat with egg-beater until fluffy. Turn vegetables and venison into a casserole and spread mashed potatoes over mixture. Bake in a moderate oven until potatoes are browned on top.

VENISON MARSALA.

This requires the following ingredients: 2 pounds of sliced venison (slices should be ⅓ inch thick, about 2 inches wide, and 4 or 5 inches long), 1 pound of fresh mushrooms (or 2 cups of canned mushrooms), ⅔ of a cup of tomato paste.

Dust meat slices with salt and pepper, roll in flour, and sauté until browned in skillet with ½ cup of olive oil. Remove meat from skillet and add sliced mushrooms. Cook mushrooms until brown over medium heat, return meat slices, and add tomato paste, which has been thinned with 1 cup of marsala wine. Add 1 clove of garlic diced *very* fine. Simmer very gently for 30 minutes with cover on skillet. Turn meat every 10 minutes.

VENISON BARBECUE.

Cut meat into 2-inch cubes (enough for the number to be served), dust with salt and pepper, and roll in flour. Place a large iron skillet on the fire and lightly brown the venison cubes in butter. (The amount of butter depends upon the size of the skillet and the amount of meat.) Slice very thin enough onions to half cover the cubed venison, which has been separated in the skillet. Add 1 cup of barbecue sauce (p. 932) and place in a medium-hot oven. Check the progress occasionally, and add more barbecue sauce as it is needed. The meat should be thoroughly cooked in about 1 hour. Remove meat cubes to a warming oven, then add 1 wineglass of sherry to the gravy, stirring well, then 1 cup of heavy cream. When this has been blended, pour over the cubes and serve.

Chipped Venison.

There is one method of cooking venison that will recommend itself to the man in the woods, as well as the man who likes a quick snack with a glass of ale before going to bed.

With a sharp knife cut off a few slices of almost any cut of meat. The slices should be 4 or 5 inches long and not more than 1/4 inch thick. Place a lump of butter the size of an egg in a large skillet, and apply heat. When the butter is lightly smoking, drop in the slices as rapidly as possible. After NOT MORE than 15 seconds, turn the slices. After another 15 seconds remove the pan from the fire, add salt and pepper, decant the contents of the pan on a plate, and fall to. Between two slices of bread, previously spread with the gravy, this is a tasty if somewhat indelicate feast. The greatest drawback to the above recipe is this: One pan of these slices leads to another, and the first thing you know there is not enough butter for breakfast and not enough venison left for a roast.

Many woodsmen claim that the above method is the only one which should be employed in cooking fresh-killed venison.

Curing.

This section would not be complete without instruction as to the proper curing of venison. If you happen to be fortunate enough to locate a butcher who understands and has the proper facilities for curing venison you will not be interested. But such butchers are not to be found in every neighborhood. The curing will determine the quality of the meat, whether it be moose, elk, antelope, deer, or caribou.

In many instances some of the curing (or aging) will have been accomplished before the meat reaches your local freezer. For the purposes of illustration and expanation, we will consider that the meat arrives at your freezer the day after it is killed. (This would be rare indeed.) In this event, the meat should be hung, with the hide removed, for not less than 24 days in a curing box where the average temperature is about 32° F. This temperature should not vary more than 3 or 4 degrees either way, if possible. Many large freezers have such a curing box, and if you remove the hide of the animal and have it properly dressed, they will not object to hanging it in the curing room.

For *each* day of delay in getting the meat to the freezer, the best rule is to subtract *two* days from the curing process. If the meat has hung in temperatures between 35 and 40 degrees while in the woods and en route to the freezer, subtract *three* days for each day after it was killed.

When the curing process has been completed, cut the meat into sections desired and have it frozen solidly. This will halt all curing and will preserve the meat in proper condition until it is desired for use. (For preservation of meat in the field see p. 991.)

## WATERFOWL

Coot Stew.

One of the most misunderstood birds, where cooking is concerned, is the lowly coot, the misnomer for the various members of the scoter family. Here is a recipe for coot stew that will remove this bird from the "lowly" list.

Skin (removing all adhering fat) two scoters (coots to you) and cut out the breast and legs and thighs. Prepare a large pot, preferably of thick iron with a heavy cover, with the following: 6 egg-sized onions, 5 carrots (cut in 1-inch sections), 5 diced tomatoes (peeled), 1 hefty pinch of marjoram, 2 tablespoons of chopped parsley, 1 tablespoon of salt, 1 teaspoon of pepper, 2 bay leaves. Add 1 quart of water and 3 tablespoons of wine or cider vinegar. Bring to a simmer. Then salt and pepper the coots, dredge sections thoroughly with flour, and brown in a large skillet with 1/8 pound of butter. Tilt browned coot sections and butter gravy (thinned out with a little water) into pot with vegetables, and simmer *very slowly* in covered pot for about 2 hours or until coot is tender. Do not be misled by the popular superstition that "coot will not get tender." It will, and if you can eat this stew and not ask for another helping you had better have a doctor examine the taste buds on your tongue.

Coot Sauté.

Skin out 2 scoters, removing all the adhering fat. Remove breasts, legs, and thighs. Soak these overnight in the refrigerator in a strong saltwater solution to which has been added 1/2 cup of vinegar and 1 sliced onion. Before cooking, dry the sections, rub with salt and pepper, and dredge with flour. Place 1/8 pound of butter in a skillet, heat until butter is smoking, and put in sections. Brown both sides quickly, then reduce flame and cook the meat slowly. When tender, remove meat to warming oven, and add 1/2 wineglass of sherry to gravy, then stir in 4 tablespoons of Merrymeeting sauce. Blend thoroughly. Remove meat from warming oven, pour the gravy over it, and serve. Believe it or not, the meat has something of the flavor of venison.

For those who are sated with roast duck, any duck is delicious prepared according to the above recipe, and is an excellent method of preparing pheasant or grouse.

Roast Duck (or Goose).

Pick the duck (or goose) dry, singe thoroughly, then draw. Remove heart, liver, and gizzard. Cut the meat from the gizzard, eliminating outer and inner skin. Place liver, heart, and gizzard sections in small stewpan with 3 tablespoons finely diced celery, 1 tablespoon finely diced onion, salt, pepper, and 1/2 teaspoon of mustard. Wipe the duck dry, inside and out, rub outside with salt and pepper, then with melted butter. Stuff according to taste (see stuffing recipes on p. 932), and place in open roasting pan in very hot oven for 5 minutes, to sear properly. Reduce heat to about 400°, and baste every 5 minutes until tender, using the following basting.

*Basting:* Melt 1/8 pound of butter. To this add 1/2 cup lemon juice, 2 tablespoons of catsup, 1/2 teaspoon prepared mustard, 1 teaspoon Worcestershire sauce, salt and pepper. Blend over mild heat. This should be kept warm for basting.

While the fowl is roasting, simmer the gizzards, liver, and heart until tender, remove and dice, then return to liquor. Add 1 cup of Espagnole sauce (see p. 932) and blend thoroughly.

When duck is cooked, remove to warming oven and blend the sauce, with the gizzard, heart, and liver, with the drippings in the roasting pan.

Some prefer to carve slices of the duck, place them in large skillet, cover with the above gravy, simmer for 2 or 3 minutes, then serve.

Broiled Duck.

Prepare the ruck exactly as in the recipe above, but instead of placing in the oven, place under the grill, which has been heated for 10 minutes. Grill without basting, close to the flame, for about 5 minutes. Reduce flame and continue the grilling, turning the bird each time it is basted. This turning and basting must be done above every 2 minutes for 20 minutes. Then remove bird to oven until tender. When tender, place under the grill again for 2 minutes, basting frequently, The gravy is prepared the same as for roast duck.

This recipe calls for more effort and attention on the part of the cook, but for an old duck, it can accomplish wonders. When cooked, the duck will be crisp outside but tender and juicy inside. The Pruyn stuffing (see p. 932) is recommended for this method of cooking.

Stewed Duck.

Most epicures will stew a duck only as a last resort, but there are times when an old bird demands this method of preparation. The recipe given under "Coot Stew" is extremely satisfactory. The recipe given for "Venison Cacciatore" (p. 927) also will find favor, with sections of duck substituted for venison.

## UPLAND GAME BIRDS

*(Pheasants, Grouse, Quail, Doves, Woodcock, Rail, Pigeons)*

Purlough (also known as Pilaf, Purleau, etc.).

There is a story in connection with this recipe. A Northern rod and gun editor was shooting quail in South Carolina many years ago. The weather was dry, the dogs worked badly, and everyone was discouraged. The host suggested that the editor attend a dove shoot on a near-by plantation. "If you gather in an even dozen doves," he promised, "I'll have Henry turn out a dove purlough for you." The doves were obtained, Henry made the purlough, and the editor was so impressed upon tasting this dish that he obtained the recipe and wrote about it in his daily column. The word "purlough" had rather stumped him, and so he inquired about its spelling. The above spelling was the one agreed upon by the host and other local sportsmen. In the fullness of time a column written by one of the reporters on a Charleston paper reached his desk. The writer took to task a "Yankee" rod and gun writer who, after tasting one of the famous South Carolina "dove pilafs" had, with typical Yankee indifference, spelled it "purlough." However, pilaf or purlough, it is quite a dish, so here is the recipe.

Skin (or pluck) 1 dozen doves (quail, woodcock, pigeons, rail), draw them, putting aside the hearts and livers. In a heavy two-gallon pot, with a cover, place the following: 2 quarts of stock (8 bouillon cubes dissolved in 2 quarts of water), 1/2 pound of butter, 6 medium onions diced very fine, 1 cup of chopped parsley, 6 diced (peeled) tomatoes, a large pinch of marjoram, 1 teaspoon of pepper, 1 teaspoon of chile powder, 3 tablespoons of salt, 2 1/2 cups of rice. When this has been brought to a slow simmer, add the birds, hearts, and livers. Place the cover on the pot and simmer slowly for 3 hours. At the end of this time almost everything has merged into a gravy but the rice and the doves. Serve this with a green salad with a tart French dressing, hot "rizzen" bisquits, and a glass of light claret, and Lucullus will spin in his grave.

(Three rabbits, divided into sections, can be substituted for the birds, and the epicure will remain content. Even a grouse or pheasant, cut into sections, will serve admirably.)

Pheasant Murray (grouse, partridge, ptarmigan).

Pluck, draw, and split the bird. Remove the heart and liver, and place to one side. Divide each half into two sections, rub with salt and pepper, dredge with flour, and sauté until brown in a skillet with 1/8 pound of butter. Dice up heart and liver and add to skillet when bird is almost browned. Remove the browned sections to a casserole. Add 1/2 cup of finely diced onion to the diced heart and liver in the skillet, and cook over moderate flame for sufficient time to brown the onions lightly, then add 1 cup of finely diced mushrooms, and 1 wineglass of white wine. Simmer gently for 5 minutes, then pour contents of skillet over the pheasant sections in casserole. Add enough heavy cream to cover all, and place in a moderate oven. When pheasant is tender, remove from the oven, sprinkle with 1 cup of finely grated American cheese, and place under broiler until cheese has melted and is lightly browned. Serve immediately.

Roast Quail (doves, woodcock, pigeons, rail).

Pluck and dress 6 birds, placing the hearts and livers to one side. Place the hearts and livers, finely diced, in a saucepan with 1 tablespoon of butter, 1 teaspoon finely diced onion, 1 tablespoon finely diced celery, salt and pepper to taste, and 1 cup of water. Simmer for about 1/2 hour.

Meanwhile, prepare the stuffing for the birds. In a saucepan place 1/2 cup of butter, 1 cup of heavy cream, 1 cup of finely diced mushrooms, 1 tablespoon of parsley, 1 tablespoon of finely diced onion, salt and pepper. Simmer gently for 10 minutes, then add bread crumbs or cracker crumbs until proper firmness is obtained.

Rub the birds with flour to which salt and pepper has been added, and stuff them with the above stuffing. Place the birds in a roasting pan, cover each breast with a thin slice of bacon, add 1/2 cup of water to the pan, and place in a medium oven. Baste frequently for about 30 minutes, and remove the birds to a warming oven. To the drippings add the prepared gizzards and hearts, 1 cup of sour cream, and stir this gravy until sufficiently thick. Place birds individually on a square of buttered toast and cover with the gravy.

GAMEBURGER.

Run 2 cups of cold venison, rabbit, pheasant, grouse (or other game, regardless of how originally prepared) through a coarse meat grinder. Place in a bowl, and add ½ cup of finely diced onion, 1 teaspoon of prepared mustard, salt and pepper. Blend this mixture thoroughly, and to it add 2 beaten eggs, and stir until blended. Place a small lump of butter in a large iron skillet, and place over a moderate flame. When the skillet is well greased, dip out the mixture with a pancake spoon, and brown on both sides. As a sandwich filler, this gameburger will be really popular.

GROUSE CASSEROLE.

Pluck and draw 2 grouse (or pheasants, partridge) and remove hearts, livers, and gizzards. Remove outer and inner skin of gizzards, and simmer with hearts and livers in 1 cup of water, salt, pepper, and a pinch of celery seed for 20 minutes. Meanwhile divide birds into eating sections, rub with salt and pepper, dredge with flour, and brown the section thoroughly in a skillet with ⅛ pound of butter. Remove sections and place in a greased casserole. Turn cooked gizzards, hearts, and livers (diced), and broth in which they were cooked, into the skillet and stir into butter in which sections were browned. Pour this gravy over sections in casserole. Add 15 tiny onions, 1 cup of shredded carrots, 2 teaspoons of salt, and ½ teaspoon of pepper. Cover sections and vegetables with sour cream and place in a medium oven. Cook slowly until meat is tender. This will serve six hearty eaters or three men who have been hunting all day.

ROAST PHEASANT.

Pluck and draw the birds, clean gizzards, and place, with hearts and livers, in a saucepan with 1 cup of water, salt and pepper, 1 small diced onion, a pinch of celery seed, and ½ teaspoon of prepared mustard. Wipe the inside of the birds with lemon juice and stuff. (For stuffing see p. 932.) Rub the outside of the birds with salt and pepper and dust lightly with flour. Place each bird in a greased brown-paper bag, tie mouth of bag, and place in shallow pan in a moderate oven. Meanwhile, simmer down the gizzards, hearts, and livers until little water remains. Remove and dice up the sections. Place a lump of butter the size of an egg in a small skillet and to it add the diced-up hearts, gizzards, and livers and the broth. To this add ½ cup of white wine and stir in 1 cup of Espagnole sauce. After 1 hour, check the pheasant's progress. Cooked in this manner, the skin should be brown and crisp and the meat juicy and tender. Serve the gravy separately, preferably on wild rice.

## RABBIT

FRIED RABBIT.

Cut rabbit into eating sections and soak in refrigerator for 24 hours in the following solution: 2 cups of white wine, 1 cup of vinegar, 4 tablespoons of salt, 4 peppercorns, 1 finely sliced onion. Just before cooking remove sections, dry thoroughly, and dust with salt, pepper, and flour. (Take 1 cup of flour, 1 teaspoon of salt, ½ teaspoon of pepper, and place in large, stout brown-paper bag. Shake sections, one at a time, in this bag.) Take a large skillet, and in it render out a heaping cup of salt pork cubes. Remove pork, and with grease smoking hot, add sections of rabbit. Cook over hot flame until well browned, then reduce heat and cook until meat is tender. Remove rabbit sections to warming oven. To the remaining grease in the pan add 1 cup of Espagnole sauce (p. 932) and ½ cup of white wine and wine vinegar (half and half). Stir and blend until gravy is of proper consistency. Place rabbit sections on hot platter and pour gravy over them. Scatter crisp cubes of salt pork on top, and sprinkle with chopped parsley.

RABBIT CASSEROLE.

Prepare exactly as for Grouse Casserole.

RABBIT STEW.

Prepare exactly as for Coot Stew (p. 928) or Venison Cacciatore (p. 927).

## PIT COOKERY

STEW.

This calls for a heavy iron pot with a tight cover (a Dutch oven will do). First dig a pit 6 inches deeper and 6 inches greater in diameter than the pot to be used.

Line the bottom and a few inches up the side of the pot with thin slices of bacon or salt pork. On this place 5 cups of cubed meat (venison, beef, other game), 6 or 8 halved onions, ½ dozen medium potatoes (2 cups of dried beans that have been soaked overnight may be substituted for potatoes); 2 cups of any other vegetable you happen to have may be placed on top. The meat and vegetables should be leveled, and enough water or stock to cover them completely should be added. Place the lid on the pot and mix up a thick, pasty dough of flour and water with which to seal the rim of the lid.

Place about 3 inches of glowing coals in bottom of pit and place pot on top, leaving about 3 inches of space between the sides of the pot and the sides of the pit. Line this space with coals; place about 3 inches of coals on top of pot, then cover with earth.

If this is done before you leave camp in the morning, the evening meal will be ready and piping hot when you return late in the day. Remove the earth, remove the pot, and brush dirt from cover. Remove the dough seal and the pit stew is ready to eat.

PIT SQUIRREL, RABBIT, OR GROUSE.

Prepare pit as previously described. Line bottom of pot with thin strips of bacon or salt pork, then put in a layer of diced ham (2 cups diced in ½-inch cubes). On this place eating sections of game. Top this with a ½-inch layer of sliced onions. Top the layer of onions with a 1-inch layer of inch-thick slices of potato (or a layer of soaked dried beans or peas). Add sufficient water or milk to barely cover (if beans or peas are used, cover completely), and seal cover as explained above. Place in pit, and cover with earth. Because of the salt in bacon and salt pork, no salt should be used in the cooking. It may be added when served.

## MACARONI AND CHEESE

Place 1 quart of water and 1 tablespoon of salt in a large kettle and bring to a boil. Add ½ pound of macaroni broken into 2-inch sections. Allow this to boil for 20 minutes. A greater part of the water will have been absorbed by the macaroni. Remove to a point where the contents barely simmer. Make a thin paste from ½ cup of flour and 1 cup of milk, turn into a saucepan, stir in 1 cup of shredded or finely diced cheese, allowing the mixture to barely simmer while blending. Add ½ teaspoon of black pepper. Stir this into the cooked macaroni, and allow the contents of the pot to simmer but not boil for 5 minutes. It is then ready to serve.

In the event this is to be the main course of the camp meal, diced cubes of *meat* (1 to 2 cups) may be added immediately after the cheese sauce has been stirred in.

*Dried beef* also adds to the savory qualities of this dish. Take ¼ pound of dried beef slices and break up into inch squares. Place in a small saucepan or skillet with 2 cups of water and simmer it for 10 minutes. Drain off the water and add the dried beef to the macaroni after the cheese sauce has been blended in it.

## SOUPS

Few camps bother with soup, considering it a course that can very well be passed up, as it merely delays a hungry man who wants to get his teeth into some solid food. There are some soups, however, that not only may be considered as really "solid," but will warm a cold hunter down to his toes when he arrives back in camp.

The thick *pea soup* of the Quebec back country is one of these, and it is not only delicious, but filling. The hunter who takes a quart thermos of this soup to the duck blind spends a good part of the day patting himself on the back for his foresight.

Soak overnight, in 3 quarts of water to which 2 tablespoons of salt have been added, 1 pound of split peas. (If you are back-packing and are using dried vegetables, soak ½ cup of dried carrots and ¼ cup of dried onion flakes in another pan for the same length of time.) The next morning, cut into ½-inch cubes ½ pound of salt pork or bacon. In a large pot place 2 quarts of water, the soaked peas (which have been drained), 2 medium carrots in ½-inch cubes, 2 onions diced fine, and the diced bacon. Put this pot on the back of the stove, where it will barely simmer, and let it simmer gently all day. If you are in a tent or lean-to camp without a stove, open up a hole in the center of the breakfast fire coals, place the pot there, bank it almost to the cover with coals and ashes, cover these coals and ashes with earth, and uncover the pot when you return. If more water is needed, add it carefully, stirring well, then let the pot simmer again until the time comes to sample the contents. In many sections of the North Country this pot is never empty. Each day more peas, onions, carrots, and pork are added and the simmering continues on the back of the stove. If cooked in a pit (see p. 930) the ingredients should be covered with 2 inches of water before the pot is placed in the pit.

## CAMP BREADS

**Corn Bread.**

Place 1 cup of corn meal, 1 cup of flour, ½ teaspoon of salt, 4 tablespoons of sugar, 3 teaspoons of baking powder in mixing tin. Blend these dry ingredients thoroughly. Add 1 cup of milk (milk powder and water) and stir until lumps have disappeared (add ¼ cup of egg powder if available), then add ¼ cup of bacon grease or other shortening and blend thoroughly. Bake in square tin in reflector oven, or in Dutch oven. Grease the tin or Dutch oven thoroughly before pouring in batter. In emergency (lacking either oven) a heavy iron skillet with a cover can be used.

If you happen to be in the woods during the berry season, a pint of berries dumped in the batter just before pouring into tin and stirred in *very* gently, will add a real touch to the corn bread. In northern Maine this berry-enriched bread is known as "bang-belly."

**Bannock.**

Place 1 cup of flour, 1 teaspoon baking powder, ¼ teaspoon of salt, and 1 tablespoon of sugar in mixing pan. Blend these dry ingredients thoroughly and add 2 tablespoons of bacon fat. Mix this until lumps have disappeared, and add from ⅓ to ½ cup of milk or water. The resultant dough should be a dry rather than wet dough. Flatten the dough to a 1-inch patty, doing this on a plate dusted with flour. Grease a skillet thoroughly and place it 1 or 2 inches above the coals. Place bannock carefully in the skillet and let it remain until browned on the bottom, which should require about 10 minutes. (Not burned, browned.) Then turn bannock and brown the other side. It may be necessary to add a bit more grease to the pan before turning the bannock. Bannock seems to remain fresh for 2 or 3 days, which is not true of most yeast-risen camp breads, which may turn sour.

**Pancake Bread.**

This is much like bannock, except that normally only one day's supply is made. Take 1 cup of flour, 1 teaspoon baking powder, ¼ teaspoon of salt, 1 tablespoon of sugar, and blend thoroughly. Add ½ to ⅔ cup of water or milk, then stir in 2 tablespoons of bacon grease. This mixture will pour rather thickly, but it will pour. Grease a skillet, heat it, and pour in about ¼ inch of this batter. Brown the bottom, add a touch more grease to skillet, and turn. Brown other side slowly and the cake is done. This can be made in small cakes if desired, rather than a large cake the size of the skillet.

**Camp Biscuits.**

Take 1 cup of flour, 2 teaspoons of baking powder, ½ teaspoon of salt, 1 tablespoon of sugar. Blend these ingredients, then work in 2 tablespoons of bacon grease or other shortening. Place on board or pan that has been dusted with flour and flatten with the hand until ¾ inch thick. Cut out circles with a baking-powder tin or cup. Place in greased tin and bake in reflector oven or Dutch oven.

## SAUCES

### Barbecue Sauce.

1 cup wine or cider vinegar, 4 tablespoons olive oil, 2 teaspoons chili powder, 1 teaspoon hot pepper sauce, 1 teaspoon black pepper, 2 tablespoons Worcestershire sauce, 2 finely diced cloves of garlic, 2 tablespoons prepared mustard, 2 tablespoons finely grated lemon peel, juice of 2 lemons, 2 tablespoons salt, 2 tablespoons sugar. Mix this thoroughly, then place in saucepan and simmer slowly for 15 minutes. This sauce can be prepared in larger quantity and kept in refrigerator until desired. Amount to be used for basting can be removed and heated. The sauce should be kept hot when used for basting.

### Quick Hollandaise.

Empty small can of evaporated milk into double boiler (about ⅔ of 1 cup), add yolk of 2 eggs, salt, pepper, and ⅛ pound of butter. Place over medium fire, and stir constantly. When sauce begins to thicken add 2 teaspoons of lemon juice or vinegar and continue stirring until proper thickness. There is but one secret to the proper preparation of this sauce: *constant* stirring.

### Horseradish Sauce.

Thoroughly mix 2 cups of butter with 1 cup of grated horseradish, adding salt and pepper to taste. When blended force the mixture through a fine sieve and spread into square glass dish. Place in refrigerator until wanted. Small squares may be cut as needed. Small square placed on portion of any broiled or sautéed game will receive acclaim.

### Orange Sauce.

Grate the peel of 1 orange and 1 lemon, and simmer in the strained juice of both, after adding 1 teaspoon sugar and 1 winegass of sherry. Simmer for 15 minutes, then add 3 cups of Espagnole sauce, stir thoroughly until smooth, and place in refrigerator until wanted.

### Espagnole Sauce.

Take ¼ pound of butter and ¼ pound of flour. Melt butter in skillet and add flour; stir constantly until flour is browned. Add 5 cups of stock. (Stock may be made by dissolving 5 bouillon cubes in 5 cups of boiling water.) Stir until mixture is smooth and store in refrigerator until wanted.

### Merrymeeting Sauce.

Grate the skin of 2 oranges, simmer lightly with 1 wineglass of sherry, then stir in 3 tablespoons of prepared mustard. When thoroughly blended, stir in 1 cup of currant or beach-plum jelly. When blended, turn into glass jar and place in refrigerator until wanted. (Four tablespoons of this, blended with duck gravy, will add a real touch.)

## STUFFINGS

The following stuffings may be used for waterfowl, or any of the upland game birds.

### Pruyn Stuffing.

Shred, as thin and fine as possible, 4 heaping cups of cabbage. Slice, as thin as possible, 2 cups of onion. Place the cabbage and onion in a large mixing bowl and mash them together with a large wooden spoon or paddle. The mashing should take 3 or 4 minutes. Beat up 3 eggs to which has been added 1 wineglass of sherry, 2 teaspoons of salt, 1 teaspoon of black pepper. Add this mixture to the cabbage and onion and mix thoroughly. Add bread crumbs or cracker crumbs, mixing with the fingers, until the stuffing is firm. This is an unusual stuffing, but is especially fine for duck or goose. It must be tried to be appreciated.

### Barnegat Stuffing.

Dice into ¼-inch squares 8 strips of bacon. Place in large skillet and render out until bacon is lightly browned. Remove bacon to brown paper to drain. To the bacon grease add the following: 2 heaping cups of finely diced onion, 1 finely diced clove of garlic, 2 tablespoons prepared mustard, ½ cup of catsup, 3 tablespoons of vinegar, 1 cup of finely diced apple, ½ cup of sherry. Simmer slowly, with frequent stirring, for 20 minutes. Add 1 teaspoon of black pepper and 2 teaspoons of salt. Stir in diced bacon, turn into a large bowl, and add diced stale bread until proper firmness is attained. Merging of the bread should be done with the fingers. This stuffing is excellent for most of the diving ducks.

### Chestnut Stuffing.

Boil until tender 4 cups of chestnuts. Mash 2 cups of chestnuts to a paste, adding 2 teaspoons of salt and ½ teaspoon of pepper. Place ⅛ pound of butter in a skillet and in this brown 1 large onion, diced very fine. To this add 1 wineglass of sherry and 1 cup of cream. Stir in the mashed chestnuts, and add 1 tablespoon finely chopped parsley, 1 pinch of marjoram. Turn into large mixing bowl and add cracker crumbs or bread crumbs until proper firmness is attained. Then add whole chestnuts.

### Apple Stuffing.

Dice into ¼-inch squares 4 slices of bacon. Place in large skillet over medium fire and render out bacon until lightly browned. Remove bacon to brown paper and drain. To bacon grease add 4 cups of diced apples, ½ cup diced onion, ½ cup diced celery, 4 tablespoons chopped parsley, ½ cup of sugar. Stir mixture thoroughly and simmer slowly with cover on the skillet. When apples are tender, uncover and add bacon scraps. Turn into mixing bowl and add bread crumbs or cracker crumbs until proper firmness is attained. This is an excellent stuffing for pheasant, grouse, and small waterfowl.

### Nut Stuffing.

Place ⅛ pound of butter in a skillet; to this add 1 cup of heavy cream, 1 tablespoon sugar, 2 tablespoons salt, ½ teaspoon pepper, a pinch of nutmeg. Stir thoroughly with merely enough heat to melt the butter. Add 1 cup of nutmeats (pecans, walnuts, peanuts) and turn into a mixing bowl. Add cracker crumbs or bread crumbs until proper firmness is attained. This stuffing is especially fine for the smaller upland game birds, such as quail, woodcock, and doves.

# CANOE TRIPS AND CANOE HUNTING

Throughout North America there is a vast extent of wild country, plentifully supplied with game and fish, that can be reached only by canoe. Canada east of the Rockies and the plains is an intricate network of lakes and rivers, almost as much water as land, abounding in moose, caribou, deer, bear, and grouse, with virgin fishing everywhere. In the United States, Maine, Wisconsin, and Minnesota are famous for their canoeing waters leading into fine game country, while the long rivers of the South, easily navigable by Indian canoe, are fringed by game country and have never been exploited.

**Canoeing.** For such waters the canoe is really the only practical craft for the sportsman. It can be easily portaged around rapids and falls, and between lakes, on one man's shoulders and can be paddled noiselessly to approach game. It can be paddled, poled, steered, and swung by its occupants facing forward and is therefore the only satisfactory craft for running rapids and white water, or ascending swift streams.

The American Indian has given us three articles which have never been equalled for their particular use—the snowshoe, the teepee, and the canoe. For all wilderness use the closer these approach the original Indian design the better.

Modern canoes are made of wood, canvas, plywood, and aluminum. On the whole, the best are those constructed of canvas stretched taut over a light wood shell, this type being sold by a number of firms in the United States and Canada, and in many varieties and lengths. Collapsible canoes with light metal or wood frame over which a waterproof canvas cover is stretched, are convenient, as when taken down they can be packed inside a car, checked as baggage, or carried by hand, and can be assembled in a few minutes, but they lack the maneuverability, liveliness, speed, and seaworthiness of the best canvas and wood canoes. Canoes are now being made of aluminum, of the conventional "summer resort" type, and with air chambers to make them unsinkable. It is perhaps too early to predict the practicability of these for wilderness travel and hunting, although they appear very promising. In what follows we will consider modern canvas and wood canoes as made by the best United States and Canadian makers.

For practical purposes of hunting and fishing, canoes vary in length from 10 to 20 feet, in width amidships from 30 to 40 inches, and in weight from 40 to 120 pounds. They also vary much in type. The typical pleasure canoe, almost the only type made in the United States, is rather narrow, not deep amidships, high at bow and stern, with slightly rounded bottom. It is speedy and pleasant in quiet waters, but not well adapted as a weight carrier or for navigating large lakes and white water. Our "guide" canoes are slightly better in these respects, being wider and deeper. The best wilderness designs, however, are made only in Canada. There the "prospector" type is generally considered by experienced wilderness hunters to be the best. This is generally about 17 feet long, 37 inches wide, and 14 inches deep, with a rather flat bottom.

The size of canoe to be chosen depends largely on the weight to be carried, outfit and occupants, and on whether many large lakes must be negotiated. The canoe must not be loaded so heavy that it will be loggy, hard to turn, and slow to paddle. It must ride large waves rather than plough through, and there must be sufficient freeboard so that the waves encountered on fairly windy days on fairly large lakes will not swamp it. No canoe will weather a serious storm on a large lake—you simply go ashore and wait for calmer weather—but the canoe should not be loaded so heavily that it will be unsafe in ordinary windy weather.

PLATE I. The Loaded Canoe, Ready to Leave.

**Plate II.** A Rest on Quiet Waters.

**Canoe Loading.** A 10-foot canoe will carry two men for a day's hunting or fishing, and can be transported on the top of a car, but it is too small for cruising with an outfit. A 12-foot canoe will safely carry one man and his outfit, to a total loading of a little short of 400 pounds. A 14-footer will safely take two men and a light "week-end" outfit, its safe lading being about 500 pounds. All of the above lengths are very easily portaged by the average sportsman, as they will not weigh over 60 pounds. The most practical length for two men, a hunting outfit, plenty of grub, with capacity to also return with a load of meat and perhaps a big moose head, is 16 to 18 feet, with a width of at least 36 inches, and depth amidships of at least 13 inches. The safe lading for the usual 16-foot pleasure-resort canoe as made in the United States is about 600 pounds, while the 17-foot Canadian prospector canoe will take almost 1000 pounds, and itself weighs about 80 pounds.

It will not take many days to convince anyone that a cruising canoe should be at least 36 inches wide and 13 inches deep amidship. This makes for stability and carrying capacity. For just one small reason, consider sleeping bags. They usually roll up about 36 inches long, and they can easily be squeezed crosswise into a craft that is that wide, but if you have to stow two sleeping bags lengthwise, along with three or four packsacks and perhaps a couple of duffle bags you will have a load that piles up dangerously high in the canoe.

A canoe should always be loaded when it is afloat or nearly so, never when pulled high up on a beach. Place the heavier packs amidships and right on the bottom. Allow space for the occupants' feet. Anything you want to get during the day, such as lunch, a kettle, or raincoat, tuck conveniently into a side space. The weight should be so distributed that when both men get in the canoe it will ride just noticeably deeper at stern than bow, and of course the side balance should be absolutely central. If you expect to run rapids during the day, crowd the weight as close to the center as possible; loaded thus, the canoe will turn much quicker. If you expect rain or rough water, place four light poles or spruce boughs in the bottom before loading to keep articles an inch high out of water that might come aboard. Any water will then run back where the stern paddler can bail it out from time to time and keep the outfit dry.

An old-timer usually has a light rucksack containing certain indispensables such as camera, matches *(in a waterproof container)*, fishline and hooks, and a small supply of ammunition. This he stows under his seat, buckling one shoulder-strap fast. He also ties his rifle and ax to a thwart or the gunwale. Then in case of an upset he saves the things most necessary for existence. If the sleeping bags are packed in waterproof duffle bags with sealer cloths at the opening, and if packsacks likewise have these sealer cloths, they will float.

For the novice it may be well to mention certain precautions and "don'ts" about canoes and canoe travel. (1) *Keep the center of gravity as low as possible* and the craft well balanced. Thus loaded a canoe is very steady and can hardly be upset except by gross carelessness or an extremely heavy curling wave taken side on. (2) *Never attempt to change places* with the other canoeist without going ashore. *Never stand up* in a canoe. This applies to everyone except the real expert using a pole, or rising to get a view of a rapid ahead. (3) *In approaching a landing, if it is a sand beach, just touch the bow to the beach.* The front paddler then gets out, *lifts* the bow and carries it up the beach a little, and steadies the canoe while the stern paddler climbs over the load and comes ashore dry-footed. *If it is a rocky shore, bring the side of the canoe to the shore.* One man then steadies it while the other throws out the outfit, and then gets out himself. (4) *Never pull a canoe over a beach or rocks;* this will wear, tear, and ruin the bottom. (5) When the canoe is empty, carry it up on the shore and turn it over; it will then keep dry inside, and things not needed for that night's camp can be stored under it. (6) A dirty or sandy canoe can be cleaned by throwing a couple of buckets of water into it, rocking gently to stir and loosen the dirt, and then turning it over to drain.

**Travel and Portaging.** A party hunting by canoe may often have to travel by water two or more days from the outfitting point on the railroad or motor road to the good hunting country. There the sportsmen may find a log camp, or they may pitch their own tents at a locality from which they hunt each day. Or their hunt may be in the nature of a long canoe trip in which they travel and camp almost every day, hunting as they go. The motive power for the daily cruising may be either paddles or outboard motor.

Two good men can average 3½ to 4 miles per hour paddling in quiet waters with no wind. Twenty miles a day is good going with paddles and a canoe loaded no heavier than indicated above. In ascending, and sometimes in going down, swift rivers and rapids it will often be necessary to pole the canoe, and sometimes in ascending swift rivers the canoe must be roped up, one or two men pulling with a long rope from the shore, while another in the canoe steers it just free from the bank. No progress can be made with paddles up a river that flows more than 4 miles per hour, nor with outboard motor over one flowing about 7 or 8 miles.

Canoes are now quite generally being used with light outboard motors; a special attachment permits these to be secured to the pointed stern. An outboard motor will get you there and back faster, it does not tire, and when speed and time are considerations it is a great advantage. Because of its noise it cannot be used in hunting, and during a day of motoring little wild life is seen. With a motor, to many of us, the abominable noise, smell, and trouble at every portage completely ruins most of the pleasures we look for in the silent places. Also, with a motor there is no healthy exercise, and one is cramped more or less in one position in the canoe for long stretches of time. Two men in a 17-foot canoe can normally carry about three months' food supply, and can paddle as far as the food lasts. With an outboard motor they can cover an equal distance in about one-fourth the time, but due to the weight of motor and gas only about three weeks' food can be carried, so that nothing is saved but time.

On a given water route there is seldom clear paddling or motoring all the way. Most days there will be some rapids or carries between lakes that must be portaged. The length of a portage may be anything from a mere lift around a falls to five miles or more. Here is one of the advantages of the light Indian canoe; it can be carried easily by one man. A 12-foot canoe usually weighs not more than 40 pounds, and an 18-footer about 80 pounds. It is carried turned over, bottom up, resting on the man's shoulders. For portaging, the two paddles are tied to the bow and middle thwarts as shown in Plate IV. When the canoe is inverted the carrier thrusts his head between the paddles where the junctions of the handles and blades rest naturally on the shoulders. The right distance apart to lash the two paddles to the thwarts is soon learned by experience. To pad the shoulders the carrier usually drapes an extra shirt, shawl fashion, over his neck, or wears his mackinaw coat. Special padded yokes are also provided by city outfitters for portaging, but to experienced men these are merely an added item, useless for any other purpose, as the paddles answer perfectly.

A canoe presses straight down on the top of one's shoulders, and therefore it is easier, in a way, to portage then a back pack of equal weight. But one should never attempt to take a canoe on the first trip over a strange portage. The first man over should carry a light pack and the ax so that he can do any clearing that is necessary to allow the easy passage of the canoe. In portaging a canoe the view of the trail ahead is restricted to about 30 feet, so one should be familiar with the portage in advance. Some skill and strength are necessary to get a canoe on and off one's shoulders unaided. For the average sportsman, it is usually best first to turn the

PLATE III. The End of the Portage—bed roll with tump line attached.

canoe over; then one man lifts the bow high, while the carrier gets under it, places his head and neck between the paddles, and stands erect. At the end of the portage it is taken off and lowered by reverse procedure.

Because of the portaging, all baggage, outfit, and foods should be packed in packsacks with shoulder straps, or in bundles, bed rolls, or duffle bags of such form that they can be conveniently carried with a tump line. These packs and bundles should not be too heavy to be carried by one man, for beginners not over 60 to 75 pounds each. If two men can get all their outfit in two packsacks and one bed roll with tump line, then it means only two trips for each man across the portage. On the first trip the two packsacks are taken over, and on the next trip one man takes the bed roll and the other the canoe.

Throughout all of northeastern United States and Canada, where canoeing with portaging has been done for many generations, the preferred type of packsack is that known as the Northwester, Duluth, Woods, or Porier, as shown in the section on "Back Packing." It consists of a waterproof canvas sack about 22 inches high, 16 inches wide, and 6 to 8 inches deep. Wide leather shoulder-straps are secured to the center of the top and the bottom corners. A tump line is also usually secured to the top of the sack. When the tump line is used in addition to the shoulder-straps it eases the pull on the shoulders, and also results in the top of the sack forming a sort of shelf on which additional articles in the form of duffle bags or even boxes can be perched and carried on top, the whole balancing well so that these top loads do not fall off.

A tump line is a band of soft leather about 2½ inches wide and 18 inches long to the ends of which are secured leather thongs or ropes about 9 feet long. The band goes over the forehead, centering about the hair line, and the thong or rope is so tied around the roll, bundle, or box to be carried that it rests on the middle of the back, rather sagging down on top of the hips. The weight is thus borne by the head and muscles of the neck, the hips steadying it. The northern Indians and voyagers, "born to the tump line," can carry unbelievable weights with it. Records of 400 to 500 pounds taken across several miles of portage without a rest have been recorded. But the average sportsman will find the tump line an exquisite form of torture at first, and he had better confine his portaging to the packsack with a loading not to exceed 60 pounds at the start. Stand the packsack straight up on the gorund, sit down back to it, place the arms through the shoulder-straps and settle them on the shoulders; then turn over onto the knees and stand up. If the sleeping bag and air mattress in their duffle bag do not weigh over 30 pounds, then it is easy, when the lightest packsack with its tump line are in place on the shoulders, to lift up the roll, carry it over the head and settle it on top of the packsack, and take the two across together.

A regular routine makes everything go smoother, faster, and with less labor on a day's canoe journey and the attending camping. Arriving at the selected camp site for the night, both men unload the canoe, carry it up on the shore, and turn it over. The site for the tent and campfire are then selected, the ground cleared and smoothed, and the packs are carried up, both men working together. The cook then gathers wood, unpacks the cook packsack, gets water, and starts the fire and the cooking. The other man puts up the tent, makes the beds, and gets everything shipshape about camp. Then he gathers firewood for the evening and next morning. Kindling wood and shavings (or birch bark) for starting next morning's fire are always prepared the night before, and stowed in the tent where they will not get wet in case of rain. In the morning a reversal of the procedure and division of labor follows, and last thing of all a good look is taken all around to see that none of the precious outfit is being left behind, *and then the campfire is drenched, put absolutely out, so that not even a trace of smoke remains.* In packing the canoe in the morning a teakettle, a lunch, and the ax are tucked in conveniently, and the sportsmen usually land about noon, have lunch, and "bile the kittle." In traversing a strange country it is best to stop at the first good camp site one sees after 3 P.M. so as to have plenty of time to make a comfortable camp and get a good supper before dark.

**Canoe Hunting.** In most country that one enters by canoe for hunting, the game will be deer and moose. In September and early in October, these will usually be found early in the morning and late in the afternoon feeding on pond lilies and water grasses along the shallow shores and in the little bays and swamps, while in the middle of the day they go back in the hills and forests. Thus there is little hunting luck from the canoe in the middle of the day. When traveling every day, and hunting while going along, an entirely different routine is a decided advantage. Most of the combined traveling and hunting should be between first dawn and 8 A.M., and between 4 P.M. and twilight. In clear weather no attempt is made to make a regular camp at night. Instead, only beds are made on the shore. When it gets too dark to see rifle sights, the hunters go ashore, make their beds, boil a kettle of tea and have a sandwich and turn in. They arise at the first streak of dawn (an alarm clock is handy), roll up and load their beds, and start off in the canoe traveling and hunting as they go. About 8 A.M., when the sun strikes the shores, they land, get a good breakfast, clean up, have a nap, followed by a good dinner about 3 P.M., and then start off again on their journey and hunt. This gives them six hours a day of canoeing at the time when game is most likely to be seen.

In hunting with the canoe during the early season when big game feeds along the rivers and lake shores, the hunters should start from camp very early so as to be on good hunting ground by the time it gets light enough to see rifle sights, and should hunt carefully until about 8 A.M. or possibly 9 A.M. on cloudy days. Then they might as well lay off until 4 P.M., as it is hardly likely that they will see any game in the heat of the day unless mosquitoes and black flies are unusually bad, forcing the game to water to escape them.

They should plan the direction of their hunting, so far as possible, so that they will approach the probable feeding localities of game up-wind or

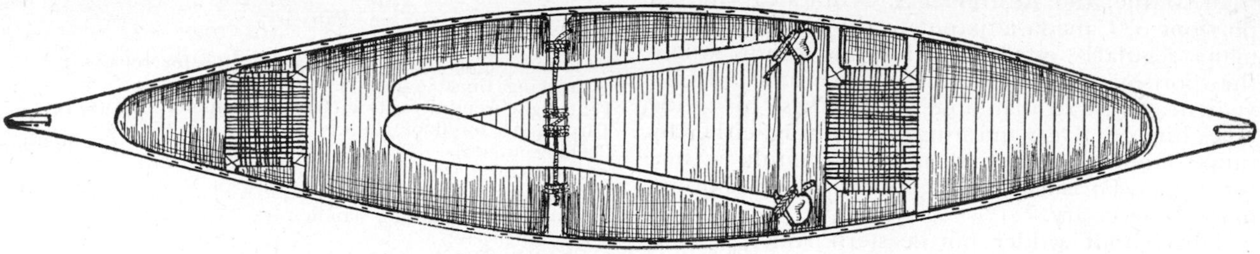

PLATE IV. Method of Lashing Paddles for Carrying Canoe on Shoulders.

across the wind, to avoid giving their scent to game. Of course there will be places where they have to travel with the wind, which under most favorable (or unfavorable) conditions can carry man scent to game for about a mile. On such courses they will hardly ever see game because their scent has alarmed it before they come in sight, and they can therefore paddle over such courses fast and without trying to avoid noise.

On stretches where wind and feeding conditions are favorable, the hunters should paddle slowly and noiselessly, and avoid talking above a whisper, keeping a sharp lookout. Where a long stretch of shore comes into view, or where a point of land is rounded and a view is offered into a deep bay, the shores should be carefully searched with binoculars. Often it pays to poke the bow of the canoe ashore so the binoculars can be held steady for such examination. Do not expect always to see game standing in full view on the shore. An occasional move of antlers or ears above a sea of grass, a brown or black movement of hide in the shadowed edge of the forest, or even the withers only of a moose, about the size of a muskrat, sticking up among lilies or grass, may be the first and only indication of game; or the hunter may hear the "slosh, slosh" of an animal walking through water or swamp.

When game is sighted, plan the stalk in the canoe. If possible skirt the edge of the shore out of sight of the game to as close as cover continues. At any rate, try to approach so that from the game's viewpoint, the canoe will appear against a forest or shore background, and thus not be so easily seen by the game. The bow man keeps his eyes on the game, and the stern man paddles noiselessly, not taking the point of his blade out of water, and paddling on the side of the canoe away from the game.

How close one can get in the canoe without disturbing the game depends upon circumstances. Sometimes a point of land jutting out or long water grass will form a screen which will allow a very close approach, close enough for the shot. At other times it may be necessary to land and make the stalk through the woods fringing the shore, and this perhaps in some circumstances for as long as half a mile.

A canoe is a very unsteady platform from which to shoot, even in absolutely calm weather with the rear paddler holding the craft as steady as possible. Sometimes it is possible to edge the canoe against the shore, a log, or a rock, or to push it into thick water grass or boggy swamp to hold it steady for the shot. But generally speaking, accuracy is a problem when shooting from a canoe at a greater distance than 50 or 75 yards—too much tremble. Always, if possible, it pays to step ashore for the shot. Take advantage of everything that can add to the steadiness of the rifle.

When an animal is killed in water over 2 feet deep it is usually necessary to tow the beast ashore or into shallows for butchering. The canoe must be up against the shore before attempting to load the head or quarter of a moose into it. These may weigh 200 pounds each, and getting them in and balanced in the canoe is a job for a strong man.

Then there is the matter of moose calling, the hunter imitating the call of the cow moose during the rutting season, which usually extends from about the first week in September to the first week in October. Calling, like water hunting, is done early in the morning and late in the afternoon, and in calm weather only. Taking up a position close to good feeding ground, where there is an extended view, and where the game must approach up-wind so as not to scent the hunter, the hunter calls at short intervals until a bull is heard to answer. Then the enticing of the bull to come to the call takes a lot of skill and experience. The bull may eventually come in sight anywhere along the shore. If close, it may be shot from where the caller sits; or it may have to be stalked from a distance. The shooting of game after dark with a light is illegal almost everywhere.

Later in the season, when nightly frosts begin and mosquitoes cease, game no longer comes down to feed at the water's edge, and must be still hunted back in the woods and hills. Then the hunters lay off from traveling for several days and woods-hunt at promising localities.

Throughout the northwest, in British Columbia, Yukon, and Alaska there are large rivers extending sometimes hundreds of miles back into splendid and almost virgin mountain hunting country. Most of these rivers can be ascended a long way, almost to their source, in canoes. Along them there is little game except an occasional moose, or bear when the salmon are running up to spawn. In these areas the hunters ascend the rivers by canoe, usually with the assistance of an outboard motor, until opposite or close to good hunting country, and from there the outfit—light bedding, featherweight tents, and food—is back packed for 10 to 20 miles into the mountain habitat of sheep, goat, caribou, moose, and grizzly. The food to be packed in can usually be kept to a minimum, as the country will afford an ample supply of fresh meat. Such a long trip is really an expedition, to be planned long in advance, and to be undertaken only by experienced and strong hunters.

In Maine, the Adirondacks, Minnesota, and in portions of Canada adjacent to the roads there are many regularly established hunting camps where the sportsman has almost all the comforts and conveniences of a regular hotel. From these his guide takes him out every morning for hunting, either by canoe or afoot, and he returns every evening in time for supper. For such hunting, of course, no camping outfit is necessary.

Throughout wilder northeastern America it is usually customary for the sportsman to employ a guide who also acts as cook. The guide or outfitter supplies the canoe, tent, cooking utensils, and food, making a per-diem charge for the lot. The sportsman supplies his bedding, personal effects, rifle, ammunition, fishing tackle, and license. The guide paddles in the stern of the canoe, and the sportsman in the bow. The sportsman helps to carry the lighter packs across portages, and assists in all the other work according to his physical capability and skill. A good sport takes pride in doing his full half of all the work, and in doing it well. He is never ashamed to ask his guide to show him how. All financial and other arrangements are made in advance, and thereafter the relationship of sportsman and guide should be as though they were two good friends. There is no surer way to spoil a trip than for the sportsman to treat his guide as a servant.

On long expeditions, particularly into the mountain country of the northwest, the sportsman will usually require two men, one as guide and one as cook, both to act also as packers. Usually a 20-foot canoe with outboard motor is taken as there are few portages, the trip being commonly ten days or more of motoring, poling, and tracking up swift rivers, and then several days of packing into the mountains.

**Check Lists.** The following check lists of essential equipment and supplies are divided in two parts. The *camp list* includes the outfit necessary for camping in the wilderness beyond sources of supply. The articles on this list are usually supplied by the guide or outfitter, but must be supplied by the sportsmen when they go without a guide. The *personal list* includes the articles worn and taken by each member of the party. The guide also will usually require most of these articles.

Superior figures (thus: [1]) refer to footnotes. Where an article is followed by a question mark it is to be regarded as not usually essential, but is included as a reminder, as under certain circumstances it may be desirable.

The lists have been formulated with a view to safety, comfort, and well-being in the canoe and in camp. Old-timers can dispense with many articles. Sportsmen should not overload themselves with unnecessary and heavy equipment, but "the less a man carries on his back the more he must carry in his head."

### Camp List

Canoe, of proper size and capacity.
- 2 paddles.
- Canvas, copper tacks, and marine glue for repairs.
- Tracking line, 50 feet (?).

Tent, light weight, easily erected. (See under "Tents.")
Tarp, light, for floor cloth.
Cooking utensils, in packsack or fiber box. (See "Camp Foods and Cooking Utensils.")
- 3 kettles to nest.
- 2 frying pans, folding handles.
- 1 mixing pan.
- 1 folding aluminum baker.
- 1 plate, cup, bowl, knife, fork, teaspoon, and tablespoon for each man.
- 1 large spoon.
- 1 butcher knife.
- 1 cream pitcher.
- 2 salt and pepper shakers.
- 1 can opener.
- 2 dish cloths.
- 1 dish mop.
- 1 cake turner.
- 1 cake kitchen soap (per week).

Ax, 3 lb., 28" handle, with sheath.
Mill file, 8-inch, and carborundum stone.
Flashlight or candle lantern [1]
Wash basin.
Cheesecloth meat safe.
Salt for curing hides, 10 lbs.
Matches in friction-top cans (3 boxes per week).
DDT bombs (?)
Food in packsacks (about 20 lbs. per man per week). (See under "Camp Foods.")

### Personal List

*Worn:* Felt hat, light wool underwear, blue denim pants,[2] belt, wool shirt, wool socks, leather-top rubbers or moosehide moccasins with moccasin rubbers, sun glasses,[3] binoculars. (See "Hunting Clothing.")

*Pockets:* Jackknife, watch, compass, handkerchief, waterproof match box, 5 cartridges, pipe, tobacco.

*Firearms:* Big-game rifle, .22 rifle (?), shotgun (?). (Featherweight rain and dew cover for each arm.)

*Rucksack:* Camera and films, exposure meter, skinning knife, cartridges, tape measure, matches in waterproof can, notebook, pencil, maps, warm gloves, fish line, hooks, sinkers, extra tobacco, hand ax (?). (See "Back Packing.")

*Packsack:* Containing personal effects as follows: Wool pants, wool shirt, wool undershirt, wool drawers, 3 pr. wool socks, light leather camp slippers, 2 handkerchiefs, small bath towel, toilet articles, toilet paper, repair kit, medicine kit, cleaning rod, oil, flannel cleaning patches, 20 rifle cartridges, cartridges for .22 rifle and shotgun (?), extra camera films, wool mitts, spectacles.[4]

*Sleeping Bag:* (See "Camp Bedding.") Air mattress, air pillow, pillow case.

*Loose:* Light water-repellent jacket or mackinaw coat, raincoat or poncho.[5]

---

[1] A 2-cell flashlight is suggested. Per hour of light its batteries do not bulk or weigh more than candles.

[2] Light pants on the assumption that weather will be warm at the start; the wool pants in packsack can be put on as it gets colder.

[3] If the sportsman requires spectacles to correct vision, at least two pair should be taken.

[4] Have small cotton bags to contain various kits, one for all underwear, one for toilet articles, slippers, repair kit, medicine kit, cleaning kit for rifle, camera films, etc.

[5] These may be needed during the day, hence are carried loose in the canoe.

# CLOTHING FOR HUNTERS

The complete redesign, on both scientific and practical lines, of all of the articles of uniform for our Army and Navy during World War II provides an excellent guide for the selection of clothing for hunters and outdoorsmen, for after all war is but hunting outdoors in all climates. Let us therefore first examine into the principles on which such ideal clothing was designed.

A man doing the relatively hard work of fighting or hunting perspires freely, and his clothing becomes more or less wet. Cotton garments are best for all hot and warm climates for they are coolest. But the perspiration which they absorb makes them so cold that they chill one as soon as perspiration ceases. Therefore when cotton is worn the hunter should have a rub-down and change to dry clothing as soon as he gets back to camp. This is not difficult in a warm climate. In an excessively hot climate perspiration does not cease, and such change is not so necessary. But if, during a day's hunting, one has occasion to stop for long in a wind, as to sit down on a lookout to watch for game, or to journey by canoe or motorboat on a windy lake, then cotton underwear would not be good.

For a cold or even only slightly cold climate the clothing should be wool throughout. Wool also gets wet from perspiration, but much of the water passes through it to be evaporated on the outside, and moreover wet wool does not feel cold and does not chill like wet cotton except when the wind is blowing strongly, in which case a thin, closely woven outside jacket of cotton may be needed to slip on as a windbreak. Wool is warm chiefly because of the insulating effect of the dead air contained. Two light wool garments are warmer than a heavy one of the same total weight because of the air contained between them.

In extremely cold weather it is very necessary to keep from perspiring as one would freeze very quickly in wet clothing as soon as strenuous exercise stopped. This is easily accomplished by shedding the layers of wool clothing as one begins to warm up, so as always to remain moderately cool. The garments removed can be stowed in the rucksack (see "Back Packing," p. 900) to be put on again when active exercise ceases and one begins to feel cold.

One article should *always* be of wool. Experience in the infantry, where men have to march long distances, has shown conclusively that socks should always be of wool to avoid sore and abraded feet—light wool socks for warm weather, heavy wool for cold.

**Footwear.** Let us begin from the ground up, with the footwear, because that is the most important. Crippled or frozen feet can bring a hunting trip to a sudden end. When one walks any considerable distance over rough ground his feet swell from the exercise of the foot muscles and the increased blood supply drawn to them. In an hour of such walking they will swell to just about one size longer and two sizes wider. If the shoe will not accommodate this enlarged foot, pinching, abrasions, blisters, and sore feet will result quite promptly. Therefore the hunter's shoe to be worn with light wool socks should be one size longer and two sizes wider than the shoe he properly wears in the city. For heavy wool socks they should be still larger. Shoes made on the Munson Army last are anatomically correct for practically all young men, can be had from almost all dealers of sporting shoes, and are the style that should almost always be chosen. When the Munson last was adopted by the Army in 1911, with proper regulations for fitting, and wool socks were made compulsory, most foot troubles ceased at once.

Weight on the feet will tire one quicker than the same weight carried anywhere else. There is no sense whatever in high-topped boots. Their extra weight tires, the tops sag down and, wrinkling, press on and cause a very painful inflammation of the Achilles tendon on long walks. Shoes should be not less than 6 inches or over 7 inches high.

For upland bird shooting and for tropical or desert hunting the Army and Navy marching shoe, of heavy leather, unlined, rough side of the leather outside, and with a composition or rubber sole, is ideal. So are the slightly more expensive sportsmen's shoes of oil-tanned leather and similar soles made on the Army last.

For autumn big-game hunting in northern countries where one is likely to encounter snow, and much marshy and boggy ground, and yet wants to be shod noiselessly, rubber hunting shoes with corrugated soles and leather uppers are best. The rubber will keep one's feet dry from outside water. No leather shoe is entirely waterproof, as water will leak in at the seams as soon as the grease rubbed into these seams wears off. These rubber hunting shoes should always be worn with felt insoles and heavy wool socks, and extra insoles and socks should be in camp drying. Insoles and socks will get damp from perspiration, but usually not inconveniently so during the day. There are a few men, however, who cannot wear rubber shoes as they gall and scald the feet. For these the bird hunter's shoe mentioned above is best—large enough to be worn with heavy wool socks.

Leather-topped rubbers with insoles and two pairs of heavy socks will keep one's feet warm while walking down to 20° below zero, at which temperature rubber freezes stiff and is no longer practical. Rubber soles can also be worn with snowshoes, while leather shoes cannot. For extreme cold, where naturally there is no water or dampness, Indian tanned moosehide moccasins with three pairs of wool socks are best, but these can be procured only at the trading posts in northern Indian country.

For the high, steep, often snow and ice-covered mountains of the Northwest—sheep, goat, and grizzly hunting in the fall—there is only one kind of footwear that will insure against dangerous slipping and falls: alpine boots. These are simply oil-tanned leather shoes with rather stiff counters, 7 inches high, studded sparsely in the centers of soles and heels with cone-headed hobnails, and every inch around the extreme edge of soles and heels with Swiss edging hobnails. The soles must be of oak-tanned leather, as only this will hold the nails. These shoes should be large enough to wear with insoles, as otherwise the nails would conduct the cold to the feet. It is usually a mistake to wear more than one pair of heavy wool socks with leather shoes, as the socks may wrinkle inside and cause rubbing and blisters.

Always back in camp there should be an easy pair of slippers to don when returning after a day's hiking. These had best be moccasin style and oiled leather, as the ground around camp may be damp.

All leather footwear should have boot grease rubbed in thoroughly every four or five days. Have the shoes dry and warm them slightly before using it. *Never* dry shoes close to a hot fire; just place them where they will remain comfortably warm to the hand.

D. T. Abercrombie, N. Y.

PLATE I. The favorite type of hunting and game coat, now made in light-weight, briarproof, windproof material.

In the North in the late fall the hunter may have to wear snowshoes with his leather-topped rubbers or moccasins. For general use the conventional pattern with slightly upturned toes are best, but for very thick brush and heavily wooded country the type known as "bear paw" should be taken. Snowshoes are usually made in three sizes; hunters weighing 150 pounds or less should use the medium size, big men the largest. Much has been written to the effect that the lacing should be of caribou-hide babiche, unprocurable except from Indians in the remote northern wilderness. Recently our Arctic explorers have found that snowshoes made by several makers in the State of Maine are much superior to all others, including the Indian-made ones. These makers also provide the best foot-harness to wear with them. (See p. 1011.)

We have left the duck hunter to the last because his is a special case. He does not have any long-distance walking to do, but he hunts in or close to swamps or swampy shores, and often he has to wade to put out his decoys, or to retrieve birds or decoys. This calls for hip-topped rubber boots with heavy, roughly corrugated soles, and large enough to be worn with felt insoles and heavy wool stockings.

**Garments.** The hunter in warm or tropical countries, the bird shooter, or the big game hunter in the desert country of Arizona and Mexico, should wear cotton clothing—cotton underwear and khaki trousers. The day of the knee-constricting riding breeches is past. Long trousers are much more comfortable, and much easier to walk and climb in, but they should be three inches shorter than city trousers, have no cuffs at the bottom, and not be baggy. In lieu of khaki, blue denim work pants are very good. In a country with many briars canvas leggings and even briar (snag) proof pants furnished by some city outfitters may be desirable. Either a khaki or light flannel shirt may be worn as desired. The bird shooter usually wears a hunting coat of khaki, duxback, or light canvas, with many pockets, including a large game pocket in the rear. In very hot weather this coat may be worn immediately over the undershirt. In cooler weather a khaki shirt, or in colder climates one or more woolen shirts, may be worn under it. For the bird hunter the hunting coat takes the place of the rucksack, and in its large pockets he carries his supply of shells.

The desert and plains hunter of big game will dispense with the coat and will wear either a khaki or a wool flannel shirt. He should also have a rucksack in which, among other daily necessities, he will carry a canteen of water. If he wears a khaki shirt he should carry a flannel shirt in his rucksack, for most desert country gets very cold as soon as the sun goes down.

The least comfortable and most handicapping places to carry anything are on the belt or by straps across the shoulders. If anything is carried on the belt, limit it to a little leather pouch carrying five extra cartridges and the case of the binoculars. Any greater weight restricts the circulation at the worst place. The place for lunch, cameras, extra cartridges, skinning knife, etc., is in the rucksack.

The hunter of big game in colder regions often makes the mistake of wearing extremely heavy clothing. Except for the canoe hunter whose guide does all the paddling, or for the late fall duck hunter who does not stir around much, this is always a mistake. Very heavy garments, such as mackinaws, etc., induce profuse perspiration, reduce one's energy, and make him cold when he stops. Very heavy trousers will gall between the legs on a long hike. Sensible clothing consists of light or medium-weight wool underwear, wool trousers of about the same weight one would wear in the city in winter, and a medium-weight wool shirt. This is enough for any man when actively hunting on foot in temperatures above zero. In the rucksack there should be carried another wool shirt, and perhaps a light cravenetted cotton wind-breaking jacket. The shirt can be donned when one stops, or when the single shirt is not warm enough; the jacket is called for in rain, snow, or strong wind. In early morning when leaving camp the hunter may need two shirts, but one usually can be taken off after the first mile, not to be put on again until he halts for lunch or for the thorough glassing of a large stretch of country.

**Gloves.** Gloves may also be a necessity—large, heavy, lined ones for medium cold, woolen gloves covered with roomy leather mittens for extreme cold. A more practical scheme than one-finger mitts is to tie one's mitts together by a long thong that goes over the shoulders behind the neck. In case of a sudden shot at game presenting itself, jerk off the right mitt with the teeth. It is not lost because of the thong. In extreme cold, however, it may be necessary to take the shot in the wool gloves, for the skin of the bare hand might freeze instantly to the metal parts of the rifle.

**Safety Precautions.** In any country that is much frequented by big-game hunters, in practically all of the United States, everywhere except in extremely remote wilderness, all of the hunter's clothing (except possibly trousers) should be red—red shirt, red coat, red cap, and a red back on the rucksack. The pocket handkerchief should not be white. This is very necessary in order not to be mistaken for game by other hunters, and in some states red clothing is compulsory by law. If the rucksack, as usual, is of drab canvas, one can baste a red bandana handkerchief over it.

**Raincoats.** In hunting on foot in the rain, which is often the best time for still hunting, it is usually best to just take it. It takes a heavy rain to wet one through when wearing wool clothing, and anyhow wet wool feels warm. Getting wet will do no harm if one keeps moving. If a raincoat were worn when actively hunting on foot the hunter would soon be soaking wet from perspiration as well as very uncomfortably warm. But for riding horseback, for traveling or hunting by canoe, or for duck hunting, a raincoat that will cover one down to below the knees may be very desirable. The raincoat for use on horseback with a slit down the back of the skirt, is called a "pommel slicker," and is habitually carried rolled up and tied on the saddle. Featherweight raincoats weighing only a few ounces may be obtained and can be carried in the rucksack.

**Parka.** In extreme cold, avoid heavy perspiration at all costs, because if the clothing gets wet one may freeze to death in a few minutes if he stops. When climbing mountains or running with a dog team, if necessary strip naked to the waist, placing the shirts in the rucksack. These dry shirts can be donned when one slows up or stops. Also avoid getting wet from snow. Sometimes it is desirable to wear an ordinary pair of blue denim overalls over the wool trousers to keep the snow from melting on them and in the socks above the moccasins. The Arctic and sub-Arctic hunter also carries a parka instead of the light wind-breaker jacket advised above. A parka is simply a light but rather tightly woven cotton or khaki garment, *not waterproof,* like an old-fashioned nightshirt, reaching to the knees, *with no opening in front,* being put on over the head. It should have a hood which may be edged with fur, preferably wolverine fur, but this hood should not come further forward than just in front of the ears. If the face or chin were partly covered, the congealing breath would soon cover the entire face with a sheet of ice. For the same reason one should keep clean shaven. The parka is worn only in extreme cold, or when one stops hard exercise, or in a strong wind. The hunter wearing medium-weight wool underwear, wool trousers with denim trousers over them, and two wool flannel shirts, and with a parka over all, will be warm and comfortable in any temperature he would be likely to be outdoors in, down even to 50° below zero.

The armholes of the parka, where the sleeve joins the body, should be extremely large. Then if the hands get so cold that there is danger of their freezing, the whole arm can be withdrawn inside the parka, and the hand can be warmed by thrusting it inside the shirts against the naked breast. If the nose or cheek freezes, as they may frequently in a wind—freezing is discovered by making faces and noticing a hard lump—similarly withdraw the arm inside the parka and, thrusting the warm hand up through the neck, massage the part until it thaws out. As the hand becomes cold in the process, place it against the breast to warm up, then repeat. NEVER *try to thaw out any part of the body by rubbing snow on it;* this is a perfectly idiotic theory long since exploded, one which would cause prompt freezing.

**Washing.** A cake of soap weighs and bulks less than a suit of underwear. It may be desirable to wash socks and wool underwear in camp. Wash in lukewarm, never hot, water, using Ivory or toilet soap; rinse in clear lukewarm water; press out the surplus water, but do not wring out; and hang up to dry.

**Headgear.** We started off from the ground up. Let us now end with the headwear. The essentials are that it should shade the eyes, should offer protection from hot sun, and should if necessary, shelter the face and back of the neck from rain or snow. All of this is best accomplished by a rather broad-brimmed felt hat of good quality. Sometimes a broad-brimmed hat may be objectionable in forest country because it is so often knocked off by branches. In that case a cap with a good visor may be worn. Some caps are reversible, drab on one side and red on the other for deer hunting. Others, of wool, have ear-tabs for cold weather or for wearing under the hood of the parka. Leather or fur caps are entirely too warm, and send a continuous flow of perspiration down over the face, but fur ear-tabs are desirable in extreme cold. Englishmen and Germans insist that a helmet is necessary in the tropics to avoid sunstroke. Fifty years experience of our Army in the tropics has not borne this out, a broad-brimmed felt hat being all the sun protection necessary. Neither have we found orange-colored spine pads or flannel belly bands of any advantage. In the more northern parts of North America in the early summer mosquito head nets, gauntlet gloves, and a rather tightly woven cotton coat are absolutely necessary protection from the vast swarms of mosquitoes that will bite through even a rather heavy flannel shirt.

D. T. Abercrombie, N. Y.

PLATE II. The Light Parka.

# COMPASS AND MAPS IN HUNTING

Every hunter visiting unfamiliar wilderness country should carry a compass and a map of the region surrounding his cabin or camp. Properly used, they can keep him from being lost while stalking or pursuing game and thus avoid the privation or real disaster which is sometimes the penalty for getting confused over direction. Besides this important function, they will help keep appointments to meet guide or companions at prearranged places and to find game killed and hung in the woods while the shooter goes back to camp for aid in packing it in. Under many circumstances these pathfinding tools are as necessary as gun and ammunition to enjoy successful safe hunting.

Many models of compasses are available and knowledge of their specifications is needed to help the hunter choose one suitable for his purpose. Size is an important distinction. Sizes vary from the small "pocket" instruments with one-inch dials to the large engineering types fitted with faces twice as wide and with special sighting devices which are invaluable to lay off true courses and follow them precisely.

A small pocket compass can be selected when it is only necessary to know the general direction. If the hunter has sound knowledge which way his destination lies and merely must distinguish north from east or west, small compasses will suffice. Fine work, however, is difficult with them and they are not advised to run long accurate lines, take bearings from maps, or to make necessary allowance for the natural declination of the needle.

Pocket compasses use two different means to indicate direction, a revolving needle that swings above a printed stationary dial, and a revolving dial which replaces the needle and turns as the body of the compass is moved. The latter is fast to use because the instrument need not be adjusted to bring needle and "north" in line. No confusion can exist either over which point of a movable dial indicates north, because it is plainly lettered. Movable-dial models should be supplied with a sighting line if the user plans to take bearings or make declination allowances with them.

The bigger engineering-type compasses with wide dials and sights or sighting lines are recommended for exacting service and for working in conjunction with maps. This type should also be chosen if the hunter intends to map and sketch the country in which he shoots. Less skill is required to use large compasses and the results obtained are more accurate. The needle in some of these instruments is surrounded by a dampening fluid which blocks the fast oscillation present in dry-dial types. Liquid compasses are quickly put in use and their pivot bearing has long life. The liquid also acts to cushion needle and bearing against shock.

All compasses except the liquid-filled type need a brake to lock the needle when not in actual service. Otherwise the jeweled bearing wears loose.

A compass dial is divided into 360 degrees called "azimuth directions" and numbered consecutively in a clockwise direction. The letter *N* designating north is placed at numbers 0 and 360 ("0" is not shown) which occupy the same position. Thus the direction of south falls at 180 degrees, west at 270, and east at 90. A degree-numbered dial is necessary for safe, accurate pathfinding. Compasses with dials marked with just the eight main directions are practical for only the very roughest work.

Hunters use three main types of maps for finding their way through wilderness country; regular printed, homemade, and mental. Printed maps can be secured from the sources listed below. Homemade maps are drawn on the scene by the hunter himself from data secured by observation and measurements or from the knowledge of his companions or guide. Mental maps are merely memories of the direction and approximate distance of the turns made during the day's travel.

Woodsmen with extensive experience can keep these details orderly filed inside their minds and when it is necessary to backtrack, can call the turns with amazing accuracy. This ability forms what some call a "homing" or "direction" instinct, though it is actually nothing of the kind. Hunters with less woods experience will be safer from getting lost if they rely on compass and printed or self-made maps instead of memory.

Among printed maps, the topographic sheets sold for about 15 cents each by the Geological Survey, Washington, D. C., are most popular with hunters. These maps are approximately 16½ by 20 inches and are drawn to scales varying from ½ to 2 inches to each mile, depending upon the character of the country charted. Topographic maps are very accurate and present a wealth of detail. Bodies of water are printed in blue, man-made works like towns, cities, roads, railroads, and boundaries in black, and features of relief (hills, mountains, and valleys) are indicated by brown contour lines. After some experience in reading contours, a hunter can quickly determine from his map the height of elevated spots and the steepness of their slopes.

To order topographic maps first write for the free index of the state (including Alaska and Hawaii) in which you are interested. This index lists the quadrangles available. Canadian topographic maps are equally useful and can be obtained from Surveys and Engineering Branch, Department of Mines and Resources, Ottawa, Canada. Before ordering write for the key price list showing sections covered.

The U. S. Forest Service, Department of Agriculture, Washington, 25, D. C., publishes maps of many of the lake and forest regions which may be obtained from the above address or from Regional Headquarters. With these, a key map is available which indicates areas covered and gives regional addresses. The conservation departments of some states also issue maps, particularly of the hunting and canoe-cruising country inside their boundaries. It is wise to obtain as many different maps of the same region as possible. Prices are low, and one chart might show useful details not carried by the rest.

The top of standard maps is usually north. When it is not, the map carries a compass rosette or arrow indicating that direction. Large maps are easier to handle in camp and on trails if cut into pocket-sized rectangles which are then pasted in proper order on muslin. Map sections should be spaced about one-eighth inch apart so the cloth between acts as a hinge and permits folding without creasing any of the print. Map faces can be protected from rain with a coat of transparent varnish. Note, however, that this prevents the hunter from marking his trail or making notes on them as he travels.

Hunters should carry their maps and not leave them at camp, because they have many uses afield. For instance, bearings can be taken from a map which give the true course to walk in order to reach any place listed upon it. A map shows the direction in which rivers and mountain ridges or valleys run, valuable help when one has lost himself. Contour lines of topographic sheets warn of steep hills or ravines ahead and also show how the hunter can detour around them if he likes. And when one has finally killed game after a 6-mile tramp, the map may disclose a short cut home which saves much tedious packing.

The first lesson in compass use is to know which end of its needle points north. This may sound unnecessary, but the fact remains that hunters have, in the sudden panic of realizing they were lost, forgotten this important fact or have refused to trust their memory of it. The north end of most compass needles is colored red or blue or is shaped like an arrowhead to distinguish it from the other end that bears south. If a different marking exists to puzzle the hunter, he can test the needle on objects about his home whose true direction is known. Then the data can be scratched on the bottom of the instrument or, if it is the hunting-case watch type, written on paper pasted to the inside of the compass cover.

When using a compass its dial must be held horizontal or the needle may bind and register untrue. The instrument must be kept away from metal objects—several feet from a gun, ax, or knife, much farther from metal bridge girders or railroad rails. Merely holding a compass against one's belt buckle can distort its action. Hidden bodies of certain ores act similarly, and when one of these is believed to lie close, the hunter should move to a different position for his bearing.

A simple and common function of the compass occurs when the hunter decides to hunt game in some general direction away from camp. For instance, he elects to stalk deer in a range of hills about 2 miles distant. A sight over the compass shows that their direction is southwest. When he has finished hunting there, he knows he must travel northeast to return. This direction is determined by compass and checked at intervals along the way.

Variations of this practice are encountered at times and must be solved by the hunter. For example, if after reaching the hills lying southwest from camp, he turns to the right and walks in that direction for several miles, the chances are that he will then be almost straight west from home and must travel east in order to arrive. This illustrates why some attention should be given to the angles of the turns made while hunting.

While the above type of direction finding is not exceedingly accurate, it is usually sufficient when the hunter has walked only a few miles away, because it will bring him close enough home to recognize landmarks about it that point the exact way in. The same procedure can be used when camps are situated on base lines like rivers, roads, or railroads. When the shooter hunts north of this base line, he knows that as long as he does not cross it again he should turn back south to return.

A problem may arise when the hunter finds his way back by compass to some base line. Then he may not know whether to turn right or left along it. To prevent this confusion, many hunters take exploring trips in both directions from camp over the base as soon as they arrive. On these trips they either map or memorize distinctive landmarks, such as waterfalls, bridges, windfalls, bends, etc., and their position in relation to camp, or they make blazes every 200 or 300 yards along the line. Blazes are cut so one glance shows the puzzled person which way lies home.

Either tree or brush blazes serve. The tree blaze is made by slicing a piece of bark from the side of the trunk facing the direction to camp. Some woodsmen cut two blazes because it is easy to remember that *two* point *to*ward home. Brush blazes can be employed in regions without trees or where it is illegal to chop into them. The stem of a bush is cut almost through and the top bent over until it touches the ground and points toward camp.

In rugged wilderness country, or wherever the hunter is apt to tramp more than 2 or 3 miles from camp, it is scarcely enough to merely know the general direction he has come. Now it is safer to record the directions of the main turns made and their approximate length. To do this, the compass must be freely consulted. For example, a hunter strikes out north from his base. After a mile he swings northeast to follow a ravine. When the ravine ends, he turns east, climbs the right-hand ridge, and drops into a

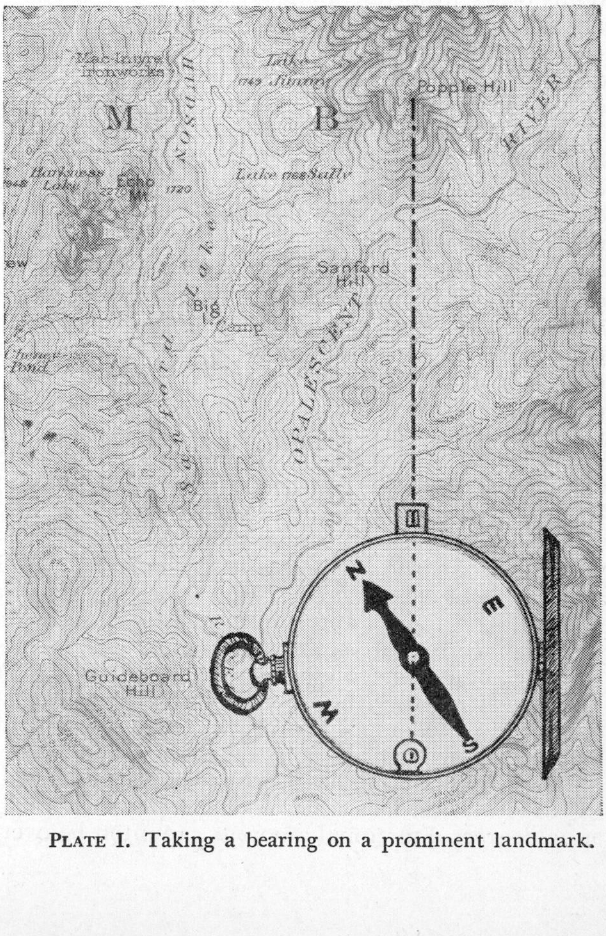


**PLATE I.** Taking a bearing on a prominent landmark.

little valley below. Another turn is made farther ahead to miss the edge of a swamp.

If the hunter notes the azimuth bearing of each turn with his compass and measures its approximate distance by consulting his watch (measuring distance in minutes is easier and just as practical as counting paces) he can always know his approximate position in relation to camp. And he will know how to proceed when he wants to return. As stated before, an experienced woodsman will often memorize these details, but hunters who visit wilderness country for only a few days each season should record them in a notebook or on a map.

A popular use of the compass consists of roughly surveying the ground about the hunting camp and making a map from the data. For instance, a flat-topped hill is visible some 2 miles away. The hunter levels his compass (in some northern latitudes it may be necessary to tilt the dial slightly to prevent the needle from sticking on account of magnetic dip) and points its sighting line at the hill. The dial (if movable) is turned until its letter *N* and the north end of the needle coincide. The hunter notes that the sighting line falls across the azimuth degree figure 225. This means the hill lies at a bearing of 225 degrees, which is southwest.

This fact is recorded on the homemade map. Then the hunter knows that should he ever become confused about direction when this hill is visible, a straight northeast course from it will take him home. If several visible landmarks lying in different directions can be charted on the home-prepared map, it will have real value as insurance against being lost in that region.

When taking bearings with compasses without sights or sighting line and which may also not possess a movable dial (meaning a dial which turns separately from the base), the hunter sights across the face of the instrument through its center to check which degree figure points at the object being mapped. For extreme accuracy the compass should be laid on the level top of a stump, log, or rock. The user then steps 2 feet away, so that any small metal object in his pocket will not affect the needle, and reads the direction.

So far no mention has been made of the natural declination of compass needles because no allowance for this factor is necessary when hunters draw their own maps or when they take bearings on natural objects like trees, hills, rocks, lakes, etc., and follow courses to or from them. But when printed maps are used, this allowance is important if it exists in any appreciable amount. Declination occurs because the compass needle points toward the magnetic pole instead of toward true north (the north pole). In only a few spots do these directions coincide.

Places where the needle points both magnetic and true north lie on a crooked line connecting a point above Lake Superior and running southeast near the southeast corner of Georgia. At points east of this line the compass needle bears west of true north, at points west of the line it bears east of true north. Because printed maps are drawn to conform with true north, declination must be compensated for to obtain absolute accuracy. Declination varies according to location from a fraction of a degree to as much as 22 degrees. Fractional amounts can often be overlooked in practical pathfinding, but one or more degrees should be compensated for to avoid following an inaccurate course.

Printed maps usually carry a note telling the amount of declination present in their area. The Government issues a chart periodically that shows these amounts in the different sections. A copy can be obtained by sending 20 cents (not postage stamps) to the Government Printing Office, Washington, D. C. Ask for latest "Map of the Compass Declination in the U. S."

A west declination requires correction toward the east, east declination requires correction toward the west. Correction can be made by adding or subtracting the declination in degrees to the regular compass dial reading. If the bearing course reads 105 degrees and 5 more must be added to correct, the true line of travel will fall over the 110-degree figure. Correction can also be made by twisting the map underneath the compass without moving the latter. The map is first placed so that its meridians run north and south by compass. The compass is laid with its center covering the hunter's position and the map is twisted clockwise to add declination, counterclockwise to subtract it. This puts the map in line with true north and accurate bearings can be taken from it in any direction.

The question of when to add and when to subtract declination depends on the problem at hand. When working from terrain to map, as when locating one's position on the map by sighting on physical objects actually visible to the eye and which are also shown on the map, then eastern declination is added and western subtracted. On the other hand, when the hunter has picked out some spot on the map to which he will walk, he reverses the above, and subtracts eastern and adds western declination to the compass-dial reading.

Detailed instructions for handling this factor are sometimes provided with high-grade compasses. Hunters lacking them should write the rules as given on a margin of their maps.

Hunters can locate their position or the position of their camp on a printed map if they can see two or more objects (mountains, towers, lake ends, etc.) which can also be recognized and located on the map. Suppose such an object lies toward the east. The map is oriented so that its meridian lines lie true north and south. This means aligning them with the compass needle and then correcting for declination. An accurate bearing is taken on the object and transferred with pencil on the map so the line starts at the object and runs toward the hunter's position. A bearing is next made on a second landmark in a different direction and drawn on the map. The point where the two lines intersect is the approximate location of the hunter or his base.

Knowing where he stands, the hunter can easily walk off to chosen points on a map without becoming lost and without wasting time and strength. The map is oriented true north (some makes of compass are constructed so that this is not always necessary), the compass is moved until the north end of its needle and the letter *N* coincide, and a sight is made toward some landmark. Then, as long as needle and letter *N* are parallel, the sighting line of the compass points the way to travel.

To follow a straight compass bearing course the hunter may carry the instrument in his hand and refer to it constantly. Or he can sight ahead, pick out some object like a rock or tree that lies exactly on his course and walk to it. On arriving at the marker, he picks up a new one in the distance by consulting the compass. In timber one can walk straight ahead by keeping in line with two trees. Just before the first tree is reached, a new one farther on is sighted in to take its place.

Some compass models have special features—such as sights, adjustment pointers, and graduated bases for projecting courses and estimating mileage—which make their use easier and more accurate. Instructions that accompany these instruments should always be followed.

Barring an accident or misuse, a compass seldom goes inaccurate. Nevertheless, every hunter should check his compass before he leaves for the game fields. It can be tested with another or by bearings taken on familiar objects whose true direction is definitely known. The best test is a comparison with the large instrument used by surveyors and county engineers.

# DECOYS

Wildfowl decoys are an indispensable part of the wildfowler's equipment. Wherever ducks or geese are shot by the American sportsmen, decoys, locally called "stools" or "blocks," are generally used to lure birds within shotgun range. The one outstanding exception that should be noted is when the hunter is "pass" shooting. Formerly decoys were widely used for shorebirds such as yellow-legs, marlin, curlew, and plover; many of the old decoys still in existence prove that fact. To a lesser extent swan and blue heron were also brought within range of the hiding gunner by the use of decoys. The use of shorebird and swan decoys was confined almost entirely to those who shot for the market and not for sport.

When and where man first discovered that a replica of the species he was seeking helped him obtain his supply of food and feathers is unknown. Before the white man came to North America, the Indians had discovered and profited by the trusting and gregarious nature of many kinds of ducks. They made crude ducklike forms out of woven reeds and also placed the feathered skin of a duck over a birdlike form. That such crude decoys must have been effective is attested to by the fact that the Indian depended for success on a single arow.

Wooden decoys as they are known today were a part of the American sporting scene by 1850. Since then improvements have concerned themselves with making decoys lighter, more easily transported, or from materials that offer certain advantages. Decoys of cork, balsa wood, rubber, and other materials are available. The conventional models, generally made of cedar with white pine heads seem to hold their own, particularly with those users who gun day after day, such as the professional guide. Two reasons are generally given by the professional for his preference for wooden stools: (1) they suffer less when the novice sprays them with shot, and (2) they stand more general abuse.

The duck hunter must have clearly in mind the two broad classifications of ducks when using decoys. The diving ducks, such as bluebills or scaup, canvasbacks, redheads, and golden-eyes, decoy best to large rigs. As a general rule the more decoys properly used, the better the result. This is readily understandable since these ducks congregate in large numbers, called rafts, and are generally gunned on the larger bays and lakes.

On the other hand, the puddle ducks, such as the black duck, mallard, and pintail, find no particular attraction in mere numbers, and many successful puddle-duck gunners use only a dozen or so decoys. At the most, about 30 puddle-duck decoys are all that are ever necessary. There is an interesting but improbable theory that for mallards and black ducks an uneven number of stools will attract better than an even number, the reasoning being that the odd duck on the water is not paired up and presents an additional appeal. Whatever the logic, many shooters rig out seven or nine wooden blocks in front of the blind.

PLATE I. Early Indian Reed Decoy.

Goose decoys along the Atlantic seaboard, whether of canvas or wood, generally are used in conjunction with a rig of duck stools, the geese being grouped and placed to one side of the ducks. The continuance of this practice through the years speaks for its effectiveness. On the other hand, geese are hunted by goose specialists throughout the rest of our flyways who use only a rig of geese decoys. Some of the so-called goose decoys look weird and far-fetched to the human eye, but they prove reasonably efficient. The mud lumps used along the Mississippi to lure these birds are just one of the crude local methods in use.

How perfect and exact a replica is needed to lure fowl within shotgun range is a subject of never-ending controversy. At times the crudest possible imitations seem irresistible to the flying birds, and again a perfect rig fails to bring a single bird near the blind. So many factors influence every given situation that no one conclusive answer can be given. For instance, the perfect effect of a splendid set of stools may be ruined by an unnoticed tin or bottle glistening near the blind. Conversely, a poor set of stools may be so well arranged, the blind be so perfectly concealed, and the hunter be so skilled

PLATE II. Mud Decoy.

that a good day's hunting is the result. Thus in many cases decoys should receive neither the praise nor the blame for a day's sport or lack of it. Realize that any decoy should copy as closely as possible the live bird in color pattern, size, and appearance on the water; with those requirements met, your decoys will serve their general purpose. Further refinements—such as glass eyes, intricate carving, and color jobs that are painstaking in detail—probably give a greater feeling of confidence to the proud owner than to the passing waterfowl, who apparently are influenced by an over-all impression rather than minor details.

## DECOY CONSTRUCTION

**Wood.** The first consideration in the production of decoys is the availability of satisfactory wood. Balsa, which is coming into great favor today because of its extreme light weight and ease of working, can be obtained without difficulty, but those who are unable to obtain it locally and must order it from a distant point will find it practical to decide what size blocks are required and have the blocks sawed at the mill where it is purchased. Such cutting will add a bit to the final cost, but balsa shipped in plank form is easily split and damaged.

Balsa can be worked easily with a sharp knife or even a motor sander. It also has another advantage. Because of its porous quality it soaks up paint readily and results in a more natural dull finish. Balsa should have a waterproof-plywood base, 1/2 or 5/8 inch thick, fastened by a good waterproof glue rather than screws. The keel and weight may be fastened to this wooden base by screws. Some decoymakers eliminate the base by fastening the keel to the balsa with long dowels and glue.

The old-time decoy makers preferred cedar and cypress for their wooden decoys, and although some of these were made of solid blocks, the majority were hollowed out, both to reduce weight in handling and to insure the proper flotation of the decoy. Hollow decoys, however, should have at least 1/4 inch more of keel depth and about 30 per cent more lead to insure greater steadiness in rough water.

The diagrams showing the construction methods are self-explanatory. A good power bandsaw and a power sander disk (fixed to a drill press or on a flexible shaft) will be a great labor saver. The bodies of many types of pressed-cork or composition-cork decoys are turned out with no other tools than those mentioned above.

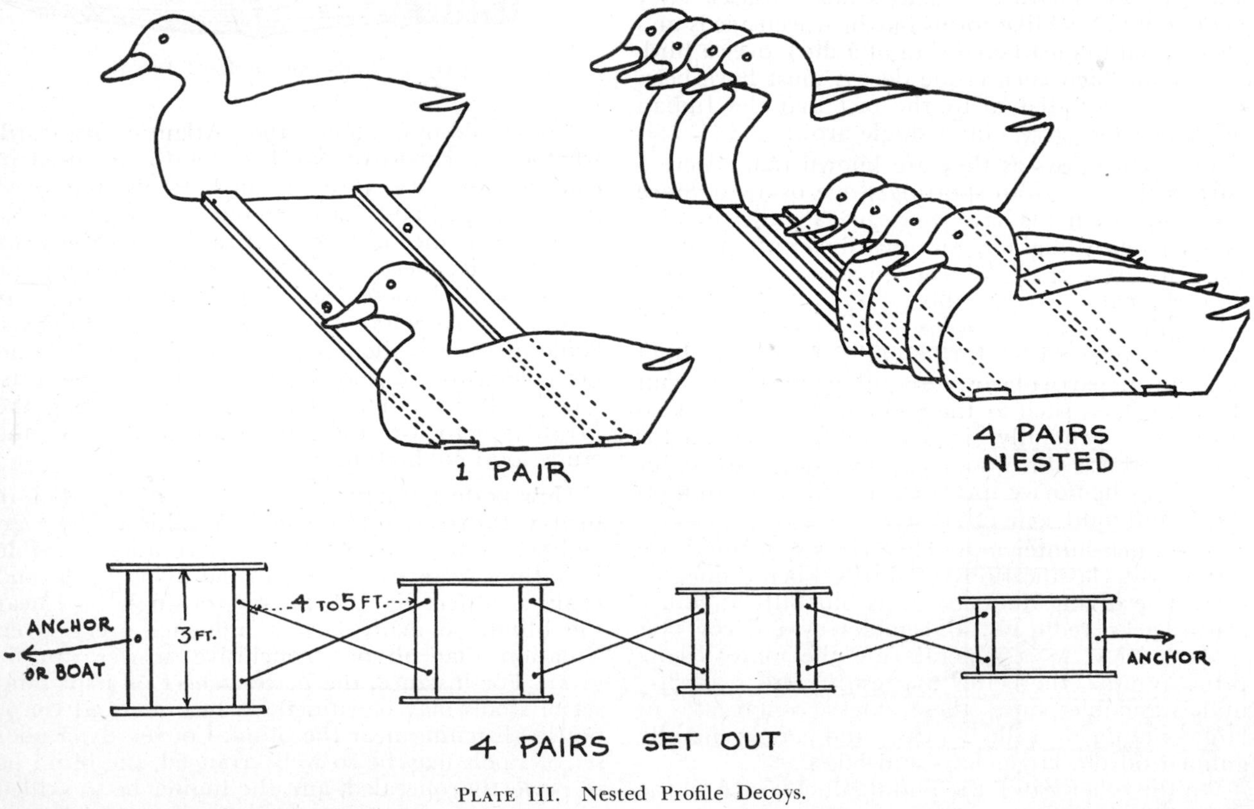


PLATE III. Nested Profile Decoys.

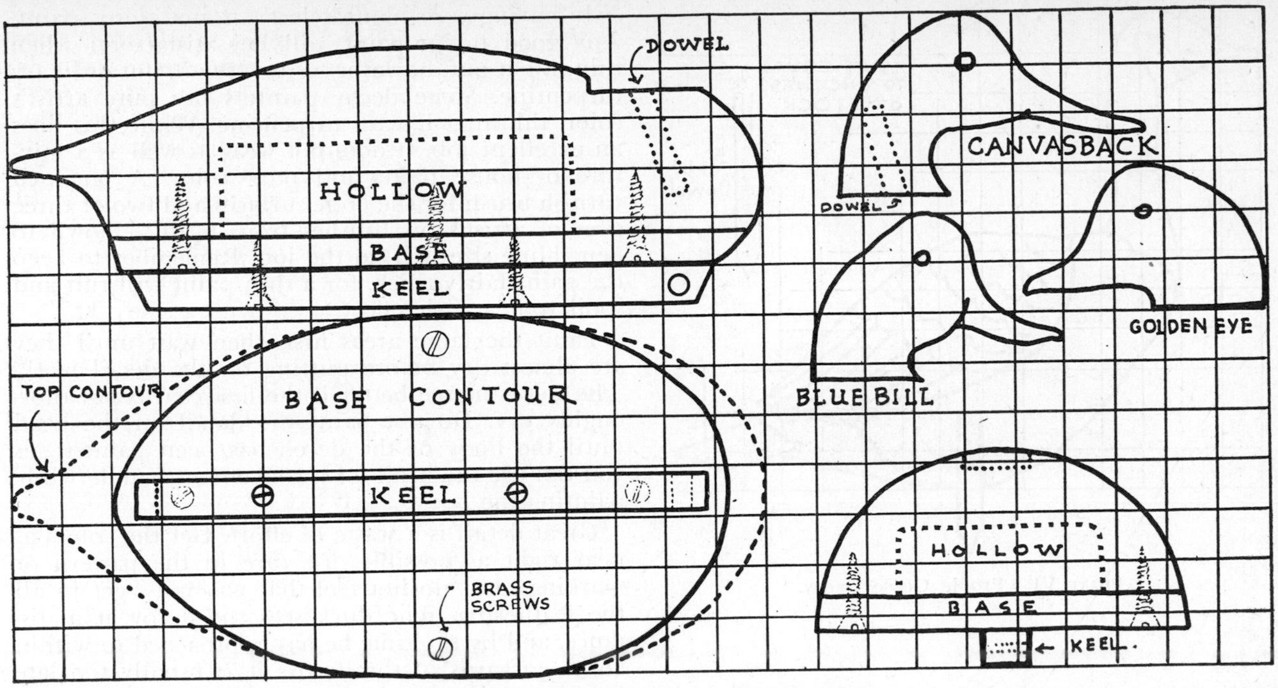


PLATE IV. Decoy Construction—diving ducks.

The base of the pressed-cork decoys quite definitely calls for a plywood or 5/8 inch wooden plate, for without this protection the decoy will not stand rough usage. The baseboard should be glued to the body with a good waterproof glue.

Regardless of the body material, all decoy heads must be of wood. Many amateur decoy makers favor white pine because of its ease of working. Whitewood also is used. In making the head remember that the excess wood under the neck should not be cut off until the head is finished and the hole for the dowel is bored, for this wood is required to hold the head in the vise or bench clamp while the carving is being done.

In order to determine the dimensions of the various decoys, the following length measurements should be used in making the patterns. Length at base, front to rear:

| *Decoy* | *Inches* | *Decoy* | *Inches* |
|---|---|---|---|
| Blue Goose | 15 | Mallard | 12 |
| Canada Goose | 19 | Old Squaw | 10 |
| White-Fronted Goose | 15 | Pintail | 11 |
| Snow Goose | 15 | Redhead | 10 |
| Brant | 15 | Ring-Necked Duck | 10 |
| Baldpate | 11 | Scaup | 11 |
| Black Duck (oversize) | 14 | Scoter | 12½ |
| Black Duck (average) | 12 | Shoveller | 11 |
| Eider | 10 | Teal | 9 |
| Gadwall | 11 | Widgeon | 11 |
| Golden-eye | 10 | | |

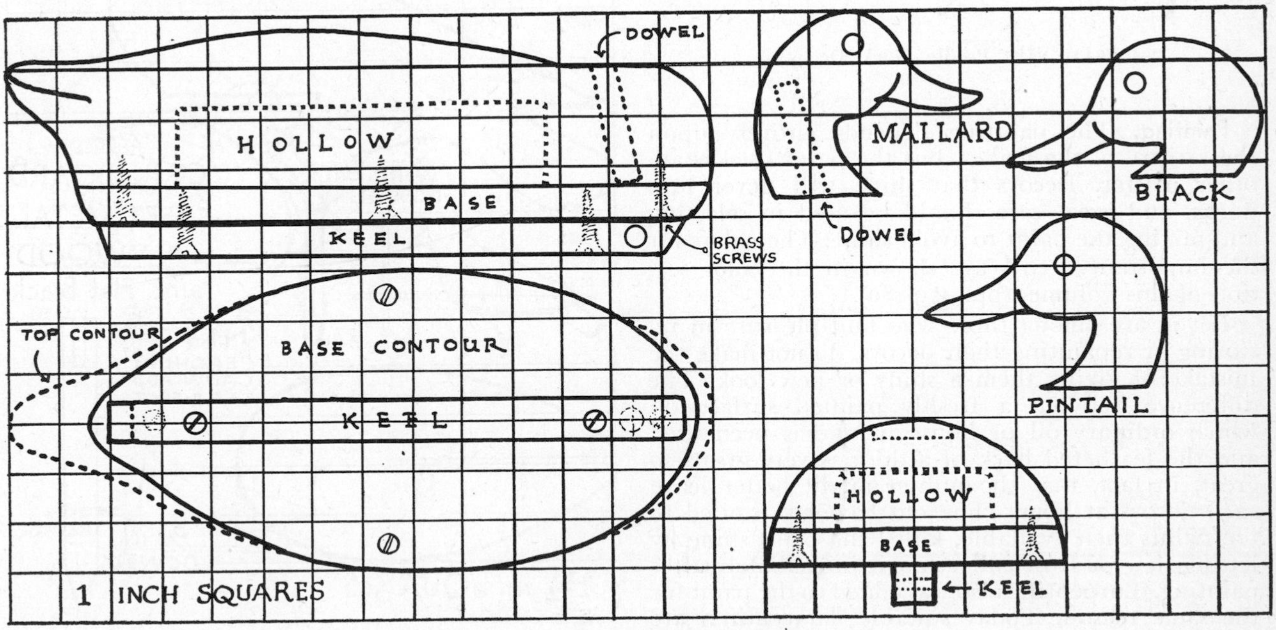


PLATE V. Decoy Construction—puddle ducks.

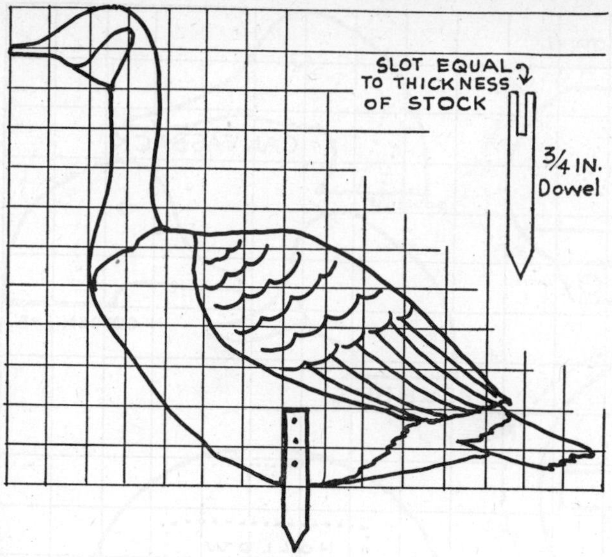


PLATE VI. Profile Goose Decoy.

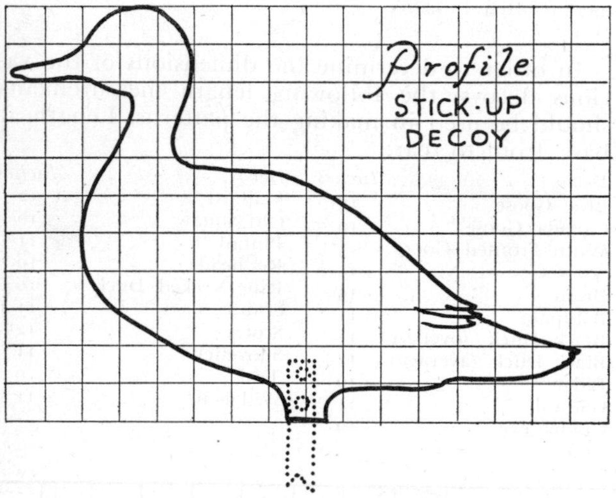


PLATE VII. Profile Duck Decoy.

**Painting.** The painting depends entirely upon the artistry of the maker, but the paint used is another matter. Decoys that shine will never lure ducks, and great care should be used in selecting and mixing the paint to avoid shine. The colors for the important decoys are shown in the color section of this volume (pp. 479-480).

If you are among those who find pleasure in restoring or repainting their decoys, do not make the mistake of giving them a shiny or new look. The difference between a freshly painted surface on which ordinary oil or house paint has been used and the feathered back of a duck is very great—so great, in fact, that the hunter might better leave such decoys at home. The old baymen, limited to the paints then available, killed the paint shine by letting dew or frost collect on it immediately after painting, Turpentine also was added to the paint for the same reason. Today suitable flat coatings are commercially available.

In buying your paint, select *flat,* not *glossy,* paint. Any good house paint will be satisfactory; when thinning it out, however, *never* use oil, but ordinary turpentine. Some decoy painters use pure artist's color, thinning it with turpentine. While this does an excellent job, it does not wear as well as a mixture of house paint and pure color. A one-inch varnish brush for the large surfaces and two or three sizes of artist's oil brushes from 1/4 inch down to pencil-line size will do the job. Remember to keep the paint fairly thick, for a thin paint will run and spoil your artistic effect.

Paint the large areas first, then wait until they are almost dry before putting on the detail work. The colors merge better if the first coat is not thoroughly dry. Do not paint the detail on the head until the body of the decoy has been painted, as you can use the head for a convenient handle while painting the body.

Great detail is a waste of effort. Get the colors as near right as possible, use care in the pattern or markings, but do not feel that you must get in all the feathering. The duck sees the decoy at a distance, and by the time he has approached to within 20 or 30 yards of the decoys it is usually too late for him to discover he has been deceived.

By adding ordinary powdered lampblack to any of the dark paints used, you will reduce to a minimum the paint's tendency to shine, even when splashed with water. In making black duck decoys of cork, or even of balsa, many decoy makers obtain the brown and black coloring by the use of a blow torch, burning the wood or composition to the desired shade. This eliminates all possibility of

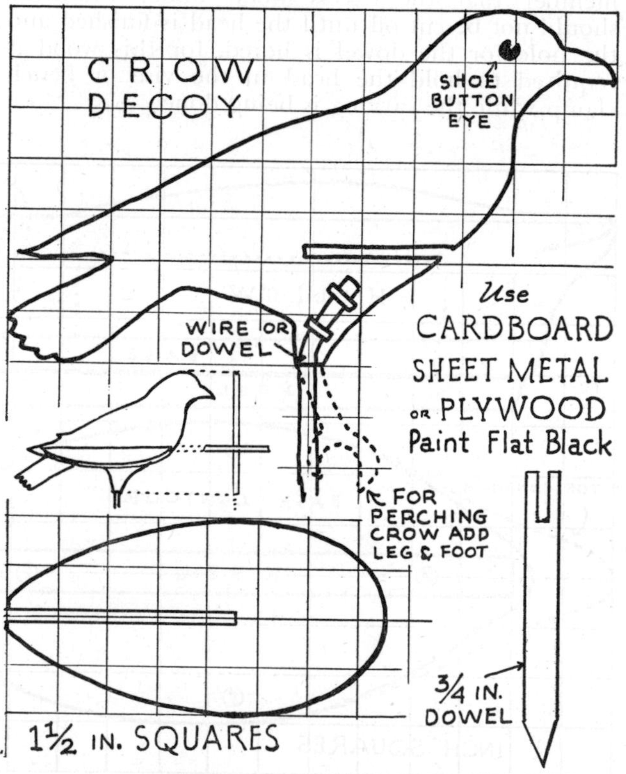


PLATE VIII. Profile Crow Decoy.

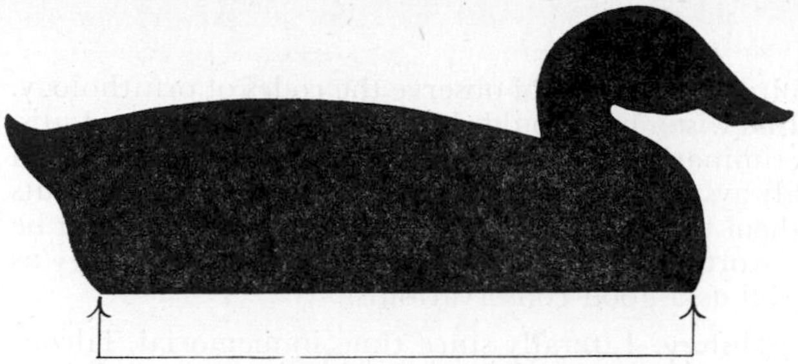

PLATE IX. Profile Duck Decoy.

paint shine. All decoys will shine to some degree, especially when splashed with water, but every effort should be made to reduce this shine to the minimum. Ducks themselves have a certain amount of "shine," and so they will not turn tail if your decoys send out only an occasional faint gleam.

In buying the paint, buy large cans of both black and white, and small cans of the other colors required. For a varied puddle-duck rig you will want black, white, tobacco brown, yellow ocher, and burnt umber in the flat house paint; also 2-ounce tubes of the following artist's colors: Prussian blue, crimson, green, chrome yellow, and vermilion.

After the paint is dry, some makers brush it over lightly with a very fine steel wool, others rub it lightly with a wet cloth and one of the household abrasives or scouring powders. This tends to reduce the shine.

**Lines.** Decoy lines are the subject of much controversy. One shooter will prefer the heavy, limp cord (braided nylon is now popular) and another will insist that the tarred line, stiff and less likely to become tangled, is best. All agree that the rawhide or plastic thong is best for attaching the line to the decoy. A metal eyelet, though it may look better, is not satisfactory. As to length of line required, to prevent excessive dragging in the event of heavy winds, a good rule to follow is to have the decoy lines three times as long as the depth of the water. In other words, if you do most of your shooting in an area where the water is 10 feet deep, use decoy lines 30 feet long. This rule should be followed except in those instances where unusually heavy decoy anchors are used.

**Anchors.** Anchors are of many types, and those favoring one type will never agree that any other is as satisfactory. Lead has proved to be the only satisfactory metal for anchors. The design of the anchor often proves more important than its weight, although the weight factor cannot be ignored. The mushroom type and the lead-ring type seem to be most popular. The mushroom anchor with a heavy copper ring is favored by some as it tends to give firm anchorage and also can be slipped over the head of the decoy when not in use, thus avoiding tangles. The lead ring, which can also be slipped over the head of the decoy, is used extensively in deep coastal waters.

**Weights.** There also are two theories on the matter of decoy weights, fastened either to the bottom of the decoy or to the keel, when a keel is used. Most hunters seem to prefer sheet lead, from 3/16 to 1/4 inch thick, but others go to more trouble and make a mold for a lead keel. The sheet lead is quite satisfactory, and certainly is much simpler, as a strip of the length desired may be readily cut from the sheet. It is important, however, to check the placing of the lead before nailing it to the decoy or the keel. This may be done by filling a bathtub or a washtub with water, and holding the weight in position with two heavy rubber bands cut from an old inner tube. Keep rocking the decoy and shifting the weight until the decoy rides properly. Only copper or brass nails should be used to fasten the weight to the decoy.

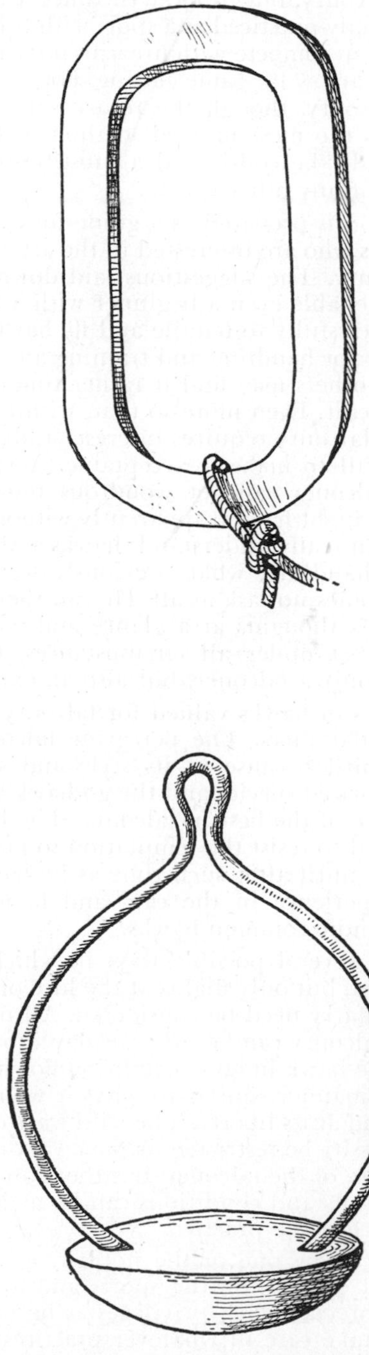

PLATE X. Decoy Anchors.

# FALCONRY

**Introduction.** Falconry is the art of getting control over the natural habits of hawks or falcons so as to turn their proclivities to the use of the falconer. The mere keeping of hawks in captivity or making pets of them could not properly be called falconry; likewise, every possessor of a hawk is not rightly titled a falconer.

In the times before the invention of gunpowder, the chief object of falconry was for hunting purposes to obtain game. The gun, of course, when and where it was widely used, made falconry obsolete for hunting purposes. In certain parts of the world, the securing of food has always been the main objective of falconry, but in modern times it has been more commonly practiced as a sport with full knowledge that it can compete with firearms no better than the bow and arrow for game getting. For small game hunting, falconry, though the returns are small, is undoubtedly the most natural method of hunting. It could hardly be considered a substitute or a replacement for any other sport.

This section is prepared as a guide for sportsmen and falconers who are interested in the art and practice of falconry. The suggestions laid down in this treatise will enable even a beginner with a little experience successfully to handle and fly hawks. Some with a knack for handling and training animals will find it easy, others may find it rather time consuming and difficult. Even more so than with the working of dogs, falconry requires interest, study, experience, and skill to make it acceptable. A really experienced falconer can get wondrous results with even newly caught hawks, apparently without effort. Once a person really understands hawks and gets the feel of the handling, what previously seemed impossible becomes no task at all. He can then almost read a hawk's thoughts at a glance and will know what to expect under all circumstances, thus becoming not only a falconer, but also an expert.

The species of hawks valued for falconry are fast and spectacular fliers. The peregrine falcon is the bird-man's bird because of its style and speed of flight. This prized species and the goshawk are most representative of the best in falconry. The beginner would do well to resist the temptation to possess the rarer falcons until after such time as he has gained sufficient experience in the care and handling of some of the more common hawks.

There are several possible ways in which hawks might be used, but only flights at the lure or fist and at natural quarry need be considered. All of the attributes of falconry can be fully displayed only with a manageable hawk in good condition flown at wild quarry in a manner similar to what it would do if untrained and at its liberty. The wild ways of hawks must of necessity be restricted or somewhat modified to the purpose of the falconer, but the more natural the bird's habits and conditions can be maintained, the more perfect the practice.

Falconry can be one of the noblest, fairest, and most natural of the hunting sports and a falconer ought to appreciate such privileges as he may have and should take care in whatever practices he may indulge. He should be genuinely interested in other birdlife and should observe the codes of ornithology. Likewise, he should be most particular and discriminating in the taking of hawks, in keeping them always in good order, and, finally, in the use he puts them to. A falconer deserving of the title should be a worthy contributor to the cause of ornithology as well as a good conservationist.

**History.** Literally since time immemorial, falcons have been used by man. There are sculptural records from Egypt and Persia associating hawks with man's activities dating back to perhaps 1000 B.C. From ancient days to the present, falconry has been practiced extensively in parts of India and other places in Asia and Africa. In fact, it has been practiced in nearly every country in the world; the United States is one of the few countries where it has been scarcely known except in literature.

Falconry was once considered the sport of kings and indeed was practiced by many of them. For example, Louis XIV, during his reign, spent many, if not most, of his days afield with a troop in the practice of falconry. During the two or three days of the week in which he was occupied with affairs of state and thus prevented from going afield, he watched his hawks fly at sealed pigeons high over the courtyard.

It has been said, with apparent authority, that there was a time in England when an educated man was not considered a gentleman unless he was fluent in the knowledge of falconry. The wide knowledge of falconry in England, at that time, is further substantiated by the frequent use of falconry terms scattered throughout the works of Shakespeare.

Volumes have been written on the history and practice of falconry, but since all that has been done on this subject cannot be reviewed in this space, the reader would do well to refer to the libraries for further enlightenment.

**Present Status of Falconry.** Before World War II, there was a rising interest in falconry, especially in Europe where it was quite widely practiced.

In this country, The American Falconers' Association was formed by Edward F. Reid in the spring of 1941 with 27 charter members from 12 states. In April 1942, this was transferred to The Falconers' Association of North America under the direction of Captain R. L. Meredith and Dr. R. M. Stabler who issued *The American Falconer* journal. By July 1942, the association had 107 members with others listed as being interested. The membership reached 150 by January 1943 and by that time there were perhaps some 200 people with at least a passing interest in the practice of falconry. There surely were many others also who had some reading knowledge of the subject. If the war had not interrupted, it might have been more widely known by this time, yet up to this writing there probably have not been over a dozen really experienced and proficient falconers in the United States at any one time. The interest in falconry apparently has not greatly diminished and it seems likely that a Falconers' Association will again become active.

To be engaged in falconry today, one must have: (1) sufficient time, (2) enough skill, (3) good hawks, and (4) a suitable place for flights. Unfortunately, there are few people so situated as not to be hampered in one or more of these requirements.

Falconry, being almost an unknown sport in this country, has scarcely been recognized by most of the state conservation departments, though many of them have some provision for the keeping or use of hawks. Most of the states would likely do more for the sport if reasonable requests were made to them by falconry groups in good standing.

Some conservation departments are aware of the desirability of harvesting limited game crops of certain species which show a surplus, but which, for one reason or another, cannot support the heavy harvest of a regular open season. The bow and arrow has been used in this manner for the taking of big

Photo by Pix.

PLATE I. A Hooded Duck Hawk (Peregrine), the Falcon of Antiquity. Note falconer's rhinoceros-hide glove.

game, and falconry might well be used for a light harvest of certain limited species in restricted areas. This mainly would amount to a provision for falconers which would otherwise go unused. Falcons could also be used in the outskirts of municipalities and other places where firearms are prohibited. Likewise, as far as the taking of game is involved, there could be no valid objection to hunting with a hawk during the regular game seasons, provided the falconer could find a place where he could dare risk releasing a hawk without danger of its being shot down by some over-ardent hunter.

The general outlook for all hunting is that it will likely become more costly and somewhat more restricted. The falconer will surely have to do his share for whatever he gets. He must be a contributor to the final hope of sportsmen—good conservation and better game management.

**Suitable Species of Hawks.** In North America there are about 35 species of hawks, eagles, and related species (sub-species and vultures not included).

The hawk groups proper are divided into:

(1) Accipitrinae, short-winged, or bird hawks.
(2) Buteos, or soaring hawks.
(3) Harriers, or marsh hawks.
(4) Falcons, or long-winged hawks.

Hawks of the first and last groups are the only ones with suitable nature, natural habits, and speed enough to be practical for training. The golden eagle is also used.

There are three species of short-winged or yellow-eyed hawks:

(1) Goshawk (universal).
(2) Cooper's hawk (no European counterpart).
(3) Sharp-shinned hawk (about same as European sparrow hawk).

Of the long-winged or dark-eyed hawks there are five principal species:

(1) Gyrfalcon (universal in northern latitudes).
(2) Peregrine falcon or duck hawk (universal).
(3) Prairie falcon.
(4) Pigeon hawk or merlin (very similar to European merlin).
(5) Sparrow hawk (about same as European kestrel).

(The sakers, lanners, hobbies, and other foreign falcons are also used.)

All of the above hawks may be further described as male or female (the male falcon is a "tiercel" and the female a "falcon"), and as adult—"haggard"—or immature. The immature are birds of the year in their first plumage. They are either nestlings, "eyases" (that is, taken from a nest), or "passage" (taken from the fall or spring migration). A "hack bird" is one taken from a nest but reared at liberty. Each species has its own characteristic sizes and behavior. Furthermore, there is a great difference between the size of the male and female of each species, the female being usually about a third larger than the male. There are also conspicuous differences in the individuals' behavior.

1. Goshawk *Astur atricapillus*

The goshawk nests in Canada and scattered along the northern border of the United States, but it is common during late migrations on most of the flyways in the northernmost part of the United States. Males and females are similarly marked, though the adult males are somewhat bluer-backed than the females. They are distinguished from Cooper's hawks by their larger size, stockier legs and feet, whitish line over the eye, and their legs are feathered one-third of the way down on the tarsus. The adults are bluish-backed and red-eyed, with light breasts barred in black. Immatures are yellow-eyed, brown-backed, with brownish or blackish streaked breasts. Both adults and immatures have dark banded tails with white tips. Males weigh from 25 to 33 ounces, females 30 to 37 ounces or more.

These hawks, like all woods-going bird hawks, have conspicuously long tails and comparatively short, stocky wings with five-notched primaries. Their most typical habit of flight is a few rapid wing beats with intermittent glides. They are fast and vicious, and as game getters probably outclass other hawks. They can be flown to either the lure or the fist, but should be flown to the fist. An inexperienced hawker may find it more difficult to fly short-wings to the fist than to the lure. These birds are generally more nervous, more flighty, and less docile than falcons, but they can be flown successfully when still apparently quite wild. The female goshawk can take such game as pheasants, ducks, grouse, rabbits, hares—in fact, almost anything up to the size of small geese. The male, being smaller and shiftier, is better for the smaller quarry.

2. Cooper's Hawk *Accipiter cooperi*

This hawk is similar to the goshawk but smaller. Males weigh from 11¼ to 14½ ounces, females from 16½ to 22 ounces. Adults have reddish barred breasts instead of black and none has the white line over the eye. The legs or tarsi are thinner. The bird's temperament is usually less dependable than the goshawk's, but it can be trained and flown in the same manner as the goshawk. Female Cooper's have been trained to take cottontail rabbits but this size prey is out of its class. It will sometimes take birds the size of European partridge. Both the male and female Cooper's are rated as efficient quail hawks, and they can be flown at ground squirrels and other small mammals.

3. Sharp-Shinned Hawk *Accipiter velox*

The sharpshin's behavior and coloration is similar to the Cooper's but the adult barring is more brownish than reddish. It is much smaller than the Cooper's; the male weighs from 3¼ to 3¾ ounces, the female from 5½ to 7¾ ounces or more. The end of the tail is described as more square or less round in flight. Training is about the same as for all other short-wings. This species naturally takes small mammals and small birds up to the size of mourning doves. Wild sharpshins will sometimes tackle pigeons and commonly harass bluejays and flickers. They could be flown at English sparrows and the female might be flown successfully at quail or woodcock. This bird, being small and of a delicate constitution, is difficult to keep in good flying condition, especially the little males.

4. Gyrfalcon *Falco rusticolus*

There are three varieties of the gyrfalcon—white, gray, and black. The female weighs about 52 ounces;

the male is somewhat smaller. These, the largest of the falcons, breed in Canada and other northern zones. Occasionally they migrate into the United States in winter. This falcon, because of its rarity, its difficulty to obtain, and its inadaptability to warm climates, cannot be considered very practical for use in the United States. Formerly in Europe and Britain, the gyrfalcon was used to take herons and other large fowl. Under certain conditions it should be excellent for taking geese.

5. American Peregrine Falcon *Falco peregrinus*

The adult is blue or blue-black above, barred gray ventrally; first-year plumage is brownish above with brownish streaks beneath. Males weigh from 17 to 22 ounces, females from 26 to 40 ounces. Individual birds vary in temperament, but almost any one properly trained will serve for the purposes intended. This species breeds irregularly throughout North America. Like all falcons, peregrines have long, rather slim, pointed wings like those of the swallow. Fast and high-flying, it is used in prairie regions and open sections. An open space of a square mile or more is none too much. The nestling is usually referred to as an "eyas" and the nest of the falcon is called an "eyrie." The male and female are distinguished by size and the adults from immature by plumage coloration markings. The tiercel will fly at woodcock, quail, teal, European partridge, magpies, crows, and birds up to the size of small pheasants and grouse. The falcon can take crows, ducks, pheasants, grouse, and birds up to the size of herons.

6. Prairie Falcon *Falco mexicanus*

This bird is light brown above, light with brownish marks below. Males weigh from 17 to 22½ ounces, females from 26 to 30 ounces. This falcon is similar in ability to the peregrine, but is also inclined to take mammals on the ground. Its range is the western half of the United States.

7. Pigeon Hawk *Falco columbarius*

The females and young are dark brown above with brown streaking beneath. Adult males are blue-backed. Males weigh from 5 to 6½ ounces, females from 7 to 8¾ ounces. The North American varieties of pigeon hawks, being similar to the European merlin, can be used for the same purposes. The flight is martinlike, but more steady. They breed in Canada but migrate through all the flyways of North America. These falcons train very well, but when hunted they tend to carry their quarry and they are limited to comparatively small species. The male "jacks" may be flown at sparrows and blackbirds. The females can take sparrows, larks, quail, woodcock, and birds up to the size of a pigeon.

8. Sparrow Hawk *Falco sparverius*

All males are light beneath, with blue wings, brown backs, and rufous tails with black and white terminal band. Females are barred brown with brown-streaked under parts. Males weigh from 4 to 4½ ounces, females from 4½ to 4⅔ ounces. This species trains well and will fly to the fist or the lure. but is more or less a toy and has a comparatively delicate constitution. It can be flown successfully at sparrows, but could be used on small game only with difficulty and special training. Its natural feed is chiefly grasshoppers, beetles, and other insects. If not underfed, it makes a good falcon for beginners to practice with.

**Hawk Furniture.** Tackle-makers in Germany, France, Britain, and India are now, for various reasons, unable to furnish tackle without delay, if at all. However, it is reported that A. Ondet of 17 Rue des quatre vents, Paris, France; Otto Kals, Falkenzeugmeister, of Düsseldorf, Germany; J. G. Mavorgordato, British Falconers' Club, 11 D Queensdale Rd., London, England; and Ch. Mohad Din Co., Hawk Merchants, Amritsar, India, are all still living and possibly may be able to supply some tackle in the future. Karl Th. Mollen, son of the famous Adrian Mollen of Valkenswarrd, by Eindhoven, North Brabant, Holland, is apparently no longer making hawk furniture, though this has not been definitely confirmed. Previous copies of the *American Falconer* list several new American tackle-makers, some of whom do a fairly commendable job. A falconer will probably get best results by making his own equipment except for bells and Dutch hoods, yet anyone accustomed to working with leather should be able to turn out good hoods with a little practice.

Jesses or leg straps. These can be made from soft, pliable leather or tough buckskin by cutting out strips usually ⅜ to ½ inches wide and 4 to 9 inches long, depending on the size of the hawk. About ¼ inch from each end the strap is slit in the middle for about ¾ inch. At one end a second slit is cut about ½ inch or so from the end slit. The double slitted end is fastened more or less permanently around the hawk's leg. Only very pliable leather should be used, as stiff leather may cut or bruise the hawk's legs. The leather used must be strong so that the loops attached to the leash will not tear out. Beginners may practice on a pencil.

Leash and Swivel. A leash is attached, by means of a swivel, to each jess so that the hawk can be tethered to a perch, or held securely. A piece of ¼ to ½-inch belt lacing or some pliable leather 3 to 4 feet long will do. A slit similar to that made in the jess should be placed near one end of the leash. If the old-fashioned falconer's swivel is used, a leather button is made on one end of the leash; nothing more is needed. It is more convenient to attach two swivel hooks to a sufficiently large barrel swivel (such as used in heavy fishing) and the swivel in turn to the end of the leash by means of split copper rings of a suitable size. Fairly heavy tackle should be used on goshawks and large peregrines. When a hawk is fastened to a screen perch, the leash should be tied as short as possible and on a bow perch only long enough to amply allow for clearance of the hawk's tail, so that it does not rebound into the perch. On a block perch, the leash must be tied long enough to allow the hawk's feet to reach the ground no matter which way she jumps off the perch. Too long a leash will be inconvenient and likely to tangle and if tied too long a hawk may injure its tarsi, or, in the case of sharpshins, may paralyze the legs from too much hard jerking.

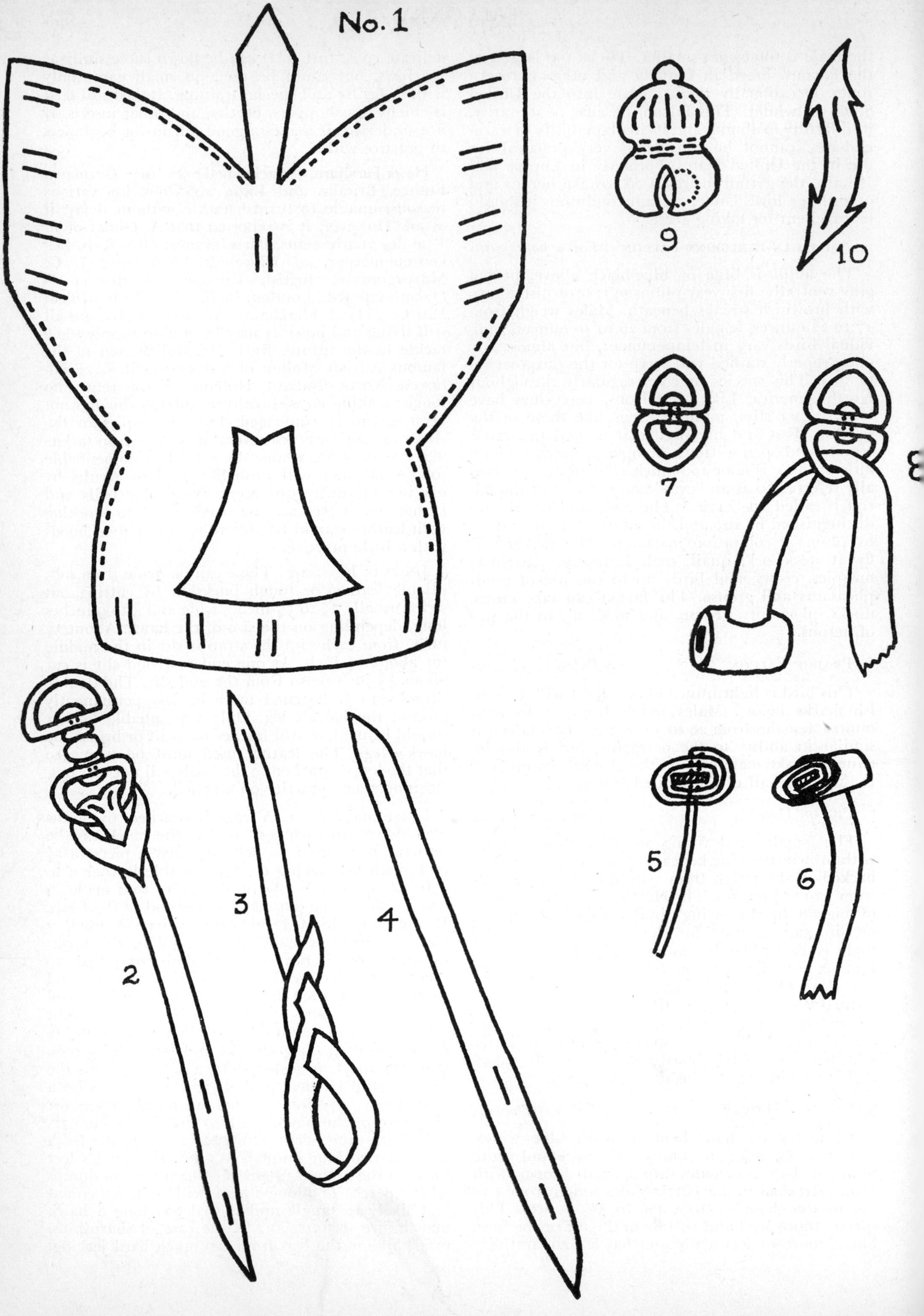
No. 1
2
3
4
5
6
7
8
9
10

The falconer's knot is always used when tying a hawk to a perch.

HOODS. There are two principal kinds of hoods—the Indian style and the Dutch style. The modified Indian style with drawstring will not easily come off and is especially useful on newly caught hawks. It is more difficult to manipulate in the usual method of hooding and if not properly made and fitted it may injure the hawk's eyes. If an Indian-type hood is used, it should be checked frequently to see that it is not pressing against the hawk's eyeballs. The Dutch hood is made from either one or three pieces of fairly stiff leather. It is comparatively easy to manipulate and should be used when necessary on peregrines. A hawk can get this type of hood off, but after the bird is once trained, this hood will be found excellent for all ordinary purposes. With a Dutch hood of the right size and shape, there is no danger of eye injury, but if it is much used the beak aperture may rub a hawk's mandibles some, especially if the leather is hard or dirty or not well fitted. Hooding should never be overdone; the less a hood is used, the better. The principal purpose of a hood is to serve, as do blinders on a horse, to keep the hawk from becoming excited or unruly when being transported or for otherwise keeping her quiet and unable to see disturbances.

METHOD FOR HOODING. One of the most difficult tasks in the handling of hawks is the mastering of the manipulation of hooding. When properly done it is easy, but it is difficult to describe and for various reasons most new falconers have trouble in doing it well. The hawk should be held on the left hand at ease and facing towards the falconer's right hand. The hood is held in the right hand firmly but gently by the base of the plume. Upside down with aperture side close to the hawk's breast, it is brought deftly and gently up, under and over the hawk's beak and rotated up onto the hawk's head. The hawk is then moved closer to the face and with the teeth on the near side and the right hand on the far side both draw straps are pulled simultaneously, so as to close the hood without putting pressure on the hawk's head and neck. There are other methods of using a dutch hood, any of which will do so long as the hood can be put on with the least possible disturbance. If done as it should be, there will be no commotion or wild movements on the part of either the hawk or the falconer. The feeding of a few bits of meat while taking the hawk on the fist and immediately preceding the hooding is an advantage, until both the hawk and the falconer are accustomed to the technique.

HAWK BELLS. Bells are especially made of copper or brass alloy so as to be light in weight yet of good bell quality; they are clearly audible at a reasonable distance. Bells are fastened to the falcon's legs by means of "bewits" or short leather straps. Goshawk bells are either fastened at the base of the tail on a small piece of leather tied between the two central "deck" feathers or sometimes on a cord around the hawk's neck. A falcon will make the most noise by having the bell attached to the legs, whereas the short-winged hawk's habit of switching its tail frequently will give better results. Bells are not necessary, but when a hawk goes out of sight in a cornfield, marsh, or woods, a bell is very helpful and may prevent the loss of a hawk. When bells are scarce, it is best not to use them in the early training of hawks. One bell will do, but two are generally used on falcons. It is advisable to have one's address engraved on the bells used. No doubt someone in this country will be marketing satisfactory bells to meet the demand, especially if foreign supplies are not obtainable.

PERCHES. There are three principal kinds of perches. The *block perch* is the common outdoor perch for a falcon and the *bow perch* is the common ground perch for a short-wing. Sparrow hawks and pigeon hawks can use either. A *screen perch* is best for all hawks when kept inside. Hawks should always be tied short on screen perches. A new hawk should be watched to make sure that it will not hang but come back quickly to the correct position whenever it should fly off. A sick hawk should never be placed on a screen perch because once off, it may not have the strength to climb back up and thus may hang and die in the falconer's absence.

A screen perch can easily be made by padding a 2″ x 2″ or pole of suitable length. Several folds of burlap tacked on top and covered with light canvas or some durable material would serve. The canvas underneath is long enough to extend nearly to the floor. The bottom corners should be weighted or tied down so as to provide a firm supporting apron for a hawk to climb back onto the perch after it has flown off. The "screen" also prevents the hawk from entangling itself round and round the perch pole. Holes are punched in the canvas just below the pole and the leash run through and the hawk tied as close as possible, right up to the swivel end of the leash. Also, the canvas apron should extend at least 18 inches each side of the fastening point. If two or more hawks are tied on a long perch, they should be spaced far enough so as not to be able to entangle each other. The proper height of a screen perch is 44 to 48 inches high, so that a hawk in falling off will not break or damage the tips of the primaries by beating them against the floor. The perch should be no nearer than 30 inches from a wall.

A block perch can be made by cutting a 6- or 8-inch diameter section from a cedar pole, etc., and by driving a 3/8-inch iron rod, 18 to 20 inches long, into the base and padding the flat top heavily with burlap or other cushioning material (cork is also used), and covering with canvas or some durable material. A harness ring is slipped over the rod and the perch pushed into the ground, leaving a few inches space between the bottom of the perch and the ground so that the leash tied to the ring will have freedom

PLATE II. Falconry "Furniture." (1) Pattern for "Indian" hood, right size for female Peregrine or Goshawk. Edges are sewn where dotted. Edge slits are for draw string or strap. Center slit for plume or leather tab. (2) Jess is put through one ring, then loop pulled over swivel and back down on itself. Thus swivel may easily be attached or removed while other end of jess is attached to hawk's leg. (3) Jess as attached to hawk's leg. (4) Jess pattern. (5 & 6) Method of putting leather button on end of leash for use with old fashioned swivel. (7) Old-fashioned swivel. (8) Method of drawing leash through swivel. (9 & 10) Bell and bewit.

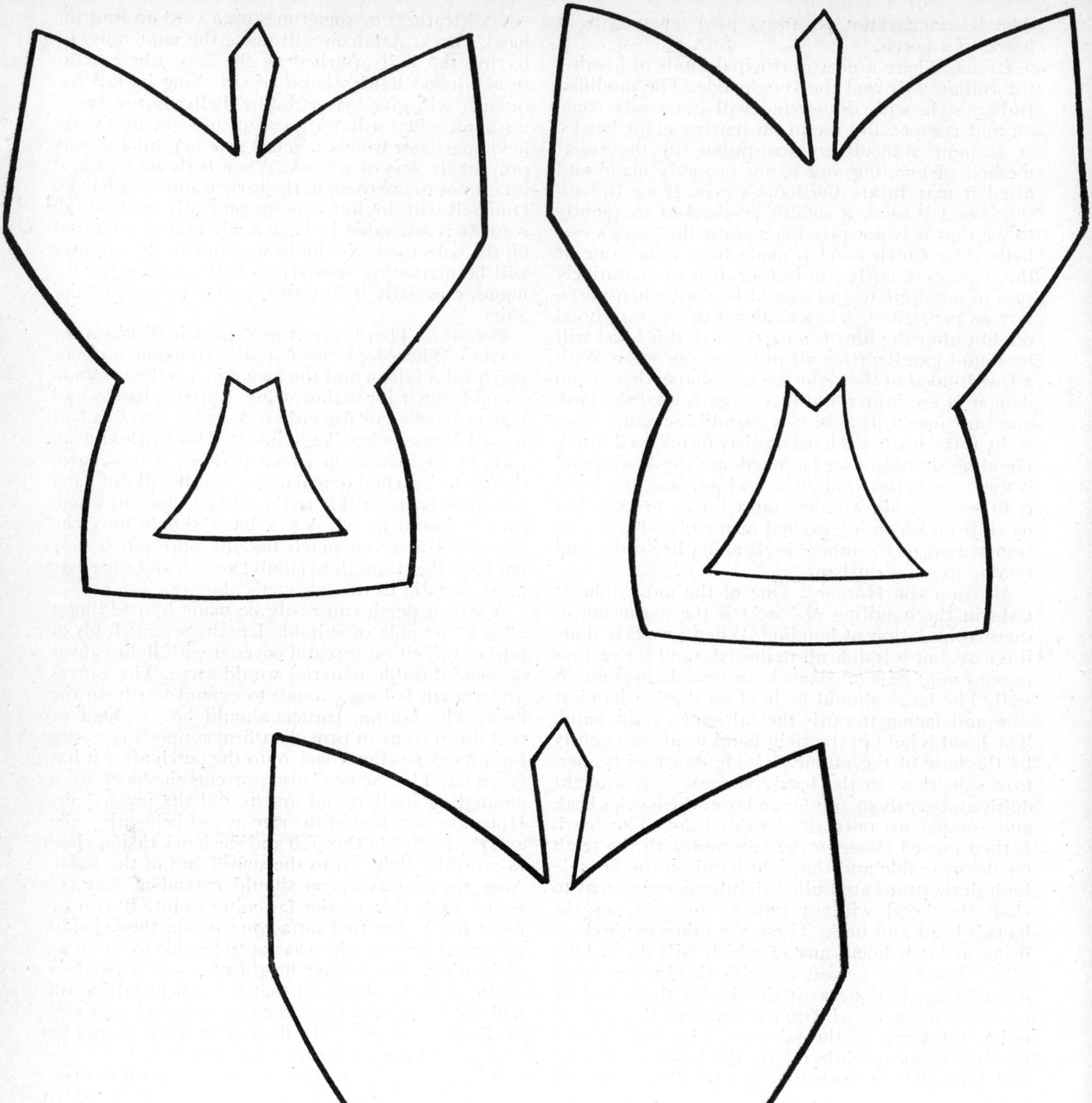

**PLATE III.** Hoods. *Upper left:* Pattern (actual size) of hood for female Pigeon Hawk. *Upper right:* Pattern (actual size) of hood for male Cooper's Hawk. *Lower:* Pattern (actual size) of hood for male Duck Hawk.

Photo by Pix.

PLATE IV. Duck Hawk About to be Hooded.

of action. This will take care of the hawk without danger of entangling, provided the leash is tied 15 to 20 inches long, or long enough so that the hawk can always reach the ground.

A bow perch can be made from a small cedar sapling or other smooth and straight wood of suitable diameter, sharpened at both ends. It is bent into an arc and held into position by means of a wire strung like a bow several inches from each point. One end is forced into the ground, the perch arched a little more, and the other end pushed into the ground so that the wire is taut and on the ground level. A loose-running ring for tying the leash is usually placed on the perch before attaching the wire.

A car perch can be made by nailing one or two blocks, as described for a block perch, on a suitable-sized piece of plywood, etc. In this case the blocks should be tall enough to prevent the hawk's tail from touching the board and a staple should be nailed on top of the block to tie in the hawk's leash. Hawks can also be carried hooded on the fist or on the back of a car seat.

Though hawks may derive much good exercising while attached to out-of-door perches, the principal object of any perch is to provide a place where a hawk can repose and be kept clean and free from entanglement or damage to the plumage. No perch should be placed near any obstructions and the hawk should not be distressed by being tied in the

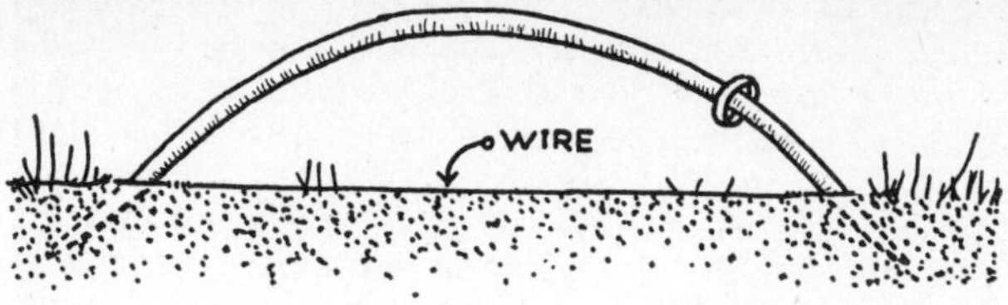


Plate V. Bow Perch with Ring.

heat of the sun during hot days, or kept out long in disagreeable cold weather.

Lure. For the training of large falcons a lure is needed; this may be used for any species of hawk. However, it is better to train all the short-wings as well as sparrow hawks and pigeon hawks to the fist. Training both to the fist and the lure may be desirable in some cases. A lure can be made from a horseshoe, padded and covered and wrapped with red cloth or leather to make it most conspicuous (hawks can distinguish the color). As an added attraction, wings of wildfowl or pigeons are usually attached to the lure. A lure made entirely of a bundle of wings, with or without red stringers, is also good. Short thongs are attached for tying on pieces of meat and a fairly long length of leather or cord is tied around the center of the arc so that the lure may be swung or thrown. A lure should never be left in the hawk's view except when calling or being fed.

Creance. A long, light, but stout line wound on a stick with a swivel snap on one end is used for training new hawks or at any time when the handler is not sure of the hawk's response to the lure. The creance should not be used any more than is necessary to prevent the escape of a partly trained hawk. It is seldom needed after the first week or two. An experienced falconer can get along without it entirely if he chooses.

Bathing Pan. A pan about the size of a washtub but only 4 or 5 inches deep is useful. Peregrines, especially, should be allowed to bathe on warm days. If they are flown loose without being bathed, they will often "rake off" to the nearest water—particularly on mild days.

Glove. Some sort of leather gloves are needed for carrying the hawk on the fist to prevent being scratched by the talons.

Halsband. Where short-winged hawks are much flown, the halsband is often used. This is a silk cord or thong placed around a hawk's neck and held in the hand so that hawks may be thrown with increased momentum on the getaway.

Imping Needles. For repairing feathers, small double-pointed three-sided needles about 1 to 2 inches long are used. These should be moderately tempered and of a diameter just the right size to fit into the shaft of the feather to be spliced without splitting it. If a feather is broken sharply off, anywhere near the midpart of the quill, it may be joined back to the butt shaft by inserting a needle halfway into it and the other half of the needle into the feather on the hawk so that the two sections come together and match as they were before being broken. A badly bent feather which cannot be straightened by steaming or wetting may be cut off and imped back. If the feather tip is lost, too badly damaged, broken too near the tip, or split at the junction, the torn end of the butt feather will have to be trimmed back to a place where it is sound and a new tip of proper length cut from a feather which matches the one damaged. The imping of a tail or primary feathers is painless and if well done is scarcely discernible. Needles soaked in salt water or dipped in waterproof glue will hold better. If regular imping needles cannot be procured, they can be filed from small wire nails or other material and tempered if necessary. All hawk flight and tail feathers ought to be saved and put in a box of mothballs or paradichlorbenzene crystals for future repairing.

**Ways to Procure Hawks.** Hawks can sometimes be secured by making arrangements with game farm operators. Since there is no hawk market, hawks can seldom, if ever, be purchased outright for a price. Nestlings are comparatively easy to get but

Plate VI. Three Types of Hoods.

no one need bother with a nestling. They are much more troublesome, difficult to get into good flying condition, and at best are inferior to a good "passage" hawk and hardly worth the time consumed. Hawks can sometimes be obtained through other falconers, but the most satisfactory way of securing a hawk is by trapping one during the fall migration. The autumn is the best time of the year to fly a hawk and nothing can beat a good passage hawk for style, appearance, and performance. There are plenty of surplus passage birds of all species to take care of all the needs of falconers. Of course, it is not everyone who has facilities to trap a hawk, and the few hawk trappers in existence are almost always unwilling to trap a hawk for sale. In other words, at the present time, there is no sure way of obtaining a suitable hawk unless one has the interest, time, and ingenuity to trap one for himself, or get a friend to do so. This is one of the falconer's first problems. A group of falconers could probably work out satisfactory ways and means, but they should be discriminating in so doing.

Most states have some laws protecting hawks and consequently, unless one can obtain the necessary permits, the trapping or keeping or hunting of a hawk may not be legally possible. However, those who have attained a knowledge of falconry and who can demonstrate their ability to handle and care for hawks properly will probably have no great difficulty in getting such permits, where they are required.

Most of the falconry books describe various net contrivances for trapping hawks, usually with a live pigeon for a decoy. Modern hawk trappers should take care to arrange their rig so as to protect the pigeon as much as possible. Many hawks, of several species, can be taken with a single pigeon without harm if the nets and lines are strung in such a manner as to give the pigeon sufficient protection. When a pigeon is used, it should be tethered by means of soft buckskin jesses. It is advisable to have several pigeons on hand so that no single pigeon will have to be kept out long enough to become tired. One of the best methods is the use of a "du-gaza" net stretched between two collapsible cane poles set up between the pigeon decoy and the oncoming hawks so that a hawk coming in will hit the net and be entangled before reaching the pigeon. Fine but strong linen "gill netting," if properly hung as fishermen hang it, is best. Five feet by 7 feet, when rigged, is ample. It is also well to have an inconspicuous inch-mesh chickenwire guard (painted black) opposite the center of the net where the pigeon can be brought to rest in comparative safety after attracting a hawk, thus giving it double protection. Extra nets well placed on all approaches are desirable also. These rigs should be set up 30 or 40 yards in front of a good blind.

The old-fashioned bow net, modified, is effective but more risky for pigeons and not quite as good as a "du-gaza." It may be made from fishermen's "pond netting" strung on two half-circle wires hinged together. It extends about 30 inches across the center and is set in a semicircle and pulled over with an off-center line. When this net is used, a suitable chickenwire guard should be placed over the glass ring in the center so as to protect the pigeon from the talons of hawks, without interfering with the action of the net or line. It is well also to place one or more "du-gazas" strategically about the bow net so as to protect the pigeon from any hawk. One should be on the alert for red-tailed hawks, goshawks, and Cooper's hawks, as they will kill a pigeon almost instantly, if it can be reached. One should also be practiced in timing the pull of the bow net so that the instant a hawk strikes the guard, the net will be sprung on any hawk missing the "du-gazas."

Pole traps are sometimes used for catching hawks, but to prevent injury they should never be left unwatched. In any case a No. 0 or No. 1 trap should

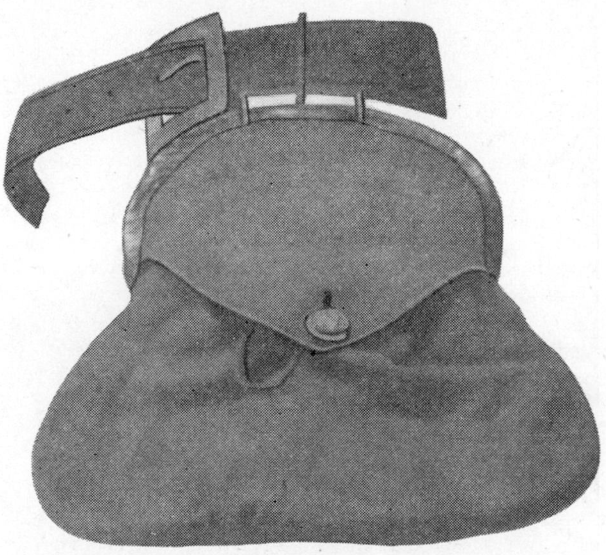

PLATE VIII. A Falconer's Bag.

be heated red hot in a fire and let cool in the air in order to remove much of the spring temper. Each jaw should be well wrapped with burlap so the hawk's legs will not be injured. Sparrow hawks are easily taken, when they are present, by placing a padded trap on top of a post set in an open field. Prairie falcons can be taken with pole traps, as can also any hawks visiting game farms. A goshawk or Cooper's flushed from fresh prey will usually return within an hour and can be taken in a padded trap or foot snares, if the trapper retreats out of view.

Prospective falconers should make it a rule to stay away from the nest of duck hawks and keep the egg collectors away also. Remember it is the peregrine's eyrie that is the source of the bird which gives delight to ornithologists and supplies falconers with the principal long-wing. An unmolested peregrine nest will go on producing three to five splendid falcons annually for many decades. Obviously, it is a foolish falconer or collector who would be so indiscriminate as to clean out the nest of a peregrine.

**Care of Hawks and Falcons.** All species of hawks can be kept indefinitely on a diet of good lean beef without anything else to eat or drink, but some individuals may be more sensitive to diet than others and will not do best on a straight beef diet. Fresh chuck-beef, stew meat, round steak, heart, etc., with fat and gristle cut away, is preferred. Pork or tainted meat will not do. Large hawks need to be fed only once a day, small hawks two or three times. From 2 to 8 ounces of red meat or equivalent is required, depending on the size of the hawk. All hawks should be given a sizable meal at least once a day, but the larger hawks may be pinched a little—enough to keep them keen—during the early training. A passage sparrow hawk, if it is underfed or suddenly has its diet changed from insects to beef, will sometimes get dumpy, lose its sleek appearance, and die in a few days before an inexperienced handler can discover what is wrong. It is all right to feed a variety of natural quarry containing feathers or fur when these are available. However, a would-be falconer ought not to engage in any unethical methods of obtaining food for a hawk, lest he incur a bad reputation. It is taboo and unnecessary to be indiscrimi-

Photo by Pix.

PLATE VIII. Hooded Duck Hawk, with Leash, Jesses, Bells, on a Block Perch.

nate in securing food for a hawk. It is much better to rely on beef, supplemented by legitimate and natural quarry taken by the hawk, or use game-bird and waterfowl heads and necks, etc., which happen to be the product of someone's hunting. Another possible supplement for beef can be found in fresh rabbits, squirrels, and birds lying dead on highways and roads.

Hawks may be kept without any "casting" material whatever, but they do better if feathers and fur or even strings of burlap are mixed with the food. These indigestible parts are "cast" out or regurgitated the next morning. These help to keep a hawk's crop and stomach clean and are healthful. The appearance of castings and "mutes" are indicators of a hawk's condition. A hawk should not be flown before she has cast her pellet.

Any outbuilding or even one's basement can be rigged to serve as a hawk house ("mews") to keep the hawk at night or in bad weather, or when one is away from home. It is not advisable to leave a hawk in a yard at all times unguarded. A hawk may be kept in a "mews" or any shed even during the coldest weather if it is free from draft or dampness and if the hawk is sufficiently fed. A screen perch is necessary for the hawk house and a block perch or bow perch for the yard.

No other hawk should ever be permitted to come within reach of a goshawk. Neither should small hawks be exposed to the reach of a large falcon because when hungry the larger hawk may attack the smaller.

Hawk tackle should always be in good repair, especially perches, leashes, swivels, and jesses. Swivel snaps are never left open in the jess loops, except immediately before a release. The leash is always held tightly while handling a hawk and never is a hawk permitted to fly with the leash on or in any manner that would hinder it, if lost.

Old jesses may be clipped off with scissors while the hawk is feeding and new ones replaced without disturbance.

Soiled feathers may be cleaned with a toothbrush and warm water.

When imping feathers, a hawk should first be hooded. Then a cloth is draped over her shoulders and at the same time both legs taken in the hand and she is partially "mailed" or bound with feet held back while the tail is imped. With wings, one wing at a time is drawn out and repaired.

There are other occasions when it may be necessary to "mail" a hawk. This is done by wrapping the feet together and rolling the hawk up in a cloth, wings closed and legs extending beneath the tail. A few crisscross wrappings with a cord over the cloth will keep the hawk still without harming the feathers. The wrapping should be snug, but not so tight as to make breathing difficult.

A passage hawk in perfect condition, obtained a few weeks before it is hunted, is easily kept in form, but a bird held for more than one season is difficult to recondition. In fact, it is almost impossible to get a falcon in anything like its natural style unless one has a good deal of time to work and fly it. About a half-hour a day of actual flying may keep a passage hawk in good flying order, if "weathered" long hours daily in the yard where it can exercise its wings hopping off and on the perch. Short-wings do not require as much perch weathering as long-wings. The weathering plus hunting every few days will suffice, but in the training process daily exercising to the lure once or twice giving some strong flight is recommended. Some falconers fly their hawks at pigeons, but the dubious practice of training hawks and dogs on pigeons might better be avoided. If ever a pigeon is flown, the wing feathers should not be bent or clipped. The use of pigeons will cause a hawk to be less attentive to the lure, which is another good reason for not training on pigeons.

PLATE IX. A Gyrfalcon on a Block Perch.

One of the secrets of having good hawks in good plumage is to get the hawks from the wild in the fall when they are at their best and release them at the close of the hunting season before too severe weather sets in. A sluggish hawk with battered plumage is a disgrace to any falconer, besides being a sure sign of either carelessness or amateurish bungling. It sometimes may be advisable to keep a good

PLATE X. Immature Male Goshawk on Bow Perch with Indian Hood.

hawk for more than one season if a falconer has the time and adequate facilities.

**A Short Training Method.** *First day:* The hawk is hooded immediately when caught, jesses and leash put on, and then placed on a perch or log in a smooth place for the remainder of the day. A good modified Indian hood is best. A hawk must not be left alone where she will become entangled, hang, or be harmed by owls or other animals. No training is needed the first day except to avoid frightening. Some may be unhooded and fed the first evening but it is usually not advisable.

*Second day:* If possible, it is best to place the hawk on a screen perch bare-faced in a room or some place where people are moving about. When removing a goshawk's hood for the first time, it is best to have the hawk in a darkened place and remove the hood while she is feeding. If she bates from the perch, she should recover herself and come back to the perch readily. If she does not do this in the presence of the falconer, he should depart for five or ten minutes. If the hawk is still hanging, she will either have to be rehooded or removed from the screen perch, as it might kill a hawk to hang from a perch for an extended time. No one should move too fast or too close around the hawk for the first few days. Meat is fed from the hand or in some way, once or twice. Rubbing a hawk's feet or putting the meat to her shoulder may help.

*Third day:* Continue as on second day, but hawk may be fed two or three times daily. At each feeding, it should be allowed a fairly good crop, particularly the last meal. At these meals the hawk should be coaxed to walk along the screen perch or jump up to the fist, if she will. Progress can be slowly made at each meal, if there are no retarding incidents. A peregrine may be fed on a lure near the block perch. If placed in the yard, children playing fairly near by is good, but no one should approach except with caution within ten yards. Always at night the hawk should be placed on the screen perch. Moving after dark the first few days is best, although the hawk can be moved while feeding. If one is adept at the use of the hood, it is best to use it when carrying the hawk about. Advancement should be made as fast as the hawk will allow it, but care should be taken at all times not to set the hawk back in the training process by any unnecessary excitement. All training should be done so as to give the hawk full confidence. A little handling a few times a day is all right, but much handling and carrying is not really necessary and if not properly done will do more harm than good. If the hawk seems frightened and resentful, the handling is probably doing no good. If the hawk is willing and unafraid, progress is being made.

*Fourth day:* Continue as before, but lengthening the distance the hawk will come to the fist or lure each feeding. The coaxing to the lure or fist is repeated with increasing distances about half a dozen times each feeding, if she has not eaten too much. The falconer always whistles when offering feed, or calling a hawk, to help keep her attention. When removing meat from a hawk, it is not pulled away roughly or too obviously, but while the hawk is

Photo by Pix.

PLATE XI. A Falcon Returning to the Lure Swung by the Falconer.

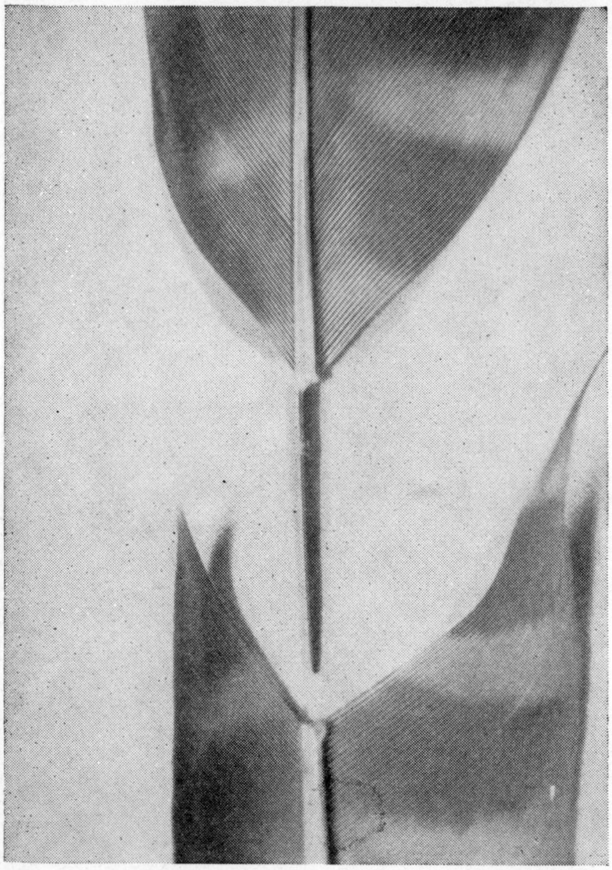

Photo by Pix.

PLATE XII. Feather Prepared for Imping—underside view.

held on the fist with one hand the meat is pulled down through the partially closed fist and concealed in such a manner as to leave the hawk wondering where it went.

*Fifth day:* Continue as before, placing the hawk in the yard on a bow perch or block perch before feeding. At each meal, feeding should be started at the hawk's feet or very close and then lengthened little by little as far as the hawk will come without much delay. Keep short-wings and small falcons on a screen perch and work inside until they will respond quickly when the fist is held up. If the hawk will come more than the length of the leash, a creance of suitable length not exceeding 50 yards—may be attached. After the feeding, and flying if possible, the hawk may be left out for the rest of the day. At the second feeding the calling is repeated, and after this is finished she is returned to the screen perch. Goshawks probably will not fly well outside before a week or more of training.

*Sixth to tenth days:* When the hawk will come quickly and surely to the fist or lure about 25 or 50 yards, she may then be flown loose, increasing the distance little by little as far as she will come without much hesitation. When flying hawks to the outstretched arm, care should be taken to keep a strong grip on the meat on the fist to prevent the hawk from striking it off and carrying it away. Training is continued for about one-half hour to one hour a day until the hawk will fly well to the lure or fist and permit handling and hooding without alarm. Two flight periods are better than one. During the first ten days, the falconer should practice walking up to the hawk while she is feeding, so that when she is flown loose there is no difficulty in approaching her. In ten days to two weeks, more or less, depending upon the progress made, it may be safe to make a falcon wait a little. This is done by calling her at a distance and hiding the lure before she takes it, making her circle and wait as much as she will without getting tired and sitting down or wandering off out of control. She will not wait much, if at all, to begin with.

In about ten days or two weeks, the hawk should be thoroughly acquainted with the trainer and seemingly at ease. By this time she should be flying unhesitatingly and keenly to the fist or lure a distance of 100 yards or more without the use of a creance. The time it takes to get a hawk flying well depends upon the individual disposition of the hawk and more particularly the experience of the falconer. An accomplished falconer may have a falcon flying loose in three or four days, but a beginner would be disappointed if he tried it. It should be remembered that hawks have off days and setbacks and times when they are indifferent. Whenever a hawk is not eager for her food, she should not be flown loose. A hawk may be carried to the field either barefaced on the fist, or hooded and on a perch or the back of a car seat, or in a dark compartment. All similar species of hawks may be trained in a corresponding manner, except that more care should be taken to feed small hawks two or three times a day so that they can be kept in a high condition.

When the hawk will fly regularly to the lure or fist, will permit handling and hooding without fear, and will allow approach while on the ground, she is ready for the hunting practice or whatever use is to be made of her. Beware of clear warm days in the fall, as the hawk may soar away and be lost. One must be cautious at all times for at least a month.

Besides good daily feeding, give a hawk all she will eat at least once a week, more often if in doubt.

**Hunting with Hawks.** There are two principal ways to hunt hawks: (1) By flying directly from the fist at quarry within range (including "downhill" hawking), and (2) by putting a hawk up and flushing game beneath, while the hawk flies, soars, or "waits on" high overhead. A good dog is most helpful for this kind of hunting.

All short-wings, as well as pigeon hawks or merlins, are flown from the fist with or without the halsband. Such hawks may be flown by this method at any suitable quarry on almost any type of terrain, except dense woods.

The long-wings or large falcons are sometimes flown at birds of passage such as crows, which do not hide on the ground, but they are more often put up high over game to be flushed beneath them. A good falcon, well trained for hunting, will mount rapidly to a height of several hundred feet and follow or wait for several minutes overhead until the falconer flushes the quarry beneath. For such hunting, falcons must be well trained to the lure so that their attention can be held by showing the lure if necessary, and so that they can be called in if they should be unsuccessful at taking game.

Besides having a falcon well trained to an attractive lure, it is advisable, when going afield, to carry a live pigeon with soft buckskin jesses on its legs and a hawk-type leash attached. The pigeon is used only when necessary. When a falcon must be called from a long distance or when she fails to respond readily to the regular lure, the pigeon, held by the end of the leash in one hand, may be tossed up a little. The fluttering of the pigeon will get the hawk's attention if anything will, but the pigeon should be put under cover and the lure thrown out when the hawk is coming in. A pigeon is not otherwise needed in the management of falcons.

Falcons can be flown successfully only in fairly open country—the more open and unobstructed the better. An open space of a square mile is none too much, although in some cases they may be flown without difficulty in smaller spaces. Falcons work well over dogs when trained to do so; consequently a good pointer or setter is most desirable when hunting game with a falcon.

A peregrine at a height of 1000 to 2000 feet has command over nearly a quarter section and can fold up and stoop at the prey like a falling meteor at a speed approaching 200 miles an hour. Judging from the comparative speeds of homing pigeons and duck hawks, it appears that a duck hawk in a straightaway flight can attain a speed of nearly 70 miles an hour. A homer can fly about 50 miles an hour without the drive of a wind.

A goshawk is much faster on the getaway than a falcon and can easily outfly a falcon on a short flight. They are built for comparatively brief, fast rushes at prey whereas the falcon is adapted to diving or "stooping" from a height at its quarry. The shortwings can also drop from a height or down a hill, but they are not as fast and spectacular in this respect as the long-wings. Flushing dogs may be used with goshawks if trained to hunt together.

Falcons nearly always take their prey in flight in open places, whereas short-winged hawks frequently catch their prey on the ground and are adept at speeding through brush and around trees. Goshawks can take practically anything that a peregrine can, as well as ruffed grouse, rabbits, etc., not suitable for a falcon. The goshawk probably has no equal among the hawks as a game getter, and some prefer the short-winged type of flight. Short-wings all kill their prey quickly with their talons. Falcons use their talons merely to grip their prey. They either knock their quarry out in the air by a tremendous blow with the feet and back talon, or dispatch it when down by severing the neck with the notched beak constructed for this purpose.

Merlins or pigeon hawks have characteristics of both the short-wings and the long-wings and can be flown either in the open or in semi-closed country. If well trained they can be flown singly at the larger quarry in their class. However, they used to be flown mostly in casts of two to offset their habit of carrying small prey out of reach. If flown in pairs at sparrow-sized prey, they will "crab" or clutch together and be forced to the ground where the falconer can get hold of them.

Hunting with hawks, no matter how it is done, is definitely a handicap. It requires skill and good timing in every detail to make it succesful, though

Photo by Pix.

PLATE XIII. A Falcon Hitting the Lure.

there is really nothing mysterious about hunting with a hawk. It is simply a matter of getting a hawk to perform in a manner she is naturally accustomed to. The main difference is that the hawk must be "manned"—fearlessly acquainted with means of transportation, carrying on the fist, hoods if used, the presence of dogs and people—and permit the falconer to "make in" or approach after a flight. Above all, she must be keenly interested in the lure at mealtime or when taken out, but not so "sharp-set" or eager that she will not "ring" up. A very experienced falconer in some instances may successfully fly a nearly wild hawk, but it is best to have the hawk willingly familiar with all circumstances demanded.

It is commonly supposed that hawks retrieve—but they do not. They take their prey wherever they can and proceed to "plume" or pluck it preparatory to a feed while the falconer approaches. The falconer walks up carefully and allows the hawk to eat a part of the quarry or deftly substitutes a piece of meat and puts the game in his pocket. The hawk is then hooded or put away and the hunt is completed. It is sometimes possible to get a falcon to make two or even three flights before being fed up. Short-wings have been flown five or ten times in a day, but usually one or two good flights is considered satisfactory.

If a hawk is lost or disappears out of sight, she may later return to the lure if well trained, or be found at the nearest water taking a bath. The badgering of martins, robins, crows, or other birds may reveal her whereabouts. On migration days, a hawk may depart speedily, but she may remain in the vicinity for a few days. An all-out search will usually bring results, if she be within a mile.

For successful flights, quarry to be flown at should be previously spotted or "marked down." Almost the exact location must be known before putting up a long-wing. To do this a dog may be essential.

Briefly, if a pheasant is spotted or found in a field, preferably with the aid of a dog, the falcon is unhooded and unleashed and after a moment is tossed up perhaps 50 to 100 yards from the pheasant. After she "rings up" to her "pitch" about as high as she will go, nearly overhead and looking in the right direction, the pheasant may be flushed. The hawk will then "stoop" or dive down head first at a terrific speed, easily overtaking the pheasant. If a goshawk is used, the pheasant should be approached as closely as possible and the bare-faced hawk, held by jesses only or with halsband, is thrown after the pheasant the instant it flushes. Goshawks will also start after prey on the ground, if visible.

The above paragraphs barely hint at the procedure, but space does not permit discussion of all of the details of hunting the many types of quarry with the various types of hawks. Each species of hawks has its characteristic abilities and habits of hunting. Allowances also have to be made for weather conditions. Different types of terrain must be worked in various manners. Each species of quarry, depending on its particular habits, must be approached accordingly. Some reading, well sifted, will help but some actual experience will do more than volumes. If one has the fortune to know an experienced falconer, he will learn many short cuts which otherwise might take him a long time to discover. The type of country one lives in or can get to, and the game laws of his state, will determine largely the kind of hawk one should keep and the species of quarry which may be hunted.

# FERRETING

Although a popular sport in Europe for several centuries, ferreting originated in Asia and was practiced by the ancient tribes of that continent at least as early as the first century after Christ. It is not a common sport in America as the laws of many states prohibit its practice. Ferreting can briefly be defined as a form of hunting where ferrets are used to drive rats and rabbits from their subterranean retreats. The ferret is about the only animal in the weasel family that has been thoroughly domesticated. It was originally derived from an Asiatic strain of polecats but has been crossed with the European species, resulting in variable size and unstable coloration. The polecat is still found in the wild state both in Europe and Asia. The marten is one of its nearest relatives in America.

Most weasels are figured in folklore and the ferret is no exception. Superstition in Europe has it that the ferret possesses great healing powers and a pan of milk which has been blessed by the ferret's tasting it will cure whooping cough. One old peasant who had great faith put it this way: "Doctor's given er up, and she comin to directly by a drop o' the milk the blessed little craythurs had been a-lappin' at; and it's the only rale remedy ye can put ye're intire faith in."

Ferreting was well known to the Romans; Strabo stated that the ferret was originally brought from Africa into Spain. Pliny was familiar with the sport in his time and refers to it as practiced in hunting rabbits.

In selecting and breeding ferrets, the smaller they are the greater service can be expected of them. The training consists of little more than bringing the ferret into top condition by restrictive feeding and breaking it to handling. Where dogs are used along with the ferret, it is the dog that must be familiarized with and taught to respect his co-worker.

There are three practices used in ferreting: two for rabbits and one for rats. In rabbit hunting the ferret is muzzled with a "cope" made by looping a piece of twine around the muzzle and over the back of the ferret's head. The cope is knotted to regulate the tension. The ferret is then turned loose in the hole with a back door. The rabbit, escaping through the bolt-hole, is either shot by a gunner, caught in a net, or run by the dog. Where there is a dead-end hole, the ferret has a stout line attached to his neck and is traced by sinking holes a yard apart and following the line until the rabbit is reached.

The most popular form of ferreting is hunting for rats along hedgerows and stone walls around cornfields or farm buildings. The ferret is turned loose without a muzzle or any other encumbrance at the entrance of a rat hole. Terriers, in leash, on either side of the fence, are held in check until the opportune moment arrives, when the rat, sensing his arch-enemy at his heels, bolts for the open. Sometimes three or four rats spring out in quick succession; then for a few moments action is fast and furious and excitement runs high. The ferret continues to work the entire network of subterranean channels until satisfied that all have been dislodged. After that he has no further interest and emerges. When a ferret refuses to go down a hole you can be assured there is nothing there.

Ferrets are best carried in a burlap bag, usually two or three together, for a morning's rat hunt. They work hard and need a rest between operations. Ferrets dislike wet ground and do not work well in wet weather.

Should a ferret make a kill himself he will immediately devour as much as he can hold on the spot, and then curl up and go to sleep. Nothing will disturb his slumber until he feels the pangs of hunger again, eight or nine hours later, and not before then can you hope to retrieve the lost ferret from the labyrinth of subterranean runways.

In general, ferrets are white with pinkish eyes or yellowish white in color, often with a fine admixture of black. In some, the black predominates, the eyes are black, and they closely resemble the wild polecat of Europe. Ferrets vary in size from that of a rat to almost as large as a house cat. However, the average length for head and body is about 14 inches and the tail 5 inches. The male ("Hob") is larger than female ("Jill"). The ferret has a long body but his strength lies in his jaws and neck. Once the needle-pointed teeth are clamped on a victim nothing but the will of the ferret can pry them loose. With a twist from the bulging muscles of his neck he can throw any creature on its back, up to twice his own size.

When not actually in use ferrets are kept in a pen, a compact, well-built wooden structure, 6 feet long, 4 feet high, and 4 feet wide with a slanting waterproof roof. The pen is divided into two compartments, one 2 feet long, the other 4 feet long, with a 4-inch hole close to the floor in the partition to permit free access from one to the other. The large section is faced with half-inch wire mesh. The smaller division is the nest box or sleeping compartment: this is enclosed in front with wood, to make it dark, and filled with clean straw. The whole structure is raised on legs 3 or 4 feet from the ground to insure dry, comfortable quarters. The pen or pens are kept outside in a shady place in summer but must have a warm southern exposure or be brought under cover in winter. Ferrets have been domesticated for many centuries and will not survive cold, hard winters if not given suitable protection and shelter.

Ferrets are carnivorous animals and under natural conditions eat raw meat but when not being used for hunting may be fed much the same food as a house cat. They readily devour cooked meat, potatoes, and vegetables, with gravy or bread and milk. However, before hunting, the ferret must be brought into top condition. The rations must be cut to eliminate excess fat because it promotes laziness; feeding is restricted to raw meat and no fat. Two or three days before hunting, the ferrets are fed hot blood—that is to say, animals just killed while the blood is still hot in them. Poultry or rabbits are suitable for this purpose. Normally ferrets are fed two meals each day but when worked are fed little on the morning of the working day.

Photo from Pete Barrett, N. Y.

PLATE I. The Ferret at a Rabbit Hole.

Common diseases among ferrets are foot-rot, distemper, diphtheria, and influenza. Foot-rot, the most common, is directly due to dirty pens. Foot-rot attacks the claws and feet first and then spreads to the nose and tail. Distemper is nothing more than an advanced stage of foot-rot. Diphtheria is a throat trouble indicated by a swelling of the throat. In influenza, the nose runs and the eyes are affected. Ferrets are normally hardy, clean animals in themselves; with clean, comfortable quarters and proper care all ailments are practically eliminated before they can get a start. There are numerous remedies advocated for diseased ferrets but few survive to be serviceable.

Normally ferrets breed twice a year and litters vary from four to nine. The mating season is in April, May, and July; gestation takes between 42 and 45 days, but before this time is up the male is removed. At birth the young ferrets are without hair and their eyes are closed for the first ten days. During the time the mother ferret is nursing her young she must be kept well supplied with food and the nest compartment not opened. Young ferrets will be ready to work when they are about seven weeks old.

Ferrets should be picked up by the shoulders, bringing the hand up from behind when the ferret is moving forward with his attention fixed in front. The movement of the hand shold be deliberate and the grip firm but not tight. Taken so, the body goes limp and there is no struggle or attempt to get away. If taken by the neck he will try to back out and will probably manage to do so; taken behind the shoulders he may reach around and bite. Beginners should practice first with a thick glove. Always bear in mind that it requires considerably more tact and skill to pick up an alert, blooded ferret than a sluggish, milk-fed one.

Hunting rats with a ferret and terriers is the only sport that can be practiced the year round. Furthermore, it is the only form of hunting that can be operated within city limits and in public parks. Ferreting is an exhilarating and entertaining pastime that has much to recommend it. The house rat is the most destructive animal in the world. There are more rats in North America than people, probably twice as many. The destruction wrought by this vast horde of rodents exceeds that of all other injurious animals combined. Losses from depredations of the house rat amount to millions of dollars annually, and the rat (principally as a disease carrier) is responsible for more human deaths than all the wars of history. A sport that is such an asset to our national economy should be not only popular but encouraged. The hunter that shoots a ferocious wildcat or a wolf has in reality accomplished little, and in fact he has got very little fun out of the incident, but a morning's sport at ferreting is not only entertaining but has aided in the elimination of man's most deadly enemy.

# HUNTING KNIVES

The legitimate uses for a hunter's knife are first and chiefly whittling—all kinds of woodwork around camp; second, skinning game; third, butchering game; and then a little of slicing bread and bacon and doing various jobs with leather and canvas. For all these purposes the knife should be of medium weight, keen shaped, very sharp, and of good steel. The one thing a knife will not be used for, and for which, strange to say, many of them are exclusively designed, is self-defense. Opening cans is sheer abuse.

The steel should be such that it can be sharpened fairly easily on a whetstone, and will then keep its edge for a reasonable time. Most American knives, and most of those made in Sheffield, England, have good steel. Stainless steel is almost impossible to sharpen in the field.

If the knife is not kept keen and sharp all work with it is greatly prolonged, and good work is impossible. With continued use in camp it will need sharpening every three or four days. Skinning animals dulls it very quickly. In skinning a deer it will probably need sharpening about three times during the operation, and for a Rocky Mountain goat about ten times. So a pocket whetstone is a necessity. A carborundum stone, coarse on one side, fine on the other, is best, as it can be used with either

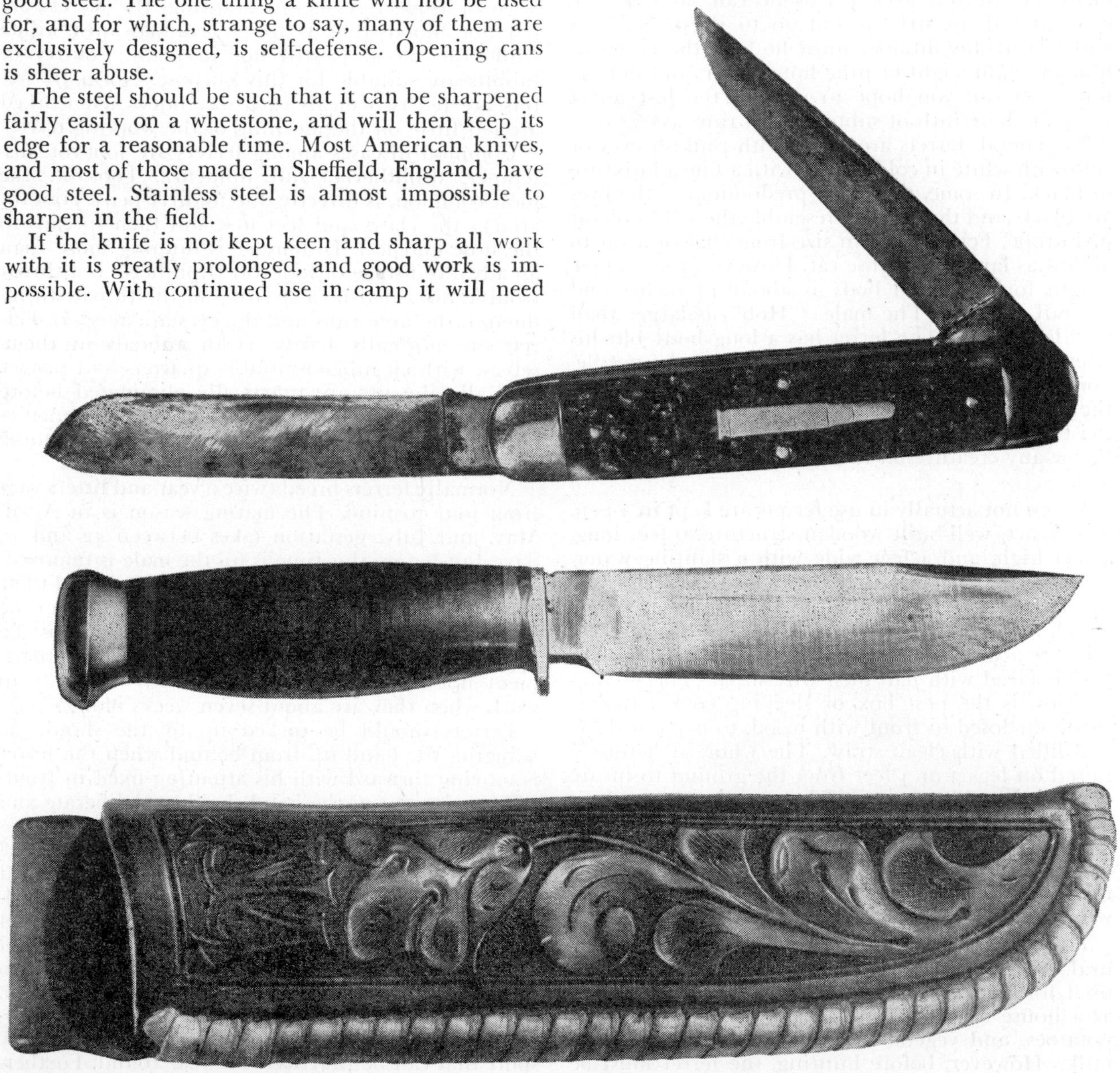

PLATE I. Satisfactory Types of Hunting Knife and Clasp Knife.

oil or water. The blade should be held on the stone at a slight angle, which will vary with individual types of knives and must therefore be learned from experience. When the edge is sharp, push, don't pull, the edge over the stone, first on one side and then on the other alternately for about 20 strokes to take off the feather edge. A sharp knife should easily shave the hairs on one's forearm.

Much can be said both for and against sheath knives and pocket knives. The choice is purely a personal one. Perhaps the best idea would be to take both, as the loss of one's only knife would be serious to a hunter. Then soon one will form a personal preference for one type or another.

A sheath knife, having but one blade, must have that of a general-purpose type, good for whittling, skinning, and butchering. The illustration on p. 968 shows the best compromise shape. The blade should be short, about 4 inches, certainly not over 5 inches. Larger knives are unhandy, slow, and useless for fine work. The leather sheath should enclose all but the extreme end of the handle. Those enclosing only the blade, with a snap buckle around the handle, are responsible for many lost knives. The seam of the sheath near the point should be sewed with copper wire so the blade cannot penetrate the sheath and cut one in case of a fall.

The pocket knife should be a large, strong one—*not* a pen knife. There had best be two blades between 2½ and 3 inches long. The illustration on p. 968 shows the best shape for the blades, the sharp-pointed one for slitting and fine work, the rounded one for straight skinning.

Have a kitchen knife, a hand-ax, and a can opener in your camp-kit and don't ask your hunting knife to do the work of any of these.

In tropical jungles and rain forests another type of knife is absolutely essential—the machete. Besides clearing trails, cutting underbrush, pegs, and tent poles, it does all the work of an ax for which there is little need in the tropics. It should be a regular machete of the type used by natives everywhere throughout the tropics, not one of the short, heavy brush knives recently offered in the United States. The blade should be broad and thin to give a good cutting edge. The best, procurable in almost all tropical countries, are made by Collins & Co., Collinsville, Conn. They usually come too long; the experienced bush native always shortens the blade to about 15 inches with a file. Besides the whetstone, a small flat file should be taken to keep the machete sharp. In its leather sheath it is much more conveniently carried on the back of the rucksack than on the belt.

# NATIONAL FORESTS AND THE HUNTER

Every citizen of the United States owns some first-class hunting ground. He is a shareholder in the world's outstanding public forest system—the National Forests. His individual share in this great public estate is equal to about an acre and a third, but he is entitled to hunt over almost any part of the 180,000,000 acres of National Forest land. His custodian and manager on the ground is the Forest Service of the U. S. Department of Agriculture. His "Board of Directors," which sets up the broad policies and appropriates the funds for administration, is the United States Congress, which he and his fellow-shareholders elect.

The National Forests are the home of a large share of the country's wildlife. Although they include less than one-tenth of the country's total land area, they harbor more than one-third of all the big-game animals in the United States. The density of big game in the National Forests is more than twice as great as on lands in any other general class of ownership. There is also a wide variety of small game and birds.

A total of 1,345,000 hunters used the National Forests in 1946. Many of these hunters were also among the 2,730,000 fishermen who availed themselves of the 90,000 miles of national forest fishing streams and 1,500,000 acres of fishing lakes that are open to the public. Hunters and fishermen combined used the National Forests for a total of more than 16,000,000 man-days. The number of hunters has been increasing before the war and since, and the Forest Service believes the trend will continue upward for some years to come.

There are National Forests in 40 of the states and in two territories—Alaska and Puerto Rico. On June 30, 1947, the gross area within the designated boundaries of National Forest units was 228,810,442 acres, of which 179,314,756 acres were publicly owned and under Forest Service administration. This net area changes from time to time as a result of purchases and land exchanges. The gross area includes several National Forest purchase units where development has only recently started, and within these units some 24,000,000 acres still need to be purchased to complete their development as public forests. There are also an additional 10,000,000 acres of intermingled private lands within the boundaries of other National Forests, chiefly west of the Great Plains, which the Forest Service hopes will eventually be consolidated with the surrounding publicly owned lands.

Establishment of the National Forest system was the first great step in the conservation movement in America. The National Forest system began in 1891, when Congress authorized the setting aside of forest reserves from the public domain. It was not until 1905, however, when these early forest reserves were placed under the jurisdiction of the Department of Agriculture and the U. S. Forest Service was set up in that Department, that development of the National Forest system really got under way. The earliest National Forests were largely in the western states where most of the remaining public domain land was located. In 1911, Congress enacted the Weeks Law which authorized federal purchase of lands for National Forest purposes, and development of a number of National Forests began in states east of the Great Plains.

Many persons confuse National Forests with National Parks. National Parks are separate and distinct areas, under separate jurisdiction. They are maintained for the preservation of unique and outstanding areas of scenic, geologic, or historic interest. Hunting is not permitted in these parks. The much larger National Forest area is administered for the production and use, in the public interest, of a variety of resources, including timber, range forage, game, and recreational values. Watershed protection is a major objective in most National Forests.

In the management of our National Forests, the Forest Service has two keynote principles. One of these is what foresters call "sustained yield." Although the techniques of sustained-yield forest management are varied and complex, the objective is simple enough—to keep forest land yielding maximum returns continuously. The principle applies not only to timber crops but to wildlife—and to range forage, recreational values, water supplies, and other forest products and services as well.

The other keynote principle in National Forest management is "multiple use." This means simply that the various uses and services of a given forest area are co-ordinated in one over-all management plan. The great bulk of the forest land can be used for a number of purposes—such as timber growing, livestock grazing, wildlife habitat, watershed protection, and recreation. Under multiple-use management, such uses can be combined and co-ordinated on the same forest unit. It may be necessary to provide special limitations for certain areas within the forest—livestock grazing, for instance, must usually be kept away from heavily used recreation areas; or timber cutting must be restricted where it would damage important scenic values. But conflicts of various interests or uses can be adjusted by carefully worked out over-all planning, and the greatest sum total of contributions to the economic life of the nation can be realized.

Under such multiple-use management, wildlife gets full recognition and consideration along with all other resources of the National Forests. Game management plans are prepared for every forest unit, and are co-ordinated with timber, recreation, and other resources-management plans. Within many of the National Forests there are certain areas where wildlife is considered the major resource, and on such areas other uses are subordinated to wildlife management. The effects on wildlife habitat and welfare of game herds is considered in planning and conducting timber-cutting operations and other activities.

**Big-Game Populations.** The 1946 estimate of big game population in the National Forests indicated a total of at least 2,300,000 animals. Deer are by far the most numerous. The 1946 "census" showed 1,170,000 mule deer, 576,000 whitetail deer and 287,000 Columbia blacktail deer. There were 159,000 elk, 83,000 black bear, 6200 grizzly or Alaska brown bear, and 27,000 antelope. In addition there were estimated to be 20,000 mountain goats, 10,000 moose, 9700 bighorn sheep, 11,000 javelinas or peccaries, and 1500 wild boar. There are countless thousands of small game animals and upland birds.

In the National Forests throughout the East and the Middle West are found cottontail rabbits, raccoons, squirrels, and the Virginia or whitetail deer. Wild turkeys are found from Virginia, Kentucky, and Missouri southward. Wild boars are available to a limited extent in the southern Appalachians. Ruffed grouse is highly prized in the cooler parts of the country, as is the woodcock in the Northeast. Black bear and opossum have a fairly general distribution.

While many kinds of small game are also available in the National Forests of the western states, the main interest has always been centered on the numbers and variety of big game animals available. Despite an expanding hunter removal the western mule deer in one or more of its several variations is found in slowly increasing numbers on nearly every National Forest in the West. Whitetail deer are found in New Mexico and Arizona, the northern Rocky Mountains, and the Northwest; and the mule deer's close cousin, the Columbia blacktail, is common in the Northwest and much of California. Wapiti or elk are found on many of the National Forests of the West and range in spectacularly large herds in Montana, Wyoming, Colorado, and Idaho. Less important numerically but of great interest to the naturalist and hunter is America's largest representative of the deer family, the moose, which is found in National Forests of Montana, Idaho, and Wyoming. A few are also found in Minnesota, but because of their scarcity are not hunted there. Mountain goats live in the more remote and inaccessible areas of Idaho, Montana, and Washington; and the bighorn or mountain sheep ranges in limited numbers in all the western states. In Arizona and New Mexico is found the native wild pig, known locally as peccary or javelina. The native pronghorn or antelope has made a remarkable recovery in the past two decades and is now found on and adjacent to many of the western National Forests. Black bears are taken both as game and predators throughout the West, and grizzlies or silvertips are hunted in Idaho, Montana, and Wyoming.

In the Southwest, many fortunate hunters get the thrill of a lifetime when they first bag a magnificent Merriam's wild turkey. Gambel's, scaled, and desert quail are found in the Southwest, and mountain quail are enthusiastically sought in California. The dusky grouse is found in the Rocky Mountain states, and the closely related sooty grouse ranges mostly in the fir forests of the Pacific Northwest. Ruffed grouse is found to a limited extent in all the West as far south as Colorado, Utah, and northern California; and the large gray sage hens are encountered in practically all of the sagebrush country east of the Cascades and as far south as Colorado, Utah, and Nevada.

Blacktail deer, elk, moose, mountain goats, bighorn, and black bear are hunted in the two National Forests of Alaska, but it is the great Alaska brown bear, largest of carnivorous game animals, that is the prize attraction in the northern territory.

At the time of their creation, there was a general depletion of wildlife in the National Forests of the western states. Similarly, the eastern National Forests, although of later development, were for the most part understocked at the time of their establishment. The first wildlife work on the National Forests was therefore concerned with the protection of the decimated wild animal populations. Forest

Service officers took an active part in enforcement of game laws and helped materially in establishing a public respect for such measures—a difficult task, since game laws were often new and inadequate, state game departments poorly financed, and public attitude often uninterested or even hostile.

The National Forests in many cases provided almost the only retreat for elks, mountain goats, bighorn, grizzlies, and other species that were being pushed off their former range by the encroachment of agriculture and settlement. Forest officers undertook to control predatory animals, and gave support to the efforts of state authorities to establish game refuges. Some game species, such as elk, had been eliminated from large portions of their native range. The Forest Service and state game departments co-operated in a number of transplants of game animals.

In the East, the period of depletion had extended over a longer period of time than in the West. People had lived in and adjacent to the forest areas for more than a century so that when National Forests were set up through purchase of private lands, wildlife problems of long standing were encountered. Deer had been completely wiped out in some areas. Throughout the South, the promiscuous running of hogs and dogs was a widespread practice with local residents. The discouragement of this practice, plus good law enforcement, was therefore a preliminary step to any program of wildlife development on many national forest areas in the South, the southern Appalachians, and the Ozarks.

The first big job was restoration and protection of wildlife. Later, as wildlife populations increased through protection, it became apparent that a program of wildlife management was necessary—that attention should be given to habitat, and that game should be managed and cropped in accordance with the capabilities of the land and in correlation with the other resources of the land.

Some attempts to estimate game numbers were made by the Forest Service as early as 1913. Systematic game census work began in 1921, and has continued yearly ever since. It is, of course, impossible actually to count noses of all game animals. The national forest game "census," however, is based on careful estimates by local Forest officers who watch closely the conditions and trends of wildlife in their areas. Actual counts of some of the big-game herds are made from the air when there is snow on the ground and the animals can easily be spotted from an airplane. There is every indication that the annual estimates of game populations come very close to what actual counts would show, if such counts were possible on a nation-wide basis.

Since 1921 the number of big-game animals has nearly quadrupled. Deer have multiplied four times over, and elk are more than three times as plentiful as in 1921. Antelope made a phenomenal come-back of more than 900 per cent. Black bear, moose, and Alaska brown bear have nearly doubled in numbers; mountain goats have more than held their own. Only bighorn have decreased—to about 70 per cent of the number estimated in 1921; but in the past few years they have been making small gains.

**Hunting in the National Forests.** Generally, all National Forests are open to hunting, with no restrictions other than those imposed by the state game laws. The Forest Service makes no charge for hunting, and requires no special license. The hunter must have a state hunting license, however, to hunt on national forest land as well as on any other land. The state game laws as to seasons and bag limits apply on the National Forests.

There are some exceptions. In some of the National Forests, certain areas have been designated as federal or state game refuges, within which hunting is either prohibited or is governed by special rules. Sometimes, because of extreme fire hazard, it is necessary to order temporary closure of certain areas. The Forest Service and the states co-operate in conducting regulated deer or elk hunts from time to time in some of the western National Forests. These may be extended-season hunts, or special hunts in refuge areas, to reduce excess deer or elk populations. In such cases, a special fee may be charged, and the number of hunters may be limited, those permitted to hunt being selected on a first-come-first-served basis or by drawing lots.

In Virginia, the legislature passed a law in 1938 requiring that a special $1 stamp be purchased in addition to the regular state license by persons hunting or fishing in the George Washington and Jefferson National Forests. The stamp money is expended to improve hunting and fishing conditions on the forest areas, in accordance with a co-operative agreement between the state and the Forest Service. In other National Forests in the Southeast and South, some 30 more or less similar co-operative wildlife management units totaling over 1,500,000 acres have been set up. These special wildlife areas are under specific co-operative agreements between the Forest Service and the states. A special fee is collected by the states and shared with the Forest Service to pay the salaries of patrolmen and defray the cost of wildlife management work. The agreements also provide for an annual revision of the hunting and fishing program so that the game and fish take can be kept in accord with the harvestable wildlife surplus or crop.

The Grand Canyon National Game Refuge in Kaibab National Forest of Arizona is a deer-management area under a federal-state co-operative plan. Following an annual census to determine the size of the herd and its condition, and a study of the adequacy of the forage supply, an annual hunting program is prepared, based on the number of animals of either sex to be taken by hunters. Special fees are collected in addition to the regular state license, the special fees being used to defray costs of management of the herd and conduct of the public hunt. Hunters are limited to the predetermined number, and on arrival are assigned to hunting areas in accordance with the distribution of the deer and other management considerations. Check stations are maintained to obtain data on the success of the hunt and the condition and character of the animals taken. Thus, a continuing record is maintained of the range, the deer herd, and the hunter success, so that annual revisions can be readily made to obtain the best results.

Regulated deer and bear hunts along similar lines are conducted from time to time in the Pisgah National Forest of North Carolina, which is also a national game preserve. Advance announcement of such special hunts is made through the press.

**Wild Boar Hunting.** Around the turn of the century, a group of wealthy sportsmen imported a few European wild boars with the idea of developing a herd of these animals on a private hunting preserve in the southern Appalachians. The animals broke out of their enclosure and took to the woods. They thrived and multiplied in their new environment, and more than 1300 animals now range in parts of what are now the Nantahala National Forest of North Carolina and the Cherokee National Forest of Tennessee. (See p. 39.)

Most of the wild boar are found in the Tellico division of the Cherokee. This area is one of the special co-operative wildlife management units described above; and in recent years the Forest Service and the State of Tennessee have permitted a limited amount of boar hunting. The number of hunters issued permits is limited, so that the number of boars killed will not exceed the annual increase of animals, and the boar population will be maintained at approximately its present size.

European wild boar are ferocious and dangerous animals. The hunters are usually organized in parties conducted by experienced local guides, with dogs.

As the result of another importation many years ago, a small number of European wild boar have also established themselves in the Monterey division of Los Padres National Forest in California.

**Facilities for Hunters.** There is no charge for entering National Forests. Most of them can be reached via regular state highways, and many of the National Forests are traversed by forest highways which are links in the state and transcontinental highway systems.

The Forest Service has constructed thousands of miles of secondary roads, which provide access to many parts of the National Forests not served by the main highways. Additional highway and secondary road mileage is being completed from year to year as funds are appropriated for this purpose by Congress. The planned system of secondary or development roads for the National Forests totals 138,000 miles. Of this planned system, some 53,000 miles have been completed and are now of satisfactory standard; an additional 47,000 miles are of unsatisfactory standard; and some 37,000 miles are still non-existent.

A network of horse and foot trails also is being developed. The planned trail system is approximately 165,000 miles, of which 88,000 miles are of satisfactory standard, 56,000 unsatisfactory, and 21,000 as yet only on paper.

Substantial areas, however, will always remain roadless. More than 70 areas, totaling more than 13,000,000 acres, have been designated within the National Forests as permanent "wilderness" or "wild" areas. (Wilderness areas are 100,000 acres or more in extent; a wild area is a small wilderness of less than 100,000 acres, but of at least 5000 acres.) No roads will be built in these areas. Free of nearly all artificial influences, accessible only by trail or water, wilderness and wild areas covering in all an area larger than the State of Connecticut will be maintained permanently in their original primitive status.

More than 4500 camping areas are maintained by the Forest Service. Facilities provided at these areas vary, but the minimum usually includes camp stoves or fireplaces, tables and benches, safe water supplies, garbage pits, and toilet facilities. Tent sites are usually spaced far enough apart so that campers may have privacy. The camper must provide his own tent and camping equipment. Many of the areas have special provisions for trailer parking. The improved camping areas cover 52,773 acres and can accommodate at one time about 43,000 family-sized groups or more than 200,000 individuals. Use of these areas is free to the public. Heavily used during the summer vacation season, these areas also in many cases provide convenient camping places for hunters in the fall.

Camping may be permitted elsewhere, but in some of the National Forests it is necessary to obtain a campfire permit from the forest ranger before pitching camp or building a fire. No charge is made for these permits.

In many of the National Forests certain areas are designated where individuals may lease sites on which they may build summer homes or recreation cabins, under a "special use" permit from the Forest Service. More than 18,000 summer home site permits are now in effect. In many cases, the cabins are used both for summer outings for the family and for hunting lodges in the fall season.

The Forest Service leases only the site. The lessee must build his own cabin. Since certain standards of sanitation, fire safety, and appearance are required, the plans must have prior approval of the local National Forest Supervisor. The permits authorize use as a recreation residence, not as a permanent residence. The fee for a summer home site is generally from $20 to $30 a year.

Since a summer home or a recreation residence is an exclusive private use of public land it can be permitted only in a location where it will not interfere with public or semi-public uses. The Forest Service has found it both impracticable and undesirable to permit individual summer homes in isolated, scattered locations. Usually from five to thirty or more sites are located in one area in such a way that there is ample space between the individual summer homes and the forest environment is preserved. The individual sites are usually about one acre in size.

Leasing of summer home sites cannot satisfactorily be handled at long distance. Persons desiring a summer home site should get in touch with the Supervisor of the particular National Forest in which they are interested. If summer home sites are available in that Forest, the Supervisor will arrange for an inspection of the area and the prospective summer home owner may take his choice of unoccupied sites. If no sites are available in that National Forest, the Supervisor will, if possible, direct him to another Forest in which sites are available.

Also operating under special use permits in many of the National Forests are resort hotels, cabin camps, stores, garages and service stations, and other commercial enterprises serving tourists and recreationists. The Forest Service permits facilities of this type to the extent necessary to serve the public. Many of the resorts and cabin camps remain open in the fall to provide service for hunters. In addition to resorts on national forest lands, there are plentiful accommodations at cabin camps, tourist homes, ranches, and hotels on private lands within or adjacent to the Forests.

Within or near many of the National Forests, local establishments have horses and pack animals for hire. Guides may be employed for trips into the back country. They usually serve also as cooks, packers, and horse wranglers. A number of popular dude ranches, located near National Forests in the West, cater to big-game hunting parties during the hunting season.

**Wildlife Management.** A great deal of the game and wildlife management work in the National Forests is of a co-operative nature. The Forest Service has a co-operative agreement with the Fish and Wildlife Service under which the latter agency aids the Forest Service with fundamental research and special investigations on wildlife problems. The Fish and Wildlife Service is responsible also for predator and rodent control work on the National Forests. For many years co-operative agreements have been in effect between the Forest Service and the several states, and these have been strengthened from time to time.

Three national forest regulations pertaining to wildlife are primarily concerned with co-operative efforts with the States. The first regulation, dating back to the early days of the Forest Service, provides that Forest officers shall assist the states in the enforcement of state game laws. The second regulation, issued in 1941, provides that the Forest Service will be responsible for determining the place of wildlife in adjustment with the other services of national forest land, and that plans of wildlife management will be developed in co-operation with the states, and realized through application of state laws. The third regulation provides for administration of federal refuges in the national forest system, preferably by co-operative agreement with the States.

One of the fundamental developments which the Forest Service encouraged was the creation of state fish and game commissions with discretionary powers in the handling of wildlife resources. The general growth of the commission system throughout the United States has been of great benefit to wildlife, since it is much more flexible than the former method of fixed seasons and bag limits set through legislative action.

In general, the kind of forest management applied on the National Forests maintains favorable habitat for game. In sales of national forest timber the Forest Service requires the use of partial, or selective, or block cutting methods, and this creates openings and forest "edge" where food plants and cover are abundant. As new timber growth occurs after cutting and the forest canopy closes, other areas are cut, and thus a shifting checkerboard of dense forest, partially opened forest, and forest openings result.

Where needed, the Forest Service has in some cases undertaken special habitat improvement work. Upland birds have been benefited by attempts to create or maintain cover types required for their welfare. In portions of the National Forests in the Lake States, open grassy areas have been reserved for sharptail grouse. On a few National Forests in the East, dense stands of second-growth timber have been deliberately opened at selected sites to create forest edges and herbaceous ground cover for ruffed grouse, turkey, and other game birds. Where turkeys have been reintroduced, food patches have sometimes been developed as a means of helping them to become established. During the period of the Civilian Conservation Corps and other emergency work programs, considerable work was done for the improvement of waterfowl habitat. A number of dams were built in National Forests of the Lake States for the purpose of stabilizing lake levels, and structures were placed on some streams to provide more marsh and duck habitat through flooding of grassy lowlands.

Domestic livestock graze under permit on range areas in many of the National Forests. There is less conflict between livestock and big game animals than might be thought, since they differ materially in feeding and ranging habits. Deer, for instance, prefer browse, while cattle prefer grass. But, where conflicts do occur, the Forest Service attempts to make adjustments in line with its guiding principle in national forest management—"the greatest good of the greatest number in the long run." Livestock have been reduced or eliminated from some deer and elk range. This has been especially true of important winter-range areas. Range areas totaling 3,620,760 acres have been specifically reserved for game within the national forest system.

To satisfy game animals' needs for salt, co-operative salting programs have been developed in several states.

The Forest Service, independently or in co-operation with state authorities, has maintained check stations in some National Forests during hunting seasons. Information obtained shows where the hunters can be expected to go of their own volition, how dependent they are on roadways, the degree of success, location of kill, age and condition of animals taken, and many other facts. A backlog of such data helps Forest officers and state authorities to work toward a proper and sustained yield of game on national forest areas.

**Overpopulation Problems.** In the early days of the National Forests the big wildlife problem was restoration and building up of game populations. In some of the refuges and certain other areas where hunting pressure has been low and habitat favorable, the Forest Service is now confronted with excess numbers of animals. On some areas deer and elk herds have increased beyond the ability of the range to support them. Serious damage to soil and vegetation has resulted, as well as starvation and disease loss in the herds.

The Forest Service early recognized the dangers of overstocking. Many deer and elk overpopulation problems were reported to the state game authorities—sometimes five or ten years before public sentiment and state laws would permit corrective action. Consequently, the Forest Service incurred much disfavor in some quarters, but in so doing helped materially in ushering in a new period of wildlife work—when game would be managed and cropped in accordance with the capabilities of the land.

Kaibab National Forest was one of the earliest problem areas. Overstocking of deer was reported here as early as 1918. Controversy over the question of reducing the herd raged for several years. Meanwhile the deer population was decimated by starvation and disease. Subsequent management plans worked out co-operatively by the Forest Service and the State of Arizona are now maintaining the herd in satisfactory condition and the depleted natural food supply is gradually improving. Co-operative management has likewise greatly improved an overpopulation situation that existed for some years on the Pisgah National Forest in North Carolina.

Deer or elk overpopulation problems still exist on national forest areas in a number of states, including California, Montana, Wyoming, Colorado, Utah, Oregon, Michigan, Wisconsin, and Minnesota.

In many cases the limiting factor is winter range. Generally the National Forests could support greater numbers of big game during the summer season than are now present. But much of the national forest country in the West is high country, where winter snows are heavy, and the animals must migrate to lower elevations during the winter months. It is on the limited areas of national forest winter range that some of the worst cases of overcrowding exist. Frequently winter range areas outside the National Forests are not available to the herds. Hungry deer and elk are not welcomed on neighboring farms and ranches. The Forest Service hopes that it will be possible eventually to acquire additional winter range areas to help relieve some of the most troublesome situations.

Within many of the National Forests are intermingled private lands. A checkerboard of diverse ownership does not always make for the most effective wildlife management or for efficient protection and management of other forest resources. Through land exchanges and through purchases of additional lands suitable for forestry purposes as funds become available, the Forest Service is endeavoring to consolidate national forest holdings.

The Forest Service believes that overpopulation problems can best be solved by increased sportsman-hunter take. The only sound alternatives would be slaughter by professional hunters or letting starvation reduce the herds. Hunting animals of both sexes is sometimes necessary to check excessive increase Since the states set the hunting seasons and bag limits, realization of proper big game utilization in the National Forests is dependent upon state action. In some cases where big game surpluses have occurred, the state game laws have remained too restrictive for best results. On the whole, however, notable progress has been made in making adjustments to meet the needs for proper utilization of the game crops.

During the war years, wildlife work in the National Forests was greatly curtailed. A heavy backlog of game inventory work, studies of wildlife habitat conditions, and other game management work has accumulated. As rapidly as available funds and other factors permit, however, the Forest Service, in cooperation with the states, is working toward its objective of building up wildlife populations where they are understocked, bringing excess populations into balance with their natural food supply, and maintaining wildlife as a permanent resource of the National Forests.

**Hunters Are Welcomed.** You are welcome to hunt in the National Forests. The Forest Service asks only that you observe the state game laws and state and federal fire regulations, leave a clean camp, and in general practice the principles of good sportsmanship. Hunters can help prevent public expense, destruction of game and timber, and occasional loss of life, by refraining from flipping lighted matches, cigarettes, cigar stubs, and pipe heels out of automobile windows or into the brush and litter along forest roads, trails, and streams; by keeping campfires small and by drowning them dead out before leaving them.

You can get information on hunting opportunities, local facilities, roads and trails, etc., in any National Forest by writing to the local Supervisor. Most of the National Forests have map folders or descriptive booklets which are available for the asking. Information on license requirements, seasons, and game laws in any state may be obtained from the state game commission.

See Appendix, pp. 1044 ff., for maps of National Forest areas by states.

# NATIONAL PARK SERVICE

National Parks and Monuments are absolute sanctuaries for all native wild animals. As such, they are closed to hunting and trapping. Nevertheless, they are of great interest to sportsmen and contribute to the game supply on open areas adjacent to the parks.

There are 171 areas in the National Park System. They cover 20,775,082 acres and include some of the greatest remaining wilderness in the United States. The largest unit, Katmai National Monument in Alaska, contains almost 2,700,000 acres. These areas are the homes of numerous important wildlife species, including great herds of game. Even in the small Eastern battlefield and historical monuments that cover only a few acres, there are numerous small game such as rabbits and quail. In dispersing, the increase becomes available to sportsmen in the surrounding countryside.

Some of the western National Parks are high mountain areas or plateaus which furnish lush summer herbage. These are the breeding grounds of many thousands of elk and deer. As winter snow becomes deep, however, these animals are forced to seek food at lower elevations. The migrations frequently extend beyond the park boundaries into country that is open to hunting. The northern elk herd of Yellowstone Park, for example, supports an annual kill of 2000 to 3000 animals. In rare instances, the harvest has run as high as 7000 elk. This hunting, in the Yellowstone River Valley and in the Absaroka and Gallatin Mountains north of the park boundary is enjoyed by thousands of Montana residents and hundreds of out-of-state sportsmen. Yellowstone also is the summer range of a considerable portion of the 15,000 elk in the so-called southern or Jackson Hole elk herd. This herd is about twice as large as the northern herd and affords a greater kill in an even more rugged wilderness.

Other parks which supply important numbers of elk to hunting areas are Olympic in Washington

State, Glacier in Montana, and Rocky Mountain Park in Colorado. As in Yellowstone, the winter range within all of these parks is not adequate to support any large percentage of the elk herds which summer therein. Hunting in the surrounding regions, therefore, is an important factor in park wildlife and range management in order to prevent serious abuse and destruction of the vegetation.

Glacier National Park is estimated to have a summertime population of 2200 western whitetail deer, many of which must migrate to open hunting country in winter. Parks which contribute large numbers of mule deer to lowland hunters are Glacier, Rocky Mountain, Yellowstone, and Yosemite and Sequoia-Kings Canyon National Parks in California.

The range of the grizzly has been so restricted within the continental United States that few localities still furnish hunting for this prized species. Glacier and Yellowstone-Grant Teton National Parks are refuges for the two largest groups of survivors. Many sportsmen annually visit northwestern Montana or the Jackson Hole-Cody region of Wyoming to try their luck at bagging one of these great bears. This good hunting is largely the result of natural protection which is afforded by the rugged, roadless country, and to the overflow of grizzlies from the three parks named.

The more common black bear is also plentiful in these parks, as well as in Yosemite and Sequoia-Kings Canyon and in Great Smoky Mountains National Park in North Carolina-Tennessee. Although less migratory than the grizzlies, these black bears wander from the sanctuaries at times and so aid in restocking other forests.

National Parks have served an important function in restoring elk to localities where the species had been exterminated or so greatly reduced that there was little likelihood of natural recovery. Surplus elk thus have been live-trapped in Yellowstone, Rocky Mountain, and other parks and planted in a number of western states from Montana to Arizona. When the population had increased sufficiently, public hunting was permitted to harvest the excess. Many hundreds of buffaloes have been transferred from Yellowstone and Wind Cave National Parks to game preserves, refuges, and zoos throughout the United States as well as foreign countries. While few of these animals or their descendants have been made available for hunters, the fact that this once almost-extinct species has been widely distributed from the parks is of interest to sportsmen.

Although the National Parks are closed to gunning, the camera hunter is always welcome. He will find these areas rich hunting grounds. Because animals and birds are protected from all molestation, they are abundant in favorable places and are generally unafraid. Extreme care in stalking, or the use of blinds, is often unnecessary. Pictures of animals and birds going about their daily lives and in their unspoiled surroundings can be made in the parks with far greater ease than elsewhere. Many of the best wildlife photographers and lecturers have obtained their material in the National Parks.

Unusual species such as the mountain lion, the mountain sheep, and the trumpeter swan can be found in the National Parks. The only place in the United States where the buffalo live in a completely wild, unfenced state is in Yellowstone. That vanishing species, the wolf, and also vast herds of caribou, are seen in Mount McKinley National Park. From the mighty moose with its 6-foot spread of antlers to the tiny shrew that poisons its victims, there are a hundred species to challenge the interest of the camera hunter.

The more notable game and the National Parks in which they are most readily hunted with the camera are as follows:

*Elk*—Yellowstone, Olympic, Rocky Mountain.
*Mule Deer*—Grand Canyon, Rocky Mountain, Sequoia-Kings Canyon, Yellowstone, Yosemite, Zion.
*Moose*—Glacier, Grand Teton, Isle Royale, Mt. McKinley, Yellowstone.
*Caribou*—Mount McKinley.
*Antelope*—Wind Cave, Yellowstone.
*Buffalo*—Wind Cave, Yellowstone.
*Bighorn*—Glacier, Mt. McKinley, Rocky Mountain, Yellowstone.
*Mountain Goat*—Glacier, Mt. Rainier.
*Black Bear*—Glacier, Mt. McKinley, Yellowstone.
*Grizzly*—Glacier, Great Smoky Mountains, Sequoia-Kings Canyon, Yellowstone, Yosemite.
*Waterfowl*—Everglades, Mt. McKinley, Yellowstone.

Many campers visit the National Parks, there to live in the open among scenes of unsurpassed beauty. Vacations spent in these areas bring to the benefits of camping the added enjoyment of intelligent understanding of the surroundings. Naturalists and historians of the park staffs explain the geology, botany, and zoology, and visitors are afforded ample opportunity to further their knowledge of the out-of-doors. In 1947, a total of 9319 free campsites existed in the National Parks. These could accommodate 37,276 people at a given time. The most popular camping parks are in the West—particularly Yosemite, Yellowstone, Rocky Mountain, and Sequoia-Kings Canyon.

# PACK-HORSE TRIPS

Throughout all the mountainous portions of western North America, from Mexico to the Arctic Circle, almost all the good big-game hunting country is at least two or three days' travel from the railroad or the nearest auto or wagon road. Sportsmen have to pack their outfit and supplies into these regions, and the most common method of packing is with pack animals.

A large pack mule will carry 250 pounds, and a burro about half that amount, but the disadvantage of both mules and burros is that it is almost impossible to make them ford rivers or even fair-sized creeks, or to traverse boggy country, so that their use is confined almost exclusively to desert regions. For general packing on hunting trips the pack horse is commonly used; a good horse will pack about 150 pounds pay weight. To load horses heavier makes for all kinds of trouble including sore backs. Bear this limiting figure in mind, as it indicates how many pack animals will be needed for necessary outfit and supplies.

Pack horses and mules can travel from 5 to 25

PLATE I. The shape of wooden panniers is important.

PLATE II. Adjustment and balance are important.

miles a day in Western mountains, depending on the country, trails, and weather. On fairly good trails the average pack train will average about 15 miles a day, starting about 10 A.M., and camping about 4 P.M. Burros are much slower. However, the location of good horse food usually dictates the camp sites and the duration of each day's travel.

Most of the good mountain hunting country in the United States is in the Forest Reserves, with good horse trails along almost every valley and across the passes. But even in wilder country it is possible to take a pack train through almost any country where steep cliffs, peaks, very heavy timber, and down timber do not prevent. Almost all the forests except on the northern slopes of mountains are open enough to ride through anywhere. Also throughout most of this Western country good grass for horse feed occurs in many places. It is necessary that the camp sites be chosen where there is good horse feed, as otherwise the horses, when turned loose at night, will stray for miles in search of feed even though, as is usual, they are hobbled.

The typical sportsman's outfit for extended big-game hunting with a pack train in this Western country consists of a guide, a horse wrangler, and a cook. The sportsman usually arranges for his trip with an "outfitter" who supplies these men, and also a riding horse for each member of the party including the man, the necessary number of pack horses to carry the outfit and supplies, all the saddles, pack saddles, horse blankets, panniers, tents, cooking and eating utensils, food, and other equipment. Each man supplies his own personal effects and bedding. The sportsmen supply their arms, ammunition, binoculars, clothing and personal effects, sleeping bag and air mattress, and purchase their hunting license. Such an outfit and method of hunting is necessarily expensive; on the basis described above, outfitters today commonly charge from $25 to $50 a day for one sportsman, with a slight reduction for two or more.

**Packing and Travel.** One who has not previously hunted with a pack train should understand certain details about the pack horse and his load, and the procedures of traveling, camping, and hunting.

The horse is packed normally as follows: First the saddle blanket is laid smoothly across its back, and then the pack saddle is laid on this and cinched in place. The usual pack saddle is of the "sawbuck" type, with double cinches and breech and breast straps, although improved military types of pack saddles are now coming into quite general use. Each horse also has a halter with neck rope, or neck rope alone, and a bell (cowbell) attached by a strap to its neck. The bell is stoppered except when the horse is turned loose to feed. The pay load usually consists of two side packs, usually panniers, weighing 50 to 60 pounds each, which are lashed on either side of the saddle, and a smaller top pack, usually bedding, a duffle or flour bag, box, or a nest of pans, laid on and also lashed on top and between the tops of two panniers. A heavy canvas pack cover, about 5 feet square, is then laid over all, and with a strong rope having a cinch at one end, a diamond hitch is thrown over the entire pack, binding the whole load tight to the horse.

An outfitter will usually assign one pack horse to each sportsman to carry his personal outfit, except his rifle, rain or mackinaw coat, and camera. The camera is usually carried on the sportsman's saddle horse, the rifle in a leather saddle scabbard. The sportsman will thus usually be furnished two panniers in which to pack all his personal effects except his bedding. The inside dimensions of a pannier are approximately 22 inches long, 8 or 9 inches wide, and 15 inches deep. They often taper to less width at the bottom so that this bottom edge will not stick out so far beyond the horse and be continually crashing into trees and brush. These panniers are usually made of plywood, wood, canvas, rawhide, or fiber. They give excellent protection to the contents except that fragile articles and bottled liquids should be wrapped in clothing. They are usually quite rainproof, but if the horse were to fall in fording a river the contents would probably get wet. There should be waterproof cotton sacks for cameras, and films should be packed in pry-up tins. The weight placed in each pannier must not exceed 50 pounds, and should be the same in each so they will balance on the animal.

The sportsman's bedding—sleeping bag, air mattress, and pillow—are usually rolled in a tarpaulin about 8 feet square and tied with a rope, so that the bundle will measure about 3 feet by 18 inches, by 7 or 8 inches thick, flat rather than round. It can thus be conveniently laid on top of the saddle and panniers as a top pack. The pack cover of heavy canvas, laid over all before the diamond is thrown, protects the load from rain or snagging in the brush.

Nowadays outfitters usually furnish a tent for each one or two sportsmen, commonly a wall tent with a small heater stove. Another larger tent with cookstove is also provided for cooking and eating, and probably a small portable table for this tent, panniers serving as seats. Occasionally one will find an outfitter who, for younger sportsmen, will furnish only a large canvas fly for shelter. This is pitched each night as a lean-to, all making their beds under it, and the fire in front serves for both warmth and cooking. Many prefer this arrangement, as it gives the pleasure and romance of a campfire, and a view out of the shelter.

Assume now that the party is already under canvas, and they are going to break camp and travel on this day. At first streak of dawn the horse wrangler starts out to find and drive in the saddle and pack horses which were turned loose the afternoon before to feed. Most of the horses, when turned out, probably had hobbles strapping their front legs close together, and their bells were unstoppered to facilitate finding them. Nevertheless, the horses may be feeding anywhere from a few yards to 5 miles from camp, and may also be scattered in several bunches, so that it may be from 8 to 10 A.M. before the horse wrangler has found them all and driven them into camp to be in time to move camp that day, and every once in a while delays of this kind must be exepected. When the wrangler drives the horses in everyone but the cook turns out to catch them, tie them to trees, and saddle them.

In the meantime the cook, also arising at dawn, starts to prepare breakfast, and wakes the sportsmen at the proper time. Immediately after breakfast each sportsman packs his panniers, rolls his bedroll, sees that he has everything needed on his person for his day's travel or hunting, and that his rifle, coat, and camera are ready to place on his riding saddle. The cook, after washing the dishes, packs the kitchen and food panniers, and then everyone turns in to take down and roll up the tents, so that when the wrangler gets back with the horses everything is ready to be packed on them.

It takes about three minutes to saddle a horse, and two men working together will pack one in about ten minutes when everything is at hand. From this one can figure out how long it will take to pack up and get on the trail after the horses arrive. The actual packing of the horses is usually done by the horse wranglers and cook, two men working together. Every sportsman, however, should learn how to pack a horse, as one can never tell when it may be very necessary for him to lend a hand. Anyone can learn to throw the various lashes and hitches in two or three lessons.

Usually the sportsmen and their guide will start off right after breakfast on their saddle horses, either to hunt, or just to ride through the most interesting country, arriving at the next camp after the train has pulled in and the wrangler and cook have camp almost pitched, and probably supper under way. On some occasions the sportsmen will travel with the pack train.

After each horse is packed it is either tied up again, or turned loose, according to the training and disposition of the animal. When all are packed, and everything is ready to hit the trail, the tied horses are turned loose, the wrangler starts ahead, and the cook drives the pack horses after him—if there is a trail, usually in a single long line. Occasionally a horse bolts out of line, the rear man driving him back, or a pack may turn or a horse bog down or get snagged up in brush, necessitating a halt to rectify the trouble. Some days may be full of all kinds of trouble and little distance may be covered, and on others the train may make as much as 20 miles.

The horse wrangler is the man to say where the next camp shall be made. He is responsible for the horses, and he must camp where the feed (grass) is good, and where he can hold the horses reasonably close to camp. Where the feed is poor the horses may travel as much as 10 miles to reach good grazing. Also, during the first day or two of a trip horses must be watched or some may wander right back to their home range when turned loose. Although the horses may be hobbled, they can nevertheless cover a couple of miles an hour in that condition. Thus a day's travel may be anywhere from 5 to 20 miles, and the sportsmen must not interfere with this. Of course, in certain localities water and wood are also paramount considerations in locating the next camp site.

**Hunting.** As regards hunting, the more or less open regions of the West are different from the wooded country of the East, Northeast, and Southeast. In the eastern woods white-tailed deer are adept at getting along close to habitations, and even moose when disturbed do not travel long distances before quieting down, and thus one can hunt one locality for a long time. But in the West when game is disturbed it often travels right out of that region, possibly 15 or 20 miles, to another feeding ground with which it is familiar. Caribou may travel much farther, and goats and sheep seek the most inaccessible fastnesses. Hence in mountain hunting one usually travels until he finds a good hunting country where fresh signs of game are plentiful, and then hunts it for perhaps three or four days until it has been thoroughly exploited. On a day's hunt the sportsman can examine a very wide stretch of country from the heights with his binoculars. Then the journey with the pack train is continued until another promising hunting country is reached. A guide can hardly guarantee that in a certain country, perhaps close to the outfitting point, he can find game for his patrons—it may have been disturbed recently. Though it may have been plentiful there in past years, the food conditions may not be to the liking of game this year. Indeed, in some cases he may have to take his party five or ten day's travel before finding a really good hunting country, or the particular game that is desired. For these reasons a successful hunting trip usually takes longer in the West than in the East. Guides do not like to book a party for less than three weeks, and a month is better for success. These facts are truest of mountain game, they do not apply so much to mule deer, which may be plentiful on certain ranges for long periods.

Western hunting differs from eastern hunting in that it is mainly done by stalking the game rather than by still hunting, or by lake or river hunting. The game is mostly sighted from afar, often from several miles away with binoculars. It is then approached under cover, and if practical up-wind, although wind does not make so much difference in the West as in the East, for among mountains it is circling and eddying, and in the day usually blowing up valleys; except at close distances the hunters' scent is often carried above the game. As the hunter approaches closer to his game, cover from sight becomes more important. Advantage must be taken of clumps of trees, rises in the ground, valleys, and depressions to keep out of sight, and often the hunter must crawl for long distances. If he has to cover a short stretch of ground in sight he must watch the game, "freezing" when the game is watching or alert, moving only when it lowers its head to graze. Sometimes when the game is moving it is possible to get to a position where it can be intercepted or ambushed. Often the roughness of the ground is a great handicap to the hunter, increasing his exertion and slowing his approach, and sometimes he has to make wide detours either to get past ground so rough he cannot cover it, or where he would be in plain sight of his game. During the last part of the stalk the hunter must go slow so as not to be winded and shaky when it comes to the shot. How close a sportsman must approach to game to be sure of hitting it depends on his marksmanship and the rifle he is using. A hunter should have thoroughly tested himself and his rifle on the range before the trip. Generally his sure hitting distance in the hills is that distance on the rifle range where he can be sure of hitting an 8-inch bull's-eye.

Western hunting is often done more or less on horseback. There are many reasons for this. The sportsman and his guide can cover much more country in a day on horseback than afoot, and consequently have a greater chance of discovering desirable game. Because of horse feed, camps may have to be made in a deep valley, and the game may all be up around timber line 5 miles away. Game is much less disturbed at the sight of horses than of men afoot, and a close approach can often be made by riding. Further, when riding the sportsman and his guide can use their eyes continually to search the country for game, while when afoot their eyes would be on the ground half the time.

It is seldom however, that game is shot from horseback, or even that one jumps off his horse and takes the shot. Usually the saddle horses are used to find the game. The hunters then usually ride as close to it is they can without danger of being seen. There the hunters dismount, tie up their horses in cover, and proceed to the stalk afoot. This final stalk may be anywhere from several hundred yards to several miles, and may involve a very rough climb of several thousand feet over rough country, and in some cases may also involve rather dangerous rock or ice work. One never knows what is in store for him in a day's hunt in wild western country. He may make an easy kill of a fine trophy before the sun is much more than up, or he may strike a grizzly trail in fresh snow, the trail may lead up a mountain impassable for horses, and before he gets back to camp at dusk on the following day he may have covered 30 miles on foot over terribly rough country, with many thrills from steep cliffs and ice-covered slopes, as well as from the bear—and all on a couple of sandwiches.

For these reasons western mountain hunting is rather a sport for young, vigorous, strong men. But there is no reason why an older sportsman need deny himself its pleasures. In almost all areas a horse can be ridden over most of the ground, and while an older man may have to pass up some of the stalks a youngster could make, sooner or later a chance within his physical capabilities will turn up. In the meantime he is riding each day in a wonderful country, and in a fine climate, surrounded by the most beautiful scenery in the world.

What has been written so far applies largely to a hunt with a guide and other helpers as it is usually conducted in the West today. However, there is no reason why two young men, thoroughly accustomed to handling horses, to camping, and to traveling with a map, should not take such a trip by themselves. It means a lot of work, for if they hunt persistently during the day they will have cooking, repairs, and odd jobs to do often late into the night, and horse wrangling will frequently interfere with a day's hunt. But it can be, and often is, done. Two men can borrow or rent a couple of saddle and pack horses, and live the life for months at a time. Their outfit will be much like that given below, but somewhat simpler and lighter. If they have two pack horses, one will carry the entire outfit, and the other just about enough food for two men for a month. Often lone trappers and prospectors travel with from one to six pack horses. In many states, however, and in some of the provinces of Canada, the law requires a non-resident sportsman to be accompanied by a registered or licensed guide. Before young sportsmen attempt such trips alone they must make sure, by experiments in country close to civilization, that they are competent; and, generally speaking, they must be of a temperament which gets as much delight from the traveling, handling horses, camp work, and cooking, as from the actual hunting of game.

Photo from C. E. Hagie.

PLATE III. Packing in the Head and Half of an Elk.

**Check Lists.** The following check lists of equipment and supplies needed for hunting in the West with a pack train are divided into two parts. The first, the *Camp and Horse Outfit,* which is usually furnished by the local outfitter or guide is included in his per-diem charge to the sportsman. Sportsmen going without a guide would have to provide most of this outfit. Some of it can be obtained from city outfitters, some only in small towns adjacent to wild mountain country where pack horses are commonly used, and some of it must be made.

The *Personal Outfit* includes those articles which it is suggested the sportsman take himself, and which the outfitter or guide does not provide. These he can usually purchase from the larger city outfitters or sporting-goods stores. Perhaps the most important single item in this personal outfit is the mountaineering boots. They must afford absolutely secure footing on steep snow, ice, and rock slopes, and they must be comfortable and light. Success and safety depend more on them than on any other single item. They cannot usually be bought, but must be made to order. For the necessary lightness they should be only six inches high. *Remember* that the composition rubber soles seen on many sportsmen's boots will not hold hobnails; soles *must* be of oak-tanned leather. (See "Clothing.")

The outfit for pack-horse trips may seem heavy and bulky to those used to the much lighter canoe outfits. There are several reasons for this. Unfortunately a horse cannot be educated to care for light and fragile articles, and the rough and tumble of pack-horse traveling both demand strong articles and make frequent repairs necessary. In high mountain country quick changes in weather from heat to blizzards are likely to occur. Trips of this kind are often taken far from sources of supply and replacement. (Question marks indicate items which are optional.)

CAMP AND HORSE OUTFIT

Tents with camp stoves, or large canvas fly.
Axes, 3-lb. head, with sheaths.
Bucksaw, with takedown frame (for stove wood).
Camp table and chairs (?).
For each saddle horse:
- Saddle blanket.
- Western stock saddle.
- Bridle, halter, and halter rope.
- Bell and strap, hobbles.
- Army saddlebags.

For each pack horse:
- Saddle blanket.
- Pack saddle with lash and hitch ropes.
- Halter and halter rope.
- Bell and strap, hobbles.
- Canvas pack cover.
- Panniers.

Repair kit:
- Horse shoes and nails.
- Files, pliers, awls, rivets, sewing kit.
- Extra rope and leather.

Cooking utensils (for 4 men, packed in pannier) (See "Camp Foods and Utensils.")
- 4 kettles to nest.
- 2 frying pans, 12-inch.
- 1 folding baker (unless stove has oven.)
- 6 plates, 6 bowls, 6 enamel cups.
- 1 cream pitcher.
- 6 knives, forks, tea spoons, table spoons.
- 1 large cooking fork and spoon.
- 1 cake turner, butcher knife, can opener.
- 1 salt and pepper shakers.
- 1 large mixing pan (goes on as top pack).
- 1 tin wash basin. " " " " "

Water bucket (canvas).
Flashlight or candle lantern.
Alarm clock, carborundum stone, file.
Dish cloths.
Cans of matches, sugar, salt, pepper, lard, and soap for daily use.
Food (see "Camp Foods"). Most of it packed in small cotton bags and then in panniers. Sacks of potatoes, onions, and flour are usually carried as top packs.

PERSONAL OUTFIT

*Worn:* Wide-brimmed hat, wool shirt, light pants, light wool underwear, wool socks, mountaineer shoes, riding gloves, belt with cartridge pocket and five cartridges, binoculars. (See "Clothing.")

*Pockets:* Watch, compass, hunting knife, handkerchief, dark glasses, map, pipe, tobacco, matches, waterproof match-box.

*On saddle horse:* Rifle (magazine but NOT barrel loaded) in leather saddle holster.
Rain or mackinaw coat on cantle (according to weather).
Army saddlebags with lunch and camera.

*On pack horse:* Top pack: Sleeping bag, air mattress, pillow, rucksack, rain or mackinaw coat.

In panniers:
- 1 wool shirt, 1 medium weight wool pants.
- 2 suits wool underwear.
- 4 pairs wool socks.
- 1 camp slippers or moccasins.
- 1 leather top rubbers (in wet country).
- 3 handkerchiefs.
- 1 pair warm gloves.
- 2 flannel pajamas.

Toilet articles. Small bath towel.
Medicine kit.
Rifle cleaning kit.
Flashlight, extra batteries and lamp.
Films for camera (in pry-up tin).
Extra cartridges.
Tobacco and extra pipe.
Boot grease.
Notebook, pencil, game license.

The guide, wranglers, and cook will require a very similar personal outfit for themselves. They must be well shod, with plenty of dry, comfortable clothes to work efficiently. and particularly if they smoke, they must have plenty of tobacco. If any of them have food they are particularly fond of it is well to cater to them in making up the food list. And so the sportsman must not be surprised if, when he starts out, he is followed by a pack train of over a dozen animals.

# PHOTOGRAPHY FOR THE HUNTER

**Camera Types.** Most hunters want clear pictures of their days afield, and they want to make these pictures with the least possible fuss and bother. Unfortunately, far too many of these photographic records are miserable failures for two simple reasons: (1) Unsuitable equipment is used, and (2) it is operated thoughtlessly, without prior planning. One of the biggest problems is just what type of camera to get, and so the matter of equipment will be taken up first.

For all-round usefulness, it is hard to beat a 35-mm. camera. Its small size and consequent lightness make carrying it hardly noticeable. This type of miniature camera is small enough to stuff easily into a coat pocket, and invariably comes in an ever-ready carrying case which may be opened quickly to permit the camera's operation from within the case. Thus the hunter carrying one of these cameras slung from his shoulder can get into action quickly to take such scenes as his dog pointing or retrieving.

All 35-mm. cameras have short-focal-length lenses, which in turn have a large depth of field. This means that most outdoor pictures taken with them will be sharp, even the extreme close-ups. It also means that a hunter can leave his camera focused on infinity—represented on the distance scale by this sign: oo—and take general scenes with the foreknowledge that the pictures will be fairly sharp over-all. What makes this possible is the fact that when a 50-mm. lens, common to most 35-mm. cameras, is focused on infinity and set at *f*.11, a typical daylight setting, everything from about 11 feet ahead of the camera and beyond will be in focus.

Such information can be found instantly by glancing at the depth-of-field scale found on most 35-mm. miniatures. Other desirable features include a full 36 exposures for each loading of film and, in all but the most inexpensive models, a built-in range finder for quick, accurate focusing. Fast shutter speeds as high as 1/500, 1/1000, and even 1/1250 of a second are standard with several 35-mm. cameras, and are used by hunters to "stop" the rapid wing-beats of flying game birds.

Many miniature cameras have a delayed-action device on the shutter to trip it some 15 seconds after the mechanism has been cocked and set off. This permits a hunter to place his camera on a rock or stump, touch off the delayed-action mechanism, and then hurry before the lens to get into the picture. Sportsmen hunting alone find this method excellent

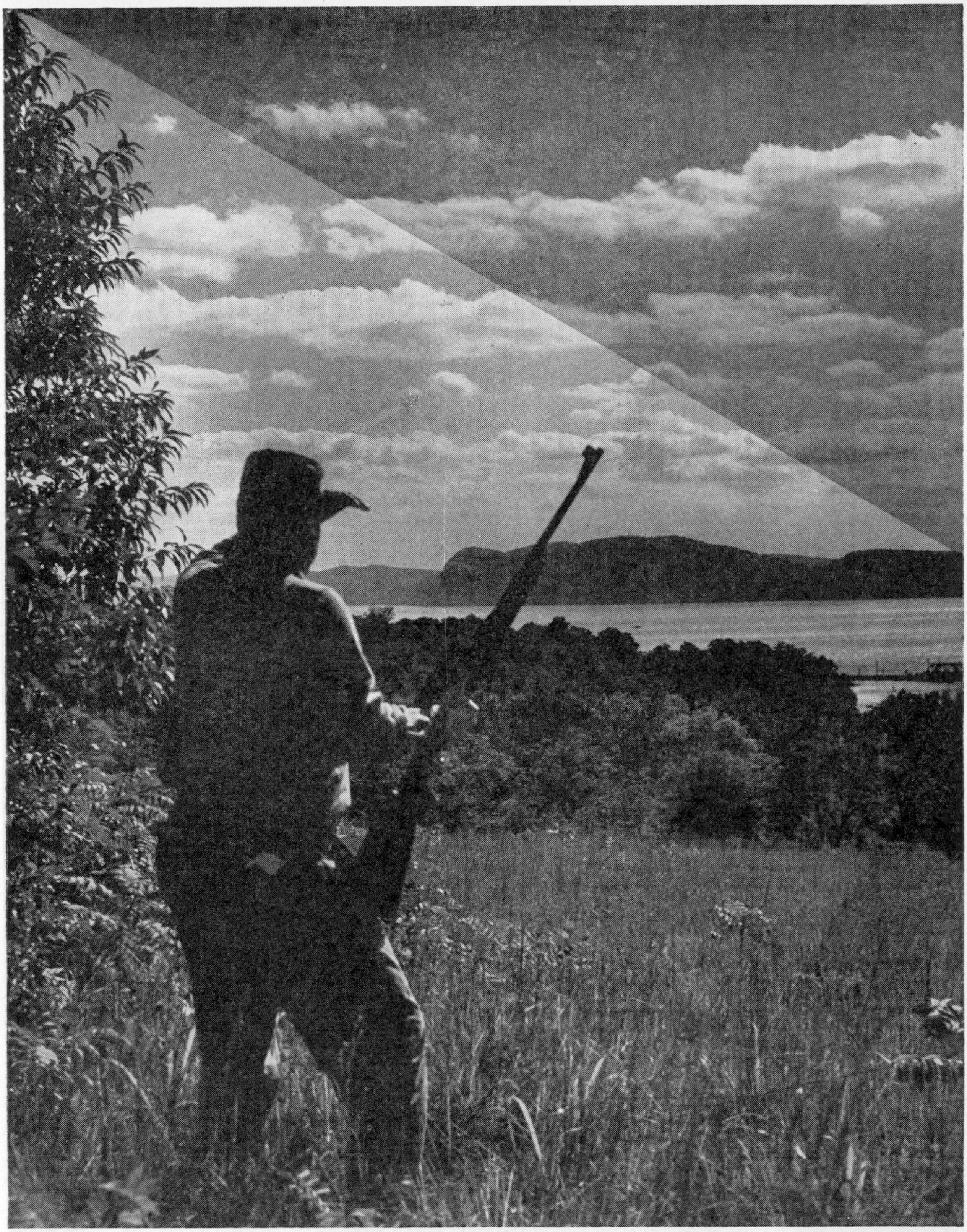

All photos in this section from Pete Barrett.

PLATE I. How Filters Bring Out Cloud Effects. Data: 35-mm. camera, yellow filter lower ¾, red filter upper ¼, speed 1/25, opening *f*.11.

for taking otherwise-impossible pictures of themselves and their trophies.

The main drawback to the 35-mm. camera is its small negative size, about 1 x 1½ inches. This requires careful processing of the film, and enlargements to be made from the desirable negatives. The cost of the camera must also be reckoned with. At present most American models with built-in range finders cost about $100, with imported models ranging from about $200 to $350. It should be mentioned here that range-finder units, suitable for use with *any* camera—and hence with the inexpensive 35-mm. models—can be bought for $5 or $6.

Also well suited to hunting conditions are many roll-film cameras of the folding type, particularly those making negatives 2¼ inches square. The focusing must be more critical with these cameras, as their lenses are of greater focal length than those of the 35-mm. models, and hence have a shallower depth of field. However, there is no great chore to being careful about the focus, although it can slow up operation of the camera somewhat, especially

PLATE II. Data: 2¼ by 2¼ roll-film camera, speed 1/400, opening *f*.4.5, Super XX film.

in cases where any auxiliary range finder is used.

A camera taking a square picture is fast to operate in this respect, though—you can shoot without ever bothering to consider which might be best: a vertical or a horizontal picture. Most folding cameras making 2¼ x 2¼, and even 2¼ x 3¼-inch negatives are compact, and many are classed as true miniatures, as easy to carry in ever-ready cases as 35-mm. models. No folding roll-film camera will take even half as many pictures at one loading as a 35-mm. camera. However, the former produces negatives large enough to make suitable and inexpensive contact prints, fine for an album.

Thus it can be seen that each type has its advantages, with folding cameras lacking some of the refinements of the 35-mm. miniatures. Most inexpensive American roll-film models selling for $50 or less do not have shutter speeds faster than 1/200 of a second, or built-in range finders. But models in the $200 class do, and most models will take the color films from which album-size color prints can be made cheaply. You can take more pictures faster with a 35-mm. camera, but a folding, roll-film model will also do the job.

As for roll-film cameras of the reflex type, they have not been discussed simply because they are not nearly so comfortable to carry, owing to their bulky shape. The same goes for press-type cameras, which are even heavier and larger. If a hunter can afford to own one of these types as an *extra* camera, and leave it with flash gun attached in his car, then he can make flash pictures of the highest quality at the start and end of each trip. This equipment will cost about $150 at the very least.

**Exposures.** Besides his camera with a built-in or auxiliary range finder, no one should go afield without some sort of light meter, and a filter or two. Ordinary films have a wide "latitude" which permits considerable under- and over-exposure, but even so it is far too easy for the average person to make a poor guess at light conditions and so lose what might have been a priceless picture. A glance at a light meter is sufficient to figure proper exposure.

There are two types of light meters; both are easy to use, and both are worth every cent of their cost. Least expensive is the extinction type, priced from about $2 to $10. One model is smaller than a booklet of paper matches. Extinction meters give fair results, but are not suited to the exacting demands of color photography because a certain amount of guesswork must be used to operate them.

A photoelectric meter costs more—from about $15 to $30—but it can be relied upon to indicate the perfect exposure every time, for all types of film. Most of these meters are about the size of a pack of cigarettes, and weigh perhaps half a pound. They are ruggedly built and unless dropped should last for several years. The beauty of all meters is that they show simultaneously all the combinations of lens stops and shutter speeds for any exposure problem.

Filters are used to "bring out" clouds against the sky. Without a filter, sky and clouds usually merge in the negative and produce a blank, white area in the finished picture. Natural sky and cloud effects are assured with the use of a yellow filter such as the Wratten K2, and many hunters keep one of these

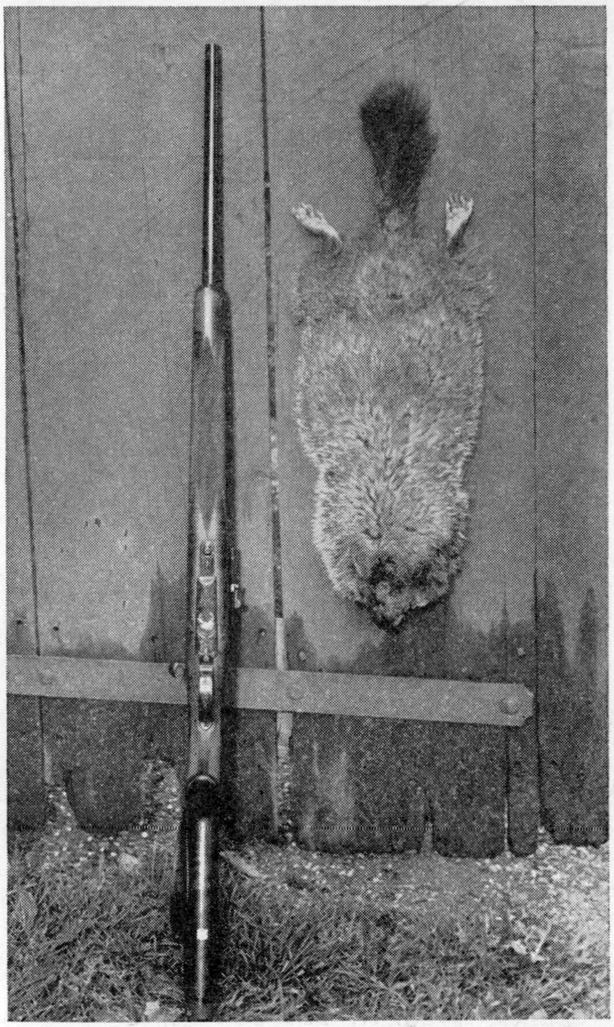

PLATE III. Data: 2¼ by 2¼ press-type camera, flash, speed 1/100, opening *f*.16, Super XX film.

in place over the lens all day long. A K2 filter will also help to eliminate haze in distant landscapes. For more dramatic results, such as a dark sky and fleecy-white clouds, and greater haze elimination, a red filter is used, like the Wratten A. Most hunters get along nicely with the K2 only—price, about $2.

All filters have a "factor," which is a number indicating how many times the normal exposure must be increased to compensate for using the filter. The pamphlet contained in each film carton always lists these filter factors, which vary with the type of film. When used with Kodax Plus-X in daylight, for instance, a K2's factor is 2, which means the exposure must be *doubled*. This can be done by *halving* the shutter speed from say 1/50 to 1/25, or by *increasing* the lens opening one whole "stop," say from *f*.11 to *f*.8. (As the lens is "opened," each larger stop *doubles* the light intake.) A simple setting on any exposure meter will make allowance for the filter factor.

Medium-fast panchromatic or "pan" films are well suited for average outdoor work. Examples are: Kodax Plus-X, Ansco Superpan Supreme, and duPont Superior 2. Similar orthochromatic or "ortho" films are Kodak Verichrome and Ansco Plenachrome. Pan films seem to be most favored. When

PLATE IV. Data: 2¼ by 3¼ roll-film camera, speed 1/5, opening *f*.5.6, cloudy day, Plus-X film.

extreme speed is needed, as for flying-bird pictures and other fast action, use of the fastest pan film is advisable. Some use this type at all times, but must be content with some "graininess" in enlargements, and often a lack of sparkle—two faults not common to medium-fast films.

Color film is the only way to capture the brilliant colors of autumn, and it is eminently suited to hunting photography. However, it *must* be used with a light meter, for an accurate exposure is needed every time, else the colors will not be reproduced faithfully. Flat lighting is best, and hazy or overcast days are particularly good for taking close-ups of hunters. Late morning or afternoon sun provides good flat lighting for close-ups of people, though flesh tones are apt to come out on the ruddy side then. However, this is not usually noticeable enough to be found objectionable.

As to technique, the rules are few and simple. A shutter speed of 1/50 is fine for most static scenes and close-ups, and 1/100 will "stop" men walking. When dogs are running, an exposure of 1/200 is sufficient. Flying birds are in a class by themselves. Sometimes a shutter speed of 1/500 will give fair results, particularly when the birds are more than 50 yards from the camera. Experts usually expose at 1/1000 or 1/1250 for sure results on all occasions.

There is just one occasion when flying game birds may be photographed successfully at a relatively slow shutter speed—say 1/200—and that is when they are approaching on set wings. Thus a duck gunner in a blind often has a perfect chance for a beautiful picture when a flight coasts in over the decoys.

Unless game birds can be photographed quite close to the hunter, they will appear rather small in the picture. To overcome this it is best to use a telephoto lens. It is available for expensive miniatures, and press-type cameras, and is itself expensive. A telephoto with a focal length of 135-mm. (5⅜ in.) and speed of *f*.4 produces excellent results with a 35-mm. camera: The birds will appear nearly three times larger than when taken with the regular lens.

Though it is desirable to stop motion in pictures and hence avoid blurs, it is nevertheless pleasing to convey the impression of motion. This is achieved by snapping the shutter when man or animal is at the mid-point of an action. To do this with animals is often difficult, but it is easy to catch a man just as he has lifted a foot in walking, or with a sandwich halfway to his mouth, and so on. When two or three hunters are walking, it is a good idea to have them get in step before you take their picture.

Veteran sportsman-photographers generally use the smallest lens stop or opening possible for most outdoor scenes, because this is the best guarantee of picture sharpness. There is an old axiom, "The

PLATE V. Data: 35-mm. camera, speed 1/200, opening *f*.4.5, Plus-X film.

smaller the stop, the sharper the focus," and it certainly holds true here.

About the only times a larger-than-usual stop need be used is for action shots, and for certain close-ups. For instance, a hunter taking a close-up of a companion posed near an undesirable background should open the lens wide and focus on the man. In the resulting picture the companion will stand out clearly, but the background will be blurry and subdued. An *f*.3.5 or *f*.4.5 lens should meet most hunters' requirements.

Though the lens may be left focused on infinity

PLATE VI. Data: Press-type camera, speed 1/50, opening *f*.11, Plenachrome film.

for many scenic shots, careful focusing should be done when near-by hunters are the most important part of the picture, and for all close-ups. This takes but a second or two if the camera has a built-in range finder coupled to the lens. Otherwise, a pocket range finder should be used, and the lens then be focused for the calculated distance.

As it is difficult to focus upon anything moving

PLATE VII. A "Framed" Picture. Data: 35-mm. camera, speed 1/50, opening *f*.8, Du Pont Superior 2 film.

toward or away from the camera, most veterans focus upon a point *ahead of* whatever is approaching or leaving, and take the picture when the moving subject has reached the point focused upon. Thus in the case of hunters walking toward the photographer, the camera is focused on a stick, rock, log, or bush ahead of and in the path of the hunters, and the shutter snapped when they reach the prefocused point. The applications are endless, and are even used in the high-speed photography of birds—the outer decoys near a duck blind often being selected for prefocusing.

**Composition.** We said earlier that lack of a plan ruins many a pictorial record. When a hunter works out a schedule of pictures to be taken, pictures to tell the whole story of a hunt, he finds himself an-

PLATE VIII. Data: 2¼ by 3¼ roll-film camera, speed 1/25, opening *f*.5.6, Verichrome film.

PLATE IX. Data: $2\frac{1}{4}$ by $2\frac{1}{4}$ roll-film camera, speed 1/50, opening *f*.8, Plus-X film.

ticipating the scenes as they unfold, and so is ready with his camera for each "right" moment. This way, the results will appear natural and the hunt itself will proceed smoothly, without unwanted interruptions.

For instance, a partner climbing over a particularly difficult fence is a candidate for a good human-interest shot—provided the action is photographed as it occurs. But ask Joe to climb back over that fence because you missed your chance the first time, and you will be unpopular.

In any hunt there are times when natural pauses occur, and these often offer opportunities for good pictures. When a hunter has just shot a pheasant, he usually takes a little time out to admire the bird before putting it away. A picture should be taken then, while the man is interested in the pheasant, and before it stiffens into shapelessness. Similarly, hunters generally pause at the crest of a hill just climbed and present the cameraman with a chance for a skyline shot and a picture of the view.

Here are a few ideas to help plan the picture story of a hunt. Scenes of the initial preparations: Letting the dogs out of the car or trailer, saddling up, or tightening the ropes on a pack horse, checking and loading guns near the car. A long and a close shot of hunters riding or walking a trail, and in the hunting country itself. Medium close-ups of hunters in natural and interesting poses, such as examining game signs, climbing a fence, crossing a stream, drinking from a spring, checking a compass near dogs on point.

Be sure to catch hunters in the act of firing, even if this must be posed. For pictorials: a man on a lone deer stand, a hunter glassing the countryside from a hilltop, two hunters carrying a deer against the skyline, a gunner picking up decoys and silhouetted against the evening sky. For close-ups: a wildfowler with his call, a hunter and his trophy, the game itself with the gun, dogs pointing and retrieving, mealtime around the campfire, and so on.

There are certain ways to get the best out of every picture set-up, and a few of these will be discussed here. For instance, a picture of a pretty view is somewhat purposeless and dead unless there is a human figure in it somewhere. In color shots particularly it helps to have a hunter walking across that empty meadow or admiring the view from the hilltop. And regardless of the type of film used, "framing" a picture—taking it so that branches, tall grass, even whole trees sometimes, appear in the foreground and slightly out of focus—serves to throw attention on the main scene.

Any picture including sky just about demands the use of a filter to bring out cloud contrast on black-and-white film. Dramatic effects can often be

PLATE X. Data: 2¼ by 2¼ roll-film camera, speed 1/100, opening f.5.6, Plus-X film.

attained by shooting almost directly into the sun. In this case a sunshade should be used, or a hat should be held above the lens to shade it from direct sunlight. If the view is attractive, but the sky has no clouds and there is no tree in just the right place to frame the picture, a branch broken from a tree and held above and slightly ahead of the camera will frame the view nicely. This is an old Hollywood trick.

Another standard type of picture, usually taken as a medium close-up, is the silhouette. In this the hunter, and possibly his game or his dog, should be pictured against a bright background, such as light-struck water or a brilliant sky. The camera should be focused sharply upon the hunter, and then an exposure made about four times longer than normal. It should be remembered that everything outlined by the light will show up in the minutest detail, and for this reason care should be used in posing the subject in a natural position, away from anything with a distracting outline. As color film lacks the wide latitude of ordinary film, silhouettes in color are best not attempted by amateurs.

Shutter speeds and focusing technique for most action shots were discussed earlier. But there is a way to take one particular type of action picture, and the method must be mentioned here, because it is not too difficult and the results are often spectacular. Though a bird's rapid wing-beats require a shutter speed of 1/500 or better for a successful picture, a *slower* speed may be used a moment after the bird has been shot.

The system is used when a bird is known to be just ahead of a hunter. The cameraman should stand with cocked and focused camera about 20 yards to one side of the gunner, and snap the picture just after the bird has been hit. If the exposure is made very soon after the gun's roar, the camera will usually catch a puff of feathers near the hit bird. Otherwise there will just be the falling bird—stopped cold when taken at 1/400. But often 1/200 or 1/250 will do the job, so the technique is possible with most inexpensive 35-mm. and folding cameras.

It is in the close-ups that most hunting pictures fall short, with hunters staring glassily at the camera while holding up game, or doing any of half a dozen things. To be convincing and appealing, such pictures should show people looking natural in what they are doing. When a man has just downed a high-flying duck, he is doing the natural thing when he looks at the duck—and not the camera. The same goes for the hunter and his big-game trophy.

What ruins many a close-up of a hunter is a distracting background, such as half of an automobile, tree branches, or the side of a house. A simple backdrop like a grassy hillside will not clash with the subject, and as a last resort there is always the sky; just take the latter picture from a low angle—and be careful of hat shadow on your friend's face.

Close-ups of the dead game itself are often desired, and here again a simple background is best. Game looks most natural when photographed at or near the spot where it was shot rather than at a roadside or in the backyard. This is particularly true in the case of big game, and photographing it "on the spot" helps to bring back the details of the hunt later. Small game, on the other hand, besides looking well on forest floor or atop a broad log, is also suited to still-life setups against a rustic background. Thus a brace of grouse hung from a peg on the barn wall—with the gun included for size comparison—makes a pleasant picture.

**Flash photography** is in a class by itself. If a hunter cares to invest from $15 to $30 on a flash gun, he can count on getting many excellent pictures otherwise impossible to take. Nowadays flash equipment is available for all modern cameras, and it is easy to use. Exposure instructions are to be found on every flash-bulb container. The extra cost for each flash exposure will run from about 10 to 30 cents, depending upon the size of bulb used.

The hunter with flash equipment can take pictures inside a tent or cabin any time; at night on a coon hunt, beside or inside a car in the dark, and in the deepest woods—day or night. With a little ingenuity he can set up his camera near camp and take night pictures of raccoons, porcupines, possums, and even bears by attaching a baited pull string to the flash gun on the camera. A trip line similarly hooked up and stretched across a game trail is all that is needed for a surprise portrait of the wiliest buck.

It is easy to make a picture of friends around a campfire at night with flash. The cameraman himself can get in the picture by using an electric extension cord to set off his flash camera set up several feet away. Flash may also be used in daytime for clear, needle-sharp close-ups that eliminate harsh face shadows. The applications are endless, and the results are usually pleasing, for flash photography can be depended upon.

# PRESERVATION OF MEAT

Wild meat is good meat. Many times, however, it does not reach the table with all its inherent fine qualities, or in a condition comparable to domestic meats. This is due, primarily, to two causes. First, the average hunter is not a professional butcher or meat processor. Secondly, the hunting field does not afford the tools or the ideal conditions for dressing out and caring for an animal, which the meat-packing establishment has as standard equipment.

On the other hand, the hunting field does provide several conditions favorable to the preservation of wild meat. Big-game hunting seasons are ordinarily set for fall, when the weather may be expected to get progressively colder. Big-game animals, by nature of their habits and habitat, are found in relatively high country during such hunting seasons. This means that such animals will be killed in high altitudes, as a rule.

Couple this to the fact that all the tools *necessary* to the proper field care of meat may handily be carried along with the hunter, while he hunts, and it becomes apparent that there is no real need for bringing home any wild meat that is not fresh, sweet, and fine-eating.

**Preparation.** The best elementary tools for caring for meat in the field are probably human intelligence and observation. The hunter must have a conception of the varied conditions (as to terrain, weather, and distances to transportation) under which he may kill his game; and also, he must be possessed of an understanding of the basic factors involved in meat spoilage, and how to thwart them.

Equipped with this fundamental knowledge, the hunter needs but few additional tools for preserving meat in the field. Generally speaking, he will need in addition only a knife, cheesecloth, small rope, belt ax (for the larger specimens), can of black pepper, and four cotton meat bags. Set down individually, this sounds like quite a list; but packed tightly together, the whole will fit neatly, and with little noticeable weight, into a rucksack, or small pack-board, along with the hunter's lunch for the day. The cotton bags, the most bulky item, may be left at camp until the day after the game is actually killed.

With this simple equipment, the intelligent hunter can keep wild meat in fine condition for at least a week, during relatively warm weather; and indefinitely, if the weather turns from cool to cold and freezing. This, in either case, is usually long enough to serve the hunter's purpose.

Immediately upon the death of a game animal, the agents of meat spoilage begin their work. Bacteria in the alimentary canal rapidly multiply. Gases form, causing the animal to bloat and to emit odors. The downed carcass provides both of the two conditions ideal and necessary to such bacterial growth—heat and moisture. These odors, at first unnoticeable to the human sense of smell, at once attract blowflies and predatory birds and animals. If undeterred, the blowflies will immediately lay their eggs, which within a few hours will become maggots, which in turn will shortly decompose the animal flesh. This, coupled to the gorging of predators, increasingly attracted by the odors of decay, will serve to dispose of the entire animal within a matter of days. This is nature's way of scavenging the landscape of its dead.

To the hunter wishing to save such an animal, this means simply that he must combat the three basic factors of meat spoilage: animal heat, blowflies, and predators. To the extent that he accomplishes this, he successfully saves his game for the table.

**Field Dressing.** Broadly, field care of meat for all kinds of game is similar; and the hunter who knows how to care for elk or antelope meat, for example, will have no trouble with deer or moose. The differences in handling, as between species, are only minor.

The field care of elk meat, therefore, will serve as an example. As with any species of wild game, the animal should be killed as quickly and cleanly as possible. Wounded game that lives for any length of time before being dispatched, or that travels any distance during such an interim, becomes fevered; and its meat is never as good as that from a beast which is quickly killed during a period of relative inaction.

With the possible exception of moose, elk meat requires the most attention and effort. This is due

All photos in this section from Clyde Ormond, Rigby, Idaho.

PLATE I. Upon reaching the fallen game, the hunter should first decide whether or not he wishes to save it for a trophy.

PLATE II. This big bull elk was draped over blowdowns, off the ground, and covered with cheesecloth. The hunter can return with help the next morning, to quarter and hang the animal.

to the animal's great size; to the high rugged terrain he inhabits and is consequently killed in; and to the fact that the elk is a spooky beast, and is often killed in such places by a hunter working alone.

The first step is to field-dress the animal. Animal heat is the first and biggest factor in meat spoilage, and the quick, clean removal of the animal's insides will greatly hasten the escape of such heat. Before beginning this, however, the hunter should determine if he wishes to save the head for a trophy. If so, the actual cleaning operation must be accomplished so as not to injure either the head or the animal's cape. Briefly, this means that the abdominal incision used in dressing must not extend much beyond the sternum at the beginning of the rib-cage, before the cape is removed. And the throat must not be cut.

To facilitate dressing out, the beast should first be placed on its back. This can be accomplished by rolling the animal belly upward, and placing rocks or chunks of wood along the underside, at the hip and shoulder areas. The animal's head should be uphill. Shot game will emit blood and excreta; and in such a position, blood will not run onto the trophy, and both blood and excreta will drain away from the carcass.

With bulls, the testicles are first removed by slicing off the entire scrotum. In the case of bull elk, too, there will be a pronounced sweet, musky odor about the abdomen, genitals, and lower hind legs. This stench, which is worse in old bulls, comes from the urine. The disagreeable odor will be transferred to the meat if such areas are allowed to touch the animal's flesh. The best way of preventing this is next to tie off the penis with a bit of cord, or strand of light rope; encircle the area with a skin incision including *all* the black curly hair surrounding the genital; then peel both the genital and the section of skin backward between the hind quarters at the pelvis, to where it can be temporarily laid behind the carcass.

The anal vent is then encircled with a knife stroke, to a depth of about 2 inches, and the vent is tied off with cord. No excreta can now be emitted, and the musky-smelling areas cut away should not be allowed to touch the flesh thereafter. With cows, the genital is tied off with the anus.

Next, the hunter's hands should be cleaned—washed, if a creek or spring is available, otherwise wiped of the musky odor upon grass and a piece of the cheesecloth.

The abdominal incision is begun at the forward end of the pelvic bone, and continued to the sternum. The knife point follows two fingers inserted in the opening, and holding the abdominal wall upward, away from the intestines. Care should be used not to puncture either intestines or stomach. The pelvis is best split between the two hams, using the small ax, to facilitate cleaning. The rib-cage is split its entire length with the same tool, and the neck skin (unless the cape is to be saved for a trophy) is split all the way to the jawbone, so that the gullet may be removed in its entirety, by cutting along either side. This is important.

An elk's gullet sours first—often, if left in the carcass, within a matter of hours. Where a trophy is to be saved, the animal is first dressed without splitting the rib-cage. The cape is next skinned out, after which the ribs are split at the sternum and the gullet removed.

With the animal's belly-line split from tail to jaw, and the carcass partially opened, the viscera is pulled and cut free along the spine and at the diaphragm (at its junction with the ribs, all around), until both the abdominal and chest contents may be removed. The heart and liver are cut out, for saving. The remainder of the insides had best be dragged some distance away from the carcass, since they will offer some "inducement" for the predatory birds, away from the meat.

Field-dressing the animal is the first step in cooling the carcass and greatly speeds up the escape of the beast's natural body warmth. The process is by no means complete at this point, but it is wise here to digress and take advantage of another tool for fighting meat spoilage—the animal's own blood.

Blowflies, during mild weather, represent the hunter's second danger to keeping his meat. Blowflies lay eggs, which turn to maggots, which feed upon the flesh, and change again to flies. This metamorphosis requires both moisture and warmth. Destroy either, and the blowfly hazard can be elim-

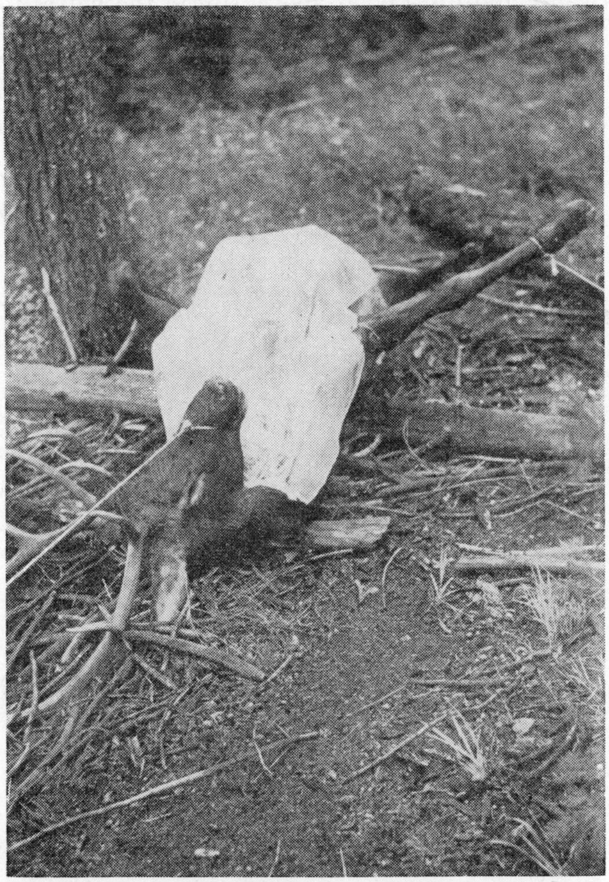

PLATE III. Even where the hunter is alone, it is always possible somehow to get the animal completely off the ground. Note chunks of blowdown under the shoulder and neck (a similar chunk is under the hams), and the way the carcass is tied, spread apart for cooling, and covered with cheesecloth to protect from blowflies.

PLATE IV. The extra effort is required to get a carcass hung in trees is always worth while. Where there is hard snow, as here, it does no harm to drag the heavy quarters, with the grain of the hair.

inated. Consequently, it is wise at this point to spread the carcass as widely as possible, even if the animal is in full sunlight, and allow the inside to dry and air out as much as possible. Contrary to the novice's opinion, such sunlight will not spoil the meat. It is animal heat, not weather heat, which does the damage.

Areas such as inside the rib-cage will dry considerably in 20 minutes. It is not safe to let the carcass lie on the ground for much longer. While such drying is taking place, the hunter should smear all exposed areas of flesh with a coating of fresh blood. If the animal has been dressed out, supine, enough blood will have been left in the chest cavity for this purpose. The most moist areas, such as between the hams, should be coated the heaviest.

Fresh blood will coagulate rapidly, upon direct contact with air and sunlight. Placed upon the surface of fresh meat, it forms a rind, or "glaze," which dries hard and seals the flesh beneath, and through which blowflies will not work. Certain areas, however, cannot be made to glaze sufficiently to make the carcass entirely flyproof. On account of heavy layers of muscle beneath, plus a natural draining of flesh, certain areas will remain moist despite blood-smearing. These areas should be sprinkled

PLATE V. A sacked quarter and one that is blood-glazed, trimmed, cooled, and ready for sacking.

heavily with black pepper. Blowflies will not work through a coating of black pepper. Consequently, fresh blood and black pepper become two invaluable tools against the blowfly hazard.

With the smearing and peppering done, the hunter continues with his efforts aimed at cooling out all possible animal heat. It is a safe conclusion to assume *always* that any game animal killed must be somehow raised off the ground, in any kind of weather, or it will quickly spoil. Elk quarters will weigh in the neighborhood of 100 pounds each. They represent large quantities of sealed-in warmth. The large porous bones of hams and shoulders, and the heavy coating of hair about the neck and shoulder areas, are the finest of heat insulators. The body heat of an elk may last 48 hours.

**Quartering.** If two or more hunters are together, the best possible procedure is to quarter and hang the carcass in trees as soon after it is dressed as possible. The beast is split lengthwise with the ax, and the halves separated at the third rear rib, into quarters. The quarters are best hung as high off the ground and in as much shade as possible. If the shady side of a ridge is anywhere near, it is always worth the additional effort to carry the quarters to such a cooler side, and hang them on the northern slope. Care is used to see that no two quarters touch, so that air may circulate freely around all sides. Quarters are proppped also away from heavy tree boles. Pines and spruce are good hanging trees.

**Preservation.** The hung quarters are then covered all over the flesh side with pieces of cheesecloth. A five-yard package is ample for an elk, and is conveniently carried. One-fourth of it will completely cover the flesh side of an elk quarter. Cheesecloth has the property of sticking well to bone splinters and matting to fresh blood. With care, this porous covering can be made to cover the quarters completely flyproof. Caution must be used, however, as blowflies will find any possible opening.

With the quarters hung and covered with cheesecloth, it is best to loosely cover them further with a canopy of several pine boughs or similar branches. These are thrust into the rope loops and among other limbs above the quarters, so that they hang downward over the meat and with the grain of the branches. Such a loose covering serves to keep predatory birds from getting to the meat, and also helps shed snow or rain, if it storms.

In many instances where the hunter makes a kill while alone, or late in the day, or in terrain devoid of suitable trees for hanging the quarters, it often is impossible to quarter an elk immediately after it is dressed. Under one, or a combination of such conditions, elk meat is often lost through souring before it can be quartered and hung. There is no need to lose a kill under these conditions, even during mild weather.

The best procedure is to dress out the animal cleanly and quickly, as above, spread the halves to

PLATE VI. The clean, porous, cotton bags are placed over the quarters after the animal heat has cooled and the quarters are hung.

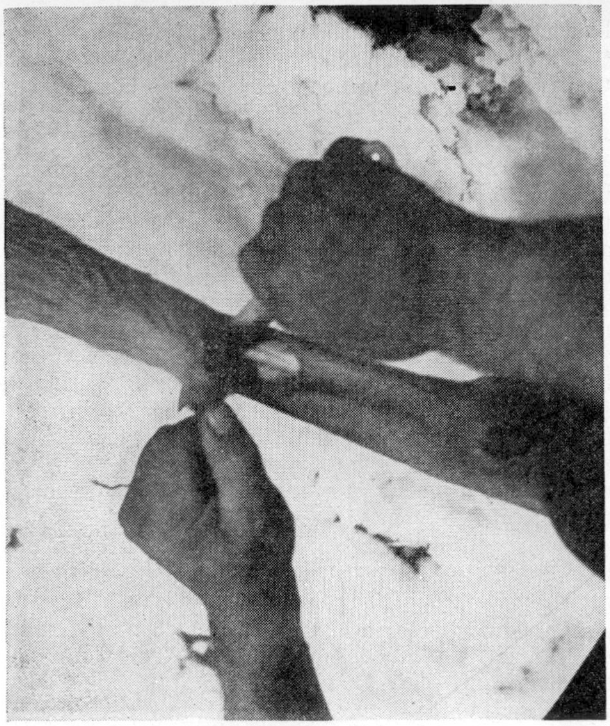

PLATE VII. The first step with deer, is to remove the musk glands found on both hind legs of either buck or doe.

get it as open as possible for airing, and then in some manner, get the animal *completely off the ground,* so that no part of it touches the earth. This is not so impossible as it would at first seem. Elk country is ordinarily timber country. In local absence of trees, there are still apt to be blowdowns or chunks of dead wood. If not, there will be large rocks within a carrying range.

If a beast cannot be hung, the next best device is to drape it over a blowdown, the higher from the ground the better. Often a beast is killed on a side-hill, where with a bit of planning it can be pulled, or rolled, a few rods, so that it may be placed over a blowdown situated below—by utilizing gravity. This, despite an elk's great size, can often be accomplished by a lone hunter.

The animal is best draped over the blowdown so that the head is highest. This way, blood and body juices will drain downward and out through the anal opening. Too, with the blowdown situated midway of the carcass, there is less danger of souring where the heavy meat areas of shoulders and hams occur, since air will be free to circulate all about them. The flesh side is blood-glazed, and peppered as before.

With the belly cavity spread to its greatest width, the hunter then spreads the five yards of cheesecloth over it, beginning at the lower jaw and folding the remaining cloth under, at the tail. Rocks and sticks may be used along either side where the cloth does not stick to bone slivers or mat to blood-coated areas. The point is, the cheesecloth must cover the entire cavity so that at no point can a single blowfly enter the abdominal cavity.

In instances where neither trees nor blowdowns are immediately available, the last resort is simply to dress out the beast, spread the carcass as widely as possible, and get it entirely off the ground—always in a belly up position. Rocks or chunks of wood are used under the back at hip, neck, and shoulder areas, so that the carcass does not touch the ground, and air will circulate all about it. Often, in such cases, the legs and head must be tied outward, with sections of the small rope, to bushes, etc., to keep the beast from rolling.

With the carcass spread, the cheesecloth is placed over the cavity, as above.

With any of these three procedures, the meat will keep safely until the following morning; but it is never safe to leave it longer without further attention. The next morning, the hunter should return to the carcass, with the necessary tools and help (from hunting companions) to quarter and hang the meat, and with the four cotton bags. Daybreak is the best time, since the night's coolness will still be on, and in, the meat. Too, if working alone, the hunter will have all day for the chore.

Most of the animal heat will now have gone from the meat. Unless previously done, the animal is now quartered. A careful check is made to see that no blowfly has laid eggs either on the flesh side or in the hair. If so, such areas are cut away. Remaining blood clots, gun-wound areas, and any soiled spots are carefully trimmed from the meat. The four sacks, of clean cotton cloth at least as porous as muslin, and roughly a yard by a yard and one-half in size, are tied over the quarters. This is best done after hanging the meat, and by tying the sack tops

PLATE VIII. Even in treeless antelope country it is always possible to find something over which a carcass can be draped or hung for temporary draining and cooling.

PLATE IX. Occasionally, for expediency, meat is skinned out and brought out to camp, without the heavy bone areas, in clean sacks on packboards.

around the hanging rope. The thin canopy of boughs is placed over the quarters as above.

The two worst bird predators are the jay and the magpie. Neither will peck through the cotton bags.

Hung and sacked in this manner, the meat is safe for another day. The remaining animal heat will now cool out from the heavy hip and shoulder bones; the blowfly hazard has been licked by blood-glazing, cheesecloth, and trimming. The problem of predator birds has been solved by the cotton bags. There remains but the problem of predatory animals.

If the distance from camp is not too great, the hunter should return to his kill each day, both for a check-up of the meat and to leave man-scent. Coyotes will come to a kill the second night, their tracks showing that they have circled, but not touched, the hung quarters. The third night, during ideal weather for man-scent to evaporate, coyotes are likely to begin eating on a kill, if the hunter has not returned during the interim.

The best way of thwarting coyotes at a kill is to handle the quarters with the bare hands and leave some item, or "scare-piece," which the coyotes associate with man. A lunch wrapper, empty rifle cartridge, or handkerchief tied to a quarter is sufficient.

In the rare instance where a black bear finds a kill there is no way of scaring him from the meat except by removing the kill or killing the bear. Black bears are suspicious of man-smell, but will come quicker than coyotes, once they have smelled fresh meat. Grizzlies will come to a kill the moment they smell it.

Once in a great while a hunter makes an elk kill too far from available trees to hang the quarters, or is hunting alone and kills a big bull whose quarters are too heavy for him to hang alone. In such cases his best bet is to use the "brush-heap." This means that he places the quarters side by side on a heap of brush, sacks them, cools them completely, and protects the meat from predators exactly as above, with the single exception of tree-hanging them.

The brush-heap is exactly what its name implies. It is best built as much in the shade as possible, and from any available brush, limbs, twigs, and small trees at hand. The coarser limbs are placed closest to the ground, the smaller stuff on top. The important thing is this: The brush-heap must be large enough so that four elk quarters will lie on top of it, side by side, but without their edges touching; it must also be of sufficient height so that when 400 pounds of meat are placed on top, the pile will still be at least 18 inches high or deep. Built in such a fashion, and of coarse enough material, the brush-heap allows the air to circulate all through itself, all about the quarters, and permits a "chimneying" effect, which keeps the meat from souring—even during relatively mild weather.

To use the brush-heap, the hunter first cools out the elk carcass for one night previously—getting it off the ground, blood-glazing it, and utilizing the pepper and cheesecloth. Cooled out to that extent, the carcass is quartered, checked, sacked in the cotton bags, and placed with quarters hair side downward on the brush heap. A very thin covering of

PLATE X. All the field requirements of a hunter may be carried easily on his back in a rucksack or a small packboard.

PLATE XI. Deer of this size are usually brought in whole, on a pack animal.

boughs is placed over the quarters, as a protection against the sight (the white bags show up prominently from the air) and action of predator birds.

The brush-heap requires more subsequent attention than a kill that is hung, since it cannot be kept quite as cool—until the meat can be moved back to transportation. It is not so ideal a method as tree-hanging the quarters, but does make a fine substitute in instances when a substitute is the only alternative.

A moose kill is best handled in the same manner and method as an elk, utilizing more manpower, since it is bigger.

The same factors regarding meat spoilage occur in the case of deer. Most of the differences in handling venison in the field come about because of a difference in animal size. The largest mule deer are, roughly speaking, about one-third the size of an elk. Consequently, their handling, after a kill is made, is easier.

A deer should be cleaned as quickly as possible after killing. A deer is dressed in the same manner as an elk, except that it is not usually necessary to make the abdominal incision further than the point of the rib-cage. Neither is it necessary to split the pelvic bone between the hams, though doing so makes it more convenient for the inexperienced to remove the genitals and lower colon. Only in cases of exceptionally big bucks, long distances back to transportation, or warm weather, is it necessary to quarter a deer. Deer, because of their smaller size, cool out much quicker than elk; they are more easily handled; and usually it is possible to get venison back to camp much more quickly than the meat of elk.

One important difference in the field dressing exists. Deer, both the does and the bucks, have musk glands on their hind legs. The glands occur in the hock area, one gland on the inside of the leg, another lower down on the outside. They are detected by the upraised or "tufted" hair covering the glands.

These musk glands contain a sweet-smelling, greenish fluid, nauseating in odor. In cases where the deer has run or rolled any great distance after being shot, the smell is pronounced. The hunter should remove these glands by "peeling" or slicing off the entire skin surrounding them, as soon as the fallen animal is reached—then carefully washing his hands of the smell before further dressing the beast. This prevents a possible flesh contamination from the musky secretion spreading through the lymph ducts, and direct tainting by the hands on the flesh after touching such gland areas while handling the carcass.

The three principal sources of venison-taint are: (1) musk which has in some manner been transferred from the glands to the flesh; (2) blood which is allowed to collect, and later putrefy, between the layers of muscle; and (3) contamination from intestinal fluid or contents which in any way comes in contact with the animal flesh. Gut-shots are a primary cause of the last, and careless field-dressing may be responsible for all three.

Tree-hanging is the rule for deer. The carcass is best hung by the head or antlers and unquartered. Blood and body juices will drain better from this position and away from the head and cape which may be wanted for a trophy. Possible rains or snow run off the carcass better too, since it is with the grain of the hair, and water does not get into the body cavity to make the meat sleazy. Too, the exposed flesh of hams and cavity are then in a position harder to get to, and peck, by predator birds.

Once hung, the carcass is spread widely at the abdominal cavity with 12-inch spreader sticks, sharpened at each end and thrust into flesh at each edge.

PLATE XII. Elk quarters are left with the hair on, and often packed in, in canvas mantas, a pair of quarters to each pack animal.

The cheesecloth is tied over the entire body cavity, blowfly-proof. Boughs are loosely draped over the cache as with elk.

Antelope are similar in size to deer, and their meat is cared for in somewhat the same manner. There are a few important differences. First, an antelope has a very pronounced "mousy" smell, due to the excretion of the cutaneous glands, especially in the hock and hip areas. This disagreeable odor is easily transmitted to the animal's flesh either from direct contact with the hands (after touching), or by allowing the hair itself to touch the warm flesh.

The best procedure with antelope, consequently, is to field-dress the animal quickly. Do not allow the hair to touch the flesh; keep the hands cleaned of all hair-contamination during the dressing operation; cool the carcass as quickly as possible; then get the animal back to camp and skin it out—rolling the hair side of the hide under as the animal is skinned so that the hair never gets to touch flesh.

Another difference in the handling of antelope is that antelope country is nearly always treeless country. It is still a cardinal rule, however, as with any game, to get the carcass off the ground. Often the enterprising hunter can find sagebrush high enough to drape the animal over while it cools and drains. Juts of rocks or even cut-banks may be utilized. Cheesecloth is used as with deer.

**Packing Out.** All these methods of handling are based on the assumption that some time and distance do separate available transportation and the spot where the kill is made. Elk and moose usually are moved over such distances by packhorses. Deer are brought to camp, either by horses or manpower, as are antelope. In all such cases the hide is best left on during packing, as it protects the meat.

In instances where kills are made close to auto or boat transportation, it sometimes hastens the cooling-out process, and otherwise expedites matters, to skin out the carcass at the kill and pack the meat in, in clean cotton bags, on pack-boards. In either case it is a basic rule never to move fresh meat until it is thoroughly cooled.

Once back at car transportation, the chore of saving meat does not end. The wise hunter has previously provided clean burlap or gunny sacks to slip over the cotton bag covering already on the meat. Meat is best packed into trailers or autos in layers not over one quarter, or one whole carcass deep, for the ride home. Meat, for the home trip, is best hung overnight, packed at daylight, and moved immediately. In cases where overnight stops en route are inevitable, the meat should be unpacked, hung high in available trees, or on meat-rack or pole, and repacked when it is coolest, at daylight. Where meat reaches camp and must lay over for several days, it is best hung overnight, then rolled in canvas or quilts at daylight and placed in the shade during daylight hours. The cool acquired during the night will often last the entire day.

**Storage and Curing.** When a hunter reaches home with his game there are several ways of preserving it until it can all be eaten. These depend largely upon climate and weather. Possibly the very best way under any and all conditions is to have the meat cut up, quick or "blast" frozen, and stored at the local cold-storage plant. These plants are mushrooming all over the country. Hunters in most areas nowadays have access to one, and they are almost the perfect answer to saving completely the meat a hunter has worked so hard to bring home in good condition. Hunters wishing to avail themselves of such services had best make the necessary arrangements in advance so that the processing plant may be prepared to care quickly for meat which perhaps cannot be saved much longer otherwise.

Wild game for storage, canning, or to be eaten fresh should first be hung for approximately eight

PLATE XIII. Antlers, unless exceptionally large, can be brought in as a top pack with a pair of quarters.

days after killing at temperatures of from 40 to 50 degrees. Hanging or aging breaks down the muscle fibers and renders such meat tender. Fibers will not break further after freezing.

In hunting areas having weather as cool as 50 degrees, whole quarters or carcasses can often be eaten before any spoilage occurs. Many hunters hang the meat in the shade of cool outbuildings or meat houses without skinning it. Steaks, roasts, etc., are cut from the whole as they are used, with only enough skinning to remove that particular piece—the skin serving to keep the remainder both clean and moist.

Another method of quickly working up meat which will not last is to can it with a pressure cooker. The meat is first cut into chunks half the size of a fist, soaked in salt water overnight, cold-packed into jars or cans, and then pressure cooked for about 70 minutes at 15 pounds pressure for quart-sized jars (at medium elevations above sea level).

Deer or elk hams can often be saved whole for at least 30 days in reasonably cool weather by sewing them up in clean cotton bags and dipping the entire ham into a heavy boiling salt brine for two to three minutes and then hanging them up to dry. The salt brine dries the outer coating of meat into a dark rind which seals the juices in and bacteria out.

Perhaps the best way of making fine meat out of old, tough game animals is to have the meat cut off the bones and double-ground into "burgers." This works with any species from deer to elk or moose. Double-grinding thoroughly breaks the fibers of the toughest of wild meat, making it edible if it has been kept sweet, clean, and untainted. Wild meat is comparatively "dry" meat. Consequently, during the grinding a quantity of fat pork should be added and mixed. From 15 to 20 per cent by weight supplies enough fat for the finished meat to fry itself well, and makes a fine flavor for "elk-burgers," "moose-burgers," or "deer-burgers." Special sausage seasonings help while frying.

Another advantage of this type of curing is that all scraps and trimmings from other choice cuts can be completely utilized, and the finished product is all meat—free of bones—and can be stored in locker boxes in a minimum of space.

PLATE XIV. A car fender, near the motor's heat, is a poor place to carry an animal in the deer class. It is better to place the carcass on top of all the duffle, spread widely and tied securely.

# PRESERVATION AND CARE OF TROPHIES

The best foundation for a knowledge of the field care of trophies is a basic understanding of the art of taxidermy. The hunter who is acquainted with the various steps in making up the finished trophy is the one best equipped to see that it reaches the taxidermist's studio in perfect shape.

Most big-game trophies take the form of mounted heads, rugs made from pelts, or some combination of both. Generally speaking, all that remains in the finished trophy of the original animal is the skin and its covering. In the case of heads, this includes the horns or antlers. With such animals as bears, goats, and sheep, it may include the claws or the hoofs. In most instances all other animal tissues, bones, and such organs as the eyes, tongue, etc., are replaced by artificial forms.

In preparing a cape or pelt for mounting, the taxidermist first scrapes, or "fleshes," the hide until it is completely free of all fat, muscle, and cartilage. In the case of heavy hides, the hide is then literally shaved down, by paring, until it is very thin. Next it is placed in a pickle bath consisting of alum and all the salt that will go into solution. After the hide has been pickled for several weeks, it is poisoned with an arsenical mixture further to preserve it and keep off such insects as moths. Lastly, the cured hide is stretched over an artificial form and shaped to approximate the appearance of the original animal; or, in the case of a rug, the finished skin is sewed to a backing of blanket or felt and trimmed into a finished piece.

The one ever-present danger in the mounting process of any trophy is the hazard of the hair loosening from the hide, or "slipping." Many of the careful steps followed by the taxidermist are aimed at thwarting this constant menace.

**Skinning and Cleaning.** The hunter who wants a trophy finished up into a perfect mount, then, must do two things: (1) He must bring to the taxidermist a cape or pelt that is undamaged as to hide or pelage; and (2) such a hide must be in such a condition that the hair will not slip. Where minor damage does occur, despite every effort to prevent it on the part of the hunter, a good taxidermist can often work seeming wonders at repairing it. The one thing impossible to repair, however, is hair slippage.

Very few tools are needed for the field care of trophies. A sharp knife of good quality, a few pieces of absorbent cotton, and a small bottle of acetone are all the equipment necessary. Quantities of salt, of course, will be available after the trophy is back to camp. Cold water makes a fine substitute for the acetone, if water happens to be near the spot where the trophy is dropped.

Most hunters fail to carry acetone, depending instead upon the availability of water for cleaning off stains. With such animals as pronghorn antelope and mountain sheep, however, acetone is almost a must, since the hair on such beasts is brittle and tubular. It has the property of immediately soaking up blood and other staining fluids. If not removed at once, such material will set permanently inside the hairs, causing dark stains in the finished mount, which cannot be removed. The simon-pure trophy hunter carries a small bottle of acetone as a matter of course. Since its weight is virtually nothing, the

All photos in this section from Clyde Ormond, Rigby, Idaho.

PLATE I. Shot animals will bleed. The first step, as with this goat, is to check the pelage for blood spots.

PLATE II. Trophy animals should be placed with heads uphill before skinning.

average hunter might well do the same; the chance for exceptional heads often comes to the novice as well as to the expert.

A cardinal rule with trophy hunters is never to make a head shot. Head shots with today's rifles are impossible to repair. Neck shots, too, are out except as a last resort.

The actual field care of all antlered or horned animals, which are to be preserved for head mounts, is similar. The objective is to remove and preserve both the cape and the "headgear." The work begins the minute the lucky hunter comes upon his fallen quarry.

Shot game animals will be bleeding animals. Too, death causes relaxation of all body muscles; and more often than not, such beasts will emit excreta —especially during the action of moving them about. In addition, regardless of where a beast is hit, it will often bleed at the nostrils and mouth. This takes place not only in cases of lung shots, but often from the sheer hydraulic action of bullets.

Any blood or excreta occurring on the cape or head should immediately be swabbed off with cotton and acetone. The nostrils, throat, and any possible bullet holes in the cape should then be plugged. The throat should *never* be cut.

The next step is to move the beast about so that the head and cape are removed from any blood puddles (on the animal's underside), and so that the head is *uphill*. This keeps subsequent blood and emission from running onto the parts desired for mounting. Care must be used in moving the animal. No beast desired for a trophy should ever be dragged, as the animal's weight and movement will cause hair to be rubbed off on the underside. This is especially true with antelope—any dragging will cause great patches of hair to rub off, thereby ruining the trophy. Instead, the animal should be lifted by the antlers or horns and gently set down again. Caution must be used here, too, to see that no blood is on the hands while doing so. Such blood will set on the antlers, turn dark, and be almost impossible to remove later.

At this point it is wise to take four simple measurements: (1) the circumference of the neck immediately behind the ears; (2) another such measurement midway of the neck; (3) another around the neck at the point of the shoulders; and (4) a measurement from the tip of the nose to a point midway between the antlers or horns. Optimistic hunters often carry steel tapes in order to measure trophies which possibly may be record heads; and they wish the measurements to be recorded on the spot, since antlers and horns will shrink slightly with the passing of time. The average hunter will find that a length of fishline, or any other unstretchable cord, does nicely, knots being tied in it for each measurement.

If the hunter has a camera he should also take several pictures from different angles of the head-and-shoulders area. Mounted heads are made either

PLATE III. With the trophy head down, it is carefully checked for blood about the nose and mouth, then carefully lifted, not dragged, out of blood puddles, with the head uphill.

PLATE IV. The white line indicates where the skin incisions for trophy removal should be made.

upon a form constructed of the actual bones and skull of the animal and built to shape, or on a shaped form made of papier-mache or plaster. Most taxidermists currently prefer the artificial papier-mâché form. But in either case, these definite animal measurements, and possibly pictures, help materially in duplicating the original size of the animal.

Most trophy animals are field-dressed and their carcasses kept for meat. Field-dressing is ordinarily done before the cape is removed; and great care should be used during this operation, so that the cape is neither cut nor injured by moving the carcass, and no blood or body excretion is smeared on it.

To remove the cape, the beast is best turned on its belly, or approximately so, in order to make the skin incision. Since head mounts are viewed from beneath, the incision in the neck skin is always made along the back of the neck—never down the under, or throat, side. The skin incision is begun far back upon the shoulders, at a point exactly between the withers. The cut is continued midway of the neck line, and forward to a point where an X-intersection between ears and opposite antlers would occur. From this point, two cuts are made, one to the center of each antler. Beginning once more at the uppermost point of the withers, the incision is continued downward on each side of the animal, midway of the shoulder and until such opposite cuts meet at a point far down under the brisket. This more or less continuous incision is the only cutting of the skin necessary to the entire cape removal.

Novices err on the side of leaving the neck skin too short. It is always better in this respect to have too much than too little. Shoulder head-mounts are impossible if too little skin is left. Many a fine potential head-mount has been ruined because the hunter cut the animal's throat crosswise, split the neck skin up the front instead of the back, or left too short a cape. It is true that a skillful taxidermist can sew up such wrong incisions. But the seams in the finished mount inevitably show; and the hunter careless enough to make these initial mistakes is also very apt to make subsequent errors as well, with the aggregate result that he brings back a trophy unfit for mounting.

After the incision is completed, the cape is skinned from the neck all around, and to a point behind the ears where the skull proper joins the uppermost vertebrae of the neck. The head is cut and twisted free at this juncture, after the two ear cartilages have been cut as close to the skull as possible.

During this entire operation, care should be used to see that no unnecessary cutting of the skin occurs; that all flesh and tissue is removed from the skin itself; that the ear skin is not cut or torn; and that the neck incision is made by running the knife beneath the skin, cutting outward through it. Cutting from the hair side inward destroys the hair, making the sewing-up job difficult and the resultant appearance unnatural.

In instances where the weather is cold and the trophy can be taken immediately to the taxidermist,

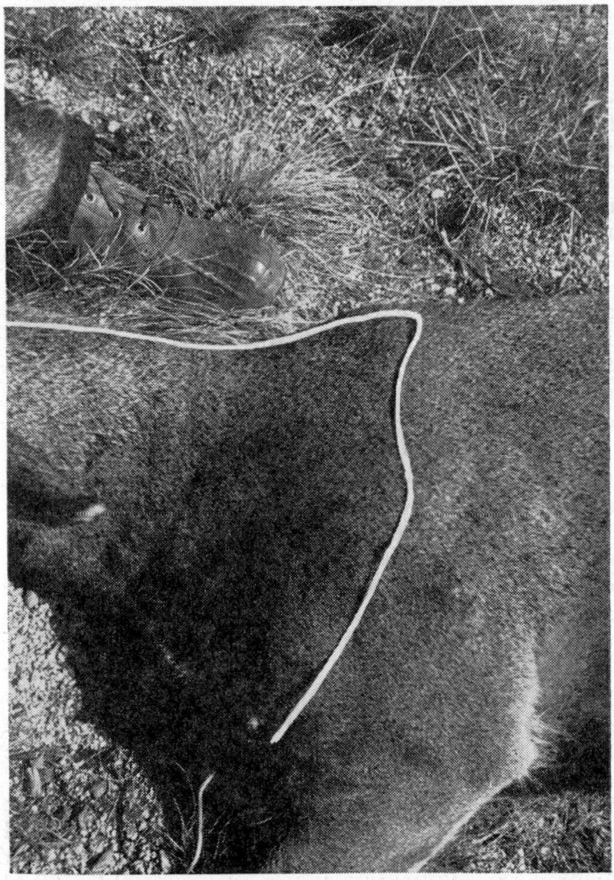

PLATE V. The shoulder cut of a cape should be well back upon the center of the shoulder as indicated here.

PLATE VI. This shows the only necessary skin cuts for an antlers-and-cape trophy.

the entire head may be taken in with the cape with no further skinning. If, however, several days will elapse before this can be done, or if the weather is at all warm, the head also must be skinned out completely, or the hair is very apt to slip. It is always best to be safe rather than sorry in this respect.

To skin out the head, the antlers are first girdled with a prying, cutting motion of the knife, which separates the skin from the antlers, leaving no hair attached to them. The hide is rolled forward and skinned from the skull. In the case of most game animals, the skin here will not skin off freely as it did along the neck, but must be cut away. Patience and care should be used to see that the thin skin in this area is not cut. Especial care must be used at the eyes. The eyelids themselves are never cut. Instead, the membraneous conjunctiva, which connects the bony eye orbit with the edge of the eyelid all around, is separated by cutting. At the eye's forward end, the skin joins tightly to the bone, and is carefully cut and pried away.

When the mouth is reached, the complete lips are left with the skin, the separation from the teeth being made by cutting through the thin black membrane at the teeth roots. The lower lip is completely removed by a continuation of this cutting. The upper lip and nose come off together by cutting through the gristly end of the nose itself, well behind the nostrils.

With the skin free of the skull, the ears should be carefully skinned out. This is a ticklish, tedious bit of effort, but well worth the time. The ears of a mounted animal are the most important part in giving the finished head character and a lifelike expression. If the ear cartilages are not removed, the finished ears will be wrinkled, unnatural, and lifeless. Worse is the danger of hair-slippage, if such cartilage is not skinned out, all the way to the ear tips.

The ears are most easily skinned when the hide is fresh. A blunt, rounded knife-point such as a table knife is useful, since the delicate skin is rather pried, or pushed, loose. The rear of each ear is completely skinned to its tip, before the front of the ear is skinned—the ear skin being folded upward and forward over the ear tip, as the work progresses. The frontal plane of the ear is then skinned, the completed ear skin resembling a pouch or purse.

In instances where the head is completely skinned out, the antlers may either be taken in along with the whole skull, or a "plate" containing the antlers and a section of skull may be taken. This plate is chopped with an ax, or sawed, from the skull, in the shape of a rough triangle. The rear cut is made squarely across the skull, 2 inches behind the antlers or horns. The side cuts begin at each end of the rear cut, pass between antlers and eye orbits, and come together at a point in the center of the face.

A packboard is useful for carrying the cape and horns back to camp, since it places their weight solidly upon the back, and will injure neither the carrier nor the cape. With heavy antlers, such as elk or moose, it is much better to carry them in as a top pack on a packhorse. When pack animals

PLATE VII. A packboard is an excellent means of back-packing in a cape and head.

PLATE VIII. Capes should be thoroughly soaked and rinsed in cold water as soon as possible after skinning, as these goats have been.

are not available, it is often necessary to split the antler-plate through the center and pack the antlers out in two parts. In finishing up the head, the taxidermist bolts both parts back together and fastens the plate onto the artificial form, preserving original measurements and symmetry.

With the cape and antlers back at camp, the hunter still must continue the effort against hair-slippage. The enemies of trophy capes are skin moisture, heat, blowflies, predators, and sharp objects which may gouge the hide or hair during transit. Any areas of a cape which retain either the hide heat or moisture will soon cause the hair to slip. Too, all such areas and creases and folds are potential blowfly hazards. Any outside moisture, such as rain or snow, is hard on capes. So is direct sunlight, as it causes them to "burn."

The procedure to thwart these dangers is apparent. The fresh cape must be cleaned thoroughly of all remaining blood, excreta, and viscera stains. This may be done by a complete soaking and rinsing in clean, cold water. Cold water will not injure a fresh cape.

With all stains washed out, the cape is squeezed and shaken dry of water and spread out to dry. A cape should never be spread upon the ground, but instead, as high off the earth as convenient, and over some such object as a willow or thin pole, where air can easily circulate all around it on both sides. Often such a pole can be erected handily where the cape can be watched. A good spot is a position in open shade, where direct sunlight cannot strike, and where some kind of protecting canopy can be placed over the trophy, in case of rain.

With the cape temporarily spread, it is then best to remove all excess bits of tissue, fat, and flesh which might remain on the hide. This is a good time, too, to remove the ear cartilages, if not already done, and to cut away, or thin down, all excess tissue about the nostrils and lips.

The next step is to work copious quantities of common salt over and into every part of the surface of the hide. Salt has the qualities both of causing moisture to drain from the hide, and of shrinking the skin so the hair will not slip. It is impossible to use too much salt.

A stretched hide will dry out much faster than a loose one. Stretching too, if only simply pulling the hide out to shape with the hands, will remove the creases and folds. A green hide has a tendency to roll inward; such creases refuse to dry rapidly, and present dark, moist pockets where blowflies will lay their eggs.

When the cape has dried out for an hour or so, it is wise to turn it hair side out, brush out any possible blowfly eggs, and sprinkle salt in such areas as the ear pockets, nostril orifices, and lips. Most of the drying will occur while the cape is hung, or stretched, with the hide out. But occasional turning of the cape inside out will hasten the cooling and drying process, and is necessary for a constant check upon every square inch of the trophy.

The procedure from then on is simply a continuation of salting, drying out moist areas, removing any possible fly "blows," and seeing that the cape remains uninjured until it can be taken back to the taxidermist.

Field care of the pelts of animals such as goats and bear, which are to be made into rugs, follows much the same pattern. It begins with a good job of skinning out the pelt of the beast.

The trophy hunter usually knows in advance what type of trophy he wishes to have made up. Yet often the animal itself determines this, and a final choice is not made until the killed beast is reached and its trophy qualities observed. A hunter, for instance, may have decided upon a head mount, if he is lucky enough to get a billy; but upon actually killing one he discovers the entire hide to be of fine quality, unrubbed, and entirely suitable for a head-and-rug mount. As with capes, it is always wise here to take too much, rather than too little; and taking the entire pelt is usually best. However, occasionally a goat, for example, might be killed in early season when the hide is not at full prime and would be worthless as a rug. In such an instance, a head mount might be the best trophy, and would be cared for as with deer or antelope capes. The point is, the hunter should never begin cutting the pelt, or skinning, until he has definitely decided upon the type of trophy he wishes.

The same precautions are necessary for pelt trophies as for cape trophies. The nostrils and mouth are checked for blood emission, then plugged with bits of cotton. Bullet holes are swabbed free of blood and plugged. Possible excreta is removed from the pelage, and the beast's under side is checked for blood puddles.

Skinning off the pelt of any game animal takes

an hour or so if done properly. It is often best to move the fallen animal out of accumulations of blood and into a better position for skinning. Care should be used, during such moving about, not to drag hair from the pelt.

The beast should be rolled onto its back and anchored solidly in such a position, by piling rocks or sticks along its sides at the hip and shoulder areas. Such anchoring is important. Freshly killed animals are jellylike during handling, and hard to make stay put. Too, unless the beast stays in the desired position, the hide incisions are likely to be off center, causing subsequent unbalance in the finished trophy, or an unwanted trimming down of hide edges, to give symmetry.

Hides of bears, goats, etc., are removed "split," or open—not "cased" as with beasts such as coyotes, foxes, or marten. Three hide incisions are necessary. The first incision is made the full length of the belly, from the anal vent to the point of the throat. With mountain goats, it is best to stop the incision at this point, since further cutting would split the beard or "whiskers"—endangering its appearance in the finished mount. The pelt, with goats, can be folded back, or cased, on over the head from this point sufficiently to permit severing the head at the base of the skull. With bears, it is all right to continue the incision, splitting the hide all the way to the terminal point of the lower jaw. Care should be exercised here to make absolutely certain that the cut is precisely in the center.

The other cuts are made across the belly of the carcass, from a point at the hoof, or claw, on one foot, down the exact inside of the leg, at right angles to the belly incision, and on across the opposing leg to a similar point on the opposite foot. Such an incision is made across between the two fore feet, and another between the two hind feet. It will be observed that the hair of the entire pelt is thinnest along the lines of these three incisions. Care should be used in making the cut between the two hind feet, to see that such a cut follows well forward along the underside of the two hind legs, and not back into the thick hair at the posterior, and somewhat natural, hair-line at the rear edge of the legs. When making up the trophy, the taxidermist will trim these thin-haired, square corners so that the finished rug will lie flat.

In cases where the belly incision is made "off-center," one edge has to be trimmed off to match the other, with resultant gaunt appearance in the finished piece. Leg incisions that run off course result in unbalanced pelage in the flattened-out rug.

With these three incisions properly made, the entire beast may be skinned out without further cutting of the hide. A small knife that will hold a keen edge is necessary to do the job correctly, especially with bears, since the fat of bears during the approaching-hibernation period (when they are usually hunted) is heavy and sticks tenaciously to the hide. In skinning a bear the hide is literally cut away, all over the beast, from this layer of fat. In the case of deer and elk capes, the excess flesh, fat, etc., may handily be removed after the cape is in camp. With bears, however, the very best time to remove all excess fat is during the actual skinning. A little extra time spent then pays big dividends later, because once a skinning cut is made, it is difficult to make a similar second one, separating the hide and the thin layer of fat which clings to it. Too, leaving all possible fat with the carcass eliminates the weight to be carried in.

The hardest part of skinning a bear is the work about the feet. The footpads are left on the carcass,

PLATE IX. Bear hides are best skinned closely of all fat, then spread to air and dry, then thoroughly salted.

the hide being separated at these points at the junction of hide-and-pad all the way around. The small terminal pads containing the claw on each toe are left with the hide. It is sufficient to skin out the feet to a point equivalent to the second joint from fingertip, on a human hand. Few average hunters can successfully skin out a bear foot beyond this.

With goats, the same three skin incisions are made. Cuts at the hoofs continue midway between the two black dew-claws, and to a point at the base, or lower joint of each hoof. The dew-claws are left on the skin, being separated at their junction with the leg bones by cutting the cartilage. These jet-black, bony appurtenances give a pleasing effect in a finished full-hide mount, and balance the black of the animal's horns. The leg skin is folded back out of the way at the feet, and the hoofs themselves are severed at the last joint downward, equivalent to the fetlock in a horse. The hoofs (as with bear claws) are left attached to the pelt.

With bears, it is best to skin the entire skull out and leave it attached to the carcass. An artificial form will be substituted in the finished trophy, and there is no need for the skull unless the hunter wishes it for some special purpose. With goats, it is best to disjoint the head and take it in with the hide, since the horns must be taken along anyway. A last precaution before taking the pelt to camp, especially with goats, is to see that no blood or excreta remains on the flesh side of the pelt. There is no way to get a pelt to camp without portions of the hair side touching the hide. The movements of carrying will transfer any such staining matter to the hair.

Unless horses are available, the best way of toting a pelt to camp is a packboard. The pelt is lashed tightly on such an implement, and there is no rubbing.

Lacking either, the hunter simply has to carry the pelt in. It is never safe to leave a pelt out overnight. Either a bear or goat hide will weigh from 25 pounds on up, when green. It has a tendency to slip and roll upon itself, and is a most awkward bundle to carry. The best way is to wipe the hide side free of all blood, etc., then, beginning at one side, roll the pelt tightly in a full-length roll, and tie tightly at each end and the center with cord or pieces of rope. The rolled pelt is then carried in over the shoulders like a horse collar.

The same hazards exist with pelts as with capes. Once they are safely in camp, the same procedure is followed to keep them perfect. The pelt is scraped and pared of all fat and tissue. It is salted heavily, the salt being worked into every part and crevice with the hands. The pelt is then stretched free of folds, and hung up where air can circulate freely about every part—out of both possible storm and full sunlight. The pole over which a pelt is hung should be as slender as possible to sustain the weight, especially in mild weather. A thin pole has less area-of-contact with the pelt—where air cannot circulate.

Heavily furred pelts hold both the skin's moisture and its heat longer than capes, increasing the blowfly hazard. In warm weather, hundreds of blowflies will begin at once to dig down into the hair and lay their eggs. They especially favor skin folds, hide pouches about the feet, nostrils, ear pockets, and eyelids. The pelt must constantly be turned, such areas checked, eggs removed, and more salt worked in as the moisture of the hide drains it off. In areas hard to free of blowflies, black pepper is used in conjunction with salt. Accumulations of blowfly eggs are best removed either by brushing, or by combing them out with a fine-toothed hair comb—such spots being heavily re-salted afterward.

Often during extended hunting trips, a hunter will wish to preserve the skull-and-horns of an animal in addition to the cape, instead of taking but an antler-plate, and must keep such a full skull in good preservation for several days or even weeks. This is especially true with such beasts as mountain sheep, pronghorn antelope, and other similar game whose horn measurements, or perhaps even the horns themselves, might be jeopardized in the process of cutting out a skull-plate.

In order to preserve the skull, it is necessary to remove everything except the skull bones—the eyes, tongue, brains, and all remaining muscle and tissue. The tongue and eyes may be removed with a knife. The brains are handily scooped out after a cut has been made across the rear of the skull bone, behind the horns. The best way of removing the remaining tissue is by boiling. The skull is placed in a bucket of cold water, and heated until it boils. This will loosen all tissue still attached to the skull.

Extreme care must be used while doing this, to see that the horns themselves never touch the water. Boiling will loosen horns upon their cores. It will also soften the horns themselves.

When the skull has been boiled, it is scraped free of tissue and dried.

Once a pelt or cape is entirely dried of every trace of moisture, the danger of hair-slipping is largely over. Care should still be exercised, to see that the dried and stiff hide is not tightly rolled, or folded. Such folding may easily break the skin enough to damage the finished mount.

The field care of smaller animals such as coyotes and foxes, which are used for trophies, is similar. One difference exists. In skinning out these lesser furred animals, the skin is "cased," not split. One incision is made from a hind foot, down the leg's inside to the anus, then across the opposite hind leg to the opposing foot. The hide is girdled around at each foot, and peeled forward and off, over the animal's head without further skin cutting. The same procedure for skinning around the ears, eyes, and mouth area is used as for larger animals.

With beasts of this class, the tail bone is also removed and left on the carcass. To do this, it is necessary to skin around the tail root sufficiently so that a boot toe may be inserted between the hide and the tail root, at the animal's back. A pair of split willows, boards, or a pair of pliers are placed around the tail bone below the hide. Gripping such a device tightly around the bare tail root, the skinner easily pulls, or strips, the tail fur free of the bone.

Such pelts are usually dried upon some sort of frame or stretcher, hide side outward, until thoroughly dry. The ears of such beasts are not ordinarily skinned out in the field. Before stretching, however, it is best to rinse all blood and excreta from the green pelt, with cold water. Bullet holes are sewed up with a needle and either linen or silk thread. Once such a hide is stretched and dried, it is reversed to hair side out, and the original luster and gloss are restored by a vigorous brushing, with the grain of the hair.

Often a hunter wishes to keep the feet of such animals as deer, antelope, or moose, for mounting into gun-racks, or novelties. In such instances, the legs are best cut off at the knee and hock joints. The bones are removed by splitting the skin its full length on the rearward side, and severing the bone cartilage at the hoof. The same care to prevent hide-spoilage and hair-slipping as with pelts and capes is used until the parts are turned over to the taxidermist.

In instances where one wishes to save the whole hide of an animal such as a deer, moose, elk, or antelope, to be made into "buckskin," he simply skins it out intact, uncased, and preserves it identically as he would a cape or pelt.

**Transportation and Care.** Field preservation of trophies is not completed until the trophy is home: and often an otherwise fine trophy is ruined the last few hours because it molds, heats up, or is rubbed during transit.

The best containers for field trophies are clean, porous burlap bags such as are used for potatoes. The cape or pelt is *loosely* folded, placed in the bag, and tied fly-proof. During transit, such bags are best placed on top of all other duffle, so that no weight is upon them. Care should be used for horned or antlered capes, to see that such appendages are not placed where they may be broken, or themselves dig into and ruin capes or pelts. Too, care should be used to make sure such parcels are not put where any heat (such as from a car motor) or moisture from other items will get at them, thereby undoing all the care the hunter has exercised while in the field to keep them perfect. During overnight stops, the burlap packages should be unloaded, checked, and hung up overnight, so air can circulate all about them.

Back at the taxidermist's—and it is always better to take trophies in person, if possible, than to ship them—a hunter can usually get invaluable suggestions on how to have his trophies made up. The taxidermist will have specimens of the various types of mounts, from which to choose. Such a person is almost always willing also to offer good advice and tips as regards future trophies. Such suggestions should be jotted down, or thoroughly remembered.

Well-mounted trophies will be moth- and bug-proof. The best way of keeping them dusted, after wall-hanging, is to vacuum-clean them carefully, with the grain of the hair. After such cleaning, bear rugs are best hung for a time out in the fresh air, after which their original luster may be restored by lightly brushing the fur with a rag *thinly* coated with such a fine oil as neatsfoot oil.

The white of a goat trophy will dull with age and the accumulation of dust, smoke, etc. Most of the original whiteness can be brought back by either dusting Bon Ami into the fur and brushing it out, or by mixing the same cleanser into a mild

PLATE X. Exceptional "billies" make good head mounts.

paste, rubbing it into the fur, and then brushing it out after it has become dry.

Small mammals, such as squirrels, raccoons, etc., require the same care as the larger trophies. However, many of these are thin skinned and require considerable care in the proper removal of the pelt. For this reason, whenever practicable, it is best to bring the whole animal to the taxidermist and let him do the skinning. Shot holes should be plugged with cotton and all blood and excreta cleaned from the fur. It is seldom necessary to plug the vent, although it will do no harm and is worth the trouble. The mouth and throat should always be plugged, as some blood and possibly body juices may exude after death. Smooth the fur down and wrap carefully in burlap or some other porous material. The trophy need not be frozen but should be kept at a temperature of about 40 degrees or less until it can be delivered to the taxidermist.

Game birds should *always* be delivered intact. Few sportsmen are capable of the delicate work required to remove the skin for mounting, and besides it is always helpful to the taxidermist to have the original body for approximate measurements. Plug the mouth and all shot holes with cotton and clean the feathers of all blood, dirt, or other matter. Prepare a paper cone (newspaper is satisfactory) large enough to accommodate the bird. Smooth out the plumage and place the bird in this cone head first. Close the large end of the cone carefully in order not to break the feathers and make sure that the cone is not crushed in transportation. Broken legs or wings usually offer no problem to the taxidermist, but he cannot restore broken feathers, and the better condition in which the bird reaches his hands the better the finished mount. Keep all birds as cool as possible while in transit and get them to the taxidermist at the earliest possible moment.

Remington Arms Co., Inc.

PLATE I. Dangerous Business. One slip and the doctor or the undertaker will be needed.

PLATE II. This is the way it should be done.

# SHOOTING SAFETY

A careful study of the hunting accident reports of the various states proves quite conclusively that they may be attributed to three general causes: in the order of importance, *carelessness, ignorance,* and *selfishness.*

It is only under very rare circumstances that any hunting accident can be labeled "unavoidable," for in almost every instance one or all three of the factors mentioned above is responsible for the death or injury. The drafting of laws to insure more drastic punishment of offenders will have little if any effect on the accident rate, for the careless, ignorant, or greedy shooter cannot be legislated out of his nature. The initiation of regulations requiring each applicant to pass an examination concerning his knowledge of the weapon he will use and the proper method of handling it might result in some reduction in the rate. Even this, however, would be but a partial cure. Education is the answer, but the promotion of shooting education rests with the various states, and few of them have assumed the obligation.

Many of the hunting accidents that come under the classification of "carelessness" might more accurately be termed "ignorance," for too many hunters are careless as a result of their ignorance of the correct procedure. It has been proved quite conclusively that red clothing is only a partial protection. The deer hunter who violates both the law and the safety regulations by firing at a rustling in the brush, does not see his victim, who would be in no less danger if he were clad from head to foot in bright crimson. Each year hunters are killed or injured when other hunters mistake them for woodchucks, gray squirrels, foxes, deer, or bear.

An unnecessarily high percentage of the total accidents are the result of the accidental discharge of a rifle or shotgun by a man who either is unfamiliar with the firearm he is using or is not sufficiently familiar with any firearms. In a few instances a mechanical fault in the firearm is to blame, but this does not relieve the shooter from his responsibility. A careful shooter checks his arm before loading it.

In one instance a hunter sent a shotgun to a local gunsmith for thorough overhaul and cleaning. The gun was returned to him, and he used it for three seasons. A broken firing pin caused him to return the gun to the factory for repair. The head of the factory repair department wrote the shooter, asking him how much time had elapsed since that particular gun had been in the hands of a gunsmith, pointing out that during that period the gun had been without a safety. The shooter who takes the mechanical safety of his gun for granted is asking for trouble, and too often his request is granted.

All kinds of safety rules and regulations have been

Remington Arms Co., Inc.

PLATE III. Never lean a gun up against a rounded surface. It might be knocked over, and even if unloaded, a damaged gun may result. Only one of these guns has the action open.

Remington Arms Co., Inc.

**PLATE IV. Lay the guns flat, with actions open.**

Remington Arms Co., Inc.

PLATE V. This is an excellent way to lose a father.

Remington Arms Co., Inc.

**PLATE VI. Keep muzzles high and pointed away from your companion.**

advanced, but actually a few simple procedures, if followed until they become second nature, will insure safety.

(1) Be familiar with your gun.
(2) Treat every gun at all times as though it were loaded.
(3) Insure that the gun, empty or loaded, is never pointed at yourself or another.
(4) Except while carrying the gun in anticipation of its immediate use, have the breech open.
(5) Be certain at all times that the barrel is free of any obstruction.
(6) Never discharge the gun without knowing exactly where the charge is directed and with full knowledge of the identification of the target.
(7) Examine every cartridge or shell before inserting it in the magazine or chamber.
(8) Never carry a loaded gun in a vehicle.
(9) Never put down a loaded gun.

In almost every instance, carelessness in the handling of a rifle or shotgun is the mark of the novice or the unskilled shooter. The experienced shooter, the man who is recognized as a capable hunter, always handles his gun in a safe and careful manner. Only the fool and the novice indulge in "horseplay" with a gun.

# SNOWSHOES

There are three general types of snowshoes, with many slight variations in each type. The various northern Indian tribes in particular have many slightly different patterns. The conventional type shown in the following illustration is the pattern most commonly used over all our wooded and partly wooded North Country when the snow gets over about 8 to 10 inches deep. It is made about 13 to 14 inches wide by about 48 inches long; the 14-inch width is best for men over about 180 pounds. A smaller shoe about 12 inches wide by 40 to 44 inches long is also made for ladies and youths. Long experience has proved this type to be the best for general use, and this is the type that guides will generally be found using, and which the hunter should generally select, particularly if he has not had much experience. Less skill is required with this type than with other patterns. A slight but worth-while variation, introduced by the well-known outfitter L. L. Bean of Freeport, Maine, and known as the "Maine Guides" model, has the toe slightly turned upward, and has proved very popular, as the toe does not dig in so much on slopes and is less likely to trip one up.

In very thickly wooded country, particularly rough ground where the snow-covered surface has many ridges and hollows, the "bear paw" pattern is best. It has no tail, and is only about 30 inches long; consequently when one steps into a slight depression the shoe bears on the snow almost throughout, and does not "bridge" the depression as the conventional type would, with danger of breaking.

The "barren ground" type is long and narrow, about 9 to 10 inches by 5 feet long. It is used chiefly in the Far North on the barren grounds and in clear going along frozen but deeply snow-covered rivers and lakes, but is very inconvenient in the bush. One can travel faster on these long, narrow shoes, but the hunter will seldom encounter conditions where they would be advantageous.

On a long trip perhaps it is best to take two pairs, the conventional or Maine Guide pattern, and the bear paw, for one would be in a serious fix if a shoe should break.

The snowshoe is tied or strapped to the moccasin or rubber so that the ball of the foot in rear of the toes comes just above the heavy cross lacing of the web in rear of the rectangular opening. Only the ball of the foot is tied tight to the shoe here, but a thong or strap goes from here around the heel to prevent the foot from coming back out of the lacing. The heel must rise and fall with the stride, and the toes must be able to reach down through the rectangular opening into the snow below to hold the shoe more or less in place where one treads so as to give a purchase for the forward reach of the other foot. The Indians use a simple lashing or tie of babiche (rawhide thongs), but most white men use an oiled leather harness as shown in Plate IV (page 1012). The front cap portion is tied at its sides to the web of the shoe; the toe of the moccasin is then inserted in this tip, the long strap being brought around the heel and buckled. When the strap is unbuckled the shoe can be kicked off quickly and easily.

In the older writings of travelers and hunters in the North we frequently come upon the warning that the webbing of snowshoes should always be

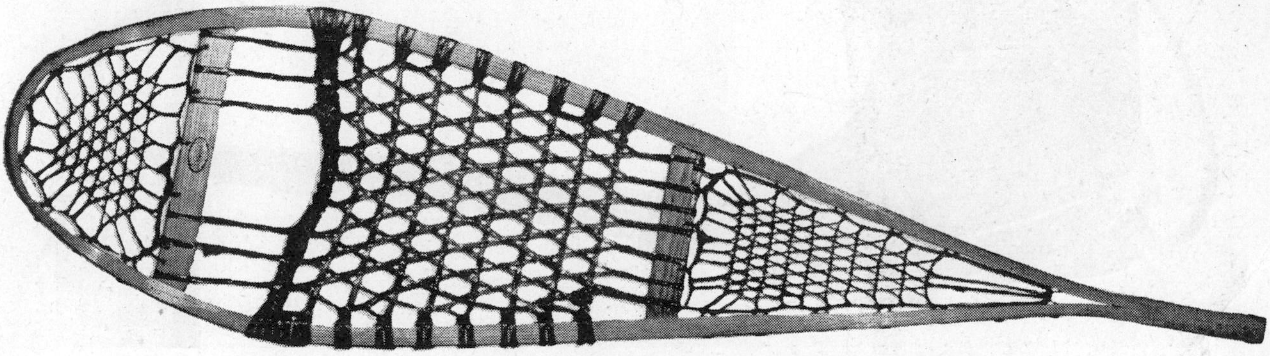

PLATE I. The conventional type of snowshoe, and the one most widely used.

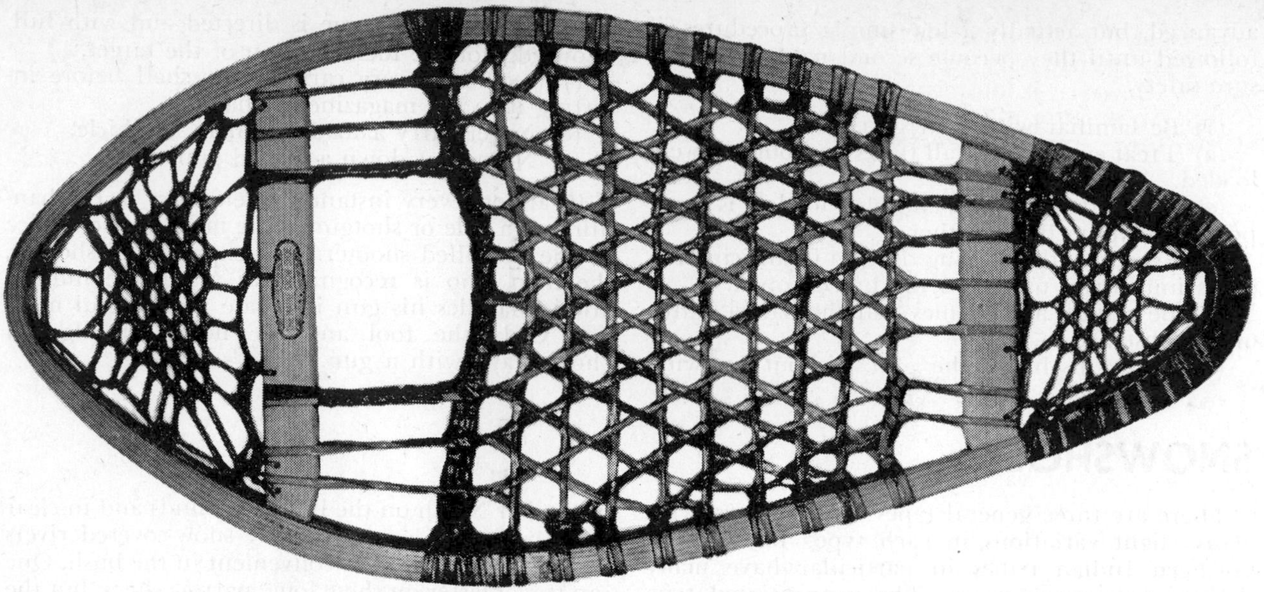

PLATE II. The "bear paw" type of snowshoe.

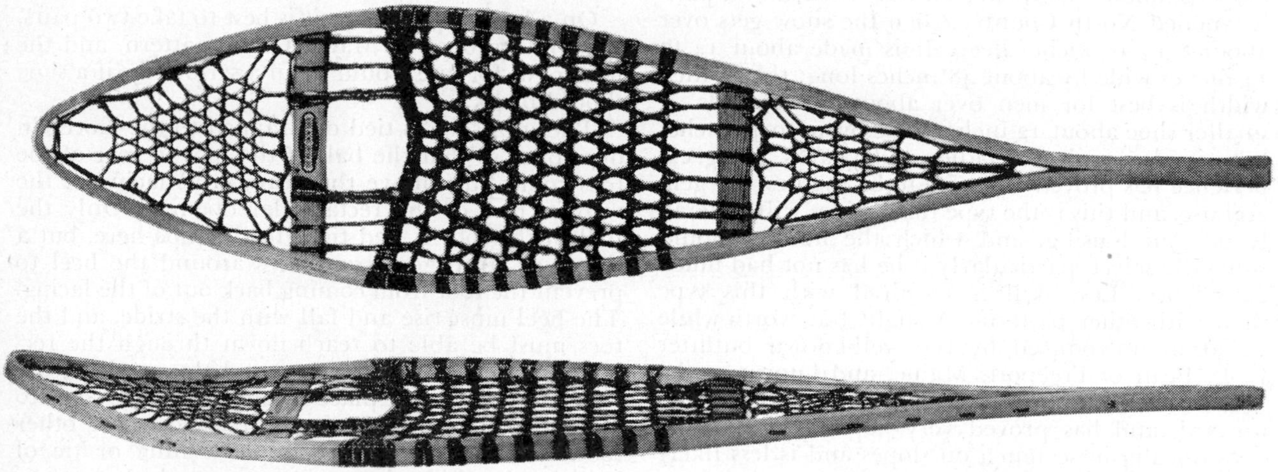

PLATE III. The "Maine Guide" snowshoe, a slight variation from the conventional type.

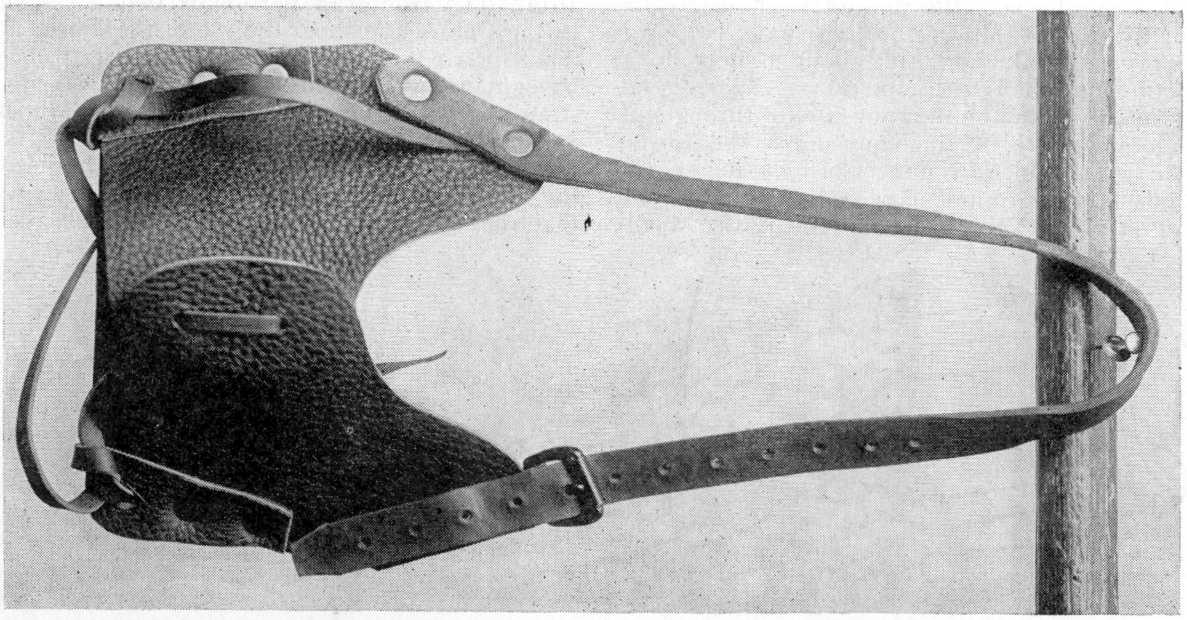

PLATE IV. The rigging or lacing required to fasten snowshoe to moccasin or boot.

made of caribou babiche, and that all other webbing will soon stretch, sag, and be worthless. Caribou babiche, however, is unprocurable except in the Far North. As a matter of fact, the recent experience of all our large Arctic expeditions has been that the snowshoes made by three or four makers in the State of Maine are superior in utility and durability to those of Indian make.

Snowshoeing is not at all difficult to learn, and can be mastered in a day or two. But it brings into use muscles in the front of the leg that are seldom used vigorously otherwise, and if one travels a long distance on the first day and is not hardened he may come down with what the northern voyageurs call "Mal-de-Racquette," and be completely incapacitated for three or four days. It is wise to harden up the muscles used in advance by two exercises. Stand with the heels on an inch board and raise the toes as high as possible. With the knee stiff, raise the leg straight to the front as high as possible. Repeat each exercise until the muscles fill with blood and begin to tire.

# TANNING HIDES AT HOME

It is not advisable for the amateur to attempt the home tanning of valuable pelts. Rare and costly skins will fare better in the hands of a professional tanner. However, the sportsman can try his hand at the home tanning of the sturdier and more common skins and by following a few simple instructions may often achieve excellent results with the very first attempt. With a little experience the work becomes relatively easy. It can be done without special tools or equipment other than those articles generally at hand, and the necessary ingredients are very inexpensive.

The process begins with the skinning of the animal, whether in the field or at home. The same care should be used as outlined above under "Preservation of Trophies," and as much flesh and fat as possible should be removed at the time of skinning. All blood and stains should be washed away immediately. Unless the tanning process is to begin at once, liberal quantities of salt should be rubbed into the flesh side of the skin, after which it should be dried in a cool, airy place. This is especially important in warm weather, as salt preserves the hide. The skin must be inspected frequently during the drying process and more salt must be added if necessary. This "curing" of a green hide aids in its preservation.

**Softening.** Next, the stiffened animal hide must be softened in a solution of salt and water. Soft water, or rain water, should always be used in such solutions. One-half pound of salt to each gallon of water is the accepted formula for this bath, and the hide should remain completely immersed therein for six to eight hours. After removal from the salt solution the pelt should be hung to permit the liquid to drain off and then have more salt rubbed on the flesh side. The pelt is then folded once, flesh side in, rolled in a bundle and left that way overnight. This permits a thorough penetration of the salt and loosens all the remaining flesh and fat.

**Fleshing.** The skin is now ready for scraping, or "fleshing," to free it from all bits of fat, gristle, and membranes. Professional tanners use a "fleshing board" for this purpose, but the home tanner can construct a board of his own. All that is necessary is a wide, smooth plank set at an angle of about 45 degrees. The top surface of the plank should have the corners removed with a plane until it is slightly convex as it is easier to work over a skin on a curved surface. The width and length of such a plank will be determined by the size of the pelts for which it will be used. A sawhorse or other convenient rest may be used to support one end of the plank while the other rests on the ground. The angle of the plank is merely to make the work easier. A section of tree trunk with the bark removed, smoothed and split in half, makes an excellent "fleshing board."

The damp pelt is thrown over this board and the operator stands at the high end to work on one area at a time. Regular fleshing tools may be purchased from a dealer in taxidermists' supplies, but these are not necessary. On small skins an old spoon will be found useful and on larger pelts several dull-edged tools, such as the back of a butcher knife, a very dull draw-shave, an old saw with the teeth ground off, or an old skate blade will work very well. Sharp-edged tools are not advisable for this work since it is important not to cut the skin. When the entire pelt has been thoroughly scraped, it is again hung in a shady place to dry. At NO time during the entire process should the pelt be exposed to the sun, as this will cause "burn spots" which may ruin the skin.

**Tanning.** The next step is to prepare the tanning solution. A vessel, tub, or barrel large enough to hold at least ten gallons of solution, plus the hide, is required. Larger hides will, of course, require a larger container, but even for small skins it is best to have at least ten gallons of the mixture. On the basis of ten-gallon units the solution is prepared as follows: Two pounds of alum are dissolved in boiling water. This is allowed to stand while ten gallons of salt solution is prepared as before, i.e., at a ratio of one-half pound of salt to each gallon of water. The alum solution is then added to the salt bath and the whole stirred until the salt and alum have been thoroughly mixed and dissolved. For a greater volume of solution, the amounts of alum and salt are increased proportionately.

The pelt is immersed in this bath and allowed to soak for a few days. The length of time will vary according to the size, weight, and thickness of the hide. The skins of small mammals require about three days, fox, coyote and wolf pelts about five or six, and large thick pelts such as bear should be left to soak for at least a week or ten days. No harm will come from leaving the pelt, or pelts, overtime, but if they are removed too soon the process will be incomplete. Therefore, it is better to let the skins soak a few days longer than to remove them too soon. During the soaking period the pelt should be doused up and down and stirred about in the bath two or three times daily to insure the solution reaching all parts of the skin evenly. The tanning process may be tested by cutting off a small strip of the hide along one edge and noting if it is the same color through and through.

At the end of the soaking period the pelt is removed and allowed to drain. It must be rinsed in cold water until *all* salt has been removed. Running water will accomplish this task much easier, and if a stream or brook is convenient the pelt may be submerged, skin side up, and anchored with rocks for a time. Water from the garden hose may be flowed over the skin or allowed to run into a vessel in which the skin is submerged. It is most important that *no* salt remains in the skin; this can best be determined with the tongue.

When sufficiently cleansed the pelt should be hung over a wooden pole to dry. The smallest-diameter pole that will support the hide is best for the purpose because more of the hide will then be exposed to the air. The pelt should be reversed every day or two, first skin side out and then fur side out for the same length of time. In this manner the pelt will dry evenly and be ready for the next step.

When completely dry the hide should be taken down and dampened with warm *(not hot)* water. A sponge or cloth dabbled over the hide will dampen it evenly; care should be taken not to get it too wet. This done, it should be folded once, flesh side in, and rolled in a piece of loosely woven cloth, such as burlap, and allowed to sweat for about 12 hours.

At this point the skin is ready for the softening process, the most laborious part of the entire procedure. The hide must be pulled, stretched, and worked; this is most easily done over some dull edge. The edge of the plank used as a "fleshing board" will serve, or a narrow board may be nailed at some convenient height. A smooth piece of two-by-four held in a vise is often most convenient, or a two-by-six plank may be driven into the ground, cut off at the desired height and the top edge rounded and smoothed so as not to tear the hide. Small hides may be stretched and pulled over one of these devices by one person, but large hides are best done by two persons pulling the skin back and forth somewhat like a crosscut saw. The time element will vary with different hides, but the pulling and stretching should continue until the pelt has been well worked over.

Most of the moisture will have been worked out during the preceding manipulations, and it is now necessary to oil the hide to keep it from becoming stiff. For this purpose any clean vegetable or animal fat such as lard, goose grease, or peanut or cottonseed oil may be used, but oils with a mineral content should be avoided. Warming the oil will give it greater penetration and facilitate working it into the pores of the hide. It may be rubbed in with the hands on small skins, but with larger hides it is easier and more efficient to place them in a barrel or box and tread on them with the bare feet. Turning the hide frequently while so working on it will assure its complete coverage and the pressure of the feet will force the oil well into the fibers.

Upon removal from this treatment the hide will look like nothing that might ever be used as a rug, clothing, or a wall hanging, but the next step will remedy that. Here again a barrel becomes the most useful apparatus for the job at hand. If it is possible to mount the barrel so that it will spin or "tumble," this step will be made easier. The pelt is placed in the barrel along with a large bagful of hardwood sawdust and the barrel is spun or "tumbled" until the sawdust has gathered all the excess oil from the hair and skin. If much oil has remained in the hair it may be necessary to discard the first sawdust and add fresh. Rabbit skins and other small animal pelts may be "tumbled" by placing them in a large paper bag with a quantity of sawdust and shaking the bag vigorously.

The pelt should now be clean and nearly ready for whatever purpose is desired. All that remains is to finish off the skin side to a smooth, suedelike finish. Sandpaper of varying grades will do this very nicely. Thin skins must be gone over very carefully, but the larger, thicker hides will stand considerable sanding. Care should be taken to sand as evenly as possible, however, in order not to create any thin spots.

The pelt is now ready to be made up into whatever article is desired. Several small pelts may be sewn together to make a robe, a parka, a cap, or other articles of clothing. This is a difficult job for the amateur, however, and it is advisable to take the skins to a professional furrier or taxidermist for best results.

A rug is relatively simple to make. The hide or pelt should be trimmed of all ragged edges; the natural contours may be preserved or the skin cut to any desired shape. Such cutting should always be done with a sharp knife and on the flesh side of the pelt. When the hide has been trimmed to the preferred size and shape, it is usually backed up with a piece of felt about 1½ inches larger all around than the skin. This felt backing is attached to the hide by catch-stitching along the edges. The sewing should be done from the back, of course, with shallow stitches that do not go clear through the hide.

The bordering edges of the felt are generally scalloped or "pinked." Regular pinking shears, which cut notches in the cloth, may be purchased, or such notches can be cut with ordinary shears—with considerably more work. Sometimes such rugs or robes are made thicker and warmer by basting in an inner lining of cotton wadding between the skin and the felt backing.

One of the warmest blankets known can be made from common rabbit skins (either wild or domestic). After tanning as described above, the skins should be cut into strips about 1½ or 2 inches wide. These are then joined end to end to form longer strips which will be the "warp" and the "woof" of the blanket. The joining should be done with an overhand stitch (such as used by furriers), with care taken to see that the fur runs the same way on each. The number of strips so joined will be determined by the over-all dimensions desired for the finished blanket. When a sufficient number of strips have been prepared for both the length and width required, they are then woven in a "basket weave," i.e., over and under each other. A pair of lace-curtain stretchers makes an excellent "loom" for this purpose. The strips forming the "warp" should be fastened in place and the lateral strips or "woof" woven through them. It is not advisable to weave these too tightly and the crossing strips may be "tacked" to each other with a few stitches at intervals of about 12 inches. A piece of outing flannel, or like material, makes an excellent backing. This should be trimmed to the size of the woven skins and the outer edges of the fur and backing should be bound together with tape or other stout material.

Innumerable practical uses for small and medium-sized pelts will be found. The pelts of raccoons, muskrats, rabbits, skunks, and others may be sewn to the back of woolen mittens for additional warmth. Fur collars, caps, vests, and other warm items of clothing are easily fashioned and are a worth-while reward for the amount of effort spent in preparing them.

**Buckskin.** We have so far considered only the tanning of pelts with the hair or fur left on. By an additional process the hair may be easily removed to make rawhide or "buckskin."

Rawhide may be fashioned from various skins. Moose, elk, caribou, deer, or domestic cow hides all furnish good basic material for this purpose. The hide should be prepared in the manner described above, but if possible it should be put into work immediately, and not salted unless it is necessary to prevent spoilage during hot weather. The hide should be well soaked in clear water to render it soft, after which it is ready for the lime bath which will remove the hair. This bath is prepared by slaking 5 pounds of lime (add the water slowly and a little at a time); when thoroughly slaked in a wooden tub or barrel, add about 30 gallons of water (lesser amounts in proportion).

The hide should remain in this solution until the hair pulls away easily. The time required for this will vary, but it is usually a week or ten days, especially in cold weather. During this soaking period the hide should be stirred around with a wooden paddle three or four times each day; this will insure the lime's acting equally on all parts of the hide. The hide should be tested occasionally; when the hair slips off readily in the hands the hide is ready for scraping. The "fleshing plank," previously mentioned, will serve as a scraping board and the same tools used for "fleshing" a green hide will remove the hair. When all the hair has been removed, the hide should be returned to the lime bath for two or three days to loosen the grain. This grain is a very thin layer on the hair side of the pelt which should be removed in order to make good buckskin. Care should be taken not to cut the skin during this scraping process. When all the grain has been carefully scraped away, the hide should be reversed and scraped on the flesh side and as much of the lime-water as possible forced out of the hide. The lime solution must be removed from the hands as soon as possible by washing them in soap and water and then rubbing them with vinegar.

The next step is to remove the lime from the hide. This may also be accomplished with vinegar. One gallon of vinegar to about 25 gallons of water makes a good solution for the purpose. If desired, lactic acid, 3 ounces (U.S.P.) to 25 gallons of water, may be used instead of vinegar. Either of these solutions will neutralize the lime after a couple of days of soaking. During the soaking period the hide should be stirred and sloshed around frequently, and after removal from the solution it should be washed repeatedly in clean cold water until free from the vinegar or lactic acid.

The hide is now ready to be worked over a smooth board until thoroughly soft. Small hides may be worked by the hands, but large hides are best worked by two people pulling them over a beam or plank. This step requires some patience and the hide should be stretched and pulled until it is thoroughly soft and pliable.

The final step for a finished buckskin is the smoking. This imparts a pleasing dark-gray color to the hide and makes it almost waterproof. Large hides may be fastened together to form a sort of tent, with a small fire built under them. Smaller hides may be placed in a barrel or covered by a tarpaulin where the smoke can circulate around them. Green hardwood should be used for the small fire. Resinous woods should be avoided because they give off an unpleasant soot. A day or two should be sufficient to smoke the average hide.

The result of these efforts should be a fine piece of finished "buckskin" ready to be made up into whatever article is desired.

# TENTS AND CAMP SHELTERS

Ever since man began to slay wild beasts and skin them tents have been the homes of all migratory people, including the modern camper. First they were made of skins, then of heavy canvas, and now often of waterproof cotton weighing scarcely five ounces per yard. The function of a tent, of course, is to keep you and your belongings dry, warm, and protected from mosquitoes, flies, and other bugs.

Tents are not needed in all climates. In the Sierra Nevada mountains it does not rain in summer or early fall, and the only shelter needed is a tarpaulin about 8 feet square. You make your bed on half of it, and fold the other half over to keep off the dew. This answers also for the deserts, although there another tarp may come in handy for a windbreak. So too in wooded countries in fall and winter when there are no mosquitoes, a plain tarp makes a most convenient and comfortable shelter, pitched at an angle of 40 degrees. Beds are made and duffle stowed under it, and a fire in front thoroughly warms the interior. If winds blow or rain beats in the ends, this is easily cured by felling and standing a few small spruce there. A tarp is also handy for many purposes in camp; for example, it may be pitched as a dining or kitchen fly, or to cover stores and saddles; so it is well to include one or more in every outfit where transportation is adequate. It is merely a rectangle of canvas or waterproof cotton, any size desired, usually with rings called "grommets" inserted every 2 feet or so around the edge for erecting or tying.

**Types.** Tents of every conceivable design and size have been and are being made, from the diminutive mountaineers' tent designed to accommodate one man and weighing only three pounds, to enormous circus tents. There are, however, certain designs and sizes which have, as a rule, proved the best for the use of hunters and sportsmen. The oldest forms were the conical Indian teepee and the dome-shaped Tibetan yort which could be warmed by an open fire in the center. Both are practically obsolete today because of the difficulty of erecting. A teepee, for example, required at least 11 long, straight poles.

The most common form of small and medium tent

D. T. Abercrombie, N. Y.
PLATE I. A-Wall Tent with Tape Ridge and Sod Cloth.

used the world over is that known as the "A-Wall." If made of suitable size it has plenty of headroom in the center with beds or cots at each side; it can be warmed with a tent stove. In hot weather the walls can be rolled up allowing free circulation of air, and it can be made mosquito-proof with a netting at the door end. If it is furnished with an outside tape ridge it is comparatively easy to erect with shear poles at each end to support the ridge pole. Often one end of the ridge can be lashed to a tree, or poles can be dispensed with entirely and the tent be suspended from a rope stretched between two trees. The ordinary commercial "A-Wall" tent does not have the tape ridge, being arranged for commercial poles. To facilitate pitching it in the woods where store poles are not carried, merely cut a 5-inch hole through the front and back walls at the peak of the tent; a ridge pole can then be stuck completely through the tent.

This tent has three slight disadvantages, which, however, may not loom up very high in your camping plans. It is rather tedious to erect, it can be warmed effectively only by a stove inside, and it is rather heavy for the amount of floor space it covers.

To determine the practical capacity of a tent, draw a plan of its floor on a scale of one inch to one foot, and lay out on this plan what you propose to put in the tent. For each bed allow a space 3 x 7 feet, and remember that there must be 2 feet headroom at the head of this space to allow you to get into a sleeping bag without bumping your head. In locating a tent stove, remember that no canvas or bedding must come within 18 inches of it.

An "A-Wall" tent 9 feet square and 7 feet high at the ridge will accommodate two men very comfortably, with cots or sleeping bags at each side, a headroom passage between the beds large enough to dress or work in, and plenty of room for personal duffle at the foot of each bed. Such a tent of light waterproof cotton will weigh about 16 pounds. If it is to be warmed by a wood-burning sheet-iron tent stove inside, then this tent had better be 12 feet long, the stove being located about 2 feet inside the door, and a little to the right or left. An asbestos stovepipe hole is sewed in the roof of the tent at the proper location. The stovepipe must project a foot above the ridge of the tent so that wind will not blow sparks onto the roof. Sometimes tin stovepipe holes are sewed in, but they rattle abominably in the wind.

All tents should have a sod cloth, or else a sewed-in waterproof canvas floor. A sod cloth is a strip of canvas about 12 inches wide, sewed to the bottom of the tent all around. It is stretched on the ground inside as shown in the picture of the "A-Wall" tent, and then weighted down with poles, stones, logs, or tucked under the bedding. With it a tarp may be spread over as much of the dirt floor as desired to make a floor cloth or carpet. The sod cloth makes a wind- and bugproof seal at the junction of the walls and the ground.

A floor cloth of waterproof canvas, covering the entire floor, and sewed to the side and back walls, is often incorporated in tents. This, with the mosquito bar in front, makes the tent absolutely bug-, wind-, and waterproof, but it has certain disadvantages. It considerably increases the weight of the tent, a wood-burning stove or a balsam-bough bed cannot be used, mud and dirt tracked into the tent are continual problems, and there must be a smooth, level site on which to pitch the tent.

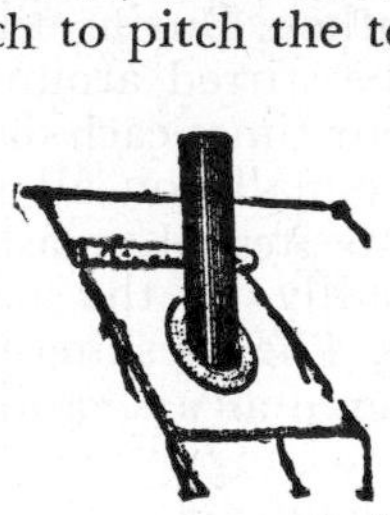

D. T. Abercrombie, N. Y.
PLATE II. Asbestos Stovepipe Hole in Tent Roof.

A tent that fastens close to the ground with sod cloth or ground cloth is made mosquito-proof by a curtain of mosquito netting or cheesecloth, covering the entire front entrance to the tent, sewed fast at the junctions of the roof and walls, but loose at the bottom. It is made very full and long so that it can be weighted down at the bottom with a pole, or tucked under the ground cloth. To enter, raise it and walk in. If made very full it can be tied up with tapes to the junction of roof and walls when not needed. This is a much better opening than the mosquito fronts with zipper opening, or a hole in the netting with a puckering string, which are great nuisances in entering or leaving the tent, and terribly in the way when there are no mosquitoes.

A tent up to about 9 x 12 feet can be made of one of the light waterproof cotton materials weighing about 5 to 6 ounces per square yard, thus economizing in weight and bulk when transportation is limited. But larger tents had best be made of 8- or 10-ounce canvas, as in high winds the lighter materials may rip. Very large tents should be of 12-ounce canvas. If the cotton or canvas is dyed light green or khaki color the tent will be cooler and the glare will not be objectionable in bright sunlight. There is, however, a very dark green canvas that is sometimes used, which makes the tent so dark inside that even in broad daylight lantern illumination is needed to do any work inside.

D. T. Abercrombie, N. Y.
PLATE III. Explorer's Tent.

The advantage of an "A-Wall" tent with stove is that in inclement weather, even in Arctic cold, it makes an entirely habitable room in which to live or carry on any kind of activity. The stove must be kept going, however, as five minutes after it is out the tent is as cold as outdoors. Perhaps the only reasons for tents of other design than the "A-Wall" are the desirability of lighter weight for the space covered, greater ease and shorter time in pitching, and being able to warm the tent by a campfire in front.

One of these tents which has become very popular is the "Explorer's Tent," which seems to have, to some extent, all the above advantages over the "A-Wall." One of these tents 7 feet square and 7 feet high at the 18-inch ridge, will accommodate two men's sleeping bags nicely with space to stow personal duffle, and in light waterproof cotton with sod cloth will weigh about 11 pounds. It requires only two long poles and one very short one to erect it. First, stake down the walls in truly rectangular form, then erect with the poles; drive the longer stakes for the rear wall, and then slightly move the butts of the long poles to make it taut and shipshape. A fire 4 feet before the entrance will warm the interior very well except in very cold and blowing weather.

The "Lean-to Tent" is a type that can be warmed more effectively by a campfire in front. The sloping roof reflects the heat of the fire down on the campers' beds, and in rainy or very sunny weather the fly can be stretched out in front or it may be lowered completely to close the tent. In the rain, by stretching the front out just so it does not get overheated by the fire, the campers can cook over the fire without getting wet. It is the most cheerful of all tents with the fire going in front and a view of the woods or lake beyond. It is, however, about as tedious to erect as the "A-Wall," with very little economy in weight over that old form.

The simple pyramidal tent is the easiest of all to pitch, and hence is popular with those who have to change camp each day and do not need heat inside the tent. Simply stake down the walls and erect with a center pole inside or two shear poles outside. Another form of this tent, about 14 feet square, and with 5-foot walls, is very popular as a cook tent for pack-horse trips in the West, with a cookstove inside. It has the advantage of headroom for a standing man practically up to the walls, the peak being about 10 feet high. It is erected with a long center pole, and a 5-foot pole at each corner.

The "Forester's Tent" is about the lightest that can be made, and can be warmed effectively by a campfire in front. The fire can be built closer to the opening than with any other tent, and the tent can be made comfortable even in extremely cold weather. It is easy to erect on a tripod of three poles; the back or ridge pole is longer than the others, and hence in the event of a continued rain which beats in front it is possible to turn the tent to face the other way in a couple of minutes.

The "Mountaineer's Tent" is intended for mountain climbers who have to carry their entire outfit on their backs. It is 6½ by 4 feet on the ground, 4 feet high, and rolls in a bundle 11 inches long by 4½ inches in diameter. With its sewed-in ground cloth it is entirely mosquito-tight, and weighs only 3 pounds 12 ounces. When one places his sleeping bag in it and crawls in there is only just room to go to bed. It would be stuffy inside in warm weather.

D. T. Abercrombie, N. Y.
PLATE IV. Pyramidal Tent.

The best tent for the tropical jungle or for woods in extremely warm countries is an "A-Wall" tent with walls and ends entirely of mosquito netting and with a ground cloth. The roof extends 6 inches beyond the walls so the mosquito netting does not catch the drip. For the very high altitudes of the Himalayas where wood for campfires cannot be ob-

D. T. Abercrombie, N. Y.

PLATE VI. Forester's Tent.

tained British sportsmen use a Wymper tent, which is an "A" tent without walls, about 5 by 7 feet, and 5 feet high, with a ground cloth and an outside sod cloth. In localities where tent pegs cannot be driven, the tent is weighted down with stones piled on the sod cloth. The 5-foot poles erect it. In the high veldt country of Africa, the "A-Wall" tent is used almost exclusively, with a large fly pitched over it, extending to the ground at the sides, and 6 feet in front to form a veranda, thus making the tent livable in the daytime.

In a tent that is not mosquito-proof it is always possible to erect a common mosquito netting over any camp bed. Simply drive stakes at the corners of the bed to erect the net on, and tuck the bottom of the net under the mattress or sleeping bag. City outfitters sell nets of the correct size for cots and sleeping bags. A "bomb" of DDT or an atomizer with Flit or similar insecticide is a good thing to eliminate the few mosquitoes that gain access to the tent when it is being put up, or when it is entered many times a day.

While on the subject of mosquitoes it might be well to mention malaria, which is borne by the Anopheles mosquito. This mosquito is night-flying only, and unless carried by strong winds, never gets more than a mile from where it is born. To inoculate a person with malaria it must first have bitten a person having malaria in his blood. It therefore follows that if one camps in the jungle several miles from any human habitation there is little danger of malaria. Or if one must be in a native habitation or village after nightfall, he should retire to net protection at dark, and not emerge until morning.

**Waterproofing.** Early tents were made of plain canvas. When it rained, if the inside of the roof were touched a drip started at that spot, and when wet the canvas and ropes shrank temporarily so much that if guy ropes were not loosened the tent pegs were pulled out. Also, a plain canvas tent increases greatly in weight when wet, and makes quite a load to pack when one has to break camp immediately after or during a rain. All these troubles are avoided in the modern tent of waterproof material. Any closely woven cotton goods can be waterproofed by painting with a transparent waterproofing solution sold by tent and awning makers, or such a solution may be home made by dissolving paraffin in gasoline. After painting or soaking, hang the tent up until the gasoline evaporates. A spot that has lost its waterproofing can be "healed" by simply ironing it cold with a block of paraffin. A fire should not be built too near such tents. Tears in tents can be

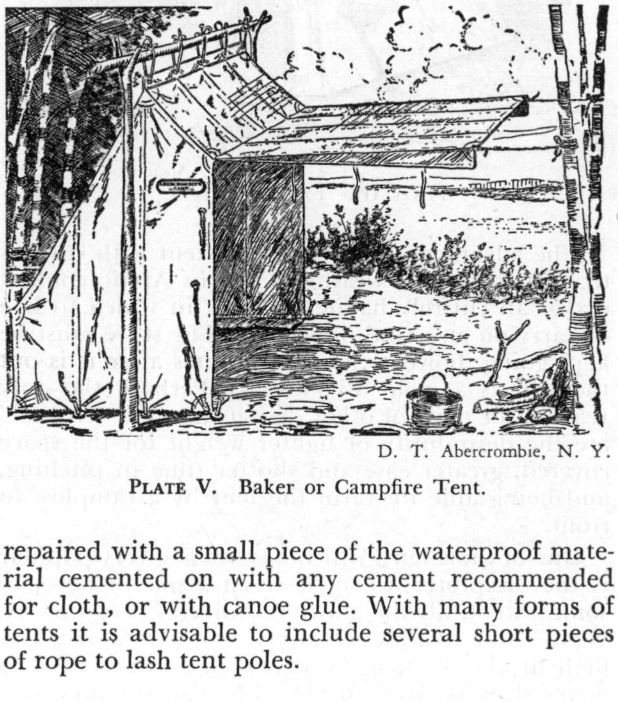

D. T. Abercrombie, N. Y.

PLATE V. Baker or Campfire Tent.

repaired with a small piece of the waterproof material cemented on with any cement recommended for cloth, or with canoe glue. With many forms of tents it is advisable to include several short pieces of rope to lash tent poles.

# UNITED STATES FISH AND WILDLIFE SERVICE

The Fish and Wildlife Service of the Department of the Interior is the agency of the Federal Government primarily responsible for the production, conservation, and management of the valuable fish and wildlife resources of the nation. When it is realized that the hunters and fishermen of this nation are responsible for the expenditure of funds that may total as much as four billion dollars per year, it is readily understandable that sound management of the resource is highly important. It is a big and complicated job.

In a civilization as complex as ours, wildlife needs must be interwoven with all other forms of land and water use. Wildlife is secondary. But our American traditions of hunting and fishing, the envy of the entire world, are so deeply ingrained that means of furnishing fish and game for an ever-increasing army of outdoorsmen must be provided. After all, there is more to life than the mere making of a living. To 20-odd million people who buy hunting and fishing licenses each year, there is the relaxation and contentment that can come only from the out-of-doors. In fact, it sometimes seems that ducks and geese and deer and trout are much more important than stocks and bonds and a stuffy old office.

It is the job of the state and Federal administrative agencies to see that every possible opportunity is taken to produce fish and game consistent with the other calls on our expanding population. There is a growing realization that with the constant pressure of civilization, the wild things of the streams and forests must have areas dedicated primarily to their own use if these needs are to be supplied. Rapid strides are being made by the states, through the Pittman-Robertson Federal Aid program to provide such places for wildlife. Federal agencies which administer public lands, such as the Forest Service, Fish and Wildlife Service, Park Service, Bureau of Land Management, and Soil Conservation Service, keep wildlife needs prominently in their programs. Some progress is being made with the owners and users of privately owned land, which produces the great bulk of game taken by American hunters. Let us hope that the progress of recent years will increase to the point where we may keep pace with the destruction of habitat. That has never yet been accomplished.

Our forefathers took wildlife for granted. Beaver trappers led the vanguard of the exploration of every frontier in America. The wild birds and animals of the forests and plains, the fishes of the streams, provided the basic supplies of meats for the hardy settlers who followed the trappers westward. Fish and game were taken as a matter of course, and as agriculture progressed and developed, there was little concern when the wild things began to fade. In the light of present-day needs, we now know that a wiser course would have been the preservation and maintenance for wildlife of certain of those original areas that were rich in wildlife. Such a policy would have avoided heavy expenditures and heart-breaking toil that went to drain many marshes that later proved entirely unfit for agricultural use. They should have been left as the good Lord originally intended them to be—homes for ducks and geese and muskrats and mink—natural reservoirs. Now we must go back and spend additional millions in the attempt to reflood areas that should never have been drained in the first place.

This concept that agriculture must always be the highest use of land has extended also to the use of waters. Practically every western state legally defines the highest use of the waters of the rivers and streams to be for agriculture and domestic purposes. Even though it can now be shown that the most productive use of water in certain areas would be the maintenance of marshes for fur-bearers, and for ducks and geese, the basic laws still stand. Our forefathers also developed a philosophy that rivers were of little use execpt for navigation and for the disposal of every sort of trash and rubbish that looked unsightly on the land. As a result, many of our finest streams have been turned into open sewers, aquatic life choked out, and disease-laden filth so thick that even swimming was unsafe. We of the present generation must now make unremitting efforts to see that domestic sewage and the effluents of industry are kept out of waters that should be providing wholesome recreation. As civilization becomes more complex, the correction of these early concepts of land and water use becomes more difficult. Progress is being made—but slowly. Perhaps, with the increase in the number of people who enjoy hunting and fishing, and who look to the out-of-doors for healthful pleasure, there may be an awakened consciousness of the need for reversing the trends.

**History.** In typically American fashion, the Fish and Wildlife Service was born of a crisis. The people of this country historically fail to worry about national problems until the eleventh hour. The black storms whirling from the dust bowl of the prairie states finally awakened the public consciousness to the need for soil conservation, and led to the organization of the Soil Conservation Service. Similarly, the Fish and Wildlife Service can trace its beginning to early alarm over decreases in fish, game, and insectivorous birds.

The Bureau of Fisheries was established in the Department of Commerce in the year 1871 on the basis of a joint resolution of the Congress which began as follows: "Whereas, it is asserted that the most valuable food fishes of the coast and lakes of the United States are rapidly diminishing in numbers to the public injury and so as materially to affect the interests of trade and commerce, therefore Be it Resolved, etc." Thus, the decrease in food fishes back in 1871 led to the creation of a Bureau which is now an integral part of the Fish and Wildlife Service. A few years later, in 1885, those who were interested in the protection of birds were alarmed at the rapid decimation of the passenger pigeons and the virtual extermination of the buffalo of the western plains. They saw other forms going the way of the dodo, and secured a small appropriation for the conduct of economic investigations of birds in relation to agriculture. From this start the Bureau of Biological Survey was organized in the Department of Agriculture, and throughout the years has expanded into various lines of activity, each springing from a new need brought on by the struggle of wildlife against a growing human population. In 1940, these two scientific conservation bureaus of the government were merged into the present Fish and Wildlife Service, which is now a strong central organization of the Federal Government dealing with problems pertaining to fish and wildlife conservation. We are still experiencing crises, and as the needs of wildlife must continue to compete with the other uses of land and water, we will have more of them in the future. Our task is to preserve the resources for future generations of hunters and fishermen.

**What the Fish and Wildlife Service Does.** The Fish and Wildlife Service:

Has primary responsibility for the management of migratory birds under treaties with Great Britain and the United Mexican States. This includes the setting of the seasons, bag limits, and prescribing methods for the hunting of ducks, geese, woodcock, doves, and other migratory game birds. It also includes the enforcement of the Federal regulations.

Operates a nation-wide system of refuges for waterfowl. Areas are also set aside for the protection of certain species of big game. Refuges are located in practically every state, and in Alaska, Hawaii, and Puerto Rico.

Secures appropriations, allocates funds, and approves all projects under the Federal Aid to Wildlife Restoration Act. Appropriations for the fiscal year ending June 30, 1948, amounted to more than $9,000,000, the full amount of the receipts from the excise tax on sporting arms and ammunition.

Under the terms of Public Law 732, studies the probable effects of impoundments to be made by Federal agencies on the river systems of the United States. In co-operation with the state fish and game departments, prepares reports to the construction agencies and the Congress, and advises means by which wildlife losses may be minimized and additional values may be secured by alterations in plans.

Supervises the work of ten research and training units financed co-operatively by the Fish and Wildlife Service, the state fish and game departments, the Wildlife Management Institute, and the land-grant colleges of the respective states.

Enforces the Lacey Act which is designed to prevent the shipment across state boundaries of game or fur taken or possessed contrary to state laws.

Conducts predatory-animal control operations in co-operation with livestock associations, fish and game departments, and private individuals, primarily in the western range states.

Performs research and gives technical advice on game management problems to the Forest Service, Soil Conservation Service, Park Service, Indian Service, the Bureau of Land Management, Bureau of Reclamation, and the Corps of Engineers.

Co-operates with the state fish and game departments in special studies dealing with game management problems. Serves as a general clearing house for conservation departments and wildlife organizations in matters pertaining to legislation affecting the entire conservation program.

**Protection of Migratory Birds.** Some, at times, may not agree that the regulations under the Migratory Bird Treaty Act governing the taking of migratory birds are a service to the hunter. A few disgruntled duck hunters have even suggested that the control of the take of migratory waterfowl should be restored to the states. Occasional comments of this sort were heard when the Federal regulations for 1947 prescribed a 30-day season for the eastern half of the United States and a 35-day season for the western, with a daily bag limit of only 4 ducks.

The regulation of the take of migratory waterfowl came about originally because of a demonstrated lack of ability on the part of the several states adequately to promulgate such regulations. No single state was able to obtain an over-all picture of waterfowl conditions, and naturally issued regulations based upon the populations of birds and the desires of the hunters within that state's own boundaries. The natural result was that those areas in the far South which winter the bulk of the waterfowl had long seasons and large bag limits. The northern states which produced the birds likewise had similar regulations. The states in between them extended their seasons to be sure that they took their share. The big trouble was that the states alone could not make laws or regulations which would fit into a pattern of management required by wildlife that moves annually from the far northern breeding grounds to the wintering marshes of the Gulf, to Mexico, and to the Caribbean.

This inability, coupled with early abuses and noticeable rapid decline in numbers, led to an urgent demand by conservationists and hunters alike for a better management machinery. A law passed in 1913 giving the Federal Government the right to prescribe closed seasons for waterfowl in migration across state borders was promptly challenged in the courts on constitutional grounds. Conservationists persevered in their attempt, however, and in 1916 a treaty was signed with Great Britain which gave the governments of the two countries authority to regulate the taking of birds migrating between the United States and Canada. This was later implemented by the Migratory Bird Treaty Act in 1918 which established the basic legislation entrusting the making of regulations governing the taking of migratory birds to the Federal Government. The Supreme Court has upheld both the treaty and the Act to give it effect (State of Missouri *vs.* Ray P. Holland, 252 U. S. 416).

As soon as the Federal law was established, the sale of ducks, geese, and other migratory birds was prohibited. This practice in the early days had led to disastrous inroads on the supply. Some of the old accounts of market hunters and the sale of game by the barrel and the wagon load are almost unbelievable when viewed through the eyes of present-day sportsmen. Spring shooting was stopped. This practice had been particularly damaging because many of the birds had already paired and mated before leaving the southern wintering areas.

The Treaty specified that no season could exceed 3½ months' duration; that no season for migratory game birds could begin earlier than September 1 or continue beyond March 10, except that hunting of shore birds might be permitted between August 16 and January 31 in the Maritime Provinces of Canada and in the states bordering on the Atlantic Ocean wholly or in part north of Chesapeake Bay. The Migratory Bird Treaty Act provided that the hunting of all migratory birds was prohibited except as might be permitted through regulations adopted by the Department and signed by the President of the United States. The privilege of hunting is thus purely permissive, and is not the birthright of any citizen. A subsequent treaty was signed between the United States and the United Mexican States in 1936. This further strengthened the authority of the Federal Government and gave protection to a few species that migrate across the southern border but do not go to Canada. A great deal of progress has resulted from that original treaty sponsored and won by the conservationists of a generation ago.

A means has been found effectively to control hunting—one of the factors in waterfowl management. True, it is only one part of a complicated job, but it is important. The regulation of the take by hunters is of more importance when waterfowl are on the decline than it is when birds are on the increase. When they are declining, every factor tending to reduce the numbers becomes of greater significance.

Decreasing the take by hunters is the only means of making rapid adjustments. There is little man can do in a hurry to change breeding conditions or to influence the elements of nature—the prime factors in waterfowl production. When two or three or four years of successive droughts have lowered the water tables; when the dry, hot summer winds have sucked the ponds and potholes dry; when the grasses wither and burn while the ducklings are too small to travel and the old birds are in their flightless moult, disaster strikes. Then, the reduction from any cause of the remnants of the flocks that find strength enough to move southward is of great importance. It makes little difference whether ducks die of drought, disease, predation, or No. 6 shot. The result is the same.

When on the other hand the years are good, when the marshes and ponds and potholes are filled with water and the vegetation is lush and green, when there are no late freezes or floods to destroy nests and young, then waterfowl can increase at a rapid rate. The clutches are large, and with good water conditions through the spring and summer large numbers of young can be brought through to the point where they will start winging southward in the fall. When those conditions prevail, the take by hunters is not so important.

This common-sense approach has guided the making of waterfowl regulations from the day of the passage of the Migratory Bird Treaty Act. It has not always been possible to keep the hunting pressure in exact tune with the supply of waterfowl, but that has been the sincere effort. In some years, admittedly, the restrictions may have been more severe than necessary, but in others they have not been restrictive enough. The latter was particularly true during the early years of the recent decline in waterfowl populations. The Federal regulations did not reduce the take by hunters as soon as they should have. This we know in the light of later experience. This is one reason why the regulations needed to be so severe for the hunting seasons of 1946 and 1947.

**Duck Depressions.** The present sorry plight of waterfowl represents the third duck depression within the memory of the older generation of waterfowl hunters. The first occurred around 1915 when conservationists became alarmed at the decreasing numbers of waterfowl. They forced through the treaty with Great Britain, and later the Migratory Bird Treaty Act. For a period of years following the passage of the Act and the initiation of Federal regulations, it appeared that the situation might be satisfactorily handled. However, with increasing agricultural development leading to the drainage of more and more marshes, and the cultivation of greater and greater areas of lands in the prairie states, and with increasing human population and hunting pressure, waterfowl populations continued to decline gradually. Then came the drought of the early 30's. Thousands of sloughs and potholes went dry, the water tables receded over the entire Great Plains area and the Prairie Provinces of Canada. Both sections have always been the cradle of production for the bulk of the ducks and geese of North America. We had approached another crisis, and the public again awakened to the necessity for action.

Out of the crisis of the early 30's came a demand for a more positive approach to waterfowl management. It was realized that the mere regulation of the annual take was not enough, that something needed to be done to restore the marshes that were being taken away from waterfowl. The nesting grounds must be safeguarded.

Out of that crisis came the enactment of the Migratory Bird Hunting Stamp Law, commonly known as the "Duck Stamp Act." This provided that each hunter over 16 years of age must acquire and have with him when hunting waterfowl a $1 Federal stamp in addition to his state hunting license, and that the money should be used for the establishment of sanctuaries and refuges, for law enforcement, and for research. Out of this crisis also came the public interest which resulted in the enactment of the Federal Aid to Wildlife Restoration law setting aside the 10 per cent excise tax on arms and ammunition for use by the states in wildlife restoration. Out of it came the move by American sportsmen for the restoration of marshes in Canada that led to the organization of "Ducks Unlimited." All of these programs have gone a long way toward providing basic requirements for the protection and production of waterfowl, but they are still wholly inadequate. Recently, three successive years' drought over the breeding marshes of the north central states and southern Canada, followed by a wet year with late freezes and floods in many areas, again brought the waterfowl population over much of the continent to a serious situation. In 1947 we were, in fact, experiencing another duck depression.

**Adjusting Harvest to Supply.** Annual regulations under the authority of the Migratory Bird Treaty Act have now been made for some 30 years. They have reflected the effort of the Federal Government to adjust the take by hunters to the yearly supply of birds. In the early days of the regulations, bag limits and seasons were liberal. Back in 1929 it was legal to kill 25 ducks and 8 geese daily during a 3 to 3½ month season. The year 1930 saw the first large reduction in bag when the duck limit was cut to 15 birds per day and geese to 4, and possession limited to not over two days' kill. As the waterfowl populations continued to decline, the limit was reduced to 12 ducks in 1933. In 1935, with the drought at its worst, and with waterfowl at the lowest point in history, the season was cut to 30 days, the bag limit to 10 ducks per day; goose limits remained at 4 per day. Hunting was permitted only between 7 A.M. and 4 P.M. The use of bait and live decoys as a means of taking waterfowl was outlawed, and an intensified program of law enforcement was initiated. The shooting of canvasbacks and redheads was completely prohibited in 1936, and the closed season on ruddy and bufflehead ducks continued. No hunting of brant on the Atlantic coast was permitted.

This crisis led to better co-operation on the part of sportsmen in general, and to closer correlation between the activities of the Federal Government and the various state fish and game departments. Many feared that waterfowl shooting was soon to be a thing of the past, and faced with a critical situation were then willing to see severe restrictions imposed where previously they had objected strenuously to curtailments. Again, this shows the normal American pattern of taking positive action in conservation matters only as the eleventh hour approaches.

The refuge program was actively initiated. Through the dynamic endeavors of J. N. ("Ding") Darling, then Chief of the Bureau of Biological Survey, $6,000,000 were obtained for the restoration of breeding marshes. The first duck stamp sales brought in added moneys. During the first year (1935), $635,000 came into the fund, and was promptly spent for the acquisition of lands which could be developed in the refuge program. The CCC and WPA programs furnished men and materials to construct dikes and dams and water-control structures looking to the day when rains would come again. Then the drought cycle broke, rains and spring snows again filled the prairie potholes and backed against the man-made impoundments, and the birds found them.

The waterfowl began to build back in numbers. From the low of 27,000,000 in the year prior to 1935, the next inventory showed a gradual increase. Later counts revealed an unexpectedly satisfactory upswing. The annual surveys showed populations coming back steadily until finally in 1944 the tally showed 125,000,000 birds.

As the waterfowl populations increased, so did the hunting privileges. The season was extended to 45 days in 1938, to 60 days in 1940, to 70 days in 1942, and 80 days in 1944 and 1945. The ban on the shooting of canvasbacks, redheads, buffleheads, and ruddies was lifted in 1938. In 1944, when there was considerable crop damage in certain localized areas, 5 mallards, widgeons, or pintails, in addition to the regular bag limit of 10 ducks, were permitted to be taken. The regulations were constantly adjusted to permit the taking of what was considered to be a safe margin of the annual increase.

Since the early 30's, one factor became increasingly important. That was the number of hunters. Duck stamp sales gradually increased from the 635,000 in 1934 to more than 1,400,000 in 1941. During the following two war years they dropped back. In 1944 they were around 1,450,000. This, remember, was the year when there were an estimated 125,000,000 birds, and when the season extended for 80 days and permitted an extra 5 ducks of certain then abundant species. Shells were scarce because of wartime restrictions and the demand for munitions to fight the battles abroad.

Unexpectedly, the number of duck stamps for 1945 increased to 1,725,000. More ammunition was made available for hunting purposes than anyone thought would be possible. Drought struck the breeding grounds again. Waterfowl production tumbled, and the result was disastrous. The next annual inventory showed a falling off from 125,000,000 birds to 105,000,000. Optimists who felt that the favorable waterfowl situation would continue indefinitely were incredulous that the official counters should have lost 20,000,000 ducks. The drought continued, but the hunting pressure increased. The duck stamp sales in 1946 totaled more than 2,000,000 while the curve of waterfowl populations took another nosedive. The inventory for that year showed a further reduction of 25,000,000 birds to an estimated continental population of about 80,000,000. The regulations reflected this decline. The season was reduced from 70 to 45 days, the bag limits were reduced from 10 ducks per day to 7.

But the end was not in sight. The inventory in January 1947, which covered the birds surviving the 1946 season, indicated another tumble. The population had by that time dropped to an estimated 54,000,000 birds while the hunting pressure had risen. Even though the census figures indicated twice as many birds as in 1935, the hunting population had in the meantime more than trebled. And surely and inexorably the march of agriculture had progressed. The demands for grains had again made serious inroads on the waterfowl nesting areas.

Faced with these facts, the Fish and Wildlife Service adopted the only course open: to recommend further drastic curtailments on the take by hunters during the fall of 1947. The season was reduced to 30 days for the states in the eastern half of the United States, and to 35 for the states in the western. This was based upon a more liberal supply of birds and less hunting pressure west of a line extending from Minnesota to Louisiana. To compensate for the inequalities that always result during short seasons where the migration of birds depends upon unpredictable weather conditions, a new plan was evolved which would permit the states to select, within limits, two periods of 12 days each in lieu of the 30-day consecutive season, or two seasons of 14 days, for states having the 35-day consecutive season. The bag limit was reduced to 4 ducks per day throughout the entire country. In addition, the shooting day was changed from a half-hour before sunrise to a half-hour before sunset to the period from sunrise to one hour before sunset, and hunting on the first day of any waterfowl season was not permitted before noon.

**Enforcement of Federal Regulations.** No law or regulation is better than its observance, and it takes effective law enforcement to make the protective measures really effective. The average hunter wants to abide by the rules of the game. The bulk of them do. Yet, when they see someone else exceeding the bag limit, shooting out of season, or taking wildlife contrary to established rules of the game, they too may feel inclined to do likewise. Nothing is more aggravating to a duck hunter than to be sitting in his blind on a cold, frosty, morning patiently waiting for the opening hour, and then to have someone a few hundred yards distant open fire on the fleeting targets in the dim morning light. With the first shot the whole marsh is alive with fluttering birds. The mallards that were "in the bag" promptly move to safer waters miles away.

Again, when the average hunter hears of the baiting and trapping of birds on his favorite marsh after the season has closed, and he knows full well that they are going into the illegal market in some large neighboring city, his natural feeling is "What's the use!" He is sorely tempted to get his share while the getting is good, regardless of what his own conscience and the administrators say.

Enforcement of the Federal regulations is a difficult task with the manpower that has been possible under present appropriations. Only 70 Federal agents can be employed. If it were not for the wholehearted co-operation of the vast majority of the state fish and game departments, reasonable enforcement of the Federal regulations would not be possible. The states, with the exception of one or two, do co-operate wholeheartedly. Many states have laws which provide that the state regulations governing the taking of migratory birds will automatically be the same as the Federal regulations, while others enable the state game departments to do so by regulatory action. Large numbers of violations where state offenses are also involved are prosecuted in state and local courts, and the remainder in the Federal courts.

Because of the inadequacy of the staff of Federal game management agents, they must concentrate on co-operation with the state enforcement officers and on specializing in particularly difficult situations. "Flying squadrons"—several Federal officers teamed together—often descend en masse on areas where serious violations of the Federal regulations are reported. Under-cover agents or co-operating state officers have preceded these crews and obtained in advance positive leads and definite information regarding illegal killing.

During the winter of 1947, four agents moved into Georgia where there were reported to be frequent violations of the regulation prohibiting the shooting of mourning doves over baited fields and in closed season. Wholeheartedly assisted by state rangers, the result was 156 arrests within a very short time. 115 offenders, some of them very prominent individuals, were hailed into Federal court and paid fines amounting to $2,982. Eight others were judged not guilty by a jury, and cases against 33 hunters are still pending.

Several years ago rumors persisted that there was a ring of violators making large hauls of quail in northern Mississippi, central Arkansas, and southern Tennessee. After painstaking effort, a large shipment of birds was seized en route to market in Chicago. A man and his sons were convicted of the trapping and illegal taking of quail. This gang had removed thousands of birds from the fields of the South and sold them in the markets of the big cities of the North.

The eastern shores of Maryland and Virginia have long been notorious for illegal traffic in waterfowl. Duck trapping has been common and most difficult to eradicate. The courts have held that the duck trapper must be caught in the act of taking the birds from the trap, which has made apprehension most difficult. Much has been done in recent years, however, through the use of airplanes for spotting and ground crews for the destruction of these illegal devices. Wartime radio developments have now provided communication between the airplanes and the wardens on the marshes below, and are putting a definite crimp in the duck-trapping racket.

A few years ago under-cover work resulted in the arrest of 54 violators on the eastern shores of Maryland and Virginia. It was found that waterfowl, taken illegally by trapping and by the long-barreled and powerful punt and battery guns, were dressed, packed in barrels with a layer of innocent-looking oysters on the top, and trucked with shipments of sea foods to Philadelphia and New York. Clever under-cover work resulted in the conviction of a large number of the violators who had taken part in this illicit traffic. The cases were terminated in Federal court as follows: Jail sentences, 20 days (1); 30 days (4); 60 days (2); 3 months (2); 3 months suspended (2); 3 years suspended (2). Fines, $2815 (25); not guilty (5); dismissed (11).

Funds for enforcement of the Federal regulations have fallen far behind the need. Although the number of duck hunters has more than trebled since 1935, the Congressional appropriations for enforcement of the regulations have actually decreased. There is strong sentiment among conservationists for an improvement in this situation.

**Wildlife Refuges.** Refuges are an essential part of a sound wildlife management program. Federal refuges administered by the Fish and Wildlife Service on July 1, 1946, totaled 291 with an aggregate of 17,819,495 acres. Of these, 271 are in the United States and 20 in Alaska, Hawaii, and Puerto Rico. All kinds of wildlife are protected on the refuges although all are especially designed for the primary benefit of a few species. For instance, 201 with 3,213,658 acres are primarily for migratory waterfowl, 49 with 91,043 acres are for colonial birds of non-game species, 16 with 10,642,015 acres are for big game, and 24 with 3,870,156 acres are for migratory birds other than waterfowl and for miscellaneous forms of wildlife. One refuge, the Patuxent Research Refuge in Maryland, near Washington, D. C., containing 2623 acres, is maintained for wildlife experimental purposes.

Refuges have been established by various means. Many were acquired with duck stamp and other special funds. This has been particularly true of those established for the protection of waterfowl. Many of the big-game refuges were set aside on public domain and their use is shared jointly by game and livestock. The large Alaskan refuges are set aside for various species of game and in the main provide restrictions controlling settlement and other uses by man, although some prohibit hunting. Some refuges are superimposed upon impoundments created by the Bureau of Reclamation and the Corps of Engineers. Others have been set aside from lands acquired by the former Resettlement Administration. In fact, the Federal program has taken advantage of the acquisition of areas particularly suited for wildlife regardless of the original methods of acquisition by the Federal Government. Several Federal areas are held in custody by the Fish and Wildlife Service but are actually administered by state fish and game departments under co-operative agreements.

**What Refuges Do.** The Federal refuges, while forming an important part of the wildlife management program, provide many incidental uses. They furnish fishing and recreation for the local communities. They serve as reservoirs for the production of birds and animals, the surpluses of which are live-trapped and transplanted to other areas. Some are managed in co-operation with the state fish and game departments as public shooting grounds for waterfowl. Others that are closed to waterfowl hunting are open for the taking of upland game such as quail, squirrels, and deer. Some are used for the holding of field trials, others for bow-and-arrow hunting for deer. All are open to nature lovers who find them interesting places to photograph and study the wild things of the areas.

There is a popular misconception about refuges, particularly those devoted to the protection of waterfowl. Many hunters feel that the refuges merely take away the best hunting areas of the local community. They see birds in great masses within the refuge boundaries and resent the fact that there are not just as many on the outisde. They do not stop to think that one of the main reasons why there are birds in the sanctuary is that the hunters have been kept out. Otherwise, the ducks and geese would long since have gone elsewhere. Refuges provide food, environment, and habitat as well as protection from the gun, and it is little wonder that the birds find them acceptable and use them. Refuges would not serve their fundamental and basic purpose if that were not the case.

Experience has shown, however, that after a waterfowl refuge has been established and permitted to operate for a few years, the local hunters who originally resented its establishment swing around to its support. They find that the refuge holds the birds in the vicinity longer and that as the ducks and geese use it the whole community gets better and longer hunting. Thus, a refuge serves as a benefit to the local hunter and at the same time provides the environment the waterfowl populations need as they move along the flight lanes.

Of the entire wildlife refuge system, the waterfowl areas are probably of more importance to the average hunter than are the other refuges. Here the Government has attempted in small measure to reverse the trend of agricultural drainage and either to protect from destruction natural marshes that are productive of waterfowl and other marsh-loving birds and animals or to restore them where agricultural drainage has run its course and proved to be unsuccessful. On many refuges the Government has restored marsh lands to their former status, to the delight of the ducks and the geese. The waterfowl refuge program has to date emphasized the restoration of breeding marshes. This was a natural result of the efforts in the early stages of the program when production was so essential. Considerable progress has been made, however, in the establishment of areas to accommodate the birds on their wintering grounds and along the flight lanes.

**Waterfowl Breeding Refuges.** Space will not permit the description of all of the refuges but a few outstanding examples will serve to emphasize the progress that has been made. The Malheur National Wildlife Refuge in Oregon, for instance, stands as a landmark of restoration—a reminder of how a once-productive area can be completely destroyed in a futile attempt to make it agriculturally profitable and how it can again be restored to wildlife. Malheur contains almost 175,000 acres including Malheur Lake. This body of water once produced myriads of ducks, geese, shore birds, and other aquatic forms of life. Then the waters from the Silvies and Blitzen Rivers which kept the lake alive were diverted for irrigation. The great Malheur Lake was turned into a veritable desert with the western whirlwinds twisting alkali dust skyward. After years of Herculean effort, a few staunch conservationists, including Dr. Ira N. Gabrielson, former Director of the Fish and Wildlife Service, were able to secure funds to purchase the Malheur lake bed and the P Ranch which owned the rights to the water that flowed into it. Life-giving water again flowed into the dusty lake bed. It is now one of the finest producing areas of the West. Somewhere near 2000 pairs of Canada geese nest there and some 8000 young are raised each season. Every species of waterfowl previously known to nest in the area has returned. More than 200 species of birds and approximately 50 mammals, including antelopes, mule deer, and beavers, are found on the refuge.

Another major project was the establishment of the Souris Refuges in north central North Dakota. At one time, the potholes bordering the Souris River, together with the natural marshes and sloughs along its banks, produced hundreds of thousands of waterfowl. The river heads in Canada, swings southward and eastward into the United States, and eventually returns to Manitoba. The entire loop was formerly exceedingly productive of marsh life before it fell into the hands of the drainage enthusiasts. The restoration of the Souris was one of the first large projects undertaken during the active period when Biological Survey Chief "Ding" Darling was at the helm. Burnie Murek, then State Director of the North Dakota Fish and Game Department and later Regional Director for the Biological Survey, was one of the moving spirits in the restoration of this great marsh. The bottom lands were acquired, a dam was constructed which provides storage for 112,000 acre feet of water in a reservoir now known as Lake Darling, and low cross dikes were constructed across the floor of the valley. The drainage ditch that cuts a straight line down the middle of the Souris Valley was plugged and water returned to the land. The results were astonishing! Ducks that had known no haven in this vicinity since the drainage of the valley years before returned in large numbers. Canada geese were brought in from other refuges and the Souris is again producing the hosts of wildlife that it did in the days of our forefathers.

The Horicon Marsh in northern Wisconsin is another striking example of the restoration of an area unwisely, unprofitably, and unsuccessfully drained for agriculture. It is a large, saucerlike basin in the heart of highly productive farm lands in central Wisconsin. It, too, was gutted with drainage ditches and suffered utter destruction. It was, for years, too wet to farm and too dry to produce anything but sedge grasses and willows. Peat fires burned over much of it.

When the Pittman-Robertson funds became available, a co-operative arrangement was entered into between the State of Wisconsin and the Fish and Wildlife Service whereby the state acquired the southern portion of the marsh and the Federal Government the northern. The land has now been acquired and as soon as funds are available, dikes will be constructed, the drainage outlet will be plugged, and this marsh will again return to its virgin state. But wildlife has lost 50 years of production in the interim.

Other refuges scattered across the northern tier of states are designed to produce waterfowl and other marsh-loving forms of life. They replace in small measure the habitat that has been taken away from them over the years. Many more are needed. Also, funds must be provided to make those that are already in public ownership more productive than they are at present. Even in the present unfinished state of the program, these breeding refuges produce an important segment of the waterfowl population each year.

**Wintering Refuges.** Because of early emphasis on the restoration of breeding areas, the wintering refuge portion of the program is far from complete. Winter habitat is just as important as breeding areas. After all, the birds that are produced in our own northern tier of states and in Canada and Alaska, spend six months of their lives either in migration or in winter quarters. Merely providing a place to nest is not enough. There must also be furnished food and protection during the long winter months when there is constant danger from predation and poaching.

Some of the more important wintering refuges are St. Marks, located on the northwest coast of Florida, the magnificent Mattamuskeet Refuge of 50,000 acres in eastern North Carolina, Back Bay in Virginia, the Wheeler Refuge in northern Alabama, the Sabine and Lacassine Refuges in Louisiana, the White River in Arkansas, Bitter Lakes and the Bosque del Apache in New Mexico, and the Sacramento, Colusa, Sutter, and Salton Sea areas in California.

**Intermediate Refuges.** Scores of refuges have been established for the accommodation of waterfowl on their flights to and from the nesting and wintering refuges. These include the magnificent Bear River Marsh in Utah which is also a great producer of ducks and geese, the Camas and Mud Lake Refuges in Idaho, the Valentine in Nebraska, Union Slough in Iowa, the Chautauqua in Illinois, and the Bombay Hook, Parker River, Black Water, Susquehanna Flats, and numerous others along the Atlantic Coast.

All have an important place in waterfowl management. Every acre restored and maintained for the birds adds just that much to the program. It is still only half completed, and as the inroads of agriculture and industry progress, the situation will become more acute.

**Public Shooting.** Refuges are established and maintained not only as sanctuaries for wildlife. Portions of some of the larger of the migratory waterfowl areas also provide public shooting. The Bear River Refuge in Utah, for instance, provided more than 4500 man-days of hunting in the 1946 season and the duck hunters took home an average of about 2¼ birds per day. Mattamuskeet, in North Carolina, has become one of the famous goose-shooting areas of the Atlantic coast. Here, the State Fish and Game Department manages the public shooting under a co-operative agreement with the Fish and Wildlife Service. 1550 man-days of hunting on this refuge was the tally for 1946. Portions of Bowdoin and Medicine Lake in Montana, Deer Flat in Idaho, Havasu and Imperial along the California and Arizona borders, Lower Klamath and Tule Lakes in California, Ruby Lakes, Nevada, the Snake River in Idaho, and the Upper Mississippi extending through Minnesota, Wisconsin, Illinois, Iowa, and Missouri furnish public shooting for waterfowl. The Upper Mississippi Refuge, extending through five states, has about 20 per cent of the area set aside as refuge while the balance is open to the hunting of waterfowl and upland game and the trapping of fur animals.

Deer hunting is permitted under state laws and in accord with state seasons on the Desert Game Range in Nevada, the Hart Mountain Antelope Refuge in Nevada, Pend Oreille in Washington, Lostwood and Lower Souris in North Dakota, Necedah in Wisconsin, San Andreas in New Mexico, Seney in Michigan, and Trempeleau in Wisconsin. Quail hunters have had access to three refuges in the Southeast, the Carolina Sand Hills in South Carolina, the Piedmont Refuge in Georgia, and the Wheeler Refuge in northern Alabama. Elk hunting has been permitted on a portion of the Elk Refuge in western Wyoming. Squirrel hunting has been permitted on the Kentucky Woodlands in western Kentucky. A portion of the Charles Sheldon Antelope Range in Nevada has been set aside for the taking of antelope.

**Bow-and-Arrow Hunting.** Bow-and-arrow hunting is coming into prominence in many sections. The Federal refuges have furnished the locale for this age-old sport. The Arrowwood Refuge in North Dakota, the Necedah in Wisconsin, and Blackbeard Island off the coast of Georgia have been used for bow-and-arrow hunting of deer. Some remarkable kills have been made. At Necedah the take during the first week end of the 1946 season amounted to 86, while archers for the entire season accounted for a total of 129 on this refuge.

**Live-Trapping.** Refuges not only serve as sanctuaries for wildlife. In some states the Federal refuges have proved to be the chief source of supply for species that are desired for live-trapping and transplanting into areas where they have been extirpated through overshooting. Take the Aransas Refuge in Texas, for instance. 6469 whitetailed deer, 296 turkeys, and 166 raccoons have been live-trapped by the State of Texas and transferred to other areas. The Kentucky Woodlands has furnished deer, raccoon, and turkeys for transplantation. The National Bison Range in Montana has furnished 315 deer and 264 elk for stocking purposes, mainly in Montana. The Wichita Refuge in Oklahoma has provided deer, wild turkeys, and raccoon. Blackbeard Island, off Georgia, has supplied whitetailed deer, the Seney Refuge in northern Michigan, muskrats, and the Elk Refuge in Wyoming has furnished elk that have gone to many different states.

**Field Trials.** One of the principal jobs of a Superintendent of a Federal Wildlife Refuge is to restore habitat, not only for the species for which the area is primarily suited, but for all other indigenous forms of birds and animals as well. This means the providing of food, cover, and environment. Quail, pheasants, grouse, and other upland birds find Federal refuges a welcome home.

As a result, these areas are rapidly becoming attractive for field trials. The Salt Plains Refuge in north central Oklahoma now provides a place for the spring field trials of the Northwest Oklahoma Sportsmen's Association. The White River Refuge in Arkansas is used by the Arkansas Field Trial Club, while the Wheeler Refuge is the locale for the semi-annual beagle trials for the State of Alabama. The Crab Orchard Refuge in southern Illinois, recently transferred to the Fish and Wildlife Service by an act of Congress, is to be the home of the National Retriever Trials. This area is destined to have wide use for various types of outdoor recreation while at the same time supplementing the sorely lacking basic needs of waterfowl in the Mississippi flyway.

**Federal Aid in Wildlife Restoration.** The Pittman-Robertson Act of 1938 was proclaimed by its sponsors as the most constructive piece of Federal legislation since the enactment of the Migratory Bird Treaty Act. Its 11 years of operations have verified the earlier predictions and it has, in fact, become one of the most potent tools in the national wildlife conservation program. This legislation set aside, in a special fund, the excise tax on sporting arms and ammunitions to be apportioned annually to the states on the basis of land area and the number of hunting-license holders in each state. It provided that the Federal funds should be spent in the ratio of $3 of Government moneys to $1 of state funds. The type of work to be undertaken was limited to the acquisition of lands, the development of those areas, and studies leading to improved management of the wildlife resources. Before a state may participate, it must insure that none of the license funds are diverted from the administration of the state fish and game departments.

Although the funds were to be derived from the annual income of the excise tax, they were still subject to appropriation by the Congress. During the fiscal years 1939 to 1948 inclusive, the receipts from the tax amounted to $36,898,742. Appropriations for the same period, on the other hand, totaled only $23,431,273. Thus, more than $13,000,000 of receipts now remain in this special fund because the Congress had never, before the fiscal year 1948, appropriated the entire income. On July 1, 1947, however, which marked the beginning of the fiscal year 1948, the Congress appropriated the entire income from tax. This amounted to slightly more than $9,000,000. This amount, when augmented by the 25 per cent supplied by the states, gave a greater impetus to the wildlife restoration program than for any single earlier year in history.

Although the state fish and game departments have the responsibility for the selection and execution of the projects, the Fish and Wildlife Service must approve them. As a result, the Service exerts a great influence on the over-all program. The Pittman-Robertson Act is a truly co-operative approach to wildlife conservation.

**Surveys and Investigations.** The Pittman-Robertson program is practical. Its survey and investigation projects are designed to find the answers to problems which constantly harass the state administrators. South Dakota, for example, shortened the pheasant season in 1946 when the findings of the Federal Aid personnel showed such action to be desirable. The Arizona game department closed the season on Gambel quail for the first time as a result of a Pittman-Robertson study. Minnesota has known for some time of an overpopulation of deer in two of the large state parks but it remained for the Federal Aid personnel to gather the indisputable evidence of the serious overbrowsing of the range so that the administrators could carry their story to the public and gain approval for opening of the areas to hunting. Montana is now opening specific areas to big game hunting on special permits to keep the elk and deer in proper balance with the food supply. These were based on Pittman-Robertson studies. Nebraska has applied the findings of these investigations to the management of the deer herd on the Nebraska National Forest. Several states have wanted to open seasons on doe deer to keep the herds in balance with the food supplies but have been balked by public sentiment against the killing of females. Studies made by the Federal Aid crews have in several instances provided the data on which the departments could move with assurance. Louisiana and other Gulf Coast states are now forming large-scale development projects to restore coastal marshes for waterfowl and fur animals. Many southern states are carrying on projects to establish lespedeza and other soil-binding legumes which are beneficial to quail. The New England states are using Pittman-Robertson findings to guide their policies on the management of woodcock, grouse, and deer.

During 1946, 103 projects of this nature were under way in 40 states. The published findings from these activities are becoming more numerous annually. Fifty-three publications telling of the results of these studies were issued during the fiscal year ending June 30, 1947.

State wildlife technicians display a fine spirit of co-operation. There is no tendency among them to hoard newly devised improvements in methods and procedure. By publication, correspondence between workers, and personal contacts, anything new that will help the other fellow solve his problem is promptly and generously passed along. The state workers in Federal Aid maintain close co-operation with the research workers of the Fish and Wildlife Service.

**Purchase of Game Lands.** In our American economy, where the wild things of the forest and plains find increasing competition with human uses, the purchase of lands is becoming more important. Wildlife must have places devoted to its primary use if the American tradition of public hunting is to survive. The Federal Aid program has furnished the wherewithal to do that job of land acquisition. Since 1939 the states have acquired about 750,000 acres of land at an average cost of a little more than $6 per acre. Pennsylvania, which has the finest record for the production and harvest of deer of any state in the Union, has acquired slightly more than 147,-

000 acres of land with Pittman-Robertson moneys. Tennessee has purchased more than 80,000 acres and Washington around 48,500. Thirty-six states have acquired lands with Federal Aid funds. Those states that are buying land with the aid of Federal funds were in a land-purchase program prior to the initiation of the Pittman-Robertson Act. They are working on a sound foundation and the future records of hunting in those states will justify their bold approach to the perpetuation of public hunting in those states.

**Development Projects.** Projects of this nature are concerned chiefly with the restoration and improvement of land and water areas to provide food, cover, and water for wildlife. The activities are varied and dependent on the problems at hand.

During 1947, 32 states improved game refuges and public shooting grounds by fencing, posting, plowing of fire breaks, seeding of food patches, planting trees, shrubs, and vines and constructing service roads, buildings, and water-control structures.

Construction work on the Ogden Bay project in Utah, the first project approved under Federal Aid in 1938, was resumed after suspension during the war. This is a combination refuge and public shooting ground. The State of Utah reports that more than 8500 hunters used it in 1946 and that they took around 23,000 ducks and geese from the area. Soil improvement projects were popular, particularly in the southern states. Five southeastern states continued the distribution of lespedeza seeds and other seedlings. About 1,500,000 trees, shrubs, and vines were planted on public and private lands through Federal Aid. Approximately 45 miles of fence were constructed to protect wildlife plantings from grazing. Restocking of game and birds on depleted ranges was carried on by 12 states. Montana set an all-time record by successfully trapping and transplanting 772 antelope under the Pittman-Robertson program. Texas moved 628 antelope to suitable but vacant ranges. Eight states transplanted and released 2137 deer. Five hundred beaver were live-trapped and restocked by seven states. Alabama, Arkansas, and Kentucky transplanted 108 raccoons, Colorado and Montana 70 bighorn sheep; Wyoming transplanted elk. Game birds, including wild turkeys, pheasants, grouse, and quail, were transplanted. All of these projects will lead to better hunting in the future.

**River Basin Studies.** Most river systems of the United States have been surveyed for dams at some future time to be constructed to create hydroelectric power, irrigation, or to supply water navigation. Though not all of the plans will materialize, many will eventually be adopted in the course of human progress. Every change in the flow of a river means an alteration in its suitability for aquatic life—fish, birds, and plants. Many impoundments, particularly in the slow, sluggish rivers of the central United States, will benefit wildlife. Dams will check the spring floods, will permit the deposition of silt that has been stripped from the fertile soils by spring floods. Water that is now too murky for fish or birds will become clear and cool. If present plans materialize, the Missouri River, which has had a reputation since frontier days of being "too thin to plow and too thick to drink," will be altered by a series of impoundments which, it is hoped, will make of it a clear, cool stream. Bass, bluegills, pickerel, pike, and perhaps even trout, will be a welcome change to the sucker and cat fishing now found infrequently along the Missouri.

At the same time, the plans for the control of the rampaging Missouri will wipe out certain waterfowl refuges that have already been established at heavy expense of duck-stamp and other hard-won conservation moneys. It is inevitable that any change in a major river system will alter the natural conditions with some benefit and some loss to wildlife. The flooding of some waterfowl refuges in the Missouri River basin, the diversion of existing water rights from others, and the general upset in the existing scheme of things will most assuredly alter the present waterfowl conservation program.

In the development of the Columbia River of the Northwest for hydroelectric power and for navigation, it is entirely possible that the dams to be constructed on the main stream will wipe out the valuable runs of salmon and steelheads in the upper reaches of the river. These have already been eliminated above the Grand Coulee Dam. Future dams now in prospect will, in the opinion of many fishery technicians, likewise eliminate the salmon migrations for many more miles of the upper Columbia and the Snake.

In order that the construction agencies and the Congress might have the benefit of expert guidance in matters pertaining to the fish and wildlife resources influenced by the alteration of the river systems, Public Law 732 was enacted. This provides that the Fish and Wildlife Service, in co-operation with the fish and game departments of the various states, shall review the plans of the construction agencies and submit reports dealing with the wildlife aspects of each project. Probable damage and benefits are evaluated. Suggestions are made as to how alterations may be made in the plans to change wildlife losses to gains. As an example, fluctuating reservoirs are not productive of either wildlife foods or of suitable conditions for spawning fish. The draw-downs leave the submerged aquatics high and dry, killing them and exposing the spawning beds of fishes. The construction of low-sill dams along inflowing tributary streams, however, can provide shallow marshes with stable water levels productive of environment suitable for both ducks and fish. In other instances, fishery values can be increased if an adequate flow of waters below the dam is released throughout the season. If a refuge is submerged, plans are made to replace it at some other point. The cost of replacing a fish hatchery or a waterfowl marsh, either state, Federal, or privately owned, should be a part of the cost of the project just the same as the cost for moving of a highway or a railroad that is to be flooded by the impoundment.

A great deal of progress has been made. The Fish and Wildlife Service has a staff of biologists and engineers in each of its five regional offices. These people work in close collaboration with the Corps of Engineers and the Bureau of Reclamation, and with the personnel of the state fish and game departments. They attempt to find how the impoundments created with public funds can be made of greatest benefit to the public.

**Training the Experts.** The job of providing suitable environment for the wild birds and animals of the forest and the prairies requires a great deal of skill and "know-how." Here we are working with forms of life that are difficult to observe and with conditions that are often beyond the control of man. Trained observers and research workers must find the answers to many of the complex problems if wildlife management is to be a success, and if live targets are to be supplied for the ever-growing army of hunters going afield each fall.

Realizing that the existing schools were not turning out graduates rapidly enough, "Ding" Darling, when Chief of the Biological Survey, perfected a plan for a co-operative approach to the problem. Through co-operation of the Wildlife Management Institute, a scientific organization financed by private contributions, the state fish and game departments, and the Fish and Wildlife Service, ten co-operative Research and Training Units were established at land-grant colleges distributed from Maine to Oregon, and from Ohio to Texas. These units provide practical courses in wildlife management, and are equipped to award Ph.D. degrees. More than 500 graduates have left these co-operative training units since their establishment. These men have gone into every phase of wildlife management. They have staffed the Pittman-Robertson program. They occupy numerous positions with state fish and game departments, with the Fish and Wildlife Service, and with other Federal agencies administering lands and waters. The Wildlife Training Unit program has been one foundation of scientific wildlife management. The field is far from saturated. There is still room for capable workers, and from present indications this demand will continue for years to come.

**Conclusions.** The average man who buys a hunting license once a year and spends either a few days or the entire season afield usually thinks little about the fundamental requirements of keeping his favorite sport alive. He seldom pauses to reflect that the state hunting license he buys, the duck stamp, or the few dollars of taxes that he pays on shells, or on that new gun he has bought for the season, are the only contribution he makes toward supplying the birds and animals that he seeks when he goes afield. He may spend a hundred dollars or more for boats, or clothing, or guns, or guides, or something to keep him warm on a frosty morning, and never complain. Yet his only contribution to production has been the wholly insignificant license fee and the minor hidden taxes on his equipment. He never sits down to think about the complicated machinery required to keep the sport alive in this complex civilization which is our American way of life.

The state fish and game departments are doing a magnificent job in attempting to provide wildlife in reasonable numbers. The land-use agencies, such as the Forest Service, the Soil Conservation Service, the Bureau of Land Management, and others, contribute in great measure. The Fish and Wildlife Service, through the regulations governing the take of migratory birds, through the program of refuges, through close co-operation with the states and all the others that make up this complicated machine, attempts to keep the needs of wildlife constantly in every program of land and water use. This task will become more difficult as time goes on but a thorough understanding on the part of the hunting public of the many interrelationships and problems will go far toward improved management of the resource.

# Waterfowl Regulations

"How in the name of common sense," many duck hunters ask, "can a bunch of swivel-chair biologists in Washington make sensible regulations governing my favorite sport—duck hunting? How do they know there were 54,000,000 waterfowl in January 1947 as against 125,000,000 in January 1944? How? I ask you. How?" The same question might just as well be posed by a goose, woodcock, or dove hunter. All are equally enthusiastic about their own favorite brand of hunting, and equally positive in their ideas about bureaucrats.

The answer is that the bureaucrats do not know, nor do they claim to know, that there were those exact numbers of birds, and they deny emphatically that the regulations are based upon the star-gazing propensities of swivel-chair biologists. They are not. The migratory bird hunting "privileges" (and they are just that under the terms of the treaties with Great Britain and Mexico) are based each year on a mass of data collected from January 1 to December 31, and covering the continent from Point Barrow to Yucatan. The annual inventories, made at the close of each hunting season and representing the potential breeding population for the following year, are mere yardsticks. They are not accurate counts, so hunters should not start figuring their share on the basis of those millions. These annual surveys give trend figures which are valuable guides when it comes to making regulations. But they are only one of many indices used in determining the seasons and bag limits each year.

Perhaps the best way to describe the method of determining migratory bird regulations is to show how they were made in 1947. Here it is:

**Winter Inventory.** The idea of attempting to estimate the continental waterfowl population originated at the time of the duck depression of the early 1930's. Everyone knew the birds were at a dangerously low level, but just how low was problematical. Observers were mobilized in all parts of the country and asked to estimate the waterfowl populations on the wintering areas where the birds were concentrated. January was chosen as the logical month, because then the birds are most concentrated on their wintering grounds. The entire staff of trained field workers of the Biological Survey—biologists, wardens, and refuge supervisors—participated. Adjustments were made in the figures to compensate for the areas not covered, and the figure that came out of the adding machine was 27,000,000. That was in 1934.

The same system has been used annually each year since that date, although refinements have been made. More areas have been covered; airplanes, blimps, and autogyros have been pressed into service. Aerial photographs have been used to check, verify, and correct ground estimates. New techniques have been evolved. Adjustments in the method of calculation have followed, but basically the principle is the same. The inventory in January 1947 was based upon the participation of approximately 1300 individuals. It included almost the entire field force of the Fish and Wildlife Service, co-operators in state game departments, the Army Air Forces, the Naval Air Service, the Coast Guard, Forest Service, Soil Conservation Service, and National Park Service, besides many individual volunteers. These selected observers estimate waterfowl concentrations on areas with which they have been familiar for years. By conducting the survey simultaneously, then assembling and analyzing the reports, a reasonably accurate over-all showing of trends in population is possible. If anyone knows a better way, the Wildlife Service would be glad to have it.

During the 1947 inventory, an amphibious plane with two trained observers flew down the east coast of Mexico past Yucatan to Panama and returned along the western shore of Latin America to California. For the first time in history, an extensive coverage of this important wintering ground was possible. These two biologists flew a total of 13,650 miles.

**Spring Flights.** The winter inventory is far from being the only data used to judge waterfowl trends. Each of the managers of the 200 waterfowl refuges, scattered along the migration lanes from California and the Gulf states to the Canadian border, supply information about the spring flights. They report constantly on whether the birds moving northward to the breeding grounds appear to be more numerous or fewer in numbers. The 70 Federal game management agents and a host of state wardens send in their observations. The numerous interested private observers tell the Service what they see.

**Summer Observations.** As the migratory hordes of waterfowl in good years, and the trickle of birds in poor seasons, reach the breeding grounds, the Fish and Wildlife Service intensifies its efforts to learn the facts. Trained observers with airplanes, autos, and canoes are dispatched to Canada and Alaska. The refuge managers of all of the Federal refuges, where waterfowl rear their young, keep a constant watch. The Federal game management agents, in close co-operation with state game department field personnel, exert special efforts to keep abreast of what is happening in the private homes of the ducks and geese. Reports come in to Washington regularly. Surface water conditions, weather data, precipitation records, temperatures, and drought prospects are carefully checked and weighed against the all-important element of the time when waterfowl pass the helpless stage of the summer moult. If they can survive on the nesting grounds until mid-July they are reasonably safe.

Not only waterfowl receive this special attention. Observers from the co-operative research units and the field staff report on the singing ground censuses of woodcock, and the nesting success of mourning doves.

During the critical summer of 1947, the Fish and Wildlife Service, in co-operation with the Canadian Department of Mines and Resources, arranged for 14 trained observers to spend the summer in Canada, and two in Alaska. These men were not all Service biologists. The State of Illinois sent one of its crack observers to work with the Federal personnel. All, however, worked as a team. Two airplanes were used, which carried observers 32,000 miles over the breeding ranges. Twenty-eight thousand additional miles were covered by auto, by canoe, and on foot. In Alaska, two observers in Service airplanes covered 7000 miles. Not only was the coverage more extensive in 1947 than ever before—it was also more intensive. New techniques in sampling were developed. Aerial photography was brought into play more than ever before. Out of all this came quantitative data on the number of potholes, on the number of breeding pairs of ducks per square mile of the different types of breeding area, and on other factors important to breeding ground appraisal.

The work in Canada is closely correlated with observations by Canadian officials. Some of these men go by canoe far northward into sections which cannot be serviced with present airplane equipment. The provincial and central government officials of Canada work in complete harmony and unity with the observers from the United States. The Wildlife Management Institute, too, aided greatly in this investigation and co-operated in the intensive coverage of Manitoba and eastern Canada. Ducks Unlimited has been furnished copies of all reports of the American observers. Their conclusions are their own.

**Public Hearings.** As soon as the January inventory figures have been assembled and the total struck, it is plainly evident whether the waterfowl population has increased, or, as in recent years, taken another nosedive. It is then safe, on the basis of current knowledge, to start discussing the next season's regulations. The spring observations serve as a check on the winter inventory and the breeding ground studies tell what the population is running into in the way of nesting conditions and producing young.

In 1947 the procedure was as follows: Two meetings of the National Waterfowl Advisory Committee were held. This Committee consisted of representatives from the following organizations:

International Association of Game, Fish, and Conservation Commissioners
Wildlife Management Institute
National Wildlife Federation
Wildlife Society
Ducks Unlimited
Izaak Walton League of America
Friends of the Land
National Audubon Society
Outdoor Writers Association of America

A nation-wide series of public conferences was organized, at which representatives of the press, sportsmen's organizations, and individual hunters were given an opportunity to express their opinions of the situation and to recommend regulations for the forthcoming season. Every attempt was made to inform the people attending these meetings of the situation confronting waterfowl, as the Service saw it, and to hear their recommendations.

Meetings were held in Chicago, New York City, Washington, Boston, Jacksonville, New Orleans, San Antonio, San Francisco, Portland, Denver, St. Louis, Madison, and St. Paul.

**The Take by Hunters.** Extra effort was made to determine the kill and cripple losses during the 1946 fall hunting season. This is a most difficult task, and requires the hearty co-operation of the individual hunter if it is to be anywhere near accurate. Two approaches were followed. One consisted of the use of "score cards," published widely by all of the outdoor magazines. This provided space for the kill of birds, the cripple loss, and the hunter's own comparison of the 1946 season with the previous year. It was disappointing to see how few duck hunters were willing to spend a few moments' time and a three-cent stamp to send in the report of their kills. Only about 3500 responded with this information which is so important to intelligent management. The Service receives that many or more letters each year complaining about the regulations, yet few of these same disgruntled individuals are willing to do this simple chore of filling out a "score card." The other data were secured by the game management agents of the Fish and Wildlife Service, and the kill estimates of the various state game departments. These were based upon personal interviews with hunters, either in the field or through sportsmen's clubs.

The net result of combined surveys of waterfowl kill and cripple loss showed a take of 19,000,000 birds, and a loss by crippling of another 5,000,000, making a net reduction by hunting of 24,000,000 birds.

**Analyzing the Data.** Days on end were spent by personnel in the Service's five Regional Offices and in the Central Office, compiling, reviewing, and digesting the material that had come in from all sources. The data on the three basic elements—the potential breeding population, as determined by the January inventory, the estimated take by hunters in the various parts of the country, and the number of hunters as indicated by "duck stamp" sales in each state, formed the basis for the preliminary calculation of what the season and bag limit should be. These initial regulations were subject to modification by further restrictions if the breeding ground data gave evidence of the need.

Briefly, here is what the figures showed in 1947:

The Atlantic flyway had 15% of the waterfowl, 14% of the hunters, and killed 9% of the birds in 1946.

The Mississippi flyway, with only 25% of the birds and 42% of the hunters, took 37% of the entire kill. Obviously this flyway was in bad shape.

The Central flyway came the closest to being in balance. It had 33% of the birds, 25% of the hunters, and registered a 29% kill.

The Pacific flyway was not far out of line. The waterfowl figure showed 27% of the birds, as against 19% of the duck stamps and an estimated 25% take of birds.

**Determining the Restrictions.** On the basis of these findings, it was decided that for 1947 the season should be shortened from 45 to 30 days, and the bag limit reduced from 7 to 4 ducks per day. However, because of the more favorable conditions in the two western flyways, both as to bird populations and hunting pressure, it was decided that an extra five-day season could be granted there for all waterfowl, and that the restrictions on the hunting of geese need not be severe.

Because shortened seasons lead to difficulties in spreading the hunting privileges to all parts of a state, it was decided to permit a split season for states desiring such an arrangement. This was handled by permitting two 12-day seasons for the states granted the 30-day season, and two 14-day shooting periods for the 35-day season states.

The responsible officials of the state fish and game departments were then notified of the Service's ideas on the hunting season, were told that no season could begin earlier than October 7 or extend beyond January 6, and that their ideas were desired as to the seasons that would best suit their conditions. It was stated that, for the sake of uniformity, seasons should begin on days two weeks apart, that is October 7, October 21, November 5, etc. Shooting on all opening days was to begin at noon. Hunting hours were to be from sunrise to one hour before sunset. They were told that reports from the corps of observers on the breeding grounds in the United States, Alaska, and Canada, together with current western reports indicating nesting conditions, could alter the basic conclusions at the last moment. That has happened on more than one occasion in past years.

**Issuing the Regulations.** After hearing from the state fish and game directors, and making minor adjustments to compensate for special conditions in some states, the Migratory Bird Hunting Regulations were drafted and submitted to the Secretary of the Interior. After his approval, they cleared through the Department of Justice, the Department of State, the Archives, and finally went to the President for signature. The law requires that only the President of the United States may sign the regulations. During the war years, when the late President Roosevelt was called to far places on affairs of state, the waterfowl regulations followed him. One year, they were signed aboard ship in the South Pacific, and on another occasion they were flown to him and signed during his attendance at a foreign conference. After publication in the Federal Register, they become effective. This complicated process of making regulations accounts, in part, for the reluctance of the Service to recommend changes after they have been adopted.

**The Aftermath.** As soon as the regulations have been published the Director and staff of the Fish and Wildlife Service brace themselves for the attack, knowing full well that there will be a barrage of criticism and complaint and name-calling—regardless. It always happens. In fact, the criticism was louder in 1944 when there was an 80-day season and 10-duck daily limit—with an extra 5 mallards, pintails, and widgeons thrown in—than in 1947 with a 30- or 35-day season and 4 birds a day. In 1944 the hunters wanted 90 days and insisted on bait and live decoys to boot.

The officials find solace in one fact: They can deny, with perfectly clear conscience, the charge that the migratory bird regulations are the result of snap judgment decisions by swivel-chair biologists.

# Ducks Unlimited

"Co-operation unlimited" well might be used in descriptive paraphrase of one of the most colorful and widely representative conservation agencies in the world of sport, for the combined efforts of men literally in all corners of the North American continent are making it possible for Ducks Unlimited, as one great unit, to aid substantially in the fight for perpetuation of wild waterfowl.

International Ducks Unlimited is the only organization working entirely to increase these birds and maintain their number. Its only function is to help keep these classic birds at greatest numbers possible and to assure the permanency of the venerable sport of wildfowling.

This useful conservation group, guided by member-sportsmen of the United States, Canada, Mexico, and Cuba, has gone to the very heart of waterfowl production, where it feels the greatest return can be had in bird numbers. That is in western Canada where extensive air and ground surveys by scientists and sportsmen in the middle 1930's revealed that most North American ducks nest and breed.

The area of operations is within the Dominion's far-reaching borders of Alberta, Saskatchewan, and Manitoba. These are "prairie provinces" whose marshland nesting and feeding advantages have been favored for as long as man remembers by parent ducks in the age-old, instinctive purpose of rearing feathered youngsters.

Ducks Unlimited's program is a giant one. Application of this program is a many-sided task. It means a fight against drought which can parch lush marshlands, turn them into desert wastes, and cause the destruction of millions of helpless nesting waterfowl caught in such death-traps. Stabilized water levels lessen this killing factor. Controlled water levels made possible by dam construction also can check the loss of legions of wild breeding ducks by floods born of melting snow waters during the early spring breeding season. Predators must be fought—predators such as crows which rob nests and destroy millions of ducks in embryo. Marsh fires, which sweep their devastation over nesting areas, must be beaten down and offset by the construction of fireguards. Advantages of duck nesting areas developed by engineering must be maintained. These all are part of Ducks Unlimited's program to keep wild water birds winging southward from the Dominion's sprawling range.

To counter adversity and to maintain production at highest levels possible, Ducks Unlimited develops in every conceivable way the most efficient use possible by man of land and water resources. This experienced sportsmen's conservation organization knows that Nature can be helpful, but that she can be destructive, too. Its program has been designed to capitalize on Nature's better moods and to fight her when she becomes unkind.

The program calls for the strategic placing of dams to stabilize water levels in vital duck-nesting areas in all of the three Canadian prairie provinces. Marsh restoration and management has become one of Ducks Unlimited's most useful and effective weapons.

Examples of different types of construction and area developments that have become a part of this conservation agency's record are the Bracken and Knapp dams, the Big Grass Marsh, and the Louisiana Lakes. These are representative of many other mediums of duck production established by the organization in the field in all three provinces.

Bracken Dam (Project No. 50) and Knapp Dam (Project No. 63) were built jointly by Ducks Unlimited and the Manitoba government to improve wildlife production on 131,000 acres of Saskatchewan River Delta marsh. This area is operated by the Manitoba Government as a wildlife production block. Development is designed to protect water levels against drought and flood.

An outstanding example of restoration is Big Grass Marsh (Project No. 1) in Manitoba. This marsh had been drained unwisely in a land-promotion scheme. Municipalities, government, and private owners co-operated with Ducks Unlimited to build dams to hold snow runoff waters and to restore lakes and ponds. Municipalities and private owners have organized a co-operative to manage the 50,000-acre marsh, under Ducks Unlimited's guidance, and to harvest the annual muskrat crop by which the area is kept self-supporting.

In its basic program of putting water to work Ducks Unlimited has developed a vast number of areas throughout the great duck-nesting range—or "Duck Factory," as it is called. One of these developments is known as Louisiana Lakes (Project No. 112-128) in southern Alberta. Land and water were provided by authorities and ranchers. Surplus irrigation water for this development is led over the prairies to create 14 lakes and ponds for the ducks. Many others have been created similarly.

In addition to the establishment strategically during its first decade of more than 225 water-fowl-producing projects from south-central Canada westward and to the north of Manitoba, Saskatchewan, and Alberta, and the improvement of more than 1,300,000 acres of nesting territory in the heart of duckland, Ducks Unlimited has many other accomplishments to its credit as a restoration agency.

Canadian sportsmen's groups and this agency, co-operating in seasonal wars on predators, such as crows and magpies, have reduced numbers of these birds by over 1,500,000 in Canada's chief waterfowl-breeding areas. More than 50,000 ducks have been banded by the organization's men in the field. Information obtained through returns of the numbered leg-bands enables Ducks Unlimited to establish special donor nesting sites with assurance that ducks will fly from them across the international border to sponsor states where groups or individuals underwrite projects in the interest of wildfowling. Bands also furnish important migration and ornithological data. Many miles of barbed-wire fencing have been erected in the three prairie provinces to protect nesting areas from trampling by cattle. Miles of fireguards have been cleared to prevent harmful marsh fires. Furthermore, Ducks Unlimited has made the people of Canada and the United States more conservation conscious.

These all are extensive accomplishments which will be enlarged upon with a future program of expansion assuring even more producing acreages and projects than those which already have become identified with this eminent restoration movement.

Ducks Unlimited, Inc., or DU, an appellation used by legions of sportsmen in friendly recognition, was incorporated in the District of Columbia on Jan. 29, 1937. It is non-profit and non-political. The pressing need for a game restoration organization such as Ducks Unlimited became manifest with disclosures that climaxed a series of surveys and investigations into causes of a sweeping decrease in the wild duck population during the early 1930's. Those surveys were sponsored by More Game Birds in America, Inc., A Foundation, of New York, and actually the parent of Ducks Unlimited. More Game Birds was formed by a group of nationally known businessmen and sportsmen who financed extensive research into the general status of game birds and waterfowl.

This survey undertaking, begun in 1930, was operated on a five-year plan to check conditions on principal wild duck breeding grounds in the north-central United States and in the provinces of Canada. The investigations disclosed that drought was rampant. Millions of ducklings were found to be perishing annually as enormous marsh areas dried up each summer. Predatory birds and animals were also taking a heavy toll.

It was on these findings that More Game Birds in America advocated an extensive program in the United States and Canada for restoration and management of wildfowl breeding grounds. But a disastrous depression had hit the United States and legislation to finance such a program was defeated. Further, the Foundation's report revealed that more than 70 per cent of North America's ducks favored Canadian prairie breeding grounds. The conservation-minded sportsmen behind More Game Birds agreed that the job should be done privately by sportsmen wanting to help preserve these birds and wildfowling.

The Foundation agreed for a three-year period to sponsor and finance their newborn association so that it could start its restoration and management job in the Dominion's duck-breeding areas. A new conservation idea had been put upon the ways and was ready for launching but it needed a suitable identification. A number of names were suggested. None of them, however, seemed appropriate. Finally, at a gathering of four leaders of the group, the cue came from an observation by one of those present that to operate in Canada a Canadian affiliate organization or company would be necessary. Such a company, in order to take legal title to lands, must be incorporated under laws of the Dominion. Legal designation of a Canadian corporation is the word "Limited." The name "Ducks, Limited" was suggested, but one of the quartet exploded: "Ducks, Limited? Never! What we want is Ducks Unlimited." Thereupon sprouted the name which has become a byword among sportsmen from one coast of the United States to another and from Canada to Mexico and Cuba. Newly tagged Ducks Unlimited rolled up its sleeves and went to work.

DU has two units. One is Ducks Unlimited, Inc., the United States association. The other Ducks Unlimited (Canada), the field organization.

Ducks Unlimited, Inc., the American organization, is governed by a Board of Trustees comprising more than 50 of the country's most representative business and professional men and sportsmen. This board elects national officers, has general direction of the work of the corporation, and administers its affairs. The Board meets annually for two-day sessions at cities chosen from year to year. All national officers and trustees serve without remuneration.

The Trustees elect vice-presidents who, in turn, take over the reins of six especially assigned regions in various sections of the country—North Atlantic, Middle Atlantic, Gulf, Mississippi, West Central, and Pacific.

Actual work of fund-raising is done by voluntary committees in the various states. These committees have raised, and there has been sent to the Canadian affiliate for waterfowl restoration work, over $1,500,000. Additional large sums are catalogued annually to meet future field expansion work.

Ducks Unlimited (Canada), as the field organization, applies funds contributed by sportsmen where they will do the most good. It is incorporated under the laws of the Dominion as a non-profit company and, like its parent organization in the United States, is guided by a carefully chosen Board of Directors composed of the same representative overseers.

Expansion of DU in the field is being met by a steady growth in membership to swell the already widespread list, during the first decade of operation, of more than 30,000 active, subscribing members and, in addition, an equal number of contributors.

In 1947 DU chapters also were organized in Mexico and in Cuba with representative sportsmen who, like their fellow wildfowlers in Canada and the United States, are working in an international cause that, clearly, has become one of the finest co-operative efforts among men in the whole, wide world of sport.

National Headquarters of Ducks Unlimited, Inc., are at 342 Madison Ave., New York, 17, N. Y.

# Federal Laws Relating to the Protection of Wildlife

## CONVENTION BETWEEN THE UNITED STATES AND GREAT BRITAIN FOR THE PROTECTION OF MIGRATORY BIRDS IN THE UNITED STATES AND CANADA[1]

### BY THE PRESIDENT OF THE UNITED STATES OF AMERICA

A PROCLAMATION

Whereas a convention between the United States of America and the United Kingdom of Great Britain and Ireland for the protection of migratory birds in the United States and Canada was concluded and signed by their respective plenipotentiaries at Washington on the 16th day of August 1916, the original of which convention is word for word as follows:

[1] Signed at Washington, Aug. 16, 1916; ratification advised by the Senate Aug. 29, ratified by the President Sept. 1, and by Great Britain Oct. 20; ratifications exchanged Dec. 7, and proclaimed Dec. 8, 1916; 39 Stat. 1702.

Whereas many species of birds in the course of their annual migrations traverse certain parts of the United States and the Dominion of Canada; and

Whereas many of these species are of great value as a source of food or in destroying insects which are injurious to forests and forage plants on the public domain, as well as to agricultural crops, in both the United States and Canada, but are nevertheless in danger of extermination through lack of adequate protection during the nesting season or while on their way to and from their breeding grounds;

The United States of America and His Majesty the King of the United Kingdom of Great Britain and Ireland and of the British Dominions beyond the Seas, Emperor of India, being desirous of saving from indiscriminate slaughter and of insuring the preservation of such migratory birds as are either useful to man or harmless, have resolved to adopt some uniform system of protection which shall effectively accomplish such objects and to the end of concluding a convention for this purpose have appointed as their respective plenipotentiaries;

The President of the United States of America, Robert Lansing, Secretary of State of the United States; and

His Britannic Majesty, the Right Hon. Sir Cecil Arthur Spring Rice, G.C.V.O., K.C.M.G., etc., His Majesty's ambassador extraordinary and plenipotentiary at Washington;

Who, after having communicated to each other their respective full powers, which were found to be in due and proper form, have agreed to and adopted the following articles:

Article I. The high contracting powers declare that the migratory birds included in the terms of this convention shall be as follows:

1. Migratory game birds:

(a) Anatidae or waterfowl, including brant, wild ducks, geese, and swans.

(b) Gruidae or cranes, including little brown, sandhill, and whooping cranes.

(c) Rallidae or rails, including coots, gallinules, and sora and other rails.

(d) Limicolae or shorebirds, including avocets, curlew, dowitchers, godwits, knots, oyster catchers, phalaropes, plovers, sandpipers, snipe, stilts, surf birds, turnstones, willet, woodcock, and yellowlegs.

(e) Columbidae or pigeons, including doves and wild pigeons.

2. Migratory insectivorous birds: Bobolinks, catbirds, chicadees, cuckoos, flickers, flycatchers, grosbeaks, humming birds, kinglets, martins, meadowlarks, nighthawks or bull-bats, nuthatches, orioles, robins, shrikes, swallows, swifts, tanagers, titmice, thrushes, vireos, warblers, wax-wings, whippoorwills, woodpeckers, and wrens, and all other perching birds which feed entirely or chiefly on insects.

3. Other migratory nongame birds: Auks, auklets, bitterns, fulmars, gannets, grebes, guillemots, gulls, herons, jaegers, loons, murres, petrels, puffins, shearwaters, and terns.

Article II. The high contracting powers agree that, as an effective means of preserving migratory birds, there shall be established the following close seasons during which no hunting shall be done except for scientific or propagating purposes under permits issued by proper authorities.

1. The close season on migratory game birds shall be between March 10 and September 1, except that the close season on the Limicolae or shorebirds in the Maritime Provinces of Canada and in those States of the United States bordering on the Atlantic Ocean which are situated wholly or in part north of Chesapeake Bay shall be between February 1 and August 15, and that Indians may take at any time scoters for food but not for sale. The season for hunting shall be further restricted to such period not exceeding 3½ months as the high contracting powers may severally deem appropriate and define by law or regulation.

2. The close season on migratory insectivorous birds shall continue throughout the year.

3. The close season on other migratory nongame birds shall continue throughout the year, except that Eskimos and Indians may take at any season auks, auklets, guillemots, murres, and puffins, and their eggs, for food and their skins for clothing, but the birds and eggs so taken shall not be sold or offered for sale.

Article III. The high contracting powers agree that during the period of 10 years next following the going into effect of this convention there shall be a continuous close season on the following migratory game birds, to wit:

Band-tailed pigeons, little brown, sandhill, and whooping cranes, swans, curlew, and all shorebirds (except the black-breasted and golden plover, Wilson or jacksnipe, woodcock, and the greater and lesser yellowlegs); provided that during such 10 years the closed seasons on cranes, swans, and curlew in the Province of British Columbia shall be made by the proper authorities of that Province within the general dates and limitations elsewhere prescribed in this convention for the respective groups to which these birds belong.

Article IV. The high contracting powers agree that special protection shall be given the wood duck and the eider duck either (1) by a close season extending over a period of at least 5 years, or (2) by the establishment of refuges, or (3) by such other regulations as may be deemed appropriate.

Article V. The taking of nests or eggs of migratory game or insectivorous or nongame birds shall be prohibited, except for scientific or propagating purposes under such laws or regulations as the high contracting powers may severally deem appropriate.

Article VI. The high contracting powers agree that the shipment or export of migratory birds or their eggs from any State or Province, during the continuance of the close season in such State or Province, shall be prohibited except for scientific or propagating purposes, and the international traffic in any birds or eggs at such time captured, killed, taken, or shipped at any time contrary to the laws of the State or Province in which the same were captured, killed, taken, or shipped shall be likewise prohibited. Every package containing migratory birds or any parts thereof or any eggs of migratory birds transported or offered for transportation from the United States into the Dominion of Canada, or from the Dominion of Canada into the United States, shall have the name and address of the shipper and an accurate statement of the contents clearly marked on the outside of such package.

Article VII. Permits to kill any of the above-named birds, which under extraordinary conditions may become seriously injurious to the agricultural or other interests in any particular community, may be issued by the proper authorities of the high contracting powers under suitable regulations prescribed therefor by them, respectively, but such permits shall lapse or may be canceled at any time when, in the opinion of said authorities, the particular exigency has passed, and no birds killed under this article shall be shipped, sold, or offered for sale.

Article VIII. The high contracting powers agree themselves to take, or propose to their respective appropriate law-making bodies, the necessary measures for insuring the execution of the present convention.

Article IX. The present convention shall be ratified by the President of the United States of America, by and with the advice and consent of the Senate thereof, and by His Britannic Majesty. The ratifications shall be exchanged at Washington as soon as possible, and the convention shall take effect on the date of the exchange of the ratifications. It shall remain in force for 15 years, and in the event of neither of the high contracting powers having given notification 12 months before the expiration of said period of 15 years of its intention of terminating its operation, the convention shall continue to remain in force for 1 year and so on from year to year.

In faith whereof, the respective plenipotentiaries have signed the present convention in duplicate and have hereunto affixed their seals.

[seal] Cecil Spring Rice.

[seal] Robert Lansing.

And whereas the said convention has been duly ratified on both parts, and the ratifications of the two Governments were exchanged in the city of Washington on the 7th day of December 1916:

Now, therefore, be it known that I, Woodrow Wilson, President of the United States of America, have caused the said convention to be made public, to the end that the same and every article and clause thereof may be observed and fulfilled with good faith by the United States and the citizens thereof.

In testimony whereof I have hereunto set my hand and caused the seal of the United States to be affixed.

Done at the city of Washington this 8th day of December in the year of our Lord 1916, and of the independence of the United States of America the 141st.

[SEAL] WOODROW WILSON.

By the President:

ROBERT LANSING,
*Secretary of State.*

## CONVENTION BETWEEN THE UNITED STATES OF AMERICA AND THE UNITED MEXICAN STATES FOR THE PROTECTION OF MIGRATORY BIRDS AND GAME MAMMALS[1]

## BY THE PRESIDENT OF THE UNITED STATES OF AMERICA

A PROCLAMATION

Whereas a convention between the United States of America and the United Mexican States providing for the protection of migratory birds and game mammals was concluded and signed by their respective plenipotentiaries at the city of Mexico on the seventh day of February, one thousand nine hundred and thirty-six, the original of which convention, being in the English and Spanish languages, is word for word as follows:

Convention Between the United States of America and the United Mexican States for the Protection of Migratory Birds and Game Mammals

Whereas some of the birds denominated migratory, in their movements cross the United States of America and the United Mexican States, in which countries they live temporarily;

Whereas it is right and proper to protect the said migratory birds, whatever may be their origin, in the United States of America and the United Mexican States, in order that the species may not be exterminated;

Whereas for this purpose it is necessary to employ adequate measures which will permit a rational utilization of migratory birds for the purpose of sport as well as for food, commerce, and industry;

The Governments of the two countries have agreed to conclude a convention which will satisfy the above-mentioned need and to that end have appointed as their respective plenipotentiaries: The Honorable Josephus Daniels, representing the President of the United States of America, Franklin D. Roosevelt, and the Honorable Eduardo Hay, representing the President of the United Mexican States, General Lazaro Cardenas, who have exhibited to each other and found satisfactory their respective full powers, conclude the following convention:

ARTICLE I. In order that the species may not be exterminated, the high contracting parties declare that it is right and proper to protect birds denominated as migratory, whatever may be their origin, which in their movements live temporarily in the United States of America and the United Mexican States, by means of adequate methods which will permit, insofar as the respective high contracting parties may see fit, the utilization of said birds rationally for the purpose of sport, food, commerce, and industry.

ARTICLE II. The high contracting parties agree to establish laws, regulations, and provisions to satisfy the need set forth in the preceding article, including:

(A) The establishment of closed seasons, which will prohibit in certain periods of the year the taking of migratory birds, their nests or eggs, as well as their transportation or sale, alive or dead, their products or parts, except when proceeding, with appropriate authorization, from private game farms or when used for scientific purposes, for propagation, or for museums.

(B) The establishment of refuge zones in which the taking of such birds will be prohibited.

(C) The limitation of their hunting to 4 months in each year, as a maximum, under permits issued by the respective authorities in each case.

(D) The establishment of a closed season for wild ducks from the 10th of March to the 1st of September.

(E) The prohibition of the killing of migratory insectivorous birds, except when they become injurious to agriculture and constitute plagues, as well as when they come from reserves or game farms: *Provided, however,* That such birds may be captured alive and used in conformity with the laws of each contracting country.

(F) The prohibition of hunting from aircraft.

ARTICLE III. The high contracting parties respectively agree, in addition, not to permit the transportation over the American-Mexican border of migratory birds, dead or alive, their parts or products, without a permit of authorization provided for that purpose by the government of each country, with the understanding that in the case that the said birds, their parts or products are transported from one country to the other without the stipulated authorization, they will be considered as contraband and treated accordingly.

ARTICLE IV. The high contracting parties declare that for the purpose of the present convention the following birds shall be considered migratory:

Migratory game birds:
- Familia Anatidae.
- Familia Gruidae.
- Familia Rallidae.
- Familia Charadriidae.
- Familia Scolopacidae.
- Familia Recurvirostridae.
- Familia Phalaropodidae.
- Familia Columbidae.

Migratory nongame birds:
- Familia Cuculidae.
- Familia Caprimulgidae.
- Familia Micropodidae.
- Familia Trochilidae.
- Familia Picidae.
- Familia Tyrannidae.
- Familia Alaudidae.
- Familia Hirundinidae.

Migratory nongame birds—*Continued:*
- Familia Paridae.
- Familia Certhiidae.
- Familia Troglodytidae.
- Familia Turdidae.
- Familia Mimidae.
- Familia Sylviidae.
- Familia Motacillidae.
- Familia Bombycillidae.
- Familia Ptilogonatidae.
- Familia Laniidae.
- Familia Vireonidae.
- Familia Compsothlypidae.
- Familia Icteridae.
- Familia Thraupidae.
- Familia Fringillidae.

Others which the Presidents of the United States of America and the United Mexican States may determine by common agreement.

ARTICLE V. The high contracting parties agree to apply the stipulations set forth in article III with respect to the game mammals which live in their respective countries.

ARTICLE VI. This convention shall be ratified by the high contracting parties in accordance with their constitutional methods and shall remain in force for fifteen years and shall be understood to be extended from year to year if the high contracting parties have not indicated twelve months in advance their intention to terminate it.

The respective plenipotentiaries sign the present convention in duplicate in English and Spanish, affixing thereto their respective seals, in the City of Mexico, the 7th day of February of 1936.

[SEAL] JOSEPHUS DANIELS.
[SEAL] EDUARDO HAY.

And whereas the said convention has been duly ratified on both parts and the ratifications of the two Governments were exchanged in the city of Washington on the fifteenth day of March, one thousand nine hundred and thirty-seven, on which day the convention entered into force in accordance with an understanding reached by an exchange of notes signed on February 10 and February 11, 1936, by the Minister of Foreign Affairs of the United Mexican States and the Chargé d'Affaires of the United States of America at the city of Mexico.

Now, therefore, be it known that I, Franklin D. Roosevelt, President of the United States of America, have caused the said convention to be made public to the end that the same and every article and clause thereof may be observed and fulfilled with good faith by the United States of America and the citizens thereof.

In testimony whereof, I have hereunto set my hand and

---

[1]Signed at Mexico City, Feb. 7, 1936; ratification advised by the Senate Apr. 30, 1936, ratified by the President Oct. 8, 1936, and by Mexico Feb. 12, 1937; ratifications exchanged and proclaimed Mar. 15, 1937; 50 Stat. 1311.

caused the Seal of the United States of America to be affixed.

Done at the city of Washington this fifteenth day of March, in the year of our Lord one thousand nine hundred and thirty-seven and of the independence of the United States of America the one hundred and sixty-first.

[SEAL] FRANKLIN D. ROOSEVELT.

By the President:

CORDELL HULL,
*Secretary of State.*

## MIGRATORY BIRD TREATY ACT[1]

An act to give effect to the conventions between the United States and Great Britain for the protection of migratory birds concluded at Washington August sixteenth, nineteen hundred and sixteen, and between the United States and the United Mexican States for the protection of migratory birds and game mammals concluded at the city of Mexico February seventh, nineteen hundred and thirty-six, and for other purposes.

*Be it enacted by the Senate and House of Representatives of the United States of America in Congress assembled,* That this act shall be known by the short title of the Migratory Bird Treaty Act.

SEC. 2. That unless and except as permitted by regulations[2] made as hereinafter provided, it shall be unlawful at any time, by any means or in any manner, to pursue, hunt, take, capture, kill, attempt to take, capture, or kill, possess, offer for sale, sell, offer to barter, barter, offer to purchase, purchase, deliver for shipment, ship, export, import, cause to be shipped, exported, or imported, deliver for transportation, transport or cause to be transported, carry or cause to be carried, or receive for shipment, transportation, carriage, or export, any migratory bird, or any part, nest, or egg of any such birds, included in the terms of the conventions between the United States and Great Britain for the protection of migratory birds concluded August 16, 1916, and the United States and the United Mexican States for the protection of migratory birds and game mammals concluded February 7, 1936.

SEC. 3. That, subject to the provisions and in order to carry out the purposes of the conventions, the Secretary of Agriculture is authorized and directed, from time to time, having due regard to the zones of temperature and to the distribution, abundance, economic value, breeding habits, and times and lines of migratory flight of such birds, to determine when, to what extent, if at all, and by what means, it is compatible with the terms of the conventions to allow hunting, taking, capture, killing, possession, sale, purchase, shipment, transportation, carriage, or export of any such bird, or any part, nest, or egg thereof, and to adopt suitable regulations permitting and governing the same, in accordance with such determinations, which regulations shall become effective when approved by the President.

SEC. 4. That it shall be unlawful to ship, transport, or carry by any means whatever, from one State, Territory, or District to or through another State, Territory, or District, or to or through a foreign country, any bird, or any part, nest, or egg thereof, captured, killed, taken, shipped, transported, or carried at any time contrary to the laws of the State, Territory, or District in which it was captured, killed, or taken, or from which it was shipped, transported, or carried. It shall be unlawful to import any bird, or any part, nest, or egg thereof, captured, killed, taken, shipped, transported, or carried contrary to the laws of any Province of the Dominion of Canada in which the same was captured, killed, or taken, or from which it was shipped, transported, or carried.[3]

It shall be unlawful to import into the United States from Mexico, or to export from the United States to Mexico, any game mammal, dead or alive, or parts or products thereof, except under permit or authorization of the Secretary of Agriculture in accordance with such regulations as he shall prescribe having due regard to the laws of the United Mexican States relating to the exportation and importation of such mammals or parts or products thereof and the laws of the State, District, or Territory of the United States from or into which such mammals, parts, or products thereof are proposed to be exported or imported, and the laws of the United States forbidding importation of certain live mammals injurious to the interests of agriculture and horticulture, which regulations shall become effective as provided in section 3 hereof.

SEC. 5. That any employee of the Department of Agriculture authorized by the Secretary of Agriculture to enforce the provisions of this act shall have power, without warrant, to arrest any person committing a violation of this act in his presence or view and to take such person immediately for examination or trial before an officer or court of competent jurisdiction; shall have power to execute any warrant or other process issued by an officer or court of competent jurisdiction for the enforcement of the provisions of this act; and shall have authority, with a search warrant, to search any place. The several judges of the courts established under the laws of the United States, and United States commissioners, may, within their respective jurisdictions, upon proper oath or affirmation showing probable cause, issue warrants in all such cases. All birds or parts, nests, or eggs thereof, captured, killed, taken, shipped, transported, carried, or possessed contrary to the provisions of this act or of any regulations made pursuant thereto shall, when found, be seized by any such employee, or by any marshal, or deputy marshal, and, upon conviction of the offender or upon judgment of a court of the United States that the same were captured, killed, taken, shipped, transported, carried, or possessed contrary to the provisions of this act or of any regulation made pursuant thereto, shall be forfeited to the United States and disposed of as directed by the court having jurisdiction.

SEC. 6. That any person, association, partnership, or corporation who shall violate any of the provisions of said conventions or of this act, or who shall violate or fail to comply with any regulation made pursuant to this act, shall be deemed guilty of misdemeanor and upon conviction thereof shall be fined not more than $500 or be imprisoned not more than six months, or both.

SEC. 7. That nothing in this act shall be construed to prevent the several States and Territories from making or enforcing laws or regulations not inconsistent with the provisions of said conventions or of this act, or from making or enforcing laws or regulations which shall give further protection to migratory birds, their nests, and eggs, if such laws or regulations do not extend the open seasons for such birds beyond the dates approved by the President in accordance with section 3 of this act.

SEC. 8. That until the adoption and approval, pursuant to section 3 of this act, of regulations dealing with migratory birds and their nests and eggs, such migratory birds and their nests and eggs as are intended and used exclusively for scientific or propagating purposes may be taken, captured, killed, possessed, sold, purchased, shipped, and transported for such scientific or progagating purposes if and to the extent not in conflict with the laws of the State, Territory, or District in which they are taken, capured, killed, possessed, sold, or purchased, or in or from which they are shipped or transported if the packages containing the dead bodies or the nests or eggs of such birds when shipped and transported shall be marked on the outside thereof so as accurately and clearly to show the name and address of the shipper and the contents of the package.

SEC. 9. That there is authorized to be appropriated, from time to time, out of any money in the Treasury not otherwise appropriated, such amounts as may be necessary to carry out the provisions and to accomplish the purposes of said conventions and this act and regulations made pursuant thereto, and the Secretary of Agriculture is authorized out of such moneys to employ in the city of Washington and elsewhere such persons and means as he may deem necessary for such purpose and may cooperate with local authorities in the protection of migratory birds and make the necessary investigations connected therewith.

[1] Act of July 3, 1918, 40 Stat. 755, as amended by Act of June 20, 1936, 49 Stat. 1555—16 U. S. C. 703-711.

[2] Full text of regulations governing the taking, possession, shipment, etc., of migratory game birds may be obtained upon request to the Fish and Wildlife Service, U. S. Department of the Interior, Washington, D. C.

[3] Sec. 4 applies to both migratory and nonmigratory birds.

SEC. 10. That if any clause, sentence, paragraph, or part of this act shall, for any reason, be adjudged by any court of competent jurisdiction to be invalid, such judgement shall not affect, impair, or invalidate the remainder thereof, but shall be confined in its operation to the clause, sentence, paragraph, or part thereof directly involved in the controversy in which such judgment shall have been rendered.

SEC. 11. That all acts or parts of acts inconsistent with the provisions of this act are hereby repealed.

SEC. 12. Nothing in this act shall be construed to prevent the breeding of migratory game birds on farms and preserves and the sale of birds so bred under proper regulations for the purpose of increasing the food supply.

SEC. 13. That this act shall become effective immediately upon its passage and approval.

## FEDERAL AID TO WILDLIFE RESTORATION ACT[1]

An act to provide that the United States shall aid the States in wildlife restoration projects, and for other purposes

*Be it enacted by the Senate and House of Representatives of the United States of America in Congress assembled,* That the Secretary of Agriculture is authorized to cooperate with the States, through their respective State fish and game departments, in wildlife-restoration projects as hereinafter set forth; but no money apportioned under this Act to any State shall be expended therein until its legislature, or other State agency authorized by the State constitution to make laws governing the conservation of wildlife, shall have assented to the provision of this Act and shall have passed laws for the conservation of wildlife which shall include a prohibition against the diversion of license fees paid by hunters for any other purpose than the administration of said State fish and game department, except that, until the final adjournment of the first regular session of the legislature held after the passage of this Act, the assent of the Governor of the State shall be sufficient. The Secretary of Agriculture and the State fish and game department of each State accepting the benefits of this Act shall agree upon the wildlife-restoration projects to be aided in such State under the terms of this Act and all projects shall conform to the standards fixed by the Secretary of Agriculture.

SEC. 2. For the purposes of this Act the term "wildlife-restoration project" shall be construed to mean and include the selection, restoration, rehabilitation, and improvement of areas and land or water adaptable as feeding, resting, or breeding places for wildlife, including acquisition by purchase, condemnation, lease, or gift of such areas or estates or interests therein as are suitable or capable of being made suitable therefor, and the construction thereon or therein of such works as may be necessary to make them available for such puposes and also including such research into problems of wildlife management as may be necessary to efficient administration affecting wildlife resources, and such preliminary or incidental costs and expenses as may be incurred in and about such projects; the term "State fish and game department" shall be construed to mean and include any department or division of department of another name, or commission, or official or officials, of a State empowered under its laws to exercise the functions ordinarily exercised by a State fish and game department.

SEC. 3. An amount equal to the revenue accruing during the fiscal year ending June 30, 1939, and each fiscal year thereafter, from the tax imposed by section 610, title IV, of the Revenue Act of 1932 (47 Stat. 169), as heretofore or hereafter extended and amended, on firearms, shells, and cartridges, is hereby authorized to be set apart in the Treasury as a special fund to be known as "The Federal aid to wildlife-restoration fund" and is hereby authorized to be appropriated and made available until expended for the purposes of this Act. So much of such appropriation apportioned to any State for any fiscal year as remains unexpended at the close thereof is authorized to be made available for expenditure in that State until the close of the succeeding fiscal year. Any amount apportioned to any State under the provisions of this Act which is unexpended or unobligated at the end of the period during which it is available for expenditure on any project is authorized to be made available for expenditure by the Secretary of Agriculture in carrying out the provisions of the Migratory Bird Conservation Act.

[1] Act of Sept. 2, 1937, 50 Stat. 917—16 U. S. C. 669.

SEC. 4. So much, not to exceed 8 per centum, of the revenue covered into said fund in each fiscal year as the Secretary of Agriculture may estimate to be necessary for his expenses in the administration and execution of this Act and the Migratory Bird Conservation Act shall be deducted for that purpose, and such sum is authorized to be made available therefor until the expiration of the next succeeding fiscal year, and within sixty days after the close of such fiscal year the Secretary of Agriculture shall apportion such part thereof as remains unexpended by him, if any, and make certificate thereof to the Secretary of the Treasury and to the State fish and game departments on the same basis and in the same manner as is provided as to other amounts authorized by this Act to be apportioned among the States for such current fiscal year. The Secretary of Agriculture, after making the aforesaid deduction, shall apportion the remainder of the revenues in said fund for each fiscal year among the several States in the following manner, that is to say, one-half in the ratio which the area of each State bears to the total area of all the States and one-half in the ratio which the number of paid hunting-license holders of each State in the preceding fiscal year, as certified to said Secretary by the State fish and game departments, bears to the total number of paid hunting-license holders of all the States: *Provided,* That the apportionment for any one State shall not exceed the sum of $150,000 annually; *Provided further,* That where the apportionment to any State under this section is less than $15,000 annually, the Secretary of Agriculture may allocate not more than $15,000 of said fund to said State to carry out the purposes of this Act when said State certifies to the Secretary of Agriculture that it has set aside not less than $5,000 from its fish and game funds or has made, through its legislature, an appropriation in this amount, for said purposes.

SEC. 5. Within sixty days after the approval of this Act the Secretary of Agriculture shall certify to the Secretary of the Treasury and to each State fish and game department the sum which he has estimated to be deducted for administering and executing this Act and the Migratory Bird Conservation Act and the sum which he has apportioned to each State for the fiscal year ending June 30, 1939, and on or before February 20 next preceding the commencement of each succeeding fiscal year shall make like certificates for such fiscal year. Any State desiring to avail itself of the benefits of this Act shall notify the Secretary of Agriculture to this effect within sixty days after it has received the certification referred to in this section. The sum apportioned to any State which fails to notify the Secretary of Agriculture as herein provided is authorized to be made available for expenditure by the Secretary of Agriculture in carrying out the provisions of the Migratory Bird Conservation Act.

SEC. 6. Any State desiring to avail itself of the benefits of this Act shall by its State fish and game department submit to the Secretary of Agriculture full and detailed statements of any wildlife-restoration project proposed for that State. If the Secretary of Agriculture finds that such project meets with the standards set up by him and approves said project, the State fish and game department shall furnish to him such surveys, plans, specifications, and estimates therefor as he may require: *Provided, however,* That the Secretary of Agriculture shall approve only such projects as may be substantial in character and design and the expenditure of funds hereby authorized shall be applied only to such approved projects and if otherwise applied they shall be replaced by the State before it may participate in any further apportionment under this Act. Items included for engineering, inspection, and unforeseen contingencies in connection with any works to be constructed shall not exceed 10 per centum of the cost of such works and shall be paid by the State as a part of its contribution to the total cost of such works. If the Secretary of Agriculture approves the plans, specifications, and estimates for the project, he shall notify the State fish and game department and immediately certify the fact to the Secretary of the Treasury. The Secretary of the Treasury shall thereupon set aside so much of said fund as represents the share of the United States payable under this Act on account of such project, which sum so set aside shall not exceed 75 per centum of the total estimated cost thereof. No payment of any money apportioned under this Act shall be made on any project until such statement of the project and the plans, specifications, and estimates thereof shall have been submitted to and approved by the Secretary of Agriculture.

SEC. 7. When the Secretary of Agriculture shall find that any project approved by him has been completed or, if involving research relating to wildlife, is being conducted, in compliance with said plans and specifications, he shall cause to be paid to the proper authority of said State the amount set aside for said project: *Provided,* That the Secretary of Agriculture may, in his discretion, from time to time, make payments on said project as the same progresses; but these payments, including previous payments, if any, shall not be more than the United States' pro-rata share of the project in conformity with said plans and specifications. Any construction work and labor in each State shall be performed in accordance with its laws and under the direct supervision of the State fish and game department, subject to the inspection and approval of the Secretary of Agriculture and in accordance with rules and regulations made pursuant to this Act. The Secretary of Agriculture and the State fish and game department of each State may jointly determine at what times and in what amounts payments, as work progresses, shall be made under this Act. Such payments shall be made by the Secretary of the Treasury, on warrants drawn by the Secretary of Agriculture against the said fund to such official or officials, or depository, as may be designated by the State fish and game department and authorized under the laws of the State to receive public funds of the State.

SEC. 8. To maintain wildlife-restoration projects established under the provisions of this Act shall be the duty of the States according to their respective laws.

SEC. 9. Out of the deductions set aside for administering and executing this Act and the Migratory Bird Conservation Act, the Secretary of Agriculture is authorized to employ such assistants, clerks, and other persons in the city of Washington and elsewhere, to be taken from the eligible lists of the Civil Service; to rent or construct buildings outside of the city of Washington; to purchase such supplies, materials, equipment, office fixtures, and apparatus; and to incur such travel and other expenses, including purchase, maintenance, and hire of passenger-carrying motor vehicles, as he may deem necessary for carrying out the purposes of this Act.

SEC. 10. The Secretary of Agriculture is authorized to make rules and regulations for carrying out the provisions of this Act.

SEC. 11. The Secretary of Agriculture shall make an annual report to the Congress of the sum set apart in "The Federal aid to wildlife restoration fund," giving detailed information as to the projects and expenditures therefor.

# WHAT TO DO WHEN LOST

**Precautions.** Intelligent use of compass and map will normally prevent hunters from becoming lost from their headquarters. But when unusual conditions exist, such as being caught in a sudden snowstorm or losing one's sense of direction in the excitement of pursuing game, it is quite possible to get confused and forget the way back. Because there is no guarantee against the occurrence of such an emergency, every hunter should know how to cope with it when it does occur.

A conference with companions or guide to discuss measures which can be followed should one of the party fail to return at night should be held on the first day. This is also a good time to be sure each hunter is supplied with essential pathfinding material that will help him survive such a mishap.

**Equipment.** Everyone needs a compass and a map. (See above, p. 942.) Should some lack maps, sketches of the surrounding country can be made for them by a guide or hunter familiar with the region. Or the individual can make his own map (see pp. 942-944) by taking exploring hikes out in each of the main directions.

Besides compass and map, each hunter should always carry a stout knife and a waterproof matchbox. The knife can be pocket or belt type. Either will cut poles for emergency shelter and fuel for signal and warming fires as well as skin out big game. Four and one-half inches is a good length for sheath blades; one inch shorter will serve in pocket models. The knife should be keenly sharp and so carried that it cannot be lost. A safety strap about the handle of the belt knife holds it securely in the sheath. Smaller models can be stored in a pocket with button-down flap or tied to the belt with a rawhide thong.

The matchbox must be genuinely waterproof to resist rain and perspiration. A good test is to submerge it in water overnight. If the matches inside strike readily next morning, the box is tight. It is vitally necessary to keep this box filled. To guarantee that it is, hunters should carry an extra supply for smoking and other ordinary purposes.

These four articles comprise the very minimum of equipment one should pack to avoid being lost. Some add a light belt or pocket ax which speeds up the work of building shelters and cutting enough firewood to last an entire night. It is useful also to chop bone framework when dressing out big game. Axes add to one's load but should certainly be carried when freezing and colder temperatures prevail. Several sandwiches or candy bars or both can be profitably added to these bare essentials. If the hunter does not get lost he will eat and enjoy them anyway. But in case misfortune does strike, the food will be a big morale builder, especially if darkness prevents him from finding small game after the shelter is built.

**Self-Control.** Just as vital as these items to help a lost hunter master his predicament is a cool head. He must not submit to fear or panic when he suddenly realizes that he does not know in which direction to go. Fear and panic only make things worse. Unless a lost man forces himself to remain calm, he cannot think clearly and will have two strikes called on him at the start. After all, **what is there to fear?** Wilderness ground holds no dire hidden danger. The hunter wears warm wool clothing, he has a gun, ammunition, knife, matches, and sandwiches. Exploring pioneers have in the past traveled great unmapped spaces with no more.

Lost people who retain their self-possession are invariably found or find their own way out. A night spent under the stars may bring small discomforts but nothing serious or fatal. One can easily survive a day or two without food. But that is seldom necessary, since the hunter has his gun and small game like rabbits, grouse, or a porcupine can usually be killed. The worst thing is a blizzard or driving rain, and many times the lost man is able to build protection against that.

The first thing to do when lost is to climb a tree or hill and look for some familiar landmark. Many cases of being lost never go beyond this stage because the hunter sights a recognizable landmark and from it orients his position and that of home.

But if he does not do so he should sit down and, by thinking hard, try to recall incidents, facts, or objects encountered along his back trail that furnish clues to the direction of camp. Other lost cases end here when the hunter succeeds in unraveling enough of his route to return along it. The importance of remaining calm and unworried can be realized now. Scared minds are incapable of logical, accurate thought.

Several actions can help induce calmness. Smoking is one. Drinking water and eating a sandwich (one only now) are others. A little vigorous exercise like climbing a tree and gathering wood for a fire also assist. If he is at all jittery—and a lost hunter has plenty of reason for feeling that way—he should briskly busy himself for a few minutes or until he has been able to conquer and dispel his fear.

If a lost man decides with reasonable certainty that he is north of camp, he can produce his compass, take a southerly bearing across the country and follow it back. Should he through some dire misfortune have lost the compass or left it at camp, he can use the sun to determine direction roughly. During hunting seasons the sun usually sets considerably south of west. How much can be checked on the hunter's first evening in camp.

Even when it is covered by thin clouds the sun still casts a faint shadow and can be located by it. A match stick or knife blade stood erect on some bright surface like a thumbnail or scrap of paper will throw a dim shadow behind it. The sun lies out in front of the object and in line with this shadow.

Direction can also be determined with a watch. When the hour hand is pointed at the sun, the point halfway between that hand and the figure 12 is south. The accuracy of this stunt should also be checked on the hunter's first day in camp if he wants to play them very close to his chest.

If the hunter lacks both compass and watch he can check with certain nature signs. They are not infallible but usually prove fairly accurate when the evidence of two or more are averaged together. Moss usually (but not always) grows thickest on the side of a tree that receives the least sun because more dampness exists there. Moss deposits are accordingly thicker on the north or nearly north sides of the trunk. Good trees to test stand out by themselves where they are not heavily shaded by others. Moss can be thickest on the south face of a tree if that side is continually in deep shade.

The thickness of a tree's bark and the width of its growth rings will also help determine direction. Both are greater on the north and northeast sides of the trunk. Tests can be made with knife or ax; notches must be cut on opposite sides for comparison. The extreme top branches of pines and hemlocks sometimes point toward the rising sun or a little south of east. This sign is not so reliable as the others named and should be used only to supplement them. Better still, the hunter should make certain he never leaves camp without his compass.

When a lost man is unable definitely to figure out which way to proceed, he should stay right where he is until his companions find him or until he can see or hear the signals they will make when they realize his plight. To wait is safer than to struggle along an unknown course, because this blind travel might result in his being more lost than before. The thing he should do now is make himself as comfortable as possible for the coming night.

**Shelter.** Some shelter not too far from water is needed. It can be a big log, rock, cave, windfall, or thick clump of young trees, preferably evergreens. Sticks can be leaned against the log or rock or against a pole held by stakes driven in the ground and coniferous branches woven between them to thatch a roof. Or pieces of easily peeled bark like cedar and birch can be used in place of boughs. Sometimes a fallen log will yield large sheets of bark. Boughs are tight enough to shed snow, bark will often turn rain. Small hollows in the side of a bank or hill can be enlarged for shelter. They prove very comfortable because they are easily heated with an open fire.

When dry foliage or grass is available, a quantity should be gathered for a bed. If nothing better is possible, the hunter can sit with his back against a tree and maintain a fire several yards away. CAUTION: Extreme care must be exercised with fires kindled near thatched or bark shelters or browse beds. Their material is highly inflammable and if accidentally ignited while the hunter sleeps, could cause disaster. Especially beware of wood that tosses out burning coals while it burns.

**Fire.** As soon as the shelter is made, the hunter should gather fuel for his all-night fire. Much will be needed, much more than he probably realizes. Lacking an ax, he must rely on loose limbs lying on the ground. With an ax, sounder, easier-burning fuel can be chopped from deadfalls and lightning-killed trees. Hemlock and birch bark and rich pine make fine kindling. So do the small dead limbs projecting from the lower trunks of pines. If it has rained recently, the soaked exteriors of the limbs must be shaved off to expose their dry cores to the match.

The hunter's matchbox should be well filled because numerous trials may be necessary to ignite damp, stubborn kindling. If he runs out of matches, he can still produce a fire with a cartridge and his rifle. The bullet must first be removed; this can be loosened by laying the neck of the cartridge case on a solid surface and pounding it with the back of a knife or stone. This stretches the brass so the projectile slips out.

Discard about two-thirds of the powder in the case, stuff a piece of dry cloth in the neck, load, point the rifle into the air, and fire. Then retrieve the smouldering rag, lay it on finely shaved kindling or bark, and blow the spark into flames. Some of the discarded powder will help the spark grow, but use this cautiously to avoid being burned.

**Signals.** With his shelter and a fire, the lost hunter can be very comfortable in normal hunting-season weather. In the morning he should climb a tree or hill and look around for the signal fire his companions have kindled. Failing to discover it, he should make his own signal. The fire should be started on high ground if possible and its flames smothered with damp, sappy fuels that produce a thick smoke. Green pine branches are good. So is the damp sawdust found at abandoned logging camps. Fires started at sunrise are especially effective be-

PLATE I. A Brush Lean-to.

cause early morning air is often still and the vapor rises in a tall column visible for miles.

A lost hunter can signal with his rifle if he has enough ammunition. Some cartridges should be saved for shooting food if that proves necessary. Standard distress signals consist of three quick shots. Other signals that are used under varying circumstances include loud shouts, whistle blasts, flashes from mirror (daytime) or flashlight (night), and waves of shirt, coat, or blanket, all in series of three. The standard response is two of the same kind.

When one hunts without companions upon whom he can depend for aid if lost, he will have to work his way out alone. His best help now is hard thinking about the back trail. Every effort should be made to recall details which will help point the way home. Old trails in the forest lacking signs of recent use should be ignored. They are probably abandoned logging roads that lead nowhere. It is safer to follow a river, even a mountain range or ridge, walking downhill if possible. A map is invaluable now to show where these things lead.

**Rescue.** A lost person knows that some recognizable landmark exists off in *some* direction from him. The problem is to find it. When leaving an emergency overnight camp to search, he should walk in a straight line, using sun or compass as a guide to avoid circling to one side in a gradual curve as unobserving hikers sometimes do. It may be wise to blaze the trail as he goes. Then if he fails to sight a familiar object that shows his position, the hunter can return to the starting point and try again in a different direction.

Hunters who pack in with horses have often found camp after being lost by merely giving their mount its head and permitting it to choose the trail. On the other hand, it is unwise to trust an ordinary dog's instinct, as his nose is likely to lead him anywhere. Trained animals, of course, are a different matter.

It is equally important that the hunters back in camp remain cool and think clearly when a companion fails to appear at sundown. They should *not* light signal fires or fire signal shots if the hour is late, for that would encourage the lost man to struggle on in the darkness, which is dangerous because mishaps occur more easily and frequently at night.

But rescue work should start promptly in the morning. A signal fire should be kindled and when the early mist is gone, someone should climb a tree or high point to look for the lost person's rising column of smoke. One hunter should stay in camp to guard and feed the fire. This watchman can also fire a signal shot every ten minutes. If he times each exactly by watch, the missing hunter will recognize the sounds as signals by their regularity.

The rest of the party should begin their search as soon as the horizon has cleared. Some delay is usually necessary to obtain good visibility and to allow time for the lost man's signal smoke to show up conspicuously. If his general location is known, all can concentrate on that area. Otherwise every quarter must be combed. The most likely, of course, are covered first.

Searchers should proceed in a straight line, using a compass if necessary to prevent straying. If a crooked trail must be followed because of rough ground, rescuers can blaze their path to be sure of finding their own way home. They should also fire a gun or shout loudly at intervals and then stand still for a minute, listening for a reply. This may prevent them from passing the lost hunter unnoticed on his way in.

After each half-mile rescuers should climb a tree and look for smoke signals. NOTE: Before a lost hunter leaves his emergency camp to seek his way home, he should carefully extinguish both signal and warming fires to eliminate danger of their spreading through the timber and also to save his rescuers unnecessary steps in walking to the place he has quitted.

If a hunter has been missing overnight, rescuers can carry food and a thermos bottle of hot coffee for his refreshment.

Getting lost is a very unsatisfactory business for all concerned and the hunter should do everything in his power to avoid it. Caution, keen observation, and the judicious use of compass and map should be employed. As with other misfortunes, prevention is better than cure. But should a cure ever be required, the hunter should remember that a cool head coupled with clear thinking is the best at his command.

# APPENDIX

## OPEN SEASONS

## GAME CONDITIONS AND REGULATIONS

## GLOSSARY

## INDEX

# OPEN SEASONS

The following schedule lists the various big game, small game, upland game birds and shorebirds with the various American states and Alaska, Canadian provinces, and Mexico, which have open hunting on this game. (Waterfowl shooting is governed by Federal regulations which vary from year to year.)

## BIG GAME

### Antelope

Idaho
Montana
Nevada
New Mexico
South Dakota
Texas
Utah
Wyoming

Alberta
Saskatchewan

### Bears

Alaska
California
Colorado
Florida
Georgia
Idaho
Louisiana
Maine
Michigan
Minnesota
Montana
New Hampshire
New Mexico
New York
North Carolina
Pennsylvania
Tennessee
Texas
Utah
Vermont
Virginia
Washington
West Virginia
Wisconsin
Wyoming

Alberta
British Columbia
Manitoba
New Brunswick
Northwest Territories
Nova Scotia
Ontario
Quebec
Saskatchewan

Mexico

### Boars

North Carolina
Tennessee

### Caribou

Alaska

Alberta
British Columbia
Manitoba
Northwest Territories
Quebec
Saskatchewan
Yukon

### Deer

Alabama
Alaska
Arizona
Arkansas
California
Colorado
Florida
Georgia
Idaho
Louisiana
Maine
Maryland
Massachusetts
Michigan
Minnesota
Mississippi
Missouri
Montana
Nevada
New Hampshire
New Jersey
New Mexico
New York
North Carolina
North Dakota
Ohio
Oklahoma
Oregon
Pennsylvania
South Carolina
South Dakota
Tennessee
Texas
Utah
Vermont
Virginia
Washington
West Virginia
Wisconsin
Wyoming

Alberta
British Columbia
Manitoba
New Brunswick
Northwest Territories
Nova Scotia
Ontario
Quebec
Saskatchewan
Yukon

Mexico

### Elk

Colorado
Idaho
Montana
New Mexico
Oregon
South Dakota
Utah
Washington
Wyoming

Alberta
British Columbia
Manitoba
Saskatchewan

### Moose

Alaska
Idaho
Montana
Wyoming

Alberta
British Columbia
Manitoba
Northwest Territories
Ontario
Quebec
Saskatchewan
Yukon

### Mountain Goat

Alaska
Idaho
Montana

Alberta
British Columbia
Northwest Territories
Yukon

### Mountain Sheep

Alaska
Wyoming

Alberta
British Columbia
Northwest Territories
Yukon

### Peccary

Texas

Mexico

## SMALL GAME

### Foxes

Alabama
Arkansas
Connecticut
Delaware
Florida
Georgia
Illinois
Indiana
Iowa
Maine
Massachusetts
Michigan
Mississippi
Missouri
Nebraska
New Hampshire
North Carolina
North Dakota
Ohio
Pennsylvania
South Carolina
Tennessee
Virginia
West Virginia
Wisconsin

Quebec

Mexico

### Hares

Alaska
Colorado
Connecticut
Florida
Louisiana
Massachusetts
Michigan
Minnesota
Nebraska
Nevada
New Hampshire
New Jersey
Pennsylvania
Rhode Island
Vermont
Washington
West Virginia
Wisconsin

Nova Scotia
Prince Edward Island
Quebec

Mexico

#### Opossum

Florida
Maryland
Massachusetts
Michigan
Mississippi
Missouri
Montana
Ohio
Oklahoma
South Carolina
Tennessee
West Virginia

#### Rabbits

Alabama
Alaska
Arizona
Arkansas
California
Colorado
Connecticut
Delaware
Florida
Georgia
Illinois
Indiana
Iowa
Kansas
Kentucky
Louisiana
Maine
Maryland
Massachusetts
Michigan
Minnesota
Mississippi
Missouri
Montana
Nebraska
Nevada
New Hampshire
New Jersey
New York
North Carolina
North Dakota
Ohio
Oklahoma
Pennsylvania
Rhode Island
South Carolina
Tennessee
Vermont
Virginia
Washington
West Virginia
Wisconsin

Nova Scotia
Ontario
Prince Edward Island
Quebec
Saskatchewan

Mexico

#### Raccoon

California
Connecticut
Maine
Maryland
Massachusetts
Michigan
Minnesota
Mississippi
Missouri
Nebraska
New Jersey
Ohio
Oregon
Pennsylvania
Rhode Island
South Carolina
Tennessee
Vermont
West Virginia
Wisconsin

Nova Scotia
Ontario
Quebec

Mexico

#### Squirrels

Alabama
Alaska
Arkansas
California
Connecticut
Delaware
Florida
Georgia
Illinois
Indiana
Iowa
Kansas
Kentucky
Louisiana
Maine
Maryland
Massachusetts
Michigan
Minnesota
Mississippi
Missouri
Nebraska
New Hampshire
New Jersey
New Mexico
New York
North Carolina
Ohio
Oklahoma
Oregon
Pennsylvania
Rhode Island
South Carolina
Tennessee
Texas
Vermont
Virginia
Washington
West Virginia
Wisconsin

Ontario
Prince Edward Island

#### Woodchuck

Connecticut
Indiana
Iowa
Massachusetts
Michigan
Missouri
Montana
Nebraska
New Jersey
New York
Ohio
Pennsylvania
Tennessee
West Virginia
Wisconsin

## UPLAND GAME BIRDS

#### Chukar Partridge

Nevada

#### Doves

Alabama
Arizona
Arkansas
California
Colorado
Delaware
Florida
Georgia
Idaho
Illinois
Kansas
Kentucky
Louisiana
Maryland
Minnesota
Mississippi
Missouri
Montana
Nebraska
Nevada
New Mexico
North Carolina
Oklahoma
Oregon
Pennsylvania
South Carolina
Tennessee
Texas
Washington

#### Grouse

Alaska
Colorado
Connecticut
Georgia
Kentucky
Maine
Maryland
Massachusetts
Michigan
Montana
Nevada
New Hampshire
New Jersey
New Mexico
New York
North Carolina
North Dakota
Ohio
Oregon
Pennsylvania
Rhode Island
South Dakota
Tennessee
Texas
Vermont
Virginia
West Virginia

Alberta
British Columbia
Manitoba
New Brunswick
Northwest Territories
Nova Scotia
Prince Edward Island
Quebec
Yukon

#### Hungarian Partridge

Idaho
Indiana
Iowa
Minnesota
Montana
North Carolina
Ohio
Oregon
Pennsylvania
Wisconsin

Alberta
British Columbia
Nova Scotia
Ontario
Prince Edward Island

Mexico

#### Pheasants

California
Colorado
Connecticut
Delaware
Idaho
Illinois
Indiana
Iowa
Kansas
Maine
Maryland
Massachusetts
Michigan
Minnesota
Montana
Nebraska
Nevada
New Hampshire
New Jersey
New Mexico
New York
North Dakota
Ohio
Oregon
Pennsylvania
Rhode Island

South Dakota
Utah
Vermont
Virginia
Washington
Wisconsin
Wyoming

Alberta
British Columbia
Manitoba
Saskatchewan
Yukon

PIGEONS

Arizona
California
New Mexico
Oregon
Washington

British Columbia

QUAILS

Alabama
Arizona
Arkansas
California
Colorado
Connecticut
Delaware
Florida
Georgia
Idaho
Illinois
Indiana
Iowa
Kansas
Kentucky
Louisiana
Maryland
Massachusetts
Minnesota
Mississippi
Missouri
Nebraska
Nevada
New Jersey
New Mexico
North Carolina
Oklahoma
Oregon
Pennsylvania
Rhode Island
South Carolina
Tennessee
Texas
Utah
Vermont
Virginia
Washington
West Virginia
Wisconsin

British Columbia

SPRUCE PARTRIDGE

New Brunswick

TURKEY

Alabama
Arkansas
Florida
Georgia
Louisiana
Maryland
New Mexico
North Carolina
Pennsylvania
South Carolina
Texas
Virginia
West Virginia

Mexico

WOODCOCK

Arkansas
Connecticut
Delaware
Georgia
Indiana
Louisiana
Maine
Maryland
Massachusetts
Michigan
Minnesota
Mississippi
Missouri
New Hampshire
New Jersey
New York
Ohio
Oklahoma
Pennsylvania
Rhode Island
Vermont
Virginia
Washington
West Virginia
Wisconsin

New Brunswick
Nova Scotia
Ontario
Prince Edward Island
Quebec

## SHOREBIRDS

GALLINULES

(Open season in every state *except* California, Idaho, Montana, Nevada, Oregon, Tennessee, Washington)

Quebec

RAILS

(Open season in every state *except* California, Idaho, Montana, Nevada, Oregon, Tennessee, Washington)

Alberta
Manitoba
Northwest Territories
Ontario
Quebec
Yukon

SNIPES

Alberta
British Columbia
New Brunswick
Nova Scotia
Ontario
Prince Edward Island
Quebec
Saskatchewan

# GAME CONDITIONS AND REGULATIONS

## ALABAMA — AREA: 51,609 square miles

**General Summary.** Game conditions for Alabama are good on the whole, with an exceptional increase in quail, the most important of all game to the hunter, as well as a rise in the dove and turkey population.

Second to the upland game birds in popularity are the small-game animals, rabbits and squirrels, which furnish much sport and table food in this state. In anticipation of more hunters, the Conservation Department has established restrictions for rabbit shooting by limiting the bag and shortening the season. This is the first bag limit ever placed on rabbits since game protection was inaugurated in Alabama about 40 years ago. The squirrel population is presently at a low period in its normal fluctuation.

Alabama has only fair waterfowl shooting, for the state is a little too far inland for the birds which travel the Atlantic flyway, and too far east of the Mississippi flyway. Of the migratory birds, ducks, geese, brant, coot, and sora rail are taken in fair numbers each year.

Deer are the only big-game animals hunted in Alabama, and despite increased hunting pressure the species has increased.

**State Conservation.** Alabama is endeavoring to educate the public on the need and methods of conservation by information and instruction in the importance of caring for its forests. One of the educational channels is directed at the farm youths of F.F.A. and 4-H Clubs. They are taught timber management, planting, and fire-control methods. In recent years Alabama has suffered an increased loss from forest fires. In 1946, for example, a total of 15,683 fires burned on 879,845 acres—the great bulk of which was unprotected land. The total fire loss to the forests was nearly $1,000,000. Normally, as care of the forests goes, so goes much of the natural habitat for wildlife, and the resultant abundance or scarcity.

Alabama started a farmer-sportsman co-operative program in 1946 which proved to be popular among both the sportsmen and the farmers.

The Conservation Department formerly raised birds in captivity for restocking purposes on a state quail farm, but that farm has been closed. However, game management includes a deer and turkey sanctuary in Clarke County where both turkey and deer are trapped for restocking purposes. The Department also supervises a program where lespedeza bicolor and partridge pea seed are distributed free of charge

to sportsmen who are interested in providing food and cover for wildlife. In one year seed sufficient to plant 575 miles of food strips 15 feet wide was given away. This method of providing a natural habitat has proved more successful than trying to stock areas with pen-raised birds.

**Licenses.** License fees are as follows:

| | |
|---|---|
| Resident state | $ 3.00 |
| Resident county | 1.00 |
| Non-resident annual | 25.00 |
| Non-resident seven days | 5.00 |

Hunting licenses are sold in each county seat by the office of the Judge of Probate and, in towns other than the county seat, they are sold at sporting-goods stores which are required to have special permission from the Director of Conservation.

**Regulations.** Game birds or animals may be taken with a shotgun not larger than 10 gauge. They may not be taken by means of an automatic-loading or hand-operated repeating shotgun capable of holding more than three shells, the magazine of which has not been cut off or plugged with a one-piece metal or wooden filler incapable of removal through the loading end, so that the capacity of the gun is not more than three shells at one time in the magazine and chamber combined.

Dogs are used for all kinds of hunting except for turkeys. Bird dogs may be trained during the closed hunting season, but not with the use of a gun.

No person is allowed to hunt wild turkey by means of a live decoy.

**Seasons.** Game animals and birds for which there are open seasons are:

| | |
|---|---|
| Deer | Coot (poule d'eaux or mud hen) |
| Opossum | Ducks |
| Rabbit | Geese |
| Raccoon | Mourning dove |
| Squirrel | Sora rail |
| Bobwhite quail | Wild turkey |
| Brant | |

There is no closed season on fox.

## ALASKA

AREA: 586,400 square miles

**General Summary.** If Alaska's big-game herds had anything to say about it, they would call an immediate halt to further talk about settling a population of two million people in their country. Already they have taken heavy losses from newcomers pouring in over the new Alaska Highway, flying in over the peaks, or coming the slow but sure steamer routes. The giant moose, the wandering white-necked caribou, the snow-colored mountain sheep, and the ambling grizzly, have learned one terrible fact about the Territory's increasing number of human beings; nearly all of them carry guns.

The result of all this is that Alaska's wild game is deserting the highways. The moose have pushed deeper into wilderness bogs; the sheep and the goats have mounted higher into the snow-capped peaks; the caribou's nomadic way of life is leading them away from the smell and sound of man into the still unexplored Arctic fastnesses. No longer are bears a setup for passing motorists; their camp plundering now takes place at dead of night. Unquestionably, the doubling of Alaska's white population in six years by an influx of airfield workers, road builders, and defense planners has created a profound change in big-game habits.

It is still good hunting land, of course, as compared with most areas in the states. Any region that has a half-million bears, moose, caribou, sheep, goats, and deer is bound to be highly attractive to rifle-bearing sportsmen. Any place that produces 8 species of grouse, three of which turn white in winter, cannot fail in its appeal to upland bird hunters. Any section of the continent that raises 7 species and subspecies of geese and 26 kinds of ducks, the whole totaling into the millions, must necessarily provide exciting waterfowl shooting. Newcomers to the Territory find no fault with the wildlife. To many of them it is like hitting the jackpot. Only the old-time resident is aware of what is happening as more and more guns ride the shoulders of the new sportsman army in a postwar invasion of America's last frontier.

Alaska is a large expanse stretching over an area large enough to blanket the United States from North Dakota to South Carolina and westward to California. For descriptive purposes it needs to be broken down into four main segments, Southeast Alaska, Central Alaska, the Arctic Plains, and the Aleutian Islands. Each of these has its own climatic conditions, its own type of game.

The best-known part of the Territory is Southeastern Alaska, which is only 650 miles north of Seattle, Washington. Its rugged, glaciated coastal valleys and mountains and its hundreds of heavily timbered islands are more or less a continuation of Puget Sound and British Columbia terrain. Clouds rolling in from the North Pacific bathe the barrier peaks with fog and much rainfall. Rivers born of the heavy precipitation furnish ideal spawning grounds for salmon which in turn provide irresistible attraction to black, brown, and grizzly bears. No other part of Alaska has such amazing concentrations. One cannot go ashore on any of the larger islands between Ketchikan and Juneau without seeing their padded trails. Some islands, notably Prince of Wales, Dall, Kuiu, and Kupreanof, harbor only black bears. Others, such as Admiralty, Baranof, and Chichagof, have only grizzlies and brownies, while on the mainland there is a mixture of all three, plus the blue glacier bear, which is merely a rare color phase of the black bear. Famous for its bears is Admiralty Island where scientists have named four kinds of grizzlies and one species of brown. Oddly enough, Admiralty's brown bear actually is nearly coal black. Here on Admiralty Island, density of bear population probably exceeds any other place in Alaska, or the world, because its 1600 square miles hold at least that many bears.

Scattered through all the timbered islands is the small Sitkan deer, a sub-variety of the blacktail which here reaches the natural northern limit of its range. Along the high cliffs of the mainland and on Baranof Island where it was transplanted many years ago, the white mountain goat is found in fair abundance. In the larger river valleys of Southeast Alaska a few moose, mostly strays from near-by Canada, wander down to tidewater. Timber wolves, most of them black or darkly grizzled, forage in such numbers over some of the islands and mainland as to call forth a bounty of $25 from the territorial legislature.

Thousands of shallow bays, tidal flats, and river mouths provide excellent waterfowl shooting. A very dark form of the Canada goose nests in this region, and rarely leaves even in severest winters. A number of greenhead mallards also stay throughout the year, while in the fall additional thousands of widgeons, pintails, green-wing teal, gadwalls, shovelers, scaups, and golden-eyes sweep through on their way south to western states. A flight of approximately 50,000 snow geese down from the Arctic loiter for a month or more at the mouth of the Stikine River before moving down to Oregon's grain stubbles.

Upland bird shooting is only fair in Southeastern Alaska; there are a few big blue grouse, a scattering of Franklin "fool hens" on Prince of Wales and Zarembo Islands, odd flocks of ptarmigan along the hillsides. Rainfall is too heavy.

Northwesterly across the Gulf of Alaska in the great mainland mass of the Territory lie the principal big game fields of the Territory. Here the country is more open, with rolling hills and bare mountaintops. Kenai Peninsula, long famed for its giant moose, also pastures mountain sheep and goats, as well as black, brown, and grizzly bears. The Kenai grizzly is the largest of its kind in existence. Along both sides of the Alaska railroad which runs from the seaport of Seward 471 miles northward to Fairbanks, the high mountain slopes hold scattering bands of caribou as well.

Anchorage, 114 miles from the coast, and the largest city in Alaska, is a favorite outfitting center. From this busy airport hunters fly not only to Rainy Pass, Talkeetna, Wood River, and other noted game fields, but also to the island home of the great Kodiak brown bear. A somewhat longer flight lands sportsmen far out on the Alaska Peninsula where another huge bear fully as large as the Kodiak variety is found. Many guides who have hunted both species claim that the Peninsula giant bear is the larger of the two. Actual measured hides and skulls show little difference between big males of either variety.

In the past few years the bears have shown better ability to adapt themselves to increasing human activities than most big-game animals. A law passed in 1925 prohibiting the sale of brown or grizzly hides, and the further fact that the flesh is inedible, has left little incentive for a native Alaskan to kill one. The black bear, in particular, has in some places such as Kenai Peninsula and the Yukon Flats become a pest and is currently believed to be killing many moose calves. At the same time the moose is extending its range into remoter areas in an effort to push beyond the reach of hunters sallying forth from sizable communities like Anchorage and Fairbanks. The worst of its foes unquestionably is the man who scouts wide stretches of country in a small, pontoon-equipped airplane, locates his bull, and lands on a near-by pothole for the kill. Some states have been driven to considering legislation curbing this kind of hunting. Alaska must do the same.

Hard hunting has forced the white mountain sheep back from the highways but not far enough to escape the eyes of an airplane pilot. It has dwindled in numbers, although not entirely through hunting, because in McKinley National Park, where it is afforded complete protection, the Dall sheep has also decreased. Wolves, coyotes, and moose have claimed many. Today, a non-resident hunter may journey to Alaska with a fair assurance that his guide will show him a full curled head, but it is likely to be an expensive back-country trip, employing both planes and pack horses.

There was a long period in Alaskan history when caribou hunting was no more exciting than shooting a cow in a barnyard, but those days are gone forever. In the early 1920's herds by the tens of thousands migrated across the railroad right of way between Broad Pass and Cantwell, occasionally holding up trains. In the same lush years other armies of the antlered legion totaling past the million mark swarmed across the upper Yukon River between Circle and Dawson. Auto drivers in the vicinity of Eagle and Summit Passes, Donnelly Dome, and Black Rapids Glacier often could not avoid hitting them with their cars. One summer near Jack Wade Creek miners watched the swaying, rocking-chair heads march by for 25 straight days.

Nobody knows what happened. Possibly the routes of migration would have changed in any event. More probably, stepped-up auto traffic in the war years, extensive, still-continuing road building and airfield construction are the chief reasons for drastic declines among Alaska's most abundant game animal. The situation has been likened to that which reduced buffalo populations in the plains from 60,000,000 to a few scattered hundreds within a human generation. At any rate, Alaska's caribou are far below normal and the herds appear to be drifting northward through low mountain passes to the unsurveyed Arctic tundra. Small groups numbering several thousands still provide thrills for newcomers along the highways north of Fairbanks. But old sourdoughs, shoveling thin pay dirt in their sluice boxes, look up from their labor long enough to tell you these are just ragged remnants of early-day runs when the "brush on the mountains seemed to be moving" and the Yukon River was "filled bank to bank" with swimming animals.

Little affected so far by Alaska's developmental pains is the polar bear of the Arctic Ocean rim. Spending a good part of its life far from land on the floating ice packs, only a few of them wander close enough to Eskimo villages to be shot. Occasionally, a hardy white hunter flies to distant Point Barrow, Wainwright, Point Hope, or Cape Prince of Wales to pick up a trophy, though on the whole Nanook, the ice bear, is faring well. It is noteworthy that the caribou, most abundant of Alaska big game, is causing grave concern on the part of local game commissioners, while the polar bear, always least numerous, has not been hurt to any measurable extent.

Another game animal found in its usual numbers is the white mountain goat. It takes a real man to get a goat, say Alaska's guides. There are no shortcuts—no escalators leading up the precipitous, icy slopes where Billy clings to ledges on which a man can scarcely find a fingerhold. In Southeastern Alaska, on the Kenai, and on the square-cut faces of the jagged mountains at the head of Cook Inlet, the mountain goat is safe from all but the nerviest, and perhaps the luckiest, of hunters. Where their ranges overlap, there is considerable evidence to support the belief that the goats are taking over some of the mountain sheep ranges.

Shotguns, once scorned by most old-time residents, are coming into common use in recent years. Throughout nearly all of interior and northern Alaska upland game birds are plentiful. But all the species—ruffed, spruce, and sharp-tailed grouse, willow, rock, and white-tailed ptarmigan—vary greatly in abundance from year to year. In a more or less regular cycle extending over a period of nine or ten years the birds build up into immense flocks totaling into the tens of millions. Suddenly, disaster strikes among them, and for a season or two only a few strays are found. Then the flocks increase steadily, affording excellent shooting until an epizootic disease similar in effect to the better-known rabbit sickness lays them low once more. For this reason, shotgunners contemplating upland bird shooting trips to the Territory will do well to consult with the Alaska Game Commission at Juneau to make sure they have picked a big year.

While the vast Bering Sea and Arctic Ocean marshes furnish ideal nesting grounds for several millions of ducks and geese, residents north of the Gulf of Alaska have but little opportunity to gun them. On September 1, which is the earliest day of shooting permitted under the Migratory Bird Treaty Act and Regulations, the birds are mostly winging southward. Ice forms on the northeastern Alaska potholes by September 10. Nor do southeastern Alaska gunners get a crack at these Arctic-nesting birds. Their shooting consists for the most part of ducks and geese breeding locally. The great bulk of northern nesters avoid the flight down through the timbered islands of Southwest Alaska and favor, instead, numerous routes which carry them eastward into Canada before swinging south through inland valleys to wintering grounds extending all the way across the southern United States from California to Florida.

Many attempts have been made to stock Alaska with various types of pheasants. Hardy, though little-known, varieties such as cheer, reeves, kaleege, and brown-eared pheasants have been tried with little success. Ring-necked and Mongolian species turned loose around the farms in the Matanuska Valley have survived, but give little promise of extending their range into natural cover.

The most successful game transplantation in Alaska was that of taking buffaloes from the National Bison Range in Montana and liberating them near Big Delta, 100 miles south of Fairbanks. In prehistoric times a giant bison ranged widely over Alaska—in fact, the great herds of our western plains came originally from the Old World through Alaska—but in modern times there were no bison this far north until 1928. Now the Alaska herd has increased from 19 to 500 or more. Because the pasturage there is practically unlimited, this northern group may some day outnumber all others. It is planned in time to permit supervised shooting of surplus bulls.

Also an item for future consideration is elk shooting on Afognak Island. In 20 years a small shipment of Olympic elk secured by trading mountain goats to the State of Washington has grown to 500, and these show a tendency to swim across the turbulent salt-water straits to larger Kodiak Island. On Nunivak Island in Bering Sea, a herd of musk-ox imported from Greenland to replace native Alaska stock wiped out by whalers a century ago is slowly building up. From this base flock it is planned to reseed these queer, shaggy beasts to various points along the Arctic coast where they were formerly found.

There are two principal reasons why Alaska rates as a great game field today. First is its size—one-fifth as large as the 48 states. Second is the fact that it has always been sparsely inhabited. If it carried human population comparable to any of the individual states, its big game might have been whittled down to the vanishing point long ago. Because of severe winter conditions which may limit the carrying capacity of the winter ranges to less than a tenth of summer pasturage, big-game animals increase but slowly in Alaska and soon show the effects of what could in other places be termed "moderate hunting." Throughout most of the area timber wolves ravage the herds without mercy.

In spite of these natural hazards, in spite, even, of increasing tolls taken by unprecedented human settlement, the Territory still rates highest among the big-game fields of the continent. Nowhere else, certainly, will the sportsman find 32 species and sub-species of bears—black, white, blue, brown, and grizzly—totaling in all over 100,000. No other region can produce a moose to match the dark giant of the Kenai and Rainy Pass. No other waterfowl breeding grounds excel the tremendous stretches of the Yukon-Kuskokwim Delta.

For the non-resident, big-game hunting has been strictly regulated ever since passage of the Alaska Game Laws in 1925. The license fee is $50 and the hunter must be accompanied in the field by a registered guide. From a list which may be procured by writing to the Alaska Game Commission at Juneau, the prospective hunter makes his selection and writes to the guides concerning length of hunt and terms. It is well to do this several months ahead of time. Bear hunting is usually best in the spring, from late April to early June. All other big game must be taken in the fall period which extends, for the various species, from late August to winter.

**Conservation.** The Alaska Game Commission enforces the regulations set forth in the Alaska Game Law, the Migratory Bird Treaty Act, and other Federal laws relating to the protection of wildlife in the Territory of Alaska. On Alaska's bird and animal refuges, most of which are administered by the Fish and Wildlife Service through its representatives in Alaska, wild animals and birds are specially protected. In addition, all hunting is prohibited in any national park, monument, or posted national forest area. In other areas where birds and animals are protected in the Territories, emphasis is placed on the hunting curtailment of moose, caribou, mountain sheep and goat, also large brown and grizzly bears.

Several years ago the U. S. Fish and Wildlife Service, acting through its operating agency in the Territory, the Alaska Game Commission, set aside certain areas for the protection of important species. Bear refuges total 3864 square miles; mountain sheep, 5096 square miles; mountain goats, 7444 square miles; moose, 11,307 square miles; caribou, 8829 square miles; Sitkan deer, 4860 square miles. But additional protection in the way of law enforcement and predatory-animal control lags far behind current demands. While the Service there has stretched its funds by the use of light aircraft for patrols and game counts, there is no denying the acute need for larger appropriations if it is to meet the impact of many thousands of new resident hunters. The wildlife refuges include the Aleutian Islands, the chain of islands extending westward 1200 miles from the Alaska Peninsula, which is maintained for the protection of native birds and game animals, the encouragement of fisheries, and the propagation of reindeer and fur animals. Chamisso Island is a reservation about 1¼ miles long and ½ mile wide, and is one of the most important breeding rookeries of Arctic birds along the northwest coast of Alaska. Forrester Island is a breeding place for various kinds of sea birds. Hazen Bay refuge comprises the islands of Nunivakchak and Krigegag and was established for migratory birds and other wildlife. A great many of the ducks and geese nest on these islands. Hazy Islands are a group of islands in southeastern Alaska which have been set aside as a breeding place for numerous sea birds. Kenai National Moose Range is an area of 2,000,000 acres on Kenai Peninsula set aside to protect the natural breeding and feeding range of the giant Kenai moose. Kodiak National Wildlife Refuge is an area of 1,957,000 acres set aside to protect the natural feeding and breeding ranges of brown bears and other wildlife on Kodiak and Uganik Islands. Nunivak Island, located in the Bering Sea off the west coast of Alaska, has been set apart for use in conducting experiments in the crossing and propagation of reindeer and native caribou and also as a preserve and breeding ground for native birds, wild game, and fur-bearing animals. A herd of 115 musk-ox, reintroduced from Greenland, is now maintained on this refuge.

**Licenses.** License fees are as follows:

| | |
|---|---|
| Resident | $ 2.00 |
| Non-resident general | 50.00 |
| Non-resident small game and fishing | 10.00 |
| Alien general | 100.00 |
| Registered guide | 10.00 |

Application for a hunting license or permit should be addressed to the Alaska Game Commission at Juneau.

**Regulations.** Game animals may be taken only with a shotgun (not larger than 10 gauge and not capable of holding more than three shells), or rifle or pistol using center-fire cartridges only. Grouse and ptarmigan only may be taken with a shotgun (not larger than 10 gauge and not capable of holding more than three shells), rifle, pistol, bow and arrow, or spear. Non-game birds may be taken by any means, except by the use of poison.

Non-residents of the Territory or aliens taking game animals (except Federal officials engaged in wildlife investigations) are required to employ a registered guide. To be eligible for a guide license a person must be a resident citizen who has lived in Alaska for five years prior to application. The Game Commission tests an applicant by written and oral examination. The license must be renewed annually.

**Seasons.** Game animals and birds for which there are open seasons are:

| | |
|---|---|
| Bear (large brown, grizzly, and black) | Moose |
| Caribou | Mountain goat |
| Deer | Mountain sheep |

There is no closed season on:

| | |
|---|---|
| Coyote | Rabbit |
| Hare | Squirrel |
| Marmot | Wolf |
| Polar bear | Wolverine |

## ARIZONA AREA: 113,909 square miles

**General Summary.** Arizona, like most of the other southwestern states, is faced with game problems resulting from vast arid areas and sparsely timbered mountains. The primary problem facing the hunter, at least so far as big-game hunting is concerned, is the inaccessibility of the areas where the game is most plentiful.

The whitetail and the mule deer are the two species of importance to the hunter. Mule deer range practically the entire state, with the best areas lying in the Kaibab National Forest, the Mogollon Rim, and along the eastern border. Whitetail deer are found primarily in the southeast, although they are fairly plentiful along the central section of the Mogollon Rim and in the extreme eastern area. The desert mule deer are most plentiful along the margin of the Colorado River, which forms the western boundary of the state.

Approximately 35,000 hunters hunt deer in the state, but the success ratio is only about 15 per cent, which is well under that of several other states. The Arizona deer are not easy to hunt, for they are more plentiful in the open terrain, where long shots are the rule rather than the exception.

The antelope, once very plentiful in Arizona, is a popular game animal with hunters, but hunting pressure has resulted in reducing the numbers to a point where more rigid regulations have become necessary. The principal antelope range is a strip running from east to west across the northern third of the state. As a result of increased protection and intensive predator control, the antelope is making a slow but definite recovery. Until the animal has made a more positive recovery it will remain on the protected list.

Another popular game animal, the desert bighorn sheep, has been on the closed list for many years, but two Federal refuges which have been created for their preservation offer hope for their future.

Native elk have been introduced by local sportsmen, and these animals, followed by subsequent shipments from Yellowstone National Park, were released in the mountainous east central section of the state. They increased sufficiently to allow a limited hunt in 1946, but an open season apparently is not probable until they are more widely distributed.

Almost every year approximately 50 Arizona hunters participate in a hunt for wild buffalo. The original herd acquired by the state numbered about 80, but is now about 250. This figure is the generally accepted maximum for the available range, and the natural increase each year is taken off by sport hunting. The Arizona buffalo comprise the only herd in the United States today roaming at large on unfenced land. This animal is capable of absorbing a lot of ill-placed lead, and his uncertain temper and massive build make near misses a source of real danger.

The mountain lion is not protected, but although pursued as a predator it is excellent and strenuous hunting in rough country where an excellent pack of lion dogs and hardy horses are necessary.

In spite of a growing interest in hunting the peccary, or javelina, an animal peculiar to the Southwest, his numbers are gradually increasing. The peccary inhabits practically all of the southeastern quarter of Arizona. His natural range varies from swamp land to mountain elevations up to 6500 feet, but he usually is found in desert foothills and along watercourses. The javelina is cautious, alert, and speedy afoot, and so is difficult to hunt.

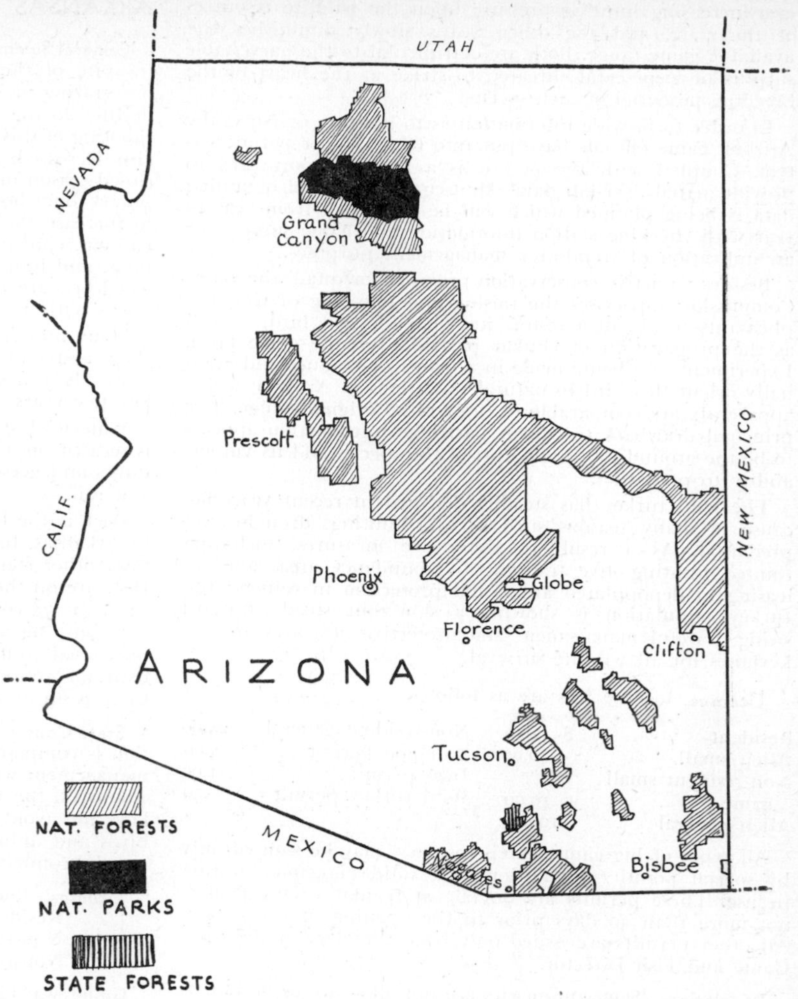


Neither upland game birds nor waterfowl are plentiful in Arizona, as water, food, and cover are all inadequate. Of the upland birds, the Gambel quail is most widely hunted as both the Mearns and scaled quail have decreased almost to the point of extinction for sport hunting purposes. Water diversions for irrigation have resulted in some restriction in the range of quail in Arizona, and clean farming methods and range utilization have tended to decrease both ground forage and protective cover for the birds. The Arizona Game and Fish Commission is working on an effective range-extension program for the conservation of quail. In some places water is the only natural factor lacking to provide a suitable range, and water-holding devices have been constructed, or wells drilled. In the vast Cochise County region quail-development plots have been instituted, where plots are fenced off to prevent access by livestock. Livestock growers have entered into cooperative agreement with the Game Commission, thus guaranteeing ground cover and forage.

Of the migratory doves, the mourning or turtle dove is the most prominent, being plentiful throughout the state. The white-winged dove is neither as widely distributed nor as numerous.

The population of the migratory band-tailed pigeon varies with the existing food conditions. These birds offer excellent shooting when conditions attract enough of them into the state.

Restoration programs on the popular ringneck pheasant have not been successful enough to provide sport hunting, partially because not enough birds have been released to stock a natural habitat; also, there is apparently a lack of suitable range in Arizona. The state now has a game-bird farm in operation which is hatching and raising moderate quantities of ringnecks with a plan to offer enough birds for limited hunting.

Arizona does not offer much in the way of waterfowl shooting, being about halfway between two general migratory-bird flyways, the Pacific and the Rio Grande. Probably the greatest concentration of both ducks and geese appears along the Colorado River at the western boundary. In common with other arid southwestern states, Arizona lacks resting areas for the birds; a scarcity of natural food is another limiting factor. Except for the Colorado River region, the state requires considerable artificial development before any good migratory bird shooting will be enjoyed.

**State Conservation.** The Arizona Game and Fish Commission consists of three non-salaried members appointed by the Governor to serve a six-year term of office. The Commission elects one of its members chairman for a two-year term. The members of the Commission are well informed on the subject of wild life and the requirements for the conservation of animals, birds and fish. They meet at least once quarterly, and meetings may be held at the call of the chairman or a majority of the Commission. The Commission makes rules and regulations concerning the control and management of the propagation and distribution of wild birds and animals.

Game management in Arizona emphasizes a constant and unremitting predatory animal control program. In this work the state co-operates very closely with the U. S. Fish and Wildlife Service. The two agencies maintain a crew of professional predator hunters who are particularly active during the critical winter-months period. They utilize strychnine drop-baits, thallium sulphate, and cyanide guns, known as "coyote getters." The results of this program have been quite satisfactory.

Another game-management problem is the rapidly growing population of the state and the constant development of new lands for agricultural purposes. The first factor exerts on ever-increasing hunting pressure upon the wildlife resources of the state, and the other factor slowly diminishes the available game range. Both are detrimental to the harvestable surplus of game, and threaten to strike at the heart of the breeding potential of each species.

In order to provide information as to hunting pressure, the Arizona game officials have put into effect a deer permit system. Coupled with the permit is a hunter report card to provide actual deer-kill data. An accurate system of obtaining data is being planned which will be correlated from year to year with checking station information and game surveys for an indication of trends for management purposes.

Besides an active conservation program for quail, the Game Commission supervises the raising and releasing of ringneck pheasants to aid in a restoration plan for that bird, as well as the propagation of chukar partridge on the game farm. Experiments are being made in a plan to introduce and gradually orient this bird to natural conditions in Arizona, which apparently are comparable to those of its original range. The principal drawback to chukar partridge introduction appears to be the ground-roosting habits of the species and its vulnerability to predation.

The wild turkey has steadily declined in recent years because of many reasons such as over-hunting, drought and predation. As a result of restorative measures, including limited hunting, live trapping in abundancy areas and releasing in depopulated areas, and protection in refuges; the turkey population is showing a slow but steady upward swing. Careful management and protective measures are the keynotes for all wildlife survival.

**Licenses.** License fees are as follows:

| | | | |
|---|---|---|---|
| Resident | $ 2.50 | Non-resident general | 25.00 |
| Alien small | 40.00 | Antelope permit | 5.00 |
| Non-resident small game | 10.00 | Deer permit | 1.00 |
| Alien general | 100.00 | Wild turkey permit | .50 |

All types of big game, except peccary, may be hunted only by special permit in addition to a valid big-game hunting license. These permits are on sale at regular license dealers not more than 30 days prior to the opening of the season. All other permits are issued only from the office of the State Game and Fish Director.

**Regulations.** Semi-automatics are not allowed (as of Jan. 1, 1948), in Arizona; however, a special permit to use semi-automatic rifles may be issued at any time to persons incapable of manual loading for physical reasons. Semi-automatic rifles are limited to magazine capacity of five cartridges.

Deer may be taken only by rifle propelling bullet weighing 87 grains or more, delivering energy of 950 foot-pounds or more at 100 yards from muzzle. Bow and arrow may be used provided bow has pull of 50 pounds or more and arrow has broad-head of one inch or more in width. Elk may be taken only by rifle using a cartridge with other than a full metal jacket or altered full metal jacket, bullet of not less than 130 grains in weight with an energy at 100 yards from the muzzle of not less than 1800 foot-pounds factory rating. Javelina and wild turkey (in this state wild turkey is considered as big game) may be taken by rifle using center-fire cartridge. Cottontail rabbits may be taken by any gun or bow and arrow.

Dogs may not be used to run or take big game animals.

No hunting may be done with the aid of an artificial light, except for bullfrogs.

No gun may be carried on a refuge except when the person is in possession of a special permit.

It is not permissible to shoot within one-fourth of a mile of a house or building without permission of the owner.

No wild animal or bird may be taken from an aircraft or automobile.

All commercial guides must be licensed, and no person acting as a guide is allowed to carry firearms other than a revolver or pistol while acting as a guide.

**Seasons.** Game animals and birds for which there are open seasons are:

Cottontail rabbit
Deer
Band-tailed pigeon
Doves
Ducks
Geese
Quail

## ARKANSAS

AREA: 53,102 square miles

**General Summary.** Arkansas offers excellent quail hunting in spite of the fact that modern agricultural methods and overgrazing of livestock have caused the number of quail to decline during the past 25 years. Many areas are open to the shooting of this popular upland game bird. Wild turkeys have also decreased; a steady decline in the last ten years forced a closed season on the bird in 1947. The protection was a temporary one, however, for the one-year closed season helped to increase the population in some areas. Pheasants, prairie chicken, chukar and Hungarian partridge were also at a low point and hunting remained closed on them. Both doves and woodcock are shot in this state; the method of taking conforms with Federal regulations on migratory birds.

Many hunters pursue squirrels and rabbits and, because of their abundance, rabbits may be taken at any time of the year. There has been no important population change in the last few years.

Waterfowl shooting is excellent in Arkansas, for this state is located on a direct line with the Mississippi flyway. Beside ducks and geese, gunners take the migrating shorebirds, coot and rail.

Deer is the only big game animal which is legally hunted in Arkansas, but the deer herd is small compared to that of most other states which have an open season on the species. Deer are on the increase in most areas and are now found in 74 of the 75 counties, but almost half of the state is closed to deer hunting while it is being restocked. Deer formerly were purchased from a game farm in Wisconsin, but the animals used for restocking are now being trapped in areas where there is an overabundance.

**State Conservation.** The Arkansas Game and Fish Commission is composed of eight men who are responsible for game management within the state. To maintain the state's wildlife resources, the Commission urges the observance of the game laws and avoidance of destructive forest fires. To protect game birds and animals a constant war against predators, including the common house cat, is necessary.

**Licenses.** License fees are as follows:

| | |
|---|---|
| Resident | $ 1.50 |
| Non-resident | 25.00 |
| Non-resident (except deer and turkey) | 15.00 |

Game wardens do not sell licenses in Arkansas, but they can be purchased from the Game and Fish Commission's office in Little Rock, from the county clerk of each county, or from

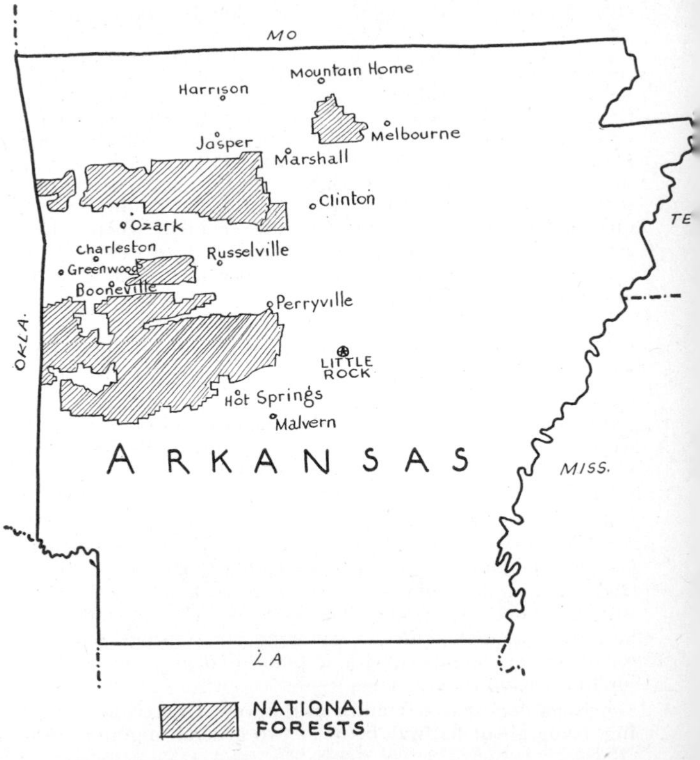

approximately 625 license dealers (drugstores, hardware stores, sporting-goods stores, and restaurants in all large towns) scattered throughout the state.

The non-resident hunting license has three tags, each good for shipment of one day's bag. The holder may carry a day's bag from the state. One bag per day, or two per week, on all game, may be shipped or carried out of the state.

Chicot and Desha counties are the only counties in the state which require a special county license in addition to the regular state license.

**Regulations.** The use of an automatic or hand-operated repeating shotgun capable of holding more than three shells is prohibited in hunting quail and other game birds.

Dogs may be used to hunt deer or game birds, and a special license ($1.50) is required. The license cost for dogs used exclusively for chasing fox is 50 cents. Bird dogs may be trained to hunt quail without guns 45 days prior to the open season.

An annual guide hunting and fishing license costs $10.00. Clubs which charge fees for hunting or fishing privileges must be licensed.

**Seasons.** Game animals and birds for which there are open seasons are:

| | |
|---|---|
| Deer | Geese |
| Raccoon | Quail |
| Squirrels | Rail |
| Coot | Turkey |
| Doves | Woodcock |
| Ducks | |

There is no closed season on:

Rabbits (no license required)
Fox (hunting license required)

## CALIFORNIA — AREA: 158,693 square miles

**General Summary.** Of California's approximately 100,000,000 acres only a small percentage is highly developed agricultural land. The Game Commission argues that there is no valid reason why the greater portion of the remainder should not be open to sportsmen provided that cooperation between the sportsman and landowner is established.

Deer are the most important big-game animals on which there is an annual open season in California. In some areas they have done extensive damage in orchards, gardens, and grain fields. To control this damage repellent sprays have been used as a temporary measure, but the ultimate plan is to thin the herds by trapping animals in those limited areas where they are congregated in considerable numbers and releasing them where they are less numerous. The annual deer kill is approximately 45,000. California has one of the largest black bear populations in the nation, and hunters take about 250 each year. There has been a closed season on antelope for several years, but the popular annual hunts are expected to be resumed at some time in the future.

Rabbits and squirrels are the only small-game animals hunted.

The quail (valley, desert, and mountain) is California's most popular game bird, but doves, band-tailed pigeons, and pheasants are also favored upland game birds.

The state is well situated for waterfowl shooting, being right on the Pacific flyway. There has been no open season, either by state or Federal law, on shorebirds for many years.

**State Conservation.** California's Division of Fish and Game is administered by a board of five commissioners with staggered terms. The commissioners are appointed by the governor for five-year terms. The work of the Division is carried on through the executive director and five bureaus—Patrol and Law Enforcement, Marine Fisheries, Fish Conservation, Game Conservation, and Bureau of Licenses. The Commission works at all times in close cooperation with sportsmen's organizations.

In conjunction with Federal Aid in Wildlife Restoration, the state has made a successful game-management study on the valley quail. The problem of quail management is strictly a problem of local land management, with the apparent solution an improvement of local habitat conditions, such as water, cover, feed and predation. Provision has been made to supply water in dry areas without the benefit of springs, seeps, pipelines, etc., by a device known as the "gallinaceous guzzler" which collects rainwater and stores it underground. The areas in which this device was set up were formerly devoid of quail but are now established centers of these birds. Other methods of improving quail habitat include control of cover by planting native and introduced shrubs, by thinning extensive brush areas, by proper management of food patches, and by predator control. Similar management is planned for the mountain quail and ring-necked pheasant, for experiments on the valley quail have shown that merely raising birds in pens and dumping them into unsuitable habitat is worthless.

Around 70,000 pheasants, partridges, and other species are liberated annually from the state game farms for restocking new areas and replenishing depleted stock in other areas. Sportsmen assisted in this work by helping to maintain holding pens where the young birds were kept until ready for liberation.

**Licenses.** License fees are as follows:

| | |
|---|---|
| Resident license | $ 2.00 |
| Junior resident | 1.00 |
| Non-resident | 10.00 |
| Alien license | 25.00 |
| Deer tags | 1.00 |

Hunting licenses can be secured from some 4000 license agents scattered throughout the state, such as hardware stores, sporting-goods stores, service stations, and other mercantile establishments.

**Regulations.** Shotguns larger than 10 gauge are prohibited and no automatic or repeater is allowed to carry more than three shells. Rifles cannot be used to take pheasants and quail.

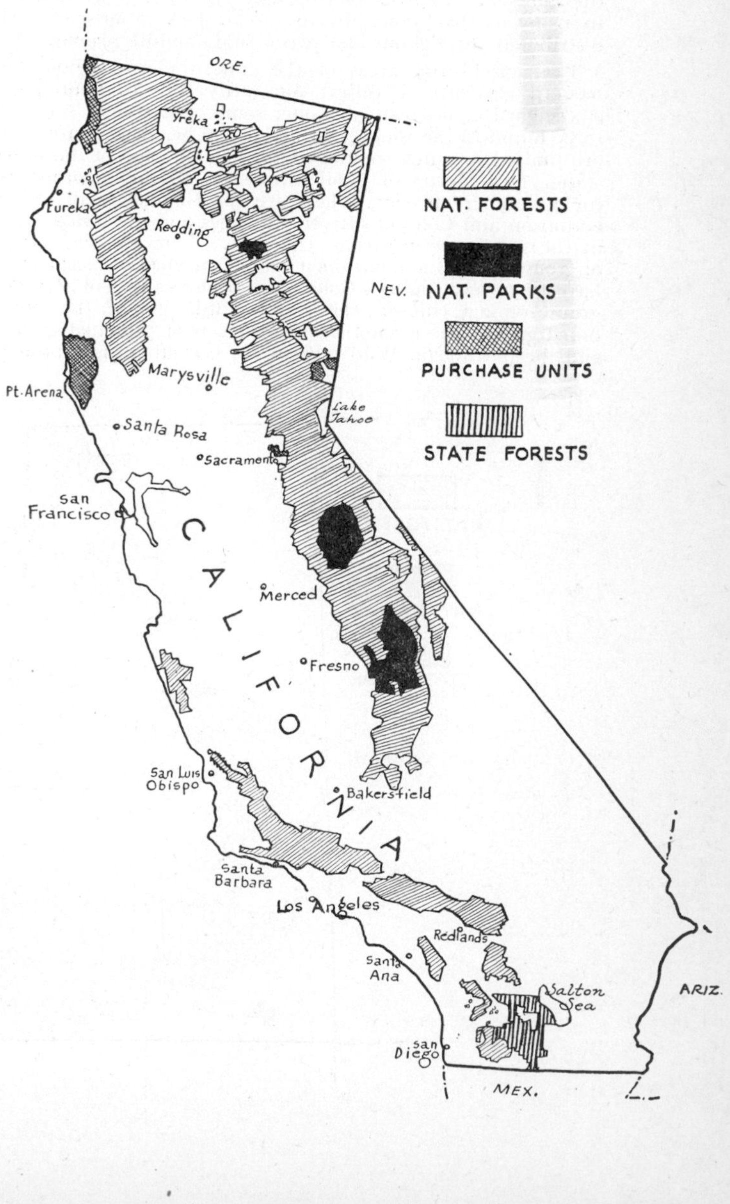

As of July 1, 1948, in taking big game no rifle smaller than .25 caliber or carrying a bullet of less than 100 grains or of less than 1300 foot-pounds of energy may be used. Also, no .22 rim-fire or full-jacket bullet may be used in taking big game. Effective July 1, 1948, no shotgun can be used in deer hunting using shot or round ball cartridges.

There is no guide license law in the state and no law that requires guides to register.

There is no state law making it necessary to have a dog license. However, in many stock counties licenses are required by county ordinance. There are no restrictions on the use of dogs in hunting during the open season other than in deer hunting, where only one dog per person is allowed to be used.

**Seasons.** Game animals for which there are open seasons are:

Bear
Brush rabbit
Cottontail
Deer
Tree squirrel
Band-tailed pigeon
Doves
Pheasant
Quail

There is no closed season on:

Cougar Coyote Raccoon Wildcat Wolf

## COLORADO AREA: 104,247 square miles

**General Summary.** Colorado is well supplied with a wide selection of game. Small-game animals are plentiful. Cottontail rabbits are to be found throughout most of the state, and the snowshoe rabbit or varying hare occurs in great numbers in many of the higher-altitude areas. Jack rabbits are well distributed throughout the plains and foothill regions.

The agricultural areas of the eastern plains region and western agricultural valleys are fairly well to abundantly stocked with pheasants and offer some of the finest shooting to be found in the country, although the heavy concentrations are limited to much smaller areas than in some of the other states. Two species of quail have been on the shooting list for a number of years. These are the Gambel quail of the Gunnison and Colorado River drainages and the scaled quail in the southeastern part of the state. There are five species of grouse in the state, but open seasons on them in recent years have been very limited. Colorado's grouse consist of the sage grouse or sage chicken, the blue or dusky grouse, the sharp-tailed grouse, the greater prairie chicken or pinnated grouse, and the ptarmigan. Wild turkeys are becoming more numerous year by year and are being reintroduced to most of their original range. The stock consists exclusively of the original "Merriam" strain.

Colorado is an important big-game state and deer (exclusively the large western mule deer) are the chief animals hunted. During the past eight or ten years the management of the deer herds has brought about their general distribution over 50% to 70% greater area than they occupied previously. Today they are found in nearly all of the state west of the eastern edge of the foothills, and are even finding their way into the valleys of the plains regions. The present population probably would justify an annual harvest in the neighborhood of 50,000 to 60,000 head. They are more easily hunted than the eastern whitetails, and every year sees an increase in the number of out-of-state sportsmen who come to Colorado to hunt them.

The second most important big-game species in Colorado is the wapiti or American elk. They are well distributed throughout the mountainous areas of the state and in some localities they occur in considerable concentrations. The annual harvest of these animals has been running from 4000 to 6000 head.

The black bear can also be found in most of the areas where deer and elk are hunted. Because the present state law does not permit them to be hunted with dogs, the getting of a bear is considered more a matter of luck than the result of a serious hunting expedition for bears. The open season for bear in Colorado for a number of years has coincided with the open season on deer and elk, and the licensing system has permitted the hunter to take one bear on either a deer or an elk license, in addition to the species for which the license was written. However, no hunter is entitled to kill more than one bear even though he may have licenses for both deer and elk.

Colorado has a considerable population of antelope and the largest population of Rocky Mountain bighorns in the United States. Under existing state laws, however, these may be hunted only by residents of the state. There has not been an open season on sheep for many years.

Many fine trophies are taken each year in Colorado, and the state has some of the most competent taxidermists to be found anywhere in the United States. Colorado big-game licenses for non-residents provide, without additional charge, shipping permits for taking the legally killed game out of the state.

**State Conservation.** A State Game and Fish Commission composed of six men has complete authority, under the law, to determine seasons, bag limits, and all other problems es-

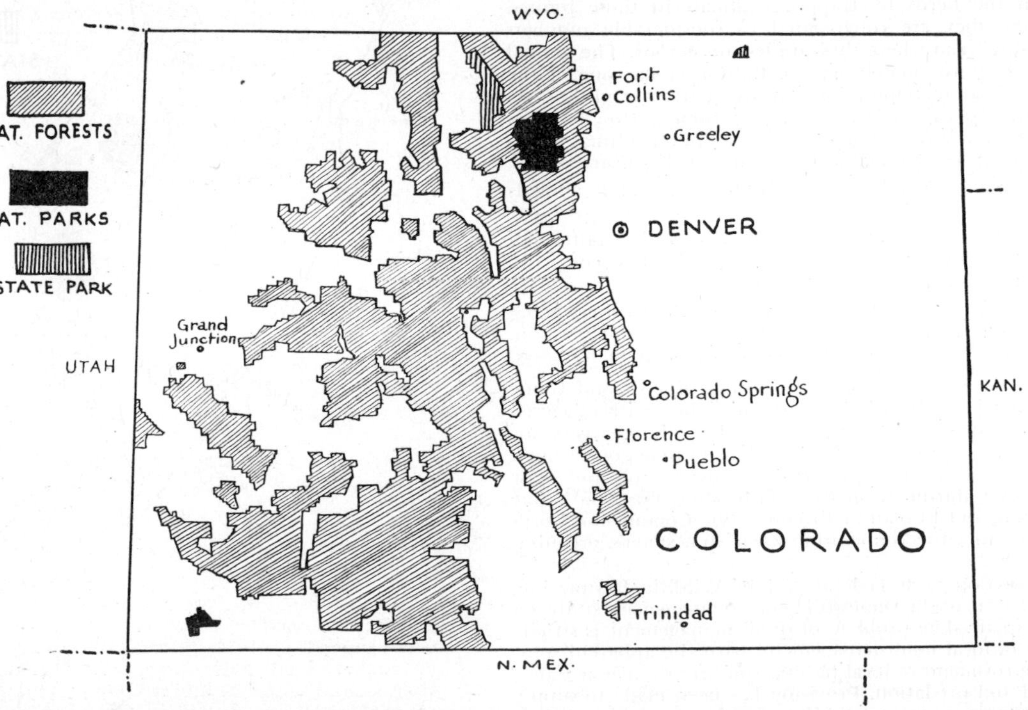

sential to systematic management of the state's game and fish populations.

Management of the state's big-game herds is based upon the principle of allowing hunters' choice between an antlered and an antlerless animal in areas of overpopulation, and of antlered animals only in districts where no winter food shortage exists.

**Licenses.** License fees are as follows:

| | |
|---|---|
| Resident deer license | $ 7.50 |
| Resident elk license | 10.00 |
| Non-resident deer | 40.00 |
| Non-resident elk | 50.00 |
| Resident small game | 3.00 |
| Non-resident small game | 10.00 |

**Regulations.** The Colorado Game and Fish Department regularly lists guides and ranch accommodations available for non-resident hunters. Colorado law does not require that non-resident hunters employ a professional guide, but doing so is highly desirable and usually results in a much more satisfactory hunt.

All rifles with a bullet weight of less than 70 grains and a rated energy of less than 950 foot-pounds at 100 yards are excluded in the hunting of big game.

**Seasons.** Game animals and birds for which there are open seasons are:

Bear
Cottontail rabbit
Deer
Raccoon
Snowshoe rabbit (Varying hare)
Wapiti (elk)
Grouse
Pheasant
Quail

There is no closed season on:

Bobcat
Coyote
Lynx
Mountain lion
Wolf

## CONNECTICUT

AREA: 5009 square miles

**General Summary.** The small herd of white-tailed deer in Connecticut is protected by very restricted hunting. Under a special permit system about 450 animals are taken each year.

More rabbits and squirrels are taken annually than any other type of game. Squirrels maintain their abundance in population and their wide distribution, but rabbits are more "spotty," being plentiful in some areas while scarce in others. The cottontail rabbit has a regular open season, but the hares are given no protection and can be taken throughout the year. Raccoon hunting is popular sport and may be done at night with the permission of the landowner. No permit is required to hunt raccoons on state forests which are open to hunting. Over 3000 foxes (red and gray) are killed yearly by hunters, although the animal is classed as a predator and may be taken by gunner or trapper at any time. The fox population is high in a few areas, but has recently decreased over the state as a whole from a recent peak in abundance.

The pheasant is the most numerous and popular upland game bird in this region. The birds have shown a recent decrease in numbers, and during the hunting season there is added emphasis on liberation so that the population generally is sustained. The ruffed grouse is showing an increase, as well as the woodcock and quail. Quail are limited in range to New Haven, Middlesex, and New London Counties.

Connecticut has excellent waterfowl shooting on the coastal area. Some species are just holding their own after several years of steady decline, while others, principally the scaup or broadbill, show a decided increase.

**State Conservation.** The Connecticut State Board of Fisheries and Game, composed of a three-man commission, is actively concerned with a program to increase the supply of fish and game in the state through improved game habitats, expanded plant facilities, and increased enforcement activities. Because of the increase in the numbers of hunters afield, there is need for more intensive stocking of game, a provision of more hunting areas, and additional warden personnel.

The Board is developing an effective program of land management, emphasizing the close alliance between forestry and wildlife—that any operation designed to benefit one is certain to affect the other to a greater or lesser degree. Considering that the pattern of the vegetation is a basic influence on the abundance and distribution of woodland game, it is of definite value to plan forest operations with a view toward providing the most desirable wildlife environment.

In recent years, the Game Board has made intensive study of several game species. A survey was made of pheasants, specifically of their mortality and nesting success, and the value of food patches of field corn surrounded by small refuge areas as a pheasant-management measure. Also, certain areas were observed for the success and effect of hunting pressure and the results of stocking those particular areas. A census of the ruffed-grouse population was made as a prerequisite to game management, and a drumming-site count was taken. A complete scientific study was done on the cottontail rabbit by a group of biologists.

Connecticut does not operate any game farms, but purchases its pheasants and quail for release from commercial game breeders both within the state and as far west as Wisconsin. Connecticut ranks high in the nation in the production of pheasants on private game farms. In 1947, the production was upward of 50,000 pheasants of which the Department purchased over 30,000.

The Connecticut Regulated Shooting Program is a farmer-sportsman co-operative program. The program involves 170,000 acres of game areas. Season permits are issued to members of the club sponsoring an area, and daily permits are issued on the area at designated points. These issuing agencies are published prior to the hunting season and posters in the hunter area also give the address of the issuing agency. The Department liberates approximately one-half of its pheasants on these regulated areas; in addition, the clubs sponsoring the area liberate from 100 to 500 birds. This program has been in operation since 1933 and is increasing in popularity. It provides ideal opportunities for gunners living in the larger cities, who are not acquainted with rural landowners, to spend enjoyable days afield. A printed list of names and locations of Regulated Permit-Required Shooting areas is available at the State Board of Fisheries and Game, State Office Building, Hartford, Connecticut.

In addition, the Department leases approximately 50,000 acres in the best pheasant covers where no permits are needed, and the signs read "State Leased—Hunting Permitted."

**Licenses.** License fees are as follows:

| | |
|---|---|
| Resident | $ 4.35 |
| Non-resident | 10.35 |
| Resident's and non-resident's one-day—private shooting preserve | 1.35 |
| Non-resident's license to hunt foxes for six days | 2.35 |

All hunting licenses are issued in the town clerks' offices.

**Regulations.** No rifle may be carried which uses ammunition larger or heavier than .22 long rifle.

A license for owners of packs of hunting dogs costs $25.00.

**Seasons.** Game animals and birds for which there are open seasons are:

Rabbit
Raccoon
Squirrel
Pheasant
Quail
Ruffed grouse
Woodcock

There is no closed season on:

Belgian hare
European hare
Fox
Jack rabbit

## DELAWARE

AREA: 2057 square miles

**General Summary.** The present game picture in Delaware is very satisfactory, although there is far from an abundant supply of game at any time. The most important game to the hunter are rabbit and squirrel, followed by upland game birds, quail and pheasant. There is fair waterfowl shooting.

**State Conservation.** The Board of Game and Fish Commissioners is composed of three salaried commissioners, one from each of the counties of Delaware. The Board is authorized to make expenditures out of funds received by it from the sale of licenses, fines, and forfeitures imposed and received for violations of the game and fish laws. Besides salaries and educational publicity, money in this fund is spent on wildlife protection, conservation, and propagation, purchase of game for stocking and propagation purposes, and the administration of refuges. Serving under the chief warden are ten game wardens authorized to enforce the regulations on wildlife.

The state has an organized farmer-sportsman co-operative program, and under this system the Board stocks farms and privately owned land provided the landowners allow public hunting. It is still necessary for the hunter to ask permission to shoot over private land. There are no state-owned game farms, but game is bought for restocking purposes.

**Licenses.** License fees are as follows:

| | |
|---|---|
| Resident | $ 1.25 |
| Non-resident (season) | 15.50 |
| Non-resident (five days only) | 5.50 |

Game wardens, justices of the peace, and specially appointed agents sell non-resident and resident licenses. No counties require a special license, and a state-wide license will cover the entire state.

**Regulations.** The only regulation concerning rifles and shotguns in this state is that no shotgun may be used that is capable of holding in the chamber and magazine combined more than three shells.

Dogs used in hunting may not wear bells or any other noise-producing device, except in pursuit of raccons and opossums.

Ferrets may not be used in hunting rabbits or hares. Game birds and animals may not be hunted while there is snow on the ground so that the game may be tracked.

**Seasons.** Game animals and birds for which there are open seasons are:

| | |
|---|---|
| Opossum | Ducks |
| Rabbit | Geese |
| Raccoon | Pheasant |
| Red Fox (chase only) | Quail |
| Squirrel | |

when drought followed by excessive rains hit the state during the breeding season. To offset this loss, the Commission purchased approximately 40,000 live-trapped wild quail and liberated them in every section of the state. A good increase in quail is expected unless unfavorable climatic conditions again prevail. The Commission favors the liberation of live-trapped quail, for although pen-raised birds have been released the percentage of survival was not high enough to warrant the expenditure.

The dove, fully migratory in some states, is a resident game bird in Florida, particularly in the northern section. There is a large migration of doves into Florida during the month of October, but this affects only four counties. Most of the doves found in the other sections of this state remain there the year round.

Ducks and geese are the principal waterfowl found in Florida, and Florida, like all other states in the union, has suffered from the reduction in duck population. The best duck-hunting areas are in the upper coastal region and in the marshes surrounding the Everglades area. Geese are found only in the upper west coastal region.

**State Conservation.** The Game and Fresh Water Fish Commission in Florida was created by a constitutional amendment passed by the 1941 session of the legislature and ratified by the voters in November 1942. The constitutional amendment calls for the appointment by the governor of a five-man commission; the first appointments were for staggered terms and subsequent appointments are to be for periods of five years each. The Commission employs a director who represents it in all matters pertaining to the operation of the Commission. The director, with the approval of the Commission, employs qualified persons to assist in carrying out the provisions of the amendment. This includes all office personnel, the enforcement officers, and trained biologists in both fish and game fields.

During the past five years an average of $21,000 has been

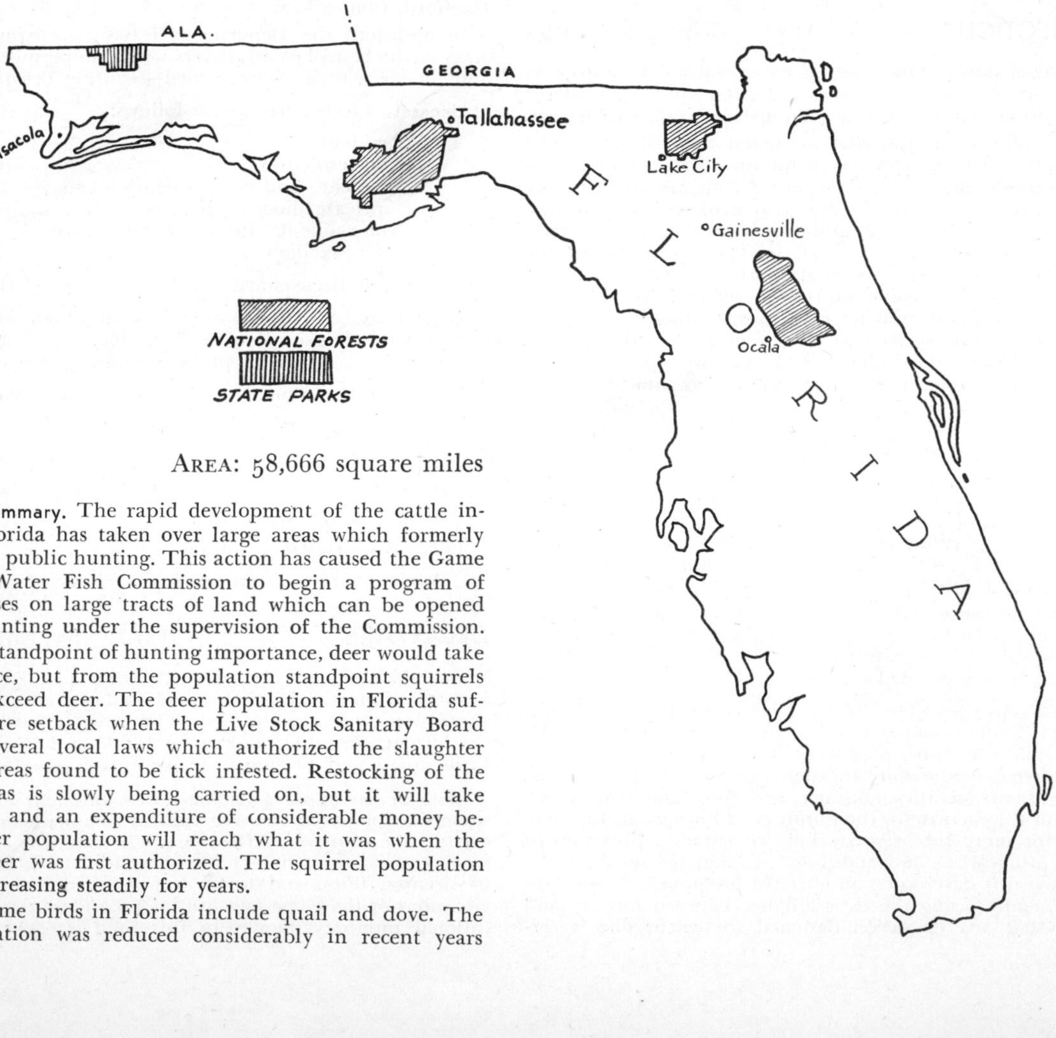


## FLORIDA

AREA: 58,666 square miles

**General Summary.** The rapid development of the cattle industry in Florida has taken over large areas which formerly were open to public hunting. This action has caused the Game and Fresh Water Fish Commission to begin a program of securing leases on large tracts of land which can be opened to public hunting under the supervision of the Commission.

From the standpoint of hunting importance, deer would take the first place, but from the population standpoint squirrels would far exceed deer. The deer population in Florida suffered a severe setback when the Live Stock Sanitary Board instigated several local laws which authorized the slaughter of deer in areas found to be tick infested. Restocking of the shot-out areas is slowly being carried on, but it will take several years and an expenditure of considerable money before the deer population will reach what it was when the killing of deer was first authorized. The squirrel population has been increasing steadily for years.

Upland game birds in Florida include quail and dove. The quail population was reduced considerably in recent years spent yearly on game restocking and an average of $34,000 has been spent yearly on game management, other than the portion of game management which is regularly carried on by the field enforcement officers.

There is no farmer-sportsman co-operative plan in operation in Florida, but before the war there was a Pittman-Robertson Project which operated in that way. This project was carried on in co-operation with the Soil Conservation Service and farmer landowners. Food strips were planted on co-operating farms with seed and fertilizer furnished by the Game and Fresh Water Fish Commission, to be distributed by the Soil Conservation Service among the co-operating farmers in the various Soil Conservation Districts. The necessary labor in putting in the strips was done by the farmer. The war brought this project to a close, but is was subsequently reinstated.

**Licenses.** License fees are as follows:

| | |
|---|---|
| Resident state | $ 7.00 |
| Resident county | 1.75 |
| Non-resident season | 26.00 |
| Non-resident 10 days | 11.00 |

State law requires that all hunting licenses be issued by the several county judges in Florida.

**Regulations.** Shotguns not larger than a 10 gauge and limited to three shell capacity may be used for taking game in Florida.

Nothing in state law prohibits the use of dogs while hunting, and no license is required for residents or non-residents for dogs used in hunting.

The use of guides is not required, but there are licensed guides for hunting purposes. Application blanks for guide licenses come from the office of the Commission and the license is issued from this office. No examination is required prior to issuing the license, the fee for which is $10 per year.

**Seasons.** Game animals and birds for which there are open seasons are:

| | |
|---|---|
| Deer | Geese |
| Squirrel | Marsh hen |
| Doves | Quail |
| Ducks | Wild turkey |

There is no closed season on:

| | |
|---|---|
| Bear | Panther |
| Bobcat | Rabbit |
| Hare | Red and gray fox |
| Opossum | Wildcat |

## GEORGIA

AREA: 58,876 square miles

**General Summary.** Approximately 60 per cent of Georgia's area has from good to excellent hunting open to the public, and approximately 2 per cent of the remaining land is owned by private hunting clubs.

Upland game birds are the most important game, and the bobwhite quail is the most productive and most hunted. In spite of heavy hunting, this bird has been able to hold its own, but as a precautionary measure the Commission recently cut 15 days off the latter part of the quail season.

The mourning dove is also widely hunted, but this bird is showing a noticeable decrease. The game department doubts that the bird will be able to support the increasing pressure.

Both the fox and cat squirrel, and the cottontail rabbit, are the principal small game. Both of these species are holding up well under heavy hunting.

The Virginia whitetail deer is very well adapted to this state, both in the coastal and in the Blue Ridge Mountain areas. Both areas have about reached their carrying capacity in spite of the heavy hunting.

With the exception of a very limited area on the Atlantic coast, Georgia does not have much hunting for waterfowl. However, marsh hens have been found in abundance off the coast. Recent hunting restrictions have been made on this bird by the Commission to insure their numbers.

**State Conservation.** The Georgia State Game and Fish Commission was established under the act of the General Assembly in February 1943, and amended in 1945, setting up the present Game and Fish Commission. The governing body of 11 members, one from each congressional district, and one from the state at large, is appointed by the governor. These appointments are on a staggered basis, and during a four-year term, the governor can make only five appointments to the Board of Commissioners. The Board of Commissioners hires the director, and the management of the department is left to the director, handled with the approval of the commissioners. The Commission is empowered to set the seasons, methods, and regulations for the taking and protection of game and fish. All funds collected by the department from sale of hunting, fishing, and other special licenses are set aside by the state treasurer for use by this department only.

The state operates one quail farm, at an annual expense of $3500, and produces about 3000 quail yearly, as well as 8000 to 9000 quail eggs. Both eggs and quail are used in an educational program carried on through the 4-H and F.F.A. clubs. The department has not used hatchery birds for a number of years for restocking of hunting lands, as experience has proved this to be entirely unsatisfactory.

Georgia does not at present have a farmer-sportsman co-operative plan, but such a plan is expected to be presented soon to both farmers and sportsmen.

**Licenses.** License fees are as follows:

| | |
|---|---|
| State resident | $ 3.25 |
| County resident | 1.00 |
| Non-resident state | 12.50 |
| Non-resident county | 5.00 |

Resident and non-resident hunting licenses are sold in sporting-goods stores, fishing camps, and courthouses throughout the state.

**Regulations.** Automatic shotguns may be used provided they are plugged to accommodate only three shells. Both rifle slug and buckshot are permissible. No rifle using ammunition less than .32 caliber is permitted in taking deer.

No licenses required for dogs, either by residents or non-residents.

There are no licensed guides in Georgia, for there is no form of hunting there which requires the help of guides.

It is unlawful to take sea turtles or their eggs, to kill alligators, or to use a light of any kind in hunting game animals and birds.

No game may be held in cold storage longer than five days after the season has expired without a permit from the Game and Fish Commission.

**Seasons.** Game animals and birds for which there are open seasons are:

| | |
|---|---|
| Bear | Squirrel |
| Deer | Dove |
| Opossum | Quail |
| Rabbit | Ruffed grouse |
| Raccoon | |

There is no closed season on fox.

## IDAHO — AREA: 56,280 square miles

**General Summary.** The majority of the 80,000 big-game hunters in Idaho kill deer, the most numerous big-game animal in the state. The annual kill is about 25,000. The game department adjusts the season each year to prevent an excessive kill. Elk have been declining in the last few years and more limited hunting has been necessary, since the 1945 and 1946 hunts nearly exterminated the herds. A swift-recovery is expected and a return to an annual take of approximately 4000. Other big-game animals include bear, mountain goat, antelope, mountain sheep, and moose, but the latter three species are hunted by special permit only. Public drawings for residents, non-residents, and aliens are conducted to determine the winners of a specified number of permits.

Game birds include quail, Hungarian partridge, mourning dove, and Chinese, Mongolian, and mutant pheasants. There are indications that the Chinese pheasant, the Hungarian partridge, and the sage hen are definitely on the decrease in Idaho. Blue grouse have decreased in certain sections almost to an extermination point. In a few sections of the state they have increased. Ruffed grouse have shown a definite increase in most of their habitat. The bobwhite quail population is still at a low ebb, but both mountain and valley quail have shown an increase.

**State Conservation.** The administration of fish and game resources in Idaho is in charge of a five-man Commission which was established by the people through initiative act in 1938. The Commission sets the policies. Management is carried on by the Fish and Game Department under the executive authority of the director who is appointed by the Commission. They make and declare rules and regulations for the preservation, protection, perpetuation, and management of wild life. The Commission is a non-salaried board of directors considering problems of the state as a whole. They are appointed by the governor for terms of six years each.

With Federal aid from the Pittman-Robertson fund, this state has endeavored to restore and aid some of its wildlife. Idaho has an abundance of summer range, but lacks winter range for all types of big game, and to meet this problem, refuges and winter ranges have been established. Land has been leased from counties, the state, and private individuals to form winter ranges for deer, antelope, and elk, as well as for pheasants and migratory birds.

The Idaho Fish and Game Department operates two bird farms, one at Lapwai, serving northern Idaho, and one in the south at Jerome. An average production from both plants is 32,000 to 35,000 each year. The department, however, works on the policy that the habitat is the deciding factor in permanent game supply, and that it is more practical for the hunter to move to the habitat of game than to attempt to create an artificial habitat at great expense in unsuitable game areas. It is an established fact that pheasants costing from 45 cents to 86 cents per bird cannot be released in the field for immediate shooting. It is impossible to plant enough hand-released birds to make any appreciable difference in the face of Idaho's heavy hunting pressure.

Predator control is handled co-operatively by the U. S. Fish and Wildlife Service, the predatory-animal control boards, and the Idaho Fish and Game Department. In one year about $117,000 was spent to kill over 17,000 predators at an average cost of $6.80 per predator. Of this number, about 16,500 were coyotes. In 1943 the Department spent for predator control approximately 7½ cents for every big-game animal in the state. About 50,000 magpies are taken annually at a cost of 2 to 3 cents per head.

From a game-management point of view, the increased use of airplanes for transporting hunters to isolated areas and

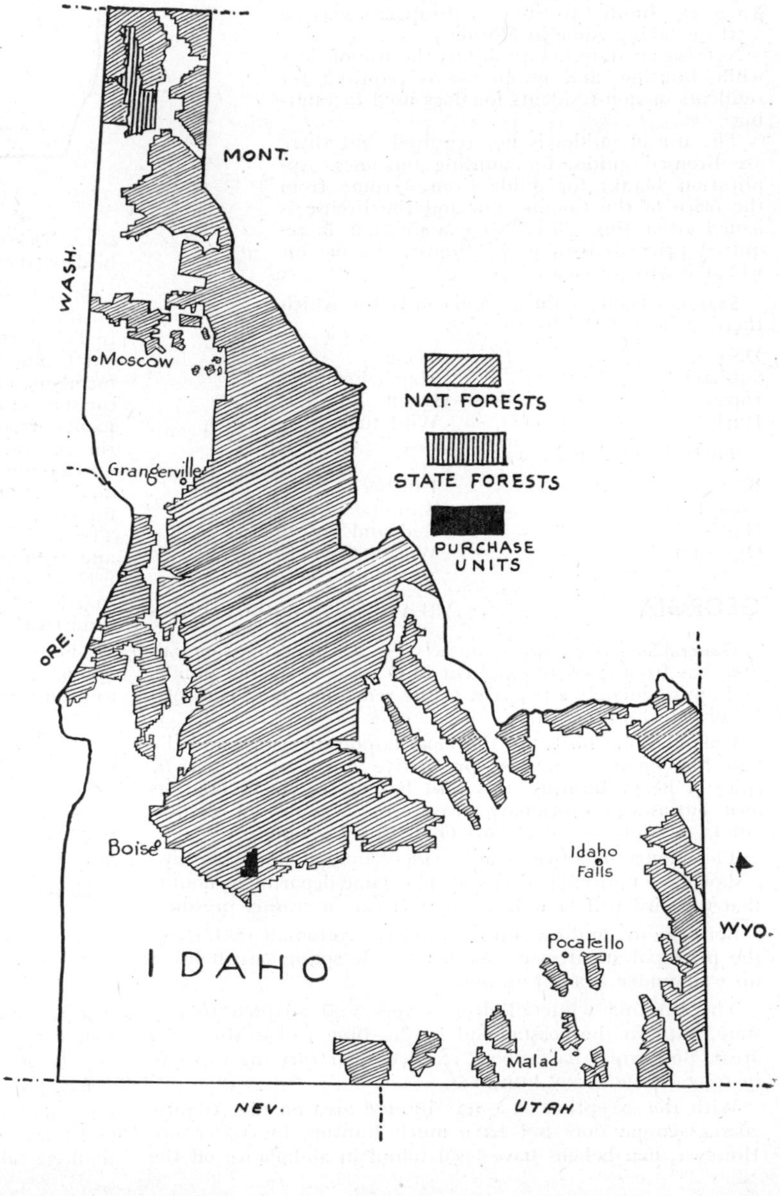

for removing their kills from these areas is not objectionable. Road and pack-string hunting tend to limit hunting to the perimeter of an isolated herd. By the use of airplanes landing in the middle of these herds, there is a tendency to keep the animals scattered over a wider area and not driven into one central location where congestion would otherwise result. With a resultant higher percentage of kill, however, a closer check must be made on herd numbers.

Sportsmen throughout the state strongly advocate farmer-hunter co-operative relations, but there is no organized farmer-sportsman plan in the state, and the informal program operates differently in different sections.

**Licenses.** License fees are as follows:

| | |
|---|---|
| Resident | $2.00 |
| Non-resident big game | 50.00 |
| (one game animal plus $25.00 for each additional species) | |
| Non-resident bird | 20.00 |
| Alien big game | 75.00 |
| (one game animal plus $25.00 for each additional species) | |
| Alien bird | 25.00 |
| Elk tag | 2.00 |
| Deer tag | 1.00 |
| Goat tag | 10.00 |

Licenses of all classes may be purchased at sporting-goods stores, etc., in all communities. There are more than 500 vendors. A license for resident or non-resident is valid throughout the state. There are no county fees. Seasons are set annually by the game commission—fishing in January and game in July.

**Regulations.** The .22 rim-fire is prohibited in taking of big game, and all rifles are prohibited in the taking of game birds.

It is unlawful to hunt deer, elk, mountain sheep and goats with dogs, but the hunting of bear and predatory animals with dogs is permissible. Any dog running at large in deer territory may be killed by a conservation officer.

No game may be killed with the aid of a spotlight, flashlight, or artificial light of any kind, and it is unlawful to kill any deer, elk, mountain sheep and goats at any deer lick.

**Seasons.** Game animals and birds for which there are open seasons are:

| | |
|---|---|
| Antelope | Bobwhite quail |
| Bear (except grizzly) | Hungarian partridge |
| Deer | Mourning dove |
| Elk | Chinese Pheasant (Chinese, Mongolian, Mutant) |
| Moose | Valley quail |
| Mountain goat | |

## ILLINOIS — AREA: 56,400 square miles

**General Summary.** Department game biologists describe the present wildlife situation in Illinois as normal, noting, however, that the state is just emerging from the low of a normal cyclic fluctuation. There has been no important change in the numbers of any game species.

Illinois does not allow hunting of any big-game animals. Although the most recent census indicated approximately 5000 deer in the state, there is no open season on them. In the order of their importance to the hunter, small-game animals, particularly rabbits, rank first, followed by upland game birds (pheasants and quail), with waterfowl third. Technicians have noted an increase in the number of prairie chickens, but this species will remain under strict protection.

**State Conservation.** The Department of Conservation enjoys the fullest co-operation of the Illinois Federation of Sportsmen's Clubs. An important part of the program of that organization is the improvement of farmer-sportsman relationship, and it is through that organization that the greater part of the farmer-sportsman program is effected. In addition, the Department supplies, upon request, speakers, motion-picture films, and other program material, for Farm Bureau groups and Sportsmen's Club meetings. The Department, through the Division of Forestry, has direct contact with many farmers and landowners in the course of reforestation projects. The Division of Game Management carries on an extensive and popular program of food and cover plantings, in direct relationship with farmer-landowners, as a part of the Pittman-Robertson program.

The Department of Conservation operates three game farms in Illinois. One, located at the State Fair Grounds in Springfield, is devoted exclusively to quail propagation; both pheasants and quail are produced at the Mount Vernon game farm; and the Yorkville farm is devoted exclusively to pheasants. The average total production of these farms is 92,968 quail, and 134,926 pheasants.

**Licenses.** License fees are as follows:

| | |
|---|---|
| Resident | $2.00 |
| Non-resident | 15.00 |

All Illinois hunting licenses are valid throughout the entire state, and there are no special county or regional licenses. The only special license fee is the Federal migratory waterfowl stamp.

Resident and non-resident hunting licenses are obtainable from county, city, village, township, and incorporated-town clerks, and are also sold by such sporting-goods stores as may be designated by those authorized to handle the licenses.

**Regulations.** No shotgun may be used which is larger than 10 gauge or capable of firing more than three consecutive shots unless the gun is fitted with a plug or otherwise altered to render it incapable of firing more than three consecutive shots. No shotgun or rifle may be carried in a vehicle unless it is enclosed in a case or is taken apart to render it incapable of being fired. It is unlawful to take game birds or migratory game birds with a rifle or pistol.

No firearms may be used in training dogs during the closed periods on individual game birds or animals.

**Seasons.** Game animals and birds for which there are open seasons are:

| | |
|---|---|
| Fox squirrel | Ducks |
| Gray squirrel | Geese |
| Opossum | Quail |
| Rabbit | Pheasant |
| Raccoon | |

There is no closed season on gray or red fox.

## INDIANA

AREA: 26,291 square miles

**General Summary.** Rabbits are the most common game animals in Indiana, with an estimated kill of over 3,500,000 in 1946. In order of importance come the fox and gray squirrel, with an annual kill of about 2,500,000, followed by the bobwhite quail, with about 1,000,000, then migratory birds (ducks, geese, coots, and woodcock), about 180,000, pheasants, 71,000, and lastly Hungarian partridge, 15,000. Formerly, deer were among the commonest of Indiana's mammals, but by 1895 all native wild deer were gone. There has been some restocking in the Brown County State Park. The bear and wild turkey have gone and there are but a few ruffed grouse left. The wild ducks largely have disappeared with the drainage of great areas. On the other hand, there are many more quail and cottontail rabbits than the pioneers ever saw.

From a hunting standpoint, the introduction of the ringneck pheasant provides a limited number of birds for the gun in counties in northern Indiana. The pheasant population reached a low in 1947, forcing a closed hunting season. Hungarian partridges, which have recently shown a decided increase, are not so popular as the ringneck, and they do not provide hunting for as large a cross-section of sportsmen. Both birds, however, have supplemented the kill in an area where the bobwhite quail, most hunted of all game birds, and the prairie chicken could not hold their own. However, quail have shown more increase throughout the state, especially in the southern section, than any other upland game bird, and the prairie chicken (upon which there has been a closed season for some time) is showing a slight increase.

**State Conservation.** The Division of Fish and Game is one of six major divisions of the Conservation Department. The conservation officers in Indiana hold a position similar to game wardens of other states. The basic activities of the Division of Fish and Game are artificial propagation of game, fish, continuation of wildlife investigation, fisheries research, and conservation organization contracts.

This state has two game farms and two preserves, but expensive and relatively unsuccessful experiments in artificial propagation for restocking have caused a lessening of emphasis on this means of stimulating wildlife. There is still pen breeding of pheasant, quail, and raccoons on the Wells County Game Farm (about 1000 acres), and artificial propagation of pheasants and quail on the Jasper-Pulaski Game Farm (about 9000 acres). The average production of these farms is 40,000 pheasants and 12,000 quail, but the accent today is on improving the habitat of game birds and animals. Figures on the cost of raising pheasants and quail run high. Since 1899 approximately 1,250,000 game birds of various species have been released in Indiana, at an approximate cost to the Department of Conservation of $40 per quail bagged, and $20 per male pheasant bagged. Pen-reared pheasants provided only 6 per cent of the total bag, and pen-reared quail provided less than 1 per cent of the total kill.

The Kankakee Game Preserve, around 2300 acres, is maintained as a waterfowl refuge, and by attracting thousands of waterfowl during the migration period provides waterfowl hunting to the surrounding area. The 900-acre Hovey Lake Game Preserve is a natural waterfowl refuge. The Beaver Lake Prairie Chicken Refuge is a sanctuary for prairie chickens.

State-owned lands have been of considerable value, but by far the greater amount of land is still in the hands of private landowners. It is primarily the farmer who holds the key to wildlife production in the state. Today, more attention than ever is given to providing better conditions of food and cover on private farms and forests, and there is a growing interest in conservation on the part of the public.

**Licenses.** License fees are as follows:

| | |
|---|---|
| Resident hunting and fishing | $1.50 |
| Non-resident hunting and fishing | 15.50 |
| None-resident archer | 2.00 |

There are no counties in Indiana which require a special county license. All hunting and fishing licenses are sold by county clerks and various agents established thorughout the state. No conservation officer is permitted to sell any type of license.

**Regulations.** It is unlawful to hunt rabbits with artificial light.

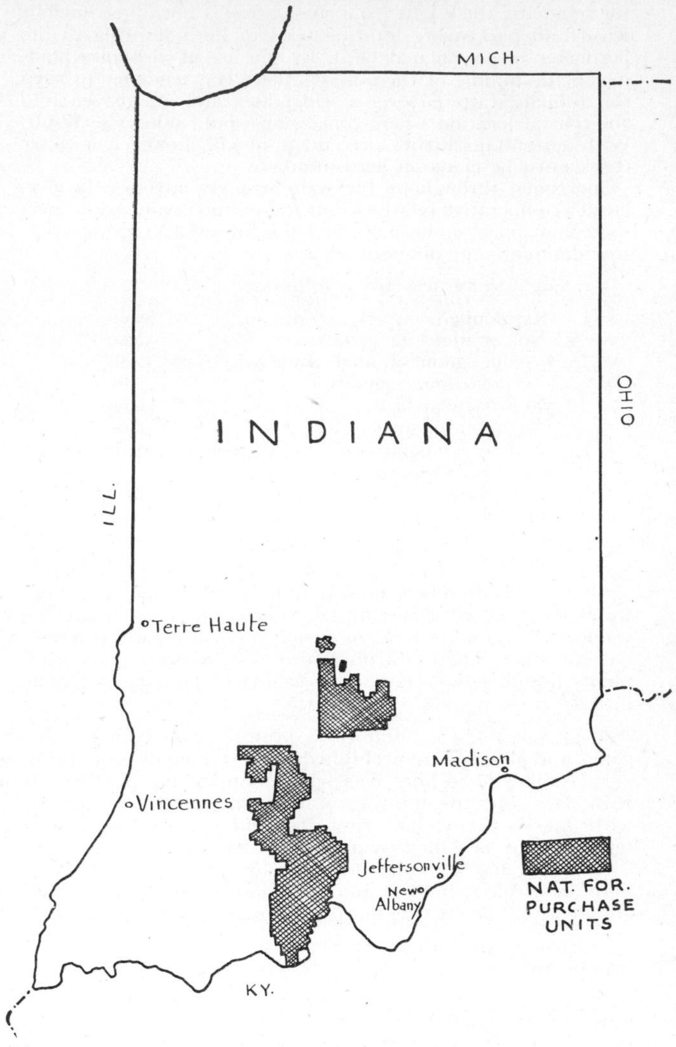


**Seasons.** Game animals and birds for which there are open seasons are:

| | |
|---|---|
| Fox squirrel | Raccoon |
| Gray squirrel | Hungarian partridge |
| Opossum | Pheasant |
| Rabbit | Quail |

There is no closed season on fox and woodchuck.

## IOWA

AREA: 56,280 square miles

**General Summary.** Game conditions in the state are good on the whole, with most species showing an increase in numbers. Small-game animals, squirrels and rabbits, are probably the most important game. Squirrels are holding their own, and cottontails in 1947 were at a high point of their cycle. Raccoons reached their highest recorded population peak.

Upland game birds provide good hunting in Iowa, and the popular quail is on the increase, although pheasants are at a comparative low. There is a fair annual take of Hungarian partridges.

Waterfowl shooting is fair. There is no open season on big game, although deer have shown a recent upswing in population.

**State Conservation.** The State Conservation Commission consists of seven members appointed by the governor, with the approval of the senate, for a term of six years. During his term no member can hold any other state or Federal office. The members are non-salaried but are compensated for expenditures to an amount not exceeding $600 a year. The Commission appoints an administrative head or director who is responsible to the Commission for the execution of its policies. The director, who receives a salary not to exceed $4800 a year, does not serve any special term but is subject to removal at the discretion of the Commission. The director employs such assistants, including a professionally trained state forester, as may be necessary. The financial resources of the Commission consist of the state fish and game protection fund (the bulk of which comes from license fees), the conservation fund, and the administration fund. The three divisions of the department of conservation are: fish and game, lands and waters, and administration. The duty of the Commission is to protect, propagate, increase, and preserve the fish, game, and fur-bearing animals, and the protected birds of the state, and to enforce pertinent rules and regulations. The Commission has specific power to provide public huntin grounds, to control, by killing, wildlife or protected birds which are damaging property, and to provide for protection against fire on state and privately owned forest and wildlife areas. This department works in close co-operation with the Federal conservation agencies.

State game refuges are established to protect wildlife, and there is no hunting in these areas. There is one game farm in Boone County, on which are raised pheasants and quail, and in 1947 approximately 12,000 quail and 20,000 pheasants were raised for hunting and natural propagation on depleted areas.

Iowa does not have a farmer-sportsman co-operative plan, but the state does have a co-operative game-management area system, and at the present time there are 698 areas totaling over 302,000 acres.

**Licenses.** License fees are as follows:

| | |
|---|---|
| Resident | $1.00 |
| Non-resident | Reciprocal (South Dakota is not eligible) |

**Regulations.** There is no state law governing shell capacity for a shotgun, but no person may use a swivel gun, and no gun may be larger than 10 gauge.

It is unlawful to train any bird dog on game in the wild from March 15 to July 15 of each year. A pistol or revolver shooting blank cartridges may be used while training bird dogs during closed season, but it is unlawful to train any foxhound, raccoon hound, or trailing dog on any fur-bearing animal between sunset and sunrise for 30 days just prior to the open season on raccoon.

**Seasons.** Game animals and birds for which there are open seasons are:

Rabbit
Raccoon
Squirrel
Ducks
Geese
Hungarian partridge
Pheasant (Chinese, Mongolian, and ringneck)
Quail

There is no closed season on:

Coyote
Fox
Groundhog (woodchuck)
Weasel
Wolf

## KANSAS

AREA: 82,276 square miles

**General Summary.** Quail and pheasant are the only game in Kansas on which there is an annual open season. Both of these upland game birds are showing a satisfactory increase. Rabbits have been less abundant in recent years, but there is no closed season on them and they provide a popular Kansas sport.

**State Conservation.** Kansas has three game farms in operation, and their combined capacity is about 50,000 birds divided equally into pheasant and quail propagation.

**Licenses.** License fees are as follows:

| | |
|---|---|
| Resident | $1.50 |
| Non-resident | Reciprocal cost basis with a $5.00 minimum charge |

Kansas licenses are good throughout the state. Non-resident hunting licenses are issued by the county clerks and their sub-agents, which include hardware and sporting-goods stores and other places of business.

**Seasons.** Game animals and birds for which there are open seasons are:

Squirrel
Pheasant
Quail

There is no closed season on coyote and rabbit.

## KENTUCKY

AREA: 40,395 square miles

**General Summary.** The game situation in Kentucky indicates an increase in most species. After a closed season on deer for about 40 years, hunting is now allowed on the state's only big game. The whitetail are becoming more numerous in the state, and in some areas the imported European red deer have become too plentiful and damaged crops. To solve this problem hunting has been allowed and the deer herds have been scattered and transplanted to many sections of the state. These deer are being protected by a system of big-game refuges, and increased numbers over a larger area are anticipated.

Dogs may be used to hunt deer, because hunters contended that on account of the heavy underbrush and inaccessibility of the areas to be hunted, dogs should be permitted to aid hunters in "flushing" their quarry.

Rabbits and squirrels are the local small-game animals. The rabbit population is excellent in some sections, but just "good" in others.

The bobwhite quail and the wild turkey are showing an increase. There is good dove shooting.

**State Conservation.** The Game and Fish Commission is composed of nine members who are appointed by the governor to serve for four-year terms. The Commission appoints a salaried director who serves for an indefinite term and is subject to removal by the Commission. The director appoints as many conservation officers as may be required efficiently to enforce the game and fish laws. All money derived from the sale of license or from any other source connected with the administration of this department is paid over to the state treasurer who deposits it in a special fund known as the Game

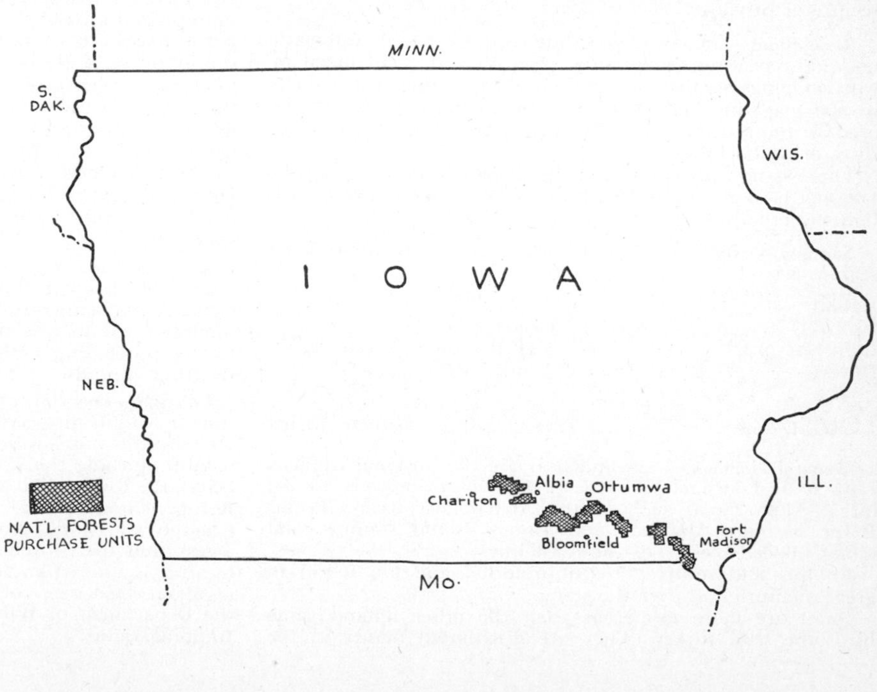

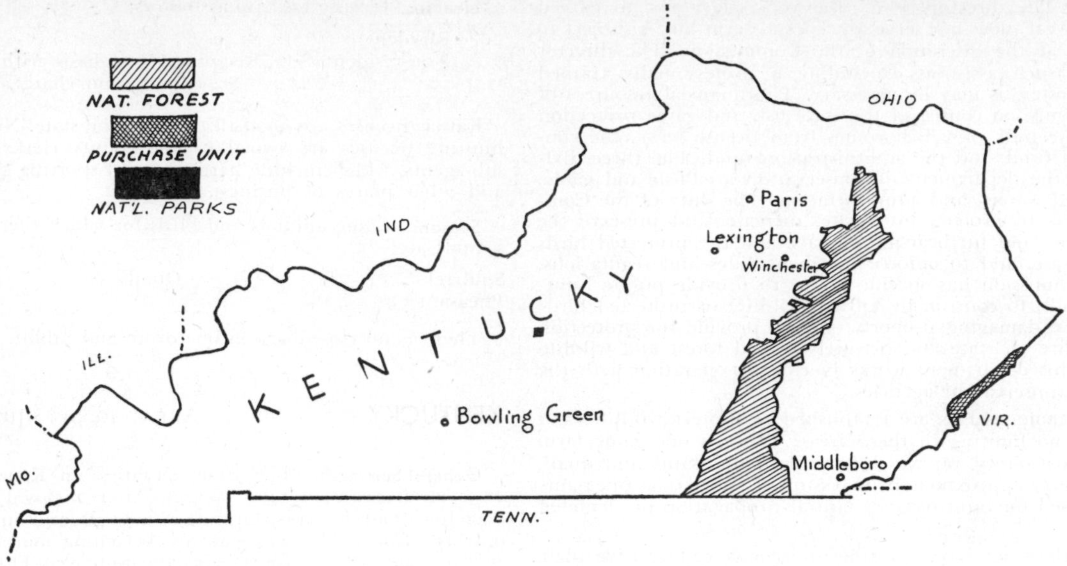


and Fish Fund. Proceeds from the seizure and sale of contraband are also paid into this fund, as well as 60 per cent of the fines levied in violation of the rules of this department.

Kentucky has a farmer-sportsman co-operative program which has been well received by the farmers and has created a better feeling between the man who owns the land and the man who owns the gun.

A state game farm raises bobwhite quail and ring-tailed raccoon. This game farm produces and releases about 65,000 quail per year. In conjunction with this game farm is a game-food nursery which supplies to the farmers different species of plants and trees that are beneficial to wildlife.

**Licenses.** License fees are as follows:

| | |
|---|---|
| Resident county | $1.00 |
| Resident state | 3.00 |
| Non-resident | 15.50 |
| Deer permit | 5.00 |

Resident and non-resident hunting licenses are on sale at county court clerks' offices, most sporting-goods houses, and hardware stores. All licenses, resident and non-resident, are regulated by the Division of Game and Fish. There are no special county licenses, although there is a county license which permits the hunter to hunt within a specified county. No hunting or fishing licenses are issued to residents of any other state which does not grant to citizens of Kentucky the reciprocal privilege.

**Regulations.** The law of this state requires that all automatic or hand-repeating shotguns be plugged with solid metal or wooden plugs so they will not hold more than three shells in the magazine and chamber combined. No rifles may be used to hunt deer. The only permissible shotgun loads are slugs or 00 buckshot.

There is no restriction on using dogs in season, but ferrets may not be used in hunting. Rabbits may not be hunted with lights or other means to blind them at night.

**Seasons.** Game animals and birds for which there are open seasons are:

| | |
|---|---|
| Rabbit | Ducks |
| Squirrel | Geese |
| Bobwhite quail | Ruffed grouse (native pheasant) |
| Doves | |

## LOUISIANA  AREA: 48,523 square miles

**General Summary.** Deer and bear are the big-game animals hunted in Louisiana. They are confined principally to the large swamp areas such as the Atchafalaya Basin, Tensas River bottoms, Manchac and Honey Island swamps, and along wooded regions of the coast line.

Rabbits and squirrel are unprotected and are found in great quantities all over the state.

Quail are more numerous than the other upland game bird, the wild turkey. They are distributed mostly in the "Florida parishes," east of the Mississippi River, and in the northern and western parts of the state.

Doves range all over the state, but the woodcock, another bird subject to the Migratory Bird Act, is found only in damp areas, especially in St. Tammany Parish and in the central part of the state.

Waterfowl shooting is excellent. Ducks and geese are found principally along the coastal areas, with occasional flights along all the major waterways.

The predatory gray fox abounds in large numbers in the northern part of the state and is the object of many a hunt.

Although the majority of hunting clubs presently operating within the state are private organizations, there are few commercial shooting groups. The State of Louisiana operates one such fraternity, the Pass-à-Loutre Public Hunting Grounds, located at the mouth of the Mississippi River. Reasonable fees are charged for guide service, board, and lodging at this 66,000 acre preserve.

**State Conservation.** Within recent years sportsmen, civic and business leaders, and the general public have joined forces with officials of the Department of Wildlife and Fisheries in an attempt to check and revive a diminishing game stock by creating stringent conservation laws.

Despite floods, forest fires, droughts, predators, and an unprecedented number of hunters, wildlife agents report an ever-increasing supply of small game roaming the flatlands, swamps, and hills of the state. Years of planning, scientific experiments, surveys, and investigations are resulting in a greater supply of quail, doves, and woodcock. Game preserves which total 500,000 acres of state-owned refuges are aiding greatly the restocking program now in effect. For years the Louisiana marshes, wintering grounds of northern ducks and geese, have been reseeded with plant life necessary for the continued existence of mallard, pintail, blue and green-winged teal, baldpates, and ruddy ducks. Approximately 50,000 sportsmen annually hunt wild ducks and geese in the watered areas of the state.

Resident game regulations are fixed by the Louisiana legislature, which sets the dates and bag limits for hunting legal game. A recent increase in the resident hunting fee has given monetary aid to predator control, to Ducks Unlimited, and for the purchasing, establishment, and maintenance of public shooting grounds.

Louisiana lays claim to being the first state in the Union to start a wildlife preserve or refuge. Refuges owned and operated by the state, which are devoted to the propagation of wildlife, include the Louisiana State Wildlife Refuge (75,663 acres), the Rockefeller Refuge (86,000 acres), the St. Tammany Refuge, known also as Fontainbleau State Park (6000 acres), Chicago Mill and Lumber Co. Wildlife Refuge (44,675 acres), and the Morehouse Game Refuge (58,000 acres). No hunting is allowed on any of the preserves, with the exception of about 1300 acres of the St. Tammany Refuge, in which the Department of Wildlife and Fisheries holds hunting and trapping rights.

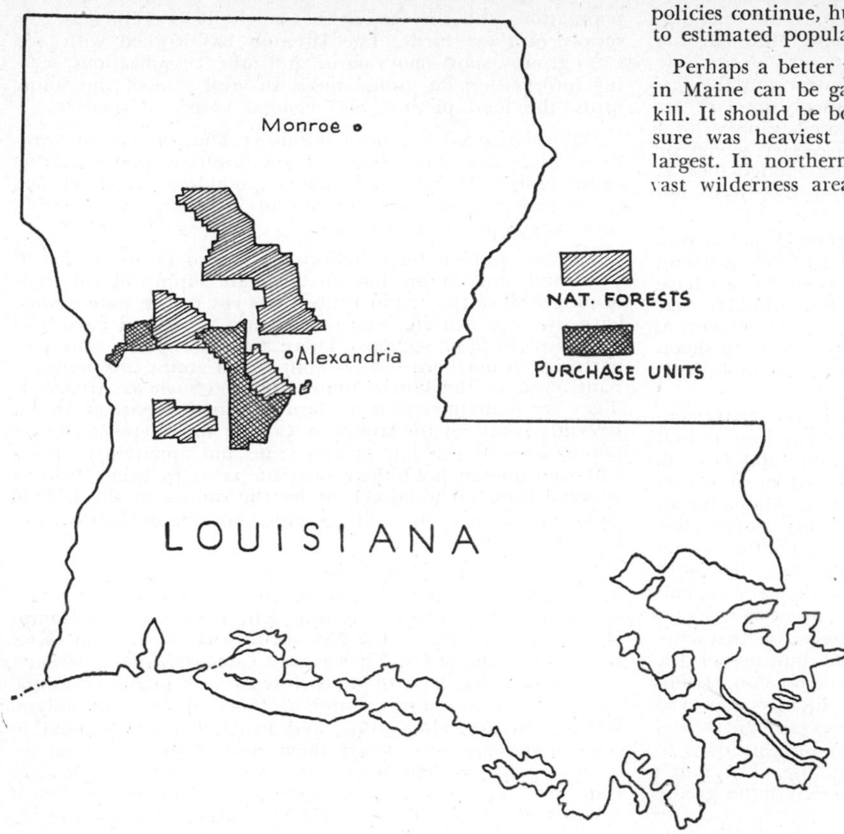


**Licenses.** License fees are as follows:

| | |
|---|---|
| Resident | $2.00 |
| Non-resident | 25.00 |

**Regulations.** Dogs may be used in hunting deer.

**Seasons.** Game animals and birds for which there are open seasons are:

| | |
|---|---|
| Bear | Doves |
| Chipmunks | Ducks |
| Deer | Geese |
| Hares | Quail |
| Rabbits | Turkey |
| Squirrels | Woodcock |

## MAINE

AREA: 33,215 square miles

**General Summary.** The general picture of all species of game animals and birds in Maine is satisfactory. Law enforcement through an efficient warden force, careful planning of open seasons through legislative action on a fish and game committee's suggestions, and stocking of such birds as pheasants are all helping to maintain a healthy crop that should reproduce indefinitely and allow a reasonable amount of shooting without serious depletion of any species.

Deer in Maine have shown a surprising increase in population since large-scale lumbering operations began about 1900. According to most observers, the present population seems to be holding its own in northern counties, particularly where lumbering continues. In central and southern counties, where farming is practiced, deer have continued to increase, despite heavy hunting pressure each fall and control-hunting as practiced by farmers.

The deer kill during the open hunting season in 1946 was 31,728, an all-time high mark for this state. In 1947, the season was cut short 20 days by a woods ban because of extreme fire hazard, but early returns showed a kill of 30,116, with three bucks for every two does taken. There should be a good crop of deer for several years at least. Maine should enjoy excellent whitetail hunting for many years to come, because, if present policies continue, hunting seasons will be regulated according to estimated populations.

Perhaps a better picture of the density of deer populations in Maine can be gathered from a recapitulation of the 1946 kill. It should be borne in mind, however, that hunting pressure was heaviest in the counties where the kill was the largest. In northern counties, hunters did not penetrate the vast wilderness area in anywhere near such large numbers as they did the more readily accessible coastal and central counties.

Androscoggin County recorded 344 deer; Aroostook, 1990; Cumberland, 1349; Franklin, 1757; Hancock, 4162; Kennebec, 1131; Knox, 462; Lincoln, 798; Oxford, 2354; Penobscot, 4608; Piscataquis, 1973; Sagadahoc, 301; Somerset, 2300; Waldo, 1111; Washington, 5047; York, 2041. Total 31,728.

Another factor, in addition to the large number of hunters concentrating in those counties showing largest kill, is cover. In Washington County, where the 1946 deer kill was heaviest, cover is ideal for hunting. Old farms and large stands of head-high growth afford excellent view for the hunter. In Aroostook County, on the other hand, away from the potato section, cover is dense. The growths are fir, spruce, and few hardwoods in this northern section.

Winter feed is an important factor in the size of deer herds. Here again the apparent population density is reflected in those counties which contain the most winter feed. In northern sections, deer are prone to follow lumbering operations around, as these operations assure winter feed.

Although moose are protected in Maine and no open season is in sight, the range of these big animals is increasing within the state, specifically around Shirley and Ross lakes, and about Fort Kent. In the coastal and central counties moose are also increasing.

Black bear are such wary animals that it is difficult to estimate their population. However, most Maine observers believe that bear are increasing or holding their own wherever they normally are to be found. With the possible exception of southeastern Maine, bear inhabit most of the state.

Not only has the range of bobcats increased but the population of these animals is showing an upward trend. Cats, like black bear, are unusually wary, and only their tracks in the snow or the kills they leave behind indicate their numbers. Sportsmen who like to follow hounds and who can do so on snowshoes will find no want of game so far as cats are concerned.

Maine has a few Canadian lynx in northern Aroostook County.

Despite the fact that rabbit hunters have increased in number about 30 per cent, observers feel that snowshoe hares have increased or are holding their own in most parts of the state. In southeastern Maine there are a few cony rabbits but the larger hare is Maine's most important rabbit. Unusually healthy, they are active runners and afford excellent sport for a large number of sportsmen and beagle owners. At least one breeder of rabbit dogs has developed a strain of his own. Termed the Canibas strain, and line-bred for many generations, these dogs are particularly adapted to hunting on the deep snow which covers most of Maine during the long open season on rabbits.

Maine allows a high rate of kill on rabbits, but populations continue high so far, and surplus rabbits afford feed for cats, hawks, and other predators which otherwise would prey on upland game birds. Foxes also find rabbits a ready source of food, and therefore ruffed grouse in Maine have been able to hold their own far longer than in some states where rabbit populations are less dense.

In organized townships, foxes are numerous. In unorganized territory they probably have decreased, although too few observers frequent Maine's wild lands to give an accurate picture of that territory. Certainly fox hunters and the few men who trap foxes in organized townships do not lack for game. The low price of fox pelts has decreased trapping to a point which may make control of foxes necessary sooner or later. As has been stated, however, foxes find enough food at present in the large rabbit population and they have not reduced bird numbers too greatly.

All counties of Maine have an open season on gray squirrels. Squirrels are most abundant where oaks afford food, as would be expected. Coastal towns and large islands in the sea have heavy to normal populations of squirrels. It is unlikely that hunters ever will decrease them to any appreciable extent, as they are targets mostly for young boys just learning to shoot. Nevertheless, they do afford shooting for a considerable body of sportsmen who enjoy the sport.

The range of another game animal has increased tremendously in Maine. The raccoon is spreading out over coastal counties and working inland to central Maine and beyond. Protected as a game animal with a restricted open season for night hunting, the coon is affording sport in Maine for an increasing number of hunters, yet the pressure is kept low by a small bag limit. With this wise control on the species and its ability to adapt itself to its surroundings, it should continue to increase both in range and population throughout the state.

Maine sportsmen are allowed an open season on that king of native birds, the ruffed grouse. Careful hunting of the species, as directed by a foresighted game commission, should keep grouse populations at a constant or slightly improved level for a great many years. More than 16,000 ringneck and mutant pheasants were stocked in Maine covers in 1947, to help reduce hunting pressure on ruffed grouse. The state's Wildlife Division has directed a survey to determine grouse populations and the factors that might help to increase the supply of these birds. The Division has worked with 4-H Club groups, sportsmen's clubs, and other organizations, seeking information on grouse nests, survival rate of the young birds, the food picture, and general cover information.

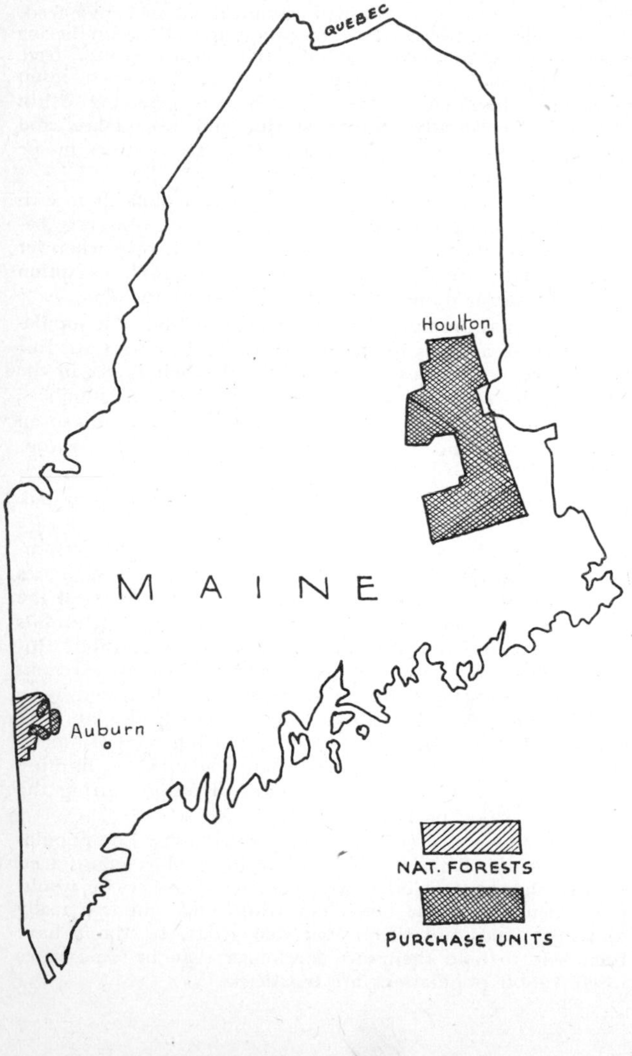


Maine has good flights of woodcock and, in normal years, these birds also take some of the hunting pressure from ruffed grouse. Maine is a breeding ground for woodcock and the state has cleared singing grounds for them in order that they may continue to increase.

The best habitat for ruffed grouse is near farms or on cut-over land, and Maine has an adequate supply of this type of range. Since the virgin timber was cut in the state, grouse have shown a definite increase in many areas and have held their own in most sections. There are some spruce grouse or partridge in northern sections, but ruffed grouse are predominant, even in the northernmost counties such as Aroostook. They are sometimes seen in the roads in that part of Maine. Recently, wardens in Aroostook County have reported heavy populations in the fall of the year, and apparently grouse will continue to hold their own for years to come. With a seasonal limit on woodcock under the control of the Federal government, these game birds should continue in their present large numbers.

Maine pheasants, though not native to the state, have taken hold fairly well, particularly in coastal counties. They are stocked in covers all the way from Kittery on the New Hampshire line to Calais on the New Brunswick border and as far inland as Farmington. They seem to do particularly well on salt marshes that have uplands close by with plenty of annual gardens, but are also gaining a foothold in some inland sections. Swales, alder runs, and fields that are planted to corn or other grains attract them, and Maine is hoping for a permanent population of pheasants in the future. With a state game farm at Gray that raises not only an ever-increasing number of pheasants for stocking but also a large part of the grain to feed them, the state should be in a satisfactory position so far as stocking of this species is concerned.

Under the Wildlife Division, a pheasant survey is progressing satisfactorily. In one experiment some 16,000 birds were banded prior to release in Maine in order that data might be gathered on types of cover best suited to pheasants there, migrations from points where birds are stocked, percentage of birds killed by hunters and other factors. With knowledge and hard work, it is believed that pheasants eventually will become widely established throughout the state. As things stand at present, they are an excellent game bird and may be found over a wide area by hunters, As elsewhere, dogs are practically essential to a successful pheasant hunt.

The range of waterfowl in northern areas is somewhat limited by weather conditions. Large numbers of birds frequent northern bogs, lakes, and rivers, but late October usually brings a freeze-up and the ducks and geese move out. However, the coastal salt-water bays and rivers, and the open sea, afford plenty of room for waterfowl of all kinds. Besides the black duck and bigger redlegs which come down from the north, there are numerous fresh-water species that stop off in Maine from the eastern flyway. Among these are the whistler (golden-eye), bluebill (scaup), green-winged and blue-winged teal, wood duck, ringneck duck, and large numbers of so-called sea ducks, such as scoters and eider ducks. The black duck leads in popularity with most Maine hunters because of its numbers, its food value, and its sporty shooting. Bluebills and whistlers also provide exciting shooting, both pass shooting over points and blind shooting in bays. Flanders Bay at Sorrento and similar spots offer excellent pass shooting. Merrymeeting Bay and Casco Bay, farther southwest, give blind shooters their chance, and on the former (Merrymeeting) scull floats are widely used. Large areas of wild rice attract black ducks and other freshwater birds to spots like Merrymeeting Bay. Heavy populations of geese also frequent Merrymeeting Bay near the mouth of the Kennebec River. Diving ducks have found eelgrass in Casco Bay, and the blacks visit this spot for the mussels at low tide. Eelgrass is making a comeback in Casco Bay, and duck hunting is expected to improve there, although it is already excellent. Sea ducks, scoters, and eiders provide good shooting all along the coast of Maine from Kittery to Calais. The scoters are shot by a comparatively small number of hunters who go offshore a short distance during seasonably good weather. Eiders fly over offshore ledges.

Maine is making further waterfowl studies and a planting of wild rice in the Penobscot River near Old Town has shown excellent results. At least one trial bog will be reclaimed near the coast and water held back to form a pond, which will be planted with duck foods. If this is as successful as anticipated, additional land will be reclaimed for the same purpose.

**Licenses.** License fees are as follows:

| | |
|---|---|
| Resident | $ 2.25 |
| Non-resident | 20.25 |
| Non-resident (small game) | 10.25 |

Resident licenses are available only from town clerks. Non-resident licenses may be purchased from agents appointed by the commissioner, including any store or other agent. Wardens do not sell licenses.

Indians over 18 years of age of both the Passamaquoddy and Penobscot tribes may procure a free license to hunt, trap, and fish from the commissioner.

**Regulations.** No automatic firearm may be used for hunting. No autoloading firearm may be used which has a magazine capacity of more than five cartridges. All autoloading firearms having a magazine capacity in excess of five cartridges must have the magazine permanently altered so as to contain not more than five cartridges before it may be used in Maine, but this ruling does not apply to firearms using the .22 caliber rim-fire cartridge, or to any autoloading pistol with a barrel less than 8 inches long.

Guides must procure a certificate from the commissioner. Those who qualify for a Class A certificate are required to pay an annual fee of $7.50, and for Class B $6.00. The commissioner has the power to suspend a certificate if a guide violates any of the fish and game laws.

It is not necessary to employ a licensed guide when hunting or fishing, but non-residents may not kindle fires in any unorganized township while engaged in camping, fishing, or hunting from May 1 to November 30, without being in charge of a registered guide except at public camp sites maintained by the forestry department. No guide may be employed by more than three non-residents while hunting at the same time.

No dogs may be used to hunt deer.

**Seasons.** Game birds and animals for which there are open seasons are:

| | |
|---|---|
| Deer | Pheasant |
| Gray squirrel | Ruffed grouse (partridge) |
| Rabbit | Woodcock |
| Raccoon | |

There is no closed season on:

| | |
|---|---|
| Bear | Canada lynx |
| Bobcat | Fox |

## MARYLAND — AREA: 10,577 square miles

**General Summary.** The cottontail rabbit is the most important game animal in Maryland. It is subject to fluctuation in numbers each year, due mainly to weather conditions, hunting pressure, predators, and farming practices. Surplus rabbits are live-trapped and removed to underpopulated public shooting areas. Squirrels provide fair shooting in the state. The Virginia whitetail deer is the only large game animal of any consequence in the state. About 450 are taken every year. They are fairly abundant in some counties and apparently the species will soon inhabit every section.

The upland game birds include bobwhite quail, wild turkey, ruffed grouse, mourning dove, and imported pheasant, but the most important is the quail, which continues to show an increase in some sections in spite of increased hunting pressure.

Waterfowl shooting of ducks and geese is excellent in the state. The Chesapeake Bay region is one of the most famous waterfowl shooting grounds in the United States. The birds are attracted to the abundant food supply of wild rice, oats, and pondweeds which grow in the marshes, leads, guts, ponds, and sloughs of the bay area.

**State Conservation.** The Game and Inland Fish Commission is appointed by the governor, and each member of the Commission serves for a five-year term, receiving no compensation other than traveling expenses. The Commission appoints a salaried director, who in turn appoints the game wardens. The power and authority of the Commission includes the hunting, taking, possession, sale, purchase, shipment, transportation, and export of any wild bird, wild animal, or fish from within the state.

Maryland has an organized farmer-sportsman program which has proved very successful. There are six field technicians whose only duty is to visit the farmers and endeavor to sell them the idea of setting aside unfarmable areas as wildlife habitats. In co-operation with county agents and others, large numbers of farm ponds have been established successfully. The Game Commission is firmly convinced that in this way it can establish small game more successfully than by artificial propagation.

As a part of the wildlife conservation measures, the state districts have employed over 30 soil conservation practices to fit the widely varying conditions of soil, topography, climate, erosion, and type of agriculture found in Maryland.

More than 4000 farmers are co-operators with the Soil Conservation districts. They operate nearly 700,000 of the approximately 7,000,000 acres of land in Maryland, of which more than 4,000,000 acres are farmland. Those co-operators have put close to 2000 acres into wildlife refuge and management areas, and nearly 3000 acres in food and cover-producing shrubs, grasses, eroding-field borders, woodland borders, and gullies. One of the activities of greatest importance to wildlife welfare has been the elimination of domestic stock grazing from over 24,000 acres of woodland and wildlife areas. Strip cropping is another soil conservation practice that has greatly increased the interspersion of different food and cover types for farm wildlife. Drainage of quality crop land is the main conservation problem on the Eastern Shore, and more than 2,000,000 lineal feet of ditches have been constructed.

The state operates two game farms, one at Gwynnbrook and the other in Wicomico. The Gwynnbrook farm (290 acres) raises deer, wild ducks and geese, wild turkeys, bobwhite quail, and chukar partridge. The Wicomico farm raises bobwhite quail and wild ducks. These two farms are augmented by smaller units on two of the state game refuges, one in Montgomery County, where quail and ducks are raised, and another in Washington County which specializes in the rearing of wild turkey. The chief attention in rearing birds in captivity is given to the native bobwhite. The game farms maintain from 300 to 500 laying pairs of birds and from these are raised annually from 12,000 to 15,000 birds. Experimentation with the chukar partridge did not begin until 1938, and it is not yet possible to tell whether the species will take hold in the available habitats. Seventeen game refuges totaling 6,293 acres are maintained on the 100,000 acres of state forest lands to provide production and assure a nucleus of breeding stock for the surrounding public shooting grounds, or to protect critically reduced species, such as deer, wild turkey, and the Bryant fox squirrel.

**Licenses.** License fees are as follows:

| | |
|---|---|
| Resident county | $ 1.25 |
| Resident state | 5.25 |
| Non-resident | 15.50 |
| Non-resident (4 days waterfowl only) | 5.50 |

Resident and non-resident licenses are sold by the clerks of the courts in each county, and by a number of agencies which are easily accessible to the sportsmen. A hunting license is required to take wild waterfowl.

**Regulations.** For hunting game birds and animals, no shotgun is permitted which is larger than 10 gauge, or capable of holding more than three shells. In hunting deer it is unlawful to use any gun except one propelling all-lead or lead-alloy or soft-nosed or expanding bullet or ball at a single discharge. It is also unlawful to hunt or shoot at a deer with a rifle using cartridges giving a muzzle energy of less than 1,200 foot-pounds.

Dogs may not be used in hunting deer, but are permitted to retrieve doves during the open season. The trainer may not have firearms in his possession while training dogs during the closed season, and every person training dogs must have in possession a hunter's license and tag displayed on outer garment.

**Seasons.** Game animals and birds for which there are open seasons are:

| | |
|---|---|
| Deer | Mourning dove |
| Opossum | Quail |
| Rabbit | Ruffed grouse |
| Raccoon | Waterfowl |
| Squirrel | Wild turkey |
| Imported pheasant | Woodcock |

## MASSACHUSETTS — AREA: 8257 square miles

**General Summary.** No game species are in danger of serious population losses in Massachusetts. Deer, the only big-game animal hunted, are showing an increase in spite of increased hunting pressure in recent years. About 3500 whitetails are taken annually.

The majority of about 300,000 hunters pursue small-game animals—rabbits, squirrels, and white hares—or upland game birds—pheasants, ruffed grouse, quail, and woodcock. Pheasants are the most numerous of the game birds and vie with the popular native ruffed grouse in importance. There are very few quail in the state.

There is fair waterfowl shooting in Massachusetts; black duck are the most important. Scoter or "coot" shooting is a favorite among many sportsmen along the coastal regions. The larger inland lakes and rivers attract some puddle ducks, particularly mallards.

**State Conservation.** The game-management program of the state's Department of Conservation includes setting aside areas in which a sufficient supply of natural food and adequate cover is available throughout the year. Massachusetts has 71 state forests and 9 wildlife sanctuaries which aid in the natural propagation of the state's wildlife. An active propagation plan is taking place on four state game farms where approximately 30,000 pheasants and 3500 quail are liberated yearly. An increase in production is planned. The Fish and Game Department, in its policy of keeping game distributed, transfers rabbits from areas that are closed to hunting and releases them in open areas. The Division has purchased hares from Canada, and some sportsmen's clubs have imported cottontail rabbits from the dominion.

There is no organized farmer-sportsman co-operative program in Massachusetts, although the Division encourages the idea through its conservation officers and sportsmen's clubs. A start has been made on cover-improvement areas and a number of these areas have been leased from the owners, usually farmers, and plantings of crops and shrubs for winter feeding of birds have been made by the farmer and paid for by the Division.

**Licenses.** License fees are as follows:

| | |
|---|---|
| Resident hunting | $ 2.00 |
| Resident hunting and fishing | 3.25 |
| Non-resident hunting | 10.25 |

Licenses are sold only by city and town clerks and at the office of the director of the Division of Fisheries and Game. No special county licenses are required.

**Regulations.** A rifle of any caliber may be used except for migratory game birds and deer. When hunting deer and migratory birds, a shotgun not larger than 10 gauge may be used. Rifles must be chambered to take ammunition not larger than .22 long rifle. Pistols or revolvers cannot be larger than .38 caliber.

Dogs may be used in hunting except during the open season on deer. No sporting or hunting license is necessary.

No person may hunt any bird or animal in any county open to the hunting of deer after having killed a deer during the current season.

**Seasons.** Game animals and birds for which there are open seasons are:

| | |
|---|---|
| Deer | Ducks |
| Gray squirrel | Geese |
| Hares | Pheasant |
| Opossum | Quail |
| Rabbits | Ruffed grouse (partridge) |
| Raccoon | Woodcock |

There is no closed season on:

| | |
|---|---|
| Fox | Wildcat (bobcat) |
| Skunk | Woodchuck |

## MICHIGAN — AREA: 96,791 square miles

**General Summary.** The southern third of Michigan is predominantly agricultural, and hunting there is mostly for farmland game—pheasants, cottontail rabbits, fox squirrels, and raccoon—and access to hunting lands is often a problem. The northern two-thirds, down to a line crossing the Lower Peninsula roughly west from the head of Saginaw Bay (the notch between the "thumb" and the rest of the "mitt"), is predominantly forested. Its hunting is mostly for deer, bear, snowshoe hares, and grouse, and access to hunting lands is seldom a problem.

Excluding water area, Michigan has 36,437,435 acres, according to the General Land Office Survey. Publicly owned lands total 6,457,000 acres, of which 2,200,000 are in national forests, 3,200,000 in state forests, and the remainder in state parks, game areas, and other state holdings. Hunting is permitted on 99 per cent of state and Federal lands and on much privately owned land, especially in the north.

Michigan offers a varied selection of both large and small game, with hunting of deer, bear, cottontail rabbit and snowshoe hare, fox and gray squirrel, raccoon, pheasant, ruffed grouse, prairie chicken, sharp-tailed grouse, ducks, geese, coot, and woodcock.

Deer are abundant; Michigan has the second largest herd in the United States. In some localities there are more of them than the winter food supply can support and so in such "trouble spots" there is starvation each winter. At the fringe of agricultural land they cause considerable crop and orchard damage. The annual kill by gunners and archers is approximately 100,000. The annual take of bears is about 1000.

There is some winter hunting for bobcat and fox, which are not considered game animals. Occasionally a deer hunter may kill a wolf or coyote, but most of these predators are taken by trappers.

The yearly cottontail kill, mostly in the southern counties, is about 1,300,000, and no concern is felt for the present supply. Hunters take about 300,000 snowshoe hares each season in northern counties. The annual fox-squirrel kill is estimated at about 700,000, that of gray squirrels at about 300,000. In some seasons the raccoon take by hunters (around 70,000) is higher than the number taken by trappers.

The duck harvest has been relatively low in recent years. About 350,000 are killed seasonally. As much of the shooting is furnished by flight ducks, the dark continental outlook affects Michigan duck hunting directly. Pheasant hunters take about 900,000 birds a year. The pheasant decrease is causing much concern because of the heavy hunting pressure this bird supports. The annual bag of ruffed grouse is roughly 180,000, and this bird is on the upswing of its cycle, but prairie chickens are disappearing with closing in of much northern woodland. Because of their scarcity in some sections, certain areas currently are closed to hunting of both prairie chickens and sharptails.

**State Conservation.** In Michigan the agency which handles fish affairs and the agency which handles game affairs are two divisions of a unified Conservation Department that includes also a law-enforcement staff, forest fire-fighting force, and divisions of forestry, lands, geology, parks, education, licensing, and other general operations.

Hunting and fishing license income, which amounts to about $2,000,000 each year, supports the game and fish divisions, the law-enforcement staff, and educational work, and another $100,000 or more for game work is received from the Federal government under the Pittman-Robertson act. The other units of the Michigan Conservation Department are financed out of the state's general fund.

The Game Division maintains trained game specialists in all districts of the state to co-ordinate forestry practice with good game management on more than 3,000,000 acres of state forests. It maintains wildlife experiment stations at Cusino in the Upper Peninsula, Rose Lake near the state capital, and Swan Creek in southwestern Michigan. In the southern third of the state where there is only one state forest, the Division manages a dozen state game areas open to public hunting. The state game farm at Mason has been producing about 10,000 pheasants and 30,000 pheasant eggs for "educational" distribution, but the current pheasant slump has prompted an increase in this output. The farm also produces some experimental releases of Hungarian partridge. Sportsmen's opinions are expressed through club resolutions, and a dozen club magazines. Several hundred selected sportsmen-observers are consulted periodically, through questionnaires, in surveys of game conditions.

Michigan's principal farmer-sportsman co-operative scheme is the Williamston plan, named for the town of Williamston where it originated. Designed to reduce hunting pressure and hunter damage to farm crops and fences, it provides for hunting by permission only, but without charge. Farmers on a section or so of land form a club, and determine how many tickets each shall issue daily; hunters who get the tickets park their cars in the farmer's yard as promise of good behavior. In prewar days the acreage covered by Williamston plan clubs totaled as much as 500,000. For the practical benefit of all southern Michigan farmers the Conservation Department maintains a typical farm at Rose Lake wildlife experiment station, where new ideas are tested and then recommended if they are beneficial to farm game and good farm management; fortunately, the practices found good for farm game have been good for the farms also.

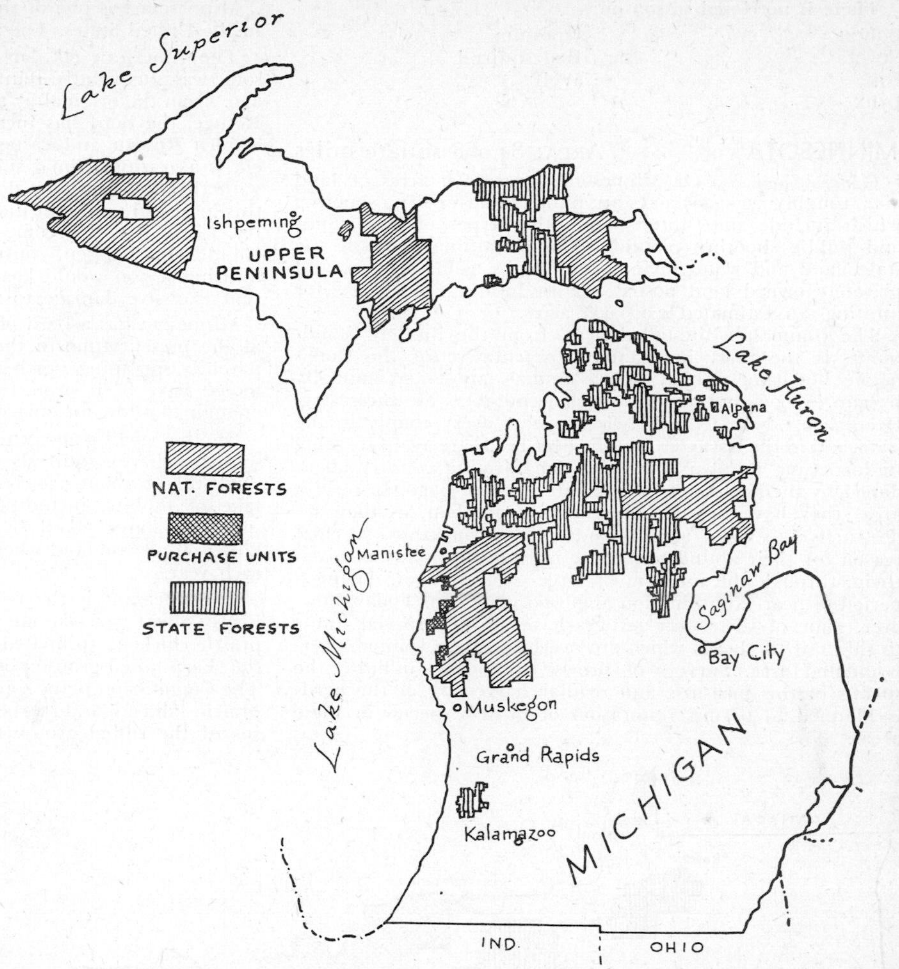


Sportsmen's clubs are well organized in Michigan, and direct co-operation between club members and local farmers is encouraged as an independent venture in each case. Farmers also are assisted by Federal, Conservation Department, and state college specialists on questions of land use, and Conservation Department farm-foresters give detailed assistance on woodlots that include broad views of farm-game matters. Farmers also may obtain reforestation stock from the Conservation Department, Federal services, and the state college at nominal costs.

**Licenses.** License fees are as follows:

| | |
|---|---|
| Resident small game | $ 2.00 |
| Non-resident small game | 15.00 |
| Resident deer and bear | 3.50 |
| Non-resident deer and bear | 35.00 |
| Resident bow-and-arrow deer and bear | 3.50 |
| Non-resident bow-and-arrow deer and bear | 10.00 |
| Camp permit for deer (general season) | 3.50 |
| Camp permit for deer (special bow-and-arrow season) | 3.50 |

Resident and non-resident deer and bear licenses are, in a sense, special licenses. Small-game licenses, resident and non-resident, cover all other game that may be taken legally in Michigan.

Resident and non-resident licenses may be obtained from the Conservation Department's regional and district offices (not from conservation officers), county clerks, sporting-goods, hardware, drug, and grocery stores, and service stations. There are some 3200 license dealers in the above classifications.

**Regulations.** No automatic, semi-automatic, or autoloading shotgun or rifle larger than .22 caliber rim-fire, capable of holding more than six shells at one time in magazine and barrel combined, may be used in hunting game birds or animals. No person is allowed to possess such firearms in any hunting area.

There is no limitation on caliber of rifle that may be used in hunting game.

No rifle larger than .22 caliber, or shotgun with buckshot, slug load, ball load, or cut shell, may be in a person's possession while in deer area during five days preceding the opening of season for the taking of deer with firearms, except for transporting hunting arms to hunting camps.

During the open season for taking deer with firearms, it is unlawful to possess a rifle larger than .22 caliber rim-fire or shotgun with buckshot, slug load, ball load, or cut shell unless the person possessing such firearms and ammunition has secured and has in possession his license to hunt deer with firearms.

During the open season on small game, in any area frequented by deer, no person may possess a rifle larger than .22 caliber rim-fire or a shotgun with buckshot, slug load, ball load, or cut shell.

No dogs are allowed in hunting deer or bear except in counties where bear are unprotected.

Michigan law does not require the employment of a guide in any type of hunting, and there is no licensing of guides in Michigan. Local chambers of commerce, tourist headquarters, etc., often are able to supply the names of local guides.

**Seasons.** Game animals and birds for which there are open seasons are:

| | |
|---|---|
| Bear | Ducks |
| Cottontail rabbit | Geese |
| Deer | Pheasant |
| Fox and gray squirrels | Prairie chicken |
| Raccoon | Ruffed grouse |
| Snowshoe hare | Sharptailed grouse |
| Woodchuck | Woodcock |
| Coot | |

There is no closed season on:

| | |
|---|---|
| Bobcat | Opossum |
| Coyote | Red squirrel |
| Fox | Wolf |
| Lynx | |

## MINNESOTA

AREA: 84,068 square miles

**General Summary.** Of Minnesota's 51,500,000 acres of land area, roughly 5,000,000 acres are public lands open to shooting which include state forests and other types of state lands and public shooting grounds. The remaining acres of the state, land and water, except state parks, game refuges, and privately owned land posted against hunting, is opened for hunting—an estimated 2,000,000 acres.

The common white-tailed deer, from the hunter's standpoint, is the most important representative of the state's native big game. About 65,000 animals are taken annually by gun or bow and arrow, but their numbers are increasing. Deer have now extended their range to every county in the state, and in the last few years the deer herds are again roaming in increasing numbers over the rich farming country abandoned by their ancestors about half a century ago. In certain areas they have become an economic problem, as they are destructive to corn, alfalfa, and other farm crops. A chief reason for their abundance is the rigid protection, first given them, through the medium of large game refuges, during a period of near-extermination about 60 years ago. Today, however, some of these deer refuges have allowed special hunts to thin out the herds which are overbrowsing a limited, overpopulated area. Surveys of browse conditions indicate the success of this measure, and regular harvesting of the herds is planned to permit restoration of browse species in these areas.

Minnesota has one of the largest populations of black bear in the United States. The annual kill totals about 1500.

The American elk, or wapiti, once abundant in Minnesota, was successfully reintroduced into the state a few years ago. From the original 27 animals confined to Red Lake Game Refuge, the herd has increased and spread over into southeastern Roseau and eastern Marshall Counties. Because the elk is a grazing animal subsisting upon food almost identical with that consumed by domestic cattle, any large increase in this herd will no doubt induce it to encroach upon farm country, where it will become a competitor with domestic cattle. Should this happen, control of the species by an occasional hunting season would keep their numbers in check and prevent excessive damage to the farmer's land and crops.

Minnesota has a herd of native moose which are increasing at the present time in the Red Lake Game Refuge and apparently spreading north and west from that area. Although moose have been protected since 1922, their increase is not enough to allow an open hunting season.

Of the small-game animals (squirrels, cottontail rabbit, snowshoe hare), squirrels are hunted the most, with an annual kill of about 250,000, but it is estimated that the total take of rabbits, including cottontail and jack rabbits and snowshoe hares taken by hunters and trappers, and those killed on private land where damage is done, exceeds 2,000,000 each year.

The pheasant is the most hunted of all the upland game birds; about 700,000 are taken each year. In recent years prairie chickens (pinnated grouse) have shown a decrease, but the sharp-tailed grouse population has remained fairly steady. The Commission plans conservation for some of the remaining prairie land as undisturbed habitat for these species. A census of the ruffed grouse reveals a rising period of its cycle which will last for several years. Hungarian partridge have suffered severely in northwestern Minnesota in recent years because of abnormally high rainfall. The annual kill is about 5000 birds. The Commission has made a study of the distribution, abundance, reproduction, and habitat requirements of both the bobwhite quail and the Hungarian partridge with a view to bettering their management. About 500 bobwhite quail are taken annually.

**State Conservation.** The Conservation Department is composed of six divisions—Lands and Minerals, Water Resources and Engineering, Forestry, Game and Fish, State Parks, and Tourist Bureau—all these co-ordinated through the commissioner's office, with a Bureau of Information and Legal Bureau performing special services.

Minnesota boasts a greater acreage in wildlife refuges than any other state, with more than 150 refuges comprising 3,300,000 acres established by the state to protect and propagate its wildlife in natural habitats.

There is no official farmer-sportsman co-operative plan in Minnesota, but various sports organizations have set up their own working agreements.

The Department of Conservation has promoted thousands of game-food patches through the state in a plan to improve game habitat by supplying farmers with the seed and soliciting their co-operation in the planting and cultivation. "Clean farming" operations during the

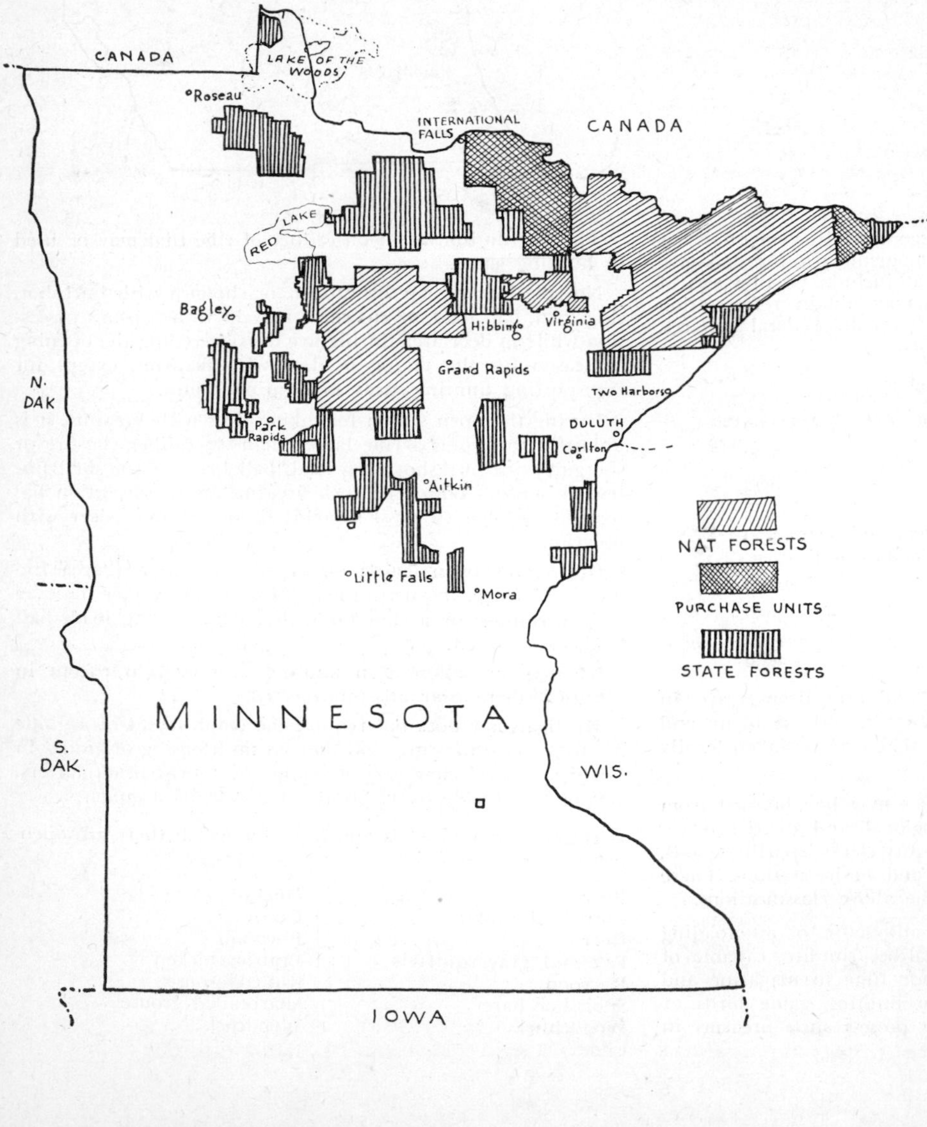

war had erased nearly all of the game cover on the best farm lands in Minnesota, leaving little cover or winter food for game birds.

The Madelia Game Farm, since its establishment in 1930, has been producing all of the pheasants used for restocking burned, frozen, or shot-out areas and for adding to the slower reproduction in the southeastern counties. Production of pheasants for release was reduced during the war years and the birds were reared principally to keep up brood stock with only a small surplus available for release. An open season on pheasants is expected when increased numbers are released and when such birds maintain higher production in restocked areas. About 10,000 bobwhite quail and 12,000 chukar partridges are released each year from the Carlos Avery Game Farm.

**Licenses.** License fees are as follows:

| | |
|---|---|
| Resident big game | $ 2.25 |
| Resident small game | 1.00 |
| Non-resident big game | 50.25 |
| Non-resident small game | 25.00 |
| Non-resident bow and arrow | 10.25 |

**Regulations.** Semi-automatic shotguns and rifles are permitted to be used for hunting in the state.

No deer may be taken with a rifle of smaller caliber than .23 or with any other caliber rifle that uses a cartridge less than 1¾ inches long, unless the gun is of .35 caliber or larger. All cartridges must contain a soft-point or expanding bullet. Shotguns may be used only with a single slug (buckshot or finer shot is prohibited). Bow and arrow may be used during a special deer-hunting season. No deer may be taken by the use of dogs, or from any artificial scaffold or platform higher than six feet above the ground. When hunting deer 50 per cent of the hunter's cap and 50 per cent of his jacket, excluding the sleeves, must be red or covered with red.

**Seasons.** Game animals and birds for which there are open seasons are:

| | |
|---|---|
| Bear | Geese |
| Cottontail rabbits | Hungarian partridge |
| Deer | Mourning doves |
| Gray and fox squirrels | Pheasants |
| Raccoon | Quail |
| Snowshoe hare | Woodcock |
| Ducks | |

There is no closed season on jack rabbits.

## MISSISSIPPI — AREA: 47,716 square miles

**General Summary.** Upland game birds are the most important game in the state. The popular bobwhite quail is hunted in every county, but is most numerous in the northern half of the state, particularly in the northeastern counties around the Black Prairie belt. There is some dove shooting, but a recent drop in the wild turkey population has forced a temporary closed season on that bird.

Small-game animals (rabbits, squirrels, opossums, raccoons) are commonly hunted. The squirrels are decreasing in number, but many gray squirrels are found among the large tracts of hardwoods, and the fox squirrel is common in the Yazoo delta. Rabbits are abundant and well distributed throughout the state. The opossum, raccoon, and fox are all numerous.

Of the big-game animals, the deer is hunted the most and is increasing in numbers, with the best hunting in the delta counties. There are a few black bear, but they are given complete protection. The bobcat is classed as a predator but provides good hunting.

Fair numbers of waterfowl are taken annually. Some good duck hunting is found on the Mississippi River and good goose hunting on the sandbars along the Mississippi.

**State Conservation.** Besides 25 state refuges, Mississippi has six Federal-aid development projects and a co-ordination project for the restoration of wildlife. The State Game and Fish Commission reports that as a result of this Federal aid, coupled with its own restocking program, there are greater numbers of deer, turkey, and quail in Mississippi now than at any time since the creation of the Game and Fish Commission in 1932.

Surplus game grown on the refuges is allowed to leave the refuge area to stock the surrounding territory for hunting, or is trapped and released in other suitable areas where it is needed to improve hunting or trapping for the sportsmen. The largest refuge (33,000 acres on U. S. forest lands) was virtually barren of wildlife in 1939. After food planting, stocking, and breeding—especially of deer, turkey, and quail—a census in 1945 revealed 353 deer, 100 turkeys, 5000 quail, 3000 doves, and 3000 squirrels.

Mississippi has no farmer-sportsman co-operative program in operation, but most landowners and farmers will permit hunting on their land upon request. The Game and Fish Commission points up to the farmers the mutual benefit to be derived if they will leave cover adequate to protect wildlife, particularly the insect-eating bobwhite quail.

**Licenses.** License fees are as follows:

| | |
|---|---|
| County resident (except deer) | $ 1.25 |
| State resident hunting and fishing (all game) | 3.25 |
| Non-resident (all game) | 25.25 |
| Non-resident (small game) | 15.25 |
| Non-resident 7-day (small game) | 5.25 |

Hunting licenses are on sale at sporting-goods stores, sheriffs' offices, and certain places of business; they may also be obtained from the game wardens.

**Regulations.** Shotguns used for hunting game birds and animals must be restricted to three-shell capacity.

Dogs may be used to hunt all game except deer. It is unlawful to hunt any game animal or bird when snow is on the ground to a depth of 2 inches.

Local people familiar with particular hunting ranges can usually be engaged as guides by non-residents.

**Seasons.** Game animals and birds for which there are open seasons are:

| | |
|---|---|
| Deer | Doves |
| Opossum | Ducks |
| Raccoon | Geese |
| Rabbit | Quail |
| Squirrels | |

There is no closed season on bobcat and fox.

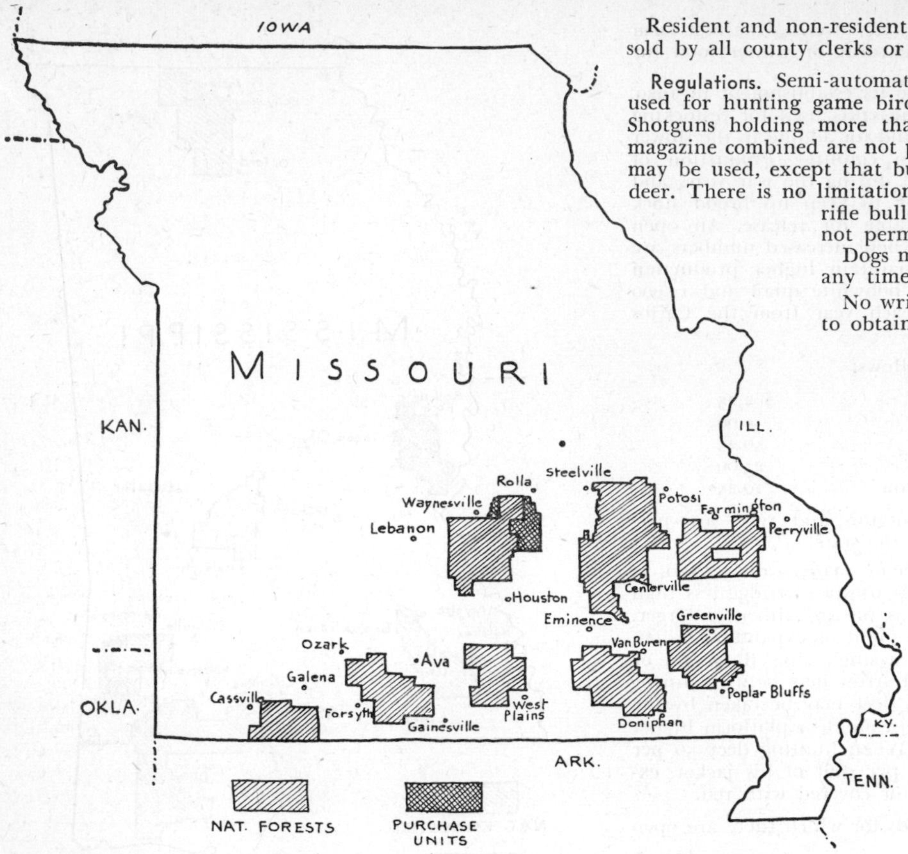

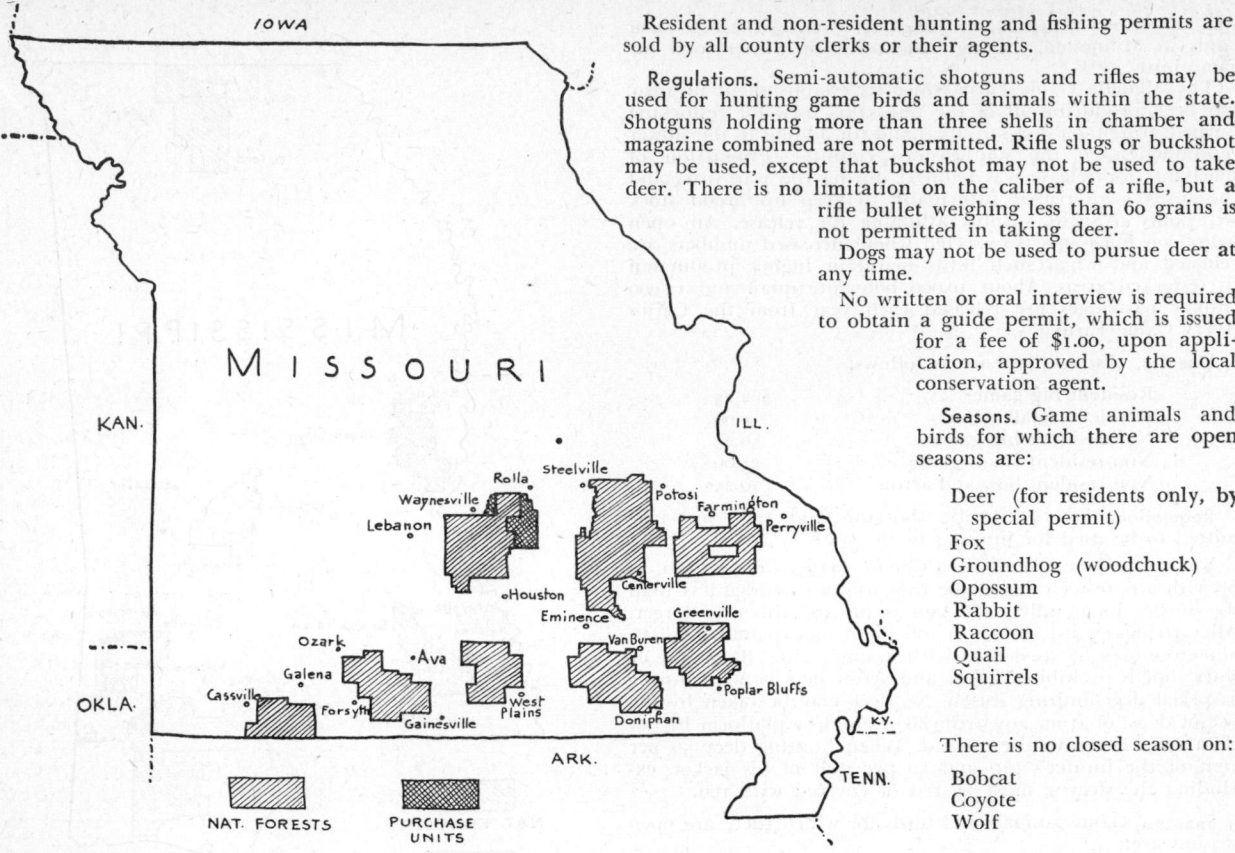

Resident and non-resident hunting and fishing permits are sold by all county clerks or their agents.

**Regulations.** Semi-automatic shotguns and rifles may be used for hunting game birds and animals within the state. Shotguns holding more than three shells in chamber and magazine combined are not permitted. Rifle slugs or buckshot may be used, except that buckshot may not be used to take deer. There is no limitation on the caliber of a rifle, but a rifle bullet weighing less than 60 grains is not permitted in taking deer.

Dogs may not be used to pursue deer at any time.

No written or oral interview is required to obtain a guide permit, which is issued for a fee of $1.00, upon application, approved by the local conservation agent.

**Seasons.** Game animals and birds for which there are open seasons are:

Deer (for residents only, by special permit)
Fox
Groundhog (woodchuck)
Opossum
Rabbit
Raccoon
Quail
Squirrels

There is no closed season on:

Bobcat
Coyote
Wolf

## MISSOURI

AREA: 69,420 square miles

**General Summary.** All land in the state, with the exception of established refuges, is available for hunting, either public or private.

Present game conditions in Missouri are encouraging in regard to everything but wild turkey. There may be a resurgence of this species but at present their numbers are still very small, approximately 4000. They are carefully protected, and there is no hunting season on them.

The state's big-game animal is deer, which has recently shown a sharp increase. There are about 25,000 animals spread over an area about twice the size of that inhabited ten years ago. Small game (in order of importance to the hunter) are squirrels and rabbits. Upland game birds are quail and dove. Virtually all waterfowl are found in Missouri during certain seasons of the year.

**State Conservation.** The Fish and Game Division is a part of the State Conservation Commission; wildlife is considered a part of the entire picture of conservation, with emphasis on suitable natural habitat rather than on artificial propagation of game. Game management is practiced, however, by live-trapping game in over-productive areas and releasing it in depleted areas. Sportsmen are represented in such matters; the Division consults with them through their various organizations in Missouri, the largest of which is the Conservaion Federation. A field census is taken each year in an effort to determine proper regulations and bag limits for the next season.

Missouri has no official farmer-sportsman plan, although the Division runs educational campaigns on the benefits of co-operation. As conservation methods are based upon restoration of natural habitat so that the game may propagate itself, this requires close co-operation between the farmers and the personnel of the Game Division.

**Licenses.** License fees are as follows:

| | |
|---|---|
| State resident | $ 2.15 |
| County resident | 2.00 |
| Non-resident (small game) | 15.00 |
| Deer hunting permit (residents only) | 5.00 |

## MONTANA

AREA: 146,316 square miles

**General Summary.** The game situation in Montana is generally satisfactory, and the population of all species of big game, except mountain sheep, has reached the maximum number which the range will support. Winter range is the limiting factor. Of the state's exceptionally wide selection of big game, deer, both whitetail and mule, are the most important species to the hunter. Recently, a good many deer have been moved from overpopulated ranges and redistributed. Second to deer in numbers and favor with the sportsman is the elk, followed by antelope, mountain goat, moose, grizzly, and black bear. This order has been maintained for a good many years, and since there has been no sharp increase or decrease recently in populations the present order probably will exist for some years to come. The mountain sheep has shown some decrease, and the problem is receiving study by the Restoration Division of the Game Department. The antelope has shown the greatest increase of all the big game, and in the last few years about 900 have been trapped and transplanted to take the pressure from limited, overgrazed ranges and to widen the distribution. Mountain goats have been transplanted in a like manner. Montana has one of the largest bison herds in the United States, but there is no regular open season.

Small-game animals hunted are jack, cottontail, and snowshoe rabbits, woodchuck, and prairie dog.

Montana has a variety but a small number of upland game birds, and there is very limited hunting on those species which have an annual open season. The most numerous upland bird is the pheasant; fewer in number are the sage hen, blue grouse, ruffed grouse, and Hungarian partridge. Partridge have shown an increase, but are still not so numerous as in previous years.

The mallard is by far the most common duck killed, with the other species better distributed. Canada and snow geese are the two species of geese commonly taken.

**State Conservation.** The State Department of Fish and Game is composed of five members, appointed by the governor for a four-year term, experienced in the subject of wildlife and the requirements for their conservation and protection. The state fish and game warden is appointed and employed by the Department for an indefinite term. The warden employs deputy wardens, not in excess of 27, who have passed the required examination to assist him in enforcing the game laws. The warden also may appoint anyone who is a resident of the state as a non-salaried special deputy fish and game warden.

Deep winter is a major concern to the game animals and birds of Montana, for at that time many die of starvation and lack of suitable coverage. Checking on game conditions, forage, snow depths, and any other factors that affect game in the depth of winter is one of the duties of the Department. The motor toboggan has greatly speeded winter patrols, and foot patrols often travel by ski-equipped planes to their starting points.

The Department has not sponsored a definite farmer-sportsman co-operative program, but by press and radio releases it attempts to explain the viewpoints of each group so as to foster a better understanding. Upon farmer-sportsman co-operation depends much future hunting, especially for pheasants, which are the most hunted upland game birds.

At the present time the state operates three game farms and releases about 40,000 birds annually. Since bird banding and certain biological studies indicate a low survival rate of birds released from game farms, it is difficult to predict the number which will be released in the future.

**Licenses.** License fees are as follows:

| | |
|---|---|
| Resident big game (available after purchase of small-game license) | $2.00 |
| Resident small game | 3.00 |
| Non-resident big game | 100.00 |
| Non-resident small game | 25.00 |
| Alien big game | 100.00 |
| Alien small game | 25.00 |
| Moose permit (special drawing) | 25.00 |
| Antelope permit (special drawing) | 5.00 |

Hunting licenses are on sale by some 450 authorized license dealers in the state and by game wardens. Many of the dealers are operators of sporting-goods stores.

**Regulations.** The only law governing firearms in the state indicates that a "set-gun" is illegal and that anything larger than a 10 gauge may not be used.

Dogs may not be used to chase any game animals. Exceptions are granted for stock-killing predatory animals.

A state resident wishing to become a commercial guide must obtain a license (fee for which is $10.00) from the state fish and game warden.

Any person hunting big-game animals must wear red on his clothing.

**Seasons.** Game animals and birds for which there are open seasons are:

| | |
|---|---|
| Antelope | Blue grouse |
| Bear | Ducks |
| Deer | Geese |
| Elk | Hungarian partridge |
| Moose | Pheasants |
| Mountain goat | Ruffed grouse |
| Rabbits | Sage hen |
| Woodchuck | Sharp-tailed grouse |

There is no closed season on:

| | |
|---|---|
| Civet cat | Wild cat |
| Coyote | Wolverine |
| Mountain lion (bobcat) | |

## NEBRASKA    AREA: 77,237 square miles

**General Summary.** A large portion of Nebraska's area is under cultivation, produces game, and is open to hunting.

Game conditions in this state are from fair to excellent, depending on the species. Waterfowl is one of Nebraska's most important types of game, for 23 species of ducks and 4 species of geese either breed in Nebraska or frequent the state. Waterfowl populations in general have held up very well despite the shortages on the East and West coasts. In addition to those birds breeding within the state, the fall and spring migrations bring about one-fourth of the North American waterfowl population through the state, which is situated on the central flyway and in the path of many birds traveling to and from the great nesting grounds of the Prairie Provinces. The Nebraska Sand Hill lake region, particularly in the western portion, has long been famous for waterfowl shooting. The Platte River west from Lexington in Dawson County also provides good duck hunting. The rainwater basins from Clay County west through Phelps County furnish good duck hunting and fair goose hunting, as does the section where the Missouri River forms the northern boundary of the state.

Jack snipe, Wilson's snipe, greater and lesser yellowlegs, curlew, willet, avocet, and phalarope are found within the state, but Federal law forbids killing them.

The pheasant, chief upland game bird, has been decreasing in numbers since about 1943, but the gradual decline apparently is a phase of a normal cyclic fluctuation. A contributing factor to this population drop in recent years has been changing land-use practices which resulted in more intensive farming methods and a consequent reduction of game cover. Also, more hunters have been in the field each year, harvesting

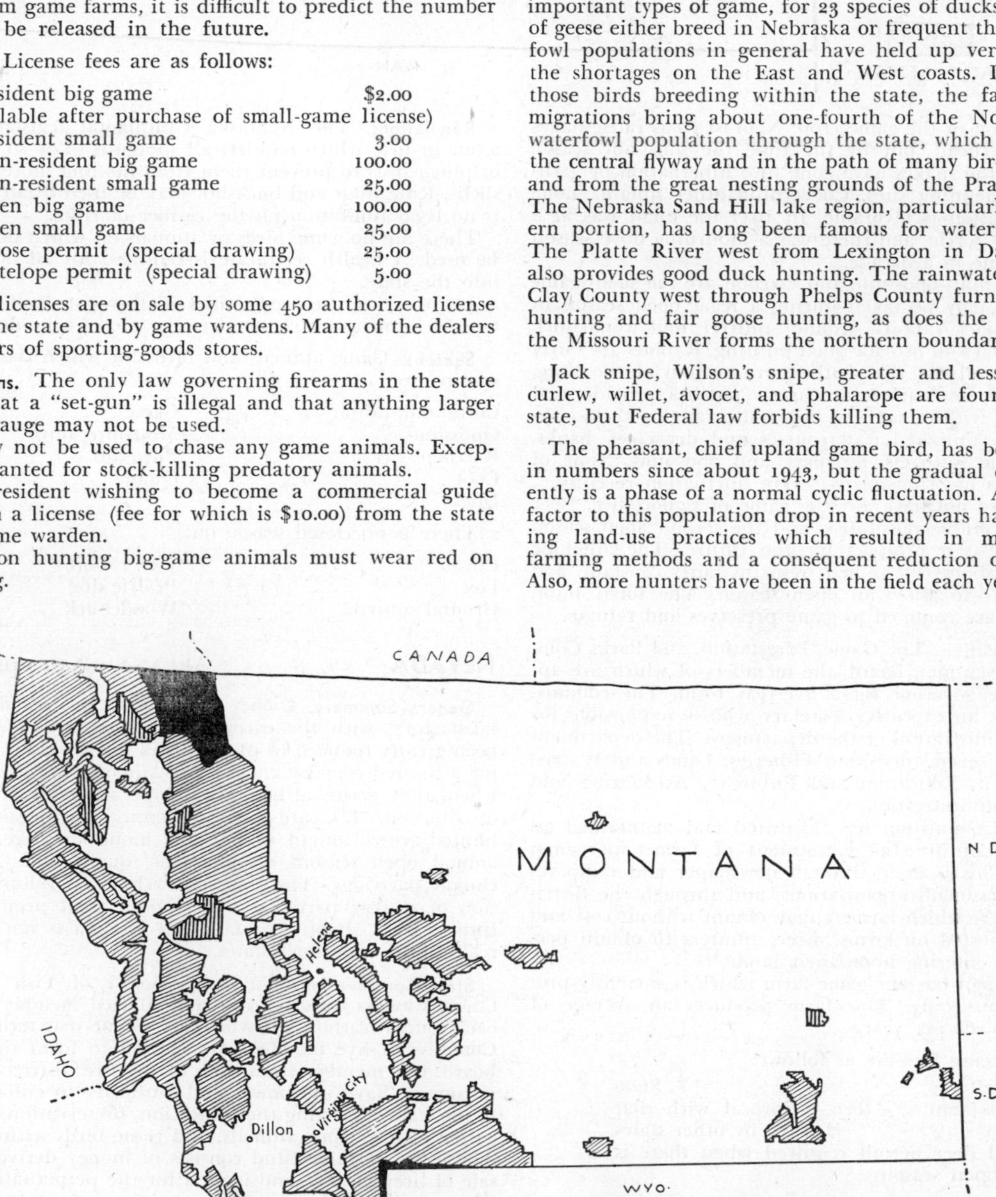

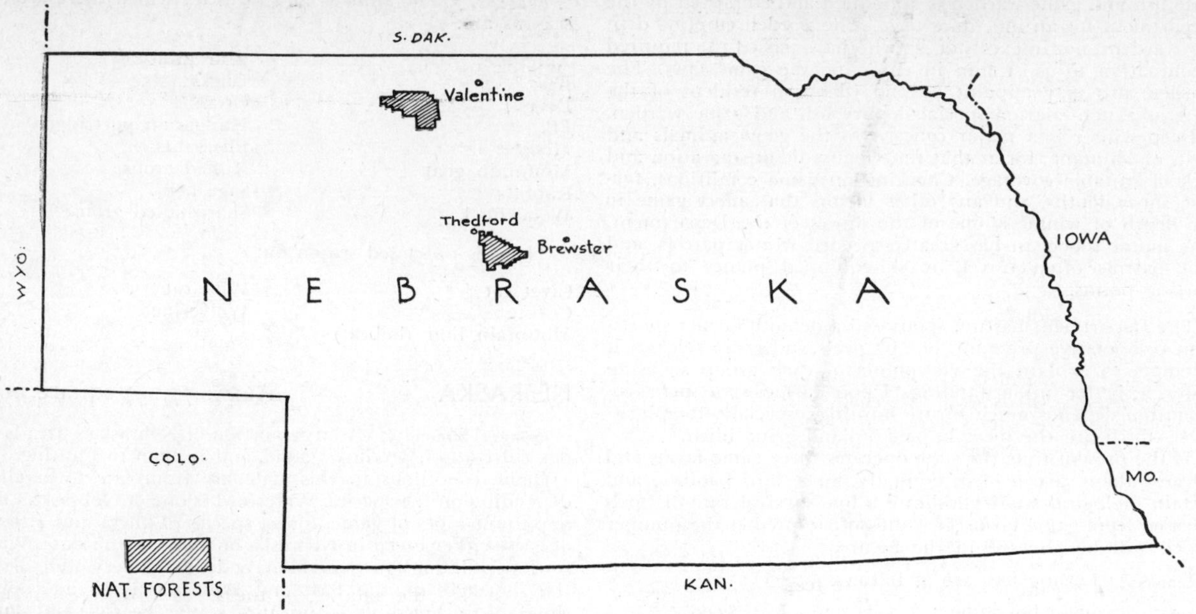


a greater portion of the game crop. Nebraska has rattlesnakes and the copperhead, but by the time the pheasant season opens most of the snakes have gone into hibernation or gathered at their denning sites. Concerning other upland game birds, the situation is favorable. In 1947 the quail was at a high peak in its cycle, and there was a mourning dove season for the first time in a decade.

Cottontail r bbit, opossum, and raccoon are the small-game animals which may be taken during a legal open season in the state, but jack rabbits, ground squirrel, and woodchuck are not protected and provide good hunting. Rabbits are fairly plentiful, especially in the southeastern section of the state. The hedgerows and numerous brush patches provide real rabbit hunting with or without dogs. Also ranging the southeast, along the timbered watercourses and dry creek banks, are most of the squirrels, raccoons, and opossums. None of the small game has shown any severe fluctuation recently.

Nebraska does not have any big game of importance. Deer is the most favorable possibility, and the second open season in many years is a prospect for the future. The antelope population of about 900 animals remains fairly constant, and is not sufficient to allow an open season. The small bison and elk herds are confined to game preserves and refuges.

**State Conservation.** The Game, Forestation, and Parks Commission is a seven-man board, the members of which are appointed by the governor for a five-year term. The commissioners appoint an executive secretary who is responsible for the direct administration of the department. The department is composed of several divisions: Fisheries, Lands and Waters, Game, Research, Education and Publicity, Accounting and Supply, and Administration.

The Game Commission has instituted and maintained an intensive program for the betterment of farmer-sportsman relationship. This is done through newspaper and radio releases and sportsmen's organizations, and through the distribution of posters which farmers may obtain without cost and which, when posted on farms, direct hunters to obtain permission before entering upon their land.

The department has one game farm which is currently producing pheasants only. This farm produces an average of about 13,000 birds per year.

**Licenses.** License fees are as follows:

| | |
|---|---|
| Resident | $1.00 |
| Non-resident | Fee reciprocal with that charged by other states |
| Special deer permit required when there is an open season | |

Resident and non-resident hunting permits are sold at the offices of county clerks and by any reliable retail dealer in the state who meets necessary qualifications. Many of the larger sporting-goods stores handle licenses, as do hardware stores, druggists, and grocers in smaller towns.

**Regulations.** The Nebraska Unicameral legislature passed a law in 1947 which requires all shotguns to be so constructed or plugged as to prevent them from holding more than three shells. Rifle slugs and buckshot may be used legally and there is no legal limitation on the caliber of rifles.

There are no game birds or animals on which dogs may not be used. A health certificate is required for all dogs brought into the state.

There are no licensed guides in this state and there is no type of hunting which requires the use of a guide.

**Seasons.** Game animals and birds for which there are open seasons are:

| | |
|---|---|
| Cottontail rabbit | Geese |
| Opossum | Mourning dove |
| Raccoon | Pheasant |
| Coot | Quail |
| Ducks | |

There is no closed season on:

| | |
|---|---|
| Coyote | Jack rabbit |
| Fox | Prairie dog |
| Ground squirrel | Woodchuck |

## NEVADA — AREA: 110,540 square miles

**General Summary.** Game populations in Nevada are very satisfactory, with the exception of sage hen. This bird has been greatly reduced in number and distribution, but is making a limited comeback. Deer and antelope are very abundant where they occur, although antelope are rather restricted in distribution. Elk are less numerous. Small-game animals hunted are cottontail rabbits and mountain hare. There are annual open seasons on pheasant, quail, blue grouse, and chukar partridge. The state has a large, developing population of chukar partridge which gives great promise for the future. Duck shooting is fair, but Nevada is not one of the really good waterfowl states.

**State Conservation.** The state Board of Fish and Game Commissioners consists of 17 non-salaried members, one from each county of the state, who serve a four-year term. From the Commission five members are elected to form the executive board, one member from each of the five districts. The commissioners have the power and authority to enforce all laws of the state respecting the protection, preservation, and propagation of fish, game animals, and game birds within the state. The fish and game fund consists of money derived from the sale of licenses, etc., and is used for the perpetuation of wildlife as well as related expenses, such as the salaries and expenses of the fish and game wardens. The commissioners are responsible for the maintenance of the 17 game refuges.

Each county has a County Game Management Board, consisting of three non-salaried members, which works in co-operation with the state Fish and Game Commission. It may take individual action on fish and game management, however, such as the shortening or closing of a season entirely, except as to migratory birds which are under Federal regulation.

The state operates one game farm, producing pheasants only. The annual production is approximately 12,000 birds.

Nevada has no formal farmer-sportsman program in operation. Written permission must be obtained from a landowner before entering his land to hunt.

**Licenses.** License fees are as follows:

| | |
|---|---|
| Resident | $ 2.50 |
| Non-resident | 10.00 |
| Alien | 30.00 |

Licenses are handled by county clerks and their agents, usually sporting-goods stores. However, non-resident deer tags must be obtained from the general office of the Commission.

Fees for big-game tags, other than buck deer, are set annually.

For hunting deer, non-residents must obtain a license specific for any one county or special area and they are not permitted to hunt in any other area. On all other big-game hunts and on some deer hunts, special tags are available, limited to a specific area for both residents and non-residents.

**Regulations.** In hunting big game it is unlawful to use a shotgun, any pistol or revolver, any .22-caliber rim-fire rifle, any .22 high-power, .218 bee, and .219 zipper rifle, or any gun or firearm capable of firing two or more rounds with one continuous pull of the trigger. Three-shell capacity on a shotgun is required on migratory game only.

Dogs are not allowed in hunting big-game animals, but may be used in tracking a wounded deer.

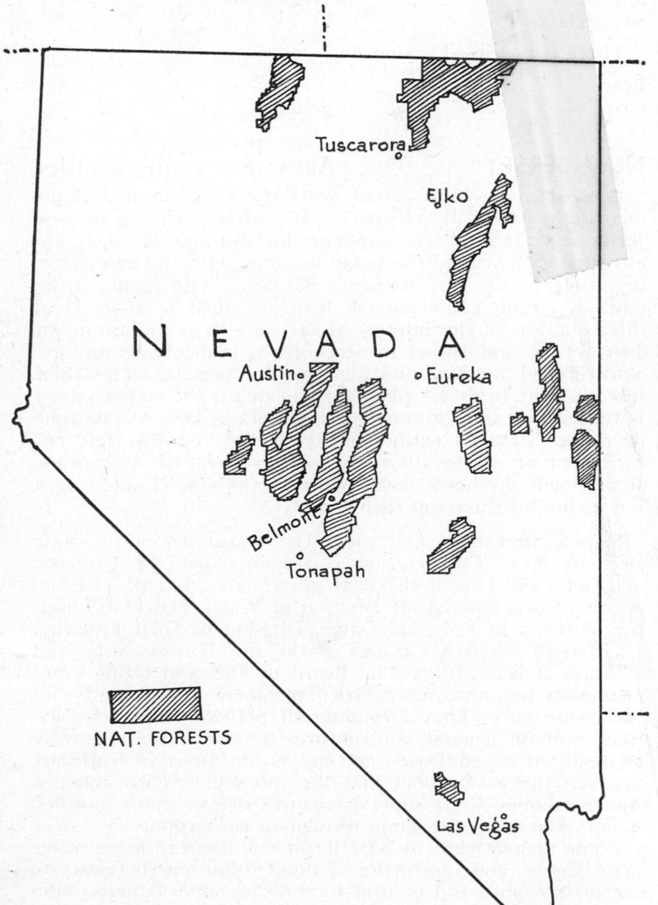


**Seasons.** Game animals and birds for which there are open seasons are:

| | |
|---|---|
| Antelope | Grouse |
| Cottontail rabbit | Mountain quail |
| Mountain hare | Pheasant |
| Mule deer | Sage hen |
| Chukar partridge | Valley quail |

The seasons on game in this state vary with each county, and should be checked locally or with the Fish and Game Commission at Reno.

## NEW HAMPSHIRE — AREA: 9304 square miles

**General Summary.** At least 90 per cent of New Hampshire's land is open to public hunting. Exceptions are urban centers, one private game park of a few thousand acres, and a few other smaller private holdings. Large areas included in waterways furnish some duck hunting.

New Hampshire's extensive forests make it possible for deer to be found in every township of the state. The Game Department believes the best management under present conditions is the proper harvest of deer. On the basis of annual kill data, and of forest browse conditions, New Hampshire's deer-harvest policies seem to have been entirely beneficial to the state's deer herd. Recently, the annual kill has shown a steady increase despite long seasons and the harvest of both bucks and does. A research staff stands by, however, to watch for any signs of deterioration in the deer herd or for signs of over-population, in which event an educational program would be launched to appeal for a larger harvest. The Department opposes periodic attempts to close the season on does, since yearly analyses of the deer sex ratios has shown this to be best for the health of the deer herd. A co-operative study with the U. S. Forest service is aimed at learning what type of lumbering operations will be most beneficial to deer, since it is realized there is no other concern in the state that can have as much influence on the deer habitat.

Former attempts at habitat improvement for the popular ruffed grouse have not been sufficiently effective in New Hampshire. The state now stresses population analyses in order to guide proper legislation.

The pheasant is considered an exotic to the state, and is treated as such. Large numbers are released annually with the expectation that they will be harvested, since present agricultural practices are inadequate to maintain many of these birds. The state also considers the pheasant a buffer between the hunter and the grouse, since the presence of pheasants supposedly removes some of the hunting pressure on the more difficult to manage grouse. A state-wide survey by the research division has mapped all pheasant cover as to location, size, and suitability. Stocking programs are based on the results of this survey.

The state has nesting woodcocks and is also in the line of these migrating birds. Therefore, the numerous alder coverts offer some attractive opportunities to the woodcock hunter.

New Hampshire does not lie in the direct line of waterfowl migration routes. The state is, however, the nesting ground for black ducks, wood ducks, American mergansers, and golden-eyes. The research staff has consequently made a statewide survey of all waterways with a view to improving habitat for the native duck population by increasing nesting areas, improving food conditions, and creating sanctuaries.

**State Conservation.** The Fish and Game Department is composed of a salaried director appointed by a rotating five-man commission which is appointed by the governor and council. Almost all regulations concerning wildlife stem from the legislature. Considerable funds are expended each year on purchase, planting, research, and management to benefit game populations in the state, and the sum is climbing yearly. Previous to 1947, the Department operated entirely on its earnings, chiefly from license sales.

Because of geographic factors—locations within easy striking range of densely populated areas, and scenic attractions provided by the White Mountains, thousands of acres of forested country, interspersed with hundreds of lakes and streams which form the headwaters of three major watersheds of New England—and the accessibility provided by a network of good motor roads throughout the state, New Hampshire's supply of game depends for its very existence upon expert control.

A highly specialized force of 28 conservation officers is entrusted with the task of safeguarding the welfare of the state's wildlife. While adequate enforcement of fishing and hunting laws is one of their functions, there are other equally vital aspects to their work. Special courses provide them with a knowledge of current research on wildlife and its application to New Hampshire species. Other study trains them for work in education and public relations which is essential under present-day conditions.

Each officer is equipped with two-way radio to insure maximum efficiency in co-ordination with headquarters and with other officers. Each has an assigned territory within which he lives and familiarizes himself with day-to-day problems of game species as well as human beings. New Hampshire conservation officers are picked for individual initiative and for their interest in their profession. Through this combination of trained specialist with practical field man, and through years of working together toward a common purpose, this field force has built up an *esprit de corps* which is the best possible insurance that New Hampshire wildlife will be protected and encouraged to increase.

There is no official farmer-sportsman co-operative program in operation in New Hampshire. Good relations are maintained through the initiative of the sportsmen themselves, sponsored by many sportsmen's clubs, and fostered by Department personnel. The careful balance of values required

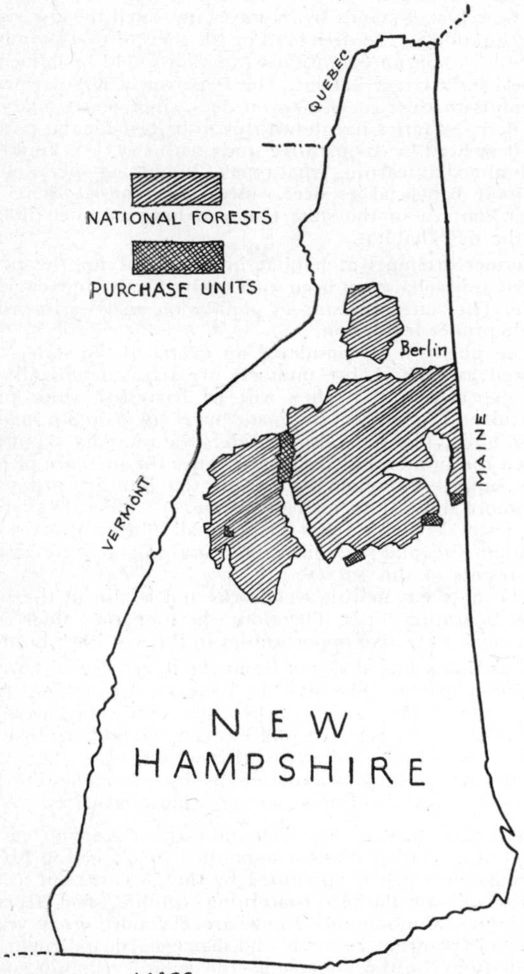


to satisfy legitimate claims of farmers against damage done by game and still preserve the maximum stock for hunting is an important factor in keeping these relations good. New Hampshire is fortunate in still being a public hunting state throughout the greatest part of her territory. Some clubs go so far as to publish signs and posters exhorting the sportsmen to good behavior and invite all local landowners to a banquet once a year.

There is at present no game farm in New Hampshire, but one is contemplated in the near future. The state buys and plants about 7000 pheasants and 2400 snowshoe hares a year. The sportsmen play an important part in game management through clubs, legislative influence, and direct contact with the Department. One of the major goals of the Game Department is to encourage them to share in the responsibility and labor wherever possible, as this is the best way to avoid uninformed or adverse pressure.

**Licenses.** License fees are as follows:

| | |
|---|---|
| Resident—general | $ 3.75 |
| Non-resident—hunting | 15.25 |

Fishing and hunting licenses are sold from the office of the Fish and Game Department or by license agents appointed in each town. These may be sporting-goods store proprietors or other merchants.

**Regulations.** Automatic rifles may not be used, and semi-automatics are limited to five shells for deer hunting. For waterfowl, automatics must be plugged so that they cannot hold more than three shotgun shells—to conform with Federal regulations. Rifled slugs, buckshot, etc., may be used. Any rifle may be used for deer hunting except a .22 rim-fire. However, the law prohibits the use of full-jacketed metal-cased bullets, whether original or altered. Certain towns are restricted to the use of a shotgun for deer hunting. Their numbers are growing less with each legislative session.

Dogs may not be used to hunt deer.

The use of a hunting guide is never required, but there are many licensed guides in the state. They obtain license application forms from the office of the Department. The fee is $2.00 for a resident license and $20.00 for a non-resident. There is no examination. A list of guides may be obtained from the office of the Department.

**Seasons.** Game animals and birds for which there are open seasons are:

| | |
|---|---|
| Deer | Grouse |
| Hares | Pheasant |
| Rabbit | Woodcock |
| Squirrels | |

There is no closed season on:

| | |
|---|---|
| Bear | Lynx |
| Fox | Wildcat |

## NEW JERSEY AREA: 8224 square miles

**General Summary.** In recent years there has been a slight increase in practically all species. Waterfowl shooting in New Jersey has always been excellent, for millions of birds are attracted each year to the broad marshes, with the best shooting being in the vast Barnegat Bay area. The rabbit is the most important game animal, being pursued by more than three-quarters of the hunters of the state. It is ubiquitous in distribution, and, aided by stocking, is multiplying rapidly. Squirrel and raccoon hunting also are popular. The chief upland game birds are pheasant and quail; the ruffed grouse is very scarce, and gunning for woodcock is fair. At one time deer were virtually extinct in New Jersey, but by rigid enforcement of conservation methods by the Fish and Game Department the herds have increased and spread, allowing a kill of several thousand each year.

**State Conservation.** The salaried commissioner of the State Department of Conservation is appointed by the governor and holds office until the next governor is elected. The Department is composed of: Division of Water Policy and Supply, Division of Fish and Game, Division of Shell Fisheries, Division of Forestry, Geology, Parks and Historic Sites, and Division of Navigation. The Board of Fish and Game Commissioners has nine non-salaried members, representative of the entire state. They formulate all policies, suggest legislation, exercise general control over administration, approve all financial expenditures, and act as the direct intermediary between the government and the sportsman. Each commissioner assumes direct supervision over two or more counties. There is at least one game warden in each county.

Game management in New Jersey emphasizes the restoring, maintaining, and improving of those conditions necessary to the maintenance and natural increase of game. It necessitates the planting of shrubs, trees, and grass. Food patches are planted to supplement a diminishing food supply and winter feeding is an active program during periods of emergency. Parts of woodland are sometimes altered to allow more light, and fence rows, etc., are created and planted. Ponds are constructed in the marshland. To facilitate a difficult task, public interest in conservation of wildlife is growing.

The "Plainsboro Hunter Co-operative Plan" represents the workable arrangement between hunter and farmer in New Jersey. The posting of private lands had previously caused a serious shortage of hunting places, and the object of this agreement was to provide mutual benefit for hunter and landowner. Hunting is allowed without cost and by registration. By this procedure the landowner receives protection against damage to livestock and property and knows who is on his land, and the sportsman is allowed to hunt on land which otherwise would have been closed to him. Any group of landowners, sportsmen, or civic organizations can make application for participation in this plan.

The Forked River Game Farm and the Rockport Game Farm both raise pheasants. Of 30,835 pheasants liberated for the year 1946, about 10,000 were propagated and distributed from these state-owned farms. Of more than 12,700 quails released in that year, the majority were propagated and distributed from the state quail farm; a few were purchased and liberated.

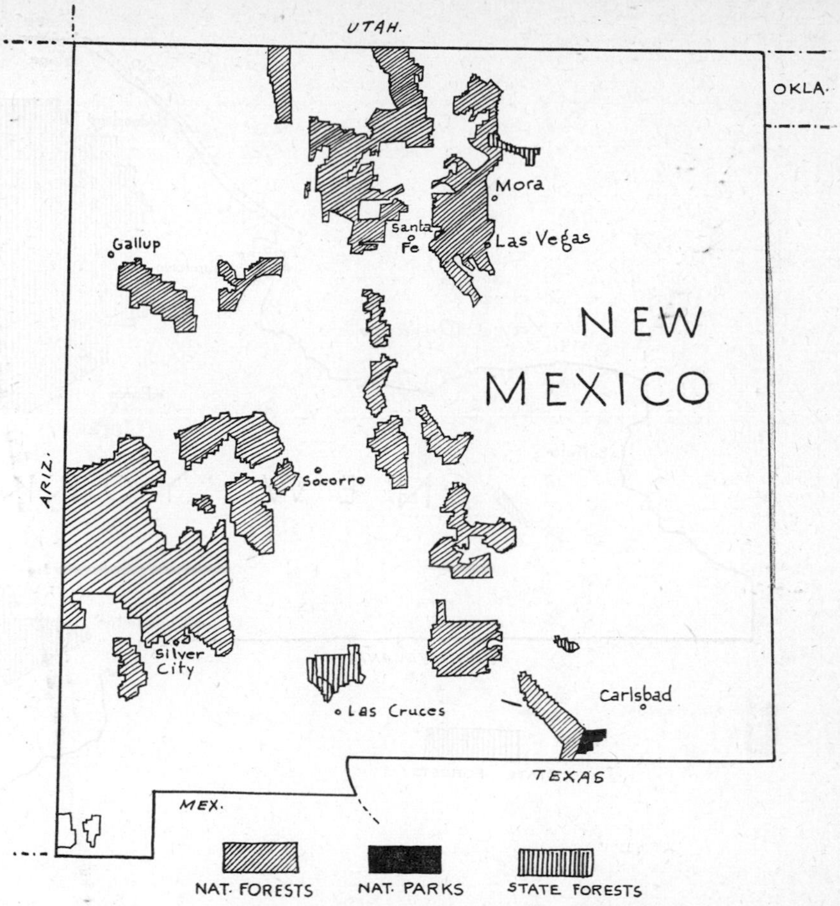


**Licenses.** License fees are as follows:

| | |
|---|---|
| Resident | $ 2.10 |
| Non-resident (general) | 10.50 |
| Alien (general) | 10.50 |
| Special woodcock permit | 2.00 |

Licenses are sold by county and municipal clerks and by game wardens.

**Regulations.** No shotgun in New Jersey may be larger than 10 gauge, be capable of holding more than two cartridges at one time, or be able to be fired more than twice without reloading. No rifle or firearm of any kind may be used to hunt deer which has a smaller caliber than 12 gauge, nor may the hunter have in his possession any shot shells except buckshot.

Dogs may not be used in hunting deer.

Hunting is not permitted in a tracking snow, and no game bird or animal (except raccoon) may be hunted by the use of artificial light.

**Seasons.** Game animals and birds for which there are open seasons are:

| | |
|---|---|
| Deer | Ducks |
| Gray squirrels | Geese |
| Hares | Grouse |
| Rabbits | Pheasants |
| Raccoon | Quail |
| Woodchuck | Rails |
| Coot | Woodcock |

## NEW MEXICO

AREA: 122,000 square miles

**General Summary.** Of New Mexico's approximately 78,000,000 acres there are about 9,000,000 acres within National Forests and 15,000,000 acres of public-domain lands, all of which, except for state game refuges, are open to public hunting. In addition, there are about 15,000,000 acres of state land of which perhaps half are open to public hunting. An estimated 10,000,000 to 15,000,000 acres of privately owned lands are open to hunting if one obtains permission from the landowner.

As in all arid and semi-arid southwestern states, game of all kinds is often reduced from time to time by the ever-recurring droughts. During the past few years antelope have been seriously affected by drought in some parts of the state. Quail also have suffered from drought as well as disease. Deer and elk, for the most part, are in good condition and holding their own, perhaps increasing some. Other game is about normal although waterfowl showed a decrease last year.

In the order of their numbers, the big animals of New Mexico are: mule deer, pronghorn antelope, elk, whitetailed deer, bear, javelina, and mountain sheep. Javelina and mountain sheep have no regular open season. Special seasons are set on elk, antelope, and deer where special problem areas exist on crowded ranges.

The only small-game animals are squirrels and whistling marmots, although beaver in this state are classed as game animals rather than fur-bearers and may be taken only under special permits.

Upland game birds are the scaled quail, Gambel quail, blue grouse, wild turkey, pheasants, prairie chickens, sage chickens, pintail grouse, doves, and band-tailed pigeons.

**State Conservation.** The State Game Commission consists of five game commissioners appointed by the governor for five-year overlapping terms. The Commission selects the state game warden, who is executive head of the department and is given a free hand. The State Game Commission has full regulatory power over the management of wildlife in the state including the right to set seasons, bag limits, etc., on any kind or sex of game animals. The Commission operates entirely upon its own receipts. The receipts and expenditures have both increased steadily since the beginning of World War II and have practically doubled in the past few years.

In an effort to maintain its supply of game, New Mexico has set aside more than 200 game refuges where all hunting is prohibited. The Department has restocked elk in a half-dozen areas of the state to re-establish that animal, which was exterminated during the early 1890's. The elk herds have been

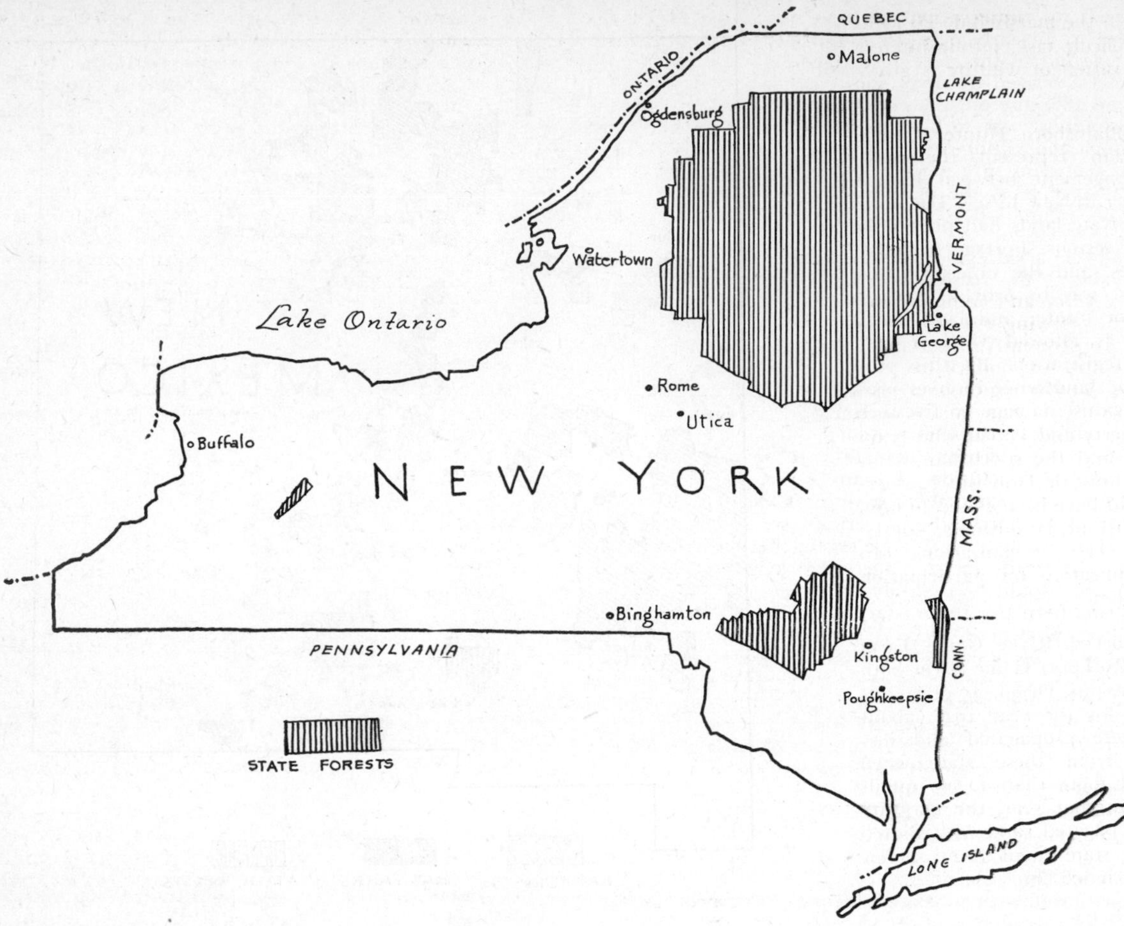


built up from meager stockings to about 4500 head at present. The antelope herds were protected and managed to increase from a low point in 1916 of about 1700 to approximately 25,000 head. The New Mexico Game Department developed and perfected a technique for the trapping and transplanting of antelope and from 1937 to 1942 trapped and moved over 1600 head to start more than 50 new herds. Where over-populations of deer occur special local seasons are held and does often are permitted to be taken. Sometimes the season provides for either a buck or a doe; at other times only does are permitted to be taken. In such areas a number of permits are issued equal to the number of deer to be removed for the good of the range. The Department has also reintroduced sage hens, which once occurred in the northwest part of the state but were exterminated about 1900.

The state has one game farm in operation that produces about 10,000 birds a year, mainly pheasants, but includes a few scaled, Gambel, and bobwhite quail, and chukar partridge.

**Licenses.** License fees are as follows:

| | |
|---|---|
| Resident big game | $ 3.00 |
| Non-resident big game | 50.25 |
| Resident bird | 2.50 |
| Non-resident bird | 15.25 |
| Resident general hunting | 4.50 |
| Non-resident general hunting | 60.25 |
| Resident special antelope permit | 10.00 |
| Non-resident special antelope permit | 40.00 |
| Resident special elk permit | 15.00 |
| Non-resident elk permit | 50.00 |
| Non-resident bear license (good only before and after regular big-game season) | 25.00 |

Resident and non-resident hunting licenses are sold by the office of the Game Commission, by field wardens, and by about 450 vendors, mainly at hardware stores, sporting-goods stores, and at some drugstores in virtually every town in the state.

**Regulations.** The only state limitation on the use of fire-arms is that shotguns larger than 10 gauge may not be used, and all shotguns used in taking birds of any kind must be plugged so they are not capable of holding more than three shells in the chamber and magazine combined. The restriction on rifles is that no rifle using rimfire cartridges may be used and no rifle using a bullet lighter than 46 grains can be used in taking big game. The M-1 .30-caliber carbine is barred entirely.

A non-resident is not required to employ a guide, although for bear or mountain lion hunting (lions are not classed as game animals) it is highly desirable, if he expects to get any game, to employ a guide with good trained dogs. There are guides available; they pay a fee of $5.00 for their licenses.

**Seasons.** Game animals and birds for which there are open seasons are:

| | |
|---|---|
| Antelope | Blue grouse |
| Bear | Doves |
| Deer | Pheasant |
| Elk | Prairie chicken |
| Squirrel* | Quail |
| Band-tailed pigeon | Wild turkey* |

There is no closed season on:

| | |
|---|---|
| Bobcat | Mountain lion |
| Coyote | |

## NEW YORK

AREA: 49,576 square miles

**General Summary.** The white-tailed deer is the game animal which provides New York with the most sport, the greatest economic return to the state, and the greatest potential headache to agriculture. Under reasonable protection deer have increased to make a reasonable match for the ever-increasing army of deer hunters which in the last 20 years has increased by 275 per cent and is now about 300,000 strong. Fortunately, in the same period the deer has extended its range so that legal hunting territory has increased by 88 per cent—and the annual take by 150 per cent.

*There is no small-game license in this state. Squirrel and wild turkey are considered big game.

The need for conservation measures of the deer herd was recognized at an early date. In 1886 the first bag limit was established, and in the same year "crusting" (taking deer in winter when bogged down in snow) in deer yards was prohibited. In 1895 the open season was shortened and the next year "hounding" was forbidden, followed by the outlawing of "jacking" and killing deer in the water. Finally, the "buck law" was passed in 1912. Deer have increased and spread, but the abundance is at the present date still far short of the demand. A record kill was made in 1947 of 20,000 antlered deer.

The Adirondacks region provides comparatively poor deer range. Some of the reasons are that plants growing in soil low in fertility and in many minerals are of low nutritive value; the growing season is short and the winter climate severe. Consequently, mortality, especially winter-kill, is heavy among Adirondack deer.

In the Catskill region there is a greater chance of conflict with agriculture than in the Adirondacks. Where local crop-damage problems occur they cannot be ignored. The present policy of issuing permits to landowners to take offending animals affords a solution in many instances. Experiments with a type of electric fence give promise that it can be recommended for orchards, nurseries, and truck crops. Beyond this, if serious crop damage should become more widespread in the future, herd reduction through the taking of anterless deer would be the only cure.

In the southern tier there is a problem very different from that existing elsewhere. Here is the best deer range in the state. Likewise farmland is also superior over the region as a whole. Unlike the other two regions, the problem here has become one of too many deer—not too many deer for immediate sporting purposes, but too many deer to live in harmony with agricultural interests and, in the wilder sections, too many deer for the range to support without overbrowsing. The only effective and practical way to keep the population within tolerable limits is to provide open seasons from time to time for taking antlerless deer.

Black bear are found in the state and an annual open season is allowed.

A large number of cottontail rabbits, snowshoe rabbits, gray squirrels, raccoon, and red and gray fox are taken each year. The foxes are considered predators but provide good sport for many enthusiasts in the state.

Modern hunting methods and land-use practices, plus unfavorable breeding conditions, have resulted in a serious setback to pheasants. Restoration, however, is limited by favorable natural factors plus adequate funds for management and stocking. In New York's many areas of excessive gunning pressure, nature can never be expected to provide adequate natural reproduction. If pheasant hunting is to be provided in such areas, the birds must be stocked. Ruffed-grouse populations continue at normal levels, subject, of course, to local fluctuations, and are a close second in number and importance to the gunner. Woodcock are also hunted in an open season.

Black duck, scaup (both varities), mallard, blue-winged teal, green-winged teal, ringneck duck, canvasback, redhead, pintail, golden-eye and the Canada goose pass over the state and provide good waterfowl shooting in some areas. The mallard duck seems to be staging a comeback due, at least in part, to a long-time policy of liberating artificially propagated breeders in favorable areas.

**State Conservation.** The Division of Fish and Game is a unit of the Conservation Department. The Commissioner of conservation appoints a director of fish and game as well as an assistant director, a superintendent of law enforcement, not less than 11 district game protectors and not less than 150 game protectors. He may also appoint such additional game protectors and other employees as are needed in the organization of the Division. The positions of director, assistant director, superintendent of law enforcement, district game protectors, and game protectors are in the competitive class of the classified civil service. Civil-service examinations for game protectors are confined to the counties, and special game protectors must first pass a non-competitive examination conducted by the Department.

In its duties of maintaining and propagating the wildlife resources of the state, the Conservation Department supervises game refuges, game management areas, and game farms. It is now actively concerned with the problem and hope of reclaiming 5,000,000 acres of farmland, or one-sixth of the land in New York State, which has been abandoned.

The state has seven large game farms in operation. In 1947 they produced for distribution 106,142 full-winged pheasants, 100,625 pheasant chicks (for rearing and release by co-operators), 36,696 pheasant eggs (for hatching and rearing), 2598 full-winged quail, and 1618 mallard ducks. This production was a record, but future plans call for even greater production.

New York has no formal farmer-sportsman co-operative program in operation at present. Special farmer-sportsman co-operative controlled public hunting areas were abandoned several years ago because the cost was believed excessive and in favor of the comparative few who used them. Sportsmen's clubs in co-operation with game-management workers and farmers have planted trees and set up fences in an effort to restore the natural game habitat in certain areas.

**Licenses.** License fees are as follows:

| | |
|---|---|
| Resident hunting | $1.65 |
| Resident combination hunting and fishing | 2.25 |
| Non-resident and alien hunting | 10.75 |
| Non-resident and alien combination hunting and fishing | 15.50 |
| Resident special deer | 1.25 |
| Non-resident special deer | 10.50 |
| Alien special deer | 10.50 |
| Indian resident, or a member of the Six Nations living on a New York State reservation, special deer | 1.25 |

Hunting licenses are sold by town clerks, game wardens, and a large number of sporting-goods stores, provided the salesman is a bonded special game protector.

**Regulations.** No rifle may be used for hunting or carried afield on Long Island or in Westchester County. In counties where the taking of deer is restricted to shotguns, no person is allowed afield during such open season with a rifle larger than a .22-caliber rim-fire.

No person is allowed to use in hunting any automatic firearm or any autoloading firearm with more than six shells in the magazine and chamber combined, or which has not been altered to reduce the capacity to not more than six shells.

Dogs may be used in hunting birds and all quadrupeds except deer. An owner may take his dog afield from September 1 to April 1 provided he does not carry a firearm loaded with other than blank ammunition or does not injure game birds or quadrupeds. Dogs may be trained by special permit at any time on special dog-training areas which have been licensed by the Department.

Any person wishing to engage in guiding in forest-preserve counties must obtain a special license from the Department.

**Seasons.** Game animals and birds for which there are open seasons are:

| | |
|---|---|
| Bear | Squirrel |
| Deer | Grouse |
| Rabbit | Pheasant |

## NORTH CAROLINA — AREA: 52,712 square miles

**General Summary.** Of the state's 31,450,880 acres, there are 4,611,922 acres on which public hunting is prohibited by law. The potential huntable agricultural land is 26,838,958 acres.

No single county in North Carolina gives a "typical" game picture of the state, but the hunting districts can be roughly divided into three principal regions: the coastal plain, Piedmont area, and the mountains. Most big game is found on the extreme coast or mountains, but the small game is comparatively well distributed. The deer population is on the increase, and good deer and bear hunting are found in both the eastern and western parts of the state. Both animals are most numerous on the lowlands of the eastern coast. Public deer and bear hunts are held in national forests, but many hunts are organized on private lands. Wild boar hunting, however, is confined mostly to the western mountains, when special hunts are allowed in the National Forest of Graham County.

Consistent with the duck situation throughout most of North America, North Carolina reports fewer ducks, but there has been an increase in geese. Migratory waterfowl abound in the coastal plain. Currituck and Hatteras are noted for all varieties of ducks, while Mattamuskeet excels in goose shooting. Rabbits and squirrels are found in every county, and there is good quail and turkey hunting in both the coastal plain and Piedmont districts, but grouse shooting generally

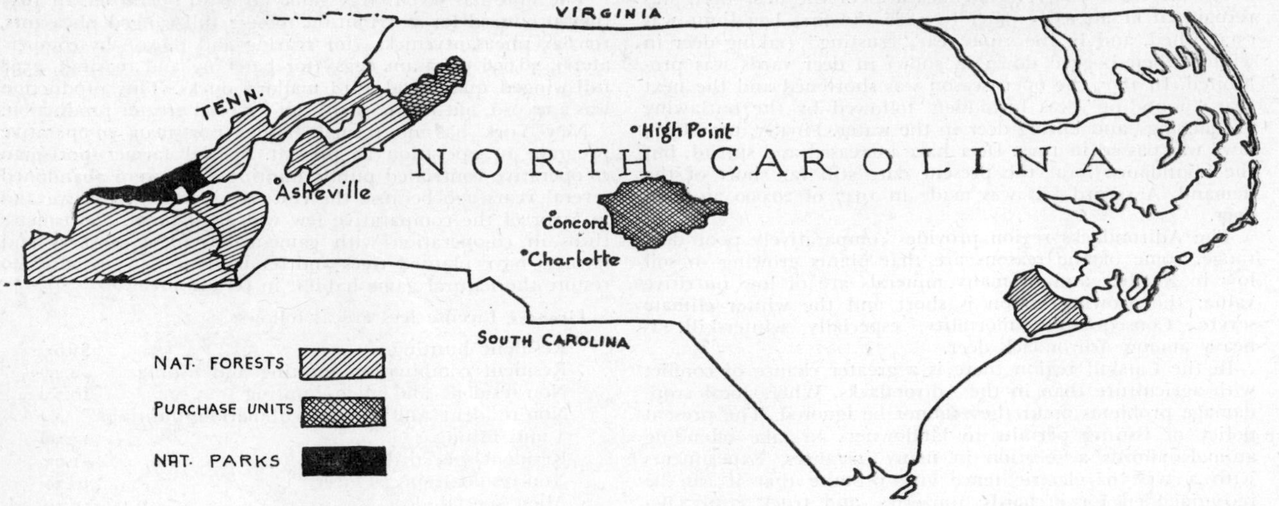


is limited to the mountains, specifically in the heatherlike land of Ashe and Avery counties. The numbers of rabbits and quail are definitely down, but grouse and wild turkey are holding their own. The red and gray fox are on the increase.

**State Conservation.** In 1947 North Carolina abolished the Division of Inland Game and Inland Fisheries of the Department of Conservation and Development, and transferred the Division's functions to an agency known as the Wildlife Resources Commission. The Commission is made up of nine members—one each from nine districts established by the Wildlife Resources Act—appointed by the governor to serve a six-year term. The Committee appoints an executive director as its chief administrative officer. The purpose and duties of the agency include the management, restoration, and protection of the wildlife resources of the state. The enforcement of game laws is directed by qualified persons who have knowledge or training in wildlife management.

In reference to the sportsmen's voice in game matters, the Commission respects interests and problems of the state's sportsmen, and most of the activities of the Commission are directly attributable to suggestions or complaints from sportsmen. At the present time North Carolina does not have the farmer-sportsman co-operative plan but is stressing work with the Federal Aid, portions of which are concerned with farmer-sportsman co-operation.

An increase in appropriated funds for Federal Aid in wildlife restoration in the postwar years allows for expansion of the state's restoration program, besides operation of the management areas. Some of the co-operative projects include:

A state-wide investigation of wildlife habitat and distribution, by which the entire state is being mapped in the field as to cover type and which will assimilate this information with a study of land-use practices, hunting pressure, and other factors in each county which are pertinent to game administration and management.

A state-wide project of deer trapping and transplanting is in effect. For many years past, deer hunting in western North Carolina had been almost non-existent. Now deer are being trapped in overcrowded national forests of the western part of the state, and released in other western areas where there are millions of acres of forested and potentially good deer range.

The farm-game habitat restoration links game habitat improvement with soil conservation practices promoted by state and Federal agricultural agencies. The state has furnished co-operating farmers with seed for lespedeza plantings on the field borders. This perennial plant retards soil erosion and water runoff and adds materially to the farming profits, as well as serving the sportsman in providing feed and cover where most needed, being especially beneficial for quail.

A study of deer management is taking place at Holly Shelter, a section typical of many shrub-covered, peat-bog areas in the southeast coastal region which is of little economic value but has valuable wildlife potentialities. The ultimate goal is the improvement of the habitat for huntable deer inhabiting the fringes by constructing ditches to stabilize the water table and by the practice of controlled burning.

Wild turkey restoration has been set up in selected areas to permit the building up of the turkey population. It should be practical to permit turkey hunting around the refuges in a few years. The surplus can move into, or be transplanted to, favorable habitat for restocking or introduction.

**Licenses.** License fees are as follows:

| | |
|---|---|
| Resident state | $3.10 |
| Resident county | 1.10 |
| Non-resident | 15.75 |

Hunting licenses, resident and non-resident, are sold by agents and usually in sporting-goods stores as well as at Commission headquarters.

**Regulations.** Automatic shotguns must be plugged to a three-shell capacity, including chamber and magazine, for shooting of upland game birds, rabbits, and waterfowl. Rifle slugs or buckshot may be used. There is no limitation on rifle calibers except some restrictions in effect on managed hunts on public land. Shotguns larger than 10 gauge are not permitted.

The western section of the state forbids chasing of deer by dogs.

No one is required to use a guide in the state, but there are many areas where a guide is recommended. Hunting guides are licensed, but licenses are granted only to local residents of close activity in the area. A list of guides is available at the State News Bureau, Raleigh, N. C.

**Seasons.** Game animals and birds for which there are open seasons are:

| | |
|---|---|
| Bear | Gallinules |
| Deer | Geese |
| Fox | Mourning dove |
| Rabbit | Rails |
| Squirrel | Ruffed grouse |
| Wild boar | Sora |
| Bobwhite quail | Wild turkey |
| Ducks | |

## NORTH DAKOTA — AREA: 70,837 square miles

**General Summary.** According to North Dakota's big game census of 1947, a total of 15,210 deer inhabit the state. Practically every county contains deer, the only big-game animal which has an annual open season. There are some elk (39), buffalo (on a Federal refuge and game farm), moose, Rocky Mountain sheep and goat, and antelope distributed throughout the state, but the numbers are not sufficient to allow hunting.

Rabbits are ubiquitous and need no protection in spite of a high yearly kill.

The upland game birds, Chinese pheasants, Hungarian partridges, and pinnated, sharp-tailed, and ruffed grouse are widely distributed. The pheasant and Hungarian partridge populations are at a low point, and there has been a large closed area on pheasants as a result of a recent decline in their numbers. Sharp-tailed grouse apparently are holding their own.

There was an excellent waterfowl hatch in 1947, and the population of ducks and geese is on the rise. Beside those birds which breed in the waters of North Dakota, great numbers migrate over the state, which is in the line of several northern flights of ducks and geese. It is one of the better waterfowl shooting states.

**State Conservation.** The state Game and Fish Department is headed by a commissioner who is appointed by the governor for a term of two years. He appoints such technical and biological experts, clerks, or other assistants as may be necessary in performing the duties of his office. About 12 district wardens work for the Department.

Because of the importance of the upland game birds in North Dakota, a considerable amount of the total research effort of this state's Conservation Department is spent on these species. The work is now carried on throughout the entire year in one form or another. Studies of winter conditions and populations are made, sex ratios are determined, and population fluctuations are watched as carefully as present facilities and knowledge allow. In addition, detailed nesting studies are made during the spring season. The crow, one of the most serious predators on the upland game birds, is attacked in organized hunts when bounties are paid. In one county, almost 2500 crows were eradicated by 25 4-H clubs which consider conservation of wildlife as an active part of their program.

There is no definite farmer-sportsman co-operative plan in existence in this state. Although landowners frequently post land with "no hunting" signs, most of the suitable hunting area is not posted.

**Licenses.** License fees are as follows:

| | |
|---|---|
| Resident | $1.50 |
| Non-resident | 25.00 |
| Resident deer permit | 5.00 |
| Non-resident deer permit | 50.00 |

Resident and non-resident hunting licenses are sold at the office of the State Game and Fish Department and by the 53 county auditors in the county seats. The county auditors usually distribute resident licenses to sporting-goods and hardware stores throughout their counties, but make a practice of selling the non-resident licenses directly from their own offices.

**Regulations.** No game birds may be shot with a rifle. It is unlawful to use a shotgun capable of holding more than three shells at one loading. The magazine of the gun must be plugged with one-piece wood or metal filler, not removable through loading end of magazine.

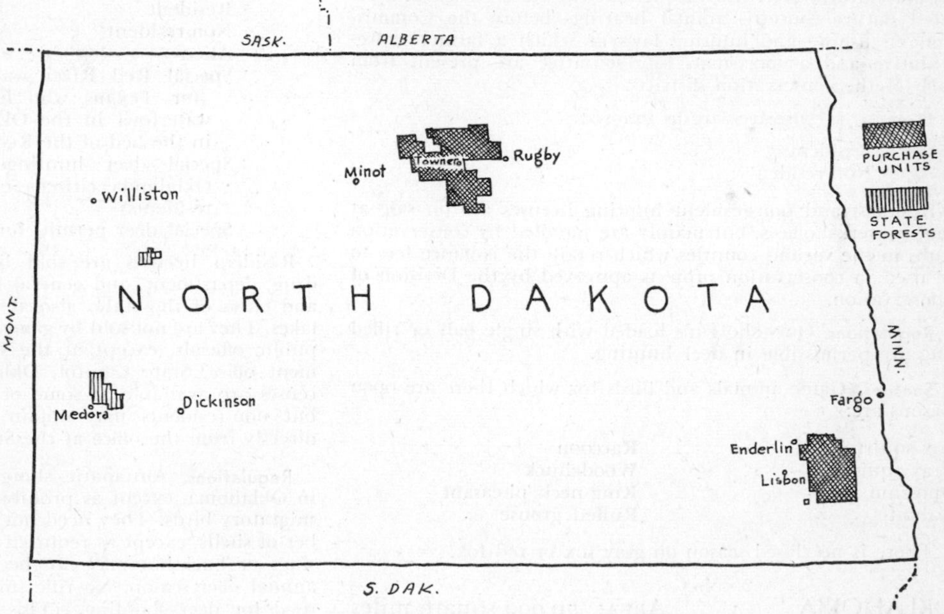


Dogs may be used for retrieving and pointing upland game, but may not be used on deer.

A non-resident hunter need not employ a guide unless he chooses to, for the highways are clearly marked and there is no agency providing guides. Occasionally, a local sportsman will volunteer to accompany out-of-state visitors. Sometimes a charge is made for this service.

**Seasons.** Game animals and birds for which there are open seasons are:

| | |
|---|---|
| Deer | Hungarian partridge |
| Ducks | Pheasant |
| Geese | Sharp-tailed grouse |

There is no closed season on:

| | |
|---|---|
| Coyote | Rabbit |
| Fox | Wildcat |
| Lynx | Wolf |

## OHIO

**AREA: 41,222 square miles**

**General Summary.** The game situation is at a low ebb in Ohio, though game-management practices and favorable weather are expected, in a few years, to produce normal conditions. The principal game bird is the pheasant, with ruffed grouse next. Although pheasants have been distributed in numbers in every county, they have failed to establish themselves in much of the unglaciated section of eastern and southeastern Ohio. They became abundant in parts of northwestern Ohio. In the unglaciated area of southeastern Ohio, habitat conditions are such that pheasant-management practices usually do not produce practical results. Hungarian partridges make a weak third on the hunting list, but recently they have been protected by a closed season. Quail are on the songbird list in Ohio, and no shooting is permitted. Opossum is the most numerous of the small-game animals, but there is good rabbit and squirrel hunting. The deer population has dropped off, and there is a closed season on them.

**State Conservation.** There is a marked trend throughout Ohio toward fundamental conservation and wildlife restoration. Sportsmen, allied conservation agencies, landowners, the public in general, and the Conservation Division itself have learned much in recent years as to the magnitude and importance of this problem. The conservation program embraces not only game and fish restoration, but forests, water, erosion control, and pollution eradication in building the habitat and sustenance required by wildlife.

Experience has taught that game farms and refuges act as an insurance policy in times of game shortages. Ohio operates three game farms for rearing and stocking of game birds. The annual production is about 65,000 birds. (A pheasant breeder's permit, costing $5, may be secured from the conservation commissioner to propagate pheasants as well as mallard and black ducks.) Raccoon production at the Miland Farm has been outstanding. Rabbit-propagation areas have been planned to insure a better distribution of rabbits as well as to encourage natural propagation. Game refuges total about 7500 acres, and the acreage under refuge agreement totals over 82,000 acres. Plans have been made to improve the waterfowl flyway. Public relations keep the public informed of the conservation activities via radio, bulletins, and the press.

One of the most difficult problems in the wildlife game management is the fox. There is an unprecedentedly large population of foxes, both gray and red. They have been building up for several years and this year apparently reached the top of the cycle, while pheasants by similar processes of nature reached the low ebb. The Conservation Department urges trapping, however, rather than promiscuous use of poison and dynamiting to curb the cycle, which will decline in the next few years.

The Conservation Division has an agricultural extension

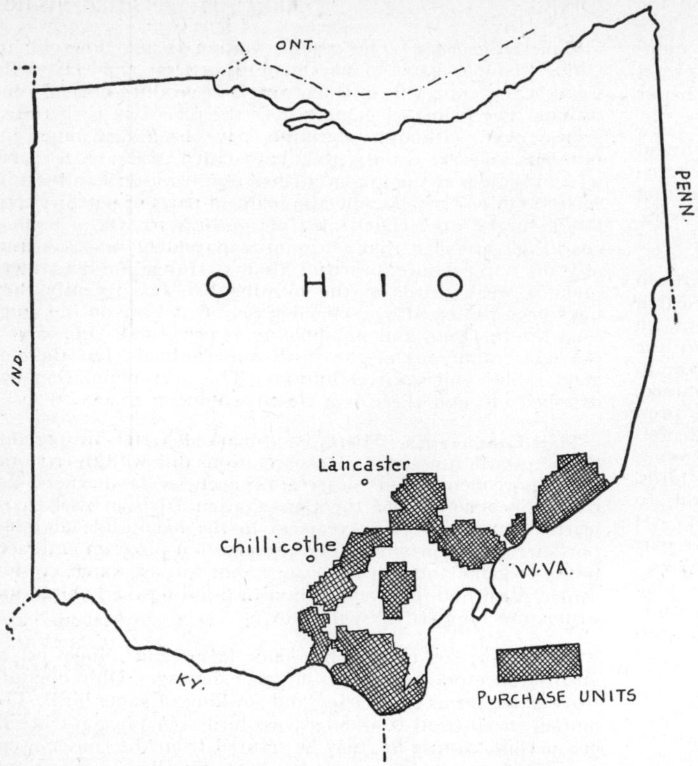


section with a chief and seven field workers who concentrate on agricultural activities throughout the state. Work of a related nature concerns annual hearings before the Commission on fishing and hunting laws at which a farmer representative and a sportsman representative are present from each of the conservation districts.

**Licenses.** License fees are as follows:

| | |
|---|---|
| Resident | $1.25 |
| Non-resident | 15.25 |

Resident and non-resident hunting licenses are on sale at county clerks' offices, but mainly are handled by conservation clubs in the various counties which retain the issuance fees to be used in conservation projects approved by the Division of Conservation.

**Regulations.** Only shotguns loaded with single ball or rifled slug are permissible in deer hunting.

**Seasons.** Game animals and birds for which there are open seasons are:

| | |
|---|---|
| Fox squirrel | Raccoon |
| Gray squirrel | Woodchuck |
| Opossum | Ring-neck pheasant |
| Rabbit | Ruffed grouse |

There is no closed season on gray fox or red fox.

## OKLAHOMA AREA: 70,000 square miles

**General Summary.** There are no extensive public hunting lands in the state, but the Game Department is acquiring, through Federal Aid funds, lands that will eventually be turned into public hunting areas. They are now in the process of being improved and will soon be open to hunting.

No species of game are in danger of serious population reductions in Oklahoma, but the supply is far from abundant. A decline has been noted in rabbits and squirrel the last few years. No species have shown any exceptional increase, but white-tailed deer are showing an upward swing in population, enough to allow the opening of new areas to hunting.

Upland birds (quail and doves) are the game most important to hunters, followed by small-game animals (rabbits, squirrels, and raccoons), then waterfowl (ducks and geese), and lastly big-game animals, represented by the white-tailed deer.

**State Conservation.** The State Game and Fish Commission consists of eight members, each of whom is a qualified elector of the state, a well known game and fish conservationist, and a man interested in the propagation of Oklahoma's wildlife resources. Members of the Commission are appointed by the governor, with the consent of the senate, and the governor selects such commissioners from diversified sections of the state in order to provide true representation.

There are 658 state game refuges in Oklahoma, covering 203,159 acres, and no hunting is permitted upon this land. Beside protection, propagation, and distribution (by trapping in abundancy areas and releasing on depopulated ranges) of game, the Commission is concerned with predators. The legislature appropriates approximately $25,000 annually for bounties on wolves, coyotes, and bobcats. The bounty on each of the three species is $2.50, but the bulk of the money is spent on coyotes.

There is one game farm in operation where bobwhite quail are raised along with a few ring-neck pheasants. In 1947 there were about 25,000 bobwhites and about 5000 pheasants produced and distributed. The plan is to produce an annual release of 40,000 to 45,000 bobwhites and about 5000 pheasants from the farm. The state manages one white-tailed deer farm, although the distribution from it has been negligible to date. Most of the restocking efforts on white-tailed deer are concentrated on live-trapping them from overpopulated areas, and transplanting the stock to depopulated areas, in addition to habitat improvement and management.

**Licenses.** License fees are as follows:

| | |
|---|---|
| Resident | $ 1.25 |
| Non-resident | 15.00 |
| Alien | 25.00 |
| Special Red River waterfowl license (for Texans who hunt migratory waterfowl in the Oklahoma season in the bed of the Red River) | 2.50 |
| Special deer hunting licenses (for Oklahoma citizens but non-county residents) | 7.50 |
| Special deer permits for non-residents | 15.00 |

Resident licenses are sold by some 1600 sporting-goods, drug, department, and general mercantile stores in all towns and cities of the state; also at concession stands at all large lakes. They are not sold by game wardens, town clerks, or other public officials, except at the state Game and Fish Department office, State Capitol, Oklahoma City. Non-resident licenses are available at some of the border towns and cities, but non-residents may obtain quicker service by ordering directly from the office at the State Capitol.

**Regulations.** Automatic shotguns and rifles may be used in Oklahoma, except as prohibited by Federal regulations on migratory birds. They need not be plugged to limit the number of shells, except as required by Federal regulations. Rifled slugs or buckshot may not be used in shotguns during the annual deer season. No rifle smaller than .25 caliber may be used for deer shooting. (This is a regulation fixed by the Oklahoma Game and Fish Commission—not by law—and may be changed at any time the Commission sees fit.)

Usually deer-hunting regulations prohibit the use of dogs in any manner, but this rule is fixed by the Commission and subject to change at its discretion. Dogs may not be trained or allowed to run in the fields during April and May, the nesting season for most game birds.

Hunting guides are not required for any type of hunting, and there are no licensed guides in the state.

**Seasons.** Game animals and birds for which there are open seasons are:

| | |
|---|---|
| Deer | Doves |
| Opossum | Ducks |
| Rabbits | Geese |
| Squirrels | Quail |
| Coot | Woodcock |

Since 1933 the taking of elk has been permitted in northeastern Oregon. Comparatively large herds of the Rocky Mountain elk and Roosevlet elk are found mostly in Baker, Wallowa, Union, Grant, Umatilla, and Morrow counties. In most years open seasons also are held in the coastal sections, for elk are most numerous in Clatsop, Coos, and Douglas counties.

The areas of concentration for deer and elk are largely open country and in most instances can be reached by automobile if the hunter does not desire to utilize pack horses. Many camp sites are available within the game country.

Oregon's antelope herd is one of the largest in the United States. The first open season was held in 1938, and hunting was allowed annually in southeastern and south central Oregon until the 1946 season when a temporary closure was made.

The small-game population of the state consists largely of migratory and upland game birds. Of the latter, the most numerous are Chinese pheasants, with a more limited supply of California or valley and bobwhite quail, Hungarian partridge and sooty and blue and ruffed grouse. The most popular territory for pheasant and partridge shooting is in Malheur and Umatilla counties.

Migratory birds hunted in Oregon include ducks, geese, band-tailed pigeons, mourning doves, brant, and coot. Some of the best duck shooting is to be found on Klamath Lake, along the Snake River in Malheur county, and at Summer Lake (Lake County) where a game-management area is maintained by the Oregon State Game Commission. Numerous other lakes in various parts of the state also offer migratory waterfowl hunting. The relative importance of waterfowl and shorebird species to hunters in Oregon is listed as follows: mallard, widgeon (baldpate), pintail (sprig), green-

## OREGON

**Area:** 96,981 square miles

**General Summary.** Approximately 31,710,298 of 61,664,000 acres are Federally owned. Of this Federal land, all but about 1,700,000 acres are open to hunting, and practically all of the state's big-game range is on this public land. Most of the upland game hunting is in areas that are largely privately owned.

Oregon offers a diversified selection of game species, and the state ranks high as far as big-game populations are concerned.

The mule deer, most numerous of the deer family and most popular with big-game hunters, is found in the area east of the Cascade Range in both heavily forested and open-type country. Hunting is found mainly in an area extending from the crest of the Cascade Range to the eastern border of the state. In some years the taking of does is permitted in areas where there is an overpopulation of a range:

The black-tailed deer is distributed west of the summit of the Cascades, which serves as the dividing line for mule and blacktail species. The heaviest concentration of blacktail deer is found in Jackson, Josephine, Douglas, Land, Lincoln, Clatsop, Coos, and Curry counties.

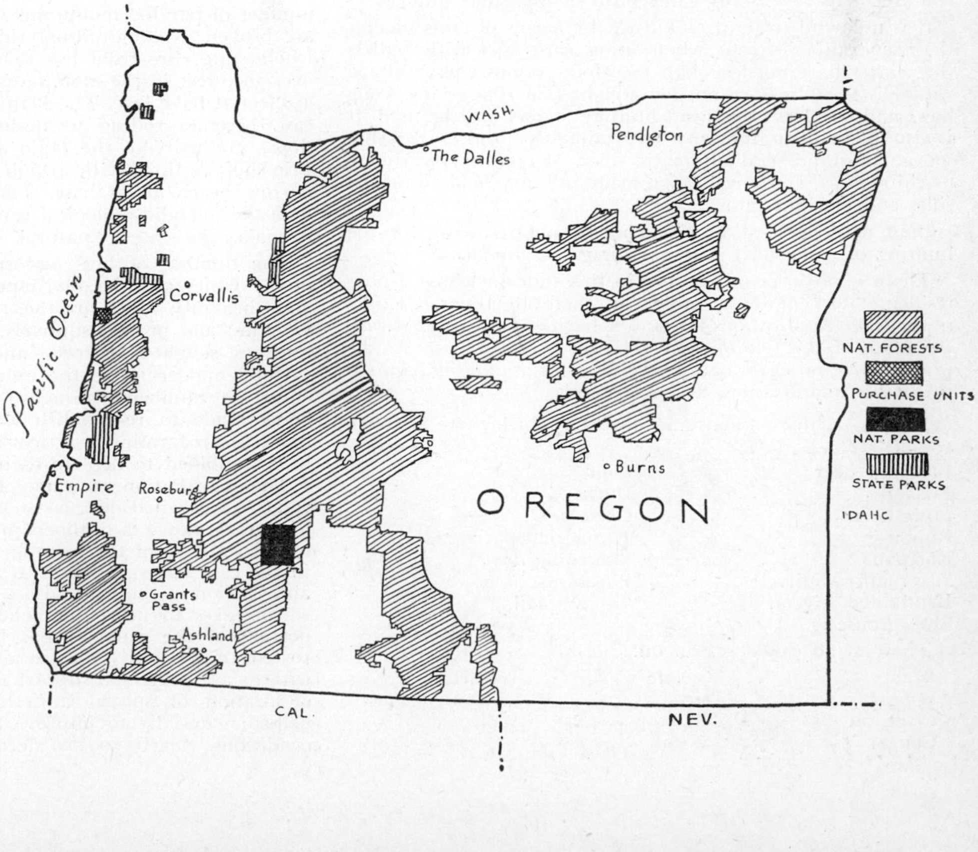

wing teal, snow goose, cackling goose, white-fronted goose (speckle-bellies), Canada geese, scaups (bluebills), wood duck, Buffleheads (butterballs), gadwalls, spoonbill (shoveller), can-vas back, black brant, redhead, golden-eyes, ruddy duck, cinnamon teal, coot, scoters, and harlequin.

**State Conservation.** Jurisdiction over the game fish, game birds, game animals, and non-game birds is under the Oregon State Game Commission. It is composed of five members appointed for staggered terms of five years each by the governor. The chief executive officer under the Commission is the state game supervisor and under him come the various divisions.

The state is divided into 13 game districts with resident biologists in each district studying conditions the year around.

The conservation methods of a cautious state Game Commission include: Hunting seasons based on a density index obtained by annual state-wide census for all species; the shooting of males only of polygamous species except where reduction is desired; the release of upland game species only in, and in proportion to, available habitat; the maintenance of a seed-stock refuge system; the utilization of an ecological succession of vegetative recovery on large logged-off or burned-over areas to build up game populations by temporary complete closures; habitat development; and an intensive appraisal of forage conditions and the maintenance of big game within their carrying capacity.

The Game Commission has in operation four pheasant farms on which from 60,000 to 80,000 pheasants, 8 to 12 weeks old, are released annually. (The open-field system of rearing pheasants is used.)

**Licenses.** License fees are as follows:

| | |
|---|---|
| Resident | $ 3.00 |
| Non-resident | 15.00 |
| Resident elk permit | 15.00 |
| Non-resident elk permit | 25.00 |

Hunting licenses are sold by authorized license agencies stationed in most of the towns in the state, usually located in sporting-goods stores. County clerks also handle licenses, but the game wardens do not.

**Regulations.** No rifle or shotgun capable of holding more than three shells may be used to kill any upland game birds, nor may any shotgun larger than 10 gauge be used in hunting game.

State law does not allow the use of any full metal-jacketed, solid-nosed bullet or of any shotguns loaded with buck or bird shot to kill big game. It is also prohibited to use .22 rim-fire shells to kill any game birds or big-game animals.

It is unlawful to hunt or kill elk by means of guns smaller than .30 caliber except when using cartridges with bullets that either have not less than 1400 foot-pounds energy at 100 yards distance, or have not less weight than 150 grains. Long bows and barbless broadhead hunting arrows may be used. It is also unlawful to hunt any wild animals or birds with Johnson and Garand semi-automatic rifles, M-1 military carbines, machine guns, and any foreign-made military semi-automatic rifles and machine guns.

Dogs may be used by residents or non-residents for the hunting of game birds but not for game animals.

There is no form of hunting in this state in which a non-resident must employ a guide, but there are licensed guides in the state. Applications for guides' licenses must be filed with the office of the Commission. The fee is $15 a year. At the present time no examination is given, but a guide is required to list his qualifications and references.

**Seasons.** Game animals and birds for which there are open seasons are:

| | |
|---|---|
| Blacktail deer | Coot |
| Elk | Ducks |
| Mule deer | Geese |
| Rabbit | Hungarian partridge |
| Raccoon | Mourning dove |
| Silver gray squirrel | Pheasants |
| Bandtailed pigeon | Valley quail |
| Blue grouse | |

There is no closed season on:

| | | |
|---|---|---|
| Bear | Coyote | Weasel |
| Bobcat | Fox | Wildcat |
| Civet cat | Lynx | Wolf |
| Cougar | Skunk | |

## PENNSYLVANIA AREA: 45,333 square miles

**General Summary.** Within the Commonwealth's 29,000,000 acres there are approximately 15,000,000 acres of forest and potential forest land and 13,000,000 acres of farm land comprising more than 170,000 farms. More than 1,665,000 acres of the forest lands are owned and controlled by the State Department of Forests and Waters, nearly all are open to public hunting, and 850,000 acres, chiefly forested, are owned and controlled by the State Game Commission. The latter constitute the largest acreage of such lands ever purchased by any state with hunters' license fees for wildlife purposes. These areas, designated as State Game Lands, are widely distributed throughout the mountainous sections and are open to public shooting, except within the numerous well-posted game refuges they contain.

The Game Commission also controls the hunting rights on nearly 300,000 acres in co-operative farm-game projects scattered chiefly throughout the thickly populated agricultural regions. It eventually hopes to expand this program, which is increasing tremendously in popularity, to a million acres or more.

Included in the all-over forest area are the Allegheny National Forest containing approximately 447,000 acres, and the Tobyhanna Military Reservation comprising around 30,000 acres. All of the former and 20,000 acres of the latter are open to public shooting.

Most of the farm land is cultivated to cereals and hay, although in recent years there has been a notable increase, in parts of the southeast as well as the southwest, in the numbers of western cattle brought east to graze and fatten for market. Thus grain crops have given way to grazing and to the growing of alfalfa, to the great detriment of wildlife food and cover. In the mountain areas only the valleys and the more gentle slopes are suited to agriculture, and in the higher plateau region only the level areas and the river bottoms are adaptable to farming.

Pennsylvania, despite its comparatively small size, its large population, and its mammoth industries, furnishes a wide diversity of hunting and trapping to about 1,000,000 of its citizens. This is due to a considerable variation in its topography. For example, the Piedmont belt crosses the southeastern part of the state, succeeds to the northwest by a broad stretch of limestone valleys, and beyond that the whole Appalachian Mountain system runs in a general northeast-southwest direction. Northwest of the mountains lies the Allegheny Plateau, succeeded by a small area of lake plains at Lake Erie. The mountain region is composed of a large number of parallel mountains with intervening valleys which are broken by longitudinal ridges and ranges of hills. The whole state rises from less than 20 feet at the Delaware to over 3000 feet in the mountains, and descends again to about 250 feet at Lake Erie. The Plateau, considerably broken in the east, becomes rolling to undulating toward the west and slopes gradually to the Ohio and the southwest. The Lake Erie shore is lined with a high wall of sand and clay, with a narrow beach at its base. The varied topography, coupled with the splendid ecological conditions which exist because of it, makes the state a "natural" for both big and small game.

The number of big- and small-game animals taken annually varies considerably, especially such species as rabbits and pheasants, which are the most popular of the farm-game varieties; and grouse, squirrels, and wild turkeys, which are the most sought-after forest and woodland species.

Quail appear to be the only game birds which have declined in numbers through the years, and every effort is being made to re-establish their numbers on a shootable basis. Clean farming practices and severe winters apparently have combined to deplete their numbers.

The distribution of game, both big and small, is quite wide. White-tailed deer occur in every county but their most productive range is confined principally to the northern half of the state, from the counties of Wayne, Pike, and Monroe in the east across the state to and including Warren, Forest, and Clarion in the west; also the entire lower mountain area, which takes in nearly the entire central and south central portion of the state. It has been necessary upon occasion to reduce drastically the size of the deer herd commensurate with its available food supply, and to balance the sexes, by the declaration of special antlerless deer seasons which have helped materially to improve both biological and ecological conditions. Nearly 500,000 deer have been taken by hunters.

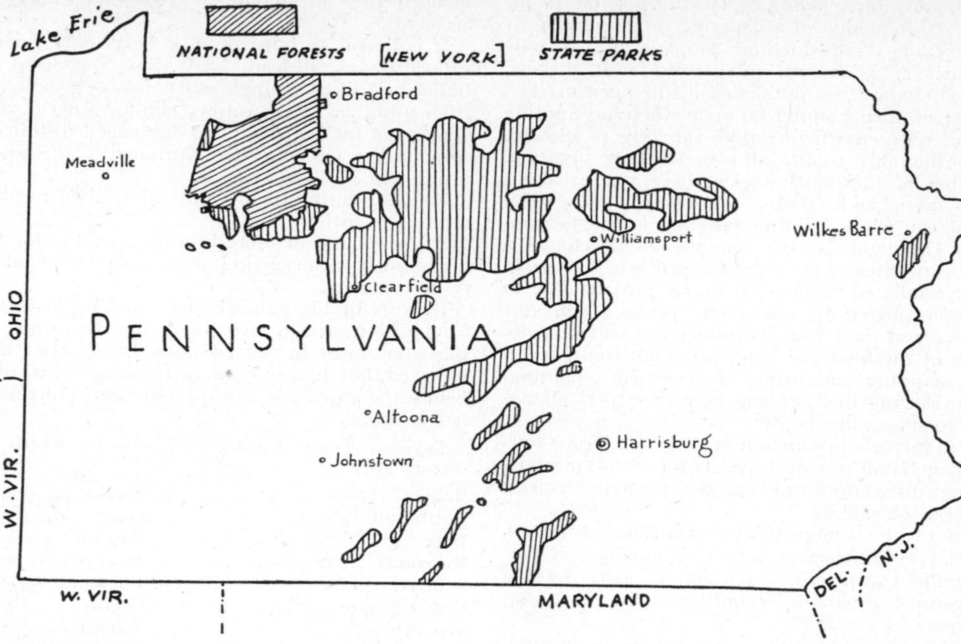


during the past 30 years, the largest number in 1940 when 40,995 bucks and 145,530 does, or a total of 186,525, were bagged. The average annual buck kill for the past few years has been around 25,000.

Black bear are found chiefly in the central and north central counties. Pennsylvania was one of the first states to recognize the black bear as a game animal, and gave it protection as such in 1905; in 1925 cubs also were protected. More and more hunters are beginning to rate Bruin very highly, and consequently he is hunted now under a special season.

Wildcat are classed as predators, but they are hunted chiefly for sport. They are found only in the remote wilderness areas of the central and north central counties.

Cottontail rabbits generally are abundant throughout the entire state, especially in the agricultural sections. The remote forest areas provide a substitute in the varying hare, although its numbers are limited and it is just about holding its own under special restricted seasons. Anywhere from 2,500,000 to 3,000,000 cottontails and from 3000 to 4000 hares are taken annually.

Of the three types of squirrels (gray, black, and fox), the gray is by far the most abundant and is found throughout all the forested and wooded areas. The black phase of the gray is found principally in the northern-tier counties, whereas the fox is more scouthern and western in its distribution. From 700,000 to 1,000,000 are bagged every year.

Raccoon are common throughout nearly all of the forested and wooded areas suitable to its existence. In recent years from 70,000 to 100,000 have been taken by hunters and trappers each season.

Wild turkey chiefly range to central and southern mountainous areas, although in recent years experimental stockings in other wooded portions of the state are beginning to bear fruit. The wild turkey is not so abundant as it was in pioneer days. Even though blended with wild farm-reared stock, it is holding its inherent wild quality, and turkey shooting, where found, is of the best. The annual take ranges from 3000 to 4000 birds.

Ruffed grouse are fairly abundant throughout all the forested and woodland areas, but are chiefly confined to the central and north central counties. Governed apparently by cycles and a tendency to gravitate from one environment to another, this popular game bird fluctuates considerably in numbers each year, with a consequent variation in each season's kill. In 1946 the season was closed; in 1947 it was opened for one week; but in 1945 around 46,000 were taken during a full month's season. Where once these birds were found almost altogether in the ravines and on the benches of the remote forest areas, now it is common to find them in the more outlying wooded areas adjacent to marginal farmlands. They are an unpredictable quantity.

Ring-necked pheasants inhabit mainly southeastern, southwestern, and northwestern Pennsylvania where grain crops, especially field corn, are grown extensively. The ringneck has well filled the gap between the rabbit hunter on one hand and the quail and grouse hunter on the other by furnishing a profitable compromise sport. From 200,000 to 400,000 are taken annually.

Bobwhite quail are not numerous enough to furnish good shooting. The bobwhite lacks its onetime abundance due to a number of unfortunate circumstances, principally clean farming and severe winters, but rehabilitation of the bird is planned.

The woodcock is an uncertain quantity. There are goodly numbers of resident birds as a rule, supplemented by transients when migration occurs. Woodcock hunting is about as erratic as the weather and the bird's flight. From 15,000 to 25,000 are taken annually.

Waterfowl are taken on Lake Erie, Pymatuning and Conneaut Lakes, and other waterways in the northwest; the Susquehanna River and its tributaries, with heaviest concentration along the "flats" of the river where it enters the Chesapeake; the marshes of the Delaware; and the lakes and ponds in the northeastern part of the state. Pennsylvania is not regarded as a good waterfowl state, yet in favorable seasons some excellent sport may be enjoyed. From 40,000 to 50,000 are taken annually.

**State Conservation.** The Pennsylvania Game Commission was established in 1895 and began functioning a year later. Although originally six, there are now eight members appointed from as many geographical districts, all of whom serve without any remuneration, except the expenses they incur in connection with official duties. The members are appointed by the governor for staggered terms of eight years. They in turn appoint their own executive director (subject to the approval of the governor), who is responsible for the administration of all the departmental activities. He and his subordinates are all salaried employees. The organization at present consists of three major bureaus: Administration, Public Relations, and Field Management. The state is divided into 150 districts, each administered by a district game protector.

The Commission holds stated meetings in January and July in its offices at Harrisburg, and at such other times and places within the state as seem necessary, usually four to five annually. It maintains an extensive public relations program with sportsmen's, women's, youth and civic groups, and cooperates extensively with all Federal, state, and private conservation agencies. It has numerous motion pictures, publications, and placards for free distribution, a list of which can be obtained by writing to Harrisburg. It also publishes a 32-page monthly magazine devoted to hunting, trapping, and the outdoors in general.

The Game Commission is doing everything possible to increase the natural production of all species, supplementing it by annually restocking those which are propagated at its four game farms, such as pheasants, quail, and wild turkeys. Pheasants and rabbits are also purchased in the open market, and are live-trapped during winter on areas where no hunting is permitted and released where public shooting is allowed, thus adding considerably to the all-over stocking program. The total number of pheasants stocked in a year is about 114,546, turkeys, 2519, and rabbits, 111,728.

The future of the whole wildlife program is briefly summarized below. To finance it the Commission developed a wartime reserve fund during the years when it was impossible to utilize all accumulated moneys on major projects due to lack of manpower, materials, etc. These projects will cost around $6,000,000, and their principal objectives will include:

(1) Expansion of the food and cover program; construction of dams; cover-mapping and future management planning; growing and purchasing food-bearing planting stock—all applicable mostly to state game lands.

(2) Facilities to increase production at the game farms; purchase of more game from private breeders for restocking purposes; increasing distribution of day-old pheasant chicks; larger importations of rabbits.

(3) Expansion of the Co-operative Farm-Game Program.

(4) Intensified law-enforcement activities; purchase of new uniforms and radio equipment; expansion of game feeding and predator control program; rendering more aid to interested landowners.

(5) Further development of the present field research projects and the initiation of new ones with aid from Federal funds.

(6) Expand educational programs currently in effect and provide for additional facilities to inform more fully sportsmen's groups, schools, service clubs, and the public in general concerning wildlife restoration needs.

Probably the most important single long-range undertaking is the development of the Co-operative Farm-Game Program to provide more open shooting territory in agricultural sections adjacent to large population centers and to better game conditions. Established in 1936, it has grown in popularity and acreage and is now being encouraged in all farming areas. At present there are over 3200 farms aggregating more than 281,000 acres incorporated, with at least 1,000,000 acres as the ultimate goal.

Landowners have subscribed to the program because of the protection it affords them. Safety zones are posted within 150 yards of all occupied buildings (this law applies state-wide whether the zone is marked by posters or not); the areas are patrolled during the gunning season by deputy game protector; patches of grain, mostly uncut, are purchased for game food; numerous small sanctuaries are established on the areas where game can find a haven when closely pursued; farmers and members of their families are encouraged to raise day-old pheasant chicks; co-operators are furnished advice on soil conservation and other profitable farm practices (the Commission employs two full-time soil-conservation experts for this purpose alone); and aid is given in planting waste spots with vines or shrubs which provide food and cover for wildlife, including insectivorous birds so beneficial to farmers.

**Licenses.** License fees are as follows:

| | |
|---|---|
| Resident | $ 2.00 |
| Non-resident | 15.00 |

Resident hunting licenses can be secured from all county treasurers and most sporting-goods and hardware stores. Non-resident licenses may be secured from county treasurers or from the Department of Revenue at Harrisburg. They entitle the owner to the same hunting privileges as residents, except where special regulations prevail, as, for example, where antlerless deer hunting is limited to a prescribed number of residents within certain counties.

It is not necessary to employ guides to hunt in Pennsylvania, nor are those local residents who serve in this capacity required to be licensed. The State Department of Commerce, Harrisburg, issues a small pamphlet annually listing hunting accommodations.

**Regulations.** Automatic or semi-automatic guns are absolutely prohibited. Magazine shotguns may not contain more than three shells at one time in the magazine and chamber combined for hunting other than big game. It is recommended that a plug be inserted in the magazine to avoid accidents.

It is lawful to hunt deer or bears only when using a gun propelling an all-lead, lead alloy, soft-nosed or expanding bullet or ball at a single discharge, or a bow and arrow. No rifles using .22 or .25 caliber rim-fire cartridges may be used. Guns used for big game may be loaded to full capacity. Telescope sights are permitted. Automatic guns and silencers are prohibited.

Parties hunting small game are limited to five persons as a safety precaution.

Parties of five or more hunting together for big game must maintain a roster giving their names and addresses and license numbers.

Reports of big game killed must be mailed to the Game Commission within five days after the close of the season. Big game must be tagged immediately after the entrails are removed, but in any event within one hour after killing and before the carcass is transported in any manner from where it was killed.

**Seasons.** Game animals and birds for which there are open seasons are:

| | |
|---|---|
| Bear | Ducks |
| Cottontail rabbit | Geese |
| Deer | Grouse |
| Raccoon | Hungarian partridge |
| Squirrel | Pheasant |
| Varying hare | Quail |
| Woodchuck | Woodcock |
| Dove | Wild turkey |

There is no closed season on:

| | |
|---|---|
| Chipmunk | Weasel |
| Fox (red or gray) | Wildcat |
| Porcupine | |

## RHODE ISLAND AREA: 1214 square miles

**General Summary.** Game populations of all species of game in Rhode Island are spotty. Small-game animals are of chief importance to the sportsmen of the state, for about 45,000 rabbits are taken annually, and approximately 9000 squirrels. Rabbit populations are indicative of the conditions facing game species. Where good habitat is available and predation and hunting pressure is not too severe, this species shows its ability to maintain good populations. Such areas, however, are few and widely distributed. With the exception of Newport County, rabbit population in Rhode Island shows a steady yearly decline.

Pheasants, the most important upland game birds, have been unevenly distributed, depending upon suitable habitat, low predation, and stocking operations. Around 2000 birds are released a year for stocking. The total seasonal kill is approximately 6000. Quail, despite several years of stocking efforts (averaging about 500 a year), have failed to increase materially. It is evident that suitable habitat for this species is decreasing yearly, but they have maintained sufficient numbers to allow an annual open season, at which time about 3000 are taken. Grouse have not shown an ability to recover from cyclic low periods and while hunting pressure on this species has been somewhat lighter than on some others, it is obviously because of low population of the species and resultant discouragement to hunters, who bag about 1800, yearly. The migratory woodcock are showing a decline in numbers, and only about 900 birds are bagged annually.

There is fair waterfowl shooting along the coast, however, and waterfowl conditions have remained good.

**State Conservation.** Rhode Island is suffering from an annual decrease of all its native wildlife. The chief reason appears to be a loss of suitable habitat because of changing agricultural economy. Concentrations therefore occur, and predation takes a very high toll. Restocking on areas unsuitable for game propagation is proving to be useless. Between 1939 and the present day there has been at least a 50 per cent drop in the seasonal kill of legal game. The aim of the Conservation Department is to improve the habitat, reduce predation, and limit hunting pressure to available surpluses to insure a future game population.

**Licenses.** License fees are as follows:

| | |
|---|---|
| Resident | $ 2.25 |
| Non-resident | 10.25 |
| Alien | 15.25 |

All hunting licenses are issued by city and town clerks and various special agents (sporting-goods stores, etc.) throughout the state. The game wardens do not issue licenses.

**Regulations.** The use of high-powered rifles or shotguns with slugs is prohibited for hunters in taking game birds or animals.

**Seasons.** Game animals and birds for which there are open seasons are:

| | |
|---|---|
| Gray squirrel | Geese |
| Hares | Partridge |
| Rabbits | Pheasant |
| Raccoon | Quail |
| Coot | Scoters (sea coots) |
| Ducks | Sora rail |
| Gallinules | Woodcock |

## SOUTH CAROLINA — AREA: 31,055 square miles

**General Summary.** The present game situation in South Carolina is satisfactory in the lower half of the state, but the upper half needs improvement and restocking. There is no danger of serious population losses, but no species are showing any exceptional increases.

The state has a good-sized herd of white-tailed deer which are hunted annually, and some black deer are killed each year. Rabbit, squirrel, raccoon, and opossum are distributed throughout most of the state. Partridge (quail) and wild turkey represent the upland game birds. There is fair waterfowl shooting along the inland marshes, and the year-round mild, equable climate along the coast attracts many ducks and geese.

**State Conservation.** The state department of Game and Fish maintains a 6000-acre wild turkey refuge along the Savannah River in South Carolina. The property is well stocked, but the surplus is not sufficient to begin trapping and distributing birds to other parts of the state.

**Licenses.** License fees are as follows:

| | |
|---|---|
| Resident state | $ 3.10 |
| Non-resident state | 15.25 |
| Resident county | 1.10 |

Both resident and non-resident hunting licenses are put on sale with the county game wardens, and they are allowed to select their agents such as sporting-goods stores, hardware stores, and other places for the convenience of the hunter.

**Regulations.** Except for Federal restriction on firearms and magazine capacity, the state allows any kind of firearms to be used in hunting, and there is no limit on magazine capacity.

Night hunting is not allowed except for raccoons, opossums, foxes, mink, and skunk, and these may not be hunted with artificial lights.

**Seasons.** Game animals and birds for which there are open seasons are:

- Deer
- Fox
- Opossum
- Rabbit
- Raccoon
- Squirrel
- Blackbird
- Ducks
- Geese
- Partridge (quail)
- Wild turkey

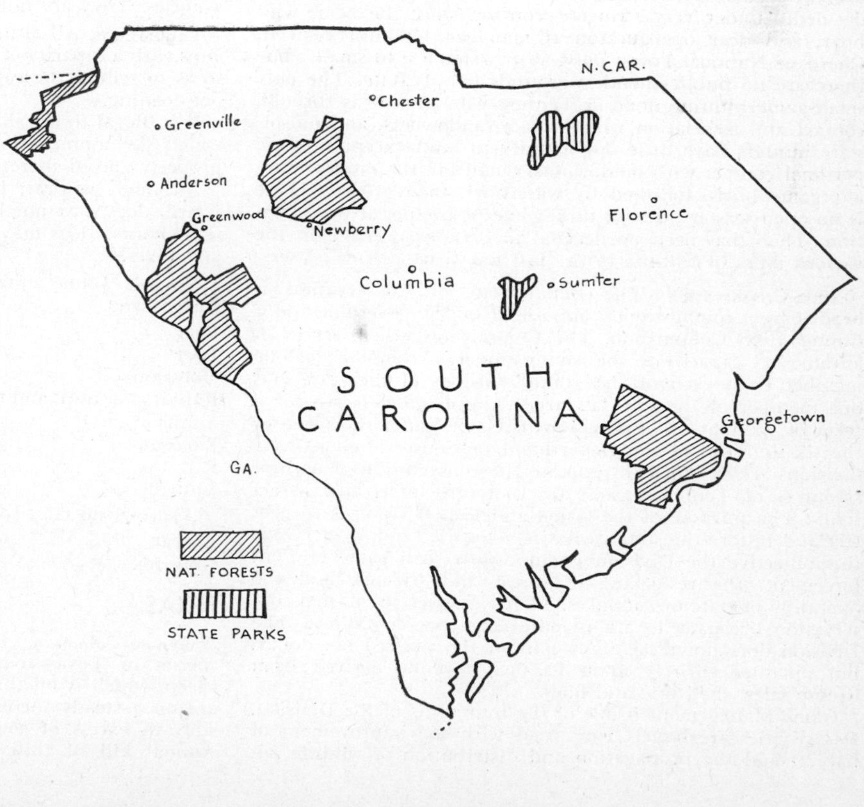


## SOUTH DAKOTA — AREA: 77,047 square miles

**General Summary.** Pheasants are of chief concern to the game hunters in this state and many pheasant enthusiasts throughout the United States. There are approximately 200,000 licensed pheasant hunters each year—one-half of them non-residents. Pheasants are numerous, inhabiting every county in the state, and although not very plentiful in some counties, they are too abundant in others. In the past several years pheasants have slowly migrated westward. The eastern counties, therefore, do not offer as good hunting as the central counties. The present pheasant population has shown a decline, as it has in all surrounding states, as compared to 1943 and 1944. The Game Commission believes the decrease is attributable to unfavorable hatching seasons, particularly in 1945 and 1946. The popular pinnated grouse is showing no improvement in South Dakota and is apparently near the extermination point because of the loss of desirable habitat. Ruffed grouse and sage grouse also have shown a decline during recent years.

There is an annual open season on white-tailed and mule deer, on antelope and elk, but hunting of these is confined to residents of the state. Waterfowl conditions are fair throughout the state, but excellent in some areas.

**State Conservation.** South Dakota is a leading state in the number of artificial dams created to conserve run-off water. The state also has instituted programs for tree planting, soil conservation, public relations and conservation education, fish hatcheries, game reserves, wildlife research and survey, and law enforcement. The Game and Fish Commission has played an active part in these conservation programs. The non-salaried, eight-man Commission, appointed by the governor to serve a term of six years, also regulates the hunting seasons, bag limits, and enforces the laws which protect wildlife.

**Licenses.** License fees are as follows:

| | |
|---|---|
| Resident small game | $ 1.00 |
| Resident deer permit | 5.00 |
| Resident antelope permit | 5.00 |
| Resident elk permit | 10.00 |
| Non-resident small game | 23.00 |

(No big-game licenses are available to non-residents.)

All hunting licenses are for sale at the office of Game and Fish Commission and by county treasurers or agents appointed by them. Game wardens do not handle hunting licenses.

**Regulations.** It is unlawful under Federal regulations to

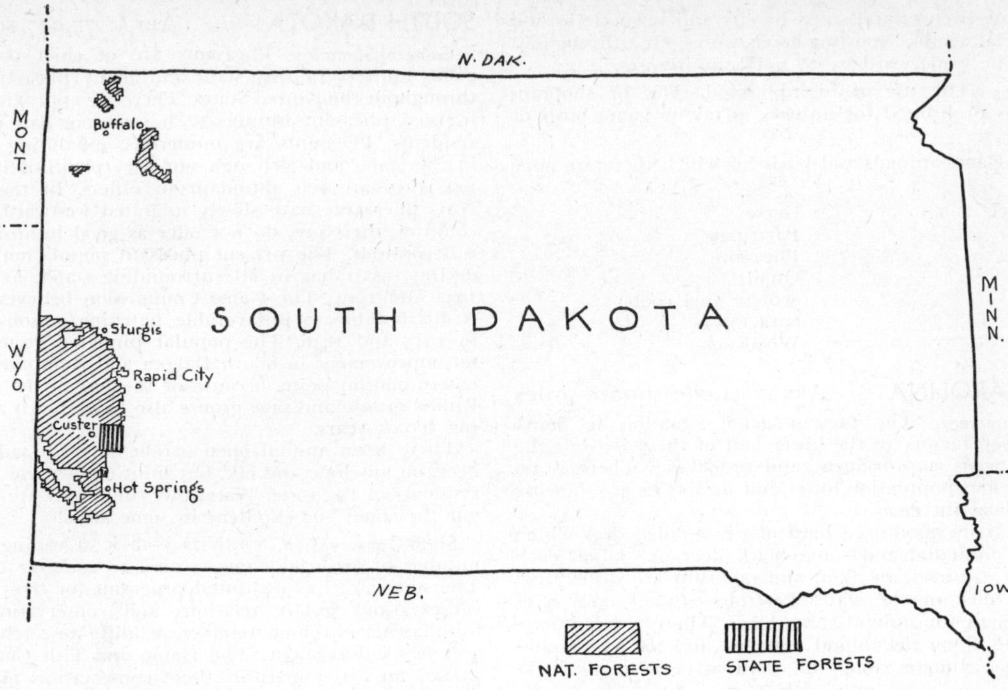


take migratory waterfowl with a shotgun larger than 10 gauge or with a shotgun capable of holding more than three shells. Deer and antelope may be taken by bow and arrow.

No game bird or animal may be taken by the use of an artificial light.

No dogs may be used in hunting deer.

**Seasons.** Game animals and birds for which there are open seasons are:

| | |
|---|---|
| Antelope | Ducks |
| Deer | Geese |
| Elk | Grouse |
| Coot | Pheasant |

## TENNESSEE

AREA: 42,246 square miles

**General Summary.** At the present time big game hunting is decidedly under very stringent control, since the bear, wild boar, and deer open season is managed by hunt plan in Cherokee National Forest only. With reference to small game there are no public shooting grounds in this state. The only small-game hunting done in Tennessee by anyone is through contact and association with private landowners, and out-of-state hunters have little opportunity to hunt except through personal contact with landowners. Quail are the most abundant game birds, followed by waterfowl, then grouse. There is no open season for wild turkey except by special proclamation. There has been no decided increase or decrease in the various types of wildlife in the last few years.

**State Conservation.** The Department of Conservation is headed by a commissioner, appointed by the governor, and a Conservation Commission. The Commission, which serves in an advisory capacity to the commissioner, is composed of one member from each of the grand divisions of the state and one member of the state at large. The members serve for a term of six years. The Division of Game and Fish is one of the six divisions of the Department of Conservation. All six divisions are designed to promote the conservation of natural resources of Tennessee, and are therefore interrelatd in activity. The purpose of the Game and Fish Division is to protect and restore the state's wildlife resources, and to carry out this objective the Division is empowered wih game law enforcement, the restocking of forest and streams, and the operation of state-owned lakes. There are over 70 salaried conservation officers who aid in enforcing the regulations. The Division does not receive any part of the assessed tax dollar, but operates entirely upon its own revenue derived from license sales, shell tax, and fines.

Game Management is one of the four units of the Division. Its activities are largely concerned with the improvement of habitat and the propagation and distribution of wildlife, although management is recognized by this unit as being only a partial substitute for the natural, wild conditions that once existed in this state.

A game farm is operated in Grainger County which annually distributes approximately 30,000 birds. In addition, the state owns and administers three large areas totaling over 80,000 acres. There is management co-operation with TVA, U. S. Fish and Wildlife Service, U. S. Soil Conservation Service, and farmer-sportsman organizations.

**Licenses.** License fees are as follows:

| | |
|---|---|
| Resident | $2.00 |
| Non-resident annual | 15.00 |
| Non-resident 2-day | 5.00 |

Resident and non-resident licenses are on sale by county court clerks, sporting-goods stores, and a few other special agencies. They are not sold by game wardens.

**Regulations.** All automatic or hand-operated repeating shotguns with a capacity of more than three shells must be plugged so as to reduce the capacity to not more than three shells at one loading.

It is illegal to use shotgun shells or other ammunition upon which the ammunition tax has not been paid and stamps properly affixed thereto.

Although wildcat, bobcat, and ground hog are not protected, dogs may not be used to hunt or chase them in daylight hours. Dogs may be used in hunting raccoon, opossum, and foxes.

**Seasons.** Game animals and birds for which there are open seasons are:

| | |
|---|---|
| Bear | Wild boar |
| Deer | Bobwhite quail |
| Opossum | Doves |
| Rabbit (swamp and cottontail) | Ducks |
| Raccoon | Geese |
| Red fox | Ruffed grouse (mountain pheasant) |
| Squirrel | |

There is no closed season on:

| | |
|---|---|
| Bobcat | Wildcat |
| Gray fox | Woodchuck |

## TEXAS

AREA: 267,339 square miles

**General Summary.** Population trends for various big-game species in Texas remain favorable except for the bighorn sheep, which is on the verge of extinction. White-tailed deer are on a steady increase, with an estimated population possibly in excess of 300,000 distributed widely over the state. Annual kill of this species totals about 40,000. There are

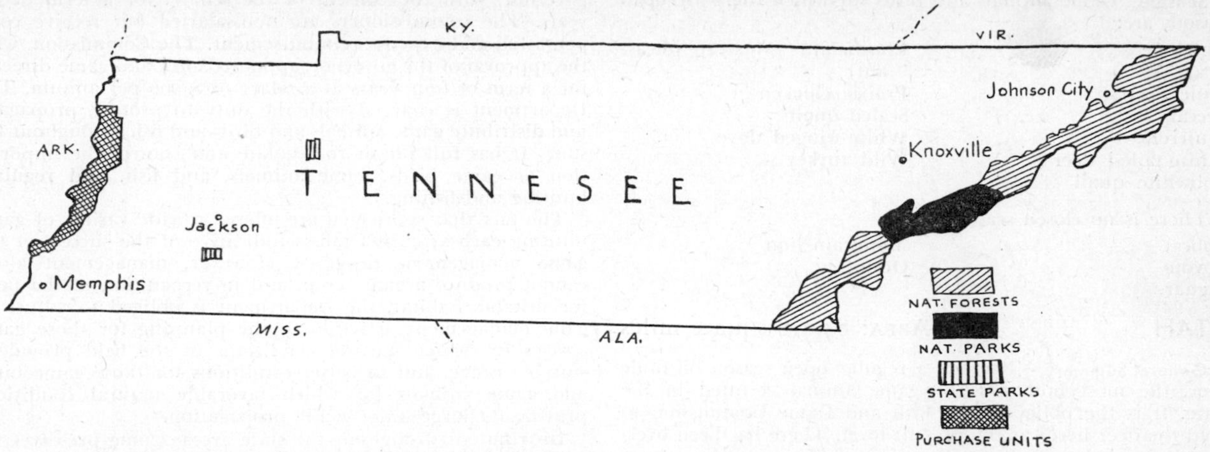


about 8000 mule deer, almost entirely in the Trans-Pecos, also on the increase under an annual harvest of about 500 animals. A near-stabilized antelope population of 12,000 has shown no decrease following three controlled hunts since 1944, in which approximately 1100 animals were harvested. Peccary are common over all the brush country of southwest Texas, but are subject to only a light kill, perhaps 5000 each year out of a 100,000 population. Black bear occur only in the Trans-Pecos, and number possibly 200. The principal hunting pressure is by stockmen, as protection against damage to sheep and calves.

Wild turkey are less widely distributed than deer, and 70 per cent of the total population, calculated at 100,000 birds, occurs in the Edwards Plateau. Beside wild turkey, the other upland game birds on which there is an annual hunting season are bobwhite quail, scaled quail, white-winged dove, prairie chicken, and chachalaca (Mexican pheasant).

**State Conservation.** Since August 1938, most of the positive game conservation efforts of the Game, Fish, and Oyster Commission have been particularly emphasized through its Division of Wildlife Restoration. This Division operates under the Federal Aid in Wildlife Restoration Act as passed by Congress in 1937, and deals entirely with game restoration problems. Its first major objective was a thorough five-year survey of the game resources of the state, and findings of the completed survey were subsequently compiled in book form, entitled *Principal Game Birds and Mammals of Texas*. Each species is treated as to distribution, status, and management needs.

Additional investigational work has been carried out with regard to relations of land use and other critical factors to game species, including bighorn sheep, antelope, whitetailed deer, bobwhite quail, scaled quail, lesser prairie chicken, Attwater prairie chicken, wild turkey, whitewinged dove, squirrels, wintering waterfowl, beaver, and muskrat. Marsh areas in southeastern Texas increased greatly in muskrat production following management work, with a corresponding rise in carrying capacity for waterfowl.

Of outstanding note has been the game trapping and transplanting program in Texas. This applies especially to whitetailed deer, wild turkey, and pronghorned antelope, for which species special trapping methods have been perfected to facilitate large scale operations. Under this program, the annual restocking of 1500 deer on selected areas in depleted sections of deer country is making a marked change in the state-wide deer distribution picture, and is providing hunting where none existed for a generation or more. Similarly, antelope and wild turkeys are being re-established on former ranges from which they were extirpated by the close of the past century.

**Licenses.** License fees are as follows:

| | |
|---|---|
| Resident county and state | $2.00 |
| Non-resident and alien | 25.00 |

**Regulations.** No shotgun larger than 10 gauge may be used for taking any game bird, and if magazine-loaded, it must be plugged to render it incapable of holding more than two shells.

No dogs may be used in hunting deer.

It is unlawful to hunt deer or any other animal or bird by the aid of an artificial light.

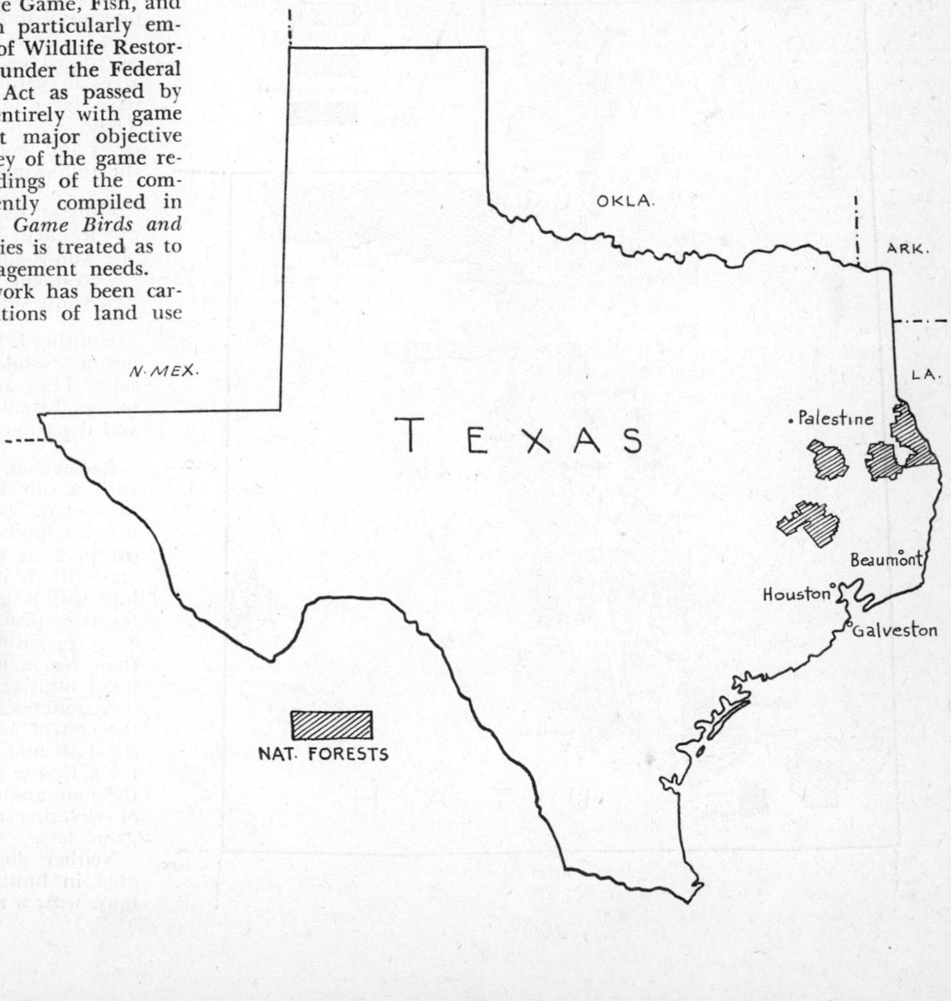

**Seasons.** Game animals and birds for which there are open seasons are:

| | |
|---|---|
| Antelope | Chachalaca (Mexican pheasant) |
| Bear | Prairie chicken |
| Mule deer | Scaled quail |
| Peccary | White-winged dove |
| Squirrel | Wild turkey |
| White-tailed deer | |
| Bobwhite quail | |

There is no closed season on:

| | |
|---|---|
| Bobcat | Mountain lion |
| Coyote | Ocelot |
| Jaguar | |

## UTAH

AREA: 84,916 square miles

**General Summary.** There is a regular open season on mule deer, the most numerous big-game animals hunted in the state. It is the policy of the Fish and Game Commission to hold the deer herds at the present level. There has been over-population in certain areas, but most of these areas have been brought under control by special hunts. Elk and antelope are less numerous than the popular mule deer, but hunting is allowed when there is sufficient increase and a surplus exists.

On the whole, Utah has good waterfowl shooting, with birds being attracted to its large river and lake marshes. Duck and goose shooting has shown a recent improvement.

Upland game birds, pheasant and quail, are in a precarious condition because there are more hunters in the field to take birds on a more limited habitat. Until a satisfactory population increase appears, there is a closed season on pinnated grouse, blue grouse, ruffed grouse, willow grouse, sage hen, Hungarian partridge, and mourning dove.

Small-game animals have no protection in spite of intensive hunting.

**State Conservation.** The Department of Fish and Game is directed by a commission of five members appointed by the governor, with the consent of the senate, for a term of six years. The commissioners are non-salaried but receive compensation and expense reimbursement. The Commission, with the approval of the governor, appoints a fish and game director for a term of four years at a salary of $4000 per annum. The Department is charged with the duty to protect, propagate, and distribute game animals and birds and fish throughout the state. It has full power to regulate and control the importation of game birds, game animals, and fish, and regulate hunting and fishing.

The fact that sportsmen are offered a wide variety of game hunting each year in Utah is indicative of the success of the game management program. However, management alone cannot produce a game crop, and in recognition of the need for suitable habitat, the Department is obliged to adjust its game-management activities to the planning for those game species for which natural conditions in the field provide a suitable range, and to better conditions for those game birds and game animals for which favorable natural conditions provide for large-scale "wild" propagation.

Distributed throughout the state are 13 game preserves for the better protection of birds and animals, and for the establishment of breeding places. In these areas hunting or the carrying of arms is forbidden. The Commission maintains public hunting grounds and protects those districts set aside as bird and game sanctuaries. A part of the special fund of the state treasury for range and game management is formed from the sale of non-resident licenses to hunt deer, since $15 of the $30 fee is contributed to that fund. Big-game animals doing damage to property are killed and sold, and the money placed in the fish and game fund.

A section of the fish and game laws of Utah provides that a group of landowners controlling at least 1000 acres may establish what is known as a posted hunting area and charge $1 per season for each hunter going onto his property. Where this program has been put into effect, it is functioning satisfactorily. Sportsmen realize that they must have a closer co-operative program with the landowner if they are going to maintain adequate wildlife.

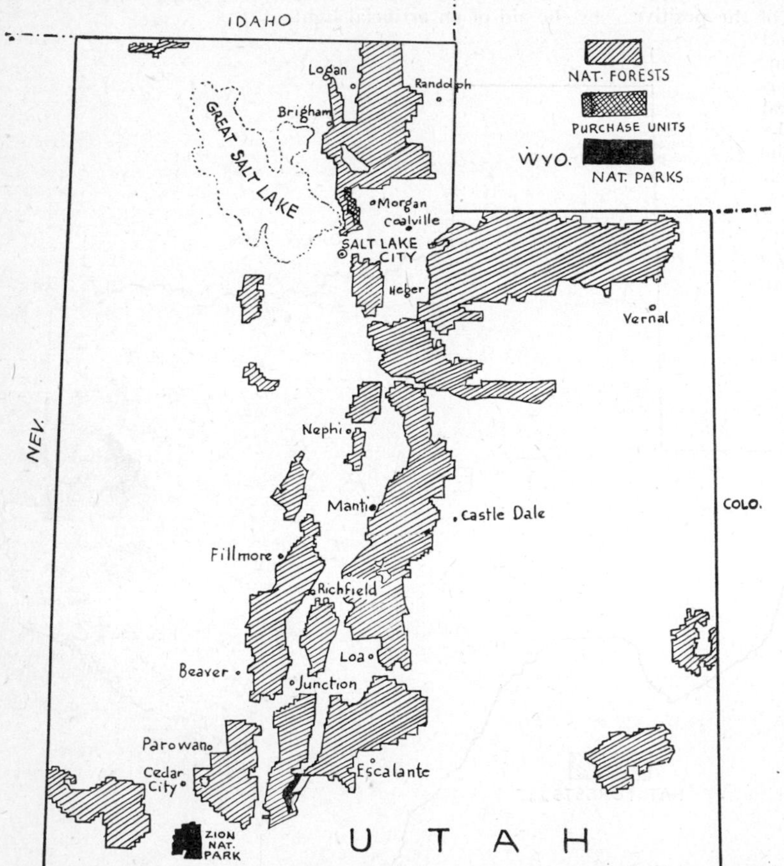


The state has in operation two game farms, each of which produces approximately 15,000 pheasants annually. In addition to the game farms, the Fish and Game Commission has purchased small plots ranging from 30 to 50 acres in various sections of the state which have been made into inviolate sanctuaries. These are planted with suitable food and cover and fenced against predators, as aids in the restocking program.

**Licenses.** License fees are as follows:

| | |
|---|---|
| Resident deer | $4.00 |
| Non-resident deer | 30.00 |
| Resident game birds | 3.00 |
| Non-resident game birds | 15.00 |

Hunting licenses may be secured at various business establishments in each town in the state. They are handled primarily by sporting-goods houses and, in some instances, drug and department stores.

**Regulations.** It is unlawful to hunt deer with a shotgun of any gauge, or with any kind of revolver, pistol, or with a .25-20 caliber, .22 special, or any other .22 caliber rifle except a .22 High Power, a .22 Hornet, or a .22 Swift. It is unlawful to hunt elk or antelope with a shotgun of any gauge, any kind of revolver, pistol, or with a rifle smaller than a .25-35 caliber. No shotgun pellets larger than No. 2 may be used for pheasant and quail hunting.

A commercial guide must obtain a license, the cost of which is $5, from the director of the Fish and Game Department. To qualify for a license a person must be a resident of the state and one who has not been convicted of violating any provision of the fish and game law.

Neither dogs nor artificial light may be used in hunting deer or elk. Every person must wear a red cap while hunting deer.

Aliens may not hunt game animals or have any type of gun in their possession.

**Seasons.** Game animals and birds for which there are open seasons are:

| | |
|---|---|
| Antelope | Ducks |
| Deer | Geese |
| Elk | Pheasant |
| Brant | Quail |
| Coot | Sora rail |

There is no closed season on:

| | |
|---|---|
| Small-game animals | Coyote |
| Bear | Mountain lion |
| Bobcat | |

## VERMONT — AREA: 9609 square miles

**General Summary.** A large percentage of Vermont's land is accessible for public hunting. Of the total area of the state, about 90 per cent is huntable, the remainder being taken up by cities, towns, roads, and waters.

The favorite big-game animal in Vermont is the white-tailed deer. Black bears are a second-choice large-game animal. Both deer and bears are on the increase, and in some sections more deer will be detrimental to the habitat.

Of the small-game species, the hunter's choices are snowshoe hare, cottontails, squirrels, fox, and coon in the order named.

The only upland game bird on which there is an annual open hunting season is the popular ruffed grouse. There is little pheasant hunting and there never will be much more in Vermont because of a combination of factors working against pheasants.

Good duck shooting is to be had along rivers and on inland ponds and lakes, but Lake Champlain is an excellent duck hunting area. The vast marshes of the eastern side provide some of the best shooting found in New England. There are two refuges, a Federal one at Missisquoi Bay and a state refuge at Sand Bar Bridge, that contribute to the duck population, particularly blacks, although teal, wood ducks, ring-necked ducks, and golden-eyes are also raised on the refuges.

**State Conservation.** The Fish and Game Department is an independent, self-supported agency. There is a five-man Fish and Game Commission and the director also acts as executive secretary for the Commission. The sportsmen have a voice in the operation of the Department since the Commission is required by law to hold county meetings once each year in each county. At these meetings the Board and the public discuss all phases of the Department's operation plans and policies. This New England town meeting system has worked out very well. The state operates no game farms, but it does purchase pheasants for liberation and has wintered birds for spring release.

The population of the state is largely rural and there is an excellent relationship between landowners and license holders, since most of the landowners are sportsmen. The Department works with sportsmen's clubs and landowners on food patch planting, winter feeding, and other practices to aid wildlife. In certain sections the Department works with the landowners to protect crops and gardens from depredations by deer.

**Licenses.** License fees are as follows:

| | |
|---|---|
| Resident (hunting) | $ 1.75 |
| Resident (hunting and fishing) | 3.00 |
| Non-resident (hunting) | 12.50 |
| Non-resident (hunting and fishing) | 15.50 |

Licenses are sold by town and city clerks, or may be obtained from the office of the Fish and Game Service, Montpelier, Vt. While sporting-goods stores may sell three-day non-resident fishing licenses, they cannot deal in hunting licenses.

**Regulations.** Semi-automatic rifles and shotguns may be used, but the full automatic is not permitted. There is no limitation on caliber or rifled slugs or buckshot.

No dog may be used to hunt deer, nor can a person have one in a camp or in the woods during deer season.

Bow and arrow may be used to hunt game.

There are no licensed guides in the state.

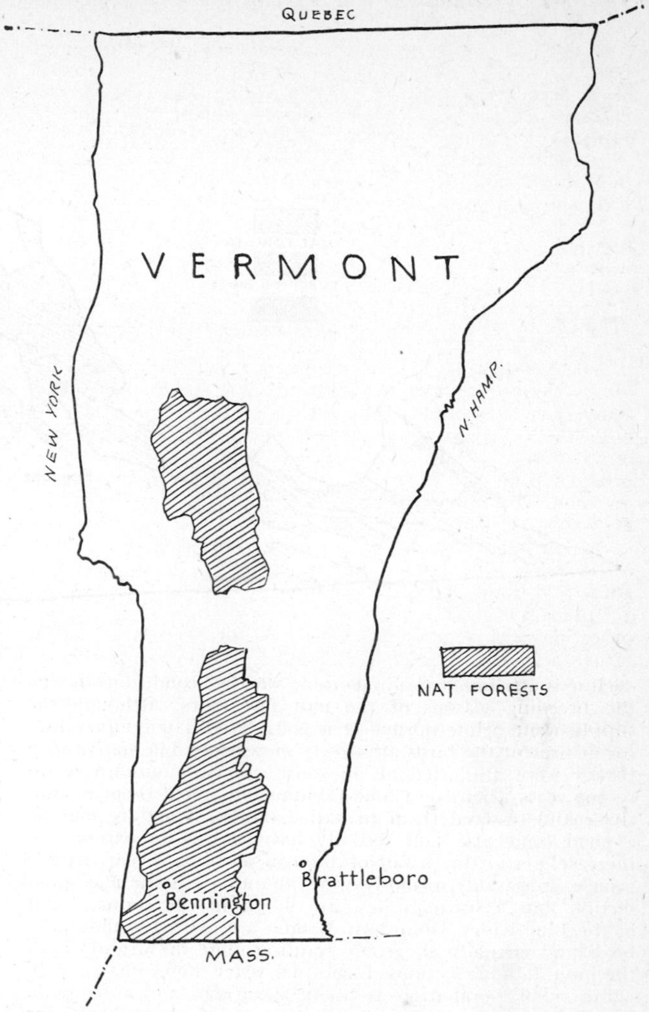


**Seasons.** Game animals and birds for which there are open seasons are:

| | |
|---|---|
| Bear | Ducks |
| Raccoon | Geese |
| Snowshoe hare | Partridge (ruffed grouse) |
| Squirrel | Woodcock |
| White-tailed deer | |

There is no closed season on cottontail rabbit.

## VIRGINIA — AREA: 39,899 square miles

**General Summary.** White-tailed (Virginia) deer are the most important big-game animal hunted in Virginia. They are widely distributed, and today there is good hunting in big swamps and large rivers. In almost all of the mountain counties they had been killed out completely until recent years when the state systematically restocked the suitable areas with about 1800 animals and protected them. Now they are rapidly becoming as abundant on their native ranges as in past years.

There is a closed season on elk at present. They were introduced to three mountainous counties in 1917 and thrived, allowing a short open hunting season for a good many years. Virginia was the last place east of the Rockies where elk were legally shot.

About 125 black bears are killed each hunting season. The range is restricted to some of the heavily wooded mountainous sections and the Dismal Swamp.

There is a good deal of small-game hunting throughout the state. Rabbits are abundant, and furnish more meat for the table than any other game animal. Squirrels—mostly gray—are found in every county. About 496,000 animals are killed by hunters annually.

The upland game birds are below normal in numbers, but no species are in danger of serious population losses. The

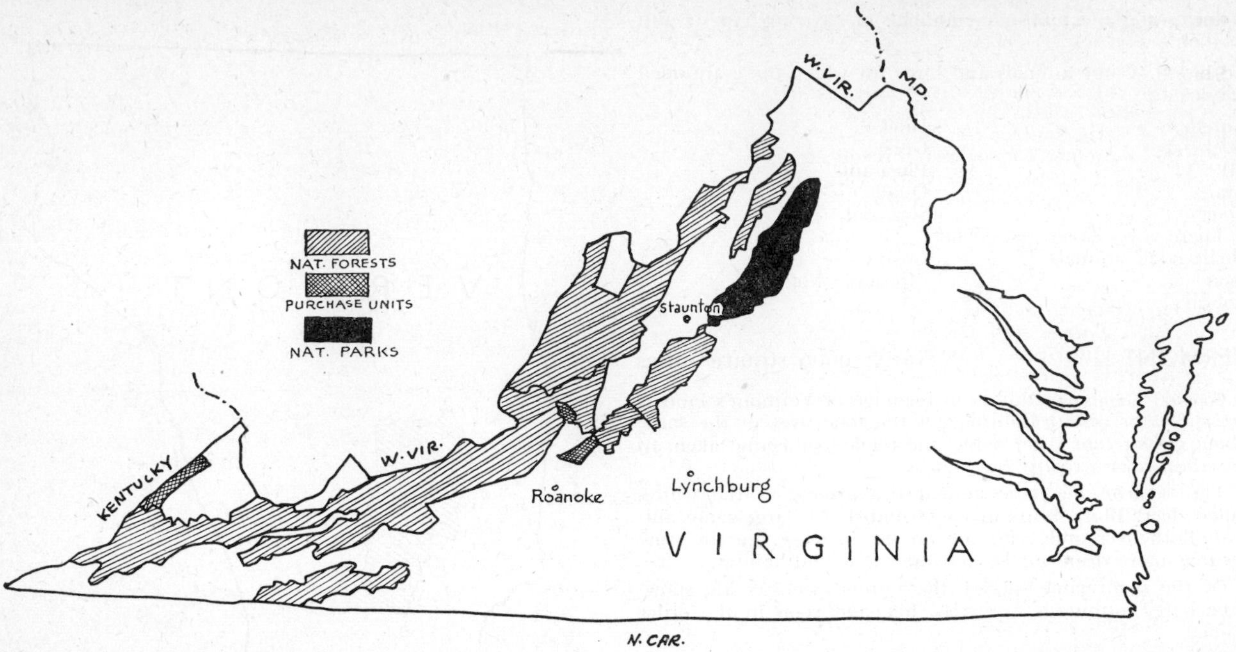


decline is attributed to unfavorable weather conditions during the breeding seasons of the past few years. Although the supply went below normal it is considered a temporary loss, for at present the birds are slowly increasing. The native wild turkey were all killed off in southwestern mountains until recent years when the Game Commission raised them in captivity and restored them to native ranges. They are making a good comeback, and recently have shown an exceptional increase, permitting a kill of about 6800 birds a year. Ruffed grouse (pheasant) formerly were abundant in the Piedmont section, but a scattered few are killed in the counties east of the Blue Ridge Mountains. Grouse are primarily mountain birds and virtually all grouse hunting done in Virginia is in the mountainous sections. In normal years the estimated bob-white quail population is about 4,000,000, and during an average hunting season about 400,000 of these birds are bagged. There is also an open season on three types of pheasants, the ringneck, Mongolian, and Chinese, but partridge, both chukar and Hungarian, are completely protected.

Waterfowl shooting in parts of the state are excellent, specifically the coastal area. Many ducks migrating along the Atlantic flyway through Virginia are attracted to its fresh- and salt-water areas. There is good goose shooting on land and over water. The clapper rail provides fine salt-water shooting, especially on the Eastern Shore.

**State Conservation.** The Virginia Commission of Game and Inland Fisheries, composed of nine members, has laid plans for the most intensive wildlife conservation in its history in order to meet the insistent demands for more adequate protection, rehabilitation, and development of Virginia's wild-lilfe resources. The Commission strongly advocates the policies set forth by the U. S. Wildlife Management Institute concerning the improvement and restoration of habitat for game birds and animals. The basic problems confronting the sportsmen of Virginia, as in many other states, are how to produce more game on less productive habitat for more hunters. Every new building constructed shrinks the potential productive range for wildlife. Eroded and burned lands also exact their toll from the total habitat. In this state intelligent wildlife administration and management is aided by scientific research at Virginia's Co-operative Wildlife Station at Virginia Polytechnic Institute. This scientific study is co-ordinated with a wide range of interests, including agriculture, forestry, and grazing, which are all a part of land management. The farmer, for example, can do much to restore wildlife by providing hedgerows which serve as travel lanes, food, and cover for game birds and animals. For years, timber and wildlife interests were in direct conflict with each other. Wholesale clearing of the land left areas in a wasted, useless condition, offering no browse or coverage for years to come. Today, wise cutting practices give better results from the standpoint of both game and timber.

Education in conservation is a most important factor in improving game conditions. The hunter must understand the reasons for strict enforcement of game laws and controlled hunting in order to co-operate in the restoration.

The state has no official farmer-sportsman co-operative program in operation. However, through bulletins and educational public-relations data, the Commission stresses the fact that hunters should respect the property rights of farmers and obtain permission to hunt before going on private property.

The state maintains one game farm in Cumberland County where wild turkeys and quail are raised. The annual production of birds is roughly estimated at 2500 quail and 400 turkeys. No game animals are reared in captivity.

**Licenses.** License fees are as follows:

| | |
|---|---|
| County resident | $ 1.00 |
| State resident | 2.50 |
| Non-resident | 15.50 |
| Non-resident 2 days | 5.00 |
| Big game stamp for bear and deer in addition to regular season license (except county residents): | |
| Resident | $ 1.00 |
| Non-resident | 2.50 |

Hunting licenses, resident and non-resident, are sold by the clerks of the circuit courts in the counties and corporation courts in the cities. Where a clerk desires to be relieved of this duty the Commission is privileged to appoint sale agents.

**Regulations.** The use of a rifle less than .25 caliber in deer hunting west of the Blue Ridge Mountains is barred. No shotgun larger than 10 gauge or one that can be shot more than three times without reloading is permissible to hunt birds and animals.

No game birds or animals may be hunted in the snow, except that bear may be hunted in counties west of the Blue Ridge in snow, and foxes may be hunted with dogs only in the snow.

A sportsmen's guide has been compiled and is available at the Commission of Game and Inland Fisheries, Richmond, Va. Accommodations for hunting, cabins, boats, blinds, horses, dogs, and guides have been listed.

**Seasons.** Game animals and birds for which there are open seasons are:

| | | |
|---|---|---|
| Bear | Rabbits | Geese |
| Deer | Squirrels | Quail |
| Foxes | Ducks | Pheasant |
| Clapper rail (marsh hen) | | Turkey |

## WASHINGTON

AREA: 68,192 square miles

**General Summary.** Washington is currently carrying a maximum deer herd and elk herd, and an excellent upland game bird population. Ducks in this area, as in the rest of the United States, are limited in number, as the majority of birds are of the migratory nature and consequently this condition finds a solution outside of the state. This state is showing a greater harvest of game than ever before. However, because of the great increase in number of hunters, the kill per hunter has dropped. This condition does not indicate the extinction of any game species, but does indicate that the game resources are being shared by a larger number of persons.

The largest demand by hunters is for Chinese pheasants; next is quail. Grouse and Hungarian partridge recently decreased and required the protection of a closed season, but reports from the field suggest that these birds are recovering sufficiently to authorize an open season within a few years. Chukar partridges were recently introduced into this state and are showing a very marked increase. A season is anticipated on these birds in the near future.

Washington's big game is composed mostly of deer of two general species which are divided into four sub-species or races. These are mule deer, Columbia black-tailed deer, Pend Oreille white-tailed deer, and Columbia River white-tailed deer. There is also a regular open season on elk. In Chelan County Bow and Arrow Area (Natapoc Mountain) firearms are not allowed. Bear can be taken throughout the year in counties lying west of the summit of the Cascade Mountains with the exception that bear may not be hunted during the general open season on elk. One may also find such big-game animals as moose, antelope, mountain sheep, and caribou, but these are definitely a minority and no season is set for their open hunting. Washington also boasts one of the largest herds of mountain goat, but because of the ranges and climatic conditions these animals are protected by a permanent closed season.

The small-game animals are rabbits (cottontail, snowshoe, and Washington hare), and squirrels (gray and black). Squirrels have recently shown a decrease and have been protected.

Another group of animals frequently hunted are the predators. Generous bounties are paid for coyote, cougar, and bobcats. The lesser predators can be listed as wolverine, skunk, civet cat, weasel, mountain beaver, badger, red squirrel, ground squirrel, rat, jack rabbit, mole, and wild house cat.

Along with the other Pacific coastal states, Washington has its full share of waterfowl that inhabit the grain fields and coastal flats.

**State Conservation.** To improve the habitats for upland birds, small tracts are being developed complete with food, water, and cover. These areas are designed to be permanent game-bird population centers. Sixty-four such regions, averaging approximately 10 acres each in size, are under management at this time. Of these areas, 43 tracts are on land purchased by the Game Department, and 21 of them are co-operative projects between the Department and the landowners.

Special hunts are held on deer and elk to control the herds in certain agricultural areas where they damage crops. These hunts and additional special seasons are only partially-corrective measures for checking big-game damage, and since 1943 the Department of Game has used the more effective method of fencing off the game from the crops.

Acting on the suggestion of the six-man Game Commission and interested sports groups, biologists of the Washington State Game Department plan an expanded waterfowl study. The study is designed to show what can be done to improve duck and goose hunting in the state and will include a survey of the principal waterfowl areas. Biologists, aided by game protectors, are gathering information concerning duck flights, nesting conditions, and other factors. In addition, a program of banding waterfowl has been started in the Skagit Flat area to determine their migratory habits.

The Department of Game maintains co-operative agreements with the farmers in the establishment of game-habitat areas and public shooting grounds. Since a great part of the game of the state is located upon private farm lands, the attitude of the farmer towards sportsmen generally governs whether or not this game is made available to the general public. The Department is now in the process of investigating farmer-sportsman co-operative programs in other states with a view to establish a larger and more concise program than there is at present.

There are in full operation ten state game farms which raise and release about 80,000 Chinese pheasants annually. In addition to these farms is a 4-H Club pheasant-raising program from which approximately 900 birds are received a year. As the figures show, Chinese pheasants are the major industry of the state game farms; however, as a sideline or experiment, 75 wild turkeys, 55 quail, 6 Hungarian partridges, 6 deer, and 1 elk were liberated in the year 1946.

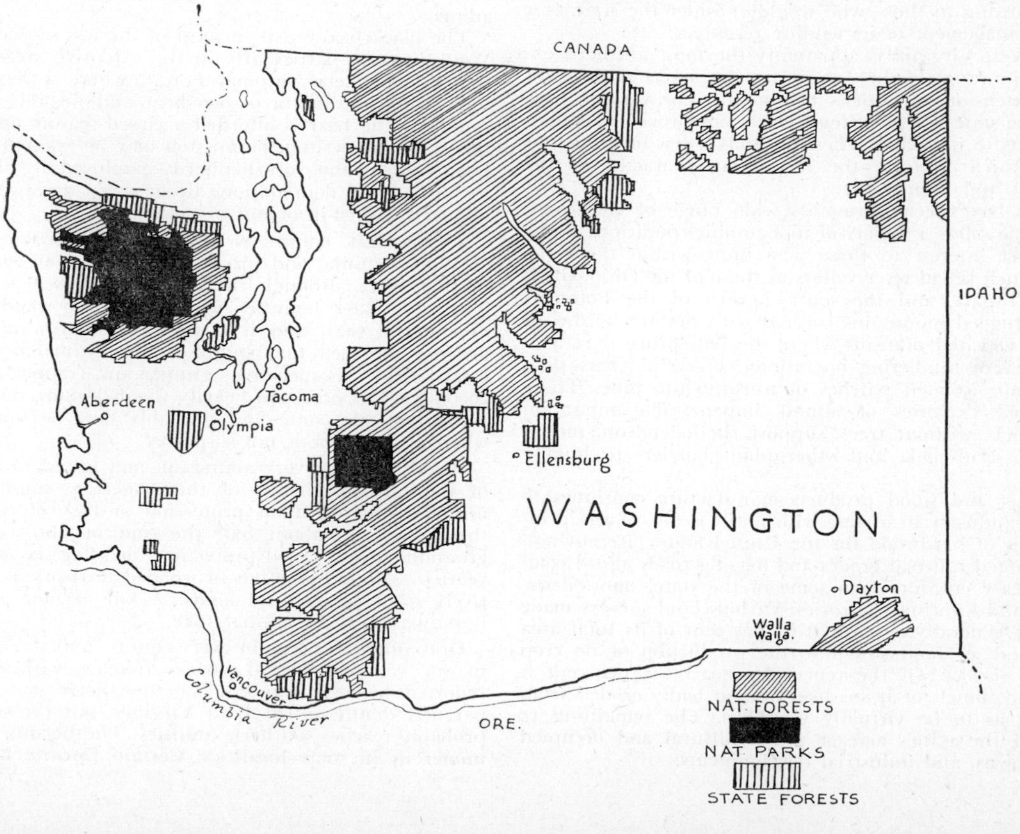

**Licenses.** License fees are as follows:

| | |
|---|---|
| Resident county | $ 2.50 |
| Resident state | 5.00 |
| Non-resident | 25.00 |
| Alien | 25.00 |
| Non-resident game bird | 15.00 |
| Resident elk permit | 5.00 |
| Non-resident elk permit | 25.00 |
| Alien elk permit | 50.00 |

Game licenses are handled by license dealers all over the state, principally operators of hardware and sporting-goods stores.

**Regulations.** No person may hunt any deer, elk, or bear with any firearm which fires any of the following loads of cartridges: Any and all rim-fire cartridges, .218 Bee, .25-20, .38-40, .30 U. S. Army Carbine, .45 A.C.P., .22 Hornet, .32-20, .44-40. No person may hunt any deer, elk or bear with any pistol or revolver, or with any fully automatic firearm.

No dogs may be used to hunt deer or elk.

**Seasons.** Game animals and birds for which there are open seasons are:

| | |
|---|---|
| Bear | Band-tailed pigeons |
| Deer | Chinese pheasants |
| Elk | Ducks |
| Rabbits | Geese |
| | Quail |

There is no closed season on:

| | |
|---|---|
| Bobcat | Jack rabbit |
| Civet cat | Red squirrels |
| Cougar | Skunk |
| Coyote | Wolverine |
| Ground squirrels | |

## WEST VIRGINIA AREA: 23,643 square miles

**General Summary.** West Virginia is a border state in a biological sense in far greater degree than in respect to its geographical, historical, or political situations. Extremes in elevation, with attendant extremes in temperature and rainfall, combine to create within the state a diversity of biological life zones. Parts of West Virginia support typically Carolinian life-zone flora and fauna. Much of the state ranges through sub-divisions of the transition zone; part of it is typically Canadian insofar as its plant and animal life is concerned. Inevitably, under these conditions, there occurs an intermingling of northern and southern forms as surprising to naturalists as it is confusing to those who would consider the state as a whole in management of its wildlife resources.

Within West Virginia is apparently the most southern extension of the range of the American tamarack, and the most northern extension of Fraser's balsam fir. The varying hare occurs in the state where extreme elevations provide northern environments to its liking. These are only a few of numerous examples which indicate the interesting character of the state's plant and animal life.

As might be expected from its wide range of elevations, West Virginia offers a variety of topographic conditions which are of direct interest to those who hunt within the state. There are such broad river valleys as those of the Ohio, Great Kanawha, Tygart, and the south branch of the Potomac. There are rugged mountains covered with mature hardwood forests and elevated plateaus where the red spruce is returning after severe lumbering operations of several years past. There remain isolated patches of uncut white pine. There are extended expanses of almost impenetrable mountain "balds" which, without trees, support rhododendron, mountain laurel, scrub oak, and other plant barriers to human intrusion.

Lumbering and wood products manufacture continues to be a major industry in a state which still is one of the principal sources of hardwood for the United States. Recent and long-abandoned railroad grades and logging roads afford comparatively easy entrance into some of the state's most desirable woodland hunting territories. Various land surveys made in the state generally agree that 60 per cent of its total area is forest land, or land suited to the production of no crop other than timber. Of the remainder nearly 35 per cent is grazing land, much of it so steep and so badly eroded from overgrazing as to be virtually worthless. The remaining 15 per cent of the state's acreage is agricultural and occupied by cities, towns, and industrial developments.

Within the state lies the Monongahela National Forest, more than 800,000 acres in extent in 1946, and with a total purchase area of 1,700,000 acres. A portion of the George Washington National Forest takes in parts of three eastern counties of West Virginia. Some 60,000 acres are in state forests and some 35,000 acres in state parks. A policy which encourages multiple use of the National Forest promises a perpetual hunting territory for the public, and quota hunting is permitted within state forest lands where game supplies permit.

There is a dearth of bibliographical material on animal life in West Virginia, more particularly concerning game species on which there is an annual open season. Records of the Conservation Commission afford some indications of game supply, but even these data afford poor yardsticks for measurement, with rare exceptions. Annual return of forms attesting game kill, for example, is not required in this state, with the exception of reporting turkey and deer. There is reason to believe that turkey are not fully reported despite this legal requirement, but that deer reports are comparatively accurate, so far as legal kill is concerned. As to small game, it is possible to estimate only the probable kill for each season.

Virginia deer is the state's most important big game. West Virginia's first legal deer season of modern times (1931) produced a kill of 282 legal bucks in two days. The six-day open season of 1946 resulted in a legal kill of slightly more than 4000 deer, of which 222 were legally-taken antlerless deer. Seven of the total killed were taken by bow-and-arrow hunters in a special two-week season preceding the firearms season. This was the fifth such successive archery season for the state, and was confined to a single state park of some 11,000 acres. Archers are free to hunt elsewhere during the regular firearms season on this species. Deer occur in every county of the state, even the smaller, heavily industrialized counties. The best kills ordinarily occur in Tucker, Preston, and Pocahontas Counties but 23 counties were open to deer hunting in the 1946 season, and plans to extend the open deer territory are being made. Original replacement stock came from the South and appears to have been even smaller than native stock remaining at the time. For example, 47 bucks killed in Seneca State Forest in 1946 (a controlled hunting area) averaged only 95 pounds field-dressed. Bucks weighed at Cooper's Rock State Forest averaged approximately 145 pounds field-dressed. Replacement stock added to the state herd in more recent years has been secured from Wisconsin; these larger, northern deer are scattered throughout the state, occasionally producing exceptionally large animals.

The black bear exists in most of the less settled counties of West Virginia, particularly in the extensive areas covered by the Monongahela National Forest, where a recent estimate indicated a minimum of 600 bear and possibly double that number. The bear is afforded a closed season (as of 1946) in this state, but written permission may be granted landowners, bona fide tenants, or shepherds employed by sheep owners to kill bear if depredations upon sheep are proved to have occurred, either in or out of season.

The wildcat, bobcat, or bay lynx still occupies large areas of West Virginia, and provides some hunting for enthusiasts of that sport although the animal is classed as a predator. The state pays bounties upon some 300 of these animals during the year, and it is probable that numerous others are not reported for bounty claim. Estimates are that the total kill of this species by gunner and trapper actually tops 2000 a year. It occurs in heavily wooded, more remote sections throughout the state and probably may be found in areas where its presence is not suspected.

Woodchuck are very abundant, and found in every county of the state. Residents of the respective counties are permitted to decide upon protection or lack of protection for this species. In about half the counties the woodchuck, or groundhog, is afforded protection for some six months of the year. It is found as often in wooded territory as in comparatively scant agricultural lands. A kill of more than 200,000 is estimated as an annual take.

Gray squirrels occur in every county, and the estimated kill in one year exceeded 1,000,000 animals, with 8191 actually reported by 1027 hunters. The northern gray squirrel apparently dominates in West Virginia, but the southern race probably reaches southern counties. The big fox squirrels are numerous in some localities. Certain favorite habitats, such as comparatively open farm woodlots, regularly produce a crop of these animals, while other areas, which appear to provide equivalent conditions for food and shelter, are barren of fox squirrels. An estimated 280,000 of these animals are taken annually in the state.

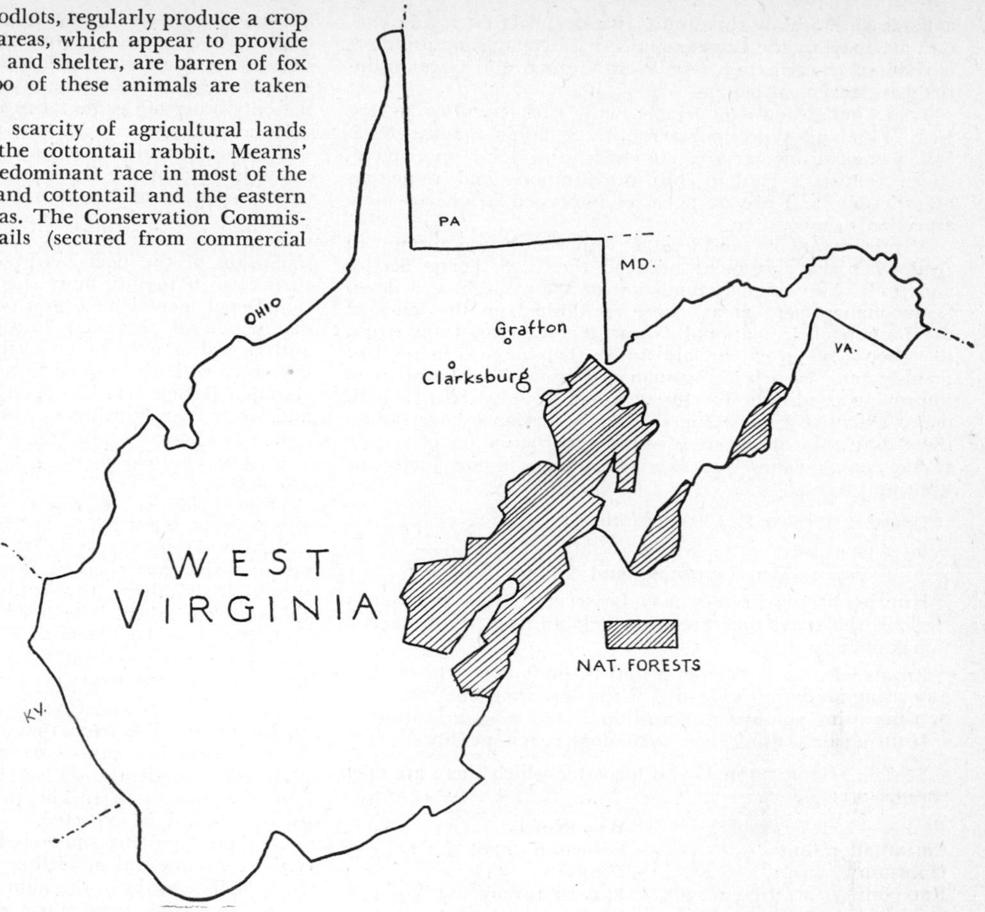


West Virginia's comparative scarcity of agricultural lands works against abundance of the cottontail rabbit. Mearns' cottontail apparently is the predominant race in most of the state, although the New England cottontail and the eastern cottontail occur in limited areas. The Conservation Commission regularly restocks cottontails (secured from commercial dealers) in an effort to supplement natural reproduction. In the past several years such purchases have been confined to Mearns' cottontail. An estimated 700,000 are killed each year.

The varying hare or "snowshoe rabbit" is confined to the state's highest mountain areas and is protected from hunting. Habitat conditions in the state probably forbid its ever becoming numerous enough to permit an open season, although in a few isolated localities it is relatively common.

Year in and year out the ruffed grouse offers the best shooting in West Virginia, sharing this distinction with the gray squirrel. It occurs in every county of the state, more abundantly in the mountainous, wooded sections of West Virginia. In West Virginia, as elsewhere, this bird is subject to cycles of abundance and scarcity. Approximately 75,000 birds are bagged annually.

The bobwhite quail is primarily a bird of agricultural land and, since land of that character is comparatively scarce in this state, the species cannot be called common in a state-wide sense. Certain territories, however, such as the South Branch, Ohio, Tygart, Great Kanawha, and other rivers and larger stream valleys usually afford good hunting for this fine game bird. The State Conservation Commission operates a quail farm which releases about 10,000 birds annually. This source of supply is supplemented by purchases from commercial dealers. About 80,000 birds are taken each hunting season.

West Virginia remains one of the few eastern states which affords good wild turkey hunting in virtually all its eastern and southeastern counties. Flocks are known to be in numerous additional counties where hunting is not now permitted, pending the building up of the breeding stock. Approximately 1200 turkeys are the average take for the season. The Conservation Commission is endeavoring to rear turkeys at its Huttonsville (Randolph County) game bird farm using the breeding plan of permitting wild gobblers to mate with wing-tipped hens enclosed in large 10- to 15-acre pens) in "turkey country," inside the state. These eggs are gathered by custodians and hatched artificially. This project was initiated in the state in 1946.

Numerous attempts have been made to introduce the ring-necked pheasant in West Virginia, and none can be termed successful. Two brief open seasons on cock birds were conducted in four northern counties of the state in past years, but these have not been repeated. A few pheasants are to be found scattered in various localities within the state, but it is improbable that this species ever will afford even fair hunting in West Virginia.

Presumably few hunters are aware of the woodcock. There are numerous breeding records for the species in West Virginia, and there are occasionally good flights of this bird in the fall hunting season. A few hunters regularly hunt this species, but such kills as are reported generally have been made by accidental contact with the birds by gunners actually seeking other upland game.

West Virginia regularly is last in the list of states in the purchase of Federal duck stamps. Some 2400 West Virginians bought such stamps in 1945 but it is believed that virtually no waterfowl hunting, as such, takes place in this state. Hunters occasionally encounter isolated flights, or flocks of waterfowl within West Virginia, or go elsewhere for this form of hunting. The protected wood duck is making a genuine comeback in this state as a breeding bird. There is at least one authenticated breeding record for the mallard, and there is the possibility that other shallow-feeding species eventually will be found nesting within the state.

As with waterfowl, shorebirds in general find small inducement even to visit West Virginia, although some regularly appear in migrations along streams, at the edges of the state's scant marshy land, about artificial lakes and ponds, and the like.

**State Conservation.** The Conservation Commission of West Virginia is headed by a director of conservation appointed by the governor. Six advisory commissioners, one member for each of the state's six congressional districts, meet quarterly with the director, and at such other times as he may call special meetings, and consult with him upon matters of policy and operation of the Commission. The director receives a salary of $6000 annually and travel expenses. Advisory commissioners are non-salaried but receive expenses incident to attendance upon their official duties.

Under the director, headquarters offices of the Commission are in the State Capitol Building, Charleston, W. Va. The executive secretary has charge of office help, supplies, equipment, etc. At headquarters, also, are offices of the chiefs and principal assistants in each of the six divisions, into which the work of the Commission is divided. The divisions are Education and Publicity, Law Enforcement, Fish Management, Game Management, Forestry, and State Parks. Field personnel includes law enforcement officers, district forest protectors, forest and park custodians, hatchery and game farm superintendents, and others responsible to these field leaders or to division chiefs.

The Commission holds statutory meetings each January, one in each of the six congressional districts, at which time sportsmen or others are encouraged to submit recommendations for open seasons, bag limits or other conservation law changes and amendments. Seasons, bag limits, parks and forest regulations, etc., are fixed by the Commission. At least one game protector is resident in each county of West Virginia and larger counties have two such officers.

The Commission co-operates with such agencies as the U. S. Fish and Wildlife Service, U. S. Forest Service, U. S. Soil Conservation Service, statewide and local sportsmen's clubs, the state garden club organizations and numerous other public and private agencies interested in one or more aspects of conservation.

A movement of considerable importance was begun in 1946 when, by agreement between the U. S. Forest Service and the Conservation Commission of West Virginia, a dozen "game-management areas" were established on the lands of the Monongahela National Forest. These areas, from 20,000 to 35,000 acres in extent, are under the charge of a resident manager and each is being managed from the standpoint of improving conditions for forest game. Coupled with a half-dozen extensive game refuges (state or national forest lands) these developments promise well for perpetuation of certain of the state's game birds and mammals despite increasing hunting pressure.

**Licenses.** License fees are as follows:

| | |
|---|---|
| Resident | $ 2.00 |
| Non-resident (hunting and fishing) | 15.00 |

Hunting-fishing licenses may be secured from any county clerk in the state; they are not available from the Conservation Commission.

**Regulations.** It is not permitted to hunt deer with a shotgun using ammunition loaded with more than one solid ball, or rifles using rim-fire ammunition of less than .25 caliber.

Hunting or chasing deer with dogs is not permitted.

**Seasons.** Game animals and birds for which there are open seasons are:

| | |
|---|---|
| Bear | Woodchuck |
| Cottontail rabbit | Bobwhite quail |
| Opossum | Ducks |
| Raccoon | Eastern turkey |
| Squirrels | Geese |
| Varying hare | Ruffed grouse (native pheasant) |
| White-tailed (Virginia) deer | |

There is no closed season on fox, coyote, and lynx.

## WISCONSIN — AREA: 56,343 square miles

**General Summary.** Approximately 5,500,000 acres (8620 square miles) of public and private lands and waters are open to public hunting.

The game census in Wisconsin has been made over the years on its most important game birds and animals, and the record showing the fluctuation in the kill is particularly interesting for this state. In 1917 about 18,000 white-tailed deer were taken, and after a slight rise in 1919 they dipped to a low of 7000 in 1924, thus demanding a closed season. For the next 12 years open and closed seasons were alternated, and there was a steady increase until 1936 when the closed seasons were terminated, and 30,000 deer were killed in that year. By 1942 the kill was 45,000, but there was an all-time high the next year when the figures soared to 128,000, followed by as dramatic a change the next season when it dropped back to 29,000, or a difference of about 100,000 from the previous year. In 1946 the number started to climb again, with 56,000 deer reported taken.

The sale of deer tags roughly paralleled the number of deer killed, with a few notable exceptions. Starting with a purchase of 54,000 in 1917, the course was followed, with corresponding fluctuations, until 1923 or the first closed season. As the number of deer taken went up, the sale of tags went down, from 50,000 to 47,000 two years later; then a sharp rise to almost 77,000 was followed by a sudden drop two years after that. The rise and fall during the intermittent open and closed season did not follow the deer kill, since a drop in deer tags (67,000) in 1932 opposed one of the highs in deer kills (36,000), and a rise in deer tags (84,000) during the next open season in 1934 was the opposite of the dipping deer figure (21,000). The most interesting variation, however, was in the peak of the deer kill of 1943 when the tag sales rose slightly (from 120,000 to 158,000) as compared to the sudden increase in deer kill (from 45,000 to 128,000); nor was the tag drop so violent the next season. Conversely, the deer kill rose to 56,000 in 1946 but the tag figure rose to an all-time high of 200,000, apparently indicating postwar intensification on big-game hunting. Deer are of chief interest to the big-game hunters of the state and are increasing. Black bears, the only other big game taken in an annual open season, also show an increase.

An open season of antlerless deer (does and fawns) was called in 1946 by the Game Management Division to thin out the overpopulated Necedah National Wildlife Refuge. This 40,000-acre Federal refuge was suffering from heavy browsing. reforestation, deer damage, and the probability of winter starvation of the deer herd which had increased from less than 2000 in 1941 to more than 6000 in 1946. The Conservation Department issued 3000 permits to be used over a nine-day season of three-day hunting periods. A total of 1637 antlerless deer were taken during this season which ran concurrently with the forked antler season on the outside. The Necedah Refuge was last open to gun hunting in 1939. Bow-and-arrow deer hunting was permitted in 1945, and the next year was allowed again when 6000 bowmen (763 were from 17 states) hunted during a 45-day season, taking a total of 258 deer.

From a kill of 1,560,000 cottontail rabbits in 1931, the game census reported an all-time peak the following year of 2,474,000. From that year to 1937, there was a steady decrease which was checked in 1937 with a kill of 529,000. A second high during this study was in 1942 when 1,397,000 rabbits were taken. The low of 658,000 in 1944 marked the end of a second cycle lasting seven years, and, according to this orderly rise and fall, the kill of 755,000 in 1946 should be higher for the next few years.

The census on the snowshoe hare shows a steady decline in the annual kill from 1931 to 1946. After the abrupt drop from 634,000 in 1931 to 60,000 in 1937, the rises and falls were more moderate, with a high of 174,000 in 1941 and a low of 27,000 in 1944. The 1946 kill was 57,000, but a cyclic swing upward is expected.

The gray and fox squirrels have gone through consistently violent fluctuations according to the game census from 1931 to 1946. The peaks in the numbers killed were: 1932 (854,000), 1935 (1,174,000), 1939 (1,073,000), 1942 (762,000), 1944 (696,000), and 1946 (1,014,000). The lows were: 1931 (660,000), 1933 (750,000), 1937 (451,000), 1941 (668,000), 1943 (589,000), and 1945 (668,000). At present they are showing a slight increase. Squirrels and rabbits are of equal importance to the hunters of this state.

The raccoon census begins in 1932 with a kill of 10,000, and the figure rises to 19,000 the next year, to drop below the 1932 mark with 9000 killed in 1934. From that date to the present, however, there has been a gradual rise, with brief setbacks. The peak was in 1943 when 26,000 were taken, but within two years the number slid to 16,000. It rose to 24,000 in 1946, and is now at a high point in population. It is significant that the kill for 1946 and 1943 is larger than the peak reached in 1933.

From 1932 to 1946 there has been a startling rise in the number of red fox, one of the most serious animal predators. From a low of 1500 in 1932 there were fewer setbacks than marks of increase until 1943 when there was a direct spurt upward from 6000 to an unparalleled high in 1944 of 24,000. The numbers were on the decrease in 1945, with 18,000, but were still greater than any year other than 1944. Though the census on the gray fox from 1932 to 1946 demonstrates that this species has generally been more abundant than the red fox, there has been no such menacing increase. From 3000 in 1932, the kill rose straight to 21,000 by 1935, then declined to 4000 by 1942. In 1944 a peak of 12,000 was reached but fell off to 6000 in 1946, and they are still decreasing.

The wolves and coyotes are treated as one animal in the game census taken from 1923 to 1945. The kill shows a spiraling rise from an all-time low of 885 in 1943 to a new peak of 4000 in 1945. Other low points during this study were marked at 2000 for 1923 and 1926, 1300 for 1932, and 2000 for 1936. Other high points were: 2500 in 1924, 2700 in 1928, and 2300 in 1935. Recently wolves have shown a population drop, but coyotes are at a high point.

The census on pheasants covers a period from 1932 to 1946 and indicates (after a rise in 1933 from 40,000 to 155,000 and a drop back in 1934 to 104,000) a continual increase in the number of pheasants taken until 1942. At this time, a high point was reached, 802,000 being bagged, but there was a sharp decline two years later to 447,000 which rose to about 471,000 the following year, but slipped back to 437,000 in 1946, or was roughly on a par with the number bagged in 1939. More sportsmen hunt pheasants than any other game bird, but they are holding their own against increased hunting pressure.

The record of the ruffed grouse between 1931 and 1946 marks the typical five-year cycle of the species. Beginning in 1931 with a bag of 56,000, the figure soared the following year to 317,000 for the annual bag. That number was virtually maintained the next year, then fell off in 1934 to 132,000 (or about a 2/3 loss) and declined to 73,000 in 1935, and a closed season was required for two years. When the season was opened in 1938, over 81,000 grouse were taken and the number leaped to a peak in 1942, at which time it was 422,000. Faster than it rose to its two-year height, it fell to 115,000 within two years, completing another five-year cycle and warranting a closed season beginning in 1945. Following this pattern, presumably an increase begins again around 1947. It is interesting to note that in spite of an increased number of hunters, the peak of the cycle in 1942 is higher than that reached in 1932, which indicates an increase in the species as a whole.

The census of the prairie chicken and sharp-tailed grouse considers these two game birds as one. There have been six closed seasons and ten open seasons on them during the recorded 1931 to 1946 period. These hunting seasons are guided somewhat by the abrupt fluctuations or cyclic changes in the population of the species. Almost 53,000 were bagged in 1931, presumably at a low point in the cycle, but in the peak year, 1933, 140,000 were taken. Within two years the number slipped back to a low of 33,000 and a two-year closed season was declared. In 1938 the climb upward began again, starting with 43,000, hitting 76,000 in 1939 and maintaining this high up to 1942 when 77,000 were bagged. Presumably in anticipation of the population drop, set by the pattern of the five-year cycle, a closed season was effected in 1943. After several years, the species should begin to revive again, although the effect of changing environmental conditions is a very uncertain quantity.

The number of Hungarian partridges taken between 1932 and 1946 shows a violently fluctuating kill for that bird, which apparently is indicative of the partridge population during that span of time. From 1932 to 1935 there was an increase from 11,000 to 23,000, but this steady rise fell off in 1937 to 15,000. A sharp up-sweep to 50,000 in 1939 revealed a peak in the partridge kill, but dropped within two years to a low of 30,000, then rose in 1942 to 40,000, only to go down into a steady decline in 1945, reaching the lowest recorded figure—less than 3000—and necessitating a closed season in 1947.

From 1932 to 1946 the game census on the bobwhite quail reflects a violent rise and fall in the number of birds taken each season. In 1932 only 550 quail were bagged, but the census reveals a rise to over 10,000 in 1933 and still higher the next year to 12,000. The following year, or 1935, saw the last quail shooting for five years (until 1941) when the season was opened again. The kill for that year dropped to 5000, apparently indicating a corresponding population decline during the closed season. In 1942 the number rallied to reach 8000, but sank again the following year to 3000, and by 1945 to 2000. The peak of 1942 was nearly the same in 1946, for 7000 birds were bagged that year.

Although the number of stamp sales made for waterfowl shooting shows a steady increase in gunners from 41,000 in 1934 to 98,000 in 1946, the census on the waterfowl kill indicates more violent changes in population. Low points were in: 1931 (462,000), 1934 (571,000), 1937 (633,000), 1944 (534,000), and 1946 (739,000). High points were in: 1933, 1938, 1939, and 1945, when over 1,000,000 birds were bagged. Local waterfowl breeding conditions have been poor on all species except wood duck and blue-winged teal, where it has been fair. Lack of sufficient breeding stock apparently has caused this condition of low population.

**State Conservation.** The Conservation Commission is composed of six members. In order to carry out a large and comprehensive conservation program, the Department receives funds from the sale of licenses (hunting, fishing, trapping, etc.), the mill tax, Federal aid, and by direct appropriation from the state general fund.

The eight state forests of Wisconsin now contain approximately 254,000 acres. With a view to encouraging reforestation and the planting of trees for forestry purposes on both public and privately owned lands, in Wisconsin, the Conservation Department is producing planting stock. The production of game-food-bearing shrubs, vines, and trees has continued, and the demand for this type of planting stock has been met by the nurseries.

Each winter the Department operates a winter game-bird feeding program to help carry the wild birds through these critical months. Feeding activities concentrate mainly on the pheasant, Hungarian partridge, and quail. A part of the revenue from deer tags supports a program for winter feeding of deer.

The state game farm raises and distributes, stocks, and plants ringneck pheasants as well as indulging in experimental plantings of chukar partridges and reeves pheasants. Experiments and trapping also involve deer.

The only farmer-sportsman co-operative plan in operation in Wisconsin is the Public Hunting Grounds program. This program operates largely by securing leases from farmers to set up large blocks of private land for hunting, and includes a total of approximately 160,000 acres. These areas vary in size from less than 1000 to nearly 10,000 acres and are located in 27 counties, with emphasis placed on the southern half of the state. There is active participation of the sportsmen in game management activities. In 1933 a program of large public hearings gave way to a more compact grouping or a system of county committees. The elected representatives take part in public hearings by counties. Every practical means has been employed to urge large numbers of citizens representative of all groups interested in conservation to attend the election and public hearing.

**Licenses.** License fees are as follows:

| | |
|---|---|
| Resident | $ 1.50 |
| Non-resident (exclusive of deer) | 25.00 |
| Non-resident (including deer) | 50.00 |
| Resident deer tag | 1.00 |
| Non-Resident archer (for deer only) | 5.00 |

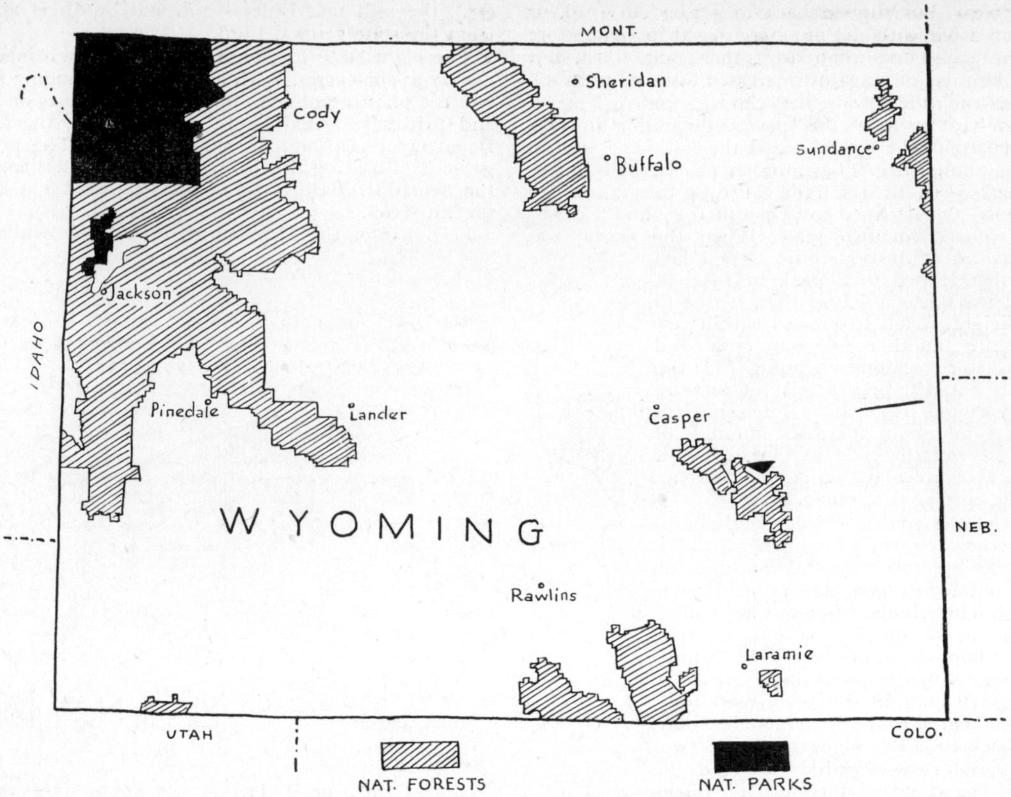


Resident hunting licenses are sold by county clerks and sub-stations they may use, such as sporting-goods stores. Non-resident licenses are sold by the main Department office at Madison, by field personnel of the Department, and by some county clerks.

**Regulations.** No firearms may be carried in a territory where there is open season for deer for a period of five days prior to the opening of such season unless such firearms, whether rifle or shotgun, are unloaded and taken apart or unloaded and enclosed within a carrying case. Exception: Before and during open deer season waterfowl hunters are permitted to hunt waterfowl only with shotguns (except the .410 bore and using shot not larger than No. 1 fine).

No person may carry or have in his possession five days prior to and during the open deer season any .22 rim-fire rifle or any .410-bore shotgun, unless such rifle or shotgun is unloaded and taken apart or unloaded and encased in a carrying case, or any shotgun loaded with ammunition other than a single ball or slug. No shotgun ammunition other than a single ball or slug may be carried during that time.

No person may hunt or pursue any deer or bear with any .22 rim-fire rifle or any .410-bore shotgun.

No person may hunt deer or bear with a bow having a pull of less than 40 pounds.

Dogs may not be used to hunt deer under any conditions or bear except under special permit. It is unlawful to use a light for the purpose of shining deer while hunting or while in possession of firearms or bow and arrow.

Non-residents are not required to have a guide for any type of hunting. There are licensed guides available and a list of about 1000 guides is available at a cost of one cent per name. Licenses are obtained from the Conservation Department headquarters at a fee of $1, and no examination is required.

**Seasons.** Game animals and birds for which there are open seasons are:

| | | |
|---|---|---|
| Badger | Raccoon | Ducks |
| Bear | Skunk | Geese |
| Cottontail rabbit | Snowshoe hare | Hungarian partridge |
| Deer | Woodchuck | Pheasant |
| Fox squirrel | Bobwhite quail | Rails |
| Gray squirrel | Brant | Woodcock |
| Jack rabbit | Coot | |

There is no closed season on fox.

## WYOMING

AREA: 97,914 square miles

**General Summary.** The game picture in Wyoming, one of the leading big-game areas, is very encouraging. Game populations in all animal and bird species have been brought back through wise management to a maximum of what can be carried under the state's present land-use policy, and no species of big game is in serious threat of depletion. There are approximately 35,000 elk, 70,000 deer, 50,000 antelope, 3500 moose, and 2500 bighorn mountain sheep. Several years ago bighorn sheep were on the decline, but at the present time they are holding their own even though their numbers have decreased somewhat over previous years. A comparatively large bison herd is protected. The hunters in Wyoming kill approximately 10,000 deer (mule and whitetails), 10,000 antelope, 6000 elk, 200 moose, 30 bighorn mountain sheep, and 100 bear each year. Antelope hunting is the most popular because it is least expensive and least strenuous. Deer and elk hunting are very popular and it is difficult to determine just which would take second place in the sportsman's interest.

Hunting of small game, rabbits, hares, rockchucks, squirrels, etc., is unlimited, for the animals are abundant and need no protection.

The ring-necked pheasant is the most hunted upland game bird. The native sage grouse, which was once so common throughout the West, is now threatened. This decrease was brought about during the drought period of a few years ago and by disease and hunting. The season has now been closed for nine years and some improvement is shown. Large numbers of these birds are being trapped and transplanted in areas where they had become depleted. There is very limited hunting of Hungarian partridge.

**State Conservation.** The Wyoming Game and Fish Commission is composed of seven members appointed by the governor for a term of four years. The duties of the Commission include the management of all game birds and animals in the state, the fixing of hunting seasons, and the provision of public hunting grounds. The Commission appoints a salaried state game and fish commissioner, and also appoints a salaried game warden for the state. With the advice of the game warden, the Commission appoints as many deputy wardens as necessary to enforce the laws of the Department. The Game and Fish Commission works in close co-operation with Federal agencies, including the Forest Service, Grazing Service, and the Predatory Animal Division of the Fish and Wildlife Service. Yearly conferences are held at which the representatives from the various agencies pool information in order to improve the effectiveness of wildlife management in Wyoming. A part of their joint efforts is the feeding of game animals during periods of emergency, and their protection and maintenance on refuges.

There is one Game Bird Farm located at Sheridan, Wyoming, that produces approximately 10,000 pheasants and about 1000 chukar partridges each year. This farm apparently is adequate for state needs since only a small part of the state is suitable pheasant habitat.

Wyoming has no farmer-sportsman co-operative program operating other than that which is established by the sportsmen's organizations themselves. There is, however, a co-operative arrangement with all the large ranches in the state where antelope graze. This permits the Wyoming Game and Fish Department to reimburse the ranch owner by refunding to him $3 of the $5 resident license fee paid for the hunting of antelope, but $5 of the $25 charged for a non-resident antelope license. This has worked out very satisfactorily, since a large part of the antelope in Wyoming at some time during the season are found grazing on privately owned land.

**Licenses.** License fees are as follows:

| | |
|---|---|
| Resident hunting and fishing | $5.00 |
| Non-resident hunting and fishing | 100.00 |
| Resident game birds | 2.00 |
| Non-resident game birds | 10.00 |
| Resident mountain sheep permit | 15.00 |
| Non-resident mountain sheep permit | 75.00 |
| Resident moose permit | 15.00 |
| Non-resident moose permit | 75.00 |
| Special resident bear permit (1 bear) | 5.00 |
| Special non-resident bear permit (2 bears) | 25.00 |
| Resident antelope permit (1 antelope) | 5.00 |
| Non-resident antelope permit (1 antelope) | 25.00 |
| Special non-resident deer permit (1 deer) | 20.00 |
| Guide license | 5.00 |

All licenses are handled by the Wyoming Game and Fish Commission at Cheyenne. Both resident and non-resident licenses are on sale in a number of localities in each county by selling agents designated as representatives of the Game and Fish Department. In some cases these licenses are for sale at sporting-goods stores, drugstores, and gasoline stations.

**Regulations.** Shotguns used in bird hunting must be properly plugged to allow not more than two shells in the magazine.

Game animals may not be hunted or killed with any rifle less than 23/100 inch in bore, or which takes a cartridge less than 2 inches in length.

A person wishing to become a guide must have a working knowledge of the game and fish laws of the state and apply to the Commission, or its authorized agent, for a license, upon payment of $5 fee. The license is valid for a year unless revoked by the Commission. All non-resident hunters for any big game, other than antelope, must be accompanied in the field by a licensed guide.

Bow and arrow may be used to take deer, elk, antelope, and bear, provided the hunter has a special archery permit in addition to a hunting and fishing license or a special deer, bear, or antelope license. He must be accompanied in the field by a licensed guide. The hunter must be equipped with a bow of not less than 60 pounds pull and an arrow the cutting head of which is not less than one inch in width.

No person may hunt any of the game animals of Wyoming without wearing a red cap or having a red cloth tied over his hat or cap.

No dogs may be used in the hunting of big-game animals.

**Seasons.** Game animals and birds for which there are open seasons are:

| | |
|---|---|
| Antelope | Mountain sheep |
| Bear | Ducks |
| Deer | Geese |
| Elk | Ringneck pheasant |
| Moose | |

# Canada

The relation of the Department of Mines and Resources to the wild life of Canada is comparable to that of the Fish and Wildlife Service to the wildlife of the United States. The Canadian department (which also includes the National Parks Bureau, Dominion Forest Service, National Museum, Indian Affairs Branch, and Bureau of Northwest Territories and Yukon Affairs) is one of the major links between the Dominion Government and the game and fish commissions of each of the nine provinces, the Northwest Territory, and the Yukon. It works in close co-operation with these commissions, being concerned with the enforcement of all laws relative to the preservation of the Dominion's wildlife in unprotected areas as well as in national parks and other Federal reserves. It contributes the results of research gathered by its scientists and furnishes financial aid. The Advisory Board on Wildlife Protection, composed of government officials whose duties as scientists or administrators are concerned with wildlife, is an active agent in handling the conservation problems of Canada. Of particular concern to Canada is the study of the rise and fall of certain species, especially the predatory fox, coyote, and wolf which have caused serious destruction to the Dominion's wildlife in recent years. Research is necessary to understand these cyclic phenomena in order to anticipate and control them.

An overabundance of certain big-game animals (specifically elk, bison, and white-tailed deer) is checked by killing off the excess on a range where the food supply will no longer support the population. Conversely, those birds and animals, such as the trumpeter swan, whooping crane, eider ducks, and prong-horned antelope, which are scarce or show a serious decrease are protected in sanctuaries or refuges, or by closed seasons.

Hunting is closely supervised in the cold and comparatively barren Northwest Territory, where wildlife is incapable of maintaining the rate of reproduction necessary to survive unrestricted hunting. In this area five preserves, aggregating over 9,000,000 square miles, are for the exclusive use of the aboriginal Indians and Eskimos; the qualifications for other hunters are strict. In the more fertile Yukon Territory, however, non-residents are allowed to hunt.

Canada is well aware of its responsibility of maintaining the great waterfowl nesting grounds on its prairies. Since 1935, when the Prairie Farm Rehabilitation Administration—a division of the Canadian Department of Agriculture—was established, $20,000,000 has been spent on 25,000 water projects on the Canadian prairies. Severe drought, however, has destroyed some of the breeding areas, principally in Saskatchewan and Alberta.

**Entering Canada.** As a general rule, entering Canada is a simple process with no difficulty or delay at the border. Permanent residents of the United States entering Canada as tourists do not require passports. It is suggested, however, that the possession of identification papers will facilitate entry into Canada in case the examining officer should require documentary evidence to satisfy himself as to the bona fides of the tourist. Citizens of the United States by naturalization should be prepared to present their certificates of naturalization, and residents of the United States who are not citizens thereof should be prepared to present proof of their legal entry into that country.

Any information regarding entry of persons into Canada may be obtained from the Immigration Branch, Department of Mines and Resources, Ottawa, Canada.

**Leaving Canada.** On their departure from Canada, which may be made either by the port of entry or any other port, visitors from the United States may have to prove to the United States immigration officers that they are legal residents of that country. To facilitate re-entry identifying documents should be carried, such as birth or baptismal certificates, tax bills, personal letters, car license, or driver's license. It is suggested that naturalized citizens carry with them their naturalization certificates.

**Regulations Governing the Importing of Firearms.** Pistols and revolvers are not permitted to be carried by non-resident aliens. (For complete details on the granting of pistol permits in Canada see p. 724.) Automatic firearms are not allowed, but autoloading guns and rifles will be admitted into Canada provided they are plugged so as to be incapable of holding more than three shells, one in barrel and two in magazine. A person who is not a British subject must have a weapon permit (Form 76B) to have a shotgun or rifle in his possession in Canada.

**Regulations Governing the Importing of Hunting Dogs.** Hunting dogs may be entered as part of a tourist's outfit, without deposit. All dogs must be accompanied by a certificate either signed by the veterinary inspector of the United States Bureau of Animal Industry certifying that the dog has been inspected and found free of any contagious disease, or by a certificate signed by a licensed veterinarian of Canada or the United States certifying that the dog has been vaccinated against rabies during the preceding six months.

**Regulations Governing the Importing of Automobiles.** Automobiles may be brought into Canada under the Travelers' Vehicle Permit by non-residents for their personal transportation for a period up to six months without the payment of duty or deposit.

**Exporting of Game Kill.** Game killed by non-resident licensees may be shipped out of Canada. Americans planning to hunt migratory birds in Canada should communicate in advance with the National Parks Bureau, Ottawa, Ontario, concerning Canadian regulations. No person may lawfully export from Canada into the United States during one calendar week migratory game birds of the species for which open seasons are prescribed in that country in excess of the numbers permitted to be possessed under regulations enforced by the U. S. Fish and Wildlife Service, from which current information on the subject should be obtained.

The exportation of game from Canada is a simple process requiring the presentation of a Declaration Form (copy of which can be secured from any Express agent) to the Canadian Collector of Customs. The approved form is then sent to the Express Company which ships the game from the Dominion. For information regarding the importation and possession of all game, hunters should write in advance to the State Game Department of the state into which the game is to be imported.

## ALBERTA — AREA: 255,285 square miles

**General Summary.** The big-game situation in Alberta is good in spite of the inroads of an enlarged population of wolves and a shortage of hunters and ammunition to keep down these predators. The population of elk has increased in certain areas and has spread out, allowing an increase in the area over which they may be taken by the hunter, and it may be necessary in the near future to increase the bag limit so that this animal will not increase to the proportion where it becomes a menace to settlers and ranchers. This is particularly true in the southwest corner of the province, where they have encroached upon farms and ranches and destroyed or eaten large quantities of feed. Reports on sheep, goat, deer, and caribou are all fairly good. There appears to be a decrease in the number of deer in certain areas, possibly because of the increase and spread of the elk population. This may also, in part, be the cause of a decrease in the moose population in certain areas. The decrease, however, in each of these species is not particularly alarming, and it is hoped that both will recover as the wolf menace decreases, which is expected to be soon. The antelope population in southeastern Alberta continues to increase, and they are in a very healthy condition. It has been found that the British Government Experimental Station north of Medicine Hat, which was causing some concern, has turned out to be a blessing in disguise as these animals are using the area more as a game preserve than as a place to shun on account of the possibility of running foul of experiments carried on in the area.

The migratory bird situation continues to improve, and statistics show that the number of ducks, geese, and other waterfowl are still on the increase throughout this province during the summer months. The majority of this increase is due to natural causes, although some assistance has been given in the reclaiming of areas to water which had dried up during the drought years.

The supply of upland birds is somewhat less gratifying. The ruffed grouse stocks have been depleted to the extent that it has been found necessary to put a closed season on this bird. The stocks of prairie chicken and Hungarian partridge in some areas of the province have been depleted, and it has been necessary to confine the hunting of these two birds to limited areas, particularly in the southern part of the province. The pheasant has managed to increase in most areas and the season is being extended each year, although the bag limit remains the same.

**State Conservation.** The lieutenant governor in council appoints the game commissioner, the fish and game commissioner, game officers, and other officers necessary to enforce the duties of the Game Commission. All members of the Royal Canadian Mounted Police, all forest officers, all fire rangers, and all postmasters are *ex officio* game guardians and have the same powers and duties as are conferred or imposed upon a game guardian appointed by the minister.

The lieutenant governor in council has the power to declare any area a game preserve or bird sanctuary and may prescribe the regulations controlling it and may alter or cancel the area as such. He also makes regulations concerning hunting licenses, their issuance and limitations, as well as the setting of open seasons and type game to be taken, and the use of firearms in designated areas.

**Licenses.** License fees are as follows:

| | |
|---|---|
| Resident big game | $5.00 |
| Special antelope | 5.00 |
| Resident game bird | 2.50 |
| Guide's license | 2.50 |
| Taxidermist's license | 10.00 |
| Tanner's license | 10.00 |
| Non-resident general | 50.00 |
| Non-resident big game | 25.00 |
| Non-resident special antelope | 15.00 |
| Non-resident game bird | 25.00 |

TROPHY FEES:

| | |
|---|---|
| Mountain sheep | $25.00 |
| Mountain goat | 25.00 |
| Moose | 25.00 |
| Caribou | 25.00 |
| Elk | 25.00 |
| Deer | 15.00 |
| Grizzly bear | 25.00 |
| Black, cinnamon, or brown bear | Free |
| Antelope | Free |

**Regulations.** No automatic shotguns are allowed for hunting game in this province. A rifle firing a .22 rim-fire cartridge is not allowed in hunting big-game animals. No rifles or any shotgun loaded with a single bullet or any other weapon using ball cartridges may be used to hunt any migratory birds.

All non-residents must be accompanied by a licensed guide while hunting big game.

No person is permitted to hunt big game unless he is clothed in a coat and cap of scarlet material.

In order to train dogs as bird dogs, including pointers, setters, and retrievers, a person must obtain a license. No person may allow a bird dog to run at large at any time between the first of May and the first of August in any year. Dogs may not be used in hunting big game and any dog at large in a district where big game is usually found may be killed.

For general information on entering and leaving Canada, rules on firearms, admission of hunting dogs and automobiles, and exportation of game, see "Canada," p. 1093.

**Seasons.** Game animals and birds for which there are open seasons are:

| | |
|---|---|
| Antelope | Mountain sheep |
| Black bear | Coots |
| Brown bear | Ducks |
| Caribou | Geese |
| Deer | Hungarian partridge |
| Elk | Rails |
| Grizzly bear | Ring-necked pheasant |
| Moose | Wilson's snipe |
| Mountain goat | |

## BRITISH COLUMBIA — AREA: 359,279 square miles

**General Summary.** For the purpose of defining the open seasons on big game and game birds, British Columbia is divided into two districts, western and eastern. The western district is roughly that region west of the Cascade Mountains, and the eastern district is the remainder of the province. In the eastern district the big-game animals hunted are deer, moose, caribou, elk, mountain sheep, mountain goat, and bear, but in the west only deer, moose, mountain goat, and bear are taken. Except that the prairie chicken is hunted only in the west, the upland game birds shot in both regions are the same, being California quail, pheasant grouse, European partridge (Hungarian partridge), and ptarmigan. Wilson's snipe, ducks, and geese are killed in either region.

**State Conservation.** Natural conditions in the greater part of British Columbia are most favorable for the preservation of its wildlife resources. Since approximately 85 per cent of the population of the province is concentrated in the southern section, the bulk of the land has few settlements. Game birds and animals thrive in those areas which are free from the pressure of civilization and where the hereditary range and habitat are unchanged. In the more northern sections predation, especially of wolves, has taken some toll of game.

Although there is no real need for an organized farmer-sportsman co-operative plan, the Game Department of British Columbia urges that the hunter respect the landowner's property and request permission to shoot over his property.

**Licenses.** License fees are as follows:

| | |
|---|---|
| Resident general | $6.00 |
| Non-resident general | 50.00 |
| Non-resident (except pheasants) | 25.00 |
| Non-resident Canadian | 15.00 |
| Non-resident game bird Canadian | 3.00 |

In addition to the license fees, trophy fees are payable on all big-game animals killed (whether for export or otherwise).

| | |
|---|---|
| On each caribou, grizzly bear, mountain sheep, or wapiti (elk) | $25.00 |
| Moose | 40.00 |
| On each mountain goat, mule or white-tailed deer | 15.00 |
| On each black or brown bear, coast or Columbian deer | 5.00 |

A non-resident may secure his license by forwarding the necessary fee to the Game Commission, 650 Burrard St., Vancouver, B. C.; at the same time the applicant should advise as to the manufacturer's name, serial number, and caliber of each firearm that he proposes to use or to bring into the province. This information is necessary in order that the applicant may be issued not only his firearms license, but his weapon permit as well.

**Regulations.** It is unlawful to use any swivel, set-gun, machine gun, or battery in the province, or any gun larger than a 10 gauge, or a pump or automatic shotgun without a permanent plug—magazine to hold one shell.

License holders hunting in a municipality are advised to acquaint themselves with any by-laws covering the discharge of firearms that may be in effect therein.

No dogs are allowed to hunt or run any caribou, moose, wapiti, or deer at any time or to run at large hunting game birds between April 1 and July 31.

Non-residents of the province hunting big game (including deer) must be accompanied by a British Columbia licensed guide, or a resident under special permit. A guide is not allowed to kill the game for the hunter.

Upon payment of the trophy fees and before leaving the province, non-residents are required to obtain a permit to export their game, whether as a trophy or as meat. Export permits may be obtained from any government agent, provincial constable, game warden, or from the Game Commission at Vancouver. In cases where licenses are issued at the border, trophy fees and export permits may be obtained at the same place. Owing to a variation in trophy fees collectible on game killed in certain parts of the province, it is advisable that the hunter be in a position to supply the name and address of the guide employed, and to be able to prove the place where the game was obtained, so that the officer collecting the trophy fee may be able to decide the fee payable.

For information on entering and leaving Canada, rules on the importation of firearms, admission of hunting dogs and automobiles, and the exportation of game, see "Canada," p. 1093.

**Seasons.** Game animals and birds for which there are open seasons are:

- Bear
- Caribou
- Deer
- Elk
- Moose
- Mountain goat
- Mountain sheep
- Band-tailed pigeon
- Brant
- California quail
- Coot
- Ducks
- European partridge (Hungarian partridge)
- Geese
- Grouse (blue, Franklin's, ruffed)
- Pheasant
- Prairie chicken
- Ptarmigan
- Wilson's snipe

There is no closed season on:

- Bears (black or brown)
- Wolverine

## MANITOBA — AREA: 246,512 square miles

**General Summary.** White-tailed deer are plentiful throughout the southern part of the province. Mule deer, although not numerous, show a slight increase, particularly in the Duck Mountain area. The hunting of both sexes of deer has been permitted. Licensed hunters take about 7000 each year. Moose are not plentiful, and in order to increase their numbers a closed season was temporarily declared, but restricted hunting under a short open season has recently been allowed. About 150 animals are killed annually. Elk show a noticeable increase in the Duck and Porcupine Mountains. Their distribution in the province generally is, however, very limited, and after some increase an open season was allowed for residents. There is a closed season on woodland caribou, but Barren Ground caribou are hunted. Recently the Barren Ground caribou have migrated farther south than usual in the winter and extended their winter range eastward to such points as God's Lake, Oxford House, and Cross Lake, where they had not been seen for many years. While this widening of the caribou range has been welcomed by the residents of the northern communities as providing a ready source of fresh meat, their appearance in the vicinity of these communities has meant a marked increase in the toll taken of the herd during its winter dispersal in the northern wooded district of Manitoba. The farther south these animals range, the greater will be the toll. The caribou is so vitally important in the northern latitudes of the province that its too frequent occurrence in the middle latitudes should be the cause of some concern.

At present there is a closed season on all upland birds except ptarmigan. Sharp-tailed and pinnated grouse have recently shown a slight increase in their very low numbers. Severe winter conditions, however, have caused some mortality and, when followed by a poor nesting season, the result is a small yearly hatch. Hungarian partridge and ruffed grouse remain very scarce. In 1945, 800 adult ring-necked pheasants, imported from the United States, were released in suitable areas of the province in a continuation of the effort to establish these splendid game birds over a wider area of Manitoba. This work has received enthusiastic support from residents in the various districts involved. The birds have increased sufficiently to allow very restricted hunting and for several years the annual bag averaged 4000 birds.

The establishment of winter feed plots for upland game birds was started in the spring of 1946. The purpose of these plots is to supplement available winter feed by providing additional feed and shelter in close proximity. Plots are between one and two acres in extent and planted with a variety of fruit or berry-producing shrubs interspersed, during the first few years, with temporary plantings of corn and sunflowers to provide feed until the permanent shrubbery becomes productive.

The waterfowl situation is about the same in Manitoba as in most other parts of the continent. There has been better hunting of geese than ducks, but only about 90,000 ducks and geese have been taken in each of the last few years as compared with approximately 130,000 in 1933.

**Licenses.**

| | |
|---|---|
| Resident deer (Virginia or mule) | $2.50 |
| Resident moose or caribou | 5.00 |
| Special resident elk (restricted to residents of Manitoba only) | 5.00 |
| Resident game birds | 2.25 |
| Non-resident deer (Virginia or mule) | 25.00 |
| Non-resident caribou or moose | 40.00 |

(One bear may be taken on all big-game licenses)

| | |
|---|---|
| Non-resident game bird (British subject) | 10.00 |
| Non-resident game bird (other than British subject | 25.00 |

Resident game licenses may be secured from the Game and Fisheries Branch, Winnipeg and The Pas, and at various hardware and sporting-stores throughout the province. Non-resident game licenses may be obtained in advance from the

Game and Fisheries Branch, Winnipeg, by forwarding bank draft or money order for amount of license. They may also be obtained from the Game and Fisheries Office at The Pas or at Manitoba ports of entry.

**Regulations.** No person may hunt big game with a .22-caliber rifle requiring a rim-fire cartridge. A big-game hunter must be clothed in a complete outer suit of some white or bright red material. No dogs may be used in hunting big-game animals.

In taking migratory game birds no person may use an autoloading shotgun or rifle, or a shotgun loaded with a single bullet, or any gun larger than 10 gauge, or a pump or repeating shotgun with a magazine that has not been plugged or altered so that it cannot carry more than two shells in the magazine, or any weapon other than a gun or a bow and arrow.

A non-resident weapon permit is issued by Royal Canadian Mounted Police, Winnipeg. Application forms are available from Mounted Police or from Game and Fisheries Branch, Winnipeg. A permit should be obtained in advance if possible.

An export permit is required for big-game. It is issued with the license and there is no fee. Export permit tags are issued with the hunting license and there is no fee. According to United States regulations it is understood that all migratory game birds must be exported from Manitoba by the end of the open season in Manitoba, but five days transit in the United States is allowed. Each shipment is limited to possession limit in effect in the state to which it is being forwarded. More than one shipment may be sent, but only one shipment in any calendar week. Manitoba regulations permit the export of possession limits only.

For general information on entering and leaving Canada, rules on firearms, admission of hunting dogs and automobiles, and exportation of game, see "Canada," p. 1093.

**Seasons.** Game animals and birds for which there are open seasons are:

| | |
|---|---|
| Barren Ground caribou | Ducks |
| Deer | Geese |
| Elk | Ptarmigan |
| Moose | Rail |
| Coot | |

## NEW BRUNSWICK — AREA: 27,985 square miles

**General Summary.** More waterfowl are killed each year than any other type of game. About 29,000 ducks are bagged annually, and approximately 240 geese. Indications are that brant have not recovered from the severe depletion during the past ten years. Of the big-game animals about 15,500 red deer are taken annually. The black bear is also classed as a big-game animal and hunted on a complimentary license. Upland game birds include ruffed grouse and woodcock, and, despite an increase in hunting pressure, both species are increasing, as well as the jacksnipe. New Brunswick has no small-game animals.

Recently there has been no marked fluctuation in the game population of this province. Moose have been a protected animal since 1936, and the population of this animal has not shown any decided increase during the past few years. The two main factors to be considered in the establishment of moose in any given area are feed and cover. The reproduction of fir or balsam since the devastation of the spruce budworm in the period of 1915 to 1920 should provide sufficient winter feed for all requirements. To offset this, however, extensive lumbering and pulpwood operations have seriously affected the cover in the big woods with the result that the moose apparently do not become definitely established in those areas where the cover has been heavily lumbered over. There are approximately 7700 moose in this province at the present date. With the large increase in beaver, however, and the establishment of new colonies by them which promote aquatic plant food for the moose, there should be an increase in the moose population.

**State Conservation.** The Game Division of New Brunswick is a unit of the Department of Lands and Mines. Certain other units of this Department are interrelated in their activities with those of the Game Division or indirectly affect the wildlife resources of the province.

Unlike the more northerly sections of Canada, New Brunswick does not suffer from such serious predator losses. The highly destructive timber wolf, for example, is a casual in this province. The province, however, does pay an annual bounty of approximately $5000 on 100 bobcats, $14,000 on 1400 bears, and $18,000 on 37,000 porcupines. Concomitant with the policy of the Dominion government, however, they do not recognize bounty payments as a cure-all for the predator problem.

Ducks Unlimited of Canada is making plans for improving conditions for ducks frequenting the Atlantic flyway.

**Licenses.** License fees are as follows:

| | |
|---|---|
| Resident | $3.25 |
| Resident game birds | 1.25 |
| Non-resident deer and ruffed grouse | 21.00 |
| Non-resident deer | 15.50 |
| Non-resident game birds (including ruffed grouse) | 15.50 |
| Complimentary license to hunt four bears during months of April, May, and June | Free |

Licenses may be obtained from local vendors in all principal cities, towns, and villages.

**Regulations.** Non-resident alien hunters must apply to a vendor of hunting licenses for permit on Form 76-B authorizing the carrying of firearms. Such permits are also issued by high sheriffs and chiefs of police within the province.

Dogs may not be used in hunting deer. Except for hunting game birds in season, no hunting is allowed at any time with dogs except by special permit.

Any competent British subject, resident of New Brunswick, may become a registered guide on application to the Department of Lands and Mines. The registration fee is $2, with an annual license fee of $1. All licensed guides are sworn game, fire, and fishery wardens.

A non-resident hunter must employ a licensed guide when he enters the woods, forest, or wild land to hunt. A guide may not accompany more than one hunter at the same time, except when hunting game birds. At such a time a guide may accompany two hunters. A guide may not carry firearms when guiding.

A list of licensed and registered camp-owning guides and outfitters is available upon request to: New Brunswick Government Bureau of Information and Tourist Travel, 454 King St., Fredericton, N. B.

For general information on entering and leaving Canada, regulations on importation of firearms, automobiles and hunting dogs, see "Canada," p. 1093.

**Seasons.** Game animals and birds for which there are open seasons are:

| | |
|---|---|
| Bear | Jacksnipe |
| Deer | Ruffed grouse (birch partridge) |
| Ducks (including eider ducks) | Spruce partridge |
| Geese | Woodcock |

## NORTHWEST TERRITORIES — AREA: 1,309,682 square miles

**General Summary.** Some years ago the serious depletion of the wildlife of the Northwest Territories forced the decision to restrict the issue of hunting and trapping licenses to those British subjects who, prior to May 3, 1938, had taken up permanent residence in the Northwest Territories and who are dependent upon hunting and trapping for a living. The supply of wildlife has not increased everywhere as hoped because of the fires which destroyed the forest cover. In the past two years the administration has made substantial progress in organizing forest protection and the problems of wildlife resources management are now under intensive investigation. Extensive hunting and trapping areas have been reserved in the Northwest Territories for the exclusive use and benefit of the Indians and Eskimos to encourage them to observe their usual conservation practices and to carry out the promises made to them.

A license to shoot game birds during the open season may be issued to any person who is ineligible for the regular hunting and trapping license.

**Licenses.** License fees are as follows:

| | |
|---|---|
| Hunting and trapping license | $2.00 |
| Resident British subjects game bird | 2.00 |
| Non-resident British subjects game bird | 5.00 |
| Other non-residents | 10.00 |

**Seasons.** Game animals and birds for which there are open seasons are:

| | |
|---|---|
| Bear (Barren Ground, grizzly and polar) | Mountain sheep |
| Caribou | Ducks |
| Deer | Geese |
| Moose | Grouse |
| Mountain goat | Prairie chicken |
| | Ptarmigan |

## NOVA SCOTIA — AREA: 21,068 square miles

**General Summary.** The peninsula of Nova Scotia is a comparatively new sporting area. Large tracts of forest land harbor moose, deer, black bear, and raccoon; uplands and intervales shelter grouse and rabbits; in the lowlands, snipe and woodcock abound; ducks and geese haunt the marshes.

Moose and caribou are given complete protection in this province, but about 20,000 deer (white-tailed or Virginia deer) are taken by hunters each year. Deer are plentiful in each of Nova Scotia's 18 counties. From a small importation made several years ago, they have spread to every woodland and are a common sight in meadows or along forest edges. The black bear is the other big-game animal of Nova Scotia and has a regular big-game hunting period, but may be trapped at any time. Approximately 350 are killed annually.

The varying hare (commonly referred to as a "rabbit") is a native to almost every section of Nova Scotia, although indiscriminate snaring of them as food at fox ranches has seriously reduced their numbers in some areas. In scattered districts, however, the rabbit is still plentiful, and in some areas is showing an increase.

Nova Scotia is a noted breeding ground of American woodcock, the popular upland game bird, and is also a favored stopping place on the bird's line of flight during the southward migration. Many of the rivers of the province are broadly margined by intervale meadows studded with alder and willow thickets, the favorite haunts of this retiring bird. Nova Scotia is one of the chief concentration points in North America, and a number of counties offer excellent woodcock hunting. It is generally found, however, that the best hunting opportunities are provided during the latter part of the season in the western and southwestern sections where the birds congregate before taking off on their long trek southward. Another migratory bird hunted in Nova Scotia is Wilson's snipe. These birds start moving to the south as the severe frosts set in, but are later overtaken by the bigger flights from the north. The diked areas of the Bay of Fundy and the marshlands of the broad Tantramar in Cumberland County, afford noted snipe grounds, as do also the meadows of the Annapolis, Stewiacke, and Musquobodoit Rivers, and the muddy beaches around Lawrencetown, Cole Harbour, and Martinique. Ruffed grouse are in fair numbers in Nova Scotia, and are found in almost every county of the province. The Hungarian partridge, introduced and thriving in this area, are hunted in fair numbers, but pheasants are on the decrease and there is a closed season at the present time.

Waterfowl shooting is fair, with the blue-wing or black duck considered as the best game duck in Nova Scotia and the most numerous. Both native and migrant black ducks are found in this area. Blue-winged and green-winged teal also afford sporty shooting.

Wildcats (bobcats or bay lynx) are found in numbers in Nova Scotia, and are very destructive to game of all kinds. The damage wrought by these predators on game birds and animals is hard to estimate. There is a bounty payable on the snout of any wildcat killed within the province.

**Licenses.** License fees are as follows:

| | |
|---|---|
| Resident | $ 3.00 |
| Non-resident (big game and birds—except woodcock and snipe) | 50.00 |
| Non-resident deer | 25.00 |
| Non-resident small game and birds (except woodcock and snipe) | 15.00 |
| Woodcock and snipe | 25.00 |

Hunting licenses may be had at the Department of Lands and Forests, Halifax, and from the rangers and other agents.

**Regulations.** In those areas where there is a closed season on big game it is permissible to hunt small game with a shotgun carrying a load no larger than BB or a rifle of a caliber not greater than .22. During the open season on big game it is illegal to have a .22-caliber rifle or shotgun shells loaded with shot larger than BB.

Any person may lawfully kill any dog found hunting or pursuing any moose, caribou, or deer.

Guides are required to register and take out licenses, paying a fee of $2. Any hotel proprietor will put the visitor in touch with a licensed guide. Rates for guides range from $3.50 to $5 per day. For information about guides available in any particular section of Nova Scotia, write to the chief forest ranger of the county in question.

A tag issued with the license and bearing the name and address of the licensee must be attached to the head or other portion of a deer exported by a non-resident licensee.

For general information on entering and leaving Canada, rules on the importation of firearms, admission of hunting dogs and automobiles, and exportation of game, see "Canada," p. 1093.

**Seasons.** Game animals and birds for which there are open seasons are:

| | |
|---|---|
| Deer | Geese |
| Hares | Hungarian partridge |
| Rabbits | Ruffed grouse |
| Raccoons | Wilson's snipe (jacksnipe) |
| Ducks | Woodcock |

There is no closed season on:

| | |
|---|---|
| Bear | Wolves |
| Wildcat | |

## ONTARIO — AREA: 412,582 square miles

**General Summary.** White-tailed deer are the most hunted of the big-game animals in this province, and they are holding their own satisfactorily. There is an annual open season on moose, but they are decreasing to a new low and may require special protection. The black bear is unprotected throughout the year.

Small-game animals include European and varying hare, cottontail rabbit, and squirrels. Rabbits and hares are very plentiful and widely distributed. No protection of them is necessary despite the fact there are more hunters in the field in recent years.

Upland game birds are increasing, with ruffed grouse the most numerous, followed by sharp-tailed and spruce grouse, woodcock, and willow ptarmigan. The prospect for an open season on partridge is very favorable. Wilson's snipe is also a legal game bird.

The recent local hunts of waterfowl have been fair in this province, but the flight has been very unsatisfactory. Black ducks, mallards, and teal are the most abundant.

**State Conservation.** Ontario's wildlife conservation policies have been actively carried out by a group of sportsmen's clubs, over 60 of which have joined to establish the Ontario Federation of Anglers and Hunters which meets yearly. The Federation has been successfully engaged in reforestation, stream improvement, and the raising and distributing of game birds. Through educational publicity the citizens of Ontario are being made increasingly conservation conscious.

Apparently influenced by the efforts of the Federation, the government of Ontario has merged the Department of Game and Fisheries with the Department of Lands and Forests to make for a closer interrelation of activities since the protection of the wildlife resources of the province is a concern of both Departments.

Northern Ontario is very favorable hunting territory since the section is composed of several hundred thousand square miles of virgin forest, lakes, rivers and streams.

**Licenses.** License fees are as follows:

| | |
|---|---|
| Resident gun | $ 1.00 |
| Resident deer | 4.00 |
| Resident moose | 6.00 |
| Non-resident bear, deer, moose, rabbits, birds | 75.00 |
| Non-resident bear, rabbits, birds | 15.50 |
| Non-resident bear, deer, rabbits, birds | 25.75 |
| Non-resident bear permit | 5.25 |

**Regulations.** No automatic or autoloading shotgun may be used unless plugged so as to be incapable of holding more than three shells. It is unlawful to carry other than a .22-caliber low-powered rifle during the open season for deer or moose in areas which these animals inhabit unless in possession of a license to hunt deer or moose.

No dog may be used to hunt deer, moose, or caribou. Greyhounds are not allowed to pursue game.

All hunting guides must have a license.

For general information on entering and leaving Canada, rules on firearms, admission of hunting dogs, automobiles, and exportation of game, see "Canada," p. 1093.

**Seasons.** Game animals and birds for which there are open seasons are:

| | |
|---|---|
| Deer | Geese |
| Moose | Hungarian partridge |
| Raccoon | Ptarmigan |
| Squirrel | Wilson's snipe |
| Ducks (including eider ducks) | Woodcock |

## PRINCE EDWARD ISLAND

AREA: 2184 square miles

**General Summary.** Prince Edward Island, Canada's "vest pocket" province, has no large game such as deer and moose. Wildcat or bobcat are unknown, but an occasional bear is reported every year or so from the densely wooded wilds of eastern Kings County.

Snowshoe rabbit (varying hare) afford good sport at all times, and as they are now nearing the peak of their cycle, hunting improves with each successive year. Hunters may be assured of splendid sport with this species of game. Action has been taken among sportsmen's organizations to curtail the practice of snaring rabbits and thus guarantee still better shooting. The annual hunters' kill of squirrels is high. Red squirrels are very common, but black and gray squirrels are unknown in this region. Flying squirrels are more plentiful than generally thought.

Raccoon are present in fair numbers, being plentiful in a few favored districts. This animal was introduced in 1912 when the fur-farming craze was at its peak and turned loose when the cost of feeding proved prohibitive. The raccoon is blamed for destruction of black duck nests as well as those of upland game birds. In short, the status of the raccoon is considered among conservationists as a liability rather than an asset, and as a predator rather than a game animal.

Before the eelgrass failure in 1933 goose shooting in this province ranked second to none. Up until this calamity thousands of geese thronged the tidal flats, bays, and estuaries. When the flight was at its peak, the clamor raised by the massed flights kept farmers living along the shoreline awake at nights. Today, the situation is changed. There is still a heavy flight of Canada geese that stops over in the province every spring on is way to the northern breeding grounds, but for every thousand geese that visit in the spring only a bare one hundred stop over in the fall flight. One factor may account for this. Once the eelgrass died, the geese had either to feed on marsh grass and sedge roots on the inshore marshes or to resort to the stubble fields. In a thickly settled province where the farms average approximately 100 acres, the feeding geese were vulnerable to attack from almost any quarter, if not while actually feeding, then while passing to or from the feeding grounds. The casualties were too heavy, and the wily geese moved on southward. The eelgrass has been making a slow but apparently steady recovery for several years, but not until the fall of 1946 were the flocks of geese known to feed in the eelgrass beds. Until the eelgrass returns in all its luxuriant growth and the geese resume their old feeding habits, goose shooting in this province is practically a waste of time and energy.

The same situation exists with the brant as pertains to the Canada geese. There is a sizable flight of brant in May and early June but only a few score birds visit in the fall. Legal brant shooting is nonexistent. Whereas the spring flight of Canada geese appears to be holding up fairly well but is definitely not increasing, the flight of brant is on the ebb.

The duck situation is giving provincial sportsmen considerable concern, and drastic curtailment of the shooting season is advocated. The black duck is the most eagerly sought game bird in the duck family. It is highly valued for the table and rates high as a sporting bird. Blue-winged and green-winged teal are fairly plentiful, with the blue-wing showing a slight preponderance in numbers. In addition, American goldeneyes (whistlers), greater and lesser scaup (bluebill), and ringneck ducks are fairly common in certain inland lakes and large mill dams, and furnish good sport in season. Pintails fluctuate in numbers, but are found quite frequently in gunners' game bags. Wood ducks (protected) are observed occasionally, and only a few mallards are bagged each season. There are also records of ruddy duck, bufflehead, gadwall, widgeon, and spoonbill, all of which are rare or decreasing.

The black duck furnishes 80 per cent of the duck shooting and the annual bag reached a high peak in 1944. It showed a noticeable decline in local breeding stock in 1945, and a sharp decline in 1946, but there was no appreciable diminution in its late fall flight. Splendid black duck shooting may be had all through the month of November, at which time the gunners should be properly equipped with a sunken "tub" and a large "stool" of decoys, for the ducks frequent the tidal flats and rivers as well as the bays and estuaries. Inland shooting of black ducks lasts for about two days after the opening date. The birds take such punishment on the inland marshes, creeks, and ponds that they move offshore and remain there for the duration of the season.

The ruffed grouse, native to the province, is fairly plentiful and increasing. The introduced Hungarian partridge has taken much of the hunting pressure from the grouse. The Hungarian partridge was introduced by a group of Charlottetown sportsmen in 1927. This gamey bird is considered the province's "ace in the hole" both as to numbers and sporting qualities. The initial import of ten pairs was a decided success, and aided by additional stock, the birds multiplied and spread rapidly. In 1933 there were thousands of Huns in Queens County with a considerable number overflowing into the adjoining counties of Kings and Prince. In the severe winter of 1933-1934, however, approximately 80 per cent of the birds died. Fortunately the recovery was quick, and by the fall of 1938 an open season was declared. Hunting has been allowed every year since that time, thanks to the cooperation of farmers and sportsmen who maintained the bird population by providing gravel and coarse sand during the calamitous winter of 1941-1942 when deep snow covered their grit, which is necessary as digestive grinding matter. At the present date Hungarian partridge are very plentiful and are reaching a new peak in numbers. It has been definitely established that the toll taken by gunners in season has little effect on the Hun crop. Winter is what actually controls the population of Huns, and heavy migrations of snowy owls throw an added strain on the partridges during the winter months.

The ring-necked pheasant was first introduced by sportsmen in 1920, but this planting failed. Succeeding introductions gradually began to take hold, and the birds were plentiful enough in 1945 and 1946 to have an open season declared on them. It is doubtful if this species will ever compete in numbers with the ruffed grouse or the Hungarian partridge, and they are not considered in the same class as the Huns as a sporting proposition.

From a small planting of five pairs of prairie chicken introduced in 1943 from western Canada, the birds are struggling to secure a foothold. Additional plantings are planned.

Woodcock are plentiful during the breeding season in this province, which ornithologists consider to be the northern limit of the bird's breeding range. Only in recent years has accent been placed on this province's contribution of woodcock to the general conservation picture. Following the heavy loss to woodcock wintering on their southern range, principally in the state of Mississippi, presumably because of unseasonable winter conditions, biologists from the United States visited the province in the month of May and conducted "singing ground" checks on special areas. These areas have been checked regularly for several years and the results have been most gratifying to the experts interested in woodcock, showing a comparatively constant population. Despite the prevalence of this valuable game bird in the province, only an occasional gunner bothers to hunt them. It is doubtful if the annual kill by sportsmen exceeds 50. This is due to a number of factors—first, the birds start migrating early in October before the leaves are off the trees; and secondly, there are no good woodcock dogs in the province. Woodcock are seldom found in the alders during the day in this province except in late October. During the summer and early fall they spend the day in second-growth hardwoods and mixed growth well inland. In the late evening they fly out to the alders and boggy swales to feed. Although local sportsmen are not greatly interested in the woodcock from a hunting standpoint they are keenly concerned in the preservation of this sporting and mysterious game bird. The main enemy of the woodcock in this province is the common house cat, and a constant war is maintained on this predatory feline. The general opinion is that the house cat and the telephone wires kill uncounted hundreds of woodcock in this province every year.

The current scarcity of the Wilson's snipe in the United States and some sections of Canada has not been noticed as yet in this province. They are found in good numbers over the length of the country. Early in the season they patronize the salt marshes and boggy intervales, but later on they favor the alder swales fed by meandering brooks. If the fall is unseasonably wet, they are to be found almost anywhere, such as turnip patches, boggy sections of stubble fields, etc. It is common sport in October to flush from 40 to 50 in an afternoon with the help of a good dog.

The Hudsonian curlew is protected throughout the year. It is very plentiful in August and has increased slowly but steadily for the past 20 years. The black-bellied plover and greater and lesser yellowlegs are also on the protected list but are not increasing as they should. They build up to a sizable flight and then the following year suddenly dwindle in numbers. The hazards of migration are assumed to be the cause.

**State Conservation.** Prince Edward Island sportsmen and interested nature lovers are active conservationists who are strong on the construction of dams which retain beneficial moisture, attract wild ducks, and many species of birds. In addition, the Provincial Department of Agriculture and the various sportsmen's organizations put on crow contests and shoots to eliminate this winged predator. Sportsmen and farmers work in co-operation, particularly in providing a winter food supply for game birds.

Thousands of dollars have been spent by sportsmen in the purchasing of adult ring-necked pheasants for liberation in the province. Among this number were 500 secured from the MacFarland Pheasant Farms, Janesville, Wis. Thousands of eggs have also been purchased and hatched in incubators. The results obtained so far do not justify the expenditure and labor involved. Prairie chickens were introduced in 1943 and this initial planting is aided by annual restocking, Hungarian partridges, introduced in 1927, have been successfully planted.

**Licenses.** License fees are as follows:

| | |
|---|---|
| Non-resident | $10.00 |

Licenses are procurable from the Royal Canadian Mounted Police at Charlottetown, Summerside, Souris, Montague, Alberton, Borden, or from the Department of Agriculture, Charlottetown. License holders are requested to study the provisions of the P.E.I. Fish and Game and the Migratory Birds Acts.

**Regulations.** It is against the law to shoot any game birds with a rifle in this province.

Permission to shoot cranes is granted only under license from the Department of Mines and Resources.

For general information on entering and leaving Canada, rules on firearms, admission of hunting dogs and automobiles, and exportation of game, see "Canada," p. 1093.

**Seasons.** Game animals and birds for which there are open seasons are:

| | |
|---|---|
| Snowshoe rabbit | Hungarian partridge |
| Squirrel | Ruffed grouse (native partridge) |
| Brant | Wilson's snipe |
| Ducks | Woodcock |
| Geese | |

## QUEBEC — AREA: 594,534 square miles

**General Summary.** Big-game animals are of chief concern to the sportsmen of Quebec. Deer is quite abundant in some districts, and, where agriculture advances, more suitable habitat is furnished for this animal which thrives alongside of cultivated land. Moose and caribou, however, have recently shown serious population losses. Both of these species prefer far-away wilderness, and decline near civilization where hunting pressure contributes to the acuity of the problem. Bears may be taken during the major part of the year.

Waterfowl are second to big game in importance to the hunter. The situation for these migratory birds is about the same as on the rest of the North American continent in general.

Upland game birds which are hunted annually include ruffed grouse, ptarmigan, and woodcock. As in the other Canadian provinces, the shorebird, Wilson's snipe is legal game.

There is seasonal hunting of the snowshoe hare, but, like the ruffed grouse of this province, its population status is more dependent on the rise and fall within its established cycle than on the aid of game management.

**State Conservation.** To carry out the regulations of the Migratory Bird Act established between Canada and the United States, the minister appoints game officers and authorizes them to exercise the powers of a police constable. All members of the Royal Canadian Mounted Police qualify as game officers.

The duties of the Fish and Game Department are executed by the minister, deputy minister, and superintendent. Every crown land agent or crown timber agent, every forest ranger, superintendent, fire ranger, and every officer of the provincial police and every revenue officer is, *ex officio*, a game warden for the Division under his respective superintendence. Every inspector and game warden sends a monthly report of his activities to the Fish and Game Department.

**Licenses.** License fees are as follows:

| | |
|---|---|
| Resident | $ 1.00 |
| Non-resident | 41.00 |
| Non-resident game club members | 20.00 |
| Non-resident game birds | 15.50 |
| Non-resident bear | 5.25 |

Licenses may be obtained from any game warden, city or town clerk.

**Regulations.** No automatic rifle may be used for hunting in this province, nor may any automatic repeating shotgun, or any type of rifle, be used to hunt migratory game birds.

Moose or deer may not be hunted or killed while in their winter yards or by taking advantage of snow crusting.

No dogs are tolerated in the forests where there are deer, moose, and caribou, but they are allowed in places where there is only ruffed grouse.

Game must be shipped with a tag and with the names and addresses of shipper and consignee as well as a full description of contents indicated on the parcel.

For information on entering and leaving Canada, rules on firearms, admission of hunting dogs and automobiles, see "Canada," p. 1093.

**Seasons.** Game animals and birds for which there are open seasons are:

| | |
|---|---|
| Bear | Brant |
| Caribou | Ducks |
| Deer | Geese |
| Fox | Ptarmigan |
| Moose | Ruffed grouse |
| Raccoon | Wilson's snipe |
| Snowshoe hare | Woodcock |

## SASKATCHEWAN — AREA: 251,700 square miles

**General Summary.** With the Department of Conservation field staff covering vast territories in the northern country of Saskatchewan by aircraft, a more complete picture of the big-game resources in that region has been established, while through the central and southern districts the observations of interested individuals and organizations have assisted the Department greatly in determining the present status of big game. The over-all big-game outlook is dark in Saskatchewan; there has been a sharp decrease in big game in recent years, chiefly as a result of timber wolf depredation.

The opinion of all observers definitely agrees that the present numbers of moose are badly depleted. Timber wolves have been mainly responsible for this decline. However, in the southern areas the hunter has taken a fair share. The district in and around Hudson Bay Junction and farther south, a usual habitat, showed a marked decline, and the same was true throughout the Pasqua and Porcupine Provincial Forests. The range of the moose is very extensive, from the present populated areas north to the Churchill. This steady decrease in the last few years forced a closed season in 1947, as recommended by the Game Advisory Committee.

The elk and woodland caribou are two big-game animals that also are showing a marked decrease, likewise probably because of extended depredations of the timber wolf. The woodland caribou is uncommon in Saskatchewan, as it habitually ranges the swamp and muskeg country fringed by spruce forest. Elk have been found in the settled areas which formerly were their range, but in some cases they have been found to move farther north with the advance of civilization. In recent years there have been fewer complaints in connection with elk destroying grain and haystacks. The elk ranges in the vicinity of the Fort à la Corne and southeast of that area, while there are a considerable number in the Moose Mountain Park and Cypress Hills area. No reports have been received that the elk is ranging in the northwest portion of the province. The Advisory Game Committee has recommended a closed season on elk for several years, but it is expected that when the enormous numbers of timber wolves decrease there will be a revival of the elk population and the regular annual hunting seasons.

The Barren Ground caribou ranging from the north of Canada to the Churchill does not mix with the woodland caribou. They are not hunted extensively by sportsmen but are an important source of food for the natives of the north. The Barren Ground caribou is found in the Reindeer Lake, Cree Lake, Lake Athabaska and Fond du Lac districts; timber wolves destroy large numbers of these animals, and in some cases many are taken by the wanton destruction of natives. The numbers of these caribou in the northern country are gradually decreasing, but there are still herds of a thousand or more. Large migrations southward in the fall and northward treks in the spring are considered an annual event by the residents of the northern districts.

The white-tailed (Virginia) deer or the black-tailed (mule) deer are found in almost all parts of the province. In the northern areas their numbers have definitely been affected by predators but they are more numerous than other members of the deer family, and a population increase is noted throughout the southern portion of Saskatchewan. During the fall and summer months a number of special permits were issued in cases where deer were causing a considerable amount of damage to crops. These special permits have been issued in all parts of the province. With the increased number throughout the province, the Department found it possible to open a shooting season in the southeastern part of the province for a two-week period under special deer licenses. The deer definitely will stay in the settled areas provided there is sufficient food for them and with proper control measures all parts of the province might enjoy the presence of this common big game animal.

The antelope, a big-game animal frequenting only the southwestern and central portion of the province, provides sportsmen with a high type of big-game hunting. Antelope hunters have been restrained, however, by recent closed seasons necessitated by a steady drop in the antelope population throughout the province. The annual reported kill was approximately 280. There was a closed season on antelope in 1947.

The province has had a decrease in ducks, as have most parts of North America. Some areas have reported good goose hunting, however, with the lesser Canada goose being much more abundant than the Canada goose. The general situation on migratory waterfowl, however, indicates a sharp decline and past season reports received from the U. S. Fish and Wildlife Service reveal that more birds were shot than had been raised. The number of licensed game hunters in the province is on the increase and the number of birds taken in Saskatchewan was far below average. The Saskatchewan Fish and Game League, through its predator-control campaign and educational work, has assisted greatly in overcoming the natural enemies of waterfowl. Ducks Unlimited has carried out water-development projects and improved water conditions to further the well-being of waterfowl resources. This work has been in progress for a number of years.

The numbers of sharp-tailed grouse, a popular upland game bird, have fallen off drastically, and the bird is considered to be at a low point of the cycle. Reports received suggest that large numbers have migrated farther north, and according to reports north of Meadow Lake and in the vicinity of Nipawin their numbers are greatly improved.

The Hungarian partridge was not affected quite so badly as the sharp-tailed grouse. However, it also shows a marked decline throughout almost all parts of the province. In some areas of concentration, however, they are causing considerable damage. The Hungarian partridge has retained its numbers, in areas where the ring-necked pheasant has infiltrated, to a much better degree than the sharp-tailed grouse.

The ring-necked pheasant has continually held its own; it was expected increased hunting pressure would certainly reduce their numbers, but they have shown a population increase. These birds are gradually adapting themselves to new parts of the province and the conservation department is anticipating the establishing of a game farm at Beaver Creek for the propagation of cock pheasant for distribution throughout the province. This excellent game bird and the shooting it offers has been received with considerable interest by the hunters of Saskatchewan, and as a result has taken a considerable pressure from other types of game birds now showing a decline. The district around Weyburn and Estevan is the largest of the open areas and the most populated, while the Moose Jaw district reports considerable numbers and has made representations to narrow down the Moose Jaw Wild Animal Park Game Preserve, in order to scatter the large abundance of birds in reserve in that area.

**State Conservation.** The Department of Conservation in Saskatchewan follows a sound policy to protect and increase its wildlife by providing or maintaining suitable natural habitat for its game birds and animals, checking serious predation, and guarding against over-shooting.

The Canadian Forestry Association makes an annual tour to educate the public on forest-fire prevention and to secure co-operation in protection and conservation of forests and wildlife. Since the Canadian prairies are the breeding grounds for 90 per cent of North American ducks, the protection of these grounds is vitally important for the outlook of duck shooting as a whole. To aid migratory waterfowl, by mitigating drought conditions, dams have been constructed in forest reserves and other wooded sections by the provincial department. Small water-development projects completed by the Federal authorities and Ducks Unlimited provide resting places for birds evacuating south. Ducks Unlimited, an organization formed to preserve and increase duck population, has made a valuable contribution to wildlife conservation in Saskatchewan, as in many other breeding areas, through prevention measures to maintain breeding grounds and the reestablishing of breeding grounds which have disappeared. Their water-conservation projects have resulted in improved feeding and breeding conditions for migratory waterfowl and their extensive publicity campaign has done much to gain general public support for game conservation work.

Saskatchewan's 76 game preserves in prairie, park belt, and wooded sections of the province total 7792 square miles. In addition there are 12 large bird sanctuaries. This vast area provides a haven and nesting place for hundreds of thousands of waterfowl, upland game birds, and big game. To discourage shooting in public park areas 12 public shooting grounds are set aside where the hunter may shoot without danger of interfering with the rights of property owners.

Farmers throughout the province have shown a continuous interest in game conservation by winter feeding of game birds and game animals during the severe winter months, and in a large number of instances have propagated various types of game birds on a small scale.

Timber wolves are increasing rapidly and in some areas have caused serious destruction of big game as well as other smaller animals. The bounty method of elimination (1237 wolves were taken over a two-year period between 1943-1945 at a cost of $12,368.) at its present rate apparently is not sufficient. Trapping and hunting have proved ineffective, but it is hoped that the use of poison will increase the kill.

To check the trend toward depletion of both game birds and big game, a closed season was declared on moose, woodland caribou, antelope, and elk, and also on prairie chicken (sharp-tailed grouse), Hungarian partridge, spruce grouse, and ptarmigan.

**Licenses.** License fees are as follows:

| | |
|---|---|
| Resident big game | $ 5.00 |
| Non-resident Canadian big game | 25.00 |
| Non-resident alien big game | 40.00 |
| Resident game bird | 2.00 |

| | |
|---|---|
| Non-resident Canadian game bird | 10.00 |
| Non-resident alien game bird | 25.00 |
| Resident special cock pheasant | 1.00 |
| Non-resident special cock pheasant | 5.00 |

All non-resident licenses may be procured in advance of the season direct from the Game Branch, Department of Natural Resources, Saskatchewan Resources Building, Regina, Sask., upon payment of the required fee. Branch offices of the Department of Natural Resources at Prince Albert, Meadow Lake, and Hudson Bay also handle non-resident licenses.

Visitors from Manitoba and Alberta may purchase a resident game-bird license in Saskatchewan when they produce a resident game bird license for the province in which they reside.

Individuals wishing to purchase a special cock pheasant license must first be in possession of a game-bird license. Tags issued in conjunction with special cock pheasant licenses must be attached to the bird immediately it has been taken. All non-residents are required to take out a non-resident special cock pheasant license, as there is no reciprocal arrangement on this particular type of license.

**Regulations.** Automatic or autoloading shotguns are allowed, provided the magazine has been plugged or altered so that the magazine cannot carry more than two shells. Such automatic weapon must be inspected by a game guardian or a member of the Royal Canadian Mounted Police.

Non-resident alien hunters wishing to import firearms into Saskatchewan for hunting purposes must first secure a Firearm Permit from the Game Branch, Department of Natural Resources, Saskatchewan Resources Building, Regina, Sask. Permits for revolvers must be procured from the Royal Canadian Mounted Police, Regina. When making application for permit, the make, model, and serial number of the firearm should be provided.

Dogs may not be used to hunt deer.

*Export Regulations:* Non-resident hunters may export from Saskatchewan only the game birds lawfully in their possession, that is, no more than the possession limit. Export coupons are issued in conjunction with the non-resident license. Resident hunters may secure coupons from the Game Branch, Department of Natural Resources, Regina. Visiting sportsmen from the United States should ascertain from their local game department the amount of game that can be imported into their respective states.

*Unied States Customs:* Game animals and birds killed in foreign countries by residents of the United States, if not imported for sale or other commercial purposes, may be admitted free of duty upon the filing of a Declaration (on U. S. Customs Form 3315). No bond or cash deposit to insure the destruction or exportation of the plumage of such birds shall be required.

For general information on entering and leaving Canada, rules on firearms, admission of hunting dogs and automobiles, and exportation of game, see "Canada," p. 1093.

**Seasons.** Game animals and birds for which there are open seasons are:

| | |
|---|---|
| Barren Ground caribou | Geese |
| Deer | Pheasant |
| Coot | Wilson's snipe |
| Ducks | |

There is no closed season on:

| | |
|---|---|
| Badger | Rabbits |
| Bear | Timber wolf |
| Coyote | Wolverine |

## YUKON

AREA: 205,346 square miles

**General Summary.** Game conditions in the Yukon are about parallel with those in the Northwest Territory. The opening of the Alaska Highway has made parts of this wilderness area more accessible, but as travel on this highway can be called only "very light," it has had as yet no bad effect on the game populations.

The game laws and regulations are rather complex, as they apply to the non-resident hunter, and anyone planning a hunting or fishing trip to this area should write in advance to the Controller of the Yukon Territorial Council, Dawson, Y.T. For general information on entering and leaving Canada, rules on firearms, admission of hunting dogs and automobiles, as well as exportation of game, see "Canada," p. 1093.

**Licenses.** License fees are as follows:

| | |
|---|---|
| Resident general | $ 1.00 |
| Resident moose and caribou | 25.00 |
| Non-resident British | 75.00 |
| Non-resident alien | 100.00 |
| Non-resident permits for each additional big-game species | 25.00 |
| Non-resident game bird | 5.00 |

**Seasons.** Game animals and birds for which there are open seasons are:

| | |
|---|---|
| Caribou | Geese |
| Deer | Grouse |
| Moose | Pheasant |
| Mountain goat | Prairie chicken |
| Mountain sheep | Ptarmigan |
| Ducks | |

# Mexico

AREA: 758,057 square miles

**General Summary.** Sportsmen have been rather slow in awakening to the hunting possibilities of Mexico, and although a number of American hunters from the border states have been taking advantage of the sporting opportunities offered there, this area has never approached the popularity of even one Canadian province.

The waterfowl and upland game shooting is unusually fine in many areas, due in part to the fact that the majority of the local residents do little hunting. In the mountainous and wooded areas, many varieties of big game offer a real inducement to the visiting hunter, and guides may be obtained for the hunting in most areas at extremely reasonable prices.

Game animals and birds of Mexico are distributed as follows:

*Lower California:* On coasts, great variety of marine fowl. Interior: Antelope, black bear, cougar, deer (blacktail and whitetail), hare, and rabbit, lynx, mountain sheep, wildcat; dove, pheasant, quail.

*Sonora:* Antelope, bear (gray and black), boar, cougar, coyote, deer (whitetail and blacktail), fox, lynx, Mexican leopard, mountain sheep, opossum, puma, wolf; wildcat, wild turkey.

*Chihuahua:* Bear (gray and black), boar, cougar, coyote, deer (blacktail and whitetail), jaguar, Mexican panther, mountain sheep, wolf; duck, geese, heron (light and dark), wild turkey.

*Nuevo Leon:* Black bear, boar, cougar, coyote, deer, hare, lynx, puma, rabbit, wildcat; Mexican dove, quail, wild turkey.

*Tamaulipas:* Alligator, Boar, cougar, coyote, deer, jaguar, opossum, puma, wildcat; dove, duck, geese, pheasant, quail, wild geese, wild turkey.

*Sinatoa:* Alligator, antelope, bear (black and gray), boar, cougar, deer, fox, hare, jaguar, Mexican leopard, mountain sheep, otter, puma, rabbit, wildcat, wolf; waterfowl.

*Tepic* and *Jalisco:* Alligator, boar, coyote, deer, hare, opossum, otter, puma, rabbit, wildcat; blue pheasant, crane, duck, geese, heron, macaw, quail, wild turkey.

*Colima:* Alligator, cougar, deer, jaguar; dove, quail, waterfowl, wild turkey.

*Michoacan:* Alligator, boar, cougar, coyote, crocodile, deer, hare, jackal, jaguar, otter, puma, rabbit; dove, duck, geese, macaw, parrots, pheasant, quail, waterfowl.

*Guerrero:* Alligator, boar, cougar, deer, fox, jaguar, opossum, puma, wildcat, dove, pheasant, quail, waterfowl.

*Oaxaca:* Alligator, boar, cougar, coyote, deer, fox, jaguar, lynx, monkey, mountain lion, opposum, otter, puma, rabbit, royal pheasant, squirrel, tapir, wildcat; dove, heron, parrot, pheasant, quail, waterfowl, wild turkey.

*Isthmus of Tehuantepec:* About the same as tropical Oaxaca.

*Chiapas:* Boar, coyote, deer, monkey, puma, tapir; dove, egret, macaw, parakeets, parrots, pheasant, waterfowl, wild turkey.

*Veracruz:* Alligator, black fox, boar, cougar, deer, hare, jaguar, marten, monkey, puma, squirrel, tapir, wildcat; dove, macaw, parakeets, parrots, pheasant, waterfowl, wild turkey.

*Tabasco, Campeche* and *Yucatan:* Agouti, alligator, armadillo, boar, cougar, deer, jaguar, monkey, oposum, puma, goose, macaws, parrots, pheasant, quail, quetzal, waterfowl, wild turkey.

*Durango:* Antelope, bear (gray and black), coati, cougar, coyote, deer, fox, jaguar, lynx, rabbit, squirrel, wildcat, wolf; black swan, dove, duck, eagle, geese, heron, ibis, macaw, parakeets, parrots, pelican, pheasant, quail.

*Zacatecas* and *Aguasalientes:* Antelope, black bear, cougar, coyote, deer, hare, rabbit, wildcat; dove, duck, geese, quail.

*San Luis Potosi:* Alligator, boar, cougar, coyote, deer, fox, hare, lynx, otter, rabbit, wildcat; dove, geese, pheasant, quail, wild duck.

*Guanajuato* and *Queretaro:* coyote, fox, hare, otter, puma, rabbit, wildcat; dove, pheasant, quail, waterfowl.

*Hidalgo:* Cougar, coyote, hare, opossum, rabbit, squirrel, whitetail deer; dove, quail, upland plover.

*Federal District:* Fox, deer, hare, rabbit, wildcat, wolf; dove, quail, waterfowl.

*Mexico:* Boar, cougar, coyote, deer, jaguar, puma, rabbit, wildcat; dove, duck, geese, pheasant, quail, upland plover.

*Morelos:* Armadillo, boar, deer, hare, rabbit; dove, duck, partridge, quail, snipe.

*Puebla:* Game similar to Oaxaca; whitetail deer; duck, geese, pheasant, quail, snipe, wild turkey.

*Quintana Roo:* Alligator, boar, deer, puma.

All that is needed to enter Mexico is a tourist card obtainable at the nearest Mexican consulate or at the border. This is valid for six months. The sportsman should specify, when getting his tourist card, that he wishes to hunt, so that it may be stated on the card; then, when taking firearms into Mexico for hunting purposes, the visitor has to apply for a special permit. To obtain this he must be provided with (*a*) a letter of recommendation from a bank, chamber of commerce, police department, or other recognized institution, stating that the applicant is a respectable, law-abiding citizen, and (*b*) two passport-size pictures. The permit entitles a person to take four guns, each of a different caliber, into Mexico. Only one gun (either shotgun or rifle) is admitted duty free; the others must be bonded. The Mauser 7-mm. rifle and Colt .45 automatic, the caliber arms used by the Mexican military forces, are not allowed. A duty deposit of $20 Mexican money is required for each extra gun brought in. The amount is refunded on leaving the country. Parties who wish to enter foreign-made guns should register them with the U. S. customs officials before entering Mexico. This insures against collection of duty on return to the United States. Ammunition up to 100 cartridges, or 500 grams of powder, for each gun is allowed duty free.

Application for a hunting license must be made in writing. On the blanks provided for that purpose the appplicant agrees to abide by the Mexican laws and that, so far as hunting is concerned, he will temporarily consider himself a Mexican citizen. Hunting licenses may be applied for at the office of the game warden *(Oficina de Caza)* at the border port of entry. Licenses may also be obtained by applying at the office of the Secretaria de Agricultura y Fomento in any state capital; at the main office of the Secretaria de Agricultura y Fomento, Direccion General Forestal y de Caza, Av. Edison 145, Mexico City, or from any local game warden *(guardia forestal y de caza).* In making his application, the sportsman must present his tourist card; he must also be prepared to furnish a bond, which may be secured from a reliable Mexican bonding company or from a responsible business firm. If the applicant is a member of an officially licensed hunting club or association of sport hunters, membership in such a club includes the furnishing of a bond.

The cost of a hunting license for the entire Mexican Republic, for six months, is $80 Mexican. A license for one state, which may not exceed 30 days, costs $50 Mexican.

A list of hunting and fishing clubs (licensed by the Hunting and Fishing Department of the Mexican government and authorized according to the hunting and fishing laws) is available by writing to the Mexican Government Tourist Department, International Building, 630 Fifth Ave., New York.

**Seasons.** Game animals and birds for which there are open seasons:

Armadillo, bear, deer, (blacktail, whitetail, and mule), fox, hare, rabbit, raccoon, wild hog (peccary), chachalaca (Mexican pheasant), chichicuilote or yellow leg, crane, curassao, doves, geese, mountain chicken, partridge, quail, snipe, upland plover, wild turkey, waterfowl.

There is no closed season on:

Coyote, jaguar, Mexican leopard, Mexican panther, mountain lion, ring-tail cat, wildcat, wolf.

# GLOSSARY

Account For. When the fox or other game is killed or run to ground or treed, it is said to be "accounted for." (Fox hunting.)

Acorn Duck. A local name for the wood duck.

Action. The breech mechanism of a gun, by means of which it is loaded, and which secures the cartridge in the chamber, preventing it from discharging to the rear.

Also, the manner in which a dog moves in the field. (Field trials.)

Adaptability. That quality which enables a bird dog to conform his speed and range to various types of country. (Field trials.)

Alaska Game Commission. Located at Juneau, Alaska.

All-Age. A bird dog over 30 months of age. (Field trials.)

Alligator *(mississipiensis)*. A lizard-like reptile, having a broader but shorter snout than a crocodile. Found in southern U. S. from the Gulf of Mexico to central North Carolina. Large specimens attain a length of 16 ft.

American Round. An archery contest established in 1879 by the National Archery Assn. The round consists of 90 arrows fired as follows: 30 arrows at 60 yds., 30 arrows at 50 yds., and 30 arrows at 40 yds. (Archery.)

Anatidae. The family of which the geese, ducks, and swans are members.

Angle of Departure. The angle of the bore (prolonged), which is determined by the setting of the sights for the range. Thus, the raising of the rear sight to increase range will depress the breech and raise the muzzle, elevating the angle of departure.

Annealing. The subjection of metal to intense heat and gradual cooling, in order to increase the strength and reduce the brittleness of the metal.

Anserinae. The subfamily of *Anatidae* which embraces the varied species of geese.

Antlers. Solid, deciduous growths, normally branched, on the head of a mammal, shed annually, and normally present only on the male. Male and female caribou are antlered.

Anvil. A component part of the primer, against which the priming composition is crushed by the impact of the firing pin, causing the explosion which ignites the powder.

A.O.U. American Ornithologists' Union.

Aplondontiidae. The family of which the beaver is a member.

Arboreal. Adjective used of birds or mammals which live in trees.

Arisaka Rifle. A Japanese military rifle, an excellent arm for the cartridge designed for it, but unsatisfactory for conversion to a highpower sporting rifle, as it was not designed to handle high-power loads with their resultant heavy pressures.

Armadillo *(Tolypeutes tricinctus)*. A small armored mammal found in Mexico, southern Texas, and Arizona. This animal has the top of the head and the body enclosed in armor formed of small bony plates. When frightened the Armadillo curls into a ball, thus giving itself all-around protection.

Armguard. A piece of leather or other substance that protects the wrist from the slap of the bowstring. (Archery.)

Arrow Plate. A small piece of bone, horn, pearl, ivory, or other substance inlaid at the right point for the arrow to pass across when bow is shot. (Archery.)

Arrow Rest. A piece of leather or other substance directly under the shooting plate for the arrow to rest on when being shot. (Archery.)

A.T.A. Amateur Trapshooting Assn., Vandalia, Ohio.

Attitude. The posture of a dog on point. (Field trials.)

Autoloader. *See* Semi-automatic.

Automatic. Any firearm which continues to fire, to the extent of the capacity of its magazine, as long as the trigger is depressed.

Babbler. A hound that is unnecessarily noisy; one which opens without cause when not on the trail or line.

Babiche. Indian term for rawhide.

Back. The flat side of the bow which is away from the archer when in shooting position (Archery.)

Backbreaker. An unusually heavy rifle or shotgun.

Back-Cast. A cast on which the dog works to the rear of the handler. (Field trials.)

Backing. A form of expressing the dog's pointing instinct: Honoring at sight or command another dog's point by coming to point also. (Field trials.)

Baffle. A rectangle of canvas, usually 8′ x 10′, with strips of 1″ x 2″ lath tacked to it crosswise. The baffle is used to break the small waves ahead of an anchored duckboat. Because of the extremely low freeboard and low coaming of the average duckboat it cannot remain anchored in rough water without the baffle. Also known in some areas as a "buffer" or "breaker."

Bagman. A fox which has been released. (Fox hunting.)

Baiting. The scattering of grain in a shooting area to attract and hold a number of birds. Now prohibited by law.

Balance. The point on the under-part of a rifle or shotgun at which the gun is balanced. A gun may be "muzzle heavy" or "butt heavy."

Ball. A solid metal projectile, usually for rifle or handgun; used with muzzle-loaders or ball cartridge. Often also used loosely for "bullet."

Ballistic Coefficient. This term, as applied to bullets, concerns the shape, length, weight, diameter, and nose design of a bullet, which have a definite effect upon its stability, velocity, and range.

Ballistics. A term covering the science of bullet velocity, trajectory, force, impact, and penetration.

Bandolier. A belt, worn around the waist or slung across the shoulder, normally containing six pockets, each holding one clip of cartridges.

Bang-Belly. A Maine term for corn bread with blueberries.

Bannock. A form of camp bread, unleavened and made of oatmeal, baked on a griddle.

BAR. *See* Browning Automatic Rifle.

Barrel. That part of a rifle, shotgun, revolver, or pistol through which the bullet or shot charge passes.

Barrelled Pile. Point for target and roving arrows. (Archery.)

Barrel Time. The time involved in the movement of the bullet from the neck of the cartridge to its arrival at the muzzle.

Barrens. Term for a flat wasteland with low, stunted vegetation; also, a broad, flat marsh.

Base Wad. A compressed fiber or paper filler inside the head of a shotshell, which keeps the powder in position in front of the primer.

Basset Hound. A short-legged hound, originally bred in France. (*See* Dogs.)

Battery Cup. *See* Primer Cup.

Beach Buggy. A large-tired automobile used to negotiate the coastal beaches for fishing and shooting.

Beavertail. An oversized fore-end on a rifle or shotgun, employed both to improve the balance of the arm and to offer a better grip for the hand.

Bedding. The fitting or "bedding" of the barrel and action in the stock. The most accurate barrel made, if incorrectly bedded, will fail to produce uniformly satisfactory results.

Bee (.218 Bee). A .22-caliber high-velocity cartridge developed by Winchester, primarily for vermin shooting. Originated from a necked-down .25/20 cartridge.

Beef Shoot. A shooting contest held in several parts of the South during the muzzle-loader days, now revived in Asheville, N. C. It is limited to the muzzle-loading rifle and the shooters use a black cross with 2″ arms as a target. The four high-score shooters divide the steer which is the prize. The winner may sell his share or there may be a shoot-off, with high man keeping the entire steer.

Bell Point. A term originating with the practice of placing a small bell on a dog while hunting woodcock in heavy cover. The hunter is unable to see the dog but can follow his movements by the light tinkle of the bell. When the sound ceases he knows the dog is on point.

Belly. The side of the bow toward the archer when bow is held in shooting position. (Archery.)

Belted Cartridge. A cartridge, primarily in heavy-caliber high-velocity types, which is rimless at the base but has a rim or belt larger in diameter than the base just forward of the extraction groove.

Belton. A type of color formed when two colors blend so closely as to lose individual identity. Blue belton is a combination of black and white; orange belton a combination of orange and white. (Dogs.)

BENCH REST. A wooden shooting bench, heavily constructed and firmly placed, with suitable "rests" for the rifle muzzle or barrel, at which the shooter may sit to engage in accuracy tests of the firearm.

BERDAN PRIMER. A primer without a separate anvil, employing a raised section in the base of the pocket of the primer as an anvil, and having two flash holes.

BEVY. A group of game birds, generally a brood, such as quail.

BEWITS. Short leather straps for fastening bells to hawks. (Falconry.)

BEZ. The second point of antlers, after the *brow* and before the *trez.*

BIG-BORE. A rather loose term, normally applied to rifles of calibers larger than .25.

BILLET. The droppings of a fox.

BINOCULAR. An instrument employing lenses and prisms for the purpose of magnifying normal vision.

BIRD DOG. A dog bred for the purpose of hunting upland game birds. In this book the term refers to pointers and setters.

BIRDS. As used in this book, game birds—more specifically, quail, pheasants, ruffed grouse, woodcock, and prairie chicken.

BISLEY. The range of the National Rifle Assn. of Great Britain, scene of many international matches.

BITCH. A female dog.

BLACK. The bull's-eye or black portion of a target.

BLIND. A natural or man-made hiding place from which a hunter shoots ducks, turkeys, or other game.

BLINKER. A term commonly used to denote a dog which points game and then leaves it before the flush. Some blinkers hunt for and find game but skirt around it, resuming hunting without pointing it. (Dogs.)

BLOCKS. Decoys.

BLOODED. When hounds kill their quarry they are said to be "blooded." "Blooding" a novice is to anoint him with fox blood at his first "kill."

BLOWBACK. A type of automatic or semi-automatic action, in which extraction, ejection, and reloading are accomplished by means of the force exerted rearward by the fired cartridge.

BLOWDOWN. A thick tangle of fallen trees and brush, usually the result of severe winds which topple large trees whose falls smash other trees to the ground.

BLOWN PRIMER. A cartridge case in which the primer was blown out during firing. Can cause serious injury, even blindness, to the shooter; one good argument for use of shooting glasses.

BLUEBIRD WEATHER. A term for sunny, windless days which are the bane of the wildfowler's existence, as waterfowl normally do not move in such weather.

BLUE PILL. A high-pressure test cartridge employed to test the strength of a rifle. This cartridge develops pressures more than one-third greater than those of the normal cartridge.

BLUNDERBUSS (originally Dutch = "thunder box"). A muzzle-loading weapon of extremely large bore diameter, with a bell-shaped muzzle, designed for use at extremely short ranges, and normally charged with several balls, pellets, or pieces of scrap metal.

BLUNT POINT. A point of the arrow that is cut off squarely across the end. (Archery.)

BOAT-TAIL BULLET. A special type of bullet designed to obtain greater efficiency at longer ranges.

BODY SCENT. Scent emanating from the bodies of game birds.

BOLDNESS. Aggressiveness in hunting. (Field trials.)

BOLTER. A dog which refuses to handle the prescribed course. Sometimes a bolter will leave the course because he does not want to hunt for his handler; sometimes because he is seeking country more to his liking. (Field trials.)

BORE. The inside of the barrel of a shotgun, rifle, revolver, or pistol, the diameter of which is determined by the caliber or gauge of the weapon. The term is sometimes used as a synonym for "gauge."

BORE SIGHTING. A means of making the initial sight adjustment on a rifle at less ammunition cost. Remove the bolt or breechblock, rest the rifle on some firm support, then look through the bore toward a target 50 or 100 yards distant. When you have moved the rifle sufficiently to center the bull's-eye in the bore opening, look through the sights, being careful not to move the rifle. Adjust the sights so that they center on the bull's-eye. The first shot will be several inches low, but this can be corrected with two or three test shots.

BOUNCE-OUT. An arrow that has hit the target but has failed to stick in it. In target archery it counts five, regardless of what ring the arrow has hit.

BOW GUARD. A piece of leather or other substance that protects the wrist from the slap of the bowstring. (Archery.)

BOWYER. One who makes bows. (Archery.)

BRACE. Standard term for two quail, partridge, pheasant, grouse, hares, or dogs. Also (archery), a wrist-protector; *see* Bow Guard.

BRACE-MATE. When dogs are worked in pairs, each is called the brace-mate of the other.

BRACING A BOW. Putting the string in the nocks of the bow.

BREAKER. *See* Baffle.

BREAKING TO SHOT. Dashing in after the shot is fired. (Field trials.)

BREECH. The base (as opposed to the muzzle) of a firearm; the rear, the portion of which, in a modern arm, is chambered to hold the cartridge or shell.

BREECHBLOCK. The metal *block* at the breech (rear) of the bore of a firearm which serves to plug the rear of the bore, thus blocking the force of the powder gases to the rear. In modern firearms this block may take the form of a bolt, the face of which is cammed firmly against the base of the chamber.

BREEDING. The ancestry of a dog.

BREEDS. Races, varieties, or families of dogs.

BROADHEAD. Steel blade on a hunting arrow—formerly made of flint. (Archery.)

BROKEN. Term for a finished performer. (Field trials.)

BROOD. A single hatching of game birds.

BROW. The first, or brow, point of antlers.

BROWNING AUTOMATIC RIFLE. A rifle with a magazine capacity of 20 rounds, gas-operated, capable of being fired full or semi-automatic.

BROWSE. Lower branches of trees, small saplings, or low brush, which serve as food for members of the deer family and other ruminants.

BROWSE BAG. A heavy cotton bag which, stuffed with leaves or pine needles, may be used as a pillow.

BROWSER. A game animal which feeds primarily on browse (as opposed to a grazer).

BRUIN. A colloquial term for any member of the bear family.

BRULÉE. *See* Burn.

BRUSH. The tail of a fox.

BRUSH-CUTTER. A bullet, usually of large caliber and considerable weight, having enough velocity and weight to continue its normal course without being deflected by light brush.

BRUSH GUN. A rifle or shotgun with a barrel shorter than average, designed to give greater ease in movement through heavy brush.

B. T. *See* Boat-Tail Bullet.

BUCK. The male of various mammals, including antelope, goat, deer, rabbit.

Also, an accessory used in teaching retrieving. (Field trials.)

BUCK FEVER. A nervous ailment which often afflicts the novice hunter when he is first offered the opportunity of a shot at big game. It takes various forms, usually causing such trembling that an accurate shot is impossible.

BUCKLING. The bending, as it leaves the bow, of an arrow that is too light of spine; this movement or buckling causes the arrow to whip to the left of its mark. (Archery.)

BUCKSHOT. Lead or alloy shot used in shotgun shells, principally for large game.

BUCKSKIN. In some parts of the West, a general term for members of the deer family.

BUFFER. A term used by biologists to designate some small form of animal life upon which predators will feed, thus reducing the mortality of game. If a sufficient abundance of these "buffers" is present to keep predators supplied with food, the game population will increase. *See also* Baffle.

BULK POWDER. Smokeless powder which gives results equal to a similar bulk of black powder.

BULL. The male of certain mammals—including bison, elk, moose, and whales.

Also, colloquial shortening of "bull's-eye."

BULLET. A spherical ball or cylindro-conodial slug, for small arms, formed entirely of lead or having a core of lead inside a jacket of some tough metal, which is propelled by means of gunpowder or some other propulsion medium.

BULLET SEATER. A device used by hand-loaders to seat the bullet in the cartridge case.

**Bullet Sizer.** A device employed by hand-loaders through which a cast bullet is forced, insuring the correct diameter.

**Bull Gun.** A heavy-barreled rifle, usually stocked in an unconventional design.

**Bull Pup.** *See* Bull Gun.

**Bump.** Slang for a flush. (Field trials.)

**Burn.** An area which has been burned over by a forest fire.

**Buros.** A native name used in Mexico for the mule deer.

**Burr.** The crown, or burr, at the base of antlers.

**Burst.** Generally the first part of the run, when hounds are close upon the fox; any fast part of a chase. (Fox hunting.)

**Butt Plate.** The metal or plastic plate covering the rear of a gunstock, usually checkered or corrugated to prevent slipping.

**Butts.** Backing (usually of hay) behind the target face that stops the arrows in target shooting. Also, bullet-stopping to backing of a rifle range, to the rear of the targets.

**Cache.** A hiding place for food, equipment, or any valuable material.

**Caliber.** The diameter of the bore of a rifle in hundredths of an inch, or in millimeters, usually measured from land to land, which gives the true diameter of the bore prior to the cutting of lands.

**Calks.** Hobnails on the soles of boots.

**Caller.** *See* Judas Duck.

**Camp Perry, Ohio.** The scene of the National Rifle Matches and the National Pistol Matches.

**Camp Robber.** *See* Moose Bird.

**Canidae.** The family which includes wolves, coyotes, and foxes.

**Canis.** The genus of the sub-family *caninae* which includes the coyote.

**Cannelure.** A groove around the circumference of a bullet, such as the lubrication groove around a lead bullet; also the extraction groove around the base of a cartridge.

**Cant.** The tilting of the rifle, shotgun, or handgun to one side or the other, off the true vertical sighting plane, causing the impact point of the bullet to be low and to one side.

**Cap.** The percussion cap used on the percussion-lock gun which, upon being struck by the hammer, caused the ignition of the powder charge.

**Capercailzie.** The largest living member of the grouse family *(Tetrao urogallus),* also known as the Caillie, found in parts of Europe and in Asia. The bird became extinct in England but was later re-introduced. Several pairs have been brought to this country for release in wooded areas but the reproduction rate has been very slow. The bird weighs up to 12 pounds and is dark gray and black in color. The male is about one-third larger than the female.

**Cap Lock.** A muzzle-loading firearm using a percussion cap (primer), usually of copper or brass. This cap fits over a nipple or tube which leads to the powder chamber. The falling of the hammer on this cap causes the ignition of the powder.

**Cape.** The hide and pelage covering the head, neck, and fore-shoulders of an animal, often removed for mounting as a trophy.

**Captain of the Green.** Official judge at target tournaments for men. (Archery.)

**Carbine.** A short-barreled rifle, normally much lighter in weight than the standard rifle.

**Carnivora.** Flesh-eating animals.

**Carry the Line.** When hounds are following the scent they are "carrying the line." (Field trials.)

**Cartridge.** A metal or paper cylinder containing the primer, propelling charge, and bullet.

**Case.** The cartridge body, containing the primer, charge, and bullet. Also used to describe the cartridge body *without* the primer, charge or bullet. (*See* Hull.)

**Cast.** The spreading out, or reaching out, of hounds in search of scent. (Dogs.)

**Cast.** The speed with which the bow will throw an arrow. (Archery.)

**Cast.** A group or flight of hawks. (Falconry.)

**Caution.** A warning given to the dog. (Field trials.)

**Center-Fire.** A cartridge whose primer is contained in a pocket in the center of the cartridge base.

**Center of Impact.** The center of the group of holes made in the target.

**Cervidae.** The family to which deer belong.

**Chalk.** The white excreta of the woodcock, indicating the presence of birds in a cover.

**Chamber.** The enlarged portion at the breech of a rifle, shotgun, or handgun in which the cartridge or shell fits when in the proper position for firing.

**Charge.** The amount of powder contained in a cartridge or shell for the propelling of the bullet or shot.

**Chasing.** Dashing after the birds when they are flushed; unsteadiness to flush. (Field trials.)

**Cheechako.** Alaskan name for a tenderfoot or greenhorn.

**Check.** A break, or interruption, in the run, due to the loss of scent. (Fox hunting.)

**Cheekpiece.** A raised portion of the side of the gunstock near the comb, against which the shooter may rest his cheek when aiming.

**Cherry.** A tool employed in machining the cavity of a bullet mold.

**Chink.** The ring-necked pheasant.

**Chilled Shot.** This shot contains a greater percentage of antimony than soft (drop) shot. All shot except buckshot is dropped from a tower. Buckshot of the large sizes is cast, as are the single balls.

**Choke.** Term for the constricted diameter of the muzzle of a shotgun which determines the diameter of the shot pattern at varied ranges. Chokes range through: full, modified, improved cylinder, cylinder, skeet.

**Choke Constriction.** The amount of constriction at the muzzle of various gauges, which produces choke, is as follows:

| *Gauge* | *Full Choke* | *Modified Choke* | *Imp. Cyl.* | *Full Cyl.* |
|---|---|---|---|---|
| 10 | .035 | .017 | .007 | 0 |
| 12 | .030 | .015 | .006 | 0 |
| 16 | .024 | .012 | .005 | 0 |
| 20 | .021 | .010 | .004 | 0 |
| 28 | .017 | .008 | .003 | 0 |

**Choke-Collar.** A collar made in the form of a noose for the purpose of applying force in a humane manner. (Field trials.)

**Chronograph.** An instrument used by ballisticians to measure the time required by a bullet to pass between two given points.

**Claimer.** A derogatory term for a hunter who "claims" game killed by others by stating this game fell to his shot.

**Class.** A term denoting high quality of performance. (Field trials.)

**Cleaning Worm.** A small, corkscrew-like instrument used in cleaning the muzzle-loading rifle. The worm was fixed to the small end of the ramrod, a greased patch or bit of tow wrapped around it, and passed up and down the bore three or four times.

**Clip.** A metal container designed to contain a given number of cartridges for insertion in the magazine of a rifle. The term originally meant a clip or container which was inserted in the magazine with the cartridges, but has now come to mean any cartridge container, whether or not it is inserted in the magazine with the cartridges. The five-round Springfield "clip" does not enter the magazine, whereas the M1 (Garand) "clip" does.

**Coat.** A dog's hair.

**Coiled Cartridge.** A cartridge developed around 1856, originally in England for the .577 caliber rifle. The case had a base of combined brass and steel and a body of alternate layers of paper and brass foil, glued together. One British factory still produces these cartridges.

**Cold Line.** The faint scent of the quarry. (Fox hunting.)

**Comb.** The upper and forward edge of a gunstock against which the shooter rests his cheek.

**Company.** A flock or group of widgeon. (British.)

**Condition.** The state of well-being. (Field trials.)

**Conseil International de la Chasse.** An organization comprising members from various European countries, which assumes responsibility for the classification and measurement system employed in measuring European game.

**Cope.** Muzzle for a ferret.

**Core-Lokt.** Trade name for an expanding bullet produced by the Remington Co.

**Corrosion.** The eating away of the bore of a rifle, handgun, or shotgun by rust caused by the action of salts from the powder or primer, which is increased with an increase in humidity.

**Couple.** Two woodcock, snipe, waterfowl, shorebirds, or rabbits. (British.) Also used to describe two hounds.

**Course.** To run by sight and not by nose. (Fox hunting.)

**Course.** The territory to be covered in the hunt. (Field trials.)

**Cover.** Vegetation. A certain area of wooded land to be hunted.

COVER DOG. Generally, a dog of close or limited range. (Field trials.)
COVERT. A place where fox may be found.
COVERTS. The feathers which cover the base of the flight feathers of birds.
COVEY. A group of game birds, generally a brood, such as quail; a bevy. Also (British), a single hatching of partridges.
COW. The female of bison, moose, caribou, and elk.
CRAMP. To force a dog's training.
CRAWLING (also called "creeping"). Allowing the hand that pulls the string back to creep forward just before loosing. (Archery.)
CRASH. When hounds give tongue all together upon finding a fox. (Fox hunting.)
CREANCE. A line wound on a stick for hawk training. (Falconry.)
CREEDMOOR TARGET. The early Creedmoor targets used in match-shooting were square and made with bull's-eyes of varying sizes for varied ranges. The "A" target had a bull's-eye 8" square, with a count of 4. This target was soon eliminated in favor of the round bull's-eye with a count of 5.
CREEP. *See* Trigger Creep.
CREST. A tuft on the head of a bird.
CRIMP. The forward portion of a cartridge case or shotshell, which is turned inward to grip the bullet—or, in the shotshell, to hold the end wad in place.
CRIPPLE. A game bird that has been shot down but not killed, normally employed in duck shooting. (In upland shooting, the term "winged" is used.)
CROPPER. A bad fall. (Fox hunting.)
CROSSBRED. A term denoting mixed ancestry, as a cross between two setter breeds.
CROSS HAIRS. The cross hairs of a good telescope sight are not hairs, but threads from the inner lining of the cocoon of the field spider, which measure approximately .001" in diameter. These threads are uniformly fine and very strong; also, they do not tend to break as a result of recoil.
CROSSING BIRD. A bird crossing directly in front of the shooter.
CROTCH-BUCK. A deer with antlers, at least one of which is forked.
CROTCH WALNUT. When used in reference to gunstocks, means a stock with fine figuring and feathering of the grain. Usually the blank was cut at the junction of two branches.
CRY. The voice of a hound. The cry of the hound varies at various stages of the chase. By its tone his mates can tell how strong the scent is and how sure he is of the line.
CUTTER. A hound which has become surly and will not hunt (called "cutting"). (Fox hunting.)
CUTTING BACK. A dog which casts back toward his handler is generally faulted for "cutting back." (Field trials.)
CYCLES. Periodic fluctuations in the populations of certain species of game birds and animals.
CYGNET. A young swan.

DAMASCUS BARRELS. Barrels made by forging iron or steel (or a combination of both) strips around a solid iron core to form a barrel. The strips are forged until they form a solid tube. Better-grade Damascus barrels are called "laminated" barrels. These barrels were not designed to withstand the great pressures created by modern smokeless powders.
DANGLE STICK (or *dingle stick*). A green branch, cut at a crotch, and about 1" in diameter, used as a pothook for use over the campfire.
DASH. Enthusiasm, spirit, quickness in action. (Field trials.)
DEFLECTION. The number of minutes of angle, right or left, to be adjusted by moving the rear sight, to compensate for the force and angle of the wind and the "drift" of the bullet.
DEN DOG. A hound which is especially determined at worrying the earth. His peculiar cry is of great assistance to the hunters in locating the spot at which the fox has gone to earth. (Fox hunting.)
DENSE POWDER. Smokeless powder normally colloided with nitroglycerine; it has more power and less bulk than black powder.
DERBY. A bird dog more than 18 months and less than 30 months of age.
DETERMINATION. The will to try and keep on trying. (Fox hunting.)
DIDELPHIDAE. The family to which opossums belong.
DISTANCE FLIGHT RECORD. The longest recorded flight ever made by a bird was that of an Arctic tern, which was banded at Turnevik Bay, Labrador, and was found at Margate on the east coast of Africa. The shortest distance between these points is 8000 miles.
DOG. A male dog.
DOG FOX. A male fox.
DOGGING DEER. Driving deer, not necessarily with the aid of dogs.
DOG HOUND. A male hound.
DOUBLE. Any shotgun with two barrels, whether the standard double-barreled gun or the over-and-under.
Also, when the fox turns short back on his course. (Fox hunting.)
DOUBLE-BASE POWDER. Powder containing approximately 30% nitroglycerine, as opposed to "single base," which contains about half that amount. Double-base powder develops more heat and consequently causes more barrel erosion than single base.
DOUBLES. The killing of two birds with two shots, or the breaking of two clay birds which are thrown from the trap simultaneously.
DOUGHNUT TARGET. A round target butt made of straw to which the target face is secured. (Archery.)
DRAG. The scent left by the fox as he returns to his den; or an artificial trail. (Fox hunting.)
DRAG HOUNDS. Hounds used to run an artificial trail.
DRAM. A unit of measurement of weight, which is the equivalent of 27.5 grains. There are 256 drams in one pound avoirdupois.
DRAW. The manner in which the string is held when drawing or pulling the string back, just before shooting an arrow; sometimes called the "loose." (Archery.)
DRAWING. The process of moving up to locate game; also called roading. (Field trials.)
DRIFT. The deviation of any projectile from the plane of its departure, caused by the rotation of the bullet.
DRIVING. A method of hunting in which the hunters are divided into two groups. One group moves to an area for distribution to points covering a wide terrain; the other group moves toward the first, making sufficient noise to frighten or drive the game ahead of it and toward the group on watch. The individuals on watch are termed "standers," those driving the game, "drivers."
DROP. The distance below the line of sight of a rifle or shotgun from an extension of this line to the comb and to the heel.
DROPPER. A cross between a pointer and a setter.
DROP TO SHOT. Dropping to the ground as the shot is fired. (Field trials.)
DRY FIRING. A form of shooting practice in which all the motions of actual firing are followed, but with an unloaded firearm.
DUMDUM. The original "dumdum" bullet was originated about 1895, and was the 215-grain jacketed .303 British army bullet, which was altered by filing off the point. This caused the bullet to break up on impact, inflicting a terrible wound. The bullet was outlawed for military use at the Hague conference of 1899. Several types of "expanding" bullets have been incorrectly termed "dumdum" bullets.
DUSKING. The dusk or early evening shooting of waterfowl, now illegal. Waterfowl or shorebirds were shot when outlined against the light western sky.
DWELLING. Lingering on the scent after the pack has gone ahead. (Fox hunting.)

EARTH. The hole of some burrowing animal, such as a woodchuck, appropriated by a fox.
ECLIPSE PLUMAGE. The plumage of a male bird before the time when he takes on his full plumage.
ELEVATION. The number of minutes of angle which the rear sight must be raised or lowered to compensate for the trajectory of the bullet and insure the desired point of impact at varied ranges.
ELIGIBLE. A dog is eligible to registration in the various stud books when he comes from registered ancestry or possesses a certified pedigree.
END OF ARROWS. Six arrows. (Archery.)
ENERGY. The amount of work or force which a bullet with a given charge can perform, expressed in foot-pounds.
ENTER. When young hounds are first put in a pack they are said to be "entered."
EOCENE AGE. The major subdivision of the Tertiary Age, prior to the Oligocene Age. Also the term used for the period preceding the Miocene Age.
ERETHIZONTIDAE. The family to which the porcupine belongs.

EROSION. The wearing away of the bore of a rifle, handgun, or shotgun as a result of the friction of bullets, shot, or powder gases.

EVEN-TOED UNGULATES. Hoofed mammals having an even number of toes on the hoof. The sub-order of *Artiodactyla,* such as deer, elk, antelope, etc.

EXALTATION. A flock or group of larks. (British.)

EXOTIC. Any game bird which has been imported from another country.

EXTERNAL (or *exterior)* BALLISTICS. The movement of the bullet after it leaves the barrel.

EXTRACTION GROOVE. A groove just forward of the base of a cartridge, permitting the extractor on the rifle to withdraw the cartridge from the chamber for ejection.

FALSE MUZZLE. An attachment for use on the muzzle-loading rifle. Actually a 2" length of barrel, fitted with four pins at the base. The pins fit four holes drilled into the end of the barrel, causing the bore of the false muzzle to line up with the bore of the rifle. The grooves and lands of the false muzzle meet those of the barrel. The bullet is placed in the false muzzle and a plunger or "starter" is struck with the heel of the hand, thus starting the bullet in the barrel of the rifle without deformation.

FALSE-POINTER. A dog which frequently points unproductively. (Field trials.)

FARQUHARSON. A falling-block rifle action, made in England, used in some single-shot match rifles.

FAULT. A check, an interruption in the run caused by loss of scent. (Fox hunting.)

FEATHER. The long hair on the setter's legs.

FELIDAE. Members of the cat family.

FIELD DRESSING. The minimum dressing out of a game animal in the field, merely enough to insure preservation of the meat and trophy.

FIELD OF VIEW. The width of the area which may be viewed through the telescope or binocular at varied ranges. The greater the magnification, the smaller the field of view.

FIGURE. In reference to gunstocks, this means the irregular waving, mottling, or variation of color of the wood. Cross-grain areas, firm knots, burls, or rays all are classified as "figuring."

FIND. When hounds first smell the line of the fox, they are said to "find." (Fox hunting.)

FINGERTIPS. Separate stalls for each of the three fingers—used for same purpose as shooting tab. (Archery.)

FINISHED. Thoroughly trained; broken. (Field trials.)

FIRE. Dash, enthusiasm, spirit. (Field trials.)

FIRELIGHTING. *See* Jacklighting.

FLAG. The tail of a deer, often all of the animal that is seen by a careless hunter.

FLAG. The long hair on a setter's tail.

FLAREBACK. Any bow that is concave on the back when it is unstrung. (Archery.)

FLAT TRAJECTORY. A term used to describe certain high-velocity, specially designed bullets, which travel for a long distance at a *flatter* or *lower arc* than other bullets of lower velocity. Scientifically an incorrect term, for no trajectory is truly *flat.* (For an example see "Development of the .220 Swift," p. 742.)

FLETCHER. One who fletches an arrow. (Archery.)

FLETCHING. Putting feathers on an arrow. (Archery.)

FLINCHING. A nervous reaction afflicting some shooters, which usually results in inaccurate shooting. The origin of flinching is often difficult to ascertain, but excessive recoil and muzzle-blast are among the major causes for the formation of this bad shooting habit. Also (Archery), the movement of either or both hands in the act of loosing the string.

FLING. Generally a period of aimless running before the enthusiastic dog settles to hunting. (Field trials.)

FLINTLOCK. A gun lock which superseded the wheellock. A piece of flint contained in the jaws of the hammer falls against a rough iron or steel surface, causing sparks to be directed into the pan containing priming powder, thus igniting the powder train to the charge.

FLOCK. A flight, group, or collection of teal. Also used generally to indicate a flight of several birds.

FLUSH. To cause game birds to fly. The rise of game birds.

FLUSHING WILD. The flush of game birds which have not been obviously or deliberately disturbed.

FLY CAMP. A temporary camp set up some distance from the base camp.

FLYWAY. The migration route of birds from the nesting and breeding grounds to the wintering grounds, and return.

FOOT-SCENT. Scent emanating from the feet of game birds.

FOOT-SECONDS. A term used to designate the speed of bullets, the number preceding the term indicating the number of feet the bullet travels per second.

FORE-END. That portion of the wooden gunstock forward of the receiver and under the barrel, which serves as a grip for the shooter.

FRAME. The wooden framework to which a target is tacked or stapled.

FRESH LINE. Opposite of "cold line"—a fresh or "hot" scent of game.

FULL CRY. The chorus of the pack. (Fox hunting.)

FULVOUS. Tawny, or yellow-brown.

GAGGLE. A flock or group of geese. (British.)

GAIN TWIST. A method of rifling a barrel in which the length of the twist of the rifling is not constant, but decreases as it approaches the muzzle. For example, the twist in the rifling may be one turn in 16" at the breech and one turn in 14" at the muzzle.

GAIT. The manner of movement. (Field trials.)

GAME. Upland game birds. (Field trials.) Also, any creature or creatures hunted for food or sport.

GANG. A flock or group of brant. Also (British), a group of elk.

GAS-OPERATED. Any firearm which utilizes the gases generated by the powder explosion, before the bullet emerges from the muzzle, to operate a piston which extracts, ejects, and reloads the arm to the extent of the number of rounds in the magazine.

GASPIPE. A colloquial term for the single-barreled shotgun, autoloader, or slide-action shotgun.

GAUGE. A term used to designate the bore of a shotgun. The number of the gauge has no relation to the linear measurement of the bore. Gauge is determined by the number of perfect spheres which may be obtained from one pound of lead. For example: a 12-gauge gun has a bore diameter the same as one of the 12 perfect spheres which could be made from a pound of lead. If 20 perfect spheres are made from one pound of lead, the diameter of one of these spheres would be the same as the diameter of the 20-gauge gun. (*See* Bore.)

GAUGE MEASUREMENTS. The bore diameters of various gauges are as follows:

| | |
|---|---|
| 10 gauge | .775" |
| 12 gauge | .725" |
| 16 gauge | .662" |
| 20 gauge | .615" |
| 28 gauge | .550" |
| .410 gauge | .410" |

GESTATION. The period covering the formation, growth, and birth of the young of any animal.

GLASS. To look over terrain with binoculars or a telescope to locate game.

GRAIN. Weight measurement. One ounce is the equivalent of 437.5 grains. There are 7000 grains in 1 pound.

GRAIN. In reference to gunstocks, this means the direction of the fibers on the surface of the stock. Stocks are taken from planks that are both "plain" sawed and "quarter" sawed. The plain sawing is to be preferred.

GRAM. A weight measurement, the equivalent of 15.43 grains.

GRAND AMERICAN HANDICAP. The national trapshooting tournament, held at Vandalia, Ohio.

GRAZE. Grasses, weeds, and similar low growths upon which deer and other ruminants feed.

GRAZER. A game animal which feeds primarily on graze (as opposed to a browser).

GREGARIOUS. Having a tendency to gather in large groups, or to avoid being alone.

GRIP. That part of the stock of a rifle or shotgun which is grasped by the trigger hand when firing the gun.

GROUND CLOTH. A light waterproof cloth used as a "flooring" in several types of tents. Also any waterproof cloth used under a camp bed or sleeping bag to prevent the penetration of moisture.

GROUND QUIVER. Any receptacle that holds the arrows in place when resting on the ground. Used only by target archers.

GROUND-WORK. The manner in which a dog works a given area, irrespective of game found. (Field trials.)

GROUP. A series of shots fired at a target with a constant sight setting and point of aim. The diameter of the group is measured from the centers of the outer holes.

GROUP DIAMETER. The distance between centers of the two shots most widely separated in a group.

GRUB. Outdoorsmen's colloquialism which includes food of all kinds.

GUN CRANK. An individual who is primarily interested in the extreme of accuracy possible with any rifle or handgun and is not particularly interested in shooting in competition or at game.

GUN-DOG. A shooting dog.

GUN-SHY. Afraid of the report of a gun.

HABITAT. The environment in which an animal or bird finds conditions satisfactory for a normal existence.

HACKED. Term for a dog which has been habitually restricted in speed and range. (Field trials.)

HAIR TRIGGER. A trigger requiring only extremely light pressure for the release of the hammer.

HALSBAND. A silk cord tied to a hawk's neck, used for throwing the hawk to a quick getaway. (Falconry.)

HAND-LAPPING. The process of lapping or polishing the bore of a rifle, to insure the maximum smoothness. Accomplished by means of a rotating metal plug and an extremely fine abrasive suspended in oil.

HANDLING. Responding to the trainer's commands, signals, and directions. (Field trials.)

HANDLOADS. Cartridges loaded by hand for precision shooting; as opposed to "factory loads" which may vary minutely in powder charge and in exactness of bullet seating.

HANG-FIRE. Delayed explosion of the powder in a cartridge after the hammer has fallen and the primer struck. This happens rarely, but can cause serious injury if the breech of the arm is opened immediately after a cartridge has failed to fire. Instances have been recorded in which there was a time-lag of several seconds between the falling of the hammer and the explosion of the powder charge.

HARD-HEADED. Headstrong; hard to control. (Field trials.)

HARD-MOUTHED. A dog which chews or crushes his birds when retrieving. (Field trials.)

HART. The male of a member of the deer family. (European.)

HEADED. When the fox is forced to turn back. (Fox hunting.)

HEADED TO DEATH. When the fox is unfairly killed by being headed. (Fox hunting.)

HEAD SPACE. The space between the head of the bolt or breechblock and the base of the cartridge. Excessive headspace is exceedingly dangerous, and can result in the bursting of the receiver. If, after firing, you note a swelling or crack in the cartridge case immediately above the base, have the headspace of the firearm checked by a reliable gunsmith. Great care should be used in the assembling of takedown rifles or shotguns to insure that the barrel makes a tight junction with the receiver. Late models insure the proper fit, but a few early models may be assembled without a tight junction, which will result in excess headspace. This can be fatal.

HEADSTAMP. The letters or number, or both, on the base of a cartridge.

HEAT. The length of the period in which the dog is hunted in training or field trials. (Field trials.) "In heat" refers to that period in which a bitch is willing to breed, or is said to be "in season."

HEATH HEN. The *Tympanuchus cupido*, also known as the eastern prairie chicken, greatly resembling the present pinnated grouse, once plentiful along the Atlantic seaboard but now extinct. At the turn of the century a few birds were located on the eastern tip of Long Island and on Martha's Vineyard, but had completely disappeared by 1920.

HEEL. The upper part of the butt of a shotgun or rifle. Also, to walk quietly by the side or at the heel of the trainer or handler. (Field trials.)

HERD. A group of bison, deer, stags, moose, caribou.

HIDE. The *skin* of any animal, as opposed to *pelage*, which is the skin WITH the fur, hair, bristles, or wool.

HIGH INTENSITY. A term designating any rifle or cartridge having a velocity of more than 2500 foot-seconds.

HIGH POWER. A term used to designate a rifle or cartridge having a velocity of more than 2000 foot-seconds.

HIND. The female of the red deer. (European.)

HOCK. The joint found on the hind legs of some animals, similar to the ankle joint on humans, but reversed.

HOGLEG. The Colt Frontier Model revolver. (Southwestern U. S.)

HONING. A process of honing or polishing the sear and sear notch of a firearm to insure a smooth, or lighter, release of the hammer. A fine oilstone, well lubricated, should be employed, and care taken that the pull is not too greatly reduced by over-honing.

HONKER. The Canada goose.

HOOD. A head covering (blinder) for a hawk, kept on until the hawk is to be unleashed. (Falconry.)

HORNET. The .22 Hornet is a high-velocity cartridge developed by several designers, introduced as a factory load by Winchester. It originated from a .22 WCF cartridge.

HORNS. Hollow, excrescent, hard growths on the head of a mammal, normally unbranched, permanently attached, and present on both the male and female.

HULL. A cartridge or shell—sometimes the term is used only when the cartridge or shell has been fired.

HUNTING. Searching for game. (Field trials.)

HURDLE. A group of three hounds. (British.)

IGNITION TIME. The time involved between the impact of the hammer or firing pin on the primer and the formation of sufficient powder gases to start the bullet up the barrel.

IMPING NEEDLE. A double-pointed needle used in repairing damaged feathers. (Falconry.)

INCOMERS. Birds approaching the shooter from the front, either high overhead or low.

INDECISIVE POINT. One in which positiveness is lacking. (Field trials.)

INDEPENDENCE. Initiative. (Field trials.)

INDIAN WALKER. A term still employed in some parts of the country to indicate a good woodsman or one who can cover much distance through the woods in a day. Originated in early colonial times when colonists bargained for land grants of "as much land as a man can encircle on foot in one day." Colonists then blazed the route and employed the fastest walker in the area to do the walking.

INSTRUMENTAL VELOCITY. The velocity of a bullet measured at some definite point ahead of the muzzle of the rifle.

INSULATED BULLET. A bullet designed by Charles Newton. A paper lining between the jacket and the lead core protected the core against the intense heat generated by friction during the passage through the bore.

INTERNAL (or *interior*) BALLISTICS. The movement of the bullet before it leaves the barrel.

IVER-JOHNSON ARMS & CYCLE CO., Fitchburg, Mass.

JACKLIGHTING. The illegal practice of killing game at night by means of artificial light, which is reflected by the eyes of the game. Jacklighting or "firelighting" accounts for a large deer kill each year and undoubtedly loses more sleep for game wardens than any other illegal practice.

JESS. Leg strap for a falcon. (Falconry.)

JOHNSON AUTOMATICS, INC., Providence, R. I.

JUDAS DUCK. A live decoy—when the use of live decoys was permissible.

JUMP SHOOTING. A form of hunting upland game birds or animals without a dog. Also, a method of duck hunting, in which the hunter drifts downstream in a boat, getting occasional shots when ducks are frightened into flight at his approach, or in which the hunter is poled through a marsh, flushing the birds ahead of the boat.

JUVENILE. A bird which, though having attained full growth, has not attained full adult characteristics or plumage.

KEEPER. A small string that keeps the bowstring in place when the bow is unstrung. (Archery.)

KENNEBAGO LIGHTNING. An extremely potent but highly potable drink concocted in northern Maine.

KENNEL. Shelter for a dog or dogs.

KENNEL-BREAKER. A dog which attempts to escape from his kennel.

KENTUCKY WINDAGE. A term used by riflemen to describe the process of "holding off" to the left or right of a target to allow for the effect of the wind on the bullet, but making no change in the sight.

KEYHOLE. A term used to describe the tumbling or end-over-end movement of a bullet in flight, which, when passing through the target, makes an elongated hole resembling a keyhole.

**Kid**. The young of the antelope and the goat.

**Killick**. A term used in parts of New England and eastern Canada for a small anchor, or a stone used as an anchor.

**Killing Power**. The ability of a bullet to destroy tissue and deliver shock. This is determined by the velocity, weight, energy, rotation speed, shape, design, and sectional density of the bullet—not by any one but by all of these factors.

**Lady Paramount**. Official judge at target tournaments for women. (Archery.)

**Laminated Barrels**. *See* Damascus Barrels.

**Laminated Case**. A cartridge case which shows places where the metal has separated. *Do not use such a case.*

**Lands**. The raised portions between the grooves of a rifled barrel.

**Lapping**. *See* Hand-Lapping.

**Lap-Weld**. A type of welding employed by gunsmiths in making early rifle barrels, in which a strip of flat bar iron was hammered around a core until it overlapped, then welded and smoothed.

**Lay**. In reference to game birds, the act of remaining still.

**Lead**. A term used to designate the amount of distance it is necessary to hold ahead of any game bird or animal to compensate for the speed of the target and the time required for the bullet or shot charge to reach the target.

**Lead**. To cause a dog to follow under restraint. Also, a cord or leather attached to the dog's collar by which he can be restrained.

**Leading**. Small particles of lead or bullet metal torn off as a bullet passes through the bore; these particles adhere to the bore. With jacketed bullets, it is termed "metal fouling."

**Leash**. A group of three quail, partridge, pheasant, grouse, or hares.

**Lee Straight Pull**. The U. S. Navy Model 1895 6-mm. or .236, invented by J. P. Lee. A box-magazine, clip-fed, high-velocity rifle, employing a rimless cartridge with a 112-grain copper-jacketed bullet. The bolt was so cammed that a pull rearward on the bolt handle uncammed the action, extracted and ejected the cartridge. The bolt and cam were so designed that the recoil shoulder securely locked the bolt in place.

**Leporidae**. The family which includes hares and rabbits.

**Limbs of Bow**. The two portions of the bow above and below the handle. (Archery.)

**Line**. The track or trail of the quarry, indicated by scent. (Fox hunting.)

**Line of Sight**. The *straight* line between the eye of the shooter and the target, as opposed to the trajectory, which is the curving path of the bullet, and the line of the bore, which normally is at a more acute angle upward to compensate for the trajectory of the bullet.

**Line-Running**. Casting in straight lines rather than hunting all the birdy places. (Field trials.)

**Line Shooting**. A form of scoter or "coot" shooting employed along the Atlantic coast. Several boats line up a gunshot apart across a known scoter flyway for pass shooting at the birds.

**Litter**. The collective young of one animal born at the same time.

**Live Weight**. The computed weight of a deer before it is dressed out. The computation is based on the following: A dressed deer normally weighs .78612 of its live weight; or, to put it more simply, it weighs approximately 21% less after being dressed.

**Lob Tree**. A tree used as a marker in designating a portage, trail, or good camp site. Tree usually is trimmed of branches except at the extreme tip.

**Lock Time**. The time involved between the release of the hammer by the sear and the impact of the firing pin on the primer.

**Loftiness**. A quality of high action in the field or high attitude on point. (Field trials.)

**Logan**. A lowland swamp or watery bog. (New England.)

**Long Rifle**. Term designating a .22-caliber cartridge developed by Col. W. A. Tewes of the Peters Cartridge Co., now manufactured by all munition companies. Average bullet weight is 40 grains, velocities from 1000 to 1400 foot-seconds.

**Loosing**. Letting the string go, or turning the string loose in the act of shooting. (Archery.)

**Loping**. Deviation of an arrow up and down on its flight in the air. (Archery.)

**Loss**. When hounds can no longer follow the scent they have come to a "loss." (Fox hunting.)

**Lure**. Any object, live or inanimate, used to attract an animal, bird, or fish. *See especially use of lures in* "Falconry."

**Machine Rest**. A device employed to check barrel or bullet accuracy, which holds the firearm in a firm, steady cradle for test firing.

**Magazine**. The tube, box, or container which holds cartridges or shells in position for mechanical insertion into the chamber of a repeating firearm.

**Magazine Plug**. A wooden plug or dowel placed inside the magazine spring of a slide-action shotgun to limit the capacity of the magazine in order to comply with the law. Under Federal law regarding the shooting of migratory birds, no shotgun may have a maximum capacity of more than three shells. If three shells can be forced into the magazine the gun is illegal, as this would permit a fourth shell to be inserted in the chamber.

**Maggie's Drawers**. A term used in target shooting to indicate that the shooter completely missed the target.

**Magnum**. When used in reference to a rifle, shotgun, or load, it refers to a high-speed, high-power, or high-velocity arm or cartridge. The majority of the "magnum" rifles or shotguns are designed to withstand the increased pressures which magnum loadings produce. Fortunately, most of the magnum cartridges are readily recognizable, as they are larger in diameter than the standard cartridges for the firearm of similar caliber which is designed for the standard load.

**Mailed**. Said of a hawk bound for immobility. (Falconry.)

**Manners**. The actions of a dog on point and at the flush and shot. The thoroughly broken dog displays "perfect manners."

**Mark**. A term used to warn another shooter of the flushing or approach of a game bird. The term often is supplemented by a direction, such as "mark right" or "mark left."

**Mark Down**. A term designating the use of some terrain feature to mark the location of a fallen game bird in order to facilitate retrieving it.

**Market Gunner**. One who hunted for the purpose of selling the game he killed. Now illegal.

**Markings**. Spots or patches of color on a dog's body.

**Mark to Ground**. When the fox has been run to earth, and the hounds give the peculiar cry known as the "den bark." (Fox hunting.)

**Mask**. The fox's head or pate.

**M.F.H.** Master of Fox Hounds.

**Maximum Ordinate**. The summit or highest point in the trajectory of a bullet. This summit, contrary to popular belief, is not near the center of the trajectory, but is beyond the center.

**Meat Dog**. A term generally applied to the slow, methodical plodder which can find and handle birds, but whose work does not approach brilliancy.

**Mechanical Dog**. One which has been placed under such restraint in training that he has become entirely dependent upon the trainer for instructions, or which quarters the ground in the same methodical way always. (Field trials.)

**Meet**. The rendezvous of those who will take part in the hunt. (Fox hunting.)

**Melanistic**. A term used by biologists to indicate an abnormal black plumage.

**Merry**. Quick, snappy, lively, attractive. (Field trials.)

**M.C.** A term designating a bullet with a metal case, in which the entire bullet is encased.

**Mid-Range**. A point midway between the muzzle and the impact point. Also used to designate a lighter-than-standard powder load.

**Migratory Game Birds**. Doves, pigeons, woodcock, rail, sora, and similar migratory birds other than waterfowl.

**Millimeter**. A metric-system measurement commonly employed in Europe. Most European rifles are described by millimeters (mm.) rather than by caliber. A millimeter equals .03937". The American .30 caliber rifle, for example, is of approximately the same bore diameter as the European 8-mm. rifle, which has a bore diameter of .314960, or slightly larger than .30 caliber.

**Mil Scale**. A scale etched on the left eyepiece of some binoculars, to aid in computing angles and judging range. The average scale is marked off by fine vertical lines, 5 mils high and 5 mils apart. For example, an object 5′ high if seen from a point 1000′ distant would measure 5 mils. The mil is a unit of angular measure.

MINIÉ. An early cylindro-conoidal bullet developed by Captain Minié, a French ordnance officer.
MINUTE OF ANGLE. The scale on a rear sight is graduated with fine lines, each one a *minute* of angle. In other words, the elevation of the rear sight 1 minute will raise the point of impact of the bullet 1″ at 100 yds., ½″ at 50 yds., ¼″ at 25 yds. Some click adjustments require four clicks to change the elevation 1 minute; therefore each click represents a quarter-minute of angle.
MIXING BOX. The typical duckboat used along the upper Mississippi River. Pointed at bow and stern, the hull normally is formed of three boards, and is partially decked over at bow and stern.
MOB. To surround and kill a fox without giving him a chance to run. (Fox hunting.)
MOCCASIN. A snake of the pit viper family, found in the southern lakes, streams and swamps. Its venom is fatal if injected in sufficient quantity into the bloodstream.
MOOSE BIRD *(Perisoreus canadensis)*, also known as whiskey jack, camp robber, and Canada jay. A member of the jay family with dark gray plumage; it has little fear of man and gathers in camps to steal bits of food.
MORAINE. The jumble of boulders, stones, and earth left by the withdrawal of a glacier.
MOUTHY. A hound that gives tongue falsely. (Fox hunting.)
MUSH. A term used in the north meaning to walk; also a command given to a dog team to start them forward.
MUSHROOM. The tendency of a bullet to expand upon impact and penetration; the bullet's shape becomes similar to that of a mushroom.
MUSKEG. A flat, lowland marsh or swamp, some of which can be negotiated only when frozen over. *See* Logan.
MUSTELIDAE. The family which includes the badger, marten, mink, otter, skunk, weasel, and wolverine.
MUSTER. A group of peacocks.
MUTE. When a hound does not open up on trail. (Fox hunting.)
MUZZLE BANDAGE. An aid to quick gun pointing for those who use a single-barrel shotgun. Several turns of ¾″ adhesive tape are made around the muzzle, just behind the front sight. As the gun comes up this bandage catches the eye.
MUZZLE BRAKE. A device for the muzzle of a shotgun or rifle which, by means of vents and baffles, deflects gases to the rear, thus reducing recoil.
MUZZLE ENERGY (M.E.). A term designating the muzzle energy of a bullet, i.e., the capacity of the bullet for striking a blow of a certain force (designated in foot-pounds).
MUZZLE VELOCITY. The estimated speed of a bullet at the point of departure from the bore of the rifle, or the velocity of the charge of shot as it emerges from the muzzle. (Expressed in foot-seconds.)

N.R.A. National Rifle Assn., 1600 Rhode Island Ave., Washington, D. C.
N.S.S.A. National Skeet Shooting Assn., 816 Barr Bldg., Washington, D. C.
N.M.L.A. National Muzzle-Loading Assn., Portsmouth, Ohio.
NATURAL INSTINCTS. Those inborn qualities characteristic of the bird dog.
NECK. The forward part of a cartridge case, normally smaller in diameter than the base of the cartridge; it serves as a sleeve to hold the bullet.
NIDE. A single hatching of pheasants. (British.)
NIPPLE. The short tube extending from the powder chamber on which is placed the percussion cap which ignites the powder in a muzzle-loading arm.
NOCK. The groove in each end of the bow into which the loops of the bowstring are fitted. Also, the notched end of the arrow that fits onto the string. (Archery.)
NOCKING POINT. The spot on the string where the nock of the arrow is fitted on the string. Many archers wrap another service below or above this point, to make it easier to nock the arrow. (Archery.)
NONMERCURIC PRIMER. A primer that does not contain fulminate of mercury, an agent employed in early primers which had a highly corrosive effect on bores.
NORTH CANOE. A large freight canoe used in parts of Canada, formerly used by *voyageurs* in bringing out fur catches.
NOSE. The ability to smell game birds.
NO-SEE-UMS. Tiny midges or gnats able to penetrate the finest mosquito bars.
NUTCRACKER. A name sometimes applied to the early, single-ball bullet mold.
NYROCINAE. The sub-family of diving ducks, sea ducks, or bay ducks.

OBEDIENT. Quick response to the trainer's commands. (Field trials.)
OCELLATED. A term for eye-like markings on birds.
ODD-TOED UNGULATES. Hoofed mammals having an odd number (one) of toes on the hoof. The sub-order of *Perissodactyla* (such as horses, tapirs).
OFFHAND. The standing position in shooting, without the use of a rest or sling, in which the left arm is pressed to the side, the weight of the rifle resting on the thumb and the tips of the fingers. This is not to be confused with the "standing" position, in which the left arm is partially extended with the left hand grasping the fore-end of the rifle.
OLIGOCENE AGE. A period or epoch, part of the Tertiary Age, between the Eocene and the Miocene Ages.
OLYMPIC RULE. This is the rule laid down by the International Olympic Committee concerning the definition of "amateur," regarding shooters: "Competitors whose connection with the sport is for pleasure and recreation and not for material gain may be certified as amateurs. Rifle and pistol competition has, in the past, afforded no shooter sufficient prize money which might be termed 'material gain.'" No definite sum is specified which would result in the disqualification of a shooter.
OMNIVOROUS. Descriptive adjective for a mammal which will eat both vegetable and animal matter.
O.P.E. Abbreviation for the open-point expanding bullet.
ORNITHOLOGY. The study of birds. (Ornithologist.)
OUTLAW. An individual who tends to ignore the game laws.
OVAL RIFLING. A method of rifling employing only two shallow but wide grooves, initiated in 1830 and employed around 1900 by Charles Newton, outstanding American ballistician.

PACE. The rate of speed at which a dog hunts.
PACK. A group of wolves. Also (fox hunting), a number of hounds hunted together regularly. Also (British), a group or flock of grouse.
PALMATED. A term used to describe the shape of the antlers of moose or caribou, similar to the shape of the palm of a hand with fingers outspread.
PALMETTO BUGGY. A converted Model A Ford used in hunting quail on the Florida palmetto barrens.
PALM REST. A short rod fixed to the fore-end of a rifle by means of a flexible coupling, at the end of which is a small wooden ball or rounded disk about 3″ in diameter. Normally used only in Schützen matches. In using the palm rest, the shooter rests his left elbow on his hip and holds the ball or disk in his left hand. This permits steadier holding than is possible by the conventional grasp of the fore-end of the rifle.
PARADOX BULLET. A bullet developed by British ballisticians just before 1900, for use on African big game. It was made in 8, 9, and 10 *bore* sizes and embodied a mushroom-shaped steel core covered with lead, cylindro-conoidal in shape. The bullet weighed about 1100 grains.
PARTRIDGE. A name loosely applied to various members of the grouse family, as well as to the various quails. More properly applied only to the Hungarian partridge and the chukar partridge, both imported from other countries.
PASSENGER PIGEON *(Ectopistes migratorius)*. This bird at one time numbered in the billions on this continent, has been extinct since about 1900. Flights of these wild pigeons more than a mile wide and estimated to be 300 miles long were seen during the early 19th century. The market in squabs, taken from the nests, was one of the factors responsible for the decline. Michigan reported the last flight of these birds in 1900.
PASS SHOOTING. A form of waterfowl shooting in which the hunter places himself in position under a known flyway or travel route of the ducks, and which does not require the use of decoys.
PATCH BOX. A container or pocket, usually with an ornate hinged cover, inletted into the stock of early muzzle-loaders, designed to contain the bullet patches.
PATCHED. A term originally applied to the bullet used in a muzzle-loading rifle. A cloth patch enclosed the bullet, which served as a greater gas seal and caused the bullet to flatten at the base and expand in the grooves while moving up the barrel, thus insuring greater velocity and accuracy. Now applied to any jacketed bullet.

PATTERN. The pattern of the shot made by one shot shell at a given range.

PATTERN CONTROL. Control of the shot pattern by means of choke.

PEABODY-MARTINI ACTION. A rifle action designed by Peabody and Martini around 1880. This was a hammerless, tilting block action, and was favored by many exacting match shooters. It was and is a fine action, and many are in use today on singleshot match rifles.

PELAGE. The coat or covering of a mammal, such as hair, fur, bristles, or wool.

PELLET. The round shot or pellet, of any size, a given number of which make up the shot charge.

PEMMICAN. A form of concentrated food, originally made of beans, corn, and dried meat, mixed and compressed in a roll, which served as trail rations for the Indian. Several forms of pemmican are now on the market.

PERCUSSION. *See* Cap.

PEREGRINE. A species of hawk used in falconry.

PETTICOAT. That small portion of a target face outside of the scoring area. (Archery.)

PINWHEEL. A bullet hole in what appears to be the exact center of the bull's-eye.

PIN-WHEELER. An arrow that has hit dead center of the bull's-eye. (Archery.)

PITTMAN-ROBERTSON ACT. A Federal law through which an 11% excise tax is levied on the sale of sporting arms and ammunition. The fund thus obtained is appropriated, in part or in full, each year for apportionment among the states for the development and restoration of wildlife resources. Apportionment is made on the basis of the number of huting licenses issued by the state.

PISTOL. A name originally applied to a gun which could be fired with one hand, but which later became a conflicting term. In modern usage, any magazine-fed handgun, other than a handgun employing a cylindrical magazine, or any single-shot handgun, is termed a "pistol." The handgun employing a cylindrical magazine is termed a "revolver."

PISTON. As applied to automatic or semi-automatic arms, a metal plunger activated by the powder gases which, when forced down a cylinder, operates a mechanism which extracts and ejects the fired cartridge, reloads and cocks the arm.

PIT. A depression, caused either by corrosion or fouling, similar to a small pockmark, in the bore of a rifle or shotgun. Also (shooting), the deep trench or pit in which the target markers stand while marking and patching targets.

PITCH. The angle of the barrel of a rifle or shotgun off the angle of the stock.

PIT SIGNALS. The signals given from the pit at a range, indicating the scoring of the shot:

White disk moved across bull's-eye—hit in X-ring.

White disk held in front of the bull's-eye—hit in 10-ring.

Red disk held just below bull's-eye—hit in 9-ring.

Black disk with white cross held below bull's-eye—hit in 8-ring.

Black disk held below bull's-eye—hit in 7-ring.

Black disk with white cross moved across face of bull's-eye —hit in 6-ring.

Black disk moved across the face of bull's-eye—hit in 5-ring.

Red flag waved across front of target—missed the target.

PLEISTOCENE. The epoch or age which followed the Tertiary age; it preceded the present age.

PLINKER. Any light .22 caliber rifle.

PLUG SHOOTING DOG. One whose manners are acceptable but whose performance fails to measure up to high standards.

PLUMP. A flock or group of ducks. (British.) A smaller number of birds than a "team" (*q.v.*).

POCKET HUNTING. Seeking game in isolated terrain pockets, small areas in which certain groups or types will confine their range and which are off the beaten track.

POINT. The motionless pose assumed by the dog which indicates the proximity of game birds.

POINTER. One of the larger, smooth-haired hunting-dog breeds, which hunts by scent and indicates the location of the game by assuming a rigid stance and "pointing" with its head.

POINTING OUT. A method of shotgun shooting in which the shooter selects a point ahead of the moving target at which to shoot, selecting this as the point at which the shot charge and target will meet. Opposed to "swinging past" (*q.v.*).

POINT OF AIM. The bottom edge of the bull's-eye for the target shooter, using iron sights; the center of the bull's-eye for the shooter using a telescope sight.

POISON ASH. *See* Sumac.

POISON ELDER. *See* Sumac.

POISON IVY. A trailing ivy, the leaves of which are always in groups of three. Physical contact with the leaves of this plant is harmful to some individuals, causing a serious skin disorder which results in the emission of a fluid causing the disorder to spread to other parts of the body on contact. A variety of this plant is the *poison oak,* a small shrub, the leaves of which somewhat resemble oak leaves, are also in clusters of three. An emergency treatment is the smearing on of yellow laundry soap.

POISON OAK. *See* Poison Ivy.

POLYANDRY. Having more than one male mate at the same time.

POLYGAMY. Having more than one female mate at the same time.

PORTAGE. The carrying of supplies, equipment, and canoe from one stretch of navigable water to another; also termed "carry."

POSSUM SNIPE. The woodcock.

POT-HUNTER. One who hunts primarily for meat rather than for sport.

POTTERER. A dog which spends a good deal of his time on foot-scent or in nosing about where birds have been, or is unable to distinguish between old and fresh scent. (Field trials.)

PRAIRIE CHICKEN. The pinnated grouse.

PRECISION LOADS. Cartridges which have been handloaded with precise instruments and great care.

PREDATOR. An animal or bird which lives by preying upon other animals or birds.

PRESSURE. The outward pressure of the powder gases against the cartridge or shell case, chamber, and bore. This pressure usually is measured 1" from the breech of the arm and is designated in pounds per square inch.

PRESSURE GUN. An instrument which determines the pressures developed by any given load. A special gun is employed, which has a hole leading up to the chamber. A piston enters the powder chamber; upon receiving pressure from the powder gases, this is forced up the cylinder, compressing a small copper cylinder. The amount this copper cylinder is compressed is measured; then a similar copper cylinder is subjected to the pressure of increasing dead weight until it has been compressed to the same size. The weight required to equal this compression gives the amount of "pound pressure" of the load.

PRIMARIES. The outer and longest flight feathers of a bird; quill feathers.

PRIMER. Collective term for the primer cup, priming compound, and anvil, which, when struck by the hammer, ignites the powder of the cartridge or shell.

PROCYONIDAE. The family of the raccoons.

PROSPECT. An untrained dog.

PULL. The distance, in a straight line, from the face of the trigger to the center of the butt of the gunstock. Also, the amount of pressure, in pounds, which must be placed on the trigger to cause the sear to disengage and permit the hammer to fall.

PULL-BANG. A trap which throws clay targets.

PUMPKIN (PUNKIN) BALL. The solid ball, or the rifled slug, used in a shotgun for big-game hunting.

PUMP GUN. Common name for the slide-action rifle or shotgun; also called "corn sheller," "gas pipe," and "husker."

PUNCTURED PRIMER. A primer which has been penetrated by the firing pin.

PUPPY. A bird dog is known as a puppy until he reaches the age of 18 months.

QUARTERING. The act of ranging back and forth across the course. (Field trials.)

QUARTERING BIRD. A bird which approaches the shooter at an angle, either right or left.

QUIVER. Leather bag for carrying arrows. (Archery.)

RABBIT FUR TERMS. The fur of rabbits, when tanned and processed, is known by several names, including French seal, French beaver, beaverette, chapchilla, coney, cony, ermiline, erminette, marmotine, moline, near seal, polar seal, lapin, sealine, squirrellette, and squirrelline.

RACK. The antlers of a member of the deer family.

RAMP. A metal ramp, the top of which usually is checkered to prevent glare, holding the front sight. Widely used on tapered barrels.

RANGE. The distance a dog hunts from his handler. (Field trials).

RAT-TAILED. Lacking long hairs on the tail. (Fox hunting.)

RECEIVER. The frame of a rifle or shotgun including the breech, locking, and loading mechanism of the arm.

RECOIL-OPERATED. Any firearm which utilizes the recoil, or rearward force exerted by the explosion of the powder, to operate the action and extract, eject, and reload to the extent of the number of rounds in the magazine.

RECORDS. The records of North American game are preserved by the Boone and Crockett Club. Send detailed measurements, photographs, and other pertinent data to the Secretary, Boone and Crockett Club, American Museum of Natural History, New York City.

RECORD TARGET. The target with the bull's-eye at which the shooter fires, which is backed by a cardboard "backing target." The double target is used to eliminate argument in the event a shooter puts a shot on his neighbor's target. The holes on the record and backing target will match only when placed there by the correct shooter.

RECURVED TIPS. (Also known as "recurved ends"). Ends of a bow so built that they curve away from the belly of the bow. (Archery.)

REDUCED LOADS. Cartridges which have been loaded with a smaller than standard powder charge, for use at short ranges and primarily for target shooting.

REFUSE. When a horse refuses a jump or leap. (Fox hunting.)

REFUSAL TO BACK. Ignoring the brace-mate's point or refusing to stop until the scent of game birds registers. (Field trails.)

REGISTERING. Recording a dog's ancestry in a recognized or official stud book.

RETICULE (OR RETICLE). The crossed wires, picket, post, or other divisional system installed in front of the eyepiece of a telescope sight to permit its use as a gunsight, or in binoculars to permit the use of a a mil scale.

RETRIEVING. The bringing of an object to the handler. Generally applied to the finding and fetching of dead or wounded game birds.

REVOLVER. Any handgun employing a cylindrical magazine, as opposed to a single-shot or so-called "automatic" handgun, both of which are termed "pistols" (*q.v.*).

RIB. The vane or rib extending from the breech to the muzzle of a shotgun or rifle (also found on some revolvers), usually checkered to eliminate glare.

RIB-CAGE. The outer circumference of an animal's ribs.

RIFLE. Any long-barreled firearm, the bore of which is rifled (cut by two or more grooves which spiral from the breech to the muzzle), causing the projectile which is forced through the bore to rotate in its flight.

RIFLING. Parallel grooves cut into the bore of a rifle or pistol, spiraling from the breech to the muzzle, causing the bullet to rotate in its flight.

RIG. A setting of decoys in front of a boat or blind; also used to describe the entire outfit.

RIM-FIRE. A cartridge in which the priming compound is contained in a rim at the base of the cartridge.

RING HUNT. An early colonial form of driving game, in which a large number of shooters formed a ring, gradually closing in and driving the game toward the center. Still occasionally used for wolves, jack rabbits, and other "pest" animals.

RINGNECK. The ring-necked pheasant.

ROADING. Exercising a dog by leading him upon a road, path, or highway. Also, a method of locating game (*See* Drawing).

ROCK TRIPE. A lichen or moss adhering to rocks in the northern part of the continent; correct name *Umbilicaria,* or *Gyrophora.* Can be boiled and eaten but is not too palatable.

ROD. A measure of length, 5½ yds. or 16½'. In early shooting matches the rod was often used as range measurement.

ROLLING BLOCK. A rifle action with a rolling breechblock, first made by Remington and patented in 1863. It employed a rim-fire cartridge. This action also was called the "split breech" action.

ROTTENSTONE. A fine abrasive, mixed with oil or water for the smoothing of the surface of a gunstock prior to waxing or oiling.

ROUGH INLETTING. This term applies to a gunstock that has been shaped roughly to a design and size, roughly inletted for the barrel and action to be used, but still requires considerable fitting and finishing.

ROUND. One cartridge or one shot, or any single unit of ammunition. (Guns.)

A competition in which several arrows are directed at a target at varied stated ranges. *See* American Round. (Archery.)

ROYAL. The fourth point, after the *trez* and before the *fifth,* of antlers.

RUFOUS. Reddish-brown coloration.

RUPTURE. A swollen or cracked cartridge case, usually the sign of excessive head space.

RUN. A term used in some areas for a gametrail or path created by certain animals over a period of time.

RUTTING PERIOD. A period, normally beginning early in the fall, in which the male deer, elk, caribou, or moose seeks a mate or mates for breeding. Such an animal is described as "rutting" or "in rut," and usually is at the peak of physical condition.

SCAPULARS. The feathers on each side of the back of a bird on the shoulder.

SCATTERGUN. A shotgun. (Colloquial.)

SCENT. The odor given off by a fox. If it is so good that the hounds do not have to stoop to it, it is called "breast high." A "burning" scent is when it is strong or good; if it is variable, it is called "flighty"; if it is good enough but not very strong it is called a "holding" scent; when it is good and at the ground level it is known as "lying."

SCHUTZEN RIFLE. The single-shot match rifle with a heavy, ornate stock, special action and triggers, and unconventional buttplate. It is primarily designed for extremely accurate target shooting at medium ranges.

SCOOTER. A term used for the Long Island duckboat.

SCORING. When the whole pack speaks to the strong scent they are said to be "scoring." (Foxhunting.)

SECONDARIES. The wing feathers inside the primaries.

SECTIONAL DENSITY. The relation between the weight, length, and diameter of a bullet. (Ballistics.)

SEDGE. A plant of the *carex* family, a tall form of grass growing in marsh or swamp areas. Also, name for a flock of herons.

SEGMENTAL RIFLING. A type of rifling somewhat similar to "oval" rifling, except that the shallow grooves, segments of a circle, were five in number and resulted in the creation of lands. It produced an extremely smooth rifling and was easy to clean.

SELF-HUNTING. The dog which habitually leaves his kennel to go hunting without his master is a self-hunter. Also the dog which refuses to stay on the course but hunts other areas, ignoring his handler and hunting to suit himself.

SELF-LOADING. *See* Auto-loading.

SEMI-AUTOMATIC. Any firearm which will fire, extract, eject, and reload by means of pressure on the trigger, but requires pressure on the trigger to fire each round. In other words, this firearm requires a separate pressure on the trigger for the firing of each round, and will not continue to fire if the initial pressure on the trigger is maintained.

SERVICE. Section of string tightly wrapped around bowstring to protect bowstring from the nock of arrow. (Archery.)

SET. A "rig" or setting of decoys.

SETTLE. When hounds, coming from different directions to a hound that has indicated he has made a find, pick up the line and go away together they have "settled to the line." (Fox hunting.)

SETTER. One of the larger, long-haired, flat-coated hunting dog breeds, originally trained to "set" or crouch after it had located game, which hunts by scent and indicates the location of the game by assuming a rigid stance and pointing toward the game with its head.

SET TRIGGER. A trigger, the sear of which is "set up" by pressure on another trigger, permitting the sear to disengage the hammer at the slightest touch or pressure on the trigger itself. The majority of these set triggers are adjustable for the amount of pressure desired.

SHEARS. Two poles lashed together, normally for use as a tent frame.

SHOOTING BLOCK. A wooden, plastic, or fiber block employed as a cartridge container, used largely by match shooters. The block has a number of perforations, each perforation approximately one-half the length of the cartridge in depth, and with the perforations sufficiently spaced to permit the unhampered withdrawal of a cartridge. The block sometimes has a hinged cover which holds the cartridges in place during transportation.

SHOOTING GLOVE. Used for same purpose as shooting tab. (Archery.)

Shooting Plate. A small piece of bone, horn, pearl, ivory, or other substance inlaid at the right point for the arrow to pass across when bow is shot. (Archery.)

Shooting Tab. A flat piece of leather used on the three fingers that hold the string to protect the fingertips when the arrow is released. (Archery.)

Shot-Breaker. A dog which dashes in when the shot is fired.

Shotgun Range. The formula (known as the Journee formula) for the extreme range of shotgun pellets, for the standard load, is based on the following: the maximum range in yards is 2200 times the shot diameter in inches. The range in various shot sizes would be: No. 2 shot, 330 yards; No. 4 shot, 286 yards; No. 6 shot, 242 yards; No. 7½ shot, 209 yards; No. 8 shot, 198 yards; No. 10 shot, 154 yards. Balled shot (2 or more pellets fused together) will travel a greater distance.

Shot Load Ratios. The ratios of powder and shot in the average shot shell are as follows:

| Gauge | *Standard* Powder dram | Shot oz | *Express* Powder dram | Shot oz |
|---|---|---|---|---|
| 10 | 4¼ | 1¼ | 4¾ | 1⅝ |
| 12 | 3 | 1⅛ | 3¾ | 1¼ |
| 16 | 2½ | 1 | 3¼ | 1⅛ |
| 20 | 2¼ | ⅞ | 2¾ | 1 |
| 28 | 1¾ | ⅝ | 2¼ | ¾ |

Shot Size Key. The key to determining the diameter of dropped or chilled shot pellets is based on an arbitrary constant of 17. For example, No. 9 shot is .08 inches in diameter. In other words, the diameter will always be the number of the size subtracted from 17.

Shot String. The longitudinal or lengthwise dispersion of a charge of shot after it leaves the muzzle, caused by the deformation of some of the pellets, which makes them offer more resistance to air and thus travel slower than pellets not deformed.

Sibley Stove. A simple tent stove, merely a metal cone with a stovepipe fitting at the apex and a hinged door on one side to admit fuel. It is a *heating* and not a *cooking* stove.

Side Cast. The way a bow will throw an arrow if one limb of bow does not line up with the handle. (Archery.)

Side-Stepping. A form of blinking. Finding birds but passing them by without pointing or flushing. (Dogs.)

Siege. A group of herons.

Sighted in for Six O'clock. A term indicating that the rifle has been sighted in to place the point of impact of the bullet not at the point of aim on the target but above it. Were the bull's-eye a clock face, the point of aim would be at 6 o'clock, but the impact point would be at the exact center, midway between 6 and 12 o'clock. Target shooters prefer this when using iron sights, as it permits them to "rest" the bull's-eye on the top of the front sight and center the bull's-eye in the rear sight aperture.

Sight Picture. The correct alignment of the sights.

Sighters. The sighting shots used to test the correctness of the zero of the rifle prior to the shooting of a match. Some matches permit unlimited sighting shots (within reason); others impose a strict limit.

Sight Rule. To *lower* the point of impact of the bullet, *lower* the rear sight; to *raise* the point of impact of the bullet, *raise* the rear sight.

Sign. Any indication of the presence of game. Sign may include tracks, droppings, marks on trees, or any other indication that the area is or has recently been visited by a game animal.

Silver Tip. Early name for the grizzly bear. Also the trade name of the Western high-velocity game cartridge.

Simp. A newly hatched crow.

Singing Ground. An open area used by the woodcock for his courtship display.

Single-Base Powder. Powder containing approximately 15% nitroglycerine, as opposed to "double-base" containing twice that amount. Single-base powder develops less heat and consequently does less damage to the barrel.

Skirter. A hound which runs wide of the pack, allowing others to carry the trail. (Fox hunting.)

Skylining. *See* Dusking.

Sloppiness. Lack of intensity. (Field trials.)

Sluggish. Latent. Slow in developing. (Field trials.)

Small-bore. A term rather loosely employed, but specifically applied to the .22-caliber rifle chambered for the rim-fire cartridge. Also applied to rifles chambered for center-fire cartridges up to .25 caliber.

Smoked Sights. Sights after they have been blackened by soot from a candle or blackening lamp, thus eliminating any shine or glare.

Snaphaunce. An early flintlock gun (Dutch *snaphaan* or gun).

Sneakbox. A term for the Barnegat Bay duckboat.

Sourberry. A form of cranberry found in the Far North.

Spaying. Removing or extirpating the ovaries of a bitch. (Dogs.)

Speak (of a hound). To cry or open when on trail. (Fox hunting.)

Speed. Rate of motion. (Field trials.)

Spike-Buck. A deer with antlers that have not yet branched.

Spike-Collar. A training accessory. A slip collar with small spikes on the inside, used to force obedience to commands. Not recommended for amateurs.

Spine. The stiffness of an arrow shaft. (Archery.)

Spitzer. A term for the pointed bullet.

Split Body. A crack in the cartridge case above the base after firing, indicating a defective and dangerous cartridge.

Spirit. Enthusiasm, boldness, dash. (Field trials.)

Spook. A term used by a hunter, indicating that a game bird or animal flushed or jumped from cover at his approach, or when it winded or heard him.

Spooky. A term used for any animal or bird that is extremely wary or is frightened of man, one that normally is constantly alert.

Sport. A biological term referring to a variation from the normal type, being different than both parents, *e.g.*, an albino. The mating of two sports would not necessarily result in an offspring of the same type, but probably would result in an offspring similar to the grandparents.

Spotting Scope. A telescope used by match shooters which has sufficient magnification to permit the identification of a bullet hole in the target at long range. Also used by hunters in mountainous and open terrain for locating game. The average sporting scope is 20 power.

Sprue. The finger or excess lead protruding from a bullet after it has been cast. Bullet molds are equipped with sprue cutters, which shear off this excess metal.

Squealer. A half-grown bird—usually used of quail, grouse, or partridge.

Stag. The male of a member of the deer family.

Stager. An old and wary deer, elk, caribou, or moose.

Stagged Pants. Trousers worn by some woodsmen, so called because they are cut off midway between the ankle and the boot-top.

Stale. Overworked. (Field trials.)

Stalking. A method of hunting in which the game animal sought is first located, by glasses or otherwise, after which the hunter follows a predetermined route to arrive within rifle range of the quarry.

Stamina. Endurance. (Field trials.)

Stanch. Describes the dog's actions while pointing. The dog which will establish a point and hold it, without caution or admonition, until his handler flushes his birds, may be regarded as stanch. Also spelled "staunch."

Stand. A group or flight of plovers.

Standard Stock. The stock dimensions followed as a standard by the manufacturers of inexpensive shotguns. Although there is some variation, the average standard stock measures as follows: length of pull, 14"; drop at comb, 1½"; drop at heel, 2½".

Start. To make a find. (Fox hunting.)

Steady. Refers to the dog's actions *after* the birds are flushed. The dog is "steady to shot and wing" when he retains his position after the birds are flushed and the shot is fired. (Field trials.)

Stern. The tail of a hound. (Fox hunting.)

Stifle. The joint, similar to the knee joint on humans, found on the hind legs of some animals. On dogs it is the joint above the hock.

Still Hunt. A method of hunting in which one or more hunters, separated but usually within sight or sound of each other, move through a game cover in search of big game. The procedure calls for slow, quiet, and watchful movement, with frequent pauses to scan the terrain within visual range.

Stool. Another name for a decoy.

Stoppage. Any malfunction of a firearm which prevents it from being fired. A stoppage may be caused by broken part, non-ejection, non-extraction, a defective magazine, a defective cartridge, or by excessive dirt in the chamber, magazine, or mechanism.

STRAIGHT PULL. *See* Lee Straight Pull.

STRAIN YOUR BARREL. Term used to deride a shooter who shoots at game at a distance well beyond the range of the gun.

STREAMING. Going across country at a fast pace. (Fox hunting.)

STRIDE. The leap of a dog while running.

STRING MEASURE MATCH. A shooting match in which each shooter fired a specified number of shots at his target. Wooden pegs were inserted in the bullet holes and a string was passed around the pegs to determine the diameter of the group. The shooter with the shortest string (best group) won the match.

STYLE. The dog's general appearance while hunting or on point. (Field trials.)

SWAMP CABBAGE. The edible heart of the cabbage palm, one of the most delicious wild vegetables available.

SWIFT. The .220 Swift is a .22 caliber high-velocity cartridge developed by Winchester, primarily for vermin shooting. Originated from a necked-down .250 Savage cartridge.

SWINGING PAST. A method of shotgun shooting in which the target is overtaken and passed by the sight and the swing "with" the target is continued as the trigger is pressed. As opposed to "pointing out."

SWING LOOSE. The letting go of the arrow while the drawing hand is still moving or in the act of pulling the string back. This loose is often used when the archer is making a flight shot. (Archery.)

SWING TO. To turn a dog in the desired direction while hunting. (Field trials.)

SWIVEL. A turnable fastening for attaching a leash to a jess. (Falconry.)

SUMAC. A shrub or small tree of the *rhus* or *toxicodendron* family. Physical contact with the leaves or bark of this plant is harmful to some individuals, causing a serious skin disorder which results in the emission of a fluid causing the disorder to spread to other parts of the body upon contact. Also known as *poison elder* and *poison ash.*

TAIL HOUNDS. Hounds near the end of the pack. (Fox hunting.)

TAILING. When the pack is not together but straggling out on the trail. (Fox hunting.)

TALLY-HO. The cheer used in organized pack hunting when a fox is viewed. (Fox hunting.)

TANG. The projection or extension of the breech or action of a firearm to which the stock is fastened.

TANG SIGHT. A rear sight mounted on the tang of the rifle.

TARGET STAND. A tripod made of wood that holds a doughnut target at the proper height from the ground. (Archery.)

TAYASSUIDAE. The family of the peccary.

TEAM. A flock or group of ducks. (British.)

TEMPERATURE BALLISTICS. This term refers to the effect of temperature on the trajectory of a bullet. For example, a rifle sighted in during midsummer with the thermometer reading 90° will not have the same zero when fired in midwinter with the thermometer reading 10°. Variation in atmospheric density is the cause. A rifle employing a 170-grain bullet with a muzzle velocity of 2700 f.s. with a midsummer zero for 500 yards, will shoot 7" low on a midwinter day. Cartridges in the magazine and chamber will be cold, and as cold cartridges have less "punch" the bullet will drop still lower than the calculated 7".

TENDERFOOT. A novice or greenhorn, one unskilled in woodcraft, a stranger to an area.

TERMINAL VELOCITY OF BULLETS. It has been claimed that a bullet, if shot straight upward, would be traveling at the same velocity when reaching the point from which it was fired as it had when it left the muzzle of the rifle. This is not correct. The speed of the bullet on its return journey is limited by the terminal velocity of the bullet itself, regulated by the shape of the bullet, and its air resistance. When the resistance to the air of any falling body becomes equal to the force of gravity the body falls at a constant speed. The bullet's terminal velocity is much less than its velocity at the muzzle.

TERTIALS. The wing feathers inside the secondaries, closest to the body.

THREE-FINGER SPUR. A finger lever (combined finger lever and trigger guard) used on the Schützen match rifles, having inletted finger rests for three fingers.

THROAT. A term designating the forward part of the chamber of a rifle, where it tapers to conform to the diameter of the bore.

THROWING OFF. A term referring to a rifle which is performing erratically, or failing to give even reasonable accuracy. This often results from the improper *bedding* of the barrel.

TILLERING A BOW. Working on a bow to get the limbs to balance correctly. (Archery.)

TIMBER. Any forest growth. Also, a term used by woodsmen in felling a tree, shouted in warning as the tree begins to fall.

TIMBERDOODLE. The woodcock.

TIMBERLINE. An extreme in altitude marking the end of forest growth.

TIN-CAN RIFLE. The light .22-caliber rifle. (Colloquial.)

TOE. The lower part of the butt of a shotgun or rifle.

TOLLER. *See* Decoys, *in text.*

TOLLING DOG. A dog once widely used in Europe, now used in Nova Scotia, to entice waterfowl to enter a trap or to lure them within range of the hunter's gun. The action of the dog in running back and forth on the shore stimulates the curiosity of the waterfowl. In Nova Scotia these dogs are bred to resemble a red fox.

TONGUE. The cry of a hound. (Fox hunting.)

TOWERING. A term describing the tendency of some game birds, especially puddle ducks, to fly almost straight upward when frightened. A wounded bird often *towers.*

TOXOPHILITE. Greek for a lover of archery; anyone who shoots archery or loves the sport.

TRADE. A term indicating the movement of game back and forth over a given area, as: "The ducks were trading along the far shore."

TRAILING. A dog which continually or frequently follows his bracemate is called a trailer. One which continues to cast in front of his bracemate and challenge him to a race is called a "head-on trailer." A dog may also trail birds by foot-scent.

TRAJECTORY. The curving path of an object (a bullet, for example) in traveling through space.

TRIANGULATION. A sighting exercise, employed primarily to teach the novice marksman to find the correct sight picture.

TRIGGER CREEP. Roughness or harshness noticeable in the trigger pull. Lack of smooth, even pull.

TRIGGER PULL. The amount of pressure, measured in pounds, required to bring about the release of the sear notch on the hammer, permitting the hammer to fall.

TRIP. A very small flight, group, or flock of widgeon.

TREZ. The third point, after the *bez* and before the *royal,* of antlers.

TUBE SIGHT. A sight used on the flintlock rifle of colonial times, consisting of a long tube of brass or iron running the entire length of the barrel, with a pin sight at the muzzle end, and an aperture at rear.

TULAREMIA. A virulent disease, known also as "rabbit disease" but which is known to affect other game birds and animals. Rabbits are the major victims of this disease, and great care should be exercised in the skinning of rabbits. The disease can be communicated to humans if a cut or scratch on the hands or arms makes contact with an infected animal. The disease can be fatal to humans. No harmful effects result from the eating of an infected bird or animal, as thorough cooking destroys the virus.

TULE. (pronounced *tooley*). A tall bulrush, *Scirpus lacustris* or *S. acutus,* found in abundance in the southwestern states and Mexico.

TUMP LINE. A flat leather band, about 3" by 12" with 3/4" leather strap firmly stitched to each end, the straps often 10' or 12' in length. The wide band is a *head* or *brow* band; the straps are used to make up a pack. Tump lines are used in carrying heavy loads when a regulation pack is not used. A tump often is used on a pack, to take some of the weight off the shoulders.

TURKEY SHOOT. The original turkey shoots, held during muzzle-loader days, had the turkey as a target as well as a prize. The bird was placed behind a bulletproof shield with only its head protruding. Contestants were permitted one shot, in the standing position at 10 rods (55 yds.). Ranges varied with shoots. At modern turkey shoots a regulation target is used, the turkey going to the shooter with the best score.

TURNING TO WHISTLE. Breaking the cast and swinging in response to the handler's whistle. (Field trials.)

TWIST. The angle or inclination of the rifling grooves off the axis of the bore. Twist is designated by measuring the number of turns or fractions of turns to the inch of barrel length. For instance, a "14-inch twist" means that the grooves make one complete turn inside the bore every 14".

TWIST BARRELS. *See* Damascus barrels.

TYPE. The dog which measures up to, or near to, the standards of bird-dog conformation is said to possess good type or be "typey." (Field trials.)

UNGULATES. A zoological term for the family of hoofed mammals.

UNITED BOWMEN ROUND. The oldest archery round still in existence, initiated by the United Bowmen in 1835. It consists of 84 arrows fired at a range of 80 yds.

U.S.R.A. United States Revolver Assn., 5 Oak St., Springfield, Mass.

UPLAND GAME. A general term for rabbits, squirrels, woodchucks, and similar small mammals.

UPLAND GAME BIRDS. A general term for quail, pheasants, grouse, and similar game birds.

URSIDAE. Members of the bear family.

USE. A term indicating that a bird or animal has been feeding or inhabiting an area.

VARMINT. A general colloquial term for a predator. Also includes the various members of the chuck family.

VARMINTER. Term for one of the small-caliber, high-velocity rifles employed primarily on varmints. (E.g., the .220 Swift.)

VELOCITY. The speed at which a bullet or shot charge travels, designated in foot-seconds (feet per second).

VELVET. The soft, vascular tissue which covers the antlers of members of the deer family until the antlers have attained their full growth and form, at which time the tissue dies and is removed by the animal's rubbing its antlers against brush and trees.

VERMICULATIONS. Thin, irregular lines which mark the plumage of some birds, usually in irregular waves.

VENADO. Native Mexican name for the Coues deer.

VERNIER SIGHT. A rear sight, the aperture of which is raised or lowered by means of a threaded post with a knurled knob, the threads engaging those of the sight carrier. Turning the knob right or left raises or lowers the carrier (with aperture), and a vernier scale on the frame indicates the elevation. The vernier scale is graduated in hundredths of an inch.

VIXEN. The female fox.

VULPES. The genus of the sub-family *Caninae* which embraces the foxes.

WALK. Where puppies are placed out on a farm to accustom them to poultry and other livestock. (Fox hunting.)

WANGAN. A term used in the North Country to describe personal duffle or outfit.

WATERFOWL. A general term for ducks and geese.

WATER TURKEY. The snakebird (*Anhinga anhinga*) found on the ponds, waterways, and swamps of the southern states. The bird resembles the cormorant in appearance and size, dark brown in color, mottled on the back and upper wings with light gray.

WHANG. Another name for rawhide.

WHEELLOCK. The lock mechanism of an early firearm. The depression of the trigger caused an iron wheel to spin against a piece of flint or pyrites causing sparks to ignite the powder train leading to the powder-charged chamber.

WHELP. A very young puppy. (Fox hunting.)

WHISKEY JACK. *See* Moose Bird.

WHISP. A flock or group of snipe. (British.)

WHITENESS. A flock or group of swans. (British.)

W.C.F. Winchester Center Fire. Term given originally to the .22 W.C.F., a high-velocity .22-caliber rifle cartridge. Now almost obsolete.

WIKIUP. A framework made by driving the pointed butts of light saplings in the ground and lashing the sapling tips at a common center. By interlacing pliable branches through the framework and covering the structure with bark or green boughs a warm hut can be made.

WILD FLUSH. The rise of game birds for no apparent reason.

WINDAGE. *See* Deflection.

WIND-PLANING. The action of an arrow as it goes through the air if it deviates up and down from a true course, or right and left. This action often occurs when a broadhead is not properly designed and constructed. (Archery.)

WINGED. A term indicating that a game bird has been hit but not killed. Used primarily by the upland game shooter. Waterfowl hit but not killed are termed "cripples."

WIRE-POINT BULLET. A bullet patented by Charles Newton in 1914, employing a copper wire at the point. The bullet was a spitzer type with a soft point, and the wire served to protect this point from damage prior to firing. The advantage of this bullet was to give good ballistic performance and also give some expansion and mushrooming quality upon impact.

WOOD-SALT. Sorrel *(oxalis* or *xanthoxalis)*, a sour grass which can be employed as a salt substitute in an emergency.

WORRIED. Torn to bits by hounds. (Fox hunting.)

WRIST GUARD. A piece of leather or other substance that protects the wrist from the slap of the bowstring. (Archery.)

X. A term which has many meanings in shooting, including the following:

Describing the *power* of a telescope sight, spotting scope, or binoculars. For example, 12X binoculars.

Meaning *Out of;* used in scoring; for example, 93 x 100.

*X-ring,* the 10-ring in a target.

YARD. An area, usually within a forest, in which a large number of deer, moose, elk, or similar mammals herd together, tramping down the snow and feeding on the browse supplied by the low branches.

YARD-BREAKING. That part of the dog's training given him in the yard.

YAW. A bullet which does not travel exactly "nose on," but slightly sideways, is said to "yaw."

YOICKS. An old hunting cry. (Fox hunting.)

ZERO. The adjustment of the sights on a rifle which will cause the bullet to arrive at a calculated impact point at a certain range. For example: a rifle with the sights *zeroed* for 100 yds., will, under normal conditions, place the bullet in the center of the target at that range.

ZIPPER. A .22-caliber high-velocity cartridge, introduced as a factory load by Winchester. Originated from a .25/35 cartridge, necked down.

# INDEX

Words in *italic* are names of magazines and newspapers, titles of books, and personal names of dogs.

## C

D

## E

## G

**H**

## I

**J**



**K**

## L

**M**

**N**

## O

**P**

**Q**



**R**

## S

## T

**Z**